PSEUDO-MANETHO,
APOTELESMATICA

Pseudo-Manetho, *Apotelesmatica*

*Books Four, One, and Five:
Edited with Introduction, Translation,
and Commentary*

J. L. LIGHTFOOT

Great Clarendon Street, Oxford, OX2 6DP,
United Kingdom

Oxford University Press is a department of the University of Oxford.
It furthers the University's objective of excellence in research, scholarship,
and education by publishing worldwide. Oxford is a registered trade mark of
Oxford University Press in the UK and in certain other countries

© J. L. Lightfoot 2023

The moral rights of the author have been asserted

All rights reserved. No part of this publication may be reproduced, stored in
a retrieval system, or transmitted, in any form or by any means, without the
prior permission in writing of Oxford University Press, or as expressly permitted
by law, by licence or under terms agreed with the appropriate reprographics
rights organization. Enquiries concerning reproduction outside the scope of the
above should be sent to the Rights Department, Oxford University Press, at the
address above

You must not circulate this work in any other form
and you must impose this same condition on any acquirer

Published in the United States of America by Oxford University Press
198 Madison Avenue, New York, NY 10016, United States of America

British Library Cataloguing in Publication Data

Data available

Library of Congress Control Number: 2022950537

ISBN 978-0-19-286847-3

Printed and bound by
CPI Group (UK) Ltd, Croydon, CR0 4YY

Links to third party websites are provided by Oxford in good faith and
for information only. Oxford disclaims any responsibility for the materials
contained in any third party website referenced in this work.

In memoriam

NMS

Das Gras ist verdorret und die Blume abgefallen.

Preface

Λοιπόν μοι Μοῦσαι δότ' ἀεῖσαι πλείονα τούτων
εἰς ἑτέραν βίβλον...

John Ma once floated the idea of writing an article about Louis Robert's unwritten articles, the countless ones he promised but never published. And then he never wrote it. Words like 'I hope to return to this in a future article', or even 'see *x*, forthcoming', are more often than not ominous, though it usually takes twenty frustrating minutes of searching to confirm that the promised work never appeared. Here, however, is the fulfilment of the promise in the preface of my first volume. I found the Manethoniana so absorbing that I could not leave them before working through the whole corpus.

I did not, in truth, expect to find the second half as enticing as the first. I was expecting catastrophic disorganisation and frustrating *impasse*. In fact, what I found was even richer and more rewarding than in the first volume. It is no exaggeration to say that I have not spent a single minute working on the Manethoniana when I have been anything other than completely absorbed, and usually enthralled. I do not apologise for the length of the commentaries. Had these texts been newly discovered they would have generated a good deal of attention once scholars realised how rich their implications were, into how many areas they reached. I have provided a slightly modified version of my usual form of commentary. The first part takes on the social and cultural dimension (an expansion of vol. i, part III). The second turns to the texts themselves, following the convention established in the first volume that the poet of books 2, 3, and 6 is referred to by shorthand as M^a, of book 4 as M^b, of book 1 as M^c, and of book 5 as M^d. I first present the main comparanda (~ i. I.5), then discuss matters of composition and style that allow the various poets in the corpus to be compared and quite clearly distinguished one from another. Finally, there is a detailed treatment of the language and style of book (~ i. II, carried out on a small scale for each book). The third part is the edition and translation of the new material, and the fourth is the commentary. For each book I provide what I call a Pinax, which for ease of reference tabulates the charts in each book against their main comparanda. The critical apparatus also contains a lower register in which the most important of the comparanda are printed in full, again for ease of comparison.

Because they are so rich and so little-read they are in many ways a commentator's paradise. They are infinitely granular and crowded with detail.

A literary scholar is always delighted when the opportunity arises to use the work of Louis Robert. They know that their response to a text will be enhanced by the demonstration that its details are not whimsical at all, but embedded in ancient usage which he so meticulously documented. With the Manethoniana it is a constant pleasure to be able to show how closely they tie in with the evidence, not only of other literary genres (epigram and satire and invective and curses and invocations and hymns), but also of other media. It has been a particular joy to be able to show that they can be used to shed light on ancient cultures with the same degree of intimacy, precision, and bright colour that Robert elicited from the inscriptions of Lycia and Pisidia and Caria. There are specialist terms and trade names and titles and honorific formulations demanding a context, and of course they are packed with problems of interpretation as well, which it is the task of any responsible commentary to tackle. One line calls for comment on a problem of Homeric interpretation. The next line sends one off to the Radcliffe Science library to elucidate ancient embryotomy or the prevalence of leprosy or some particular problem of ecliptic longitude. I quote a colleague, who puts it exactly: 'Writing a commentary is very, very enjoyable… I like the combination of sustained focus on a single text and the huge variety of things one always needs to be thinking about' (Barney Taylor, Twitter, 29 March 2021).

At the same time—and precisely for many of these reasons—this project has prompted particularly acute reflection on the philosophy of commentary. Why do commentaries have the conventions they do, and why do we retain so many of them in a digital age when not all of them have retained their usefulness?

To begin with, any commentator has to think hard about narrative voice.[1] The genre tends to elicit a magisterial quasi-neutral informativeness—which, if it does, should give immediate pause for thought, as should the mindless bulk of bibliographical virtue-signalling. On the other hand, the Manethoniana are so full of uncertainty that one can often only make reasonable inferences and best guesses. How many times did I find myself having recourse to 'presumably', and disliking it intensely? In practice the narrative voice is required to steer an unsteady course between the Scylla of quasi-certainty and pseudo-authoritativeness and the Charybdis of barely concealed admission of defeat. Every assertion, every caution, every doubt, is a matter of what the evidence can be pressed to say, and this, too, is something a commentator, any commentator, has to think hard about. What are acceptable standards of evidence? A commentator talks of numbers of occurrences and parallels, and makes another uneasy choice, this time between

---

[1] C. S. Kraus, 'Introduction: Reading Commentaries/Commentaries as Reading', in R. K. Gibson and C. S. Kraus (eds.), *The Classical Commentary: History, Practices, Theory* (Leiden, 2002), 1–27, at 4–5.

hand-waving 'often', 'common', 'frequently', and a list of loci which any search-engine can generate.

There is more. There are problems of quality, of assortment and consistency and coherence. The commentator is trained to find parallels, establish contexts, and present as multi-dimensional and adequate an account as she can. But an ancient morsel presents itself for which parallels are scattered and of variable quality. The commentator tries her best, but all she ultimately achieves is the ahistorical and decontextualised accumulation of little bits of stuff.[2] As Keith Hopkins and Mary Beard put it:

> This is a trap modern students of Roman culture often fall into: pick up one reference in a letter written in the first century AD, combine it with a casual aside in a historian writing a hundred years later, a joke by a Roman satirist which seems to be referring to the same phenomenon, plus a head-on attack composed by a Christian propagandist in North Africa; add it all together and—hey, presto!—you've made a picture, reconstructed an institution of ancient Rome.[3]

Fortunately there is a possible response to this. One can suggest that the patient accumulation of data, properly controlled within an appropriately robust framework, serves to establish patterns beyond localised instances.[4] One may not have reconstructed an institution of ancient Rome, but one *has* found repeated evidence of an attitude, the persistence of a topos or cultural pattern. And that is particularly important for astrology, whose contents usually (genitures apart) cannot be dated because astrological texts inveterately repeat each other with a few localised tweaks and updates which effect no more than cosmetic changes, but which in principle are all about norms and archetypes and replicability. Hence the difficulty when Cumont claimed that this or

---

[2] Norman Maclean, *Young Men and Fire* (Chicago, 1992), 262: 'Unless you have some good idea of what you are looking for and how to find it, you can approach infinity with nothing more than a mishmash of little things you know about a lot of little things.' See also C. A. Kraus and C. Stray, 'Form and Content', in iid. (eds.), *Classical Commentaries: Explorations in a Scholarly Genre* (Oxford, 2016), 9, on the 'Wunderkammer' effect of commentaries.

[3] K. Hopkins and M. Beard, *The Colosseum* (London, 2005), 70.

[4] Morgan, 38–9: 'The picture which will develop will derive cumulatively from thousands of individual references in literary sources, inscriptions, and papyri, and on coins. This kind of survey has both advantages and risks. Its main risk is that it puts side by side, as in some sense comparable, passages from very varied texts and objects, without doing full justice to differences of context, author, genre, or audience which may affect their meaning. Its main advantage is that, carefully handled, it allows one to see beyond the immediate contexts of texts and objects, the imaginations of individual authors, and the demands of genre, to assumptions and habits of thought which are shared between texts, objects and their audiences, and arguably among populations more widely. The historiography of *mentalités* depends on the possibility of detecting such patterns of thought and assumption, and some qualities of the evidence give us confidence in doing so…The sheer breadth of material we will survey also acts as a control on individual examples.'

that detail reflected life in Ptolemaic Egypt. But if one is documenting attitudes and manners and cultural patterns the chronological range of the cited material is less problematic, and the geographical range becomes an interesting artefact in its own right if it turns out that details in the presumably Egyptian Manethoniana find their best parallels in the epigraphy of Anatolia. It becomes less of a desperate attempt to solder x onto y, and more of an interesting reflection on the standardisation of public and private discourse across the Roman Near East.

What needs most reflection of all is antiquarianism. The Manethoniana are full of notaries and sewer workers, graving tools and Roman brickwork, sponge-divers and caulkers of ships, birthing stools and nails for crucifixion, acclamations and—since there is nothing astrology does not have a bearing on, even the ancient smellscape—rotting fish. Suppose one is absorbed by the detail, which after all not many literary texts offer in anything like this plenitude. Suppose one sets out to provide a little exegesis of each topic. At best, you have come up with something that Daremberg–Saglio did so much better over a century ago. At worst you have walked into a nightmare Prussian seminar:

> As you see, gentlemen, the porter shut the gate [on Socrates and his companions]. At this passage anyone would be struck by the question of how this gate was constructed, and also by the important, still unsolved problem of door-shutting in antiquity.[5]

Can one be true to the text's granularity without being sidetracked into footling antiquarianism? Are we so mesmerised by the ancient world that it is a sacred duty to explore even the most sapping banality? Once again, one presumably *can* mount a vigorous response to this. It is up to us as critics to show how and why something matters, what it implies for social or economic or political or institutional life, or for the Greek language, or for literary culture, or whatever; the onus is on us to find that enlightening moment, and if we fail it is our fault; no-one calls Robert an antiquarian. But about the granularity itself? Is that a blessing or a curse? The answer to the tweet I mentioned above was thought-provoking. On the pleasure of commentary-writing the correspondent, David Scourfield, tweeted back: 'In all sorts of ways—not least, not having to worry about an overarching argument!…And one learns about all sorts of interesting things in the process, even if some of them can't be pursued very far.' Is it enough just to be interested or interesting? Should a commentary be a collection of *morceaux*, even (especially) if that is the character of the

---

[5] Ludwig Hatvany, *Die Wissenschaft des nicht Wissenswerten* (Ein Kollegienheft, 2nd edn, Munich, 1914), 14, cited by A. Grafton, 'Prolegomena to Friedrich August Wolf', *Journal of the Warburg and Courtauld Institutes*, 44 (1981), 101–29, at 101.

commented text? Should we not in fact worry *very much* about the lack of an overarching argument?⁶

All my commentaries are deliberately half exegesis and half extended discussion, and the two halves are integrated into one another, or at least an effort is made that they should be. In this case, the commentary also makes an effort to highlight certain running themes (sources and models, the use and poetic abuse of astrological vocabulary, the adaptation of Homer and the creation of a hybrid idiom, and so on). But the particular subject-matter in this case happily facilitates a novel and more interesting answer to the challenge of what a commentator is doing, line by relentless line. For a commentary answers to the nature of astrology; it understands its character as bricolage and turns its liabilities into advantages. One might in general feel distinctly sceptical about the rationale for accumulating parallels in commentaries, which is what the genre is all about. What earthly conclusion is one supposed to draw from the fact that x is more, or less, like y or z in another text? But it so happens that astrology is well placed—almost uniquely well placed—to defend itself in this regard. The heaping-up of parallels demonstrates precisely what it is, the accumulation of commonplaces. It has to appeal to common experience; that is its whole point. And the sources of those parallels, all the way from the Homeric poems to semi-digested Hippocrates to curse tablets, help us to place it, and in the present case to measure the cultural range and competence of the readers of the poems on which I have commented.

Suppose we consider what else was going on in intellectual life at the time our texts were produced, which I take to be the high to later empire, the second to fourth centuries AD. Suppose, in particular, we compare and contrast it with the Second Sophistic, when the high literary culture of élites took its inspiration from what were now acknowledged as the classics. The first part of this book will propose viewing astrology as an imaginary, a collection of tropes. Instead of full-on intellectual engagement with the grand genres of drama, historiography, rhetoric, and philosophy, one could instead suggest that it is a poor-man's version of that, a rag-bag of motifs, not underpinned by any thought-through ideas (or barely digested at best); that cultural capital is sourced, not from reworkings of Thucydides and Demosthenes, but from second-hand attitudes and platitudes about cleanly conduct and domestic decency; that instead of reworking big political themes about politics and agency and identity, astrology retreats from the grand stage of the polis and public conduct and the role of the citizen to petty day-to-day concerns about

---

⁶ J. Ma, 'Black Hunter Variations', *PCPS* 40 (1994), 49–80, at 75 '...it just plows through the text and tackles problems in an inert, atomistic fashion, lemma after lemma...it does not have a strong line of argument and does not stand or fall with a conclusion'.

individual coping; that instead of even trying to engage in big debates about the nature of goodness, it just shrugs and passes responsibility over to the stars. Suppose, in short, we suggest that this is what the Second Sophistic looks like in the hands of *hoi polloi*. But that we are empowered, too, by seeking out the very important areas where the two cultures meet, ethically on the issues of community, friendship, the social network, and culturally on the unchallengeable centrality of Homer.

This may or may not be my sign-off from astrology. Whether it is or not it is patent how much more is left to do, and specifically on astrological poetry. If a classicist is prepared to venture into Byzantine Greek, then surely Camaterus' poems are another goldmine waiting for someone to sink a shaft into them, and if a Hellenist ventures into Latin, there is still a great deal to do with Firmicus, especially, I sense, with the eighth book. It is clear even from the revision of LSJ how unfamiliar this material still is; in the course of my commentary I have had occasion to supplement or criticise so many entries, not only on astrological *termini technici* themselves,[7] but also in the incidental material which the apodoses throw up.[8] We badly need a dictionary of astrological technical terms. It is beyond my competence to do it, but someone with a training in the history of science could, or could assemble a team of people with the appropriate expertise. This is just a sample of what might be done. It was while writing this book that I stopped even trying to characterise my specialism to anyone who cared to ask about it in terms of a particular subject area, and started saying that there is so much classical literature that no-one reads and my particular interest is in reclaiming it.

This book was my lock-down project, which I was able to complete so expeditiously largely because of the magnificence of Oxford's librarians, even when the buildings themselves were inaccessible. The thought I kept coming back to throughout all the pandemic, the thought to which everything seemed to return, was the question St John put into the mouth of Pontius Pilate: What is truth? This applied to the epidemiology, the statistics, the political implications of the pandemic at every point, and above all it applied to the basic epistemology of why we think what we think and how we know what we know. Caring about truth, determining that there is such a thing, testing methodologies, and

---

[7] e.g. 4.38 δέσποσμα; 189 σελάγισμα 'lightning', which seems to betray a complete ignorance of what the Manethoniana are about; 421 καταθρῇ (their interpretation not necessarily wrong, but uncertain); 572 βιοτοσκόπον; 1.353 παρόδοισιν; 5.79 παλίνορσος.

[8] p. 7 n. 5 εὐφαντασίωτος; p. 121 τάξις; p. 76 n. 23 καθαιρετικός; 4.75 ἀλλότυπον; 4.104 θρονισμός; 4.277 θεατρομανοῦντας; 4.301, the secular meaning of θίασος; 4.345 λίπασμα; 4.364 ἐπαγωγή; 4.412 (apropos of Epit. IV) δυστοκία; 4.556 μηνύματα; 4.559 θάμβημα; 563 ἀλλόφρων; 1.54, on lepromatous leprosy; 1.189 ἐγγάστριον; 1.199 μετατρεψέμεν; 5.78 πανήμερος; 5.85 ὑψηλούς; 5.138 μεθοδεύεται as verb of motion; 5.320–3 ἀσελγοπύγους.

simply getting the facts right, seem to me the most important things a scholar can do, despite a certain one who, in a review of my second book, seemed to regard my desire to get at it as an amiable but slightly embarrassing eccentricity.[9] I would like to thank the people who have helped cleared some of the brambles out of my path, which, if I still missed it, is entirely my own fault: Mark Griffith, Georgy Kantor, Robin Lane Fox, Andy Meadows, Harry Samuels, Barnaby Taylor, Peter Thonemann, and Nigel Wilson. A special technological thank-you goes to the papyrologist Konstantine Panegyres and to Hongyu Sun, who showed me how to position Greek characters with diacritics directly suprascript above letters by means of a Pinyin keyboard: such are the unexpected benefits of confirmation-of-status interviews. And Amin Benaissa deserves my heartfelt thanks for drawing my attention to the existence of three Manethonian papyri from the second, fourth, and first books, due to be published in P.Oxy. LXXXVII, and for most generously taking time out of his schedule to supply preliminary information about them. I also thank the librarians, especially Charlotte Goodall, Clare Hills-Nova, Isabel Holowaty, and Christopher Skelton-Ford in New College, who did so much to keep the knowledge chain intact during the pandemic. And I thank OUP, now that the whole Manethonian project is at an end, for being prepared to invest in something whose enormity was not clear at the outset, least of all to me.

The excerpt on p. 997 from *Pale Fire* by Vladimir Nabokov (copyright © 1962, Vera Nabokov and Dmitri Nabokov, copyright renewed 1990 by the Estate of Vladimir Nabokov) is used by permission of The Wylie Agency (UK) Limited and Vintage Books, an imprint of the Knopf Doubleday Publishing Group, a division of Penguin Random House LLC. All rights reserved.

In a sense this book was always for Noel Swerdlow, who would have treated it with fathomless contempt. I lack the data to cast his horoscope, as I did for Martin West. But in the end his combative nature encountered the sanguinary planet Mars, which attacked his blood. Now, alas, it is in his memory, and in memory of the Trinity Term he spent in All Souls in 1995.

J.L.L.

---

[9] *SCI* 23 (2004), 298–301.

FAUSTUS. Now would I have a book where I might see all characters and planets of the heavens, that I might know their motions and dispositions.
MEPHISTOPHILIS. Here they are.
    Christopher Marlowe, *The Tragical History of Doctor Faustus*

Contents

Conventions and Citations	xxv
Abbreviations	xxix
Editions	xxxiii

PART ONE: THE WORLD OF ASTROLOGY (REVISITED)

1. Viewpoint	3
2. Character of the Value System	7
3. Élite and Mass	18
Kings and Big Men	18
Mass	26
4. Work	34
Introduction	34
Lexicography	38
Distortions and Blind Spots	41
Comparative Excursus: Manetho (and the Related Material in Ptolemy/Θ) and Firmicus	52
Mental Structures	58
Organising Principles	58
Values	62
Interim Conclusions	70
5. The Poor	73
6. Slaves	84
Further Comparisons	96
Astrology and Oracles	96
Astrology and Dreams	98
7. Conclusions and Further Reflections	106
Letters	106
Games, Spectacles, Entertainments	110
So What About Egypt?	117
Middlingness?	119

PART TWO: THE LATER BOOKS OF MANETHO

The Later Books	127
1. Comparanda, Common Sources, Underlay	129
Evidence from Types of Material Found within the Books of the Corpus	129
Evidence from Order of Planets	134
Pingree's Epitomes: The Manethoniana and Antiochus/Rhetorius	135
Conclusions	146
2. Organisation of Sequences	149
Book 1	151
Book 5	154
3. Internal Patterning	156
4. Stylistic Markers in Each Poet	163
Asyndeton	163
Delayed Particles	164
Definite Article	165
Types and Moods of Clauses in the Protasis	166
Verbs in the Apodosis	167
Conclusions	169
5. On the Presentation of Work	171
Book Four	178
4.1. Preliminaries	178
4.2. The Original Poem: Inferences about Shape and Structure	182
Proem and 4.107–9: Planets and Fixed Stars	182
4.109–69: Signs of Birth, or from the Place of Birth	183
4.170–End: Γενεαί and Τέχναι	184
4.3. Phonologica et Morphologica	186
Phonologica	186
Morphologica	187
Conclusions	188
4.4. Word-Formation	188
Parts of Speech	189
Conclusions	195
4.5. Syntax	197
Particles	197
Definite Article	198
Third-Person Pronouns and Adjectives	198
Prepositions	199
Nouns	202

Verbs	203
Adverbial Neuters Plural	204
4.6. Style	205
Composition	205
Verbiage	210
Use and Recycling of Earlier Poets	214
4.7. Metre	220
Outer Metric	220
Inner Metric	226
Prosody	232
Summary and *Obiter Dicta*	237
4.8. Narrator and Addressee	239
4.9. Astrologica	239
Characteristics of M^b's Protases	239
Characteristics of M^b's Apodoses: Combinatory Technique	252
Planetary Names and Epithets	255
4.10. The Relationship of M^b and M^a, and of Each with Θ	259
Patterns of Correspondence	260
Register of Similarities	262
Register for *Lib. Herm.*	268
Book One	270
1.1. Preliminaries	270
1.2. The Composite Character of Book 1	273
M^b, M^c, and P.Oxy. 2546	274
Pentameters	276
A, B, C, D …	281
Conclusion	283
1.3. Phonologica et Morphologica	284
Phonologica	284
Morphologica	285
1.4. Syntax	286
Particles	286
Definite Article	287
Third-Person Pronouns and Adjectives	287
Prepositions	287
Verbs	288
Negations	290
1.5. Style	290
Use and Recycling of Earlier Poets	291

Hapax and *Proton Legomena*	294
Composition	294
1.6. Metre	297
Outer Metric	297
Inner Metric	301
Prosody	306
Summary and Final Implications	309
1.7. Narrator and Addressee	311
1.8. Astrologica	312
Treatment of Technical Terms	312
Charts Involving the Malefics and a Phase of the Moon	313
Planetary Names and Epithets	315
Book Five	317
5.1. Preliminaries	317
5.2. Multiple Authorship?	319
Correspondences	324
Conclusions	326
5.3. Phonologica et Morphologica	327
Phonologica	327
Morphologica	328
5.4. Syntax	329
Particles	329
Definite Article	330
Third Person Pronouns and Adjectives	331
Prepositions	331
Verbs	333
Negations	334
5.5. Style	334
Use and Recycling of Earlier Poets	336
Composition	341
5.6. Metre	343
Outer Metric	343
Inner Metric	348
Prosody	352
Summary	357
5.7. Narrator and Addressee	358
5.8. Astrologica	360
Treatment of Technical Terms	360
Planetary Names and Epithets	362

Addenda	365
1. Pinax of Θ Against Manetho (M^a, M^b, M^c, M^d)	365
2. Pinax of Anubion Against Manetho, Firmicus	368
3. Metre Overview	369
Outer Metric	369
Inner Metric	374
Prosody	378
Note on Metrical Licence	381
4. Planetary Rank Orders	383

PART THREE: TEXT

The Text of the Later Books	387
Palaeographical Notes	387
The Editor's Problem	388
Stemma	391
Evaluating the Quality of Readings	393
Conclusion	395
Register of Differences Between the Texts of Lightfoot and De Stefani	398
Sigla	402
Book Four (Text, Apparatus, Translation)	405
Book One (Text, Apparatus, Translation)	454
Book Five (Text, Apparatus, Translation)	480

PART FOUR: COMMENTARY

Book Four	507
4.1–13 Proem	507
4.14–109 *Kentrothesiai*	514
4.14–34 Saturn	515
4.35–43 Jupiter	521
4.44–52 Mars	525
4.53–68 Venus	528
4.69–76 Mercury	534
4.77–92 Moon	538
4.93–106 Sun	545
4.107–9 Transition	550

4.110–69 'Signs of Birth'	551
4.110–20 Charts Involving *Kentra*	551
4.121–64 Mostly Πρᾶξις Charts	555
4.165–9 Transition	571
4.170–end Γενεαί and τέχναι	574
4.170–346 Sequence of Mainly τ- Charts	574
4.347–65 Group on Harms	651
4.366–413 Group on Nurture and Parentage	655
4.414–49 More τέχναι	671
4.450–90 Miscellanea	683
4.491–507 More *Kentrothesiai*	697
4.508–36 Luminaries in Gendered Signs	704
4.537–59 New and Full Moon	712
4.560–92 Aspects Across *Kentra*	721
4.593–626 Miscellanea	734
Book One	749
1.1–15 + 16–17 Proem	749
1.18–361 The Book Proper	759
1.18–25 Charts Involving Venus	759
1.26–33 Luminaries in Places of Gender	762
1.34–44 Three Mars-Related Charts?	764
1.45–138 Miscellanea	766
1.139–52 *Schetliasmos* of Mars	796
1.153–95 Miscellanea	801
1.196–207 Protreptic	817
1.208–76 Miscellanea	828
1.277–80 + 281–3 + 284–5 Royal Charts	846
1.286–326 Τέχναι	849
1.327–33 + 334–8 Parents	852
1.339–58 Miscellanea	854
1.359–61 Sign-Off	860
Book Five	862
5.1–26 Introduction	862
5.1–24 Proem	866
5.25–6 Words and Thought	880
5.27–340 Charts	882
5.27–43 Miscellanea	882
5.44–129 Good and Bad Stars	889
5.130–6 Compilation on Mars' Oppositions	914

5.137–88 The Περὶ μίμων Sequence (from Θ pp. 217.5–218.8)   916
5.189–312 Miscellanea   939
5.313–40 Charts Specifically for Women   987

Epimetrum   997

APPENDICES

Appendix I: Pinakes   1009
Appendix II: Roster of Trades   1025

Addenda and Corrigenda to the First Volume   1059
Bibliography   1069
Index of Passages Discussed   1087
Index of Greek Words   1099
General Index   1103

Conventions and Citations

This second volume follows the conventions of the first, to which cross-reference is often made in the short form i. 000. All the conventions discussed there, on pp. xxiv–xxix, remain valid here. In particular, the various poets of the corpus continue to be referred to as M^a (books 2, 3, and 6), M^b (book 4), M^c (book 1), and M^d (book 5). The various poets identified by Koechly within book 1 may be further differentiated by letter, e.g. M^c(A) for the poet Koechly identified as the biggest contributor to the book. Anubion is now cited from Paul Schubert's edition rather than Dirk Obbink's.

The various epitomes of Rhetorius continue to be very important, and it is a matter of regret that this volume was completed before the publication of Stephan Heilen's completion of David Pingree's edition. As it is, I cite these epitomes using the letter-names given to them in Pingree's article on Antiochus and Rhetorius (1977), and my own abbreviation of the most important of them, Epit. III, as Θ (as explained in i. xxv, and further discussed in this volume, pp. 136–46). For Ptolemy's *Tetrabiblos*, I no longer cite the numbers of the 1553 edition in brackets. Citations of Artemidorus' text on the interpretation of dreams, which becomes an important comparison in certain parts of this volume, use the subparagraph numbers conveniently introduced into the text in the new translation by Martin Hammond for Oxford World's Classics (Oxford, 2020).

An author who becomes newly important in this volume is Teucer of 'Babylon' (probably the one in Egypt) who lived perhaps in the first century BC. His significance for the Manethoniana is that his work on the Paranatellonta (the constellations that rise along with the zodiacal signs), which he gave in their Egyptian forms (the *Sphaera Barbarica*), was influential on the text group to which the Manethoniana belong. His original work does not survive, but is reflected in a couple of redactions known since Boll, who published them, as the first and second Teucer texts (Boll 1903), as well as a number of other witnesses (Feraboli), of which those most immediately helpful for Manetho are Firmicus 8 and *Lib. Herm.* xxv. Parallel passages in Θ can sometimes show where Teucer has been elided from the Manethoniana themselves. For further literature on Teucer, see Heilen 2015, 568 n. 937.

Where secondary literature is concerned, in general I have used the same system as in my other commentaries. I refer to frequently cited works by author's name alone. These are listed in the final bibliography. The name–date system is used to distinguish works by authors cited twice or more. The details of works cited only once are given in the passage in question. Deeming itemised lists of standard editions and commentaries on classical texts supererogatory (e.g. West on Hes. *Op.* 247), I have not included them in the bibliography unless I also refer to them by page number.

GLOSSARY OF ASTROLOGICAL TERMS

benefic	planet with good effects: Jupiter, Venus, sometimes Mercury
malefic	planet with bad effects: Saturn, Mars, sometimes Mercury
exaltation	sign (other than the planet's own) in which it exercises maximum power; Greek ὕψωμα
dejection	sign in which a planet has least power; Greek ταπείνωμα
rejoice	exercise maximum power
aspect	(noun) an angular relationship of planets; (verb) to occupy such an angular position in respect to another planet
conjunction	strictly the location of planets in the same degree of longitude, more loosely proximity within about 6°
opposition	angular relation of 180° between planets
trine	angular relation of 120° between planets
quartile	angular relation of 90° between planets
right quartile	position of 90° ahead in diurnal motion
sextile	angular relation of 60° between planets
dodecatopos	the system of twelve houses into which the circuit of the heavens is divided; also *dodecatropos*
kentron	centre; one of the cardines or cardinal points, i.e.:
ASC	Ascendant
DESC	Descendant
IMC	Imum Caelum
MC	Medium Caelum
epanaphora	the next place to rise after a *kentron*
apoklima	the place that has risen before a *kentron*
cadent	'falling away', located in the house preceding a *kentron*
succedent	located in the house following a *kentron*
synaphe	approach of one planet, especially the Moon, to another; also called application
aporrhoia	departure of the Moon from another planet; also called defluxion
kenodromia	the Moon's motion towards no other planet
decans	divisions of a sign into 10° portions
dodecatemories	twelfth parts: divisions of a sign into twelve parts each of 2°30′
phase	a planet's position vis-à-vis the Sun
eastern	setting before the Sun

western	setting after the Sun
sect	one of two categories (day or night) to which each planet is assigned and in which it is most effectual, Saturn, Jupiter, and the Sun being day planets, Mars, Venus, and Mercury night
tropic signs	Cancer and Capricorn; sometimes also including equinoctial signs, Aries and Libra
solid signs	Taurus, Leo, Scorpio, Aquarius, following the tropic and equinoctial signs
double-bodied signs	Gemini, Virgo, Sagittarius, Pisces, placed between tropic and solid signs
native	the subject of the birth chart; the person for whom the horoscope is drawn up
nativity	birth chart
katarche	inception: a chart cast to determine the prospects for an undertaking at its outset

Finally, an apotelesma, which is what the Manethoniana are all about, is literally a 'rendering', a 'bringing to completion', the product or effect of a certain configuration of stars. In my own jargon, an 'executive' verb is one which renders the stars' causative effects with a neutral verb of making (ποιεῖ, τεύχει, ῥέζει), while a factitive verb is one whose meaning is more specific (e.g. ὀπάζει, δῶκε(ν), φθείρει, ὀλέκουσιν).

Abbreviations

Astrological

CCAG	*Catalogus Codicum Astrologorum Graecorum*
Lib. Herm.	*Liber Hermetis*
'Par. Anub.'	Paraphrasis Anubionis (Heilen's Paraphrasis Anubionis ⟨et Dorothei⟩), in D. Pingree, *Dorotheus*, pp. 345-67.
Περὶ κέντρ.	Περὶ κέντρων = 'Par. Anub.', pp. 361-7.
Περὶ κράσ.	Περὶ κράσεως καὶ φύσεως τῶν ἀστέρων = Valens, App. I, pp. 369-89 Pingree.
Περὶ σχημ.	Περὶ σχηματισμῶν = 'Par. Anub.', pp. 345-57.
Pingree[1]	Δωροθέου Σιδωνίου τῶν ἑπτὰ ἀστέρων ἐπίθετα, in Marcianus Graecus 313, fo. 30^r (in D. Pingree, *Dorotheus*, p. 435, Appendix III A).
Pingree[2]	Ἐπίθετα ὀνόματα τῶν ζ′ ἀστέρων, in Laurentianus 28.34, fo. 144^v (in D. Pingree, *Dorotheus*, p. 435, Appendix III A 1).
Π.σ.α.	Astrol. Anon. 379, Περὶ συναφῶν καὶ ἀπορροιῶν τῆς Σελήνης πρὸς τοὺς ἀστέρας, ὅσα ἐν τοῖς γενεθλίοις σημαίνει; ed. F. Cumont, *CCAG* viii/1. 181-6.
Π.τ.δ.	Περὶ τοπικῶν διακρίσεων = 'Par. Anub.', pp. 357-61.

Other

BGU	*Aegyptische Urkunden aus den Königlichen (Staatlichen) Museen zu Berlin, Griechische Urkunden*.
BNJ	*Brill's New Jacoby*, general editor Ian Worthington.
B.-P.	C. D. Buck and W. Petersen, *Reverse Index of Greek Nouns and Adjectives* (Chicago, 1945).
CA	*Collectanea Alexandrina*, ed. J. U. Powell (Oxford, 1925).
CAAG	*Collection des anciens alchimistes grecs*, 3 vols., ed. M. Berthelot and C. É. Ruelle (Paris, 1887-8).
CFHB	*Corpus Fontium Historiae Byzantinae*, edd. var. (Berlin, 1967-).
CLE	*Carmina Latina Epigraphica*, ed. F. Buecheler, 2 vols. (Leipzig, 1895-7).
CMG	*Corpus Medicorum Graecorum*, edd. var. (Leipzig *et al.*, 1908-).
DNP	*Der Neue Pauly: Enzyklopädie der Antike*, ed. H. Cancik and H. Schneider, 16 vols. in 19 (Stuttgart, 1996-2003).
D.-S.	C. Daremberg, E. Saglio, and E. Pottier, *Dictionnaire des antiquités grecques et romaines d'après les textes et les monuments*, 5 vols. (Paris, 1877-1919).

DVC	S. Dakaris, J. Vokotopoulou, and A. P. Christidis (eds.), *Τα Χρηστήρια Ἐλάσματα της Δωδώνης των ἀνασκαφών Δ. Εὐαγγελίδη/The Oracular Tablets of Dodona from the Excavations of D. Evangelides*, 2 vols. (Athens, 2013).
EGHP	Early Greek Hexameter Poetry.
FGE	*Further Greek Epigrams: Epigrams before A.D. 50 from the Greek Anthology and Other Sources not Included in 'Hellenistic Epigrams' or 'The Garland of Philip'*, ed. D. L. Page, rev. R. D. Dawe and J. Diggle (Cambridge, 1981).
Garland	*The Greek Anthology: The Garland of Philip, and some Contemporary Epigrams*, ed. A. S. F. Gow and D. L. Page, 2 vols. (Cambridge, 1968).
GVI	*Griechische Vers-Inschriften*, ed. W. Peek, i: *Grab-Epigramme* (Berlin, 1955).
HE	*The Greek Anthology: Hellenistic Epigrams*, ed. A. S. F. Gow and D. L. Page, 2 vols. (Cambridge, 1965).
IGLS	*Inscriptions grecques et latines de Syrie*, edd. var. (Paris, 1929–).
IGR	*Inscriptiones Graecae ad Res Romanas Pertinentes*, ed. R. Cagnat, 3 vols. (Paris, 1906–27).
IGUR	*Inscriptiones Graecae Urbis Romae*, ed. I. Moretti, 4 vols. (Rome, 1968–90).
IK	*Inschriften griechischer Städte aus Kleinasien*, edd. varr. (Bonn, 1972–).
ILAlg	*Inscriptions latines de l'Algérie*, edd. varr. (Paris, 1922–).
K.-B.	R. Kühner, rev. F. Blass, *Ausführliche Grammatik der griechischen Sprache, Erster Teil: Elementar- und Formenlehre*^{3}, 2 vols. (Hanover, 1890–2).
K.-G.	R. Kühner, rev. B. Gerth, *Ausführliche Grammatik der griechischen Sprache, Zweiter Teil: Satzlehre*^{3}, 2 vols. (Hanover, 1898–1904).
Lampe	G. W. H. Lampe (ed.), *A Patristic Greek Lexikon* (Oxford, 1961).
LfgrE	*Lexikon des frühgriechischen Epos*, ed. B. Snell, H. J. Mette, *et al.* (Göttingen, 1955–2010).
LGHP	Late Greek Hexameter Poetry.
LIMC	*Lexicon Iconographicum Mythologiae Classicae*, ed. L. Kahil *et al.* (Zurich, 1981–99).
MAMA	*Monumenta Asiae Minoris Antiqua*, edd. varr., 11 vols. (1928–2013).
OCD[4]	*The Oxford Classical Dictionary*, ed. S. Hornblower, A. Spawforth, and E. Eidinow (Oxford, [4]2012).
OMS	L. Robert, *Opera Minora Selecta: Épigraphie et antiquités grecques*, 7 vols. (Paris, 1969–90).
PDM	*Papyri Demotici Magici*, transl. H. D. Betz, *The Greek Magical Papyri in Translation Including the Demotic Spells* (Chicago, 1986).
PGM	*Papyri Graecae Magicae = Die griechischen Zauberpapyri*, ed. K. Preisendanz and A. Abt, 3 vols. (Leipzig, 1928–41).
PHI	Packard Humanities Institute: https://inscriptions.packhum.org/ and https://latin.packhum.org/
RAC	*Reallexikon für Antike und Christentum*, ed. T. Klauser *et al.* (Stuttgart, 2003–).

RE	*Paulys Real-Encyclopaedie der classischen Altertumswissenschaft*, ed. A. F. von Pauly, rev. G. Wissowa *et al.* (Stuttgart, 1893–1972).
SB	*Sammelbuch Griechischer Urkunden aus Ägypten*, ed. F. Preisigke (Berlin, 1915–).
SEG	*Supplementum Epigraphicum Graecum* (Leiden, 1923–).
SH	*Supplementum Hellenisticum*, ed. H. Lloyd-Jones and P. J. Parsons (Berlin, 1983).
SSH	*Supplementum Supplementi Hellenistici*, ed. H. Lloyd-Jones (Berlin, 2005).
SVF	*Stoicorum Veterum Fragmenta*, ed. H. A. von Arnim and M. Adler, 4 vols. (Leipzig, 1903–24).
TAM	*Tituli Asiae Minoris*, edd. var. (Vienna, 1901–).
TDNT	*Theological Dictionary of the New Testament*, ed. G. W. Bromiley, G. Friedrich, G. Kittel, and R. Pitkin, 10 vols. (Grand Rapids, MI, 1964–74).
TLG	*Thesaurus Linguae Graecae: A Digital Library of Greek Literature* (University of California, Irvine, 2017).
TLL	*Thesaurus Linguae Latinae* (Leipzig, 1900–).
UPZ	*Urkunden der Ptolemäerzeit (ältere Funde)*, ed. U. Wilcken (Berlin, 1927–57, repr. Berlin, 2016).
WBC	Word Biblical Commentary, cited by volume number and editor.

Editions

1. Of ps.-Manetho

ΜΑΝΕΘΩΝΟΣ ΑΠΟΤΕΛΕΣΜΑΤΙΚΩΝ ΒΙΒΛΙΑ ΕΞ/*Manethonis Apotelesmaticorum Libri Sex, nunc primum ex Bibliotheca Medicea editi cura Jacobi Gronovii qui etiam Latine vertit ac notas adjecit* (Lugduni Batavorum apud Fredericum Haaring, 1698).

ΜΑΝΕΘΩΝΟΣ ΑΠΟΤΕΛΕΣΜΑΤΙΚΩΝ ΒΙΒΛΙΑ ΕΞ/*Manethonis Apotelesmaticorum Libri Sex, recognoverunt commentationem de Manethone eiusque carmine brevesque annotationes criticas adiecerunt C. A. Mauritius Axtius et Fr. Antonius Rigler. Additus est Index Verborum locupletissimus* (Coloniae ad Rhenum, Typis et Sumtibus [sic] Joannis Petri Bachemii, 1832).

H. Koechly, *Arati Phaenomena et Prognostica. Pseudo-Manethonis et Maximi Carmina Astrologica, cum fragmentis Dorothei et Anubionis,* in *Poetae Bucolici et Didactici, editore Ambrosio Firmin Didot* (Paris, 1851, reissued 1862).

——*Manethonis Apotelesmaticorum qui feruntur Libri VI. Accedunt Dorothei et Annubionis Fragmenta Astrologica* (Leipzig, 1858).

R. Lopilato, 'The Apotelesmatika of Manetho' (Diss. Brown, 1998).

C. De Stefani, *Ps.-Manethonis Apotelesmatica: Einleitung, Text, Appendices* (Wiesbaden, 2017).

J. L. Lightfoot, *Pseudo-Manetho, Apotelesmatica: Books Two, Three, and Six: Edited with Introduction, Translation, and Commentary* (Oxford, 2020).

2. Of other Astronomical and Astrological Texts

'Antiochus'	Ἀντιόχου ὅσα οἱ ἀστέρες ἐν τοῖς τόποις τοῦ θέματος τυχόντες σημαίνουσιν, ed. A. Pérez Jiménez, 'Antiochi *De stellarum in locis thematis significationibus fragmentum epicum*: Edición, traducción española y comentario', *MHNH* 14 (2014), 217–89 [previously A. Olivieri, *CCAG* i (Brussels, 1898), 108–13].
Anubion	P. Schubert, *Anoubion: Poème astrologique: Témoignages et fragments* (Paris, 2015).
Apomasar	D. Pingree, *Albumasaris De revolutionibus nativitatum* (Leipzig, 1968). Cited by page and line-number.
De astrologia dialogus	W. Kroll and P. Viereck, *Anonymi christiani Hermippus De astrologia dialogus* (Leipzig, 1895), 1–71.
Dodecatopos	Ἀποτελέσματα τοῦ πίνακος τῆς ⟨δωδεκατόπου⟩, ed. F. Cumont, *CCAG* viii/4 (Brussels, 1921), 126–75 (within Θ below).
Dorotheus	D. Pingree, *Dorothei Sidonii Carmen Astrologicum: Interpretationem Arabicam in linguam Anglicam versam una cum Dorothei fragmentis et Graecis et Latinis* (Leipzig, 1976).

Firmicus	W. Kroll and F. Skutsch, *Julii Firmici Materni Matheseos Libri VIII*, 2 vols. (Leipzig, 1897–1913). Cited by book, chapter, and section-number.
'Heliodorus'	A. Boer, *Heliodori, ut dicitur, in Paulum Alexandrinum Commentarium* (Leipzig, 1962). Cited by page and line-number.
Hephaestion	D. Pingree, *Hephaestio Thebanus Apotelesmatica*, 2 vols. (Leipzig, 1973–4). Cited by volume and page-number.
Liber Hermetis	Simonetta Feraboli, *Hermes Trismegistus: De triginta sex decanis* (Corpus Christianorum, Continuatio Mediaevalis, 144) (Turnhout: Brepols, 1994). Cited by chapter and section-number.
Maximus	N. Zito, *Maxime, Des Initiatives* (Paris, 2016).
Nechepso–Petosiris	E. Riess, 'Nechepsonis et Petosiridis fragmenta magica', *Philologus Supplement* 6 (1892), 325–94.
Paul of Alexandria	A. Boer, *Pauli Alexandrini Elementa Apotelesmatica* (Teubner, 1958). Cited by page and line number.
Ptolemy	J. L. Heiberg (ed.), *Syntaxis Mathematica*, 2 vols. (Leipzig, 1898–1903).
	W. Hübner, *Claudii Ptolemaei Opera Quae Extant Omnia*, iii/1, *ΑΠΟΤΕΛΕΣΜΑΤΙΚΑ* (Teubner, 1998).
Teucer, I	ed. Boll 1903, 16–21, from codd. TR (cited by page and line).
Teucer, II	PL cited from W. Hübner, *Grade und Gradbezirke der Tierkreiszeichen: Der anonyme Traktat De stellis fixis, in quibus gradibus oriuntur signorum: Quellenkritische Edition mit Kommentar* (Stuttgart and Leipzig, 1995), i. 109–27.
	V cited from Boll 1903, 41–52 (by page and line).
Θ	Ἐκ τῶν Ἀντιόχου θησαυρῶν ἐπίλυσις καὶ διήγησις πάσης ἀστρονομικῆς τέχνης, ed. F. Cumont, 'Excerpta ex codice 82 (Paris. 2425)', *CCAG* viii/4 (Brussels, 1921), 115–225.
Valens	D. Pingree, *Vettii Valentis Antiocheni Anthologiarum Libri Novem* (Leipzig, 1986). Cited by chapter and section number.
'Valens'	F. Cumont, 'Vettii Valentis fragmentum novum: Τοῦ σοφωτάτου Οὐάλεντος περὶ τὰς ἐπεμβάσεις τῶν ἀστέρων κατὰ θεματίου καὶ γενεθλίου', *CCAG* viii/1 (Brussels, 1929), 161–71.

3. Other Editions

Achmet	F. Drexl, *Achmetis Oneirocriticon* (Leipzig, 1925).
John of Gaza, Ἔκφρασις τοῦ κοσμικοῦ πίνακος	D. Lauritzen, *Jean de Gaza: Description du tableau cosmique* (Paris, 2015).
Sortes Sangallenses	A. Dold and R. Meister, 'Die Orakelsprüche im St. Galler Palimpsestcodex 908 (Die sogennanten "Sortes Sangallenses")', *Sitzungsberichte der Österreichischen Akademie der Wissenschaften, phil.-hist. Klasse*, 224: 4 (Vienna, 1948).

Part One

The World of Astrology (Revisited)

In all social systems there must be a class to do the mean duties, to perform the drudgery of life. That is, a class requiring but a low order of intellect and but little skill. Its requisites are vigor, docility, fidelity. Such a class you must have, or you would not have that other class which leads progress, refinement, and civilization.

James Henry Hammond, *Congressional Globe*, 35th Congress, 1st Session, 4 March 1858, 962

1

Viewpoint

This volume is an edition of the later books of the Manethoniana (4, 1, 5). These books are enormously detailed and rich, still more so, in my view, than the first three. But one will not get lost in the detail. This first part tries to draw out some of the biggest implications, not just of these books, but of astrology in general. The rather fundamental question is one that was not directly asked in vol. 1. Is astrology focalised? Is it meaningful to ask through whose eyes its mass of detail is seen?

All the Manethoniana turn out to draw on basically similar material; the grounds for thinking this are laid out more fully in Part II. This shared underlay transmits to all the authors who continue to reflect certain core preoccupations, especially about work ($\tau\acute{\epsilon}\chi\nu\alpha\iota$) and generally about how activity ($\pi\rho\hat{\alpha}\xi\iota\varsigma$) is essential to identity. Much of this material in turn proves to have parallels in (i) Ptolemy's *Apotelesmatica* and (ii) a prose summary of another text (Θ) which runs very closely parallel to the Manethoniana and essentially bears witness to even more forms in which this material circulated. And it is from these corpora of closely related material, which circulated in prose and poetry, that the enquiry takes its beginning. This enquiry concerns astrology's social, economic, intellectual, and cultural horizons, its values, the appropriateness of interrogating it for class attitudes, and indeed about how one reads astrology in order to make these kinds of inference possible in the first place.

Astrology covers the whole social spectrum. Anyone who wanted to know what awaited them in old age, how and when they would die (or even more importantly when their parent or childless rich uncle would), whether their son would be rich, what their daughter's marriage prospects were, had an interest in it—in other words everyone. If there was any *a priori* idea that 'superstition' or debased forms of religion would be the preserve of an underclass,[1] astrology certainly gives the lie to that. As an imaginative exercise, think your way into the ancient city—the people who walked in the streets and stoas, drank from the fountains, oiled themselves in the gymnasia with oil supplied by benefactors (or themselves supplied the oil), bought and sold in the shops, and attended

---

[1] Kudlien 1991, 20–1.

the theatre are all to be imagined among its potential consumers. It was not the preserve of any one class.

At the same time our astrological texts—the Manethoniana, Ptolemy, as well as Firmicus, author of the Latin *Mathesis*, which will be important in this part and throughout—*represent* all these people. It is an *imaginary* of a population. It portrays well-known types. To return to the ancient city, a walk through the stoa will reveal 'priests and magistrates, benefactors and sporting champions, star-performers and Roman officials, precocious youths as well as virtuous women'[2]—another image-repertory, of the culturally valued. We meet them all again in astrology. Putting it the other way round, every one of the bigwigs in 1.100–5—the donor of oil to the *palaestra*, the high priest, ἀγορανόμος, general, consul, judge, sponsor of public buildings—is a statue in the stoa, gymnasium, odeion, *bouleuterion*.[3] But astrological texts represent the fishmongers and vegetable-sellers as well, and especially they represent the merchants and manufacturers and retailers whose shops clustered in the commercial districts of towns and cities, the textile merchants and jewellers and to some extent the carpenters and potters, and the funerary professionals who at some point would come to sweep it all away. The statue of the asiarch Marcus Fulvius Publicianus Nicephoros of Ephesus, who held many civic offices and adorned his city with many splendid public-spirited works, was erected by the clothes-sellers of the agora (εἱματιοπῶλαι οἱ ἐν τῇ ἀγορᾷ πραγματ[ευ]όμενοι).[4] Astrology admits them, as well as the beggar who was beneath the attention of both.

I chose statues as a context or offset for astrology in order to reinforce the notion that these textual and sculptural populations were both the real inhabitants of cities and also the product of image-making and trope. In what follows the job of contextualising astrology will shift more to literary texts, which will extend the image-repertoire beyond the great and the good and the celebrities to those who made their livings from intellectual and artisanal skill, commercial nous, and physical labour, and further still to a rogues' gallery of pirates and prostitutes and pimps. Statues and literary texts alike have a kind of genericity and replicability, topoi for intelligibility.[5] The official commemorated in the agora was a sort of distillation of officialdom fashioned for general consumption. But much the same can be said for literary tropes as for the 'public

---

[2] Van Nijf 2015, 233.
[3] Van Nijf 2000, 27–32: a good impression of the honorific landscape of one particular city (Termessos in Pisidia), with the places where particular kinds of honorific inscription were clustered.
[4] *IEph* 3063 (AD 222–35); compare ll. 8–10 πολλοῖς καὶ μεγάλοις ἔργοις κοσμήσαντα τὴν πατρίδα with 1.105.
[5] 'Intelligibility' comes from Ma, 332.

semiology'[6] of statues; not only socially valued persons but also murderers and bandits and autocastrates, as well as acrobats and mimes and disreputable performers, have image-repertoires of their own. No less than statuary, astrology uses a 'social language',[7] generated by a culture of honour and shame, which affirms communal values by promoting types for approbation or its opposite. One question, however, might be whether there is anything distinctive about astrology's particular selection of tropes. Can anything be inferred about clientele? Do astrological texts reflect fears, hopes, expectations—and whose? Given that it presents such a strong temptation to talk about averageness and middlingness, can astrology contribute anything new to the extraordinarily conceptually difficult question of class in ancient society?

These are understudied questions. The representation of prestige, (dis-) advantage, power and disempowerment in divinatory texts is almost completely underresearched, but could be a very fruitful topic, given astrology's ultra-sensitivity to hierarchy and status. A still fairly recent volume on power—specifically Roman power—is entirely typical: one draws a complete blank here for anything involving popular literature and subliterary texts.[8] Attention in this first part extends far beyond that—to the representation of the whole social hierarchy, perceptions of social value, the obsessive attention to social standing, all of which keep coming back to the question whether astrology just represents a kind of Chaucerian richness or is tilted towards the perspective of a particular class and implies attitudes that differ from those in privileged literary sources. There are sections on mass and élite, work and occupations, the poor, and slaves, and, at the head of these, on the values of the consultants. The ultimate aim will be, not so much to ask whether there is any evidence for a value system other than that of the élites, or whether the hegemons have imposed their values on their subalterns, or whatever, but whether such questions are even meaningful in the first place, or whether astrology's universe would be better off conceptualised in different terms. (Yes, I will ultimately suggest: it would.)

Comparisons are important in what follows, especially with oneiromancy, which constitutes our second largest literary corpus of ancient divinatory texts after astrology. 'Oneiromancy' means Artemidorus, whose five-book *Oneirocritica* Peter Thonemann has recently dated to the years between about 180–210,[9] and Achmet, who now needs to be properly introduced. These

---

[6] Ma, 332.   [7] Ma, 337.
[8] P. Erdkamp, O. Hekster, G. de Kleijn, S. T. A. M. Mols, and L. de Blois (eds.), *The Representation and Perception of Roman Imperial Power: Proceedings of the Third Workshop of the International Network Impact of Empire (Roman Empire, c. 200 B.C.–A.D. 476), Rome, March 20-23, 2002* (Leiden, 2003). The review by David Potter (*JRS* 96 (2006), 226-7) notes the absence of the Sibylline Oracles as witnesses to the 'provincial reaction to the imperial message'.
[9] Thonemann 2020, 9–11.

authors are especially important for this enquiry because their shared method of targeting dream interpretations at a clientele defined by class and occupation makes them an important comparison for an enquiry into social status and perspective. Achmet is credited with a Greek *Oneirokritikon* datable to the late ninth or tenth century, of undeterminable provenance. This latter is, in its present form, despite its attribution to the seventh-century Muslim scholar Mohammed Ibn Sîrîn, Christian. Purporting to cite Indian, Persian, and Egyptian sources, in practice it is a compilation of earlier, Arabic, material on dream symbols. There are similarities with Artemidorus in method (the use of analogies and word-play), in particular dream symbols, and especially in their social and economic segregation of dreamers, but the current view of the matter is that this is not because Artemidorus is among the compiler's direct sources. Or at least, he did not use the Greek original. But he will have shared in the general influence on Islamic dream interpretation exerted by the Arabic translation.[10]

---

[10] This information is drawn from Mavroudi. See also A.-M. Bernardi, 'L'Oneirocriticon d'Achmet et la christianisation de la tradition grecque d'interprétation des rêves', *Kentron*, 27 (2011), 81–98; S. Buzzi, 'Byzantine Society and Gender Mirrored in Dreams: Achmet's *Oneirocriticon*', *Semitica et Classica*, 11 (2018), 155–66. The edition I cite is that of Drexl, although Mavroudi pronounces it inadequate. It is that used on the TLG.

2

Character of the Value System

This section sets the context by sketching astrology's communitarian value-system. It continues to urge that astrology can be contextualised with other evidence for communal life in the ancient city, by pointing to topoi shared with inscriptions (this is what everybody thought). But it also shows ways in which astrology is idiosyncratic, by turning this communitarian value-system inward and focusing it on the individual (this is what I, the individual subject, have internalised).

The argument is that the value system is mediated in two ways: (i) exemplarily, by giving instances of those held worthy of approval or disapproval, thereby inviting the reader to participate in this collective judgement (I register it, and stand shoulder to shoulder with those who feel this way) and (ii) emotively (by inducing a strong response, whether revulsion, pity, perhaps fear, or conversely warm approval). Both are in service of an ethical system which was discussed in the first volume and needs no repeating here, one based on social cohesion, friendship (φιλία), and trust (πίστις). Astrology portrays a world of individuals shorn of the horizontal connections between them. But that does not stop it espousing the same values that lubricated cooperative life that emerge, for instance, from associational inscriptions, and stigmatising disruptiveness, isolationism, and uncooperativeness.

To begin with honour and shame. Both have wide vocabularies, especially associated with being seen and being heard: astrology represents ancient morality's public-facing character in a particularly concentrated form. Honour,[1] for instance, is associated with derivatives of βοάω,[2] φήμη,[3] κλέος,[4] with derivatives of φαίνω,[5]

---

[1] δόξα (with its derivatives ἔνδοξος, ἐπίδοξος), τιμή, ἀξίωμα; associated words include ἔπαινος; σέβας, σεβάσμιος. Men themselves are never τίμιοι, though crafts are in 'Heliodorus', p. 84.15–16.

[2] ἐπιβόητος/περιβόητος (which can be in either sense, good or bad, unlike περιβοησία); Περὶ κράσ. 139 σεβασμίους καὶ τῇ πόλει περιβοήτους.

[3] εὐφημία (Hephaestion, i. 209.16–17...καὶ σύστασιν πρὸς ὑπερέχοντα πρόσωπα καὶ εὐφημίας ὀχλικάς); εὐφημεῖσθαι (Apomasar, De Rev. p. 61.24–5 καὶ φημήσει τοῦτον ὁ κοινὸς λαὸς τοῖς ἐπαίνοις).

[4] εὐκλεής (incl. 11× in Mᵃ books 2 and 3; Περὶ κράσ. 115 εὔφημον καὶ εὐκλεές, reflecting Dorotheus' hexameter diction?; 3.353 ἀγακληεῖς τ' ἐνὶ λαοῖς). From ὄνομα: ὀνομάζεσθαι, ὀνομαστούς, περιωνύμους (Paul, p. 67.3).

[5] ἐμφανής; εὐφαντασίωτος (Valens, I 19.25; I 20.24 εὐφαντασιώτους μὲν καὶ ἐπιδόξους; V 1.20 εὐφαντασίωτον καὶ ἐπίδοξον; Θ p. 209.4–5 εὐκλεεῖς καὶ εὐθύμους καὶ εὐφαντασιώτους τὰς πράξεις ποιεῖ; LSJ wrongly renders 'gifted with a vivid imagination'); φανέρωσις.

and with other words for sound[6] and visibility,[7] while shame[8] likewise has its own words for exposure[9] and audible outrage.[10] Some of this vocabulary is special, or almost so, to astrology,[11] and many passages hammer home the message through sheer accumulation of semantically related words.[12] The platitudes of astrology's narrative voice serve as a proxy for collective opinion, and poetic astrology turns up the volume because it has the extra resources of emotive language to draw on.

Honour is one of the greatest goods. As we saw in the first volume, the earliest Manethonian poet formulaically associates it with wealth (the wealth–renown nexus), and it is just an extension of that to say that throughout astrology in general honour is strongly correlated with words indicating accomplishment and success ($προκοπή$, $ἐπίτευξις$, $ἄνυσις$),[13] derivatives of $πρᾶξις$ and $πράσσειν$,[14] gain,[15] or some combination thereof.[16] That does not make it a zero-sum hostile encounter with an opponent, but it does treat the honourable individual as the one who stands out from, is ahead of, the rest.

---

[6] εὐ-/πολυθρύλλητος.
[7] θηητός (2.224 θηητοὺς λαοῖσι); λαμπρός; περίβλεπτος.
[8] διαβολή/διαβάλλεσθαι; ἔγκλησις/ἔγκλημα; κατηγορία/κατηγορεῖσθαι; κακολογεῖσθαι; μέμψις; (ἐπί)ψογος.
[9] δειγματισμός (Achmet, Oneir. 12.52 ἐὰν δὲ γύναιον τοῦτο ἴδῃ, θέατρον αἰσχύνης ἔσται παντὶ τῷ λαῷ).
[10] κραυγαί; περιβοησία/περιβόησις (Valens, IV 23.9 εὐθρυλλήτους περιβοήσεις); 4.592 αἰσχεόφημοι.
[11] Of 22 literary instances of δειγματισμός, all but three are in astrological writers (mostly Valens); περιβοησία and περιβόησις are strictly confined to astrological writers (above all Valens, to a lesser extent Ptolemy) and Artemidorus (eight instances of -ία, another two of -ις).
[12] 3.337–8 αἶσχρ' ἔτλησαν ... φήμη δὲ κακὴ περιδέδρομεν αἰεί; 5.322–3 ἐπ' ἔργοις | ἐκ στομάτων αἰσχροῖς διαβαλλομένη κακοφήμως; Valens, I 20.8 ψόγοις ἐπαίσχροις ... περιτρέπονται, καὶ περιβοησίας καὶ δειγματισμοὺς ἀναδέχονται; App. X 8 τινὲς δὲ ... ἐπαίσχροις τισὶ πράγμασι καὶ ἐπιψόγοις περιτραπέντες ... περιβοησίας ἢ δειγματισμοὺς ἀναδέχονται; App. X 15 ψόγους, δειγματισμούς, ἀθεμίτους πράξεις. Valens often combines stigma words (διαβάλλεσθαι, περιβοησία) with ὄχλος, ὀχλικός, underscoring the public nature of the condemnation (e.g. II 17.66 καὶ γὰρ αἰσχροποιοῦσι καὶ διαβάλλονται ὑπὸ ὄχλων).
[13] Περὶ κράσ. 112 προκοπῆς καὶ κτήσεως αἴτιος καὶ τιμῶν πολιτικῶν καὶ ἡγεμονίας λαοῦ καὶ συνεχῶν ἐπιτεύξεων ~ Περὶ σχημ. 10 δράστας, παρ' ἡγεμόσι τιμωμένους; Περὶ σχημ. 103 προκοπτικούς, εὐκτήμονας, τιμωμένους ἐν πόλεσιν, ἡγεμόνας, ἐπιτευκτικούς; Περὶ κράσ. 192 προκοπὰς καὶ τιμάς; Valens, IV 21.3 ἀρχάς τε καὶ προκοπάς, καὶ τιμῶν καὶ στεμμάτων καταξιοῖ; Ptol. 4.8.4 προκοπαὶ καὶ δωρεαὶ καὶ τιμαί; Hephaestion, i. 224.28 δόξαν καὶ κέρδη καὶ ἐπίτευξιν; CCAG iii. 37.27–8 τὰ γεννώμενα ... εἰς τιμὴν καλὴν προκόπτοντα ἔσονται; Hephaestion, i. 159.20–1 τὸ γὰρ δοξαστικὸν ... καὶ ἀνυστικόν.
[14] Περὶ κράσ. 139 ἐμπράκτους καὶ σεβασμίους καὶ τῇ πόλει περιβοήτους, ὑπὸ πολλῶν τιμωμένους; Additamenta Antiqua, IV 24 πρακτικός, δοξαστικός; Apomasar, De Rev. p. 65.1–4 προστεθήσεται ἡ δόξα αὐτοῦ καὶ ἡ ἀξία καὶ ἐπικτήσεται παρὰ ἀνθρώπων εὐφημίαν καὶ ἔπαινον καὶ οἱῳδήποτε ἐπιχειρήσει ἔργῳ ἢ οἱᾳδήποτε πράξει, τελειωθήσεται; 'Heliodorus', p. 71.4–5 τὸν περὶ πράξεως καὶ δόξης καὶ συστάσεως καὶ ἀξιώματος καὶ προεδρίας ...
[15] Hephaestion, i. 219.15 ἐπικε‹ρδὴς καὶ δοξαστικὸς›.
[16] Hephaestion, i. 203.14–15 δόξας ... καὶ κέρδη καὶ προκοπὰς καὶ πράξεις; i. 209.14–17 ἔμπρακτος εἰς πάντα καὶ ἐπικερδὴς καὶ δοξαστικὸς καθέστηκεν (ποιεῖ γὰρ προκοπὰς ...); i. 224.13–14 κέρδη καὶ δόξας δὲ καὶ ἱλαρίας καὶ πράξεις.

Character of the Value System

Honour tends to be treated as something self-evident. Unlike in inscriptions, where there is a contract-clause to spell out what deserved the honour, astrological honour simply parades its manifestations. Yet the thoroughly conventional way in which it is conceived is brought home by various overlaps with these same honorific inscriptions. This does not mean that astrology is usually echoing inscriptional formulations (though sometimes the Manethoniana do that), only that it is conceived in the same way and is associated with the same visible rewards, which include δωρεαί,[17] εἰκόνες and ἀνδριάντες,[18] στέφανοι,[19] προεδρία,[20] and even ἰσόθεοι τιμαί.[21]

Gifts have to be given by a giver, which is sometimes explicitly the city.[22] And insofar as astrology echoes this whole repertoire of communitarian tropes, it shares in their generic and reproducible character—like that of the portrait statues that the inscriptions once accompanied, and, like them, allowing for little dabs of individuation. This is the ancient city's stock repertoire of public virtue. There are even some passages in the later books of the Manethoniana that echo inscriptional formulae for the great and the good still more closely, and insofar as they do giving the honour some rare content: 4.514 πάτρης κηδέστορες ἰθυδίκαιοι; 1.105 κοσμητῆρας ἑῆς...πόληος; 5.308 σιτοδόται, κτίσται,[23] μὴ φειδόμενοι φιλοτίμως; 1.102 εὐδόξως (of an ἀγορανόμος); see too a reference to acclamations in 5.296.

At the same time, there are also some important differences between the astrology's given, self-evident honours and the hard-won, intently scrutinised

---

[17] e.g. Ptol. 4.3.6 ἐπὶ χάρισι καὶ δωρεαῖς καὶ τιμαῖς, etc.

[18] Valens, I 1.1 ἔνδοξα πρόσωπα, τιμὰς εἰκόνων, ἀνδριάντων, στεμμάτων, ἀρχιερατείας πατρίδος; I 2.16 ἀρχιερεῖς, γυμνασίαρχοι, στεμμάτων καὶ πορφύρας καταξιούμενοι, εἰκόνων τε καὶ ἀνδριάντων; I 19.13 ἀρχιερωσύνας, προστασίας ὄχλων, στεμματηφορίας, χρυσοφορίας, ἀνδριάντων καὶ εἰκόνων καταξιουμένους; I 20.21 τινὰς μὲν οὖν ἀθλητικούς, στεφανηφόρους, τιμῶν, εἰκόνων, ἀνδριάντων καταξιουμένους; Περὶ κράσ. 119 τῆς ἐν εἰκόσι τιμῆς, 184 εἰκόνων, ἀνδριάντων, στεμμάτων, ἀρχιεραρχίας, πατρίδος; Hephaestion, i. 27.18 εἰκόνων καὶ ἀνδριάντων ἀξιωθήσεται.

[19] 5.294–5 τιμῶνται...αὐχοῦσιν στεφάνοις; Ptol. 4.4.4 ἀθλητάς, στεφανηφόρους, τιμῶν καταξιουμένους; Valens, I 3.42 ἔνδοξοι, νικητικαί, στεφανηφόροι, τιμωμένων ἀνδρῶν ἐν ὄχλοις καὶ παρ' ἡγεμόσιν.

[20] There are fourteen mentions of this in astrology and one of προέδρους (Θ p. 154.14). προεδρία is usually combined in the same sentence with δόξα, though it is unclear whether it is ever the literal grant of the right to sit in the front seats (perhaps, if it all, Θ p. 174.13–14 ἐπὶ προεδρίαις τεταγμένους), rather than prominence more generally (e.g. Περὶ κράσ. 146 ἐπὶ προεδρίας λαοῦ τεταγμένος).

[21] Hephaestion, ii. 157.2 ἰσοθέοις τιμαῖς τιμηθήσεται.

[22] Περὶ σχημ. 103 τιμωμένους ἐν πόλεσιν; Περὶ κράσ. 139 τῇ πόλει περιβοήτους, ὑπὸ πολλῶν τιμωμένους; Θ pp. 167.4–5 τιμωμένους ἐν πόλεσι καὶ μεγάλους ὀνομαζομένους, 169.1 ἀπὸ πόλεων τιμωμένους.

[23] The title κτίστης was generally conferred by a decree of the *boule* (or of a provincial *koinon*), as noted by Erkelenz, 69–70. It is not unknown for the titles to be used on private monuments, but in those cases the question remains open whether a civic or provincial decree nevertheless underlies it.

honours of the ancient city. These are not necessarily differences in the value system itself, but differences in the way that it is articulated or realised. For the whole transactional side of the commemoration has gone. Recent scholarship has shifted the focus from the rhetoric of élites and notables and their self-image towards the transactions that took place between these people and their communities. It emphasises the city's role: the polis' decree of the honours in the first place, the negotiation between city and honorand and/or his or her family, the role of the decree in motivating desired behaviour from the honor-and and, explicitly in the hortatory clause, from others in the future.[24] Astrology is having none of this.

In the first place, astrological honours are not necessarily conferred by the city any more. It is characteristic of astrology to adopt a hierarchical as well as/instead of a communitarian outlook, which will become still clearer in the next section. The result is that the honours are *also* conferred by 'big men'[25] or by alternative 'populace' words, including, disconcertingly, ὄχλος[26]—at which point one has to wonder whether to attribute this to casual variation, or whether there can be any carry-over of the negative connotations of this word (explored in the next section). If there were, it would imply that the narrative voice were somehow *dissociating* itself from the givers of the honours, quite unlike inscriptional parlance.

In the second, astrology has its own rhetoric, which is not normative (behave like this, it is expected of you) or agonistic (you are encouraged to enter into a competition for merit) but presumptive (here is a template into which it is presumed that an individual of a given type will fit). So the focus is on individual personalities even more squarely than it was before the 'transactional turn' in recent scholarship. Love of honour has become a descriptor of character. Astrological language represents the degree to which it had been internalised: these individuals want what they are supposed to want (whether the ruling power goes under the name of the *polis* or whoever the overlords are supposed to be). The texts present these honours as *eo ipso* desirable, and presumably astrology's clientele agreed. So there is an apparent convergence between

---

[24] e.g. J. Ma, 'Public Speech and Community in the *Euboicus*', in S. Swain (ed.), *Dio Chrysostom: Politics, Philosophy, and Letters* (Oxford, 2000), 108–24, at 121–2; id. 332; van Nijf 2000, 2013.

[25] Περὶ σχημ. 1 ὑπὸ μεγάλων ἀνδρῶν τιμωμένους; CCAG xii. 131.23–4 τιμώμενος παρὰ βασιλέως καὶ μεγιστάνων.

[26] Περὶ κέντρ. 79 δοξάζει ἐν ὄχλοις; Valens, I 3.42 τιμωμένων ἐν ὄχλοις καὶ παρ' ἡγεμόσιν; I 19.10 ὑπὸ ὄχλων τιμωμένους; II 17.7 ὁ γεννώμενος ἐν ταῖς μεγαλειότησι καὶ δόξαις ὄχλων γενήσεται; Hephaestion, i. 12.4 δοξασθήσεται ὑπὸ ὄχλων, 214.25 ἐξ ὄχλου δόξας πολιτικὰς; Θ pp. 153.19–20 ἐνδόξους τε ⟨καὶ⟩ ὑπὸ ὄχλων ⟨τιμωμένους⟩ καὶ γνωστοὺς ἄρχουσιν, 168.7–8 ὑπὸ ὄχλων τιμωμένους; Critodemus, CCAG viii/1. 257.24 ἐν ὄχλοις εὐδοξοῦσιν. Other: Achmet, *Oneir.* 11.29 τιμώμενος ὑπὸ λαοῦ; Valens, II 26.12 τιμηθέντες ὑπὸ πολλῶν; Apomasar, *De Myst.*, CCAG xi/1. 184.10–11 παρὰ πάντων τιμωμένους; CCAG x. 171.7 ὑπὸ πάντων τιμώμενος.

honorific public language and personal ambition, between communitarian values and private desire. Indeed, with the native's behaviour predetermined instead of volitional, there is no scope for negotiation. From the Manethoniana, 1.102 is a nice example. It is the planet that crowns a benefactor εὐδόξως; there is nothing anyone else can do about it.

But making it a personal characteristic diminishes the role of any third party. The citizenry are just a blurred background against which the native stands out, and in 5.296 μαρτυρίαις δόξῃσί τ' ἀγαλλόμενοι κελαδοῦνται they are not even that. The passive construction completely elides the makers of the acclamations. Shortly after that passage comes a reference to an individual who acts φιλοτίμως (5.309), but the quality of φιλοτιμία[27] has now become an idiosyncrasy; the individual acts unilaterally, and the quality that would have launched inscriptional tributes now, instead, redounds to personal liability and financial loss, as the language pivots from that of euergetism to formulations suggestive of the individual vice of profligacy. Astrology's relatively few other instances of φιλοτιμία confirm this pattern of depoliticisation and personalisation.[28] Inscriptions praise the honorand for φιλοτιμία εἰς, περί, πρός, or ὑπέρ,[29] in other words the quality is relational. But in astrology it exists in and of itself, having no relationship to a third party, and in one passage in Ptolemy is even aligned with a set of distinctly *un*-cooperative characteristics. Unyielding, relentless, unforgiving, disputatious, and grasping, these are hardly the epigraphic heroes of selfless public service.[30]

The final point is the utter banality to which fame and glory have been reduced. Their association with efficacy and success (p. 8) already entrains a connection with material wealth, with the possession of estates and slaves; the wealth–renown nexus that was so well documented in M[a] is simply a banality of the astrological world-view. It brings on further associations with a happy family

---

[27] Van Nijf 2013, 359; J. Miller, 'Euergetism, Agonism, and Democracy: The Hortatory Intention in Late Classical and Early Hellenistic Athenian Honorific Decrees', *Hesperia*, 85/2 (2016), 385–435, at 397–9, 414–15.

[28] Note especially Ptol. 3.14.3 [qualities of hard signs] βεβαίας, συνετάς, ὑπομονητικάς, φιλοπόνους, σκληράς, ἐγκρατεῖς, μνησικάκους, ἐκβιβαστικάς, ἐριστικάς, φιλοτίμους, στασιώδεις, πλεονεκτικάς, ἀποκρότους, ἀμεταθέτους, 3.14.22 [combination of Jupiter and Mars] μεγαλοψύχους δὲ καὶ φιλοτίμους καὶ θυμικοὺς καὶ κριτικοὺς καὶ ἐπιτευκτικούς; Astrol. Anon. 379, CCAG v/1. 200.9–10 [certain bright stars in ASC and MC] πλουσίους, μεγαλοψύχους καὶ φιλοτίμους, with parallel versions in 222.3 and Θ p. 177.20.

[29] For the preposition, see Miller (n. 27), 398.

[30] Inadvertently, by omitting the preposition and hence the relational aspect of φιλοτιμία, astrology reverts to the state of affairs analysed by Thucydides (2.65.7; cf. Miller, art. cit. 398, and Hornblower ad loc.) where unbridled and self-indulgent ambition was a disruptive quality. Moreover, the εὔνοια that is so often combined with φιλοτιμία in inscriptions disappears in astrology as a public quality altogether; it appears, if at all, among family relationships.

life (a happy marriage, εὐτεκνία) as well as a well-lubricated social network. All this is really so trite as to be barely worth documenting. Ptolemy, eccentric in many ways, is not eccentric in this. His description of the powers of Venus (very similar to those of Jupiter, with a dash more warmth and charm thrown in) can represent this whole nexus:

2.9.14 δόξας καὶ τιμὰς καὶ εὐφροσύνας καὶ εὐετηρίας εὐγαμίας τε καὶ πολυτεκνίας καὶ εὐαρεστήσεις πρὸς πᾶσαν συναρμογὴν καὶ τῶν κτήσεων συναυξήσεις καὶ διαίτας καθαρίους καὶ εὐαγώγους καὶ πρὸς τὰ σεβάσμια τιμητικάς, ἔτι δὲ σωματικὰς εὐεξίας καὶ πρὸς τοὺς ἡγεμονεύοντας συνοικειώσεις καὶ τῶν ἀρχόντων ἐπαφροδισίας.[31]

'fame, honour, happiness, abundance, happy marriage, many children, satisfaction in every mutual relationship, the increase of prosperity, a neat and well conducted manner of life, paying honour to those things which are to be revered; further, she is the cause of bodily health, alliances with the leaders, and elegance of rulers' (transl. Robbins).

To turn from honour to shame. Shame is not only the counterpart of honour; it has been seen as the main driver in the enforcement of social norms.[32] Which of the two is the more important in astrology might not seem like a very meaningful question. After all, how would one go about answering it? Yet it is perhaps possible to argue that astrology has a view of shame that is both deeper and more differentiated than its view of honour, that its effects are wider-reaching, that it gives us perhaps better insights into the social constraints on behaviour at least as astrology imagines them. Honour and shame complement one another, but they are also asymmetrical in various ways. Because so little is left of the conventional public basis for honour, what remains looks solipsistic, narcissistic, desirable, but not necessarily with a very firm grounding. Shame

---

[31] Creature comforts: Ptol. 2.9.9 δόξας ἀποτελεῖ καὶ εὐετηρίας καὶ εὐθηνίας καὶ καταστάσεις εἰρηνικὰς καὶ τῶν ἐπιτηδείων αὐξήσεις εὐεξίας τε σωματικὰς καὶ ψυχικάς, ἔτι δὲ εὐεργεσίας καὶ δωρεὰς ἀπὸ τῶν βασιλευόντων αὐτῶν τε ἐκείνων αὐξήσεις καὶ μεγαλειότητας καὶ μεγαλοψυχίας καθόλου τε εὐδαιμονίας ἐστὶν αἴτιος. Any TLG search for e.g. -δοξ-/-πλου- or -δοξ-/-κτημ- shows how trite all this really is. Children: Dorotheus, p. 382.4 πράξεις καὶ δόξαν καὶ τέκνα; Valens, I 19.13 τέκνων γονάς; V 6.20 τέκνων γονὰς καὶ εἰκόνας προλείψαντες, περιόντες μὲν δοξάζονται, θανόντες δὲ αἰωνίας φήμης καταξιοῦνται; V 6.58 δόξας, κληρονομίας, περικτήσεις, παιδοποιίας, προκοπάς, συστάσεις μειζόνων; Περὶ κέντρ. 30 ἐμφανείας καὶ δόξης αἴτιος καὶ εὐτεκνίας; Περὶ κράσ. 119 ὁ δὲ τοῦ Διὸς καὶ τῆς Ἀφροδίτης δόξης περιποιητικοὶ καὶ ἐπικτήσεων καὶ δωρεῶν καὶ κόσμου σωματικοῦ, τέκνων τε γονῆς καὶ ἀρχιερωσύνης καὶ στεμματοφορίας, ὄχλων προστασίας, τῆς ἐν εἰκόσι τιμῆς; Valens, V 6.58 δόξας, κληρονομίας, περικτήσεις, παιδοποιίας, προκοπάς, συστάσεις μειζόνων; Antiochus, CCAG xi/2. 109.13–15 μεγαλοπρεπείας καὶ δόξης, σεμνότητος, ἀπολαύσεώς τε καὶ εὐτροφίας, ἀρχῆς τε καὶ τιμῆς, εὐτεκνίας τε καὶ τῆς παρ' ἡγεμόσι καὶ ὄχλοις ἀποδοχῆς. Wives: 5.294; Hephaestion, i. 27.18–19 ὑπὸ γυναικὸς εὐνοηθήσεται. Both: Περὶ σχημ. 11 πλουσίους, ἐνδόξους, ἀρχικοὺς ποιεῖ, καὶ τέκνων ἐστὶ δοτὴρ καὶ εὐγαμίας αἴτιος, καὶ βίον ἐπίσημον παρέχει.

[32] Elster, 140 '…social norms in general operate through the emotions of shame and contempt'; 145 'Roughly, I now think that the emotion of shame is not only a support of social norms, but *the* support.'

comes out looking more contentful, and a more meaningful insight into the communitarian nature of the value-system.

In astrological grammar, shameful behaviour can be divided between Saturn, who produces behaviour of a kind of indurated, contemptible meanness, and Mars (and sometimes Mercury), who produces shocks and scandals, outrages of decency, infringements that disturb the peace.[33] Both disrupt normal, healthy social functioning, the circulation of trust. All kinds of behaviour, public and private, are constrained by fear of shame. That seems to mark an important difference from honour which, although associated with other kinds of (private) felicity, is expressed in the public sphere and for public virtues, and rarely for anything else.[34] What draws down shame is any kind of offence against the community, beginning, once again, with what disrupts trust networks. Offences involving the circulation of wealth[35] take the form of both professional improprieties (maladministration, malfeasance in public office) and personal meanness/misanthropy, which are both matters that evoke revulsion in the onlooker and hence stigmatise the guilty individual. Sexual offences are particularly, obviously, prominent.[36] But shame does not stop there. In a telling passage Ptolemy refers to diseases which are πολυθρύλλητα καὶ ἐπιφανέστατα, and epilepsy that involves the sufferer in περιβοησίαις (3.15.5). In other words, in a characteristically Greek turn, something that is by no means the fault of the sufferer is still a source of shame and scandal.[37]

Another asymmetry between honour and shame is that the former emanates from particular sources. Shame, on the other hand, although there are some expressions involving ὄχλος or ὀχλικός,[38] need not be, and is not usually, formulated like this. Honour is bestowed by a specified constituency; shame just *is*. The speaking voice in astrology takes it upon itself to articulate something supposedly self-evident. In the words of John Elster, 'in any system of norms, there must be some unmoved movers—sanctioners whose disapproval of others cannot itself be explained by the fear of disapproval' (155). The astrological speaking voice is a strong, hard-line embodiment of community

---

[33] e.g. Ptol. 4.4.12, 4.5.10, 4.7.8.

[34] A rare exception: Astrol. Anon. 379, CCAG v/1. 202.28–203.1 ἱερωσυνῶν τινων μεταλαμβάνοντας, διὰ θρησκείαν τινὰ θεϊκὴν ἢ ἐγκράτειαν τιμωμένους (other versions in CCAG v/1. 224.25–6; Θ p. 180.13–14).

[35] e.g. Valens, I 19.22, I 20.5; IV 16.3.

[36] e.g. Valens, I 20.8; II 17.66; IV 23.2 ψόγους καὶ δειγματισμοὺς καὶ μοιχείας, 8 δειγματισμούς, ψόγους τε ἢ μοιχείας; IV 25.9. In the female chart in 5.322–3, the public censure that results from sexual offences is presented with notable emphasis.

[37] Cf. Elster, 161–3, on the Greek tendency to treat even things over which one has no control, such as disfigurement, as shameful.

[38] e.g. Valens, II 11.2 ἐν ὄχλοις κακολογουμένους, II 17.66 διαβάλλονται ὑπὸ ὄχλων; IV 21.10 ἐν ὄχλοις διαβάλλονται.

norms, all the more effectively in that shame is elicited by behaviour (not just disposition) and what stars produce are of course *outcomes*. It seems plausible to argue, too, that astrology is working harder to make *us*, the reader, shudder in revulsion than nod in approval. How might astrology elicit approval? It records the fact of prosperity (i. 169 'lip-smacking overviews of landed property'), lists honours and plaudits, gestures at a few literary topoi,[39] but hardly seeks to promote enthusiastic endorsement, let alone emulation, by a reader. Towards the shameful and loathsome, on the contrary, it seeks to stir up feelings of revulsion. That is particularly conspicuous with poetic astrology, which cultivates emotional *Affekt*. The poet who makes this particularly clear is M^b, with his long-winded and lugubrious catalogues of transgressors—consider the highly charged language which mixes shame with revulsion for the adulterer in 4.56–8, the pimps of 4.314–16, the homosexuals of 4.590–2. It holds good in general that rhetorical effects are most readily piled on for negative images in astrology's repository of commonplace. Insistence, repetitions, the use of the basic components of the hexameter, hammer home messages about what to loathe, what to scorn, what to shudder at.[40] The admirable rarely receives comparable treatment.

The other main way we, the readers, are encouraged to respond is through pity. As was argued in the first volume, poetic astrology has a particularly affective tone because it mobilises emotive language from poetry. It is appropriate to call these universal emotional 'scripts', not only because these are stereotyped responses to certain triggers, 'approved' attitudes which all right-thinking people are supposed to adopt, but also because they are literally scripted insofar as they have an ultimate source in Homer, and are subsequently repeated *ad nauseam* by the astrological writers themselves. Take the parents genuinely torn about whether to expose a newborn; early Greek hexameter poetry gives a ready-made voice to their heartache. Another nice instance is 1.274 ἠδ' ἐλεεινός, where we are asked to feel pity for the wretches born when malefics join with the Moon across a line in which, in Homer, a named individual had hoped for pity from a source about which he was apprehensive. In its new context, the response has become generalised; it is incumbent on all of us to feel it for all members of a category. 'Real world' illustrative material here comes, not from honorific inscriptions, but from sepulchral epigram. Vocabulary that finds its best parallels in epitaph is used for childlessness or loss or just unspecified harm. The same script works for individual private grief and for generic

---

[39] Particularly in passages of Firmicus' eighth book which draw on Manilius, where the dependence on trope is particularly obvious (p. 55).

[40] For instance the sociopath in 4.529–33: dense vocabulary for violence (θρασύθυμα, λυμάντορες), hostility (ἐχθροί), unreliability (ἀκριτόβουλοι, οὐ μίαν εἰς ἀτραπόν, ἄλλοτε δ' ἀλλοίην … εὔτρεπτον, ἀλλάσσοντες); the scold in 5.335–9.

categories—and occasionally for distinctly strange situations, as if reaching for pity had become such a reflex for some poets that it overrode weirdness.[41] Maybe the most important point here is, not that sepulchral epigram and astrology share topoi, but that the Manethoniana use these scripts in the first place, and court and demand such an emotional response. This is not private sorrow, but a text that presents human life itself in tropes and seeks to elicit stereotyped responses.

And although it would be hard to quantify, it is surely pity that poetic astrology makes the most concerted efforts to elicit from us as private individuals (rather than, say, envy or even fear). Pity seems to work much as Aristotle described it: it is elicited by undeserved misfortune, by situations that are not self-elected (which is exactly the case with stars), and to which one is aware of one's own vulnerability.[42] True, we might not ourselves be vulnerable to that precise outcome if we were not originally born under that configuration, but we *are* equally at the mercy of the same remorseless stellar physics, and when we read about bodily pains, successive crises, and violent death, we assuredly do not breathe a sigh of relief when we consult our own chart and see that Saturn is not in conjunction with Mars in the Ascendant; we pity, rather, because we are in principle fabricated of the same stuff and subject to the same stellar actions. That is why the Manethonian poets, M[a] in particular, lay on the miserabilism so thick,[43] for it applies *tout court*. The many 'grievous' epithets in the Manethoniana[44] work exactly on an Aristotelian analysis because of our relationship to the sufferer and our equal vulnerability with her. The Homeric pastiche λύπας γὰρ στονάχας τε in 1.356 has antecedents whose subject (the source of the scourge) is Zeus (*Il.* 2.39) or the gods in general (*Od.* 14.39); the poet reached for this script because he could rely on its universalism and efficacy. The change of context is immaterial. Seen in this light the switch of agency, which looks at first sight like a sea-change in intellectual history, proves merely superficial. As in the case of 1.274, the basic situation that evokes the pitying response—humans helpless against an inscrutable higher power—and the dynamics of that response still pertain.

The first takeaway, which is commonplace, is that astrology promotes uncontroversial attitudes, and pushes them hard with the language of collective honour

---

[41] At 1.138 λύπην αἰείμνηστον, the disabled person staring dolefully at his prosthetic limb does so in the language of sepulchral epigram. The marginal variant πανόδυρτον at 1.120, for a self-castrator, produces a similar effect.

[42] *Rhet.* 2.8.2, 1385^{b}13–16; discussed by D. Konstan, *Pity Transformed* (London, 2001), 128–36; id., 'Affect and Emotion in Greek Literature', in *Ancient Prose Literature* (Oxford Handbooks Online: Classical Studies), Online Publication Date Oct. 2015, consulted 12 Jan. 2022, unpaginated.

[43] i. 58–9.   [44] i. 365–7.

and—especially—censure. Communitarian values are pressed; people are evaluated according to the degree to which they uphold them; what is expected, and what guarantees trust from one's fellow-men, is scrutability; and, by contraries, for this reason, astrology has a veritable obsession with secrecy, hiddenness, and lack of candour. Saturn is the icon of all those qualities. Saturnian individuals conceal their cunning, have a hypocritical demeanour.[45] They keep everything under wraps.[46] Worst of all are those born under the last six degrees of Scorpio, which belong to Saturn: these have every characteristic of the sociopath, including few relatives, universal unpopularity, a tendency to poison people, melancholy (an 'inner' disease?), and hidden wounds.[47] This pathological aversion to secrecy does not seem to be a feature of Artemidorus, though the physiognomists draw dire prognostics about lack of candour from eyes that are too small, or blinking, or shifty, or are suspiciously merry.[48] But it is astrology that elevates lack of candour, clandestineness, into a fetish.[49] There are secretive individuals, secret texts (below, pp. 106–7, on secret books), and other sorts of arcane knowledge.[50] A particularly interesting category, apparently not attested in any other medical literature, is pathological—hidden parts of the body,[51] hidden diseases,[52] secret

---

[45] Valens, I 1.7 ἀποκρύπτοντας τὴν δολιότητα…ὑποκρινομένην τὴν ὅρασιν ἔχοντας.

[46] Valens, I 2.67 ἀποκρυπτόμενοι πάντα, under Aquarius, which belongs to Saturn.

[47] Valens, I 3.40 κολαστικῶν, σπανοτέκνων, σπαναδέλφων, μισοϊδίων, φαρμακευτῶν, μελαγχολικῶν, μισογυναίων, κρυπτὰ σίνη ἐχόντων, καθόλου κολαστικωτάτων, μεμψιμοιροτάτων· μισοῦνται δὲ καὶ ὑπὸ θεῶν καὶ ὑπὸ ἀνθρώπων.

[48] Merry: ps.-Polemon, 20, 24 ~ Adamantius, 1.17/Epit. Matrit. 7, 21. Blinking: ps.-Polemon, 24 ~ Adamantius, 1.21. Small: ps.-Polemon, 12 ~ Adamantius, 1.8; cf. ps.-Polemon, 19 ~ Adamantius, 1.16/Epit. Matrit. 6 κρυψίνους. Shifty: ps.-Polemon, 11 ~ Adamantius, 1.7.

[49] As does the NT, in a different way, with hidden things brought to light (Matth. 10:26, Mark 4:22, Luke 12:2), that which is hidden in the heart being known to God and judged (Romans 2:16, 1 Cor. 4:5, 14:25).

[50] Lib. Herm. xxvii. 19 absconditorum vel futurorum scientiam, 30 caelestia addiscentes vel ea quae sunt in absconsis scientes, xxxi. 10 caelestia scientes, perversarum vel absconditarum rerum scientes, xxxii. 12 absconditorum secretorum conscios.

[51] Valens, IV 14.6 and App. XIX. 11 κρυπτῶν τόπων πόνους; Θ pp. 149.9–10 κρυπτῶν τόπων πόνους, 159.22 κρυπτῶν τόπων σίνη, 185.5–6 ὑπὸ κρυφίμων τόπων ὀχλοῦντα; Π.σ.α. p. 183.14–15 περὶ τοὺς ἀπορρήτους τοῦ σώματος τόπους κρυπτὰ πάθη καὶ σίνη; Apomasar, De Rev. pp. 185.4–5 ἔν τισι δὲ μορίοις κρυφίοις τοῦ σώματος ἀρρωστίαν ἕξει, 200.5–6 καὶ τὴν κοιλίαν ἀλγήσει ἢ τόπον κρύφιον, 204.21–2 καὶ ἔν τινι κρυφίῳ τόπῳ ἀλγηδόνα ἕξει; Firmicus, 4.9.5 absconsarum partium adsiduos dolores, 5.3.38 et absconsorum et latentium locorum assiduos dolores, 5.3.48 Dolores vero et valitudines aut in extremis partibus corporum, aut in absconsis, 7.21.7 in absconsis locis a medicis secabuntur; Lib. Herm. xxxii. 6 quidam vero et laesiones et passiones habent in absconditis, xxxii. 14 dolorem absconditorum locorum. In 1.159 a noun has to be supplied with κρυφίμων, which is presumably τόπων, because what follows in the next line is a list of organs (liver, spleen, kidneys, heart, lungs); see too Θ pp. 129.15 σῖνος ἕξει ἀπόκρυφον ἢ εἰς τὸν σπλῆνα, 155.27 κρυπτὰ πάθη τῶν σπλάγχνων; Camaterus, Intr. 606–7 ὑποτάσσει δὲ [sc. Cancer] τοῦ σώματος στήθους τε καὶ καρδίας, σπληνός, στομάχου καὶ μαστῶν καὶ τόπων ἐγκρυφίων.

[52] 1.252; Περὶ κράσ. 85 κρυπτοὺς πόνους; Hephaestion, i. 176.1 κρύφια τὰ πάθη; Apomasar, De Myst., CCAG xi/2. 192.19 κρυφίαν νόσον; Π.σ.α. p. 183.14–15 (n. 51); Apomasar, De Rev.

pains.⁵³ Although this never becomes explicit, the category suggests a contrast in inner logic with the conditions that produce striking visual effects (skin diseases; paralysis, spasms, epilepsy, dropsy) towards which astrology normally gravitates (i. 356–7): here, instead of shocking public demonstrations, is private pain.⁵⁴ In a more positive sense, the discovery of secret treasure brings about economic transformation which no amount of good, candid, plain-spoken business dealing could ever have achieved.⁵⁵

This section should also have begun to illustrate one of astrology's idiosyncrasies. That is the combination of a narrative voice whose attitudes are deeply normative with an intent focus on personalities that somewhat unbalances the relationship between individual and community in which those norms were embedded in the first place. Not that the result is very different. Individuals are born into the categories society has scripted for them, and we, too, the readers, are tapped for the appropriate emotions, which are aroused not just by obvious triggers like bereavement and pain, but also by matters of status. We are therefore schooled to look down on those who toil away in humiliating conditions (4.252 οἰκτρούς τ' ἀμαρησκαπτῆρας, 1.80 βαφέας μογερούς, 1.84 ἀργαλέους ὑδραγωγούς, 1.85 ὑδροφόρους πολυπήμονας, 1.86 ἀεικέος εἵνεκα μισθοῦ), and personal emotions are harnessed to the end of reinforcing the sense of a hierarchy of labour (section 4). It is the relationship between the individual and the community—his social superiors and inferiors and especially his peers and his co-workers in the world of work—that the next sections will continue to explore. The focus continues to be on social standing.

---

p. 184.24 νόσον κρυφίαν; Achmet, Oneir. 266.6 κρύφιον πάθος; Firmicus, 3.12.11 absconsarum valitudinum vitia.

⁵³ 4.413 κρύφιμ' ἄλγε'; 5.107 κρύφιμα στομάχων ἀλγήματα; Θ p. 160.2 κρυπτῶν πόνους; Firmicus, 3.2.9 ex latentibus doloribus, 13 latentes corporis dolores, 14 latentium vero corporum dolores; 3.4.19 absconsos corporum...dolores; sim. 4.9.5; 4.15.2 qui latentibus vitiorum doloribus torqueantur; 5.3.18, 59; 7.9.4 absconsis pater et latentibus aegritudinibus interibit; 7.20.8 latentium et absconsorum locorum dolores; 8.26.1 latentes dolores; Lib. Herm. v. 3 dolores absconditi, xxxii. 14 dolorem absconditorum locorum, 35 absconditorum dolorum, 46 absconditas vero passiones habentes vel interiorum dolorem, 62 Plures autem et stomachici vel splenici fiunt vel in locis absconditis dolorem habentes. See 4.413 n.

⁵⁴ Presumably this is how you would categorise cancer, if at all: Valens, II 41.31 ἐπὶ δὲ θηλυκῶν μαζῶν ἀλγηδόσιν, καρκινώμασιν, κρυπτῶν πόνοις; Θ p. 189.24 κρυπτὰ πάθη...καὶ καρκίνου ἕλκος; cf. Hippocr. Aphorismi 6.38 κρυπτοὶ καρκίνοι; Prorr. 2.11 οἱ δὲ καρκίνοι οἱ κρυπτοί, 13; De Mul. Affect. 133. For hidden disease and haemorrhage, see 1.338 n.

⁵⁵ i. 280, 321 n. 1; Θ pp. 141.23–4 κρυπτὸν καὶ λαθραῖον πλοῦτον, 149.12 ἀπὸ κρυπτῶν ἔργων ὠφέλειαν φέρει.

3

Élite and Mass

This section is about what social level astrology launches itself from, where it implicitly positions itself in a social hierarchy. It analyses astrology's own language of status. Class—which is much more problematic, because imposed on the material top-down and outside-in—is treated in the next section.

In the absence of any bibliography to speak of, evidence was derived in the first instance by investigating the use of individual words for 'big men', on the one hand, and for 'populace', on the other, and looking for patterns. And patterns do emerge. At the same time, however, astrology is a large corpus and one must be very cautious, indeed suspicious, of generalising. Different authors have different interests, and there is no one narrative voice, not even in specifically natal astrology. Each author has his pet phrases, his own mannerisms.

KINGS AND BIG MEN

To start with some facts. On the matter of quantity: even on a crude count, references to overlords far outnumber words for the populace; more of this later. On that of quality, there is also a large vocabulary (ἄρχων, αὐτοκράτωρ, δυνάστης, ἐξουσιάστης, ἡγεμών, κοσμοκράτωρ, κύριος, μεγιστάν, στρατηγός, τύραννος), with βασιλεύς by far the most frequent at all periods. The preferred terminology is unspecific. Some of astrology's bland Greek terms can indeed sometimes double as titles for Roman authorities (βασιλεύς; στρατηγός can mean a praetor, an urban magistrate in Roman Greece,[1] or nomarch in Egypt). But because it so habitually shuns specificity it is rare that a term can definitely be taken to evoke Roman titulature, except in the case of αὐτοκράτωρ, and even that is vastly outnumbered by βασιλεύς.[2] It does not use official titulature for

---

[1] Mason, 155–63. Perhaps most famously in Acts 16:20 (Philippi).
[2] So too Artemidorus, who has only three instances compared to forty of βασιλεύς. Apropos of Antigonus' single use of βασιλεύς, Heilen 2015, 1194, notes this as an oddity against his three instances of αὐτοκράτωρ, but his general preference for the latter seems to me more noteworthy. Otherwise there are occurrences in Hephaestion, i. 14.4 δυνάστης, βασιλεύς, αὐτοκράτωρ (source

emperors (there are no instances of σεβαστός; Καῖσαρ is used only in dating formulae or in epistolary address). The sense of στρατηγός is either undeterminable, or the word has its usual military associations, although is clearly a Roman office-holder in *CCAG* ix/1. 180.23. In the exceptional passages in Θ pp. 221.5-6, 224.13 the references to κουέστωρ, ὕπατος, πατρίκιος are precisely in historical charts. These are the only uses in Greek astrology of πατρίκιος, the only one save 1.104 of ὕπατος, and the only one save Θ p. 223.9 of κουέστωρ. There are no references to the senate (σύγκλητος), save in Glycas, and once each in a *tonitruale* and in Achmet.

There are different genres of astrology. This is fundamental. While a fixation on big men is common to most if not all types, they range all the way from charts of individuals with kingly characteristics including physiognomy (5.286 n.), through to the natal charts of those who *interact* with such individuals (for weal or woe), to general astrology which sees kings as just the most obvious twigs swept along on the tides of massive international events. Each type has its own perspective. Thus, natal charts tend to see big men as figures either to fear or, with relentless instrumentalism, to extract benefit from. That is not to say that an alternative perspective does not exist—the ideal king, the king of justice—but it is found in a different kind of chart. It is a matter of genre and viewpoint. It is also a matter of resources. It is, in fact, a chicken-and-egg situation: the aspects that receive emphasis are those that are coralled under the influences and prerogatives of the planets in question, while the planets are marshalled to express the aspects of kingship in which the writers are interested. So, if you want the good king, you choose Jupiter. If you want unpredictability, upsets, war, violence, you choose Mars.

The various words for 'big men' have overlapping associations (as is about to become clear), but some are more restricted or specialised, while others are more capacious. μεγιστᾶνες, for instance, 'great men', revolves very largely around 'persons desirable to cultivate' (the leitmotifs being φίλος, φιλία), and this seems to change very little over time or across genre.[3] The operative concept with δυνάστης seems, unsurprisingly, to be power itself; it is often qualified

unknown); *CCAG* ii. 192.9; Julian of Laodicea, *CCAG* iv. 105.33, 152.4; Theophilus, *De Rebus Praesertim Bellicis, CCAG* xi. 223.3; Camaterus (3×). The adjectival form occurs in Valens, I 3.19 and 21 αὐτοκρατορικαί.

[3] Antiochus, *CCAG* vii. 108.18 ὁμιλεῖν μεγιστᾶσιν, sim. 109.4, 30, 110.28 συναυλίζεσθαι μεγιστᾶσιν, 114.24; Valens, II 12.6 μεγιστάνων φίλους, sim. II 33.7; Hephaestion, i. 23.3 ἐγγὺς μεγιστάνων; *CCAG* vii. 216.29 ἀποδοχήν τε ἔχοντας παρ' ἀλλήλοις ἢ βασιλεῦσιν ἢ μεγιστᾶσιν; *CCAG* viii/1. 245.11 γνώσεις μεγιστάνων; *CCAG* viii/2. 144.15 φέρουσα εἰς ἀγάπην αὐθεντῶν καὶ μεγιστάνων; Θ pp. 126.1–2 μεγιστάνων φίλοι, 148.12 ἐν μεγιστᾶσιν ἀναστρέφονται, 167.7–8 φίλα μεγιστᾶσιν, 211.8–9 προσφιλὴς παρὰ μεγιστάνων ἢ βασιλέων; Camaterus, *Introd.* 725 προκοπὴν, φιλίαν μεγιστάνων, 1374 καὶ συναναστραφήσεται μεγιστάνοις ἀνδράσι. Astrobotany prescribes means to guarantee their goodwill.

by appropriate epithets.[4] τύραννος can have its traditional negative associations, or anyway military ones, but can just be used alongside other big men.[5] βασιλεύς on the other hand, is far richer in association. It is also more ambiguous, for there are kings and there are Kings. Some passages list a range of socially prominent individuals ('kings and big men', kings and *strategoi*),[6] whereas others really do mean an exceptional individual, a King or an emperor; and where such an individual is in question, it becomes a question of reading kingship against a number of overlapping backgrounds, including, but not necessarily limited to, the mythopoeic and imaginative, philosophical (kingship framed by Greek political theory), and Roman imperial (an available meaning for βασιλεύς from at least the second century in prose, and earlier in poetry[7]). The massive preference for βασιλεύς over αὐτοκράτωρ is thoroughly consistent with astrology's preference for fuzzy suggestibility, although the latter has much the same associations as the former. The advantage of less determinate terminology is richness of association.

To begin with the ways the king impinges on communities. His power and might are not in question, although given astrology's oriental origins one is rather struck by the shortage of kingly mirage, for instance the low incidence of the 'king of kings'[8] and 'kings of many nations' tropes. One also misses much of the formal public language that the Greek political communities might direct towards their rulers, the rigmarole of diplomatic language and official courtesies. The absence of official titulature for the Roman emperor has been noted. Ruler cult does receive some slight mention. There are a couple of passage of undetermined origin in Hephaestion, in one of which he refers to an individual who enjoys ἰσόθεος τιμή (i. 14.7), and another in which an individual is 'sown by the gods, a great man, who will be worshipped among the gods, ruler of the

---

[4] μέγας, μεγάλοι: Θ pp. 153.21, 169.18, 170.6, 13, 173.2. Other words for 'powerful' include 1.28 ὑπερθύμους τε δυνάστας; *Π.τ.δ.* 8 δυνάστας, φοβερούς; Camaterus, *Introd.* 2946 δυνάστης ὑπὲρ δύναμιν ὀξύς τε καὶ ἀνδρεῖος; Theophilus, Περὶ προβολῆς ἄρχοντος, *CCAG* iv. 94.1 ἰσχυρὸν ὄντα δυνάστην καὶ δραστήριον καὶ ἐπωφελῆ; efficacious: Hephaestion, i. 224.29–30 καὶ δριμεῖς ἔσονται ἐν ταῖς πράξεσιν ὡς δύνασθαι πολλὰ ἀνύοντες.

[5] Military associations: Valens, I 20.15, II 8.3. Especially in connection with Mars: Valens, II 12.4, 17.5; Θ pp. 144.11, 152.13, 164.7. Combined with other big men: Valens, II 7.2 τύραννοι ἢ βασιλεῖς (with a benefic in the MC); even a person to be cultivated: *CCAG* viii/2. 144.15–16 εἰς ἀγάπην αὐθεντῶν καὶ μεγιστάνων καὶ τυράννων.

[6] One example among many: Valens, I 2.41 λαμπροί, ἔνδοξοι, τυραννικοί, βασιλικοί. Artemidorus also uses βασιλεύς in lists where Harris-McCoy (548) suggests that he is the greatest of great men along a spectrum of power, although still not necessarily a literal king.

[7] Heilen 2015, 1194–5.

[8] Valens, II 17.23, 31 βασιλεῖς βασιλέων; a spurious letter of Petosiris to Nechepso, *CCAG* vii. 161.7.

cosmos, to whom all shall be subjected.[9] Given that astrology's normal procedure is to repeat tropes, 'sown by the gods' is surprisingly hard to parallel, unless it is simply a very highly coloured rendering of *divi filius*. κοσμοκράτωρ is presumably a vaguely evocative description which suggests (rather than specifies) an emperor, as it does again in its other occurrence in Ptolemy.[10]

It is less surprising that there is so little trace of the tradition of theoretical writing περὶ βασιλείας,[11] which credited the ideal king with qualities such as law-abidingness and justice, ἐπιείκεια (clemency), εὐσέβεια, φιλανθρωπία, εὔνοια, εὐεργεσία and πρόνοια for his people, self-regulation, and so on. What little there is about justice depends to a great extent for its slant on the type of text in question. Natal astrology, in all its relentless careerism, occasionally mentions royal appointees in law courts (see on 2.264–5); general astrology, on the other hand, with its grand-sweep catastrophising, has many an arbitrary despot who oppresses his subjects.[12] Neither has any time for the generic figure of the just king, who is present, if at all, in texts less embroiled in tricky and perilous interactions and more amenable to mythological thinking.[13] A sadly

---

[9] i. 28.9–11 ἐκ θεῶν σπαρήσεται καὶ ἔσται μέγας καὶ μετὰ θεῶν θρησκευθήσεται καὶ ἔσται κοσμοκράτωρ καὶ πάντα αὐτῷ ὑπακούσεται, cf. ii. 157.1–3 ὁ δὲ τόν γ' ἔσται μέγας καὶ ἰσοθέοις τιμαῖς τιμηθήσεται καὶ κοσμοκράτωρ ἔσται καὶ πάντα αὐτῷ ὑπακούσεται; whence Camaterus, *Introd.* 1528–9.

[10] 4.3.2 ~ Hephaestion, i. 155.12, where, aligned with the equally unspecific μεγάλοι καὶ δυναμικοί, it is presented as an aggrandisement of those who are already βασιλεῖς. The other occasions in astrology where it refers to big men rather than (as it normally does) luminaries are *Lib. Herm.* xxvi. 5, xxviii. 8, and Camaterus, *Introd.* 2804. There is a clear link between the standard astrological usage κοσμοκράτορες = luminaries, on the one hand, and, on the other, the connection of luminaries with kings (often born when luminaries are on centres: 1.26–8 n.). The use of κοσμοκράτωρ as a term in art history for gods and emperors—sometimes going back as early as Augustus (P. J. E. Davies, *Death and the Emperor: Roman Imperial Funerary Monuments from Augustus to Marcus Aurelius* (Cambridge, 2000), 92)—is confusing, first because it does not seem to be iconographically well defined, and second because when applied to emperors it reaches far earlier than any attested application of the term that is known to me. In Greek inscriptions it begins to be attested in the reigns of Caracalla (*IGR* I,5 1063) and Gordian III (*IGR* III 387). The whole subject needs a proper investigation. For the astrological/magical/demonological application of κοσμοκράτωρ, see Lincoln on Ephesians 6:12 (WBC 42).

[11] Xenophon, *Cyropaedia*; Isocrates, *Ad Nicoclem* and *Evagoras*; Letter of Aristeas, 187–294 (G. Zuntz, 'Aristeas Studies 1: "The Seven Banquets"', *JSS* 4/2 (1959), 21–36, esp. 24–30; O. Murray, 'Aristeas and Ptolemaic Kingship', *JTS* 18 (1967), 337–71); H. Sidebottom, 'Dio Chrysostom and the Development of *On Kingship* Literature', in D. Spencer and E. Theodorakopoulos (eds.), *Advice and its Rhetoric in Greece and Rome* (Bari, 2006), 117–57.

[12] e.g. Camaterus, *Introd.* 1032 καὶ δίκαιον οὐχ ἕξουσιν ἐκ τῶν αὐτοκρατόρων.

[13] Valens describes Jupiter's degrees within Cancer as βασιλικαί, αὐτοκρατορικαί, ἔνδοξοι, πολύδικοι (I 3.19); Apomasar tells his interlocutor that Aries (sign of Mars) stands for τοὺς φιλοδικαίους βασιλεῖς καὶ τοὺς τὰ συμφέροντα τοῖς ὑπηκόοις ἐργαζομένους (*De Myst.*, *CCAG* xii. 99.20–1). But these are not actual charts, and none of the following is from natal astrology: *CCAG* ix/2. 173 col. ii. 32–3 βασιλεὺς ἀναφανῇ δίκαιος, καὶ οἱ κριταὶ δίκαιοι (a dodecateris, for which this is the entry under Libra); *CCAG* xi/1. 177.10 βασιλεῖ φιλοδικαίῳ καὶ φοβερῷ (a comparison for the

eloquent reference to kings dispensing injustice to their subjects who receive it, perforce, as *justice*, is surely a more realistic vision of political power.[14] In that connection it is also notable that the king is scarcely to be seen personally dispensing justice to his subjects.[15] In the old Millar *versus* Hopkins controversy about who or what the Roman Emperor was, astrology—always supposing that emperors underlie its hazy terminology—has much to contribute on the side of perceptions, image-making, what the emperor meant to his subjects in terms of the mental categories they used when they thought about him. But although there are some references to distinguished individuals whose communities choose them to serve as ambassadors,[16] the day-to-day grind of receiving petitions and issuing responses—central in Millar's version—contributes practically nothing at all.

Euergetism does have at least a marginal presence. This was an, if not *the*, expectation of kings in the περὶ βασιλείας tradition,[17] and it is too basic to the image of well-ordered power for astrology to ignore, whether in its presentation of Jovian characteristics,[18] or in association with Saturn (foundations presumably being an 'earthly' business),[19] or the Sun.[20] Certainly it is a kingly activity, and for Hephaestion, a foundation is successful and guaranteed the support of great kings when it is made with the Moon in the royal trigon.[21] Where astrology specifies (as it usually does not), it takes the form of 'places', villages, or cities themselves. It is a top-down idea. The king does not institute public works. He does not stimulate economic activity. What he does is to

Sun in Aries); *De septem mundi aetatibus*, CCAG iv. 117.3–4 ἐγένοντο βασιλεῖς ἰσχυροί, δυνάσται μεγάλοι, ἔνδοξοι, ἔχοντες δικαιοσύνην (a vision of the fourth age under the Sun).

[14] CCAG xi/1. 175.5–7 σημαίνει ἀδικίας βασιλέων πρὸς τὸ ὑπήκοον, καὶ λογίσονται τὰς ἀδικίας ὡς δικαιοσύνην (conjunction of Jupiter and the Sun in the DESC: presumably the Sun obliterates Jupiter's good qualities). See too Ptol. 4.9.14 ... πάλιν ἀπόλλυνται κατακρίσεσι καὶ χόλοις ἡγεμόνων ἢ βασιλέων, again involving damage to Jupiter.

[15] One historical case (8 May 107) in Valens, V 6.88 (no. L 107 Neugebauer–Van Hoesen) καὶ ἐπὶ βασιλέως ἐλθὼν δίκην ὑπὲρ φίλου ἀρχιερωσύνης ἐνίκησεν ('and going before the king he won a lawsuit for a high-priesthood on behalf of a friend').

[16] Περὶ κράσ. 207 τοὺς εἰς δημοσίας χρείας ἢ πρεσβείας στελλομένους; Firmicus, 8.26.12 *illis legatio patriae credetur*, and 13 *legati mittentur ad imperatorem, et complebunt omnia quaecumque illis fuerint in legatione mandata*; embassies an honourable function: CCAG v/1. 189.1–2 ὁ δὲ Ζεὺς ἄρχουσι, βασιλεῦσι, υἱοῖς, δόξαις, τιμαῖς, πρεσβείαις. The context of Valens, IV 21.4 καὶ ἐντεύξεις ποιουμένους suggests that petitions were seen as hassle.

[17] D. M. Jacobson, 'King Herod's "Heroic" Public Image', *RB* 95 (1988), 386–403, at 389–91, 394–9.

[18] Ptol. 3.14.20, 26; associated with men of the millennium governed by Jupiter in CCAG iv. 116.14–15 ἄρχεσθαι δίκην βασιλείας καὶ κτίσεις πόλεων καὶ δικαιοσύνην.

[19] In the fifth place: Valens, II 12.5 κτίζοντας κώμας καὶ τόπους; Θ p. 152.15–16 θεμελίων κτίστας ἢ χωρῶν ἢ πόλεων.

[20] Ptol. 2.3.16 ἡγεμονικοὶ μᾶλλον οὗτοι καὶ εὐεργετικοί; Valens, II 17.22 βασιλεύσει καὶ πολλῶν χωρῶν ἐπικρατήσει, γίνονται δὲ εὐεργετικαί (Mars, Sun, benefics, female chart).

[21] i. 256.3–6 ὑπὸ μεγίστων βασιλέων ἤτοι ἀρχόντων τὸ κτίσμα καὶ τὴν τούτου ἐπιμέλειαν καὶ φροντίδα ἔσεσθαι μηνύει καὶ ἐνδιαίτημα βασιλέων καὶ θεοῖς προσφιλές.

impose himself. But there are two very big qualifications. First, exactions go hand-in-hand with donations (Hephaestion, i. 14.5 ~ Camaterus, *Introd.* 695–6): the king and the king's men (*Π.τ.δ.* 11 φοροπράκτορας βασιλέων) are extractors at least as often as they are benefactors. And second, even a motif which might have formed part of a positive presentation is inflected to bring out the bare fact of power. The motif of founding cities is combined with the power to destroy[22] or subjugate[23] them; the ability of the mighty to subdue (ὑποτάσσειν) cities, lands, and peoples[24] is merely the most visible and spectacular realisation of astrology's general propensity to see the world in terms of uppermost and underlings (the ὑποτεταγμένοι: p. 94).

That makes great men formidable, a quality which rarely appears in a positive context.[25] One is struck when, in an otherwise favourable scheme (Saturn trine with Jupiter), Valens describes founders of vineyards, villages, and cities, as 'lowering (oppressive?) and wearing a frown' (II 17.69 βαρεῖς δὲ καὶ ἐπισκύνιον ἔχοντας). The phrase is graphic to the point of humorousness if it is meant to evoke the Homeric simile of a menacing lion, where ἐπισκύνιον (*Il.* 17.136) is a *hapax legomenon* meaning the skin of the forehead that is drawn downwards in a frown; it may be, however, that ἐπισκύνιον is simply meant to suggest a severe deportment.[26] Those described explicitly as φοβεροί are usually military men, generals (warlords?),[27] 'lords of life and death', an interesting rendering into Greek of the Latin *vitae necisque potestas* which is almost

---

[22] e.g. Valens, II 8.3 ὁ γεννώμενος τύραννος ἔσται· κτίσει πόλεις, ἑτέρας δὲ διαρπάξει; Firmicus, 3.4.30 *reges, imperatores, potentes, maxime terribiles, periculosi, civitatum eversores vel fabricatores.*

[23] Hephaestion, i. 14.4–5 βασιλεύς, αὐτοκράτωρ ἀναγορευθήσεται καὶ πολλοὺς ὑποτάσσει καὶ κτίσει πόλεις; Camaterus, *Introd.* 2500–1 περιβόητον ἄνδραν καὶ μεγιστᾶνον | εὐτυχῆ τε καὶ πλούσιον, ὑποτάσσοντα πόλεις; *Lib. Herm.* xxvi. 30 *et ipse natus erit rex maximus autocrator, insignis, potentissimus, civitatum terrarum et climatum aedificator et gentes ei subicientur.*

[24] Hephaestion, i. 23.26–7 ἡγεμόνας, βασιλέων διαδόχους, πόλεις ὑποτάσσοντας; Firmicus, 7.22.1 *subiugantes*; Camaterus, *Introd.* 694–5 ἀποτελεῖ αὐτοκράτορας ὑποτάσσοντας πλείστους | καὶ φόρους ἀπελαύνοντας ἐκ δυναστῶν προσώπων; 1232–3 ἐνδόξους καὶ βασιλικοὺς, δοξασθῆναι ἐν βίῳ | καὶ πόλεις ὑποτάσσοντας ἐν πολλῆς τῆς ἰσχύος; 2500–1 (quoted in n. 23), cf. *CCAG* v/1. 221.13–14 μεγιστᾶνα εὐτυχῆ, πλουσιώτατον, ὑποτάσσοντα πόλεις; Θ p. 177.16–18 ἐνδόξους στρατηγικούς, χώρας καὶ πόλεις καὶ ἔθνη ὑποτάσσοντας καὶ διοικοῦντας, καὶ φοβεροὺς ἀνθρώπους καὶ ἡγεμόνας καὶ στρατηλάτας.

[25] Apomasar, *De Myst., CCAG* xi/1. 177.9 βασιλεῖ φιλοδικαίῳ καὶ φοβερῷ.

[26] Polyb. 25.3.6. For the combination of βαρύς and ἐπισκύνιον see Plut. *Mor.* 45 D βαρύτης ἐπισκυνίου ('frowning': Babbitt); Adamantius, 1.16 (a sign of <θυμὸν>... καὶ ἀλκὴν μετ' ἀβουλίας).

[27] Θ pp. 153.21–2 μεγάλους δυνάστας, φοβεροὺς ἐπὶ στρατοπέδου, 168.14 στρατοπεδάρχας φοβεροὺς, 173.2–3 μεγάλους δυνάστας, φοβερούς, ἐπὶ στρατοπέδων ἢ μαχαίρας τασσομένους, 177.17–18 φοβεροὺς ἀνθρώπους καὶ ἡγεμόνας καὶ στρατηλάτας; *CCAG* v/1. 221.28 ἐνδόξους στρατηγικούς, ἔθνη ὑποτάσσοντας, φοβερούς, ἡγεμονικούς; Theophilus, *De Rebus Praesertim Bellicis, CCAG* xi/2. 205.12–13 ἐπανδροτέρους καὶ φοβερωτέρους τοὺς στρατηγούς; Camaterus, *Introd.* 2444 καὶ βασιλεῖς καὶ στρατηγοὺς καὶ φοβεροὺς σατράπας. Exceptions: Θ p. 170.13–14 μεγάλους δυνάστας, ἀρχικούς, βασιλεῖς φοβερούς, Camaterus, *Introd.* 2948 ἀνδρεῖος, μέγας, ἔμπρακτος καὶ φοβερὸς ἐν πᾶσιν.

confined to astrology[28] (though there is also an instance in Galen, who appears to be thinking of Mithridates VI[29]). In astrology these men are usually holders of military and/or political power,[30] but sometimes simply rich and powerful men.[31] Even if the applications of the motif to the latter are simply lazy and unthinking transferences, they are eloquent in their own way about the existential effects of economic as well as military might.

And so, to move finally to interactions with individuals, natal astrology reflects the focalisation of natives for whom what matters is danger to the person, on the one hand, but benefits extractable from their environment, on the other. For the careerist in search of positions as administrator, steward, scribe, teacher, the receipt of honourable and prestigious 'trusts', that environment might be a royal or imperial court, or the provincial administration.[32] It might also be a civil magistracy. The glamorous prospects—the δωρεαί, εὐεργεσίαι,

---

[28] The Greek is usually ζωῆς καὶ θανάτου κύριος/κυριεύειν or ἐξουσίαν ἔχειν, corresponding to Latin *potestas*. Exceptions are Valens, I 2.2 ζωῆς καὶ θανάτου παρρησίαν ἔχοντες; id. II 41.92 = Critodemus, *CCAG* v/2. 53.2, with ἄρχειν. Those described thus are βασιλεῖς, βασιλικοί, δυνάσται, ἐξουσιαστικοί, ἡγέμονες, ἡγεμονικοί, στρατηγοί, στραταρχικοί (and other military words: πολεμάρχους, στρατιώτας, στρατοπεδάρχας), τύραννοι, or just μέγας—or have no specific word at all: they are just born lords of life and death. Firmicus applies the motif to *duces* (Appendix II, VIII.1), *iudices* (3.5.10; 8.26.4), and the *potentes* (3.13.9 *administratores*, 8.26.7; 8.31.5, 8), and there is an adaptation of the motif in Manilius, 4.549 *iudex examen sistet vitaeque necisque* (alluding to Augustus' birth under Libra). In other words, astrology selects only one of the three contexts in which the power is exercised in Roman sources (by a ruler over subjects, by a master over slaves, and by a father over his children), but precisely that one which is also found in Ancient Near Eastern texts (cf. R. Westbrook, 'Vitae Necisque Potestas', *Historia*, 48 (1999), 203–23, at 213). As an expression of political power, it can be compared to another favourite astrological polar statement, founding and destroying cities (Firmicus, 3.4.30, *al.*). Firmicus' extension of the motif to judges can be seen as a latter-day realisation of the king's divine mandate to do justice (Westbrook, art. cit. 216), but his association of the motif with arbitrary violence (3.5.10, 8.31.8) is a more cynical reflection of Roman power. At 3.4.13, 29, it is associated with the *ius gladii*, the right to execute civilians (P. Garnsey, 'The Criminal Jurisdiction of Governors', *JRS* 58 (1968), 51–9). It may indeed connote tyranny (Cic. *De Re Publ.* 3.23), but also a power, bestowed by Fortune, which is fragile; see Boyle on Sen. *Thyest.* 608.

[29] Galen, *De Theriaca ad Pisonem*, xiv. 214.18–215.1 Kühn τῶν ἀρχόντων τινὲς, ἐξουσίαν θανάτου καὶ ζωῆς ἔχοντες (the context is those who fortify themselves in advance with antidotes against poisons). ἐξουσία θανάτου alone is commoner (e.g. Plut. *Sull.* 33.1), and ἐξουσίαν ἔχειν standard Greek.

[30] e.g. *Π.τ.δ.* 8 βασιλεῖς ποιοῦσιν ἢ δυνάστας, φοβερούς, ζωῆς καὶ θανάτου ἐξουσίαν ἔχοντας. In Ptol. 4.3.2 they are ἡγέμονες, one step down from the top slot occupied by μεγάλοι καὶ δυναμικοὶ καὶ κοσμοκράτορες.

[31] Hephaestion, i. 23.21–4 τραφήσεται ὡς πλούσιος καὶ ἔσται ἐκ μεγάλων γονέων, ὀξύς, πεπαιδευμένος καὶ δημοσιεύσει καὶ κύριος ἔσται ζωῆς καὶ θανάτου; cf. Firmicus, 8.26.7 *erit magna potentia felicitatis ornatus; vitae et necis habebit maximam potestatem*. Great men also wear a threatening aspect in Artemidorus: see Klees, 60.

[32] A rare addition to the usual hangers-on: the man who makes his living from royal portraits (Valens, IV 15.3 οἱ δὲ καὶ ναοὺς ἢ ἱερὰ ἢ βασιλέων τύπους κατασκευάσαντες ἀείμνηστον φήμην ἀναλαμβάνουσιν; are the temples those of imperial cult?). That does not break the unrelieved run of instrumentality, but at least adds a flash of artistry to it.

κέρδη, πίστεις, τιμαί—are what shimmer in the imagination in this way of thinking. These are the operative ideas, and big men are time and again the conduits through which they come, but so, too, is the city, whose career structures offer rewards of their own. So too with harms: big men can bring fatal harms, but so can the city; in both cases, astrology so often uses formulations in which βασιλ- and ὀχλ- appear harnessed together as alternatives.[33] The difference inheres in the character that comes from a personal source. The king confers not only πίστεις (so does the city), but also gifts (δωρεαί, εὐεργεσίαι), personal benefits which are rarely specified but which keep company with other items that leave us in no doubt about the eye-wateringly lucrative and status-heightening nature of what is meant.[34] But the same men who confer the gifts can also display their displeasure.[35] One might have to defend oneself before them.[36] Libanius, for one, knew the risks of offending one who was invested with state power, knew, too, that it could amount to more than a passing cloud (Or. 33.2). This is reflected in astrology's vocabulary of anger—χόλος, usually, for the anger of the princes and kings which is often combined with references to condemnations and death;[37] θυμός, usually, in characterisations of the bare effects of Mars (5.74 n.), but also for the anger of kings in Achmet and some short, late extracts; and ὀργή, singular or plural, for ominously unattached 'anger' that could strike from any source, but again sometimes for the anger of kings.[38] All this is thoroughly congruent with Artemidorus, for whom (though he has significantly less than astrology to say about them) kings and rulers are potentially dangerous, figured in dreams as wild animals whose lack of aggression comes as an unexpected bonus but is by no means to be

---

[33] e.g. Ptol. 2.9.11 ὄχλων ἐπαναστάσεις καὶ χόλους ἡγεμόνων.

[34] Valens, II 21.2 ἄργυρον καὶ κόσμον καὶ πλείστην ὕπαρξιν καὶ ἀπὸ μειζόνων τε καὶ βασιλέων δωρεάς; IX 2.14 συμπάθειάν τε βασιλικὴν κεκτημένοι δωρεὰς καὶ δόξης καταξιοῦνται; Apomasar, De Rev. pp. 184.7–8 ἐπικτήσεται χρυσὸν καὶ ἄργυρον καὶ λίθους τιμίους καὶ δῶρα βασιλικά, 189.6–7 καὶ βασιλεῖς αὐτῷ ἱματισμὸν δωρήσονται, 201.14–15 λήψεται γυναῖκα περιφανῆ καὶ δῶρα βασιλέων δέξεται; Camaterus, Introd. 943 τιμὰς πολλὰς δὲ λήψεται καὶ δῶρα βασιλέων.

[35] Anger an existential quality of rulers: Lib. Herm. xxxii. 49 iracundi tamen. Irascibility figures among the qualities of the great-souled individual (born under Leo): Firmicus, 5.3.21 Erunt sane cordatissimi, peregrinorum inimici, iracundi, boni, benivoli docti, et qui incorruptam fidem in omnibus contractibus servent, boni consilii, integri et incorrupti animi, multorum amici, et qui omnia validissimis viribus compleant.

[36] Περὶ σχημ. 87/Περὶ κράσ. 179.

[37] Περὶ κράσ. 151 χόλων ἡγεμονικῶν; ps.-Palchus, viii/1. 248.21 κατακρίσεις ἢ χόλους ἡγεμόνων ἢ βασιλέων. Risk of death: Ptol. 4.9.14...πάλιν ἀπόλλυνται κατακρίσεσι καὶ χόλοις ἡγεμόνων ἢ βασιλέων; Valens, II 41.33 τελευτῶσι...χόλῳ δυναστῶν, 37 τελευτῶσι...χόλῳ βασιλέως ἢ δυναστῶν.

[38] Valens, II 17.19 ἐξ ὑπερεχόντων ὀργάς; CCAG x. 143.24 ὀργῆς κυρίου ἐπίτασις; CCAG ix/2. 172 col. a 12–13 ὀργὴ βασιλέων κατ' ἀρχόντων/b 11–12 ὀργὴ βασιλέων κατ' ἀρχόντων; Apomasar, De Rev. p. 82.4–5 ὀργῆς βασιλικῆς πειραθήσεται; Achmet, Oneir. 145.34–5 ἔσται τὸ πάθος καὶ ἡ ἀπώλεια...δι' ὀργῆς βασιλέως.

relied on.[39] To dream of fighting with a king or grandee is *ipso facto* a prediction of being worsted (3.9 κακῶς διατεθῆναι).

In conclusion, there is a disparity between the treatment of kings/big men and the treatment of honourable members of the community. The latter tends to reflect inscriptional topoi, the vocabulary of honour, more often. Presumably the man honoured by his city was among the potential consumers of astrology, or he was a relatable type for the astrologers' clients, whereas the king was not (there are lots of royal charts, but the images they contain are vaporous). Or rather, the effect of interactions with the 'king' (or emperor) was likely to be on the community at large rather than on individuals, and so his image was correspondingly more generic.

MASS

The words on which this survey rests are ὄχλος, δῆμος, λαός, and πλῆθος, and the derivatives of the first two (ὀχλικός, δημοτικός). ὅμιλος is not used in the astrological corpus in the relevant sense.[40] Also included are πόλις and πολιτικός. The picture on a raw count is that λαός is much the commonest of the 'populace' words, but is heavily skewed towards Achmet and general astrology, leaving a residue of approximately the same number as δῆμος (36 cases), though that, too, is heavily skewed, in that case towards the Manethoniana (15 instances, of which 13 are in M^a). Overall numbers therefore differ significantly, but we do find marked variations in different authors, with Valens, for instance, far more massively preferring ὄχλος to δῆμος than does the corpus as a whole, the Manethoniana (poetic, of course) strongly preferring δῆμος, and Ptolemy notably apolitical except in the use of a scattering of adjectives.[41] So much

---

[39] 2.12 (a tame lion, an elephant). In 2.30 the king is ἀνυπότακτος, which is also an astrological word (specifically of kings in Camaterus, *Introd.* 2443–4 ἀνυποτάκτους ἄνδρας | καὶ βασιλεῖς; elsewhere of tyrants or just spirited men).

[40] *De Astrologia Dialogus* has a throng of stars and a throng of angels.

[41] (i) Valens has ὄχλος 59 times, ὀχλικός another 17 times, but δῆμος and δημοτικός only once each. (ii) The Manethoniana have 15 instances of δῆμος (of which 13 are in books 2 and 3), five of λαός (all in books 2 and 3), two of ὄχλος (in M^b) plus ὀχλοχαρεῖς (in M^d), all of popular entertainments, and none of πλῆθος in the relevant sense. (iii) 'Par. Anub.' has no settled pattern. δῆμος: Περὶ σχημ. 14, 90, Περὶ κέντρ. 28; ὄχλος: Περὶ σχημ. 60, 80, Περὶ κέντρ. 79; λαός: Περὶ κέντρ. 57; πλῆθος: Περὶ σχημ. 60 (~ Περὶ κράσ. 219), 90. λαός also occurs in Περὶ κράσ. 112, 132, 146, suggesting its presence in the poem that underlies both texts. But the fragments of Dorotheus other than 'Par. Anub.' contain one instance of δῆμος, none of λαός, ὄχλος, or πλῆθος in this sense. (iv) Ptolemy has no δῆμος, ὅμιλος, λαός, no πλῆθος in the relevant sense, and only three instances of ὄχλος, though he also has three of δημόσιος, a couple of ὀχλικός, and one each of δημοτικός, δημηγορικός, δημοκρατικός.

for quantities. In what follows one object of interest is in how words capable of meaning simply undifferentiated 'people'[42] (in contradistinction to their leaders, βασιλεῖς, ἄρχοντες, ἡγεμόνες, and so on) carry more nuanced meanings, for instance how δῆμος and ὄχλος divide the semantic labour of representing the people—populace, mob—between them. In the formulation of Nicholas Purcell, the former presents the population in institutional terms, the latter in behavioural ones.[43] ὄχλος is the commonest word in the corpus once the evidence for λαός is put in its proper context, which on the face of it suggests that what preoccupies astrology—natal astrology, anyway—is the individual's ability or inability to negotiate turbulent forces rather than his relations with a regulated community.

A healthy dose of scepticism is always a good starting-point. Is astrology even *interested* in society?

The fact that this is natal astrology *ipso facto* means that the focus is on the native, with 'the people' that against which he is thrown into high relief. General astrology, about which less will be said, also has its own focalisation, whereby the populace is on the receiving end of earthquakes, famines, pestilences, tyrants, and countless other banes. But they do not figure there as foils for the deeds of a lone individual. With regard to natal astrology, one can legitimately ask about its politics, but the first observation is that it does share this type of offsetting with various kinds of politically motivated writing. Whether it is a contrast between the 'rabble' and 'the few', 'the better sort', the oligarchs,[44] or a (good) people being led by a first citizen, or a rabble being led astray by a demagogue,[45] it is a contrast between the many and the few, and sometimes between the many and a specific individual. Astrology in its turn makes the crowd a foil for the natives on whom attention is fixed. They are the blurry mass against whom the native emerges in sharp focus, whether to control them (the conjuncture in Ptol. 4.4.6 παίδων διδασκάλους, ὄχλων προεστῶτας is eloquent about the implied infantilisation of a mass which needs a leader) or to court them (Ptol. 3.14.14 ὀχλοκόπους). In any case, an individual or small group is pitted against, or thrown into relief against, a somewhat unpredictable mass. Indeed it is much the same in the evangelists as well, for whom the ὄχλος is the

---

[42] For instance, Apomasar, *De Myst.*, CCAG xi/1. 169.20–1 τὸν χυδαῖον λαὸν; Hephaestion, i. 233.2 τὰ δὲ πολύσπερμα καὶ πολύγονα (sc. signs, representing) ὄχλους καὶ δήμους: the implication here is simply that of multitude.

[43] N. Purcell, 'The Populace of Rome in Late Antiquity: Problems of Classification and Historical Description', in W. V. Harris (ed.), *The Transformations of Urbs Roma in Late Antiquity* (Portsmouth, RI, 1999), 135–61, at 135.

[44] A. Garzya, 'Il Sicionio di Menandro e la realtà politica del tempo', *Dioniso*, 43 (1969), 481–4; S. Karpyuk, 'Crowd in Archaic and Classical Greece', *Hyperboreus*, 6/1 (2000), 79–102, at 101–2.

[45] C. Magdelaine, 'Le vocabulaire du peuple et de la démocratie chez Euripide', *Ktèma*, 28 (2003), 105–21.

wavering—sometimes pitiful, sometimes menacing—mass who can be swayed either by Jesus' message or by his enemies.[46]

That being so, it is not surprising that things are not seen from the people's point of view. Although it does parasitise attitudes which emanate from 'the people' in inscriptions (see the discussion of honour, above), natal astrology mostly fails to identify *with* the people: the narrative voice is not that of the δῆμος. 4.566 is unusual in that *we* are implicitly the δῆμοι who condemn the misanthrope and sociopath. Otherwise the δῆμος is not us. Nor does astrology recognise the category of citizenship, unless Περὶ κράσ. 132 τῇ πόλει κοινοῦται ἢ τῷ λαῷ gestures at the difference between the strict citizen body and the people as a whole. If the main determinant of identity in the ancient world, at least before 212, was the possession of citizenship, one would struggle to find any reflection of this in astrology. πολίτης does not occur in a single astrological text except for Glycas, who is not even writing about astrology; the only other mention is of the dual citizens of 5.291, where having dual citizenship is a curiosity. The possession or otherwise of citizenship is not treated as an important principle of identity.[47]

But does astrology advance a particular picture of society? To that the answer is yes. Themes tend to emerge in clusters (including within authors, presumably as they draw on different sources), but repeated patterns emerge.

Just because it is the foil or backdrop, the people is far from passive. On the contrary, the people both gives and receives. It confers honour[48]—or conveys reproach. But it also guzzles payments, gifts,[49] and especially entertainments.[50] This forms the greatest contrast with inscriptions issued by the δῆμος, wherein the latter proudly constitutes itself the *giver* of δωρεαί. ὄχλος is the main word used for the populace as consumer, although λαός is used in 3.38 (which is of course poetry). Of those who enjoy or court popular favour, Valens, I 2.38,

---

[46] P. S. Minear, 'Jesus' Audiences, According to Luke', *NT* 16 (1974), 81–109, esp. 84–7 (ὄχλος); J. Murphy O'Connor, 'The Structure of Matthew XIV–XVII', *RBi* 82 (1975), 360–84, at 371–6, 381–2.

[47] Firmicus' rare mentions of *cives* are in connection with the native's fellow-citizens (who fear or revere him or send him on embassies), never with the native himself. *Lib. Herm.* lacks *civis* altogether (unsurprisingly if its Greek source lacked πολίτης). In Manilius I find only 3.106–7, where the third in a series of 'lots' (i.e. twelve places) which are labelled differently from the normal *dodecatopos* is devoted *ad urbanos... labores*, which are presented as a matter of transactions (*civilibus actis | compositum*, 'made up of civil engagements': Goold) based on friendship and trust. Thus not even here is it a matter of juridical status. Manilius' language is similar to Cicero's description of civil law in *Pro Muren.* 19 *urbanam militiam respondendi, scribendi, cavendi.*

[48] e.g. Paul, p. 69.24 καὶ ὑπὸ ὄχλων τιμῆς καταξιουμένους.

[49] e.g. Valens, II 21.2 εὐπροαιρέτους ἐξοδιασμοὺς [payments] εἰς ὄχλους; II 22.35 δωρηματικὸς ἐγένετο καὶ ὄχλοις ἀρεστός; IV 21.8 δωρεὰς εἰς ὄχλους; IV 23.3 εἰς ὄχλους δωρεάς.

[50] Valens, I 3.24 ἀκροαματικαί, ὀχλικαί.

Élite and Mass 29

places θεατρικοί in the vicinity of both ὀχλικοί and δημόσιοι, but closer to the former.

There is a strong tendency to associate the crowd with upset and turbulence (θόρυβος, στάσις, ἐπαναστάσεις, ἔφοδοι),[51] and crowd words are associated with the effects of the tropic signs, places in the zodiac where change and upheaval comes about.[52] This association is most appropriate for ὄχλος, which is etymologically connected with ὀχλέω 'trouble'/'be troublesome',[53] but extends to the other crowd words as well, and seems to be the main or only association for πλῆθος.[54] Ptolemy's combination of 'upheavals from crowds and generals' anger'[55] brackets together the kinds of harm that come from their respective sources (see p. 25 on the anger of great men). It is not, however, entirely the case that emotion-words are only ever attached to a personal source, any more than that the imagery of inscrutable elements is only ever attached to the mob: crowds can react personally, and dynasts with tempestuous rage.[56]

It is the populace in general that spells trouble, whatever word is used for it. No single writer seems consistently to be making the distinction that other writers, including Artemidorus, do, and have done since the classical period, between δῆμος, the populace when it is functioning in an orderly way as the citizen body, and ὄχλος, the rabble.[57] There are, it is true, suggestions of such a

---

[51] e.g. Περὶ σχημ. 90 ἀπὸ πλήθους καὶ δήμου στάσεις ἐγείρει καὶ κραυγάς; Hephaestion, i. 206.17–18 κρίσεις καὶ φθόνους καὶ μερίμνας ἕνεκεν δημοσίων, 208.11–12 ἐξ ὄχλων λύπας καὶ θορύβους καὶ ζημίας καὶ κρίσεις καὶ μερίμνας, 210.3 ἐκ δημοσίων βλάβας καὶ κινδύνους, 210.9–10 μετεωρισμοὺς χάριν ὀχλικῶν ἢ δημοσίων πραγμάτων, 211.2–3 δήμου ἐπηρείας [abuse] καὶ κατακρίσεις, 212.5–6 κινδύνους, ταραχάς, δικολογίας ἕνεκεν δημοσίων πραγμάτων καὶ ζημίας; CCAG viii/1. 245.12–13 στρατείας, δημόσια πράγματα, θράσος, δίκας, θορύβους, αἰφνιδίους πολέμους. Consider also passages where it is aligned with other types of injury: Ptol. 4.9.10 τοὺς κατὰ θλῖψιν [Hephaestion, i. 187.29 καταθλίψει] ὄχλων ἢ ἀγχόναις ἢ στραγγαλιαῖς ἀπολλυμένους; CCAG viii/1. 167.12–13 ἀπὸ ὄχλου καὶ πυρὸς καὶ αἵματος ‹καὶ› κακούργων φόβους; Hephaestion, i. 238.11–12 τὸ δὲ γ΄ περὶ ὄχλου ἢ μάχης καὶ ἀηδίας ἐπικινδύνου.

[52] Ptol. 3.14.3 δημοτικωτέρας ποιεῖ τὰς ψυχάς, ὀχλικῶν τε καὶ πολιτικῶν πραγμάτων ἐπιθυμητικάς; CCAG v/1. 187.7–10. δημόσιοι: Valens, I 2.1 (Aries), 37–8 (Cancer), 51 (Libra); Camaterus, *Introd.* 898 (Libra). But natives born under non-tropic signs can also be δημόσιοι (Valens, I 2.66; Teucer, CCAG vii. 201.6).

[53] Karpyuk (n. 44), 81.

[54] Περὶ σχημ. 60 δι᾽ ὄχλον καὶ πλῆθος λυποῦνται ~ Περὶ κράσ. 219; Περὶ σχημ. 90 ~ Περὶ κράσ. 220 ἐκ πλήθους στάσεις ἐγείρει καὶ ταραχὰς καὶ βοάς; Θ p. 200.12–13 ἀπὸ δήμου ἢ πλήθους ἢ βασιλέων ἀναιρεῖ σταυρουμένους ἢ ἀποκεφαλιζομένους ἢ θηριομαχοῦντας.

[55] Ptol. 2.9.11 ὄχλων ἐπαναστάσεις καὶ χόλους ἡγεμόνων.

[56] Valens, IV 21.3 ὀχλικὰς εὐημερίας ἐπάγει is rendered 'popular success' by Riley, but inasmuch as it literally means calm weather it suggests the possibility of the opposite, storms—which duly break out in 'Rhetorius', CCAG vii. 218.24 ὑπὸ ὄχλων ἢ μεγιστάνων χειμαζομένους.

[57] Euripides: Magdelaine (n. 45), 116–20 (ὄχλος), *et passim*. Herodian: D. Motta, 'Il « demos » in Erodiano', *Incidenza dell'Antico*, 15 (2017), 49–81, at 69–74. Artemidorus' usage strongly implies a difference between ὄχλος (30 instances) and δῆμος (five instances), with the former having something uncontainable and above all *noisy* about it (1.51.4 περιβοησίας…καὶ ὄχλων

distinction, for instance in Valens' telling formulation associating δῆμος and ὄχλος respectively with glory and with expenditure,[58] and in a certain tendency to prefer δημόσιος where it is a question of distinctions and trusts and personal integrity.[59] The values attached to each term emerge quite plainly in the rare (but separate) passages where democracy and ochlocracy appear as more or less fully-fledged political categories.[60] Such passages, however, run against a counter-tendency to run 'populace' words together in an undifferentiated way, in which astrology's preferred listing idiom overrides nuance.[61]

That is not quite the case with πόλις (see i. 294–6). There are continuities, it is true. A city, like the populace, is the background for the native's actions, the arena in which he operates (rules, controls, is general, fulfils administrative functions, holds positions of responsibility, wins fame and glory). To some extent its intrinsic sense of place sets it apart from other 'crowd' words. This perhaps functions even more clearly in passages of severance (loners live beyond city boundaries, offenders are expelled from them, congenital wanderers live in foreign ones) than in those of belonging. There seems less overlap than one might have expected with the themes of honorific inscriptions (1.105 κοσμητῆρας ἑῆς ἐποίησε πόληος is an outlier) given the emotional and ethical commitment that inheres, or might have inhered, in the city. Cities are not, however, sources of turbulence like the people, except in an unusual little cluster in Valens.[62] Or at least, the noun πόλις is not. The adjective πολιτικός, has a

---

συνδρομὰς; 2.20.7 Ψᾶρες ὄχλον σημαίνουσι καὶ ἄνδρας πένητας καὶ ταραχὴν ματαίαν; 2.27.2 σημαίνουσιν...ὄχλον διὰ τὸ βίαιον καὶ μεγαλόφωνον; 3.16.2 ἔοικε γὰρ καὶ ὄχλῳ ἡ θάλασσα διὰ τὴν ἀταξίαν; 3.62 Ἀγορὰ ταραχῆς ἐστι σημαντικὴ καὶ θορύβου διὰ τὸν ἐν αὐτῇ ἀγειρόμενον ὄχλον). This is the word used in connection with popular entertainments (5.104 n.), and with the faintly damning phrase ἐξ ὄχλου πορίζεσθαι (1.64.4, 68; 2.15; 3.6, 16.2, 47.2, 48, and especially 3.52 Κόπρια συνάγειν ἀγαθὸν τοῖς ἐξ ὄχλου πορίζομένοις καὶ τοῖς τὰς ῥυπώδεις ἐργασίας ἐργαζομένοις). As in astrology, it is the foil of a prominent and strong character (2.12.1, 3.42.1). δῆμος, on the other hand, is used when the people has more agency and more dignity (1.2.12, where they are a collectivity whose combined weight is no less than that of a civic leader; 1.78.8, where the δῆμος has the same symbolic significance as a father; 2.30.6, where it confers priesthoods; 3.56.2, the recipient of portions of meat at a sacrifice; 4.44.1, that which is not deserving of contempt).

[58] Valens, IV 16.22 φιλοδοξούντων εἰς δήμους καὶ ἀναλισκόντων εἰς ὄχλους.

[59] Valens, I 19.12, V 6.84; Περὶ κράσ. 139 δημοσίας διοικήσεις πιστευομένους ἐκ βασιλέων καὶ ταῖς πράξεσιν ἀμέμπτους; Θ p. 151.1–2.

[60] Ptol. 2.3.19 φιλελεύθεροι δὲ καὶ αὐτόνομοι καὶ δημοκρατικοὶ καὶ νομοθετικοί (the people of Greece); Hephaestion, i. 57.2–3 ὠμότητα πολλὴν γενέσθαι ὑπὸ ὀχλοκρατησίας καὶ φόνους, 60.22–6 ἐμφύλιον πόλεμον καὶ ὀχλοκρατίαν καὶ τοὺς πρώτους κατακοπῆναι καὶ ἀποστατῆσαι δὲ ἄλλους τοῦ ἡγουμένου καὶ ἄλλον ἄλλου ἀφελέσθαι τὰ κτήματα, 63.1 ὄχλων ἀκαταστασίας καὶ ταραχὰς καὶ ἔρεις. The whole of this section, which is attributed to οἱ παλαιοὶ Αἰγύπτιοι, appears as Nechepso and Petosiris, fr. 6 Riess.

[61] e.g. Περὶ σχημ. 60 πλὴν δι' ὄχλον καὶ πλῆθος λυποῦνται, 90 ἀπὸ πλήθους καὶ δήμου στάσεις ἐγείρει καὶ κραυγάς; Valens, I 3.29 δημοτικῶν, ὀχλαγωγῶν; Ptol. 3.14.3 (quoted in n. 52).

[62] IV 15.4 ὄχλων ἐπαναστάσεις ἢ πόλεων, 16.4 πόλεων ἢ ἐχθρῶν ἐπαναστάσεις, 22.5 πρὸς ὄχλον ἢ πόλιν ἐπιτάραχος.

Élite and Mass 31

generally similar range of reference to other crowd words (changeability, nuisance, vain and idle pastimes),[63] while Θ p. 217.7-8 unflatteringly couples πολιτικοί with mimes under the sign of the Ape.[64] Yet there is also a more positive dimension, for the πολιτικοί are also those equipped to live the associative and cooperative life, and it is here that we find the characteristics of urbanity and sociability which leaven political, economic,[65] social, cultural, and intellectual life in a way that crowds and mobs do not.[66] It happens to be in second-century sources, in Ptolemy and Valens (and in a passage of 'Rhetorius' somehow related to Valens), that the sociable character (κοινωνικός) makes his slick appearance.[67] One can well imagine him steering his way to every sort of private and public success in the well-lubricated cities and commercial networks of that period.

Those who are involved with the populace stand both to gain and to lose. They are obliged to court (or 'serve'[68]) it. It can be a source of profit,[69] but it is also the

---

[63] Nuisance: Hephaestion, i. 220.22 πολιτικὰς ἀηδίας, 238.6-7 φορτίου πολιτικοῦ. Changeability (again linked to tropic signs): Ptol. 2.8.11 τὰ δὲ τροπικὰ ταῖς τῶν ἀέρων καὶ ταῖς τῶν πολιτικῶν ἐθισμῶν μεταβολαῖς; 3.14.3; Teucer, CCAG vii. 204.1-2 εὐμετάβολον... πολιτικόν and Camaterus, Introd. 898 πολιτικὸν, εὐμετάβλητον ὅλον (Libra); Περὶ κράσ. 44 ἐν τροπικοῖς δὲ μάλιστα ἔσονται αἱ πολιτικαὶ ἀρχαί... ἐπεὶ καὶ πολιτικὰ φαμεν τὰ τροπικά; Valens, I 2.1 (Aries) and 37 (Cancer) εὐμετάβολον... πολιτικόν (also 40, Leo, but this is not tropic, whence ἀμετάβολον Kroll). Vain and idle pastimes: Apomasar, De Myst., CCAG xi/1. 182.16-17 καὶ τὰ διὰ τῶν ταυλίων παίγνια [board-games], ἔτι δὲ τὸ ζατρίκιον [chess] καὶ τὰς ἀργίας καὶ τὰς νωχελίας καὶ τοὺς πολιτικοὺς λόγους.

[64] The imitative Ape (Πίθηξ) is an obvious sign for actors and mimes (see on 4.271-85 + 286-9, p. 618). But other imputed characteristics better suit the association with politicians—trickery, mendacity (Aesop, Fab. 14, 75), flattery (Plat. Rep. 590 B: note the reference to the ὀχλώδει θηρίῳ which represents the base part of the soul to which such flattery panders; Plut. Mor. 52 B, 64 E; Lucian, Pisc. 34 κολακικώτεροι δὲ τῶν πιθήκων; Hubbard, 75), and demagoguery (Ar. Ran. 1085 δημοπίθηκοι; Phrynichus, F 21 K.-A.; cf. S. Luria, 'Der Affe des Archilochos und die Brautwerbung des Hippokleides', Philologus, 85 (1929-30), 1-22, esp. 1-15). More on the semantics of apes: S. Lilja, 'The Ape in Ancient Comedy', Arctos, 14 (1980), 31-8.

[65] Observe how rarely words for the populace are associated with economic activity. This is not even certainly the case in Θ p. 209.6-7, where δημόσια πράγματα are listed along with metallurgy under the general rubric of Mars.

[66] Ptol. 3.14.26 ἀγαθόφρονας, καλοσυμβούλους, πολιτικούς, εὐεργετικούς...; Περὶ κράσ. 43 πολιτικὰς ἀρχὰς... διὰ τὸ κοινωνικόν; Valens, I 20.31 ἀγαθούς, εὐσυμβιώτους, ἁπλοῦς, μεταδοτικούς, φιλογέλωτας, πολιτικούς, παιδείας ἢ ῥυθμῶν μετόχους, sim. Appendix X 36.

[67] Ptol. 2.3.14, 16, 19, 41, 44; Valens, I 19.21, II 33.9, IV 17.7, 24.2; Περὶ κράσ. 43, 217; CCAG vii. 222.3.

[68] Valens, I 20.26 δωρηματικούς, φιλοδόξους, ὄχλων ἡδοναῖς ἐξυπηρετοῦντας could be seen as a subversion of epigraphic language, where this verb is used of civic benefactors who have exerted themselves τῇ πατρίδι or εἰς τὴν πατρίδα. (Similarly I 20.19 ἀθλητικοὺς ἢ ἱερῶν προεστῶτας ὄχλων ἡδοναῖς ἐξυπηρετουμένους; Pingree added a second disjunctive from App. X 17 ἀθλητικοὺς ἢ ἱερῶν προεστῶτας ἢ ὄχλων, ἡδονῇ ἐξυπηρετουμένους.)

[69] Valens, I 20.18; Hephaestion, i. 18.22-3 [~ Camaterus, Introd. 961-2], 223.10-12, 224.6-7.

object of sometimes thankless expenditure.[70] The cynicism of a comment by Valens on the fruitless life of currying favour and keeping up appearances, whether at court or in public service, almost persuades us that the focalisation is authorial.[71] In presenting euergetism from the point of view of the donor, astrology acknowledges the possibility of ingratitude, gifts that misfire: Valens has a series of charts aimed at benefactors in which the malefics produce their characteristic ill effects, Saturn a sordid spirit in the giver which attracts resentment, Mars a bumpy outcome whereby even the generous come to regret their outlay (IV 16.22). Artemidorus agrees: to dream of making donations (ἐπιδόσεις … δημοσίας) from your own funds signifies upsets and scandals (2.30.4). There are indeed those who thrive in this environment; but they are themselves suspect, ambitious, trouble-makers.[72] And this provokes reflections, at least interim ones, on the social level from which astrology pitches itself.

Taking stock, one is impressed by the massive disproportion between numbers of references to kings (raw count 719) and references to the δῆμος (without the Manethoniana, around 20) or even the ὄχλος. The astrologers' clientele appear to be looking up far more than often than they are looking down, and when they do the latter it is with contempt. There is no trace so far of a counter-view, a subaltern conception of the world, nor of a divided consciousness, as if the ὄχλος were struggling to articulate an independent politics and assert a more self-confident or challenging view of itself. The readers of this material would have rejected the label of ὄχλος with indignation.

Yet, suspicious of demagogues and contemptuous of the mob, astrology can hardly be said to project an élite hauteur either. Kings and big men are never far from the consciousness, but attitudes towards them range through the intimidated, the resigned, the deferential, to the standardly communitarian, modelling them as euergetai and benefactors. Whatever else it is, the focalisation is not that of upper classes looking down at the populace, any more than is it that of a populace which, having adopted the values of the élites as hegemonic,

---

[70] Valens, II 21.4 εἰς δημόσια ἢ εἰς βασιλικὰ πράγματα ἀναλίσκοντας; IV 22.1 ἔχθρας καὶ βλάβας καὶ δημοσίων πραγμάτων ἐπηρείας ἢ εἰς δημόσια ἀναλίσκοντας.

[71] Valens, IX 2.14 … ἢ ἐν βασιλικαῖς αὐλαῖς καὶ δημοσίοις τόποις ὀψωνίων μετέχουσιν, οὐ τοσοῦτον περὶ τὸν βίον συγκεκοσμημένοι ὅσον τῇ κακοδόξῳ φαντασίᾳ καὶ πολυμερίμνῳ καὶ εὐθραύστῳ κακοπαθείᾳ ('… They are not however elevated so high in their livelihoods as they are sunk in inglorious display and in careworn, broken misery': Riley).

[72] Valens, I 19.20 πολυφίλους καὶ ὑποκριτικοὺς ποιοῦσιν, ποικίλους δὲ καὶ ἐγκρατεῖς καὶ ἐν δημοσίοις τόποις τὰς ἀναστροφὰς ἔχοντας (cf. Περὶ κράσ. 189 εἰσὶ πολύφιλοι καὶ ὑποκριτικοὶ καὶ ποικίλοι καὶ ἐν δημοσίοις τόποις ἀναστρεπτικοί); I 20.17 θρασεῖς, δημοσίους, πολυφίλους, ἐν προβιβασμοῖς γινομένους καὶ ἀπὸ μικρᾶς τύχης ὑψουμένους, 28 ἁδρεπηβόλους (ambitious), καταφρονητάς, πλανήτας, θρασεῖς, δημοσίους; Hephaestion, i. 146.12–14 δημοτικωτέρας ποιεῖ τὰς ψυχάς, ὀχλικῶν τε καὶ πολιτικῶν πραγμάτων ἐπιθυμητικάς.

looks upon itself with self-loathing.⁷³ Rather, it is an 'average' discourse capacious enough for any member of the political community to adopt, a value-system of cleanly respectability, one which Theocritus' comically limited but self-respecting and self-important Gorgo and Praxinoe could still comfortably adopt in an Alexandria three or four hundred years later than their own. A local bigwig would find a familiar repertory of images to cultivate and to shun. But if we imagine that astrology's consumers were numerically more likely to be represented by the clothes-sellers of the agora than by Marcus Fulvius Publicianus (p. 4), then astrology ventriloquises them with a voice that is conformist, average, self-seeking, materialist. One reaches for the word 'bourgeois',⁷⁴ but that is to presuppose an urban setting, the applicability of a modern class descriptor, and a particular disposition towards work. All of which are the topics of the next section.

---

[73] Or, on the other hand, loathes the rich and looks forward to their downfall: see R. MacMullen, 'Social History in Astrology', *AncSoc* 2 (1971), 105–16, at 110, contrasting the attitude of apocalyptic prophecy.

[74] On the adoption of bourgeois values by *die kleinen Leute*, see Kudlien 1991, 155, 159–60.

4

Work

> ' "Work! work! work!"… "Let us be *doing* something!" '
> Samuel Smiles, *Self-Help*, p. 216.

INTRODUCTION

That, according to Samuel Smiles at least, was David Wilkie's watchword—not a bad epigraph for a genre which is all about 'people doing things', about enterprise and exertion. Whether or not they use formal trade names, or whether their aim is simply to give an impression of busy activity, various astrological corpora seem to have specialised in this. Our main focus is the group that consists of Ptolemy, Manetho, and Θ, but its evidence is enriched by a second one, the group including Firmicus 8 (the *paranatellonta* of 6–17 and the *monomoiriai* of 19–30 which give a more minute degree-by-degree account) and the various witnesses to Teucer (including *Lib. Herm.* xxv). Miscellaneous others include Firmicus 3 (the *dodecatopos*) and 4 (movements of Moon). The partial similarities between Firmicus 4 and the text on the movements of the Moon in *CCAG* viii/1. 181–7 ($Περὶ\ συναφῶν\ καὶ\ ἀπορροιῶν\ τῆς\ Σελήνης$ = $Π.σ.α.$), which in Firmicus' rendering is fleshed out with occupations and in the Greek version with a great deal of material on disease and harm, suggests that it was possible for authors to make their own thematic selections of what to include. Some decided to make economic activity their special interest.

But how does such material work in a real horoscope? Charts involving very specific predictions about jobs are for obvious reasons impractical. No forecaster wants to be boxed in. Anubion is quoted as instructing $οἶνος$ to be considered before $πρᾶξις$, lest a career as an athlete be predicted for a gouty individual, a man with a non-functioning hand be made into a shoemaker, or a blind man a tailor (fr. 7, ap. Θ ch. 82, p. 208.2–8). Reasonable enough—but such evidence as we have for predictive charts, in other words charts where the interpretation is given in the future tense,[1] do not commit themselves to specific occupations *at all*. More interestingly, it is not even clear what function a precise prediction about an occupation would serve. The many charts for historical individuals quoted by Valens use the same motifs as his theoretical discussions; in retrospective, past-tense analyses, he points to changes of status in vague and periphrastic terms,[2] showing in a subsequent γάρ-clause how the stars produced or foresaw that effect, but never claiming (for instance) that they made a man a linen-worker, or foresaw his change of career to a travelling salesman.[3] The most specific labels occur at the beginning of a chart, in the scene-setting introduction (ὁ τοιοῦτος γέγονε, *vel sim.*): one individual is said to have been a eunuch priest; another a soldier; a third a dancer; in the same idiom, the retrospective chart for Pamprepius identifies him as a poor Theban grammarian.[4] These are preparatory notices. They set the context for what follows, but do not press the hard implication that the stars mandated this exact calling.

An over-specific indication of career is not only a risk for the forecaster; it also over-simplifies the complex reality of changing employments in response to opportunity or need. More consideration needs to be given to what these jejune labels—reductive enough even before the familial and social aspects of the world of work are factored in as well—were actually meant to achieve. Indeed, the question arises for all catalogic material, not just on the subject of employment. In the first volume the assumption, possibly naive, was that what the catalogues offer is a store or well-stocked repository from which the forecaster simply picked the items he wanted when producing his overall interpretation. But it is not at all clear that it worked like that, or that (as in Tamsyn Barton's modern experiment: i. 41) charts were constructed by the accumulation of micro-segments from a pre-script. For the purposes of this section, though, that does not matter. Rather, the argument is that what astrology's trade names

---

[1] The Old Coptic Horoscope (no. 95 Neugebauer–Van Hoesen). Antigonus' chart for a member of Hadrian's family (no. L 40) begins with a future tense, but then reverts to the past.
[2] II 22.11 ἡγεμονική, στρατηγική (sc. γένεσις), 14 ἡγεμονικὴν καὶ ἐξουσιαστικὴν τύχην, 18 ἐν στρατιωτικαῖς καὶ προκοπτικαῖς τάξεσιν, 23 ἡγεμονίας καὶ τάξεως ἐξουσιαστικῆς; II 27.1 and 6 ἡγεμονικός, τυραννικός, 4 ἡγεμονικός, ζωῆς καὶ θανάτου κύριος; V 6.84 ἀρχὴν ἐπίσημον ... δημοσίων χάριν πραγμάτων, 108 ἀρχὴ ἐπίσημος; VII 3.31 ἐν ἐπισήμῳ τάξει στρατευσάμενος, 41 ἡγεμονίας κατηξιώθη. High-priesthood (ἀρχιερωσύνη): II 22.25, 27, V 6.107, and acquisition of a high priesthood and στεμματηφορία in VII 6.188.
[3] The only precise office, as far as I can see, that is laid to the stars' door is II 37.34 χρησμοδότης. This reluctance to make the stars responsible for specific careers supports Riley's interpretation of II 22.32 θησαυροφύλακα as 'miserly' (an ethical term) rather than (with LSJ) a treasury guard.
[4] II 22.47 εὐνοῦχος, ἱερεὺς θεᾶς; V 1.20 στρατιώτης; V 6.121 ὀρχηστής; Θp.221.2 Οὗτος γέγονε Θηβαῖος γραμματικὸς πένης (Pamprepius). In Hadrian's chart (no. L 76 Neugebauer–Van Hoesen) the implication *is*, presumably, that the stars brought about his specific calling, but emperors are exceptional.

provide is above all an imaginary of work. The disjunction between the catalogic material which predicts and pigeonholes, and the actual historical charts which seem more interested in providing an unspecific overview of advancement and downturn, is rather disconcerting. But the interest here is in astrology's collective picture of work, based on a mixture of observation and representation and trope, and the question is, *whose*. Whose sensibility, whose outlook is this?

The end of the last section used words like 'averageness'. But once the discussion moves to the world of work we can hardly avoid introducing the concepts of class and status. The old question is whether there were class-based attitudes to work in antiquity, specifically whether there was a middle-class attitude that differed from the élite one. Astrology's extraordinarily rich and still under-exploited evidence might at first sight seem to give the resounding answer yes, but terminological and above all theoretical problems come crowding in. On the other hand, one cannot just shut the question down by stating the obvious fact that 'class' is a modern concept.[5] 'Status' rather than 'class' was the ancient category of analysis, and astrology promotes that relentlessly, but it does have its own version of the tripartite hierarchy of wealth and status that goes back to Aristotle,[6] only now, instead of constructing the μέσοι as a contentless middle between the marked extremes of wealth and poverty, it marks them specifically as associated with labour. It even has its own word for them, the μεσόβιοι, and however sketchily defined these people are, Valens does at least make it perfectly clear that they are firmly associated with activity, business, lack of leisure.[7] This meshes nicely with the fact that Dio concludes a discussion of honourable and dishonourable trades with the term μέτριοι. This is precisely what and whom we will be talking about, working people. It is not in contradiction with the fact that up until that point the term he has been using is in fact πένητες, which in ancient authors simply means the not-rich (p. 73).[8]

Dio's discussion will be important below, and still more so will be Paul Veyne's analysis of the *plebs media*. That remains true even though Veyne was

---

[5] Even if one is reluctant to go as far as Emmanuel Mayer by importing the notion of a 'middle class' into the ancient world. Against Mayer's quest for specifically middle-class values, see the review by A. Wallace-Hadrill, *JRA* 26/2 (2013), 605–9.

[6] *Pol.* 1295^{b}2–3, etc.

[7] Sarapion, *CCAG* viii/4. 229.14, 16; Valens, V 7.16 πλουσίοις, μεσοβίοις, ἀσχοληματικοῖς, πένησιν, ἐργαστηριακοῖς. But how do ἀσχοληματικοῖς and ἐργαστηριακοῖς relate either to each other or to μεσοβίοις and πένησιν? For astrology's concepts of class, see i. 287–90.

[8] *Or.* 7.127 ἡ γὰρ περὶ ἐργασιῶν καὶ τεχνῶν σκέψις καὶ καθόλου περὶ βίου προσήκοντος ἢ μὴ τοῖς μετρίοις; compare 7.104 εἶεν δή, περὶ τῶν ἐν ἄστει καὶ κατὰ πόλιν πενήτων σκεπτέον ἂν εἴη τοῦ βίου καὶ τῶν ἐργασιῶν, πῶς ἂν μάλιστα διάγοντες καὶ ποῖ' ἄττα μεταχειριζόμενοι δυνήσονται μὴ κακῶς ζῆν. μέτριος also figures in Artemidorus' dream interpretation—but only rarely (2.20.3; also as part of a three-tier scheme in 2.34.3 and 4.84.4; Klees, 58–9). For him, the two way rich/poor classification is more important.

specifically concerned with what he took to be the upper échelons of the *plebs* of the city of Rome.⁹ Rome is not the crucible in which astrology was forged, and even astrologers who give their material an Italian make-over (Manilius, Firmicus) can hardly be said specifically to have Rome in mind. Veyne's sampling of the evidence for this social group—their values, aspirations, cultural level—nevertheless remains extremely suggestive, although these were people who could pay for commemorative inscriptions and commission reliefs on their gravestones depicting themselves at work, not, according to Veyne, vulgarly obliged to work for their daily bread in the way Dio's subjects (~ the *plebs vulgaris?*) were. We have to consider both groups, and it may not be very meaningful to bundle them together under a baggy label like 'middle'. Or perhaps we can get away without talking about 'middlingness' at all? What we mean, after all, are *all* the categories of person who worked for their living, in all their diversity, and what we really want to know is whether we can go into this enquiry expecting to find anything different from what most classical sources assume about work. Can astrology show us what the world looked like to the *homines tenuiores*,¹⁰ the *popolo minuto*, or some other term that simply aims to evoke the mass of people whose voice does not dominate our prestigious literary texts? These, at any rate, are questions that the traditional agenda would have laid down. Do we see different attitudes to work, ones that allowed for more craftsmanly pride than élites would ever have countenanced? And/or: do we see signs of the sub-élites emulating the values of their hegemonic superiors, those they aspired to join, sneering at those lower than themselves in a hierarchy of prestige? Then again, for that matter, is 'élite' any better as an analytical label? Or are any of these the right questions at all? There is a turn in recent scholarship towards the idea of a single Roman *culture*, which is entirely compatible with the existence of different *ordines* and economic classes and well-policed hierarchies of prestige. But the first question we need to tackle is terminological, that of the ancient occupational labels themselves.

---

⁹ Veyne 1990–1; 2000, updated in Veyne 2005, 117–61; Courrier, part 2 (chs. 4 and 5); C. Burgeon, 'La classe moyenne commerçante et l'"économie-*taberna*" aux premiers siècles de l'Empire romain', *Folia Electronica Classica*, 35 (2018), 2–22; and criticised by P. Wojciechowski, 'In Search of the Roman Middle Class: An Outline of the Problem', *Palamedes*, 7 (2012), 109–16. Ancient evidence for the term is collected by Courrier, 305–10 (the prime example being Plin. *NH* 26.3); some, but not all, witnesses are also capable of being understood in the sense 'from the midst of', 'from the bosom of'. For the *pars populi integra* vs the *plebs sordida* in Tac. *Hist.* 1.4, see C. Badel, '*Pars populi integra*: Clientèle et régulation chez Tacite', in M. Molin, *Les Régulations sociales dans l'Antiquité* (Rennes, 2006), 71–84, at 72–4.

¹⁰ Van Nijf 1997, 3 and *passim*.

LEXICOGRAPHY

Astrology is full of what appear to be occupational terms, both categorising and specifying. To take examples from Ptolemy, a list will characteristically begin or end with the umbrella-category, which is then filled in with exemplifying detail, for instance 'scribes, men of business, calculators, teachers, merchants, bankers, soothsayers, astrologers, sacrificers, and in general those who perform their functions by means of documents, interpretation, and giving and taking' (4.4.3, transl. Robbins), or 'persons whose activities lie among the perfumes of flowers or of unguents, in wine, colours, dyes, spices, or adornments, as, for example, sellers of unguents, weavers of chaplets, innkeepers, wine-merchants, druggists, weavers, dealers in spices, painters, dyers, sellers of clothing' (4.4.4, transl. Robbins). The interest in labels immediately suggests a certain similarity to the epigraphic habit of specifying occupations on tombstones, as if work were seen by the person or person who formulated the inscription as essential to the identity of the deceased (whether the deceased himself, or those who honoured him, or even the stone-mason[11]). The implicit pride of those whose tombstones boast of being 'best of' even suggests astrology's sensitivity to status within professions (not just doctors, but *top* doctors; not just merchants but those who have attained the highest esteem in their profession).

All of which takes us back to the need to contextualise this value-system. We might want to press harder, certainly for evidence of bias (what is over- and under-represented, and why), and potentially, though somewhat positivistically, about the economy (horizontal differentiation of a variety of crafts and trades in an increasingly specialised economy; vertical differentiations, whether of stages within an industrial process or of hierarchy). All of that will follow. But astrological usage needs to be considered first. And what seems the obvious question—whether astrological authors use real trade names, which would warrant the comparison with inscriptions in the first place—comes up against immediate frustrating difficulties.

How do we identify a real trade name? Evaluating the testimony of a literary author is not necessarily straightforward:[12] his labels might not represent anything workers in question would have recognised, and at the outside he might even be joking.[13] Hence, in the quest for parallels to establish usage, is the

---

[11] K. Bradley, 'History and Fiction: A Review Essay', *CJ* 90/4 (1995), 445–50, at 448.

[12] T. Erb, 'Prolegomena einer Untersuchung der handwerklichen Arbeitsteilung in der römischen Antike, anhand der überlieferten lateinischen Berufsbezeichnungen', *Klio*, 64 (1982), 117–30, at 127.

[13] Erb (n. 12), 127, and Petrikovits, 69, adduce Plautus, *Aulul.* 508–21, a joke list of all the creditors who descend on a house demanding payment (makers and vendors and menders of women's clothes and footwear and accessories—mostly -*arii*, also some in -*ones*, -*ores*); cf. Holleran, 244. For 'literarische Augenblicksbildungen', see also Drexhage 2004, 43.

testimony of a literary author as valuable as that of an inscription or papyrus? How reliable are the latter, or are they, too, stylised in certain ways?[14] What about lexica and glossaries? What if other attestations of a word are only later than the text in question? If a word subsequently turns up in Hesychius, say, does that establish that it was already a technical term in a second-century source? But—perhaps the most serious difficulty—with all types of source there arises the question whether the word in question is a trade name at all, or rather describes a habitual activity. The former, the *Berufsbezeichnung*, may be defined as what the person in question would use to describe how he made his living. The latter, the *Tätigkeitsbezeichnung*,[15] is something to which astrology in principle is particularly liable. Indeed, because astrology represents a universe of 'people doing things', it has in principle *more* motivation to find words for activities than to use specific job-titles, let alone be remotely concerned with specifying what precise stage of a production process an individual was involved in. It needs to show how the disposition inculcated by the stars produces action in a certain domain, and prefers formulations with a certain spread and multi-applicability. An extreme case is 'workers in fire and iron', governed by Mars (rather than cutlers or armourers or blacksmiths), although astrology usually prefers to flesh this out with more specific examples. Context also affects how the labels are interpreted. For example, in a highly differentiated economy, the label 'carpenters' might underspecify workers who in fact specialised in a particular kind of product. Conversely, 'coffin-maker' might well be a good choice for a themed list of funerary workers, but in a small-town environment where a man did whatever joinery came his way might be an unduly limiting way to describe a particular individual's activities (4.191 n.).

To cut through all the difficulties, I compared the occupational descriptions in the Manethoniana with the least possible controversial trade names, drawing heavily on the papyri and inscriptions documented by Ruffing 2008. From the study of the earliest Manethonian poet's preferences (i. 169–70, 175–6), it can now be seen that all poets have the same techniques at their disposal, but very different patterns of preference. There is a sixfold difference between the poets who most (M^b) and least (M^c) often make reference to occupations, and at the bottom end of the scale (M^c and M^d) numbers are low enough to make statistics questionable, but in order to facilitate comparisons I converted numbers for each category (using my judgement over what to assign to each one) into percentages rather than using raw totals. The results were as follows:

---

[14] Tran 2013, 225–8, on names which are likely to overspecify professional activities (e.g. sculptor of the eyes of statues).
[15] Drexhage 2004, 42; Ruffing 2008, 23, 212.

	straight	morphological adaptations	same root	epic paraphrase	unsure	total
M^a	9 (14.52%) 3	3 (4.84%) 4	27 (43.55%) 1	22 (35.48%) 2	1 (1.61%) 5	62
M^b	30 (24.39%) 2	25 (20.33%) 3	50 (40.65%) 1	9 (7.32%) 4=	9 (7.32%) 4=	123
M^c	11 (52.38%) 1	3 (14.29%) 3	6 (28.57%) 2	1 (4.76%) 4		21
M^d	8 (32%) 2	1 (4%) 4	9 (36%) 1	7 (28%) 3		25

By 'morphological adaptations' I mean for instance poetic forms of a name, like ἰητήρ for ἰατρός (indicated in the Roster of Trades with 'cf.' after the standard trade name), and by epic paraphrase I mean for instance ἐχυρῶν δωμήτορας οἴκων (6.415) for οἰκοδόμος (indicated in the Roster of Trades by 'Periphrasis'). Rather counter-intuitively, the wordy and paraphrastic M^b turns out to be significantly fonder than M^a of the straight trade name (or trade name modified only by change of dialect). But he is less so than M^d, and not nearly so much as M^c, slightly over half of whose occupational references are attested trade names, usually with parallels in Θ. No surprise, though, that M^b is much the fondest of all the poets of morphological adaptations using his favourite -τωρ and -τήρ suffixes, which he not infrequently expands with a dependent genitive to enhance the sense of agency exercised *upon* something (p. 212). The favourite technique of all the poets except M^c, who relegates it to second place, is to build a little expansion around the root of the original trade name; this leaves the basic term visible amid the poetic encrustations. Where M^a comes into his own, however, is in his liking for paraphrasing trade names with epic wadding that overwrites the underlay altogether. This constitutes his second favourite technique, and if there is a way of distinguishing between M^c and M^d it consists in the latter's liking for this device as well. I have assigned instances to this category where it is possible to be confident that there is such an underlying term. There are a number of cases, however, especially in the fourth book, where it not clear whether this is the right explanation, or whether the poet is simply freewheeling.

Firmicus is a different matter. Although no claim is made to provide a comprehensive study, the *Mathesis* turns out to include a remarkably large number of ordinary trade names—everyday names that figure in inscriptions[16] as well as in literary authors—alongside typical astrological circumlocutions and umbrella-categories (for instance, those who work with fire and iron). Like the Greek poets, Firmicus mostly shuns the over-specific (for instance, there are no *sitularii*, *capsarii*, or *anularii*), but he will as soon or sooner name broad and basic categories as wrap them in diffuse and indirect verbiage. Moreover,

---

[16] Convenient lists in Petrikovits, 83–130; Joshel, app. II, 176–82 (the city of Rome); Varga, 17–20 (Moesia Inferior).

although it is extraordinarily difficult to impose robust categories that are accurate, not anachronistic, and not prejudicial ('skilled'/'unskilled'),[17] it turns out that they particularly cluster in some sectors—manufacturing, especially handicrafts;[18] secondarily retail;[19] and that luxury goods are well represented. Only a few specifically pertain to domestic service, but several more are compatible with it.[20] These patterns will receive attention in what follows.

DISTORTIONS AND BLIND SPOTS

The closer reading of the astrological texts which follows rests on two premises. One is that, as was said above, they offer an imaginary of work. The second, however, is that astrology is also and above all a consumer activity, and that astrological texts are *Fachtexte*, meant to be useful and used. So without losing sight of the tropes and stock images which should give some insight into the mental frameworks of its users, it is fair to ask how astrology's occupations relate to those in the real-world economy, about the selection biases of the texts' authors, and whether any inferences can be made about their clientele. The task, accordingly, will be to navigate between the Scylla of a positivist reading that takes the texts as transparent sources for economic history and the Charybdis of treating them as purely a repository of literary tropes.

Either way calls for a reckoning with the matrix that generated them. No one, presumably, will argue that any astrology envisages a village economy. Papyri show us what that would look like,[21] and it is very clearly not the world of Manetho or Ptolemy. Papyri feature bakers, butchers, and brewers—producers of basic foodstuffs—as well as carpenters and workers in brick and ceramic. Apprenticeship contracts are a particularly good source for the trades

---

[17] 'Literate': *grammaticus, philosophus*; presumably *notarius, scriba, tabularius*. 'Technical': *architectus, geometres, herbarius, medicus*. Care of animals: *armentarius, asinarius, equitarius, mansuetarius, porcarius*. Transport: *navicularius, veredarius*. Other: *aquarius* (unless this is 'technical', depending on the nature of the work), *balneator, clavicularius, cornicularius, funerarius, laturarius*.

[18] *artifex; opifex; faber; organarius*. Metal: *aerarius, argentarius, aurifex, bra(c,t)tiarius, inaurator, caelator, monetarius, ferrarius, ferramentarius, scutarius*. Stone work, construction: *lapidarius, marmorarius, parietarius, politor, structor*. Textiles: *textor, lanarius, linteo, fullo, infector, tinctor, plumarius*. Leather, skins: *caligarius, coriarius, gallicarius* [*ex emend.*], *pellarius*. Ceramic: *figulus*. Decorative arts: *musivarius, pictor, sculptor*.

[19] *negotiator, nauclerus, navicularius, mercator, tabernarius*. Of wares: *margaritarius, pigmentarius, turarius, sericarius*. Of services: *popinarius*.

[20] *mediastinus, minister*. Potentially also *actor, coquus, pistor, tonsor, unctor, obstetrix*.

[21] Ruffing 2008, 84–7.

needed for day-to-day subsistence.[22] These are dominated by weavers, but also include carders of wool, masons, basket-weavers, a maker of nails, a smith, a doctor, someone involved in the funeral industry, as well as stenographers and even a musician. They hardly indicate the clientele with the purchasing power for the astrological luxuries and refinements we shall be discussing, perfumes and mechanical toys and luxury cloth in purple and gold.[23] Presumably for these texts we should envisage a setting, if not in Alexandria itself, then in one of the bigger nome capitals.[24] We are on firmer ground for Firmicus, for whom we have to assume a sophisticated city economy in the western Empire in the fourth century (or, rather, source-material reaching back to Hellenistic Egypt which has been updated to reflect that environment). One must not overspecify. Firmicus was a Sicilian, maybe from Syracuse;[25] he practised as an advocate in Rome.[26] These are not the 'settings' of the *Mathesis*. But they provide the background for the imaginary of work presented therein.

Some more caveats: a genre which strangely blends *Realien* with stylisation needs delicate judgement, and there are major blind spots where any enquiry is bound to fail. The first of these is not unique to astrology. There is enormous interest in manufactures—but hardly any in the natives' relations to the product, whether they produce it or retail it or both. Ancient job descriptions habitually blur this distinction (the *-arius* suffix is notoriously hard to interpret), which was in any case barely meaningful for the small craftsman who marketed his own goods from a shop in the front room of his own house (the so-called *Produzentenhändler*).[27] But astrology has even less interest in making precise distinctions insofar as its real concern is the sphere in which a person operated and the ethical values attached to that sphere. It does make occasional distinctions, but these are incidental and inessential.[28] For that same reason it is utterly

---

[22] Bergamasco, esp. the list of professions in 96–8, and discussion in 104–6; Freu, 32–3 (mainly textiles).

[23] Although one of the contracts (SB XIV 11982, Oxyrhynchus, AD 554) does concern the art of embroidery with gold thread (cf. Appendix II, II.7.viii.c, Firmicus, 3.3.14, 3.13.23).

[24] For Oxyrhynchus, capital of the 19th nome, see Alston, 275 (citing figures of 90 different crafts and a bare minimum of 33 guilds in the fourth century); P. van Minnen, 'Urban Craftsmen in Roman Egypt', *MBAH* 6/1 (1987), 31–88, at 37–8, estimating 30–50% of the population occupied in crafts in the late Roman/Byzantine city; Venticinque, 17–18. An impressive range of goods was apparently available in a modest settlement like Corycos (Drexhage 2012, 167).

[25] Cf. 6.30.26 for Archimedes as *civis meus* [F. Skutsch, *ex emend.*]: Boll, *RE* s.v. Firmicus, 2365.27–31; T. D. Barnes, 'Two Senators under Constantine', *JRS* 65 (1975), 40–9, at 40 n. 4; R. Turcan (ed.), *L'Erreur des religions païennes* (Paris, 1982), 10; P. Monat (ed.), *Mathesis*, i (Paris, 1992), 8; Frakes, 77.

[26] Turcan (n. 25), 14. Bram, 2, conjectures that he was active in Constantinople as well, if that is where he exercised a senatorial office—on which Turcan is, however, agnostic (12).

[27] Petrikovits, 69–70.

[28] Take the example of perfume. Sometimes natives are explicitly sellers (Appendix II, III.4.vii), sometimes makers (II.8.ix), but other formulations are open to interpretation (3.9.5

unconcerned with the size and scale of an operation in which a worker was involved, anywhere on the spectrum from lone artisan to part of a large work-team or organised industry. This kind of factor simply does not register.

Secondly, astrology does not concern itself with the legal or contractual conditions under which work is done. There is no way of distinguishing the self-employed from the wage labourers ($\mu\iota\sigma\theta\omega\tau o\iota$/*mercennarii*[29]), nor among the latter any way to distinguish those secure individuals who worked maybe for yearly contracts in great houses as tutors or tame intellectuals or artisans from the seasonal labourers who queued in the agora for a day's work at harvest time. Casual labour performed in, say, building sites or the docks is formulated in such a way as to make it indistinguishable from professional labour, for instance as 'load-bearers', 'hauliers', 'builders'. The men treated like pack animals in 6.383–4 are possible candidates. For all we know, Firmicus' *pastinatores* (5.4.18) were hired on the same terms as the $\dot{\epsilon}\rho\gamma\acute{a}\tau a\iota$ by the owner of the vineyard in Matthew's proverb (Matt. 20:1). But we cannot deduce that from the language used to describe them, where the poet is more interested in his miserabilist pitch and the prose-writer inscrutable.

But the most important distinction, to which astrology is blind, is between the juridical status of slave and free. This turns out to be quite different from esteem within a profession, in which astrology is very interested indeed, with frequent references to status within a métier.[30] In practice, this could vary enormously. The gamut ran all the way from local notables to the peddlar on the street pavement, from the wool barons[31] to the sweated labour who wove and fulled and dyed their products in doubtless reeking workshops for poor pay. Above all, it ran from the baker M. Vergilius Eurysaces to the slaves shown running his business on his extraordinary bread-basket of a tomb outside the

---

aromatum...praepositos; 3.11.18 *aromata...tractantes*; 3.13.5 *actus...de aromatibus*; 4.11.2 *artes...aromatum*; 5.5.6 *per ipsos aromatum odor suavitatis adfertur*). It barely matters, and Venus oversees both.

[29] Treggiari 1980; P. A. Brunt, 'Free Labour and Public Works at Rome', *JRS* 70 (1980), 81–100; Veyne 2000, 1171. Finley thought the contribution to the economy of wage labourers was small (1981, 166 = 1989, 13: the self-employed were probably 'much the larger class' than casual labourers, except for the city of Rome and possibly Alexandria). But see the bibliography cited in Lis and Soly, 265 n. 18.

[30] Firmicus, 3.6.3 *tinctores maximos*; 5.2.14 *sculptores sed quos operis sui gratia commendet*; 5.2.21 *artifices, sed qui omnibus artificibus praeferantur*; 8.7.5 *pictorem...sed quem hoc studium famoso honore nobilitet*; 8.24.3 *pistores, sed qui inter collegas suos habeant principatum*; 8.26.12 *medici, sed quos professionis suae nobilitet ingenium*; 8.27.8 *auriga regius, sed qui ob hoc maxima gloriae consequatur insignia*; 8.28.3 *curiosi artifices, sed quos artificii sui nobilitas commendet, amici regum*; successful athletes in 6.31.3, 8.24.4, 5; see too Teucer, II 12.8 πολυκρίτους ἐργάτας (presumably the sense of the epithet is 'singled-out', i.e. select, special).

[31] P. J. Thonemann, *The Maeander Valley: A Historical Geography from Antiquity to Byzantium* (Cambridge, 2011), 188–90, on the purple dyers of Hierapolis.

Porta Maggiore.[32] This man, who made his money from supply contracts with the government as *pistor redemptor*, is the very icon of such status differentials; he may well himself have passed through the ranks of those whose labour he depicts. But when astrology talks about status, it is in terms of intangible qualities and matters of sentiment. These are the result of a particularly happy alignment of stars (being in sect, having a benefic in aspect) which adds a dash of prestige. It is not in terms of the very real and practical matter of whether one was slave, freed, or free.[33]

The more we contextualise astrology in a world of élites with big spending power, the more likely the artisans are to be slaves or ex-slaves simply in virtue of the fact that élite status is so closely associated with slave-ownership.[34] But the likelihood of slaves or ex-slaves practising a particular occupation is presumably also to a high degree a matter of location. There would be different demographics in Rome, Alexandria, Antioch; cities would differ from towns, and both from villages; areas dominated by rural villas from regions dominated by smallholdings.[35] The implications are that the likelihood of finding slaves and ex-slaves and descendants of slaves among the tradesmen and professionals listed so inscrutably in astrology will differ according to the presumed context of the text in question. We know that Firmicus reflects that of a sophisticated fourth-century city. Many professions are compatible with freedmen in a Roman setting, where freed *opifices* and *tabernarii* are legion.[36] But the artisans in the common source of the Manethoniana and Θ are perhaps rather less likely to have been so against an Egyptian background, where slave artisans are

---

[32] Zimmer 1982, 21, and 106–9, no. 18; Joshel, 80–1; Petrikovits, 66; Veyne 2000, 1173; L. Hackworth Petersen, 'The Baker, His Wife, His Tomb, and Her Breadbasket: The Monument of Eurysaces in Rome', *The Art Bulletin*, 73 (2003), 230–58; Mayer, 112–13; MacLean, 5–15. See D.–S. s.v. Pistor, 499–500 (M. Besnier), on the wide spectrum of statuses in the profession of *pistor*.

[33] Tran 2013, 68–72, on the tendency of Roman trade names to refer to the manager of a business ('l'entrepreneur'), not those who worked under him (or those who merely put up the money for a business, and drew profits without having any further involvement in it). This state of affairs results from the skew in the evidence away from slave labourers who could not, in any case, afford to commemorate themselves.

[34] K. Harper and W. Scheidel, 'Roman Slavery and the Ideal of a "Slave Society"', in N. Lenski and C. M. Cameron (eds.), *What is a Slave Society? The Practice of Slavery in Global Perspective* (Cambridge, 2018), 86–105, at 99–100.

[35] Regional variation in Harper and Scheidel (n. 34), esp. 98–9.

[36] Strictly, what inscriptions tell us is not that freedmen dominated a particular industry, only that they were the ones likeliest to want to commemorate themselves with reference to it (Joshel, 125, 162–3). In practice, many freeborn will simply have lacked the skill-set to compete with trained slaves and ex-slaves in many crafts, forcing the former back on unskilled and/or part-time labour. But freeborn sons continuing their fathers' trades will have swelled the free artisanate. See Huttunen, 124; Garnsey 1980, 44, 45; Hasegawa, 51.

poorly represented, and the great majority of the slave population is located in the household.³⁷

Why is astrology—unlike Artemidorus, and unlike the oneirocritical as opposed to astrological writings ascribed to Achmet—so blind to juridical status? If it were supposed to represent the viewpoint of the élites and to reflect their attitudes, the obvious answer is that work is demeaning anyway, so distinctions of status are beside the point.³⁸ Likelier, however, is that it was not relevant to a class or classes who saw work, not juridical status, as the essential part of their and others' identity. That was all the more so where boundaries were permeable, and the free, freed, and enslaved might be working cheek by jowl. In that connection it is very suggestive to compare astrology's attitude with that of Roman work reliefs.³⁹ Unlike Athenian commercially produced vases showing images of workmen,⁴⁰ the Roman work scenes are mostly from

---

³⁷ For Egyptian papyri mentioning slave occupations, see I. F. Fichman, 'Sklaven und Sklavenarbeit im spätrömischen Oxyrhynchus', *Jahrbuch für Wirtschaftsgeschichte*, 2 (1973), 149–206 (tables 3 and 5–6 show how few out of the total numbers of slaves have any indications of profession, and table 2 indicates what those professions, if any, were: the only one that recurs to any significant degree is that of weaver); Bieżuńska-Malowist 1977, ii. 78–108, esp. 85–91; 103–4; 107–8 ~ 1984, 192–7, 207–8, 229–30; Straus 1988, 867–76; Bagnall 2003, 232–3 (little evidence for them in craft production). Where slaves are artisans (as opposed to agricultural workers, managers, wet-nurses, or prostitutes), they are most often textile workers: see Harper, 128–35, and, for apprenticeship contracts, Bergamasco, 124; carpentry in Freu, 35–6.

³⁸ J. Bodel, 'Slave Labour and Roman Society', in Bradley and Cartledge, 311–36, at 317; Bernard, 84–5.

³⁹ Zimmer 1982; 1985; R. Turcan, *Messages d'outre-tombe: L'iconographie des sarcophages romains* (Paris, 1999), 80–8; Béal; Courrier, 253–62.

⁴⁰ Some basic points to inform the comparison. (i) The Athenian vases (which cease in the 460s) are far more selective in the trades they represent (above all, metalworkers and potters) than either the Roman reliefs or astrology; the same is true of Etruscan gems of the classical and Hellenistic periods, which prefer shipbuilding, the manufacture of armour, and sculpting (L. Ambrosini, 'Images of Artisans on Etruscan and Italic Gems', *Etruscan Studies*, 17/2 (2014), 172–91; see her n. 15 for recent bibliography on the Athenian images). (ii) The context of the image is presumably all-important. For the role of the export market in the Athenian vases, see S. Lewis, 'Images of Craft on Athenian Pottery: Context and Interpretation', in *Bollettino di Archeologia*, online, 2010/Volume speciale, 12–26. As for the Etruscan gems, there is an orientation towards naval and military activities, as well as a focus on lone artisans outside a workshop context which, whatever else it may imply, does not suggest self-portraiture. (iii) The Athenian images possess conventions which are able *both* to idealise (heroic nudity; presence of Athena) *and* to bring out banausic or even slave status. The former is stressed by S. von Reden, 'Arbeit und Zivilisation: Kriterien der Selbstdefinition im antiken Athen', *MBAH* 11 (1992), 1–31, at 24; the latter by Finley (1980, 101: 'upper-class ideology...prevails throughout, even when a potter-painter is depicting his own craft and his own workshop: the craftsman himself is denigrated in one way or another, and his slave still more, either by his physiognomy or by his "slavish" posture'; cf. N. Himmelmann, 'Archäologisches zum Problem der griechischen Sklaverei', in *Abhandlungen der Akademie der Wissenschaften und der Literatur in Mainz, Geistes- und Sozialwissenschaftlichen Klasse*, 13 (1971), 1–49, esp. 16–34 on physiognomy and physiology, and 35–8 on the natural slave indicated by a squatting position), though M. Pipili, 'Wearing an Other Hat: Workmen in Town and Country', in B. Cohen (ed.), *Not the Classical Ideal: Athens and the Construction of the Other*

funerary or votive monuments which showcase the ways in which workers wanted posterity to remember them. To some extent their reasons can be reconstructed or hypothesised: for slaves, this was their best way of asserting personhood; for *liberti* it was their best route to wealth, status, and becoming an insider.[41] Yet the freeborn chose this type of commemoration as well, even if in numbers not quite so high as for freedmen.[42] Work itself seems to have acquired merit. Perhaps the values associated with it in astrology—an enterprising spirit, πίστις/*fides*, social connections, and the comfort and reassurance of transmissible prosperity—can help us understand something of the moral climate in which that has happened.

Yet astrology is also peculiar. Astrology has its own ethics and adheres to conventions which are sometimes weirdly stylised, and this section is really about trying to decipher them. We begin with the 'what' and 'how' rather than the 'why'. The focus is on occupations not offices, hence on producers and distributors and to some extent providers of service. It is not on administrators, hence not primarily the civic élites of the Greek East, the senators (in Rome) and knights, except insofar as they owned the land that provided the raw materials, or owned the slaves and freed the freedmen who manufactured and distributed the products, or put up money for the *negotiatores* and *naucleri* who shipped them. But on what basis can we even begin to make comparisons for the occupations on which the enquiry turns? How is it possible to determine what is over- or under-represented? Given its repetitive nature, one cannot simply produce raw totals for particular kinds of occupations in an astrological text or across astrological texts. One can of course count the number of trades and register their types in text A vis-à-vis text B. But vis-à-vis the real economy?

---

in *Greek Art* (Leiden, 2000), 153–79, at 158, warns that not all features of banausic iconography are necessarily meant to denigrate the craftsman; so too N. Himmelmann, *Minima Archeologica: Utopie und Wirklichkeit der Antike* (Mainz, 1996), 46–53. For both approaches, see A. Chatzidimitriou, 'Distinguishing Features in the Rendering of Craftsmen, Professionals and Slaves in Archaic and Classical Vase Painting', in V. I. Anastasiadis and P. N. Doukellis (eds.), *Esclavage antique et discriminations socio-culturelles: Actes du XXVIIIe colloque international du Groupement international de recherche sur l'esclavage antique (Mytilène, 5–7 décembre 2003)* (Bern, 2005), 131–45, at 134–8. Figures on the Etruscan gems are even potentially confusable with Hephaestus or Daedalus.

[41] Joshel, 52–61.

[42] In Zimmer's collection, which is restricted to Italy and Cisalpine Gaul, 34 of the 107 readable inscriptions (= 31.78%) were set up by those who can certainly be identified as freeborn (Zimmer 1982, 6–7). This is less than the bare minimum of 36 (= 33.65%) set up by freedmen, which is likely to be a very significant underestimate, but still not negligible. However, the pattern changes when the entirety of Gaul is taken into account, where the majority of monuments with work scenes whose owners can be identified commemorate the freeborn (Béal, 162–3, 165–6).

An urban environment might go some way towards explaining what is an egregious underrepresentation, obvious even without recourse to other literature or papyri or epigraphy to shore up the comparison. That is agriculture, in which, drawing partly on comparative data, Keith Hopkins estimated that as much as 90% of the population outside Italy was engaged.[43] One would get little sense of this from astrology. It is not that farming is altogether overlooked (Appendix II, I.1.i): there is even a Lot of farming and planting. But its scattered mentions are dissipated among so many different taxonomies (below) that it rather gets lost as a category in its own right, and land-based occupations altogether lack the specificity of those in, say, manufacturing or retail, let alone offices associated with religion, temples, and divination. There is some mention of the cultivation of cereals, but those staples of the Mediterranean landscape, the olive and the vine, barely register at all, the former not in the slightest, the latter barely.[44] It is interesting that the Roberts noted that farmers were underrepresented in inscribed epitaphs as well.[45] Gardeners occur, however, perhaps not on a scale to match the λαχανοπῶλαι in papyri,[46] but far more prominently than other cultivators (I.1.iii). To explain this, one is reluctant to fall back on the ready availability of water as a taxonomical category, though it may matter more that the gardener was a literary topos (4.257, 258 nn.). Might visibility also have contributed to the higher profile of market gardeners than farm labourers? Astrology's urban clientele were more familiar with them.[47]

And yet this appeal to clientele will hardly do as a general explanation for the underrepresentation of farming and food-production, because there is *also* so little trace of the secondary and tertiary sectors which produced and distributed food products (Appendix II, VII.1). There are *pistores* in Firmicus (but not *Lib. Herm.*), but only a couple of bakers (VII.1.ii), and scarcely more butchers (VII.1.i).[48] And given the Egyptian origin of so many of our texts, another notable absence are beer-makers and -sellers.[49] As for luxuries, Firmicus does have a confectioner,[50] but from a culture of infamous élite gourmandising you might have expected endless scope for honeyed eggs or sows' wombs or

---

[43] Hopkins 1978, 6.
[44] Appendix II, I.1.ii. Valens, I 2.51, makes Libra preside over καρπῶν, οἰνικῶν, ἐλαϊκῶν, and texts on eclipses and brontology pay attention to what harms or helps their cultivation. When Firmicus mentions wine, it is mostly as a lifestyle choice (3.12.3, 4.19.10, 8.7.1, 8.12.3).
[45] J. Robert, 284–5, 289–90; L. Robert, 'Une épigramme de Carie', *Opera Minora Selecta*, i (Amsterdam, 1969), 373–401, at 384–7, 389; *BE* 1979, nos. 556, 567.
[46] Ruffing 2008, 84, 628–31.
[47] See too Patlagean, 164, on the market gardeners (κηπουροί) of Corycos.
[48] This is a way in which astrology parts company with inscriptions: cf. Joshel's table on 175, in which butchers and bakers may not approach metalsmiths or textile workers, but do outnumber jewellers.
[49] Ruffing 2008, 83, 86, 529–33 ζυτᾶς, ζυτοποιός, ζυτοπώλης.
[50] 8.11.3 *pistores dulciarii*; on confectioners see D.-S. s.v. Pistor, 499 (M. Besnier).

lampreys' milk. Not a bit of it. Astrology is, however, fascinated by garum, an extraordinarily niche item in comparison to the cereals and wine and olives which are so underrepresented. It is simultaneously a must-have Roman food, an aspirational item, but also disgusting, one that seems to have made moralists no less ethically than digestively queasy;[51] nor does it seem to have struck the astrologers as in any way odd to bracket it together with the Egyptian practice of mummification (see on 6.456–64). Somehow that seems like a suitable emblem for the pretensions, contradictions, and cultural complexities of astrology's implied setting.

With the move into the secondary and tertiary sectors, and a presumable urban environment, more robust comparisons are needed. For Ptolemy/Θ/the Manethoniana, that comparative material is furnished especially by the Egyptian papyri, and in Kai Ruffing's massive study of their evidence for manual labour and trade.[52] That study extends to empire-wide Greek inscriptions as well,[53] and astrology can be complemented by the associational inscriptions of the Greek East, on the one hand, and by grave inscriptions on the other, especially (though it is somewhat later than one would want to go even for the latest of the Manethoniana) the corpus from Corycos in Cilicia Trachea,[54] which constitutes evidence for a small-to-middle ranking city in the Greek East. Ruffing's particular interest is in professional specialisation, both horizontal and vertical. To some extent his questions can be applied to astrology as well, and though it would not be the most obvious source from which to launch an enquiry into the sophistication of the ancient economy, its practice of listing related items under a grand heading might have some useful insights into diversification within given sectors.

For Firmicus, there is the enormous documentation for the city of Rome. The most recent studies of this known to me are still those of Huttunen and Joshel. Huttunen took every fifth epitaph from *CIL* vi (*Inscriptiones Urbis Romae*), where that was possible, but occupations were not his main interest: only about a tenth of his corpus indicated the occupation of the deceased,[55] and as a result, although from a larger sample size, he ended up studying a much

---

[51] Aspirational: Drexhage 1993, 29 'in sehr konkreter Weise Ausdruck römischer Lebensart'. Disgusting: Sen. *Ep.* 95.25. Both: Purcell 1995, 145: '... the dissonance between the squalor of the producer and the desirability of the product'.

[52] Ruffing 2008; see the review by D. W. Rathbone, *BASP* 47 (2010), 365–7 (one problem is that the tabular presentation conceals the local context of each document); also, K. Ruffing, 'Driving Forces for Specialization: Market, Location Factors, Productivity Improvements', in Wilson and Flohr (eds.), 115–31.

[53] Not tabulated, but footnoted. Ruffing indexes his sources at the end of the second volume.

[54] Patlagean, 156–69; Drexhage 2008, 2012.

[55] Huttunen, 48 (Table 4): occupation is indicated for 9.5% of the deceased, and for 4.4% of dedicators.

smaller total than Joshel, who concentrated on occupational inscriptions, mainly *CIL* vi itself, but supplemented from other sources. Joshel also had many important exclusions, not only senators and knights, but also imperial freedmen and slaves, actors and actresses, charioteers, gladiators, and the military and military support staff. That left as her principal categories building, manufacture, retail (distribution), baking, professional or educated services (architects, doctors, teachers), skilled services (barbers, entertainers), domestic service, transport, and administration. That constitutes most of the areas of interest in the present discussion, though entertainers deserve some separate attention as well (pp. 111–16).

None of these sources will give us a neutral and representative picture of the economies from which they derive. They have their own selection biases. One cannot match astrology up against them as against a transparent and self-evident representation of the 'Roman economy'. What one *can* do, however, is ask whether they share any of the same biases as astrology. Some of these biases will be different. Inscriptions are affected by the physical location of the sector in question, for instance agricultural occupations will be underrepresented in an urban cemetery. Epitaphs are also affected by the type of burial, for instance burial inside a Roman *columbarium* which limited space and might squeeze out indications of the deceased's occupation. But one might want to know how, or whether, prestige affects what is recorded—whether astrology is focusing ambitions and aspirations which also manifest themselves in commemorative display, or, to put it the other way round, whether the same occupations that had bragging rights for the owners of tombs or allowed petty tradesmen to parade with collegiate grandeur also have cachet in astrological predictions.[56]

Not necessarily, seems to be the answer. In the first place, the enormous coverage of occupations in associational inscriptions, which is well known, is a better parallel for the broad spread of occupations mentioned in astrology than for its particular patterns of concentration in certain areas. Associational inscriptions include many overlaps with astrology, including stonecutters, marble masons, interior decorators, metalworkers, textile workers a-plenty

---

[56] See Treggiari 1975, 57; M. B. Flory, 'Family in *Familia*: Kinship and Community in Slavery', *AJAH* 3 (1978), 78–95, at 80, for the presumption that prestige affects which professions are named on tombstones. It does seem a plausible factor in a society so concerned with 'face'—note the same reticence about *mediastini* in the tomb of Livia (Treggiari 1975, n. 122) and in Firmicus (App. II, VII.3.vii). But Joshel qualifies the idea with the different meanings work had for those who undertook it; see too Hasegawa, 31; Varga, 16: 'The complexity and multitude of the occupational titles is the hard proof for the fact that certain people identified with their profession regardless of which [*sic*] it was and that sometimes, even if modest, it became an important part of one's life and being'; Courrier, 260–2 (noting that even a slave's humble job-title might be staking a claim to be part of an aristocratic household); J.-M. Carrié, rev. of Joshel, *Annales*, 50/5 (1995), 1109.

(linen-workers, tailors, fullers[57]), shoemakers, ragmen (*centonarii*; compare the sellers of bric-a-brac in 4.322?), bakers and butchers, transport workers (porters, muleteers[58]), and workers in the funeral industry (νεκροτάφοι; *libitinarii*). But there is a yawning image gap between astrology, which barely conceals its disdain for some of these arduous, smelly, tawdry businesses, and the members of the corporations, who represent themselves in inscriptions with all the pomp and circumstance and procedural decorum that any self-respecting commemorator did in antiquity. What the associational inscriptions do is simply testify to the same diverse economic landscape that astrology is embedded in, but inscribes with its own peculiar values.

Epitaphs and dedications by individuals are more interesting. Their patterns are not identical to astrology's, and different corpora seem to have very significantly different distributions within them. For instance Joshel's figures imply that only $46/1470 = 3.13\%$ of her occupational inscriptions involve distributors of food (meat, fish, produce, oil, wine), whereas in Corycos that rises to almost a quarter.[59] But where they do agree is in the overrepresentation of luxuries, such as precious metals, jewellery, quality textiles, and unguents. These form a disproportionately large part of the (itself large) combined category of manufacturers and salesmen in Rome,[60] and constitute the most obvious bias of the whole astrological corpus, which seems to reflect the interests of specialist craftsmen who served élites with massive purchasing power. Conversely—what is even more striking—both bodies of material tend to look away from cheap mass-produced goods. Contrast the legions of artisans in luxury crafts (Appendix II, II.8) with the paucity of workers in wood and makers of ceramic products (Appendix II, II.7.iii),[61] which had so many applications, architectural and domestic, functional and decorative, that their meagre astrological presence (save the odd reference to brick-makers in M^b, lamps in Θ, and *figuli* in Firmicus) is truly glaring.

It is not altogether self-evident that the same factors are at play in inscriptions and grave-reliefs as in astrology, but it would seem that the banal ubiquity of ceramic products, in particular, is the reason for their underrepresentation in the latter. This fastens attention on the gold- and silversmiths, the chasers

---

[57] Guilds of textile workers: Poblome, 499.   [58] Huttunen, 120 (on transport workers).

[59] Joshel: figures from 174–5; Patlagean, 159–60; it makes little difference even if the seven individuals involved in *droguerie* are subtracted from the 97 or 98 (Patlagean gives both figures) involved in the super-category *alimentation et droguerie*.

[60] Joshel, 69–70 and table on 175. The same tendency was already evident in Huttunen's much smaller corpus (Huttunen, 122). On the overrepresentation in epigraphy of those who work in precious materials, see Tran 2013, 213–14.

[61] Zimmer 1985, 215. The pattern in Corycos is different, and rather puzzling (Patlagean, 162–3). The workers in ceramic (34) about equal the combined total of goldsmiths (13), workers in bronze (18), and engravers of gems (2 καβιδάριοι), but carpenters are still desperately few (2).

and engravers and embroiderers in gold thread, the jewellers, ivory-carvers, parfumiers, even makers of expensive toys. It has little time for the makers of bricks, tiles, pipes, amphorae, tableware, lamps (neither did Hyperbolus' detractors, for that matter), or cheap terracottas. That simple contrast seems to be the nub of it. One might want to invoke other factors too, like a largely servile workforce,[62] or the setting or nature of the workplace, as if such workers were simply less visible.[63] It is presumably true that the goldsmiths and all the luxury retinue were indeed very visible within their cities, lined up in *tabernae* opening onto the prime shopping streets, known to shoppers as 'the pearl-dealer', 'the engraver', 'the parfumier', and represented as such on their shop-signs. But the matter clearly cannot be reduced to the extra-urban location of big pottery manufactories, for there is no shortage of smaller urban artisanal outfits in the ceramic industry (like the one in the Via di Nocera in Pompeii, which made lamps and die-holders among other wares). Nor, despite the potential interest of bringing to bear the 'spatial turn' in recent archaeology, can it be a matter of the visibility or otherwise to the public of ceramic workers in the workplace, whether they worked in large production halls or in cellular production units. There is just too much variability in the evidence to make that possible.[64] The status of the product seems to count for more than the visibility of the producer here.

Some of the best-known sources of occupational inscriptions from Rome are the *columbaria* of Livia and the Statilii Tauri, which contained the ashes of the serving staff of these members of the imperial élite (Livia's in use from late in Augustus' reign till after Livia's deification in AD 41; that of the Statilii again between the reigns of Augustus and Claudius).[65] That opens the possibility of comparing the jobs attested in these great houses with Firmicus (or even with Greek-language astrology). If there were any significant degree of overlap, it

---

[62] Zimmer 1985, 208 and n. 15; Petrikovits, 78, on slaves in terra sigillata manufacture; P. Mayerson, 'The Economic Status of Potters in *P.Oxy.* L 3595–3597 & XVI 1911, 1913', *BASP* 37 (2000), 97–100. On the social status of the potter (mostly Palestinian evidence), F. Vitto, 'Pottery and Pottery Manufacture in Roman Palestine', *BIAL* 23 (1986), 47–64, at 60–1.

[63] For the importance of visibility in fostering a sense of professional identity, see e.g. Flohr 2011, 96–7.

[64] For case-studies of environments in which ceramic workers lived and worked, see E. A. Murphy, 'Roman Workers and their Workplaces: Some Archaeological Thoughts on the Organization of Workshop Labour in Ceramic Production', in Verboven and Laes (eds.), 133–46 (La Graufesenque and Scoppieto); see too M. Flohr, 'Constructing Occupational Identities in the Roman World', ibid. 147–72. Anyone so minded could work through the list of pottery production sites in Asia Minor in Poblome, 495–6. There is also wide variability among the working environments of fullers (Flohr 2011), who are slightly less well represented in astrology even than ceramic workers (Appendix II, II.7.viii.f.).

[65] S. Treggiari, 'Domestic Staff at Rome in the Julio-Claudian period, 27 B.C. to A.D. 68', *Histoire sociale*, 6/12 (1973), 241–55; ead. 1975; Joshel, 74; Hasegawa; S. R. Joshel and L. H. Petersen, *The Material Life of Roman Slaves* (Cambridge, 2014), 215–16.

might suggest the representation of slaves and freed persons among the clientele of the latter, or at least that it reflected their outlook and horizon of expectations. Common sense would counsel not to expect precise forecasts for a *libraria*, *cellaria*, or *ab ornamentis*, for instance, but astrology might, in its less precise way, refer to waiters or bearers or simply to servants. That particular enquiry, however, turns out not to be particularly fruitful. Astrology does, obviously, refer to the service sector (Appendix II, VII), occasionally specifically to servants (VII.3.vii), to managerial and administrative (VII.6.ii) and clerical (IV.2.vi) posts,[66] and to very many other professions which are compatible with a great-house context, or with alternating between public and private employment, like builders, gardeners, textile workers, cooks, barbers and masseurs, doctors, teachers, or musicians and entertainers. But the setting is not explicit, the location of the labour not usually identified.[67] Once again, it is the type of activity that furnishes the interest, not its social setting or any relationships of dependence or interdependence it may have entailed.

Comparative Excursus: Manetho (and the Related Material in Ptolemy/Θ) and Firmicus

This section sophisticates the assumption that the Manethoniana and related texts (Ptolemy, Θ) reflect Egypt in the early to mid Empire, Firmicus the western Empire in the mid fourth century. We should expect to find some differences between them, and do, but it is far more complicated than that they present snapshots of particular economies at given moments in time. The first explanation for that is astrology's tralatician character. Earlier texts are transcribed, but also modified and updated. On the one hand, the Manethoniana share material with Ptolemy that presumably, on chronological grounds, predates him.[68] This material turns up in each of the several Manethonian poets and then again in Θ, allowing us to see how it has been supplemented, including with some -άριος trade names (p. 144), potentially from a date as late as, if not later than, Firmicus himself. On the other hand, there are some distinctive items in Firmicus' eighth book whose sources (Teucer of Babylon and Manilius)[69] take them even further back than the earliest of the Manethoniana. Astrological texts are palimpsests, in no way snapshots of a given author's life and times. Secondly, they are individually styled. Ptolemy gives deadpan lists. Firmicus is hospitable to long lists as well, but entirely capable of rhetoric and emotionalisation. The Manethoniana have poetry's essential *Affekt*/emotivity,

---

[66] Firmicus has *procuratores*, *actores*, a *scriba tabularius*, but no *vilici* or *dispensatores*.
[67] p. 56, on imperial functionaries. [68] i. 785–6.
[69] Hübner 1984, 139–43, and id. on Manilius 5, i. 20–1.

but also share its hospitality to vivid little particularisations.[70] Can we nonetheless make any inferences, if not about the economies they represent, then about their emphases in what they select for attention?

Let us begin with construction (Appendix II, II.5) and handicrafts (Appendix II, II.7). On construction, the Greek sources have a generally wider vocabulary for workers with stone and builders (stone-cutters and quarrymen: 6.416, 419, 4.325; dressers of stone: 4.326; stone-carvers: Θ p. 212.28; builders of houses: 6.415, 4.325; of walls: 4.291; shinglers: Θ p. 215.15; and apparently specialists in coping: 4.151-2 ~ 1.299-300). Firmicus' offerings (*lapidarius, marmorarius, structor, architectus*) are mostly more generic, with the striking exception of *parietarius*.[71] Ship-building—what little there is of it (II.5.vi.f)—is somewhat more detailed in the Manethoniana as well, with carpenters (4.323-4), painters (4.342), and caulkers (4.345-6). As for handicrafts, while sharing certain blind spots (if anything, Firmicus pays ceramics and carpentry even scanter attention than the Greek sources), they all refer to basic manufactures such as leather-working (II.7.v: tanning, shoe- or boot-making) and especially textiles (II.7.viii). All also have the basic categories of weavers, dyers, and fullers, to which Firmicus adds one of antiquity's most celebrated manufactures, that of purple cloth (8.19.7), a sumptuous specialism. From that point on, they diversify. If M^a refers to embroidery (2.320-1, 322-3, to which Θ adds πλουμαρίους), Firmicus has embroidery specifically with gold thread (3.3.14, 3.13.23), as well as weavers or dealers of silk (8.19.12 *siricarius textor*, which could be taken together or separately[72]), while M^d/Θ seem to refer to the Egyptian specialism of jacquard-style weaving with multiple threads (5.168 πολλοῖσι μίτοις/ πολυμιταρίους). Do these add-ons straightforwardly reflect increasing technological progress? Jacquard technique perhaps might, but in general any expectation of finding a linear increase in professional specialisms would be naïve. We should rather allow for different authors having different thresholds for detail.

Other luxuries (parfumiers, florists, craftsmen of precious stones) are pretty much six of one and half a dozen of the other. All sources refer to those who craft (engrave, polish, even paint) precious stones (Appendix II, II.8.vii); Θ and Epit. IIIb add the late antique technical term καβιδαρίους.[73] Firmicus has pearl-dealers

---

[70] i. 170.

[71] *TLL*: attested also in the tomb of the Statilii (*CIL* vi. 6354) and a *pictor parietarius* in Diocletian's Price Edict (7.10); D. Esposito, 'Il sistema economico e produttivo della pittura romana: Esempi dall'area vesuviana', in Monteix and Tran (eds.), 65-85, at 66, 68.

[72] Feraboli, 216. The parallel transmission in Teucer, II 1.10, and *Lib. Herm.* refers to χλαῖναι or *tunicae*, not to silk, but I doubt whether we are entitled to infer updating by Firmicus. On *sericarii*, see Veyne 2000, 1183 (representative of the *plebs media*); Dumitrache, 25-6 (with an example from the second half of the second century AD).

[73] *TLL* s.v. *cavidarius* (perhaps in Justinian and in glossographers).

(Appendix II, III.4.vi, *margaritarii*), and a more differentiated vocabulary for workers in gold (*aurifex, inaurator, bra(c)tiarius,* and variants) (Appendix II, II.8.vi.a). He is also more inclined than the Manethoniana to specify (at least occasionally) that he has retailers as well as, or instead of, manufacturers in mind (below). It is a strange idiosyncrasy of the Manethoniana that they refer to petty traders or altogether more disreputable forms of commerce, but not to the merchants of boutique wares that so captivated the other astrologers (Appendix II, III.4.iv–x). On the other hand, the Manethoniana have slightly more specificity on the visual and plastic arts: M^b has colossi (4.570), and M^a panel-painters and workers in the encaustic technique (6.524–5, cf. 4.342), which is unsurprising in Egypt if mummy-portraits are meant. Incidentally, the higher degree of specialisation in the funeral industry in Manetho/Ptolemy/Θ (Appendix II, V.6), with their eviscerators (6.461, 4.267), embalmers (4.267), coffin-makers (6.496), professional mourners (6.498), cremators (6.497), grave-diggers (Θ p. 215.11), and doubtless even worse ghouls from whom only textual corruption spares us, is also readily explained by an Egyptian context (pp. 117–18).[74]

But if there is little to choose between the luxuries in the Greek and Latin texts, one interesting difference reveals itself in categorisation, which extends over and beyond luxuries and into therapeutics (that is, medicine). This is the 'chemical' industry (Appendix II, V.2),[75] for which Firmicus has a word (*pigmenta*; not in *Lib. Herm.*) and the Greek texts do not. *Pigmenta* could be rendered 'granular substances', or just 'ingredients', and include dyes (hence with a link to the textile industry), flowers, perfume, wine, precious stones, and medicaments.[76] But the difference between the Greek texts and Firmicus seems to consist just in the availability of an umbrella term to the latter ($\varphi\acute{\alpha}\rho\mu\alpha\kappa\alpha$ is not used in the same way). All the individual items subsumable under the category are familiar in the Greek texts. The Manethoniana generally itemise them in isolation (in 5.167, $\chi\rho\acute{\omega}\mu\alpha\tau\alpha$—pigments in the modern sense—figure alongside embroidery, statuary, and waxworks, in other words under the notional rubric of 'media'), but Ptolemy, 4.4.4, has a cluster of professions which exactly match the concept with the sole difference that he fails to use a label.

---

[74] For the necrotaphoi see 4.192 n. The ἐνταφιαστάς in Ptol. 4.4.8 are also well documented in Egyptian papyri: N. Reggiani, 'Ispezionare cadaveri: Mummificatori, medici e anatomisti nell'Egitto greco-romano (a proposito di P. Oxy. III 476)', *MBAH* 33 (2015), 75–86.

[75] Schmidt; Ruffing 2008, 115, 120 'Chimie'; 122 'd.h. die Verarbeitung und Herstellung von Mineralien, Drogen und Aromata, Seifen, Salben, Farben und Klebstoffen'.

[76] For *pigmenta*, see L. R. LiDonnici, 'Single-Stemmed Wormwood, Pinecones and Myrrh: Expense and Availability of Recipe Ingredients in the *Greek Magical Papyri*', *Kernos*, 14 (2001), 61–91, at 73. It is easy to see how several functions could come together in one product from the case of Corycian saffron, which had properties as a cosmetic, drug, spice, and colorant: see Drexhage 2008, 25, and 2012, 168–9.

It is also instructive to compare the trades of the Manetho/Ptolemy/Θ group with those of the 'Teucer' group (the various witnesses to Teucer himself, as well as Manilius 5, Firmicus, 8.6–17 (paranatellonta) and 19–30 (*monomoiriai*), and *Lib. Herm.* xxv). Comparing the various witnesses to Teucer with one another (helpfully done by Feraboli for Firmicus, 8.19-30) shows both what is common to the tradition and the individual choices that different users have made. My focus here is on Firmicus book 8, on which there is a great deal of work to do. It is hard to judge when there is no correspondence at all (given how patchily, and in how abbreviated a form, the various witnesses are transmitted), but one can be more confident when there is a basis for comparison. Best of all is when the other sources have something in that exact same degree position. The force of the comparison is blunted somewhat, though not completely nullified, when the item is not exactly matched.

Where Firmicus departs from the Greek comparanda, it is sometimes because he has Manilius' verbiage as a sort of heady brew from which he can extract more precise trade names (such as the *aurifices, bracteatores, inauratores, margaritarii*, and very likely also the *emplastratores* from Manilius, 5.505–30). Manilius has also supplied him with some of his specialist types of fishermen (Appendix II, I.2.ii), as well as his workers in saline products and garum (Appendix II, VII.1.v). Firmicus is sometimes influenced, too, by Manilius' sentimental-moral tropes, which is clearest in his treatment of the little agricultural idylls (n. 104). Where Firmicus lacks the support of Manilius as well as of the other comparanda, it *might* be because he is thinking of the Rome and western empire that he knew, with its highly sophisticated and diverse economy,[77] the imperial court at the centre,[78] but also what Professor MacHugh called its cloacal obsession.[79] But we cannot be confident about this, in the light of the incomplete and discrepant state of our sources for Teucer.

Is there anything that can be shown to differentiate Firmicus from the Greek sources? The point of this section was never to conduct a general head-to-head between the two, merely to show that the kinds of difference that *do* occur are not matters of fundamental re-orientation. So far they have been matters of detail or of individual weighting. It is hardly surprising, for instance, that Firmicus the lawyer extends his legal terminology beyond the range of anything

---

[77] For Deltoton (25° Aries) Teucer, II 1.10 has κατασκευαστὰς χλαινῶν καὶ παντοίας ἐσθῆτος and *Lib. Herm.* xxv. 1.38 *aptatores tunicarum vel cuiuscumque vestis* (24°–25°). For this position Firmicus has goldsmiths (8.19.11 *aurifex, bracteator*), while textile-workers appear in a more specialist form at 27° (8.19.12 *siricarius*).

[78] e.g. 8.24.1 the lettered who enjoy royal favour ~ Teucer, II 6.3 εὐπαιδεύτους; 8.29.14 *muliones regis*, cf. Feraboli, 228; 8.26.1 (4° Scorpio), where the court dwarfs find no parallels.

[79] The sewer-workers in 8.19.12 (28° Aries) and 8.20.1 (2° Taurus) seem to do double duty for what appear in Teucer, II 2.2 (7° Taurus) as ὑδραγωγούς, περιχύτας; cf. Feraboli, 231.

offered by the Greek sources (Appendix II, IV.2.v: *advocati*; *causidici*; *iudices*, and references to popular courts; *iuridici*; *iuris periti/interpretes*; *legum interpretes/inventores/latores*). More important for the discussion of the world of work in this section is the range of offices explicitly set in the ambit of the imperial court.[80] These are both scattered and pervasive, though they belong in the domains of service (including transport and entertainment) and administration and make very little difference to the world of trades and crafts and manufactures; the master-weavers in the imperial textile mills seem the only instance where the latter have been relocated in the world of the court.[81] No manufactures, on the other hand, are set explicitly in the context of the military, although in Firmicus' day that was becoming an increasingly important sector.[82] The economy itself, the financial system, barely registers as different. There are stampers of coins/men who work in the mint (*monetarii*), money-changers and money-lenders (*feneratores*), bankers (*mensis praepositi*), tax-men—and now tax-farmers,[83] and accountants (*rationales*). It is hardly surprising that the private wealth-managers have now been almost entirely subsumed into imperial business. But the chief distinction between 'private' and 'public' wealth that Greek astrology makes—between 'royal' (βασιλικά) and public (δημόσια) or civic (πολιτικά) revenues[84]—does not in practice figure very differently in Firmicus' consistent distinction between the *fiscus* and 'public' funds.[85] Firmicus here seems to use traditional terminology[86] to reflect a

---

[80] Qualified as *regii* for specifically imperial functionaries: administrators, scribes and secretaries (Appendix II, IV.2.vi: *scribae*; 6.23.6), interpreters, doorkeepers (8.14.1), couriers (3.11.18), entertainers (3.6.3), a dwarf (8.26.1), a charioteer (8.27.8), muleteers (8.29.14).

[81] 3.6.4 *textores... regis textrinis... praepositos*. See Jones 1960, 189–90; Quintana Orive, 335–8. In Italy there were imperial *fabricae* for woollen cloth at Milan, Aquileia, Rome, Canosa, and Venosa, for linen at Ravenna, for dye in Taranto and Syracuse: K. Randsborg, *The First Millennium AD in Europe and the Mediterranean: An Archaeological Essay* (Cambridge, 1991), 94–102, esp. fig. 53; B. Ward-Perkins, *The Fall of Rome and the End of Civilization* (Oxford, 2005), 102–3 and n. 24.

[82] Petrikovits, 74–5.

[83] Appendix II, IV.1.v *vectigalarii* (no *redemptores*), but perhaps also the sense in 4.330 ἐργολάβους (see ad loc.).

[84] Royal/civic: e.g. Περὶ σχημ. 2 βασιλεῦσιν ὑπηρετουμένους ἢ πόλεσιν; Π.τ.δ. 22 ἐν πολιτικαῖς πράξεσι ἢ βασιλικαῖς ἀναστρεφομένους; Valens, I 20.15 δημοσίων, πολιτικῶν, βασιλικῶν πραγμάτων προεστῶτας; I 20.18 βασιλικὰ ἢ πολιτικὰ πράσσοντας, II 19.3 ἀρχῆς πολιτικῆς ἢ βασιλικῆς, etc. Royal/public: Περὶ σχημ. 13 δημοσίων χρειῶν ἢ βασιλικῶν ὑπηρεσιῶν, 36 οἱ δὲ ἐν βασιλικαῖς αὐλαῖς ἀναστρέφονται ἢ ἐν δημοσίαις πράξεσι, 37 ἔν τε δημοσίαις ἢ βασιλικαῖς πράξεσι διαβαλλομένους; Valens, II 21.4 εἰς δημόσια ἢ εἰς βασιλικὰ πράγματα; IV 8.17 καὶ δημοσίας καὶ βασιλικὰς πράξεις; IX 2.14 ἐν βασιλικαῖς αὐλαῖς καὶ δημοσίοις τόποις.

[85] Appendix II, IV.1.i; cf. also 8.14.1 *Huic opes regiae credentur aut aerarium populi*.

[86] F. Millar, 'The Fiscus in the First Two Centuries', *JRS* 53 (1963), 29–42, at 41 and n. 171, and 1977, 190 and n. 5 (τὸ βασιλικόν v. τὸ δημόσιον). The *fiscus* is associated with the emperor in Firmicus, 3.10.7, 3.11.17.

distinction that was no longer, in practice, enormously meaningful.[87] Astrological writers reflect the world they lived in, but not to the extent of radical overhaul of their inherited material or of abandoning idioms which characterise the genre and provide its distinctive, unmissable argot. Work and its values remain for Firmicus much as the Greek sources present them.

* * * * *

The matter at stake in this section has ultimately been the rather fundamental one of how to read astrology. The richness of its treatment of work, the precision of some of its details, is seductive, but positivism is ultimately a danger because, as has been suggested, astrological texts should also be seen as an imaginary of work, a repository or treasury of tropes about it. The selection of professions in the various texts has at best an oblique relationship to the real world of work. The goods and services they refer to are indeed those to be had in Alexandria, Rome, Corycos, or Oxyrhynchus. But aspiration, fascination, dread, and above all literary-philosophical commonplaces are what drives astrologers' selection of material, not the occupational structure of the real economies in which they lived. Why is there such a glut of fishermen (and huntsmen) in comparison to butchers and bakers? Very likely because the fisherman was a figure loaded with cultural resonance, he and his products ripe with metaphor;[88] the butcher hardly was. Why else so much garum? And it is against the background of huge discursive interest in luxuries of all kinds that the singling-out of Venereal crafts such as garland- and perfume-making must be seen (Athenaeus allows us to gauge something of the vast literature generated by both subjects[89]). Conversely, there must have been any number of midwives and wetnurses[90] in Manetho's and Firmicus' worlds, but (save for the sole reference to *obstetrices* in Firmicus) they were simply too uninteresting to register in their texts. Yet there are pimps and prostitutes a-plenty, and the odd

---

[87] Millar (n. 86); id. 1977, 189–201.

[88] Purcell, esp. 135–8. In Firmicus, the main associations of fishermen are *labor* (3.3.11, 3.10.8, 4.13.6, 8.30.8) and other words for hardship (4.14.14 *gravia, misera et scelerata...officia*), the low status of the trade (8.22.1), and antisociality (5.2.14). The contrast between the imaginary and real worlds is clear: Patlagean, 164, contrasts the plentiful documentation of Corycos' market gardeners with that of its very few fishermen. Astrology's urban setting failed to lower the latter's profile.

[89] Athen. 15.669 C–686 B (garlands), 686 C–692 F (perfumes). Athenaeus' discussions have a lexicographical motivation and geographical dimension, but also suggest the extraordinary specialisation the crafts no doubt entailed. For a likely commercial flower garden in Pompeii producing material for the perfume and perhaps garland industries, see W. F. Jashemski, '"The Garden of Hercules at Pompeii" (Appendix II, II.viii.6): The Discovery of a Commercial Flower Garden', *AJA* 83 (1979), 403–11.

[90] A 'highly regulated' business in Egypt: cf. A. Ricciardetto and D. Gourevitch, 'The Cost of a Baby: How Much did it Cost to Hire a Wet-Nurse in Roman Egypt?', in L. Totelin and R. Fleming (eds.), *Medicine and Markets in the Graeco-Roman World and Beyond* (Swansea, 2020), 41–69, quotation on 55.

procuress for whom one would look hard and long among gravestones commemorating the honest dead, or in the epigraphy of work associations.[91] Again, any number of women might be included tacitly among the textile-workers. But there are no spinners, which was specifically women's work, unskilled, deeply repetitive,[92] and simply of insufficient interest to merit a mention. In short, astrology both embeds conventional attitudes and commonplaces, and reformulates them in its own strange idiolect. It needs to be studied alongside literary and philosophical texts which do not necessarily replicate its attitudes, but revolve around the same themes, agree about what merits attention and discussion, in other words participate in a shared 'discourse'. It is here that we reach the heart of the matter.

MENTAL STRUCTURES

> To study trade (or agriculture, or manufacturing, or money) in purely economic terms may be intellectually convenient, but it completely misses all the other dimensions, all the other meanings of the activity, most of which were far more important to the ancients than the purely economic…The ancient *agora* was firmly embedded in the value-system of the *polis*.' (Morley, 47)

Organising Principles

Professions are not cited in and of themselves, but as representatives of mental categories, which broadly hold good across different writers. You cannot ask astrology to reflect the organisation of the Graeco-Roman economy. But you can expect arrangements to reflect certain mental structures and logics. Investigating them starts off as a formal exercise, but soon passes over into the much more complicated and interesting question of how astrological categories (which are constrained by the elements of the system, planets and constellations) interact with/reflect social attitudes to work, which once against brings up the question of whose value-system is implied here.

    Astrology, arguably, does two things: it lists categories associatively or 'horizontally', e.g. members of the funeral industry,[93] and it links them 'vertically' by

---

[91] A point made by Diana Delia (review of Joshel), *American Historical Review*, 98/4 (1993), 1217.
[92] Jones, 190; Poblome, 499 (no guilds); Harper, 129–30.
[93] 4.190–2, 267; Firmicus, 3.9.3; Ptol. 4.4.8.

association with some superordinate category, whether a 'given' of astrology, for instance Martian or Saturnian professions,[94] or an aesthetic or moral category, for instance noisome professions including tanning, fulling, woolworking, baking, and cookery.[95] Each method has a story to tell. It is interesting to reflect which professions seem to be categorisable together in ancient terms and which do not. Funerary workers, for instance, are envisageable as a group, but 'medical' professionals are split between various sub-specialisms (Mercury for doctors, Mars for surgeons, the category for *pigmenta* for druggists), suggesting the contingency or artefactuality of the modern category of medicine.

Signs and planets both provide ready organising categories for certain professions (for instance, Equus, paranatellon of Aries, organises 'all things horses'; Mercury everything involving intelligence or dexterity), though there is plenty of scope for complication even here.[96] Most obviously, to underscore an earlier point, the fact that there is an at-hand planetary icon or mascot does not guarantee the elaboration of the category in question: cultural choice comes first and determines what is of taxonomical or 'discursive' interest. There is enormous investment in the delightsome Venus and her combinations with Mercury. We are attracted to this group of professions on account of their appeal to the senses (colourful dyes[97] and gems; fragrances and flowers; wine; music; perhaps even the sense of touch if one includes textiles) and in the *esthiopolis*[98] that is their implicit setting. Yet the Martian professions are puzzlingly under-represented and under-differentiated.[99] Surely, one might have thought, the military profession cultivated a kind of fatalism to which astrology would have been congenial. Mithraism suggests that pop astrology played very well to soldiers. Is it that *our* astrology, the version that has survived, is dominated by the urban shop-keepers, and the military had a culture of its own?

---

[94] Resulting in some arbitrary-seeming collocations. Mars drags into association military men, athletes, hunters, and artisans whose trade involves fire and iron. For Saturn, see e.g. *Lib. Herm.* xxviii. 13 (pilots, fishermen, drawers of water, farmers, ship-builders, undertakers). Artemidorus employs a similar procedure, except that the god is a dream symbol rather than a planet, e.g. Dionysus linking vine-growers, tavern-keepers, and Dionysiac artists (2.37), Athena *cheirotechnai*, philosophers, farmers and soldiers (2.35), and Aphrodite a very mixed range of professions (2.37 ἀγύρται, κάπηλοι, ζυγοστάται, θυμελικοί, ἰατροί, σκηνικοί, ἑταῖραι).

[95] Firmicus, 3.8.7 (Tran 2013, 187).

[96] For instance, why are gold- and silversmiths assigned to 'glamorous' Venus rather than metallurgical Mars (Firmicus, 7.26.10)? Why are dyers so wretchedly Martian in 1.80 when they are normally charmingly Venereal (n. below)?

[97] Ptol. 4.4.4, where the category seems to be 'things decorative', Valens, I 1.29 χρωμάτων κράσεις καὶ ποικιλτικήν, πορφυροβαφίαν; for dyeing, Appendix II, II.7.viii.e.

[98] To use the term of Morley, 28.

[99] Natives in Firmicus are *milites*, sometimes *militares*, occasionally praetorian prefects or commanders of legions, but they are more often ranked horizontally among related professions (athletes, hunters) than vertically within a military hierarchy (no *manipulares, legionarii*, centurions, let alone (military) *principales, optiones, tesserarii, signiferi*).

Particularly interesting is the organisation of material for which there was no ready-made principle. The underrepresentation of farming and foodstuffs has already been noted. We can now add the under- (or perhaps over-?) theorisation of land, which, vacillating between categories (functional, symbolic, ethical, but tending towards the economic[100]), hardly exploits the possibility which the planet Saturn offered for a category of 'land' itself.[101] It is the same with gardening. Instead of mobilising terrestrial signs for 'landed' professions,[102] astrology ranks gardeners alongside sailors, undertakers, and so on, among 'watery' ones. Land is not an organising category at all in this way of thinking. In that respect, astrology contrasts with other systems of thought (Dicaearchan cultural history,[103] or indeed the élite consensus that land was the only occupation for a gentleman) which dignified it as a conceptual category. There is a certain amount of mileage to be had out of agriculturally themed paranatellonta, where the most extensive treatments of landed professions are in Firmicus' eighth book, with a background in Manilius (not Teucer), embracing sowing, harvesting, and storing cereals, gardening, grafting, the pruning of vines, as well as pastoralism.[104] But it is precisely at the point where constellations, with all their fruitful possibilities for analogy (Spica, Falx, Crater, and so on), are used in place of planets that the presentation of the land is most encrusted with literary topoi. Astrology itself has nothing new to offer here. Presumably, once the élites had theorised farming as the only honourable profession for a gentleman, they

---

[100] Functional (rare): γεωργούς among Martian professions that use iron in Ptol. 4.4.5. Symbolic: Ptol. 4.4.9 puts farming among tropic signs, metaphorised as exchange (you give to the earth and it gives back) or mediation (between the lower world and our own). Ethical: *agrorum cultores* among the effects of the Sun, also physiological and ethical, in Firmicus, 4.19.32; cf. 3.2.20 *honestos honestis moribus agricolas*. *Labor* in 8.11.3, 8.29.10. Economic (a good Roman attitude, cf. Finley 1973, 58): associated with wealth in Firmicus, 3.2.20, 3.3.4, with *patrimonium* in 4.19.32, 6.32.10, and otherwise the generation of wealth in 6.22.11, 8.11.3, 8.26.15(?); in 7.26.10 *negotiatores, agricolas, feneratores, nauclerosque*, with Jupiter in the Lot of Fortune, the organising category seems to be those who make money by handling other people's goods, as also in 6.489–90. γειοπόνους, ξείνοισι γεγηθότας and Hephaestion, i. 235.22-3 περὶ ξένων ἢ ξενιτείας ἢ γεωργίας, 236.7 περὶ γεωργίας ἢ ξενιτείας. Managerial: Hephaestion, i. 239.1-2 περὶ γεωργίας ἢ οἰκονομίας. 'Grounded' things seem to be the theme in Hephaestion, i. 237.13 περὶ γεωργίας καὶ οἰκοδομῆς. Farming among very miscellaneous Mercurial occupations in Valens, I 1.40.

[101] Valens, I 1.9; *CCAG* vii. 214.15; Apomasar, *De Myst.*, *CCAG* xi/1. 178.26.

[102] Rarely: in ps.-Palchus, *CCAG* v/1. 188.2.

[103] N. Purcell, 'The Way We Used to Eat: Diet, Community, and History at Rome', *AJP* 124 (2003), 329–58, at 346–52.

[104] Agriculturalists under Spica (Firmicus, 8.11.3 ~ Manilius, 5.270–84; this passage combines the primary and secondary sectors—cereal-growing and baking—under a single heading). An *arator* under Falx (8.29.13; cf. Hübner on Manilius, 5.22 *falce*). Gardeners under Crater (8.10.6 ~ Manilius, 5.236–44, gardening, grafting, topiary, trimming vines: remarkably extended, and over-writing the usual classification of gardeners by watery, toilsome activities). Pastoralism in 8.6.5 ~ Manilius, 5.115–17: tootling shepherds overwrite disdain for the real-life version (Reynolds and Tannenbaum, 118; Pleket 1988, 270).

left the messy business to their farm-managers (*vilici*) and withdrew into their precious *otium*. What is left of agriculture is caught between pragmatism on the one hand, sentimental cliché on the other.

Then there is manual work. Intellectual professions have an icon in Mercury. There is none for manual labour, although it does not follow that the astrologers have no category for it. That category is both explicitly invoked[105] and emerges empirically from passages in which physical labourers are aligned with artisans under what appears to be the general category of 'toil' (6.410–24, 4.437–43).[106] At the same time, there are only ambiguous signs of any category of manufacturing. Groups that seem to maintain a conceptual coherence can be counterpoised to those that do not (4.125–30). Any impression which arises from lists of cobblers or carpenters or statue-makers[107] is undercut when add-on factors turn the outcome in a direction suggesting that manufacture was not the organising principle after all.[108] Perhaps 'dexterity' or other ingenious *ad hoc* combinations are undergirding the arrangement; even then, 'dexterity' is invoked only patchily. Textiles form a category whose various subspecialisms, including manufacture, retail, cleaning, and repair, are readily grouped together (6.431–5; 4.420–4), but textiles as a whole are 'delightsome' Venereal trades, not 'dexterous' ones. Trades involving 'fire and iron' are not restricted to manufacturing (might a planet Vulcan have made a difference?), and show just the same eclecticism as those involving water. The ancient absence of a manufacturing category is hardly surprising in light of the insensitivity of the *-arius* suffix to the modern distinction between the secondary and tertiary sectors. But we might perhaps be struck by the preparedness to lump together hod-carriers and makers of precision instruments in a crude category of 'labourers'. Taxonomic brutalism runs up against the impressive particularity of the listed trades, not to mention the poetic investment of (especially) M^a and M^b in fleshing them out. It starts to raise the question of the values attached to work, and it is to these that we now turn.

---

[105] Appendix II, II.7.i. Add Valens, App. XVI 1 ἡ διὰ χειρὸς τέχνη, and other references to banausic arts in Apomasar, *De Myst.*, *CCAG* xi/1. 197.9. The Latin equivalent *artes sordidae* in Firmicus, 3.8.7. It is unclear whether the location of banausic arts in the centre of signs in *CCAG* xi/1. 134.6–7 implies a judgement about their social level, but the *banausoi* are the lowest property-class in Apomasar, *De Rev.* p. 64.12.

[106] Perhaps also note M^b's use of παλάμῃσιν for makers of pitch (4.346), of statuary (4.569), and ἐργοπόνους (4.442).

[107] 6.341–7 ~ 4.567–79; 6.520–5 ~ 4.146–52; 4.317–26 (contrast the treatment of shoemakers in 4.320–1 with Firmicus, 3.10.8, where they are organised under trades *gravibus odoribus*) and 4.14.13 (*ex igni vel ex ferro*); 4.341–6.

[108] 6.476–9 + 480–3; 4.271–89 + 290–3; 4.333–40 + 341–6; 4.437–43 + 444–9; Θ pp. 215.13–17, 216.8–16 (connection ζω-, living creatures?), 217.1–4 (dexterity?).

Values

From all the schemes which astrology's mania for classification elicits from its endlessly flexible organising principles, group attitudes and social judgements are implicit over and over again. This is a communitarian genre. Suspicion of the antisocial and untransparent, so patent in the references to misanthropes, secret books, and even in the category of 'hidden disease' (pp. 16–17), is equally visible in the alignment of tomb guardians with shepherds and herdsmen who live outside the city's bounds (6.407–9, and the additional note). These people raise a slight shudder. Some implicit judgements cause a certain amount of head-scratching. What conceivable set of prejudices could have aligned the legal and clerical professions with gardening and water-management as instances of the *malitiosi*?[109] But the focus of this section is less on community ethics, and more on hierarchy within it. It is about the perennial obsession with status, and respectability, and esteem. The more astrology speaks about this, the more interesting and distinctive does its voice become. While agreeing with astrology in its general valorisation of work and fear of idleness, dream interpretation has little to match it.[110] Once again we drive at the basic question of this whole first part, and maybe this is the best way of all to address it. Whose values are these? Whose version of respectability is this?

This is not a single or simple enquiry. In what follows, astrological value-judgements stated or implied[111] about professions are compared with other ancient theorists of work in order to try to isolate astrology's peculiar outlook. In virtue of the enormous attention it has attracted, the notorious passage from Cicero's *De Officiis* shoulders its way to the forefront of the discussion. Yet to focus too exclusively on that is to miss out on other discussions of labour which have shades and emphases of their own, so the following discussion also takes account of Xenophon, Aristotle, Posidonius, Musonius, Dio's *Euboicus*, and Pollux.[112] It is important, though, that the type of work is not the be-all and end-all. Astrology so far adopts the worm's-eye view, that of the little man who wants to know how he is doing vis-à-vis his peers, that it often notes

---

[109] Firmicus, 3.5.25.
[110] Pomeroy, 67: 'there is surprisingly little status distinction according to occupation indicated in Artemidorus'; on (in)activity, Thonemann 2020, 185–7.
[111] Deterioration of status brought about by unfavourable new factor: Firmicus, 4.21.7–8; 4.10.3 (*duces/milites*); 4.14.1–2 (watery trades); 7.26.5 (*oratores/causidicos*: for the disparaging tone of the latter, see Wilkins on Cic. *De Or.* 1.202).
[112] Xen. *Oec.* 4–5; Posidonius, F 90 Kidd/447 Theiler (ap. Sen. *Ep.* 88.21–8); Musonius, fr. xi Hense; Dio, *Or.* 7 (*Euboicus*), esp. 109–24; Pollux, 6.128 (Βίοι ἐφ' οἷς ἄν τις ὀνειδισθείη); Cic. *De Off.* 1.150–1. See Brunt 1973, and specifically on Cicero, e.g. Finley 1973, 41–3, 44, 51–8; Biliński; Brunt 1973, 26–34; Treggiari 1980, 48–9; S. Mrozek, 'Die gesellschaftliche Rolle der Arbeit in der Augusteischen Zeit', *Klio*, 67 (1985), 65–9, at 66–7; Joshel, 66–8; M. Valencia Hernández, 'Ética y economía en *De Officiis* 1. 150', *Veleia*, 10 (1993), 85–94; Ruffing 2004, 87–8; Scherberich.

status-differentials *within* professions. It is eloquent that Firmicus more often notes that a man surpasses his peers than that he has surpassed his ancestors.[113] From this point of view what matters is not *only* the business you are in, but also and especially your place in a pecking order.

The risk of a conducting a head-to-head between astrology and other sources is that the former comes off looking oppositional, as if it simply up-ends the élite disdain that Cicero best articulates. It would be all too easy to set sneering élites in one scale of the balance, and petty craftsmen with all their artisanal pride and sensitivities in the other. The reality is more interesting. On the one hand, astrology is not completely divorced from certain élite attitudes. As for esteemed professions, there is consensus from Xenophon to Cicero that farming is the only thing for a gentleman, but not perfect clarity about whether this involves getting one's hands dirty (it does for Xenophon and Musonius, but not clear that it does for Cicero, let alone for Rome's ultra-rich). But insofar as it implies a view at all, astrology does not seem to demur. Firmicus' references to agriculture associate it with wealth or wealth-creation considerably more often than with *labor* (n. 100), sometimes with virtue as well.[114] Land both produces crops and generates investment; a good sound conservative ethic is erectable on both. The image is a generally positive one. In astrology's few references to farmers, it is very rare for hands-on labour to be specified. Conversely, members of the élite like Cicero were perfectly capable of expressing contempt for manual work while appreciating and admiring the work of the skilled *artifex*[115]—in this respect validating that artisanal pride which astrology seems so strongly to channel.

The Greek authors involved in the comparison—Musonius, Dio, also Lucian—use the categories of seemly and unseemly (εὐσχήμονα, εὐπρεπῆ, πρέποντα as opposed to ἀσχήμονα, ἀπρεπῆ).[116] These are not the preferred

---

[113] Peers: 3.11.6 (*superiores*); 3.14.3, 5.2.21 (*praeferri*); 8.24.3 *pistores, sed qui inter collegas suos habeant principatum*; see also n. 30 (high status within métier). Subordination in 3.7.5. Ancestors: 6.3.4, 6.23.7.

[114] 6.32.10 vaguely suggests the old myth of the peasant patriarch (Garnsey 1980, 36–7; Lis and Soly, 266); the hint of complacent pleasure at the accumulation of wealth is one from which Cato the Elder would probably not have demurred.

[115] Biliński; Tran 2013, 214–17, 222–5, and 2017, 252–5, 260–1; Lis and Soly, 270. Craftsmen themselves boasted of their *ars, doctrina*, and *peritia* (Ruffing 2004, 97–8; Courrier, 270–2; Lis and Soly, 269; Tran 2011, 2013, 208–12, 2017, 255–6). Firmicus himself does not use terms of approbation like *callidus, doctus, peritus*, or *magister* for artisans, although his *callidi* (8.17.4) correspond to 8.30.9 *aurifex, caelator, pictor* (25° Pisces) and to Teucer, II 12.8 πολυκρίτους ἐργάτας. He uses *magister* (Tran 2011, 128–9 and 2017, 257–60) of those who practise the liberal arts, or train athletes or animals, not, say, of goldsmiths or architects.

[116] Musonius, fr. xi Hense ἐλευθέρια...καὶ ἀνδράσιν ἀγαθοῖς πρέποντα; Dio, Or. 7.110 ἀσχημοσύνην τε καὶ ἀνελευθερίαν, cf. 125–6 μυρίας ἀφορμὰς πρὸς τὸ ζῆν...οὔτε ἀσχήμονας οὔτε βλαβεράς; Lucian, Somn. 13 σχῆμα εὐπρεπές; Brunt 1973, 9, 13, 14, 19–26.

terms of astrology. It is Firmicus who comes closest, with his oppositions of *nobilis* and *honestus* to *ignobilis, inhonestus, vilis,* and *servilis.*[117] But the basic opposition is not the philosopher's or educational theorist's, between honourable and dishonourable in the sense of liberal *versus* illiberal. Esteem and disesteem for the purposes of astrology turn out, on the one hand, to correlate with the degree of physical effort that was in accordance with human dignity.[118] It was all very well for Xenophon or Dio to condemn arts that led to physical enervation,[119] but someone faced with the prospect of backbreaking labour might well take a different view of sedentary trades. And, on the other hand, the astrological value-system also has an aesthetic component, or rather an aesthetic component that also takes on an economic as well as moral dimension. Astrology is fond of opposing 'pure'—mostly Venereal, occasionally Mercurial[120]—arts (τέχναι καθάριοι or καθαραί, *artes mundae*[121]) to 'impure' ones (ῥυπαραί, cf. 6.459 τέχνησιν μυσαραῖς). These categories seem almost, though not quite entirely,[122] astrological, and rather look like a reframing of the conventional distinction between *liberalis* and *sordidus* from the point of view of skilled labourers themselves. 'Pure', or 'clean', arts include goldsmithing, painting, weaving, and trade in perfume and precious stones. They are not only free of grinding labour, but have an economic value which comes of sensory

---

[117] Indeed, the categories may cut across one another, so that your profession may be *honestus* while you remain *ignobilis* (4.21.2); one wonders whether the converse is also possible. Presumably *collegia*, which use *honestus* in their self-appellations (J.-P. Waltzing, *Étude historique sur les corporations professionnelles chez les Romains depuis les origines jusqu'à la chute de l'Empire d'Occident*, ii (Louvain, 1896), 190: *honestissimus, dignissimus, splendidissimus*) would never have admitted this, but Cicero might have done. In *De Off.* 1.151, *honestae artes* have to be certain kinds of thing in the first place (his examples are *medicina, architectura,* and *doctrina rerum honestarum*) and have to be compatible with one's *ordo* (in other words might be ignoble for a senator, but fit for someone more lowly).

[118] 2.356 σκληρὰς καὶ ἀπηνέας...τέχνας ~ *Lib. Herm.* xxxii. 36 *rigidas artes*; Valens, I 20.9 πράξεων ἐπιμόχθων, 33 ἐπιμόχθων τεχνῶν; ps.-Palchus, CCAG v/1. 187.13 πράγμασι δὲ βεβαίοις, σκληροῖς, ἐπιμόχθοις; Firmicus, 4.15.5 *laboriosas artes* ~ *Lib. Herm.* xxxiii. 6 *artes laboriosas*; for ἐπίμοχθος, see on 4.248. See also Firmicus, 3.8.7 *quibus artibus vigiliae perpetuae ab operantibus exigantur.* Dream interpretation implicitly agrees about the undesirability of grind: Thonemann 2020, 188–9.

[119] Xen. *Oec.* 4.2; Dio, *Or.* 7.110.

[120] Περὶ Πράξεως, CCAG v/3. 88.22–3 βελτίους καὶ καθαρὰς παρέχει τέχνας, οἷον σοφιστικήν, ῥητορικήν, γραμματικήν, διδασκαλικήν.

[121] Valens, I 1.29; App. II 30; Περὶ κράσ. I 192; 'Rhetorius', CCAG vii. 220.7, Apomasar, *De Myst.*, CCAG xi/1. 182.25.

[122] Porphyry, *FGrH* 260 F 8 καθάρειος γὰρ ἡ τέχνη καὶ οὐ πρὸς ὀνείδους, who is talking about ἑρμογλυφία; Neophytus Inclusus (12th/13th c.), Πεντηκοντακέφαλον, 48.6, who ingeniously manages to take Malachi's refiner's fire as the work of a τεχνίτου ἀρίστου κεκαθαρμένου. The καθαροπώλης/καθαρουργός (Ruffing 2008, 557–9) has nothing to do with this: he is an artisan baker. And Plat. *Phileb.* 62 B is completely different: geometry and music are impure arts insofar as they are this-worldly rather than divine.

attractiveness and are perhaps underpinned by a sense of social possibilities.[123] In practice, a nexus constitutes itself between the honourable, pure, and physically undemanding, on the one hand, and the dishonourable, impure, and laborious, on the other,[124] which have Firmicus reaching for his profoundest tones of miserabilism and gloom.[125]

Cicero's list of disesteemed (*sordidi*) professions contains five categories. The discussion below adheres to them. Cicero is discussing these occupations—as is Dio—from the perspective of allowable ways of making money,[126] not of what is most or least conducive to the philosophic life. Astrology's framing is economic as well.

The first category consists of those that incur *odium*, such as tax-collecting. While Pollux uses no labels, he lists various types of tax-men (τελώνης δεκατώνης, δεκατηλόγος εἰκοστολόγος πεντηκοστολόγος ἐλλιμενιστής) as well as the πορνοβοσκός. These are conventional attitudes, though no doubt extreme wealth or shamelessness might sometimes override or confuse them.

The second is wage labour, consisting of those who sell their *operae*. Cicero distinguishes between these and those who sell their *artes*, and he reserves the comparison to slavery for this type of occupation (*est enim in illis ipsa merces auctoramentum servitutis*). Although at first sight this sounds like Marx, Marx made no distinction between corporal and specifically manual (artisanal) labour. No-one else formulates it quite like this. It would correspond well to Pollux's ὑπηρέτης, though since Pollux follows this immediately with two types of leather-worker it is unclear whether he means to put them in different conceptual categories or not. What astrology misprises is specifically physical labour, and only because it is hard, not because it is sold.[127] Not everyone took this view. Xenophon and Dio have no objection to physical labour at all: what they care about is the opposite, physical enervation. Again, physical labour might have been discussed by some of the Stoics, given the topos of Cleanthes' work as a drawer of water (see on 4.257); it was possible to regard this as an entirely acceptable occupation for a rich man fallen on hard times.[128] One suspects that to be sanguine about hard labour required either the dissociation of those never threatened with it, or the fortitude of philosophy. Astrology has neither.

---

[123] See Pleket 1988, 267 and n. 3 for goldsmiths and purple-dealers.

[124] Θ p. 209.5–6 ῥυπαρὰς καὶ ἐπιμόχθους καὶ ἐπονειδίστους and Anubion ap. *CCAG* ii. 191.5 ῥυπαρὰς καὶ ἐπιμόχθους καὶ ἐπονειδίστους (sc. πράξεις).

[125] The aesthetic component is particularly clear in 3.8.7 *artes aut sordidae aut squalidae aut gravi odore*.

[126] Brunt 1973, 28; Scherberich, 88.

[127] For changing attitudes to working for money, see Graßl, 111–28 (in practice, for all but die-hards, it came to be recognised as a necessity).

[128] Epictetus, 3.26.7 (cf. 23); Brunt 1973, 26.

The third group is retail, those who buy wholesale and then sell at elevated prices. Pollux likewise lists the κάπηλος after the brothel-keeper. Disdain for the small-time profiteer who grasps after petty gain is an attitude that goes back to Aristotle,[129] and in *Lib. Herm.* xxv. 4.26 *mercatores, avaros, usurarios*, merchants appear next to skinflints.[130]

That attitude, though, is rare in astrology. In general we are hard-pressed to find any stigma. Greek astrology in general is more inclined to refer to ἔμποροι (long-distance traders, wholesale dealers, *Großhändler*)[131] than to κάπηλοι (small-scale traders),[132] just as Firmicus has far more *negotiatores* than *mercatores* (only a single instance, a pearl-dealer) (3.12.10). Firmicus' usage could be attributed to a general tendency for the title *negotiator* to proliferate at the expense of *mercator* (which sounded less ambitious and more parochial[133]). But when astrology refers to ἔμποροι and *negotiatores* it often makes obvious that it really does intend their original meaning, overseas traders who carry merchandise in ships. The astrological coding—Saturn for water, Jupiter or Mercury for lucre, and the Moon for wandering—brings out the main themes here, rich rewards weighed up against the pathos of severance from home. From this nexus of ideas astrology extracts as much mileage as it can about lifestyle choice. It is a good instance of how it is the moral dimension that exercises ancient writers on economic topics.

Yet the silence about κάπηλοι and *mercatores* is far from implying that astrology is uninterested in specialist or local dealers, petty wares, or the artisan who markets his own products. In the Manethoniana mention is made of trade in clothes (4.424), bric-a-brac (4.322), slaves (6.447), while sex (4.313–14) and grave-robbery (4.268) are also spoken of in commercial terms.[134] Firmicus is somewhat more forthcoming about specialist traders (identified by reference to *merces* or part of the verb *mercari*, or through *-polae* compounds; but of course *-arii* may be manufacturers, dealers, or both). The largest category turn out to be luxuries—precious stones, perfumes, incense, metals—followed by

---

[129] *Nic. Eth.* 1121^{b}31–1122^{a}13 αἰσχροκέρδεια.
[130] See too *Hist. Apoll.* 10 for disdain for the *mercator*; Treggiari 1969, 89.
[131] Ruffing 2008, 53, 84, 516–22.   [132] Maximus, *Epit.* 2, l. 22 ~ Camaterus, *Introd.* 1739.
[133] P. Kneissl, 'Mercator–negotiator: Römische Geschäftsleute und die Terminologie ihrer Berufe', *MBAH* 2/1 (1983), 73–90, at 75–81.
[134] So interpreting κακεμπορίης τε ματευτάς, although a reference to funerary professionals in general is not impossible in the light of the self-interested legalism in papyrus archives concerning them. For the necrotaphoi, see 4.192 n. For the Ptolemaic *choachytai*: M. Chauveau, *Egypt in the Age of Cleopatra: History and Society under the Ptolemies*, transl. D. Lorton (London, 2000), 139–49; on the legal case of the Theban *choachytai*, in and before 117 BC, see P. W. Pestman (ed.), *Il processo di Hermias e altri documenti dell'archivio dei choachiti (P. Tor. Choachiti): Papiri greci e demotici conservati a Torino e in altre collezioni d'Italia* (Turin, 1992). On the many sources of revenue of Ptolemaic mortuary workers, see Cannata 2020, ch. 7, 'Services, Income and Taxation of Funerary Priests', 122–58.

consumables (Appendix II, III.4.xi). Ptolemy and Θ offer support: when they use -πώλης compounds it is for sellers of perfumes, flowers, wine, or clothing, including purple.[135] In other words, retail items are the very things that most exercised the moralists, as we are about to see, but it seems that astrology has no problem with the vending of luxuries at all, and the only type of sale that elicits positive condemnation from Firmicus is sex (6.11.7, 6.30.16, al.). Most often he sees trade as the source of benefit. One waxes rich from it, and/or it is an opportunity to display professional probity (3.6.23; 4.19.29; 5.5.6). The auctioneer is a figure with a poor reputation in classical literature,[136] but Firmicus, who seems not to have inherited him from Greek astrology, has not seen fit to introduce him, for either weal or woe.

It is the fourth category, that of *opifices*, that best focuses the characteristics of astrology. Almost all discussions of work have something to say about this. For Cicero, the *officina* can have nothing liberal (*ingenuum*) about it.[137] Posidonius/Seneca say much the same (all manual work is illiberal), but formulated in light of the Stoic concern with what was requisite for the truly philosophical life. Pollux objects to leather-workers (βυρσοδέψης, σκυτοδέψης: were they too smelly?). Dio takes a quite different view. Luxuries are out (*Or*. 7. 117), but handicrafts *per se* are not only allowable, but even preferable to arts that imply the disingenuousness of speech and sophistry.[138]

Do the astrologers simply reject this view of the matter? For all their exuberance about manufactured products, it cannot be quite as straightforward as that they simply up-end élite attitudes, for several charts in Firmicus apply the logic that some sort of worsening produces handicrafts.[139] They are clearly not, though, the basest occupations.[140] But what seems most distinctive of astrology is that it exploits the in-principle porousness of the boundary between this and the next category—that of arts which minister to pleasure—and springs it wide open. For instance, it knows nothing of any theoretical boundary-line between

---

[135] Ptol. 4.4.4 μυροπώλας, φαρμακοπώλας, ἀρωματοπώλας, ἱματιοπώλας ~ Θ p. 211.17–20, which adds οἰνοπώλας (for οἰνεμπόρους) ἢ ἀνθοπώλας; Θ p. 209.9 πορφυροπώλας. Valens, I 1.29 adds trade in emeralds, fine stone, and ivory. See too *Lib. Herm.* xxxiii. 10 *emptores rerum pretiosarum regum vel principum*.

[136] Dio Chrys. *Or*. 7.123 ἐν ὁδοῖς καὶ ἐν ἀγορᾷ φθεγγομένους μετὰ πολλῆς ἀνελευθερίας; Holleran, 252–5; D. Lowe, 'Loud and Proud: The Voice of the *Praeco* in Roman Love Elegy', in S. Matzner and S. J. Harrison (eds.), *Complex Inferiorities: The Poetics of the Weaker Voice in Latin Literature* (Oxford, 2018), 149–68, at 150–5.

[137] *Off*. 1.150; see too *Flacc*. 18 *Opifices et tabernarios et illam omnem faecem civitatum*.

[138] 124 χειροτέχνας μὲν γὰρ ἐξ αὐτῶν τινας ἀνάγκη γενέσθαι, γλωσσοτέχνας δὲ καὶ δικοτέχνας οὐδεμία ἀνάγκη. Brunt 1973, 25–6 suggests that some early Stoic writers—specifically Cleanthes and Chrysippus—might have preceded Dio in less than blanket condemnation of banausic trades.

[139] 4.10.3; 4.19.18; 4.21.6; 4.14.17 (the Moon is implicitly out of sect).

[140] In Firmicus, 8.7.5, *pictores* are born under a middling outcome, gladiators under a worsened one.

textiles and dyeing or embroidery, or between construction and ornamental masonry or interior decoration (mosaics: Firmicus, 3.3.23), which latter for Dio rank among adornment rather than manufacture, and which he tellingly combines with the meretricious arts of the beautician (*Or.* 7.118). In general, the manufactures to which astrology is most drawn are fine crafts, or outright luxuries—weaving,[141] embroidery,[142] painting, sculpting, and marble-working,[143] gold- and silver-smithing[144]—the very categories the moralists found most problematic. Some writers say that we may prize luxury goods themselves but despise their manufacturers.[145] One step further, and moralists denounced the products altogether. Astrology is having none of this. While acknowledging such trades as a sort of *Mittelstand*, it applies its closest focus and directs its best rhetorical efforts to arts which are, in its view, *honestae et mundae*.

Cicero's fifth and final category consists of professions *quae ministrae sunt voluptatum*. For Cicero, these are producers and sellers of consumables; parfumiers; dancers; and the denizens of the gaming-house (*totumque ludum talarium*). Pollux's fruiterer (ὀπωρώνης, ὀπωροπώλης), sausage-seller (ἀλλαντοπώλης ~ Cicero's *fartores*), and inn-keeper (πανδοκεύς ~ Cicero's *popinarii*) will belong in this category. Dio agrees about parfumiers (*Or.* 7.117), and has much more on the performing arts (7.119). Indeed, *voluptas* is a natural for Venus, and astrology, too, has a category of 'panderers to pleasure' with many of the same associations.[146] Interestingly, Ptolemy names providers of pleasure (ἐμπόρους τῶν πρὸς ἀπόλαυσιν καὶ κόσμον) as an afterthought to the professions that might have been thought to typify them (florists, dyers, druggists, wine-merchants, etc.), under an aggravating factor which makes it look as if he wants *both* to list the professions in question *and* to acknowledge the category, but to have the former escape the taint of the latter (4.4.4). Luxury is what most problematises this category for the moralists (although note the contrarian view of Maximus of Tyre, *Or.* 15.3, who is entirely happy, not only with painters

---

[141] Sen. *Ep.* 90.19.   [142] Plat. *Rep.* 373 A τὴν ποικιλίαν; Dio, *Or.* 7.117 ποικιλτικῇ πάσῃ.

[143] In Seneca's rigorous restriction of liberal arts to the truly philosophic, these necessarily fall short (*Ep.* 88.18, where *pictores, statuarii*, and *marmorarii* count as *luxuriae ministri*). They are not singled out by name in the fourfold Posidonian classification of 21–3, but where even mathematics and astronomy fall short, the visual arts hardly stand a chance. Yet Philostr. *Gymn.* 1 allows that ζωγραφία, statuary, gem-cutting and metal-engraving may count as branches of σοφία, as distinct from banausic arts which have τέχνη alone.

[144] Plut. *Lyc.* 9.3, *Mor.* 527 C, 830 E χρυσοχόους καὶ ἀργυροκόπους.

[145] Plut. *Per.* 1.4; Lucian, *Somn.* 9 and Graßl, 101–7; T. Pekáry, 'Welcher vernünftige Mensch möchte schon Phidias werden? Das Ansehen des Künstlers im antiken Rom', *Boreas*, 18 (1995), 13–18; Drexhage–Konen–Ruffing, 302.

[146] Ptol. 4.4.4 ἐμπόρους τῶν πρὸς ἀπόλαυσιν καὶ κόσμον; Firmicus, 4.13.2...*et qui alienarum voluptatum et delectationum curam sollicitudinemque sustineant*; Lib. Herm. xxvii. 18 *operatores colorum vel cibi aut poti aut ad voluptates pertinentium vel lenones fiunt*.

and sculptors and musicians, but also perfume-sellers and cooks, who can still plead that they are contributing pleasurable things—ὅσα πρὸς ἡδονὴν δημιουργεῖται—to the common good). There is also the potentially servile aspect of the business, since attending to their masters' *voluptas* was only what slaves did (Sen. *Ep.* 47.2-3, 5-8; Joshel, 152).

Here astrology seems to meet the moralising attitude (barely) halfway. Innkeepers, for instance, are somewhat equivocal. Firmicus' two instances of *popinarii* are produced by worsened set of circumstances which reduce optimal conditions to those involving (merely) the production of pleasure.[147] These are at least coded as Venereal professions, of a déclassé variety. But culinary arts, which also attract the condemnation of the moralists,[148] are not so coded at all (App. II, VII.1.iii). Firmicus does take a dim view of cookery, ranking it among *artes aut sordidae aut squalidae* (3.8.7), but it counts (along with tanning and fulling) as a smelly and laborious trade, not one that ministers to pleasure.[149] Perfume, on the other hand, is the Venereal trade *par excellence*. Dio happens to list it next to dyes, the same combination that is produced by astrology's category of 'granular substances' (*pigmenta*).[150] But the qualities that troubled the moralists[151] rarely seem to trouble the astrologers. Apart from Firmicus, 8.11.1, a passage which takes on, and indeed enhances, the censoriousness of its source (Manilius, 5.267-8) towards *users* (not manufacturers or vendors) of perfume, those in the trade are generally mentioned without aspersion or negativity.

But finally there is one area on which all are agreed, one area in which astrology, especially the Manethoniana, musters every bit as much disdain as the most sneering of the moralists. That is popular entertainment. Dio is the most sweeping in his condemnation of performing artists, which extends beyond tragic and comic actors, mimes, dancers, and *choreutai*, to instrumentalists as well, citharodes and auletes.[152] For others, however, the problem centres more

---

[147] 4.13.2, 4.21.6. *Caupones* also suspect in 3.6.4, though the logic in 4.11.2, which connects them to the Moon, seems to imply that their business involves some kind of conversion or transformation (along with dyeing and *metalli... commercia*).

[148] Plat. *Rep.* 373 A πέμματα; Plut. *Mor.* 527 C μαγείρων; Cic. *Fin.* 2.23 *optimis cocis, pistoribus*; Sen. *Epist.* 90.19 *odores coquentium*; Musonius, fr. xvIII B Hense (against γαστριμαργία καὶ ὀψοφαγία). Luxury chefs: Lucian, *Gall.* 27 ὀψοποιόν. On chefs, see Graßl, 104–5. That the chef is treatable as an *opifex*, indeed an *artifex*, is illustrated by Trimalchio, who calls his Daedalus in recognition of his creativity (Petron. *Sat.* 70).

[149] Associated with fire in Ptol. 4.4.5 ~ Θ p. 211.26; Firmicus, 4.14.13. Venus is involved in Firmicus, 7.26.6 (Mars and Venus in each other's terms), but this is a modification of a chart involving doctors; luxury is not involved here.

[150] Dio, *Or.* 7.117 βαφεῖς... μυρεψούς.

[151] Dyes: Plut. *Mor.* 830 E, ἀνθοβάφους ~ 2.326. Perfumes: Plut. *Mor.* 1096 A μύρα καὶ θυμιάματα, 527 C μυρεψῶν.

[152] *Or.* 7.119; Brunt 1973, 16–17. Aristotle had objected to musicians as well, but on the grounds that the trade is banausic (*Pol.* 1339^{b}9; 1341^{b}15), not because it caters to luxury.

specifically on mimetic dancing (Cicero singles out *saltatores*; problems with dancers go back as far as Plat. *Rep.* 373 B), or indeed taints the very business of stage machinery (Posidonius/Seneca, *Ep.* 88.22 *machinatores*). These arts elicit disdain for the mob (Arist. *Pol.* 1341^{b}17; Dio, *Or.* 7.122; Sen. *Ep.* 88.22) and disgust at the performers' effeminacy (Sen. *Ep.* 90.19). Much of this can be found in the Manethoniana as well. But how come it is precisely here, and not elsewhere, that they reproduce élite attitudes? Astrology's stone-masons and instrument-makers, goldsmiths and jewellers, are presumably *also* the crowd who love an afternoon at the theatre, have their own favourites among the rock-star pantomimes, and laugh heartily at the antics of the mimes. This is a big question. It reaches beyond attitudes to work to the culture of entertainment in the Roman world, and the politicisation of attitudes towards it. It deserves a separate treatment. I return to this at the end.

INTERIM CONCLUSIONS

This section began with some fairly broad-brush questions about astrology's value system. It is time to sophisticate them. It is not really satisfactory to say either that it should be seen as an alternative or rival to that of upper classes who could afford the pose of a 'liberal' lifestyle, or that excellence was simply a common goal, whatever one's métier. No doubt a life well-lived was constituted by the expenditure of well-directed effort and a show of probity, whether for a decurion or a shopkeeper.[153] But more needs to be said.

What makes Paul Veyne's picture of the mental universe of the *plebs media* so compelling for this analysis is how well suited it is to astrology's comfortably banal aspiration to prosperity. The combination of hauteur towards certain trades with craftsmanly pride in others is compatible with attitudes held by respectable artisans, men who thought well of themselves, who had boutique outlets on the Sacra Via, who aspired to join the élites or anyway serviced them by providing the luxury goods they wanted to show off with, and in turn were patronised by them.[154] So too the importance of social relations, of πίστις, σύστασις, a well-lubricated social network, and the importance attached to

---

[153] A. Wallace-Hadrill, *JRA* 26/2 (2013), 605–9, at 607; Lis and Soly, 263–71 (celebrating the value of effort in whatever sphere that constituted a productive life dedicated to the common good).

[154] K. Verboven, 'The Associative Order: Status and Ethos among Roman Businessmen in Late Republic and Early Empire', *Athenaeum*, 95 (2007), 861–93. On the Sacra Via: Holleran, 245–6, 255–6; on prestigious trades addresses: Courrier, 202–31.

receiving a return on an investment.[155] So too the idea of excellence within a métier. Firmicus' notations of this run nicely parallel to epitaphic boasts of distinction, and one imagines the *pistores* who were *principes* among their associates (8.24.3) resting very complacently beside the *cocus optimus* and *popinaria nota*.[156] Still, Veyne formulates the distinction between the attitudes to work of the Roman *plebs media* and *plebs sordida* as between the conception of work as exploit and as identity.[157] Firmicus, it is true, takes a rather jaundiced view of those who had to work for their daily bread,[158] but it will not do to say that astrology regards work *only* as exploit. It is all very well if one reaches excellence within one's craft, but the whole procedure is to essentialise that employment: these people *are* their work (see 5.175 n.!), it is not something they do from art, show, or dilettantism. The perspective of a Cicero who could regard certain types of work as 'slavish' (*Off*. 1.150) is completely absent. Activity ($\pi\rho\hat{a}\xi\iota s$) is the watchword. Unemployment, as dream interpretation makes clearer still, is a thing of dread.

Does that mean we should still accept that the attitudes of a particular social class or classes can be read off from astrology, only that we should extend the search beyond Veyne's group of well-heeled professionals? Or is it more complicated? I postpone the final discussion until the end of the first part, but emphasise here the all-important complicating factors of conventional attitudes, commonplaces, posturing, in a word, trope. It is misleading to take the attitudes of *De Officiis* 1.150-1 as representative of the views of 'the élite' (whoever 'the élite' were—and the most exclusive among them in Rome would hardly have accepted Cicero anyway), as opposed to a set of philosophical commonplaces that could be adopted by someone who wanted to attitudinise in that particular way.[159] There was nothing inevitable about them. Cicero was quite capable of expressing himself differently on the subject of the *artifex*.

---

[155] Firmicus, 3.4.10 *Faciet etiam eos sine gratia praestare quod dederint; nam quicumque aliquid ab ipsis fuerit consecutus ingratus illis semper existit*; 5.1.2 *et beneficia sua praestabit ingratis, ut numquam ei pares gratiae rependantur*. Compare the complaints of an individual who had a right to expect a better return from his friends: *CIL* vi. 9659 and 33814 = Dessau, *ILS* 7519 (Rome), ll. 5-8 .... *Qui negotiando locupletem | se speravit esse futurum | Spe deceptus erat et a mult|is bene meritus amicis*; this inscription is discussed by Panciera and Zanker, with notes on these lines at 370 [385] and n. 22. For ungrateful amici see i. 312 and n. 45 and 5.308-12, 312 nn.

[156] Petrikovits, 79; Tran 2013, 242-3, and 2017, 256; Veyne 2000, 1183, n. 77.

[157] Veyne 2000, 1183 '... à son heure dernière, la classe moyenne imite l'aristocratie. En somme, le métier n'était pas une identité, mais un exploit : on n'en faisait état que si l'on s'était distingué par une réussite personnelle.' See also Zimmer 1985, 218, for grave inscriptions which replace *labor* with terms like *studium* and *officium*.

[158] 3.2.5, 22; 3.8.7; 3.9.4; 3.14.3; 4.8.1; 4.13.6; 4.15.7; 5.3.30, 35; 6.30.13, 16. Compare Tac. *Hist.* 4.38 *vulgus alimenta in dies mercari solitum*.

[159] So too Ruffing 2004, 88, 99-101, and for variable and contradictory attitudes, Tran 2013, 251.

From that point of view, then, it would be preferable not to hammer away at questions whether astrology adopts the point of view of a specific class, as if this were something reified and reifiable, but to see the whole as a field of possibilities, a field within which there was 'discursive space', here for one set of tropes, there for another. We can certainly read craftsmanly *amour propre* between the lines of astrology, but what it is expressly articulating are the attitudes its consumers had imbibed from authors and texts they had been taught to approve, and these become signalling and rhetorical manoeuvres. These include distant respect for agriculture insofar as they had anything to do with it, which was very little, as well as pity for the hod-carrier and contempt for the pimp. *Collegium* inscriptions routinely launder the professions that publicly commemorate themselves, whatever they are, through the language of institutional integrity, courtesy, and high-mindedness.[160] Astrology does not do that. What it does, more interestingly, is to combine a store of commonplace on the ethics of professional life with a rather distinctive vision of its aesthetics which may well reflect the focalisation of the craftsman. Perhaps the last word in this section should go to the poet of the fourth book, who is fascinated with the word πόνος, which he explores in all its complex significance (4.72 n., and p. 174). It means hard labour, physical unpleasantness, mean and humiliating at worst, but also, the pleasing craftsmanly and artistic products of those labours, and the effort which the good man directs to the common weal. The poet reflects much of the range of, and reproduces many of the tropes associated with, what Hesiod had already taught us was mankind's common lot.

---

[160] A dramatic example: in Dorotheus, p. 342.25, a slave-dealer is a type you really would not want to seduce your daughter. Yet those involved in the slave-market in Thyateira honour a slave-dealer (σωματέμπορος) with a statue for his exemplary management (ἀγορανομήσαντα... ἁγνῶς) of that market (*TAM* v. 932; cf. Ruffing 2004, 91–2; P. A. Harland, *Greco-Roman Associations: Texts, Translations, and Commentary*, II. *North Coast of the Black Sea, Asia Minor* (Berlin, 2014), 222).

5

The Poor

'The less said of beggars...the better' (Lightfoot, i. 344).

It is time to revisit that.

The poor are always with us, unless you are a wealthy benefactor working out how to disburse your funds in one of the cities of the Greek east, in which case the poor barely register at all. They are very present in astrology, but the terminology needs to be clarified. The commonest word is πένης (some 53 instances), but in ancient usage this (like Latin *pauper*) simply means not-rich,[1] not necessarily the out-and-out destitute. A person in that state of economic hardship is more likely to be called a πτωχός, of which there are a further 23 instances, and another 16 of πενιχρός, with no particular clusters in any particular author. There are no instances of προσαίτης or μεταίτης, but three of ἐπαίτης.[2] The very disparate nature of the astrological corpus makes it impossible to generalise about usage. Some authors only use the one term,[3] and on the very rare occasions where πένης and πτωχός occur together, the authors in question seem to differ over whether the words are contrastive or interchangeable.[4] The only passage where πτωχός is certain to mean a beggar seems to be 3.249, though elsewhere it is associated with mendicants and slaves.[5] But in texts which reflect the Christian or Islamic ethics of charity, πτωχός is the normal word for 'poor', and the same is true of Achmet. The difference between his usage and Artemidorus' when both of them want to refer to the broad class of dreamers that stands opposed to the rich exemplifies the general difference between Christian and pagan usage: Artemidorus' usual word is πένης, with

---

[1] G. Nenci, 'Pratiche alimentari e forme di definizione e distinzione sociale nella Grecia arcaica', *ASNP* 18 (1988), 1–10, at 4; Osborne, 11.

[2] Valens, II 11.2, VII 6.193; Hephaestion, i. 241.2.

[3] Neither Dorotheus nor Valens has any instances of πτωχός, but two and six respectively of πένης. Ptolemy uses neither.

[4] Paul, p. 58.17–18 ἢ πτωχῆς ἢ πενιχρᾶς (the disjunctive implies a distinction). πένης is the usual word in the trivially common distinction of rich and poor (every instance of πένης in M^c belongs here, ll. 247, 264, 269), but πτωχός at *CCAG* vii. 225.20–1, xi/1. 133.22. Interchangeable in Hephaestion, i. 70.11–12 (from Nechepso–Petosiris, fr. 12 Riess) τούς τε πένητας πλουτήσειν καὶ τοὺς πλουσίους πτωχεύσειν and *CCAG* x. 210.28–9.

[5] Mendicants: *CCAG* x. 239.24–5. Slaves: Paul, p. 58.17; Camaterus, *Introd.* 2821–2, 2892.

only three instances of πτωχός (none of them for categories of dreamer), while Achmet's overwhelming preference is for πτωχός.[6] He does not thereby mean the out-and-out destitute. His πτωχοί stand opposed either to the rich in the two-tier scheme, or to kings and the middling[7] in the three.

So astrology does have specific words for the poor, although one must look carefully at each author to see what he means, and sometimes the precise meaning is rendered difficult by the practice of listing, which makes it hard to gauge whether juxtaposed items are synonyms or meant to be contrasted. But the terminology of poverty is expanded and enhanced in a number of ways. The poor are accompanied by other related types, for instance the exile (ἔκπτωτος). There are many looser words for those in a state of neediness or lack: ἄβιος, ἄπορος, ἐνδεής (including 4.32, 340), κακόβιος; δυσπερίκτητος ('unsuccessful in acquiring property'), a particular favourite of Paul. And there are endless sketchy words for wretchedness (κακοδαίμων, δυσδαίμων, ἄθλιος, ἀτυχής, δυστυχής, 1.274 ἐλεεινός) which just convey *Affekt*. This effect is still more pronounced, of course, in poetry, which can avail itself of a ready-made formulary for 'emotive pity'.[8] Much the same applies to abstract nouns: as well as πενία (23/39 instances of which are in the Manethoniana themselves) and a smattering of πτωχεία[9] and ἔνδεια (1.172) there are many other words for lack, loss (ἀποβολή), deprivation (ἔκπτωσις: 2.482 n.), overthrow (καθαίρεσις), oppression (θλῖψις), narrowing of opportunity and straitened circumstances (στενοχωρία), humiliation (ταπείνωσις), and general harm (βλάβη) and suffering (μόχθος, λύπη).[10] These words, stretching from reduced means to destitution, were never meant to classify a condition, but to evoke it subjectively. They are also serving more purposes than that of simply emoting. The vague terminology allows listeners to hear what they want to hear, and to apply the prediction to their own circumstances, both the rich man whose investments have taken a tumble, and the out-and-out beggar. Put otherwise, it means that astrology

---

[6] Artemidorus: 3 instances of πτωχός, at 1.1.4 (Irus), 1.78.6, 3.53.2 (both dream symbols). Achmet: 70 instances of πτωχός, 7 of πένης.
[7] For which the usual expressions are ἐκ τοῦ λαοῦ or τοῦ κοινοῦ λαοῦ (other variations include ἐκ τῶν μέσων τις).
[8] The phrase is that of Holman, 7 (cf. 11, the 'discourse of emotion').
[9] Only five, without Glycas and Achmet. In Achmet it occurs in predictions, often combined with θλῖψις or other highly coloured words which suggest that the abstract noun is more loaded than πτωχός itself.
[10] Valens, II 21.5 ἐκπτώσεις, ἀφαιρέσεις, ναυάγια, ἐνδείας, χρεωστίας, II 23.26 ἐκπτώσεις τῶν πράξεων καὶ μειώσεις καὶ βλάβας; Valens, App. XI 25 ἐκπτώσεις καὶ καθαιρέσεις, sim. 39; Paul, pp. 55.2–3 ἔκπτωσιν βίου καὶ χρημάτων ἀποβολάς, 62.12–13 ἔκπτωσιν βίου καὶ καθαίρεσιν πραγμάτων καὶ ἀποβολάς, 66.8 ἐν πενίᾳ καὶ στενότητι βίου, cf. 'Heliodorus', pp. 69.27–70.1 ἔκπτωσιν γὰρ βίου καὶ καθαίρεσιν πραγμάτων ἢ ἀποβολάς; Hephaestion, i. 23.11 ἐν κακοπαθείαις καὶ πενίαις; Camaterus, *Zod.* 1171 πενίαν καὶ στέρησιν πραγμάτων.

The Poor

can talk of both absolute and relative poverty and all positions between. It can even use the same words to do it.

But absolute poverty is easy to recognise and has its own topoi. As in other classical (and Judaeo-Christian) literature,[11] the genuinely destitute figure as those unable to feed[12] or clothe[13] themselves. There are a few references to exigents literally stretching out their hands,[14] but apart from 4.113 ἀμελάθρους astrology has surprisingly little to say about homelessness. Wandering, however, is an essential part of the literary image of beggary for anyone brought up on the *Odyssey*, and so it appears here. Although people are on the move throughout astrology, either for economic reasons or because they are just drifters, there are constant references to mendicants,[15] who are often connected to exiles,[16] *peregrini*,[17] and slaves.[18] Not that there is any particular merit attached to relieving them, which suggests a possible cleavage between the popular ethics represented by the astrological texts and the day-to-day reality, for it is perfectly possible, indeed likely, that people gave out of common humanity.[19] Almsgiving does not appear as a virtue until astrology that is demonstrably influenced by Christian and/or Islamic values.[20]

---

[11] Ecclus. 29:21 Ἀρχὴ ζωῆς ὕδωρ καὶ ἄρτος καὶ ἱμάτιον καὶ οἶκος καλύπτων ἀσχημοσύνην. Cloak: *Od.* 14.460; Hipponax, frr. 32, 34 W. Bed: Ar. *Plut.* 540–1, Epictet. 1.24.7; Juv. *Sat.* 5.8–9. Hearth: Cat. 23.2. All three: Martial, 1.92.5–10, 11.32. On the archaic and classical image of the πτωχός, see H. Kloft, 'Gedanken zum Ptochós', in Weiler and Grassl, 81–106.

[12] 2.454, cf. 456; Valens, II 5.3. Lack of βίος: 4.113; Hephaestion, i. 241.2; Paul, p. 66.9 and 'Heliodorus', p. 72.3.

[13] Valens, II 9.3, 11.2 γυμνῆτας; Firmicus, 3.9.2, 4.8.3, 4.14.3, 4.15.7, 8.11.4 (motifs: *nudus, pannis obsitus, vel sim.*).

[14] Valens, II 5.3 ἐνδεεῖς τῆς ἐφημέρου τροφῆς, πολλοὶ δὲ καὶ τὰς χεῖρας ὑφέξουσιν, II 9.4 ὁ γεννώμενος τὰς χεῖρας ὑφέξει καὶ προσαιτήσει; Firmicus, 8.11.4 *et eum, usque ad extremum ‹diem› vitae, perducit praesidio publicae miserationis alimenta poscentem*. Compare Epictetus, 4.1.4 ὀρεγόμενος καὶ ἀποτυγχάνων.

[15] *Misera mendicitas, vel sim.*: Firmicus, 1.7.3; 4.8.1; 4.10.2; 5.3.6; 6.30.17; 6.31.2, 13, 28.

[16] 6.581–2, 5.129 ἀλήτην. Theme words include ἀποδημία; μετάστασις (Περὶ κέντρ. 5), μετανάστασις (CCAG i. 137.17), μετοικισμός (Περὶ κέντρ. 43); φυγή (Περὶ κράσ. 150), φυγαδεία (Valens, I 1.21); ξενιτεύειν (Hephaestion, i. 23.11). See e.g. Paul, p. 60.3–4 δυσπερικτήτους ἢ ἐν ἀλλοδαπῇ γῇ διατελοῦντας ἢ μετανάστας ἢ ξενιτεύοντας; 'Heliodorus', p. 68.22 πενιχροὺς καὶ ξενιτεύοντας καὶ ἀστάτους; CCAG x. 239.24–5 περιπολεύσει ἀπὸ τόπου εἰς τόπον· βίον πτωχὸν ἔχῃ; Θ p. 166.25–6 πλανήτας καὶ πένητας.

[17] Firmicus, 3.8.12; 4.14.15; 4.15.3, 6, *Lib. Herm.* xxvii. 26, xxxiii. 7.

[18] Paul, p. 58.17–18 μητρὸς δούλης ἢ πτωχῆς ἢ πενιχρᾶς; Firmicus, 4.10.2, 4.15.6; *Lib. Herm.* xxxiii. 7 *pauperes, peregrinantes, errantes vel servilem vitam peragentes*.

[19] A. Parkin, '"You Do him No Service": An Exploration of Pagan Almsgiving', in Atkins and Osborne, 60–82.

[20] CCAG x. 107.33–4 τὴν ψυχὴν αὐτοῦ θύσει ὑπὲρ τοὺς ξένους καὶ πτωχοὺς καὶ φίλους, 117.13–14 ἐλεημονητικὴ εἰς τοὺς ξένους καὶ πτωχούς (sim. 218.3–4, 222.25–6) καὶ εἰς τοὺς πτωχοὺς εἶναι ἐλεήμων; 227.6–7 ἀγαπᾷ καὶ τοὺς πτωχούς (all from various Zodiologia); Apomasar, *De Rev.* p. 162.22–3 πλῆθος εὐποιιῶν καὶ μεταδόσεων πρὸς πένητα; Achmet, *Oneir.* 224: a clean and not malodorous sock means giving to the poor!

Indeed, astrology is relatively well equipped to go beyond the rehearsal of topoi, by imputing agency to planets in such a way as to distinguish between existential condition and precipitous change. In other words to some extent it can anticipate the modern distinction between structural and conjunctural poverty. Mars represents sudden catastrophe (Valens, II 22.39), Saturn grim indurated misery (Valens, I 1.7; Περὶ κράσ. 1). This is how poverty can be both σίνος (acute harm), and πάθος (settled state).[21] ἀνωμαλία, unevenness, is the bread and butter of the astrological universe: a catastrophic plunge from a height is an obvious life-event in a birth chart, and the desperate pitfall that *catarchai* are deployed to avert. Words for loss and damage present this view of the subject, as do verbs of reversal,[22] and adjectives for 'perilous' and 'risky'.[23] Astrology has a veritable obsession with loss of wealth, which it can present, once again, as either a dramatic loss of everything, or 'relativised', so that it was up to the native to decide just how it applied to his or her own circumstances.[24] It may also be temporary or permanent. Although alternating fortunes,[25] or even loss and restoration,[26] are rarer than outright loss, astrology is perfectly capable of conceiving of transient poverty,[27] the idea of which is facilitated by metaphorising wealth as moonlight which waxes and wanes in relation to the luminary's motions (5.120–6, 307–12 nn.; Valens, II 21.3). One of Valens' occasional passages of fleetingly brilliant metaphor figures wealth as illusory or rotten, a mirage that vanishes or something that just crumbles away.[28]

Where causes are given for loss or immiseration, it is usually general astrology that looks to environmental causes, natal astrology to social ones, failures of cooperation, wherever the fault lies—to lawsuits,[29] failed business enterprises (Valens, II 21.5), misplaced trust (Valens, IV 8.18). But this 'wherever the

---

[21] Paul, p. 46.21-3 πένητας καὶ δυσπερικτήτους ... ἢ ἐμπαθεῖς ἢ ἐπισινεῖς; 'Heliodorus', p. 64.7–8 ἄτροφα γὰρ καὶ πτωχὰ καὶ ὀρφανὰ τὰ τικτόμενα γενήσεται, προσέτι δὲ καὶ σεσινωμένα ἢ ἐμπαθῆ.
[22] Valens, I 20.9 ἐνδείαις περιπίπτοντες, sim. IV 15.4; II 35.3 ἐναντιώμασι καὶ ὑποταγαῖς καὶ ἐνδείαις περιτραπήσονται.
[23] ἐπικίνδυνος, ἐπισφαλής, often paired; σφαλερός. Particularly eloquent is Θ p. 202.14–15 (from ch. 78 Καθολικὰ σχήματα ἐκπτώτων) ἐπισφαλεῖς καὶ ἐπικινδύνους καὶ καθαιρετικὰς ποιεῖ τὰς γενέσεις, where I take καθαιρετικὰς to mean 'prone to downfall', a sense not recognised by LSJ.
[24] e.g. Apomasar, De Rev. p. 57.22–3 στενοχωρίαν ἐν τῇ ὑποστάσει, p. 68.20–1 ὑποστήσεται αὐτός τε καὶ οἱ γονεῖς αὐτοῦ ἔνδειαν καὶ στενοχωρίαν ἐν πλούτῳ.
[25] 3.307; 5.301; Valens, II 22.29 ἡ δὲ περιποίησις ἀνώμαλος καὶ ἄστατος, ὁτὲ μὲν ὑπερπλεονάσασα, ὁτὲ δὲ ἐνδεής; Firmicus, 6.18.1, 6.36.7.
[26] Valens, VII 6.118 μετὰ τὴν ἔκπτωσίν ἐστιν ἀνάσφαλσις [recovery] καὶ ἀποκατάστασις.
[27] Valens, I 20.20 ἐνδεεῖς κατά τινας χρόνους γινομένους.
[28] Valens, II 23.25 (cf. App. XI 107) ἐὰν μὲν ἀγαθοποιοὶ ὦσι (sc. Lord of Fortune and of Accomplishment) τὰς ὑπάρξεις πεφαντασιωμένας ('a mirage': Riley) ποιοῦσι καὶ ἐπισάθρους καὶ ἐπικινδύνους, ἐὰν δὲ κακοποιοὶ ὦσιν ἐκπτώσεις ποιοῦσιν.
[29] 3.290–1; Valens, IV 22.15; Additamenta Antiqua, IV 25; κρίσεις (lawsuits) connected with debts in I 19.4, 18, 20.5. False accusations, lawsuits, and poverty in Firmicus, 3.11.16.

fault lies' is the nub of it. As we shall see with slavery, poverty can be a stroke of ill fate, against which the native is powerless.[30] But more interesting than mere fatalism is the implication that a faulty disposition causes it, which can be seen, ultimately, as a reworking of the old Hesiodic idea that the acquisition and loss of wealth were matters of individual temperament and self-help.[31] The Hesiodic echoes in M[a] are no accident: these characters are unable to shift for themselves. Mars contributes his usual share of instability and Saturn of ineffectuality, but other factors such as places, sect, and more complicated aspects of the planets are involved as well. Whether because of mental attitude[32] or because of physical incapacity, these natives have no talent for acquisition; things slip through their hands. There is no trace of the hostility and contempt which some classical sources indicate that paupers received (and which some of them display),[33] although there are words for humility, ignobility, baseness, and lack of repute, with a particular tendency in certain authors to associate poverty with status terms (ταπεινός, εὐτελής, κακός, ἀγεν(ν)ής, ἄδοξος, etc.).[34]

If the outlook of astrology were oriented to commercial life, loss of wealth might have been more strongly associated with business ventures. As it is, it is formulated in terms of the destruction and squandering of what one has,[35] and the greater preoccupation is with loss of patrimony.[36] The problem goes beyond that of individual (ir)responsibility, as the words by which it is denoted, τὰ πατρῷα and τὰ πατρικά, makes clear. By connecting it with hostile relations with the family,[37] some passages lay bare how its implications extend beyond the individual. Whether the loss of it is caused by external events beyond the

---

[30] Paul, p. 46.21–2 πένητας καὶ δυσπερικτήτους καὶ κακοδαίμονας ἀποδείκνυσιν; Antiochus, CCAG vii. 114.38 κακοδαιμονοῦντας καὶ ἐκπτώτους.
[31] Osborne, 13. Hesiod's attitude to work cited approvingly by Dio Chrys. Or. 7.110–11, 116. On Hesiod's influence (also apparent in IK Klaudiu Polis, 75.5, on γεωπονία), see Lis and Soly, 264; and, in Polish, B. Biliński, 'L'antiquité à la manière d'Hésiode', Annales de la Société archéologique polonaise, 2 (1948), 31–104, id., 'Le problème du travail dans la Rome antique: L'époque royale et les premiers temps de la République', Annales de la Société archéologique polonaise, 3 (1949), 45–111.
[32] See Favorinus, fr. 105 Barigazzi = fr. 14 Amato πενίας διττὸν εἶδος· ἢ γὰρ διὰ τὴν γνώμην ἄνθρωποι πένονται ἢ διὰ τὴν τύχην.
[33] Tyrtaeus, fr. 10.3–12 W.; Ar. Ach. 854–9; Sen. Clem. 2.6.2, on the contempt with which alms are normally given; Juvenal, Sat. 3.152–3; Martial, 11.32 and 12.32, with Watson and Watson on the latter (their no. 64); Gell. 9.2.6, with Holford-Strevens, 142 and n. 64.
[34] Hephaestion, i. 241.2; Paul, pp. 58.17–18, 71.3–6; 'Heliodorus', pp. 67.6–7, 74.29; Θ pp. 128.18–19, 155.8; CCAG ix. 155.1–2.
[35] (ἀπο-, ἐκ)βάλλειν, (ἀπ)ολλύναι, ἀφανίζειν, διαφθείρειν, μειοῦν, ὀλοθρεύειν, σκεδαννύναι, σκορπίζειν.
[36] e.g. Περὶ κέντρ. 13; Θ pp. 140.9–10, 149.13–14; Firmicus, 5.3.6, 31; 5.6.2; 6.9.11; 6.17.1; 6.22.10; 6.36.4; Lib. Herm. xxxiii. 1 (and passim).
[37] Περὶ κράσ. 60, 69.

power of the individual (as usually it is not),[38] by incompetence,[39] by recklessness,[40] or by the specific lifestyle choice of profligacy and whoring[41]—a fault of which we hear a great deal in invective and moralising literature, and might perhaps have expected to hear more in astrology[42]—astrology's view of it does not depart from the standard one in classical sources. It was fearful because it involved more than financial loss: it meant social annihilation.[43] But it tends to be treated as such a self-evident harm that no further elaboration is necessary.

The alternative view is that poverty is a chronic state, linked to ineffectuality, shiftlessness, and debility.[44] This will prove to have a certain similarity with the treatment of slaves, which, in turn, raises the question how far the latter really has anything to do with any notion of 'natural slavery', or how far it arises from an even more deeply rooted view of human inadequacy; slaves and the poor are thus nature's losers. Both share a lack of capacity, a similar temperamental languor and sluggishness. But there is also a difference insofar as poverty is far more liable to be connected to physical harms which go beyond a lack of stamina to wasting, limb disabilities, humoral conditions, and blindness.[45] By

---

[38] Περὶ σχημ. 115 εἴτε ἀπὸ πυρὸς εἴτε ἀπὸ πολέμου.
[39] Περὶ κράσ. 58 τῷ τε σώματι φρικαλέους ποιεῖ καὶ πυρέττοντας καὶ πυκνῶς νοσοῦντας, ἀπράκτους δέ, καὶ τὰ πατρικὰ κτήματα ἀφανίζει.
[40] 5.232; Valens, I 20.9; CCAG i. 164.12–14 ~ ii. 192.2–5; Teucer, CCAG vii. 208.7–10.
[41] The spendthrift in 5.232–6 (first prostitutes himself, then spends his money on women); Dor.^ARAB II 4.12; Περὶ κέντρ. 34; women in Apomasar, De Rev. p. 156.15–16 (though not explicitly loss of patrimony).
[42] Manil. 4.537–41 has the topos of eating away one's inheritance (as in Juv. Sat. 11.35–49, Pers. Sat. 6.21–2, Cic. Phil. 2.67 devorare; Luke 15:30).
[43] Holman, 121–2, on loss of patrimony as 'a form of social death: the end of family land, the end of a stable civic identity, the end of all political rights that may be tied to land ownership'. See Veyne 1987, 139–59, on the ideology of making it grow, though not on the ignominy of wasting it.
[44] Περὶ σχημ. 84 ἀδρανεῖς... καὶ τῷ βίῳ ἐκπτώτους ~ Περὶ κράσ. 171 ἀδράνειαν καὶ ἔκπτωσιν βίου; Περὶ κράσ. 1 ἐνδείας, ἀπραξίας, νωχελίας; Valens, II 17.77 ἐπισφαλεῖς μὲν τῷ βίῳ καὶ ἀφερεπόνους... ταῖς δὲ πράξεσι νωθροὺς καὶ βιαίους; Paul, p. 62.10–11 πένητας, ἀθλίους, δυσπερικτήτους τε καὶ ἐμπαθεῖς ('subject to passivity'), cf. 'Heliodorus', p. 69.23 πένητας, ἀθλίους καὶ ἐμπαθεῖς; p. 65.15–16 δυσπράκτους δὲ καὶ δυσπερικτήτους καὶ ἀπροκόπους καὶ ἀδρανεῖς, p. 69.18–19 ἀργοπράκτους δὲ καὶ δυσεπιβούλους καὶ δυσπερικτήτους; Apomasar, De Rev. p. 81.24–7 ἔσται ῥάθυμος καὶ μηδὲν κατορθῶν, ἀλλὰ καὶ εἴ τινος κατάρξεται ἔργου, οὐ τελειώσει αὐτό· καταναλώσει δὲ πλοῦτον καὶ ὑποστήσεται στενοχωρίαν ἐν τοῖς ἀνὰ χεῖρα; Firmicus, 5.6.2 tales quorum desideria et actus numquam prospere sequatur eventus, et qui, amissa patrimonii facultate, misero paupertatis onere deprimantur, tardos in omnibus actibus et languidos animo pariter et corpore.
[45] Περὶ σχημ. 96 ἐκπτώτους καὶ ἐπινόσους καὶ ἐξ ὑγρῶν ὀχλουμένους καὶ τοὺς ὀφθαλμοὺς βλαπτομένους; Valens, II 11.2 σίνη καὶ πάθη κατὰ τὸ μέλος ἀποτελεῖ τοῦ ζῳδίου... ποιεῖ δὲ καὶ γυμνῆτας, ἐπαίτας; Valens, App. XIX 5 νόσον ἢ πενίαν; Θ p. 162.23 ἐκπτώτους, φθινώδεις; Π.σ.α. p. 183.4–5 νόσους τε γὰρ καὶ ἐκπτώσεις; Camaterus, Introd. 1214 πένητας καὶ ἀρρώστους, 2899–2900 ἔκπτωσιν τῶν βιωτικῶν πραγμάτων... καὶ παθικὸν τὰ μέλη; Firmicus, 4.10.2 misero onere mendicitatis oppressos, vitiis ac valitudinibus implicatos, 6.17.1 fractis viribus, substantiam omnem fatigati corporis imbecillitate debilitat, et lacerato ac dissipato patrimonio, egestatem mendicitatis

astrology's standards this is fairly specific, and behind all the stylisation we can perhaps discern something of the real practical consequences of inability to work in the ancient world. There is little suggestion that poverty is connected with intellectual deficit (as opposed to attitude or motivation), but occasional connections with a lack of education.[46] On the other hand, it was perfectly possible for the educated to be impoverished too.[47] Astrology does not theorise about lack of opportunity. There are very many references to having a *parent* who is poor, from which one could infer that parentage affects life chances, or simply the existence of a familial disposition. Sometimes the loss of a parent really does precipitate into poverty:[48] that was a matter of observable fact.

Astrology lays the responsibility for their distress at the door of either the stars or of individuals themselves, and although there are certain local causes that precipitate crises, there is no idea of an economic system that keeps people poor and immiserated.[49] Debt is a subject that is variously handled by the different divinatory methods that treat it (and they all do: Plutarch regards the subject as one of the trivialities that oracles dealt with[50]). The *Sortes Astrampsychi* contain an approximately equal number of responses for lenders worried about getting their loan back and from borrowers worried about timing or their credit rating. Catarchic astrology advises about the timing as well. It also envisages lawsuits on the subject; their outcome can be read from the strength of the position of the luminaries, whose identification with the parties in the suit differs according to Moon phase.[51] Some of the charts for historical individuals in Valens single out debt as a life-event.[52] But wherever the fault lies, in the hated loan-shark (2.309; 4.330), or in some temperamental fault in the native himself

---

imponit, 6.31.28 caecitatem et debilitatem corporis ‹cum› misera mendicitate decernunt, 7.5.4 debiles, caecos servos efficient, qui, in publicis deiecti locis, vitam suam mendicitate sustentent.

[46] Intellectual weakness: Valens, II 9.5 καὶ ἄφρων καὶ πένης ἔσται: but the chapter from which this is taken, which has much to say about intellectual deficit, does not make it an appurtenance of poverty, and this particular case is the result of an aggravating factor. Lack of education: Teucer, CCAG vii. 198.4 ἀπαιδεύτους, ἐργοπόνους (husbandmen? not explicitly paupers); Θ p. 144.1–2 ἄφρονας, σκολιούς, ἀλλοτρίους γραμμάτων, καὶ τοῖς βίοις ἐνδεεῖς ~ Firmicus, 3.7.4 *homines obscuros, sceleratae mentis, alienos ab scientia litterarum et qui sint ab omni vitae subsidio destituti*. Either/both implications possible in Basil, PG 29.257 c Πενίαν δὲ, ἢ δυσγένειαν, ἢ ἀμάθειαν, ἢ σώματος ἀρρωστίαν ὀνειδίζειν πάντη ἄλογον, and 260 B κἂν πένητες ὦσι, κἂν ἀγενεῖς, κἂν ἰδιῶται τῷ λόγῳ, κἂν ἀσθενεῖς τῷ σώματι.

[47] Impoverished grammarian: Θ p. 221.2 γραμματικὸς πένης. Teaching γράμματα shameful: Dio Chrys. Or. 7.114.

[48] 'Heliodorus', p. 64.7–8; CCAG ix. 154.33–155.2; Lib. Herm. xxxiii. 1.

[49] General astrology can make the connection between civil wars, enemy incursions, famines, earthquakes, and poverty on a population level. Even so, these are disastrous events rather than a stagnant economy.

[50] Mor. 408 B–C.   [51] Hübner 2003, 161–3; Hephaestion, i. 279.4–13, 299.13–19.

[52] Valens, II 22.34, 45 (= nos. L 95,V,14, 109 Neugebauer–Van Hoesen), VII 3.36 (no. L 117,VI Neugebauer–Van Hoesen).

(impetuosity, gullibility, sluggishness, failure of self-help[53]), or whether the blame lies simply in the inscrutable stars themselves, it is hard to find a middle term, a conception of an economy which makes it impossible for people to thrive. Telling, however, is the prominence of debtors among categories of dreamer in dream interpretation. Many a nightmare must have been haunted by money worries.[54]

To the astrologers and their clients, the state of not working, which the privileged call σχολή and regard as an opportunity to cultivate refined dilettantism, is ἀργία, ἀπραγία, and associated with words for 'misery' and 'wretchedness'— almost exactly the same as in Artemidorus.[55] It is produced by the same conditions as those that produce poverty.[56] One might perhaps have expected the connection between them to be drawn more tightly,[57] but it was obvious enough, and immiserated old age, when one cannot work, is always an anxiety (and a literary commonplace, too).[58] Can you be in work and *still* a πένης?[59] This is not just about classification, but another way of approaching the question whether astrology has any notion of an economic system which keeps people just getting by, struggling, but unable to rise. By and large it is true that astrology shows little interest in the poor working man, although the beggar

---

[53] A moralising tone in Firmicus, 3.9.7, 3.11.8, 6.17.3; only in 3.11.16 does the native himself not seem implicated.

[54] Artemidorus, 1.26.7, 31.3, 35.3, 42.4, 67.2; the κατάχρεως alongside the slave in 1.14.2, 80.1; 2.3.7; anecdotes about debtors in Artemidorus, 1.15; 4.41.2; 5.31, 33 (both suicides). Achmet often associates χρέος and χρεωστεῖν with θλῖψις/θλίβειν (Oneir. 35.12, 43.7–8 and 16–17, 120.4).

[55] Pleket 1988, 272; Klees, 61–2; Hahn, 21. For instance, CCAG ii. 158.26 βλάβης, δίκης, ἀργίας, φόβου ~ Artemidorus, 1.53.1 ἀπραξίας ἅμα τοῖς φόβοις καὶ πόνοις; Maximus, Epit. 1 ἀπραξία γὰρ καὶ βλάβη ~ Artemidorus, 2.55.1 ἀπραξίαν καὶ βλάβην; Valens, Additamenta Antiqua IV, 16 ἀπραξίας... πένθη, νόσους ~ Apomasar, De Myst., CCAG xi/1. 203.2 νόσου ἢ ἀπραξίας; Valens, CCAG viii/1. 164.16–17 κινδύνων ἐπαγωγὰς καὶ ζημίας καὶ ἀπραξίας ~ Artemidorus, 2.36.3 ἀπραξίας... νόσον ἤ τινα κίνδυνον; Valens, I 1.8 ταπεινότητας, νωχελίας, ἀπραξίας; Camaterus, Zod. 535–6 ἀργίαν φέρει, | Λύπην τε δηλοῖ ~ Artemidorus, 2.8.1 πρὸς ταῖς ἀπραξίαις καὶ λύπας σημαίνει.

[56] But only occasionally caused by harm to Mercury (Hephaestion, i. 207.13, 208.19), as one might have expected if, as seems obvious to us (and as is suggested in De Astrologia Dialogus, p. 28.13 ἡ πρᾶξις τῇ ἀργίᾳ ἀντίκειται), it had been mentally bracketed as 'damage to trade' and coded accordingly.

[57] Περὶ κράσ. 1 ἐνδείας, ἀπραξίας, νωχελίας; Valens, I 1.8 ταπεινότητας, νωχελίας, ἀπραξίας; Apomasar, De Rev. p. 45.3–6; by contraries, Valens, App. X 31 οὐκ ἀπόρους... οὐδὲ ἀπράκτους ποιεῖ.

[58] 2.464; 3.205–6; Valens, II 11.1, 11.2 ἐπαίτας, κακῶς τὸν βίον καταστρέφοντας; Artemidorus, 1.21.2 (Pomeroy, 65), 76.4; Menander, Sent. 656 Jäkel = 647 Liapis; Epictetus, 3.26.6; Macedonius, AP 6.30.5–6; Anon. AP 7.336.1; Cic. De Senect. 8 Nec enim in summa inopia levis esse senectus potest (with the comment of Finley 1981, 165 (= 1989, 11): it is true that Cicero himself is utterly unattuned to this eventuality, but other sources are); Juv. Sat. 9.139–40 sit mihi tuta senectus | a tegete et baculo.

[59] You cannot, apparently, in Artemidorus, for whom, according to Hahn, 18–19, the πένης belongs outside the various classes of people in work. The πένης is someone who lacks means, support, needs a lucky break, but is not an impoverished *worker*.

and the workman, perhaps tellingly, are aligned at 5.129 πτωχόν, χερνήτην (prose astrology, however, does not use χερνής at all). The poor and the hired man are *distinguished* in Dorotheus, p. 413.28 δοῦλος ἢ πένης ἢ μισθωτός, but here we confront the problem of the relatedness of items in lists, and how to interpret disjunctives. Still harder is the distinction (because they are produced by different conditions) between the free πένης on the one hand, and δοῦλος or μισθωτός on the other on p. 409.31–2 εἰς ἐλεύθερον μέν, ἀλλὰ πένητα/δοῦλον ἢ εἰς μισθωτόν: slave v. free is clear enough, but πένης v. μισθωτός is not.[60] Firmicus has a 'daily bread' motif for poor workmen,[61] and there are scattered references to manual workers struggling for a livelihood.[62] Poverty does sometimes intersect with trades involving hard labour, which is sometimes described as servile,[63] but the artisan, the handicraftsman, is not presented as a figure who is immiserated *per se*.[64] The many qualifications in this paragraph suggest the range of positions, and the generally untheoretical approach, though it also suggests, once again, a generally 'middling' position which is slung low enough to appreciate the economic difficulties of the just-managing.

And so we can conclude with the question whether poverty can be called a 'discursive field',[65] in the same way that (for instance) sexuality obviously is, or luxury in Latin literature. The question, that is to say, is whether it develops a repertoire of motifs and tropes, of conventional stances, attitudes, and

---

[60] The same difficulty about the disjunctive renders uncertain the relationship between δοῦλος and μισθωτός (who are at least on the same side of the opposition against the free poor; this is not necessarily so in Lucian, *Fugit*. 12 ἐδούλευεν γὰρ ἢ ἐθήτευεν). For the hired man *in loco servorum*, see Treggiari 1980, 52; K. Hopkins, 'Economic Growth and Towns in Classical Antiquity', in C. Kelly, *Sociological Studies in Roman History* (Cambridge, 2017), 160–206 [repr. of P. Abrams and E. A. Wrigley (eds.), *Towns in Societies: Essays in Economic History and Historical Sociology* (Cambridge, 1978), 35–77], at 193 (the legal point of view); W. Scheidel, 'The Hireling and the Slave: A Transatlantic Perspective', in P. Cartledge *et al.* (eds.), *Money, Labour and Land: Approaches to the Economies of Ancient Greece* (London, 2002), 175–84 (élite sentiment). The other contentful reference to μισθωτοί is in Θ p. 131.1–3 μεγάλων πραγμάτων ἀντιλαμβανομένους γεννήσει ἢ καὶ μισθωτὰς δημοσίων, ὑπὸ ἄλλων [ἀλλοτρίων conj. Dr L. Holford-Strevens] κινδυνεύοντας πραγμάτων. The point here is not that they are badly off, but that they work for others.

[61] p. 71; good examples are 3.2.5, 4.15.7, 6.30.13.

[62] *De mansionibus Lunae*, *CCAG* ix/1. 146.7–8 τὸ ἀρρενικὸν γενέθλιον πτωχὸν καὶ ζῶν δι' ἐργοχείρου, πολλὰ μηχανώμενον πρὸς τὸ πορίζεσθαι τὰ πρὸς τὸ ζῆν ἀναγκαῖα; Firmicus, 6.30.14 *laboriosos pauperes et vitam manu quaerentes*.

[63] Firmicus, 6.15.12 *aut... certe laboriosae vitae pondus... aut egestatis angustias*, 6.30.13 *laboriosos, pauperes, misero onere paupertatis oppressos*; servile: Dorotheus, p. 328.4–5 τὸ μὲν γένος ἐλεύθερον, πενιχρὸν δὲ καὶ ὑποτεταγμένον καὶ δούλια ἔργα ποιεῖν σημαίνει.

[64] Specific circumstances cause harm to particular economic sectors in Achmet, *Introductio et fundamentum astrologiae*, *CCAG* ii. 125.4–6. The ἐργοπόνος is gainfully employed in 4.150 ~ 1.298 and 4.442, if boorish in Teucer, *CCAG* vii. 198.4, and Valens has a positive idea of Hesiod's work-stimulating Eris in IX 15.1 ἐργοπόνον τε καὶ φιλόκαλον (which is not, however, an apotelesma).

[65] Osborne, 15 ('in Rome... there was only a discourse of wealth, not a discourse of poverty'); Woolf, 'Writing Poverty in Rome', in Atkins and Osborne, 83–99, at 86–7, denying that there is a unified discourse of poverty in Latin literature.

value-judgements. Arouse attention it certainly does. There seems to be a broad consensus that lack of wealth is a matter of temperament, which, it was suggested, is simply the latest reworking of the sturdy old Hesiodic idea of self-help and the lack of it. Loss of wealth is a matter of temperament too,[66] but also a misfortune. Either idea tends to present the poor as individual unfortunates. They are conceived in rather limited terms. Here are some things that they are not:

(i) A class. Poverty is presented as a state of wretchedness, but not consistently or coherently connected with lack of economic or educational opportunity, or with lack of social capital[67]—most unlike its opposite, where wealth is very closely linked with high-status professions and with social connections and leverage.

(ii) A mob, the undeserving ὄχλος or *vulgus*, the urban trash sneered at by Roman sources for hanging around wine shops and gambling dens and racecourses.[68]

(iii) An 'other'. There is not an 'us', a collectivity, from which the poor are excluded. Connections are rarely if ever drawn between poverty and lacking a stake in the community,[69] and, although poverty and failure to marry are sometimes connected,[70] the further step of connecting this to a loss of personhood is not taken either.

(iv) An 'us'. There is no alternative poor man's value system. There is no valorisation of poverty for its own sake, as *per* the Cynics. Nor are there complaints about wanton *luxuria*, or posturing—itself a feature of

---

[66] There is even such a thing as being 'poor in spirit' (Firmicus, 3.2.6 *animo pauperes*; Θ p. 142.19 πενιχροὺς ταῖς ψυχαῖς), which is independent of material poverty, but different again from the poor in spirit (οἱ πτωχοὶ τῷ πνεύματι) of Matt. 5:3, and most certainly not a matter for beatitude.

[67] Contrast Martial, 5.19, on the poor man's lack of *amicitia*. Conversely, Libanius, *Or.* 8: no man is truly poor who still has friends.

[68] Sallust, *Cat.* 37.5; Ammianus Marcellinus, 14.6.25 *Ex turba vero imae sortis et paupertinae*. The discrimination of deserving from undeserving poor (Pleket 1988, 272, 274–5; Holman, 52, 111, citing Basil, *Ep.* 150.3) is not a feature of astrology.

[69] A wandering lifestyle is inimical to having a steady commitment to the community in 4.89–90, 521–6, and especially 282 ἀπόλιστα γένεθλα, but poverty is not involved in any of these passages. In Martial, 11.32, a man who is utterly destitute nevertheless aspires to be a *pauper*, which would at least qualify him as a member of the *populus*, and Martial ridicules this.

[70] Paul, p. 65.15–17 δυσγάμους καὶ σπανοτέκνους καὶ πένητας, cf. 'Heliodorus', pp. 71.20–1 πένητας δὲ καὶ δυστυχεῖς καὶ ἀγάμους καὶ σπανοτέκνους, 72.2–4 τοὺς δὲ γεννωμένους πένητας, δυστυχεῖς, ἀστάτους τε καὶ ἀβίους καὶ ἀγάμους ἐπὶ τῆς νεότητος; Valens, VII 6.193 ἄτεκνος... τρόπον ἐπαίτου ζήσεται. In the eyes of Libanius, precisely this condition is a disqualifier from membership of the community (on moral if not juridical grounds): *Or.* 41.11 πόλιν τοὺς ἀοίκους, πόλιν τοὺς ἀγάμους (sc. ἡγῇ;) (do you seriously think these worthless types constitute the city?) (Patlagean, 179).

upper-class sources—about virtuous poverty, save for gesturings in Manilius, who reflects some of the topoi of élite verse (5.374–7, cf. 400, 524–6).

And it is perhaps connected to the failure to see them as a category in the same way as the ὄχλος is a category that the poor do not have the same presence as they do in some Christian texts where they appear shaking their palsied guilt-inducing limbs at the gates of the rich.[71] (The startlingly phenomenological verb ἰνδάλλονται for the beggars at the gate at 3.249 turns out to anticipate their Christian visibility, but only through the happenstance of an Aratean borrowing which makes it *look* as if the point were their 'spectacular' presence.) In sum: the poor *are* always with us. They just do not have the same political presence as the masses, or, although they overlap with them to a certain extent, attract the same interesting and conflicted responses as slaves—to whom we now turn.

---

[71] Greg. Nyss., PG 46.477 c develops an extended metaphor of the poor as a tragic chorus on stage in a theatre (the treatise from which the passage derives is translated by Holman, 199–206, 'On the Love of the Poor: 2 "On the Saying, 'Whoever Has Done It to One of These Has Done It to Me'"'; this passage on 202). On the poor as spectacle, see L. Grig, 'Throwing Parties for the Poor: Poverty and Splendour in the Late Antique Church', in Atkins and Osborne, 145–61, at 148–9; Holman, 96–7, 155 (lepers).

6

Slaves

Slave stewards facing charges of malfeasance (like the one in the Gospels); the half-suppressed murmurings of 'freedmen' who are not, in practice, all that free;[1] the complex situations of slaves who, all things considered, might in fact be better off remaining so,[2] and of free men for whom becoming a slave might be a smart career move;[3] the anxiety of sale, of a new master, in which case pity the man sold a dozen times (4.606); the runaway who found himself in makeshift accommodation in a sanctuary, or shivering with cold on the highway, or who turned bandit and evaded capture for some time, living comfortably off the plunder.[4] There is no doubt that astrology provides a series of fine snapshots of ancient slave life. But can it do more than that?

The project in the first part as a whole concerns perspective and focalisation. Who speaks? If it is true that the attitude to work differs from that of élite sources, not by according *all* work dignity, but at least by replacing the ideal of aristocratic leisure with a graded set of attitudes depending on the nature of the work, then astrology's treatment of slavery would seem to be promising grounds on which to search for further possible lower-class focalisation. If astrology reaches as far as the handicraftsmen with pride in their labour, does it reach still further and embrace the perspective of slaves (which many of those same handicraftsmen were)?

But for slaves more is at stake. Divination, which includes astrology, dream interpretation, and now some of the lead tablets from Dodona, which take the inquiry back to the classical period, can tell us about what was preoccupying masters and slaves when they sought more-than-mortal guidance or insight. It sends a series of shafts of light—occasional, dispersed—into matters that were

---

[1] 4.600; Dor.ᴬᴿᴬᴮ I 10.41: 'he will be manumitted, but he will not escape from servitude which is like slavery'.

[2] Dorotheus, p. 390.13–16. On the preferability of slavery under a good master: Menander, fr. 787 K.–A. Not a possibility contemplated by dream interpretation: Klees, 65.

[3] Valens, II 35.6; presumably this individual opted to become a slave in order to serve as an administrator. On slavery *ad actum gerendum/administrandum*, cf. Veyne 1987, 145; J. Ramin and P. Veyne, 'Droit romain et société: Les hommes libres qui passent pour esclaves et l'esclavage volontaire', *Historia*, 30 (1981), 472–97, at 493–7; Garnsey 1996, 98. On self-enslavement, Scheidel, 300 and n. 36.

[4] Maximus, 344–5; Valens, VII 6.67 (= no. L 129 Neugebauer–Van Hoesen).

of day-to-day concern in master–slave relations. Its insights come at the individual, not the population level. They cannot be quantified. Those from astrology are particularly hard to historicise because of the perpetual problem of dating. They cannot address structural or macro-economic questions or questions about the historical development of slavery. So the question comes down to the usefulness of a historiography of slavery that can *only* be a 'humanist' one. Yet that is not the same thing as 'soft', 'sentimental'[5]—or indeed anecdotal. Joseph Vogt's work, derided by Finley for its unquantifiability,[6] looked in particular at ancient slave nurses (105–9) and *paedagogoi* (109–14), but whatever type of evidence divinatory texts contain, it is not sentimental anecdotage; I have not found a single slave nurse, a single *paedagogos*, in any of the texts (or oracles) treated here. It does, on the contrary, deal with practical matters, and although they are separated by half a millennium or more, the Dodona texts and catarchic astrology show masters and servants preoccupied with a similar set of concerns. The evidence of dream interpretation perhaps adds a psychological dimension as well, though it will be argued that that is very hard to interpret. Fridolf Kudlien's study of ancient divinatory texts from the perspective of slaves, the poor, the disadvantaged, tried to make them a way of nuancing Finley's picture of systemic brutalisation of ancient slaves—not by showing that the latter was wrong, but by changing the focal length, by looking at individuals rather than institutions, by taking a psychological rather than a demographic or economic or historical approach. Let us see how viable that is.

The first question is what situations astrology addresses. Natal and catarchic astrology have complementary, sometimes overlapping, areas of interest. Natal charts are interested in the first place in free/slave status itself: who is born into the latter, who falls into it, who is liberated from it (a subject of which one might perhaps have expected to hear more[7]); what is the status of the native's parents. M^a's section on slavery further includes the number of masters, relations between masters and slaves, the threat of being chained. A lot more material on slavery derives from catalogues (i.e. not individual charts, but

---

[5] Vogt, esp. chap. 5, 'Human Relationships in Ancient Slavery', whose peroration reads 'From deep and indestructible human feelings, a sort of self-purification of the whole polluted system took place in some small but decisive respects, as a reminder of the eternal truth that man is something sacred to man' (121).

[6] Finley 1980, 107: 'I can make nothing of all this, at least not until the documentation is removed from anecdotage and converted to a form that lends itself to significant analysis.'

[7] In 6.684–731, 4.597–611 (imperial freedmen in 4.600), Valens, II 35, and Firmicus, 7.6, freed slaves figure among other questions of status (who is born into or falls into it). It is interesting that Nicholas Pruckner (*Iulii Firmici Materni… astronomicōn libri VIII, per N. Prucknerum nuper ab innumeris mendis vindicati*, Basel, 1551), among his other additions to Firmicus' text, saw fit to append to Firmicus' chapter 7.4 (on the number of masters) a chapter of *libertinorum et liberorum geniturae*. If the source of the additions in book 7 is known, it is not mentioned by Bouché-Leclercq, 441–2 n. 3.

surveys that review the kinds of thing that happen in two or three-factor situations). From the point of view of the freeborn, these include marriage or sexual relations with slaves. Specifically from that of masters, it includes various bothers of slave-owning: troubles, losses, that stem from slaves; sicknesses; conspiracies, abuse, and attacks (the situation that so worried Roman slaveowners and precipitated spectacular campaigns of revenge), and of course runaways. Running away is one of the main preoccupations of catarchic astrology as well, the concern of both the slaves who were desperate enough to undertake it, and of the masters who wanted their valuable property back. It also counsels the owner on the right time to buy; and, at the opposite end of the slave's career, it advises both parties on emancipation,[8] whether it was advisable for the slave himself, and on the state of relations between him and the person freeing him. Other situations in catarchic astrology involve slaves as third parties, for instance, concerning stolen goods, where the thief, or the recipient of the goods, is a slave; where a slave is party to the concealment of a will; or—sexual anxieties again—whether a wife will consort with slaves.

Astrology can also tell us a lot more. For one thing, it makes reference to the main historical sources of slaves. They are both home-grown (4.603) and bought (4.605–6), born and made. All sources, especially the Manethoniana, are very alert to slavery as the outcome of child exposure and/or loss of parents.[9] Firmicus, on the other hand, makes reference far more often than Greek texts to prisoners of war (*captivi*),[10] although it seems unlikely that this is to be accounted for simply by the Latin writer being more attuned to Roman militarism, or by the military situation in Firmicus' own day.[11] Although catarchic astrology does address the time to buy them, it is not very interested in the dealers that sold them (Appendix II, III.3).[12] It is not particularly interested in their activities, either. Astrology's chief association for slaves is, not their function, but the misery of their situation. There are innumerable references to slaves along with other wretches, the poor, the unfortunate (pp. 75, 78, 81), and

---

[8] Dorotheus, pp. 389.21–390.25.

[9] 6.58–9, 67–8; 4.368–73; 4.379–83; Firmicus, 4.3.3, 7.2.18, and associated at 4.10.2, 11, 4.13.10, 4.15.3. Slavery and loss of parents: e.g. 1.342.

[10] *Passim*. There are also αἰχμάλωτοι in Valens, II 2.21, 35.5; Θ pp. 130.12, 164.21, 205.17; Camaterus, *Introd.* 2821, 2892, and they are presumably what *captivi* renders in *Lib. Herm.* xxvi. 23 and xxxiii. 4.

[11] The references to *captivi* are especially in the *dodecatopos* of book 3 and the *synaphai* and *aporrhoiai* of the Moon in book 4, for which Firmicus appeals to Greek sources (4 *Praef.* 5 *Omnia enim quae Aesculapio Mercurius et Hanubius tradiderunt, quae Petosiris explicavit et Nechepso, et quae Abram, Orfeus et Critodemus ediderunt [et] ceterique omnes huius artis antistites…*). Firmicus' own writing career coincided with the civil wars of the Tetrarchy (306–24) and then the Perso-Roman wars of 337–61, although there is also the possibility of slaves reaching the Roman market from perennial third-party wars.

[12] See 6.447; i. 731 n. 26, and the Addenda to 6.19–112.

it is perhaps a correlate of the fact that they are seen in terms of debility that they are very rarely mentioned in connection with employment.[13] Treatments of slaves show no more interest in the slave, or ex-slave, who is an artisan than treatments of $πρᾶξις$ show in the artisan who is a slave, or ex-slave (pp. 43–6). This applies equally from the point of view of the slave who has his own *peculium* to manage and from that of the master who may be considering how profitably to employ him: you went, it seems, to the astrologer to ask about getting your runaway back, but not what to do with him when you had him. Astrology does, however, when it implies anything at all, imply situations where the slave lived in close contact with the master and his family, so presumably a domestic setting, although this is not always very overt. We should not look to astrology to tell us what slaves did all day. Astrology does not overtly concern itself with agricultural[14] or industrial slaves, although one can draw one's own conclusions from the wretches whose business involves cleansing, refuse, water-carrying,[15] heavy lifting, and general hard physical labour. There are no chain gangs, although chains are sometimes mentioned as a specially dreadful fate (4.609 n.). There is a rare reference to a public slave in Maximus, 380 ὃς δήμου θεράπων κοινὸς πέλει.

The questions here are: whose perspective or perspectives are reflected; what (if anything) we can learn from them about private preoccupations on either side; and beyond that, what it all contributes to ancient slavery and ancient ideology. Can we generalise about ancient astrology? How does its attitude to slaves compare with its treatment of the ὄχλος? Do we find the same contempt (perhaps for people from whom we are all the more anxious to distance ourselves the closer to them we are)? Do astrology and other forms of divination constitute a form of social control? Or, if it is even remotely meaningful to call astrology a 'popular' medium, does it ever—against a hopeless background where the institution is written into the fabric of the universe by the stars themselves—allow the underdog his occasional, cheering, little victories?

If we find that anywhere at all, we find it in catarchic astrology, which in the first volume was contrasted with natal astrology as offering everyday pragmatic workability (i. 13–14). It shows that pragmatism here, above all in its treatment

---

[13] At 1.275 it is characteristically unclear what the λάτρια ἔργα are, or whether they are literal or metaphorical. Manufactures seem to be completely absent; so too 'humane' professions, such as teaching and medicine (on slave doctors, see Vogt, 114–20). Anubion, F 12.26–7 = 12 Perale κ]άρα [suppl. Boll] δούλους συνελ[αύνειν] | μουνομάχας [π]οι[ε]ῖ τλήμονας ἐσσομέ[νους] is apparently a reference to a slave gladiator. (Boll appealed to Firmicus, 3.4.23, which has simply *gladiatores*, but it is unclear that this is the appropriate parallel, as the planets are differently placed.)

[14] Very rare counter-example: Maximus, *Epit.* 2 γεωργὸν δοῦλον.

[15] (Domestic) slaves juxtaposed with an *aquarius* in Juv. *Sat.* 6.332.

of the perennial theme of runaways.¹⁶ Generally, it proceeds by selecting entities which represent the slave and the master, and then permitting inferences about the runaway and the success of his enterprise through the contingencies that affect those entities. We learn a lot from the analogies, prejudicial or otherwise, through which the writer has chosen to work out his theme. Often it is the Moon that represents the slave (obvious enough, for the wanderer), with the Sun or MC as master, though other symbolism is possible.¹⁷ It can readily be seen from the Moon whence and in what direction the runaway went, the distance he has travelled, and within how many days he will be found;¹⁸ the character of signs indicates the kind of terrain the slave has fled to,¹⁹ and their shape the straightness or crookedness of his course.²⁰ At the New Moon he will be temporarily concealed.²¹ So too, where a planet represents the slave, if that planet is ὕπαυγος the slave is hidden; if it emerges from the sun's rays he comes to light;²² if it retrogrades, the slave returns.²³ You can see from this kind of simple-minded analogy-making how useful this information would be to masters who wanted their valuable property back—but perhaps also to a clever slave if it occurred to him to have a chart cast for the day of his flight and then did precisely the opposite of what the chart forecast. Indeed, some aspects of the coding in catarchic charts are interestingly ambiguous about whose perspective they represent. When it is a matter of aspect, benefics and malefics are good and bad respectively from the point of view of the slave: malefics represent chains, imprisonment, death, benefics happy outcomes.²⁴ Crucifixion has obvious disadvantages for the slave himself, but also for the master who loses a valuable commodity. More striking is when benefics represent, not only a change of heart and rehabilitation between slave and master,

---

¹⁶ For writing Περὶ δραπετῶν, see Hephaestion, i. 317.11–323.3 (= Dorotheus, pp. 414.30–418.22), 323.4–329.18 (citing Protagoras of Nicaea at the beginning); Timaeus Praxidas, *CCAG* i. 97–9; Serapion, ibid. 101; Demetrius, ibid. 104–6 (Bouché-Leclercq, 472–4); 'Palchus', *CCAG* xii. 192–5; Protagoras of Nicaea, *CCAG* iv. 150–1; Maximus, 320–438; Hübner 2003, 191–202. The subject is also treated in *Sortes Astrampsychi*, *Sangallenses*, and was a specialism of Alexander of Abonouteichos. For slaves running away, see Bagnall 2003, 234.

¹⁷ Moon: Dorotheus (Hübner 2003, 193); Timaeus Praxidas, *CCAG* i. 99.19–20 (Hübner 2003, 191–2); Protagoras of Nicaea, *CCAG* iv. 151.11–12. The Moon is not only swift, but strays furthest outside the ecliptic: Hübner 2003, 199. Lord of the ASC in Protagoras of Nicaea, in Hephaestion, i. 323.6–12.

¹⁸ Hephaestion, i. 323.13–25, 324.18–325.8; *CCAG* iv. 150.2–17, 151.13–19.
¹⁹ Hephaestion, i. 324.1–11; *CCAG* iv. 150.18–151.7.
²⁰ Hephaestion, i. 325.6–10.
²¹ Hephaestion, i. 329.14–17. Also on Moon phase: Timaeus Praxidas, *CCAG* i. 99.19–25.
²² Hephaestion, i. 329.4–7.
²³ Hephaestion, i. 323.6–8 (Hübner 2003, 198); *CCAG* iv. 150.2–3.
²⁴ Dorotheus, pp. 416.19–417.10. Punishments include hanging, crucifixion, and burning alive (*bestiae* are not mentioned in this passage): see Bradley, 131–2, and for burning as a slave punishment, cf. Artemidorus, 4.24.3.

Slaves 89

which is obviously good news for the property-owner, but also escape and freedom,[25] which suggests a medium which is dangerously available for slaves who risk putting it to their own subversive interests.

But the coding and its application is up to the astrologer, and our ultimate impression is how it fortifies the prejudices of a slaveowning class. Some of its strongest articulations are found in a little section from Timaeus Praxidas[26] and in Maximus. The slave's thoroughly debased character is clear to see: not only does he abscond, but the likelihood is that he will be taking stolen goods with him (*CCAG* i. 97.10–12); not only does he take stolen goods, but he wastes the proceeds (i. 99.13–14); and what impelled him to flight in the first place was whoring after women (99.15–16). Maximus' decorative epithets simply spell it out with dreary lugubriousness (320 δμώων ὀλοφώια ἔργα, 323 δρῆσται ἀταρτηροί, 334 δμὼς ὀλοός, 368–9 αἰσυλοεργὸν | δμῶ᾽, 384 δρήστῃ ἀταρτηρῷ, 426 θεράπων ὀλοφώιος, 437 θεράποντι δολόφρονι); and after all that, look how much trouble the master took to reclaim the good-for-nothing (336)! Indeed, a master could consult his slaves' birth charts and see, from the location of devious Mercury, their temperamental disposition to abscond in the first place.[27] Knowing that in the first place, a master only had himself to blame if he expected better.

In short, this way of proceeding makes slaves things of scrutiny, trackable, and despite the occasional opportunities for slaves to turn things to their own advantage, the texts that we have reflect the attitudes of owners who suspect and distrust them—but would rather not see them damaged or lost. Is it really surprising, though, that none of our extant sources is subversive enough to preserve charts that positively advise slaves on running away? A less explosive topic, emancipation, better illustrates astrology's instrumental character, how, tool-like, it could be recalibrated for different users. Dorotheus' method posited that the Ascendant represented the person whose interests were being consulted, whether the owner or the slave himself, so presumably one simply made the necessary adjustments.[28] It mentioned, also, how the state of relations between master and slave could be determined, a matter of interest for both parties. Ptolemy dealt with this as well, but if we were expecting any insight into the anxieties and insecurities of the parties in a delicate relationship (*shall I be*

---

[25] Dorotheus, p. 417.5–10.
[26] Generally dated to the first century BC; see W. Kroll, *RE* s.v. Timaios, 9), 1228.61–7; Hübner, *DNP* s.v. Timaios, 4); Heilen 2015, 691 n. 1473, 794, 1344. Gundel and Gundel, 111–12, treat Antiochus of Athens (at the earliest 100 BC) as the *terminus ante quem*.
[27] Hephaestion, i. 328.27–329.3.
[28] As noted by Hübner 2003, 205. See Dorotheus, pp. 389.21–390.3.

promoted? shall I receive a whipping? is he plotting against me?), we shall only be disappointed by an account that is over in a few, frustratingly obscure, lines.²⁹

On the matter of slave charts themselves, those that simply spell out that x will be a slave, it is not self-evident what they are in principle *for*. Did the hungry slave in waiting at his master's dinner table need reminding he was a slave? Parents considering whether to expose a child might want to know what would become of it; you might also, especially if you were living somewhere at risk of pirates or foreign incursions or civil war, be worried about the prospect of captivity for yourself or your children. But a lot of this would seem to be stating the obvious. Likewise, charts that cover the status of parents ('slaves born of slaves', 'having a slave mother', in other words a house-born slave). Who needed to be told their offspring was a slave? A slave mother had no need to be told that, though she might want to know whether the child would be emancipated in later life, or would remain a slave for ever.³⁰ The pregnant slave who had had no choice but to submit to her master's advances had no need to be reminded that her offspring's father was free; neither did he. Still, the same question arises for charts that specify noble parentage, which was equally obvious (if fuzzier). One can envisage cases like the suspicious householder whose wife or daughter was mysteriously pregnant, or the many slaves who had been separated from their families and just wanted to know who they were.³¹ But one also wonders about the extent to which such astrology was rhetorical rather than informational, aiming to give a comprehensive suite of 'predictions', or rather just descriptions of the way things were.³² An individual was born to wretchedness, or he might entertain the hope of dying in freedom, but either way there was no point in trying to change matters; all this against a background in which the stars themselves guaranteed that slavery was written into the pattern of the universe. That was not even in question.

Other kinds of chart deserve attention as well, and two other characterisations of slaves which are very broadly associated with them. They might be classified as respectively (i) the miserabilist and (ii) the paternalistic. It is worth spending a little time on these because they reflect, not only astrology's most

---

²⁹ Ptol. 4.7.10 (at the end of a chapter on friends and enemies).
³⁰ Firmicus, 7.4.13; cf. Artemidorus, 4.67.6, a slave whose child became a runaway.
³¹ Cf. Firmicus, 7.4.7 *et qui a parentibus suis alienentur*. Comedy and oratory presuppose the situation in which a woman smuggles a slave woman's child into the house and passes it off as her own (M. Golden, 'Slavery and the Greek Family', in Bradley and Cartledge, 134–52, at 137). For children separated from parents, see Bradley, 57–62 (and ch. 2 in general on the instability of the slave family). More exotically, in Xen. *Anab.* 4.8.4, a man who had been a slave at Athens only accidentally discovered that he came from the country of Macrones when he was with Xenophon's army who were passing through the area.
³² As in retrospective charts, e.g. Valens, II 22.44 ὁ τοιοῦτος δοῦλος γεννηθεὶς καὶ εἰς γένος εἰσελθὼν πολιτικὰς ἀρχὰς ἀνεδέξατο καὶ ἐφιλοδόξησεν (no. L 109 Neugebauer–Van Hoesen).

characteristic stances with regard to slaves, but possibly those of ancient society at large.

The first, the miserabilist, usually occurs, not in individual charts (*x* will be born a slave), but in reviews and systematic catalogues, such as the *dodecatopos*, the *topikai diakriseis*, the *synaphai* and *aporrhoiai* of the Moon, although there are also examples in some themed chapters, for instance on parents or *biaiothanatoi*. This type of chart enumerates generic categories of native rather than specific individuals, and it is here that astrology's penchant for listing comes into its own. Slaves appear alongside the wretched, the incapable, the downtrodden and subjugated, including exiles and prisoners of war. In other words, not only are they 'vertically' challenged (by being low down in a hierarchy, ὑποτεταγμένοι), they are also 'horizontally' so by being outsiders, sometimes specifically enemies.[33] This type of chart makes of them an out-group. They are treated with distant pity rather than with contempt, like the ὄχλος, but they are not us.

The other kind of chart is quite different. This time they are not outsiders, but at the very heart of the family. The slave's proper place, as οἰκέτης, is in his master's household, a level which is both political, familial, and even somatic. Slaves, seen from the point of view of the master, are threats (at worst),[34] nuisances (in all probability),[35] chattels (in juridical terms), but also an extension of himself, a tool, even a body-part. This attitude, which can be seen already in the *Odyssey*[36] and is implied by Plato (*Leg.* 6.777 D–E), was theorised by Aristotle, of course to a far higher degree of sophistication than anything found in astrology,[37] which is highly unlikely to have been aware of his treatment anyway. What is found in the latter are conventional attitudes—the same which are carried by Seneca's approval of the ancestral Roman custom of calling the master *paterfamilias* and his slaves *familiares* (*Ep.* 47.14), the same mentality which

---

[33] Parallel to enemies: Firmicus, 2.19.13 *inimicorum qualitas et servorum substantia* (both illustrated by the Evil Demon).

[34] *Pericula*: Firmicus, 3.2.26, 3.4.34, 3.7.26, 3.11.7–8, 4.14.9, 7.23.27. On fear of slaves, see the essays collected in Serghidou. (But also, *against* fear of slaves by their owners in classical Greece, N. McKeown, 'Resistance among Chattel Slaves in the Classical Greek World', in Bradley and Cartledge, 153–75.)

[35] Firmicus, 3.2.26 *tumultus servilis*; on (real-life) troubles caused by slaves, see Bagnall 2003, 234–7.

[36] Eumaeus would rather see Odysseus again than his own parents (14.138–44); ἤπιος is habitually used of both masters (14.139, 15.490) and fathers (2.47, 234, 5.12, 15.152), as well as of the slave's attitude to his master (13.405 = 15.39, 15.557).

[37] *Pol.* 1252^{a}24–^{b}15: the household is the natural locus of the relationship of ruler and ruled (man/wife and master/slave). But master/slave, husband/wife, father/son all imply different types of governance (*Pol.* 1259^{a}37–1260^{b}24, *EN* 1160^{b}24–1161^{a}1 and *EE* 1242^{a}27–1242^{b}1). See also *Pol.* 1278^{b}32–9 (master/slave treated differently from man/wife and father/son). But rule of man over wife, father over sons, and master over slaves, are collapsed once again by Augustine, *Civ.* 19.14.

is found in inscriptions,[38] the same which was certainly also internalised to some extent by slaves themselves. It is characteristic of ancient attitudes to slavery that everyone proceeded as if these goodwill sentiments legitimated an institution that violated basic human rights—of which they had no concept.

This, the paternalistic, attitude, like the miserabilist one, occurs in catalogues and surveys,[39] as well as in themed discussions, for instance of slaves, parents, marriage, or wills. It is also found over and over again in discussions of astrological doctrine, in Valens, Hephaestion, Paul, Firmicus, and elsewhere. Slaves are mentioned alongside other household members—children, occasionally wives[40]—but also with beasts of burden.[41] Seen in this light, they are σώματα, possessions to buy and sell, and Valens, in particular, has a series of charts in which slaves (σώματα) figure as trophy possessions, regularly coupled with κόσμοι (which Riley renders as 'adornments', 'jewels'). This is the attitude of a *paterfamilias*. Valens has a genial example, where masters who treat their servants as εὐεργέται are mentioned in parallel (the eloquent list again) to those who bring up foster-children.[42] A heavier form is adopted by Maximus' narrator in his finger-wagging attitude to runaways (323–5, φιλίην λείποντες ἐδητύν etc.), and is implied generally by the EGHP-inflected idiom which expresses pious disapproval of sin and transgression. But it also seems that slaves had internalised it too, even if their focalisation is hard to prove in astrology itself;[43] and it is at least the desired result of a magic stone in *Orph. Lith.* 41–2 (cited by Schubert on Maximus, 320–6) which makes slaves love their master like a father. They may be a headache, but are still his chattels, a measurable index of his status, and even, on a good day, a quasi family-member, which is how a loyal (or self-interested) slave might see it.[44]

Intermediate between these two types of perspective, the miserabilist and the paternalist, are those that involve sexual relations with slaves.[45] Many charts strongly discountenance marriage with slave wives, who appear alongside

---

[38] Kudlien 1991, 15 and n. 24.
[39] For instance, in Hephaestion, of signs and decans, or the planets as chronocrators.
[40] Περὶ κέντρ. 25/Dor.ᴬᴿᴬᴮ II 23.11; Valens, I 19.11, 13; I 20.4, 14, 19; IV 11.63; Hephaestion, i. 210.25–6, 212.12–13, 219.19–20, 220.7–8, 224.21–2. In parallel configuration to children, implying equivalence: Valens, V 1.13. Among familial relationships which in principle *should* be harmonious (parents/children, brothers, husband/wife): Paul, p. 25.14–19.
[41] Paul, pp. 70.19–71.1 τὸν περὶ...δούλων ἀρσενικῶν καὶ τετραπόδων λόγον, 71.15–16 ἐν τῷ περὶ δούλων καὶ τετραπόδων, 72.1–2 τὸν περὶ δούλων καὶ τετραπόδων λόγον.
[42] IV 12.15 αὐτοὶ δὲ εὐεργέται εἰς αὐτοὺς [sc. slaves] γενήσονται ἢ καί τινας ἀναθρέψουσιν ἐν τέκνων μοίραις.
[43] e.g. in Firmicus, 7.6.9 *nati servi libertatis praemia consequentur, aut in filiorum loco nutrientur.*
[44] On the accommodation of ancient slaves with their servitude, see Finley 1980, 116–17; Bradley, 139.
[45] Bradley, 117–18; further bibliography in Edmondson, 361.

other categories of undesirable female (the disfigured, the elderly and infertile, the prostitute).[46] A few others, though not nearly as many, worry about sexual relationships between women and domestic slaves.[47] On the one hand, slaves are again an out-group—only it now looks much less pitiable, and the more undesirable the greater the risk of *our* being infiltrated by its members. On the other, they are a threat from within the house itself. All reflect the concerns, either of the free about the behaviour of their womenfolk (free female, slave male[48]), or of a society as a whole that condemns the indignity of marrying beneath one (free male, slave female[49]). We are told that as a matter of historical fact casual sexual relations between master and female slave were taken for granted.[50] But there are many passages in astrology that possibly allude to such relations (they use verbs such as ($ἐπι$)μίσγεσθαι, ἐπιπλέκεσθαι, συνέρχεσθαι, rather than γαμεῖν), and do so in less than approving tones.[51] Does astrology police social boundaries with unusually outspoken rigour?

One might suggest that astrology runs through some of the chief ancient positions on slavery. This cuts across the question of whether slaves are born into the status or fall into it. It reaches further back to what made them slavery-prone in the first place, to what created the liability. On the one hand, it sees them as casualties of the stars, Fortune's victims, whatever one wants to call them. Astrology would not be expected to formulate its position in terms of the Stoic belief in the brotherhood of man, but it can formulate it in terms of a

---

[46] 2.179; 1.20, 258; 5.236; Anubion, F 8 ii. 31; Dorotheus, p. 330.22–3 δούλην... ἢ σεσινωμένην, Περὶ σχημ. 70 δούλας ἢ σεσινωμένας, Π.τ.δ. 19 γυναιξὶ λυγραῖς ἢ ἐπιψόγοις ἢ δούλαις; Hephaestion, i. 21.3–4, 176.13–14; Paul, p. 72.6–7 and 'Heliodorus', p. 75.14; Θ pp. 155.15–16, 156.14–15, 158.12–13, 185.20–1; CCAG ii. 210.16–17; Firmicus, 3.12.6, 5.1.14, 5.3.32, 6.15.15.

[47] Anubion, F 4 ii. 4 ἥττονος ἢ δούλ[ου] ὕπο χείρονος ἠὲ πενιχροῦ; Maximus, 128; Valens, II 38.78; Hephaestion, i. 178.2 γυναῖκας ποιεῖ ῥυπαίνεσθαι παρὰ δούλων; 250.1 ἡ νύμφη δούλοις μιχθήσεται; Firmicus, 6.29.23 aut a patre ‹a› patruo aut a vitrico stuprum virgini praeparatur, aut a sene aut a servo; Ptol. 4.5.17. Although he does not mention the evidence of astrology, this tends to confirm the argument of H. Parker, 'Free Women and Male Slaves, or Mandingo Meets the Roman Empire', in Serghidou, 281–98, that Roman sources are in fact rather reticent on the subject in comparison to the scare-mongering and scandal that it *might* have occasioned; it is epigram and satire that pay it the most attention. He argues that it probably did not happen all that often; when it did, sources tend to use it to score points off other men (which is *not* the case in astrology).

[48] Edmondson, 351; Fountoulakis, 259–60.

[49] The option that involved the worse derogation of dignity: Kudlien 1991, 42–3, citing Plat. *Leg.* 841 D–E; cf. Klees, 70.

[50] A historical chart in Valens, V 6.85, in which a master frees his slave παλλακίδας (no. L 111, IV Neugebauer-Van Hoesen). Artemidorus, 1.78.5, regards sex with a male or female slave as a good sign (Klees, 69).

[51] See 1.20; Valens, II 38.22, 59 ἐπὶ δούλαις ψογηθήσονται; Hephaestion, i. 26.2 διαβληθήσεται; Θ pp. 158.12–13 τὴν δὲ νεότητα ἄστατον, καὶ δούλαις ἢ πόρναις μίγνυσι, 185.20–1. Maximus, 121–2, regards concubinage with a slave as a λέκτρον ἀεικέλιον imposed by Libra perforce in place of legitimate marriage.

commonality of suffering: there but for the grace of God go I. This is astrology's stock-in-trade, the miserabilist register. On the other, however, they are Nature's losers. The idea that people are simply born this way conjures up the idea of natural slavery, which evokes thoughts of Aristotle.[52] But once again his highly theorised treatment is an interesting sidelight to astrology, whose real basis is rather in what look like ancient and deeply rooted assumptions about an essential slavery grounded in the nature of things.[53] Astrology's concern is with spiritual subalternity rather than juridical status—to such an extent that it often prefers to speak of the ὑποτεταγμένοι (who may even be of free birth, but are so downtrodden that they might as well not be[54]). It associates them with physical and mental defect,[55] making them congenitally poor specimens with an emphasis that differs from *both* the complaints about slaves' mentalities, capacities, and attitudes that run throughout ancient sources *and* from Aristotle's treatment of the natural slave. It is not that mental inferiority is completely foreign to Aristotle's idea of the natural slave, but his postulate of slavish semi-brutishness crashes against the observation that nature often makes it far from obvious which categories men should be sorted into, thinkers or beasts of burden. Astrology knows no such inconcinnity. There is a certain likeness between its perception of slavish mental deficiency and the rewrite of *Od.* 17.322–3 in Plato's *Laws*, where the speaker goes on to connect the brutish treatment of slaves with their spiritual brutalisation. But for astrology this is congenital, not contingent, better explained by sub-philosophico-medical theories about the sluggish soul (i. 353–4).

And insofar as this is the case, it extends beyond individuals to whole races. Two passages in Ptolemy describe entire peoples as δουλόψυχοι. One of them,

---

[52] Arist. *Pol.* 1253^{b}15–1255^{b}40.

[53] It is not hard to find illustrations of this assumption (on Plato: Vogt, 24, 33; W. G. Thalmann, 'Despotic Authority, Fear, and Ideology of Slavery', in Serghidou, 193–205, at 197; Finley 1980, 118–19, on Hdt. 4.1–4), but whether embedded in narrative or presented as argument they seem to make the case for certain people or peoples needing to be ruled by others. Astrology is not doing that: it confines itself to the wretched condition to which the stars have reduced them.

[54] Hephaestion, i. 101.23–5: free by birth, but πενιχρὸν, ὑποτεταγμένον, and performing δούλια ἔργα.

[55] Valens, II 11.2 ἀδύνατος; Περὶ κράσ. 76 τὰς μὲν βουλὰς ἐκκόπτει, ψύξεις δὲ ‹περὶ› τὰς πράξεις ἐπάγει, αὐτοὺς δ' ἑτέροις προσώποις ὑποτεταγμένους (not categorically slaves, but subjugated) ... καί τινες τραυλοὶ ἔσονται ἢ μογιλάλοι καὶ ψελλίζοντες ἢ βρυχιῶντες ἢ κωφοί (where the harm to Mercury categorises this as a mental deficit). *Pigritia*: Firmicus 3.8.6 *pigros...tardos in actibus, et qui nihil consequi possint*, 6.32.11 *pigris semper conatibus haesitantem*. *Debilitas*: Firmicus, 7.4.16, 7.5.4 *debiles, caecos servos*, cf. 7.8.7 *debiles, captivos*; Lib. Herm. xxxvi. 18. *Aegritudo*: Firmicus, 5.4.4. *Valitudo*: Firmicus, 4.10.2, 4.13.12, cf. 4.22.5 *minori corpore, deiecti animo, invalidis viribus, semper potentioribus servientes et in omnibus aequalibus subiacentes*. Lib. Herm. xxxii. 10 *servos, sine semine, steriles* implies ἀσπέρμους in the original, but I do not find this (or στεῖρος) coupled with δοῦλος in Greek astrology. See too Firmicus, 7.4.17 *servi lunatici*; 8.27.10 *nanus, gibberosus, captivus*.

which evokes treacherous Semitic traders (2.3.30), has in mind an ethical or spiritual quality. But the second, which includes those who voluntarily enslave themselves,[56] recalls the well-known instance of a historical tribe who did precisely that, the Mariandynoi, who subjected themselves to their neighbours the Heracleotae of the southern Black Sea coast, in other words, precisely the geographical area Ptolemy is discussing.[57] Various sources mention them, but Posidonius attributes their action to mental incapacity (διὰ τὸ τῆς διανοίας ἀσθενές), as if, weak and debilitated, they acceded to a kind of serfdom which they could see was in their self-interest.[58] This proves a perfect, if presumably fortuitous, fit for astrology's mental framework. Might the intellectual Ptolemy, whose ideas are not necessarily less 'popular' than those of other astrologers but who at least encases them in a more intellectual armature, be thinking directly of Posidonius here?[59]

All this proves to have similarities and dissimilarities with the treatment of the poor. Both poverty and servitude are statuses into which the native can be born or can be precipitated. Both are sometimes associated with bodily and mental defect, with wandering and displacement, and both are emotionalised with the language of miserabilism. Both include information about parents, as if the status of the previous generation is relevant to this one as well, although it is true that the same applies at the opposite end of the social spectrum. The proneness to lump together slaves and the 'poor'[60] may or may not reflect the perception of the

---

[56] 2.3.38 (Asia Minor, Commagene, Syria).

[57] Another alleged case of voluntary self-subjugation: the Thessalian Penestae, on the account of Archemachus of Euboea, *FGrH* 424 F 1 (Eidinow 2011, 255).

[58] Posidonius, ap. Athen. 6.263 c = F 60 Kidd, cf. P. Garnsey, 'The Middle Stoics and Slavery', in P. Cartledge, P. D. A. Garnsey, and E. S. Gruen (eds.), *Hellenistic Constructs: Essays in Culture, History, and Historiography* (Berkeley, 1997), 159–74, at 166–72, and id. 1996, 146–8, 149–50. Garnsey reads this as Stoic rather than Aristotelian thinking (Posidonius may not have known the *Politics*). But if so, Posidonius has reapplied Stoic ethical theory in an ethnographic sense that the Stoics themselves never intended (nor did they intend its application to slavery, as Garnsey notes). Stoic theory has more plausibly coloured the story of Esau, one of the exemplars of natural slavery, in Philo and his follower Ambrose (Garnsey 1996, 163–71, 196–8, cf. 204 and n. 10); see too Basil, *De Spiritu Sancto*, 20.51; J. Glancy, 'Slavery and the Rise of Christianity', in Bradley and Cartledge (eds.), 456–81, at 473. Philo describes Esau as ἄφρων, suffering mental turbulence, in need of governance (*De congress.* 175, 176). Better parallels for the terms in which astrology's dullards are described is to be found in *Quod Deus*, 63 οἱ δέ γε νωθεστέρᾳ μὲν καὶ ἀμβλείᾳ κεχρημένοι τῇ φύσει, of fools who need a master to admonish them.

[59] And it *would* be specifically Posidonius, because other versions of the subjugation of the Mariandynoi (principally Strab. 12.3.4) do not have them putting themselves into subjection *voluntarily*. See A. Paradiso, 'Sur la servitude volontaire des Mariandyniens d'Héraclée du Pont', in Serghidou, 23–33; M. Manoledakis, 'Greek Colonisation in the Southern Black Sea from the viewpoint of the Local Populations', in P. Adam-Veleni and D. Tsangari (eds.), *Greek Colonisation: New Data, Current Approaches: Proceedings of the Scientific Meeting Held in Thessaloniki (6 February 2015)* (Athens, 2015), 59–71, at 63.

[60] Also found in dream interpretation (below, Klees, 62–3, and Thonemann 2020, 185): in that case, Artemidorus speaks of poverty and wretchedness (abstract nouns, not persons) in predictions

poor themselves,[61] but astrology adopts a generally cool, unfocalised, though not clinically distanced,[62] narrative voice. It relates, or fails to relate, to each group in a different way. The poor may be dislocated from their homes, or not have a stake in the city, and hence constitute an internal out-group in that way. Slaves are both more and less subtle. They may be ethnic foreigners; they may have real subversive tendencies. Yet they are in our homes, they belong to us, they are part of us, are treated with a greater intimacy than astrology extends to the poor.

Note, finally, how little astrology has to say about freedmen. Some authors do mention the fifth and eleventh places in the *dodecatopos* as having to do with slaves and freedmen,[63] but in practice no one seems to make much use of them. There are natal charts for slaves being freed,[64] but when astrology mentions ἀπελεύθεροι, they are usually categories of person involved in a catarchic outcome (e.g. as recipients of legacies, or of stolen objects, or as thieves themselves, or sexual partners, or as the sources of harm). Firmicus never refers to *liberti*; neither does *Lib. Herm*. The surprise can be mitigated when it is considered that the total lack of interest in juridical status in its treatment of work will have eradicated one of astrology's main potential occasions for treating them. That explanation is not available, however, for Artemidorus. He mentions ἀπελεύθεροι rarely; what attracts his attention is manumission more often than the ongoing condition of the freedman.[65]

FURTHER COMPARISONS

Astrology and Oracles

Turning to the slave material that has come to light from Dodona, which extends back to the classical period,[66] we are at first struck by the extent of

---

for persons who, at the time of dreaming, are presumably not yet in those lamentable states: 1.20, 24.3, 37 δουλείαν καὶ ταλαιπωρίαν, 56.4 ταλαιπωρίαι καὶ δουλεῖαι [NB Harris-McCoy has a different text, reading ἀπωλίαι]; 1.45 πενίᾳ δὲ καὶ δουλείᾳ καὶ δεσμοῖς; 3.18 δουλείαν καὶ κάματον καὶ νόσον (even for someone well off).

[61] O. Patterson, *Slavery and Social Death: A Comparative Study* (Cambridge, MA, 1982), 92, citing Hopkins 1978, 112: even the free Roman poor felt superior to slaves. But apropos of the story in Tacitus, *Ann*. 14.42–5, Finley 1980, 103, noted that the Roman *plebs* rioted in support of the slaves threatened with execution.

[62] Very far from it, in some of Firmicus' contemptuous references (1.7.5, 3.13.13, 4.12.1, 6.15.15, 6.32.11).

[63] Valens, IV 12.1; *CCAG* ii. 158.22, 30; cf. ps.-Palchus, *CCAG* xi/1. 202.26, 203.11.

[64] Dor.^ARAB I 10.26, 34–41; Firmicus, 7.4.1, 4, 11, 12, 17; 7.6.9.

[65] But see 1.47.3, 2.31.2, noting that in practice it often equates to continued enslavement; Klees, 76.

[66] Corpora: Lhôte, DVC.

overlap in the subjects covered. The consultations at Dodona come from both masters and slaves, though comparison is hindered to some extent by the lack of clarity about the identity of the slaves at Dodona (were they domestic slaves who accompanied their masters to the oracle and found some opportunity of consulting it on their own account, or were they some other kind?[67]). However that may be, the same practical questions arise about purchase and, from both points of view, manumission. Several might refer to *paramone*, the semi-free state wherein an 'emancipated' slave had to remain semi-indebted to his/her master;[68] a few permit the inference that a slave in that state was chafing at continuing restriction (see on 4.600 ἡμισύδουλοι). But masters had worries of their own. One asks 'what god should he pray to concerning his slaves?',[69] suggesting anxieties that become all too specific in the astrological record over half a millennium later. It might be worth asking whether anything has changed about the purview of divination over that span of time. But while that kind of enquiry can be conducted on a subject like sales, against the background of changes and developments in Egypt's economy and legal institutions (narrowing down the scope of uncertainty and hence what people needed to ask about),[70] with masters and slaves it is largely a matter of human irreducibles. It has been noted how some of the Dodona slave texts ask the 'open' question 'shall I become free?' rather than the 'closed' one available to those who know that a certain course of action is open to them and want only to know how to go about it, 'By doing *what* shall I become free?'[71] Natal astrology continues to address itself to the question in that open form, for those who simply wanted a window into their life prospects. The more precise formulation is answered, if at all, by the *katarche*, but the mechanics of escape are one place astrology takes us that the Dodona texts do not. Although some of the latter can be construed in this way, it is not at all certain that the Dodona corpus really shows slaves ruminating about running away.[72] There is nothing to prove that the institutional framework would have permitted that kind of question, which the *Sortes*

---

[67] One Dodona text has been interpreted perhaps to refer to 'slaves who live apart' (i.e. in their own establishment) [no. 60 Lhôte]: Eidinow 2007, 100; 2011, 266.

[68] Eidinow 2007, 100, 101; 2011, 262; Parker, 84; E. A. Meyer, 'Slavery and Paramonē in the Dodona Lamellae', in K. Soueref et al., *Dodona: The Omen's Questions: New Approaches in the Oracular Tablets* (Ioannina, 2018), 151–7; cf. Dorotheus, p. 390.1; Hephaestion, i. 264.18.

[69] DVC 2287, end of 5th c.; cf. Parker, 84.

[70] D. M. Ratzan, 'Freakonomica: Oracle as Economic Indicator in Roman Egypt', in A.-M. Luijendijk and W. E. Klingshirn (eds.), *My Lots are in Thy Hands: Sortilege and its Practitioners in Late Antiquity* (Leiden, 2019), 248–89.

[71] Eidinow 2007, 100–1, 2011, 264–5; Parker, 83–4.

[72] Speculated by Eidinow (2011, 262–3) for her nos. 10, 11 [= 35 Lhôte], 12 [= 62 Lhôte], 15 [= 63 Lhôte], 16 [= 64 Lhôte], but Lhôte takes the first (about whether to 'remain') as a question about marriage, and the last three (about 'going' or 'going away') as posed by freedmen not subject to *paramone*. See Parker, 85: 'There is no sign that slaves would have been allowed to pose

Astrampsychi do permit, and to which catarchic astrology is apparently prepared to lend itself as well (pp. 88–9). It seems that astrology reaches to more private concerns, anxieties (including about slave sexuality), and wishes. Is that down to context? Are private diviners more relatable intermediaries than priests in temples, backed by all the public authority of a prestigious institutional setting?

Astrology and Dreams

This is the most obvious comparison, and ideological, sociological, psychological questions come crowding in. Do they share the same preoccupations, concerns, anxieties, about slaves? Do they reflect the same perspectives, values, speak from and to the same social levels? What does each contribute to a 'humanist' historiography of slavery? But we had better first be clear what assumptions underlie the questions in the first place. Are we assuming that two bodies of 'popular' literature are likely to contain ideological similarities in the first place? What does 'popular' mean? Who were their respective users? If there *are* similarities, what does it tell you? If there are not, is that because clientele differs, or the relationship between expert and said clientele, or because of the way each method generates its data, or what?

In the first place, astrology and dream interpretation are not necessarily doing the same jobs. The two types of astrology most relevant to the present discussion are natal (this is the sort of person born at the present moment) and catarchic (is it an auspicious time to do this?). Dreams predict outcomes, for individuals, at certain moments. The non-contingent basis of oneiromancy is therefore shared with natal astrology, its occasional basis with catarchic. Natal astrology is about profiling an individual, his or her very identity, including parentage.[73] Dream interpretation, on the other hand, assumes the identity in the first place in order to make the prediction.

Like any other category of person involved in divination, slaves are involved at different stages of the process: (*a*) as recipients of the prognostic; (*b*) in the protasis, that is, in the material from which the prediction is drawn; and (*c*) in the apodosis, the prediction. In both astrology and oneiromancy, apodoses include both predictions and observed outcomes that have taken place in the past. Slaves and slaveowners are embedded at every stage of the process in dream interpretation, as dreamers, as the subjects of the dream, and in their

---

a question found in a late antique oracle book "Will my running away go undetected?"' (= *Sortes Astrampsychi*, qu. 89).

[73] It is rare to hear about more than one generation in dream interpretation, though Artemidorus, 4.67, follows the careers of several women's offspring.

interpretations. In astrology it is overwhelmingly (*c*), the apodosis, in which they appear, although there is such a thing as a House of slaves, which earns them a place in (*b*) as well. Of course they might theoretically be recipients of the prediction, (*a*) as we have discussed above, for both natal and catarchic astrology, although determining the recipient of slave charts is generally a matter of inference rather than explicitation, as on the other hand it is in oneiromancy. These distinctions will be useful in the discussion below.

In applying dream to dreamer, Artemidorus has two ways of proceeding. He mainly takes a known type of dream and accommodates it to various categories of person (slaves, the poor, debtors, merchants, shipowners, and so on). Less often, he cites specific instances of dreams that have happened in the past and then shows how they turned out. In the first place, the dream has to be made to apply to a dreamer with a determined social identity (rich, middling, poor; potential slave-owner, potential or actual slave).[74] In the second, a dreamer generates the data, whose interpretation is shown to apply to his or her situation. Either way, there is a specific context, one that either determines the interpretation, or *ipso facto* arises with the dream itself. This differs from much astrology, which simply announces that 'slaves are born' under such-and-such circumstances; the data come first, float free of context. The 'embeddedness' of oneiromancy matters for two reasons, one social, the other—potentially—psychological.

The 'social' dimension, which is the more straightforward of the two, is that dream interpretation's slave material, concerning both slaves and their owners, comes explicitly from domestic settings. This is much more clearly the case than for slave horoscopes. It is very easy to assume that both come from the same background, and it is true, as noted above, that one looks more or less in vain for agricultural and industrial slaves in the astrological corpus, so that a domestic setting tends to go by default. Nonetheless, much astrology just waves nebulously at 'slaves', along with 'the poor', 'exiles', 'the wretched', and so on. For dream interpretation, on the other hand, the household setting matters at every level. Slaves belong to their master's *familia*, are listed alongside biological family members,[75] are located in dreams in very specific domestic settings,[76] are

[74] Many dreams can be had by either slaves or the poor (1.14.2, 50.3, 80.1; 2.3.3, 8.2, 12.5, 56.3; 3.13, 59.1; 4.15.1). Some can only be had by a dreamer who is non-free, or a particular meaning is applicable to a slave which is not available to anyone else (1.54.1: dreaming of the ephebate). In 2.30.2, serving as a στρατηγός has dramatically different implications for a poor man (disturbances and scandals) and for a slave (freedom). Dreams of clothing can fall into either category. The loss of an enveloping garment signifies the riddance of an oppressive nuisance, but where a certain type of dress signifies a precise status it applies to a specific group (2.3).

[75] 1.5.2 γονεῖς φίλους οἰκέτας, 24.1 γυναῖκα τέκνα οἰκέτας, 41.2 τέκνων ἅμα καὶ σωμάτων ἐπίκτησιν, 42.2 γυναῖκα μητέρα ἀδελφὴν θυγατέρα δούλην, 48.5 παίδων καὶ δούλων; 2.11.3 γυναῖκα...καὶ οἰκείους καὶ τὰ πεπορισμένα κτήματα; 3.47.2 οἰκέτης...παῖς...γυνή (among τῶν οἰκείων); Klees, 68.

[76] 5.53: a woman dreams that her slave girl borrows her mirror and garments to attend a procession.

repeatedly metaphorised as household utensils (on which more below). It is also worth noting, a fact which is easily missed, that Artemidorus (although not Achmet) has a wide vocabulary for them, considerably wider than astrology's, even within a single work of limited scope.[77] Overwhelmingly the most frequent term in astrology (and in Achmet) is δοῦλος. Limping way behind come ὑπηρέτης (about a dozen instances, depending on what is counted, and in any case not always clearly slaves), θεράπων, which is exclusively poetic (3× M^a, 8× Maximus), and ἀνδράποδον (barely any)[78]. Valens, in particular, uses σώματα when he views them as possessions the acquisition of which heightens the owner's standing.[79] δοῦλος is the commonest word in Artemidorus as well (93 instances, three in Achmet), with five of ὑπηρέτης and three of ἀνδράποδον. Artemidorus also has nine instances of θεράπων, and a further eleven of θεράπαινα (Achmet has neither, though he has a single θεραπαινίς at *Oneir.* 45.14), having no intuition, as the astrologers apparently do, that this is a poetic word: its advantage for him would seem to be the degree of personal care and tendance that it implies (cf. 1.48.5, 64.6, 3.54). But the most striking divergence is his liking for οἰκέτης (29 instances, three in Achmet), which by contrast is very rare in astrology, figuring only in Dorotheus, and in Hephaestion, who uses him.[80] Moreover, it is very clear from the contexts in which Artemidorus uses the word, sometimes aligned with other household members or in proximity with the word οἶκος itself, that it designates specifically house-slaves, which is not the case in the exiguous number of instances in the astrologers, nor indeed in Egyptian papyri.[81]

The psychological implications of the 'embeddedness' of dream interpretation are much more complicated. 'As has long been recognized' (writes Peter Thonemann[82]), 'Artemidorus is an exceptionally important source for the mentalities of both slave-owners and slaves in the high Roman imperial period.'

---

[77] One thing they have in common, however, is that both use language flexibly, to fulfil different functions—precise when it is a matter of ensuring that interpretation is matched to client, but also vaguer, more suggestive, when it is a matter of allowing room for subjective interpretation. Both speak of 'the subjected', 'subordinates' (ὑποτεταγμένοι) beside 'overlords' (οἱ ὑπερέχοντες, *passim* in astrology, and in Artemidorus, 1.27, 77.6; 2.9.2, 12.5; 3.9.1), i.e. using the same vertical hierarchy.

[78] Five instances, none of which is in natal or catarchic astrology except for *CCAG* xii. 179.11, a woman who will own property including ἀνδράποδα. For papyri, see Bieżuńska-Małowist 1977, 9 ~ 1984, 18: again it is rarer than δοῦλος, which tends to appear in private documents, ἀνδράποδον in official ones.

[79] σώματα and κόσμος: I 19.11, 13; IV 17.6, 21.8, 11, 23.3, 24.10. Always in the plural, as in papyri: Bieżuńska-Małowist 1977, 10 ~ 1984, 18–19.

[80] Dorotheus, pp. 387–8 (five times in a passage on the purchase of slaves); Hephaestion, i. 219.19–20, 248.26, 278.19.

[81] For papyri, see Bieżuńska-Małowist 1977, 12, 94 ~ 1984, 19, 199, where (i) δοῦλος can mean a household slave and (ii) οἰκέτης can mean a slave in general (but does not necessarily designate a slave at all).

[82] Thonemann 2020, 181.

And there is a great deal of interest in, and for, both parties. Topics in Artemidorus' dream interpretations include being made to work harder, being beaten, tortured (by lash, whip, treadmill).[83] A master takes away the slave's pay.[84] Masters are represented by chaotic and capricious natural forces.[85] What happens if slaves get on the wrong side of them?[86] Will they be forgiven?[87] Dreams predict promotion, positions of trust.[88] They also warn of demotion and upheavals—being sold,[89] the death of a master (what comes next)?[90]—but life-changing events (giving birth, turning into a woman, turning into a god; being blasted by a thunderbolt, crucified, or eaten by a wild beast; being murdered by their master[91]) symbolise longed-for change. Above all, dreams predict freedom, whether this comes about through escape, or, much more often, through the legal channels of emancipation.[92] Some just want to go home.[93]

But before we start celebrating the reclamation of an ancient source that offers us all these priceless psychological insights, we need to listen, as usual, to Finley. 'I have sedulously avoided any reference to overt statements in ancient literature about the psychology of slaves', he wrote, 'for the simple reason that they represent the views and hopes of the slaveowning class, not of the slaves themselves, and have no unequivocal standing as evidence, except about the ideology of the free.'[94] The very basic, methodological, point, is that Artemidorus is not saying, and cannot be read to be saying, that slaves *have* these hankerings, or anxieties. He is making the presumption that these dream symbols are to be interpreted for them in this way; he is presuming that this is what they will want, or fear, to hear. Slavish preoccupations and anxieties can only be only suppositions based on reading back from the interpreter's forecasts. Both Artemidorus and Achmet proceed by taking dream symbols and interpreting them in the way they deem appropriate for the social level of the dreamer. So strictly we cannot say Artemidorus offers evidence that slaves thought a single

---

[83] Harder work: 1.50.4 (Klees, 72). Torture (βάσανοι), blows (πληγαί): 1.76.4; 2.14.3, 25.1, 28.1; 3.59.1; Thonemann 2020, 182. Lash and whip: 1.70.1 (Klees, 71; Bradley, 119). Bradley, 137: 'The frequent recourse to physical coercion produced pain and hardship in the lives of countless slaves... of which virtually nothing is heard in conventional sources.' It is here.

[84] 3.41; for ἀποφορά, see Bieżuńska-Małowist 1977, 106–7 ~ 1984, 209.

[85] A bull: 2.12.5; a river: 2.27.2; Klees, 70–1.   [86] 4.69.   [87] 1.13.2.

[88] Promotion: 2.15.1, 30.2, 31.2, 47, 68.5; 4.61 (Thonemann 2020, 184). Demotion: 1.35.5; 2.9.5. See Klees, 68, 73–4.

[89] 1.35.5, 50.5; cf. also *Sortes Astrampsychi*, P.Oxy. 1477.3 (no. 74) εἰ πωλοῦμαι.

[90] 2.20.4; 5.23 (retrospective: the slave got another one); cf. Klees, 75.

[91] Respectively 1.14.2, 50.3; 3.13; 2.9.5, 53.2, 54; 4.64.

[92] Escape: 2.14.6 (Klees, 72); cf. also *Sortes Astrampsychi*, P. Oxy. 1477.15 (no. 86) εἰ φυγαδεύσομαι, 18 (no. 89) εἰ λύεταί μου ὁ δρασμός. Freedom: see Klees, 74–6; Thonemann 2020, 183, cites a figure of 32/89 dream outcomes for slaves on this topic.

[93] 4.56.4; Klees, 72.

[94] Finley 1980, 117.

one of these things. We can only say that Artemidorus thought that they *ought* to have thought them, or that it was plausible that they would have thought them. As a matter of fact there is only a tiny number of actual dreams which are imputed to slaves (4.69, one plays ball with Zeus; 5.91, one has three sets of genitals), and it is only the interpretation that brings them to bear on their slavehood. As it happens, there is an equally small number of historical dreams imputed to slave-owners,[95] but these do at least concern the master–slave relationship, and *do* imply that it involved perplexity and tension.

Artemidorus is not a psychoanalyst. What he is, if Peter Thonemann's recent identification is correct, is one of his city's élites, a mint-magistrate who also held at least twice the chief civic magistracy of Daldis, that of 'first archon'. A number of issues arise here. One is the surprise that such an elevated figure should include this kind of material at all, and that, granted his elevated standing, he stoops to trivia about slaves at all. Yet, given that he does, some of the questions suggest a sensitivity on the part of the dreamer to delicate situations—to slaves worried about being forgiven, or wanting to be liked; or slaves engaging in power-play with their masters (4.69). If any of these dreams can be salvaged for 'slave psychology', as opposed to that of their more acute masters, should we take Artemidorus to be reflecting, or at least refracting (though at that point it becomes hard to say how much stylisation or distortion has entered the picture), the concerns of slaves, or what he *believed* to be the concerns of slaves, as they emerged from his, or other practitioners', dealings with them in the course of consultations? Could slaves afford his fees? Did he really sit, as he claims to have done, with the downmarket, the quacks and mountebanks of the marketplace, and listen to their dealings with their sordid clientele (1 Praef. 2)? Or is he at least reflecting a *literary* tradition of dream interpretation which had accrued material that gives, or seems to give, a slave's-eye view? On the other hand, there is also the distinct possibility of divination being used to insinuate a form of social control. Slaves are allowed to hanker after freedom, or at least the interpreter assumes that they will care about this. But the great majority of Artemidorus' freedom charts involve the legal channel of emancipation, not running away—precisely the opposite way round from astrology. And when a dream 'admonishes him [the slave] to obey this master and to do the things that he delights in' (2.33.2, transl. Harris McCoy), is this—far from being a penetrating psychological shaft into the mind of a slave who had internalised the code so effectively that he felt guilty about not adhering to it—a way of gently insinuating to a potentially mutinous cook or gardener or litter-bearer what he really *ought* to do?

---

[95] 4.59, a mistress who is jealous of her θεράπαινα dreams of her reciting words by Euripides (Klees, 69); 5.53 (n. 76).

We are on firmer ground in claiming that the dream interpreter can speak more eloquently *about* them than astrology can. We understand why by considering how the two methods convert their respective signifiers (planetary configurations, dreams) into signifieds. Astrology comes from the cosmos, dream interpretation from the soul.[96] Both sets of data, from sources at opposite poles of externality/interiority, have to be brought to bear in some way. It is only by undertaking some kind of process of conversion that they can operate at all, but they go about it in different ways. It is attractive, in principle, to want to draw a clean contrast between the sclerotic, highly formalised, and rule-governed system that is astrology with the more plastic and versatile business of the dream interpreter, but it is hard to make it as neat as all that, not least because we do not have Artemidorus' predecessors in order to be able to conduct a comparison between one practitioner and another and discover what the ground-rules (if any) were. It seem fair to say that the dream interpreter is not shackled, as the astrologer is, by a system which consists of a series of game-pieces with fixed meanings (there is little room for manoeuvre with the planets' associations), although it is moot whether having a matrix based on the complicated geometry of the cosmos allows the interpreter scope for more or less creativity than one that comes from all the incalculable chaos of the human psyche. Perhaps it is better to say that they are just different. The point here is how meaning is produced. In the first volume it was suggested that the astrologer's techniques are analogy and affinity, those of the dream interpreter analogy and *association*.[97] That still seems right: the dream interpreter uses analogy (x is like y) and association (x belongs in the same semantic field as y). But he has greater scope for metaphor because anything in a dream can be suggestive; with astrology, on the other hand, after stars have been compared to eyes, not much remains. Dream metaphor is infinitely richer.

The domestic is one of its favourite domains. Artemidorus expressly locates slaves in the household. The men's quarters of a house represents kinsmen and menservants, the women's quarters maidservants.[98] Household slaves (οἰκέται) are represented by mice, which cohabit with us and eat our food[99]—an image eloquent about the domestic nuisance slaves were expected to cause. Blood means στάσις with one's household slaves (1.33.2)—to which is added the indignity that only a *small* amount signifies it (were slaves too trivial to merit more than a trickle?). Most eloquent are the metaphors that represent them: tools, utensils, animals[100] (or indeed pests), or functional body-parts (hands, feet, which at least makes them integral to the functioning of a complex

---

[96] As Artemidorus, 1.2.3, himself tells us: Thonemann 2020, 44.
[97] i. 22 n. 31.   [98] 2.10.1.   [99] 3.28.1; Thonemann 2020, 181–2.
[100] 4.56.3 τὰ ⟨δὲ⟩ ἐργατικὰ καὶ ταλαίπωρα [sc. ζῷα] ἐργάτας καὶ ὑποτεταγμένους, ὡς ὄνοι καὶ βόες ἐργάται; four-footed beasts: 1.37, 3.18.

mechanism[101]). Aristotle had already foreshadowed most of this,[102] but Aristotle's point was the 'naturalness' of having the inferior ruled by the superior to the mutual benefit of both parties. For Artemidorus, the point is exploitability; for him, the images simply appear, particularised, to suggest the various kinds of function slaves were expected to fulfil. On the other hand, although the semantic domains themselves are demeaning, the associations were presumably intended to express constructive aspects of the relationship. Scrapers and cloths represent the personal care domestic helps provided (1.64.6 στελγίδες ‹δὲ› καὶ ξύστραι καὶ καταμαγεῖα). Physical intimacy as well as hierarchy is also suggested by the image of the feet of a bed, where the bed is the wife herself (1.74.3). Oil-flasks and boxes (1.64.6 λήκυθος δὲ καὶ ξυστροφύλαξ) represent stewardship. So does a key (3.54), and baskets presumably express a similar idea (2.24.4 κόφινοι). Faithful servants are represented by mill-stones (2.42 μύλος) and dishes (3.30 λεκάνη): the former presumably implies thoroughness, fine-grained attention to detail (and labour-saving), the latter perhaps reliable functionality (though they can be broken). A wine-jar represents a public slave (δημόσιος), being accessible to all (5.25).[103]

Achmet takes this further. His basic type of slave chart symbolises the slave in some way, and then makes the condition of the object symbolising the slave represent the master's relations with the slave, whether for weal or woe. His favourite symbols are serviceable animals, which include the horse, camel, sheep, bees, and birds (doves, cocks, geese, a caged nightingale),[104] and body-parts,[105] which he particularises to a greater extent than Artemidorus. A rod or a staff, that upon which one leans for support, symbolises a dependable, cherished servant.[106] But in Artemidorus, the idea of slave as body-part extends to dreams in which the slave is a corporeal extension of the master himself, implying a still greater degree of interdependence—and potential conflict. A 'sympathetic' dream in which the slave's fever prognosticates the master's illustrates, less the principle that they have a body–soul relationship in which one

---

[101] Hands: 1.42.2, 78.7. (Epictetus, 4.1.78, has it the other way round: the hand is a slave.) Feet: 1.48.2, 74.3 (of a bed). See Klees, 66–7.
[102] Slaves as ὄργανα: Pol. 1253ᵇ30–2 (von Reden, 1–2), EN 1161ᵃ34–5, 1161ᵇ4–5, EE 1241ᵇ17–24, 1242ᵃ28–30; cf. Varro, Re Rust. 1.17.1, slaves an instrumenti genus vocale; Pol. 1254ᵃ8 διὸ καὶ ὁ δοῦλος ὑπηρέτης τῶν πρὸς τὴν πρᾶξιν; Garnsey 1996, 119–20, 122–3. Slaves as ζῷα: Plat. Polit. 289 B 8; Arist. Pol. 1254ᵇ2–26, esp. 25–6 (conversely, Philo, Spec. Leg. 2.69: dumb beasts like slaves). Body-parts: Arist. Pol. 1255ᵇ11–12 (and 1254ᵃ8–13 on part to whole).
[103] Images for the functionality of slaves: Klees, 67.
[104] Horses: 231.22. Camels: 235.15–16. Flocks and herds: 240.52–3. Bees: 241.12, 282.18. Birds: 250.3–4. Doves: 291 passim. Cocks: 292 passim. Geese: 293.2. Nightingale: 286.13–15.
[105] Hands: 17.13–14, 107.12–13, 115.15–16, 131.91–2, 149.20–1. Nails: 75.3–4. Arm: 135.7–8. Arms and legs: 71.2–3, 155.26–7. Feet, legs: 116.6–7 and 14, 117.13–14. Feet: 189.8–9 (the lowest of the slaves), 224.6–7, 242.6–9.
[106] 211.18–19 ποθητὸν δοῦλον καὶ ἰσχυρόν.

'naturally' governs the other, and more the presence of some kind of psychosomatic equivalence.[107] In another, the master is indeed represented in the dream by the head,[108] but its severance is the happy occasion of the emancipation of the servile body.

Let us conclude with that bird that cannot fly. Dream interpretation can be both stunningly insulting and pitifully sad. The bird is a solace ($παρηγορίαν$) for its owner: the narrative voice seems oblivious to the pathos this implies. Artemidorus does rather better, but the problem with his evidence at the end of the day is that it *is* a projection; the slaves themselves remain as mute as ever. What we have in his dream book is a source that beggars astrology for psychological perspicuity, but *is* the stylisation of an external party. Suppose we give it some credit. It had to be plausible to a clientele, after all, or the interpreter would be out of business. Kudlien took issue with what he saw as Finley's sledgehammer approach. There is no point harping on about brutalisation, but nothing gained by eliding it either. How reduced must one be to dream of crucifixion and be persuaded that it represented *an improvement*? But in the absence of ancient slave memoirs the evidence of divination, especially dream interpretation, complicates the documentation of brutalising attitudes and effects with apparent testaments to sensitivities and sense of pride. Dreams, in particular, *both* reveal the profound wish to be free *and* suggest, hardly surprisingly, Stockholm syndrome.[109] This is not to be overtly empathetic, or roseate about affectivity between masters and slaves. This is not a revival of Vogt's project. But dreams give perhaps the best idea that we are likely to attain of what humanity managed to make of the shackles it had wrought for itself, both literal and psychological.

---

[107] 4.30.3; Klees, 66; Kudlien 1991, 72; Thonemann 2020, 182.

[108] Artemidorus, 1.35.5; Kudlien 1991, 73. See also 3.51 (Thonemann 2020, 184), where a master lame in one leg dreams that his slave is lame in the same leg; in practice, both are in love with the same woman. Aristotle had the soul ruling the body and the rational part the emotional: *Pol.* 1254^{b}6–9 and other passages in Garnsey 1996, 119–22.

[109] Bradley, 142–3.

7

Conclusions and Further Reflections

Astrology is a repository of images. These images extend across the whole social spectrum, with the implied point of view launched from a position of middlingness. Disdain for the ὄχλος contrasts with the tone adopted towards superiors. Occasional dabs of adept use of diplomatic language suggest *savoir-faire* with negotiating relationships with ruling powers, yet real power is too remote to be seen through anything other than a haze of ambition on the one hand, menace on the other. Work is one of the basic categories of existence, alongside physical and mental health (with which, in truth, it sometimes overlaps). Astrology manages to compartmentalise it in such a way as to be independent of juridical status: one's existence as *grammatikos* or muleteer is not coextensive with one's existence as slave, but the two are equally essential and intrinsic. Conventional attitudes are policed with language of shame still stronger than that of honour. Before we try to draw any conclusions from all this, two further topics call for comment, which also circle round the question of middlingness, not from socio-economic points of view, but from intellectual and cultural ones. Both continue to exemplify the principle of bricolage, motifs grabbed from a storehouse of classical culture and commonplace—with little to mark it as specifically Graeco-Egyptian.

LETTERS

There are not very many references to books in astrology (i. 329–30); Achmet, whose dreams involve the reading of sacred scripture, is moving in a very different world. They do not figure where they might have been expected, alongside members of literary professions. Given astrology's predilection for luxury goods, they might have figured there, too,[1] but do not. Apart from miscellaneous references to their acquisition or loss in catarchic texts, references are mostly in connection with 'secret books' (5.304 n.), for which Firmicus prefers

---

[1] Holleran, 246–8 (in 2nd-c. Rome bookshops were located in the near vicinity of the shops for other luxury goods, not in the Sacra Via itself, but on the Vicus Sandaliarius parallel to it).

the formulation 'hidden letters'. These are associated with τελεταί, secret rites (2.197-9, 204-5), magic (5.304, Firmicus, 3.12.6 *magos*), divination (3.293-4), religious secrets (Firmicus, 4.19.28; *Lib. Herm.* xxxii. 13), and arcane knowledge (*Lib. Herm.* xxxi. 35 and xxxii. 12 *caelestia*). These associations are not distinctive of astrology: the association of books with magic, rituals/initiations, and indeed philosophic lore can all be paralleled. They can be found contexts in Greek (the secret books in the mysteries of Andania), Roman (pontifical, augural, and prophetic books), and Egyptian (magical papyri; Hermetic texts) traditions. It is doubtful whether the motif of 'secret books' can be used to identify a particular cultural strand in astrology. But Saturn's morose, introverted nature and uncanny character gives them especial purchase there.

There is more to say about 'letters'. Not surprisingly, astrology reflects the cachet attached to them, to the distinguished profession of grammarian, to *paideia*. It sees them as a source of emolument which would have pleased Gaisford,[2] a means to proximity to the powerful,[3] and soft power.[4] But there are also several apparently off-colour references. On a number of occasions, literary professionals are among the ill-willed,[5] and Firmicus has a number of motifs which cast letters as problematic in some way—*malitiosae* (5.5.3), *laboriosae* (3.7.4, 5.5.3), *difficiles*.[6] These pejorative epithets raise the question whether, beside the conventional deference towards those endowed with *paideia* (cultural capital), there is *also* a trace of the nervousness or suspicion or insecurity on the part of those who are less competent or incompetent in letters (unless, as Dr Holford-Strevens suggests, it is the μελαγχολία to which the learned are notoriously subject that gives letters their unsettling quality). The question does not depend on defining literacy and then putting a figure on what proportion of the population we think possessed it or lived in its

---

[2] e.g. Valens, II 23.14 ὁ τοιοῦτος εὐτυχήσει ἀπὸ γραμμάτων καὶ παιδείας; *Περὶ κράσ*. 177 οὗτοι δὲ καὶ ἐκ γραμμάτων καὶ λόγου καὶ παιδείας τὸν βίον αὔξουσιν; *CCAG* iv. 169.9 ἐὰν μάθῃ γράμματα, μεγάλως προκόψει. Gaisford: i. 344-5.

[3] Appendix II, IV.2.iv; IV.2.vi *scriba*; Firmicus, 3.7.13; 4.14.5.

[4] *CCAG* v/3. 92.16-17 Ἀββά· καλὸν ὁμιλεῖν γραμματικοῖς καὶ μεγιστᾶσιν καὶ κτᾶσθαι δωρεάς.

[5] Paul, p. 72.14-15; Firmicus, 3.5.25 (*malitiosos*); Rhetorius, *CCAG* vii. 222.13-15 ψεύστας, κλέπτας, γράμματα εἰδότας (al.), which is particularly interesting because these are among the bare effects of Mercury, not vitiated in any way.

[6] 3.5.22, 3.7.15, 3.9.10, 4.12.4, 5.5.3. Not clear what these 'difficult' letters are (listed along with other technical subjects in 3.7.15, and with meteorology in 4.12.4), but intriguing in any case to set this alongside Richard Gordon's observation (apropos of the use of writing in Roman religion) that 'in effect, writing offered a sovereign means of institutionalizing unintelligibility' (R. Gordon, 'From Republic to Principate: Priesthood, Religion and Theology', in M. Beard and J. North (eds.), *Pagan Priests* (London, 1990), 179-98, at 189). Even if Firmicus does not mean religious writings, he seems to give the non-expert's focalisation of technically demanding branches of literature, arcane and exclusionary.

penumbra.⁷ It matters more whether we are persuaded by Youtie's view (that functional illiteracy was just too prevalent to be stigmatised) or Hopkins's (that even if only a minority could read and write, literacy was so obviously advantageous and so obviously part of a system of power and control that it created a new kind of culture, 'a larger store of knowledge, a system of laws and a market in cultural skills and values', that might have fostered feelings of suspicion and estrangement in those who did not partake of it).⁸ Astrology does occasionally mention the 'illiterate' (or whatever is meant by ἀγραμμάτους—unable to read, less competent in letters, or just not interested in *belles-lettres*?).⁹ But for what this very small number of passages is worth, they code illiteracy as an intellectual defect (a badly placed Mercury) and associate it with lack of intelligence (not lack of opportunity or resources) and definitely not neutrally. There is also a passage which seems to acknowledge what many papyri show to have been the *de facto* reality: those who muddled through, even in lettered professions, without having a very secure grasp of the medium.¹⁰

As a matter of fact it is hard to attribute these pejorative epithets to an attitude about literacy that emanates from sectors that had a precarious grasp of it.¹¹ It was surprising to find no obvious Greek equivalents that Firmicus' *malitiosae*, *laboriosae*, and *difficiles* could be rendering. Nor is there anything similar in Artemidorus, who represents dreams involving letters as signifying the cultural adeptness and competence (or the opposite) of the reader (1.53), yet without failure turning into hostility towards the medium itself.¹² What is clear is that astrology presents the problems as arising from private relationships

---

⁷ Hopkins 2017, 365 accepted Harris's figure of about 10% (where 'literacy' is not, however, defined), but interpreted the figure differently.

⁸ H. C. Youtie, '*βραδέως γράφων*: Between Literacy and Illiteracy', *GRBS* 12 (1971), 239–62; id. '*Ἀγράμματος*: An Aspect of Greek Society in Egypt', *HSCP* 75 (1971), 161–76; Hopkins 2017 (the quotation on 389).

⁹ Valens, II 15.9 ἀνοήτους καὶ ἀγραμμάτους ~ Θ p. 140.17–18 ἀμυήτους … καὶ ἀγραμμάτους (Mercury ὕπαυγος, its effect nullified); Valens, II 9.5 μωροὺς καὶ ἀνοήτους καὶ τῷ λόγῳ ἐμποδιζομένους καὶ ἀγραμμάτους ~ Θ p. 161.10 ἀνοήτους καὶ ἀγραμμάτους καὶ νωχελεῖς (Mercury in eighth house).

¹⁰ Θ p. 185.18–19 οὐκ ἔσται ἐμπαίδευτος, ἀεὶ δὲ ἐν γράμμασιν καὶ λόγοις ἔσται.

¹¹ A thought-experiment, unfortunately uncontrollable, to marry it up with evidence from dedications and epitaphs, and from craft (and other) associations, whose members might be expected to represent a good part of astrology's tradesmanly clientele (pp. 49–50). Hopkins 2017, 387, provides evidence from one particular club in 1st-c. Tebtunis which had 9/15 literate members, and a 'literate' culture insofar as it had a set of written regulations (*P.Mich.* V 243, AD 14–37). Contrast the less sanguine appraisal of likely levels of literacy among tradesmen by W. V. Harris, 'Literacy and Epigraphy, I', *ZPE* 52 (1983), 87–111, at 93–5 (Corycos and Tyre), and 108 (Pompeii).

¹² For Artemidorus himself, a large part of his art consists in converting dreams into texts which can be manipulated to produce interpretations (1.11.1, and Harris-McCoy, 435). Some interpretations are produced by noting letters in a name (5.26) or converting numbers to letters (2.70) or letters to numbers (3.28.3, 3.34, 4.22.7), or by the transposition of letters (1.11, 4.23).

between letters and individuals. The same is true of its preoccupation with forgery (πλαστὰ γράμματα, πλαστογραφία, *falsae literae*[13]), which has, obviously, nothing to do with the Platonic Socrates' old suspicions, launched from within an oral culture, about a medium which *in principle* could not be held to account.[14] The problem seems, as so often in astrology, to be about isolation, separateness, failure to circulate—those skilled in 'laborious' letters 'who are unwilling to compare their nature with other people' (3.7.4); the association of 'difficulty' with 'malice' (3.5.22, 5.5.3), of secrecy with illicitness (4.9.8, 4.12.4). For that reason, attitudes about malicious and difficult letters are not necessarily incompatible with respect for grammarians and rhetors (not strongly associated with a bookish culture anyway: i. 329–30), who could be heard exercising their golden tongues in assemblies and on embassies, at weddings and funerals and congratulatory gatherings, and for public delectation in the odeion. And this supports, by contraries, the interpretation of the epigraphic habit itself, the prominent display of public inscriptions, as conveying a sense of settled permanence and established order.[15] Public display implies a consensus and scrutability (even if in practice an inscription was little-read or hard to read) which the private, secretive, inaccessible letters challenge and threaten.

And then there are *polite* letters, *belles-lettres*, an issue raised specifically by poetic astrology. Perhaps there is a sense in which it is helpful to think of astrology, with its rag-bag of motifs, as a kind of poor man's Second Sophistic (pp. xi–xii, 1004–5). At the same time, however, the Manethoniana and Maximus are right in the mainstream Greek literary tradition of Great Authors and Great Books—weighed more heavily, it is true, towards the Homeric poems over and above the Hellenistic masters than in the case of their contemporary Dionysius the Periegete, but in any case deriving prestige and cultural capital from demonstrating mastery in a game of interwoven allusion. The question would be where exactly they were pitched among that great ocean of 'middlingness' which the astrological texts reflect. For if one can make any inferences at all about readership from the poems' content and style, this is assuredly not the sturdy outlook of a *plebs media* which sees learning letters as a practical business, and advocates a kind of homespun wisdom in opposition to belletristic fawning over the great masters (Veyne drew attention to the prologue of the second book of the *Disticha Catonis*, whose narrator set himself up as the plain-spoken man's answer to Virgil, Ovid, and Lucan[16]). On the contrary, this is a

---

[13] Firmicus, 3.9.6; 6.24.7; Lib. Herm. xxvii. 24; cf. xxviii. 5 *perversarum...litterarum... exquisitores*.

[14] Plat. *Phaedrus*, 275 C, D–E, cf. *Protagoras*, 329 A.

[15] Van Nijf 1997, 25–7.

[16] Veyne 2000, 1193. Veyne's interpretation of 1 Prol. 38 *Litteras disce* 'learn to read' suits his argument better than the Loeb's 'study literature' (*Minor Latin Poets*, vol. ii). His view that 'En

readership that reaches beyond basic literacy in Homer and Greek tragedy (staples of the schoolroom in the fifth book), but to Aratus, Callimachus, and even, briefly, Nicander (5.185, 185–6, 187–8). Reflecting on the papyrus archives from which literary texts are absent or in short supply, Eric Turner wondered whether we were 'to accept the depressing conclusion that the ordinary man cared little for literature, even if he could read it'.[17] Amin Benaissa draws attention to a papyrus of the later second century concerning the education of orphans, which distinguishes between those for whom a literary education (*paideia*) is appropriate, on the one hand, and the middling, who are to learn a craft (τοὺς δὲ μετρ[ι]ωτέρους τέχνας τινὰς ἐκμα[νθάνειν), on the other.[18] The problematic words here are 'ordinary' (in the Turner quotation) and 'middling' (in the papyrus). Inheriting astrology's capacious presentation of the everyday, the poets invest it with an art that draws on considerable cultural competence and resource, implying a readership that appreciated the dexterous adaptation of classic texts[19]—not that that helps very much with actually pinning it down.[20] May we hope for more papyrological evidence from archives that permit some eventual insight into *Sitz im Leben*?

GAMES, SPECTACLES, ENTERTAINMENTS

The *plebs media* played as well as worked hard. Veyne cited the epitaph of a merchant from south-central Spain, a self-made man who prided himself on professional integrity (*colui f(id)em*) and loved his friends and the games (*ludo[s soda]les amavi*).[21] This is almost point-for-point like Horace's Volteius Mena, an auctioneer (*praeco*) of modest fortune (*tenui censu*) but blameless life

---

somme, les *Dicta Catonis* sont un « Miroir de bourgeoisie »'' contrasts with what he had written ten years before, 'Une littérature pour plèbe moyenne? Ce n'est pas le cas des *Disticha Catonis*' (1990–1, 726), noting that the taste for sententiousness cut across classes. But the two positions can be reconciled if the claim is that the 'plèbe moyenne' were more inclined to verbalise and ground their identity in these kinds of homespun pieties, and to strike up an attitude of anti-intellectualism.

[17] *Greek Papyri* (Oxford, 1968), 78. Update with Benaissa, 534: literary papyri newly provenanced by association with documentary archives prove, unsurprisingly, to establish the link between literary culture and high socio-political status.

[18] *P Mich.* IX 532 (Karanis, AD 181–2); Benaissa, 530–1.

[19] See too Courrier, 356–64 on the capacity of the *plebs media* to read not just for *utilitas* but also for *voluptas*.

[20] R. L. Hunter, 'Ancient Readers', in T. Whitmarsh (ed.), *The Cambridge Companion to the Greek and Roman Novel* (Cambridge, 2008), 261–71, at 265: 'Can one move in any simple way from the demands which a text makes upon its readers to the identity of those readers?'

[21] Veyne 2000, 1185; *CIL* ii. 3304 = Buecheler, *CEL* 1556 (Castulo).

Conclusions and Further Reflections 111

(*sine crimine*), who well knew how to work and to unwind, and loved his friends, his home, the games, and the Campus (*gaudentem parvisque sodalibus et lare certo | et ludis et post decisa negotia Campo*).²²

Is this a class attitude? Of course, the upper classes were funding these spectacles even as they were holding their noses (or purporting to) at having to sit through them, if in a posher block of seats, and some astrology even notes them, the civic worthies, clad in purple, who bankroll the pleasures of the people (3.38 τερπωλῆς ... λαῶν ἡγήτορας ἄνδρας²³). There were kinds of culture that were truly popular in that the whole community shared in them,²⁴ but it seems to have been particularly important to tradesmen, at least on the evidence of the western empire, to want to represent their merry, affable side, and to picture their lives as a combination of hard work and well-earned leisure. This corresponds very well to astrology's own range of interests. There is an entirely expected emphasis on traditional Greek musical, theatrical, and sporting activities,²⁵ but the Greek texts also witness how Roman forms of entertainment had colonised the eastern provinces.²⁶ And astrology reaches further still, to the fringe entertainers who existed on the informal edges of the festival circuit and were hired in as additional crowd-pleasers (ἀκροάματα) without being admitted to the contests proper—the conjurers (Appendix II, VI.6.iii), strong-men (VI.6.vi), tightrope-walkers and petauristae (VI.6.iv), ball-players (VI.6.iii), and trick-riders (VI.6.v). Other texts do, of course, pay attention to many of these performers, especially those with 'ideological' weighting like mimes (VI.6.i) and pantomimes (VI.4), on whom more below. But it bears reflection that the astrology is the literary genre that takes most notice of some of them, for instance the tumblers and strongmen and petauristae, for whom one looks otherwise mainly to inscriptions (epitaphs, records of payments, honours) and visual art (terracottas, mosaics, the occasional fresco).²⁷ Authors like Pliny and

---

²² *Epist.* 1.7.55–9; Treggiari 1969, 100–1. Nicholas Horsfall chose Volteius as the icon of the Roman *plebs* in his study of that class, *The Culture of the Roman Plebs* (London, 2003).

²³ See ad loc. for 'joy', and add the epitaph of the mime Protogenes *que(i) fecit populo soveis gaudia nuge(i)s* (*CIL* ix. 4463, Amiternum, late 2nd c. BC; for the date, see A. Kuznetsov, 'Sweet Protogenes' Grave', *ZPE* 187 (2013), 132–43).

²⁴ C. Courrier, '"Une" culture populaire dans l'antiquité romaine? Quelques remarques sur l'ouvrage de J. Toner, *Popular Culture in Ancient Rome*, Cambridge/Malden, Polity Press, 2009', *AnTard* 19 (2011), 333–8, at 336.

²⁵ Instrumentalists: players on cithara (2.332; 6.370, 506; 4.185; 5.163), aulos (6.370, 506; 5.160); on panpipes (5.161), trumpets (5.162), cymbals (5.164); a *nabla* player (4.185). Singers: 2.331; 6.369, 506. Dancers: 6.507; 4.186. Reference to the *thymele*: 6.510; 4.186; 5.141. Tragic (6.509) and comic (4.183) actors. Sporting: running (4.173); wrestling, boxing (3.356–7); trainers (4.178–9); crowned victors (3.353–4).

²⁶ Charioteers (5.170–2); gladiators (6.375 n.), animal-fighters (Θ p. 212.22–3 θηριομάχους), as well as hunters and tamers.

²⁷ Inscriptions: see Tedeschi 2002, 137–42. Visual art: Dunbabin 2016, chs. 4 (pantomime) and 5 (mime); Tedeschi 2002, 141, 142–3.

Seneca offer the odd anecdote, or glance at the whole entertainments culture (Dio, condescendingly[28]). But it is hard to think of another genre that returns with such a fine eye, and mostly un-stern tone, to the variety of performers who enlivened classical festival life.

The same texts and groups of texts that paid such keen attention to occupations do the same for entertainers. What follows is just a foray into a subject that deserves an extended treatment, but what matters is the extent of overlap between Manetho/Ptolemy/Θ, on the one hand, and the witnesses to Teucer (including Manilius, Firmicus, and *Lib. Herm.*) on the other. This makes the very obvious and basic point that all are part of an enduring interest in artists and performers which manifests across Greek and Latin astrology and across many centuries of adaptation. But the various witnesses are even more alike in their treatment of entertainments than in their treatment of occupations, and there are signs that they are working from a common basis. There is clearly a great deal more work to be done on comparing the many witnesses with one another, but here is a start.

The argument begins with Firmicus' eighth book, which stands out from the rest in its minute treatment of entertainers. It does so both quantitatively—for instance, five out of seven explicit references to pantomimes are found in book 8, plus another paraphrastic reference in an earlier book—and qualitatively, in the professional names, largely based on the Greek, under which it identifies them.[29] These performers seem to derive from a series of backgrounds or layers or levels in his text. Some are drawn from Manilius, whose influence on Firmicus is clear.[30] But the interesting ones are those with transcribed Greek names, suggesting that in addition to Manilius Firmicus had a Greek source, presumably some version of Teucer. These popular performers are produced by the effects of planets, which Manilius obviously does not specify, but which turn out to have interesting correspondences in the Manethoniana and Θ

---

[28] *Or.* 32.86, 66.8 (Tedeschi 2002, 141).

[29] 8.8.1 *stadiodromos... pyctas,* ‹pan›*macharios* [rest. Robert 1938, 89–92]... *praestigiatores aut pilis ludentes... pantomimos aut mimologos* [under the paranatellon Lepus; Firmicius has used Manilius, but the only linguistic overlaps are 5.162 *stadio* and 165 *pilam*, 168 *pilarum*: the Graecisms come from another source, and Firmicus' *praestigiator* as a choice to render the presumable original ψηφοπαίκτης is paralleled in glossaries]; 8.10.4 *arenarii, parabolarii* (on the evidence of Gloss. III 240.45 ff., cited by *TLL* s.v. *parabolarius*, the second word glosses the first); 8.15.2 *petaminarios, ephalmatores, orchestopalarios, petauristarios*; 8.17.4 *funambuli,* †*olibatae* [*oribatae* Aldine, *calobatae* F. Skutsch], *neurobatae*; 8.20.7 *tragoedi, comoedi, ceryces* (cf. Robert 1938, 92–3).

[30] e.g. the trick-riders of 8.6.3 ~ 5.85–8 (*desultor, stabilis, arma movebit*); the runners, wrestlers, ball-players, and prestidigitators of 8.8.1 ~ 5.162–71; the various acrobats of 8.15.2 ~ 5.438–445; the tightrope-walkers of 8.17.4 ~ 5.652–5. The tragedians of 8.15.5 (Cepheus, 15° Capricorn) are paralleled partly by Manilius, 5.458–61 (though Cepheus is now under Aquarius: pp. 618–19) and *Lib. Herm.* xxv. 1.6 *scenici* (Cepheus under 6° Aries).

Conclusions and Further Reflections 113

themselves. Hübner lists some of them, but when it is supplemented the pattern only becomes clearer: the planetary agencies specified by Firmicus correspond either fully or partially with those that bring the corresponding types of entertainer to birth in the Manethoniana and/or Θ.[31] The argument for a connection between the corpora can be strengthened by pointing to specific affinities between the two Teucer texts and the Περὶ τεχνῶν section in Θ, especially the sequence in the final chapter Περὶ μίμων (96). They rest on Θ's actual naming of certain paranatellonta, or, failing that, specification of the signs of the zodiac that accompany the outcomes, and on verbatim correspondences among the outcomes. Not all concern performing artists (fuller references can be found in Part II, p. 141). But mimes (~ 4.280), pantomimes (~ 5.137–43), various instrumentalists (~ 5.159–64), and charioteers (~ 5.169–72) are all part of the great accumulation of craftsmen and members of leisure and entertainment professions which characterise the avocations and diversions of Veyne's *plebs media*.

A secondary question is the extent to which authors are able to innovate on their own account—whether they are at liberty to substitute different types of performer from what they found in their source. There are a few passages, lacking an immediate background in Manilius, where Firmicus can be shown to reference a figure with an exact or near-exact correspondence of degree position with one of the other witnesses, but with a slight modification,[32] and one wonders whether he was the one responsible for changes, for instance, from mimes to pantomimes,[33] or the numerous *citharoedi* who appear under different

---

[31] Hübner 1984, 140–2. A fuller list is as follows: runners 8.8.1 *stadiodromos* (Mars) ~ 4.171–3 (the aspect or terms of Mars are involved); boxers 8.8.1 *pyctas* (Moon with Mars) ~ 3.356 (Moon and Mars both involved); conjurers 8.8.1 *praestigiatores* (Mercury) ~ 4.448 ψηφοπαῖκται (Mercury in aspect to Venus, Moon, Mars) [*aut pilis ludentes* corresponds to Manil. 5.165 *pilam*, but Dr Holford-Strevens suggests that <la>pi<l>lis might render the pebble-conjurer]; mimes and pantomimes 8.8.1 *pantomimos aut mimologos* (Venus) ~ 5.138–41 pantomimes, 6.508–9, 4.184, and Valens, II 17.60 mimes (Venus and Mercury involved in all cases); *petauristae* 8.15.2 *petaminarios, ephalmatores, orchestopalarios, petauristarios* (Mars and Mercury) ~ 6.444–5 (Mercury joins Mars, Venus, and Sun), 4.278–9 (Sun aspects Mars); tragedians 8.15.5 *arte tragica carmina aut legunt semper aut faciunt* (Venus and Mercury in aspect) ~ 6.509–10 (Mercury and Venus in each other's houses and terms); tightrope-walkers 8.17.4 *funambuli, oribatae, neurobatae* (Mars and the Moon) ~ 6.439–40 (Venus with Mars and Sun), 4.286–9 (Venus joins Sun and Mars); Θ's various tightrope-walker charts involve Mars as well. I have failed to find correspondences only for 8.10.4 *arenarii, parabolarii* (malefics, with Moon aspecting Saturn) and 8.20.7 *tragoedi, comoedi, ceruces* (benefics *in situ* or in trine).

[32] Feraboli, 215–29.

[33] Teucer, II 3.5 [11–12° Gemini] σκηνικούς, μιμηλούς and *Lib. Herm.* xxv. 3.13 [11–12° Gemini] *scenicos, mimos, ioculatores* ~ 8.21.6 *pantomimi* [16° Gemini]. See Feraboli, 217; Hübner 1984, 142. In 8.8.1 [7° Gemini, Lepus], the mimes and pantomimes are without parallel in Manilius.

renderings in other sources.³⁴ There are also cases, albeit a certain number of degrees apart,³⁵ where the various witnesses offer what seem to be different realisations of one and the same underlying entity.³⁶ Sometimes what one finds across the various sources are different degrees of detail rather than basically different conceptions. The crowned wrestlers of Firmicus, 8.24.4 [9° Virgo], correspond to *Lib. Herm.* xxv. 6.14 [13–15° Virgo] *athletas fortes* (Feraboli, 233), and the *athleta oplomachos* of 8.27.3 [10° Sagittarius] to *Lib. Herm.* xxv. 9.14 [17° Sagittarius] *certatores* (Feraboli, 234, 238). A seemingly unusual example of Firmicus losing specificity in comparison to the other sources are the *musicos* of 8.28.2 (4° Capricorn, with Mercury), corresponding to *Lib. Herm.* xxv. 10.7 (6° Capricorn) *tubatores*³⁷ *vel tibicines vel citharoedos magnatum*.

What ultimately matters in all this is astrology's sharp eye for these performers. Its labels are presumably their own labels, the designations under which the audience knew them, under which they advertised themselves and put themselves forward as contenders at games (if they ever got that far). It acknowledges their world, indeed sometimes evokes it with a zest which matches their own energy: take the little *morceaux de bravoure* elicited by the petauristae as they soared into the air from their springboards like an avian species (6.443–4, 4.278–9). The inscriptions which attest these performers are either epitaphs (which show how they wanted to be remembered) or honorific decrees (which again use formalised courteous language of public commemoration). Here and there the Manethoniana reflect these tropes of public acknowledgement and self-worth, just as they evoke the tropes of inscriptional commendation for bigwigs and grandees—the gladiators whose favourite term of self-praise is echoed in 6.375 σθεναροὺς ῥοπάλοισι γεγηθότας; the performative εὐδοκιμεῖν (4.175); the inscriptional formula ἐνδόξως, transferred by a tiny sleight of hand to their crowns (4.175 στέμματα μυριόδοξα). These are the approved attitudes, those the performers themselves adopted and the community adopted towards them when the frame of reference was commemoration and courtesy.³⁸

---

³⁴ 8.21.9 [22° Gemini] ~ Teucer, II 3.10 [25° Gemini] κιθαριστάς and *Lib. Herm.* xxv. 3.29 [25° Gemini] *musici*, cf. Feraboli, 218; 8.24.6 [13° Virgo] ~ Teucer I, p. 18.6 [2nd decan] Μοῦσα λυρίζουσα, II 6.3 [7°–10° Virgo] ἡ Μοῦσα βαστάζουσα τὴν μικρὰν λύραν, cf. Feraboli, 223; 8.27.4 [14° Sagittarius] ~ *Lib. Herm.* xxv. 9.16 [13°–17° Sagittarius] *amatores musicae*, cf. Feraboli, 225.

³⁵ Feraboli, 229–34 (her examples are 8°–10° apart).

³⁶ The *pantomimi* of 8.23.3 [8° Leo] appear to be an individual realisation of a figure noted by Teucer in the *second* decan with its arms stretched out in a gesture that could be construed as theatrical or religious (Feraboli, 232–3). The *insignia coronarum* of the *scaenici* in 8.20.1 [4° Taurus] correspond, *qua* circular objects, to the wheel held by the charioteer in Teucer, II 2.4 [14° Taurus] and *Lib. Herm.* xxv. 2.13 [12°–14° Taurus] (Feraboli, 231).

³⁷ So Feraboli, 227, though *turbatores* in her text.

³⁸ *ITral.* 110, decree for the βιολόγος Flavius Alexandros Oxeidas of Nicomedia, honouring him for τὸ κόσμιον τοῦ ἤθους (Robert 1936, 245); toga-clad statue of a *parasitus Apollonis* at Nemi: K. Dunbabin, 'Problems in the Iconography of Roman Mime', in Hugoniot et al. (eds.), 161–81, at 175–6.

But there is another possible set of attitudes towards popular performers, which is elicited when the *plebs media* turn (behaviourally) into an ὄχλος. Take, on the one hand, Claudian's communitarian posturings when he puts the Muses themselves in charge of all the stage, circus, theatre, and amphitheatre events that get Manlius' consulship off to a flying start.[39] Then contrast that with Dio's sniffy treatment of all the vulgarities with which the wealthy office-seeker has to court the mob's favour.[40] This is another, and very good, instance of trope; which set of attitudes you strike up is a political choice. The interest for us is that the Manethoniana are wide open to both. For all their receptivity to entertainers, they too (especially M[b]) are entirely capable of sniffing at the ὄχλος (4.277, see ad loc.; 4.448, 5.104),[41] as well as raising distant suggestions of pity and disapproval for the itinerant lifestyle of the popular performer (6.510 ἀλωομένους, 4.281–2, 449).

It is the mime who most consistently evokes the tone of sneering disdain. No reference to mimes in the Manethoniana is commendatory; the tropes, all familiar from at least the times of the Attic orators, are all about lewd laughter, smutty speech, scandalous conduct, and the language used to stigmatise them is the same as that for sexual offence (αἰσχρ-: see i. 343). None of this is very interesting in itself. But the question why it is particularly *these* performers who trigger the change from communitarianism to élitism, from δῆμος to ὄχλος, has wider implications for astrological politics, ethics, and aesthetics. Perhaps it was because these performers mounted the most obvious challenge to a culture of honour and decorum, a culture of great sensitivity to the semiotics of clothing and deportment; a culture which could just about tolerate the fun of the prestidigitator and acrobat, but simply could not digest the indignity of the buffoon, and was uneasy, too, about the hyper-sexualised mannerisms of the slinky pantomime (5.139–41). To put it otherwise, the mime (and pantomime) was more politicised,[42] or more politicisable, than the acrobat or tightrope-walker, the former, perhaps, because his art was *verbal* (see on 4.280),

---

[39] *Carm.* 17.276–332 = *De Consulatu Flavii Manlii Theodori* (the Muse herself proposes horse-racing, wrestling, hunts in the amphitheatre, clowns, mimes, actors, an organist, acrobats, fake fire, and naval battles).

[40] Dio Chrys. *Or.* 66.8 αὐλητὰς δὲ καὶ μίμους καὶ κιθαριστὰς καὶ θαυματοποιοὺς συνακτέον, ἔτι δὲ πύκτας καὶ παγκρατιαστὰς καὶ παλαιστὰς καὶ δρομεῖς καὶ τὸ τοιοῦτον ἔθνος, εἴ γε μὴ μέλλει φαύλως μηδὲ ἀγεννῶς ἑστιάσειν τὸ πλῆθος.

[41] Firmicus' language for crowd-pleasing entertainers is less strident (6.8.2 *alios dulci modulatione cantantes popularibus deputant voluptatibus*, 6.26.2 *musicos faciunt, sed popularibus voluptatibus deputatos*, 8.27.4 *citharoedi erunt publicis voluptatibus deputati*).

[42] On the politics of mimic and pantomimic performance, see J. Ingleheart, 'Et mea sunt populo saltata poemata saepe (*Tristia* 2.519): Ovid and the Pantomime', in Hall and Wyles, 198–217, at 201–2. Pylades' quip to Augustus (Dio Cass. 54.17.5 συμφέρει σοι, Καῖσαρ, περὶ ἡμᾶς τὸν δῆμον ἀποδιατρίβεσθαι) uses δῆμος rather than ὄχλος, but recognises the 'vulgar' nature of the entertainment. See also the epitaph of Protogenes (n. 23), for 'popular' entertainment.

the latter because of the explosive combination of marginal status (Roman *infamia* for stage-performers) with an overt sexiness to which no class was immune. The man who made pebbles disappear simply could not compete.[43] And it seems significant that when the Manethoniana have the opportunity to strike up a class attitude, they come firmly down on the side of respectability.

Either way, all this is trope. Left- or right-wing, these are attitudes that can be donned or doffed at will. Suppose we do locate the Manethoniana in Egypt. Papyri from Oxyrhynchus and elsewhere give some insight into popular entertainments, their management and finance if not much else. We discover performers being hired in for local festivals, games, by dining societies.[44] A pair of papyri often cited together show, respectively, a series of payments in connection with a festival of the Nile to performers including a μῖμος, Ὁμηριστής, ὀρχηστής, σαλπικτής, and other unspecified musicians, and another series of payments on an occasion that involves judges and a theatre to performers who include ball-players (13 σφαιρομαχ(ούντων) [ζε(ύγει)), an acrobat (19 μανγαναρ[ίῳ), aulete (20), mime (25 μείμῳ), and Homerist (26 Ὁμηρισ[τῇ), apparently a type of performer who acted out Homeric tableaux.[45] These are not the only sources in which Homerist and mime keep company.[46] The boundaries of the two types of performance have attracted attention,[47] and the relationship between them and the literary performers in the Manethoniana certainly needs a critical appraisal as well (the papyri and the literary texts cannot just be assumed to be referring to the same thing). But that is precisely the point. Mimetic dancing seems to have been entirely at home in Egypt. But whatever local colour is missing from the papyrological record is certainly not recoverable from the literary one. All is drowned out by conventional gesture and trope. We would barely know we were in Egypt.

---

[43] In Athen. 1.19 E, it is reported in indignant tones that the Athenians permitted the use of the Euripidean stage to a mere νευροσπάστης, but the point is the city's decadence; it is not about lower-class taste.

[44] Tedeschi 2002, 122–3; Alston, 245–6; S. Nervegna, *Menander in Antiquity: The Contexts of Reception* (Cambridge, 2013), 186–7. Earlier bibliography: T. Grassi, 'Musica, mimica e danza: Secondo i documenti papiracei greco-egizî', *Studî della Scuola Papirologica*, 3 (1920), 117–35; W. L. Westermann, 'The Castanet Dancers of Arsinoe', *JEA* 10 (1924), 134–44; id. 'Entertainment in the Villages of Graeco-Roman Egypt', *JEA* 18 (1932), 16–27; M. Vandoni, *Feste pubbliche e private nei documenti greci* (Milan, 1964), nos. 14–28.

[45] P.Oxy. 519 fr. a (2nd c. AD), P.Oxy. 1050 (2nd/3rd c. AD); E. Wüst, *RE* s.v. Mimos, 1755.34–42; Tedeschi 2011, 110–11 and 116–17; S. Tsitsiridis, 'Greek Mime in the Roman Empire (P.Oxy. 413: *Chariton* and *Moicheutria*)', *Logeion*, 1 (2011), 184–232, at 220 and n. 93; E. Greensmith, *The Resurrection of Homer in Imperial Greek Epic: Quintus Smyrnaeus' Posthomerica and the Poetics of Impersonation* (Cambridge, 2020), 70–1.

[46] Tedeschi 2002, 138 (*Corpus Glossariorum Latinorum*, ii (Leipzig, 1888), 22, ll. 40–2); Tedeschi 2011, 31.

[47] Greensmith, n. 45.

Conclusions and Further Reflections 117

SO WHAT ABOUT EGYPT?

The Manethoniana are Egyptian. No-one, presumably, will quarrel with that. The first and fifth books fictively address King Ptolemy in their opening lines. The speaker in the first includes himself among Egypt's denizens (1.2) and among its learned men (1.15). They insert themselves into the literary tradition associated with (Nechepso and) Petosiris, whom both books name (1.11; 5.10), and whose authenticating devices they evoke.[48] The fiction of texts discovered in temples, especially in a pillar, and carried to the king, is Egyptian (5.1–2); the motif of secret books in general is especially at home in Egypt (5.304 n.).

The technical methods employed in the texts are not especially revealing, but are completely compatible with Egyptian practice. The data in M^a's horoscope (6.745–50; i. 868–9) follow exactly the format of papyrus horoscopes. Their mostly nursery-school astrology seems not to contain specifically Egyptian methods: there are no decans, and while it is suggestive that Manetho's close cousin, Θ, knows of the Egyptian *dodecaoros* (p. 141), traces of this have been ironed out of the poetic versions. However, 1.203–4 present a version of qualitative planetary order which is paralleled in a Demotic ostrakon. It is possible that 4.24 contains a suggestion of the year beginning with Cancer (not Aries), as it did in Egypt. The separate section on women in 5.315–end reflects the practice of some Demotic manuals.

But would you get any sense of this from the world that is depicted? Only a very few of the offices and occupations look specifically Egyptian. The ἀρχιδικαστής is an Egyptian official (1.104). Quarrymen could belong anywhere with stone, but Louis Robert brilliantly saw in 4.325 a reference specifically to the granites and marbles of Egypt. The snake-charmers of 5.185 have hooded cobras—a nice case of the modifiability of astrology's generic detail, for the equivalents in Firmicus are the Italian Marsi. The greatest source of plausibly Egyptian details is, unsurprisingly, temple culture: the location of dream interpreters in temples (1.237–8), combined with the hangers-on known as κάτοχοι (1.239); astrologers in temples, too (i. 337), and in general the image of temples thronged with prophets (4.428–9), which sounds at least Near Eastern, and could well evoke Egypt in particular. Funerary culture has a distinctly Egyptian complexion as well, especially M^a's warmed-over Herodotean account of embalming (6.461–2; more cedar-wood in 4.191), the νεκροτάφοι (4.192), professional mourners (4.190 θρηνήτορας ἄνδρας evoke papyrological θρηνηταί,

---

[48] i. 54–7; J. L. Lightfoot, 'Stars of a Lesser Magnitude: Some Glimmerings from the Corpus of Astrological Poetry Ascribed to Manetho', in B. Kayachev (ed.), *Poems without Poets: Approaches to Anonymous Ancient Poetry* (CCJ Supplement 43) (Cambridge, 2021), 32–48, at 35–7.

although it would be bold to claim they existed nowhere else), and encaustic painters, perhaps of mummy portraits (6.524–5).

None of this is urged in support of the position that the Manethoniana are Egyptian as opposed to that they are not. (A hardline sceptic might, it is true, object that the fiction of Ptolemy and all the Petosirian rigmarole could have been adopted in order to authenticate a text written by some shivering *Graeculus* on Hadrian's Wall.[49]) Rather, the question is which aspects of Egyptian culture have been allowed into the texts, and why. The enquiry, in effect, is the opposite way round from Cumont's, whose starting-point was that the whole thing was embedded in the world of Ptolemaic Egypt. The starting-point instead is that astrology prefers a non-restricting lack of specificity and labels that tend to the generic, which make portraiture of either Ptolemaic or Roman Egypt something of a forlorn hope. The great majority of astrology's professions, the fullers and carpenters and metalworkers are perfectly bland. Some labels are more interestingly specific, and do indeed sort well with an Egyptian background,[50] without being in any way exclusive to it. But even then, the point is not to establish the texts' origin, or to pin down astrology's habitually unspecific idiom, but rather to note the cultural choices their authors are making. It makes sense for texts that come out of a temple-based tradition to be especially sensitive to that environment.[51] But temple offices and the professions that temples support, like the whole mortuary business,[52] emerge looking rather like the jetsam left high on the beach after the tide has receded into the great homogeneous sea of Graeco-Roman culture, leaving everything else immersed in the great wash of ubiquitous labels, generalising topoi, and universally approved sentiments. In other words, trope.

What else is there? No need to repeat has been said about the world of work. Leisure time is represented by the culture of the gymnasium (4.178–9), and by entertainers as familiar to Roman satire and the novel as to Egyptians. We have already seen the extent to which the Manethoniana, especially the later poets in

---

[49] But would, as Dr Holford-Strevens observes, have to explain the use of λίψ (3.18), 'the Libyan wind', by someone writing outside Egypt to mean 'west'.

[50] e.g. 4.160 λογισταί; 4.213, practitioners of lecanomancy; 4.252 ἁμαρησκαπτῆρας, ditch-diggers, i.e. diggers of irrigation channels, and 256, market gardeners (see on 256–8 for the encrustation of trope); 1.84–5 water-carriers; 1.102, the ἀγορανόμος as an honorific position, though this is more likely to carry the empire-wide associations of the market official rather than refer to the Egyptian notarial office; 5.168, the πολυμιτάριοι; perhaps 5.289 ἀρχικυνηγοί.

[51] Benaissa, 534–5, notes that 'some of the Greek literary texts from the villages of the Fayum were discovered in temple areas and belong to archives that include Egyptian literary and religious texts': a milieu that supports both Greek literary culture and Egyptian mortuary practices certainly suits these parts of the Manethoniana.

[52] Cannata 2012, 608–9, notes that the names of necrotaphoi remain stubbornly Egyptian rather than Greek. Astrological writers have preserved this little ethnic enclave (even as Mᵃ overlays Egyptian mortuary practices with garbled Herodotus).

Conclusions and Further Reflections   119

the corpus, use or evoke the epigraphic language of commendation,[53] but these inscriptions are of course predominantly from Asia Minor, except for the Egyptian corpora edited by A. and E. Bernand, where occasional parallels can indeed be found (cf. 1.102, the ἀγορανόμος). To this public language can be added that of conventional attitude and private sentiment, the commendation of virtuous wives (4.43), and the rehashing of sepulchral platitude (1.48 τέκνοις γλυκεροῖς, 276 πρόμοιροι, 340 αἴλινος (adj.), 356 λύπας γὰρ στοναχάς τε), even if, on some occasions, the way the poet has decided to apply them is distinctly weird (1.120 vl πανόδυρτον, of a castrating weapon or even the severed member itself; 138 λύπην αἰείμνηστον, of a crippled foot). These are formulae rehashed from a thousand grave inscriptions across the Greek East. If, or since, the corpus is Egyptian, all this could be fodder for a dauntingly large project, which would aim to show the degree of integration of Egypt's institutions, public language, and culture, into the rest of the empire. Such a project would conduct a more broadly based comparison with inscriptions, beginning, perhaps, with the material shortly to become available for the Ptolemaic period.[54] The point here is more modest. For all its presumable origins in temples, astrology—or at least the tradition represented by the Manethoniana—has a retina that is sensitive to a wide spectrum of classical motifs, but only very, very limitedly to Egyptian ones. Anything that might, in the first instance, have been locally specific is drained of that distinctiveness, and coloured, instead, in a wash of topoi. The market gardeners in 4.256 might just as well be in Corycos as in the Fayyum; the writer of 4.493–4 seems tone-deaf to the implications of locating 'foreign spells' in Egypt, the home of magic; and, perhaps the biggest giveaway of all, the temple-based dream interpreters in 1.237–8 pivot to *galli*, the stuff of Lucian, Catullus, and epigram.

MIDDLINGNESS?

Let us return to the image-repertoire of the ancient city, its physical statues and its literary tropes. By so relentlessly peddling the latter, even as it overlays them with an argot which constituted its professional brand, astrology ensures an instant intelligibility. The types are repeated over and over again; astrology has a basic code which promotes similar outcomes under similar circumstances; and they are transmitted from text to text in manuals which offer general rules

---

[53] 4.175 ἐνδόξως, εὐδοκιμεῖν, for athletes; 4.512 ἀριστοπονῆες, 514 πάτρης κηδέστορες, ἰθυδίκαιοι; 1.100–5, the various euergetes; 5.309 σιτοδόται, κτίσται, μὴ φειδόμενοι [~ ἀφειδῶς] φιλοτίμως; see too 5.269–73, the cultural attainments for which the 'iatrosophist' is praised.

[54] Corpus of Ptolemaic Inscriptions; prequel: C. V. Crowther and A. K. Bowman, *The Epigraphy of Ptolemaic Egypt* (Oxford, 2020).

and principles and guidance on how to interpret configurations of stars that occur over and over again. The readings in the whole of Part One are based on such manuals. They do not derive from the interpretations of individual charts (though the interpretations of individual charts which Valens provides are designed to illustrate his own rules, so simply reinforce the same values on a micro-level). Manuals cannot tell you what to do. But the speaking voice encourages conformism through the unvarying promotion of 'average' values, and poetic astrology, through its use of emotive colour, all the more so. The everyday workability of catarchic astrology sometimes runs up against attitudes that float free of any concrete situation. It is quite happy to explain to the loan-shark when to lend to a needy client, or apparently when would be a good time for the discontented slave to make his escape. Such pragmatism is no surprise at all. The generalising procedure of the manuals articulates conventional values and sentiment. The diviner faced with a client—perhaps untrammelled by any institutional setting—engages with a particular consumer, to whose requirements he adapts his technique.

'He.' That is an assumption about both diviner and consumer; it may or may not be true in either case. Not all Valens' charts for historical individuals are for males,[55] but the generalising voice of the manuals either elides female outcomes into male ones[56] or ignores the former altogether; those pitched explicitly at women reduce them to the reproductive function (5.316–31; Valens, II 38.77–89; IV 20.11, etc.). Such little interest is taken in gender (though even that is more than the zero interest in race) that class becomes the most obvious category of analysis. It is promoted by astrology itself, which uses—when it uses anything at all—a three- (or occasionally four-) tier status scheme, which, short as it is on content, suffices to make the point that its basic model is socio-political. There is a basic idea of stratification, which manages to coexist with astrology's alternative model, that of moving up and down a vertical axis of status, from lower to higher or the reverse. Some later writers use τάξις, 'rank', in a socio-political sense, which, for all its 'obviousness' in the increasingly

---

[55] VII 6.36–44, 51–7 (nos. L 134,VI and L 110,XII Neugebauer–Van Hoesen), but only as adjuncts to those of husband and brother, as parties in a lawsuit. Women/wives mentioned as adjunct to a male nativity: V 1.20, VII 3.20, VII 6.84, 165 (nos. L 121, 120,XII, 102,XII,14, 142 Neugebauer–Van Hoesen).

[56] There were, for instance, female weavers (see on 4.422–3), shoemakers (see on 4.320–1, n. 228), and even fullers (Ruffing 2008, 501; Gourevitch 2011, 45) and glass-blowers (Stern, 457). Women are highly likely to be represented among the clothes-menders in 6.434–5 (Larsson Lovén, in Wilson and Flohr (eds.), 209). Wives also participated in their husbands' businesses, or took over after their husbands' deaths (Tran 2013, 77–82). Not that you would ever have learned this from the texts (or, as a rule, from the inscriptions) themselves.

Conclusions and Further Reflections 121

hierarchical society of later antiquity, still seems distinctive and important:[57] it is not registered at all by LSJ, and the parallels in Lampe are for hierarchies of juniority and seniority, or within the Trinity (8), or within the ecclesiastical order (11), not the social order in general. These suffice to show, however, that the conception is of a tidy, self-contained system, as natural and self-evident as that of the stars themselves (for which τάξις is also common), with a structure of deference and authority that envisaged no challenge. All the characteristics of astrology's world-view in the earlier imperial period show up in Valens' chapter of illustrative examples concerning the Lot of Fortune and its influence on εὐδαιμονία (II 22): the vertical axis ascending from low to high through middling (μετριότης, μετρία τύχη); the crucial importance of social capital, proximity to power; the inexorable language of status (ταπεινός, ἔνδοξος), and the signification of high status through badges and insignia (στέμματα), a basic visual code which everyone understood. Valens particularly loves the word τάξις, which he uses in the sense of 'rank', 'post', 'appointment', 'appointed place' (in a hierarchy).[58]

Much of this fits astonishingly well with the culture whose pen-portrait Veyne sketched in his study of the *plebs media*. First, that work is a massive component of an individual's identity: Veyne even suggested that specifying an occupation on an epitaph was a sufficient criterion for belonging to the *plebs media*.[59] Not that astrological texts restrict their scope to 'middle-class' occupations, but they see the world of work from this perspective, drawing attention again and again to the skilled trades and barely suppressing a shudder at the poor labourer who had to work for his daily bread. Then there is the whole associated value-system of *fides* and *amicitia*,[60] which lubricated business dealings and shored up credit, and, at the same time, combined business integrity with a healthy attitude to sociability and leisure. Take the freedman M. Publicius

---

[57] Apomasar's *De Revolutionibus*, e.g. p. 25.17–19...ὅτι δ' εἰσὶν αἱ τῶν ἀνθρώπων τάξεις· καὶ πρώτη μὲν ἡ τῶν βασιλέων, δευτέρα δὲ ἡ τῶν ‹εὐγενῶν›, καὶ τρίτη ἡ τῶν μέσων, καὶ τετάρτη ἡ τῶν πενήτων. Of defined high rank: Hephaestion, i. 240.3 Τὴν βασιλικὴν τάξιν καὶ ἡγεμονικὴν δύναμιν (source unknown); Achmet, CCAG ii. 128.3–4 τῆς τάξεως τῶν ἀρχιερέων καὶ μεγιστάνων. Artemidorus, 4.77.1, uses τάξις of the hierarchy of gods, as it relates to the human social classes who dream about it.

[58] Sometimes with qualification, e.g. I 1.10 δόξας...μεγάλας καὶ τάξεις ἐπισήμους, I 1.45 μειζόνων τάξεων, but sometimes alone (I 20.29 πίστεων ἢ τάξεων μεταλαμβάνοντας, 30 πίστεων καὶ τάξεων καταξιουμένους), as if τάξις per se = 'honorable rank', in which sense it is sometimes paired with the idea of προκοπή, 'advancement' (I 1.45, IV 19.4); so too Θ p. 148.6 ἐν ἱεροῖς τάξεις ἢ δωρεάς, sim. 151.4, 165.13.

[59] 1990–1, 723.

[60] Veyne 1990–1, 724: 'l'amicitia jouait, pour la plèbe moyenne, le rôle que jouait la clientèle dans l'aristocratie'; on *fides*: 1990–1, 725, and 2000, 1187; Tran 2013, 244–5. Combining both: AE 1991 (1994) 122 (Rome, epigraph for a *bublarius* [butcher])...*fide et amicitia sanctissimus* (cited by C. Courrier, 'Plebeian Culture in the City of Rome, from the Late Republic to the Early Empire', in L. Grig, *Popular Culture in the Ancient World* (Cambridge, 2017), 107–28, at 118).

Unio, whose grave inscription was discovered at Tusculum.[61] Almost every single one of his boasts finds a parallel within astrological ethics. He wanted to be remembered for returning deposits, bringing his friends together, enjoying a continent marriage with a chaste wife, not being tight-fisted, and above all for never getting involved in lawsuits. Or a silversmith from Cirta, proud of his professional integrity (*mira...fides...veritas omnis*), accessibility (*Om/ni{s}bus communis ego*), and happy amenability to life's pleasures in the company of his friends (*Ubique risus, luxuria(m) semper fruitus cun/caris amicis*).[62] Veyne laid emphasis on the representations of feasting on his subjects' grave monuments.[63] Astrology has no literal equivalent, but it is very clear from Mᵃ, in particular, that the blessed existence is conceived in materialist terms.

Two other points are also suggestive, if less precisely mappable onto our texts. Veyne tried to contrast the plebeian 'culture sapientiale' (represented, for him, by the sententiousness of the *Disticha Catonis*) with the 'culture livresque' of the élites.[64] This is hard to square exactly with the Manethoniana, which do a pretty good job of enforcing conventional norms, but do so by means of a curious combination of distant suspicion towards books with deference to grammarians and ventriloquism of literary classics on which their whole idiom rests. Second, reflecting on the differences between the ancient and modern middle classes, he noted that, because of the small size of what he took to be the *plebs media* (as opposed to the huge amorphous *plebs* in general), he noted that there was nothing to create class tensions between, on the one hand, the poor who might respect the magnates and even have a sentimental attachment to their rulers, but lack the same deference towards the bourgeois, and, on the other, the bourgeois no longer willing to obey a master and determined to govern themselves.[65] This offers a good account of astrology's absence of class tension, or at least, its deference towards kings and big men even as its speaking voice seems to articulate disdain for the sweaty masses below.

But what to do with all this? Veyne's vision of the *plebs media* was of a small class,[66] and Cyril Courrier, in his refinement-cum-critique of Veyne, reduced it still further to a small élite, just below the equestrians in assets, and largely overlapping with them in culture. Both scholars, of course, were talking specifically about Rome. Whatever else astrology is, however much it adapts itself in

---

[61] *CIL* xiv. 2605 = *CLE* 477 (Veyne 2000, 1187 n. 95).
[62] *CIL* viii. 7156 = *ILAlg.* II, 820 = *CLE* 512 (Veyne 2000, 1189 n. 110; Panciera and Zanker, 370 [385]).
[63] Veyne 2000, 1180–2; Courrier, 409–20.
[64] Veyne 1990–1, 726; 2000, 1183, cf. 1194.
[65] Veyne 2005, 161 (a couple of crucial paragraphs added to Veyne 2000).
[66] Veyne 1990–1, 'une classe moyenne, réduite en nombre'; 2005, 'la mince plèbe moyenne romaine'.

the hands of different writers, its basic attitudes to work emerge from the Greek East. One very easy approach would be to argue that these values were far from simply confined to Rome. We find the evidence there because that is where the evidence happens to be preserved, but Courrier's reviewers already pointed out that the analysis could profitably be extended to, say, the culture of the *Augustales*, wealthy freedmen (including Trimalchio) who paraded themselves as civic benefactors in the pomp of quasi-magistracies which, in the real world, they were ineligible to hold;[67] or to the *decuriones* of cities other than Rome.[68] But one might also wonder whether the question should be turned on its head. It is perfectly legitimate to ask whether attempting to define classes and attitudes associated with them is a useful approach at all; whether we should instead be starting off, not with the class, but with the value-system, so that it is no longer a question of 'who thought like this' (which presumes the possibility of defining), but of beginning from a certain, characterisable, attitude to life, for which material evidence has been found among certain economic sectors because they could afford to leave traces of themselves, but which may, for all we know, have been characteristic of a great deal more besides. More, in a society with no class tensions, where firm class lines cannot be drawn, where boundaries of status and class (in an economic sense) are so permeable, it is entirely possible that these attitudes of mingled self-respecting pride, deference, conservative personal morality, sociability, and hedonism towards licit pleasures, extended well beyond a *plebs media* in one particular city, and were a kind of common currency.[69] Astrology is witness to a broad commonality of values, *and* at the same time to a status-conscious, hierarchical mindset where people were very keen to mark themselves off from their perceived inferiors. Everyone went to the games—yet sneered at an ὄχλος which, whoever else it

---

[67] L. Vandevoorde, *Annales*, 70/4 (2015), 981–3. Numerous honorands in Zimmer's corpus of work reliefs are named or identified by symbols as *Augustales* or *seviri Augustales* (Zimmer 1982, nos. 25, 59, 103, 148, 157, 168; see too Index s.v. Sevirat/Sevir).

[68] E. E. Mayer, 'Was there a Culture of the Roman Plebs?', *JRA* 29 (2016), 653–8, at 656. Examples would be the family of the Umbricii Scauri at Pompei, among them A. Umbricius Scaurus, the son of a garum merchant who rose to the rank of *duumvir*, and the Secundinii, cloth merchants, who erected the Igel column near Trier, though they said nothing on it about municipal offices (J. France, 'Les monuments funéraires et le "capitalisme" des élites Trévires', in J. Andreau, J. France, and S. Pittia (eds.), *Mentalités et choix économiques des romains* (Bordeaux, 2004), 149–78).

[69] Mayer (n. above), 658: 'indeed the evidence presented by Courrier does not suggest that we are dealing with a distinct aristocratic *versus* a bourgeois culture of businessmen, but instead with milieu-specific expressions of the same culture in distinct but overlapping life-worlds'; 659: 'There was just one language of achievement and dignity that expressed itself differently in different life-worlds, just as there was only one repertoire of images that could be employed in a variety of ways'.

was, was not them. These two attitudes are entirely compatible.⁷⁰ Economic situations no doubt limited opportunities, but the ethical codes the various economic classes would have signed up to no doubt looked very similar, peddled by sententious literature which everyone had been brought up with and everyone loved.⁷¹ Beyond a certain point, elaborate conceptual modelling collapses for a genre which is entirely blind to *ordo* and relentlessly keyed into the idea of status. We can talk about 'middlingness' with the risk of getting sucked into the definitional and demographic problems which bedevil discussions of ancient middle classes and attempts to pin them down. But at the end of the day I suggest that what matters most to astrology is a capaciousness which absorbs the mental images and commonplaces of its society, rendering familiar attitudes in a conventionally authoritative voice, and, in the case of poetic texts, with the additional sanction of the literary classics. Anyone familiar with those images and commonplaces was primed to receive its message.

---

⁷⁰ A. Wallace-Hadrill, *Athenaeum*, 106/2 (2018), 747: 'They (sc. the members of the École Française) have shown how implausible it is to imagine a deep divide between the values and expressions of elite and popular culture, when the norms and actions of the elite penetrate so deeply into the world of the poor—what form of popular entertainment did not depend on elite sponsorship?'

⁷¹ Veyne 1990–1, 726–7 '... la Sagesse était étudiée aussi bien par les fils de sénateurs que par les fils de plébéiens: la société romaine toute [*sic*] entière (sénateurs et philosophes compris) était très sententieuse, pesante, amoureuse de proverbes...', and more.

Part Two

The Later Books of Manetho

…increasingly obscure and desperate pieces of late Antique learning
(Nicholas Purcell, address given at the funeral of
Donald Russell, 8 March 2020, his italics)

The Later Books

This part returns to ground covered in the first volume, but is now redirected towards the peculiar properties of the later books. The format for the analysis of each book is similar, but in the cases of the first and fifth the analysis cannot get off the ground without first discussing the question of authorship (single or multiple?) and, especially for the first, establishing a model for the kind or kinds of recycling and reworking in evidence in the book. The relation of the fourth book to books 2, 3, and 6 also needs separate treatment, but because that does not involve modelling that determines the rest of the analysis it stands at the end rather than at the beginning (4.10). The phonology and morphology, syntax, style, narratorial voice, and handling of the astrological content (treatment of technical concepts, formulary of the planets) are discussed for each poet, with particular attention being paid to metre. This is not only a particularly robust way of differentiating the poets, but makes a contribution to late antique poetics in general, which can only be furthered by the patient and systematic collection of data for individual authors and corpora. The Manethonian corpus has been particularly badly served in this respect.[1]

There is so much to say about every individual book that there is a risk of getting lost in the detail. So to establish that wider perspective this section opens by addressing some bigger questions. First, the comparanda and the relationships between them need to be described (Section 2); this corresponds to the fifth section of Part One of the first volume, and is necessary to establish the terms of reference for what follows. The next two sections (3 and 4) are more literary, and take their departure from the literary aesthetics for astrological poetry that were established in the first volume, and that bear some elaboration here. For in its essence as catalogue poetry which *ipso facto* consists of a series of clearly defined segments (and in the case of systematic catalogues follows a given order), and which accumulates parallel items to illustrate a particular state of affairs, astrological poetry can be seen, not as some strange

---

[1] Chalcenteric his labours may have been, but by lumping the whole corpus together as 'Manetho' La Roche limited their usefulness. Comparisons can be conducted with his other authors (Quintus, Coluthus, Triphiodorus, Musaeus, Nicander, and ps.-Oppian) only if the data are properly quantified.

outlier, but as responding to aesthetic trends that can be discerned in a huge variety of Greek and Latin literature, poetry and prose, indeed in some ways (formalism, segmentation, the microscopic as opposed to macroscopic approach, the *enumeratio* or even *congeries* of thematically related material) to be their perfect expression. The third section, accordingly, concerns external arrangement. The three later books at first sight look completely chaotic, but that first impression is not completely correct, not even for the first and fifth. How are they arranged? On what principles does one apotelesma follow from another, or are blocks of related charts organised? Whose mind is behind this? Are we to think of poets or editors, and is that a helpful distinction? Complementarily, the poets have taken infinite pains to hold each individual apotelesma together as a coherent and aesthetically pleasing unit. This tells a rather different story from that of the frustrating and sometimes dispiriting quest to find external links. The perfect fit between the poetry of apotelesmata and the late-antique aesthetic of *Medalliondichtung*, the construction of a whole out of a series of micro-managed segments, brings out their best qualities, their *internal* cohesion (Section 4). It is also possible to form a sharper awareness of the character and mannerisms of individual poets by comparing them across a series of metrics such as the use of connective particles (their presence or absence, the inhibition or lack of inhibition about delaying them), the formal treatment of the *if–then* structure (moods and tenses), and the presence or absence of the definite article. There are many other possible metrics as well, but because these target what is essential to the structure of the apotelesma, they offer a way of profiling individual poets and of reaching such confidence as is possible about authorship *across* and *within* books. For example, did the same poet write books 1 and 5? Might the same poet have been responsible for *all* the τέχναι charts, which only the efforts of a later editor distributed across different books? Is there good reason to dissect the first and fifth books into different sections? Stylistics is at least one way of attacking these questions (Section 5). Finally I have added a short section on a matter of content, not of style, which all books share. This is their outlook on work, on toil (on the one hand) and productivity, manufacture, and exploit (on the other). This forms a link with Part One; at the same time it points up small individual emphases within different poets (Section 6).

There are four appendices at the end of Part Two. The first two tabulate matching charts in different collections, (i) Θ against the Manethoniana, in which some of them appear more than once, and (ii) Anubion against Manetho and Firmicus. The third and fourth collate figures arrived at in the analyses of individual poems, again for the purposes of comparison and profiling. The third tabulates metrical facts and figures. It makes it easier to see how poets differ, where individual differences lie—and also collects some of the metrical licences they all avail themselves of, to a greater or lesser extent, to accommodate their intractable subject-matter to the hexameter. Dorotheus, Maximus, and 'Antiochus' are included for maximum context; one foreseeable disappointment is that they do not arrange themselves in a linear way which can establish relative chronology or timeline. The fourth is more of a curiosity. I decided out of interest to tabulate the number of references to each of the planets in each of the books, simply to see how different their profiles were, and I turned back to book 6 to include that in the comparison as well.[2] Book 6, because that has the most comparable kind of material: the systematic catalogues of books 2 and 3 would presumably produce results that were more evenly distributed, although skewed by mentions of additional factors. The findings took me rather by surprise, but perhaps should not have done. Ratios between planets remain remarkably steady; it is maleficence that the poets are drawn to over and over again, not benignity. The Devil has all the best lines.

1. COMPARANDA, COMMON SOURCES, UNDERLAY

From now onwards attention turns to the Manethoniana themselves. The first task is to prepare for the analysis of the individual books and the commentary by laying out the most relevant comparanda and by drawing what inferences can be drawn about their sources. The attention then shifts to the three books themselves and becomes more linguistic and stylistic in focus. Deathless prose is not to be expected from this section. But it will be important for reference, and for laying out the armature of what follows.

Evidence from Types of Material Found within the Books of the Corpus

A Common Stock

Now that the scope has widened beyond the first volume and it is possible to take stock of the collection as a whole, the four identifiable authors in the collection can be seen to share a large amount of material.

---

[2] There were certain methodological difficulties. I decided to count references to luminaries and malefics even when the poets did not mention them by name; I did not, on the other hand, include references in the form of anaphoric pronouns, even though this sometimes led to inconsistency (when, of two entities that had been previously mentioned, one was referred to by name and the other was not).

(i) Charts on life outcomes, work, activities[3]

Every poet in the corpus has this kind of chart; indeed it often elicits their best poetic efforts. Almost all are affiliated to a chapter in Ptolemy (4.4 Περὶ πράξεως ποιότητος), which is much reworked and appears in a number of later epitomes with important supplements. Its principles are also put into practice and used in a series of worked-out charts for individual occupations (all to be discussed below). I call these respectively πρᾶξις and τέχναι charts. The material on πρᾶξις stands on a different footing from the bundle of material (*topikai diakriseis, kentrothesiai*, and aspects) inherited from Nechepso–Petosiris, whose distribution across M[a], Anubion, Dorotheus, and Firmicus was discussed in i. I.5. πρᾶξις was indeed treated by Dorotheus and Anubion,[4] using the same three planets as Ptolemy but departing from him in similar ways.[5] But I have found no definite evidence that supports the idea that their system, as opposed to Ptolemy's, underlies the Manethonian material on πρᾶξις.[6]

(ii) Charts on harm (σίνος)[7]

There is a close relationship between this category and the previous one. It is especially clear in M[a], where they are juxtaposed as self-contained sections, in M[b] where whole blocks and sometimes individual charts are juxtaposed,[8] and in Θ, where the epitomator has treated them almost contiguously.[9] The relationship is not so clear in the other books, though three σίνος configurations follow the block of τέχναι in M[d].[10] Σίνος charts are interspersed among the τέχναι in M[b],[11] and a few charts concerning those who lead a problematic or deviant lifestyle even have a double tradition.[12]

---

[3] 6.339–543; 4.121–52, 157–60, 170–92, 201–13, 230–346, 395–401, 420–49, 466–71; 1.38–9, 58–65, 75–88, 129–33, 180–1 + 184, 286–326; 5.134–5, 137–88, 243–5, 274–81.

[4] Dorotheus, p. 431 = fr. 38 Stegemann; Anubion (T 9, a composite text based on Θ pp. 207.26–208.25 and Epit. IV, *CCAG* ii. 190–1). A scratch collection of τέχναι charts in Firmicus, 7.26.

[5] More is said about Anubion's method, but both involve the ASC, MC, IMC, Lot of Fortune. Both attach importance to *synaphai* of the Moon. Dorotheus is also said to have recommended the use of *synaphai* with the Sun if all else failed.

[6] Though 4.571, where Jupiter in the MC aspects the New Moon, is at least compatible with Anubion's method.

[7] 6.544–631; 4.153–6, 193–200, 214–23, 347–65, 472–7, 537–59, 613–18; 1.89–91, 229–44, 250–5; 5.136, 189–201, 217–21, 246–55, 320–3.

[8] Blocks: 4.170–346 + 347–65; perhaps also 4.537–59 + 560–81; individual segments: 4.466–71 + 472–7.

[9] Though chapters on Moon phases, the ascending and descending nodes, and καθολικὰ σχήματα εὐτυχούντων, intervene between σίνος and πρᾶξις in Θ chs. 79–81 (pp. 203–7), Epit. IIIa, chs. 72–4 (*CCAG* viii/3. 109–10).

[10] 5.137–88 + 189–201.

[11] 4.153–6; 214–17 + 218–23. For M[a], see i. 785.

[12] 4.230–7, including bodyguards; 294–308 + 309–16, those with a louche lifestyle; 4.478–90, a chart for thieves and murderers who come to a violent end.

(iii) Effect of signs' gender on luminaries[13]
This is an interesting group because it is small enough to show in what ways the books are related and large enough to show how much they differ. Comparative material is in Ptolemy, 3.15.7–12 and 4.3; Paul of Alexandria, p. 19.15–20; Epit. II. = 'Antiochus', *CCAG* i. 145.12–22 (also quoted and discussed on i. 702). All the Manethonian poets are interested in the relationship of the gender of the luminary to that of the sign in which it is located. All organise their material by the permutations of the luminary and the gender of its location, and all begin with the principle of concord, which produces the ideal (as is assumed, but not discussed, by Ptolemy), then explore deviations. There is a particular relationship between M^a, M^b, and Epit. II (see on 4.508–36); in a pattern which proves to be characteristic of this poet, M^b seems to have drawn on both the earlier Manethonian poet and additional material as well. At the same time, each poet has his individual emphasis. M^b concentrates on outcomes for one gender (males). M^d concentrates on the specific theme of sex-reversal (effeminacy for males and masculinisation for females). M^c (like Ptol. 4.3.1, but unlike his double-dose of masculinity) deals with kings, lesbians, and effeminate men.

Other sorts of subject-matter are shared across several books, but not all: *kentrothesiai*;[14] material on aspects;[15] the effect of the Moon's *synaphe* and *aporrhoia* (*de coniunctionibus et defluxionibus lunae*). All Manethonian poets except M^b contain this last kind of chart. Perhaps a little more should be made of this, in view of Gundel's remark that systematic charts of the Moon's contact with planets are rare in antiquity. He pointed to Firmicus book 4 and *Lib. Herm.* xxvii and xxxiii,[16] though he missed another passage in the Anonymous Astrologer of 379, Περὶ συναφῶν καὶ ἀπορροιῶν τῆς Σελήνης πρὸς τοὺς ἀστέρας, ὅσα ἐν τοῖς γενεθλίοις σημαίνει (*CCAG* viii/1. 181–6), referred to hereafter as *Π.σ.α*. Cumont thought the doctrine ancient, and traced it to Petosiris or Hermes.[17] Gundel suggested the latter. Whatever its ultimate origins, the presence of pentameters in a couple of passages in M^c (1.208–14, three elegiac couplets; 158–66, with one pentameter) suggests that Anubion may have treated this material as well, how systematically we do not know (p. 278).

The poets who treat this material share a number of common features.

---

[13] 3.363–98; 4.508–36; 1.26–33 [cf. also 115–18 and 277–80 + 281–5]; 5.209–16.
[14] One-factor: 3.8–131; 4.14–72, 83–108, 116–20, 491–8, 503–7; 1.176–9. Two-factor: 3.132–226; 4.73–6, 77–82, 110–15, 499–502; 1.339–40.
[15] 3.227–362; 4.161–4, 472–7, cf. on 558; 1.215–22, 327–33, 334–8.
[16] Gundel 1936, 323: 'Ausgearbeitete Gutachten in der so ganz ausführlichen Form, wie sie unser Fragment des hermetischen Corpus bietet [sc. *Lib. Herm.* xxvii], finden sich sehr selten in der astrologischen Literatur der Antike.'
[17] *CCAG* viii/1. 181.

First is organisation by quality of planet, rather than the usual Manethonian principle of location in the *heptazonos*. M^a contains a systematic or semi-systematic list organised in this way (see i. 632–4). There are traces of such a system in a short section on the Moon in M^d, and the first five of the relevant charts in M^c, although as things stand they are split apart by intervening material, also look very much as if they were once arranged in the same way as well (p. 314).[18]

Second is that the charts characteristically begin with a preliminary notice of goodness and badness. Examples are to be found in M^a (2.442 κρείσσων, 447 ἐσθλή, 453 κακίστη, 462 δεινή, 465 φαύλη); M^c (1.246 κακὴ κατὰ πάντα); and M^d (5.109 ἀγαθὴ κατὰ πάντα, 111 καλή, 112 κακίστη, 113 ἀρίστη). This feature is also found in the Moon catalogue of *Π.σ.α.*, although often that author specifies what it is good or bad in respect of.[19]

Third is that outcomes in these charts show distinct affiliation with Firmicus' catalogues of the Moon's contacts (4.2–8 + 9–14) and with *Π.σ.α.*, even though neither Firmicus nor *Π.σ.α.* is organised in the same way.[20] This applies to M^a and M^c, though not to 5.109–29. Furthermore, even though M^b (as mentioned above) does not contain this type of chart, the outcome of 4.478–90 (which involves the Moon's aspect with Mars) is related to Firmicus, 4.14.7.

These combined witnesses not only add to the evidence that different poets are returning again and again to the same foundational texts. They also suggest how the material could be individuated in different treatments. While the abbreviated nature of the catalogue in M^a has denatured the outcomes to the point of contentlessness, M^c has decided to specialise in medical features in his Moon charts (pp. 313–15) to an even greater extent than *Π.σ.α.*, in whom this material was already fairly well represented.

(iv) Sample charts

These charts are affiliated to Firmicus, 6.29–31 (i. 718), and to the parallel versions, as far as we have them, in Anubion (i. 66).[21] Once again the outlier is M^b. Almost all parallels with Firmicus in this book[22] lie outside 6.29–31 with the exception of the very last one.[23]

---

[18] 2.438–79; 5.109–29; 1.50–7, 134–8, 153–7, 158–66, 185–95, 208–14, 245–9.

[19] *CCAG* viii/1. 182.8–9, 15; 183.4, 6; 184.23–4, 25–7; 185.1, 4, 11–12, 13–16, 30, 32; 186.15–16.

[20] They adhere to *heptazonos* order, although, like 2.483–5 and 498, *Π.σ.α.* puts the Moon's *aporrhoia* from the Sun (p. 186.14–16), and Moon at node (p. 184.7–9; see on 5.127–9), at the end of his sequences.

[21] i. 717–22; 1.45–9, 106–28, 339–52 (cf. 42–4); 5.192–6 (but otherwise apparently not represented).

[22] 4.180–6 ~ Firmicus, 7.26.7; 4.366–71 + 372–3 + 373–8 ~ Firmicus, 7.2.15–16 (though cf. 4.372–3 ~ 6.31.19); 4.379–83 ~ Firmicus, 7.4.5; 4.478–90 ~ Firmicus, 4.14.7.

[23] 4.613–18, which has a parallel in 6.29.10, except that the malefics are on different *kentra*.

In sum, all the books appear to have a similar background, although their organisation is fundamentally different. M^a is a more or less original composition which retains a good degree of integrity. M^b, or at least parts of this book, is interpretable as a single composition as well, only the *membra* are a good deal more *disiecta*. M^c and M^d are partly chaotic. Koechly took M^c as a multi-author compilation (although it will later be argued that his view needs to be modified). But irrespective of arrangement, all are drawing on a common stock of material, from which they make different selections.

Of the most important comparanda, Anubion, Dorotheus, and Firmicus were extensively discussed in the first volume. Θ (Epit. III) was introduced there too. But it will now be subjected to a much more thorough analysis; what is at issue are the different patterns of affiliation between it and the poets who run parallel to it.

The model proposed by Stephan Heilen for the material shared between M^a, Anubion, Dorotheus, and Firmicus (not for the πρᾶξις material related to Ptolemy) still holds good. But it needs to be modified in a number of small ways.

1. Though it is barely possible to construct a stemma, allowance has to be made for the distinct likelihood that some members of the tradition do directly descend from others (rather than all on an equal footing from Nechepso–Petosiris). Not Manetho from Dorotheus, certainly, but probably M^b from M^a, and parts of M^c from Anubion. This coexists with the certainty that M^b has other sources beside M^a. Whatever else this book is, we can now see further than Koechly's original hypothesis that it reworks a single model.

2. Individual poets (or editors) have made different selections of what to include. M^b has gone overboard on πρᾶξις and οἶνος material related to Θ, while M^c is especially receptive to material related to Firmicus' sample charts. It is indeed curious that while M^a and M^b are otherwise so closely related, M^a has so much material related to Firmicus—not just the sample charts of 6.29–31, but other themed material as well—while M^b has so little.[24]

---

[24] Οἶνος. In 6.544–631 there are 22 charts (not including add-ons, which would bring the number to 28). Of these, I have found Firmican parallels for 8, and the only one which is also present in 4 (6.548–50 ~ 4.153–6) is not a specific chart but a matter of general logic, which is also used by Θ. *Nurture* (6.19–112) is strongly Firmican; only a few charts have no Firmican background. But few find correspondences in the fourth book—only 6.46–50 ~ 4.366–71, which corresponds, if imperfectly, to Firmicus, 7.2.16. *Marriage* (6.113–223) is strongly Firmican. The charts come especially from Firmicus, 6.29–30, and are mostly disaster-laden (adultery, incest). Only one has a significant parallel in M^b (6.124–5 ~ 4.386–9), and it is not Firmican. *Slaves* (6.684–731). M^b's charts on slaves in 4.597–611 all have correspondences in M^a's section on the birth of slaves, but none with parallels in Firmicus. There are also slavery-related charts in 6.57–9 + 53–6 ~ 4.372–3 + 373–8, which have partial correspondences in Firmicus, 7.2.15–16 (see p. 656), but also a background in Dorotheus.

Finally, some books have material that is peculiar to them. For instance, M^a on length of life (at least partly related to Ptolemy); 5.44–129, on Good and Bad Stars. These sections are discussed at the relevant point in the commentary, not in this section.

Evidence from Order of Planets

The order in which the various sources present the planets is of some diagnostic value in establishing relationship. To some extent it corroborates affiliations which were already established in the first volume. It will now help to establish others.

Saturn... Mercury + luminaries

Topikai diakriseis, 2.141–398: Saturn... Mercury, Sun + Moon. M^a affiliates with 'Par. Anub.' (no evidence in M^b). *Kentrothesiai*: 3.8–131: Saturn... Mercury, Sun + Moon; 4.14–106: Saturn... Mercury, Moon + Sun. 'Par. Anub.' puts Moon + Sun first (so does Dor.^{ARAB}, but he omits the Sun). This evidence clearly places M^b among the same group of texts as M^a and Dorotheus.

Qualitative

By qualitative order I mean that malefics and benefics are grouped together instead of occupying their place in a positional arrangement. It is found mostly in M^c and M^d, suggesting a relationship between them, though also in the eccentric passage at the end of book 2, which in combination with 5.109–29 suggests it was used for the Moon in particular.

(a) Malefics first
2.441–502 (*synaphai* with Saturn, Mars, Sun; *aporrhoiai* and *synaphai* with benefics nested within each). But the order in $\Pi.\sigma.\alpha.$ is *heptazonos* for the Moon's *synaphai* and *aporrhoiai* (pp. 182–184.6), and mostly also for two-factor charts involving *aporrhoia* + *synaphe* (pp. 184.12–186.19), except that *aporrhoia* from Mars is promoted ahead of *aporrhoia* from Jupiter. In Firmicus, 4, the order is entirely *heptazonos*.
1.16–17: Sun, Moon; Saturn, Mars; Mercury; Jupiter, Venus; 1.203–4: Saturn, Mars; Mercury; Venus, Jupiter; Moon, Sun.
5.44–129 (Good and Bad Stars): Saturn and Mars... Moon (but with some disruption).

(b) Benefics first
1.100–5 (short section on prominent persons): Jupiter, Venus; Saturn, Mars; Sun, Moon; Mercury.

5.109–29 (compilation on the Moon): Jupiter, Venus; Mars, Saturn; Sun; node.
5.316–19 (schemes for women): Venus, Jupiter, Mercury, Saturn.

The clearest outcomes are the relatedness of M^b to M^a and his comparanda, which comes as no surprise, and the affinity of M^c and M^d. The latter will be corroborated on other levels as well (including stylistic), although not necessarily to the extent of making common authorship probable.

Pingree's Epitomes: The Manethoniana and Antiochus/Rhetorius

Among the richest sources of parallels for the Manethoniana are a series of texts which either give themselves out as being excerpts from the Θησαυροί of Antiochus (i. xxv–xxvii), or overlap with treatises so headed. Antiochus, according to David Pingree, was active in the later second century. This is too late to have served as a source for M^a. It is not too late for putatively later books, but given his unavailability to the earliest poet in the corpus, and the close-knit nature of the corpus as a whole, it is not clear what would be gained by positing that even the later books were using Antiochus himself—quite apart from the serious doubts about how much in the texts does in fact go back to Antiochus. Whatever the origins of the material they share with the Manethoniana, this section reviews those epitomes. It relies, perforce, on the versions published in *CCAG*, since Heilen's completion of Pingree's edition of Rhetorius remains unpublished.

Epit. II

Pingree called this the 'fundamental epitome' of Antiochus' Θησαυροί, although it is still unclear how much is really based on him. It was published by F. Boll, principally from Laur. Plut. 28.34, in *CCAG* i. 140–64 ἐκ τῶν Ἀντιόχου Θησαυρῶν ἐπίλυσις καὶ διήγησις πάσης ἀστρονομικῆς τέχνης.[25] It has some short chapters on the harmful effects of signs (on scaly diseases, on lewd persons, and on eyes), but nothing on τέχναι.

The only material in the Manethoniana that is connected specifically with Epit. II rather than Θ concerns the gendered luminaries (*CCAG* i. 145.12–22, there called *Epit. Antioch.*): see on 3.363–98 and 4.508–36. There is also non-specific partial overlap with 5.246–51, on scaly diseases (*CCAG* i. 147.4–10).

---

[25] Strictly, Rhetorius' name is attached only to Epit. IIb, though the editors of *CCAG* then extended it to the related texts.

Epit. III (Θ)

This remains the most important and useful of the comparanda for the second half of the Manethoniana. Headed ἐκ τῶν Ἀντιόχου Θησαυρῶν ἐπίλυσις καὶ διήγησις πάσης ἀστρονομικῆς τέχνης, it was published in large part by Cumont in *CCAG* viii/4 from Paris. gr. 2425 (the only complete witness), with adjuvant material from Paris. gr. 2506 and Marcian. gr. 335.[26]

The first 53 chapters of this treatise correspond to Epit. II. Pingree 1977, 210–12, held that ch. 54 onwards, those that concern us, were additions to the original epitome, taken from a variety of sources including Dorotheus, Valens, Paul, Firmicus, and others, and he dated the whole to the early seventh century. There are significant modifications to this picture in the latest appraisal by Levente László. According to him, the later chapters are no less likely (or unlikely) to derive from Antiochus than the earlier ones, and the whole can be seen as a 'heavily reworked and supplemented version' of Antiochus' other work, the Εἰσαγωγικά. He thinks that the treatise as it stands is incomplete, and that the original was composed by an anonymous astrologer working for the emperor Zeno in 504 or shortly thereafter. But this astrologer in turn was working from an earlier treatise. Its author was Rhetorius, whom László would date to the fourth century (much earlier than Pingree's sixth or seventh); he it was who assembled the congeries of Antiochus, Teucer, Dorotheus, Valens, and the rest. László seems to imply (p. 340) that the material relevant to us in what he calls the 'genethlialogical treatise' that is extant as Epit. III goes back to Rhetorius.

Some of the material in Epit. III chapters 54 ff. also appears in Pingree's Epitome IV, extant in four manuscripts, from which very little was published in *CCAG*.[27] It will add little to Θ until we reach a chapter on the prior death of parents (below, p. 145), for which the relevant part of Θ was not published in *CCAG*.

Does this leave us any the wiser about the ultimate origins of the material relevant to the Manethoniana? I fear it does not, but let us review the important correspondences. The crucial overlaps are in chapters concerning οἶνος

---

[26] Of the epitomes derived from this [= IIIa–c], some are partly published in *CCAG*. Epit. IIIa = *CCAG* viii/3. 104–11 consists of chapter headings which indicate content corresponding to Epit. III, though sometimes divided up differently (see Pingree 1977, 213, table 1). Of the three main codices of Epit. IIIb, relevant chapters from Monac. gr. 287 were partly published by Boll in *CCAG* vii. 111–13, 115–16, 117–18. Vienna, Phil. gr. 179 is missing the chapters on τέχναι.

[27] Pingree 1977, 216–19; László, 335. The corresponding material is as follows: *Dodecatopos* (Epit. IV ch. 1 ~ Epit. III ch. 57); harms (Epit. IV chs. 4–7 ~ Epit. III chs. 61–8); violent death (Epit. IV ch. 8 ~ Epit. III ch. 77); πρᾶξις (Epit. IV ch. 27 ~ Epit. III chs. 82–3); 'family' configurations (Epit. IV chs. 24–6 ~ Epit. III chs. 97, 99–102, 104–5; missing are chs. 98, 103, 106–7).

(physical, mental, and moral harms) (Θ pp. 186–97.12, chs. 61–8), πρᾶξις (the business of life) (Θ pp. 207.25–213.34, chs. 82–3),[28] and τέχναι, trades and crafts (Θ pp. 214.1–218.8, chs. 84–96). Note that the two chapters on πρᾶξις also appear, condensed, in Epit. IV, about which there is otherwise little to be said,[29] and that the chapters which give specific instances of τέχναι (that is, chs. 85–96, omitting the first) likewise appear, much abbreviated, and without adding anything of interest, in a single chapter under the heading Περὶ ῥητόρων καὶ παιδευτῶν καὶ ἑτέρων ὑποθέσεων in Monacensis graecus 287, whence they were published by F. Boll in CCAG vii. 117–18 (Pingree's Epit. IIIb[30]).

There are various points of interest. The first is obviously to analyse the parallels between Θ and the Manethoniana, their distribution, the preservation or otherwise of sequences, the presence or absence of detailed similarities in protasis and apodosis, of correspondences in diction, and whether patterns are discoverable across the several books. Some observations can be made immediately. Θ has very miscellaneous material on harms: after a desultory miscellaneous chapter (61), it ranges across injuries to the eyes (62), the bald (63), the gouty (64), madmen and epileptics (65), the lecherous, drunkards, and homosexuals (66), and the places, degrees, and decans that produce them (67–8). In practice, no Manethonian poet strays beyond chs. 61, 65, and 66. They have nothing to say about eye-injuries, the bald, or the gouty, though *every* book has something to say about madmen and epileptics; beyond that, they are selective. The pattern for the chapters about πρᾶξις and τέχναι is not very different. The subjects are clearly interrelated. The former is about employment, what one does in life. Τέχναι are the same thing, only they give more individual instances of it, each with charts of their own. Their interrelatedness is acknowledged by their combination in the Manethonian poets; M^a even makes this almost explicit in 6.14 τέχνας... ἰδὲ πρήξιας and 542 πρήξιας ἢ τέχνας. However, the poets of different books make different selections, as we shall see. *All* contain material on πρᾶξις from ch. 83, but the τέχναι material is distributed selectively across different books.

---

[28] Σίνος and πρᾶξις were also treated by Anubion, apparently one after the other (CCAG ii. 190.15–21 ~ Θ p. 208.2–8 = T 9 Schubert). Θ follows his recommended order of presentation (σίνος first), though M^a and M^b do not.

[29] The chapters on πρᾶξις were published by Olivieri from Marcianus gr. 335 in CCAG ii. 190–1. This matches Epit. III, sometimes in abbreviated form, as far as the reference to Ptolemy on 191.14 = Θ ch. 82, p. 209.20 (with some slight expansions on the effects of the signs). At that point they diverge. Then 191.15–27 (miscellaneous charts involving one, two, or three planets mostly in the ASC and/or MC) ~ Θ ch. 83, p. 212.9–24 (an expansion of Ptolemy), and 191.27–30 ~ Θ p. 213.28–34. This version of the material adds nothing except an additional detail to an outcome on watery occupations, for which see on 1.84–5.

[30] Pingree 1977, 214; László, 334.

Another object in what follows is to advance, if possible, the source criticism of Θ by pressing harder at comparanda. The most straightforward comparison will prove to be between Θ's chapters on πρᾶξις and τέχναι, Ptolemy's underlying chapter on πρᾶξις, and the Manethonian versions. But it might also be possible to expand Pingree's observations about Θ's other sources. In particular, we might want to look for signs of a verse underlay, as evidence for yet another circulating poem with content related to the Manethoniana. On the other hand, we might decide that it was only ever a prose version, or a digest of a longer prose version. The enquiry is a reasonable one given the traces of verse that are often found in astrological prose digests, for instance the traces of Dorotheus' verse in Περὶ κράσ. and in 'Par. Anub.', and in a couple of versions of Teucer's treatise on paranatellonta (Boll 1903, 35–6). One would have to reckon with the possibility of complex transmission. Θ itself might not be, or contain, first-generation paraphrase of a poem, but might do so by a stage or stages of intermediaries.

The chapters containing material parallel with the Manethoniana are as follows.

Ch. 57, Θ pp. 126.12–182 Ἀποτελέσματα τοῦ πίνακος τῆς ‹δωδεκατόπου› [Ἑρμοῦ τοῦ Τρισμεγίστου περὶ τῆς τῶν ιβ′ τόπων ὀνομασίας καὶ δυνάμεως]. This chapter contains material from two sources, (i) related to (sharing a common source with) Valens, II 5–14, and (ii) related to Firmicus, 3.2–7 and 13 (although Firmicus arranges by planet, not place).[31] It cannot be proved that the common source of this chapter and Firmicus is Antiochus. Sometimes the material derived from (i) disagrees with the material derived from (ii). Paul's treatment of the *dodecatopos* overlaps, now with (i), now with (ii). Pingree also detected the influence of Dorotheus (Dor.^{ARAB} I 27.5–24) and Critodemus.

There are mostly non-specific correspondences between this chapter and M^b's *kentrothesiai*, and otherwise as tabulated in the Pinax. The most distinctive are between 1.83–8 and Θ p. 166.22–4, and 4.248 = Θ p. 151.7 ἐπιμόχθους. The next word on p. 151.7 ἐρημοβάτας is a *hapax*, which looks to correspond to 4.247 ἐμβασικοίτας. Does it reflect a hexameter source (Dorotheus)?

Ch. 59, Θ p. 183 Περὶ σχημάτων Σελήνης καθολικῶν. Parallels are limited. See especially on 5.224 ~ p. 183.16–17 ἀτίμους, μετανάστας: insofar as there is a recollection of the *Iliad*, there may be a verse underlay.

Ch. 61, pp. 186.1–190.18 Καθολικὰ σχήματα περὶ σινῶν καὶ παθῶν. Pingree identified the use of Dorotheus in this chapter. The most pronounced correspondences within it are with M^c and M^d, and there are a few applications of

---

[31] Cumont, *CCAG* viii/4. 116–18; Pingree 1977, 211.

general rules, of interest because one of the lines in M^c certainly contains a pentameter, and another is restorable as one.³² That does not suffice, of course, to trace Θ's own material to Anubion.

Ch. 65, pp. 192.8–194.8 Περὶ μαινομένων καὶ ἐπιληπτικῶν. Most of the parallels for this chapter, both precise and approximate,³³ are in M^a, M^b, and M^c. One overlap is with a passage containing a pentameter (1.91). There is a strikingly poetic epithet on p. 194.7 ἀκριτόβουλοι, otherwise in 4.530 (see ad loc.), though the chart does not otherwise match.

Ch. 66, pp. 194.9–195.14 Περὶ ἀσελγῶν καὶ μεθυστῶν καὶ ἐμπαθῶν. Pingree has identified Dor.^ARAB II 7.2–6 (the beginning of the chapter 'knowledge of sodomy'), as the source of at least parts of this chapter. In practice the parallels reach to approximately p. 195.2, though the last chart in this sequence finds no perfect correspondence in Dorotheus.³⁴ Nonetheless, the Dorothean ambience of this section makes it the more possible that he underlies 4.354–8, a chart which runs parallel to Θ p. 194.17–18 (even though once again there is no precise match in Dor.^ARAB), and contains the Dorothean epithet Διωναίη for Venus (i. 906–7 n. 7).

Ch. 77, Violent death = Θ pp. 199.1–202.10 Καθολικὰ σχήματα βιαιοθανάτων Some precise correspondences in M^d and M^c, and less precise in M^b.

Ch. 82, pp. 207.25–210.19 Περὶ πράξεως καὶ ἐπιτηδεύματος. This section describes Anubion's method for forecasting πρᾶξις (T 9 Schubert; see n. 5). According to Anubion, what mattered was the Moon's application to planets after the phase, Full or New, that preceded the birth. Unlike Ptolemy (below) and Dorotheus, he did not confine his attention to Mars, Venus, and Mercury. After Θ p. 208.25 admonishes the reader that these things are to be found ἐν τῷ περὶ πράξεως λόγῳ, the epitomator then moves on to a discussion (obviously not Ptolemaic) of the effects of the planets governing πρᾶξις in their own and in others' houses (p. 209.1–16), which he says is taken ἐκ τῆς τοπικῆς διακρισέως. If he is still talking about Anubion, this would seem to confirm the evidence of Julian (F 3) that Anubion did indeed have a section on that subject (see Heilen 2010, 170–1, and i. 66 n. 6).

Ch. 83, pp. 210.20–213.34 Περὶ τῶν γ' ἀστέρων τῶν σημαινόντων τὰς πράξεις. Each poet in the corpus has charts affiliated to this chapter. The compiler has

---

[32] pp. 186.5–6 (lone malefics in *kentra*) ~ 1.167–75 (pentameter possible at 1.169); 186.8–9 (Moon's *aporrhoia* from a malefic) ~ 1.158–66 (pentameter at 159); 187.17–18 (malefics on *epanaphora* of luminaries) ~ 4.153–6; 189.13–14 ~ 5.252–5 and 25–6 ~ 5.246–51.

[33] Among the latter (not included in Pinax of Θ against Manetho): pp. 192.13–14 ~ 4.537–44; 193.13–15 ~ 4.362–5; 193.16–17 ~ 4.545–51; 193.20–2 ~ 4.537–44, 6.599–600, 1.229–34; 194.17–18 ~ 4.354–8.

[34] In Θ pp. 194.18–195.2, Venus and the Moon are both on the DESC; in the parallel 4.219 they are at least in conjunction; but in Dor.^ARAB II 7.6 only Venus is on the DESC and the Moon is in opposition.

said that he has made a selection from various ancient authors (p. 208.1 τὴν ἐπιλογὴν ποιούμενος ἐκ διαφόρων ἀρχαίων). But in practice this chapter is an expanded version of Ptolemy, 4.4 Περὶ πράξεως ποιότητος, which concentrates on the planets Mercury, Venus, and Mars, and their effects as Rulers of πρᾶξις, first singly, then with each other (Mercury + Venus, Mercury + Mars, Venus + Mars), and combined with the influence of other planets (Saturn and Jupiter). The Ruler or Rulers of πρᾶξις, Ptolemy explains, is or are the planet whose morning appearance is closest to the Sun, and the one in the MC, especially receiving the application of the Moon. Ptolemy explains ways in which the basic configuration may be modified: (i) through zodiacal signs (4.4.9); (ii) through the additional presence of the Moon (4.4.10); and through other factors such as phase, position on *kentra*, aspect of benefics and malefics, and opposition of malefics. The chapter is essentially a catalogue, which, presenting a series of unfleshed-out possibilities, I call Π- charts, for πρᾶξις. This is in contrast to τ- charts (for τέχναι), or worked-out realisations, discussed below. (My capitalisation reflects that πρᾶξις is the superordinate category.)

In Θ Ptolemy is modified and expanded in various ways. Θ presents the planets in the order Mercury, Mars, Venus; then Mars + Mercury, Venus + Mars, Mercury + Venus. For almost all he gives, like Ptolemy, the additional aspects of Saturn and Jupiter, but also a good deal more; this is why some Π- charts come close to being worked-out examples like τ-. (In the Pinakes for each book I indicate this supplementary material with an asterisk *.) In addition to outright supplements, Θ frequently offers fuller or different trades and professions than Ptolemy's, even where they do overlap. Finally, Ptolemy's supplementary information (4.4.9–12) is much condensed in a final chapter which also tells how to calculate the Lot of πρᾶξις and how to draw predictions from it.

Can anything be said about the origin of the new material in Θ? If it represented a later reworking of Ptolemy, it would suggest the efforts of an interpreter active in or after the third century, which it seems is when the *Tetrabiblos* started to attract interest.[35] But it cannot be that, or at least not all of it, for several of the supplements vis-à-vis Ptolemy are already represented in M^a in the early second century (see Pinax). The inference is that at least some of the material is pre-Ptolemaic, and for some reason not represented in him. It need not all come from one and the same source, of course. There is one passage where Θ has a verbatim correspondence with M^c (p. 211.11 ~ 1.77 λαξευτὰς ἢ τέκτονας ἢ λιθοεργούς): the epitomator has not even bothered to contract the

---

[35] Heilen 2015, 59–60, and n. 293: the first evidence for the reception of the *Tetrabiblos* is Porphyry's Εἰσαγωγὴ εἰς τὴν Ἀποτελεσματικὴν τοῦ Πτολεμαίου, but for doubts about the extent to which this treatise derives from Porphyry, see L. László, 'Revisiting the Authenticity of Porphyry's *Introduction to Ptolemy's "Apotelesmatics"*', *CPh* 116 (2021), 392–411.

vowels in the last word. Moreover, this line is immediately preceded in M^c by a pentameter, which might suggest not only that Θ is drawing on a verse source at this point, but that that source might be Anubion. M^c has nothing else to offer that is quite so egregious, but almost immediately after the stone-carvers, Θ p. 211.12 χαλκοτύπους ἢ ἱερουργοὺς ἢ βαφέας corresponds to 1.79–80 χαλκοτύπους, ἢ φυσητὰς ὑέλοιο, | ἢ βαφέας, where to complete the run of handicrafts I conjecture that ἱερουργοὺς is corrupt for ὑαλ- or ὑελουργούς (see ad loc.). If one accepts verse origins (Anubion?) for 211.11, this line, which follows on its heels, might also derive from the same source.[36]

Chs. 84–96, pp. 214.1–218.8 Περὶ τεχνῶν. These can be seen as worked-out 'realisations' of the basic principles which Ptolemy laid out in 4.4. I call them τ- charts, after τέχναι.

The workings-out include specifications about constellations which are not inconsistent with, but go beyond, what Ptolemy himself says about constellations in 4.4.9. Rather, they seem to have connections with a source like (i) the first Teucer text, which divides each sign of the zodiac into its three decans and lists their respective paranatellonta, and (ii) the second Teucer text, which lists the effects of the paranatellonta. In a couple of places Θ seems to be aware of the Egyptian *dodecaoros*, and either names (p. 217.7–8, the Ape) or implies the name of (p. 216.15 ἱερακοτρόφους, the Hawk) one of its members. Otherwise, what Θ does is to name, not the paranatellon itself which Teucer specifies as producing the effect, but the zodiacal sign which it accompanies. Yet the connections are strong and consistent enough to support the idea that Θ knows a version of Teucer. This holds good for the construction workers of p. 215.12–16 (~ 4.290–3), the manual workers of p. 216.1–6 (~ 4.317–26), the hunters and predators of p. 216.8–15 (~ 4.333–40), and above all for the Περὶ μίμων (ch. 96) sequence which finds its closest matches in book 5 (mimes, p. 217.5–7 ~ 5.137–43, cf. 4.280; instrumentalists, p. 217.12–13 ~ 5.159–64; artists and craftsmen, p. 217.14–15 ~ 5.165–8; charioteers, p. 217.16–18 ~ 5.169–72; hawkers, p. 217.19–20 ~ 4.339 and 5.175–6; root-cutters and snake-charmers, p. 217.21–3 ~ 5.181–8).[37] A few correspondences among the outcomes are verbatim, or almost: p. 215.15 οἰκοδόμους, p. 216.5 τέκτονας, p. 216.6 λιθοξόους, p. 217.17 ἡνιόχους, p. 217.23 θηριοδείκτας.

---

[36] Also close, but inconclusive about a possible verse source, are: (i) Epit. IV = CCAG ii. 191.22 κηπουρούς, ἁλιεῖς, ὑδραγωγούς (cf. Θ p. 166.22 κηπουροὺς καὶ ὑδραγωγούς) ~ 1.84 κηπουροὺς ἠδ' ἀργαλέους ὑδραγωγούς [Θ p. 212.17 has κηπουροὺς ἢ ἁλιεύοντας]; (ii) Θ p. 209.13 ἢ λόγων ἢ καλάμου ~ 1.131 ἢ ἐκ λόγου ἢ καλάμοιο. This latter falls within a section (p. 209.10–16) that involves location in another planet's houses, in other words *topike diakrisis*, a subject treated by Anubion (p. 139). But the apotelesma in M^c (1.129–33) does not involve houses, nor contain any pentameters (though the previous one does: 124, 128).

[37] Reinforcing the suggestion that the items at the end of this list are rag tag and bobtail taken from other sources, the reckless Leonines of pp. 217.24–218.2 find their best parallels, not in the Teucer texts, but in Manilius, 5.220–2, and Firmicus, 8.10.1.

The representation of these chapters in the Manethoniana is different from that of ch. 83. Whereas that was represented in all of M^a, M^b, M^c, and M^d, chs. 85–95 are confined to M^a and M^b (plus those charts of M^c which are shared with M^b), while ch. 96 Περὶ μίμων is confined to M^b and M^d.[38] In particular, we find long sequences where both M^b and M^d run parallel to Θ (the former with interpolations, the latter substantially without), which, whatever else they do, show that the arrangement in the Manethoniana is not a higgledy-piggledy mess produced by the editors of the books in question; they have, on the contrary, stayed faithful to sequences which are retained elsewhere, although they may well have packed them with additional material. The division of labour is particularly intriguing. M^b leaves off just where M^d takes over; they have just one chart in common, the mime chart of p. 217.5–7. This mime chart is a curiosity. In Θ the rest of the material in the substantial chapter that goes under the title Περὶ μίμων is a miscellaneous assemblage that for the most part has nothing to do with mimes (pp. 217.9–218.8). Cumont prints these miscellanea with a half-line after p. 217.8, but this corresponds to nothing in the manuscript (Par. gr. 2425, fo. 132 recto), where p. 217.9 follows on continuously, without line-break. It is also curious that although the parallel sequence in M^d and Θ begins with the mimes, the former starts to run strictly in line with the latter only from p. 217.9 onwards; the mimes themselves find their best correspondence, not with 5.137–43, but with 5.103. It appears there was a series of charts with individual titles (up to and including the mimes), which is what M^b is following, and a separate collection of miscellanea, reproduced by M^d. Somehow the mimes make their appearance in the latter book as well. It is hard to explain why.

(i) The charts in Θ chs. 85–96 (pp. 214.9–217.7) run essentially in the same order as the matching material in M^b, from 4.170, i.e. the beginning of the τέχναι after the transition, until 449. There are many intrusions in the latter, but the sequence holds strong, and its members are underlined for convenience in the Pinax of book 4. It carries through the main τέχναι section up to and including 4.346, although it is frequently interrupted by other Π-, τ-,[39] and οἶνος charts. It then resumes and is completed with 395–401 (although this is stranded in the middle of charts about parents), 420–4, and 437–49. The parallels in Θ are extensive, but they do not seem to include traces of metre or poetic diction, as they did in the previous chapter. The most reasonable conclusion is that Θ represents

---

[38] Plus one imprecise correspondence with 1.38–9: why?

[39] Including alternative versions of τ- charts which are themselves later parts of the sequence. 4.187–92 anticipates 263–70 as a version of Θ p. 215.8–11. The outcome of 238–48 anticipates 333–40 as a version of Θ p. 216.8–15, and that of 271–85 + 286–9 anticipates 444–9 as a version of Θ p. 217.5–9.

a prose source from which both M^a and M^b drew material, poeticising it to fit their idiom (rather than that Θ strips back a poetic source).

(ii) The charts from p. 217.5–23 are exactly parallel with 5.137–88, although <5.154–8>, on divers, and <5.177–80>, on the *gallus*, are not represented in Θ. The remaining charts in the chapter, pp. 217.24–218.8, are also paralleled in M^d at some further remove (pp. 217.24–218.2 also has correspondences in M^b and M^c, notably more distant than M^d's), and the penultimate one (p. 218.3–6) recurs, elaborated, in one of M^d's long discursive charts. In almost every case the protases in Θ and M^d correspond closely. This holds good despite the fact that on a couple of occasions Θ has extra details, and on another occasion M^d (and M^b) have a different agency.[40] The only oddity, mentioned above, is that the mime chart that best corresponds with Θ p. 215.5–7 is in fact the isolated one in 5.103–4, not the one that stands at the head of the main sequence in 5.137–43. Otherwise, the similarity gains from two contrasts:

(a) The relationship between Θ and M^d in their 'sequence' charts is far closer than that which subsists between Θ and M^b in theirs.

(b) Where there are points of correspondence between M^b and Θ ch. 96 [see Pinax], these consist almost entirely in the apodoses, with major differences in protases. An extreme case is Θ pp. 217.24–218.2, where Θ matches the protasis of 5.252–3, while the apodosis is much more like 4.232–7.

Yet in spite of the close correspondence of their sequences and the shared details of their charts, Θ ch. 96 still shows no sign of being a redaction of poetry. Even if one argued that a paraphrast simply reduced the outcomes to their essentials, omitting all the wadding, Θ adds further detail (such as p. 217.7–8 on the Ape as a paranatellon of Capricorn) which, if this came from a poem at all, would have had to be a poem of a very different character from the Manethoniana. As it is, there are no traces of poetic diction. Once again, a more plausible analysis is that Θ represents (a reduction of) the kind of source M^d has versified, in which case M^d has been remarkably careful to retain, in most cases, the detail of the protasis, while wadding, in typical poetic fashion, the apodosis (146–7, the tightrope-walker; 152–3, the sailor's life; 160–4, more musical instruments than are mentioned in Θ; 170–2, the charioteer; 175–6 the technique of the

---

[40] Protases match at 5.103–4, 149–50, 169, 173–4. Extra details vis-à-vis 5.159 (Θ: οἴκῳ Ἡλίου…μάλιστα ἐπίκεντροι) and 165–6 (Θ: ἐπίκεντροι ἢ ἐπαναφερόμενοι ἔξαυγοι). Θ suggests the presence of a missing line before 170. 5.144–5 is very similar, but swaps Venus for Mercury (as does 4.286, which is, however, less close), and adds an extra factor (148). 5.181–2 is corrupt, and I have remade 181 to correspond more closely, but the paradosis does suggest a reference to scaly signs (181), and confirms the content of 182.

bird-catcher; especially 184–8, the snake-handler). It is Θ that in general preserves the specialist terms; see Θ p. 217.13 (~ 5.160), 15 (~ 5.168), 19–20 (~ 5.176).

In sum, the correspondences in sequence between Θ chs. 84–95 and 96 and M^b and M^d do not indicate that those chapters are likely to be, or to contain, the remains of a poem. It is only in ch. 83 that our very few indications of a poetic source or sources can be found. To conclude this discussion of the πρᾶξις and τέχναι chapters in Θ, and what can be gleaned about their character, I note one small further detail. A distinctly *prosaic* feature which both πρᾶξις and τέχναι chapters contain is the -άριος ending for occupational titles, lent by Latin.[41] There are instances both of the -άριος suffix attached to Greek stems, and of outright Latin loans;[42] indeed, this text contains more examples of the -άριος formation than any other Greek astrological prose work known to me, except the second Teucer text.[43] Now this can barely be used as a dating criterion for Θ, certainly not one that is in any way precise. There is no clearly defined point at which -άριος formations start to be found in Greek,[44] and there are epigraphical examples from as early as the first century BC.[45] However, the first words of this type to be attested tend to be army (and perhaps clerical) terms, with other trade-names only starting to be attested in later antiquity.[46] They do not occur in Ptolemy's πρᾶξις charts. Nor do they occur in the alternative version of Epitome III that has come down to us as Epit. IIIb (see p. 137), where it is not the case that the material is present but alternatively phrased; rather, it is absent

---

[41] Palmer, 48–9; Cavenaile, 201–2; Adams 2003, 495; Ruffing 2008, 54–6, 88–93, 96. For -άριος in astrology, see Robert 1938, 84, 90.

[42] Ch. 83: pp. 213.1 μαγγαναρίους, 213.26 πλουμαρίους [*plumarius*]. Chs. 84–95: pp. 215.15 σκανδουλαρίους [*scandularius*], 216.7 καβιδαρίους [*cabidarius*]. Not, however, p. 216.12 μαρμαρίους, where the suffixed form is μαρμαράριος/*marmorarius*. There is another Latin loan in p. 216.12 βηνάτορας; this corresponds to M^b κυνηγητῆρας (4.337) and Epit. IIIb = CCAG vii. 117.33 κυνηγούς. Ch. 96: pp. 217.9 μαγγαναρίους, 217.15 πολυμιταρίους, 217.20 ἱερακαρίους.

[43] For Teucer, see Boll 1903, 36–7, 38–9 (he seems to find a date in later antiquity, from the 3rd or 4th c. onwards, likeliest for a text which contains these forms). Otherwise, νοτάριος is by far the best represented in Greek astrological texts, and there are a couple of attestations of σκρινιάριος (Paul, p. 67.11 and 'Heliodorus', p. 72.22). Unsurprisingly, there are several dozen in Firmicus: *aerarios, armentarios, argentarios, bratiarios, caligarios, coriarios, dulciarios, equitatros, ferramentarios, funerarios, gallicarios, herbarios, lanarios, lapidarios, laturarios, musivarios, notarios, operarios, orchestopalarios, organarios, pellarios, petaminarios, petauristarios, pictomacharios, pigmentarios, plumarios, popinarios, porcarios, scutarios, statuarios, tabernarios, venenarios, veredarios, victimarios*.

[44] In Latin they are very early, and already in Plautus' *Aulularia*, of about 190 BC, many of the items in the list of joke-formations at 508–21 (p. 38 n. 13) already have a Greek basis.

[45] *IK* Ephesos, 1687, 2a, ll. 3–4 (c. 31 BC) συμβολάριος *bis*; the form is unexplained. For papyri, see Ruffing 2008, 89–90 (very rare in the 1st c. AD, gathering pace thereafter).

[46] Among trade names a rare early example is *IG* IX,2 16 (Thessaly, Hypata, AD 131–3) ὑποδηματάριος (shoemaker). For those attested in the cemetery of Corycos, see Robert 1969, *passim*.

altogether. That would suggest the chronological order Epit. IIIb—M^b (which has charts not yet present in Epit. IIIb[47])—Θ (which, as it stands, dates from later antiquity).

Supposing that Θ does represent the kind of thing the poets of the Manethoniana were versifying, it seems unlikely that M^a, at least, was working from a text which already contained these forms, although, since it is his way to offer poetic paraphrase, little can be inferred from the complete effacement of the καβιδαρίους (gem-engravers) by poetic verbiage in 6.343–4. Likewise the σκανδουλαρίους (shinglers) receive a total rewrite in 4.292–3. More interesting are the πολυμιταρίους (Θ p. 217.15) who correspond to 5.168 πολλοῖσι μίτοις. In this case the poetic form looks distinctly likely to be secondary to the prosaic one (it is followed immediately by πλάσμασιν, which also looks likely to be a rendering of Θ's ἀνδριαντοπλάστας): it is hard to see it as anything other than a versification of that.[48] If so, then although we are no nearer to an absolute date for M^d, the poet is late enough to reflect a text itself late enough to contain such a formation.

Chs. 97–108 'Family' configurations = Θ pp. 218.9–221.9. These are relevant to M^b, not to M^c (except in lines shared with M^b) or M^d. M^a had placed sections on nurture, marriage, children, and siblings before the τέχναι and harms in book 6. M^b, on the other hand, follows his main τέχναι series with miscellaneous charts on matters of birth, upbringing, siblings, and the status, marital history, and prior deaths of parents. What Θ contains are matters concerning parents (chs. 97–8), their relations with their offspring (ch. 99), their mortality (chs. 100, 102), and on siblings (number, seniority, relations between) (chs. 103–8). Not all were published by Cumont in CCAG viii/4, and that makes it hard to assess the extent of the overlap with the chapters. But it is at least suggestive that the main τέχνη sequence, which finishes in 4.346, is followed, after a short mainly οἶνος cluster, with charts about nurture and parentage (4.379–413), at least one of which (4.379–83) can be shown to have a parallel with ch. 97 περὶ γονέων. It may well be that when the complete publication of the various epitomes of 'Antiochus' becomes available, more of M^b's family charts will prove to have parallels there. Pingree had already seen that Dorotheus underlay several of Θ's family chapters, including περὶ γονέων. It may be that there is more Dorotheus behind both Θ and M^b. We will have to wait and see.

For the time being, a little more help is to be had from Epit. IV, parts of which were published by Olivieri from Marcianus gr. 335 in CCAG ii. 187–8 Περὶ γονέων, 188–9 Περὶ προτελευτῆς γονέων, and 189–90 Περὶ ἀδελφῶν. From the second of these emerges an impressive parallel with 4.402–8 + 409–13, where

---

[47] M^a's τέχναι section *also* contains charts with parallels in Θ but none in Epit. IIIb (6.362–5^a, 415–18, 419–21, 431–5, 484–6). But those parallels are more distant, so it is hard to infer much from the absence of the charts in question from Epit. IIIb.

[48] 5.176 ἴρηξ also corresponds to p. 217.20 ἱερακαρίους, but it less conclusively versifies it.

we can see the application of a principle attested also in both Dorotheus and Firmicus that malefics harming the Sun and Moon annihilate fathers and mothers respectively. Dorotheus could underlie Epit. IV, though if he does he has left no trace in the epitomator's diction. Intriguingly, however, the verses parallel to 4.409–13 in 1.334–8 contain a pentameter, so it is possible that Anubion treated the material as well.

Conclusions

Almost all the material in the Manethoniana with parallels/overlaps in the 'Antiochus' epitomes turns out to come from Epit. III (Θ) chs. 54–96, and only very little from our best (or least worst) witness to Antiochus, namely Epit. II. The most interesting and extensive material, on activities, comes both directly from Ptolemy and from expansions of Ptolemy, but also apparently from the tradition Ptolemy himself inherited. Dorotheus seems to have had a sizeable influence on family themes. The compiler of the treatise that is represented by Θ has drawn on both prosaic and poetic sources, among which a very few traces of poetic diction continue to show through. Parallels between Θ and the Manethoniana subsist at the level of individual charts (set-up, outcomes, diction), themed sequences (on τέχναι, to a much lesser extent on οἶνος), and also, perhaps, though we wait to have this confirmed by the publication of more of the 'family' charts from Epit. III and IV, sequences across larger groups (τέχναι followed by family relations?). We can be reassured that the later books of Manethoniana are not total chaos. Editors will have redacted, interpolated, and doubtless curtailed on principles that we no longer understand. But enough is left to show that the poets are following sequences that have been preserved elsewhere, and are perhaps working from prose manuals, alongside (or even instead of?) earlier poets who had already been epitomated in those very manuals.

What can we make of all these comparative versions, now that we have so painfully traced them? One result of the enquiry is to reveal the extent to which charts transmitted by multiple pathways vary in tiny and not-so-tiny ways. It is not the goal of this section to investigate precise patterns of variation between one source and another. Later sections will look at individual books in more detail. But it does seem appropriate to draw out some general reflections on the implications of this variation. It seems highly unlikely that textual corruption accounts for more than a very small proportion of it.[49] Rather, reflections on the allowability of variation and its limits encourage further thoughts on what

---

[49] *Pace* Heilen 2010, 166 n. 92 (who gives examples of disparities between M^c with Firmicus): 'complex astronomical protases are more likely to be corrupted than the rather simple astrological apodoses'.

The Later Books 147

is involved in generating astrological charts in the first place. From there it is a short step to the purposes of the authors and the nature of their project.

The degree to which one chart differs from another varies enormously. The simplest type of transmission is plain copying. The correspondences between M^d and Θ in the τέχναι charts suggest that the poet invested his efforts in wadding the outcomes. He did not expend any creativity in changing the details of the configuration; his enterprise was essentially a rhetorical one. To judge from his bloated prolixity, M^b's enterprise was most certainly a rhetorical one as well, but he is also more given to altering details in the protasis. The correspondences between M^b and Θ in their own 'sequence' charts are less strict than in the former instance, though it is still the case that when a number of similar charts are available for comparison (as, say, with the tightrope-walkers of 4.286–9) it is the one in the Θ sequence that offers the closest parallel; also that, where M^b himself has more than one version of the same chart, it is usually the one that stands in the sequence that has the closest likeness to Θ.[50] The differences tend to involve position, not the planetary entities themselves, which remain the determining influences. It is not necessarily right to assume that a poetic treatment is poorer at handling detail than a prose one. By comparing the Manethoniana with a prose source like Firmicus it is easy to see how, and why, a poet will have wanted to strip out masses of minute and complex details from the protasis.[51] Yet comparisons with Θ itself tend to show, now that Θ has more detail, now the matching poetic charts, and often they are simply different (pp. 240–2; see also i. 79–80).

A common type of variation involves the application of basic principles to produce variations. A student would be expected to have imbibed the theory from elsewhere. Themed charts would then provide him with examples to mull over (Dorotheus, p. 336.21 ὑποδείγματος χάριν), and the opportunity to generate more on the same lines (hence the topos of 'a wise man could deduce more', i. 184). This is fully borne out by the τέχναι charts which are realisations or instantiations of Ptolemaic theory about πρᾶξις. Many involve the basic rulers of πρᾶξις (we have seen how astrology returns over and over again to combinations of Mercury and Venus which govern 'clean' and prestigious crafts[52]) further inflected by the presence of an additional planet (especially the Moon,[53] an important item in Anubion's as well as Ptolemy's own method of determining

---

[50] Θ p. 216.17–22 ~ 4.395–401 (closer than 131–8); Θ p. 216.8–15 ~ 4.333–40 (closer than 238–48). Not, however, Θ pp. 214.22–215.2 ~ 4.206–13, 425–30.

[51] See on 4.93–100 + 101–6. Of all the sources for the chart of Oedipus (6.160–9, 1.106–11, Anubion, F 4 ii. 11–16, and Firmicus, 6.30.1), Firmicus has the most detail (including the locations of the Sun and the ASC). Of the poetic realisations, 6.160–9 looks to be independent of the others, but 1.106–10 and fr. 4 ii. 11–15a are almost similar enough to be companion renderings into different metres.

[52] 6.366–70 and 504–10 ~ 4.180–6; 6.465–71 ~ 4.206–13; 1.58–61 + 62–5; 1.180–4; 5.159–64 and 165–8.

[53] 6.398; 4.146 ~ 6.521; 4.195; 4.334–5; 4.437; 4.467; 4.478 ~ 1.306; 4.568; 4.571; 5.149; 5.169.

πρᾶξις), or by qualities of sign. Ptolemy already envisaged signs as a factor, but the differentiating potential of signs seem to have been further extended by the application of Teucer's theory of paranatellonta. This is clear from Θ, and acknowledged almost explicitly in p. 213.28–9 Πλέον δὲ πάντων ζήτει τὰ ἀποτελέσματα... τῶν ζῳδίων καὶ τῶν παρανατελλόντων. It is all but invisible in M^b, but the greater fidelity of M^d to his source still lets it rise to view in 5.137 (bent signs), 5.154 (slippery signs and mute Pisces; see also on 5.156), and according to my emendation 5.181 (scaly signs). Another factor which allowed Ptolemy's system to be creatively complicated, and has left more traces of itself in the Manethoniana, are degrees and terms. The MC has obvious metaphorical potential for determining the business of adulthood, and Ptolemy had laid particular emphasis on it.[54] But in practice the significance of *kentra* is far outdone by that of terms, a factor in Θ but still more in *Lib. Herm.* xxxiv. *De terminis in quibus fuerint planetae locati*, to which both M^a and M^b, especially the latter, show affinities.[55]

Why rake through all this tedious detail? One object might be to see whether comparison of one author or one corpus with another allows inferences about rules to which astrologers adhere, but more importantly from that to what they understand their project or projects to be. And it seems that multiple answers emerge. Where the reader or user is concerned, it is perhaps helpful to imagine a spectrum that runs from didaxis to exclusion, at one extreme simplifying, reassuring, and handholding, at the other complicating, offputting, and deliberately baffling. The medium of *poetic* astrology would seem to draw it towards the former end of the spectrum. With poetry it is a matter of rhetorical display, demonstrating command of a prestigious idiom, a fashionable aesthetic (segmented poetics, *Medalliondichtung*), and allusions which showcase the authors' familiarity with, and ability to manipulate, approved sources. This is meant to draw a reader in, not to exclude her, and in the first volume it was suggested that the earliest books in the corpus could be seen as an attempt to ease her into the basics in a companionable and aesthetically pleasing way (i. 84–5). Even so, that is not incompatible with indulging in a little gentle variation according to the rules of the game. Where M^a, M^b, and Θ have common ground, they repeatedly vary each other's offerings in small ways (pp. 262–4); it is a matter, not only of steering a novice through new territory, but also of demonstrating expertise through a little gentle variation of astrology's ground-rules, and perhaps, in the process, of showing her how to do the same. Different poets seem to assign their priorities differently between *enumeratio* of what has been transmitted to them,

---

[54] MC in τέχναι charts: 4.131–2 (equating with ASC in 6.484–5); 4.263 ~ 6.456. Also in 4.560, 567–8, 571 (oppositions across *kentra*, of which the first two are connected with Θ ch. 83, πρᾶξις).

[55] Terms in τέχναι charts: 4.172; 4.177; 4.181–2 ~ 6.504–5; 4.189–90 ~ 6.494; 4.195; 4.202 ~ 6.476–7; 4.265 ~ 6.457; also, 6.466–7, 487, 586.

and *variatio* or elaboration of traditional material. Subsequent sections move on to the three later books in the corpus, paying more attention to their individual characteristics and what gives each their distinctive idiom and style of approach. The introduction to Part Three complements and complicates this by drawing out the implications of *Fachliteratur* which is in a constant state of overhaul and manipulation. From this perspective, it may be harder to be sure where polite games of *variatio* end, and updates to meet a specific set of circumstances begin. The distinction between poets and editors itself will also start to look less secure.

2. ORGANISATION OF SEQUENCES

The poetry of apotelesmata consists of micro-segments (endlessly repeated *if-then*) strung together. It is happily attuned to a particular taste or compositional principle or even way of thinking, *Blockbildung*, the creation of macro-structures out of self-contained segments (i. 181, 212). But they must make cumulative sense for the whole not to fall into chaos, which is the impression the later books of the Manethoniana too often leave. M^a made it relatively easy to grasp what was going on, or rather the editor who was responsible for the final form of the collection left it easy to deduce, because catalogues were retained in their original order and themed sequences were preserved. This is not always the case in later books.

Koechly tackled this question for books 1 and 5, both of which he believed to be multi-authored. He tried to explain why an editor arranged the sequences of charts as he did. He did not address it for book 4, which he (rightly) considered single-authored. But in principle the questions do not differ. In the first place, book 4 also seems to have been subject to curtailment and apparent reshuffling. In the second, books 1 and 5 no less than 4 retain, to different degrees, the groupings of material that has been transmitted to their authors. One asks whether a poet was responsible for *this* collocation, an editor for *that*, resting (it would seem) on the assumption that the more ham-fisted the joins, the more likely blame is to be directed towards an editor. But the distinction between poets and editors starts to look less clear when it is realised that they are both essentially facing the same set or spectrum of choices, namely the transmission of inherited material on the one hand, and wadding or reordering it on the other. It is a false dichotomy to conceive of the one as creative, generative artists, the others as mere shufflers of blocks of text.

Let us be clear what this is not. At first sight, Fakas's term 'das assoziative Kompositionsprinzip' looks useful. He applied it to his analysis of Aratus,[56] who is a model for astrological poets, and whose weather-signs are another specimen of *if–then* literature. But with Aratus it is a matter of imitating archaic poetry, especially Hesiod. In the Manethoniana one is dealing with various possible principles of association which are a matter of the recycling of sub-literary lists: by elements of protasis, by outcome, by shared formal devices, and potentially in all cases by the retention of inherited clusters. Of these, the first two already came into play in the organisation of the τέχνη section in book 6 (i. 789–90). There appeared to be a tendency for groups to be organised around astrological set-up *within* an overall group that was subject-themed. But M^a turned out not to be following Θ- based sequences. These now become more important.

Koechly may have been unaware of the comparanda, but it is worth noting 5.137–88 ~ Θ p. 217.5–23 Περὶ μίμων as an instance of the excellence of his instincts. He could see that 5.137 seems to begin a τέχναι sequence, and suggested a group consisting of 5.137 καμπτομένοις ζῴοις + 149 ἐφ' ὑγροῖς + 154 ζῴοις ἐν ὀλισθηροῖσι—'nisi iam hic [sc. 149] aut supra [sc. at 137] longior continuarum figurarum series incohata est', which is precisely what it is. He even suggested that the charts as far as 201 were 'iam ab auctore hoc similive ordine disposita' (1851, lix), and that is exactly confirmed by Θ.

In the case of 4.170–449 ~ Θ chs. 85–96 we can now probe the places where M^b expands Θ's τέχναι sequence and suggest reasons for those insertions (which, given that there is no sign that book 4 is anything other than single-authored, *may* be the poet's choices, though could of course be those of an editor who is chopping and changing the text in front of him). The ordering principles are sometimes so hazy that suggestions about the rationale for the 'interpolations' vis-à-vis Θ can only be speculative.[57] But some rationale, or rationales, can be discerned, and what emerges is that several principles are in play:

(i) The most interesting cases are where M^b retains a sequence from M^a. We first leave the Θ sequence at 4.187–200 with two charts that are contiguous in M^a, in whom they directly *precede* the one that corresponded to 4.180–6. Later, 4.425–30 has no correlate in Θ's sequence, but does follow

---

[56] C. Fakas, *Der hellenistische Hesiod: Arats Phainomena und die Tradition der antiken Lehrepik* (Wiesbaden, 2001), 72–6, on Aratean 'digressions' which turn out to be very planned, and about shorter organised passages; 77–84, on the evocation of archaic catalogue poetry.

[57] Particularly unclear is the rationale for the long sequence from 4.347–94, a mixture of οἶνος, *trophe*, and parents. No one principle will explain this. Within the οἶνος mini-cluster we seem to see a couple of charts which preserve (in reverse) a sequence in Θ (4.347–58 ~ pp. 194.17–195.2) to which 4.359–61 could be a thematic add-on (sexual chicanery). The *trophe* charts (4.366–78) adhere closely to a mini-sequence in M^a (= 6.46–50 + 53–9). 4.431–6 also remains unaccounted for.

on from the previous chart in M^a. Note also that the three charts in 4.125–45 have their best matches in 6.480–90.

(ii) Some seem to be thematic add-ons. With the five charts inserted at 4.214–48, the rationale at least for the first three is thematic: they add various sorts of inspired person to the diviners of 4.210–13, though that does not hold good for the last two. Likewise, the rationale for the addition of 4.271–85 is clear; it is the chart of another type of popular entertainer (mime), though it is inserted ahead of, and made superordinate to, the 'original' items in the sequence (4.286–9 and thereafter).

(iii) Only a few are better explained by planetary agency or set-up. For the three charts inserted at 4.402–19, the link with the first two appears to be the set-up (conjunction of both malefics with a luminary) rather than the outcome, though 4.414–19 cannot be explained on that hypothesis.

Perhaps in some cases it is appropriate to think of poet-compilers who have several sources in front of them, and are trying to balance the competing considerations of fidelity to a transmitted original and compendiousness. Appealing to the evidence of Θ, and assuming it to represent the kind of source on which M^b drew, does, it is true, only push the problem one stage further back. But it suggests that the question is not always, 'Why did the poet (or editor) order a sequence in this way?' He was following tradition. Fidelity to a transmitted *Urtext* also shows up in a small way in the charts carried over from M^b to M^c. While most of them are reordered, 4.395–413 corresponds to 1.321–38, which has been preserved despite the entirely non-rational leap from professions to parents.

Book 1

Book 1 poses a different problem, whether or not one fully endorses Koechly's thesis of multiple authorship. Themed groups, which Koechly did not know, can still be found there, most sustainedly a group of Π- charts (58–88, oddly divided by two on kings and their friends in 66–9 + 70–4). But the fewer the correspondences with sequences elsewhere, the harder it is to defer the problem by pushing it back to a source ('the poet was just copying'), and the harder to find any alternative to Koechly's original method. In proportion as sequences with underlying parallels become shorter, and the disjuncts between groups become harsher, the more one finds oneself asking questions about the rationale of the arranger.

Koechly was, as always, asking the right questions, but his approach in this book faces certain methodological difficulties. He noted that many charts shared key words, phrases, and motifs. He used lexical similarities to argue for common authorship,[58] which is entirely reasonable. But he often also used lexical similarities to explain editorial arrangement, and it is not always apparent why the similarity was taken to be evidence of the one thing rather than the other. That said, there is at least a cogency to the claim to editorial intervention when the charts are in immediate or very close proximity to one another.[59] But it is more difficult, and harder to know what to think, when they are not; the more widely separated the charts, the less plausible editorial jiggery-pokery becomes.[60] Sometimes it is not clear from hand-waving at similarities ('cf.'; 'similia vide haec') what we are supposed to think, or what conclusions to draw.[61] Sometimes his strictures at arbitrary collocations turn out to be within sequences which he attributes to one and the same poet, so that the problem is as soon compositional as editorial.[62]

Koechly posited that certain sequences were based on shared subject-matter. That is not very easy to sustain. He identified clusters on *res venereas* (1.18–25, 29–33, 42–9) and kings (1.26–8, 34–6, 41), but they are vague, not very impressive, and overlap in a confusing way. But his connection of 106–14 (incest) with 115–28 (eunuchs) is more convincing, since the three basic charts involved here, if not their add-ons, are all attested in Firmicus, 6.30.[63] It is the common

---

[58] Koechly 1851, lv. The difference between author and editor emerges clearly from the placement of 1.262–76, sundered from 1.215–28 (with which it has similarities of diction) and linked instead to 250 and 256 through the presence of Mars and Saturn in 263.

[59] 1.130 βαίνοντες ὁμοῦ + 134 συμβάλλουσα; 271 κερόεσσα Σελήνη + 277 ἡ Κερόεσσα; 272 μοίρης ἐντὸς ἐοῦσα + 278 κατὰ μοῖραν ἰοῦσα. He explained the placement of 1.196–207 (why sacrifice?) after 1.185–95 (miscarriage) through the references to birth and infancy (1.199 γένεσιν ... ἀνδρῶν, 200 νηπιάχοις) as well as by the presence of Zeus (p. 154).

[60] Non-contiguous charts: 1.41 Ζηνὸς ἄτερ + 56 ἄτερ Ζηνός ('locus huc illatus'); 66 κέντρων + 75 κέντροισιν ἐπὼν + 90 κεντρωθείς; 70 μεσουρανέοντες + 83 μεσουρανέων; 74 + 108 συναφὴν; 85 πολυπήμονας + 110 δυστλήμονες; 91 ἐμμανέας + 111 μαινόμενοι; 123 κέντρον ἔχοι + 130 κέντρα λαβόντες; 115 ἐπεμβαίνουσα τόποισιν + 135 ἔχοντι τόπον; 120 ἀποτμήξειε σιδήρῳ + 136 τέμνονται ὑπ᾽ ἀνδροφόνοιο σιδήρου.

[61] (i) 1.175 Ζεὺς δ᾽ ἐσιδὼν ~ 182 εἰ δὲ Ζεὺς ἐσίδοι ~ 194 εἰ δὲ Ζεὺς ἐσίδοι: it turns out from his later analysis that he regards 182 and 194 as the work of the same poet, but not 175. (ii) He compares various lines within 1.167–75 + 176–9 to previous passages ('in singulis quibusdam antecedentibus appropinquant') which turn out, from his subsequent dissection of the poem, partly to emanate from the same hand (174 θνήσκουσι σιδήρῳ ~ 136 ὑπ᾽ ἀνδροφόνοιο σιδήρου), and partly from different ones (178 σίνος αἰνόν ~ 135 σίνος ἀνδράσιν αὐτίκα ῥέξει; 179 ἢ πάθος, ἢ πλώουσιν [ἢ πέλαγος πλώουσιν K] ~ 143 καὶ νῆες πελάγεσσιν ἐπιπλώουσαι). (iii) He compares the effects of Mars in 1.178–9 λύπας καὶ θορύβους, ἐγκλήματα καὶ σίνος αἰνόν | ἢ πάθος and 220–1 πενίη τε κακὴ θόρυβοί τε μάχαι τε, | ἐγκλήσεις μεγάλαι, περὶ σώματος ἔσθ᾽ ὅτ᾽ ἀγῶνες, but does not regard the poets as identical (although those of 183 and 228 are).

[62] 1851, li (apropos of the link between 129–33 with 115–27: 'hoc postremum mirum, immo incredibile videatur ei, qui talia non investigavit; nobis quidem hoc ipsum vel maximum est signum aliud in his anthologiis vinculum frustra quaeri. Similia passim Lehrsius in Hesiodo notavit' [intriguing; there is no reference]. On the analysis of the book which he advances in lv, these are both by poet 'A'.

[63] Koechly proposed the same thematic linkage in 5.202–8 + 209–16, which would be a collocation of two different types of chart (the second, but not the first, is in the gendered luminaries series).

source rather than the vaguely similar domain that lends this conviction—and makes it likelier to be poetic than editorial.

On the other hand, linkage by agency and by set-up is apparently much more important in this collection:

1.58–61 + 62–5. Two Venus/Mercury charts, yielding musicians. This looks editorial.

1.96–7 + 98–9 (elegiac couplet). On the mitigation of Mars by the Sun. Koechly's transposition of 114 to form part of this mini-series is defensible (and followed by De Stefani), but he thought that they were concatenated here because of a non-existent mention of Mars before 1.77.

1.229–62. A group of five charts on malefics (*only* Mars in 245) with the Moon or Venus, whose outcome is mental or moral defect, or impoverishment.

1.262–76. Three more charts involving both malefics positioned together, along with both benefics, Jupiter alone, or the Moon, producing impoverishment or instability.

1.339–40 + 341–52 (elegiac) + 353–6 + 357–8. A possible sequence involving Mars and Saturn. Curiously, although as it stands 1.334–8 (the last of the charts shared with M^b) involves only Mars, in its original form (4.409–13) it, too, involved both malefics.

These are sufficient to establish the point, even setting to one side what Koechly considered to be editorial collocations by planet, some of which are very loose indeed.[64] Were these latter to be accepted, they would imply an even fuzzier model than my own, ie. an editor whose concern is not with strict sequencing or the retention of items juxtaposed in a source, but with putting a chart in only the right *approximate* vicinity.

Conversely, linkage by agency provides the only discernible explanation for the sundering of a group of charts which patently belong together (the medical charts of 1.50–7, 134–8, 153–7 + 158–66, 185–95). In these, *synaphe* and *aporrhoia* from the Moon to and from malefics causes a range of bodily diseases and harms, and what demonstrates their cohesion, apart from the shared theme, are parallels in *Π.σ.α.*, and the retention, despite so much tampering, of an underlying order (p. 314). Ad hoc reasons for the severance can be found in

---

[64] Some involve items that are directly juxtaposed (1.45 and 51, Saturn). Others do not (1.58, 62 Ἑρμῆς and 70, 89 Ἑρμείας; 1.115 (Moon), 119 (Mars), and 134 (both); 1.186, 194, and 208, the Moon's *synaphe* with Mars, then Jupiter; 1.208 and 224, the Moon), or imply just an imprecise perception that a planet is receiving particular prominence in a section (1.215 Mars, 'de quo tam multa iam habuimus'), or involve so many entities that it is far from clear that the net is fine enough to catch a genuine association (1.58–9 and 62–5, Mercury, the Moon, Venus, and Jupiter, 'eosdem qui supra memorati sunt planetas').

each case; put together they imply an editor who would happily rupture continuity in the interests of making connections by planet.[65]

To complicate matters, however, there are other instances where agency-based groups have been sundered.

> (i) 1.26–33 are two continuous charts on gendered luminaries which look as if they will begin a sequence from which subsequent members seem to have been disaggregated. (*a*) 1.115–18 has been sundered from its sister-chart in 1.29–33. Why? In its new environment it is run together with another eunuch chart (121–8) which contains two elegiac couplets. Did an editor choose to override coherence of set-up in favour of shared theme (for once), and then draw together miscellaneous material, some of it potentially Anubion-based?[66] (*b*) The royal charts in 1.277–85 are also related to 1.26–8 (both have a common stock in Firmicus, 7.22), but widely separated from them. Here it is not at all easy to understand the rationale for their current placement (kings follow impoverishment and precede τέχναι).
> (ii) The 'why sacrifice' passage (1.196–207) also sunders Jupiter-related material between 1.194–5 and 1.208–14 (and persisting in 1.215–28). Koechly (1851, lii) suggested that it might have been the effective uselessness of the (traditional) king of the gods (1.195) which led to the full-blown tirade about the gods as a collective. It is hard to think of anything better.

Book 5

This book is slightly less dispiriting than the previous one insofar as the identification of sequences makes it possible to advance a little beyond Koechly. It is in the last third of the book, especially, that a sense of order tends to fall away and one is left with the unsatisfying and inconclusive connections by agency[67] and shared diction or motifs.[68] But before that, we have the τέχναι sequence in

---

[65] Saturn in 45–9 + 50–7; Mars in 134–8 rolled over into the *schetliasmos* of 139–52; Mars in 158–66 rolled over into 167–79 before returning to more diseases in 185–95, though the τέχναι charts of 180–4 strike an odd note, even if they *are* doctors.

[66] Koechly made it even more complicated and thought the same material had been treated, first in hexameters, and then in elegiacs.

[67] 5.139a and 145, Venus; 5.198 and 202, Saturn (and indeed all of 192–208); 5.217–18 malefics, 222 Moon, 225 malefics and Moon, 249–50 malefics + Moon.

[68] 239 γραφαῖς + 242 γραφαῖς + 245 εὔγραμμον; 254 ὀφθαλμὸν + 257 ὄμμα (even though these are different sorts of eye). Non-contiguous: 5.212 ταλαπείριον, 224 ἀτιμήτους, 231 πολύτλητον.

5.137–88, to which nothing need be added to the earlier discussion, and the long section in 5.44–129, which I have called the Good and Bad Stars because it consists of a list of their good and bad qualities. Koechly saw that 5.44–108 belonged together. But he did not grasp the qualitative ordering principle, which is still just about discernible. Instead, by applying his usual associative method,[69] he produced the unnecessarily complicated hypothesis that it was a multi-author compilation,[70] and for once failed to see that 109–29 belonged in the same block. The truth is considerably more consoling. This is a single-author sequence. It is held together by formal means, so that although most segments are asyndetic they are linked by the pattern that each begins with the entity (5.84, 93, 103, 115, 120), mostly in the nominative, and often a comment on its quality (5.62, 66, 74, 81, 100, 105, 108, 109, 113, 127). This suggests a conscious and purposeful procedure to keep them together as a group, even though the departures from the qualitative principle (p. 890) indicate a certain amount of disruption.

Nothing else quite matches this, but a short sequence of almost[71] contiguous charts in 5.211–12, 214–15, 222–4, has the pattern 'if you should see/find, know/forecast that', which is a refinement of the *if–then* sequence (similar to Anubion, F 3a, d). Each employs the didactic verb νόει. Koechly apparently thought that this was an editorial combination (on 222–4, 'adiectum ad'), but the charts, all concerned with the placement of luminaries in signs of the opposite gender, or the Moon in the Sun's, look as if they belong together. I would look instead to Hellenistic didactic, first for the technique of opening sections with didactic verbs ('see', 'understand', 'forecast'),[72] and, second, for aligning parallel segments with similar opening phrases. If that is the right place to look, this would be a mildly striking finding. Instances of apotelesmata being linked together by formal devices at the beginning, drawing attention to sequences of items meant to be taken together, are generally rare. Aratus uses such alignments from time to time, using the same conditional incipit in the weather signs,[73] but though it might seem an obvious device for astrological poets to

---

[69] 5.108 + 110 ἐπὶ τὸν Δία; 113 Πλησιφαὴς Μήνη ἐπὶ τὸν Κρόνον + 115 Πλησιφαὴς δ' ἀκτῖσιν ἀπορρείουσα Κρόνοιο ('adnexum antecedentibus', as if through a casual similarity of diction); 114 πλοῦτον + 125 πλούτῳ.

[70] lvi: 'a variis poetis particulas fere minores continet, eodem sive sententiae sive vocum similitudinis artificio consertas'.

[71] Somehow 217–21 (which also has 'if you see', but no νόει) has intruded. There is one subsequent example in 5.231, where σύ νόει γε (unaccompanied by 'if you find') is stranded in a completely different kind of chart; Koechly was right to suspect an interpolation.

[72] On didactic verbs (φράζεο, πιφαύσκεο, τεκμαίρευ, etc.) as segment-openers in Nicander, see Bone, 34–5.

[73] Fakas, 83, citing εἰ δέ [κε] in Aratus, 788, 792, 794, 811; Bone, 30–1 for Nicander and 31–2 for Aratus.

flag sequences and encourage the reader, it is not a feature cultivated in the Manethoniana, not even in M^a, whose poem looks most like a worked-up artefact which is meant to have a certain integrity. There are some cases where broadly groupable charts begin in broadly similar ways,[74] but not strong enough to thrust themselves on the attention, and it looks like an uninterpretable tick. It is very far from the case that *all* groupable charts have a distinctive style of beginning.[75]

Finally, 5.49 δείμαινε and 5.54 τάρβει are a matching pair, combining (with a modest degree of art) line-initial ἀρχαί (for Mars) with final τελευτήν (for Saturn). But these stand within a segment. In general, as far as we can see, it is within, rather than across, segments that poets direct their best efforts at connection. They seem more interested in how individual items are held together, in unity *within* than in continuity *across* components. And that is the subject of the next, and one hopes more conclusive, section.

3. INTERNAL PATTERNING

Astrological poetry consists of a series of self-contained segments, mostly apotelesmata, but other material as well (such as the procedural rules in M^a and the proems, polemics, and asides in M^c). There is scope for marking off both their beginnings and ends.

An extensive analysis of the *if–then* structure of apotelesmata was already given in i. 213–16. I add here that they produce an *ipso facto*[76] version of a

---

[74] For instance, the long discursive charts in M^d (p. 321) stand out from their contexts by beginning, not with a conditional or temporal clause, as most of the charts in their vicinity do (few exceptions: 159, 246, 316), but with asyndeton and a proper name (or minor modification): 5.225 (epithet αὐξιφαής comes first), 260 (definite article), 284 (prepositional phrase precedes nominative), 332 (proper name in accusative). But as the book stands, they are separated. In M^b there is a tendency for certain mainly τέχναι charts to begin with the name of the planet in the nominative (4.131–64 [5/6 charts]; 4.395–449 [4/6 τέχναι charts; of the exceptions, 437 has the name in the accusative instead, which leaves only 431, while 444 is an add-on, and 402 and 409 are 'parent' charts anyway, so do not count]; 4.560–81 [3/4 charts]. Yet this is not a feature of the main τέχναι block running from 170–346 (only in 4.230, 271, and in the accusative at 4.201). The nominative personal name incipit is also bunched within the Good and Bad Stars (5.39, 66, 84, 93, 103; 260, with article).

[75] Medical charts: 1.50–1 μή + prohibition; 153 εἰ, 158 ἤν; 185 relative clause; 134 and 229 nominatives with executive verb. The Περὶ μίμων sequence has mostly 'if' or 'when' clauses, but a genitive absolute in 5.159 and perhaps a declarative statement in 5.103 (the outlier).

[76] Or almost *ipso facto*, except where the author deliberately flouts the traditional format by placing the apodosis first (i. 215).

device which Hellenistic didactic poets invest with more art and self-consciousness. This is the technique of 'front-loading' each segment by placing the key entities—in this case, the proper names of planets and constellations—at the head. Hellenistic didactic which employs this technique has a choice whether to use it or not. In astrology, however, it is totally routine, and that is why I suggest that it is segment-end that offers scope for rather more distinctive literary effects. It has been observed that Aratus likes to end sections with 'impressive' formal devices, including tetracola, spondeiazontes, and rhyme, homoeoteleuton, and parallelism.[77] These devices are all the more striking when they fill the line with homogeneous content, adding sonorousness and insistence to the message.[78] Aratus set a standard for subsequent star poetry, and every poet of the corpus draws on this basic stylistic repertoire with his own preferences and mannerisms. It is more important, it seems, to create series of closed units than to signal to the reader that items are to be read sequentially. So much so that they go much further than Aratus in using parallelisms, repetitional devices, and rhyme, to hold entire, or almost entire, segments together.

To begin with specifically closural devices, we can be reasonably confident that the spondeiazon is being used in this way if, of their total occurrences in each poet, respectively 27.6% (8/29) in M^b, over a third (8/21) in M^c (A), and no fewer than two out of five in M^d are at segment end. Bone is impressed enough by a figure of 23% of Aratean spondeiazontes at section- or sub-section end to regard it as significant, so presumably the figures for the Manethoniana are even more so. Indeed, 1.227–8 is both a double spondeiazon and a double tetracolon, rounding off a section on bigwigs whose pomp and circumstance (they include priests) the devices might be thought to evoke (p. 305); likewise the tetracolon 5.24 impressively concludes the proem on Homer with a reference to precious sea-purple. We find a rather different pattern in M^a. They increase as the work progresses. In book 2, a figure of merely 5/35 (= 14.3%), one of which is double, defies expectations that Aratean imitation might have brought out this mannerism (on the contrary, there is only a single instance in the Aratea).[79] There are 2/10 in the third book, but almost a third in the sixth, including one to round off the poet's own horoscope.[80] This marked increased in ambition from the less 'artistic' books to the more artistic one runs entirely parallel to the other stylistic niceties (including more involuted word-order) in which M^a increasingly invests as the poem progresses.

---

[77] Bone, 39–41; he contrasts Nicander, who prefers content to formal devices for closure.
[78] Bone, 40, notes Aratus, 401 δινωτοὶ κύκλῳ περιηγέες εἰλίσσονται.
[79] 2.100, 208–9, 265, 409 (5/35).
[80] 3.35, 379 (2/10); 6.50, 59, 98, 310, 455, 493, 603, 750 (end of horoscope) (8/25).

As for tetracola themselves, the later books are less revealing. In M^b the tetracolon is too blunt an instrument for it to be clear that the poet is using it as a closural device.[81] In M^c there are only ten (one repeated) tetracola with grammatical words, of which 227–8 constitute the end of a unit and 228 = 183, which is not much. And in M^d, there is only the spondeiazon at 24, which was noted above as a stand-out. In M^a, on the other hand, the pattern reinforces that of the spondeiazontes. In book 2, 1/8 stands at segment end (308), and in book 3, 2/6 (20, 252), but 8/19 in the sixth book (42, 68, 204, 226, 428, 435, 512, 525), once again signalling more stylistic ambition.

These devices are important, but even more so is parallelism. This is a useful effect when it comes to closure, but it is far from confined to that. It happens within lines (across hemistichs) and across lines, and can link together part or even the whole of an apotelesma (the entirety of an apodosis, or even protasis and apodosis). Ultimately, the structure of the hexameter itself is friendly to it and the style has its origins in EGHP, though it is instructive to consider precisely which aspects are anticipated there (noun-attribute pairs and line-internal *parisa*) and which aspects have been developed since EGHP (sustained isocola and self-conscious parallelisms that reach across two or more lines, which EGHP, in contrast, tends to avoid).[82] Perhaps the most telling difference of all is that what, in EGHP, had tended to accompany divine names, predications, descriptions of mythological subject-matter or remote places, and especially the *locus amoenus* or earthly paradise, now, in astrological verse, is used for stars, on the one hand, but also for their innumerable earthly effects, on the other. What had been a marker of exceptionalism is now transferred to the everyday. Or perhaps, in the astrological universe, there is no such thing as the everyday in which every tiniest event is a manifestation of cosmic force.

As far as star-poetry is concerned, the parallelistic style has particularly useful antecedents in Aratus, and ultimately in Hesiod.[83] Aratus uses word-patterning (noted by Kidd, 28–9, as a feature of his style) to model layout or location, in the paranatellonta especially for constellations that lie adjacent or opposite, while the opposite and balancing motions of rising and setting are

---

[81] 192, 346, 419, 514 (well nigh), 518, 570, 592 = 7/45 instances.

[82] Fehling, 308–25. *Il.* 1.157, 18.576 are nice examples of line-internal *parisa* with noun + epithet (Fehling, 322–3). Formally correct parallelisms across lines like *Od.* 5.331–2 (simile), 6.43–4 (earthly paradise), and *HHom. Aphr.* 97–8 (divine predication) are unusual (Fehling, 313–14, 316); more obtrusive examples are found in later verse (Call. *Hymn* 4.84–5; Fehling, 322). On the other hand, astrological poetry has no instances of parallelisms consisting of balancing couplets, of which there are occasional examples in EGHP (West on Hes. *Th.* 721–5; Fehling, 314).

[83] *Op.* 383–4, a chiasmus on the rising and setting of the Pleiades as the signals for reaping and ploughing.

modelled by parallelisms and chiasmus, especially of δύνειν and ἀντέλλειν.[84] Wordplay serves other purposes as well,[85] including achieving closural effects.[86] But the needs of the astrological poets are not those of Aratus, and, especially in the hands of the later poets in the corpus, the rudiments of the idiom with which he was associated have been developed into something like a house style for astrological poetry, a formal expectation, a genre feature.[87] Content and form are mutually supportive. Content contributes to the parallelistic style because apodoses consist of lists of like material; the parity of the outcomes is figured literally in the phonology, morphology, syntax, and metre of the poet's choice of words. The style is less common in the protasis, but there, too, it can suggest how each part of a configuration makes its contribution to the whole; doubtless it helps with the mnemonic effect as well. And form supports parallelism too, because these poets take a workmanlike approach to the hexameter in which it often breaks down into its two constituent hemistichs, each occupied with a unit of meaning, or even into the four units into which Fränkel

---

[84] At caesura and line-end: 341 καί οἱ ἐπαντέλλει, καί μιν κατιόντα δοκεύει; 534 καὶ τὰ μὲν ἀντέλλει καὶ αὐτίκα νειόθι δύνει; 571 τοὶ μὲν δύνοντες, τοὶ δ' ἐξ ἑτέρης ἀνιόντες; 617 ἀμφότερον δύνοντα καὶ ἐξ ἑτέρης ἀνιόντα; at successive caesurae: 555–6 ἐξ αἰεὶ δύνουσι δυωδεκάδες κύκλοιο, | τόσσαι δ' ἀντέλλουσι; 597–8 Παρθένος ἀντέλλουσα. Λύρη τότε Κυλληναίη | καὶ Δελφὶς δύνουσι; cf. 659–60 ἡ μὲν ἄρ' εἰς ἑτέρην φέρεται· τὰ δὲ νειόθεν ἄλλα | οὐρανὸς ἀντιφέρει. Successive parallel line-beginnings: 601–2 δύνει δ' Ἱππείη κεφαλή, δύνει δὲ καὶ αὐχήν | ἀντέλλει δ' Ὕδρη. 577–8 κατάγει… κατάγει models the parallel settings of two constellations. Chiasmus: 540 (ὅσσον ἀπάντη) ἀντέλλων ἐπέχει, τόσσον γε μὲν ἀλλόθι δύνων; 690–1 ἦμος καὶ Προκύων δύεται, τὰ δ' ἀνέρχεται ἄλλα, | Ὄρνις τ' Αἰητός τε τά τε πτερόεντος Ὀϊστοῦ; chiasmus of the constellation's own name in 693–4 Ἵππος δ'… ἀντία δ' Ἵππου.

[85] Anaphora and polyptoton may suggest quantity or duration (377–8 πολλοὶ γὰρ πάντη, πολέων δ' ἐπὶ ἶσα πέλονται | μέτρα τε καὶ χροιή, πάντες γε μὲν ἀμφιέλικτοι; 458–9 μακροὶ δέ… μακρὰ δέ), and—approaching more closely the literary concerns of the Manethoniana—itemisation in an inventory (481–2 ἐν δέ οἱ… ἐν δέ τε; 572 δύνει μὲν Στέφανος, δύνει δὲ κατὰ ῥάχιν Ἰχθύς; 573 ἥμισυ μέν κεν ἴδοιο μετήορον, ἥμισυ δ' ἤδη… models the semi-visible nature of the constellation). Parechesis is used for related constellations or their parts in 665 Τόξῳ καὶ σπείρη Ὄφιος καὶ σῶμ' Ὀφιούχου; 673 τόξῳ ἀνέρχονται καὶ Τοξότη ἀντέλλοντι. Chiasmus at 507–9 τὸν πύματον καθαροῖο παρερχόμενος βορέαο | ἐς νότον ἠέλιος φέρεται· τρέπεται γε μὲν αὐτοῦ | χειμέριος models the turning of the Sun at the winter tropic. A series of parallel verbs located at the caesura in 444–7 (καλέουσι)… εἰλεῖται… ἱκνεῖται… κρέμαται models the elongated shape of the constellation Hydra.

[86] Couplets at 237–8 εὐάστερός ἐστιν / ἀστέρες εἰσίν (rounding off a little section on Deltoton); 266–7 χείματος ἀρχομένοιο / ἐπερχομένου τ' ἀρότοιο (rounding off the Pleiades, a double effect with assonance and homoeoteleuton) (both noted by Bone, 40). Both items connect one item (star-cluster) to another. Possibly 384 φαίνονται ~ 385 φέρονται at opposite ends of the line (at the end of Lepus and the digression on stars not formed into constellations). The intended effect of the homoeoteleuton across segments in 394–5 εἰλίσσονται | φορέονται is unclear, at least to me.

[87] Taken as a whole Aratus is not a model for the strong end-stopping found in M^c and M^d. There are examples where bites of information are allocated to metrical units (halflines in 487–8 ὁπλαὶ δ' Ἵππειοι, καὶ ὑπαύχενον Ὀρνίθειον | ἄκρῃ σὺν κεφαλῇ, καλοί τ' Ὀφιούχεοι ὦμοι; whole lines in 471–2), but enjambment, liberally employed by Aratus, works against such neat apportionment (see Kidd on 97 for enjambment with proper names; at 691–2 Ὄρνις τ' Αἰητός τε τά τε πτερόεντος Ὀϊστοῦ | τείρεα the enjambed word is a common noun).

divided it, each again occupied with a unit of meaning.[88] Such-and-such a combination of stars produces a series of instances of a given type, each severally enumerated, and/or elaborated with decorative detail.

Astrological poets have no monopoly on any of these devices. They sit very happily in other genres, such as hymn.[89] They suit the sing-song style of an oracle. Some of the Sibylline poets weaponise accumulations of parallel elements (units of the line, or half-lines, or full lines) for accusatory jabs, indictments, threats (and more rarely promises), and woe-sayings,[90] and they pack the hexameter with like content to stay on message about anger, outrage, and atrocity. Yet even here it is hard to find anything quite like the enmeshment of sense, syntax, and metre which produces the characteristic effects of the Manethoniana. It is in demand to close segments, but also to suggest a momentum towards closure which is diverted by what a Scorpio might call the sting in the tail:[91] a parallelism stretching over two or more lines is broken off by a sudden change of rhythm. It is worth suggesting that the sting in the tail, which is used by all poets in the corpus, is a useful mode of sign-off because it combines a sense of drawing a line in an aesthetic (phonic) sense without suggesting that the set is *de facto* closed or bounded[92] (which, given the infinite variety

---

[88] H. Fränkel, *Wege und Formen frühgriechischen Denkens: Literarische und philosophiegeschichtliche Studien* (Munich, 1968), 100–56. Strictly, Fränkel's schematisation of the hexameter will not work as a template for the many lines with a feminine caesura and a caesura after the fifth longum (why did he not allow for a C_3 in this place?), nor for the much rarer hexameters without a third-foot caesura. Otherwise it serves well enough.

[89] Used sparingly by Isidorus: see *Hymn* 3.20–5 (the last three ἢ καί); jingles at line-end: *Hymn* 1.13–17, five lines ending in an [i] sound. Scale up to Greg. Naz. *PG* 37.507, Ὕμνος εἰς Θεόν, ll. 2–7, a series of couplets whose singsong parallelism puts even M^d to shame. Presumably a case like this is to be seen as a hybrid of Greek rhetorical isocolon with Hebrew parallelism, which has already borne fruit in the New Testament (E. Norden, *Agnostos Theos: Untersuchungen zur Formengeschichte religiöser Rede* (Leipzig, 1913), 254–63, noting that Hes. *Op.* 1–8 already helped to entrench the style in hymn).

[90] Weaponisation: e.g. 5.72, 80–4, 228–45 (indictment of Hybris), 390–3 ἐν σοὶ γὰρ μήτηρ τέκνῳ ἐμίγη ἀθεμίστως, | καὶ θυγάτηρ γενετῆρι ἑῷ συζεύξατο νύμφη· | ἐν σοὶ καὶ βασιλεῖς στόμα δύσμορον ἐξεμίηναν, | ἐν σοὶ καὶ κτηνῶν εὗρον κοίτην κακοὶ ἄνδρες, an *enumeratio* of sexual outrages of equal and parallel heinousness. Woe-sayings: 5.289–90. Promises: 5.266–7. The fifth book also shows a strong tendency to construct the line out of two halves, each containing an information unit. This is well illustrated by the battle of the stars in 512–31 (main verbs, aorist and imperfect, stacked at the caesura in 514, 518, 522, 523, 524, 525, 526). Formal parallelisms with rhyme across whole lines are not found evenly throughout the book, but consider the series of prophecies against named places in 118–23 (six self-contained lines, four asyndetic, five ending with future indicative verbs, three with rhyme; Gorgianic jingle in 121 βαθὺν εἰς βυθὸν), or 204–5.

[91] To the examples cited in i. 219 add Isidore, *Hymn* 1.6–8 (1st c. bc): καὶ θεσμοὺς κατέδειξας, | ἵν᾽ εὐδικίη τις ὑπάρχῃ, | καὶ τέχνας ἀνέδωκας, ἵν᾽ εὐσχήμων βίος εἴη, | καὶ πάντων τε φύσιν εὐανθέα εὗρεο καρπῶν; *Or. Sib.* 5.80–5, 118–21. Antecedents in Aratus, 202–4 (end of the section on Andromeda), τετάνυσται / ἀνέχονται / ἐκεῖναι [ἐκείνῃ *ex emend.*], and 364–6 (end of section on the chains binding Pisces) φορέονται / πειραίνονται / ἀκάνθῃ.

[92] On the bounded set: Galjanic, 105–6 (and *passim*); Lightfoot 2014, 94–5.

theoretically producible by the stars, it is presumably not). However, the parallelism may also bind together most or all of a segment, reinforcing the cohesiveness of the outcome with a cohesiveness of morphology and syntax; and it is useful as well for self-contained soundbites, for instance, lists of zodiacal signs of a given type, or 'apophthegms'.

One might expect this style to be correlated with the practice of end-stopping, and so, at least to some extent it proves. I sampled several hundred-line sections from each poet in the corpus and concentrated on the proportion of lines within each section which clearly coincided with sentence, colon, or phrase end, as opposed to lines where pauses were marginal or absent, and cases where a clause or phrase is syntactically complete but re-opened by an add-on in the next line. The parallelistic style is least obtrusive in M^a (hence far less was said about it in vol. i). The clearest contrast within the corpus is between this poet, on the one hand, who has lower proportions of clear-cut clause- and phrase-end, more marginal cases, and more instances of outright enjambment and add-ons, and M^c and M^d, on the other, in whom line-end tends much more strongly to coincide with colon- and sentence-end, with fewer marginal cases, and with much less enjambment. But the evidence of M^b, who proves far more like M^a in the variability of his line-end pauses, and yet who strongly exhibits the parallelistic style as well, shows that matters are more complicated. Not all of M^b's parallelisms are picked up by simply looking at pause at line-end. Rhymes need not imply a sense-pause (especially when they are not located at line-end, as at 4.196–7); chiasmus may be elegantly worked out, but need not correspond to line-divisions (e.g. 4.508–10); metrical parallelisms do not necessarily map onto syntax, and do not guarantee alignment of sense pauses (e.g. 4.222–3, 315–16). That suggests different poets (unsurprisingly) have different practices, have different 'voice-prints', are more or less mechanistic or more or less flexible in the way they construct their parallelisms.

Indeed, granted this style of composition, it is sometimes a fine call—perhaps not even very meaningful to ask—whether a given parallelism is 'intended' or 'inadvertent', a result of cellular technique. All the poets make use of the style I already analysed for the Sibylline oracles, where each of the four units of the hexameter is occupied by a unit of sense.[93] Very often these consist of parallel parts of speech, typically epithets or nouns, which are aligned, with or without connectives, all in the same case. Two, three, four (and more[94]) items can be stacked up in this way, depending on how much padding is used, and whether one of the units in the verse is occupied by a verb.[95] But essentially these are

---

[93] Lightfoot 2007, 196–7; i. 217.

[94] Five items in 5.67 (asyndetic); six in 5.133 (asyndetic); seven in 5.34 (asyndetic, planetary names).

[95] e.g. verb in second place in 4.31, 85, 178–9; 5.183. Verb in fourth place: 5.251, 283.

variations on a listing formulary which had taken the favoured form of the expanded tricolon in EGHP,[96] and now finds its ideal form in the 'rule of four'. Married up with the (also Sibylline) technique of cramming each verse unit with material of like content,[97] and finding its ideal expression in the tetracolon,[98] this produces a particularly forceful effect, not lugubrious, like the Sibyl, but crowded and multifarious, suggesting endless possibilities for variation on basic scripts. M^b and M^d both have particular likings for relentless lists of juxtaposed units (e.g. 4.277–84, 300–1, 305–7, 311–16, 342–3; 5.286–9, 335–8) which are better seen as particulate than parallelistic composition.[99] But the more the style gives rise to loud and ringing homoeoteleuta, rhymes, and half-rhymes (whether at caesura and line-end, in which case the line is called Leonine, or across successive lines); the more it gives rise to formal isocola; the more it builds itself into sequences terminated by the sting in the tail; and the more it is played off against its natural twin, the chiasmus—the more secure we can be that these parallelisms are self-consciously meant.

Syntax interacts in formal parallelisms with metre. The poets align units of sense (especially agent nouns and epithets, but also verbs) which are also parallel in syntax and scansion. But metre can also hold items together (mostly in adjacent, but sometimes also in non-adjacent, lines) even in the absence of strict syntactic parallelism. Some sequences are too formally perfect and too

---

[96] Where the last item has an ornamental epithet: 4.261, an epic pastiche (see ad loc.); 1.219 (a fairly feeble example); 5.308. Otherwise 4.284, 378, 540; 1.137 (from a medical chart); and cf. 4.358.

[97] Good examples in 4.199 (crucifixion), 427 (priests); 5.199–200 (modes of suicide) and 246–8 (scaly signs), but the style is *ipso facto* illustrated by any of the lists of related items discussed here.

[98] 4.57, 307, 563–4; 1.172, 178 (polysyndetic); 5.85, 286, 288–9.

[99] Koechly 1851, xxxviii, compares the asynetic lists of epithets in the Orphic Hymns stretching across even more lines at a time than the Manethoniana. A by-product of this syntactic and stylistic similarity is that both types of verse need to find ways of introducing verbs by other means, the Manethoniana in order to evoke the busy activity of the natives, the *Hymns* the divine narratives which the absence of the *pars epica* of the normal hymn withholds. The *Hymns* do this through verbal adjectives in -τός, deverbative adjectives, and participles (Galjanic, 216). The Manethoniana do it through agent nouns, participles, and compound adjectives with a verbal component (i. 214). The *Hymns* also employ sound-effects and jingles, especially homoeoarchon, anaphora, and parechesis (on their style, see Galjanic, 213–27). But they do so to completely different effect. Their incessant use of παν- as the repeated element expresses the god's totalising power, as does the chiasmus of 4.2, 15.7 ἀρχὴ πάντων πάντων τε τελευτή; the argument + negated argument motif in (e.g.) 10.10 αὐτοπάτωρ, ἀπάτωρ; 12.13 πολύπειρος, ἀπείριτος; 32.3 ἄρρητε, ῥητή implies a kind of boundlessness and lack of containment. Homoeoarchon (10.3–4, 16; 12.6; 25.1–2; 26.2; 66.5) suggests sameness/homogeneity, which is the opposite of the multiplicity the Manethonian apodosis wants to convey. Another device in which hymn is invested, and which astrology has little use for, is the merism, in which two components suggest a totality. There is an example at 1.139, but the slew of items in the succeeding lines suggests that the poet was not very comfortable with the device.

perfectly aligned with content to be anything other than purposeful. Sometimes they reinforce an analogy (or even sharpen a disanalogy: these things are only alike up to a point...). Sometimes they are aligned with other signs of high and ambitious style (metrical parallelisms are very strongly marked in the medical charts of M^c). In other cases, however, they spill across protases and apodoses or indeed across segments (from the end of one chart to the beginning of another), and so it is not *ipso facto* the case that metre is meant to draw parallelisms to our attention. Sometimes it may genuinely be that a rhythm (especially a popular one like 5d) has invaded the poet's ear.

The question of the degree to which individual poets have their own styles is addressed further in the sections on each separate poet, but clearly they do. M^b, as indicated above, is less mechanistic than either M^c or M^d. The Leonine hexameter is not absent from M^b, but is positively fetishised by both M^c and M^d. De Stefani found the last two so similar that he suggested they were the same poet. This is not completely untenable on stylistic grounds, though perhaps M^d has a particular fondness for isocola over two or more lines (especially elaborate in 5.160–4, the capriccio on musical instruments), while metre is a firmer criterion by which the two can be separated. One other particular mannerism is the relative and gnomic sign-off in M^b, a specialised form of the sting in the tail. Once again he shows that his range is somewhat wider than that of the latest two poets in the corpus.

4. STYLISTIC MARKERS IN EACH POET

Ut sua cuique facies, ut sua cuique vox, ut suus cuique mos et genius, ita suus cuique stilus.
                    Preface of Erasmus to the fourth Tome of Jerome

This section aims to see whether one can determine a 'voice print' for different poets in the collection. (Spoiler alert: the answer is to a large extent 'yes'.) The criteria used to distinguish between the styles of books are syntactical, in other words a matter of the deep structure of how the poets have decided to present their material. They are: asyndeton; delayed particles; the use of the definite article; temporal and conditional clauses and their moods in the protasis; and tenses in the apodosis.

Asyndeton

Connectives and lack of connectives do allow us to distinguish between, on the one hand, the usages of M^a (almost invariably connected) and M^b (connected the great majority of the time), and, on the other, M^c and M^d (both variable and inconsistent). They do not take us much further with the question of multiple authorship within M^c, save for the special case of the block shared with the fourth book; indeed, if anything, they undermine the thesis that multiple poets were responsible for the rest. Frustratingly, they are not a completely reliable guide to sequencing either, with the stand-out exception of M^d's τέχναι group. Their presence and absence in M^c and M^d does not correlate with particular kinds of chart (save the long ones in M^d).

M^b. The charts are almost all connected (see p. 197). Even the sequences that begin in 14 and 170 do so with Πρῶτα μὲν οὖν, though there is no particle at the beginning of the sequence in 110 (σήματα θεῖα γενέθλης). Two of the other four exceptions likewise stand at identifiable moments of transition. 193 stands at the turn from a series of mainly τ- charts to a partly οἶνος chart, and 560 at the beginning of the oppositions across *kentra*. But 362 continues a group of οἶνος charts (sundered only by 359–61[100]), and for 567 there is no obvious reason.

M^c. This book, in contrast, is highly asyndetic, which is unsurprising in view of its disjointed character. In fact, the presence or absence of connection does not clearly support Koechly's distinctions between poets, except that (i) the material borrowed from M^b and (ii) the second two sections of 'C' (176–9 and 353–8) are connected, and the rest generally not. Poet A is mostly asyndetic except for add-ons, but there are connectives in 129, 235, 245, and then a run of five charts (267, 271, 277, 281, 284) directly before the M^b borrowings. For the relationship between subject-matter and the presence or absence of connection, see further on p. 286.

M^d. There are a few clear patterns in this book. Asyndeton generally prevails in the first half, with connectives used mostly for add-ons (but also in 28, 72, 109). That holds good until the sequence of τέχναι (137–88) and three following οἶνος charts (189–201), all of which are connected. Thereafter lacks of connection prevails over connection,[101] but not so as to reveal any clear pattern; for more detailed discussion, see pp. 329–30.

Delayed Particles

The willingness to delay particles does spread poets clearly across a spectrum. Overall, M^b is much the fondest of delayed particles, M^c least, and there is a sizeable gap between M^c and M^d. Once again, it provides no criterion for

---

[100] Unless τὸν in 362 is supposed to pick up Mercury from the chart before?
[101] Connection: 217, 243, 252, 256, 300, 324, 326. Asyndeton: 202, 209, 222, 225, 246, 260, 274, 282, 284, 316, 320, 332.

distinguishing between poets within the first book. Occurrences simply reflect the distribution of verses across the poets of the corpus.[102]

M^a: with δέ 1 per 78.8 lines;[103] with τε 1 per 90.92 lines;[104] with γάρ 2; total 30 = 1 per 39.4 lines.

M^b: with δέ 1 per 62.6 lines;[105] with τε 1 per 27.2 lines;[106] with γάρ 1; with μέν 2; total 36 = 1 per 17.4 lines.

M^c: with δέ 1 per 120.33 lines;[107] with τε 1 per 90.25 lines;[108] none with γάρ or μέν; total 7 = 1 per 51.57 lines.

M^d: with δέ 1 per 56.67 lines;[109] with τε 1 per 113.33 lines;[110] with γάρ 1 per 170 lines;[111] with μέν 1 per 340 lines; total 12 = 1 every 28.33 lines.

Thus, from most to least frequent the order for δέ is d,b,a,c, with M^d a little over twice as likely to do it than M^c (in other words these two poets differ in this respect). For τε it is b,c,a,d, with M^b about four times more likely to do it than M^d, while c and a are very close.

Definite Article

The use of the definite article is another good differentiator. M^d is the king of the definite article, and opens up a particularly sharp divide between him and the first book. The poet most loth to use it is, by a wide margin, M^a (except in the Aratea). Within each book, it does not usefully distinguish between one type of chart and another (I took τέχναι charts and found that the average was barely different for the average in their respective books as a whole). It does, on the other hand, seem to distinguish very clearly between strata and hence possibly poets in M^c, with three examples in pentameters (76, 99, 211) and another three concentrated within Koechly's poet F (277–85, including two instances of the name ἡ Κερόεσσα and one of the technical term τῶν ὀλοῶν), but only a single instance within the main poet, A, which is in the prose phrase τὴν πρᾶξιν (181).

---

[102] 30, 56, 82, 222, 235 are A; 339 is the *ineptus versificator*; 4 is the proem.
[103] Article–noun: 2.378. Preposition–noun: 2.422, 442, 494; 6.36, 583, 589, 649, 672. Noun–epithet: 2.425; 3.409. Other: 2.139; 3.253; 6.528, 554. In all, 15/1182.
[104] Noun–epithet: 2.99, 122, 173, 205, 239, 331 [*ex emend.*]; 3.240 (poss.); 6.423, 474. Preposition–noun: 6.11, 17. Preposition–epithet: 2.238. Other: 2.286. In all, max. 13/1182.
[105] 10/626. Instances on p. 197.
[106] 23/626 (excluding editorial restorations). Instances on p. 198.
[107] 3/361 (excluding ἔσθ' ὅτε δ'). Instances on p. 286.
[108] 4/361. Instances on p. 286.
[109] 6/340 (three others the result of emendation or restoration). Instances on p. 330.
[110] 3/340 (one other restored). Instances on p. 330.
[111] 2/340. Instances on p. 330.

M^a: see i. 115–16. The range is from 1 *per* 94 lines (book 6) to 1 *per* 214 lines (book 3), with the exception of the Aratea (1 *per* 15.56 lines).

M^b: see p. 198. 1 *per* 30 lines (1 *per* 37.57 lines among τέχναι).

M^c: see p. 287. 1 *per* 51.57 lines overall (1/43 lines among τέχναι), but see above: the average is not a meaningful figure.

M^d: see pp. 330–1. 1 *per* 5.15 or 5.67 lines (1 *per* 6.88 or 1 *per* 5.63 lines among τέχναι).[112]

Types and Moods of Clauses in the Protasis

(i) All poets in the corpus prefer conditional clauses to temporal, with the exception of M^b.

(ii) Books 1, 2, 4, and 5 prefer ἤν over εἰ to varying degrees, and M^b does not use εἰ at all. But from the fact that book 2 contains four and a half times as many instances of ἤν as εἰ, whereas books 3 and 6 contain respectively about 50% and 20% more instances of εἰ, it seems that choice of conditional conjunction *per se* does not necessarily offer any insight into a given author's preferences.

(iii) All poets in the corpus prefer the subjunctive to the optative, but only in the case of M^b is this so marked as to enable emendation of transmitted optatives with a clear conscience. Note that in the table below, the numbers given for the verbs of each mood are not necessarily equal to the headline numbers of εἰ and ἤν clauses because it is clearly not the case that there need be one verb *per* clause. There are also clauses containing more than one verb which begin with one mood then drift into another, indicated in the table with opt. > subj. or *vice versa*.

(iv) All books except 2 contain ἤν with the optative, but to varying extents. In book 3, only 1/16 verbs is 'wrong'. In book 6, 16/58 are 'wrong'. In book 4, only 2/40 are 'wrong' (assuming that indicatives can be emended with a clean conscience), and one is an 'honorary subjunctive' (i. 135–6) anyway. In book 1, overall 9/24 are 'wrong', while within poet A himself no fewer than 7/15 are 'wrong' (the highest percentage within the corpus, though four of them occur within a single clause). In book 5, 7/24 are 'wrong'.

---

[112] Maximum (including all transmitted) 66/340. Minimum (only those used in my text); 60/340.

Table 1. Temporal and conditional clauses and their moods in the protasis

	Book 2	Book 3	Book 6	Book 4	Book 1	Book 5
εἰ	2, of which	19, of which	52, of which	—	9, of which	17, of which
	subj. opt.	subj. opt.	subj. opt.	subj. opt.	subj. opt.	subj. opt.
	2 —	4 15	14 38	— —	3 6	6 10
	+ 1 opt. > subj.	+ 1 opt. > subj.	+ 4 opt. > subj.			+ 1 indic.
			+ 1 opt. > subj. > opt.			
			+ 3 subj. > opt.			
			+ 1 indic.			
ἤν	9, of which	13, of which	41, of which	31, of which	20, of which	24, of which
	subj. opt.	subj. opt.	subj. opt.	subj. opt.	subj. opt.	subj. opt.
	11 —	15 1	31 7	36 2	14 8	17 7[i]
			+ 5 opt. > subj.	+ 2 indic.	+ 1 subj. > opt.	
			+ 4 opt. > subj.			
			+ 1 subj. > ind.			
'When'	2, of which	14, of which	49, of which	39, of which	9, of which	6, of which
	subj. opt.	subj. opt.	subj. opt.	subj. opt.	subj. opt.	subj. opt.
	2 —	15 3	53 7	52 1	9 —	3 2
			+ 5 subj. > opt.			+ 1 indic.
			+ 2 opt. > subj.			
			+ 3 indic.			

[i] Including 169 [*ex emend.*].

(v) There is a similar pattern of wrongness in temporal clauses. Books 1, 2 contain no 'wrong' verbs, and book 4 only 1/53. On the other hand, book 3 contains 3/18 (in two clauses), book 6 15/80, and book 5 2/6 (or out of 7 including a Homer quotation).

Verbs in the Apodosis

It seems to me that the results of this investigation are particularly robust and revealing.

The first question is who the actors actually *are*, the stars or the natives. One poet might like to concentrate on the stars' effects, while another might want to elaborate on the natives acting out the results (or at least, might want to present those activities in verbal form rather than as nouns, epithets, or even participles). And we do indeed find differences. M[a] has many more references to stars (110) than natives (38). M[b], on the other hand, has more references to natives (103) than to stars (74 or 75), which is presumably a reflection of his very wordy apodoses. In the first book, there are somewhat more references to stars than natives (80/62), while M^d has significantly fewer references to stars than to natives in apotelesmata (respectively 35/61), but numbers would be made about even if one included his many generalisations about the stars (a further 26 verbs, twelve of which are in the Good and Bad Stars).

But one achieves a finer degree of differentiation by considering what the various tenses are used for. Although the stars repeatedly arrange themselves in similar ways, and natives are accordingly born with the appropriate characteristics, there might be differences, suggesting nuance in meaning, in the tenses the poets use to represent the one and the other. In the tabulation below, figures are given separately for stars (including both executive and factitive verbs, and where the stars bring about direct, specific effects) and for natives. The figure added to the natives (e.g., for M^a, 18 + 4) is for verbs whose subject is not the natives themselves, but which describe activities closely linked with the natives.

If one begins by asking what tenses are preferred for stars and natives respectively, the answer is that in each case there is a general pattern to which one book is an outlier. For stars, the general preference (to differing extents) is for presents over futures. This is not very surprising, for the protasis deals with recurrent states of affairs, not specific predictions; for that purpose the gnomic aorist is a ready alternative which actually supersedes the present in M^d and at least approaches it in M^a (but is not popular with M^b). For natives, again the general preference is for the present. M^a uses it slightly more often than the aorist; M^c has nearly three times as many presents as futures; and M^d has over six times as many present as futures.[113] The outlier is M^b, who likes to present his charts as predictions (i. 142) and uses the future over twice as often as the present.

Turning the question around and asking what the various tenses are used for partly restates the matter, but also adds further precision. The only real fan of the future tense is M^b, who uses it mainly for natives; in this way, the forecasts are presented as prophecies rather than timeless descriptions (i. 142). No one favours it for the stars, though numbers are kept up in M^b by the ἔσσεσθαι δείκνυσι construction. The various strata of M^c use it (10/80 verbs for stars), but do not prefer it. But in both M^a and M^d there is only a single use of the future tense for a star.

The present, on the other hand, presents a somewhat more complex picture.

In M^a, while there are numerically many more references to stars than natives, within each category the present is almost exactly as likely to be used for stars (58.18%) and for natives (57.89%); there is no bias towards the one or the other.

---

[113] On the few occasions where M^d uses the future, it tends to cluster (4/7 possible instances in one of the long discursive charts).

M^b, on the other hand, who has more references to natives than to stars, is very considerably more likely to apply the present to stars: 91.25% of verbs used for stars are present,[114] but only 29.13% of sentences referring to natives are.

M^c has 80 references to stars and 62 to natives. 65% of the stars, 69.35% of natives, are present.

M^d has 35 references to stars and 61 to natives in apotelesmata. 42.86% of the former, 78.69% of the latter, are present, but including generalisations about the stars alongside the apotelesmata would bring the figure for the present tense to around 67%, in other words to a very similar level to that in M^c(A).

These characteristics run *through and within* their respective books. They do not correspond to any particular kind of chart distributed *across* different books. There may be particular concentrations of one type of thing within a particular apotelesma (e.g. the present tense description of the natives within 5.225–42, 284–99, and 300–12, which together make up over half the total number of present tenses used of natives in that particular book; or the future tenses used for the natives in 1.312–20). But that finding remains localised. There are no similarities across charts in different books; it is not the case (for instance) that the τέχναι charts across the different books all manifest a particular tendency or pattern.

	Book 2 (ex 148)		Book 4 (ex 177 or 178)		Book 1 (ex 142)		Book 5 (ex 96)	
Present	86 = 58.11%		71(72) = 41.01%		95 = 66.9%		63 = 65.63%	
…of which	stars	natives	stars	natives	stars	natives	stars[115]	natives
	64	18 + 4	41(42)	12 + 18	52	43	15	48
Future	4 = 2.7%		75 = 42.13%		25 = 17.61%		8 = 8.33%	
…of which	stars	natives	stars	natives	stars	natives	stars	natives
	1	3	7 + 2	60 + 6	9 + 1	15	1	6 + 1
ἔσεσθαι δείκνυσι	—		24 = 13.48%		1		—	
Aorist	58 = 39.19%		7 = 3.93%		21 = 14.79%		25 = 26.04%	
…of which	stars	natives	stars	natives	stars	natives	stars	natives
	45	13	2	2 + 3	17	2 + 2	19	4 + 2

Conclusions

This investigation has shown that some types of analysis reveal particularly clear voice-prints among the poets of the collection. If the hypothesis that all

---

[114] Including the ἔσεσθαι δείκνυσι construction (56.76% without that).

[115] Significantly fewer than in other books because M^d is so fond of the 'who whom' construction (i. 215).

τέχναι charts were by one author and scattered by an editor across different books of the collection needed refutation, this analysis decisively achieves that end. It also (more constructively) fleshes out our idea of the activity of astrological poets. It is clear that there is a common stock of material which authors realise in their idiosyncratic ways. In other words the analogy with 'evolved' literature (i. xxiii), whereby tradents hand down a (religious, philosophical, dogmatic) tradition in which there is certainly editorial activity, but in which imposing a personal stamp on the material in question is most certainly not the aim, is only very limitedly helpful. These poets have very individualisable styles.

Of the various criteria, asyndeton is perhaps the least helpful, since what it differentiates is presumably, in the first instance, methods of organisation rather than personalities of narrator; the same poet could adopt or jettison connectives according to need. But delayed particles, the definite article, and the tenses of the apodosis are very good differentiators. Temporal and conditional clauses in the protasis further illustrate the peculiarities of M^b (who prefers ἤν and the subjunctive over and above all else), although some of the variation here may be the result of distortions that have come about in transmission (such as confusions of mood and even of conjunctions; for this whole thorny subject, see i. 135–41).

The poet who consistently stands out is M^b, while the books that stand closest together are the first and the fifth. Even there, M^d has far more definite articles, is much fonder of delaying δέ after second position, is wedded to the 'who whom' construction' (and hence has fewer verbs in the apodosis whose subject is the stars), and is less fond of the future in the apodosis (even allowing for the fact that their number in M^c is inflated by the borrowings from M^b).

Given that stylistic criteria differentiate so clearly *between* books, it is possible that they might, in the case of M^c, be brought to bear *within* them. The problem is the dearth of what survives for anything other than $M^c(A)$, and for the lines borrowed from M^b, whose extraneous character was clear already. Conditional and temporal clauses and moods within them are only meaningful for A, who simply replicates the tendencies found throughout the corpus, and the excerpts from M^b.[116] The same is true for tenses in the apodosis, where for A we find 72.83% presents, 15.22% gnomic aorists, and the rest futures, and for M^b the same pattern as in book 4 as a whole. The rather high representation of the definite article in the pentameters of book 1 comes as no surprise, though it might, for what the very small statistical sample is worth, throw into question the authorship of F (three in nine lines).

---

[116] A has 4 temporal clauses with 4 subjunctive verbs; 7 εἰ clauses with 4 optatives and 3 subjunctives; 12 ἤν clauses with 8 subjunctives and 7 optatives. In other words he replicates the preference for conditional over temporal clauses that we see in other poets, and within the former for ἤν over εἰ. The lines from M^b have two conditional and three temporal clauses (all subjunctive).

Additional note on the use of the second person in conditionals ('if you see') and imperatives ('forecast'). For the most part this is so distinctive of M^d, and to a lesser extent M^c, that I treat it there. The one feature on which I comment here is the 'be very afraid' motif, found in 5.49 δείμαινε, 5.54 τάρβει, 1.250 δείμαινε, and in the third person in 4.618 ταρβείτω. There are weaker forms in 1.51 μὴ Κρόνῳ ἀντήσειε and still weaker in 5.202 μὴ λαθέτω σε. It is not found in M^a.

This motif makes of the Manethoniana an affiliate of other 'guidance' literature. It is at home in didactic,[117] astrology,[118] and in other divinatory literature. In the *ecdosis altera* of the *Sortes Astrampsychi*, the instruction *not* to fear is far commoner than the positive version, but there is one instance of the latter at 47.8 βλαβῆναι ἕξεις. φοβοῦ καὶ σαυτὸν τήρει.[119] It is occasional in the *Sortes Sangallenses*: III.1 (*non poteris in expeditionem ire.*) *cave*; XXIV.11 *cave tibi*. One also thinks of Eliot's parody of tarot, 'Fear death by water' (The Waste Land).

5. ON THE PRESENTATION OF WORK

To finish with, let us return to content. Form and stylistics have served very well to distinguish poets and strata within them, but the final emphasis needs to be on the values and outlook that inform the collection as a whole. The next sections take the later books one by one, their language and mannerisms and more on style. All, however, come out of a single stable, all have a vision of human life which is expressed with more pungency by some poets than others, but combines a contemporary ethics of work with an agenda derived from its poetic inheritance (which is why it is treated here rather than in the chapter on work in Part One). The important words are about work, ἔργον, πόνος, κάματος, and others in the same domain which have a nexus that includes laborious effort, suffering, but also the outcome of those efforts, the product of labour, and the achievement or exploit that comes from endurance. I argue that some of the core values, perhaps *the* core values, of the Manethoniana come to them already

---

[117] Hes. *Op.* 736a = 758 ἐξαλέασθαι (after a command not to do something: West calls it a line-filler), 802; Aratus, 430 δείδιθι (although this is time-limited: fear *until* something happens to stop it). Nicander has various forms: μή σύ γε; forms of the optative/imperatival infinitive; *Ther.* 121 ἐξαλέασθαι. He also has 'do NOT fear': *Al.* 443 ἄσσα σὺ μὴ δείδιχθι.

[118] Maximus, 220–1 δείδιθι Χηλάων ἐνὶ τείρεσι χρυσοέθειραν | Μήνην; also of outcomes at 55 δείδιθ' ὁδοιπλανίην (and negative command in 148–9 μή νύ τι πῆμα | δειδέχθαι); 491 οἴνας δ' ἐξαλέασθαι; Propertius, 4.1.150 *octipedis Cancri terga sinistra time*; Manilius, 4.464 *timendus*, 471 *timenda est* or *timendae*; cf. 4.482 *fuge et octavam*; zodiologia, which repeatedly use Προσεχέτω αὐτόν/αὐτὴν + ἀπό or μή... and/or (παρα)φυλασσέσθω (e.g. CCAG x. 102–21; CCAG xii. 173–91). P.Oxy. 804 (Heilen 2015, 972) has the instruction φυλάττου, of unspecified dangers.

[119] On addresses to the petitioner, see Naether, 178–88; 179 on (μὴ) φοβοῦ.

scripted into their EGHP diction, that the same domains continue to dominate their thinking, only inflected, now, by the contemporary world of work which was discussed in Part I.4. The basic vision of human life continues to triangulate between suffering, effort, and exploit; indeed, the vocabulary and the concepts have weathered the millennium since EGHP with startling applicability to the economic life in the Roman Near East. The difference between poets is between the rhetorical and stylistic ways they work out this programme, not in its content. Once again, M^b stands out.

Using archaic and classical evidence (up to and including Xenophon), Nicole Loraux discussed the nexus that connects suffering and exploit for words like πόνος and κάματος. There is no need to repeat any of that. It remains firm, only shifted from the heroic world where Iliadic heroes performed their labours on the battlefield, and Heracles was the mythological paradigm of endurance, to Roman ateliers and *officinae* and sweatshops. It can be illustrated by the use of κάματος and κάμνειν *both* in connection with words for suffering (ἀνία, etc.) *and* in connection with the world of labour. In EGHP it was mostly a matter of verb forms, only rarely of nouns.[120] One shift that has come about is that nouns are far more important, and that μόχθος, which barely figured in EGHP (two verb forms, one noun), has now been added to them, wobbling in precisely the same way from suffering to effortful labour (hard, heavy jobs), but occasionally also with a sense of productivity from which satisfaction is derivable.

The sense of productive labour is the important one here. Mankind's lot is suffering and there is little point hand-wringing about that. It is astrology's reflection of the working man's attitude to his labour that matters, and here in fact it is *not* a simple story of democratisation from EGHP, for alongside the divinities Hephaestus and Athena, and alongside Odysseus who had showed the way to incorporate technological prowess into the repertoire of a hero,

---

[120] κάμνειν: of metalwork, *Il*. 2.101 … σκῆπτρον ἔχων τὸ μὲν Ἥφαιστος κάμε τεύχων; 4.187 = 216 ζῶμά τε καὶ μίτρη, τὴν χαλκῆες κάμον ἄνδρες; 8.195 δαιδάλεον θώρηκα, τὸν Ἥφαιστος κάμε τεύχων; 18.614 Αὐτὰρ ἐπεὶ πάνθ' ὅπλα κάμε κλυτὸς ἀμφιγυήεις; 19.368 δῶρα θεοῦ, τά οἱ Ἥφαιστος κάμε τεύχων, of the arms of Achilles. Carpentry: *Od*. 9.126–7 οὐδ' ἄνδρες νηῶν ἔνι τέκτονες, οἵ κε κάμοιεν | νῆας ἐϋσσέλμους, 11.523 ὃν κάμ' Ἐπειός (wooden horse); also *Od*. 23.189 τὸ δ' ἐγὼ κάμον οὐδέ τις ἄλλος (Odysseus' bed, which involves various kinds of craftsmanship, including masonry, carpentry, metalwork, and ivory inlay). Leather work: *Il*. 7.220–1 ὅ οἱ Τυχίος κάμε τεύχων | σκυτοτόμων ὄχ' ἄριστος (Ajax's tower shield). Textiles: *Il*. 5.338 ἀμβροσίου διὰ πέπλου, ὅν οἱ Χάριτες κάμον αὐταί, 5.735 = 8.386 [πέπλον] ὅν ῥ' αὐτὴ ποιήσατο καὶ κάμε χερσίν; *Od*. 15.105 πέπλοι παμποίκιλοι, οὓς κάμεν αὐτή. The noun is used of the labour of bees in Hes. *Th*. 599 and *Op*. 305 μελισσάων κάματον (semi-craftsmanly, and unheroic, but the point is hard labour from which drones unfairly profit). πονεῖσθαι: of Hephaestus' technology, *Il*. 18.380 ὄφρ' ὅ γε ταῦτ' ἐπονεῖτο ἰδυίῃσι πραπίδεσσι and 18.413 τοῖς ἐπονεῖτο; the construction of Patroclus' tomb, *Il*. 23.245; the construction of Hesiod's plough, *Op*. 432 δοιὰ δὲ θέσθαι ἄροτρα, πονησάμενος κατὰ οἶκον.

Epeius who made the horse, and Tychios who manufactured Ajax's tower-shield, there are anonymous craftsmen who build Paris' house and women who make textiles.[121] In this respect the Manethoniana simply normalise the deheroisation or secularisation which had already been grounded in EGHP.

How, then, does it differ? For it is not, presumably, simply a matter of rehearsing EGHP tropes in a Graeco-Roman setting. The first point is political (or the opposite). In her study of πόνος, which is first and foremost the labour of a hero on the battlefield or of a worker on the soil, Loraux emphasises that it is available only to a free man, who has scope for merit; it differs from forced labour, or even wage labour which is done for another, and it is not applicable to slaves. But astrology knows no juridical distinctions between types of labour and labourer. Work is a matter of self-realisation for the individual, and the activity constitutes his identity, whether free, freed, or slave.

Yet there remains scope for merit. It is no longer exactly heroic merit, although it may sometimes borrow its vocabulary. Rather, it seizes upon what basis EGHP provided to cast excellence and skill in terms of the craftsmanly *amour propre* of the goldsmith, the carpenter, the master weaver (pp. 70–1). The best of the carpenters who built Paris' apartments,[122] the leather-worker who made Ajax's shield,[123] establish the motif of 'best in show' (ἄριστος) which M^a extends to pilots (6.364 κυβερνητῆρας) and wrestlers (3.356 παλαισμοσύνῃσί τ' ἄριστοι), and M^b further still to tailors (4.423), makers of colossi (4.570), and even mere porters (4.442–3) and general labourers (4.150); and it is only one small step further to claims of 'mastery' (ἄρχειν) and 'pre-eminence' (προφέρειν) which very nicely reflect the real-life boasts (*magister, princeps*) which Roman craftsman were making on their gravestones (p. 71).[124] Again, it is the same two poets who see the potential of the verb δαιδάλλειν, which the *Iliad* and *Odyssey* use for Hephaestus and Odysseus respectively, for the ordinary artisan,[125] and M^b extends yet again with μέλειν/μελεῖσθαι, a verb not found in other books, which suggests the craftsman's painstaking care and vigilance, as if their work were the object of devotion.[126] Finally, in one remarkable passage M^b, who is

---

[121] The *Odyssey* gives the action of πονεῖσθαι to the labours of the Cyclops (*Od.* 9.310, 343), ordinary mariners (12.151), Eumaeus (16.13), and the servants in the palace in Ithaca (17.258, 20.159, 281); πόνος of cooking *chez* Eumaeus, *Od.* 16.478.

[122] *Il.* 6.314–15...τά ῥ' αὐτὸς ἔτευξε σὺν ἀνδράσιν οἳ τότ' ἄριστοι | ἦσαν ἐνὶ Τροίῃ ἐριβώλακι τέκτονες ἄνδρες.

[123] *Il.* 7.221 σκυτοτόμων ὄχ' ἄριστος.

[124] 6.482 πάσης τέχνης ἄρχοντας ἐν ἔργοις; 4.323, 440 τεκτοσύνης τ' ἄρχοντας; 4.186, 233, 344 προφέροντας.

[125] *Il.* 18.479 δαιδάλλων; *Od.* 23.200 δαιδάλλων χρυσῷ τε καὶ ἀργύρῳ ἠδ' ἐλέφαντι: 6.401 ὄργανα δαιδάλλοντας; 4.441 θαύματα δαιδάλλοντας; 6.552 αἰόλα δαιδάλλοντας; the participle again in 2.320, 4.321.

[126] 4.124 ἄκμοσι ῥαιστοτύποις μεμελημένοι ἠδὲ καμίνοις ~ 1.289, 4.321 σκυτείῃ τέχνῃ μεμελημένα; 4.338 σταλίκεσσιν ἐϋσταθέεσσι μέλοντας; 4.430 σηκῶν τε νεωκορίῃσι μέλοντας.

speaking, to all appearances, of ordinary porters, burden-bearers, manages to present them turning their toils into pleasure (4.443 καμάτων τε πόνους εἰς τέρψιν ἄγοντας). An astonishing transformation of the old idea of effort as self-realisation, if even the hod-carrier now finds his own special dignity in the excellent fulfilment of haulage!

What we can see so far is that astrology combines productive activity with the idea of autonomous and potentially meritorious effort. This is available to everyone. Work is an identity; it may fulfil, it may satisfy; and the idea that the free man, or self-employed worker, has a capacity for self-realisation that the slave or wage labourer lacks is completely lost to view. It is M^a who first explores the space between suffering and exploit that EGHP had already opened up in the idea of work. M^b extends it further, by particularising the trades and crafts so minutely, by straining his rhetoric to present the extremes of misery and mastery that work embraces—and especially through his particular obsession with πόνος (4.72 n.). He democratises it; he particularises it; and insofar as Loraux was right that πόνος commemorated in words becomes a source of glory,[127] the poem itself becomes a sort of poor man's encomium.

However, there is another concept in the world of work that needs unpacking, and that is ἔργον. This too has EGHP antecedents, and this too has a spectrum of meanings exploited by the Manethoniana. But it is a different spectrum from the suffering/exploit words κάμνειν/κάματος and πονέεσθαι/πόνος. In the first place, EGHP already uses ἔργον in the sense of craftsmanship. It applies it to the same basic technologies of metalworking, carpentry, and textiles as the verbs κάμνειν and πονέεσθαι (a range that will extend much further in later sources[128]), and once again the makers of ἔργα are not only divine craftsmen,[129] but already include human artisans.[130] A second domain in which EGHP uses ἔργον, or rather ἔργα, plural, is agriculture. This is not relevant to the present argument, but the related sense, especially closely bound to agriculture in the *Works and Days*, is deeply relevant, and that is ἔργα (qualified by an epithet) as deeds calling for moral appraisal (σχέτλια ἔργα, ἀθεμίστια ἔργα, and so on).[131] What the Manethoniana do is to retain and elaborate both senses, and introduce a major new one.

---

[127] Loraux, 172–3, citing Pindar, Herodotus, 1.177 τὰ δέ οἱ παρέσχε τε πόνον πλεῖστον καὶ ἀξιαπηγητότατά ἐστι, τούτων ἐπιμνήσομαι, and Thucydides' Pericles (2.63.1).

[128] LSJ III.1 gives examples of woodwork (Theocr. 24.45 μέγα λώτινον ἔργον), masonry (Ar. *Av.* 1125), and statuary (Xen. *Mem.* 3.10.7 ἀνδριάντες).

[129] *Il.* 19.22 ἔργ᾽...ἀθανάτων; *Od.* 4.617 ἔργον δ᾽ Ἡφαίστοιο; *Od.* 10.223, of the works of Circe's loom.

[130] *Il.* 6.289, the anonymous weavers of Trojan textiles; 9.128 = 270, Lesbian craftswomen; 9.390.

[131] *Op.* 124 δίκας καὶ σχέτλια ἔργα; 146 ἔργ᾽ ἔμελε στονόεντα καὶ ὕβριες; 254 σχέτλια ἔργα; 334 ἔργων ἀντ᾽ ἀδίκων.

To begin with moral appraisal, this is found (ἔργα with epithet) in the second, third, and fourth books, mostly adopting the piously shocked tone of EGHP towards transgression, but tellingly also adapting the pattern for deeds productive of worldly success—which *ipso facto* demands approval.[132] Related to this (because obviously calling for the strongest possible condemnation) is the particular matter of sexual behaviour. Every single book contains examples of ἔργα qualified with 'male', 'female' (for deviant sexual practices) or adjectives like 'lewd', 'unseemly', and so on,[133] which is simply to restate points already made, and at length, about how astrology's narrative voice polices personal morality with the sanction of communal censure. There is much more to say about ἔργον as work or economic activity. Almost all uses are of the noun; the verb ἐργάζεσθαι occurs only in the rather workaday (in lexical terms) 1.82, 87. A few lack specificity. They refer just to activity itself (3.96, 6.427), or to labour as a source of wealth (6.397). But although that view of the matter is implicit throughout M^a's banal worldliness, the great majority of the references to ἔργα look, not to the pay-off, but to the activity itself. M^a sometimes connects the word with τέχνη.[134] He and still more M^b develop it into little periphrases which specify the area of activity (which in M^b's hands are both scabrous and fanatically detailed).[135] And all of M^a, M^b, and M^c frequently connect it with manufactures, from the wondrous to the banal, from automata to loaves of bread, but all tangible products of the artisan's workshop.[136] That these are not just whimsies of individual Manethonian poets is indicated by the presence of similar themes in Mesomedes. Glass (1.79) and sponges (5.154–8) reappear, both times as the toil of ἐργάται, for whom, whether they are intrepid (9.12) or the opposite (13.10), work is an exploit. Mesomedes' extravagant language gets

---

[132] 2.301 ἀθεμίστια ἔργα, 470 ἀπηνέα ἔργα, 484 ὑπείροχα ἔργα; 3.116 εὐκλέα ἔργα, 343 ὀλοοῖσιν ἐπ' ἔργοις; 4.270 οἰκτρότατ' ἔργα (the only example outside books 2 and 3).

[133] 2.242 γυναικείοισιν ἐπ' ἔργοις; 2.276 μάχλοις ἔργοισιν; 3.395 γυναικῶν ἔργα; 6.130-1 ἀνάξια μαχλοσύνησιν ἔργα μετερχομέναις; 1.31 ἀρσενικοῖς ἔργοισιν; 4.358 ἀνδρόστροφα ἔργα; 5.213 ἔργα γυναικῶν; 5.216 ἀνδρῶν ἔργα; 5.318 ἀσχήμονα ἔργα; 5.322-3 ἀρρήτοις ἔργοισι μιαίνεται, ἠΰτ' ἐπ' ἔργοις | ἐκ στομάτων αἰσχροῖς; 6.296 ἀεικέα ἔργα (of castration).

[134] 2.356 τοῖς δ' ἔργοις σκληρὰς καὶ ἀπηνέας ὤπασε τέχνας; 3.62 τέχνας ... βαναύσους, ἔργα βίοιο; 6.14 καὶ τέχνας μέλποιτ' ἰδὲ πρήξιας, ἔργα θ' ὁποῖα...; 6.339-40 τέχνας δ' ἐγὼ αὐτίκα λέξω | ἔργα θ' ὁποῖα νέμουσιν; 6.482 πάσης τέχνης ἄρχοντας ἐν ἔργοις.

[135] 3.79 γυναικείοισιν ἐπ' ἔργοις (female industries—not, for once, sexual behaviour); 6.374 παλαίστρης ἔργ', 452 ἁλίων ... ἔργων; 4.88 ἔργα τε πλαγκτὰ [ex emend., life of merchant, cf. 136 ἐργασίην]; 4.160 λογιστονόμοισιν ... ἔργοις; 4.276 ἰσχυρῶν ἔργων ... πονοπαίκτορας; 4.278-9 πηκτοῖσι πεταυριστῆρας ἐν ἔργοις, | αἰθέρι καὶ γαίῃ μεμετρημένα ἔργα τελοῦντας; 4.306 μάστροπά τ' ἔργα; 1.275 λάτρια ἔργα.

[136] 6.402 θαυματόεντ' ἔργ', 418 ἔργων τεκτοσύνης; 4.149-50 ἐλέφαντος | ἐργοπόνους, 191 σορόεργα τέχνης κανονίσματ', 320 δεροεργέας, 324 πελεκήτορας εὐξυλοεργούς; 1.77 λιθοεργούς, 78 πυροεργέας ἄνδρας, 80 κλιβανέας σκοτοεργούς; cf. also 4.442 ἐργοπόνους παλάμαισι (along with various manufacturers).

more mileage than Manetho out of the wondrousness of the production process itself (13.8) and the picturesqueness of the object's uses (9). But the same imaginary of Roman consumer products elicited these treatments from the workmanlike astrologers and from the Hadrianic citharode.

Poetic astrology therefore particularises and concretises work; it makes its products very specific and tangible. But it operates in the opposite way as well, to turn ἔργον into an abstraction which is often combined with πρᾶξις in the sense of action, activity, achievement, accomplishment, effectuality, as opposed to inefficacy, frustrated purposes, feebleness, and unmanliness.[137] This use is especially found in books 2 and 3. But whether one calls it ἔργον or πρᾶξις, the abstract notion of action complements the specific and concrete details of particular activities to correlate strongly with prosperity (3.76–7 ἔργοις | τρισμάκαρας; 4.27 εὐδαίμονας ἔργοις). This is how one forges ahead; no Manethonian poet demurs. It might be worth noting 2.386 μύθοις... ἔργοις, the old opposition between words and deeds. In astrology's universe of busy activity, this commonplace only gets a single mention. The emphasis is all on the latter.

We need finally to take stock of the general presentation of work, business, life activity. Aristotle had distinguished between πράττειν and ποιεῖν, activity which is an end in itself, and making which has an object, and he denied that the one was a subset of the other.[138] This now looks completely irrelevant. Πρᾶξις is instantiated by τέχναι, a large part of which involves manufacturing. Equally irrelevant is the distinction which Plato's Critias, leaning on Hesiod, draws between invariably honourable ἔργα and πρᾶξις, on the one hand, and potentially dishonourable ποίησις, on the other, though this looks like a sophistic capriccio, nothing that corresponds to normal usage.[139] Πρᾶξις is the headline category, but one's life's business can and very often does, in the Roman economy, involve making things. There is no opposition between the two. The concept of 'work' extends in two directions, both traditional. On the one hand, labour reaches towards difficult effort, hence suffering; on the other, it

---

[137] Along with πρῆξις: 2.162, 173, 250, 339–40; 3.23–4, 242, 368, 373; along with parts of τελέω: 2.173, 340; 3.368; 3.210 δρηστήρας ἐν ἔργοις. And inefficacy: e.g. 2.375; 2.455 ἔργοις... καμάτοισι, 2.471 ἔργμασιν.

[138] J.-P. Vernant, 'Work and Nature in Ancient Greece', in Vernant, 275–92, at 275–6, citing Arist. EN 1140ᵃ1–7; ibid. 291: 'The domain of praxis excludes all technical operations performed by men with trades... The ponos of the artisan in his work cannot acquire the value of an active virtue.'

[139] Plat. Charmides, 163 B–D (cited by Vernant, art. cit. 275). ποίησις here includes manufacture (shoemaking) but also retail (selling salt fish) and selling services (prostitution). If ἔργον ends up on the same side as πρῆξις in 3.23–4, as it did in Plato, it is only by accident, for in 3.23–4 ἔργον is used alongside τέχνας χειρῶν.

subsumes productivity and exploit. Astrology democratises, adds specificity, and enhances. It ditches social context, disregards civic and juridical status; as far as astrology is concerned, this is all about individuals and self-realisation. But it also creates new connections which EGHP had not foreseen and which are proper to the experience of real workers. It creates a strong link between suffering, on the one hand, and occupations, on the other, as some sorts of work themselves now become the source of suffering (κάματος, μόχθος), and certain τέχναι are themselves low, repulsive, and punishing in astrology's hierarchy of labour (pp. 64–5).[140] Conversely, it enhances the sense of *amour propre*, to such an extent that even suffering words can be drawn into the nexus of self-realisation and pride (3.20 μόχθοισιν ἰαινομένους σφετέροισιν; 4.443, cited above). If EGHP had incorporated (for Odysseus and a few rare individuals) productivity into the heroic register, poetic astrology now does it the other way round, integrating the heroic into the craftsmanly. Craftsmen—high-status ones, anyway—enjoy their *kudos*.[141] From a literary perspective it is an astonishing, and marvellous, reversal. From a cultural one, it gives an epic idiom to the attitudes their own monuments have left behind.

---

[140] For κάματος used of manual/physical labour, see 4.293 n., adding 3.322 (the merchant); also the verb in 4.340 κάμνοντας ἐπ' ἔργοις (the life of the hunter). For μόχθος or ἐπίμοχθος of hard, heavy jobs see 4.248 n.; 6.383 (men like beasts of burden). τέχναι are qualified as σκληρὰς καὶ ἀπηνέας (2.356), βαναύσους (3.62, 6.527), μυσαραῖς (6.459).

[141] i. 344: 6.347, 6.403–4.

Book Four

4.1. PRELIMINARIES

Koechly saw that the fourth book was later than, and dependent on, M^a (which he had dated to the reign of Alexander Severus). More precisely, following Tyrwhitt's interpretation of 561–6 as a hostile reference to Christians,[1] he found the most plausible setting to be the reign of Julian (mid-4th c.),[2] which was further supported by the absence of any reference to persecutions of diviners. In his view, the *terminus ante quem* was the persecution of magicians under Valens mentioned in Ammianus, 29.2.2–4.

W. Kroll, *RE* s.v. Manethon (Astrologe), 1104.17–25, had already thrown out the Julianic dating, though he had also denied that the poet was dependent on M^a at all, insisting on the tralatician and traditional character of astrological doctrine. The latter point is undeniable, but Koechly was right about the poet's use of M^a. He simultaneously reworks his predecessor *and* expands him with fresh material from another source or sources.

A more solid *terminus ante quem* for this book was supplied by papyri published in the second half of the twentieth century. The main evidence is P.Oxy. 2546, corresponding to 4.384–433 + 564–604, published by John Rea in 1966 (P.Oxy. XXXI); a second short fragment, P. Amsterdam Inv. No. 56, 4.231–5, was published by P. J. Sijpesteijn, 'Ps.-Manetho, Apotelesmatika IV 231–235', *ZPE* 21 (1976), 182. Both papyri were dated on palaeographical grounds by their publishers to the third century. Rea reported (p. 57) that examples of the hand[3] in the Oxyrhynchus fragments extended from the second to the fourth centuries, with a preponderance in the third, and also (p. 58) cited the opinion of Eric Turner that the hand in question should be assigned to the early third century. A short new Oxyrhynchus fragment of the fourth book (P.Oxy. 5590, containing lines 233–6, 285–91) has now been dated to the third century as

---

[1] Tyrwhitt, xiii f.
[2] 1851, xxxix f., xlvii; still accepted by T. Mommsen, 213.
[3] A representative of the severe style, in common use for literary texts, most famously the London Bacchylides (E. Turner, *Greek Manuscripts of the Ancient World* (*BICS* Suppl. 46) (London, 1987), 22–3; I. Gallo, *Greek and Latin Papyrology* (BICS Suppl. 54) (London, 1986), 86–7.

well.[4] This has interesting implications for the history of poetics, for there are various features of the poet's metre and style which commentators have repeatedly seen as anticipating Nonnus.[5] It now turns out that some aspects of his style are anticipated by a couple of centuries, if he is located in the fifth century. See further II.4.11, on metre.

Beside the connections with Nonnus' style and metre, the book is nothing if not a grand accumulation of tropes, one after the other, and a couple of them turn out to echo the rhetoric of late antique inscriptions (see on 4.512 ἀριστοπονῆες; 4.514 ἰθυδίκαιοι). Parallels for both motifs—the euergete who 'labours' for his city (πόνος), and the good official who enacts 'straight' justice— are from later antiquity (4th c. and thereafter). But these are not dating criteria; the discovery of more inscriptions could change the picture, or it could simply be that a literary text anticipates them.[6] One further peculiarity is the number of overlaps between this book and Christian literature. This is different from diagnosing a reference to Christians in 561–6, which seems to me unprovable and unlikely. Rather, it speaks, not only to a shared cultural background (which is unsurprising), but also to a certain sensibility, which is more notable. This sensibility is particularly attuned to pain, wounding, torture. *All* the later books have something to say about crucifixion, sometimes using vocabulary and motifs that overlap with those in Christian writers (see on 4.197–8, 197 βασανηδόν, 198 στρεβλὰ κολαζόμενοι, σκολοπηίδα κτλ; 1.149; 5.219). This is perhaps simply a function of astrology taking cognisance of matters too unsavoury for élite sources to register, or perhaps it reflects the outlook of lower classes for whom heavy-handed officialdom and its brutal violations of the person, from which *honestiores* were spared, were very real threats. At the same time, there are also certain convergences of moral sensibility, with strongly worded disapproval of mimes (4.283 ἀσχήμονας) and of homosexuality (4.590 ἀρσενομίκται) that reflect New Testament attitudes and even vocabulary; still more striking is the apparent aesthetic-moral disgust at the human body, if that is what this passage really means (4.254–5). The elderly gardener (4.257) is a topos well represented in Christian literature, but with classical antecedents that leave it requiring no particular explanation here.

---

[4] The hand is an informal bookhand distantly related to the severe style. There are no divergences from L in what is extant.

[5] Koechly 1851, xxxix, xli (style and metre); T. Mommsen, 213 (various stylistic mannerisms); W. Kroll, *RE* s.v. Manethon (Astrologe), 1104.26–9 ('artistic character'); Gundel and Gundel, 161–2 ('spiritual world'); De Stefani 2016, 183–4, and 2017, 31 (placement of -ηδόν adverbs and development of prepositions), cf. 27 on late antique style.

[6] For other parallels with the language of inscriptions, see on 4.43 εἰς ἀρετὴν νεύουσα; 118 ἀώρους.

The proem of the book seems to glance at the late antique motif of material brought to light from hidden recesses, perhaps temples (9). But it lacks the overt references to Ptolemy and to the (Nechepso and) Petosiris tradition that books 1 and 5 both contain. There are, nonetheless, a few tell-tale suggestions of an Egyptian setting—above all, in the references to funerary workers (192, the νεκροτάφοι, now well attested in papyri) and mummification (4.191 κεδροχαρεῖς, 4.267 γαστροτόμους). The sharp eyes of Louis Robert also spotted a reference to workers in hard Egyptian granite, the σκληρουργοί, in 4.325 λαοτόμους τε πέτρης σκληρώδεος. Other details are at least compatible with Egyptian setting, though not enough on their own to establish one: 4.213, lecanomancy; 4.252 ἀμαρησκαπτῆρας, if these are irrigation channels; 4.342, the use of wax in caulking ships (mentioned in papyri); 4.160, λογισταί. De Stefani 2017, 28, interestingly suggests that the Gorgianic jingle in 4.495 works better with the Egyptian pronunciation of ὕβρις as *hypris*.[7] But in general this book exhibits the internationalism typical of astrology that smooths out local peculiarities and is unfriendly to limiting specificity. See on 4.256–8 on the treatment of market gardeners, and 4.493–4 on magic.

Much of what follows will concern the most remarkable aspect of this poet, which is his wholly distinctive idiolect. But one feature which deserves mention at the outset is his 'theological' outlook. The conception of a divinely planned or controlled universe—the underpinnings of the whole astrological system that ultimately go back to the *Timaeus*—are particularly pronounced in this book. Part and parcel of the poet's bombast is a certain hierophantic tone, which goes further than his predecessor in making planets deities, and astrology a divine mystery.

Bouché-Leclercq eloquently set out the reasons why the *Timaeus* was so important for astrologers.[8] It personifies the stars as living beings who are also visible gods, made out of fire, and although it obviously does not anticipate the full-blown system of natal astrology as it would be worked out in the late Hellenistic period, it does envisage the motions of the stars (specifically, conjunction and opposition) having general significance as portents.[9] The Manethoniana habitually apply to the stars vocabulary which implies some degree of personification (i. 886, 895), and it seems possible that it was the *Timaeus*, which calls stars divine and immortal living creatures, which inspired Mᵃ's systematic use of ζῷον (strictly, a living being) instead of ζῴδιον.[10] The

---

[7] In general, Agosti (Agosti and Gonnelli, 352) is sceptical of Egyptian influence on late-antique prosody, but he is discussing 4th-c. Christian material.
[8] Bouché-Leclercq, 19–24; 77; 545 n. 1 'le livre de chevet des philosophes astrologisants'.
[9] 40 C–D, esp. ὁποῖοι τῶν θεῶν κατ'ἀλλήλους γιγνόμενοι καὶ ὅσοι καταντικρύ.
[10] 40 B ζῷα θεῖα ὄντα καὶ ἀΐδια, cf. 39 E τὰ πάντα ζῷα, of which the stars are the first category. Mᵃ has ζῷον 62 times in all; otherwise 6× in Mᵈ; in Mᵇ only in 4.509. Not in Maximus.

occasional references to planets as gods in later books of the Manethoniana certainly evoke the *Timaeus*' elevated conception of their nature,[11] and the preferred recourse to epithets of fire and radiance (rather than, say, those evoking the planets' mythological characters) could also be residues of the *Timaeus*' outlook. One wonders, too, whether this is the reason for a couple of references to the ἀήρ (4.37, 214; 5.29) instead of the usual αἰθήρ, for Plato treats ἀήρ as the basic category of which the αἰθήρ is the most rarefied kind (58 D); if so, then instead of being a 'late' use (37 n.), it could, in fact, be an early one. Above all, the *Timaeus* establishes a direct link between stars and individual souls, each of which is assigned a star upon its creation. It does not fully flesh out the character of each star, but does at least adumbrate the idea of an affinity between them and human beings. As Bouché-Leclercq put it, it has the effect of making the stars 'une collection de types fascinant à distance ou pénétrant de leurs effluves les générations terrestres' (24).

The influence of the *Timaeus* is more or less explicit at the end of this book (4.625–6), where the poet refers to the planets as measurements of time, past, present, and future, and also exploits Plato's word αἰών for its mysterious grandeur, even without the particular theory of the universe and cosmic time that underpins it. This is by far the most impressive reference, but in retrospect connections with the *Timaeus*, more or less traditional or mediated, become possible at other points as well. One of the poet's mannerisms is his biological language (e.g. 483 ἐκφύσει, subject Mercury), and especially his connection of birth with the ASC, which is presented as having generative powers (p. 246; 4.577, 597). In the *Timaeus*, the Demiurge, not wanting to create living beings himself, leaves their generation to the stars,[12] although it is true that the most biological language (σπείρειν, at 41 C, 41 E, 42 D) is used for his own actions in creating the divine part of the soul, while the stars' actions are described instead with metaphors of construction and craftsmanship (joining, riveting), not of parturition.[13] The poet repeatedly refers to the Moon's course as 'spiral' or 'twisted', but also apparently to that of the ecliptic as well; the ἕλιξ of *Tim.* 39 A was interpreted by Proclus, at least, as a reference to the same thing (see on 4.298). The *Timaeus* has a chorus of the stars (40 C χορείας δὲ τούτων αὐτῶν, cf. 4.11 χορείη), but that is a *topos*.[14] Finally, one feature of this book is the

---

[11] 4.170 φανερὸς θεός, sc. Mercury; also 1.176 δεινὸν θεόν, sc. Mars; 5.29 Ἀστέρες ἑπτὰ θεοί; 5.122 ἡ θεός, sc. the Moon. For the planets as gods in the *Timaeus*, see 40 A–D, esp. 40 C (in the very passage where he is talking about their motions as interpretable signs), 40 D καὶ τὰ περὶ θεῶν ὁρατῶν καὶ γεννητῶν εἰρημένα φύσεως.

[12] 41 C–D τρέπεσθε κατὰ φύσιν ὑμεῖς ἐπὶ τὴν τῶν ζῴων δημιουργίαν, μιμούμενοι τὴν ἐμὴν δύναμιν περὶ τὴν ὑμετέραν γένεσιν...ἀπεργάζεσθε ζῷα καὶ γεννᾶτε τροφήν τε διδόντες αὐξάνετε.

[13] 41 C δημιουργίαν, 41 D προσυφαίνοντες, ἀπεργάζεσθε; 42 D πλάττειν; 43 A ξυγκολλεῖν; and the metaphor of joinery, *passim*.

[14] Already attested, pre-Plato, in Eur. *El.* 467 and fr. 593 = Critias, 43 F 4.5 Snell.

enormous popularity of the word κόσμος (thirteen times; otherwise only twice in lines shared with this book in M^c, three times in the Aratea of the second book, and dubiously in 3.323, which in any case I emend). This can hardly be laid directly at the door of the *Timaeus*. But it *is* a word Plato uses especially often, and the 'holistic' conception of the universe which it implies, unique to this book in the corpus, at least calls for comment.[15]

4.2. THE ORIGINAL POEM: INFERENCES ABOUT SHAPE AND STRUCTURE

The consoling feature of this book is that it is, to all appearances, by a single author. But, as with M^a, the original poem is truncated, and indeed in a worse state than anything we had to face in the first three books. It was Koechly who recognised all this. He saw that that poet was an imitator of M^a, who reworked material that corresponded to much that is found in books 2, 3, and 6. But unlike what has survived of M^a, which retains its original organisation, it was apparent that M^b is *both* incomplete *and* disordered: the fourth book consists only of *disiecta membra* (1851, xxxviii, xlviii).

I essentially agree. Before going further with the analysis, in this section I lay out what can be said about the present state of the poem, and what inferences can be made about its original organisation. The advances proposed here arise from the availability of much more comparative material than Koechly had access to. The discussion will have two foci. In the first place, clues are derivable from transitions dispersed throughout, and from their rationale or lack of fit with the contents of the poem. Second, there are the *de facto* groupings, which Koechly could perfectly well read for himself, as he could read the transitions, but not against the evidence of Dorotheus, Firmicus, *Lib. Herm.*, and above all Θ.

Proem and 4.107–9: Planets and Fixed Stars

4.3–4 promises (if one accepts Koechly's correction ἐξονομήνω in l. 4) an account of the wandering and fixed stars (πλάνα φέγγη | ἀπλανέων τ' αὐγάς). It is true that the poet is very fond of words for pathway, but if we can take it literally, this looks like an announcement of a treatment of cosmic motion. Planets

---

[15] So too 4.9 φύσις αἰθερόπλαγκτος, but the conception in *Timaeus* is different, with the created world designed to imitate the eternal nature (38 B κατὰ τὸ παράδειγμα τῆς διαιωνίας φύσεως; 39 E πρὸς τὴν τῆς διαιωνίας μίμησιν φύσεως); on this view, φύσις is not located in the aether.

are fair enough: the whole book is about them. But fixed stars? Taken on its own, 4.4–5 might just about have been taken to anticipate the poet's many references to zodiacal signs—or even suggest the existence of a fuller version where they played an even larger role (pp. 240–1). But the sign-off in 4.107–9, which links back to 4.3–4, suggests the existence of a systematic and self-contained discussion of planets and fixed stars. It does this without paying the slightest attention to the fact that the subject of the intervening section has, in practice, been about the planets in the centres (*kentrothesiai*).

What might a putative section about fixed stars and planets have looked like? This is to enter the realms of pure speculation. One could envisage an introductory treatment, say, of the ecliptic (the circle of fixed stars within which the planets move), which in turn would suggest some kind of similarity with M^a. There is absolutely nothing to confirm or disconfirm that (though see on 4.107–8, on ῥομβηδόν). But perhaps it is worth noting that the transitional formula in 107 is ὧδε (thus) rather than ταῦτα (4.165). For what it is worth, in its transitional formulae the sixth book uses τόσσα and never ὧδε. It does not look like the sign-off of a mere enumeration. It suggests a passage, not on 'what', but 'how'.

4.109–69: Signs of Birth, or from the Place of Birth

4.109 need not follow 107–8, and is separated from that couplet in both of Koechly's editions. Its promise of σήματα γενέθλης presumably means, not 'sign of birth' ('and now I will tell you other divine omens of birth': Lopilato)—for what in natal astrology is not a sign of birth?—but 'signs from the (place of) birth', the ASC. I augur this from the language and imagery of birth which frequently clothes references to the horoscope in this author (p. 246), and from the topos (in Θ, Paul, Camaterus, and elsewhere) that the ASC is the gateway of life and breath (ζωή, πνεῦμα: 5.262 n.): the poet has (I surmise) chosen a word that suggests both birth itself and specifically the ASC. This is then recapitulated by 4.165 ὡράων σκεπτήρια. One can only speculate about the rationale for the placement of a (putative) section on the ASC at this point. Might it have been designed to follow the fuller but more scattergun treatment of all four *kentra* that has just preceded? Might that even be the point of ἄλλα ('you've had some already, now here are some more')? In which case, 109 belongs with 14–106, and 107–8 are intrusive.

Once again, however, the section-markers do not correspond to the material they enclose. The first two charts in the section (110–20) do mention the ASC, but most of those thereafter do not. On the contrary, the ASC is more prominent in the *previous* section, which was not labelled in this way. In particular,

116–20 (Mars in ASC in signs not its own) looks as if it would have been more at home in the vicinity of 4.44–52. The ASC is also the common factor in the little section at 4.491–507 (which locates Venus, Jupiter, and Saturn there). Is this a remainder of what *once* stood in this (putative) section? However, it is not as straightforward as deciding that 4.491–507 has simply got separated from the section that it once belonged to. For at least *two* of the charts consist of varied or remixed versions of what was found in the earlier section. 4.496–8 remixes 4.35–6 + 39–43, and 491–5 corresponds to 4.59–64, with different emphases, though 4.499–502 is novel, and 4.503–7 is specifically for women, as 4.14–27 was not. The idea that they are by different poets is to be rejected. But under what circumstances does a poet return to the same material and recast it, and under what circumstances does an editor split the two treatments apart? I certainly cannot explain their current placement, but their existence does suggest a possible theme-and-variations procedure by astronomical poets (and maybe by astrologers in general), the kind of altered emphases that were possible from the same basic elements. This departure from the Koechly model (one set-up one outcome, and only one per poet) does seem an important gain.

At the same time, the transitions, 'irrelevant' though they may be, are not completely arbitrarily placed. After the first two (about the ASC), most of the charts in this section are Π- charts, except for one τ- chart, one σίνος chart, and the last one, which seems to be a straightforward aspect. In other words it is very loosely πρᾶξις material before what follows in the next section, which can be more definitely identified as τέχναι. The section does not have perfect integrity, but it does not completely lack it either.

4.170–End: Γενεαί and Τέχναι

After the previous section the poet in 165–9 promises a transition to (*a*) aspects, which he calls ἀκτινηβολίαι, (*b*) terms, and (*c*) (again) the zodiac, and to the areas covered by these prognostics, namely γενεαί and τέχναι. There are no further formal transitions in the book. *De facto* groupings can be discerned, but the poet does not section them.

τέχναι are very reassuring. Indeed, this is precisely the point where the sequence corresponding to Θ chs. 84–96, Περὶ τεχνῶν, begins. M[a] uses the same label for the same material (6.14, 339, 542), although of course he presents it in a completely different sequence. But what does γενεαί mean, and which charts in the following material is it supposed to cover? If τέχναι is a title, and corresponds to one in Θ, then perhaps the same is true of γενεά. This is indeed used as a section-heading in book 6, where it always has a dependent genitive (12 τέκνων γενεῆς, 225 ἀμφὶ τέκνων γενεῆς, 260 Ἀμφί γε μὴν τεκέων γενεῆς), meaning something like 'the birthing-time of children'. In any case what the label refers to is the section on the birth of children from 6.224–261. Charts within this section do find correlates at 4.450–65, while the appendix on sterility (6.262–305) has further correlates in 4.582–92. Yet if that is what M^b has in mind it hardly seems enough to warrant turning it into a joint section-heading for almost three-quarters of the poem. Alternatively, γενεά can mean 'race', 'family', and if one takes it in that sense (M^b of course is not following the usage of the earlier poet in narrowing its scope by the addition of 'children') it would also embrace the material on parents (4.379–94, 402–13) (corresponding to various chapters Περὶ γονέων in Θ), and perhaps *trophe* (4.366–78).

That is at least limitedly helpful in making sense of the book's structure. One of the abiding impressions of this (and the other two late books) is the chaotic interleaving of different kinds of chart. The mix-up of Π-, τ-, and οἶνος charts already had precedent in book 6, but now we find the main τ- sequence broken up, not only with other τέχνη, πρᾶξις, and οἶνος charts, but also with nurture, parentage (4.366–413), and the prior deaths of parents (4.402–13). The joint title γενεαί and τέχναι does not explain *why* this arrangement was adopted, but at least seems to give advance notice *that* it has been adopted; the pell-mell miscellany of charts in the main section reflects the conception of the person who gave it this title. Not that the title is in any way an adequate summation of what follows. Even on the expanded sense of γενεά, γενεαί and τέχναι hardly do justice to the material in question. What of οἶνος? What of slaves?

Can any structuring principles be discerned *apart* from the explicit indications of titles? It is true that very vaguely catalogic material (on *kentra*) precedes the long roster of themed charts, but there is little sign of any consistent attempt to obey the *prima facie* logic of having simpler charts precede the more complex ones, for had that been the case, it is hard to see what principle separates the block of aspects across *kentra* (560–92) from 110–65.[16] Still less sign is there of a poet or editor trying to shape a collection in a way that generally corresponds to M^a. Had the intention been to erect a structure on the same basic armature of the earlier books, the gendered luminaries (4.508–36) should have come well before the τέχναι, while the charts that deal with the birth of children (4.582–92) and nurture (4.593–6) are also delayed with respect to their corresponding position in the sixth book (namely 6.286–94 and 6.60–3). The position of a group of slave charts almost at the end (4.597–611) does correspond to 6.684–731, the last block of themed charts, but by now, with so much other disruption, that looks as if it might be happenstance.

In short, it is hard to be satisfied with any analysis of the main section of book 4.

---

[16] They would even have been *better* placed there from the point of view of source-criticism, given that most of 560–81 are Π- charts which would have been in good company with 4.121–60.

4.3. PHONOLOGICA ET MORPHOLOGICA

Phonologica

α/η

4.195 ἐπὰν (implied); 204 λαμπράν L (corr. K.)
Standard epic Ἑρμείας: 4.126, 194, 386, 444, 567 Ἑρμείας, 161 Ἑρμείᾳ, 230 Ἑρμείαν, but Hesiodic Ἑρμείην at 147, 414 [both times corr. K]. At 4.157 Ἑρμείας and Ἑρμείης are both products of emendation.
4.143, 533 πρήξιας
4.14 Τιτάν, and only there; this is expected.
4.485 = 1.312 φωραθέντες [corr. A.–R., D]

ρρ/ρσ

4.458 ἄρρενες, 515 ἄρρεν, 369 ἀρρεγόνων, but 461 ἄρσενος

ττ/σσ

No instances of Attic -ττ- (4.105 φυλάσσει; 163 ἥσσονα, 385 ἥσσονες; 189 and 473 δισσά, 527 δισσοί; 184 θρασυγλωσσέας; 346 πισσήεντα; 464 περισσομελής; 533 ἀλλάσσοντες)

Contractions

ε + α: see i. 95, and correct to 4.555 νεκροειδῆ.
ε + ι: for the dative singular see i. 95.
ε + ο > ου: this occurs in verbs *passim*. To those in i. 96 n. 44, add 4.149 Ἰνδογενοῦς. The poet finds it useful to accommodate words of shape ⏑ — — at line-end: 4.15 καλοῦσιν, 279 τελοῦντας, 361 φανοῦνται, 498 φρονοῦντας, 609 φοροῦσιν; before caesura: 306 τελοῦντες.

In addition, M[b] has ten epithets of choriambic shape, mostly at line-beginning, with the ending εῖς (originally from ε + ε, thence extended into the accusative): 4.162, 470, 521 πουλυπλανεῖς, 191 κεδροχαρεῖς, 221 γαλλομανεῖς, 277 ὀχλοχαρεῖς, 284 κρατοπλαγεῖς, 364 ὑπνοφανεῖς, 476 νουσομελεῖς, 503 θηλυγενεῖς; of other shapes: 4.105 ἀφανεῖς, 120 παναγεῖς, 569 ἀγαλμοτυπεῖς.[17] M[a] had only 2.171 πανθαρσεῖς, 470 ἀστεμφεῖς, cf. 4.244 τοξελκεῖς.

---

[17] One might have expected this pattern more often in Nonnus, but there are a mere eighteen examples in the entire *Dionysiaca*, or 1/1135 lines, as against 1/63 in M[b] (2.429 ὀξυβελεῖς, 5.362 ἀμφιπαγεῖς, 6.36 θυμοδακεῖς, 13.421 ἰσοφανεῖς, 14.136 ὀξυτενεῖς (+ one more at line-end), 4x ἀμφιλαφεῖς (+ one more at line-end), 21.218 ἀλλοφυεῖς (+ one more at line-end), 21.268 ἡμιτελεῖς, 25.107 χαλκοβαρεῖς, 41.120 αὐτοφυεῖς, 42.495 χρυσοφαεῖς, 43.341 ταυροφυεῖς, 46.151 ἀγχινεφεῖς, 2x οἰνοβαρεῖς; *Par.* 2x ζηλομανεῖς, 9.180 ὀξυφαεῖς, cf. 19.161 καὶ ζαμενεῖς (metrical word).

Vowel quantities

καλός: long at 4.148 κᾱλῷ.

Morphologica

κεῖνος/ἐκεῖνος

See i. 98. Epic κεῖνος (4.30, 296, 416, 612) appears twice as often as ἐκεῖνος (381, 554), although 381 is the result of emendation, and restorable differently (ἔσσυτο κείνων).

Dative plural

-αις, -αισι(ν), -ῃσι(ν)
See i. 100. There are 13 instances of -αισι(ν)[18], 23 of -ῃσι(ν),[19] but even more examples of -αισι in Π¹ (4.396, 569, 570) where L has -ῃσι. There are also 27 instances of -αις.

ἀστράσι, ἄστροις
One instance of the latter (4.516), none of the former.

'Aeolic' endings (-εσσι)
With precedent in EGHP and/or Mª: 4.82b σινέεσσι; 143 χείρεσσι; 162 μερόπεσσι; 207, 431 ἀκτίνεσσι; 275 ὠδίνεσσι; 360 ἄνδρεσσι. The only innovation is 338 ἐϋσταθέεσσι.

Declension of Ares

Almost all the forms and *sedes* are attested in either EGHP, Mª, or both. The exceptions (where the location, not the form, is new) are Ἄρεα at line beginning and Ἄρεϊ at the bucolic diaeresis. The fact that Ἄρευς, produced by Koechly's emendation in 391, is unprecedented in either, is suspicious: see ad loc. Three of four instances of Ἄρεος are transmitted as Ἄρεως (4.112, 171, 462; the exception is 44), and Ἄρεως is metrically guaranteed at 4.121, 366 (where Ἄρεος is corrected by L¹).

---

[18] 4.2, 122, 129, 130, 174, 228, 390, 399, 442, 470, 471, 494, 556.
[19] 4.101, 127, 129, 225, 235*bis*, 254, 284, 306, 346, 378, 396, 421, 430, 440, 469, 476, 498, 499, 568, 569, 570, 588.

i-stem accusative plural

-ιας: 4.322 ἴδριας; 211 μάντιας, 212 ὑδρομάντιας; 143, 533 πρήξιας, 617 πτώσιας.
-εις: none.

Forms of εἶναι

The poet uses this rarely. He prefers to indicate location in other ways than banal 'being in'.
Epic forms in ἐ- (4.73 ἔῃ, 319 παρέῃ; 295 ἐοῦσα, 351 ἐόν; and restored by D at 598 συνέῃ) are well outnumbered by non-epic forms (4.126, 403 ᾖ; 148 συνῇ [Κυθέρῃ συνέῃ A.-R. xxix]; 193 συνών; 407 προόντων; 625 ἐπών).
Future indicative: 4.458, 579 ἔσσονται, and transmitted at 390 [*Π*¹ ἔσται]; 528, 599 ἔσονται; 461, 561 ἔσται.

Conclusions

The salient points are: a somewhat higher tolerance of Attic forms (including 4.282, 523, 580 πόλεως, which I retain; εἰς in 372 and perhaps formerly in 94; implied in 231 and in *Π*²; required by metre at 386; corrupt at 157, 472); contractions of all sorts readily admitted, the most striking result of which is how εἶ facilitates the inclusion of epithets of choriambic shape, mostly at line-beginning. There are many more instances of -αισι(ν) relative to -ῃσι(ν) than there were in M^a, though not as many as in the later books. On the other hand one notes the absence of some of the most striking features of M^a (subjunctive in -ῃσιν, a feature of Dorothean style that M^b does *not* take up); the irrational iota adscript in εἴῃι, though there is an example in 4.546 φανίῃι (i. 103–4). The poet avoids the optative, so there is nothing to be said about the endings -αις, -αι, and -ειε(ν).

4.4. WORD-FORMATION[20]

This section concentrates on the poet's innovations. The categories under consideration are: (i) nouns, other than agent nouns (mostly abstract); (ii) agent nouns; (iii) other epithets; (iv) verbs; (v) adverbs. In each section I list first

---

[20] See Axtius and Rigler, xxiv f.; Koechly 1851, xxxviii f.; Palmer; James.

Book Four

those items which are previously attested; then those which are *proton legomena*; and those which are absolute *hapax legomena*. Where relevant, simplex forms are presented before compounds (and derivatives from compounds), though in some cases only compound forms will be of interest. In some cases, compounds are alphabetised by the second rather than first element. Indications are also given where a new form varies a previously attested form by means of modifying stem or suffix.

Parts of Speech

Nouns, other than Agent Nouns

-ίη
Attested. Simplex: 288 γειτονίη; 606 κυρείαις; 430 νεωκορίῃσι. 585 ἀσπορίη (Or. Sib. 3.542; Byzantine prose) is corrupt. Compound: 600 ἀπελευθερίης; 447 ἀρεταλογίῃ; 376 διωνυμίῃ; 270 δυσοσμίῃ; 331 ἐπήρειαι; 344 λινοστολίης; 332 ψευδοκατηγορίαι.
Proton: 260 δυσπονίης.
Hapax. 510 ζωφορίην; 245 θηροδιδασκαλίης; 268 κακεμπορίης; 72 καλαμογραφίης; 213 λεκανοσκοπίη; 130 λιθογλυφίαισι; 412 μογοστοκίῃ; 64 φυγαρσενίης; 433 φυτοσπορίας; 353 χαμαιτυπίης. Varying stem: ἀκτινηβολία (166, 396, 421, cf. 1.322) vs. ἀκτινοβολία. Varying suffix: 312 ἀναστροφίῃ vs. ἀναστροφή; ἐκθεσίην (368, 381, 596) vs. ἔκθεσις.

-σύνη
Attested. Simplex: 566 ἀφροσύνην; 383 δεσποσυνάων [though the gen. pl. is new]; 440 τεκτοσύνης. Compound: 462, 475, 594 κακοδαιμοσύνη.
Hapax: 505 ἀξιοπιστοσύνη; 394 μοιχοσύνην; 378 παιδοσύνῃσιν; 222 πολυπλαγκτοσύνης; 314 πορνοσύνης. Varying suffix: 460 θεωροσύνην vs. θεωρία; 436 μετεωροσύνης vs. μετεωρία.

-μός
Attested: 319 διωγμοῖς; 104 θρονισμούς; 448, 533 πορισμῶν; 580 τοκισμοῖς.
Proton: κανονισμός (151, 292); σελασμός (36, 171, 231, 266, 351).
Hapax: 41 κτεανισμῶν; 213 νεκυϊσμός. Varying suffix: 189, 250 ἀλλαγμοῖσι vs. (ἐν)αλλαγή; 332 τεχνασμοί vs. τέχνασμα.

-ημα
Proton: 559 θαμβήματος.
Hapax. Varying suffix: 553 δινήματι vs. δίνη; 522 μεταβλήμασι vs. μεταβολή.

-σμα
Attested: 200 ἑλκύσματα; 191 κανονίσματα; 345 λίπασμα; 269 τεχνάσμασι.
Proton: σελάγισμα (189, 240, 473); 601 σελάσματα.
Hapax. Varying suffix: 38 δεσπόσμασι vs. δεσποσύνη.

-(ε)υμα
Attested: 447 μυθεύματα; 556 μηνύμασι.
Hapax: 479 λοξεύματα.

-ήριον
Hapax: 550 ἀποφθεγκτήρια; 165 σκεπτήρια (~ τεκμήριον).

Agent nouns and adjectives, substantival and adjectival

See i. 109–12.

First declension
M^b has no examples of -ᾶς, though he does have the accusative plural νεκρονώμας (192, *hapax*) apparently from νεκρονώμης. We should not be surprised: -ᾶς does not fit the poetic register. Drexhage notes that to ancient ears it connoted low-status trades, and that in literary texts this taint does not wear off until the Byzantine period.[21]

-της
Attested. Simplex: 259 μεταλλευταί; 448 παίκτας; 236 ψέκτας. Compound: 278 αἰθρο-βάτας; 397 ναυσι-βάτας; 569 θεο-πλάστας; 300 ζωρο-πότας.
Proton: 287 σχοινο-βάτας; 243 ἰχθυο-θηρευτάς.
Hapax. Simplex: 258 ἀρδευταί; 268 ματευτάς; 305 μοιχευταί. Varying stem: 329 τελωνητάς vs τελώνης. Compound: 305 μοιχ-απάται [L, but emended by A.–R.]; 307 αἰσχρο-διδάκται; 234 θεο-λωβήτας; 590 ἀρσενο-μίκται; 311 γονο-πώτας; 342 ὁλκαδο-χρίστας.

Second declension
I focus on compounds. There are no examples of the -άριος suffix (p. 144).
Attested: 291 τειχο-δόμους; 330 ἐργο-λάβους; 405 νεκυο-στόλος; 192 νεκρο-τάφους.
Proton: δολο-εργός (57, 243, 394, 563); 291 κεραμ-ουργούς; 185 μελ-ουργούς; 320 βυρσο-τόμους; 313 ἑταιρο-τρόφους; 343 ζωο-τύπους; 258 λαχανη-φόροι.

---

[21] Drexhage 2004, and id., 'Vorläufige Liste der bislang ausschließlich literarisch belegten Berufs- bzw. Tätigkeitsbezeichnungen', *MBAH* 23/1 (2004), 41–65.

Hapax: 243 ἰξο-βόλους; 342 ὑλο-γράφους; 324 εὐ-ξυλο-εργούς; 300 εἰλαπιν-ουργούς; 259 ὀνθο-λόγοι [*ex emend*. D, for ἀνθολόγοι]; 343 εἰκονο-μόρφους; 569 εὐ-ξοάνους; 244 τροφο-ποιούς; 570 κολοσσο-πόνους; 256 καρπο-σπόροι; 134 φορτο-στόλος; 267 γαστρο-τόμους; 232 σωματο-φόρβους. With verbal first element: 280 μιμο-βίους; 325 ἐγρεσι-οίκους. With two nominal elements: 160 λογιστο-νόμοισιν.

Third declension
-εύς
Hapax: ?342 κηρ-αγγέας; 185 ναβλιστο-κτυπέας; 512 ἀριστο-πονῆες; 569 ἀγαλμο-τυπεῖς. Varying stem: 251 ὑδρέας vs ὑδρευτής.
-ής
Hapax: 244 τοξ-ελκεῖς (badly formed, for τοξουλκούς; as it is, the second element should come from ἕλκος, for which observation I thank Dr Holford-Strevens); 320 δερο-εργέας.
-τήρ
A *koine* background offsets the outlandishness to at least some extent: the suffix lived on there, unlike in Attic-Ionic, where it became specialised in the vocabulary of law and religion.[22]
Attested: 173 ἀθλητῆρας [Homeric]; 257 ἀντλητῆρες; 603 γενετήρων; 158 ἰητῆρα [Homeric]; 251, 253 καθαρτῆρας; 398 κυβερνητῆρας; 264 ὀπτῆρα [Homeric]; 559 πλάστειρα; 329, 424 πρηκτῆρας; 149, 229 ῥεκτῆρας [Hesiodic].
Proton: 339 ἰξευτῆρας [also ps.-Opp.].
Hapax. Vowel stem: 56 ἀατήρ [*ex emend*. K]. -ε- stem: 47 φρουρητῆρα; 337 κυν-ηγητῆρας. -ευ- stem: 267 ταριχευτῆρας. Consonant stem: monosyllabic: 119 ψευστῆρας [but cf. *Or. Sib*. 3.816 ψεύστειρα]; 192 κλαυστῆρας; 304, 484 κλεπτῆρες; 423 ῥαπτῆρας [*ex emend*.]; polysyllabic: 221 ἀγυρτῆρας; 178 ἀλειπτῆρας; 278 πεταυριστῆρας. Compounds: 40 δι-ιθυντῆρας; 235 κατ-ονειδιστῆρας; with adjectival or nominal first element: 11 βροτο-κλώστειρα; 252 ἁμαρη-σκαπτῆρας; 232 σωματο-φρουρητῆρας.
-τωρ
-τωρ was less productive than -τήρ until the spreading influence of Latin popularised it,[23] and a high proportion of instances in papyri, inscriptions, and literary texts (among which astrology is prominent) consist of Latin loans. This is not, however, the case with M[b], whose resolutely Greek vocabulary, with its basis in Homer and the usages already established by M[a], suggests that for him it was the suffix's associations with hexameter poetry that mattered.

---
[22] Palmer, 108-9.
[23] Adams 2003, 495; Palmer, 118-19, with many loans from Latin; Cavenaile, 200-1, whose evidence comes from papyri.

Attested. Simplex: 404 γεννήτορα; 446 ἡγήτορας [Homeric]; 197 θηρήτορας [Homeric]; 196, 349, 482 ληίστορας [Homeric]; 530 λυμάντορες; 247, 314 σημάντορας [Homeric]; 422 τεύκτορας. Compounds. 223 διαδέκτορας; 222, 245, 280, 281, 339, 471, 521 ἐπιβήτορας [Homeric]; 227, 428 προφήτορας.
Proton: 236 δια-βλήτορας; 307 κακο-μήστορες.
Hapax. Simplex. -α- stem: 324 πελεκήτορας. Denominative: 514 κηδέστορες; 114 χερνήτορας. -ε- stem: 190 θρηνήτορας; 120 ποθήτορας. -ευ- stem: 580 ταμιεύτορες; 568a τορν[εύτορας [*ex emend.*]. Consonant stem: monosyllabic: 422 γνάπτορας; 183 μελπήτορας; 397 νήκτορας; polysyllabic: 493 κωμάστορας. Compound: 220 ἀπ-αμήτορας; 483 ἐπ-αν-οίκτορας; 343 ἀπο-πλάστορας; with adjectival or nominal first element: 276 πονο-παίκτορας; 439 ὀργανο-πήκτορας; 160 πολυ-πρήκτορας; 39 χρυσο-στέπτορας; 58 παμ-ψέκτωρ.

Note on -τήρ and -τωρ
See i. 110–12. The following reviews the kinds of stem to which the poet's new formations are affixed.

M^b operates with a mixture of awareness of Homeric patterns and disrespect for Homeric precedent. For example, κλεπτῆρες and ψευστῆρας are technically correct, insofar as the suffix is added to a simplex verb stem: it is just that they ride roughshod over Homeric κλέπτης and ψεύστης. [24] But the latter look too common; the poet wants to do better. Correct, too, are κλαυστῆρας and ἀγυρτῆρας. M^b also has several forms from -ᾶν and -εῖν verbs, from which the lion's share of –τήρ and -τωρ formations derive in the Homeric poems;[25] from -εύειν (Homer has ἀρνευτήρ); and from -άζειν (κωμάστορας[26]) and -ίζειν (κατονειδιστῆρας, πεταυριστῆρας,[27] πονοπαίκτορας) verbs, whether or not they originally came from -αδ- or -ιδ- stems (as regularity requires). πονοπαίκτορας, which does, is still wrong because it is a nominal compound. Not that that was in the poet's mind: he just wanted to defamiliarise -παίκτης, a common element in the names of popular performers. The desire to defamiliarise shows itself in the number of words which are elsewhere attested with a different suffix:

ἀγυρτήρ (ἀγύρτης); ἀλειπτήρ (ἀλειπτης); ἀμαρησκαπτήρ (σκαφεύς; σκαφευτής in glossographers); ἀπαμήτωρ (ἀμητήρ is Homeric); ἀποπλάστωρ (πλάστης); γνάπτωρ (κναφεύς); διθυντήρ ((δι)ιθυντής Hesychius, but simplex ἰθυντήρ already Hellenistic Poetry); ἐπανοίκτωρ ((θυρ)επανοίκτης); θρηνήτωρ (θρηνητήρ, θρηνητής in Aeschylus); κατονειδιστήρ (ὀνειδιστής, but simplex ὀνειδιστήρ already in Euripides); κηδέστωρ (κηδεστής); κλεπτήρ (κλέπτης); κυνηγητήρ (κυνηγέτης); κωμάστωρ (κωμαστής); ὀργανοπήκτωρ (for ὀργανοποιός); νήκτωρ

---

[24] Fraenkel, i. 75–6, 123, 131. [25] Fraenkel, i. 9. [26] Fraenkel, i. 136.
[27] Fraenkel, i. 135–6.

(νήκτης); παμψέκτωρ (ψέκτης: Fraenkel, i. 127); πελεκήτωρ (πελεκητής in glossographers); πεταυριστήρ (πεταυριστής); πονοπαίκτωρ (-παίκτης); ῥαπτήρ (ῥάπτης); ταμιεύτωρ (ταμίας); ταριχευτῆρας (ταριχευτής); τορνεύτωρ (ex emend., for τορνευτής); φρουρητήρ and σωματοφρουρητήρ (φρουρός; φρουρήτωρ an alternative poetic form in AP 9.812.1); χερνήτορας (χερνής, χερνήτης: Fraenkel, i. 127); ψευστήρ (ψεύστης).

In sum, the poet uses these suffixes in every kind of situation. He has no preference for any particular type of formation, and no inhibitions at all in creating compounds, using prepositions, adjectives, adverbs, and nouns. This is the greatest contrast with M[a], whose few compounds were prepositional, and partly earlier attested (ἐπιίστορες, ὑποφήτορες—though not 3.98 ὑφηγητῆρας, προφήτορας).

Other compounds
Hapax: 330 χρε-άρπαγας; 287 καλο-βάμονας.

Adjectives

I focus on compounds, but not to the exclusion of simplex forms when newly attested.

First declension
Hapax: 304 πλαστο-κόμαι; 196 ἐμπεδο-λώβας.

Second declension
Attested. Simplex: 274 ἀσθματικοῖο. Varying suffix: 324 καγκανέης vs κάγκανος. Compounds: 390 σπαν-άδελφον; 421 πυρι-βλήτοισι; 438 πυρσο-βόλοις; 614 θηρο-βόρου; 530 ἀκριτό-βουλοι; 557 ὀξύ-γοοι [ex emend. K]; 233 πλαστο-γράφους; 600 ἡμισύ-δουλοι; 478 σκολιό-δρομος; 516 πολυ-ζώοισιν; 446 μωρο-λόγους; 423 ἱστο-πόνους; 597 τεκνο-σπόρον; 467 πυρσο-τόκος; 313 ἑταιρο-τρόφους. Double compound: 477 δυσ-εκ-φεύκτων.
Proton. Simplex: 564 ἀτράπεζος; φαρμακτός (52, 540). Compounds: 175 μυριό-δοξα; δολο-εργός (57, 243, 563); (?)9, 182 αἰθερό-πλαγκτον; (?)*509 ἠερό-πλαγκτον; (?)*623 οὐρανό-πλαγκτον; ἑλιξό-πορος (437, 467); 255 ἀρνο-φάγοισι; 78 σκολι-ωπά.
Hapax. Simplex: 113 ἀμελάθρους; 184 μαχλικῶν; 282 ἀπόλιστα; 368 ἀτίθηνον. Compounds: 224 ἑλικ-άστερον; 298 αἰθρο-δόνητον; 394 δολο-εργέα; 191 σορό-εργα; 529 θρασύ-θυμα; 540 νοσό-θυμον; 74 ἀντι-κέλευθον; 222 οἰκτρο-κελεύθους; 247 ἐμβασι-κοίτους; 301 ἀει-κώμους; 322 θηλυ-λάλους; 227 ἱερο-λήπτους; 33 οἰκτρο-μελάθρους; 504 ὀλβο-μέλαθροι; 234 ἀφθιτο-μίσους; 513 ἀξιό-μορφοι; 555 νερτερό-μορφα; 452 δι-μορφώτοισι; 57 αἰσχεό-μυθος; 501 νευρο-νόσους; 252 ἀμφ-οδικῶν; 572 βιοτο-σκόπον; 577 μεροπο-σπόρον; 358 ἀνδρό-στροφα; 590 διδυμό-στροφοι [ex emend. K]; 339 αἰθρο-τόκου; 102 πλειστο-τόκους [L]; 281 ὀθνιο-τύμβους;

124 ῥαιστο-τύποις; 564 ἀθεσμο-φάγος; 592 αἰσχεό-φημοι; 128 θεο-φήμους; 514 δοξο-φόροι; 333 σελαη-φόρος; 316 παμ-ψέκτους; 326 λιθο-ψώκτῳ; 316 μυσαρ-ωπά. With verbal first element: 500 φθινο-κώλους; 325 ἐγρεσι-οίκους. Varying suffix: 56 παν-αθέσμιος [L] vs. πανάθεσμος; 514 ἰθυ-δίκαιοι vs. -δίκης and -δικος; 75 ἀλλο-τυπώτων vs. ἀλλότυπος; 316 ἀπό-φωλα vs. ἀποφώλιος; 261 κελαινό-χροος vs. κελαινόχρως. Prepositional compounds: 161 προσ-μάρτυρα, 176 προσ-μάρτυρος; 83, 126 ἐπί-φοιτος. Double compound: 305 νεο-μορφο-τύπωτοι.

Third declension
-*ής*
Attested: 472 βλαβερ-αυγέος; 464 περισσο-μελής; 311 παμ-παθέας; 586 αἰθρο-πλανής; 277 ὀχλο-χαρεῖς.
Proton: 415 λαμπρ-αυγέσι; 555 νεκρο-ειδῆ [ex emend. K²]; 510 νεο-λαμπέα.
Hapax: 122 παντ-αυγές; 500 ἰχνο-βλαβέας; 31, 76 παμ-βλαβέας; 184 θρασυ-γλωσσέας; 583 μεσο-δερκέα; 555 νεκρο-δερκῆ [L]; 394 δολο-εργέα; 29 αἰθερο-λαμπῆ; 221 γαλλο-μανεῖς; 476 νουσο-μελεῖς; 284 κρατο-πλαγεῖς [ex emend. K: κρατοπαγεῖς L]; 249 αἰπυ-πλανής; 484 νυκτο-πλανέας; 364 ὑπνο-φανεῖς; 191 κεδρο-χαρεῖς. Varying stem: 314 αἰσχεο-κερδεῖς vs. αἰσχροκερδής. Varying suffix: 323 ναυ-πηγέσι vs. ναυπηγός, ναυπηγικός.
-*ήεις*
Attested: 485a σιδηρήεντα.
-*όεις*
Attested: 489 ἀλγινόεντα; 305 μυρόεντες; 273 οὐρανόεσσαν; 346 πισσήεντα.
Hapax: 156 ἀμβλυόεσσαν; 275 εἰαρόεντος; 373 πονόεντα; 51 σφονδυλόεντα.
-*ως*
Proton: 77, 274 ἀμφί-κερως.
-*μων*
Attested. Simplex: 584 ἀτέκμονας. Compound: 77 βιο-τέρμονος. Prepositional compound: 526 ἐπι-λήσμονας.
Hapax. Simplex: 501 ἀχθήμονας. Compound: 318 βαρυ-βάμονος; 300 μεθυ-χάρμονας; βαθυ-χρήμων (66, 504, 579). Varying suffix: 445 αἰσχεο-ρήμονας vs. αἰσχρορρήμων.
-*φρων*
Proton: 563 ἀλλό-φρων.
Hapax: 283 μωρό-φρονας; 580 πιστό-φρονες.
-*άς, -άδος*
Attested: 357 μαχλάδας.
Hapax: 63 ὀργιάδεσσιν.
-*ής, -ῆτος*
Hapax: 6 ἡμι-τμῆτι.
-*ις, -ιδος*

Attested: 603 οἰκέτιδος.
Proton: 91 κερατ-ώπιδος.
Hapax: 201 λαμπρ-αύγετις; 616 αἱματο-πώτιδες; 177 φαιν-ώπιδα.
-ηίς, -ηίδος
Attested: 98 ἡγεμονηίδας.
Hapax: 198 σκολοπηίδα; 376 δι-πολήιδι.
-γέλως, -ωτος
Hapax: 283 αἰσχρο-γέλωτας; 280, 446 ὑβρι-γέλωτας.
-παις
Hapax: 585 λιπό-παιδα.
-πους
Proton: 118 χωλό-ποδας.

Verbs

Attested: 277 θεατρο-μανοῦντας. Prepositional compound: 302 μετα-κοσμηθέντα. *Proton*: 216 λυσσο-μανοῦντα. Prepositional compound: 419 δια-ποιμαίνοντες. *Hapax*. Simplex: 269 σηπεύοντας. Compound: 272 βολ-αυγῶν, 431 βολ-αυγῇ; 224 αἰθρο-βολήσῃ, 214 πυρσο-βολοῦσα; 520 τερμο-δρομούσης; 581 ὀλβο-νομοῦντες; 25 αἰθερο-νωμῶν; 79 ἀκρο-πολεύῃ. Prepositional compounds: 84 ἀμφι-θοάζῃ; 131 ὑπερ-ορμαίνων. Varying stem: 217 σεληνάζοντα vs. σεληνιάζειν; 217 προφητάζοντα vs. προφητίζειν, προφητεύειν; 229 ὀργιόωντας vs. ὀργιάζειν.

Inflectional novelties
51 ἀκροτομηθείς, 260 ἀκροτομοῦνται; 65 μεσόωντα; 82b πεπληθώς (though Aratus and later poets have πεπληθυῖα); [87 δύναντος L]; 119 κυρτιόωντας; 481 ὁραθῇ; 518 νενεφωμένα.

Adverbs

Those that concern us all have the suffix -ηδόν. See De Stefani 2017, 31.
Attested: 424 ἀγεληδόν; 621 στοιχηδόν.
Proton: 429 στεφανηδόν.
Hapax: 486 ἀλυσηδόν; 197 βασανηδόν; 622 καματηδόν; 449 ῥεμβηδόν [*ex emend.*]; 108 ῥομβηδόν.

Conclusions

In general, the poet prefers to innovate in the most familiar categories, not, as an initial reading might suggest, in the most recherché ones. So, innovations take place mainly:

(i) among nouns, with -ίη, followed by -σύνη, then by -σμός;
(ii) among agent nouns, with -της, -ος and -ός, and -ωρ ahead of -ήρ;
(iii) among adjectives, with -ος and -ης compounds, and others far behind, though -μων is prominent among the also-ran suffixes. Dental stems get only a few instances each. Striving for a poetic effect accounts for the dearth of forms (new and old) in prosaic -ικός.

New compound verbs are far outnumbered by nouns and adjectives. The poet has a niche interest in adverbs in -ηδόν.

As we saw from the study of -τωρ and -τήρ suffixes, morphological proprieties are not this poet's concern.[28] That point has already been made. More interesting is the basic question of what he innovates *for*. There is a basic division of labour, it seems, between protases, where most of the innovations in verbs are to be found, and apodoses, where it is mostly a matter of abstract and agent nouns and adjectives. This suits the jobs the two halves of the apotelesma are called upon to do. The apodosis needs to specify activities, which it does in the form of lists and accumulations. These can indeed develop into little tableaux, but the preference remains for parallelistic forms of expression within clauses. This does some of the work in explaining why nouns and epithets are the focus of interest, not verbs, but given that the actions of the natives are the *sine qua non* of the outcome, the nominal and adjectival innovations are usually verbal derivatives, and the formations employed are not those used for outcomes or products or locations of actions (hence, not suffixes like -ιον and -εῖον), but for actions themselves. Furthermore, the popularity of -ίη and -σύνη and to a lesser extent of -μός speak to a liking for abstract forms of expression ('practitioners of animal training', 'affected to the sowing of seed') which perhaps enhance the professional and technocratic rhetoric. -σύνη is used, according to Palmer, 107, 'to form abstract nouns denoting personal qualities'. That remains true for ἀξιοπιστοσύνη and μετεωροσύνη (absent-mindedness), and it is very harnessable for types of behaviour to which astrology is particularly attentive (πολυπλαγκτοσύνη; μοιχοσύνη, πορνοσύνη). These are now served up as abstract categories of quasi-theoretical interest which can sometimes tip over into mannered excess (παιδοσύνη = the quality of being brought up).

The poet uses suffixation to create 'impressiveness' for ordinary vocabulary. This is readily seen from cases like 522 μεταβλήμασι χώρης, 550 ἀποφθεγκτήρια

---

[28] 234 θεολωβήτας also falls foul of the strict rule that derivatives from -άω and -έω verbs should not be compounded with a nominal first element, but in practice the rule was not always observed (Palmer, 110–11).

κρυπτά, and especially 4.41–2 κτεανισμῶν | δεσποσύνους, where there is a familiar and shorter prose equivalent to which the suffix adds pomp and circumstance and a sense of abstraction (as if the poet had said 'proprietorships' instead of 'goods' or 'belongings'); modern English that seeks to impress (and obfuscate) does the same. There are also cases where the poet uses suffixed forms which already exist, but have meanings of their own. Such appears to be the case for 4.104 θρονισμούς (for θρόνους); 4.151, 292 κανονισμός (for κανών); 4.202 ὁρισμούς (for ὅρους); and 4.462 κακοδαιμοσύνη (for κακὸς δαίμων). One can only wonder about the effect on the native Greek ear. Presumably it was not malapropic enough to offend or amuse or dent credibility. Intended archaism is not an obvious explanation when some of the suffixes in question are clearly not archaic, unless readers had a very different perception of their own language. Was it intended to mystify or to impress the 'simple'? Did it sound particularly impressive if being declaimed aloud?

4.5. SYNTAX

Particles

Asyndeton

It is not the norm (see p. 164). Rationales can be provided for some examples, but charts in comparable circumstances do not behave in the same way (for instance, 193 breaks off a τέχνη sequence, but so does 347, which is connected to what precedes). 362 is a slightly marginal example. It thematically continues what has gone before (harms), but at the same time stands apart because it lacks any reference to rays or striking, two key (though not absolutely invariable) characteristics of this section (pp. 248–9).

Postponed Particles

δέ is most often postponed after a prepositional phrase (nine instances, of which one involves three words and a temporal conjunction before the preposition).[29] There is one example after a noun and its epithet.[30] Four of the

---

[29] Two words: 4.55 ἐν τούτῳ δέ, 303 πρὸς τούτοις δ', 383 ἐκ γενέτου δέ, 436 ἐκ μετεωροσύνης δέ, 462 ἐν κακοδαιμοσύνῃ δ', 525 εἰς ἰδίην δέ, 594 ἐν κακοδαιμοσύνῃ δέ, 607 εἰς γῆρας δ'. Three words: 83^b ἐπὴν κατὰ γῆς δέ. Also 68 ἐκ τοίης τιμῆς δέ [ex emend. De Stefani].

[30] 77 ἀμφίκερως Μήνη δ'.

postponements occur at the main caesura (one is elided, the others create a feminine caesura). This is true for the majority of instances of delayed τε (often involving phrase- or segment-end, and followed by καί),[31] both of those with μέν (4.46, 178), and the one example of γάρ (4.541). For comparisons with other books, see p. 165.

Clusters

The wadding with gnomic τε that is characteristic of M^a (i. 113–14) is absent, except for ἦν δέ τ' (4.28, 116, 515).

Definite Article

Of the 21 instances, half are either in expressions for 'the native' or with a planet's name or name of *cardo*.[32] Most are discussed in i. 117–20, and for most of them (except as noted below) it is not worth trying to appeal to Homeric precedent. There are no articles as demonstratives.

Third-Person Pronouns and Adjectives

There are no examples of μιν; ἑ, σφε, ἑός, σφέτερος; dative οἱ, σφιν. The Attic reflexives ἑαυτοῦ (16, 157), ἑαυτῶν (250), ἑαυτούς (288) depart from epic usage

---

[31] (i) *Noun + genitive*: 4.186 ὀρχηθμῶν ἴδριάς τε; 4.448 ψηφάων παίκτας τε; 4.204 ζηλωτὰς σκολιῶν τε λόγων. (ii) *Preposition + noun (or adj.)*: 4.135 ἐν χρέεσίν τε; 4.286, 450 σὺν Ἡελίῳ τε; 4.441 ἐν ἀλκήεντί τε θυμῷ; 4.605 ἐξ ἑτέρων τε δόμων. (iii) *Noun + epithet*: 4.173 ἀθλητῆρας ἀελλόποδάς τε; 4.251 ἀχθοφόρους ὑδρέας τε (unless the epithet functions as a substantive); 4.292 πηλαίης πλίνθου τε; 4.369 θηλυτέρων βρεφέων τε; 4.434 ὀθνείης χώρης τε; 4.551 ἐσσομένων ἔργων τε; 4.603 οἰκέτιδος γενεῆς τε; 4.611 κινδύνων κρυερῶν τε. (iv) *Prepositional phrase + noun + epithet*: 4.534 ἐκ δ' ἐνύδρων μόχθων τε. (iv) *Noun + participle*: 4.567 Ἑρμείας δύνων τε. (v) *Executive verb*: 4.31 παμβλαβέας ῥέξει τε; 4.233 πλαστογράφους τεύχει τε; 4.439 μηχανικοὺς τεύχει τε. Also restored by editors in 4.60 αἰμυλίους τεύχει <τε>, 4.76 παμβλαβέας τεύχει <τε>, 4.118 χωλόποδας τεύχει <τε>, 4.445 μυθολόγους τεύχει <τε>. (vi) *Other*: 4.19 εὐτυχέας ζωῇ τε; 4.604 οὗτοι δεσποσύνων τε. Separated by a lacuna in 4.90 ... τὸ πλεῖστον ζωῆς <> τε.

[32] *The native* (8 examples): 46, 80 ὁ φύς, 87 ὁ λοχευθείς, 299 τοὺς τεχθέντας, 351 τὸ πεφυκός, 387 ὁ φυόμενος, 463 ὁ τικτόμενος, 617 ὁ γεγώς. *Planet's name* (2 examples): 271–2 τὸν πυρόεντα | ἀστέρ' Ἐνυαλίοιο (unless this is anaphoric, inasmuch as the previous configuration involves Mars, or demonstrative: 'the fiery one, you know the one I mean, the star of Mars'); 362 τὸν συνετόν. *Cardo*: 69 ἐπὶ τὴν δύσιν. Others as follows. *With noun*: 285 ὁ βίος; 289 ὁ πόρος; 319 τοῖσι διωγμοῖς(??); 625 ὁ πάλαι καὶ ὁ νῦν καὶ ἐπῶν χρόνος (cf. i. 120). *With αὐτός + noun*: 297–8 τὸν αὐτὸν...δρόμον (cf. i. 117). *With particle + noun*: 208 τάς τ' αὐγὰς (possibly anaphoric). *With neuter part.*: 236 τὸ τεχνασθέν. *With neuter adj.*: 90 τὸ πλεῖστον ζωῆς (cf. i. 120, but the genitive makes it unlike Homeric οἱ πλέονες). *In predicative position*: 24 Κριὸς ὅ τ' οὐρανίου κορυφῆς ὄρος.

Prepositions

Protasis

M^b has a quite different pattern of usage from that of M^a (whose sixth book is used as the comparison in what follows). He avoids certain prepositions, but does not avoid prepositional expressions *per se*; rather, those he uses fall short of giving nice positional notations, as they did in M^a. M^b can be sketchy.

To begin with ἐν, which is used copiously. Several instances are accounted by normal prose usages ('in these aspects',[33] 'in the nativity',[34] 'in a sign' (or type of sign),[35] 'in its own signs/terms',[36] 'in the Evil Demon'[37]). Even here, though, some of M^b's uses are vague,[38] others catachrestic.[39] They contrast with M^a's more frequent and succinct uses of ἐν for positional data, most conspicuously, fourteen instances with being-in certain types of sign (as against M^b's two: n. 35), as well as being-in houses,[40] being-in places (6.36), and being-in *kentra*.[41] Moreover, when it comes to the epic form ἐνί (4.205), M^b's single use occurs in a pastiche Homeric expression, not in a protasis, whereas M^a has some 35(!) instances in all, a dozen of which refer to being-in terms, houses, signs, or *kentra*.[42]

The use of ἐς/εἰς by M^b exceeds that of M^a by a greater margin, with over twice as many occurrences in almost 20% fewer lines.[43] These are accounted for by both protasis and apodosis, but especially the former, where he has a dozen instances against M^a's four (two of which represent the same stylisation

---

[33] 4.80 ἐν σχήματι τοίῳ, 444 φαύλοις ἐν σχήμασιν, 617 σχήμασι δ' ἐν τούτοις.
[34] 4.390, 568 ἐν γενέθλαισιν/-ῃσιν.
[35] 4.97 ἐν Διδύμοισι φαανθείς, 452 ἐν ζῳιδίοισι διμορφώτοισι; routine in book 6.
[36] 4.20 ἐν οἰκείοισι, 265 ἔν θ' ὁρίοις ἰδίοισι δυωδεκατημορίοις τε; cf. 6.430, 487.
[37] 4.462, 594 ἐν κακοδαιμοσύνῃ; cf. 6.61, 151, 220.
[38] Wadding: 4.208 ἐν οὐρανῷ ἀστερόεντι, 516 πολυζῴοισιν ἐν ἄστροις, 553 ἐν κύκλοισι θοοῦ δινήματι κόσμου.
[39] 4.45 ἐν καθέτῳ κόσμου (for κατὰ κάθετον); 63 προστήσονται ἐν; 82^b ἐν σινέεσσι πεπληθώς; 122 ἐν ἡμεριναῖσι λοχείαις (for ἐπὶ ἡμερινῆς γενέσεως); 189 ἐν ἀλλαγμοῖσι... ὧν ὁρίων; 250 δωδεκατημορίοισιν ἐν ἀλλαγμοῖσιν ἑαυτῶν (for e.g. ἐναλλάξαντες); 431 ἐν ἀκτίνεσσι βολαυγῇ (for dative of agent). 351 ἐν ἤματι would normally be ἡμέρας (or καθ' ἡμέραν), though there are instances of ἐν ἡμέρᾳ.
[40] 6.107, 160, 265, 283, 301, 302. [41] 6.230, 355, 526, 610.
[42] 2.379; 3.363, 365, 398; 6.111, 176, 181, 214, 272, 282, 451, 535.
[43] 17 instances in M^a book 6, 36 instances in M^b.

for 'setting').[44] M[b] uses it directionally for aspect (171, 317, 472) and the casting of rays (214), and renders other expressions for aspect (231, 479) and location in (519, 577) in the form of motion towards. But he also uses it instead of 'being-in', where one would sooner expect ἐν,[45] and a passage like 452–4, where the prepositions ἐν, κατά, and ἐς are ranged in parallel, show that *variatio* is prized more highly than precision.

He is also fond of κατά, where a similar pattern arises. In raw numbers, he uses it more frequently than M[a] in book 6, and many of these passages do convey a specific meaning (in a sign;[46] in a planet's own houses or degrees;[47] in *kentra*[48]). On the other hand, and contrasting with M[a], who uses it considerably more often for being-in *kentra* (ten instances), he has many more which are simple waffle ('in the heavens', etc.),[49] and a couple which ought to convey a precise meaning but succeed only in obfuscating it (4.335, perhaps meaning 'in the same position in the dodecatemories of', and 4.457, apparently for the simple meaning 'in equal degrees').

The pattern is less pronounced with ἐπί, although it is still there. In absolute terms M[a] uses this more frequently (37 instances to M[b]'s 21), but numbers in the protasis itself are similar (15 in M[b], 17 in M[a]). Both poets have a similar preference for the dative (about two-thirds of instances in both books), though M[a] also has four instances of the genitive and M[b] none. The difference is that once again, while both poets use this preposition in positional notations to mean 'on', 'in', 'at', or (with acc.) 'towards',[50] M[b] has more instances that are nebulous (335, apparently a tortured expression for 'at the Full Moon'), strange (410, 586 with μάρτυς, where a bare genitive or dative would have sufficed, presumably to be regarded as a quasi-tmesis of ἐπιμάρτυρος), or just wadding (35, 275).

Of other prepositions which are used less frequently, there are three uses of ἀνά with the accusative ('in heaven').[51] περί is used twice with the accusative (4.108 'around', in circular motion, and 242 'in the vicinity of'), contrasting with the three more precise uses with accusative or dative apropos of location in *kentra* in M[a] (3.18, 6.227, 276). The single use of ὑπέρ (4.131, accusative), which means apparently 'to the right of' (and is *de trop* with a ὑπερ- compound verb[52]),

---

[44] 6.22, 76; 381 = 642. [45] 4.17, 94, a *kentron*; 182, terms.
[46] 4.96, 240, 241, 454; also 6.48, 78, 495, 499, 534.
[47] Houses: 4.16, 157; also 6.372, 520, 526 (gen.), 641 (gen.). Degrees: 4.38, 172 (gen.).
[48] 4.65, 70, 367 (periphrastic). With gen., for IMC/underground: 4.82, 480, 582.
[49] 4.139, 140, 147, 239, 295, 310, 367, 453, 466, 509, 537, 589.
[50] Also, without ambiguity, 'following on from' (89).
[51] 4.111 and 403 ἀν' οὐρανόν, 273 ἀν' οὐρανόεσσαν ἀταρπόν. Contrast 6.199 μέσσον ἀν' οὐρανόν, a precise indication of the MC, though the datives in 2.3 ἀν' οὐρανῷ, 105 ἀν' ἀστράσιν are evocative rather than precise. Vague ἀν' οὐρανόν is also found five times in Quintus.
[52] Other examples are 4.345 συνασκοῦντας σὺν ἐλαίῳ; 575 μέτ' εὐτυχίης μετέχοντας (as transmitted); and 4.598 συνέῃ... σὺν αὐτῷ. Redoubled prepositions are a feature of prose (T. Mommsen, 762–4).

contrasts with the copious occasions when M^a used it with the genitive to mean location in a *kentron*. Finally, only one of the four examples of ὑπό is in a protasis (578), where it is used with the accusative of descending motion. This once again contrasts with M^a, who uses it extensively in expressions for 'aspected by [the rays of]',[53] and 'under the rays of' (3.301, 6.712), always in the dative except in 3.301.

For comitative expressions, of which any astrologer has great need, the essence of the matter is that M^b has a broad spectrum, ranging from bare datives (e.g. 28) to exotic and composite phrases, or hazy expressions which do not specify the precise relationship between two entities (4.226–7, 420, both with κοινῶς).[54] Some of his borrowings of unusually constructed verbs from poets expand the range further. In theory this range of options reduces his need for prepositions, and among those in common use elsewhere in the corpus the poet limits himself to σύν (9×) and μετά (4.231), with no ἅμα or ὁμοῦ. Of the nine instances of σύν, seven are in protases. Of these, 4.219, 238, 552, 598, and possibly 319 (regarded by T. Mommsen, 213, as a *Häufung*, not necessarily correctly), are in accordance with M^a's practice, that is, they indicate an add-on element. The use of σύν in 450 also corresponds to that of ἅμα in 6.249. Perhaps for deliberate effect, 4.286 reverses normal procedure (it is used for existing items to which a third is added).

The poet expands his limited range with a number of μίγ- words (all with precedent in Nicander) which hover between adverbs and prepositions (in which case they take the dative) and which Mommsen calls *Casusadverbien*, but which do not necessarily denote a straightforward relationship of conjunction, as one might at first have supposed.[55] Without anticipating the later discussion (pp. 217–18), the point here is that they contribute to the nebulous comitative statements which the poet favours above conciseness. He employs redundant adverbs (219 κοινὰ σὺν), wadding compound verbs where a bare dative would have sufficed (290 τούτοις δ' ἄμμιγα πᾶσι Κρόνου συναλώμενος ἀστήρ), and other types of comitative phrase (499 μίγδην ἰκέλῃσι πορείαις).

Apodosis

Other than to note that, so far from over-using ἀπό (i. 122), M^b is not even particularly fond of it (five instances), the main interest here is the uses of ἐν.

---

[53] 2.390; 3.6, 115, 265, 272; 6.136, 138, 382, 400, 521.
[54] T. Mommsen, 212–15.
[55] μίγα: 4.219 (prep.), 527 (adv./prep.). μίγδην: 4.202 (adv.), 499 (adv./prep.). ἄμμιγα: 4.215, 290 (prep.); of these, 290 is an add-on, as is 458 in an apodosis. συμμίγδην: 4.266 (adv.).

Some are unexceptionable.[56] Some are EGHP hand-me-downs.[57] Some continue favourite usages from the earlier poet: 'among' a population, including the 'best in show' motif;[58] 'in' an area of distinction.[59] Most distinctive of this poet is a group of passages that refer to life circumstances.[60] As we should expect, some are otiose or clumsy,[61] while others are constructed with verbs with which this would not be the expected preposition.[62] See also De Stefani 2017, 31, on possible instances where εἰς is used for ἐν.

Other remarks

There is no anastrophe (N x) with ἄνα, ἄπο, ἔνι, ἔπι, μέτα, πέρι, ὕπερ, ὕπο (ἅμα, ἄτερ, ὁμοῦ are in any case absent), and the poet is very sparing with the prior placement of an epithet (4.117 γονίμην ἐπὶ γαστέρα; 263 κορυφὴν ἐπ' Ἀρήιον; 273 τετράγωνον ἀν' οὐρανόεσσαν ἀταρπόν). He also uses tmesis extremely parsimoniously, if at all. An indication of this is 4.220 μηδέων ἀπαμήτορας, doing away with the tmesis in the Hesiodic model (*Th.* 180–1) which M^a at 3.396 retains. If it happens at all, it happens eccentrically with the epithet ἐπι-μάρτυρος (see above).

Nouns

For the poet's uses of the genitive, see s.v. Style. Genitives of place are found in 4.5 πόλοιο and 396 φαεσφόρου Οὐλύμποιο (though not 110, 449). See also on 4.81 νόοιο.

---

[56] 4.89, 281 ἐν ξενίῃ, 397 ἐν ὕδασι, 401 ἐν πελάγεσσιν.
[57] 4.143 ἐν χείρεσσι, [150 ἐν πραπίδεσσιν L], 155 ἐν ὀφθαλμοῖσι, 208 ἐν οὐρανῷ, 375 ἐν μεγάροισιν, 401 ἐν πελάγεσσιν, 492 ἐν εἰλαπίναις (Hes. fr. 305.3 M.–W., in this *sedes*). ἐνὶ στέρνοισιν is not Homeric, but ἐνὶ στήθεσσιν is (4.205 n.).
[58] 4.138 ἔν τε γυναιξίν; 4.516 (among the stars). 'Best in show': 4.46 ἐν ἡγεμόνεσσιν ἄριστος; 233 ἐν ψεύσταις προφέροντας, 511 ἐν ἀνθρώποισι κράτιστοι.
[59] In a certain field: 4.127, 129*bis*, 130, 150, 175 εὐδοκιμοῦντας ἐν ἄθλοις, 186 ἐν θυμέλαις προφέροντας, 228 ἐν τελετῇσιν ἀρίστους.
[60] With a verb: 4.135 ἐν χρέεσίν τε ... βιώσεται; 376–7 ἐν διπολήιδι φήμῃ | ζήσεται; 580–1 ἔν τε τοκισμοῖς | καὶ χρείαις ζήσουσι; 257 ἐν ὕδατι γηράσκοντες; 487 ἔν τε βιαιοτάτῳ θανάτῳ βίον ἐκλείψουσιν; 556–7 ἔν τε καταγγελίῃσι θεῶν ... βιότου τέλος ἀθρήσουσιν. With a word for 'actions': 4.160 ἔν τε λογιστονόμοισιν ... ἔργοις; 278 πηκτοῖσι ... ἐν ἔργοις; 323 ἐν ναυπηγέσι τέχναις. Other: 4.82^b ἐν σινέεσσι πεπληθώς (noted by Koechly 1851, xli); 61 λάμποντας ἐν ὄλβοις, 106 ἐν ὄλβῳ; 447 ἔν τ' ἀρεταλογίῃ; 471 ἐν προκοπῇσιν.
[61] 4.235 ἐν ἀλλοτρίῃσι βλάβῃσιν (unless ἐπ' is correct); 390 ἐν γενέθλαισι or γενετῆρσι: odd either way (see ad loc.). ἐν θυμῷ is Homeric, but 441 ἐν ἀλκήεντί τε θυμῷ sits oddly in its context.
[62] 4.63 προστήσονται ἐν ὀργιάδεσσιν ἑορταῖς (for genitive); 82b ἐν σινέεσσι πεπληθώς (for genitive or dative, respectively Homer and Hellenistic poetry); 199 προσαρτηθέντες ἐν ἥλοις (for instrumental dative); 257 ἐν ὕδατι γηράσκοντες (contrast e.g. Θ p. 121.19–20 ἐξ ὑγρῶν πραγμάτων ... ἐπικτήσεται); 431 ἐν ἀκτίνεσσι βολαυγῇ (for instrumental dative).

Verbs

Number

The dual is introduced in 4.599 as a result of light emendation.

Voice

311 ὀπυιομένους: passive, perhaps to make an effective point (see ad loc.).
473 ἐναντιόωντα: active for middle.
480 ἐπὶ δυομένῳ: middle for active τὸ δῦνον.

Mood

In temporal clauses M[b] so decidedly prefers the subjunctive that deviations can be corrected with confidence. See pp. 166–7 for comparisons with other authors in the corpus.

These subjunctives are generally accompanied by ἄν. Of eleven instances of ἡνίκα, ten are accompanied by the particle; only 4.170 is not. Particle-less are also 386 ἦμος, and 73, 466, and 527 ὁππότε; otherwise there are four instances of ὁππότε δ' ἄν, ten of ὅτ' ἄν, nine of ἐπήν (one of which, at 83[b], is transmitted with an optative which is not metrically guaranteed and duly corrected by Koechly), and one of εὖτ' ἄν. The poet does not use κε or κεν.

In conditional clauses the poet's only conjunction is ἤν; he does not use εἰ. Once again his preference is for the subjunctive; of the four exceptions, the indicatives (i) 452 πέλονται (following ἀμφιπολῶσιν) and (ii) 589 λάμψει meet the criteria (i. 390) laid down in M[a] for emendation [-ωνται and -ῃ A.-R.], while (iii) 552 φανείη is presumably an 'honorary subjunctive' (i. 135–6), and (iv) 147 ἔχοι (followed by συνῇ) should be corrected [-ῃ A.-R.]. The corresponding passage in 1.294–5 has εἰ + optative.

Tense

Protasis
Aorist and present tenses are about evenly split. That is, in temporal clauses there are 23 aorists and 30 presents, in conditional clauses 23 aorists and 17 presents.

Apodosis
Formal matters (the clause- and phrase-patterns in which apodoses are presented) are discussed in the next section. The focus here is on the choice of tense within those clauses.

(i) Gnomic aorist. Seven in apotelesmata (plus one in a naming formula), two of stars and five of natives and their circumstances.[63]

(ii) Future. 75 in all, six of the stars, in addition to which an aorist optative can be taken as proxy for the future (546); two of fate; the remainder of natives and their circumstances.[64]

(iii) Present. 71 or 72 in apotelesmata, 41 or 42 of the stars, 30 of natives, and 8 more outside apotelesmata.[65]

(iv) Of the hybrid construction ἔσσεσθαι δείκνυσι, which combines present and future, a further 24 examples.[66]

Thus, of a total of 177 or 178 verbs (the uncertainty is caused by 141), 3.93% are gnomic aorists, 42.13% are futures, 41.01% are presents, and 13.48% are the hybrid ἔσσεσθαι δείκνυσι. The pattern is distinctive. The hybrid construction is unique in this poet. The future is not, but the extent to which it predominates over the present is remarkable. The resulting presentation is like that of an oracle, but in the absence of evidence for gathered oracle collections other than the highly idiosyncratic Sibyllina, it is hard to say whether the rather scattergun collection either does or is intended to resemble a collection of oracles.

Unusual Constructions

See notes on 4.74 διαμετρεῖν; 95 βάλλειν; 310 συννεύειν (w. dat.); 508–10 ἐλθεῖν (w. dat.); 575 μετέχειν.

Adverbial Neuters Plural

These are not unique (cf. 1.184 ἀνώδυνα φαρμάσσοντας, 192 ἀνηλέα κωκύουσαι), but become a mannerism of this poet.

---

[63] Stars: 4.115 ὤλεσε, 212 ἔρξεν. Natives: 248 ἔφυ, 285 ἀπεμάξαθ', 377 ἔβλαστεν (with sense of anteriority), 381 ἔσσυτ' [ex emend. K], 413 ἔδωκεν. In naming formula: 54.

[64] Stars: 104, 344, 363, 483, 492, 584. Fate: 405, 406. Natives: 46, 50, 52, 56, 63, 88, 89, 90, 123, 134, 135, 136, 137, 138, 143, 254, 256, 303, 352, 353, 361, 372, 374, 377, 388, 389, 390, 393, 400, 408, 411, 433, 435, 455, 458, 459, 461, 464, 475, 485a, 486, 487, 490, 504, 506, 511, 528, 538, 546, 554, 557, 561, 579, 581, 590, 592, 596bis, 599, 604, 605, 607; and their circumstances: 43, 237, 370, 566, 612, 615.

[65] Stars: 18, 21, 27, 31, 34, 60, 66, 71, 76, 85, 100, 102, 105, 113, 118, [141], 142, 178, 179, 184, 190, 196, 203, 215, 228, 233, 244, 276, 287, 291, 320, 340, 357, 369, 416, 439, 445, 468, 497, 568a, 602, 609. Natives: 81, 92, 198, 365, 371, 385, 407, 417, 474, 517, 535bis; and their circumstances: 62, 64, 68(?), 72 (present perfect), 213, 246, 260, 262, 270, 289, 308, 331, 382, 383 (present perfect), 385, 495, 543 (present perfect), 559. (Not in apotelesmata: 14, 15, 20, 169, 242, 543 (present perfect), 620, 622.)

[66] 39–40, 99, 128, 150–1, 155–6, 158–9, 162–3, 173–4, 210, 221, 228–9, 252–3, 268, 299, 313, 329–30, 337, 349–50, 397–8, 423 (see the correction by Massimilla), 428–30, 501–2, 521–2, 573–4.

In protasis: 78 σκολιωπὰ περῶσα; 79 ἰσόμοιρα...ἀκροπολεύῃ; 359 ἰσόμοιρα φανῇ; 380 διάμετρα φανῇ; 409 ἰσόμοιρα πελάζῃ; 520 τετελεσμένα τερμοδρομούσης; and possibly 367 φεγγοβολῶν ἰσόμοιρα κατ' Οὐλύμποιο κέλευθα.

In apodosis: 164 ἀνάξια θηλυμανοῦντας; 198 στρεβλὰ κολαζόμενοι; 277 φιλόμοχθα θεατρομανοῦντας; 303 πουλὺ κακώτερα βλαστήσουσιν; 394 δολοεργέα νυμφευθεῖσα; 506 ἐπίψογα νύκτας ἄγουσαι; 529 θρασύθυμα μεμηνότες; 602 ὁμόζυγα λατρεύοντας. Internal accusatives at 498 τὰ βέβαια φρονοῦντας; 518 νενεφωμένα βουλεύοντες.

Outside apotelesmata: 7 πλαγκτὰ διχαζόμενος; 10 ὀρθὰ τεκμαιρομένοισι; 92 λοξὰ ταλαντεύουσα.

4.6. STYLE

Composition

All poets have their preferences in the ways they handle the skeletal *if–then* pattern of the apotelesma; this one has a particularly varied way of handling the limited range of options available to him. These are:

(i) 'the stars bring about', with an executive verb[67] followed by accusative nouns (especially, in this case, agent nouns), adjectives, and participles;

(ii) the ἔσσεσθαι δείκνυσι construction, that is, a revelatory or annunciatory verb followed by the future infinitive, of which there are 24 examples, although in some the infinitive follows the first accusative as something of an afterthought (150–1, 173–4);

(iii) the announcement of birth ('there will be born', 'there will be'), which comes close to the use of ἐκφύσει as executive verb in 483.[68]

The simplest form of the list that follows these announcements is nominal. But it is readily diversified with clauses containing finite verbs for the natives' lives and activities. Finite verbs may round off what began as nominal constructions (accusative nouns after executive verbs, and nominative nouns after 'there will be born' etc.),[69] or the whole entry may take verbal form.[70] Sometimes the

---

[67] For the terminology, see i. xxviii.

[68] 'The native will be/be born/be seen' (46, 87–8, 387–8, 463–4). 'There will be born' (455 φύσεται; 256, 504, 511, 590 φύσονται; 417 λοχεύονται; 459 τεχθήσεται), 'grow' (303 βλαστήσουσιν), 'appear' (361 φανοῦνται), 'live' (433 ζήσουσι). 'He/there/they will be': 56, 88, 134 ἔσσεται; 538 ἔσσετ', 461, 561 ἔσται; 528, 599 ἔσονται; 579 ἔσσονται.

[69] 62–4, 143–4, 254–5, 485–90, 604–7 (after accusatives); 505–7 (after nominatives).

[70] 88–92, 123–4, 351–3, 372–3, 374–8, 381–3, 385, 387–90, 393–4, 411–13, 433–6, 554–9, 596.

verbal round-off takes the form of a relative clause,[71] and in this case there is a rather remarkable parallel with the syntax of Rom. 1:29–32, where Paul is enumerating and denouncing the unrighteous among men:

²⁹ πεπληρωμένους πάσῃ ἀδικίᾳ πονηρίᾳ πλεονεξίᾳ κακίᾳ μεστοὺς φθόνου φόνου ἔριδος δόλου κακοηθείας, ψιθυριστάς, ³⁰ καταλάλους, θεοστυγεῖς, ὑβριστάς, ὑπερηφάνους, ἀλαζόνας, ἐφευρετὰς κακῶν, γονεῦσιν ἀπειθεῖς, ³¹ ἀσυνέτους, ἀσυνθέτους, ἀστόργους, ἀνελεήμονας· ³² οἵτινες τὸ δικαίωμα τοῦ θεοῦ ἐπιγνόντες, ὅτι οἱ τὰ τοιαῦτα πράσσοντες ἄξιοι θανάτου εἰσίν, οὐ μόνον αὐτὰ ποιοῦσιν ἀλλὰ καὶ συνευδοκοῦσιν τοῖς πράσσουσιν.

²⁹ Being filled with all unrighteousness, fornication, wickedness, covetousness, maliciousness; full of envy, murder, debate, deceit, malignity; whisperers, ³⁰ Backbiters, haters of God, despiteful, proud, boasters, inventors of evil things, disobedient to parents, ³¹ Without understanding, covenantbreakers, without natural affection, implacable, unmerciful: ³² Who knowing the judgment of God, that they which commit such things are worthy of death, not only do the same, but have pleasure in them that do them.

The list of delinquents consists of a vast asyndetic accumulation of adjectives and nouns, ending with a relative clause introduced by οἵτινες.[72] One wonders whether there was a common source for this and astrology, or at least whether the listing style had a parallel manifestation in e.g. diatribe.[73]

To align the items in his lists, this poet uses more kinds of parallelism than the latest two, and more creatively. Like them, he has rhymes/jingles across the caesura (200, 348) and line-end (even in a protasis at 139–40). But he is much more sparing than they of the former; conversely, he is much readier to place the jingles at different points in the line (at line-beginning 191–2, 382–3, 445–6; before the caesura 80–3, 357–8; across the caesura 345–6; before the bucolic caesura 135–8, 196–7), and is capable of separating parallelistic material by an intervening line, which arguably makes the effect less cloying (50 + 2; 127 ἐν σοφίῃσιν ἀρίστους + 129 ἐν τελεταῖσιν ἀρίστους; 149 ῥεκτῆρας + 150 ἐργοπόνους

---

[71] 42–3, 197–200, 213, 236–7, 260–1 (and 262 on Koechly's restoration), 270, 285, 289, 308, 331–2, 382–3, 399–401, 413, 495, 559, 565–6, 615–16 (a relative clause whatever the corrupt 614 was). A relative clause occurs mid-entry at 246. There were already examples of the sign-off relative clause in 2.216–17(?), 231, 262 (interim), 311–12; 3.94–5; 6.347, 354, and very briefly in 2.183, 245; 6.679.

[72] Cf. too 1 Tim. 1:9–10, where the last item in the *Lasterkatalog* is verbal if not specifically in a relative clause: εἰδὼς τοῦτο, ὅτι δικαίῳ νόμος οὐ κεῖται, ἀνόμοις δὲ καὶ ἀνυποτάκτοις, ἀσεβέσι καὶ ἁμαρτωλοῖς, ἀνοσίοις καὶ βεβήλοις, πατρολῴαις καὶ μητρολῴαις, ἀνδροφόνοις, (10) πόρνοις, ἀρσενοκοίταις, ἀνδραποδισταῖς, ψεύσταις, ἐπιόρκοις, καὶ εἴ τι ἕτερον τῇ ὑγιαινούσῃ διδασκαλίᾳ ἀντίκειται. Rev. 22:15 ends a nominal list with two participles. In *Or. Sib.* 3.36–40 the relative clause is in the *pen*ultimate line.

[73] For a vindication of diatribe as a genre, and a discussion of its stylistic features (although not this particular one), see C. Song, *Reading Romans as a Diatribe* (New York, 2004).

+ 152 κοσμήτας; 245 ἐπιβήτορας + 247 σημάντορας; 62–4, where 62–3 are linked by line-initial demonstratives but 62 and 64 also by middle-passive verbs and κρυπτά/ἄπυστα at line-end). More conventionally, he has chiastically constructed single lines (130; 332, where parechesis reinforces the chiasmus; 385), and sometimes longer passages (508–10).

Parallelisms are brought about by any or all of morphology, syntax, and metre,[74] but are sometimes reinforced by phonology,[75] even of two different parts of speech which nevertheless sound alike (85–6 τίθησι/τέκνοισι; 200 κατάδειπνα/δεινά; 445–6 τεύχει/χλεύης, no doubt enhanced in pronunciation by itacism). That the items are in question are so often agent nouns[76] arises from the subject-matter, but the poet's favourite formations in -(ή)τορας, and -τῆρας prove a particular godsend (196–7, 245 + 247, 280–1, 579–80; at 220–3 and 422–4 he rings the changes by *avoiding* an exact alignment).

The poet uses parallelisms as he pleases. Some consist of isolated lines. But the poet also builds more extensive sequences, even structures which hold together entire segments, a useful way of creating a sense of cohesiveness not only for the items in an apodosis (31–4, 80–3, 85–6, 135–8, 178–9; moreover, all of 98–106 and 276–85[77] are loosely parallelistic) but also for comprehensive bite-size lists of various types of sign (22–6, 96–7, 240–2, 274–5). The same is true of chiasmus, which, in the case of 508–10, holds together a complete protasis. Both techniques can create a sense of closure (the restoration of the end of 357 should take into account the likelihood that the poet was trying to create some sort of jingle with 358 ἔργα τελούσας; chiasmus: 130, 616), but the sting-in-the-tail technique, whereby a parallelism is disturbed by a sudden change of syntax and/or rhythm, does this with an arguably greater sense of finality, not only at the end of an entire chart (113–15, 118–20, 127–30,[78] 523–6, 579–81), but also to round off a sense-unit within it (531–3, which formulates the idea of career-change three times over).

All these effects are made to work in interesting tension with one another. For instance, in 127–30, the first three lines have parallel endings, but the last

---

[74] e.g. 85–6, 178–9, 183–4, 243–4, 569–70 are almost metrically identical; 31–2, 33–4, 49–51, 57–8, 184–6, 222–3, 279–80, 388–9, 405–6, 439–40, 464–5 are metrically identical; 563–4, 579–80 are identical after the caesura; 245 + 247 are almost identical after the caesura.

[75] But can we swallow 33–4 λύπης *bis*?

[76] Of the same metrical shape and in same *sedes*: 184–5 θρασυγλωσσέας ᾠδούς/κιθάρης τε μελουργούς; 191–2 κεδροχαρεῖς/νεκροτάφους; 243–4 δολοεργούς/τροφοποιούς; 311–12 γονοπώτας/ἐφυβρίστους; 315–16 ἔχθιστον/παμψέκτους; 464–5 σῶμα περισσομελῆς/πὰρ φύσιν ἡμερίην; 513–14 ἀξιόμορφοι/ἰθυδίκαιοι [ex emend. K]; 569–70 θεοπλάστας/παναρίστους.

[77] Cf. —⏑⏑— compounds at line-beginning in 277–8, 280, 283–4; 280–1 ἐπιβήτορας; 280 ὑβριγέλωτας and 283 αἰσχρογέλωτας.

[78] A gentle example, shifting a line-end from accusative to dative.

two also have parallel first halves, so that the sting in the tail is strictly confined to the second half of the line. At 183–6, a more or less strictly parallel first couplet is followed by one arranged around an accusative/dative—dative/accusative chiasmus. In 324–5 near-identical metre reinforces near-parallelism of syntax, but the accusative + dependent genitive expressions are also constructed chiastically. In 345–6, the jingle words συνασκοῦντας and πονήσοντας are exactly parallel, but the first halves of the lines consist of a noun + -ήεις adjective arranged opposite ways round, even as their phonology continues to support the isocolon. In 382–3, ἐκ γενέτου is phonologically parallel with ὧν γένεσις but syntactically with πρὸς μητρὸς.

The poet engineers the shift, swerve, or change of tack in ways that, though not unique to him, harden in his hands to the point of mannerism. As we have seen, the relative clause is a particular favourite after inventories of nouns (listed above), and some of them *also* involve disrupting a more or less strongly marked syntactic/rhythmic and/or metrical parallelism: 197–200, 213, 260–1 + 262 (on Koechly's restoration), 270, 285, 399–401, 565–6. In 382–3, where it follows a verbal construction, the relative clause is itself constructed as a parallelism.

Much of the time these are formal games. But sometimes they reinforce sense. The whole of 98–106 is loosely parallelistic, but the position of the verbs underscores the similarities and contrasts in the outcomes (100 ἔρδει ~ 102 τεύχει ~ 105 φυλάσσει at line-end, but 104 οὐκ ἄξει before the caesura). In the family charts of 382–3, 385, 393, parallelisms and chiasmus are both useful when it comes to comparing and contrasting the mother's and father's sides of the family. And depending on how charitable one is prepared to be to the poet, the metrical parallelism of 485–6 might reinforce the sense of corollary: imprisonment is the outcome of being apprehended in other people's houses. Conversely, the poet is seeking an effect of deliberate variety when he chooses to end a sequence with a change of tempo. The relative clauses make generalising remarks about the natives, and some are more general still (413, 495); there are even a few gnomic conclusions with γάρ (91–2; 541–3 + 544) or which consist of a self-contained *bon mot* (248, with gnomic aorist). Such sign-offs move away from circumstantiality to eternal verities, and create a sense of neat, formal conclusiveness.

One final aspect of the poet's compositional technique is his tendency to think in information units and to construct his hexameters accordingly. These units usually occupy whole or half lines, and explain why there are so many occasions in both protasis and apodosis when a line is re-erected over the same framework, sometimes with minimal change, sometimes with more substantial differences (change of agency, different epithets, different positional data), but in such a way that the component parts occupy the same positions in the hexameter.[79] This is a matter of compositional convenience. It means that data can be swapped in and out in blocks without having to rethink a ground-plan that remains basically stable. The same tendency to think at the level of the line also determines the poet's formulary, but it can have curiously opposite effects in the protasis and apodosis. In the former, when the unit of thought is short (for instance, name of the planet, type of aspect, or identification of *kentron*), the poet leans heavily on decorative epithets, and where another poet less sensitive to information overload (i. 203–4) might sandwich this together with other data into a single line, this one produces an effect of word-spinning. The line-by-line approach is a bonus for composition, and presumably also for memorisation if that comes into question, but its by-product is an impression of loadedness and encumbrance; the poet seems constitutionally incapable of leaving a noun unadorned. In the apodosis, on the other hand, one can have the impression of bombardment (this *and* this *and* this *and* this), where it is sometimes unclear whether the extensions to the basic notion in a line are to be regarded as decorative epithets or appositional nouns with some additional information value or shade of meaning (for unrelenting Focus, see i. 204–5).

The tendency to over-egg the pudding by aggregating epithets is just a particular instance of the one-line-at-a-time approach. Double epithets, with and without connectives, are of course entirely at home in epic.[80] Patterns like 4.26 πολυάστερος ἔμπυρος οἶκος and 146 ἑλικοδρόμος ἄστατος ἀστήρ are formally and even rhythmically very similar to (say) Τελαμώνιος ἄλκιμος Αἴας, while 298 ἑλικὸν δρόμον αἰθροδόνητον (on either side of the noun) is perhaps most like *Od.* 4.393, 483 δολιχὴν ὁδόν ἀργαλέην τε (despite the connective). On the other hand, patterns like 4.11 πλαγκτὴ...βροτοκλώστειρα χορείη and 94 οὐρανίης...πυριλαμπέος αἴθρης, where the epithets are separated and distributed across both halves of the line, cannot be found exact Homeric matches, and such aggregations might, together with the poet's borrowings from tragedy and apparent attempts to strike up a tragic register, suggest a simultaneous striving towards a kind of pseudo-lyric, even pseudo-dithyrambic effect.[81]

---

[79] *Protasis.* 16 ~ 157; 45 ~ 132; 59 ~ 491–2; 95 ~ 110; 176 ~ 290 ~ 309; 180 ~ 356; 182 ~ 509–10; 189 ~ 473; 201 ~ 496 (first half of line); 271–2 ~ 420–1; 420 ~ 613; 437 ~ 467; 595 and 608 Ἡελίου δ' ἀκτῖνες. *Apodosis.* 33 ~ 222; 85 ~ 497, cf. also 113, 142; 89 ~ 135 (cf. 138, 388); 151–2 ~ 292–3; 152 πεπονημένα τεχνάζοντας ~ 321 μεμελημένα δαιδάλλοντας, 518 νενεφωμένα βουλεύοντες; 162 and 521 πουλυπλανεῖς ξενίης, 470 πουλυπλανεῖς ξενίῃσιν; 186...τε, καὶ ἐν θυμέλαις προφέροντας, 233...τε καὶ ἐν ψεύσταις προφέροντας, 344...τε λινοστολίης προφέροντας; 222 ~ 245 (cf. 33, 280–1, 339, 471); 280 ~ 446; 283 ~ 446; 326, 525 βίον ἰθύνοντας, 507 βίον ἰθύνουσαι; 470 ἀρήια λήματ' ἔχοντας, 512 ἐλεύθερα λήματ' ἔχοντες; 477 ~ 611; 504 ~ 590.

[80] J. La Roche, 'Die Stellung des attributiven und appositiven Adjectives bei Homer', *WS* 19 (1897), 161–88, at 175–7 (before the noun), 178–80 (on either side of the noun).

[81] 'Aggregation' comes from R. Hamilton, 'The Pindaric Dithyramb', *HSCP* 93 (1990), 211–22, at 215–16.

Nevertheless, their function remains what it so often was in the Homeric hexameter, and continues in line with this poet's consistent practice, namely that of stretching a simple information unit out across a full line. That is why many occupy the second half of it;[82] it is also why one epithet is often informational, the other decorative, in other words provides the wadding to complete the metrical unit (4.273 τετράγωνον ἀν᾽ οὐρανόεσσαν ἀταρπὸν, 415 ἀκτῖσιν φαέθουσι... λαμπραυγέσι κόσμου, where the first epithet hints at Jupiter's lightname, 583 οὐρανίην ἀτραπὸν μεσοδερκέα, 586 αἰθροπλανὴς... μάρτυρος ἀστήρ; across a line-division, 4.454–5 σταχυηφόρον ἁγνὴν | Παρθενικήν).

Verbiage

This poet has the most extravagant style in the corpus. All poets to some extent take the opportunity of elaborating circumstances in the apodosis, even if only with trope; the game is to achieve maximum colour within the severely restricted form. This one elaborates more than most; he brings to bear a rhetorician's training on the *amplificatio* of stock themes. He enjoys the grit of economic life (4.134–7: trading, the life of a merchant; 323–4: ships' carpenters), deviant and especially salacious behaviour (4.56–8: adulterers; 220–3: *galli*; 280–5 and 445–6: mimes; 300–2: partying; 304–8: adulterers; 311–12: oral sex; 313–16: pimps; 521–6: congenital wanderers), violence (4.50–1: throat-cutting, 197–200: crucifixion), and situations from which it is possible to extract a high-pitched pathos (4.399–401: shipwrecked sailors; 554–9: seeing ghosts/visions of the dead). This section further analyses how he produces his distinctive effects, and especially his two hallmarks, wordiness and obfuscation.

We have touched on the poet's tendency relentlessly to package the units of the line with like content (i. 216–17); the feature is shared with the Sibylline Oracles. In protases, any number of over-egged light expressions, often involving parechesis, are either oblivious to repetition or make a virtue of it, once again with the sole aim of filling the line.[83] Apodoses are less monotonous. Their repetitions are synonymic, and, apart from word-spinning, achieve the ends of intensification and sometimes pathos or atrocity; the stars in this poet's universe bring about outcomes that are in no way nuanced.[84] The underlying

---

[82] Not so 4.478 Μήνη δ᾽ ἀμφίκερως σκολιόδρομος (two post-posed epithets are not discussed by La Roche).

[83] 201 λαμπραύγετις ἀκτίς; 214 ἀκτῖνας... πυρσοβολοῦσα; 218 ἀκτῖσιν... πυριλαμπέσι; 426 ἀκτῖσι, στίλβουσι φλογὸς λαμπτῆρσι (στίλβουσι is informational, but the apposition is redundant); 508 Ἥέλιος δ᾽ ἀκάμας, πυρόεν σέλας. For parechesis, see p. 213.

[84] 50 λαιμοτόμου φάρυγος, 51 σφονδυλόεντα τράχηλον, 566 ἀφροσύνην ἀλόγιστον; 199 n. Pleonastic genitival expressions: 49 μοιριδίου θανάτοιο... πολυτήμονι πότμῳ; 67 δόξης ἀπλέτου κοσμήτορα κόμπον; 553 ἐν κύκλοισι θοοῦ δινήματι κόσμου. Tautology: 603 πεφυκότας ἐκ γενετήρων.

aim of stretching sense units to coincide with metrical units has in this poet produced a weird symbiosis between the formal parsimony of the apotelesma and the amplitude of the rhetor.

The discussion of word-formation already noted one important feature of the poet's style, his penchant for abstract expressions.[85] This is generalisable well beyond neologisms to a standing feature. The poet uses a pseudo-academic jargon, especially for habitual activities and in professional expressions which catch him out between the rhetorician's drive to particularise and the theoretician's to taxonomise and idealise. It produces some remarkable hybrids. Periphrastic expressions may also suggest that the poet was striving for impressive indirection, but with welcome suggestions of the tragic and lyric manner (6 αἰθερίην τε κέλευθον; see 52 n. on φαρμακτοῖο δόλου and 339 n. on αἰθροτόκου τε γονῆς).

Some of the poet's periphrastic expressions involve the genitive (n. 84). The type of planetary name in which the mythological name is dependent on the light-name (e.g. the Shining One, star of Hermes) is nothing new, but sits well in a style that already courts pleonasm and lends itself to ever more embellishment (i. 898 n. 4). The poet is particularly given to expressions involving κόσμου (whirl, path, sign, rays, and so on), where either κόσμου is redundant or the whole expression is, but the very fact of it adds a nebulous grandeur perhaps very distantly evoking the *Timaeus* (p. 182).[86] The use of multiple genitives, where one is dependent on another, did not produce a particularly wordy effect in the hands of M^a.[87] If it does in M^b, it is partly because some are pleonastic (5 ζῳδίων τε πόλοιο περίδρομον; 167–8 δωδεκατημορίων τ' ἄστρων... Ζῳδιακήν = the zodiac consisting of the twelve-parts of the stars) and partly because this poet more complicatedly combines genitives in different senses (110 ὡράων πανεπίσκοπα φέγγεα Μήνης = rays of the Moon, beholders of the ASC (below, p. 213); 48–9 ἐπὴν δ' εἰς τέρμα βίοιο | μοιριδίου θανάτοιο: the end of life, obj., consisting in death, subj.).[88]

---

[85] See examples of expressions for habitual activities expressed in abstract terms on pp. 212–13. Professional expressions: 88 ἐμπορίης ἐμπείραμος, 179 διδασκαλίης τε παρέδρους, 245 θηροδιδασκαλίης τ' ἐπιβήτορας, 259–60 ὑπουργοὶ | δυσπονίης, 344 μεθόδῳ τε λινοστολίης προφέροντας, 353 χαμαιτυπίης, 418 παιδείης ἡγήτορες (contrast M^a's favourite παίδων ἡγητῆρας), 433 φυτοσπορίας ἀγαπῶντες, 495 μοιχείας τ' ἀγαπῶντας. Other examples: 64 φυγαρσενίης μυστήρια, 332 κατηγορίης τε τεχνασμοί, 494 στοργῇσι κεκασμένα φίλτρα, 600 ἀπελευθερίης (rare and otherwise prosaic).

[86] κόσμου redundant: 45 = 132 (perpendicular line); 482 (sign); 336, 415 (rays). Entire expression redundant: 553 (whirl); 147, 380 (path).

[87] i. 230; K.–G. i. 337 Anm. 4.

[88] Also 253 λουτρῶν τε καθαρτῆρας βαλανείων (if βαλανείων is a noun rather than unattested epithet); transmitted in 40 πόλεών τε διθυντῆρας ἀέθλων, but universally corrected to πολέων.

Another type of genitive which M^b has learned from M^a is in combination with an agent noun. At its simplest, even when the morphology is mannered, an agent noun with a defining genitive is how one would naturally express the idea. This is well attested in the earlier poet.[89] Examples are 4.183 μελῶν μελπήτορας, 244 ὀρνίθων τροφοποιούς, 247 κτηνῶν... σημάντορας, 251 καθαρτῆράς τε κελεύθων, 253 λουτρῶν τε καθαρτῆρας, 343 μακάρων ἀποπλάστορας, 422 τεύκτορας αὐτῶν [sc. clothes], 514 πάτρης κηδέστορες, 580 πόλεων ταμιεύτορες. In closely related examples, the genitive is epexegetic (it simply fills out what was already implicit in the agent noun) or redundant. Once again there were examples in M^a,[90] but the poet who seeks bulk extends the category: 4.114 πενίης χερνήτορας, 158 ἰητῆρα... βροτῶν, 259 γαίης τε μεταλλευταί, 267 νεκρῶν τε ταριχευτῆρας, 300 ζωροπότας οἴνου, 324 ὕλης πελεκήτορας, 398 σκαφέων... κυβερνητῆρας (cf. 6.364 νηῶν τε κυβερνητῆρας), 399 πρῳράρχους τε νεῶν, 422 γνάπτορας εὐσήμων πέπλων, 493 θιάσων κωμάστορας. Others, again with precedent in M^a,[91] are periphrastic versions of occupational terms or titles: 4.40 πολέων τε διιθυντῆρας ἀέθλων (agonothetes), 134 ἐμπορικοῦ πλοίου φορτοστόλος (~ ἔμπορος), 149 ῥέκτρας χρυσοῖο, 151–2 θριγκῶν τε καὶ εὐτοίχων κανονισμῶν | κοσμήτας, 183 λυρικῶν τε μελῶν μελπήτορας, 185 κιθάρης... μελουργούς, 192 κλαυστῆρας ἀποφθιμένων, 257 ληνῶν ἀντλητῆρες, 258 ἀρδευταί φορβῆς (gardeners), 276 ἰσχυρῶν ἔργων... πονοπαίκτορας, 292–3 πηλαίης πλίνθου τε καὶ εὐτοίχων κανονισμῶν | θριγκῶν τ' εὐθυντῆρας, 339 αἰθροτόκου τε γονῆς ἐπιβήτορας, 483 θυρέτρων ἐπανοίκτορας (θυρεπανοίκτας); further examples in n. 85. But where M^b's usage has developed furthest from that of M^a is in cases where the expression does not refer to a trade or occupation, but to other kinds of activity expressive of character; the fact that the poet has chosen nominal rather than verbal forms of expression when the same content might have been conveyed with participles or relative clauses has the effect of turning them into quasi-occupational labels, as if this is what the natives customarily do: 56 ἀλλοτρίων λεχέων πανάθεσμος ἀατήρ [ex emend. K], 349 ἀλλοτρίων θαλάμων... ληίστορας, 75 χειρῶν μιμήτορας ἀλλοτυπώτων, 220 γονίμων μηδέων ἀπαμήτορας ἄνδρας. They become, in other words, a sort of *Tätigkeitsbezeichnung* (p. 39). Several combine deverbative agent nouns with abstract nouns, in a characteristic manoeuvre which makes an abstract outcome the object or result of an active process: 4.33 λύπης ἐπιβήτορας, 67 δόξης ἀπλέτου κοσμήτορα κόμπον,

---

[89] 2.152–3 δασμῶν | πρήκτορας; 6.357 χρεῶν νωμήτορας, 408 ἵππων... σημάντορας, 415 δωμήτορας οἴκων, 447 παίδων πρηκτῆρας, 453–4 ὀρνίθων... θηρήτορας, ὠμοβόρων θηρήτορας.
[90] 6.364 πλωτῆρας νηῶν; 2.259, 6.479 ῥητῆρας μύθων.
[91] 3.98–9 ὑφηγητῆρας... παιδείης; 2.333 μολπῆς... τεύκτορας; 2.327 μύρων... τεχνήτορας; 6.358 κτεάνων ἰθύντορας; 2.332 κιθάρης ὑποφήτορας; expressions of expertise, 6.509 ἴστορας and ἐπίστορες, *passim*.

120 ὄλβου τε ποθήτορας, 197 κέρδεος...θηρήτορας, 222 πολυπλαγκτοσύνης ἐπιβήτορας, 223 καμάτου τε κακοῦ διαδέκτορας, 268 κακεμπορίης τε ματευτάς, 280 χλεύης τ' ἐπιβήτορας, 281 γήρως ἐπιβήτορας, 446 χλεύης θ' ἡγήτορας, 530 φιλίης λυμάντορες.

The poet seeks to defamiliarise his expressions through various means. Words are used in unusual senses,[92] including several agent nouns,[93] or applied in unusual ways (606 καινισθέντες: the people are 'innovated'), or used in unusual combinations (55, 133 γονὰς...φέρειν; 164 παρὰ κῦδος 'dishonourable'). The voice of a verbal root is different from normal (455 διδυμάτοκα passive, not active; 58 παμψέκτωρ and 525 ψογερὸν both mean blame*worthy*, not blam*ing*), and there are occasional syntactical fudges where sense requires that a part of speech be other than what at first sight it seems to be (at 17 ἐπίσκοπον ἐς βίου ὥρην, the meaning should be 'the horoscope, overseer of birth', which requires ἐπίσκοπον to be a noun, not an epithet; similarly at 4.110 ὡράων πανεπίσκοπα).

On a syntactical level, the poet seeks *variatio*. Throughout the book he varies the constructions of ἐλθεῖν;[94] likewise of ἰσόμοιρος (normally dative, but in 4.386 and 601 with genitive, in 194 with ἐπί, in 231 with μετά; in 589 with κατά); and there are numerous passages where the same technique is practised on a small scale with the construction following a verb (4.18, after δείκνυσι; 99–100, after φράζει) or with prepositional phrases to express location (4.96-7; 452-4) or agency (4.199 πικροτάτοις κέντροισι...ἐν ἥλοις or ἔνηλοι, 435 δίχα γράμματος, οὐχὶ νόμοισιν). A particularly highly wrought example is 4.508–10, where different constructions are used for the complementary locations of Sun and Moon.

On a phonetic level, on the other hand, he is either indifferent to repetition or positively cultivates it, which is most apparent in the parecheses for fire, rays, vision, and striking in the protasis (4.44 πυρόεις Ἄρεος πυριλαμπέος ἀστὴρ, 93–4 πυριμάρμαρος ἀστήρ...πυριλαμπέος αἴθρης, 187–8 Ἄρεος αὔγλη...αἰγλοβολήσῃ, 125 σκοπιὴν ὡροσκόπον, 421 ἀκτινηβολίῃσι πυριβλήτοισι, 438 πυρσοβόλοις ἀκτῖσι βαλών). It is difficult to see what this achieves, other than give the impression of a dearth of invention; or are jingles supposed to serve as a memory-aid—or perhaps add resonance in oral performance? In the apodosis, some repetitions are certainly artful (a *figura etymologica* in 463–4 ὁ τικτόμενος τότε θνητῶν | σῶμα περισσομελὴς τεχθήσεται; paradox in 58 ἀδίδακτος, ἀεὶ

---

[92] 4.123 ἐκ πυρὸς αὐχήσουσι τέχνας (αὐχεῖν here means 'profess' a trade); 196 δρῶσιν 'make', 'produce'; 516 πολυζώοισιν ἐν ἄστροις: not 'consisting of many animals', but 'arranged in many constellations'; 535 τελέουσιν: 'farming' taxes, not 'paying' them.

[93] 4.257 ἀντλητῆρες (a person not an instrument); 258 λαχανηφόροι (a person not a soil-type); 293 θριγκῶν τ' εὐθυντῆρας (a builder not a moral guide); 568a παντευχούς ('manufacturing all kinds of thing', rather than 'armed to the gills': a resemanticisation).

[94] 4.112, 121, 577 εἰς; 121, 263, 327 ἐπί + acc.; 560, 568, and in Π[1] at 577 with straight accusative; 327, 508-9 with dative.

δεδιδαγμένος, 282 πόλιος πάσης ἀπόλιστα γένεθλα, 625–6... χρόνος ἐκμεμέτρηται | ἐκμέτροις αἰῶσι [ex emend. K], fortified with polyptoton), and puns and jingles reach Gorgianic levels of infantilism (4.88 ἐμπορίης ἐμπείραμος, 146 ἄστατος ἀστήρ, 289 ὧν ὁ πόρος μόρος ἐστίν, 495 ὕβρις, οὐ κύπρις). On the other hand, there are passages which betray a casual indifference to repetition (192 νεκροτάφους... νεκρονώμας, with different scansion, 251–3 καθαρτῆρας... καθαρτῆρας, 280–1 ἐπιβήτορας... ἐπιβήτορας, 315–16 μυσαρόν... μυσαρωπὰ γένεθλα, 332 ψευδοκατηγορίαι τε κατηγορίης, 354–5 ἐπὴν... ἐπὴν, 535–6 ἐκ λιμένων τελέουσιν, | δημοσίων τελέων), or may represent dittography in the manuscript (33–4 λύπης... λύπης; 278–9 ἐν ἔργοις... ἔργα τελοῦντας).

The poet employs various metaphors, none of which is original to him, but some of which he embellishes in a lively way. His favourite is that of the pathway for cosmic and planetary motion, the most inventive application of which is that of the Moon's labyrinth (334 λαβύρινθον), and the most peculiar the idea that Venus and Mars 'leap' (297 θρῴσκωσι) upon their cosmic path with a thrusting motion and perhaps sexual innuendo. He also invokes the idea, going back to the *Timaeus*, that the stars measure out human lifespans (2) and cosmic time (625–6); life has a delimited course, which divination can foresee (551). Nature, too, has a path (591), an old ethical metaphor; by narrowing it down to specifically sexual conduct, the poet affects a censoriousness that in no way contradicts his tabloid relish for perversion and deviant acts. The apodosis also yields the trite yoke of slavery (602), governance as shepherding (419 διαποιμαίνοντες), adultery as piracy (56, 164, 304), and a moderately interesting variation on the trope of liquid money (92 ἀντλούμενος ὄλβῳ).

Use and Recycling of Earlier Poets

EGHP

The ways in which the poet exploits EGHP can be categorised in much the same ways as for M^a, but the same is presumably true for almost any poet; this will not tell us what is distinctive about him. It is a matter of which types he prefers, and where his attentions are directed.

First, he recycles a small number of Homeric hapaxes (51 ἰνίον < *Il.* 5.73; 108 ἁματροχίῃ < *Il.* 23.422; 173 ἀθλητῆρας < *Od.* 8.164 ἀθλητῆρι; 424 ἀγεληδόν < *Il.* 16.160 (but also in Ap. Rhod.); see too on 406 ἐξολέσει. 449 ἀλήμονας (see ad loc.) is *dis legomenon* in *Od.* 17.376, 19.74. But in general he is more interested in redeploying them in his own outlandish innovations, e.g. *Il.* 20.483 σφονδυλίων becomes 51 σφονδυλόεντα; *Il.* 17.577 εἰλαπιναστάς becomes 300 εἰλαπινουργούς; πολύπλαγκτος contributes to 222 πολυπλαγκτοσύνης; *Il.* 11.385

λωβητήρ contributes to 234 θεολωβήτας; Od. 18.54 κακοεργός becomes 599 κακοεργέϊ (third-declension).

He recycles phrases from EGHP, whether non-specific and formulaic,[95] or from particular passages.[96] Mostly this is a matter of opportunism, not meaningful allusion (though see on 144). So too the use of verse-patterns, based on the partial or total substitution of metrically equivalent material,[97] and the regeneration of formulae through variations of case,[98] *sedes*,[99] number,[100] or the use of cognates[101] and synonyms.[102] All this is pretty routine and barely meaningful, other than as a compositional tool. There are some passages of more deliberate and determined engagement. 374 ἦμαρ ἐλευθερίης ἕξει obviously reverses Iliadic ἐλεύθερον ἦμαρ ἀπούρας (3×); 223 διαδέκτορας is possibly a play on Od. 4.248 δέκτης in the sense of 'beggar'; and the line-end of 614 has something to do with Od. 7.197 ἄσσα οἱ αἶσα κατὰ Κλῶθές τε βαρεῖαι, however it is emended. Hesiod's sturdy, down-home, wholesome world has provided material which the poet can usefully vary,[103] as well as a passage of grotesque enormity too good to miss, to which M[a] was already drawn (see p. 219).[104] Perhaps the most interesting comparison or rather contrast between them is that while M[a]'s habitual technique of combinatory allusion—the threading together of two separate passages, usually linked by some common word or root—is clearly within M[b]'s range, he does it to a lesser extent, and only very rarely to combine passages from EGHP and Hellenistic Poetry.[105] He never

---

[95] 79 δι' αἰθέρος; 413 ἄλγε' ἔδωκεν; 549 κατ' ἀνθρώπους [*ex emend*. K]; 500, 537 κατὰ κόσμον, which is now made meaningful.

[96] 144 ἀλλοτρίων κτεάνων; 302 ἤματα νύκτας; 588 ἀνδράσιν ἠδὲ γυναιξίν; 618 ἀφ' ὑψηλοῖο μελάθρου, and, with minor modifications, 542 μὴ φρονέῃ κατὰ θυμόν, and 615 ὀρέστεροι ἠὲ λέοντες. See ad loc. in each case.

[97] See notes on 16 κατὰ δώμαθ' ἑαυτοῦ; 22 νεφελώδεος Οὐλύμποιο; 24 εἴαρος ἀρχή; 40 πολέων τε διθυντῆρας ἀέθλων; 46 ἐν ἡγεμόνεσσιν ἄριστος; 51 σφονδυλόεντα τράχηλον; 152 μάλα τοι πεπονημένα; 190 θρηνήτορας ἄνδρας, ἀσέμνους; 194 ἐπ' ἀμφοτέροισι φαανθῇ; 264 κακὸς κακόν, αἰγλάζοντες; 270 οἰκτρότατ' ἔργα τελεῖται; 273 ἀν' οὐρανόεσσαν ἀταρπόν; 331 ἐκδύσιες τελέθουσιν; 447 μυθεύματα ποικίλ' ἔχοντας; 470 ἀρήια λήματ'; 489 βρόχον ἀλγινόεντα; 524 μεμετρημένα πράγματ' ἔχοντας ; 545 πάμμηνα κέλευθα; 546 σεληνιόωντα φανείη.

[98] See notes on 93 ἡελίου ἀκάμαντος; 271 Ἥλιος δ' ἀκάμας; 349, 482 ληίστορας ἄνδρας.

[99] See note on 616 ἢ σύες ἀργιόδοντες.

[100] See notes on 5 ὃς κατὰ γαῖαν; 622 μερόπων γενεή.

[101] See note on 485a σιδηρήεντά τε δεσμά.

[102] See notes on 205 ἐνὶ στέρνοισιν ἔχοντας; 246 ἀγρίη γενεή; 503 θηλυγενεῖς δὲ γυναῖκες.

[103] See notes on 103 βιοτὴν πλήθουσαν; 123-4 black iron; 149 ῥεκτῆρας; 442 ἀδροτάτους; 514 ἰθυδίκαιοι [*ex emend*. K].

[104] See note on 220 μηδέων ἀπαμήτορας.

[105] With shared item or element: see notes on 123-4 μέλανός τε σιδήρου; 208 ἐν οὐρανῷ ἀστερόεντι; 222 πολυπλαγκτοσύνης; 261; 360; 367 ἰσόμοιρα κατ' Οὐλύμποιο κέλευθα; 374-5 (something similar already attempted at 6.56); 578 λοίσθια τέρματα γαίης. EGHP and Hellenistic Poetry: 123-4.

manages anything as targeted and witty as Mᵃ's allusion to Nausicaa apropos of fullers, nor as sophisticated as his combinations of Homer, Apollonius, and Aratus to self-construct a tradition in epic and didactic poetry concerned with stars, locations, and mapping. Nor is this very surprising. His extravagant diction and high emotional tone suggest that he has no particular investment in constructing himself as a continuator of Homeric epic, which is certainly useful for the building blocks of his verse (and we have seen how he creates a pseudo-formulaic style of his own aided by certain Homeric verse-patterns: pp. 208–9, and see too p. 215 n. 97). But the real interest lies elsewhere.

Tragedy

Once again, the techniques themselves are very comparable to those of Mᵃ (i. 159–60), but the boot is now on the other foot: *this* is where the poet directs his best efforts, and there are far more of them in a much narrower compass. True, with individual words it is sometimes hard to know whether something is distinctive enough to be confident that the poet intended a specifically tragic effect,[106] but there are also oddities of usage and mannered types of phrase[107] which seem to want to evoke the tragic idiom, and a handful of possible allusions to particular passages.[108] Nothing is as extravagant as Mᵃ's stand-out tragic pitch for Oedipus (6.167–8), but this poet's interest is not in creating isolated tragic moments. Rather, it is in using tragedy to create a thoroughgoing idiom characterised by dithyrambic compounds,[109] circumlocution,[110] and unexpected constructions.[111] Grief,[112] madness,[113] and deviancy are bonuses, as, on the other hand, are words and phrases that can be ingeniously redeployed for heavenly bodies and their motions. But the main interest is in the style itself, which is more marked, mannered, and bombastic than the merely routine *presque homérique*.[114]

---

[106] Demonstrable or likely for 84 ἀμφιθοάζῃ; 453 συνωρίζουσι, of siblings; 521 αὐδῶσιν.
[107] See notes on 282 πόλιος... ἀπόλιστα; 455–6 σώματα + genitive.
[108] See notes on 103 ἀλύπητόν τε δίαιταν; 131 φοράδην; 190 θρηνήτορας ἄνδρας; 223 διαδέκτορας (possibly); 239 ῥόμβῳ; 262 (the inauguration of mining); 555 νερτερόμορφα.
[109] See notes on 50 λαιμοτόμου φάρυγος; 261 κελαινόχροός τε σίδηρος; 339 αἰθροτόκου τε γονῆς; 445 αἰσχεορήμονας; 461, 503 θηλυγενής; 477 δυσεκφεύκτων; 555 νερτερόμορφα; 557 ὀξύγοοι [ex emend. K]; 616 αἱματοπώτιδες. Nouns: 433 φυτοσπορίας; 556 κακαγγελίαισι.
[110] See notes on 52 φαρμακτοῖο δόλου; 198 σκολοπηΐδα μοῖραν; 339 αἰθροτόκου τε γονῆς.
[111] See notes on 229 ὀργιόωντας; 297–8 θρώσκωσι + straight accusative; 425–6 πελάζειν + accusative.
[112] See note on 585 λέχη λιπόπαιδα.   [113] See note on 539 λυσσαλέῃ μανίῃ.
[114] See also notes on 178 ἀστεφάνους; 179 παρέδρους; 335 λαμπάς; 526 οἰκείων... θυραίων; 588 θυραίους vs kin.

Hellenistic Poetry

M^b quarries the Hellenistic poets, as had M^a before him, but again with different patterns of exploitation.

Apollonius continues to furnish verse-patterns[115]—hardly surprising, since he survives in bulk—but no positional expressions; Apollonian precision proves to be at odds with M^b's impressionism and gesturing. There are no other marked patterns, though 1.1099 νιφόεν θ' ἕδος Οὐλύμποιο was nicely chosen when the poet wanted to evoke the heavens with gently mythological coloration (22 νεφελώδεος Οὐλύμποιο, alluding to a catasterism myth). Again, it is hard to marshal such evidence as there is from Callimachus into any kind of order,[116] and the most important result is that this poet, unlike M^a, is generally *not* quarrying him for his exotic *lexeis* and wonderfully granular view of human existence. There are, however, apparently a few opportunistic reworkings,[117] especially and most interestingly that of Callimachus' picture of the Cyclopes at work in their forge in Lipara for the workers in fire and iron in 123-4. The poet does not do what M^a would have done and splice two passages together, but the imitation is sustained and does exploit the quiddity (hammers and furnaces) which otherwise constituted Callimachus' fascination for the earlier poet.

No surprise that Aratus has been used for the prologue and transitions,[118] and for 'phenomenal' details of light and appearance[119] (of which Nicander perhaps furnishes another example in 318 σελάοντι, *ex emend.*). A telling difference between M^a and M^b that while the former uses Nicander for the narrator–addressee relationship and for paragraphing (i. 160-1, 191-2), the latter quarries him especially for comitative expressions, as he repurposes adverbs or prepositions meaning 'with' for apotelesmata with multiple components.[120] Given the remarkable proliferation of -μιγ- words it is presumably also

---

[115] See notes on 194 ἐπ' ἀμφοτέροισι φαανθῇ; 257 ἐν ὕδατι γηράσκοντες; 296 φάος ἄπλετον, ἀστέρι κείνῳ.

[116] Irregular morphology not provably from Callimachus himself: 42 ὀλβίστῃ; 448 ψηφάων. Likewise the verse-pattern at 23 ἀμφίβιος θήρ; and the kenning in 339 αἰθροτόκου τε γονῆς (for which there are much closer Euripidean parallels).

[117] 334 σκολιὸν λαβύρινθον (not beyond the bounds of possibility that this is accident); 472 ἐς Ἄρεα φέγγος ἀθρήσῃ.

[118] See notes on 7 πλαγκτὰ διχαζόμενος; 8 ἐξ ἠοῦς ἐπὶ νύκτα; 10 διώρισεν ἀνδράσιν ἄστρα; 109 Ἄλλα δέ τοι λέξω; 167-8 ἐνισπεῖν.

[119] See notes on 25 αἰγλήεις; 26 πολυάστερος; 528 ἀνάστερον; 545 πάμμηνα κέλευθα. Verse-pattern in 58.

[120] See notes on 219 μίγα; 202 μίγδην; 215 ἄμμιγα; 266 συμμίγδην. Although only the last of these is unique to Nicander and M^b, the comitative sense of μίγδην is distinctive of Nicander as well. Nicander also has other 'mingling' adverbs beside those M^b exploits (ἀμμίγδην; μιγάδην; ἀνάμιγδα).

significant that M^b is the only poet in the corpus to speak of stellar configurations in the language of 'mixing' (621 μιγνυμένων), perhaps a novel interpretation of the concept of κρᾶσις in which stellar powers are figured as components in a Nicandrian recipe (*Al.* 574 μίγμενος; fr. 72.8 μιγήμεναι; cf. fr. 68.4 μιγῇ).[121]

Other Astrological Poets

The extent of the influence of Alexander of Ephesus is one of the great unknowns of the Manethoniana; his importance is suggested by the unambiguous echo of *SH* 21.26 θεομήστορος εἰκόνα κόσμου in the proem (7 θεομήστορα κόσμον: no longer an image of the cosmos, but the cosmos itself).

Dorotheus is a different matter. Even though the great part of the surviving fragments are catarchic, not natal, there is a promising number of overlaps. Planetary epithets are discussed separately (p. 256), but to the already fairly impressive number of parallels there can be added the circumlocution for Saturn which avoids the planet's proper name (4.131 ἀστέρα πατρός), the combined light-and-proper name for Hermes at 4.206 στίλβων δ' Ἑρμάωνος ὅτ' ἂν Κυλληνίου ἀστήρ, and the reference to Virgo at 4.454–5 σταχυηφόρον ἁγνὴν | Παρθενικήν. There are Dorothean cadences at 4.545 πάμμηνα κέλευθα (with an Aratean background) and 4.593 Κρόνος ὡρονομεύων,[122] and a smattering of occasions where Dorotheus has supplied or helped to furnish technical or pseudo-technical terminology (4.79 ἀκροπολεύῃ; 4.181 ἐναλλάγδην; 4.599 κακοεργέϊ, 3rd decl.). We should like to be able to dig beyond the incidental to evidence for more systematic use by M^b of Dorotheus' catalogues (in other words, of material which they have in common). At least one passage with overlaps in the witnesses to Dorotheus' catalogue of aspects suggests that he made use of that (4.163–4, for 'unworthy' wives and the metaphorical use of θηρᾶν in connection with sexual predators), and διευθυντῆρας, uniquely shared between 4.106 and Περὶ κράσ. 141, with Dorothean underlay, is also suggestive. 4.80 τηνίκα (after ὁπότ' ἂν) also has a Dorothean background. It raises the possibility that Dorotheus also influenced the formal presentation of apotelesmata.

The only poet whose influence on M^b we are really in a position to analyse, however, is of course M^a. Their diction has a lot in common. Quite apart from the shared items in their apodoses in the τέχναι and σίνος charts, which are

---

[121] Sporadic connections otherwise. Subject-matter in 123–4 (possibly). Usage in 453 συνωρίζουσι (intrans.); morphology in 485a σιδηρήεντα; verse-patterns/cadences in 273 ἀν' οὐρανόεσσαν ἀταρπόν; 543 ὄμμασι λεύσσῃ. See notes.

[122] 4.26 ἔμπυρος οἶκος ~ p. 383.8 ἔμπυρος Ἄρης is less distinctive.

likely to derive from a common source, there are words unique to M^a and M^b among the Manethoniana,[123] including some rare enough to be striking,[124] or even unique to these two authors.[125] Several shared phrases are also best explained by direct imitation, perhaps even where there is a possibility of a shared source.[126] More interesting are passages where M^b seems to be reacting to M^a in some way, and the curiosity here is that, apart from the routine business of element-for-element metrical substitution (4.398 σκαφέων τε κυβερνητῆρας ἀΰπνους ~ 6.364 νηῶν τε κυβερνητῆρας ἀρίστους; 4.441 θαύματα δαιδάλλοντας ~ 6.401 ὄργανα δαιδάλλοντας), the type of imitation one *might* have expected— verbose wadding (4.222 πολυπλαγκτοσύνης ~ 6.539 πλάζονται, 4.297–8~6.587)— in fact seems to be less important than light-touch reversals, where the items match each other point for point, but word-order, sense, or both, have been reversed.[127]

Perhaps it is possible to follow this through into the way they tiptoe around each other in passages where they share a common source, a kind of astro-poetic version of Monro's Law. At 4.517 and 3.377–8, both pick out different words from the description of feminised individuals in Epit. II, and at 4.618 and 3.262 the two poets are apparently using opposite ends of the same Homeric line (*Od.* 11.278). As with the examples above, this seems to be a game of complementarity rather than raised stakes in a competition of horror.[128] Otherwise, what we see are the two poets translating common material into their respective favourite idioms. At 4.220/3.396, both M^b and M^a are using Hes. *Th.* 180–1, the famous passage on Cronos' castration of his father. Here, M^a had substituted a different verb for Hesiod's, but retained the verbal construction with tmesis (ἀπὸ μήδε᾽ ἔκειραν ~ ἀπὸ μήδεα...ἤμησε). M^b, on the other hand, creates a suitably monstrous agent noun from the same root (μηδέων ἀπαμήτορας). It is a similar picture at 4.252, where the same Homeric gardening simile (*Il.* 21.257–9) supplies the ὀχετηγοί directly to 6.422, but also water-channels (ἀμάρης) to the morphological monstrosity ἀμαρησκαπτῆρας, helping the latter equivocate, perhaps usefully, between gardeners and the distasteful activity

---

[123] Reference to birth-pangs (ὠδῖνες) in the protasis: 4.125, 275, and in particular the phrase ἀπ᾽ ὠδίνων in 4.459 and 6.33, 100, 165; the phrases 4.139 κατὰ κύκλα, 454 κατὰ κύκλον and 2.394–5 κατὰ κύκλον. See also on 4.13 ἀμείβεται (even if the context is uncertain), 18 εὐκτεάνους, 19 ἀμόχθ-, 114 λιτῆς [ex emend. K], 119 ἀθέσμους, 611 κρυερῶν; i. 906 n. 1, on Ἀφρογενῆς.
[124] See notes on 6.16 πολυχρήμον-; 4.31 ἀκτεάνους, 56 παναθέσμιος or πανάθεσμος, 300 ζωροπότας, 325 λαοτόμους, 597 τεκνοσπόρον; i. 887–8 for 4.188 καταντίπερ᾽.
[125] See on 2.317 προφήτορας; 4.85 ἐπόλβους.
[126] See on 2.1 κατ᾽ αἰθέρα; 2.16 φῦλα βροτῶν (later also 4× ps.-Apollinaris); 4.47, 113 ἐνσινέας τε τίθησιν, 144 ἀλλοτρίων κτεάνων, 186 ὀρχηθμῶν ἱδριάς, 234 θεολωβήτας, κακοεργέας.
[127] See notes on 4.144 and 4.433–4 ~ 6.489; 4.532 εὔτρεπτον ~ 3.370 ἀτρέπτους; and above all 4.593–6 ~ 6.60–3.
[128] For which, however, see perhaps 4.270 οἰκτρότατ᾽ ἔργα ~ 6.464 οὐλοὸν (garum)?

of sewer-cleaners (not that repulsiveness usually deters him). Although the exercise is somewhat complicated by uncertainty about the exact status of Θ, we see once again that where M^a and M^b have a common correlate in that prose witness, M^b repeatedly takes the agent noun option, while M^a has recourse to some combination of synonymity, Homeric diction, and a verbal paraphrase.[129] The variation between 4.594 ἐν κακοδαιμοσύνῃ and 6.61 δαίμονι δ᾽ ἐν λυγρῷ is of a similar nature, while the yoke of slavery cliché elicits a choice Hellenistic vocable from the one poet (6.59 ἀτμενίης), more prosaic vocabulary but a little flourish on his favourite πόνος theme from the other (4.372–3).

Finally, my discussion of the poet's astrology will note various conventions and mannerisms which the later poet seems to have borrowed from the earlier one. In the protasis, these include a predilection for the physical language of birth (pp. 251–2); this is one respect in which M^a already showed the way to M^b's grossness. He also gave him the language of rays (ἀκτῖνες) in connection with aspect, which M^b worked up so as almost to sound as if he meant the technical notion of ἀκτινοβολία (pp. 248–9, and see too on 4.272 θοαῖς ἀκτῖσι βολαυγῶν). And he may have taught him how to model opposition through the use of chiasmus (4.74; 567, ex emend. A.-R.). The correlation of protasis to apodosis by means of τῆμος may have been taught by M^a to M^b, though the latter has formalised it (4.46 n.); and in the apodosis itself, he uses the 'best in show' motif,[130] the occasional possible portmanteau expression,[131] and, most importantly, converts what were originally EGHP formulae for the Olympians into expressions for the power of the stars.[132]

4.7. METRE

Outer Metric

Hexameter Schemes

In the following table, 86, 90 + 90a, 175 + 175a, 568a, 611, 614, 621 are omitted through uncertainty. The total number of verses included is therefore 620. 357 is counted as DDSSD, 585 as DSDDD, 590 as SSDDD.

---

[129] 4.149–50 ἐλέφαντος | ἐργοπόνους/Θ ἐλεφαντουργούς/6.523 πριστοῦ ἐλέφαντος; 4.423 ῥαπτῆρας/Θ ῥάπτας/6.434–5 ἰσχαλέαις βελόνῃσιν | ῥωγαλέους πέπλους ἀσκηθέας ἐκτελέοντας; 4.614 θηροβόρου/Θ θηριόβρωτον/3.260 θήρεσσιν ἕλωρ καὶ κύρμα.

[130] ἄριστος + noun or dative expression; see i. 155; p. 173.

[131] See notes on 4.39 (gold and chaplets), 52 (poison and disease); i. 174–5.

[132] See notes on 4.400 χείματος ὀρνυμένοιο, 406 ἐξολέσει, 413 ἄλγε᾽ ἔδωκεν, 490 ὑπ᾽ ἀνάγκης, 619 Μοῖραν ἄφυκτον; i. 62.

	no.	%
5D		
DDDDD	112	18.06
4D, 1S		
SDDDD	66	10.65
DSDDD	102	16.45
DDSDD	42	6.77
DDDSD	51	8.23
DDDDS	11	1.77
3D, 2S		
SSDDD	52	8.39
SDSDD	11	1.77
SDDSD	26	4.19
SDDDS	6	0.97
DSSDD	20	3.23
DSDSD	51	8.23
DSDDS	5	0.81
DDSSD	10	1.61
DDSDS	2	0.32
2D, 3S		
SSSDD	11	1.77
SSDSD	29	4.68
SSDDS	2	0.32
SDSSD	1	0.16
SDSDS	2	0.32
DSSSD	6	0.97
DSSDS	1	0.16
1D, 4S		
SSSSD	1	0.16

Of 32 possible schemes, 23 occur, of which the eight most popular are:

DDDDD	18.06
DSDDD	16.45
SDDDD	10.65
SSDDD	8.39
DDDSD	8.23
DSDSD	8.23
DDSDD	6.77
SSDSD	4.68

Every combination involving 4D except DDDDS occurs in the top seven. Conversely, the schemes that do *not* figure are DDDSS; DDSSS, DSDSS, SDDSS; DSSSS, SDSSS, SSDSS, SSSDS; SSSSS. As usual, what is being avoided are schemes where the fourth and fifth feet are both spondaic.

Accounting for 86% of the poem, the eight most favoured hexameter schemes exert a stranglehold greater than in any other astrological poet except

'Antiochus' (87.29%); in third place is Dorotheus (81.17%), with M^a well behind (67.8% in books 2 and 6; see i. 235). By pre-Nonnian standards the figure is high, in the same range as Callimachus (86.8%). If one takes the three most popular schemes instead (Zito, lxxv f.), these make up 45.16% of lines, which is well behind 'Antiochus' (53.48%), but again above Maximus (42.57%), Dorotheus (43.81%), the first book (42.93%/45.04%), and well above M^a (33.2, 35.27, 30.45%). But the tail, the percentage of the poem that is constituted by the seventh and eighth most favoured schemes, is not so distinctive (11.45%; book 6: 11.84%; book 2: 11.98%; Dorotheus: 12.9%). What that implies is that it is the most popular rhythms that enforce themselves. That proves to be the case, with holodactylic feet (18.06%) way ahead of all but 'Antiochus' (21.43%), and even the second favoured pattern, DSDDD, ahead of Maximus' first two (DDDDD and DSDDD both on 16.31%; in book 2, by contrast, both stand at a mere 11.6%).

There are inevitable runs of the same pattern. Of DDDDD: four at 472–5; three at 49–51, 82–4, 361–3, 427–9, 599–601. Of SDDDD: three at 184–6. Runs of two are trivial. In some cases it is hard to believe that any literary effect is intended, especially since the runs do not coincide with sections of the poem, but cut across protases and apodoses and between apotelesmata. In others, though, metrical repetitions (or near-repetitions) can help to reinforce parallelisms of sense and sometimes of syntax (see pp. 162–3). Or patterns can pull slightly against one another: while 49–51 are metrically identical, the syntactical parallelism is between 50 and 52.

Ratios and Percentages

1. *Dactyls to spondees* (i. 236)

Numbers (out of 3100 feet)	%
2302 : 798	74.26 : 24.74

Dactyls per verse: 3.71

2. *Dactylic feet per line* (i. 236)
Percentages of lines with *n* dactylic feet:

5	18.06
4	43.87
3	29.52

Book Four

2	8.39
1	0.16[133]

3. Percentages of spondaic feet by position in line (i. 237–8)

1	33.39
2	45.16
3	17.26
4	28.26
5	4.65

4. Distribution of metra in line by numbers of dactyls in line (i. 238–9)

Four dactyls	(% ex 272)
SDDDD	24.26
DSDDD	37.5
DDSDD	15.44
DDDSD	18.75
DDDDS	4.04

Three dactyls	(% ex 183)
SSDDD	28.42
DSDSD	27.87
SDDSD	14.21

Two dactyls	(% ex 52)
SSDSD	55.77
SSSDD	21.15
DSSSD	11.54

5. Location of successive spondees (i. 239)
With two successive spondees:

1 + 2	15.32
2 + 3	6.29
3 + 4	2.9
4 + 5	—

---

[133] The one line with four spondees puts the single dactyl in the fifth foot. For this occasional pattern, see La Roche, 42 (4.444 misrepresented as 3.444, but correct on 48); Agosti and Gonnelli, 312–13.

With three successive spondees:

$$\begin{array}{ll} 1+2+3 & 1.94 \\ 2+3+4 & 1.13 \\ 3+4+5 & — \end{array}$$

Discussion of 1–5
In view of his hexameter schemes, it is no surprise that of all the astrological poets, M^b has the second highest overall average number of dactyls per verse (3.71) and the second highest ratio of dactyls to spondees (74.26%), in both cases trailing 'Antiochus' (3.79 and 75.71%, respectively), and trailed by Dorotheus and Maximus. He has the second highest number of holodactylic lines (behind 'Antiochus', with over twice as many as M^a book 6); of lines with at most one spondee (again behind 'Antiochus'); and with precisely four dactyls (43.87%, narrowly beaten by Dorotheus at 44.35%, but running 'Antiochus' and Maximus into third and fourth places respectively). On the other hand, he has the second lowest (after 'Antiochus') percentage of lines with three dactyls (29.52%) and lowest with one dactyl (0.16%). For two dactyls, Dorotheus, Maximus, and 'Antiochus' all undercut him.

To turn to spondees, and to their distribution within the line, it is no surprise that M^b is strongly disinclined against runs of three, which are not common in any poet. Only Dorotheus and Maximus admit them even more rarely ('Antiochus', however, more so, despite his greater dactylicity), while there are fewer than half as many of either $1+2+3$ or $2+3+4$ as there are in M^a. In runs of two, his figures for $2+3$ and $3+4$ are again well down on those of M^a, down on Dorotheus too, and only slightly higher than those of Maximus. The figure for $1+2$ (15.32%) is also well down on that of M^a book 2, but in fact slightly elevated over M^a book 6, and in absolute terms closest to both Dionysius the Periegete (15.57%) and the Sibylline Oracles (15.6%), themselves of course very different. Since this combination is admitted even by dactyl-loving poets (except 'Antiochus'), it is less diagnostic of spondaicity.

As regards the placement of spondaic feet within the line, his pattern comes closest to Dorotheus in the first foot (33.39% and 33.06%), to Maximus for the second (45.16% and 45.51%), and to 'Antiochus' for the fourth (28.26% and 28.47%). In the third (17.26%) he is least distant from M^c (15.66/14.89%), while in his use of the spondeiazon he falls into mid-range among astrological poets (4.65%), and in absolute terms very close to the *Odyssey* (4.74%); this is not a metric by which he shows himself to be very distinctive. Nor do the distributions of metra within the line produce any very startling correspondences (as in general they tend not to do), although in lines with four dactyls, his figures for the location of the single spondee in the first and second feet come closest to those of Maximus (respectively M^b 24.26% and 37.5%, Maximus 23.92% and 39.22%). Relative to other astrological poets, M^b is particularly fond in tridactylic lines of DSDSD (27.87%, followed by the third book, at 23.61%) and in bi-dactylic of SSDSD (55.77%, followed by Dorotheus, at 50%).

6. *Spondeiazontes*

There is a total of 29, or 4.65% (excluding 86, 90, 175, 568a, 611, 621 from a total of 630 lines).[134] But the overall percentage is not particularly revealing, since there is wide fluctuation within astrological poets themselves and M^b's own figure turns out to be closest to the undiagnostic *Odyssey*.[135]

Sixteen, or two-thirds, are accounted for by participles (152, 264, 269, 302, 321, 326, 394, 419, 489, 507, 518, 525, 531, 572, 602, 606), mostly present active (489 aorist active; 302, 394, 606 aorist passive). Of the rest, six are main verbs (111, 303, 408, 487, 557, 605), one an infinitive (576), and five nouns (22 and 396 Οὐλύμποιο; 125, 339, 359).

Only two do not consist of bucolic diaeresis + tetrasyllable (302, 419).[136] Even there, the two instances consist of a compound verb, of which the prefix, if considered as semi-detached from the root, would leave the root to stand as a 'normal' tetrasyllable. There are none with trisyllables (e.g. -ῳ δεικήλῳ). In only ten cases—about a third—does the tetrasyllable *not* begin with a vowel (152, 269, 303, 321, 394, 518, 577, 602, 605, 606). This is different from M^a (about half in books 2 and 6, almost all in book 3).

On the composition of the line as a whole, none is unaccompanied by a fourth-foot dactyl. Only five stand in lines with two dactyls (321, 408, 518, 576, 606), a pattern which tends to be avoided elsewhere too. Twenty (= 68.97%) are accompanied by a masculine caesura, as opposed to 43.54% in the book as a whole:[137] in other words they are about one and a half times as likely as average to have a masculine caesura. Both figures are considerably higher than in M^a, where 56–60% are so accompanied, representing a 5–10% increase on the average; the figure for Dorotheus is very similar (57.14%), which represents a 10.7% increase on the average. Only four (302–3, 605–6) occur in pairs (13.79%); it is not a pattern on which the poet wants to insist. But eight occur at the end of their respective apotelesmata (152, 326, 394, 408, 419, 507, 518, 576). It is a useful conclusive device (p. 157).

---

[134] 22, 111, 125, 152, 264, 269, 302, 303, 321, 326, 339, 359, 394, 396, 408, 419, 483, 487, 489, 507, 518, 525, 531, 557, 572, 576, 602, 605, 606.

[135] i. 240–1; to the comparisons, add Nieto Ibáñez, 240 and 241, and Agosti and Gonnelli, 316–17.

[136] Agosti and Gonnelli, 327–9.

[137] Feminine caesurae: 111, 264, 269, 302, 303, 396, 419, 489, 602.

Inner Metric

Caesurae

In the following, I continue to adhere to the Cantilena/Magnelli definition of appositives. Figures are produced from a theoretical maximum of 630 lines (626 + 90a, 175a, 485a, 568a). From this total, I subtract 68, 90, 614 from the analysis of B = 627 lines; and 68, 90, 175, 614 from the analysis of C = 626 lines. The following cautions are also to be observed. In 53, 77, 139, 402, 420, 613 ὁπότ' ἄν is longer than *tre more*, and I post a word-division after it. A series of appositives in 72, put together, results in something much longer than *tre more*, and I post a word-division after καὶ ὅσ' |. In 481 ἢ καὶ I treat καί as adverbial not conjunctive (which would be over *tre more* anyway) and post a word-division after it.

B_1		B_2	No B	C_2
43.54% (273), of which		56.46% (354)	—	39.14% (245[138])
$B_1 + C_1$	31.5% (86)			
$B_1 + C_2$	49.08% (134[139])			
$B_1 + C_1 + C_2$	15.02% (41[140])			
Neither	4.4% (12)			

Discussion

1. The ratio of B_1 to B_2, that is, of the masculine to feminine caesura, is very much as it was in the *Iliad*.[141] By astrological standards, however, the figure for B_1 is rather low—not as low as the first book (30.66/33.57%) or Maximus (31.59%), but lower than the rest, most of whose percentages stand in the low 50s, let alone M^d at 79.13%. Conversely, the figure for B_2 is rather high, though still significantly lower than the first book (67.45%) and Maximus (67.43%).

2. The combination of $B_1 + C_1$ (31.5%) stands between extremes represented by M^a, on the one hand (50–60%), and 'Antiochus' (15.18%), on the other. His figure is closest to that of Maximus (32.64%).

3. M^b much prefers $B_1 + C_2$ to $B_1 + C_1$. For M^a it was the other way round, while Dorotheus had each combination in equal numbers. In this respect

---

[138] These figures employ my restoration at 568a, and assume that καί is not conjunctive at 617. There are a further 27 lines where C_2 is bridged by a metrical word.

[139] Employing my restoration at 568a. Excluded are 11 cases where C_2 is bridged by a metrical word.

[140] Assuming that καί is not conjunctive at 617.

[141] Full set of figures in Agosti 2004b, 66–7 (cf. Agosti and Gonnelli, 317–19), who for the *Iliad* quotes 44% : 54.9%, with 1.1% of lines having no third-foot caesura at all. Another late antique author close to the Homeric norm is that of the Orphic *Argonautica* (43% : 57%).

M^b comes closer to Hellenistic taste, though he is nowhere remotely as high as Callimachus and Theocritus (i. 246). He shares his preference for $B_1 + C_2$ with Maximus, and in reasonably comparable numbers: the latter has 32.64% $B_1 + C_1$ and 50.26% $B_1 + C_2$.

4. M^b is among the most sensitive of astrological poets to Meyer's Third Law, in other words to the desirability of a second caesura accompanying the masculine one in the third foot. His figure of 4.4% of violations is very close to that of 'Antiochus' (4.46%), and is undercut by only Maximus (3.11%).

5. There are no lines without a caesura in the third foot. The only other astrological poet of whom this is true is M^d. M^a ranges from 1.4% to 3.26%. That, too, suggests a certain punctiliousness.

6. While the figure for the bucolic diaeresis, C_2 (39.14%), is higher than that of M^a (26.26–34%), it is less high than that of the first book (46.7%/47.35%), 'Antiochus' (43.75%), Maximus (45.33%), Dorotheus (50.54%), or indeed than Homer (47%), and nowhere near the Hellenistic poets who are mostly at 50% or higher.[142]

7. Eleven instances of C_2 are preceded by a spondee, in other words violate Naeke's Law, that is, 4.49% of lines with C_2, or 1.76% lines in the whole book. This is a low number: of all astrological poets only M^d proves more adherent to this law (2.44% and 0.93%). The poet who stands at the opposite extreme is M^a, in whom 12.94%–18.6% of relevant lines are non-compliant, and 4.18%–5.59% of all lines.

8. The Hellenistic trend for combining C_2 with a spondaic third foot is one nicety to which the poet is not sensitive, but that is no surprise; the rest of the astrological poets are the same. There are 59 cases among 245 spondaic third feet = 24.08% (~ 17.26% in the book as a whole). In other words fewer than a quarter of relevant lines are spondaic—although, given that in the poem as a whole only 17.26% of third feet are spondaic, 24.08% when C_2 is present at least represents an increase on that.

9. Runs of the same type of caesura are common. The likelihood of recurrence increases with the number of instances. So:

Of 39.14% instances of C_2 (161/245), 65.71% are in the immediate vicinity of another.
Of 43.54% instances of B_1 (197/273), 72.16% are in the vicinity of another.
Of 56.46% instances of B_2 (297/354), 83.9% are in the vicinity of another.

---

[142] i. 245; add Agosti and Gonnelli, 321.

This looks like a steady trend. Although it remains for a statistician to calculate the probability of a cluster of any given length occurring by chance, the more instances of a given type of caesura, the longer the clusters of it tend to be.[143] There are also runs of a given pattern within a line, which tend to increase the greater the number of instances of that pattern: four cases of $B_1 + C_2$ at 576–80, and runs of three at 196–8, 571–3; $B_1 + C_1$ at 166–8.

Word-Break and the Second Foot

In calculating percentages, 90a, 175a were deemed uncountable, producing a countable total of 628 lines. The first percentage is for all lines; the second is with grammatical words only.

Meyer I	37 (9 + 28[144])	5.89% (1.43%)
Meyer II	17[145]	2.71%
Meyer I and II	15 (5 + 10[146])	2.39% (0.8%)
Meyer I or II	24	3.82%
Giseke	1[147]	
Hilberg	—[148]	
Giseke & Hilberg	—	
Giseke *or* Hilberg	1	

Discussion

The impression of punctiliousness that had started to arise from the treatment of the caesura (never lacking in the third foot, treatment of Naeke's and Meyer's Third Law) is now reinforced.

---

[143] B_2: one run of ten instances (199–208), one of nine (426–34), two of eight (288–95, 436–43), two of seven (154–60, 264–70), three of six (15–20, 328–33, 607–12), nine of five (39–43, 79–83a, 96–100, 147–51, 173–6, 225–9, 309–13, 344–8, 367–71), and a dozen of four (10–13, 46–9, 127–30, 140–3, 183–6, 241–4, 272–5, 489–92, 509–12, 540–3, 548–51, 601–4). B_1: one run of nine instances (404–12), six of five (74–8, 279–83, 362–6, 377–81, 455–9, 576–80), and eight of four (165–8, 280–3, 324–7, 356–9, 399–402, 444–7, 524–7, 622–5). C_2: one run each of nine (501–9), eight (524–31), seven (576–82), and six (392–7) instances, as well as five runs of five (22–6, 324–8, 468–72, 589–93, 599–603) and four of four (2–5, 17–20, 410–13, 493–6).
[144] Grammatical words: 47 φρουρητῆρα, 171 εἰς ἀκτῖνα, 294 ἰσόμοιρα, 295 τρίγωνος, 359 ἰσόμοιρα, 380 διάμετρα, 559 πλάστειρα, 589 ἰσόμοιρος, 601 ἰσόμοιρα. Metrical words: 26, 85, 86, 91, 113, 140, 142, 244, 249, 291, 325, 339, 340, 345, 371, 379, 383, 395, 399, 435, 460, 497, 503, 517, 525, 575, 602, 605 (very often before τίθησιν).
[145] 26, 91, 171, 215, 249, 325, 339, 359, 379, 380, 399, 435, 457, 525, 559, 589, 605. Saved by metrical word: 21, 499.
[146] Grammatical words: 171 εἰς ἀκτῖνα βλέπῃ, 359 ἰσόμοιρα φανῇ, 380 διάμετρα φανῇ, 559 πλάστειρα θεά, 589 ἰσόμοιρος Ἄρης. Metrical words: 26, 91, 249, 325, 339, 379, 399, 435, 525, 605.
[147] 39 χρυσοστέπτορας. Saved by metrical words: 96, 108, 310, 425, 625.
[148] Saved by metrical words: 42, 163, 168, 195, 238, 382, 519.

1. The figure for violations of Meyer's First Law is most comparable to that of the sixth book (5.71%), followed by 'Antiochus' (5.36%). But there are a little over three times as many violations with metrical words as with grammatical words; hence there are only 9/628 = 1.43% of genuine cases, which would compare better with the second book (1.39%). And of those genuine cases, two-thirds are technical terms (ἰσόμοιρ-, τρίγωνος, διάμετρα), with which violations are also licensed with M^a and Dorotheus (i. 249). This implies that the poet is sensitive to the difference, and does it only when he considers it licensed in some way ('Antiochus' has *no* instances with grammatical words at all).
2. The figure for violations of Meyer's Second Law (2.71%) is most comparable with book 2 and Dorotheus, both at 2.99%.
3. For combined violations of Meyer's First and Second Laws the figure is 2.39% (out of a total of 628), for grammatical words alone a mere 0.8%. These figures compare best with 2.59% and 0.8% in book 2, and following that with 3.04% and 0.93% in book 3, and 2.92% and 1.59% in book 6.
4. There was a pattern in M^a for single violations of Meyer I to be about twice as common as double violations of Meyer I and II. M^b remains comparable, though there are proportionately rather more of the former, with 37 (28) single violations of Meyer I, as against 15 (10) double violations.
5. The extreme reluctance to violate the laws of Giseke and Hilberg represents a contrast with M^a (as well as with Maximus). This time, the poet is in line with the first and fifth books, as well as with 'Antiochus' (even Dorotheus is slightly less purist).

Bulloch's Law[149]

The medial position is often bridged by a metrical word (involving copula, disjunctive, negative, preposition (including 219 μίγα), relative, article, or other appositive). Excluding those, I find a dozen instances (109, 126, 187, 296, 571, 575, plus six instances with μέσον οὐρανόν: 29, 45, 84, 451, 560, 568; there were already three instances of this in the third book, and there is another in Dorotheus, p. 386.12).

All have a third-foot caesura. Two (126, 575) lack a bucolic diaeresis, but that is a far smaller proportion (16.67%) than in M^a, where (deviantly) over half of medial caesurae lack one. On the other hand the poet seems indifferent to punctuation at either point, whereas in M^a half (15/30) had punctuation,

---

[149] i. 250–1; add Agosti and Gonnelli, 322.

usually in the third foot. The only case where punctuation is certain is 126 (in the third foot), but this, as noted, lacks a bucolic diaeresis. Otherwise one struggles to find any punctuation at all. The poet instead favours the alternative scenario, whereby, in the absence of punctuation, there is a close syntactic relation between the words on either side of the medial caesura (noun-epithet, noun + dependent genitive, preposition + noun); all are thereby accounted for except 109 and 575.

Hermann's Bridge[150]

The only violation is 193 Φαίνοντι, a technical name. I find no weak examples caused by appositives. The poet does not use μάλ' or τόθ', which produce marginal instances in M^a. Taking 68, 568a, 614 for these purposes as uncountable, this results in 1 per 627 lines = 0.16%. No astrological poet is more loth to violate the Bridge than this; even Dorotheus and Maximus have two violations each to his one.

Tiedke's Law

Taking five lines to be uncountable (68, 90, 357, 568a, 614, producing a total of 625 lines), there are four 'hard' instances each of spondaic[151] and anapaestic[152] violations = 1.28% of all lines. Again, this is the lowest figure among the astrological poets, about half of the Homeric figure, though still not as low as Callimachus (0.21% in the *Hymns*), and dramatically lower than M^a, whose range is 11% (in book 2) to 16.45%(!) (in book 6). M^b either avoids altogether the words that trigger the violation in M^a (Φαίνων; καλή) or at least does not place them in the relevant *sedes* (Μήνη; ὥρη; ζῷον, which anyway he uses only once and in the dative plural). In practice his figure stands closest to that of Maximus (1.63%[153]). Zito, lxxx, calls this a 'dérogation... remarquable', but in context the figure remains low. Dorotheus' is relatively high (7.61%) if one includes the lines on *klimata* etc., but if one does not, the figure is the same as that of Maximus.

---

[150] i. 251; add Agosti and Gonnelli, 325.
[151] 121 ἐλθοῦσ', 145 καρπὸν, 148 καλῷ, 490 Μοίρης. Rescued by appositive: 72 εἰς μοῦσαν, 130 νηῶν τε, 168 τέχναι τε, 551 ζωῆς τε, 561 τιμήν τε.
[152] 52 νοσερὸν, 113 ἀβίους, 126 Κυθέρη, 427 ζακόρους. Rescued by appositive: 15 μέροπές τε, 47 φυλακάς τε, 55 μερόπων τις, 71 προκοπήν τινα, 83b κατὰ γῆς δὲ, 123 μέλανός τε, 133 μερόπων τις, 141 σοφίη τε, 144 ἰδίων δὲ, 185 κιθάρης τε, 186 ἐν θυμέλαις, 203 σοφίης τε, 355 ἐπὴν ἐφορῶσ' (just!), 535 ἐκ λιμένων, 574 ἐκ σοφίης.
[153] Seven anapaestic (203, 218, 304, 344, 495, 543, 546), three spondaic (119, 254, 377).

Tetracola

These were already discussed in i. 254–5. Revised figures are presented here.

On a strict interpretation of tetracola (with no appositives, not even elided τ'), there are 45 tetracola in 628 lines (omitting 175a and 621 though an abundance of caution, but including 614 which cannot have been a tetracolon however it is restored) = 7.17% = one every 13.96 lines, which is dramatically higher than M^a (1.6% = 1/62.75 lines, 1.4% = 1/71.3 lines, 2.52% = 1/40 lines), and even higher than Maximus (4.92% = 1 in 20.33 lines). Including appositives inflates the number still further. There would be an additional 87 lines with a single appositive, and an additional 92 with two appositives. These would produce respective new totals of 132 = 21.02%, or one every 4.76 lines, including single appositives, and 224 = 35.67%, or one every 2.8(!) lines, including both single and double appositives. I add this to supply a comparison for Maximus, for whom Zito provides a grand total of 85 tetracola, or 14% of lines, for single appositives. M^b on that count would overtop even Maximus by 50%. He achieves these remarkable totals partly by permutations of certain favourite verse-patterns which prove to be based on the component that follows the third-foot caesura. Foremost among them are (before the bucolic diaeresis) -έας, -ώδεος, -μονες, and -μονας, reduplicated perfect participles in -μένα, -σεται verb endings, and above all -τορες and -τορας; and, before the final bacchius, agent nouns in -τῆρας and the cadence ... τε ⏑ — —.

The following analysis of content is based on strict cases of tetracolon. The four-word hexameter confers instant weight and impressiveness, and it is no surprise, therefore, that the great majority (36) are in apodoses, enhancing the sense both that each item has sharp individual contours and that it contributes cumulatively to a total outcome. The tendency of the late antique hexameter to regularise itself and emphasise the cola from which it is composed (below, p. 238) thus serves astrology's turn very well. Most examples of adjacent tetracola are in apodoses as well, where they heighten already-emotive content (300–1, the indictment of hedonists; 554–5, hair-raising visions of the dead; 563–4, the sociopath; so too, with enclitics, 252–3, the wretched life of the water-pourer, 267–9, the frisson of those whose business is with the dead) or, conversely, reinforce a sense of down-to-earth 'thinginess' (342–3 and 569–70, carpenters and carvers). At the same time, a further eight figure in protases, and one case straddles both protasis and apodosis (as does the double example in 336–7). In these cases it is not necessarily that each item is informationally important, though the style shows its utility for itemisation in the list of Saturn's own houses in 22–7: the first item is a perfect tetracolon, and the second and fourth are tetracola as well if metrical words are counted in. Of the instances in the apodosis, nine contain a main verb (mostly executive, factitive, or be 'born'; only in 554 of other activities of the native),[154] seven a participle, and twenty no verb, of which five (but only five) consist of asyndetic single-item lists (57, 283, 307, 563, 564). Koechly 1851, xxxviii, rightly compared the asyndetic heaping up of epithets with the style of the Orphic Hymns (p. 162 n. 99), although asyndetic four-item tetracola, the purest form of this style, are even better represented in the latter (12.2% reported by Magnelli 2002, 85). More characteristic of M^b is for tetracola to fall into two halves, with noun + epithet, or noun + dependent genitive, or word + dependent case, on one side of the caesura. Some twenty of the genuine examples fall into this pattern.[155]

There are also tricola at 227, 396, 421 (grammatical words), plus 222, 232, 234, 245, 250, 600 (with one appositive), 213, 224, 235, 243, 265, 332, 436 (with two appositives).

Final Monosyllables

These occur at 23 ἀμφίβιος θήρ (see ad loc.), 170 ἡνίκα καὶ Ζεύς (where καί is not conjunctive). 287 ὑψόθεν εἰς γῆν is arguably spoiled by the appositive. All have the usual rhythm (most popular in Hellenistic poets, but also before them) ⏑⏑ | — ⏑⏑ — | —.[156]

Prosody

Muta cum liquida

There are 281 cases of *muta cum liquida* in the first 500 lines. The following table profiles M^b in the same way as was done for M^a in the first volume, establishing in which positions the combinations make and fail to make position, and in what proportions.

---

[154] Including appositives has the biggest effect on this category.
[155] Noun + epithet: 188, 225, 266, 321, 324, 342, 346, 416, 530, 550, 554, 570; see too 22 (apposition), 592 (participle + epithet). Dependent genitive: 288, 300, 518, 546 [*ex emend.*]. Other dependent case: 433, 555. The tendency is also noted for Nonnus by Agosti 2004a, 44.
[156] Agosti and Gonnelli, 327; Magnelli 2016, 367.

Table 2. *Muta cum liquida* in M[b]

Word-boundary		Internal	
position	correption	position	correption
1.78%	22.06/23.13%	38.08/37.72%	38.08/37.02%
princeps: 1.78/2.14%[1]	‿|‿: 18.15/18.86%[2]	princeps: 33.81/33.45%[3]	‿|‿: 19.22/18.51%[4]
biceps —	‿‿|: 3.91/4.27%[5]	biceps: 4.27%[6]	‿‿|: 18.86/18.51%[7]

[1] Five or six instances, depending on 242.
[2] 51 or 53 instances, depending on 104 and 295.
[3] 94 or 95 instances, depending on 242.
[4] 54 or 52 instances, depending on 104 and 295.
[5] 11 or 12 instances, depending on 435.
[6] 12 instances (including 86, although ἀτρέπτους is uncertain).
[7] 52 or 53 instances, depending on 435.

Discussion

M[b] partakes in the general trend for word-boundary position to shrink from its high of 26.83% in the *Iliad*. His very low figure of 1.78%, all in the princeps, is very close to that of the first 500 lines of *Or. Sib.* 3. His figure for word-boundary correption is fairly high, though slightly overtopped by the first and fifth books (and dwarfed by 'Antiochus', at 47.73%). Many instances are accounted for by a limited number of forms—especially Κρόν- (all the more in that he does not use Φαίνων), parts of βροτ-, and θνητ- preceded by a short syllable. M[a] had used these too, of course, but for his *five* uses of part of Κρόνος preceded by a short syllable M[b] has *thirteen* in the same number of lines; for θνητ- the figures are four and seven, and for βροτ- five and eleven. There are also 3 instances before προφήτ-, and 2 before προφαίνει.

The treatment of *muta cum liquida* word-internally is unusual: the figures for position and correption are identical, or nearly so. In the astrological poets cited in i. 257, position outnumbers correption by a factor of at least 2.5, and sometimes very appreciably more than that: in Dorotheus the figures are 74.17% and 6.67% (similar figures, as it happens, to Antimachus). 'Antiochus' is quite different: he has over twice as much correption as position, but his figure for word-internal correption is, in absolute terms, closest to that of M[b], which is the highest among all the poets surveyed. Certain triggers repeatedly elicit it.[157] It is not so much that the poet innovates as that he presses harder at options that were already available to earlier poets, although he himself sometimes fluctuates, for instance in his treatment of τέχν-.

---

[157] ἀλλότρι- (7 instances); Ἀφροδίτη (6 instances); Κύπρις (7 instances); τέχν- (7 instances); parts of -πλαν- (4 instances); πατρ- (4 instances); parts of τετρα- (3 instances); ὀθν- (3 instances).

Hiatus

1. After princeps

		per *n* lines	no hiatus	% of possible instances
1st foot	—	—	—	—
2nd foot	95 -η	630	12	7.69
3rd foot	171, 392 -η	315	19	9.52
	597 -η	630	6	14.29
4th foot	73, 379 -η	315	12	14.29
	294 -η	630	4	20
5th foot	126 -η	630	2	33
	486 -οι	630	28	3.45

Overall, there are 9 instances, one in 70 lines (allowing the full count of 630 lines, although this is generous). This is as restrictive as astrological poetry gets. It stands at the opposite extreme from the fifth book (one in 6.48 lines). M^a forms a less dramatic contrast, for his practice differs across books (see i. 259–63), but the most comparable, the sixth, has an instance every 15.39 lines.

In practice the poet almost restricts it to -η (twice at the main caesura, and both instances in the fourth foot before ἰσόμοιρος) and to the proper name Κυθήρη (for which 597 has a different reading in the papyrus, while Koechly corrected 294), in other words to situations where greater leniency is brought to bear. There are no instances of the also-licensed hiatus with the disjunctive (although there is where one of M^b's lines reappears in 1.337). Of a total of 123 instances of -η in the whole book, five have hiatus, and so 4.07% of them are realised, which is lower than any of M^a books 2 (5%), 3 (9.76%), or 6 (10.26%). Of a total of 53 instances of -η (excluding disjunctives), three are realised, or 5.66%. Of a total of 62 instances of -οι, one is realised = 1.62%. These figures are produced using TLG. In other words, the much lower overall percentage of hiatus in this book comes *both* from its avoidance with most qualities of vowel and diphthong *and* because the poet is fairly sparing even with the few he does use. *None* of the 27 possible instances of ω or ῳ employs hiatus, as opposed to 2.27%, 2.86%, 13.58% in the books of M^a.

There is not enough evidence to speak of a tendency for hiatus to become commoner in the second half of the line, as there is in M^a, merely a mild and hardly statistically significant increase in the third, fourth, and fifth feet. Presumably that is either because the poet is not putting locatival expressions there, or because he *is* putting them there but is avoiding hiatus with them. One would expect ω to be used in locatival expressions, and as we have seen there is *no* hiatus with this long diphthong; this contrasts with Maximus, eleven of whose 36 instances of hiatus involve -ῳ, with all but two of those eleven cases involving a prepositional expression (e.g. αἰπυτάτῳ ἐνὶ Καρκίνῳ, though not all are locatival). In practice the failure of M^b to replicate M^a's pattern seems to be a mixture of (i) fewer locatival expressions in the first place, (ii) the shortage or absence of constructions which produced hiatus in M^a (this poet does not use anastrophic prepositions, and is very sparing with the construction n *x* N: p. 202), (iii) the failure of those that exist to be concentrated at the end of the line (-ῳ in the princeps tends to stand in the second foot or at the main caesura[158]), and (iv) the avoidance of hiatus with dative endings anyway.

2. After contracted biceps

Three instances with καί in the third foot: 60, 76, 118.

3. After uncontracted biceps

One is transmitted at 230 διαλαμπάδα ἀκτινιβάλλων, which is corrupt.

4. In middle of contracted biceps

None.

Crasis

Very meagre gleanings indeed here. With καί only 86 κ' ἀτρέπτους, which is already suspect and even more so since it proves to be unique. 226 ταὐτό, 335 ταὐτόν, 612 ταὐτό are Homeric.

Elision

1. Parts of speech

Nouns 11 [16 δώμαθ', 21 ζωίδι', 157 δώμαθ', 191 κανονίσματ', 272 ἀστέρ', 413 ἄλγε', 470 λήματ', 502 δάκτυλ', 512 λήματ', 524 πράγματ', 618 σφάλματ']
Adjectives 3 [270 οἰκτρότατ', 413 κρύφιμ', 447 ποικίλ']
Pronouns 1 [72 ὅσ']
Main verbs 9 or 10 [-ι: 355 ἐφορῶσ'; -ο: 54 ἐπεφράσσαντ', 381 ἔσσυτ', 285 ἀπεμάξαθ'; -αι: 64 τεύχετ' [and 68 τεύχετ'], 246 πρηΰνετ', 371 ὑποβάλλετ', 411 ἵξετ', 538 ἔσσετ']
Participles 1 [121 ἐλθοῦσ']
Adverbs 3 [188 καταντίπερ', 528 τότ', 575 μέγ']
Numerals —

---

[158] These are the figures for *all* instances of ῳ in the princeps (whether in locatival expressions or not). In second foot: 9 instances (45, 133, 138, 239, 348, 482, 538, 546, 560). In third: 10 instances (55, 78, 115, 132, 286, 326, 344, 480, 488, 537). In fourth: 3 instances (302, 326, 488). In fifth: 2 instances (450, 542). This contrasts with a total of 81 instances of -ῳ (or ῷ) in book 6, of which 11 are in hiatus, and 7 of those 11 in the fifth foot.

There are thus 28 or 29 instances of elision (depending on the inclusion of l. 68), that is, one every 22.5 lines, or 4.44 every 100 lines. Among astrological poets, this is low, which adds to the overall impression of metrical nicety: only Dorotheus (1 per 26.57 lines, or 3.76 every 100 lines) avoids elision even more stringently. M^a is at the opposite extreme, at around fifteen instances per 100 lines. Further comparisons in i. 269–71, and in Lightfoot 2014, 62–3.

2. *Location in the line*
On the following scheme (reproduced from i. 271), the examples of hiatus are located as follows. Beside the line number, the part of speech involved is indicated in abbreviated form.

— ⏑ ⏑ — ⏑ ⏑ — ⏑ ⏑ — ⏑ ⏑ — ⏑ ⏑ — —

1 1.5 2 3 3.5 4 5 5.5 6 7 7.5 8 9 9.5 10 11

1	272N
2	21N
5.5	618N
6	72PR
	575ADV
8	270, 413ADJ
	188ADV
9	54, 355V
	121PART
9.5	16, 157, 191, 413, 470, 502, 512, 524N
	447ADJ
	64, [68,] 246, 285, 371, 381, 411, 538V
	528ADV

This is a remarkably distinctive pattern. The extraordinary dominance of elision at position 9.5 comes at its expense in positions favoured elsewhere, above all 9 (which has the lion's share of elisions in M^a and constitutes a quarter of all elisions in M^c(A) and M^d, although numbers in both cases are small), 5 (the masculine caesura), as well as 1.5, 2, and 3 (of which last there are no examples at all). Elision at 9 in M^a is at least partly accounted for by expressions of place which, as we have already seen, M^b does not use to the same extent; conversely, in M^b, the great majority of cases at 9.5 (which would only be increased if one included the four instances of ἡνίκ' ἄν in this position, which, as a conjunction, I do not include) are accounted for by elisions of third-person middle verb endings (-το, -ται) and neuters plural. Exiguous as the numbers are, the poet who is most comparable is Dorotheus, five of whose 14 elisions are in this same position (pp. 402.13 ἄλγε', 403.1 ἀνέρ', 369.3 and 389.3 ἔσσετ', 399.16 εἴδετ'), with a mixture of nouns and verbs. In Dorotheus' case, too, elisions happen here at the expense of elisions in position 9 (in fact Dorotheus and M^b have the same, low, percentage in this position; Maximus is close as well, but without so much of a rise at 9.5). There is a well-established tendency for elision to dwindle over time, which could account for some of the difference between M^a and M^c, but the similarity with Dorotheus' pattern cuts across that; perhaps literary imitation is playing a part.

Lengthening in Arsi of Syllables Closed with -ς or -ν

564 ἀθεσμοφάγος, ἀτράπεζος [5th foot]. Others are healed by emendation: 106 ἀβλαβέας ‹τ› οἴκων [K, 2nd foot]; 358 τριβάδας ‹τ› ἀνδρόστροφα [K; 3rd foot].

Summary and *Obiter Dicta*

M^b leaves us with an impression of a certain scrupulosity, an impression which is enhanced when it is seen that violations of rules to which the poet is otherwise adherent are sometimes caused by technical terms or names, as if these stood outside normal practice. Two-thirds of the strict violations of Meyer's First Law (i.e. with grammatical words) involve astrological technicalities. Hermann's Bridge is violated only with Φαίνων in 193. Hiatus, to which the poet is less hospitable than any astrological poet except Dorotheus, is permitted in the vicinity of Κυθέρη/Κυθήρη and ἰσόμοιρος. Κυθέρη is once allowed to violate Tiedke's Law as well.

The constant reference to Dorotheus, 'Antiochus', and Maximus, and the repeated contrasts with M^a (non-admission of no B; adherence to the Laws of Naeke, Giseke, Hilberg, Bulloch, Tiedke; restriction of hiatus and elision), will have been apparent throughout this discussion. But Dorotheus is presumably very considerably earlier, and Maximus somewhat later. This implies that poets are not shunted along a pre-set track depending purely on their date. It also means that there is no chronological framework into which 'Antiochus' can be fitted from a metrical point of view. Conscious literary imitation could be playing a part in the similarity to Dorotheus.

Finally, Koechly (who wanted to date the poet to the time of Julian) saw the metre as a staging-post on the way to Nonnus.[159] Certainly his dactylicity stands out in comparison to the other poets except 'Antiochus'. But even the latter pales in comparison with Nonnus, who has 85.1% dactyls overall, 38.07% of lines holodactylic, and an average of 4.25 dactyls per verse; as a result,

---

[159] 1851, xxxix: 'versuum pangendorum ratio, accedens illa iam ad Nonni severam puritatem'; cf. xli, on the poet anticipating 'volubilitatem illam liquidam'.

Nonnus is far more monotonous, with a mere 9 hexameter schemes, and a 90% stranglehold exerted by the top *five* (let alone eight).[160] One respect in which M^b equals or even outdoes him, however, is in the use of the *versus tetracolus*. For M^b, as we have seen, this constitutes over 7% of lines, rising to 21% if lines containing single appositives are included. For Nonnus, various figures are quoted (and the *Dionysiaca* and *Paraphrasis* are very different), but for the *Dionysiaca* they hover at or below 7% for pure tetracola and 18% including single appositives.[161] M^b's extraordinary penchant for the tetracolon is such that it puts him among Nonnus' heirs and successors (Pamprepius, Agathias, John of Gaza)—a good (approximate) two or three centuries before any of them. If this is combined with other features of M^b's line—the invariable presence of a third-foot caesura, the low incidence of elision, and its near-avoidance at the main caesura (save 618), the almost invariable presence of mitigations when Bulloch's Law is set to be breached, the low incidence of violations of Meyer's Third Law (in other words, the regular combination of B_1 with C_1 or C_2)—then we see clear signs of the tendency of the late antique hexameter to fall into a regular structure which emphasises the cola on which it is based.[162] Whether that implies for M^b in particular the utility for oral performance and declamation that the style implies for late antique poetry in general is an interesting question.[163] It would certainly be compatible with the Gorgianic jingles, and with the resonant sound effects produced by the parallelisms, rhymes, and semi-rhymes inherent in the style. Seen in this light, such devices might be useful, not only for the effects of segmentation and cohesiveness which we have analysed, but also for enhancing the impact on a live audience. The astrologer/rhetor/literary man whose chart is presented in 5.260–73 might have found them very useful—provided his speech defect (5.263) did not let him down.

---

[160] Figures from Magnelli 2016, 356–7. Nieto Ibáñez, 231, gives a slightly higher figure for Nonnus' top five feet.

[161] Single appositives: Magnelli 2002, 86 n. 113: 6.6%; Agosti 2004a, 42: 7%. With appositives: Agosti, ibid. and 2010, 91, quotes 18% (repeated by Zito, lxvii), and 20% or above for Nonnus' successors. F. Vian, *Nonnos de Panopolis: Les Dionysiaques, Chant XLVIII* (Paris, 2003), 215–16 reports 1 in 9 lines specifically for book 48. Further literature on tetracola in Nonnus in Agosti and Gonnelli, 322–4; Magnelli 2016, 368 n. 99. M^b's tetracola do not exhibit the tendency, noted by Agosti, for two shorter words to enclose two longer ones.

[162] Agosti 2004b, 64–6; 2010, 89–98.

[163] Agosti and Gonnelli, 356; Agosti 2004a, 40–1; id. 2004b, 63–4; id. 2010, 94; id. 2012, 377–8; id., 'Nonnus and Late Antique Society', in D. Accorinti (ed.), *Brill's Companion to Nonnus of Panopolis* (Leiden, 2016), 644–68, at 667. The use of accentuation to reinforce caesura and line-end, which, it is suggested, would have helped a live audience increasingly unfamiliar with classical prosody to perceive structure and rhythm, is not yet an issue in M^b, and neither is uncertainty about vowel quantities.

4.8. NARRATOR AND ADDRESSEE

If M^a was sparing with his narratorial interventions, M^b is vanishing. First persons occur only in transitional formulae (4 ἐξονομήνω, 109 Ἄλλα δέ τοι λέξω, 165 νῦν δέ με χρειώ), never in apotelesmata themselves. Nor does the narrator make a parade of the conventional virtues of informational writing (clarity, comprehensivity, organisation). There is indeed a reference to clarity in 12, ironically in an extremely unclear sentence terminated by a lacuna which obfuscates whether the σαφῆ... ἔλεγχον is what is being provided by the present work or not. Transitions at 107-9 and 165-9 offer the conventional summary plus prospect, but not in such a way as adequately either to overview what has just been presented or to introduce what follows (pp. 182-5).

The quest for an addressee finds itself restricted to the marginal evidence of the particle τοι, in which respect this is indeed the most 'communicative' of the Manethoniana (1 instance in 104 lines), although this is still a low number relative to other didactic poetry (i. 192 and n. 64). Five are transmitted, one (109) the product of emendation by Koechly, for transmitted σοι. That and 624 are in transitional passages, while the remaining four are in apodoses. Two are accompanied by a verb of communication (66 φράζει τοι; 584 στείρας τοι δείξει), while the remaining pair in some sense buttonhole the reader, drawing attention to the Focus word (80 τηνίκα τοι θεόλημπτος; 152 μάλα τοι πεπονημένα). Still, it can hardly be described as a concerted attempt to draw them in. So little sense is there of a narrator trying to stir up his reader's ratiocinative facility that in 4.66 and 99 it is the sign itself which φράζει a certain effect (as opposed to the reader's being instructed to φράζεσθαι from within the range of its several meanings). 4.583 ἀτραπὸν μεσοδερκέα at least implies something to be seen, if not an actual observer. Not that M^a himself had made much of an attempt to engage the didactic addressee in the earlier books. But there is a particularly glaring contrast in this one between disinvestment in the didactic fiction, that is, in developing the relationship of teacher and pupil, and, on the other hand, the poet's strained efforts to overwhelm his reader, or perhaps listener, through extravagant diction and bloated style.

4.9. ASTROLOGICA

Characteristics of M^b's Protases

Handling of Detail

The two things any astrologer is repeatedly called upon to express are (i) location (in *kentra*, signs, and terms) and (ii) aspect. This poet stands out for nothing if not for his verbiage, which encrusts details, though does not necessarily smother them altogether.

Location

(*a*) Place. On first reading M^b gives the impression of haziness about place. But this is not altogether fair. πρᾶξις configurations concentrate in the πρακτικοὶ τόποι anyway, so indications of place are sparing in M^a and Θ as well. In practice, although M^b tends to *omit* detail that is present in Θ, he also tends to *include* positional data that M^a lacks.

~ Θ. (i) In 4.201–2, 206–9, and 425–6, M^b is missing specifications in Θ that the planets are favourably placed. (ii) 4.218–19 fails to specify DESC. (iii) *Both* 4.347–8 *and* 6.583 miss the reference to the DESC in Θ p. 194.18. (iv) 4.354–6 fails to locate Venus in MC, if the parallel with Θ p. 169.4 holds. (v) 4.613 fails to specify that Mars is in the MC ~ Θ p. 201.22.

~ M^a. (i) 4.379–80 has no indication of *kentron* vis-à-vis 6.698–9, and (ii) 4.601 lacks the reference to the ASC ~ 6.724. On the other hand, (i) 4.193 contains an indication of *kentron* which 6.193–4 lacks; (ii) 4.396 (~ Θ p. 216.18–19) preserves a reference to the MC ~ 6.362–3; (iii) 4.480–1 preserves a reference to the DESC ~ 6.499–500; (iv) 4.595 has the Sun cadent from the MC, whereas in 6.62 no *kentron* is specified; (v) 4.597 specifies the ASC, whereas 6.692–3 does not.

As compared with Firmicus, 7.2.16, 4.368 indicates a different *kentron*, but not none at all.

(*b*) Signs. This poet has a penchant for listing signs of the zodiac by name.

Such lists are found across different types of chart, which suggests that this is the poet's own contribution; only in the first case (Saturn's own signs) is there a match in M^a.

Saturn's own: 4.20–6 ~ 3.12–15; *Sun's own*: 4.96–7 ~ Firmicus, 3.5.1 and Περὶ κέντρ. 8 (without names).

Winged signs: 4.240–2 (without label) ~ 6.450–1 (label without names) ~ Θ p. 216.13–15 (label + names).

Four-footed signs: 4.273–5 (names) ~ Θ p. 215.13–14 (names without label, but a non-identical chart); absent from 6.439.

Double-bodied signs: 4.452–5 (label + names) ~ 6.250 and *Lib. Herm.* xxxiv. 39 (label only).

This is a distinctive aspect of the poet's style, but in some cases it can also be shown, and in others suggested with a good degree of probability, that the poet has *omitted* references to signs. Any mention of watery signs has been lost in

4.87 ~ Paul, p. 61.2; of human signs in 4.230–1 ~ 6.446; of male signs in 4.317–19 ~ Θ p. 216.4; of wet signs in 4.395–6 ~ 6.362 and Θ p. 216.18; of signs for the birth of monsters in 4.462–3 ~ Ptolemy (various kinds) and *Lib. Herm.* (many-seeded) (see on 4.464–5 περισσομελής); (perhaps) of signs productive of gout in hands and feet in 4.501–2; of signs that produce different kinds of violent death in 4.613–18 ~ Firmicus, 6.15.4–8 and 6.29.10–11. One wonders also whether signs would have produced the differentiated outcomes in 4.129–30, 149–52, and 155–6, although in these cases not preserved in any source.

This has the effect of leaving the apodosis a tumble of outcomes which lack the analogical rationale they might have had in a fuller source.

(c) 'Ownness'. One scenario which obliges the poet to use expressions of location is when a planet is (or is not) in its own or another planet's houses or terms.

The poet in the *kentrothesiai* distinguishes several times between being in one's own signs and not being in them (Saturn, 16, 20, 28, cf. 3.12; Sun, 98, 101; 'own' in Jupiter, 38; 'not own' in Mars, 116). 'Own' places are mentioned in some of the τέχναι as well (4.139, 157, 310, 328, 341; own terms in 172), but otherwise only once, among the σίνη (608).

As for the *kentrothesiai* themselves, it looks, from repeated references to 'own' and 'other' signs in Περὶ κέντρ.[164] as well as *Lib. Herm.*,[165] as if M^b preserves more detail from a source that M^a has all but eradicated (save for 3.12–15). There is no trace of this system in 4.491–507 or 560–92 (which anyway uses short, snappy formulations with no room for reference to anything other than the *kentra* themselves). But where we are in a position to compare such annotations with those in another source, they do not necessarily concur. The only match among the τέχναι is for Mars' terms in 4.172, where Θ agrees.

The poet's preferred word for 'own' in this sense is οἰκεῖος (= ἴδιος, or possessive pronoun) and its negative ἀνοίκειος. He did not innovate this terminology,[166] but even where other books have corresponding details (which is not always the case[167]) they use different expressions.[168] The poet also extends it, so

---

[164] 2 οἴκῳ ἰδίῳ (Moon in ASC/MC), 8 ἰδιοτοπεῖ (Sun in ASC), 12 ἐν δὲ ἀλλοτρίῳ τόπῳ (Sun in DESC), 14 ἰδίῳ τόπῳ ἢ συναιρέτου (Saturn in ASC/MC), 39 ἐξ ἰδίων (Mars in ASC), 45 ἐπὶ ἀλλοτρίου τόπου, 47 ἐν δὲ ἰδίοις ζῳδίοις (Mars in DESC), 67 ἐν ἀλλοτρίῳ οἴκῳ (Venus in DESC).

[165] *Lib. Herm.* xxvi. 5 Sun on ASC *in domo propria vel triplictate aut exaltatione*, 36 Moon on ASC *in domo propria vel exaltatione vel triplicitate*, 70 Saturn on ASC *maxime in domo propria vel triplictate vel exaltatione*.

[166] Valens has οἰκεῖα ζῴδια, e.g. I 19.3, I 20.40, II 2.2, III 7.7, al.; ἀνοικεῖος likewise very common in Valens and Ptolemy.

[167] 4.38 ~ 3.32, 36; 4.101 ~ 3.117 (different factor: influence of malefic); 4.116 ~ 6.574–5 (a more complex chart); 4.172 ~ 6.511–12; 4.310 ~ 6.591; 4.608 ~ 6.728. Other references (using ἴδιος) without parallel in Θ: 4.177, terms; 265, terms and signs.

[168] 4.16, 20, 28 ~ 3.12 ἀλλοτρίοις οἴκοισιν... ἐν ἑοῖσιν; 4.139 [= 1.290] ~ 6.488 ζῷον ἔχων ἐόν; 4.341 ~ 6.520 χῶρον καθ' ἑόν.

Aspect

(*a*) There are differences in treatment of aspect from other sources, but not so as to leave an overriding impression that he is less precise than they. Sometimes M^b's indications of aspect are indeed foggier than those of the comparanda: (i) 4.170–5 ~ Θ p. 214.9–13 (conjunction) and 4.176 ~ Θ p. 214.12 συσχηματισθῇ; (ii) 4.366–71 omits being-in-same-sign and opposition ~ 6.46–50; (iii) 4.379–80 omits quartile ~ 6.699, and 4.384 opposition and quartile ~ 6.701–2; (iv) 4.395 has lost all specification of aspect, whereas 6.363 has conjunction and Θ p. 216.18–19 that, quartile, and opposition; (v) 4.552–3 has lost opposition and quartile ~ 6.601–2 (and Περὶ σχημ. 52). But in some cases this imprecision is shared with M^a: (vi) 4.180–6 and 6.371–2 omit quartile ~ Θ p. 214.13–14, and (vii) 4.420–1 and 6.431 omit quartile ~ Θ p. 216.24.

But details of aspect are *added* at (i) 4.230 (opposition) ~ 6.446–9 and Θ; (ii) 4.266 (trine) ~ 6.456; (iii) 4.273 (quartile) ~ 6.439 and Θ p. 213.1; (iv) 4.362 (quartile) ~ Θ p. 193.13; (v) 4.380 (opposition) ~ 6.57; (vi) 4.479 (quartile) ~ 6.499. In 4.294–6 ~ Θ, it is 6.586–7 which has omitted the information about aspects.

(*b*) Although the poet likes comitative expressions, they often fail to specify a precise relationship. So, although in 4.219 μίγα corresponds to καί in Θ and means conjunction, in 527 it just means that the same condition pertains for the two entities, namely that both luminaries are in male signs. In 4.499 μίγδην suggests conjunction, but in 4.202 μίγδην has a loose idea of a swap or vaguely commingled power (see ad loc.). Finally, although at 4.215 ἄμμιγα corresponds to conjunction in M^a (while Θ has the somewhat more elaborate situation of ἐμπερίσχεσις), and in 4.290 to equal degrees in Θ, συμμίγδην in 266 is once again vague. Whatever else it means it does not mean conjunction, for trine is mentioned immediately afterwards. What emerges from the study of comitative expressions is that the poet's main interest is in agencies and their combinations (in other words κρᾶσις or σύγκρασις: 2.400 n.) rather than the minutiae of how they come about. Personification is not necessarily implied. μίγα and ἄμμιγα may be used of persons, but may also be used of combinations of substances, for instance commingled waters (Ap. Rhod. 2.983, 4.628) or elements (Plut. *Mor.* 399 c); Nicandrian didactic relishes them; so too Andromachus the Elder. This, I suggest, is what enables the poet to exploit recipe-didactic for the language of combination (p. 218).

Terminology, Style, and Mannerisms

To repeat: the two things the poet is repeatedly called upon to express are (i) location (in *kentra*, signs, and terms) and (ii) aspect. What characterises him is a minimal amount of technicality and verbiage around the residue—verbiage which sometimes obfuscates the simple point at issue (e.g. 4.208-9, 335-6; also 154 νέρθε, 165 ὡράων, 266 συμμίγδην, 297-8 τὸν αὐτὸν ... δρόμον, 319 διωγμοῖς, 327 τέρμονας, 609 νεύουσαι). He favours, on the one hand, an impressionistic kind of grandiosity, with references to the cosmos for notional perpendicular lines to the cardinal points (45, 132) and in connection with the circle of the heavens (7, 11, 108, 147, 336, 380, 553), aspect (415, 482, 500), and the Moon (phase: 537; node: 546 [*ex emend.*]).[169] On the other, he has derived from Mᵃ a natalist idiom which derives ultimately from the ordinary prose term for the native (ὁ γεννηθείς) and from the standard term for nativity (γένεσις, poetic γενέθλη) but burgeons into the language of begetting, sowing, and obstetrics (see pp. 251-2). In Mᵃ, this is part and parcel of the miserabilist discourse about mortality. Mᵇ has less of that, and more of a rather weird contrast between sublimity and the grossly physical.

Specifications of location and relationship between one entity and another involve him in more or less endless permutations on the themes of visibility and motion.

(a) Expressions for 'being in' a location range from the very bland ('being in'[170]) through expressions of station,[171] proximity,[172] motion,[173] and appearance.[174] We are not consistently invited to see the planets as either figured on a chart or carried around in an Aratean cosmic whirl. There is little general sense that

---

[169] This has nothing to do with Ptolemy's use of κοσμικῶς (as opposed to κατὰ τὴν γένεσιν) (3.4.7). Robbins explains (n. 3 on p. 239) that the cardinal points change for each nativity, but the signs, houses of the planets, terms, etc. 'are cosmic, as being related to the universe itself and therefore fixed'. That will work for the reference to the zodiac in 482, but it will not work for references to *kentra* in 4.45, 132, and 537, let alone references to aspect without further indication of location.

[170] 157 τυχών; 181 γένωνται; 379 ὑπάρχῃ; 403 ᾖ.   [171] 177 φαινώπιδα τάξιν ἐπίσχῃ.

[172] 341 οἰκείων ὁρίων ψαύσωσιν.

[173] Coming/going: 327 (terms?) ἐπὶ τέρμονας ἡνίκ' ἂν ἔλθῃ; 508 (signs) ἡνίκ' ἂν ἔλθῃ; 519 (sign) καταντήσωσιν ἰόντες; 560 (MC) ἢν Κρόνος ἔλθῃ; 568 (MC) Μήνης ἐρχομένης; 583 (MC) οὐρανίην ἀτραπὸν μεσοδερκέα βαίνῃ.

[174] 16 (house), 154 (under rays of Sun), 189 (exchange of terms), 359 (equal degrees) φανῇ; 53 (setting signs), 139 (own houses), 194 (equal degrees) φαανθῇ; 69 (DESC) φανείς; 97 (in a sign) φααανθείς; 38 (own degrees), 94 (MC) προφανῇ; 111 (in ASC) αὐγάζηται; 65 (MC), 172 (own terms), 594 (Evil Demon), 601 (equal degrees) ὀφθῇ; 444 (in a bad aspect) ὀφθείς (cf. 2.357); 481 (conjunction or opposition) ὁραθῇ, 587 (aspect) δερχθείς.

the poet is using different kinds of verb for different kinds of place (terms, houses, signs, *kentra*), although expressions for 'frequenting' are proper to *kentra*, and seem to show the influence of M^a.[175] 'Ruling' applies to a *kentron* (78 κρατέῃ), but the concept apparently extends to terms as well (above, 4.38). There is a particular idiom whereby planets located *in* the ASC are said to 'regard' it.[176]

A rich but unthinking eclecticism is betrayed by verbs of motion which range in their implications from controlled, linear progress (466 στείχωσι, cf. 177 τάξιν ἐπίσχῃ), through the Aratean notion of carriage along the cosmic whirl (83b φέροιτο, 108 πεφόρηται; i. 895), to expressions borrowed from divine kinesis (37 ἠέρα τέμνῃ), and the startlingly dynamic 297 θρώσκωσι. The poet seeks *variatio*, not only through the verbs themselves and their semantics, but also through construction.[177] One particular favourite is the notion of carriage along a heavenly pathway, a commonplace traceable back to the paths (κέλευθοι) of day and night in *Od.* 10.86 (see on 4.6). M^a has already shown the way to synonymic enrichment of that founding instance, and to its use in expressions for conjunction ('on a common path').[178] M^b takes it further. He diversifies the vocabulary, using 'pathway' words both in proems, syllabuses, and advertisements,[179] and in quasi-technical expressions, sometimes with a sense of strain (the path of the terms),[180] but also where it sits happily, as it does for the twisted path of the Moon.[181] The semantic range of 'path' extends to steps, embarcations, tracts, courses, and trajectories;[182] and as an added bonus the same vocabulary can be used for the path of life, which is the human correlate of the motions of the stars (4.169 βίου θνητοῖο πορείην).

---

[175] 30 (see ad loc.), 45, 132 ἀμφιπολεύῃ (i. 879; 3.36, 114, 6.199, and cf. 6.273, of location in a house); 451 ἀμφιπολῶσιν; 79 ἀκροπολεύῃ; 84 ἀμφιθοάζῃ; 593 γενέθλην ἐφέπῃ ... ὡρονομεύων (3.32 ὥρην ἐφέπων; 6.156 δύο κέντρ' ἐφέπωσιν, 618 ὥρην ἐφέποντος).

[176] λευσσ-: 4.35–6 κυδόσκοπον ὥρην | εἰσλεύσσῃ; 59 μερόπων ὡροσκόπα φέγγεα λεύσσῃ; δερκ-: 491–2 ὡροσκόπα φέγγη | δερκομένῃ; σκοπ-: 110 ὡράων πανεπίσκοπα φέγγεα Μήνης; cf. 116–17 ὡροσκόπον ... φέγγος ἐπιτρέψῃ, 496 ὡροσκόπον ὄμμα τιταίνῃ.

[177] For ἐλθεῖν see n. 94; accusatives (4.297 θρώσκωσι, 583 βαίνῃ); ἐν (466 στείχωσι); ἐς (519 καταντήσωσιν ἰόντες).

[178] 6.140 ξυνὰς ἀνύωσι κελεύθους; 2.431 ξυνὴν βαίνων κατ' ἀταρπόν, 6.206 μίαν κατ' ἀταρπόν.

[179] κέλευθος: proem: 4.3, 6; syllabuses: 107, 166; cf. 3.232, 6.114. ἀταρπός: in syllabuses etc.: 4.147 = 1.295 κατὰ κόσμου ἀταρπόν; cf. 6.545. πορεία: proem: 4.6 ἡμιτμῆτι πορείῃ; in padding: 380 πλαγκτῷ κόσμοιο πορείῃ. πόρος: in *excipit*: 4.620 ζῳδίων κύκλιος πόρος. δρόμος: in padding: 297–8 τὸν αὐτὸν ... δωδεκατημορίων ἑλικὸν δρόμον αἰθροδόνητον.

[180] κέλευθ-: 4.74, 294, 310, 367, 545; ἀταρπός: 4.73, 273; τρίβος: 182; δρόμος: 231; πορεία: 499.

[181] 4.78 σκολιωπὰ περῶσα; 334 σκολιὸν λαβύρινθον; 467 εἰλιξόπορος; 478 σκολιόδρομος.

[182] 4.209 δωδεκατημορίων ... βάσιν εἵλικα; 295 κατ' ἔμβασιν; 318 ὁλκῷ; 319 διωγμοῖς; 510 ζῳοφορίην.

(b) To express the notion of aspect the poet uses, and varies, the language of witness,[183] is capable (though it is not his preference) of specifying geometrical relationship,[184] and continues M^a's practice of diversifying words for gazing and regarding, with different semantic implications for the verbs in question.[185] But his efforts lie mainly in two directions. In the first place, planets are visible phenomena, observed in their relationships by an observer;[186] they are invariably radiant; and more than being isolated points of brilliant light, that radiance is actively extramitted in ἀκτίς expressions which I examine below. In the second, these configurations are not just static presentations into which the planets have fallen and remain preserved,[187] but are schemes which they approach,[188] enter (or even mount),[189] into which they incline,[190] converge,[191] rush,[192] or through which they wander[193] or pass.[194] As with expressions of location, in striving to give maximum variety to a basically simple notion, the poet ranges across an entire spectrum from pure impersonality (a planet is observed in such-and-such a relationship by an anonymous annotator) to a high degree of personification, both implicit in his choice of verbs, and as a consciously cultivated effect.

Sticking to aspects and location in *kentra* and terms rarely embroils the poet in more complicated terminology. Where he does tackle technicality, he typically does so with some kind of defamiliarisation, for instance by altering constructions, wadding with verbiage, or through some other deformation.[195] A telling

---

[183] 4.121–2 ἐπὶ μαρτυρίην... ἐλθοῦσ'; 140 μαρτυρίη... πελάζῃ; 161 προσμάρτυρα φέγγεα βάλλῃ; 176 προσμάρτυρος ἀστήρ; 348 μαρτυρέουσα; 384 προσμαρτυρέουσα γένηται; 410 μάρτυς δ' ἐπὶ σήματι τῷδε γένηται; 451 μάρτυρες ἀλλήλων; 586–7 ἐπὶ τούτοις μάρτυρος ἀστήρ.

[184] 4.148 συνῇ; 598 συνέῃ; 380 διάμετρα φανῇ; 481 διάμετρος ὁραθῇ (cf. 6.701 διάμετρος ὁρῷτο); 295 τρίγωνος ἐοῦσα κατ' ἔμβασιν ἢ τετράγωνος; 273 ζῳδίων τετράγωνον ἀν' οὐρανόεσσαν ἀταρπόν; 362 διὰ τετράδος; 479 εἰς τετράγωνα πόλου λοξεύματα βᾶσα.

[185] ἀθρεῖν: 4.271 (see n.), 395, 472; also 421 καταθρῇ; 597 ἐσαθρῇ. ὁρᾶν and compounds: 355 ἐφορῶσ', 392 εἰσορόωντος, 362 κατιδών. δέρκεσθαι: 373 ἐπιδερκομένοιο, 492 δερκομένη (see n.). Other: 59 λεύσσῃ (see n.); 171 βλέπῃ (see n.); 372 ἐπισκοπέῃ; 460 θεωροσύνην ἐπέχοντος.

[186] ὀφθῇ (7×); 587 δερχθείς. Also φανῇ (6×); προφανῇ (2×); 552 φανείη.

[187] 4.319 παρέῃ.   [188] 4.140, 409, 426 πελάζῃ; 249 πελάζων.

[189] 4.266 συμμίγδην ἐπιβῶσι.   [190] 4.609 νεύουσαι.

[191] 4.310 συννεύῃ, 392 συννεύσῃ.   [192] 4.219 ὁρμώσῃς, 387 ὁρμήσῃ.

[193] 4.290 συναλώμενος.   [194] 4.226 κοινῶς ἐπὶ ταὐτὸ πόλου διὰ κύκλα περῶσιν.

[195] Technical language defamiliarised through suffixation/use of cognate forms: 4.167–8 κυκλόεσσαν... Ζῳδιακήν, for ζῳδιακὸς κύκλος; 202 ὁρισμούς (ὅρια); 295 κατ' ἔμβασιν (ἐπέμβασις); 460 θεωροσύνην ἐπέχοντος (θεωρίαν); 462 κακοδαιμοσύνη. Use of synonyms or poetic circumlocution: 122 ἡμεριναῖσι λοχείαις (contrast 1.282 ἡμερινοῦ θέματος); 368 ἀκροτάτοις κέντροισι (on my interpretation MC and IMC); 595 ἀποκλίνωσιν Ὀλύμπου; 481 διάμετρος ὁραθῇ (prose would probably have used the verb 'to find', e.g. Valens, App. XVI 11 εὑρέθη διάμετρος). With wadding: genitival expressions, such as 546 συνδέσμῳ κόσμοιο (the prose construction would involve a preposition or e.g. σύνδεσμον πανσεληνιακὸν ἔχων, ἔχουσα); 479 τετράγωνα πόλου λοξεύματα; with

illustration of his preference for circumventing technical terms is the noun *kentron* in its astrological sense, which he uses a mere three times in the entire book, that is, over seventy times less often than M^a.[196] His treatment of the names of the individual *kentra*, especially the two most often mentioned, the ASC and MC, further illustrate his *modus operandi*. For the former (see i. 879–80) he is the only Manethonian poet not to shun the technical name ὡροσκόπος, but he transforms it into an epithet and transfers it to the light or notional gaze which the planet brings to bear on the location.[197] Otherwise he has his own repertoire of themes (oversight; generation; fame; boundary) associated with the traditional poetic form ὥρη,[198] or makes occasional use (always in connection with Saturn) of poetic ὡρονομεῖν/ὡρονομεύειν, with perhaps some underlying input from 'Antiochus' or Dorotheus.[199] He is (as mentioned above) especially given to mentioning the ASC in connection with birth, life, generation, sowing, and birth-pangs,[200] although this is maybe, less an individual quirk, than a grotesque inflation of an association found in M^a (p. 251). For the MC, he generally takes the opportunity to vivify the standard prose μέσον οὐρανόν, with cognates, or epithets, or by making the expression genitival,[201] though he also finds periphrastic forms which avoid the technical form altogether.[202]

---

prepositional expressions: 147 σύμφωνον ἔχῃ κατὰ κόσμου ἀταρπόν, 537 σύνοδον κατὰ κόσμου ἐχούσης. Pseudo-technical: 4.38 δεσπόσμασι (hapax); 327 τέρμονας ('terms'?); 500 σχηματίσῃ (apparently intrans.); 515 ἐναλλάξωσι (intrans.); 519 καταντήσωσιν (technical, but not used in the expected way); 520 τερμοδρομούσης; 528 ἀνάστερον ('unaspected'). Rare examples of technical language: οἰκεῖος, ἀνοικεῖος, *passim*; 45, 132 κάθετος; 53–4 δύνουσι…ζῳδίοις; 193 ἐπίκεντρος; 503 ὡρονομήσῃ; 567 ὡρονομῶν; terms for aspect (examples in nn. 183–4).

[196] Three times in 628 lines = 1 every 209 lines, contrasted with 89 in 1,684 lines in M^a = 1 every 18.92 lines. Figures for M^c are 12 in 361 lines = 1 every 30.08 lines, and for M^d 10 in 340 lines = 1 every 34 lines.

[197] 4.59 μερόπων ὡροσκόπα φέγγεα, 70 ὡροσκόπον (with a missing noun likely in the previous line), 116–17 ὡροσκόπον (adj.)… | φέγγος, 125 σκοπιὴν ὡροσκόπον, 491 ὡροσκόπα φέγγη, 496 ὡροσκόπον ὄμμα.

[198] ἐπίσκοπ-: 4.17 ἐπίσκοπον ἐς βίου ὥρην, 30 κείνην ὥρην πανεπίσκοπον, 95 γονίμῃ ὥρῃ πανεπίσκοπα φέγγεα, 110 ὡράων πανεπίσκοπα φέγγεα Μήνης. Sowing, generation: 577 ὥρην μεροποσπόρον, 597 τεκνοσπόρον ὥρην, and life itself: 572 βιοτοσκόπον. Fame: 28 κλυτοτέρμονος ὥρης, 35 κυδόσκοπον ὥρην. Boundary: 28 κλυτοτέρμονος ὥρης, 77 βιοτέρμονος ὥρης. See Hübner 2001, 233–4, and on the root σκοπ-, Prévot, 239–46 (basic sense 'observation attentive', and ἐπί- with the sense of surveillance).

[199] 503 ὡρονομήσῃ, 567 ὡρονομῶν, 593 ὡρονομεύων; Hübner 2001, 229–31.

[200] Birth: 16–17, 28–30, 35, 70, 95, 110–11, 116–17, 593. Birth-pangs: n. 123. Conception: 577, 597–8. Life: 77, 572. Mortality (implied): 59, 491–2. Most for obvious reasons are in the *kentrothesiai* or oppositions across *kentra*; only a few are in connection with themed charts (593, 597).

[201] 29 μέσον οὐρανὸν αἰθερολαμπῆ, 37 μέσον οὐρανίης ἀτραποῦ…ἠέρα, 65 μεσόωντα κατ' οὐρανόν, 70–1 κατὰ μέσον | οὐρανόν, 94 ἐς μέσον οὐρανίης…πυριλαμπέος αἴθρης, 132 μέσον <>, 583 οὐρανίην ἀτραπὸν μεσοδερκέα. But plain μέσον οὐρανὸν in 45, 84, 451, 560, 568.

[202] 263 κορυφὴν ἐπ' Ἀρήιον; 367–8 κατ' Οὐλύμποιο κέλευθα | ἀκροτάτοις κέντροισι; 571 n.

The DESC and IMC are referred to less often, again with either poetic derivations of the normal prose forms or periphrasis.[203]

A few terminological peculiarities deserve slightly more extended discussion.

(a) 'Dodecatemories' meaning 'signs of the zodiac'. We get to this point by ruling out the more technical astrological meaning.[204] Of its various occurrences, 4.167–8 uses it in a reference to the zodiac, either as a very untoward epithet for ἄστρων, or in a double genitive (the zodiac [consisting] of the twelve parts of the stars), while 4.209 and 298 refer to their 'twisting path' in what sounds like one of the poet's wadded expressions for 'zodiac' (clearly so in 298, by comparison with 6.587). 4.227 and 335–6 (see n.) κατὰ ταὐτόν…δωδεκατημορίων need no greater degree of precision than a reference to signs. 4.250 and 265 are discussed below. In all these cases it appears that M^b is simply using 'dodecatemory' to mean a sign of the zodiac, but no further subdivisions of them.

Most of M^b's references to dodecatemories are paralleled in Θ (not, however, 4.209, while the chart containing 4.227 has no parallel that I have found in Θ). What is curious, however, is that when Θ uses dodecatemory, he means it—not just in the harms and τέχναι, but throughout. One can see this because he is referring to scenarios which clearly involve detail that is finer-grained than signs. There is a single mention of them in the Πρᾶξις chapter, p. 213.4–5, then another four in the Περὶ τεχνῶν and succeeding chapters on work—all of them paralleled in M^b. So, if Θ is a reduction of a poem, it was a poem that included a technicality of which no trace remains in M^a, and barely more than the terminology in M^b. Alternatively, if it renders or reflects a source which they both used, it looks as if M^b (but not M^a) was struck by the terminology but retained it only in a more anodyne way. That is just what seems to be happening in Θ p. 215.20 ~ 4.298 and p. 216.11 ~ 4.336. And it *could* be in pp. 215.4–5 ~ 4.250[205] and 215.9 ~ 4.265, both of which refer to two entities being in each

---

[203] (i) DESC. With some part of δύνειν: 53–4 δύνουσι…ζωιδίοις, 87 δύνοντος, 480 δυομένῳ, 560 Ἄρεϊ δυομένῳ, 567 Ἑρμείας δύνων, 578 δυνούσης Μήνης ὑπὸ λοίσθια τέρματα γαίης. With some part of δύσις (or cognate): 69 ἐπὶ τὴν δύσιν, 112 εἰς δυσμάς. Other: 582 κατὰ γῆς ἕλκῃ δρόμον. (ii) IMC: 83b ἐπὴν κατὰ γῆς δὲ φέροιτο; 582 ἦν δὲ Κύπρις κατὰ γῆς ἕλκῃ δρόμον; 613 Ἀντιμεσουρανέων δ' ὁπότ' ἂν Κρόνος Ἄρεϊ λάμψῃ; implied in 4.368 ἀκροτάτοις κέντροισι.

[204] Bouché-Leclercq, 299–304; G. P. Goold, *Manilius: Astronomica* (Cambridge, MA, 1977), li–liv; Hübner 2005, 198–217, and 192–4 on δωδεκατημόριον = sign (Geminus, Ptolemy, Paul).

[205] Note that the Moon here has dodecatemories of her own, which she lacks in Manilius' system (2.741–2).

other's dodecatemories—where 'in each other's signs' is a familiar specification—and both of which involve a change and simplification vis-à-vis Θ. That is interesting: a willed simplification which we can demonstrate in both M^a and M^b, while the latter has at least turned to good account a polysyllable which suits his wordy style.

(*b*) References to rays. At 165–9 the poet introduces an entire section—not formally concluded until the end of the book—to be devoted to ἀκτινηβολία. This merely lightly Ionicises the technical term ἀκτινοβολία, which according to Heilen might already have figured in Nechepso–Petosiris. The basic idea of ray-casting was that a planet shot hostile rays at the planet behind it, while the planet behind regarded the planet in front in virtue of its ordinary motion, but did not shoot rays at it; this directionality of vision was reflected in the distinction between normal ὄψις and hostile ἀκτίς.[206] This happened when the planets were in quartile. Bouché-Leclercq cites 4.165 ff. as an illustration of the theory,[207] and it is true that (i) the poet lards what follows with words for 'ray' or other words for light, and with parts of βάλλειν or compounds of βολεῖν (αἰγλο-, πυρσο-, αἰθρο-, φεγγο-, ἀκρο-, βολαυγεῖν) + 'light' words; (ii) quartile is expressly mentioned in 4.272.[208]

But it is generally not clearly the case that the planets are in quartile when ἀκτινηβολία is mentioned, and sometimes clearly not the case. In most cases the relationship is not specified, but in some the poet possibly or certainly means conjunction,[209] in one case specifies trine (4.266), in another opposition.[210] Moreover, although 264 φεγγοβολῶν ὀπτῆρα seems to be making a distinction between ἀκτίς and ὄψις, the poet would be riding roughshod over that distinction in other passages where part of ἀθρεῖν is used in parallel with a reference to ἀκτινηβολία as if both mean the same thing (271–2 ἀθρῇ...ἀκτῖσι βολαυγῶν, 395–6 ἀθρῶν | ἀκτινηβολίῃσι, 421 ἀκτινηβολίῃσι...καταθρῇ). And sometimes the ἀκτίς is not even that which is doing the looking, but that which is the object of a gaze (4.171).

It seems much likelier that in using this vocabulary the poet is simply picking up on (i) the combination of ἀκτῖνες with βάλλειν, which is already Homeric

---

[206] Heilen 2015, 1215–26.   [207] 247 n. 6.
[208] And is a possible position in 4.180–1, to judge from Θ, while at 4.420 Θ mentions conjunction or quartile. See also on 4.273, where emendation produces a possible reference to quartile.
[209] Inferred from parallels in M^a or Θ: 4.180–1 ~ 6.371–2; 4.206 ~ 6.466–7; 4.214 ~ Θ p. 194.3; 4.272, cf. 6.439; 4.347–8 ~ 6.583; 4.366–7 ~ 6.46–8 (which specifies conjunction or opposition); 4.396 ~ 6.363, Θ p. 216.18–19.
[210] 4.188; so too at 4.230 (with Axtius' emendation, which, however, gets rid of the reference to ἀκτίς). *Rays*, but not the *casting* thereof, are also mentioned in connection with opposition at 473 ἐναντιόωντα...σελαγίσματα.

Book Four

(Livrea on Ap. Rhod. 4.885), and (ii) the usage of his predecessor, who had already spoken of ἀκτῖνες if not of ἀκτινοβολία in connection with aspect. Note in particular 3.327, 6.53, and 6.293, where ἀκτῖσιν is used together with a verb of seeing (ἀθρήσῃ, ὁρώῃ), and 3.115, where 'rays' and 'witnesses' are parallel. This continues to be the case in M^b:

(i) In 272–3, aspect and the casting of rays seem to be mentioned in parallel.

(ii) In 395–6 ἀστέρας ἀθρῶν | ἀκτινηβολίῃσι..., they are bound together in a portmanteau expression.

(iii) The text transmitted at 354–5 might seem to imply a difference between ἀκροβολῶσιν and ἐφορῶσί τε, but τε τοῦτον at the end of 355 is in need of emendation, and with Koechly's reading the two verbs are in parallel and mean the same thing.

Although the technical meaning has been effaced, one might still wonder whether any implication remains concerning the physics of planetary influence. The incessant emphasis on light rays is at least consistent with ancient theories of vision, which see it as the extramission of 'radiative visual force',[211] and the frequent omission of any word for aspect might be more comfortable if the poet thought it more important merely to gesture at visual theory than to specify a precise angular relationship. It is hard to advance beyond the suggestion, however. When ancient authors, sympathetically or sceptically, try to explain what force it is in the heavens that brings about terrestrial effects,[212] they are trying to explain the influence of the planets on the earth, not on each other, and they do not locate this force in the rays of light themselves. Even when Manilius refers to *visus* (see Housman on 2.356) within the heavens, it is not a matter of rays, but of the angular relationship of one zodiacal sign to another (a line of sight, for instance along a square or a triangle).

What yields a much clearer result is noting the patterns in the distribution of 'ray' charts throughout the book (see on 4.165–9). They turn out to be strongly associated with the τέχνη theme, although, given that charts of this theme are usually correlated with either Ptolemy or with the corresponding Π- charts in Θ or their τ- developments, it is not at all apparent from the language in which Ptolemy and Θ discuss occupations why that association should have arisen. Nor is there a denser concentration of 'ray' language in the τέχναι section of M^a.

---

[211] D. Lehoux, *What Did the Romans Know? An Inquiry into Science and Worldmaking* (Chicago, 2012), 111–16 (quotation on 112).

[212] Cic. *De Div.* 2.89 *vim quandam* in the zodiac, according to the Chaldaeans; Manilius, 2.352 *vis* (in the trigon); 2.801–2, 822 *vires, effectus* (in the cardinal points), Sext. Emp. *Adv. Gramm.* 5.4, συμπάθεια and ἀπόρροια.

The congruence of the language of 'rays' and 'striking' with the τέχνη theme, and especially within 4.165–365, emerges in comparison with the far less strict adherence to the pattern in the remainder of the book. The charts that continue to adhere to it are mostly τέχναι-themed charts anyway (431, 438, and 415, a strange mixture of incest and τέχναι; 396 and 421 both have ἀκτινηβολίῃσι). 426 ἀκτῖσι...πελάζῃ has rays but no 'striking' verb, but its formulation is almost identical to that of 249 ἀκτῖσι πελάζων. On the other hand:

(i) Among τέχναι charts in 4.110–65, *only two* have a 'striking' verb (4.122, 161 βάλλειν) and none has rays (though 122 has ὄμμα...παντανγές and 161 φέγγεα). There are no τέχναι charts from 4.366–end which have not been accounted for by what has already been said.

(ii) Of the remaining charts, *the great majority* have neither a 'striking' verb nor rays. Two, however, employ φεγγοβολεῖν (527, luminaries in gendered signs, and 571, oppositions across *kentra*), and it is notable that both have outcomes that are τέχνη-themed as well (the former strikingly so: see on 534–5). The only anomalies—that is, charts which are clearly *not* τέχναι-themed but do use 'ray' language—are therefore 366–7 ἀκτῖσι...φεγγοβολῶν (on the theme of *trophe*) and 409 ἀκτὶς ἰσόμοιρα πελάζῃ (on the mortality of parents). At 4.479 ~ 1.307, the latter passage has ἀκτίνεσσι but M^b himself offers a different detail (εἰς τετράγωνα).

So closely is the *absence* of the language of striking and rays associated with charts that are *not* τέχναι in the closing stages of this book that it becomes doubtful whether to classify the apparent exceptions—those that look τέχνη-themed, but fail to mention rays or striking—among τέχναι charts at all. 466–71 looks like a τέχνη chart (for bodyguards and mercenaries), but is sandwiched between charts on children and harms, so its position perhaps indicates that it should be treated otherwise. The anomalies here are the three oppositions across *kentra* in 560–6, 567–70, and 577–81, for although they do not contain references to striking or rays they do nevertheless appear to be affiliated to Π- charts in Θ and sometimes Ptolemy.

What of other light words? The poet ekes out his limited vocabulary through the use of nouns, epithets, and verbs of the same root; his favourites are λαμπ- (and compounds), σελα-, and φέγγ-, augmented by αἴγλη, αἰθ-, αὐγ- (little used), μαρμαρ-, and πυρι- compounds. Despite the morphological variation, what strikes us is a sense of sameness. With the exception of ἀκτίς, which is reserved for aspect in the sense discussed above, and is not used as the basis of rhetorical variation, the vocabulary is barely differentiated for function, save that φέγγ- is sometimes combined with the notion of 'casting' and σελα-, for whatever reason, rarely is (4.240). A peculiarity of σελα- words is that they are sometimes used metonymically of the planet itself (4.231; 189, 473), as if the planet *is* its radiance, and vice versa. Again, πυρι- is specialised for the Sun and fiery Mars, μαρμαρ- for the same two plus Mercury, but apart from that the vocabulary is not particular to any heavenly body. On the contrary, λαμπ-, σελα-, and φέγγ- are used so often that it is a mere matter of chance if they happen *not* to be used for any one of the planets.[213] The writing is even lazy at times (for parecheses see p. 213).

M^b and M^a

Plenty of evidence has accrued so far that the later poet has been influenced by the earlier one in his adaptation of technical astrological concepts and vocabulary to the poetic idiom. To notations of position (being-seen-in: n. 174; ἀμφιπολεύειν, ἐφέπειν, of *kentra*: n. 175), rays (ἀκτῖνες) and the path metaphor, can be added variations on parts of ἐναλλάσσειν (4.515 n.) to refer to *x* being in the terms, or signs, or *y* (see on 4.181 ἐναλλάγδην; novelties are 4.189, 250 ἐν ἀλλαγμοῖσι and 4.202 = 1.302 μίγδην τε διαλλάξωσιν ὁρισμούς). I now add that M^b has drawn on M^a for what might be called the aesthetics of parturition.

M^a and M^b stand out from the other two books for their references to human birth. Poets across the corpus refer to 'mortals',[214] which is banal. Rather, what is meant here are strong statements like 'when persons are born...', 'to natives at their birth', and so on. When M^a does this it is mostly in the sixth book, but much more restrainedly, and largely where the context mandates it—in references to birth, and where there is a need to specify the sex of the native. This is then picked up by M^b and turned into something of a fetish.

Some specific patterns in M^a, which are either absent from other books or etiolated in comparison, are copied by M^b: references to γενέθλη, in the combined sense of birth and birth chart;[215] the dative of interest, 'to men at their birth';[216]

---

[213] λαμπ- and compounds are applied to everything (including the MC in 4.29); φέγγ- happens not to be used for Venus or Mercury (it is not particularly associated with the Moon, which, as Dr Holford-Strevens notes, is τὸ φεγγάρι in modern Greek); σελα- for Mars, Venus, or the Moon.

[214] βροτοί: 3.51; 6.484, 550, 608, 616, 634; 5.127. θνητοί: 3.96; 5.74 [ex emend. De Stefani]. ἄνθρωποι: 1.216a, 257. Characteristically M^b makes these at least a little more elaborate than the rest: 4.59 μερόπων ὡροσκόπα φέγγεα, 162 μερόπεσσι, 215 μεροπήια ἔργα, 538 βροτῶν γένος, 547 φῦλα βροτῶν.

[215] 3.114 ἐν γενέθλῃ; 6.213 ἀνδρὸς γενέθλην ἠδ' αὖ κείνοιο συνεύνου, 296 ἀνδρὸς...γενέθλη, 682 γενέθλη; 4.101 γενέθλῃσιν ἐφεστὼς, 372 ἐπισκοπέῃ γενέθλην, 568 ἐν γενέθλῃσιν, 593 γενέθλην ἐφέπῃ.

[216] 3.135, 159 γεινομένοισι, 146 γεινομένοις; 6.20 τοῖσπέρ τ' ἀπὸ γαστέρος ὀρνυμένοισιν, 25 ὅσσοις γεινομένοισιν, 100 ὁπόσοισιν ἀπ' ὠδίνων προθοροῦσιν, 108 τοῖσιν ζωὴν πόρε Μοῖρα; 4.17 γεινομένοις θνητοῖσιν, 29 φυομένοις θνητοῖς, 35 ἐπὶ γεινομένοισιν, 65 ἀνδράσιν (no participle), 102 τικτομένοις [ex emend. K], 111 φυομένοις μερόπεσσιν, 154 λοχευομένοισι βροτοῖσιν.

genitive absolute, 'when men are born';[217] and references to 'the native', standard in astrology, which M^b elaborates.[218] More striking is their shared obstetric language,[219] using the verb φύεσθαι[220] and the nouns γοναί[221] and, especially, ὠδῖνες.[222] A couple of these were already in M^a incorporated into references to the ASC (6.75 ὥρης... ὑπὲρ βροτέης, 618). This elicits certain patterns in M^b, in expressions in which the ASC is both designated by nouns (4.77 βιοτέρμονος ὥρης, 95 γονίμῃ ὥρῃ, 572 ὥρην... βιοτοσκόπον, 577 ὥρην μεροποσπόρον, 597 τεκνοσπόρον ὥρην) and folded into adjectives (4.59 μερόπων ὡροσκόπα φέγγεα, 125 σκοπιὴν ὡροσκόπον ὠδίνεσσιν, 491 βροτῶν ὡροσκόπα φέγγη).

Note also the strongly marked patterns and stylisation when M^b mentions natives (which is not observed in M^a). Very broadly, he does this in the *kentrothesiai* (4.14–120 + 125, 133, which are τέχναι in theme, but continue the references to *kentra*). They occur only rather rarely in the themed charts among the γενεαί (ironically) and τέχναι section.[223] Where they do occur among the γενεαί they are not dative participles (except the very first; after that the dative participle peters out). They then reappear when *kentra* configurations return towards the end of the book (4.491–507, which continues with 511, an oddity among the luminaries in places of gender; 560–600). M^a does not obviously explain why M^b has so strong and distinctive a tendency to refer to natives where *kentra* are involved. There *are* indeed such passages among the *kentrothesiai* and oppositions in book 3,[224] but by no means as regular or formulaic as they will become in M^b.

Characteristics of M^b's Apodoses: Combinatory Technique

A number of M^b's τέχναι charts contain not only τ- realisations but parallels with Π- charts and/or Ptolemy himself. It looks as if the schematic original has been back-fed into the worked-out version, which, given the latter is based on

---

[217] 6.115 γεινομένοιο βροτοῦ (in 205 ἀνδρὸς γεινομένου it specifies gender); 4.70 γεινομένων βρεφέων, 404 φυομένων βρεφέων (but conditioned by mention of the father).

[218] 6.697 n. ὁ φύς and n. 32.

[219] Absent from other books: contrast 5.144 φαίνοιτό τις ἀνήρ.

[220] 3.108 γεγαὼς τότε φύσεται ἀνήρ; 6.530 τῆμος ὅσοι φῦσαν, 576 φύντες; 4.504, 511, 590 φύσονται; 598 φυομένων.

[221] 6.618 γονῆς ὥρην ἐφέποντος (apropos of ASC); 4.55 ἐν τούτῳ δὲ γονὰς μερόπων τις ἐνέγκῃ, 133 τῆμος δὲ γονὰς μερόπων τις ἐνέγκῃ. Also 2.288 γονίμης ὥρης, 4.117 γονίμην ἐπὶ γαστέρα θνητῶν.

[222] 6.33 ἀπ' ὠδίνων καὶ γαστέρος ἐκπροθορόντες, 100 ὁπόσοισιν ἀπ' ὠδίνων προθορούσιν, 165 ἀπ' ὠδίνων ὁπόσοι φάος ἔδρακον ἠοῦς (Oedipus); 4.125–6 Ὁππότε δ' ἂν σκοπιὴν ὡροσκόπον ὠδίνεσσιν Ἑρμείας κατάγῃ, 275 ἐπ' ὠδίνεσσι βροτείαις.

[223] The only strongly marked ones are 154 and 275; also 372, 404.

[224] 3.15 ἐξεγένοντο, 107 βροτὸς ἐς φάος ἔλθῃ, 108 γεγαὼς τότε φύσεται ἀνήρ, 114 ἐν γενέθλῃ.

the former, would be hardly surprising. Examples are 4.170–5, 206–13, 230–7, 249–62, 263–70, 341–6, 437–43.

The technique is especially characteristic of book 4, but not necessarily confined to it, for the wax-workers who figure in both 4.342 and 6.524 seem to be the result of pivoting from a τ- chart in Θ to a Π- chart in Ptolemy, both involving Mars (but with different partners) via the word ζωγράφους. The ivory-carvers in 6.421 seem to be an infix from Mercury and Venus (Θ p. 213.23) into something like Θ p. 216.6.

This turns out to be an analytical clue to other charts which seem to be composite.

Linkage is by similar agents in the protasis:

4.125–30: Venus is the link connecting the intellectuals in the first part of the configuration (4.125–9 ~ 6.476–81) to the craftsmen of the second (4.130 ~ 6.482–3), though the same connection is made in M^a, and indeed is even clearer there;

4.193–200: Mars and Mercury link crucifixion (Θ p. 201.2–5) to thieves and murderers (Θ pp. 192.20–193.1);

4.206–13: for the geometers and diviners here, M^b seems to have anthologised Mercury-based material—for Mercury alone, or Mercury and Venus—and perhaps infilled further detail (sub-types of diviner) on his own initiative;

4.317–26: the initial chart concerns Saturn, Mars, and Venus, onto which are threaded items for Mars alone and for Saturn and Mars, and perhaps for Mercury (not Mars) and Venus with Saturn;

4.333–40: hunters are combined with fowlers, the subject of a related but non-identical chart including two of the same agents (Mercury and the Moon);

4.414–19: one way of explaining the otherwise bizarre link of incestuous marriages and offspring who are educators is via the combination of Jupiter and Mercury;

4.420–4: clothes vendors are added to clothes makers and menders, the common element being Venus.

This may be reinforced by a kind of midrashic procedure, where one link-word causes two passages to be spliced together:

4.196, where a Π- chart is threaded to a οἶνος chart sharing the elements Mercury and Mars through the common word λῃστάς;

4.249–62, where the operative planet is Saturn, but ἀντλητάς has served as a link-word to authorise the inclusion of material listed by Ptolemy and Θ under Mars;

4.333–40 (above), where the link was perhaps facilitated by ἱερακοτρόφους and ἱερακαρίους;

4.341–6: the outcome combines types of artisan whose common elements in Θ are Mercury in the protasis and ζωγράφους in the apodosis (M^b himself uses, not ζωγράφους, but ζωοτύπους).

Sometimes it seems simply to be a matter of the association of ideas:

4.271–85: the basic chart (the one in the sequence M^b is following) has tightrope-walkers. M^b has added strongmen, petauristae, mimes, which seems to be *via* his own association of ideas (not midrash): the mime chart in Θ is produced by a different agency;

4.437–43: the outcome threads together a Π- and a τ- chart for Mercury and Venus, combining mechanics with instrument-makers, but adds carpenters, who are purely Martian, and nothing to do with Mercury/Venus.

Some of the other types of chart in M^b may be composite as well. In 478–90, the thieves and those who die a violent death are linked by the presence of Mars; these items are also combined in M^a, Firmicus, and Valens. Other possibilities are 4.366–71 (exposure and rescue, the latter redundant because also in 377–8); 379–83 (exposure and slavery); 386–90 (noble parents, shortage of brothers); 402–8 (prior death of fathers, elder brothers, inheritances: also in Θ). But these are hard to assess without full publication of the relevant chapters in Θ.

In sum, there are various signs from both protases and apodoses that M^b's charts are secondary—secondariness being diagnosed through the presence of the combinations of charts that are separate in other sources, by the absence of factors which might have supplied a needed rationale, and through illogicalities.

4.271–85 + 286–9: in Θ, four-footed signs produce builders, as they do in Ptolemy. M^b retains them, but in a new connection (performers and entertainers) which makes little sense.

4.355 ἐπὶ τούτῳ: the prepositional phrase only makes sense if there has been a fuller chart to which this one marks an additional factor. Such a situation pertains in Θ, where there was a basic chart with Saturn and Venus, and then Mars is an add-on.

4.406 + 408: the combination of loss then gain of wealth appears strange, and one suspects the patching of two similar charts.

4.414–19 (noted above): strange combination of outcomes, incest and pedagogy.

4.437–43: it seems illogical to exclude Mercury, who is present in the corresponding chart in M^a, from an apotelesma involving fine crafts.

4.589–92: the addition of Mars should not produce passive homosexuals.

The poet's effort has gone into his strangely contorted rhetoric. Sometimes this is at the expense of detail; sometimes the peculiar idiom does a very effective job of obfuscation. The poet does seem to understand the rules of the astrological game,[225] yet seems quite prepared to override them. Omissions sometimes leave the reader short of a rationale. Apparently novel combinations provide scope for the kind of packed and crowded outcomes that the poet clearly enjoys, but once again are sometimes head-scratchingly short on astrological logic. The question is what purpose, whose turn, is served by informational poetry that seems to place that information *behind* stylistic self-advertisement and (undoubted) mastery of the rhetoric of the inventory. The illogicalities will remain in any medium, but would they be likelier to sweep over the heads of an audience in an auditorium, agog at a declamation?

Planetary Names and Epithets

The second appendix of the first volume and its tables already presented the basics. One of the main new points is that the contribution of a poet so mannered in so many ways is in the way he varies his references to the planets.

One might have expected, given M^b's engrossing love of epithets in general, that it would consist in his elaboration of a formulary to embellish their names. It does not. Table 3 in i. 901–2 already showed that he is not markedly out of line with other poets in his application of epithets to planetary names. He is fonder than M^a of epithets for Mars and Saturn, but in both cases very close to the figure of Dorotheus, and, like all the Manethonian poets, well behind Maximus. His choice of epithet is not very adventurous. Like the other poets, he generally prefers to evoke observable qualities—light; the distance and slowness of Saturn's orbit; the 'wandering' path of the Moon. Rather more distinctive is his 'fiery' vocabulary for Mars (πυριλάμπης, πυριμάρμαρος, πυρσοτόκος, αἰθαλόεις) which seems to have been elaborated out of πυρόεις, the light-name, possibly with some impetus from Dorotheus, who supplied πυριμάρμαρος. No other Manethonian poet treats this theme so sustainedly, although M^a has πυρφόρος (6.692) and M^d πυρβόλος (5.93).

It could already be seen from Table 1 (i. 897) how much fonder M^b is than M^a of mythological as opposed to light-names (except in the marginal case of

---

[225] Contrast W. Kroll, *RE* s.v. Manethon (Astrologe), 1104.29–34 ('Von seinem Gegenstand scheint er wenig zu verstehen...man wird daher die herrschende Unordnung ihm selbst und nicht einem späteren Bearbeiter zuschreiben müssen'), and Gundel and Gundel, 162 ('Das Buch zeigt das konfuse Durcheinander, das für spätere Astrologoumena typisch ist, deren Verfasser von dem Gegenstand selbst herzlich wenig verstehen'). These are, I think, uncharitable, but the characterisation of the book as 'l'opera di un letterato puro, ben più disinteressato al tema astrologico dell'autore...dei libri II-III-VI' (De Stefani 2016, 180 n. 11) still rings true.

Phosphorus): this can be read at a glance from the ratios of the former to the latter. M^b also is fondest of all the Manethonian poets of the name Selene, of which there is a bare majority over Mene (17: 16 instances).²²⁶ Yet it remains the case that mythological associations in his choice of epithets are secondary. True, there are a few EGHP appropriations (laughter-loving Venus: 4.225; mighty Mars: 4.362; Saturn of crooked counsel: 4.425) and other recastings from literary sources (4.356 Διωναίης Κύπριδος, a by-name of Aphrodite first in Hellenistic poetry; 4.355 Ἄρεά τ' ἐγρεκύδοιμον, a repurposing for Mars of pugnacious Athena's epithet in the *Theogony*). Venus is lovely, Mars warrior-like. None of this is newsworthy. It is hard to show that in his choice of epithets this poet is markedly *more* susceptible than any other to the influence of Dorotheus, but that there *is* a relationship is suggested by a number of commonalities unique to M^b among the Manethoniana.²²⁷ These include: for Saturn, *ἀγκυλομήτης, ‡βλαβεραυγής, and *βραδύς; for Mars, ‡Ἐννάλιος and †‡ὄβριμος as well as ‡πυριμάρμαρος, which M^b also applies to the Sun; for the Sun, ‡ἀκάμας; for Venus, ‡Διωναίη and ‡λαμπροφαής; and, as a general label for malefics, κακοεργέϊ (599, cf. Dorotheus, p. 326.6). Furthermore, σεληφόρος for Mercury (4.333) is very like †‡σελασφόρος (but of the Moon), and the Moon's epithet *ἑλικῶπις is matched in 1.294, although the corresponding 4.146 has ἑλικοδρόμος. He also has a Dorothean-type periphrasis for Mercury (4.362 τὸν συνετόν; cf. 4.65 ἐρατή for Venus, *ex emend.* K), and ἀστέρα πατρός for Cronos (4.131) is somewhat redolent of the earlier poet as well.

Rather, the poet's main contribution consists in his pursuit of *variatio* in the ways the planets are named. The choice is not just between mythological names and light-names. He varies these by all means at his disposal. Both mythological names (4.187 Κρονικοῦ ... ἀστέρος, 207 Κυθερηΐδος αἴγλης) and light-names (4.201 Ζῆνα ... φαέθοντα, 496 Ζεὺς ... φαέθων, 432 Ἄρεα ... πυρόεντα) can become epithets. There was already an established usage whereby light and mythological names could be combined in a genitive construction (i. 898 n. 4); the poet avails himself of this and extends it by a new construction in which the mythological name appears in the nominative and the light-name as an epithet in a dative expression,²²⁸ or occasionally taking some other grammatical role in a sentence (176–7 Κρόνου ... ἀστὴρ | φαινώπιδα τάξιν). Table 2 (i. 899) already showed that he is fonder than any other poet in the corpus of the 'star of' construction.²²⁹

---

²²⁶ Selene: Mene. Book 2: 2: 11; book 3: 4: 10; book 6: 30: 54; book 4: 17: 16; book 1: 15: 20; book 5: 8: 16.
²²⁷ Evidence comes from the verse quotations (asterisked*), from Pingree¹ (marked with dagger †), and from Pingree² (marked with double dagger ‡).
²²⁸ 4.425–6 Ἑρμάων ... στίλβουσι φλογὸς λαμπτῆρσι; 35–6 Ζεὺς ... φαέθοντι ... σελασμῷ; 170–1 Ζεὺς | φαέθοντι σελασμῷ; 414–15 Ζεὺς ... ἀκτῖσιν φαέθουσι; 238–9 Κρόνος ... φαίνοπι ῥόμβῳ; 317 φαινούσαις δ' ἀκτῖσιν ... Κρόνος; cf. also 77–8 ἀμφίκερως Μήνη .... | φωτὶ Σεληναίῳ.
²²⁹ Moon: 87, 146; Venus: 180, 356; Sun: 93; Mars: 44, 112, 328, 366, 391, 395, 552–3; Jupiter: 586; Saturn: 176, 290, 309, 395, cf. 131 ἀστέρα πατρός.

This is seen on a simple numerical basis for Mars and Saturn, and by the fact that he alone of the poets in the corpus uses it for Mercury, Venus, and the luminaries. To this we can add that he is fonder still of 'star of' than appears from that table because he extends it with (i) star or 'light' words accompanied by the planet's name in the form of an epithet (4.187, 207), and (ii) 'light' words (in place of 'star') followed by the genitive of the planet's name (αἴγλη, ἀκτῖνες, σέλας, φάος, φέγγος, etc.).[230] It seems most unlikely that he thought that 'star of' was an archaising construction; he simply deploys it as part of his arsenal of *variatio*. There are also a couple of naming formulae ('which men call') to introduce a planet's name in a more ceremonious way (4.14–15, Saturn; 53–4, Venus).

Of 174 planetary mentions, the malefics are named oftener than benefics. It is not immediately obvious why that should be the case, although Mars would be expected to have a prominent role in both τέχναι charts (because he is one of the Rulers of πρᾶξις) and in σίνος charts (because he is a malefic), while Jupiter would not be expected to have much of a role in either. That does not altogether explain, though, why Saturn is so popular (not one of the Rulers of πρᾶξις), nor why Mercury (another Ruler of πρᾶξις) is not more popular. It was also surprising to find how similar the results were to those of M[a], with the top four identical but for the swapping of the Moon and Saturn, and Jupiter demoted from third-last to last place. The proportional mentions of each planet (expressed as percentages of the total number of occurrences) even turned out to be fairly similar, especially for Mars. This outcome defied expectation because book 6, while containing similar kinds of material to book 4, represents it in very different proportions; there is much more about birth in the former, which might have been expected to favour the Moon more than it did.

Sun

15 instances (8.67%), of which four are ornamented (4.93 πυριμάρμαρος ἀστήρ; 271, 420, 508 ἀκάμας).

Moon

33 instances (19.08%) (16 of Μήνη, 17 of Σελήνη/Σεληναίη), of which nine are ornamented (wandering: 4.91 πουλυπλανὴς ... ἕλιξ Μήνης; 146 Σεληναίης

---

[230] 110 φέγγεα Μήνης; 249 Μήνης ἀκτῖσι; 347 Ἀκτὶς δ' αἰγλήεσσα Σεληναίης; 335 λαμπάσι Μήνης; 409 Σεληναίης ἀκτὶς; 594 Σεληναίης φάος; 201–2 ἀκτὶς | Ἑρμείου; 354 Ἑρμείου δ' ἀκτῖνες; 601 σελάσματα Κύπριδος; 171 ἀκτῖνα ... Ἄρεος; 187 Ἄρεος αἴγλη; 153 αὐγῶν Ἠελίοιο (unless this is part of an expression for ὕπαυγος); 403 Ἠελίου σελάεσσι; 595, 608 Ἠελίου δ' ἀκτῖνες; 215, 410 φωτὶ Κρόνου; 187 Κρονικοῦ σέλας ἀστέρος; 472 Κρόνου βλαβεραυγὲς ... φέγγος.

ἑλικοδρόμος ἄστατος ἀστήρ; 224 ἑλικάστερος; 437, 467 εἰλιξόπορος; horned: 77, 478 ἀμφίκερως; 91 κερατῶπις; New: 510 νεολαμπής).

Mercury

19 instances (10.98%) (17 mythological, 2× Στίλβων + 1× στίλβων as epithet), of which three are ornamented (light: 4.333 σελαηφόρος, 4.201–2 λαμπραύγετις ἀκτὶς | Ἑρμείου; character: 4.362 τὸν συνετόν).

Venus

27 instances (15.61%) (6× Ἀφροδίτη, 2× Κυθέρεια, 2× Κυθέρη, 1× Κυθερηιάς, 1× Κυθερηίς as adj., 1× Κυπρογενής, 14× Κύπρις; 4.65 ἐρατή [ex emend.] is not included in the count), of which seven are ornamented (light: 4.53 λαμπροφαὴς δ᾽ ἀστήρ; character: 414 ἱμερτής; epic/mythological: 356 Διωναίης Κύπριδος, 225 φιλομμειδής; two names combined: 180 ἀφρογενοῦς Κύπριδος θοὸν ἀστέρα, 437 Κύπριν δ᾽ ἀφρογένειαν, 491 Κύπρις δ᾽ ἀφρογένεια).

Mars

38 instances (21.97%) (35× Ἄρης, 1× Ἐννάλιος, 2× Πυρόεις + 1× πυρόεις as epithet), of which 14 are ornamented (light: 4.153 αἰγλήεις, 187 Ἄρεος αἴγλην; fire: 44, 112, 172 πυριλαμπής, 218 ἀκτῖσιν Ἄρης πυριλαμπέσι, 391 πυριμάρμαρος, 467 πυρσοτόκος; smoke: 319 αἰθαλόεις, 366 Αἰθαλόεις δ᾽ ἀστὴρ Ἄρεως, 552–3 αἰθαλόεις ἀστὴρ... Ἄρεος; character: 438 τευχεσφόρος; epic: 355 ἐγρεκύδοιμος, 362 ὄβριμος).

Jupiter

13 instances (7.51%) (12 mythological, 1× Φαέθων + 2× φαέθων as epithet), of which one is ornamented (4.148 καλῷ Φαέθοντι).

Saturn

29 instances (16.76%) (28 mythological, including 187 Κρονικοῦ... ἀστέρος; 1× Φαίνων + 1× φαινῶπις as adj.), of which ten, possibly eleven, are ornamented (orbit: 4.249 αἰπυπλανής; maleficence: 309, 472 βλαβεραυγής; slowness: 318 φλογὸς βαρυβάμονος, 432 βραδύς; senescence: 402 πολιός; mythological: 14 Τιτάν, 238, 460 Οὐρανίδης; epic: 425 ἀγκυλομήτης; possibly another epithet to be restored in 567, e.g. αἰνός, αἰπύς).

4.10. THE RELATIONSHIP OF M^b AND M^a, AND OF EACH WITH Θ

An earlier section compared the structure of book 4 with that of books 2, 3, and 6. This one turns to source criticism. Many similarities have already been noted between M^a and M^b. I now press harder at the relationship between both and Θ.

(i) As far as macro-content is concerned, M^a and M^b are related in their coverage, especially concerning *kentrothesiai*, aspect, and the themed charts in book 6, namely nurture, marriage, τέχναι, harms, slaves, indeed everything except loss of wealth.
(ii) They uniquely share details absent from other comparanda, especially in charts involving *kentrothesiai* and τέχναι.
(iii) As noted earlier (p. 134), they exhibit a similar and distinctive planetary order in the *kentrothesiai* (*pentazonos* + luminaries).

This is not to say, however, that M^b is simply working from M^a. If that had been the case, it is hard to see why M^b should so systematically have selected against material with parallels in Firmicus' sample charts (6.29–31). As it is, this is a stratum strongly represented in M^a and all but absent from M^b, whose Firmican material, such as it is, is found outside these chapters (p. 133). Even in shared material, M^b contains additional details in the protasis and circumstances in the apodosis which are not derived from M^a:

(i) in the *kentrothesiai* (including 'own' houses);
(ii) in the aspects across *kentra*;
(iii) in the luminaries and gendered signs (see introduction to 4.508–36).

M^b is either not working directly from M^a himself, or is working from him but has combined elements from a separate source or sources.

The most sustained parallels are found in their treatment of themed charts. In i. 787–8 it was already shown that M^a and M^b are related to each other, and each to Θ, in respect of their material on πρᾶξις (Θ ch. 83), τέχναι (Θ chs. 84–96), and madmen (Θ ch. 65), in such a way that M^b tends to be more closely related to Θ in both protasis and apodosis. This section adds to the evidence. The arguments are that (i) M^a and M^b have a common source that is like Θ; but also (ii) they have material in common which could (*a*) go back to a source that only *they* share and/or (*b*) be directly imitated by M^b from M^a. And, importantly, that (iii) M^b seems to have returned to Θ or a Θ-like source and is generally closer to that than M^a is.

Arguments from coverage are as follows.

(i) There is almost, but not quite, perfect correlation in the material they cover. A handful of πρᾶξις/τέχναι charts appear in M^b and Θ but not M^a (4.157–60, 327–32, 333–40, 560–6), or in M^b alone (4.224–9, if indeed this is a τέχναι chart). But there are no τέχναι charts where M^a and Θ have common ground which are not also shared with M^b.

(ii) M^a and M^b have the further peculiarity that they contain hybrid charts that blend details from both Θ ch. 83 (an enriched version of Ptolemy's Π- charts) and chs. 84–96 (the τ- realisations).

(iii) Both also mix up οἶνος and τέχναι charts.
   (a) With a single tradition in Θ (among οἶνος), but among τέχναι in M^a and M^b: 4.193–200 ~ 6.499–503; 4.214–17 (+ 218–23) ~ 6.491–3.
   (b) With a double tradition in Θ: 4.230–7 ~ 6.446–9 (both among τέχναι); 4.294–308 + 309–16 (among τέχναι) ~ 6.586–90 + 591–2 (among οἶνος).

But it does not necessarily follow that M^b is *only* derivative from M^a. Both have their own distinctive affiliations. M^a, on the one hand, is more closely affiliated than M^b to *Lib. Herm.* xxxiv *De terminis in quibus fuerint planetae locati*, a chapter on planets in each other's degrees (pp. 268–9). These detailed correspondences are not represented in M^b, as we should expect were M^b simply a copy. M^b, on the other hand, tends to have more in common with Θ, which simply reinforces the affinity that can be seen from their shared sequence of charts (Θ pp. 214.9–217.7). M^b seems to have access to other material as well. In the case of 4.558 εἰδώλων there is also a common link with περὶ σχημ. 52, i.e. Dorotheus.

Patterns of Correspondence

These are the implications of the correspondences tabulated below.

(a) In those charts where they share common ground, Θ is not the direct source of either M^a and M^b. Nor were they the source of Θ. Rather, all have a common source. In the τέχναι charts, that common source is related to Ptolemy's treatment of πρᾶξις, apparently an enriched version of it (see p. 140).

(b) In the details of their apodoses, M^a and M^b both exhibit parallels with the 'original' Ptolemy (group (i)(1), (2)). But there are far more of them that are restricted to Ptolemy and M^b (group (iii)(1), (3)). That should not matter: it causes no chronological difficulties. The single unique parallel between M^a and Ptolemy (group (iv)(1)) is harder. One can only infer that Ptolemy's material is already traditional, and not original to him. The substantial similarities between his method of calculating πρᾶξις and that of Dorotheus and Anubion (who

Book Four   261

agree on the three principal planets involved: p. 130) suggest that this may indeed have been the case.

(*c*) Both M^a and M^b also have correspondences with Θ (group (i) (3, 4, 5)), so although our extant version of Θ seems to be late (as demonstrated by the -άριος endings discussed on p. 144), it contains material early enough to have been used by M^a in the early second century.

(*d*) Interestingly, although the category is not large, M^a has far more overlaps with Θ against M^b (group (iv)(2)) than it has overlaps with Ptolemy against M^b (group (iv)(1)). A couple involve items which are simply absent in M^b, though in most cases it is a matter of more similar diction. Unless Θ is simply a paraphrase of a poem which happened to overlap with M^a in these particular items, this is compatible with the suggestion that Θ might be preserving pre-Ptolemaic or para-Ptolemaic material, thereby allowing us largely to circumvent the chronological impossibility of making M^a 'use' Ptolemy himself.

(*e*) Notwithstanding the previous point, details in both protases and apodoses and the lexis of the latter indicate that M^b is more closely affiliated with Θ than is M^a. On this model, Θ, M^a, and M^b ultimately go back to a common source (which we cannot, unfortunately, identify with Antiochus, because of the unknown origin of the relevant chapters in Θ). But M^b *also* goes back directly to a source like Θ for many individual details.

(*f*) There are no straightforward, clear, or consistent patterns of correspondence with Θ. For instance, it is not the case that the similarities with M^a are with the Π- charts, in M^b with the τ- realisations, or *vice versa*.

(*g*) Despite the demonstrable relationship between Θ and M^b, it is not an egregiously close one. The striking similarities, especially in the protases, that subsist in the series of charts shared between M^d and Θ ch. 96 fail to materialise in those shared between M^b and Θ. The mere fact that the charts appear in the same sequence does not necessarily mean that their details are more closely related to each other than either is to M^a. To consider their protases, it is true that the majority of the charts in the sequence belong to group (iii) below (where M^b stands with Θ against M^a), but a few belong to group (ii), where M^a and M^b side together against Θ.[231]

(*h*) The possibility that Θ represents the remains of a poem was viewed sceptically in II.2. The most reasonable interpretation of the correspondences is that Θ represents some version (quite possibly truncated) of the prose underlay which M^a and M^b poeticise in their several ways. This is suggested by:

(1) the generally more detailed and technical protases (including the preservation of the more technical meaning of 'dodecatemory' in Θ);

---

[231] Group (ii): 4.206–13; 286–9; 420–4. Group (iii): 4.170–5 + 176–8; 249–62; 294–308 + 309–16; 317–26; 437–43. Group (i): 4.180–6; 201–5; 263–70; 341–6; 395–401.

(2) the character of the shared material in the apodoses. Typically, the overlaps between either or both of M^b/M^a and Θ are with key nouns, especially agent nouns and trade names. Either Θ represents the kind of prose version from which the poets take their departure, or, in the less likely event that Θ is a reduction of another poetic version, an epitomator has chosen to single them out because they are *ipso facto* the most important words.

(*i*) At the same time, there are commonalities between M^a and M^b unshared by Θ which could show that M^b was drawing on M^a but could also indicate a common ancestor (conceivably itself poetic).

(1) They share set-ups and details and diction in the apodosis more closely related to each other than to other comparanda in τέχναι and harms (group (ii)).

(2) There are cases in which M^b demonstrably contains elaborated versions of M^a's diction (4.297–8 ~ 6.587; p. 219).

Insofar as M^b uses M^a plus another source close to Θ, this pattern of affiliation is similar to what has been established for Firmicus' *Sphaera Barbarica* (8.6–17), which uses the fifth book of Manilius' *Astronomica*, plus their common source, Teucer. See Hübner 1984, 139–43; 2010, 20.

Register of Similarities

~ means 'there is a correspondence with'.
/ means 'dissimilar to the previous item or items'.

Protases

(i) Agreement

M^a ~ M^b ~ Θ *(no match in Ptolemy)*

4.131–8 ~ 6.484–6 ~ Θ p. 216.17–22. In M^b and Θ the MC is involved, but differently populated; in M^a and M^b Jupiter is involved, but differently located; in M^a and Θ watery signs are involved.

4.146–52 ~ 6.520–5 ~ Θ p. 213.22–4.

4.180–6 ~ 6.366–72 ~ Θ pp. 213.9–13, 214.13–17. M^a has houses and terms, M^b aspect and terms (both using ἐναλλάγδην); these options, and more, are included within Θ.

4.201–5 ~ 6.476–9 ~ Θ p. 214.18–21. M^b and Θ have aspect then exchange of terms; M^a and Θ have exchange of terms, then friendly beams/a good place (καλῷ τόπῳ ἑστῶτα).

4.238–48 ~ 6.450–5 (both additive) ~ Θ p. 216.8–15 (both M^b and Θ name the signs).

4.263–70 ~ 6.456–64 ~ Θ p. 215.8–11. M^a and M^b involve the MC; M^b and Θ refer to dodecatemories; 6.458 shares with Θ that there is no benefic in aspect, and reciprocal placement.

4.341–6 (Moon and Mercury in their own terms) ~ 6.520–5 (Moon with Mercury in its own place) ~ Θ p. 216.15–16 (Moon and Mars in terms of Mercury).

4.395–401 ~ 6.362–5 ~ Θ p. 216.17–22. M^a and M^b make the Sun aspect malefics, but also reflect different facets of Θ (respectively, watery signs and location in MC).

(ii) M^a closer to M^b than either or both of Ptolemy and Θ

4.139–45 ~ 6.487–90 (M^a and M^b introduce terms, though differ over whose)/Ptol. 4.4.3, Θ p. 210.29–31.

4.187–92 ~ 6.494–8 (in each other's terms; 4.188 καταντίπερ' ~ 6.495 ἀντιπέρην)/Θ p. 215.8–11.

4.206–13 ~ 6.465–71 (Mercury aspects Venus)/Θ pp. 214.22–215.3.

4.214–17 ~ 6.491–3 (Saturn, Venus, and Mars together)/Θ pp. 192.16–18 (ἐμπερίσχεσις ~ 1.235–40), 194.2–4 (involving IMC).

4.286–9 ~ 6.439–40 (Venus aspects Sun + Mars)/Θ pp. 215.16–17 (Venus as add-on, to Saturn + Mars), 213.1 (Sun as add-on, to Mars + Venus).

4.347–53 ~ 6.583–5 (Moon, Venus, and Mars)/Θ pp. 194.18–195.2 (Mars an add-on), 215.19–21 (no Mars).

4.420–4 ~ 6.431–5 (Sun involved)/Θ p. 216.23–5.

4.425–30 ~ 6.436–8/Θ pp. 214.22–215.2 (involves the aspect of Mars and mentions the house of Saturn).

4.537–44 ~ 6.599–600/Θ pp. 192.13–14, 193.20–2 (Θ involves Saturn, and 192.13–14 locates the luminaries in the ASC).

4.567–70 ~ 6.341–7/miscellaneous τ- charts in Θ.

4.577–81 ~ 6.355–6 (M^a and M^b equip Mercury with a location and relation to the Moon)/Ptol. 4.4.3, Θ p. 210.26–7.

(iii) M^b closer to Θ than to M^a

4.121–4 ~ Θ p. 211.13–14 (Venus aspects Mars; M^b adds day birth)/6.518–19 (no Mars; Venus aspects ASC).

4.170–5 ~ Θ p. 214.9–11 (Jupiter, Mercury, with Mars)/6.511–14 (Sun with Mercury).

4.230–7 ~ Θ pp. 193.1–3 and 212.2–5, 217.24–218.2/6.446–9 (Mᵃ adds human sign).

4.249–62 ~ Θ p. 215.4–7/6.422–4.

4.294–308 + 309–16 ~ Θ pp. 195.5–10 and 215.18–22/6.586–90 (simplified).

4.317–26 ~ Θ p. 216.1–7 (Saturn, Venus, Mars in mutual aspect)/6.415–18. Mᵇ ~ Θ σίνος/Mᵃ

4.193–200 ~ Θ pp. 192.20–193.1 (Mars in DESC; Mercury and Moon involved).

4.613–18 ~ Θ p. 201.22–3 (Saturn in IMC)/3.260.

(iv) Mᵃ closer to Θ than to Mᵇ

6.484 Ζηνὸς δ᾽ ἐν καθύγρῳ ζῴῳ ~ Θ p. 216.18 τοῦ ὡροσκόπου ὄντος ἐν καθύγρῳ ζῳδίῳ: but presumptively missing in lacuna after 4.132.

Apodoses

(i) Agreement

(i)(1) Mᵃ ~ Mᵇ ~ Ptol., Θ Π

4.127 ῥήτορας ~ 6.479 ῥητῆρας ~ Ptol. 4.4.3, Θ pp. 211.1, 212.19–20 ῥήτορας

4.144 ἀλλοτρίων ~ 6.489 ξείνοισι ~ Ptol. 4.4.3, Θ p. 210.30 ἀλλοτρίων οἰκονόμους

4.203–4 σοφίης τε κρατίστους | ζηλωτὰς ~ 6.479 σοφίῃσί τε πάμπαν ἀρίστους ~ Ptol. 4.4.3, Θ pp. 211.1, 214.21 σοφιστὰς

4.252 ἀμαρησκαπτῆρας ~ 6.422 ὀχετηγοί ~ Ptol. 4.4.5, Θ p. 211.30 ὑπονομευτάς (both poets find different solutions for the unscannable prose term)

4.257 ληνῶν ἀντλητῆρες ~ 6.424 ἄντλοις ~ Ptol. 4.4.5, Θ pp. 211.30, 212.17 ἀντλητάς

4.439 ὀργανοπήκτορας ~ 6.401 ὄργανα δαιδάλλοντας ~ Θ p. 213.12 ὀργανοποιούς ~ Ptol. 4.4.6 ὀργάνων

(i)(2) Mᵃ ~ Mᵇ ~ Ptol. (no match in Θ)

4.175 στέμματα μυριόδοξα ~ 6.514 πολυστεφέες ~ Ptol. 4.4.4 στεφανηφόρους

4.267 γαστροτόμους ~ 6.461 γαστέρας ἀμπτύξαντες ~ Ptol. 4.4.5 παρασχίστας (unless Θ p. 215.11 νεκρεπάρτας is also relevant)

4.342 κηραγγέας ~ 6.524 ἀπὸ κηροῦ ~ Ptol. 4.4.6 κηροπλάστας

4.441 θαύματα δαιδάλλοντας ~ 6.402 θαυματόεντ᾽ ἔργ᾽ ~ Ptol. 4.4.6 ὀργανοποιούς, 3.14.5 ὀργανικάς

(i)(3) Mᵃ ~ Mᵇ ~ Θ Π (no match in Ptol.)

4.123–4, 6.519 πυρὸς … σιδήρου ~ Θ p. 211.12–13 ἀπὸ πυρὸς ἢ σιδήρου

4.149–50 ἐλέφαντος | ἐργοπόνους ~ 6.523 ἐλέφαντος ~ Θ p. 213.23 ἐλεφαντουργούς

Book Four

4.185 κιθάρης τε μελουργούς ~ 6.370 κιθάρης ἐπιίστορας ~ Θ p. 213.12–13 κιθαρῳδούς (cf. p. 217.13 κιθαριστὰς)

4.190 θρηνήτορας ~ 6.498 θρηνοῦντας ἀεὶ κεραοῖς ἐπιτύμβιον αὐλοῖς ~ Θ p. 212.30 θρηνῳδούς

4.300 μεθυχάρμονας ~ 6.588 ἔν τε μέθῃσιν ~ Θ p. 213.6 (cf. 215.21) μεθυστάς

(i)(4) M^a ~ M^b ~ Θ τ

4.185 κιθάρης τε μελουργούς ~ 6.370 κιθάρης ἐπιίστορας ~ Θ p. 214.16 κιθαρῳδοὺς

4.186 ὀρχηθμῶν ἴδριας ~ 6.507 ὀρχηθμοῦ βητάρμονας ἴδριας ~ Θ p. 214.16 ὀρχηστὰς

4.278, 6.440 αἰθροβάτας ~ Θ p. 215.16 (cf. 213.1, 217.9) νευροβάτας

4.398, 6.394 κυβερνητῆρας ~ Θ p. 216.20 κυβερνήτας

4.427, 6.437 ἱερῆας ~ Θ p. 215.2 ἱερεῖς

(i)(5) M^a ~ M^b ~ Θ σίνος

4.196 ἀνδροφόνους ~ 6.500 ἀνδροφονῆας ~ Θ pp. 192.24–193.1 ἀνδροφόνους

4.196, 6.500 ληίστορας ~ Θ p. 192.24 λῃστάς (cf. Ptol. 4.4.7)

4.484 κλεπτῆρας ~ 6.500 κλῶπας ~ Θ p. 192.21 κλέπτας

4.539 λυσσαλέῃ μανίῃ ~ 6.599 λυσσήρεις ~ Θ p. 192.14 λυσσῶντας

(ii) M^a and M^b, with no evidence in Θ or more distant wording

Professional terms or labels

4.134 ἐμπορικοῦ ~ 6.486 ἐμπορίῃ (but see Ptol. 2.3.41 ἐμπορικοί, also 4.137 κοινωνὸν ~ κοινωνικοί)

4.178 ἀστεφάνους ~ 6.517 ἀστεφέες

4.183 μελπήτορας ~ 6.369 μολπῇσιν

4.210 γαιομέτρας ~ 6.479 μέτρα…χθονὸς ~ Lib. Herm. geometros

4.221 ἀγυρτῆράς ~ 6.538 ἀγείροντες

4.232 σωματοφρουρητῆρας ~ 6.449 φρουρούς θ' ἥβης ἐρατεινῆς

4.243 ἰχθυοθηρευτάς ~ 6.452 ἰχθυβόλους/Θ p. 212.17 ἁλιεύοντας in a different chart

4.253 λουτρῶν…βαλανείων ~ 6.422 λοετροχόοι/Θ p. 215.6 βαλανεῖς

4.259 ὀνθολόγοι ~ 6.423 ὄνθον δηθὰ φέροντες

4.278 πεταυριστῆρας ~ 6.444–5 ἐπ' ἠνεμόεντι πετεύρῳ

4.300, 6.588 ζωροπότας/Θ p. 215.21 μεθυστάς

4.342 ὑλογράφους ~ 6.524 ἐϋξέσταις σανίδεσσιν

4.422 γνάπτορας ~ 6.433–4 ῥυπόεντα πλυνοῖσιν | εἵματα καλλύνοντας

4.423 ἱστοπόνους ~ 6.432 ἱστουργούς

4.427 ζακόρους…430 σηκῶν τε νεωκορίῃσι ~ 6.437 ζακόρους σηκῶν

4.433 γειοπόνοι ~ 6.489 γειοπόνους, cf. 4.145 γαίης

4.568a τορν[εύτορας ~ 6.346 τορείαις

See also: 4.267 γαστροτόμους ~ 6.461 γαστέρας ἀμπτύξαντες/Ptol. 4.4.5 παρασχίστας

Ancillary words
4.144 ἰδίων, 6.489 ἰδίοισιν
4.150 [ex emend. De Stefani], 6.525 γραφίδεσσιν
4.174, 6.514 νίκ-
4.184, 6.508 μαχλ- (of mimes)
4.191, 6.462 κεδρ-
4.222 πολυπλαγκτοσύνης, 6.539 πλάζονται
4.246, 6.455 τιθασ-
4.270 δυσοσμίη, 6.460 ὀδμῇ
4.311, 6.592 στομάτεσσιν
4.558 εἰδώλων, 6.603 εἰδώλοις
4.581, 6.356 ὀλβ-

(iii) M^b corresponds with Ptolemy and/or Θ (M^a absent, or more distantly worded)

(iii)(1) With Ptolemy and Θ
4.128 ἀστρολόγους ~ Ptol. 4.4.3, Θ pp. 210.27, 212.20
4.135 ναυκλήρου ~ Ptol. 4.2.2 ναυκληριῶν, Θ p. 216.20 ναυκλήρους
4.183 μελῶν ~ Ptol. 4.4.6, Θ p. 213.10 μελῳδιῶν
4.211 ἀστρολόγους...μάντιας ~ Ptol. 4.4.3 μάντεις, ἀστρολόγους, Θ p. 215.1–2 ἀστρολόγους, μάντεις
4.233 πλαστογράφους ~ Ptol. 4.4.7, Θ pp. 193.3, 218.2
4.234 κακοεργέας ~ Ptol. 4.4.7, Θ p. 212.5 κακοπράγμονας
4.259 μεταλλευταὶ ~ Ptol. 4.4.5, Θ p. 211.26–7 μεταλλευτάς
4.260 λᾶες...ἀκροτομοῦνται ~ Ptol. 4.4.5, Θ p. 211.28 λατόμους
4.261 σίδηρος ~ Ptol. 4.4.5, Θ p. 211.27 διὰ σιδήρου
4.322 ῥώπου τε γυναικῶν ~ Ptol. 4.4.6 γυναικείους κόσμους, Θ p. 213.14 κόσμους γυναικείους(?)
4.332 κατηγορίης ~ Ptol. 4.4.7, Θ p. 212.4 κατηγόρους
4.343 ζωοτύπους ~ Ptol. 4.4.6, Θ pp. 213.13, 216.16, 217.15 ζωγράφους
4.397 ναυσιβάτας ~ Ptol. 4.4.5, Θ p. 211.30 ναυτικούς, Θ p. 216.20 ναύτας
4.439 μηχανικοὺς ~ Θ p. 217.3; μηχανικάς also in Ptol. 3.14.5
4.440 τεκτοσύνης ~ Ptol. 4.4.5, Θ p. 211.11, 28 τέκτονας
4.579 τραπέζαις ~ Ptol. 4.4.3, Θ p. 210.27 τραπεζίτας

(iii)(2) With Θ alone
4.124 ἄκμοσι ~ Θ p. 211.14 ἀκμόνων
4.130 λιθογλυφίαισι ~ Θ p. 212.28 λιθογλύφους
4.149 ῥεκτῆρας χρυσοῖο, 152 κοσμήτας ~ Θ p. 213.24 χρυσοχόους ἢ κοσμητάς
4.158 ἰητῆρα ~ Θ p. 210.27 ἰατροὺς

Book Four 267

4.175 μυριόδοξα ~ Θ p. 214.13 ἐνδόξους/6.514 κυδάλιμοι
4.192 νεκροτάφους ~ Θ p. 215.10
4.205 γραμματικήν τ' ἄσκησιν ~ Θ p. 214.21 γραμματικοὺς
4.210 μαθηματικούς ~ Θ p. 215.3
4.237 ἀπάτην δολόεσσαν ~ Θ p. 218.2 δολίους
4.244 ὀρνίθων τροφοποιούς ~ Θ p. 216.15 ὀρνιθοτρόφους
4.250 δωδεκατημορίοισιν ~ Θ p. 215.5 δωδεκατημόριον
4.251 ὑδρέας ~ Θ p. 166.22, Epit. IV (*CCAG* ii. 191.22), 1.84 ὑδραγωγούς
4.253 βαλανείων ~ Θ pp. 211.31 βαλανέας, 215.6 βαλανεῖς
4.258 ἐπίμοχθοι ~ Θ p. 212.18 μετά…μόχθου
4.265 δυωδεκατημορίοις ~ Θ p. 215.9 δωδεκατημόρια
4.280 μιμοβίους ~ Θ p. 217.7 μίμους
4.291 τειχοδόμους ~ Θ p. 215.15 τοιχοβάτας ἢ οἰκοδόμους
4.291 κεραμουργοὺς ~ Θ p. 213.3, cf. p. 215.16 κεραμεῖς
4.305 μοιχευταὶ ~ Θ pp. 195.8, 213.6, 215.21 μοιχούς
4.320 βυρσοτόμους ~ Θ p. 216.5 βυρσεῖς
4.325 ἐγρεσιοίκους ~ Θ p. 215.15 οἰκοδόμους
4.326 λιθοψώκτῳ ~ Θ p. 216.6 λιθοψήκτας
4.337 κυνηγητῆρας ~ Θ p. 216.12 κυνηγοὺς
4.339 ἰξευτῆρας ~ Θ p. 217.19 ἰξευτὰς
4.343 μακάρων ἀποπλάστορας ~ Θ p. 217.15 ἀνδριαντοπλάστας
4.350 μοιχευτὰ ~ Θ p. 215.21 μοιχούς
4.483 θυρέτρων ἐπανοίκτορας ~ Θ pp. 192.21, 211.15–16 θυρεπανοίκτας
4.561 μισέλλην ~ Θ p. 212.25 μισέλληνας

The following cases occur among σίνος charts:

4.156 ἀμβλυόεσσαν ὀμίχλην ~ Θ p. 187.18 ἀμβλωπίαν
4.198 σκολοπηίδα μοῖραν ~ Θ p. 201.4–5 ἀνασκολοπίζονται
4.233 ψεύσταις ~ Θ pp. 193.3, 218.2 ψεύστας
4.332 ψευδοκατηγορίαι ~ Θ p. 193.3 ψευδοκατηγόρους
4.487 ἕν τε βιαιοτάτῳ θανάτῳ ~ Θ p. 202.6, 10 βιαιοθανάτους, Θ p. 201.4 βιαιοθανασίαν
4.539 λυσσαλέῃ μανίῃ ~ Θ p. 192.14 λυσσῶντας καὶ μαινομένους
4.548 θεόληπτα ~ Θ p. 193.16 θεολήπτους
4.550 φοιβητοῖς ~ Θ p. 193.17 φοιβαζομένους
4.554 δαιμονίοισι ~ Θ p. 193.17 δαιμονιοπλήκτους
4.614 θηροβόρου ~ Θ p. 201.24 θηριόβρωτον

And on prior death of parents:

4.412–13 μογοστοκίῃ…κρύφιμ' ἄλγε' ~ Epit. IV (*CCAG* ii. 189.14) δυστοκίας ἢ κρυπτῶν ἀσθενειῶν

(iii)(3) With Ptolemy alone
4.160 λογιστονόμοισιν ~ Ptol. 4.4.3 λογιστάς
4.211 θύτας ~ Ptol. 4.4.3

(iv) M^a corresponds with Θ or Ptol. against M^b

(iv)(1) With Ptolemy
6.498 θρηνοῦντας ἀεὶ κεραοῖς ἐπιτύμβιον αὐλοῖς ~ Ptol. 4.4.8 τυμβαύλας/4.190 θρηνήτορας

(iv)(2) With Θ
6.419 λιθοξόοι ~ Θ pp. 211.28, 216.6 λιθοξόους/4.325–6 —
6.509 τραγικῆς τε βαρυβρόμου ἵστορας οἴμης ~ Θ p. 213.13 τραγῳδούς/4.183 κωμῳδούς

The rest are cases where M^a's diction is closer to Θ than is that of M^b:

6.415 δωμήτορας οἴκων ~ Θ p. 215.15, cf. p. 213.2 οἰκοδόμους/4.291 τειχοδόμους
6.424 κοσμῆται κήπων ~ Θ p. 166.22 κηπωρούς ~ 1.84 κηπουρούς/paraphrase in 4.256–8
6.433 φάρεά θ' ὑφανόωντας ~ Θ p. 216.25 λινοΰφους/4.422–3 τεύκτορας, al.
6.438 μαντοσύνας ~ Ptol. 4.4.3, 10, Θ p. 215.2 μάντεις/4.428 προφήτορας
6.478 παίδων ἡγητῆρας ~ Θ p. 214.21 παιδευτάς/4.204 νεότητά τε λαμπρὴν
6.493 φοιβάζοντας ~ Θ pp. 192.18, 193.17 φοιβαζομένους/4.216–17 λυσσομανοῦντα, etc.

Register for *Lib. Herm.*

(i) M^a, M^b, Lib. Herm. all have a relationship

4.139–45 ~ 6.487–90 ~ *Lib. Herm.* xxxiv. 31.
4.180–6 ~ 6.504–10 ~ *Lib. Herm.* xxxiv. 29.
4.263–70 ~ 6.456–62 ~ *Lib. Herm.* xxxiv. 4.

(ii) M^a ~ Lib. Herm./M^b

4.180–6/6.366–70 + 371–2 ~ *Lib. Herm.* xxxiv. 29. All have swapped terms (4.181, 6.368 ἐναλλάγδην, cf. Θ p. 214.15 ἀλλήλων τὰ ὅρια ὑποδέξωνται), but only M^a and *Lib. Herm.* swapped houses and conjunction as well.

4.206–13/6.465–71 ~ *Lib. Herm.* xxxiv. 29. The set-up in M^b is simpler than the others (unless I misunderstand 209); both the others speak of (*a*) conjunction, (*b*) houses, and (*c*) an exchange of terms. Both M^a and *Lib. Herm.* have their diviners produced by the add-on aspect of Saturn.

4.431–6/6.487–90 ~ *Lib. Herm.* xxxiv. 31.

4.437–43/6.398–404 ~ *Lib. Herm.* xxvi. 62.

(iii) M^b, M^a/Lib. Herm.

4.187–92 ~ 6.494–8/*Lib. Herm.* xxxiv. 4.

4.201–5 ~ 6.476–9/*Lib. Herm.* xxxiv. 33.

(iv) M^b, Lib. Herm./M^a

See commentary on 4.450–6 + 457–9 + 460–1 + 462–5 (the sequence on multiple births). Unusually, M^b is more closely affiliated to *Lib. Herm.* xxxiv. 39 than is 6.249–55.

Book One

1.1. PRELIMINARIES

The main matter for discussion in this book is its composite character. The two most obvious features of its content, apart from its chaotic state, are the chunk of verses shared with the fourth book (286–338) and the presence of pentameters scattered throughout the whole. But once these are granted as intrusions there is the possibility of more, and Koechly detected as many as eight separate hands in the book. Was he right, and are the methods and models he used still valid? Those questions impinge on every section below.

A dating criterion has just come to light for this book, more precise than anything known hitherto, in the form of a papyrus which Amin Benaissa generously shared with me before its scheduled publication as P.Oxy. LXXXVII 5588. It consists of the lines 26–34 + 36–48, in what Dr Benaissa describes as a fair-sized official cursive of the 'chancery' type (that is, a documentary rather than book hand, which sorts with the character of astrological poetry as *Fachliteratur*), and which he dates to the fourth century. The papyrus contains numerous variants with respect to L, but the line sequence is identical, which is important, because it contains material which Koechly attributed to more than one poet.[1] If, therefore, the book does constitute a compilation, this takes that compilation back to at least the fourth century.[2]

Until this papyrus came to light, the *terminus ante quem* of the first book, or at least parts of it, was supplied by Hephaestion, two of whose three citations of the Manethoniana (and the most certain ones) are from this book. Although the *Apotelesmatica* were not composed until about 415,[3] Hephaestion's testimony remains valuable. One is a direct quotation (1.167–9), important evidence that the manuscript version represents a recension that has been hexametrised

---

[1] The papyrus acknowledges section breaks by *ekthesis* (26, 34, 38, 42), without bearing, of course, on editorial activity.

[2] And would thereby vindicate Massimilla, 264–5 n. 2, who dated the compilation (as opposed to composition) of books 1 and 5 already to the fourth century.

[3] Pingree, edn. i. v.

from an earlier version that contained more pentameters than we can now see.⁴ The other is a paraphrase (1.250–2) which runs closely parallel to the diction of 251 but adds additional specifications about the set-up.⁵ Hephaestion attributes both passages to Manetho, which implies that the portions of the book from which 1.167–9 and 250–2 both come (Koechly's poet A) were already connected with the current proem, or something very like it, in which an Egyptian sage addresses himself to King Ptolemy, by the early fifth century.

The setting in the proem is fictive,⁶ but an Egyptian origin for at least parts of the book is strongly implied by the reference to the ἀρχιδικαστής, an Egyptian legal official, in 104 (less so by the ἀγορανόμος of 102, who took a special form in Egypt but is widely attested throughout the Greco-Roman world). Above all, it is implied by the remarkable outcome in 1.237–9 which not only locates dream interpreters in temples, but connects them with the well-known (if still mysterious) Egyptian practice of κατοχή. It further combines them with the very rare agent noun φοιβητάς, unique in literary tests, but also attested in an Egyptian papyrus (1.237 n.), together with other temple personnel (παστοφόροι) who are themselves connected elsewhere with dream interpreters. In other words, the whole nexus of 237–9 is entirely plausible in an Egyptian temple setting, and hard to imagine anywhere else. In a move typical of astrology, however, the chart soon pivots, via mention of their physical condition, to long-haired self-wounding ecstatics who are presumably *galli*, and in that case are a topos mentioned in literature empire-wide. Elsewhere there are also references to dignitaries and civic worthies in language of bland, empire-wide commendation (101 high priests, 105 κοσμητῆρας... πόληος). Admittedly this segment was attributed by Koechly to a different poet, but it is typical of the Manethoniana in general (pp. 117–19).

I noted a certain affinity between the fourth book and the sensibility and to some extent language of early Christianity. There is rather less of that here,

---

⁴ Citation discovered by A. Engelbrecht, *Hephaestion von Theben und sein astrologisches Compendium: Ein Beitrag zur Geschichte der griechischen Astrologie* (Vienna, 1887), 37–42, though his discussion is vitiated by his failure to realise that Manetho is a pseudepigraph.

⁵ Heilen 2017, 226 n. 19. The third citation apparently glances at 3.399–428 (see i. 42–3).

⁶ Gundel and Gundel, 162–3 were sufficiently impressed to expect more Egyptian material to come to light from a closer inspection of the context. They also wondered whether the chaotic state of the book was in fact a fair specimen of Egyptian priestly literature. At the time they were writing (their book was published in 1966), the astrological material from the temple library at Tebtunis was known, but it really only began to be published from the 1990s. Its interpretation, it is true, is hindered by the fragmentary condition of the papyri, but the manuals published so far suggest conventions of orderly structure, even if they are not exactly the same from one text to another (framing device/general rules or instructions/predictive material/colophon), and systematically organised catalogues (Winkler 2009, esp. 362–3 on the historiography of publication, and 366–74, on structure; id. 2016, esp. 247–52).

perhaps because there is less interest in the infliction of pain—though there is, on the other hand, very considerable interest in morbidity. A nice case of shared territory and contrasting sensibility occurs at 1.157, where, somehow, both the poet and St Jerome have got hold of the same conceit, that of the dropsical man who is 'pregnant with his own death' (i.e. is suffering from ascites). For the medically minded poet, this concludes a passage which has been overlaid with typical poetic miserabilism, but basically consists of a neutral list of pathologies produced by corrupted humours. Jerome, on the other hand, has a political and spiritual purpose in portraying the scene—beggars at the rich man's gate—in the lurid colours appropriate to a drama of suffering and redemptive almsgiving. Crucifixion is mentioned again here (1.149), though the verb that is used of it, $\tau\epsilon\acute{\iota}\nu\epsilon\iota\nu$, is found in both pagan and Judaeo-Christian writers. 'Tribulations' in 1.171 sound at first rather Christian, but the plural is more characteristic of pagan writers ($\theta\lambda\hat{\iota}\psi\iota\varsigma$ is Judaeo-Christian). The unkempt holy men of 1.241–2 are not Christian ascetics. There is a tirade about the vanity of sacrifice (1.196–207) for which parallels can be found in Christian polemicists, but that is because they go back to a common form of argumentation concerning petitionary prayer which we find fully developed in Maximus and Porphyry. The poet who wrote this, the Christian polemicists, and indeed Firmicus, who has something similar, are all exploiting a set of tropes for their individual ends.

There has always been a suspicion that the first book and the fifth somehow belong together. Tyrwhitt first supposed this, on the basis of their similar style and metrical defects, their chaotic conditions, and their prefaces addressing Ptolemy.[7] Koechly significantly modified this: he agreed that both collections were the casualties of incompetent editing, but found the first to contain the remnants of what was once the better and more competent poem;[8] the fifth was simply a mess. But De Stefani (2017, 32–3) continued to find aspects of the style and prosody of the first and fifth books sufficiently similar to merit the suggestion that they have the same author; ingeniously he suggested that the new book that is being announced in 1.360–1 is in fact the fifth. He is certainly right that they have a similar compositional style, based on parallelisms and jingles, though on other metrics (grammatical and metrical criteria) they come out looking rather more different. Stylistic analysis is important in what follows, and I introduce what I think is the important concept of 'ownership' (whereby a poet inherits material but, in taking it over and rewriting it, imposes his own stylistic mannerisms thereon). We shall see that it is quite characteristic for separate segments to be alike in some respects (shared diction and phrases) but unalike in others (metrical practice). Such is the synthetic character of

---

[7] Tyrwhitt, xiv.   [8] 1851, lvi ('quaedam adeo et antiquiora et elegantiora'); 1858, vii.

astrological poetry, such are the labile characters of its authors, that one must operate a fine balance between aspects of 'house style' and individual poets' traits.

1.2. THE COMPOSITE CHARACTER OF BOOK 1

The questions that guide the whole discussion of the first book arise from the certainty that it contains multiple strata. But we have to get the model straight before we can proceed. Are we right to think of multiple authors and an editor/compiler who pulls them all together? It was Koechly who first pronounced the book a compilation. He laid out the groupings, which he arrived at on the basis of shared phrases ('propter sermonis similitudinem', 'dicendi ratio') as well as theme (a group of medical charts; 'res venereas'), as follows:[9]

A 18–25, 26–33, 42–4 + 45–9, 50–7, 62–5, 66–9, 70–4, 77–88, 89 + 92–95, 106–13, 115–27, 129–33, 134–8, 153–7 + 158 + 160–6, 167–8 + 170–4, 180–4, 185–95, 215–28, 229–61, 262–76.

This includes six 'medical' charts (50–7, 134–8, 153–7 + 158–66, 185–95, 229–34). Comparison with $\Pi.\sigma.a.$, which Koechly of course did not know, confirms that all but the last of these do indeed belong together.

B 139–51 (*schetliasmos* of Mars), 196–207 (why sacrifice?). Koechly ascribed these to a 'carmen antiquius'.
C 34–6, 176–9, 353–8.
D 100–5.
E 36b + 37, 75–6, 90–1, 97b + 114, 98–9, 114, 122–8, 152, 159 + 174 + 175, 208–14, 341–52 (elegiac material).
F 277–85 ('a recentiore quodam').

To which he added:

(i) the verses shared with M^b (286–338);
(ii) those credited to an *ineptus quidam versificator*, 16–17; 38–9 + 40–1; 58–61; 96–7 ('misellus poeta'); 339–40; 359 and 360–1.

In this section I argue that Koechly was both right and wrong. A great deal of material is now available that was not available to him (the manuscript material published in *CCAG*, and above all the Manetho and Anubion papyri), yet even now it seems that scholars have not properly grasped its full implications. My

---

[9] Koechly 1851, lv.

eventual argument will be that it is simultaneously possible for the corpus to contain both a medley of different poets and the *disiecta membra* of the same one.

Koechly was clearly right in principle that the book is a compilation. He may or may not have been right in the details of his dissection, but the section shared with (lifted from?) M^b and the irregular presence of pentameters throughout are the two unassailable pieces of evidence. I tackle them in that order, adding the evidence that Koechly did not know, and pressing harder for its full implications.

M^b, M^c, and P.Oxy. 2546

At issue here is the block of text from 1.286–338, all of which is also present in M^b, but mostly not in the same order. Based on what was available to him, the comparative versions in the two books, Koechly regarded M^c as a hack, a careless transcriber.[10] He used words like *consutor, consarcinator, ineptus concinnator* (1851, liii); his model was one of repeating, copying, or stealing, for which he used the verbs *repetere, depromere, exscribere, omittere, surripere* (*subreptos*). He repeatedly disparaged M^c, as if degeneracy followed from borrowing (e.g. 1851, liv 'ineptum et stolidum'). And indeed, his model is by no means completely invalid. It is supported by demonstrable editorial hack-work, of which the worst example is probably the interpolation of a couple of lines from 4.50–1 in the middle of a sequence from 4.481–90, involving an inept swerve from plurals to singulars and back to plurals again, and requiring some patching to get the two sequences to hang together (see on 1.318–20). And although I reserve discussion of minutiae for a later section, there are many occasions where M^c's reading is clearly inferior to than M^b's—even as there are *also* occasions where neither is obviously superior and some seem to be equally valid alternatives (p. 395).

Our understanding of the relationship between the two books was transformed by the publication in 1966 of P.Oxy. 2546 (3rd c.), which overlaps with the version in book 4, including in several of the charts with a double transmission in books 4 and 1. What this showed was a complex situation which cannot be straightforwardly stemmatised, but which tends to suggest a situation in which each version goes back to a common source (including occasions where M^c agrees with the papyrus' reading against M^b). In other words, it is not simply the case that M^c represents a vitiated version of M^b; sometimes (in a minority of

---

[10] 1851, xlix '…et quidem cum mutationibus quibusdam et variationibus, quales excidere solent fugitivo calamo aliquid transscribentibus'.

cases, it is true), it has the better form. More important still, comparison of the three witnesses suggested that each user of the text was capable of making independent variations, tailored, presumably, to individual taste and to the need of the moment; this is the way of *Fachschriften*, which are not museum-pieces but in active use. But my argument here is that it was already available to Koechly to see that M^c is doing something more than lifting passages from M^b and botching him in the process. He is making independent little adjustments—or perhaps, adding in the evidence of the papyrus, we should now say that those responsible for the recensions of the poem in the first and fourth books are intervening in a vulgate and each tailoring it to his own style.

4.146 ἦν/1.294 εἰ (although even ἦν in 4.146 is followed by an optative). εἰ is not *more* characteristic than ἦν of M^c, but it is securely attested.

4.146 ἑλικοδρόμος (cf. this poet's other 'journey'/'pathway' words, as well as his tolerance of multiple epithets glossing a single noun)/1.294 ἑλικώπιδος.

4.150–1 δείκνυσι... ἔσσεσθαι/1.298–9 ῥέζει... εὐφυέας. This is a very good example. In the first place, M^b has his characteristic executive verb + future infinitive. In the second, M^c has his characteristic line-internal parallelism in 1.299 εὐφυέας θριγκῶν τε καὶ εὐτυπέων κανονισμῶν. εὐτυπέων corresponds to 4.151 εὐτοίχων (υ/οι look like phonetic variants), but the supralinear variant εὐτυπέας would draw the formal parallelism still closer, balancing εὐφυέας.

4.397 and Π^1 ἐν ὕδασι νήκτορας (agent noun)/1.323 ὕδατος ἵστορας (although this is not straightforward, because the reading in M^b and Π^1 in turn depends on φαίνει καὶ, and that of 1.323 on δείκνυσι καὶ, an executive verb which is normally characteristic of M^b).

4.402 ὁπότ᾽ ἂν πολιοῖο (Π^1 πλαγκτοῖο)... ᾖ/1.327 κυανοχρόοιο... ἦν, cf. 1.35 κυανόχροον.

4.478–9 Μήνη δ᾽ ἀμφίκερως σκολιόδρομος... βᾶσα (cf. 146 ἑλικοδρόμος)/ 1.306–7 Μήνης δ᾽ ἀμφίκερως [-ω Hal^{mg}] σκολιὸς δρόμος... βαίνων (cf. 1.359 δρόμος οὐράνιος).

4.483–4 ἐκφύσει, θυρέτρων... τε λαθραίους/1.310–11 καὶ θυρέτρων δεινοὺς... τελέουσιν. Each version has a different verb, with an extra epithet vis-à-vis the other. Both verb and tense are accommodated to each book's preferences. M^b likes 'generative' verbs, while M^c has several other instances of τελ- (5, 76, 213, 270, 284); M^b has far more future tenses, although M^c does not altogether lack them. Further differences of tense occur in 4.406 ἐξολέσει/1.331 ἐκβάλλει/Π^1 ἀπόλλυσιν and 4.411 ἵξετ᾽/1.336 οἴχεται.

4.486 ἀλυσηδόν (other -ηδόν adverbs in 108, 197, 424, 429, 449, 621, 622)/1.314 ἀλύσεσσιν.

Although there is less evidence, there are signs of the same relationship between M^b and the papyrus, which would be confirmation of a tendency in the curatorship of shared material:

4.385 λοχεῖαι/Π¹ τοκειαι.

4.390 ἔσσεται δ'/ Π¹ ἔσται δ' (unless L's version is an unintelligent scribal attempt to normalise to M^b's usual practice, for clearly it is at the cost of scansion).

4.412 and 1.337 δεδαιγμένη (cf. 488 δεδαϊγμένοι)/Π¹ δεδαμασμένη.

(possibly) 4.572 βιοτοσκόπον (cf. ἐπίσκοπον, πανεπίσκοπον, κυδόσκοπον; μεροποσπόρον, τεκνοσπόρον)/Π¹ βιότου σκοπ. But it is unclear if the genitive in Π¹ is sound.

The evidence of Π¹ complicates matters considerably. But it was already available to Koechly to observe that if M^c is directly sourcing his text from M^b he is also actively 'owning' it as well, and insofar as the papyrus makes anything clearer it tends to confirm that the various poets, so to speak, share a common language, but inflect it with their own accent, impose their own mannerisms. The importance of intervention and 'ownership' will become still clearer below.

Pentameters

This is the second case where M^c can be shown to contain material sourced from elsewhere. The immediate question is whether there are good reasons to suppose that 'elsewhere' to be Anubion. In the course of answering it we will find further evidence that supports what has just been argued about textual 'ownership'.

The best evidence for supposing a connection with Anubion comes right at the end, in the sign-off which can only derive from a poet who envisaged adding a second book in elegiac metre to an existing book (n. on 1.360–1). That clearly does not apply to *our* book 2; we owe these lines to an incompetent editor who preserved the lines despite their irrelevance. Except for two sequences (208–14 and 341–52) the pentameters in the first book are occasional, and that leaves us with the problem of trying to deduce whether they were only ever isolated—it is easy to find irregular sequences in inscriptional verse, especially sepulchral epigram—or whether they are the flotsam and jetsam of what were once elegiac sequences which were partly converted to hexameters. If so, it raises the further possibility that what present to us now as entirely hexametric sequences might themselves be overwriting elegiac couplets, their potentially Anubionic pentameters having been lost to view. We do know that such conversions took place; they are documentable for antiquity (169 vis-à-vis the version quoted in Hephaestion; 1.334–8 vis-à-vis 4.409–13), Byzantium (L¹ at 1.213, 342), and indeed the early modern period (Axtius and Rigler).[11]

---

[11] De Stefani 2017, 24.

The recent expansion in our knowledge of Anubion came from a series of papyri that provide evidence for an elegiac poem, presumptively attributed to Anubion as the only known astrological elegist, which shadowed parts of Firmicus 6.29-31, the sample charts.[12] Each of the charts within the more or less elegiac sequence within 1.341-52 turns out to contain parallels with these chapters of Firmicus, which *prima facie* suggests that they, too, could derive from such a poem, even though they do not represent a continuous sequence as some of the Anubion papyri do.[13] Two narratorial interventions, for what they are worth, are very much in the style of Anubion (p. 312). On the other hand, the possibility of comparing two of these charts with material preserved on papyri illustrates the complex transmission of astrological material, and is an early lesson that we can *never* expect material to be reproduced without chopping and changing. With regard to F 7 Schubert (from the same papyrus roll as F 8, and therefore with the same claim to be Anubionic), 1.350-2 has a shortened protasis; with regard to F 11, on the other hand, the version in 1.341-5 appears to be prior, with the papyrus' version a lazy and truncated remake. This material was susceptible to constant remodelling, and in this case the manuscript's version turns out to be, if not closer to a putative 'original', then at least more coherent than the papyrus', in which charts have been dislocated and turned into a series of individually titled epigrams.

If one accepts, nonetheless, the existence of an elegiac version of the sample charts, we might also be able to connect a couple of other passages with it. The first is 1.121-8, which, although not in straight elegiacs, contains pentameters at 124 and 128. No papyri this time are at hand, but the content overlaps with both M^a and Firmicus, 6.30.5, in other words with Anubion's 'siblings' in common descent from Nechepso-Petosiris on the model proposed by Heilen. We could potentially add 1.106-11 as well, the hexametric chart of Oedipus which has a couple of tight parallels with Anubion's version of the chart in F 4, although it also contains a coda (including a pentameter) of which there is no sign in Anubion, and which actually gainsays Anubion's own treatment of the subject (see on 112-13 (+ 114?)). The particular local detail is tangled and frustrating, but what matters are the inferences we are able to draw so far about the possible or likely use of Anubion in this book. As far as the compilation of the whole is concerned, it is clear that from 286 (at the latest) extraneous material is being appended to the book's main core.[14] The Anubion material of 341-52 (and

---

[12] The first papyri attributed to Anubion were F 11 = P.Oxy. III 464 and F 12 = PSI III 157, followed by F 8 = P.Schubart 15; the new material (F 4-6) turned out to be of a piece with the last of these. See Heilen 2010, 129-30.

[13] F 4 ~ Firmicus, 6.29.23-30.3; F 6 ~ 6.30.20-2; F 7 ~ 6.31.51-5; F 8 ~ 6.31.75-86.

[14] The pentameter at 336 is particularly difficult to deal with, and Koechly tried to eliminate it. It occurs almost at the very end of sequence taken over from M^b, where the subject has turned

potentially all of 339–52) is consistent with that: it is another appendage. So far so clean, so separable. But it looks possible, even likely, that Anubion has leaked into the main body of the book as well, to a degree that is hard to determine because of overwritings and adaptations. All this is an illustration of how complicated the transmission of astrology truly is.

To make matters even more obscure, there are far less certain and scrappier suggestions of an elegiac or partly elegiac treatment of material on the *synaphai* and *aporrhoiai* of the Moon (~ Firmicus book 4 and $Π.σ.α.$). The evidence, such as it is, consists of (i) 1.208–14 ~ Firmicus, 4.3.1–2 and (ii) 1.159 ~ $Π.σ.α.$ and Firmicus, 4.11.7. There is also a correspondence between 1.169 (subsequently hexametrised) and Firmicus, 3.4.32, from the *dodecatopos*. If there ever was such a poem or poems—the evidence is particularly frail—it strictly need not have been by Anubion or (if not he) the author of the poem on the sample charts. In particular, if 1.158–66, the medical chart in which 159 is embedded, was ever more systematically elegiac than it currently is, the baroque and pathetic treatment implies something very different and far more discursive from the workaday style of the Anubion fragments on papyrus (and also, be it noted, from the succinct 1.208–14, although they represent the same kind of chart).[15] We are arguing from the slenderest of scraps, but there probably needs to be more willingness than there has been in the past to concede that not all the elegiacs necessarily came from a single source. Some might be Anubion (or modified Anubion), some might not be. The attribution of astrological elegiacs to Anubion by default, simply because the name of no other astrological elegist has been transmitted, should not go unchallenged. He was not necessarily the only writer of astrological elegiacs in antiquity.

Nor does it make theoretical sense to insist that he was. The direction of attack here is from the concept of authorship in principle. The verifiable fact that M^c is a compilation should not predispose the scholar to think in terms of *mechanical* copying. That is not the correct model, even for the lines adapted from M^b, and the evidence of the papyri certainly does not support the idea that this is how Anubion's poem circulated. What we have seen with M^b and M^c is a good deal of overlap, but also many cases where subtle changes have brought each passage into line with that poet's personal style. Under circumstances of such textual fluidity, one can certainly name individual authors, because the

---

from τέχναι to parents. There is a possible background in Dorotheus (p. 145), and, if Dorotheus, then conceivably Anubion as well. This at the moment is completely without confirmation, but if there ever was an Anubionic background it would mean that there was already thoroughly hexametrised material in M^b himself, lying completely concealed from view.

[15] Or, to put it more kindly, they would imply a very different use of the elegiac metre from the spare and economical apportionment of protasis and apodosis across single lines or couplets, well analysed by Monteventi, 199–202.

ancient tradition does so, and it may be that, from time to time, we do have access to an 'original' form of their works (an optimist's view of the Oxyrhynchus and Berlin fragments of Anubion). In practice, however, when one author takes over verses from another it is not reasonable to expect that he will not have imposed himself in some way. Passive compilation is not a useful model for understanding the process of borrowing and transformation, and even if the arguments presented here about Anubion are accepted, it does not follow that we can draw forth nuggets of the pure source text, as if by applying a magnet to a pile of iron filings. The chart of Oedipus is a particularly salutary instance. If one thinks of the kind of exercise by which modern editors (Axtius and Rigler, Koechly, and De Stefani himself)—and indeed ancient critics as well—try to convert five feet into six by minimal jiggery-pokery, the practice looks increasingly dubious in light of the very close correspondences of *detail* between 1.106–11 and Anubion, F 4, but the almost completely different phraseology.

There are three features of the elegiacs in the first book that militate strongly against any notion it contains undigested lumps of Anubion. These are as follows.

(i) Significant overlaps between the passages containing pentameters and the straight hexameters. This is discussed below.

(ii) The reasonable popularity of the pattern whereby an epithet and its noun are placed at mid-line and line-end, what Slings called parallel word-end.[16] Of course one must exert due caution when the sample is so small, but for what it is worth there are four instances among 20 pentameters, or 20%.[17] This contrasts with only a single instance in Anubion, which involves, moreover, a decorative epithet (F 10 (f) 3 κερδαλέην... ἐμπορίην), whereas three of these four instances in Mᶜ involve colourless adjectives ('own', 'former', 'same'). This could be an important difference, and it nudges the book 1 pentameters in the direction of the parallelistic style the main poet otherwise favours.

(iii) The significantly different patterns with *muta cum liquida* and Attic correption. With all due caveats, once again, for sample size, the two corpora[18] produce particularly notable differences when it comes to word internal

---

[16] S. R. Slings, 'Hermesianax and the Tattoo Elegy (P.Brux. inv. E 8934 and P.Sorb. inv. 2254)', ZPE 98 (1993), 29–37, at 33–4 and table II ('parallel word-end'); G. O. Hutchinson, 'Pentameters', in Sistakou and Rengakos, 119–37.

[17] 37 ἰδίης... πραγματίης, 99 προτέρην... κακοφροσύνην, 128 ἀχρήστους... φύσεις, 211 αὐτὴν... δύναμιν. For these purposes I do not include 169 among the pentameters.

[18] The comparison was conducted on the basis of the 20 pentameters in Mᶜ, together with the whole of 208–14 and 341–52 (since these passages are more or less consistently elegiac) and, on the other hand, the fragments that stand the best chance of being Anubion, or F 1–10 Schubert.

correption. The total figure of 38.46% for M^c's pentameters is high and may be partly statistical fluke, but it is compatible with the fact that M^c(A) otherwise has the second highest figure for word internal corrrption (37.97%) among all astrological poets surveyed. The figure of 12.82% in Anubion, on the other hand, brings him into a range occupied by M^a, Maximus, and Dorotheus. As for correption at word boundary, Anubion seems only to employ it in restricted circumstances (4/5 times with Κρόνος, once with τρίγωνος), a limitation that does not seem to be observed in the pentameters of M^c (Κρόνος and τρίγωνος once each of five). The figures for internal position are also significantly out of kilter (M^c's pentameters 23.08%/Anubion 46.15%).

In short, the evidence suggests either that Anubion was transformed far more thoroughly than M^b was transformed by M^c, or that the pentameters are 'after' Anubion, rather than 'by' Anubion, or perhaps, some of them, simply compositions *de novo*. Most likely, they are some combination of all three. And on the possibility of composition *de novo*, the possibility should also be raised that lone pentameters can be deliberate stylemes. The argument so far has proceeded mainly from sequences or individual pentameters that can be connected with Anubion, either through papyri, or through affiliation with the group of sources to which Anubion belongs (especially Firmicus), or both. Nonetheless, it is also possible that isolated pentameters were all a poet ever intended, that they are self-conscious, purposeful, and were only ever meant to stand alone. The clearest example of this is the one at the end of the commination of Ares in 152. There are also pentameters at the end of sequences in 37, 91 (but only a weak pause, for a complementary chart follows), 114 (but its position is challengeable), 128 (but I have argued that this may be Anubion), 175 (the pentameter itself ends with τέλος), and of course 361, at the end of the book itself. Inscriptional examples of both closural pentameters after sequences of hexameters, and of generally irregular sequences of hexameters and elegiac couplets, are readily found.[19] In other words, isolated pentameters may, but need not always, be the débris of an incomplete conversion.

---

[19] K. Flower-Smith, 'Some Irregular Forms of the Elegiac Distich', *AJP* 22 (1901), 165–94, at 184–92. He had used Kaibel for Greek and Buecheler for Latin; the Greek evidence is now massively expanded and made easy to consult by Merkelbach and Stauber, among whom closural pentameters are trivially easy to find, e.g. 09/08/04, 09/09/16, 09/12/04 (a pentameter to close two elegiac couplets), 10/02/11, 10/02/16, 11/01/01, 11/05/04. See too Trimalchio's efforts in Petron. *Sat.* 34.10 and 55.3 (which Trimalchio calls an *inscriptio*, as if acknowledging the verses' epigraphical character), both doggerel on fatalism consisting of two hexameters + pentameter: see Smith, art. cit. 187–9, and bibliography in Schmeling on both loci; add N. Horsfall, ' "The Uses of Literacy" and the *Cena Trimalchionis*: I', *G&R* 36 (1989), 74–89, at 79; L. Edmunds, 'Rules for Poems in Petronius' *Satyrica*', *SyllClass* 20 (2009), 71–104, at 81, 88. There is a question whether the inscribed epigram is an appropriate comparison for astrological verse, but perhaps (*a*) the ready

Finally, there is Anubion, F 12 = 12 Perale (PSI III 157), which contains pentameters at 3, 27, 39, and possibly 41. This fragment has a large number of correspondences with the later books of the Manethoniana, especially with the first and fifth (see on 4.80, 207; 1.34, 50–7, 230; 5.78–80, 162, 197, 260, 324; l. 14 ἡνίκα δ' ἄν, restored by Perale, occurs 4× in book 4 and 5.243), and was even ascribed to Manetho by its first editor, Boll, because he discovered various parallels with Firmicus' third and fourth books. The textual history of this fragment is completely unclear, but it shows that whatever process led to the metrical mess in the first book is not a unique state of affairs there, and occurs in other material with Firmican parallels.

It does, in conclusion, seem likely that Anubion substantially underpins at least parts of this book, but that is without prejudice to the poet's own creativity. We are fooling ourselves if we think the processes of ancient textual requisitioning will allow us to recover more than a travestied sense of Anubion's work.

A, B, C, D...

But there is another thorny problem. Even on his own limited terms, Koechly did not carry his method far enough. He could have done better even with the material he had, which at that point was confined to the published editions of L. He arrived at his groupings on the basis of shared words and phrases, but he spotted certain parallels and missed others. There are overlaps in diction beyond the ones he identified, and these include overlaps between groups that he identified as separate. Using internal likenesses within book 1 as a basis for ascribing lines to an individual poet seems to me a valid enough principle, but if pursued thoroughly it weakens Koechly's whole approach.

To begin with the elegiac material, there are numerous examples of similar wording between pentameters—both lone pentameters and pentameters in sequences that putatively depend on Anubion—and hexameters:

The former:

91 ἐμμανέας τεύχει ἠδὲ φρενοβλαβέας ~ 231 ῥέζουσ' ἐμμανέας, πάσας φρένας ἐξολέσαντες

159 (ἐκτήκει) ἐκ κρυφίμων ~ 252 τρύχει γὰρ ταύτας κρυφίμων ἄπο (the adjective is not unique, but the constructions are parallel, and the situations alike)

---

disaggregability of astrological poetry into bite-size portions (even into separately entitled epigrams in the case of F 11), and (b) the tropes that are shared with epigraphical verse, in this and other books, help to bridge the gap between the two. The counterparts of closural pentameters are closural hexameters, of which there seem to be instances in Anubion, F 7 (ii) 7, 24: see Schubert, 412–13.

193 εἰς Ἄϊδος κατίασιν ~ 336 οἴχεται ἐς Ἀΐδην (gynaecological context)

The latter:

45–6 πολιὸς Κρόνος ἀγκαλίσαιτο... ῥέζουσι ~ 351 Κρόνον φίλον ἀγκαλίσαιτο... ῥέζει
185–6 ὑπὲκ συνόδοιο... Μήνην ~ 351 Μήνη δ' ἐκ συνόδοιο
208 Πλησιφαὴς Κρονίωνι συναντήσασα Σελήνη ~ 245 πλησιφαὴς δ' Ἄρηι συναντήσασα Σελήνη
267 εἰ δ' Ἄρης ὥρην κατέχοι Φαίνων τε σὺν αὐτῷ ~ 281 Ἑρμείας δὲ μεσουρανέων, Τιτὰν δὲ σὺν αὐτῷ ~ 347 Ἑρμείας δέ τ' ἐφ' ὡρονόμου Μήνη τε σὺν αὐτῷ[20]

The last of these examples involves Koechly's poets AEF, and further similarities can be found between his groups which he himself did not acknowledge. So, AEF are also precisely the poets who use κατεναντίον before the bucolic caesura (90, 215, 268, 285, 342), whose only other occurrence in the corpus is at 3.137. Other similarities between groups are as follows. They include Koechly's *ineptus versificator* (whose existence thereby becomes problematic), and their number is presumably significant given the small sample size:

AC: 36 + 72 ἀνέρας ἡγεμονῆας; 158 + 176 Ἄρεα δ' ἦν (unique in the Manethoniana); 83 Κρόνος αἰνὸς ~ 187 Κρόνῳ αἰνῷ, 273 Κρόνου αἰνήν, 357 Κρόνον αἰνόν; 256–7... οὐ καλοεργός | οὕνεκεν ἀνθρώποισι... ~ 354–5... οὐ καλοεργός | ἔσσεται ἀνθρώποις...

AF: 116 + 282 ὡρονόμοιο τυχοῦσα; 153 + 278 κατὰ μοῖραν; as well as 267 ~ 281 ~ 347, noted apropos of the overlaps with elegiac couplets

A + *ineptus*: 58 + 224 Μήνης μέτα καὶ Κυθερείης

M^b + *ineptus*: 306 σκολιὸς δρόμος ~ 359 δρόμος οὐράνιος

There is less evidence for B, which does not, in any case, contain apotelesmata, though even then one can compare 203 ῥέζε Κρόνῳ καὶ Ἄρηι with 271 εἰ δὲ Κρόνῳ καὶ Ἄρηι, and the ending καὶ Κυθερείη/-είης in each of 58 (*ineptus*), 203, and 224. The only poet who yields no internal cross-references is D, who Koechly assigned only six lines anyway.

In the light of all this, I would query the separate existences of poet C and probably B, and while acknowledging the likely Anubionic underlay of at least some of E would treat it for all practical purposes as emanating from the same hand as A, so thoroughgoing has been the makeover. The most theoretically difficult set of overlaps is with group F, which, despite the similarities of *lexis*, packs in so many stylistic and metrical peculiarities within the short space of nine lines that one would otherwise doubt their ascription to the same poet as

---

[20] Otherwise 4.598 has Ἄρης τε σὺν αὐτῷ, but not the rest of the formulation.

A. There are three definite articles in the space of nine lines, whereas A only uses the definite article once; two of them are in the phrase ἡ Κερόεσσα, whereas A always (three times) uses this as an epithet of Mene or Selene, and never with an article; Hermann's Bridge is down in 278, which A never does in what is extant, and there is no third-foot caesura in 281. The question is whether the model I favour, whereby a poet overwrites inherited material in his own idiom, can cope with this peculiar pattern of similar diction and stylistic/metrical idiosyncrasy. It is worth, in any case, pondering the fact that the new Oxyrhynchus papyrus consists of a sequence which contains a series of segments ascribed by Koechly to different poets (A: 26–33, 42–8; C: 34–6; E: 37; 'Ineptus': 38–41— although the presence of 16–17 is uncertain). Assemblage or the work of a single poet, these lines stood together already in the fourth century.

Conclusion

This book is a salutary lesson in the complexities of the transmission of poetic astrological material. I have argued for the concept of 'ownership' or 'curatorship', whereby a poet takes over matter from a predecessor and imposes his own idiom upon it. It requires all the more flexibility from a critic in that that appropriation seems to have been much more far-reaching in the case of Anubion than in that of M^b; and it is not completely straightforward to deal with in cases where lexical and metrical homogenisation do not seem to pull together. The implications of Π^1 are particularly challenging, for insofar as it encourages the idea of separate recensions, it suggests that what we have in book 4 is, not so much the *Urtext* of a highly eccentric voice from whom M^c borrowed, but a worked-over version in which some of the mannerisms were exaggerated and carried to even further extremes, as opposed to the version in M^c in which they are somewhat muted.

For the purposes of deriving statistics for this book's usages, the only portion that can certainly be excluded are the lines shared with M^b. F is borderline. The *ineptus* is a ragged category. I would be inclined to reassign 1.16–17 from the *ineptus versificator* to B on the grounds of an eccentric planetary order shared with 1.203–4; but, if to B, then to A as well. (The new papyrus, however, may complicate this.) The case against 58–61 and 96–7 rests on the argument from doublets. The mere existence of a doublet does not *ipso facto* mean that multiple authors are in play, though there are metrically suspect features in both passages. On the other hand, as a matter of principle, it is not clear why the undoubted metrical difficulty in l. 60 should override the 'protective' effect of 224 (A) on 58: in other words, if ὁμοῖον ἐς τὸν ὁμοῖον is a reasonable guide for what goes with what, it should be applied consistently, and not jettisoned when a difficulty presents itself that emendation could, potentially, solve. 339–40 should be taken with 341–52; 359 should presumably be attributed to the writer of 4 (although ἀπλανῶν τε πλάνων τε would be mindlessly easy to replicate); and 360–1 seems to be Anubion, if anything in this book is (though see p. 278). For metrical statistics on the 'main' poet, then, I would include almost all of the *ineptus* except for the corrupt 41 and perhaps, out of an abundance of caution, 58–61 and 96–7, for want of sound theoretical reasons to exclude him.

1.3. PHONOLOGICA ET MORPHOLOGICA

The following notes, supplementing i. 89–105, illustrate the Attic forms that permeate the book.

Phonologica

α/η

Attic forms transmitted: 1.181 πρᾶξιν (πρῆξιν D), 304 λαμπράν (as also at 4.204, K λαμπρὴν), 352 εὐπράκτους, 361 ἑτέραν. There are some divergences within the lines shared with M^b: 1.295 Ἑρμείαν (but 4.147 Ἑρμείην), 315 ἔν τε βίᾳ (4.487 has a different text); and particularly the Doric forms in 320 πικρᾶς Μοίρας ὑπ' ἀνάγκας (L^1; but 4.490 πικρῆς Μοίρης ὑπ' ἀνάγκῃ), for which see De Stefani 2017, 33 n. 119.

ρρ/ρσ

120 ἄρρενα (-ρσ- K), 125 ἄρρενας (-ρσ- K).

ἐς/εἰς

Of the three occasions where neither ἐς nor εἰς is metrically guaranteed, εἰς is transmitted at 68 and 313, ἐς at 269.

Contractions

See i. 94–7; A.–R. xxx: they are ubiquitous, and nothing is gained by occasional editorial tampering. But A.–R. substitute σεῦ for Attic σου at 1.142.

Vowel quantities

καλός
The quantity is simply inconsistent (cf. A.–R. xx f.): 45 καλήν and 256 κᾰλοεργός are both Koechly's poet A. Otherwise: 96 κᾰλόν, 354 κᾰλοεργός; but 17 κᾱλή, 296 κᾱλῷ.

Morphologica

αις, -αισι(ν), -ῃσι(ν)

-ῃσι(ν) is associated with the lines shared with M^b, with a little raggedness at the beginning of the section. αισι(ν) is transmitted or implied by -εσσι at: 171 πενίεσσιν, 172 ἐνδίεσσιν, 190 θηρίεσσι, 239 κατοχαῖσι; 241 οὐ[..]ρῇσιν L¹; 251 μογεραῖσι; 258 δούλαισιν; 292 σοφίεσσιν [M^b σοφίῃσιν]. -ῃσι(ν): 241 οὐρῇσιν L; 287 ἡμερινῇσι; 322 ἀκτινηβολίῃσι; 324 ναυφθορίῃσιν ~ 4.399 ναυφθορίαισιν; 326 Μοίρῃσιν; 338 αἱμηρῇσι.

Declension of Ares

The Attic form Ἄρεως is metrically guaranteed in 1.286, and transmitted at 1.220; certainly to be corrected at 1.307, but restorable at 1.273 Ἄρεος to avoid a lengthening in arsi.

Miscellanea

Attic forms at 1.140 πόλεσιν καὶ ναυσὶ (νηυσὶ A.–R.).
The heteroclite plural 1.126 ἄχνοας is unique.

Forms of εἶναι

A very narrow majority of forms are epic,[21] but Attic forms are transmitted (across the various strata) at 22, 57, 66 ὦσιν; 26, 27 παρών; 75 ἐπών; 78, 271, 296 συνῇ; 332 προόντων. A.–R. xxix would emend all of them (having initially read 235 ᾖ for L's ἦν). 150 ἦν is Attic-Ionic.

---

[21] 8, 354 ἐών, 32 ἐοῦσαι; 38, 284 ἔωσιν, 49 ἔασιν; 29, 62, 81 ἐόντες, 126, 133 ἐόντας; 106 παρεοῦσα. Restored by Axtius at 272 ἐοῦσα.

1.4. SYNTAX

Particles

Asyndeton

There are distinct patterns, but they do not necessarily carry implications for authorship (p. 164). Asyndeton is found throughout the book.[22] The only segment which sets itself off from the rest is the block shared with M[b], all of whose τέχναι charts as well as the two parental charts at the end stay connected. This is the more distinctive in that, outside this block, τέχναι charts are divided.[23] But this is the only instance where connectivity hints at a different source. Charts themed on οἶνος are ordinarily asyndetic (50, 89, 134, 229, 250; not 235), which contrasts markedly with the οἶνος charts in M[b]. But the last three charts of the medical group are connected (153, 158, 185), and so is a later chart which also belongs to the type 'Moon encounters x' (245). This is presumably not an issue of authorship (all the charts belong to A); it looks, instead, as if they were designed as a sequence, later broken up, although that does not explain why the *second* chart should be missing a particle (134).

There is no consistent pattern in the elegiac couplets, some of which are connected and some of which are not.

Postponed particles

This feature is also occasional and not distinctive of any one segment. Postponements of δέ occur throughout A (preposition + noun: 1.82 ἐν ἤματι δ', 1.222 ἀπ' εὐπορίης δέ; subject + verb: 1.339 Πυρόεις δύνῃ δέ; 1.127 ἔσθ' ὅτε δ' is normal in prose). τε is postponed in the prologue poet (1.4 ἄστρων οὐρανίων τε φάσεις); possibly B (1.206); otherwise in A (1.30 θηλυτέρης Κύπριδός τε καί; 1.171 θλίψεσιν οὐλομέναις τε καί; 1.235 ἦν δὲ Κρόνου μέσσῃ τε καὶ Ἄρεος). Further examples would be 1.91 ἐμμανέας τεύχει ‹τ'› ἠδὲ suppl. K (in pentameter), 1.141 καὶ καρποῖς γαίης ‹τε› καὶ suppl. A.–R. (poet B). γάρ and μέν are not postponed.

Clusters

Gnomic τε is used for wadding, once again throughout the book, at 1.27 Μήνῃ δέ τ', 332 καί τε, 341 Μήνῃ δέ τε, 347 Ἑρμείας δέ τ'. The last two examples are in

---

[22] 18, 22, 26, 29, 34, 38, 42, 50, 58, 62, 66, 70, 83, 89, 96, 100, 106, 112, 115, 119, 134, 139, 167, 180, 208, 210, 215, 224, 229, 250, 256, 262, 339, 341, 346.

[23] Connective: 75, 129 [NB *ex emend.* K for θ'], 180 (very delayed); asyndeton: 38, 58, 62, 83.

elegiacs. There are no certain examples in extant Anubion, but τῶν δέ ⟨τε⟩ φαύλων is restored in F 11.15 (among the *incerta*, and certainly showing signs of textual manipulation: see on 1.341-2 + 343-5).

Definite Article

Three out of seven are in elegiacs (76 τὴν πρᾶξιν, a technical phrase also in 181 and 5.182; 99 τὴν προτέρην...κακοφροσύνην, 211 τὴν αὐτὴν...δύναμιν). The definite article is quite normal in Anubion, but the pattern with parallel word-ends is not (p. 279). Three are in the paired charts on kingship which Koechly ascribed to F, all of planets (277 and 282 ἡ Κερόεσσα, 285 τῶν ὀλοῶν), which suggests the distinctiveness of this segment.

Third-Person Pronouns and Adjectives

1.10 σφέτερος is used of the first person by the prologue poet, and not otherwise. See K.-G. i. 573; Schwyzer, ii. 204-5; Gow on Theocr. 25.163.

Less distinctive is the use of ἑός of a plural subject (111, 138, 214, 240, 320). See i. 121-2, adding Vian 1987, 60.

Prepositions

Anastrophe

This is limited to poeticising planetary configurations (1.41, 246 Ζηνὸς ἄτερ; 1.58 and 224 Μήνης μέτα) or stock phrases (1.252 κρυφίμων ἄπο; contrast e.g. Θ p. 185.5-6 ὑπὸ κρυφίμων τόπων ὀχλοῦνται). There are no examples with ἅμα, ἔνι, ἔξ, ἔπι, ὁμοῦ, ὕπερ, ὕπο (except in Koechly's remade hexameter 1.97b αὐγῇσιν ὕπ').

Tmesis

No examples, unless 1.217 ἐκ φιλίης ἐλάσουσιν is taken in this way (Monaco, 42).

n x N (i. 128-32)

Prior placement of epithets, mostly decorative, occurs throughout the book: 1.25 χαλεπῇ ἐπὶ κύπριδι, 48 γλυκεροῖς ἐπὶ χείλεσι, 101 πορφυρέοισιν ἐν εἵμασιν, 144 ξηροῖσιν ἀνύδατοι ἐν στομάτεσσιν. The epithet is informational only in

1.266 πυμάτην περὶ μοῖραν (and in Koechly's remade hexameter at 1.159 κρυφίμων ἄπο πολλάκι νούσων). Genitives are pre-posed in 1.201 Μοιράων... ἀμφὶ μίτοισιν, 234 Σεληναίης ὑπὸ ῥιπῆς, 320 πικρᾶς Μοίρας ὑπ' ἀνάγκας.

Expressions for 'with'

Figures are given in the chart in i. 125. See T. Mommsen, 212, noting that the two instances of μετά + genitive (58, 224) disguise its prosaic quality with anastrophe. Also to be noted is that of the six instances of σύν, which properly suggests that the item is an add-on or adjunct, half (267, 281, 347) are used where the items in practice seem to have parity, so that it effectively means simply 'and'. In 107 the phrase runs parallel to 6.161, and in 110 Saturn is an add-on ~ Anubion, F 4 ii. 15a. The other is 62.

ἐν

The pattern in this book is quite different from that of M^d in that only five (perhaps six) of the 25 instances are in technical expressions,[24] the great majority in apodoses.[25] Misuse is not a characteristic. Neither are the phrases typical of M^a except in 292 (excellence in a given domain).

I find no examples of prepositions reduplicated after a compound verb (the overkill construction).

Verbs

Protasis

In all nine temporal clauses in the book (22, 38, 43, 57, 66, 277, 284, 301, 306) the mood is subjunctive. Conditional clauses are more variable:

With εἰ, there are six optatives (AE: 153, 182, 194, 210, 267; M^b: 294–5: contrast 4.146–7) and three subjunctives (all of which lack a particle) (92, 266, 271).

With ἤν, in addition to eight subjunctives in A (18, 64, 78, 108, 119, 180, 223, 236), two in M^b (287, 334, as well as γένηται in the corrupt 335), three in C (176,

---

[24] 5(?), 27, 29, 279, 287, 357.
[25] 82 (see n.), 101 (Archilochus, F 9.11 W. ἐν εἵμασιν and Bion, Epit. 79), 144, 170, 173, 177, 214 (Ap. Rhod. 2.214 ἐν καμάτοισιν), 239, 253, 255 (Ap. Rhod. 3.876 ἐν ὕδασι), 264bis (adaptation of Il. 11.65), 269 (ἐν νεότητι prosaic, but also Anubion, F 11.39), 292, 305 (presque homérique ἐνὶ στέρνοισιν), 312, 326 (Od. 5.335 ἐν πελάγεσσι). A couple of others: 8, 198.

339*bis*), and another in 40 (from Koechly's *ineptus*), A employs four clauses which contain optatives (45, though Π^3 disagrees; 121–4, involving a sequence of four verbs; 158; 225), one of which is metrically guaranteed (158), and appears to have been modelled consciously on Dorotheus (see n. ad loc.)—an interesting endorsement of the principle that poetic precedent can override grammar when choosing a mood (i. 138–9). Not even Axtius and Rigler correct the optatives at 45 (though ἀγκαλίσηται is available, and now attested in Π^3), 225, or 353 (C), and cannot correct those at 121–3 because they remake 124 as a hexameter which requires an optative for the cadence. There is one further sequence in 343–4 containing a shift from the subjunctive to optative (an intervening pentameter may have been lost). There is a parallel passage in Anubion, F 11.5, but it appears to be secondary to this one (see on 1.344). Again, not even A.-R. correct 344 ἴδοι.

Tenses are more or less evenly split. In temporal clauses, there are four aorists (A 43; F 278; M^b 301, 306) and five presents. And in conditional clauses there are sixteen aorists (eleven in A) and seventeen presents (ten in A). No distinctive and statistically significant patterns emerge.

Apodosis

(i) Gnomic aorist. 21 in apotelesmata, seventeen of stars, four of natives or in association with them. Three more are outside apotelesmata.[26]

(ii) Future. 25 in all, nine of the stars, one of Fate, fifteen of natives (including one aorist optative which I take as a proxy future).[27]

(iii) Present. 95 in all, 52 of stars and 43 of natives.[28]

Thus, of a total of 142 verbs, 14.79% are gnomic aorists, 17.61% futures, 66.9% presents (the remainder is ἔσεσθαι δείκνυσι). But this is across the book as a whole. Different patterns emerge for Koechly's segments, but with tiny numbers involved not all figures are obviously significant. The results are these:

---

[26] Stars: 36, 69, 70, 93, 94*bis*, 102, 105, 161, 168, 170, 175, 214, 248, 249, 253, 358. Natives: 48, 240, and associated generalisations: 218b, 338. 191 is imperfect. Outside apotelesmata: 99, 114, 143.

[27] Stars: 117, 195*bis*, 213, 217b, 342*bis*, 355, 356. [Also 293 ἔσεσθαι δείκνυσι.] Fate: 330. Natives: 52, 54, 120 (aor. opt.), 274, 276*bis*, 288, 313, 314, 315, 318, 320, 333, 340; I include also 57.

[28] Stars: 19, 23, 28, 31, 36, 43, 44, 46, 63, 67, 68, 69, 72, 76, 79, 84, 85, 91, 100, 131, 135, 154, 155, 159, 167, 169, 177, 181, 209, 211, 212, 216a, 217a, 222, 231, 237, 247, 251, 252, 258, 270*bis*, 280, 283, 284, 298, 303, 311, 323, 331, 352, 358. 257 present perfect. Natives: 20(?), 21, 25, 33, 39, 41, 47, 49*bis*, 53, 59, 60, 61, 82*bis*, 86, 87, 95*bis*, 111, 113, 136, 157, 163, 174, 179, 188, 193, 222*bis*, 223, 232, 234, 238, 242, 244, 259, 260, 261, 265, 325, 332, 336.

	Total	Aorist	Future	Present
A	of 92	15.22% (14)	11.96% (11)	72.83% (67)
C	of 7	28.57% (2)	28.57% (2)	42.86% (3)
D	of 3	67% (2)	—	33% (1)
E	of 13	15.38% (2)	23.08% (3)	61.54% (8)
F	of 3	—	—	100% (3)
M^b	of 17	5.88% (1)	47.06% (8)	47.06% (8)
ineptus	of 6	—	16.67% (1)	83.33% (5)

But it was always clear that the very high number of futures in the M^b segment would drag down the average in A, and conversely that the lower number of presents in M^b would push A's presents up. With small numbers involved, E's figures are not so very different from A's. But it is worth making the comparison with the fragments of Anubion, even if, to get sufficient numbers to make the comparison worthwhile, one has to include A as well as E. Many of the verbs in Anubion cannot be pronounced on with any degree of confidence. But among those that can, it is clear that, in line with the general practice in M^c and M^d, he reserves gnomic aorists for the stars (four examples),[29] tends to use the future for natives (perhaps six examples, with perhaps two for stars),[30] but also—the clearest difference from the first book—reserves the present almost exclusively for stars (at least thirteen examples in apotelesmata, with none certainly of a native).[31] Restricting the comparison to the strictly elegiac sections of the first book, however, there is no difference between them and Anubion, for only one line uses the present of natives, and that is the difficult case at 336.

Negations

285 μηδένα for οὐδένα
(Also 6.6 μή; 6.723, or has this gen. abs. a sense of conditionality?)

1.5. STYLE

The style of the book is far less extravagant than that of the fourth. Attention can therefore concentrate on the use and recycling of earlier poetry, on the one

---

[29] Stars: 5b 12 ἔδωκ'; 10(a) ὤλεσεν, 10(f) θήκατο, δῶκε.
[30] Natives: 4 ii. 3 πάσεται, 16 μείξεται, 18 λέξεται; 8.17 ἔσσεται (?), 36 μείξεται. [Also F 9 Obbink ἔσσεται in connection with native.] Stars: 4 ii. 5 ὀλέσει,11.54 δώσει (star?).
[31] Stars: 3c προλέγει, 3e ἐπάγει; 4 ii. 8 ἐπάγει, 19 γίνονται; 5b 9 δίδωσι; [6a 4 φέρει restored]; 8.33 ἵεται, 40 ῥέζει; 10a φέρει, 10b διδοῖ (presumably), 10e φέρει; 11.47 δηλοῦσι (?); 12.21 τεύχουσιν, 27 ποιεῖ. Not apotelesmata: 10c and d χαίρει. [Natives: F 10 Obbink εἰσίν.]

hand, and compositional technique, on the other. Once again we shall want to know whether the style is uniform, or whether it supports the idea of different poets.

Use and Recycling of Earlier Poets

Use of Homer extends from the formal emptiness of metrical patterns through the trivia of phrase-endings and opportunistic grab-and-snatch to more intelligent and perhaps pointed reworking. The poet(s) use Homer to communicate meaning in an idiom of which they are keen to demonstrate mastery, but the approach is essentially one of appropriating the compositional facility and communicative possibilities of the Homeric language. It is not about engaging with Homer in a sustained way. The closest any part of the book comes to that is in the commination of Ares (see on 139; 139–52, for 146–7; 150–2), and even that is really more an appropriation of Homeric models for *schetliasmos* and of the EGHP idea of destructive deity than a challenge to Homer's worldview; it is shored up with pastiche Homeric vocabulary (p. 797), not to ram home a point, but for stylistic authenticity. The second passage of polemic, where a formula of prohibition (198 n. ἴσχεο) is turned against pagan sacrifice, formulated in Homeric language (197 n.), has more bite, but that is what it is, polemic. The approach is not basically a philological one in any section. There is little interest in Homeric rarities and *hapax legomena* for their own sake (145 ὠλεσίκαρπα; 227 καρήατα was *hapax* at *Il.* 17.437).

There are endless instances where Homeric phrase-patterns are recycled over and over again as nothing more than rhythmic armature, and the more doggedly one uses the TLG the more one finds.[32] The point is not this or that particular echo, but that this is presumably a kind of composition which either came naturally to composers who were still steeped in Homer—a few instances suggest memory of sound[33]—or wanted to advertise Homeric credentials to their readers, or both. Beyond the mere formalism of patterns, the other

---

[32] The following list is guaranteed not to be exhaustive (see notes ad loc. where there is no comment here): 13 ἑξαμέτροις ἐπέεσσιν (many Homeric examples of epithet + ἐπέεσσιν); 51 τίς ἂν τότε φῶς ἐσίδοιτο; 55 νηλέϊ λύθρῳ; 75 κορυθαίολος Ἄρης; 104 Μήνη δέ τοι ἀρχιδικαστήν ~ *Il.* 4.314 βίη δέ τοι ἔμπεδος εἴη, 16.725 δώη δέ τοι εὖχος Ἀπόλλων, al.; 157 ἑὸν μόρον ἐντὸς ἔχοντες; 161 ἢ κραδίην παρέτριψε νοήμονα, μητέρα βουλῆς; 162 πνεύμονά θ' ἑλκήεντα, κακὴν νόσον ἀνθρώποισιν; 185 ὑπὲκ συνόδοιο φυγοῦσαν; 193 εἰς Ἄϊδος κατίασιν ἀνοστήτοιο μέλαθρον; 199 οὐ γάρ τις δύναται γένεσιν μετατρεψέμεν ἀνδρῶν; 200 συγγίγνεται ἀνθρώποισιν; 218 ἐπεὶ Διὸς ἔπλετο πλοῦτος; 223 τέλος αἰνὸν ἔχουσιν; 232 νεκύων σκιοειδέα μορφήν; 233 ἀεικέα πήματ' ἔχοντες; 257 κατὰ λέκτρα τέτυκται ~ *HHom. Herm.* 196 περὶ θαῦμα τέτυκται; 280 θεὸν βροτὸν ἀνθρώποισιν; 315 κακοεργέϊ θυμῷ.

[33] 177 ἐν ἀνθρώποισιν ἀνιῶν ~ *Od.* 17.419, 19.75 ἐν ἀνθρώποισιν ἔναιον.

ubiquitous technique is the constant purloining of phrases, especially at line-end, sometimes with opportunistic tweaks such as a change of case or number. The poet of the prologue applies the grab-and-snatch method to an extent that becomes almost predictable, but it is found throughout the book; it is a routine and not in the least distinctive technique.

Usually it is simply a matter of the suitability of sense and/or rhythm.[34] Toil and suffering, fate, divine formulary that lends itself to planets, luminaries, and fire,[35] all go down well, but it is rarely the case that the poet seems to want to activate any recollection of the original context. That claim is justified because the echoes so rarely seem 'meaningful'. Recognising the original context might provoke reflection on the sheer distance between the world of the heroes and that of today, or simply a wry smile, but neither seems to have been the poet's usual purpose in redeploying the phrase or clausula.[36] If there *is* any carry-over, it is not exactly because the poet was deliberately setting out to trigger the associations of the original line, but rather because, by recycling it, he *ipso facto* carries over some intrinsic feature of it. For instance, by describing planets in opposition using formulary adapted from Homeric warriors, he implies both

---

[34] 'Flagship' concepts: 1.1 n. βασιληίδα τιμήν; 2 n. γαίης ἡμετέρης; 10 μέγ' ὄνειαρ; 47 κουριδίους ἄνδρας (irony possible: see n. ad loc.); 118 n. καὶ φιλότητα; 168 λέχος αὐτῶν (*Il.* 15.39); with modifications: 147 n. ἔλωρ θήρεσσιν; 181 n. ἀμύμονας ἰητῆρας; 184 n. ἤπια φάρμακ' (ἔχοντας); 220 θόρυβοί τε μάχαι τε (4× EGHP πόλεμοί τε μάχαι τε); 356 n. λύπας γὰρ στοναχάς τε. Prepositional phrases: 153 n. κατὰ μοῖραν; 154 κατὰ σῶμα (Hes. *Op.* 540); 326 (τρόμον) ἐν πελάγεσσιν (*HHom. bis* (ἁλὸς) ἐν πελάγεσσιν). Verbal phrases: 94 n. παρέπλαγξεν δὲ νόημα; 146 ὤλεσας ἄνδρας (Hes. *Op.* 372 ὤλεσαν ἄνδρας;* Theogn. 43 ὤλεσαν ἄνδρες); 166 n. ἦτορ ἔχοντες (irony possible: see n. ad loc.); 167 τάδε ῥέζει (*Od.* 22.158); 199 n. οὐ γάρ τις δύναται. Supporting phrases: 123 ἠδὲ καὶ αὐτὸς (EGHP ἠδὲ καὶ αὐτοί, *passim*); 281 δὲ σὺν αὐτῷ (*Il.* 15.353); 146 οὓς μὲν γὰρ (*Il.* 11.341 τοὺς μὲν γάρ); 155 οἳ καὶ ἔπειτα (*Od.* 2.60 ἦ καὶ ἔπειτα).

[35] Suffering: 6 δειλοῖσι βροτοῖσι (EGHP *passim*, and *Or. Sib.*); 8 πολλὰ μογήσας (EGHP); 52 κακὰ πολλὰ παθών (3× *Od.*); 338 ἄλγε' ἔδωκεν (EGHP, subj. Κρονίδης Ζεὺς/Ὀλύμπιος); with modifications: 162 n. κακὴν νόσον ἀνθρώποισιν; 194 n. μάλα πολλὰ παθοῦσαν; 255 πολλὰ παθόντας (*Od.* 13.131 πολλὰ παθόντα); 274 n. ἠδ' ἐλεεινός. Fate, necessity, death: 52 Ἀϊδόσδε κάτεισιν (see n. on 51–2); 275 n. μοῖρα κακή; 320 ὑπ' ἀνάγκας (8× EGHP); with modifications: 174 n. θανάτῳ στυγερῷ; 193 n. εἰς Ἄϊδος κατίασιν; so too accomplishment (284 n. ταῦτα δέ τοι τελέουσιν, a particularly arch borrowing of *Od.* 2.306 for the purposes of an apotelesma). Supernatural powers: 176 n. δεινὸν θεόν; 195 n. ἔσσετ' ἀρωγός (ironic); with modification: 129 n. Υἱὸς δ' υἱωνός τε Κρόνου Ζεὺς ἠδὲ καὶ Ἑρμῆς; 205 n. ... θεῶν, κρατέουσι καὶ ἀνδρῶν. Sun or Moon: 97 n. ὑπὸ αὐγαῖς Ἠελίοιο (also Tyrtaeus, fr. 11.6 W. αὐγαῖς ἠελίοιο); 98 n. καθορῶν φάος Ἠελίοιο; with modification: 204 n. Ἠελίῳ βασιλῆι; 277 n. Ἡνίκα δ' ἡ Κερόεσσα μέσον πόλον ἀμφιβεβῶσα; cf. 322 φαεσφόρου Οὐλύμποιο ~ πολυπτύχου, θυώδεος, πολυδειράδος Οὐλύμποιο. Another category is that of phrases that further the construction of the narrative voice, communication between narrator and reader: 12 n. μάλ' ἀτρεκέως καταλέξω; 14 ἀνέρες εἰμέν (*Il.* 21.586, cf. *Od.* 16.236 ἀνέρες εἰσί); 73 αἴ κεν ἴδηαι (*Il.* 17.652).

[36] The inexperience of the sexless freaks and of Aphrodite playing *ingénue* are comically different: 1.126 ἀπειρήτους φιλότητος ~ *HHom. Aphr.* 133 ἀπειρήτην φιλότητος; likewise the godlikeness of the hermaphrodites and the divinely privileged: 127 ὁμώνυμον ἀθανάτοισιν ~ EGHP ἐπιείκελον ἀθανάτοισιν.

hostility and the purposeful movement of personified agencies (24, 215, and 343 nn.). There is a particularly nice instance at 270, where the adaptation of a line from Hesiod encapsulates—whether the poet intended it or not—the transformation from a meaningful world of actions and consequences to the astrological universe of meaningless upheaval. One also finds several more examples of the pattern that was already familiar from M^a and M^b, the use of divine formulae for gods in general or Zeus in particular being reapplied to the stars (see on 139–52 (on 146–7), 195, 205, 222, 247–8, 358). Recognise the source of any individual instance of this technique and it looks arch. Put them together, magnify their effect across the collection, and it becomes a systematic overhaul whereby the old system is ventriloquised by the new, a true project of cultural appropriation.

One can move forward through more purposeful and intelligent creation of *presque homérique* effects. These include passages where more than one Homeric model is juxtaposed (51–2, 241, 254–5), and passages which create convincing new syntheses by imbricating two (or even more) separate passages, generally linked (as in M^a: i. 152) by a key word.[37] I find one, but only one, example of Dionysius' signature technique, also used by M^a in the Aratea at his moments of greatest stylistic ambition, where a passage from EGHP is threaded together with a Hellenistic master (86 n. ἀεικέος εἵνεκα μισθοῦ). Hellenistic poetry is in evidence from time to time, not in a consistent way, but ranging from 'meaningless' phrase-ends (214 ἐν καμάτοισιν and Ap. Rhod. 2.214—if this is even an example) through cases where it can be pressed into service for polemic (142 n. εἵνεκα σοῦ; 198 n. ἀθανάτοισι or -οιο θυηλαῖς) to isolated curious factoids, for which no-one was more suitable than Callimachus (190–1 σαρξὶ δὲ θηρείῃσι). The author of the polemic against Mars, who for the most part is pressing hard on Homeric and Hesiodic themes, also mobilises Callimachus for one of the ruinous outcomes Mars brings about. It consists, apparently, of two separate Callimachean passages threaded together by keyword (143 n. πελάγεσσιν ἐπιπλώουσαι), both on the topic of sailing, but neither remotely catastrophic, on the contrary, each having a rather gladsome air about it. The poet seems, on this rather incongruous occasion, to be showing off—unless he is deliberately setting out to take a wrecking ball to the graceful or magical effect that Callimachus was trying to conjure.

Tragedy is not exploited very much, nothing like to the extent seen in the fourth book. A woe-saying comes in nicely in the first medical chart (n. on 51–2 δύσμορος, ὅς), and the imagery of madness reaches a high pitch in 93. For emotive vocabulary, the poet or poets also reach for phrases which are best attested in inscribed epitaph (see notes on 48 τέκνοις γλυκεροῖς; 120 (*vl*)

---

[37] See notes on 1 λαχὼν βασιληίδα τιμὴν; 145 δένδρεά τ' ὠλεσίκαρπα; 193 εἰς Ἄϊδος κατίασιν; 358 νῖκος ὀπάζει.

πανόδυρτον; 138 λύπην αἰείμνηστον; 276 βίοτον λείψουσι (also tragic), πρόμοιροι; 340 αἴλινος (adjectival); 356 λύπας γὰρ στοναχάς τε).

Connections with M^a (in Apodoses)

Several words or phrases are unique to M^a and this book, which might indicate that the poet—Koechly's poet A in almost all cases—knows the earlier one, but it is only a matter of odd shared items, not sustained exploitation.[38]

Hapax and Proton Legomena

Lexical innovation is not a large part of the book. The clearest pattern is that the poet of the medical charts is the most innovative, combining suggestions of technical precision (162 ἑλκήεντα) with the emotive effect of adjectival compounds (54 κακοελκέας; 55 λιποσαρκέα (3rd decl.); 166 ἀειθανές) and the extraordinary quasi agent noun 155 ὑδρογάστωρ). For whatever reason there is also a little moment of ambition for the workers with fire (78 πυροεργέας, 80 σκοτοεργούς, 81 ἀγρυπνητῆρες); τέχναι charts do of course attract interest, but it is not completely clear why this particular one does. There are also innovations throughout the commination of Mars (Koechly's poet B), but these are mostly of a different kind, less adventurous, and more in the style of Homeric pastiche (141 εὐρρείθροις, for εὐρρείτης; 144 ἀνύδατοι, for ἄνυδροι; 145 αἰνογένεθλοι; 146 μογερῶς, also in Greg. Naz. *PG* 37.562.11; most adventurous is 149 ἡλοπαγής). Other, desultory, innovations are in 260 ὀργιόωντες = be angry (A), 212 ῥεκτεῖρα (E), and the decorative epithets 100 ἐλαιορόοιο (D) and 327 κυανοχρώτοιο (also *Or. Sib.* 11.289).

Composition

The elements of the parallelistic style have by now been well established. All that is needed here is to illustrate the special mannerisms in this book, and to see whether there is any evidence for the hands of multiple poets.

The poet(s) of this book particularly enjoy formal parallelisms with isocolon and rhyme. There are line-internal parallelisms (below) and chiasmus (65, to conclude protasis; 94, 171, 184, 264, within apodosis). And there are specifically Leonine (internally rhyming) hexameters at 29, 108, 115, 130, 134 (in protases);

---

[38] 1.60 n. λύρης εὐρύθμοιο; 63 n. ῥέζουσιν, μούσης ἐπιίστορας, εὔφρονας; 182 n. πολυόλβους; 241 n. εἵματα μὲν ῥυπόωντα. ῥέζουσιν (23, 46, 63, 68, 181, 231, 270) is otherwise mainly (save for a couple of instances in book 4) in M^a, in the same *sedes* save for 23 and 46. For the transformation of nuisance-causing adjectives to nuisance-suffering see i. 367.

95, 133, 166, 216a + 217a, 233 (in apodoses), and 207 ('why sacrifice'?). A particularly telling case is 299, one of the lines 'shared' with M^b, where the two versions of the line show the idiosyncrasies of their respective poets (p. 275). M^b has his favourite ἔσσεσθαι construction, which in this book is replaced by an accusative epithet of κοσμήτας in the following line. But εὐτοίχων, epithet of κανονισμῶν, reappears as εὐτυπέων with a supralinear variant, εὐτυπέας, that would create a perfect and totally characteristic intralinear parallelism.

Parallelisms are good for complementarity and contrast. 269, for instance, suggests the complementarity of youth and age. Hence they are favoured for rounding off an apodosis in a pithy, aphoristic way. Single-line parallelisms oppose night and day (82), sanity and madness (95), eating and emaciation (166, a particularly strong jingle effect), riches and impoverishment (222). They associate the merchant with his trade (133), the doctor with his drugs (184), and, using chiasmus to shore up the effect, book-end wealth and honour (183 = 228). Two-line parallelisms round off apodoses at 94–5 (mental instability), 165–6 (consumption), 254–5 (modes of violent death), and there is a pathetic anaphora of οὐδέ in 47–8 for the familial delights from which the childless are excluded, followed by a sting in the tail.

Among the most distinctive charts in this book are those of the medical group, and the stylistic ambition which is plain enough from the poet's fascination with gore turns out to be underscored by syntactic and metrical parallelism as well. The rheumatic and dropsical are shackled together at 154–5 (τεύχει), a trick the poet repeats for the water-workers of 84–5 (ῥέζει): perhaps it appealed to a taste for watery pathos. The lunatics get a little treat in 94–5, a chiasmus followed by a Leonine jingle, which Koechly's transposition of l. 94 would obscure. The leprous enjoy a sophisticated little sequence in 53–5, with an accusative–main-verb construction in the first two lines that shifts to a participle and dative in the third, while retaining an accusative noun at the beginning of the line. And the consumptives are rounded off with a nice couplet (165–6) consisting of two lines each of which contains a parallelism with a particularly strongly marked jingle in the second line, but together form a kind of chiasmus of sense (spiritual/corporeal/corporeal/spiritual). As for metre, repeated patterns are more or less obvious according to whether inner metric corresponds, as well as outer (in other words, whether the pattern of caesurae matches the mere run of dactyls and spondees). Parallelism is used to close the apodosis (156–7, dropsy), or lead into the sting in the tail (53–4, leprosy; 164–5, consumption), or hold together items in the protasis (185–6, miscarriage), or even to provide an overlap between protasis and apodosis (51–2, leprosy;[39]

---

[39] At risk of overreading there is even a parallel here between 'seeing the light' and going down to Hades, the un-seen.

187–8, miscarriage). Indeed, the whole run of 253–5 (on violent death) plus 256 (the first line of the next chart) is held together by outer metric, but only the first two lines share a caesura; 254–5, the couplet which is the more obviously syntactical parallel, do not.

Can we identify this style with any specific poets that Koechly distinguished in this book, or, to rephrase the question, can we use stylistics to confirm Koechly's apportionment of the book among different poets? But stylistics only confirms the separate identity of poets we already knew to be distinct, i.e. M^b from the rest of the book. Otherwise, the poet who produces a list of the kinds of leader severally engendered by the planets in 100–5 (D) holds his list together with parallelisms across (100–1, 103, 105) and within (104) lines, together with a midway sting in the tail (102). Poet B (he of the *schetliasmos* and 'why sacrifice') is indistinguishable in this respect from A—unless one wanted to argue (not impossibly) from the sheer persistence and concentration of his efforts that he is more like A than A himself. The Mars passage presents a series of loose parallelisms, marked at line-beginning (anaphora in 140–1, 143–4, 146–7) or end (139–41 with metrically identical datives plural; 142–3 with main verbs parallel in sense and syntax; 147–8 with main verbs parallel in syntax), with 143 sharing in both the pattern of the line before and that of the line after, and a sting in the tail in 149 to round off 146–8 (and the whole). Again, from the 'why sacrifice' passage, consider the parallelism in 205, the Leonine hexameter in 207, and the buttonholing anaphora of Τίπτε μάτην in 196–7. Astrological poetry does develop a house style, it is true, but these devices reinforce the evidence of diction to suggest that Koechly's hubbub of poets might be reduced to a much smaller number. And as we have seen, the parallelistic style is also more characteristic of the pentameters of this book than they are of the fragments of Anubion himself. They suggest that if there ever was a hypothetical Anubionic underlay, this was a way the poet asserted his own stylistic 'ownership' of the material.

Note: Separate from artfully designed parallelism is the unthinking repetition of words that share the same root. This book is as oblivious as others to casual recurrence:

81–2 οὗτοι γὰρ καὶ νυκτὸς ἀγρυπνητῆρες ἐόντες | νύκτα μὲν ἐργάζονται
184 ἤπια φάρμακ᾽ ἔχοντας, ἀνώδυνα φαρμάσσοντας
297–8 ῥεκτῆρας χρυσοῖο καὶ Ἰνδογενοῦς ἐλέφαντος | ἐργοπόνους ῥέζει (absent from 4.149–50)
315–20 ἔν τε βίᾳ θάνατον λείψει…318 βίον αἵματι λείψει…320 πνεῦμά θ᾽ ἑὸν λείψουσι (~ 4.487–90 ἐκλείψουσιν…λείψουσι, but aggravated by the poet of the first book, since 318 is imported from 4.50).

1.6. METRE

Two sets of figures are given, distinguished in the tables below by (i) and (ii):

(i) For A + E (except 360) = 198 lines.
(ii) For the whole book, with the following exclusions: the two doublets, 58–61 (60 is corrupt) and 96–7 (which contains two peculiarities); M^b (286–338) = 198 + 84 = 282 lines.

Outer Metric

In addition to the exclusions above, I omit 41 (corrupt). At 141 I scan ἐϋρρείθροις rather than εὐρείθροις.

Hexameter Schemes

	no.		%	
	(i)	(ii)	(i) *ex* 198	(ii) *ex* 282
5D				
DDDDD	31	49	15.66	17.38
4D, 1S				
SDDDD	28	42	14.14	14.89
DSDDD	26	36	13.13	12.77
DDSDD	8	11	4.04	3.9
DDDSD	16	23	8.08	8.16
DDDDS	3	4	1.52	1.42
3D, 2S				
SSDDD	12	16	6.06	5.67
SDSDD	8	10	4.04	3.55
SDDSD	15	21	7.56	7.44
SDDDS	8	9	4.04	3.19
DSSDD	5	8	2.53	2.84
DSDSD	12	16	6.06	5.67
DSDDS	5	7	2.53	2.48
DDSSD	1	1	0.5	0.35
DDSDS	—	1		
2D, 3S				
SSSDD	5	7	2.53	2.48
SSDSD	8	12	4.04	4.25
SSDDS	3	4	1.52	1.42
SDSSD	2	2	1.01	0.71
SDSDS	1	2	0.5	0.71
DSSDS	1	1	0.5	0.35

Of 32 possible schemes, 20 or 21 occur, of which the eight most popular are:

	(i)		(ii)
DDDDD	15.66		17.38
SDDDD	14.14		14.89
DSDDD	13.13		12.77
DDDSD	8.08		8.16
SDDSD	7.56		7.44
SSDDD	6.06		5.67
DSDSD	6.06		5.67
DDSDD/SDDDS/SSDSD	4.04	SSDSD	4.25

Every combination of 4D except DDDDS occurs in the top four. The top eight (or in practice the top ten in (i)) account for 82.81% or 76.23% of the poem. The former figure is a similar proportion to that in the Homeric poems,[40] while the latter is very close to M^d and then Maximus. The absent schemes are: DDDSS; DDSSS, DSSSD, DSDSS; SDDSS; DSSSS; SDSSS; SSDSS; SSSDS; SSSSD, SSSSS (except in the suspect line 60). The only runs of the same pattern longer than two lines are: DDDDD at 253–6, 277–9, and SDDDD at 166–9. Some short runs reinforce syntactic parallelisms, though the fact that some straddle protasis and apodosis (or even reach into the next chart, as in 166–9) gives pause for thought about intentionality. See p. 163.

Ratios and Percentages

1. Dactyls to spondees (i. 236)

Numbers (i) out of 990 feet	%	Numbers (ii) out of 1410 feet	%
717 : 273	72.42 : 27.58	1032 : 378	73.19 : 28.81
Dactyls per verse:	3.62	3.66	

2. Dactylic feet per line (i. 236)

Percentages of lines with n dactylic feet:

	(i)	(ii)
5	15.66	17.38
4	40.91	41.14
3	33.32	31.86
2	10.1	10.39

---

[40] Nieto Ibáñez, 231.

3. Percentages of spondaic feet by position in line (i. 237–8)

	(i)	(ii)
1	45.45	44.31
2	38.89	37.93
3	15.66	14.89
4	27.27	26.58
5	10.6	9.57

4. Distribution of metra in line by numbers of dactyls in line (i. 238–9)

Four dactyls	(i)	(ii)
	(% ex 81)	(% ex 116)
SDDDD	34.57	36.21
DSDDD	32.1	31.03
DDSDD	9.88	9.48
DDDSD	19.75	19.83
DDDDS	3.7	3.45
Three dactyls	(% ex 66)	(% ex 89)
SDDSD	22.73	23.26
SSDDD	18.18	17.98
DSDSD	18.18	17.98
Two dactyls	(% ex 20)	(% ex 28)
SSDSD	40	42.86
SSSDD	25	25
SSDDS	15	14.29

5. Location of successive spondees (i. 239)

With two successive spondees:

	(i)	(ii)
1 + 2	14.14	13.82
2 + 3	5.55	5.67
3 + 4	1.52	1.06
4 + 5	—	—

With three successive spondees:

	(i)	(ii)
1 + 2 + 3	2.53	2.48
2 + 3 + 4	—	—
3 + 4 + 5	—	—

Discussion of 1–5

In terms of dactylicity, figures of 72.42% or 73.19% of dactyls, and averages of 3.62 or 3.66 dactylic feet per verse, place this book second in the Manethoniana, behind M^b, and also behind Dorotheus, Maximus, and 'Antiochus'. The favourite hexameter scheme is DDDDD (15.66% or 17.38%), which tells the same story. The second commonest, SDDDD (14.14% or 14.89%), is more distinctive, and more popular than in any other astrological poet (it is the outright favourite pattern in the third book, but with fewer overall instances; other astrological poets favour DSDDD over SDDDD).[41] Indeed, it is striking that this book has more spondees in the first foot than any other astrological poet, even though it is more dactylic in general than they are (the figure of 45.45% or 44.31% is followed closely by M^d's 44.54%, but the first book is far more dactylic than the fifth). This is compensated by the notable drop-off in spondees in the second, third, and fourth feet. Parallels can be found in imperial poetry, yet it remains an unusual pattern.[42]

In the second, third, and fourth feet the poet or poets adhere to the norm whereby 2, 4, and 3 have decreasing percentages of spondees. Absolute figures (38.89/37.93%, 27.27/26.58%, and 15.66/14.89% respectively) are perhaps closest to those of the *Iliad*. Among astrological poets his closest counterpart, although there is a sizeable gap in the second foot, is Maximus (45.51%, 27.73%, and 12.23%), with the consequence that the pattern for the location of two successive spondees in the line (i. 239, Table 5) is also closest to that of Maximus. A low number of spondees in the third foot should, and does, correlate with a low number of masculine caesurae, and the first book's figures for both third-foot spondees (15.66/14.89%) and for masculine caesurae are the second-lowest among all astrological poets, trailing only Maximus.

6. *Spondeiazontes*

There is a total in (i) of 21 = 10.6%, to which (ii) adds a further 6 = 9.57%.[43] The popularity of the spondeiazon was not necessarily to be predicted from the other trends in the verse. The rate is over twice that of M^b (4.65%), and falls behind only Maximus (12.07%); as an absolute figure it comes close to that of Dionysius the Periegete (10.39%).

As usual, it is participles (42, 134, 138, 184, 189, 190, 192, 227, 230, 238) and main verbs (24, 39, 49, 82, 87, 95, 142, 148, 244) that account for most examples (otherwise nouns: 2, 15, 162, 172, 200, 228; pronouns: 215). All but two (96 and 148) consist of a tetrasyllable preceded by bucolic diaeresis, and of these the

---

[41] A range of comparative figures in Nieto Ibáñez, 220–1 and 222: Gregory, Theocritus, Quintus, and Dionysius (in decreasing order) are higher.

[42] For comparisons, see i. 237, Table 3; Ludwich 1885, 327–9; Magnelli, 61; Nieto Ibáñez, 240 and 241. The first foot outdistances the second in spondaicity in Quintus, Dionysius, and Oppian; and in 'Dorotheus' (i.e. from the Bodmer Papyrus) and Eudocia (Agosti and Gonnelli, 313) by far more dramatic margins than here (respectively about 16% and 14%). The most similar absolute numbers are found in *Or. Sib.* 8, with 42.7% and 37.6% respectively.

[43] (i): 24, 42, 49, 82, 87, 95, 134, 138, 162, 172, 184, 189, 190, 192, 215, 227, 228, 230, 238, 240, 244. (ii): 2, 15, 39, 142, 148, 200.

latter consists (with Koechly's emendation, accepted in my text) of a compound verb (ἀνεσταύρωσας), as in similar cases in M^b; the former is one of the reasons the couplet in which it stands is suspect. Of the tetrasyllables, all but eight (95, 134, 138, 184, 190, 192, 227, 238) begin with a vowel.

As for the composition of the rest of the line, all are accompanied by a fourth-foot dactyl (the only exception being 60, one of the lines I have excluded). Six stand in lines with two dactyls (2, 24, 42, 138, 148, 189), a generally disfavoured pattern. There is a strong pattern in (i) for spondeiazontes *not* to be accompanied by a masculine caesura, with six times as many feminine as masculine (the latter only in 42, 189, and 215, i.e. in 14.29% of cases). This is completely different from other Manethonian poets, and from Dorotheus, where there is a mild-to-significant preference for masculine, and from Maximus, where the type of caesura more or less matches their incidence in the poem as a whole.[44] ('Antiochus' has too few to make comparison worthwhile.) Given 85.71% of spondeiazontes with feminine caesurae in (i) and 67.45% in lines in (i) overall, there is an approximately 27% *increased* likelihood of spondeiazontes with a feminine accompaniment. This, too, is very distinctive. Including the extra sections (2, 15, 39, 142, 148, 200) dilutes the effect, and brings the number of spondeiazontes with masculine caesurae (29.63%) closer to the average for (ii) as a whole (33.57%), though still below it.

Only four spondeiazontes occur in pairs (189–90; 227–8). The second of these ends its chart, and a further seven single lines round off theirs (49, 82, 95, 138, 184, 228, 244). This suggests that the poet is making moderate use of the spondeiazon as a closural device (p. 157).

Inner Metric

Caesurae

	B_1	B_2	No B	C_2
(i) total lines = 212		67.45% (143)	1.89% (4[45])	46.7% (99)
30.66% (65), of which				
$B_1 + C_1$	27.69% (18[46])			
$B_1 + C_2$	46.15% (30)			
$B_1 + C_1 + C_2$	12.31% (8[47])			
Neither	13.85 (9[48])			

---

[44] L. Ruggeri, 'Osservazioni sulla metrica del Περὶ Καταρχῶν di Massimo', in F. Guidetti (ed.), *Poesia delle stelle tra antichità e medioevo* (Pisa, 2016), 337–74, at 343–4.
[45] 46, 88 (overridden by metrical word), 219, 347.
[46] Taking καί in 132 as not connective.
[47] Metrical words preclude this at 22 and 66, 25, 194, 266 [otherwise $B_1 + C_1$]; 224, 252 [otherwise $B_1 + C_2$].
[48] C_1 overridden by metrical word at 69.

(ii) total lines = 283[49]

33.57% (95),[50] of which   64.31% (+ 39[51])   2.47% (+ 3[52])   47.35% (+ 35[53])

     $B_1 + C_1$ 25.26% (+ 6[54])
     $B_1 + C_2$ 47.37% (+ 15[55])
     $B_1 + C_1 + C_2$ 13.68% (+ 5[56])
     Neither   13.68% (+ 4[57])

Discussion

1. The figures for B_1 are very low, and for B_2 very high. These figures are the stand-out item here. The book has the highest incidence of B_2 in the Manethonian corpus (67.45/64.31%), almost identical to that of Maximus (67.43%). The figure for this book vis-à-vis that of the fourth might seem surprising in a book which is generally less dactylic, but that is because the higher incidence of spondees occurs in the first and last feet, and not in the third.

2. As in all three later books, $B_1 + C_2$ is favoured over $B_1 + C_1$.

3. The figure for violations of Meyer's Third Law, which is relatively high (though still only half the figure for M^d), is most comparable to that for the third book. Supplements of ⟨τε⟩, which I have not accepted, designed in themselves to heal hiatus, would bring the numbers down somewhat (to 10.78% and 11.58%). This Law is also violated by 169, a reconstructed hexameter.

4. The number of lines without a third-foot caesura almost doubles (from four to seven) if the sections attributed to poets other than A are included. This has slightly disconcerting, but not conclusive, implications for anyone who wants to reduce the number of strata within the book.

---

[49] That is, excluding 58–61, 96–7, 286–338, and 19 pentameters (i.e. all except 336).

[50] For the 18 lines of prologue + epilogue, B_1 stands at 43.75%. For the 25 lines of B, B_1 stands at 38.46% (for 139–51) and 41.66% (for 196–207). For the 13 lines of C, B_1 stands at 46.15%. Three of the nine lines of F are B_1. For the 6 remaining lines of the *ineptus versificator* (those that I have not reassigned to other categories), B_1 stands at 16.67%.

[51] Prologue + epilogue: 1, 3, 4, 5, 7, 11, 12, 13, 14 (B_2 stands at 50%). B: first extract: 139, 140, 142, 143, 144, 145, 147, 150 (B_2 stands at 61.54%); second extract: 196, 197, 198, 202, 203, 205, 207 (B_2 stands at 58.33%). C: 36, 177, 179, 353, 354, 356, 357 (B_2 stands at 53.85%). D: 100, 101, 105. F: 277, 279, 280, 282, 284 (B_2 stands at 55.55%). [*Ineptus*: 59, 61, 96 (B_2 stands at 41.16%).]

[52] Prologue + epilogue: 6, 359. F: 281.

[53] Prologue + epilogue: 2, 8, 9, 14, 15, 360. B: 16, 17; first extract: 139, 140, 142, 144, 145, 146, 149, 150, 151 (C_2 stands at 69.23%); second extract: 197, 200, 201, 203, 207 (C_2 stands at 41.67%). C: 35, 36, 176, 178, 354, 355 (C_2 stands at 46.15%). D: 101, 102, 104. F: 277, 280, 283, 285 (C_2 stands at 33.33%). [*Ineptus*: 58, 60(?), 61, 96, 97 (C_2 stands at 83.33%).]

[54] Prologue: 10. B: 199, 206. C: 34, 358. D: 103.

[55] Prologue + epilogue: 2, 8, 360. B: 16, 146, 149, 151; 200, 201. C: 35, 178. D: 102, 104. F: 283, 285. [*Ineptus*: 58, 60(?), 97.]

[56] Prologue + epilogue: 9, 15. B: 17. C: 176, 355.   [57] B: 141, 148; 204. F: 278.

5. The figure for C_2 is highest in the Manethonian corpus, much higher than M^a (26.26%–34%), and closest to Maximus (45.33%). Yet that is to say only that it reaches the Homeric norm (West 1982, 154: also 47%): the incidence of C_2 in astrological poetry is in general low, and Dorotheus (50.54%) is the only poet who exceeds the Homeric rate. Further instances of C_2 are prevented by a metrical word in 246, 257, 261, 275, and there is elision across it in 188.

6. Violations of Naeke's Law occur in (i) in 6.06% of lines with C_2,[58] or 2.83% of the total lines. They occur in (ii) in 5.99% of lines with C_2,[59] or 3.18% of the total lines. Three of the six instances in (i) involve proper names (Ζεύς, Σελήνη). Observance of Naeke's Law is at levels most similar to Dorotheus; there is a general pattern for all poets other than M^a to be more or less heedful of this constraint.

7. 14.14% of lines with C_2 in (i), or in 17.91% (ii) are combined with a third-foot spondee.[60] This constitutes an insignificant variation on the respective averages (15.66%, or 14.89%) of all lines with all types of caesura. This is unsurprising: no Manethonian poet is responsive to this Hellenistic fashion.

8. There are runs of B_2, inevitable when B_2 is so frequent, for instance six at 48–53, 183–8, 260–5, seven at 161–7, eight at 26–33. There is a run of six C_2 at 85–90, five at 180–4 and 186–90, nine at 223–31.

Word-Break and the Second Foot

The first percentage is for all lines; the second is with grammatical words only.

		(i)	(ii)
Meyer I	7 (5 + 2)([61])	3.3% (2.36%)	2.47% (1.77%)
Meyer II	2([62])	0.94%	0.71%
Meyer I and II	2 (1 + 1)([63])	0.94% (0.47%)	0.71% (0.35%)
Meyer I or II	4 (5)	2.36%	1.77%
Giseke	—		
Hilberg	—[64]		
Giseke & Hilberg	—		
Giseke *or* Hilberg	—		

---

[58] 6/99 (129, 173, 182, 225, 262, 272).   [59] 9/134 (above, + 97, 150, 360).

[60] That is, 42, 71, 73, 88, 93, 110, 125, 160, 189, 224, 226, 231, 237, 247 + 2, 9, 17, 104, 151, 176, 178, 200, 201, 355.

[61] Grammatical words: 87 ἢ παρύγροισι, 112 ἣν δ' ἀκτῖνα, 118 πάντα γυναικὸς, 135 ἕκτον ἔχοντι; 269 ἐν νεότητι. Metrical words: 49 στειρώδεις γὰρ; 97 νικᾶται γὰρ.

[62] 97, 135. Saved by metrical word: 54 ἀμφὶ δέμας.

[63] Grammatical words: 135 ἕκτον ἔχοντι τόπον. Metrical words: 97 νικᾶται γὰρ Ἄρης. Both violations of Meyer II involve a technical word or proper name.

[64] Saved by metrical word: 219 καὶ δόξαι καὶ.

Already in (i) these numbers are low, fairly comparable to Dorotheus, and including (ii) does not produce any more cases. The fact that the small number of violations of Meyer I consists mostly of grammatical words does not suggest that the poet is indifferent to the rule: it suggests that he tries to steer clear of violating it altogether, and exceptions are so exceptional that they might as well be the one thing as the other. Notable, given this indication of punctiliousness, is that the grammatical words are mostly not accounted for by technical terms (only 87 ἢ παρύγροισι, unless 112 ἢν δ' ἀκτῖνα also counts); it is the other way round with Dorotheus.

Bulloch's Law

Excluding those involving a copula, disjunctive etc. in the medial position, there are five examples (88, 117, 135, 168, 169), with (ii) contributing a sixth (16). Three have a sense-pause at C_2 (16, 117, 168), two at B_1 (169, 135). All have a third-foot caesura save 88, where it is bridged by a metrical word. This line, which lacks a sense-pause at either of the requisite places, and 169, which lacks C_2, are non-compliant; the second is a reconstructed hexameter. In other words, very few cases present themselves, and the poet is mostly compliant in those that do.

Hermann's Bridge

The only example in (i) occurs with a metrical word: 69 τιμήν τε. (ii) adds 278 κατὰ μοῖραν, from F, a technical term. Koechly's emendation at 148 μετέωρον (which I have accepted) would add one to B. 169, suspect anyway, is rescued by the disjunctive.

Tiedke's Law

There are three anapaestic violations in (i) (21 ἕνεκεν, a preposition, but one that exceeds the *tre more* limit, 47 κατέχουσ'; 92 καθέτου, a technical term), to which (ii) adds a couple more (10 σφετέρων, B: 206 ῥοθίων[65]). There are six spondaic violations, all in (i)[66] (43 τεύχουσ'; 74 τούτοις; 64, 109 Μήνην; 122 καλὴν, epithet of Ἀφροδίτην; 273 ἠδέ, a copula, but exceeding *tre more*), making eleven in all. That makes 4.25% of lines affected in (i), and 3.89% in (ii). The conditions which disinhibit other poets about breaking this law (the use of proper names and of technical terms) do not seem to have disinhibited this

---

[65] Saved by metrical word: 4, 359 ἀπλανῶν τε; 97 ὑπὸ αὐγαῖς.
[66] In (ii), saved by metrical word: 281 Τιτὰν δέ.

one, for numbers are low, and liable proper names are otherwise 'rescued' by metrical words.[67] In general, the pattern across the Manethoniana with Tiedke's Law is somewhat similar to that for Naeke's Law, i.e. a happy-go-lucky approach in M^a which is not shared by any other poet; book 1 lies between M^b and M^d in this regard.

Tetracola

There are ten full tetracola in (i) (4.72%, or 1 every 21.2 lines),[68] to which (ii) adds another example (2) (3.89%, or 1 every 25.73 lines). This is similar to Maximus (4.92), and the second highest number in the Manethonian corpus after M^b. Only two are in protases (115, 208). Another two or three are closural (183 = 228; 172). The first of these adds pomp and circumstance to the bigwigs it describes (and the double tetracolon at 227–8 amplifies the *gravitas* for these priestly personages). 172 is an asyndetic list; the accumulation mimics the effect of piling woe on woe. Of the rest, 164 has obvious pathetic effect in the medical chart on consumptives, which also contains a number of 'near-misses' (163, if δή is allowed as a metrical word; 165; 160, with two metrical words). 31 and 260 are fairly similar, both courting a sense of pathos and atrocity for sexual crime (respectively lesbianism and wife-murder). The others are 238 (dream interpreters) and 2, where it is a suitably momentous opening, whoever wrote the line.

The effect of including additional appositives is precisely the same as in M^b: that is, percentages shoot up to the extent that it casts doubt on the value of the exercise. Allowing one appositive brings (i) an additional 31 (19.34%, or 1 every 5.17 lines), and (ii) an additional seven (17.31%, or 1 every 5.78 lines). Allowing two brings (i) a further 24 (30.67%, or 1 every 3.26 lines), and (ii) a further 5 (27.56%, or 1 every 3.69 lines). Allowing three brings (i) a further five (33.02%, or 1 every 3.03 lines), and (ii) a further three (30.39%, or 1 every 3.29 lines). Allowing four adds a further one each. There is no point in calculating further.

Final Monosyllables

Three examples, all from (ii), and all preceded by tetrasyllables: 149 ἡλοπαγὴς χείρ, 150 αἰγίοχος Ζεύς (B), 176 αἰθέριος λίψ (C). The first and third have the ⏑⏑ | — ⏑⏑ — | — rhythm, but not the second.

---

[67] 27 Μήνη δέ; 119 Ἄρης τε; 217b; 220; 267 Φαίνων τε; the other example is 179 ἐὴν πάτρην.
[68] 31, 115, 164, 172, 183 = 228, 208, 227, 238, 260.

Prosody

Muta cum Liquida

(i) has 79 instances, including 13 in the elegiac sections; (ii) has 111.

Discussion

The most distinctive feature of the first book's prosody is the profile produced by the treatment of *muta cum liquida*. Apart from a low incidence of word-boundary position in the *princeps* (comparable to M^b, M^d, and 'Antiochus'), there are comparable rates of correption at word-boundary, and position and correption internally, with each category accounting for about a third of instances. The most similar profile to this is that of M^b, especially in respect of their percentages for word-internal position and correption. M^b falls slightly behind on word-boundary correption, which is highest among the Manethoniana in this book, though nowhere near the extreme of 'Antiochus'. It is especially accounted for by $Kρον$-, to an even greater extent than in other poets (in (i), 10/17 or 11/21 instances, which gives one instance every 21.2 or 19.27 lines). But in general, M^c and M^b belong in similar territory, and differ

Table 3. *Muta cum liquida* in M^c

Word-boundary		Internal	
position	correption	position	correption
(i) 2.53%	24.05/29.11%	35.44%	37.97/32.91%
princeps: 2.53%[1]	◡|◡: 21.52/26.58%[2]	princeps: 32.91%[3]	◡|◡: 26.58/21.52%[4]
biceps —	◡◡|: 2.53%[5]	biceps: 2.53%[6]	◡◡|: 11.39%[7]
(ii) 1.8%	23.42/27.92%	42.33%	32.43/27.93%
princeps: 1.8%	◡|◡: 20.72/25.22%[8]	princeps: 38.74%[9]	◡|◡: 21.62/17.12[10]
biceps —	◡◡|: 2.7%[11]	biceps: 3.6%[12]	◡◡|: 10.81[13]

[1] 71, 273 (would count as word-internal in a metrical word, but ἠδέ exceeds *tre more*).
[2] 17 or 21 instances, depending on 189, 263; 91, 346. The majority involve $Kρον$-.
[3] 26 cases.
[4] 21 or 17 cases, depending on 189, 263; 91, 346.
[5] 2 cases (218; 37).
[6] 2 cases (106; 361).
[7] 9 cases.
[8] Prologue, epilogue: 4, 6, 359. Also treatable as word-internal: 5. B: 203. C: 353, 356. Total: 7 or 6.
[9] Prologue, epilogue: 2, 5, 8, 11*bis*, 12, 13, 14. B: 17; 143, 145, 148, 151. C: 35, 354. D: 101. F: 283. Total: 17.
[10] Prologue and epilogue: 4,359. Also treatable as word-boundary: 5.
[11] B: 197.
[12] Prologue and epilogue: 9. C: 179. [Also 60.]
[13] Prologue and epilogue: 13. B: 199, 202.

strikingly from the massive disproportions in favour of internal position found in M^a, Maximus, and (especially) Dorotheus. The higher this disproportion, the closer a poet comes to Homeric practice. With their tolerance or mild preference for internal correption, which tends to be elicited over and over again in the same situations (Κύπρις in 30, 45, 121, 246, 256, Ἀφροδίτη in 122, 235, cf. 127, τετράγωνος in 122, 236; also ἀλλοτρ-, πατρ-; Dorotheus goes the opposite way, and avoids Ἀφροδίτη), the first and fourth books are not like this at all. Their figure is similar to that of 'Antiochus', who disfavours internal position still more strikingly.

For comparison, in Table 4 I present the figures for the elegiac portions of M^c (the pentameters themselves, 208–14, and 341–52), and for Anubion (F 1–10). Respectively they yield 13 and 39 examples of *muta cum liquida*. They show marked differences, especially in regard to word-internal position in the princeps and word-internal correption in both princeps and biceps: see pp. 279–80.

Table 4. *Muta cum liquida* in elegiacs

Word-boundary position	correption	Internal position	correption
Eleg. princeps: —	ᴗ|ᴗ: 15.38/30.78%[1]	princeps: 23.08%[2]	ᴗ|ᴗ: 38.46/23.08%[3]
biceps: —	ᴗᴗ|: 7.69%[4]	biceps: 7.69%[5]	ᴗᴗ|: 7.69%[6]
Anub. princeps: 0 or 2.56%	ᴗ|ᴗ: 10.26/12.82%	princeps: 46.15/43.59%	ᴗ|ᴗ: 12.82/10.26%
biceps: 0 or 5.13%	ᴗᴗ|: —	biceps: 10.26/5.13%	ᴗᴗ|: 20.51%

[1] 212, 351. Also treatable as word-internal: 91, 346.
[2] 91, 99, 128.
[3] 341, 344, 346. Also treatable as word-boundary: 91, 346.
[4] 37.
[5] 361.
[6] 361.

Hiatus

Hiatus after the *princeps* is so rare as to make it impossible to generalise about individual poets' usage. In 25 χαλεπῇ ἐπὶ κύπριδι (4th foot), it occurs in the n *x* N prepositional phrase pattern, which exposes a case-ending to the initial vowel of the following preposition; in 235 ᾗ Ἀφροδίτη the planetary name may smooth the licence.[69] Both occur in A. There are also two instances mid-pentameter (91 -ει ἤ-, 336 -η οἴ-), an eventuality not found in the fragments of Anubion. Including all of them produces a total in AE of one instance per 49.5

---

[69] For what it is worth, these constitute 2/22 = 9.09% instances of final η/ῆ/ῇ in the portions of the book I assign to AE.

lines, a figure most comparable to that of the second book (50.2) and, after that, to Dorotheus (43.33). This enables the reflection that prosody is not something that comes as a bundle: two poets may have very similar practices in some respects and entirely different ones in others. In respect of *muta cum liquida*, Dorotheus behaves completely differently, and yet is comparable on this criterion.

Hiatus occurs after a contracted biceps in the third foot in 106, 171 (A); 141, [203 reading Ἄρη], 204 (B); and 321 (M^b). In all cases ⟨τε⟩ has been proposed to remedy it, but, like Gerhard, who discountenanced these stopgaps, I have not adopted them.

Finally, there are instances within an uncontracted biceps in 282 Κερόεσσα ἐπ' [corr. Gerhard, al.], and after an uncontracted biceps in 16 Ἄρεα, Ἑρμέα, 97 ὑπὸ αὐγαῖς, 178 ἐγκλήματα ἢ [corr. Spitzner], 187 ἀνηλέϊ ἢ, 198 ἴσχεο· οὐ, 270 ἀνώμαλα ἔργα.

Elision

1. Parts of speech

Nouns   (i) 2 [184 φάρμακ', 233 πήματ']
Adjectives   (i) 1 [188 μινυνθάδι']; (ii) 2 [adding 10 μέγ']
Pronouns   (ii) 1 [151 σ']
Main verbs (i) 6 [43 τεύχουσ', 47 κατέχουσ', 113 μίσγοντ', 149 τέτατ', 195 ἔσσετ', 231 ῥέζουσ'];
                (ii) 7 [adding 360 δότ'; from *ineptus*, 60 ἄπτοντ']
Adverbs   (i) 3 [186 ἔτ', 221*bis* ἔσθ' + ὅτ']; (ii) 4 [adding 12 μάλ']

The rate of elision in (i) is thus once every 16.5 lines, or 6.06 every hundred lines; this is most comparable to M^d (16.15) but also, more reassuringly, similar to Maximus (14.19). The specific rate of elision of main verbs is most comparable to that of the poet of book 2.

2. Location in the line

	(i)	(ii)
2	149vb, 231part	[60vb]
3.5	184n	
5	113vb	
5.5		360vb
6	186adv	12adv
8	188adj	
9	43vb, 47vb, 221adv	
9.5	195vb, 221adv, 233n	10adj
10		151prn

Lengthening

142 ὑπὸ πυρὸς [ὑπαὶ H^h, D'Orville]
175 (pentameter) τοῦτον L [τούτων D'Orville; cf. Ludwich 1904, 132–3]
273 Ἄρεος [Ἄρεως A.-R.]
332 θάνατον (θανάτους Axtius)
359 οὐράνιος (οὐράνιός γ' vel οὐρανίων Axtius)

Summary and Final Implications

In general this book makes a good impression. For comparisons one finds oneself looking soonest to Dorotheus and/or Maximus, to the former in terms of the percentage of the poem dominated by the top eight schemes (A = 82.81%, compared with 81.17%), to the latter in the range of the eight most favoured hexameter schemes (A = 15.66%–4.04%, compared with 16.31%–4.08%), in the proportion of the poem accounted for by the three top schemes (A = 42.93%, compared with 42.57%), in the percentage of lines with no more than one spondee (A = 56.57%, compared with 57.91%), in the numbers of spondees in the third through fifth feet, and in the distribution of adjacent spondees. And in inner metre, it is again most comparable to Maximus in respect of feminine caesurae; bucolic diaeresis; and the use of tetracola. Adherence to Naeke's Law and to rules concerning word-break in the second foot are particularly similar to Dorotheus. It will be worth bearing all this in mind in the analysis of the metre of the fifth book.

As for what this implies for the book's internal composition, one can ask the question two ways round. First, does metre support Koechly's assignation of different segments of the book to different poets? Conversely, are there any particular metrical features which are potential discriminators between different segments?

To take the second question first, some potential discriminators noted above include the rate of spondeiazontes with masculine caesurae; the tolerance of hiatus; and violations of Hermann's Bridge. On the other hand, the incidence of the feminine caesura is not as decisive as it might have been. The rate is very high in (i) (AE). Adding the extra sections brings it down somewhat, but rates in the extra sections are still on the high side (see n. 53).

To take the first question:

(i) Koechly would make his poet B violate Hermann's Bridge in 148. (Nothing can be built on the treatment of *muta cum liquida* in 197: this is only very occasional in all poets.)

(ii) Koechly's poet 'F' violates Hermann's Bridge (278) and lacks a third-foot caesura in 281.

(iii) The *ineptus versificator* is a difficult category, and at risk of circularity (bad metre goes into it by default, thus proving the existence of the category). Some of the lines I have reassigned,[70] but among what is left is the wholly spondaic line in 60; a spondeiazon which is not a tetrasyllable in 96 ἀλλ' οὐκ Ἄρην; and, directly following it, the hiatus of 97 ὑπὸ αὐγαῖς.

(iv) The poet of prologue and epilogue twice cancels the third-foot caesura (6, 359), which is either idiosyncrasy or statistical fluke, but perhaps the former in combination with other eccentricities (p. 287, on σφέτερος). He has a lengthening *in arsi* in 359 οὐράνιōς, though it is not without parallel.

In sum, there *are* metrical peculiarities and idiosyncrasies in particular segments of this book, and that is why two sets of figures are presented in this chapter, (i) for the 'core' and (ii) for the sections which are vulnerable to challenge. In practice there is usually little difference between the two sets of figures, but that is because the number of additional lines in (ii) is insufficient to make a big impact, however different their practice. The real problem is in deciding how much weight to assign competing criteria—similarities of diction, on the one hand, which for Koechly were enough to join like with like, and metrical practice, on the other, which sometimes cuts across phraseological likeness. In any case, the underlying model may need to be revised, inasmuch as the old idea of separate contributors who can be teased apart like cell cultures in a petri dish no longer suits what we can see of the practice of astrological poets, how they appropriate and purloin (macrophages might be a more appropriate cellular metaphor). If a poet has inherited material and is trying to 'own' it, how likely is he to retain lines that conflict with his own metrical preferences? The lines shared between books 4 and 1 are a case study in the kinds of manipulation that occur; small tweaks occur throughout, though metrical differences are, for some reason, concentrated in the last three charts, with most of the

---

[70] In lines I have reassigned to B, 16 Ἄρεα, Ἑρμέα, Ζῆνα, exhibits both hiatus and prosodic licence, but the latter is Dorothean (i. 232 n. 3; p. 381), and the former is perhaps occasioned by the exceptional nature of the list.

irregularities in the first book.[71] They are compatible with the generally degraded condition of the text in M^c, though 1.335-6 complicatedly combines textual degradation in 335 with an apparently sound pentameter in 336.

In short, the idea that eight poets are separable in this book seems hard to sustain, even on Koechly's own method. In this section an attempt has been made to strike a workable balance between proceeding as if the traditional technical methods of scholarship could establish, with a reasonable degree of likelihood, who wrote what (in other words, as if authorship were a meaningful notion), and the *de facto* situation that in astrology things are a good deal more complicated. On the former principle, it is not unreasonable to distinguish the poet of the prologue, F, and the most intractable lines of the *ineptus*, from A, but there are insufficient grounds to distinguish A from C, D, or E. M^b is a separate matter.

1.7. NARRATOR AND ADDRESSEE

This book is more complex than others because of its apparently different strata.

In the proem the narrator addresses Ptolemy, offering him plural books in which he claims to be presenting a version of the work of Petosiris; in the concluding elegiac couplet he rounds off one book and invokes the Muses for aid in composing another in the same metre, i.e. elegiacs. Presumably the narrators are different, with the second representing a straight quotation of Anubion (if anything is straight in this book). They *have* to be different if l. 13, which refers to hexameters, is not an interpolation. De Stefani's theory that ll. 11–15 of the proem were once upon a time also elegiac and go back to Anubion would ultimately imply a complex set-up if it also accepted and tried to accommodate the closing couplet (on which, after all, much of the evidence for Anubion is grounded). It would imply that a frame established the didactic relationship between sage and king and then that *within* that fiction the poet invoked the traditional Muse–poet relationship, which, if the speaker in the final couplet is still supposed to be an Egyptian sage, seems to me at any rate to tax cultural credibility. So is 360-1 a *different* Anubion from the hypothetical Anubion of 11–15? The theory involves too many complications.

---

[71] Lengthening in 1.332 θάνατον ~ 4.407 θανάτους; hiatus in 1.321 καὶ Ἄρεος, unlike 4.395; 1.337 ἢ ὑπὸ ~ 4.412 ἢ διὰ (but 1.328 ἦν ἰσόμοιρος ~ 4.403 ᾖ ἰσόμοιρος). Also crasis in 1.333 κἀκ, unlike 4.408 δ' ἐκ.

312   *The Later Books of Manetho*

After the proem, the pattern does not seem markedly different from that of M^a or M^b, at least at first sight. Narrator and addressee are minimally present. Nevertheless, within Koechly's poet A there are two tiny interventions which exceed M^a's norm, namely an additional stipulation built into the first with 'if you see' (73 αἴ κεν ἴδηαι), and an example of the 'be very afraid' motif (p. 171) (1.250 δείμαινε, cf. 1.51 μὴ Κρόνῳ ἀντήσειε). Both features are also found in the fifth book (pp. 358-9). And in the run of elegiacs towards the end there is at least one and probably two imperatives ('know', 'forecast') in the style of Anubion (1.345 νόει, 348 †εσειτε†, perhaps corrupt for ἔννεπε), which is consistent with other indications of the Anubionic character of this section (p. 277).

1.8. ASTROLOGICA

Treatment of Technical Terms

Many are prose terms, not confined to this book in the Manethoniana,[72] but there are also a good few more which are unique to this book.[73] There is a little non-standard usage or catachresis, but no such straining to defamiliarise as we find in the fourth book.[74] Then there are standard poeticisms,[75] and several shared specifically with M^a, which add to the words and phrases the two books have in common in the apodosis (p. 294).[76] But what is distinctive about this

---

[72] ἀρσενικοὶ τόποι (279; 5.209); ἐπεμβαίνειν (115; M^{a,c,d}); ἐπίκεντρος (34, 279, 284; M^{b,c,d}); ἑστάναι, of location (230, 344; M^a); κάθετος (92; 4.45, 132); κατέχειν, with planet as subject and place as object (267; M^a); κεντρωθείς (90, though prose constructs with σύν, as in 5.252, not the dative); λείπειν 'wane' (212; 5.111); μεσουρανεῖν (223, 281; M^{a,c,d}); παρεῖναι σύν (106; M^{a,b,d}); Πλησιφαής (208, 245; M^{c,d}); συνάπτειν (225, 272; M^{a,c,d}); συνεῖναι + dat. (78, 271, 296; M^{a,b,c}); φάσιν λύειν (50; 5.128); ὡρονομεῖν (58, 339, 350; M^{a,b,d}). Also εἰ μή πως (266; 3.253).

[73] ἐναλλάξ (27); ἔχειν τὴν πρᾶξιν (180-1; see n.); ἡμερινὸν/νυκτερινὸν θέμα (283, 278, cf. 3.409 νυκτερινῇ γενέθλῃ; prose would probably use ἐπί); κατὰ μοῖραν (153, 278); κατοπτεύειν (357); μοίρης ἐντὸς ἐοῦσα (272; cf. e.g. Hephaestion, i. 40.1, 'Heliodorus', p. 12.18); πάροδος (353, 357; prose would probably have κατά, ἐπί, ἐν); συμβάλλειν, of synaphe (134, 187); συναντᾶν (208, 245; cf. 3.424 συναντόμενοι); συναφὴν ἐπέχειν (74); τόπον ἔχειν (135; prose, but also Dorotheus, p. 386.12); φωστῆρες (29). Also 353 ἐπ' Ἄρηος τόπον ἔλθοι: cf. e.g. Dorotheus, pp. 338.32-339.1, 382.7, 383.2 ἐλθεῖν εἰς τόπον; 'Valens', CCAG viii/1. 165.19 ἐλθεῖν ἐπὶ τόπου.

[74] νυκτερινός, ἡμερινός, of natives (83, 167); φωσφορεῖν, of Moon phase (65 n.). The context of λείπειν, used of aporrhoia in 158, 210, saves it from confusion with λείπειν 'wane' and ἐκλείπειν 'be eclipsed' (contrast 2.452 προλιποῦσα, 483 ἀποχαζομένη).

[75] Words for aspect: εἰσορᾶν, passim; ἐποπτεύειν (34); καθορᾶν (18; see on 4.362); λεύσσειν (236). Other: κακοεργός (139); ὡρονόμος (30, 90, 116, 262, 282, 347). See also on 185 (ὑπ)ἐκ συνόδοιο, 123 κέντρον ἔχοι.

[76] κερόεσσα as epithet of Mene (1.26, 64, 2.465, 6.44) or Selene (1.271, 6.593, 640 κερόεσσα Σελήνῃ: M^b has ἡ Κερόεσσα as p.n.; M^d does not use it); 1.83 and 6.64 Κρόνος αἰνὸς (also 6.450 in different sedes). See also 5 n. τελέουσιν; 42 n. κοινὴν ὁδὸν ἰθύνοντες; 57 n. ἀπόστροφοι; 65 n. λιποφεγγέα; 75 n. κέντροισιν ἐπὼν; 90 n. κατεναντίον ὡρονόμοιο; 282 n. καθ' ὡρονόμοιο.

book? The poet or poets extend technical vocabulary through the use of synonyms, mostly poetic,[77] and introduce some new constructions, which are usually intuitive enough even if they turn out not to be documented elsewhere in astrology.[78] Perhaps the most striking is a little sub-group in A, which uses confrontational vocabulary for opposition (30 n. κατιθύ; 339 n. κατ' ἰθύν), and especially derivatives of ἀντί which can indeed be used of geographical location (Lightfoot 2014, 81), but which are formulated in such a way as to represent the planets as encountering one another in the style of Homeric antagonists (nn. on 230 καταντίον; 90, 215, 343 κατεναντίον; 24 n. ἀντήσειε(ν), 51). There are other expressions for motion, too, whose poetic antecedents imply personification (42 n. κοινὴν ὁδὸν ἰθύνοντες; 185 n. ὑπὲκ συνόδοιο φυγοῦσαν, for e.g. ἀπὸ συνόδου φέρεσθαι/δρόμον ποιεῖσθαι; 277 n. μέσον πόλον ἀμφιβεβῶσα, where the EGHP model already implied personification of Helios), and the affective metaphors for witnessing and contact in 45 + 351 ἀγκαλίσαιτο (AE) and 124 μαρτυρίην ... ἀμφιβάλοι imply an emotional engagement.

Charts Involving the Malefics and a Phase of the Moon

All books in the corpus except M^b contain charts in which the Moon comes into contact with, or leaves, a malefic. The situation is pregnant with disaster. *Aporrhoia* from a malefic is said by Θ p. 186.8–9 to cause σίνη ἢ πάθη, and the charts that deal with it flesh this out in various ways, whether in terms of mental or of physical harm. From 1.208–14, it appears that Anubion may have treated this kind of chart; this short passage looks like an excerpt from an overview, which concentrated on the nature of the contact (first *synaphe*, then *aporrhoia*, and the additional factor of phase), but is limited to Saturn. There are also isolated hexameter passages in 245–9 and 271–6 which have slightly more circumstantial detail and are less parsimonious about the outcome. But the most interesting charts form a series on illness and physical mishap in which the outcome is developed at gory length.

They deal, in order, with 'elephantiasis' (leprosy), lameness, dropsy, 'internal' diseases including consumption, and finally abortions and miscarriages, which

---

[77] 22 n. κέντρων ... ἄνακτες; 24 n. ἰσόρροπος; 109 n. εἰσβλέψαντος; 186 ὀρνυμένην τε; 344 n. ὑψόθεν; 256, 354 καλοεργός, for ἀγαθοποιός.

[78] διάμετρον ἔχειν (89, 121, cf. also 5.334); τετράγωνον ἰδεῖν (122, 346; prose would be κατὰ τετράγωνον, but there is precedent or analogy in 6.266 διάμετρος ὁρῆται, 4.481 = 1.308 διάμετρος ὁραθῇ); κατέχειν, with place as subject and planet as object (176); φέρεσθαι, of the Moon (158 n.). With λαμβάνειν: 108 συναφὴν ... λάβῃ for 'receive application/contact' (6.79–80, 162, and Apomasar have δέχεσθαι); 112 ἀκτῖνα λάβωσι; 130 κέντρα λαβόντες.

can be treated pathologically, and is so treated for instance by Ptolemy in his chapter on bodily diseases (3.13.10 and 15). They have parallels in Firmicus book 4 (a one-factor catalogue of *synaphe* followed by a two-factor catalogue of *aporrhoia* and *synaphe*), *Π.σ.α.*, which Cumont attributed to the Anonymous Astrologer of 379 and ultimately to Hermes or Petosiris,[79] and in Θ ch. 61, from Καθολικὰ σχήματα περὶ σινῶν καὶ παθῶν. Of these three witnesses the first two are in the form of systematic catalogues, arranged in *heptazonos* order, and although the charts are separated in the current arrangement of the first book it looks very much as if they originally stood together, and in much their present order, which is as follows:

Synaphe (best parallels in Θ, Firmicus): 1.50–7: Waning Moon meets Saturn; 1.134–8: Full (φωσφορέουσα) Moon meets Mars in 6th house
Aporrhoia (best parallels in *Π.σ.α.*, Firmicus): 1.153–7: Moon leaves Saturn κατὰ μοῖραν; 1.158–66: Moon leaves Mars
Aporrhoia + *synaphe* (best parallels in *Π.σ.α.*): 1.185–95: Moon regains light after New, meeting either malefic.

Koechly already saw that they belonged together (1851, l, lv), but he also grouped 229–61 along with them (1851, lii f.). The members of this latter group all concern mental or moral disturbance or other kinds of mishap, involving one or both malefics and the Moon and/or Venus, but while they no doubt derive from the same author they do not strictly belong to the same sequence, nor do they focus on physical disease. Those that remain, however, are in almost exactly the right order for a putative *heptazonos* sequence, save that 134–8 and 153–7 have been reversed. And they are in perfect order if the arrangement were first by *synaphe* and then *aporrhoia*, as in both *Π.σ.α.* and Firmicus, whether the planets were in *heptazonos* or qualitative order. True, the *aporrhoia* charts in *Π.σ.α.* and Firmicus are two-factor (the Moon leaves x and meets y), but the Mars chart in 158–66 strongly implies the presence of Saturn as well, suggesting that a two-factor chart did indeed once underlie it. Also suggestive is that the last three charts are asyndetic, although that does not explain the connective at 1.153.

Σίνος charts of this type can apparently be particularised in various ways; the poet of this sequence has decided to specialise in disease. Some give more than one outcome (154, 160–1), but all latch onto one particular condition and elaborate it. The first begins with a form of the 'be very afraid' motif (1.51;

---

[79] Cumont, *CCAG* viii/1. 181: 'totus sermonis color doctrinam quae hic profertur ex antiquis fontibus haustam esse prodere videtur, fortasse ex Hermete vel Petosiride'. See on 2.443 and 469–70 for parallels within the *synaphe/aporrhoia* catalogue at the end of the second book.

p. 171), which is not restricted to medical literature, but is very appropriate to it (much used by Nicander, and the instance in Maximus, 220-1, is from his section on disease). The baroque treatment some of these charts receive makes them a kind of halfway house between (say) Nicander, for whom accurate description serves a purpose and hence detail is functional, and rhetorical elaboration for its own sake.

Planetary Names and Epithets

Of a total of 214 instances of planetary naming, the order is identical with that of M^a save that Jupiter and Venus are reversed, and the occupancy of the top three positions by the malefics and the Moon is also shared with M^b. After the top three, there is little to choose between the four remaining planets, but Jupiter, for obscure reasons, is considerably more frequent than in other books. As in all four poets, the Sun is in one of the bottom two places.

A similar approach to formulary can be seen as in the other books, with EGHP epithets replaced by new ones (for the Sun, πυραυγής; for Mars, κακοεργός), or EGHP epithets repurposed for planetary purposes (for Venus, ἐϋπλόκαμος; for Mars, κορυθαίολος). ἀνηλεής (Mars) is interesting if the background is indeed Callimachus, and κυανόχρωτος is the most adventurous. Perhaps what deserves most note is that the epithets are mostly not light epithets (except πυραυγής for the Sun and Jupiter's conventional φαέθων). Rather, they refer rather to moral qualities (ἀνηλεής, αἰνός, βλαβερός) or are quasi-anthropomorphic (ἐϋπλόκαμος, καλή, κορυθαίολος, κυανόχρωτος, πολιός; αἰγίοχος too, though this is not a reference to the planet). This tendency might lead one to suspect a connection with Dorotheus, although the only positive detectable connections are κορυθαίολος for Mars and βλαβερός for Saturn, along with κερόεσσα for the Moon (shared with M^a). Little difference can be detected between different parts of the book. Most obviously fall within the sections ascribed to poet A. κορυθαίολος falls to E (75), and is considerably more adventurous than the bland αἰνόν (357) and predicative epithets within the 'purer' section of Anubion at the end. Others replicate (301), or tweak, those shared with M^b (294, 327); 17 (B) ἐϋπλόκαμος is shared with 56 (A); and 139 κακοεργέ (B, the commination of Mars) has its own internal logic as a substitute for Homeric βροτολοιγέ.

Sun

22 instances (10.28%) (21 Helios, 1 Titan), of which two are ornamented (112 πυραυγέος Ἡελίοιο, 204 Ἡελίῳ βασιλῆι).

Moon

37 instances (17.29%) (20 of Μήνη, 15 of Σελήνη, and two of ἡ Κερόεσσα as p.n.), of which three are ornamented (1.26 κερόεσσά τε Μήνη, 271 κερόεσσα Σελήνη; 294 Σεληναίης ἑλικώπιδος).

Mercury

23 instances (10.75%) (22 mythological, one light-name), none of which is ornamented.

Venus

25 instances (11.68%) (4× Ἀφροδίτη, 9× Κύπρις, 5× Παφίη, 7× Κυθήρη or Κυθέρεια), five of which are ornamented (17 Κύπριδά τ' εὐπλόκαμον; 56 εὐπλοκάμου Κυθερείης; 30 θηλυτέρης Κύπριδός; 45 Κύπριν καλήν; 122 καλὴν Ἀφροδίτην).

Mars

42 instances (19.63%) (38 mythological, four light-names), five of which are ornamented (75 κορυθαίολος Ἄρης, 119 Ἄρης τε κραταιός, 263 Ἄρηος... ἀνηλέος, 187 Ἄρεϊ... ἀνηλέϊ; and outside apotelesmata, 139 Ἄρες Ἄρες, κακοεργὲ).

Jupiter

26 instances (12.15%) (16× Ζεύς, 3× Κρονίδης, 7 light-names), two of which are ornamented (1.301 Ζῆνα... φαέθοντα, including 150 αἰγίοχος Ζεύς, not of the planet).

Saturn

39 instances (18.22%) (36 mythological, 3 light-names), of which 8 or perhaps 9 are ornamented (1.45, 180 πολιὸς Κρόνος, 108 πολιοῖο Κρόνοιο; 83 Κρόνος αἰνός, 357 Κρόνον αἰνόν, 187 Κρόνῳ αἰνῷ; 110 Κρόνῳ βλαβερῷ; 327 κυανοχρώτοιο Κρόνοιο; predicative at 351 Κρόνον φίλον, 354 ψυχρὸς ἐών). At 263 ἀνηλέος certainly applies to Mars, but the word-order would allow it to apply to Saturn or to both planets ἀπὸ κοινοῦ, along with δύνοντος.

Book Five

5.1. PRELIMINARIES

The book has attracted little but contempt. Koechly described it as a congeries of poetry and prose, defective and inconsistent in diction and dialect, and was sometimes hesitant to correct the text, so uncertain was he of what he was emending and of what an editor could be supposed to aim for.[1] In his second edition he poured scorn on the compilers of both this and the first book, who left them in such a state;[2] a hundred years later, the Gundels were still making essentially the same complaint (163 'ein unerfreuliches Gewirr von Planetenkonstellationen und Tierkreisaspekten'). Particular parts of the book have also drawn particular ire.[3]

There is no real way of dating it. For Koechly, there was nothing which did not smack of late antiquity,[4] and no later critic has found grounds to disagree. De Stefani finds the style hard to classify, with both late antique features (Chaldaean Oracles, early Byzantine prosody) and echoes of Hellenistic poetry.[5] Massimilla went as far as to put a definite date on the compilation (the fourth century, the same as the first book),[6] although in this case there are no convenient quotations in Hephaestion to produce a *terminus ante quem* (a form of 5.27 is quoted twice, anonymously, in the sixth century by John Philoponus, which proves nothing). I see no details in the text which allow a finer determination. In a few cases, usage suggests a date as late as comfortably possible (109 n. on

---

[1] Koechly 1851, lvi 'multa, in quibus tam aperta deprehenduntur scabrae pravaeque dictionis vestigia, ut vel apertissima vitia corrigere subinde dubites, incertus, num librariorum errores reprimas an ipsius auctoris manui vim inferas... Taedet dictionem bonis malis raris vulgaribus, poeticis prosaicis varie mixtam in singulis excutere, aut formarum dialective inconditam vicissitudinem componere'.

[2] 1858, vii.

[3] W. Kroll, *RE* s.v. Manethon (Astrologe), 1105.27–8 'törichte Verse über Homer als Prophet des Sternglaubens'.

[4] 1851, lvi 'nihil invenitur, quod non recentiora tempora redoleat'.

[5] 2016, 181, and 2017, 25; his alleged example of Hellenistic poetry is Callimachus at 5.172, but Nicander in 185–8 is far more impressive.

[6] 264–5 n. 2.

αὐξιφαής; 137, sigmatic aorist of εὑρίσκειν; perhaps 168 πολλοῖσι μίτοις, insofar as this reflects the trade name πολυμιτάριος). On the other hand, granted an Egyptian setting—which seems likely, from the proemic fiction and ongoing addresses to Ptolemy (35–8, 207–8)—the reference to double citizenship in 291 makes most sense at a date before 212, with the citizenships in question being one municipal and the other Roman. But given the tralatician nature of astrological poetry, this does not prove anything about the poem in its present state. The same objection could presumably made about any other detail that was supposed to offer a fixed date or *terminus ante quem*; at best all they could be would be flecks and spots of earlier strata of composition, like Cumont's (alleged and controversial) Ptolemaisms.

Late antique details, *mœurs*, and sensibility, on the other hand, are readily found. I interpret the individual described in the long chart in 260–73 (despite possible interpolations) as an iatrosophist, one of the late antique showman-intellectuals who blinded crowds with pseudo-science and rhetoric. 296 is a clear reference to late antique acclamations, the practice of publicly hailing benefactors with concerted sing-song chants. A little later, the σιτοδόται and κτίσται of 309 are precisely the municipal bigwigs who elicited such plaudits, and of course did so empire-wide; this book reflects the same homogeneous culture of the eastern empire, with many parallels in the epigraphy of Asia Minor, as the others do. On the other hand, confirmation that the setting is in reality Egypt comes from the reference to the hooded cobra in 185,[7] and perhaps from the ἀρχικυνηγοί in 289: this was both a court title and a military command in Ptolemaic Egypt, though it is far from clear that the poet continues to reflect usage so old. References to exorcisms (303 τὰ πνεύματα φεύγειν), to 'unclean' Attis (180 δυσαγῆ...Ἄττιν), and above all an extraordinary line describing crucifixion in language pitch-perfect for Christian usage (219 ἁπλώσας παλάμῃσιν ἐπὶ ξύλου ὑψόθι σῶμα) suggest the late antique interface between pagan and Christian superstition and morbid fascination with pain. If the reference to hanging in 133 βρόχους is to judicial punishment, as the context suggests, and not to a method of suicide, that also suggests late antiquity. See 4.489 n., where it is claimed that hanging on the gallows gradually took the place of crucifixion in and after the time of Constantine and the Christian emperors of the fourth century.

The question of authorship will not be settled here, but it should be raised. At the end of the eighteenth century Tyrwhitt already noted similarities between books 1 and 5, above all their chaotic state, and their opening prefaces. He attributed them to a single poet (who was also, in the first book, the 'plagiarist' of book four), responsible for both the diction and metre which he found

---

[7] De Stefani 2017, 28.

equally objectionable in both books.⁸ Koechly's advance was to attribute the mess to editors, separate for each book (and equally contemptible), the first book including some good material, the fifth nothing but late antique dross.⁹ But the idea of a single author did not go away. In 1928 Kroll opined that 'es ist ganz dieselbe Stümperei [as the first book], und wir werden denselben Verfasser dafür annehmen dürfen'.¹⁰ Gundel and Gundel agreed (163), and the possibility has been revived most recently by De Stefani 2017, 33 (cf. Heilen 2017, 222).

Some of the similarities with book 1 speak only to their external condition as (putatively) edited collections. This is true not only of their chaotic state but also of the curious fact (already noted by Tyrwhitt) that book 5 apparently also contained isolated pentameters, not nearly as many as book 1, but at least one at 292. And although he did not print it this way, Lopilato was also inclined to restore the corrupt 55 as a pentameter ψυχρὸς γάρ τε πέλει τῇ δὲ Κρόνοιο βολή, 'for you see, Saturn is cold, and so, too, is its ray'. Both have prefaces addressing Ptolemy, situating their efforts, implicitly or explicitly, in native Egyptian wisdom, and both mention Petosiris. But that would seem to have no bearing on authorship (if anything it would tell against it: the reference to Petosiris in book 1 is disparaging, in book 5 more friendly; and why would the same author repeat the same trope in different ways?). Rather, both are recycling a motif with which Manetho's name had apparently become associated.¹¹ If a case is to be made for common authorship, it should have regard to the main bodies of the poems, and be based most soundly on criteria which identify poets, not editors. Such are the stylistic criteria on which De Stefani bases his case. The following chapters will gather possible evidence each way, and I will eventually return to the question in the Epimetrum.

But the prior question is the attribution of the book to a single writer in the first place. That needs to be addressed straight away.

5.2. MULTIPLE AUTHORSHIP?

This book is unusually varied in the types of chart it contains. The question is whether it derives from one and the same poet or is a miscellany, like the previous book.

---

⁸ Tyrwhitt, xiv; repeated by W. C. L. Ziegler, 'De libris apotelesmaticis, Manethonis nomini vulgo addictis, commentatio', *Neues Magazin für Schullehrer*, ed. G. A. Ruperti et H. Schlichthorst, ii/1 (Göttingen, 1794), 99–126, at 114.

⁹ Not dissenting in this from Axtius and Rigler, xxxiv: 'Liber quintus est farrago, in qua alia sunt antiquiora, alia recentiora, ut multo peior eius sit conditio, quam libri primi, qui per se satis est antiquus; sed maxime mutilatus et interpolatione depravatus.'

¹⁰ W. Kroll, *RE* s.v. Manethon (Astrologe), 1105.37–8.

¹¹ Or the poet of the proem of the fifth book is imitating that of the first: Monteventi, 150.

Koechly thought the latter (1851, lvi, cf. lxi). The first part runs from 1–108:[12] this consists of fragments of multiple authors ('a variis poetis particulas fere minores') threaded together, mostly on the theme of good and bad stars. The second, from 109 to the end, consists of material on τέχνας and σίνη from no more than two poets in late antiquity ('et vix ad plures quam ad duos diversos auctores referenda ultimis paganismi temporibus ascribenda sunt').

Koechly numbered the charts, as he had done for the first book. In the main he did not attempt the kind of analysis into separate layers that he had carried out for the first book, but he did identify a few individual contributors. In the first place, 202–8 fairly clearly belong with the fictional address to Ptolemy and hence to the same writer as 35–8. Secondly, the style of 84–92 reminded him of the poet of the fourth book, and he gave both that section and (without comment) 332–40, with its cascade of partly asynctic epithets and tetracola, the marginal label 'IV', the only such identifying label within the book. Its implications are unfortunately not exactly clear. Was it meant as a positive ascription to the author of the fourth book, or simply as a descriptive label? Another potential source of confusion were his other marginal indications. He used the obelos (†) to stigmatise lines he particularly disliked ('pessima quaeque'),[13] and square brackets ([ ]) for passages where he detected editorial intervention or interpolation. But against a background where the whole book was a piece of editorial hackwork, it was not clear what notions like authenticity, spuriousness, and interpolation could really mean.[14]

My own view of the book is rather different. It is based in the first place on an analysis of content, fortified by the evidence (once again) of Θ, and with style to back it up. There are, I suggest, at least a few clear groups here.

(i) From 44–129 there seems to be a sequence (not necessarily uninterrupted) on Good and Bad Stars, to which 44–7 is the preface, and within which 78–80 stand as a general rule. Each one begins with a statement whether a star is good or bad in a particular position; entries are asynctic, with

---

[12] So too T. Mommsen, 208.

[13] i.e. 25–43, 202–8, 222–4, 293–8, apparently simply an aesthetic judgement; but he disliked the whole book.

[14] These all occur within what I call the long discursive charts (below), which are unusually detailed, crowded, and sometimes discrepant in detail and style. Thus, he diagnosed as interpolations 231 + 232–3 (from different sources), similarly 265–7 + 268 (the latter having already been suspected by A.-R.), and 270–1. He held that 286–92 and 293–9 were two alternative apodoses (he calls them 'duarum recensionum vestigia, quae toto caelo distant'), the first a list of epithets, the second verbal clauses; the former he bracketed, the second he obelised except for 299, which looks as if it belongs with 293 and which he bracketed as well. This is all rather confusing, but implies that he thought 293–8 were 'genuine', just not very good.

Book Five 321

a copula for occasional add-ons. My title for this section comes from Koechly (lvi: 'quae fere omnes in stellis *malis bonis*ve explicandis versantur' [his italics]), except that we differ over the extent of the sequence, which he thought ended at 108: in my view the closing section on the Moon (109–29), which has some of the most sustained and systematic comment on the planet's quality, should certainly be included. In any case, 120–6 + 127–9 should presumably be attributed to the same author as 300–12, which also concern New Moon and σύνδεσμος, and involve the same explanatory mechanism on the Moon's gain and loss of light.

(ii) The book contains a complete set of correspondences for Θ ch. 96 Περὶ μίμων, although distributed in a strange way which is hard to explain. Mostly these are miscellaneous τέχναι charts. The first chart, an exact match, is found already within the Good and Bad Stars (103–4). Next come a series of partial matches over three charts in 137–53 (repeating the first one, only second time round in a more approximate form). Then there is a series of particularly close correspondences in 159–88, notable for the fidelity with which the poet repeats the detail found in the prose witness, which includes specifications about types of sign glossed over elsewhere. Then two final outliers (252–5, 260–73) to complete the sequence, with demonstrably similar details in the protasis but differently developed apodoses. Why this strange spread? We have only isolated snapshots and cannot explain the whole tradition, but the closing charts in Θ ch. 96 are themselves outliers, especially p. 218.3–6, which is the main basis of 260–73. In other words, book 5 simply gives clearer expression to what was already internally evident from Θ itself.

(iii) In *later* stages of the book there are native-focused apotelesmata which vividly imagine the native's activities and personality (225–42, 260–73, 284–99, 332–40). All are long. All are asyndetic. All say at least something about the native's physical appearance, and in 229–30 and 286–7 that is very circumstantial. I call them long discursive charts. As mentioned, one of them (260–73) exists in Θ (p. 218.3–6), now much wadded out, especially in the last four lines; no other book in the Manethoniana versifies this chart. All involve relatively elaborate protases. All involve lists of epithets: 229–32 (to some extent); 263–9; 286–92; 335–9. Most develop into verbal clauses at the end: 233–42, including parallelisms at 234–8; 270; 293–9.

These seem to me the most obvious groups. In other words, it is not just a matter of differently themed charts (for instance on τέχναι, on οἶνος, on parents), but of different kinds of prediction, from general admonitions ('x is bad'[15]) to very specific charts which in certain cases look as if they might have originated from descriptions of individuals. The book is not as miscellaneous as the first (no rants about Ares or about sacrifice), but what is interesting, and might help with an analytical account of it, is the range of constructions used in the protasis and apodosis of the predictive material, in other words variations on the *if–then* formula.

Normally one would expect some kind of continuity between *p* and *q* to be provided by an executive or factitive (or 'declarative') verb: *x* in such a place brings about, or reveals, such-and-such an outcome. That is so whether the protasis has a finite verb, as it usually has, or consists of a participle (e.g. 39, 130) or prepositional phrase (41), of which there are occasional examples here outside the systematic catalogues which are their normal home. But charts in the fifth book are unusually prepared to dislocate the two halves of the construction. The least abnormal occur in the last third of the book, where there is an unsignalled change of subject between protasis and apodosis ('when the star does this, the native does that'). In other books, even where there is no executive verb to link protasis and apodosis, the apodosis is introduced by a word for 'native' (ὁ γεννηθείς, etc.) or there is *deixis* (ἐκεῖνοι, οὗτοι).[16] Here, however, a number of charts just launch into the apodosis construction (mostly in the singular) without advertisement that the subject has changed.[17]

There is a certainly an oddity at 278–9, where the star itself performs the action of the apodosis, implying an elision of star into native, but one cannot generalise from it except to rank it among the book's many eccentricities. Much more distinctive and characteristic is what I have already called the 'who whom' construction (i. 215), where the apodosis launches straight into accusatives for the outcome, without a factitive or executive verb to govern them.[18] A handful of examples were noted in the first and second books, but of none is it more characteristic than the fifth—in which it occurs throughout, including in the Good and Bad Stars, τέχναι, and long discursive charts (66–7, 84–5, 103–4, 115–16, 130–1, 132–3, 134–5, 136, 155–6, 262–3, 316–17, 318–19, 334–5). That

---

[15] General rules are formulated throughout the Good and Bad Stars: 44–7 (introductory/proemic), 59–61 (after apodosis), 78–80. Consider the number of 'x is good' or 'x is bad' statements followed by a γάρ clause: 62 Μειλίχιος + γάρ, 74 Ἄστοργος + γάρ, 105 Οὐ καλός + γάρ, 113 ἀρίστη + γάρ. Later in the book, a statement of a general rule is followed by its exemplification (209–10, 246–8, 284–5).

[16] 'Native': 4.87, 351, 381, 387, 432; *deixis*: 4.554, 5.138b, part of ἐκεῖνος, cf. 4.381; 4.393, part of οὗτος.

[17] Singular: 159–64, 217–21, 280–1, 300–2, 320–3, 324–5. Plural: 307–12. M^b has some examples, mostly of the plural: 4.123 αὐχήσουσι, 385 ἥσσονες ... τελέθουσι, 407 ὁρόωσι, 596 ἕξουσι. Singular at 4.134 ἔσσεται ... ἴδρις (but the suddenness of the transition in this case is offset by 133).

[18] Also noted by Massimilla, 269 n. 30.

seems a good initial indication of continuity, and it is supported by a handful of verbless nominatives in the apodosis implying the verb 'to be' or 'to be born' or 'to come to light' which are distributed across the τέχναι (169–72), one of the later miscellanea (274–5), and one of the long discursive charts (286–92).

Another peculiarity of ps and qs in the book is the unusually high profile of second-person verbs. In the protasis, these take the form of conditional 'if you see/find', imperative 'look out for' (or alternatively 'let not x escape you'); in the apodosis, of 'reckon/forecast as follows'. Once again, these tend to be distributed throughout the book, though there are certain types of chart where one would not expect, and does not find, them. 'If you see/find' (5.137, 149, 154, 177, 211, 214, 218, 222–3, 280, 282, 321) is found throughout the τέχναι and later charts, but not in the Good and Bad Stars, where it does not really fit, or in the long discursive charts, where the description is too particular for it to be describable as a generic repeatable outcome. Second-person imperatives are found once in a τέχνη chart, but mostly in the miscellanea at the end of the book (138 Ἑρμείαν σκέπτου; 207 γίγνεο μάρτυς (NB Ptolemy's chart); 212, 224, 231 σὺ νόει (interpolated, according to Koechly); 215 νόει τὸ σχῆμ' ὅ τι δηλοῖ; 202 μὴ λαθέτω σε; 222 Τὴν Μήνην σκέπτου; 324 λογίζου). The instances of 'be very afraid' in the Good and Bad Stars are not necessarily to be classified in the same way (49 δείμαινε, 54 τάρβει); an instruction to fear bad stars arises naturally out of the context. Still, it *is* a narratorial intervention, and so is 81 γίγνωσκε.

Syntax will be discussed in a later section, but one of the strongest arguments for the book's cohesiveness is surely the pervasiveness of the definite article. It occurs, in similar contexts (see pp. 330–1) throughout the Good and Bad Stars (44, 47, 48, 54, 81, 84, 90, 91, 102, 108, 110, 113, 122, 126, 128), τέχναι (139a, 150, 152, 154, 155, 167bis [but corrupt], transmitted at 182, where I do not accept it), the long discursive charts (228, 234, 235, 237, 240 [but corrupt], 260, 262, 264bis, 269, 270bis, 272, 284, 285, 340), the introductory material (8, 13, 23, 25, 28, 30), and remaining miscellaneous charts (42, 197, 207, 208, 215, 222, 247, 275, 277 (transmitted, but corrected by Koechly), 282, 303, 307, 311, 313, 315, 316, 318, 321, 331). Other books of course employ the article, but nowhere nearly as pervasively as here. No other syntactic peculiarity is as sustained as this. There are a couple of periphrastic tenses (see on 4.384) in 5.189 αὔξουσα τύχῃ, 320 ᾗ στείχουσα. The use or omission of connective particles does fluctuate throughout the book (see pp. 229–30), with Good and Bad Stars being asyndetic and τέχναι being linked. But the same will apply here as in the first book. The use or omission of connectiveness is not an intrinsic part of a poet's 'voice-print', merely an indication of what he wanted to do with that particular body of material.

Then there is the matter of repeated vocabulary. In the first book, this was pronounced enough seriously to undermine some of Koechly's proposed groupings. Even though he had based those very groupings on an incomplete sampling of the evidence, it was a sorting principle he accepted. In this book, most of the terms of the comparison turn out to be single words or very short phrases rather than the part- or whole-line rewritings found in the first book. Although no one instance carries a great deal of weight, they do produce a cumulative effect. There are also a few more impressive correspondences of entire phrase-patterns, of the kind far more pervasive in the first book, at 152 + 270 and 218 + 280.

Correspondences

Found throughout the Book

Parts of καθευρεῖν, unique to this book, of the addressee finding a star in a chart (211, 321), of one star finding another (120, 317, 326), or the narrator finding enlightenment (8).

Compounds of δείκνυμι: 37 ἀνέδειξαν, 39 ἐπιδείξει (executive); 73 ἐπέδειξε, 220 ἐπέδειξεν (non-executive).

39, 189 μεσσουραν- (rhythm of the first half of the next line is the same as well).

56, 211, 255 εἰ δ' ἄμφω, and nowhere else in the corpus.

69, 130, 217, 284 ⏑ ⏑ — ⏑ ὑπάρχ — at line-end, but also 4.379, 1.34, and not wholly distinctive.

Connecting Good and Bad Stars with Later Material

62, 111, 274 συνοδεύειν (and nowhere else in the corpus).

100, 249 λοίγιος Ἄρης.

Connecting τέχναι with Later Material

137 and 300 ποτε in protasis (same *sedes*), unique in corpus.

165, 320 στείχουσα (also 58 στείχωσι, but cf. 6.277, 4.466).

Connecting Long Discursive Charts with Other Material

207 τῷ σχήματι γίγνεο μάρτυς ~ 227 ἐν σχήματι τῷδέ γε μάρτυς.

248 καὶ λεπίδων πολλῶν λεπτῶν θ' ἅμα καὶ πολυχρώμων ~ 291 δισσολόγοι, δίγαμοι, δίγονοί θ' ἅμα καὶ διπολῖται.

Connecting τέχναι with Long Discursive Charts

143 σοβαρήν, 288 σοβαροί, 305 σοβαραῖς (otherwise only 4.468).

152 ὧν ὁδός ἐστιν ὕδωρ, οἱ δ' ἀστέρες εἰσὶν ὁδηγοί (one of the τέχναι) ~ 270 οὗ πόρος ἐστὶ φύσις, ἡ δ' αὖ φύσις ἐστὶν ὁ δαίμων.

Connecting Good and Bad Stars, τέχναι, and Long Discursive Charts

109, 174, 225, 257 αὐξιφαής, unique in corpus.

Other Correspondences

These are within sections one would probably have ascribed to a single poet in the first place.

22, 28 δόγματα θεῖα (δόγμα also 4.12).

218 καὶ δέ τ' Ἄρην ἐσίδοις γε μεσουρανέοντα ἄνωθεν and 280 εἰ δ' Ἄρην ἐσίδοις, 324 εἰ δ' Ἄρης ἠοῦς γε μεσουρανέοιτο.

Within the Good and Bad Stars

Confirming that there is no break at 108.

45–6 ἀστὴρ ἀργαλέος, ἀργαλέοις ἀστήρ; 81 Ἀργαλέων ἄστρων.

54, 62, 109 κατὰ πάντα (trivial, not confined to this book).

86, 114 ἐπὶ δόξῃ, though in different senses: (i) over, because of, for the sake of, (ii) attended with.

Within the Long Discursive Charts

226 ψυχρήν τ' ἀκτῖνα Κρόνοιο ~ 334 δνοφερὴν ἀκτῖνα Κρόνοιο.

242 βίοτον διοδεύει ~ 271 βίοτον μεθοδεύων.

Finally there are stylistic criteria, again to be examined below.[19] The sing-song style characterised by parallelisms and jingles is particularly marked in the long discursive charts, but not confined to them. It links them with τέχναι, Good and Bad Stars, and much of the miscellaneous matter that does not fall into any of these groups. This is why Koechly's ascription of a couple of sections

---

[19] De Stefani 2017, 32: 'Im ganzen genommen weist dieses Buch eine gewisse stilistische Einheit auf' (though not as consistently as M^a and M^b).

to M^b, or a poet very like him, was evidence of a good ear, but ultimately arbitrary. A more pertinent question is whether there is anything to *separate* the poets of the first and fifth books in this respect. Παφίη, the poet's preferred designation for the planet Venus, runs throughout the book, though there is a curious gap between 165 and 282 (that is, the second half of the τέχναι and miscellaneous charts thereafter). One final criterion that is (semi-)stylistic, or at least a mannerism, are the repeated mythological references to paradigms of a particular activity. I have argued that astrological literature pictures the world through trope. The contract between astrological producers and consumers simply assumes that everyone has a shared cultural repertoire in which mythological characters, icons, and archetypes are embedded (i. 227–8). But no book makes this clearer than the fifth. The τέχναι give us Icarus (147), Attis (180), and Tantalus (187); these are self-consciously fine writing, but a little later we get Thyestes and Jocasta (203, 204) in an incest chart, and insofar as the poet of the last of these contrives a further connection with Ptolemy and Arsinoe, it also links up with 35–8, on Ptolemy and Alexander. The reference to autophagy in 117 also suggests, though does not name, Erysichthon as a paradigm. This stands within the Good and Bad Stars but, the reference being at best implicit, the procedure is less distinctive and cannot advance the case for common authorship.

Conclusions

As we found with book 1, stylistic analysis will not provide tools for neatly teasing apart one level of the book from another. Some criteria are particularly impressive, especially the use of the definite article, and the spread of the various protasis/apodosis constructions across all types of chart. And although verbal repetitions are not as pronounced across this book as they were in the first, there are enough to show significant continuities.

There are apparently distinctive sections within the book, it is true. The main τέχνη section sticks to the sequence in Θ's chapter Περὶ μίμων, and its cohesiveness is marked by the sudden shift from asyndeton to connection. In stylistic terms it is particularly elaborate, its apodoses crowded out with lively particularisms and topical detail. There is also a certain sense of aesthetic closure after the last chart in the sequence (181–8), because the last item, on snakes and snake-charmers, is much the most elaborate, a tour de force of Nicandrian collage. Nothing on this level of stylistic ambition is found elsewhere in the book. That said, the next two charts (189–91 and 192–6) seem to be linked associatively to what precedes, and lest we conclude too hastily that this is *merely* evidence of an editor stringing charts impressionistically together the compositional technique of 194–6 (Homeric rather than Hellenistic, but still a tessellation of related passages) does not look terribly different from that of what has gone before. There may well be editorial reshuffling, but it is not necessarily evidence of different poetic hands.

This provides a unitarian response to the analyst case in very general terms ('there is an overall stylistic homogeneity', or rather a unity in diversity). It does not supply answers to Koechly's specific *ad lineam* objections, but these can be tackled on a case-by-case basis. Thus: (i) the parallelisms of 84–92 are in fact characteristic of much of the book, and the rhyming parallelism of 87–8 followed by the sting in the tail of 89 are more characteristic of M^d (and M^c) than of M^b. And, as to his objections to the long discursive charts: (ii) on grounds of theme and content rather than of style, 232–3 (and possibly 231) are not from a different source from what follows (see commentary ad loc.). (iii) Parallels with Θ and Epit. IIIb show that 265 is not an interpolation. My commentary ad loc. argues for the likely conflation of several charts here, but if material has been jumbled together in this section, it is the work of the poet rather than of an editor. (iv) Koechly objected to the juxtaposition of 286–92 + 293–9, but both styles are represented in this category of chart, as I have shown (p. 321).

No doubt one *could* apply the idea of 'ownership' to this book—that is, the idea that a single poet has imposed his hallmark on material of extraneous origin—but the case is different from that of book 1, where Anubion and the M^b material were given, or as good as given. There is no reason to assume that kind of background here. On the contrary, there is a great diversity of material within the book, but no evidence of previous poetic treatments, only a single approach that cultivates variety within a set of specifiable parameters.

5.3. PHONOLOGICA ET MORPHOLOGICA

The following notes, supplementing i. 89–105, illustrate the Attic forms that permeate the book.

Phonologica

α/η

5.70 πράξεις, 182 πρᾶξιν
80 ἰδίαν, 85 δράστας, 222 Τιτάνος (corr. D), 337 βληχρὰν
Ἑρμείας transmitted at 93, 138, 260, but Ἑρμείης at 274, Ἑρμείην at 178.

ἐς/εἰς

On the five occasions when neither form is metrically guaranteed, εἰς is transmitted (5.118, 240, 272, 301, 310).

ττ/σσ

5.237 κρείττοσιν.

Contractions

At 5.296 I have introduced κελαδοῦνται in place of κελαδεῦνται (A.-R.), σελαγεῦνται (Koechly). εο is cheerfully contracted (180 μιμοῦνται, 184 ζητοῦντας, 295 αὐχοῦσιν, γηθοῦσιν) except for 218 μεσουρανέοντα, 324 μεσουρανέοιτο, where diaeresis is a necessity, and 234 φιλέοντι, a curiosity which violates Hermann's Bridge with no mitigating circumstances.

See i. 95 for adjectival neuter plurals in -ῇ (all are contracted).

Vowel Quantities

The treatment of καλός is opportunistic: 44 καλόν, but 46, 105 κᾱλός (cf. Axtius and Rigler, xxi), 111 κᾰλή.

Axtius and Rigler themselves restored un-Homeric ἴσον at 245.

Morphologica

ἐκεῖνος/κεῖνος

i. 98: 5.139b ἐκεῖνος (not guaranteed), 138b (guaranteed); 64 κείνῳ (guaranteed).

-αις, -αισι(ν), -ῃσι(ν)

An overall majority of forms are Attic:

-αισι(ν): 5.48 συναφαῖσιν, 99 οὐρανίαισι, 103 μοίραισι, 119 θείαισι, 120 συναφαῖσι, 132 μοίραισι, 239 πλασταῖσι, 244 μελέταισι, 264 ἀκοαῖσι, 296 δόξαισιν. Also implied by: 5.121 ἀρχέσιν, 141 θυμέλεσσιν, 233 δαπάνεσσι, 273 ἰδίαισι implied by ηενιδιεστι, 278 χώρεσσιν, 299 στρατίεσσιν [all A.-R. -ῃσι].

-ῃσι(ν): 5.131 γενέτῃσι, 163 παλάμῃσιν, 187 γαμφηλῇσιν, 205 μητρυιῇσιν, 219 παλάμῃσιν, 271 σοφίῃσι, 305 μεγάλῃσι.

ἀστράσι, ἄστροις

5.63 and 97 ἄστροις (i. 100).

Declension of Ares

The Attic form Ἄρεως is metrically guaranteed at 5.41, and transmitted but in need of correction at 198.

Forms of εἶναι

Even in this most workaday of books, a majority of forms continue to be epic,[20] but Attic forms are transmitted at 320 ᾗ [ἔῃ, ἔοι A.-R. xxix], 142 ᾖι [ἔῃ A.-R.], 159 οὔσης, 261 οὖσαν, and restored by Koechly at 182 ὄνθ' (whose text I do not follow).

Verb Endings

Note 5.124 ἔλησιν, 262 κρατῆσι (i. 102), the only instances of this Homeric ending outside Mᵃ. The third person optative ending is -ειε (5.43 λεύσσειε) (i. 103).

5.4. SYNTAX

Particles

Asyndeton

There are different patterns in different parts of the book, implying that if this is one and the same poet his use of particles is not consistent. Some of the particles (many are δ') could be editorial, but others are metrically guaranteed.

There is a strong preference for asyndeton in primary charts (with connectives only for add-on items) all the way through to the Περὶ μίμων sequence.[21]

---

[20] 5.47, 60, 64, 140, 276 ἐών; 94 ἐόντες; 227 ἔῃ; 178 παρέοντα. Restored by Koechly at 56 ἔωσιν.

[21] Asyndetic: 39. In the Good and Bad Stars: 44, 48 (add-ons in 53, 54–6, 56–7, 58–61), 62, 66, 74, 78, 81, 84 (add-on in 90–2), 93, 103, 105, 108, 113, 120 (add-on in 124), 127. Thereafter 130 (add-ons in 132–3, 134–5, 136). But there are connectives in 69 (preceded by a lacuna, so hard to judge), 72 (add-on to theme of wealth?), 100 (add-ons in 101–2), 109 (add-ons in 111, 112), 115.

This opens in 137 with asyndeton. Thereafter (from 144) it is connected, although the τέχνη chart that opens the sequence but stands among the Good and Bad Stars is, like them, asyndetic (103). Connection remains consistent until 201; the presence of connectives in the σίνος charts in 189, 192, and 197 reinforces the sense that though the τέχναι may have come to a grand rhetorical finale in 188, associative links persist (pp. 326–7, 939–40). Finally, from 202 until the end of the book, connection and lack of connection alternate.[22] The long discursive charts are all asyndetic (225, 260, 284, 332).

Postponed Particles

δέ, τε, and γάρ are postponed throughout the book, in habitual situations including set phrases (5.311 τὸ πλέον δέ), article + noun (5.102 ἡ Παφίη δέ), preposition + case (5.64 σὺν κείνῳ γάρ), noun + epithet (259 εἵμασι πορφυρέοις τε), and a few others (conjunction + verb: 5.58 ἢν στείχωσι δ'; 5.128 κὴν λύσῃ δέ; modifier + adj.: 5.122 οὐκ ἰδικὴν γάρ; 226 λίην ψυχρήν τ'; other: 5.38 καὶ σὺ δέ γ', 42 καὶ τούτων δέ). There are longer postponements at 29 Ἀστέρες ἑπτὰ θεοὶ μέν and 319 ἐν διθύροις αἰεί τε. A few are the result of emendation: 5.11 οὐ βαιὸς κάματος ⟨δ'⟩, 5.28 Ὥρῃ ἀκριβοῦται δέ, 245 ἐν γυμνασίοις ⟨τ'⟩, 5.236 ζηλώσει δούλην ⟨δ'⟩.[23]

Clusters

There is a little of M^a's tendency to wad particles with pseudo-gnomic τε (i. 113): 55 γάρ τε; 218 καὶ δέ τ' (vl in Il. 20.28); 33, 129, and 232 ἠδέ τ'; 300 Ἢν δέ τ' (and *ex emend.* in 169); 254 μέν θ' [*ex emend.* R].

Definite Article

This notorious feature of the book is ubiquitous, and weakens the case for multiple authorship unless an editor has somehow assayed to find multiple poets with the same fetish (pp. 165, 323). It occurs throughout every section and in protases and apodoses, perhaps especially in the former on account of its association with technical or pseudo-technical terminology and planetary

---

[22] There could still be said to be a tendency to asyndeton (202, 209, 222, 225, 246 [presented as a generalisation], 260, 274, 282, 284). Women's charts mostly unconnected (316, 320, 332; exception 324). Most of the connected charts could be described as σίνος, τέχνη, or τέχνη-related: 217, 243, 252, 256, 278 (add-on in 280–1), 300 (add-on in 307).

[23] Excluding manipulations at 5.71 εὐπορίην δηλοῖ ⟨τε⟩ καί, 301 ἐκ πενίης πλουτεῖ ⟨τε⟩ καί (suppl. Gerhard).

names,²⁴ but that is not to suggest any inhibition about using it elsewhere.²⁵ It is marked in the long discursive charts, but it would be, because their apodoses are so long. Some lines involving articles are corrupt, but allowing for that I count a minimum of 60 instances and a maximum of 66, in other words one instance every five or six lines. Some are capable of being given 'charitable' readings (i. 116–21). Some, for instance, are capable of being taken as anaphoric: to my earlier discussion add planetary names at 102 (cf. 100), 110 (but already 108 has an article), 165 (cf. 159), 340 (cf. 332). But given that there are so many that are simply prosaic²⁶ that exercise is of questionable value. The fact that a few stand at line-beginning (54, 91, 102, 167(?), 182, 222, 228, 234–5, 260, 264, 313) is a matter of happenstance, not Homeric imitation.

Third-Person Pronouns and Adjectives

No irregularities noted, contrasting with the misuse of ἑός in the first book. But ἴδιος may be used for the first-person possessive in 5.25.

Prepositions

Anastrophe

There are no certain examples. At 5.240, a *locus corruptissimus*, λύπης δίχα is transmitted [μέτα Koechly]; other than that, all possible instances involve emendation: 32 σφαίρωμ' ἄνα [K], 83 γονῇ ἔπι [A.-R.], 146 σχοίνοισί τ' ἔπ' [K], 181 ζώοις ἔπι [A.-R.]. There are no cases with ἅμα, ἄπο, ἄτερ, ἔνι, ἔξ, μέτα, ὁμοῦ (presumably not 37), ὕπερ, ὕπο.

---

²⁴ With technical or pseudo-technical terms: 48, 331 τὴν φάσιν, 91 τὸν δεσμὸν (?), 128 τὰ τελέσματα (?), 307 τὴν λύσιν. Kentra: 84, 154 τὰ κέντρα, 321 τὴν ὥρην, cf. 262 τοῦ πνεύματος (horoscope). Signs: 150, 155, cf. 247. Aspects: 44 μεγάλοις τοῖς σχήμασι, 47 and 315 τοῖς σχήμασιν, 90 τούτῳ τῷ σχήματι, 207 τῷ σχήματι, 215 τὸ σχῆμ'. Houses, spheres of influence: 182 τὴν πρᾶξιν (transmitted, though not used in my reconstruction), 228 τὸν βίον. Planets' names: 54, 102, 108, 110, 113, 139, 165, 182 (transmitted, not used in my reconstruction), 222, 260, 282, 284, 316, 318, 340. As title of the Moon: 122, 197. Luminaries: 42, 285 τὰ φῶτα.
²⁵ In apodoses: 126, 152, 167bis (L, corrupt), 208, 234, 235, 237, 240 (corrupt), 264bis, 269, 270bis, 272, 275, 277 (transmitted, but corrected by Koechly), 303, 311. In introductory material: 8, 13, 23, 25, 28, 30. Elsewhere: 81, 313.
²⁶ 272 τὸ νοῆσαι, articular infinitive; 311 τὸ πλέον δέ. With adjective in attributive position: 13 ὁ σοφώτατος Ὅμηρος, 25 τῇ ἰδίῃ διανοίῃ, 30 τὰς ἑπτὰ πόλοιο, 234 τὴν δ' ἰδίην ἀκμήν, 313 τὰς αὐτὰς δυνάμεις. Adjectives in predicative position are mostly apt (8 λάλον τὸ μάθημα, 42 ἐπίκεντρα τὰ φῶτα, 44 μεγάλοις τοῖς σχήμασι, 84 σύμφωνα τὰ κέντρα, 285 ἐπίδοξα τὰ φῶτα), though 28 τὰ δόγματα θεῖα is bad grammar.

Tmesis

No examples.

n x N (i. 128–32)

Prior placement of epithets is not beyond the poet's reach, but minimal, and rarely decorative (5.118 ἐπίψογον εἰς νόσον, 325 πολλοῖς [ex emend. K]…ἐπὶ δάκρυσι). Informational in 210 θηλυτέροισιν ἐν οἴκοις, and with genitive at 333 Στίλβοντος ἐν οἴκοις; otherwise in 98 ἐὴν διὰ πίστιν, and 240 τοῖς ἐπὶ τέκνοις [locus corruptissimus; ταῖς ἐπὶ τέχναις K]. N x n: 117 σαρκῶν ἐξ ἰδίων.

Expressions for 'with'

Figures are given in the chart in i. 125. T. Mommsen, 215–16, reports five instances of σύν; in fact there are seven.[27] The two certain instances of μετά occur in protases (169, 316), uncamouflaged by anastrophe. The third, which occurs in an apodosis of some stylistic pretension, is the result of emendation (240).

ἐν

Here is another difference from the first book. Of 39 instances, the majority (24) are in technical expressions.[28] Of the remainder, some are epic cribs, some patently prosaic, and the rest somewhere in between.[29] The issue in this book is not so much the misuse of ἐν, though there are examples at 25 and 273 (where the sense anyway is opaque), and of redundancy in 263 τραυλὸν ἐνὶ γλώσσῃ. There are no instances of ἐν used for agency; nor are there any of M^a's characteristic uses of ἐν (for example, outstanding among a population or in a given quality, the 'best in show' motif). It is simply the preparedness to use prose expressions.

Other

In a prosaic style one might expect prepositions redoubled after a compound verb. This proves not to be the case. In 5.63–4 συνοδεύων | σύν τ' ἄστροις πᾶσιν, the preposition is in the next clause.

---

[27] 5.63, 64, 145, 173, 178, 190, 252.

[28] In terms, houses, places, signs: 33bis, 40, 41, 154, 159, 210, 211, 214, 222, 249, 260, 278, 284, 321, 333. At a given time: 38 ἐν ὥρᾳ (astrological prose); 35, 36, 38, at synodos; 48 at synaphe; 44, 227 ἐν σχήματι; 79 ἐν γενεῇ.

[29] In apodoses: 65 (epic ἐν νήεσσι), 68 (ψόγον ἐν λέκτροις: fine in prose), 70, 163 (epic ἐν παλάμῃσιν), 238, 244, 245, 263, 293, 299, 319. Other: 25, 51 (epic ἐν ὕλῃ), 82 (in respect of: LSJ A.I.7, attested in epic), 273.

Verbs

Protasis

Conditional clauses greatly outnumber temporal clauses (41 : 6). At 39–41 there is also a short list of outcomes, one per line, which employs a participle and two prepositional phrases, which is a standard form, used in Mᵃ and elsewhere, in systematic catalogues (i. 213); this is not a systematic catalogue, but neither is it a series of formal charts. The use of the participial construction at 130 is more surprising.

Of the half-dozen temporal clauses, four are unexceptionable (197 ἡνίκα + opt.; 44, 137, 165 ὅτ' ἄν + subj.); the indicative with ὅτ' ἄν at 77 is readily emended. That leaves just one optative (not metrically guaranteed) with ἡνίκα δ' ἄν in 243 συνάπτοι (A.-R. συνάπτῃ).

Among the conditional clauses, of the seventeen which employ εἰ, most have the optative. 56, 90 (if this is εἰ not ἤν), 142, 189, and 320 use the subjunctive without a particle, and I include 257 ὑποδέξεται as a short-vowel subjunctive. (139b is an indirect question.) Among the 24 clauses which employ ἤν, seven use the optative, on two occasions (43 and 252) metrically guaranteed. (A.-R. emend those at 261 and 274, but not at 149 and 174.) The other arises from emendation of 169 (transmitted unmetrically as subjunctive). In other words, eccentric as this book is in many ways, it is not particularly aberrant with regard to 'wrong' moods, and in fact has rather fewer instances of this than the first book (29% of verbs with ἤν are optative, as against 37.5%).

Four out of six verbs in temporal clauses are present, and 14 out of 41 in conditional clauses.

Apodosis

Gnomic aorist: 25 in apotelesmata, 19 of stars, six of natives and their circumstances. Three more stand outside apotelesmata.[30]

Future: eight in all, one of stars, six of natives, one generalisation.[31]

Present: 63 in apotelesmata, 15 of stars, 48 of natives and their circumstances. A further 26 generalisations about stars and four about human lives.[32]

---

[30] Stars: 37, 41, 73 bis, 91, 92 [imperf.], 125, 128 [ex emend. K], 142, 146, 148, [164 and 167, too uncertain to include], 199, 201, 205, 229, 251, 255, 258, 283. Natives and their circumstances: 98b, 99, 195, 216, 220, 331. Outside apotelesmata: 43, 124, 125.

[31] Stars: 39. Natives: 163, [transmitted at 164, not accepted in my text], 235, 236, 238bis, 325. Generalisations: 46.

[32] Stars: 35, 64, 65, 71, 106, 114, 121, 175, 183, 193, 206, 244, 254, 259, 285. Natives and their circumstances: 87 (present perfect), 88 (present perfect), 89, 95, 97, 140, 157, 160, 161, 162, 176, 180, 191, 194, 233, 234, 237, 239, 241, 242, 276, 279, 281, 293bis, 294bis, 295bis, 296 [ex emend.], 297,

Thus, of a total of 122 verbs, 20.49% are gnomic aorists, 6.56% are future, and 72.95% are presents. This particularly high percentage of presents is explained by the large number of generalisations about the stars' behaviour (especially in the Good and Bad Stars) which are not formal apodoses but nevertheless describe the stars' effects. The table on p. 169 gives numbers for verbs in apotelesmata alone.

Negations

μή for οὐ in 75 (not required by metre), 309.

5.5. STYLE

This book is often seen as the collection's ugly duckling. Whether or not it knows and responds to the earliest poet in the collection,[33] it adheres to the literary house style of the Manethoniana, characterised by cut-and-paste Homerism and occasional raids on later sources. Like the other poets, this one targets *Realien* on the one hand and emotional *Affekt* on the other; the epics provide the requisite qualities of granularity and pathos. At the same time, this book has distinctive features, above all its notoriously 'prosaic' quality. That obviously applies to some aspects of its syntax (definite articles; 272, articular infinitive), and it is one way of characterising its variously tortuous and lumbering expressions (below). In respect of diction, however, not all prosaic vocabulary is born equal. All poets use or modify prose vocabulary to some extent for technical terms in the protasis (see pp. 360–1). In apodoses, too, prose jargon forms the basis of outcomes, and few poets feel much inhibition about simply rehashing it from time to time without any attempt at concealment (e.g. 5.67, 133). There are particularly extensive examples of this in the shrew's chart (5.332–40), which tumbles EGHP and tragic epithets together with many descriptors paralleled in Ptolemy, 3.14 (his chapter on the planets' effects on character). These uses of prose are not very interesting or distinctive,

---

298, 299*bis*, 301*bis*, 302, 303 (present perfect), 304, 305, 306, 310, 312, 322, 327, 328, 330, 340. Generalisations about stars: 45, 50, 53*bis*, 55, 59*bis*, 60, 61, 66, 76, 78, 82, 83, 101, 102, 108, 109 (present perfect), 113, 122, 123, 127, 209, 210, 247, 314; about human lives: 152*bis*, 270*bis*.

[33] 5.64 and 6.80 πατρώιον οἶκον; 5.201 συνθλωμένῳ ὀστᾶ ~ 3.263 ὀστέα συνθλιφθέντες; 5.220 οἰωνοῖσι βορήν ~ 6.98 βορήν τ' ἔμεν οἰωνοῖσιν; 5.232 οἶκον μὲν φθείροντα πατρώιον ~ 2.463 οἴκων γὰρ φθείρει κτῆσιν and 6.80 πατρώιον οἶκον; 5.328 ψευδομένη δ' ὠδῖνας ~ 6.291 ψευδέσιν ὠδίνεσσι; (perhaps) 5.330 στεῖρα λοχός ~ 3.278 στείρας τ' ἀλόχους.

and indeed complaining about them might be missing the point when the desired effect is positively that of establishing a professional idiom, e.g. in τέχνη or medical charts (examples of this in 157 ὑπονήχεται, 191 φρυγομένων, ὑποτήκεται, 201 συνθλωμένῳ, 330 λοχός) and to sound commandingly technocratic (e.g. in 60-1 on the physics of heat and cold).

I would suggest that what is distinctive about this poet is not *per se* that he uses an untypically large number of prose forms—although he does use prose forms, including 'gratuitous' forms not determined by the astrological idiom (e.g. 122 ἰδικήν; 311 τὸ πλέον), and some that are attested rarely if at all before Byzantine prose (5.8 n. καθευρεῖν, *passim*; 126 ἀποδωκαμένη; 27, 43 συνεξώλισθεν). Rather, it is the breadth of the spectrum between determinedly prose forms on the one hand, and epic ones on the other—and not only the usual type of epic remix, but highly recherché and effect-seeking adaptations which will be examined a little later. It is also the related spectrum between the particularisms in which astrology delights and the poet's individual penchant for abstract nouns (four instances of διάνοια, unique to him in the corpus) and expressions (270 οὗ πόρος ἐστὶ φύσις, where the urge to create a jingle has overridden clarity of sense), which is particularly in evidence in noun/epithet combinations (14 νεκταρέῃ διανοίῃ; 187 Ταντalική κολάσει, 273 ἀνθολόγοισι τροφαῖς, 302 Ἑκατησίου εἵνεκα κέρδους, 303 μαγικῇ συνέσει; 221 μοίρης νευροτόμου is somewhat different, a type of tragic periphrasis.

Corruption clearly does not help matters (e.g. 5.99, 240-1, 267). Neither does the book's mangled state, which deprives a couplet like 5.25-6—highly abstract, and characterised by a mixture of Homerism (πραπίδων) and prose (εἴρηται; the preface-writer's boast of *synthesis*)—of context and clues about the speaker. But even where the sense is continuous and the reading appears sound, the book is characterised by opaque pronouncements, whether because of obscurity of referent (242 εὐτραπέλοισι γραφαῖς), vagueness (285 οὕτως παρέχει, 311 καιροῖσιν πάμπαν), the abstract nature of the pronouncement (31 αἰῶνός τε γένος καὶ ῥίζα φύσεως), or sheer semantic and syntactical difficulty (118 ἐπίψογον εἰς νόσον ὀργῆς, and above all the whole of 270-3).

So too, if there is a problem with the poet's vocabulary, it is not so much that it is obscure in itself (but what is 277 ψηφών?) as that words are used in strained (271 σοφίῃσι λόγων φυσικῶν, 'by learned pursuit of'?; 322 ἠΰτ᾽, 'such as') or unfamiliar (183 παραβαλλομένους) senses. He seems especially to enjoy stretching the meaning of ὁδεύειν and its compounds (306 ὁδεύει, of social advancement; 139b μεθοδεύεται, of planetary motion; 271 βίοτον μεθοδεύων, of the quest to make a living). There are a couple of interesting possible instances of grammarians' forms, in other words artifices constructed in accordance with theory rather than following normal usage (somewhat after the manner of Lexiphanes and his ilk, some centuries earlier): 119 βωμολόχους, literally lying in wait at altars; 337 βληχρὰν, meaning 'forceful', of which the Homeric poems supposedly have the alpha privative. There are also a few catachreses, by no means ineffective or necessarily the product of incompetence: 268 ἐπώδυνον, of an individual *suffering* chronic pain, 340 ἀμβλυνομένη of a person who *is* a pain. Poetic vocabulary, finally, offers few surprises. Innovations, as one would expect, are almost entirely in apodoses,[34] adding little touches of verbal charisma to the τέχναι[35] and long discursive charts,[36] and pathos to charts about harm.[37] The morpho-syntactical novelty κοχλίδεσσιν (24) is also in a passage of self-consciously fine writing.

Use and Recycling of Earlier Poets

The use of Homer stays mainly in familiar territory, except that the poet, or perhaps editor, has chosen to position him overtly as a figurehead in a way the other books do not. The proem is directly followed with a string of Homeric commonplaces, perhaps taken from an anthology, because Valens and other authors have hold of much the same material. To the writer of these lines Homer mattered for intellectual, professional, and literary reasons. He first embeds the astrological universe in the original Homeric world-view, then deprecates his own work besides that of the master (raiding and reversing *Il.* 6.236 χρύσεα χαλκείων ~ 5.22 in the process), and finally (which is presumably what he is really about) slithers from that to the claim that he offsets or complements Homer, like a gold trim bordering a purple cloth (5.23 ~ *Od.* 6.232 = 23.159). Can he carry it off? Assuming that the same poet is still involved, he does his best in a simile comparing Ares to a forest fire, constructed from mainly simile material or narrative involving fire and flood (see on 5.51, 52a, 52b, 53); it is the poet's most sustained Homeric effort, but all the techniques (straight transcription, changes of case, context-related material blended with opportunistic pilfering) should by now be wholly familiar. A more candid fabric metaphor would involve Homer providing the warp and weft and entire texture of the writing of his epigoni.

And so it continues. There is nothing here we have not seen before. Phrases are copied for mere shape and form (see on 5.229), or lifted or lightly modified

---

[34] Except 78 πανήμερος, proton legomenon, which reinforces ἥμερος (108).
[35] Proton legomena: 143 μουσῳδόν; 185 αἰνομανοῦς; 185 πλατυαύχενος; 187 Τανταλικῇ (note the density in the climactic member of the τέχνη sequence). Hapax legomena: 163 νευρένδετος; 279 ἀνεφέλκεται.
[36] Proton legomenon: 337 εὔκνιστον. Hapax legomena: 237 ἐκπτώσσει; 337 πρόλαλον.
[37] Hapax legomena: 220 ἐπανιπταμένοις; 221 νευροτόμου; 308 χρυσοφορητά is not from a σίνος chart, but is from a pen-portrait of a self-harming individual (see n.).

to provide wadding,[38] content for the narratorial persona (5.10 πολὺ φίλτατος), or filler for passages of authorial direction and structuring.[39] Opportunism raises the occasional eyebrow.[40] One particular species of it is the reapplication of phrases to the astrological cosmos, to describe the heavens (5.29 ἠέρα πουλὺν), for planetary identities (5.245 ἶσον Ἑρμῇ, ex emend. A.-R.), appearance,[41] locations,[42] and behaviour.[43] Two passages in the *Iliad* which involve the literal conveyance of a physical object are now applied to the stars' gifts or their effects.[44] As in the first book, the Homeric poems are also the source of vocabulary for the everyday stuff of the astrologers' universe—native land, vagrancy and wretchedness, childbirth, women's works.[45] Iliadic solemnity, grandeur, and Odyssean wonder are downgraded to the workaday (or the workaday acquires something of their cachet): Circaean enchantment becomes tawdry crime, heroic *Todesverkündung* becomes (perhaps) the antics of the snake-charmer, and the shattering impact of Diomedes' attack becomes a calamity of shoddy Roman building technique.[46] And all this is found throughout the book, not restricted to particular sections of it, except that it is, if anything, particularly pronounced in the ambitious writing of the τέχναι charts. Here, in a manoeuvre we saw especially often in M[a], *Realien* in the Homeric poems are especially frequently mobilised for those of the contemporary world.[47]

The poet uses the same combinatory techniques as the others in the corpus. Line-ends are always among the likeliest places to find epic flotsam and jetsam; some are straight pilferings but others are created by splicing together related or sometimes completely distinct cadences.[48] In some cases the entire line

---

[38] 5.224 διὰ πάντων, 263 εἶδος ἔχοντα [ex emend. A.-R.], 325 ἢ πολλοῖς.

[39] In the introduction to the women's charts: 5.313 εἴτ' ἀνδράσιν εἴτε γυναιξὶν, 315 ἀλλὰ καὶ ὡς ἐρέω.

[40] Or rather it knits them together at 5.230 εὖ ἀραρυίαις (from a physiognomic description of the individual with joined eyebrows), which is taken from expressions for well-fitted gates and doors (see n.).

[41] 5.122 ἀλλά τιν' αὐγὴν ~ Od. 13.325 ἀλλά τιν' ἄλλην.

[42] 5.40 οἷς ἐνὶ οἴκοις: repurposed for planetary houses from Homeric ᾧ (σῷ) ἐνὶ οἴκῳ.

[43] 5.59 δῆριν ἔχουσι ~ Od. 24.515 (ἀρετῆς πέρι) δῆριν ἔχουσι.

[44] 5.92 ἐπέχευε, 125 ἐπέθηκε φέρουσα.

[45] See notes on 5.64 πατρώιον οἶκον, 96 τεύχεσι θωρηχθέντες, 129 χερνήτην ταλαπείριον ἠδέ τ' ἀλήτην, 213 ἱστοῖς, ἠλακάταις and ἔργα γυναικῶν, 327 ἐκ νηδύος.

[46] See notes on 5.106 φάρμακα δεινά, 186 θάνατον †δὲ καλούντων, 201.

[47] *Realien*: 5.158 σφόγγους...πουλυτρήτους; 163 ἐν παλάμῃσιν; 172 ἵππον ἐλαύνων; 176 ἴρηξ ὠκύπτερος; 179 φάσγανον ὀξύ. Hes. *Th.* 40 ἐκ στομάτων appears twice, in 5.162 (different *sedes*), but also 323 (same *sedes*), where the mouths make a very different sort of contribution; this could be comic, depending on one's view of the poet's sense of humour. Filler-material in 5.144 τις ἀνήρ || (relocated in line, and with lengthened alpha); pattern in 5.146 ἠερόφοιτον.

[48] See notes on 5.7 ἀνὰ νύκτα μέλαιναν, 9 ἐμήσατο κῦδος, 153 κύματα μακρὰ κέλευθα, 187 ὑπὸ γαμφηλῇσιν ὀδοῦσιν, 255 πηρὸν ἔθηκεν. Line-beginning: 118 θυμῷ μορμύροντας.

consists of a splice (5.237). One of the most ambitious examples is the outcome concerning the victims of wild animals, which the poet apparently saw as an opportunity for clawing together lines on beasts, boars, tusks, and mountains from wherever he could find them in EGHP (see on 5.194, 195–6). Still more ambitious, however, is the astonishing conclusion of the τέχναι sequence (184–8), a *morceau de bravoure* weaving together largely impressionistic Homerism with very specific allusions to Nicander's *Theriaca*, and a little Theocritus thrown in (why not?).[49] The passage can be added to other evidence of the strange fascination exerted by Nicander's poisonous snakes, whose influence deserves more detailed consideration than the overviews which it tends to receive.[50] Like Lucian, on the one hand, the poet exploits the conceit of the διψάς inflicting torments like those of Tantalus. But like Lucan's offering in book 9 of the *Bellum Civile* on the other, this is also a catalogue of different species of snake, or at least it is an *extremely* condensed one. (Two are expressly distinguished, but others are embroiled in the comparison to intensify the effect; Lucan, for his part, sets out to sound more sciency and iological, but at the same time takes liberties and combines his snakes for rhetorical ends, like M[d].) What distinguishes this passage is that it is here that the poet has decided to employ a technique which in the hands of Dionysius—who would have been proud of it—advertises the 'active tradition' of his verse by weaving together his most respected authorities.[51] But Hellenistic poetry is *not* among M[d]'s usual models; it does not otherwise enlarge his image-repertoire. This cross-period mishmash is certainly something of which M[a] is capable. In this book it appears as gratuitous, if rather splendid, ostentation.

One final point on the use of classical models: the exploitation of tragedy. This poet, like that of the first book, goes in for the occasional moment of plangency which recalls both tragedy and the high pathos of inscribed epitaph (83 πένθιμον ὄμμασι δάκρυ); he also strikes up a generally tragic idiom (98 πίστιν ἄπιστον). 95 ἐλπίσιν ἀπλήστοις shows the possible influence of Euripides' *Iphigenia in Tauris*. But there is also a group of passages, none particularly consequential in itself, which, cumulatively, make it seem possible that a small core of canonical tragedies was in his repertoire: *OT* at 204 ἀσεβῆ (and/or *OC*), 302 κέρδους, 331 πλαστὴ μήτηρ; *Medea* at 102 ἐπὶ λέκτροις, 339 λυγρῷ γαμέτῃ;

---

[49] From Nicander the poet draws together allusions to the asp/cobra (157–89), the viper/dipsas (334–58, one of the best-known passages in the *Theriaca*, containing the acrostic, and 826), the Cocytos (another viper) (232), and the chelydros (436); the additional allusion to Theocr. 24.18 αἱμοβόρους is decorative. Homerism: 184, 188, and see above on 186.

[50] Overduin, 128–31. Add P.Köln VI 244 (3rd c., unknown provenance) = 13 Perale, a classification of vipers which reflects Nicander, and which, according to Perale (172), imitates him, rather than being the work of a more distinguished Hellenistic master.

[51] Lightfoot 2014, 38–40; i. 165 n. 47.

Orestes at 330 κλίνασα δέμας. Except for the bribable seers of the second passage, all concern grievous or criminal family relations, for which tragedy would be *the* go-to source: wretched spouses, blighted sexual relationships, fictitious parenthood, incest. They extend throughout the book and, provided they are not chimerical, once again suggest a consistency of approach that argues for a single author, and a different author from that of the first book, who has the plangent moments but not the core texts.

One other distinctive and apparently consistent feature of the book is the poet's rather interesting use of metaphor. It opens with one, the idea of the anthologising bee (6), though the only thing that is likely to strike us as unusual about this realisation of an old trope, which had already been deployed by Dorotheus in his own proem, is the obscurity with which it is formulated. From this point onwards tropes abound, but the particular issue raised by the subject-matter is not so much when metaphor is still metaphor and when it has been troped to the point of death, but the more interesting one of whether personalised language is figurative when it applies to stars in the first place, or not. Is it metaphor, or does it stay just below the level of metaphor, if EGHP vocabulary throughout the corpus habitually describes the rays, motions, and aspectual relationships of the planets in ways which implicitly credit them with agency and intentionality? For if the planets really are personalities who marshal their forces and feel attractions and antipathies, then their hostile stances are not figurative but literal. Ancient optics, moreover, gave stars *qua* sources of rays the quality of eyes (4.122, 496; 5.45–6, 257 ὄμμα), and it is a nice question how to regard the language that not only makes them sighted but endows them with affective types of gaze (friendly, baleful, and so on). Minimally, this could be taken as the enabling metaphor that, according to Philodemus, technical language needed to get off the ground at all.[52] But it could also be taken as conceptual metaphor, that is, a basic organising system that gives rise to an unlimited number of local realisations (life as a path, or a thread, and so on). M^a has a far wider range of terms for aspect which imply certain types of regard (fixed, concentrated, hostile, wary; see i. 885 and Prévot). The idea of Mars 'raising his eyes' to Venus (5.77 ὅσσ' ἀνέχων), nevertheless, implies a lively personal interest, and as for planetary motion, this poet applies some bold new images which do seem to tip over into metaphor proper. The Sun, rather oddly, 'lurks', as if embedded in a den (5.223 φωλευόμενον, but also in Θ, so perhaps in a common source?); Venus takes Mars into her embrace (282 περιπλεξαμένην).

---

[52] Philodemus, Περὶ ῥητορικῆς, 4, xv. 15–18, i. 175 Sudhaus, πᾶσα τέχνη φων[ὴ]ν οὐ δύναται προ[ίεσ]θαι στερ[η]θεῖσα τῆς ἐκ τῶν μεταφορῶν εὐχρησ[τίας, cited by A. Novokhatko, 'Metaphor (metaphorá), Ancient Theories of', in G. K. Giannakis (ed.), *Encyclopedia of Ancient Greek Language and Linguistics* (Leiden, 2014), ii. 414–18, at 416.

Most metaphors, however, apply to human life or individual human lives. The familiar ones presumably trigger a set of scripted associations, for instance the reflex of hostility to the sexual predator (297–8), or outrage against the violator of domestic commonality (339, if that is a reference to table salt); very differently, efflorescences on the skin (287) strike a tone of quasi-clinical precision. Life's path is a cliché, but its deployment in 242 possibly strives for effect in repurposing a technical term for heavenly bodies; social ascent (276) is very familiar to us, but possibly more eye-catching to a Greek (as opposed to a Roman). The poet is seeking to cast human lives as cosmic dramas, and to give them that momentous and universal quality he reworks metaphors for which tragedy is one possible source, or apparently finds inspiration in the heavens themselves. One man's career of turbulence is brought to an end like the calm after a storm; the metaphor is not new, but calls attention to itself through the repurposing of a verb which was used of literally poured-out water in the source passage (92 ἐπέχευε). Another man apparently plummets to the earth after a meteoric career like a fallen star (98–9, strictly a simile); this seems to be the poet's happy inspiration, and Koechly's brilliant insight in recovering it from a *locus corruptissimus*. Again, individuals seethe in spirit (118), consign their money to the winds and waters (310), or even, apparently, put it into circulation (275). The first is familiar; the second an idiosyncratic reworking; the third new and altogether startling in its accidental anticipation of something so familiar to us. It is very difficult to generalise about all this, but the poet is using metaphor both to vivify *ethos* (of individuals, and even of planets) and to bathe human life itself in a glamorous light of consequence and melodrama. He is an adept reworker of trope and a daring innovator at the same time. Ancient theories of metaphor wobble between commending it as part of a pleasant and non-routine style and discomfort with what is sourced πόρρωθεν.[53] The poet is more enamoured of extravagance than inhibited by austere prescription.

I have already (p. 326) commented on the mythological references strewn throughout the book (Icarus, Attis, Tantalus, Thyestes, and Jocasta), but perhaps it is worth suggesting that they complement the metaphors by lifting the subject-matter onto the plane of universals. One can see what is going on from the tightrope-walker's chart (146–7), which begins routinely enough with the trade name, καλοβάτην, follows it up with the conceit of treading the air, and then evokes the full-blown Icarus myth (even surpassing it, because here are no

---

[53] Arist. *Rhet.* 1405ᵃ8–9 τὸ σαφὲς καὶ τὸ ἡδὺ καὶ τὸ ξενικὸν ἔχει μάλιστα ἡ μεταφορά, 33–5 (against the recherché); for advocates of common usage, see Novokhatko, op. cit. 416 (Theophrastus), 417 (Demetrius).

faux wings); the reference to Attis obviates the need to name the *galli* at all. Myths evoke archetypes, metaphors elicit scripted responses. Both raise the humdrum onto a plane which we regard with enhanced attention.

Composition

The book exhibits formal features very similar to those of the first book. Repetitions of words and phrasal and metrical patterns are of the essence, the casual repetitions of the same or very similar words in close proximity being tightened to the point where it is hard to draw any kind of line between insensitivity and deliberate parallelism.[54] There are Leonine hexameters at 59, 86, 238 (aided by itacism), 293, 299. There are many parallelisms of two lines or more, including rhyming couplets for closural effect at 171–2, 175–6, 311–12 (convincingly restored by D'Orville). Many examples of chiasmus are presented below; the device can be illustrated line-internally by 14, 92, 116,[55] 330, and as a couplet by 23–4, or 254–5 which constitutes the entire apodosis, and neatly wraps up the one-eye/two-eye effect (a parallelism would have done just as well). The sting in the tail is well illustrated by 44–6 + 47; 87–8 + 89. I have introduced another example in 160–1 + 162–3 + 164.

Metre reinforces parallelism, although it is not always easy to be sure that the effect is not casual, especially in passages that lack precise congruence of sense and/or where the rhythm is anyway a common one. There are examples in protases at 217–18, 227–8, 256–7; in certain passages of heightened colour in apodoses at 185–6 (snakes), 219–20 (crucifixion), and in couplets that round off apodoses in 152–3 (relative closure), 163–4 (the whole segment is highly wrought), and 311–12 (rounding off an ignominious career). One instance binds together a short two-line chart (324–5); another aligns two parallel outcomes (40–1). This poet likes maxims and apophthegms, and metrical parallelisms certainly advance the aphoristic feel in 110–11 (when the Moon approaching benefics is good), 122–3 (on the Moon's borrowed light), 209–11 (on luminaries and gender), 247–8 (on the scaly signs). There is also a non-astrological example in 35–6 (the birth of kings in *synodos*) which nicely points the flattering comparison between King Ptolemy and Alexander the Great; as if to hammer the point home, line 38 even repeats the pattern as far as the

---

[54] De Stefani 2017, 34, gives examples (5.108–10 ἐπὶ τὸν Δία; 113–15 Πλησιφαὴς; 141–3 ἐραστάς; 335–6 κακοπράγμονα/πολυπράγμονα), to which could be added e.g. 149–50 δύνουσαν; 247–8 ἐκ φολίδων πολλῶν/καὶ λεπίδων πολλῶν; 322 ἔργοισι … ἐπ᾽ ἔργοις [*ex emend.*].

[55] The poet is so loth to spoil his formal structure that he dispenses with an executive verb.

analogy holds and then diverges at the point where the kings' hours of birth do the same. Although they cluster there, it is hard to be confident about examples in the poet's long discursive charts which do not overlap with the syntactically parallel lines,[56] still less about other segments which are less obviously meaningful.[57]

Once again, these are mostly formal games, serving to highlight precious passages, which means they are especially concentrated in the long charts, both incidentally within them (267 σχήμασιν/χρώμασιν beginning hemistichs; 270, a chiastic Gorgianic jingle) and to round them off (Leonine hexameters end apodoses in 273, 299). The entirety of some charts illustrate the technique. In 234–42, 234–5 are parallel, 238 Leonine, and although the last three lines are heavily restored, it looks as if a chiastic effect was intended with λύπης δίχα [μέτα Koechly]/δίχα λύπης, and εἰς στεινὸν ζωῆς/τερπνὸν βίοτον. 263–73 contains accumulations (three parallel instances of the same part of speech in each of 264, 265, 268, 269), line-internal parallelisms (267, apparently, though ἀπροφίδητον is recalcitrant; 273) and a Gorgianic jingle (270). And in 286–99, the whole passage consists of parallelisms, loose and strict: asyndetic lists (286 + 288–9, and 291 with connectives), Leonine lines (293, 299), isocola (296–7), and chiasmus (294; more approximately in 295). Each line is strongly end-stopped, and all of 293–9 contain one or more main verbs.

Other passages, too, can be singled out where the poet has made a special effort. The musical instruments of 160–4 consist of two sequences of parallel structures, one immediately following the other.[58] The second varies the first; in the first, the native is the subject of the verb and his instrument in the dative, while in the second it is the opposite way round. The second sequence also somewhat relaxes the strict isocolon of the first couplet, with the verb varying its place in the hexameter. (Compare and contrast the much simpler parallelism in *Or. Sib.* 8.114–17.) The snakes of 184–8 consist of two sets of chiasmus, the first a particularly elaborate specimen in which two species of snake in the genitive are enclosed within an accusative armature extending from θάνατον κακοδαίμονα (184) to φοβερὸν θάνατον (186); piquantly, the poet pays tribute to Nicander in a style whose formalism ultimately derives from Aratus. And the

---

[56] 233–4 (though 234–5 are the more obvious syntactic parallel, and in Koechly's view 233 and 234 anyway derive from different sources), 235–7 (though 234–5 are the more obvious pair in sense), 264–5 (though 263–4 are the more obvious pair in sense). Perhaps 338–9 (an accumulation of epithets) is more plausible.

[57] 61–2, 70–2, 108–9, 198–9, 251–2, 314–16.

[58] For two successive sequences of parallelistic structures in ps.-Oppian, *Cynegetica*, see E. Norden, *Die antike Kunstprosa: Vom VI. Jahrhundert v. Chr. bis in die Zeit der Renaissance* (Berlin, 1923), ii. 837–8, adding 1.386–8 + 389–90, 2.102–4 + 105–7.

marauding wild animals of 194–6 are enumerated in a little list which combines chiasmus (genitive of animal–verb–tooth (accusative)/nails (nominative, *ex emend.*)–verb–genitive of animal) with parallelism (194–5 ἤ...ἤ) and a sting in the tail. The specification of detail in an astrological outcome has tipped over particularly clearly here into rhetorical *enumeratio* and *elaboratio*, and the formal devices shape a potentially extendable list into a neat and self-contained structure.

I have noted this poet's especial liking for maxims. Formulating them in a parallelistic style makes for neatness and memorability. Mostly they are astrological in subject-matter: in 44–7, a chiasmus brings out the complementarity of good and bad stars and their counteracting aspects; in 59 + 60–1, a Leonine hexameter followed by an isocolon brings out the malefics' mutually tempering influence; at 209–10, a strict isocolon encapsulates the antithetical characters of the luminaries. There is also one 'ethical' example, an almost Eddaic little caprice on the roadsteads of the sea in 152–3 (four hemistichs, arranged chiastically). Would Snorri have appreciated art of this kind?

Although these are largely virtuosic formal exercises, they do serve occasionally to reinforce sense. In astrological material, we have seen their utility in modelling parallel or complementary agencies. To the maxims already cited can be added 40–1, where chiasmus models swapping of terms, and, very straightforwardly, 75, the parallel naming of the two benefics. Otherwise, a line-internal parallelism suggests the false self-reliance of those who think themselves invulnerable (96), and—an old trick used by other poets—both chiasmus and parallelism encode the arc from poverty and back again (121, 301, cf. 1.222). The techniques, in themselves, are little different from those used by the poet of the first book. It is rather that this one brings them to bear on his own individually favoured types of utterance.

5.6. METRE

Outer Metric

Calculations are based on the following assumptions. To be excluded are lines that are incomplete (52a, 52b), hopelessly corrupt (55, 151, 167, 194, 231, 240 + 241, 292), remade (98b + 99, 141, 181 + 182), and Homeric quotations (15–17, 18–19, 20). That leaves a total of 321 countable lines. The cadences of 191 and 267 are taken as $-\,\cup\cup\,-\,-$.

Hexameter Schemes

	no.	%
5D		
DDDDD	35	10.9
4D, 1S		
SDDDD	31	9.66
DSDDD	39	12.15
DDSDD	37	11.52
DDDSD	11	3.43
3D, 2S		
SSDDD	27	8.41
SDSDD	29	9.03
SDDSD	15	4.67
SDDDS	2	0.62
DSSDD	28	8.72
DSDSD	13	4.05
DSDDS	2	0.62
DDSSD	8	2.49
2D, 3S		
SSSDD	20	6.23
SSDSD	5	1.56
SDSSD	7	2.18
SDSDS	1	0.31
DSSSD	5	1.56
1D, 4S		
SSSSD	6	1.87

Of 32 possible schemes, 19 occur, of which the eight most popular are:

DSDDD	12.15
DDSDD	11.52
DDDDD	10.9
SDDDD	9.66
SDSDD	9.03
DSSDD	8.72
SSDDD	8.41
SSSDD	6.23

This is a fairly unusual pattern. DDDDD is neither top nor second, DDDSD does not appear (in each of the other Manethonian poets every one of 4D, except DDDDS, appears in the top eight), whereas SSSDD unexpectedly does. There are also half a dozen instances of the very unusual rhythm SSSSD (149,

222, 238, 251, 252, 258).⁵⁹ The absent schemes are: DDDDS; DDDSS, DDSDS; DDSSS, DSDSS, DSSDS, SDDSS, SSDDS; DSSSS, SDSSS, SSDSS, SSSDS; SSSSS. Runs of a couple of a pattern at a time are common. There are runs of three SSDDD at 209–11; of DSSDD at 70–2; of SSSDD at 235–7.

The percentage of the poem accounted for by the eight most favoured schemes (76.71%) is in approximately the middle of the range of the astrological poets, and most comparable to Maximus (77.98%). But the spectrum is narrower than in most other poets other than Mᵃ, with relatively low percentages at the top end and relatively high ones lower down. The percentage accounted for by the seventh and eighth most favoured patterns (14.64%) is higher than in any other except Mᶜ(A), where the last place is in any case shared between three schemes. Late antique this poet may be, but in this respect he pulls in quite the opposite direction from the Nonnian school, with the massive disparities that open up between the most favoured schemes and the rest.⁶⁰ Yet neither can he (nor Mᵃ) be said to be pulling back towards a Homeric or Hesiodic norm,⁶¹ and instead the best parallel turns out to be the Sibylline Oracles (spectrum of top eight schemes: 13.3%–5.8%; seventh and eighth schemes: an average of 10.6%, and 14.2% in book 6).⁶²

Ratios and Percentages

1. *Dactyls to spondees* (i. 236)

Numbers (out of 1605 feet)	%
1101 : 504	68.59 : 31.41

Dactyls per verse: 3.43

---

⁵⁹ Agosti and Gonnelli, 312–13. At one instance per 53.5 lines, his rate is even higher than his closest competitor Mᵃ (i. 234; 23 instances, or 1 in 73.22 lines).

⁶⁰ Magnelli 2016, 356 (the *Dionysiaca* has a range from 38.07% to 0.43%). Other figures are calculable from the data supplied by Ludwich 1885, 321–2 and Nieto Ibáñez, 217–22. Another wide range is that of Quintus of Smyrna, from 35.45% to 2.77%.

⁶¹ The Homeric poems range from 19.3%–4.1% and 18.6%–4.2% (J. M. Foley, *Traditional Oral Epic: The Odyssey, Beowulf, and the Serbo-Croatian Return Song* (Berkeley, CA, 1990), 72), and Hesiod's *Theogony* from 19.86%–4.3% (figure from Ludwich).

⁶² Figures from Nieto Ibáñez, 217–22 and 233; Lightfoot 2007, 155 n. 11. Another parallel are the 4th-c. epigrams in Fantuzzi and Sens, 108 (15.28%–5.21%), a very different corpus, although the similarity suggests the utility of drawing comparisons with another body of material uninfluenced by Hellenistic trends.

2. *Dactylic feet per line* (i. 236)
Percentages of lines with *n* dactylic feet:

5	10.9
4	36.76
3	38.61
2	11.84
1	1.87

3. *Percentages of spondaic feet by position in line* (i. 237–8)

1	44.54
2	45.17
3	43.91
4	21.81
5	1.55

4. *Distribution of metra in line by numbers of dactyls in line* (i. 238–9)

Four dactyls	(% ex 118)
SDDDD	26.27
DSDDD	33.05
DDSDD	31.36
DDDSD	9.32
DDDDS	—

Three dactyls	(% ex 124)
SSDDD	21.77
DSDSD	10.48
SDDSD	12

Two dactyls	(% ex 38)
SSDSD	13.16
SSSDD	50
DSSSD	15.79

5. *Location of successive spondees* (i. 239)
With two successive spondees:

1 + 2	18.07
2 + 3	18.38
3 + 4	8.1
4 + 5	—

With three successive spondees:

1 + 2 + 3	8.1
2 + 3 + 4	3.43
3 + 4 + 5	—

Discussion of 1–5
The average number of dactyls per verse (3.43) is towards the bottom of the range, above only M^a books 2 (3.4) and 6 (3.39), and percentages of lines with *n* number of dactylic feet are most similar to M^a as well. There is admittedly some variability between books 2, 3, and 6, but the figures for 2 and 5 dactyls are closest to book 3, and for 1, 3, and 4 dactyls to book 6. Put otherwise, he is the poet with the lowest number of holodactylic lines (although individually the sixth book, on 8.91% is lower still) and with the second-lowest number of lines having no more than a single spondee (ie 5d or 4d).

Turning to spondaic feet by location in line yields another interesting pattern. No other poet, not even M^a, brings out almost equal numbers for the first three feet (though book 3 has very similar figures for at least the first and second). This poet has the second highest number, behind only poet A in the first book, of spondees in the first foot (some books of the Sibylline Oracles produce some high figures in this position as well: i. 237 n. 13) and, conversely, the lowest number of spondees in the fourth and fifth feet. Yet the numbers of spondees in the first and second feet still remain within the range of EGHP.[63] What does not, and what stands way beyond the range of any body of comparative material, is the extraordinary incidence of spondees in the third foot (43.91%), which implies proportionately high numbers of masculine caesurae. No other poet comes near this (the least distant, book 6, trails behind on 30.59%)—least of all the poet(s) of the first book (15.66 or 14.89%).[64] After all this, it is no surprise at all to discover how fond this poet is of successive spondees, especially early in the line, where his figures for 2 + 3 and 1 + 2 + 3 are beyond any other astrological poet. For 1–2 (18.07%) he is somewhat behind the second book (21.4%), but for 2 + 3 (18.38%) his rate is about half as high again as his nearest rival, book 6 (12.23%), and for 1 + 2 + 3 (8.1%) he has almost twice as high a rate as the nearest contender, book 2 again (4.6%). At the other end of the line, however, his figure for the fourth foot is the lowest of all the astrological poets, well below the range of EGHP, and closer to that of the Hellenistic poets, among whom a comparable figure of about 21% is found in the 'New Posidippus' and Alexander of Aetolia.[65] This is related to his (surprising?) sensitivity to Naeke's Law (below, p. 349).

---

[63] Figures in Fantuzzi and Sens, 111; for instance, they quote 42.5% for the first foot in *Od.* 1, and 48.1% for the second in the *Works and Days*.

[64] Comparisons in Nieto Ibáñez, 240 and 241: the closest is *Or. Sib.* 6 (39.2%), followed by 8 (33.9%).

[65] Magnelli, 61; Fantuzzi and Sens, 112.

6. Spondeiazontes

There are only five examples, of which three are participles (24, 96, 216), one a main verb (97), one a noun (159). Only two consist of bucolic diaeresis + tetrasyllable (96, 159), of which only one begins with a vowel (159), though all do have a dactylic fourth foot. Three out of the five (not 24, 216) are in lines with masculine caesurae, and 96 is in a line with only two dactyls.

Such as they are, two have a clearly closural effect (p. 157): 24 occurs at the end of the discursive paragraph about Homer, and 216 occurs at the end of the little sequence about luminaries in places of gender. An explanation can be cobbled together for the two that are adjacent (96 and 97: the grandeur of the characters, the solemnity of their fall), but not one that is beyond special pleading.

Inner Metric

Caesurae

The following figures are produced by excluding 15–20 (Homer), 52a (but assuming 52b is $B_1 + C_2$), 55, 98b + 99, 141, 151, 167, 181, 186 (whether it has a bucolic diaeresis is unclear), 194, 204, 231, 240–1, 292 = 19. That leaves a countable total of 321.

B_1		B_2	No B	C_2
79.13% (254), of which		20.87% (67)	—[66]	35.83% (115[67])
$B_1 + C_1$	30.71% (78)			
$B_1 + C_2$	37.01% (94)			
$B_1 + C_1 + C_2$	2.76% (7[68])			
Neither	29.53% (75[69])			

Discussion

1. The figure for B_1 is extraordinarily high, and for B_2 correspondingly low. B_1 constitutes almost four-fifths of all lines, which is simply out of the range of other astrological poets, and beyond that of even the most extreme books of the Sibylline Oracles (i. 243).
2. There are no lines that lack a third-foot caesura.

---

[66] Although 78 is straddled by a metrical word.
[67] There are a further 20, perhaps 21 (depending on the treatment of 291), cases where C_2 is bridged by a metrical word, and 8 by enclitic parts of the verb 'to be'.
[68] A further 10 examples are precluded by metrical words.
[69] C_1 overridden by metrical words at 38, 75, 196, 238, 244, 273, 294, 301, 311, 314; C_2 at 84.

Book Five   349

3. As in all three later books, $B_1 + C_2$ is favoured over $B_1 + C_1$. The figure for $B_1 + C_1 + C_2$ (2.76%) is much the lowest of all the poets surveyed, at the opposite extreme from Dorotheus (22.4%).

4. The poet treats Meyer's Third Law with gay abandon, with over twice as many violations (29.53%) as the otherwise-worst offender, the third book (13.89%). In this respect he stands at the opposite extreme from Maximus and M^b, who are most punctilious about it.

5. The figure for C_2 is middling, closest to that of the second book (34%).

6. Three instances of C_2 (2.44%) are coupled with a spondaic fourth foot, in other words violate Naeke's Law. At 0.93% of all lines, this is much the lowest among all the astrological poets, lower even than M^b, and at the opposite extreme from M^a (i. 245–6). This is clearly related to the fact that M^d also has the lowest proportion of fourth-foot spondees in the first place (21.81%), and yet there is still a measurable difference between him and Dorotheus, who has the second-lowest number of fourth-foot spondees, but is more tolerant of the licence (3.27% of all lines). Yet this one feature apparently shared with a Hellenistic metrical sensibility[70] remains isolated: it runs up dramatically against the first and fourth observations above.

7. 59 instances of C_2 are coupled with spondaic third foot = 51.3%. In other words, this poet, like the others, is somewhat more inclined to use a spondee in this position than across the poem as a whole (43.91%).

8. There are runs of patterns, some of which are certainly not coincidental, because they correspond to one of the poet's parallelistic structures. Above all, there are remarkable runs of $B_1 + C_2$ at 263–70(!) [with the exception of 268 B_2] and 335–8. Another holds a sequence together at 256–8, while at 171–3 the last line spills over the parallelistic content, and 279–81 is independent of content. Also independent of content are runs of $B_1 + C_1$ at 56–8, 119–21, 132–4, 332–4.

Word-Break and the Second Foot

The following calculations make the following assumptions. Treated as uncountable are 15–20, 52b (but 52a is taken at face value), 98b, 141, 151, 167, 181, 194, 204, 292. Some lines as a whole are suspect, but the verse-patterns at the beginning are entirely characteristic, so their inclusion is moot: 55, 99, 231, 241 ἀλλοτρίαις τε γοναῖς. Thus, a minimum of 13 and a maximum of 17 lines are

---

[70] Though for the spectrum of different poets' behaviours see Magnelli, 77.

excluded. The first percentage is for all lines; the second is with grammatical words only.

Meyer I	53 (33 + 20)[71]	16.21% (10.09%)
Meyer II	47 or 48[72]	14.37% or 14.68%
Meyer I and II	43 (29 + 14)[73]	13.15% (8.87%)
Meyer I or II	14 or 15	4.28% or 4.59%
Giseke	—	
Hilberg	—[74]	

Discussion

1. The extraordinarily high figures for violations of Meyer's First and Second Laws are simply out of the range of the other poets, including that of the first book, and instead in the range of some of the Sibylline Oracles (i. 248, where a figure of 15.5% is cited for *Or. Sib.* 8 from Nieto Ibáñez, although my own figure is lower). There are obvious triggers, but they are not always technical expressions or planetary names (Κρόνος, Ἄρης scanned iambically). Rather, they are metrical schemes that the poet fills with content, whether in protases or in apodoses (of which I count 26 instances, plus another in the proem).

2. The poet is evidently indifferent as to whether the violations involve metrical words or grammatical words. With double violations, over twice as many involve grammatical as metrical words, and some are formed in the

---

[71] In addition to those in n. 73. Grammatical words: 8 μοιραίοισι, 83 καὶ διδόασι, 166 Ἑρμείαο, 230 ὀφθαλμοῖσι. Metrical words: 7 ἀνὰ νύκτα, 42 καὶ τούτων δέ, 61 ψυχροτάτη δέ, 145 καὶ σὺν τῷδε, 262 ὡρονόμου τε, 297 πενθερικοῖς δέ.

[72] 212 εὐνοῦχον σὺ νόει, 224 καὶ φυγάδας σὺ νόει, 231 μηχανικὸν σὺ νόει (caesura uncertain), 270 οὗ πόρος ἐστὶ φύσις, 228 τὸν βίον αὐτὸς ἔχων. Obviated by appositives: 29 Ἀστέρες ἑπτὰ θεοὶ μέν, 156 καθ' ὕδωρ, 198 ἠδὲ Κρόνου, 318 ὁ Κρόνος.

[73] (i) *With grammatical words.* Datives plural: 82 Ἐν δὲ τέκνοισι μόνοις, 99 οὐρανίαισι βολαῖς (accepting at least the line-beginning), 168 ἢ πολλοῖσι μίτοις, 239 καὶ πλασταῖσι γραφαῖς, 242 εὐτραπέλοισι γραφαῖς, 273 ἀνθολόγοισι τροφαῖς, 281 καὶ δολίοισι βρόχοις, 333 Ἡελίοιο τόποις. Dative plural + iambic word: 220 οἰωνοῖσι βορήν, 249 ἐν τούτοισι τυχών, 264 ταῖς ἀκοαῖσι βαρύν, 271 καὶ σοφίῃσι λόγων. Dative singular + iambic word: 92 καὶ χειμῶνι πικρῷ, 279 ἀγρευτῆρι λίνῳ. Participle + iambic word: 111 καὶ λείπουσα καλή, 330 καὶ κλίνασα δέμας. Technical expressions: 47 ἢ τετράγωνος ἐών; 227 Ζεὺς δὲ τρίγωνος ἔῃ; 132 καὶ διάμετρος Ἄρης, 134 ἢν δ' ἀπόκεντρος Ἄρης, 190 καὶ διάμετρος Ἄρης, 334 ἢν διάμετρον ἔχῃ; 110 ἢν φεύγουσα Κρόνον; 58 ἢν στείχωσι δ' ὁμοῦ, 94 ἢ δύνοντες ὁμοῦ. Semi-technical: 142 εἰ δὲ γυναικὸς ἔῃ, 189 εἰ δ' αὔξουσα τύχῃ, 214 εἰ δὲ γυναῖκα λάβοις. Other: 199 τῷ μὲν ἔδωκε βρόχον. Saved by a metrical word: 83 καὶ διδόασι γονῇ ἔπι. (ii) *With metrical words.* 60 θερμότατος γὰρ ἐών, 64 σὺν κείνῳ γὰρ ἐών, 276 σμικρολόγος γὰρ ἐών; 178 καὶ σὺν τῷδε Κρόνον, 202 Μὴ λαθέτω σε Κρόνος, 217 Νυκτερινὸς δὲ Κρόνος, 241 ἀλλοτρίαις τε γοναῖς, 329 ἀλλοτρίην τε γονήν; 55 ψυχρὸς γάρ τε πέλει (suspect line); 102 ἡ Παφίη δὲ πικρή; 122 οὐκ ἰδικὴν γὰρ ἔχει; 128 κἢν λύσῃ δὲ φάσιν; 108 Ἥμερός ἐστιν Ἄρης, 152 ὧν ὁδός ἐστιν ὕδωρ (but excluding 270 οὗ πόρος ἐστὶ φύσις).

[74] Except 105 οὐ καλός Ἄρης D[666], which I have not accepted.

same basic way (e.g. 47 ἢ τετράγωνος ἐών/64 σὺν κείνῳ γὰρ ἐών) irrespective of whether they are metrical or grammatical.

Bulloch's Law

Treatment of Bulloch's Law is entirely unremarkable. Excluding those involving appositives (conjunctions, disjunctives, prepositions, relative pronouns, articles etc.) in the medial position, there are five examples. Two are fully compliant (122, 199). 83 and 210 are non-compliant, with 210 lacking C_2 and a sense-pause at B_1, and 83 lacking a sense-pause in either place. (In other words, 20% of affected lines lack C_2, which is exactly the same as the first book, in the same range as M^b and the Hesiodic poems, and well below the once-again aberrant M^a.) 174 has a bridge across the diaeresis (κλυτὸν Ἥλιον).

Hermann's Bridge

This analysis excludes 15–20, 52a, 55, 98b + 99, 151, 181, 204, 240–1, 292, but allows 141, 167, 194. The total countable is therefore 326.

Here is another stand-out item. There are eleven full violations (9 σοφίης ἔτ', 28 βροτοῖσι, 31 ῥίζα, 62 and 109 κατὰ πάντα, 84 σύμφωνα, 142 πολύκοινον, 216 γυναιξὶ [ex emend.; Nauck's further correction seems unnecessary], 234 φιλέοντι, 274 Ζηνὶ, 276 πολλοῖσι), and only a further two involving metrical words (311 τὸ πλέον δὲ, 314 ὥρη δὲ),[75] suggesting disinhibition about what type of word produces it; nor are cases dominated by technical vocabulary with which it is licensed. Thus, 3.37%/3.99% of lines are affected, which simply soars above any other astrological poet, and is in the same range as the figures for *Or. Sib.* 6 and 8 (i. 251; Lightfoot 2007, 162).

Tiedke's Law

Excluding 15–20, 52a, 55, 98b + 99, 181, 204, 240, 241 (δίχα τοῖς), but including 141, 151, 167, 194, there are 327 countable lines. There are eighteen anapaestic and three spondaic violations, producing a total of 21 = 6.42% affected lines[76]—

---

[75] Saved by metrical word: 112 πρὸς Ἄρηα, 169 μετ' Ἡελίοιο.

[76] Anapaestic: 248 and 291 ἅμα καί, 1 βασιλεῦ and 36 βασιλεὺς, 242 and 271 βίοτον, 134 and 298 ἰδίων, 316 ἰδίοις, 228 καθορῶν, 175 καλάμοις τ', 161 κεφαλὴν, 21 παρέθηκ', 35 and 182 παρέχει, 111 Παφίη, 121 πενίην, 235 ποθέων. Rescued by appositive: 25 τῇ ἰδίῃ, 294 ἐξ ἀλόχων, 301 εἰς πενίην, 314 ὥρη δὲ φύσιν. Spondaic: 37 σκήπτροις, 95 ἀρχὰς, 275 κυκλῶν. Rescued by an appositive: 38 οὐκ αὐτῇ, 114 ἀλλ' οὐκ ἐπὶ δόξῃ (caused by one appositive, rescued by another), 238 ἐν ξείνῃ.

a high figure (2.5% in the Homeric poems) which is not dominated, as in other poets, by planetary names (the only one in fact is 111 Παφίη). The poet remains, however, far below the range of the arch-culprit M[a] (from 11–16.45%).

Tetracola

The following figures exclude 15–20, 52a–b (though it is possible that 52a *was* an example), 98b–99, 141, 181, 182 (remade), 241 (too corrupt), 292 (too uncertain), but include 55, 151, 167, 194, 204, 240 (where it is possible to rule out the presence of tetracola). 327 lines are thus countable.

There are nine true examples (2.75%),[77] while including lines with one appositive adds an additional 25 and with two a further 20; the step-up is far less than in the first or fourth books, though far more than in Dorotheus or 'Antiochus'. Two of the poet's five spondeiazontes are in true tetracola (24, 97) and another among the expanded set (96). All the true examples are in apodoses apart from the first, which is in the proem, but other than that they fail to form obvious patterns. One is clearly closural (24). One constitutes a four-item asyndetic accumulation of epithets (289), and the long discursive charts add other examples with metrical words (236–7, 265, 267–9, 272, 287, 296–7, 291, 293, 335, 337–8). But the poet is not in general striving for weighty effects by this means.

Final Monosyllables

The only example is 123 (-εται) οὐ μόνιμον φῶς, with the characteristic ⌣⌣ | — ⌣⌣ — | — rhythm.

Prosody

Muta cum liquida

From the following figures are excluded 15–20, 98b–99, 141, 181, 182 (restored), 267 †ἀπροφίδητον†. But 55 Κρόνοιο (dubiously), 151 ὑγρήν, 194 καπρίοιο, 241 ἀλλοτρίαις are included. There is a total of 158 instances.

---

[77] 5, 24, 39, 97, 116, 170, 183, 220, 289.

Table 5. *Muta cum liquida* in M^d

Word-boundary		Internal	
position	correption	position	correption
0.63/3.16%	23.4/26.58%	54.43/51.9%	21.52/18.35%
princeps: 0.63/2.53%[1]	‿|‿: 19.62/21.52%[2]	princeps: 38.61/36.71%[3]	‿|‿: 20.25/18.35%[4]
biceps: 0/0.63%[5]	‿‿|: 3.78/5.06%[6]	biceps: 15.82/15.19%[7]	‿‿|: 1.27/0[8]

[1] One (205) or four instances, depending on 196, 260 (*Κρόν-*), 263.
[2] 31 or 34 instances, depending on 198, 311, 318. Cases involve *Κρόν-*, and more rarely *βρόχ-, βροτ-, γραφ-, τρί-*.
[3] 58 or 61 instances, depending on 196, 260 (*Κρόν-*), 263. Cases involve *inter al. μετρ-, τέκν-, δάκρ-, δόγμ-, ψυχρ-, τέχν-, ὑγρ-*.
[4] 29 or 32 instances, depending on 198, 311, 318.
[5] Also treatable as word-internal: 303.
[6] Six or eight instances, depending on 160, 330.
[7] 24 or 25 instances, depending on 303.
[8] Also treatable as word-boundary: 160, 330.

Many words are scanned differently: ἀκριβ- (position: 275; correption: 28); ἀκρ- (position: 221; correption: 177); ἀθρ- (position: 254; correption: 44); πατρ- (position: 64, 238, 293; correption: 89, 232); τέκν- (position: 268; correption: 82), τετρ- (position: 171, 320, 321; correption: 47).

This poet's profile proves to be closest overall to that of M^b for word-boundary. Word-internally, his pattern does not closely shadow that of anyone else, but does have a very similar absolute percentage of internal position in the biceps, and a fairly similar figure for correption, to M^a.

Hiatus

1. After princeps
1st foot: 1
 η: 88 ἢ ἀλόγους
2nd foot: 2
 ου: 235 ἄλλου [ἄλλων S] ὥρην; 253 Ἡελίου οἴκῳ (with digamma)
3rd foot: 26
 η: 83 γονῇ ἔπι [*ex emend.*]; 227 ἔῃ ἐν; [261 ἐσίδῃ ὑψώματι A.–R.]; 263 γλώσσῃ, ἀχαρίστατον
 ῳ: 5 κηρῷ ἀπομαξάμενος [*ex emend.*]; 38 συνόδῳ, ἀλλ'; 155 Ὑδροχόῳ ἠδ'; 279 λίνῳ ἀνεφέλκεται [*ex emend.*]
 ει: 54 τάρβει αἰεί; 126 νεμέσει ἀποδωκαμένη; [157 πελάγει ὑπονήχεται Rigler]; 187 κολάσει ὑπό; 254 βλάπτει, εἰ; 285 παρέχει, ἢν [*ex emend.*]
 οι: 261 ἐσίδοι ὑψώματι; 289 πινυτοί, εὐσχήμονες
 ου: 94 ὁμοῦ ἢ; 221 νευροτόμου ἐσφιγμένος [*ex emend.*]; 222 σκέπτου, εἰ

η: 103 Παφίη ἰδίαις; 111 καλή, ὁπότ'; 113 Μήνη ἐπὶ; 120 Μήνη ὁπότ' ἂν; 165 Παφίη Ἑρμῇ; 173 Σεληναίη ὑψώματι; 243 Μήνη Ἑρμῇ; 316 Παφίη οἴκοις
ω: 314 προλέγω, ὥρη
4th foot: 11
η: 25 τῇ ἰδίῃ
ῳ: 60 ψυχρῷ ἀνακίρναται
αι: 69 καὶ ὑπόγειος; 94 καὶ ὑπόγειοι
ει: 74 ἀεὶ ὁλοώτατος; 114 παρέχει, ἀλλ'; 206 ἐπάγει ὁμογάστριον
η: 61 βολὴ ὑποθάλπεται; 100 κακή, ὡς; 204 ἀσεβῆ υἱὸν [ex emend.]; 298 λέχη ἰδίων [ex emend.]
5th foot: 10
η: 38 αὐτῇ ἐνὶ
ῳ: 190 Ἠελίῳ ὑπόγειος [ex emend.]
αι: 285 καὶ ἐπίδοξα [ex emend.]
ει: 182 παρέχει ὑπόγειος [ex emend.]
ευ: 230 εὖ ἀραρυίαις [Homeric]
οι: 97 ἐπιπειθόμενοι ἀτῶνται
ου: 260 Κριοῦ ἐνὶ
η: 166 ἀγαλλομένη, ἐπὶ; 198 συνθλιβομένη ἰσόμοιρος; 204 ἢ Ἰοκάστην [as transmitted]

Reckoning 52a and 52b as two half-lines that together constitute a whole, and excluding 15–20, 55, 151, 167, 240–1, 292, 98b + 99, 141, 181–2, there are 324 countable lines, and 50 affected lines = 15.43%, or 1 in 6.48 lines. That includes the disjunctive; recalculating without that, since it is licensed (and one of them is doubtful anyway) there are 48 instances, a remarkable figure. The demonstrable mania for hiatus quashes any inhibitions about accepting additional instances which are the result of emendation. The rate is about double that of the Homeric poems, and about three times that of M[a] (i. 260).

As far as location is concerned, it is the same pattern that one sees in Homer and in astrological poets other than book 6 (where they concentrate in the fourth and fifth feet), or book 3 (where they concentrate in the first and fourth): just over half of the total number of instances is at the main caesura. Yet the disproportion, a factor of 26, between the most and least favoured *sedes* (the first) is far greater than anything found in any other poet or in the Homeric poems. Of those in the third foot, ten involve a sense-pause, and another ten occur in expressions giving positional information (seventeen overall involve a preposition or a prepositional compound, ἀν-, ἀπο-, ἐν-, ἐπί-, ὑπό-). These are clearly significant factors, but not ones that encourage the poet to do something he would otherwise avoid. Two out of eleven in the fourth foot involve punctuation, but another two immediately follow καί, and the one instance with punctuation in the fifth book is likewise counteracted by another instance with καί.

Hiatus is most frequently produced by η (fourteen realised out of 62 possible instances, excluding disjunctives), followed by ει (9/89), then ου (6/44), the Homeric favourites ῳ (6/44) and ῃ (5/61), and αι (3/154) and οι (3/53). So η has the highest number of instances outright and the highest percentage of realisations. This is clearly a different pattern from that in EGHP, where the long diphthongs are most commonly involved, and from M[a], where -ου is commonest; the triggers in this book (9/11 instances of η) are nominative endings of the Moon or Venus or adjectives/participles qualifying them.

2. After contracted biceps

Third foot καί, remediable with ⟨τε⟩: 65, 71, 178, 238, 301

Fourth foot: 58 ἢ εἰς

3. After uncontracted biceps

Third foot: 79 ὅτε οἱ [169 μετὰ Ἡελ. D'Orville, not accepted here]

Fourth foot: 67 ἐγκλήματα, ὕβριν; 173 ὑψώματι οὖσα; 261 ὑψώματι οὖσαν; 318 ἀσχήμονα ἔργα (Homeric treatment of digamma)

Fifth foot: 38 ἐνὶ ὥρῃ; 159 ἅμα Ἑρμάωνι; 40 ἐνὶ οἴκοις and 222 ἐνὶ οἴκῳ (digamma, and Homeric)

4. In middle of uncontracted biceps

Second foot: 42 δὲ ἕκαστος

Third foot: 145 γένοιτο ἰοβλέφαρος; ??194 καπρίοιο ὑφίσταται

Fifth foot: 218 μεσουρανέοντα ἄνωθεν [μεσουρανέοντ' ἐπάνωθεν R]

Crasis and Synizesis

The former only at 299 κἄν; the latter only at 31 φύσεως.

Elision

Excluding 15–20, 55, 98b, 99, 141, 151, 167, 181–2, 231, 240–1, 292, that is, in 323 countable lines:

1. Parts of speech

Nouns   6 [32 σφαίρωμ', 46 ὄμματ', 57 πῆμ', 72 Στίλβοντ', 77 ὄσσ', 215 σχῆμ']
Adjectives   1 [123 χείρον']
Pronouns   1 [195 σφ']
Main verbs   7 [21 παρέθηκ', 23 ἐσθ', 78 πέλετ', 102 ἐστ', 140 κοσμεῖτ', 255 κατίδοιτ', 330 ἐστ']
Participles —
Adverbs   5 [9 ἔτ', 52a λάβρ', 57 ἔνθ', 108 πάντοτ', 138 τότ']
Numerals   —
Total: 20.

2. Location in the line

1   52aADV, 57ADV, 77N
2   123ADJ, 140V
3   195PR
4   78V
5   72PN, 255V
7   32N, 57N
7.5 9ADV
9   21V, 23V, 102V, 215N, 330V
9.5 46N, 108ADV, 138ADV

The rate of elision, at 1 in 16.15 lines, is very comparable to that of the first book (1 in 16.5); the tendency for it to be located, if at all, in positions 9 (of which three of five examples are of ἐσθ') and 9.5 is broadly similar to that book as well.

Lengthening in Arsi of Syllables Closed with -ς or -ν

3rd foot:

11 κάματος οὗτος L [⟨δ'⟩ K, ⟨γ'⟩ A.–R.]; 45 ἀργαλέος, ὑπό; 110 Κρόνον ἐπὶ [⟨γ'⟩ ἐπὶ R.: πρὸς A.–R.^conj]; 202 Κρόνος ἰσομοιρήσας [⟨γ'⟩ A.–R.]; 217 Κρόνος ὁπότᾱν [μὲν ἐπὴν R]; 245 πινυτόν, ἐν L [⟨τ'⟩ A.–R.]; 270 φύσις, ἡ; 318 Κρόνος ἀσχήμονα [⟨γ'⟩ A]

4th foot:

26 κάματος εὐσυνθέτῳ [κάματος πραπίδων A.–R.]; 42 ὅτ' ἂν ἐπίκεντρα; 56 δῆριν ἐπὶ [ex emend.; D'Orville ⟨γ'⟩]

5th foot:

[204 υἱὸν Ἰοκάστην K; cf. his note ad loc.]; 222 Τιτῆνος ἐνὶ [Τιτῆνος ⟨γ'⟩ A.–R.]

These are exaggerations of licences familiar since EGHP,[78] and they are circumscribed, so there is no need to appeal to phonetic developments or a loss of sensitivity to the quantity of /o/.[79]

---

[78] For their persistence in later poets, see A. Rzach, 'Neue Beiträge zur Technik des nachhomerischen Hexameters', *SB Wien*, 100 (1882), 307–432, at 354–8 for ι- stems and 399–414 for -ος and -ον.

[79] Agosti and Gonnelli, 338.

Other

133 ἀσχήμονα ζωήν, 316 μετὰ Ζηνός, 338 λυσσάδα, ζηλότυπον: cf. Dorotheus (but already ὑλήεσσα Ζάκυνθος); G.–P. on *HE* 4199; De Stefani 2017, 32.

5.70, 214 εἰν in *thesi*: De Stefani 2017, 32.

Summary

This poet stands out for the spondaicity of the verse (the second lowest average number of dactyls per verse, higher only than M^a; the lowest proportion of DDDDD except for the sixth book; the highest proportion of spondees in the third foot). The last of these implies a high percentage of masculine caesurae, which indeed proves extraordinarily elevated—not only an un-Hellenistic and anti-Nonnian feature, but beyond even the most extreme of the Sibyllina. Insensitive to Meyer's Third Law, untroubled about whether violations of Meyer's First Law and Hermann's Bridge involve metrical words or grammatical ones, and casual about Tiedke's Law, the poet's treatment of inner metre suggests an off-handedness set against which the relative sensitivity to Naeke's Law is an isolated nicety. For many of his mannerisms one can look to M^a. In respect of outer metric, these include the low numbers of holodactylic lines and low numbers of verses with only a single spondee; high numbers of lines with two successive spondees in the first three feet, with three spondees,[80] and preparedness to admit the eccentric pattern SSSSD; the interesting restrictedness in the range of the favoured hexameter schemes; and high proportions of lines with a third-foot spondee.[81] In respect of inner metric, they include low numbers of bucolic caesurae[82] and insensitivity to Tiedke's Law. But in some mannerisms M^d is completely alone, and in respect of prosody he positively

---

[80] Compare with the tables in Nieto Ibáñez, 225 and 226 (two successive spondees) and 228 and 229 (three successive spondees). Figures for M^a and M^d are well beyond the ranges of those quoted for archaic poetry, and most comparable, if at all, to certain books of the Sibyllina (especially the sixth). So, for spondees in 1 + 2 *Or. Sib.* 6 and 7 (respectively 28.5% and 24.6%) overtop even books 2 (21.4%) and 5 (18.07%), while for spondees in 2 + 3 the best comparisons for M^d (18.38%!) are *Or. Sib.* 6 (17.8%) followed by *Or. Sib.* 8 (15.9%). For spondees in 1 + 2 + 3, the best comparison for M^d (8.1%!) is *Or. Sib.* 6 (7.1%), while M^a (3.99–4.6%) is best compared to *Or. Sib.* 2 (4.8%). For spondees in 2 + 3 + 4, the highest figure occurs in book 6 (4.39%), though this is beggared by *Or. Sib.* 8 (7.7%).

[81] Although interestingly they differ when it comes to the fourth. There is a general post-Homeric trend, even in the Sibylline Oracles, to reduce the number of spondees in this *sedes* (Nieto Ibáñez, 244, 245), and among astrological poets M^d in fact represents this tendency most strongly. But M^a goes in quite the opposite direction, and the sixth book reaches a high of 44.55% (Homer has 29.5%).

[82] The remarkably divergent numbers quoted for other authors (West 1982, 154; van Raalte, 86–7; Nieto Ibáñez, 158–9) add to the difficulty of contextualising this, but the numbers are again most comparable to some books of the Sibyllina (8: 35.3%; 12: 32.9%; 13: 32.7%).

cultivates hiatus after the *princeps* and lengthenings *in arsi* (De Stefani 2017, 31–2) to the point where they become almost an aspect of house style. In short, comparing and contrasting this poet's metrical technique with the rest, and especially the relatively refined M^b, is one of the best ways of appreciating the diversity within the Manethonian corpus.

5.7. NARRATOR AND ADDRESSEE

This book has a wider range than others in that it combines apotelesmata with abstract rules and generalisations, and similarly combines lofty *ex cathedra* pronouncements with more personal interventions.[83]

The speaker of the proem presents himself in some kind of continuity with the arcana of Egyptian temples, as having friendly relations (though apparently not contemporary ones) with Petosiris, and as being in a position to address the king in courteous professional terms according to the customary style of the prose preface. In the next section, concerning Homer, the focus shifts away from antique σοφίη and Egyptian traditions to Greek ones; whatever was in those *adyta*, Homer now becomes the originator of the world-view, and the poet's task is to add embellishment or the technical refinements of his discipline (which he calls δόγματα θεῖα) to the understanding of the world that Homer had already promulgated. Whether the cultural swerve is credible in a single poet is debatable. The δόγματα θεῖα linger over into 28; the courtly address to the king persists into 35–8 (βασιλεῦ; an analogy with Alexander) and 207–8 ('be witness to this incest configuration, mindful of your own marriage'). But if the book consists wholly or mainly of a single poet's work, he has kept up the fiction with which he began only very patchily indeed.

There is another narratorial intervention at the end when the speaker breaks off to announce that everything he has said so far applies equally well to men and women, but that the last section is for women alone. This is neutral and colourless save insofar as one is willing to activate the original contexts of the EGHP formula (ἀλλὰ καὶ ὣς ἐρέω) which the poet mobilises at this point (315 n.); I see the poet in general as more opportunistic than subtle. More interesting and characteristic of this book, and more capable of supporting an argument for its (substantial) cohesion, is the formula 'if you find'/'if you see' in the protasis. This is more distinctive.[84] 'If you find' is a common way of expressing

---

[83] The narratorial interventions are noted by Monteventi, 148.
[84] To the examples below add 5.177 Ἄρεα δ' εἰ γνοίης; 214 εἰ δὲ γυναῖκα λάβοις.

location in prose astrology, but not normal in the Manethoniana.[85] 'If you see' is found otherwise only in 6.213–14 εἰ...κατίδοις ἄμφω ζώοιν ἔνι Μήνην and for an additional stipulation in 1.73 αἴ κεν ἴδηαι; otherwise, if verbs of vision or discovery are used at all, passive constructions are preferred.[86] 'If you see' is found in the τέχναι (154) and the second half of the book (218, 280—though not in the long discursive charts), and three examples (211–12, 214–15, 223–4) contain the full form 'if you see, then be apprised of/expect/prognosticate', which is also in Anubion (F 3a, d). The first τέχνη chart is also linked to a later one by the instruction to look (138, 222 σκέπτου, cf. 314 σκεπτόμενος), a verb not just suitable for attentive regard, but at home in prognostics (so, not just 'look', but 'look *whether*'); Aratus uses σκέπτεο in both senses, and, as in 222, to broach a new topic.[87]

There are other 'didactic' verbs as well. Individually they are more miscellaneous, but the point is simply that the narrator is making more efforts than the others in the corpus to buttonhole his reader. There is a little cluster of νόει, 'recognise' what the configuration means (215) or a particular kind of native (212, 224, and 231);[88] 'reckon' or 'calculate' (324 λογίζου);[89] and its negative version, 'let not *x* escape you' (202 Μὴ λαθέτω σε: see ad loc.). Not much in this vein is to be had from the Good and Bad Stars save an instruction to recognise their gifts (81 Ἀργαλέων ἄστρων δυνατῶς γίγνωσκε τὰ δῶρα); there are also two instances of the 'be very afraid' motif (49 δείμαινε, 54 τάρβει; see p. 171). Gestures towards the addressee thus go considerably further than the minimally involved τοι (i. 192), of which there is a single instance in 209 Χαίρει τοι Τιτὰν μὲν ἐπ' ἀρσενικοῖσι τόποισιν. The variation in l. 27 is particularly interesting, for John Philoponus (who notionally quotes the line in verse regardless of

---

[85] 'If/when you find': 5.137 ὅτ' ἂν εὑρήσῃς; 149 Ἢν δ' εὕροις Μήνην; 211–12 εἰ δ' ἄμφω τούτους ἐνὶ θηλυτέροισι καθεύροις; 223 κἢν εὕρῃς τοῦτον; 282 ἢν Παφίην εὕρῃς; 321 εἰ καὶ τὴν ὥρην ἐν τετραπόδεσσι καθεύροις. The simplex is the standard prose term (Heilen 2015, 713) for the location of an entity in a chart. M^d is the only poet in the corpus to use it. The commoner passive use is illustrated by the *pinax* of the third book, but the second person 'if you find' is also attested in astrological prose (e.g. CCAG viii/1. 140.9; xi/2. 112.1; Theophilus, *De rebus praesertim bellicis*; Apomasar, *De myst.* 5×), and in Anubion, F 4 ii. 2 εὕροις (vl). M^a had 3.416 εὕρῃς of the *aphaeretes* in the calculation of the length of life (where it is a matter of determination, not of 'finding' a planet), and in 6.338 (τις) ἀνεύροι 'infer', in a transitional formula.

[86] For the passive, see 4.65, al. ὀφθῇ, 4.481 = 1.308 ὁραθῇ; 6.116, al. ὁρῆται; 2.145, al. ὁρῶνται; 6.164 ὁρόωνται; 3.248 ὁρῶντο; 3.369, al. ὁρῷτο; 2.357, al. ὀφθείς.

[87] 'Look whether' in Aratus, 832–4, 881–2. Otherwise to introduce new topic in 778, 799, 892, 994.

[88] Of making forecasts about natives also in Camaterus, *Introd.* 2810–11, 2828, 2891–2, 2944; cf. Θ p. 150.1. There are also many examples in Dorotheus and Ptolemy of ὑπονοητέον used in the same way. Another very common formulation is 'say' (λέγε, φάσκε; Valens, V 1.13 δεήσει...λέγειν), as if instructing the practitioner in what to say to his client.

[89] Compare Aratus, 801, 1129 τεκμαίρεο (also used for closure at 1154); 803–4 δοκέειν; 795, 907 δειδέχθαι (see Kidd on 795: according to sense, from δέχομαι); 813, 908, 1128 δοκεύειν.

defective scansion) gives it its expected meaning, 'if the horoscope goes wrong' (then the whole calculation is thrown out).[90] But in the version transmitted by L the verb is apparently a second person middle, 'if you make a mistake with regard to the horoscope' (27 ἢν δ᾽ ὥρην ψεύσῃ τι). The speaker positions himself as having oversight over the adept's bungling efforts, a far more involved relationship than that envisaged by the other books. The chasm which had opened in the fourth book between the poet's massive efforts towards his reader and the didactic narrator's minimal ones towards his addressee has closed at least somewhat.

5.8. ASTROLOGICA

Treatment of Technical Terms

This poet incorporates a good deal of technical vocabulary, not only terms shared with other poets in the corpus (or with Dorotheus),[91] or terms which are not prosaic but which are attested in other astrological poets,[92] but also prose expressions which are newly included here.[93] The last group includes specialised nouns (εὐκρασία, ἐπέμβασις, σύνδεσμος, ἀκρονύκτιον), and set

---

[90] The second quotation, Ἢν δ᾽ ὥρη ψεύσηται, ἐξώλισθεν ἅπαντα, in fact scans according to the unusual rhythm (SSSSD), and the hiatus is entirely allowable by the poet's standards, but the verb needs to be compounded with συν.

[91] 5.134 ἀπόκεντρος (also 3.269); 115 ἀπορρέουσα (also M^a); 169 ἐπαμφορέοιτο [ex emend.] (cf. 6.104 ἐπαμφορίῃσιν); 209 ἐπ᾽ ἀρσενικοῖσι τόποισιν (also 1.279 ἐν ἀρσενικοῖσι τόποισιν); εὑρίσκειν, of location (see n. 85); 32 ζωδιακοῦ κύκλου (also 2.14–15, 55, 129); 42, 76 ἐπίκεντρος (M^{b,c}); 252 κεντρωθείς (also 1.90); 111 λείπουσα = waning (also 1.212); 39, 189, 218, 324 μεσ(σ)ουρανεῖν (all books except M^b); 178 παρεῖναι σύν (2.438, 4.319(?), 1.106–7); 115 πλησιφαής (M^c); 243 συνάπτειν (all books except M^b); 58 σύνοδος (M^{b,c}); 69, 94, 144, 182, 190, 217 ὑπόγειος (M^a); 227 τρίγωνος (all books); 48 φάσις (M^{a,c}); 192 ὡρονομεῖν (all books). Shared with Dorotheus: 103 ταπεινοί (cf. Dorotheus, p. 324.5 ταπεινώσεις); 33, 173, 261 ὕψωμα (cf. Dorotheus, p. 324.5 ὑψώματα).

[92] 5.166 ἀγάλλεσθαι (2.404, 501; 3.17, 351, 358); 44, 254 ἀθρεῖν (all books); 48 ἀντολίη (M^{a,b,d}); 134 ἀπόκεντρος (3.269); 53, 72, 148, 261 ἐσορᾶν (all books); 75, 174, 228, 255 καθορᾶν (all books); 77 λεύσσειν; 76 ὁδεύων (M^{a,c}); 58, 165, 320 στείχειν (6.277, 4.466); 110 φεύγειν, of Moon (6.613, 1.185); ὥρη, passim (all books); 262, 278 ὡρονόμος (M^{a,c}). Possibly βολή (5.55, 61, 99; 2.364; 6.314) should be included here too, but there is also a single example in Ptol. 3.10.3. εὑρίσκειν used of συναφή (subj. the Moon in 307 εὕρῃ, 332 εὑροῦσα; subj. the planet in 132 εὑρών) seems unusual, but there is a part-parallel in Dorotheus, p. 326.8, 13 ἀστὴρ οὐκέτι φαῦλος ἐπὴν ἀγαθὸν τόπον εὕρῃ.

[93] 108 ἄκεντρος; 177 ἀκρονύκτιον (for ἀκρόνυχος/ἀκρόνυκτος); 43 ἀτόνως; 228 τὸν βίον (ἔχειν); 280 ἐκ διαμέτρου; 80 κατ᾽ ἐπέμβασιν; 284–5 ἐπίδοξος; 59 εὐκρασίη; 49 ἑῷος; 202 ἰσομοιρήσας (prose uses the present participle); 112 μεστή, of the Moon; 49, 217 νυκτερινός, used of planet; 182 πρᾶξιν...παρέχειν; 127 σύνδεσμος, 300 σύνδεσμον ἔχειν; 62, 111, 274 συνοδεύειν.

phrases (πρᾶξιν...παρέχειν, τὸν βίον...ἔχειν). Yet it is not enough to say that it is his use of technical vocabulary *per se* that characterises him. He not only uses it but also deforms and varies it.

By deformation I mean technical language that is 'not quite right'. The right words are used, but not in quite the usual applications.[94] More often, novelty is produced through variation, whether of vocabulary, construction, or both. Cognates suggest the technical term by sharing its root,[95] while synonyms (53 κενοῦται for e.g. ἀτονεῖ or ἐξασθενεῖ or θραύεται; 66 κοινούμενος for 'in conjunction with'; 278 χώρα for χῶρος for τόπος: see i. 877) or periphrastic expressions (112 μεῖον...ἢ μεῖζον μεστή for ἀμφίκυρτος) circumvent it. Throughout the Good and Bad Stars, adjectives of quality for benefics and malefics ring the changes on plain old ἀγαθοποιοί and κακοποιοί (45–6 and 81 ἀργαλέος; 45, 102 βάσκανος; 78 πανήμερος; 100 λοίγιος; 108 ἥμερος). A few such substitutions are Homerisms or other poeticisms (79 παλίνορσος, for 'retrograde'; 174 Ὠκεανίτην, which is not itself epic, but suggests the epic conceit of the Sun rising from or sinking into the Ocean; 226 προφύγῃ, enhancing φεύγειν which is itself poetic), but that is not the only source of variation. The poet ranges widely, most strikingly with a couple of bold metaphors (pp. 339–40) φωλευόμενον (223) and περιπλεξαμένην (282). συνθλιβομένη (198) is a bold metaphor as well, but paralleled in Timaeus Praxidas (see ad loc.); the priority is not clear.

As for varying constructions, all poets do this. Dorotheus already did. The point is that it is not just a matter of establishing where or how deviantly a poet uses technical vocabulary, but more importantly of identifying the new constructions to which he subjects it. To take expressions of aspect, some are attested in astrological prose, others are not.[96] It is not always obvious which are which (although it is likely to have been more so to an ancient adept with an attuned ear), but presumably it was always apparent that 90 μάρτυς ἐπέλθῃ (of

---

[94] 5.63 ἄστροις, 81 ἄστρων for stars (not constellations); 105 ἐπεμβαίνων 'aspecting'; 165 συνοικῇ 'be in the house of'; 84 σύμφωνα used of *kentra* (as opposed to aspect); σύνοδος and συνοδεύειν used for conjunction of planets other than luminaries (see on 5.35–8); 122 φάσιν = light (i.e. shining), not phase. In 48 συναφή is used for the conjunction with the Sun of planets other than the Moon. συναφή in practice refers mostly to the Moon, but in principle nothing so restricts it (for instance, Ptol. 1.24 makes no such restriction). Obscurity rather than catachresis is represented by 128 κῆν λύσῃ δὲ φάσιν τὰ τελέσματα, and 260 κατέχων is probably imprecise rather than catachrestic too. Pseudo-technical: 139b–139a μεθοδεύεται...σχήματι τῆς Παφίης.

[95] 109, 174, 225, 257 αὐξιφαής for αὐξιφωτοῦσα; 197 μέσῃ συνέχοιτο paraphrases ἐμπερίσχεσις; 282 περιπλεξαμένην suggests συμπλοκή; 32 σφαίρωμα for σφαῖρα, but paralleled also in Or. Sib.

[96] Attested in prose: 5.136 Παφίη διάμετρος, 280 ἐκ διαμέτρου. Not: 5.130 Ἡελίου...διάμετρος; 5.334, cf. 1.89, 121 διάμετρον ἔχειν; 5.132 διάμετρος...εὑρὼν + acc.; 5.228 καθορῶν διάμετρος. Dorotheus, p. 394.6 πρὶν Μήνην διάμετρον ἐς Ἡελίοιο περῆσαι comes from catarchic astrology, and an analogy is being drawn between the motions of the heavenly body and the human being it represents.

which both words are represented in astrological prose) have been reassembled into a familiar hexameter cadence (αὐτὸς ἐπελθών, υἱὸς ἐπελθών, ἦμαρ ἐπέλθῃ, ὕπνος ἐπέλθοι, οἷος ἐπελθών, etc.). So too with expressions of location: some tweak standard formulations in a new direction (144 ὑπόγειον ἔχων) which is not always very clear (50 δύνουσαν τὰ βόρεια).

In general, this book handles technical terminology in a fairly similar way to the first, with both obviously different from the windy verbiage of the fourth book. Both are quite happy to introduce prose terminology alongside conventional poeticisms, though they make different choices about which terms to include. This one, however, seems to push technical terminology further over into catachresis, which would likely produce a double impression on an ancient reader of precision in the detail transmitted and wilful eccentricity, occasionally to the point of obscurantism (44 μεγάλοις τοῖς σχήμασι; 128 κῆν λύσῃ δὲ φάσιν τὰ τελέσματά γ'), in the way it is formulated.

Planetary Names and Epithets

Eccentric this book may be in many ways, but it is absolutely on-trend in placing Mars at the head of the list of 147 occurrences of planetary names. Indeed, it pushes the runner-up into second place by a wider margin than in any other book. In this case that planet is the Moon (16.33%), followed by Venus (15.65%), who, for reasons that are not obvious, pushes the other malefic into fourth place (14.97%). Jupiter's dismal showing (8.16%) is only worsted by his showing in the fourth book (7.51%).

A few light-names are turned into epithets (curiously, the Sun is φαέθων but Jupiter φαεσίμβροτος; Mercury στίλβων; Mars πυρβόλος). Quasi-anthropomorphic epithets are used for Mercury and Venus (εὔσφυρος, εὐπλόκαμος, ἰοβλέφαρος), but the main emphasis in this book is on moral qualities, for the Sun (κακοεργός), Mercury (κακότεχνος), Mars (ὀλοώτατος, λοίγιος, ὀβριμοεργός, θυμούμενος), and Jupiter (ἀγαθός, σωτήρ). One might be tempted to connect the remarkable preference for 'the Paphian', as well as Titan for the Sun, to the poet's penchant for mythological allusion, but the epithets in general are not strongly mythological. Possible connections with Dorotheus are to be found in Mars ὀβριμοεργός and Dorotheus ὄ(μ)βριμος; Saturn βραβεύς and Dorotheus βραβευτής. Τιτάν of the Sun, ψυχρός of Saturn, are banal.

Sun

17 instances (11.56%) (14 Helios, 3 Titan), of which three are ornamented (5.63 Ἡλίου κακοεργοῦ, 148 Τιτὰν φαέθων, 174 κλυτὸν Ἥλιον).

Moon

24 instances (16.33%) (16 of Μήνη, 8 of Σελήνη), of which one is ornamented (250 Μήνη κεραή), five described by phase (113 πλησιφαὴς; 109 and 225 αὐξιφαὴς, 189 αὔξουσα, 257 αὐξιφαοῦς), and one further entitled 197 ἡ βασίλεια.

Mercury

17 instances, excluding 2 and 245 (11.56%) (13 mythological, four light-names + one light-name used as epithet), three of which are ornamented (93 κακότεχνος, 243 στίλβοντι, 274 εὔσφυρος).

Venus

23 instances (15.65%) (3× Ἀφροδίτη, 17× Παφίη, 2× Κυθέρεια, 1× Κυθήρη), of which three are ornamented (75 εὐπλόκαμον Κυθέρειαν, 145 ἰοβλέφαρος Κυθέρεια, 250 γλαυκιόωσα Κυθήρη).

Mars

32 instances (21.77%) (31 mythological, 1 light-name), of which at least five are ornamented (75 ὀλοώτατος Ἄρης, 93 πυρβόλος Ἄρης, 177 Ἄρεα...ὀβριμοεργόν, 225 θερμὸν...Ἄρηα, but 60 θερμότατος is predicative; 249 λοίγιος Ἄρης, but 100 λοίγιος is predicative; 280 θυμούμενον predicative).

Jupiter

12 instances (8.16%) (9 Ζεύς; 3 Κρονίδης; no light-names), of which there is a single line containing four epithets (256 ἀγαθὸς σωτὴρ φαεσίμβροτος οὐράνιος Ζεύς).

This remarkable line has an overall similarity with 'Antiochus', l. 84 (CCAG i. 112.2) πλούτου καὶ καρπῶν δωτὴρ μέγας οὐράνιος Ζεύς, which also fills up a whole line with Jupiter's benevolence; and even, in the heaping-up of epithets of the/a supreme deity, a general similarity with the style of Or. Sib. (Lightfoot 2007, Appendix A).

For σωτήρ as epithet of Zeus, see C. F. H. Bruchmann, *Epitheta Deorum quae apud poetas graecos leguntur* (Leipzig, 1893), s.v.; A. B. Cook, *Zeus: A Study in Ancient Religion*, ii/1: *Zeus, God of the Dark Sky (Thunder and Lightning)* (Cambridge, 1925), 1123–5 n. 7; Arnott on Alexis, fr. 234.1–2. From the literary evidence the epithet is found above all in tragedy and comedy (also Pindar); the earliest examples are Aesch. *Sept.* 520, *Suppl.* 26 (see Sommerstein ad loc.). In Aeschylus of course the main association is with the third libation, and that would make the transference seem all the more arbitrary. However, the cult of

Zeus Soter in fourth-century Athens was a popular focus for everyday concerns (Robert Parker, *Athenian Religion: A History* (Oxford, 1996), 239–40)—indeed, concerns of the sort which astrology itself would later focus (Ar. *Plut.* 1179–81 includes trade and lawsuits).

ἀγαθός is not part of the title σωτήρ (a couple of Christian writers refer to the 'good saviour', but it is not a formal expression nor cult title), and seems to be unique. It recalls Ἀγαθὸς Δαίμων on the one hand, Zeus Soter on the other, but the composer of the line was not clearly thinking of that, as opposed to a way of filling the hexameter.

For φαεσίμβροτος, remarkably transferred to Jupiter given its (presumably) perceived strong association with the Sun, see i. 910 n. 8.

For οὐράνιος Ζεύς (omitted from Table Four in i. 910) see Nonn. *D.* 21.4 (and Hopkinson ad loc.), 25.348, 31.44, Dioscorus (XLII Heitsch), fr. 22.11 Heitsch, and Lightfoot 2007, 537–8.

Saturn

22 instances (14.97%), all mythological, of which four are ornamented (61 ψυχροτάτη δὲ Κρόνοιο βολή, 226 λίην ψυχρήν τ' ἀκτῖνα Κρόνοιο, 334 δνοφερὴν ἀκτῖνα Κρόνοιο; also 262 βραβεὺς τοῦ πνεύματος, properly a description rather than an epithet).

Addenda

1. PINAX OF Θ AGAINST MANETHO (M^a, M^b, M^c, M^d)

Θ ch. 57. Ἀποτελέσματα τοῦ πίνακος τῆς ‹δωδεκατόπου›

149.9–11			5.132–3
151.1–5			5.69–71
151.7	4.248		
159.24–5			5.69–71
166.22–4	4.249–62	1.83–8	
167.7–8			5.39
168.14			5.40
169.4–8	4.354–8		5.137–43

Θ ch. 59. Περὶ σχημάτων Σελήνης καθολικῶν

183.2–3		5.246–51
183.14–16	4.233	
183.16–17		5.222–4

Θ ch. 61. Καθολικὰ σχήματα περὶ σινῶν καὶ παθῶν

189.6–8	1.134–8	
189.10–13	1.50–7	
189.13–14		5.252–5
189.25–6		5.246–51

Θ ch. 65. Περὶ μαινομένων καὶ ἐπιληπτικῶν

192.9–11			1.89–91	
192.11–16	6.554–65 (see i. 835)			
192.13–14		4.537–44	1.229–34	
192.16–18			1.235–44	
192.23–193.1	6.499–503	4.193–200		
193.1–3	6.446–9	4.230–7		
193.5–6				5.115–19
193.16–17		4.545–51		
193.17–18	6.601–3	4.552–9		

Θ ch. 66. Περὶ ἀσελγῶν καὶ μεθυστῶν καὶ ἐμπαθῶν

194.18–195.2	4.218–23	
195.5–8		5.136
195.5–8 + 8–10	4.294–308 + 309–16	
195.12–14		5.320–3

Θ ch. 77. Καθολικὰ σχήματα βιαιοθανάτων

200.1–2		1.250–5	5.197–201
201.2–5	4.193–200		
201.20–2			5.192–6
201.22–3	4.613		5.217–21
201.23–4	4.614–18		

Θ ch. 82. Περὶ πραξέως καὶ ἐπιτηδεύματος

209.10–13	1.129–33

Θ ch. 83. Περὶ τῶν γ′ ἀστέρων τῶν σημαινόντων τὰς πράξεις

* = material supplementary to Ptolemy

210.26–7		4.211, 577–81		
210.26–9		4.157–60		
210.27–8	6.468–71	4.127–9		
210.27		4.579–80		
210.29–31		4.139–45	1.290–1, 303	
210.29–30	6.489–90			
210.30–211.1	6.479	4.127		
211.10–13			1.75–82	
*211.10–11	6.401–4	4.440–1		
*211.13–14	6.518–19	4.121–4		5.135
*211.27–9	6.415–18, 419–21	4.320–6, 440		
*211.29–31	6.422–4	4.251–9	1.85–8	
212.2–4		4.332		
212.5–6	6.499–503	4.193–200; 478–90	1.306–20	
*212.11–12				5.280–1
*212.16–18	6.422–4	4.257–8	1.85–8	
*212.18–20		4.127–8		
*212.23–4				5.149–53
*212.24–5		4.560–6		
212.27–8	6.343–7	4.570		
212.29–31	6.496–8	4.190–2		
212.28		4.130		
*213.1	6.439–40, 441–5	4.286–9		
*213.4–7		4.287–9		
*213.7–8			1.180–1 + 184	
213.9–13	6.366–70, 480–3, 504–10	4.206–9	1.58–61, 62–5	
213.10	6.401–3			
213.13		4.344		
213.13–14		4.322		
*213.22–4	6.522–5	4.146–52	1.294–300	
*213.26–7	6.344–7	4.569–70		

Θ ch. 84. Περὶ τεχνῶν

214.9-11	6.512	4.170-5
214.12-13		4.176-9
214.13-17	6.366-70 + 371-2	4.180-6

Θ ch. 85. Περὶ ῥητόρων καὶ παιδευτῶν

| 214.18-21 | 6.476-9 | 4.201-5 | 1.301-5 |

Θ ch. 86. Περὶ μαθηματικῶν ἢ μάντεων

| 214.22-215.3 | 6.436-8, 468-71 | 4.209-13, 425-30 |

Θ ch. 87. Περὶ βαλανέων

| 215.4-6 | 6.422-4 | 4.249-62 |

Θ ch. 88. Περὶ νεκρεπαρτῶν

| 215.8-11 | 6.494-8 | 4.187-92 |
| | 6.456-62 | 4.263-8 |

Θ ch. 89. Περὶ οἰκοδόμων ἢ κεραμέων

| 215.12-16 | 6.415-18 | 4.290-3 |
| 215.16-17 | 6.439-10 | 4.286-9 |

Θ ch. 90. Περὶ μεθυστῶν καὶ κιναίδων καὶ γοήτων

| 215.18-21 | 6.586-90 | 4.294-308 |
| 215.21-2 | 6.591-2 | 4.309-16 |

Θ ch. 91. Περὶ τεκτόνων καὶ βυρσέων καὶ λιθοξόων καὶ καβιδαρίων

| 216.1-5 + 5-6 + 6-7 | 6.415-18, 419-21 | 4.317-26 |
| 216.7 | 6.343-4 | |

Θ ch. 92. Περὶ κυνηγῶν καὶ ἱερακοτρόφων καὶ ὀρνιθοτρόφων καὶ ζωγράφων

| 216.8-15 | | 4.238-48, 333-40 |
| 216.15-16 | 6.520-5 | 4.341-6 |

Θ ch. 93. Περὶ ναυτῶν καὶ κυβερνήτων

| 216.17-22 | 6.362-5 | 4.131-8, 4.395-401 | 1.321-6 |

Θ ch. 94. Περὶ ῥαπτῶν

| 216.23-5 | 6.431-5 | 4.420-4 |

Θ ch. 95. Περὶ μηχανικῶν καὶ ψηφάδων

| 217.1-3 | 6.526-7 | 4.437-43 |
| 217.3 | 6.401-4 | |

Θ ch. 96. Περὶ μίμων

217.5–7	4.445–6, cf. 4.280–5		5.103–4, 137–41
217.9	4.287–9		5.144–7
217.10–11			5.149–53
217.12–13	4.185		5.159–64
217.14–15	4.343		5.165–8
217.16–18			5.169–72
217.19–20	4.339		5.173–6
217.21–3			5.181–8
217.24–218.2	4.230–7	1.38–9	5.252–3
218.3–6 + 7–8			5.260–73

2. PINAX OF ANUBION AGAINST MANETHO, FIRMICUS

The table shows where there are parallels in Anubion and/or Firmicus for the pentameters in M^c, which are highlighted in **bold**.

Anubion	Firmicus	Manethoniana
	Books 3–4	
	3.4.32	1.167–74 (**169** as transmitted by Hephaestion but not L)
	4.3.1	1.208 + **209**
	—	1.210 + **211**
	4.3.2	1.212–14 (L¹ tries to make a hexameter out of **213**)
	4.11.7	1.158–66 (**159**)
	Book 6	
	6.29.3	1.341 + **342** (L; L¹ attempts hexameter)
	6.29.4	1.343–**345**
	6.29.5	1.346–7, **348–9**
F 4 ii. 1	6.29.23	6.171–5
F 4 ii. 2–4	6.29.23	6.176–9
F 4 ii. 5	6.29.24	—
F 4 ii. 6–9	6.29.24	6.180–4 + 185–6
F 4 ii. 10–12 + 13–16	6.30.1	6.160–9; 1.106–11
F 4 ii. 17–18	6.30.1	6.170–1
		1.112–**114**
F 4 ii. 19–24	6.30.2–4	
	6.30.5	Cf. 6.276–81; 1.121–8 (**124, 128**)
	6.30.18	Cf. 6.534–40, 1.115–18
F 6	6.30.20–2	
F 7	6.31.51–5	Cf. 1.350–**352**
F 8	6.31.75–86	

3. METRE OVERVIEW

Outer Metric

Eight Most Popular Schemes

M[a]	2	3	6	4	1(i)	5	Dorotheus	Maximus	'Antiochus'
	DDDDD (11.6%)	SDDDD (13.08%)	DSDDD (10.9%)	DDDDD (18.06%)	DDDDD (15.66%)	DSDDD (12.15%)	DDDDD (16.13%)	DDDDD (16.31%)	DDDDD (21.43%)
	DSDDD (11.6%)	DDDDD (11.21%)	DDDSD (10.24%)	DSDDD (16.45%)	SDDDD (14.14%)	DDSDD (11.52%)	DSDDD (15.05%)	DSDDD (16.31%)	DSDDD (20.44%)
	SSDDD (10%)	DSDDD (10.98%)	DSDSD (9.31%)	SDDDD (10.65%)	DSDDD (13.13%)	DDDDD (10.9%)	SDDDD (12.63%)	SDDDD (9.95%)	DDDSD (11.61%)
	SDDDD (8.8%)	DDDSD (10.28%)	DDDDD (8.91%)	SSDDD (8.39%)	DDDSD (8.08%)	SDDDD (9.66%)	DSDDD (8.87%)	DDDSD (9.14%)	SDDSD (10.71%)
	DDDSD (7%)	DSDSD (7.94%)	SDDSD (8.38%)	DDDSD (8.23%)	SDDSD (7.56%)	SDSDD (9.03%)	SSDDD (8.06%)	SSDDD (9.14%)	SDDDD (8.93%)
	SDDSD (6.8%)	SSDDD (7.01%)	SDDDD (8.24%)	DSDSD (8.23%)	SSDDD (6.06%)	DSSDD (8.72%)	DSDSD (7.53%)	DSDSD (6.69%)	SDSDD (6.25%)
	DSDDD (6.2%)	DDSDD (6.54%)	SSDDD (6.65%)	DDSDD (6.77%)	DSDSD (6.06%)	DSSDD (8.41%)	DSSDD (6.72%)	SDSDD (6.36%)	DSSDD (4.46%)
	DSDSD (5.8%)	DSDSD (6.31%)	DDSDD (5.19%)	SSDSD (4.68%)	DDSDD (4.04%)	SSSDD (6.23%)	DSDSD (6.18%)	DSSDD (4.08%)	SSDDD (3.57%)
					SDDDS (4.04%)				
					SSDSD (4.04%)				

% of poem accounted for by the eight most favoured schemes

M^a:	67.8, 73.35, 67.82
4	86
1(i/ii)	82.81 (with a three-way tie in position 8)/76.23
5	76.71
Maximus	77.98
Dorotheus	81.17
'Antiochus'	87.29

% of poem accounted for by the seventh and eighth most favoured schemes

M^a:	11.98, 13.08, 11.84
4	11.45
1(i/ii)	18.18 (with a three-way tie in position 8)/9.92
5	14.64
Maximus	10.44
Dorotheus	12.9
'Antiochus'	8.03

Dactyls to Spondees

Book	Numbers	%	Dactyls per verse
2	1701 : 799	68.04 : 31.96	3.4
3	1498 : 642	70 : 30	3.5
6	2533 : 1227	67.37 : 32.63	3.39
4	2302 : 798	74.26 : 24.74	3.71
1(i)	717 : 273	72.42 : 27.58	3.62
1(ii)	1032 : 378	73.19 : 28.81	3.66
5	1101 : 504	68.59 : 31.41	3.43
Dorotheus	1374 : 486	73.87 : 26.13	3.69
Maximus	2250 : 815	73.41 : 26.59	3.67
'Antiochus'	424 : 136	75.71 : 24.29	3.79

Percentages of Lines with n Number of Dactylic Feet

	2	3	6	4	1(i)	1(ii)	5	Dor.	Max.	'Antiochus'
5	11.6	11.21	8.91	18.06	15.66	17.38	10.9	16.13	16.31	21.43
4	34.8	41.59	35.51	43.87	40.91	41.14	36.76	44.35	41.6	42.77
3	37.4	33.88	40.96	29.52	33.32	31.86	38.61	32.26	35.24	29.45
2	14.6	12.15	12.77	8.39	10.1	10.39	11.84	6.99	6.53	5.36
1	1.6	1.17	1.86	0.16	—	—	1.87	0.27	0.33	0.89

Percentages of Spondaic Feet by Position in Line

	2	3	6	4	1(i)	1(ii)	5	Dor.	Max.	'Antiochus'
1	43.4	42.29	40.56	33.39	45.45	44.31	44.54	33.06	35.4	34.81
2	47.6	42.76	44.15	45.16	38.89	37.93	45.17	44.08	45.51	35.62
3	27.4	26.17	30.59	17.26	15.66	14.89	43.91	25.55	12.23	19.64
4	34.4	36.91	44.55	28.26	27.27	26.58	21.81	24.18	27.73	28.47
5	7	2.33	3.32	4.65	10.6	9.57	1.55	2.97	12.07	2.68

Distribution of Metra in Line by Numbers of Dactyls in Line

Four dactyls

Pos. of spondee	2 (% ex 174)	3 (% ex 179)	6 (% ex 267)	4 (% ex 272)	1(A) (% ex 81/116)	5 (% ex 118)	Dorotheus (% ex 165)	Maximus (% ex 255)	'Antiochus' (% ex 48)
1 (SDDDD)	25.29	31.28	23.22	24.26	34.57/35.34	26.27	28.48	23.92	20.83
2 (DSDDD)	33.33	26.26	30.71	37.5	32.1/31.03	33.05	33.94	39.22	47.92
3 (DDSDD)	17.82	15.64	14.61	15.44	9.88/10.34	31.36	20	7.06	4.17
4 (DDDSD)	20.11	24.58	28.84	18.75	19.75/19.83	9.32	15.15	21.96	27.08
5 (DDDDS)	3.45	1.68	2.62	4.04	3.7/3.45	—	2.42	7.84	—

Three dactyls

Pos. of spondees	2 (% ex 187)	3 (% ex 144)	6 (% ex 308)	4 (% ex 183)	1(A) (% ex 66/86)	5 (% ex 124)	Dorotheus (% ex 120)	Maximus (% ex 216)	'Antiochus' (% ex 33)
1 + 2 (SSDDD)	26.74	20.83	16.23	28.42	22.73/23.26	21.77	25	25.93	12.12
2 + 4 (DSDSD)	15.51	23.61	22.73	27.87	18.18/18.6	10.48	19.17	18.98	6.06
1 + 4 (SDDSD)	18.18	18.75	20.45	14.21	18.18/18.6	12	10.83	18.06	36.36

Two dactyls

Pos. of dactyls	2 (% ex 73)	3 (% ex 52)	6 (% ex 96)	4 (% ex 52)	1(A) (% ex 20/28)	5 (% ex 38)	Dorotheus (% ex 26)	Maximus (% ex 40)	'Antiochus' (% ex 6)
3 + 5 (SSDSD)	36.98	42.31	32.29	55.77	40/42.86	13.16	50	47.5	—
4 + 5 (SSSDD)	20.55	25	16.67	21.15	25/25	50	15.38	10	33.33
1 + 5 (DSSSD)	15.07	17.3	20.83	11.54	15/14.29	15.79	19.23	5	33.33

Location of Successive Spondees (as % of All Lines)

	2	3	6	4	1(i)	1(ii)	5	Dor.	Max.	'Antiochus'
Lines with two successive spondees										
1 + 2	21.4	16.59	14.89	15.32	14.14	13.82	18.07	13.17	14.19	6.25
2 + 3	12.2	10.98	12.23	6.29	5.55	5.67	18.38	10.22	5.71	8.93
3 + 4	9.2	7.24	12.37	2.9	1.52	1.06	8.1	4.03	1.96	4.46
4 + 5	0.2	—	—	—	—	—	—	0.27	0.65	—
Lines with three successive spondees										
1 + 2 + 3	4.6	4.21	3.99	1.94	2.53	2.48	8.1	1.35	0.82	2.68
2 + 3 + 4	3.4	3.04	4.39	1.13	—	—	3.43	1.34	0.33	2.68
3 + 4 + 5	—	—	—	—	—	—	—	—	0.16	—

Inner Metric

Types of Caesura (as % of All Caesurae)

	2	3	6	4	1	5	Dorotheus	Maximus	'Antiochus'
B_1	53	50.35	51.06	43.54	30.66/33.57	79.13	51.61	31.59	50
of which:									
$B_1 + C_1$	50.94	50.93	60.52	31.5	27.69/25.26	30.71	35.42	32.64	15.18
$B_1 + C_2$	29.81	22.69	6.75	49.08	46.15/47.37	37.01	35.42	50.26	22.32
$B_1 + C_1 + C_2$	7.55	12.5	11.95	15.02	12.31/13.68	2.76	22.4	13.99	8.04
Neither	11.7	13.89	8.57	4.4	13.85/13.68	29.53	6.77	3.11	4.46
B_2	45.6	46.39	46.02	56.46	67.45/64.31	20.87	47.31	67.43	48.21
No B	1.4	3.26	2.79	—	1.89/2.47	—	0.81	0.98	1.79
C_2	34	30.07	26.26	39.14	46.7/47.35	35.83	50.54	45.33	43.75
of which									
3rd foot spondee	31.89			24.08	14.14/17.91	51.3			22.45
[% in all lines]	27.4	26.17	30.59	17.26	15.66/14.89	43.91	25.55	12.23	29.45]
4th foot spondee	12.94	18.6	17.68	4.49	6.06/5.99	2.44	6.38	7.58	8.16
% of all lines	4.18	5.59	4.64	1.76	2.83/3.18	0.93	3.27	3.44	3.57

Word-Break in the Second Foot (as % of All Lines)

	2	3	6	4	1	5	Dorotheus	Maximus	'Antiochus'
Meyer I	4.38	6.07	5.71	5.89	3.3/2.47	16.21	2.17	5.07	5.36
grammatical only	1.39	2.1	3.98	1.43	2.35/1.77	10.09	0.54	2.78	—
Meyer II	2.99	4.44	3.98	2.71	0.94/0.71	14.37	2.99	2.13	0.89
Meyer I & II	2.59	3.04	2.92	2.39	0.94/0.71	13.15	0.82	1.31	6.25
grammatical only	0.8	0.93	1.59	0.8	0.47/0.35	8.87	0.27		1.79
Meyer I *or* II	2.19	4.4	3.85	3.82	2.36/1.77	4.28	3.53	4.58	6.25
Giseke	0.8	0.93	0.93	0.16	—	—	0.27	2.29	—
Hilberg	3.78	1.64	2.39	—	—	—	0.82	1.31	—
Giseke & Hilberg	0.4	0.93	0.4	—	—	—	—	0.49	—
Giseke *or* Hilberg	3.78	0.7	2.52	0.16	—	—	1.09	2.95	—

Bulloch's Law (% of Lines Affected)

2	3	6	4	1(i)	1(ii)	5	Dorotheus	Maximus	'Antiochus'
2.19	2.34	1.2	1.91	2.36	2.12	1.53	4.93	2.93	6.14

Hermann's Bridge (as % of All Lines)

	M^a	4	1	5	Dorotheus	Maximus	'Antiochus'
Full	0.36	0.16	—/0.71	3.37	0.27	—	1.77
+ metrical	1.01	0.16	0.47/1.06	3.99	0.54	0.33	2.66

Tiedke's Law

	2	3	6	4	1	5	Dorotheus	Maximus	'Antiochus'
% of all lines	11	12.82	16.45	1.28	4.25/3.89	6.42	7.61 (1.63)	1.63	2.61
of which:									
% spondaic	54.55	45.45	62.1	50	33.33/45.45	14.29	53.57	30	33.33
% anapaestic	45.45	54.55	37.9	50	66.67/54.54	85.71	46.43	70	66.67

Tetracola (as % of All Lines)

	2	3	6	4	1	5	Dorotheus	Maximus	'Antiochus'
True	1.6	1.4	2.52	7.17	4.72/3.89	2.75	1.34	4.92	1.74
+ 1 appositive	10.96			21.02	19.34/17.31	10.4	3.49	14	3.48
[+ pl. appositives	28.09			35.67	30.67/27.56	18.04	3.76		17.39]

Prosody

Muta cum liquida[1]

	Il.	2.1–500	4	1 (i)	5	Dorotheus	Max. 1–500[2]	'Antiochus'
Word-boundary								
position	**26.83**/37.4	**3.21**/8.02	**1.78**/2.14	2.53	0.63/3.16	7.5/14.17	**5.49**/12.64	2.27
princ.	**26.02**/36.59	all princeps	all princeps	all princeps	0.63/2.53	6.67/13.34	**4.95**/12.09	2.27
bic.	0.81	—	—	—	0/0.63	0.83	0.55	—
correption	3.25	15.51	22.06/23.13	24.05/29.11	23.4/26.58	11.67/12.5	**10.99**/14.84	47.73
∪|∪	2.44	13.37	18.15/18.86	21.52/26.58	19.62/21.52	9.17/10	**4.94**/7.69	38.64
∪∪|	0.81	2.14	3.91/4.27	2.53	3.78/5.06	2.5	6.04/7.14	9.09
Internal								
position	**69.92**/59.35	**64.71**/59.89	**38.08**/37.72	35.44	54.43/51.9	74.17/67.5	**67.03**/59.89	15.9
princ.	**61.79**/51.22	**48.13**/43.43	**33.81**/33.45	32.91	38.61/36.71	62.5/55.83	**60.44**/53.3	13.63
bic.	8.13	16.58	4.27	2.53	15.82/15.19	11.67	6.59	2.27
correption	—	16.58	**38.08**/37.02	**37.97**/32.91	21.52/18.35	6.67/5.83	**16.48**/12.64	34.09
∪|∪	—	9.63	19.22/18.51	26.58/21.52	20.25/18.35	4.17/3.33	**4.95**/2.2	25
∪∪|	—	6.95	18.86/18.51	11.39	1.27	2.5	**11.54**/10.44	9.09

[1] Treating appositives as creating metrical words, i.e. treating such cases as word-internal not word-boundary; thus the preferred figures (as used in vol. 1) are marked in **bold**.

[2] NB Figures revised from those presented in i. 257 (calculated out of a new total of 182).

Hiatus in Princeps per n Lines

	2	3	6	4	1(A)	5	Dorotheus	Maximus
1	502	61.14	125.67	—	—	324	—	—
2	502	428	68.55	630	—	162	184	76.75
3	107	142.67	150.8	210	—	12.46	73.6	51.17
4	167.33	85.6	58	210	198	29.45	368	68.22
5	502	214	50.27	315	198	32.4	368	76.75
all lines	50.2	23.83	15.39	70	49.5	6.48	43.33	16.59

Vowels in Hiatus in Princeps (as % of all Hiatus[3])

	M[a]	4	1(A)	5 (ex 48)	Dorotheus (ex 8)[4]	Maximus
-η	9.52	33.33	25	29.17	12.5	16.22 + 2.7 α
-ω	3.17	—	—	2.08	—	—
-ῃ	20.6	55.56	50	10.42	—	13.51
-ῳ/ῷ	20.6	—	—	12.5	—	29.73
-αι	6.35	—	—	6.25	12.4	8.11
-ει	3.17	—	25	18.75	—	8.11
-οι	9.52	11.11	—	6.25	12.5	10.81
αυ	1.59	—	—	—	—	2.7
ευ	—	—	—	2.08	—	—
ου	30.16	—	—	12.5	50	8.11

As percentage of total possible instances

	2	3	6	4	1(AE)	5	Dorotheus	Maximus
η	5	9.76	10.26	4.07	15.38	8.2	—	5.68
ῳ	2.27	2.86	13.58	—	—	13.64	—	13.41
ου	4.44	9.09	14.61	—	—	13.64	10	4.35
αι	4.76	5.56	5.56	—	—	1.95	0.56	1.19
ει	5.56	—	—	—	5	10.11	—	1.75
οι	3.85	8.33	4.69	1.62	—	5.66	3.03	3.92
η	3.33	5.26	5.13	5.66	3.85	22.58	2.82	2.82

[3] Excluding the disjunctive on the grounds that this is licensed (cf. i. 261 n. 107).
[4] Does not add up to 100 as there is also a single deviant instance with o(!).

Elision: Frequency

	1 per n lines							
	2 (500)	3 (428)	6 (753)	4 (630)	1 (198/273)	5	Dorotheus	Maximus
Nouns	38.46	30.57	41.83	57.27	99/136.5	53.83	124	76.25
Adjectives	45.45	85.6	94.125	210	198/136.5	323	372	305
Pronouns	250	53.5	83.67	630	—/273	323	—	83.33
Verbs (finite)	31.25	19.45	17.93	70	33/39	46.14	46.5	87.14
Participles	33.33	428	150.6	630	—	—	—	83.33
Adverbs	31.25	25.2	25.1	210	66/68.25	64.6	372	67.78
Numerals	166.67	—	—	—	—	—	372	305
Total	6.58	6.49	6.72	22.5	16.5/17.06	16.15	26.57	14.19

Elision: Location in the Line (as % of All Elisions)

	2 (ex 76)	3 (ex 66)	6 (ex 112)	4 (ex 28)	1 (ex 12/16)	5 (ex 20)	Dor. (ex 14)	Maximus (ex 43)
1	2.63	3.03	3.57	—	—	15	—	4.65
1.5	5.26	3.54	8.93	3.57	—	—	7.14	6.98
2	13.16	9.09	10.71	3.57	16.67/12.5	10	—	9.3
3	9.21	12.12	10.71	—	—	5	14.29	2.33
3.5	—	3.03	1.79	—	8.33/6.25	—	7.14	4.65
4	—	—	—	—	—	5	—	2.33
5	7.89	13.64	15.18	—	8.33/6.25	10	—	9.3
5.5	9.21	7.58	3.57	3.57	0/6.25	—	—	2.33
6	3.95	9.09	2.68	7.14	8.33/12.5	—	7.14	18.6
7	5.26	1.52	2.68	—	—	10	7.14	18.6
7.5	3.95	4.54	0.89	—	—	5	—	—
8	7.89	6.06	6.88	10.71	8.33	—	7.14	—
9	14.47	10.61	22.32	7.14	25	25	7.14	6.98
9.5	17.1	12.12	8.04	64.29	25/25	15	35.71	11.63
10	—	3.03	1.79	—	0/6.25	—	7.14	2.33
11			0.89					

Note on Metrical Licence

Greek astrological poetry permits itself certain kinds of conventional licence to accommodate planetary names and technical terms (West 1982, 44–5; R. Kassel, 'Quod versu dicere non est', ZPE 19 (1975), 211–18). I find no equivalent in Manilius.

Prosody

(i) 1.16 Ἑρμέα, Ζῆνα; 5.316 μετὰ Ζηνός; Dorotheus, p. 430.124 ἑπτὰ δὲ Ζεὺς φαέθων; see Housman 1972, 743–4. Extended to 5.133 ἀσχήμονα ζωήν, 338 λυσσάδα, ζηλότυπον. Not in M^a or M^b.

(ii) Hiatus in *princeps*: M^b with Κυθήρη and ἰσόμοιρος; M^d at the masculine caesura with Μήνη, Παφίη, Σεληναίη; of Dorotheus' nine instances of this kind of hiatus, the majority involve technical terms (p. 361.22 ἢ ὕψος; p. 386.17 οἱ ὅριον; p. 394.8 παμμήνου ὁπότ'; p. 407.15 Ἐνυαλίου οἴκους), numerals (p. 430.144 Παφίη, ὀκτώ), or are in notations of planetary motion or position (pp. 391.19 ἐπεσσυμένου ἢ, 407.21 Ἡελίου ἐν χώρῳ).

(iii) Lengthening *in arsi*: M^d, Κρόνος/-ον before masculine caesura; potentially also 1.273 Ἄρεος, as transmitted, although A.-R.'s emendation Ἄρεως is available, and 1.321 Κρόνου, although their Κρόνοιο is available.

Not only the other instances of lengthening in the same poet, but also the range of measures used to accommodate proper names across all poets, suggests no need to intervene.

Inner Metric

(i) Violation of Meyer I, often in combination with violation of Meyer II, to accommodate διάμετρος, τρίγωνος, τετράγωνος, sometimes other (ἀπόκεντρος, ἰσόμοιρος) in the first half of the line: M^a, with planetary name + μέν or δέ: i. 247 n. 44; M^b; M^d; Dorotheus, p. 399.2 τρίγωνος, p. 432.9 Αἰγοκέρωτα: i. 249; 'Antiochus', τρίγωνος; less often M^c(A), save for 1.87 ἢ παρύγροισι and perhaps 112 ἦν δ' ἀκτῖνα.

(ii) Violation of Meyer II, often in combination with violation of Meyer I, to accommodate Κρόνος, Ἄρης before the masculine caesura (M^a: i. 247 n. 44; M^c(A), 1.97; M^d, 5.132, 134, 190 Ἄρης, 110 Κρόνον; Dorotheus: i. 249) or other technical language (1.135 ἕκτον ἔχοντι τόπον); with disyllabic part of verb 'to be', ἀεί, βροτ-, δόμ- in M^a (i. 247 n. 44).

(iii) Violation of Giseke's Law: M^a, 2.36 ὄντε Βόρειον, 47 ὅς δέ Μεσημβρινός, 114 ὅς ῥά θ' Ὁρίζων, 123 ἠδὲ Θυτήριον, all proper names or technical terms; Dorotheus, p. 428 καὶ κλίμ' Ἀχαιικόν: i. 249.

(iv) Violations of Hilberg's Law: Dorotheus, p. 323.19 Ἑρμείας· εἶς: i. 249.

(v) Violations of Bulloch's Law: with name of Zeus (3.186, 6.70, 395; already EGHP); μέσον οὐρανόν (3.36, 61, 114; Dorotheus, p. 386.12; M^b (6×)).

(vi) Violation of Hermann's Bridge: 4.193 Φαίνοντι συνών; 1.278 κατὰ μοῖραν; 5.274 Ζηνὶ μόνῳ.

(vii) Violation of Tiedke's Law: M^a, esp. with Μήνη, Φαίνων, καλὴ (epithet of Venus), ζῶον, ὥρη; Dorotheus, esp. with Στίλβων, Παφίη, Ἄρης, Πυρόεις, Φαέθων, Φαίνω, ἴσας, μοίρας: i. 252–3; 1.92 καθέτου. To a much lesser extent in M^b (4.126 Κυθέρη) and M^d (5.111 Παφίη).

(viii) Violation of Naeke's Law: M^a, esp. with Ζεύς (also in M^c) and Ἄρης in the fourth foot; Dorotheus, esp. with numerals; Maximus, esp. with planetary names (Θεαντίς, Ἄρης) or epithets (ἀγαυή, ἀγνή) or in their vicinity. See i. 245–6.

(ix) No third-foot caesura, a trick used by M^a to accommodate proper names (2.116 Γαλαξίεω, 417 Τιτῆνος; 3.14 Ὑδροχόῳ, 47, 6.695 Ἡελίῳ; 6.95 Ἡελίου; 6.708, 747 Σεληναίη, 583 Σεληναίην) or epithets (6.29 ἠΰκερων, 535 θηλυτέρῳ, a specification of sign); indications of place (3.181 ἀντολίης; 6.83 ὡρονόμῳ, cf. 1.346 ὡρονόμου; 6.126 μεσουρανίου,

667 μεσουράνιον, cf. 1.281 μεσουρανέων; 3.44 ἀντιμεσουρανέων); participles specifying aspect (6.195 δερκομένη; 3.272 ἐπιδερκόμενος, 6.103 ἐπιδερκόμενοι, 137 ἐπιδερκομένων; 3.424 συναντόμενοι). The first of these is an established licence: three of Aratus' eight instances involve the proper names of stars or constellations (D. Kidd, 33); both of Apollonius' two examples are with proper names (West 1982, 153); and many of Homer's examples are too (Lehrs, 396–403).

4. PLANETARY RANK ORDERS

M^a		M^b		M^c		M^d	
Mars	114 (22.57%)	Mars	38 (21.97%)	Mars	42 (19.63%)	Mars	32 (21.77%)
Saturn	94 (18.61%)	Moon	33 (19.08%)	Saturn	39 (18.22%)	Moon	24 (16.33%)
Moon	92 (18.22%)	Saturn	29 (16.76%)	Moon	37 (17.29%)	Venus	23 (15.65%)
Venus	65 (12.87%)	Venus	27 (15.61%)	Jupiter	26 (12.15%)	Saturn	22 (14.97%)
Jupiter	57 (11.29%)	Mercury	19 (10.98%)	Venus	25 (11.68%)	Mercury	17 (11.56%)
Mercury	46 (9.11%)	Sun	15 (8.67%)	Mercury	23 (10.75%)	Sun	17 (11.56%)
Sun	37 (7.33%)	Jupiter	13 (7.51%)	Sun	22 (10.28%)	Jupiter	12 (8.16%)

Part Three

Text

And with their *deleaturs, alii legunt sic, meus codex sic habet*, with their *postremæ editiones*, annotations, castigations, &c., make books dear, themselves ridiculous, and do nobody good.

Robert Burton, *Anatomy of Melancholy*, 'Democritus to the Reader'

The Text of the Later Books

PALAEOGRAPHICAL NOTES

The question to be addressed first is whether the formatting that accompanies the three books edited here suggests any particular relationship between them in their textual history (for instance, whether there is anything in particular to connect 4 and 1, or 1 and 5).

Each book in the corpus contains marks in the left-hand margin separating apotelesmata, but only the first book and the fourth (down to 165, the section on ἀκτινοβολία) do so by alphabetic numerals. The rest of the time sections are separated by paragraphoi. Corresponding to the divisions of the charts there are also summaries of the protasis in the right margin (using a mixture of words and symbols for planets and aspects) for each book except the sixth. Dividers and summaries are both by L^1 (see i. 375), using majuscule for the latter.

L^1 is also responsible for additional material in tabular form, principally the long table at the beginning of the first book which occupies the whole of 8^v after the conclusion of the poem of Maximus and all of 9^r. Unique in format, this table lists all seventy of the apotelesmata of the first book, using numbers that correspond to the marginal annotations and offering somewhat fuller summaries, including summaries of the outcome. At the end of the same book, L^1 adds a short table of the exaltations (ὑψώματα) and dejections (ταπεινώματα) of all seven planets (13^v). This is rather odd, given that it is only the fifth book that uses these concepts by name, although exaltations are implied in others (see on 5.33). So, while it is not the case that any two books (except the second and third, headed by similar pinakes) share distinctive formatting which suggests they were particularly closely associated in transmission and exegesis, it *is* the case that book 1 is accompanied by exegetical material which is more appropriate to book 5. This is a possible, if weak, argument for some sort of prior association. But it is hard to go further.

L^1 continues to offer various kinds of marginalia, already discussed in the first volume. There are γρ variants (left margin, unless otherwise stated) at 1.120 (10^v), 217 (12^r), 316 (13^r); 4.67 (26^v, right margin), and other variants or glosses at 1.24 (9^v), 25 (apparently ἁρπαγέτηι, looking back to 23 ἁρπακτῆρας), 338 (13^v); 4.28 (26^r, majuscule, and accompanied by another majuscule note in the right margin), 526 (32ʳ, right margin). These are mostly recorded in the apparatus. There are also longer glosses at 4.78 (26ᵛ) ἐπειδὴ περὶ τῶν ἄλλων διαλαμβάνων ἐν ἰδίοις οἴκοις ὡροσκοποῦντας τοὺς πλάνητας ἀποτελεῖν ταῦτα, followed by four characters of uncertain significance (φησί fits the sense of the first one, but the accent is wrong for the context), and 87–9 οὐ μεταβάλλοντας ἐπὶ τὸ χεῖρον· οὐδὲ μείωσίν τινα τῶν προγενομένων αὐτοῖς ἀγαθῶν ὑφισταμένους (thanks to Nigel Wilson for help with deciphering these). Then there are marginal signs, some of clear meaning, others less so. A paragraphos with cedilla (i. 377) marks obvious transitions at 4.164/5 (27ᵛ) and 5.312/13 (37ʳ). There are asteriskoi throughout, some for sections of unusual form (1.100–5) or content (1.139–52, 196–207) or involving signs (4.22–3, 25–6, 96–7; 5.246–8) or special names (4.55) or *gnomai* (4.91; 5.27, 42–6, but not the more obvious 44–7, 55, 62, 75), or simply of uncertain meaning (4.200, 247, 472). The diple › is used throughout the fourth book (i. 379 n. 39). Other signs include a slightly angled cross, at the end of 4.263 and at the beginning of 4.264 (28ᵛ); at the end of 349 (30ʳ); at the beginning of 325 (29ᵛ), 359 (30ʳ), 494 (31ᵛ); a neat × against 4.283, 289, 302, 311 (i. 380 n. 40); a large, wide-angled bracket ⟨ against 4.485 (31ᵛ); a colon against 4.584 (32ᵛ), and a heavy colon against 5.265 (36ᵛ); a long vertical bar against 5.111 (34ᵛ); a small cross with thick strokes against 5.273 (36ᵛ, right margin); and a division sign at an angle at the end of 5.288 and beginning of 289 (36ᵛ). Darts in each margin indicate that a verse is missing between 4.428 and 4.429 (30ᵛ); that verse (4.430) has been displaced overleaf, where it is enclosed between similar darts (i. 379).

De Stefani continues an excellent editor.[1] My apparatus is rather leaner, though I distinguish the readings of Hal's marginalia more pedantically. The textual differences between us are largely attributable to my greater reliance on the astrological prose comparanda. As in the first volume, I have supplied an additional register of parallels.

THE EDITOR'S PROBLEM

This section, which belongs closely with the discussion of Mᵇ, Mᶜ, and P.Oxy. 2546 (= Π¹) on pp. 274–6, continues to explore the implications of the three

---

[1] Tiny misreportage of marginal note at 1.24; of Hal at 1.292, where A.–R. report σοφίεσσιν; 5.181, not ἐπιφωλεύοντα. He continues to confuse the Liber Halensis and Holsten's annotations in it (Hal and Hol) at 1.142 ὑπαί, 5.325 ἔσται; Hal^mg and Hol are not distinguished at 5.330. He infers Hal's reading at 1.191 (φέρον), 291 (κατ' αἰθέρα τῷδε), 5.176 (οὔποτε), 5.208 (γενεῇ, with question mark).

The Text of the Later Books 389

recensions of the same material which are available for comparison in M^b, M^c, and $Π^1$. For the purposes of the discussion, M^b means the recension of the poem provided in the fourth book, not necessarily implying that that is the 'original' or 'definitive' version of the material.

For convenience the overlaps are as represented in the following table:

4.121–4	1.286–9	—
4.127–8	1.292–3	—
4.139–40	1.290–1	—
4.146–52	1.294–300	—
4.201–2 + 141 + 203–5	1.301–5	—
4.384–5	—	$Π^1$ fr. 1
4.386–9/390	—	$Π^1$ fr. 1
4.391–4	—	$Π^1$ fr. 1
4.395–401	1.321–6	$Π^1$ fr. 1
4.402–8	1.327–33	$Π^1$ fr. 1
4.409–13	1.334–8	$Π^1$ fr. 1
4.414–19	—	$Π^1$ fr. 1 to 415, $Π^1$ fr. 2 (from 417)
4.420–4	—	$Π^1$ fr. 2
4.425–30	—	$Π^1$ fr. 2
4.431–6	—	$Π^1$ fr. 2 (to 433)
4.478–9 + 481–8 + 50–1 + 490	1.306–20	—
4.560–6	—	$Π^1$ fr. 3 (from 564)
4.567–70	—	$Π^1$ fr. 3
4.571–6	—	$Π^1$ fr. 3
4.577–81	—	$Π^1$ fr. 3
4.582–5	—	$Π^1$ fr. 3
4.586–8	—	$Π^1$ fr. 3
4.589–92	—	$Π^1$ fr. 3 (to 590), fr. 4 (from 592)
4.593–6	—	$Π^1$ fr. 4
4.597–600	—	$Π^1$ fr. 4
4.601–7	—	$Π^1$ fr. 4 (to 604)

L presents us with the state of the text in the ninth century, or rather in its exemplar (fifth/sixth century?). The Byzantine attitude to technical (as opposed to literary or dogmatic) material could be cavalier,[2] but the text transmitted by L has been subject to critical scrutiny and annotation, i.e. converted into an *objet d'art*, rather than being treated as a technical manual which still has practical application and is modified accordingly.

The first Oxyrhynchus Manetho papyrus, $Π^1$, which is third-century, contains 4.384–433 (frr. 1–2), 4.563–90 (fr. 3), 4.592–604 (fr. 4). This was a manuscript of book 4 *in extenso*, not some haphazard collection of charts that just happened to cohere with book 4 in what has been preserved, because frr. 1–2 constitute a

---

[2] Mavroudi, 91–2.

column of the right number of lines for fr. 3 (which begins with traces of the end of 520 and subsequent lines) to rejoin book 4 at an appropriate place, viz. after the loss of two intermediate columns. The preserved lines include 4.402–8 ~ 1.327–33 + 4.409–13 ~ 1.334–8; in other words the papyrus version, too, made the apparently arbitrary leap from τέχναι to parents. The papyrus show us how the material was circulating in the high or late Roman empire, a very different kind of transmission from what the manuscript documents. The readings of this Manetho papyrus have been the subject of scrutiny by Radici Colace[3] and Monaco, who have concluded that the recensions of the text are simply different, in a way that would be accounted for by the circumstances in which *Fachliteratur/Gebrauchsliteratur* in antiquity was produced and consumed.[4]

I accept the *Fachliteratur* model and its implications that material was constantly being revised and updated, but a closer look at the kinds of difference that subsist between the different versions suggests a more complicated situation. The *Fachliteratur* model ought to imply a principle of 'equal valence', where each version has its own validity (even if the choices made by particular 'realisers' of the tradition are not necessarily of equal merit). But in practice this is not always the case. The equal-valence principle subsists side by side with the traditional model of lineal descent and textual degeneracy (as is in practice acknowledged by those who have engaged with the text). What one tends to find is a series of relationships that can be partly, but only partly, stemmatised, and do not result in a totally consistent pattern of affiliation. And the problem for the editor is how to tell corruption from purposeful, if perhaps inept, variation.

---

[3] P. Radici Colace, 'P.Oxy. 2546: Per una nuova edizione degli Apotelesmatiká di Manetone', *Analecta Papyrologica*, 2 (1990), 45–51, and 'Gli Ἀποτελεσματικά di Manetone tra editori e copisti antichi e moderni', in S. Sconocchia and L. Toneatto (eds.), *Lingue tecniche del greco e del latino: Atti del I Seminario internazionale sulla letteratura scientifica e tecnica greca e latina, Trieste, 5-7 Ottobre 1992* (Trieste, 1993), 273–86.

[4] Monaco, 71: 'Π ed M non attestano due momenti di una stessa tradizione, ma due tradizioni affatto diverse'. To some extent parallels could be drawn with the *Sortes Astrampsychi*, on which see Naether, 107–8: the relatively simple idea of two separate recensions (the first edited by G. M. Browne and the second by R. A. Stewart) is complicated by papyrological evidence (P.Oxy. LXVII 4581) which does not fit it, and which suggests the existence of local versions answering to local needs: as Naether writes (108), '…jede Version des Orakels hatte wohl ihre Relevanz innerhalb ihrer lokalen Anwendung. Die Frage des Urhebers zweier Editionen stellt sich insofern nicht, als der mantische Spezialist entscheidend war, der das Losbuch für die Petenten bediente und die erhaltenen Ordale mündlich noch weiter ausdeuten konnte. Durch die Praxis und die unterschiedlichen Anliegen der Menschen enstanden die Erfahrung und das Wissen, womit man den Text noch besser auf die Bedürfnisse und Situationen zuschneiden konnte.' It would not (she adds) be surprising if more witnesses were discovered which turned out to complicate the picture still further.

Stemma

Insofar as the relationships of the witnesses can be represented stemmatically, it looks like this:

The recensions differ in various ways.[5] Errors shared between M^b and M^c imply descent from a common source:

4.50, 1.318 φάρυγγος
4.408 αὐχήσωσιν, 1.333 αὐχήσουσιν
4.479, 1.307 Ἄρεως
4.483, 1.310 ἐπανύκτορας ὀθνιάων
4.485 φωραθέντες, 1.312 φοραθέντες
4.488, 1.316 ξίφεσι (but corr. L¹)

Phonetic errors might have arisen independently, but the two contiguous errors in 4.483 = 1.310 make this harder to sustain.

---

[5] (i) Phonetic variants: 4.479 λοξεύματα ~ 1.307 λαξεύματα. (ii) Morpho-syntactic variants: 4.124 καμίνοις ~ 1.289 καμίνῳ; 4.139 οἰκείως ~ 1.290 οἰκείοις; 4.147 κόσμου ~ 1.295 κόσμον (ante corr.); 4.202 Ἑρμείου ~ 1.302 Ἑρμείᾶ; 4.389 θαλάμους ~ Π¹ θαλάμων; 4.390 ἔσσεται ~ Π¹ ἔσται; 4.395 and Π¹ Κρόνοιο ~ 1.321 Κρόνου (which leads to one of five instances of hiatus after καί in the biceps: there are three in M^b); 4.407 θανάτους ~ 1.332 θάνατον (the latter entails a lengthening *in arsi*, of which there are three other examples in the hexameters of M^c (p. 309); none, by contrast, in M^b); 4.490 ὑπ' ἀνάγκῃ ~ 1.320 ὑπ' ἀνάγκας (both diverge from Homeric ὑπ' ἀνάγκης). (iii) Syntactic variants: 4.146 ἦν ~ 1.294 εἰ (both transmitted with optative); 4.205 τ' ~ 1.305 — ; 4.407 δέ ~ 1.332 τε. (iv) Other minor differences: 4.51 ἐς ἰνίον ~ 1.319 ἢ ἰνίον; 4.385 ἤ ~ Π¹ αἱ; 4.386 ἤ ~ Π¹ εἰς; 4.412 and Π¹ διά ~ 1.337 ὑπό. For the hiatus in 1.336 see p. 307: it is too rare to claim it is more typical of M^c than of M^b. 4.413 κρύφιμ' (Π¹ κρύφιμα) ~ 1.338 κρύφι' (κρύφιμ' in marg.); 4.489 ἐκδήσαντες ~ 1.317 ἐνδήσαντες. (v) Dialectal differences, which more often show M^c with the koine forms: 4.127 σοφίῃσιν ~ 1.292 σοφίεσσιν; 4.147 Ἑρμείην ~ 1.295 Ἑρμείαν; 4.490 πικρῆς Μοίρης ὑπ' ἀνάγκῃ ~ 1.320 πικρᾶς Μοίρας ὑπ' ἀνάγκῆς; but 1.324 ναυφθορίῃσιν ~ 4.399 ναυφθορίαισιν [Π¹ damaged at this point]. (vi) Alternative epithets: 4.146 ἑλικοδρόμος ~ 1.294 ἑλικώπιδος; 4.151 εὐτοίχων ~ 1.299 εὐτυπέωῦ (οἱ ~ υ confusion?); 4.402 ὁπότ' ἂν πολιοῖο (Π¹ πλαγκτοῖο) ~ 1.327–8 κυανοχρόοιο; 4.405 and Π¹ νεκυοστόλος ~ 1.330 νεκυηπόλος; 4.406 πολὺν ~ Π¹ βαθὺν ~ 1.331 μέγαν; 4.488 φοβεροῖς ~ 1.316 σφαγίοις; 4.489 ἀλγινόεντα ~ 1.317 ἀγχονόωντα; 4.490 πικρὸν [λυγρὸν K] ~ 1.320 θ' ἐόν; 4.564 κακόθυμος ~ Π¹ κακόθοινος (if not another phonetic variation based on the confusion of ‹οι› and ‹υ›). (vii) Difference in executive or factitive verb: 4.150 δείκνυσι ~ 1.298 ῥέζει; 4.397 and Π¹ φαίνει ~ 1.323 δείκνυσι; 4.406 ἐξολέσει ~ Π¹ ἀπόλλυσιν ~ 1.331 ἐκβάλλει; 4.483 ἐκφύσει ~ 1.311 τελέουσιν.

Other alignments are as follows.

M^b and Π^1 ~ M^c

4.397 and Π^1 ὕδασι νήκτορας ~ 1.323 ὕδατος ἵστορας
4.401 and Π^1 Μοίρης βαιὸν χρόνον ~ 1.326 Μοίρησιν ὑπὸ τρόμον
4.402 and Π^1 ὁπότ' ἂν πολιοῖο (Π^1 πλαγκτοῖο) ~ 1.327 κυανοχρόοιο
4.405 and Π^1 νεκυοστόλος ~ 1.330 νεκυηπόλος
4.410–11 and Π^1 φωτὶ Κρόνου, μάρτυς δ' [τ' Π^1] ἐπὶ σήματι τῷδε γένηται | καὶ Πυρόεις ~ 1.335 μάρτυς δ' ἐπὶ τοῦτο γένηται καὶ Πυρόεις
4.111 and Π^1 μήτηρ προτέρη πατρὸς ἵξετ' ἐς Ἀίδην ~ 1.336 ἡ μήτηρ προτέρη οἴχεται ἐς Ἀίδην
4.412 and Π^1 διὰ νούσου ~ 1.337 ὑπὸ νούσου

M^b and M^c ~ Π^1

4.395 and 1.321 ἀθρῶν ~ Π^1 αἴθων
4.405 μητέρας εἰς Ἀίδην and 1.330 μητέρος εἰς Ἀίδην ~ Π^1 μ]ητρὸς ες Αιδεω
4.409 and 1.334 ἀκτὶς ~ Π^1 ἀκτεὶς (spelling variant)
4.412 and 1.337 δεδαϊγμένη ~ Π^1 δεδαμασμένη

M^b ~ Π^1 and M^c

4.400 λείψουσι ~ Π^1 ζησουσι and 1.325 σώζουσι (different verbs, but agreement that the swimmers are saved)
4.403 ᾖ ~ 1.328 ἦν and Π^1 ην
4.413 ἀμβλώσσους δ' ~ Π^1 αι]μηρης and 1.338 αἰμηρῇσι
4.413 κύπρις ~ Π^1 and 1.338 φύσις

M^b ~ Π^1 ~ M^c

4.399 πρωτάρχας τε νεῶν ~ Π^1 πρωράρχους τε νεῶν ~ 1.324 πλωτάρχας σκαφέων
4.400 ὀρνυμένου βίοτον ~ Π^1 ὀλλύμενοι τε βίον ~ 1.325 ὀρνυμένοιο βίον
4.406 κτήματά τ' ἐξολέσει ~ Π^1 κτήματ' ἀπόλλυσιν ~ 1.331 κτήματά τ' ἐκβάλλει
4.406 πολὺν ~ Π^1 βαθὺν ~ 1.331 μέγαν
4.413 κρύφιμ' ~ Π^1 κρύφιμα ~ 1.338 κρύφι' (κρύφιμ' in marg. sin.)

Plus and minus lines point every way:

M^b habet/Π^1 caret: 4.392. Π^1 therefore adjusts 391 to supply a verb. On the other hand, nominative Ἄρης is correct in Π^1 but needs emendation in L.
M^b habet/M^c, Π^1 carent: 4.398.

M^b, Π^1 habent/M^c caret: 4.410 ~ [1.334b]

M^b, M^c habent/Π^1 caret: 4.407–8, 1.332–3. Lines guaranteed by Epit. IV.

M^b habet/M^c caret: 4.480. But 4.481 has connective δ', which is appropriate in 1.308, but not after 4.480. Could 4.480 be a plus-verse, rather than a loss between 1.307 and 308?

M^c habet/M^b caret: <4.485a> ~ 1.313. In sense the line is a doublet of the following one (chains and imprisonment). Valens in a similar chart also has συνοχαί.

Π^1 habet/M^b caret: <4.568a>.

The stemma works, by isolating a deviant version against the rest, in the following cases:

Π^1 in error against the consensus of M^b and M^c: 4.395 αἴθων, 4.405 μ]ητρός, 4.409 ἀκτεῖς; omission of 4.407–8, 1.332–3; though 4.412 δεδαμασμένη is viable. Π^1 in error against M^b with no evidence from M^c: 4.387 μέν ~ Π^1 γάρ; 4.388 ᾧ ~ Π^1 ὡς.

M^b in error against M^c and Π^1: 4.413 κύπρις.

M^c in error against M^b and Π^1: 1.326 (less error than eccentricity); 1.335.

Where the stemma does not cope well is with the concurrence of Π^1 and M^c in error against M^b:

4.398, which contains an ἔσσεσθαι construction, is absent in the other two witnesses, but is more than an idiosyncrasy of M^b, because steersmen are guaranteed by Θ; also, σκαφέων is retained in 1.324. 4.398–9 is arguably better than the other versions because it mentions both prow and tiller.

4.400 λείψουσι, as against the other versions in which the shipwrecked are saved (see commentary on 4.400–1).

4.403 ᾖ against 1.328 ἦν and Π^1 ην.

Evaluating the Quality of Readings

This complicates what has already been said and implies a non-stemmatic approach.

(i) M^b's readings are more often preferable to those of either or both of the other two recensions than either of the others is to the rest,

(a) because they include necessary information:

4.410–11 and Π^1 ~ 1.335–6 (no mention of Saturn, τοῦτο in 335 lacks an antecedent, and the line is unmetrical)

4.479 εἰς τετράγωνα ~ 1.307 ἀκτίνεσσι

(b) because they make better sense or are simply less inept:

4.479 λοξεύματα ~ 1.307 λαξεύματα

4.400 ὀρνυμένου βίοτον λείψουσι ~ 1.325 ὀρνυμένοιο βίον σώζουσι ~ Π¹ ὀλλύμενοι τε βίον ζησουσι. Was M^c's inept formulation (their lives are saved) devised for a particular consultation?

4.401 and Π¹ Μοίρης βαιὸν χρόνον ~ 1.326 Μοίρησιν ὑπὸ τρόμον

4.478–9 Μήνη δ' ἀμφίκερως σκολιόδρομος…βᾶσα ~ 1.306–7 Μήνης δ' ἀμφίκερως [-ω Hal^mg] σκολιὸς δρόμος…βαίνων

(c) because there are syntactic problems with M^c and/or Π¹:

4.51 ἐς ἰνίον ~ 1.319 ἢ ἰνίον

4.147 κόσμου ~ 1.295 κόσμον

4.204 σκολιῶν τε λόγων ~ 1.304 τεύχει [τέχνης K] τε λόγων

4.205 τ' ~ 1.305: a connective is needed

4.389 θαλάμους ~ Π¹ θαλάμων

4.487 ἔν τε βιαιοτάτῳ θανάτῳ βίον ἐκλείψουσιν ~ 1.315 ἔν τε βίᾳ θάνατον λείψει κακοεργέϊ θυμῷ. M^c's version is secondary because (i) θάνατον λείψει makes no sense, and (ii) sing. λείψει is sandwiched between two plurals (but how did it arise?).

(d) because there are editorial problems with M^c:

4.50–1 ~ 1.318–19: singulars interpolated in M^c into the middle of a sequence of plurals.

(e) other (more subjective):

4.489 ἐκδήσαντες ~ 1.317 ἐνδήσαντες

(ii) Some of the instances where Π¹ is superior to M^b are trivial:

4.385 ἤ ~ Π¹ αἱ

4.386 ἤ ~ Π¹ εἰς

4.390 ἔσσεται ~ Π¹ ἔσται

But in 4.385 τελέουσι λοχεῖαι ~ Π¹ τελέθουσι τοκειαι, 4.390 ἐν γενέθλαισι ~ Π¹ γενετῆρσι (neither of which is easy), 4.402 πολιοῖο ~ Π¹ πλαγκτοῖο, 4.412 and 1.337 δεδαιγμένη ~ Π¹ δεδαμασμένη, and 4.577 Ἑρμῆς δ' εἰς ὤρην ~ Π¹ Ἑρμείης δ' ὤρην (since ἐλθεῖν can be constructed with a straight accusative) it is a matter of true alternatives, and in 4.399 πρωτάρχας ~ 1.324 πλωτάρχας ~ Π¹ πρωράρχους, Π¹ is to be preferred. Π¹ preserves 568a, missing in L itself.

(iii) M^c is rarely superior.

The only instance where it is, in fact, is at 4.413 κύπρις, where the correct reading, φύσις, is shared by M^c (1.338) and Π¹, showing that this is to be regarded as M^b's isolated corruption of the vulgate.

Nonetheless, it is certainly not as simple as that M^c has used M^b directly (*contra* Monaco, 71), for there are cases where M^c and M^b are equally valid (with $Π^1$ supporting different sides), and M^c's version has an interest of its own:

1.298 ζωγραφίης μεδέοντας [supported by Θ] ~ 4.150 ἐν πραπίδεσσιν [γραφίδεσσιν S] ἀρίστους
1.303–4 ῥήτορας ἐμφαίνουσι βροτούς... τέχνης [K, for τεύχει] τε λόγων ~ 4.203–4 ῥητορικῆς φαίνουσι τέχνης... σκολιῶν τε λόγων (but cf. 4.141)
1.314 ἀλύσεσσιν ~ 4.486 ἀλυσηδόν
1.316 σφαγίοις ~ 4.488 φοβεροῖς
1.317 ἀγχονόωντα ~ 4.489 ἀλγινόεντα
1.323 ὕδατος ἴστορας ~ 4.397/$Π^1$ ἐν ὕδασι νήκτορας
1.330 νεκυηπόλος Αἶσα ~ 1.405 νεκυοστόλος Αἶσα
1.333 κἀκ πολλῶν θανάτων πλοῦτον ~ 4.408 πλοῦτον δ' ἐκ θανάτων πολλῶν
1.338 αἱμηρῇσι, $Π^1$ αι]μηρης ($Π^1$'s version preferable to M^c's) ~ 4.413 ἀμβλωσμοῦ θ', ἅ

In sum, the evidence of $Π^1$ and the complicated interplay of inheritance and appropriation (pp. 274–6) in the transmission of astrology throws into question the status of what we have in the fourth book—original poem, or merely another redaction. So, some of M^b's mannerisms are present in lines shared with M^c and/or the papyrus; others are absent. If we were to accept M^b as the source and M^c the borrower, we would suppose that the latter took over material, but stripped out <some of[6]> what he saw as eccentricity (for example the ἔσσεσθαι construction) and replaced it with something less mannered or something more typical of him. But the fact that *both* M^c *and* $Π^1$ seem consistently to favour present indicatives where M^b favours futures suggest that the former might (at least in some ways) represent a vulgate on which a redactor imposes his own stylistic choices. In 1.299, εὐφυέας is a perfectly respectable option, which a redactor could have ousted in favoured of his own preferred ἔσσεσθαι in 4.151; εὐφυέας in no way makes the impression of a stop-gap. We would need more witnesses to develop a clearer picture.

Conclusion

As I wrote in the first volume, Robert Kraft's model of 'evolved' literature, devised for the early Christian pseudepigrapha, is an intriguing and initially attractive comparison.[7] The radicalism of being able to throw out the notion of authorship in the first place might seem to hold a certain allure. With our

---

[6] Not all. Many of what we take to be M^b's mannerisms are present in M^c as well, such as 1.307 λαξεύματα, for λοξεύματα, the agent noun in 1.310 ἐπανοίκτορας. But we lack the evidence of any papyrus for these lines and without a third witness we cannot be certain whether they go back to a common source or not.

[7] Cited in i. xxiii n. 1.

material that would go too far, but one might still want to argue that this is not authorship in the conventional sense. Material circulates and is recast by poets who are not originators, but can still impose their own stylistic stamp, and sometimes even change the sense. They can modify details of the protasis, and they can tinker with the outcome. They are also free to reorder. The recension in Π^1 adheres to the same textual sequence as M^b, although the readings frequently differ. But the recension in M^c substantially re-orders, as well as imposing readings which are more integrated into the general style of the book.

This state of affairs, it should be said, is not really comparable to the Sibylline Oracles, although they might at first sight seem to be most comparable among Christian texts, being pseudepigraphically transmitted repositories of partly ancient material which is demonstrably patched and gerrymandered over time. There are three classes of manuscript among the Sibylline corpus, Φ, Ψ, and Ω, representing different recensions of the oracles, but those differences are of an editorial nature: they concern (i) the ordering of books, with evidence of the ancient partitioning of the collection; (ii) interpolated material (the pseudo-Phocylidea in Ψ + S in *Or. Sib.* 2); (iii) 'corrections', where Ψ with respect to Φ presents many readings which restore standard Greek prose forms and often fail to scan.[8] But it does not represent a separate ancient recension with equally valid alternative forms. The corpus does not suggest the presence of separate tradents of the same material with individual, analysable stylistic (let alone doctrinal) profiles.

Editorial policy is therefore a complex matter, and one that previous editors have not properly confronted. (It is possible that the situation will become even more complicated, as more Manethonian papyri emerge from Oxyrhynchus; we can already see that P.Oxy. 5588 (book one) contains new variants in lines 32 and 43, P.Oxy. 5589 (book two) several new readings, both superior, inferior, and of uncertain value, although it is true that P.Oxy. 5590 (book four) has no divergences from L.)

Koechly knew nothing of ever-adaptable *Fachliteratur*; he proceeded according to traditional methods. It was Radici Colace who, with her detailed comparisons of the different recensions, gave us the new model. Like Monaco and De Stefani,[9] in principle I accept this model.

Yet Monaco, who has provided critical apparatuses for each passage that he studies, pays it lip-service, but continues to operate in the traditional way, habitually using the language of 'choice' (*scelta*) and preference. So does De Stefani. The complication is that that is not wholly wrong. If it were, one could

---

[8] See the editions of Geffcken, xlix–lii, and Rzach, viii f.   [9] 2016, 205; 2017, 26.

simply throw it out, but one cannot. What is confusing, or frustratingly ragged, about the situation in the Manethoniana is that one cannot jettison the old model of transcription and relationships between texts which are modelled in a linear, quasi-stemmatic way, any more than one can throw out the notion of authorship. On the one hand, the principle of equal valence implies that each recension should be represented on its own terms; that follows from accepting that each version of the text represents something viable in its own terms. In that light, 'choosing' one reading over another means nothing more than favouring one poet on aesthetic grounds—not a method one would want to adopt. On the other, however, M^c can so often be weighed in the balance against M^b (and sometimes Π^1 as well) and found wanting that it is not unreasonable to conclude that this version represents something secondary; conversely, there are occasions where M^b can be corrected against it and/or the papyrus. One must *simultaneously* proceed as a traditional textual critic, pronouncing some readings better than others, *and* acknowledge instances of equally valid alternatives. It is a question *both* of textual degradations that arise from traditional causes (corruption, copying errors), *and* of creative or manipulative poet-editors who remake texts as they use them. We must reconcile the idea of one version being secondary to another, which implies copying, with that of magpie poet-practitioners who possess more agency and creative power. This can be complicated for a modern editor, who is both trying to respect the integrity of a recension and operating with an editor's instincts for correction where something is demonstrably wrong.

The real question—not really faced by Monaco or De Stefani—becomes whether to represent a recension in all its fallibility and ineptitude—after all, it was what the poet meant at the time—and reserve corrections only for outright errors of transmission (phonetic confusions, errors of transcription, and so on). The editor of a papyrus, after all, is called on to reproduce the transmitted text, and it is not clear why the same principle should not apply to M^c vis-à-vis M^b—or indeed to M^b vis-à-vis M^c, on the smaller number of occasions where this applies. So I print ἀμβλωσμοῦ θ' at 4.413 because it is the linchpin of my approach, and allow that 1.299 εὐτυπέων is at least a possibility. I retain L's ἀμφίκερως (as well as σκολιὸς δρόμος) at 1.306, taking it to be what the poet inherited and what he intended (albeit rather ineptly), rather than a misguided attempt by a later copyist to restore the nominative form in 4.478. At 1.315 I (like De Stefani) print θάνατον λείψει even though it is patently nonsensical. I have also respected the fact that M^c's recension is more Atticising than M^b's. On the other hand I have corrected obvious impossibilities (1.295 κόσμον, 307 λαξεύματα), have allowed metre to prevail in accepting Axtius and Rigler's κυανοχρώτοιο at 1.327, and have added ‹τ'› at 305. I retain 4.485a, which is supplied from 1.313, though I do so with a slightly uneasy conscience in the light of a principle that requires the representation of what the manuscript carries. My best justification is that an angled bracket by a later hand in the left margin at 4.485 possibly indicates that *someone* thought something was to be supplied at that point.

REGISTER OF DIFFERENCES BETWEEN THE TEXTS OF LIGHTFOOT AND DE STEFANI

	L	S
Book 4		
2	αἷσιν	ᾗσιν
17	ἐς	εἰς
43	οἴσεται οἴκοις	ἔσσεται οἴκου
49	πότμῳ	θεσμῷ
56	πανάθεσμος ἀατήρ	πανάθεσμιος [sic] †ἀνήρ
65	ἣν δ' ἐρατὴ	ἣν †μὲν γὰρ†
post 69	lacunam indicavi	—
80	θεόλημπτος	θεόληπτος
83b	φέροιτο	φέρηται
86	†κ' ἀτρέπτους	καὶ ἀμέμπτους
88	τε πλαγκτὰ	τ' ἔπολβα
94	ἐς	εἰς
102	τικτομένοις	πλουτοτόκος
114	λιτῆς	⟨χα⟩λεπῆς
122	ἡμεριναῖσι	ἡμερινῇσι
127	ἀρίστους	κρατίστους
129	τελεταῖσιν	τελετῇσιν
130	λιθογλυφίαισι	λιθογλυφίῃσι
174	ἱεραῖσιν	ἱερῇσιν
175–175a	lacunam indicavi	—
200	κατάδειπνα	κακὰ δεῖπνα
216	λυσσομανοῦντα	λυσσομανούντων
228	τελεταῖσιν	τελετῇσιν
262	πάντα θ' ἅτ' ἐκ	†πάντ' ἐπὶ†
post 269	lacunam indicavi	—
274	ἀσθματικοῖο	αἰθοτόκοιο
282	πόλεως	πόλιος
285	ἑτοίμην	ὁμοίην
294	Κυθήρη	Κυθηριὰς
318	σελάοντι	σελαγεῦντι
320	δεροεργέας	δοροεργέας
363	ὀρίνει	†ὁρίζου†
390	γενέθλαισι	γενέθλῃσι
395	ἀθρῶν	αἴθων

The Text of the Later Books 399

	L	S
399	ναυφθορίαισιν	ναυφθορίῃσιν
406	πολὺν	βαθὺν
413	ἀμβλωσμοῦ θ'	αἱμηρῆς
422	αὐδᾷ	αὐτῶν
423	ἰδὲ ῥαπτῆρας	ἰδ' ἡγητῆρας
442	παλάμαισι	παλάμῃσι
449	ῥεμβηδὸν	βομβηδὸν
470	ξενίαισιν	ξενίῃσιν
471	προκοπαῖσιν	προκοπῇσιν
473	ἐναντιόωντα	ἐναντίον ἄστρα
494	στοργαῖσι	στοργῇσι
514	ἰθυδίκαιοι	ἠδὲ †βίαιοι
536	ἦθος	ἦτορ
546	συνδέσμῳ κόσμοιο	†συνδέσμους ῥυσμοῖο†
548	θεόλημπτα	θεόληπτα
556	κακαγγελίαισι	κακαγγελίῃσι
557	ὀξύγοοι	ὀξύχολοι
566	δι'	ἰδ'
568a	τορν[εύτορας	τορν[
575	μέτ'	μέγ'
577	Ἑρμῆς δ' εἰς	Ἑρμείης δ'
597	Κυθέρη ἐσαθρῇ	Κυθερειὰς ἀθρῇ
612	πάθος	σίνος
post 614	lacunam indicavi	—
621	†τε δικήλων	τ' εἰδώλων
Book 1		
8–9	non traieci	traiecit
77b	[non dedi]	ῥέζει
post 89	—	lacunam indicavit
96	Ἄρην	Ἄρηα
97	ὑπὸ αὐγαῖς	ὑπ' αὐγαῖς
post 99	—	lacunam indicavit
114		post 99b traiecit
120	ἄρρενα	ἄρσενα
	δεινῷ	κεῖνος
123	ἠδὲ καὶ αὐτὸς	εἰ δέ κεν οὕτω
125	ἄρρενας	ἄρσενας
140	ναυσὶ	νηυσὶ
141	ἐϋρρείθροις	εὐρείθροις
142	σου	σεῦ
146	μογερῶς	σμυγερῶς
148	μετέωρον ἀνεσταύρωσας	†μεθ' ἑοῦ μόρου† ἐσταύρωσας
169	θανάτῳ κακῷ	θανάτῳ
	διχοστασίῃσιν	διχοστασίῃ
173	ἄστεγον	ἄστεγοι
	ἀγύναιον	ἀγύναιοι
	ἄτεκνόν τ'	ἄτεκνοί τ'
179	ἢ	ἢ‹ν›
	πλώουσιν	πλώωσιν

	L	S
181	πρᾶξιν	πρῆξιν
	ῥέζουσιν	τεύξουσιν
188	μινυνθάδι' οἶσι	μινυνθαδίοισι
203	Ἄρηϊ	Ἄρη
222	ἀπ' εὐπορίης	ἐν εὐπορίῃ
239	κατοχαῖσι	κατοχῇσι
post 240	lacunam indicavi	—
251	μογεραῖσι	μογερῇσι
258	δούλαισιν	δούλῃσιν
273	ἠδὲ	⟨τ'⟩ ἠδὲ
282	καθ'	ἐφ'
283	γενέθλη	γενέθλης
292	σοφίαισιν	σοφίῃσιν
304	λαμπρὰν	λαμπρὴν
306	ἀμφίκερως	ἀμφίκερω
post 334	lacunam indicavi	—
335	ἐπὶ τοῦτο	⟨ἣν⟩ ἐπὶ τοῦτο
	Πυρόεις	Πυροειδής
345	τούσδε	τῇδε
Book 5		
4,3	traieci	
3	ἰδίαις	ἰδέας
6	βλύζον	βαιῶν
11	οὐ βαιὸς κάματος δ' οὗτος	οὐδ' οὗτος βαιὸς κάματος
37	ὁμοῦ	ὅλων
43	λεύσσειε	λεύσσειε
48	συναφαῖσιν	συναφῇσιν
56	δῆριν	δι' ἔριν
	περὶ κέντρον	λιπόκεντροι
	ἔχωσιν	ἔωσιν
63	Ἡελίου κακοεργοῦ	Ἡελίου· κακοεργός
74	θυμοῖσιν	θνητοῖσιν
79	ἐπειχθεὶς	ἐπαχθεὶς
80	ἰδίαν	ἰδίην
83	γονῇ ἔπι	γονὴν ἰδὲ
85	δράστας	δρήστας
97	ἐπαειρόμενοι	ἐπιπειθόμενοι
	ἀτῶνται	⟨ἀπ⟩ατῶνται
98	ψευσθέντες	φυσῶντες
98b	—	
99	οὐρανίαισι	οὐρανίῃσι
103	μοίραισι	μοίρῃσι
119	θείαισι	θείῃσι
120	συναφαῖσι	συναφῇσι
121	ἀρχαῖσιν	ἀρχῇσιν
128	ἔφυσεν	†ἔασιν
132	μοίραισι	μοίρῃσι
post 136	—	lacunam indicavit

The Text of the Later Books 401

	L	S
141	ἴδμων τ' ὀρχηθμοῦ ⟨τέρψει⟩	καὶ τούτων †ἄρχι† δήμου
	θυμέλαισιν	θυμέλησιν
161	νομίᾳ	νομίῃ
164	χαλκόκτυπον ἐξετέλεσσαν	†χαλκῶι τε παρέξεται πνεῦμα†
169	δέ τ' ἐπαμφορέοιτο	δ' †ἐπαναφέρηται
post 169	lacunam indicavi	—
172	σύρδην	†συρτηι†
181	ὥρη	Ἄρης
	εὑρίσκηται φολιδωτοῖς	ἔπι φωλεύων κατὰ κέντρα
182	καὶ	τὴν
	πρᾶξιν	πρῆξιν
	ξὺν Ζηνὶ	κρίνῃ κατιδὼν
	Κρόνος	Κρόνον
	παρέχει ὑπόγειος	⟨ὄνθ⟩ ὑπόγειον
184	αὔτως	αὐτοῖς
186	†δὲ καλούντων	προκαλοῦντας
195	γναμπτοί σφ' ὄνυχες	†γναμπτοῖς ὀνύχεσσι
	διόρυξαν ὄρεσσιν	ἀνόρυξεν ὀρίοις†
203	τέκνῳ	τέκνοις
204	εἰς	†ὡς†
	υἱὸν	⟨β⟩ίον
216	γυναιξὶ συνευνάζουσα	συνευνάζουσα γυναιξίν
231	†τε†	γε
233	δαπάναισι	δαπάνῃσι
235	ἄλλου	ἄλλων
239	πλασταῖσι	πλαστῇσι
243	συνάπτοι	συνάπτῃ
244	μελέταισι	μελέτῃσι
254	εἰ μέν θ' ἕνα	†καὶ τενι
	ἀθροῖ	αἴθρει†
261	ἐσίδοι	ἐσίδῃ
263	εἶδος ἔχοντα	†ἠθάδ' ἐόντα
264	ἀκοαῖσι	ἀκοῇσι
273	ἰδίαισι	ἰδίῃσι
274	συνοδεύοι	συνοδεύῃ
278	χώραισιν	χώρῃσιν
285	ἦν καὶ	†καὶ ἦν
296	δόξαισί	δόξῃσί
	κελαδοῦνται	†λελάληνται†
299	στρατιαῖσιν	στρατιῇσιν
304	περιέργει	περιείργει
315	ἀλλὰ καὶ ὣς	†ἄλλως δ' ὥς†
322	ἠΰτ' ἐπ' ἔργοις	ἠΰτε πόρνη
323	αἰσχροῖς	αἰσχρῶν
335	κακοπράγμονα	κακοπρήγμονα
336	αὐστηρὰν	αὐστηρήν
	πολυπράγμονα	πολυπρήγμονα
337	βληχρὰν	βληχρὴν

SIGLA

Codices

L	Laur. Plut. 28.27
L^1	corrector principalis (i. 376–6)
L^{ac}	L ante correctionem
L^{ras}	correctio supra rasuram scripta
L^{sl}	varia lectio vel correctio supra lineam scripta
	Sic intelligenda: γήρα¹ L^{1sl} = γήρα L, γήρα¹ L^1
L_{sl}	varia lectio vel correctio sub linea scripta
$L^{γρ}$	γράφεται varia lectio in L
L^{mg}	varia lectio vel correctio in margine scripta
L^{rec}	corrector recentior (p. 382)

H	Hamburg. philol. 4
H^h	Consensus H cum lectionibus Holstenio attributis
Hal	Liber Halensis A 91
Hal^{mg}	Lectiones in margine libri Halensis, non Holstenio attributae
Hol	Holstenii variae lectiones in margine codicis Halensis A 91

Papyri

Π^1	P.Oxy. 2546 (3rd c.)
Π^2	P.Amst. Inv. No. 56
Π^3	P.Oxy. 5588

Editores atque critici
De editionibus, cf. i. 387–8

A	Axtius (solus)
A.-R.	Axtius–Rigler in contextu
A.-R.^{c}	Axtius–Rigler in corrigendis
conj.	coniecit (neque in contextu recepit)
D	J. P. D'Orville, *Animadversiones in Charitonis Aphrodisiensis de Chaerea & Callirrhoe Narrationum Amatoriarum Libros VIII* (Amstelodamii, editio altera, 1783)
Ger	E. Gerhard, *Lectiones Apollonianae* (Lipsiae, 1816)
Gr	Gronovius (in contextu)
Gr*	Gronovius (in annotationibus in marg. inf.)
Gr^n	Gronovius (in annotationibus post contextum)
Gr^v	Gronovii interpretatio
Head	W. Headlam, *Journal of Philology*, 26 (1899), 110
Heil	Heilen 2010
Heph	Hephaestion
Herm	J. G. Hermann, *Orphica* (Lipsiae, 1805), 716–17, 749–50
Hop	N. Hopkinson, *Eos*, 73 (1985), 65–8
Jac	F. Jacobs, *Anthologia Graeca*, iii (Lipsiae, 1817)
K	Koechly in editione Didotiana (1851, ²1862)
K^2	Koechly in editione Teubneriana (1858)

Key	R. Keydell, *Kleine Schriften zur hellenistischen und spätgriechischen Dichtung (1911–1976)*, ed. W. Peek (Lipsiae, 1982)
Lehrs	K. Lehrs, *Quaestiones Epicae* (Regiomontii, 1837)
Lob	C. A. Lobeck, sic:
	Para. = *Paralipomena Grammaticae Graecae, Pars Prior* (Lipsiae, 1837)
	Phryn. = *Phrynichi Ecloga Nominum et Verborum Atticorum* (Lipsiae, 1820)
	Rh. = *Rhematikon; sive, Verborum graecorum et nominum verbalium technologia* (Regimontii, 1846)
Lop	Lopilato
Luc	C. M. Lucarini, *BMCR* 2018.08.29, rev. of De Stefani 2017
Lud	A. Ludwich, *Philologus*, 63 (1904), 118–34
Mon	Monaco 2013
Nauck	J. A. Nauck, *Mélanges gréco-romains*, 6 tomm. (Petropoli, 1849–1894)
Pin	Pingree (ap. Lopilato)
R	Rigler (solus)
S	De Stefani, edn
Sp	F. Spitzner, *De versu Graecorum heroico, maxime homerico* (Lipsiae, 1816)
Span	K. Spanoudakis, *YAGE* 1 (2016), 206–9
Wa	G. Wakefield, *Silva Critica: Sive, in auctores sacros profanosque commentarius philologus* (Cantabrigiae *et alibi*, 1789–95)

Μανέθωνος Ἀποτελεσματικῶν Βιβλία Δ', Α', Ε'

Βιβλίον Δ′

Οὐρανίων ἄστρων ἀτραπούς, πλάστιγγας Ἀνάγκης
αἷσιν ἐφημερίων μερόπων γένος ἐκμεμέτρηται,
Μοιράων τε κέλευθα βροτήσια, καὶ πλάνα φέγγη
ἀπλανέων τ' αὐγὰς πυριλαμπέας ἐξονομήνω,
ζῳδίων τε πόλοιο περίδρομον, ὃς κατὰ γαῖαν   5
αἰθερίην τε κέλευθον ἐν ἡμιτμῆτι πορείῃ
πλαγκτὰ διχαζόμενος διέπει θεομήστορα κόσμον
ἐξ ἠοῦς ἐπὶ νύκτα καὶ ἀντολίης ἐπὶ δυσμάς.
ταῦτα γὰρ ἐξ ἱερῶν ἀδύτων φύσις αἰθερόπλαγκτος
ὀρθὰ τεκμαιρομένοισι διώρισεν ἀνδράσιν ἄστρα,   10
οἷς πλαγκτὴ κόσμοιο βροτοκλώστειρα χορείη
δόγματος ἐξ ἱεροῖο σαφῆ πρὸς ἔλεγχον ἰοῦσα,
⟨   ⟩
ἐξ οὗ μὲν καὶ ἐς οἷον ἀμείβεται εἶδος ἕκαστον.
  Πρῶτα μὲν οὖν Τιτὰν παντὸς Κρόνος αἰθέρος ἄρχει,
ἀστήρ, ὃν Φαίνοντα θεοὶ μέροπές τε καλοῦσιν·   15
οὗτος, ἐπὴν οἰκεῖα φανῇ κατὰ δώμαθ' ἑαυτοῦ
γεινομένοις θνητοῖσιν ἐπίσκοπον ἐς βίου ὥρην,
εὐκτεάνους δείκνυσι καὶ ὄλβου πλείονος ἄρχειν,
εὐτυχέας ζωῇ τε καὶ ἐς τέλος αἰὲν ἀμόχθους·
ἔστι δ' ἐν οἰκείοισι τεταγμένα ταῦτα Κρόνοιο   20
ζῳδί', οἷστε φανεὶς τεύχει πολυχρήμονας ἄνδρας·
Ὑδροχόος, ταμίης νεφελώδεος Οὐλύμποιο,
Αἰγόκερως, γαίης τε καὶ ὕδατος ἀμφίβιος θήρ,
Κριὸς ὅ τ' οὐρανίου κορυφῆς ὅρος, εἴαρος ἀρχή,
καὶ Ζυγὸς αἰγλήεις πρὸς Σκορπίον αἰθερονωμῶν,   25
τετραπόδης τε Λέων, πολυάστερος ἔμπυρος οἶκος·
οὗτοι ἀεὶ τεύχουσι βροτοὺς εὐδαίμονας ἔργοις.

14–27. Cf. 3.12–17.

fo. 25ᵛ
1 πλάστιγγος L: corr. Hal   2 αισιν L: αἷσιν H: ἧσιν A.-R.   3 β̄ροτήσια L¹ˢˡ
4 ἐξονομήνας L: corr. K: ἐξονόμηνα A.-R., post ἐξονόμηνα D³³⁵   6 ημιμηταπορρειηι L: corr.
Lob. Para.²³⁷, A.-R.ᶜ (ἡμιτμῆτι), Halᵐᵍ (πορείῃ)   7 διεπει, -ει L¹ʳᵃˢ   θεομήτορα L: corr.
Lob. Para.²¹³ⁿ· ⁷   9 φάτις Sᶜᵒⁿʲ   10 τεκμαιραμένοισι L: corr. Hal

Book Four

The ways of the heavenly stars, Fate's balances,
By which man's transient life is measured out,
The mortal paths of Fate, the wandering lights,
And the fire-bright fixed stars' rays shall be my theme,
And the orb of heaven's signs, which under ground   5
And through the ether on a cloven path
Cut slantwise, rules the god-appointed whole,
From dawn to nightfall, east to setting-place.
From sacred alcoves heaven's natural force
For men who judge aright spaced out the stars   10
Whose roving cosmic choir spins Fate for men
By ordinance divine, to clear proof put,
⟨   ⟩
Whence and to what each species[1] is transformed.
   Now, first, Saturn the Titan rules the sky,
The star which gods and humans Phainon call.   15
This star, when it appears in its own homes
In the hour with oversight of life in births,
Shows forth the propertied, who rule great wealth,
Blessed in life, and leisured till the end.
The following signs are reckoned Saturn's own,   20
Those where, when he appears, he makes men rich:
Aquarius, steward of the cloudy heaven,
Capricorn, by land and sea amphibious beast,
The Ram that marks heaven's summit, start of Spring,
The bright Scales by the Scorpion, sky-possessing,   25
And four-foot Leo, spangled fiery house.
These always make men wealthy by their works.

---

[1] Or 'species each'!

11 ὡσπλαγκτη L: corr. Gr   κόσμου βιοτοκλ. S^{conj}   χωρείη L: corr. H, Gr   12 post hunc versum lacunam indicavit K   17 ἐς βίον ὥρης L: corr. D⁶⁵⁵

fo. 26^r
20 οἰκίοισι L: corr. L¹   21 ζωϊδίοιστε L: dist. K   22 νεφελώδεος Οὐλύμποιο L¹
25 αἰθερονομῶν L: corr. Gr, Hal^{mg}   26 ἔμπυρος, υ L^{1ras}

ἢν δέ τ' ἀνοικείοισι τόποις κλυτοτέρμονος ὥρης
φυομένοις θνητοῖς μέσον οὐρανὸν αἰθερολαμπῆ,
ἢ κείνην ὥρην πανεπίσκοπον ἀμφιπολεύῃ, 30
παμβλαβέας ῥέξει τε καὶ ἀκτεάνους καὶ ἀδόξους,
ἐνδεέας ζωῆς καὶ ἐφημερίης βιότητος,
καὶ πάσης λύπης ἐπιβήτορας οἰκτρομελάθρους
τεύχει, καὶ λύπης καὶ ἀλημοσύνης μετέχοντας.

Ζεὺς δ' ἐπὶ γεινομένοισιν ὅτ' ἂν κυδόσκοπον ὥρην 35
εἰσλεύσσῃ φαέθοντι πυρὸς θερμοῖο σελασμῷ,
ἢ μέσον οὐρανίης ἀτραποῦ δρόμῳ ἠέρα τέμνῃ,
ἠδὲ κατ' οἰκείων προφανῇ δεσπόσμασι μοιρῶν,
χρυσοστέπτορας ἄνδρας ἢ ἀρχιερῆας ἀϋτεῖ
ἔσσεσθαι, πολέων τε διιθυντῆρας ἀέθλων, 40
ἠδὲ μεγιστάνας τε καὶ ἀλλοτρίων κτεανισμῶν
δεσποσύνους, οἷς τέκνα καὶ ὀλβίστη παράκοιτις
εἰς ἀρετὴν νεύουσα πολὺ κλέος οἴσεται οἴκοις.

ἡνίκα δ' ἂν πυρόεις Ἄρεος πυριλαμπέος ἀστὴρ
ἐν καθέτῳ κόσμου μέσον οὐρανὸν ἀμφιπολεύῃ, 45
τῆμος ὁ φὺς ἔσεται μὲν ἐν ἡγεμόνεσσιν ἄριστος,
φρουρητῆρα σίδηρον ἔχων, φυλακάς τε κρατούντων
πίστιν τ' ἀλκήεσσαν· ἐπὴν δ' εἰς τέρμα βίοιο
μοιριδίου θανάτοιο μόλῃ πολυπήμονι πότμῳ,
ἢ διὰ λαιμοτόμου φάρυγος βίον αἵματι λείψει 50
σφονδυλόεντα τράχηλον ἐς ἰνίον ἀκροτομηθείς,
ἢ διὰ φαρμακτοῖο δόλου νοσερὸν τέλος ἕξει.

λαμπροφαὴς δ' ἀστὴρ ὁπότ' ἂν δύνουσι φαανθῇ
ζωιδίοις, ὃν πάντες ἐπεφράσσαντ' Ἀφροδίτης
φωσφόρον, ἐν τούτῳ δὲ γονὰς μερόπων τις ἐνέγκῃ, 55
ἔσσεται ἀλλοτρίων λεχέων πανάθεσμος ἀατήρ,
ὀρφνήεις, δολοεργός, ἀνέστιος, αἰσχεόμυθος,
παμψέκτωρ, ἀδίδακτος, ἀεὶ δεδιδαγμένος αἰσχροῖς·

28–34. Cf. 3.21–6.
Paul, p. 65.13–19. ἐπὶ δὲ τῶν νυκτερινῶν γενέσεων τὸν τόπον τοῦτον ἐπέχων ἐν παρύγροις μὲν τὰς πράξεις ἀποτελεῖ· δυσπράκτους δὲ καὶ δυσπεριοκτήτους καὶ ἀπροκόπους καὶ ἀδρανεῖς καὶ δυσγάμους καὶ σπανοτέκνους καὶ πένητας ἀποτελεῖ, ὅτὲ δὲ καὶ πολὺν χρόνον ξενιτεύοντας ἢ ἐκτὸς τῆς ἰδίας πόλεως οἰκοῦντας καὶ πλανωμένους ἐπὶ πολὺν χρόνον ποιήσει.
35–43. Cf. 3.36–8.
44–52. Cf. 3.61–71.
53–8. Cf. 3.84–9.

---

28 εἰ δ' ἐν ἐναντι(οις) in marg. sin., εἰ δε ἐν ἀνοικ(είοις) τόποις ὥρης ἢ ⊙ [id est MC] Κρόνος in marg. dextr. L¹   33–4 λύπης…λύπης L: pro λύπης¹ λύμης R^conj, K: pro λύπης² πενίης S^conj

But in alien places on the Hour's famed bounds
Should it roam Midheaven, shining in the skies,
Or that all-seeing Hour when men are born, 30
It blights them utterly, takes wealth and fame,
Makes them want livelihood and daily means,
Acquainted with all grief, in wretched homes,
Familiar with distress and wandering.
   When Jupiter at birth the famous Hour 35
Regards with shining rays of torrid fire,
Or cleaves mid-air pursuing heaven's path,
Or shows forth governing his own degrees,
He presages men crowned with gold, high priests,
Who oversee their many festivals, 40
Great personages, of others' estates
Directors, whose offspring and wealthy wife
Disposed to virtue bring their houses fame.
   When the flaming star of Mars, blazing with fire,
On the cosmos' plumb-line occupies Midheaven, 45
The native will be foremost among chiefs,
With iron encompassed, guards of those in power,
And sure in his own strength. But when life's end
He reaches through death's lamentable lot,
He'll leave life bloodily through jugular cut, 50
Cervical vertebrae cleft to the occiput,
Or meet a sickly end through poisoned fraud.
   When in setting signs the radiant planet shines
Which all men have entitled Venus' star,
Light-bringer, and a mortal birth occurs, 55
He'll ravage wedlock, all-unscrupulous,
Shady, deceitful, hearth-less, lewd of speech,
All-culpable, past mending, schooled in shame.

---

35 γεινομένοις ὁπότ' ἂν S^{conj} 36 εἰσλεύσῃ L: corr. K   37 δρόμον L: corr. D^{656} 38 ἠὲ M: corr. K   40 πόλεών τε L: corr. H, Hal, D^{650}: πολέμῳ τε K^2 43 πολύκλεος L: corr. Hal   οἴσεται οἴκοις L: πολὺ κλέος...οἴκου Gr^n: οἴσετ' ἐς οἴκους R: ἔσσεται οἴκου K   44 περιλαμπέος L: corr. D^{671} 45 ἀμφιπολεύει L: corr. H^h 49 κόσμῳ L: corr. K post Letronne: θέσμῳ S   50 λαιμοτόμου L^{1sl} φάρυγγος L: corr. D^{407} 51 ἰνίον, ἱ- L^{1ras} 52 νοσερῶς L: corr. K   53 δύνουσα L: corr. K   56 παναθέσμιος ἀνήρ L: corr. K: παν. ἅρπαξ Neri: λῃστὴρ πανάθεσμος S^{conj} 57 ὀ‹ρ›φνήεις L^1 αἰσχρεόμυθος L: corr. K post A.-R.^{conj} αἰσχιόμυθος   58 μεμελημένος αἰσχρ. Nauck$^{iv.162-3}$

ἢν δὲ Κύπρις μερόπων ὡροσκόπα φέγγεα λεύσσῃ,
αἱμυλίους τεύχει καὶ εὐμούσους καὶ ἀμόχθους, 60
ἔκ τε γυναικείων χαρίτων λάμποντας ἐν ὄλβοις·
τούτοις θηλειῶν πιστεύεται ὅρκια κρυπτά,
οὗτοι προστήσονται ἐν ὀργιάδεσσιν ἑορταῖς,
ἔνθα φυγαρσενίης μυστήρια τεύχετ' ἄπυστα·
ἢν δ' ἐρατὴ μεσόωντα κατ' οὐρανὸν ἀνδράσιν ὀφθῇ, 65
φράζει τοι βιοτὴν βαθυχρήμονα, χιλιάδας τε
ἀρχάς, καὶ δόξης ἀπλέτου κοσμήτορα κόμπον,
ἐκ τοίης τιμῆς †μυστήρια τεύχετ' ἄπιστα†
στίλβων δ' Ἑρμείαο φανεὶς ἐπὶ τὴν δύσιν ἀστὴρ
⟨   ⟩
γεινομένων βρεφέων ὡροσκόπον ἢ κατὰ μέσσον 70
οὐρανόν, ἔκ τε λόγων τεύχει προκοπήν τινα θνητοῖς,
καὶ καλαμογραφίης, καὶ ὅσ' εἰς μοῦσαν πεπόνηται·
τούτῳ δ' ὁππότ' Ἄρηος ἔῃ ἰσόμοιρος ἀταρπός,
ἢ διαμετρήσῃ φάεσιν φάος ἀντικέλευθον,
πλαστογράφους, χειρῶν μιμήτορας ἀλλοτυπώτων 75
παμβλαβέας τεύχει καὶ ὠχρήεντας ἰδέσθαι.
ἀμφίκερως Μήνη δ' ὁπότ' ἂν βιοτέρμονος ὥρης
φωτὶ Σεληναίῳ κρατέῃ σκολιωπὰ περῶσα,
τῇ δ' Ἄρης ἰσόμοιρα δι' αἰθέρος ἀκροπολεύῃ,
τηνίκα τοι θεόληπτος ὁ φὺς ἐν σχήματι τοίῳ 80
γίνεται, ἔκπληκτός τε, σεληνάζων τε νόοιο,

59-64. Dor.^{ARAB} II 26.1. If Venus is in the ascendant or in what follows the ascendant, eastern [and] rejoicing in its light, he will be praiseworthy, handsome, a master of women, well known among kings and lords of men, well known in metropolises and cities, and some of them will have intercourse with the women of the rich, but they will not profit or excel by means of this, and some of them will occupy houses of worship [and will be] pure (we have seen something like this), great, one whom praise will lift up and his head will be crowned, and he will be good in [his] character [and] will love wealth, especially if the Moon aspects.

Περὶ κέντρ. 52. Ἡ Ἀφροδίτη ὡροσκοποῦσα ἢ ἐπαναφερομένη τῷ ὡροσκόπῳ ἀνατολικὴ πολυγυναίους, γνωστούς, βασιλεῖς, εὐμόρφους, λογίους, ἐνδόξους, ἀγαθούς, θεοσεβεῖς, καὶ τῇ πόλει γνωστοὶ ἔσονται· πλουσίων γυναικῶν ἄνδρας, ἀλλ' ὄνησιν τούτων οὐχ ἕξουσιν· τινὲς ἱερῶν προΐστανται, στεφανηφοροῦντες· μουσικούς τε καὶ φιλολόγους καὶ προσηνεῖς ποιεῖ.

Firmicus, 3.6.1. *Venus in parte horoscopi partiliter constituta, si per noctem in hoco loco fuerit, divinis ingeniis homines faciet; amicos imperatorum aut potentium reddit et quibus imperatorum ac magnorum virorum negotia credantur. Faciet etiam oratores maximos et bonos, secundum naturam*

---

60 ⟨τε⟩ καὶ A.-R.   κατὰ μόχθους L: corr. A^{conj}

fo. 26^v

65 ἢν μὲν γὰρ L: ἢν δ' ἐρατή K   μεσόεντα L: corr. A.-R.^{c} ὀφθῇ L: corr. Hal^{mg}, D^{563}
66 χειλιάδας L: corr. A.-R.   67 ἀπλάτου L: corr. H, Gr (cf. ἀπλέτοι Hol)   διάκοσμήτορα, ια L^{1ras}, dein ' L^{1sl} tamquam δὲ κοσμ. voluit: corr. Gr   γρ. θεομήτορα κόσμον L^1 marg. dextr.   68 μυστ. τεύχ. ἄπιστ. ex 64: τοίης δ' ἐκ τιμῆς πλούτου κυδήνορα κόσμον K^2: ἐκ τοίης τιμῆς δὲ τέλους τεύξονται ἀνιγροῦ S^{conj} 69 post hunc versum lacunam statuit K   72 ἐκ καλαμογρ. L: corr. K

If Venus sees men's horoscopic rays,
She makes the wily, cultured, those at ease,   60
Basking in wealth attained through female aid;
To them are trusted women's secret oaths,
And over cultic rituals they'll preside
Where secret mysteries refused to males are held.
If in Midheaven the fair one's seen by men,   65
She signals affluent means, thousandfold rule,
Self-praise that marshals glory without bounds;
From such honour...
When Hermes' star appears towards the setting
⟨   ⟩
When births occur, in the Horoscope or Midheaven,   70
It brings advancement through the power of words
And penmanship, and what pertains to Art;
When Mars' path's in degrees equal with his,
Or rays to rays directly are opposed,
Then forgers who feign scripts of others' hands   75
Are born—guilty, and pallid to behold.
When the two-horned Moon with her selenious light
Rules the Hour, margin of life, in devious course,
And Mars in like degrees visits Midheaven,
The one born in such schemes is god-possessed,   80
Out of his natural wits, moonstruck in mind,

qualitatemque signorum. Si enim in humanis signis partiliter in horoscopo fuerit inventa, faciet sacerdotum principes et qui in ipsis sacerdotiis purpureis aut auratis vestibus induantur et qui futura praedicant. Faciet autem gratos, venustos, divites, si nulla malivola stella sic positae Veneri aliqua se potestate radiationis obiecerit.

69–72. Cf. 3.96–100.

Paul, p. 67.9-13. Ὁ δὲ τοῦ Ἑρμοῦ τὸν κατὰ κορυφὴν τόπον ἐπέχων ἀπὸ λόγων ἢ ἐπιστήμης ἢ γραμμάτων ἢ προφορῶν λόγων διαζῶντας ποιήσει, ὁτὲ δὲ καὶ ἐπισκέπτορας ἢ σκρινιαρίους ἢ ἀντιγραφέας ἢ νοταρίους ἢ δικολόγους ἢ συνηγόρους ἢ νομικοὺς ἢ ἑρμηνέας ἢ τραπεζίτας ἀποδείκνυσι.

73–6. Paul, pp. 67.13–68.4. τοῦ δὲ Ἄρεως συσχηματισθέντος ἤτοι κατὰ συμπαρουσίαν ἢ τετράγωνον ἢ διάμετρον ψεύστας, ἀθέους, ἀσεβεῖς, ἱεροσύλους, τὸ θεῖον ἀφαιροῦντας πρὸς ἐπὶ τούτοις ἢ φαρμακοὺς ἢ φαρμάκων συνίστορας καὶ πλαστογράφους ἢ παραχαρακτὰς ἢ λῃστὰς ἢ φονέας ἢ τούτοις συνειδότας καὶ τὸ παράπαν κακωνύμους καὶ περιφήμους τούτων ἕνεκεν ἐσομένους, ὁτὲ δὲ καὶ δημίους ἢ δεσμοφύλακας ἢ μεταλλάρχας ἢ τελώνας ποιήσει. κακῶν γὰρ ἔργων πάντοτε καὶ εἰς τὸ κακὸν ἄξονας ἡ σύγκρασις Ἄρεως πρὸς τὸν τοῦ Ἑρμοῦ χωρὶς τῆς τῶν ἀγαθοποιῶν ἐπικουρίας παρασκευάζει.

77–82ᵃ. Θ p. 193.16–18. ἡ Σελήνη σύνδεσμον πανσεληνιακὸν ἔχουσα ποιεῖ θεολήπτους, ἐνθέους, φοιβαζομένους· ἐὰν δὲ καὶ Ἄρης ἐπιθεωρήσῃ, ποιεῖ δαιμονιοπλήκτους ἢ μαινομένους.

Θ p. 192.18–20. ἡ Σελήνη ὡροσκοποῦσα καὶ Κρόνος μεσουρανῶν καὶ Ἑρμῆς δύνων παραπληκτικοὺς καὶ φρενοβλαβεῖς.

76 ⟨τε⟩ καὶ K   ἀχρήεντας L: corr. K²   78 κρατέῃ] κατὰ γῆς L: corr. K   σκολιοπὰ L: corr. L¹
79 δ'] δὲ L: corr. A.-R.   80 θεόλημπτος L, μ puncto del. L¹   81 σεληνιάζων L: corr.
D⁶⁴⁴   νόοιο] νόσοισι L: corr. K

καὶ μανίης ἀνάμεστος· ἐπὴν κατὰ γῆς δὲ φέροιτο, 82a/83b
δυστυχίῃ τ' ἐπίφοιτος ἰδ' ἐν σινέεσσι πεπληθώς· 83a/82b
ἢν δὲ μετ' ἀντολίην μέσον οὐρανὸν ἀμφιθοάζῃ,
παμπλούτους τε τίθησι καὶ ἐντρυφέας καὶ ἐπόλβους, 85
θηλυγόνους δὲ τέκνοισι καὶ εὐπάτορας †κ' ἀτρέπτους·
δύνοντος δ' ἄστροιο Σεληναίης ὁ λοχευθεὶς
ἔσσεται ἐμπορίης ἐμπείραμος, ἔργα τε πλαγκτὰ
ναυκλήρου βιοτήν θ' αἱρήσεται, ἐν ξενίῃ τε
τὸ πλεῖστον ζωῆς ⟨ 90
⟩ τε διευθύνων βιοτεύσει— 90a
πουλυπλανὴς γὰρ ἕλιξ Μήνης κερατώπιδος αἰεὶ
λοξὰ ταλαντεύουσα—μένει δ' ἀντλούμενος ὄλβῳ.

Ἡελίου δ' ἀκάμαντος ἐπὴν πυριμάρμαρος ἀστὴρ
ἐς μέσον οὐρανίης προφανῇ πυριλαμπέος αἴθρης,
ἢ γονίμῃ ὥρῃ πανεπίσκοπα φέγγεα βάλλῃ, 95
Τοξότεω κατὰ χῶρον ἰδ' εὐστέρνοιο Λέοντος,
Κριοῦ τ' εὐκεράοιο, καὶ ἐν Διδύμοισι φαανθείς,
ζῳδίοις ἰδίοισιν, ἐς ἡγεμονηίδας ἀρχὰς
ἵξεσθαι καὶ σκῆπτρα βροτοῖς βασιλήια φράζει,
πλοῦτόν τ' ὀλβήεντα δόμους τ' εὐδαίμονας ἔρδει· 100
ἐκτὸς δ' οἰκείων μοιρῶν γενέθλῃσιν ἐφεστὼς
27ʳ τικτομένοις κτῆσιν μὲν ἄγαν πολυχρήμονα τεύχει
καὶ βιοτὴν πλήθουσαν ἀλύπητόν τε δίαιταν,
ἀρχὰς δ' οὐκ ἄξει βασιληίδας οὐδὲ θρονισμούς,
ἡσυχίῃ δ' ἀφανεῖς σκήπτρων δίχα τούσδε φυλάσσει, 105
ἀβλαβέας τ', οἴκων τε διευθυντῆρας ἐν ὄλβῳ.

83ᵇ–82ᵇ. Cf. 3.126–9.
87–92. Paul, p. 61.1–5. Ἡ δὲ Σελήνη τὸ ἕβδομον ἀπὸ ὡροσκόπου λαχοῦσα ξενιτείας ποιήσει. ἐὰν δὲ ἐν παρύγροις ζῳδίοις εὑρεθῇ, ἡμερινῆς οὔσης τῆς γενέσεως, ναυκλήρους ἢ κυβερνήτας ἢ ναύτας ἢ ἐμπορικὸν βίον διάγοντας, πολυπλάνους καὶ ἐν ὑψηλοταπεινώματι τὴν τύχην ἔχοντας τελευτήσει.
93–100. Cf. 3.114–16.
Περὶ κέντρ. 8–9. Ὁ Ἥλιος ὡροσκοπῶν ἐν ἡμέρᾳ, Διός, Ἀφροδίτης ὁρώντων, ἀγαθός, καὶ μάλιστα εἰ ἰδιοτοπεῖ καὶ ἐν ἀρρενικῷ ζῳδίῳ ἐστίν. πολὺ δὲ κρεῖττον εἰ ὑπὸ ἀγαθοποιοῦ ἐπιδεκατεύοιτο· ἡγεμονικαὶ γὰρ αἱ τιμαὶ ἢ στρατοπεδαρχικαί.
Firmicus, 3.5.1. Sol in parte horoscopi constitutus... in masculino autem signo constitutus, in domo sua aut in altitudine sua, et benivolae stellae radiatione coniunctus ⟨aut a⟩ benivolis protectus, magnae nobilitatis largitur insignia.
Firmicus, 3.5.34. In decimo loco Sol ab horoscopo partiliter constitutus in diurna genitura, id est in MC., in domo sua, aut in domo Iovis, aut in ea parte in qua exaltatur, faciet reges quibus a patre

---

82–3 καὶ μανίης ἀνάμεστος· εἰ δ' [corr. Grⁿ] ἐν σινέεσσι πεπληθώς | δυστυχίῃ τ' ἐπίφοιτος ἐπὴν κατὰ γῆς τε [δὲ K] φέροιτο L: distichia permutavit K   φέρηται K   85 τίθησιν L: corr. Gr   ἐνόλβους L: corr. K   86 κ' ἀτρέπτους, κ L¹ʳᵃˢ] εὐθρέπτους Halᵐᵍ: κ' εὐτέκνους D⁶⁵⁷: καὶ ἀτρέπτους A.–R.: καὶ ἀμέμπτους S   θηλυνόους δὲ τρόποισι καὶ εὐτρέπτους καὶ ἀπρήκτους K   87 δύναντος L: corr. K

And full of madness; when borne underground,[2]	82a/83b
That man's misfortune's friend, and full of harms.	83a/82b
If, after rising, she [the Moon] visits Midheaven	
She makes the rich, luxurious, and flush,	85
Fathers of females, having noble sires...	
When Selene's star is setting, the newborn	
Will be well-versed in commerce, undertake	
Itinerant trade, in shipping; overseas	
Most of his life ...⟨	90
⟩ regulating, he will live;	90a
For the horned Moon's ever-mobile gyre remains	
Obliquely poised—but stays awash with wealth.	
When the blazing star of tireless Helios	
Shines forth midmost in the clear celestial air,	
Or casts all-seeing rays on the hour of birth,	95
In the Archer's place, or noble-breasted Lion,	
Or the well-horned Ram, or appearing in the Twins—	
Its own signs—then to ranks of high command	
And kingly sceptres it predicts attainment;	
And makes substantial wealth and blessed homes.	100
But governing births outside its own degrees,	
The natives it grants copious wealth indeed,	
A generous income, comfortable life,	
But kingly rank it will not bring, nor thrones.	
It keeps them hid in private life, remote	105
From sceptres, safely tending private wealth.	

[2] Sc. the Moon.

tradatur imperium, aut duces quibus hoc honoris simili modo paternis cum honoribus conferatur, aut administratores et consules et proconsules, sed quibus hoc ex paterno dignitatis merito deferatur.
  101–6. Cf. 3.117–18.
  Firmicus, 3.5.2 ... *quodsi vires eius leviter fuerint impeditae, consulares faciet ⟨et⟩ proconsulares et dat ordinarios consulatus.*

---

88 ἔσσεται L, σ¹ L¹, σ² L^ras   ἐμπείραμος L^isl   πλαγκτά] πολλά L: corr. K: ἔπολβα S
89 ξενίῃσιν K   90 lacunam inter ζωῆς et τε statuit K²   91 κεραώπιδος Meineke
(1856 edn) ad ps.-Theocr. 25.146   94 ἐς μ L^1ras (εἰς L?)   95 γονίμην ὥρην L: corr.
K   96 ἰδ'] εἰδ' L: corr. H, Gr   98 ἐς L¹
fo. 27^r
102 τικτομένοις] πλειστοτόκους L: corr. K: πλουτοτόκος K²: πλεῖστα διδοὺς S^conj   τεύχῃ
L: corr. H, Hal   104 οὐχ ἕξει, χ L¹: corr. K   105 ἡσυχίης L: corr. R   106 ⟨τ'⟩ add. K

Ὧδε μὲν ἀπλανέων τε πλανητάων τε κέλευθα
ῥομβηδὸν περὶ κόσμον ἁματροχίῃ πεφόρηται.
Ἄλλα δέ τοι λέξω πάλι σήματα θεῖα γενέθλης.
Ἡνίκ' ἂν ὡράων πανεπίσκοπα φέγγεα Μήνης 110
φυομένοις μερόπεσσιν ἀν' οὐρανὸν αὐγάζηται,
ἀστὴρ δ' εἰς δυσμὰς Ἄρεος πυριλαμπέος ἔλθῃ,
ἐνσινέας τε τίθησι βροτούς, ἀβίους, ἀμελάθρους,
καὶ λιτῆς πενίης χερνήτορας, ἀκτεάνους τε·
πολλάκι καὶ θανάτῳ κακομήχανος ὤλεσε δεινῷ. 115
Ἢν δέ τ' ἀνοικείοισι τόποις ὡροσκόπον Ἄρης
φέγγος ἐπιτρέψῃ γονίμην ἐπὶ γαστέρα θνητῶν,
χωλόποδας τεύχει καὶ ἀσθενέας καὶ ἀώρους,
νῶτά τε κυρτιόωντας, ἰδὲ ψευστῆρας ἀθέσμους,
καὶ παναγεῖς ὄλβου τε ποθήτορας ἀλλοτρίοιο. 120
ἢν δ' ἐπὶ μαρτυρίην Ἄρεως ἐλθοῦσ' Ἀφροδίτη
ὄμμα βάλῃ πανταυγὲς ἐν ἡμεριναῖσι λοχείαις,
ἐκ πυρὸς αὐχήσουσι τέχνας μέλανός τε σιδήρου,
ἄκμοσι ῥαιστοτύποις μεμελημένοι ἠδὲ καμίνοις.
Ὁππότε δ' ἂν σκοπιὴν ὡροσκόπον ὠδίνεσσιν 125
Ἑρμείας κατάγῃ, τῷ δ' ᾖ Κυθέρη ἐπίφοιτος,
δὴ τότε ῥήτορας ἄνδρας ἰδ' ἐν σοφίῃσιν ἀρίστους
ἔσσεσθαι δείκνυσι, καὶ ἀστρολόγους θεοφήμους,
ἔν τε γεωμετρίῃσι καὶ ἐν τελεταῖσιν ἀρίστους,
ἔν τε λιθογλυφίαισι θεῶν νηῶν τε θεμέθλοις. 130
Ζεὺς δ' ὑπερορμαίνων φοράδην ὑπὲρ ἀστέρα πατρὸς
ἡνίκ' ἂν ἐν καθέτῳ κόσμου μέσον ἀμφιπολεύῃ
⟨   ⟩
ζῳδίῳ, τῆμος δὲ γονὰς μερόπων τις ἐνέγκῃ,
ἔσσεται ἐμπορικοῦ πλοίου φορτοστόλος ἴδρις,
ναυκλήρου τέχνας θ' αἱρήσεται, ἐν χρέεσίν τε 135

116-20. Cf. 6.574–7.
125-30. Cf. 6.476–83.
Θ p. 210.26-7 [Ptol. 4.4.3]. Ὁ μὲν γὰρ τοῦ Ἑρμοῦ τὸ πράσσειν παρέχων ποιεῖ γραμματέας, πραγματευτάς, τραπεζίτας, μάντεις, ἰατροὺς καὶ ἀστρολόγους.
Θ pp. 210.31-211.1 [Ptol. ibid.]. ὁ δὲ τοῦ Διός, νομογράφους, ῥήτορας ...
Θ p. 212.18-20. ὁ δὲ Κρόνος καὶ Ἄρης καὶ Σελήνη ὡροσκοποῦντες ἢ μεσουρανοῦντες ποιεῖ φιλοσόφους, ῥήτορας ἢ ἀστρολόγους.
Θ p. 212.26-8. Ἀφροδίτη καὶ Ἄρης τὸν οἶκον δεσποτεύοντες, τὴν οἰκοδεσποτείαν τῆς πράξεως εἰληφότες, ποιοῦσιν ... λιθογλύφους.

107 πεπλανητάων L: corr. L[1sl]   108 πεφόρηται L[1sl]   109 σοι L: corr. K
112 ἄρεως L: corr. A.-R.   113 ἀβίους τ' L: corr. A.-R.   114 λιτῆς] λεπτῆς L: corr. K: χαλεπῆς Massimilla   115 ὤλετο L: corr. K   116 τόποις⟩ L[1]   ὡροσκόπου Hal[mg]

The paths of fixed and mobile stars are thus
Borne whirling round the world, concurrently.
I'll tell you further heavenly signs of birth.
When the Moon's all-seeing rays upon the Hours(?)   110
Are radiant in the sky at mortal births,
And the star of fiery Ares comes to set,
He makes men damaged, homeless, indigent,
Menials of slender poverty, destitute,
And often kills, cruel one, by painful death.   115
   If Mars in alien places turns his rays
Horoscopic to teeming human wombs,
He makes the halt, the weak, those out of season,
With crooked backs; unrighteous liars too,
Accursed ones who covet others' wealth.   120
   If Venus comes to testify to Mars,
And casts her shining eye on daytime births,
They'll boast of trades from fire and swarthy iron,
Of hammer-blows on anvils, furnaces.
   When Hermes brings his horoscopic watch   125
To birth-pangs, Venus in his retinue,
Then orators and men supremely wise
Are shown, astrologers who voice God's plan,
Best in geometry and religious rites,
In carving divine statues, founding shrines.   130
   Zeus borne aloft above his father's star
When on the cosmos' plumb-line he is centred...
   ⟨   ⟩
In a sign, and then a child is brought to birth,
Of merchant ships and cargoes he's apprised,
Will know the business of ship-owning, live   135

131–8. Cf. 6.484–6.

Θ p. 216.17–22. λγ΄. Περὶ ναυτῶν καὶ κυβερνήτων. Κρόνος μεσουρανῶν ἐν καθύγρῳ ζῳδίῳ Ἄρεος καὶ Ἡλίου συμμεσουρανούντων ἢ ἐπιθεωρούντων κατὰ τετράγωνον ἢ διάμετρον, ναύτας ποιεῖ ἢ κυβερνήτας ἢ ναυκλήρους, μάλιστα καὶ τοῦ ὡροσκόπου ὄντος ἐν καθύγρῳ ζῳδίῳ ὁρίοις Κρόνου καὶ τοῦ κλήρου τῆς τύχης ἢ τοῦ κυρίου αὐτοῦ.

Ptol. 4.2.2. ἀλλ' ὁ μὲν τοῦ Κρόνου [sc. τοῦ κλήρου τὴν οἰκοδεσποτείαν λαβών] διὰ θεμελίων ἢ γεωργιῶν ἢ ναυκληριῶν.

Ptol. 2.3.41. οἱ δὲ περὶ τὴν Λυδίαν καὶ Κιλικίαν καὶ Παμφυλίαν τοῖς τε Ἰχθύσι καὶ τῷ τοῦ Διός, ὅθεν οὗτοι μᾶλλον πολυκτήμονές τε καὶ ἐμπορικοὶ καὶ κοινωνικοὶ καὶ ἐλεύθεροι καὶ πιστοὶ περὶ τὰς συναλλαγάς.

---

118 ⟨τε⟩ καὶ¹ Gerhard (dub.), A   121 Ἀφροδίτηι L: corr. H, Gr   122 ἡμερινῆσι A.-R.   126 ᾗ] ἦν L: corr. Hal^mg: ἥν H, Hal   127 σοφίῃσι κρατίστους K²   129 γεωμετρίῃσιν L: corr. H, Gr   τελετῇσιν A.-R.   130 λιθογλυφίῃσι A.-R.   θεμίθλοις L^1sl   132 post hunc versum lacunam statuit K²   134 ἐμπορικοίου L: corr. Gr   135 θηράσσεται L: corr. A   χρέεσσίν τε L: corr. Gr

ἥμενος ὠνητοῖσι βιώσεται, ἐργασίην τε
κοινωνὸν πολλῶν συστήσεται, ἄστατα δ' αὐτῷ
ἐν θαλάμῳ νυμφεῖα γενήσεται ἔν τε γυναιξίν.
Ἑρμῆς δ' οἰκείως ὁπότ' ἂν κατὰ κύκλα φαανθῇ,
μαρτυρίῃ δὲ Κρόνοιο κατ' αἰθέρα τῷδε πελάζῃ, 140
[ῥήτορας ἐμφαίνουσι βροτοὺς σοφίῃ τε κρατίστους,]
ἑρμηνεῖς τε τίθησι καὶ ἀστρολόγους τότε θνητούς,
27ᵛ χρήματα δ' ἐν χείρεσσι καὶ ὄλβου πρήξιας οἴσει
οὐ μόνον ἀλλοτρίων κτεάνων, ἰδίων δὲ μάλιστα
⟨   ⟩
ὀφθῆναι, γαίης τε τεμεῖν καρπὸν περὶ νῶτα. 145
ἢν δὲ Σεληναίης ἑλικοδρόμος ἄστατος ἀστὴρ
Ἑρμείην σύμφωνον ἔχῃ κατὰ κόσμου ἀταρπόν,
καὶ μούνη Κυθέρεια συνῇ καλῷ Φαέθοντι,
ῥεκτῆρας χρυσοῖο καὶ Ἰνδογενοῦς ἐλέφαντος
ἐργοπόνους δείκνυσι, καὶ ἐν γραφίδεσσιν ἀρίστους 150
ἔσσεσθαι, θριγκῶν τε καὶ εὐτοίχων κανονισμῶν
κοσμήτας, μάλα τοι πεπονημένα τεχνάζοντας.
Ἄρης δ' αἰγλήεις ὅτ' ἂν αὐγῶν Ἡελίοιο
νέρθε φανῇ Μήνης τε, λοχευομένοισι βροτοῖσιν
πήρωσιν στονόεσσαν ἐν ὀφθαλμοῖσι τίθησιν 155
ἔσσεσθαι κείνοισι καὶ ἀμβλυόεσσαν ὀμίχλην.
Ἑρμείας δ' οἰκεῖα τυχὼν κατὰ δώμαθ' ἑαυτοῦ
ἰητῆρα τίθησι βροτῶν, Παιώνιον ἄνδρα,
εἴσεσθαι μάλα δεινὰ καὶ εἰς πανάκειαν ἑτοῖμα,
ἔν τε λογιστονόμοισιν ἀεὶ πολυπρήκτορας ἔργοις. 160

139–45. Cf. 6.487–90.
Ptol. 4.4.3. κἂν μὲν ὁ τοῦ Κρόνου αὐτῷ (sc. τῷ τοῦ Ἑρμοῦ) μαρτυρήσῃ, ἀλλοτρίων οἰκονόμους ἢ ὀνειροκρίτας ἢ ἐν ἱεροῖς τὰς ἀναστροφὰς ποιουμένους προφάσει μαντειῶν καὶ ἐνθουσιασμῶν; cf. Θ p. 210.29–31 ... ἐνθουσιασμῶν ἢ μαθημάτων.
Lib. Herm. xxxiv. 31. Mercurius in terminis Saturni contingens... Si vero Saturnus aspexerit eum, facit agricolas vel conductores terrae.
146–52. Cf. 6.520–5.
Θ p. 213.22–4. ὁ Ἑρμῆς καὶ ἡ Ἀφροδίτη ἐν τοῖς πρακτικοῖς τόποις τυχόντες καὶ ὑπὸ Διὸς θεωρούμενοι ποιοῦσιν ἐλεφαντουργούς, ζωγράφους ἢ χρυσοχόους ἢ κοσμητάς.

---

136 ἥμενος] ἵμερον L: corr. A^conj: ἥμερον K: ἥμερος Luc   ὠνητοῖσσι L: corr. H, Gr
137 πολλῶν] πάντων L: corr. K   συστήσεται L: corr. Hal   138 ἐκ θαλάμων L: corr. K   νυμφεῖα] υμφεῖ supra litteras priscas, crasso stilo, atramento fusco, scr. L^rec
140 μαρτυρίῃι L: corr. Gr   141 del. K, ut intrusum e 1.303

fo. 27ᵛ
143 χείρεσι L: corr. H, Gr   144 μόνων L: corr. H, Gr   post 144 lacunam stat. S: inter 145 τεμεῖν et καρπόν, vel καρπόν et περὶ νῶτα K², qui ὀφθῆναι in προσθῆναι mutavit   145 περὶ] παρά L: corr. K²   147 Ἑρμείαν K   ἔχοι: corr. A.–R.

[136–160] Book Four 417

On goods purchased with loans, and undertake
A business shared with many; changeable
Are his liaisons[3] with the female sex.
   When Hermes shows in the circles domiciled,
And Saturn's witness nears him in the sky,   140
[They show forth orators, men most astute,]
He makes interpreters and astrologers,
Will hand them goods and traffickings in wealth,
Not merely those of others, but their own
⟨   ⟩
(To be seen), and from the earth's broad back reap fruits.   145
   If Selene's roving star that twists and turns
Finds Hermes friendly on the cosmic path,
And Venus joins with fair Phaethon alone,
Goldsmiths and artisans of Indus-born
Ivory are shown, masters of graving tools,   150
Of cornices and walls built true and square[4]
The artisans, hard-working in their crafts.
   When radiant Mars appears beneath the rays
Of Sun and Moon, for natives brought to birth
He sets a mournful blindness in their eyes   155
To be on them, and dark opacity.
   Should Mercury be found in his own homes,
He makes a healer, Paian's devotee,
One with imposing knowledge, prompt to cure;
And those engaged in rendering accounts.   160

---

[3] Or, espousals.
[4] Or, measurements of decorative walls (if, say, fresco painters are meant)?

153–6. Cf. 6.548–50.
Θ p. 187.17–18. τοὺς φωστῆρας ἐπαναφερόμενοι οἱ κακοποιοὶ μόνοι ὀφθαλμοὺς ἀδικοῦσιν ἢ ἀμβλυωπίαν ποιοῦσι.
157–60. Θ p. 210.26–9. Ὁ μὲν γὰρ τοῦ Ἑρμοῦ τὸ πράσσειν παρέχων ποιεῖ γραμματέας, πραγματευτάς, τραπεζίτας, μάντεις, ἰατροὺς καὶ ἀστρολόγους, θύτας, νομικούς, ῥήτορας καὶ ὅλως τοὺς ἀπὸ γραμμάτων καὶ δόσεως καὶ λήψεως γινομένους ἢ ἐργαζομένους.
Ptol. 4.4.3. ὁ μὲν γὰρ τοῦ Ἑρμοῦ τὸ πράσσειν παρέχων, ὡς ἄν τις εἴποι τυπωδῶς, ποιεῖ γραμματέας, πραγματευτικούς, λογιστάς, διδασκάλους, ἐμπόρους, τραπεζίτας, μάντεις, ἀστρολόγους, θύτας καὶ ὅλως τοὺς ἀπὸ γραμμάτων καὶ ἑρμηνείας καὶ δόσεως καὶ λήψεως ἐργαζομένους.

---

150 δείκνυσιν L: corr. H, Gr   γραφίδεσσιν] πραπίδεσσιν L: corr. S   154 Μήνη τε L: corr. K   λοχευομένη τε L: corr. Hal, Herm[811]   155 ὀφθαλμοῖσιν L: corr. H, Gr   156 κενεοῖσι K: κεινοῖσι S   157 Ἑρμῆς δ'εἰς οἰκεῖα L: corr. D[250] (-ης: -ας A.-R.)   158 τίθησιν L: corr. H, Gr   159 ἔσσεσθαι L: corr. D[657]   δεινὰ] κεῖνα L: corr. D[657]   160 πολυπράκτορας L: corr. A.-R.

$$Z\epsilon\grave{\upsilon}s\ \delta'\ \ddot{o}\tau'\ \ddot{a}\nu\ `E\rho\mu\epsilon\acute{\iota}a\ \pi\rho\sigma\mu\acute{a}\rho\tau\upsilon\rho a\ \phi\acute{\epsilon}\gamma\gamma\epsilon a\ \beta\acute{a}\lambda\lambda\eta,$$

πουλυπλανεῖς ξενίης φαίνει μερόπεσσι κελεύθους
ἵξεσθαι, καὶ λέκτρα γυναικῶν ἥσσονα πολλῷ
θηρήσειν παρὰ κῦδος ἀνάξια θηλυμανοῦντας.
Ταῦτα μὲν ὡράων σκεπτήρια· νῦν δέ με χρειὼ   165
ἀκτινηβολίας ὁρίων τ' αἰθωπὰ κέλευθα
δωδεκατημορίων τ' ἄστρων κυκλόεσσαν ἐνισπεῖν
Ζῳδιακήν, ἐξ ὧν γενεαὶ τέχναι τε βροτοῖσιν
κλωστὴν ἐκπληροῦσι βίου θνητοῖο πορείην.
Πρῶτα μὲν οὖν Στίλβων, φανερὸς θεός, ἡνίκα καὶ Ζεὺς   170
εἰς ἀκτῖνα βλέπῃ Ἄρεος φαέθοντι σελασμῷ,
ἠὲ κατ' οἰκείων ὁρίων πυριλαμπέος ὀφθῇ
Ἄρεος, ἀθλητῆρας ἀελλόποδάς τε προφαίνει
στερροτάτους τ' ἔσσεσθαι, ἰδ' ἐν νίκαις ἱεραῖσιν
στέμματα μυριόδοξα, ⟨   175
⟩ καὶ εὐδοκιμοῦντας ἐν ἄθλοις.   175a
ἄμφω δ' ἢν τούτοισι Κρόνου προσμάρτυρος ἀστὴρ
εἰν ἰδίοις ὁρίοις φαινώπιδα τάξιν ἐπίσχῃ,
ἀστεφάνους τεύχει μέν, ἀλειπτῆρας δὲ κρατίστους
παιδότριβας δείκνυσι διδασκαλίης τε παρέδρους.
ἢν δὲ καὶ ἀφρογενοῦς Κύπριδος θοὸν ἀστέρα βάλλῃ   180
ἀκτὶς Ἑρμάωνος, ἐναλλάγδην τε γένωνται
εἰς ἰδίων ὁρίων ἄμφω τρίβον αἰθερόπλαγκτον,
κωμῳδοὺς λυρικῶν τε μελῶν μελπήτορας ἄνδρας
δείκνυσιν, μαχλικῶν τε λόγων θρασυγλωσσέας ᾠδούς,
ναβλιστοκτυπέας τε χοροῖς, κιθάρης τε μελουργούς,   185
ὀρχηθμῶν ἴδριάς τε, καὶ ἐν θυμέλαις προφέροντας.
ἡνίκα δ' ἂν Κρονικοῦ σέλας ἀστέρος Ἄρεος αἴγλη
πορφυρέαις ἀκτῖσι καταντίπερ' αἰγλοβολήσῃ,
δισσά τ' ἐν ἀλλαγμοῖσι φανῇ σελαγίσματα τῶνδε

28ʳ (margin)

161–4. Cf. 3.321–2.
170–5. Cf. 6.511–14.
Ptol. 4.4.4. (ὁ δὲ τῆς Ἀφροδίτης τὸ πράσσειν παρέχων)...ἐὰν δὲ ὁ τοῦ Διὸς [sc. μαρτυρήσῃ] ἀθλητάς, στεφανηφόρους.
Θ p. 214.9–10. Ζεὺς καὶ Ἑρμῆς μετὰ Ἄρεος ἢ ὁρίοις Ἄρεος ἀθλητικοὺς ἢ καὶ φιλοπαλαίστρους ποιοῦσι...
176–9. Cf. 6.515–17.
Θ p. 214.12–13. εἰ γὰρ Κρόνος τούτοις συσχηματισθῇ, οὐκέτι ποιεῖ ἀθλητὰς καὶ ἐνδόξους, ἀλλὰ σπουδαίους περὶ τὰ μουσικά.
180–6. Cf. 6.366–72; 6.504–10.

---

164 θηράσσειν L: corr. A.–R.   165 ὡράων] οὐρανίων Lop   166 αἴθρωπα L: corr. K
167 ἀστρωκυκλόεσσαν L: corr. D³³⁵⁻⁶   169 θνητοῖσι L: corr. D⁶⁵⁸   πορείην, η L¹ʳᵃˢ
171 βλέπῃ] βάλῃ L: corr. K   Ἄρεως L: corr. A.–R.   φαίνοντι L: corr. D²⁶⁴ ᶜᵒⁿʲ   173 Ἄρεος]
αἰθέρος L: corr. K   ἀελλόποδάς τε] αἰολαπάλαστε L: corr. A.–R.   προφανει L (ā L¹): corr. Hal, D⁶⁴³

[161–189] Book Four 419

    When Jupiter casts rays which witness Hermes,
He shows much-wandering paths in foreign lands
To come, and the pursuit of low amours,
Woman-mad beyond what's decent or correct.
    These signs are from the Hours. Now I'll describe   165
Castings of rays, the shining paths of terms,
And, of the twelve parts of the stars, the round
Zodiacal path, whence births and crafts of men
Fulfil the fated course of human life.
    Now Stilbon, manifest god—when he and Zeus   170
Look to the ray of Mars with radiant light,
Or in the terms of fire-bright Mars are seen,
They mark the birth of athletes swift of foot,
Most hardy, who in sacred victories
Illustrious garlands 〈   175
                         〉 distinguished in the games.   175a
If Saturn's star in aspect to these two
In its own terms maintains its shining course,
Uncrowned it leaves them, yes; but good with oils
And rubbing down, and supervising drill.
    If Venus' swift star, foam-born one, is struck   180
By Hermes' beam, and mutually in
Each other's terms they tread the ethereal lanes
Comedians, songsters of lyric airs
Are shown, lewd minstrels of lubricious words;
Who thrum the *nabla*, sound the lute, for choirs,   185
Skilled in the dance, and excellent on stage.
    When Ares' ray to Cronos' lambency
Is cast opposed with his rubescent beams,
And both these lights appear in mutual change

Ptol. 4.4.6. ἐὰν μὲν ὁ τοῦ Ἑρμοῦ καὶ ὁ τῆς Ἀφροδίτης λάβωσι τὴν οἰκοδεσποτείαν ἀπὸ μούσης καὶ ὀργάνων καὶ μελῳδιῶν ἢ ποιημάτων καὶ ῥυθμῶν ποιοῦσι τὰς πράξεις καὶ μάλιστα ὅταν τοὺς τόπους ὦσιν ἀμφιλελαχότες· ἀποτελοῦσι γὰρ θυμελικούς, ὑποκριτάς, σωματεμπόρους, ὀργανοποιούς, χορδοστρόφους, ὀρχηστάς, ὑφάντας, κηροπλάστας, ζωγράφους...

Θ p. 213.9–13. Ἑρμῆς καὶ Ἀφροδίτη τὴν πρᾶξιν παρέχοντες ποιοῦσι τὰς πράξεις ἀπὸ μουσικῆς καὶ ὀργάνων καὶ μελῳδιῶν ἢ ποιημάτων ἢ ὀρχήσεων καὶ ῥυθμῶν, καὶ μάλιστα ὅταν τοὺς τόπους ὦσιν ἐναλλάξαντες. ἀποτελοῦσιν οὖν θυμελικούς, ὑποκρίτας, σωματεμπόρους, ὀργανοποιούς, κιθαρῳδούς, τραγῳδούς...

---

174 〈τ'〉 A.-R.   ἱερῇσιν A.-R.   175 post hunc versum lacunam statuit K: inter μυριόδοξα et καί K²   178 ἀλιπτῆρας L: corr. L¹   179 παιδοτρίβας Holford-Strevens   183 λυρικῶν] λογικῶν L: corr. A^conj   μελπίτορας L: corr. H^h

fo. 28^r

185 ναβαιστοκτύπεας L: corr. Gr   187 αἰθέρος L: corr. Hal^mg   αἴγλη L: -ν L¹: corr. S   188 πυρφερέαις L: corr. H, Hal, D³⁰⁸   ἀκτίνεσσι L: corr. D³⁰⁸   189 -ῆ σελαγίσματα̈τῶνδε L^1ras

ὧν ὁρίων, τεύχει θρηνήτορας ἄνδρας, ἀσέμνους, 190
κεδροχαρεῖς, σορόεργα τέχνης κανονίσματ' ἔχοντας,
νεκροτάφους, κλαυστῆρας ἀποφθιμένων, νεκρονώμας.
ἢν Πυρόεις δύνῃ Φαίνοντι συνὼν ἐπίκεντρος,
Ἑρμείας δ' ἰσόμοιρος ἐπ' ἀμφοτέροισι φαανθῇ,
εἰν ὁρίοις καὶ κέντρῳ ἐπὴν ἴσχωσι Σελήνην, 195
ἀνδροφόνους δρῶσιν, λῃίστορας, ἐμπεδολώβας,
κέρδεος ἐχθροτάτου θηρήτορας, οἳ βασανηδὸν
στρεβλὰ κολαζόμενοι σκολοπηίδα μοῖραν ὁρῶσιν
πικροτάτοις κέντροισι προσαρτηθέντες ἐν ἥλοις,
οἰωνῶν κατάδειπνα, κυνῶν θ' ἑλκύσματα δεινά. 200
Ζῆνα δ' ὅτ' ἂν φαέθοντα βάλῃ λαμπραυγέτις ἀκτὶς
Ἑρμείου, μίγδην τε διαλλάξωσιν ὁρισμούς,
ῥητορικῆς φαίνουσι τέχνης σοφίης τε κρατίστους
ζηλωτὰς σκολιῶν τε λόγων, νεότητά τε λαμπρὴν
γραμματικήν τ' ἄσκησιν ἐνὶ στέρνοισιν ἔχοντας. 205
στίλβων δ' Ἑρμάωνος ὅτ' ἂν Κυλληνίου ἀστὴρ
φωσφόρον ἀκτίνεσσι βάλῃ Κυθερηίδος αἴγλης,
τάς τ' αὐγὰς ἐπέχοντες ἐν οὐρανῷ ἀστερόεντι
δωδεκατημορίων σχῶσιν βάσιν εἴλικα, θνητοὺς
γαιομέτρας δείκνυσι μαθηματικούς τε φανεῖσθαι, 210
ἀστρολόγους, μαγικούς τε θύτας, ἰδὲ μάντιας ἐσθλούς,
οἰωνοσκοπικούς τε, σαφεῖς θ' ὑδρομάντιας ἔρξεν,
οἷς λεκανοσκοπίη πιστεύεται ἢ νεκυϊσμός.

193-200. Cf. 6.499-503.
Ptol. 4.4.7. κἂν μὲν ὁ τοῦ Κρόνου αὐτοῖς [sc. τῷ τοῦ Ἑρμοῦ καὶ τῷ τοῦ Ἄρεως] μαρτυρήσῃ, φονέας, λωποδύτας, ἅρπαγας, λῃστάς, ἀπελάτας, ῥᾳδιουργούς.
Θ pp. 192.20-193.1. Σελήνη καὶ Ἄρης καὶ Ἑρμῆς ἐπίκεντροι τυχόντες δίχα Διὸς καὶ Ἀφροδίτης ποιοῦσι λῃστάς, κλέπτας, θυρεπανοίκτας· εἰ δὲ καὶ Κρόνος ὢν ἐν τῷ ὑπογείῳ τούτους ἐπιθεωρήσει, τυμβωρύχους ποιεῖ. ἐὰν Ἄρης καὶ Ἑρμῆς ἐν τῷ δυτικῷ κέντρῳ τύχωνται, [καὶ] ὑπὸ Σελήνης θεωρούμενοι κατὰ διάμετρον ἢ τετράγωνον, λῃστάς, ἀνδροφόνους ποιοῦσι σταυρουμένους ἢ κρημνιζομένους.
Θ p. 201.2-5. ἐὰν ὁ Ἀναβιβάζων τύχῃ ἐν τῷ ὀγδόῳ τόπῳ ‹καὶ› ἐπιθεωρήσωσι Ἄρης καὶ Κρόνος καὶ Ἑρμῆς, βιαιοθανασίαν ποιοῦσι· ἢ γὰρ ἀποκεφαλίζονται ἢ ἀνασκολοπίζονται.
201-5. Cf. 6.476-9.
Θ pp. 210.31-211.2. ὁ δὲ τοῦ Διός, νομογράφους, ῥήτορας, σοφιστάς, μετὰ μεγάλων προσώπων ἔχοντας ‹τὰς› ἀναστροφάς.
Ptol. 4.4.3. ἐὰν δὲ ὁ τοῦ Διός, νομογράφους, ῥήτορας, σοφιστὰς μετὰ προσώπων μειζόνων ἔχοντας τὰς ἀναστροφάς.

---

191 ὀρόεργα L: corr. Gr   καινίσματ' L: corr. Sp[158]   ἔχοντες L: corr. Gr   194 ἐν L: corr. K   195 ἐπανίσχωσι L: corr. A.-R. post D[336] ἐπὰν   197 αἰσχροτάτου Nauck[IV,163]   οἳ] L: ἢ L[1sl]   198 κολαζόμενοις κολοπήιδα L: corr. L[1]   199 κέντροισιν L: corr. H, K   ἔνηλοι H. Cancik (ap. Hengel, 9)   200 οἰωνῶν [spatium c. 3 litt.] κατάδιπνα L: corr. L[1]: κακὰ δεῖπνα Wa[IV,192], K[2]   ἑλκύσματα L: -στματα L[1]: σ (non, ut oportebat, τ) del. L[rec]   δεινά] λυγρά K[2conj]

[190–213]   Book Four   421

 Of terms, they make dirge-singers, unrefined, 190
Cedar-oil-loving, squaring coffins' sides,
Morticians, mourners, handlers of the dead.
 If Mars with Saturn sets upon the centre,
With Mercury in degrees equal to each,
And in their terms, centred, they hold the Moon, 195
They make assassins, bandits, harms to all,
In quest of vicious gain, who under lash
And rack of torture meet their end impaled
In bitter torments fastened up by nails,
Banquets for birds, for dogs a ghastly spoil. 200
 When radiant Zeus is struck by the bright beams
Of Hermes, in reciprocal change of terms,
Great adepts of the rhetor's skill are born,
And art in devious words, the brilliant youth
And lettered culture closest to their heart. 205
 When Hermes of Cyllene's shining star
Strikes with his rays the Cytherean's beam,
And in the starry sky holding(?) their rays
They keep their twisted path through the twelve parts,
He shows geometers and men of science, 210
Astrologers, mage-sacrificers, seers,
Those who divine by birds or watery signs,
Who scry the dish, or summon up the dead.

Θ p. 214.18–21. πε′. Περὶ ῥητόρων καὶ παιδευτῶν. Ἐὰν ὁ τοῦ Ἑρμοῦ ἐπιθεωρήσῃ τὸν Δία ἐν καλῷ τόπῳ ἑστῶτα καὶ ἀλλήλων ὑποδέξωνται τὰ ὅρια, ἔξαυγοι ὄντες καὶ ἐπίκεντροι καὶ ἐπαναφερόμενοι, ποιοῦσι σοφιστάς, γραμματικοὺς ἢ παιδευτάς.
 Lib. Herm. xxxiv. 33. Si vero permutatos habuerint terminos seu domos vel oppositi sint sibi ad invicem, fiunt sophistae, grammatici vel puerorum magistri.
 206–13. Cf. 6.465–71.
 Ptol. 4.4.3. ὁ μὲν γὰρ τοῦ Ἑρμοῦ τὸ πράσσειν παρέχων … ποιεῖ … μάντεις, ἀστρολόγους, θύτας …
 Θ p. 210.26–7 … μάντεις, ἰατροὺς καὶ ἀστρολόγους, θύτας …
 Θ pp. 214.22–215.3. πς′. Περὶ μαθηματικῶν ἢ μάντεων. Ἐὰν ὁ Ἑρμῆς ἐν καλῷ τόπῳ τύχῃ, μάλιστα καὶ Κρόνου οἴκῳ, ἔξαυγος καὶ θεωρηθῇ ὑπὸ Διὸς καὶ Κρόνου καὶ Ἄρεος, ποιεῖ ἀστρολόγους, μάντεις ἢ ἱερεῖς. εἰ δὲ Κρόνος ὡροσκοπῶν τύχῃ οἴκῳ Ἑρμοῦ ἢ ὡροσκοπῇ Ἑρμῆς, ἀπαραβάτους μαθηματικοὺς ποιεῖ.
 Lib. Herm. xxxiv. 29. Si vero permutatos habuerint terminos sive domus vel simul fuerint, geometros, astronomos, tragoedos vel citharoedos, musicam artem tangentes facit; si vero Saturnus aspexerit, vaticinatores, somniorum iudicatores, augures.

---

201 λαμπραύγετις A.–R. 204 λαμπράν L: corr. K post hunc versum lacunam statuit K 206 Κυλλήνιος L: corr. K 209 εἵλικα] ἡνίκα L: corr. R 210 γαιωμέτρας L: corr. K: γεομέτρας Nauck[IV,163] 211 μάντιν ἔθηκαν L: corr. K 212 ὑδρομάντις ἔρεξεν L: corr. D[658]

422   Βιβλίον Δ'   [214-244]

   Κυπρογενὴς δ' ἀκτῖνας ἐς Ἄρεα πυρσοβολοῦσα
   ἄμμιγα φωτὶ Κρόνου τεύχει μεροπήια ἔργα   215
   δοῦλα θεῶν ἱερῶν τε νεωκόρα λυσσομανοῦντα,
   νοῦν τε σεληνάζοντα προφητάζοντά τε θνητοῖς.
   Ἥλιον δ' ἀκτῖσιν Ἄρης πυριλαμπέσι βάλλων,
   Μήνης ὁρμώσης μίγα Κύπριδι κοινὰ σὺν αὐτοῖς,
   θηλυτέρους, γονίμων μηδέων ἀπαμήτορας ἄνδρας   220
   γαλλομανεῖς τ' ἔσσεσθαι ἀγυρτῆράς τε προφαίνει,
   καὶ πολυπλαγκτοσύνης ἐπιβήτορας, οἰκτροκελεύθους,
   δυστυχέας, καμάτου τε κακοῦ διαδέκτορας αἰεί.
   ἢν δὲ Σεληναίην ἑλικάστερον αἰθροβολήσῃ
28ᵛ ἀκτῖσι χρυσέῃσι φιλομμειδὴς Ἀφροδίτη,   225
   ἢ κοινῶς ἐπὶ ταὐτὸ πόλου διὰ κύκλα περῶσιν
   δωδεκατημορίοισι, προφήτορας ἱερολήπτους
   ἀνέρας ἐμφαίνουσι, καὶ ἐν τελεταῖσιν ἀρίστους
   μυστιπόλους ῥεκτῆρας ἰδ' ὀργιόωντας ἔσεσθαι.
   Ἄρης δ' Ἑρμείαν διὰ λαμπάδος ἀντία βάλλων,   230
   ἢ δρόμον εἰς ἰσόμοιρον ἰὼν μετὰ τοῦδε σελασμοῦ,
   σωματοφρουρητῆρας ἰδ' ἔμπαλι σωματοφόρβους,
   πλαστογράφους τεύχει τε καὶ ἐν ψεύσταις προφέροντας,
   καὶ θεολωβήτας, κακοεργέας, ἀφθιτομίσους
   καὶ κατονειδιστῆρας ἐν ἀλλοτρίῃσι βλάβῃσιν,   235
   ψέκτας ἀνθρώπων διαβλήτορας, οἷς τὸ τεχνασθὲν
   εἰς ἀπάτην δολόεσσαν ἀληθείης πέλας ἥξει.
   ἡνίκα δ' ἂν σὺν τοῖσι καὶ Οὐρανίδης Κρόνος ὀφθῇ
   ζῳδίῳ, βαίνων τε κατ' αἰθέρα φαίνοπι ῥόμβῳ
   ἢ κατὰ Τοξότεω βάλλῃ σελάγισμα μέλαθρον,   240
   ἠὲ κατ' ἰχθυόεντα βορειοτάτην τε χορείην,
   ἔνθα τε Παρθένος ἐστὶ περὶ Πλάστιγγα Λέων τε,
   ἰχθυοθηρευτάς τε καὶ ἰξοβόλους δολοεργούς,
   τοξελκεῖς τε τίθησι, καὶ ὀρνίθων τροφοποιούς,

214–17. Cf. 6.491–3.
Θ ξε'. Περὶ μαινομένων καὶ ἐπιληπτικῶν, p. 192.16–18. ἐὰν ἡ Ἀφροδίτη ἐμπεριέχηται ὑπὸ Κρόνου καὶ Ἄρεως ἐν ἑνὶ ζῳδίῳ, τετραγωνίζηται δὲ ὑπὸ Σελήνης καὶ Ἑρμοῦ, ποιοῦσι θεοφορουμένους καὶ φοιβαζομένους καὶ ἐνθέους.
Θ p. 194.2–4 ὁ Ἄρης ἢ ‹ὁ› Κρόνος ἐν τῷ ὑπὸ γῆς δαιμονιοπλήκτους ἢ ὑπὸ εἰδώλων φοβεριζομένους· εἰ δὲ καὶ Ἀφροδίτη συνῇ, ποίει θεοφορουμένους ἢ ἀποφθεγγομένους.
230–7. Cf. 6.446–9.

---

214 Ἄρεα] ἤερα L: corr. S   216 ἱερέων A^conj   λυσσομανόυντων L: corr. K
220 παίδων ἰσομήτορας: corr. A^conj   221 ἔσεσθαι L: corr. H, Gr   ἀργυρτῆράς L: corr.
Gr   223 διαδέκτορας L: δ² L¹   224 Σεληναί ̔ͮ L¹ˢˡ
fo. 28ᵛ
225 χρυσῆσιν L: corr. A.-R. post χρυσῆσι Gr, Hal   φιλομειδὴς L: corr. A.-R.   Ἀφροδίτηι L:
corr. H, Gr   227 ἱερολήμπτους, μ puncto del. L¹: ἱερολάμπρους K²   228 τελετῆσιν
A.-R.   229 μυστι[.]πόλους L, rasura inter ι et π

>When the Cyprian casts her firebrand rays to Mars
>Conjunct with Saturn's light, she makes her sons 215
>Slaves of the gods, or crazed keepers of shrines,
>Minds moonstruck, hurling prophecies abroad.
>
>When the Sun is struck by fiery beams from Mars,
>And the Moon rushing with Venus joins with them,
>Then women-men who dock their seminal parts, 220
>Mad *galli*, beggars—such births are foretold,
>Who lead nomadic lives, tread wretched paths,
>Sad types, for whom toil always is in store.
>
>If Selene's devious star is struck mid-ether
>By laughter-loving Venus' golden beams, 225
>Or jointly through the circles' twelve divisions
>Combined they travel, seers divinely seized
>Are brought to light, experts in ritual,
>Mystic practitioners and celebrants.
>
>Mars striking Hermes with opposing beams, 230
>Or in gradation with that source of light,
>Custodians or nurturers of the person,
>But forgers, too, mendacious types, are born,
>Perjurers, evil-doers, misanthropes,
>Who dispense blame, to other people's hurt, 235
>Scolders and slanderers, whose contrivances
>In sly deceit will come nigh to the truth.
>
>When Uranus' son Saturn's seen with these
>In a (winged) sign, airborne in his shining gyre,
>Whether he casts his rays from the Archer's house, 240
>Or from the troupe of Pisces and far north,
>Where lies the Virgin, near the Scales, and Leo,
>Trappers of fish, masters of limed deceit,
>Drawing the bow, are born, and bird-keepers,

Θ p. 212.2–5. Ἄρης καὶ Ἑρμῆς τὸ πράσσειν παρέχοντες ποιοῦσιν ἀνδριαντοποιούς … κατηγόρους, μοιχικούς, ἱερογλύφους, ζῳοπλάστας, ἰατρούς, χειρουργούς, κακοπράγμονας, πλαστογράφους.

Cf. Ptol. 4.4.7. ἐὰν δὲ ὁ τοῦ Ἑρμοῦ καὶ ὁ τοῦ Ἄρεως ἅμα τὴν κυρίαν λάβωσι τῆς πράξεως, ποιοῦσιν ἀνδριαντοποιούς, ὁπλουργούς, ἱερογλύφους, ζῳοπλάστας, παλαιστάς, ἰατρούς, χειρουργούς, κατηγόρους, μοιχικούς, κακοπράγμονας, πλαστογράφους.

Θ p. 193.1–3. Ἄρης καὶ Ἑρμῆς ἐπίκεντροι τυχόντες καὶ ἰσόμοιροι δίχα τῆς τῶν ἀγαθῶν ἐπιθεωρίας ποιοῦσι ψεύστας, ψευδοκατηγόρους, πλαστογράφους, ἐπιόρκους.

Θ pp. 217.24–218.2. Ὁ Ἄρης καὶ ὁ Ἑρμῆς ἐπίκεντροι ἐν Λέοντι δίχα Διὸς καὶ Ἀφροδίτης καὶ Ἡλίου ποιοῦσι τολμηρούς, τὸ ἴδιον αἷμα ἐκχέειν εἰς οὐδὲν λογίζοντας ἢ ψεύστας, ἐπιόρκους, ἀσεβεῖς, πλαστογράφους, δολίους.

---

230 διαλαμπάδα L: corr. Wa^{iv.33}: διὰ λαμπάδας R   ἀκτινιβάλλων L: corr. A   πυριφεγγέι λαμπάδι βάλλων Key¹²: Ἑρμείᾳ λαμπρὰς ἀκτῖνας ἰάλλων S^{conj}   231 εἰς] ἢ L: ε̣ἰ[s] Π² ˢˡ (iam corr. K)   232 [σωμ]ατοφρουτητ[ῆρας Π²   233 ψεύστοις K²   234 ἀφθιτομίσους: ἰ̈ L¹ʳᵃˢ (μείσ Lᵃᶜ ut vid.)   235 κατανειδιστῆρας L: κατονειδ[- Π² (iam corr. D³⁰¹)   239 βαίνων] φαίνων L: corr. K   240 Τοξότεῳ τε βάλῃ L: corr. R^{conj}   σελάεσσι μελάθρου L: corr. K   242 Λέοντος L: corr. D⁶⁵⁸

θηροδιδασκαλίης τ' ἐπιβήτορας ἡμεροέσσης, 245
οἷς ἀγρίη γενεὴ τιθασῷ πρηΰνετ' ἀγωγῇ,
κτηνῶν δ' ἀγρονόμων σημάντορας ἐμβασικοίτους·
τούτων οὐκ ἀτυχὴς μὲν ἔφυ βίος, ἀλλ' ἐπίμοχθος.
αἰπυπλανὴς δὲ Κρόνος Μήνης ἀκτῖσι πελάζων
δωδεκατημορίοισιν ἐν ἀλλαγμοῖσιν ἑαυτῶν 250
ἀχθοφόρους ὑδρέας τε καθαρτῆράς τε κελεύθων
ἀμφοδικῶν, οἰκτρούς τ' ἀμαρησκαπτῆρας ἔσεσθαι
ἀγγέλλει, λουτρῶν τε καθαρτῆρας βαλανείων,
ἔν τε παραιχυσίῃσι μέλη μωλυτὰ καθέψει
καὶ πτηνοῖσιν ἄβρωτα καὶ ἀρνοφάγοισι λύκοισιν· 255
πρὸς δ' ἔτι φύσονται τούτοις καρποσπόροι ἄνδρες,
ληνῶν ἀντλητῆρες, ἐν ὕδατι γηράσκοντες,
ἀρδευταὶ φορβῆς, λαχανηφόροι, ἠδ' ἐπίμοχθοι
ὀνθολόγοι, γαίης τε μεταλλευταὶ καὶ ὑπουργοὶ
δυσπονίης, οἷς λᾶες ἀπ' οὔρεος ἀκροτομοῦνται, 260
χαλκὸς κασσίτερός τε κελαινόχροός τε σίδηρος,
πάντα θ' ἅτ' ἐκ γαίης μερόπων ἐπίνοια ματεύει.
ἢν δ' ἀκτὶς Κρονικὴ κορυφὴν ἐπ' Ἀρήιον ἔλθῃ,
φεγγοβολῶν ὀπτῆρα κακὸς κακόν, αἰγλάζοντες
ἔν θ' ὁρίοις ἰδίοισι δυωδεκατημορίοις τε 265
29ʳ συμμίγδην ἐπιβῶσι τριγωνίζοντι σελασμῷ,
γαστροτόμους, νεκρῶν τε ταριχευτῆρας ἀπηνεῖς
ἔσσεσθαι φαίνουσι, κακεμπορίης τε ματευτάς,
καὶ μυσαροὺς σηπτοῖσι τεχνάσμασι σηπεύοντας
⟨   ⟩
ἔνθα δυσοσμίη τε καὶ οἰκτρότατ' ἔργα τελεῖται. 270

249-55. Θ p. 215.4–6. πζ'. Περὶ βαλανέων. Ἐὰν ὁ Κρόνος ἐπιθεωρῇ τὴν Σελήνην καὶ τὸ δωδεκατημόριον αὐτῆς τῆς Σελήνης οὔσης ὁρίοις Κρόνου, βαλανεῖς ἢ περιχύτας ποιεῖ.
251-9. Cf. 6.422–4.
251-62. Ptol. 4.4.5. ὁ δὲ τοῦ Ἄρεως μετὰ μὲν τοῦ ἡλίου σχηματισθεὶς τοὺς διὰ πυρὸς ἐργαζομένους ποιεῖ οἷον μαγείρους, χωνευτάς, καύστας, χαλκέας, μεταλλευτάς· χωρὶς δὲ τοῦ ἡλίου τυχὼν τοὺς διὰ σιδήρου οἷον ναυπηγούς, τέκτονας, γεωργούς, λατόμους, λιθοξόους, λαοξόους, λιθουργούς, ξυλοσχίστας, ὑπουργούς. κἂν μὲν ὁ τοῦ Κρόνου αὐτῷ μαρτυρήσῃ ναυτικούς, ἀντλητάς, ὑπονομευτάς, ζωγράφους, θηριοτρόφους, μαγείρους, παρασχίστας.
Θ p. 211.24–31. ὁ δὲ τοῦ Ἄρεως αὐτῷ [sc. τῷ τῆς Ἀφροδίτης] συμπαρὼν μετὰ μὲν Ἡλίου ‹συ›σχηματισθεὶς τοὺς διὰ πυρὸς ἐργαζομένους ποιεῖ, μαγείρους, χωνευτάς, καύστας, μεταλλευτάς· χωρὶς δὲ Ἡλίου ἑστὼς τοὺς διὰ σιδήρου τὰς ἐνεργείας ἔχοντας, ναυπηγούς, τέκτονας, γεωργούς, λατόμους, λιθοξόους, λιθουργούς, ξυλοσχίστας. κἂν μὲν ὁ τοῦ Κρόνου αὐτῷ μαρτυρήσῃ, ποιεῖ ναυτικούς, ἀντλητάς, ὑπονομευτάς, θηριοτρόφους, μαγείρους, περιχύτας, βαλανέας.
Θ p. 166.22–4 [Saturn in MC]... κηπωροὺς καὶ ὑδραγωγοὺς ἢ ναύτας ἢ ἁλιεῖς ἢ πορθμ(εῖς) καὶ ὅλως πένητας καὶ περὶ ὑγρὰς ὕλας ἀναστρεφομένους.

245 ἱμεροέσσης L: corr. K² 247 δ'] τ' L: corr. K 250 ἀλλήλοισιν L: corr. R 251 ὀχθοφόρους L: corr. D³²² 252 ἀμάρης σκαπτῆρας D³²², Lob. Phryn.⁶⁵⁴ 254 παραγχυσίησι D⁶⁴⁷ 255 ἄβροτα L: corr. H, Hal, D⁶⁴⁷ 256 φύσσονται L: corr. D⁶⁵⁹ 259 ἀνθολόγοι L: corr. D⁶⁵⁹ 261 κελαίχροός L¹ˢˡ

Directors of a brutish mansuefaction, 245
By whom the beasts are tamed to docile ways,
Wild creatures' keepers, entering their lairs.
Their lives, though not unfortunate, are hard.
   High-wandering Saturn nearing the Moon's rays,
In mutual exchange of their twelfth parts, 250
Gives burdened water-drawers, road-sweepers
Diggers of ditches (lamentable trade!),
Who clean the sluices of the public baths;
He'll[5] soften bodies tenderised in saunas,
Refused by birds and lamb-devouring wolves. 255
What's more, sowers of fruit will come to birth,
Who draw from troughs, grow old in watery trades
Who nurture plants, grow vegetables, sweat
In gathering dung, or mine the earth, servants
Of toil, by whom from mountains rocks are hewn, 260
Bronze, tin, or swarthy iron, all things which
Man's ingenuity wrests from the earth.
   If Saturn's ray strikes Mars in heaven's summit,
Ill beams meeting an ill regard, ablaze
In their own terms and portions of the twelve, 265
They make their joint way in trine radiance,
Slitters of bellies, and embalmers grim
Are shown, practitioners of a vile trade,
Foul ones, who by their putrid arts make rot…
⟨   ⟩
Where foul stench and most wretched works are wrought. 270

[5] The native.

Θ p. 212.15–18. ἐπὰν ὁ Κρόνος παραιρέτης καὶ ἐν ἀλλοτρίῳ ζῳδίῳ τύχῃ ἐν τῷ μεσουρανήματι, τὰς δι' ὑγρῶν ποιεῖ τέχνας, τοῦτ' ἐστι ἀντλητάς, κηπουροὺς ἢ ἁλιεύοντας καὶ τὰς παρύγρους πράξεις παρέχει μετὰ κόπου καὶ μόχθου κάμνοντας.
Epit. IV = CCAG ii. 191.20–2. ὁ Κρόνος παρ' αἵρεσιν ἐν ἀλλοτρίῳ ζῳδίῳ ἐν τῷ μεσουρανήματι τὰς δι' ὑγρῶν δίδωσι τέχνας, οἷον ἀντλητάς, κηπουρούς, ἁλιεῖς, ὑδραγωγούς; cf. 1.83–8.
263–70. Cf. 6.456–64.
Ptol. 4.4.5. κἂν μὲν ὁ τοῦ Κρόνου αὐτῷ [sc. τῷ τοῦ Ἄρεως] μαρτυρήσῃ ναυτικούς, ἀντλητάς, ὑπονομευτάς, ζωγράφους, θηριοτρόφους, μαγείρους, παρασχίστας.
Θ p. 215.8–11. πη'. Περὶ νεκρεπαρτῶν. Κρόνος ἰσόμοιρος Ἄρει καὶ Ἑρμῇ, θεωρούντων τὰ δωδεκατημόρια ἀλλήλων δίχα τῆς τῶν ἀγαθοποιῶν θεωρίας, νεκροτάφους ἢ νεκροθάπτας ἢ νεκρεπάρτας ἢ τυμβωρύχους ποιοῦσι.

262 πάντ' ἐπὶ γαίης L, τ supra ras. c. 2-3 lit. L¹: corr. K: πάντ' ἐπεὶ ἐν γαίῃ R: πᾶν γὰρ ὑπαὶ γαίης R^conj: πάνθ' ἃ τ' ἐνὶ γαίῃ vel sim. requiritur

fo. 29ʳ
268 καὶ ἐμπορίης L: corr. Lob. Rh.¹⁹⁶ⁿ·²   269 μυσεροὺς L: corr. D⁶⁵⁹   παμμυσαροὺς Lob. Rh.¹⁹⁶ⁿ·²   σηπτοῖσι] σηπτάστε L: corr. K post D⁶⁵⁹ σηπτοῖς τε   post hunc versum lacunam statuit K, quam complendam sic fere K² censuit: ἰχθύας ἔν τε λέβησιν ἅμ' ἅλμῃ μελδεύοντας

Ἥλιος δ' ἀκάμας ὅτ' ἂν ἀθρῇ τὸν πυρόεντα
ἀστέρ' Ἐνυαλίοιο, θοαῖς ἀκτῖσι βολαυγῶν,
ζῳδίων τετράγωνον ἀν' οὐρανόεσσαν ἀταρπὸν
ἀμφίκερω Ταύροιο καὶ ἀσθματικοῖο Λέοντος
Κριοῦ τ' εἰαρόεντος ἐπ' ὠδίνεσσι βροτείαις,   275
ἰσχυρῶν ἔργων τεύχει πονοπαίκτορας ἄνδρας,
ὀχλοχαρεῖς, φιλόμοχθα θεατρομανοῦντας, ἴχνεσσιν
αἰθροβάτας, πηκτοῖσι πεταυριστῆρας ἐν ἔργοις,
αἰθέρι καὶ γαίῃ μεμετρημένα ἔργα τελοῦντας,
μιμοβίους, χλεύης τ' ἐπιβήτορας, ὑβριγέλωτας,   280
ἐν ξείνῃ γήρως ἐπιβήτορας, ὀθνιοτύμβους,
ὄρνεα γῆς, πόλεως πάσης ἀπόλιστα γένεθλα,
μωρόφρονας, λιτούς, ἀσχήμονας, αἰσχρογέλωτας,
κρατοπλαγεῖς, ἀχίτωνας, ἀεὶ κορυφῇσι φαλακρούς,
ὧν ὁ βίος χλεύῃ τέχνην ἀπεμάξαθ' ἑτοίμην.   285
ἢν δὲ σὺν Ἡλίῳ τε καὶ Ἄρεϊ καὶ Κύπρις ὀφθῇ,
σχοινοβάτας τεύχει, καλοβάμονας, ὑψόθεν εἰς γῆν
γειτονίῃ θανάτοιο καταρριπτοῦντας ἑαυτούς,
ὧν ὁ πόρος μόρος ἐστίν, ἐπὴν εἰς σφάλματα νεύσῃ.

τούτοις δ' ἄμμιγα πᾶσι Κρόνου συναλώμενος ἀστὴρ   290
τειχοδόμους τε τίθησι, καὶ εὐτόλμους κεραμουργοὺς
πηλαίης πλίνθου τε καὶ εὐτοίχων κανονισμῶν
θριγκῶν τ' εὐθυντῆρας, ἀεὶ καμάτοισι συνήθεις.

ἢν δ' ἰσόμοιρα κέλευθα Κυθήρῃ Ἄρεϊ βαίνῃ,
ἠὲ τρίγωνος ἐοῦσα κατ' ἔμβασιν ἢ τετράγωνος,   295
ἢ διαμετρήσῃ φάος ἄπλετον ἀστέρι κείνῳ,
ἄμφω δ' αὖτε τὸν αὐτὸν ἅμα θρῴσκωσι τυχόντες
δωδεκατημορίων ἑλικὸν δρόμον αἰθροδόνητον,

271-9. Cf. 6.439-45.
280-5. Θ p. 217.5-8. Περὶ μίμων. Ἑρμῆς καὶ Ἀφροδίτη ταπεινούμενοι ἐν ὁρίοις ἰδίοις ἢ ἀλλήλων μίμους ἢ πολιτικοὺς ποιοῦσιν, μάλιστα ἐν Αἰγοκέρωτι διὰ τὸ παρανατέλλειν τὸν Πίθηκα.
286-9. Θ p. 213.1. ἐὰν δὲ ὁ Ἥλιος αὐτοῖς [sc. Ἀφροδίτῃ καὶ Ἄρει] μαρτυρήσῃ, νευροβάτας ποιεῖ, μαγγαναρίους.
Θ p. 213.4-7. Ἄρης καὶ Ἀφροδίτη ἰσομοίρως τυχόντες, εἰ καὶ τὰ δωδεκατημόρια τύχωσι τετράγωνα [ἐν] αὐτοῖς ἢ τρίγωνα ἢ διάμετρα, ποιοῦσι μοιχούς, μεθυστάς, ἀπατεῶνας. Ἄρης καὶ Ἀφροδίτη ἐν τοῖς ὑπογείοις ποιοῦσι σχοινοβάτας ἢ θεοφορουμένους.

272 Ἐνυᾱλίοιο L[1sl]   273 an τετράγωνος?   274 ἀσθμοτόκοιο L: corr. A.-R.: αἰθοτόκοιο K[2]   275 ἰαρόεντος L: corr. D[301]   276 πονοπέκτορας L: corr. Gr   277 ἴχνεσιν L: corr. H, Gr   278 πηκτοῖσιν L: corr. H, Gr   πετευριστῆρας L: corr. A.-R.   ἔργοις] ἄκροις K[2]: οἴμοις S[conj]   282 πόλιος A.-R.   284 κρατοπαγεῖς L: corr. Lob. Para.[288]: κρατοπαλεῖς K[conj], K[2]   285 χλεύης L: corr. A.-R.[conj]   ἀπεμάξατ' L: corr. L[1]   ὁμοίην L: corr. K   288 καταριπτοῦντας: corr. H, Hal, D[608]   289 μό[.]ρος L   νεύσῃ, ηι L[1ras]   290 δ'] δὲ L: corr. Gr   292 πλήνθου L: corr. H, Gr   κα[..]νονισμῶν L[ras] (κατα- ante ras. u.v.)

When the tireless Sun beholds the igneous
Star of the Warlike, striking with swift beams,
Along the quadrate path of heavenly signs,
In the horned Bull and Lion panting hard
Or vernal Ram, in pangs of mortal birth,   275
He fashions men whose sport with mighty toils
Delights the theatre mob, crazed by their feats;
Who tread the air, gymnasts on jointed frames,
Achieving feats portioned 'twixt air and earth,
Mime-actors, lords of jest, outrageous clowns,   280
Spending old age abroad, in foreign tombs,
Earth's birds, in every town a townless folk,
Fools, meagre, ugly, raising laughs at shame,
Slap-headed, tunicless, bald in their pates,
Whose lives mimic an art inclined to jest.   285
  If with the Sun and Mars Venus, too, shows,
She makes rope-walkers, ambulants on twine,
Hurled to the ground in death's vicinity,
Whose trade's the grave when tending to a fall.
  The star of Saturn wandering with these linked   290
Makes those who build walls, sturdily make tiles
Of baked brick, and of walls expertly squared,
And cornices the levellers, sons of toil.
  If Venus' paths match Ares' in degree,
Whether her transit's trine or square with him,   295
Or she opposes light to light with his,
And both being together course across
The anfractuous path of twelve ethereal parts,

Θ p. 215.12–17. πθ'. Περὶ οἰκοδόμων ἢ κεραμέων. Κρόνος ἰσόμοιρος Ἄρει Κριῷ ἢ Ταύρῳ ἢ Λέοντι ἢ τετράγωνος ⟨signum planetae deest⟩ ὑπάρχων καὶ ὑπὸ Ἄρεος θεωρούμενος χωρὶς τῆς τῶν ἀγαθοποιῶν ἐπιθεωρίας σκανδουλαρίους ποιεῖ ἢ τοιχοβάτας ἢ οἰκοδόμους ἢ κεραμεῖς ἢ λυχνοποιούς. εἰ δὲ καὶ Ἀφροδίτη ἐπιθεωρήσῃ, νευροβάτας ποιεῖ.
Θ p. 217.9. Ἄρης καὶ Ἑρμῆς ὑπόγειοι νευροβάτας ἢ μαγγαναρίους ποιοῦσι.
290–3. Cf. 6.415–18.
Θ p. 213.1–3. εἰ δὲ καὶ Κρόνος καὶ Ἥλιος αὐτοῖς [sc. Ἀφροδίτῃ καὶ Ἄρει] μαρτυρήσωσιν, οἰκοδόμους ποιοῦσιν ἢ κεραμουργούς.
Θ p. 215.12–16. πθ'. Περὶ οἰκοδόμων ἢ κεραμέων. Κρόνος ἰσόμοιρος Ἄρει Κριῷ ἢ Ταύρῳ ἢ Λέοντι ἢ τετράγωνος ⟨signum planetae deest⟩ ὑπάρχων καὶ ὑπὸ Ἄρεος θεωρούμενος χωρὶς τῆς τῶν ἀγαθοποιῶν ἐπιθεωρίας σκανδουλαρίους ποιεῖ ἢ τοιχοβάτας ἢ οἰκοδόμους ἢ κεραμεῖς ἢ λυχνοποιούς.

294 ἰσόμοιρα, ι' L¹ʳᵃˢ   Κυθήρῃ L: Κυθηριὰς K   βάλλῃ L: corr. D⁶⁵⁹   296 ἄπλατον L: corr. J. Pierson, *Moeridis Atticistae Lexicon*, ed. G. A. Koch (Leipzig, 1830), 23, dein A.-R.   297 θρώ'σκωσι L¹ˢˡ   298 ἑλικὸν] ἴκελον L: corr. Aᶜᵒⁿʲ

τηνίκα τοὺς τεχθέντας ἀναγγέλλουσιν ἔσεσθαι
ζωροπότας οἴνου, μεθυχάρμονας, εἰλαπινουργούς, 300
δαιτυμόνας, θιάσοισιν ἀεικώμους, ἀκολάστους,
ἤματα νύκτας ἄγοντας ὕπνῳ μετακοσμηθέντα·
πρὸς τούτοις δ᾽ ἔτι πουλὺ κακώτερα βλαστήσουσιν,
πλαστοκόμαι, νομίμων λεχέων κλεπτῆρες ἄθεσμοι,
μοιχευταὶ μυρόεντες ἀεί, νεομορφοτύπωτοι, 305
μάστροπά τ᾽ ἔργα τελοῦντες, ἀεὶ κακίῃσι γυναικῶν

29ᵛ   σύμβουλοι, δόλιοι, κακομήστορες, αἰσχροδιδάκται,
ἴδμονες, ὧν ἄλοχοι θαλάμους πωλοῦσι συνεύνων.

ὁππότε δ᾽ ἂν τούτοισι Κρόνου βλαβεραυγέος ἀστὴρ
συννεύῃ κατὰ χῶρον ἀνοικείοισι κελεύθοις, 310
παμπαθέας, στομάτεσσιν ὀπυιομένους, γονοπώτας,
μήδεα μασθὸν ἔχοντας, ἀναστροφίῃ τ᾽ ἐφυβρίστους
ἐκφαίνει φύσεσθαι, ἑταιροτρόφους τε γόητας,
πορνοσύνης ἀκρατοῦς σημάντορας, αἰσχεοκερδεῖς,
ἔχθιστον, μυσαρόν, μεμαχλευμένον ἦτορ ἔχοντας, 315
παμψέκτους, ἀπόφωλα βίου μυσαρωπὰ γένεθλα.

φαινούσαις δ᾽ ἀκτῖσιν ὅτ᾽ ἂν Κρόνος εἰς Ἀφροδίτην
λαμπάζῃ, σελάοντι φλογὸς βαρυβάμονος ὁλκῷ,
Ἄρης δ᾽ αἰθαλόεις παρέῃ σὺν τοῖσι διωγμοῖς,
βυρσοτόμους τεύχει, δεροεργέας, ἔν τε καθέδραις 320
σκυτείῃ τέχνῃ μεμελημένα δαιδάλλοντας,
θηλυλάλους, ῥώπου τε γυναικῶν ἴδριας αἰεί,
τεκτοσύνης τ᾽ ἄρχοντας, ἰδ᾽ ἐν ναυπηγέσι τέχναις
καγκανέης ὕλης πελεκήτορας εὐξυλοεργούς,
λαοτόμους τε πέτρης σκληρώδεος, ἐγρεσιοίκους, 325
ἠδὲ λιθοψώκτῳ καμάτῳ βίον ἰθύνοντας.

τούτοις δ᾽ Ἑρμάων ἐπὶ τέρμονας ἡνίκ᾽ ἂν ἔλθῃ
οἰκείως, εὔσχημον ἔχων φάος Ἄρεος ἄστρῳ,
πρηκτῆρας δείκνυσι, τελωνητάς τε βιαίους
φύσεσθαι, δεινούς τε χρεάρπαγας ἐργολάβους τε, 330

309-16. Cf. 6.591-2.
Θ pp. 195.8-10 = 215.21-2. εἰ δὲ Κρόνος ἐπιθεωρήσῃ, ποιεῖ κιναίδους, ἀσελγεῖς, μάλιστα ἐν θηλυκοῖς ζῳδίοις.
327-32. Ptol. 4.4.7. ἐὰν δὲ ὁ τοῦ Ἑρμοῦ καὶ ὁ τοῦ Ἄρεως ἅμα τὴν κυρίαν λάβωσι τῆς πράξεως, ποιοῦσιν ἀνδριαντοποιούς, ὁπλουργούς, ἱερογλύφους, ζῳοπλάστας, παλαιστάς, ἰατρούς, χειρουργούς, κατηγόρους...
Θ p. 212.2-4. Ἄρης καὶ Ἑρμῆς τὸ πράσσειν παρέχοντες ποιοῦσιν ἀνδριαντοποιοὺς ἢ τέχνην τινὰ ἀπὸ πυρὸς ἢ σιδήρου, ἢ πάλιν ὁπλουργούς, κατηγόρους...

---

302 μετακοσμηθέντας L: corr. A.-R.   303 πολὺ L: corr. A.-R.   βλαστήσωσιν L: corr. A.-R.   305 μοιχαπάται L: μοιχευταὶ A.-R.   μοιρόεντες L: corr. A.-R.   νεομορφ[.]οτύπωτοι Lʳᵃˢ

> Then they declare the progeny to be
> Bibbers of neat wine, sots, founders of feasts, 300
> Diners, inveterate roisterers, uncontrolled,
> Who turn night into day by ousting sleep;
> As well as these, far worse types are born:
> False-haired, unlawful thieves of marriage-beds,
> Perfumed adulterers, formed as if anew, 305
> Doing procurers' works, of women's guilt
> Confidants, sly, who teach and contrive shame,
> Knowing whose wives traffic their husbands' beds.
>   When with these baleful-gleaming Cronos' star
> Tends to one place in houses not his own, 310
> Passives, mouth-wedded, swallowers of seed,
> Cock-suckers, in lubricity depraved
> Are born, and charlatans who maintain whores,
> Chiefs of unbridled lust and shameful gain,
> With hateful, loathsome, vitiated hearts, 315
> All-blameful, null in life and foul of face.
>   With shining rays when Saturn on Venus
> Gleams in the radiant path of his slow flame,
> And smoky Mars shows with them in pursuit(?),
> He makes hide-cutters, tanners, at their bench 320
> Those given to pattern-cutting leather arts,
> Womanish gossips, versed in female trash,
> Masters of joinery, in shipwrights' crafts
> Plying the axe with skill on sapless wood,
> Who hew recalcitrant stone, and buildings raise 325
> Guiding their lives by stonework-smoothing toils.
>   When Hermes comes into the terms of these,
> In his house, well-disposed with Ares' star,
> He shows the birth of dealers, and unloved
> Taxmen, dread loan-sharks, also profiteers, 330

Θ p. 193.1–3. Ἄρης καὶ Ἑρμῆς ἐπίκεντροι τυχόντες καὶ ἰσόμοιροι δίχα τῆς τῶν ἀγαθῶν ἐπιθεωρίας ποιοῦσι ψεύστας, ψευδοκατηγόρους, πλαστογράφους, ἐπιόρκους.
Epit. IIIb [*CCAG* vii. 112.15–16]. Ἄρης καὶ Ἑρμῆς ἐπὶ κέντρῳ τυχόντες ψευδοκατηγόρους ποιοῦσιν, ἐπιόρκους.

fo. 29ᵛ
307 κακομήτορες L: corr. K² 310 ἀνοικίοισι L: corr. L¹ 311 στομάτεσσι L: corr. H, Gr 312 μασθὸν L¹ˢˡ 313 ἐταιροτρόφους L¹ˢˡ 314 αἰσχρεοκερδεῖς L: corr. K 316 πανψέκτους L: corr. L¹ 318 σελάοντι] σελάεσσι L: correxi post σελαγεῦντι S 319 τοῖσι] ἑοῖσι Aᶜᵒⁿʲ 320 δοροεργέας L: corr. K 322 ῥωπουστε L: corr. Grⁿ 323 ἰδ'] ἠδ' L: corr. H, Gr 324 καγκανέης L¹ᶜᵒʳʳ 325 λαοτόμουτε L: corr. A.-R. σκιρώδεος Span²⁰⁶⁻⁷ ἐγρεσιδόμους L: corr. Sp²²³ 327 ἀνέλθηι L: corr. Gr

ἔνθεν ἐπήρειαί τε καὶ ἐκδύσιες τελέθουσιν,
ψευδοκατηγορίαι τε κατηγορίης τε τεχνασμοί.
μαρμαρυγὴν δ' ἀκτῖνος ὅτ' ἂν σελαηφόρος Ἑρμῆς
ἀμφὶ Σεληναίης σκολιὸν λαβύρινθον ὀρίνῃ,
ἠὲ πέλῃ κατὰ ταὐτὸν ἐπ' αὐταῖς λαμπάσι Μήνης   335
δωδεκατημορίων ἀντώπια φέγγεα κόσμου,
ἀγραύλους δείκνυσι κυνηγητῆρας ἔσεσθαι
ἄρκυσι καὶ σταλίκεσσιν ἐϋσταθέεσσι μέλοντας,
αἰθροτόκου τε γονῆς ἐπιβήτορας ἰξευτῆρας,
ἐνδεέας τε τίθησι τροφῆς κάμνοντας ἐπ' ἔργοις·   340
ἢν δὲ καὶ οἰκείων ὁρίων ψαύσωσιν ἅμ' ἄμφω,
ὑλογράφους ἄνδρας, κηραγγέας, ὁλκαδοχρίστας,
ζωοτύπους, μακάρων ἀποπλάστορας, εἰκονομόρφους
θήσονται, μεθόδῳ τε λινοστολίης προφέροντας,
πευκῆέν τε λίπασμα συνασκοῦντας σὺν ἐλαίῳ,   345
μόχθον πισσήεντα πονήσοντας παλάμῃσιν.
Ἀκτὶς δ' αἰγλήεσσα Σεληναίης Ἀφροδίτην
30ʳ   φωτὶ νέῳ βάλλουσα καὶ Ἄρεϊ μαρτυρέουσα,
ἀλλοτρίων θαλάμων φαίνει λῃστορας ἄνδρας
ἔσσεσθαι, μοιχευτὰ λέχη μελάθροισιν ἔχοντας·   350
θῆλυ δ' ἐὸν τὸ πεφυκὸς ἐν ἤματι τοῦδε σελασμοῦ
πάγκοινον κέρδος θηρήσεται ἀνδράσι μιχθέν,
ἔκ τε χαμαιτυπίης ἕξει βίον εὔπορον αἰεί.
Ἑρμείου δ' ἀκτῖνες ἐπὴν Κρόνον ἀκροβολῶσιν,
Ἀρεά τ' ἐγρεκύδοιμον ἐπὴν ἐφορῶσ' ἐπὶ τούτῳ,   355
ὃς δὲ Διωναίης Κύπριδος θοὸν ἀστέρα βάλλῃ,
τηνίκα δὴ μαχλάδας τεύχει †ταστοια φυείσας,
πόρνας τε τριβάδας τ' ἀνδρόστροφα ἔργα τελούσας.

333–40. Θ p. 216.8–15. 4β'. Περὶ κυνηγῶν καὶ ἱερακοτρόφων καὶ ὀρνιθοτρόφων καὶ ζωγράφων. Ἐὰν ὁ Ἑρμῆς ἔξαυγος ὢν ἰσόμοιρος γένηται τῇ Σελήνῃ καὶ ἐπιθεωρήσωσι τὰ δωδεκατημόρια ἀλλήλων ‹καὶ› Ἄρης καὶ Κρόνος διαμετροῦντες ἑαυτοὺς ἐπιτύχωσι τῶν κέντρων, κυνηγοὺς καὶ βηνάτορας. εἰ δὲ ἐν τοῖς πτερωτοῖς ζῳδίοις τύχωσιν ὁ Ἑρμῆς καὶ ἡ Σελήνη, λέγω δὴ ἐν Παρθένῳ καὶ Τοξότῃ καὶ ταῖς πρώταις μοίραις τῶν Ἰχθύων διὰ τὸν Πήγασον, ἱερακοτρόφους ποιοῦσι ἢ ὀρνιθοτρόφους.
Θ p. 217.19–20. Ἡ Σελήνη ἐν Ταύρῳ μετὰ Ἑρμοῦ καὶ Ἡλίου αὐξιφαὴς ἰξευτὰς ποιεῖ καὶ ἱερακαρίους.
341–6. Cf. 6.520–5.
Ptol. 4.4.6. ἐὰν μὲν ὁ τοῦ Ἑρμοῦ καὶ ὁ τῆς Ἀφροδίτης λάβωσι τὴν οἰκοδεσποτείαν,...ἀποτελοῦσι...ὑφάντας, κηροπλάστας, ζωγράφους...
Θ p. 213.13...ὑφάντας, πλάστας, ζωγράφους.

331 ἐπήριαί L: corr. A   333 μαρμαρυγὴ L: corr. R   ἀκτῖν' L: corr. R   σελατηφόρος L: corr. A.-R.: σελαγηφόρος S[conj]   334 Σεληναίῃ L: corr. R   335 πέσῃ L: corr. D[660]   336 ἀντώπεα L: corr. Hal   338 ἐυσταθέεσι L: corr. H, Gr   340 ἔργοις] ἀγροῖς D[648]   342 κηραγγέας] κηρουργούς Luc[conj]   343 ζωοτύπης L: corr. A.-R.   344 θήσοντ' ἢ L: corr. Hal (θήσονται ἢ H)   μεθόδων L: corr. R   λινοστολίῃ L: corr. A.-R.   345 λήπασμα L: corr. Hal, D[660]   346 πονήσονται L: corr. K

[331–358] Book Four 431

    Whence violations, asset-strippings, false
Denunciations and complaints arise.
    When radiant Hermes lifts his lustrous beam
Around Selene's twisted labyrinth,
Or in the Full Moon's beams, in the same place   335
Of the twelve parts, their lustres stand opposed,
They shadow forth huntsmen, who in the wild
Tend nets and stakes implanted in the ground,
Who trap the ether's denizens with lime:
Hard work, to meet hunger's imperative.   340
Should both also touch their own terms, they make
Those who paint panels, work with wax, coat hulls,
Carve forms, sculpt gods, and fashion effigies,
Or in the linen-worker's art excel,
Or else compound from pine a gum with oil,   345
Making a pitchy labour with their hands.
    If Selene's shining beams when she is New
Strike Venus, bearing witness, too, to Mars,
She shows marauders of the marriage-bower,
Having adulterous couches in their homes;   350
But if the birth is female, and by day,
She'll spoliate gains from coupling with men,
From lowly tumblings earn a ready wage.
    When Hermes' beams strike Saturn up on high,
And with him witness Mars, bringer of war,   355
Who strikes Dionean Venus' rapid star,
She makes lascivious persons...
Whores, tribades, whose torsions mimic men's.

Θ p. 216.15–16. ἐὰν δὲ καὶ Σελήνη καὶ Ἄρης εὑρεθῶσιν ὁρίοις Ἑρμοῦ, ζωγράφους ποιοῦσι.
Θ p. 217.14–15. Ἀφροδίτη οἴκῳ Ἑρμοῦ μετὰ Ἑρμοῦ ἐπίκεντροι ἢ ἐπαναφερόμενοι ἔξαυγοι ζωγράφους ποιοῦσι ἢ ἀνδριαντοπλάστας ἢ πολυμιταρίους.
347–53. Cf. 6.583–5.
Θ p. 215.19–21. Ὁ Ἄρης τῇ Ἀφροδίτῃ ἰσόμοιρος ⟨ ⟩ κατὰ τετράγωνον ἢ διάμετρον ἐπιθεωρούντων ἀλλήλων τὰ δωδεκατημόρια ἐκτὸς τῆς τῶν ἄλλων ἐπιθεωρίας ποιοῦσι μεθυστάς, λῃστάς, μοιχούς, ἀναστάτους (cf. 195.5–8).
Θ pp. 194.18–195.2. ἡ Ἀφροδίτη καὶ ἡ Σελήνη ἐν τῷ δύνοντι τὰς μὲν γυναῖκας ἀσελγεῖς ποιοῦσι, τοὺς δὲ ἄνδρας μαλακούς, πλέον δὲ εἰ καὶ ὑπὸ Κρόνου ἢ Ἄρεως θεωρηθῶσιν.
354–8. Θ p. 169.4–8 ... ἐὰν δὲ καὶ ὁ τοῦ Ἄρεως κατοπτεύσῃ τὸν τῆς Ἀφροδίτης ... ἐπαίσχρους καὶ περιβοήτους ἀποτελεῖ. εἰ δὲ γυνὴ τύχῃ ἐπὶ τοῦδε τοῦ διαθήματος, πολυκοινήσει ἑταιριζομένη καὶ ἐπὶ τέγαις σταθήσεται ταῖς διὰ ζωῆς.

---

fo. 30ʳ
351 ἐὸν] επηνL (ἐπ' ἦν L¹): corr. A.–R. (δὲ ὂν Hal)   352 πάνκοινον L: corr. Hal   θηράσσεται L: corr. A.–R.   355 ἐφορῶσί τε τοῦτον L: corr. A (ἐφορῶσ'), K (ἐπὶ τούτῳ)   356 ὅς δὲ] ἠὲ L: corr. K   357 ταστοια φυείσας L: τάστεῖα φυ. Gr, Hal^mg: τάστεῖα φρονοῦσας Herm⁷¹⁶: παντοῖα μιγείσας vel παθούσας K: sub ταστοια latere τ'αἰδοῖα suspicatus est S   358 τε] καὶ L: corr. Herm⁷¹⁶   ⟨τ'⟩ Herm⁷¹⁶   357–8 τηνίκα δὴ πόρνας ... καὶ μαχλάδας, τριβάδας τ' K

ἢν δ' ἰσόμοιρα φανῇ Κυθερηιὰς Ἑρμάωνι,
ἄνδρεσσι ξείνοισι καὶ ἀλλοδαποῖσι μιγεῖσαι   360
δεσποτίδες μεγάλων τε βίων μελάθρων τε φανοῦνται.
τὸν συνετὸν κατιδὼν διὰ τετράδος ὄβριμος Ἄρης
οὐκ ἀγαθὸν τελέσει, βλαβερὸν δ' ἐπὶ πᾶσιν ὀρίνει,
σκυλμοὺς ὑπνοφανεῖς, φαντάσματά τ' ἠδ' ἐπαγωγάς·
καὶ διεγείρονται νεκύων θάμβησιν ἔχοντες.   365
Αἰθαλόεις δ' ἀστὴρ Ἄρεως ἀκτῖσι Σελήνην
φεγγοβολῶν ἰσόμοιρα κατ' Οὐλύμποιο κέλευθα
ἀκροτάτοις κέντροισι, πρὸς ἐκθεσίην ἀτίθηνον
θηλυτέρων βρεφέων τε καὶ ἀρσενικῶν βίον ἕλκει·
οὐ μὴν εἰς θάνατόν γε πορεύσεται ἔκθεσις ἥδε,   370
ἀρνυμέναις δὲ γυναιξὶ τροφοῖς θ' ὑποβάλλετ' ὀθνείαις·
κἢν μὲν ἐπισκοπέῃ γενέθλην Κρόνος, εἰς ζυγὸν ἥξει
λατρείης πονόεντα· Διὸς δ' ἐπιδερκομένοιο,
ἦμαρ ἐλευθερίης ἕξει ποιητὸς ὀθνείων,
συληθεὶς γονέων, οὐ γνήσιος ἐν μεγάροισιν,   375
σὺν δὲ διωνυμίῃ τε καὶ ἐν διπολήιδι φήμῃ
ζήσεται ἀλλοτρίων γονέων, οὐχ ὧνπερ ἔβλαστεν,
χρήμασι καὶ στοργαῖς καὶ παιδοσύνῃσιν ὀθνείων.
αὐτὰρ ἐπήν γε Κρόνος Μήνῃ ἰσόμοιρος ὑπάρχῃ,
ἢ διάμετρα φανῇ πλαγκτῷ κόσμοιο πορείῃ,   380
πάμπαν ἐς ἐκθεσίην βρεφέων γένος ἔσσυτ' ἐκείνων,
ὧν γένεσις πρὸς μητρὸς ἐλέγχεται ἀνδράσι δούλη,
ἐκ γενέτου δὲ πέφυκεν ἐλεύθερα δεσποσυνάων.

362-5. Θ p. 193.13-15. ὁ Ἑρμῆς πάντοτε ἀπόστροφος ὢν τοῦ ὡροσκόπου καὶ τῆς Σελήνης ἐπιληψίας ποιεῖ· εἰ δὲ καὶ κακοποιὸς ἐπιθεωρήσῃ, δαιμονιοπλήκτους ποιεῖ.
366-71. Firmicus, 7.2.16. *Si Luna in occasu fuerit inventa, et Mars aut cum ipsa in isdem partibus fuerit inventus aut in horoscopo partiliter constitutus, et sit diurna genitura, is qui natus fuerit exponetur.*
372-3. Cf. 6.57-9.
Firmicus, 6.15.9. *Nam si geniturae cardines possidentes [sc. Saturnum, Martem] Luna in quocumque cardine constituta hac eadem radiatione [sc. opposition] respexerit vel quadrata, tunc graviora pericula tunc fugitivos errores, tunc exilia publicasque decernit mortes ista coniunctio, tunc honore libertatis erepto iugum miserae servitutis imponunt.*
Firmicus, 6.31.19. *Si Luna in MC. fuerit inventa, et in IMC. Saturnus et Mars et Iuppiter sint pariter constituti, is qui sic ‹eos› habuerit de patriis la[bo]ribus retractus grave iugum captivitatis accipiet.*
373-8. Cf. 6.53-6.
Firmicus, 7.2.16. *Sed et Iuppiter hos sic collocatos in alio cardine positus respexerit, aut si Venus hoc idem fecerit, exposito vitae praesidia per alium conferuntur, scilicet ut ab his collectus nutriatur.*

359 φαν[..]ηῖL, accent. L¹ (olim φανειηι?)   360 ἄνδρεσσιν L: corr. H, A.-R.   361 τε βίων: τ' ὄλβων S^conj   362 κατιδὼν L: τ L¹corr   363 τελέσσει L: corr. H, Gr   ὀρίνει] ὁρίζου L: corr. K: ὁρίζει Hal: an ⟨πᾶσι⟩ κομίζει?   365 καὶ δι- L¹   366 Ἄρεος L: corr. L¹   368 ἔχθεσιν ἢ L: corr. Gr (ἔκθ-), K (-ίην)   369 θηλυτόκων L: corr. K²   ἀρσενικῶν] ἀρρεγόνων L: corr. A.-R. (ἀρρ-)   371 ⟨θ'⟩ K   ὀθνίαις L: corr. L¹   372 ἐς H, Gr

> If with Hermes Venus is in like degree,
> Then, joined with aliens and with outlanders, 360
> Ladies of assets and estates are born.
> If mighty Mars squares with the wily one,
> No good he does, but causes harm for all,
> Dreaming night-horrors, phantasms, and spells,
> And waking apparitions of the dead. 365
> Mars' smoky star, when he irradiates
> The Moon in like degrees of heaven's paths
> In the top centre, leads to nurtureless
> Exposure of both male and female births.
> Yet this exposure's not as far as death, 370
> But hands the child to alien fosterage.
> And if Saturn should view the birth, he comes
> To servitude's hard yoke; if Zeus looks on,
> A child adopted, he'll have freedom's light,
> But torn from parents, bastard in the home, 375
> With two names and enrolment in two towns
> He'll live with foreign parents, not his own,
> With others' goods and love and sustenance.
> But when Saturn equals the Moon's degrees,
> Or shines opposed in the cosmos' slanted course, 380
> That brood speeds to exposure, without fail,
> Whose birth is proved slave on its mother's side,
> But on its father's free from masters' rule.

Dor.^ARAB I 7.14. If the Moon is as I told you and is in its own triplicity and the benefics aspect the malefics from trine, he is not ruined but he is brought up in another house than his parents' because he is expelled and is brought up in the house of strangers, and sometimes he will be a slave and will be employed and will be miserable.

Dor.^ARAB I 7.19. If you find the Moon with a malefic in a cardine or what follows a cardine and benefics aspect it, the native will be brought up but his parents [will cast him out].

Dor.^ARAB I 10.22. If Jupiter or Venus aspect the Moon with this, he is born [but] then he grows up in the house of strangers.

379-85. Cf. 6.57-9 [ad 372-3]; 6.698-702.

Firmicus, 7.4.5. *Sed et si Luna in IMC, vel in occasu fuerit inventa, et eam de dextro quadrato Saturnus respexerit, aut Mars ex eodem quadrato aut de diametro hos eosdem videat [aut certe de quadrato], servos efficient.*

Θ p. 219.13-14. ἐὰν δὲ τύχῃ ἡ Σελήνη διάμετρος κακοποιοῦ ‹καὶ ὁ κλῆρος αὐτῆς ἀποκλίνῃ›, δούλην λέγε τὴν μητέρα.

Dor.^ARAB I 10.23. If you find the Lord of the triplicity of the ascendent cadent and you find the Moon [with] a malefic opposing it and the Sun in an evil place, the native's parents are slaves.

Dor.^ARAB I 7.10. There is no good for the native in the matter of his upbringing if Saturn and Mars strike the Moon, then especially when the Moon is in a cardine and one of the two malefics aspects it from opposition and the degrees of the ascendant from the degree.

---

373 λατρίης L: corr. H, Hal, D^446   πονέοντα L: corr. D^446: στονόεντα Nauck^V,169
374 ἐλευθέριον L: corr. A: ἦμαρ ἐλεύθερον ἕξει ἀνὴρ ποιητὸς ὀθνείων Herm^716   376 δὲ] τε L:
corr. K   378 χρήμασι καὶ] χρηματίαι L: corr. D^279   ὀθνείων pro suspecto habet S
379 Μήνης L: corr. R   380 πλαγκτοῦ L: corr. R   πορίηι L: corr. Gr, H   381 ἐχθεσίην
L: corr. Gr   ἔσσεται κείνων L: ἔσσετ᾽ ἐκείνων L¹: corr. K   382 ἐλέγχεται, -αι L^1ras
383 ἐκ] καὶ L: corr. A

ἢν δὲ Κύπρις τούτοις προσμαρτυρέουσα γένηται,
ἥσσονες αἱ πατέρων μητρὸς τελέθουσι λοχεῖαι. 385
ἦμος δ' Ἑρμείας Ζηνὸς φάος εἰς ἰσόμοιρον
ὁρμήσῃ, τῆμος μὲν ὁ φυόμενος τότε θνητῶν
σεμνοτάτων γονέων ὀφθήσεται, ᾧ πατρὶ μήτηρ
30ᵛ παρθένος εἰς θαλάμους ζευχθήσεται ἀνδρὸς ἄπειρος,
ἔσται δ' ἐν γενέθλαισι φάος σπανάδελφον ἐσαθρῶν. 390
σχῆμα δ' Ἄρευς ἐπὶ τοῖσιν ὅτ' ἂν πυριμάρμαρος ἀστὴρ
Κύπριδι συννεύσῃ, ἔτι καὶ Κρόνου εἰσορόωντος,
ἢ μετὰ χηρείην μήτηρ πατρὶ τοῦδε συνήξει,
ἢ διὰ μοιχοσύνην δολοεργέα νυμφευθεῖσα.
Ἥλιος δὲ Κρόνοιο καὶ Ἄρεος ἀστέρας ἀθρῶν 395
ἀκτινηβολίῃσι φαεσφόρου Οὐλύμποιο,
ναυσιβάτας φαίνει καὶ ἐν ὕδασι νήκτορας ἄνδρας
ἔσσεσθαι, σκαφέων τε κυβερνητῆρας ἀΰπνους,
πρωράρχους τε νεῶν, οἳ πολλάκι ναυφθορίαισιν
χείματος ὀρνυμένου βίοτον λείψουσι δι' ἅλμης, 400
νηχόμενοι Μοίρης βαιὸν χρόνον ἐν πελάγεσσιν.
Παμφαίνων δ' ἀστὴρ ὁπότ' ἂν πολιοῖο Κρόνοιο
Ἡλίου σελάεσσιν ἀν' οὐρανὸν ᾖ ἰσόμοιρος,
τηνίκα φυομένων βρεφέων γεννήτορα πρῶτον
μητέρος εἰς Ἀΐδην πέμψει νεκυοστόλος Αἶσα, 405
κτήματά τ' ἐξολέσει πατρῴα καὶ πολὺν ὄλβον·
καὶ δὲ κασιγνήτων θανάτους ὁρόωσι προόντων,
πλοῦτον δ' ἐκ θανάτων πολλῶν μέγαν αὐξήσουσιν.

386–90. Cf. 6.124–5.
395–401. Cf. 6.362–5.
Ptol. 4.4.5. ὁ δὲ τοῦ Ἄρεως μετὰ μὲν τοῦ ἡλίου σχηματισθεὶς τοὺς διὰ πυρὸς ἐργαζομένους ποιεῖ... κἂν μὲν ὁ τοῦ Κρόνου αὐτῷ μαρτυρήσῃ ναυτικούς...
Θ p. 216.17–22. λγ'. Περὶ ναυτῶν καὶ κυβερνητῶν. Κρόνος μεσουρανῶν ἐν καθύγρῳ ζῳδίῳ Ἄρεος καὶ Ἡλίου συμμεσουρανούντων ἢ ἐπιθεωρούντων κατὰ τετράγωνον ἢ διάμετρον, ναύτας ποιεῖ ἢ κυβερνήτας ἢ ναυκλήρους, μάλιστα καὶ τοῦ ὡροσκόπου ὄντος ἐν καθύγρῳ ζῳδίῳ ὁρίοις Κρόνου καὶ τοῦ κλήρου τῆς τύχης ἢ τοῦ κυρίου αὐτοῦ.

385 αἱ] Π¹ : ἢ L: ἐκ D⁶⁶⁰   τελέθουσι] Π¹ (iam D⁶⁶⁰): τελέουσι L: θαλέθουσι K   λοχείαις K: τοκειαι Π¹   386 φάος εἰς] φαέεσσ' D⁶⁶¹   εἰς Π¹: ἢ L   387 μὲν] γὰρ Π¹   τότε θνητῶν] θηητῶν K   388 ᾧ] ὡ L: corr. L¹: ὠσ Π¹: οὗ A.-R.ᶜᵒⁿʲ
fo. 30ᵛ
389 θαλάμων Π¹   390 ἔσται Π¹ (iam A): ἔσσεται L   γενέθλαισι, αισ L¹ʳᵃˢ: γενέθλῃσι A.-R.: γενετῆρσι Π¹   ἦσται δ' ἐν μελάθροισι conj. S   ἐσαθρεῖν Halᵐᵍ   391 Ἄρευς] Ἄρης Π¹, L: corr. K   ἀστὴρ] ἔλθῃ Π¹   392 om. Π¹   395 ἀθρῶν] αἴθων Π¹   396 ἀκτεινηβολίαισι Π¹: ἀκτινι- L, corr. L¹   397 ὕδασι νήκτ[ο]ρας Π¹ : ὕδασιν ἥκτορας L: corr. Hal, Gr (in corrigendis, p. 294)

If Venus should be witnessing to these,
The father's is more mean than mother's stock.   385
   When Hermes into like degrees with Zeus
Should speed, the son of man born at that time
Shall be of honourable parents, whose
Mother came virgin to her husband's bed;
For all his birth, few brothers light his life.   390
   When the fiery star of Ares joins to these
Aspect with Venus, Saturn looking on,
Either his mother's widowed when she weds,
Or joined in love through sly adultery.
   When Helios views Cronos' and Ares' stars   395
From bright Olympus emanating rays,
He shows the birth of sailors, those who swim
In water, sleepless guardians of the helm
Or of the prow, who, when ships come to grief
In rising storms, consign life to the waves,   400
Swimming a little time allowed by Fate.
   When hoary Saturn's all-resplendent star
Meets Helios' rays in heaven in like degree,
The father of the infants that are born
Is first despatched by Fate the layer-out   405
And all ancestral goods and wealth are lost;
They see the deaths of brothers born before,
But opportune decease augments their wealth.

402–8. Epit. IV [CCAG ii. p. 189.8–12]. ἐὰν Ἥλιος καὶ Κρόνος ἰσόμοιροι ὁμοῦ ὦσι, τὸν πατέρα προαναιροῦσι καὶ τοὺς προτέρους ἀδελφούς, ποιοῦσι δὲ καὶ κληρονομίας. ὁ Ἥλιος ἐν μοίρᾳ Κρόνου ἐν παντὶ ζῳδίῳ μετὰ κακοποιῶν νεκρὰ ἢ ἐπίσινα δηλοῖ τὰ γεννώμενα καὶ τὸν πατέρα ταχὺ ἀναιρεῖ.
Περὶ σχημ. 96. ὁ Κρόνος σὺν Ἡλίῳ τὸν μὲν πατέρα κακοθάνατον, τὰ δὲ πατρικὰ φθείρει, καὶ πλεῖον τὸ κακὸν ἐν νυκτερινῇ γενέσει εἴτε ἑῷος εἴτε ἑσπέριος· τότε γὰρ οὐ τῷ πατρὶ μόνῳ, ἀλλὰ καὶ τῇ γενέσει ἔσται τὰ δεινά, ἑτέρως δὲ καὶ τοῖς ἀδελφοῖς, καὶ μάλιστα τοῦ Ἡλίου πλειόνων μοιρῶν ὄντος· τότε γὰρ ἀναμφίβολος ἡ βιαιοθανασία τοῦ πατρός, καὶ αὐτοὺς δὲ τοὺς γεννηθέντας ἐκπτώτους καὶ ἐπινόσους καὶ ἐξ ὑγρῶν ὀχλουμένους καὶ τοὺς ὀφθαλμοὺς βλαπτομένους, ἐπὶ δὲ ταῖς γεωργίαις μόνον εὐτυχοῦσιν οἱ τοιοῦτοι· ἐν γὰρ τοῖς ἄλλοις πᾶσι δυστυχεῖς.
Lib. Herm. xxxi. 2. Sol Saturno coniunctus eiusdem condicionis paternorum deminutor fit et laesiones et peregrinationes inducit, in nocte vero deteriora mala facit et patrem ante matrem perimit et paterna corrumpit.

398 om. Π¹ ⟨τε⟩ A.-R.   399 πρωράρχους Π¹: πρωτάρχας L: πρωράτας iam Nauck^{V.169}   οἳ L^{1ras}   ναυφθορίησιν A.-R. (de Π¹ non liquet)   400 ὀρνυμένου βίοτον] ὀλλύμενοι τε βίον Π¹: ὀρνυμένοιο βίον S^{conj}   λίψουσι L: corr. L¹: ζησουσι Π¹   401 Μοίραις A^{conj}, K   402 πολιοῖο] πλαγκτοῖο Π¹   403 ᾗ] ἣν 1.328: ην Π¹   405 μητέρᾱς L^{1sl}: μ]ητρὸς Π¹   ἐς Ἀιδεω Π¹   406 κτήματ' ἀπόλλυσιν Π¹   πολὺν] βαθὺν Π¹   407–8 om. Π¹   407 προόντων] προώρους Nauck^{V.169}: προμοίρων S^{conj}   408 αὐχήσωσιν L: corr. Hal: αὐχήσουσι D^{661}

ἢν δὲ Σεληναίης ἀκτὶς ἰσόμοιρα πελάζῃ
φωτὶ Κρόνου, μάρτυς δ' ἐπὶ σήματι τῷδε γένηται 410
καὶ Πυρόεις, μήτηρ προτέρη πατρὸς ἴξετ' ἐς Ἀίδην,
ἠὲ μογοστοκίῃ δεδαϊγμένη, ἢ διὰ νούσου
ἀμβλωσμοῦ θ', ἃ γυναιξὶ φύσις κρύφιμ' ἄλγε' ἔδωκεν.
Ζεὺς δ' ὅτ' ἂν Ἑρμείην τε καὶ ἱμερτὴν Ἀφροδίτην
ἀκτῖσιν φαέθουσι βάλῃ λαμπραυγέσι κόσμου, 415
αὐτοκασιγνήτας ῥέζει κείνοισι βροτοῖσιν
νύμφας συγγενικάς τε, λοχεύονται δ' ἀπὸ τούτων
ἄνδρες παιδείης ἡγήτορες, ἔν τε καθέδραις
γραμματικαῖς δήμοιο βίον διαποιμαίνοντες.
Ἥλιος δ' ἀκάμας ὁπότ' ἂν Κύπριν Ἄρεϊ κοινῶς 420
ἀκτινηβολίῃσι πυριβλήτοισι καταθρῇ,
γνάπτορας εὐσήμων πέπλων, καὶ τεύκτορας αὐδᾷ
ἱστοπόνους ἔσσεσθαι, ἰδὲ ῥαπτῆρας ἀρίστους
πρηκτῆράς τ' ἀγεληδὸν ἀλωομένους διὰ παντός.
Ἑρμάων δ' ὁπότ' ἂν Δία καὶ Κρόνον ἀγκυλομήτην 425
ἀκτῖσι, στίλβουσι φλογὸς λαμπτῆρσι, πελάζῃ,
νηοπόλους ἱερῆας, ἰδὲ ζακόρους θεοσέπτους,
γραμματέας, τεμενῶν τε προφήτορας ἄνδρας ἀϋτεῖ
ἔσσεσθαι σηκῶν τε νεωκορίῃσι μέλοντας 430
μυστιπόλους, ἱερῶν τε προϊσταμένους στεφανηδόν. 429

31ʳ ὁππότε δ' ἂν Κυθέρειαν ἐν ἀκτίνεσσι βολαυγῇ,
Ἀρεά τ' αὖ πυρόεντα βραδὺς Κρόνος, οἱ τότε φύντες
γειοπόνοι ζήσουσι φυτοσπορίας ἀγαπῶντες
ὀθνείης χώρης τε καὶ οἰκείης διὰ παντός·
λήψονται δὲ λέχη δίχα γράμματος, οὐχὶ νόμοισιν, 435
ἐκ μετεωροσύνης δὲ συναντήσαντες ὁμεύνοις.

409-13. Epit. IV [CCAG ii. p. 189.12–14]. ἐὰν δὲ Κρόνος γένηται τῇ Σελήνῃ ἰσόμοιρος, τὴν μητέρα προαναιρεῖ, εἰ δὲ καὶ Ἄρης ἐπιθεωρήσῃ, ποιεῖ τὸν θάνατον ἢ ἀπὸ δυστοκίας ἢ κρυπτῶν ἀσθενειῶν.
Περὶ σχημ. 100. ὁ Κρόνος σὺν Σελήνῃ ἀδρανεῖς καὶ τὰ μητρικὰ φθείροντας, αὐτούς τε ἐπινόσους καὶ τὰς αὐτῶν μητέρας.
420-4. Cf. 6.431-5.
Θ p. 216.23-5. μδ'. Περὶ ῥαπτῶν. Ἄρης καὶ Ἀφροδίτη ὁμοῦ ἢ τετράγωνοι ἐν ὁρίοις ἀλλήλων ποιοῦσι ῥάπτας, λινούφους, ὀθονιακούς.

---

409 ἀκτεὶς Π^1 410 δ'] τ' Π^1 411 προτέρι L: corr. L^1 412 δεδαμασμένη Π^1 413 ἀμβλωσμοῦ θ'] ἀμβλώσσους δ' L: corr. K: αι]μηρης Π^1 (suppl. Rea), cf. 1.338 αἰμηρῆισι   ἀγυναιξὶ L   φύσις] κύπρις L: corr. iam K   κρύφιμα Π^1 414 Ἑρμείαν K εἱμερτὴν Π^1, necnon L ut vid.: ἱμερ- L^{1ras} κρύφιμ' ἄλγε L: -ν add. L^1 418 παιδίης L: corr. H, Hal   419 διαποιμένοντες L: corr. H, Gr: δαπο [....] τε[Π^1 421 ἀκτινηβολίῃσι] βλήθροισι Π^1 καταθρῇ] κατ' αἴθρης Π^1 422 εὐνήτων A.-R.^{conj}: εὐσχήμων Nauck$^{IV.163-4}$: εὐπήνων S^{conj} αὐδᾷ] αὐτῶν L: corr. Massimilla, Prometheus, 46 (2020), 271   423 ἔσεσθαι L: corr. H, Gr   ἰδὲ ῥαπτῆρας] ego: ἰδ' ἡγητῆρας L: ἰδὲ σμητῆρας K, qui et πλυντῆρας conj.   426 ἀκτῖσιν στίλβουσιν L: corr. H, Gr (στίλβουσι)   427 θεοσέπτους] θεολήπτους A.-R.

>   If Selene's ray comes near in like degree
>   To Saturn's light, and Mars joins witness too,   410
>   Before the sire the mother will succumb
>   Rent by the pangs of labour, or disease,
>   Or feticide, nature's dark female pangs.
>   When Zeus strikes Hermes and lovely Venus
>   With radiant rays bright with the cosmos' beams,   415
>   The very sisters of the men born then
>   Become their brides, kinswomen; from them spring
>   Leaders of culture, who from teachers' chairs
>   On public life have civilising sway.
>   When the tireless Sun descries the Cyprian   420
>   Jointly with Mars with missile rays of fire,
>   It speaks of those who full and make plush robes,
>   Who work on looms, are experts with the thread,
>   And those who swarm abroad to sell their wares.
>   When Hermes' rays meet Jupiter and him   425
>   Of crooked counsel with bright-gleaming rays,
>   Priests who tend shrines and holy sacristans,
>   Prophets and scribes in sanctuaries are foretold,
>   Devoted temple-wardens, mystagogues,   430
>   The chiefs of shrines who wear a holy crown(?).   429
>   When both the Cytherean with her beams
>   And also fiery Mars slow Saturn strikes,
>   The natives till the ground, loving to plant
>   The seed through others' land, and in their own.
>   Their unions are lacking script or law,   435
>   In adventitious couplings finding mates.

425–30. Cf. 6.436–8.
Ptol. 4.4.3. ὁ μὲν γὰρ τοῦ Ἑρμοῦ τὸ πράσσειν παρέχων, ὡς ἄν τις εἴποι τυπωδῶς, ποιεῖ... μάντεις, ἀστρολόγους, θύτας...
Ptol. 4.4.10. ἐὰν ἡ σελήνη τὸν πρακτικὸν τόπον ἐπισχῇ τὸν ἀπὸ συνόδου δρόμον ποιουμένη σὺν τῷ τοῦ Ἑρμοῦ, ἐν μὲν τῷ Ταύρῳ καὶ Αἰγοκέρωτι καὶ Καρκίνῳ ποιεῖ μάντεις, θύτας, λεκανομάντεις. ἐν δὲ Τοξότῃ καὶ Ἰχθύσιν νεκρομάντεις καὶ δαιμόνων κινητικούς, ἐν δὲ Παρθένῳ καὶ Σκορπίῳ μάγους, ἀστρολόγους, ἀποφθεγγομένους, προγνώσεις ἔχοντας, ἐν δὲ Ζυγῷ καὶ Κριῷ καὶ Λέοντι θεολήπτους, ὀνειροκρίτας, ἐξορκιστάς.

Θ pp. 214.22–215.2. πϛ΄. Περὶ μαθηματικῶν ἢ μάντεων. Ἐὰν ὁ Ἑρμῆς ἐν καλῷ τόπῳ τύχῃ, μάλιστα καὶ Κρόνου οἴκῳ, ἔξαυγος καὶ θεωρηθῇ ὑπὸ Διὸς καὶ Κρόνου καὶ Ἄρεος, ποιεῖ ἀστρολόγους, μάντεις ἢ ἱερεῖς.

431–6. Cf. 6.487–90.

---

428 αὖτι L: corr. L¹   430 hunc versum post 441 transmissum, post 428 inserendum indicavit L¹, Hal^mg (post 429 iam A.-R. transposuerunt); in hoc loco servavit Π¹

fo. 31^r

431 ἀκτείνεϛϛ[ι]ν Π¹   433 ζήσωσι L: corr. D^661   434 οἰκίης L: corr. L¹
435 λή[.]ψονται L: λήμψ- L^ac ut vid.

Κύπριν δ' ἀφρογένειαν ἑλιξοπόρον τε Σελήνην
πυρσοβόλοις ἀκτῖσι βαλὼν τευχεσφόρος Ἄρης
μηχανικοὺς τεύχει τε καὶ ὀργανοπήκτορας ἄνδρας,
τεκτοσύνης τ' ἄρχοντας, ἰδ' αὐτοδίδακτα τέχνῃσιν 440
θαύματα δαιδάλλοντας, ἐν ἀλκήεντί τε θυμῷ
ἐργοπόνους παλάμαισι καὶ ἁδροτάτους καὶ ἀρίστους
ἀχθοφόρους, καμάτων τε πόνους εἰς τέρψιν ἄγοντας.
   τούτοις δ' Ἑρμείας φαύλοις ἐν σχήμασιν ὀφθεὶς
μυθολόγους τεύχει καὶ αἰσχεορήμονας ἄνδρας, 445
μωρολόγους, χλεύης θ' ἡγήτορας, ὑβριγέλωτας,
ἔν τ' ἀρεταλογίῃ μυθεύματα ποικίλ' ἔχοντας,
ψηφάων παίκτας τε καὶ ἐξ ὄχλοιο πορισμῶν
ῥεμβηδὸν ζώοντας, ἀλήμονας ἧς χθονὸς αἰεί.
   Ἢν δὲ Κύπρις Μήνη τε σὺν Ἡελίῳ τε καὶ Ἑρμῇ 450
μάρτυρες ἀλλήλων μέσον οὐρανὸν ἀμφιπολῶσιν,
ἠδ' ἐν ζῳδίοισι διμορφώτοισι πέλωνται,
Ἰχθύσιν ἢ Διδύμοισι συνωρίζουσι κατ' αἴθρην,
Τοξότεω κατὰ κύκλον ἢ ἐς σταχυηφόρον ἁγνὴν
Παρθενικήν, τῆμος διδυμάτοκα φύσεται ἀνδρῶν 455
σώματα καὶ τριδύμων παίδων θαυμαστὰ γένεθλα·

437-43. Cf. 6.398-404.
Lib. Herm. xxvi. 62. *Luna in ascendente cum Mercurio vel in occidente vel in medio caeli vel in angulo terrae matris rationalibilis natos ostendit; maxime si Iupiter aspexerit aut Luna plena cum Mercurio et Iove iungatur, matris divitis et ipsos mechanicos vel instrumentorum annexores vel statuarum plasmatores, amicitias habentes cum magnatibus viris.*
   Ptol. 4.4.6. πάλιν δὲ δύο τῶν τὰς πράξεις παρεχομένων εὑρεθέντων ἐὰν μὲν ὁ τοῦ Ἑρμοῦ καὶ τῆς Ἀφροδίτης λάβωσι τὴν οἰκοδεσποτείαν, ἀπὸ μούσης καὶ ὀργάνων καὶ μελῳδιῶν ἢ ποιημάτων καὶ ῥυθμῶν ποιοῦσι τὰς πράξεις καὶ μάλιστα ὅταν τοὺς τόπους ὦσιν ἀμφιλελαχότες· ἀποτελοῦσι γὰρ θυμελικούς, ὑποκριτάς, σωματεμπόρους, ὀργανοποιούς...
   Θ p. 213.9-12. Ἑρμῆς καὶ Ἀφροδίτη τὴν πρᾶξιν παρέχοντες ποιοῦσι τὰς πράξεις ἀπὸ μουσικῆς καὶ ὀργάνων καὶ μελῳδιῶν ἢ ποιημάτων ἢ ὀρχήσεων καὶ ῥυθμῶν, καὶ μάλιστα ὅταν τοὺς τόπους ὦσιν ἐναλλάξαντες. ἀποτελοῦσιν οὖν θυμελικούς, ὑποκριτάς, σωματεμπόρους, ὀργανοποιούς...
   Θ p. 211.10-11. Ἄρης τὸ πράσσειν παρέχων καὶ μαρτυρῶν ἢ ὡροσκοπῶν ποιεῖ λαξευτὰς ἢ τέκτονας ἢ λιθοέργους.
   Ptol. 4.4.5. χωρὶς δὲ τοῦ ἡλίου τυχὼν [sc. ὁ τοῦ Ἄρεως] τοὺς διὰ σιδήρου οἷον ναυπηγούς, τέκτονας, γεωργούς, λατόμους, λιθοξόους, λαοξόους, λιθουργούς, ξυλοσχίστας, ὑπουργούς.

---

442 παλάμῃσι A.-R.   ἀνδροτάτους L: corr. D[322,661]   443 τέψιν L: corr. L[1sl]   444 ἐν] σὺν L: corr. K   445 ‹τε› dub. Ger[163], R   αἰσχρεορήμονας L: corr. K   447 ποικίλ' ἔχοντας] ποικίλλοντας S[conj]   448 ψηφίδων K[2conj]   πέκτας L: corr. Gr   449 ῥεμβηδὸν] ego: βομβηδὸν L: ῥομβηδὸν A.-R.[conj]   452 ἠδ' ἐν] ἢν μὲν L: corr. K   πέλονται L: corr. A.-R.   453 αἴθρῃ L: corr. Hal, D[374] (qui et κατ' αἴθρης conj.)

> The foam-born Cypris and the deviant Moon
> When struck by torch-like rays of warlike Mars
> Make artisans, builders of instruments,
> Masters of carpentry, and self-moved machines   440
> Contrived as wonders, and, with sturdy hearts,
> Workers by hand, most strapping and robust
> Porters who turn their labours to delight.
> 　By these aspected poorly, Mercury
> Makes story-tellers, men of shameful speech,   445
> Stage fools, leaders of jest, outrageous clowns,
> Who fabricate assorted famous yarns,
> Conjure with pebbles, and from popular doles
> Live as eternal nomads from their land.
> 　If Venus, Moon, and Mercury with the Sun   450
> Tenant Midheaven, witness each to each,
> And occupy the double-bodied signs,
> The Fish or Twins, conjoint in the clear sky,
> In the Archer's Circle, or the Holy Maid
> Who bears the sheaf, then double births of men   455
> And even threefold prodigies take place:

Θ p. 211.27–9. χωρὶς δὲ Ἡλίου ἑστὼς τοὺς διὰ σιδήρου τὰς ἐνεργείας ἔχοντας, ναυπηγούς, τέκτονας, γεωργούς, λατόμους, λιθοξόους, λιθουργούς, ξυλοσχίστας.
　Ptol. 3.14.5. [ἐφ' Ἑρμοῦ καὶ Ἀφροδίτης] ὀργανικάς, μηχανικάς, θαυματοποιούς…
　Θ p. 217.1–3 ἧε΄. Περὶ μηχανικῶν καὶ ψηφάδων. Ἑρμῆς καὶ Ἄρης καὶ Ἀφροδίτη καὶ Σελήνη ἐπίκεντροι ἢ ἐπιθεωροῦντες ἀλλήλους κατὰ κέντρον, μηχανικοὺς ποιοῦσι.
　444–9. Ptol. 3.14.29. τῷ δὲ τῆς Ἀφροδίτης συνοικειωθεὶς [sc. ὁ τοῦ Ἄρεως ἀστὴρ] ἐπὶ μὲν ἐνδόξων διαθέσεων ποιεῖ ἐπιχάριτας, εὐδιαγώγους, φιλεταίρους, ἡδυβίους, εὐφροσύνους, παιγνιώδεις, ἀφελεῖς, εὐρύθμους, φιλορχηστάς, ἐρωτικούς, φιλοτέκνους, μιμητικούς, ἀπολαυστικούς…
　Θ p. 217.5–7. ἧϛ΄. Περὶ μίμων. Ἑρμῆς καὶ Ἀφροδίτη ταπεινούμενοι ἐν ὁρίοις ἰδίοις ἢ ἀλλήλων μίμους…
　450–6. Cf. 6.249–51.
　Lib. Herm. xxxiv. 39. *Luna cum fuerit in domo Mercurii et Sol cum aliquo de planetis in terminis Iovis ac Mercurii in bicorpore signo in angulis, bigamus erit. Semper enim luminaria in terminis Iovis vel Mercurii in signis multi seminis plura generant et in bicorporibus ‹in› angulis.*

---

454 ἠὲ σταχ. L: corr. Gr　　455 διδυματοκαταφυσετ᾽ L: corr. D[336,374]　　διδυμήτοκα Lob. *Phryn.*[661], Schneider ad Call. *Hymn* 2.54

κἢν μὲν Ζηνὶ Κύπρις κατὰ φῶς ἰσόμοιρον ἐνεχθῇ,
ἄρσενες ἔσσονται δισσοὶ γένει, ἄμμιγα δ' αὐτοῖς
κούρη ἀπ' ὠδίνων τεχθήσεται ἐσχατόωσα·
Οὐρανίδου δὲ Κρόνοιο θεωροσύνην ἐπέχοντος,   460
θηλυγενὴς διδύμων ἔσται τόκος ἄρσενος ἐκτός·
ἐν κακοδαιμοσύνῃ δ' Ἄρεος κατεναντία Μήνης
μαρμαρυγὰς φαίνοντος, ὁ τικτόμενος τότε θνητῶν
σῶμα περισσομελὴς τεχθήσεται, ἔκμετρα γυῖα
πὰρ φύσιν ἡμερίην δεικνὺς μερόπεσσιν ἀθρῆσαι.   465
Ὁππότε δ' εἰν ἀγαθοῖσι τόποις στείχωσι κατ' αἴθρην
Ἄρης πυρσοτόκος θ' εἰλιξόπορός τε Σελήνη,
τεύχουσιν σοβαροὺς πολυΐστορας ἄνδρας ὑπουργούς,
ἡγεμόνων φιλίῃσι γεγηθότας, ἀμφὶ δὲ μισθῷ
πουλυπλανεῖς ξενίαισιν ἀρήια λήματ' ἔχοντας,   470
καὶ πάσης στρατιῆς ἐπιβήτορας ἐν προκοπαῖσιν.

ἢν δὲ Κρόνου βλαβεραυγὲς ἐς Ἄρεα φέγγος ἀθρήσῃ,
δισσὰ δ' ἐναντιόωντα φανῇ σελαγίσματα τῶνδε,
τῆμος ὅσοις γενεὴ μεροπήιος ἄρχεται ἀνδρῶν,
ἐν κακοδαιμοσύνῃ καματώδεϊ πᾶσα βιώσει,   475
νουσομελεῖς τεύχουσα βροτούς, ὀδύνῃσι συνήθεις,
κινδύνων βλαβερῶν τε δυσεκφεύκτων τε παρέδρους.

457–61. Cf. 6.252–5.
Lib. Herm. xxxiv. 40. Et si Iuppiter, Saturnus et Mercurius in angulis occidentales in signo bicorpore ‹sunt›, tres erunt, feminae duae et masculus unus; si vero orientales, masculi duo et femina una.
462–5. Lib. Herm. xxxiv. 40. Luna, Sol et Mercurius cum locati fuerint in signis multi seminis, Iove existente remoto, tria monstra faciunt.
472–7. Περὶ σχημ. 63. ὁ Κρόνος Ἄρην διαμετρῶν, περιστάσεσι βιωτικοῖς περιπίπτουσι καὶ ἐναντιώμασι χαλεποῖς καὶ φθόνοις καὶ ἐνδείαις καὶ σωματικαῖς ὀχλήσεσι καὶ κινδύνοις ζωῆς τε καὶ τέκνων.
Cf. Περὶ κράσ. 62. σωματικὰς κακώσεις καὶ κινδύνους ζωῆς ... ἐκ πόνων πόνους ἤτοι ἐκ μόχθων μόχθους.
Firmicus, 6.15.4. Si Saturnus et Mars diametra se radiatione respexerint, et in contrariis constituti locis longa se invicem virium suarum potestate pulsaverint et corpus assiduis aegritudinum et assiduis laborum faciet continuationibus fatigari.

458 ἄρρενες L: corr. K   459 ὠδείνων L[ac] ut vid.: corr. L[1ras]   460 οὐρανίου L (per compendium): corr. D[661]   462 Ἄρεως L: corr. A.–R.   465 φύσιν L, -ν L[1ras]   467 θ' εἰλιξ-] ἰδ' ἑλιξ- L: corr. A.–R.   468 σωβαροὺς L: corr. H, Gr   ὑπουργούς] ὑπὲρ γῆν L: corr. K: ἐννοῦς S[conj]   469 μισθῷ] κόσμωι L: corr. K   470 ξενίῃσιν A.–R.   λή[μ]ματ' L[1sl]

Should Venus' light equate with Zeus' degrees,
Two offspring will be male, but linked with them
A girl, last of the birth-pangs, will emerge.
If Uranus' son Cronos aspects too, 460
Twin females will be born, besides one male.
With Mars in the Evil Demon shining rays
Contrary to the Moon, that son of man
Shall have redundant body-parts, spare limbs,
A monstrous sight for mortals to behold. 465
    When in good places in the radiant sky
The torch-bright Mars and wandering Moon progress,
They make men fearless, knowing, quick to act,
Enjoying rulers' friendships, and for pay
Roaming abroad with martial temperament, 470
Of every regiment the advance guard.
    If Saturn's harmful beams are turned to Mars,
And their twin phosphorescence stands opposed,
The human lives inaugurated then
Will pass in every harsh adversity, 475
Sickly of limb, companions of distress,
Exposed to harmful dangers, hard to flee.

fo. 31ᵛ
471 προκοπῇσιν A.–R.   472 ἐς Ἄρεα] εἰς αἰθέρα L: corr. Hal^{mg}   473 ἐναντίον ἄστρα
L: corr. K   ἐναντίον ἄστρα...σελαγίσμασι A^{conj}   δισσὰ δ' ἔναντα φανῇ ἄστρων σελαγίσματα
τῶνδε R^{conj}   474 μεροπηιας L: corr. R   476 νουσωμελεῖς L^{ac}: corr. L^{1ras}   συνήθεις
L^{1sl}

Μήνη δ' ἀμφίκερως σκολιόδρομος ἡνίκ' ἂν ὀφθῇ
Ἄρεος εἰς τετράγωνα πόλου λοξεύματα βᾶσα,
ἢν δ' ἐπὶ δυομένῳ κατὰ γῆς ἀπὸ τέρμονος αἴθρης 480
Στίλβων ἀμφ' αὐτοῖς ἢ καὶ διάμετρος ὁραθῇ
ζωιδίῳ κόσμοιο, κακοὺς ληίστορας ἄνδρας
ἐκφύσει, θυρέτρων ἐπανοίκτορας ὀθνειάων,
κλεπτῆρας φαύλους, νυκτοπλανέας τε λαθραίους·
οὗτοι φωρηθέντες ἐν ἀλλοτρίοισι μελάθροις 485
⟨ εἰς συνοχὰς ἥξουσι σιδηρήεντά τε δεσμά ⟩, 485a
εἱρκτὰς δ' οἰκήσουσι φυλασσόμενοι ἁλυσηδόν,
ἔν τε βιαιοτάτῳ θανάτῳ βίον ἐκλείψουσιν,
ἢ φοβεροῖς ξίφεσιν δεδαϊγμένοι ἢ πελέκεσσιν,
ἢ βρόχον ἀλγινόεντα δι' αὐχένος ἐκδήσαντες
πνεῦμα λυγρὸν λείψουσι πικρῆς Μοίρης ὑπ' ἀνάγκῃ. 490
    Κύπρις δ' ἀφρογένεια βροτῶν ὡροσκόπα φέγγη
δερκομένη, θήσει μὲν ἐν εἰλαπίναις φιλομούσους,
ἡδυπότας, θιάσων κωμάστορας, ἔκ τε γυναικῶν
ὀθνείων στοργαῖσι κεκασμένα φίλτρα φέροντας,
μοιχείας τ' ἀγαπῶντας, ἐν αἷς ὕβρις, οὐ κύπρις ἄρχει. 495

478-90. Cf. 6.499-503.

Firmicus, 4.14.7. *A Mercurio defluens Luna si feratur ad Martem, in diurna genitura, et sit Luna crescens vel plena luminibus, faciet irreligiosos, periuros, fallaces et quorum malitia ad omne facinus per dies singulos crescat. Erunt effractores, fures, et qui templa sacrilego furore semper expilent, erunt latrones, homicidae, et ad neces hominum semper armati; sed in his comprehensi facinoribus custodiae vinculis carcerisque traduntur, et gladio severa iudicis animadversione plectuntur aut quolibet genere ob haec facinora biothanata morte depereunt.*

Valens, II 17.57-8. [Ἑρμῆς Ἄρει τρίγωνος ἢ δεξιὸς ἑξάγωνος] γίνονται δὲ καὶ κλῶπες καὶ ἐπίορκοι καὶ ἀσεβεῖς καὶ ἐπίβουλοι τῶν ὁμοίων, αἰσχροκερδεῖς, ἀποστερηταί, ἁπλῶς οὐδὲν ἔχοντες ἐλεύθερον, ὅθεν κακοῖς πλείστοις περικυλίονται καὶ ἐπαγωγῆς ἢ φυγαδείας ἢ συνοχῆς πεῖραν λαμβάνουσιν. [58] μάλιστα δὲ ἐν τοῖς ἀχρηματίστοις ζῳδίοις ἢ μοίραις τυχόντες χείρονα ἀποτελοῦσιν, ἐν δὲ τῷ ὑπὸ γῆν ἢ δύνοντι ἀμφότεροι ἢ ἐὰν ὃς μὲν δύνῃ, ὃς δὲ ὑπὸ γῆν τύχῃ, φόνους ἐπιτελοῦσιν ἢ συνίστορες ἔσονται καὶ ἀπὸ ληστείας τὸν βίον διάγοντες, ἔνιοι δὲ καὶ ἀδελφοκτονοῦσιν, καὶ βιαία ἔσται ἡ ἐσχάτη αὐτῶν τελευτή, μάλιστα ἐὰν καὶ τὴν Σελήνην προσλάβωνται· βιαιοθάνατοι γὰρ καὶ ἄταφοι γίνονται.

Valens, II 10.5. εἰ δὲ ὁ τοῦ Ἑρμοῦ σὺν τῷ Ἄρει ἐπὶ τὸ δυτικὸν τύχῃ ζῴδιον, λῃσταῖς καὶ φόνοις συνιστορήσει, διὸ κακῷ θανάτῳ ἀπολοῦνται ὕστερον.

Θ p. 211.14-16. ὁ Ἄρης καὶ ἡ Σελήνη καὶ ⟨ἡ⟩ Ἀφροδίτη ἐπικείμενοι ποιοῦσι λῃστὰς καὶ θυρεπανοίκτας.

Ptol. 4.4.7. κἂν ὁ τοῦ Κρόνου αὐτοῖς [sc. τῷ τοῦ Ἑρμοῦ καὶ τῷ τοῦ Ἄρεως] μαρτυρήσῃ, φονέας, λωποδύτας, ἅρπαγας, λῃστάς, ἀπελάτας, ῥᾳδιουργούς...

Θ p. 212.5-6. κἂν ὁ τοῦ Κρόνου αὐτοῖς μαρτυρήσῃ, φονέας, ἅρπαγας, ἀπελάτας, λῃστάς.

Θ p. 192.20-3. Σελήνη καὶ Ἄρης καὶ Ἑρμῆς ἐπίκεντροι τυχόντες δίχα Διὸς καὶ Ἀφροδίτης ποιοῦσι λῃστάς, κλέπτας, θυρεπανοίκτας· εἰ δὲ καὶ Κρόνος ὢν ἐν τῷ ὑπογείῳ τούτους ἐπιθεωρήσει, τυμβωρύχους ποιεῖ.

---

479 Ἄρεως L: corr. H, A.-R.   481 Στίλβων δ' L: corr. Gr   αὐτοῖς ἢ] αὐτοῖσι L: corr. Hal[mg], D[315,336]   483 θυρέων K[2conj] (p. xxx)   ἐπανύκτορας L: corr. H[h]   ὀθνιάων L: corr. H, Hal   485 φωραθέντες L: corr. A.-R.   ⟨ in marg. sin. L   485a ex 1.313 suppl. Hal, K   486 οἰκήσωσιν L: corr. Hal, D[661] (iam -σι H, Gr)   ἁλυσηδόν L: corr. K   487 ἐκλίψουσιν L: corr. L[1]

> When the horned Moon's seen in her meandering path
> In heaven's convolutions square with Mars,
> And if at the descending edge of heaven   480
> Mercury's seen nearby, or in a sign
> On the opposed side of the cosmos, bandits vile
> Are born, forcers of other people's doors,
> Base thieves and furtive wanderers by night,
> Who, apprehended in another's home,   485
> ⟨End in confinement and in iron chains⟩,   485a
> And live in prison bound with manacles,
> And perish by a sanguinary death,
> Cloven by fearsome swords, or by the axe,
> Or tying a grievous noose around their necks
> They'll quit a wretched life though grim duress.   490
>   When foam-born Cypris sights the rays of birth
> On the Horoscope, then urbane dinner-guests
> Are born, tipplers and roisterers, and from strange
> Females acquiring philtres charged with lust,
> Prone to affairs where outrage rules, not love.   495

Θ p. 215.8–11. πη′. Περὶ νεκρεπαρτῶν. Κρόνος ἰσόμοιρος Ἄρει καὶ Ἑρμῇ, θεωρούντων τὰ δωδεκατημόρια ἀλλήλων δίχα τῆς τῶν ἀγαθοποιῶν θεωρίας, νεκροτάφους ἢ νεκροθάπτας ἢ νεκρεπάρτας ἢ τυμβωρύχους ποιοῦσι.

Θ p. 201.2–5. ἐὰν ὁ Ἀναβιβάζων τύχῃ ἐν τῷ ὀγδόῳ τόπῳ ‹καὶ› ἐπιθεωρήσωσι Ἄρης καὶ Κρόνος καὶ Ἑρμῆς, βιαιοθανασίαν ποιοῦσι· ἢ γὰρ ἀποκεφαλίζονται ἢ ἀνασκολοπίζονται.

Firmicus, 3.11.12–13. *In octavo loco ab horoscopo Mercurius cum Marte partiliter constitutus: si per diem sic fuerit inventus... Quidam vero erunt insani ac furiosi; alii in custodia coiciuntur aut damnabuntur ad finiunt frequenti ratione biothanati.* [13] *Si vero per noctem in hoc loco fuerint inventi... erunt fures aut effractores... sed mors eis cum violentia aut cum quibusdam tormentis gravibus proveniet, aut moriuntur gravis insaniae vitio laborantes.*

Firmicus, 6.31.64. *Si in VIII. ab horoscopo loco Mars et Mercurius simul fuerint collocati, malos fures efficient.*

Firmicus, 7.23.3. *Sed et si Mars, in cardinibus constitutus, vel in anaforis cardinum positus, per quadratum Lunam crescentem de loco superiore videat, nec benivolae radius respicit, biothanatum simili ratione perficiet. Et sicut frequenter diximus, secundum differentiam signorum exitus decernitur mortis. In humanis enim signis gladio mors inferetur aut a latronibus aut in pugna aut [in] aliqua licentia potestatis...* cf. 7.23.1.

Θ p. 202.4–6. ἡ Σελήνη μεστὴ ὑπὸ Ἄρεος δεκατευομένη ἐν τοῖς μελεοκοπουμένοις ζῳδίοις δία Διὸς καὶ Ἀφροδίτης βιαιοθανάτους ποιεῖ.

Θ p. 202.9–10. ὁ Ἑρμῆς ἐναντιούμενος τῇ πανσελήνῳ καὶ ὑπὸ κακοποιῶν θεωρούμενος βιαιοθανάτους ποιεῖ.

Critodemus, CCAG v/2. 112.34–8 / Valens, IV 25.11. Ἄρεως δὲ καὶ Ἑρμοῦ ἐπόντων ἢ ἐπιμαρτυρούντων ἢ παραλαμβανόντων τὸν χρόνον κακούργων πραγμάτων ἢ λῃστρικῶν ἐρῶσι· γίνονται γὰρ πλαστογράφοι ἅρπαγες θυρεπανοῖκται κυβευταὶ τεθηριωμένην τὴν διάνοιαν ἔχοντες.

491–5. Cf. 4.59–64.

---

488 φονίοις K²   ξίφεσι L: corr. H, A.-R.   490 λυγρὸν] πικρὸν L: corr. K: φίλον Nauck^IV,165   λίψουσι L: corr. L¹   492 ἐνὶ λαπίναις L: corr. Gr   494 στοργῇσι A.-R.

Ζεὺς δ᾽ ὁπότ᾽ ἂν φαέθων ὡροσκόπον ὄμμα τιταίνῃ,
εὐμόρφους τε τίθησι καὶ εὐτυχέας καὶ ἐπόλβους,
ἔν τ᾽ ἀρχαῖς πλειστῇσι πάτρης τὰ βέβαια φρονοῦντας.
τούτῳ δ᾽ εὖτ᾽ ἂν Ἄρης μίγδην ἰκέλῃσι πορείαις
σχηματίσῃ κατὰ κόσμον, ἰχνοβλαβέας, φθινοκώλους,   500
νευρονόσους, ποδαγρούς, ἀχθήμονας ἄνδρας ἀϋτεῖ
ἔσσεσθαι, κατὰ μικρὰ νεκρούμενα δάκτυλ᾽ ἔχοντας.
θηλυγενεῖς δὲ γυναῖκες, ἐπὴν Κρόνος ὡρονομήσῃ,
φύσονται λαμπραί, βαθυχρήμονες, ὀλβομέλαθροι,
ἀξιοπιστοσύνῃ μεμελημέναι, ἀλλὰ πρὸς ἄνδρας   505
παγκοίνως ζήσουσιν ἐπίψογα νύκτας ἄγουσαι,
ἀλλοτρίου θαλάμου κέρδει βίον ἰθύνουσαι.
Ἥλιος δ᾽ ἀκάμας, πυρόεν σέλας, ἡνίκ᾽ ἂν ἔλθῃ
ἀρσενικοῖς ζῴοισι κατ᾽ αἰθέρος ἠερόπλαγκτον
ζωφορίην, θήλεια δ᾽ ἔχῃ νεολαμπέα Μήνην,   510
τῆμος ὅσοι φύσονται, ἐν ἀνθρώποισι κράτιστοι
ἄνδρες, ἀριστοπονῆες, ἐλεύθερα λήματ᾽ ἔχοντες,
εὔσημοι γενεήν, ἀγαθοὶ φύσιν, ἀξιόμορφοι,
δοξοφόροι, πάτρης κηδέστορες ἰθυδίκαιοι.
ἢν δέ τ᾽ ἐναλλάξωσι, Σεληναίη μὲν ἐπ᾽ ἄρσεν,   515
Ἥλιος δ᾽ ἐπὶ θῆλυ πολυζῴοισιν ἐν ἄστροις,
νωχελέες τε πέλουσι, καὶ ἄπρηκτοι καὶ ἄτολμοι,
πηρώσει ψυχῆς νενεφωμένα βουλεύοντες.
αὐτὰρ ἐπὴν ἐς θῆλυ καταντήσωσιν ἰόντες
ἀμφότεροι, Μήνης τετελεσμένα τερμοδρομούσης,   520
πουλυπλανεῖς, ξενίης ἐπιβήτορας ἄνδρας ἔσεσθαι
αὐδῶσιν, χαίροντας ἀεὶ μεταβλήμασι χώρης,
καὶ πόλεως σπουδαῖα πρὸς ὀθνείους φορέοντας,
ἤθεα καὶ τιμῇ μεμετρημένα πράγματ᾽ ἔχοντας,
εἰς ἰδίην δὲ πάτρην ψογερὸν βίον ἰθύνοντας,   525
οἰκείων ἔργων ἐπιλήσμονας, οὐχὶ θυραίων.

496-8. Cf. 4.35-6, 38-43.
508-14. Cf. 3.365-8, 5.209-10.
515-18. Cf. 3.372-5, 376-9; Epit. II (CCAG i. 145.19-20) ἀτόλμους.

498 πλειστισι L: corr. L¹   502 ἔσεσθαι L: corr. L¹   νεκρούμεν L: corr. L¹
506 ἄγουσαι, -αι L¹ʳᵃˢ   507 ἀλλοτρίους θαλάμους L: corr. D⁵⁵⁵: ἀλλοτρίοις θαλάμοις
A.-R.   509 ἱερόπλαγκτον L: corr. D³⁶¹   510 ἔχηι νεο-, -ι ν L¹ʳᵃˢ   Μήνη L: corr. D³⁶¹
fo. 32ʳ
513 γενεήν τ᾽ L: τ᾽ del. A.-R.   514 ἰθυδίκαιοι] ἠδὲ βίαιοι L: corr. K: ἠδὲ βέβαιοι D³¹⁵: ἠδὲ
δίκαιοι Aᶜᵒⁿʲ   515 ἄρρεν L: corr. K   516 ἐν] ἐπ᾽ L: corr. K

When Phaethon Zeus tends horoscopic eye
He makes the handsome, fortunate, and blessed,
The mainstays of their country's offices.

When Ares joins with him in like career
Upon the cosmic path, then halt, or lame, 500
Or nerve-sick, gouty, ailing men are born,
Their fingers necrotising inch by inch.

Daughters of Eve, when Saturn's in the Hour,
Are born distinguished, rich, of happy homes.
Their honour's true, but with regard to men 505
They live promiscuous lives, spend scandalous nights,
Profit from others' beds their guiding rule.

When the fiery glare of the untiring Sun
Goes in male signs through the aether's aerial path
And a female sign contains the Moon's new light, 510
Those born at that time are the mightiest men,
Most efficacious, having liberal souls,
Of noble race, fine stature, handsome form,
The just and glorious guardians of their homes.

But if they swap, the Moon in a male sign, 515
The Sun a female 'mid the figured stars,
They're sluggish, unavailing, faint of heart,
Dim souls in vaporous musings occupied.

But if it's in a female sign that both
Are lodged, the Moon reaching its ordained bounds, 520
They foretell migrants, wanderers abroad,
Rejoicing in the constant change of place,
Bearing their city's chief affairs afield,
Their conduct, their affairs, by honour ruled,
But in their own homelands not free from blame, 525
Minding external business, not their own.

519–26. Cf. 3.376–9.

519 εἰς K   καταντήσουσιν L: corr. L^{1sl} ἰόντες, ἰ L^{1ras} 523 πόλιος A.-R.
524 τιμὴν L: corr. K   526 οὐχὶ θυραίων] ἄγχι θυραων L^{mg}

ὁππότε δ' ἀρσενικοῖς δισσοὶ μίγα φεγγοβολῶσιν
ζωιδίοις κατὰ χῶρον ἀνάστερον, οἳ τότ' ἔσονται
τολμηροί, θρασύθυμα μεμηνότες, ἐχθροὶ ἑταίρων,
πιστοτάτης φιλίης λυμάντορες, ἀκριτόβουλοι,   530
οὐ μίαν εἰς ἀτραπὸν βιότου νόον ἐκνεύοντες,
ἄλλοτε δ' ἀλλοίην ζωὴν εὔτρεπτον ἔχοντες,
πρήξιας ἀλλάσσοντες ἀεὶ μεθόδους τε πορισμῶν,
ἐκ δ' ἐνύδρων μόχθων τε καὶ ἐκ παράλοιο διαίτης
δώματα ποιμαίνουσι καὶ ἐκ λιμένων τελέουσιν,   535
δημοσίων τελέων ἐμπείραμον ἦθος ἔχοντες.

Μήνης δ' Ἡελίῳ σύνοδον κατὰ κόσμον ἐχούσης
ζωιδίῳ δύνοντι, βροτῶν γένος ἔσσετ' ἀμυδρόν,
ἢ καὶ λυσσαλέῃ μανίῃ δεδαμασμένον αἰεί,
φαρμακτόν, νοσόθυμον, ἀεὶ θανάτοιο πάρεδρον·   540
πᾶσα βροτῶν ψυχὴ γάρ, ἐπὴν τά γε κοινὰ βίοιο
μὴ φρονέῃ κατὰ θυμόν, ἀναισθήτῳ τε παλαίῃ
δυσκρασίῃ, προτέθνηκε, καὶ ἢν φάος ὄμμασι λεύσσῃ·
ψυχὴ γὰρ μερόπων ἀμαθὴς νεκύεσσιν ὁμοίη.

ἢν δὲ Σεληναίη κατέχῃ πάμμηνα κέλευθα   545
συνδέσμῳ κόσμοιο, σεληνιόωντα φανείῃ
φῦλα βροτῶν τάδε πάμπαν, ἰδ' εἰδώλοισιν ὅμοια,
καὶ κραδίῃ θεόληπτα, καὶ ἀκρατέοντι λογισμῷ
ἔνσοφα, πολλὰ δ' ἄβουλα κατ' ἀνθρώπους προλέγοντα
φοιβητοῖς μύθοισιν ἀποφθεγκτήρια κρυπτὰ   550
ἐσσομένων ἔργων τε βίου, ζωῆς τε κελεύθων.

ἢν δὲ καὶ αἰθαλόεις ἀστὴρ σὺν τοῖσι φανείῃ
32ᵛ Ἄρεος ἐν κύκλοισι θοοῦ δινήματι κόσμου,
φάσμασι δαιμονίοισι συναντήσουσιν ἐκεῖνοι,
ψυχῇ δερκόμενοι νεκροειδῆ, νερτερόμορφα,   555
ἔν τε κακαγγελίαισι θεῶν μηνύμασί τ' αἰεὶ
ὀξύγοοι λυπρὸν βιότου τέλος ἀθρήσουσιν,

527-36. Cf. 3.369-71.
537-44. Cf. 6.599-600.
Θ p. 192.13-14. ἐὰν ὁ Ἥλιος καὶ ἡ Σελήνη ὡροσκοπῶσιν, ὁ δὲ Κρόνος δύνῃ δίχα Διὸς καὶ Ἀφροδίτης, λυσσῶντας καὶ μαινομένους ποιοῦσιν.

---

527 μέγα L: corr. D⁵⁶⁴   529 μεμηνότες L¹ˢˡ   ἑταίρο]ις fort. Π¹   531 ἀτραπὸν, ἀτ-L¹ʳᵃˢ (fort. ἀρ- ante ras.)   533 πορισμῶ L: -ῶι L¹: corr. Gr   534 δ'] τ' L: corr. K   535 ποιμένουσι L: corr. Gr   τελέοντες K   536 τελέων] τε λόγων L: corr. K   ἐμπίραμον L: corr. L¹   ἦθος] ἦτορ S, fort. recte   537 ἐχούσης] ἔχοντες L: corr. Halᵐᵍ, D⁶⁶¹   538 ἀ[.]μυδρόν L   539 καὶ] τοι L: corr. A.-R.   δεδαμασμένοι L: corr. Hal   540 μαρφακτόν L: corr. Halᵐᵍ   544 an ἀπαθής?   546 συνδέσμῳ] ego: συνδέσμους L: συνδέσμου K: σύνδεσμον K²   κόσμοιο] ego: ῥυσμοῖο L: Κρονικοῖο K: τε Κρόνοιο K²   φανίῃι L: corr. H, Hal (φανείῃ Gr)   547 ἰδ'] ἐν L: corr. A.-R   548 θεόληπτα L: μ del. L¹ puncto, dein A.-R.   ἀκρατόεντι L: corr. A.-R.ᶜ,ᶜᵒⁿʲ

When both of them together cast their rays
In male signs in a starless place, those born
Are daring, fearless-hearted, their friends' foes,
Who violate true friendships, reckless ones,   530
Turning their thoughts into no single path,
Their lives veering from one thing to the next,
Changing their occupations and their means;
From watery works and seaside avocations
They tend their homes and extract harbour dues,   535
Being well-versed in public revenues.
    But if the Moon's synodic with the Sun
In setting signs, the race of men is weak,
Or subject to enraged insanity,
Poisoned, diseased at heart, death's intimate.   540
For every human soul, when common ties
Are overlooked in apathetic, grey
Distemper, dies, though it beholds the day.
For an unfeeling human soul is like a ghost.
    But if Selene's course is at the full   545
At the cosmic node, that race of men appears
In all respects moon-struck and phantom-like,
Their hearts possessed, with rambling intellect
Inspired, whose inconsidered flow of words
Broadcasts occult discourse in maddened speech   550
Of things to come and of the paths of life.
    But if with these the smoky star appears
Of Ares in the heavens' wheeling gyres,
Those men will meet daemonic images
In spirit viewing death-like, hellish forms.   555
In grim signs and prognostics from the gods
With keening shrill they'll see their life's grim end,

Θ p. 193.20–2. ἡ Σελήνη συνοδικὴν ἔχουσα φάσιν ἢ πανσεληνιακὴν καὶ ὑπὸ Κρόνου θεωρουμένη δίχα Διὸς ἢ Ἀφροδίτης δαιμονιοπλήκτους ποιεῖ.

545-51. Θ p. 193.16–17. ἡ Σελήνη σύνδεσμον πανσεληνιακὸν ἔχουσα ποιεῖ θεολήπτους, ἐνθέους, φοιβαζομένους.

549 πολλὰ] πάντα K   δ'] τ' L: corr. A.-R.   κατ'] καὶ L: corr. K   550 ἀποφεγκτήρια L: corr. D³⁰⁶   551 βίου] βίων L: corr. A   κελεύθους L: corr. K²

fo. 32ᵛ

553 δεινήματι L: corr. L¹ˢᵗ   555 ψυχῇ L: corr. Gr   νεκροειδῆ] νεκροδερκῆ L: corr. K²: νεκροειδέα Sᶜᵒⁿʲ   556 κακαγγελίαισι] κατ' ἀγγελίαισι L: κακαγγελίῃσι Lobeck ad Soph. Aj. 704 (Lips. ³1866, 265 n. 1): comprobavit Hop⁶⁸   μηνίσμασί L: corr. D³⁰³, qui et μηνύσμασί conj.   557 ὀξύχολοι L: corr. K: ὀξύφοβοι K²   ἀρθρήσουσιν L ante ras. ut vid.

εἰδώλων στονόεντα τύπον διὰ παντὸς ὁρῶντες,
ὧν πλάστειρα θεὰ πικροῦ θαμβήματος ἄρχει.
Ἄρεϊ δυομένῳ μέσον οὐρανὸν ἢν Κρόνος ἔλθῃ, 560
ἔσται μισέλλην γενέθλη, τιμήν τε θεοῖσιν
οὐχὶ νέμων, ἄνομός τε φρεσὶν λήθοντι λογισμῷ,
ἀλλόφρων, δύσμικτος, ἀμετροεπής, δολοεργός,
αὐτόνομος, κακόθυμος, ἀθεσμοφάγος, ἀτράπεζος,
ὀθνείων κτεάνων ἐπιθύμιος, ὃν διὰ θυμὸν 565
δῆμοι μισήσουσι δι' ἀφροσύνην ἀλόγιστον.
Ἑρμείας δύνων τε καὶ ὡρονομῶν Κρόνος †ἄνδρας
Μήνης ἐρχομένης μέσον οὐρανὸν ἐν γενέθλῃσιν,
παντευχοὺς τεύχει τορν[εύτορας 568a
εὐξοάνους παλάμῃσιν ἀγαλμοτυπεῖς, θεοπλάστας,
χαλκοτύποις τέχνῃσι κολοσσοπόνους παναρίστους. 570
Ζεὺς δ' ὑψοῦ φοράδην νέον ἀστέρα φεγγοβολήσας,
ὥρην Ἡελίου βιοτοσκόπον αὐγάζοντος,
ἐκφαίνει γενεῆς βασιληίδος ἄνδρας ἔσεσθαι
κοινωνοὺς μετόχους τε, καὶ ἐκ σοφίης κλέος ἕξειν,
ῥητορικοῖς τε λόγοισι μέτ' εὐτυχίης μετέχοντας 575
ὄλβον καὶ βιοτὴν εὐδαίμονα καρπώσεσθαι.
Ἑρμῆς δ' εἰς ὥρην μεροποσπόρον ἡνίκ' ἂν ἔλθῃ,
δυνούσης Μήνης ὑπὸ λοίσθια τέρματα γαίης,
ἀνέρες ἔσσονται βαθυχρήμονες, ἔν τε τραπέζαις
πιστόφρονες πόλεως ταμιεύτορες, ἔν τε τοκισμοῖς 580
καὶ χρείαις ζήσουσι βίον πολὺν ὀλβονομοῦντες.
ἢν δὲ Κύπρις κατὰ γῆς ἕλκῃ δρόμον ἀστερόεντα,
καὶ Κρόνος οὐρανίην ἀτραπὸν μεσοδερκέα βαίνῃ,
στείρας τοι δείξει καὶ ἀτέκμονας ἀνδράσι νύμφας
†ἀσπορίῃ τέκνοισι† λέχη λιπόπαιδα φερούσας. 585

560-6. Θ p. 212.24–5. (Ὁ δὲ Ἄρης καὶ ὁ Κρόνος καὶ ὁ Ἥλιος ἐν τοῖς πρακτικοῖς τόποις τυχόντες) ὁ Κρόνος μεσουρανῶν Ἄρης δύνων μισέλληνας, ἀλλοφύλους ποιοῦσιν.
567-70. Cf. 6.341–7.
Θ p. 212.27–8. [Ἀφροδίτη καὶ Ἄρης] χωνευτάς, χρυσοχόους, λιθογλύφους, ἀργυροκόπους; 213.26-7. Ἀφροδίτη οἴκοις Ἑρμοῦ μετὰ Ἑρμοῦ ποιεῖ ζωγράφους ἢ πλουμαρίους ἢ γλύπτας ἢ ἀνδριαντοπλάστας; 216.7 εἰ δὲ καὶ Ζεὺς καὶ Σελήνη ἐπιθεωρήσωσι [sc. τὸν Κρόνον καὶ τὴν Ἀφροδίτην καὶ τὸν Ἄρη], καβιδαρίους ποιοῦσιν ἢ μαρμαρίους.

560 ἔλθῃ] ὄφθῃ L: corr. K   561 μείσέλλην L: corr. L[1sl]   562 πλήθοντι L: corr. S: an πλαγχθέντι?   563 ἀλιτροεπής S[conj]   563-4 δολοεργός...ἀτράπεζος transp. dub. Herm[717]   564 κακόθυμος] κακόθοινος Π[1]   565 διὰ θυμὸν] διὰ παντὸς K: περίαλλα S[conj]   566 μισήσωσι L (μεισ- L[ac] ut vid.): corr. Hal[mg] δημονελωντειμωντα[Π[1]   δι'] (-ιν) ἰδ' S   567 ἄνδρας] immo αἰνός, αἰπύς?   567-8 transp. A.-R.[c-]   568[a] om. L: iam K lacunam post 570 indicaverat   τορν[εύτορας restitui: τορν[εύοντας Lop[13n.18]

[558–585]   Book Four   449

    Beset by lamentable casts of ghosts
Sent by the infernal queen of bitter dread.
    When Ares sets, if Saturn's in Midheaven,   560
He'll hate his fellow-man, paying the gods
No honour, lawless through deficient sense,
A dissident, a misfit, loose-tongued, sly,
Self-willed, malign, eschewing common board,
Desiring others' goods, whom cordially   565
The people hate for rude neglectfulness.
    When Hermes sets and Cronos rises [ ],
And Moon in the Midheaven at the birth,
He makes all-purpose turners...   568a
Of hewn and chiselled statues, forms divine,
Or adepts in colossal works of bronze.   570
    When Zeus on high casts rays at the New Moon,
And the Sun irradiates the natal Hour,
He shows the men to be of royal race,
Its partners, sharers, eminently wise,
Sharing good fortune through their skill in words,   575
Whence wealth and lucky means of life are reaped.
    With Hermes in the Hour that sows men's births,
The Moon sinking beneath earth's furthest bounds,
Men will be steeped in wealth, and in their banks
Trusted paymasters of the state; 'mid loans   580
And debts they'll live, controlling ample funds.
    If Venus draws her starry train to set,
And Saturn treads the heavens' central path,
They give men barren and infertile wives,
Their beds through seedlessness(?) devoid of young.   585

577–81. Cf. 6.355–6.
Ptol. 4.4.3, Θ p. 210.26–7. ὁ μὲν γὰρ τοῦ Ἑρμοῦ τὸ πράσσειν παρέχων...ποιεῖ...τραπεζίτας.
582–5. Cf. 6.286–9.

569 εξοχανοις Π¹: ἐν χοάνοις vel εὐχοάνοις S^conj   παλάμαισιν Π¹   570 χαλκοτύπους
Π¹   τέχναισι Π¹   571 νέον] θοὸν K^2conj   572 βιοτόσκοπον L: corr. A.-R: βιότου
σκοπο[Π¹   575 μετ᾽] μέγ᾽ K   576 καρπώσασθαι L: corr. K   577 Ἑρμείης δ᾽
ὤρην Π¹   579 ἔσονται Π¹   βαθυχαρ.[Π¹   580 πόλεως L: πόλεων Π¹: πόλιος
A.-R.   581 ζήσουσι Π¹: -ωσι L: iam corr. D^294,661   βιων[Π¹   583 φαίνῃ L: corr.
D^659   584 ἀκύμονας Nauck^IV,165-6   585 ἀσπορίῃ]]ην Π¹   τέκνοισι] κείνοισι R:
τέκνων τε D^661: τε τόκοιο K

450　　　　　　　　　　Βιβλίον Δ'　　　　　　　　　[586–612]

Ζηνὸς δ' αἰθροπλανὴς ἐπὶ τούτοις μάρτυρος ἀστὴρ
δερχθείς, ἀλλοτρίων τέκνων ὑπόβλητα γένεθλα
ἀνδράσιν ἠδὲ γυναιξὶν ὑπὸ στοργῇσι θυραίους
⟨   ⟩
ἢν δ' ἰσόμοιρος Ἄρης κατὰ σήματα τοιάδε λάμψῃ,
φύσονται μάχλοι, †διδυματόκαιτ, ἀρσενομίκται.　　　　590
μεμφόμενοι φύσεως ὀρθὴν ὁδόν, ἔν τε πόλεσσιν
ἀλλοτρίαις ζήσουσιν ἀλώμενοι αἰσχεόφημοι.
　ὁππότε δ' ἂν γενέθλην ἐφέπῃ Κρόνος ὡρονομεύων,
33ʳ　ἐν κακοδαιμοσύνῃ δὲ Σεληναίης φάος ὀφθῇ,
Ἡελίου δ' ἀκτῖνες ἀποκλίνωσιν Ὀλύμπου,　　　　　　595
ἐκθεσίην ἕξουσι, τραφήσονται δ' ὑπ' ὀθνείων.
　Ἡνίκα δ' ἂν Κυθέρη ἐσαθρῇ τεκνοσπόρον ὥρην
φυομένων, συνέῃ δὲ Κρόνος τ' Ἄρης τε σὺν αὐτῷ
φέγγεϊ λαμπομένῳ κακοεργέϊ, τῆμος ἔσονται
ἐξ ἀπελευθερίης βασιληΐδος ἡμισύδουλοι.　　　　　　600
　ἢν δ' ἰσόμοιρα Κρόνοιο σελάσματα Κύπριδος ὀφθῇ,
πανδούλους τε τίθησιν ὁμόζυγα λατρεύοντας,
οἰκέτιδος γενεῆς τε πεφυκότας ἐκ γενετήρων·
οὗτοι δεσποσύνων τε πικρὰς ἕξουσιν ἀνάγκας,
ἐξ ἑτέρων τε δόμων ἑτέροις πάλι δουλεύσουσιν,　　　605
ἑπτάκι κυρείαις καὶ πεντάκι καινισθέντες,
ἐς γῆρας δ' ἥξουσιν ἀνασσόμενοι διὰ παντός.
　Ἡελίου δ' ἀκτῖνες ἀνοικείως ἐπὶ τούσδε
νεύουσαι δεσμούς τε κατηγορίας τε φοροῦσιν
ἀνδράσιν οἰκονόμοισι, καὶ ἔμπαλιν ἔκλυσιν ἄτης,　　610
κινδύνων κρυερῶν τε καὶ ἀλγεινῶν τε †καὶ ἐχθρῶν.
　ταὐτὸ πάθος κείνοισι καὶ ἄρξεται, ἢν ἀπολήγῃ
⟨   ⟩

586–8. Cf. 6.290–2.
589–92. Cf. 6.293–4.
593–6. Cf. 6.60–3.
597–600. Cf. 6.692–4.
601–7. Cf. 6.724–7.
608–11. Cf. 6.728–9.

---

587 δειχθείς L: corr. K　　　588 θυραίοις A　　　post 588 lacunam (quod Π¹ non novit) statuit K　　589 λάμψει L: corr. A.-R.　　590 διδυμάστροφοι K: διδυμόστροφοι K²: διδυμάτομοι Pin: διδυμέκτομοι S^conj　　592 ζήσωσιν L: corr. D⁶⁶¹　　αἰσχρεόφημοι L: corr. K fo. 33ʳ
594 δὲ] τε Π¹　　595]ακτεισιναπ[Π¹, ut ἠέλιος δ' ἀκτεῖσιν ἀποκλίνησιν lectionem fuisse S suspicatus sit　　596 ἐκθεσίμην L: corr. D⁶⁶¹　　]ἔξουσιν Π¹: ἔξωσι L: corr. Hal
597 Κυθεριασα[Π¹　　598 συναίῃι L: corr. D³¹⁵: συνεχῃ Π¹　　⟨τ'⟩ Ἄρης A.-R.ᶜ

> With Zeus' air-wandering star witness to these,
> Of others' stock a substituted brood
> For men and women, through non-kindred love
> ⟨   ⟩
> If Mars shines in these signs in like degree,
> Those born are lewd, twice(-gendered?), couched with males,   590
> Nature's straight path disdaining; foreign lands
> They'll haunt as wanderers of ill repute.
>   When horoscoping Saturn rules the birth,
> And in the Evil Demon shows the Moon,
> And Helios' rays decline from heaven's height,   595
> They'll be exposed and reared by foreign hands.
>   With Venus in the Hour that sows the seed
> Of birth, Saturn attending, Mars with him,
> Both shining with malignant light, they'll be
> By royal emancipation semi-slaves.   600
>   If in Saturn's degrees Venus' light shines,
> She makes them slaves to all, yoked man to man,
> And house-born ones of servile parentage.
> From masters they'll endure severe duress,
> And pass from house to house for ever slaves,   605
> Seven times and five(?) renewed in servitude,
> And reach old age their bondage unrelieved.
>   And if the Sun's rays, not in his own house,
> Incline to these,[6] they bear chains and abuse
> From householders, but then relief from harm,   610
> From dangers chill and bitter and [ ].
>   The same fate will befall them, if declines...
> ⟨   ⟩

---

[6] Sc. Saturn and Venus.

---

599 φέγγεῖ L¹ˢˡ   ]αμπασμω. Π¹ (i.e. λαμπασμῷ): λαμπομένωι L: corr. K²: λαμπόμενοι K   κακοεργεῖ L: corr. A.-R.   600 ἀπελευθερίης L¹ˢˡ   601 Κρόνου .[Π¹, ut consequatur σελαγίσματα pro σελάσματα   602 λατρ[.]εύοντας L   603 οἰκέτιδος, ι¹ Lʳᵃˢ   604 δεσποσύνων L¹ˢˡ: δεσποσυννοιπικρ[Π¹   ἕξουσιν] στέρξουσιν Sᶜᵒⁿʲ   605 δουλεύσωσιν L: corr. L¹   606 κυρίαις L: corr. D⁴⁴⁶   καὶ] ἐπὶ Sᶜᵒⁿʲ   πεντάκι...τε καὶ ἑπτάκι K²ᶜᵒⁿʲ   607 εἰς K   609 νείουσαι L: corr. A.-R.   610 οἰκονόμοισιν L: corr. H, Gr   611 καὶ¹] μάλ' A.-R.ᶜ   ἀλγινῶν L: corr. H, Hal, Gr   ἀλγεινῶν ἐχθράων A.-R., unde ἐχθράων ἀλεγεινῶν Lehrs³¹²ⁿ·***: εἱρκτάων ἀλεγεινῶν K: ἀλγεινῶν εἱρκτάων K²   612 πάθος] γένος L: corr. K: σίνος S   ἦν δ' L: corr. K   ἀπολήγεῖ L¹ˢˡ   post 612 lacunam statuit K

Ἀντιμεσουρανέων δ' ὁπότ' ἂν Κρόνος Ἄρεϊ λάμψῃ,
†θηροβόρου θανάτου φωσὶν κλωσθέντα βαρεῖαν†
⟨   ⟩
ὧν σάρκας δαίσονται ὀρέστεροι ἠὲ λέοντες,   615
ἢ σύες ἀργιόδοντες, ἢ αἱματοπώτιδες ἄρκτοι·
σχήμασι δ' ἐν τούτοις ὁ γεγὼς καὶ πτώσιας οἴκων
ταρβείτω, καὶ σφάλματ' ἀφ' ὑψηλοῖο μελάθρου.
Πάντα γὰρ ἀνθρώποισι πέλει κατὰ Μοῖραν ἄφυκτον·
ὡς μὲν ζῳδίων κύκλιος πόρος αἰθέρα τέμνει,   620
μιγνυμένων στοιχηδὸν ἀφισταμένων †τε δικήλων,
οὕτω καὶ μερόπων γενεὴ καματηδὸν ἀλᾶται,
ἢ βίον ἢ θάνατον διζημένη οὐρανόπλαγκτον.
Ταυτά τοι οὐρανίων ἄστρων στοιχεῖα τέτυκται,
οἷς ὁ πάλαι καὶ ὁ νῦν καὶ ἐπὼν χρόνος ἐκμεμέτρηται   625
ἐκμέτροις αἰῶσι, καὶ εἰς αἰῶνας ὀπηδεῖ.

ΜΑΝΕΘΩΝΟΣ ΑΠΟΤΕΛΕΣΜΑΤΙΚΩΝ ΒΙΒΛΙΟΝ Δ'

613–18. Cf. 3.260–3.
Θ p. 201.22–4. ὁ Κρόνος ὑπογείῳ, Ἄρης μεσουρανῶν νυκτὸς ποιοῦσιν ἐσταυρωμένους καὶ ὑπὸ ὀρνέων βεβρωμένους. ἐὰν ὁ κύριος τῶν ὁρίων τοῦ διέποντος κακοδαιμονήσῃ, θηριόβρωτον ποιεῖ τὸν γεννηθέντα.

613 ἀντιμεσουρανέων L¹   614 θηροβόλου θανάτου L: θηροβόρον θάνατον A.-R.   κλωσθέντα] κλωθῶα K, qui post hunc versum lacunam statuit   βαρεῖαν] βραβεύει A.-R. e D⁵⁴⁰   615 δαίσονται L (diaeresim L¹): corr. Nauck^(V.169-70)   ἠδὲ L: corr. Sp¹⁵⁴, R   620 μὲν...τέμνει] ἂν...τέμνῃ L: corr. K   621 τε δικήλων, λ L^(1ras), supra ω punctum L^(rec): τ' εἰδώλων K   623 διζημένη, ι L^(1ras)   οὐρανόκραντον S^(conj)   625 ἐπῶν L: corr. A   626 ἐν μέτροις L: corr. K: νηρίθμοις Magnelli   ἀγῶσι L: corr. H, Hal, Gr^(v.n)

If Saturn underground shines upon Mars,
A grievous fate to be the prey of beasts(?)...
⟨   ⟩
Their flesh devoured by mountain-haunting lions, 615
Or white-tusked boar, or blood-consuming bear;
Born in these charts let natives also fear
Collapse of buildings, falling from a height.
    For all things come to man by certain Fate.
As the cyclic path of figures cleaves the air, 620
Whose elements converge and separate,
So too do humans transit painfully,
Encountering life or death by cosmic round.
    These are the elements of the heavenly stars,
By which past, present, future time is measured, 625
For ages measureless, and still to come.

Βιβλίον Α´

Χαίροις, ὦ Πτολεμαῖε, λαχὼν βασιληίδα τιμὴν
γαίης ἡμετέρης, κοσμοτρόφου Αἰγύπτοιο·
ἄξιά σοι τάδε δῶρα φέρω βασιληίδος ἀρχῆς,
ἄστρων οὐρανίων τε φάσεις ἀπλανῶν τε πλάνων τε,
ὅσσα βροτοῖς τελέουσιν ἐπιβλέψαντες ἐν ἀρχαῖς,   5
σπειρομένοις καὶ τικτομένοις δειλοῖσι βροτοῖσιν,
Μοιρῶν ἀρρήκτοισι μίτοις θεσμοῖσί τ' Ἀνάγκης,
νύκτας ἄϋπνος ἐὼν καὶ ἐν ἤμασι πολλὰ μογήσας,
ὅππως σοι βίβλους, ἅσπερ κάμον, ἅσπερ ἔτευξα,
τάς σοι ἐγὼ πέμψω καμάτων σφετέρων μέγ' ὄνειαρ,   10
ὄφρα κεν, ὅσσαπερ αὐτὸς ἐπιτροχάδην Πετόσιρις
εἴρηκεν, τάδε πάντα μάλ' ἀτρεκέως καταλέξω
ῥυθμοῖς ἡρωικοῖσι καὶ ἑξαμέτροις ἐπέεσσιν,
ὄφρα μάθῃς, ὅτι πάντα δαήμονες ἀνέρες εἰμέν,
οἳ λάχομεν ναίειν ἱερὸν πέδον Αἰγύπτοιο.   15
    Ἥλιον, Μήνην, Κρόνον, Ἄρεα, Ἑρμέα, Ζῆνα,
Κύπριδά τ' εὐπλόκαμον καλὴ λέγε Καλλιόπεια.
    Ἢν Κρόνος Ἥλιός τ' ἄμφω κατίδωσι Κυθήρην,
δυσγαμίην παρέχουσι καὶ ἀστασίην ἐπὶ λέκτροις·
καὶ δούλαις μίσγουσιν ἑταιρίσιν, ἠδὲ λάφυρα   20
αἰσχίστως διδόασι κακῆς ἕνεκεν κυθερείης.
    Ἄρης καὶ Παφίη κέντρων ὅτ' ἂν ὦσιν ἄνακτες
μοιχοὺς ἁρπακτῆρας ἀεὶ ῥέζουσι γυναικῶν.
    Ἑρμείας δ' ἢν τοῖσιν ἰσόρροπος ἀντήσειεν,
τέρπονται παίδων χαλεπῇ ἐπὶ κύπριδι κεῖνοι.   25
    Ἥλιος κέντροισι παρὼν κερόεσσά τε Μήνη,
ὃς μὲν ἐν ἀρσενικοῖσι παρών, Μήνη δέ τ' ἐναλλάξ,
γεννῶσιν βασιλῆας ὑπερθύμους τε δυνάστας.
    ἀμφότεροι φωστῆρες ἐν ἀρσενικοῖσιν ἐόντες
θηλυτέρης Κύπριδός τε καὶ ὡρονόμοιο κατιθύ,   30

---

fo. 9ᵛ

2 κουροτρόφου Nauck[v.168]   4–7 pro interpolatis habuit K: 6 deletum vult Luc
8 ἄϋπνο[.]ς, ο L^ras (pro -ους ut vid.)   9–10 pro interpolatis habuit K; 8–10 S, qui tamen 8 et
9 traiecit   14 ὄφρα] ἠδὲ S^conj   15 Αἰγύπτοιο, -οιο L^1ras   16 Ἑρμεῖα L^rec (Ἑρμῆ- L^ac)
18 κατίδωσι L, τ- L^1ras   20 ἑταιρίσιν, ί L^1ras, ρ puncto signavit L^rec   τ' ἠδὲ L: corr. Gr
λαφύραις L: ις del. L^1 punctis necnon accentum in λάφυρα correxit: λαφύροις K

Book One

Hail Ptolemy, holder of the royal rank
In this our land, Egypt that feeds the world.
I bring gifts worthy of your royal state—
Phases of heavenly stars fixed and unfixed,
What they effect when viewing mortal births, 5
The engendering and birth of wretched men,
By the Fates' unbroken threads, and Fate's decrees—
Sleeping the night out, labouring hard by day,
So that the books I laboured o'er, and made,
I might despatch as harvest of my pains, 10
That what great Petosiris passingly
Did treat, I'd tell the whole most carefully
In verse heroic, hexametric lines,
To show you how all-knowing are we men
Who dwell in Egypt's consecrated plain. 15
    The Sun, Moon, Saturn, Mars, Hermes, and Zeus,
And fair-haired Venus—tell, fair epic Muse.
    If Sun and Saturn both view Cythera,
They give ill wedlock and unstable beds,
Couplings with slave-girl mistresses, and spoils(?) 20
Of shame they give for basest venery.
    Mars and the Paphian, Lords of centres, make
Adulterers, and predators of wives.
    If Hermes meets these equal (in degree?),
They revel in the vicious love of boys. 25
    The Sun in centres, and the hornèd Moon,
He in male places, she in the reverse,
Engender kings and mighty potentates,
    Both luminaries being in male signs
Facing the Cyprian and the Horoscope, 30

20–1 uncis inclusit K   22 κέντρον L: corr. Gr   24 τοῖσιν] τούτοις L: corr. D[314-15]
δ' ην ταιπισ ϊσορρ L[1mg]   26–7 κέντροισιν ἐπὼν aut ἀρσενικοῖσι τυχών vel ἐών S[conj]
27 αρϲενικοιϲι εων Π[3]   28 γεννηϲι βαϲιλεαϲ Π[3]   30 κατεἰθὺ L[1corr]: κατ] ιθψν Π[3]

ἀρσενικοῖς ἔργοισιν ἀναγκάζουσι γυναῖκας
τέρπεσθαι, μέγα θαῦμα· γυναιμανέες γὰρ ἐοῦσαι
ἀργαλέως γαμέουσιν ἐς ἀργαλέην φιλότητα.
Κριὸν ἐποπτεύων Κρονίδης ἐπίκεντρος ὑπάρχων,
ἢ καὶ σκόρπειον κυανόχροον οἶκον Ἄρηος,   35
ἐσθλὸς ἔφυ, ῥέζει δὲ καὶ ἀνέρας ἡγεμονῆας
ἄρχοντάς τ' ἰδίης πάντοτε πραγματίης.
Ἑρμείας καὶ Θοῦρος ἐπὴν τετράγωνοι ἔωσιν,
πολλάκι κινδύνους περὶ σώματος εὑρίσκουσιν·
ἢν δ' ἄρα καὶ δύνωσι, κακίονες οἷδε μάλιστα·   40
Ζηνὸς ἄτερ, μόρον αἰνὸν †οὐκ ἐκφεύγουσι δυναστῶν.
10ʳ Ἄρης καὶ Παφίη κοινὴν ὁδὸν ἰθύνοντες,
Μήνην εὖτ' ἂν ἴδωσι, λέχος τεύχουσ' ἀθέμιστον,
συγγενικὰς δ' αὐτοῖσιν ἐφαρμόζουσι γυναῖκας.
ἢν δὲ Κύπριν καλὴν πολιὸς Κρόνος ἀγκαλίσαιτο,   45
δυσγαμίην καὶ δυστοκίην ῥέζουσι γυναιξίν,
οὐδέ τι κουριδίους ἄνδρας κατέχουσ' ἄχρι γήρους,
οὐδὲ τέκνοις γλυκεροῖς ἐπὶ χείλεσι μαζὸν ἔθηκαν·
στειρώδεις γὰρ ἔασιν ἀχρηιά τ' ὠδίνουσιν.
Ἀντίον Ἡελίοιο φάσιν λύσασα Σελήνη   50
μὴ Κρόνῳ ἀντήσειε· τίς ἂν τότε φῶς ἐσίδοιτο;
δύσμορος, ὃς κακὰ πολλὰ παθὼν Ἀϊδόσδε κάτεισιν·
χροιὴν μὲν φορέουσιν ἀμετροβίων ἐλεφάντων,
ὄχθους δ' ἀμφὶ δέμας κακοελκέας ἀμφιβαλοῦνται,
δάκτυλα σηπόμενοι λιποσαρκέα νηλέϊ λύθρῳ·   55
ταῦτα δ' ἄτερ Ζηνός τε καὶ εὐπλοκάμου Κυθερείης
ἔσσεται, ὁππότ' ἐκεῖνοι ἀπόστροφοι ὦσι Σελήνης.

45-9. Firmicus, 6.22.12. Si Saturnus et Venus unum hospitium partis acceperint, et in eodem pariter loco constituti aequabili societatis potestate iungantur, indignarum mulierum nuptias decernit ista coniunctio, et misera matrimoniorum infortunia semper excitat. Aut steriles enim aut debiles decernit uxores, quarum insigne vitium omnem formam corporis dedecoret, aut gravi pulsat infamia, aut, ex istis infortuniis, etiam filiorum illis soboles denegatur.
Firmicus, 6.31.43. Si in MC. Venus fuerit collocata, et ei Saturnus in MC. aequata partium societate iungatur, Luna vero in IMC. constituta hos eosdem diametra radiatione respiciat, aut steriles aut certe provectae aetatis decernit uxores, ut ex ista matrimonii copulatione filii in perpetuum denegentur.

32 [γ]υναιμανεc[[αc]] Π³, id est γυναιμανὲc post corr.   [ἐρ[η[τ]ορ]γα] ἔουcαι Π³, corr. manus altera^d, tamquam γυναιμανὲc ἦτορ ἔχουcαι voluit corrector   35 σκορπίον L: corr. A   36 post hunc versum ‹Ἐσθλὸς ἔφυ Κρονίδης, ῥέζει δὲ καὶ ἡγεμονῆας› suppl. K   37 πραγματείης L: corr. H, Hal, Gr   38 Θοῦρος L^rec   39 κινδυνοιc Π³   χρώματος L: corr. D⁶⁴¹ (vel χρήματος)   ευριcκονται Π³   40-1 κ. οἵ. μάλιστα· | Ζ. ἄ. μόρον (χόλον S) αἰνὸν οὐκ ἐκφεύγουσι L: κακίονες οἷδε, μάλιστα | Ζηνὸς ἄτερ, μοῖραν δ' οὐκ ἐκ. K ('maiore quam opus erat molimine' K²), qui etiam μόρον αἰνὸν δ' οὐ φεύγουσι conj.: μόρον αἰνὸν ὑπεκ. D⁶⁷⁸: μόρον αἰνὸν ὑπ' ἐμφαίνουσι K²   40 κακειονεc Π³   ὅττι μάλιστα S^conj

>   Make females take delight perforce in male
>   Proceedings—strange to tell—for woman-mad
>   They make foul marriages for loathsome love.
>   Beholding Aries, Zeus upon a point,
>   Or the Scorpion, house of Mars, of livid hue,   35
>   Has good effects, and makes men who command
>   And men who manage their own businesses.
>   Hermes and Mars, when they in quartile stand,
>   Engender many dangers for the person;
>   And if they set, they're worse still; without Zeus,   40
>   They don't escape a dread fate from their lords.
>   Ares and Venus on a common path,
>   Viewing the Moon, make godless marriages,
>   And couple with kinswomen as their wives.
>   Should grey-haired Saturn the fair Cypris clasp,   45
>   They make ill wedlock, painful parturition,
>   Nor do they keep their spouses till old age,
>   Nor press their breasts to cherished sucklings' lips,
>   For barren are they, sterile in their pangs.
>   Facing the Sun, when the Moon moves from her phase,   50
>   Keep Cronos from her! Who'd then see the light?
>   A wretch, who, sorely tried, goes down to hell;
>   Their flesh is that of long-lived elephants,
>   Their forms encased in ulcerated welts,
>   Their stunted fingers weeping with foul pus.   55
>   This much when Zeus and fair-haired Cythera
>   Are absent, from the Moon's face turned away.

50–7. Θ p. 189.10–13. ἡ Σελήνη ἐξ ἀποκρούσεως πρὸς Κρόνον φερομένη μετὰ τὴν λύσιν τοῦ συνδέσμου δίχα Διὸς καὶ Ἀφροδίτης ποιεῖ κελεφούς, ἐλεφαντιῶντας, λελωβημένους, ῥευματιζομένους.

Firmicus, 8.21.7 [Gemini 19°]. *Quodsi Luna, in squamosis signis posita, plena lumine feratur ad Martem, vel minuta ad Saturnum, elephantiaci fient.*

Π.σ.α. p. 182.14–16. ἐὰν δὲ ἐκτὸς τῶν κέντρων Κρόνος τυγχάνῃ καὶ ὑπὸ τὰς τοῦ Ἡλίου αὐγάς, πολλῶν κακῶν αἴτιος ἔσται· νόσους γὰρ ἀπὸ ὑγρῶν ἢ ὀχλήσεις ἐπάγει.

---

fo. 10ʳ

43 Μήνην εὖτ᾽ ἂν ἴδωσι] ευσταν‚γενεεϲϲι Π³, e.g. ἐϋγενέεϲϲι, sed non satis clarum   λεχος τ᾽ ἐχουϲιν αθε[[ϲ̔μον]] Π³ u.v., corr. manus altera^{sl}   44 συγγενίδας A^{conj}   δ᾽ om. Π³   αὐτοῖσιν] ἄνδρεσσιν K^{2conj}   45[η]ν [δ]ε Κυπριν τε κα[λ]ην Π³   αγ᾽καλιϲηται Π³, a³ fors. post corr.   46 δυϲτοκιην ῥε[[ζουϲι]] Π³ˢˡ ut vid.   γυναιξι Π³   47 οὐδέ, οὐ L¹ʳᵃˢ   κρατέουσ᾽ L, κρατεουϲι Π³: corr. K   γήρους L, Π³: γήρως A.-R.   49 ὠδείν- L: corr. H, Hal   52 ἄϊδος δὲ L: corr. Hal, D³³²   54 ὄγκους A.-R.^{conj}   55 σειπόμενοι L: corr. H, Hal   λιποσαρκέα L¹ˢˡ   56 δ[.]᾽[.] ἄτερ L, ᾽ L¹ʳᵃˢ   εὐπλοκ., ε L¹ʳᵃˢ   57 ἔσσεται ὀπ- L, αι ὀπ L¹ʳᵃˢ

Ἑρμῆς ὠρονομῶν Μήνης μέτα καὶ Κυθερείης,
δύνοντος Κρονίδαο, θεῶν μυστήρια δρῶσιν·
†ἢ μούσης ἅπτοντ' ἢ λύρης εὐρύθμοιο,† 60
ἠὲ πάλην φιλέουσιν ἀμύμονα παγκράτιόν τε.
Ἑρμῆς καὶ Κυθέρεια σὺν ἀλλήλοισιν ἐόντες
ῥέζουσιν μούσης ἐπίστορας εὔφρονας ἄνδρας,
ἤν πως καὶ κερόεσσαν ὁμοῦ Μήνην ἐσίδωνται,
Ἑρμῆς φωσφορέουσαν, ἀτὰρ λιποφεγγέα Κύπρις. 65
Ζεύς, Κρόνος, ἀμφότεροι κέντρων ὅτ' ἄν ὦσιν ἄνακτες,
ἀνθρώποις διδόασι τύχης πολυήρατα δῶρα,
καὶ μεγάλους ῥέζουσι, καὶ ἐς βασιληίδας αὐλὰς
πολλάκις ἤνεγκαν, τιμήν τε φέρουσι μεγίστην.
Ἑρμείας Φαέθων τε μεσουρανέοντες ἔθηκαν 70
ἄνδρα μέγα πλούτῳ γαυρούμενον εὐτεκνίῃ τε,
καὶ φιλίην παρέχουσι πρὸς ἀνέρας ἡγεμονῆας
καὶ δόξῃ μεγάλῃ γαυρούμενον, αἴ κεν ἴδηαι
εὐκέραον Μήνην συναφὴν τούτοις ἐπέχουσαν.
Πάντοτε μὲν κέντροισιν ἐπὼν κορυθαίολος Ἄρης 75
τὴν πρᾶξιν παρέχων τοιάπερ ἐκτελέει·
ἤτοι λαξευτὰς ἢ τέκτονας ἢ λιθοεργούς.
Ἥλιος δ' ἢν τῷδε συνῇ, πυροεργέας ἄνδρας
ῥέζει χαλκοτύπους, ἢ φυσητὰς ὑέλοιο,
ἢ βαφέας μογερούς, ἢ κλιβανέας σκοτοεργούς· 80
οὗτοι γὰρ καὶ νυκτὸς ἀγρυπνητῆρες ἐόντες
νύκτα μὲν ἐργάζονται, ἐν ἤματι δ' ὑπνώουσιν.
πάντοτε νυκτερινοῖσι μεσουρανέων Κρόνος αἰνὸς
ῥέζει κηπουροὺς ἠδ' ἀργαλέους ὑδραγωγούς,
ῥέζει δ' ὑδροφόρους πολυπήμονας, οἵθ' ὑπὸ γαίης 85
κευθμῶνας δύνουσιν ἀεικέος εἵνεκα μισθοῦ,
ἢ παρύγροισι τόποισι παρήμενοι ἐργάζονται,
μήποτε τῶν ἰδίων τι κτώμενοι ἐκ καμάτων γε.

70-4. Firmicus, 3.10.12. *In decimo loco ab horoscopo Mercurius et Iuppiter magnos actus et magnas administrationes et magnas decernunt potestates, pro mensura geniturae.*
75-7. Θ p. 211.10-11. Ἄρης τὸ πράσσειν παρέχων καὶ μαρτυρῶν ἢ ὡροσκοπῶν ποιεῖ λαξευτὰς ἢ τέκτονας ἢ λιθοέργους.
Cf. Ptol. 4.4.5. ὁ δὲ τοῦ Ἄρεως...χωρὶς δὲ τοῦ ἡλίου τυχὼν τοὺς διὰ σιδήρου οἶον ναυπηγούς, τέκτονας, γεωργούς, λατόμους, λιθοξόους, λαοξόους, λιθουργούς, ξυλοσχίστας, ὑπουργούς.

60 ἅπτοντ' L: -αι L[1] per compendium, deinde H, Hal   λύρης] πηκτίδος D[571]   ἅπτονται εὐρρύθμοιο λύρης τε A: ἠὲ λύρης ἅπτονται εὐρρύθμοιο τε μούσης S[conj]   61 πάλιν L: corr. Gr   παγκράτιόν, γ L[1ras] (παν- L)   63 ἐπιΐστορας, ἐπιΐ L[1ras]   67 πολυπείρατα L: corr. D[643]   68 εἰς L: corr. Gr   73 γαυρούμενον] τιμώμενον S[conj]   76 πρῆξιν A[conj], K   post hunc versum lacunam statuit K, post 77 S

    Hermes with Moon and Venus on the Hour,
As Zeus descends, make holy mysteries:
They cultivate the Muse, the rhythmic lyre,   60
Or love to wrestle and the all-in sport.
    Hermes and Cythereia when conjoined
Engender gracious votaries of the arts,
If they should also aspect the horned Moon,
Hermes when Full; Cypris when on the wane.   65
    Zeus, Cronos, both of centres being Lords,
To men give Fortune's most aspired-to gifts,
Create great persons, who to royal courts
Often advance, and garner great prestige.
    Hermes and Phaethon in Midheaven make   70
A man proud in his wealth and progeny,
And friendships give with those who hold command,
One proud of great renown, if you should see
The horned Moon in companionship with them.
    When Mars of flashing helm is on a point   75
Controlling action, these are his effects:
Stone-masons, carpenters, or quarry men.
    If the Sun is with him, men who work with fire
Are born, casters of bronze, or who blow glass,
Or wretched dyers, bakers at dark stoves,   80
Who keep awake during the hours of night,
Who work by night and take their rest by day.
    When in night births dread Saturn's in Midheaven,
He makes men who keep gardens, toil on ducts,
Or—arduous work!—bear water, or descend   85
Into the earth's depths for a meagre wage,
Or do their work in waterside locales,
From labours gleaning nothing of their own.

78–82. Θ p. 211.11–13. εἰ δὲ Ἥλιος αὐτῷ συμμαρτυρήσῃ, ποιεῖ χαλκοτύπους ἢ ἱερουργοὺς [sic M: immo ὑελουργοὺς?] ἢ βαφέας ἢ ὅσα διὰ πυρὸς καὶ σιδήρου.
    Cf. Ptol. 4.4.5. ὁ δὲ τοῦ Ἄρεως μετὰ μὲν τοῦ ἡλίου σχηματισθεὶς τοὺς διὰ πυρὸς ἐργαζομένους ποιεῖ οἷον μαγείρους, χωνευτάς, καύστας, χαλκέας, μεταλλευτάς.
83–8. Cf. ad 4.251–62.

---

fo. 10ᵛ

85 οἵ τ' ἐπὶ γαίης, αἱ L¹: corr. K (θ'), A^conj (ὑπό)   87 πανύγροισι A^conj: πανήμεροι D³²⁹   88 μήποτέ τοι ἴδιόν τι R^conj   τι κτώμενοι] κεκτημένοι Ger¹³⁸, unde κεκτημένοι...τι (pro γε) Magnelli

Ἑρμείας διάμετρον ἔχων Κρόνον ἠδὲ Σελήνην
κεντρωθεὶς δ' αὐτοῖς κατεναντίον ὡρονόμοιο, 90
ἐμμανέας τεύχει ἠδὲ φρενοβλαβέας.
εἰ δὲ ῥοπῆς μὴ μοῖρα τύχῃ, καθέτου δ' ἀποκλίνῃ,
ἐσκότισεν μούνῳ κλεψίφρονι ῥεύματι κείνους·
καὶ φρένας ἠλλοίωσε, παρέπλαγξεν δὲ νόημα·
ἔσθ' ὅτε σωφρονέουσι, καὶ ἔσθ' ὅτε μαργαίνουσιν. 95
Πάντας ἀπ' Ἡελίοιο φυγεῖν καλόν, ἀλλ' οὐκ Ἄρην·
νικᾶται γὰρ Ἄρης ὑπὸ αὐγαῖς Ἡελίοιο.
Αἰδεῖται δ' Ἄρης καθορῶν φάος Ἡελίοιο,
οὐδ' ἔτι τὴν προτέρην ἔσχε κακοφροσύνην.
Ζεὺς ῥέζει κρατέοντας ἐλαιορόοιο παλαίστρης, 100
Κύπρις πορφυρέοισιν ἐν εἵμασιν ἀρχιερῆας,
καὶ Κρόνος εὐδόξως ἀγορανόμον ἐστεφάνωσεν·
Ἄρης δ' εὐτόλμους στρατιῆς ἡγήτορας ἄνδρας,
Ἥλιος δ' ὕπατον, Μήνη δέ τοι ἀρχιδικαστήν,
Ἑρμῆς κοσμητῆρας ἑῆς ἐποίησε πόληος. 105
Αἰγόκερῳ Κύπρις καὶ Ὑδροχόῳ παρεοῦσα
σύν τε Κρόνῳ καὶ Ζηνὶ κακὴ κατὰ πάντα τέτυκται,
ἢν συναφὴν πρώτοιο λάβῃ πολιοῖο Κρόνοιο,
Ἄρεος εἰσβλέψαντος ὁμοῦ Μήνην Παφίην τε
σύν τε Κρόνῳ βλαβερῷ· δυστλήμονες ἀνέρες οὗτοι 110
μαινόμενοι βαίνουσιν ἑῆς ἐπὶ λέκτρα τεκούσης·
ἢν δ' ἀκτῖνα λάβωσι πυραυγέος Ἡελίοιο,
μητρυιαῖς μίσγοντ' ἢ παλλακίσιν γενετήρων,
καὶ προτέρην κακίην ἔσβεσεν Ἥλιος.
Μήνη θηλυτέροισιν ἐπεμβαίνουσα τόποισιν 115
ἀντίον Ἡελίοιο, καὶ ὡρονόμοιο τυχοῦσα,
ἀνέρα γεννήσει μόνον οὔνομα, πάντα δὲ θῆλυν,
πάντα γυναικὸς ἔχοντα καὶ αἴσχεα καὶ φιλότητα.
ἢν δὲ μεσουρανέῃ Φαίνων Ἄρης τε κραταιός,
καὶ στάχυν ἄρρενα δεινῷ ἀποτμήξειε σιδήρῳ. 120

89-91. Θ ξε'. Περὶ μαινομένων καὶ ἐπιληπτικῶν, p. 192.9–11. Ἐὰν ἡ Σελήνη καὶ ⟨ὁ⟩ Κρόνος ὡροσκοπῶσιν, ὁ δὲ Ἑρμῆς δύνῃ κατὰ κέντρον, μαινομένους καὶ φρενοβλαβεῖς ποιοῦσιν, δίχα τῆς τῶν ἀγαθῶν ἐπιθεωρίας.
Epit. IIIb = CCAG vii. 112. κ'. ⟨Ἀντιόχου⟩ περὶ σινῶν, φαλακρῶν, ποδαλγῶν, μαινομένων, ἀσελγῶν καὶ τῶν λοιπῶν παθῶν, ll. 11–13. εἰ δὲ Σελήνη καὶ Κρόνος ὡροσκοποῦσιν, ὁ δὲ Ἑρμῆς κατὰ κέντρον ⟨ἐστίν⟩, μαινομένους καὶ φρενοβλαβεῖς ποιεῖ.

---

89 + 91, dein 89 iterum + 90 K: lacunam post 89 statuit Heil[168], nequiquam; cf. commentaria ad loc.   91 ⟨τ'⟩ ἠδὲ K   92 ἀποκλείνῃ L: corr. Hal (ἀποκλίνει H)   94 post 90 transp. K   96 Ἄρηα L: corr. D[496], qui et Ἄρεα δ'οὐχί conj.   97 νικᾶται, -ι et -αι L[1ras]   ὑπ°αὐγαῖς L[1sl], -αῖς L[1ras]   μὲν ὑπ' Sp[156]: ὅθ' ὑπ' Ger[181]

> When Hermes faces Saturn and the Moon
> He in a centre, on the Horoscope, 90
> He makes the maddened, blasted in their wits.
> If his degree's not poised, but falls from true,
> He darkens them in tides of lunacy,
> And takes their wits, and causes loss of mind:
> One moment sane, the next they rant and rave. 95
>   To flee the Sun is good for all but Mars,
> For Mars is overborne by the Sun's rays,
> And is inhibited by the Sun's light,
> And does not hold his erstwhile ill-intent.
>   Zeus makes the oily wrestling-school's heroes, 100
> The Cyprian high-priests in their purple robes,
> And Saturn crowns the market's clerks with fame;
> Mars makes stouthearted leaders of the troops,
> The Sun a consul, Moon a leading judge,
> And Hermes those who beautify their towns. 105
>   Venus in Capricorn and Aquarius,
> With Zeus and Saturn, in all ways is bad,
> If first with grey-haired Saturn she's in touch,
> And Mars aspects both Moon and Paphian
> With baleful Cronos: wretchedly those men, 110
> Distracted, enter in their mothers' beds,
> But if they take the fiery Sun's ray, mix
> With stepmothers or fathers' concubines,
> And Helios quells his erstwhile ill effects.
>   The Moon stationed in feminine domains 115
> Facing the Sun, and in the Horoscope,
> Makes men only in name, else womanish,
> With all a woman's shame and acts of love.
>   If mighty Mars and Saturn are mid-heaven,
> They shear their male stock with a vicious blade. 120

106-11. Cf. 6.160-9; Anubion, F 4 ii. 10-16; Firmicus, 6.30.1.

---

post 97 hexametrum confecit K, sic fere νικᾶται δ' Ἄρης αὐγῇσιν ὑπ' Ἡελίοιο, dein hic traiecit 114   97-8 νικᾶται δ'...αἰδεῖται γὰρ A^{conj} hos duos versus (non, ut S praefert, 96-7) traiectos voluit R   100 ἐλαιοφόροιο L: corr. K: ἐλαιοφίλοιο S^{conj} παλαίστρης, -αίστρης L^{1ras} 101 πορφυρέοι[.]σιν L (-νσιν ante ras. u.v.)   εἵμασιν: εἴ- L^{1ras} 106 ⟨τε⟩ καὶ Ger^{162} (noluit)   108 πρώτοιο] τὰ πρῶτα S^{conj} 109 Ἄρηος L: corr. H^{h} 112 λάβωσι] βλέπωσι S^{conj} 113 παλλακίσιν, -σι- L^{1ras} 114 ante 98 traiecit K (cf. supra)   115 θηλυτέροισιν L^{1sl} 117 θῆλυ L: corr. D^{249} τἆλλα δὲ θῆλυν S^{conj} 120 στάχυν] σ del. puncto L   in marg. sin. καὶ ταχυνον vel σταχυνον πανόδυρτον ἀ. σ., unde κ. στ. ἄν π. R^{conj}, κ. στ. ὃν π. Mon^{41} ἄρσενα K   δεινῷ] δεινὸν L: corr. A.-R.: κεῖνος S

11ʳ

ἢν δὲ Κύπρις διάμετρον ἔχοι Κρόνον ἠδὲ Σελήνην,
Ἄρης δ' ἢν τετράγωνον ἴδοι καλὴν Ἀφροδίτην,
Ἑρμείας δ' ἄρα κέντρον ἔχοι μέσον, ἠδὲ καὶ αὐτὸς
μαρτυρίην τούτῳ καὶ Κρόνος ἀμφιβάλοι,
εὐνούχους στείρους, οὔτ' ἄρρενας οὔτε γυναῖκας, 125
ἄχνοας, αἰὲν ἐόντας ἀπειρήτους φιλότητος,
ἔσθ' ὅτε δ' ἑρμαφρόδιτον ὁμώνυμον ἀθανάτοισιν,
δισσάς, ἀχρήστους εἰς ἓν ἔχοντα φύσεις.

Υἱὸς δ' υἱωνός τε Κρόνου Ζεὺς ἠδὲ καὶ Ἑρμῆς
ἀμφότεροι βαίνοντες ὁμοῦ καὶ κέντρα λαβόντες, 130
τεύχουσιν ῥητῆρας, ἢ ἐκ λόγου ἢ καλάμοιο
γραπτῆρας πινυτούς, ἢ καὶ πολυκερδέας ἄνδρας,
ἐμπορίην φιλέοντας, ἀεὶ πρηκτῆρας ἐόντας.

Μήνη φωσφορέουσα καὶ Ἄρεϊ συμβάλλουσα
ἕκτον ἔχοντι τόπον, σίνος ἀνδράσιν αὐτίκα ῥέζει· 135
ἀμφὶ πόδας τέμνονται ὑπ' ἀνδροφόνοιο σιδήρου,
χωλοί, μουνόποδες, ξύλινον προσκείμενοι ἄρθρον,
λύπην αἰείμνηστον ἐὸν πόδα παπταίνοντες.

Ἄρες Ἄρες, κακοεργὲ καὶ ἀνδράσι καὶ μακάρεσσιν
καὶ πόλεσιν καὶ ναυσὶ καὶ ἠέρι καὶ πελάγεσσιν 140
καὶ καρποῖς γαίης καὶ ἐΰρρείθροις ποταμοῖσιν·
εἵνεκα σου πόλιες μὲν ὑπαὶ πυρὸς ἐμπίμπρανται,
καὶ νῆες πελάγεσσιν ἐπιπλώουσαι ὄλοντο,
καὶ ποταμοὶ ξηροῖσιν ἀνύδατοι ἐν στομάτεσσιν,
δένδρεά τ' ὠλεσίκαρπα καὶ ἀνέρες αἰνογένεθλοι· 145
οὓς μὲν γὰρ μογερῶς πυρικαέας ὤλεσας ἄνδρας,
οὓς δὲ καὶ ὠμοβόροισιν ἕλωρ θήρεσσιν ἔδωκας,
ἄλλον δ' ἀκλειῶς μετέωρον ἀνεσταύρωσας,
οὗ τέτατ' ἀνδροφόνοις περὶ δούρασιν ἡλοπαγὴς χείρ·
νηλεές, οὐκ ἄρα σοί γε πατὴρ ἦν αἰγίοχος Ζεύς, 150

121-8. Cf. 6.276-81.
Firmicus, 6.30.5. *Si Mars et Luna diametra sibi fuerint radiatione contrarii, et easdem ambo in diametro constituti partes accipiant, Venus vero in dextro eorum quadrato fuerit constituta, et Venerem de diametro Saturnus respiciens per sinistrum quadratum Lunam Martemque pulsaverit, ut Venerem quidem de diametro, Lunam uero et Martem de quadrato respiciat, et Mercurius MC. possederit, post ex hac stellarum mixtura aut steriles aut hermaphroditi aut certe generantur eunuchi.*

---

123 εἰ δέ κεν οὕτω L: corr. K, qui et εἰ δ' ἐπὶ τούτῳ conj. exempli gratia

fo. 11ʳ

124 ἀμφιβάλοι L: βάλλοι L¹   125 ἄρσενας K   126 αἰνοτέρ' ὄντας L: corr. A
128 ἔχοντα᾿ L¹ˢˡ   129 δ'] θ' L: corr. K   136 ἀμφιπόλας L: corr. Hal, Gr
138 ἀείμνηστον L: corr. Hal, D⁶⁴³   140 νηυσὶ A.-R.ᶜ   141 ⟨τε⟩ καὶ A.-R.ᶜ   εὐρίθροις L: correxi: εὑρείθροις H, D⁶⁴³   ποταμοῖσιν, -οῖ L¹ʳᵃˢ   142 σεῦ A.-R.ᶜ   ὑπὸ L: corr. Hʰ,
D⁶⁴³   ἐμπίπρανται L: corr. K²

[121–150]   *Book One*   463

> If Venus faces Saturn and the Moon,
> And Ares views from quartile Venus fair,
> And Hermes holds the mid-point, while Saturn
> Himself embraces him in his regard,
> Then sterile eunuchs, nor female nor male,   125
> Beardless, with no part in the works of love,
> And some hermaphrodites, named for the gods,
> Of double nature, neither sex of use.
>
>   Saturn's son Zeus, and Hermes his grandchild,
> Upon a common path, and centred both,   130
> Make orators, in words or with the pen
> Skilled in the scribal art, and profiteers,
> Who thrive on trade and traffic merchandise.
>
>   The radiant Moon, when she encounters Mars
> In the sixth place, brings detriment to men—   135
> Disabled in their feet by murderous steel,
> One-footed, lame, propped on a wooden crutch,
> Viewing their foot, an endless source of woe.
>
>   O Ares, Ares, vile to men and gods,
> To cities, ships, by air and in the sea,   140
> To fruits of the earth and to fair-flowing streams,
> For your sake, cities are consumed with fire,
> And on the sea ships founder in their course,
> And rivers at their arid source run dry,
> Trees lose their fruit, and men are born to pain.   145
> For some you slay consumed in pain by fire,
> Some give as prey to flesh-devouring beasts,
> Impale another, raised aloft in shame,
> His nailed hand stretched upon a murderous cross.
> Your father, wretch, not aegis-bearing Zeus,   150

129-33. Θ p. 209.10–14. εἰ δὲ καὶ Ζεὺς ἐπίδοι τὸν κλῆρον τῆς πράξεως...ἐν οἴκοις Ἑρμοῦ, ποιεῖ τὰς πράξεις ἀπὸ παιδείας ἢ σοφίας ἢ λογογραφίας ἢ ψήφων ἢ λόγων ἢ καλάμου ἢ ἐμπορίας ἢ ἀπὸ σταθμοῦ καὶ ζυγοῦ τὸν βίον ἔχοντας.

Ptol. 4.4.3. ἐὰν δὲ ὁ τοῦ Διός [sc. τῷ τοῦ Ἑρμοῦ μαρτυρήσῃ], νομογράφους, ῥήτορας, σοφιστὰς μετὰ προσώπων μειζόνων ἔχοντας τὰς ἀναστροφάς, cf. Θ pp. 210.31–211.2. ὁ δὲ τοῦ Διός, νομογράφους, ῥήτορας, σοφιστάς, μετὰ μεγάλων προσώπων ἔχοντας ⟨τὰς⟩ ἀναστροφάς.

134-8. Θ p. 189.6–8. οἷον Σελήνη μεστὴ ἐν τῷ ϛ′ τόπῳ πρὸς Ἄρεα φερομένη κατὰ σῶμα ἢ κατὰ διάμετρον κυλλοὺς ποιεῖ ἢ χωλοὺς ἢ ξυλόποδας.

Firmicus, 4.4.2. *Si vero diurna fuerit genitura et sic [sc. crescens lumine] se Marti Luna coniunxerit, omni faciet parte corporis debiles aut parte corporis amputatos...4.4.3 In his enim signis quae aliena esse a societate horoscopi diximus, id est in sexto ab horoscopo vel in duodecimo loco, si crescens lumine Luna se Marti coniunxerit...aliorum corpus ferri laceratione conciditur.*

---

144 ξηροὶ μέν L: corr. R   146 σμυγερῶς S   148 μεθ' ἑοῦ μόρου ἐσταύρωσας L: corr. K: μεθ' ἑὸν μόρον ἐστ. D³⁸¹: μυσαρὸν μόρον ἐστ. K^conj: ἀπολούμενον vel sim. S^conj   149 οὗ τέτατ'] οὔτι τάδ' L: corr. Wa^iv.191, A.-R.   ἡλοπαγῆ L: corr. H, Wa^iv.191, D³⁸¹

οὐδ' Ἥρη μήτηρ, ἀλλ' οὔρεα πικρά σ' ἔτικτεν,
καὶ Λύσσα στυγερὴ καὶ Χάος οὐλόμενον.
Εἰ δὲ Κρόνον λείψειε Σεληναίη κατὰ μοῖραν,
τεύχει ῥευματικοὺς ἠδ' ἀσθενέας κατὰ σῶμα,
τεύχει δ' ἀργαλέους ὑδρογάστορας, οἳ καὶ ἔπειτα   155
ὀστέα χαυνωθέντες ἀφ' ὕδατος οὐλομένοιο
ἔγκυον ὠδίνουσιν ἑὸν μόρον ἐντὸς ἔχοντες.
Ἄρεα δ' ἢν λείψασα Σεληναίη φορέοιτο,
ἀνέρας ἐκτήκει πολλάκις ἐκ κρυφίμων,
ἥπατος ἢ σπληνὸς τρυχουμένου ἠὲ νεφροῖο,   160
ἢ κραδίην παρέτριψε νοήμονα, μητέρα βουλῆς,
πνεύμονά θ' ἑλκήεντα, κακὴν νόσον ἀνθρώποισιν,
οἵπερ δὴ μογέοντες ἀποπτύουσιν ὄλεθρον
βηχὸς ἀνιάτοισιν ἐλαυνόμενοι στροφάλιγξιν,

11ᵛ   λεπταλέοι θυμοῖσι καὶ ἀδρανέες μελέεσσιν   165
πίνοντες καὶ ἔδοντες, ἀειθανὲς ἦτορ ἔχοντες.
Ἄρης ἡμερινοῖσι μεσουρανέων τάδε ῥέζει·
πρῶτον μὲν γονέων βίον ὤλεσε, καὶ λέχος αὐτῶν
χωρίζει θανάτῳ κακῷ ἠὲ διχοστασίῃσιν·
αὐτοὺς δ' ἐν πολλοῖσιν ἐγύμνασε πήμασιν αἰεί,   170
θλίψεσιν οὐλομέναις καὶ ἀργαλέαις πενίῃσιν,
κινδύνοις, βλαβέεσσι, δανείσμασιν, ἐνδείῃσιν·
⟨   ⟩
ἄστεγον ἠδ' ἀγύναιον ἄτεκνόν τ' ἐν νεότητι.
⟨   ⟩
πολλάκι καὶ θανάτῳ στυγερῷ θνήσκουσι σιδήρῳ·
Ζεὺς δ' ἐσιδὼν τούτων ἐσθλὸν ἔθηκε τέλος.   175
Ἄρεα δ' ἢν κατέχῃ, δεινὸν θεόν, αἰθέριος λίψ,
πολλῶν αἴτιός ἐστιν ἐν ἀνθρώποισιν ἀνιῶν·
λύπας καὶ θορύβους, ἐγκλήματα καὶ σίνος αἰνόν

153-7. *Π.σ.α.* p. 182.16–22. Σελήνη Κρόνου ἀπορρέουσα σημαίνει τινὰ πρὸ αὐτοῦ γεγονέναι ἄχρηστον, ὡς αὐτὸν πρωτότοκον τοῦ οἴκου νομίζεσθαι· ποιεῖ δὲ σωμάτων ψῦξιν καὶ σίνος καὶ νεύρων κακώσεις καὶ ὑγρῶν ὀχλήσεις. ἀφαιροῦσα δὲ τῷ φωτὶ ποιεῖ ψυχροκοιλίους, φλεγματώδεις, κατίσχνους, ἀσθενεῖς, ἀπὸ ὑγρῶν ἐνοχλουμένους, συντηκτικούς, ἀποστήματα, διαστήματα, πυρώματα ἔχοντας, μικροῖς χρόνοις † συνερικομους.

Firmicus, 4.15.2 ...*circa ventrem frigus adsiduum, quos Graeci psychrocoelios vocant, et infinitis flegmatum vitiis laborantes, macros, splenicos, dysentericos, hydropicos, pleumaticos vel dysuriacos, et qui latentibus vitiorum doloribus torqueantur.*

---

151 ἔτικ⸢εν Lˢˡ   152 χᾶός ⟨τ'⟩ L¹   οὐλόμενον ad σ' referri, potius quam ad Χάος, monuit S   153 λίψειε L: corr. L¹   Σεληναίην fort. ante rasuram L   154 σάρκα Gr   155 τεύχει δ'] ἄλλοτε Sᶜᵒⁿʲ   καὶ] κεν L: corr. K, nisi κατάσηπτα pro καὶ ἔπειτα   157 ὠδείνουσιν L: corr. H, A.-R.   158 λίψασα L: corr. L¹   160 τρυχώμενον L: corr. A.-R. post Grⁿ   τρυχωμένου   162 θ'] τ' L: corr. A.-R.   164 βηκὸς L: corr. R

fo. 11ᵛ

165 λεπταλέοις L: corr. D⁶⁴³   166 πείνοντες Lˢˡ   167-9 cit. Hephaestion, i. 102.9–11

[151–178] Book One 465

    Nor mother Hera, but the heartless rocks,
And hateful Rage and Discord, noxious fiend.
    If the Moon withdraws from Saturn by degree,
She makes rheumatic persons, weak of limb,
She makes the dropsical of belly, their   155
Bones rendered flaccid by pernicious rheum,
Who suffer pangs in birthing their own death.
    If leaving Mars the Moon is carried free,
She wastes her victims with concealed disease,
Of liver, ravaged spleen, or else of reins,   160
Wears down the thinking heart, volition's seat,
Or ulcerates the lung, a vile disease,
Whose sufferers expectorate their deaths,
Pressed hard by hacking coughs without a cure,
Attenuated hearts, feeble of limb,   165
Who eat and drink and yet die by degrees.
    In day-births, Mars mid-heaven does these things:
He first wrecks parents' livelihoods, their beds
Sunders by hateful death or by divorce;
Then makes the natives prey to constant pains,   170
To cruel travails and wretched poverty,
To dangers, harms, to creditors, and want;
⟨   ⟩
Homeless and wifeless, childless in his youth.
⟨   ⟩
They often die a violent death, by steel;
But Zeus, regarding, makes the outcome good.   175
    If western skies hold Mars, that fearsome god,
He causes much vexation to mankind,
Sorrows and uproars, summonings and wounds,

Θ p. 193.5–6. ἡ Σελήνη μεστὴ κατὰ σῶμα ἀπορρέουσα τὸν Κρόνον ἀποπλήκτους ἢ μαινομένους ποιεῖ, ἔσθ' ὅτε δὲ καὶ τυφλούς.
158–66. Π.σ.α. p. 183.5–11. Ἐὰν δὲ ἡ Σελήνη ⟨τύχῃ⟩ ἀπὸ Ἄρεος τὴν ἀπόρροιαν ποιουμένη, κακὴ πρὸς πάντα... εἰ δὲ καὶ τῷ φωτὶ ἀφαιρεῖ ἡ Σελήνη ἢ καὶ τοῖς ἀριθμοῖς, τὰς διὰ χολῆς μελαίνης ὀχλήσεις ποιεῖ καὶ αἵματος ἀναγωγὰς καὶ δαιμόνων πάθη καὶ αἱμορροΐδας καὶ τομὴν καὶ χωρισμούς.
Firmicus, 4.11.7. Si vero deficiens lumine, a Marte defluens, ad Saturnum feratur, fames, aegritudines valitudinesque decernit; facit, lunaticos, aemorroicos, claudos, paralyticos, gibberosos; oligochronios aut, si nihil horum fuerit, facit biothanatos.

---

167 ἡμερινοῖσι L: ἡμερινῇσι Heph: ἡμερίοισι S   168 ὤλεσε Heph (iam A.-R.): ὄλλυσι L
169 κακῶι ἠὲ διχοστασίη τε L¹ʳᵃˢ: hexametrum corr. A.-R. κακ. ἠὲ διχοστασίῃσιν χωρίζει θανάτῳ ἢ καὶ διχοστασίῃ Heph: pentametrum corr. Heil¹⁶⁵ χωρ. θαν. ἠὲ διχοστασίῃ
170 πολλοῖσιν, λ¹, οἱ L¹ʳᵃˢ ἐγύμνασεν ἤμασιν L: corr. Hal, D³³²   171 ⟨τε⟩ καὶ vel οὐλομένῃσι A.-R.ᶜ   πενίεσσιν L: corr. D³³²   172 ἐνδίεσσιν L: εἰ- L¹: corr. D³³²   post 172, 173 lacunas statui propter syntaxin   173 ἄστεγοι ἠδ' ἀγύναιοι, ἄτεκνοί D³³² ἐν νεότητι, ἐν ν L¹ʳᵃˢ   174 στυγεροῦ Κ   σιδήρου D³³²   175 τοῦτον L: corr. D³³²   176 λίψ L¹ˢˡ
178 καὶ²] ἢ L: corr. Sp¹⁵⁷

ἢ πάθος, ἢ πλώουσιν ἑὴν πάτρην προλιπόντες.

Ἑρμείας, Παφίη, πολιὸς Κρόνος ἢν μὲν ἔχωσιν 180
τὴν πρᾶξιν, ῥέζουσιν ἀμύμονας ἰητῆρας,
ἤπια φάρμακ' ἔχοντας, ἀνώδυνα φαρμάσσοντας· 184
εἰ δὲ Ζεὺς ἐσίδοι, πολυόλβους εὐτυχέας τε, 182
πλούτῳ τιμήεντας, ἀγακλέας ἀνθρώποισιν.

Ὅσσαι δ' ἄν κεν ἔχωσιν ὑπὲκ συνόδοιο φυγοῦσαν 185
Μήνην, φωσφορέουσαν ἔτ' ἔμπεδον, ὀρνυμένην τε,
Ἄρεϊ συμβάλλουσαν ἀνηλέϊ ἢ Κρόνῳ αἰνῷ,
ἔμβρυα μὲν φθείρουσι μινυνθάδι' οἷσι χρόνοισιν,
μηδὲ βροτῶν μορφὴν ἐγγάστριον αὐξήσαντα,
σαρξὶ δὲ θηρείῃσι πανείκελα †ῥυζήσασαι 190
ὠμοτόκοις ὠδῖσιν ἐς ἠελίου φέρον αὐγάς·
αὐταὶ δ' ἀμφὶ πόνοισιν ἀνηλέα κωκύουσαι
εἰς Ἄϊδος κατίασιν ἀνοστήτοιο μέλαθρον·
εἰ δὲ Ζεὺς ἐσίδοι, ψυχὴν μάλα πολλὰ παθοῦσαν
ἐκσώσει θανάτοιο, κακῶν δ' οὐκ ἔσσετ' ἀρωγός. 195

Τίπτε μάτην, ἄνθρωπε, θυηπολέεις μακάρεσσιν;
τίπτε μάτην τρισέλικτος ἀν' οὐρανὸν ἤλυθε κνῖσα;
ἴσχεο· οὐ γὰρ ὄνειαρ ἐν ἀθανάτοιο θυηλαῖς.
οὐ γάρ τις δύναται γένεσιν μετατρεψέμεν ἀνδρῶν,
ἥθ' ἅμα νηπιάχοις συγγίγνεται ἀνθρώποισιν, 200
εὐθύ τε Μοιράων εἱλίσσεται ἀμφὶ μίτοισιν,
κλώσμασιν ἀρρήκτοισι σιδηρείοισί τ' ἀτράκτοις.
ῥέζε Κρόνῳ καὶ Ἄρηϊ καὶ Ἑρμῇ καὶ Κυθερείῃ
καὶ Διὶ καὶ Μήνῃ καὶ Ἡελίῳ βασιλῆι·
οὗτοι γὰρ κρατέουσι θεῶν, κρατέουσι καὶ ἀνδρῶν, 205
πόντου καὶ ποταμῶν πάντων ῥοθίων ἀνέμων τε,
καὶ γῆς καρποφόροιο καὶ ἠέρος ἀενάοιο.
Πλησιφαὴς Κρονίωνι συναντήσασα Σελήνη

180–4. Θ p. 213.19–22. εἰ δὲ εἰς τὸν τῆς πράξεως τόπον τύχωσι Ἑρμῆς καὶ Κρόνος καὶ Ἀφροδίτη, ποιοῦσιν ἰατροὺς ἢ ἐπαοιδοὺς ἢ βοτανικούς· εἰ δὲ καὶ Ζεὺς ἐπιμαρτυρήσῃ αὐτοῖς, ἐκ τούτων τὰς εὐτυχίας ἕξουσιν.
CCAG v/1. 199.9–11. ἐὰν δὲ ὁ Κρόνος ἐπίδῃ τινὰ αὐτῶν τῶν ε' λαμπρῶν ἀστέρων ὡρονομοῦντα, ἰατρικῆς ἔμπειροι γίνονται καὶ προγνῶσται, ἀποκρύφων βιβλίων ἢ τελετῶν πολυΐστορες.

---

179 sic dedi, post D³³²: ἢ⟨ν⟩ πλώωσιν Wa^{iii.93}: ἢ πάθος ⟨...⟩ | ἢ πέλαγος πλώουσιν K   180 Παφίην L: corr. Hal, D⁶⁴³   ἢν μὲν] ἢν κεν L: corr. Hal: εἰ κεν Mon⁴¹   181 πρῆξιν D⁶⁴³   ῥέζουσιν] ἕξουσιν L, qui τευ add. (id est, τεύξουσι) in marg. sin.: corr. A.-R.   ἀμύμονες ἰητῆρες L: corr. L¹ˢˡ, Hal   182 ἐσίδοι, ί L¹ʳᵃˢ   184 post 181 trans. K post A   185 ὅσσοι L: corr. D⁶⁴³   ἄν] αὖ Head   ὑπεξυνόδοιο L¹ˢˡ   187 καὶ Sp¹⁵⁷   188 φθείρουσι L: corr. H, A.-R.   μινυνθαδίοισι L: corr. K   189 ἐμγάστριον L¹ˢˡ   αὐξήσαντα L: corr. K   190 θηρίεσσι L: corr. D⁶⁴³   πανείκελα L¹ˢˡ: an πανίκ- voluit (cf. 6.346)?   ῥυζήσασαι L: ῥοιζήσασαι K: ῥυστήσασαι K²: αὐξήσασαι Sᶜᵒⁿʲ   191 ὠδεῖσιν L: corr. H   φέρων L: corr. H, Gr   192 αὐταί L: corr. Hal, D⁶⁴³   194 μάλα] κακὰ Hal^{mg}   195 κακῶν] τέκνων Sᶜᵒⁿʲ   δὲ οὐκ L: corr. H, Hal

>   And harms; they go to sea, quitting their homes.
>   Hermes, the Paphian, Cronos, governing   180
>   Activity, make excellent physicians,
>   In soothing drugs, in painless treatments skilled.   184
>   If Zeus looks on, they're rich and fortunate,   182
>   Honoured with wealth, persons of public note.
>   Women whose Moon's departing from the Sun   185
>   And bearing light once more, and on the rise,
>   With pitiless Mars or grey-haired Saturn joined,
>   Destroy their foetus, not yet brought to term,
>   Nor in the womb assuming human form,
>   Discharging them, inhuman gouts of flesh,   190
>   In raw birth-pangs into the light of day,
>   While they, with shrieks of unrelenting pain,
>   Go down to Hades' halls of no return.
>   If Zeus looks on, he saves from death a soul
>   That's suffered much, but brings no rest from harm.   195
>   Why vainly, man, give sacrifice to gods?
>   Why rises curling smoke in vain to heaven?
>   Desist. In god's oblations there's no good,
>   For what's assigned at birth none can avert,
>   What was engendered in his infant state,   200
>   And was entangled in Fate's filaments,
>   With iron spindles, webs no man can tear.
>   Serve Saturn, Mars, Venus, and Mercury,
>   And Zeus, the Moon, and Helios the king;
>   For these rule over gods, rule men alike,   205
>   The sea, all rivers, dashing waves, and winds.
>   Fruit-bearing earth, and everlasting sky.
>   The Moon Full in her light with Cronos' son

185-93. Cf. 6.46-50.
Π.σ.α. p. 182.12. (Σελήνη Κρόνῳ συνάπτουσα)...τῇ δὲ μητρὶ ψύξεις καὶ νόσους ποιεῖ.
Firmicus, 7.2.15. *Si Luna aequis partibus cum Marte iungatur in eodem signo posita, aut si in diametro constituti aequas partes teneant in ‹MC. et in› IMC., nec eos aliqua benivola stella respiciat, Saturnus vero sic positam cum Marte Lunam qualibet ratione videat, matres eorum in ipso partu constitutae moriuntur.*
Π.σ.α. p. 183.11-12...ἐπὶ δὲ γυναικῶν ἐμβρυοτομίας καὶ τῆς ὑστέρας κίνδυνον.
194-5. Firmicus, 7.2.15. *Si vero aliqua benivola stella sic cum Marte positam Lunam respiciat, conciso infante particulatim prolato mater ex mortis periculo liberatur.*

198 ἀθανάτοισιν θυήλης L: corr. K 199 μετ᾿τρεψέμεν, μετ L¹ʳᵃˢ 202 σιδηρίοισι L: corr. L¹ 204 ‹τε› καὶ Ἡελίῳ Ger¹⁶² (nol.), K 205 ρατέουσι καὶ ἀνδρῶν L¹ʳᵃˢ
fo. 12ʳ
206 πάντων...τε L¹ʳᵃˢ: τῶν μετὰ ψόφου κυμάτων L¹ˢˡ

εὐτυχέας ῥέζει καὶ μακαριστοτάτους·
εἰ δὲ λίποι Κρονίωνα φάει πλήθουσα Σελήνη, 210
οὐκέτι τὴν αὐτὴν ἐντὸς ἔχει δύναμιν·
ἀλλὰ κακῶν ῥεκτεῖρα πέλει λείπουσα πρὸς αὐτόν·
ἔκφρονας, αἰνομόρους ἢ νοσεροὺς τελέσει,
ἀμβλύτερόν τ' ἐτέλεσσεν ἑὸν βίον ἐν καμάτοισιν
⟨   ⟩
Ἄρης καὶ Φαέθων κατεναντίον ἀλλήλοισιν   215
ἄμφω κέντρον ἔχοντες, ἀνωμαλίην βιότοιο   218a/216b
ἀνθρώποις ἐπάγουσι καὶ ἐκ φιλίης ἐλάσουσιν, 216a/217b
καὶ προκοπῆς στερέουσιν, ἐπεὶ Διὸς ἔπλετο πλοῦτος 217a/218b
καὶ δόξαι καὶ σωφροσύναι καὶ πίστιες ἐσθλαί,
ἐκ δ' Ἄρεος πενίη τε κακὴ θόρυβοί τε μάχαι τε,   220
ἐγκλήσεις μεγάλαι, περὶ σώματος ἔσθ' ὅτ' ἀγῶνες·
οὗτοι δ' εὔποροί εἰσιν, ἀπ' εὐπορίης δὲ πένονται·
ἢν δὲ μεσουρανέῃ Πυρόεις, τέλος αἰνὸν ἔχουσιν.

κέντρον ἔχων Φαέθων Μήνης μέτα καὶ Κυθερείης,
ἤν πως φωσφορέουσα Σελήνη τῷδε συνάπτοι,   225
ἄρχοντας μεγάλους, εὐδαίμονας, ἔμφρονας ἄνδρας,
ἐνδόξους, στροφίοισι καρήατα κοσμηθέντας,
πλούτῳ τιμήεντας, ἀγακλέας ἀνθρώποισιν.

Ἀμφότεροι δύνοντες ὁμοῦ Κρόνος ἠδὲ καὶ Ἄρης,
Μήνης Ἡελίου τε καταντίον ἑστηώτων,   230
ῥέζουσ' ἐμμανέας, πάσας φρένας ἐξολέσαντες·
οἴονται δ' ὁράαν νεκύων σκιοειδέα μορφήν,
οἱ δὲ καὶ εὐφρονέοντες ἀεικέα πήματ' ἔχοντες
πίπτουσιν συνόδοισι Σεληναίης ὑπὸ ῥιπῆς.

215-22. Cf. 3.306-8; Περὶ σχημ. 77; Περὶ κράσ. 129; Firmicus, 6.16.1.
229-34. Valens, II 37.43. Κρόνος δὲ καὶ Ἄρης ἐν τῷ ὑπογείῳ ἤτοι ὁμόσε ἢ κατὰ μόνας ἐπισκιασμοὺς ἢ καταπτωτικοὺς ἢ θεῶν ἢ νεκρῶν εἰδωλοποιητὰς καὶ ἀποκρύφων ἢ ἀπορρήτων μύστας· τὸ δ' ὅμοιον κἂν τὴν σύνοδον ἢ πανσέληνον καθυπερτερήσωσιν ἢ διαμετρήσωσιν ἢ καὶ κατὰ μόνας τὴν Σελήνην, [ἢ] τῆς Σελήνης φάσιν τινὰ λυούσης, κατοπτεύσωσιν, μανιώδεις, ἐκστατικούς, πτωματικούς, ἀποφθεγγομένους ἀπεργάζονται.
Θ p. 192.13-14. ἐὰν ὁ Ἥλιος καὶ ἡ Σελήνη ὡροσκοπῶσιν, ὁ δὲ Κρόνος δύνῃ δίχα Διὸς καὶ Ἀφροδίτης, λυσσῶντας καὶ μαινομένους ποιοῦσιν.

---

212 λίπουσα L: corr. L¹   213 νοσερούς L¹ˢˡ (sed cum puncto supra σ)   τελέσει L: -εν add. L¹, nec non ποιη- supra lineam   214 ἐὸν] ἔμεν K: νέων Sᶜᵒⁿʲ (aut ἐτέλεσσαν ἐὸν)   post 214 lacunam statuit K

Makes prosperous men, with every bounty blessed.
But if the Full Moon parts from Cronos' son, 210
No more does she exert that self-same power;
But drawing near him when she's on the wane
Makes mad men, sick men, doomed to a bad end,
Leading a faint existence in their woes
⟨   ⟩
Ares and Phaethon facing each to each 215
And both on centres, bring vicissitudes 218a/216b
In livelihood to men, end amities, 216a/217b
And curb success, since wealth is Zeus' domain, 217a/218b
And glory, self-control, and noble trust;
But Mars brings penury, alarums, wars, 220
Grievous indictments, fighting for one's life;
Such men are wealthy, but from wealth turn poor,
And, Mars midheavened, meet an evil end.
Zeus centred with the Moon and Cythera,
If the Moon was shining when she joined with him, 225
Great leaders, fortunate men, endowed with sense,
Esteemed, their heads adorned with priestly bands,
Honoured with wealth, and famous among men.
When Mars and Saturn both together set,
The Sun and Moon facing them opposite, 230
Madmen they make, devoid of all their wits;
Who think they see the dead's shadowy forms,
Or even, sane, to undeserved ordeals
Fall victim on the Moon's synodic path.

Θ p. 193.9–10. ἐὰν ὁ Κρόνος διέπῃ τὴν Σελήνην διαμετρῶν αὐτήν, ἔσται τὸ γεννηθὲν θεοφορούμενον, ἐπιληπτικόν.

Θ p. 193.20-2. ἡ Σελήνη συνοδικὴν ἔχουσα φάσιν ἢ πανσεληνιακὴν καὶ ὑπὸ Κρόνου θεωρουμένη δίχα Διὸς ἢ Ἀφροδίτης δαιμονιοπλήκτους ποιεῖ.

Π.σ.α. p. 183.19-20. ἐὰν δὲ οἱ δύο φωστῆρες κακωθῶσιν ὑπὸ Κρόνου καὶ Ἄρεως μαρτυρούντων αὐτοῖς, μαινομένους, φρενοβλαβεῖς ποιοῦσιν.

216-18 ἀνθρώποις ἐπάγουσιν ἀνωμαλίην βιότοιο | καὶ προκοπῆς στερέουσιν καὶ ἐκ φιλίης οδασουσιν | ἄμφω κέντρον ἔχοντες L: corr. K   217 προκοπη L, ˆet s add. L¹   στερέουσιν L: corr. H, Gr   ἐλάσουσιν] οδασουσι L: γρ. σκεδάσουσιν, ελασουσιν in marg. sin. (ἐλάσουσι etiam [387])
220 ἐκ δ'[..] Ἄρεως L: corr. Gr   221 χρώματος L: corr. K   222 ἐν εὐπορίῃ L: corr. K
230 Ἡελίου τε] ἠελίοιο L: corr. D[644]   234 πίπτουσι L: corr. H, Hal

ἢν δὲ Κρόνου μέσση τε καὶ Ἄρεος ᾖ Ἀφροδίτη, 235
καὶ Μήνην λεύσσωσι καὶ Ἑρμείαν τετράγωνον,
δρῶσιν φοιβητὰς ἢ μάντιας, οἵθ' ἱεροῖσιν
ἑζόμενοι ζώουσιν ὀνείρατα μυθίζοντες,
οἱ δὲ καὶ ἐν κατοχαῖσι θεῶν πεπεδημένοι αἰεὶ
δεσμοῖσιν μὲν ἔδησαν ἑὸν δέμας ἀρρήκτοισιν, 240
⟨   ⟩
εἵματα μὲν ῥυπόωντα, τρίχες δ' οὐρῇσιν ὅμοιαι
ἵππων κηροπαγεῖς οὖλαι πληροῦσι κάρηνον·
οἱ δὲ καὶ ἀμφιτόμοισι σιδηρείοις πελέκεσσιν
ἔνθεα λυσσώοντες ἑὸν δέμας αἱμάσσουσιν.
πλησιφαὴς δ' Ἄρηι συναντήσασα Σελήνη, 245
Ζηνὸς ἄτερ Κύπριδός τε, κακὴ κατὰ πάντα τέτυκται·
βλάπτει μὲν βίοτον καὶ πλούσιον ἄνδρα πένητα
ῥηιδίως ἔρρεξε, μινυνθάδιόν τε χρόνοισιν
ἐξαπίνης ἀπόλεσσε βίῃ κακοεργέϊ Μοίρης.
Ἄρεος ἠδὲ Κρόνοιο μέσην δείμαινε Σελήνην, 250
οὕνεκεν ἀργαλέη πέλεται μογεραῖσι τεκούσαις·
τρύχει γὰρ ταύτας κρυφίμων ἄπο· πολλάκι δ' αὐτοὺς
ὤλεσεν ἐν θανάτοισι βιαιοτάτοισι βαλοῦσα,
ἁψαμένους βρόχον αἰνὸν, ἢ ἀραμένους ξίφος ὀξύ,
ἢ πυρὶ δαιομένους, ἢ ἐν ὕδασι πολλὰ παθόντας. 255
Ἄρεος ἠδὲ Κρόνοιο μέση Κύπρις οὐ καλοεργός,
οὕνεκεν ἀνθρώποισι κακὴ κατὰ λέκτρα τέτυκται·
μίσγει γὰρ δούλαισιν ἑταιρίσιν, ἃς φιλέοντες
ζήλῳ ἐλαύνονται κακοεργέϊ· πολλάκι δ' οὗτοι
ἀνέρες ὀργιόωντες ἀποκτείνουσι γυναῖκας, 260
καὶ μόρον αἰνὸν ἔχουσι κακῆς διὰ λέκτρα κυθήρης.
Ζῴδιον ὠρονόμοιο λαχὼν Ζεὺς ἠδ' Ἀφροδίτη
Ἄρηος δύνοντος ἀνηλέος ἠδὲ Κρόνοιο,
⟨   ⟩

235–44. Cf. 6.491–3; 4.214–17.
Θ p. 192.16–18. ἐὰν ἡ Ἀφροδίτη ἐμπεριέχηται ὑπὸ Κρόνου καὶ Ἄρεως ἐν ἑνὶ ζῳδίῳ, τετραγωνίζηται δὲ ὑπὸ Σελήνης καὶ Ἑρμοῦ, ποιοῦσι θεοφορουμένους καὶ φοιβαζομένους καὶ ἐνθέους.
Θ p. 194.2–4. ὁ Ἄρης ἢ ⟨ὁ⟩ Κρόνος ἐν τῷ ὑπὸ γῆς δαιμονιοπλήκτους ἢ ὑπὸ εἰδώλων φοβεριζομένους· εἰ δὲ καὶ Ἀφροδίτη συνῇ, ποίει θεοφορουμένους ἢ ἀποφθεγγομένους.
250–5. Cf. 4.409–13; 5.197–201.
Θ p. 125.17–19. ἡ οὖν Σελήνη...ὑπὸ τῶν κακῶν ἐμπερισχομένη δυστοκίαν ἀποτελεῖ.

235 Ἄρεῶς L¹ˢˡ   ᾖ] ἢν L: corr. A.–R.   Ἀφροδίτηι L: corr. Gr   237 μάντ[.]ας L: corr. H, Gr   238 ἐζ[.]όμενοι   L   239 κατοχῇσι A.–R.   post 240 lacunam statuit K   241 ῥυπόντα L¹ˢˡ   οὐρ[..]ῇσιν L¹ˢˡ   242 ὀλοαὶ τήρουσι L: corr. K   243 σιδηρίοις L: corr. L¹   244 λυσσόωντες L: corr. H, D⁵³³

fo. 12ᵛ
247 βίοτου Head

If Venus is between Saturn and Mars, 235
And they view Moon and Mercury in square,
They make inspired ones, prophets, who preside
Over offerings, or live by telling dreams,
Or, fettered, in detention by the gods,
They bind their persons with unyielding chains 240
⟨   ⟩
In sordid clothes, their hair trailing like manes
Of mares, thick, fixed with wax, covers their heads;
While they, with iron axes double-edged,
In sacred madness bloody their own flesh.
When the Moon in her full light encounters Mars, 245
Without Zeus or the Cyprian, all turns bad:
She injures wealth and makes a rich man poor
With ease, shortening his span of life, and slays
Him outright by Fate's swift and deadly power.
Between Ares and Cronos fear the Moon, 250
For she's a menace to those giving birth:
She injures them from unseen causes; often
Destroys men in most violent modes of death,
Fixing a noose, upraising a sharp sword,
Burning with fire, or overwhelmed at sea. 255
Between Ares and Cronos Venus brings
No good, a threat to human marriages:
She entangles men with slave-girls, loving whom
To ill will they're exposed; and often these
Persons become incensed, and kill their wives, 260
And come to grief through amorous mishap.[1]
If Zeus or Venus holds the rising sign,
While Mars the pitiless and Cronos set,
⟨   ⟩

[1] Literally, beds of evil love.

Θ p. 200.1-2. ἡ Σελήνη συνεχομένη ὑπὸ Κρόνου καὶ Ἄρεος ἐν ἑνὶ ζῳδίῳ ἐπίκεντρος ἢ ἐπαναφερομένη βιαιοθανάτους ποιεῖ.

250-2 cit. Hephaestion, i. 330.25-6. Καὶ ὁ Μανέθων δέ φησιν· Σελήνη ἐμπερισχεθεῖσα ὑπὸ Κρόνου καὶ Ἄρεως ἀργαλέα ἐστὶ ταῖς τικτούσαις, καὶ μάλιστα εἰ ἐν πλαγίοις ζῳδίοις καὶ οὗτοι οἱ ἀστέρες (ὅ τε Κρόνος καὶ ὁ Ἄρης) τύχοιεν, ἡ δὲ Σελήνη ἐπίκεντρος εἴη, ὁμοίως δὲ καὶ εἴπερ καὶ οὗτοι ἐπίκεντροι εἶεν.   250 δείμαινε, -αι-, -ε L^{1ras} 251 μογερῇσι A.-R.   252 αὐτοὺς L^{1sl} 254 ἀψαμένους...ἀραμένους L^{1sl} αἰνὸν] αἰπύν conj. Lop, cf. 3.262   255 δαιομένους...παθόντας L^{1sl} 256 Κρόνοιο μέση] Κρόνου μέση L: corr. Gr^n, D^{254}, qui et Κρόνου μέσῃ protulerunt   257 ἀνθρώποισιν L: corr. H, Gr   258 δούλαισιν, -ιν L^{1ras}: δούλῃσιν A.-R.   261 καὶ] αἳ K   αἰνὸν [...] ἐχουσι L   λέκτρα] φίλτρα K, qui etiam θέλκτρα conj.   post 263 lacunam statuit K

πλούσιοι ἐν πρώτοισι καὶ ἐν πυμάτοισι πένητες,
ἀλλ' οὐκ ἐκλείπουσι μάχας θορύβους τε δίκας τε, 265
εἰ μή πως Φαέθων πυμάτην περὶ μοῖραν ὁδεύσῃ.
εἰ δ' Ἄρης ὥρην κατέχοι Φαίνων τε σὺν αὐτῷ,
δύνῃ δ' αὖ Φαέθων κατεναντίον ἀμφοτέροισιν,
ἐν νεότητι πένητα καὶ ἐς τέλος εὔπορον ἄνδρα
ῥέζουσιν, βιότοιο δ' ἀνώμαλα ἔργα τελοῦσιν. 270
εἰ δὲ Κρόνῳ καὶ Ἄρηι συνῇ κερόεσσα Σελήνη,
μοίρης ἐντὸς ἐοῦσα, συνάπτῃ δ' αὐτίκα τοῖσδε,
ἐντὸς ἔχει κακίην Ἄρεος ἠδὲ Κρόνου αἰνήν,
αἰνός τ' ἀνθρώπων ἔσεται βίος ἠδ' ἐλεεινός,
καὶ πενίη καὶ μοῖρα κακή· καὶ λάτρια ἔργα 275
πείσονται, βίοτόν τε ῥοπῇ λείψουσι πρόμοιροι.
Ἡνίκα δ' ἡ Κερόεσσα μέσον πόλον ἀμφιβεβῶσα
νυκτερινοῦ θέματος κατὰ μοῖραν ἰοῦσα φαανθῇ,
Ἥλιός τ' ἐπίκεντρος ἐν ἀρσενικοῖσι τόποισιν,
γεννῶσιν βασιλῆα, θεὸν βροτὸν ἀνθρώποισιν. 280
Ἑρμείας δὲ μεσουρανέων, Τιτὰν δὲ σὺν αὐτῷ
αὐτή θ' ἡ Κερόεσσα καθ' ὡρονόμοιο τυχοῦσα
ἡμερινοῦ θέματος, βασιληίδος ἐστὶ γενέθλη.
ταῦτα δέ τοι τελέουσιν, ἐπὴν ἐπίκεντροι ἔωσιν,
μηδένα τῶν ὁλοῶν κατεναντίον ἐχθρὸν ἔχοντες. 285
Ἢν δ' ἐπὶ μαρτυρίην Ἄρεως ἐλθοῦσ' Ἀφροδίτη
ὄμμα βάλῃ παντανγὲς ἐν ἡμερινῇσι λοχείαις,
ἐκ πυρὸς αὐχήσουσι τέχνας μέλανός τε σιδήρου
ἄκμοσι ῥαιστοτύποις μεμελημένοι ἠδὲ καμίνῳ.
Ἑρμῆς δ' οἰκείοις ὁπότ' ἂν κατὰ κύκλα φαανθῇ, 290
μαρτυρίῃ δὲ Κρόνοιο κατ' αἰθέρα τῷδε πελάζῃ,
δὴ τότε ῥήτορας ἄνδρας ἰδ' ἐν σοφίαισιν ἀρίστους
ἔσσεσθαι δείκνυσι καὶ ἀστρολόγους θεοφήμους.
εἰ δὲ Σεληναίης ἑλικώπιδος ἄστατος ἀστὴρ
Ἑρμείαν σύμφωνον ἔχοι κατὰ κόσμου ἀταρπόν, 295
καὶ μούνη Κυθέρεια συνῇ καλῷ Φαέθοντι,
ῥεκτῆρας χρυσοῖο καὶ Ἰνδογενοῦς ἐλέφαντος
ἐργοπόνους ῥέζει καὶ ζωγραφίης μεδέοντας,
εὐφυέας θριγκῶν τε καὶ εὐτυπέων κανονισμῶν
κοσμήτας, μάλα τοι πεπονημένα τεχνάζοντας. 300

278-80. Lib. Herm. xxvi. 34. Sol in ascendente in signo masculino et Luna in medio caeli gradatim in nocturna nativitate locis in quibus gaudent, sine aspectu Saturni vel Martis, ex claris parentibus natum ostendunt et ipsum regem, deum existentem hominem humanitatis participem.
286-9. Cf. 4.121-4.

---

264 πυμάτοισι, -οι- L^{1ras} 265 ἐκλίπουσι L: corr. L^{1} 272 μοίρην...ἐχοῦσα L: corr. A (ἐοῦσα e conj.) 273 Ἄρεως D^{644}, A.-R. ⟨τ'⟩ ἠδὲ K 274 ἔσεται L^{ras} (ἔσσεται ante corr. ut vid.) 276 λίψουσι L, corr. L^{1} 280 γεννῶσι L^{1sl} 282 καθ'] ἐπ' L: corr. K: ἐφ' Ger^{179}, Key$^{11n.13}$, Pin 283 βασιληίδος, -ηί- L^{1ras} γενέθλης S 287 λο[.]χείαις L

>   Rich at the first, and paupers at the last,
>   But don't desist from fights, alarums, suits,   265
>   Unless Phaethon traverse the last degree.
>   If Ares holds the Hour, Phaenon with him,
>   With Phaethon setting opposite to both,
>   One indigent in youth, but rich at last
>   Is born, afflicted with life's ups and downs.   270
>   If horned Selene nears Cronos and Mars,
>   Within a degree, and then conjoins with these,
>   Contracting evil from that wicked pair,
>   Man's life will be abject and pitiful,
>   Poor and ill-fated. Slaves' lives they will lead,   275
>   And leave them early through catastrophe.
>   When the Horned One rides the centre of the sky,
>   Seen by degree in a nocturnal chart,
>   With Helios on a point in a male place,
>   A king is born, a god-like man on earth.   280
>   With Hermes in Midheaven, the Sun with him,
>   And the Horned One being on the Horoscope
>   In a day chart, the geniture's a queen's.
>   They have this outcome when upon a point,
>   And no malefic star opposes them.   285
>   If Venus comes to testify to Mars
>   And casts her shining eye on daytime births,
>   They boast of trades from fire and swarthy iron,
>   Of hammer-blows on anvils, furnaces.
>   If Hermes shows in the circles domiciled,   290
>   And Saturn's witness nears him in the sky,
>   Then orators and men supremely wise
>   Are shown, and stargazers who voice God's plan.
>   If Selene's roving star that twists and turns
>   Finds Hermes friendly on the cosmic path,   295
>   And Venus joins alone with Phaethon fair,
>   Goldsmiths and artisans of Indus-born
>   Ivory are made, lords of the painter's art,
>   Of cornices and well-hewn walls the gifted
>   Artisans, hard-working in their crafts.   300

290–1. Cf. 4.139–40.
292–3. Cf. 4.127–8.
294–300. Cf. 4.146–52.

---

fo. 13ʳ
290 δ'[..] οἱ. L   291 μαρτυρίηι L: corr. Hal   καθ'αιτερατωδε [..] π. L: corr. Gr
292 ἀνδράσι [.] δ' L¹ʳᵃˢ (ἀνδράσιν fort. ante ras.): corr. Gr (ἄνδρας iam H)   σοφίεσσιν L: corr. H: σοφίησιν A.-R.   295 κόσμοῦ L¹ˢˡ   299 εὐτυπέω̌ν L¹ˢˡ: εὐτοίχων 4.151: εὐτύκτων A.-R.: εὐτυχέας K: εὐγλύπτων Neri: εὐγλυφέων Magnelli

Ζῆνα δ' ὅτ' ἂν φαέθοντα βάλῃ λαμπραυγέτις ἀκτὶς
Ἑρμείου, μίγδην τε διαλλάξωσιν ὁρισμούς,
ῥήτορας ἐμφαίνουσι βροτοὺς σοφίης τε κρατίστους
ζηλωτάς τέχνης τε λόγων, νεότητά τε λαμπρὰν
γραμματικὴν ‹τ'› ἄσκησιν ἐνὶ στέρνοισιν ἔχοντας.   305
  Μήνης δ' ἀμφίκερως σκολιὸς δρόμος ἡνίκ' ἂν ὀφθῇ
Ἄρεος ἀκτίνεσσι πόλου λοξεύματα βαίνων,
Στίλβων δ' ἀμφ' αὐτοῖς ἢ καὶ διάμετρος ὁραθῇ
ζῳδίῳ κόσμοιο, κακοὺς λῃίστορας ἄνδρας
καὶ θυρέτρων δεινοὺς ἐπανοίκτορας ὀθνειάων,   310
κλεπτῆρας φαύλους νυκτοπλανέας τελέουσιν·
οὗτοι φωρηθέντες ἐν ἀλλοτρίοισι μελάθροις
εἰς συνοχὰς ἥξουσι σιδηρήεντά τε δεσμά,
εἱρκτὰς δ' οἰκήσουσι φυλασσόμενοι ἁλύσεσσιν,
ἔν τε βίᾳ θάνατον λείψει κακοεργέϊ θυμῷ,   315
ἢ σφαγίοις ξίφεσιν δεδαϊγμένοι ἢ πελέκεσσιν,
ἢ βρόχον ἀγχονόωντα δι' αὐχένος ἐνδήσαντες,
ἢ διὰ λαιμοτόμου φάρυγος βίον αἵματι λείψει
σφονδυλόεντα τράχηλον ἢ ἰνίον ἀκροτομηθείς·
πνεῦμά θ' ἑὸν λείψουσι πικρᾶς Μοίρας ὑπ' ἀνάγκας.   320
  Ἥλιος δὲ Κρόνου καὶ Ἄρεος ἀστέρας ἀθρῶν
ἀκτινηβολίῃσι φαεσφόρου Οὐλύμποιο,
ναυσιβάτας δείκνυσι καὶ ὕδατος ἵστορας ἄνδρας,
πλωτάρχας σκαφέων, οἳ πολλάκι ναυφθορίῃσιν
χείματος ὀρνυμένοιο βίον σώζουσι δι' ἅλμης   325
νηχόμενοι Μοίρῃσιν ὑπὸ τρόμον ἐν πελάγεσσιν.
  Παμφαίνων δ' ἀστὴρ κυανοχρώτοιο Κρόνοιο
Ἡλίου σελάεσσιν ἀν' οὐρανὸν ἢν ἰσόμοιρος,
τηνίκα φυομένων βρεφέων γεννήτορα πρῶτον
μητέρος εἰς Ἀΐδην πέμψει νεκυηπόλος Αἶσα,   330
κτήματά τ' ἐκβάλλει πατρώϊα καὶ μέγαν ὄλβον,
καί τε κασιγνήτων θάνατον ὁρόωσι προόντων,
κἂκ πολλῶν θανάτων πλοῦτον μέγαν αὐξήσουσιν.

301–5. Cf. 4.201–5, 141.
306–20. Cf. 4.478–9, 481–90, 50–1.
321–6. Cf. 4.395–401.
327–33. Cf. 4.402–8.

301 λαμπραύγετις A.-R.   302 Ἑρμείᾰ͞ου L[sl]: Ἑρμείῳ K   304 τέχνης] τεύχει L: corr. K (quamquam non dedit) e τέχνῃ A[conj]   λαμπρὴν K   305 ‹τ'› e 4.205   306 ἀμφίκερω Hal[mg], D[333]   307 Ἄρεως L: corr. H, D[258]   ἀκτίνεσσιν L: corr. H, Gr   λαξεύματα L: corr. Hal[mg], D[258]   309 ζω[.]ιδίῳ L   310 ἐπανύκτορας L: corr. H[h], D[257]   ὀθ[.]νιάων, ων L[ras], corr. L[1]   312 φοραθέντες L: corr. H (φωρ-), D[406]   313 σιδηρόεντά L: corr. D[406–7]

>   When radiant Zeus is struck by the bright beams
>   Of Hermes, in reciprocal change of terms,
>   They show forth speakers, wisdom's mightiest
>   Disciples and of word-craft; brilliant youth
>   And lettered culture closest to their heart. 305
>   When the horned Moon's wandering path is visible
>   In the heaven's convolutions with Mars' rays,
>   And Stilbon's seen nearby, or in a sign
>   On the opposed side of the cosmos, bandits vile
>   And dread forcers of other people's doors, 310
>   Base thieves and wanderers by night, are made,
>   Who, apprehended in another's home,
>   End in confinement and in iron chains
>   And live in prison bound with manacles,
>   And die by violence with malignant heart, 315
>   Cloven by fearsome swords, or by the axe,
>   Or tying a choking noose around their necks,
>   Or he'll leave life bloodily through jugular cut,
>   Cervical vertebrae cleft, or occiput;
>   They'll quit their lives though grim necessity. 320
>   When Helios views Cronos' and Ares' stars
>   From bright Olympus emanating rays,
>   He shows the birth of sailors, skilled at sea,
>   Captains of ships, who, when they come to grief
>   In rising storms, are rescued in the waves, 325
>   Swimming the seas in fear through Fate's decree.
>   Should swarthy Saturn's all-resplendent star
>   Meet Helios' rays in heaven in like degree,
>   The father of the infants that are born
>   Is first despatched by Fate who deals in death, 330
>   And all ancestral goods and wealth are lost;
>   They see the deaths of brothers born before,
>   But opportune decease augments their wealth.

---

315 λείψει, λ L¹ʳᵃˢ   ἐν δὲ βίῃ βίοτον λ. aut ἐν δὲ β. θάνατον βλέψει Kᶜᵒⁿʲ   316 γρ. ξίφεσσι δεδειγ. in marg. sin.   ξίφεσι L, corr. L¹   317 ἀγχονέοντα L: corr. A.–R. (qui 317 post 319 traiecerunt)   318 φάρυγγος L: corr. D⁴⁰⁷   320 πνεῦμά θ'] πνεῦματ' L: corr. Hal, D⁴⁰⁷   ἀνάγκη̃ς L¹ˢˡ   321 Κρόνοιο A.–R.: Κρόνου ‹τε› Ger¹⁶² (nol.)   325 ὀρνυμένοιο βίοτον L: corr. Gr: -ου βίοτον D⁴⁰⁷   327 κυανοχρόοιο L: corr. A.–R.

fo. 13ᵛ
332 θανάτους A   333 κὲκ L: corr. A.–R.   αὐχήσουσιν L: corr. K

ἢν δὲ Σεληναίης ἀκτὶς ἰσόμοιρα πελάζῃ
⟨   ⟩ 334b
†μάρτυς δ' ἐπὶ τοῦτο γένηται καὶ Πυρόεις† 335
ἡ μήτηρ προτέρη οἴχεται ἐς Ἀίδην,
ἠὲ μογοστοκίῃ δεδαϊγμένη, ἢ ὑπὸ νούσου
αἱμηρῆς ἃ γυναιξὶ φύσις κρύφιμ' ἄλγε' ἔδωκεν.
Ἢν Κρόνος ὡρονομῇ, Πυρόεις δύνῃ δὲ κατ' ἰθύν,
αἴλινος ὅστις ἀνήρ γε βιαιότατον μόρον ἕξει. 340
Ἡελίῳ τετράγωνος Ἄρης, Μήνῃ δέ τε Φαίνων,
δούλους ποιήσει καὶ γονέων στερέσει.
ἢν δ' ἔτι καὶ Παφίη κατεναντίον Ἄρεος ἔλθῃ,
⟨   ⟩ 343b
καὶ ταύτην τετράγωνος ἴδοι Κρόνος ὑψόθεν ἑστώς,
ἐκ δούλων δούλους τούσδε νόει ξυνέσει. 345
ἢν Φαέθων τετράγωνον ἴδοι Κρόνον ἠὲ τρίγωνον,
⟨   ⟩ 346b
Ἑρμείας δέ τ' ἐφ' ὡρονόμου Μήνῃ τε σὺν αὐτῷ,
εὐτυχὲς ἐκ γενεῆς †ἐσειτε† τοῦτο θέμα
⟨   ⟩ 348b
δόξῃ καὶ πλούτῳ καὶ φιλίαις μερόπων.
καὶ Ζεὺς ὡρονομῶν Πυρόεις θ' ἅμα καὶ τρίτος Ἑρμῆς 350
⟨   ⟩ 350b
Μήνη δ' ἐκ συνόδοιο Κρόνον φίλον ἀγκαλίσαιτο,
εὐπράκτους ῥέζει καὶ μακαριστοτάτους.
Ἢν δὲ Κρόνος παρόδοισιν ἐπ' Ἄρηος τόπον ἔλθοι,
ψυχρὸς ἐὼν θερμοῖο, μολὼν τόπῳ οὐ καλοεργός,
ἔσσεται ἀνθρώποις πολλοῦ κακοῦ αἴτιος οὗτος· 355

334–8. Cf. 4.409–13.
341–2. Firmicus, 6.29.3. *Si Lunam de diametro Mars et Saturnus pariter aspexerint, et nulla benivolarum stellarum vel Lunam vel illos qui sunt in diametro constituti, salutari radiatione conveneri[n]t, aut servos efficiet ista coniunctio, aut privatos parentum praesidio misero faciet orbitatis onere praegravari.*
343–5. Firmicus, 6.29.4. *Si Venerem et Lunam in diversis locis constitutas Saturnus et Mars quadrata vel diametra radiatione respexerint, et his omnibus Iovis oportunum testimonium denegetur, a servis parentibus natos ista coniunctio perpetuo faciet servitutis onere praegravari.*

---

335 μάρτυς δ' ⟨ἢν⟩ ἐπὶ τοῦτο γένηται καὶ Πυροειδής Lop (⟨ἢν⟩), Pin (Πυροειδής) 335–6 [φωτὶ Κρόνου,] μάρτυς δ' ἐπὶ [σήματι] τῷδε γένηται | καὶ Πυρόεις, μήτηρ προτέρη [πατρὸς] οἴχετ' ἐς Ἄδην K   336 ἀιδην, ι (ex parte), η L¹ʳᵃˢ   338 αἱμηρῇσι γυν. L: αι]μηρης ἃ γυν. Π¹   κρυφιμ'] κρύφι' L: corr. L¹ in marg. sin.   340 εἴ τις ἀνήρ...ἔξων Sᶜᵒⁿʲ 342 καὶ] ἢ L: ⟨καὶ⟩ L¹ per compendium   στερέησιν, -έησις L¹ʳᵃˢ: corr. K: an στερέσεις?   ἢν γονέων στερέῃ vel στερέσῃ Lud¹³⁰   343b pentametrum iam desideravit K; lunae mentio requiritur, cf. Anubion, F 11.5   345 τούσδε [quod confirmatur ex Anub. F 11.6]: τοὺς δὲ Lud¹³⁰: τῇδε A.-R.ᶜᵒⁿʲ   τούσδε˚νόει L¹ˢˡ, qui tamen del. ˇ puncto

[334–355]   Book One   477

      If Selene's ray comes near in like degree
    ⟨   ⟩   334b
And Mars is joined in testimony too,   335
The mother goes down first to Hades' halls
Rent by the pangs of labour, or disease
Through haemorrhage, nature's dark female pangs.
      If Cronos rises, Mars sets opposite,
Woe for that man who meets a violent end.   340
      Sun square with Mars, and Phaenon with the Moon
Makes slaves of those bereft of parents' care.
But if the Paphian comes adverse to Mars,
    ⟨   ⟩   343b
And Saturn views her quartile from on high,
Through acumen account them slaves of slaves.   345
      If Phaethon aspects Cronos square or trine,
    ⟨   ⟩   346b
If Hermes holds the hour-mark with the Moon,
Pronounce(?) that chart a happy one from birth.
    ⟨   ⟩   348b
With wealth, repute, and friendships with his peers.
Zeus rising, Mars, and Hermes as a third,   350
    ⟨   ⟩   350b
And the Moon after conjunction Saturn clasps,
He makes effective men, most affluent.
      If in his transit Cronos gains Mars' place,
Cold meeting warm, no advantageous guest,
That planet causes men excess of harm: 355

    Anubion, F 11.5-6. [ε]ἰ δὲ Κρόν[ος ἴδοι μ]ήνην καὶ [ὕ]ψ[οθεν ἑστώς] | [ἐ]κ δούλων δούλους τούσδε νοεῖ ξυ[νέσει].
    350-2. Firmicus, 6.31.55. *Si in Virgine sit horoscopus constitutus, et in eodem horoscopo Iuppiter Mars Mercurius et Venus sint collocati, Saturnus vero in Piscibus, id est in occasu, ⟨positus⟩ hos omnes quos diximus diametra radiatione respiciat, et Sol in anafora horoscopi constitutus signum Librae possideat, Luna vero in Aquario sit posita, et omnes in suis sint finibus constituti, id est Iuppiter Saturnus Mars Mercurius et Venus, ex ista genitura decretum potentissimi imperatoris ostenditur.*
    Anubion, F 7.25. Ζεὺς δ Ἄ[ρης Ἑρ]μῆ?ς Παφίη ὁ[μοῦ ὡρονομοῦντες].

---

346 Φαέθων L^{rec} 346b pentametrum excidisse vidit K   347 ἐφ'] ἐπ' L: corr. R   348 εσειτε L: supra lineam εσσται (sic) L^{1sl} u.v.: ἔννεπε malim: ἔξετε Lud^{130}: εἴσιδε Luc   ἔσσεται ἀνδρὶ θέμα S^{conj} εὐτυχὲς ἐσσεῖται τοῦτο θέμ' ἐκ γενεῆς D^{644} 348b hexametrum desiderabat K   350 πυρόεις L^{rec} 350b pentametrum excidisse vidit K; fort. Veneris mentio facta est (Firmicus, 6.31.55)   351 ἐκ συνόδοιο, κ σ L^{1ras} 352 εὐπρήκτους A.-R.^{c} 353 ἔλθοι, ο L^{1ras} 354 ἐ[.]ὼν L   θερμοῖο, ι add. L^1 355 πολλῶν κακῶν L: corr. Gr^n

λύπας γὰρ στοναχάς τε βλάβας τ' ἄξει μερόπεσσιν.
Ἄρης δ' ἐν παρόδοισι κατοπτεύσας Κρόνον αἰνὸν
ἐσθλὸς ἔφυ· κτήσεις δ' ἀγαθῶν καὶ νῖκος ὀπάζει.
Εἴρηται δρόμος οὐράνιος ἀπλανῶν τε πλάνων τε.
Λοιπόν μοι Μοῦσαι δότ' ἀεῖσαι πλείονα τούτων   360
εἰς ἑτέραν βίβλον τῷδε μέτρῳ πρὸς ἔπος.

ΜΑΝΕΘΩΝΟΣ ΑΠΟΤΕΛΕΣΜΑΤΙΚΩΝ ΒΙΒΛΙΟΝ
Α' ΠΕΠΛΗΡΩΤΑΙ

356 ⟨τ'⟩ D³³³   ἄξει] ἕξει L: corr. D³³³   357 παρόδοισιν L: corr. H, Gr   359 οὐρανίων A^conj   πλάνων τε] πλανητῶν L: corr. D³³⁵ (πλανῶν iam Hal^mg, Gr)   360 δότε L: corr. A.-R.   ἀῆσαι L: corr. H^h, D⁶⁴³   361 ἑτέρην A.-R.^c   ἔπος, -πος L^1ras

Grief, lamentations, injuries it brings.
    Ares in transit spying Cronos dread
Brings increment of good and grants success.
    The astral paths, fixed and unfixed, are told.
What's left, O Muses, grant me to sing more,   360
In a later book conjoining verse to verse.

Βιβλίον Ε′

 Ἐξ ἀδύτων ἱερῶν βίβλων, βασιλεῦ Πτολεμαῖε,
καὶ κρυφίμων στηλῶν, ἃς ἤρατο πάνσοφος Ἑρμῆς
σύμβουλον πινυτῆς σοφίης Ἀσκληπιὸν εὑρών,   4
οὐρανίων ἄστρων τ' ἰδίαις ἐχάραξε προνοίαις,   3
ἀντιτύπῳ κηρῷ ἀπομαξάμενος, κεκόμισμαι   5
ἀνθολόγου Μούσης βλύζον δώρημα μελισσῶν,
ἠδ' ἀνὰ νύκτα μέλαιναν ὑπ' οὐρανίων χοροῦ ἄστρων
μοιραίοισι μίτοισι λάλον τὸ μάθημα καθεῦρον·
οὐ γάρ τις τοίης σοφίης ἔτ' ἐμήσατο κῦδος,
ἢ μοῦνος Πετόσιρις, ἐμοὶ πολὺ φίλτατος ἀνήρ·   10
οὐ βαιὸς κάματος δ' οὗτος, Πτολεμαῖε, πέφυκεν.

 Ἀνθρώπων γενέσεις, ἃς ἤραρε μυρίος αἰών,
ἐκ στομάτων ἱερῶν ὁ σοφώτατος εἶπεν Ὅμηρος
χείλεσιν ἀμβροσίοις καὶ νεκταρέῃ διανοίῃ
«φύλλα, τὰ μέν τ' ἄνεμος χαμάδις χέει, ἄλλα δέ θ' ὕλη   15
τηλεθόωσα φύει, ἔαρος δ' ἐπιγίνεται ὥρῃ·
ὣς ἀνδρῶν γενεὴ ἡ μὲν φύει, ἡ δ' ἀπολήγει».
«μοῖραν δ' οὔτινά φημι πεφυγμένον ἔμμεναι ἀνδρῶν,
οὐ κακόν, οὐδὲ μὲν ἐσθλόν, ἐπὴν τὰ πρῶτα γένηται».
«ἀλλὰ τίη μοι ταῦτα φίλος διελέξατο θυμός;»   20
μύθοις οὐρανίοισι φέρων παρέθηκ' ἀγελαῖα,
χάλκεα χρυσείοισιν, ἐπεὶ καὶ δόγματα θεῖα
οἷα κόχλῳ χρυσὸς περικείμενός ἐσθ', ὁ δὲ χρυσὸς
κοσμεῖται κοχλίδεσσιν ἁλὸς περιπορφύροντος.

 Ἐν πᾶσιν μύθοις καὶ τῇ ἰδίῃ διανοίῃ   25
εἴρηται πραπίδων κάματος εὐσυνθέτῳ ἔργῳ.

---

fo. 33ʳ
 2 κρυφίμων, ι L¹ʳᵃˢ   ηὕρατο] L: corr. K²   4 post 3 traiecit K   3 οὐρανίων τ' ἄστρων A.-R.ᶜᵒⁿʲ   ἰδέας Key⁶⁰

fo. 33ᵛ
 5 κηρῷ τ' L: τ' del. K   κεκόσμηται L: corr. Key⁶¹, Lop: κεκόμισται D⁶³⁵   6 βλύζον] βληδων L: corr. R: βαιῶν Key⁶¹   7 ην δ' ἄρα L: corr. Wilamowitz ap. Key⁶¹: ᾗ διὰ K   οὐράνιον L: corr. K   χορὸν L: corr. K post Letronne   8 μυρίοισι L: corr. D³⁰¹   9 ἐπεμήσατο L: corr. D⁶⁶³   11 οὐ […] βαιὸς Lʳᵃˢ   οὐ Halᵐᵍ, Fabricius (ap. D⁶⁶³)   ⟨δ'⟩ K: ⟨γ'⟩ A.-R.   οὐδ'

Book Five

From sacred books' alcoves, King Ptolemy,
And hidden pillars all-wise Hermes raised—
Asclepius his sage associate— 4
And carved with forecasts from the heavenly stars, 3
And fixed with waxen countermark, I bring 5
An apian gift of fine selectiveness,
And under dark night's dance of heavenly stars
I found a speaking science, through fate's threads.
For no-one for such lore acquired the fame
Save only Petosiris, my dear friend; 10
No trivial labour, Ptolemy, was this.
   Of man's fate, which the infinite age has fixed,
The all-wise Homer spoke from holy mouth,
With lips ambrosial, nectareal thought:
'Leaves scatter in the winds, then grow again 15
In teeming woods when spring comes round once more;
So rise one race of men, another fall.'
'No man, I say, has circumvented fate,
Or bad, or good, when first it was decreed.'
'But why, my heart, discourse upon these things?' 20
To heavenly words I've counterposed mundane,
As bronze to gold, for heavenly decrees
Are like gold hemming purple, while the gold
Is graced by shells of the empurpled sea.
   At full length, with (my?) own intelligence, 25
In a well-made work I set forth my mind's toils.

οὗτος βαιὸς κάματος S   12 γενέσειας L: corr. D⁶⁶³   15 θ' ὕλη] γύλη L: corr. Hal^{mg}   16 ἔαρος, ο L^{1ras}   ὥρη, -ι add. L¹   17 ὡς L: corr. H   18 μοίρην L: corr. A   21 παρέθηκα γελοῖα L: corr. Jac⁶⁷¹   22 χρύσεα χαλκείοισιν L: corr. A.-R.   23 κόχλος χρυσῷ L: corr. K   24 κοσμῆται L: corr. H, Hal, D²⁴⁰   κοχλάδεσσιν L: corr. R   περιπορφυρούσαις K^{conj}, K²   25 πᾶσιν, -ν L¹   26 εἴρηται] αἰνεῖται S^{conj}   κάματος πραπίδων A.-R.

Ὥρῃ ἀκριβοῦται δὲ βροτοῖσι τὰ δόγματα θεῖα, 28
ἢν δ' ὥρην ψεύσῃ τι, συνεξώλισθεν ἅπαντα. 27
Ἀστέρες ἑπτὰ θεοὶ μὲν ἂν' οὐρανοῦ ἠέρα πουλύν,
οἳ ζώνας κατέχουσιν ἄνω τὰς ἑπτὰ πόλοιο, 30
αἰῶνός τε γένος καὶ ῥίζα φύσεως πολυμόρφου,
ζωδιακοῦ κύκλου σφαίρωμ' ἄνα καγχαλόωσιν
εἰν ἰδίοις ὁρίοις ὑψώμασιν ἠδέ τ' ἐν οἴκοις·
Ζεύς, Ἄρης, Παφίη, Μήνη, Κρόνος, Ἥλιος, Ἑρμῆς.
⟨   ⟩
ἐν συνόδῳ, βασιλεῦ, μεγάλους παρέχει βασιλῆας· 35
αὐτίκα δ' ἐν συνόδῳ Μακεδὼν βασιλεὺς ἐγενήθη,
ὃν πινυταῖς πραπίδεσσιν ὁμοῦ σκήπτροις ἀνέδειξαν·
καὶ σὺ δέ γ' ἐν συνόδῳ, ἀλλ' οὐκ αὐτῇ ἐνὶ ὥρῃ.
Ἥλιος σατράπας μεσσουρανέων ἐπιδείξει,
καὶ στρατιῆς Ἄρης ἡγήτορας οἷς ἐνὶ οἴκοις, 40
ἐν δ' Ἄρεως οἴκοις καὶ Ζεὺς ἀπέφηνε δικαστάς·
καὶ τούτων δὲ ἕκαστος, ὅτ' ἂν ἐπίκεντρα τὰ φῶτα·
ἢν δ' ἀτόνως λεύσσειε, συνεξώλισθεν ἅπαντα.
Ὡς ὅτ' ἂν ἐν μεγάλοις τοῖς σχήμασι καλὸν ἀθρήσῃ
ἀστὴρ ἀργαλέος, ὑπὸ βασκάνῳ ὄμματι θραύει, 45
οὕτως ἀργαλέοις ἀστὴρ καλὸς ὄμματ' ἐποίσει
ἢ τετράγωνος ἐὼν τοῖς σχήμασιν ἢ διάμετρος.
Ἀντολίην ζητῶν καὶ τὴν φάσιν ἐν συναφαῖσιν,
νυκτερινὸν δείμαινε Κρόνον καὶ ἑῷον Ἄρηα·
ἀρχαὶ γὰρ τούτῳ πάμπαν τελέθουσιν ἀηδεῖς. 50
ὡς πυρὸς αἰθομένου μαλεραὶ φλόγες εἰσὶν ἐν ὕλῃ
λάβρ' ἐπιγινομένου ⟨   ⟩ 52a
⟨   ⟩ καὶ σβέννυται εὐθὺ παρ' ἀκμήν, 52b
⟨   ⟩
ἢν δ' ἐσίδῃ Παφίην, οὐ μαίνεται, ἀλλὰ κενοῦται.
τοῦ δὲ Κρόνου τάρβει αἰεὶ κατὰ πάντα τελευτήν·
ψυχρὸς γάρ τε πέλει †τῇδε Κρόνοιο βολὴ καὶ πήγνυται† 55
ὄψιμος· εἰ δ' ἄμφω δῆριν περὶ κέντρον ἔχωσιν,

27 post 28 traiecit K   27 ἢν δὲ ὥρην ψεύσηται L: corr. K: ἢν δ' ὥρῃ ψεύσηται Joan. Philop. Op. Mund. 4.20, 6.2, A.-R. (+ ἅμ' ἐξωλίσθεν): ἢν δ' ὥρῃ ψεύσειε D⁶⁴⁴   28 ὥρη δ' ἀκριβοῦται L: corr. K (ὥρῃ iam Hal)   29 ἂν'] ἀπ' L: corr. A.-R.ᶜ   ἀρέρι L: corr. K: αἰθέρα A.-R.ᶜ   31 καὶ] γίνεται L: corr. K   32 σφαίρωμ' ἄνα] σφαιρώματα L: corr. K: an σφαιρώματι?   post 32 punxit L, dein paragraphos ad vv. 33, 39 posuit, ut 33-8 unum apotelesma fierent, nullo puncto post 33 apposito   34 ἥ[.]λιος L (ex ἠέλ-)   post hunc versum lacunam stat. K: post 35 Sᶜᵒⁿʲ   35 ὧν σύνοδος Kᶜᵒⁿʲ (sc. planetarum quorum mentio facta erat in versu antecedente cuius iacturam suspicatus est): Ζεύς συνόδῳ Sᶜᵒⁿʲ   μεγάλας L: corr. Gr   παρέχουσιν ἄνακτας Aᶜᵒⁿʲ   37 ὁμοῦ] ὅλων S   38 οὐ L, -κ L¹   39 μεσουρανέων L: corr. A   43 λεύσειε L: corr. S   44 σχήμασιν ἄλλος L: corr. A.-R.

Book Five

By the Hour divine decrees are made exact; 28
Should this go wrong, all reckonings are thrown out. 27
Seven stars—true gods—are in the sky's expanse
Who tenant heaven's seven zones above, 30
Time's children, polymorphous nature's stock,
Exulting in the zodiac's curved gyre
Within their houses, terms, and exaltations:
Zeus, Ares, Venus, Moon, Saturn, Sun, Hermes.
⟨   ⟩
It (they?[1]) makes great kings, my Lord, when it's conjunct; 35
At juncture the king of Macedon was born,
Whose sceptre and shrewd wits they showed; your birth
Was at juncture too, but in a different Hour.
    The Sun shows satraps in the Middle Heaven,
Mars in his houses leaders of the troops, 40
And in Mars' houses Zeus makes justices,
In each case when the lights are set on points;
But if they slip, the outcome fails with them.
    As when in strong aspect a kindly star
Is blasted by a bad one's evil gaze, 45
So, to a bad, a good star lifts its eyes,
Figured in quartile, or placed opposite.
    Seeking their phase and risings when they meet,
Fear Saturn vespertine, and morning Mars;
For Mars always commences with pure spite. 50
When in the woods fierce flames of raging fire
Upon a sudden violent... ⟨   ⟩ 52a
⟨   ⟩ and at its height is in an instant quenched, 52b
⟨   ⟩
At Venus' sight he's checked, and does not rage.
But Saturn's to be feared at every end;
For he is cold; his ray is hard as ice(?) 55
When late; if both contend about a point,

---

[1] Subject perhaps the Moon, or a plurality of planets.

fo. 34ʳ
48 συναφῆσιν A.-R.   50 τούτων L: corr. K   51 μαλεραί] φλογεραί L: corr. R^conj: στυγεραί K   φλόγεσισιν L: corr. L¹   52 λάβρ […] ἐπιγινομένου L: -ρ᾽ως (sic, per compendium) ἐπιγειν- L¹: λάβρον ἐπειγομένου D^665   σβέννυντ᾽ εὐθύ S^conj   lacunas post 51, 52 statuit K, inter 52ᵃ et 52ᵇ K²   54 τάρβησον ἀεί S^conj   55 ψυχρὸς γάρ τε πέλει τῇδε Κρόνοιο βολὴ καὶ πήγνυται ὄψιμος L: πήγνυται Gr (et Hal^mg), qui ὄψιμος initio v. 56 reposuit: πήγνυται ⟨ἤδη⟩ A.-R.^conj: ψ. γ. τ. π. ⟨ | ⟩ τῇδε K. β. καὶ πήγνυται ⟨αἰεὶ⟩ K: ψ. γ. τ. πέλει, τῇ δὲ Κρόνοιο βολῇ Lop^conj: ψ. γ. τ. πέλει· καὶ τῇδε πήγνυται ⟨ἀκτίς⟩ vel ⟨αἰεὶ⟩ S^conj   56 διέριν δ᾽ ἐπί κέντρον ἔχωσιν L: correxi post δῆρίν γ᾽ ἐπὶ κέντρου ἔχ. D³³⁶, δι᾽ ἔριν περὶ κέντρον ἔωσιν K: δι᾽ ἔριν λιπόκεντροι ἔωσιν S

ἔνθ' ἀκαταστασίαι καὶ πῆμ' ἐπὶ πήματι δεινῷ.
ἢν στείχωσι δ' ὁμοῦ συνόδοις ἢ εἰς ἕνα χῶρον,
εὐκρασίῃ χαίρουσι καὶ οὐκέτι δῆριν ἔχουσιν·
θερμότατος γὰρ ἐὼν ψυχρῷ ἀνακίρναται Ἄρης,   60
ψυχροτάτη δὲ Κρόνοιο βολὴ ὑποθάλπεται Ἄρει.
Μειλίχιος Κρονίδης κατὰ πάντα Κρόνῳ συνοδεύων
σύν τ' ἄστροις πᾶσιν, πλὴν Ἡελίου κακοεργοῦ,
σὺν κείνῳ γὰρ ἐὼν λύει πατρώιον οἶκον
καὶ φυγάδας τεύχει καὶ ἐν νήεσσιν ἀλήτας.   65
Ἥλιος Παφίῃ κοινούμενός ἐστι κάκιστος·
ζῆλον, δυσγαμίην, ἐγκλήματα, ὕβριν, ἀνάγκην,
καὶ ψόγον ἐν λέκτροις, ἀσχήμονά τ' ἀλλοπρόσαλλον.
⟨   ⟩
Καὶ δύνων Κρονίδης ἢ καὶ ὑπόγειος ὑπάρχων
λαμπροτέρας πράξεις εἰν ἀλλοδαποῖσι τόποισιν,   70
εὐπορίην δηλοῖ καὶ ὀψίτυχόν τινα πίστιν.
Ἢν δ' ἐσορῇ Στίλβοντ' Ἄρης ἐπὶ τέρματος αἴης,
θησαυροὺς ἐπέδειξε, καὶ ἐκ χθονὸς ὄλβον ἔδωκεν.
Ἄστοργος θυμοῖσιν ἀεὶ ὀλοώτατος Ἄρης
μὴ καθορῶν Κρονίδην, μηδ' εὐπλόκαμον Κυθέρειαν. 75
Οὗτος γὰρ κακός ἐστιν· ὅτ' ἂν δ' ἐπίκεντρος ὁδεύων
ὅσσ' ἀνέχων λεύσσῃ καταλαμπομένην Ἀφροδίτην
⟨   ⟩
Πᾶς ἀστὴρ πέλετ' ἠὲ πανήμερος ἠὲ πονηρὸς
ἐν γενεῇ· φαῦλος δ' ὅτε οἱ παλίνορσος ἐπειχθεὶς
εἰς ἰδίαν χώρην αὐτὸς κατ' ἐπέμβασιν ἔλθοι.   80
Ἀργαλέων ἄστρων δυνατῶς γίγνωσκε τὰ δῶρα·
⟨   ⟩
ἐν δὲ τέκνοισι μόνοις ἀγνώμονές εἰσι δοτῆρες
καὶ διδόασι γονῇ ἔπι πένθιμον ὄμμασι δάκρυ.
Ἄρης καὶ Στίλβων, σύμφωνα τὰ κέντρα λαχόντες,
ὑψηλούς, δράστας, μεγαλόφρονας ἠδὲ βιαίους,   85
πταίοντας τόλμῃ καὶ σφαλλομένους ἐπὶ δόξῃ·

66-8. Cf. 2.426-30.
69-71. Cf. 3.39-48.
84-9. Firmicus, 3.11.9. *In septimo loco ab horoscopo, id est in occasu Mercurius cum Marte partiliter constitutus: si per diem in hoc loco partiliter fuerint inventi, eos qui sic eum habuerint, mulierem aut uxorem suam manu propria interficere compellunt aut propter mulierem vel propter*

58 στίχωσι L: corr. D³³⁶   σύνοδοι L: corr. K   61 ἀποθάλπεται L¹ˢˡ: corr. K   Ἄρει] θερμῶι L: corr. K   63 ἄστροισιν ἅπασιν L: corr. D³¹⁵   κακοεργὸς L: corr. K   65 ⟨τε⟩ καὶ Ger¹⁶³ (nol.)   ἐν νήεσσιν] ἐν ὀθνείησιν K: ἐνὶ ξενίῃσιν K²   66 Παφίῃ L: corr. Gr   67 ζῆλος L: corr. H, Hal, D²⁷⁸: ζήλους Sᶜᵒⁿʲ   ἀνάγκην] ἀνίην K²ᶜᵒⁿʲ: ἄναγνον Sᶜᵒⁿʲ

There's turmoil, and woe comes on dreadful woe.
   If they're synodic, or come to one place,
In tempering they rejoice, and quit their strife:
For torrid Mars is mingled with the cold,   60
And Cronos' freezing ray is warmed by Mars.
   Synodic with his father, Cronos' son
Is kind—and with all stars save harmful Sun.
Being with *him*, he wrecks the father's house,
And makes men exiles, wanderers in ships.   65
   With Venus joined, the Sun is worst of all:
Spite, evil unions, charges, violence, force,
Connubial blame, unseemly tit-for-tat...
⟨   ⟩
   When Cronos' son sets, or is underground,
He makes resplendent acts in foreign parts,   70
Shows affluence, and trust that comes, though late.
   If Mars beholds Stilbon at earth's confines,
He brings treasure to light, gold from the ground.
   Loveless is Mars, vindictive in his heart,
Not seeing Cronos' son, nor fair-haired Venus.   75
For he's malign, but when he's on a point,
And raising up his eyes, sees Venus gleam,
⟨   ⟩
   For every star is noxious or benign
At birth, but turns bad when it retrogrades
And on a transit comes to its own place.   80
   The harmful stars' gifts learn as best you may.
⟨   ⟩
With only children, they give heartlessly;
They grant at birth an eye that's wet with tears.
   Stilbon and Mars, harmonious on their points:
Haughty, dynamic, valiant, men of force,   85
Felled by their daring, wrecked for honour's sake;

---

uxorem aut propter amoris cuiusdam praeposteras cupiditates semetipsos aut alios interficient, aut propter tale aliquod admissum facinus ⟨faciunt⟩ in publica custodia aut in carcere constitui et ex ista accusatione damnari; 3.11.16 (infra).

post 68 lacunam stat. K: ἀλλοπρόσαλλα A.-R.: κ' ἀλλοπρόσαλλον Head (sed quid iuvat?) 70 πρήξεις A.-R.   71 ⟨τε⟩ καὶ Ger¹⁶³ (nol.)   72 Στίλβωντ' L: corr. Gr   αὐάίης L: corr. Hal, D⁶²⁹   74 θυμοῖσιν] θνητοῖσιν S   Ἄρης, ρης L¹ʳᵃˢ   76 ὅτ' ἂν] ἐπὴν A: ⟨δ'⟩ K   'desunt aliquot versus', secundum Halᵐᵍ   77 ὅσσον ἔχων L: corr. D²⁶¹   λεύσει L: corr. A.-R. (-η), K (-σσ-)   post hunc versum lacunam statuit K   78 πέλεται πανείμερος: corr. R: πέλει ἠὲ π. Sᶜᵒⁿʲ   79 ἐπιχθεὶς L: corr. D³⁰¹ (cf. Gr 'citato reditu festinans'): ἐπαχθεὶς K²   80 ἰδίην A.-R.   83 γονῇ ἔπι πένθ.] γονὴν ἐπιπένθ. L: corr. Kᶜᵒⁿʲ (sed nol.) post A.-R. γονὴν ἔπι πένθ.: γονὴν ἰδὲ πένθ. K   85 δρήστας A.-R.

34ᵛ
ἤτοι γὰρ κολάσει συνελαυνόμενοι βεβάρηνται,
ἢ ἀλόγους μέμψεις ὑπενεγκάμενοι πεπάτηνται,
ἠὲ πάτρην φεύγουσι διωκόμενοι παρ' ἕκαστα.
ἢν δὲ Κρόνος τούτῳ τῷ σχήματι μάρτυς ἐπέλθῃ, 90
τὸν δεσμὸν λύσας δόξαν παλίνορσον ἔδωκεν,
καὶ χειμῶνι πικρῷ γλυκερὴν ἐπέχευε γαλήνην.
Ἑρμείας κακότεχνος ὁμοῦ καὶ πυρβόλος Ἄρης,
ἢ δύνοντες ὁμοῦ ἢ καὶ ὑπόγειοι ἐόντες,
⟨   ⟩
ἐλπίσιν ἀπλήστοις μεγάλας ἀρχὰς μελετῶσιν· 95
ὄλβῳ γὰρ πίσυνοι καὶ τεύχεσι θωρηχθέντες
οὐρανίοις ἄστροις ἐπαειρόμενοι ἀτῶνται,
ἠδ' ἄστρων ψευσθέντες ἐὴν διὰ πίστιν ἄπιστον
οὐρανίαισι βολαῖς ὡς ἀστέρες ἄφνω ἔλαμψαν, 98b
οὐρανίαισι βολαῖς ὡς ἀστέρες ἦλθον ὑπ' ὀρφνην.
Καὶ Παφίη δύνουσα κακή, ὡς λοίγιος Ἄρης· 100
ἀλλ' ὁ μὲν ἀλγύνει ψυχὴν καὶ σῶμα βρότειον,
ἡ Παφίη δὲ πικρὴ καὶ βάσκανός ἐστ' ἐπὶ λέκτροις.
Ἑρμῆς καὶ Παφίη ἰδίαις μοίραισι ταπεινοὶ
ξυρομένους κεφαλὰς μίμους ὄχλοισι γελοίων
⟨   ⟩
Ἄρης οὐ καλός ἐστιν ἐπεμβαίνων Ἀφροδίτῃ· 105
ζήλους γὰρ τεύχει φοβερούς, καὶ φάρμακα δεινά,
καὶ κρύφιμα στομάχων ἀλγήματα καὶ νόσον ἄρθρων.
Ἥμερός ἐστιν Ἄρης ἐπὶ τὸν Δία πάντοτ' ἄκεντρος.
Αὐξιφαὴς δ' ἀγαθὴ κατὰ πάντα πέφυκε Σελήνη,
ἢν φεύγουσα Κρόνον ἐπὶ τὸν Δία πρῶτον ἵκηται· 110
καὶ λείπουσα καλή, ὁπότ' ἂν Παφίη συνοδεύῃ·

93-9. Firmicus, 3.11.16. *Sed semper Mercurius cum Marte pariter constitutus in actibus publicis aut in administrationibus aut in occupationibus constituit, sed in ipsis actibus numquam longis temporum continuationibus perseverant; aut enim impetiti aut accusati amoventur et frequenter iudiciis adplicantur et falsis interdum accusationibus opprimuntur; ex quibus infortuniis ita eorum*

---

fo. 34ᵛ
90 ἢν δὲ] ἠδὲ L^isl (cum puncto supra η): corr. Letronne ap. K   91 δρησμὸν K   94 δύναντες L: corr. K   lacunam post 94 statuit K, qui et 96 + 95 traiecit et 97 οὐρανίοις ⟨δ'⟩ add.   96 πίσυνοι] πιννυτοὶ L: corr. D⁴³⁷   97 ἐπαειρόμενοι] ἐπιγινόμενοι L, -γειν- L¹: corr. A.-R.^conj : ἔπι γεινόμενοι D⁴³⁷: ἐπιτεινόμενοι A.-R.^conj: ἀνεπειγόμενοι K: μέγ' ἀειρόμενοι K²: ἐπιπειθόμενοι S   ⟨ἀπ⟩ατῶνται S   98 ψευσθέντες] ego, post A^conj (ad sensum ἐκ δ' ἄστρων πταισάντες R^conj): φύσαντες L: ψαύσαντες K   ἠδ' vel ἐξ ἄστρ. φυσῶντες D⁴⁸² ('superbientes ex astris')   99 οὐρανίαισι [-ῃσι A.-R.] βολαῖς ὡς ἀστέρες ἦλθον ἐπ' ἀφνωι ἀνέλαμψαν L: versus reficit K post A^conj ἐς ὄρφνην (sed monuit Hal^mg ἀνέλαμψαν pro glossa habendum esse)   102 ἐπὶ, π L^1ras (fort. ἐνὶ ante ras.)   103 μοίρῃσι A.-R.   104 γελοίους D⁶⁶⁶, K, qui post hunc versum lacunam statuit: γελοίων | ⟨ἔργων πραγματίη μέγα χάρμα φέροντας

> For either they're oppressed by punishment,
> Or trodden down by charges without base,
> Or, being persecuted, fly their homes.
>> If Saturn comes as witness to this chart, 90
>> Loosing the bounds, he brings restored esteem,
>> And sheds a grateful calm on bitter storms.
>>> Designing Hermes joined with fiery Mars
>>> Setting together, or beneath the earth,
>>> ⟨   ⟩
>>> With unfulfilled hopes they hold great commands: 95
>>> Trusting in wealth and fortified with arms
>>> Placing their faith in stars, they come to grief,
>>> Deceived in them by trust that was no trust,
>>> With heaven's bolts, like stars, they quickly flare, 98b
>>> With heaven's bolts, like stars, they're overcast.
>>>> Setting, the Paphian's bad, like noxious Mars. 100
>>>> But he injures the soul and man's physique,
>>>> While she brings harm and malice to the bed.
>>>>> Hermes and Venus in their own degrees
>>>>> Dejected, shaven mimes whose jokes the mob...
>>>>> ⟨   ⟩
>>>>>> Transiting Venus, Mars is not a friend. 105
>>>>>> He brews fearful resentments, noxious drugs,
>>>>>> Concealed pains in the throat,[2] and joint disease.
>>>>>>> Mars reaching Zeus, not on a point, is mild.
>>>>>>>> The waxing Moon is good in all respects
>>>>>>>> If fleeing Saturn first she comes to Zeus, 110
>>>>>>>> And, waning, when she joins the Paphian;

---

[2] Or stomach.

patrimonia dissipantur, ut [in] gravi fenore usurarum quatiantur; sed et sponsione aut fideiussione aliqua gravibus damnorum vel condemnationum generibus opprimuntur.
  103–4. Θ p. 217.6–8. Ἑρμῆς καὶ Ἀφροδίτη ταπεινούμενοι ἐν ὁρίοις ἰδίοις ἢ ἀλλήλων μίμους ἢ πολιτικοὺς ποιοῦσιν, μάλιστα ἐν Αἰγοκέρωτι διὰ τὸ παρανατέλλειν τὸν Πίθηκα.
  111. Π.σ.α. p. 184.23–4. πρὸς μὲν πάντα καλή; Firmicus, 4.6.2, 4.9.7.

ἔτευξαν⟩ exempli gratia K²ᶜᵒⁿʲ   105 οὐ καλός ἐστιν Ἄρης L: corr. Nauck^{IV.166}: οὐ καλὸς Ἄρης ἐστὶν D⁶⁶⁶: ⟨μὲν⟩ R: ⟨καὶ⟩ ἐπεμ. K   107 στομάχων κρυφίμων L: corr. R   108 ἄκεντρος, -ς L¹ʳᵃˢ   110 ⟨γ⟩ ἐπὶ R: πρὸς A.–R.ᶜᵒⁿʲ   111 λίπουσα L: corr. L¹

μεῖον δ' ἢ μεῖζον μεστὴ πρὸς Ἄρηα κακίστη.
Πλησιφαὴς Μήνη ἐπὶ τὸν Κρόνον ἐστὶν ἀρίστη·
πλοῦτον γὰρ πουλὺν παρέχει, ἀλλ' οὐκ ἐπὶ δόξῃ.
Πλησιφαὴς δ' ἀκτῖσιν ἀπορρείουσα Κρόνοιο 115
ψυχαῖς πλαζομένους, ἐξισταμένους διανοίης,
σαρκῶν ἐξ ἰδίων ἀπογευομένους, ἱεροῖσιν
θυμῷ μορμύροντας ἐπίψογον εἰς νόσον ὀργῆς,
βωμολόχους θ' ἱερεῖς, τιμαῖς θείαισι προφήτας.
Ἥλιον Μήνη ὁπότ' ἂν συναφαῖσι καθεύροι, 120
ἀρχαῖσιν πλοῦτον παρέχει πενίην ἐπάγουσα·
οὐκ ἰδικὴν γὰρ ἔχει φάσιν ἡ θεός, ἀλλά τιν' αὐγὴν
χείρον' ἀπ' Ἡελίοιο δανείζεται, οὐ μόνιμον φῶς·
Μήνη δ' ὡς σχομένη περ ἀπώλεσεν, ὅσσον ἔλησιν,
οὕτω καὶ πλούτῳ πενίην ἐπέθηκε φέρουσα, 125
ἀντιτύπῳ νεμέσει ἀποδωκαμένη τὸ δάνειον.
Σύνδεσμος Μήνης ὀλοώτατός ἐστι βροτοῖσιν·
35ʳ κἢν λύσῃ δὲ φάσιν τὰ τελέσματά γ', οὗτος ἔφυσεν
πτωχόν, χερνήτην ταλαπείριον ἠδέ τ' ἀλήτην.
Ἡλίου κέντροισιν Ἄρης διάμετρος ὑπάρχων 130
τέκνοις καὶ γενέτῃσι μάχας ἠδ' ἄστατον ὀργήν·
καὶ διάμετρος Ἄρης εὑρὼν μοίραισι Σελήνην,
δεσμά, βρόχους, εἱρκτάς, πολέμους, ἀσχήμονα ζωήν·
ἢν δ' ἀπόκεντρος Ἄρης μοιρῶν ἰδίων διάμετρος,
μιμηλὰς τέχνας, καμάτους πυρὸς ἠδὲ σιδήρου· 135
καὶ Παφίῃ διάμετρος Ἄρης οὐ σώφρονα μοιχόν.

115-19. Θ p. 193.5-6. ἡ Σελήνη μεστὴ κατὰ σῶμα ἀπορρέουσα τὸν Κρόνον ἀποπληκτοὺς ἢ μαινομένους ποιεῖ, ἔσθ' ὅτε δὲ καὶ τυφλούς.
130-1. Firmicus, 7.10.1. Sed et si Mars in horoscopo vel in MC. partiliter fuerit inventus, Sol vero aut in occasu aut in IMC. fuerit constitutus, hoc idem [sc. aut alienabitur a patre, aut gravia habebunt iurgia simultatum] simili ratione perficitur.

112 μείων δ' ἢ μείζων L: corr. Hal^mg, D^666   Ἄρεα L: corr. H, Hal, Gr^n   115 ἀπορρέουσα L: corr. Gr^n   116 διανοίαις L: corr. R   118 νόσου ὀργῇ L: -ι add. L¹: corr. S: νόσου ὀργήν K   119 τ' L, corr. L¹   θείῃσι A.-R.   120 συναφῇσι A.-R.   121 ἀρχέσιν L: corr. Gr: ἀρχῇσιν A.-R.   ἄρχῃ μὲν...πενίην ⟨δ⟩ Magnelli ap. S   122 οὐχιδικὴν L: corr. Gr   γὰρ ἔχει] παρέχει L: corr. Hal^mg   τιν'] τὴν L: corr. Gr   αὐγην L   123 χείρον' ἀπ'] χείρων L: corr. K   124 μιμνης ἀσκομένη δάνιόν περ ἀπώλεσεν ἰσοτέλησεν L: corr. R (Μήνη δ' ὡς), D^666 (σχομένη), A (ὅσσον ἔλῃσιν)

> But worst approaching Mars, more or less Full.
> The Full Moon joined to Saturn is benign:
> She gives great wealth, but little of repute.
> When, Full, she shrinks from Saturn with her rays, 115
> Wandering in spirit, driven from their wits,
> Consuming their own flesh, in sanctuaries
> Seething in spirit, sick with toxic rage,
> Or scrounging priests, divinely honoured seers.
> When Moon encounters Sun, and they connect, 120
> At first she vouchsafes wealth, then indigence.
> For the goddess' light is not her own, but lent,
> Inferior, by the Sun, a transient gleam.
> The Moon thus yields as much as she receives,
> And hence, to riches, she annexes dearth, 125
> With matching portion rendering up the loan.
> The Moon at node brings devastating harm,
> And if she leaves her phase, this brings to birth
> A beggar, wretched hireling, wanderer.
> When Mars upon a point faces the Sun, 130
> Discord of sons with fathers, constant strife;
> When he finds the Moon opposed in his degrees,
> Bonds, nooses, prisons, wars, an ugly life;
> If Mars, decentred, fronts his own degrees,
> Mimetic arts, labours of fire and steel; 135
> And Mars opposing Venus, unchaste rakes.

132-3. Περὶ κέντρ. 6. ἐν δὲ τῷ ὑπογείῳ, κακοποιῶν ὁρώντων, ἐκ κρυπτῶν τόπων ἐνοχλεῖ [sc. the Moon]· συνοχαί τε γὰρ καὶ δεσμὰ διὰ κρυπτὰ πράγματα...
Θ p. 149.9-11. ἡ δὲ Σελήνη ὑπὸ Κρόνου ἢ Ἄρεως ὁρωμένη, κρυπτῶν τόπων πόνους ποιεῖ ἢ χάριν τινῶν πραγμάτων κρυπτῶν· συνοχὰς γὰρ καὶ δεσμοὺς ἐπάγει.
Firmicus, 3.4.15. *Metuendum est autem, quotiens sic per diem constitutus in diametro habuerit Lunam crescenti lumine...accusationes, seditiones, turbas, damna faciet et repentina pericula...faciet etiam vincula, carceres et custodias.*
136. Θ p. 195.5-8. ὁ Ἄρης τὴν Ἀφροδίτην ἰσομοίρως θεωρῶν κατὰ τρίγωνον ἢ τετράγωνον ἢ διάμετρον ἐν τροπικοῖς ζῳδίοις καὶ ἀλλήλων τὰ δωδεκατημόρια ὑποδεξάμενοι ἢ ἐπιθεωρήσαντες, ποιοῦσι μεθυστάς, μοιχούς, ἀναστάτους.

---

125 οὕτω [.] καὶ L^ras, -ως ante ras. ut vid.   127 ἐστιν L: corr. H, Gr
fo. 35^r
128 ἔφυσεν] ἔασιν L: corr. K: ἔασεν Gr   οὗτοι ἔασιν A, dein plurales nominativi insequenti versu R^conj   132 μοίρῃσι A.-R.   133 δεσμοβρόχους L: corr. A.-R.   ζωήν] θωήν R^conj   135 μιμητὰς τέχνης καμάτου L: corr. K   post 136 lacunam statuit K

καμπτομένοις ζώοις ὅτ᾽ ἂν εὑρήσῃς ποτὲ φῶτα,
Ἑρμείαν σκέπτου, μεθοδεύεται εἰ τότ᾽ ἐκεῖνος 138a,139b
σχήματι τῆς Παφίης, θηλυνόμενος γὰρ ἐκεῖνος 139a,138b
κοσμεῖτ᾽ ἀρρενόθηλυς ἐὼν πέπλοισι γυναικῶν, 140
ἴδμων τ᾽ ὀρχηθμοῦ ‹τέρψει› θυμέλαισιν ἐραστάς·
εἰ δὲ γυναικὸς ἔῃ, πολύκοινον ἔτευξεν ἑταίρην,
μουσῳδόν, σοβαρήν, πολλοὺς τήκουσαν ἐραστάς.

Εἰ δ᾽ Ἄρην ὑπόγειον ἔχων φαίνοιτό τις ἀνήρ,
καὶ σὺν τῷδε γένοιτο ἰοβλέφαρος Κυθέρεια, 145
καλοβάτην σχοίνων ἠδ᾽ ἠερόφοιτον ἔθηκαν,
Ἴκαρον αἰθέριον πτερύγων δίχα καὶ δίχα κηροῦ·
ἣν δ᾽ ἐσίδῃ Τιτὰν φαέθων, ἐπὶ γαῖαν ἀφῆκαν.

Ἢν δ᾽ εὕροις Μήνην αἰεὶ δύνουσαν ἐφ᾽ ὑγροῖς,
πρὸς Κρόνον ἐρχομένην ἢ δύνουσαν τὰ βόρεια, 150
†ἀνθρώπων δύνουσαν ὁρᾶν ὅτι† ναυτίλοι ὑγρήν,
ὧν ὁδός ἐστιν ὕδωρ, οἱ δ᾽ ἀστέρες εἰσὶν ὁδηγοί,
ἡνίοχοι δ᾽ ἄνεμοι, καὶ κύματα μακρὰ κέλευθα.

ἢν δ᾽ ἐσίδῃς ζῴοις ἐν ὀλισθηροῖσι τὰ κέντρα,
Καρκίνῳ, Ὑδροχόῳ ἠδ᾽ Ἰχθύσι τοῖσιν ἀφώνοις, 155
δύνοντας καθ᾽ ὕδωρ δεσμευομένους θ᾽ ὑπὸ μαζῶν
⟨   ⟩
κυανέῳ πελάγει δ᾽ ὑπονήχεται, ἠΰτε δελφίν,
σφόγγους ἐκ βυθίων πουλυτρήτους ἀνερευνῶν.

Ἐν δ᾽ ἰδίοις οὔσης Παφίης ἅμα Ἑρμάωνι,
ἢ τρητοῖς καλάμοις ὑπὸ πνεύμασιν ᾆσμα μελῳδεῖ, 160
ἢ νομίᾳ σύριγγι φίλην κεφαλὴν ἐπισείει,
ἄλλῳ δ᾽ ἐκ στομάτων κελαδεῖ μυκήματα σάλπιγξ,
ᾧ δ᾽ ᾄσει κίθαρις νευρένδετος ἐν παλάμῃσιν,
ἄλλῳ δ᾽ ἁρμονίην χαλκόκτυπον ἐξετέλεσσαν.

137–41. Θ p. 217.5–8. Περὶ μίμων. Ἑρμῆς καὶ Ἀφροδίτη ταπεινούμενοι ἐν ὁρίοις ἰδίοις ἢ ἀλλήλων μίμους ἢ πολιτικοὺς ποιοῦσιν, μάλιστα ἐν Αἰγοκέρωτι διὰ τὸ παρανατέλλειν τὸν Πίθηκα.
142–3. Θ p. 169.6–8. εἰ δὲ γύνη τύχῃ ἐπὶ τοῦδε τοῦ διαθήματος, πολυκοινήσει ἑταιριζομένη καὶ ἐπὶ τέγαις σταθήσεται ταῖς διὰ ζωῆς.

137 ζώιοις [..] ὅτ᾽ ἂν L^ras   εὑρ̣ῃ̈σῃς L^sl sl   138–40 Ἑρμείαν σκέπτου. θηλυνόμενος γὰρ ἐκεῖνος | σχῆμα τό τε Παφίης, μεθοδεύεται καὶ τότ᾽ ἐκεῖνος | ἀρρενόθηλυς ἐὼν κοσμεῖται πέπλοισι γυναικῶν L: corr. A.–R. (σχήματι τῆς, κοσμεῖτ᾽ ἀρρενόθηλυς), versus rest. K (ἀρσεν-)   141 καὶ τούτων ἀρχιδήμου θυμέλεσσιν ἐραστάς L (ἐρ- H, Hal^mg, Gr): restituit exempli gratia; possis etiam τέρψει τ᾽ ὀρχηθμοῦ ‹πεδάῳ›, cf. Or. Sib. 1.342 πεπεδημένος ὀρχηθμοῖσιν, alia multa: κ. τ. ἄρχει δήμου θυμέλῃσιν ἀρεστός A.–R. (nec non ἐφεστὼς A^conj pro ἐραστάς): κ. τ. χάρισιν δαμνᾷ θ. ἑ. K   142 ᾗ L: corr. A.–R.   τεῦξεν Magnelli ap. S   143 ἐραστάς L: corr. H, Hal, Gr^n   146 σχοίνων δὲ, ‹ἰδὲ› add. L¹: corr. Sp^159: σχοίνοισί τ᾽ ἔπ᾽ K   ἱερόφοιτον, ὁ-, -οιτον L^1ras: corr. Gr^n, D^361   ἔθηκεν, -θηκ- L^1ras: corr. K   147 πτερῶν L: corr. A.–R. (πτερύχων D^608)   151 ἀνθρώπων δύνουσαν ὁρᾶν ὅτι ναυτηλον (ναύτιλον H, Hal, Gr) ὑγρήν L: ἄνθρωποι θύνουσαν ὁρῶνται ναυτίλοι ὑγρήν K: ἄνθρωποι σπεύδουσι περᾶν τότε ναυτίλοι ὑγρήν, aut λαίφεσιν οὐ δείσουσι περᾶν τότε ναυτίλοι ὑγρήν S^conj   155 Καρκίνῳ ἢ L: del. ἢ A.–R.   ἢ ἰχθ. L: corr. A

[137–164]   Book Five   491

    Should Sun or Moon be found in a curved sign,
    Consider whether Hermes moves into   138a,139b
    Aspect with Venus: rendered feminine,   139a,138b
    That woman-man is dressed in female robes;   140
    A dancer, he delights his fans on stage.
    In a woman's chart, this makes a common whore,
    A chanteuse, proud, who saps her lovers' strength.
    If one is born with Mars below the earth,
    And dark-eyed Venus should be found with him,   145
    They make a tight-rope walker, treading air,
    An Icarus on high, *sans* wings or wax;
    If Titan bright looks on, he's thrown to earth.
    When the Moon's found setting in the aqueous signs,
    Gaining on Saturn, or setting in the north,   150
    Sailors are born who brave the raging seas(?),
    Whose way is water, stars their pathfinders,
    The winds their steeds, and waves their roadsteads broad.
    If you see the centres in the slippery signs—
    Cancer, Aquarius, and the voiceless Fish—   155
    Plumbing the seas with bands around their breasts,
    ⟨   ⟩
    He swims in the dark waters, dolphin-like,
    Fetching up porous sponges from the depths.
    With Hermes, Venus in her own domains:
    He blows a melody on punctured reeds,   160
    Or to the pastoral pipes he sways his head;
    The trumpet blasts forth from another's mouth,
    Or the stringed lyre is songful in his hands,
    Or they make a concert of percussive bronze.

144-7. Θ p. 213.6-7. Ἄρης καὶ Ἀφροδίτη ἐν τοῖς ὑπογείοις ποιοῦσι σχοινοβάτας ἢ θεοφορουμένους.
149-53. Θ p. 217.10-11. Ἡ Σελήνη δύνουσα καὶ πρὸς Κρόνου φερομένη, ἐν ὑγροῖς ζῳδίοις ἢ βορεία κατιοῦσα ναυτικοὺς ποιεῖ.
    Θ p. 212.23-4. ὁ Κρόνος καὶ ἡ Σελήνη δύνοντες ἐν καθύγροις ζῳδίοις ποιοῦσι ναυτικοὺς ἢ πλευστικούς.
159-64. Θ p. 217.12-13. Ἀφροδίτη οἴκῳ Ἡλίου ἢ ἰδίῳ μετὰ Ἑρμοῦ, μάλιστα ἐπίκεντροι καλαμαύλους ἢ κιθαριστὰς ἢ μουσικοὺς ποιοῦσι.
    Θ p. 213.24-5. ὁ Ἑρμῆς οἴκοις Ἀφροδίτης μετὰ Ἀφροδίτης ποιεῖ αὐλητὰς ἢ κιθαρῳδούς.

---

156 ⟨θ'⟩ add. R   post 156 lacunam stat. K   157 δ' del. R, K, S: rest. K²
158 πολυτρήτους L: corr. D⁶⁷²   160 ἄσθμα L: corr. Hal^mg, D⁵¹⁶   161 νομίαν L: corr. Gr^n, D⁵¹⁶: νομίη A.–R.: νομίῳ K   ἐπισίει L: corr. L¹   162 κελαδι L: corr. L¹
163 ὠιδαῖσιν L: corr. R   κιθάρης L: corr. K (κιθάρῃ R)   νευρένδετοῦ L, L^1sl: corr. R παλάμῃσιν L: corr. H, Gr   164 χαλκόκτυπον ἐξετέλεσσαν] χαλκῶι τε παρέξεται πνεῦμα L: restitui: χαλκώματα πληκτὰ παρέξει K: χαλκῶν πλατάγημα παρέξει S^conj

ἀλλ' ὅτ' ἂν ἡ Παφίη Ἑρμῇ στείχουσα συνοικῇ, 165
Ἑρμείαο τόποισιν ἀγαλλομένη, ἐπὶ χώρῃ
†τὴν δ' ἄλλων μορφὴν τοῖς χρώμασιν ὧδε διώκει†
ἢ πολλοῖσι μίτοις ἢ πλάσμασιν ἢ ποτε κηρῷ.
ἢν δέ τ' ἐπαμφορέοιτο μετ' Ἠελίοιο Σελήνη,
⟨   ⟩
ἡνίοχος καμπτῆρα διερχόμενος, φιλονείκως 170
ἱπταμένων πώλων τετράζυγον ἅρμα διώκων,
καὶ νύσσῃ σύρδην ἐπινίκιον ἵππον ἐλαύνων.
ἢν δὲ Σεληναίη ὑψώματι οὖσα σὺν Ἑρμῇ
αὐξιφαὴς κατίδοι κλυτὸν Ἥλιον Ὠκεανίτην,
ἰξῷ χρησαμένην τέχνην καλάμοις τ' ἀναφαίνει, 175
καὶ ταύτην ἴρηξ ὠκύπτερος οὔ ποτε λείπει.
Ἄρεα δ' εἰ γνοίης ἀκρονύκτιον ὀβριμοεργόν,
καὶ σὺν τῷδε Κρόνον καὶ Ἑρμείην παρεόντα,
ἀράμενοι παλάμαις ὑπὸ τύμπανα φάσγανον ὀξὺ
μιμοῦνται δυσαγῆ Κυβελήιον ἔνθεον Ἄττιν. 180
ἢν δ' ὥρῃ ζῴοις εὑρίσκηται φολιδωτοῖς
καὶ πρᾶξιν ξὺν Ζηνὶ Κρόνος παρέχει ὑπόγειος,
ῥιζοτόμους τεύχει, παραβαλλομένους, ἐπαοιδούς,
ζητοῦντας θάνατον κακοδαίμονα καὶ μόρον αὔτως
ἀσπίδος αἰνομανοῦς πλατυαύχενος, ἠδ' ἄρ' ἐχίδνης 185
διψάδος αἱμοβόρου φοβερὸν θάνατον †δὲ καλούντων,
Τανταλικῇ κολάσει ὑπὸ γαμφηλῇσιν ὀδοῦσιν
ἰὸν ἐρευγομένης ὑποδίψιον ἄσθματι δεινῷ.

165-8. Θ p. 217.14–15. Ἀφροδίτη οἴκῳ Ἑρμοῦ μετὰ Ἑρμοῦ ἐπίκεντροι ἢ ἐπαναφερόμενοι ἔξαυγοι ζωγράφους ποιοῦσι ἢ ἀνδριαντοπλάστας ἢ πολυμιταρίους.
Θ p. 213.25–7. Ἀφροδίτη οἴκοις Ἑρμοῦ μετὰ Ἑρμοῦ ποιεῖ ζωγράφους ἢ πλουμαρίους ἢ γλύπτας ἢ ἀνδριαντοπλάστας.
169-72. Θ p. 217.16–18. Εἰ δὲ Ἥλιος καὶ Σελήνη ἐν ταῖς ἐπαναφοραῖς τύχωσιν Ἑρμοῦ καὶ Ἀφροδίτης ἐπίκεντροι ὄντες, ἡνιόχους ποιοῦσι, μάλιστα ἐν Διδύμοις καὶ Ταύρῳ.
173-6. Θ p. 217.19–20. Ἡ Σελήνη ἐν Ταύρῳ μετὰ Ἑρμοῦ καὶ Ἡλίου αὐξιφαὴς ἰξευτὰς ποιεῖ καὶ ἱερακαρίους.
181-8. Θ p. 217.21–3. Ἐὰν δὲ ὁ ὡροσκόπος τύχῃ ἐν Καρκίνῳ ἢ Σκορπίῳ ἢ Ἰχθύσι Διὸς καὶ Κρόνου ὑπογείων ⟨ὄντων⟩ καὶ τὴν πρᾶξιν παρεχόντων, ποιεῖ βοτανικούς, θηριοδείκτας [θηριοδείκτους cod., corr. Boll dubitanter] (sim. CCAG vii. 118.6–8 [Epit. IIIb]).

165 στίχουσα L, corr. L[1]
167 αἰόλλειν μορφὰς ἢ χρώμασι τῇδέ γ' ἔδωκεν K post R[conj] δαιδάλλειν μορφὴν ὑπὸ χρ. τῷδέ γ' ἔδ.: αἰόλ. μορφ. τοῖς χρώμασιν ἥδε διδάσκε S[conj]: pro clausula εὖ δεδάηκεν A.-R.[conj]: οἵδε διδοῦσι, οἱ διδόασι, ἥδε δίδωσιν, alia possis: etiam οὗτος ἔδειξεν (cf. 2.323)

fo. 35[v]
169 ἢν δὲ L: ⟨τ'⟩ ego: ἢν δ' H, Hal   ἐπαμφορέοιτο] ego, post D[336] ἐπάνω φορέοιτο: ἐπαναφέρηται L: φέρεται μετὰ Ἡελ. D[336] (nol.), unde φέρεται μετά ⟨γ'⟩ Ἡελ. A.-R.   ἢν δ' ἐπάνω Κερόεσσα μετ' Ἡελίοιο φέρηται S[conj]   post hunc versum lacunam suspicor

[165–188]   *Book Five*   493

  But when with Hermes Venus shares a house, 165
Rejoicing in his places, in that place(?),
To form portraits with pigments ⟨ ⟩
Or many threads, or sculpture, or with wax.
  If with the Sun Selene's borne aloft,
⟨   ⟩
A driver, chasing triumph, past the post 170
With racing steeds urging his four-horsed car,
Driving his horse to victory past the post.
  If the Moon at exaltation with Hermes,
Waxing, beholds the famed Sun Ocean-bound,
She shows an art with bird-lime and with reeds, 175
One that the swift-winged hawk does not escape.
  If mighty Mars at sunset's found to rise,
And with him Cronos, Hermes, are at hand,
Seizing a sharp sword as drums beat, they mime
Inspired, cursed Attis, Cybele's devotee. 180
  If the Horoscope is found in scaly signs,
And Zeus and Saturn underground rule Action,
They make root-cutters, spreaders(??), charm-singers,
Those rashly seeking ill-starred death and fate
From a maddened, thick-necked asp, or thirsty snake, 185
A viper sucking blood that brings grim death—
A Tantalus-ordeal under hooked fangs—
Disgorging parching gall with breath malign.

Θ p. 212.20-1. τοῦ ὡροσκόπου Καρκίνῳ ἢ Σκορπίῳ ἢ Ἰχθύσι ὄντος Ζεὺς καὶ Κρόνος ὑπογείῳ ποιοῦσι βοτανικοὺς ἢ θηριοδείκτας [θυριωδήκτας cod., corr. Cumont dubitanter].

---

170 ἡνίοχον...διερχόμενον L: corr. A.-R. 171 πώλων] ζώιων L: corr. K² 172 νύσσῃ σύρδην] νεεσει συρτηι L: corr. D⁶⁷⁵ 173 ἣν δὲ] ἡ δὲ L: corr. Hal, D³³⁶ ὕψωμ' ἀνιοῦσα K 175 χρησαμένῃ τέχνῃ L: corr. K post A^conj χρισαμένην τέχνην ⟨τ'⟩ suppl. K ἀναβαίνει, -ει L^{1ras}: corr. K 176 οὔπωτε L: corr. H, Gr 177 εἰ δ' Ἄρεα L: corr. K² ἀκρώνυκτον L: corr. D⁶⁶⁷ 178 ⟨τε⟩ καὶ Ger¹⁶³ (nol.) Ἑρμίην L: corr. L¹ 179 ἀράμεναι L: corr. Gr 180 δυσαγῆν L: corr. D⁶⁶⁷ 181-2 hos duos versus refeci e Θ p. 217.19-20. Mars nullum locum hic habet, neque istud φωλεύων, pro quo signa squamosa manifeste memorari debent: alia possis, e.g. ζῴοις φολιδωδέσιν εὑρίσκηται, ἢν δ' ὥρῃ ζῴοις ἐπί/ἔνι φαίνηται/εὕρηται φολιδωτοῖς; ἢν δ' ὥρην ζῴοισιν ἐσαθρήσῃς φολιδωτοῖς; neque in 182 Jupiter eici debebat 181 ἣν δ' Ἄρης ζῴοις ἐπιφολεύοντα κέντρα L: ἔπι φωλεύων κατὰ κέντρα A.-R. post Gr (φωλ-), D⁶⁶⁷ (ἔπι φωλ-) 182 τὴν πρᾶξιν ζηνὶ καὶ τὸν κρόνον ὑπόγειον L πρῆξιν A.-R. pro ζηνί, κρίνῃ Key⁶²: ζητῇ Hal^{mg}, K τὸν Κρόνον ⟨ὀνθ'⟩ ὑπόγ. D⁶⁶⁷ ξυνὰ Ζηνὶ ⟨λαχὼν⟩ κατίδῃ Κρόνον ὄνθ' ὑπόγ. K² 184 αὐτοῖς L: corr. K: αὐτοῖς S 185 αὐτομανοῦς L: corr. A 186 θ. καθελόντας K: θ. προκαλοῦντας K²: quidni θανατόνδε κάλουσης? 187 γαμφηλαῖς ὁλοῇσιν R^conj 188 ὑποδύψια χάσματι δεινῷ S^conj

εἰ δ' αὔξουσα τύχῃ μεσσουρανέουσα Σελήνη
καὶ διάμετρος Ἄρης σύν τ' Ἡελίῳ ὑπόγειος, 190
φρυγομένων σαρκῶν ὑποτήκεται †πένθημος† ἀνήρ.

καὶ δύνων Πυρόεις, ὁπότ' ἂν Κρόνος ὡρονομήσῃ,
σαρκοβόροις θηρσὶν παρέχει γεννώμενον ἄνδρα·
ἢ †γὰρ καπρίοιο† ὑφίσταται λευκὸν ὀδόντα,
ἢ γναμπτοί σφ' ὄνυχες λαιμὸν διόρυξαν ὄρεσσιν 195
πορδάλιος στικτῆς ἠὲ βλοσυροῖο λέοντος.

ἡνίκα δ' ἡ βασίλεια μέση συνέχοιτο Σελήνη
Ἄρεος ἠδὲ Κρόνου συνθλιβομένη ἰσόμοιρος,
τῷ μὲν ἔδωκε βρόχον, τῷ δ' αὖ βυθόν, ᾧ δὲ μελάθρων
πολλάκις ἢ πτώσεις ἢ χώματα προσκυλίσασα 200
κληΐδων ἀπέρηξε βίῃ συνθλωμένῳ ὀστᾶ.

Μὴ λαθέτω σε Κρόνος ἰσομοιρήσας Ἀφροδίτῃ,
τέκνῳ μὲν τεύχων Πελοπήιον ἠὲ Θυέστην,
ἠὲ καὶ εἰς ἄλλην ἀσεβῆ υἱὸν ἢ Ἰοκάστην,
πολλάκι δὲ προγόνους καὶ μητρυιῇσιν ἔμιξεν 205
ἠδὲ κασιγνήτοις ἐπάγει ὁμογάστριον εὐνήν.
ἐνθάδε μοι, βασιλεῦ, τῷ σχήματι γίγνεο μάρτυς,
γνωρίζων γενεῇ τοὺς Ἀρσινόης ὑμεναίους.

Χαίρει τοι Τιτὰν μὲν ἐπ' ἀρσενικοῖσι τόποισιν,
γηθεῖ δ' αὖ Μήνη πάλι θηλυτέροισιν ἐν οἴκοις. 210
εἰ δ' ἄμφω τούτους ἐνὶ θηλυτέροισι καθεύροις,
εὐνοῦχον σὺ νόει ταλαπείριον ἠὲ κίναιδον,
ἱστοῖς, ἠλακάταις μιμούμενον ἔργα γυναικῶν.
εἰ δὲ γυναῖκα λάβοις εἰν ἀρσενικοῖσιν ἔχουσαν
Μήνην Ἡέλιόν τε, νόει τὸ σχῆμ' ὅ τι δηλοῖ· 215
ἀνδρῶν ἔργα τέλεσσε γυναιξὶ συνευνάζουσα.

197–201. Cf. 4.409–13 and 1.250–5.
Θ p. 200.1–2. ἡ Σελήνη συνεχομένη ὑπὸ Κρόνου καὶ Ἄρεος ἐν ἑνὶ ζῳδίῳ ἐπίκεντρος ἢ ἐπαναφερομένη βιαιοθανάτους ποιεῖ.

189 μεσουρανέουσα L: corr. A.-R.   190 σὺν ἡλίῳ δ'ὑπόγειος L: corr. K post Gr σὺν ἠελίῳ   191 πένθημος L: ἄθλιος, αἴλινος D⁶⁶⁷, qui et ὑποτήκει πένθιμον ἄνδρα conj.: αἴθινος K: ἔμπυρος K²: ἐμμενὲς S^conj   194 ἢ γὰρ καπρίοιο ὑφίστ. λευκὸν ὀδόντα L: ἢ γὰρ ⟨υἱὸς⟩ κ. ὑ. ἀργὸν ὀ. R: ἢ γὰρ ὑ. κ. ὑφέστη λευκὸν ὀδόντα K²: ἤτοι γὰρ καπ. κτλ S^conj

> If Selene's found increasing³ in Midheaven,
> Opposed to Mars with Helios underground,   190
> With shrivelled flesh that (poor?) man atrophies.
>   Mars setting when Cronos is on the Hour
> Consigns the native to carnivorous beasts:
> Either a boar's white tusk will gore him through,
> Or in the hills the curved claws tear his neck   195
> Of dappled pard or lion shaggy-maned.
>   When the Lady Moon is held between the pair
> Of Mars and Saturn, pressed in shared degree,
> To one, she gives a noose; to one, the depths;
> On a third she tumbles ruins, falling roofs,   200
> Which break the collar-bone with shattering force.
>   When Saturn and Venus share degrees, take heed!
> For the child he makes a Thyestean sire,
> Or some such mother as Jocasta was;
> Often he joins stepmothers to stepsons,   205
> For siblings brings a bed from one same womb.
> Witness this pattern, king, from your own house,
> Seeing your sister-marriage figured there.
>   In places masculine the Sun is glad,
> In feminine, the Moon, contrariwise.   210
>   If both are found in places feminine,
> Behold a eunuch or effeminate male
> At looms, with spindles, aping woman's work.
>   If in a woman's chart the Sun and Moon
> Are in male places, understand what's meant: 215
> She'll do the works of men in women's beds.

---

³ Actually, Full.

195 ἢ γναπτοῖς ὀνύχεσσι‹ν› [add. L¹] λαιμὸν [αι L¹ʳᵃˢ] ἀνόρυξεν ὁρίοις L: corr. Hal [γναμπτ-], K: οὔρεσιν ἢ λαιμὸν γναμπτοῖς ὀνύχεσσ᾽ ἀνορύχθη S^conj   198 Ἄρεως L: corr. H, A.-R.   συνλιβομένη L: συνλειβ- L¹: corr. S: συλλαμπομένη K   199 τῶι δὲ μέλαθρα L: corr. A.-R. (ᾧ δὲ), K (μελάθρων)   200 πολλάκι δ᾽ ἢ πτῶσιν ἢ χώματι L: corr. K   201 κληΐδων] κλινηδὸν L (κλειν- L¹): corr. A   ἐπέρηξε L: corr. R: ἔρρηξε D³³⁷   συνθλώμενον L: corr. K   202 Κρόνος ‹γ› A.-R.   203 τέκνων L: corr. K: τέκνοις S   πεδοπήϊον L: corr. A.-R. post D⁶⁶⁷ Πελοπηΐαν (sc. filiam Thyestae)   204 ἠὲ καὶ ὡς ἄλλην ἀσεβήϊον ἠϊοκάστην L: locus desperatus: ἠὲ καὶ εἰς ἄλλην ἀσεβῆ υἱὸν Ἰοκάστην K: ἀσεβῆ ‹β›ίον S, qui et ἢ καὶ ὡς Ἑλένην aut ἠὲ Κλυταιμήστρην conj., sed nihil ad rem   205 ‹καὶ› suppl. D⁶⁶⁸   207 μάρτυς] μάντις L: corr. A post Gr (in interpretatione) testis, μάρτυρ D⁶⁶⁸   208 γενεὴ L: corr. H, Gr   209 Χαίρει μεν Τιτὰν ἐπ᾽ L: corr. R

fo. 36ʳ

211 θηλυτέροισιν L: corr. H, Gr   212 ἠὲ] ἠδὲ L: corr. K   213 ἠλακάταις, ἠ- L¹ʳᵃˢ   214 εἰν] ἐν L: corr. D⁶⁶⁸, qui et ἐνὶ conj.   216 τελοῦσαν γυναιξίν τε συνευνάζουσαν L: corr. K, post A.-R. τελοῦσι γυναιξὶ συνευνάζουσαι: τέλεσσε συνεύνάζουσα γυναιξίν Nauck^{V,170}

Νυκτερινὸς δὲ Κρόνος ὁπότ' ἂν ὑπόγειος ὑπάρχῃ,
καὶ δέ τ' Ἄρην ἐσίδοις γε μεσουρανέοντα ἄνωθεν,
ἁπλώσας παλάμῃσιν ἐπὶ ξύλου ὑψόθι σῶμα
οἰωνοῖσι βορὴν ἐπανιπταμένοις ἐπέδειξεν, 220
μοίρης νευροτόμου ἐσφιγμένος ἄκρα σιδήρῳ.
Τὴν Μήνην σκέπτου, εἰ Τιτῆνος ἐνὶ οἴκῳ,
κἢν εὕρῃς τοῦτον φωλευόμενον διάμετρον,
καὶ φυγάδας σὺ νόει καὶ ἀτιμήτους διὰ πάντων.
Αὐξιφαὴς Μήνη θερμὸν διάμετρον Ἄρηα 225
ἢν προφύγῃ, λίην ψυχρήν τ' ἀκτῖνα Κρόνοιο,
Ζεὺς δὲ τρίγωνος ἔῃ ἐν σχήματι τῷδέ γε μάρτυς,
τὸν βίον αὐτὸς ἔχων ἢ καὶ καθορῶν διάμετρος,
ἡλικίῃ μὲν πρῶτα μέγαν, περιμήκεα θῆκεν,
ὀφθαλμοῖσι χαρωπὸν ἰδ' ὀφρύσιν εὖ ἀραρυίαις, 230
μηχανικὸν σὺ νόει †τε† πολύτροπον ἢ πολύτλητον,
οἶκον μὲν φθείροντα πατρώιον, ἠδέ τ' ἀλιτρόν,
ὃς σκεδάσας ὄλβον πενίην δαπάναισι διώκει,
τὴν δ' ἰδίην ἀκμὴν φιλέοντι δίδωσιν ἐραστῇ,
τὴν δ' ἄλλου ὥρην αὐτὸς ποθέων ἀγαπήσει, 235
ζηλώσει δούλην δ', ἢ ψάλτριαν, ἢ πολύκοινον,
ἐχθροὺς δ' ἐκπτώσσει, τοῖς κρείττοσιν ἀντιφερίζων,
καὶ πάτρης εἴξει, καὶ ἐν ξείνῃ διατρίψει,
καὶ πλασταῖσι γραφαῖς ἀπελαύνεται ἄλλοσε γαίης
εἰς στεινὸν ζωῆς †λύπης δίχα τοῖς ἐπὶ τέκνοις 240
ἀλλοτρίαις τε γοναῖς ἐπιτέρπεται, ἢ δίχα λύπης †
εὐτραπέλοισι γραφαῖς τερπνὸν βίοτον διοδεύει.
Ἡνίκα δ' ἂν Μήνη Ἑρμῇ στίλβοντι συνάπτοι,
ῥήτορα σημαίνει, καί ῥ' ἐν μελέταισι σοφιστήν,
εὔγραμμον πινυτόν, ἐν γυμνασίοις ἴσον Ἑρμῇ. 245
Σκορπίος, Αἰγόκερως καὶ Καρκίνος ἠδὲ καὶ Ἰχθῦς

217-21. Θ p. 201.22-3. ὁ Κρόνος ὑπογείῳ, Ἄρης μεσουρανῶν νυκτὸς ποιοῦσιν ἐσταυρωμένους καὶ ὑπὸ ὀρνέων βεβρωμένους.
222-4. Anon. ap. Θ p. 222.12-14. Τὴν Μήνην καθόρα τίνος ἀστέρος ἐστὶν ἐν οἴκῳ· | κἂν εὕρῃς τοῦτον φωλευόμενον διαμέτρῳ, | καὶ φυγὰς ἔσται δὴ [ἔστι δὲ cod., corr. Delcourt] κάτιμος [καὶ ἄσιμος cod., ἄτιμος m²: κάσημος Cumont: καὶ πανάτιμος vel κατίμητος Lop] καὶ μετανάστης.

---

217 ὁπότ' ἂν] μὲν ἐπὴν R ὑπάρχηι, -ηι L[1ras] 218 μεσουρανέοντ' ἐπάνωθεν R 219 ὑψό[.]θι L[ras] 221 μοίρην νευροτόμον L: corr. K ἐσφιγμένην ἀκρι L: corr. D[398] (ἄκρα), K (ἐσφιγμένος) ἄκρα] ἄρθρα D[337] 222 Τιτάνος L: corr. D[668]: Τιτᾶνος H ἐνὶ οἴκῳ] ἐστὶν ἐν οἴκῳ L: corr. K post A.-R. Τιτηνός γ' ἐνὶ οἴκῳ 224 ἀτίμητον L: corr. K² 226 λίην] λειηντε L: del. τε D[668], λί- A.-R. 229 ἐπιμήκεα L: corr. A 230 ἰδ'] ἠδ' L: corr. Gr 231+ 232-3 pro interpolatis habuit K

When Cronos in night births is underground,
And Mars is seen in Midheaven above,
His body stretched on wood, hands out, on high,
He summons birds to swoop and make their meal, 220
Pierced hand and foot, his sinews rent by steel.
  Observe the Moon, if she's in Titan's house.
And if you find him couching opposite,
Count them as outcasts, everywhere disgraced.
  If the waxing Moon is fleeing heated Mars 225
Placed opposite, and Cronos' chilly ray,
And Zeus in trine is witness to this scheme
As Lord of Life, or viewing it opposed,
In youth he makes him tall, of lofty build,
Bright-eyed, and having eyebrows close-conjoined; 230
Behold a practical, skilled man, or wretch,
Who ruins his ancestral home, a knave,
Who scatters wealth and courts want through expense,
To ardent lovers tendering his charms,
Another's youth desiring in his turn; 235
He'll chase a slave, or lute-girl, or a whore,
Will cower if set against a stronger foe,
And quit his native land and live abroad,
Through spurious documents driven land to land,
In life's tight straits... 240
  ...or without grief
He leads a pleasant life through devious texts.
  When the Moon with twinkling Mercury joins, she shows
An orator, sophist, trained by exercise,
Lettered and shrewd, a gymnast like Hermes. 245
  The Scorpion, Horned Goat, Cancer and the Fish

243-5. Θ p. 208.19-23. ὅτι δεῖ ζητεῖν τὴν Σελήνην ἀπὸ συνόδου ἢ πανσελήνου πρὸς τίνα φέρεται καὶ πρὸς ἐκεῖνον τὴν πρᾶξιν λέγειν, οἷον ... εἰ δὲ τὸν Ἑρμέα, γραμματικὸν ἢ ῥήτορα ἢ σοφόν.
246-51. Θ p. 189.25-6. Κρόνος καὶ Ἄρης καὶ Ἀφροδίτη καὶ Σελήνη ἐν Ἰχθύσιν ἢ Σκορπίῳ ἢ

231 νόει τε [.] L, -ε L^{1ras} (fort. νόειτον ante ras.): νόει γε A.-R.: νόει πουλύ- S^{conj} 233 δαπάνεσσι L: -ῃσι A.-R.   235 ἄλλων S   ὥρην] χώρην L: corr. R   236 ⟨δ'⟩ K   237 ⟨δ'⟩ K   ἐκπτώσει L: corr. K   238 εἴξει] ἄρξει L: corr. R   καὶ²] ἠδ' R   ἐνὶ Ger^{163} dub.   239 πλαστῇσι A.-R.   ἀπελαύνεται] ἐπεριδεῖται L: -είδ- L¹: corr. K²: ἀπεπείγεται K   ὑψόσε γαίης L: corr. K   240-1 εἰς τεινον L: στεινὸν L¹   λύπης μέτα, ταῖς ἐπὶ τέχναις (post ἐπὶ τέχναις A.-R.^{conj}) | ἀλλοτρίαις τε γραφαῖς ἐπιτέρπεται, ἢ δίχα λύπης K: λύπης μέτα, τοῖς ⟨δ'⟩ ἐπὶ τέκνοις | ἀλλοτρίαις τε γοναῖς ἐπιτερπόμενος δίχα λύπης S^{conj} 243 συνάπτῃ A.-R.   244 μελέτῃσι A.-R.   245 πινυτόν ⟨τ'⟩ A.-R.   ἐν γυμνασι τὸν Ἑρμῆν L: corr. A.-R.   γυμνασίοις ⟨τ'⟩ K   246 ἠδὲ καὶ] αὐτὰρ L: corr. S: ἠδ' ἄρ' οἱ A.-R.

ἐκ φολίδων πολλῶν συγκείμενοί εἰσι τὸ σῶμα,
καὶ λεπίδων πολλῶν λεπτῶν θ' ἅμα καὶ πολυχρώμων·
ἐν τούτοισι τυχὼν Πρέσβυς καὶ λοίγιος Ἄρης
καὶ Μήνη κεραὴ καὶ γλαυκιόωσα Κυθήρη   250
ψώρην καὶ λέπρην, ἀλφούς, λειχῆνας ἔτευξαν.
κεντρωθεὶς δ' Ἄρης ἤν πως φαίνοιτο σὺν Ἑρμῇ
Ἡελίου οἴκῳ καθορώμενος, ἐχθρὸς ἐπ' ἐχθρῷ,
ὀφθαλμὸν βλάπτει, εἰ μέν θ' ἕνα φωσφόρον ἀθροῖ·
εἰ δ' ἄμφω κατίδοιτ', ἀλαὸν καὶ πηρὸν ἔθηκεν.   255
Εἰ δ' ἀγαθὸς σωτὴρ φαεσίμβροτος οὐράνιος Ζεὺς
αὐξιφαοῦς Μήνης ὑποδέξεται ἱερὸν ὄμμα,
ἀρχῇ καὶ πίστει καὶ τιμαῖς ἐστεφάνωσεν,
εἵμασι πορφυρέοις τε φέρει κοσμούμενον ἄνδρα.
Ὁ Κρόνος Ἑρμείαν κατέχων Κριοῦ ἐνὶ οἴκῳ,   260
ἤν Μήνην ἐσίδοι ὑψώματι οὖσαν ἑαυτῆς,
ὡρονόμου τε κρατῇσι, βραβεὺς τοῦ πνεύματος αὐτός,
τραυλὸν ἐνὶ γλώσσῃ, χαρίεστατον εἶδος ἔχοντα,
ταῖς ἀκοαῖσι βαρὺν καὶ τοῖς ποσὶν ἠδὲ καὶ ἄρθροις,
ἀστρολόγον πινυτὸν καὶ ῥήτορα καὶ φιλόμουσον   265
ῥυθμοῖς καὶ μέτρων ποιήμασιν, εὔστοχον ἄνδρα,
σχήμασιν εὐθαρσῆ καὶ χρώμασιν †ἀπροφίδητον†,
πουλύγαμον, τέκνοισιν ἐπώδυνον ἠδὲ πολύτλαν,
εὔμουσον, λιγυρόν, φιλοπαίγμονα τῇ διανοίῃ,
οὗ πόρος ἐστὶ φύσις, ἡ δ' αὖ φύσις ἐστὶν ὁ δαίμων,   270
καὶ σοφίῃσι λόγων φυσικῶν βίοτον μεθοδεύων,
ζωῆς καὶ μούσης εὐσύνθετον εἰς τὸ νοῆσαι
ἀνθολόγοισι τροφαῖς ἠδ' εἰν ἰδίαισι μελίσσαις.

Καρκίνῳ λέπρας ἢ ἀλφοὺς ἢ λειχῆνας ποιοῦσιν.
Epit. II = CCAG i. 147.4–10. Περὶ ζῳδίων λεπρωδῶν καὶ ἀλφωδῶν καὶ ψωροποιῶν ἢ λειχήνων. Ψώρας λέπρας λειχῆνας ἀλφοὺς ποιεῖ ἡ Σελήνη κακουμένη ἐν Κριῷ Καρκίνῳ Σκορπίῳ Αἰγοκέρωτι Ἰχθύσιν· οὐ μόνον δὲ ἡ Σελήνη ἀλλὰ καὶ ὁ κλῆρος τῆς τύχης ἢ τοῦ δαίμονος ἐν τοῖς ζῳδίοις τούτοις τετυχηκότες καὶ ὑπὸ κακοποιῶν μόνον θεωρούμενοι. ποιοῦσι δὲ καὶ ὑποκύρτους τοὺς οὕτω γεννηθέντας.
Θ p. 183.2–3. Σελήνη Σκορπίῳ ἢ Ἰχθύσιν ἢ Καρκίνῳ Κρόνου καὶ Ἄρεως ἰσομοίρων αὐτῇ ὄντων λεπροὺς ἢ ἐλεφαντιῶντας ποιεῖ ἢ φαρμάκῳ ἀναιρεῖ.
CCAG i. 166.15–19. δίχρωμα δὲ τὰ ἰχθυακά, ἐπεὶ οἱ ἔχοντες ἐν αὐτοῖς τὴν Σελήνην ἢ τὸν ὡροσκόπον ἀλφοῖς ἢ λέπραις ἢ φακοῖς ἢ λειχῆσι ἁλίσκονται· εἰσὶν δὲ τὰ λεχθέντα ἰχθυακὰ Ἰχθύες Καρκίνος Σκορπίος, ἀπὸ μέρους δὲ καὶ Αἰγόκερως. ταῦτα δὲ λέγεται καὶ λεπρώδη διὰ τὸ ἔχειν λεπίδας, διὸ σὺν αὐτοῖς τέτακται ὁ Σκορπίος.

---

247 συγκείμενοί, γ L¹ʳᵃˢ   248 τ' ἅμα L: corr. L¹   249 λύγιος L: corr. H, Hal, D²⁵⁷,⁶⁶⁹   250 γλαυκιόωσσα L: corr. H, A.–R.
fo. 36ᵛ
251 λιχῆνας L: corr. Hal   252 δ'] δὲ L: corr. Hal   254 βλάπτηι L: corr. Gr   εἰ μέν θ' ἕνα] καὶ τενι L: corr. R: καὶ ἤν πως D³³⁷   ἀθροῖ] αἰθρει L: corr R post D³³⁷ ἀθρῇ   255 κατίδοιτ', ἀλαὸν] καθίδοι ταχιλὸν L: corr. D³³⁸   257 ἱερὸν] μυρίον L: corr. A

> Have bodies laminate of many scales,
> And many platelets, fine and many-hued.
> In them, the Old Man and destructive Mars,
> And horned Moon and the fire-eyed Cythera, 250
> Make scabs and cankers, flakes and leprosies.
> If Mars is seen with Hermes on a point,
> In Helios' house, foe pitted against foe,
> He harms an eye, viewing just one light-source;
> But seeing both, he makes them wholly blind. 255
> If Zeus, good saviour, mortals' heavenly light,
> Receive the waxing Moon's sacred regard,
> He crowns with magistracies, trust, high rank,
> And makes one bedizened in purple robes.
> If Saturn holds Hermes in Aries' house, 260
> And in her exaltation sees the Moon,
> And rules the Hour, himself the judge of life,
> Of lisping speech, unprepossessing form,
> Heavy of hearing, motion, and of limb,
> A skilled star-gazer, rhetor, cultured man, 265
> Shrewd in his aim, in measured formal verse,
> In figures, bold; in colours un-...
> Much married, grieved by offspring, greatly vexed,
> Cultured, clear-voiced, of playful temperament,
> Whose means are nature, and that nature God, 270
> Whose life is ruled by nature's wise accords,
> Through life and art...
> Sustained by hand-picked flowers and his own bees.

252-5. Θ p. 189.13–14. ὁ Ἄρης ἐν Λέοντι δίχα Διὸς ἢ Ἀφροδίτης σίνη ἢ πάθη περὶ τοὺς ὀφθαλμούς.
256-9. Θ p. 208.19–22. ὅτι δεῖ ζητεῖν τὴν Σελήνην ἀπὸ συνόδου ἢ πανσελήνου πρὸς τίνα φέρεται καὶ πρὸς ἐκεῖνον τὴν πρᾶξιν λέγειν, οἷον ... εἰ δὲ τῷ Διὶ εὔπορον καὶ εὐσχήμονα ποιήσει.
260-73. Θ p. 218.3–6. Ἐὰν ὁ Κρόνος καὶ ὁ Ἑρμῆς οἴκῳ Κρόνου καὶ Σελήνη τύχῃ ἐν Ταύρῳ, ποιοῦσι σοφὸν ῥήτορα ἢ μαθηματικόν, χαριέστατον δὲ καὶ φιλόμουσον, ῥευματιζόμενον τοὺς πόδας ἢ τὰ ἄρθρα καὶ σύμμετρον τὸν βίον, ἀλλὰ μεγαλόφρονα καὶ ἡδύν.
ibid. 6-7. Ὁ Ἄρης καὶ ἡ Ἀφροδίτη ὁμοῦ ἢ τετράγωνοι ἢ διάμετροι ἐν τοῖς αὐτοῦ κλίμασιν ἰατροὺς ποιοῦσιν ἢ φιλοσόφους.

---

258 πίστι L: corr. L¹   259 πορφυρέοισι φέρει L: corr. A.-R.: πορφυρέοισι φέρων S^conj   260 Ἑρμείαν, -εί- L^ras   261 ἦν] κ'ἦν L: corr. A.-R.   εἰσίδοι L: ἐσίδη A.-R.   ὕψωμ' ἀνιοῦσαν K   262 ὡρονόμον τε: corr. D⁶³⁹   κρατεῖ L: corr. A.-R.   τοῦ πνεύματος αὐτὸς ὁ βραβεύς: corr. A   263 ἀχαρίστατον A.-R.^conj   ηθαδ' ἐόντα L: corr. A.-R.^conj   264 ἀκοῇσι A.-R.   265-7 aliunde intrusa putabat K; 268 suspectum habebant A.-R.   267 ἀπρονόητον K²   269 φιλοπράγμονα L: corr. D⁶³⁴   271 φυσικὸν L: corr. R   273 ἠδ' εἰν ἰδίαισι] ηενιδιεστι L: corr. K (ἰδίῃσι): ἰδίαισι iam Gr^n

Εὔσφυρος Ἑρμείης ἦν Ζηνὶ μόνῳ συνοδεύοι,
εὔπορος ἀκριβής τε φύσει, κυκλῶν τὸ νόμισμα· 275
σμικρολόγος γὰρ ἐὼν πολλοῖσι τόκοις ἀναβαίνει,
φειδωλὸς ψηφῶν τε φιλάργυρος ἠδὲ δανειστής.
ἐν δὲ τρίταις χώραισιν ἀφ' ὡρονόμοιο τυχήσας
ἀγρευτῆρι λίνῳ ἀνεφέλκεται ἐξ ἁλὸς ἰχθύν.
εἰ δ' Ἄρην ἐσίδοις θυμούμενον ἐκ διαμέτρου, 280
καὶ δολίοισι βρόχοις ὀρεσίτροφα πάντα κυνηγεῖ.
ἢν Παφίην εὕρῃς περιπλεξαμένην τὸν Ἄρηα,
μοιχοὺς καὶ λάγνους καὶ παντοπαθεῖς ἐποίησεν.

Ἐν Παφίης οἴκοις ὁ Ζεὺς ἐπίδοξος ὑπάρχει,
καί ῥ' οὕτως παρέχει, ἢν καὶ ἐπίδοξα τὰ φῶτα· 285
ἀφνειοί, μεγάλοι, περικαλλέες, ὄμμασι γαῦροι,
λευκοί, καὶ ξανθοῖσιν ἐπαντέλλοντες ἰούλοις,
εὐπρόσιτοι, γλυκεροί, σοβαροί, χαρίεντες ἀοιδοί,
εὔθικτοι, πινυτοί, εὐσχήμονες, ἀρχικυνηγοί,
οὐχὶ μόνον ζῴων θηρήτορες, ἀλλὰ γυναικῶν, 290
δισσολόγοι, δίγαμοι, δίγονοί θ' ἅμα καὶ διπολῖται,
†φαινόμενον πάλιν καὶ μακαριζόμενοι†
καὶ πάτρῃ χαίρουσι, καὶ ἐν ξείνοισι βιοῦσιν·
τιμῶνται συνεχῶς ἠδ' ἐξ ἀλόχων ἀγαπῶνται·
αὐχοῦσιν στεφάνοις, φιλίαις γηθοῦσιν ἀνάκτων· 295
μαρτυρίαις δόξαισί τ' ἀγαλλόμενοι κελαδοῦνται,
πενθερικοῖς δὲ δόμοισι διωκόμενοι καθορῶνται,
ἢ κλοπίμως φθείρουσι λέχη ἰδίων συνεφήβων.
κἂν ἄστει φαίνονται, ἰδ' ἐν στρατιαῖσιν ὁρῶνται.

Ἢν δέ τ' ἔχῃ σύνδεσμον ἐπ' Ἡέλιόν ποτε Μήνη, 300
ἐκ πενίης πλουτεῖ καὶ εἰς πενίην ἀνακάμπτει·
δόξαν ἔχει τέχνης Ἑκατησίου εἵνεκα κέρδους,
καὶ μαγικῇ συνέσει πέπιθεν τὰ πνεύματα φεύγειν,
καὶ κρυφίμαις βίβλοις ἐπαγαλλόμενος περιέργει·
πίστεις μὲν παρέχει σοβαραῖς μεγάλῃσι γυναιξίν, 305

280-1. Θ p. 212.11–12. καὶ Ἑρμῆς ἐν τῷ γ' καὶ Ἄρης ἐν τῷ θ' κυνηγοὺς ποιοῦσιν; Epit. IV = CCAG ii. 191.17 Ἑρμῆς ἐν τῷ γ', Ἄρης ἐν τῷ θ' κυνηγούς.
284–99. Cf. 2.221–31; Π.τ.δ. 9; Dor.ᴬʳᵃᵇ II 29.3; Lib. Herm. xxxii. 23.

274 συνοδεύῃ A.-R.   275 τε] τῆι L: corr. Gr   277 φιδωλὸς L: corr. L¹   ψήφων L: corr. A.-R.: γνίφων Nauckᴵᵇ·⁴³⁵   τε] ὁ L: corr. K²   278 χώρεσσιν L: corr. Hʰ: χώρῃσιν A.-R.   279 λίνων L: corr. Grⁿ   285 ἢν καὶ] καὶ ἢν L: corr. A.-R.   286 ἀφνιοὶ L: corr. L¹   289 ἀρχι[.]κυνηγοί L¹ʳᵃˢ (ἀρχη- ante ras. ut vid.)

fo. 37ʳ

292 φαινόμενοι πᾶσιν [post D⁵³⁹] μακαριζόμενοί τε βροτοῖσιν Aᶜᵒⁿʲ: φαινόμενοι λαμπροὶ πᾶσιν μακαριζόμενοί τε Kᶜᵒⁿʲ: τιόμενοι πᾶσιν καὶ μακαριζόμενοι Lop: σαινόμενοι π. καὶ μ. Sᶜᵒⁿʲ   296 δόξαισιν L: δόξῃσί τ' A.-R.   κελαδοῦνται] ego, post A.-R.ᶜᵒⁿʲ κελαδεῦνται: λελάληνται L: σελαγεῦνται K

>   When slender Hermes goes with Zeus alone,
>   Of ready means, keen, circulating coin, 275
>   A niggard, who mounts up through usury,
>   Cheese-paring, lending coins he loves to count.
>   When in the third place from the Horoscope,
>   He draws with angler's line fish from the sea.
>   If in opposition Ares vents his spleen, 280
>   With cunning snares he'll hunt all mountainous things.
>   If the Paphian's found in Mars' embrace, she makes
>   Seducers, rakes, those free for all abuse.
>   In the Paphian's houses, Zeus stands in good stead,
>   And duly gives should Sun and Moon do too: 285
>   Rich, tall and fine, imperious of eye,
>   Fair, with blonde stubble sprouting on their cheeks,
>   Open, engaging, proud, delightful bards,
>   Hitting the mark, shrewd, stately, chief huntsmen,
>   Not merely of wild beasts, but women too, 290
>   Double in tongue, in wives, offspring, and town,
>   But seen, felicitated, by all men (?),
>   Loving their homes, but living in strange parts;
>   They're always honoured, and loved by their wives;
>   In crowns, in great men's friendships, they exult; 295
>   Enlarged with sung acclaim and accolades.
>   Yet see them driven from their in-laws' house!
>   By stealth they spoil their fellows' marriage-beds.
>   They're seen in town, seen in the army too.
>   If Moon approaches Sun when she's at node, 300
>   From dearth he rises and to dearth returns;
>   His fame and fortune come from Hecate's trade,
>   By magic arts he's skilled to make ghosts flee,
>   Is busied avidly with secret books.
>   By having haughty ladies' confidence 305

---

297 δὲ δομοισι] δὲ τόποισιν L: corr. S: θαλάμοισι K, qui et λέκτροισι, μελάθροισι conj.   298 ἰδίων] δισσῶν L: corr. K   299 post 296 traiecerunt A.-R.   κἂν] κ' ἦν L: corr. K   στρατίεσσιν L: στρατιῇσιν A.-R.   300 ἡλιόν L: corr., spirantem add. L¹   301 ⟨τε⟩ Ger¹⁶³ (nol.)   302 Ἑκατήσιον L: corr. D⁶⁷⁰   303 πέπιθεν] πίθεται L: corr. R: πείθει D⁶⁷⁰   πείθει κακὰ πνεύμ. Wa^{II,143}   φεῦγε L: corr. Gr^n, D⁶⁷⁰   304 ἐπαγαλλομένους L: corr. A   περίεργα L: corr. A^{conj} (qui etiam περιείργει conj.)   305 πίστις L: corr. D⁴⁵⁷

ἐκ δὲ τύχης μικρῆς ἐπὶ μείζονα πίστιν ὁδεύει.
κἢν εὕρῃ Μήνη μετὰ τὴν λύσιν ἀστέρας ἐσθλούς,
σιτοδόται, κτίσται, μὴ φειδόμενοι φιλοτίμως 309
ὄλβον καὶ πλοῦτον καὶ χρήματα χρυσοφορητὰ 308
εἰς βυθόν, εἰς ἀνέμους διαπαιζόμενοι δαπανῶσιν, 310
καιροῖσιν πάμπαν, τὸ πλέον δὲ περισσὰ ‹διδόντες›
λείπονται πάντων ἐλεούμενοι οὐδὲν ἔχοντες.
Τὰς αὐτὰς δυνάμεις εἴτ' ἀνδράσιν εἴτε γυναιξὶν
σκεπτόμενος προλέγω, ὥρῃ δὲ φύσιν διορίζει·
ἀλλὰ καὶ ὡς ἐρέω τοῖς σχήμασι καὶ τὰ γυναικῶν. 315
σώφρονας ἡ Παφίη οἴκοις ἰδίοις, μετὰ Ζηνὸς
εὐμόρφους, πινυτάς τ', ἢν καὶ Στίλβοντα καθεύρῃ·
καὶ πόρνας ὁ Κρόνος ἀσχήμονα ἔργα τελούσας,
ἐν διθύροις αἰεί τε προϊσταμένας ἀναφανδόν.
τετράποσιν ζώοισιν εἰ ᾖ στείχουσα Σελήνη, 320
εἰ καὶ τὴν ὥρην ἐν τετραπόδεσσι καθεύροις,
ἀρρήτοις ἔργοισι μιαίνεται, ἠΰτ' ἐπ' ἔργοις
ἐκ στομάτων αἰσχροῖς διαβαλλομένη κακοφήμως.
εἰ δ' Ἄρης ἠοῦς γε μεσουρανέοιτο, λογίζου,
ἢ πολλοῖς μήτηρ ἐπὶ δάκρυσιν ἔσται ἄτεκνος· 325
εἰ δὲ Κρόνος Παφίην ἰδίοις οἴκοισι καθεύροι,
κἢν φάσκῃ τίκτειν ἐκ νηδύος, οὔ ποτε τίκτει,
ψευδομένη δ' ὠδῖνας ἀνώδυνός ἐστιν ἄτεκνος,
ἀλλοτρίην τε γονὴν ὑποβαλλομένη κακοτέχνως
καὶ κλίνασα δέμας στείρα λοχός ἐστ' ἐπὶ κλίνης, 330
καὶ πλαστὴ μήτηρ ἐσκήψατο τὴν φάσιν ἁγνῶς.
Ἄρεα καὶ Παφίην συναφαῖς εὑροῦσα Σελήνη
37ᵛ Ἡλίοιο τόποις ἢ καὶ Στίλβοντος ἐν οἴκοις,
ἢν διάμετρον ἔχῃ δνοφερὴν ἀκτῖνα Κρόνοιο,
ἰσχνὴν καὶ λυπρήν, κακοπράγμονα καὶ κακόβουλον, 335
αὐστηρὰν, προπετῆ, πολυπράγμονα, βάσκανον αἰεί,
εὔκνιστον, πρόλαλον καὶ βληχρὰν καὶ φιλόνεικον,
λυσσάδα, ζηλότυπον καὶ ἀγνώμονα καὶ περίεργον,
πῆμα λυγρῷ γαμέτῃ συναλιζόμενον κακόηθες·
ἀλλ' ὑπὸ τῆς Παφίης ἀμβλυνομένη μεταβάλλει. 340

ΜΑΝΕΘΩΝΟΣ ΑΠΟΤΕΛΕΣΜΑΤΙΚΩΝ ΒΙΒΛΙΟΝ Ε'

320–3. Θ p. 195.12–14. ἡ Σελήνη δὲ ὡροσκοποῦσα καὶ ἡ Ἀφροδίτη ἐν τετραπόδοις ζῳδίοις τὰς μὲν γυναῖκας ἀσελγοπύγους [immo ἀσελγοποιούς?] ποιοῦσιν, τοὺς δὲ ἄνδρας λείκτας καὶ αἰσχροποιούς.
326–31. Cf. 2.184–5; Lib. Herm. xxxii. 68; 6.286–94.

---

306 ἐκ δὲ μικρῆς ψυχῆς L: corr. D⁴⁵⁷: ψυχῆς δ' ἐκ μικρῆς Span²⁰⁷⁻⁸   309, 308 traiecit R
309 κισται L, corr., accentum add. L¹   φιδόμενοι L: corr. H, Hal, D⁶¹⁸   310 διαπεζόμενοι L: corr. Gr   δαπάνων L: corr. A.–R.: δαπανῶντες D⁶¹⁸   311 καιροῖσην L: corr. Gr   τὸ] τὰ L: corr. D⁶¹⁸   ‹διδόντες› suppl. D⁶¹⁸: ‹πόροντες› Luc

He's raised from low estate to greater trust.
   If, once released, the Moon finds kindly stars,
They give grain, build, and honourably spend 309
Their riches, wealth, convert their goods to gold, 308
Flinging them heedless to the void and winds, 310
At critical times—and by such steep expense
They're stripped of all, pitied, with nothing left.
   The same effects for women and for men
My art declares; the Hour decides the kind.
But to these schemes I'll now add women's charts. 315
   In her own houses, Venus makes the chaste;
With Zeus, the fair, with Mercury, the shrewd;
And Cronos, whores who do indecent acts,
Flaunting themselves in doorways, openly.
   If Selene wends her way in four-foot signs, 320
And four-foot signs hold the Horoscope as well,
She's soiled with deeds unspeakable, defamed
For shameful actions which involve the mouth.
   If Mars is eastern in Midheaven, count
That woman childless, prone to many tears. 325
   If Saturn finds the Paphian in his homes,
For all she doth protest, she bears no child,
But, feigning pangs, lacks pains and child to boot,
Yet slyly sneaking in another's child,
And taking to her bed, gives sterile birth, 330
A sham mother who feigns a solemn guise.
   If the Moon joins up with Mars and Paphos' queen,
In Helios' places or in Stilbon's house,
Or has Cronos' dark rays placed opposite,
Meagre and wretched, ill of deed and thought, 335
Harsh, headlong, interfering, rancorous,
A fractious gossip, slight but quarrelsome,
Pugnacious, jealous, thoughtless, meddlesome,
A malign domestic plague for her poor spouse;
Yet, melted by the Paphian, she can change. 340

---

312 ἐλεώμενοι μηδὲν L: corr. D⁶¹⁸ 315 ἀλλὰ καί] ἄλλως δ' L: corr. K 316 post ἰδίοις punxit K Ζηνός· L 317 post εὐμόρφους punxit K πινυτοὺς L: corr. D⁴¹³ (cf. 315) ⟨τ'⟩ K 318 Κρόνος ⟨γ'⟩ A 319 τε add. K ἐν τριόδοις αἰεί τε Nauck^(III,)²⁷⁶⁻⁷ 320 ἔῃ Hol στίχουσα L: corr. H, Hal 322 ἠΰτε ἔργα L: corr. K: ἠΰτε πόρνη S 323 αἰσχροῖς] αἰσχρῶς L: corr. K: αἰσχρῶν Lop, S κακοφήμων R 324 γε] τε L: corr. D⁶⁶⁷ ἠοῦς μεσσουρανέοιτο S^conj 325 πολλῶν L: corr. K ἔσται] ἔστε L: corr H^h, Gr^n: ἔστεν' K 330 κλείνασα L: corr. H^h στεῖρ' ἄλοχος L: corr. D³³⁸ κλίνης L^(1sl) 331 καί] ἢ L: corr. A

fo. 37^v
335 κακοπρήγμονα K 336 αὐστηρὴν...πολυπρήγμονα K 337 βληχρὴν K 338 λύσσαδέ, -έ L^(1ras): corr. Hal 339 κακοήθως L: corr. R 340 ἀμβλύνεται καὶ L: corr. R

Part Four

Commentary

The best way to be boring is to leave nothing out.
(Voltaire)

Book Four

4.1–13 Proem

1–13 Interpreting this passage has consequences for what kind of débris we think this book consists of. A lot hangs on ἐξονομήνας (accented thus), which is transmitted at the end of the fourth line. An aorist participle cannot be right. Axtius and Rigler followed D'Orville with ἐξονόμηνα, interpreting everything down to l. 8 as an announcement of subjects the poet has already treated in an apparently lost portion of the poem. Lopilato followed them (as does Monteventi, 140–1), further imposing a full stop at the end of 11, and by additional manipulations (ἱεροῦ δὲ…ἴοιμι) turning l. 12 into an announcement of the topic to come. The latter interventions are unacceptable on any count, but Koechly's future tense ἐξονομήνω is in any case clearly better than D'Orville's original correction, and removes the need to posit a large lost portion before the book has even started. It is easy to see how an omega might have been misread as an alpha joined to a sigma in a minuscule exemplar. But above all, on formal grounds this is clearly a proem which follows a standard pattern in antiquity, with an initial object, sometimes an apposition, a verb of speech or invocation, and then further objects (a structure in which any of the objects might be accompanied by a relative clause). The essential pattern goes back to the Homeric poems (object, verb of invocation, relative clause),[1] but there are good parallels in Call. fr. 7c.5–6 (Αἰ⌊γλήτην ⌊Ἀνά⌋φην τε = two initial objects; Λακωνίδι γείτονα Θ⌊ήρῃ = apposition; ἐνὶ μ]νήμῃ κάτθεο = substitute for the invocation, since the Muse here is speaking; καὶ Μινύας = additional objects) and in the first book of Oppian's *Halieutica*, with two objects (1–2), an apposition (2), a verb of speech (3 ἐξερέω), and after a couple of indirect questions (4–5) eventually a further seven(!) objects (5–8), then a relative clause (8–9). Triphiodorus is an additional parallel for delaying the verb of invocation, after a couple of objects, the second with an apposition (2), until the fourth line.

---

[1] Compare also *HHom. Dem.* [obj. + apposition + verb of singing + obj. + rel. cl.], *HHom. Herm.* [obj. + invocation + apposition + attributes + rel. cl.].

The first eight lines seem to promise a special treatment of the zodiac, which never happens (see p. 183).² The remaining lines before the lacuna which, as Koechly saw, must supervene after l. 12 are opaque even by this poet's standards, but seem to suggest the idea of a natural power which makes itself known to humans skilled to interpret it, possibly via the motif of texts deposited in temples (9 ἐξ ἱερῶν ἀδύτων, unless this is just verbiage intended to suggest some mysterious natural sanctum; the phrase most naturally goes with φύσις, but could at a push go with ὀρθὰ τεκμαιρομένοισι). This power regulates the chorus of stars through sacred decree and apparently can itself be put to the test, presumably through the art of the astrologers. There is a vague similarity with Cicero's sketch of Chaldaean doctrine (*De Div.* 2.89), but that talks of *vim quandam* latent in the zodiac itself, rather than a nature that directs the whole.

1 Οὐρανίων ἄστρων ἀτραπούς: for the pathway metaphor, see on 4.6. ἀτραπ- is an idiosyncrasy of this poet, also at 4.37, 583, and non-astrologically at 531, but he shares ἀταρπ- with Mᵃ (6.545, and i. 887 n. 94), cf. Mesomedes (2nd c.) (II Heitsch), 8.6. He avoids ὁδός, which occurs in all other books of the corpus and is prosaic (e.g. Plat. *Leg.* 821 B).

The poet does not consistently follow the distinction between ἄστρα 'constellations' and ἀστέρες 'stars' (for which see on 2.3). ἀστήρ, almost always in the circumlocution 'star of', is always used of planets, but ἄστρον is also used for 'planet' in 87 and 328. With the genitive plural there is of course no metrical room for manoeuvre.

1–2 πλάστιγγας Ἀνάγκης: the diction is close to Julian, *Hymn to King Sun*, 146 D μεγάλης Ἀνάγκης εἰσὶ πλάστιγγες. His thought is convoluted and not helpful to understanding the present passage, but does direct attention to the presence of other heavenly Scales (those of Virgo, and Libra itself),³ which may have helped add them to the image-repertoire of a power otherwise associated

---

[2] Greenbaum detected a similarity between the idea of the zodiac circling round the pole and a Hermetic fragment which speaks of the Bear doing the same (2016, 252, using the text and translation of Lopilato, and *Corp. Herm.* fr. 6.13, esp. παραδιδοῦσα τὸ πᾶν τοῦτο ἀπὸ μὲν τῆς νυκτὸς ἡμέρᾳ, ἀπὸ ‹δ'› ἡμέρας νυκτί), and found it 'clear' that Mᵇ was either using the Hermetic fragment, or drawing on a common source. But the unsetting Bear is simply a trope, absent in any case from Mᵇ.

[3] Julian claims that the Sun rules five circles in the heavens, two of which are the scales of Necessity. G. Mau, *Die Religionsphilosophie Kaiser Julians in seinen Reden auf König Helios und die Göttermutter* (Leipzig, 1907), 78–81, favours the interpretation that the scales are Libra (sign of the autumn equinox), and Necessity the adjacent Virgo (who, as Dike, has scales of her own), rather than that the scales are the two remaining circles left after the three traversed by the Sun in his annual course (in other words, the Arctic and Antarctic circles). The latter remains the view of A. Mastrocinque, *Giuliano l'Apostata: Discorso su Helios Re: Testo, traduzione e commento* (Nordhausen, 2011), 59–60 nn. 177–8, who suggests the scales are the North and South Pole.

with Fate-motifs (spindle, yoke, perhaps whip).[4] As symbolic attributes Fate acquires balances much later than her essential spindles (S. Eitrem, *RE* s.v. Moira (Machtgebiet), 2485.25–36), but Persius associates Fate (*Parca*) with the constellation Libra (*Sat.* 5.47–8), and the lid of a sarcophagus in the Capitoline shows Lachesis with a pair of scales and cornucopia (*LIMC* s.v. Moirai, no. 37; *RE* ibid. 2493.68). Tyche is also associated with them (Stob. 1.6.13 = *PMG* Lyr. Adesp. 1019.6 τὸ τεᾷ πλάστιγγι δοθέν).

2 ἐκμεμέτρηται: the implications of the scale metaphor vary: in *Il.* 22.209, Zeus' scales (τάλαντα) weigh one life against another; here, they mete out a set portion; otherwise, they maintain cosmic balance (Nemesis[5]) or represent the strict equity of justice (Dike[6]). The poet (or an editor) reintroduces the idea of measurement in the last couplet of the poem, but there he inflates the commonplace of individually measured human lives (the verb is quite common with βίος[7]) to the idea of aeons of cosmic time (4.625–6; see ad loc.).

3 Μοιράων τε κέλευθα βροτήσια: the expression identifies the Fates with the stars. The epithet anticipates later passages where the 'mortality' motif will be connected specifically with the ASC (4.59 μερόπων ὡροσκόπα φέγγεα, 491 βροτῶν ὡροσκόπα φέγγη, cf. 577 ὥρην μεροποσπόρον).

3–4 πλάνα φέγγη | ἀπλανέων τ' αὐγὰς πυριλαμπέας: the conventional pairs are πλάνητές τε καὶ ἀπλανεῖς or ἀπλανεῖς καὶ πλανώμενοι; for other circumlocutions for the planets see on 3.232.[8] Three of the four Manethonian poets begin their books with this motif (only M^d does not). M^a is the least problematic (2.9–16), since he does not promise a treatment of the fixed stars. But the prologue of book 1 also promises to treat the φάσεις of the fixed and wandering stars (4), and its envoi claims to have treated their δρόμος οὐράνιος (359). One might suggest this is a conventional advertisement in the proem of an astrological poem which in practice will concentrate on planets, but the amount of attention paid to the zodiac in the next lines makes it hard to dismiss it as one of those occasions where the author uses a polar statement only one half of which in practice interests him.[9] See p. 183 for speculation about an earlier

---

[4] Spindle: Plat. *Rep.* 616 C; whip perhaps in *LIMC* s.v. Ananke, no. 2. Horace's *Necessitas* has nails (Nisbet and Hubbard on *Od.* 1.35.18; Nisbet and Rudd on *Od.* 3.24.5–7).

[5] *LIMC* s.v. Nemesis, p. 769 (nos. 248–63). In Valens, VI 9.14, Nemesis has a measuring-rod (πῆχυς), μηδὲν πράσσειν ὑπὲρ τὸ μέτρον ἐμφαίνουσα.

[6] As such, among the many emblems of Virgo (*CLE* 24.5 (*Virgo...*) *lance vitam et iura pensitans*; Roscher s.v. Sternbilder (Boll, Gundel), 962.43–5).

[7] Greg. Naz. *De Vita Sua* 512 ἐκμεμέτρηκας βίον (of part of a lifespan), al.

[8] For ἀπλανής see Kidd on Aratus, 461. A variant in Timaeus, Περὶ φύσιος, ed. W. Marg, in Thesleff, p. 214.11 πολλοὶ μὲν τῶν ἀπλανέων, πολλοὶ δὲ τῶν πλαζομένων.

[9] G. E. R. Lloyd, *Polarity and Analogy: Two Types of Argumentation in Early Greek Thought* (Cambridge, 1966), 92, citing *Od.* 14.178–9 and 15.374–5.

510 Commentary on Book Four

version of the poem. Note also Nonn. *D.* 6.69, where the god Astraeus, in the act of casting a horoscope, looks at both planets and fixed stars, though the latter are relevant there, because Spica in Virgo has an important role.

For the decorative epithet see on 4.44.

ἐξονομήνω: see on 1–13 for Koechly's emendation. For the future, see also *Or. Sib.* 1.327 (riddle on the name of God), *AP* 1.102.2 (how shall I name thee?).

5 ζῳδίων τε πόλοιο περίδρομον: a double genitive (p. 211; already a mannerism of M^a), but the second perhaps a genitive of place (like 396 Οὐλύμποιο), circuit of the constellations in the heaven.

ὃς κατὰ γαῖαν: from Hes. *Th.* 346 αἳ κατὰ γαῖαν (same *sedes*), but there it means 'on the earth', and here must mean underground (not 'along the earth', Lopilato).

6 αἰθερίην τε κέλευθον: this, the standard poetic word for the paths of heavenly bodies,[10] occurs in several syllabuses and overviews in the Manethoniana (3.232; 6.114; 4.107, 166).

ἡμιτμῆτι πορείῃ: the noun suggests purposeful movement. It is used of military marches, but also of the regular paths of the stars in Ps. Sol. 18:10 ὁ διατάξας ἐν πορείᾳ φωστῆρας...καὶ οὐ παρέβησαν ἀπὸ ὁδοῦ, ἧς ἐνετείλω αὐτοῖς. It is a prosaic and unremarkable component of this poet's favourite 'path' imagery (also 4.380, 499, and of human life in 169), though it is also exploited by poets for the movements of heavenly bodies in the Hymn to Isis from Andros, *IG* XII,5 739.32 εὐκόσμοισι πορείαις (of the Sun's orderly path through the heavens), Nonn. *D.* 38.289 ἀμοιβαίη δὲ πορείη (of the Hours), cf. 1.176 παλιννόστῳ δὲ πορείῃ. As for the epithet, ἡμίτμητος is better attested, in Byzantine poetry and scholia, and -τμής compounds are rare (B.–P. 452), but *D.* 5.282 ἰθυτμῆτες ἀγυιαί (which exactly matches the rhythm) and 2.451 ἰθυτμῆτας...σπήλυγγας support the manuscript against D'Orville's correction ἡμιτμῆγι (Paul Sil. *Descr. Sanct.* 378 ἡμιτμῆγι περισταδὸν ἄντυγι κύκλου, also of a half-circle).

7–8 This couplet imitates Aratus, 532–3, who describes the ecliptic as an oblique circle, bounded by the tropics, among the circles that go spinning in diurnal motion from east to west (8 ~ Aratus, 533 ἐξ ἠοῦς ἐπὶ νύκτα). The main changes are that (i) it is now explicitly about the zodiac; (ii) the previous two lines have slightly muddied the idea by confusing the equator (which bisects the ecliptic) with the horizon (which bisects the zodiac into visible and invisible

---

[10] The application to constellations (Leonidas, *AP* 9.80.1; Or. ap. Euseb. *PE* 9.10.5; Nonn. *D.* 13.168–9; Hymn to Isis (PSI 7.844) (XLVIII Heitsch) 6–7) is later than the application to the Sun and Moon (Eur. *Helen* 342–3, Ap. Rhod. 1.500, 3.533; Aratus, 149, and *passim*), a usage presumably first suggested by *Od.* 10.86 ἐγγὺς γὰρ νυκτός τε καὶ ἤματός εἰσι κέλευθοι.

7 **πλαγκτὰ διχαζόμενος**: Aratus' epithet πλάγιος (532 πλαγίῳ...κύκλῳ) was a synonym for λόξος (527), and M^b varies Aratus a little more with an epithet which suggests both the obliquity of the zodiac and, anticipating the next line, its apparent diurnal motion from east to west (so too 509–10 ἠερόπλαγκτον | ζωφορίην, of the Sun). Of cosmic motion again in 11 πλαγκτὴ κόσμοιο...χορείη, 380 πλαγκτῷ κόσμοιο πορείη, and with impressive vagueness in 9, 623; compare the Isis hymn from Andros, *IG* XII,5 279.29 ἀτραπιτὸν πλάγκτειραν which, given that Isis is talking about discriminating the seasons, presumably is the zodiac. Of planetary motion in 182, *Π*^1 402 (cf. already Alex. Eph. *SH* 21.13 πλαγκτῶν...ἄστρων); of human journeys in 88 [*ex emend.*], cf. 222.

διέπει θεομήστορα κόσμον: the claim that the zodiac governs the cosmos is somewhat reminiscent of the Chaldaeans' claim in Cic. *De Div.* 2.89 that each part of the zodiac contains a force that influences and has an effect on the heavens, though the Chaldaeans go on to say that this force is itself affected by the planets as they wander about in it, while M^b seems to connect the effect simply with diurnal rotation. The conception is not very clear, but the phrase echoes Alexander of Ephesus, *SH* 21.26 θεομήστορος εἰκόνα κόσμου. Alexander in turn would seem to have repurposed θεομήστωρ in Aesch. *Pers.* 655 ('god-like in counsel', epithet of Darius, a condensation of Iliadic θεόφιν μήστωρ ἀτάλαντος). The recasting implies a divinely controlled universe—not necessarily one in which the stars themselves are the gods, but like that of Manilius (1.37). ἱερός in 9, 12 points the same way. The cadence is late antique, especially Nonnian;[11] adapted in 4.67 κοσμήτορα κόμπον.

8 **ἐξ ἠοῦς ἐπὶ νύκτα καὶ ἀντολίης ἐπὶ δυσμάς**: the second half of the line glosses the first with prosaic synonyms[12] instead of supplying the complement, which is, however, found in expressions concerning the cycle of hours in a day: Aratus, 842–3 ἢ ὅ γ᾽ ἐς ἠῶ | ἔρχηται παρὰ νυκτὸς ἢ ἐξ ἠοῦς ἐπὶ νύκτα and Hedylus, *HE* 1857–8 ἐξ ἠοῦς εἰς νύκτα καὶ ἐκ νυκτὸς πάλι Σωκλῆς | εἰς ἠοῦν. Another imitation of Aratus in ps.-Bion, *Epithalamium* 22 ἐξ ἀοῦς δ᾽ ἐπὶ νύκτα.

9 This hovers between the topos of scrolls or pillars discovered in temples (see 5.1–24 n.) and the metaphor of heavens as a temple from which nature herself directs operations. Despite the presence of Nechepso–Petosiris themes at the beginning of books 1 and 5, De Stefani's conjecture φάτις in place of

---

[11] Greg. Naz. *PG* 34.530.5, Nonn. *D.* 7.220 θηήτορα κόσμου, and *Par.* 14.87 θηήτορι κόσμῳ; Greg. Naz. *PG* 37.1500.7 λήιστορα κόσμον; Nonn. *D.* 12.20 νωμήτορι κόσμου, *Par.* 3.161, 5.152, 14.98 χραισμήτορα κόσμου, 5.100 παμμήτορα κόσμου, 6.57 and 8.173 ἰθύντορα κόσμου.
[12] e.g. ps.-Plat. *Def.* 411 Β Ἡμέρα ἡλίου πορεία ἀπ᾽ ἀνατολῶν ἐπὶ δυσμάς.

φύσις goes too far; this is not a single *ad hominem* revelation, in fact it is not revelation at all, but directive activity interpretable by those skilled to read the signs (compare φύσις in Ocellus, *De universi natura* 1 (Thesleff, p. 126.4–5); *Natura* in Manilius, 1.40, 2.107, 122, 4.883). The epithet is the first of the poet's -πλαγκτος compounds (B.–P. 494, originally Homeric), in most of which the first element is the space wandered over: αἰθερόπλαγκτος again in 4.182, of planetary motion, otherwise *HOrph.* 6.1 (of Protogonos); see also on 4.509 ἠερόπλαγκτος and 623 οὐρανόπλαγκτος (mobilised by the heavens, not wandering through them).

10 ὀρθὰ τεκμαιρομένοισι: implying that astrology had foes (there were those who did *not* think in the approved way on the subject)—or just referring to people who went about it in the wrong way (as in those defences of astrology which blame the practitioner when things go wrong, not the art itself, e.g. Lucian, *Astr.* 2)? Earlier hexameter examples do not have Attic correption (not even τέκμωρ and διετεκμήραντο in Mᵃ).

διώρισεν ἀνδράσιν ἄστρα: presumably 'established', 'set out', the constellations. Nature undertakes the role performed by personal agents (often with δι- compounds) in other sources, especially LXX Is. 45:18 Οὕτως λέγει κύριος ὁ ποιήσας τὸν οὐρανόν—οὗτος ὁ θεὸς ὁ καταδείξας τὴν γῆν καὶ ποιήσας αὐτήν, αὐτὸς διώρισεν αὐτήν ('For thus saith the Lord that created the heavens; God himself that formed the earth and made it; he hath established it...') and sources which (presumably) reflect its wording: Justin, *Epist. ad Diogn.* 498 D (on the maker of heaven and earth) ᾧ πάντα διατέτακται καὶ διώρισται καὶ ὑποτέτακται, οὐρανοὶ καὶ τὰ ἐν τοῖς οὐρανοῖς...; Euseb. *PE* 7.10.7 εἰ δὲ δὴ καὶ ἥλιος καὶ σελήνη καὶ ἀστέρες, τοῦ θείου νόμου καὶ αὐτοῖς διωρισμένου τοὺς οἰκείους ἀποδιδόναι δρόμους ('If then sun and moon and stars, having been appointed by the divine law to perform their proper courses...').[13] There is a lesser similarity with Aratus, 11 ἄστρα διακρίνας (subj. Zeus), with datives of advantage in 13 ἀνδράσιν and 5 ἀνθρώποισι. Martin ad loc. argues that the meaning here is not 'delimit', 'determine', but 'distinguish': Zeus causes the constellations to be picked out in the heavens by means of their bright stars (Manil. 1.469–73). (Kidd's translation, 'making them into distinct constellations', is compatible with either sense.)

---

[13] Passive also in Plut. *Mor.* 429 F ἐν δὲ τῷ παντὶ πέντε μὲν ζώναις ὁ περὶ γῆν τόπος, πέντε δὲ κύκλοις ὁ οὐρανὸς διώρισται. Other conceptions involving δια- (or *di-*): Julian, *Contra Galilaeos*, 96 D, p. 170 περὶ δὲ οὐρανοῦ καὶ γῆς καὶ τῶν ἐν αὐτῇ [καὶ] τίνα τρόπον διεκοσμήθη διέξεισι...(sc. Moses); Claudian, *Stil.* 2.434 *numeros qui dividit astris*: 'he fixes the number of the stars in each constellation' (Platnauer); 'he separates the measures of the stars' (Coombe [12 n.], 88, which she glosses 'the timings of the stars').

11 The star-chorus motif (Csapo; T. Whitmarsh, 'The Cretan Lyre Paradox: Mesomedes, Hadrian, and the Poetics of Patronage', in B. E. Borg (ed.), *Paideia: The World of the Second Sophistic* (Berlin, 2004), 377–402, at 389–90; S. Lanna, *Mesomede, Inno a Iside: Edizione con introduzione, traduzione, commento, e altri testi del culto isiaco* (Rome, 2021), 170–1) is extended to the cosmos itself. Entirely fittingly, for *kosmos* (order) was precisely what was required of a *choros* (Seaford, 273; e.g. Eur. *El.* 951). For plural worlds (*kosmoi*) engaging in a dance, see Plut. *Mor.* 422 B. βροτοκλώστειρα archly repurposes κλωστήρ, 'spindle', as an agent noun for an intelligent, or purposeful, being. The first element is sufficiently strongly paralleled by 4.3 Μοιράων τε κέλευθα βροτήσια (= paths concerning human life) not to need De Stefani's κόσμου βιοτοκλώστειρα.

12 δόγματος ἐξ ἱεροῖο: for the language of law, see i. 11–12 n. 35, adding Manilius, 4.919; Claudian, *Stil.* 2.432–6, where an 'old man' (Aion? Thoth?) writes *mansura... iura*, and has oversight of the fixed stars and planets 'whereby everything lives and dies by pre-ordained laws' (*quibus omnia vivunt | ac pereunt fixis cum legibus*) (C. Coombe, *Claudian the Poet* (Cambridge, 2018), 87–8). The epithet reinforces the divinely ordained nature of the cosmos (4.7) with the suggestion that astrology came about through divine decree, against secular accounts of its development.

σαφῆ πρὸς ἔλεγχον ἰοῦσα: the phrase is strikingly prosaic, even Valens-like.[14] That astrology can be put to the test suggests either or both of an author who wants to assert high intellectual standards for his discipline and a defensiveness and defiance of astrology's critics, as possibly implied by 10 ὀρθά. The lacuna after this line raises the possibility that the poet originally had more to say in promotion and defence of his discipline.

13 ἀμείβεται εἶδος: this line remains baffling, though the indirect question implies it is still part of a manifesto. Does ἕκαστον agree with εἶδος, or do we need to find another neuter subject? Otherwise εἶδος occurs in the corpus only in an emendation of A.–R. at 5.263, straightforwardly of physical appearance. In M^a the planets' positions are changing as they move into different configurations with one another (2.15 ἀμειβόμενοι; 2.148, 394, 3.232), but εἶδος is not a synonym of σχῆμα (aspect). Nor is it a synonym of εἴδωλον (so this is unlikely to be a reference to the Sun passing from one zodiacal sign to another). The Moon's phase undergoes successive changes, but that seems an unlikely subject for a catalogue.

---

[14] For Valens and the proper ἔλεγχος of astrological method, see VIII 5.30; VI 8.5, 9; i. 28. For the prose phrase πρὸς ἔλεγχον ἰέναι, see e.g. Demetrius, *Formae epistolicae*, 18 πάντα πρὸς ἔλεγχον ἐλεύσεται.

4.14–109 *Kentrothesiai*

This section reviews the effects of planets in *kentra*. The most immediate comparanda are the *kentrothesia* of 3.8–131 (see on 35–43, 39, 44–52, 46, 47, 48–52, 53–8, 72, 83ᵇ–82ᵇ), and those of 'Par. Anub.' and Dor.ᴬᴿᴬᴮ. A little treatise ascribed to Valens in Par. gr. 2419 and Vindob. phil. gr. 108 which reviews the planets one by one opens with a discussion of their effects in each *kentron*, taken clockwise from the ASC (*CCAG* viii/1. 163–71). All these are organised planet × *kentron*, as here, but there are also similarities with Firmicus' third book (planet × *dodecatopos*) (see on 93–100 + 101–6), *Dodecatopos* (Θ pp. 126.12–174.17) (see on 98–9), and Paul (both *dodecatopos* × planet) (see on 4.41; 73–6; 85; 87–92).

Comparisons suggests the use of a common source, rather than (or as well as) direct dependence on Mᵃ by Mᵇ. This would demonstrate that Mᵃ was not, in that section, operating unilaterally in making a selection from a larger *dodecatopos*.

(i) The planetary order, which places Moon + Sun at the end, corresponds to that of Mᵃ, except that Mᵃ puts the Sun before the Moon (p. 134). 'Par. Anub.' and Dor.ᴬᴿᴬᴮ had listed the Moon and Sun at the head of the planets.

(ii) In comparison with the earlier book, this inventory is truncated. The ASC and MC are specified for almost all of them (MC only for Mars); the DESC in addition for Mercury and Venus; only for the Moon are all four *kentra* treated. But the running-together of *kentra*, especially the ASC and MC, *as alternatives* (if *x* is in *a* or *b*) rather than as separate items, is a peculiarity that this section shares with Dorotheus against Mᵃ. See 4.28–9 (Saturn), 35–7 (Jupiter), 69–71 (Mercury), 94–5 (Sun), comparing e.g. Dor.ᴬᴿᴬᴮ II 21.1 'if the Moon is in the ascendant or midheaven good in its light', II 22.1 'if the Sun is in the ascendant or midheaven in its own house'.

(iii) Several additions vis-à-vis the third book suggest that this is a fuller version of an original source:

It gives 'own' houses (p. 241) for Saturn (corresponding to book 3) but also for the Sun, where book 3 offers no correspondence. For both configurations, both the ASC and MC are involved; in 3.8, it was only a question of Saturn in the ASC.

For Mercury it gives an additional configuration, with Mars in equal degrees (73).

For the Moon it gives an additional circumstance, with Mars in equal degrees (79).

These listings of additional planets have their best parallels in comparanda other than Mᵃ.

4.14–34 Saturn

14–27

Saturn in its own houses in ASC. In comparison with 3.12–17, this is even more limited. That has birth, the wealth–renown nexus, and the favour of kings; this has only wealth, which is stated four times.

14 Πρῶτα μὲν οὖν: this cluster opens the sequence of *kentrothesia* at 3.8 as well as the ἀκτινηβολίαι at 4.170. See n. ad loc. for the sense of orderly progression which developed from the inaugural instance in the *Odyssey*, and p. 164 for the connection which prevails throughout this section and most of the rest of the poem.

Τιτὰν...Κρόνος: this seems, in practice, to be the only instance of Titan as a title of Saturn (Bouché-Leclercq, 93 n. 2, citing this passage at 94 n. 2). *HOrph.* 13.2 addresses Cronos as ἄλκιμε Τιτάν, but he is the mythological figure, not the planet. Titan was the name given by John Herschel in 1847 to the largest of Saturn's moons, which had been discovered a couple of centuries earlier.

Calling Saturn by the Sun's title (used by all the other Manethonian poets, though not by M^b himself) suggests the possibility that the poet is thinking of the old association of the two planets.[15] Simplicius alludes to its old name 'star of the Sun' (*In Aristot. De Cael. Commentaria*, p. 495.28 Heiberg ὃν Ἡλίου ἀστέρα οἱ παλαιοὶ προσηγόρευον), and Ptolemy claims that in Asia Saturn goes directly under the name of Mithras Helios (2.3.23). Alternatively, he might have called Saturn 'Titan' because this was the mythological generation to which the god belonged, and whose leader he was; compare Οὐρανίδης at 238 and 460.

παντὸς...αἰθέρος ἄρχει: on the primacy of Saturn among the planets see Bouché-Leclercq, 94–5 and n. 2; Boll 1919, 345 n. 2; 5.262. It derives from both the planet's superior position (Diodorus of Tarsus, in Photius, cod. 223, 211 B 29 (εἰ μικροφανὴς ὁ Κρόνος), μείζων, ὥς φασι, τῶν ἄλλων ὑπάρχων πλανήτων, ὅτι τούτων ἀνώτερον διατρέχει κύκλον), and the god's mythological persona (*HOrph.* 13.1 μακάρων τε θεῶν πάτερ ἠδὲ καὶ ἀνδρῶν, borrowing a Hesiodic Zeus-formula).

15–16 The scientific or technical term elicits a naming formula (see on 2.136–7 and 6.37), which looks like an adaptation of the Homeric 'gods call *x* and men call *y*' motif (*Il.* 1.403, 20.74) to suggest that the name is so 'right' that

---

[15] Roscher, s.v. Planeten (Roscher), 2523.59–2524.21; Boll 1903, 313 n. 3 and Addenda p. 563; id. 1919; Cumont 1935, 14 n. 2; W. and H. Gundel, *RE* s.v. Planeten, 2032.35–50; Le Bœuffle on Hygin. *Astr.* 2.42.2, n. 7; Pingree 1978, ii. 233; Heilen 2015, 1051 and n. 2667.

there is universal consensus about it. That is an appropriate stance for practitioners of a divine art.

16 + 20-6 Like M^a, M^b both categorises the signs (own and other) and names them. Neither defines them. They differ only in that one calls Libra the Balances (M^b), and the other the Claws (M^a) and that this poet uses his favourite οἰκεῖος terminology for 'own' signs (16, 20, 28 ~ 3.12 ἀλλοτρίοις οἴκοισιν ν. ἑοῖσιν; see pp. 241–2). οἰκεῖα is in Focal position.

Other comparanda present similarities as follows:

(i) *Lib. Herm.* xxvi (an excerpt dealing with Sun, Moon, and Saturn in the ASC). This defines Saturn's signs but does not name them: xxvi. 70 *in domo propria* (Capricorn, Aquarius) *vel triplicitate vel exaltatione* (Libra); 71 adds that it has the same effect in the houses of Jupiter (Sagittarius, Pisces) or the Sun (Leo), which are fellow members of its sect, and the terms of Mercury. These account for four of the five mentioned in M^a/M^b—Aquarius, Capricorn, Libra, Leo. The other, Aries, is the exaltation of the Sun (despite also being Saturn's depression).

(ii) The sources for Dorotheus categorise without either naming or defining: Dor.^ARAB II 23.1 'in his own house', Περὶ κέντρ. 14 ἰδίῳ τόπῳ ἢ συναιρέτου.

There are no parallels in Firmicus, 3.2.1–3, 'Valens', *Dodecatopos*, Paul.
The pattern is different from that of the Sun (below).

16 The verse pattern recurs at 4.157 Ἑρμείας δ' οἰκεῖα τυχὼν κατὰ δώμαθ' ἑαυτοῦ. The basis is *Od.* 24.188 κατὰ δώμαθ' ἑκάστου.

17 ἐπίσκοπον ἐς βίου ὥρην: the expression combines three features of M^b: (i) -σκοπ- compounds which evoke the full technical term ὡροσκόπον (see p. 246); (ii) reference to the horoscope in connection with life/engendering (p. 246); (iii) fudges of what could be nominal or adjectival components: the genitive here should be governed by the adjectival ἐπίσκοπον (see too 110 ὡράων πανεπίσκοπα, although, regularising the construction, Hübner 2001, 233, reads ἐς βίον ὥρην). (i) is again combined with a dative expression 'when men are born' in 110–11 πανεπίσκοπα φέγγεα…φυομένοις μερόπεσσιν. (i) and (ii) are again combined in 572 ὥρην…βιοτοσκόπον.

18 εὐκτεάνους: M^a's word (i. 158–9 and n. 40); only here in the later books.

19 ἐς τέλος: also 1.269. This is astrological jargon, usually used for the retention or non-retention of wealth throughout a native's life (Περὶ κράσ. 66; 'Heliodorus' on Paul, p. 65.5; Apomasar, *De Rev.* p. 111.11).

ἀμόχθους: see on 2.173. The word is unique to M^a and M^b in the corpus, M^a always in connection with ease of action (τελ-, πρᾶξις), M^b (also 4.60) with wealth.

Kentrothesiai

21 πολυχρήμονας: see on 6.16.

22-6 The poet first names Saturn's own houses, Aquarius and Capricorn. Then he gives exaltations: that of the Sun (Aries) and Saturn's own (Libra). Finally he names Leo, house of the Sun, ruler of Saturn's sect. See on 3.14-15: M[a] does it slightly differently, promoting Leo ahead of the exaltations. Also, M[a] winds it up in a line and a half, with only a single decorative epithet (for Leo), whereas M[b] spreads each constellation out over an entire line (p. 210). The first three are asyndetic, which is not M[a]'s preference when listing planets.

22 One of the commonest types of *versus tetracolus*: self-contained, and what Bassett calls epexegetical, in this case involving a noun in apposition to a personal name (Bassett, 225). This type is most often found with a family relationship, e.g. Ἀνδρομάχη θυγάτηρ μεγαλήτορος Ἠετίωνος (2× *Il*.). But sometimes it is a 'professional' one: Bassett's Homeric examples (art. cit. n. 5) involve ἕταρον or ἑταῖρον, ἀρχός, ἡγήτορα, (ὀτρηρὸς) θεράπων or θεράποντα, θαλαμηπόλος, and ταμίης belongs to the same category. Why is Aquarius a 'steward'? Not in the first instance because his commonest mythological identification was as Ganymede, cupbearer of Zeus,[16] but because Aquarius, as a winter constellation, dispenses storms and rain; his identification as the mythological pourer of liquids stems from that. For Aquarius as a water-pourer, see Roscher, s.v. Sternbilder (Boll, Gundel), 974.38-65; Hübner 1982, 95, 120, 128; *fundens* is often part of his Latin poetic formulary (*TLL* s.v. *Aquarius*, 367.19-23); cf. French *Verseau*. For stewardship of the elements see Stephanus s.v. ταμίας, 1798 C (the idea stems ultimately from Aeolus as ταμίας of the winds in the *Odyssey*), and for Aquarius and cloud, Q. Tullius Cicero, fr. 1.13 Courtney *quem sequitur nebulas rorans liquor altus Aquari*.

νεφελώδεος Οὐλύμποιο: the verse is based on the pattern *Il*. 1.499 (al.) πολυδειράδος Οὐλύμποιο, *HHom. Dem.* 331 (al.) θυώδεος Οὐλύμποιο; for sound and sense see too Ap. Rhod. 1.1099 νιφόεν θ' ἕδος Οὐλύμποιο.

23 Again the name is expanded in an appositional phrase which contains a traditional datum (Housman on Manilius, 2.231 (Capricorn *ambiguus*), Hübner 1982, 171-6; Heilen 2015, 888). Capricorn and Cancer are both ἀμφίβια because of their habitat. This formulation could be a poeticisation of something like Teucer, *CCAG* vii. 208.14 γηθαλάσσιον, ps.-Palchus, *CCAG* viii/1. 263.13-14 ὁ δὲ Αἰγόκερως γήϊνος καὶ θαλάσσιός ἐστι, of which there is another poetic version in ps.-Emped. *Sphaera* (Anon. II.7), ll. 142-3 (p. 166 Maass) ἢ μὲν γὰρ ἐν γῆι φέρβεται χλοηφόρωι, | ὃ δ' ἐν κλύδωνι νήχεται γλαυκηπόρωι (Hübner 1982, 175-6 (§3.351.42)). θήρ monosyllables at line-end

---

[16] Roscher, s.v. Ganymedes (Drexler), 1596.65-1597.6; s.v. Sternbilder (Boll, Gundel), 976.59-977.2; Bouché-Leclercq, 146.

begin in Hellenistic poetry. But the cadence established by Call. *Hymn* 2.100 δαιμόνιος θήρ is so popular in imperial poetry that direct Callimachean influence here is unprovable.

24 No surprise that Aries counts as the beginning of spring. To indicate this the poet has lightly modified the very common (in the first instance Hesiodic) hexameter-ending εἴαρος ὥρη (fr. 70.13 M.–W. and thereafter), which most often occurs in the dative to indicate the time of an inception (equivalent to εἴαρος ἱσταμένοιο); now, in the nominative, it becomes a cosmic event in its own right. For Aries as a spring sign, see also 4.275; Hübner 1982, 83–4. But its location in the MC is more interesting. For this meaning of κορυφή, which standardly means 'zenith',[17] see Heilen 2015, 785; it recurs in 4.263 (and Dorotheus, p. 393.4–6; Ptol. 4.6.1, 4.8.1). Aries is also associated with the midheaven in Valens, I 2.1 κόσμου μεσουράνημα, Nonn. *D.* 1.181 and 38.268 κέντρον ὅλου κόσμοιο, μεσόμφαλον ἄστρον Ὀλύμπου (see Simon ad loc.). But when Aries is on the MC, the sign on the ASC is Cancer,[18] and the midpoint of that sign symbolised the beginning of the Egyptian year (Heilen 2015, 1359 n. 3573). The ASC was also in Cancer in the *Thema Mundi*, the birthchart of the cosmos itself (Roscher, s.v. Sternbilder, 934.62–935.6 (Boll, Gundel); see e.g. Firmicus, 3.1.1; illustrated in Monat, n. 3 ad loc.; Heilen 2015, 632, cf. 635). Aries could accordingly be regarded as head of the universe, either because spring began then (Hephaestion, i. 3.29 κεφαλὴν τοῦ κόσμου) or because Aries was culminating when the universe began (Macrob. *Somn. Scip.* 1.21.32...*quia medium caelum quasi mundi vertex est*). For different systems of marking the beginning of the year, see H. Diels, *Doxographi Graeci* (Berlin, 1879), 196 n. 3; F. Boll, *Studien über Claudius Ptolemäus* (Leipzig, 1894), 166; Bouché-Leclercq, 129 n. 1; L. Aurigemma, *Le Signe zodiacal du Scorpion: Dans les traditions occidentales de l'Antiquité gréco-latine à la Renaissance* (Paris, 1976), 22 n. 33.

25 Libra is the focus. Scorpio allows the poet to stretch the identifier across a full line. The technique is similar at 4.242, where Leo and Libra wad out the reference to Virgo. But Libra was originally Chelae, the claws of Scorpio, before being hived off as a constellation on its own (see on 2.136–7), so the reference to the Scorpion is not just padding.

αἰγλήεις takes a decided stance on whether the constellation was a bright one or not. In fact it is not large and does not have many bright stars. Aratus called it dim (90 ἀλλ' αἱ μὲν φαέων ἐπιμεμφέες οὐδὲν ἀγαναί and 607 Χηλαὶ καὶ λεπτὰ

---

[17] e.g. Ptol. *Synt.* 1, 1 p. 89.2 τὸ κατὰ κορυφὴν σημεῖον. In 2.44 it means the North Pole.
[18] As on two of the extant astrological boards: J. Evans, 'The Astrologer's Apparatus', *Journal for the History of Astronomy*, 35 (2004), 1–44, the Tabula Bianchini illustrated in fig. 2, and the Daressy table discussed on 9 and illustrated in F. Boll, C. Bezold, and W. Gundel, *Sternglaube und Sterndeutung: Die Geschichte und das Wesen der Astrologie* (Leipzig, ³1926), Tafel XIV.

φάουσαι, the latter rendered by Cicero, Arat. 393 *obscuro corpore Chelae*; cf. Gundel, *RE* s.v. Libra, p. 121.7-15). But it did have two bright stars and others took the view that it was, on the contrary, bright (ibid. p. 121.15-22; Cic. *Arat.* 323 *claro cum lumine Chelae*; Germanicus, 89 *insigni caelum perfundent lumine Chelae*, correcting Aratus in the light of Hipparchus' implied criticism, 1.4.18-20, and exaggerating in the process: see Le Bœuffle ad loc. and Martin on Aratus, 90-91; 416 *candentis... Chelas*). When these bright stars are pointed out at all, they are located at the tips of the claws of Chelae (*RE* ibid. pp. 120.63-121.1). On αἰγλήεις as epithet of heaven and stars (from Ap. Rhod. and Aratus onwards), see Zito on Maximus, 137, but is there a specific connection with Maximus, 552 ἐν Ζυγῷ αἰγλήεντι?

αἰθερονωμῶν: absolute *hapax* (like 4.29 αἰθερολαμπῆ, 182 αἰθερόπλαγκτον). LSJ renders 'rule the sky'. Alternatively, simply 'occupy' it. The meaning is unlikely to be more precise than that (e.g. a reference to Libra's weighing out the days into equal portions of light and darkness).

26 τετραπόδης: because it was among the four-footed signs (τετράποδα ζῴδια), in both the senses of being four-footed (as opposed to human) and of having four feet (as opposed to some other number): Bouché-Leclercq, 149; Hübner 1982, 136, 145-6. The standard astrological form is τετράποδος (though poetic τετραπόδεσσ(ι) appears at 6.415 and 5.321). τετραπόδης is a *hapax*.

πολυάστερος: in comparison to Libra, yes. In total count, not particularly. According to ps.-Eratosth. *Catast.* it has nineteen stars, the same number as Gemini and Virgo, many more than Libra (four), but fewer than Capricorn (twenty-four). But ancient lists single out four particularly bright stars that stand out from the rest. For ancient star-lists on Leo, see Gundel, *RE* s.v. Leo, 1975.63-1978.29, and on its bright stars 1978.7-23 (Hipparchus singled out ten). The nominative form is very rare (otherwise only in glosses[19]), but it and 4.224 ἑλικάστερον (unique) look to have been given impetus by εὐάστερος (Aratus, 237) and ἀνάστερος (Aratus, 228, 349, and in M[b] himself at 528).

ἔμπυρος: because it is the Sun's house, and the Sun is in it at the hottest time of the year (late July/August). The verse end casts a standard datum about the sign—its fieriness (Gundel, *RE* s.v. Leo, 1981.40-1982.40; Hübner 1982, 92)—in the form of a fashionable late antique hexameter end, seemingly attested first in Dorotheus, p. 383.8 (then Nonn. *D.* 38.232) ἔμπυρος Ἄρης.[20]

27 ἀεὶ τεύχουσι: also 6.248.

---

[19] Hesych. ε 7135 πολυάστερος νύξ; Σ Arat. 665 πολυτειρέος τοῦ πολυαστέρου. Gen. νυκτὸς πολυάστερος in an oracle quoted ap. Euseb. *PE* 3.15.3 and by John Lydus, *De Mens.* 2.5.

[20] Empedocles ap. Diog. Laert. 8.77, 31 B 117.2 D.-K. (see app. crit.); *Or. Sib.* 6.28 ἔμπυρον ὄμμα; Nonn. *D.* 36.121 ἔμπυρον αἴγλην, 47.614 ἔμπυρον αἰχμήν, John of Gaza, *Descr.* 606 ἔμπυρον ὁρμήν.

28–34

Saturn *not* in its own houses in MC or ASC. The poet pairs the ASC and MC as he had not in the previous entry. But this pairing corresponds to some of the comparanda, Περὶ κέντρ. 14 [but not Dor.^ARAB] and 'Valens', *CCAG* viii/1. 163.7–8. In practice the poet describes what 3.21–6 reports for the MC (alone): general miseritude, lack of estate, with the addition of wandering. The latter detail is shared with Paul, who reports it when the planet is out of sect (p. 65.17–19).

28 ἀνοικείοισι τόποις: for ἀνοικεῖος see p. 241. As with οἰκεῖος, although M^b is the only Manethonian poet to use this term, it is technical. τόπος here must mean 'sign' (i. 877–8: a frequent licence in later books). *Lib. Herm.* xxvi. 71 has *in signis in quibus non gaudet*; Dor.^ARAB II 23.3 has 'in the house of his enemies' and Περὶ κέντρ. 15 ἐν ζῳδίῳ ἐχθροῦ ἀστέρος. Neither identifies these signs.

κλυτοτέρμονος ὥρης: Koechly's literal translation ('terminando-celebris horae') is uninterpretable, but Lopilato understands this as ablatival ('apart from the ascendant'). τέρμ- here must mean the marker at the beginning, not the end: so too 77 βιοτέρμονος ὥρης, 480 ἀπὸ τέρμονος αἴθρης (see ad loc.). Another instance where it does not mean the final boundary is Valens, VI 2.14 τερματίζεται (of the zodiac) = 'subdivided', not 'terminated'. This poet likes foggily bombastic compounds so much it is probably idle to ask whether the epithet means the ASC itself is famous or presages fame for natives (as 4.35 κυδόσκοπον ὥρην seems to do).

29 αἰθερολαμπῆ: λαμπ- compounds, which the poet likes (i. 106 n. 90; p. 250), are usually used for stars, but also for the MC as the source of radiance when it hosts a luminary (94 πυριλαμπ-). Other innovations beside this one are λαμπραύγετις (of Mercury in 201 = 1.301, Jupiter in 415) and νεολαμπέα (of the Moon in 510). See also on 4.53 for λαμπροφαής (Venus) and 4.44 for πυριλαμπής.

30 πανεπίσκοπον: also 95, 110, again in connection with the ASC. Often epithet of God (Lightfoot 2007, 544–5), though I doubt whether this is an example of the re-appropriation of divine vocabulary. The σκοπ- element in the compound evokes 'horoscope' (p. 246), but the παν- compound grandly extends the scope; the implication is presumably that the ASC has a bearing on everything.

ἀμφιπολεύῃ, also 45 and 132: see i. 879 (3.36, 114, 6.199; Dorotheus, p. 386.12).

31 παμβλαβέας: only here and 76. Similar is 4.311 παμπαθέας (possibly *proton legomenon*). These are astrological answers to more familiar compounds like πανάθλιος, πανδάκρυτος, πανόδυρτος, πάμμορος, only substituting the astrological concept of 'harm', 'damage' (~ σίνος) for the emotive element. The sense of Lucian, *Tox.* 24 παλλώβητον is similar. For παν- compound neologisms in Mᵃ and their legacy in Mᵇ (all παμ-), see i. 108.

ἀκτεάνους: cf. 3.22 (lack of κλῆρος). The epithet is first in Antipater of Sidon, *AP* 7.353.4 = *HE* 359; then 3.118, here and at 114, then in LGHP.

ἀδόξους: Dor.ᴬᴿᴬᴮ II 23.3 'his reputation will become bad'. The epithet is unique here in the Manethoniana, though common in astrological prose. Only the later books of the corpus mention δόξα (4× Mᵇ, 5× Mᶜ, 7× Mᵈ, two of which refer to a star). Mᵃ had (massively) exploited κῦδος instead, which, conversely, only appears at 4.35 (in an epithet), 164, and 5.9. κλέος is much less used: five instances in Mᵃ of which one is in a coda, otherwise two instances in this book.

32 ἐνδεέας + gen.: also 4.340 (and Dorotheus, p. 395.28 φάος ἐνδεές, not of natives). Again prose astrological vocabulary, lightly epicised. Constructions vary: see Valens, II 2.10 ἐνδεεῖς τῷ βίῳ; II 5.3 ἐνδεεῖς τῆς ἐφημέρου τροφῆς, II 41.8 περὶ δὲ τὸν βίον ἐνδεεῖς; Paul, p. 70.2 ἀνενδεεῖς τοῦ βίου; Θ p. 144.2 τοῖς βίοις ἐνδεεῖς.

ἐφημερίης βιότητος ~ 3.251 ἐφημερίης δαίτης.

33-4 πάσης λύπης ἐπιβήτορας: the agent noun, from Homer onwards in the sense 'mounted on' (sexually, or just 'on top of'), extends to 'possessed of' or 'occupying' (e.g. land in 4.521), and in Mᵇ's hands still further to activities (222 πολυπλαγκτοσύνης, 245 θηροδιδασκαλίης, 471 στρατιῆς), experiences (281 γήρως), possession (339 αἰθροτόκου τε γονῆς), and now to mental or moral conditions (compare, too, Greg. Naz. *PG* 37.1233.6 κακίης ἐπιβήτορες), as well as other categories (280 χλεύης τ' ἐπιβήτορας = evoking it, subjected to it, or both?). It is equivalent to μετέχοντας (in the next line, and common in astrological prose). The sequence of poverty and grief is good (e.g. 3.249-52). So, if the repetition of λύπης is unacceptable, the second instance is more vulnerable than the first, and should presumably be regarded as a dittography (in support of De Stefani's πενίης see e.g. Hephaestion, i. 23.10-11 καὶ ἔσται ἐν κακοπαθείαις καὶ πενίαις καὶ ξενιτεύσει, 'Heliodorus' on Paul, p. 68.22 πενιχροὺς καὶ ξενιτεύοντας), unless Rigler's λύμης is to be introduced at this point.

34 ἀλημοσύνης: only here and Dion. Per. 716; Mᵃ already had 3.379 ἀλητύος (Callimachean). Prose terms which this would enliven include πλάναι, ἀλητεία (Valens, I 1.39), ξενιτεία, ἀποδημία, ἐκδημία.

4.35-43 Jupiter

35-43

Jupiter in ASC or MC, and in its own degrees. As with 4.28-34, this notice collapses together the ASC and MC; the corresponding entries at 3.32-5 + 36-9 run them together with a ταὐτὰ δέ notice. The high priests and agonothetes, who are not specified in the other comparanda, are a particular link with that passage; there, they are listed under the MC (3.38). They are also compatible with Θ p. 135.18–19 δοξαστικούς, πόλεων προηγουμένους, ἡδυβίους δὲ καὶ καλοψύχους (for Jupiter in the ASC). 'Own degrees' are new here.

35 ἐπὶ γεινομένοισιν: recasts prosaic ἐπὶ γενέσεως ('in a nativity'), helped by EGHP phrases such as Hes. *Th.* 218-19 βροτοῖσι | γεινομένοισι, fr. 58.14 M.-W. τοῖσι δὲ γεινομ[ένοισιν, *HHom. Aphr.* 265 γεινομένῃσιν.

κυδόσκοπον: see on 28.

36 φαέθοντι πυρὸς θερμοῖο σελασμῷ: for this kind of name see i. 903 n. 17. The light name is treated as epithet of a 'radiance' noun (p. 256),[21] the first of a number of enhancements of σέλας all of which are *proton legomena* in this book (for the others see on 4.189 σελάγισμα and 4.601 σέλασμα). Here and at 4.171 it means 'light'; at 4.231 'planet' (anaphoric); at 4.266 'aspect'; and in 4.351 the entire chart or configuration. If θερμός is not padding (it is not an EGHP formula) it makes the point that Jupiter is a warm planet (Bouché-Leclercq, 97; Ptol. 1.4.5 θερμαίνει...θερμαντικὸς).

37 οὐρανίης ἀτραποῦ: this iteration of the pathway metaphor (4.273, 583) has various parallels, not all astronomical: Antipater of Sidon, *AP* 7.241.8 = *HE* 345 οὐρανίας ἀτραπιτούς (of a lunar eclipse); Archimelus, *SH* 202.8 οὐρανίας... ἀτραπιτούς (of gigantic construction); Anon. *AP* 7.337.7 ἐς οὐρανίας...ἀταρπούς (of a departed soul).

δρόμῳ: compare 4.131 ὑπερορμαίνων (of Jupiter), though its orbit is *not* fast, and 'running' vocabulary is more often lunar (i. 892–3).

ἠέρα τέμνῃ: an unusual move away from the generally preferred noun αἰθέρα (Heilen 2011, 45–7), which is paralleled at 214 and 509. Heilen attributes it to lateness, but see p. 181; the two are also used without distinction in Hellenistic poetry (Harder on Call. fr. 110.7). The ultimate model is *HHom. Dem.* 383 ἠέρα τέμνον ἰόντες (of divine travel), whence ἠέρα τέμν- in imperial poetry moves to line-end, still for the flight of gods or demigods (e.g. Nonn. *D.* 11.131, 37.266) and birds, especially the eagle (e.g. Nonn. *D.* 3.61). Hence this is another instance of EGHP divinity-words transferred to stars. It has the somewhat strange effect of locating Jupiter in the ἀήρ, which in more precise sources means the lower atmosphere (murky in EGHP; a sublunar element, in the view of Ptolemy[22]), as opposed to the αἰθήρ (location of the stars in 2.1), but

---

[21] Otherwise only Tzetzes, *Alleg. in Il.* 20.364 ἀρεϊκοὶ δὲ σελασμοί. A secondary meaning in ps.-Zonaras, σ 1634.7 Σελασμός. ἡ ἀλαζονεία; sim. Theognostus, *Canones*, 33.

[22] *LfrgrE*, 3. b), c); Richardson on *HHom. Dem.* 383; Livrea on Ap. Rhod. 4.443. In Ap. Rhod. 4.1287 starlight reaches *us* through the ἀήρ, but the stars themselves are not *in* it. For Ptolemy, see e.g. 1.2.1.

which M^b is happy to use for the medium through which the planets move (4.214 ἐς ἠέρα πυρσοβολοῦσα), combining it casually with αἰθήρ (4.509–10 κατ' αἰθέρος ἠερόπλαγκτον | ζωφορίην, of the ecliptic), and in this case embroiling it with an adapted Homeric formula μέσον οὐρανὸν (p. 246), used for the location of the Sun. See also n. on 5.29.

38 προφανῇ: also 4.94; 'Antiochus', l. 56 (*CCAG* i. 110.33) προφανείη (the Moon). Transitive at 4.173, 221. The celestial sense goes back to *Od*. 9.144–5 οὐδὲ σελήνη οὐρανόθεν προὔφαινε (intrans.).

κατ' οἰκείων...δεσπόσμασι μοιρῶν: in its own degrees (not, with LSJ s.v. δέσποσμα, through the decrees of Fate), as in 172 κατ' οἰκείων ὁρίων. δεσπόσμασι (a *hapax*) is padding. The corpus uses the accusative with κατά far more often than the genitive. Most of the genitives are for location on *kentra* (see on 1.282). In none of the exceptions (6.526, 641 σφετέροιο κατ' οἴκου; 2.410–11 κατὰ πάντων | ζωιδίων) is it a matter of placement on a precise point, but location somewhere within a domain. For this one can perhaps appeal to a form of the Hellenistic, distributive sense of the genitive (Blass–Debrunner–Rehkopf, §225 and n. 3).

39 χρυσοστέπτορας...ἢ ἀρχιερῆας: the poet evokes the gold and chaplets which, together with purple robes (see on 1.101), are the outward marks of the high priest. At 3.37, M^a had singled out the μίτραι (head-bands) and purple robes (pp. 1062–3) of the agonothetes who, as members of the provincial élite, were very often priests and high-priests as well (G. Frija, *Les Prêtres des empereurs: Le culte impérial civique dans la province romaine d'Asie* (Rennes, 2012), 156–9). M^b may be dialoguing with the earlier poet (p. 219); he has singled out the other distinctive feature of ceremonial dress. It was available to priests to wear gold in many ways, not only in crowns, but also in ornaments and jewellery and embroidered garments (A. B. Kuhn, 56–8, 59–61, and *passim*), but this poet has combined the gold with chaplets by producing a more exotic rendering of the epithet χρυσοστέφανος (usually of goddesses, but of crowned games in Pind. *Ol*. 8.1); in 2.235 στέμμασί τε χρυσοῦ (Venus in house or terms of Jupiter) the poet has combined them into a portmanteau expression (see ad loc.). This new compound is an all-time *hapax*, and seems to be the only -στέπτωρ compound in existence at all. It not only flouts the old rule—long disused—that -τωρ and -τήρ are used with simplex verbs (and if with compounds, only prepositional ones), but also makes the suffix passive (Fraenkel, i. 126, 157).

40 The high priests of the previous line are coupled with organisers of games, as in Θ p. 138.12 ἀρχιερεῖς ἢ ἱερῶν ἀγωνοθέτας (Moon in sect on the ASC). They could be the same people acting in different capacities (*qua* provincial élites), or even the same people acting in one and the same capacity, inasmuch as the high-priest of the imperial cult, whether provincial or municipal, organised gladiatorial games.[23] For the ἡγήτορας of the earlier passage (3.38) the poet substitutes a more exotic (hapax[24]) agent noun, which enhances poetic ἰθυντήρ in the sense that ἰθύνειν may be used of organised activities (Or. ap. Demosth. Or. 21.52 ἰθύνεθ' ἑορτάς). Everyone from L's copyists onwards seems to concur in correcting πόλεων (gen. pl. of πόλις); De Stefani points out one reason to do so, namely Od. 23.350 πολέων κεκορήμεθ' ἀέθλων. I concur, although concourses of games are held in cities, and the multiple genitives which would result from this are within M^b's range (p. 211).

41 μεγιστᾶνας: see on 3.36–8: in the parallels, Jupiter in the MC produces, not μεγιστᾶνας themselves, but those charged with managing their affairs. The word, common in prose astrology (also Camaterus), is unique here in the Manethoniana.

41–2 ἀλλοτρίων κτεανισμῶν | δεσποσύνους: an attempt to disguise the banality of the expression through suffixation; cf. e.g. Valens, I 1.10 and I 19.2 ἀλλοτρίων διοικητάς, II 2.24 ἀλλοτρίων πραγμάτων προεστῶτας, Περὶ κράσ. 12 ἀλλοτρίων ἔργων καὶ κτημάτων ἐμπίστευσιν; Rhetorius, CCAG vii. 215.12 ἀλλοτρίων κτῆσιν; CCAG x. 108.12–13 χρήματα ἀλλότρια κτήσεται. κτεανισμός is a hapax; for δεσπόσυνος see Braswell on Pind. P. 4.267 (the nominal use goes back to Tyrtaeus).

42 ὀλβίστη παράκοιτις: substituting for αἰδοίη παράκοιτις (also κυδρὴ παράκοιτις), with a fatly prosperous implication that epic lacked. The irregular superlative is first attested in literary texts in Call. Hymn 5.117 (Hopkinson's note ad loc. discusses the morphology). For its application to spouses, compare Greg. Naz. AP 8.103.5 ὀλβίστης ἀλόχου, Nonn. D. 47.392 ὀλβίστῃ σέο νύμφῃ, and above all AP 1.12.5 σὺν ὀλβίστῳ παρακοίτῃ (of the founder of the/a church of the Trinity, from an inscription).

43 εἰς ἀρετὴν νεύουσα: ἀρετή has been the highest praise of a woman since Od. 24.193, and is a topos of funerary epigram,[25] but the most distinctive word is the verb, which must mean 'disposed to' (SEG 28.563, Byzantium, 6th c. πρ]ὸς θ(εὸ)ν νενούσαν) rather than 'inclined towards', as if there could be a question of hesitation (Antiphilus of Byzantium, AP 16.136.4 = Garland 1082 (ἵν' ἤθεα δισσὰ χαράξῃ,) | ὧν τὸ μὲν εἰς ὀργὰν νεῦε, τὸ δ' εἰς ἔλεον, of indecisive Medea). Koechly 1851, xli noted the preposition as odd.

---

[23] Robert 1940a, 271–5; S. J. Friesen, Imperial Cults and the Apocalypse of St John: Reading Revelation in the Ruins (Oxford, 2001), 32, 57 (modifies traditional view).

[24] But for Hesych. δ 1780 διϊθυντής· διοικητής, also hapax.

[25] For female virtue in inscriptions, see R. van Bremen, 'Women and Wealth', in A. Cameron and A. Kuhrt (eds.), Images of Women in Antiquity (London, 1993), 223–42, at 234; grave inscriptions e.g. GVI 293, 729, 893, IG XIV 2317.

πολὺ κλέος οἴσεται οἴκοις: the paradosis has been suspected, but has an implied materialism, as if κλέος were a commodity (Eur. *Andr.* 1282 μηδ' εἰ ζαπλούτους οἴσεται φερνὰς δόμοις), which does not seem entirely out of keeping with astrology. With Koechly's ἔσσεται, the line is phonetically very similar to *Or. Sib.* 3.485 πολύστονος ἔσσεται οἶκτος.

4.44–52 Mars

44–52

Mars in MC. In the corresponding chart in 3.61–71, the basic set-up produces banausic workers, while military leaders are born under the additional aspect of benefics. The apodosis, including the same two specific types of violent death, is markedly closer to M^a than to any of the comparanda, even though the topos of plunging from a height (3.67–8) has been omitted, as has the less exciting outcome of exile.

44 For the form of name, see i. 898 and n. 4; for πυριλαμπέος, 2.37 n. and i. 909 n. 19. We are rather bludgeoned by Mars' fieriness in this line (p. 213).

45 ἐν καθέτῳ κόσμου: the significance of κάθετος, 'perpendicular', which is used not only for the MC (representing an apparent confusion with the zenith), but also for other *kentra*, seems to be that it implies exact location at that point. Of the MC again in 4.132, Astrol. Anon. 379, *CCAG* v/1. 196.9–10 = 'Palchus', *CCAG* i. 113.9–10 κατὰ κάθετον ἐν τῷ μεσουρανήματι, and 200.29–30 = Θ p. 178.7 μεσουρανοῦντες κατὰ κάθετον; of the DESC in 1.92; of the ASC in *CCAG* i. 106.14 κατὰ κάθετον ὡρονομοῦντα.

ἀμφιπολεύῃ: see on 4.30.

46 τῆμος: this adverb of time is well suited to astrological poetry, since when it is coordinated with a conjunction in EGHP it is predominantly in 'when – then' clauses that involve times of day or seasons, in other words, cosmic time. This is always the case in the *Iliad*, and the connection with seasons is likewise clear in Hesiod (even when τῆμος is not formally coordinated with a time- or season-clause), though it is not invariably so in later EGHP (*Od.* 12.441, *HHom. Aphr.* 170 have no reference to heavenly bodies; *Od.* 7.318 has no coordination). Apotelesmata simply extend the use from markers of daily time (sunrise, midday, etc.) to the movement of the heavenly bodies themselves, which produce effects for the *longue durée* of human life.[26] In EGHP the correlative is usually, though not invariably, ἦμος; in the

---

[26] Surprisingly in *Or. Sib.* only in 3.471, though apparently highly appropriate for the life-cycle of the cosmos and for eschatological signs; not listed by Parke and Wormell in *Delphic Oracles*.

Manethoniana, where it is confined to M^a and M^b, it now appears in conditional as well as temporal clauses with a variety of conjunctions. At the same time, M^b has formalised it. In M^a it does not regularly stand at the beginning of its clause (6.123, 285), and indeed is not invariably coordinated with a conjunction (not at 3.169, 185, 249; 6.551 it is itself in the protasis). In M^b both are the case. Maximus uses it sixteen times (i.e. over twice as often as in M^b—seven times—in a very similar number of lines), but without the latter's formalism; much more often than not he uses it as an uncoordinated adverb (the only exception being 115).

ὁ φύς: see on 6.697 and p. 252 on references to natives.

ἐν ἡγεμόνεσσιν ἄριστος ~ 3.64 ἡγεμόνας θῆκε, recast in the rhythm of Homeric ἄμ' ἡγεμόνεσσιν ἕκαστοι (Il. 3.1; later and presumably independently Greg. Naz. PG 37.1542.2 ὑφ' ἡγεμόνεσσιν ἀρίστοις). For the 'best in show' idiom, see p. 173. Θ p. 168.13–14 has the 'lords of life and death' motif (pp. 23–4), with a note of recklessness, emphasised by the other comparanda, which is missing here (ἡγεμόνας δὲ ζωῆς καὶ θανάτου κυρίους ἢ στρατοπεδάρχας φοβεροὺς κλίμασιν).

47 Other sources have military men, but bodyguards are restricted to M^a and M^b, who partly recycles the vocabulary of the earlier passage and partly rewrites it by means of synonymity (3.64–5 φρουρούς τε τυράννων, | εὔθηκτον φορέοντας ἑὸν περὶ σῶμα σίδηρον ~ φρουρητῆρα σίδηρον ἔχων).

48–52 These two modes of violent death—by bloodshed and poisoning—are absent from other sources save 3.70–1, which they elaborate.

48–9 πίστιν τ' ἀλκήεσσαν: a position of trust in the army (e.g. Plut. Sert. 3.4), involving the exercise of valour. This man is like the types in Valens, I 20.17 (born under a combination of Jupiter, Mars, Moon) πίστεως καταξιουμένους, στρατιωτικούς. The epithet (one of only a couple of instances of the feminine of ἀλκήεις, the other being HHom. 28.3) enlivens the abstract by bringing to it a quality normally associated with persons, creatures, or their dispositions (other transferences in AP 6.277.1 ἀλκήεντας ὀιστούς; Opp. Hal. 2.27 ἀλκήεντας ἀέθλους).

ἐπὴν δ' εἰς τέρμα βίοιο | μοιριδίου θανάτοιο: combining objective and subjective genitive, each of which is a cliché. For multiple genitives, see i. 230; p. 211. For τέρμα βίου see on 3.254, and for 'the end consisting in death', on 6.502, 598; K.–G. i. 265.

49 μοιριδίου θανάτοιο: the earliest uses of the epithet (Sophocles, Pindar) do not apply to death, but it has become a topos in that connection by the imperial period (Valens, IX 9.20 uses τὸ μοιρίδιον apropos of Hector), especially in sepulchral epigrams (Fate's threads, fated days[27]), and where μοιριδίωι

---

[27] Threads: PHI s.v. μοιρίδιος; days: Eparchides, FGrH 437 F 2 φέγγει μοιριδίῳ.

θανάτωι is a convenient pentameter ending (ps.-Plut. *Mor.* 109 D; *IG* II² 7227 (Attica, 4th c. AD)). Similar diction in *Orph. Arg.* 1287-8 ἐπεὶ πότμος ᾔιε λυγρός | μοιριδίου θανάτοιο supports Letronne's correction of κόσμῳ at line-end; De Stefani's θεσμῷ does not seem superior to this. For πολυπήμονι see Livrea on Ap. Rhod. 4.228.

50 λαιμοτόμου φάρυγος: a gruesome particularisation of the motif, associated with Mars, of 'wounds from iron';[28] 3.70 had a simpler form, death from iron (σιδήρῳ; *ferro*, *passim* in Firmicus). Another Martian throat-cutting in Firmicus, 8.9.2 (Mars aspecting 1° Cancer, whose paranatellon is *Iugulae*); Valens has various individuals who were beheaded, including one who had Mars ruling the Lot of Fortune (II 41.55). As for diction, the poet fails to exploit the obvious source for throat-cutting (*Il.* 18.34 λαιμὸν ἀπαμήσειε σιδήρῳ): φάρυγος is Odyssean (9.373; 19.480), while its tragic/dithyrambic epithet most closely recalls Eur. *IA* 776 λαιμοτόμους κεφαλάς.[29] The tautology is the poet's own.

βίον αἵματι λείψει: βίον...λείπειν is unremarkable, while αἵματι underscores Mars' specialism (e.g. Antiochus, *CCAG* vii. 127.14 ἄρχει δὲ τοῦ ἐν ἡμῖν αἵματος; Valens, App. II 14 κυριεύει δὲ...αἵματος), a natural companion to iron weapons. To the passages on wounds cited above add e.g. 1.243-4, Apomasar, *De Rev.* p. 217.19, Θ p. 125.26-7, *CCAG* ii. 134.6, and especially 'Antiochus', ll. 63 and 92 (*CCAG* i. 111.9, 112.11-12), where Mars in the third and fourth places causes damage αἵμασι. Prose astrological jargon is αἱμαγμός (p. 854: used above all by Valens).

51 The line is all but a tetracolon: the poet must have been proud of it. It is semantically packed (p. 210) with anatomical vocabulary (apart from the verb), of which ἰνίον (occiput) and σφονδυλόεντα (composed of vertebrae) are both ultimately Homeric, the former *hapax* at *Il.* 5.73 (in the same *sedes*), the latter based on the *hapax* σφονδυλίων (suffixed with -ι for metrical reasons) at *Il.* 20.483. Both passages are appropriate models because they refer to blows to the head with (obviously iron) weapons. Moreover, the whole phrase σφονδυλόεντα τράχηλον, which comes close to tautology again (a vertebral or cervical neck), reproduces the rhythm of *Il.* 16.841 αἱματόεντα χιτῶνα, or *Od.* 3.177 ἰχθυόεντα κέλευθα—a pattern I do not find in Hellenistic poetry. ἀκροτομεῖν (again in 4.260), a rare verb with only eight instances (excluding repetitions), is used in a very similar context to this by Theophylactus Simocatta, *Hist.* 4.1.5 ἀκροτομήσαντές τε τὸν δείλαιον τήν τε κεφαλὴν τῶν ἐν τῷ τραχήλῳ σφονδύλων

---

[28] TLG s.v. τομή, σίδηρος, e.g. Valens, II 34.16, V 8.29, Περὶ κράσ. 150; Hephaestion, i. 209.24.
[29] Passive also in *Hec.* 208, *Ion* 1055; active in *IT* 444 λαιμοτόμωι...χειρί, Timotheus, *PMG* 791 col. iv. 130, Ariston, *AP* 6.306.4, and in agent noun Eur. *El.* 459 λαιμοτόμαν.

ἀποκοψάμενοι (though the first participle seems to mean something different from the beheading that follows: cutting off hands and feet perhaps?).

52 Poison and disease are sometimes separate items (e.g. Valens, II 41.31, IV 24.5, and Apomasar, *De Myst.*, *CCAG* xi/1. 169.2 περὶ νοσοῦντος ἢ φαρμακωμένου), sometimes combined (Apomasar, *De Rev.* pp. 189.19 νόσος ἀπὸ φαρμάκου πόσεως, 218.13 νοσήσει ἐκ φαρμακοποσίας): this could be a portmanteau expression, but need not be. Both components, of which the one depends on the other, consist of an abstract noun with qualifier (a poisoned deception; a sickly end). This poet and others cultivate such genus–species expressions (e.g. 4.198 σκολοπηΐδα μοῖραν), which, as periphrases, and especially when the epithet is a compound one (see on 4.339 αἰθροτόκου τε γονῆς, 5.221 μοίρης νευροτόμου), have a markedly tragic character.[30] Poison is often linked to other deceitful activities in astrological catalogues,[31] but the poet has managed to formulate that association here in a periphrasis involving a verbal adjective with which one can compare Aesch. *Ag.* 116 χερὸς ἐκ δοριπάλτου (the right), 1391–2 διοσδότωι | γάνει (dew), Eur. *Or.* 1357–8 τὸν Ἑλένας φόνον | καθαιμακτόν; *Alc.* 184 ὀφθαλμοτέγκτωι…πλημμυρίδι. The epithet φαρμακτός (here and at 540) is new (though restored by Korais at Strab. 11.2.19; much later in Theodorus Prodromus, 11th–12th c.). The poet seems to have devised it as a riposte to the almost equally rare φαρμακόεν (of a poisoned chalice) at 3.71.

4.53–68 Venus

53–8

Venus in DESC. This outcome concentrates on adulterers, more prominent in 3.87–9 than in the remaining comparanda, which are more fixated on promiscuous wives and female natives (see on 3.84–9); add, however, 'Valens', *CCAG* viii/1. 169.1 μοιχείας.

53–5 The naming formula demonstrates that this is not an extract from a formerly complete catalogue of planets in *kentra*, which would presumably have begun with the ASC and not have needed to reintroduce the planet at such length (contrast 3.84). The naming formula at 4.14–15 had introduced Saturn's light-name; here it introduces *both* halves of Venus' name, the mythological and the light-name, which are connected the one as a dependent genitive to the

---

[30] For periphrastic expressions as characteristic of tragedy, see W. Schmid and O. Stählin, *Geschichte der griechischen Literatur*, 5 vols. (Munich, 1929–48), i. 2.295 n. 3; Breitenbach, 197–8, 199–201.

[31] 2.305–10 = Π.τ.δ. 16, cf. 5.106–7 (poison listed next to hidden things); Περὶ σχημ. 87; Περὶ κέντρ. 83; Ptol. 3.14.15, 17, 19, 32.

other: for the type, see i. 898–9; p. 256. πάντες corresponds to gods and men in the former passage: *everyone* is agreed on this name. The verb should precisely mean 'come up with the idea of' (the relevant EGHP meaning is 'contrive' in *Od.* 15.444, Hes. *Th.* 160, and in this *sedes* in Call. *Hecale* fr. 70.13; other meanings are 'realise', 'notice', 'mark', 'perceive'). But the poet has stretched it into a synonym for 'call' (cf. Alexis, F 206.2 K.–A. ὃν πάντες εἰώθασιν ὀνομάζειν ὑγρόν; *Or. Sib.* 11.164 ὃν πάντες καλέουσι σοφώτατον, Greg. Naz. *PG* 37.1510.2 Ὃν πάντες ἐνέπουσι διδάσκαλον).

53 λαμπροφαής: i. 907.19.

53–4 δύνουσι...ζωιδίοις: cf. 4.538 ζωιδίῳ δύνοντι; also 6.26 δῦνον δέ τε κέντρον. The expression could reflect prose: Dorotheus, p. 409.7 ἐκ δὲ τοῦ δύνοντος ζῳδίου (from Hephaestion); Ptol. 4.5.6 τοῦ τε ἀνατέλλοντος σημείου τοῦ ζῳδιακοῦ καὶ τοῦ δύνοντος; 'Valens', CCAG viii/1. 165.10 and 170.6 τὸ δῦνον ζῴδιον, 168.30 τῷ δύνοντι ζῳδίῳ, Valens, II 38.41 ἐν τῷ δύνοντι ζῳδίῳ, III 2.4 ἐν τῷ...δύνοντι ζῳδίῳ; Hephaestion, i. 130.3 δύνει τὰ ζῴδια, 272.10.

55 ἐν τούτῳ δὲ γονὰς μερόπων τις ἐνέγκῃ: a very similar formula in 4.133; for the rhythm, cf. Nonn. *D.* 8.89 μερόπων τις ἐνίψῃ. The expression is very unusual, and paralleled, if at all, in late prose (Olympiodorus, *Comm. in Job*, p. 184.11 οὐ νεκρὸν καὶ ἀτελῆ γονὴν ἤνεγκε; Methodius, *Or.* 12.1.94 τὰς σὰς γονὰς ἐν ἀσπόρῳ φέρουσα νηδύι; Hippocr. *Mul. Affect.* 1.12 οὐ δύνανται φέρειν τὴν γονήν means 'unable to bear the seed', in the sense of unable to establish a pregnancy).

56 De Stefani's note explains why a noun meaning 'thief' (or despoiler, corrupter etc.) is required. The theft metaphor, already in 2.278, 6.207, recurs in 4.304, 1.23, 5.290, 298.[32] See also on 4.164 θηρήσειν. The closest linguistic parallels for the outcome are 2.184–5 λεχέων ὀλετῆρας | ἀλλοτρίων and 267 ἀλλοτρίων λεχέων κρυπτοὺς λυμάντορας (see ad loc. in both cases), though the corresponding passage at 3.89 also has ἀλλοτρίων τε μέλαθρον ὀπιπεύουσι γυναικῶν ('ogle'). In support of ἅρπαξ (Neri), add 1.23; Valens, I 1.21 ἁρπαγάς...μοιχείας; and, though not specifically about adultery, Critodemus, *CCAG* v/2. 52.33–4 ἅρπαγές τε καὶ ἀλλοτρίων ἐπιθυμηταί; *Περὶ σχημ.* 51 and *Π.τ.δ.* 43 ἀλλοτρίων ἅρπαγας; Dorotheus, p. 368.5 ἁρπαγὰς καὶ ἀλλοτρίων σ‹τ›ερήσεις. παναθέσμιος, which is transmitted, would be *hapax*, but πανάθεσμος is already in 6.158 and ps.-Opp. *Cyn.* 3.224 as well as ps.-Opp. *Cyn.* 2.438, while

---

[32] On the theft metaphor: D. Cohen, *Law, Sexuality and Society: The Enforcement of Morals in Classical Athens* (Cambridge, 2011), 113 n. 45; C. B. Patterson, *The Family in Greek History* (Cambridge, MA, 1998), 123 and n. 53.

two out of three instances of the much commoner ἄθεσμος in the Manethoniana are also about sexual behaviour (3.154, 4.304).

57 The line is a happy combination of late hexameter stylistics, with four asyndetic epithets, and the long asyndetic accumulations in prose astrology. The items are recherché, but the semantic range is entirely traditional, e.g. Ptol. 3.14.30 μοιχικούς…ψεύστας, δολοπλόκους; Π.τ.δ. 16 ψεύστας…μοιχικούς; Valens, IV 23.2 μοιχείας…καὶ δόλους γυναικῶν. See on 6.212 for shady adulterers. ὀρφνήεις is otherwise only in Quint. Smyrn. 3.657 and Hesych. ο 1359. δολοεργός is unique to M^b, here, at 243 (hunters), 563, and 3rd decl. at 394 (more adultery). ἀνέστιος has been firmly located in its present *sedes* by the much-quoted *Il.* 9.63 (though the poet has jettisoned the list of alphas privative in which it is embedded); note the shift from the man who is outcast from his community as a lover of strife to the man who has no place at the hearth because he is a wrecker of homes. Finally, αἰσχεόμυθος is also new (for αἰσχ- and social disapproval, especially about sexual matters, see i. 304, 367–8). The shameful utterances are presumably lewd suggestions: compare perhaps Apomasar, *De Myst.*, *CCAG* xi/1. 181.9–10 τὰς ἀκολάστους γλώσσας in a list which also includes τὰς πορνείας and τὰς ἀπάτας καὶ τοὺς δόλους; mimes are described in a similar way, presumably because of their smutty talk (i. 343). It might represent prose αἰσχρολόγος (Hephaestion, i. 92.20, 314.2, not of adulterers), or a compound involving -γλωσσ-.

58 παμψέκτωρ: *hapax*, other than 4.316 παμψέκτους. By comparing the simplex ψέκτης (one who blames) in Hippocrates, *De diaeta in morbis acutis*, and Plato, *Laws* and *Republic*, Fraenkel, i. 127, implicitly understands the compound, too, to be active, but it seems likelier to mean 'all-blameworthy', 'reprehensible in every way' (as in 4.316, and see too 525 n.), in which case it would be another example of a -τωρ agent noun in a passive sense (see on 4.39). Compare Valens, I 20.8 ψόγοις ἐπαίσχροις ἢ μοιχείαις περιτρέπονται ('involved in shameful faults and adultery'): this means that adulterers attract blame, not that they mete it out to others.

ἀδίδακτος, ἀεὶ δεδιδαγμένος αἰσχροῖς: if the participle is right (Nauck objected precisely *because* it repeated the root of the previous verb), it reads like a theological oracle where an alpha privative is played out against positives (*Or. Sib.* 3.12, fr. 1.8 ἀόρατος, ὁρώμενος αὐτὸς ἅπαντα): in the theological oracle the paradox has a point, but here it adds a kind of phoney resonance. δεδιδαγμένος may have been given some impetus by Aratus, 529 (though the poet does not follow the construction with the genitive), but it has been combined with the ponderous ἀδίδακτος, used of man unaided by divine wisdom (Orph. *Lith.* 75 ἀδίδακτοι; Nonn. *Par.* 1.112, in this *sedes*), and of the divinity himself (*Theos. Tüb.* 13.18 ἀδίδακτος, in this *sedes*: L. Robert, 'Un oracle gravé à Oinoanda', *CRAI* 1971, 597–619, at 603). As for the astrological stigma of shame (pp. 12–14),

Kentrothesiai 531

compare Critodemus, *CCAG* v/2. 112.30–1 αἰσχρῶν καὶ ἀσελγῶν ἔργων ἐρῶσι; *Π.τ.δ.* 7 αἰσχρονοήμονας; Ptol. 3.14.17 αἰσχροποιούς, al.).

59–64

Venus in ASC. This presents a different pattern from the previous entries, which tended to elaborate one particular theme already found in M^a; in general there is little overlap with 3.72–5. Plus factors are culture, ease, riches derived from women and female confidentiality, involvement in mystery cults. Missing with respect to M^a are fame in native land and fame of mother. The plus factors in M^b are almost all paralleled in the comparanda (Dor.^{ARAB} II 26.1; *Περὶ κέντρ.* 52; Firmicus, 3.6.1) although they do not appear in the same order; only the female confidentiality has no parallel. ('Valens', *CCAG* viii/1. 168.25–6 has only a cheerful disposition and wealth.)

59 For the protasis see p. 246. The ASC has its own light again in 4.491 ὡροσκόπα φέγγη. For λεύσσειν (far more popular in M^a), see i. 886; Prévot, 247–9.

60 αἱμυλίους: *Περὶ κέντρ.* 52 προσηνεῖς; 3.73 and Θ p. 132.17 χαρίεντας; Firmicus, 3.6.1 *gratos venustos*. For charm as an asset, see i. 311. αἱμύλιος, which applies to λόγος in EGHP, begins to apply directly to persons from Soph. *Aj.* 388, but retains a negative or ambivalent sense which the comparanda show cannot be intended here, any more than is the sense of infants 'chattering' (see Gow–Page on Crinagoras, *AP* 7.643.2 = *Garland* 1874 κούρην αἱμύλον). Perhaps better is Democritus, 68 F 104 D.-K. γέρων εὔχαρις ὁ αἱμύλος καὶ σπουδαιόμυθος.

εὐμούσους ~ *Περὶ κέντρ.* 52 μουσικούς; Θ p. 132.17 φιλομούσους; Firmicus, 3.6.2 *musicos* (with the additional presence of Mercury); see on 5.269 for its Venereal associations.

ἀμόχθους: no exact parallel in the comparanda, but associated with the easy life of prosperity (see on 4.19).

61 I infer that they profit from being in the good graces of women (material benefit from rich women: i. 310)—not necessarily that they are married to them. Dorotheus reports liaisons with women (*Περὶ κέντρ.* 52 πλουσίων γυναικῶν ἄνδρας; Dor.^{ARAB} II 26.1 'a master of women…some of them will have intercourse with the women of the rich'), which, however, bring no profit. They do here: λάμποντας is well chosen to connect (i) the radiant good fortune of the wealthy (3.112 λαμπροὺς βιότῳ καὶ ἐπόλβους; 4.504) and (ii) the radiance of attractiveness, especially sexual (e.g. Ap. Rhod. 3.925 λαμπόμενον χαρίτεσσιν, of Jason, that conspicuous beneficiary of female help[33]). γυναικείων χαρίτων,

---

[33] Other examples: Ariphron, *PMG* 813.9 λάμπει Χαρίτων ὄαροις; Diog. Laert. 5.76 Χαριτοβλέφαρον καὶ Λαμπιτώ (two nicknames given to Demetrius by a *hetaira*).

meanwhile, combines the astrological motifs of (i) the blessings of *charis* granted by friendly stars, especially Venus (e.g. Θ p. 145.29 τὰς ἀπὸ γυναικῶν χάριτας καὶ δωρεὰς) and (ii) the use of adjectival γυναικεῖος qualifying benefit (or harms) (e.g. Ptol. 4.2.2…διὰ φιλικῶν καὶ γυναικείων δωρεῶν; Hephaestion, i. 224.13 ἐκ γυναικείων προσώπων κέρδη).

62 No immediate parallels in the comparanda. But based on, and reinterpreting, Homeric ὅρκια πιστά, this perhaps elaborates a phrase about pledges or trust, like Hephaestion, i. 239.19 πίστεων γυναικείων, Θ pp. 148.19 τινὲς δὲ καὶ γυναικῶν πράγματα πιστεύονται and 166.8 ἐνίους δὲ καὶ γυναικῶν πράγματα πιστευομένους (Moon in third and ninth houses). θηλειῶν would be plausible in a prose source.

63 In Dorotheus, they are in charge of shrines (*Περὶ κέντρ.* 52 τινὲς ἱερῶν προΐστανται; Dor.^{ARAB} II 26.1 'some of them will occupy houses of worship'); in Firmicus (in human signs, and with Venus *partiliter* in the ASC), chief priests (3.6.1 *faciet sacerdotum principes*). προστήσονται ἐν represents a characteristic rewriting of a usage that normally governs the genitive[34] with a prepositional phrase (p. 202); normally in astrology it would refer to the management of temples (e.g. 4.429, where see note; Valens, I 2.16; ἱερῶν / ναῶν προεστῶτες / -ας, θηλυκοῦ ἱεροῦ προεστῶτας; Θ p. 165.3 ἐν ἱερατικαῖς ἀσχολίαις ἢ ἱερῶν προεστῶτας; etc.), and it seems unusual in connection with rituals. Needless to say, ὀργιάδεσσιν is *hapax*.

64 For women-only religious cults, see Laura McClure, 'Women in Classical Greek Religion' (Oxford Research Encyclopedias), s.v. 'Women's Religious Festivals'; for the Thesmophoria, which comes to mind first, see Hopkinson on Call. *Hymn* 6, p. 36, but there were others in Athens (Arrhephoria; Haloa; Adonia) and elsewhere.[35] The comparanda make no mention of this detail, which could just be a sensationalist add-on; how is a (presumably male) native supposed to preside over occasions which, in classical mythography at least, would normally get him lynched? φυγαρσενίη is *hapax*. ἄπυστα = unheard-of (because clandestine) reproduces the meaning at *Od.* 1.242, but the *sedes* of *Od.* 4.675 and 5.127, where the meaning is active (not knowing); the same is true at ps.-Opp. *Cyn.* 1.236 and *Or. Sib.* 7.109.

---

[34] Aristotle, fr. 424 (from Pollux 8.90) μυστηρίων προέστηκε, Σ Plat. *Euthyphr.* 2 A 3 μυστηρίων προεστηκώς, Suda, η 39 τῶν μυστηρίων…προΐσταται; Diod. Sic. 4.25.1 Μουσαίου τοῦ Ὀρφέως υἱοῦ τότε προεστηκότος τῆς τελετῆς.

[35] Men were excluded from the cults of Ares of Tegea (Paus. 8.48.5) and Dionysus at Brusiae (Paus. 3.20.3).

65-8

Venus in MC. The corresponding passage in M^a has an emphasis on wives and female works which this passage, despite the corruption in 68, appears to lack.

65 ἐρατή: Koechly's restoration produces a Dorothean mannerism (i. 920), a fact of which he would have been unaware; there is another example at 4.362.

μεσόωντα κατ' οὐρανόν: this expression for the MC (i. 881 and p. 246) refreshes standard μέσον οὐρανόν and κατ' οὐρανόν; see LSJ s.v. μεσόω in expressions of time, and for position in the sky add Hipparchus, 2.3.19 μεσούντων τῶν ζῳδίων.

ὀφθῇ: for the passive see p. 359 n. 86; perhaps prompted by 2.357, cf. 4.444, ὀφθείς, but also occasional in prose (Hephaestion, i. 64–5 *ter*).

66 φράζει τοι: perhaps adapting the idiom whereby the astrologer is instructed to make predictions to his client (p. 323): here, and at 4.99, the star itself make the announcement (p. 239), both times where great success is in store, and the particle, which is unusual in the Manethoniana (i. 192) shores up a sense of excitability/urgency.

βαθυχρήμονα: unique to this author (also 504, 579), a quick-fix variation on βαθύπλουτος (from 5th c. tragedy and Bacchylides).

66–7 χιλιάδας τε | ἀρχάς: some comparanda say efficacious (Περὶ κέντρ. 64 ἔμπρακτον), others the opposite ('Valens', *CCAG* viii/1. 168.28 ἀπραγίας), but none has this precise detail. The phrase (which awkwardly juxtaposes two nouns as if, combined, they mean 'thousandfold commands') apparently paraphrases χιλιάρχης, who strictly is a person who leads a χιλιαρχία (a Macedonian military unit, and before that a Persian unit of 1,000 men which constituted the king's bodyguard);[36] the office of chiliarch is like that of the εἰσαγγελεύς (see on 2.263), an important court position taken over by the Macedonians from the Achaemenids. Otherwise it means a Roman *tribunus militum* (Cumont, 40 n. 2, but not including this passage; Aune on Rev. 19:18; John 18:12 Ἡ οὖν σπεῖρα καὶ ὁ χιλίαρχος and Acts 21:31–24:22). χιλιάρχης/χιλίαρχος do not seem to recur in Greek astrological texts (except Michael Glycas), though Firmicus and *Liber Hermetis* refer many times to *tribunos* (not, however, in this set-up). When they do, the context is power (these men are individually terrifying and/or enjoy close proximity to the king), not riches. 'Chiliarch' is thus apparently used in a similar way to some passages in the NT, where holders of the title rank

---

[36] Recent bibliography in A. W. Collins, 'The Persian Royal Tent and Ceremonial of Alexander the Great', CQ^2 67 (2017), 71–6, at 73–4; also, Brandis, *RE* s.v. Chiliarchos; *Encyclopaedia Iranica*, V. 4, 423–4, s.v. Chiliarch (P. Gignoux).

among those who are very high up in society (Mark 6:21 τοῖς μεγιστᾶσιν αὐτοῦ καὶ τοῖς χιλιάρχοις καὶ τοῖς πρώτοις τῆς Γαλιλαίας; Rev. 6:15 οἱ βασιλεῖς τῆς γῆς καὶ οἱ μεγιστᾶνες καὶ οἱ χιλίαρχοι καὶ οἱ πλούσιοι καὶ οἱ ἰσχυροί, cf. Aune ad loc.; Rev. 19:18 βασιλέων καὶ…χιλιάρχων καὶ…ἰσχυρῶν).

67 δόξης ἀπλέτου κοσμήτορα κόμπον: padding of Περὶ κέντρ. 64 ἔνδοξον (Venus eastern, or in the *epanaphora* of the MC); Θ p. 168.20–1 δοξαστικούς; Firmicus, 3.6.21 *claros…et quibus grandis gloria…conferatur*. The second and third words depend on restoration (Monaco, 49), but the epic ancestry remains clear, with κοσμήτορα (Gronovius) redeployed in the same *sedes* as epic κοσμήτορε (-ι), with influence perhaps too from Pindar, cf. *Isthm.* 3/4.29 ἀπλέτου δόξας. I find no sign that ancient authors quote the Pindar passage in such a way as to suggest its presence in an anthology, but for traces of Pindar in M[a], see i. 160. For the cadence, see on 4.7; the poet seems to have accommodated κόμπος, which is not a word otherwise used in apotelesmata (the same is true of its presumable equivalent αὐχ-), to the usual pattern with κόσμος.

68 Possibilities for what has been lost to dittography might include yet more wealth or crowns (cf. Firmicus *coronatos…et quibus…fortuna maxima conferatur*). The comparanda, for what they are worth, do not support De Stefani's suggestion that these types come to a bad end.

4.69–76 Mercury

69–72

Mercury in DESC <>, ASC, MC. This corresponds to 3.104–5 + 90–5 + 96–100 (minus 101–3). The outcomes are generally intelligence and success. Paul, p. 67.11–13, has an interesting list of lettered professions, but the only detailed correspondence is between the scribes of 72 καλαμογραφίης and 3.97 καλάμοιό τε γραπτῶν (the MC).

69 For the planetary name, see i. 898 n. 4; p. 256. Koechly was right that there must be a lacuna after this line. ὡροσκόπον cannot follow directly from ἐπὶ τὴν δύσιν in the previous line; it needs something to govern it. It is highly unlikely to be governed by κατά, together with οὐρανόν, in the ἀπὸ κοινοῦ construction, because all other occurrences of ὡροσκόπον in M[b] are adjectival (59, 116, 125, 491, 496; Hübner 2001, 234–6, who on 236 is more open to the possibility that this is a noun than I am).[37] It seems that a line containing a noun has fallen out.

---

[37] *Contra* De Stefani, who refers to Wilamowitz on Eur. *HF* 237. In *Od.* 12.27 ἢ ἁλὸς ἢ ἐπὶ γῆς, which Wilamowitz quotes, there is anyway a disjunctive before the first member of the pair as well. See on the subject G. Massimilla, 'The ἀπὸ κοινοῦ Construction of Prepositions as a Feature of the

70 γεινομένων βρεφέων: taken by Hübner ibid. as a dependent genitive, as in 4.491, rather than genitive absolute.

71 ἔκ τε λόγων τεύχει προκοπήν τινα θνητοῖς: Dor.^ARAB II 27.5 'However you find Mercury in midheaven or the ascendent, then he will be wealthy or a scribe or possess [his] livelihood from calculation' (cf. Περὶ κέντρ. 73). For the sense compare also Valens, II 4.7 ἀπὸ λόγων καὶ ἐντρεχείας [sc. skills] αἱ προκοπαὶ ἔσονται (with aspect of Mercury and Moon); II 12.7 τὰς διὰ λόγων προκοπάς ~ Θ p. 152.18 προκόπτοντας διὰ λόγων (Mercury in fifth house); Hephaestion, i. 219.27-8 προκοπὰς διά τε λόγων καὶ γραπτῶν (Mercury distributing to Jupiter); Camaterus, *Introd.* 992 προκόπτοντας λόγων (Mercury's degrees within Libra).

72 καὶ καλαμογραφίης: as compared to 3.97-8 καλάμοιό τε γραπτῶν | πρῆξιν, this poet characteristically (p. 220) prefers a bulky compound noun, which is *hapax* (but cf. Choeroboscus, *Prolegomena et scholia in Theodosii Alexandrini canones*, GG iv/2. 52.16 καλαμογραφῶ ἐκαλαμογράφουν).

καὶ ὅσ' εἰς μοῦσαν πεπόνηται: cf. Θ p. 160.18-19 μουσικῆς...εὑρετάς and Firmicus, 3.7.15 *musicae...inventores* (both Mercury on DESC, in sect); 'Antiochus', l. 41 (CCAG i. 110.8) (on ASC) ἡμάτιος Μουσῶν δωρήσατο θέσπιν ἀοιδήν; Περὶ κέντρ. 76 μουσικούς (Mercury with Venus in ASC or MC). This poet is fascinated with the πον- root (p. 174), which in fact recurs in the Manethoniana only in the reduplicated lines in the first book, and in M^a's reference to *geoponoi* (6.489; also 4.433). As well as πόνος itself (4.443) and simplex πονέω (346), he enjoys compound adjectives (4.150, 442 ἐργοπόνους; 423 ἱστοπόνους; new are 4.276 πονοπαίκτορας and 570 κολοσσοπόνους) as trade descriptors or (pseudo-)specifiers (for -πονος compounds, see B.-P. 281). The various uses range through work which is effortful (4.259-60 ὑπουργοὶ δυσπονίης; 346 μόχθον...πονήσοντας; the strongmen in 276 entertain the crowd with physical feats) to work which is skilled and presumably more highly prized (here and presumably 4.152); in 512 the ἀριστοπονῆες are civic benefactors, so their πόνος consists in well-directed exertions, labour for the common good. Only one instance (4.372-3) refers to miseritude rather than work itself. For πόνος, which has been man's lot since Pandora (Hes. *Op.* 91, 113), see Martínez-Hernández, 106-12; Loraux; King, 124-5; von Reden, 4.

73-6

As above, with Mars in equal degrees or in opposition. This extra specification is paralleled in a number of comparanda (see Pinax), but this time it is Paul

Epigrammatic Style', in Sistakou and Rengakos, 173-91, but this has nothing to do with the present passage.

who has the closest match, with forgers among the treacherous and duplicitous natives produced by this combination (p. 67.17). Other sources speak of condemnation and exile, but do not specify the nature of their offences.

73 ἰσόμοιρος ἀταρπός: for the hypallage of the epithet, cf. already 6.125 πλευρὴν ἰσόμοιρον; also 4.231 δρόμον...ἰσόμοιρον, 294 ἰσόμοιρα κέλευθα, 367 ἰσόμοιρα κατ' Οὐλύμποιο κέλευθα.

74 φάεσιν φάος ἀντικέλευθον: M^b emulates M^a's penchant for modelling opposition through the use of chiasmus (i. 197–8, 220; p. 220). The closest parallel in the earlier poet is 3.245 κακὸς κακοῦ ἀντίον ἑστώς, and the new version continues to use an ἀντί- compound, which is often involved in polyptota (Fehling, 227; also 221–30, on juxtaposed cases of the same word). Jacob Wackernagel held that a nominative form in polyptoton precedes an oblique case,[38] and that holds good here if φάος is, not a nominative, but accusative object of διαμετρήσῃ; that is confirmed by the parallel construction in 4.296 (which also shows that the implied subject of the verb is of course the planet itself, not its path). The first syllabus of φάεσιν must be scanned short; it has, in other words, to adopt the sometime quantity of φάεσσι (Cleanthes, *Hymn to Zeus*, 13 μικροῖς τε φάεσσι) against Dorotheus, p. 399.29 φᾱεσσι, and Call. *Hymn* 3.71, Greg. Naz. *AP* 8.32.6, both φᾱεσιν. ἀντικέλευθος itself has 31 occurrences, of which 23 are in Nonn. *D.* and a further 6 in *Par.*; the only other is in John of Gaza, *Descr.* 56 (of the crossbar of the crucifix). Of celestial objects also *D.* 2.658, and 38.248 [see Simon ad loc.], 273, 285, 365 (others are geographical), but the epithet always stands before the main caesura (save in *D.* 47.307, where it begins in the fourth foot); M^b's placement is unique.

75 πλαστογράφους: an effect of Mercury combined with Mars: also Θ p. 131.12–13 (Mercury opposed by Mars in 12th house) καταδικάσει ἕνεκα ἀπορρήτων πραγμάτων ἢ πλαστῶν, p. 161.26 πλαστογράφους (Mercury with Mars in the 8th house), p. 193.1–3 ψεύστας, ψευδοκατηγόρους, πλαστογράφους, ἐπιόρκους (Mercury and Mars, centred, in equal degrees, without aspect of benefics). In the presence of malefics Mercury makes natives ἀπίστους: Περὶ κέντρ. 83.

ἀλλοτυπώτων: a sort of hypallage from a noun which is not specified (the writings are forged, not the hands). The epithet is unique, though there are numerous lexicographical sources for ἀλλότυπον (ignored by LSJ), always

---

[38] J. Wackernagel, *Lectures on Syntax: With Special Reference to Greek, Latin, and German*, transl. D. Langslow (Oxford, 2009), 644, though B. Gygli-Wyss, *Das nominale Polyptoton in älteren Griechisch* (Göttingen, 1966), 137–42, esp. 141–2, notes exceptions.

describing χρυσίον—not, however, referring to forged coin, but to decorative mounting.

76 παμβλαβέας: see on 4.31.

ὠχρήεντας: Koechly's correction is patently correct; in fact it has an overplus of signification:

- (i) In relation to Mercury. Valens, VI 3.10, makes Mercury's own coloration ὠχρός (Boll 1916, 21 'bläßlich', yellow-white), the colour of bile (Bouché-Leclercq, 314). Ptolemy agrees that Mercury governs bile (3.13.5) and without using the word ὠχρός says that those born under him are variously μελιχρόας or λευκούς... οὐκ ἐπὶ τὸ εὔχρουν (3.12.7).

- (ii) In relation to Mars. One well-established medical context for ὠχρίασις is jaundice (ἴκτερος),[39] and precisely this connection is reproduced (at least, as the result of Olivieri's textual manipulations) by 'Antiochus', l. 94 (CCAG i. 112.13), apropos of Mars in the house of parents (= the IMC), κακὸν ἴκτερον ὠχροσύνην τε. This is the more surprising in that jaundice is naturally classified in astrology among wet (and cold) diseases and therefore ought to be produced by Saturn;[40] nevertheless, the two malefics sometimes do cause each other's diseases (both occasion coughing; Saturn single-handedly can produce ῥιγοπύρετος).

- (iii) In relation to both Mercury and Mars. Some of the comparanda agree that their combination can produce physical or mental harms, and a couple, for Mercury on the DESC, specifically mention consumption: Θ p. 160.16 ὀλιγοχρονίους, φθισικούς (Mars opposing or in right quartile); Firmicus, 3.7.14 (inter al.) thisicos (Mars on ASC, MC, or DESC)—of which medical writers sometimes note ὠχρίασις as a feature (Anon. Med. De morbis acutis et chroniis, 27.2 φθίσεως σημεῖα...ὠχρίασις; Aretaeus, De Caus. et Sign. Diut. Morb. 1.8.3 ἦν γὰρ καὶ δημότης ἴδη τὸν ἄνθρωπον ὠχρόν, ἀδρανῆ, ἀναβήσσοντα, ξυντετηκότα, ἀτρεκέα μαντεύεται φθόην [= phthisis]; Andromachus the Elder (LXII Heitsch), 41–4).

---

[39] e.g. Hippocr. Aer. 15 τήν τε χροιὴν ὠχρὴν ἔχουσιν, ὥσπερ ὑπὸ ἰκτέρου ἐχόμενοι; De intern. affect. 35, 37, 45; Galen, In Hippocratis aphorismos commentarii, xviib. 658.5 Kühn τῆς χρόας ὠχροτέρας γεγενημένης, ὡς ἐν ἰκτέροις; Palladius, Commentarii in Hippocratis librum sextum de morbis popularibus, Stephanus, Scholia in Hippocratis prognosticon, 1.5 ἰκτερώδες ἢ ὠχρόν; Paul of Nicaea, Liber medicus, 62 Τί ἐστιν ἴκτερος; ἀνάλυσις χολῆς καθ' ὅλον τὸ σῶμα, ὡς καὶ τοῖς ἰδιώταις ἐμφαίνεσθαι οἷον ἴκτερος. τότε γὰρ ὅλον τὸ σῶμα ὠχρόν ἐστιν...; Leo Medicus, Conspectus medicinae, 5.24 Ἴκτερός ἐστιν, ὅταν ὅλον τὸ σῶμα ἢ ὠχρὸν ἢ μέλαν ἢ ἄλλου του οἱουοῦν χρώματος γένηται.

[40] As it is in e.g. Ptolemy, 3.13.15; and under Saturn's sign Aquarius in Teucer, CCAG vii. 210.19–20, Valens, II 41.31, 38.

4.77–92 Moon

*77–82*ᵃ

Moon in ASC, with Mars in MC in equal degrees. There is no parallel in book 3 (120–1 deals only with the Moon in the ASC without Mars), and while comparanda (see Pinax, p. 1010) have some scenarios for the Moon in the ASC with one or both malefics in aspect, they do not combine it with this outcome. Conversely, the madmen and epileptics of Θ ch. 65, 192.8–194.8, are born under some similar charts (e.g. pp. 192.18–20, 193.16–18), but not this precise one.

77 ἀμφίκερως: i. 904 n. 4. It is more likely, I think, to be decorative than to indicate phase (presumably crescent), which tends not to be a factor in *kentrothesia*.

βιοτέρμονος ὥρης: the passage competes with 'Antiochus', l. 43 (*CCAG* i. 110.11) βιοτέρμονα πλοῦτον, for first attestation of the epithet (and for its meaning, see Pérez Jiménez 2014, 263–4: 'riches lasting till the end of life'). The only later use is in George of Pisidia, *De vit. hum.* 23 βιοτέρμονος ἄνθεα φύτλης ('time-limited', mortal). The present meaning must be 'at the boundary of': see 4.28 n.

78 φωτὶ Σεληναίῳ: with the Moon the poet is unable to adopt the technique he uses for the five planets (light name + mythological name connected by genitive); instead he manages to slide in Selene's name with an epithet (first in an oracle ap. Hdt. 1.62.4 σεληναίης διὰ νυκτός). Perhaps most comparable to this passage are Nonn. *D.* 18.115, 21.204 Σεληναίῃσι κεραίαις.

σκολιωπά: also 4.478 σκολιόδρομος; otherwise only Maximus, pr. 3 σκολιωπὸν ἐπιστείχουσα κέλευθον. The epithet refers—like the many ἑλιξ- or ἑλικ- compounds applied to the Moon (i. 904, 912; 4.91n.)—to its oblique path through the ecliptic. See too on 4.334, on the Moon's labyrinthine path.

79 δι' αἰθέρος ἀκροπολεύῃ: the compound crosses ἀμφι- or αἰθρο-πολεύειν (i. 879; n. on 2.383) with ἄκρον used of the MC. There is conceivable impetus from Dorotheus, p. 386.11–12 ... καὶ αἰθέρος ἀκροτάτοιο | ζῷον ὅτι ψαύει μέσον οὐρανὸν ἀμφιπολεῦον. δι' αἰθέρος itself resides here since EGHP (incl. *Il.* 2.458, of light-rays travelling through the atmosphere).

80 τηνίκα: this is used as a coordinating adverb in the apodosis only in this book (also 299, 357, 404 = 1.329). Unlike τῆμος, which is commoner (4.46 n.), this has no prehistory of use in connection with cosmic events and motions. It was introduced into astrological poetry by Dorotheus, p. 394.9 (after ὁπότ'); also in Maximus, 216 as an uncoordinated adverb.

80–1 θεόλημπτος ... σεληνάζων τε νόοιο: the lines combine 'lunacy' with the idea of divinely sent affliction, suggesting epilepsy without spelling it out

(i. 356 and n. 54; 4.546 n.; Schwenn, *RE* s.v. Selene, 1139.40-64; Temkin, 92-6). The Moon's effect is psychic (it is the ψυχή which is afflicted by synodic luminaries in 4.537-44), and where there is a distinction between ψυχή and νόος, the Moon governs the former (Plut. *Mor.* 943 A). But in Lucian, *Philops.* 16, the healer sends his moon-struck patients away ἀρτίους τὴν γνώμην.

80 θεόληπτος: nicely placed in Focal position. Also connected with the Moon in 4.548; Epit. IIIb, *CCAG* vii. 112.19 (at node, Full) θεολήπτους καὶ φοιβαζομένους; Ptol. 4.4.10 (after New, in contact with Mercury in Libra, Aries, Leo). 6.378 (adverbial) involves Saturn.

ἐν σχήματι τοίῳ: compare especially Anubion, F 12.19 = 12 Perale σ[χήμ]ατι τοιού[τωι]; there are similar expressions in 5.90, 207, 227.

81 ἔκπληκτος: the only other astrological example is in 'Heliodorus' on Paul, p. 138.11-14, which involves precisely the Moon (just after *synodos*) and Mars (ἐκπληκτικούς), an expansion on Paul, p. 95.5-7. 'Strickenness' is compatible with both divine agency (*HOrph.* 39.10, a prayer to Corybas to be rid of ψυχῆς ἐκπλήκτου ἀνάγκας)[41] and epilepsy (Σ Eur. *Med.* 1172 τοὺς ἐξαίφνης καταπίπτοντας ᾤοντο τὸ παλαιὸν οἱ ἄνθρωποι ὑπὸ Πανὸς μάλιστα καὶ Ἑκάτης πεπλῆχθαι τὸν νοῦν).

σεληνάζων τε νόοιο: the poet (with D'Orville's correction) employs the same resource to accommodate prose σεληνιάζεσθαι as at 4.217 νοῦν τε σεληνάζοντα, which involves, however, uncanny Saturn. The genitive νόοιο (noted by Koechly 1851, xl) is like the genitive in Parthenius, *Narr. Am.* 17.7 παραπλὴξ ἦν νοῦ τε καὶ φρενῶν (unless the latter is ablatival after παρα-).

82 μανίης ἀνάμεστος: ἀνάμεστος is used in connection with mental and psychological states, for which parallels are in late imperial and Byzantine prose: Cyril, *Thesaurus de sancta consubstantiali trinitate*, *PG* 75.321.33-4 μανίας ἀνάμεστον; John Chrysostom, *Ad eos qui scandalizati sunt*, 8.13 Πῶς γὰρ οὐ μανικὸν καὶ ἐσχάτης ἀπονοίας καὶ παραπληξίας ἀνάμεστον; John of Caesarea, *Apologia concilii Chalcedonensis*, l. 93 μανίας ἀνάμεστον (of a heresy); Constantine Porphyrogenitus, *De administrando imperio* 50 ἔχθρας ἀνάμεστοι καὶ μανίας πλήρεις.

83ᵇ-82ᵇ

Moon in IMC. Mᵃ once again has the best match, but he distinguishes between the effect of good and bad stars in aspect (3.126-30, as do Dor.ᴬᴿᴬᴮ II 21.7-8,

---

[41] Although Julian, *Contra Heracl.* 234 D, distinguishes ἔνθεος from ἔκπληκτος μανία.

540   Commentary on Book Four

Περὶ κέντρ. 6–7, Θ pp. 151.28–152.1, and Firmicus, 3.13.7); tacitly M^b follows only the latter. Θ and Firmicus also discuss the status of the mother.

83 ἐπίφοιτος: unique to here and 4.126. The verb is used with persons or places; the poet seems to have created an epithet for the sake of parallelism (see p. 206), and its use in connection with an abstract quality recalls 4.33 πάσης λύπης ἐπιβήτορας. Prose mostly has δυστυχεῖς or δυστυχοῦντας (or δυστυχίας). **ἐν σινέεσσι πεπληθώς** ~ 3.129 κρυπταδίοισι σίνεσσι. See p. 202, for the redundant ἐν.

84–6

Moon in MC. This certainly contains new material vis-à-vis 3.123–4, which, in turn, shares with other comparanda additional annotations about sect and the rescuing influences of benefics (see Pinax, p. 1010).

84 ἀμφιθοάζῃ: when M^b was coining this verb, a metrical alternative for ἀμφιπολεύειν (i. 879), the simplex may have seemed to him to have a tragic character (Soph. OT 2; Eur. Bacch. 219, Phoen. 794a, Tr. 349, fr. 145 K.).

85 Riches, absent from M^a, are mentioned in Paul, p. 65.5 πλουσίους. M^b tries to enliven a worn theme. ἐντρυφέας is new, but varies the much commoner τρυφερός/τρυφητής which astrologers, especially Ptolemy, use in connection with Venus, often but not always (Θ pp. 168.8 τρυφηλούς, 175.19 τρυφεροδιαίτους) in connection with effeminacy.[42] ἐπόλβους (assuming Koechly's correction of ἐνόλβους) is from 2.413, 3.112 (and again in 4.497); παμπλούτους is not new, but transferred from wealth itself (Soph. fr. 646.5 Radt πάμπλουτον ὄλβον) to its owners (for other examples, see i. 158–9).[43]

86 θηλυγόνους...εὐπάτορας: the first epithet is not new; the second is, or almost (εὐπατόρεια is an epithet of Hecate in PGM iv. 2714). Individually each detail has good astrological precedent (for the parents' pedigree, the commonest word in astrological texts is εὐγενής and parts thereof); but it is a surprising combination. The Moon should promote the female side of the family consistently, if at all. Other sources say natives have distinguished mothers (not daughters): Paul, p. 65.8 τὰς δὲ μητέρας τῶν τοιούτων εὐγενεῖς εὑρήσεις; Περὶ κέντρ. 4 τὰς μητέρας μείζονας. For Paul, p. 65.2–3 it is, expectedly, the Sun in this position that produces distinguished fathers. It also seems to represent a

---

[42] Ptol. 2.3.26 τρυφεροὶ καὶ τεθηλυσμένοι, 3.12.6 γυναικοπρεπωδέστερον καὶ θηλυμορφώτερον... καὶ τρυφερώτερον, 3.14.25 τρυφητάς...θηλυψύχους...γυναικοθύμους.
[43] So too Ἡλιοδώρου φιλοσόφου πρὸς Θεοδόσιον τὸν μέγαν βασιλέα περὶ τῆς τῶν φιλοσόφων μυστικῆς τέχνης διὰ στίχων ἰάμβων, l. 78 ξένον πάμπλουτον; Tzetzes, Chil. 1.5.206 εἰς Ἀλκμαίονα τὸν πάμπλουτον; of the personified city of Jerusalem in Or. Sib. 5.261 πάμπλουτε.

very simplified logic. While astrological texts do deal (if rarely) with the question of θηλυγονία, the birth of daughters, they do not make the Moon the sole agency. Other factors include signs or portions thereof in Valens, I 3.47, II 37.9; bright stars and what aspects them in Astrol. Anon. 379, CCAG v/1. 199.7, 24 and 220.23 = Θ pp. 176.13, 177.3. For Apomasar, *De Myst.*, CCAG xi/1. 190.5, there is a Lot of θηλυγονία which is determined by the distance between the Moon and Venus; for Ptolemy, 3.7.2 and 3.8.2, eastern and western positions of planets determine sex at birth.

87–92

Moon in DESC. This elaborates the wandering theme, on which all comparanda (not just the corresponding 3.121–2) are agreed: cf. Περὶ κέντρ. 5 ἐκ πατρίδος μετάστασις; Θ pp. 158.24 φιλόξενον, 160.20 and 23 ξενιτείας. The best parallel for the focus on merchants and sailing is Paul, p. 61.1–5: the Moon in DESC causes ξενιτείας (~ ἐν ξενίῃ τε | τὸ πλεῖστον ζωῆς) and *if it is in watery signs* natives are ship-owners (ναυκλήρους ~ ναυκλήρου βιοτήν) or pilots or sailors or merchants (ἐμπορικὸν βίον διάγοντας ~ ἐμπορίης ἐμπείραμος), and muchwandering (πολυπλάνους ~ ἔργα τε πλαγκτά). Firmicus' entry is missing.

87 ἄστροιο Σεληναίης: this looks like a figment based on 'star of' names. There is possible precedent in Anubion, F 2.6 μέχρι Σεληναίης ἀστέρος ἱσταμένου (Bouché-Leclercq, 389 n. 2), but Schubert, with n. 381, interprets 'jusqu'à l'astre présent (occupé par) la Lune'. Much later, it is in vogue with Camaterus, *De Zodiaco* (Ἀστὴρ Σελήνης, and oblique cases), but his terminology could be no less factitious than M^b's.

ὁ λοχευθείς: synonym for ὁ γεννηθείς (see on 6.697 ὁ φύς, and p. 252 for M^b's 'natalist' language), with a poetic and perhaps specifically tragic feel. For the passive, 'be born', LSJ cites Soph. *OC* 1322 λοχευθείς and Eur. *Ion*, 455 λοχευθεῖσαν, though it seems largely post-classical.[44]

88 ἐμπορίης ἐμπείραμος: as often (Appendix II, III.1) ἔμποροι are connected with sailing. This matches the traditional understanding of them as wholesale dealers/having international business contacts.[45] By coding them with the Moon, the present passage and its parallels associate them with

---

[44] Ps.-Phocyl. 176 τέκε δ' ἔμπαλιν, ὡς ἐλοχεύθης; Cornutus, *Nat. Deor.* p. 58.6–7, HOrph. 27.7 and 56.9, Anacreont. 38.7. In Christian writers, largely of birth of Christ. Lexica also acknowledge it (e.g. Hesych. ε 2205, Suda, ε 903).

[45] For the ἔμπορος, see Pleket 1984, 17–20 (either independent, or with wealthy backers; the term could cover everything from the small-town trader to the wealthy merchant of purple); Drexhage 1991, 29–42; C. P. Jones, 'A Syrian in Lyon', *AJP* 99 (1978), 336–53, at 351 n. 60 for a list of merchants attested in inscriptions.

wandering, but others, which involve Mercury and/or Jupiter (e.g. 1.133 ἐμπορίην φιλέοντας; Venus distributing to Jupiter in Hephaestion, i. 217.24 ἐξ ἐμπορικῶν…ὠφελοῦνται), foreground business dealings and lucre (see Courtney on Juv. *Sat.* 14.267). ἐμπείραμος tends to involve the exercise of a skill (Lyc. *Al.* 1196 πάλης ἐμπείραμος; iambic lines quoted in Σ ps.-Opp. *Cyn.* 3.397 τοξικῆς ἐμπείραμος; Nonn. *D.* 39.181 ὑσμίνης ἐμπείραμος; Agathias, *AP* 10.14.7 ναυτιλίης ἐμπείραμε, though less so at 4.536 δημοσίων τελέων ἐμπείραμον); in any case the quasi-Gorgianic jingle was too good to miss.

ἔργα τε πλαγκτά: Koechly's correction for τε πολλά is corroborated by Paul's πολυπλάνους (hence, not De Stefani's ἔπολβα, despite 4.92). For the epithet see on 4.7. Periphrastic expressions for professional activities are also found in Dorotheus, p. 386.19 δομήιά τ' ἔργα; Maximus, 528 ὄμπνια ἔργα; and see p. 175 n. 135. They are modelled presumably on Homeric expressions like πολεμήια ἔργα, but also mesh helpfully with astrology's liking for periphrasis and expressions such as δούλια ἔργα (see on 1.275 λάτρια ἔργα), βασιλικὰ ἔργα (Apomasar, *De Rev.* p. 41.9), γυναικεῖα ἔργα (see on 2.242-3; 3.79; p. 175), ἀφροδισιακὰ ἔργα (Apomasar, *De Rev.* p. 93.1 *et al.*).

89 The line is built over the same structure as 135. ναυκλήρου (~ Paul's ναυκλήρους) depends on βιοτήν (life rather than pelf) with delayed connective, rather than ἔργα. For ναύκληροι (Appendix II, III.2.i), see B. Holtheide, 'Zum privaten Seehandel im östlichen Mittelmeer (1.-3. Jh. n. Chr.)', *MBAH* 1/2 (1982), 3–13; for those of the important maritime city of Nicomedia specifically, Robert 1978, 422–3; and for the standing of such men—generally low, but with upper-class backers—Pleket 1984, 10–17.

89-90 The lacuna marked in this line comes from Koechly's second, Teubner, edition. In the Didot he solved the problem with the connectives by emending L's ἐν ξενίῃ τε to ξενίῃσιν, which, although he would not have been aware of it, is in fact closer to the astrological *terminus technicus* ξενιτείας. The counter-argument is that the postponement of τε in 90a would strain at, or surpass, the limits of tolerance (p. 198), but other than that, the first solution seems to me excellent. A lacuna in which διευθύνων no longer governs τὸ πλεῖστον ζωῆς leaves open the possibility that it might be intransitive,[46] but for transitive examples of the required sense see Valens, VII 2.29 οὐδὲ τὸν βίον ὁμαλῶς διευθύνουσιν, IX 12.18 τὸν βίον…διευθῦναι.

91 πουλυπλανής: from what follows this must be predicative. The epithet is apparently *proton legomenon* here; also 162, 470, 521 πουλυπλανεῖς (all of

---

[46] e.g. Valens, IV 15.4 οὐ διευθύνουσι κατὰ τὴν ξένην 'he does not succeed abroad' (Riley); IV 24.9; V 6.64 ὥσπερ ἂν εἰ διὰ πολλῶν ὁδῶν διευθύνοντας 'as if we were travelling by many roads'; Ptol. 4.7.8 ἐπισφαλεῖς δὲ καὶ οὐκ ἐπιπολὺ διευθυνούσας 'unsure and flourish only briefly' (Robbins).

natives, in the second and third cases in configurations involving the Moon); ps.-Opp. *Cyn.* 4.358 (of the tracks of beasts in the hunt). Three later instances in Theodorus Metochites (13th–14th c.) show no signs of influence from M^b. Rather counter-intuitively, πλαν- words do not seem to form part of the Moon's formulary, and in general the Greek examples of the 'wandering' trope[47] are outdone by *vagus* and *(per)vagari, volvi, errare* in Latin (*TLL* s.v. *Luna*, 1836.3-12; V. *Aen.* 1.742 *errantem*); as a result, the only other apparent example of a πλαν- compound for the Moon is in fact a rendering of Virgilian *noctivaga*.[48] For the alternative conception, of the Moon's chariot, see on 6.711. The 'wandering' motif is not necessarily less purposeful, but implies restlessness, and hence is suitable when the Moon is analogised to those who live roving lives (see Fordyce on Cat. 64.271 for *vagus* of Latin wanderers).

γὰρ: γάρ clauses are much commoner in astrology's adumbration–precision construction (cf. i. 224-5), but the explanatory clause draws an analogy between the celestial set-up and the effect on earth. γάρ-clauses furnish similar 'explanations' in 1.81 (between the bakers who work at night and an eclipse), and 5.120-3 (between the Moon's phases, transmitting and then reducing in light, and the endowment and then withdrawal of wealth). Other γάρ clauses do not contain analogies but still provide a rationale based on a planet's character/physical characteristics: 5.54-5 ψυχρὸς γάρ τε πέλει…; 5.60-1 θερμότατος γὰρ ἐών, on the neutralising effect of the malefics on one another (cf. also Dorotheus, pp. 368.25–369.3 Pingree); and of course many apotelesmata work on the principle of analogy, but without spelling it out (e.g. 6.326-8, gender; the effects of signs in 5.149-53, 154-8, 246-51; 5.252-5, luminaries and eyes). Some γάρ clauses explain nothing (Περὶ σχημ. 52, 89), but Περὶ σχημ. 128-9 indicates that Dorotheus himself used a comparison for the Moon which explained its effect on the earth. With μένει δ' in the next line there is a sudden return to the native, which suggests that the γάρ clause should be punctuated as a parenthesis, although the other γάρ-clauses cited here are not parenthetical.

ἕλιξ: the Moon's orbit is not only oblique to the equator, like the Sun's (Diog. Laert. 7.144 τὸν·δ' ἥλιον λοξὴν τὴν πορείαν ποιεῖσθαι διὰ τοῦ ζῳδιακοῦ κύκλου· ὁμοίως καὶ τὴν σελήνην ἑλικοειδῆ), but also tilted with respect to the ecliptic, which it crosses at the nodes; so, if the path of the zodiac is ἑλικός (4.298), the Moon's is doubly so. According to Plut. *Mor.* 937 F, ἕλιξ is the word used for the

---

[47] Parmenides, 28 B 10 ἔργα τε κύκλωπος πεύσηι περίφοιτα σελήνης and 14 περὶ γαῖαν ἀλώμενον D.-K.; Alexander of Ephesus, *SH* 21.20 πολυκαμπέα.

[48] Franciscus Philelphus (15th c. humanist active in Venice/Tuscany/Lombardy), *Poema ad Georgium Gemistum*, l. 3 ὡς ἡ νυκτιπλανὴς ἄστροις ἐν ἐλάττοσι μήνη (a comparison for the addressee); V. *Aen.* 10.216.

Moon's motion against the signs on the ecliptic in latitude.[49] An early poetic application of the verb to the Moon in Lyc. Al. 305–6 χρόνος, | μήνης ἑλίσσων κύκλον will be succeeded by a late antique fashion for compound epithets (4.146 n.). Other examples are Nonn. D. 6.245 ἑλικώδεα Μήνην, and a comet in D. 2.515 ἕλιξ...κομήτης.

Μήνης κερατώπιδος: Meineke's reason for correcting to κεραώπιδος was the short α; according to him, in compounds formed with the stem κερατ- the α is long. See against this Williams on Call. Hymn 2.91—not adducing any new evidence, but simply adverting to the number of exceptions to Meineke's rule, i.e adducing all over again the passages Meineke proposed to change (NB Phaistos, FGrH 593 F 1 κερατόφορε continues to be reproduced in Brill's New Jacoby, online, and Vian prints κερατοξόος at Nonn. D. 3.76). The epithet would be *proton legomenon* if we could be confident, as we cannot be, that PGM iv. 2544 κερατῶπι (Mene) is later (J. L. Calvo-Martínez, 'Himno sincrético à Mene-Hécate (PGM IV 2522–2567)', MHNH, 10 (2010), 219–38, at 235). Also close is Maximus, 337 κεραῶπα Σελήνην. For horned epithets for the Moon, see on 4.77.

92 λοξὰ ταλαντεύουσα: λοξά of the ecliptic, as in 4.479 πόλου λοξεύματα βᾶσα (~ 1.307). See Kidd's note on Aratus, 527 λοξός: it is the standard prose term (the ecliptic is ὁ λοξὸς κύκλος); Theodorus Prodromus, Carm. hist. 38.78 ἡέλιός τ᾽ ἀκάμας λοξὴν περίεισι πορείαν. The verb is intransitive, 'in oscillating movement'. Usually that means from day to night (Nonn. D. 38.271, John of Gaza, Descr. 674, Synes. AP App. Epigr. Exhort. et Suppl. 74.5–6 τῆς ἔπι Τιτὰν | νύκτα ταλαντεύει καὶ φάος ἐρχόμενος, although these have a transitive verb), though λοξός suggests the oscillation here is from one side of the ecliptic to the other.

μένει δ᾽ ἀντλούμενος ὄλβῳ: the participial phrase means 'abounding in wealth' (Lopilato), literally, 'flooded with' it (LSJ). The poet has chosen his metaphor to suit the watery trades of these natives, extending the verb boldly from drawing water (in which sense the passive is not unique) to having it drawn over one, or being overrun with it (in which it apparently is). M^b metaphorises something harmful (and/or degrading: for watery charts where natives are ἀντληταί see on 4.257) as overflowing profit.

Metaphorical ἀντλεῖν is familiar for draining the cup of suffering.[50] This, though, is an interesting variation on the trope of riches as liquids, well known

---

[49] Earlier uses, not of the Moon: Aristotle speaks of αἱ κινήσεις καὶ ἕλικες τοῦ οὐρανοῦ (Met. 998ᵃ4–5); Timaeus, Περὶ φύσιος, 29 (ed. W. Marg, in Thesleff, p. 214.20–1) uses ἕλιξ to refer to the Sun's diurnal movement back through the fixed stars.

[50] Tragic, but also in Teucer, CCAG ix/2. 184.4–5 καὶ ἐπὶ ξένοις νοσήσει τὰς προειρημένας ἄντλων ἀνίας.

in modern languages (liquid wealth, cash flow), but with plenty of classical precedent as well. In Greek it seems that a couple of passages in the Homeric poems gave special impetus to the use of ῥεῖν and χεῖν, and their associated adverbs, for flowing assets;[51] later writers extend the trope to rivers (Plat. *Soph.* 222 A ποταμοὺς...πλούτου),[52] showers of rain or snow (Pind. *Ol.* 7.34, 48–50),[53] and deluges (Dion. Hal. 15.2.2 ὥστ' ἐπικλύσαι πλούτῳ τὴν ἑκάστου πενίαν);[54] and it exists in Latin, obviously with *affluens* (*TLL* s.v. *affluo*, II.A.2) and *abundare*.[55] All in all, we could suggest that this is one of the instances that strikes out from the banal, revitalising what was on the way to becoming dead metaphor. Alternatively, even if the metaphor was still going strong (and some of the Byzantine examples are developed with gusto: 5.310 n.), M[b] has still gone out of his way to turn it nicely to the stock figure of the merchant and his nautical existence. (Reflecting grim reality, too: this was no mere figure for the man with the Moon and Lot of Fortune in Pisces, and aspected by malefics, who ended up drowned in bilge water.[56]) Finally, although the metaphor mainly applies to being deluged with or awash with riches, M[d] anticipates (or almost anticipates) the idea of spending wealth like water (5.310 n.).

4.93–106 Sun

93–100 + 101–6

Sun in MC or ASC in its own signs and not in its own signs. The poet draws a contrast between favourable placement (in its own signs) and less favourable

---

[51] (i) *Od.* 15.426 ῥυδὸν ἀφνειοῖο (cf. ps.-Zonaras, ρ 1623 'Ῥυδὸν καὶ ῥύδην...ῥυδὸν ἀφνειοῖο ἀντὶ τοῦ ἄγαν πλουσίου. ἀπὸ τοῦ περιρρεῖν τὸν πλοῦτον), whence Call. *Hecale* fr. 48.3 Hollis ῥυδὸ̣ν ἀφνύονται (cf. Hesych. α 8709); Call. *Hymn* 1.84 ῥυηφενίην. There are many more, which are easily called up on the TLG by the search terms ρρει and πλουτ. ῥύδην can be used in the same way: Plut. *Lucullus* 39.2 τῷ πλούτῳ ῥύδην καταχρώμενος; id. *Caesar* 29.3 Καίσαρος τὸν Γαλατικὸν πλοῦτον ἀρύεσθαι ῥύδην ἀφεικότος πᾶσι τοῖς πολιτευομένοις. (ii) *Il.* 2.670 θεσπέσιον πλοῦτον κατέχευε, and more examples on TLG s.v. χρυσ/πλουτ. Once again, χύδην can be used in the same way: Plut. *Arist.* 5.6 χύδην μὲν ἀργύρου καὶ χρυσοῦ παρόντος; Basil, PG 31.541.22–3 μηδὲ εἰ χρυσὸς φαίνοιτο χύδην προκείμενος.
[52] Is the Halys an actualisation of this idea?
[53] cf. Σ Pind. *Ol.* 7.63a, 63b, D. Young, *Three Odes of Pindar: A Literary Study of Pythian 11, Pythian 3, and Olympian 7* (Leiden, 1968), 83–4; Strab. 14.2.10.
[54] Late antique/Byzantine examples of κλύζειν: *Suda*, γ 78, τ 597 πλοῦτον ἐπικλύζοντα; ps.-John Chrys. PG 64.476.43 κἂν τρυφῇ περικλύζηται, Basil, PG 85.104.16 περικλύζει τῷ πλούτῳ; Theodoretus, PG 83.653.43 πλούτου ῥεύμασι περικλύζονται, *Catenae in Joannem*, p. 188.25–7 οὐκ ἐν ἑαυτῷ συνέχων τὸν πλοῦτον, ἀλλὰ καὶ εἰς τοὺς ἄλλους ἅπαντας ὑπερκλύζων αὐτόν, καὶ μετὰ τὸ ὑπερκλύσαι μένων πλήρης.
[55] Sallust, *Cat.* 11 *divitias...quas profundant.*
[56] Valens, II 41.80 = no. L 88 Neugebauer–Van Hoesen; Heilen 2015, 890.

placement (other signs). The effect is not to harm the native (he is still rich), but to deny him the supreme advantage (kingship) that own signs contribute.

The comparanda (see Pinax), which distinguish between good and less favourable outcomes for both ASC and MC, have many similarities, and the interest lies in which of them comes closest to the specifications offered in addition to bare placement, and which has the most similar contrast between advantageous and less advantageous (or positively injurious) outcomes. So:

(a) 3.114–18 (MC). M^b is not just a reduction or elaboration of this. In the first place, kingship happens there when the Sun is in the ASC (3.111), not the MC. In the second, M^a similarly distinguishes between a good and a less good outcome, but on the basis of the aspecting planets, not the location in signs. For M^b, the native is wealthy anyway; the disadvantage comes with not being a king. For M^a, the contrast is between rich and poor.

(b) Περὶ κέντρ. 8–10 mentions 'own' places (καὶ μάλιστα εἰ ἰδιοτοπεῖ) even if it does not enumerate them. Dor.^{ARAB} II 22.1–2 also pairs the ASC and MC together. Additional factors are aspecting planets, and presence in a male sign. For this author, the disadvantage brought by an aspecting malefic is shortage of siblings.

(c) Θ pp. 136.9–20 (ASC) and 167.6–8 (MC). The factors specified for the ASC are sect (when the Sun is out of its sect the natives are of humbler parentage) and the presence of additional planets (Saturn: conducive; Mars: destabilising). Fathers are distinguished, and natives are friends of kings. It seems that the Sun in the MC produces kings as well (p. 168.18, cf. p. 170.12–14), though there is no extended discussion of this.

(d) Paul, pp. 64.17–65.3 (MC). A brief discussion in which, in the absence of malefics, natives and their fathers are of high status.

(e) Firmicus, 3.5.1–11, has the longest discussion of the ASC. Here, the favourable factors that produce kings when the Sun is on the ASC are his being in a masculine sign, in his own house or exaltation, and accompanied by benefics (3.5.1). In combination with other planets (though not the shift to other signs) their status may be reduced (to consuls, consulars, generals, judges) or they may come to a bad end, exile, violent death, etc. (3.5.2, 4). Firmicus lacks, however, the contrast between kings and the merely rich who manage their houses in obscurity; all his natives hold publicly prominent positions. His discussion of the MC, 3.5.34, mentions own house, Jupiter's house, exaltation, and the rest of his discussion (35–6) concerns the additional effect of malefics.

Kentrothesiai 547

In sum, it is not surprising that the closest correspondences are with details in Firmicus' long account of the ASC, which, first, specifies the favourable factors of exaltation and own house, and, second, parallels the slight diminution of status if the accompanying circumstances are not favourable (kings/not kings). After that, the closest is Περὶ κέντρ. Not even Firmicus, however, *identifies* the signs which are Saturn's own; he and Περὶ κέντρ only adduce the category. Mᵃ merely distinguishes malefics and benefics; Θ merely refers to sect and names Saturn and Mars.

93 Ἠελίου δ' ἀκάμαντος: see i. 908 n. 9 (to which add Empedocles, 31 B 115.11 D.-K., as quoted by Plut. *Mor.* 361 c). The Homeric formula (accusative) occupies the first half of the verse, as do most revivals (except Quint. Smyrn. 2.503, 10.197–8).

πυριμάρμαρος ἀστήρ: the poet has created a 'star of' name where none belongs (see on 4.87, 'star of Selene') to give a sense of lexical propriety—which is immediately undermined by the epithet. μαρμαίρω, according to LSJ, is used of any darting, quivering light, which is obviously not right for the Sun. Instead, the poet has transferred an epithet which Dorotheus seems to have coined for Mars (i. 909 n. 20) with his sights set on the first part of the compound, not the second.[57]

94 The quality of Homeric αἴθρη was clarity, lack of nebulosity (*Il.* 17.646; *Od.* 6.44–5). The latter passage, in virtue of the association of Olympus with οὐρανός (Hainsworth on *Od.* 6.42–7), facilitates the new meaning, the sky illuminated by the sun. For προφανῇ, see on 4.38.

95 ἢ γονίμῃ ὥρῃ πανεπίσκοπα φέγγεα βάλλῃ: as transmitted, the verb takes a double accusative, and Axtius and Rigler were happy to print that. The dative is Koechly's emendation. One might expect dative and accusative to be the other way round, but there are comparable examples of switches of case in Mᵃ (see on 3.88). As for γονίμῃ ὥρῃ, it looks like a reinterpretation of 2.288 γονίμης ὥρης, from 'the hour of birth' to 'the natal horoscope', aligning it with other birth-epithets (among which this is the only non-compound) in the protasis (p. 252). πανεπίσκοπα: see on 4.30, and Hübner 2001, 234.

96–7 The Sun's houses are given as Sagittarius, Leo, Aries, and Gemini. Leo is the Sun's own house, Aries its exaltation, and Sagittarius the other constella-

---

[57] There are no earlier uses. There are later ones, in Byzantine prose, applying to beams, beauty, majesty, and sometimes to stars (Constantinus Manasses, *Breviarium Chronicum*, 4873) or the thunderbolt (Nicephorus Basilaces, *Or.* 3 p. 50.30 πυριμάρμαρον ἀστραπήν, in an extended conceit praising the emperor).

tion in their triplicity (Bouché-Leclercq, 202–3), the royal triplicity, which produces kings. Pingree (as reported by Lopilato) found Gemini an interloper, and wanted to bracket from 97 καί to 98 ἰδίοισιν. Its inclusion presumably is to be explained on the grounds that it was the Sun's apogee at that period of antiquity (see Beaujeu on Plin. *NH* 2.64, Belles Lettres edn, p. 151, n. 2, with testimony reaching back to Hipparchus; Bouché-Leclercq, 195).

96 εὐστέρνοιο Λέοντος: see Hübner 1982, 125, especially Teucer, *CCAG* vii. 202.7, where the constellation Leo produces the εὐστέρνους, like itself; ps.-Pythagoras, *CCAG* xi/2. 137.11 τοιαῦτα ὅμοια τῷ λέοντι· εὐρύστηθοι ... Because the trope of the lion's courage located the quality in its breast (Tyrtaeus, fr. 13 W.), it was appropriate that the star in Leo that was located over the Lion's heart was the brightest in that sign.[58] The quality of being εὔστερνος or εὔστηθος becomes a motif in physiological or physiognomic descriptions of human beings, especially accounts of Byzantine emperors, but the lion also becomes an icon for having splendid foreparts but an underdeveloped behind, a category which is used both by Philostratus, *De gymn.* 37, in his physical classification of athletes (οἱ λεοντώδεις εὔστερνοι) and by Ptolemy in his discussion of human physiology (3.12.13; Hübner 1982, 190). The epithet's only earlier poetic occurrence is in Empedocles, 31 B 96 D.-K. ἐν εὐστέρνοις χοάνοισι, where it applies to pores or concavities in the earth (D. Sider, 'Empedocles B 96 (462 Bollack) and the Poetry of Adhesion', *Mnemosyne*[4] 37 (1984), 14–24, at 18–20, although Sider argues for the variant, attested in Alexander of Aphrodisias and Simplicius, εὐτύκτοις).

97 Κριοῦ τ᾽ εὐκεράοιο: Hübner 1982, 124. The epithet is new in Moschus, *Eur.* 52/153 ἠύκερως (see on 6.29–30). Bulls remain one of the referents (see Zito on Maximus, 73), but it is carried over to many other horned creatures and mythological beings, especially by Nonnus. Of the passages where it applies to goats (Nonn. *D.* 1.369, 32.276; Theaetetus Scholasticus, *AP* 16.233.2), this is the earliest.

φαανθείς: pioneered at line-end by Ap. Rhod. 2.693 (of a divine epiphany), 3.961 (of Jason, who has just been compared to a star).

98–9 Among the comparanda the best parallel for this outcome is Θ p. 136.10 βασιλεῖς ἢ ἡγεμόνας (Sun in ASC with Saturn). Specifically kings in 3.111. ἡγεμόνες and kings are parallel here, implying for the former the sense of *principes*, provincial governors, or just 'rulers', rather than holders of military commands (Mason, 144–9; 2.216 and 3.296). For the end of 98, it looks as if

---

[58] α Leonis, or Regulus; cf. Hipparchus, *Comm. in Arat. et Eudox.* 1.10.10; Lydus, *Ost.* 59 κζ´, 65 κθ´; Camaterus, *Intr.* 3451 Βασιλίσκος [i.e. *Regulus*] ὁ λαμπρὸς ἐν Λέοντος τῷ στήθει; Pachymeres, *Quadrivium*, 4.19, l. 106 ὁ ἐν τῷ τραχήλῳ καὶ στήθει τοῦ Λέοντος λαμπρός.

Kentrothesiai 549

some such phrase as in Περὶ κέντρ. 9 ἡγεμονικαὶ γὰρ αἱ τιμαί has been touched up in a popular late antique hexameter rhythm which is especially used for expressions about kingship (1.3 βασιληίδος ἀρχῆς, al.; see also on 4.207 and 1.68). Indeed, the diction of the whole couplet is best paralleled in oracles: see also Euseb. Orat. ad sanct. coet. 20 σκῆπτρον βασιληίδος ἀρχῆς; Or. Sib. 1.292–3 βασιλήιον ἀρχήν | σκηπτροφόρον; Or. Sib. 14.70 σκῆπτρον βασιλήιον. A precursor is found in the Hellenistic oracle at Or. Sib. 3.175 βασιληίδος ἔσσεται ἀρχή.

100 πλοῦτόν τ' ὀλβήεντα: the epithet recurs only in 'Antiochus', l. 109 (CCAG i. 112.31) ὀλβήεντα δόμον (δρόμον codd., corr. Kroll).

102 πολυχρήμονα: see on 6.16. The notion need not be reinforced by πλουτοτόκος (K²) at the beginning of the line. Koechly's first instincts were correct. His n. ad loc. shows that he understood that τικτομένοις follows the poet's convention of referring to birth in the protasis or apodosis (p. 252).

103 βιοτὴν πλήθουσαν: compare Hes. Op. 307 ὡραίου βιότου πλήθωσι καλιαί; 'Plenitude of livelihood' is not a usual expression (LXX Prov. 5:23 ἐκ δὲ πλήθους τῆς ἑαυτοῦ βιότητος notwithstanding).

ἀλύπητόν τε δίαιταν: another happy convergence between astrological idiom (Epit. II, CCAG i. 151.4 ἄλυπον βίον ζήσεται) and tragic diction (Soph. Tr. 168 ἀλυπήτῳ βίῳ; the word's other tragic showing is in Eur. Hyps. fr. I, i. 9 ἀ]λύ[π]ητ[ο]ι). This is one of the alphas privative meaning 'unharmed' (ἀσινής, ἀκάκωτος) in which astrology is rich. It recurs in Valens, VI 9.12 ἀτάραχοι μὲν καὶ ἀλύπητοι, IX 12.19 ἀλύπητον καὶ ἀκοπίατον, IX 12.23; see 4.106 ἀβλαβής, 6.136 ἀπήμαντος (Maximus has four instances of ἀπήμον-).

104 θρονισμούς: not a neologism, but it usually refers to the enthronement of the candidate for initiation.[59] Would this bombasticated version of θρόνος have been felt as catachrestic? Its other use is in Synesius, Epist. 66 Hercher (l. 104), where it refers to a bishopric (a see = sedes), which at least establishes the possibility in a later author of transferring the word to other types of seat.

105–6 This kind of muting of the outcome in the absence of the clinching factor can be compared to 2.218–20, where natives miss out on being great men in the retinue of kings, but still dominate their peers at a lower station (there, for want of being in a kentron).

105 ἀφανεῖς: for the meaning 'undistinguished' see ps.-Demosth. Or. 61.35 τοῖς μὲν ἀφανῆ καὶ ταπεινὴν τὴν φύσιν ἔχουσιν (opposed to τοῖς ... περιβλέπτοις

---

[59] Not properly documented in LSJ, but see Dio Chrys. Or. 12.33 = Posidonius, fr. 368 Theiler; a work Θρονισμοὺς Μητρῴους mentioned in Suda, o 654 (Orpheus, 1 A 1 D.-K.); Proclus, Theol. Plat. 6 p. 65.23–4 Saffrey and Westerink, who renders Plato's word θρόνωσιν at Euthyd. 277 D (of Corybantic initiations) as θρονισμός.

γεγενημένοις); Call. *Ep.* 12.2 Pf. = *AP* 7.521.2 = *HE* 1238 ἀφανὴς οὔτι γὰρ ἡ γενεή; Philo, *Vit. Mos.* 1.30. ('Lacking renown' in Eur. *Tr.* 1244.)

σκήπτρων δίχα: the post-positional placement is common in iambics (Schwyzer, ii. 538), then spreads to Hellenistic epigram (Mnasalcas), but not in hexameter verse before the imperial period (Greg. Naz. *PG* 37.416.2 Θεοῦ δίχα, 448.5 ἧς δίχα, 676.3 Χριστοῖο δίχα; in Nonnus, 3x *D.*, 1x *Par.*, contrasting with 8x *D.*, 2x *Par.* as preposition; the poet of 5.147 has it both ways).

106 ἀβλαβέας: see on 4.103 ἀλύπητον; this is common, including outside astrology.

διευθυντῆρας: unique to this passage and Περὶ κράσ. 141 ψήφων διευθυντῆρας (Riley: 'directors of accounts'), where it presumably reflects the underlying poem of Dorotheus.[60] In absence of any indication to the contrary, they presumably manage their own property, not that of others. For διευθύνειν, see on 4.89–90.

4.107–9 Transition

107–8 As Koechly already noted, this break-off formula, although it picks up 3–4 πλάνα φέγγη | ἀπλανέων τ' αὐγάς, is a poor fit for the preceding section. The combination of πεφόρηται and ῥομβηδόν, which evoke motion whirling around a fixed centre, might suggest a discussion of cosmic circles (p. 183), something like 2.1–140 (compare 2.13 πεφορημέν' ὕπερθεν and, of planetary orbits, an oracle ap. Euseb. *PE* 9.10.5 = Porphyry, *De philosophia ex oraculis haurienda*, p. 141.12–13 Wolff Εἷς ἐν παντὶ πέλει κόσμῳ κύκλος, ἀλλὰ σὺν ἑπτὰ | ζώναισιν πεφόρηται εἰς ἀστερόεντα κέλευθα).

107 πλανητάων for πλανήτων: πλανήτης a variant of πλάνης (e.g. Jude 13 ἀστέρες πλανῆται).

108 The line as a whole is identical in rhythm to ps.-Opp. *Cyn.* 4.407 ἀμφίβολος μάλα πάμπαν ἀτυζομένη πεφόρηται; compare also the clausula of *IG* XIV 2461.15 ἐπιχθονίη πεφόρηται (Marseille, n.d.; of the part of the body that is left behind on earth at death, the other being carried aloft among the stars). There are two highlights. First, ῥομβηδόν makes the conceit of the cosmic whirl as a *rhombos* (on which see on 4.239) even more exotic by converting it into a unique adverbial form. Second, ἀματροχίη cannot be anything other than a retooling of *Il.* 23.422 ἀματροχιάς, where it means a chariot collision. Perhaps

---

[60] The prose form in Valens, I 20.5 ψήφων διευθυντάς. At App. X 4 Pingree prints ψόγων διευθυντάς, but the surrounding context is essentially the same as the earlier one, so this seems to be a corruption.

'Signs of Birth' 551

additional stimulus came from Call. fr. 383.10 Pf., where Callimachus had deliberately crossed wires with ἁρματροχιή in *Il.* 23.505 to produce a complex interpretation,[61] but now it means synchronised movement.

109 Ἄλλα δέ τοι λέξω: ἄλλα δέ τοι occurs twice elsewhere, first in Aratus, 773 Ἄλλα δέ τοι ἐρέει (which Kidd ad loc. notes as a light adaptation of Homeric ἄλλο δέ τοι ἐρέω) and again in Dion. Per. 961 ἄλλα δέ τοι. In all cases it is transitional. In Aratus, it concludes a proem but leads on to the main body of an upcoming section; in Dionysius it is a break-off formula to terminate a list; here it opens a catalogue. The present passage may or may not have come via Aratus: all it does is employ synonymic variation of Homeric ἐρέω.

σήματα θεῖα: this appears to be calling the configurations of stars signs rather than causes; signs, moreover, sent by the gods. On the question of signification *versus* causation in astrology, see on 5.244. Taken literally, that would run up against factitive verbs that imply causation. But the poet may simply be using Aratean vocabulary and/or using the word to mean 'configuration' (extending the Aratean σῆμα from a constellation to a particular planetary set-up) as he does again in 4.410 ~ 1.335 and 4.589 (where κατὰ σήματα τοιάδε refers to 4.582-3 + 586). In a similar way, the literal meaning of σήματα is not to be pressed in 6.222-3 γάμοιο | σήματα (another transitional passage). There is a question how solemnly to take the epithet, but see pp. 180-1 on the influence of the *Timaeus* and i. 62-3 for the divinity of the stars.

4.110-69 'Signs of Birth'

4.110-20 Charts Involving *Kentra*

110-15

Moon in ASC, Mars in DESC. Does this chart belong with 4.560-92 as a relic of a section on oppositions/aspects across *kentra* which included luminaries, as Dorotheus also does (Jupiter × Moon; Mars × luminaries), but 3.132-226 does not? The best parallels, however, come from add-ons to the Moon in reviews of the *dodecatopos*, which agree on βιαιοθανασία (see on 115).

110 ὡράων πανεπίσκοπα φέγγεα Μήνης: the expression, though very nebulous, must mean that the Moon is in the ASC, using the plural ὡράων instead of the normal and expected singular (meant to match δυσμὰς in 112?). The apparent

---

[61] ἁρματροχιή is the track left by wheels; Callimachus denies that the winds left visible marks (ἁματροχίας).

parallel with the sign-off at 165 Ταῦτα μὲν ὡράων σκεπτήρια (meaning 'tokens *derived from the Ascendants*', as Lopilato renders it) is, I think, illusory. The Moon's rays are all-seeing as they strike the ASC, like the Sun's in 4.95, and -επίσκοπ- seems to govern the genitive plural, much as in 4.17, where ἐπίσκοπον seems to govern βίου.

111 αὐγάζηται: 'appears', but with the sense of αὐγή strongly residually present (Prévot, 252–3); also Maximus, 63, 114, 118, twice preceded by a prepositional phrase.

112 εἰς δυσμάς: see on 4.8: a standard prose expression, but not the standard way of expressing the DESC.

πυριλαμπέος: see on 4.44. It evokes Mars' light name Πυρόεις without spelling it out.

113 ἐνσινέας τε τίθησι: precisely as in 2.445 (*synaphe* of Moon and Saturn), the adjective's only other occurrence. By an emendation in 2.472, the Moon in *synaphe* with Mars produces σίνος.

ἀβίους, ἀμελάθρους: the second is an absolute *hapax*. The first is much commoner, but well complements the sense. One of the interpretations of Homer's Abioi in *Il.* 13.6 (see Janko on 13.4–7) was that the name was an epithet for nomadic peoples (as in Philostr. *Vit. Apoll.* 2.6), in other words, referred to the homeless; one wonders whether the redundant τ' after ἀβίους, deleted by A.-R., is due to scribal reminiscence of that passage. For homelessness (p. 75), see Greg. Naz. *PG* 35.593.8–9 Ὁρᾷς τοὺς ἀβίους τούτους καὶ ἀνεστίους; for indigence, Hephaestion, i. 241.2 ταπεινοὺς καὶ ἀβίους καὶ ἐπαίτας καὶ δυστυχεῖς; for lack of fixity, 'Heliodorus' on Paul, p. 72.3 ἀστάτους τε καὶ ἀβίους καὶ ἀγάμους.

114 λιτῆς πενίης χερνήτορας: the pompous suffixation and hazy use of the genitive are characteristic. For the agent noun, from χερνής or χερνήτης, see Fraenkel, i. 127. Ever since the simile about the γυνὴ χερνῆτις in *Il.* 12.433 the word connotes both manual labour and poverty.[62] Followers of Homer evoke the immiserated working woman (e.g. Posidippus, *Ep.* 46.1 A.-B.; Archias, *AP* 6.39.7), but this passage and 5.129 χερνήτην concentrate on poverty *per se* (without implying a miserabilist view of handicrafts themselves: see p. 81). The genitive seems to purport to take the agent noun formation at face value, as if it derived from a verb whose action resulted in pauperism (as if the meaning were e.g. 'workers-of-poverty'). Either correction of transmitted λεπτῆς has support. For Koechly's, see on 2.488 λιτός. For Massimilla's, see

---

[62] Hesych. χ 362 χερνής· πένης. λάτρις, χειροτέχνης; Eustath. on *Il.* 12.433, iii. p. 415.8–10 Φασὶ γοῦν οἱ παλαιοί· χερνήτης, λάτρις, χειροτέχνης, ἀπὸ χειρὸς ζῶν. καὶ πάλιν· χερνήτης, πένης, χειρόβιος; Σ vet. Aesch. *PV* 893c χερνήταν] Τὸν εὐτελῆ καὶ διὰ τῶν χειρῶν νήθοντα, ὅ ἐστιν ἐργαζόμενον, 893d πτωχόν, χειροτέχνην.

'Signs of Birth'   553

2.464. Either would constitute another connection between the diction of M^a and M^b.

ἀκτεάνους: see on 4.31.

115 Θ p. 138.8–11, 22–5, and Firmicus, 3.13.2, agree that with the Moon on the ASC, malefics in aspect, and no benefics in sight, one outcome is violent death.

116–20

Mars in ASC in signs not its own. Koechly rightly wondered whether this originally belonged in the vicinity of 4.44–52, which deals with Mars in the MC. It would supply for Mars an entry in the ASC, which only Mars lacks in that section. The specification 'in signs not its own' would fit with other items in the *kentrothesia* sequence (Saturn, Sun), although it is true that such comments occur throughout the book.

The chart is not directly supported by the comparanda. The *dodecatopos* charts do agree that Mars in the ASC produces σεσινωμένοι (Περὶ κέντρ. 40 and Θ p. 133.3), but have no comment at this point on 'own' or 'other' signs. Neither does 6.574–7 (with the additional presence of the Moon setting in the terms of Saturn), which agrees on hunchbacks.

116 ἀνοικείοισι τόποις: see on 4.28.

ὡροσκόπον is an epithet of φέγγος, as in 491, 496; Hübner 2001, 234.

117 γονίμην ἐπὶ γαστέρα θνητῶν: while the epithet is taken from M^a (see on 4.95 and 6.56), here and still more at 220 it is applied in a grossly physiological sense more reminiscent of the earlier poet's fancy for expressions about emerging from the womb (see on 6.33; also 6.100, 165; p. 252). A couple of parallels from rhetorical (not medical) texts: Choricius, *Or.* 23.2.38...τὸ γύναιον γόνιμον ἔχει γαστέρα; Philagathus (12th c.), *Hom.* 24.10 Ὦ μάτην γονίμου γαστρός.

118 χωλόποδας: there seem to be two main logics involved in physical deformity. The first is injury to the Moon by Mars or both malefics;[63] the second is analogy with bent signs.[64] Only here, it seems, is the Moon *not* involved. The adjective is *proton legomenon*. χωλόπους reappears in Byzantine authors

---

[63] 6.574–7 (Mars in ASC, Moon in DESC in terms of Saturn); 1.134–7 (Mars encounters the Moon in the sixth house), cf. Θ p. 189.6–8; Epit. IIIb, *CCAG* vii. 114.35–6 Σελήνη σὺν Κρόνῳ καὶ Ἄρει ἐν ὑστέραις μοίραις τῶν ζῳδίων χωλοὺς ποιεῖ, cf. Θ p. 183.4–5; Ptol. 3.13.13: damage to the luminaries by malefics, especially in certain critical places, produces κυρτώσεων ἢ κυλλώσεων ἢ χωλώσεων ἢ παραλύσεων; Θ p. 156.9–10 Σελήνη μεστὴ πρὸς Ἄρεα φερομένη χωλούς, κυλλούς.

[64] Capricorn: Teucer, *CCAG* vii. 208.17; Valens, I 2.57; Camaterus, *Introd.* 1328; Taurus: Valens, II 37.8.

(Ignatius the Deacon; Psellus). In Psellus' case it applies to Thersites, making obvious the connection with *Il.* 2.217 χωλὸς δ' ἕτερον πόδα. Thersites was already a subtext of 6.575-7 (see on 6.577), while other aspects of his anatomy become signifiers for physiognomical writers.[65] The difference from Babylonian omens involving birth anomalies is profound. In the first place they put the defect in the protasis. In the second, some are constructed to fit abstract schemata rather than real deformities[66]—let alone literary archetypes.

ἀώρους: rare in apotelesmata (Hephaestion, i. 8.8–9), perhaps for the good reason of illogicality (what do stars do if not determine the hour?), but stock in inscribed epitaphs.

119 νῶτά τε κυρτιόωντας: cf. 6.577 (similar configuration except that the crescent Moon is involved as well). For Thersites' ongoing influence in apparently procuring names like Κυρτός, Κύρτος, and Κυρτίων for hunch-backed individuals, see Robert 1960a, 41–2. The participle is new. It varies more banal expressions involving κυρτός[67] or κυρτόω[68] on the analogy of -ιάω verbs that mean 'be in the state described by the adjective' (γλαυκιόων, ἀκροκελαινιόων, etc.), and is perhaps specifically influenced by *Il.* 13.799 κυρτὰ φαληριόωντα.

ψευστῆρας ἀθέσμους: the astrologers often associate lying with rapacity (next entry). The agent noun (a false form: Fraenkel, i. 76, 123, 131) is a *hapax*, but the feminine exists in *Or. Sib.* 3.816 ψεύστειραν. Given its usual associations with murder and sexual outrage (3.154, 6.158; 4.304, and not otherwise in the corpus), the adjective seems rather exaggerated, but that is M^b's lurid outlook.

120 παναγεῖς: not 'all-hallowed', but all-accursed: Philonides, F 5 K.-A. παναγεῖς γενεάν; Philodemus, Περὶ τῶν Στοικῶν, xviii τοῖς παναγέσι τούτοις (ed. T. Dorandi, 'Filodemo, Gli Stoici (PHerc. 155 e 339)', *CErc 12* (1982), 91–133, at 102), of sectaries of whom the author disapproves.

ὄλβου τε ποθήτορας ἀλλοτρίοιο: Thersites falls into abeyance—but it is notable that venality is combined with spinal deformity and other Thersitean qualities in Anon. Med. *Physiogn.* 25 Ἄνθρωπος κοντός, κυρτός, ψεδνός, κυφοειδής, κατὰ τὸ εἶδος πίθηκι ἐοικὼς περίεργος, πονηρός, ὀχληρός, φιλάργυρος καὶ ματαιολόγος ἐστίν (with thin hair thrown in for good measure); Adamantius, 2.16 [~ ps.-Polemon, 42] κυρτὸν ὁ φέρων μετάφρενον καὶ ὤμους εἰς τὸ στῆθος ἐπικεκλασμένους κακοήθης ἐστὶ καὶ βάσκανος· εἰ δὲ καὶ τὸ σῶμα ἐπικεκλασμένον,

---

[65] ψεδνότης: Adamantius, 2.37; ps.-Polemon, 8; Anon. Med. *Physiogn.* 25 (4.120 n.); cf. also Lucian, *Dial. Mort.* 30 (25) 1. Pointed head: ps.-Arist. *Physiogn.* 812ª οἱ τὰς κεφαλὰς φοξοὶ ἀναιδεῖς; Anon. Med. *Physiogn.* 1 Φοξῇ κεφαλῇ μεστῇ ἀνοίας.

[66] F. Rochberg, 'Empiricism in Babylonian Omen Texts and the Classification of Mesopotamian Divination as Science', *JAOS* 119 (1999), 559–69, at 563–4; Pangas, 318 and 321.

[67] Aretaeus, *De Caus. et Sign. Acut. Morb.* 1.6.7 κυρτοὶ μὲν τὰ νῶτα.

[68] e.g. Eur. *Helen* 1558 κυρτῶν τε νῶτα; ps.-John Chrys. *De Spe*, PG 60.771.63 κυρτώσας τὰ νῶτα (of the posture of a farmer).

'Signs of Birth' 555

φειδωλὸς καὶ φιλάργυρος, cf. 56 Τὸν δὲ φιλάργυρον ἄνδρα τοιόνδε εἶναι λέγε· μικρομελῆ, μικρόμματον, μικροπρόσωπον, ταχυβάδιστον, ἐγκεκυφότα, ταχύφωνον, ὀξυβόην [~ Il. 2.224 μακρὰ βοῶν]. (The reason is not obvious. Thersites was not obviously venal, nor did he take bribes: on the contrary he criticises Agamemnon's greed and is a doublet of Achilles, the man who had accused Agamemnon of being φιλοκτεανώτατε πάντων. See, however, ps.-Hippocr. *Epist.* 17.159–62 νικῶνται δέ…ὑπὸ τῆς φιλαργυρίης, ὑπὸ τῶν παθέων πάντων, ἃ νοσέουσι. Θερσῖται δ' εἰσὶ τοῦ βίου πάντες.) The phrase elaborates standard astrological expressions for covetousness, involving part of ἀλλότριος/*res alienae*, which are also used, under different circumstances, in 2.306 (Mercury in the houses of Mars); Valens, I 2.52 (under Libra, oddly; see Kroll, *CCAG* v/2. 143); Firmicus, 3.5.10 (Sun in ASC, Saturn in trine or sextile, and Jupiter, Venus, Mercury in other *kentra*) *rapaces, et qui res alienas avaro rapiant cupiditatis instinctu*, 6.11.9 (Mercury in right quartile to Mars) *rapaces et qui de rebus alienis varia mentis cupiditate pascantur*.

4.121–64 Mostly Πρᾶξις Charts

These are almost all *Π*- charts. The exceptions are (i) 4.131–8, another version of Θ p. 216.17–22, which also appears in its place in the τ- sequence in 4.395–401; (ii) 4.153–6, a σίνος chart; and (iii) 4.161–4.

121–4 [= 1.286–9]

Venus aspects Mars in day births. This item serves as a pivot between the *kentron* configurations which precede and the πρᾶξις charts which follow. It adds Venus to the previous chart to produce metal-working. Koechly suggests that the link is lameness (in other words, the limping Hephaestus), though it seems unlikely that this poet would use Homeric gods as an organising principle.

As it stands, this is a πρᾶξις configuration describing the outcome when Mars and Venus are Rulers of πρᾶξις. It is closer to Θ (which employs aspect) than to Ptolemy, who gives instances of trades involving heat (Ptol. 4.4.8 βαφέας, μυρεψούς, κασσιτεροποιούς, μολυβδουργούς, χρυσοχόους, ἀργυροκόπους), but adds sect. In the sister-chart at 6.518–19, Mars, an expected presence, is absent and the effect is Venus' alone, located explicitly in the ASC. In the apodosis, M^a and M^b refer to works 'from fire and iron' (App. II, II.6.i) and decorate iron with an epithet; it is hard to say whether they have independently hit on contrasting epithets (in 6.519 πολιοῖο from EGHP), or whether book 4 is deliberate *variatio*.

122 ὄμμα βάλῃ: also 496 ὄμμα τιταίνῃ, 5.45–6 ὑπὸ βασκάνῳ ὄμματι …ὄμματ' ἐποίσει, 5.77 ὅσσ' ἀνέχων, and for the luminaries as eyes, see on

5.257. The analogy between stars and eyes[69] is no mere conceit, but based in ancient optics and physiology of vision (Rizzini, 132–42), and if both stars and eyes are fiery entities that forcefully project rays (already *Od.* 4.150 ὀφθαλμῶν τε βολαί) the astrological notions of aspect and ray-casting are a logical extension of the basic idea (see pp. 248–9; 339). In this particular iteration, as object rather than subject of the verb, the eye itself becomes equivalent to the ray, that which is cast. The phrase also implies a degree of personification.[70] Other examples of ὄμμα βαλών have a personal subject (Pindar, *Paean* XV, fr. 52p 6; Nonn. *D.* 22.56, 43.277; Greg. Naz. *PG* 37.1356.7; Meleager, *AP* 12.159.5 = *HE* 4566; Damagetus, *AP* 16.95.3), or their subject is another personification (Greg. Naz. *PG* 37.565.1, 597.9–10; John of Gaza, *Descr.* 119; *SH* 1181.1) where the point is regarding, having in purview, 'casting a glance' at.

ἐν ἡμεριναῖσι λοχείαις: prose would be ἐν ἡμερινῇ γενέσει, or ἐπὶ ἡμερινῆς γενέσεως, ἐπὶ ἡμερινῶν γενέσεων, ἐπὶ ἡμερινοῦ θέματος, in comparison to which this is startlingly earthy and physiological (see pp. 251–2). λοχεία is not nearly as rare as Mineur's lazy note on Call. *Hymn* 4.251 suggests, though in astrology it occurs only here = 1.287 and 4.385. ἐν is normal.

123–4 Vis-à-vis Θ the poet gives the hammers a decorative epithet (ῥαιστοτύποις is a *hapax*, though see Ap. Rhod. 3.1254 for a ῥαιστὴρ springing back παλιντυπές from an anvil), and adds a reference to furnaces. σιδηρ- and καμίν- also stand at the end of two successive lines in Nic. *Ther.* 923–4, but a more convincing model is Call. *Hymn* 3.59–61 εὖθ' οἵγε ῥαιστῆρας ἀειράμενοι ὑπὲρ ὤμων | ἢ χαλκὸν ζείοντα καμινόθεν ἠὲ σίδηρον | ἀμβολαδὶς τετύποντες... (of the Cyclopes);[71] this would show the poet using a similar technique to Mᵃ in purloining mythological material from prestige models to glamourise workaday activities. He is also employing the same nicety as Mᵃ and Dion. Per. in combining Hellenistic poetry and EGHP (p. 215), for iron's epithet, 'black' (however unusual a choice when it is being forged), must come from Hes. *Op.* 151 μέλας δ' οὐκ ἔσκε σίδηρος. (EGHP iron is normally 'shining', and grey in the metrically similar *Il.* 23.261 πολιόν τε σίδηρον, whereas Hesiod is visualising

---

[69] Proclus, *In Timaeum*, ii. 84.7–8 ὅπου καὶ τὸν ἥλιον ὄμμα λέγομεν καὶ τῶν ἀστέρων ἕκαστον.

[70] As do other examples of the idea, in their very different contexts. The heavenly bodies are the eyes of God (*Corp. Herm.* XXIII. 34 περιλαμπῆ τε, ὀφθαλμοὶ θεῶν, ἄστρα; *Hist. Alex. Magn.*, *Recensio* γ (Lib. 2), 35a,27 οὗ ὄμμα πάντες οἱ ἀστέρες, ἥλιος καὶ σελήνη; Orph. 243 F 16 Bernabé ὄμματα δ' ἠέλιός τε καὶ ἀντιόωσα σελήνη, from a Hymn to Zeus) or of his ministers (Synesius, *Hymn* 1.272–4 κοσμαγοὶ ὀμματολαμπεῖς νόες ἀστέριοι) or of the night (Aesch. *Sept.* 390 πρέσβιστον ἄστρων, νυκτὸς ὀφθαλμός, of the Moon, cf. Hutchinson ad loc.; *HOrph.* 34.13 ἀστερόομματον ὄρφνην; Theodorus Balsamon, *Ep.* 45.2 Ἀστέρες ὡς πολύφωτοι, ἀφεγγοῦς ὄμματα νυκτός). Radiant gaze of lovers: Aristaenetus, *Ep.* 1.10 sub fin. λαμπροῖς ὄμμασιν οἷον ἀστέρες ἀνταυγοῦντες ἀλλήλοις.

[71] An anvil and hammer in *Il.* 18.476, but no iron.

'Signs of Birth' 557

iron when it is rusty—cf. West ad loc.) Moreover, the Hesiodic epithet is threaded onto the verse pattern of Odyssean [διοϊστεύσειν, al.] τε σιδήρου (4×).

123 αὐχήσουσι τέχνας: LSJ cite one parallel for the verb with a straight accusative ('boast'). Another is a grave stele from Amisos (n.d.), *Studia Pontica*, III 7c 3–4 εὐτυχίην ἐν βροτοῖσιν αὐχ[ῶ] τοῦτο μόνον ('I claim').

124 μεμελημένοι: M^b has turned an expression elsewhere used for interest or expertise (Opp. *Hal.* 4.101, Quint. Smyrn. 4.500, Nonn. *D.* 25.424, 37.495, 48.667) into a professional label (p. 173). For the construction with the dative see Harder on Call. fr. 75.76 ἐτητυμίῃ μεμελημένος; Gow on Theocr. *Id.* 26.36 πολλαῖς μεμελημέναι ἡρωίναις; very popular after the Hellenistic period.

125–30

Mercury in ASC, Venus following. This chart is not exactly like any other, but the closest overall match for protasis + apodosis is 6.476–9 + 480–3, in which *rhetores* and the wise are produced by Venus following Mercury in the ASC (4.127 ~ 6.479). 4.127–8 (including astrologers) also recur at 1.292–3, but with a different protasis. There is no single πρᾶξις chart in Ptolemy or Θ which matches each detail in M^b, though astrologers are born under Mercury, and all three of *rhetores*, 'wise' men, and astrologers are combined at Θ p. 212.18–20, albeit under completely different agencies. As for the scratch collection of add-on professions in 129–30 (geometers, ritualists, makers of divine statues, and temple-builders), one wonders whether these represent the detritus of a fuller version which once described the effect of the Rulers of πρᾶξις in different signs (Ptol. 4.4.9; Θ pp. 209.17–210.4). On this view, geometers and ritualists belong under tropic/equinoctial signs (see on 129), while stone-carvers and builders of temples are likely progeny of four-footed signs (~ οἰκοδομικὰς καὶ τεκτονικάς). There are certainly other occasions in the *Περὶ τεχνῶν* where Θ contains mentions of signs which clarify matters in M^b (see pp. 113 and 141 for entertainers and tradesmen).

125–6 σκοπιὴν…κατάγῃ: Lopilato renders 'when Mercury gains the look-out of the ascendant for the pangs of childbirth', but the sense of the verb seems to me to be 'draws the ASC down upon the birth' (although it is hard to see what the poet gains from evoking either the nautical use of the verb—bring down something to the sea coast—or the idea of witches drawing down the Moon from the sky[72]). For σκοπιὴν ὡροσκόπον, see Hübner 2001, 235 ('die

---

[72] κατάγειν in e.g. Plut. *Mor.* 400 B; Lucian, *Dial. Meretr.* 1.2, Dio Chrys. *Or.* 47.8.

stundenprägende Warte'), and p. 213 on parechesis. Once again, ὠδίνεσσιν attracts attention by its physicality (p. 252).

ἐπίφοιτος: see on 4.83. The epithet is new, but adheres to the tendency, already established in M^a, for expressions of following to involve an ἐπί compound (i. 882). That said, the verb ἐπιφοιτᾶν itself is not used in this technical sense.

128 θεοφήμους: *hapax*. Astrologers articulate divine truths/give voice to divine will. The pietistic presentation of their role is in keeping with Firmicus, 1.6.1 *nos numen eorum maiestatemque monstramus*, 2.30.1 *Oportet enim eum qui cotidie de diis vel cum diis loquitur* (i.e. the astrologer is one who speaks of and with gods). The idea of Manilius is that the gods, above all Mercury, have willingly communicated knowledge of the discipline to human beings (1.25–39, 48–9); he does not make the latter interpreters.

129 Although the passage in question describes the effects, not of the Rulers of πρᾶξις themselves, but of the signs they are in, Ptol. 4.4.9 τὰ δὲ τροπικὰ καὶ ἰσημερινὰ πρὸς τὰς ἑρμηνευτικὰς καὶ μεταβολικὰς καὶ μετρητικὰς καὶ γεωργικὰς καὶ ἱερατικάς [sc. τέχνας] (~ Θ p. 210.1–2, replacing μετρητικὰς with γεωμετρικὰς) suggests by what mental processes land-surveying or geometry and religious rites could be combined. The categories all involve some sort of interpretation or transference or analogy. If the ἔν τε γεωμετρίῃσι…ἀρίστους are geometers, perhaps the idea is that they proceed from imperfect physical objects to eternal forms. If they are land-surveyors, then the other way round, as abstract calculations are imposed on a real landscape to measure and partition it.

130 ἔν τε λιθογλυφίαισι θεῶν: see on 4.569 for makers of divine images, and Appendix II, II.5.v for λιθογλύφος as a trade name.

νηῶν τε θεμέθλοις: that θεμέθλοις refers to the foundation of buildings and is a poetic rendering of what Ptolemy and Θ call οἰκοδομικά in their taxonomy of signs (above) is suggested by Dorotheus' introduction to his section περὶ οἰκοδομίας, p. 386.19 Ἡνίκα δ᾽ αὖτε θέμεθλα δομήιά τ᾽ ἔργα τελείοις. Firmicus has a number of *fabricatores templorum* (Appendix II,V.5.i), but only in 3.5.33, where they are combined with *fabricatores deorum*, does it seem reasonably clear that these are architects or builders, as opposed to patrons, those who put up the money (Bernard, 69).

131–8

Jupiter in MC above Saturn <in a wet sign>.

Protasis. Ptolemy gives (i) the effect of Saturn ruling the Lot of Fortune, producing profits through shipping (4.2.2), and (ii) the basic Π- configuration for

'Signs of Birth' 559

Mars aspected by Saturn, producing seamen (4.4.5 ναυτικούς). He also (iii) associates gainful, mercantile occupations with Jupiter and its sign Pisces (2.3.41). Θ has a τ- chart, involving not only Saturn and Mars but also the Sun, and giving their locations (p. 216.17–22). Mᵃ and Mᵇ have evolved in a similar way, dropping Mars, but introducing Jupiter; they disagree, however, about the latter's location. It is surprising that it was not until the second edition of Koechly that the presence of a lacuna was spotted after 132 which must have contained the words ‹οὐρανόν› (vel sim.), to complete μέσον, and ‹καθύγρῳ› (or a synonym[73]) to accompany ζῳδίῳ. K² deduced this from 6.484 (though his suggested supplement also added 'winged' from 6.450–1, which is superfluous), and it is confirmed by Θ, which he did not know. For watery signs, see on 6.362; Hübner 1982, 94. Pisces is a fixture, and Capricorn and Aquarius are usually present, but other signs may produce nautical professions through their paranatellonta (Hübner on Manilius, 5.41).

Apodosis. The forms 4.134 ἐμπορικοῦ, 6.486 ἐμπορίη (not in Θ), and 4.137 κοινωνόν, are best paralleled in Ptol. 2.3.41, from his discussion of geothesia (which constellations dominate which regions). If the connection is real, it would extend the range of pre- or para-Ptolemaic material which Manethonian poets seem to have known (pp. 140, 261).

131 ὑπεροpμαίνων…ὑπὲρ ἀστέρα πατρός: to judge from 6.484–5, presumably 'above' in the sense of being to the right of, not Mᵃ's normal usage 'in' a kentron (i. 878), which is indicated separately in the next line. The compound is a hapax; the simplex refers to motion only post-Homerically. It suggests eagerness, haste (e.g. Theocr. 24.26), which in Jupiter's case is only less strange than it would have been in Saturn's, though see on 4.37 δρόμῳ. ὑπερ-…ὑπέρ (the only occurrence of ὑπέρ in this book) is a little de trop (p. 200, though see Hdt. 4.103.3); the accusative instead of genitive has facilitated a cadence like Nonnus' ἀστέρα Μαίρης, passim, and especially D. 5.208 ἀστέρα πάτρης. 'Star of his father', without a planetary name, rather suggests Dorotheus, a periphrasis (i. 920) to avoid the proper name.

φοράδην: 'borne along', again in 4.571. The adverb, though common, does not recur in astrology, but comes from the same set of ideas as φορεῖσθαι (i. 895 and n. 150; cf. 4.108 πεφόρηται, 510 ζωφορίην; p. 244) and, given Mᵇ's tragic leanings, might evoke Soph. OT 1310 διαπωτᾶται φοράδαν, where it is again a matter of being carried through the air. It has respect only to cosmic, not planetary, motion.

132 καθέτῳ: see on 4.45. If this means precisely overhead to the exact degree, this detail is unique to Mᵇ.

---

[73] Several ὑγρ- and ὑδρ- compounds (Hübner 1982, 171–3, 176–8), and perhaps even ὑδατώδεϊ (Hübner 1982, 245 and 503); Heilen 2015, 890.

560   Commentary on Book Four

133 μερόπων τις ἐνέγκῃ: see on 4.55.

134 ἐμπορικοῦ πλοίου φορτοστόλος ἴδρις: like the abstract noun ἰδμοσύνη (i. 58 and n. on 6.744), the adjective implies knowledgeability in a craft, mastery of a body of knowledge or discipline. That craft is the art of navigation already in Od. 7.108–9, whence Orph. Arg. 727–8 ἴδριν…ναυτιλίης, Opp. Hal. 1.344–5 ἀκάτοιο | ἴδρις ἀνήρ. φορτοστόλος is unique.

135 ναυκλήρου τέχνας θ' αἱρήσεται: the context makes clear that they are not just ship-owners, but involved in trade (Drexhage 2012, 171). Trade itself is a craft in Heliodorus, Aeth. 4.16.6 Ἔλεγον δὴ οὖν εἶναι μὲν Φοίνικες Τύριοι, τέχνην δὲ ἔμποροι; see too on 88 ἐμπείραμος. The present coding employs Jupiter for wealth and Saturn for water; for ναύκληροι see on 4.89, where the Moon implies an itinerant lifestyle.[74]

135–6 ἐν χρέεσίν…βιώσεται: literally this means they make money from purchased debts. One question is whether this went on in the ancient world; another is whether it belongs here at all. It is clear that debt *could* be transferred through the procedure called *delegatio obligandi*, whereby a debt was passed on by the *delegans* to the *delegatus*, who then become liable to the original creditor.[75] But whether anyone bought up debt from creditors for a fraction of their write-down value and in the hope of recouping them is another matter. I do not know of any ancient evidence for it, but the prior question is whether this is what the text actually means. If the subjects are still merchants (since no change has been signalled since the previous line), merchants would be supposed to *contract* debts rather than purchase them,[76] and indeed, according to Dorotheus, p. 395.25–9, the right time to contract a debt is when the Moon is in two of the watery signs (Aquarius and Pisces). So perhaps we should try to interpret χρέεσίν τε…ὠνητοῖσι not, as the modern parallel seduces us into thinking, of purchasing debts, but as an elliptical expression (not untypical of this poet's

---

[74] Traders and Saturn + Moon: Valens, I 19.6, Περὶ κράσ. 41; Saturn + Jupiter: Valens, IV 20.8; Saturn + Jupiter + Moon: Valens, I 20.2, App. X 5 and XI 37; all planets + Moon: Valens, II 21.6; wet signs: Paul, p. 61.1–5; Firmicus, 8.20.10 (Argo); 8.30.5 (Pisces).

[75] M. Kaser, *Das römische Privatrecht, i: Das altrömische, das vorklassische und klassische Recht* (Munich, 1971), 651–2 and ii: *Die nachklassischen Entwicklungen* (1975), 607; R. Zimmermann, *The Law of Obligations: Roman Foundations of the Civilian Tradition* (Oxford, 1996), 60; T. Rüfner, 'Money in the Roman Law Texts', in D. Fox and W. Ernst (eds.), *Money in Western Legal Tradition: Middle Ages to Bretton Woods* (Oxford, 2016), 93–109, at 94, 98. Thanks to Georgy Kantor for these references.

[76] Cf. Philogelos, 50 ναυκλήρῳ χρεώστῃ; *OCD*[4] s.v. maritime loans, P. C. Millett, and online, D. W. Rathbone; Plut. *Cat. Maj.* 21.6–7, with commentary in E. Gabba, 'Riflessioni antiche e moderne sulle attività commerciali a Roma nei secoli II et I a.C.', in J. H. D'Arms and E. C. Kopff (eds.), *The Seaborne Commerce of Ancient Rome: Studies in Archaeology and History* (Rome, 1980), 91–102, at 92.

'Signs of Birth' 561

imprecision) for goods which the merchant has purchased and for which he is in debt (but by selling which he makes money).

136 ἥμενος: given the roving and perilous life of the merchant,[77] neither Axtius' nor Koechly's restoration is ideal, but ἥμενος is the right word for being embarked on a ship (*Od.* 17.161).

136-7 ἐργασίην τε...συστήσεται: this is a little knot of reworked astrological prose words—ἐργασία, σύστασις (alliance, 'networks'), and κοινωνίαι (cooperative ventures). κοινωνίαι are an astrological topos, often cheek-by-jowl with trade, not only in Ptol. 2.3.41 and 44 διόπερ οὗτοι κοινωνικοί τε καὶ ἐμπορικοὶ τυγχάνουσι, but in independent contexts.[78] Koechly did not know these passages, but he did, when giving reasons for emending πάντων to πολλῶν (many take part but hardly 'all'), adduce Plut. *Cat. Maj.* 21.6-7, on Cato's system of marine loans, where consortia were formed whose members shared in the risks of a voyage. For having a share in a ship's cargo, see also Philostratus, *Vit. Ap.* 3.24.1 (there, a consortium of four).

137-8 These insecure unions are not found in the comparanda. But astrology, which in general is obsessed with ἀκαταστασία (i. 168; n. on 3.81), and often connects it to marriage and the family (γάμος in Π.σ.α. p. 182.28, Θ p. 164.19), does attach it to character-types who are otherwise bright and versatile (e.g. Valens, II 38.27) and economically successful (Περὶ σχημ. 79, Περὶ κράσ. 138, 200). In particular, a wandering life joins with unstable marriages in Hephaestion, i. 25.27-26.1 καὶ δι' ὑγρῶν τὸ ζῆν ἔχων, ἀκαταστατήσει δὲ πρὸς γυναῖκα ἢ καὶ βραδυγαμήσει; in Camaterus, *Introd.* 1376, an individual who spends time away from home (πολλὰ ξενιτευόμενος) is also unstable with regard to his family (πλὴν ἔσται ἀκατάστατος πρὸς γυναῖκα καὶ τέκνοις...). See also Firmicus, 5.2.14 (of those who live from watery professions or trade)...*ab omni societatis officio separatos.*

Koechly saw that ἐν θαλάμῳ...ἔν τε γυναιξίν referred to two different kinds of union—legitimate and extra marital. This insight is confirmed by texts he could not have known, which also make it likely that the poet is paraphrasing some piece of astrological jargon involving part of γάμος and perhaps πρός (Περὶ σχημ. 79, Περὶ κράσ. 138), περί (Valens, II 38.27, Περὶ κράσ. 200; 'Heliodorus' on Paul, p. 68.28-9, Θ p. 158.10), ἐν (Περὶ σχημ. 58, Περὶ κράσ. 201), or εἰς (Hephaestion, i. 210.29). νυμφεῖα, accordingly, are 'marriages' (see

---

[77] TLL s.v. *mercator*, 788.81-3; Nisbet and Hubbard on Hor. *Od.* 3.24.40 and further references.
[78] e.g. Hephaestion, i. 217.24-5 ἐξ ἐμπορικῶν ἢ κοινωνικῶν πραγμάτων ὠφελοῦνται, 238.12-13 τὸ δὲ ε' (sc. dodecatemories of Scorpio) περὶ ὁμονοίας ἢ πλοῦ ἢ κοινῶν πραγμάτων, 239.11-12 τὸ δὲ ε' (sc. dodecatemories of Aquarius), περὶ κοινωνίας ἢ καθύγρων πραγμάτων, CCAG xi/2. 158.25 κοινωνίας ποιεῖν, πλέειν τε καὶ ἀποδημεῖν, CCAG iv. 143.33-4...ἐμπορεύεσθαι, γαμεῖν, κοινωνεῖν.

562   *Commentary on Book Four*

Davies on Soph. *Tr.* 6 ff. and refs.). The intimate little detail ἐν θαλάμῳ, restored by Koechly, is Homeric, though obviously not confined to him; four of its five uses in the *Iliad* refer to that arch-exponent of stable marriage, Paris.

139–45

Mercury in its own houses, Saturn in aspect.

Protasis. This is a lightly-realised Π- chart for Mercury as Ruler of πρᾶξις aspected by Saturn. There is a similar chart in 6.487–90. M[a] and M[b] differ slightly: in M[b], Mercury is in its own houses; in M[a], Saturn is in his own houses or terms. It seems that M[b] has only slightly added to the Π- chart in Ptolemy/Θ, while M[a], affiliated to *Lib. Herm.*, has introduced the additional factor of terms, though in the latter Mercury is in Saturn's.

Apodosis. Of the outcomes listed by Ptolemy/Θ, the logic that connects stewards and dream interpreters seems to be mediation (those who act as intermediaries for others), though dreaming one's own dreams and undergoing *enthousiasmos* are solipsistic. M[a] and M[b] both pick up on property-managers and add lessees of other people's land, while, still adhering to the underlying logic, M[b] substitutes astrologers for dream interpreters and adds interpreters (one of the outcomes of Mercury alone in Ptol. 4.4.3). Ptolemy/Θ confirm Koechly's insight that line 141 does not belong here.

139 κατὰ κύκλα: padding (as is 4.454 κατὰ κύκλον, of Sagittarius). Plural otherwise only in Orph. 338 F 4 Bernabé κατὰ κύκλα χρόνοιο (on the cycle of reincarnations), but the singular is most like 2.394–5, of the zodiac circle (in Dion. Per. 595 of the tropic of Cancer).

140 (Κρόνοιο) κατ' αἰθέρα: like 2.1 (κόσμοιο) κατ' αἰθέρα (see ad loc.); also 239, cf. 509 κατ' αἰθέρος.

πελάζῃ: used in 4.249 of Saturn approaching the Moon (one would expect the Moon to be the subject of the technical term συνάπτειν), but of the Moon approaching Saturn in 4.409 = 1.334, and Mercury approaching Saturn and Jupiter in 4.426, where it takes the accusative.

144 The same motif as 6.489, but with the opposite emphasis: it looks as if with ἰδίων δὲ μάλιστα (*their own*, not another's), the poet was deliberately fencing with οὐκ ἰδίοισιν | μούνοισιν (p. 219). The effect is odd, if the logic is supposed to be about mediation. ἀλλοτρίων κτεάνων is taken via 6.358 from Hes. *Op.* 315 (where Perseus is being firmly steered off other people's covetable goods and adjured to work). Those goods are now among the very objects of the native's business. Perhaps this is opportunism, or perhaps it is the poet's joke, but the joke was already made by M[a].

145 The question is where to mark the presumed missing line. Besides after 144 (the whole line), other possibilities are after τεμεῖν or after καρπόν, for each of which K² proposed supplements. As De Stefani notes, νῶτα and γαίης are an appropriate collocation (Nonn. *D.* 1.107), as are γαίης and καρπόν (*HHom. Ap.* 365), but τεμεῖν and καρπόν are not (one would expect φέρειν). Perhaps any missing material elaborated on the idea of *geoponia* (the word used by 6.489), which all sources agree is the contribution of Saturn,[79] for whose connection with agriculture see p. 60.

146–52

Moon in harmonious aspect with Mercury, and Venus joined with Jupiter.

Protasis. This and its parallel chart at 6.520–5 are realisations of Mercury + Venus aspected by Jupiter, a *Π*- chart present in Θ p. 213.22–4, but not in Ptolemy. Both poets place the Moon and Mercury in favourable aspect, but only M^b retains the link with Jupiter. M^a, in turn, has added *synaphe* and Mercury's houses.

Apodosis. Both M^a and M^b have links with Θ:

(i) Both have workers in ivory, though only M^b has gold.

(ii) Θ's ζωγράφους find an immediate correspondence in 1.298 ζωγραφίης μεδέοντας. De Stefani's highly plausible correction ἐν γραφίδεσσιν ἀρίστους in 4.150 could then be seen as a periphrastic version of that, while in 6.525 the same word seems to denote the graving tool of a wax-worker (De Stefani himself referred to 1.298 but not to 6.525, perhaps not realising the close affiliation between the two charts).

(iii) 6.523 adds workers in marble (~ Θ p. 215.7 μαρμαροξύστας, and especially p. 216.7 μαρμαρίους, where Mercury, Jupiter, and the Moon are all in additional aspect to a basic configuration in which Venus is involved), while 4.151 has decorators/finishers of walls, i.e. of cornices and friezes(?). These two groups are themselves related to outcomes in Firmicus, 8.24.8 *architectus, structor, parietarius vel marmorarius* (with the ASC in 19° Virgo). For the group see Appendix II, II.5.iii.

As in 4.129–30, it seems possible that these types of artisan derive from a source which distinguished the effect of planets in different signs, which Θ's version has also lost. Support comes from 6.413–21, where four-footed signs produce hard labour including building, and terrestrial signs produce finer crafts including sculpture and ivory-carving. In that case, the ivory-carvers, workers

---

[79] e.g. Dorotheus, p. 373.23, Valens, App. II 3, Rhetorius, *CCAG* vii. 214.15, Apomasar, *De Myst.*, *CCAG* xi/1. 178.26.

in gold, and painters could be born under the latter, and builders under the former.[80]

146 ἑλικοδρόμος: i. 905 n. 22 (Eur. *Bacch.* 1067 is a restoration by Reiske). The corresponding line in 1.294 has ἑλικώπιδος, on which see note ad loc. and p. 275. Similar compounds in 4.224 ἑλικάστερον and 4.437 ἑλιξοπόρον; for the Moon's 'twisted' course, see further on 4.91.

ἄστατος ἀστήρ: see on 4.87 ἄστροιο Σεληναίης, and on the Moon's mobility, i. 891–3 and 4.91 n. on ἕλιξ. The cadence follows Hellenistic and imperial trends (Aratus, ἔσχατος ἀστήρ, Ap. Rhod. ἄκριας ἀστήρ; *Or. Sib.* 2.87 = ps.-Phoc. 27 ἄστατος ὄλβος); particularly similar, with double epithet, are *HOrph.* 74.5 πελαγοδρόμος ἄστατος ὁρμή; Nonn. D. 2.196 παλίνδρομος ἄστατος αἴγλη, and even 48.573 ὀρίδρομος ἄστατος Αὔρη.

147 σύμφωνον: meaning that it is in favourable aspect (6.107–8). As Ptol. 1.14.3 explains, the harmonious aspects are those of trine and sextile.

149 ῥεκτῆρας χρυσοῖο: this circumlocution for goldsmiths—a respectable profession—does duty for χρυσοχόος, a perhaps over-familiar prosaic term (Appendix II, II.8.vi.a). The previous occurrence of ῥεκτήρ, which recurs in 4.229, was in Hes. *Op.* 191 κακῶν ῥεκτῆρα; the word's adaptation to a manufacturing process appears unique to M[b].

149–50 Ἰνδογενοῦς ἐλέφαντος | ἐργοπόνους ~ Θ ἐλεφαντουργούς (App. II, II.8.viii). Valens, I 1.29, lists ivory-carving (ἐλεφαντουργίας) last in a series of luxuries presided over by Venus, though its rarity in this context (unlike, say, dyeing or perfumes) runs quite counter to its iconic status in the moralists' repertoire of luxury (R. T. White, '*Locus classicus*: Origin Brands in Roman Luxury Markets, c. 100 BC–c. AD 130' (Diss. London, 2017), 146–76). M[b] seeks to make up some lost ground. He recycles the trope—otherwise, it seems, only in Latin authors[81]—about ivory's Indian origins, irrespective of Africa's role in the trade (perhaps undetectable to Romans who knew only that it came through the same route, up the Red Sea to Berenice and Myos Hormos, as Indian goods); and he applies (coins?) an epithet with only two other attestations (*Or. Sib.* 11.62, and Joseph Genesius, 10th c.). Most -γενής adjectives apply to persons and mean 'born in' (as do the other two examples), but for the local origins of objects compare an oracle ap. Hdt. 7.140.2 συριηγενὲς ἅρμα διώκων, Euphorion, fr. 63.1 P. Πυληγενέεσσί τε νηυσίν; Philodemus, *AP* 11.44.4 = *Garland* 3305 χιογενῆ πρόποσιν. ἐργοπόνους is mostly[82] poetic as well, at least

---

[80] Cf. Θ p. 215.15 σκανδουλαρίους ποιεῖ ἢ τοιχοβάτας (born with malefics in four-footed signs).
[81] Cat. 64.48 Indo…dente; Hor. Od. 1.31.6 ebur Indicum; V. Aen. 12.67–8 Indum…ebur, cf. Georg. 1.57 India mittit ebur.
[82] Not entirely: Artemidorus, 1.79.3 ἀγαθὸν δὲ παντὶ χειροτέχνῃ καὶ ἐργοπόνῳ.

before Byzantine authors. In Nic. *Th.* 831 the workman is a fisherman, and there is a little cluster that refer to outdoor activities (see Jacques ad loc., adding Leonides of Alexandria, *AP* 11.9.3 = *FGE* xxxiv,[83] and apparently *IG* XII,1 779 (Lindos), of a *geoponos*). In imperial poetry the domain shifts to mainly handicrafts—stone-carving (Nonn. *D.* 17.65, 37.109); masonry (Paul Sil. *Descr. Sanct.* 719); brick-making (Theodorus Prodromus, *Epigrammata in Vetus et Novum Test., Exodus*, 39b); carpentry (Colluthus, *Rapt.* 195); metalworking (Hephaestus: Nonn. *D.* 3.133, 25.563, 30.66, 43.403, cf. *SEG* 31.1284, Pisidia; Christodorus, *AP* 2.1.316); general handicrafts (*AP* 4.3.120). Of Athena: *Inschriften von Milet*, vi. 3, 1142.16; Colluthus, *Rapt.* 195. See App. II, II.1, and for πόνος on 4.72.

150 γραφίδεσσιν: see p. 563, and on 6.525.

151-2 Given the refined arts of 149–50, one might interpret these, not just as builders of walls, but as those who decorate them in some way. θριγκῶν…κοσμήτας ought to be makers of decorative coping.[84] For the κανονισμῶν which are parallel to them (unless they simply repeat the sense with a different word, as LSJ seem to think), any number of technical terms are suggested by Vitruvius' discussion of the architecture of capitals (3.5.13), but the precise meaning is hidden behind a word which suggests the straight-edged tool of a builder or carpenter (κανών)[85] without giving anything more away (architraves, ἐπιστύλια, stand out as things that particularly need to be straight). Interestingly, Teucer has a category of natives who work with precisely such measuring tools (πάντας τοὺς περὶ σταθμία ἀσχολουμένους) along with housebuilders, carpenters, and sculptors (see additional note to 6.419, p. 1065). κανονισμός itself is not an absolute *hapax*, but does seem to be so in connection with building and construction, for its other attestations are either grammatical (= κανών in the sense of 'paradigm') or ecclesiastical ('regulation', as in 'canon law'). It recurs in 4.292, once again in connection with θριγκῶν (293), with builders of walls (291 τειχοδόμους), and with heavy labour (293 ἀεὶ καμάτοισι συνήθεις); the poet also has κανονίσματ᾽ in 4.191 for coffin-makers, i.e. a species of carpenter.

---

[83] ἀγροπόνοισι is printed, though Page admits there is nothing wrong with ἐργο-.

[84] For Firmicus' *parietarius*, see p. 53. Manilius, 5.288–9 (under Spica) has a man who sculpts panelled ceilings (*laquearia*) in temples. I do not find any astrological frieze-painters, who might be expected to be indicated by something derived from *zo(o)phorus*, Vitruvius' word for a frieze.

[85] On the history of the word, Bremmer 2010, 358–9. Roman builders' tools (W. Gaitzsch, 'Werkzeuge und Geräte in der römischen Kaiserzeit: Eine Übersicht', *ANRW* II 12.3, 170–204) are illustrated on funerary plaques (Tran 2013, 233). For one which includes various instruments for producing straight edges, verticals, and right-angles, see R. Cohon, 'Tools of the Trade: A Rare, Ancient Roman Builder's Funerary Plaque', *Antike Kunst*, 53 (2010), 94–100: they include a *regula*, for which κανών would be the Greek equivalent; another including a *regula* in R. B. Ulrich, *Roman Woodworking* (Yale, 2007), 14 fig. 3.1.

εὐτοίχων: very rare (otherwise only 4.292 and Σ Pind. P. 2.107, glossing εὐστεφάνων (ἀγυιᾶν)), but presumably suggested in the vicinity of θριγκοί by the connection of -τοίχ- with θριγκός elsewhere (Od. 7.86–7, 17.267 τοίχῳ καὶ θριγκοῖσι, Ap. Rhod. 3.216).

152 κοσμήτας: LSJ II: 'adorner' (less common than the political/administrative/legislative senses).

μάλα τοι πεπονημένα τεχνάζοντας: presumably fine or exquisite, rather than effortful, labour (see on 4.72). This recalls the rhythm of Il. 23.543 μάλα τοι κεχολώσομαι (same *sedes*), Op. 799 μάλα τοι τετελεσμένον, while the cadence, which recurs at 4.321 μεμελημένα δαιδάλλοντας (see ad loc.) and 518 νενεφωμένα βουλεύοντες, goes back to Od. 11.41 βεβροτωμένα τεύχε᾽ ἔχοντες, as is even more apparent from the closer equivalent at 4.524 μεμετρημένα πράγματ᾽ ἔχοντας.

153–6

Mars beneath rays of both luminaries. This is a σίνος chart nested within the series on πρᾶξις. The general logic is that the luminaries represent eyes and are vulnerable to malefics. Many charts have variations on this situation, though when they specify the damage is usually done by one malefic *per* luminary. This passage shares with 6.548–9 the peculiarity that a single malefic, Mars, damages both, and its formulation, that Mars is 'beneath' the Sun and Moon, is also compatible with the location in the earlier passage of Mars in a 'following' sign (ἐπίοντι), in other words, on the *epanaphora* of the luminary.[86] The alternative meaning is that it is ὕπαυγος (within 15° of the Sun and thus invisible beneath its rays),[87] which fits well with the mention of rays but less well where the Moon is involved too.

154 νέρθε: of the eleven Homeric occurrences of νέρθε(ν), all are adverbial except Il. 14.204 γαίης νέρθε and Od. 11.302 νέρθεν γῆς, though there are more instances of prepositional ἔνερθε(ν), before or after the noun. There is a strong sense in these (and other) examples of 'underneathness', which would be suitable for either interpretation of what is meant by 'beneath'.

λοχευομένοισι βροτοῖσιν: not 'when mortals are giving birth', but 'when mortals are being born'. For the passive, see on 4.87.

155–6 This couplet distinguishes different sorts of eye damage. Astrology perpetuates its own form of the medical distinction between total (ἀμαύρωσις)

---

[86] Malefics on the *epanaphora* of luminaries: Θ p. 187.17–18; Firmicus, 6.30.19, 7.8.1, 6. Similar situations include malefics eastern with respect to the Sun and western with respect to the Moon (Ptol. 3.13.9) and malefics enclosed by, or enclosing, the luminaries (Θ p. 187.2–5).

[87] Heilen 2015, 742, 842, 1084 n. 2746.

'Signs of Birth' 567

and partial (ἀμβλυωπία) loss of sight (J. Hirschberg, *Geschichte der Augenheilkunde*, i: *Geschichte der Augenheilkunde im Alterthum* (Berlin, 1899), 92–7), and overlays onto that its own distinction between acute injury (Martian) and occlusion (usually the fault of Saturn).[88] Only Mars is mentioned here, but he apparently causes both types of impairment in Firmicus, 4.19.34. There are also sources which enumerate effects produced by signs with a sting or a weapon,[89] and others produced by signs with a nebula.[90] Maybe mention of signs has been suppressed here; that is unprovable. But in any case Koechly's emendation of the transmitted κείνοισι to κενεοῖσι in 156 is questionable. Empty eye-sockets[91] might look contextually appropriate, but there is nothing like this in other σίνος charts about damaged vision. κείνοισι would therefore seem sound, corresponding to the deictics in 381 and 416 (at 612 κείνοισι is anaphoric).

155 The line epicises πήρωσιν, or rather πηρώσεις (sing. only in Valens, II 41.36; Camaterus, *Intr.* 1293), with a Homeric prepositional phrase in place of the genitive (e.g. Ptol. 3.13.7 πηρώσεις γὰρ ὄψεως) and a Homeric epithet of miseritude.

156 ἀμβλυόεσσαν ὀμίχλην: a poetic rendering of ἀμβλυωπία, a dulling of vision. It is an authentic medical term, which appears from the Hippocratic corpus onwards (Hirschberg, 92–3). Ancient medical writers distinguish it from ἀμαύρωσις (blurred as opposed to darkened vision).[92] The massive and untreatable problem that vision loss must have presented in the ancient world elicits from astrology a wide vocabulary for eye conditions, of which a good example is Θ p. 187.28–9 ὑποχύσεως[93] ἢ ψύξεως ἢ γλαυκώσεως ἢ ῥεύματος.[94]

---

[88] Firmicus, 7.20.2; Θ p. 187.27–9. A schematised version of plausible sources of vision loss in ancient society: L. Trentin, 'Exploring Visual Impairment in Ancient Rome', in Laes et al., 89–114, esp. 94–106.

[89] Scorpio: Valens, II 37.15 ἀμαυρώσεις, πηρώσεις, ἐπισκιασμούς ~ Teucer, CCAG vii. 206.8 ἀμαυρώσεις, ἐπισκιασμούς; Sagittarius: Valens, II 37.16 ἐπισκιαζόμενοι ἢ ὀφθαλμοπόνοι ἢ πηρώσεις ~ Teucer, CCAG vii. 207.23–4 ὀφθαλμῶν πόνους ἢ πηρώσεις; Capricorn: Valens, II 37.17 ἀμαυρώσεις, πηρώσεις ~ Teucer, CCAG vii. 209.7 ἀμαυρώσεις καὶ πηρώσεις.

[90] Cancer, home of Praesepe: Valens, II 37.10 πηρώσεις διὰ τὸ νεφέλιον ~ Teucer, CCAG vii. 200.16 ἀμαυρώσεις διὰ τὸ νεφέλιον.

[91] Pollux, *Onom.* 2.62 ῥηθείη δ' ἂν τοὺς ὀφθαλμοὺς ἐξορύττειν, σβεννύναι, κενοῦν…; Ap. Rhod. 2.254–5 κενεὰς…γλήνας; AP 2.1.336 κενεοῖς…ὄμμασιν.

[92] So too Thessalus, *De virtutibus herbarum* (e cod. Monac. 542), 1.11.4/Harpocration, CCAG viii/3. 149.12 τὰς ἀμβλυωπίας καὶ τὰς ἐπισκοτήσεις.

[93] Cataract, Latin *suffusio* (Celsus, *Med.* 6.6.35); S. Ry Andersen, *The Eye and its Diseases in Antiquity: A Compilation Based on Finds from Ancient Times* (Copenhagen, 1994), 77–8.

[94] Perhaps what Romans call *lippitudo*; in Celsus, *Med.* 6.6.1, characterised by *crassa pituita*. B. W. Fortson, 'Bleary Eyes and Ladles of Clay: Two Liquid Sabellicisms in Latin', *Glotta*, 84 (2008), 52–71, at 52–9, argues that the basic meaning of *lip-* is not 'fatty', but 'liquid'; that works well if ῥεῦμα is a symptom.

These are labels for symptoms or groups of symptoms, not diagnostic terms, so that ἀμβλυωπία, which is the modern medical term for lazy-eye syndrome—generally a childhood condition—denotes, for ancient authors, the declining vision of old age.[95] Yet it is usually Saturn, or both malefics together, especially when they attack the luminaries, that cause eye disease like ἀμβλυωπία,[96] as opposed to acute injury; a rare exception is Π.σ.α. p. 183.5–8, where the Moon leaving Mars (not Saturn) ἀμβλυωπίαν ἀποτελεῖ καὶ πολλοῖς κακοῖς περιβάλλει καὶ ἐπὶ τέλει ἀμαυροῖ τὴν ὄψιν.[97]

157–60

Mercury in its own houses. An instantiation of Mercury ruling πρᾶξις. There is no parallel in book 6. Θ p. 210.26, but not Ptolemy, mentions doctors among the outcomes, and Ptol. 4.4.3, but not Θ, mentions λογιστάς.

158 Doctors are mentioned otherwise only in 1.181–2. Among related categories such as surgeons, druggists, and singers of charms, there is only one other passage that mentions root-cutters, charm-singers, and snake-charmers (5.183–8). Why such underrepresentation in comparison to other astrology (Appendix II, V.3.i), where they are usually categorised, as here, among Mercurial (i.e. intellectual) disciplines, especially given that doctors and astrologers could be the same people (*CCAG* xii. 168.2 Ἰητὴρ ὢν ἀστρολόγος; p. 967)? The line is rounded off with an *Ersatz* epic cadence that employs an epithet that is, in practice, first attested in tragedy (esp. Soph. *Tr.* 1208–9 παιώνιον καὶ…ἰατῆρα).

159 πανάκειαν: when not used metaphorically (e.g. ps.-Longin. *Subl.* 38.5 and Philo, *Quod det.* 123), this is used mainly as marketing ploy for drugs,[98] which might suggest, without naming, the druggists (φαρμακοποιοί) who feature in other astrology (Appendix II, V.3.iii).

160 λογιστονόμοισιν…ἔργοις: padding for λογιστάς, as in Ptolemy, where Robbins renders 'calculators'; better, accountants. They are not particularly frequent in astrology and are mentioned in connection with administrators,

---

[95] Hippocr. *Aph.* 3.31; cf. Celsus, *Med.* 6.6.32. For Valens, App. XXII, 10, it is caused, not by the Sun, but by the inherent weakness of the eyes.
[96] Saturn in Θ p. 187.28–9; Ptol. 3.13.9 ἀπογλαυκώσεις; Saturn and Moon in Firmicus, 4.19.7 and 7.8.4, *suffusiones*. In Dorotheus, p. 376.18–19/Θ p. 187.17–18, malefics on the *epanaphora* of luminaries ὀφθαλμοὺς ἀδικοῦσιν ἢ ἀμβλυωπίαν ποιοῦσιν.
[97] ἀμβλυωπία is also produced by the Full Moon in degrees of certain signs (Dorotheus, p. 376.28/Θ p. 187.26; Epit. IIIb, *CCAG* vii. 111.23 γλαυκώσεις, ῥεύματα, ἀμβλυωπίας).
[98] Applied to the root of Chiron (Nic. *Ther.* 508) and to other drugs in Galen, *De compositione medicamentorum secundum locos* (xiii. Kühn), *passim*.

sometimes royal officials, and people who occupy 'intelligent' professions, always Mercurial (Appendix II, iv.1.viii).

What do these people do? The oldest and among the best-known λογισταί were in classical Athens (Schultheß, RE s.v. λογισταί). Their successors continue to audit accounts, and there are named λογισταί of a city in the first century BC (BGU vi. 1235, 75 BC or 46 BC, a letter from the λογιστής of Heracleopolis to the λογιστής of Philadelphia concerning a payment). There are also private auditors.[99] One must assume that the astrological λογισταί are not the very important extraordinary appointees, some of them of consular rank, known in Latin as *curatores civitatis*, attested perhaps from the reign of Trajan, certainly from the later second century, and in fourth-century Egypt, who seem to have been tasked with dealing with problems of the administration of public property.[100]

Ptolemy and Θ also mention—still in Mercurial, 'intelligent' connections— the λογιστήρια which are the physical places where accounts are kept and documents deposited, or the boards of officials charged with this function:[101] Ptol. 4.4.6 δικολόγους, λογιστηρίων προισταμένους, ἐν δημοσίοις ἀσχολουμένους... (cf. Θ p. 213.15–16); Θ p. 157.24–5 ἐπὶ λογιστηρίων ἢ τραπεζῶν ἢ ἀποθηκῶν ἢ γραμμάτων ἢ ἐμποριῶν τασσομένους; p. 174.5–6 πραγματικοὺς ἢ ἐπὶ λογιστ- ηρίων θεωρουμένους. Papyri very often mention the ἐκλογισταί who work, one assigned to each nome, in the central bureau in Alexandria,[102] but astrology does not.

161–4

Jupiter aspects Mercury. Although this is appended to the τέχναι charts, and Koechly treats it as part of the same sequence, it does not reflect the Ptolemaic

---

[99] The λογισταί in the private litigation of Drusilla (M. *Chr.* 88 col. iv l. 12, 2nd c., Alexandria) are associated with the λογοθέται or auditors (P. M. Meyer, 'Papyrus Cattaoui: Kommentar', *APF* 3 (1906), 67–105, at 100–1) appointed by the στρατηγός to look into the moneys involved. Cumont, 116 n. 4 infers the existence of λογισταί in temples as well.

[100] List of known λογισταί in P.Oxy. LIV Appendix 1, p. 223; for Oxyrhynchus, see A. Bowman, 'Oxyrhynchus in the Early Fourth Century: "Municipalization" and Prosperity', *BASP* 45 (2008), 31–40 (the earliest here is attested in AD 303); and for Egypt also K. Maresch, 'Von Gau zur Civitas: Verwaltungsreformen in Ägypten zur Zeit der Ersten Tetrarchie im Speigel der Papyri', in R. Haensch, J. Heinrichs (eds.), *Herrschen und Verwalten: Der Alltag der römischen Administration in der Höhen Kaiserzeit* (Cologne, 2007), 427–37, at 434–7.

[101] Cumont, 71 n. 1; Preisigke, *RE* s.v. λογιστήριον; P. Fröhlich, 'Logistèrion: À propos d'une inscription de Kymè récemment publiée', *REG* 71 (2004), 59–81, at 71–9; B. Kramer, 'Objektschütz für das Logisterion in Herakleopolis', *ZPE* 200 (2016), 329–35, at 330–1.

[102] S. LeRoy Wallace, *Taxation in Egypt from Augustus to Diocletian* (Princeton, 1938), 32–3; F. A. J. Hoogendijk, 'Amtliche Korrespondenz zwischen Dorfschreiber und *Eklogistes*', in A. J. B. Sirks and K. A. Worp (eds.), *Papyri in Memory of P. J. Sijpesteijn* (Oakville, Conn., 2007), 128–39, at 129 and 132 (P. Sijp. 20); also Philo, *Plant.* 57 οἱ ταχθέντες τῶν φόρων ἐκλογισταί.

account of Mercury as Ruler of πρᾶξις witnessed by Jupiter (4.4.3; Θ p. 211.1–2). Of its two elements, wandering and questionable relations with the opposite sex, the first is paralleled for the aspects of Jupiter and Mercury in 3.321–2 (and in none of the comparanda that treat each aspect separately). The other motif, unworthy women, finds parallels in sources that reflect Dorotheus (nn. on 4.163–4 and 164). All involve Venus being injured by a malefic—precisely what one would expect to produce philanderers. The rationale in the present passage is much less obvious. Even if one can understand how Mercury produces wanderers (= quick off the mark) it is not easy to see why in combination with stately Jupiter it arouses lust for déclassé women.

161 προσμάρτυρα φέγγεα: prose astrology has προσμαρτυρεῖν. On the three occasions M^b uses προσμάρτυρ- it means 'witness in addition': here, Jupiter in addition to Mercury (the subject of 157–60), in 176 Saturn in addition to Jupiter and Mercury, and in 384 Venus in addition to Saturn and the Moon.

162 πουλυπλανεῖς: see on 4.91.

163–4 For the connection between a roving lifestyle and unstable relations with the opposite sex, see on 4.137–8. Without the evidence of Περὶ κράσ. 28 ἀνάξια λέκτρα γυναικῶν (Saturn in conjunction with Venus), one would have reckoned λέκτρα γυναικῶν with other overlaps between the diction of M^a (2.236 and 3.84) and M^b, but we can now see that, with ἀνάξια in 164, M^b is echoing the whole phrase. That adds some evidence for Dorotheus' influence on M^b (p. 218; for Dorotheus as the source of the traces of verse in Περὶ κράσεως see i. 679). One wonders, in turn, how many more of the shared words and phrases in M^a and M^b are owing to this common source.

164 θηρήσειν: for the theft metaphor see on 4.56.[103] Notably, in connection with the apparent echo of Dorotheus just noticed, it also occurs in Περὶ σχημ. 17 οἱ τοιοῦτοι δὲ πολλῶν γυναικῶν λέχη θηρῶσιν, ἤτοι μοιχοὶ γίνονται and Περὶ κράσ. 172 πολλῶν γυναικῶν λέχη θηρῶντας (Mars in trine with Venus). The first of these also shares with the present passage the connection between philandering and roving (the natives are ἐμπόρους), while the philanderers in 5.290 οὐχὶ μόνον ζώων θηρήτορες, ἀλλὰ γυναικῶν (Jupiter in the houses of Venus) again live overseas (5.293).

παρὰ κῦδος: apparently this poet's deliberately off-beat equivalent for what M^a would have labelled ἀεικές (i. 367).

---

[103] Specifically with this verb: Clem. Al. Paed. 3.11.75.1 τὰς παριούσας θηρώμενοι γυναῖκας; with infin., Eur. Hel. 63 θηρᾶι γαμεῖν με; also of women pursuing men (Xen. Mem. 1.2.24; Philostr. Vit. Apoll. 4.25.3; Heraclitus, Incred. 20).

'Signs of Birth' 571

θηλυμανοῦντας: parts of θηλυμανής seem to begin in Hellenistic epigram (Meleager, *AP* 9.16.2 = *HE* 4387; G.-P. ad loc.) and infiltrate imperial poetry, (becoming very common in Byzantine prose). The verb is much rarer (Philo, *Abr.* 135 οὐ γὰρ μόνον θηλυμανοῦντες ἀλλοτρίους γάμους διέφθειρον, and of animals in Julian, *Comm. in Job.* p. 225.7 Hagedorn, ps.-Clem. *Recogn.* 9.20), but what is interesting is the presence of θηλυμανίαν (among the effects of badly-placed Venus) in Περὶ κράσ. 193. This does not demonstrably reflect Dorotheus, however, because it occurs in the general characterisation of the planet before the list of aspects, which *does*.

4.165–9 Transition

Not all is well here. Koechly 1851, xliv thought it would make more sense at the conclusion of the section on the *kentra*, in place of the obviously inept 107–8. The lesser problem with that is that not even 14–106 has *restricted* itself to the ASC, the greater that 110–38 continue to discuss *kentra* (including but not restricted to the ASC). Lopilato shares the view that 165 rounds off the section that began at 14 and extended at least as far as 138, but does not want to move it from its present place. My own preference would be for analysing the structure on the basis of sources; in that case, 110–20 (involving the ASC) could be taken as still belonging to 14–106, with 4.121 beginning the long run of Πρᾶξις/τέχναι material that has affinities with Θ and/or Ptolemy. That does not, however, make the argument for shifting this transition to after 120. In the first place, 4.121 (for all its new source) has been made to segue from the previous item. In the second, and more importantly, this notice *does* demonstrably stand at a transition, even if it is not one to which the wording can obviously be made to refer. For it is precisely at this point that the miscellaneous charts on Πρᾶξις (Θ ch. 83) end, and the sequence affiliated to the Περὶ τεχνῶν begins (170–449), and that seems to be acknowledged in 168 by τέχναι τε (p. 184). A transition of some sort is appropriate here, even if the ὡράων σκεπτήρια in no way captures what has come before (p. 183).

165 Ταῦτα μὲν ὡράων σκεπτήρια: the noun is a *hapax*. LSJ renders σκεπτήρια = τεκμήρια; Lopilato 'tokens derived from the Ascendants', and it is difficult to disagree—even though it is an inaccurate description of the previous section, for the ASC is certainly not a connecting thread throughout 110–65.

165–8 These lines seems to introduce two different kinds of thing: (i) technical categories from astrology: ἀκτινηβολίας, terms, and 'dodecatemories', and (ii) types of chart, among which are mentioned birth (corresponding to the first section of book 6) and τέχναι (170–346).

There are certain difficulties with both. In the first place, ἀκτινηβολίας does not mean ray-casting in the technical sense; this is imprecise terminology (p. 249). In the second, birth and τέχναι seem a strange combination. They do not make particular sense together, unless the original intention was to have a *kentrothesia* followed by charts dealing with those two *kentra* which had obvious specialisms (ASC = birth; MC = τέχναι), but that is drastically to oversimplify the factors that operate on both kinds of outcome. There are no further break-offs between now and the end of the poem, and if we are to take 165–end as a single section it is certainly characterised by much more than 'birth' and τέχναι (i.e. there is also material on harms, nurture and slavery, parents, and the effect of gender on luminaries). Τέχναι marries up very nicely with the heading of the section in Θ to which 170–346 starts to run parallel. But 'birth' (on my reckoning) applies only to 450–65 (pp. 184–5). This seems to compromise the integrity of this section (if 165–end can be described as that).

On the other hand, if one looks more closely at the distribution of the three technical terms that this *incipit* singles out, a coherence starts to emerge that was not apparent before. In the first place, 'dodecatemories' are mentioned in 209, 227, 250, 298, 336 (i.e. all τέχναι charts), and only here in the corpus. Terms are mentioned in 172, 177, 182, 190, 195, 202, 265, 334, 327(?), 363 (i.e. mostly τέχναι charts and a couple of harms). Both, in other words, are restricted to the first half of the section (165–365), where there is a marked break between what have been exclusively τέχναι and σίνος charts and the much more miscellaneous material that follows. With ἀκτινηβολία it is not so clear-cut. But *almost all* of the charts in 165–365 either use a verb of striking (βάλλειν; αἰγλοβολεῖν, αἰθροβολεῖν, ἀκροβολεῖν, πυρσοβολεῖν, φεγγοβολεῖν; βολαυγεῖν; or ἀκτινηβολίη itself), or mention rays (usually ἀκτίς, though note also 230 λαμπάς and 240 σελάγισμα), and generally have both.[104] This section is very largely composed of τέχναι charts, but the two σίνος charts at the end conform to the same pattern. Outside this section, the great majority of charts, unless they themselves are τέχνη-themed, turn out not to have such a conjuncture (see p. 250).

Composed entirely of τέχναι and σίνος charts, there is, then, a substantial coherence to 4.170–365, which I now treat as a section. It is not clear why the poet flags it up with 'birth and τέχναι' rather than 'τέχναι and harms', but he is strongly inclined to refer to the casting of rays, to terms, and to degrees in this connection; indeed, he never mentions terms or degrees anywhere else. Has a

---

[104] 'Striking' and rays: 180–1, 188, 201, 207, 214, 218, 224–5, 230 (λαμπάς), 240 (σελάγισμα), 263–4, 272, 347–8, 354. Rays (with no striking): 249. The only charts that lack either are 193–5, 294–8, and 362, i.e. all σίνος charts or at least charts with σίνος-like characteristics. NB here I include only 'primary' charts rather than 'secondary' ones, i.e. ones that piggy-back on something previously mentioned ('and when in addition to this *x*…'); these cannot be relied upon to refer to either striking or rays.

'Signs of Birth'

section division has fallen out between 365 and 366? Or are the charts that follow 365 secondary additions to an original 'core'?

166 ἀκτινηβολίας: see pp. 248–50.

αἴθωπὰ κέλευθα: the phrase remodels Iliadic λαιψηρὰ κέλευθα. The epithet αἰθωπός is unique. In Apollonius, *Lex. Hom.* 13.30 αἴθωπα οἶνον is for αἴθοπα οἶνον from αἶθοψ.

167–8 δωδεκατημορίων...Ζωδιακήν: a long-winded promise to treat the zodiac. The present sentence is to be translated 'the circular zodiac [consisting] of the twelve parts of stars', or perhaps even 'the circular zodiac [consisting] of stars in twelve parts' (taking δωδεκατημορίων as an adjective with ἄστρων; Hübner 2005, 193, prefers the adjectival construction; see p. 247). Perhaps the poet singles out the zodiac because the signs do have some explanatory value in what follows (and precedes), and the poet likes naming them (p. 240). But it is rather puzzling that they are thus singled out when indications are that the signs have been demoted from the more important causal role that they play in Θ's version, and perhaps still more in a lost original (pp. 240–1).

κυκλόεσσαν...Ζωδιακήν varies Ζωδιακὸς κύκλος; as LSJ note, ὁδός is to be understood, which explains the feminine, and is in keeping with M^b's obsession with words for path. The epithet is new in Soph. *OT* 162 (a circular agora), and otherwise only Anyte, *AP* 7.232.4 = *Garland* 749 κυκλόεσσαν ἴτυν.

There is some interest in the verb M^b uses for his undertaking. The infinitive ἐνισπεῖν is very common, but in particular occurs in a couple of passages where an author is discussing what he is (or is not) able to say: in *Th.* 369, Hesiod was unable to name all the rivers, but Aratus, 460–1, who feels himself inadequate for dealing with the planets, does propose to deal with the circles of the fixed stars. Martin has a complex note on 461 ἀπλανέων τά τε κύκλα τά τ' αἰθέρι σήματ' ἐνισπεῖν (where the question is whether these are the circles run through by the stars in daily motion, or the ones which mark the annual path of the Sun, i.e. the tropics, equator, and ecliptic). In echoing Aratus' ἐνισπεῖν, M^b, whose own special interest is in the ecliptic, i.e. the zodiac, is perhaps supporting the second interpretation (ἀπλανέων τά τε κύκλα ~ κυκλόεσσαν...Ζωδιακήν). In that case his own ἄστρων, otherwise redundant, answers to Aratus' σήματα, the stars that are *on* this circle.

169 κλωστὴν...πορείην: as a whole the expression is typically foggy (it is less that the γενεαί and τέχναι 'fulfil' a fated path, and more that a man fulfils his destiny by following that path). The poet applies one of his favourite 'path' words (4.6 n.; 380) to life itself (4.551 n.; also John of Gaza, *Descr.* 198 βιότοιο πορείη), and gives it an epithet which is usually used of literal threads or fabrics (often but not entirely in prose: see Benaissa on Dionysius, fr. 12.2 κλωστοῖο λινοῦ). Here of course the putative connection is with Clotho.

4.170–end Γενεαί and τέχναι

There is a certain amount of method in the madness here. 4.170–449 constitutes the long sequence that runs parallel to Θ pp. 214.9–217.7, with interpolations. 4.491–507 contains a group of charts involving the ASC; 4.508–36 another self-contained section on luminaries in gendered signs; and 4.560–92 another group of oppositions across *kentra*.

4.170–346 Sequence of Mainly τ- Charts

170–5 + 176–9

Mercury and Jupiter aspect Mars, or are in his terms; and with Saturn aspecting in his own terms. The set-up of M^b is all but identical with that of Θ p. 214.9–10 + 12–13. The only difference is that with the additional presence of Saturn in Θ the natives are no longer uncrowned athletes: they are not athletes at all.

The scenario in 6.511–14 + 515–17 is different, but both produce athletes, with a contrast between athletes crowned (with the additional presence of Venus in M^a)[105] and uncrowned (with the additional presence of Saturn in both cases). M^a lacks the trainers of 4.179, while M^b lacks the wanderings that the failures undertake in 6.516. For the basic pattern—an initial situation which is then modified by further factors, for weal (victory), woe (defeat or a lesser type of activity), or both, see also on 3.346–58.

170 Πρῶτα μὲν οὖν: a strong beginning, the rhetoric of order; and indeed, whatever its logic, the forthcoming section does adhere to the sequence found in Θ ch. 84. Following *Od.* 22.448, which is succeeded by 452 αὐτὰρ ἔπειτα, some other examples of this collocation, whether in catalogues or narrative, enhance the itemisation (Orph. *Lith.* 699...703 Δεύτερον αὖτ᾽, 708 Αὐτὰρ ἔπειτα, a list of ritual instructions; *Or. Sib.* 8.459–60 πρῶτα μὲν οὖν...δεύτερα, narrative of the Annunciation). More like this passage, Archestratus, *SH* 135.1, seems to place it at the head of a macro-section (no further itemisation follows).

φανερὸς θεός: this boldly formulated claim is, it seems, one of the points in the poem where the influence of the *Timaeus* (pp. 180–1; n. on 4.625–6) becomes clearest; further in the background are generalised claims that the stars (collectively) are divine beings,[106] and the equation of planets with gods which is implicit in the shortening of the name 'star of *x*' to just *x* (Cumont

---

[105] Venus also produces victors in Θ p. 154.1 (in fifth place), and crowned athletes in Ptol. 4.4.4 (as Ruler of πρᾶξις with the additional aspect of Jupiter).
[106] Ps.-Plat. *Epin.* 981 E, 983 E; Cic. *Nat. Deor.* 2.42 (= Arist. fr. 23 Rose), 44 (= Arist. fr. 24 Rose).

1935, 35-7). Reference to a planet as ὁ θεός is occasional astrological usage (analeptic in Valens, as here it is parenthetical),[107] while the epithet[108] is a more pointed version of Plato's indirect and rather periphrastic reference to the stars as manifest gods (*Tim.* 41 A ἐπεὶ δ' οὖν πάντες ὅσοι τε περιπολοῦσιν φανερῶς καὶ ὅσοι φαίνονται καθ' ὅσον ἂν ἐθέλωσιν θεοί).[109]

171-2 βλέπῃ...ὀφθῇ: two singular verbs with plural subject: cf. K.-G. i. 80 (verb accords with the first of a series of singular subjects, so that in practice the others are treated as subordinate). See also on 4.598, where the verb, in first position, accords with the closest subject and disregards the rest. For βλέπειν, the simplex unique here in the corpus, see Prévot, 258-63 (regularly constructed with a preposition, implying a deliberate act of turning one's gaze upon a subject).

171 βλέπῃ: as Koechly noted, one could have left transmitted βάλῃ, correcting to φαέθοντα σελασμόν at line-end. That might have had the advantage of retaining the notion of ἀκτινοβολία, but the resulting construction (casting its light at the rays of Mars) would have been odd.

σελασμῷ: see on 4.36.

172 κατ' οἰκείων ὁρίων: see on 4.38.

173 ἀθλητῆρας: simply the Homeric form (*Od.* 8.164 ἀθλητῆρι, hapax) in place of Mᵃ's offering (6.512 ἀεθλητῆρας, first occurrence in Theocr. 22.24).

ἀελλόποδας: presumably runners (3.356, 6.517), or perhaps equestrian competitors (ἡνιόχους) in which case the epithet, normally of horses (or of those who move with preternatural swiftness), has been transferred to the competitors. There are similar conceits in CCAG i. 166.33-4 γίνονται δὲ καὶ δρομεῖς

---

[107] Valens, I 1.43 and IX 9.13 (Mercury), VI 3.5 (Saturn), 7 (Jupiter); *passim* throughout *Dodecatopos*; Hephaestion, i. 329.3. Also in sources which discuss the days of the week: Dio Cass. 37.19.3...τὸν προσήκοντα ἑαυτῇ θεὸν ἑκάστῃ ἡμέρᾳ λήψεται; Paul, p. 40.11-12 Περὶ τοῦ γνῶναι ἑκάστην ἡμέραν, τίνος τῶν θεῶν ἐστιν. In Mesomedes (II Heitsch), 8 εἰς ὡρολόγιον, l. 2, the stars are μάκαρες.

[108] A 'technical' religious term: Plut. *Is.* 16/*Mor.* 357 C τὴν δὲ θεὰν φανερὰν γενομένην; Ar. *Thesm.* 672 φήσει δ' εἶναί τε θεοὺς φανερῶς; 2 Macc. 9:8 φανερὰν τοῦ θεοῦ πᾶσιν τὴν δύναμιν ἐνδεικνύμενος; on the manifest god, R. Lane Fox, *Pagans and Christians* (London, 1986), ch. 4, 'Seeing the Gods', 102-67.

[109] Babylonian expressions for visible stellar gods are interesting as comparanda, but the weight of the comparison still falls on Plato. See F. Rochberg, 'Marduk in Heaven', in *Wiener Zeitschrift für die Kunde des Morgenlandes* (*Festschrift für Hermann Hunger zum 65. Geburtstag gewidmet von seinen Freunden, Kollegen und Schülern*), 97 (2007), 433-42, noting inter al. the opening of the fifth tablet of the Enuma Elish: 'He projected positions for the Great Gods conspicuous in the sky, he gave them a starry aspect as constellations'; Enuma Elish vii. 126 'Nēberu is his star which he made visible in the skies' (sc. Marduk); from Assurbanipal's hymn to Marduk, l. 41 'Your shining name is Jupiter', and other evidence for the conception of Jupiter as the visible form of Marduk shining in the heavens.

ταχεῖς πτεροῦ δίκην κινούμενοι; *IG* VII 530 (Tanagra, 3rd c. BC) ἄλλους τε ἀθλοφόρους πτανοῖς ποσὶν εἷλον ἀγῶνας.

174 ἐν νίκαις ἱεραῖσιν: for ἱερονῖκαι see Appendix II, VI.7.ii.

175 Sacred games, crowns, and glory are the topoi of athletic victory, whose language the poet partly evokes. Verse inscriptions[110] boast endlessly of κλέος and κῦδος, but μυριόδοξα, which is *proton legomenon*, more closely shadows the prose formula, that of having competed (νικήσας, ἀγωνισάμενος) ἐνδόξως (L. Robert, 'Inscription agonistique d'Ancyre: Concours d'Ancyre', *Hellenica*, 11–12 (1960), 350–68, at 351–8; see also on 1.102).[111] The use of στέμματα, normally a priest's fillet, as a synonym for στεφάνους is also found in *SEG* 19.532 (Delos, 1st c. BC) στέ[μματα δισσὰ λάβον], *SEG* 19.589.15 (Chios) στέμματα δισσά and *SEG* 41.1407 B.8 (Seleukeia on the Kalykadnos, 161–80) Παναθηναίων στέμμασι; they are also conflated in 2.235. εὐδοκιμοῦντας ἐν ἄθλοις continues to evoke honorific language, though it is hard to find examples of the verb, which is especially used for individuals who have given performances/recitals/ presentations in Delphi,[112] applied specifically to athletes.

176–7 In order to avoid the routine verb προσμαρτυρεῖν, M^b invests the weight of the sentence in his new epithet (see on 161), which governs indeclinable ἄμφω. He uses a routine prose expression τάξιν ἐπέχειν (to occupy a position, or fulfil a role) which evokes, without reproducing, the use of τάξις to describe the order of the heavens (planets, constellations) (p. 121), and dresses it up with a new epithet evoking Saturn's light-name (i. 898–9; cf. on 4.239).

178 ἀστεφάνους: the normal form is ἀστεφάνωτος, but this form has already appeared in Eur. *Hipp.* 1137 and *Andr.* 1021.

178–9 ἀλειπτῆρας ... παιδότριβας: it is only if one takes 6.515–17 as a point of departure that one infers that these characters are failures or also-rans, or that their situation is déclassé in some way as compared with the glamorous victors. These are their trainers (see too Firmicus, 7.26.3 *aut palaestrae aut*

---

[110] L. Moretti, *Iscrizioni agonistiche greche* (Rome, 1953).
[111] Also in a boxer's self-commemoration from Alabanda, δόξαν ἔχων ἔνοπλον (Robert 1940*a*, no. 169); an honorific decree for a pancratiast under Hadrian (*MAMA* 8.417.12) ἐκτήσατο τὴν εὐκλεῆ δόξαν. Elsewhere the term of commendation is λαμπρός: in a decree for a deceased athlete, *IK* Knidos I 234 (2nd–3rd c. AD) τὸ περὶ τὴν ἄθλησιν λαμπρόν; in another boxer's list of victories at Gortyn, νεικῶ λαμ(πρῶς) (Robert 1940*a*, no. 65, though restored differently in *IC* IV 375). Glory, crowns, and victory dominate commemorations of gladiators as well (Robert 1940*a*, 302–3).
[112] Including 'cultural' performers in the gymnasium (*SEG* 3.364, Haliartos, before 168 BC: a philosopher; *SIG*³ 771, 29 BC: an ἀστρολόγος; *BCH* 63 (1939), 168 [restored]: a rhetor; *FD* iii. 3, 338, n.d.: a *grammatikos*), and some in connection with the Pythian games themselves (*SIG*³ 689, 134 BC: a χοροψάλτρια).

athletarum magistri), who have a high profile in inscriptions and are highly regarded in their own right.¹¹³ The two nouns are near-synonyms,¹¹⁴ as the poet implies by aligning them without a copula: ἀλείπτης had apparently developed from the basic meaning 'anointer'¹¹⁵ in a way that is paralleled by the metonymic use of οἱ ἀλειφόμενοι for those who participated in the whole athletic culture of the gymnasia. Holders of this title are well known in inscriptions which commemorate both a successful athlete and the ἀλείπτης under whom he trained (Robert 1937, 139 and n. 1, and other examples of the formula ὑπὸ ἀλείπτην in *IEph*. 1112.18, 1130, 1611.19.; *TAM* V.2 1022 (Thyateira)); they are also commemorated in their own right (*IG* V,1 491 and 569, Sparta). The same person readily graduated from the one role to the other (*IG* V,1 666, Roman Sparta, for Marcus Aurelius Asclepiades, δὶς περιοδονείκης, ἀλείπτ‹η›ς). κράτιστος might thus be a very apposite epithet for an ex-athlete and now trainer.

Despite the importance of this profession in cultural life, no other Greek astrological text mentions the ἀλείπτης, though other trainers are mentioned (Appendix II, VI.7.ix; Cumont, 80 n. 1). The manuscript accentuates παιδοτρίβης as the exotic form παιδότριψ, also in Herodian, *De pros. cathol.*, *GG* iii/1. 246.25–6); Dr Holford-Strevens, however, suspects, perhaps rightly, that the latter is a comic insult, and that παιδοτρίβας should be restored, all the more in that the poet himself may not have used accentuation.

179 διδασκαλίης τε παρέδρους: it looks as if the παιδοτρίβαι have suggested educators in general. πάρεδροι are normally officials, assessors, or assistants in magic. This use is partly figurative (as also in 477 and 540, perhaps helped by tragedy¹¹⁶), but also evokes the idea of literally sedentary teachers (n. on 6.393–4).

180–6

Mercury aspects Venus, each in the other's terms.

---

¹¹³ J. König, *Athletics and Literature in the Roman Empire* (Cambridge, 2005), 305–15; id. 'Gymnasticus: Introduction', in id. (ed.), *Philostratus: Heroicus, Gymnasticus, Discourses 1 and 2* (Cambridge, MA, 2014), 337–40; M. Girardi, 'Chi "ha unto e preparato" (ἀλείπτης) al martirio Saba il goto? A proposito di Basilio, ep. 164,1', *Classica et Christiana*, 8 (2013), 109–28, at 120.

¹¹⁴ J. Jüthner, *Die athletischen Leibesübungen der Griechen*, i: *Geschichte der Leibesübungen*, ed. F. Brein (Graz, 1965), 161–82 (Paidotribai), 188–90 (Aleiptai). The third type of trainer, the γυμναστής (Jüthner, 183–8; König (n. 113), *Athletics*, 306, and *Gymnasticus*, 340–4), is not mentioned here.

¹¹⁵ H. Taeuber, 'Ein mysischer Athletiktrainer in Klosterneuburg', *ZPE* 99 (1993), 203–6, at 204.

¹¹⁶ Soph. *Ant.* 798 τῶν μεγάλων πάρεδρος...θεσμῶν (sc. ἵμερος); Eur. *Med.* 843 τᾶι Σοφίαι παρέδρους...Ἔρωτας, although there of abstract qualities.

Protasis. M^a (two separate charts, 6.366–72 and 504–10) and M^b both offer versions of Θ p. 214.13–17, one of many realisations of Mercury and Venus as Rulers of πρᾶξις. Θ gives an insane amount of detail (which speaks for a prose rather than poetic original). M^a retains more of this than does M^b, who has jettisoned the mutual exchange of houses and the complicated specification of 6.371–2, but agrees with M^a on the exchange of terms,[117] for which he uses ἐναλλάγδην (cf. Θ p. 213.11 ἐναλλάξαντες; Ptol. 4.4.6 ἀμφιλελαχότες), and the pathway metaphor (τρίβον ~ οἶμον).

Apodosis. Ptolemy's account of Mercury and Venus as Rulers of πρᾶξις already offers most of the detail which appears in the other sources (which for M^a implies the existence of a pre-Ptolemaic version: pp. 52, 261–2), except for the citharodes, which appear in Θ (both τ- and Π-).

Overall, the closest connections are between M^b, M^a's second chart, and the chart in Θ's τ- sequence (the cithara, dancers). Thymelic artists come from the Π- chart, though M^b has comedians instead of the tragedians shared by the other two. With M^a's *first* chart M^b shares μελπ-/μολπ-; with his *second* he shares mimes with their 'lewd' words (μαχλ-). Typically (p. 220), M^b prefers agent nouns to the Homeric derivatives of M^a (μελῶν μελπήτορας ἄνδρας ~ μολπῇσιν γλυκερῇσι μεμηλότας ἄνδρας; κιθάρης τε μελουργούς ~ κιθάρης ἐπιίστορας).

180 Cf. 4.356. For Venus' swiftness, see i. 907 n. 23. The outer planets are not called θοοί (though for Jupiter's motion see 131 n.), although the planets generically may be (6.223); otherwise θοός refers to daily motion (2.38, 109, 4.553).

181 ἐναλλάγδην: see on 6.368, though the constructions differ (there and 466–7, βεβ(α)ῶτες + dative).

182 αἰθερόπλαγκτον: see on 4.9.

183–6 The list of entertainers is particularly similar to Dio Chrys. *Or.* 7.119, who, among a list of professions he classifies as sordid and dishonourable, includes tragic and comic actors, mimes, dancers, chorus-members, citharodes, and auletes who perform in theatres. Compare also *Or.* 66.8, where mimes and citharists are entertainers to be assembled by a euergete who wanted to please the crowd, and Greg. Nyss. *De Beneficentia*, in A. van Heck (ed.), *Gregorii Nysseni opera*, ix. 1, p. 105.20–1, γελωτοποιούς, μίμους, κιθαριστάς, ᾠδούς (from a list of decadent entertainments). The third-century AD Attic inscription (*IG* II² 2153) discussed by Robert 1936 lists, among a series of entertainers (ἀ]κροά[ματα), κωμῳδοί, ἀρχαιολο- (which Robert identified as a type of

---

[117] Another source with an outcome involving musicians when Mercury and Venus undergo some kind of exchange (of house or terms or trigons) is Firmicus, 7.26.7.

mime), and κιθ]αρῳδοί (Dittenberger and Kirchner's restoration, though Robert preferred π]αρῳδοί).[118]

183 This is related to Valens, II 17.60 ἐὰν δὲ ὃς μὲν οἰκοδεσπότῃ, ὃς δὲ δεσπόζῃ [sc. Mercury and Mars], Ἑρμῆς ἑξάγωνος Ἀφροδίτῃ ἢ σὺν αὐτῇ τοὺς γεννωμένους ποιοῦσι συνετούς, ἐπιχαρεῖς, φιλομούσους, φιλοπαίκτας, σκώπτας, ἄλλοτε ποιητάς, μελογράφους, φωνασκούς [voice-trainers], ὑποκριτὰς μίμων, κωμῳδίας... In other words, this is a different aspectual relation of the same planets. For comic actors in astrology (Appendix II, VI.5), see Cumont, 81 n. 4; Hübner on Manilius, 5.471. The implication is that the comedians were in a fuller source, and are not simply M[b]'s own *variatio* of M[a].

The reference to lyric singers is a poetic periphrasis, though could also evoke a professional specialism. There are references to lyre-players, λυρισταί, in Artemidorus, 4.72.1, and in epitaphs (*SEG* 17.438 κωμῳδὸς καὶ λυριστής (Malta, 3rd c. AD); *IGUR* ii. 965 (Rome, n.d.) Σωτηρίχῳ λυριστῇ; *IDidyma*, 579 (imperial)), and periphrastic expressions in verse (*IG* X,2 2 386 (Ohrid, 2nd c.) ἐμπέ-|[ραμος] δὲ λύρης; *SEG* 12.339 (Beroia, late 2nd/early 3rd c. AD) Μουσάων θεράπαινα λυροκτύπος; *IGUR* iii. 1319 θαλίῃσι λυρόκτυπος). For those who apparently sing as well as (or instead of?) play, one looks to Antipater, *AP* 6.118.3 = *HE* 498, a λυρῳδός (female); *IGUR* iii. 1154 (Rome, n.d.) ὁ τῆς σοφίης μελῳδός, ἔντεχνος λύρης. As far as can be seen from I. E. Stephanis, *ΔΙΟΝΥΣΙΑΚΟΙ ΤΕΧΝΙΤΑΙ* (Heraclion, 1988), 608, 'lyric poetry' is not a category in contemporary thymelic festivals, other than in a highly dubious restoration in a victory list in *I. Napoli* I 54 (178–86 AD) λ[υρικῶν μελῶν].

184 ᾠδούς: that the mimes are not named as such but called 'singers' (whatever the mode of their delivery, song, sing-song, *Sprechgesang* or what) minimally reflects the same conception of their role as in the job-descriptions παρῳδός, μαγῳδός, λυσιῳδός,[119] and so on, but presumably also the real musical component in their performances, not only the percussive accompaniment, but also the songs performed by the actors in Roman mime.[120] Songs appear again alongside mimes (as examples of execrable taste) in Plut. *Mor.* 706 D ἡδόμενον δὲ μίμοις καὶ μέλεσι καὶ ᾠδαῖς κακοτέχνοις καὶ κακοζήλοις, and in Galen as examples of things that (over-)heat the blood (*De sanitate tuenda*, vi. 41 Kühn ᾠδάς... καὶ μίμους γελοίων καὶ μέλη).

---

[118] M. T. Mitsos, 'Some Lists of Athenian Ephebes: vi', in D. W. Bradeen and M. F. McGregor (eds.), *ΦΟΡΟΣ: Tribute to Benjamin Dean Meritt* (New York, 1974), 117–20, at 120, was unable to confirm either restoration.

[119] E. Wüst, *RE* s.v. Mimos, 1732.19–26; cf. Athen. 14.620 E τὰ αὐτὰ δὲ μέλη ᾄδουσιν, on the magode and lysiode.

[120] Wiemken, 207–9; G. E. M. Wootton, 'Representations of Musicians in the Roman Mime', in *Mediterranean Archaeology*, 17 (2004) = *Festschrift in Honour of J. Richard Green*, 243–52, esp. 245.

The present passage adds yet another instance to the literary dossier of the mime's scurrility (see i. 343 and on 6.508-9; p. 115);¹²¹ like αἴσχ- (i. 367), μάχλος is another word that stretches from sexual to linguistic impropriety. It stigmatises the mimes' subject-matter (Lucian, *Salt.* 2) and personal conduct (John Scylitzes, *Synopsis hist.* (ed. J. Thurn, *CFHB* V (Berlin, 1973)), Ῥωμανὸς ὁ νέος, 3 μαχλάδων καὶ μίμων καὶ γελοτοποιῶν).

185 The *nabla* was a type of West Semitic lyre which arrived in Greece at about the end of the fourth century and sometimes renders Hebrew *nēvel* in LXX.¹²² A couple of other agent nouns appear in epigraphy: (i) ναβλᾶς, on an inscription from the grotto of Buscemi, near Syracuse;¹²³ (ii) ναβλίστρια, on an plaque from imperial Macedonia.¹²⁴ The present form has to be taken as either a solecism (because the instrument is a *nabla*, not a *nablist-*) or a double agent noun (*both* a *nabla*-person *and* a *nabla*-striker). This is the only known -κτυπεύς compound, though M^b has various others in -τυπος/-τυπεύς. The normal verb for 'striking' a stringed instrument is πλήσσειν (cf. πλῆκτρον); κτυπεῖν seems to amplify this with a verb more appropriate for thunder, pounding feet, drums, cymbals, and the soundscape of ecstatic cults (Strab. 10.3.15; Philostr. *Ep.* 69). The only other application to a non-percussive musical instrument in LSJ concerns trumpets (Bacchyl. fr. 4.75 Maehler σαλπίγγων κτύπος).

χοροῖς (dative of interest?) implies that they accompany choruses, as stringed instruments often do (cf. the χοροκιθαριστής/χοροκιθαρεύς in Hellenistic and imperial thymelic festivals,¹²⁵ the χοροψαλτρίαι at Delphi and Iasos¹²⁶). For the

---

¹²¹ More ancient testimonia in E. Wüst, *RE* s.v. Mimos, 1736.32-8, 1747.8-24; Ingleheart on Ov. *Trist.* 2.497-500; Plut. *Mor.* 712 E.

¹²² J. Montagu, *Musical Instruments of the Bible* (Lanham, MD, 2002), 41, corrects West, who called it a harp; Montagu notes further that it is possibly, but not certainly, differentiated from the *kinnōr* as being of lower tessitura (42). Classical references and earlier bibliography in West 1992, 77, n. 134; Radt on Strab. X p. 471 c l. 23 (10.3.17); T. A. C. Lynch and E. Rocconi, *A Companion to Ancient Greek and Roman Music* (Hoboken, 2020), 237.

¹²³ G. Manganaro, 'Iscrizioni "rupestri" di Sicilia', in L. Gasperini (ed.), *Rupes Loquentes: Atti del convegno internazionale di studio sulle iscrizioni rupestri di età romana in Italia: Roma-Bomarzo 13-15. X. 1989* (Rome, 1992), 447-501, at 459-64, no. 5 and n. 28 (gen. Ἔρωτος ναβλᾶ). Its first editor, G. Pugliese Carratelli, 'Sul culto delle Paides e di Anna in Acre', *PP* 6 (1951), 70 no. 3, had accentuated it as νάβλα from νάβλας. The accent was corrected by L. and J. Robert, 283 n. 6.

¹²⁴ L. Heuzey and H. Daumet, *Mission archéologique de Macédoine* (Paris, 1976), 28, no. 10 (Palaeochori), cf. M. G. Demitsas, *Sylloge inscriptionum Graecarum et Latinarum Macedoniae* (Chicago, 1980), no. 979. What can be read is κιθαρῳδίστρια, ναβλίστρια, and then τετρ[α-], restored by Heuzey as τετρ[αχορδ-. Demitsas interpreted all three terms to refer to one and the same woman, the commemorand.

¹²⁵ W. Slater, rev. of Aneziri, *BMCR* 2004.02.40; P. Ceccarelli, 'Circular Choruses and the Dithyramb in the Classical and Hellenistic Period: Problems of Definition', in B. Kowalzig and P. Wilson (eds.), *Dithyramb in Context* (Oxford, 2013), 153-70, at 157 n. 17.

¹²⁶ West 1992, 379-80; S. Aneziri, *Die Vereine der dionysischen Techniten im Kontext der hellenistischen Gesellschaft* (Stuttgart, 2003), 221; W. Slater, 'Deconstructing Festivals', in P. Wilson (ed.), *The Greek Theatre and Festivals: Documentary Studies* (Oxford, 2007), 21-47, 45-6.

nabla to be used in this way sits well with the idea that it was a deeper/more resonant instrument than other types of lyre.

κιθάρης τε μελουργούς: if μελ- implies songs, this corresponds to Θ's κιθαρῳδός rather than κιθαριστής (which is all Mᵃ seems to have in mind). But it need not (cf. LSJ B.3, where μέλος can be the melody of an instrument).

186 ὀρχηθμῶν ἴδριάς τε: similarly at 2.335 and 6.507 [*ex emend.*]. Are these specifically pantomimes, the commonest word for whom is ὀρχησταί (Garelli, index s.v. ὀρχηστής; Tedeschi 2011, 37)? See also on 5.141.

ἐν θυμέλαις προφέροντας: both Mᵃ and Mᵇ replace this from the head of the list (in Ptolemy and Θ) to its closing item, which could be read resumptively (as it encapsulates all the previous artists, at least loosely, depending on the admissibility of mime to formal competitions). The poet enjoys the cadence (also 233, 344).

187–92

Mars in opposition to Saturn, each in the other's terms. This is a chart with various relatives: another follows shortly in this book (263–70), while there are likewise two affiliated charts in Mᵃ. They appear in the two books in the opposite order. Thus, this is the closer match for 6.494–8, while the later one is a better fit with 6.456–64.

Protasis. Both (or rather all four) charts have connections with the τ- chart in Θ for Saturn in equal degrees with Mars and Mercury (p. 215.8–11). In comparison with this chart, Mᵃ and Mᵇ both eliminate Mercury, narrowing down to the two malefics, for which they also specify an aspect (there was none in Θ). And both involve an exchange of terms (as does *Lib. Herm.* xxxiv. 4). It is evident that they are more closely related to each other than either is to Θ, though Mᵃ offers even more detail (6.495, the alternative scenario of the planets being in the same sign).

Apodosis. The closer parallels are again with 6.496–8 (the other chart concerns cremation, embalming, and garum, though there is one shared detail, viz. cedar oil). In both cases the outcome includes coffin-makers (not clearly specified in Θ) and mourners. The latter constitute a link, not with the τ- chart, but with the Π- chart in Ptolemy and Θ for Mars and (surprisingly) Venus as Rulers of πρᾶξις with Saturn in additional aspect. Mᵃ also mentions cremation; Mᵇ does not.

188 A palmary emendation by De Stefani of αἴγλη in the previous line correctly ascribes these beams to Mars, not Saturn. Because of iron oxide on its surface the planet does appear red to the naked eye. Sources for Mars' colour in Bouché-Leclercq, 313–14; Roscher, s.v. Planeten (Roscher), 2531–2; Boll 1916,

19–24, 50, 52–3, and *passim*; Pingree 1978, ii. 248–50. They include Plat. *Rep.* 617 A ὑπέρυθρον and Cic. *Rep.* 6.17.3 *ille fulgor rutilus, horribilisque terris, quem Martium dicitis.* Perhaps characteristically, the poet chooses an adjective that suggests intensity (of hue) rather than radiance (of light), though he might have been helped by the purple rainbow and purple cloud of *Il.* 17.547, 551. Boll 1916, 21, refers πορφύρεος to 'kaum...ein dunkleres Rot, sondern...ein Schillern', and Edwards renders the Iliadic rainbow epithet 'lurid, dark-shimmering'. For καταντίπερ, see i. 887–8.

189 ἐν ἀλλαγμοῖσι: ἄλλαγμα exists, and astrology refers to the exchange of terms and signs with ἐναλλασσ-, but the second-declension form is unique to M^b. (I do not understand De Stefani's reference 'praesertim' to 265, which has 'in their *own* dodecatemories', i.e. signs.)

σελάγισμα (*not* 'lightning', with LSJ!) is *proton legomenon* in this poet (also 240, 473, a near-identical line, and always of Saturn or both malefics), but not *hapax* (later, Paul Sil. *Descr.* 634, 849, and then in Byzantine prose, always of planets, stars, or the Sun). See also on 4.36 σελασμός and 4.601 σέλασμα.

190 θρηνήτορας ἄνδρας, ἀσέμνους: the line plunders *Il.* 9.544 θηρήτορας ἄνδρας ἀγείρας (other lines are erected on the same pattern, e.g. *HHom. Ap.* 542 σημάντορες ἄνδρες ἔσονται). The *hapax* agent noun tweaks θρηνητῆρος (also *hapax*) in Aesch. *Pers.* 937 to evoke real functionaries in the funeral industry (App. II, V.6.v.). There are θρηνηταί in papyri (Wessely, *Stud. Pal.* 22.56, l. 27, from Soknopaiou Nesos, 2nd–3rd c. AD, and *BGU* i. 34, Hermoupolis, *c*.322(?)), confirming the existence of male mourners as well as females; the latter are deplored by the fastidious young man from Hermoupolis Magna (6.460 n., i. 813 n. 90; *SEG* 8.621 (2nd c. AD), ll. 17–18 τὰς καλουμένας θρηνητρίας = Bernand, no. 97).[127] See Derda, 33–4. Still, the passage in Ptolemy and its relatives remain, as far as I can see, the only references to professional mourners in Greek astrology.

ἀσέμνους might have crept in by association with mummification, reflecting the low status of the profession, and see too Youtie, 656, but it might also be expressing disapproval for extravagant displays of mourning. ἄσεμνος can apply to words/sounds (LSJ, Stephanus; for example, four times in Dion. Hal. *De Comp. Verb.*, where it is combined with ignobility and opposed to majesty), and also to indecorous grief. On the need for mourning to adhere to a norm of propriety, see especially Basil, *PG* 31.229 C, speaking of a κανὼν ἀκριβής, καθ᾽ ὃν προσῆκε σεμνῶς καὶ εὐσχημόνως τοῖς τῆς φύσεως ὅροις ἐμμένοντας διαφέρειν τὰ λυπηρά (reference from M. Alexiou, *The Ritual Lament in Greek Tradition*

---

[127] θρηνήτρια is attested mostly in scholia or lexicographers glossing ἐγχυτρίστριαι or ἰηλεμίστριαι, and in Byzantine prose; also in an abbreviated version (δ) of Aesop. *Fab.* 221 as an alternative for τὰς θρηνούσας.

(Cambridge, 1974), 28). The poet reflects a persistent attitude, which had led to the famous sumptuary legislation of the archaic period,[128] and apparently still makes itself felt even in a context where hired mourners were a norm.

191 κεδροχαρεῖς: cedar oil was used in mummification (see on 6.461–2), though this could also be a reference to coffins of cedar wood, or even panels for mummy-portraits.[129]

σορόεργα τέχνης κανονίσματ' ἔχοντας: Disentangled and rearranged, this means 'using rulers in the construction of coffins as tools of their trade'. This detail is shared only with M^a. In Egypt one thinks first of wooden coffins, though in principle this could also refer to (stone) sarcophagi, since both carpenters and masons use the κανών. That word has been slightly exoticised here, as it has in 4.151 κανονισμός (see ad loc.), though the third-declension variant is not unique: already in Hellenistic epigram it referred to a straight-edge, a ruler, as part of a scribe's equipment.[130] Note how the funerary theme has turned craftsmen who presumably did not specialise in coffin-making but made different kinds of furniture as well (Cannata 2012, 609) into exclusively mortuary practitioners (p. 39).

192 νεκροτάφους: an everyday Egyptian job-title well represented in papyri (first certainly in P. Ryl. II 65, of perhaps 67 or 57 BC), occasionally in Egyptian epigraphy, but in no other literary sources except lexica (Hesych. τ 273, glossing ταφεῖς, and *Lexica Segueriana*, τ 308, glossing Ταφέας). The growing literature on these workers,[131] who had their own professional associations, tends to agree that the trade name is an umbrella term for all those involved in the burial of the dead, within which there were any number of sub-specialisms—quite a different approach from the (pseudo-?) specificity of the previous item.

κλαυστῆρας ἀποφθιμένων: back to lamentation (the entry is not well organised).

---

[128] Pejorative language, comparable to ἄσεμνος: e.g. Plut. *Sol.* 21.5, on Solon's legislation countering τὸ ἄτακτον καὶ ἀκόλαστον at funerals; *Mor.* 609 B ἡ δὲ θρήνων ἄπληστος ἐπιθυμία καὶ πρὸς ὀλοφύρσεις ἐξάγουσα καὶ κοπετοὺς αἰσχρὰ μὲν οὐχ ἧττον τῆς περὶ τὰς ἡδονὰς ἀκρασίας.

[129] V. Dasen, 'Mummy Portraits', *Encyclopaedia of Ancient History*, Wiley Online Library.

[130] Phanias, *AP* 6.295.3 = HE 2980, described as φιλόρθιον (ruler, as item of a scribe's equipment); in Posidippus, *Ep.* 36.7 A.–B. (col. vi. 16), the editors suggest 'striscia (di stoffa)'. Eustathius uses it to mean a grammatical rule.

[131] Derda, 26–31; Bagnall 2017; Cannata 2012, *passim*, and 2020, 47–8, 99–103. On the Christian necrotaphoi of Kysis in the Great Oasis (apropos of P. Grenf. II 73/Chr. Wilck. 127), see the earlier bibliography in S. Torallas Tovar, 'Egyptian burial practice in a period of transition: On embalming in Christian times', in P. Mantas-España and C. Burnett (edd.), *Mapping Knowledge: Cross-Pollination in Late Antiquity and the Middle Ages* (Cordoba, 2014), 129–40, at n. 27. For the court case involving the necrotaphoi of Thebes, see P. W. Pestman (ed.), *Il processo di Hermias e altri documenti dell'archivio dei choachiti: (P. Tor. Choachiti): Papiri greci e demotici conservati a Torino e in altre collezioni d'Italia* (Turin, 1992).

νεκρονώμας: 'corpse-bearer' (LSJ); or just those that handle them in some way, which could again include any part of the burial process; *pollinctor* (Stephanus). The only other -νώμης compound in B.–P. 6 is ἱππονώμας, which is rare and poetic (Rüedi, 84–6). If that register applies here as well (though see p. 190), it does not look likely to shed much light on Θ's νεκρεπάρτας (unparalleled, including in papyri; the parallel recension in Epit. IIIb, *CCAG* vii. 117.25 offers νεκροπάρτους, for which Cumont conjectured νεκρορράπτας and Boll νεκροπράτας). LSJ suggest a connection with SB 1 5774 (*AJP* 34 (1913), 448) νεκροαρτου (on a mummy label, possibly from Panopolis, AD 117–217); see also 267n.

193–200

Mars setting with Saturn, Mercury in equal degrees; Moon in their(?) terms and in a *kentron*. The main agents, Mars, Mercury, and Saturn, indicate the basis of both this chart and the corresponding 6.499–503 in an account of Mars and Mercury as Rulers of πρᾶξις with Saturn testifying (cf. Ptol. 4.4.7). But there is a further connection between both M^a and M^b with Θ pp. 192.20–193.1 (from the Περὶ μαινομένων καὶ ἐπιληπτικῶν), while M^a and M^b have novelties of their own.

Protasis. Overall, M^b is more similar to Θ than M^a is, because M^b, like Θ, locates Mars in the DESC, possibly Mercury as well, and involves the Moon. M^a, on the other hand, presents an additive chart, in which Mercury is tagged on to the entities in the previous apotelesma (6.494–8). Although M^b's previous chart (4.187–92) had also dealt with Mars and Saturn, their positions were different, and, above all, this new item is asyndetic.

Apodosis. Θ provides sufficient parallels for M^a. It includes a reference to crucifixion, which M^a follows, in veiled terms. M^b elaborates with customary lack of taste, deriving a little more stimulus in his vocabulary from a separate configuration on violent death (Θ p. 201.2–5, from the βιαιοθανάτων, another realisation of Mars, Mercury, and Saturn governing πρᾶξις; ἀνασκολοπίζονται ~ σκολοπηίδα).

193 ἐπίκεντρος: if this is not to be merely tautologous after δύνῃ, it must add greater precision—*exactly* on the cardinal point. It *can* mean this (Heilen 2015, 732, 817), although it does not obviously do so in its other uses in the Manethoniana (1.34, 279; 5.76).

194–5 There is no punctuation in L at the end of 194. Lopilato follows the manuscript, taking εἰν ὁρίοις καὶ κέντρῳ together with ἰσόμοιρος, and interprets ἴσχωσι in 195 as 'restrain' (i.e. presumably they—the two malefics—surround the Moon in the position called ἐμπεριοχή or ἐμπερίσχεσις, cf. Heilen 2015, 807–9). Koechly's punctuation, on the other hand, followed by De Stefani, takes the phrase with ἴσχωσι in the following line, and insofar as Θ is of any use here at all it supports him, for it makes the Moon ἐπίκεντρος along with Mars and Mercury (or alternatively in quartile or opposition to them), and says nothing about the Moon being enclosed by the other planets. The extra specification εἰν ὁρίοις is obscure (in *whose* terms exactly?), and the double reference to *kentron* and terms is hard to parallel, though it is apparent that Lopilato's reading would involve tautology (being ἰσόμοιρος *ipso facto* would cover εἰν ὁρίοις—at least if they are in conjunction).

194 ἐπ': 'as well as, in addition to'. Perhaps it is an import from the verse pattern ἐπ' ἀμφοτέροισι τάνυσσαν (*Il.* 13.359), ἐπ' ἀμφοτέροισιν ἔπιπτεν (*Od.* 12.239); this instance is especially like Ap. Rhod. 2.104 ἐπ' ἀμφοτέροισι κεάσθη.

196 ἀνδροφόνους δρῶσιν, λήιστορας ~ Θ p. 192.24–5 λῃστάς, ἀνδροφόνους ποιοῦσι.

ἐμπεδολώβας: active, 'ever-injurious'. There are no other -λώβης agent nouns in B.-P. or Rüedi, and this is the only ἐμπεδό- compound listed by LSJ whose second component is verbal.[132] The typical contexts for the root λωβ-, which astrology (including prose) likes, are physical harm and personal harm to, or from, spouses (see i. 368; 3.60, 6.210 nn.; 6.211 λωβήτορας continues a tradition inaugurated by the *Odyssey*), though 4.234 θεολωβήτας falls outside the pattern.

197 κέρδεος ἐχθροτάτου: cf. Maximus, 573 κέρδεος ἁρπαλέοιο.

197-8 Malefics bring about crucifixion—either both together,[133] or with the emphasis on violent Mars[134] (and only rarely Saturn: Valens, II 41.37). For crucifixion in astrology, see Cumont, 196–7, and J. G. Cook, 282–9. Like Artemidorus and the novel, it associates it with robbers (*CCAG* viii/1. 176.14–17; Firmicus, 8.22.3; Hengel, 48–50). Indeed, λῃσταί is precisely the Gospels' word for those who were crucified alongside Jesus (Matth. 27:38, Mark 15:27; Luke instead has κακοῦργοι); other crucified λῃσταί are in Plut. *Caes.* 2.7 and Jos. *BJ* 2.253. Other aspects of the passage's vocabulary too (the collocation of βασαν-, στρεβλ-, κολαζ-, σκολοπ-, and the reference to nailing) are best paralleled in Christian texts (whether martyrologies or meditations on Christ himself).[135] Once again, astrology proves receptive, not only to vocabulary, but

---

[132] -καρπος and -φυλλος (Empedocles), -μοχθος (Pindar), -μυθος (Nonnus), -σθενης (Pindar), -φρων (Phalaris).
[133] Θ p. 201.22–3; *CCAG* viii/1. 176.14–17 (pirates and murderers again involved); Theophilus, *CCAG* xi/1. 259.7–8.
[134] 1.148; Dorotheus, p. 362.11; Θ p. 200.13. σκολοπισμός: Valens, II 41.35, Apomasar, *De Rev.* p. 204.10.
[135] Theodorus Bestus, *Laud. Sanct. Euphem.* 5 σταυροί, κλῖναι πεπυρακτωμέναι, στρεβλωτῆρες μελῶν καὶ εἴ τι ἄλλο πρὸς κολαστηρίων εἶδος; Basil, PG 31.500.21-4 ἐπὶ τοῦ ξύλου στρεβλοῦσθω,

also to *Realien*, which slip from view in mainstream classical sources (p. 179). It is unsurprising that Martin Hengel, a scholar of early Christianity, cited this passage (9).

197 βασανηδόν: the adverb itself is unique, but torture is a regular enough effect of Mars,[136] and a regular enough precursor of crucifixion (Callisthenes, *FGrH* 124 F 3; Jos. *AJ* 12.256, *BJ* 5.449; Chariton, 8.8.2–3; Hengel, 26–9).

198 στρεβλὰ κολαζόμενοι: strictly the punishment of being twisted, racked, or stretched on the wheel, which might precede crucifixion.[137] Crucifixion itself could force the body into a distorted posture; the position in which Jehohanan, whose bones were discovered at Giv'at ha-Mivtar north of Jerusalem, had been crucified is controversial, but on the reconstruction of Dr N. Haas of the Hebrew University his 'torso was forced into a twisted position with his calves and thighs bent and unnaturally twisted'.[138]

σκολοπηίδα μοῖραν ὁρῶσιν: the basic noun is σκόλοψ, 'stake', and ἀνασκολοπίζεσθαι means literally 'impale', but in practice it is often synonymous with ἀνασταυροῦσθαι ('crucify') (see Asheri on Hdt. 3.125.3).[139] This is the verb used of Jesus' crucifixion by Lucian, *Peregr.* 11, and Celsus (Orig. *Cels.* 2.36), as well as for the martyrdom of Andrew in *Acta Andreae*, 51; that event, too, receives poetic make-overs (compare a Didymean oracle cited by Lactantius, *Div. Inst.* 4.13.11 γόμφοις καὶ σκολόπεσσι πικρὴν ἀνέτλησε τελευτήν = *AP* App. *Orac.* 125; Eudocia, *De martyr. sanct. Cypr.* 1.191 has the unique form σκολοπή). In this case, for the periphrastic expression for a type of death, see on 5.221.

199 The line is an excellent example of 'hammering home' the meaning across each part of the hexameter (p. 210). The usual way of saying this in prose would be with the verb προσηλοῦν,[140] Latin *cruci affigi, affigere, suffigere*;

φερέσθω τὰ κολαστήρια· τὰ θηρία, τὸ πῦρ, τὸ ξίφος, ὁ σταυρὸς...εὐτρεπιζέσθω; Theodoretus, *PG* 75.1465.34–41 ἀνέχεται...κολαφιζόμενος, ἐμπτυόμενος, ὀνειδιζόμενος, στρεβλούμενος, μαστιγούμενος, καὶ τὸ τελευταῖον σταυρούμενος, καὶ λαμβάνων λῃστὰς τῆς τιμωρίας κοινωνοὺς ἑκατέρωθεν, καὶ ἀνδροφόνοις καὶ κακούργοις συνταττόμενος.

[136] Θ pp. 159.28, 160.4, 205.6; Dorotheus, pp. 414.17, 416.20; Valens, I 1.22, I 3.29, etc.

[137] *Suda*, λ 840 (= Aelian, fr. 276); *Acta et Martyrium Apollonii*, 40; Theodoretus, *De incarnatione Domini*, *PG* 75.1465.37–8; Nicephorus Callistus Xanthopoulos, *Hist. Eccl.* 7.22.

[138] J. H. Charlesworth, 'Jesus and Jehohanan: An Archaeological Note on Crucifixion', *Expository Times*, 84.5 (1 Feb. 1973), 147–50, at 149; cf. J. A. Fitzmyer, 'Crucifixion in Ancient Palestine, Qumran Literature, and the New Testament', *CBQ* 40 (1978), 493–513, at 496.

[139] For Philo, ἀνασκολοπισμός involves nails (*Somn.* 2.213; *Post.* 61) and σταυροί (*Flacc.* 84).

[140] Demosth. *Or.* 21.105 προσηλῶσθαι; Diod. Sic. 2.18.2 σταυρῷ προσηλώσειν; Jos. *BJ* 2.308 σταυρῷ προσηλῶσαι; Col. 2:14 προσηλώσας αὐτὸ τῷ σταυρῷ; ps.-Plut. *Fluv.* 1.4 σταυροῖς προσηλώσαντες.

προσαρτᾶν is more usually used of impaling.¹⁴¹ The κέντρα and the nails reduplicate the sense, although the former can also be yet another word for tortures (LSJ 2). Either ἐν ἥλοις varies the bare dative, or Cancik's conjecture ἔνηλοι varies the noun with an epithet, also plausible in this poet. It would be new in this sense, for ἔνηλος, glossed *clavatus* in the entry cited by LSJ and Stephanus, turns out to refer to the purple stripe (*clavus*) on a toga.

200 These happened: the point of crucifixion was not just torture but the humiliation (see on 1.148 ἀκλειῶς) of the dead man and his family by leaving the body to decompose. On the fate of victims of crucifixion, and the denial of burial, see J. G. Cook, 'Crucifixion and Burial', *NTS* 57 (2011), 193–213, at 206–9. The dogs-and-birds motif occurs, *inter alia*, in a Hellenistic epigram from Amyzon for a man killed by a slave, who was punished with crucifixion and exposed to the predators *while still alive* (*GVI* 1120.9 θηρσὶ καὶ οἰωνοῖς ζωὸν ἀνεκρέμασαν = Merkelbach and Stauber, 02/03/01¹⁴²), and in a scenario in Apuleius where robbers plan a *patibuli cruciatum, cum canes et vultures intima protrahent viscera* (*Met.* 6.32); see too the treatment of suicides by Tarquinius Superbus, who had them nailed up *spectanda civibus simul et feris volucribusque laceranda* (Plin. *NH* 36.107). Birds are relatively common.¹⁴³ As for dogs, it was seriously suggested by J. D. Crossan, *Jesus: A Revolutionary Biography* (San Francisco, 1994) that this might have been the grisly reality that all the Gospels' hocus-pocus about the fate of Jesus' body is trying to conceal (154: 'In either case, his body left on the cross or in a shallow grave barely covered with dirt and stones, the dogs were waiting', cf. 158).¹⁴⁴

κατάδειπνα: The noun is unique (Wakefield's κακὰ δεῖπνα is entirely plausible); the very rare verb καταδειπνεῖν is in Plut. *Mor.* 355 c, Aelian, *Var. Hist.* 1.24. All are of 'heavy', fleshy meals (in Plutarch the Apis bull, in Aelian a bull, here human flesh). At 6.98 I wondered whether βορήν τ' ἔμεν οἰωνοῖσιν (of an

---

¹⁴¹ Tatian, *Or. ad Graec.* 21.1 applies it (derisively) to Prometheus, and in Xen. *Eph.* 4.2.1 προσαρτῆσαι σταυρῷ, cf. 4.2.3, the method involves binding not nailing.

¹⁴² Robert 1937, 388–9 n. 2; id. *Fouilles d'Amyzon en Carie*, i: *Exploration, histoire, monnaies, et inscriptions* (Paris, 1983), i. no. 65, 259–63, esp. 262–3, and *BE* 1984, no. 430; more bibliography in Hengel, 76 n. 19; Thompson, 211.

¹⁴³ 5.220 οἰωνοῖσι βορήν; Θ p. 201.22–3 ἐσταυρωμένους καὶ ὑπὸ ὄρνεων βεβρωμένους (Cumont, 197 n. 1); Horace, *Epist.* 1.16.48 *non pasces in cruce corvos*; Juv. *Sat.* 14.77–8; Petronius, *Sat.* 58 *Crucis offla, corvorum cibaria*; Priscus, fr. 8 (p. 35.9–10 Bornmann) ἔλεγεν ὡς αὐτὸν ἀνασκολοπίσας πρὸς βορὰν οἰωνοῖς ἐδεδώκει ἄν. Also threatened for Mnesilochus subjected to the punishment of *apotympanismos*: Ar. *Thesm.* 942, 1028.

¹⁴⁴ There is also the infamous case of the Laureolus mime by Catullus involving a robber-bandit and its historical re-enactment in the amphitheatre when a criminal was hung on a cross and devoured by a bear. But this was stage-managed (and partly patterned after the Prometheus myth): Martial, *De Spectaculis*, 7; references in Hijmans *et al.* on Apul. 6.32 (Groningen Commentaries on Apuleius, vol. vi–vii, p. 76), adding Carcopino, 231, 246; Coleman 1990, 64–5.

588   *Commentary on Book Four*

exposed child) was responding to Aristarchus' criticism of *Il*. 1.5 οἰωνοῖσί τε δαῖτα (Robert was also reminded of the *Iliad* proem by the Amyzon epitaph). This looks more like a positive challenge to Aristarchus, revelling in the idea of a feast of human flesh.

ἔλκυσμα is not new, though this is only one of the senses specialised from its basic meaning, that which is drawn (LSJ and Stephanus cite also dross of silver and spun wool). It comes from the Homeric atrocity-motif (*Il*. 17.558 ταχέες κύνες ἑλκήσουσιν; 22.335–6 σὲ μὲν κύνες ἠδ' οἰωνοὶ | ἑλκήσουσ' ἀϊκῶς), and Homeric lexica/scholia use it to gloss both ἑλώρια (Σ D *Il*. 1.4) and μέλπηθρα, 'sport' (Σ D *Il*. 17.255; Apollonius: τὰ σπαράγματα τῶν κυνῶν καὶ ἑλκύσματα).

201–5

Mercury aspects Jupiter, each in the other's terms. This case is very straightforward. Both this chart and 6.476–9 reflect the lightly realised τ- chart in Θ p. 214.18–21, based on Mercury as Ruler of πρᾶξις when aspected by Jupiter. Mᵃ adds 'friendly' beams, which perhaps reflects Θ's ἐν καλῷ τόπῳ ἑστῶτα. (If there is a further correspondence with *Lib. Herm.* xxxiv. 33, it shows that opposition there is treated as a favourable aspect.)

201 λαμπραυγέτις: otherwise only 4.415 λαμπραυγής (*proton*, not *hapax*, because taken up by Constantinus Manasses). The suffix, feminine of the agent noun suffix -έτης, is normally attached to verb stems, but compare HOrph. 23.1 κυαναυγέτιν ἕδρην (of the sea). This seems to have been a little astrological *tournure*, to judge from Maximus, 103 ἐριλαμπέτιν αἴγλην (cf. 'Antiochus', l. 71 (CCAG i. 111.21) Σεληναίη χαριλαμπέτις, Lucian, *Podagra* 103 λαμπέτις ἀώς) and 584 πολυωπέτις αἴγλη. In the latter case, the suffix has attached itself to another noun stem (see Zito ad loc.).

202 μίγδην looks like a very imprecise expression of the idea of a swap (as opposed to 'betwixt and between' (two categories), 'in conjunction with', apparently in 4.499, and 'indiscriminately' in Ap. Rhod. 3.1381). Perhaps there is also the suggestion that once they are related in this way their power is mingled. The poet of *HHom. Herm.* 494 uses it for sexual relations (see Thomas ad loc., n. 568), Pind. fr. 52m (Pa XII) 7 for 'in the company of', and Nicander for ingredients in a recipe (*Ther.* 932, *Al.* 179, 385). See pp. 217–18 for other comitative expressions perhaps related to Nicander, and on 2.400 for the notion of mixture.

διαλλάξωσιν ὁρισμούς: a little exercise in defamiliarisation (p. 245). ὁρισμούς for ὅρια is only here, while the normal compound in astrology would be ἐναλλάξ- (see on 4.515).

203-5 These lines refer to the two middle tiers of ancient education, grammar and rhetoric, which (whatever the solution to the continuity problem of 204-5) are associated with gilded youth. One notes a concentration of prose phrases which are lightly elaborated with *presque homérique* and hexameter rhythms. So, philosophers and scholars are often described as 'emulous of wisdom'; the rhetoric that comprises one part of ancient higher education is threaded onto this (ῥητορικῆς...τέχνης),[145] and the grammar that constitutes the other is added in a second piece of professional jargon in the next line (γραμματικήν τ' ἄσκησιν[146]). De Stefani well draws attention to a passage about the sophist Scopelian and his starstruck followers which illustrates the culture that imbues these lines: νεότης τε αὐτῷ λαμπρὰ ξυνηκολούθησεν ἐς Ἰωνίαν σοφίας ἐρῶντες (*Vit. Soph.* 1.21.6 (520)).

203-4 σοφίης τε κρατίστους | ζηλωτάς: expanding σοφιστάς with a prose phrase[147] further ornamented with an occasional hexameter cadence (Archestratus, *SH* 155.4 ἀρετῇ τε κράτιστοι; Critias, fr. B2 3 West δαπάνῃ τε κράτιστος).

204 σκολιῶν τε λόγων: 1.304 has τέχνης τε λόγων (see ad loc.). If this is M^b's modification, it seems that his penchant for this epithet and its compounds has overridden the strong EGHP associations of σκολιός with injustice (Hes. *Op.* 194 μύθοισι σκολιοῖς, 262 σκολιῶς ἐνέποντες; Theogn. 1147 ἀδίκων ἀνδρῶν σκολιὸν λόγον; Antipater of Sidon, *AP* 7.146.6 = *HE* 213 σκολιῶν μύθων), lying (Nonn. *Par.* 8.129), and, at best, riddles (ps.-Plut. *Vit. Hom.* 48 δυσξύνετον σκολιοῖσι λόγοις εἰρημένον ὕμνον).

204-5 νεότητά τε λαμπρὴν | γραμματικήν τ' ἄσκησιν: without positing a lacuna between these lines, as Koechly did, this is a zeugma, both objects depending on ἔχοντας (so De Stefani): that is, these natives care about their charges *and* about the art of grammar. They could also be taken as a hendiadys (pedagogy, i.e. the grammatical training of upper-class youth). 'Radiance' might simply be a quality of youth (John Chrys. *In SS. Martyres Juventinum et*

---

[145] The phrase is attested since the 3rd c. BC, cf. Kaster, 67. It refers to their professional competence, but the τέχνη ῥητορική in the form of the technical manual was also their 'most characteristic document' (Kaster, 34).

[146] Many examples of γραμματικὴ ἐπιστήμη on TLG, e.g. Harpocration, *Epist.* 3 ~ Thessalus, *De virtutibus herbarum*, prol. 3 Ἀσκήσας ⟨γὰρ τὴν⟩ γραμματικὴν ἐπιστήμην ἐν τοῖς τῆς Ἀσίας κλίμασι; cf. also Ramsay, 386 no. 232, A l. 2 Μούσαις ἀσκηθείς, B l. 10 γράμμασι δ' ἠσκήθην ἐκπονέσας μετρίοις.

[147] TLG s.v. (φιλο)σοφία and ζηλωτής (e.g. Athen. 3.97 F; Euseb. *Orat. ad sanct. coet.* 17.1, *PE* 11.18.26; Porph. *Abst.* 1.3); σοφίας...ἐραστής (e.g. Plut. *Sol.* 2.2, Philo, *Cherub.* 41); and other expressions of this sort, e.g. Plat. *Prot.* 343 A οὗτοι πάντες ζηλωταὶ καὶ ἐρασταὶ καὶ μαθηταὶ ἦσαν τῆς Λακεδαιμονίων παιδείας; Diod. Sic. 8.31.1 ζηλωτὴς παιδείας; Eunap. *Vit. Soph.* 5.1.4 παιδείας ἐπιθυμοῦντες.

Maximinum, PG 50.572 νεότητι λάμποντες), but it is impossible to silence the suggestion of social status (compare 6.353 ποτὲ δ' αὐτῶν παῖδες ἀνάκτων).

205 ἐνὶ στέρνοισιν ἔχοντας: LGHP hexameter ending (including in Maximus, 260; *Or. Sib.* 8.330; Quint. Smyrn. 3.595, 5.175), replacing *Il.* 4.309 ἐνὶ στήθεσσιν ἔχοντες as στέρνον tends to crowd out στῆθος in LGHP (i. 283 and n. 1).

206–13

Mercury aspects Venus.

Protasis. Although M^b continues to follow the τέχναι sequence in Θ, the set-up is quite different from the one in pp. 214.22–215.3. All they have in common is Mercury. Θ involves just about every other planet except Venus, which is conjoined with Mercury both here and in 6.465–71. But M^a and M^b are themselves different. The former offers much more detail (Venus in Mercury's houses alongside Mercury himself, or each in the other's terms), which is closer to *Lib. Herm.* xxxiv. 29. The interpretation of 4.208–9 presumably turns on ἐπέχοντες, but it is hard to see how it could have either of these meanings.

Apodosis. The combination of Mercury and Venus in M^a and M^b does not reflect the Mercury/Venus Π- chart in Ptol. 4.4.6/Θ p. 213.9–13, which concentrates on music. Instead, the material on technical specialists—geometers, astrologers, and specialist diviners—is paralleled in a mixture of sources for either Mercury alone (see on 4.211), or for other combinations of Mercury and Venus. We re-encounter the geometers and astrologers of 4.210–11 in *Lib. Herm.* (Mercury and Venus in each other's houses, terms, or in conjunction), while the specialist diviners of 210–13 are best paralleled in Ptol. 3.14.5, where the planets' western settings by day and eastern settings by night produce souls including μαγικάς, μετεωρολογικάς (cf. 6.470–1?), ἀστρολογικάς, οἰωνοσκοπικάς, and ὀνειροκριτικάς (cf. *Lib. Herm. somniorum iudicatores*), although the very niche specialisms of hydromancy, lecanomancy, and necromancy are perhaps the poet's amplification, like the *nabla* players above. There are also similarities with the list in Θ p. 166.4–6 (Mercury eastern in the ninth place) ἱερομάντεις, θύτας, οἰωνοσκόπους, ἀστρολόγους θεοπλόκους, and with Θ's τ- chart (p. 215.2–3), where Mercury or Saturn in Mercury's houses are in the ASC and μαθηματικούς are the result.

It is less clear that M^a has in mind the bare description of Mercury's effects on πρᾶξις. But his two categories—geometers and lofty thinkers on eternal verities—are reminiscent, not only of *Lib. Herm.*'s *geometros, astronomos*, but also of Mercury (alone) on the ASC in Θ p. 137.13–14 γεωμέτρας ἢ καὶ τῶν οὐρανίων μύστας.

Γενεαί and τέχναι 591

In sum, M^b seems to have produced a compilation of Mercury-based material, some involving Venus too. M^a has more a complex protasis and simpler apodosis. The influence of a source on shared houses or terms shows itself in both poets (the geometers), but only M^a's protasis reflects that explicitly.

206 Very reminiscent of Dorotheus, p. 430.124 στίλβων ἀστὴρ μέγας Ἑρμάωνος.

207 Κυθερηΐδος αἴγλης: similar cadences in Nonn. *D.* 14.10 Κυβεληΐδος ἠχοῦς, 42.60 Λιβανηΐδος ὕλης, 48.347 ποταμηΐδος ὄχθης, *Par.* 6.1 et al. Τιβερηΐδος ἄλμης, and also in Anubion, F 12.38 = 12 Perale Κυθερηΐδος οἴκ[ῳ]. Partly anticipated by Ap. Rhod. 2.548 Θυνηΐδος ἀκτῆς.

208-9 Making this couplet meaningful is not at all easy. The 'literal' translation in Koechly 1851 is 'et radios injicientes in caelo stelligero | 12-in-partes-descriptorum (siderum) habeant gradum incurvum'; Lopilato, who prints the same text, agrees with the translation of ἐπέχοντες, 'sending out their rays in the starry heaven'. It is odd that the reference to 'dodecatemories' has no match in Θ (n. on 4.167-8). But the real problem is the participle in 208, which ought to mean, not 'emitting', but 'occupying' (6.47, 200; an ἐποχή is a position), which is hard to understand with αὐγάς. One would prefer a reference to (say) swapping terms or houses ('the one occupying the house of the other'), as in M^a—but it is hard to see how to do that in the space available. At 4.460 θεωροσύνην ἐπέχοντος means 'occupying an aspecting position', but it is also hard to get that out of this, or to see what it would add to the line before.

The clausula of 208 is one of several adaptations of *Il.* 4.44 (ὑπ' ἠελίῳ τε καὶ) οὐρανῷ ἀστερόεντι, combined, for the preposition, with 8.555 ἐν οὐρανῷ ἄστρα or 22.318 ἐν οὐρανῷ ἵσταται ἀστήρ. It well lends itself to astronomical (pseudo-pagan verses ap. Clem. Al. *Strom.* 5.14.107.4/Euseb. *PE* 13.12.16, 13.13.34) and apocalyptic (*Or. Sib.* 3.758 and 758) pronouncements.

210-13 The list of diviners (which constitutes a little genre of its own) can be dismissive,[148] damning (as when Byzantine writers use it to mark bad people or bad times for the empire[149])—or self-advertising, as when Nectanebo lays claim to the whole lot.[150] The neutrally informative tone here is more like that of the lexicographers,[151] or rather encourages admiration for the rich variety of what language gives names to, or what the stars produce. In Ptol. 4.4.10 the point is differentiation by signs; the effect is somewhat obsessive.

210 As well as the passages above, note Ptol. 3.14.26 γεωμέτρας, μαθηματικούς (Jupiter with Mercury in honourable positions).

---

[148] Artemidorus, 2.69.1; Dickie 2003, 231.
[149] Cedrenus, *Compend. Hist.* 2.146.14–15/John Scylitzes, *Synops. Hist.*, Michael 3, 4.
[150] *Hist. Alex. Magn., Recensio a*, 1.4.3.
[151] e.g. Phrynichus, p. 91.7 ὀνειρόμαντις, ἀστρόμαντις, ὀρνιθόμαντις, ἀλφιτόμαντις.

211 Compare Ptol. 4.4.3 and Θ p. 210.26 (Mercury as Ruler of πρᾶξις) .... μάντεις, ἀστρολόγους, θύτας. But the magi are new here, famed as sacrificial experts,[152] a connection known to astrology (Valens, II 17.57 μάγους, πλάνους, θύτας, ἰατρούς, ἀστρολόγους; ps.-Clem. Recogn. 9.17.1 μυστηρίων ἀποκρύφων ἵστορας, μάγους, θύτας καὶ τὰ τούτοις ἀκόλουθα). It is simply a topos; one need not ask whether *echt* Persian magi are meant.[153] At the same time, the magi are a suitable presence within the list of diviners (Cumont, 158-9 n. 4, citing *Hist. Alex. Magn., Recensio a*, 1.4.3, 170 n. 3, and 175 n. 3). Further on magi, see on 6.475.

212 οἰωνοσκοπικούς: 'augural types'; the closest parallel is Ptol. 3.14.5 ἀστρολογικάς, φιλοσόφους, οἰωνοσκοπικάς, ὀνειροκριτικὰς, where the feminines agree with ψυχάς.

ὑδρομάντιας: Cumont, 161 n. 4 (no others in astrology). Bibliography in J. Heeg, *CCAG* viii/2. 141; S. Carroll, 'A Preliminary Analysis of the *Epistle to Rehoboam*', in *Journal for the Study of the Pseudepigrapha*, 4 (1989), 91–103, at 100 n. 3, to which add Y. Hajjar, 'Divinités oraculaires et rites divinatoires en Syrie et en Phénicie à l'époque gréco-romaine', *ANRW* II 18.4 (1990), 2236–2320, at 2296–8. C. B. R. Pelling, 'Notes on Plutarch's *Caesar*', *RhM*² 127 (1984), 33–45, at 39: it 'seems to have been a technique derived from the Orient and from Egypt'.

213 οἷς here is not just a lazy connective; the two species of divination in this line are expressly linked to the previous one. Lecanomancy is treatable as a subtype of water-divination (Bouché-Leclercq, i. (1879), 184–6; Hajjar (n. above), 2297), and necromancy is not infrequently combined with it.[154] Indeed, lecanomancy itself could be used to conjure illusions of the dead (*Cyranides*, 1.13 ἐν ταῖς νεκυομαντείαις ταῖς διὰ λεκάνης γενομέναις; *PGM* iv.

---

[152] Hdt. 7.191.2; Derveni papyrus, col. vi, cited by J. N. Bremmer, 'The Birth of the Term "Magic"', *ZPE* 126 (1999), 1–12, at 7; Strab. 15.3.13; Diog. Laert. 1.6 (with W. Burkert, *Die Griechen und der Orient: Von Homer bis zu den Magiern* (Munich, 2003), 130); Philostr. *Vit. Apoll.* 1.29.1; Greg. Naz. PG 36.340.14 μάγων θυτική and its commentary in ps.-Nonnus, *Scholia mythologica, Or.* 39 *hist.* 15 Οἱ Μάγοι διὰ θυσιῶν ἔλεγον τὰς προγνώσεις, διὰ τῆς ἡπατοσκοπίας. Sacrifices prescribed by Zoroaster: Dio Chrys. *Or.* 36.40. On the magi and sacrifice, see E. Bickerman and H. Tadmor, 'Darius I, Pseudo-Smerdis, and the Magi', in *Athenaeum*, 56 (1978), 239–61, at 254–5; M. Boyce, *A History of Zoroastrianism*, i: *The Early Period* (Leiden, 1975), 168–9, ii: *Under the Achaemenians* (Leiden, 1982), 117–18; De Jong, 400–1. Magi and sacrificers juxtaposed in e.g. Herodian, *Ab exc. div. Marc.* 4.12.3; Pollux, 7.188.

[153] A valid question for the Derveni passage: T. Kouremenos, G. M. Parássoglou, and K. Tsantsanoglou (eds.), *The Derveni Papyrus* (Florence, 2006), 166–7; F. Ferrari, 'Rites without Frontiers: Magi and Mystae in the Derveni Papyrus', *ZPE* 179 (2011), 71–83.

[154] Ogden 2001, 191–3, and id. 2009, 54; Strab. 16.2.39 οἱ μάγοι καὶ νεκυομάντεις καὶ ἔτι οἱ λεγόμενοι λεκανομάντεις καὶ ὑδρομάντεις; Artemidorus, 2.69.1; Cedrenus, *Compend. Hist.* 2.146.14/John Scylitzes, *Synops. Hist.*, *Michael* 3, 4 νῦν δὲ ἡπατοσκοπίαι καὶ λεκανομαντεῖαι καὶ γοητεῖαι καὶ νεκυομαντεῖαι ἐνηργοῦντο.

227; *PDM* xiv. 280–95; Nelson, 374, 380; cf. Bouché-Leclercq, i. (1879), 340–1), and water is otherwise in conjurations of the dead, for example though the use of libations (Ogden 2001, 169–70).

λεκανοσκοπίη: see too Ptol. 4.4.10/Θ p. 210.7 μάντεις, θύτας, λεκανομάντεις (Moon after New, with Mercury, in Taurus, Capricorn, Cancer). For λεκανομαντεία, divination by a dish or bowl (J. Heeg, *CCAG* viii/2. 141–3; Hajjar, 2297; W. Burkert, *The Orientalizing Revolution: Near Eastern Influence on Greek Culture in the Early Archaic Age* (Cambridge, MA, 1992), 53; Nelson, 365–9). This passage will give little insight into technique (for example, whether oil was poured onto the surface of the water), though the combination with necromancy suggests that what is envisaged is 'intuitive' divination (i.e. visions, as in e.g. Hippolytus, *Ref.* 4.35, or in an anecdote about Bishop Sophronius of Constantia, near Edessa, cf. Dickie 2003, 267–8) rather than (or as well as) inductive (i.e. the reading of signs). Above all, it is plausible in an Egyptian setting. Whatever one makes of Genesis' apparent reference to Joseph's interest in cup divination (44:5, 15),[155] the Demotic magical papyrus P.Leiden/London (*PDM* xiv, 3rd c. AD) attests the practice of scrying—by various means including liquid in a vessel—in Roman Egypt (Nelson, 365 and n. 9), and it belonged in the imaginary of Egypt as well, with lecanomancy being attributed to Nectanebo in the Alexander Romance (*Recensio a*, 1.1.3). Indeed, the word for divination in Coptic meant literally 'inquiring of cup' (Nelson, 366 n. 12).

νεκυϊσμός: Bouché-Leclercq, i. (1879) 330–43; Cumont, 166; Ogden 2001. Also mentioned in astrology in Θ p. 193.5 γόητας, νεκυομάντεις (Mars and Mercury, centred, aspected by Moon and Saturn), and in Ptol. 4.4.10/Θ p. 210.8 (Moon after *synodos* makes contact with Mercury in Taurus, Capricorn, Cancer). See above for the connection between necromancy and the other forms of divination mentioned here.

214–17

Venus aspects Mars with Saturn. From this point until 4.249–62, the poet takes a break from the τ- sequence in Θ. As with 4.193–200, it looks as if here and in the next chart οἶνος configurations have crossed over into the τέχναι. They have infiltrated the τέχναι of Mᵃ as well (i. 785), though not adjacently. Perhaps the immediate link is *via* the prophets in the last chart.

---

[155] J. Capart, 'Les anciens Égyptiens pratiquaient-ils déjà la lécanomancie?' *Chronique d'Égypte*, 19 (1944), 263, and figs. 30 and 31; J. Vergote, *Joseph en Égypte* (Louvain, 1959), 172–6; F. Cunen, 'Les pratiques divinatoires attribuées à Joseph d'Égypte', *Revue des sciences religieuses*, 33 (1959), 396–404.

Protasis. The closest cousins here are 4.214-17 and 6.491-3, involving both malefics and Venus (Θ p. 194.2 has only one malefic and adds the *kentron*). Mars in 4.214 is an emendation by De Stefani (for ἠέρα), but it makes good sense. Θ p. 192.16-18, on the other hand, is more directly represented by 1.235-44, where Venus is enclosed by malefics in the situation known as ἐμπερίσχεσις.

Apodosis. All involve some sort of divine madness. Venus' influence produces θεοφορία (Ptol. 3.15.6, on psychic harms), whence presumably Θ pp. 192.18 and 194.3 θεοφορουμένους. M^b does not reflect Θ's vocabulary, though M^a shares φοιβαζ- with Θ p. 192.18.

214 ἀκτῖνας...πυρσοβολοῦσα: compare 4.438 πυρσοβόλοις ἀκτῖσι, as well as 467 πυρσοτόκος (Mars). πυρσός is a torch, firebrand, or beacon. The poet—as again with λαμπτήρ in 426—has reconstrued a source of light as the beams which emanate from it. The same happens in Straton, *AP* 12.196.2 ἀκτῖνας... πυρσοβόλους (of the eyes of an attractive youth).

215 ἄμμιγα: also 290, 458; as one of the poet's various comitative expressions (T. Mommsen, 213; i. 125-6; pp. 201, 242) it takes the dative, which is Nicandrian only in *Ther.* 850, *Al.* 548, but also Apollonian and elsewhere. For the history of the word, see Livrea on Ap. Rhod. 4.628 (adding Theocr. *Ep.* 5.3 = *AP* 9.433.3). Dorotheus, p. 428.102, uses it as an adverb.

μεροπήια ἔργα: cf. 4.474 γενεὴ μεροπήιος. Perhaps it was the topic of slavery that prompted the turn to miserabilist language (i. 58-9). The late antique epithet distinguishes humans from beasts (ps.-Opp. *Cyn.* 1.23; 2.364, 541; 3.15), gods (or God) (Or. ap. Eunap. i. 230.2 Dindorf; *AP* 1.25.2 μεροπηίδα φύτλην), or just evokes the human condition (Christodorus, *AP* 2.1.270 μεροπήια πήματα; *Theos. Tüb.* 36 μεροπήιος Ὕπνος).

216 ἱερῶν τε νεωκόρα λυσσομανοῦντα: for νεωκόρος, see i. 336. The present passage, like 4.430 σηκῶν τε νεωκορίῃσι, which also has the relatively unusual feature of following up with the genitive of a temple (rather than the god's name),[156] conflates the idea of an administrator with that of an inspired prophet. λύσσα is a general word for frenzy without being linked specifically to prophecy, which is also clear from the epithet λυσσομανής (Hellenistic and thereafter[157]); at 6.597 it is a feature of melancholy. The agencies that cause it are different each time the Manethoniana mention it, though Mars, Venus, and

---

[156] νεωκόρος of Sarapis, and so on. Of a temple also in Nicephorus Callistus Xanthopoulos, *Hist. Eccl.* 3.37 νεωκόρος τοῦ μεγίστου ναοῦ.

[157] Antipater of Sidon, *AP* 6.219.2 = *HE* 609 λυσσομανεῖς πλοκάμους (madness inspired by Cybele); Callias the Argive, *AP* 11.232.2 λυσσομανές τι κακόν (effect of drink); Opp. *Hal.* 2.208 λυσσομανῆ βούβρωστιν.

Saturn are again involved in 5.338 (a distinctly non-inspired case). The participle is new and rare (Ephrem Syrus, *Encomium in sanctos quadraginta martyres*, p. 151.6 τὴν λυσσομανοῦσαν ἀκρίδα).

217 σεληνάζοντα: see on 4.81.

218-23

Mars aspecting Sun, together with Moon and Venus.

Protasis. The set-up is compatible with Θ pp. 194.18–195.2, except that the latter does not involve the Sun and does specify the DESC as the location of the conjunct Venus and Moon.

Apodosis. The outcome, but not the set-up, is like 6.534–40, the last of the τέχναι, but an outlier from it (dealing with *galli*), and finding its closest parallel in Firmicus, 6.30.18.

219 T. Mommsen, 214, singles this line out for its plethora of comitative expressions; μίγα itself (on which see Livrea on Ap. Rhod. 4.1345) hovers between adverbial and prepositional uses when it recurs in 4.527. ὁρμώσης (also 4.387 ὁρμήσῃ, of Mercury) strongly implies personification, but neither passage hostility; for other verbs for the Moon's motion, see i. 843–4 n. 141. Compare *Or. Chald.* fr. 61a des Places μήνης ἄπλετος ὁρμή.

220 θηλυτέρους: always accompanied by part of γυναικ- in EGHP (unless goddesses are meant). In those cases, it is oppositional (women as opposed to men: 1.30 n); here, in qualifying ἄνδρας, it suggests a different sense of the comparative ('rather', 'woman-ish'). In 3.392 it qualifies the signs under which eunuchs are born (395 γυναικῶν ἔργα τελοῦντες). That passage, however, uses a different logic: gender problems arise when the luminaries are feminised, whereas here the masculine Sun is reinforced by the very masculine Mars, and there are no signs. There is a different logic again in Valens, II 17.68 πολλάκις δὲ καὶ τῶν γονίμων στερίσκονται: this chart is purely planetary, with Venus and Saturn both in a westerly position (which feminises). The deviant gender of the *galli* is itself imagined in different ways: see on 1.125 for 'neither man nor woman', and *RAC* s.v. Gallos (G. M. Sanders), 1024, with sources for ἀνδρόγυνοι, *semiviri*. Cat. 63.27 has *notha mulier*.

γονίμων μηδέων ἀπαμήτορας ἄνδρας: the (restored) agent noun is *hapax*, but the basic verb ἀπαμᾶν is specialised for mutilation (*Od.* 21.300–1, of nose and ears), especially castration (Hes. *Th.* 180–1 φίλου δ' ἀπὸ μήδεα πατρὸς | ἐσσυμένως ἤμησε). This same passage has supplied (if Axtius was right) μήδεα to both this passage and 3.396 (see ad loc.); Mᵃ has paid tribute in a different way, by retaining a finite verb with tmesis but substituting a synonym (p. 220). A similar expression for genitals in Alcaeus, *AP* 6.218.1 = *HE* 134 Κειράμενος γονίμην τις ἄπο φλέβα.

221 γαλλομανεῖς: manic *galli* aplenty in the epigrams about the encounter with a lion (Dioscorides, *AP* 6.220.2 = *HE* 1540 μαινομένην δοὺς ἀνέμοισι τρίχα, with Gow–Page ad loc.; Antipater, *AP* 6.219.2 = *HE* 609 λυσσομανεῖς πλοκάμους); Hesych. κ 4370 κυβέβις· γάλλος. κίναιδος. μανιῶν; Eustath. on *Od.* 4.249 (i. 163.39) μαινόμενος ἄσωτος γάλλος; Cat. 63.4 *furenti rabie*, 38 *rabidus furor*. The epithet is unique. The adjectival nature of the second half of the compound, which is unique (mad, not mad for or maddening or maddened by), seems peculiar (B.-P. 721–2; James, 96–7).

ἀγυρτῆρας: see on 6.299. For ἀγύρται, see Graillot, 312–16; Blümner, 27–8; Sanders, *RAC* s.v. Gallos, 987, 997–8; Dickie 2003, 64–5.

222 The line as a whole is similar to 33, on which see for ἐπιβήτορας, but other ἐπιβήτορας lines are erected on the same foundation (incl. 245), while content is similar to 4.281 and 521. In creating πολυπλαγκτοσύνης the poet may have had an eye on 6.539 πλάζονται (another characteristic noun/verb difference between the two: p. 220). The abstract is unique, though it uses the epithet πολύπλαγκτος (*hapax* in *Iliad*, 3× *Od.*) to bolster *Od.* 15.343 πλαγκτοσύνης (also used of Odysseus in *Laudatio professoris Smyrnaei* (XXX Heitsch), l. 64, as well as of the revolution of the stars in Planudes' Greek translation of Boethius). The Odyssean passages have already set the tone—long suffering on the one hand (*Od.* 17.511, cf. 510 ταλασίφρονος; 20.195 δυόωσι), vagabondage on the other (*Od.* 17.425).

223 διαδέκτορας: already Eur. *Ion.* 478, but there in practice passive, 'received', i.e. inherited.[158] Given the Odyssean vocabulary in this passage, it would be fitting if the poet had in mind the meaning of δέκτης, 'receiver' in the sense of 'beggar' (Fraenkel, i. 76–7: *hapax* in *Od.* 4.248), where Aristarchus took it as a common noun and glossed it as ἐπαίτης, while others took it as a proper noun, a soubriquet Odysseus adopted when he entered Troy in disguise (but which still rests on the same idea). If so, M^b would be enhancing the theme of mendicancy with a suggestion of an extra, Odyssean level (4.449, 5.212 nn.). *Galli* are indeed receivers (see Cic. *Leg.* 2.22, 40 for the collection of *stips*, and Dyck on 22.4; for the priests of the Syrian Goddess cadging petty gifts, see ps.-Lucian, *Asin.* 37; Parkin, 67), but what they receive is a painful and unhappy life (of which Odysseus also had his fair share).

---

[158] Fraenkel, i. 77, nevertheless translates it as active ('vererbend', 'als Erbschaft empfangend', while in ii. 10 he renders 'Reichtum, der durch Vererbung seinen Besitzer wechselt', which obscures the issue by seeming to give the verb a double application, to the inheritance of the money and the transformative effect on the one who possesses it.

224-9

Venus aspecting Moon, or in conjunction with it. This does not seem to be a πρᾶξις configuration, but neither are there parallels in Θ ch. 65 Περὶ μαινομένων καὶ ἐπιληπτικῶν, under aspect (Firmicus, 6.26.5; Περὶ κράσ. 200), or *synaphai* (Firmicus, 4.6). One might have expected a mystic outcome to involve Saturn, but the logic is compatible with Ptolemy, who does associate Venus in certain positions with mysteries.[159] In Θ p. 145.5 a προφήτης is born when the Moon is together with the other benefic in the third house.

224 ἑλικάστερον: see on 4.26 (for the -άστερος compound) and 4.146 (for ἑλικ- compounds used for the Moon).

αἰθροβολήσῃ: this must be a synonym for αἰγλοβολήσῃ (strike *in* the aether): a sort of zero-grade of ἀκτινοβολία, which eliminates mention of rays. αἰθρο- compounds seem to be an astrological specialism. M^a already had a couple (2.383 αἰθροπολεύων; cf. Maximus, who has αἰθροπολεύσ- four times as a contraction of αἰθροπολέω; 6.440, whence also 4.278, αἰθροβάτας), to which M^b adds this and three epithets—4.298 αἰθροδόνητον, 339 αἰθροτόκου, 586 αἰθροπλανής.

225 ἀκτῖσι χρυσέῃσι: this adaptation of the χρυσέη Ἀφροδίτη formula[160] perhaps nudges it towards the phenomenology of the planet. When the quality of Venus' light is at issue it is often a question of radiance rather than colour, and when a colour is specified (Bouché-Leclercq, 314 n. 2; Roscher, s.v. Planeten (Roscher), 2531-2; Boll 1916, 20; Pingree 1978, ii. 248-50), that colour is often white. But a yellow hue is mentioned by Plat. *Rep.* 617 A ξανθότερος, Ptol. 2.10.1 ξανθά (colours of eclipses, whose effects are like those of the planets who share that colour); cf. Boll 1916, 22-3 (with a 17th.-c. text characterising Venus as *buxea* ('blaßgelb'). 'Gold' (outright) is putting it rather strongly, though in the Washington University text edited by Packman, which apparently gives instructions for the counters that represent the planets on an astrology board, Venus is represented by lapis lazuli πε]ρίχρυσος (9; rendered 'veined with gold' by Packman, 94, although the preposition would suggest 'rimmed with'). Boll (20) notes Σ German. p. 103.8 Breysig *Phosphoros colore aureo*; and there appears to be at least one similar case in a neo-Latin poem by Bartholomaeus

---

[159] 2.3.19 (occidental Venus); 3.14.5 μαγικάς, μυστηριακάς…(western settings by day and morning settings by night); 3.14.16 φοιβαστικούς, θρησκευτάς, μυστηρίων καὶ τελετῶν ἐπιθυμητάς (Saturn as Ruler of the soul allied with Venus); 3.14.25 (Jupiter as Ruler of the soul allied with Venus).

[160] West on Hes. *Th*. 822; and for πολυχρύσου Ἀφροδίτης West on *Th*. 980 and Faulkner on *HHom. Aphr.* 1. I. Ziogas, *Ovid and Hesiod: The Metamorphosis of the Catalogue of Women* (Cambridge, 2013), 33, notes that archaic poets were already capable of playing on its literal and figurative meanings.

Beverinus in praise of Queen Christina of Sweden,[161] where *Venus aurea* is the planet. See also i. 914 n. 27.

226–7 That is, conjunction ζῳδιακῶς (i. 47, 884)?

227 ἱερολήπτους must be the equivalent of θεολήπτους (see on 4.80). The latter are associated with prophets (6.378; dream interpreters: Ptol. 4.4.10/Θ p. 210.10; φοιβαζομένους: Epit. IIIb, *CCAG* vii. 112.19–20/Θ p. 193.16–17; augurs, astrologers, *et al.*: Θ p. 148.14–15).

229 μυστιπόλους: for astrology and mysteries, see on 2.197–9. From non-epigraphical texts alone this passage and the Orphic Hymns (6×, including 48.6, 68.12, of devotees, and 49.2, as epithet of τελεταί) would be contenders for first occurrence, but it is found before then on Attic inscriptions, the earliest datable one being *IG* II² 3734 (Attica, 126/7), epithet of a ἱροπόλος at the Eleusinia.

ῥεκτῆρας: see on 4.149, but here as in Hesych. ρ 139 ῥεκτῆρα. σφαγέα. ῥέκτης does not seem to have this sense, but the verb can (LSJ s.v., II).

ὀργιόωντας: the absolute form of ὀργιάζειν, which this varies, is in Eur. *Bacch.* 416; Ap. Rhod. 2.907; Herodian, *Ab exc. div. Marc.* 1.11.2, 5.5.4.

230–7

Mars in opposition to Mercury or in conjunction in equal degrees. 4.230–7 and 6.446–9 are affiliated with each other and in turn with two closely related charts in Θ, one belonging to harms (p. 193.1–3), the other among the τέχναι (pp. 217.24–218.2), but still not part of the running τ- sequence.

Protasis. All configurations involve Mercury and Mars, but each has a unique detail—Mᵃ, human signs; Mᵇ, opposition as an alternative to conjunction; Θ's τ- chart, Leo. Equal degrees are a detail uniquely shared between Mᵇ and Θ's οἶνος chart. The references to signs are another pointer to factors Mᵇ has jettisoned (p. 148); Θ's Leo is presumably a figurehead for the carnage, while Mᵃ's human signs inflect the outcome into a more 'humane' dimension by making the natives custodians—φρουρούς—of children (as opposed to the σωματοφρουρητῆρας of 4.232).

Apodosis. Mᵇ is obviously closely related to Θ's οἶνος chart and the Π- chart for Mars and Mercury (various kinds of deceiver), while the bodyguards also suggest those who are prepared to put their life on the line in Θ p. 218.1–2. Yet perhaps the best and most comprehensive parallel is Θ p. 179.15–24, part of a discussion of the powers of the fixed stars—*not* the planets—and their effect when they are exactly on *kentra* and conjoined with planets (p. 175.1

---

[161] In *Carmina illustrium poetarum Italorum*, vol. 2, ed. T. Buonaventura (Florence, 1719), 199.

Γενεαί and τέχναι 599

ἰσομοιροῦντες τοῖς κέντροις καὶ τοῖς πλάνησι). This section discusses a number of fixed stars, all said to be 'of the krasis of Mars and Mercury' (κράσεως Ἄρεως καὶ Ἑρμοῦ), in other words the same combination as here:

Οἱ τοιοῦτοι ἀστέρες πάλιν ἰσομοίρως ὡροσκοποῦντες ἢ μεσουρανοῦντες, μάλιστα ἐπὶ νυκτερινῆς γενέσεως ποιοῦσι στρατηγικούς, δεινούς, δράστας, πολυτρόπους, σοφιστικούς, πολυπράγμονας, λογίους, ἀπαρεγκλίτας, ὀξυφώνους, ἐξαπατητὰς [cf. 237 ἀπάτην], ἐπιτευκτικούς, ὀξεῖς δὲ ἅμα καὶ ἀπροσκορεῖς πρὸς τὰς ἐπιθυμίας, διαφθορεῖς ὄντας ἀθῴων καὶ παρθένων, ἐπιόρκους. ἐπὶ δὲ ἡμερινῆς γενέσεως ὡροσκοποῦντες ποιοῦσι τολμηρούς, ὠμούς, μεταμελητικούς, ψεύστας, κλέπτας, ἀθέους [cf. 234 θεολωβήτας], ἀφίλους, ἐπιθέτας, θεατροκόπους, ἐφυβρίστας, μιαιφόνους, πλαστογράφους, γόητας, ἀνδροφόνους, οὐ καλῷ τέλει ἐνίοτε χρωμένους μάλιστα, ὡς προείπομεν, ἐπὶ ἡμερινῆς γενέσεως.

Overlaps are not always word-for-word, but remain salient. The desperadoes are realised as generals, then types of deceiver follow (though not in the same order as in M^b). There are deceivers, liars, and forgers, and godless types who correspond to M^b's outragers of the gods. Only the 'blaming' motif seems to be without parallel.

230 Mars strikes Mercury from opposite with its rays. True, opposition is introduced by emendation (Axtius), but it is a better emendation than Keydell's (for whom ἀκτινι- was an intrusive gloss which led to the deletion of the epithet πυριφεγγεῖ in an attempt to restore the metre) or De Stefani's in that it makes better sense of ἢ in the following line. The alternatives are ἀντία and being ἰσόμοιρος with (presumably the distinction by sign or by degree: i. 884), exactly as in 4.73–4 and 379–80. (True, μετά is not otherwise used of conjunction in this book, but it often is elsewhere.[162]) Only M^b among the Manethonian poets uses λαμπάς, here and in 4.335; see ad loc.

232 σωματοφρουρητῆρας: σωματοφύλακες are indeed mentioned in astrology (Cumont, 31 n. 2), but not under these circumstances (Valens, I 20.29: Mercury and the luminaries).

σωματοφόρβους: if these specialists in dietetics are to be made to correspond to a known job-title it could be the γυμναστής—one aspect of whose role was nutrition, along with oversight of exercise, sleep, and sexual conduct (cf. p. 577 and n. 114; J. König, 'Regimen and Athletic Training', in G. L. Irby-Massie (ed.), *A Companion to Science, Technology, and Medicine in Ancient Greece and Rome* (Chichester, 2016), 450–64). Sources on γυμνασταί certainly mention their concern with bodily condition and εὐεξία (e.g. Isocr. *Or.* 15.181 περὶ μὲν τὰ σώματα τὴν παιδοτριβικήν [sc. ἐπιμελείαν], ἧς ἡ γυμναστικὴ μέρος ἐστίν; Xen. *Mem.* 2.1.20; Philo, *Spec. Leg.* 2.230; Plut. *Mor.* 7 D; Philostratus, *Gymn.*

---

[162] 2.417; 6.77, 191, 195, 567; 1.58, 224; 5.169, 316.

14). They do not, as far as I can see, make nutrition the lead element, though Philostratus makes clear that food was part of the training regime of the γυμναστής (44, 48), and for Galen, *De Sanitate tuenda*, 1.15 (vi. 78 K.), food is one item among four *differentiae* of hygiene. If trainers are what M^b has in mind, this is compatible with M^a's παίδων φύλακας φρουρούς θ' ἥβης ἐρατεινῆς.

233 πλαστογράφους: see on 2.305. Once again, these are the outcomes when Mercury and Mars are in aspect (cunning intelligence misapplied) in Θ p. 183.14–16.

234 θεολωβήτας, κακοεργέας: the diction appears to have been influenced by 3.289 κακοεργέα λώβην. For the first, see on 4.196. The parallels with ἀσεβεῖς (Θ p. 218.2), ἀθέους (p. 179.21), suggest that these commit outrages against the gods rather than being injured by them, and that those offences consist in perjury (Θ pp. 193.3, 218.2 ἐπιόρκους) rather than blasphemy (cf. 6.625, a different configuration). The -ήτης termination is new (Fraenkel, i. 136 n. 2). Homer had λωβητήρ (*hapax*, *Il*. 11.385); later came λωβήτωρ (see on 6.211). For its epithet see i. 909 n. 8; already associated with Mars' effects in 3.289.

ἀφθιτομίσους: possible renderings are 'eternally hating', 'eternally hated', or 'hating/hated by the immortals' (θεομισεῖς: De Stefani), according to the post-EGHP use of ἀφθιτ- for gods (see Thomas on *HHom. Herm*. 325–6; Braswell on Pind. *P*. 4.33(d)). The first half of the compound is unusual *tout court*, the second in its position,[163] but astrology has a relatively large number of μισ- compounds which attach to unintegrated individuals, sociopaths, like these.[164] Valens has a number of instances of μισοΐδιοι, μισάνθρωποι; a particularly hate-filled section in I 3.40 (the terms of Saturn in Scorpio) μισοϊδίων...μισογυναίων...μισοῦνται δὲ καὶ ὑπὸ θεῶν καὶ ὑπὸ ἀνθρώπων. More hatred at 4.561 μισέλλην, 566 δῆμοι μισήσουσι. In Ptolemy they cluster in the section on qualities of the soul, implicitly making the point that hatred is some sort of psychic pathology.[165]

235–7 Those who speak ill, for whom astrology has various words, are often mentioned alongside liars and cheats.[166] The best parallel is Θ p. 193.3 (Mars and Mercury of equal degrees in a centre; quoted in 75 n.), where

---

[163] ἀφθιτόμητις (Orph. 111 F Bernabé, epithet of Chronos, and Greg. Naz. *PG* 37.913.5, epithet of the divine Logos); ἀξιόμισος (Aesch. *Eum*. 365, passive); φιλόμισος (*EtMag* p. 793.30–1); B.–P. 737.

[164] Apomasar, *De myst*., *CCAG* xi/1. 179.2–5 σημαίνει δὲ καὶ φυγάδας καὶ πονηροὺς καὶ μνησικάκους καὶ δολίους καὶ ἀπατεῶνας καὶ βλάπτας καὶ τὸ φιλέρημον καὶ τὸ μισεῖν τὴν τῶν ἀνθρώπων ὁμιλίαν; *CCAG* iv. 118.5–7 ψεῦσται, ἄπιστοι, δόλιοι, φθονεροί, ἐπίβουλοι, προδόται, μισόκαλοι, φιλόμαχοι, πλάνοι, μὴ ἔχοντες ἀγάπην βεβαίαν.

[165] 3.14.11 μισοσωμάτους, 13 μισοτέκνους, 14 μισοπολίτας, μισανθρώπους, 16 μισογυναίους, μισοκάλους (also 17), 19 μισοϊδίους, 28 μισοικείους, 33 μισοπονήρους.

[166] Under Saturn's influence: Rhetorius, *CCAG* vii. 215.32 καταφρονητάς, Ptol. 3.14.11, 17 κακολόγους; under Mercury's: *CCAG* vii. 225.32 ψεύστας, πλαστογράφους, λοιδόρους, Valens, II

ψευδοκατηγόρους provides a plausible correspondence for the slanderers whose fabrications are believed, or almost believed, in 236-7. The vocabulary, on the other hand, is exotic—κατονειδιστῆρας unique (the verb, too, is rare before Byzantine prose, four times in Josephus and once in Dionysius of Halicarnassus), and διαβλήτορας *proton legomenon* before Byzantine prose.

238-48

As above, with Saturn in Sagittarius, Pisces, Virgo.

Protasis. This chart lines up with 6.450-5 against Θ p. 216.8-15. In the first place, all involve winged signs, but Θ locates Mercury and the Moon in them, M^a and M^b Saturn. However, both M^b and Θ name the winged signs; M^a does not. In the second place, M^a and M^b are additive, with Mercury + Mars and then Saturn.

Apodosis. All three sources list various kinds of hunter, but M^a and M^b have particular similarities. In Θ, the general domain is hunting, which is narrowed down to bird-(catching and) training by the placement of the agencies in winged signs. But in M^a and M^b, Saturn's location in a winged sign less logically effects *all* kinds of animal-catching. Fishermen stand at the head of the lists in M^a (ἰχθυβόλους) and M^b (ἰχθυοθηρευτάς); from Θ they are absent.[167] Only M^a and M^b include animal-*trainers* (4.246 τιθασῷ/6.455 τιθασοῖσιν), and although M^a organises by species, M^b by activity (hunting then training), the trainers in both stand at the end. But there is also a match between ὀρνίθων τροφοποιούς (M^b) and ὀρνιθοτρόφους (Θ), and ἐπιμόχθους, the very last word, matches Θ p. 151.7 (Mars in the IMC) in a context which implies hunting.

239-40 With the standard set of emendations (Koechly in 239 and Rigler in 240), the point is first made that Saturn is in the same sign (~ ζωιδίῳ) (perhaps implying that it is not necessarily ἰσόμοιρος), and then that it is located in one of the winged signs (Hübner 1982, 125-6) whose enumeration follows.

239 βαίνων τε κατ' αἰθέρα φαίνοπι ῥόμβῳ: the idea of a cosmic *rhombos* (whirl) becomes embedded in late antique hexameter verse (HOrph. 4.4 ῥόμβου δίναισιν ὀδεύων (Ouranos), 8.7 ῥόμβου ἀπειρεσίου δινεύμασιν οἶμον

11.2 (κακολόγους, accompanied by thieves) and Paul, p. 72.13 (κακολόγους, accompanied by thieves and δολίους).

[167] Fishermen (ἁλιεύοντας) are also present in Θ p. 212.17, among other hunting-related outcomes in a paragraph notionally under the rubric of Mars and Mercury as Rulers of πρᾶξις but which in practice includes a mass of observations not all of which involve these two planets. Thus fishermen are born with Saturn alone in the house of πρᾶξις, out of sect and in an alien sign. Has the common source of M^a and M^b produced a compilation on hunting by combining different charts which he found bundled together under the general heading of 'Mars and Mercury'?

ἐλαύνων (the Sun)), but the attribution of this motion to the αἰθήρ (also Nonn. D. 43.16 δρόμον αὐτοκέλευστον ἔχων ἑλικώδεϊ ῥόμβῳ[168]) might suggest a connection with a much-quoted excerpt from a fifth-century tragedy mentioning an aetherial rhombos (αἰθερίῳ | ῥύμβῳ) and a circular dance of the light and darkness and chorus of stars.[169] The lines are included in an anthology of what are claimed to be Greek plagiarisms from 'barbarian philosophy' (in other words, were compatible with the Judaeo-Christian world-view) which is quoted by both Clement, *Strom.* 5.14.114.2 and Euseb. *PE* 13.13.41. If the excerpt also influenced the present passage it would be testimony to the characteristic borrowability into astrology of lines that also suited a henotheistic or even monotheistic cast of mind. See also on 4.108 ῥομβηδόν, and for the phrase κατ' αἰθέρα on 2.1, 4.140. For the epithet φαίνοπι the only parallel is *IG* XII,5 739.31 (Isis inscription from Andros, 1st c. BC or AD), where φαίνοπα is epithet of ἀέλιον (less likely of πόλον), but gesturing in the present passage to Saturn's light-name (see also on 4.176–7).

240 σελάγισμα: see on 4.189.

Τοξότεω... μέλαθρον: genitive of identity (house consisting in the sign of Sagittarius). While this is the only attempt to co-opt μέλαθρον for technical terminology, M^a has already used the synonyms δόμος, μέγαρον and δώματα in connection with *planetary* houses (i. 877).

241 ἠὲ κατ' ἰχθυόεντα: this should be specifying Pisces. Does it agree with implied ζῷα/ζῴδια?

βορειοτάτην τε χορείην: the intuitive interpretation is that this refers to Cancer, location of the Summer Solstice, where the Sun reaches its furthest point north; but Cancer is not among the winged signs. Does it, then, refer to Pisces (with τε coordinating the two expressions for the same sign), or Virgo and Co. in the next line? But Pisces, though it is associated with the north wind and with winter (W. Gundel, *RE* s.v. Pisces, 1780.14–20) is nowhere near the northernmost sign, nor does it govern the northern nations in *geothesia*. Less implausible is that this is a reference to Virgo, or rather to the northern quadrant in which Virgo is located. This is how the passage is understood by both Lopilato, 376, and by Hübner 1982, 50, although taking Leo, Virgo, and Libra to constitute the northern quadrant is somewhat bizarre, and all the more so when other sources gives the northern signs more intuitively as Gemini,

---

[168] Although Chuvin and Fayant ad loc. think the reference is to the hum of the spinning body. The movement of shooting stars in D. 2.190 ἀελλήεντι δὲ ῥόμβῳ is harder to understand. Should they not move in a straight line?

[169] Five anapaestic lines from *Pirithous*, whose attribution to Critias (*TGrF* 43 F 4) rather than Euripides is controversial (C. Collard and M. Cropp (eds.), *Fragments: Oedipus–Chrysippus* (Loeb, 2008), Appendix, 629–35); see Csapo, 273; Seaford, 267.

Cancer, and Leo (Hübner 1982, 266; *Σ* Aratus, 147 σφόδρα βόρεια). At least this interpretation has the possible advantage that it takes χορείην as referring to a large group of stars, not merely to one particular constellation. Perhaps another possibility, however, is that the reference is to Gemini, which is the 'northernmost' point of the Sun's course in that this, at the relevant point in antiquity, was its apogee (see on 4.96–7). Gemini does indeed sometimes figure among the winged signs (Hübner 1982, 125).

242 περὶ Πλάστιγγα: when Libra is called Balances (as opposed to Claws: see on 2.136–7), its name is Ζύγον, not Πλάστιγγες, which is a periphrastic way of referring to the constellation, or to its parts (2.138; Dorotheus, p. 428.121; Hephaestion, i. 68.9 (source not known); Teucer, *CCAG* vii. 204.17; Camaterus, *Introd.* 986). Hephaestion uses the singular because he means only one of the pans, and that could be the case here as well (Virgo is closer to one than the other[170]); if so, a lower-case might give a less misleading impression about titulature, or lack of it. It still leaves the nominative Λέων τε surprising: this is not a winged sign, and should itself be subordinate to περί.

243–4 ἰχθυοθηρευτάς ... ἰξοβόλους ... τοξελκεῖς: the 'encyclopaedic' view of hunting, which groups fishing and fowling along with hunting proper (Varro, *De Re Rust.* 3.3, esp. 3.3.4 *aucupes venatores piscatores*), trumps strict logic, according to which only winged signs should produce fowlers (as in Θ), and wet signs (or planets) fishermen.[171] M^b and M^a (6.451–3) both bundle them all together under the winged, and conversely *CCAG* xi/2. 138.34–5 κυνηγοί, θηρευταί, ἁλιεῖς, ἰξευταί, ὀρνεοτρόφοι lumps them under Pisces. Manilius, 5.295–7 puts them all under Sagitta (8° Libra), and *CCAG* x. 197.17 combines all three as auspicious on the birthday of Nimrod; see Hübner on 5.296–7 for the association of fishing and fowling, and *TLL* s.v. *aucupium*, p. 1238.14–39.[172]

243 ἰχθυοθηρευτάς: the form is not quite unique: Hesych. α 3001 ἁλιεῦσι· θαλαττουργοῖς. ἢ ἰχθυοθηρευταῖς; cf. Apollonides (possibly late Augustan/Tiberian), *AP* 7.702.1 = *Garland* 1185 Ἰχθυοθηρητῆρα.[173]

ἰξοβόλους δολοεργούς: fowlers are born properly under winged signs (*CCAG* i. 166.3 ὀρνιθοθήρας, ὀρνεοτρόφους, ἰξευτάς; Manilius, 5.371–3, under Cycnus); see also on 5.173–6 for fowlers born under Orion. A similar evasion of the proper noun ἰξευτής in Bianor, *AP* 9.273.4 = *Garland* 1710 ἰξοβολῶν (Gow–Page

---

[170] For talking about only one pan at a time, see also Plat. *Rep.* 550 E.
[171] Θ p. 210.4; Hephaestion, i. 244.2. Cancer: Hephaestion, i. 248.17; *CCAG* v/3. 95.7. Under the influence of Saturn: Θ pp. 166.23, 212.17; *CCAG* ii. 191.22.
[172] Fishing combined with hunting: Hephaestion, i. 250.9; *CCAG* iv. 142.28, xi/1. 137.14.
[173] Abstracts at Eustath. on *Il.* 24.587–9 (iv. 263.3) ἰχθυοθηρία and Pollux, *Onom.* 1.97 ἰχθυοθηρική.

prefer the participle, Pauw the epithet ἰξοβόλων). The epithet (for which see on 4.57) could apply to one or both nouns. The first instance of the δόλος motif (*Od.* 12.252) applies to a fisherman,[174] but it is commonplace for hunting (see on 5.281) and fowling as well (for instance, in the Bianor epigram).

244 τοξελκεῖς: metonymic for hunters (~ Θ κυνηγοὺς καὶ βηνάτορας). Hunters obviously *might* use bow and arrows,[175] but they do not seem to have been particularly distinctive of them (on Dunbabin's scenes of animal capture and of *venationes* in the amphitheatre, the weapon of choice is the javelin or thrusting-spear), so the poet would seem to be using Homeric diction (*Il.* 11.375, 582-3, al.) to evoke the trademark weapons of the goddess of hunting (literary references in *LIMC* s.v. Artemis, 619; Roscher, s.v. Artemis (Schreiber), 576.27-38; Bornmann on Call. *Hymn* 2.81).

244-6 For tamers and trainers of animals, see on 6.453-4 and Robert 1940a, 320 (θηροτρόφος), and for the astrological sources, Hübner 2010, ii. 224 (on Manilius, 5.378).

244 ὀρνίθων τροφοποιούς: M^a seems to mean trainers, but τροφ- here suggests those who rear birds for the dinner-table (A. Cameron, *Callimachus and his Critics* (Princeton, 1995), 31-2, noting the use of τρεφ- in Athen. 1.22 D, apropos of birds bred for eating at the Ptolemaic court; Philostr. *Vit. Apoll.* 8.7.15, where the word is πιαίνουσιν). Both types are discussed by Jennison, 100-21; A. R. Littlewood, 'Ancient Literary Evidence for the Pleasure Gardens of Roman Country Villas', in E. B. Macdougall, *Ancient Roman Villa Gardens* (Dumbarton Oaks Colloquium on the History of Landscape Architecture; Washington, DC, 1987), 7-30, at 14-15. For Roman aviaries, see the discussion of *ornithones* in Varro, *De Re Rust.* 3.4-11; Johnson, 6-19 and 20-49. See also Robert 1937, 434-6, and 1960a, 49, for the φασ(ι)ανάριος/*fasianarius*, breeder of pheasants; L. R. Johnston, 'Birds for Pleasure and Entertainment in Ancient Rome', *The Maryland Historian*, 2 (1971), 76-92.

245-6 θηροδιδασκαλίης: διδάσκειν/διδασκαλία are the usual words for animal-training (Plut. *Mor.* 968 B, 972 F, 975 E-F; Aelian, *NA* 2.11; Philostr. *Vit. Apoll.* 6.36.1).

---

[174] And is redeployed in that context almost *ad nauseam* by Oppian: Kneebone, 123; ps.-Opp. *Cyn.* 4.221; Ov. *Hal.* 11, 26.
[175] For hunting weapons, see D.-S. s.v. Venatio (A. Reinach), 683-6. Bow and arrows in ps.-Opp. *Cyn.* 4.54; Julian, *Or.* 2.3 (53 B); Dunbabin 1999, 183 fig. 196; ead., *Mosaics of Roman North Africa: Studies in Iconography and Patronage* (Oxford, 1978), 58 and figs. 35-6; Commodus' displays of archery in the arena, in Herodian, *Ab exc. div. Marc.* 1.15.1-2, 5, cf. Ammianus Marcellinus, 31.10.19, of Gratian.

246 Very similar vocabulary in Aelian, NA 2.11 πραότατον ἀπέφηνε καὶ εὐάγωγον, of the eminently trainable elephant. ἀγρίη γενεή is *variatio* on EGHP ἄγρια φῦλα.

247 This looks very much like a poetic rendering of a phrase like Θ p. 137.7-8 (φιλοτρόφους ζῴων ‹ἢ› ζῴων ἡγεμόνας (albeit produced under entirely different conditions, Venus in the ASC in four-footed signs). The sense of σημάντορας comes from *Il.* 15.325 (where Janko ad loc. regards it as a transference from the military sphere), a herdsman. The meaning of the epithet ἐμβασικοίτους has caused trouble: 'humi-cubantes' (Koechly 1851); 'sleeping on the ground(?)' (LSJ); 'ground-sleeping herdsmen' (Lopilato). A σημάντωρ does indeed sleep in Quint. Smyrn. 13.74 εὕδοντος μογεροῦ σημάντορος, but that is irrelevant here, nor is this a synonym for χαμαιεῦναι (*Il.* 16.235). ἐμβασι- means 'entering upon'; in another sense ἐμβασικοίτας is used of a cup whose liquid contents send you to sleep (Athen. 11.469 A), i.e. cause you to embark on the process of dormition (see Schmeling on Petronius, *Sat.* 24.1: a 'night-cap', 'sleeping-draught'). Satisfactory sense is supplied by 'entering the animals' dens' (or pens or lairs or stalls) in order to train them, and doing so safely. κοίτη and κοῖτος have this meaning often enough (more than are listed by LSJ) to recognise it here. So the first translation, that of Gronovius, 'cubilia lustrantes', which was subsequently ignored, turns out to have been the best. It is all but guaranteed by Θ p. 151.7 ἐρημοβάτας, 'enterers upon desolate places', next to animal trainers—another *hapax* βαίνω compound.

For ἀγρονόμων, see on 6.407; it now becomes an epithet of livestock.

248 The topos of the hard life of the hunter goes back to *Od.* 9.120-1 (cf. Xen. *Cyn.* 12.9 on πόνοι), also 4.340 ἐνδεέας τε τίθησι τροφῆς κάμνοντας ἐπ' ἔργοις; Firmicus, 3.3.11 *venatores...et adsiduis laboribus implicatos.*[176] But the poet also notes other toilsome professions with the μοχθ- root (p. 172), whose range is more limited than that of πόνος (4.72 n.)—gardening (258), the manufacture of pitch (346), watery professions (534). This contrasts with Mᵃ, who used it eleven times in all, but for a general sense of distress, not to describe particular occupations. ἐπίμοχθος itself is a piece of astrological jargon, which reappears in Θ p. 151.7. Of 45 astrological instances on the TLG, no fewer than 20 are in Valens. In some passages there is, as here, a contrastive construction ('not...but ἐπίμοχθον', or 'ἐπίμοχθον, but...'): Valens, I 20.6 καὶ οὕτω μὲν ἐπίμοχθον, πλὴν οὐκ ἄπρακτον, II 41.8 πολυχρονίους μέν, ἐπιμόχθους δὲ καὶ λελωβημένους; Artemid. 1.18 οὐχ ἡδεῖαν ἀλλ' ἐπίμοχθον; Greg. Naz. PG 37.673.1 ἐρίδωρον ἔχων τέλος, ἀλλ' ἐπίμοχθον.

---

[176] Reversed by Opp. *Hal.* 1.12-28, esp. 28 τερπωλὴ δ' ἕπεται θήρῃ πλέον ἠέ περ ἱδρώς.

249–62

Saturn approaches Moon, each in the other's signs.

Protasis. M^b rejoins the τέχναι sequence at Θ p. 215.4–7 (Περὶ βαλανέων), and is very similar to that set-up except that for M^b 'dodecatemories' seems to mean 'signs', rather than the more technical meaning in Θ (p. 247). 6.422–4 is quite different. Its planets, Mars and Saturn, which are in watery signs, point rather to a connection with Ptolemy's Π- chart for Mars as Ruler of πρᾶξις aspected by Saturn (4.4.5).

Apodosis. Despite their different set-ups, the outcomes of M^b and M^a both contain ditch-diggers, dung-shifters, gardeners, and water-carriers; they also share some vocabulary. They go well beyond the contents of Θ p. 215.4–7. There are at least two additional comparanda:

(i) Ptolemy's Π- chart for Mars as Ruler of πρᾶξις, which reappears in Θ for Venus as Ruler of πρᾶξις with the additional aspect of Mars (p. 211.24–31). From this M^b seems to have reproduced a series of outcomes depending on the additional presence of other planets (Mars with the Sun; Mars without the Sun; Mars with Saturn). The first and second of these account for the miners (~ μεταλλευταί) and quarry-workers in 4.259–62 (absent from M^a). The third involves ὑπονομευτάς, workers on underground channels or sewers, who could correspond to 6.422 ὀχετηγοί and 4.252 ἀμαρησκαπτῆρας, and (in Θ, not Ptolemy) βαλανέας, who appear in 4.253. The higgledy-piggledy way in which the outcomes are strung together in M^b suggests that the poet had something like Θ in front of him, but stripped out the differentiations.

(ii) A group of charts concerning Saturn in the MC. This set-up is reproduced straightforwardly in 1.83–8. These consist of (i) Θ p. 166.22–4 and (ii) Θ p. 212.15–18/Epit. IV (CCAG ii. 191.20–22), the same chart in slightly different transmissions. This group of charts, in which Saturn presides over aqueous outcomes, supports gardeners (κηπουρούς ~ 6.424 κοσμῆται κήπων, and implicitly the vegetable-growers in 4.256, 258), water-carriers (ὑδραγωγούς ~ 4.251 ὑδρέας), and toilsome labourers (Θ p. 212.18 μετὰ...μόχθου ~ 4.258 ἐπίμοχθοι).

In sum, the protasis of M^b adheres closely to one particular configuration in Θ (on bath-attendants) whose effect is relevant but limited. Its extensive series of outcomes better reflects a series of other charts which strongly suggest an associative procedure by means of key words (βαλανεῖς; ἀντλητάς). There are also a couple of lexical tie-ins with M^a's chart on watery occupations (λουτρῶν ~ λοετροχόοι; ὀνθολόγοι ~ ὄνθον...φέροντες; ἀντλητῆρες ~ ἄντλοις), even though the latter's protasis (involving Mars as well as Saturn) is different.

249 αἰπυπλανὴς: i. 911 nn. 8–9 (unique, but a variant on the motif of the planet's distance from the earth). ἀκτῖσι πελάζων has the same illogicality, with the slower planet doing the approaching, at 4.140, q.v.

250 ἀλλαγμοῖσιν: see on 4.189.

251 ἀχθοφόρους ὑδρέας τε: ἀχθοφόρος can be a trade name, as in 4.443 (q.v.), like σκευοφόρος, cf. Y. Pikoulas, 'Travelling by Land in Ancient Greece', in C. E. P. Adams and J. Roy (eds.), *Travel, Geography and Culture in Ancient Greece, Egypt, and the Near East* (Oxford, 2007), 78–87, at 79. That could be the case here, though the comparanda have nothing to match; or it could be an epithet of ὑδρέας. This is unique. LSJ represents it as a poetic form of ὑδρευτής (itself a rarity, attested only in a glossary, by which LSJ presumably mean *CGL* ii. 462.12, where it is equated with *aquator*), but it seems more likely, given the cognates (Θ p. 166.22 and *CCAG* ii. 191.22), to be the equivalent of ὑδραγωγούς, which duly appears in the corresponding 1.84. For water-carriers, see Carcopino, 38–9; n. on 1.84–5; Appendix II, II.3.i.

251–2 καθαρτῆράς τε κελεύθων | ἀμφοδικῶν: see on 6.423–4 for street-cleaners, and add Carcopino, 46; A. H. M. Jones, *The Greek City: From Alexander to Justinian* (Oxford, 1979), 214 and n. 7; Courrier, 104–16 (Rome); Bernard, 69; Lane Fox, 182–3. The responsibility for street-cleaning seems to have been shared between householders, who were liable for cleaning exposed gutters in front of their own house (*Digest*, 43.10.1.3), and civic authorities, of whom we hear in a set of regulations dealing with the municipal administration of Pergamum from the late Hellenistic or imperial period. This law speaks of ἀστυνόμοι making contracts[177] with ἀμφοδάρχαι, who could fine householders who did not play their part (*OGIS* 483.49–59), and of the responsibility of the ἀστυνόμοι for the cleaning of the public toilets and sewers (ὑπόνομοι) that ran from them (ibid. 233–6)—the job of Ptolemy's ὑπονομευτάς (on whom see next note). Who were these people? If the ἀστυνόμοι did not use the corvée labour of the citizens themselves, presumably they were public slaves or convicts. Trajan proposes to Pliny the use of condemned criminals to clean sewers and baths (*Ep.* 10.32.2; Ebner 2012a, 260–1).

Firmicus has cleaners of unsalubrious public facilities (*latrinas cloacasque*) born under various degrees in the Myriogenesis (28° Aries, under the Hyades: 8.19.12; 2° Taurus: 8.20.1; 13° Aquarius: 8.29.6). καθαρτῆρας is not new, but in a totally different context in Plut. *Mor.* 302 A-B (a local term for vetch); some sort of plate-cleaner in *EtMag* and *EtGen* s.v. Λυμαντῆρα; there is also a καθαρτής in a list of individuals with trade names in *IG* V,1 209.25 (Sparta, 1st c. BC),

---

[177] See too Σ Juv. *Sat.* 3.32.

but no further clue about *what* he cleans. ἀμφοδικῶν is unique, but based on the prosaic ἄμφοδον or ἄμφοδος, as are the Pergamene ἀμφοδάρχαι.

252 ἀμαρησκαπτῆρας: Ptolemy and passages dependent on him have ὑπονομευτάς, 'workers on underground channels' (LSJ),[178] which is unique in astrology to these passages, and very rare in general.[179] So perhaps this reworks that in (semi-)epic language. The first part—which is also present in Teucer, II 5.1 ἀμαρηγούς (under Hydros, paranatellon of Leo)—comes from *Il.* 21.259 ἀμάρης, a channel in which water flows, from the same simile which supplied ὀχετηγός to the poet of 6.422. But that simile is about a gardener, and the verb σκαπτ- (in EGHP at *HHom. Herm.* 90, 207) also applies mainly to land cultivation and to surface digging, e.g. of trenches to irrigate fruit trees (cf. also Hes. *Op.* 572; specialised in the term φυτοσκάφοι, cf. Gow on Theocr. 25.27), which makes it a less than perfect rendering of a word for subterranean tunnellings.[180] So although the subject of gardeners (cf. Apul. *Met.* 9.32 *fodiens*, of a market gardener) does not 'officially' begin until 256, an alternative interpretation is that these people dig or maintain irrigation channels, for which both ἀμάρα and ὀχετοί are attested terms (Krüger, 24, 25). That would be compatible with, though not proof of, an Egyptian location. However, the epithet οἰκτρούς perhaps better suits the underground workers. For the unhappy circumstances of the (Roman) *fossor*, see Courtney on Juv. *Sat.* 11.77 (though that passage concerns slaves in chain-gangs).

253 For personnel in the baths, see on 6.422 λοετροχόοι and add M. Wissemann, 'Das Personal des antiken römischen Bades', *Glotta*, 62 (1984), 80–9 (no cleaners as such, but p. 85 on the *praefusor/profusor* who replaced the dirty water with fresh); M. Hoffmann, *Griechische Bäder* (Munich, 1999), 199 (βαλανεύς, λουτροχόος). The poet offers both the poetic word (λουτρῶν) and the prose one (βαλανείων). The construction is unclear (apposition? one genitive dependent on the other? βαλανείων an epithet, which would be a novelty?).

254–5 What is going on here? One problem is the subject of the verb (whether Saturn directly bringing the outcome about, or the native performing whatever job is being described); another is the meaning of the opening noun.

---

[178] Cf. ὑπόνομος, LSJ II.2, waterpipe, conduit, and 3, sewer.

[179] ὑπονομέων (from ὑπονομεύς) in P.Lond. 3.1177 (a list of expenses on the municipal water-supply in the city of Arsinoe, AD 131–2), ll. 312, 335; P. Cairo Zen. 4/59745 ll. 30–2 ὑπονόμους. These rare words, according to W. Habermann, *Zur Wasserversorgung einer Metropole im kaiserzeitlichen Ägypten: Neuedition von P. Lond. III 1177: Text, Übersetzung, Kommentar* (Munich, 2000), 253 and n. 538, have to do with 'unterirdische Führungen von Wasserleitungen wie z.B. durch Stollen und Tunnel'. On the former, see also A. C. Johnson, *Roman Egypt to the Reign of Diocletian* = Tenney Frank (ed.), *An Economic Survey of Ancient Rome*, ii (Baltimore, 1936), 690.

[180] A better rendering is 1.85–6 οἴθ᾽ ὑπὸ γαίης | κευθμῶνας δύνουσιν, although this locates Saturn in the MC, which in the comparanda does *not* involve ὑπονομευτάς.

Γενεαί and τέχναι 609

L reads παραιχυσίησι. When D'Orville emended this to παραγχυσίησι, he understood stagnant pools left by the receding tide (cf. ἀναχέω of floods and water spread over a wide space) in which corpses are left to moulder. That makes good sense of 255 (since Homer the birds and carnivores motif suggests dead bodies), but it is not at all clear what trade or profession would be described, let alone one with a link to Θ. Retaining παραιχυσίησι, on the other hand, continues the bath-attendant theme of the line before (~παραχύτης; Θ περιχύτας[181]), but fits less well with 255. Are there any better possibilities? Ptolemy and Θ p. 211.30 mention μαγείρους (indeed, the rotting and boiling down slightly recalls the description of garum-making in 6.463–4, μωλυτά/πυθομένοις; καθέψει/μέλδουσιν), while Ptolemy (alone) mentions παρασχίστας. In this latter case, and in connection with D'Orville's παραγχυσίησι, one might wonder about a reference to mummification, which once again involves semi-mouldered corpses which carrion might well disdain. But παρασχίστας ought to be the people who make the incisions and remove the entrails (on whom the next entry elaborates), rather than those involved with natron baths.

On balance, this seems likeliest to continue the reference to bathing. Galen uses καθέψειν of bodies softened up by hot baths (*De sanitate tuenda* 3.4 = vi. 185 Kühn). It would have to be taken as a sudden switch from Saturn, the subject of the previous verb, to the native, but perhaps the future tense (pp. 168–9), which predicts the latter's behaviour, helps, and the subject of the next verb (φύσονται) is certainly the natives. μωλυτά, which comes from the verb μωλύειν ('soften', cognate with *mollis*), then points in the same direction. (*Lib. Herm.* xxvi. 43 refers mysteriously to *dissolutiones in balneis*.) Whichever context one interprets this line in, the verbal adjective is novel,[182] and so, too, seems to be its application. Apart from a medical use in Oribasius, *Collect. med.* 44.18.2, where μωλυτικός describes some sort of swelling or tumour, μωλ- does not seem to be used in connection with bodies, let alone the preparation of corpses. But if baths are the most plausible connection it becomes a question of finding a context for the disapproval registered in 255.

255 The disapproval here does not seem to be directed against lifestyle choice—decadent expenditure on self-care, mixed-sex bathing.[183] Rather, it seems to be a disgust for bodies in general. Y. Z. Eliav, 'The Roman Bath as a

---

[181] The same fluctuation is found in the glossographers, where *mediastinus* is glossed by both περιχύτης and παραχύτης (Wissemann, art cit. (253 n.), 86, cf. 82).

[182] μωλύτης occurs in an epigram attributed to Timon in Diog. Laert. 7.170; rendered 'slow-coach' in the Loeb at *AP* 11.296.2, but in *SH* 815.2 taken by the editors with the following word, μωλυτὴς ἐπέων, in connection with Apollonius' derivation of μωλύειν from μῶλυ, hence apparently meaning a softener of words, one who takes the sting out of them(?).

[183] Not just a Jewish or Christian attitude, e.g. Sen. *Ep.* 86.4–13; *CIL* vi/3. 15258 ~ *AP* 10.112; Philostr. *Vit. Apoll.* 1.16.4; M. Zytka, 'Baths and Bathing in Late Antiquity', Diss. Cardiff, 2013,

Jewish Institution', *Journal for the Study of Judaism*, 31 (2000), 416–54, at 445, documents exceptions to the general practice of nudity at the baths (for instance the bikini girls at Piazza Armerina). Martial, 3.87 wishes that, to preserve her decency at the baths, Chione would cover, not just her private parts, but in particular her *face* (in other words her face is worse, but there is still an expectation that the rest is covered up as well). Perhaps one also thinks of Marcus Aurelius' disgust for bathing and for the human body generally (8.24; J. Perkins, *The Suffering Self: Pain and Narrative Representation in the Early Christian Era* (London, 1995), 195).

ἀρνοφάγοισι λύκοισιν: the epithet otherwise only in Nonn. *Par.* 2.112 ἀρνοφάγων ἱερήων (Livrea ad loc. refers to James, 68–9, for -φάγος compounds, which are not rare). Why wolves and lambs? Because the former's predations on the latter have been a topos ever since *Il.* 16.352 ὡς δὲ λύκοι ἄρνεσσιν ἐπέχραον and *Il.* 22.263 οὐδὲ λύκοι τε καὶ ἄρνες ὁμόφρονα θυμὸν ἔχουσιν (not to mention Isaiah 11:6).

256–8 These market gardeners could perfectly well be located in Egypt,[184] but are so encrusted with the topoi of gardening in classical literature that they are indistinguishable from, say, the κηπουρός/*hortulanus* who briefly becomes the owner of Lucius the ass, who goes to market loaded with λάχανα/*holeribus*, then returns to his digging and watering (ps.-Lucian, *Asin.* 43 καὶ ἔσκαπτε καὶ ἐφύτευε καὶ τὸ ὕδωρ τῷ φυτῷ ἐπῆγεν; cf. Apul. *Met.* 9.32 *fodiens, irrigans*). These topoi include (perhaps) ditch-digging (252), working to irrigate their little plots (258), producing vegetables (258), toil (258 ἐπίμοχθοι).

256 καρποσπόροι ἄνδρες: gardeners. After the intervening reference to water-drawing (similarly linked with gardening in 6.424 and in the charts for Saturn in the MC), the poet returns to their produce in 258. The phrase—nebulous because what is sown is obviously not *fruit* (other -σπόρος compounds in B.-P. 331-2)—is modelled on the Iliadic *clausulae* αἰπόλοι ἄνδρες, βουκόλοι ἄνδρες.

257 ληνῶν ἀντλητῆρες: water-drawers from troughs. For ἀντλεῖν as a low-status activity, see Epictet. *Diss.* 3.26.7; the tradition about Cleanthes (*SVF* i. frr. 463, 466 von Arnim, ap. Diog. Laert. 7.168 and Sen. *Ep.* 44.3); Philostr. *Vit.*

66–71, id. *A Cultural History of Bathing in Late Antiquity and Early Byzantium* (London, 2019), 41–6, 64, 90–3, 108–9.

[184] Cumont, 54 n. 3; Drexhage 1990; U. Thanheiser *et al.*, 'Roman Agriculture and Gardening in Egypt as Seen from Kellis', in C. A. Hope and G. E. Bowen (eds.), *Dakleh Oasis Project: Preliminary Reports on the 1994-5 to 1998-9 Field Seasons* (Oxford, 2002), 299–310, at 304–5; K. Blouin, 'The Agricultural Economy of the Mendesian Nome under Roman Rule', in A. Bowman and A. Wilson (eds.), *The Roman Agricultural Economy: Organization, Investment, and Production* (Oxford, 2013), 255–70, at 258, 263.

Soph. 488. With the agent noun the poet has repurposed a word that usually meant something else, a ladle, pail, or other instrument for drawing water.[185] ληνός often refers to a wine vat, but need not (watering-trough in *HHom. Herm.* 104; water-source for bees in *Geoponica* 15.2.4 καθαροὺς ληνοὺς ἢ κρήνας). The cadence of the line is like Ap. Rhod. 2.893 ἐτώσια γηράσκοντας.

The figure of the elderly gardener recalls Virgil's old man of Tarentum (*Georg.* 4.127 *Corycium...senem*), who grows cabbages and various kinds of flower, and Longus' old man (πρεσβύτης) Philetas, who tends a well-watered garden (*Daphnis and Chloe*, 2.3, esp. 2.3.5 πηγαῖς τρισὶ κατάρρυτος). Richard Thomas, 'The Old Man Revisited: Memory, Reference and Genre in Virg., Georg. 4, 116-48', *MD* 29 (1992), 35-70, argues for a common background for Virgil and Longus in Philitas of Cos, though the topos is a more widespread one. It goes back to Laertes (Aeneas Sophistes, *Epist.* 2), on whom is based Nonnus' Icarius (*D.* 47.58 = 70 γέρων φυτοεργὸς ἁλωεύς; R. Shorrock, *The Challenge of Epic: Allusive Engagement in the Dionysiaca of Nonnus* (Leiden, 2001), 100-1); there is another example in *HHom. Herm.* 90 (see Thomas on 87-94). Longus' speaker suggests that gardening is a suitable occupation for someone past tending the fields, and maybe this corresponded to reality. Among his sources for botanical lore Pliny names Antonius Castor, who continued to cultivate his *hortulus* beyond his hundredth year.[186] In the *De Senectute* Cicero gives Cato a speech in which the elderly are not only not precluded from the pleasures of agriculture, but specially suited to them (51-60); he particularly praises viticulture (52-3), which is represented as a suitable occupation for an old man in Nonn. *D.* 43.85. Other, humbler, figures of this type are represented above all in early Christian literature.[187] The elderly gardener is still a stock figure, it seems, in the Byzantine novel.[188]

---

[185] I cannot see (*contra* LSJ) that it refers to a person in Pollux 10.31.

[186] *NH* 25.9 (thanks to Robin Lane Fox for this reference); M. Wellmann, *RE* s.v. Antonius (45), and id., 'Beiträge zur Quellenanalyse des Älteren Plinius', *Hermes*, 59 (1924), 129-56, at 143-4; M. Schanz, *Geschichte der römischen Literatur*, ii: *Die römische Literatur in der Zeit der Monarchie bis auf Hadrian* (Munich, ⁴1935), 498, §495.3.

[187] In the *Martyrium Cononis*, Conon, who tends the royal gardens (2.2 βασιλικὸν ἐπαρδεύοντα κῆπον), is an old man (3.4 τὸν γέροντα τοῦτον ἐν κήπῳ τινί), and there are elderly abbatial gardeners in ps.-Athanasius, *Epist. ad Castorem*, PG 28.864.15-18 θεωρῶν τὸν τοιοῦτον ἄνδρα γεγηρακότα, καὶ δίκελλαν κρατοῦντα, καὶ γῆν ἐργαζόμενον, καὶ κόπρον τοῖς οἰκείοις ὤμοις βαστάζοντα, καὶ ταῖς ῥίζαις τῶν λαχάνων ἐπιβάλλοντα and in *Apophthegmata Patrum*, p. 409 (Περὶ τοῦ ἀββᾶ Σιλουανοῦ, 4). Further: R. Lane Fox, 'Early Christians and the Garden: Image and Reality', in K. Coleman and P. Derron (eds.), *Le Jardin dans l'Antiquité: Introduction et huit exposés suivis de discussions* (Entretiens sur l'Antiquité Classique; Vandœuvres, 2014), 363-95, esp. 385-91.

[188] Andronicus Palaeologus, *Callimachus and Chrysorrhoe*, 1639, 1655, 1831, 2340, 2432 (14th c.).

258 ἀρδευταὶ φορβῆς: the poet's elaborate periphrasis for irrigation[189] and reference to vegetables (next entry) obviate any need for part of the word κηπ- itself, which is present in Mᵃ, Mᶜ, and in the sources for Saturn in the MC; see too Appendix II, I.1.iii. The agent noun is unique.[190] But there are ἐπαρδευταί, 'irrigators', in P. Tebt. 1 108 (93 or 60 BC), 120.137 (97–64 BC), 209 (76–75 BC), and C. Pap. gr. 2.1 App. l. 4 (of a vineyard; a man who climbed a date palm and accidentally fell to his death) (Oxyrhynchus, AD 178).

λαχανηφόροι: also evoking gardens. The word is *proton legomenon*. Later passages apply it (or the verb λαχανηφορεῖν) to the land or soil itself; applied to persons, it gestures at both growing and (perhaps) transport/vending. The word's position sandwiched between irrigation and fertilisers is a fair summary of what market gardeners do (Drexhage 1990, 101–3). For the perception of vegetables as the meal of the poor see on 6.423–4, adding Hijmans *et al.* on Apul. 9.32 *holeribus* (~ ps.-Lucian, *Asin.* 43) (Groningen Commentaries on Apuleius, ix. 272). In practice all social classes consumed them, nor, given the frequency with which they did, were they necessarily cheap (Drexhage 1990, 104, 109–11).

ἐπίμοχθοι: hardship emphasised in other passages on watery occupations (Cumont, 54 n. 3: Θ p. 166.22–4; Firmicus, 4.13.6 *miseris laborum continuationibus...hortulani, sed miseri*; 4.14.2 *circa aquam semper adsiduis laboribus fatigari*; *Lib. Herm.* xxvii. 11 (Moon leaving Venus for Saturn by day) *In die vero et Luna minuente laesibiles, vitiosos, ab humidis molestatos, actus vero in aquosis locis habentes, ut superius dictum est, laboriose vitam ducentes vel aquae haustores vel aquae ductores, nautas, hortulanos*.

259 ὀνθολόγοι: see on 6.423, where they are street-cleaners. In theory they could be here, too, although the context suggests the dung is fertiliser (Theophr. *Hist. Plant.* 7.5.1, on λάχανα and κόπρος; id. *Caus. Plant.* 3.19.1 (κόπρισις); ps.- Athanasius, *Epist. ad Castorem*, PG 28.864.17–18). As Varro indicates, there was an art to sourcing and storing it (*De Re Rust.* 1.13.4, 1.38, al.).

μεταλλευταί: Ptolemy and Θ imply a distinction between μεταλλευταί and stone-cutters, for they associate the former with fire (the influence of the Sun), and distinguish them from the λατόμους, λιθοξόους, λιθουργούς who are born without that influence. But sometimes μέταλλον does indicate stone-quarries (Pollux, 7.100 καὶ λίθων δὲ μεταλλεῖαι, λιθουργίαι, λιθοτομίαι; Hesych. μ 1014 μέταλλος· λίθος), and so the label (Appendix II, II.4) covers both the (implied)

---

[189] Gardens and irrigation: *AP* 6.21.1, 7; *AP* 6.42; *AP* 9.667.1; Theophr. *Char.* 20.9; id. *Hist. Plant.* 7.5.2; LXX Deut. 11:10; Aes. *Fab.* 121; Synesius, *Epist.* 106; Meletius, *De natura hominis*, p. 131. For the Latin topos of the irrigated garden, see Bömer on Ov. *Met.* 8.646–7 (prose and poetic references to the (*ir*)*riguus hortus*).

[190] Unless in Laur. plut. 28.34 (Ludwich 1877, 120.11), s.v. Capricorn, ἀρδευτῶν is from ἀρδευτής, not ἀρδευτός, 'watered'.

λαοτόμοι of the next line and the extractors of metals after that. So too Latin *metalla* refers to both mines and quarries.[191]

259-60 ὑπουργοὶ | δυσπονίης: 'servants of hard labour'. *damnatio ad metalla* was a fate to be shuddered at (M. Gustafson, 'Condemnation to the Mines in the Later Roman Empire', *HThR* 87 (1994), 421-33). The hardship motif is not in Θ at this point, but it is obvious enough; and/or there might be a connection with 6.416-17, where stonecutters, born under four-footed signs according to the scheme laid out in Ptol. 4.4.9, are again associated with hard labour (cf. 6.411-12, and as implied by the coding with malefics). For the πόνος theme, see on 4.72; δυσπονία itself is otherwise only in Themistius, *Or*. 17, p. 216 A, p. 309.8 Downey (of the fate of being an orphan). As for ὑπουργοί, the suitable meaning is 'servants', for instance in Ptol. 4.4.5 (Appendix II, VII.3.vii), where they figure in a list together with stonecutters and carpenters, though the genitive construction also suggests the other meaning 'workers of', i.e. those who bring about an effect (normally of the planets themselves: Dorotheus, p. 397.1-2 πημάτων ὑπουργός; Valens, II 1.3 ὑπουργὸν κακίας).

260 οἷς λᾶες ἀπ' οὔρεος ἀκροτομοῦνται ~ λατόμους, which are also in Θ p. 216.6 (a τ- chart, quite different), and 6.416, 4.325 λαοτόμους (Appendix II, II.5.iii). For the verb see on 4.51. It gives the strange impression that the stones are being quarried from the summit. ἀπ' οὔρεος starts its career in Apollonius and Callimachus and then spreads throughout imperial poetry.

261 *Presque homérique*. The line combines χαλκός τε χρυσός τε πολύκμητός τε σίδηρος (3× *Il*. 1× *Od*.) with *Il*. 18.474 χαλκὸν δ' ἐν πυρὶ βάλλεν ἀτειρέα κασσίτερόν τε. If these are to be taken seriously as mineable metals, then χαλκός must be copper, not bronze. The first two metals in the line are those which are alloyed to produce bronze, and they are combined with iron (rather than precious metals) as the other metal in most common use. Egypt itself is mostly irrelevant to their extraction (closest are the copper mines in the Timna Valley in southern Israel), most of all for tin, which was sourced in the Erzgebirge and in Western Europe.[192] This looks like a case where astrology's imaginary of

---

[191] *TLL* s.v. *metallum*, I.A.1; S. Dore, 'La *damnatio ad metalla* degli antichi cristiani: Miniere o cave di pietra?', *ArcheoArte* 1 (2010), 77-84. In Greek, μεταλλεία can also refer to the digging of underground tunnels (LSJ 2, 3, adding Polyb. 16.11.2; Dion. Hal. 4.44.2), including water-channels (Plat. *Leg*. 761 C); hence μεταλλευταί are a good fit for this passage.

[192] Helpful maps in C. Domergue, 'Les mines et la production des métaux dans le monde méditerranéen au 1er millénaire avant notre ère: Du producteur au consommateur', in A. Lehoërff (ed.), *L'Artisanat métallurgique dans les sociétés anciennes en Méditerranée occidentale: Techniques, lieux et formes de production* (Rome, 2004), 129-59, at 130-9. See also id., *Les Mines de la péninsule Ibérique dans l'Antiquité romaine* (Rome, 1990), esp. 68-70 (copper), 70-1 (tin), 78-9 (iron), and 351-66 on conditions in the mines (thanks to Harry Samuels for this reference). For tin, see *OCD* online (Oxford Research Encyclopaedias), s.v. tin (O. Davies and D. W. J. Gill);

work takes precedence over local relevance, or, rather, a case where a combination of literary allusion and a casually assumed availability of metal products[193] has blithely overridden real-world extraction and distribution. For 'black' iron, see on 4.123. This particular epithet is just an uncontracted version of Aesch. *Suppl.* 785 κελαινόχρως (restored by Lachmann; epithet of καρδία) and ps.-Aesch. *PV* 1025 κελαινόχρωτον (epithet of ἧπαρ), counterpart of Homeric μελανόχροος (*Od.* 19.246, cf. *Il.* 13.589 κύαμοι μελανόχροες). See also on 1.35 κυανόχροον.

262 The line sounds very like Plat. *Pol.* 288 D Χρυσόν τε καὶ ἄργυρον καὶ πάνθ' ὁπόσα μεταλλεύεται, but it also conjures ps.-Aesch. *PV* 500–3, where of course it was the Titan, not mankind's ingenuity, that brought mining into being. Has the poet that passage in mind? Not provably, but perhaps. ἐκ γαίης matches ἔνερθε δὲ χθονὸς (500), and Prometheus begins his list with χαλκὸν σίδηρον (though includes precious metals too). Lucretius' vision is completely different (6.808–17), of human oppression and Nature's malignity, and by singling out gold and silver he implies a moralistic stance against luxury. Also negative is the Enochic tradition about mining and metalworking, where it is associated with the rebel angels (see Lightfoot 2007, 356).

263–70

Saturn aspects Mars in MC, in its own terms or signs, in trine. The comparanda offer different realisations of the situation that Mars as Ruler of πρᾶξις is aspected by Saturn (Ptol. 4.4.5).

Protasis. All involve the malefics, Θ p. 215.8–11, but only this, Mercury as well. Beyond that, all have slightly different specifications. In M^b, the planets are in their *own* terms and signs; in 6.457, they are *in each other's* degrees, i.e. terms; in Θ, they aspect each other's dodecatemories (which presumably means more than just 'signs'). Both M^a and M^b mention aspect and *kentron* (Θ does neither), but again there are slight differences: in 6.456 *both* are specifically in the MC, but in M^b, while Mars is located there, the planets are in trine, so Saturn cannot be.

Apodosis. This is an enormous elaboration of the theme of embalming (which suggests that that was *not* meant in 254–5).

R. D. Pennhallurick, *Tin in Antiquity: Its Mining and Trade throughout the Ancient World with Particular Reference to Cornwall* (London, 1986).

[193] M. L. Ratliff, 'Globalisation, Consumerism and the Ancient Roman Economy: A Preliminary Look at Bronze and Iron Production and Consumption', in D. Mladenović and B. Russell (eds.), *TRAC 2010: Proceedings of the Twentieth Annual Theoretical Roman Archaeology Conference* (Oxford, 2010), 32–46.

263 κορυφήν: for the meaning MC see on 4.24.

264 This is one of the few passages in this book which (a) seems to distinguish between the casting of rays and aspect, and (b) talks of the casting of rays as a hostile relationship. It might on first reading be taken to indicate ἀκτινοβολία proper, but the trine relationship in 266 rules that out. So it must just refer to the mutual aspect of malefics (p. 248). Other uses of φεγγοβολ- do not support the idea that this is ἀκτινοβολία (4.367, 527, 571). The epithet φεγγοβόλος (Lampe; not in LSJ) describes rays, both literal and metaphorical, in later poetry and prose, but in an evocative and non-technical way. For the second half of the line, compare *Od.* 17.217 κακὸς κακὸν ἡγηλάζει, i.e. same *sedes* and rhythm, and even a certain phonetic similarity (-γ-, -λάζ-) with the final spondeiazon.

266 συμμίγδην: the adverb (whose only earlier literary appearance is in Nic. *Ther.* 677, meaning straightforwardly 'mixed with') is unique in the Manethoniana. It cannot mean conjunction (as simplex μίγδην seems to do in 4.499), as trine is involved, and it does not appear to suggest reciprocity, unlike the other occurrence of μίγδην at 4.202, where it refers to exchange of terms. Apparently, then, it is simply an overcumbrous way of saying 'in (mingled with) their own signs'. See pp. 217–18.

σελασμῷ: see on 4.36.

267 γαστροτόμους: this corresponds to 6.461 γαστέρας ἀμπτύξαντες (see ad loc.), and both to Ptolemy's technical term παρασχίστας (6.459 n.).[194] There is no actual cutter-open of corpses in Θ unless these are the νεκρεπάρτας (192 n.; 'remover of corpses', LSJ, but could it be connected with πείρω, 'pierce'?). Diod. Sic. 1.91.4–5 reports that a scribe first marked the extent of the incision on the left flank, and the παρασχίστης then carried it out (the evidence of the mummies confirms him). The point was to remove the intestines, and the incision was on the left because it gave better access to the descending colon (B. Brier and R. S. Wade, 'Surgical Procedures during Ancient Egyptian Mummification', *ZÄSA* 126 (1999), 89–97, at 91). γαστροτόμους replaces the precision of the technical label with a word designed to shock.

ταριχευτῆρας: this lightly exoticises ταριχευτάς (a label both literary, first in Herodotus, and in papyri). Diodorus distinguishes them from the παρασχίσται, whose function is *only* to make the incision. The ταριχευταί then remove the innards and embalm them and the body itself. Herodotus, on the other hand, who has the participle παρασχίσαντες instead of the noun, has the same persons

---

[194] P. W. Pestman, *L'archivio di Amenothes figlio di Horos (P. Tor. Amenophes)* (Milan, 1981); H.-J. Thissen, *LÄ* iv (1982), 910, s.v. Paraschist; Derda, 15–19.

making the incision (2.86.4 παρασχίσαντες) *and* cleaning the bowels.[195] M[b] is not guaranteed to be distinguishing them (as opposed to amassing the various 'mortician' words in his vocabulary); there is no such distinction in M[a] (6.461); and the issue does not arise with Ptolemy, who mentions only the slitters. Either way, his *presque homérique* epithet, ἀπηνεῖς, contrasts with Diodorus' offset between the ritual humiliation/expulsion of the slitters and the honour accorded the embalmers.

268 κακεμπορίης τε ματευτάς: the seekers after evil merchandise, unless the whole funerary industry is being stigmatised, are likely to be tomb-robbers (~ Θ τυμβωρύχους) (p. 66). These are not in Ptolemy's Π- chart. But they *are* mentioned in 3.14.15, among the natives born under Saturn in alliance with Mars (i.e. the same two entities) as Ruler of the soul; and they are in a 'realised' version of this in Θ p. 192.22 (Moon, Mars, Mercury in *kentra* aspected by Saturn in the IMC, among the Περὶ μαινομένων καὶ ἐπιληπτικῶν). τυμβωρυχία is associated with Mars alone in Rhetorius, *CCAG* vii. 217.20 = Valens, App. II 15. It was to Lobeck's credit that he restored this without knowing the background. The agent noun is unique, though there is a μαστευτής in Xen. *Oec.* 8.13.

269–70 The question is what process (τέχνασμα) these lines refer to. Koechly 1851, xlv opined that this was not a return to the subject of morticians, but that there has been a shift to the manufacture of garum, as in the parallel 6.463-4— facilitated by the double meaning of ταριχεύειν as both 'mummify' and 'pickle', 'salt' (Derda, 19). In that case a line would appear to be missing after 269 containing a noun for μυσαροὺς and a reference to the place where the procedure was carried out. This is more reasonable than a return to a subject the poet has already exhausted. Indeed, 269 fits *better* with garum than with mummification, because the latter was supposed to arrest decay, while the manufacture of garum induced it. The insistence on putrefaction (σηπ-) finds its natural context in the traditional link of garum with rotten matter.[196] (For Greek see 6.464; Artemidorus, 1.66.2 ἔστι γὰρ οὐδὲν ἄλλο ὁ γάρος ἢ σηπεδών, as well as the medical nostrum, repeated in numerous writers and in the Cyranides, that garum should be used on putrefying wounds—σηπεδόνας, τὰ σηπεδονώδη τῶν ἑλκῶν—as if by sympathetic association;[197] for Latin, see Manilius, 5.673 *putris turbae strages*, 681 *liquidam tabem*; Plin. *NH* 31.93 *putrescentium sanies*; Sen.

---

[195] E. Revillout, 'Une famille de paraschistes ou taricheutes thébains', *ZÄSA* 17 (1879), 83–92, argued, not only that this was common sense, but that it was historically the case, and that the same demotic word *χer-heb* denoted persons who performed both functions.
[196] And more generally the associations of rotten fish: Antiphanes, F 159 K.-A. (ap. Athen. 6.225 E) is not about garum, but it does use the verb σήπειν of rotting fish (l. 6 σήπονθ').
[197] For garum in medicine, see Curtis, 27–37; Drexhage 1993, 44–5.

Ep. 95.25 *salsa tabe.*) Also, the reference to smell suits garum better than the preparation of mummies (although doubtless there were bad smells there too[198]): cf. Curtis, 15 and n. 29, 155, and id., 'In defense of garum', *CJ* 78 (1983), 232–40, at 232–3. For the availability of garum in Egypt, see Curtis, 137–8; Drexhage 1993.

Astrology's insights, it turns out, even reach to the ancient smellscape. Smells in its world are delicious and Venereal (2.327; Ptol. 4.4.4 τοὺς παρ' ὀσμαῖς ἀνθέων ἢ μύρων; Firmicus, 5.5.6, colours, scents, gems, 8.11.1 flowers, gardens, and perfumes); or they are noisome (smelly trades: 6.460; Firmicus, 3.8.7 *gravi odore* and 3.10.8 *gravibus odoribus*). They generally belong to the aesthetics of labour, except for references to offensive body odour (Firmicus, 3.13.13, 6.31.38, 8.20.4).

The second half of 270 is modelled on e.g. *Od.* 6.234 (al.) χαρίεντα δὲ ἔργα τελείει, 17.51 ἄντιτα ἔργα τελέσσῃ, *Th.* 89 μετάτροπα ἔργα τελεῦσι. The corresponding 'atrocity' word in 6.464 was οὐλοόν.

271–85 + 286–9

Sun quartile(?) with Mars, in Taurus, Leo, Aries; and with the addition of Venus.

Protasis. M^b has two charts, the first of which involves just the Sun and Mars, while the second adds Venus for tightrope-walkers (why Venus should be necessary for tightrope-walkers but not petauristae is unclear). M^a likewise has two, the first of which already involves all three of Mars, Venus, and the Sun (6.439–40), while the second adds Mercury for the petauristae (6.441–4).

There is nothing directly to correspond in Ptolemy. What Θ offers are five separate configurations, one for Mercury + Venus producing mimes (p. 217.5–8, Περὶ μίμων), and four others which produce tightrope-walkers and sometimes conjurers as well. Mars is involved in all of them,[199] both Venus and Mars in three. None fits perfectly, but the one that corresponds in the sequence of τ-charts, which M^b continues to follow, is Θ p. 215.16–17, which agrees with M^b's second chart in putting the whole under the auspices of four-footed signs. But Θ's chart is primarily about builders, to whom tightrope-walkers form a curious add-on with the presence of Venus. This makes good sense of the four-footed signs, given Ptolemy's association of four-footed signs with building and carpentry (4.4.9). M^b's version makes a lot less, for while he continues to treat

---

[198] Consider modern attempts to replicate ancient Egyptian mummification techniques: R. Garner, 'Experimental Mummification', in A. R. David (ed.), *The Manchester Mummy Project* (Manchester, 1979), 19–24.

[199] One additional tightrope-walking chart in Firmicus, 8.17.4, involves Mars but also, unexpectedly, the Moon, under Engonasin, which is a paranatellon of Pisces.

Venus as an add-on, the builders who give the four-footed signs their primary rationale are postponed until the next chart. This would suggest his version is secondary (p. 254).

One might have expected Mercury to be an important factor in charts which involve physical/manual dexterity (e.g. Valens, I 1.39). Yet he is present in only one of Θ's tightrope charts, and in neither of those that form the best matches for M^a and M^b, the other one being Θ p. 213.1 (where the same three agencies, but formulated as Sun together with Mars + Venus, give birth to tightrope-walkers).

Apodosis. There are four principal outcomes: (i) ἰσχυροπαίκτας (276–7); (ii) petauristae (277–9); (iii) mimes (280–5); (iv) tightrope-walkers (286–9). (i) and (ii) are unique to M^b and M^a, in whom they are both combined (strongmen first, then petauristae; for the compendious expression see on 6.441–5). The set-ups differ, however: M^b knows nothing of Mercury. (iii) is shared with Θ, not M^a, though again the set-ups differ: M^b knows nothing of Venus. As for (iv), all three sources have them. Θ calls them νευροβάτας, which seems to have been the usual term, three times, but also agrees with M^b on σχοινοβάτας on p. 213.7. This is the only other occurrence of the agent noun in Greek for another thousand years, but its presence in Θ should not be interpreted as the relic of another, parallel, poetic version (see below on 287). M^b also uses αἰθροβάτας for his petauristae—the word M^a uses for the tightrope-walkers.

The mime chart in Θ p. 217.5–8 deserves a little more comment. The interest is the connection it draws between the outcome—mimes and politicians—and the paranatellon of Capricorn identified as the Ape. While there are various implicit connections between Θ's constellations and the outcomes produced by their paranatellonta, in this case the paranatellon is explicitly named, and that name comes from the Egyptian *dodecaoros* as we know it from Teucer (p. 141). Teucer associates the Ape with Capricorn, calling it Cynocephalus in the first decan and δυσώνυμον ζῷον or δυσώνυμος in the second and third (TR, p. 20.3, 6, and II 10.9; cf. Boll 1903, 295). Its association with acting is well documented.[200] The corresponding constellation in Firmicus is Cepheus, associated (in the additional presence of Mercury and Venus) with the art of tragedy (8.15.5). Manilius himself places Cepheus in the adjacent sign, Aquarius, but once again

---

[200] J. Hammer, 'Trained Animals in Antiquity: A Portion of a Paper', *The Classical Outlook*, 20/6 (1943), 59–61, at 60; Hubbard, 75 and n. 5; D. Steiner, 'Making Monkeys: Archilochus frr. 185–187 W. in Performance', in V. Cazzato and A. Lardinois (eds.), *The Look of Lyric: Greek Song and the Visual: Studies in Archaic and Classical Greek Song*, i (Leiden, 2016), 108–45, at 117–18; E. Csapo, 'Kallipides on the Floor-Sweepings: The Limits of Realism in Classical Acting and Performance Styles', in P. Easterling and E. Hall (eds.), *Greek and Roman Actors: Aspects of an Ancient Profession* (Cambridge, 2002), 127–47, at 127–8. It elicits laughter (W. C. McDermott, *The Ape in Antiquity* (Baltimore, 1938), 109–10) and its antics involve dressing up (Diogenianus, 7.94; Apostolius, 14.32; *Suda*, π 1581).

associates him with 'mimetic' professions, and the births of both tragic and comic poets and pantomimes.[201] Finally, *Lib. Herm.* xxv. 10.13 mentions dancers (*saltatores*) and mimes under the second and third degrees of Capricorn, and Gundel, 233, suspected an underlying reference to the Ape here too.

271 Ἥλιος δ' ἀκάμας: i. 908 n. 9, 917 and n. 42. ἀθρῇ: Prévot, 246–7 (Homeric in this non-intellectual sense).

272 θοαῖς ἀκτῖσι βολαυγῶν: further suggesting the equivalence of aspect and the casting of rays. For the Sun's swiftness, see Mimnermus, frr. 11a.1–2, 14.11 W. ὠκέος Ἡελίοιο; Nonn. *D.* 33.235 Φαέθοντα ταχύδρομον, and above all the topos of his chariot (n. on 2.38–9; Richardson on *HHom. Dem.* 89; Mimnerm. fr. 12.9 W. θοὸν ἅρμα). The poet looks to be adapting a rhythm prevalent in M^a, but not otherwise in M^b (3.327 μαλεραῖς ἀκτῖσιν ἀθρήσῃ, 6.293 μαλεραῖς ἀκτῖσιν ὁρῴη, 6.477 φιλίαις ἀκτῖσιν ὁρῷεν; 6.693 κρυεραῖς ἀκτῖσιν ὁρῴη).

273 τετράγωνον: to all appearances this indicates aspect. It is hard to believe that Mars is in quadrature with the signs in question (so Hübner on Manilius, 5.650–5). But one might consider emending to τετράγωνος, agreeing with Helios. The Sun, located in the signs in question, is then in quartile with Mars, as Saturn is in the affiliated chart in Θ p. 215.13. On the other hand, it is very easy to see why Lopilato wanted to emend to produce a label for the four-footed signs in the next two lines, even though his solution does not convince; their names would then be epexegetic of the category defined here. The line-end is modelled on *Il.* 17.743 κατὰ παιπαλόεσσαν ἀταρπόν, perhaps via Nic. *Al.* 16 οὐρανόεσσαν ὑπήνην. According to the scholia there, the epithet (which is confined to these two passages) is used for the roof of the mouth. M^b has restored his favourite pathway metaphor (see on 4.37).

274–5 Taurus, Leo, and Aries constitute the hard core of the four-footed signs; other sources may add Sagittarius and/or Capricorn (Hübner 1982, 145–6).

274 ἀμφίκερῳ Ταύροιο: for the epithet see on 4.77, and for other horned epithets for Taurus, Hübner 1982, 124.

ἀσθματικοῖο Λέοντος: 'panting' (LSJ). The epithet paraphrases Ptolemy's characterisation of the sign (within a review of the signs' climatic effects) as 'stifling', 2.12.5 καυματῶδες καὶ πνιγῶδες (Hübner 1982, 89); cf. Valens, I 2.42 (the star in the middle of Leo's breast is πυρώδης καὶ πνιγώδης), 43. Doubtless

---

[201] Manilius, 5.458–85; Hübner on 5.476 and 477–85; id. 1984, 189; id., 'Das Sternbild Lychnos', *Lychnos: Lärdomshistoriska Samfundets Årsbok*, 1987, 1–13, at 5; Abry, 38–9.

a mythological construction could be put on this (Bouché-Leclercq, 139 n. 1: 'étouffé par Hercule'). 'Heat' epithets for Leo: Hübner 1982, 92.

275 Κριοῦ τ' εἰαρόεντος: Hübner 1982, 83–4 (1.321.31), cf. 85 (1.322.21) (Pisces); *TLL* s.v. *Aries*, 572.40–6. The only quoted Greek examples in fact are this and Maximus, 145 εἰαρινοῖσιν ἐν ἄστρασιν Ἀρνειοῖο. The epithet is possibly/probably a *hapax*. Ludwich restored it in Maximus, 281 Πληιὰς εἰαρόεσσ' for L's αιοερωση, which looks, however, more like the remains of αἰθερόεσσ' (Gerhard), which Zito accepts.

276 An expansion of ἰσχυροπαίκτας, strongmen, who are to be found in the company of mimes under the presidency of Mercury in Valens, I 1.39, in Delphi, *FD* iii. 1, 216 (n.d.), and in Rome, *IGUR* ii. 473 (n.d.). All four passages are assembled and discussed by Robert 1929, 436–7; id., Ἰσχυροπαίκτης, *BCH* 52 (1928), 422–5 ('un faiseur de tours de force'); id. 1936, 245; id. 1938, 102–8, where he seems to see the present verse as a direct poetic response to Valens (103: 'le vers de Manéthon est le développement du ἰσχυροπαίκτης de Vettius Valens'), proof of which is that mimes follow in both writers. He also illustrates ἰσχυρῶν ἔργων by the praise for the honorand διὰ τὴν εὐτονίαν τοῦ ἔργου in the Delphic inscription. By decoupling the two parts of ἰσχυροπαίκτας and transferring ἰσχυρῶν to the ἔργων, M^b has managed to create a new compound with oxymoronic effect: as Robert saw, -παίκτης comes from παίζειν (player, showman), while πονο- suggests physical effort and struggle (see on 4.72), here, with deliberate paradox, in a leisure context.

277 ὀχλοχαρεῖς: there are six instances of this, of which the first dateable example is in Marcus Aurelius, which well illustrates its associations: καὶ τὸ μήτε περὶ θεοὺς δεισίδαιμον μήτε περὶ ἀνθρώπους δημοκοπικὸν ἢ ἀρεσκευτικὸν ἢ ὀχλοχαρές, ἀλλὰ νῆφον ἐν πᾶσι καὶ βέβαιον καὶ μηδαμοῦ ἀπειρόκαλον μηδὲ καινοτόμον (1.16.3). There is also another astrological usage, in ps.-Palchus, *CCAG* v/1. 187.9, where it is connected with the turbulent tropic signs (i. 618), and the ὀχλοχαρέσιν οὐκ ὀρθῶς are accordingly accompanied by κούφοις, δυσκαταλήπτοις ('unpredictable'?). It is a variant on the slightly more familiar δημοχαρής, on which see on 3.38, and the Addenda to vol. 1 (p. 1063). For the use of ὄχλος of the theatre crowd see on 5.104.

φιλόμοχθα θεατρομανοῦντας: presumably active, delighting the theatre audience with their feats of strength, rather than 'mad *for* the theatre' (LSJ needs correction; add John Chrys. *PG* 51.178.40–1). Pliny claims to have seen a strongman who walked across the stage (*per scaenam ingredi*) wearing a breastplate and boots of enormous weight (*NH* 7.83), and Robert 1929, 436–7, infers that the ἰσχυροπαίκτης at Delphi performed in the theatre. M^b goes on to mention petauristae, and these, too, are a plausible theatre-act to judge from Terence's famous complaints about the fiasco at the first production of his

Hecyra, which had been interrupted by a crowd expecting to see a tightrope-walker.²⁰² For other popular performers in the theatre, see Blümner, 29, and *passim*. They include Martial, 9.38, an acrobat who performs with a shield on *pulpita*; Quint. 10.7.11-12, jugglers and conjurers (*pilarii, ventilatores*) who perform *in scaenis*; Alciphron, 2.17 [3.20], a conjurer with cups and pebbles (a ψηφοκλέπτης); Athen. 1.19 E, a νευροσπάστης in Athens; Eustathius (of Antioch, 4th c.), *De engastrimytho contra Origenem*, 9.10 ...ὅτι καὶ νυνὶ πολλῷ πλείονα καὶ μείζονα τούτων ἐν τοῖς θεάτροις οἱ ψηφοπαῖκται δρῶσιν εἰωθότως; more in Dickie 2001 (a pebble-conjurer from a seventh-century saint's life set in Emesa). The theatre is also where statues of popular entertainers were set up, e.g. for a conjurer (ψηφοκλέπτης) by the Euboeans of Histiaea (Athen. 1.19 A-B); for a mime (βιολόγον) by the people of Tralles (*ITral.* 110).

φιλόμοχθα: though suspected by De Stefani, this seems to me a nice reversal of the poet's usual semantics of μόχθος (see on 4.248) to indicate the strong-man's pleasure in his feats of strength (μόχθος can be used of the Labours of Heracles; cf. Martínez-Hernández, 82-5). Contrast the mood in Ptol. 3.14.11, where Saturn as Ruler of the soul, dominating Mercury and the Moon, produces φιλομόχθους in a typically joyless list of Saturnian miserabilism.

277-8 For *petauristae*, see on 6.441-5 and on 443, 444; for αἰθροβάτας, on 6.440 (there tightrope-walkers). ἴχνεσσιν presumably refers to the steps they took to ascend to their platform, or springboard themselves into the air, or however one envisages their apparatus.

πηκτοῖσι...ἐν ἔργοις: see W. J. Slater, 'High Flying at Paestum', *AJA* 80 (1976), 423-5, at 424, who interprets this in the light of the perch or platform reached by a ladder which is mentioned by Polybius, 8.4.8, and Petronius, *Sat.* 53.11. Presumably any structure would consist of multiple parts, and there is no particular type of structure to which πηκτός is specialised (a plough in *Il.* 10.353 and *Od.* 13.32), but it applies to a ladder in Eur. *Phoen.* 489 (a scaling ladder, used in assaulting a city) and *Bacch.* 1213 (whence *Christus Patiens*, 1263), and De Stefani would restore a word with that meaning in place of ἔργοις.

279 αἰθέρι καὶ γαίῃ: for this topos see on 6.443.

280 μιμοβίους: the word is unique, but there is a type of mime called the βιολόγος (Robert 1936, 237, 239-41; F. Perpillou-Thomas, 'Artistes et athlètes

---

²⁰² See I. Lada-Richards, 'Authorial Voice and Theatrical Self-Definition in Terence and Beyond: The *Hecyra* Prologues in Ancient and Modern Contexts', *G&R* 51 (2004), 55-82, at 56-7: the crowd did not exit the theatre, but became confused by the expectation that such entertainment was to be had in the theatre itself. C. W. Marshall, *The Stagecraft and Performance of Roman Comedy* (Cambridge, 2006), 26, is less sure that the tightrope-walkers were in the same venue, but does think the gladiatorial combat which wrecked the second production was located in the same place as the actors ('a "main stage" location').

dans les papyrus grecs d'Égypte', ZPE 108 (1995), 225–51, at 230; *Corpus Glossariorum Latinorum*, ii (1888), 22, ll. 40–2); Garelli, 131; Webb 2008, 103; Tedeschi 2011, 44. M^b's formation conceivably puns on both 'imitator of (everyday) life' (as the βιολόγος does) and 'making a living from being a mime'. In P.Oxy. 1025.7–8, a βιολόγῳ and ὁμηριστῇ mentioned together (Euergetis, AD 275–99) look as if they are a complementary pair, one doing the everyday and the other the grandiose.

χλεύης τ' ἐπιβήτορας: see on 6.508–9, adding Diod. Sic. 31.16.3 γέλωτα καὶ χλευασμόν.

ὑβριγέλωτας: also 4.446, of mimes, in the company of conjurers. The reference to *mimos ioculatores* in *Lib. Herm.* xxv. 3.13 suggests something like γελωτοποιούς for the underlying Greek. Mimes very obviously induce laughter,[203] and keep frequent company with γελωτοποιοί (Garelli, 131; Plut. *Sulla* 2.2 μίμων καὶ γελωτοποιῶν, sim. *Anton.* 9.5, *Brut.* 45.6; Diod. Sic. 20.63.2; Artemidorus, 1.76.5; Athen. 6.261 C, 11.464 E); as for ὕβρις in this same nexus, Plut. *Mor.* 67 E combines ὕβρις and γέλως with σκῶμμα and βωμολοχία as the vices of excessive freedom of speech, which was exactly the problem the mime posed (i. 343); conversely, the well-ordered society is characterised by the absence of outrageous laughter (Xen. *Cyr.* 8.1.33 ὑβριστικῷ γέλωτι). See pp. 115–16 on the hostile tone these popular entertainers elicit.

281 A life of wandering (Blümner, 6–7, on troupes of small-time actors and mimes; 8–9, on strongmen; 12–13, on petauristae; 13–15, on tightrope-walkers; Drexhage–Konen–Ruffing, 157; for vagabondage see also Dickie 2001, 602–3). The motif recurs in Valens, I 1.39 (see on 4.276) ἰσχυροπαίκτας ἢ μιμῳδούς, ‹ἀπὸ› ἐπιδείξεως τὸν βίον ποριζομένους, ἔτι δὲ πλάνης καὶ ἀλητείας καὶ ἀκαταστασίας, thereby reinforcing the affinity of the two passages, and it also recurs in the related 4.449. An entertainer, Gemellus, mentions it on his tombstone (*St.Pont.* III 143, Apameia), καὶ πολλὰς ὁδοὺς αὐτὸς ὁδεύσας. Robert 1929, 438, also notes the appositeness of an invocation to Hecate Εἰνοδία in *FD* iii. 1, 469, a Delphic honorific inscription for the dancer and θαυματοποιός Nicon. Athen. 1.20 A even uses πλάνοι as a term for mimes. (Although their members operated at a higher and more prestigious level than these popular entertainers, the same was true of the ecumenical synods of athletes and theatre performers in the imperial period, both of which had περιπολιστική in their titles; see S. Aneziri, 'World Travellers: The Associations of Artists of Dionysus', in R. L. Hunter and I. C. Rutherford (eds.), *Wandering Poets in Ancient Greek*

---

[203] Demosthenes, *Or.* 2.19; Plut. *Mor.* 477 D; Dio Chrys. *Or.* 7.119 διά τινων μίμων ἀκράτου γέλωτος δημιουργούς; Galen, *De anatomicis administrationibus*, ii. 644.10–11 Kühn; Dio Cass. 79.1.4; Sext. Emp. *Adv. Math.* 2.56; Ov. *Trist.* 2.497 *mimos obscena iocantes*; Cic. *De Or.* 2.251 al. See Webb 2017.

Culture: Travel, Locality and Pan-Hellenism (Cambridge, 2009), 217-36, at 227, and B. Fauconnier, *Ecumenical Synods: The Associations of Athletes and Artists in the Roman Empire*, forthcoming with Cambridge University Press.)

ὀθνιοτύμβους: the epithet is new, the sentiment is not. Performers and entertainers were indeed among those most likely to die outside their homeland (C. Marek, *Geschichte Kleinasiens in der Antike* (Munich, 2010), 623-4),[204] and this is among the many passages in the corpus that betray a completely internationalist outlook, with nothing distinctive of Egypt at all (p. 119). The expression is particularly reminiscent of epigram:[205] compare ἐν ξείνῃ in Dionysius of Cyzicus, *AP* 7.78.5 = *HE* 1445 and Crinagoras, *AP* 7.371.5 = *Garland* 1851, and others which carry the 'abroad' motif with ὀθνειο-,[206] if not τηλ- or ἑκάς.

282 ὄρνεα γῆς: the best parallel seems to be Ar. *Av*. 169-70 ἄνθρωπος ὄρνις ἀστάθμητος πετόμενος, | ἀτέκμαρτος, οὐδὲν οὐδέποτ' ἐν ταὐτῷ μένων (the alternative ἄνθρωπος ὄρνις = 'the man-bird', which Dunbar also considers, would not affect the underlying idea). But the present poet caps that with what Hutchinson 2009, 202, calls 'a cosmic paradox'. This is certainly not found when Nicetas Choniates uses the bird as a pathetic image for a lost people (rather than for the human condition)[207]—nor when the Son of Man makes more or less the opposite point (Matth. 8:20 'The foxes have holes, and the birds of the air have nests; but the Son of Man hath not where to lay his head').[208]

πόλιος πάσης ἀπόλιστα γένεθλα: Aristophanes' play is founded (*Av*. 172-3, 550) on the conceit that birds have no *polis*; conversely, mankind are the only animals that live in cities (Arist. *Pol*. 1252^{b}15-18, on the κοινωνία of those who share a household and *polis*). The poet phrases this with a characteristic jingle. For the alpha privative + genitive construction, see on 2.185. For the type of parechesis where the genitive contains the same root as the alpha privative, see Wilamowitz on Eur. *Her*. 114 πατρὸς ἀπάτορ'. Weir-Smyth, §1428 adds prose examples, while noting that the genitive construction in general is commoner

---

[204] Epitaphs for a different professional group—peripatetic doctors—in L. Robert, 'Épitaphes métriques de médecins à Nicée et à Tithorée', *Hellenica*, 2 (1946), 103-8.

[205] M. A. Tueller, 'Sea and Land: Dividing Sepulchral Epigram', in M. Kanellou, I. Petrovic, and C. Carey (eds.), *Greek Epigram from the Hellenistic to the Early Byzantine Era* (Oxford, 2019), 192-209, at 193-5, and n. 6; A. Bettenworth, 'The Mutual Influence of Inscribed and Literary Epigram', in P. Bing and J. S. Bruss (eds.), *The Brill Companion to Hellenistic Epigram* (Leiden, 2007), 69-93, at 75 and n. 39. Leonidas' (supposed) self-epitaph in *AP* 7.715 = *HE* 2535-40, is a good example.

[206] Diodorus, *AP* 7.74.3 = *Garland* 2172; Damagetus, *AP* 7.497.3 = *HE* 1417; Leonidas/Theocritus, *AP* 7.660.4 = *HE* 3429.

[207] *Hist. Alex*. 5, p. 578.24-5 ἀλλὰ πολύπλαγκτοι φερόμενοι ὡς ὄρνιθες οἱ ἀβέβαιοι (and *Or*. 14 p. 138.21f, 15.148.36-7).

[208] Similarly Plut. *Tib. Gracch*. 9.4-5 (but no birds). Theodoretus, *Interpretatio in Psalmos*, *PG* 80.1540.21-33 contrasts former wanderings with present settled state.

in poetry than prose. Finally, the whole thing is wrapped up in a cadence that begins with Soph. *OT* 1424–5 θνητῶν...γένεθλα and takes imperial poetry by storm (4.316 μυσαρωπὰ, 587 ὑπόβλητα; Opp. *Hal.* 1.103 and 5.366 ὑπέροπλα, 1.623 ἀμενηνὰ, ps.-Opp. *Cyn.* 2.315 ἀρίδηλα).

283 The vocabulary finds a good parallel in Ephes. 5:4 αἰσχρότης καὶ μωρολογία ἢ εὐτραπελία, which is endlessly repeated and discussed in Christian writers. John Chrysostom in particular connects these vices explicitly with mime artists and with the theatre (*PG* 61.64.42–51; cf. Halliwell, 500–2 and 505–7[209]), while Webb 2017 makes the case that the theatre was already implicit in the formulation of the author of Ephesians when he wrote the phrase (223–4).

μωρόφρονας: suggesting the mime fool, the μωρός or *stupidus* (Welborn 2002, 424–8; id. 2005, 33 and n. 64, 36–48). The association with the citiless may suggest the same nexus that produced the modern meaning 'idiot' out of the private, i.e. politically disengaged, person (LSJ ἰδιώτης, III.3; Lampe s.v. ἰδιώτης, 'unskilled', 'uncultivated'; s.v ἰδιωτικός, 'unlearned').

λιτούς: goes well with Aristotle's claim that the stateless (ἄπολις) man is a worthless individual (or a god): *Pol.* 1253ᵃ3–4 ἤτοι φαῦλός ἐστιν (ἢ κρείττων ἢ ἄνθρωπος).

ἀσχήμονας: good parallels in Christian writers (p. 179): John Chrys. *PG* 51.188.23–6 Καὶ οἱ περὶ τὴν ὀρχήστραν δὲ ἐσχολακότες, οὐκ ἐλάττω τούτων [sc. horse-fanciers], ἀλλὰ καὶ πλείω μανίαν περὶ τοὺς ἐν τοῖς θεάτροις ἀσχημονοῦντας ἐπιδείκνυνται, μίμους λέγω καὶ ὀρχηστρίας; and in company with bawdy types, *PG* 61.313.58–60 Νῦν δὲ, μίμου μὲν γελωτοποιοῦντος, καὶ πορνευομένης γυναικὸς καὶ ἀσχημονούσης; ps.-Cyril, *Mystagogiae, Catechesis* 1.6 Μὴ περισπούδαστόν σοι ἔστω ἡ θεατρομανία, ἔνθα αἱ ἀσελγεῖς εἰσι τῶν μίμων ὄψεις, ὕβρεσι πεπραγμέναι καὶ πάσαις ἀσχημοσύναις; Arethas, *Scripta Minora* 21 (Χοιροσφάκτης ἢ Μισογόης) θεάτροις καὶ μίμοις τε καὶ προδείκταις (panto-mimic actor: LSJ) καὶ τῇ ἐκεῖ πάσῃ ἀσχημοσύνῃ.

αἰσχρογέλωτας: a unique combination of two of the mimes' characteristic words, similarly combined in Demosth. *Or.* 2.19 μίμους γελοίων καὶ ποιητὰς αἰσχρῶν ᾀσμάτων; Philo, *Flacc.* 34 ποιηταῖς μίμων καὶ γελοίων διδασκάλοις χρώμενοι τὴν ἐν τοῖς αἰσχροῖς εὐφυΐαν ἐπεδείκνυντο, *Legatio* 42 ἐπὶ μίμοις αἰσχρῶν καὶ σκωμμάτων...μειρακιωδέστερον καγχάζοντα. For laughter see on 4.280 and also on 5.104 γελοίων.

284 κρατοπλαγεῖς: Lobeck's emendation of L's κρατοπαγεῖς depends on the stock figure of the bald-pated mime whose head was buffeted by blows (Webb

---

[209] Cf. 485–6 on the connection of mime artists with γελοῖα and καταγέλαστα in Clement of Alexandria.

2008, 96 and fig. 8, a relief from the theatre in Sabratha, showing a man landing a punch on a bald figure in a short tunic; Welborn 2005, 39 and n. 30; Juv. *Sat.* 5.171-2, literally a slaphead. Lobeck explained his κρατοπλαγεῖς ('ad significandos salapittarum crepitus cum stupidorum capitibus rasis conjunctissimos') with reference to Arnobius, *Adv. Nat.* 7.33.5 *Mimis nimirum dii...delectantur...stupidorum capitibus rasis, salapittarum sonitu atque plausu*; the noun *salapitta* is explained by the gloss *salapitta*: ῥάπισμα. The alternative is Koechly's κρατοπαλεῖς ('de his scurris capita ad vulgi risum effuse jactantibus'), but Juvenal's *pulsandum* much sooner suggests a compound derived from πλήσσω than one from πάλλω (notwithstanding a few other -παλής compounds in B.-P. 719).[210]

ἀχίτωνας: one of the items that the mime actor wore was, precisely, the *chiton*, albeit it might be a short one, the slave's version, as on a terracotta, probably from Alexandria, now in Hildesheim, showing two mimes (these and other mimes in short *chitones* are illustrated in Welborn 2002, figs. 1 and 2, and 2005, figs. 2, 4, and 5). Alternatively he wore the *centunculus*, a tattered garment stitched together from rags (Apul. *Apol.* 13); cf. Martial, 5.61.11-12 *Panniculus*; Wiemken, 205-6; Welborn 2002, 425, with bibliography in n. 31; id. 2005, 39.

κορυφῆσι φαλακρούς: cf. 5.104. A shaven head characterises the mime.[211] He appears in (mainly) Greek sources as the buffoon-parasite who entertains the company at the dinner-party,[212] and in Latin sources as the *stupidus*. Modern scholarship repeatedly talks about the μῶρος φαλακρός as if it is a technical term, for which I see no real proof, but see also ps.-Lucian, *AP* 11.434.2 μῶρον ὁρᾷς φαλακρόν.

285 Something like: 'whose <imitation of> life is characterised by a craft ripe for ribaldry'. As so often there is a catachresis, because the poet means that the mime artist imitates (takes the impression of, models itself on, mimics: LSJ ἀπομάσσω, III) life—obviously not that life takes the impression of his art. Despite the extravagance of the diction of *HHom. Herm.* 511 αὐτὸς δ᾽ αὖθ᾽

---

[210] Synesius, *Calv. Laud.* 13.4 describes a type of popular entertainer who showed off the strength of his skull by exposing it to battery, but this is not the *stupidus* (pace Webb, n. below), and M[b] is talking about comedians.

[211] C. J. Grysar, 'Der römische Mimus', *SAWW* 12.2 (1854), 237-337, at 266; E. Wüst, *RE* s.v. Mimos, p. 1748.27-32; Wiemken, 178; Webb 2008, 96 and nn.; J. J. Winkler, *Auctor and Actor: A Narratological Reading of Apuleius' Golden Ass* (Berkeley, 1985), 226. In art: G. M. A. Richter, 'Grotesques and the Mime', *AJA* 17 (1913), 149-56, at 149 (but see J. Masséglia, *Body Language in Hellenistic Art and Society* (Oxford, 2015), 317-18); Welborn 2005, 38 and n. 26; Dunbabin 2016, 114-23, *passim*.

[212] Juv. *Sat.* 5.171-2; Luc. *Symp.* 18 ἄμορφός τις ἐξυρημένος τὴν κεφαλήν; Alciphron, 3.7.1 [3.43] ξυράμενοι τὰς κεφαλὰς ἐγὼ καὶ Στρουθίας καὶ Κύναιθος οἱ παράσιτοι. On buffoons at dinner, Nesselrath, 26-7, 100-1, 218, 458-9.

ἑτέρης σοφίης ἐκμάσσατο τέχνην, which David Ruhnken, *Epistola critica I. in Homeridarum Hymnos et Hesiodum, ad L. C. Valckenarium*, 2nd edn (Leiden, 1781), 49, took this passage to be imitating ('hinc sumsit'), the verb is different (ἐκμαίομαι) and the meaning clearer ('he sought out the craft of a second expertise', transl. Thomas). For the vocabulary, see on 4.280 (the βιολόγος; χλεύη).

286 On the configuration, see above.

287 σχοινοβάτας: so too in Θ p. 213.7, as the outcome of Mars and Venus in the IMC, while the otherwise closely related Θ p. 215.16 has νευροβάτας. Both are standard Greek: the one is not more poetic than the other (so it cannot be inferred that Θ's σχοινοβάτας is the debris of a poetic version related to this). That it is standard Greek usage is the point of Juv. *Sat.* 3.77 schoenobates (W. J. Watts, 'Race Prejudice in the Satires of Juvenal', *AClass* 19 (1976), 83–104, at 101) and Porphyrion on Hor. *Sat.* 1.10.28. See also Σ Dion. Thrac. p. 110.14 σχοινοβατική, ἤγουν ὁ ἐν τῇ σχοίνῳ περιπατῶν; Blümner, 13; Kay, 141–2 (on *Anth. Lat.* 101 (112R), already cited on 6.443).

καλοβάμονας: cf. 5.146 καλοβάτην σχοίνων ἠδ᾽ ἠερόφοιτον ἔθηκαν (and see note for the terminology). M^b's suffix is obviously more recherché (B.–P. 217): other -βάμων compounds where the first element refers to that on which something is mounted are tragic.

287-8 For the perilous display, compare Manilius, 5.654–5. Hübner on 654 cites Scaliger's interpretation: in Manilius they only *pretend* to fall, such is their art (but *paene* saves the day[213]). In the present passage there is no *paene* equivalent, but the line can and probably should still be interpreted in the same way. Tightrope-walkers and acrobats *do* have accidents, as in 5.148, as one does in Petronius, *Sat.* 54.1, and as one did historically according to Suet. *Nero* 12.2. But they do not precipitate themselves deliberately. καταρριπτοῦντας presumably refers to the risk, or to the illusion. There is no connection with the details of the configuration, as in Valens, IV 13.6, where καταρριπτοῦσιν is linked to the notion of exaltation.

289 ὧν ὁ πόρος μόρος ἐστίν: tightrope-walkers and petauristae are spectacular instances of those who gain a livelihood at risk of death (Juvenal, *Sat.* 14.265–75). The jingle is practically Gorgianic (Hutchinson 2009, 202). Larry Kim's essay for the edited volume, forthcoming with Cambridge, on Late Hellenistic Greek Literature, '"Asianist" style in Hellenistic Oratory and in Philostratus' *Lives of the Sophists*', continues to find Gorgianic figures of rhyme in some imperial orators (Isaeus of Assyria, Pollux of Naucratis), and indeed Kim

---

[213] Unless one does away with it; Hübner conjectures *praeceps*.

suggests that the orators of this period are *fonder* of Gorgianic word-play than were their late Hellenistic counterparts, who were more sparing with rhyme.

290–3

As above, with the addition of Saturn.

Protasis. The factor on which M^b, the poet of 6.415–18, and Θ p. 215.12–16, all agree is the presence of one or both malefics in four-footed signs, as appropriate for building (Ptol. 4.4.9 οἰκοδομικάς, sc. πράξεις). These signs are identified in Θ p. 215.13, as Aries, Taurus, and Leo. This is not the usual full quota (for which see Hübner 1982, 145–6), but Aries is the important item, as his paranatellonta (from Teucer, II 1.2, 8, 10) include Athena for ἀρχιτέκτονας, ὁ τὰ λύχνα φέρων for κανδηλάπτας, λαμπαδαρίους, and Deltoton for οἰκοδόμους.

They differ in that only M^b presents Saturn as an add-on to a previous set-up; that only he includes the Sun in that set-up; and that M^a (6.410–11) has Saturn following, not aspecting, Mars.

Apodosis. The distinctive connection of tightrope-walkers and builders is shared by M^b and Θ's τ- chart, only they present it the opposite way round (Θ adds tightrope-walkers to builders; here, it is the opposite). So too there are verbal correspondences, with potters (κεραμ-) and builders of walls (τειχ-, τοιχ-). There is a further link between M^b and Θ's Π- chart in that κεραμουργούς is almost unique to them in literary texts, though Ruffing 2008, 591, adds two instances in papyri: it is a trade name (Appendix II, II.7.iii)), and should not be seen as a poeticism shared between M^b and Θ.

290 For ἄμμιγα see on 4.215. συναλώμενος is not quite unique, but not planetary in Diog. Laert. 6.20.

291 τειχοδόμους: this agent noun (which in theory ought to be capable of meaning 'builders of fortifications', though in context clearly does not) is otherwise found only in Pollux, 1.161 (next to τέκτονες) and 7.118. Pollux glosses them οἱ οἰκοδομοῦντες, which matches Θ's own οἰκοδόμους, a very standard job-title (Appendix II, II.5.vi.b).

291–2 εὐτόλμους κεραμουργοὺς | πηλαίης πλίνθου: the accusative noun suggests the common (since Hesiod) trade name κεραμεῖς (Appendix II, II.7.iii), with the genitive then tying it to a particular kind of ceramic, namely brick, whose makers are more formally known as πλινθουλκοί (the Ptolemaic term), πλινθευταί, πλινθοποιοί, πλινθουργοί.[214] What is meant are probably the makers of kiln-baked (as opposed to sun-dried) bricks facing a concrete core in

---

[214] H.-J. Drexhage, 'Einige Bemerkungen zur Ziegelproduktion und den Ziegelproduzenten im römischen Ägypten (1.-3. Jh. n. Chr.)', in R. Günther und S. Rebenich (eds.), *E fontibus haurire:*

opus testaceum, the commonest construction technique under the empire.²¹⁵ Their epithet, attested as early as Aeschylus, suggests daring/audacity (aggrandising a banal activity with shades of Prometheus?)/the overcoming of odds.

292–3 κανονισμῶν could be governed by κεραμουργοὺς or εὐθυντῆρας, but if the latter the sequence is logical: the bricks having been provided, the natives make straight walls and the coping on top.²¹⁶ The two construction terms remaining in Θ for these to map on to are σκανδουλαρίους and τοιχοβάτας. The former are shinglers (Ruffing 2008, 747; *TAM* V.3 1852 (Lydia, 3rd c.)), who fasten pieces of wood to laths on the surface of a building or its roof.²¹⁷ The latter, literally 'walkers on walls', are hard to identify unless one back-reads M^b's apparent meaning 'copers' into it. As for M^b's own vocabulary, εὐθυντήρ usually refers to (i) one who has the role of a moral corrector or chastiser (Theogn. 40) or (ii) the steerage of a ship (a rudder: Aesch. *Suppl.* 717; a wind: *EtGud* o 442, *EtMag* 642.30). In Iambl. *Theol. arithm.* p. 79.23 it does refer to a straight edge and measure, albeit a metaphorical one (the decad). For κανονισμῶν and θριγκῶν see on 4.151–2.

293 ἀεὶ καμάτοισι συνήθεις: rather as with μόχθος (see on 4.248), the poet has applied a 'toil' word (p. 172; Martínez-Hernández, 105–6), which M^a had used mostly in the impressionistic sense of suffering (though already in the world of work at 3.322), for specific kinds of labour: here, of builders; in 326, of stone-dressers(?); and in 443, of manual and physical labourers. Of watery trades in 1.88 and metal workers in 5.135.

294–308 + 309–16

Venus and Mars in equal degrees in trine, quartile, or opposition; and with the addition of Saturn in houses not his own.

Protasis. We are dealing with parallels with three charts in Θ (pp. 195.5–8, 213.4–6, 215.18–21), each of which involves Venus and Mars in equal degrees, and makes some specification about their dodecatemories.

Beiträge zur römischen Geschichte und zu ihren Hilfswissenschaften/[Heinrich Chantraine zum 65. Geburtstag] (Paderborn, 1994), 263–72, at 265–6; Ruffing 2008, 719–22.

²¹⁵ D. S. Robertson, *Greek and Roman Architecture* (Cambridge, ²1943), 235; A. R. A. van Aken, 'Lateres and Latericium', *Mnemosyne*⁴, 5 (1952), 139–48; F. Sear, *Roman Architecture* (London, 1982), 76–7; A. Wilson, 'The Economic Impact of Technological Advances in the Roman Construction Industry', in E. Lo Cascio (ed.), *Innovazione tecnica e progresso economico nel mondo romano: Atti degli incontri capresi di storia dell'economia antica (Capri 13–16 aprile 2003)* (Bari, 2005), 225–36, esp. 227–9.

²¹⁶ Unless θριγκός is just a synonym for 'wall' (LSJ II.1).

²¹⁷ J. Bardouille, 'L'importance du génie militaire dans l'armée romaine à l'époque impériale', *Revue historique des armées*, 261 (2010), 79–87, at §5.

M^b reflects Θ against the corresponding chart in 6.586–90 in various ways: (i) equal degrees instead of swapped terms; (ii) the *language* of dodecatemories, albeit in the non-technical sense of signs (p. 247); (iii) consensus on aspects, which include quartile and opposition, as well as trine in Θ pp. 195.6 and 213.5, whereas M^a specifies only conjunction. Yet M^b also looks to be embroidering M^a (or a common predecessor) because 297–8 is clearly a verbose re-rendering of 6.587 ξυνὸν ζῴων δρόμον ἐξανύοντες.

All witnesses except Θ p. 213.4–6 run on from the aspect of Mars and Venus to the additional presence of Saturn. In Θ pp. 195.9 and 215.22 ἐπιθεωρήσῃ just signifies an additional aspect. M^a agrees (6.591). M^b, however, adds a detail about alien houses, and if 4.310 συννεύῃ means conjunction—like a drawing-together of the eyebrows in the other parallel for the transitive use of the verb in 4.392—that, too, is new. (See n. ad loc.)

Apodosis. M^b offers a vastly inflated version of M^a. 3.329–34 noted the effects of the aspects of Venus and Mars with considerably less sensationalism.

294 ἰσόμοιρα κέλευθα...βαίνῃ: also 4.583 οὐρανίην ἀτραπὸν...βαίνῃ: Pind. fr. 191 Maehler Αἰολεὺς ἔβαινε Δωρίαν κέλευθον ὕμνων; similar to εἶμι + ὁδόν, but more exclusively poetic.

295 κατ' ἔμβασιν: basically a place of entering. This obviously suggests the technical term ἐπέμβασις, which means a planet's entering a sign or place in the *dodecatopos* (Heilen 2015, 521–2). But it is not itself a technical term of astrology, although it appears in codex M in Valens, I 18.79 κατὰ τὰς ἐμβάσεις, with the same meaning as ἐπέμβασις. The poet gestures both at the technical term (p. 245—redundantly, given what we have been told already) and also at his favourite pathway metaphor.

296 Compare 4.74 for the construction (διαμετρεῖν + acc. + dative). φάος ἄπλετον looks to vary Ap. Rhod. 2.669 φάος ἄμβροτον, while the clausula purloins 2.523 ἀστέρι κείνῳ, of Sirius. The epithet is a strong formulation of Venus' brightness (i. 906, 914), first in Empedocles, 31 B 17.27 D.-K. ἠέρος ἄπλετον ὕψος, and like Greg. Naz. PG 37.525.12 σέλας ἄπλετον (albeit of semi-metaphorical, divine light); see Accorinti on Nonn. *Par.* 20.6.

297–8 τὸν αὐτὸν ἅμα θρώσκωσι τυχόντες...δρόμον: the verb must govern the bare accusative (as in 294); there is a parallel in Eur. *Bacch.* 873, and in the text of Soph. *Tr.* 58 (where, however, various emendations have been attempted; see Davies ad loc., who accepts Wakefield's correction of δόμους to the dative). The verb is remarkably vigorous, to the point where one suspects (with the male Mars, anyway) a sexual metaphor. The second hand adds an iota *supra lineam* (θρώ'σκωσι), and there was disagreement about the orthography in antiquity. See West, *Ilias* i. xxxi.

298 ἑλικὸν δρόμον αἰθροδόνητον: Axtius's emendation introduces a ἕλιξ word, other forms of which are used for the Moon (see on 4.91). If it is correct, it presumably has reference to the obliquity of the ecliptic (which is how Proclus, *In Plat. Tim. Comm.* iii. 78.29 interprets Plat. *Tim.* 39 A πάντας γὰρ τοὺς κύκλους αὐτῶν στρέφουσα ἕλικα). The epithet is rare, of controversial meaning where the superlative occurs in Call. *Hec.* fr. 116.1 ἑλικώτατον ὕδωρ (Hollis ad loc. argues for the probable meaning 'black'), but certainly 'circular' (or rather 'circling', LSJ) in the Hymn to Isis, *IG* XII,5 739.155 ἑλικὰν...χορείαν. αἰθροδόνητον, while unique, is most similar to Ar. *Av.* 1385 ἀεροδονήτους, where the feel is distinctly dithyrambic (see Dunbar ad loc.; corroborated by the other -δόνητος compounds in B.–P. 486). For αἰθρο- compounds see on 4.224. δρόμος itself, of the rotation of the cosmos, is the least striking part of the expression (LSJ I.1; Mesomedes (2nd c.) (II Heitsch), 8.3, 11), but there is a fairly similar poetic transformation in *IG* IX 1, 880 = *SEG* 45.540 (Corfu, 1st c. BC/AD), epitaph for Mnaseas (of Miletus?), astronomer and agrimensor, ll. 7–8 δι' ἀστέρων | δι[ῆλθ]ε τὰν πυρωπὸν αἰθεροδρόμω[ν] | [κέλευθον...] (the epithet having been repurposed from its original occurrence in Ar. *Av.* 1394–5 αἰθεροδρόμων οἰωνῶν).

300 ζωροπότας οἴνου: see on 6.588, now wadded with a superfluous genitive (p. 211). The commoner word, especially in Athenaeus, is ἀκρατοπόται/ἀκρατοποτεῖν, especially of the Scythians. The motif especially evokes them, Satyrs, Cleomenes, and Alexander's Macedonians, but the point of the present passage is not so much the catastrophic debauch (e.g. Chares, *FGrH* 125 F 19a–b) as the decadent lifestyle, a point made vividly by Boudicca in Dio Cass. 62.6.4, who links it, as here, with gourmandising, wearing perfume, and sexual excess; see too Sen. *Ep.* 122.6. Aelian, *VH* 2.37 has a factoid about the lawcode of Zaleucus of Locri, who made non-dietetic neat-wine drinking punishable by death. This epithet occurs twice more in asyndetic lists in Gregory of Nazianzus (*PG* 37.444.12 Πλάγκται, ζωροπόται, φιλομειδέες, ἐγρεσίκωμοι and 1233.2 Ζωροπόται, πλάγκται, φιλοκέρτομοι, ἀβροχίτωνες).

μεθυχάρμονας: the only -χάρμων compound listed in B.–P. 220, but on reprehensible pleasures one can compare e.g. Arist. *EN* 1154ᵃ17–18 πάντες γὰρ χαίρουσί πως καὶ ὄψοις καὶ οἴνοις καὶ ἀφροδισίοις, ἀλλ' οὐχ ὡς δεῖ; Xen. *Mem.* 1.5.4 τῷ ὄψῳ τε καὶ τῷ οἴνῳ χαίροντα μᾶλλον ἢ τοῖς φίλοις.

300–1 εἰλαπινουργούς | δαιτυμόνας: these seem to be a pair, corresponding to hosts and guests; cf. Plat. *Tim.* 17 A δαιτυμόνων/ἑστιατόρων; Phil. *Spec. Leg.* 2.193 ἑστιατόρων καὶ ἑστιωμένων θίασος. The poet has based the first on εἰλαπιναστάς, *hapax* at *Il.* 17.577, and found the second in this *sedes* in *Od.* 4.621, 9.7; none of these is in the least pejorative in its original setting.

301 θιάσοισιν ἀεικώμους: cf. 4.493 θιάσων κωμάστορας. For the purely secular meaning of θίασος (LSJ III) one should add Plut. *Cleom.* 55.2 ἐν γυναιξὶ καὶ θιάσοις καὶ κώμοις (*Mor.* 301 F is partly religious) and Philo, *Spec. Leg.* 2.193 (as in the previous note).

302 For the topos—reversal of night and day—see A. J. Woodman, 'Nero's Alien Capital: Tacitus as paradoxographer (*Annals* 15.36–7)', in id. and J. Powell (eds.), *Author and Audience in Latin Literature* (Cambridge, 1992), 173–88, at 179–80, repr. in R. Ash (ed.), *Oxford Readings in Tacitus* (Oxford, 2012), 315–37, at 324–5; Carcopino, 265; Juv. *Sat.* 8.11–12; Sen. *Ep.* 122; Petron. *Sat.* 41. A more positive spin is attempted by Libanius in praise of Antioch's night-life, *Or.* 11.267. This version omits the riotous nights to dwell on the somnolent days; contrast Tac. *Ann.* 16.18.1 *illi dies per somnum, nox officiis et oblectamentis vitae transigebatur*, Sen. *Ep.* 122.9 *lucet: somni tempus est …. iam lux propius accedit; tempus est cenae.* The beginning of the line is taken from *Od.* 10.11 ἤματα· νύκτας, though there—the isle of Aeolus—dining takes place during the day and sleep, in due order, by night; the juxtaposition of the nouns, now without punctuation, indicates, not the succession of these two time-periods, but their confusion (and in *Or. Sib.* 2.207, there at line-end, their total disorganisation on the Day of the Lord).

303 βλαστήσουσιν: the verb (simplex and compounds) is at home describing the growth of crops, fruits, or organic material. Perhaps it ultimately belongs to the same 'natalist' style of presentation as the many references to human birth (ὠδῖνες, λοχευομένοισι βροτοῖσιν, etc.) in both M^a and M^b (pp. 251–2); what underlies all this is ultimately the idea that underlay Greek astronomy in the first place, that the cycle of generation on earth is influenced by the stars—vegetable and animal in Hesiod, and human no less in the astrologers.

304–5 With the wearers of wigs (πλαστοκόμαι) the poet segues from those who live a decadent, sybaritic lifestyle to adulterers in particular. The passage entirely reflects the tendency for ancient literary sources, when they mention wigs, to do so in a satirical or moralising way (Ackers, 176–7). Most of them refer to women, and that is what the vast bulk of modern literature is about.[218] But there are scattered references to wearers of male wigs too. Various gentlemen conceal embarrassing baldness under a false hairpiece (Luc. *Alex.* 59 φενάκη; Mart. *Ep.* 12.45; Avian. *Fab.* 10); closer to the present point are references to wigs in connection with louche or rowdy behaviour. Suet. *Nero* 26.1 describes how Nero, after twilight, would go roaming in the streets and taverns

---

[218] E. Bartman, 'Hair and the Artifice of Roman Female Adornment', *AJA* 105 (2001), 1–25; Ackers, 165–77; ead., 'The Representation of Wigs in Roman Female Portraiture of the Late 2nd to 3rd Century AD', *BABesch* 94 (2019), 211–34.

sporting a *galerus* or *galerum*;²¹⁹ Ackers glosses this as a partial hair-piece, to cover baldness, but from the context it sounds more like a disguise, as it certainly is when Caligula dons *capillamenta* in Suet. *Calig.* 11; both passages concern nefarious activities *by night*, and the second one adultery. In Petron. *Sat.* 110, Giton and the narrator, whose heads have been shaved, are adorned by a maid with their mistress' false golden curls, though this is a vaudeville, not an habitual adornment. The expression, though unique, is reminiscent of ἐπεισάκτου κόμης (Σ Ar. *Plut.* 271; there, of a woman).

The present passage is a variant on the perfumed lover topos. Other instances refer specifically to *hair*: Plaut. *Truc.* 610 *moechum malacum, cincinnatum*; *Mil.* 923-4 *cincinnatum* | *moechum unguentatum*; Hor. *Od.* 4.9.13 *comptos…adulteri crines* (Paris); a seducer with fancy hair in Ov. *Ars* 3.434. Nisbet and Rudd on Hor. *Od.* 3.24.20 *nitido…adultero* comment that he 'has a hint of hair-oil'; and cf. Ingleheart on Ov. *Trist.* 2.497-500 *cultus…adulter*. For the association of long hair with sexual availability, see Olson 2014, 188-9 and 2017, 139.

304 For the theft metaphor and for ἄθεσμοι see on 4.56.

305 μοιχαπάται is transmitted; μοιχευταὶ is the correction of Axtius and Rigler. The compound is badly formed. In other -απάτης compounds (B.-P. 547) the first element gives the object of the deception (strangers, mankind, the soul) or that wherein it consists (oaths), not the perpetrator. That kind of deformation does not, however, seem beyond the talents of a poet who could devise, say, 4.221 γαλλομανεῖς.

μυρόεντες: otherwise only Erycius, *AP* 6.234.5-6 = Garland 2260-1 μυρόεντα | βόστρυχον (of a gallus; cf. Ov. *Met.* 5.53 *madidos murra…capillos*, of Athis), but scented locks are a topos.²²⁰ Perhaps μυροβαφίαις means, or includes, this in ps.-Palchus, *CCAG* v/1. 189.9 (in Venus' domain).

νεομορφοτύπωτοι: the extravagance of the compound perhaps satirises their narcissism. νεοτύπωτα alone glosses νεοχάραχθ' in Soph. *Aj.* 6, and not otherwise except in Nicetas Choniates (of script). The nominal component seems otherwise paralleled only in the specifically Christian θεοτύπωτος (B.-P. 527).

306-8 These lines shift to those who are complicit in adultery, to the pimps and procurers who facilitate it. The conventional figure is that of the meddling

---

[219] D.-S. s.v. Galerus (S. Reinach), 1452-3.
[220] Females: Meleager, *AP* 5.147.5 = *HE* 4240 μυροβοστρύχου Ἡλιοδώρας; *Ep. Adesp.* 9 (Powell), col. iii. 9 ξανθοῖο κόμη[.] μυροβοσστρυχόεντος; 3 Macc. 4:6 τὴν μυροβρεχῆ πεφυρμέναι κόμην (the epithet also in Suet. *Aug.* 86.2). Males: Pease on V. *Aen.* 4.216 *crinemque madentem*; Gibson on Ov. *Ars* 3.443-4; Bömer on *Met.* 3.555; *Hist. Alex. Magn., Recensio* γ, 35a,53 Ἐπικουρείων ἀνδρῶν μυροβρόχων.

old *woman* (going back to the *Hippolytus*; Gyllis in Herodas 1; see also Ov. *Am.* 1.8, with McKeown on 33–4; Hutchinson's intro. to Propertius, 4.5 (Acanthis); Maltby on Tibull. 1.3.84, 1.5.47–8). This is also the case with the (one hopes) more respectable figure of the matchmaker or προμνήστρια: there *are* some male προμνήστορες, but only in Christian writers in biblical contexts (D. Noy, 'Matchmakers and Marriage-Markets in Antiquity', *EMC* 34 (1990), 375–400). In other words, the grammatically masculine forms in these lines *may*, by convention, be embracing female natives as well.

306 μάστροπά τ' ἔργα τελοῦντες: LSJ glosses μαστροπικοί. μαστροπός is a pimp or procuress (Kapparis, 252; E. E. Cohen, *Athenian Prostitution: The Business of Sex* (New York, 2015), 140–3). In Comedy they are usually the female counterparts of the male πορνοβοσκός (Arnold, 13–14, 120, 125, 144–5, 158, 174–8; in Attic orators: 42–4; in Roman comedy, i.e. the *lena*, 46–8, 233–6, 252); the latter control the slave prostitutes in their possession, the former procure for their own 'daughters'. Male μαστροποί are extremely rare, and, when they exist, figurative (Xen. *Symp.* 3.10 *et al.*, of Socrates; in Lucian, *Symp.* 32, a man is insulted by being called μαστροπός of his own wife). The periphrastic formulation here presumably permits us to understand meddlers of either sex who promote adulterous relationships among the free-born.

Elsewhere in astrology pimps figure under a wide and not completely predictable variety of circumstances: 4.314 (below); Valens, II 4.9 πορνοβοσκήσουσιν (Venus' influence queered by Saturn); Θ p. 160.15 πορνοβόσκους (Mercury in the DESC, Venus in the MC); for Firmicus, see Appendix II, VII.3.vi. As in 279, the poet transforms a very common ἔργα τελ- phrase (4.358, 1.270 nn.; p. 617) into a (quasi-)professional designation.

307 σύμβουλοι: in a much more positive light (Venus transmitting to Jupiter), Valens, IV 23.7 συμβουλὰς θηλυκῶν προσώπων καὶ φιλίας.

αἰσχροδιδάκται: compare 4.58, where the lexicon is similar; for αἰσχ- of sexual conduct, see i. 304, 367–8; and for teaching, Hesych. π 3308 προαγωγός· διδάσκαλος κακῶν. καὶ μαστροπός.

308 'Knowing whose wives sell the beds of their husbands', or 'which husbands have their beds sold by their wives'. Sell them, that is, to the adulterous buyer: Hor. *Od.* 3.6.32 *dedecorum pretiosus emptor*; see Nisbet and Rudd ad loc. for more instances of the *dives amator*, and for other adulterers who are profligate with their gifts see Dio Chrys. *Or.* 7.140, 143–4; Ant. Lib. 41.2–3 and Ov. *Met.* 7.720–40; Juv. *Sat.* 1.55 *moechi bona*; Apul. *Met.* 9.18–19; 6.212 n. I have found no parallels for the idea of wives 'selling' their marriage beds. Usually, panders sell, or hire out, their wives (Valens, II 4.9 ἑτέροις τὰς γυναῖκας αὐτῶν μισθώσουσιν; for the husband-pander, see 6.212 n.; V. A. Tracy, 'The *leno-maritus*', *CJ* 72 (1976), 62–4; S. Treggiari, *Roman Marriage: Iusti Coniuges from the Time of*

634 Commentary on Book Four

Cicero to the Time of Ulpian (Oxford, 1991), 288; Hunink on Apul. *Apol.* 75,2). Conversely, for the association between adultery and the *threat* to the husband's financial security (as opposed to the *enhancement* of his fortune through complaisance), see J. Porter, 'Aristophanes, *Wealth* 168: Adultery for Fun and Profit', *Hermes*, 145 (2017), 386–408 (classical Athens); and for Roman writers' proclivity for attributing meretricious behaviour to women of every social class, C. Edwards, 'Unspeakable Professions: Public Performance and Prostitution in Ancient Rome', in J. P. Hallett and M. B. Skinner (eds.), *Roman Sexualities* (Princeton, 1997), 66–95, at 81–2.

309 Κρόνου βλαβεραυγέος ἀστήρ: for the epithet see i. 911 n. 4, and for βλαβερός 1.110 n.

310 This specification is different from that given in Θ, and incompatible with it. Saturn's houses are Capricorn and Aquarius. Only the former ranks among the female signs (on the usual system whereby signs alternate, beginning with masculine Aries). For unparalleled references in M^b to 'own' places, see i. 648.

συννεύῃ: implies conjunction more strongly than Θ's formulation. Also 392 συννεύσῃ (which parallels the unusual construction with dative,[221] rather than prepositional phrase), and 609 νεύουσαι. These are not technical terms for location in or motion towards in astrology (which uses νεύειν, if at all, to indicate inclination, e.g. in describing the layout of a constellation; see also Perale on Anubion, F 12.30 = his no. 12, for its use of the trajectory of a comet), but the simplex is shared with 'Antiochus', ll. 60, 90 (*CCAG* i. 111.5, 112.9), where it refers to location in a house. The literal Latin version of the present passage in Koechly 1851 has 'simul-est in regione', while Lopilato has 'becomes associated with them in the (same) place'. κατὰ χῶρον (in EGHP only *HHom. Ap.* 359, of the slaying of Typho) also implies together in the sense of conjunction.

311–12 For attitudes to oral sex see on 6.592; i. 303 n. 29; add Krenkel. Martial is the king of it in Roman satire (Richlin, 132 and n. 36). Disgust in Roman satire stems from fear of the defilement of the mouth (316 n.), and it is perhaps curious that this Greek source does not reflect that.

311 παμπαθέας: rare and unique here in a sexual sense. Their juxtaposition with the devotees of oral sex reflects the common assumption that passive homosexuals 'enjoyed fellating other men' (W. A. Krenkel, 'Sex und politische Biographie', *WZRostock* 29 (1980), 65–76, esp. 75, 76; id. 83–4; Richlin, 27;

---

[221] For the meaning 'consentio', 'conspiro', Stephanus adds Greg. Nyss. *Contra Eunom.* 3.2.77, where, however, Jaeger's text reads οἱ φίλτατοι καὶ τούτῳ συνανανεύουσιν, and Nicetas Eugen. Drosill. 3.224 σύννευε τοῖς φιλοῦσι (12th c.).

Watson and Watson on Martial, 7.67.14 (= their no. 50)). An example from Pompeii in E. Diehl, *Pompeianische Wandinschriften und Verwandtes* (Berlin, 1910), no. 648.

στομάτεσσιν ὀπυιομένους: surrounded by references to passive homosexuals and seed-swallowers, this looks like performers of fellatio, although in a system which regards cunnilingus as a passive act, even if a heterosexual male performs it (H. N. Parker, 'The Teratogenic Grid', in J. P. Hallett and M. B. Skinner, *Roman Sexualities* (Princeton, 1997), 47–65, at 51–3), it could refer to that as well. ὀπυίειν is a synonym for γαμεῖν, both of which can refer to intercourse (Adams 1982, 159–61; Henderson, 157; D. Bain, 'Six Greek Verbs of Sexual Congress', CQ^2 41 (1991), 51–77, at 54; Faraone, 13; LSJ ὀπυίω, II).[222] In particular, the 'marriage' travesty with oral sex is almost exactly as in Martial, 11.61.1 *lingua maritus*, which refers to a *cunnilingus* (and similarly Martial, 3.81.6 *ore vir es*: a castrated gallus, but a *vir* with his tongue). Both verbs usually distinguish male (active γαμέω, ὀπυίω) and female (middle γαμοῦμαι, passive ὀπυίομαι). So if this line reflects the standard sentiment that passive homosexuals perform fellatio, there would seem to be an unusual but rather effective equivocation between middle and passive: these types are performing the act (rather than having it performed on them, which would make them the dominant partner), but at the same time the act is described with a formally passive verb which assigns them the feminine role.

γονοπώτας: a circumlocution for the much more obscene λαικαστάς (H. Jocelyn, 'A Greek Indecency and its Students: *ΛΑΙΚΑΖΕΙΝ*', *PCPS* 26 (1980), 12–66, n. 155), but drawing attention in its own right: according to Richlin, 123, semen is rarely alluded to in Latin humour, though there is a good parallel in Cat. 80.8 *emulso labra notata sero*. Semen there is likened to whey. Elsewhere it is like a vintage (*CIL* iv. 1391.5–6 = Diehl no. 425, a Pompeiian graffito, where Veneria sucks her lover *per vindemiam totam* and ends up with a mouth *muci...plenum*; compare also the metaphorical *vites* and *uvam* on a priapic statue in Priap. 30.3–4; both passages are quoted and translated in Krenkel, 80). There is also a type of drinking vessel with a penis-shaped spout which made the drinker appear to be performing fellatio (Krenkel, 82; Courtney on Juvenal, *Sat*. 2.95).

312 μήδεα μασθὸν ἔχοντας: Krenkel, 84–5, cites this line for its precise and technical, rather than psychological, approach to human sexuality. μασθόν implies fellatio (sucking), as opposed to cunnilingus (licking), much as in the frankly disgusting anecdote about Tiberius and the sucklings in Suet. *Tib.* 44.1 *atque etiam quasi infantes firmiores, necdum tamen lacte depulsos, inguini ceu*

---

[222] Cf. also the use of 'brother-in-law' as an insult to a male in Arabic, Urdu, Swahili, and doubtless other languages to imply that you have slept with their sister.

papillae admoveret. The same idea underpins the sexual senses of Latin *fello* and *irrumo*, which mean basically 'suck' (*fello*, an appropriate word with milk[223]) and 'insert' (*irrumo*) the teat (Adams 1982, 126, 131–2).

ἀναστροφίῃ τ' ἐφυβρίστους: 'licentious in their mode of life' (LSJ ἀναστροφή, II.3), a coy translation; στροφ- has a sexual sense (Henderson, 176), as Koechly already saw (his n. on 4.590). The epithet could go back to a prose source. Not all passages are obviously sexual (Ptol. 3.14.32, and passages dependent on it; Valens, II 17.26), but Dorotheus, p. 351.29, uses it of bad wives.

313 See Dickie 2003, 240: '...no more than a poetic way of saying *pornoboskoi goetes*... That *pornoboskoi* characteristically engaged in sorcery is hardly surprising, but it is helpful to have a text that explicitly says they did.' Dickie discusses the association between prostitutes and magic (2003, 77–85, fifth and fourth century Athens; 96–101, 103–4, the Hellenistic period; 158–9, Roman comedy; 171–5, 175–84, early imperial Rome; 239–40, provinces of Greek East; 290–2, under the Christian empire). If they dabbled in it then presumably pimps could too, although so far I have not encountered another text that says so. ἑταιροτρόφους is rare but not unique.[224]

314 In i. 368 it was noted that when Mª treats sexual matters he tends to evoke popular disapproval rather than complain of lack of self-regulation, but here is an example of the latter. *Porneia* and *akrasia* are a well-sorted pair (e.g. Clem. *Strom.* 3.18.109.2) as are harlotry and shameful gain (Arnold, 57–8, on αἰσχροκέρδεια and the pimp; Arist. *EN* 1121ᵇ33–1122ᵃ3, and Aspasius, *In Nic. Eth. Comm.* p. 102.20–2; Sopater, *Rhet. Gr.* viii. 182.27–183.2 Walz μόνον τῷ κέρδει κηλούμεναι (sc. αἱ ἑταῖραι) εἰς αἰσχρὰς ἡδονὰς δελεάζουσι τοὺς νέους, ἵνα χρηματίζωνται, κολακεύουσιν, ἀπατῶσι, πλεονεξίας, κέρδους χάριν). Theophrastus' shameless man may be a πορνοβοσκός (*Char.* 6.5), and although neither a word for shamelessness nor κέρδος occurs in Herodas 2, the whole mime is about that.

315 μεμαχλευμένον: a new part of a new verb; for μάχλος see i. 302. For the cadence see on 2.241.

316 παμψέκτους: see on 4.58.

---

[223] *TLL*, s.v. *fel(l)o*, 1; Arnobius, *Adv. Nat.* 2.39.1 *exsugerent fellitantes mammas*; cf. Krenkel, 77. As far as I know, there is no equivalent secondary meaning for Greek θῆσαι (*Il.* 24.58) (Greek words for this activity in Krenkel, 77–8), but there may be a parallel in Shakespeare (G. E. Minton and P. B. Harvey, '"A Poor *chipochia*": A new look at the Italian word in *Troilus and Cressida* 4.2', *Neophilologus*, 88 (2004), 307–14, at 313 n. 20).
[224] Hesych. π 3044, Julian, *Contra Galilaeos*, 238 E (p. 208.18 Neumann, among a list of other disreputable types, καπήλων, τελωνῶν, ὀρχηστῶν), and Athanasius, *Hist. Arian.* 20.5 (a sectarian incident in Antioch involving a harlot).

μυσαρωπὰ γένεθλα: there are many -ωπός compounds (B.-P. 396), and here as elsewhere the second element might have weakened to padding, as in 4.78 σκολιωπά, 4.166 αἰθωπά.²²⁵ If, on the other hand, it could be taken very loosely to refer to the face in general (like -οψ), rather than the eyes in particular, one might detect at least a hint of the topos of the *os impurum* (= filthy-mouthed, practitioners of oral sex), which was missing in 4.311–12 (Krenkel, 80–1; Adams, 199; Richlin, 69, and s.v. *os impurum*; Watson and Watson on Martial, 7.95.15 (= their no. 69)). For the rhythm see on 4.282.

317–26 + 327–32

Saturn aspects Venus in the presence of Mars; and with Mercury in its own house, favourably configured with Mars.

Protasis. Θ has two relevant configurations. Closest to M^b, and matching it in the τέχναι sequence, is Θ p. 216.1–7. Both include the same three entities (Saturn, Venus, Mars) in the basic configuration, and both then have an add-on involving Mercury. (Θ has a second add-on with Jupiter and the Moon.) Θ includes a reference to male signs (Aries, Leo, Sagittarius), which M^b has lost. Among these signs, particularly relevant is Aries, for the sake of its paranatellon Deltoton, under whom are born τέκτονας, λιθοξόους...ἔτι μὴν κατασκευαστὰς χαλινῶν (P) (Teucer, II 1.10). M^a, on the other hand, has a series of banausic charts beginning in 6.410. The basic set-up involves just Saturn and Mars, which is then inflected by the influence of different kinds of sign, starting with four-footed. This is closer to Θ p. 215.12–16, which formed the basis of 4.290–3, and is discussed there.

Apodosis. M^b has a scattered pattern of affiliation. (i) With Θ p. 216.5 he agrees that the basic set-up produces leather-workers and carpenters, though stone-cutters, for him part of the basic chart, for Θ are the result of adding Mercury. M^a seems to make a clearer distinction than the other sources between quarrymen and stone-cutters,²²⁶ because he makes them products of different kinds of sign (6.415–16, 419). (ii) The addition of ship-builders, not present in Θ, to carpenters, constitutes some sort of link to Ptolemy's Π- chart for Mars (4.4.5). (iii) Between the leather-workers and carpenters M^b also has a reference to feminine trifles (322), whether sellers or makers thereof. Interesting here is that although Ptolemy's Π- chart for Mars + Venus with Saturn (4.4.8) clearly has nothing to do with this, he and Θ do mention vendors (not makers, but M^b's own ἴδριας is not specific) of women's adornment (κόσμους) for

---

[225] e.g. εὐρωπός = simply εὐρύς; στε(ι)νωπός = στενός; πυρωπός, which may mean no more than πυρόεις; ἀντωπός ~ ἀντίος. For the phenomenon of 'die Verdunkelung des Hintergliedes', see Schwyzer, i. 426, where -οψ though not -ωπός is given as an example.

[226] See p. 1065. Another source that runs them together is Ptol. 4.4.5 λατόμους, λιθοξόους...

638   Commentary on Book Four

Mercury + Venus with Saturn (4.4.6). (iv) House-builders (4.325) constitute a link with Θ p. 215.15, concerning Saturn and Mars.

As for the Mercury add-on, the tax-collectors and contractors are mysterious. But false accusations are best paralleled from a οἶνος chart for Mars and Mercury (Θ p. 193.3), which is affiliated to the Π- chart in Ptol. and Θ for those same two entities (4.4.7; p. 212.4).

318 I agree with De Stefani that the manuscript's redundant dative plural should go, and my suggested alternative to his σελαγεῦντι comes from Nic. *Ther.* 691 πυρὸς σελάοντος. This is somewhat closer to the paradosis, and, as noted in i. 96, the sporadic use of the Ionic contraction -ευ- is a peculiarity of M^a. For Saturn's slowness, see i. 910; n. on 6.142. For -βάμων compounds, n. on 4.287. For ὁλκός, i. 538–9.

319 **αἰθαλόεις**: i. 909 n. 24. It does not come from the epic formulary of Ares. It is an extension of Mars' association with fire, which M^b enjoys (πυριλάμπης, πυριμάρμαρος, πυρσοτόκος, and already 6.692 πυρφόρος).

παρέῃ σὺν τοῖσι διωγμοῖς: this is very mysterious. On the one hand, παρέῃ σὺν τοῖσι is entirely coherent (Mars is with them, sc. Saturn and Venus). But the addition of διωγμοῖς changes τοῖσι into a definite article. διωγμός is *not* a technical term in astrology, but at least on M^a's idiom it ought to mean that the planet is in the place behind them, pursuing them in daily motion. It is curious that, of three references to pursuit in this sense (6.38, 572, 659), the subject of the first and third is Mars, perhaps suggesting his aggressiveness, and here, also, that his greater speed allows him to catch Saturn up (*suo Marte*, as it were). But if τοῖσι is a definite article (as opposed to anaphoric pronoun), neither it nor the preposition with it is satisfactory. Something is amiss here beyond what Axtius' limited expedient ἐοῖσι can fix. One could read διωγμῷ, but 'in pursuit' is not a suitable adjunct to being 'with' them.

320 **βυρσοτόμους**: for βυρσεῖς, leather-workers or tanners. Given the many uses of leather for military and civilian equipment (tents, harnesses, saddles, shields, bags, articles of clothing[227]), one might expect to hear of them more often (App. II, II.7.v). The single occurrence of σκυτοτόμους in Teucer, II 12.8 (under Engonasin, paranatellon of Pisces) sits directly in between ἐπιδιφρίους (sedentary workers) and λιθοξόους, who shortly appear under this name in Θ and periphrastically in 326. Boll placed a comma after ἐπιδιφρίους, separating them from the shoemakers, but Hübner removed it, citing this passage. That has

---

[227] C. Van Driel-Murray, 'Tanning and Leather', in Oleson, 483–95; C. L. Heth, 'The Skin they were in: Leather and Tanning in Antiquity', in Rasmussen, 181–96 (193 on the nastiness of the process).

Γενεαί and *τέχναι* 639

interesting possible implications for contact, not just between Teucer and Θ, of which there is ample evidence, but also between Teucer and M^b himself.

In choosing βυρσοτόμους as a poetical equivalent for these, it is interesting, in light of the fact that it is the additional presence of Mars that brings about this outcome, that M^b has chosen a word which is used (Hesych. ρ 340; Eustath. on *Il*. 21.392, iv. p. 525.27) to gloss Homeric Ares' epithet ῥινοτόρος. Yet he could also have constructed it independently, especially if he had in mind *Il*. 7.221 σκυτοτόμων (of the maker of Ajax's shield).

320-1 A periphrasis for the basic term σκυτεύς (Ruffing 2008, 751–5). The sedentary cobbler is a topos of literature (Headlam on Herodas, 7.40; Lau, 40) and visual art (where they are shown on chairs, stools, benches), especially on their grave monuments.[228] Those reliefs, and this notice, pose the habitual difficulty (pp. 42–3) of distinguishing between owners, managers, and shop-floor workers.

321 The line is of a similar general shape (while also recalling the cadence of 4.152) to 2.320 αἰόλ' ὑπὸ χροιῇ ποικίλματα δαιδάλλοντας, describing manufacturers of luxury products. M^a was especially fond of this verb in his τέχνη section, also using it of metalwork, ivory, and precious trifles (6.345, 401 [~ 4.441], 421, 522), which is now 'downgraded' to (smelly) leather-work. Yet (i) the extension is not really surprising, given the elaborateness of some Roman footwear,[229] and above all (ii) it plays well to an ethos in which workmen had real pride in their craftsmanship—including the use of Daedalus as an icon.[230] The expression adapts personal μεμελημένοι, of those with a professional commitment (see on 4.124).

322 θηλυλάλους: speaking in a feminine way, or speaking with women? LSJ assume the former and compare Antip. Thess. *AP* 9.26.7 = *Garland* 181 Νοσσίδα θηλύγλωσσον; a better comparison might be Θ p. 180.12 μαλακολάλους (the feminising effect of certain bright stars in the ASC or MC). But why? Does the passage suddenly espouse Xenophon's view that indoor banausic trades

---

[228] Zimmer 1982, nos. 47–50; id. 1985, 209; M. De Spagnolis, *La Tomba del calzolaio dalla necropoli monumentale romana di Nocera Superiore* (Rome, 2000), figs. 39, 41–2, 48, 50–1; M. Leguilloux, *Le Cuir et la pelleterie à l'époque romaine* (Paris, 2004), 61, 64, 67–8, 70, 71; Larsson Lovén, 210 and fig. 9.3 (a seated female cobbler from Ostia, *CIL* 14.4698).

[229] Leguilloux (n. 228), 94–138, esp. 127, 130–1 on decoration; C. van Driel-Murray, 'Fashionable Footwear: Craftsmen and Consumers in the North-West Provinces of the Roman Empire' in Wilson and Flohr (eds.), 132–50, esp. 134, 141.

[230] Tran 2011, 127, 129; 2013, 220, 222; 2017, 255, 260; Mayer, 6. For instance: an *Aschenkiste* from Rome: Zimmer 1982, 139 (no. 56) and 1985, 216–17. A painting from the shop of a carpenters' guild in Pompeii: T. Fröhlich, *Lararien- und Fassadenbilder in den Vesuvstädten: Untersuchungen zur 'volkstümlichen' pompejanischen Malerei* (Mainz, 1991), Index s.v. Daidalos; B. C. Madigan, *The Ceremonial Sculptures of the Roman Gods* (Leiden, 2012), 55–6.

softened the body (*Oec.* 4.2; p. 64)? Or rather, although the first epithet in -λάλος compounds usually serves as an adverbial qualifier (B.–P. 358), could it be that they speak *with* women, as they most certainly do in their second specialism, that of stitching dildos (Herodas, 6–7; see Headlam, *Introduction*, p. li)?

ῥώπου τε γυναικῶν: ῥῶπος means 'petty wares'. It can refer to nautical or military supplies (LSJ s.v.; Diphilus, F 55.5 K.–A.), although in Strab. 4.5.3 it refers to chains, necklaces, pieces of amber, and glass vessels (gewgaws), so here perhaps feminine trifles or knick-knacks or just bric-a-brac. The connection with the previous item is clear if the poet is still thinking about shoemakers with a female clientele. Hesych. ρ 583 ῥωποπώλης· ὁ ῥῶπον πωλῶν. Ῥῶπον δὲ ἔλεγον τὸν λεπτὸν καὶ ποικίλον φόρτον approaches a suitable sense. The agent noun is also attested in epigraphy, though not in papyri, to denote 'les brocanteurs, revendeurs, marchands de pacotille' (Robert 1937, 261; Drexhage and Reinard, 61; Ruffing 2002, 41, and id. 2008, 127, 735), and there is a verb ῥωποπωλεῖν (Hesych. γ 293 γελγοπωλεῖν· ῥωποπωλεῖν. παντοπωλεῖν). Secondary meanings of ῥῶπος have to do with dyes and/or with pharmacology.[231]

323–4 Ship-builders side by side with carpenters are to be found in Ptolemy's Π- chart for Mars alone. For the ναυπηγός, see Appendix II, II.5.vi.f.

323 τεκτοσύνης τ' ἄρχοντας: the poet evades the basic trade name τέκτων (Appendix II, II.7.iv) with a periphrasis ultimately based on *Od.* 5.250 εὖ εἰδὼς τεκτοσυνάων, cf. 6.418 τεκτοσύνης…ἐπιίστορας. The Homeric version already anticipates the theme of *peritia* and mastery in craftsmanly boasts (Tran 2011, 2017, and p. 63 n. 115), but replacing 'knowledge' with 'rulership' (6.482 πάσης τέχνης ἄρχοντας) enhances it.

324 καγκανέης ὕλης: dry, seasoned. The expression varies EGHP ξύλα κάγκανα. For the connection with shipbuilding (for which the proper word was κᾶλα), the poet might have recalled *Od.* 5.240 αὖα πάλαι, περίκηλα, τά οἱ πλώοιεν ἐλαφρῶς. For seasoning timber, see R. Meiggs, *Trees and Timber in the Ancient Mediterranean World* (Oxford, 1982), 349–50. Only an irritating expert would object that ships sometimes needed more pliable timber; let alone that in some emergencies there was no choice but to use green.[232]

πελεκήτορας εὐξυλοεργούς: while this form of the agent noun is new, it is facilitated by πελεκητός (πελεκητὸν ξύλον = hewn wood, Theophr. *Hist. Plant.* 5.5.6 *et al.*), and improves the basic trade names πελεκᾶς and πελεκητής

---

[231] *Suda*, ρ 261; ps.-Zonaras, ρ 1624; Hesych. ρ 582; Photius, ρ 209, 494. Galen uses ῥωποπώλης (Schmidt, 77), which lexicographers gloss μυροπώλης or μυρεψός in this sense.

[232] Theophr. *Hist. Plant.* 5.7.4; Casson, 205 and n. 21; E. N. Borza, 'Timber and Politics in the Ancient World: Macedon and the Greeks', *PAPS* 131 (1987), 32–52, at 38–9.

(Appendix II, II.5.ii). The epithet reworks familiar ξυλουργ- compounds, transferring 'excellence' (εὐ-) from the supply of wood (εὔξυλος, of territory) to craftsmanship (p. 173). For ξυλουργός as a trade name, see Ruffing 2008, 680, adding an epitaph from Rome, SEG 4.105 οἰκο|δόμον ξυλοεργόν, with Robert 1978, 418–19.

325 λαοτόμους: strictly quarrymen (Appendix II, II.5.iii; p. 1065), 'lapicides', though some evidence points to work involving a higher degree of finesse (Robert 1960a, 32 n. 3, with late antique inscriptions where it must refer to mason artisans who work on buildings). The present passage does not sneer, nor should it; the quarrymen of Mons Claudianus in the eastern desert in Upper Egypt were well paid in comparison with the average unskilled worker at the time (Bernard, 80), and their diet was probably better (though see Gourevitch 2011, 57–8). For the form see on 6.416: Latin *latomiae* and *lautumiae* is further evidence for the alternation of stem in λαοτόμ- and λατόμ-, which is much commoner. See Schwyzer, i. 578; K.–B. i. 518.

σκληρώδεος: Spanoudakis should not have meddled with this. σκιρώδεος is not more in keeping with M^b's kind of 'exquisite' vocabulary; rarities are less characteristic of him than epic (or standard) vocabulary enhanced with impressive suffixes. Not only is σκληρός the *mot juste* with rock (e.g. Strab. 17.1.50; Diod. Sic. 1.57.5), it is, as Robert 1960a, 32–3 n. 4, brilliantly saw, a reference to the hard stones of Egypt, granite and porphyry, whose workers are also known as σκληρουργοί, also mentioned in Valens, I 1.22 χειροτέχνας, σκληρουργούς, cf. I 20.33 ἀπὸ βιαίων πραγμάτων ‹καὶ› ἐπιφθόνων πορίζοντες καὶ ἐπιμόχθων τεχνῶν ἢ σκληρουργίας, I 2.66 αἴτιον μόχθων τῶν δι' ἀθλήσεως ἢ βασταγμάτων καὶ σκληρουργίας, ἐργαστικόν.

ἐγρεσιοίκους: seems to correspond to οἰκοδόμους (App. II, II.5.vi.b), in which case the poet has dipped into a related chart (Θ p. 215.15) and out again, because the next item continues the adherence to his main model (Θ p. 216.1–7). For ἐγείρειν of a building (frequent in imperial Greek), see Williams on Call. *Hymn* 2.64, but for the compound the only formal parallel is ἐγρεσίκωμος.[233]

326 λιθοψώκτῳ: this corresponds to Θ's λιθοψήκτας (Cumont, for transmitted λιθοψύκτας, which is, however, reproduced by Robert 1960a, 33 n. 1). Θ lists them separately from λιθοξόους (see on 6.419 and the supplementary note). In general, it can be difficult to know whether fine distinctions are intended (or even possible) between different kinds of mason,[234] but the second half of this compound is distinctive and seems to mean something more precise than -ξόος. λιθοψήκτας (if correct) comes from ψήχω, 'rub down'.

---

[233] *AP* 9.524.6, Greg. Naz. *PG* 37.444.12, al.
[234] e.g. in Ptol. 4.4.5 λατόμους, λιθοξόους, λαοξόους, λιθουργούς, the second and third terms are effectively identical (Robert 1960a, 36), and the first, second, and fourth are all glossed by the same Latin term, *lapidarius* (ibid. 32).

Perhaps it refers to dressing the stone, giving it a smooth surface. M^b's form, on the other hand, comes from ψώχω, which ought to mean 'rub into little pieces' (as the disciples do to the ears of corn in Luke 6:1). It does not mean 'wear smooth', and if applied to stone ought to mean 'grind into dust'. The reason for the change is unclear, unless it is simply a corruption. Still, on the assumption that dressing is meant, to judge from attempts to extrapolate ancient labour-costs from nineteenth-century builders' manuals, this—especially fine dressing—was the most labour-intensive stage of the stone-carving process,[235] hence καμάτῳ (for which see on 4.293) is right.

βίον ἰθύνοντας: one would like to comment that this turns a Hellenistic mannerism (ἰθύνειν or the agent noun forming a spondeiazon; cf. also 2.265 νόῳ ἰθύνοντες; 1.42 ὁδὸν ἰθύνοντες) to nice effect, with the squared-off effect mirroring their work. But the indiscriminate repetition of the line-end in 4.507 βίον ἰθύνουσαι and 4.525 spoils it.

327 Mercury is in its own house (οἰκείως), but τέρμονας is harder to understand, and Θ does not help (Mercury and Mars are in *kentra* and in equal degrees). Lopilato renders 'comes upon their boundaries'. Could Mercury be entering the terms of one of the aforesaid planets? If ὅριον, normally a boundary or limit, comes to mean a term, perhaps τέρμων can do so too (pp. 245–6 n. 195).

328 In a good aspect with Mars. εὐσχήμων is common in astrology, but for natives; if a good aspect is meant, the normal expression is καλὸν σχῆμα, καλῶς σχηματισθείς, etc.

329 πρηκτῆρας: see on 2.152–3, 6.447. If this a treasury official (πράκτωρ), the alteration of suffix is misleading.

τελωνητάς τε βιαίους: this passage sharpens the conventional motif of their unpopularity (i. 332 and n. 21); for Byzantine writers, the taxman and coercion (βία) go together.[236] Compare Valens, I 1.10 τελώνας καὶ βιαίους πράξεις. For their association with robbers, exponents of βία by other means, see J. R. Donohue, 'Tax Collectors and Sinners: An Attempt at Identification', *CBQ* 33 (1971), 39–61, at 52–3.

330 χρεάρπαγας: possibly rapacious lenders or bailiffs (who seize goods when a borrower defaults), but anyway an elaboration on the ἅρπαγες who

---

[235] S. Barker and B. Russell, 'Labour Figures for Roman Stone-Working: Pitfalls and Potential', in S. Camporeale, H. Dessales, and A. Pizzo (eds.). *Arqueología de la Construcción III. Los procesos constructivos en el mundo romano: La economía de las obras* (Madrid and Mérida 2012), 83–94, at 88, 91; B. Russell, *The Economics of the Roman Stone Trade* (Oxford, 2013), 30–1.

[236] Theophylactus, *Poem.* 14.67–8 Ἀκρίδες, χάλαζα, βροῦχος [locust] | μικρὰ πρὸς βίαν τελώνου; and a topos on licensed violence and shameless greed which appears in similar form in various sources, of which *Suda*, τ 290 stands as an example.

appear *passim* in connection with the rapacious, the violent, in astrology. In fact ἅρπαγες is so common there (though it exists outside it, and is much commoner than LSJ would suggest) that it becomes a piece of jargon.[237]

ἐργολάβους: normally, contractors. We hear of them especially in connection with building works and with the hiring of artists/*technitai* on the festival circuit. But what would they be doing here and why should they have a bad reputation? Valens, I 1.40 mentions ἐργολαβία neutrally, among other honourable positions and assignations, but they have a bad reputation among thieves and charlatans again in Paul, p. 72.12–14 Ὁ δὲ τοῦ Ἑρμοῦ τὸν τόπον τοῦτον ἐπέχων κλέπτας, ἀφανιστὰς, κακολόγους, κακοπράγμονας, ἐργολάβους, δολίους, ὑποκριτὰς ἀποτελέσει. Paul's epithets are generally unspecific, but one wonders if in M[b] the meaning could be pressed as hard as tax-farmers (App. II, IV.1.vi; the standard Latin rendering of ἐργολάβος is *redemptor*, which can have that specific meaning[238]). In any case ἐργολαβία/ἐργολάβεια/ἐργολαβεῖν can refer to profiteering, and that sense would also suit the context.

331–2 In this and the next line four plural abstract nouns are strung together in a recognisable, if adorned, imitation of astrological prose. The style is particularly well illustrated by a section of Hephaestion on chronocratories (source unknown), which contains numerous instances of both ἐπήρεια (abusive treatment), whose rate of occurrence in this section[239] is matched only by Valens, *and* two out of the three astrological occurrences of ψευδοκατηγορίαι.[240] In particular, a combination of Mars and Mercury (Mars as chronocrator distributing to Mercury) causes ἐπηρείας with accusations (there, ἐγκλήματα) along with onslaughts by the rapacious (λῃστρικὰς ἐπιθέσεις) and trouble on account of loans or loan-sharks (i. 211.30–212.1).

331 Unlike ἐπήρεια, ἔκδυσις is unfamiliar, but continues to recall designedly vague and multi-applicable astrological abstracts. To get to the sense, perhaps something like 'fleecing' or <asset>-stripping, one has to go back to the base meaning of the verb, irrespective of its *de facto* connection with clothing (or skin), and irrespective, too, of its extension—almost an antonym of what is required here—to wriggling out of some unpleasant imposition (for instance,

---

[237] Critodemus, CCAG v/2. 52.33, 112.37; viii/1. 258.14 λῃσταί, ἅρπαγες, 261.1 ἅρπαγες, λῃστρικοί, and so on.

[238] A. Mateo, *Manceps, redemptor, publicanus: Contribución al estudio de los contratistas públicos en Roma* (Santander, 1999), 67–8.

[239] There are twelve occurrences of this noun in Hephaestion. In only one is the source traceable (Ptolemy at i. 174.22). The section on chronocratories (pp. 202–26) accounts for nine of the remaining eleven.

[240] i. 203.27–8, 210.25. The only other is Valens, V 6.117, a historical chart (no. L 114, XI Neugebauer–Van Hoesen).

Demosth. *Or.* 20.1). The cadence is slightly reminiscent of *Il.* 23.589 ὑπερβασίαι τελέθουσι (on the genesis of another kind of wrong).

332 The line is not only not sensitive to repetition; it makes a virtue of it (p. 210). ψευδοκατήγορος glosses συκοφάντης in Hesych. σ 2238 (and elsewhere), which closes the circle with the rest of the vocabulary because συκοφαντία can be an affiliate of ἐπήρεια (ἐπηρείας καὶ συκοφαντίας πραγμάτων in the Hephaestion passage cited above). τεχνασμοί simply renovates the common third declension form (used in its other sense in 4.269, of artful contrivance or skilful technique), which is used of mendacious reports also in Xen. *Hell.* 6.4.7.

333–40 + 341–6

Mercury in contact with Moon, or in opposition in the same position in their respective signs at Full Moon(?); and with both in their own terms. This is a chart about the Moon's relationship with Mercury. In M^b and Θ p. 216.8–15 + 15–16, the chart is bipartite, in which a modification involving terms produces a different kind of outcome which, in M^b, seems to have been padded out with related items from a different configuration. M^a has *only* an entry corresponding to this second component (6.520–5), again with wadding in its outcome from a different configuration whose details are suppressed.

Protasis. For the basic set-up M^b is close to the τ- chart in Θ (both mention a direct relationship between Moon and Mercury *and* a relationship between their dodecatemories). Θ has an additional tweak, lacking in M^b, locating the Moon and Mercury in winged signs (Hübner 1982, 125; id. 2010, ii. 217) which are identified as Virgo, Sagittarius, and the first degrees of Pisces 'on account of Pegasus'.

The secondary configurations of M^b and Θ are similar as well, although they are each in their own terms in M^b (for the terms of the Moon see 6.520–5 n.; Heilen 2015, 721–2), but are both in Mercury's in Θ, which makes more sense in a configuration about craftsmanship.

Apodosis. Θ p. 216.8–16 has three outcomes logically differentiated from one another: hunting (Mercury and the Moon,[241] with the additional presence of opposing malefics), the rearing of birds (with additional factor of winged signs), and representational art (with an additional dose of Mercury). M^b has something to correspond to all three outcomes, but without the additional factors in each case. But his word for fowlers seems rather to match Θ p. 217.19–20 (where fowlers are born under Taurus, implicitly because of its paranatellon Orion, the hunter), and his treatment of artists includes not only ζωοτύπους (~ Θ p. 216.16 ζωγράφους) but also the wax-workers and weavers with whom

---

[241] For the connection of Mercury, the Moon, and hunting, see 5.278–9, where hunters are born when Mercury is in the third house, which is linked to the Moon.

Γενεαί and *τέχναι* 645

they are combined in the Ptolemaic account of Mercury and Venus as Rulers of πρᾶξις (4.4.6). Mᵃ has a similar combination (Mercury and the Moon in the protasis, but artisans who include wax-workers in the apodosis).

One item of interest here are the reflections in Θ of the Egyptian *dodecaoros* (p. 141). The equivalent of Sagittarius in that system is the Hawk, Ἱέραξ (Teucer I, pp. 19–20), which is presumably relevant to the ἱερακοτρόφους in Θ p. 216.15. As for Pegasus, the fact that Θ p. 216.14–15 locates this in ταῖς πρώταις μοίραις τῶν Ἰχθύων points specifically to Teucer, for of the many complex positions given for this well-known paranatellon of Pisces it is Teucer who has this precise location (Hübner 2010, 357; Πήγασος ἵππος listed first among the paranatellonta in I, p. 21.1–2, and II, V, p. 51.25–6 (suppl. Hübner in II 12.2); Lib. Herm. xxv. 12.1: hind parts of Pegasus in 1–3° Pisces).

Still more interesting is the very intricate network of connections that are implied between Θ, Teucer (and his witnesses Manilius and Firmicus), and Mᵇ himself. The hawk is not the only 'translation' of the bird connected with Sagittarius (Hübner 2010, ii. 217). Teucer makes the front part of that constellation rise in the closing degrees of Sagittarius (II 9.8 τὸ ἔμπροσθεν τοῦ ἱέρακος), and this position corresponds in Manilius to that of Cycnus, the Swan (5.364–88; apparently identified in Teucer, II 9.5 as ὁ τείνων τὸ ὄρνεον τὸ ὑποκάτω αὐτοῦ). Under this sign, Manilius and Firmicus (8.14.3, placing Cycnus a little earlier, at 10° Sagittarius) have three basic avian outcomes, namely bird-catchers, sellers, and rearers (or tamers), which must in turn link with Θ p. 216.15 ὀρνιθοτρόφους. Mᵇ does not himself have rearers or tamers under this sign, though Mᵃ does (6.453, under Mercury and Mars aspected by Saturn, again in a winged sign). But there is a notable similarity between his kenning for the avian species in 4.339 and Manilius, 4.368 *aërios populos* (at the beginning of his description). How to account for this? Is it conceivable that there was a (presumably) poetic version of Teucer early enough to have influenced both Manilius *and* Mᵇ?

333 μαρμαρυγήν: LSJ gives the basic meaning as gleaming or sparkling, which is consistent with Mercury's light-name (Stilbon). Both instances in Mᵇ (the other of Mars in 4.463) apply to planets, which is consistent with the idea that the word is proper for the gleam of light on reflective surfaces (B. V. Pentcheva, 'Hagia Sophia and Multisensory Aesthetics', *Gesta*, 50 (2011), 93–111, at 100–1; N. Schibille, *Hagia Sophia and the Byzantine Aesthetic Experience* (Abingdon, 2016), 22–3); even though Mars' dull red glow has a very different quality, the noun imparts a dynamic character. Yet Dorotheus, p. 397.16, had used it of the Sun itself. It is not Aratean.

σεληφόρος Ἑρμῆς: i. 906 n. 8. The model, σελασφόρος, is unspecific. Other applications to celestial light include Nonn. *D.* 38.8, the first pre-dawn light, and 27.3, the Dawn; various applications to the thunderbolt; metaphorical ἀκτῖνες or stars, in e.g. Christodorus, *AP* 2.1.362.

334 σκολιὸν λαβύρινθον: the labyrinth does not seem to be a metaphor for heavenly motion elsewhere (as opposed to tortuous astrological methods, in Valens, II 36.23, VII 5.27), but it seems to have been drawn in by their shared epithet σκολιός (see on 4.78, and for the labyrinth especially Call. *Hymn* 4.311 σκολιοῦ λαβυρίνθου, which violates Tiedke's Law, as this line does not). The comparison implies, not a confusing tangle, but an intricate circular system with concentric paths centred on a point. The Cretan labyrinth is shown like this in some ancient representations (references in Mineur ad loc.), including a famous labyrinth coin from Knossos (which even shows the path winding back upon itself seven times, though whether that implied that anyone ever had a planetary conception of the labyrinth I do not know).[242] The idea of an intricate circular labyrinth was taken over by the Christian church (illustrations in A. B. Cook, *Zeus: A Study in Ancient Religion*, i: *Zeus, God of the Bright Sky* (Cambridge, 1914), 484–5, figs. 349–50), which implies the possibility of late antique examples with which M^b could have been familiar. A labyrinth of this sort with its worm tracks might have served at least to suggest the known irregularities of the Moon's motion (cf. Plut. *Mor.* 937 F, referring to movement against the zodiac in longitude, latitude, and depth, i.e. lunar anomaly). This is entirely independent of modern interpretations of the Cretan labyrinth—lunatic or otherwise—as a 'garbled recollection of...the complex calculations necessary to chart the Sun's journey across the dome of heaven.'[243]

335–6 As punctuated by Koechly, with a comma after δωδεκατημορίων, this looks as if it should mean that Mercury and the Moon are in the same sign (interpreting dodecatemories to mean that), possibly that they are in precise *synaphe* (ἐπ' αὐταῖς λαμπάσι Μήνης), and then with some additional stipulation about φέγγεα in opposition. This is not easy, and if the entities are in close proximity it is unclear how it would constitute an alternative to 333–4. The real difficulty, however, would be how to interpret the appositional phrase; what are the φέγγεα and what are they in opposition to? D'Orville, 660, explained vaguely that the Moon and Mercury were in mutual aspect, but he offered no

---

[242] J. Svoronos, *Numismatique de la Crète ancienne* (Macon, 1890), Cnosos, no. 96, pl. VI,18; M. Mielczarek, 'More on the Labyrinth on the Coins of Knossos', *Studies in Ancient Art and Civilization*, 17 (2013), 127–38, esp. 133, where it is suggested that the Romans might have popularised the circular, as opposed to square, form of the labyrinth, which began to appear on Knossian coins from 200 BC. Among the earliest depicted labyrinths, one on an Etruscan vase (which labels itself 'Truia'), was round (Karo, *RE* s.v. Labyrinthos, 322.18–29; J. L. Heller, 'A Labyrinth from Pylos?', *AJA* 65 (1961), 57–62, at 57, and pl. 33 fig. 3).

[243] A. MacGillivray, 'The Astral Labyrinth at Knossos', in *Knossos: Palace, City, State* (British School at Athens Studies, vol. 12) (London, 2004), 329–38.

interpretation for ἐπ' αὐταῖς λαμπάσι Μήνης, nor did he explain how he took ἀντώπια φέγγεα κόσμου. He also has a mysterious full stop after 336.

None of this matches Θ, which does, however, specify an opposition between the malefics (cf. p. 201.20-1 and 212.22: Saturn in ASC and Mars in DESC produces κυνηγούς). But it is also hard to map that onto M^b because φέγγεα κόσμου can hardly refer to Mars and Saturn. I can think of two possibilities: (i) the phrase is anaphoric, referring back to Mercury and the Moon, or (ii) it means the luminaries (as in 3.369). The former is possible, because M^b is even less inhibited than M^a in applying φέγγος to all planets without distinction. Removing Koechly's comma in 336 allows the φέγγεα κόσμου to be treated as the subject of πέλη. The planets are in opposition (ἀντώπια) in the same position in their opposed signs (κατὰ ταὐτὸν...δωδεκατημορίων), presumably meaning they are in equal degrees. And this takes place, perhaps, at the Full Moon (ἐπ' αὐταῖς λαμπάσι Μήνης), which indeed it is in the Nonnus passage cited on 4.336; this would of course be an equally appropriate meaning if the φέγγεα were the two luminaries. That is the best sense I can make of this couplet.

335 For the other instance of λαμπάς see on 4.230. Tragedy sometimes applies the noun to the Sun (LSJ I.3, adding Eur. *Ion* 1467). Some reconstructions of the text of the badly corrupt Eur. *Suppl.* 993-4 make it apply to the Moon already there, but Collard ad loc. thinks it likelier to be a reference to marriage torches. However that may be, something describable as a torch is presumably bright and shining; hence it is a reasonable inference that the Moon here is Full.

336 ἀντώπια: the first instance of this adjective is in Ap. Rhod. 4.729 ἀντώπιον ἴεσαν αἴγλην and it sets the trend for it to be used of rays, whether eyes (frequent in Nonnus), or the Sun's rays (Spanoudakis on *Par.* 11.148b), or other source of cosmic or divine light,[244] although it is capable of meaning 'opposite' without rays of light being involved at all.[245] The most interesting comparison is with Nonn. *D.* 6.76-7 καὶ Φαέθων ἰσόμοιρος ἔην ἀντώπιδι Μήνῃ | κέντρῳ ὑποχθονίῳ πεφορημένος, which describes an exact opposition between Sun and Moon. So (i) the application to celestial light anticipates Nonnus, who normalises it in this connection, and (ii) Nonnus also provides a parallel for the technical astrological meaning. Nonnus also has a number of phrases which reflect the shape of this phrase more closely than Apollonius' original (*D.* 42.232 ἀντώπια νεύματα πέμπων, cf. *Par.* 1.103 ἀντώπιον ὄμμα τιταίνων, al., and De Stefani ad loc.).

337 ἀγραυλούς: mostly epithet of βόες in EGHP, but sometimes of shepherds (Livrea on Ap. Rhod. 4.317, Luke 2:8 ποιμένες...ἀγραυλοῦντες); of

---

[244] Artemis: *D.* 5.485; Christ: *Par.* 20.83 (with Accorinti ad loc.). Of personified Draco: *D.* 25.408.

[245] e.g. Spanoudakis on *Par.* 11.168c; of position across a strait of water, *Par.* 6.2 (see Franchi ad loc.).

country-dwellers in ps.-Opp. *Cyn.* 4.268; of open-air sleeping arrangements in Nic. *Ther.* 78, which suits hunters very well.

338 These two nouns go together: the latter are the stakes to which the former are fixed (ps.-Opp. *Cyn.* 4.121, 380–1; Artemidorus, 2.11.2). Hence the epithet, which Homerically applies to structures (μέγαρον, θάλαμος), here describes well-fixed nets; the στάσις (Xen. *Cyn.* 2.8, 9.16), ἀρκυοστασία (Artemid. ibid.), ἀρκυστάσιον (Xen. *Cyn.* 6.6), λινοστασίη (ps.-Opp. *Cyn.* 4.71) are words for the setting of the nets.

339 αἰθροτόκου τε γονῆς ἐπιβήτορας: as in 4.245 θηροδιδασκαλίης τ' ἐπιβήτορας. For periphrastic expressions, see on 4.52. This one, in particular, qualifies as a kenning because it falls into two larger categories of such expressions: (i) it involves a relationship, 'born from' (others in this very broad category include patronymics and expressions of the type 'wife of father'); (ii) it involves an animal (see West on Hes. *Op.* 524). The first of these considerations does not apply to Manilius' otherwise similar *aerios populos*, apropos of Cycnus in Sagittarius (5.368; see Hübner ad loc.).

The conceit (contrast Genesis 1:20, where birds are notoriously born from water like fish) is also in Eur. *El.* 897 οἰωνοῖσιν, αἰθέρος τέκνοις and fr. 839.10 K. ἀπ' αἰθερίου βλαστόντα γονῆς (I. Wærn, ΓΗΣ ΟΣΤΕΑ: *The Kenning in Pre-Christian Greek Poetry* (Uppsala, 1951), 93, 133), either of which was conceivably the direct model. The second passage, from the *Chrysippus*, was widely quoted in antiquity; the poet may have known it from an anthology, if not from the play itself. Its better-known counterpart, 'children of the sea' (sea-creatures), goes back to *Od.* 4.404 νέποδες καλῆς ἁλοσύδνης = seals (glossed); later variations include Aesch. *Pers.* 577–8 ἀναύδων…παίδων τᾶς ἀμιάντου = fish (not glossed), and especially Call. *SH* 295.2 = fr. 533 Pf. πουλὺ θαλασσαίων μυνδότεροι νεπόδων (not glossed in what is extant).[246] But the other element, earth, has 'offspring of' kennings too, in the form of both flowers (Aesch. *Pers.* 618 ἄνθη τε πλεκτά, παμφόρου γαίας τέκνα; Chaeremon, F 9 Snell ἀνθηροῦ τέκνα ἔαρος, 10.3 λειμώνων τέκνα, 13 τιθήνημ' ἔαρος ἐκπρεπέστατον) and mud (Aesch. *Ag.* 494–5 κάσις | πηλοῦ ξύνουρος, glossed).[247] The Callimachean example is a good formal match for M^b because the 'offspring' word is qualified by an epithet: genitives are much commoner. But M^b's epithet is a compound, and such formations are characteristic above all of tragedy and the New Music (examples in Wærn, 126–38, from ps.-Aesch., Sophocles, Euripides, Ion of Chios,

---

[246] Apparently also ON *sævar niðr* 'kinsman of the sea' = fire (*Ynglingatal* 4. 3).
[247] Other examples, also involving genitives: Critias, fr. 2.12 W. γαίας τε καμίνου τ' ἔκγονον (potter's wheel); Philo, *SH* 690.25 νᾶμα θυγατέρων ταύρων (honey; bees are the daughters of oxen). In Skaldic poetry: 'Offspring of Fenrir'/'The evil offspring of the she-wolf' = wolf; 'offspring of the ash vat' = bowl.

Timotheus, al.). This seems unsurprisingly to be a precious Greek stylisation; ON has some kennings in which a noun is qualified by an adjective, but not by a compound adjective, and they are not 'offspring' kennings.[248]

ἰξευτῆρας ~ Θ p. 217.19; see on 5.173–6 for the reason why fowlers are born here.

340 The presentation of hunting as a means of procuring subsistence (Arist. *Pol.* 1256ᵃ35–40) omits the motifs of animal rearing, found in Θ, and training, found in 4.244–6 and expanded extravagantly by Manilius (5.378–86), but shares with the earlier passage the motif of the hard life of the hunter (see on 4.248). The thought is presented as a *hysteron proteron*. In keeping with the workaday activity, ἐνδεέας ... τροφῆς is a prose phrase (e.g. Plut. *Mor.* 654 A, al.).

341 This seems a logical progression: (i) in 333–4 Mercury was in *synaphe* with the Moon; (ii) in 335–6 (apparently) they were in opposition but in the same position in their respective signs; (iii) now they are both in their own terms. Yet the Moon has terms only under isolated, non-standard systems (p. 644) and it seems most unlikely that M^b (or his source) is using someone else's private and idiosyncratic method. ἅμ' ἄμφω is a Homeric line-end (2× *Il.*, 1× *Od.*).

342–4 These three lines apparently offer theme-and-variation on three or four of the items in the Π- and τ- charts for Mercury and Venus (not the Moon). Wax-workers are in Ptolemy, while artists (ζωγράφους) are in the Π- and both τ- charts, and sculptors (πλάστας or a compound thereof) and weavers are in the Π- and one τ- chart.

342 The last item, ὁλκαδοχρίστας, is the clearest: ships were painted with wax either decoratively or with a protective coat (Casson, 211–12 and n. 47; Reinard, 234–5, with papyrological evidence; Plin. *NH* 35.149; Dioscor. *Mat. Med.* 1.72.5). For χρίω in the sense of smear or coat, see LSJ II; this is one of only two -χρίστης compounds listed in B.–P. 568.[249] The first item, ὑλογράφους, could be a synonym, or, perhaps more likely, correspond to the painters on wooden panels in 6.524–5. As for κηραγγέας, if this is sound (for wax-working professional names, see Reinard, 242–4), the formation (which is without parallel) implies people who have wax in a bucket—perhaps in quantities to paint a ship, those to whom Pliny (ibid.) refers as applying it with a brush (*penicillo utendi*) (App. II. II.5.vi.f. and II.8.v). One wonders how they prevented the wax from hardening.

343 The second and third items are recherché (unique) words for sculptors. The first, ζωοτύπους, could reinforce them, or could refer to painters instead:

---

[248] *fagr-drasill*, 'fair steed' = ship, *fagr-regn* 'fair rain' = 'gold' (thanks to Mark Griffith for these references).

[249] The other being ἐλαιοχρίστης in papyri (presumably an office associated with the gymnasium).

the former if the line, like the previous one, refers to workers all in the same medium, the latter (perhaps) if there is a link with the comparanda which distinguish ζωγράφους from πλάστας (or a compound) whose work consists in moulding some sort of form.[250] The word's four other occurrences could support either interpretation. One refers to sculptors (Nonn. D. 5.527), another two to painters (AP 15.1.1; Paul Sil. Descr. 611, compared to mosaicists).[251]

344 In this line I take μέθοδος to mean 'trade' (LSJ Suppl., II.6) and λινοστολίη to mean, not the cladding of statues in linen (Valens, I 1.40; Plut. Mor. 352 c = Is. 3), but its production. Aside from the Venus and Mercury charts quoted above, the textile industry, including linen workers, is involved in other charts with Venus (App. II, II.7.viii.b). As with the shoemakers of 320, it is impossible to tell whether these are the masters or the heads of workshops or owners, or the manual workers (perhaps slaves). προφέροντας (also 186, 233) suggests proficiency, but if prominence or distinction as well, these are not the people on the shop floor.

345-6 This last couplet refers to the production of pitch.[252] There is no obvious counterpart in Ptolemy or Θ, but a reference to pine pitches, which were used inter al. to caulk ships,[253] would make sense after the ὁλκαδοχρίστας of 342. πευκῆέν τε λίπασμα could be the natural sticky resin bled from the pine (Plin. NH 16.57–60), or extracted from the wood by combustion to produce pitch (NH 16.52), or boiled to produce various kinds of viscous liquid (NH 16.53 liquor crassior...pinguior, 55 pingue). At all events, μόχθον πισσήεντα refers to the finished product, the outcome of the industrial process. These same pitches were used to line transport amphoras.[254] LSJ render συνασκοῦντας in 345 as 'work up together' (sc. σὺν ἐλαίῳ), implying that the pitch and olive oil are both part of the same industrial process, but Pliny (who mentions vinegar) says nothing about oil. Could it instead be the product, or a metonym for the products, that such amphoras transported? For σὺν ἐλαίῳ M^b has repurposed the Homeric line-end, normally λίπ' ἐλαίῳ, reincorporating the epithet in the noun λίπασμα which, contra LSJ, does not mean salve. For πόνος of hard physical labour, see on 4.72.

---

[250] Ruffing 2008, 719: the πλάστης worked in clay, and/or made the mould in bronze casting.
[251] In the only other, Acta Philippi 12:4 τὴν ζωοτύπον μορφήν means 'shape in animal form' (of our corporeal part).
[252] Plin. NH 16.52–60; Theophr. Hist. Plant. 9.2–3; H. A. Orengo et al., 'Pitch Production During the Roman Period: An Intensive Mountain Industry for a Globalised Economy?', Antiquity, 87 (2013), 1–13.
[253] C. W. Beck and C. Borromeo, 'Ancient Pine Pitch: Technological Perspectives from a Hellenistic Shipwreck', in W. R. Biers and P. E. McGovern (eds.), Organic Contents of Ancient Vessels: Materials Analysis and Archaeological Investigation (MASCA Research Papers in Science and Archaeology, 7, 1990), 51–8, is a study of four samples taken from a ship (one from the ship itself, three from ceramic vessels) wrecked off the north coast of Cyprus in the 4th c. BC.
[254] Plin. NH 16.53; C. W. Beck, C. J. Smart, and D. J. Ossenkop, 'Residues and Linings in Ancient Mediterranean Transport Amphoras', in R. O. Allen (ed.), Archaeological Chemistry IV (Advances in Chemistry Series 220, American Chemical Society; Washington, 1989), 369–80.

4.347–65 Group on Harms

347–53

New Moon aspects Venus and Mars.

Protasis. The configurations here and in 6.583–5 are closer to each other than to either Θ p. 215.19–21 or the 'licentious' chart in pp. 194.18–195.2, in virtue of the fact that they include three elements, Venus, Moon, and the aspect of Mars. M^b adds that the Moon is New, and, for the female native, that the harm is done in a day birth (when Venus is out of sect). The 'licentious' chart is similar, but involves the DESC.

Apodosis. M^a and M^b agree that males are adulterers (so too Θ p. 215.21) and females whores. But in the 'licentious' chart, the men are effeminates, and in Dor.^{ARAB} II 7.6, with the Moon in the ASC and Venus in the DESC, the women are lesbians as well.

347 αἰγλήεσσα: a good multi-purpose radiance epithet for the Sun and Dawn, but of the Moon also in Nonn. *D.* 47.283.

349 For the motif of 'others' beds' (ἀλλότριος) see on i. 302 and n. 25, 2.184–5, 267. For marriage-rapine, see on 4.56. This cadence, based on *Od.* 15.427, again in 4.482 = 1.309.

350 μοιχευτά: unique, but to be compared with the agent noun in 4.305 μοιχευταί.

351 τὸ πεφυκὸς for routine astrological prose τὸ γεννηθέν (p. 198 n. 32); for σελασμοῦ see on 4.36.

352 πάγκοινον: a hypallage, properly of the common whore. cf. 4.506 παγκοίνως ζήσουσιν, Meleager, *AP* 5.175.7 = *HE* 4360 γύναι πάγκοινε, *AP* 7.218.13 = *HE* 332 πάγκοινον δούλην… κέρδεος εὐνήν (the bed of Lais); for 'common' or 'public' women see on 2.180, and more πολύκοινοι in 3.85, 5.142, 236.

θηρήσεται: for the predatory woman, see Eur. *IA* 960, 963; Eccl. 7:26 τὴν γυναῖκα, ἥτις ἐστὶν θηρεύματα καὶ σαγῆναι καρδία αὐτῆς, Philostr. *Vit. Apoll.* 4.25.3, Heraclitus, *Incredib.* 20; for chasing gain, Pind. *Nem.* 11.47; Stob. 3.10.46. This combines both.

353 χαμαιτυπίης: the abstract noun is also transmitted in the text of Alciphron, 3.28.2 [3.64], but was there corrected by Stephan Bergler to χαμαιτυπεῖα, n.pl., brothels, stews (Kapparis, 253; Hesych. χ 138 χαμαιτυπιῶν). χαμαιτύπη was a low word for a cheap whore (Kapparis, 223–4, 233), implying a squalid encounter supported by nothing more than the ground. But if these whores make money from their trade—they themselves, and not their pimps or owners—they are presumably not the very lowest type, and are being described in deliberately opprobrious, insulting terms. To apply such a label to the famous courtesans of classical Athens, the Neaeras and Plangons, whose fees funded a lifestyle that could indeed be described as εὔπορον, well-resourced (507 n.), would be deliberately offensive. But there are odd things about this claim. This chart describes wealthy prostitutes as a category, though in reality such women must have been exceptional. It seems on the one hand (especially from Pompeian graffiti) that paid sex was cheap (though even the small sums involved were beyond the reach of many), on the other that the business of prostitution involved the rapid turnover of resources, and not the kind of accumulation implied by βίον εὔπορον αἰεί.[255] McGinn points out that fourth-century sources (i.e. only a little later than the presumed date of M^b) emphasise the poverty of the prostitute, and cites Firmicus, 6.31.79 *meretrices…quae…miserum quaestum per dies singulos quaerant*. The sixth-century figure of the empress Theodora, who (allegedly) started off as a prostitute and a dancing-girl, is hardly a basis to revise the overwhelming impression of precarity at best, immiseration at worst, presented by the imperial sources (Neri, 200–3, 229–33).

βίον εὔπορον: the vocabulary itself is banal, the figure another hypallage (Isocr. *Or.* 8.19 τὰ περὶ τὸν βίον εὐπορώτεροι; Philo, *Spec. Leg.* 1.134 τῶν πρὸς ἁβροδίαιτον βίον εὐποροῦντες, etc.). Is it over-subtle to find, beside the primary meaning, a literal one, 'easily got', 'easily won', in view of the whore's accessibility (McGinn, 52 'few…start-up or marginal costs to the individual seller')?

354–8

Mercury aspects Saturn, plus Mars, which in turn aspects Venus. Similar agencies (but no Saturn) are involved in Θ p. 194.17–18 ἡ Ἀφροδίτη καὶ Ἑρμῆς καὶ Ἄρης θεωρήσαντες ἀλλήλους ἀσελγεῖς ποιοῦσι, though the outcome is not specifically for women. Another parallel is Θ p. 169.4–8: Venus is in the MC, Saturn in aspect, and Mars an add-on (which might help to make sense of M^b's otherwise rather pointless ἐπὶ τούτῳ in 355). Natives are notorious rakes, and, if female, whores. M^b's peculiarity is the presence of Mercury in the basic set-up. Saturn governs 'unclean' sexuality, but why Mercury? Did an earlier and fuller version involve an option for pederasty?

354 The verb, which means 'strike from afar', is neither unique nor new (Diodorus Zonas, *AP* 6.106.4 = *Garland* 3455, of a shepherd's staff), but the astrological context is. Is the implication that the aspect in question is not conjunction (which is not 'from afar')? In Zonas, the accusative is the thrown object (so too

---

[255] K. Ruffing, 'Wirtschaftliche Aspekte der Prostitution in der Römischen Kaiserzeit', in P. Mauritsch (ed.), *Aspekte antiker Prostitution: Vorträge gehalten im Rahmen des Symposions « Hetären. Gespräche - Aspekte antiker Prostitution » am 4. Dezember 2009* (Graz, 2013), 87–101; McGinn, ch. 2, 'Basic Economics', esp. 52–5.

Γενεαί and τέχναι 653

Evagrius, PG 79.1116.18–19 προφάσεις ἀκροβολοῦσι), here the struck one. EtGud α 74 notes that συντάσσεται μετὰ αἰτιατικῆς, but not the accusative of what. If the accusative of the target is M^b's innovation, he is constructing the verb in the same way as φεγγοβολεῖν in 4.264, 367, 571, αἰγλοβολεῖν in 188, αἰθροβολεῖν in 224, and βολαυγεῖν in 431 (but not πυρσοβολεῖν in 214, whose object is the rays).

355 Ἄρεά τ' ἐγρεκύδοιμον: *presque homérique* (since the form Ἄρεα is not in EGHP). For the epithet, see i. 909 n. 11 and Schubert on Maximus, 268.

356 Διωναίης Κύπριδος: i. 906–7 n. 7, adding Ausonius, 7.10.13 *Dionaeo... astro*.

θοὸν ἀστέρα: see on 4.180.

357 μαχλάδας: harlots (not merely lustful): see Vian on Nonn. *D.* 48.299; Kapparis, 237–8 (μάχλος, not specifically the feminine form).

358 The prose phrase is ἀνδρῶν (or γυναικῶν) ἔργα ἐπιτελεῖν. This formulation (p. 175) is especially at home in the scheme about luminaries in places of gender (5.216; 1.31; Ptol. 3.15.9 ἀνδρῶν ἔργα ἐπιτελούσας). It is not limited to it, though the curiosity remains that this configuration is so different from others in which the phrase is found (a factor shared by Ptolemy and Valens, II 17.68, is phase: male and female homosexuals are born when the female planet is eastern and male western; in Hephaestion, i. 16.27, thence Camaterus, *Introd.* 850, women do the works of men in the *mesembolema* between Virgo and Libra). Nonetheless, the phrase does conform to the wider pattern that, of the dozen occurrences of the simplex ἔργα τελεῖν in the Manethoniana, half are in connection with inappropriate sexual behaviour (3.395: passive homosexuals; 6.296: autocastrates; 4.306: pimps/madams; here and 5.216: lesbians; 5.318: whores). The epithet, ἀνδρόστροφα, is based on the specialised sense of στρέφειν for sexual intercourse, for which see on 4.312. Ptolemy and 'Antiochus' (i. 702) call these women τριβάδες, by which they refer specifically to the active partner, who committed the offence against nature.[256]

359–61

Venus in equal degrees with Mercury.

360 The line is a tissue of Homeric reminiscence, especially *Il.* 3.48 μιχθεὶς ἀλλοδαποῖσι (of Paris); *Od.* 23.219 ἀνδρὶ παρ' ἀλλοδαπῷ ἐμίγη (of Helen); *Od.* 17.485 ξείνοισιν ἐοικότες ἀλλοδαποῖσι.

---

[256] Astrology: B. J. Brooten, *Love Between Women: Early Christian Responses to Female Homoeroticism* (Chicago, 1996), ch. 4, 'Predetermined Erotic Orientations: Astrological Texts', 115–41. Satire: Richlin, 134 (Martial); ead., 'Invective against Women in Roman Satire', *Arethusa*, 17 (1984), 67–80, at 77.

361 This is an unusual outcome when one considers that, in the opposite scenario, liaisons with foreign women are usually considered a misfortune for male natives (see on 6.146–50). Before Byzantine prose δεσπότις is rare. Nicaenetus, *AP* 6.225.6 = *HE* 2694, and Philodemus, *AP* 11.41.8 = *Garland* 3267, apply it to the Muses; Antipater of Sidon, *AP* 6.160.8 = *HE* 189, to a mistress of slaves.

362–5

Mars in quartile with Mercury. The prior mention of Mars presumably places him in right quartile. No good comes from this set-up (Dor.^ARAB II 15.27; Περὶ σχημ. 50; Firmicus, 6.11.8), but the ghostly outcome does not come from the standard catalogue of aspects. There is a parallel in the chapter on madmen (Θ p. 193.13–15), which does not specifically mention quartile.

362 τὸν συνετὸν...ὄβριμος Ἄρης: the shrewdness theme is well attested in Mercury's formulary (i. 905; add Dorotheus, Pingree[1] ὀξύς, πινυτός), while the standalone epithet without personal name is in the style of Dorotheus (i. 920 and 4.65n.). For Mars' epithet see i. 909 n. 15 (also Quint. Smyrn. 11.139).

κατιδών: this is used of aspect sporadically throughout the corpus (3.289, 6.30, 554, 689, here, 1.18, 98, 5.75, 174, 228, 255), and deserved a remark in vol. i, since it is not standard astrological prose (only Hephaestion, ii. 228.16, where i. 162.19 has the simplex); also Camaterus, *Zod.* 1323. It is not a particularly poetic verb (though used of the Sun in Solon, fr. 14.2 W. and Theognis 3x). Perhaps it implies slightly more personification ('behold') than the simplex. See also on 4.420–1 for καταθρεῖν. The absence of 'ray' language is notable (p. 572 n. 104), although this aspect, quartile, would be—if anywhere—where it was at home.

363 τελέσει: see on 1.5.

364–5 It seems always to be visionary, not auditory, hallucinations which are envisaged by astrology. The implication given the coding (harm to Mercury) is that the visionaries are hallucinating, of unsound mind (compare the situation in tragedy: Harris 2013b, 292).

364 σκυλμοὺς ὑπνοφανεῖς: the noun, meaning annoyance, vexation, is common in astrological prose, where the lion's share of the occurrences are in Hephaestion and Valens. Mars is a likely culprit (Ptol. 4.10.10 μερίμνας τε καὶ σκυλμούς, *et al.*). The epithet, which is unique but fairly reminiscent of Parthenius' Εἰδωλοφανής (*SH* 630), tips the annoyances into mental disturbances and psychological upsets. Compare the nightmares that plague the Hebrews' enemies in Wisd. 18:17 τότε παραχρῆμα φαντασίαι μὲν ὀνείρων δεινῶν ἐξετάραξαν αὐτούς, φόβοι δὲ ἐπέστησαν ἀδόκητοι.

φαντάσματα: see J. N. Bremmer, 'Ghosts, Resurrections, and Empty Tombs in the Gospels, the Greek Novel, and the Second Sophistic', in J. Verheyden and J. S. Kloppenborg (eds.), *The Gospels and their Stories in Anthropological Perspective* (Tübingen, 2018), 233–52, at 236–7. One famous φάντασμα was Jesus. The word is used for the episode of walking on the water in Matth. 14:26, Mark: 6:49 (M. J. Thate, *The Godman and the Sea: The Empty Tomb, the Trauma of the Jews, and the Gospel of Mark* (Philadelphia, 2019), 171–3), and in the 5th-c. Codex Bezae at Luke 24:37 for one of his post-resurrection appearances, where other codices read πνεῦμα. See also i. 360 n. 81 for φάσματα. The word is not very common in astrology. Closest to this passage is *Περὶ σχημ*. 52 ὁ δὲ τεχθεὶς...ὑπὸ φαντασμάτων καὶ εἰδώλων ἐνοχλεῖται, where Mars is in right quartile to the Moon, a configuration which in turn is similar to 4.552–9 (the Moon with Mars and perhaps another entity, depending on the restoration of 546), esp. 554 φάσμασι δαιμονίοισι συναντήσουσιν ἐκεῖνοι.

ἐπαγωγάς: the context shows that, of the many possible meanings of this compound, the right one is 'sendings-against', and specifically conjurations of the soul of a dead person to haunt or terrify the living: see Diggle on Theophr. *Char*. 16.7 Ἑκάτης...ἐπαγωγήν; Johnston, 106 and n. 55; Dickie 2003, 41, 43.[257] The entry in LSJ 4.b needs further refinement.

365 They are roused up in terror of the dead. For terrors and visions of the dead, see i. 360, adding Harris 2013b, 297. θάμβησιν is only recorded otherwise in Aquila, Ps. 30 (31): 23 (LXX ἐν τῇ ἐκστάσει μου; KJV 'in my haste'), but it is matched by the almost equally rare θάμβημα in the related chart at 4.559 πικροῦ θαμβήματος: see ad loc. Another testimony to seeing the dead (with Saturn in IMC): Valens, II 37.51 (= no. L 85, XI Neugebauer-Van Hoesen) θεῶν καὶ νεκρῶν εἴδωλα ἐφαντάσθη.

4.366–413 Group on Nurture and Parentage

The bizarre intruder here is the τ- chart in 4.395–401.

366–71 + 372–3 + 373–8

Mars aspects Moon, in equal degrees, in MC/IMC(?); with additional aspect of Saturn; and with additional aspect of Jupiter. Versions of a sequence in which the Moon first comes into contact with Mars, and then encounters the saving

---

[257] An example (not, however, using the word ἐπαγωγή itself): *SEG* 34.1437 (Apamea, 5th/6th c.), a charm against charioteers, wishing upon them visions of the *daimones* of those who have died prematurely and by violence.

presence of a benefic (Jupiter), are found here and in 6.46–59 and 1.185–95. All are affiliated to Firmicus, 7.2.15 (which concentrates on the fate of the mother, and to which 1.185–95 is closely related) and 7.2.16 (which concentrates on the fate of the child). There are also approximate parallels in Dor.^ARAB, but they are not worked up into the tight sequence found here: I 7.10 concerns lack of τροφή, and in I 7.14 a benefic protects from 'ruin', but the child is brought up in an alien household.

In M^b, where all the outcomes bear on exposure and subsequent fate (slavery or freedom, depending on the influence of malefic or benefic), the backbone of the sequence is found in Firmicus, 7.2.16. Firmicus simply has harm (exposure), then rescue: the malefic effects the first, the benefic the second. M^b, however, has three parts. The baby is already rescued from death in 370–1, an outcome which is then modified by (*a*) malefic (slavery) and (*b*) benefic (loving and prosperous parents). The protases are similar but not identical: M^b specifies a different *kentron* (the MC as opposed to DESC or ASC), while Firmicus specifies a day birth (the Moon is out of sect). But the connection is clear.

Considerably less lucid is the corresponding sequence in 6.46–50 + 57–9 + 53–6. This is more messy because it uses the intervention of Saturn to pivot from Firmicus, 7.2.15 (the abortive mother) to 7.2.16 (the foster-child). Firmicus, 7.2.15, does mention Saturn, but the best parallel for the role ascribed to him in 6.57–9, where he makes children foundlings who grow up as slaves, is found in Firmicus, 6.31.19 and 6.15.9 (all involving malefics and the Moon), which also use the distinctive idiom of slavery's yoke. In particular, in 6.15.9 the Moon, as in 6.46, is in a *kentron* and there are two alternative aspects, one of which is opposition (although they disagree about the other). Perhaps this configuration once intervened between the two halves of Firmicus, 7.2.15, although it is now missing from our texts.

As usual it is hard to deduce who is working from whom. What M^a and M^b have in common is that there is a middle term in which an encounter with Saturn produces slavery; M^c lacks this. But it is clear enough that M^b's macro-sequence is not drawn directly from M^a, and that he has a source which stands closer to Firmicus, 7.2.16.

366 αἰθαλόεις: see on 4.319.

367 φεγγοβολῶν: see on 4.264.

ἰσόμοιρα κατ' Οὐλύμποιο κέλευθα: hybridising *Il.* 2.167 (al.) κατ' Οὐλύμποιο καρήνων with κέλευθα at line-end (e.g. ὑγρὰ κέλευθα, λιγέων ἀνέμων λαιψηρὰ κέλευθα), with resulting change of case governed by the preposition.

368 ἀκροτάτοις κέντροισι: had the MC alone been meant, it is hard to see why the poet would not just have used the singular. If the poet means simultaneously both extremes, however, in other words highest and lowest, that would align him with Kroll's restored reading at Firmicus, 7.2.15 (produced without reference to this passage) *aut si in diametro constituti aequas partes teneant ‹in MC et› in IMC.*

ἐκθεσίην ἀτίθηνον: both new, the former varying ἔκθεσις (370; see on 6.52 ἔκθετον), again in 381, 596.

369 I do not discuss the details of the emendation of both adjectives, but wonder why the poet felt it necessary to labour in this way that both sexes were meant. None of the comparanda is interested in the gender of the offspring.

βίον ἕλκει: the hexameter end (usually preceded by an epithet) goes back at least as far as Leonidas of Tarentum, *AP* 7.736.1 = *HE* 2167 (see G.–P. ad loc.).

371 A hendiadys: this configuration of stars consigns the child to women, non household-members, who take it up and nurse it. For this meaning of ὑποβάλλεσθαι, see LSJ II and 6.292 n. This is the first of nine occurrences in M^b of ὀθνεί-, his preferred equivalent for ἀλλότριος (though cf. 4.377), and used in much the same senses. Four are in connection with foster-parents (also 4.374, 378, 596; these are also precisely those scanned with Attic correption); compare Philo, *De Plant.* 15 συγγενέσι καὶ μὴ ὀθνείοις τροφαῖς. Otherwise in the Manethoniana only in 3.250 and 5.65.

372-3 The yoke of slavery cliché recurs in the parallel passages 6.59 (as well as in 6.709, 719), in Firmicus, 6.15.9 and 6.31.19, and as far as I know nowhere else in astrology (though Firmicus, 7.2.18 has *laqueis servilibus implicantur*). M^b does not seem to respond directly to M^a, but their different approaches to what is presumably a common source are typical. M^a chooses a more recherché word for slavery, which he glosses (6.59). M^b has less recherché basic vocabulary (though he chooses masculine ζυγός over ζυγόν), but renovates it with a new adjective on the πόνος theme (4.72 n.).

374 ἦμαρ ἐλευθερίης ἕξει: for this detail, absent from the parallels, the poet reverses the Iliadic formula (3×) ἐλεύθερον ἦμαρ ἀπούρας. Of the innumerable variations, a few use ἔχειν: Philitas, fr. 28.2 L. ἐλεύθερον ἦμαρ ἔχοντες; Greg. Naz. *PG* 37.598.12 ἐλεύθερον ἦμαρ ἔχοιμι. In the parallels, Jupiter confers nurture but not freedom, but has a liberating effect once again in 6.691.

374-5 ποιητὸς ὀθνείων... ἐν μεγάροισιν: the antithesis between the ποιητός and the γνήσιος offspring is conventional (e.g. Dio Cass. 49.41.2 ὅτι ποιητὸς ἀλλ' οὐ γνήσιος αὐτοῦ παῖς ἦν). But while ποιητός is a standard prose term (along with εἰσποιητός and θετός), and persists, as Jos. *AJ* 3.288 and Dio show, after classical Attic, γνήσιος, though also prosaic, is already Homeric, and the poet in these lines produces the sort of Homeric mélange that is otherwise more characteristic of M^a (by whom he was perhaps inspired): cf. *Od*. 14.201–2 υἶες ἐνὶ μεγάρῳ ἠμὲν τράφον ἠδ' ἐγένοντο | γνήσιοι ἐξ ἀλόχου, *Il*. 15.439 ἶσα φίλοισι τοκεῦσιν ἐτίομεν ἐν μεγάροισι, and the earlier effort in 6.56.

376 σὺν δὲ διωνυμίῃ: διωνυμία is not a new word; two of the main contexts for its use are discussions of the double names in Homer and in biblical genealogies. But it can mean adoption, as certainly in Valens, IV 16.26; it was routine in Roman adoption for the adoptee to take on the adopter's name, and at least occasional in Greek (where the adoptee also took on a new patronymic).[258] In Egypt, adoptees could both retain their original name and take the name of their adopter's father (i.e. their new presumptive 'grandfather') in addition.[259] This formulation is compatible with that, but nothing points specifically to it; standard Roman practice will explain it.

ἐν διπολήϊδι φήμῃ: this is not technical language. The adjective with this suffix is unique, but δίπολις (when it occurs at all) applies to places and means 'having two cities' (LSJ; Scylax, 58; *EtMag* p. 279.5). For the high-status individuals with double citizenship (διπολῖται) in 5.291 and *CCAG* viii/1. 258.1, see note ad loc. On the face of it a reference to citizenship here seems rather unlikely, given that adoptions, if they occurred at all, were likely to take place within families, and even if we are talking here about the adoption of foundlings, those foundlings were either found within the city of birth or brought into the city from the surrounding country regions. Nevertheless, Greek adoptions might involve a change of *polis*, as well of deme; there is testimony to this in the large dossier on adoption from Rhodes.[260] Perhaps the line also envisages the eventuality that a child has been trafficked by slave traders from a completely different location, but then it is unclear that a meaningful link could be retained with the city of origin (*Shepherd of Hermas*, 1: evidently the writer was brought up somewhere else and sold in Rome, but there is no record of where that somewhere else might be).

377–8 The lines paraphrase the idea of τροφή. For the θρεπτοί, among whom foundlings will have constituted a large group, see on 6.58 and 58–9, adding Boswell, 116–21. The emotive language is not belied by other literary and epigraphic evidence. στοργή, used in similar circumstances in 4.588, is the proper word for the love of parents and children. Grave inscriptions provide particularly

---

[258] M. S. Smith, 'Greek Adoptive Formulae', *CQ*² 17 (1967), 302–10, Appendix *(c)*, Change of Name, 309; for the additional patronymic, see G. Poma, 'Ricerche sull'adozione nel mondo rodio (III sec. a.C./III sec. d.C.)', *Epigraphica*, 34 (1972), 169–305, at 184.

[259] S. Remijsen and W. Clarysse, 'Incest or Adoption? Brother-Sister Marriage in Roman Egypt Revisited', *JRS* 98 (2008), 53–61, at 58–9.

[260] Poma (n. 258), 182–3, 191–206 (demes); 177, 199 (poleis).

good parallels for the use of affectionate language towards θρεπτοί,[261] which is by no means incompatible with the probability that most foundlings ended up as slaves.[262] How many were adopted is unquantifiable, but some foundlings were indeed reared ἀνθ' υἱοῦ/loco filii (Ricl, 103). χρήμασι is accurate as well, in fact to a point concealed by the sentimental tone here, in cases where the outlay on a foster-child became a bone of contention when its biological parents, or original owners in the case of a slave, wanted the child back (i. 732 and n. 27, adding Ricl, 100–1). Non-biological parents could also make foster-children their heirs if there were economic need (Boswell, 74). The presentation is emotive, but what the lines essentially drive at is the question of what parenthood is (ps.-Quint. *Decl.* 278.5 *patres enim non tantum natura…continentur*; cf. A. Casamento, 'Patres non tantum natura: l'expositio di minori nelle declamazioni in lingua latina: il caso di ps. Quint. *Decl. Min.* 278', *Camenae*, 23 (2019), 1–12). Constantine would resolve the question in favour of the rearer (*C. Th.* 5.9.1: biological parents had no right of reclaim), but what that did in practice was to cement the rights of slave-holders (Harris 1994, 20–1; Ricl, 101).

379–83 + 384–5

Saturn in equal degrees with Moon or in opposition, and with Venus in aspect. This chart combines two outcomes: (i) exposure and (ii) slave parentage, (*a*) with slave mother, (*b*) with mother's status superior to the father's (an outcome produced by Venus). The villain is Saturn, and the chart—as shown by the parallels—can be seen as a much expanded version of 4.372–3, which produced slavery in addition to exposure above.

None of the parallels has all these elements. 6.57–9 has (i), 6.698–702 (ii), but without part (*b*). Dor.^ARAB I 7.10 has (i), Dor.^ARAB I 10.23 (ii), but lacking (*a*) and (*b*). Θ p. 219.13–14 has an isolated passage for a slave-mother (iia) in the chapter Περὶ γονέων. None of the parallels involves Venus in such a way as to indicate the mother's status vis-à-vis the father's.

Of the two part parallels in M^a,

(i) 6.57–9 is less precise in the protasis (it does not specify aspect), but more in the outcome (the offspring is exposed, raised by another, and undergoes the yoke of slavery). This chart was discussed above (p. 656).

(ii) 6.698–702 is more precise in the protasis (the Moon is in the IMC or DESC, Saturn in quartile or opposition, and Mars with Venus in opposition

---

[261] Boswell, 74, 120–1; Ricl, 98–9, 103 and n. 57, 106; ps.-Quint. *Decl.* 278.10–12; *RECAM* ii. 250, a memorial of imperial date from Yamak, N. Galatia, τρεπτῷ γλυκυτάτῳ.

[262] Harris 1994, 19; M. Corbier, 'Child Exposure and Abandonment', in S. Dixon (ed.), *Childhood, Class and Kin in the Roman World* (London, 2001), 52–73, at 67–8.

660   Commentary on Book Four

or quartile) but shares only half the outcome (namely iia). The protasis has a close parallel in Firmicus, 7.4.5 (the only differences are that opposition is not mentioned for Saturn and that Venus is absent) and a looser one in Dorotheus (both malefics strike the Moon, one of them opposing it).

380 πλαγκτῷ κόσμοιο πορείῃ: for the epithet see on 4.7, and for πορεία see on 4.6.

381-2 There is no surprise that the fruits of an unwanted and shaming pregnancy should be exposed, but how surprising is the implication that the child of a domestic slave should be exposed? *Vernae* were valuable commodities, and it seems that a female slave's fertility was a consideration when she went on the market (Bradley, 55–6, 62–3). However, Dio Chrys. *Or.* 15.8 notes that slave women both practise abortion and 'destroy' their children after birth (διαφθείρειν, whatever this implies—murder? exposure?), sometimes with the connivance of their husbands, lest raising a child just added to the miseries of slavery itself. This is not, it seems, an implausible event (Harris 1994, 14).

382 πρὸς μητρὸς ἐλέγχεται ἀνδράσι δούλη: Dorotheus has δούλην λέγε τὴν μητέρα. This version is reminiscent of a formula sometimes used in papyri to indicate slave parentage, ἐκ δούλης, sometimes ἐκ δούλης μητρός (Bieżuńska-Małowist 1977, 12 ~ 1984, 20).

383 ἐλεύθερα: presumably the neuter plural agrees with βρέφεα, carried forward from 4.381.

384-5 Elsewhere it is the location of Venus in female signs that has the effect of making the mother more noble than the father. In Dor.^{ARAB} II 26.13/Περὶ κέντρ. 63, Θ p. 133.22–3, Venus in the ASC in a female sign makes the mother εὐγενεστέραν, and conversely Jupiter in a male sign ennobles the father (Dorotheus, p. 324.13–14). However, it is the sign, not the planet, that is determinative in Dorotheus, p. 324.15, Θ pp. 133.24–134.1 (Jupiter in a female sign on the ASC still ennobles the mother), and in Dor.^{ARAB} I 10.33, apparently as the result of *either* benefic, the father is more noble than the mother.

384 προσμαρτυρέουσα γένηται: the periphrastic tense[263] (as opposed to a part of the epithet προσμάρτυρος, for which see on 4.161) conveys a steady state ('x-being-in-such-and-such-a-position does this'), rather than a one-off event (K.-G. i. 39 'wenn das Partizip in der Weise eines Adjektivs…dem Subjekte ein

---

[263] See K.-G. i. 38–40; Schwyzer, i. 813; Blass–Debrunner–Rehkopf, §353 (εἶναι with present participle). Wisdom on the periphrastic tenses is that while they are attested since Homer they become much commoner in LXX and the NT through Aramaic influence.

charakteristisches Merkmal, eine dauernde Eigenschaft, einen bleibenden Zustand beilegt'; Mayser, ii/1. 223 '...um eine dauernde Eigenschaft oder einen bleibenden Zustand auszudrücken'; Blass–Debrunner–Rehkopf, §353.1 '...die dauernde Aktion zu bezeichnen'); cf. also J. Gonda, 'A Remark on "Periphrastic" Constructions in Greek', *Mnemosyne*⁴, 12 (1959), 97–112: in its quality of 'semi-nominal sentence' it is suited to a description of a settled state of affairs (including what on 99 Gonda calls 'indications of time or circumstances'). Planets move; but such expressions apparently transform the natal event into a little moment of permanence. It happens again in 5.320 ἣ στείχουσα, Maximus, 429–30 συνόδοισιν ἐπιστείχουσα...εἴη (see too Zito on 505–6 εἴη...ἐνιβληθέντα), and the construction with a verb of appearing instead of being is functionally equivalent (1.277–8 ἀμφιβεβῶσα...ἰοῦσα φαανθῇ, Maximus 282 ἐνιδρομέουσα... ἰνδάλληται).²⁶⁴ It even occurs with τυγχάνειν, not the word for a state of permanence, in 5.189 αὔξουσα τύχῃ and Maximus, 393 τύχοι...δινεύουσα.

385 πατέρων μητρός: once the poet gets this figure into his head he cannot get it out again (388, 393, cf. 411). Fehling discusses the general figure (the juxtaposition or near-juxtaposition of antithetical or complementary terms), and on 282–3 gives examples with fathers and sons and one with men and women (Aesch. *Suppl.* 477), but no others with husbands and wives. The usual form of the figure involves contrasting cases; this first instance is deviant.

λοχείαι: the required sense is <social status at> birth. Monaco, 51, proceeds as if it is a matter of 'choice' or preference between this and the papyrus' τόκειαι. I submit that this is an instance of equal validity (p. 394). Both versions employ 'birth' vocabulary, but the papyrus carries a unique noun, while Mᵇ prefers a commoner one, cognate forms of which he uses several times elsewhere (87, 122 [see ad loc.], 154, 417) in keeping with his generally more physiological approach to childbirth (p. 252).

386–9/390 + 391–4

Mercury in equal degrees with Jupiter; Mars in conjunction with Venus, with Saturn in aspect. Although I see no obvious counterparts in Θ or Dorotheus, these charts constitute a pair, on the subject of the mother's sexual history. ἐπὶ τοῖσιν (which Lopilato renders 'There is a configuration of Mars in addition to these') underscores that the second chart is a follow-on from the first in an unusually direct way (Mᵃ uses conjunctions and connective particles but not

---

[264] There are also (assuming that his Byzantine Greek continues to reflect the classical language in this respect) many instances in Camaterus where a verb 'to be' must be supplied with a participle in a protasis, for instance *Introd.* 1922 εἰ δὲ Σελήνη σύνοδον μετὰ Κρόνου ποιοῦσα, 1967 μετὰ δὲ Ἄρη Κρόνου τε ἡ Σελήνη προσοῦσα, etc.

prepositional phrases to signify sequence). That connection subsists solely on the level of theme. The entities involved in the second chart are entirely different from the first, and there is no indication of how they might fit together. In fact they do not; it is simply that the second chart produces the converse of the first.

(a) 386–90
Mercury in equal degrees with Jupiter. The set-up is exactly as in 6.124–5 (virgin marriages, but without noble ancestry or shortage of brothers). Noble ancestry is no surprise for kingly Jupiter (see on 4.384–5). But shortage of brothers (in the absence of a malefic, or *synodos* of Sun and Moon, which very often has this effect[265]), is a strange outcome, especially given that Zeus himself was not short of them. σπαναδελφία, σπαναδελφεῖν, σπανάδελφος are exclusive to astrology: this is an instance of professional jargon.

387 ὁρμήσῃ: see on 4.219.
τῆμος μὲν ὁ φυόμενος: compare, and see on, 4.46 τῆμος ὁ φύς.

388 σεμνοτάτων: a scannable equivalent for εὐγενῶν, using a word associated with Jupiter.[266]

389 The vocabulary is probably too conventional to suggest the influence of Theocr. 2.159 παρθένον ἐκ θαλάμοιο (at line-end).

390 There are differences between L and Π¹ in this line (Monaco, 51–2). At least it seems fairly clear that it is meant to offer a simple contrast to the previous four. δ' is preserved in both Π¹ and L, even if it is unmetrical with ἔσσεται in the latter. Perhaps it originally stood in both recensions, but a scribe altered ἔσται because ἔσσεται is the form the poet normally uses in this position. Its function seems to be to pit a negative outcome (few siblings) against the positive one introduced by μέν in 387 (noble parents). Otherwise, that μέν would have to be taken as contrasting with the entirety of 391–4, but if so we should sooner expect it to have been placed at the beginning of 386 to indicate that the contrast was of whole with whole.

Thereafter, the main difference is that Π¹ offers γενετῆρσι, L γενέθλαισι, which is the standard poetic term in Mᵃ and Mᵇ for a nativity. Both transmit the participle ἐσαθρῶν, although the unknown scholar who annotates Hal (i. 385) offers ἐσαθρεῖν, which seems to be a conjecture of his own. With the participle, both versions seem to mean 'he will see [i.e. experience] a life with few siblings' (an abridgement of phrases like ὁρᾶν φάος ἠελίοιο), but alongside this neither

---
[265] Heilen 2015, 866.
[266] Antiochus, *CCAG* vii. 127.12–13 Ὁ δὲ Ζεὺς ἄρχειν λέγεται μεγαλοπρεπείας καὶ δόξης καὶ σεμνότητος, id. xi/2. 109.13 Ὁ δὲ τοῦ Διὸς ἡγεῖται μεγαλοπρεπείας καὶ δόξης καὶ σεμνότητος.

ἐν γενέθλαισι (poetic plural for 'in his family'?) nor ἐν γενετῆρσι ('alongside of [or even in spite of] his noble lineage he will be short of brothers'?) is easy. The infinitive, on the other hand, permits L, at least, to be understood as 'it will be possible to see in the nativities [the usual meaning of γενέθλη] a light [sc. of life] with few children'. There are considerable problems here; the line is in any case peculiar because it uses vocabulary which one would sooner associate with a protasis, not only L's γενέθλη, but also the periphrastic tense (see on 4.384), and the verb ἐσαθρεῖν, which is otherwise used of aspect (3.285, simplex at 4.597). It seems prudent, in any case, to refrain from deeming one recension 'better' than another and correcting the other against it.

(b) 391–4

Mars applying to Venus, with Saturn in aspect. As noted by Monaco, 52, there is a similar configuration in Valens, II 38.45. If, there, the effect of Mars (along with Mercury) aspecting Venus is marriage with young women and virgins, the additional presence of Saturn presumably turns the women old.

391–2 L's version is longer. The papyrus omits 392, and finds the necessary main verb by reading ἔλθῃ instead of ἀστήρ; the construction is therefore σχῆμα ἐλθεῖν ἐπί, 'come into aspect with', which is strange, but does mean that the nominative Ἄρης transmitted by both L and Π^1, is at least correct in the latter. As a result, L and the papyrus construe ἐπὶ τοῖσιν differently. In L, it means 'super his' (Koechly), 'in addition to the above'; in Π^1, it becomes anaphoric, 'when Mars comes into aspect with the aforementioned [stars]', i.e. with Mercury and Jupiter. Either way, ἐπὶ τοῖσιν is a unique way of connecting apotelesmata. It is used for items *within* apodoses in 2.469, 3.162, 319.

There are two ways of taking L's version. In Koechly's own rendering, the genitive Ἄρευς depends on ἀστήρ, and σχῆμα is object of transitive συννεύσῃ (compare and contrast 4.309–10, the only other Manethonian occurrence of the verb, where it is intransitive, but constructed with the dative): literally, 'when the star of Mars connects an aspect with Venus'.[267] Lopilato, on the other hand, reads Ἄρεως and takes it with σχῆμα, understanding the verb 'to be': there is a configuration of Mars when its fiery star connects...'. Despite the oddity of transitive συννεύειν (which nevertheless seems far preferable to Π^1's σχῆμα... ἐλθεῖν), Koechly's rendering, with its partial parallel in 309–10, seems better. Why should a σχῆμα single out Mars?

391 Ἄρευς...ὅτ' ἂν πυριμάρμαρος ἀστήρ ~ 4.93 ἐπὴν πυριμάρμαρος ἀστήρ (the Sun). See ad loc. for the epithet. Koechly's emendation does not introduce

---

[267] Again transitive in ps.-Lucian, *Philopatr.* 1 τὰς ὀφρῦς κάτω συννένευκας, and, as quoted by Stephanus, in ps.-Alex. Aphr. *Probl.* 1.70. (Ideler's text in *Physici et Medici Graeci Minores* differs, but there is no apparatus to explain why.)

a completely unwarranted form (Opp. *Hal.* 2.667 and Leonidas, *AP* 9.322.9 = *HE* 2121), but it does introduce into M^b the only form of Ares' name that is unique within the Manethoniana themselves, and that is uneasy (p. 187).

392 συννεύσῃ: of conjunction, apparently (see on 4.310), and all the more so if a parallel is intended with συνήξει in the next line, as husband and wife join together.

393 μετὰ χηρείην: the parallelism of widows with adulteresses does not imply a high regard for second marriages—a view which emerges repeatedly in the review of the *dodecatopos*, cf. Θ pp. 157.12–13 ἢ χήραις ἢ σεσινωμέναις, 159.16–17 γυναῖκα...ἢ εὐτελῆ ἢ χήραν, 163.6–7 ἀγενεστέραις ἢ χήραις ἢ παισί. Elderly wives are the more commonly dispraised category in astrology than widows themselves: see on 2.178 + 180. Catarchic astrology, which recommends suitable times for marriages with widows, takes a more pragmatic view.[268] On the documentary evidence for second marriage in Roman Egypt, see J. U. Krause, *Witwen und Waisen im römischen Reich*: i: *Verwitwung und Wiederverheiratung* (Stuttgart, 1994), 95–100; D. Rathbone, 'Poverty and Population in Roman Egypt', in Atkins and Osborne, 100–14 at 102; M. Malouta, 'Families, Households, and Children', in Riggs 2012, 288–99, at 291–2 (noting that for the purposes of the contract itself it was irrelevant). If women survived childbearing, they were likelier to outlive their husbands than vice versa, and did remarry after both divorce and bereavement, though they were less likely to do so with increasing age.

συνήξει: rare and not otherwise used of marriage. Could it be a Latinism (*in matrimonium convenire*, cf. OLD s.v. *convenire*, 1e)?

394 This line ought to be describing the other circumstance in which second marriage took place, namely after divorce; it seems to be making the assumption that adultery was the reason for that. There is a similarly shaped line in HOrph. 29.14 ἁρπαγιμαῖα λέχη μετοπωρινὰ νυμφευθεῖσα (Persephone). Both noun and epithet are unique; for the latter see on 4.57 δολοεργός (also of adultery).

395–401

Sun aspects malefics in MC. Θ p. 216.17–22 offers a τ- chart whose protasis and apodosis are both considerably more expansive than the Π- version in Ptol. 4.4.5.

Protasis. This is a case where parallels go in every direction. With Θ, the chart in 6.362–5 shares watery signs, while M^b implies the location in the MC (φαεσφόρου Οὐλύμποιο). But against both Θ and Ptolemy, on whom Θ is based,

---

[268] Favourable in Virgo and Capricorn: Dorotheus, p. 392.14; Maximus, 115, 132 (Bouché-Leclercq, 468–9); Camaterus, *Introd.* 1808; *CCAG* ix/1. 148.17, xi/1. 167.14.

Mᵃ and Mᵇ both make the Sun (not Saturn) the subject, the aspecting planet, and the malefics the object. No source is discoverable for the note about Jupiter in 6.365. Perhaps Mᵃ himself has worked it in as an antithesis to the Saturnian outcome.

Apodosis. All of Mᵃ, Mᵇ, and Θ agree on sailors and pilots. Θ also mentions merchants (ναυκλήρους); the poets do nothing with them, and Mᵇ instead diverts his attention to a pathetic shipwreck tableau.

396 φαεσφόρου Οὐλύμποιο: a suitably cosmic version of Iliadic πολυπτύχου Οὐλύμποιο/πολυδειράδος Οὐλύμποιο. This is to be taken as a genitive of place (p. 202); ἀκτινηβολίῃσι stands alone as a dative of agent with ἀθρῶν, as in 4.421. The construction is poetic and especially Homeric (Chantraine, ii. 58–9; K.–G. i. 384–5; Schwyzer, ii. 112; Weir Smyth, §1448)—and perhaps recalls, or was at least suggested by, λελουμένος ὠκεανοῖο (*Il.* 5.6, used of a bright star). 'Shining Olympus' is a circumlocution for the MC (p. 246). This is explicit in 6.146 μέσου...ἀπ' Ὀλύμπου and almost so in 4.367–8, and inferrable again in 4.595 Ἡελίου δ' ἀκτῖνες ἀποκλίνωσιν Ὀλύμπου (~ 6.62 κέντρου Τιτῆνος ἀποκλινέος τελέθοντος; Mᵇ has understood that the *kentron* in question is the MC). The epithet is unique here in the Manethoniana; more often it is used of the Moon (Bornmann on Call. *Hymn* 3.11), and thrice in that capacity in Maximus, but also for other light deities (Zito on Maximus, 246; Livrea on Ap. Rhod. 4.885).

397 φαίνει ~ 1.323 δείκνυσι, preserving the executive verb which is characteristic of Mᵇ where Mᵇ's own version does not (p. 275).

ναυσιβάτας: possibly the first occurrence, depending on the date of *Nautarum cantiuncula* (IV Heitsch), 7, from a papyrus of the second half of the third century AD (*CA Lyr. Adesp.* fr. 33.7 P.); later in Greg. Naz. *AP* 8.209.4 (in connection with stormy seas); finally, Hesych. β 262, glossing βαρίβαν.

ἐν ὕδασι νήκτορας ἄνδρας: supported by the papyrus, against 1.323 ὕδατος ἴστορας. 'Swimming' is a euphemism for drowning in 3.255 (see ad loc., a similar chart where the harm is caused by the malefics alone without the Sun). We should not expect the theme to be pre-empted before its full treatment in 399–401. Yet Ptol. 4.9.11 distinguishes drowning from the specific fate of shipwreck, and uses this same prepositional phrase for the fate of being overwhelmed by waters. See also *Lib. Herm.* xxv. 3.34 *nautas, natatores*, the same pair as here.

398 This line is missing in both Π¹ and the corresponding passage in 1.323–3. Monaco, 53–4, gives good reason to suppose that this version is the original and that the other two represent an abbreviation. To his arguments I simply add that Mᵃ and Θ provide evidence for at least two other ancient versions which certainly mentioned steersmen, and that there is near-exact metrical equivalence between σκαφέων τε κυβερνητῆρας ἀΰπνους and 6.364

νηῶν τε κυβερνητῆρας ἀρίστους, whether that implies a direct reworking of M^a by M^b or a common source.

The topos of the sleepless helmsman originates in *Od.* 5.270-1 (Eustath. ad loc., i. p. 215, 25-7, points out that the reason he is sleepless is that he is watching the stars), but its greatest concentration (before Byzantine writers) is in rhetoric,[269] where it is used with a rather annihilating obviousness as a political metaphor. Apolitical astrology reduces it to pure trope.

399 For the initial noun, M^a, M^b, and Π^1 each has a *hapax*. Monaco, 53-4, argues that a conflated version of Π^1 and M^b produces the most satisfactory version, whereby a neat contrast emerges between the steersman at the stern of the ship and the helmsman at the front. No single version preserves this, however. My text adopts Π^1's πρωράρχους because the transmitted version in L needs emendation, although I remain sceptical of the methodology of reconstructing an original version from which the others decay.

ναυφθορίαισιν: see on 3.255-6.

400-1 In these two lines all three versions differ (discussion in Monaco, 54), but Π^1 and M^c both have the victims of shipwreck survive (in M^c in rather more coherent Greek than in Π^1). It seems to me that the problems go much further than its being simply a question of trying to work back to an original version on the basis of deductive logic from what we have. The version in M^c and Π^1, whereby they are pitched into the water and still manage to survive (despite the ominous mention of fate), is patently absurd, but even M^b's version strikes an odd note by listing the victims of shipwreck in the next breath after sailors and conscientious pilots, for why the sudden plunge into disaster (of which M^a and Θ know nothing)? My conjecture is that once upon a time there was a reference to another factor that brought about the upset—not watery signs, for the basic situation is aqueous enough already, and the malefics are already in play, but a hostile aspect, perhaps opposition (cf. Mars opposing Saturn in watery signs in Firmicus, 6.15.6 *tunc procellis gravibus tempestatibusque submersos naufragos saeviens undarum fluctus exponit*). Something needs to be mentioned between the first and second halves of 399 for the configuration fully to make sense. M^b nevertheless preserves the correct outcome; M^c and Π^1, on the other hand, betray some sort of awareness of the oddity of an unmotivated shipwreck, and try to correct by tangling themselves up in the absurdities of their respective versions.

---

[269] Dio Chrys. *Or.* 3.65, 77/78.7 (and negative in *Or.* 1.29); ps.-Hermogenes, *Progymn.* 4 Περὶ γνώμης (27; p. 10.16-17 Rabe); Themistius, *Or.* 15.195 c (p. 281.22 Downey); Himerius, *Or.* 48.32 (l. 361 Colonna); Libanius, *Progymn.* 4.2.8. In later antiquity and Byzantium it is a metaphor for the devoted duty of the ruler or emperor. Mythological examples: Stat. *Theb.* 8.269-70 *pervigil*; Val. Flacc. *Arg.* 5.49, and of course counterexamples such as Palinurus.

400 χείματος ὀρνυμένου: in Homer, gods arouse storms with the active of this verb (LSJ 3.a ὄρνυμι, adding Aesch. *Pers.* 496 χειμῶν᾽ ἄωρον ὦρσε). M^b has found a way to adapt it without implying divine agency, though that is not a problem when this very phrase recurs in Quint. Smyrn. 2.195 and the instigator is Zeus; again in Quint. Smyrn. 14.615 and John of Gaza, *Descr.* 521.

βίοτον λείψουσι: possibly their livelihoods, certainly their lives. There is nothing notable about the line-end (Nic. *Ther.* 268 δι᾽ ἅλμης, al.).

401 L's genitive Μοίρης must presumably depend on βαιὸν χρόνον. This is tortured, but M^c's version is little better. I retain the manuscript version for methodological reasons and because the transmission history of the whole passage is so uncertain.

402–8 + 409–13

Saturn in equal degrees with Sun; Moon in equal degrees with Saturn, with Mars in aspect. A pair of charts on the subject of which parent dies first. Something very like the second one appears in 1.250–5 and 5.197–201, both times involving ἐμπερίσχεσις of the Moon (see on nn. on 6.657 and 1.250–5). 1.250–5 involves death of the *mother*. But neither is couched in terms of prior deaths.

Protasis. Firmicus has a whole chapter (7.9) on the prior death of parents which explains and works out the principles employed here (so too Περὶ σχημ. 5: the Sun and Saturn rule or oversee the father's person). But the closest detailed match is in *CCAG* ii. 189.8–14 (from Epit. IV; pp. 145–6). Other set-ups present variations on the same theme. In *Lib. Herm.* xxvi. 25 the Sun and Saturn are in the ASC, and other factors are involved. Περὶ σχημ. 96 for the father speaks initially of conjunction and then adds that for the evils to be at their worst the Sun is of *greater* (not equal) degrees; for the mother (100) there is no mention of any additional factor. In Dor.^{ARAB} I 15.2 and 4, Mars in left quartile to the relevant luminary causes the prior death of each parent.

Apodosis. Of the various outcomes here (which are often combined[270]), Epit. IV has the prior death of the father and of the elder brothers, but the gaining of wealth through inheritance. Περὶ σχημ. 96, on the other hand, has the death of the father, loss of paternal wealth, and mishaps for the brothers (interpreting ἑτέρως as 'adversely'). M^b produces an odd effect by combining loss of inheritance on the one hand with testamentary gain on the other. Does this once again imply inept secondary recombination?

---

[270] All three (death of fathers, loss of paternal wealth, death of elder brothers) in Περὶ σχημ. 95; loss of paternal wealth and death of older brothers in 2.175–6, Περὶ σχημ. 26, Π.τ.δ. 12; injury to the father and the loss of his estate in Περὶ σχημ. 24.

402 Παμφαίνων: i. 911 n. 23.

πολιοῖο: the readings at first sight are the 'wrong' way round, with $Π^1$'s πλαγκτοῖο more characteristic of M^b (7n.) than πολιοῖο (which is generic: i. 911 n. 14). But in fact M^b only ever uses πλαγκτ- and its compounds of cosmic motion, never of the planets. Monaco, 55, observes that Saturn is at issue in 380, but even there the motion is cosmic, and so M^b retains its integrity. I have no particular explanation for how the papyrus' form arose, but would regard the two recensions as co-valent (p. 394).

403 Ἡελίου σελάεσσιν: the Sun's singular σέλας is normal (see on 4.508), while M^a uses σέλα (not an epic plural) for the luminaries (6.82, 127, 252, 549); now the plural means rays (transmitted at 4.318 for Saturn, too, but see ad loc.), as in Paul Sil. *Descr.* 690 (of reflective metal), 743.

ἀν' οὐρανὸν: see p. 200 and 5.29 n.

405 εἰς Ἀίδην is often at the end of a pentameter, as indeed it is in 1.336, the counterpart of 4.411. Alternatively it ends (or begins) the first half of the pentameter. Are there implications for a version which has not been preserved in M^c itself?

νεκυοστόλος: see on 6.530.

406 ἐξολέσει: M^b offers a future tense where $Π^1$ (ἀπόλλυσιν) and M^c (ἐκβάλλει) both have presents (see p. 275). All seem to be diverging in their preferred direction; it is hard to see how one would reconstruct an 'original' here. This instance showcases the difference between my approach, which sees purposeful variation by individual poets, and that of Monaco, 56, who proceeds according to the model of textual corruption, and regards ἐξολέσει as the *lectio difficilior* which the papyrus degrades. He is entirely correct, however, that M^b's choice of verb is more interesting. It is a *hapax* in *Od.* 17.597 τοὺς Ζεὺς ἐξολέσειε, and the association with Zeus persists in Archilochus, fr. 327.8 W. ὄλοιτο τοίνυν κἀξόλοιτο, Ζεῦ, and Theogn. 850 Ζεὺς ἀνδρ' ἐξολέσειεν Ὀλύμπιος. The poet avails himself of M^a's signature-technique, the repurposing of Zeus-vocabulary (i. 62), and does so again in 413 (see ad loc.).

πολὺν ὄλβον: see Monaco, 56. M^b's epithet is banal enough (the cadence again in 2.227; antecedents in Hes. *Th.* 974 πολὺν δέ οἱ ὤπασεν ὄλβον; *HHom.* 30.12 ὄλβος δὲ πολύς; Solon, fr. 6.3 W. πολὺς ὄλβος; Ibycus, S 166.11 πολὺν ὄλβον ἐδώκ[αν, etc.). 1.331 μέγαν ὄλβον is equally unremarkable (see ad loc.). Slightly more interestingly the papyrus has βαθύν, using the same metaphor as in this poet's favourite βαθυχρήμων (66 n.), though it does not, I think, undermine my view that $Π^1$ should not have readings more characteristic of M^b than M^b himself.

407–8 The absence of these two lines in the papyrus all but establishes that it is an abbreviated version (rather than that M^b is extended), since these two motifs are also present, in the same order, in Epit. IV.

Γενεαί and τέχναι 669

The normal way of saying 'elder brothers' in astrology is with some case of πρεσβύτεροι ἀδελφοί, or ἀδελφοὺς προτέρους (3.10; Epit. IV, above; Θ p. 147.3-4; Dorotheus, p. 334.6). But see too Περὶ σχημ. 95 τοὺς πρὸ αὐτῶν ἀδελφούς, from Saturn's conjunction with Mars, which is just ahead of the apotelesma quoted in the opening discussion; it may be that a source used similar phraseology.

408 This reads like a poeticisation of a phrase about legacies, which are Saturn's specialism, e.g. Valens, I 19.2 ὠφελείας ἐκ νεκρικῶν, I 20.12 ἀπό τε νεκρικῶν εὐεργεσίας, App. X 3 προβιβασμοὺς ἀπὸ νεκρικῶν ὑποθέσεων; Hephaestion, i. 202.16-17 ἀπὸ ... κληρονομιῶν ποιεῖ κέρδος.

409-11 The parallel transmission in 1.334-6 contains a pentameter, which raises the question whether either or both passages have been hexametrised, this one wholly, the other partly, from an elegiac original. The situation is typically and frustratingly unclear. On the one hand, it is clear that M^b has the better and fuller version of the protasis, which requires the presence of Saturn to make sense of ἰσόμοιρος. On the other, as a hexameter ending ἐς Ἀΐδην in 411[271] is considerably less satisfactory than εἰς Ἀΐδην as a pentameter ending in the corresponding 1.336 (see n. ad loc.), and πατρός is readily seen as a line-lengthener.

410 ἐπὶ σήματι: see on 4.109.

412 ἠὲ μογοστοκίῃ δεδαϊγμένη: a domestication of the Homeric, where the usual combination is δεδαϊγμένος ὀξέϊ χαλκῷ. Childbirth, as so often observed, is the woman's equivalent of war, and indeed, when a similar phrase occurs later in the book the subjects are males who die by violence (4.488 φοβεροῖς ξίφεσιν δεδαϊγμένοι). The substitution nicely makes that point, but presses the equivalence further in that both sexes are now equally the casualties of Mars (Il. 22.72 ἄρηϊ κταμένῳ δεδαϊγμένῳ ὀξέϊ χαλκῷ). $Π^1$ has δεδαμασμένη, a verb M^b himself uses at 4.539 λυσσαλέῃ μανίῃ δεδαμασμένον, though the present passage is supported by a very close parallel at 4.488, and so the variants do uphold the principle of internal consistency within poets.

μογοστοκίη refers, not just to birth-pangs, but to difficult ones. See LSJ μογοστόκος, 2 and 3, and add Suda, μ 1182 μογοστόκος· περὶ τοὺς τόκους κακοπαθοῦσα; Christus Patiens, 13, and George of Pisidia, De Vit. Human. 58 μογοστόκον...λύπην (both of Genesis' curse). Epit. IV has δυστοκία (see on 1.46), difficult or painful birth,[272] a standard astrological topic (Dorotheus, p. 324.6-325.17; Valens, I 22.1 ἐκτρώματα...καὶ δυστοκίαι καὶ νεκρώσεις). It is

---

[271] Cleinias ap. Stob. 4.20b.52; Theodorus Prodromus (11th/12th c.!), Carm. hist. 38.116.
[272] Add to LSJ Antipater, AP 9.149.4 = Garland 444; very common in the medical writers (Soranus, Aetius, Paul, al.).

670   Commentary on Book Four

combined, as here, with abortion/surgical removal of the foetus (Θ p. 157.14 δυστοκίαι ἢ ἐμβρυοτομίαι; Apomasar, De Myst., CCAG xi/1. 174.20 δυστοκίας καὶ ἐκτρωσμούς; 2.288-9 n.). While various factors bring it about, the same agencies as here are involved in Dorotheus, p. 324.21-4, where δυστοκία results when the Moon is surrounded by malefics. See further on 1.250-5.

413 $Π^1$ represents a form of the same recension of the text as M^c; M^b is quite different. In the papyrus, the women are afflicted with a 'bloody disease' (νούσου αἱμηρῆς); in M^c, the women themselves are bloody, or bloodied (1.338 αἱμηρῆισι γυν.); M^b refers to abortions (ἀμβλώσσους, readily corrected to some form of the noun ἀμβλωσμός).

Either version is viable. Abortion and haemorrhage/flux are independent motifs; both are mentioned in Valens, IV 22.7, where Mars is transmitting to the waxing Moon in a day birth, and the outcomes for female natives include κινδύνους σωματικούς, αἱμαγμούς τε καὶ φθορὰς ἢ ἐμβρυοτομίας. It is not a question of one version of the text being 'corrupted' into another (Monaco, 44 'niente di più facile che in questo luogo l'aggettivo raro sia stato poi sostituito dalla lezione in seguito corrottasi nell'ἀμβλώσσους trasmesso da M'), nor of taking ἀμβλώσσους as originating in a gloss to explain the 'bloody disease' (Monaco, 57). Bloody outcomes are discussed on 1.337-8. ἀμβλωσμός also has good credentials. While the noun has only one other pre-Byzantine occurrence, in Aretaeus, De Caus. et Sign. Diut. Morb. 2.11.9 (among causes of a prolapsed uterus), the verb ἀμβλόω or ἀμβλώω occurs five times in Maximus, together with 275 ἀμβλώσιμον ἦμαρ. Zito on 172 says that it is used strictly of deliberate abortion, but that sources cannot be relied on to maintain the distinction between it and miscarriage (ἐκτιτρώσκειν, ὠμοτοκεῖν). If it is objected that νούσου | ἀμβλωσμοῦ θ' (Koechly's light correction of the accusative plural) is less satisfactory (because of the indeterminate nature of the diseases) than 'bloody diseases', I would suggest it is a hendiadys for 'sickening abortion/miscarriage' (Maximus, 273 ἀμβλώσεις χαλεπάς τε δυσηλεγέας).

φύσις κρύφιμ' ἄλγε' ἔδωκεν: the author of these lines has performed a similar manoeuvre to M^a (i. 62) in adapting ἄλγε' ἔδωκεν at line-end, whose subject in EGHP is usually Zeus (Il. 2.375, 18.431, 24.241, Od. 4.722, but not Il. 1.2). It is κύπρις here, at least according to L. In the corresponding 1.338, and in $Π^1$, the subject is φύσις, a reading which satisfyingly implies both the natural world (and ultimately the whole cosmos as controlled by the stars) and women's biological nature, and which also happens to be more in keeping with M^b's own habitual references to φύσις (9, 465, 513, 591) and use of the verb φύειν/φύεσθαι. κύπρις, on the other hand, is unhappy (Koechly 1851, xlvi; Monaco, 57), on the grounds that (a) the planet Venus is not involved, and (b) as both theonym and metonym its normal context is sexual misdemeanour, not biological misfortune.

It seems that in this case we are dealing with genuine corruption, and Π^1's version on this occasion can be preferred.

I should have noted on 3.294 that κρύφιμος is almost a technical term of astrology: almost two-thirds of its occurrences (16/25) are astrological, with another five in magical papyri. κρυπτός and κρύφιος are far commoner in prose, and the latter is substituted for this more recondite form when the present line reappears in 1.338; but in general the Manethoniana prefer κρύφιμος (Monaco, 43). Of its astrological occurrences, a significant number refer to hidden parts of the body/disease therein (1.159, 252, 5.107; Paul, p. 59.14–15; Θ p. 185.6), what prose texts more often call κρυπτὰ πάθη (see pp. 16–17, and for secret books, on 5.304). If there is any sense in which Epit. IV represents an underlay, M^b/M^c have particularised 'hidden diseases' with a specific instance (either miscarriage or flux). If, on the other hand, it represents a paraphrase, it has stripped out the specific instance.

4.414–49 More τέχναι

414–19

Jupiter aspects Mercury and Venus. This chart involves a strange mixture of incest and τέχναι; was it in fact designed as a transition? The agencies seem peculiar for the former outcome, but Valens, II 38.73 has marriage with siblings or relatives (ἀδελφαῖς ἢ συγγενέσι) with Jupiter in the Evil Demon and Venus in that of Marriage-Bringer. In II 38.16–20 he also has a series of unions with relatives (συγγενικοὺς...γάμους), including siblings (ἀδελφαῖς ἢ ἀδελφοῖς), where the same two planets are involved. The Moon generally accompanies Venus, and one of the planets in additional aspect is Mars, but Mercury is mentioned in II 38.19 Ἀφροδίτη ἐν ἰδίῳ οἴκῳ ἢ ὑψώματι, Διὸς [καὶ Ἀφροδίτης] ὁρίοις, σὺν Ἑρμῇ καὶ Σελήνῃ συγγενικῷ γάμῳ ζευγνύουσιν ἀπὸ μητρός. Valens of course has nothing about pedagogues, and one wonders whether the combination, which is surprising, is the poet's own (or at least is secondary). Teachers are a much more normal and expected outcome of Jupiter with Mercury (2.255 = 3.193; 6.351–2, 478).

415 λαμπραυγέσι: see on 4.201.

416–17 This embellishes the conventional pair ἀδελφοὶ and συγγενεῖς. The same pairing of 'sibling' and 'kindred' (συγγενικός) marriage in Epit. II ('Antiochus', CCAG i. 161.27–8) συγγενικὸν τὸν γάμον δίδωσιν ἢ καὶ ἐξ ἀδελφῶν (the Moon is involved, but another planetary agency is lost); Valens, II 38.20 (Venus and Moon in IMC or opposing each other), 73 (see above); Ptol. 4.5.10 (Venus and Mars in Capricorn or Pisces).

417 λοχεύονται: for the passive see on 4.87. The preposition is presumably transferred from γίγνεσθαι used in this sense (LSJ I.1).

418 For the phrase 'leaders of youth', see on 2.255.

418–19 ἔν τε καθέδραις | γραμματικαῖς: see on 6.393–4 for the chair of the teacher, though ἔν τε καθέδραις has already been used for shoemakers in 4.320.

419 δήμοιο βίον διαποιμαίνοντες: the governance metaphor goes back to the idea of a shepherd of the people, but for its application to someone who is an educator of the youth or philosopher compare in particular an oracle ap. Eunap. *Vit. Soph.* 6.4.4. ἀνδρῶν ποιμαίνοντι νέων θεοείκελον ὁρμήν. Libanius, too, refers to his activity as teacher and leader of a school with the verb ποιμαίνειν, as he also calls his charges his ποίμνιον and ἀγέλη (*Epist.* 904.1 ῥίψας τὰ βιβλία δακρύω τὸν ὑπ' ἐμοὶ ποιμαίνοντα τοὺς νέους οὐκ ἔχων; *Or.* 55.8 ἓν ποιμαίνειν ποίμνιον, 58.19; P. Petit, *Les Étudiants de Libanius* (Paris, 1957), 21). Himerius develops the conceit in *Or.* 23.9, 24 ll. 6–7, 39.8, 54.2 (the herdsman, tendance of the flock, combined with the metaphor of τρέφειν, for which see Petit, op. cit., 31–2). The extension of their role here to the whole people, not just the youth, suggests (*a*) the embeddedness of polite letters in ancient society at large and (*b*) its extension beyond polite letters to moral suasion. (A modern example, from Jerusalem, recorded in 1988: 'the teacher is like "a shepherd, responsible for leading, caring for and watching over the flock altogether, but who moves at the pace of the slowest sheep"' (D. E. Inbar, 'The Free Educational Prison: Metaphors and Images', in *Educational Research*, 38.1 (1996), 77–92, at 86).

420–4

Sun aspects Venus in conjunction with(?) Mars.

Protasis. This and the sister-chart in 6.431–5 deviate from Θ p. 216.23–5 Περὶ ῥαπτῶν by (i) dropping any reference to terms or quartile and (ii) introducing the Sun. On the other hand, M^b hews closer to Θ by retaining the idea of Mars and Venus as a pair (to which the Sun is an addition); it is plausible that by κοινῶς in 420 he means conjunction, corresponding to Θ's ὁμοῦ (compare κοιν- in 4.219, 226).

Apodosis. All agree that Venus and Mars produce clothes-makers. Θ and M^a, but not M^b, also have clothes-menders (pp. 1065–6, additional note on 6.434–5), while M^b has stitchers (according to my restoration) and dealers (so interpreting πρηκτῆρας). In the Π- chart for Venus and Mars in Ptol. 4.4.8 Venus and Mars alone produce (*inter alia*) a cloth-related outcome (βαφέας), but not stitchers or manufacturers. But the dealers correspond to Ptol. 4.4.4 ἱματιοπώλας (Venus alone as Ruler of πρᾶξις). For the various workers in the textile industry, from spinning and weaving to finishing and retail, see A. H. M. Jones.

420-1 The couplet is constructed on the same foundations as 4.271–2. ἀκτινηβολίῃσι (p. 248) serves as an equivalent to 272 ἀκτῖσι βολαυγῶν, while καταθρῇ answers to ἀθρῇ alone. The compound is not unique, though it is in astrology. If it were taken literally (as it is by LSJ, 'look down on from above'), it could be pressed to yield the specific meaning 'regard from right quartile' (i.e. in superior position), though that is neither confirmed nor disproved by Ptolemy or Θ, which do not mention the Sun at all; perhaps it is the equivalent of κατιδεῖν (see on 4.362).

For the Sun's epithet, which is an EGHP make-over, see i. 908 n. 9. πυρίβλητος, on the other hand, is Hellenistic, first in Nic. *Ther.* 774 πυρίβλητοι (passive), but for the active meaning see Gow–Page on Meleager, *AP* 12.76.2 = *HE* 4477, Vian on Nonn. *D.* 30.238, Kost on Musaeus, 88 πυριβλήτοισι...ὀιστοῖς, and John of Gaz. *Descr.* 365 πυριβλήτοισι προσώποις.

422 γνάπτορας: for fulling, see on 6.433–4. This form renovates the old and over-familiar γναφεῖς (Appendix II, II.7.viii.f.).

εὐσήμων πέπλων: although attempts have been made to emend the epithet, it can be supported by *BGU* vii. 1564.10–11 (Philadelphia, AD 138), a set of orders for army supplies, where it is specified that certain apparel should be produced ἔκ τε καλῆς καὶ μαλακῆς καὶ λευκοτάτης ἐρέας χωρὶς παντὸς ῥύπου εὐυφῆ εὐπαγῆ εὔσημα ἀρεστὰ ἀσινῆ. LSJ render 'with fine edging'.

422-3 τεύκτορας...ἱστοπόνους: masking ὑφάντας, or, more likely in the imperial period, γερδίους (Appendix II, II.7.viii.c). The agent noun is otherwise only in 2.333, its epithet in Philip, *AP* 6.247.2 = *Garland* 2782 (of Athena; not as rare as G.-P.'s note claims), 9.778.4 = *Garland* 2669 (of the shuttle), Lyr. Adesp. *PMG* 975(a) ἱστοπόνοι μείρακες; also a great favourite in Nonnus (12×, including a title). For πόνος, see on 4.72. This is a good illustration of astrology's total inscrutability regarding the status and sex of workers (pp. 42–4, 120). A. H. M. Jones wrote his celebrated article on the textile industry on the assumption that the weavers were male (as they are in many sources, including the famously rowdy linen-workers of Tarsus[273]), but there is evidence for female weavers too, especially from papyri, who might be subsumed here among their actually and grammatically male counterparts.[274]

αὐδᾷ...ἔσσεσθαι: for the verb, introduced by Massimilla's conjecture, see on 4.521–2.

---

[273] Dio Chrys. *Or.* 34.21–3.
[274] Ruffing 2008, 470; Diocletian's Price Edict, 20.12 (cf. Groen-Vallinga and Tacoma, 113). For the Latin evidence, see L. L. Lovén, 'Women, Trade, and Production in Urban Centres of Roman Italy', in Wilson and Flohr, 200–19, at 208 (two male *textores* and one *textrix* on the Monumentum Statiliorum).

423 ῥαπτῆρας: my conjecture for L's ἡγητῆρας. Koechly had proposed σμητῆρας, which would have referred to a particular stage of the fulling process (mentioned in the previous line), either the finishing of a newly made-up garment,[275] or to the cleansing of a used, soiled one. This is defensible, although rather than reintroducing the idea of fulling (whole and part) it seems preferable that there should be references to the same three forms of clothiers' work as in the corresponding passage in book 6 (weaving, cleaning, and repairing). This would correspond to 6.434–5, and the two passages would relate to Θ's ῥάπτας in a characteristic way, the one poet with a wordy periphrasis, the other with a spruced-up agent noun (p. 220). And with a down-stroke that descends below the line, ῥαπτῆρας is not palaeographically inferior to Koechly's suggestion.

424 These itinerant vendors are either merchants in their own right or agents of merchants (Latin *circitores*) who hawk their goods. For the export of textiles, and merchants who settle overseas to organise the business, see A. H. M. Jones, 192; Dumitrache, 40–1. For long-distance trade in textiles between Rome and the east, see K. Droß–Krüpe, 'Textiles and their Merchants in Rome's Eastern Trade', in M. Gleba and J. Pásztókai-Szeőke (eds.), *Making Textiles in Pre-Roman and Roman Times: People, Places, Identities* (Oxford, 2013), 149–60, esp. 156–7, including a 2nd-c. letter in which an Egypt-based wool-merchant enquires about his presumable partner's business trip to Rome (P. Fouad. 1/77).

ἀγεληδὸν ἀλωομένους: the phrase insists on the collective nature of the enterprise; recall the activity of the ναύκληρος in 4.136–7 ἐργασίην τε | κοινωνὸν πολλῶν. The adverb, for which see Livrea on Ap. Rhod. 4.934, is a Homeric *hapax*, and *Il.* 16.160 sets a trend, to which M[b] adheres, for it to be followed more or less immediately (or in Nonnus' case preceded) by a verb of motion (examples given by Livrea); for the participle see on 3.121–2, which concerns wanderers, not specifically merchants.

διὰ παντός: 'for ever' (LSJ πᾶς, IV). Once this has invaded the poet's ear he cannot get rid of it: at line-end also in 4.434, 607, in penultimate place in 558, and restored by Koechly in 565.

---

[275] 'Rubbing' would describe how a paste was rubbed onto the soaked fabric, not only to cleanse it, but also to compact its fibres and give it strength (Soriga, 27). The substance would have been not soap—not used on garments in the ancient world—but one of the various types of fuller's earth, which would have been formed into a paste before being rubbed into the soaked textiles (Pliny, *NH* 35.196–8; see Croisille ad loc.). A scene from *fullonica* VI 8, 20–21.2 in Pompeii shows fullers at work, one of them treading the chemicals through a garment, three others holding garments in their hands in such a way as to suggest they are 'scrubbing the clothes or wringing them out' (cf. Flohr 2011, 90 fig. 51; ead. 2013, 22 fig. 2, 100; Soriga, 28 and 29 fig. 1).

425–30

Mercury approaches Jupiter and Saturn.

Protasis. This and 6.436–8 are essentially the same version of a τ- chart concerning types of diviner in Θ pp. 214.22–215.2. They differ from it in a number of details: (i) Mercury is not said to be in Saturn's house, nor to be *exaugos*; (ii) Mercury is now doing the aspecting, instead of receiving the aspect; (iii) there is no reference to Mars. Θ's τ- chart in turn is a version of Ptolemy's Π- chart for Mercury (alone) as Ruler of πρᾶξις (4.4.3). Ptolemy also has a version of the Π- chart modified by the presence of the Moon in various signs (4.4.10).

Apodosis. In the apodosis M^a and M^b both have connections to Θ (ἱερῆας; M^a μαντ-) and each to each other (ζακόρους, σηκῶν).

425–6 The verb in the Manethoniana is unique to M^b (4×, two with overlaps in M^c), and only here is it constructed with an accusative, which in general is very rare (to the point that De Stefani doubts it). LSJ A.I.4 give only one certain example, Eur. *Andr.* 1167, on which see Stevens's note. If it is sound, one explanation is that no effect is intended (as in the 'who whom' construction, the important factors are the agents and the verb linking them is a stopgap). More plausible, however, is that the poet intends us to be struck; in that case it should be seen as a bold extension of the Homeric usage with ἱκάνω, ἔρχομαι, νέομαι and others (Chantraine, ii. 45–6; K.-G. i. 311–12). Tragedy cultivates this (Stevens on *Andr.* 3), a similar case being ps.-Eur. *Rhes.* 13–14 τίνες...τὰς ἡμετέρας | κοίτας πλάθουσ' (see Feickert and Liapis ad loc. against attempts to emend).

426 λαμπτῆρσι: rays, as in Eur. *Rhes.* 59–60 φαεννοὶ...ἡλίου | λαμπτῆρες. The old IE conception of the Sun as a lamp (West 2007, 195, and passages assembled by Liapis on the *Rhesus* passage) is modified by the new plural λαμπτῆρες, meaning the rays streaming from it. See Feickert ad loc.; he compares Nonn. *D.* 2.189–90 νύχιοι λαμπτῆρες ἀκοιμήτοιο Σελήνης | ὡς δαΐδες σελάγιζον, which performs a balancing act: the plural suggests beams, but the torches point to the light source. See further on 4.214.

427 νηοπόλους: the poet has appropriated this rare epithet for a temple-warder from Hes. *Th.* 991, demythologising it in the process (as does *IG* V,1 960.8 (Boiai), an extravagant tribute to a dead maiden); Nonn. *D.* 3.262 uses it of Inachus keeper of Hera's temple in Argos. The Christian epigram *AP* 1.16.2 applies it to the restorer of a church. Only here is it attributive.

ζακόρους θεοσέπτους: the epithet occurs in classical Greek otherwise only in Ar. *Nub.* 292, as epithet of awe-inspiring thunder, and in a Didymaean oracle quoted twice by Julian, meaning 'holy'; here, as LSJ observe, it is equivalent to θεοσεβεῖς.

428 γραμματέας: the only secular item in the inventory, unless it refers to temple scribes (Appendix II, V.5.xiii). A 2nd-c. BC inscription detailing the procedure at the Oracle of Apollo Koropaios in Magnesia (*IG* IX/2. 1109) mentions a functionary (ll. 32–3 and 46 γραμματεὺς τοῦ θεοῦ) who would sit well in this context, where prophets follow. This man keeps a register of those wanting to consult the oracle, and it is he who presides over the submission of their written enquiries on a sealed tablet and subsequent return with appended responses.

430 + 429 The correctness of replacing 430 after 428 (as L¹'s insert mark indicates) is suggested by the sequence αὐτεῖ | ἔσσεσθαι (which Axtius and Rigler's placement ruptured), even if μυστιπόλους (4.229 n.) now connects with the temple-wardens (216 n.) rather than prophets.

429 ἱερῶν τε προϊσταμένους: a metrical version of ἱερῶν προεστῶτας, very common in astrology (4.63 n.), usually with the involvement of Jupiter; both Saturn and Jupiter in *Περὶ σχημ*. 1. στεφανηδόν is rather remarkable, for at first sight it seems to envisage the persons it describes encircling the temple in a ring (an alarming thought for administrators), evoking images of Near Eastern temples with their large retinues of staff. Yet I wonder whether it is in fact a deformation of στεφανηφόρους, who are associated with ἱερῶν προεστῶτας on a number of occasions (*Περὶ κέντρ*. 52; Valens, I 20.19, 26). In any case, the word has a remarkable profile (31× Nonn. *D*., a further four times in *Par*., then twice in Paul Sil. *Descr. Sanct*. and once in John of Gaza, *Descr*. 298), so this is the earliest attestation, and a notable connection with Nonnus. With the repositioning of line 430, it concludes the paragraph, presumably drawing attention to itself by its rarity and extravagant conceit.

431–6

Saturn aspects Venus and Mars.

Apodosis. I have juxtaposed 4.431–6 with 6.487–90 because both have γειοπόνοι in the outcome and the motif of 'their own and others'. But 6.487–90 is in turn related to a series of other charts (see on 4.139–45), all of which involve quite different conditions (Mercury and Saturn). There are no links with the *Π*- account of Saturn aspecting Mars and Venus (Ptol. 4.4.8/Θ p. 212.29–32) save that they, too, are somewhat 'anti-structural'.

431 ἐν ἀκτίνεσσι βολαυγῇ: the only other occurrence of the verb is 4.272 ἀκτῖσι βολαυγῶν; contrast 4.214 πυρσοβολοῦσα, where the verbal element comes second.

432 βραδὺς Κρόνος: see on 4.318.
οἱ τότε φύντες: see on 6.697.

Γενεαί and *τέχναι*   677

433 γειοπόνοι: see on 6.489 (also Saturnian; presumably because of the water element); Appendix II, I.1.i.

φυτοσπορίας: the poet literalises a compound which normally refers to human conception. The abstract noun is new, but the epithet is already in Soph. *Trach*. 359, then Lyc. *Al*. 1304. Other literalisers are Xenocrates ap. Stob. 1.1.29b φυτοσπόρον Δήμητρα; Pamprepius (XXXV Heitsch), fr. 3.104, 145; while Nonn. *D*. 21.256 plays with the literal and metaphorical meanings.

433–4 ἀγαπῶντες | ὀθνείης…οἰκείης: deliberate variation of 6.489 ξείνοισι γεγηθότας, οὐκ ἰδίοισιν? See ad loc. for owners who were simultaneously lessees. Such men were not necessarily the have-nots taking on the surplus of those who had too much land to work themselves; that is illustrated by the case of Isidorus of Karanis (P.Cair. Isid. 74; R. S. Bagnall, *Egypt in Late Antiquity* (Princeton, 1993), 119–20), who, so far from taking on additional land because he needed to, appears to have leased it from its impoverished owners to whom he allowed the capital to work it themselves, but kept the crop. Landowners could also take on short-term leases for particular purposes (M. Langellotti, *Village Life in Roman Egypt: Tebtunis in the First Century* AD (Oxford, 2020), 185). διὰ παντός in context seems rather vacuous, but at a push could mean 'throughout the totality of their holding' (consisting of both their own land and that which they held on lease).

436 ἐκ μετεωροσύνης: the Latin rendering in Koechly 1851 has 'ex conniventia', whence Lopilato's 'through connivance', which is hard to extract from the basic root. Closer to the mark are LSJ, who gloss it as equivalent to μετεωρία, 'forgetfulness', which, though itself rare,[276] is supported by astrological references (especially in Valens and Hephaestion) to μετέωροι as distracted and unsettled persons, and μετεωρισμοί as states of distraction or instability.[277] The point seems to be that their encounters are casual, opportunistic (like those of the merchants in 4.137–8), rather than that they *did* have legitimate wives, but just did not see them on a regular basis. ὁμεύνοις, 'bed-mates', pointedly does not commit to the position that these were married spouses. In that case, the suggested homology between farming, but not one's own land, and having sexual relations, but not within stable marriage, is a fascinating one, bedded down in the same metaphor that betrothed a woman to a man for the ploughing of legitimate children (Menand. *Periceir*. 1013–14 ταύτην γνησίων παίδων

---

[276] Attested in a couple of passages which refer to the absent-mindedness of an emperor or his friend (Suet. *Claud*. 39.1, and in transliteration in Fronto, *Ad M. Caesarem* 4.7.1).

[277] The noun goes together with ταραχαί (Valens, IV 16.9), ἀκαταστασίας (IV 23.5), ἀνωμαλίας, ἀστασίας (Additamenta Antiqua, IV 28). Often in proximity to mental problems (Critodemus, CCAG v/2. 112.9; Valens, IV 25.4, VII 6.171, CCAG viii/1. 168.22, 28–9, 169.27–8; Hephaestion, i. 20.28–21.1, 23.12, 207.26).

ἐπ' ἀρότωι σοι δίδωμι ~ *Dysc.* 842). See L. A. Swift, 'The Symbolism of Space in Euripidean Choral Fantasy (*Hipp.* 732-75, *Med.* 824-65, *Bacch.* 370-433)', *CQ*² 59 (2009), 364-82, at 368 and n. 17, not only on the agricultural metaphor, but on the implied identification between women and types of physical space, of which this is an unusual but logical example.

437-43 + 444-9

Mars aspects Venus and Moon; and with Mercury in unfavourable aspect. These are the final two charts of Θ's τέχναι series.

Protasis. There are two charts in M^b, the first resulting in various kinds of craftsman (mechanics, instrument-makers, carpenters, makers of automata), the second, with the addition of Mercury, mimes. While the poet continues to adhere to the τέχναι series, the corresponding charts in Θ are independent: the second (p. 217.5-7) is not an add-on to the first (p. 217.1-4). (Mercury is already present in the first, and Mercury and Venus are the *only* agencies mentioned in the second.)

6.398-404 is different. This chart is proof of concept for its special affinity with *Lib. Herm.* What they offer is essentially the same realised version of Mercury and Venus as Rulers of πρᾶξις (though *Lib. Herm.* xxvi. 62 has lost the reference to Venus herself), and what they have in common is the conjunction of Mercury and the Moon in a *kentron* and the additional aspect of Jupiter. They lack Mars, present not only in M^b and Θ, but also in another carpenter-chart in 4.319.

Apodosis. 1. In the first chart, M^b and Θ p. 217.4 agree on μηχανικούς. But the rest of the items find their best parallels in Π- charts (or elsewhere in Ptolemy). (i) Instrument-makers correspond to Ptolemy's account of Mercury and Venus either as Rulers of πρᾶξις (4.4.6 ὀργανοποιούς) or as exerting an effect on types of soul (3.14.5 ὀργανικάς). (ii) Carpenters are products of Mars alone (Θ p. 211.11; Ptol. 4.4.5 and Θ p. 211.28); Martian outcomes also include the sort of effortful labour indicated in 442-3. (iii) Makers of marvels (automata), who are also present in M^a, seem to correspond with the θαυματοποιούς who figure next to instrument-makers and μηχανικούς in Ptol. 3.14.5.

2. In the second chart, mimes are shared with (i) Θ p. 217.5-7 (a realised version of Mercury and Venus as Rulers of πρᾶξις) and (ii) Ptol. 3.14.29, on Mars and Venus as governors of the soul. This is M^b's second mime chart (after 4.280-5), and although, as we have seen, its set-up is not identical to that in Θ, it is nevertheless closer to it than the earlier one was. Despite their different inputs, the two passages have considerable overlap: 4.280 ~ 446, the wandering motif in 4.281-2 ~ 449, the motif of 'folly' in 4.283 ~ 446. Both are in turn

connected to Valens, I 1.39: the present passage supplies the Mercurial connection that former one was lacking. See on 448, 449.

In short, M^a (and *Lib. Herm.*) remain true to the agencies in Θ, but the further aspect of Jupiter explains the favour of kings and big men. So far so good. In contrast, M^b has changed and changed about, and shows marked illogicality. His chart gives a strong impression of being secondary to M^a's, with which it shares items that involve graciousness and delicacy (the instruments, which the context in Ptolemy suggests are musical; the automata) for which Mercury's presence is necessary—and yet denies his presence until 444–9. It gives the impression of using M^a (and being drawn especially to his poetic niceties) yet cobbling him together with other material in a rather higgledy-piggledy way.

437 Κύπριν δ' ἀφρογένειαν: see i. 906 n. 1.

ἑλιξοπόρον τε Σελήνην: see i. 905 n. 24, and on 4.91 for ἑλιξ- or ἑλικ- compounds used of the Moon.

438 πυρσοβόλοις: see on 4.214.

τευχεσφόρος Ἄρης: see i. 909 n. 12.

439 ὀργανοπήκτορας: perhaps simply 'makers of instruments' (ὀργανικούς), perhaps specifically musical instruments; in addition to the passages in the apparatus, there are specialists in the latter in Antiochus, *CCAG* vii. 110.11 μαθήσεις παντοίας, ἐξόχως μουσικῶν μελῶν καὶ ὀργάνων (Moon in quartile with Venus).

440 τεκτοσύνης τ' ἄρχοντας: looks at first sight as if it might be paraphrasing ἀρχιτέκτονας (Appendix II, II.5.vi.a), but Ptolemy and Θ have just τέκτονας, and this is a phrase the poet has used before: see on 4.323.

440-1 On automata, see on 6.402. θαύματα δαιδάλλοντας looks very much like a reprise of 6.401 ὄργανα δαιδάλλοντας; the verb δαιδάλλειν, for which see on 4.321, is especially appropriate in connection with fine craftsmanship, such as here. These craftsmen are a nice illustration of Vernant's point that the maker of automata is a Hellenistic translation of the archaic idea of the craftsman as wonder-worker, producing marvels of spectacular effect but limited application (works of technology, such as metalwork and weaving are formulaically pronounced θαῦμα ἰδέσθαι in EGHP; the best-known example is the Shield, *Il.* 18.549 τὸ δὴ περὶ θαῦμα τέτυκτο; cf. J.-P. Vernant, 'Some Remarks on the Forms and Limitations of Technological Thought among the Greeks', in Vernant, 299–318, at 311–12).

441 ἐν ἀλκήεντί τε θυμῷ: see on 4.48–9 for the epithet. It is at this point that the composite structure which has welded ingenious Mercurial items together with sturdier Martian ones (p. 254) shows a certain strain.

442 ἐργοπόνους παλάμαισι: perhaps a paraphrase of χειροτέχνας, whereby the Homeric dative, by conferring a little cachet, makes a positive virtue out of manual labour in place of the theoretical limitations with which Aristotle had taxed these workers (*Met.* 981ª30–981ᵇ2; 981ᵇ31–932ª1). παλάμη is apposite for craftsmanly material, ever since *Il.* 15.411 τέκτονος ἐν παλάμῃσι, *Il.* 18.600 (a potter), *Od.* 5.234 (Odysseus wielding an axe for shipbuilding), Hes. *Th.* 580 ἀσκήσας παλάμῃσι (Hephaestus crafting a wreath), ps.-Hes. *Scut.* 219, 320 (Hephaestus manufacturing the shield of Heracles). For ἐργοπόνους see on 4.149–50.

ἀδροτάτους: West on Hes. *Op.* 473, where ἀδροσύνη is the sturdy quality that makes for agricultural success, remarks that words from this root are hardly found in verse except Comedy. It is lacking from astrological prose too. Perhaps the Hesiod passage on its own was enough to license it in hexameters in the eyes of Mᵇ.

443 ἀχθοφόρους: see on 4.251 (there, Saturnian). Here it is a trade name, in 6.384 an epithet of beasts of burden (as in Hdt. 7.187.1), which makes its combination with ἀρίστους, the 'best in show' motif (p. 202), truly remarkable.

καμάτων τε πόνους εἰς τέρψιν ἄγοντας: the most remarkable expression of this poet's 'redemptive' (as opposed to degrading) view of work; see p. 174, and for πόνους see on 4.72. The haulier's work is most certainly not usually viewed in this way. See on 6.383, 384, and the supplements, and for other astrological passages see Appendix II, II.2.

444 φαύλοις ἐν σχήμασιν: for the jargon see on 2.465.

445–7 The professional term, μῖμος, gets swamped under the verbiage, but the typical vocabulary (αἰσχ-, χλεύη, ὕβρι-, γέλωτ-) makes them easy to identify. There is enormous emphasis on speech (λογ- three times, μυθ- twice, -ρημ- once), one of the most obvious differences from the earlier mime chart (which had more to say about appearance). Perhaps that is because this chart involves Mercury, and the earlier one did not. The speech theme (4.280 n.) features in the mimes' own self-presentation, only in their mouths it can sound rather different (Webb 2008, 144–5, 255 n. 9). In the epitaph for Bassilla from Aquileia, her fellow-mime Heraclides describes himself as τὸ λαλεῖν σοφός (9–10), and her as the tenth Muse (9), who has won δόξαν φωνάεσσαν (3); he has now laid her μουσικὸν...σῶμ' (15–16) to rest in the earth, while her fellow-artists also bid her (λέγουσι) farewell.[278]

445 μυθολόγους: 'fabulatores' (Koechly 1851); 'prating' (LSJ and Lopilato).

---

[278] *IG* XIV 2342 (first half of 3rd c. AD); bibliography in *SEG* 52.947, adding Webb 2008, 103 and fig. 11. For the motif of silence after speech, Webb also cites the epitaph of the entertainer Gemellus from Amaseia (*St.Pont.* III 143.2–3), ὁ πολλοῖς θεάτροις πολλὰ λαλήσας.

αἰσχεορήμονας: For the shameful speech of mimes, see i. 367. Other -(ρ)ρήμων compounds are in B.-P. 218 (in most of them the first component is adjectival, describing the quality of the words; already Aesch. Ag. 1155 κακορρήμονας). αἰσχεορήμ- is new, but only a small tweak on αἰσχρορρήμων, which is not (already in Suetonius, Περὶ βλασφημιῶν καὶ πόθεν ἑκάστη, 3, a gloss on Κυσολέσχης; Pollux, 8.80; plus the verb αἰσχρορρημονεῖν and noun αἰσχρορρημοσύνη in imperial prose).

446 The line is erected over the same foundations as 4.280 and 283. See the notes on both passages, especially on 283, for the connection of μωρ- and αἰσχρ- in connection with mimes. Lexicographers use μωρολόγος as the common Greek to gloss Attic φλήναφος. It is not, as far as I can see, the formal title of a type of mime. But it readily suggests the mime fool, the μῶρος, like its counterpart at 4.283 μωρόφρονας.

447 ἀρεταλογίη: although a familiar word in the history of religions for a narrative of a god's powers, the abstract form would be unique in Greek except for Ecclus. 36:13 πλῆσον Σιων ἀρεταλογίας σου ('praises', in parallel with δόξης, but KJV 'unspeakable oracles'). The agent noun ἀρεταλόγος is usually one whose task it is to tell forth a god's power (S. Reinach, 'Les arétalogues dans l'antiquité', BCH 9 (1885), 257–65; W. Aly, RE Suppl. VI, s.v. Aretalogoi, 13.10–15; M. Leigh, 'Two Notes on Ovid', CQ² 50 (2000), 311–13). However, the basic sense 'telling of wonder-stories' develops in directions which better fit the present context.[279] This is clearest from Juv. Sat. 15.16, where an *aretalogus* is someone who tells tall tales at dinner; μυθεύματα here makes clear that the context is also (tall) stories, and if Juvenal's suggestion is that these people sing for their supper, that would make them like the mime-buffoon-parasite of 4.284 (see ad loc.). The association with mimes is illustrated in other sources. (i) In Suet. *Aug.* 74 Augustus invites *aretalogoi* to dinner along with actors and circus performers (*acroamata et histriones aut etiam triviales ex circo ludios interponebat ac frequentius aretalogos*; cf. K. Vössing, *Mensa regia: Das Bankett beim hellenistischen König und beim römischen Kaiser* (Munich, 2004), 493 n. 6). (ii) The Lexicon of Philodemus [not on TLG] has ἀρεταλόγος...μιμογραφος (the edition of C. J. Vooys has no apparatus, but Reinach reports that ἀρεταλόγος is an emendation). These passages illustrate what the present poet must have in mind. Finally, the ancient commentators Porphyrio and ps.-Acro on Horace, *Sat.* 1.1.120 use the word in their expositions of an allusion to a prolix writer called

---

[279] Without having to distort the text to fit some derivative of ἀρρητολογία, cf. e.g. Oenomaus, fr. 11 Mullach αἰσχρορρημοσύναις καὶ ἀρρητολογίαις, of the foul-mouthed Archilochus. Indeed, Juv. *Sat.* 15.16 wrote *aretalogus*, but was taken by his scholiast to have meant ἀρ(ρ)ητολόγος (see A. Rostagni, 'Gli aretalogi e un esempio di falsa etimologia', RFIC 59 (1931), 103–4; R. Merkelbach, 'Tatian 40', VC 21 (1967), 219–20, at 219).

Crispinus. Other details (that he was a Stoic philosopher-poet) seem extraneous to the meaning established here, but wordiness (*garrule, loquacissimi*) remains relevant. For both meanings, teller of miracles and teller of tall stories, see M. Smith, 'Prolegomena to a Discussion of Aretalogies, Divine Men, the Gospels and Jesus', *JBL* 90 (1971), 174–99, at 174–6; H. C. Kee, 'Aretalogy and Gospel', *JBL* 92 (1973), 402–22, at 402–4.

The line-end, as transmitted, adapts *Il.* 13.537 = 14.431 ἅρματα ποικίλ' ἔχοντες, but De Stefani's suggestion (μυθεύματα ποικίλλοντας, cf. 2.293 βουλεύματα ποικίλλοντας, 2.325 στεφανώματα ποικίλλοντας) would reduce the similarity. Of all the senses in which ποικίλος can describe utterances, the point, given the context, is likelier to be self-interested wiliness (Eur. *Andr.* 937) than subtlety or stylistic diversity.

448 ψηφάων παίκτας: the ψηφοπαίκτης, conjurer/illusionist with pebbles (making them appear and disappear), was not mentioned in the earlier passage, but is elsewhere (Appendix II, VI.6.iii), including Firmicus, 3.7.15 *psefopaectas* (Mercury in the DESC), Valens, I 1.39 ἐπιχειροῦντας τὰ παράδοξα καὶ μεθοδικὰ ['crafty': LSJ] διὰ ψήφων, and he is what Artemidorus, 3.55, alludes to. For the type of entertainer, cf. Blümner, 19; Dickie 2001; J. Linderski, 'The Paintress Calypso and Other Painters in Pliny', *ZPE* 145 (2003), 83–96, at 88–9.

The ending of ψηφάων is one of several instances where the feminine first-declension gen. pl. ending is transferred, not only to the second-declension feminine gen. pl. (Callimachus, νησάων), but also to masculine and neuter second declensions (ps.-Hes. *Sc.* 7 βλεφάρων...κυανεάων, Xenophanes, fr. 6.4 W. ἀοιδάων), and third declensions as well (ps.-Opp. *Cyn.* 4.392 γυπάων). See Harder on her Call. 67.8, with further refs.; K.-G. ii. 581; G. J. Mahlow, *Neue Wege durch die griechische Sprache und Dichtung* (Berlin, 1926), 273–4; Schwyzer, i. 559. Vian, however, rejects μοτάων (from μοτός, lint) at Quint. Smyrn. 4.212. Pfeiffer on his Call. fr. 786 suggests that the present form might be a direct imitation of Callimachus' νησάων, and although it is not in the same *sedes* that does look possible.

ἐξ ὄχλοιο πορισμῶν: this is like Artemidorus' category of those who make their living from a/the crowd (ἐξ ὄχλου πορίζεσθαι, e.g. 1.64.4), except that in Artemidorus' case the category is a wide one that includes politicians and probably craftsmen and tradesmen (3.6 ἐργοπονούμενοι) as well as performers (Thonemann 2020, 114–15). More specifically there looks to be a connection with Valens, I 1.39 ‹ἀπὸ› ἐπιδείξεως τὸν βίον ποριζομένους. While LSJ illustrate the absolute use of πορισμός from this passage alone, it is also found in Ptol. 3.13.19, Valens, VII 6.63, and 1 Tim. 6:5 (so it is not exclusively astrological). As illustrations, Blümner, 29 and n. 229, cites Theophrast. *Char.* 6.4, a man who (argumentatively) collects the fee ἐν θαύμασι; also (n. 228) John Chrys. *PG*

57.509.22–4, an act in which the performers have blacked-up faces and demand a μισθός in abusive tones.

449 ῥεμβηδόν: I have corrected L's βομβηδόν, which would have to refer to their noisiness (for the application to a crowd, see Lucian, *Pisc.* 42 βομβηδὸν νὴ Δία καὶ βοτρυδὸν ἑσμοῦ δίκην), when what is really wanted is a word describing their wanderings. Though the word is new, it is supported by many other astrological words for wanderers such as Ptol. 3.14.19 νυκτιρέμβους and Valens, I 3.29 νυκτιρέμβων; Dorotheus, pp. 342.5 ῥεμβάδα καὶ φοιτῶσαν ὅπῃ κύρσειεν ἑταίρους (of a gadabout woman), 387.20–1 ῥεμβὸς καὶ ἀλήμων (of a gadabout slave), 392.19 ῥεμβαὶ δὲ καὶ ψεῦσται; Περὶ σχημ. 85 ῥέμβους καὶ ἀστάτους ~ Περὶ κράσ. 175 ῥέμβους καὶ ἀστατοῦντας; Rhetorius, *CCAG* vii. 215.32 ῥέμβους, not to mention others in more marginal texts.

For wandering see on 4.281, 282. ἀλήμονες is *bis legomenon* in the *Odyssey* (17.376, 19.74, of πτωχοί), reused once by Aratus (1101), and attains extraordinary popularity in Nonnus (28× *D.*, 5× *Par.*). The present passage has more in common with the *Odyssey* (and Nonn. *D.* 20.167 ἀλήμονας ἄνδρας ὁδίτας) than with Aratus, for it applies to a group of itinerants rather than humanity as a whole (see Franchi on *Par.* 6.108). The construction with a case is unusual. ἧς χθονὸς is better taken as ablatival than as a genitive of place within which movement occurs (Lopilato: 'ever wanderers within their own land'): the point must be that they wander abroad. While most ablatival genitives depend on verbs, ἀλήμονας derives from a verbal root, and more obviously so than the other examples of adjectives followed by ablatival genitive in K.-G. i. 401 (κενός, ἔρημος etc., not of physical distance).

4.450–90 Miscellanea

450–6 + 457–9 + 460–1 + 462–5

Venus and Moon with Sun and Mercury, in aspect to one another in MC, or in two-bodied signs; with Jupiter in equal degrees with Venus; with Saturn in aspect; and with Mars in the Evil Demon opposite Moon. This is a sequence on multiple births and monsters. I take the protasis and apodosis together.

A. There is a basic chart and a series of add-ons. The first deals with multiple births, the second and third with the numbers of males and females therein, and the last with *monstra* who have excess limbs.

B. Something very like this sequence is preserved in its entirety in *Lib. Herm.* xxxiv. 39–40. Details differ, but there is general agreement on the importance of double-bodied signs (which only M[b] enumerates). The outcomes are also similar, and all the more so if my interpretation of 461 is accepted. Thus, *Lib. Herm.*

has multiple births of unspecified gender/systems of triplets (two girls one boy, two boys one girl)/monsters, M^b has male twins and unspecified triplets/systems of triplets (two boys one girl, two girls one boy)/monsters.

C. Underlying both sequences are two chapters from Ptolemy, the first Περὶ διδυμογόνων (3.8), the second Περὶ τεράτων (3.9). Both M^b and *Lib. Herm.* treat monsters after multiple births. Beyond that, affiliation fluctuates.

(i) M^b is closer to Ptolemy's discussion of the determination of the sex of multiple births, 3.8.3. Ptolemy and M^b agree that it is a question of luminaries in the MC,[280] and that the number of offspring of each gender is determined by the aspecting planets. (For *Lib. Herm.*, in contrast, it is western or eastern locations on any angles.) Only from this point do the details differ. For Ptolemy, two male births and one female are produced by Saturn, Jupiter, and Venus, whereas in M^b Saturn contributes to the birth of two females and one male.

(ii) Concerning the birth of monsters, Ptol. 3.9.2–4 agrees with *Lib. Herm.* that the relevant factors are the luminaries placed in a certain type of sign in the presence or absence of benefics. For M^b, on the other hand, it is a matter of one luminary, one malefic (Mars) in the Evil Demon, and aspect. Once again, it is signs that are the missing factor for him.

D. Finally, M^a has a truncated and somewhat simplified version of the sequence (6.249–51 + 252–5, the first two items alone), sharing, however, one detail with M^b that *Lib. Herm.* lacks (the location of Mercury with the luminaries specifically in the MC). He envisages only twins, not triplets. And there are no benefics at all in the initial chart; it is the addition of both of them that makes the births male. In general, the closer affiliation of M^b than M^a to *Lib. Herm.* in this instance is unusual and striking (p. 269).

Multiple births are also treated in Firmicus, 7.3.1, 7. There are similar principles (special roles for Jupiter and Mercury; double-bodied signs), but the charts do not match those here.

450–1 The details are significantly different in *Lib. Herm.*: the other benefic is involved, and it is a matter of the location of the luminaries in houses and terms when they are positioned on *kentra*.

450 The line is nicely arranged with a mixture of parallelism (for the case-endings) and chiasmus (for planets and luminaries).

451 ἀμφιπολῶσιν: a variant of ἀμφιπολεύειν (i. 879; p. 244 n. 175), used mostly of location in the MC (3.36, 114; 6.199; 4.45, 132; ASC in 4.30), substi-

---

[280] Though Ptolemy's discussion began with the ASC, like that of Firmicus, 7.3.5.

Γενεαί and τέχναι 685

tuted for metrical reasons. The latter is Homeric, the former a favourite of Pindar (see Braswell on P. 4.158).

452 Double-bodied signs (see i. 769, 876). Signs are double-bodied in two senses, the first according to their position in the zodiacal circle (between tropic and solid signs, as explained by Ptol. 1.12.5, Manilius, 2.178-96, cf. the chart in Hübner 1982, 75), the second, the relevant one here, according to their physical form (as explained by Manilius, 2.159-72, 660-3, cf. the chart in Hübner 1982, 106). That may mean there are two of them (Pisces and Gemini are *Paarzeichen*: Hübner 1982, 108-9) or hybrid (Sagittarius is a compound of man and horse, Virgo has wings: Housman on Manil. 2.176). The label διμόρφωτα is unusual (Hübner 1982, 107; § 2.213.21), though δίμορφα is found in Serapion, Valens, and elsewhere (Hübner 1982, 109). δίσωμα and δισώματα are also used for this and the first, positional, sense of 'double-bodied'.

453 συνωρίζουσι: intransitive, as in Nic. fr. 74.23 G.-P., and applied (as in Nicander it is not) to siblings, like ξυνωρίς in Eur. *Med.* 1145, *Phoen.* 1085, 1618; Soph. *OC* 895.

κατ' αἴθρην: also 3.231, 4.466, and an epigram in praise of Aratus, Ptolemy, *SH* 712.1 (Hermippus, fr. 95 Wehrli). On αἴθρη, indicating the MC, see 4.94 n.

454-5 σταχυηφόρον ἁγνὴν | Παρθενικήν: while ἁγνὴν gestures at Aratus' myth of the Maiden (without directly quoting it), the name and epithet seem to evoke Dorotheus, specifically p. 398.15 Παρθενικὴ σταχυηφόρος. Παρθενικὴ also occurs on pp. 323.5, 8, 324.4, 402.15, and in no other astrological text. Perhaps drawing on Aratus, 97 ἥ ῥ' ἐν χειρὶ φέρει Στάχυν, Dorotheus seems to have set a fashion for poetic designations of Virgo: others include Maximus, 219 and 291 Ἀστραίη κούρη σταχυηφόρος; id. 553 Ἀστραίου σταχυηφόρῳ ἀμφὶ θυγατρὶ; Camaterus, *Introd.* 63 κόρη τις Παρθένος σταχυηφόρος; Manilius, 2.442 *spicifera... Virgo*; Gundel, *RE* s.v. Parthenos, 1937.49-56. Since συνωρίζουσι glosses the (very obvious) sense in which Gemini are double-bodied, could this epithet have the same function? Serapion, *CCAG* v/3. 96.28, explains that Virgo is among the περισσομελῆ ζῴδια because of her ear of corn (Hübner 1982, 110-11; § 2.222.11), but for him this is a super-category within which the truly δίμορφα (conjoined) form a subset.

455-6 'Human beings are born in a double *accouchement*', i.e. twins are born. -τοκ- is passive, not active (as διδυμητόκος and διδυμητοκεῖν normally are). The Doric alpha (διδυμάτοκ- is Theocritean) is surprising and suspect. Perhaps the periphrastic σώματα + genitive is another tragic idiom (LSJ σῶμα, II.1; Biehl on Eur. *Tr.* 201-2, calls it 'Ausdruck des besonderen Gefühlsgehalts der Stelle'). ἀνδρῶν should presumably be taken at face value, even though it complicates the simple twins-triplets parallelism by introducing an extra factor, and even though the offspring are gender-neutral in 6.251. The poet could have said e.g. τέκνων, but he has chosen a gendered word.

456 τριδύμων: the normal word for triplets (e.g. Dion. Hal. *AR* 3.13.4 βρέφη τρίδυμα, 3.22.10 τρίδυμοι παῖδες; Artemidorus, 5.12 τρίδυμα θηλυκά).

θαυμαστὰ γένεθλα: for the cadence see on 4.282. The normal attitude in antiquity to multiple births would have been to regard twins as a blessing[281] and anything above triplets as a prodigy, potentially sinister. Triplets themselves were borderline (Plaut. *Mil.* 717 *et tibi sunt gemini et trigemini, si te bene habes, filii*; yet *pueri trigemini* listed alongside celestial portents, potentially menacing, in Julius Obsequens, *Prodigiorum Liber*, 14), but to a Roman the legendary Horatii and Curatii constituted a happy precedent (Dion. Hal. *AR* 3.13.4; Livy, 1.24–5). Hence θαυμαστά here is genuinely 'marvellous' without any sinister shadow. See V. Dasen, 'Multiple Births in Graeco-Roman Antiquity', *OJA* 16 (1997), 49–63; ead., 'Blessing or Portent? Multiple Births in Ancient Rome', in K. Mustakallio, J. Hanska, H.-L. Sainio, V. Vuolanto (eds.), *Hoping for Continuity: Childhood, Education and Death in Antiquity and the Middle Ages* (Rome, 2005), 61–73; Doroszewska, 136–7.

457 Ζηνὶ Κύπρις: new Topic (or Focus) precedes Continuous Topic (i. 193–4): it is Jupiter who needs emphasis.

458–9 It is indeed possible for triplets to be different sexes. If they are not monozygotic (born from a single egg), i.e. if they are di- or trizygotic (and indeed, most triplets are trizygotic), then each has an equal and independent chance of being male or female. Not that biological impossibility would have deterred the Babylonian compilers of omens, but sex ratios within multiple births is one of the topics noted in the Babylonian teratomantic text *Šumma izbu* (Bottéro, 22). Bottéro notes that, as a general ordering principle, the less valuable category, the girl, is listed after the male (see next note).[282]

459 ἐσχατόωσα: in epic (and Hellenistic poetry thereafter) it is used of place, but the presumption here—unless it means 'lowest', 'least', 'meanest' (LSJ ἔσχατος, I.3; ἐσχατεύω, II)—is that it means last in birth order (see also on 3.48). But why are we told this? Ptolemy (above) does not include this information, and it is hard to see how it could matter from the point of view of inheritance (which

---

[281] Though note Lydus, *Mens.* 4.89…ὥστε μὴ διδύμους ἢ τερατώδεις γενέσθαι τοὺς τοκετούς (or does this mean multiple births of all sorts?).

[282] On the other hand, a preponderance of girls over boys among triplets is a decidedly good thing. Tablet I, 108: 'If a woman gives birth to three (children), two boys (and) one girl—the gods will…[…]; (there will be) dissension (in) the land; there will be famine, and the people […] 109. If a woman gives birth to three (children), two girls (and) one boy—the gods will…[…] (there will be) dissension (in) the enemy land; the land of the king will become happy.' (Transl. E. Leichty, *The Omen Series Šumma izbu* (Locust Valley, NY, 1970), 42.)

was partible, and extended to women under Roman law). It is hard to escape the impression of a 'last and least' quality to this birth.

460 For Cronos' patronymic, see i. 911 n. 22. θεωροσύνη, for θεωρία, is unique. For the verb, 'occupy' (see on 4.208–9) is less fitting than 'hold out to', 'present', 'offer'. The poet excels himself at padding out the simple notion of aspect.

461 I propose a different interpretation of ἐκτός from that of Koechly ('sine masculo') and Lopilato ('without a male'): ἐκτός here means 'besides', 'apart from' (LSJ I.3), in other words 'in addition to'. The cadence is Iliadic (δώματος ἐκτός, τείχεος ἐκτός), clearly reinterpreted in *some* sense, but it is hard to parallel ἐκτός meaning 'without', 'lacking'. If I am right, it restores the eventuality of two girls one boy to complement two boys one girl, and produces a more perfect correspondence with *Lib. Herm*. The periphrasis for twins has a possibly tragic tone (Aesch. *Suppl.* 28 θηλ. στόλον; Eur. *Bacch.* 117 θηλ. ὄχλος, 1156 θηλ. στολάν; *Christus Patiens* 1614 θηλ....γένος). The epithet again in 4.503.

462 κακοδαιμοσύνῃ: also 4.475, 594. The poet has perhaps reinterpreted or resemanticised an existing word in an astrological sense; cf. Aelian, fr. 110 (ap. Suda, α 3213) ἀσωτίᾳ καὶ πολυτελείᾳ καὶ ῥᾳστωνεύσει βίου καὶ κακοδαιμοσύνῃ λοιπῇ; ps.-Hippodamus, p. 101.20 Thesleff, ap. Stob. 4.1.95 οὐ γὰρ τὰν τυχοῦσαν ἀλλὰ τὰν μεγίσταν κακοδαιμοσύναν.

463 μαρμαρυγάς: see on 4.333.

463–4 τικτόμενος...τεχθήσεται: see Fehling, 135 for repetitions where a participle and main verb derive from the same root (both where there is an implied contrast between them and, as here, where there is not—in which case the participle may be almost pleonastic). He also gives instances of *figurae etymologicae* involving verb and subject (158–9); his examples are of nouns, but the nominalised participle comes close, a sort of 'internal' nominative.

464–5 περισσομελής is intriguing. Astrological jargon for humans with skeletal abnormalities (Valens, I 3.57, II 37.16, 19; Hephaestion, i. 23.2; Teucer, *CCAG* vii. 207.22), it suggests the possibility that in another version of this chart the outcome was brought about by signs of the same quality (Hübner 1982, 110–11). In other disability charts, signs have an analogical effect; Ptolemy himself invokes four-footed and bestial as well as human signs (with planets badly disposed), though does not use this particular category, and the monsters in *Lib. Herm.* are produced by *signis multi seminis*. Are signs a factor M^b has written out?

Those born with excess body parts are a sub-category of prodigious births, within both Babylonian and classical taxonomies of congenital abnormality. In Babylon, the omen series *Šumma izbu* has more to say about animal than human births, but one of its five main categories (along with animal-like features, missing parts, deformed or incomplete parts, and misplaced parts) is that of excess body parts.[283] Likewise, Aristotle's taxonomy of τέρατα includes, along with those with a part resembling that of a different species, and those with missing limbs, those with extra feet or extra heads (*GA* 769ᵇ26–7...τὰ δὲ τῷ πολυμερῆ τὴν μορφὴν ἔχειν, πολύποδα καὶ πολυκέφαλα γιγνόμενα). From a medical perspective, περισσομελής could refer to someone born with extra limbs (polymelia)[284] or to the much commoner condition of extra digits (polydactyly). The latter was noted or discussed by Aristotle (*GA* 772ᵇ13–26), Pliny (*NH* 11.244), and Galen (*De morb. diff.* vi. 862.9–12; *De causis morborum*, vii. 35.4–5 Kühn),[285] while, in the realm of the imaginary, Ctesias' ethnography runs through the various categories of malformation, including those with eight digits on each hand and foot (*FGrH* 688 F 45 (50)). At all events, the poet has used the right word. The only occurrence of περισσομελής outside astrology is in a chronicle of Theban kings in Syncellus, *Chron.* p. 109.7 Mosshammer, where it figures as a gloss on a Pharaoh's name, but περιττεύειν is Galen's word for excess body-parts (*De morb. diff.* vi. 862.7–8 Kühn ἢ ἐλλείποντός τινος μέρους, ἢ περιττεύοντος).

464 ἔκμετρα γυῖα: elsewhere this implies disproportion to extravagant excess (Soph. fr. 353.2 Radt ὄλβον ἔκμετρον; Lucian, *Pro Imag.* 18, 'over the top'), but here just 'the wrong number of', and at 4.626, if Koechly's conjecture stands, 'measureless'.

465 πὰρ φύσιν ἡμερίην: above and beyond human nature (for the adjective, 'mortal', see on 3.264–5). Ptolemy classifies monsters according to their likeness or unlikeness to the human race: 3.9.2–3 οὐδὲ ἐξ ἀνθρώπων ἔσται τὸ γεννώμενον... ὑπ' ἀνθρώπων μὲν ἢ παρ' ἀνθρώποις ἔσται τὰ γεγενημένα, τέρατα δὲ καὶ αἰνιγματώδη ('of the human race or to be classified with humans, but monsters and nondescript' [Robbins]). For Ptolemy, as for Aristotle, forms unclassifiable as human may count as bestial (*GA* 769 B 9–10 οὐδὲ ἄνθρωπος ἀλλὰ ζῷόν τι

---

[283] Tablets I–IV concern human births; wrong numbers of parts are found throughout II, III, IV. See De Zorzi, 48, 65 on excess body parts; Pangas, 321 (polydactyly). I have not seen D. Attenborough, *Birth Defects in the Omen Series Šumma Izbu* (Melbourne, 1999).
[284] *Epidemics* 5.1.13 ἔχον τὸν δεξιὸν βραχίονα προσπεφυκότα τῇ πλευρῇ (cited by D. Lenfant, 'Monsters in Greek Ethnography and Society in the Fifth and Fourth Centuries BCE', in R. Buxton (ed.), *From Myth to Reason? Studies in the Development of Greek Thought* (Oxford, 1999), 197–214, at 199 n. 9) seems to be a case of a misplaced limb rather than an extra one.
[285] For ancient sources see Z. Laffranchi *et al.*, 'Foot Polydactyly and Bipartite Medial Cuneiform: A Case of Co-Occurrence in a Celtic Skeleton from Verona (Italy)', *HOMO: Journal of Comparative Human Biology*, 66 (2015), 216–28, at 225–6; A. Lange, 'Polydactyly in Development, Inheritance, and Evolution', *The Quarterly Review of Biology*, 92 (2017), 1–38, at 7–9. An instance on a Roman-period shroud (provenance not known): Riggs 2005, 100.

μόνον φαίνεται τὸ γιγνόμενον, ἃ δὴ καὶ λέγεται τέρατα).[286] Yet in the context of foreign lands, as Lenfant notes on the Ctesias extract, these anomalies do not seem to make their possessors any less human: 'ils n'en restent pas moins des hommes tout à fait sociables, qui sont en relation avec les autres Indiens.'

466-71

Mars and Moon in favourable places. This looks like a τ- configuration, but has more in common with Ptolemy's account of Mars as governor of the soul (3.14.28). Natives are headstrong, violent, appetitive types. When Mars governs πρᾶξις, together with the Moon and Venus, he produces burglars (Θ p. 211.15-16 λῃστὰς καὶ θυρεπανοίκτας).

466 στείχωσι κατ' αἴθρην: see i. 894 n. 147 for the verb, and 4.453n. for the prepositional phrase.

467 πυρσοτόκος: see i. 909 n. 21 and 4.214 n.
εἱλιξόπορός τε Σελήνη: see on 4.437.

468 The combination of arrogance (the presumable implication of σοβαρούς) and subordination (ὑπουργούς) is initially strange, though comprehensible if the poet is describing mercenaries. The meanings of σοβαρός range from violent to haughty (see on 5.143) to fearless, but in any case are compatible with warlike dispositions.[287] For ὑπουργούς see on 4.259-60. Koechly's correction is supported, if not confirmed, by Ptol. 4.4.5, last in the list of those born when Mars rules πρᾶξις.

469 ἡγεμόνων φιλίῃσι: i. 292, 293, 309-10; again in 1.72. ἀμφὶ δὲ μισθῷ combines the stipulated wage of Il. 21.445 μισθῷ ἔπι ῥητῷ, the force of the preposition in e.g. ἀμφ' Ἑλένῃ, and cadences like ἀμφὶ δὲ κῦμα or ἀμφὶ δὲ πήληξ. Mercenaries are poorly represented in astrological texts. Ptol. 2.3.38 gives a negative pen-portrait of the peoples of Asia Minor and Levant who lend themselves out ἐν μισθοφορικαῖς στρατείαις, under the influence of Mars (among other planets), and Firmicus also has those willing to sell themselves when Mars and the ASC are in the terms of Saturn (5.2.3 *et qui se variis generibus ad varios actus aut locent semper aut vendant*).

470 πουλυπλανεῖς: see on 4.91.

---

[286] A category also found in the Babylonian omen series *Šumma izbu* (Bottéro, 15–18; De Zorzi, 61–2.
[287] Saturn allied with Mars produces this effect on the soul in Ptol. 3.14.14, but not on its own in 3.14.28.

ἀρήια λήματ': derived from Homeric Ἀρήϊα τεύχεα (HOrph. 38. 1, 7 Ἀρήια τεύχε' ἔχοντες).

471 καὶ πάσης στρατιῆς ἐπιβήτορας: for ἐπιβήτορας phrases see on 4.33 πάσης λύπης ἐπιβήτορας, which also has the closest phrasal similarity to the present line.

ἐν προκοπαῖσιν: equivalent to Ptolemy's δράστας (3.14.28), προκόπτοντας, προκοπτικούς, or a noun or verbal phrase (προκόπτουσιν, προκοπαὶ γενήσονται).

472-7

Saturn opposes Mars. Suddenly there is a straightforward opposition, with parallels from the catalogues of aspects. The two corrections in the protasis, 472 ἐς Ἄρεα and 473 ἐναντιόωντα, are to the credit of the scholars who made them, unaware of the parallels that confirm them. Axtius' σελαγίσμασι in 473 re-interprets the δισσὰ...ἄστρα (as transmitted) as the luminaries in opposition to the rays of the malefics, but the usage is doubtful.

472 ἐς Ἄρεα φέγγος ἀθρήσῃ: this imitates Call. Ep. 55.3–4 Pf. ἐς δ' ἐμὰ φέγγη | ἀθρήσας; Callimachus himself imitates the construction of ἀθρεῖν with a preposition in Il. 10.11 ἤτοι ὅτ' ἐς πεδίον τὸ Τρωϊκὸν ἀθρήσειε. Callimachus' epigram is for a lamp dedicated in a temple; the rays of the lamp are compared to those of the Evening Star. This will have attracted a poet who conflates words for natural and artificial light (cf. n. on 4.426 λαμπτῆρσι, and his many πυρσο- compounds). For Saturn's epithet, see on 4.309.

473 As an active form, ἐναντιόωντα is unique (Stephanus, writing before Koechly's emendation, noted that 'Activi ἐναντιόω ex. nullum usquam repertum est'). But as an 'information unit' it occupies exactly the same slot as 4.189 ἐν ἀλλαγμοῖσι, in a protasis which is otherwise closely parallel to this one. For σελαγίσματα, see on 4.189.

474 γενεὴ μεροπηίος: see on 4.215; the reason for the turn to miserabilism here is clear.

475 κακοδαιμοσύνῃ καματώδεϊ: for the noun, see on 4.462. The application of the epithet to a cosmic state of affairs causing physical wretchedness for human beings is rather like Hesiod's application of it to Summer (Op. 584, 664); at the same time, κάματος (p. 172) corresponds to 3.252 ἄλληκτον καμάτοισιν ὀϊζυροῖς φθινύθοντες and to Firmicus' laborum and aegritudinum (6.15.4).

477 κινδύνων...παρέδρους: once again the poet looks to be glamorising astrology's stock-in-trade with vocabulary targeting a tragic register. The basic idea here is a combination of bodily pains or weakness and dangers, which is astrological cliché (e.g. Valens, IV 5.2 σωματικάς τε ὀχλήσεις καὶ κινδύνους, IV

Γενεαί and *τέχναι* 691

10.19 ἀσθενείας σωματικὰς ἢ καὶ κινδύνους, and many such phrases), and for expressions meaning 'involved in disaster' compare e.g. Περὶ σχημ. 88 κινδύνοις περιπίπτοντας; Dorotheus, p. 414.17 κινδύνοις χαλεποῖς περιπετής, Valens, II 22.22 πολλοῖς κινδύνοις περιετράπη; cf. Ptol. 3.15.5 κινδύνοις θανατικοῖς τοὺς πάσχοντας περικυλίοντες. νουσομελεῖς is a quasi-tragic rendering of the idea that the malefics damage the limbs (Θ p. 156.26–7 εἰ δὲ Κρόνος καὶ Ἄρης [sc. are in the sixth place], ἀπαλλαγήσεται κακῶν, πλὴν σινοῦται αὐτῷ μέλος τοῦ σώματος) and perhaps corresponds to Περὶ σχημ. 63 σωματικαῖς ὀχλήσεσι and Περὶ κράσ. 62 σωματικὰς κακώσεις. ὀδύνῃσι συνήθεις means almost literally 'acquainted with grief', except that it sooner means physical pain, and suggests comparison with Περὶ κράσ. 62 ἐκ πόνων πόνους ἤτοι ἐκ μόχθων μόχθους and the strong emphasis on continuation in Firmicus (*assiduis, assiduis, continuationibus*). Finally, for παρέδρους see on 4.179, while δυσεκφευκτός is otherwise in Theodectas, *TGrF* F 10.4 and Timotheus, *PMG* 791 col. iii. 119, iv. 129 (though also Polyb. 1.78.1).

478-90

Moon (Crescent?) in quartile with Mars, with Mercury in DESC or in opposition. This configuration reappears in 1.306–20, with a couple of lines interpolated from 4.50–1 (Mars in MC). Its parallels are found in charts for both πρᾶξις and σίνος (on madness and on violent death). The same combination occurs in 6.499–503, but under a different protasis (Mercury added to the two malefics). The combination is intuitive and easy to grasp.

Protasis. The essential item is Mars. It is he who unites the main themes of πρᾶξις and violent harm. Given its highly composite nature it is not very surprising that the protasis of M^b does not exactly match any other in all its details, but it does have close affiliates.

I. The 'trade' of the robber is brought about by a combination of violent Mars and wily Mercury, which is paralleled in their respective Π- chart in Ptol. 4.4.7 and Θ p. 212.5–6. But the additional presence of the Moon is paralleled only in Θ p. 192.20–3, from the chapter on madmen and epileptics (no information about their position, except that they are centred).

II. As for violent death, there are a few related charts in Θ ch. 77, Καθολικὰ σχήματα βιαιοθανάτων:[288]

---

[288] Pingree 1977, 211, does not indicate a source. It is not Ptolemy, who does not discuss this topic, but one wonders about a connection with Dorotheus, or at least one of the texts which belong in the dossier that Heilen diagnosed as descending from Nechepso and Petosiris. Compare p. 202.4–6 with Περὶ σχημ. 121 (Moon and Mars in absence of benefic).

(a) In the first (p. 201.2–5, cf. Firmicus, 3.11.12, 6.31.64), there is a reference to the ascending node instead of to the Moon itself, but Mercury and Mars are also present, and the outcome makes reference to beheading.

(b) In the second (p. 202.4–6, cf. Firmicus, 7.23.3), the Moon is in the correct aspectual relationship (quartile) with Mars.[289]

(c) In the third (p. 202.9–10), Mercury is in (one of) the correct places, namely in opposition to the Moon, in the presence of at least one other malefic, although the Moon is Full, which 478 implies she is not.

Possibly there was once more along the same lines. The author/excerptor explains (p. 201.10–18) that he has preferred to expound general principles (the Lot of Fortune, the significance of the eighth place) rather than list isolated multi-component charts (ἀπὸ πολλῶν ἀστέρων συσχηματιζόμενα). Perhaps he means the kind of chart amassed in Firmicus, 7.23.

III. As for both combined, Firmicus, 4.14.7, and Valens, II 17.57–8, are the best witnesses. They have all three agencies—Mars, Moon, and Mercury—though for Firmicus they are configured as a *synaphe-aporrhoia* arrangement. Valens also gives an option for Mars and Mercury to be together in the DESC (cf. II 10.5) or IMC.

Apodosis. M^b, M^a, Firmicus, and Valens all combine πρᾶξις and violent death (M^b most wordily). Although M^a preserves one detail from Firmicus and Valens that M^b lacks—namely that these are murderers as well as λῃσταί—the closer match is undoubtedly between Valens, Firmicus, and M^b, and especially the last two of these. Like Firmicus, M^b distinguishes house-breakers from thieves in general; he mentions their capture (φωρηθέντες ~ *comprehensi*) and its circumstances (485 φωρηθέντες ἐν ἀλλοτρίοισι μελάθροις ~ *in his comprehensi facinoribus*), chains (δεσμά ~ *vinculis*) and imprisonment (συνοχάς, εἱρκτάς ~ *custodiae, carceris*). Of their modes of death, both mention the sword (ξίφεσιν ~ *gladio*); Firmicus spares us more, but suggests that other methods were available (presumably it was a matter of signs, as it is in Valens, Firmicus, 7.23.3–4, and Περὶ κέντρ. 45–6). βιαιοτάτῳ θανάτῳ/*biothanata morte* are a near-exact match.

There are more isolated matches for other items. λῃσταί are found in the Π-chart for Mars and for Mars and Mercury as Rulers of πρᾶξις + Saturn (Ptolemy and Θ). θυρεπανοῖκται and λῃσταί are found in Critodemus, *CCAG* v/2. 112.34–8 /Valens, IV 25.11. And all three of θυρεπανοῖκται (burglars), κλέπται, and λῃσταί are found in the madman chart in Θ p. 192.20–3.

---

[289] See too Θ p. 205.22–4; Valens, VII 6.65.

IN SUM: M^b's closest affiliation of all is with Firmicus. Indeed, they are so close here that Firmicus can serve as a control for M^b's poetic procedures (how he adds epithets, expands, retains the basic roots). It illustrates once again that charts can pass from one taxonomy to another while their basic signification remains unchanged: in Firmicus, this is a *synaphe-aporrhoia* chart, while in M^b the variables are aspectual relationship and *kentron*.

478 ἀμφίκερως: i. 904 n. 4. If one takes this at face value it means that the Moon is crescent, not Full or New. This is compatible with Firmicus' *crescens* (4.14.7).

σκολιόδρομος: i. 905 n. 26; and for σκολι- of the Moon, see on 4.78.

479 The λοξεύματα should refer to the oblique circle of the ecliptic (see on 4.92). The Moon is in quartile with Mars as they move round its slanting path. For εἰς τετράγωνα see on 1.307–8.

480 Such is the plethora of prepositional expressions in this line that at first sight it appears to be giving two separate indications: (i) in the DESC and (ii) in the IMC (for κατὰ γῆς in this sense see 4.82 and 582). (Dorotheus, p. 403.11–12 is similarly plethoric in its indications of place.) Presumably, though, the poet means that the planet is crossing the horizon on its downward course, with κατὰ γῆς used of downward motion as in Mimnerm. fr. 2.14 W. (descending to Hades, but not of location in the nethermost point). The DESC is the τέρμων or limit of the bright sky (94 n.), just as the ASC attracts -τέρμων epithets (see 4.28, 77 nn.), and for the DESC as τέρμα see further 578 n. ἐπὶ δυομένῳ renders normal astrological τὸ δῦνον, 'the setting point', in terms of Homeric δύομαι, of the setting Sun (*Il.* 7.465, etc.). For Mars in this location causing βιαιοθανασία, compare Περὶ κέντρ. 45 ἐν δὲ τῷ δύνοντι βιαιοθανάτους σημαίνει (cf. 17).

481–2 ἀμφ' αὐτοῖς...ζωιδίῳ κόσμοιο: I take it that this means conjunction or opposition by signs rather than strict degrees (i. 884). For the genitive κόσμοιο see p. 211.

481 ὁραθῇ: the use of the prose form instead of his normal ὀφθῇ (65 n.) provides the poet with a new metrical resource, but poetic examples are few and far between (Strato, *AP* 12.197.3 ὁραθείς, Camaterus, *Introd.* 1234 ὁραθείη).

482 κακοὺς λῃίστορας ἄνδρας: Boll 1898, 204, compared Firmicus, 3.13.2 *piratas crudeli feritatis atrocitate famosos*, although that passage involves both malefics and no Mercury. The cadence is like Iliadic ἡγήτορας ἄνδρας.

483 ἐκφύσει: extremely biological, and at first sight one is taken aback by the boldness of a claim that goes way beyond weaker attempts to explain the effect of the stars through 'influence' or 'sympathy' (i. 16); on reflection, however, it seems that the poet simply casts the causal relationship for which astrology

694   *Commentary on Book Four*

normally uses ποιεῖν and *facere* in his favoured physiological idiom (4.46 ὁ φύς, 4.387 ὁ φυόμενος, 4.455 φύσεται, etc.: p. 252). At that point the claim becomes much less startling than, say, Pliny's, that seeds (*semina*) fall from the sky and generate monsters (*monstrificae gignantur effigies*) (*NH* 2.7), and the question becomes one of usage, namely which other authors employ the conceit of the stars as progenitors. Another example is Manilius, for whom the universe (*mundus*) not only controls but also generates animate beings by means of the constellations (1.18 *quaque regat generetque suis animalia signis* ...). His formulations vary in strength (weaker ones use *facere, fingere, dare*, etc.), but the strongest do employ the conceit of procreative stars (e.g. 4.507 *generabit*, 518 *quos prima creant nascentis sidera Tauri*; 5.97 *hoc genitum ... de sidere*; 116 and 127 *generant*; 135 and 648 *hinc ... creantur*; 634 *dabit ... partus*; 658 *natos*), and all imply the transmission of influence (rather than mere analogy).

θυρέτρων ἐπανοίκτορας ὀθνειάων: elaborating on what the prose source presented as θυρεπανοίκτας (the word is in Θ and Critodemus/Valens),[290] glamorising the act of house-breaking with a word more at home in connection with Homeric palaces, and replaying the same trick in the genitive plural -άων ending as in 4.448.

484 φαύλους: a ready transference from the malefic Mars to the nuisances he brings about.

νυκτοπλανέας: *hapax*; for the association of thieves and the night, see *Il.* 3.11; Job 24:14; 1 Thess. 5:2 ἡμέρα κυρίου ὡς κλέπτης ἐν νυκτί, and many less famous passages, including *Or. Sib.* 3.238, 380; Artemidorus, 4.56.4. In astrology: Ptol. 3.14.19 νυκτιρέμβους ... κλέπτας. It is no mere literary topos. Many papyrus records make the reality clear (H.-J. Drexhage, 'Eigentumsdelikte im römischen Ägypten (1.–3. Jh. n. Chr.): Ein Beitrag zur Wirtschaftsgeschichte', in *ANRW* II 10.1 (1988), 952–1004, at 953; id. 'Einbruch, Diebstahl und Straßenraub im römischen Ägypten unter besonderer Berücksichtigung der Verhältnisse in den ersten beiden Jahrhunderten n. Chr.', in Weiler and Graßl, 313–23, at 313.

485a Only M^c preserves this line, but it comes from a good source, for it shares συνοχάς with Valens, the idea of imprisonment with Firmicus, and has the occasional astrological motif of 'iron chains' (Firmicus, 6.30.13 *ferrea ... vincula catenarum*; Apomasar, *De Rev.* p. 106.14–15 δεσμὰ σιδηρᾶ περιβληθήσεται). These are elaborated with a rewrite of *Od.* 1.204 σιδήρεα δέσματ',[291] using a form of the epithet whose only earlier attestation was Nic. *Al.* 51 σιδηρήεσσαν.

---

[290] Grammarians note the triple compound: Herodian, *GG* iii/2. 791.9–10; *EtMag* 459.4–6; *Commentaria in Dionysii Thracis Artem Grammaticam*, Scholia Marciana, p. 380.10–11.

[291] For others see Orac. ap. Hdt. 5.77.4 δεσμῷ ἐν ἀχλυόεντι σιδηρέῳ, ps.-Opp. *Cyn.* 4.296 δεσμοῖσιν ... σιδηρείοισιν.

486 The subjects here are thieves and bandits, in Firmicus homicides and armed assassins as well, but whatever their crimes the poet seems to have heightened the horrors by implying a long stay in prison (οἰκήσουσι). This was not how the Roman carceral system was supposed to work—it was supposed to be a place of detention for the prisoner pending trial or the execution of sentence—but it seems that under the empire judges (legally or otherwise) increasingly imposed custodial sentences that were *poenae* in themselves.[292] One of antiquity's most famous prisoners, St Paul, was imprisoned for two years in Caesarea Maritima in a state which Acts 24:27 describes as δεδεμένον. Astrology is one of our best sources for long-term durance.[293] Its usage habitually conjoins prison (for which the usual Greek words are εἰρκταί, συνοχαί, φυλακαί, rarely δεσμωτήριον) with chains (either/or, both/and, and simply as two items with an inevitable association);[294] while this pairing is not unique to astrology, it seems to be less common in Greek than *carcer* + *vincula* in Latin, including many times in Firmicus.

488 The coupling of sword and axe—sanguinary, Martian outcomes[295]— suggests these are judicial punishments. M^b is not explicit, but Firmicus is (cf. also 3.4.23 *gladio percutitur sententia iudicantis*, 4.19.27, 7.23.3). Beheading was the basic form of Roman execution without aggravations (e.g. crucifixion, the arena) intended to cause extra damage or humiliation, to which non-citizens and/or *humiliores* were liable.[296] Texts up until the first century refer to the use of the axe,[297] but it was superseded by the sword,[298] whose use is assumed in legal texts and which, to outsiders, came to look characteristic of the Roman

---

[292] Arbandt and Macheiner, 329–32; Krause, 223–47; J. Hillner, *Prison, Punishment and Penance in Late Antiquity* (Cambridge, 2015), 135–43.

[293] Dorotheus, p. 403.24 πολυχρονήσοντα ἐν τοῖς δεσμοῖς; Valens, V 1.13 τινὲς μὲν οὖν καὶ ἔτι νήπιοι ὄντες ἐν συνοχαῖς ἢ εἰρκταῖς γίνονται καὶ ἐν τούτοις τοῖς τόποις τὰς ἀναστροφὰς ποιοῦνται ('spend their lives in such places'—Riley); Hephaestion, i. 325.23–5 ἐν δεσμοῖς ἔσονται πολὺν χρόνον, ἔσθ' ὅτε καὶ ἐν εἰρκταῖς ἀποθνῄσκουσιν; Firmicus, 3.4.18 *vinculis…perpetuis*, 4.8.3 *perpetui carceris poena*, 5.5.2 *diuturna carceris custodia*.

[294] Including in 6.669; 1.239–40; 5.133. Examples to be had on the TLG s.v. εἰρκτ-/συνοχ-/φυλακ- + δεσμ-.τήρησις also in Valens, V 1.9. One of the very rare occurrences of δεσμωτήριον is Dorotheus, p. 403.33–4, who envisages the possibility of a break-out. For Greek and Latin usage see Arbandt and Macheiner, 319.

[295] Death by the sword (*gladio*) associated with Mars: Firmicus, 3.4.20; 4.6.3, 4.19.27; 6.31.18, 61, 63; 7.14.1, 7.23.3; 8.26.6.

[296] Garnsey 1970, 124, 155; Callu, 338; Ruffing 2012, 83, 84–5, and *passim*; in general on corporal punishment and torture for *humiliores*, C. Humfress, 'Poverty and Roman Law', in Atkins and Osborne, 183–203, at 201.

[297] Th. Mommsen, 914 n. 2; Cantarella, 154–67; Aune on Rev. 20:4 τῶν πεπελεκισμένων διὰ τὴν μαρτυρίαν Ἰησοῦ (WBC 52C, p. 1087), with examples from Livy, Josephus, *et al.*

[298] Th. Mommsen, 916–18 (axe), 923–5 (sword); K. Latte, *RE* Suppl. VII, s.v. Todesstrafe, 1615.27–56; Callu, 334, with a couple of throw-backs to the use of the axe; Cantarella, 167; Ruffing 2012, 79.

state.²⁹⁹ The poet seems to be preserving an archaic detail, which is all the more striking in that no other astrological text seems to mention it, despite astrology's tralatician and conservative character. The 'fearful sword' is a minor topos,³⁰⁰ but it is unlikely that the axe can be explained as simply a poetic *tournure*; this is not a remake of an EGHP or Hellenistic line-ending.

489 ἐκδήσαντες shows that this is self-inflicted, and is not a reference to judicial punishment (hanging being a method which, in any case, the Romans did not use before the late empire).³⁰¹ When classical texts refer to 'hanging' as a punishment, what they often mean is affixation to a pole, in other words impalement.³⁰² Conversely, when astrology refers to hanging, unambiguous references—those involving a noose—are generally in connection with suicide.³⁰³ In the case of 5.133 δεσμά, βρόχους, εἱρκτάς, if this refers to judicial punishment, one wonders if it is because the text is late enough to reflect the wider prevalence of the practice in the later empire.³⁰⁴ At any rate, the classification among violent deaths is normal (1.254, sword and noose; Firmicus, 7.23.10 *laqueo suspensi interibunt*, 8.25.6).

---

²⁹⁹ Legal texts: Th. Mommsen, 924 n. 2; *Dig.* 48.19.8.1. Typical of Rome: *mSanh.* 7:3: 'They would decapitate him with a sword, as does the [Roman] state.' See D. J. Halperin, 'Crucifixion, the Nahum Pesher, and the Rabbinic Penalty of Strangulation', *JJS* 32 (1981), 32–46, at 34 n. 14, and B. A. Berkowitz, *Execution and Invention: Death Penalty Discourse in Early Rabbinic and Christian Authors* (Oxford, 2006), 161–2.

³⁰⁰ Cf. *Il.* 14.385 δεινὸν ἄορ (from δέος), cf. χαλκῷ σμερδαλέῳ; Tib. 1.10.1 *horrendos...enses*; Sil. Ital. *Pun.* 7.702 *ferrumque super cervice tremiscens*; Cedrenus, *Hist.* i. 226.3 ξίφη καὶ ὅπλα φοβερά; negative in Hor. *Od.* 1.37.23, Ov. *Met.* 3.534.

³⁰¹ J. G. Cook, 3 and n. 14, 49; Cantarella, 185–6. Not even hanging on the *infelix arbor*, the penalty for those convicted of treason (Livy, 1.26.6 *infelici arbori reste suspendito*), involved death by strangulation, but rather by flogging *after* suspension on the tree (Cook, 45–8). The practice was so archaic that details are distorted already in Cicero's reference in *Rab. Perd.* 13 (Cook, 70 and n. 88).

³⁰² For 'hanging' referring to crucifixion or impalement, cf. Hengel, 71; for the conflation of hanging and crucifixion (and ambiguity in the word *crux*), J.-L. Voisin, 'Pendus, Crucifiés, *oscilla* dans la Rome païenne', *Latomus*, 38 (1979), 422–50, at 440–6. 'Hanging' is seen as characteristic of 'the kingdom', presumably Rome, in *Sifre Deuteronomy* 21:22: 'Is it possible that they hang him alive the way that kingdom does?'; Berkowitz (n. 299), 161, takes this as an allusion to crucifixion. Given the judicial context, Firmicus, 8.25.6 *in crucem iussu imperatoris tolletur, aut praesente imperatore torquebitur, aut iussu principali suspendetur*, presumably means impaling.

³⁰³ 2.459, 3.262, 1.254, 5.199; Valens, II 41.84 (= no. L. 89 Neugebauer–Van Hoesen); Firmicus, 1.7.2, 4.9.5, 8.29.4, 8.30.7 (but definitely judicial punishment in 8.25.6). Perhaps more topos than reality? The Romans apparently loathed this method, and Voisin (n. 302) found a mere six cases of hanging among some 410 historical suicides spanning a period of almost 750 years.

³⁰⁴ Hengel, 29: hanging on the gallows gradually took the place of crucifixion in and after the time of Constantine and the Christian emperors of the 4th c.; F. Parente, 'Patibulum, crux, furca: Alcune osservazioni a proposito di un libro recente', *RFIC* 107 (1979), 369–78, at 377–8; J. Harries, *Law and Empire in Late Antiquity* (Cambridge, 1999), 139; Isid. *Et.* 5.27.34. 100 Nubian victims of this method from 'late Roman and Byzantine times' were examined by F. Wood-Jones ('The Examination of the Bodies of 100 Men Executed in Nubia in Roman Times', *British Medical Journal*, 28 March 1908, 736), establishing fractures of the cervical spine as the cause of death.

As for vocabulary, ἐκδήσαντες is precise ('bind', something to oneself), but δι' αὐχένος has been maladapted from the Homeric poems, where it thrice refers to the passage of a spear-tip. On βρόχος the note on 2.459 should be expanded. It is almost exclusively the Manethoniana that use it; prose almost always uses ἀγχόνη (acknowledged by 1.317 βρόχον ἀγχονόωντα), and βρόχος otherwise only in Hephaestion, i. 205.7. βρόχον ἀλγινόεντα repeats the pattern of Hes. *Th.* 226 Πόνον ἀλγινόεντα (there, at line-end).

490 It is presumably by accident that this is reminiscent of Firmicus, 1.9.1 *Ille, cogente fato, suspenditur laqueo.* For Koechly's λυγρόν = suffering, rather than giving, grief, see i. 367. The second half of the line is a compendium of popular cliché—'bitter fate' is a trope of popular verse (sepulchral epigram, *Or. Sib.* 3.502 πικρὴν μοίρην)—and EGHP, with ὑπ' ἀνάγκης shifted into the dative presumably in order to avoid a glut of first declension genitives singular. In EGHP (except in the *Odyssey*, where it refers to Penelope's forced completion of the shroud) it refers to cosmic necessity (Atlas; Prometheus; Nemesis, raped by Zeus)—another example, therefore, of Olympian vocabulary repurposed for the astrological world-view.

4.491–507 More *Kentrothesiai*

These four charts partly overlap with the *kentrothesiai* at the beginning. The first two use the same idiom (*x* 'looking at' the ASC = 'being in' the ASC), and the additional item in 499–502 (which is not, *contra* Koechly, parallel to 4.116–20) deals with Mars, as do the add-ons in 4.73–6 and 77–82. (Another, lost, Martian add-on may be suspected in 4.493–4.) But why repeat the configurations with slightly conflicting information? Koechly (1851, xlvi f.) thought there were two options—either that they were *adaptata* from what had gone before, or that they were of different authorship, and he (doubtfully) took the second option, bracketing them in both editions. I take the first (W. Kroll, *RE* s.v. Manethon (Astrologe), 1103.64–6, objected to deletion as well). My view is that they rework the same basic material. The question why they have ended up here in the book is secondary. The important takeaway is that one and the same poet (as it surely is) can revisit a theme, now with significantly different emphases. (Were they meant for different clients?)

491–5

Venus aspects ASC. At first sight, there is an almost total contrast with 4.59–64, where, instead of being party-goers, the natives preside over religious gatherings. Conversely, it is a different means of producing drunkards etc. from

4.294–308, where Mars and Saturn are involved as well as Venus. Yet the similarity between 4.59 μερόπων ὡροσκόπα φέγγεα λεύσσῃ and 491–2 βροτῶν ὡροσκόπα φέγγῃ | δερκομένη is too close for coincidence. Nowhere else in the book is ὡροσκόπος epithet of φέγγος, and nowhere else is it used in the plural.[305] The φιλομούσους of 4.492 seem born of the same stock as the εὐμούσους of 4.60, only radically reimagined. And the relationships of both sets of natives with the opposite sex are characterised by a certain frisson of secrecy or deviance. What kind of procedure has produced such variation? Rewritings of different sources do not really explain the shared idiom of 4.59 and 491–2. More likely, it is a matter of theme and variation on a single, but broadly-based, ground; or perhaps the poet has returned to the same subject but omitted an additional factor (aspect of a malefic?) which would explain the worsened outcome (see on 4.493–4).

491 Κύπρις δ' ἀφρογένεια: see i. 906 n. 1.

492 δερκομένη is the only instance in the later books of one of Mᵃ favoured verbs for aspect (i. 885); at its strongest it implies a keen, intense regard (Prévot, 233–9). Thereafter, the line develops Venus' quality of cultivated hedonism (e.g. Valens, I 2.16 φιλήδονοι, φιλόμουσοι; Ptol. 2.3.36 φιλόμουσοι καὶ μᾶλλον ἁβροδίαιτοι) with a little touch of EGHP, though ἐν εἰλαπίναις is hardly precise enough to pinpoint an allusion to Hes. fr. 305.3 M.–W. (the only occurrence of the phrase in EGHP, and in this *sedes*). Although the word is strongly associated with secular festivities (weddings; the Odyssean suitors), insofar as it can also be used of religious occasions (Livrea on Ap. Rhod. 4.1421) it is not incompatible with the activities of the natives in the earlier passage, at 4.63. But that changes in the next line.

493 ἡδυπότας: the agent noun is a rarity: it begins in Hedylus (*HE* 1884, describing one of the subjects of a piper), and recurs only rarely (Nonn. *D*. 12.249, epithet of Ampelos; *AP* 9.524.8, anon.; *AP* Appendix, Epigr. Sepulchr. 134.8).[306] But it tessellates well with the ἡδυπάθεια (Critodemus, *CCAG* viii/1. 260.17) Venus bestows, and the ἡδύβιοι who are her offspring (e.g. Ptol. 3.14.25; Valens, I 3.56; Hephaestion, i. 264.22).

θιάσων: for the secular meaning see on 4.301.

493–4 The association of love-charms with foreigners and females is pure trope (for instance, a Massylian priestess discloses *magicas artes* to Dido in V. *Aen*. 4.478–98, cf. Sil. Ital. 8.98–9; a Syrian woman practises love magic for Athenian prostitutes living in the Kerameikos in Lucian, *Dial. Meretr*. 4.4–5). It

---

[305] p. 246. Hübner 2001, 235, misses the fact that the *two* passages share this peculiarity.
[306] Its antecedent was ἡδύποτος, EGHP epithet of drink.

is typical of astrology's strong tendency to placelessness that a text which is presumably itself Egyptian makes use of the topos of 'foreign spells' (Egypt being the land of magic in the Greek imaginary) (p. 119). If the male natives are soliciting love-charms, they are probably using *agogai* to summon the women of their desire, the typically male form of magic spell (as opposed to the *philia* spell used by the woman who wants to keep her man).[307] This wholly suits the present context with its associations, not only of adultery, but also of *hybris* (coercive behaviour): the forcible removal of the woman from her surroundings and due presentation to her lover was exactly what the magic sought to achieve. Is the poet trying to evoke a frisson of illegality, or at least to invite disapproval? Probably love magic was too trivial to attract the attention of authorities[308] unless the outcome was fatal, in which case it fell under the purview of the *Lex Cornelia de sicariis et veneficiis*, concerning *venena mala* specifically intended to kill. A shift in attitudes has been detected towards the end of the third century. Love magic and the use of abortifacients—the practices themselves, not just a fatal outcome—are now severely punished, while the actions of fixing and binding (*defixio* and *obligatio*) are ranked among *sacra impia* and to be punished with death.[309] But the present text floats free of specific legal rulings. All is commonplace about sexual laxity and underhand practices.

Other references to potions in astrology are not particularly closely related to this one, but do make it clear that they are not the pure effect of Venus, but of Venus harmed in some way, especially by a malefic: (i) Epit. IIIb, *CCAG* vii. 116.9-11 Ἀφροδίτη ἐπὶ κέντρῳ καὶ ἐν θηλυκῷ ζῳδίῳ ὑπὸ Ἄρεως θεωρουμένη πρὸς φίλτρον ἐγείρει τοὺς ἔρωτας καὶ ἐπιχαρεῖς ‹ποιεῖ›; (ii) Dorotheus and Theophilus both speak of charms for loving and hating being the result of harm to Mercury (i.e. misplaced ingenuity) and Venus (Dorotheus, p. 367.19 φιλτροπόσιμα, μισοπόσιμα; Theophilus, *CCAG* xi/1. 263.7 τὰ γυναικεῖα φάρμακα, οἷον φίλτρα καὶ μίσηθρα); (iii) Camaterus, *De Zodiaco*, 724 Ἐν τῷ τρίτῳ δὲ πορνικὰ φίλτρα φέρει. Koechly also restored φίλτρα in 1.261 (Venus surrounded by malefics). Has the poet omitted a factor explaining the bad outcome?

494 στοργαῖσι κεκασμένα φίλτρα: the sense requires 'laced with', rather than 'endowed with' (a moral or intellectual quality, as abstract nouns with

---

[307] Faraone, ch. 2.

[308] For spasmodic attempts to expel magicians from Rome, but also from time to time by governors in the provinces, see Dickie 2003, 149-51, 151-2.

[309] *Pauli Sententiae* 5.23.14. For the developing interpretation of Sulla's law of 81 BC, see Garnsey 1970, 109-11; J. B. Rives, 'Magic, Religion, and Law: The Case of the *Lex Cornelia de sicariis et veneficiis*', in C. Ando and J. Rüpke (eds.), *Religion and Law in Classical and Christian Rome* (Wiesbaden, 2006), 47-67; Bremmer 2015, 259.

κεκασμ- usually are[310]), and it is the more unusual in that στοργή is used of erotic love, not parental affection (4.378 n.). The other examples listed in LSJ are all epigrams by Meleager. Taking issue with this entry, David Konstan argues that all these cases 'exploit the primary sense of the term as a kind of familial or friendly affection', and suggests instead epigrams by Marcus Argentarius (*AP* 5.89.4, 116.3, 11.320.1), Philodemus (*AP* 5.107, 121), and Strato (*AP* 12.5) as examples of the very rare, purely erotic, use of στέργειν.[311] This passage can be added to them.

495 ὕβρις, οὐ κύπρις: another Gorgianic jingle (p. 214).

496–8

Jupiter aspects ASC. This is not dissimilar to 4.35–6, 39–43. The ἀρχαί mentioned here are specified there; the finery there (χρυσοστέπτορας) translates here as εὐμορφία.

496 ὡροσκόπον ὄμμα τιταίνῃ: M^b is possibly the earliest of the late antique poets to use the expression ὄμμα τιταίνειν, which becomes very popular (Franchi in Nonn. *Par.* 6.160; De Stefani on *Par.* 1.103; Kost on Musaeus, 336). The epithet that normally decorates ὄμμα, sometimes indicating the direction of vision,[312] or vision itself ((παν)ἐπίσκοπον ὄμμα in LGHP), now becomes fully informational (Hübner 2001, 235–6), and, in connection with the noun, exercises its full, active sense: the planet's eye is looking, and hence, according to the Greek understanding of vision, directing rays, at the horoscope, i.e. the ASC.

497 εὐμόρφους: since this is the effect of Jupiter, not Venus, the good looks are presumably physical impressiveness rather than (sexual) attractiveness (although it is true that Jupiter contributes to female beauty in 5.317, where see note). See on 5.229–30, 286, 287.

498 ἔν τ' ἀρχαῖς πλειστῇσι: not the specific Romano-Egyptian offices called ἀρχαί, whose holders were ἄρχοντες (Riggs 2005, 204; ead. 2012, 4), but the positions of power indicated in 4.39–40.

τὰ βέβαια φρονοῦντας: good conservative voters ('strong and stable'). Most astrological uses of βέβαιος refer to the certainty of an outcome; as a mental

---

[310] Ar. *Eq.* 684–5 πανουργίαις μείζοσι κεκασμένον; 2.338 χαρίτεσσι κεκασμένοι; 6.468 σοφίῃσι κεκασμένοι; al.

[311] 'Στοργή in Greek Amatory Epigrams', in F. Cortés Gabaudan and J. V. Méndez Dosuna (edd.), *Dic mihi, musa, uirum: Homenaje al profesor Antonio López Eire* (Salamanca, 2010), 363–9; the quotation on 368–9.

[312] Nonn. *D.* 2.673 (cf. 37.71), Christodorus, *AP* 2.1.225 ἐναντίον ὄ. τ.; Nonn. *D.* 4× and *Par.* 1.103 ἀντώπιον ὄ. τ.; *AP* 2.1.353 μετάρσιον ὄ. τ.

quality it equates with Jovian ἐχέφρονας (Apomasar, De Myst., CCAG xi/1. 179.29–30), σώφρονας (Π.τ.δ. 41 σώφρονας, εὐσταθεῖς), the opposite of ἀνοήτους, ἄφρονας, παράφρονας. Jupiter is again associated with stability, but political, in 6.365 Ζῆνα δ᾽ ὁρῶν, καί τ᾽ ἀπταίστους ἐνὶ πάτρῃ.

499–502

As above, when aspected by (in conjunction with?) Mars. I find no match for this chart. The details are perplexingly Saturnian (see on 4.501–2).

499–500 τούτῳ...σχηματίσῃ: the normal constructions would be active with direct object (e.g. Dorotheus, p. 425.1-3 ἐὰν...ὁ Κρόνος αὐτὴν σχηματίσῃ) or σχηματίζεσθαι with dative (or πρός, μετά), 'be in aspect with', which is much commoner than LSJ I.3 suggest. μίγδην may be exerting an influence on the dative (although at 4.202 it is purely adverbial); it seems, taken with ἰκέλῃσι πορείαις, to indicate conjunction. For πορεία, see on 4.6. κατὰ κόσμον intelligently reworks EGHP, where this phrase, especially, when it occurs at the caesura, is often preceded by the negative (or εὖ).

500 ἰχνοβλαβέας, φθινοκώλους: astrology makes much ado about foot (less often leg) problems, which are brought about by various agencies, including Mars but not restricted to him.[313] In particular, like the Gospels it makes a good deal of cripples. These two epithets are nicely paired, their nominal/verbal components arranged 'chiastically', but they are hardly specific enough to map onto the standard pair χωλοί (lame) and κυλλοί (club-footed, or deformed),[314] nor does either suggest the loss of a limb (Firmicus, 8.21.13). The second suggests wastage and weakness (compare perhaps the χωλός in Acts 3:2 and 7 παραχρῆμα δὲ ἐστερεώθησαν αἱ βάσεις αὐτοῦ καὶ τὰ σφυδρά). Valens, II 37.8, through the analogy with Taurus' bent hoof, suggests deformity.

501–2 The connection between lower limbs and hands is found over and over again in astrology, and the logical Ptolemy tries to rationalise it by having damage to the extremities caused analogically by planets in the last degree positions of the dodecatemories (3.13.17 χειράγραι καὶ ποδάγραι). But the damage is normally caused by wet agencies, which preside over humoral conditions and over nerves (see on 6.613–15), with which gout is associated. That agency is normally Saturn, which vividly causes weeping fingertips in contact with the waning Moon in 1.55 (see ad loc.). Nerves and 'gout' of feet and hands (rheumatism? arthritis?) all fall under Saturnian influence (Valens, I 1.13, Περὶ κράσ. 8;

---

[313] 1.136–8; Θ pp. 127.7, 155.1–2, 16–17, 189.4, 190.5, 201.5–6. Sore feet: Valens, II 37.47 περὶ τοὺς ἀναγκαίους τόπους οἶνος καὶ ποδῶν αἴσθησιν = no. L 106 Neugebauer–Van Hoesen.
[314] Ptol. 3.13.13; Hephaestion, i. 143.13; Θ pp. 156.10, 189.7; Matth. 15:30–1, 18:8.

702   Commentary on Book Four

Rhetorius, *CCAG* vii. 214.14 ποδάγρας, χειράγρας; Θ pp. 158.16–17 πάθη...περὶ τοὺς δακτύλους...ἢ ῥεύματα περὶ τοὺς πόδας, 192.7). Sometimes this takes place under the additional influence of signs (Dorotheus, p. 404.11–14 ἐὰν οὖν...οἱ κακοποιοὶ...μέσην περιέχωσι τὴν Σελήνην ἐν μὲν Διδύμοις ὄντες χειράγραν ἐπιφέρουσιν, ἐν δὲ Ἰχθύσι ποδάγραν; Θ pp. 155.24 ποδάγρας, χειράγρας, χειρῶν ἕλκη πρὸς τὴν τοῦ ζῳδίου φύσιν, 191.15–192.1...ῥευματικοὺς ποιεῖ περὶ τοὺς πόδας καὶ τὰς χεῖρας, especially in Gemini and Cancer). Pisces presides over feet, nerves, and gout in Maximus, 258; *CCAG* v/3. 129.16–17, Teucer, *CCAG* vii. 211.26–7. If one needs an explanation why Mars can cause gout, perhaps it is to be found in medical theory, which held that there were two kinds, hot and cold.[315] Still, astrology concentrates almost exclusively on the cold, wet type. The only non-wet agency is in Valens, II 37.50: the Sun causes ποδάγρα, because it presides over nerves (νεύρων κυριεύει).

ἀχθήμονας: for ἄχθος of a burden of physical suffering, see Maximus, 170 (there, angina).

503–7

Saturn in ASC in female births. The equivalent chart in 4.14–27 is not for females and has only one real overlap, which is that the position is fortunate (if the planet is in its own signs). There is no distinction between own and other signs here. The subjects seem to be prostitutes. The turn from prosperity in 504–5 to promiscuity in 506–7 is surprising, a far stronger version of 3.178–9, where wives are socially prominent but complaisant, but under completely different conditions (Jupiter in the ASC, Venus in the DESC). The diction points to a connection with an earlier prostitute chart (4.506 παγκοίνως ~ 4.352 πάγκοινον κέρδος), and the contrast between prosperous circumstances and a low expression for 'whore' is again replayed from the earlier passage (see on 4.353). The 'others' beds' motif (507) had also appeared in the earlier chart for the male counterparts of the courtesans (4.349 ἀλλοτρίων θαλάμων).

503 θηλυγενεῖς δὲ γυναῖκες: an intelligent adaptation of EGHP θηλύτεραι δὲ γυναῖκες (more often in dative), because the point is now, precisely, their birth.

504 The shape of the line is identical to 4.590, which comes from a different kind of chart. For βαθυχρήμονες see on 4.66 βαθυχρήμονα. ὀλβομέλαθροι, which shows the poet's willingness to cobble together eccentric compounds (contrast Philoxenus, *PMG* 836 (*e*) 23 ὀλβιόπλουτον), is unique.

---

[315] Thessalus, *Virt. herb.* 2.3.1 = *CCAG* viii/3. 155.4–5; Diocles of Carystus, fr. 138 (P. van der Eijk, *Diocles of Carystus: A Collection of the Fragments with Translation and Commentary* (Cologne, 2000)); K. C. Gritzalis *et al.*, 'Gout in the Writings of Eminent Ancient Greek and Byzantine Physicians', *Acta medico-historica Adriatica* (*AMHA*), 9 (2011), 83–8, at 84–5.

505 ἀξιοπιστοσύνη: the noun is unique. Contrary to expectation, since candour is so important in astrology, ἀξιοπιστία is mentioned mostly in connection with reliable, trustworthy methods and in respect to the moral character of natives only in Dorotheus, p. 426.26–7 (the safekeeping of a will, where it is a matter of tropic signs rather than a planet) and Valens, IV 25.10 (where it is the gift of Jupiter, not Saturn).

506–7 The accusative ἀλλοτρίους θαλάμους is transmitted in 507. One has some sympathy with Axtius and Rigler's emendation to the dative, which makes the promiscuous women spend their nights in others' chambers, but with D'Orville's genitive singular one understands that they direct their lives by means of the profits from other people's marriages ('alieni thalami lucro': Koechly's Latin)—in other words that they are not simply promiscuous, but prostitutes who predate on their clients' lives. This revises the initial impression made by βαθυχρήμονες, ὀλβομέλαθροι, and we now understand that this wealth was adventitious all along. For 'the common woman' see on 2.180 and 4.353 (also 3.85–6 πολυκοίνους | δῶκ᾽ ἀλόχους).

506 ἐπίψογα: used adverbially here, but usually adjectivally, especially reprehensible sexual behaviour. Of women in Περὶ σχημ. 98, 127; Valens, II 38.75; CCAG v/1. 207.32 ἐπιψόγους ἐν τοῖς ἀφροδισίοις; CCAG ix. 147.27 ἐπίψογον ἀπὸ τῶν ἀνδρῶν.

507 This suggests the kind of high-class prostitute, the *hetaira*, who can demand the maintenance of her household,[316] whose lovers support them at the expense of another family,[317] and who is best known from the Attic orators and comic stage. Is this a stock figure? If so, the poet simultaneously rehashes the trope of their avarice,[318] *and* lowers them to the level of the promiscuous streetwalker; he combines the private household (their βίον, the θαλάμους on which they predate) with public availability (παγκοίνως). The κέρδος motif which attached to the pimp in 4.314 now attaches to the woman herself: so too Aristaenetus, *Epist.* 1.14; Sopater, Διαίρεσις ζητημάτων, ap. Walz, *Rhet. Gr.* viii. p. 182.2 αἱ ἑταῖραι…μόνον τῷ κέρδει κηλούμεναι.

βίον ἰθύνουσαι: see on 4.326.

---

[316] See e.g. Xen. *Mem.* 3.11.4 Πόθεν οὖν, ἔφη, τὰ ἐπιτήδεια ἔχεις; Ἐάν τις, ἔφη, φίλος μοι γενόμενος εὖ ποιεῖν ἐθέλῃ, οὗτός μοι βίος ἐστί; ps.-Demosth. Or. 59, passim, e.g. 29, 42, 67. In Hellenistic Athens, maids and *parure* were an expected part of the package (E. Fantham, 'Sex, Status, and Survival in Hellenistic Athens: A Study of Women in New Comedy', *Phoenix*, 29 (1975), 44–74, at 65–6 n. 48).

[317] Ps.-Demosth. Or. 48.53–5, Menander, *Epitr.* 133–6; Athen. 13.590 c–d.

[318] L. Kurke, 'Inventing the *Hetaira*: Sex, Politics, and Discursive Conflict in Archaic Greece', CA 16 (1997), 106–50, at 109; Glazebrook, 178–80.

4.508–36 Luminaries in Gendered Signs

There are distinct connections with the treatment of gendered luminaries in M^a (see on 3.363–98). Unlike the earlier poet, this one confines himself to male natives, but, like M^a, he runs through all possibilities of alignment, beginning with perfect concord. Thereafter he follows a different order (two pairs: concord/discord; over-masculinisation/over-feminisation) and without add-ons. Both also have a discernible relationship with Epit. II (i. 702), and they adapt its explanatory model (the gendering of stars by location in signs or quadrants) to their own organising principle (the congruity of luminaries and signs) in a similar way, by stretching what is said about masculinity across concord (4.511–14) and excessive (4.529–33) forms, and likewise what is said about effeminacy across the crossed-wire (4.517–18) and excessive (4.521–6) scenarios. In so doing they abide by the same logic, whereby the ideal is attained by concord, not by the maximum dose of masculinity (as in Ptolemy, 4.3, and as partly implied by Epit. II). There are some correspondences of outcome (3.379 ~ 4.521–6). At the same time, M^b has new departures: Moon phase in 4.510, details of outcomes in 512–14, and especially the watery professions of 534–6.

508–14

Sun in male, Moon in female signs. Is there a connection with 3.365–8? Possibly 4.511 ἐν ἀνθρώποισι κράτιστοι answers to 3.365 πάντων…ἄριστον. There is no mention of πρᾶξις (3.368), but 4.512 ἀριστοπονῆες indicates efficacy by other means. Affability is missing (3.367), and there are new details about disposition, family, physique, and social status which suggest the poet has access to another source (unless he is freewheeling). In particular, we learn that the Moon is New. Whatever source supplied these details, it is not Ptolemy, who does not discuss the 'concord' scenario.

508 Ἥλιος δ' ἀκάμας: see on 4.271.

σέλας: already 6.95 σέλας Ἡελίου; cf. Il. 19.374, singular σέλας of the Moon. It seems first to be used of the Sun in tragedy (Eur. El. 866); of daylight in Pindar, fr. 108b.4 Maehler. See 4.403 n.

508–10 Variatio of constructions for each planet (p. 213): the Sun is the subject, the Moon the object, of their respective clauses. ἐλθεῖν itself elicits a novel treatment: the poet does not otherwise construct it with the dative (Dr Holford-Strevens notes the similarity with e.g. Virgil, Aen. 11.192 it caelo, etc.). None of the earlier senses for this construction seems particularly pertinent (LSJ A.III.4 come (to the aid of), with persons; A.V, including evils coming to a person or place); it is simple variatio. For this section and what follows, the poet needs the

Γενεαί and τέχναι   705

notion of signs, and it is here and here only that he revives ζῷα in Mᵃ's sense, for 'constellations' (509; i. 876); then, having gestured at the earlier poet, he innovates with his own word ζῳφορίη, exploiting the use of φορ- for cosmic motion (i. 895). The only other occurrence of its epithet is at HOrph. 7.8 ἠερόπλαγκτοι, also of the stars. For -πλαγκτος compounds, see on 4.9 αἰθερόπλαγκτος.

510 νεολαμπέα: i. 904 n. 9.

512-14 This package of qualities (efficacy, liberality, nobility, physical impressiveness, distinction, patriotism, justice) is also strongly Jovian (compare e.g. Ptol. 3.14.20 ἐλευθερίους, δικαίους…εὐεργετικούς…ἡγεμονικούς; 2.3.34 τὰ ἤθη δίκαιοι καὶ ἐλεύθεροι καὶ τὰς ψυχὰς μεγάλοι καὶ γενναῖοι, of those ruled by Saturn and Jupiter). These are kingly characteristics. At the same time, some reflect epigraphical themes which commend the activity, probity, and devotion of public officials. There is no strong implication that they are the provincial governors whom ἰθύδικος in particular describes. But the poet borrows the rhetoric associated with prestigious public figures to present the natives as embodying ideal norms.

512 ἀριστοπονῆες: the agent noun is unique. The adjective ἀριστοπόνος first, and generally, applies to crafts and manufacture,[319] but administrators in later antiquity can also be praised in inscriptional verse for their labours (πόνοι, μόχθοι) (Robert 1948, 21 and n. 3; BE 1961, nos. 536-7). The poet means they are efficacious and proactive (as in 3.368), a quality combined with others mentioned here e.g. by Ptol. 2.3.45 ἐλεύθεροί τε καὶ ἁπλοῖ τοῖς ἤθεσι καὶ φιλεργοί. For πόνος, see further on 4.72.

513 εὔσημοι γενεήν: i.e. εὐγενεῖς or γενναῖοι, which is not a normal meaning of εὔσημοι, but perhaps draws attention to the outward clues by which their birth is recognisable. Nobility is not mentioned in 3.365-8.

514 πάτρης κηδέστορες: 'patriae curatores' (Koechly 1851); 'guardians of the fatherland' (Lopilato). Both depend on taking κηδέστορες as an agent noun from κήδεσαι, 'those who care for' their cities. Fraenkel, i. 139-41, argues that the poet intended it as a pseudo-archaic form of κηδεστής, which in practice never means 'guardian'/'carer', but 'relative by marriage'. But surely what was in the poet's mind was the common praise-formula κηδεμὼν τῆς πόλεως (etc.), which is ubiquitous in inscriptions, and attested in literary texts as well, e.g. Dio Chrys. Or. 34.30 κηδεμόνα ὄντως τῆς ἑαυτοῦ πατρίδος; Julian, Περὶ τῶν τοῦ

---

[319] Pind. Ol. 7.51 ἀριστοπόνοις χερσί, of craftsmen, specifically sculptors; in ps.-Phoc. 171, of a bee; in Nonn. D. 29.350, 37.126 of Hephaestus; in Nonn. D. 44.79 ἀριστοπόνοιο…μελάθρου, Greg. Naz. PG 37.1254.13, and AP 1.10.29 (cf. 40), of construction work. But in AP 9.466.2 ἀριστοπόνοις ὑμεναίοις it presumably refers to artistry, and in John Geometres, Carm. 24.2 to Simplicius' intellectual labours.

αὐτοκράτορος πράξεων, 29 (88 Β), πόλει δὲ σωτὴρ καὶ κηδεμών; John Chrysostom, *De inani gloria*, 4 κηδεμόνα...καὶ προστάτην τῆς κοινῆς πόλεως (Roskam, 151).[320] For versions of this formula, see Mason, 151-2; H. Malay, 'Letter of the Proconsul Taurus and the People of Pylitai near Tralles', *EA* 11 (1988), 53-8 at 56 n. 3; Blume, 283-5; Roueché 2007, 190-1. All the rhetoric points in the same direction. Those praised in inscriptions for their straight justice (next word) and hard labour (512), are also praised by cities for their devotion to that city.

ἰθυδίκαιοι: this correction by Koechly is a unique remake of Hes. *Op.* 230 ἰθυδίκῃσι μετ' ἀνδράσι, which otherwise reappears as ἰθύδικος in Maximus, 13 ἔργοις ἰθυδίκοισιν, et al. If it is correct, the poet is anticipating a usage which will become conventional in late antique metrical inscriptions, to praise imperial governors in their capacity as judges (Robert 1948, 13-18, 27; Zito on Maximus, 13; *IEph* 1310 = *BE* 1961, no. 536): examples include Greg. Naz. *AP* 8.135.2 βήμασιν ἰθυδίκοις; *IC* IV 325 (Gortyn, AD 412/13) = *AP* Appendix, *Epigr. Dedicatoria*, no. 324; Roueché 1989, no. 63 = *AP* 16.35.2 (honorific inscription from Aphrodisias for Flavius Palmatus, provincial governor of Caria). Still with the same associations in John Gemetres, *Carm.* 96.3 ἰθυδίκης Θεόδωρος, an epigram for the 10th-c. jurist and official Theodore Decapolites.

515–18

Moon in male, Sun in female signs. The scenario corresponds to 3.372-5, but the outcome is a mixture of that and what the earlier poet reports for feminisation (4.517 ~ 3.378 ἄπρηκτοι). Both independently cohere with Epit. II ('Antiochus', *CCAG* i. 145, reproduced on i. 702).

515 ἐναλλάξωσι: normally of one entity in the house or terms of another (6.670 ἐναλλάξαντες ὅρους; 6.504 ὅρι' ἀλλάξωσιν; Valens, III 1.35 ἐὰν δὲ ἐναλλάξωσι τὰ ὅρια, III 7.15 ἐναλλαγέντος τοῦ ὁρίου; Apomasar, *De Rev.* p. 160.6 ἡ ἐναλλαγὴ τῶν ὁρίων; and see on 6.368 ἐναλλάγδην and p. 251), but here of the location of luminaries in a house of the opposite sect. The intransitive use can be part-paralleled in Valens, II 17.46 (but with οἴκοις ἢ ὁρίοις, derivable as objects, just before), II 17.59 ἐναλλάξαντες. The technical sense is still recognisable. See also on 1.27 ἐναλλάξ ('contrariwise').

516 πολυζώοισιν ἐν ἄστροις: repurposed to stars from livestock (to LSJ add Eustath. on *Il.* 2.605, i. 466.19, a gloss on πολύμηλον, cf. *Epist.* 9 πάνυ τι πολύζωον καὶ ἀγαθοθρέμμονα, of Cos). The epithet continues the self-conscious use of ζῷα for 'constellations' (see 508-10 n.).

---

[320] PHI s.v. parts of κηδεμών, κηδεμονία, κηδεμονικῶς.

517 ἄπρηκτοι ~ 3.378, 373–4 τοῖσιν δ' ἄρα πρήξιες ἔργων | ἄλλως ἐξανύονται ἢ ὡς φρεσὶν ᾗσι μενοίνων.

ἀτόλμοι: this word occurs in other 'inefficacy' clusters (Ptol. 3.14.33, Valens, VI 2.25), but the particular connection here is with Epit. II (see i. 702, on 3.377–8). Of the little sequence on feminisation, ἀτόλμους, παντ<u>α</u>ρβεῖς, θηλυνομένους καὶ τὸ ἐπί<u>παν</u> ἀποκόπους, 3.377–8 echoes the words here underlined. The division of labour between the two is so neat that it looks as if, from a common source, M^b has deliberately seized on what the earlier poet omitted. For this and other examples of complementarity, see p. 219.

518 Ineffectuality is presented as a blunting of the 'soul', the active and, in context, manly principle (i. 306–7) which in these individuals is disabled. It stretches the application of πήρωσις from the senses (especially sight, as in 4.155) to the principle of action and motivation itself. νενεφωμένα could extend the blindness metaphor (cf. Soph. *OT* 1314), but more precisely suggests the ineffectuality or truncation of their projects, with βουλεύοντες corresponding to 3.374 ὡς φρεσὶν ᾗσι μενοίνων. In 4.542–4, another passage concerned with badly-placed luminaries, it is apparently failure to participate in a shared existence that is spoken of as insensibility. For the verse pattern, of which the poet is fond, see on 4.152.

519–26

Both luminaries in female signs. This chart is an expansion of 3.379, where such natives are wanderers (the one detail left after 3.377–8 had been transferred to the crossed-wire scenario). There is no doubt that they are migrants, uncomfortable at home. 4.523–4 and 525–6, although not expressed as a μέν…δέ pair, are complementary.[321] I take the meaning to be that they (somehow) do well abroad—are highly motivated, punctilious—but are blameworthy and negligent with respect to their homes.

519 ἐς θῆλυ καταντήσωσιν: the basic meaning of the verb is to 'reach' a certain point, and among the ways in which astrological prose writers use this verb it is often a matter of counting off along an arc until an end-point is reached.[322] It can also be used of chronocrators entering new places (Valens, V 6.1, VI 6.7).

---

[321] Opposition of home and abroad (but not associated with the Moon): Teucer, *CCAG* vii. 196.7–9 (first decan of Aries) καταλιπεῖν δὲ ἢ φεύξεσθαι τὴν πατρίδα καὶ πολλὴν διελθόντα γῆν καὶ θάλασσαν καὶ ἐπὶ ξένης θαυμασθέντα χρόνῳ ἀντιστρέψειν; 208.8–10 (second decan of Sagittarius) τὰ πατρῷα ἀποβάλλοντας, ξενιτεύοντας ἐπὶ πολλοὺς καὶ ἀκαταστατοῦντας; *CCAG* x. 238.5 (the child born under Sagittarius) εἰς ξένην χώραν δὴ ἀπέλθῃ καὶ εἰς τὴν πατρικὴν οἰκίαν οὐ τελευτήσει.

[322] e.g. Dorotheus, p. 327.2; Ptol. *Synt.* i. p. 144.4; Hephaestion, i. 83.18, 90.18; Valens, IV 29.5, App. VI 4, App. IX *passim*; Camaterus, *Introd.* 3016.

I do not find it used of the motion of a planet into a certain position until Apomasar, *De Rev.* p. 118.16, 207.9, 11 (*et al.*); so too Camaterus, *Introd.* 3024 (of the Moon's *synaphe* with malefics). Since it is properly used of trajectories which have a natural defined limit (rather than simply reaching a location as capacious as an entire sign), it seems that this is a lax use of a technical term.

520 'While the Moon runs to the very boundary of its sign' (Lopilato). Another specification new with respect to the parallels. While -δρομ- compounds suit this poet's vocabulary of rapid motion, this verb form was perhaps inspired by κενοδρομέω (2.486 *et al.*). If there is an analogy between wandering Moon and wandering natives, it is imperfect (since the Moon stays within her bounds but the natives do not), but one grasps the basic logic: she (not the Sun) is iconic for wandering, instability, and perhaps also forgetfulness (see 4.526 n.).

521 πουλυπλανεῖς: see on 4.91.

ξενίης ἐπιβήτορας: see on 4.33, 222; also *Or. Sib.* 3.168 Ἀσίης ἐπιβήτορες.

521-2 ἔσεσθαι | αὐδῶσιν: although most examples of this construction involve a verb of revelation, there are also verbs of announcement (4.252-3 ἔσεσθαι | ἀγγέλλει; 299 ἀναγγέλλουσιν ἔσεσθαι), enunciation (4.39-40 αὔτεῖ | ἔσσεσθαι), and this same verb is introduced by emendation at 422. There are three points about it. One is the implied personification (αὐδή is a human voice; the stars are articulate); another is the implication of, or at least compatibility with, oracular utterance (LSJ I.3; Pind. *P.* 4.61; Or. ap. Demosth. *Or.* 21.52; the examples are enunciated through the human—or divine—voice, in articulate speech); the third is its strong (though not exclusive) association with tragedy.

522 χαίροντας ἀεὶ μεταβλήμασι χώρης: μετάβλημα, which is unique, renders μεταβολαί scannable.[323] Compare especially Valens, I 20.13 ἡδομένους τῇ καινότητι καὶ μεταβολῇ καὶ ξενιτείᾳ (though under different circumstances, a combination of Saturn, Venus, and Mercury).

523-4 The question of punctuation arises here. There is none in the manuscript. Axtius and Rigler (who retained L's reading τιμὴν in 524, before Koechly's correction to the dative) had punctuated after 523, and Lopilato follows them, rendering 'Those who bear the goods of the city to foreigners, having their affairs measured in character and honour' (two accusatives of respect). When Koechly emended τιμὴν to τιμῇ he also removed the comma from the end of 523 and placed it after ἤθεα, thus taking ἤθεα together with σπουδαῖα. Depending on punctuation, that collocation might be supported (although in

---

[323] Valens, IV 12.1 μετατροπαί, μεταβολαὶ τόπων; ps.-Palchus, *CCAG* xi/1. 202.24 μεταβολῆς τόπου καὶ πόλεως; Θ p. 170.1 μεταβολὰς καὶ ξενιτείας ποικίλας. Otherwise: 'Valens', *CCAG* viii/1. 167.12 οἰκίας μεταβάσεις καὶ κινήσεις, ἀποδημίας αἰφνιδίους.

a different setting) by Ptolemy, 3.14.34 εὐαρμόστους, τοῖς ἤθεσι σπουδαίους, although Hübner in his edition places the comma after ἤθεσι (and so do the editors at Θ p. 176.4–5, CCAG v/1. 198.29). πόλεως then presumably becomes an ablatival genitive, and the whole means 'betaking their earnest selves (characters) from the city to foreign peoples'. Still, 523 makes better sense taken as a unit, 'carrying the important matters of the city to outsiders'. Whatever the σπουδαῖα are, the logic is that if a luminary is in a house of the opposite sect, what belongs in a certain place is transferred somewhere else. I do not think, however, that this means betraying their country's secrets.[324] A contrast is drawn between behaviour abroad and at home, the former basically honourable, which is not compatible with treachery.

524 Koechly did not intend his emendation, τιμῇ, to be taken with ἤθεα as well as πράγματ'; the question is whether the hyperbaton with the new punctuation is acceptable. It would mean 'having both their characters and their affairs measured by honour'. For the verse pattern, see on 4.152.

525 ψογερὸν βίον ἰθύνοντας: for the verse pattern see on 4.326. This is the only astrological instance of ψογερόν, which basically means 'scolding' (to LSJ add Ael. VH 3.7, 11.10), and is so understood by Monaco, 49 ('inclini a biasimare la propria patria'). But the combination with βίον makes that difficult; 'blameworthy' or 'reprehensible' is the required sense, found in Hesych. ψ 230 ψογερά· ὡς λίαν μεμπτά and 231 αἰσχρόν, μεμπτόν, ἐπίψογον, though very rare (Eustath. on Od. 13.242, ii. 48.12 τὰ ψογερὰ τῆς νήσου). For a similar manoeuvre, see 4.58 n. 'Blameworthy' behaviour is usually sexual (4.506 n.; 5.68), where identified at all, and/or stigmatised as 'shameful'. I have not found other examples of blameworthiness with regard to the fatherland. The prose words are most often ψόγον, ψόγους, sometimes part of the verb ψογίζεσθαι, ψογιζομένους.

526 οἰκείων...οὐχὶ θυραίων: their own, as opposed to belonging to others (~ ἀλλοτρίων), or 'things at home' versus 'things abroad'. Either way, the background seems to be tragic. The first in Aesch. Ag. 836–7, Eur. Hipp. 395–7; the second in Aesch. Eum. 864–6 θυραῖος ἔστω πόλεμος...ἐνοικίου δ' ὄρνιθος οὐ λέγω μάχην (the closest to this in diction); Soph. fr. 745 Radt κατ' οἶκον/πρὸς θυραίων and Phil. 158 ἔναυλον ἢ θυραῖον. See also on 5.588.

ἐπιλήσμονας: the natives are not unqualifiedly negligent (as in Ptol. 3.14.36 and Περὶ κράσ. 207, the result of badly-placed Mercury), only of their immediate concerns. An exact correspondence is hard to find, but according to Apomasar, De Myst., CCAG xi/1. 184.9 the quality of forgetfulness, or rather of

---

[324] Greek astrology has προδόται, and Firmicus the motif of proditores suorum (3.11.13, 18; 5.6.9; 7.23.27), but not specifically of one's city.

being a *tabula rasa* which takes on the impression of its circumstances, is associated with the Moon. More examples would be welcome.

527–36

Both luminaries in male signs. Representing a contrastive sort of instability: the predominance of feminine influence caused wandering and a lack of moral compass; the preponderance of masculine causes a recklessness which violates social relationships and is unable to commit to a steady path in life. The watery professions and tax-collecting at the end come as a surprise.

527–8 ἀρσενικοῖς…φεγγοβολῶσιν | ζωιδίοις: meaning presumably simply that they are *in* male signs. This verb elsewhere means 'aspect' and takes a straight accusative of the planet concerned (4.264, 366–7, 571). For the verb see on 4.264, and for μίγα on 4.219.

528 ἀνάστερον: first in Aratus, 228 ('having no visible stars', when the Moon dims them out) and 349 (literally 'having no stars'),[325] but now in yet another sense, 'not aspected by any star'.

529 τολμηροί, θρασύθυμα μεμηνότες: cf. Epit. II ('Antiochus', *CCAG* i. 145.15) αὐθάδεις, τολμηρούς (3.370 is lexically further removed). For recklessness, normally a Martian quality, see i. 315. θρασύθυμα is unique but seems to glance at *Il.* 5.639 θρασυμέμνονα θυμολέοντα (epithet of Heracles), which is glossed, precisely, as τολμηρόν by Σ A and Σ rec. (e cod. Genevensi gr. 44) (cf. Hesych. θ 697 θρασυμέμνονα· θρασὺν κατὰ τὸ μένος. γενναῖον. εὔτολμον, τολμηρόν). L¹'s superscript annotation μεμηνότες is interesting in this connection, but hard to interpret.[326]

530 λυμάντορες: see on 2.267; for φιλία and πίστις (Ptol. 3.14.13 ἀφίλους… ἀπίστους; Hephaest. i. 213.5 πίστιν καὶ φιλίας) see i. 313, and Morgan, 55–60, 118–19. There is an illuminating contrast with Theognis, whose outlook also leans heavily on trust, in S. Johnstone, '*Pistis* and Citizens in Ancient Greece', in L. Kontler and M. Somos (eds.), *Trust and Happiness in the History of European Political Thought* (Leiden, 2018), 371–90, at 375–6. For Theognis, friendship was a civic matter, and offence against it a matter of insidious and calculating betrayal. The civic context has now fallen away, and violations of trust are aggressive, violent, and ultimately self-defeating acts of self-harm. For once, in astrology, secrecy and underhand behaviour are not the problem.

---

[325] As also in *Or. Sib.* 5.531 ἀνάστερος αἰθήρ—because the stars have fled. An overcast sky in Anon. *Sylloge tacticorum* 21.1.
[326] Did the annotator mean to suggest a connection with μένος? For the connection of μαίνομαι and μένος see *Il.* 6.100–1; on μένος and anger, Padel, 24–6, 68.

ἀκριτόβουλοι: otherwise Or. Sib. 1.110 (of the chaotic and bloodthirsty fourth generation). Cyril of Alexandria, Comm. in Joann. i. p. 611.19 knows a poem in which it was applied to the mob. With the present passage his elaboration of the word shares the emphasis on anger, fickleness, poor impulse control, and parts of θράσος and τόλμη: ἀκριτόβουλον γάρ πως, κατὰ τοὺς παρ᾽ Ἕλλησι ποιητὰς, καὶ πρόχειρον εἰς ὀργὴν ἀεὶ τὸ πλῆθός ἐστι...καὶ εἰς ἀκάθεκτον θράσος εὐκόλως ἀποταυρούμενον, γοργότερον δέ πως ἤπερ ἐχρῆν εἰς τὰς ἐπὶ τοῖς δεινοῖς ἁλίσκεται τόλμας. Finally, Θ p. 194.7 (in the section on madmen and epileptics) lists ἀκριτοβούλους along with contrarians and boasters, though the emphasis is not on instability. -βουλος compounds in general answer to astrology's interest in mentality and disposition. Those with a negative sense, suggesting either malignity (κακόβουλος, ἐπίβουλος or εὐεπίβουλος; ἐναντιόβουλος, ἀνδρεπίβουλος) or inconsistency (δυσεπίβουλος; εὐμετάβουλος, παλίμβουλος, παράβουλος, πολύβουλος; Maximus, 76 ταχύβουλον), vastly outnumber those with a positive one (καλοσύμβουλος; Περὶ κράσ. 120 τὸ εὔβουλον).

531 νόον ἐκνεύοντες: the poet seems to conflate two expressions, (i) not sticking *to* a single path and (ii) digressing or divagating *from* a steady course. Both are in Firmicus, 6.14.3 *faciet ista coniunctio levitate mentis instabiles, et consilia eorum hac atque illac varia cogitatione transvertit, nec animus eorum aliquando unius consilii ratione utatur*, though the circumstances differ (the Moon in right quartile to Mercury). In a departure from the normal construction, where the accusative is used of that which is being avoided (LSJ I.2; AP 9.371.3), ἐκνεύειν is constructed with νόον as an direct object or internal accusative.

532 ἄλλοτε δ᾽ ἀλλοίην: see on 2.381.

εὔτρεπτον: see on 3.370 ἀτρέπτους, the corresponding chart but opposite meaning.

533 μεθόδους τε πορισμῶν: see on 4.448 ἐξ ὄχλοιο πορισμῶν.

534–5 ἐκ δ᾽ ἐνύδρων μόχθων...δώματα ποιμαίνουσι: watery businesses should be Saturn's domain, as in the similar formulation by Valens, I 20.2 (the combined influence of Saturn, Jupiter, and the Moon) ὅσα δι᾽ ὑγρῶν συνίστανται μεταχειρισάμενοι διῳκονόμησαν τὸν βίον. Otherwise they should be brought about by watery signs (e.g. ἔνυδρα in Hephaestion, i. 232.24–6),[327] for which, as for watery paranatellonta, there is no scope here. It is hard to think of another rationale. For μόχθος, see on 4.248. The poet uses this elsewhere of toilsome professions; it is a loaded formulation for what would otherwise be expressed

---

[327] That is, signs whose *Lebensbereich* is water (Hübner 1982, 171–80, §3.35), not those that cause watery climatic conditions (Hübner 1982, 94–5, §1.433.2). For their impact on careers, see e.g. Ptol. 4.4.9 τὰ δὲ χερσαῖα καὶ τὰ κάθυγρα πρὸς τὰς ἐν ὑγροῖς καὶ δι᾽ ὑγρῶν καὶ τὰς βοτανικὰς καὶ ναυπηγικάς (sc. πράξεις) ~ Θ p. 210.2–4.

with πρᾶξις or πρᾶγμα (e.g. Valens, I 1.7 πάρυγρα πράσσοντας; II 21.6 καθύγρων πραγμάτων) or simply with a nominalised adjective (Valens, IV 20.8 ἐξ ὑγρῶν περικτῶνται, V 8.41 ὑγρῶν). παράλιος is not a common word in astrology, but it clearly means coastal districts in the list of the capacities of the various signs in Laur. plut. 28.34 fo. 156ᵛ Καρκίνος ἐνύδρων τόπων καὶ ἀλσέων καὶ δρυμῶν καὶ τῶν παραλίων καὶ παραποταμίων δρυμῶν καὶ ἐλαιώνων (Ludwich 1877, 119.21–3, misreports the folio as 155ᵛ and δρυμῶν as στρυμόνων).

535 δώματα ποιμαίνουσι: for the phrase pattern, cf. HHom. Dem. 156 (κατὰ) δώματα πορσαίνουσι (also Il. 1.600 (διὰ) δώματα ποιπνύοντα), but at line-end.

535–6 ἐκ λιμένων τελέουσιν…ἦθος ἔχοντες: not only is this type of outcome a surprising result of luminaries in masculine signs; it is remarkably specific. It seems these natives are connected with harbour taxes, not a subject otherwise mentioned in astrology. τελέω should mean pay tax rather than administer it (Koechly: 'ex portubus tributa-dantes'). But if that were the meaning, the poet would surely have identified the natives as e.g. mariners or ship-owners. I therefore interpret ἐκ λιμένων τελέουσιν to mean that they make their living from the farming of harbour taxes, with a catachrestic use of the verb which perhaps hints at their identity as τελῶναι (Appendix II, IV.1.v): that is compatible with 534 ἐκ παράλοιο διαίτης, which should mean making their living *beside* water (rather than *on* it), and it makes better sense of 536, which implies expertise and specialism (rather than simply paying a tax that everyone had to pay). δημοσίων τελέων (Koechly, for τε λόγων) uses δημόσια in the sense of taxes in general (LSJ III.2.b), 'public dues' (D. Rathbone, 'Egypt, Augustus and Roman taxation', *CCG* 4 (1993), 81–112, at 83). There is a similar conjuncture in Valens, I 3.18 τελωνικαί, δημώδεις, where the latter term, which is unique in Greek astrology, can mean neither 'popular' nor 'common'. Riley renders 'in the public eye', but could it be a Greek calque on *publicani*?

536 δημοσίων τελέων ἐμπείραμον: for ἐμπείραμον + genitive, of a specialism or skill, see on 4.88.

ἦθος ἔχοντες: much sympathy with De Stefani's correction to the common hexameter end ἦτορ ἔχ., though Theognis, 964 ἐπίκλοπον ἦθος ἔχοντες prevents L's reading from being completely implausible.

4.537–59 New and Full Moon

537–44 + 545–51

Moon in *synodos* with Sun in setting sign and Full Moon at node.

Protasis. The sequence of three 'mad' or uncanny configurations in Mᵇ very broadly matches up with 6.599–600 + 601–3. There are also parallels for each in

Γενεαί and *τέχναι*

Θ's ch. 65 *Περὶ μαινομένων καὶ ἐπιληπτικῶν*, the second and third in immediate succession (193.16-17, 17-18), and two close but non-exact matches for the first (192.13-14, 20-2). There is a slight difficulty about the agency or agencies involved in the middle one: see on 4.546.

Apodosis. The outcomes are described more wordily than by Mᵃ, together with four remarkable lines of gnomic content (541-5). These lines have a partly epic background in their reference to the insensible souls of the dead, but even in an author who favours tragic vocabulary there is an unusual concentration in this section (see on 539, possibly 540 νοσόθυμον, 555 νερτερόμορφα, 556 κακαγγελίῃσι, and 557 ὀξύγοοι). Firmicus, 4.5.1, for the New Moon, also has a generally depressed state (*miseros deiectos ac miseros facultatibus et ‹in› omni vita humili conversationis deiectione prostratos*) which includes madness (*insanias*).

538 βροτῶν γένος ἔσσετ' ἀμυδρόν: this adjective in astrology usually refers to the quality of the light of a star (especially the Sun or Moon), or to the strength, or rather weakness, of an outcome. That which is described as ἀμυδρόν either produces a weak impression on a sense (often vision), or is intrinsically lacking in force, and this second implication underlies the interpretation of ἀμυδρή, epithet of νοῦσος, as 'chronic' in Maximus, 209 (see Zito ad loc.), and description of an ailing infant in Camaterus, *Zod*. 1203 as living ἀμυδρῶς. If natives are ἀμυδροί, perhaps it is a consequence of the Moon's having been subsumed into the Sun, just as 'setting' planets (those losing their light by sinking into the Sun's vicinity) are repeatedly described as ἀδρανεῖς (i. 622, 623, 624).

539 λυσσαλέῃ μανίῃ δεδαμασμένον: λύσσα is also connected with synodic luminaries in 6.597; with the DESC in 6.573 (Jupiter and Mars); and with both in 6.560. Parts of both words for madness figure in Θ, only the first (in a different adjectival form) in Mᵃ. The natural pair is made slightly less routine by an epithet which is new in Apollonius (Livrea on Ap. Rhod. 4.1393), and perhaps also by the noun-epithet formation itself (with a background in tragedy, cf. Soph. fr. 941.4 Radt λύσσα μανιάς; Eur. *Or*. 326 λύσσας μανιάδος, 845 θεομανεῖ λύσσῃι; also Orph. *Hymn* 66.12 λυσσῶσαν μανίαν). λυσσαλέος is a hypallage, mostly used (and especially by Nonnus) of animate beings or of parts of animate beings (the hands, the voice), not of madness itself, though Nonn. *D*. 12.381 has λυσσαλέης...ἀνάγκης. The cadence is fairly like Nic. *Al*. 29 δεδαμασμένος οἴνῃ. See too *IGUR* iii. 1207 (Rome, undated) νούσου ὑπὸ στυγερῆς δεδαμασμένη.

540 Although the language is not technically medical, the conception is pathological (it will become ethical in 542-5). Madness in 539 perhaps suggested the conceit (which the poet has added: it is not in the comparanda) that drugs are responsible.[328] For φαρμακτόν, see on 4.52, although the referent here

---

[328] Gorgias, *Helen* 14 (they do not directly cause madness, but are compared to artifices which may produce this effect); Aesch. *Ag*. 1407-11; Eur. *Bacch*. 326-7; Quint. *Inst*. 9.2.105 (the *veneficus*

is the individual himself. νοσόθυμος is unique, though perhaps recalling Soph. Trach. 882 τίς θυμός, ἢ τίνες νόσοι (a zeugma: Jebb renders 'What disease of her mind'). Perhaps what requires comment is the choice of θυμός rather than ψυχή: it has a stronger suggestion of irrationality (for Arist. De An. 432^{b}6, the former was one of the irrational parts of the latter), and, insofar as the language is physiological (for the Homeric conception, see Bremmer 1983, 54–6), suggests also the soul's warm, febrile, element (C. Thumiger, *A History of the Mind and Mental Health in Classical Greek Thought* (Cambridge, 2017), 346; Galen, *De causis morborum*, vii. 4.13–15 Kühn). For θανάτοιο πάρεδρον, see on 4.179. As in the tragic instances cited there, one abstract quality is πάρεδρος with another.

541–4 These lines stand out as a gnomic statement which does not set out to explain the (supposed) theoretical (physical, analogical) basis for the outcome, as γάρ clauses sometimes do (4.91 n.), but simply moralises. They are also remarkably complex, for they contain ideas from several different backgrounds which are not perfectly brought together. First, the poet plays on the tension between the ψυχή as metonymic for the person (such as he is) and the Homeric ψυχή, of which we hear only at moments of crisis when it vacates the body, temporarily or permanently (Bremmer 1983, 15–16). But these souls are dead before their time because setting planets in a position of weakness produce a quasi-analogical effect of enfeeblement and insensibility. This is further combined with the medical notion of δυσκρασίη, or imbalance of temperament (cf. Galen, *De temperamentis*, ed. G. Helmreich (Leipzig, 1904), transl. P. N. Singer and P. J. van der Eijk, *Galen: Works on Human Nature*, i: *Mixtures* (*De temperamentis*) (Cambridge, 2018)), which rests on the idea of one element or elements in a mixture getting out of hand. And all this, in turn, is overlaid by an ethical disapproval of antisociality which may be connected with either or both of feebleness or imbalance, but in ways which are not fully worked out.

541–2 ἐπὴν τά γε κοινὰ βίοιο | μὴ φρονέῃ κατὰ θυμόν: when a man is not disposed in a social way (towards his fellow human-beings). The first half of 542 is built upon *Il.* 10.491 τὰ φρονέων κατὰ θυμόν, and the construction is φρονεῖν with a neuter plural adjective (LSJ II.2.a), unusually expanded with a definite article (and frankly desperate γε) and dependent genitive. This is the antisociality astrology finds so problematic, the converse of the sociable qualities which are connected with manliness and efficacy (approving references to κοινωνία and the κοινωνικός throughout Ptol. 2.3, Valens, and Hephaestion[329]),

---

is not only one who destroys a life, but also destroys a mind, *mentem*); Theophr. *Hist. Plant*. 9.11.6, with Faraone, 127–8. Associated with magic: ps.-Apollod. 1.9.26; Faraone, 117.

[329] Epit. II = *CCAG* i. 160.22 and Rhetorius, *CCAG* vii. 222.1–5 give good examples of the range of its positive associations.

and the converse, too, of what is recommended by ps.-Phoc. 30 ἔστω κοινὸς ἅπας ὁ βίος καὶ ὁμόφρονα πάντα (see van der Horst ad loc., interpreting that 'one should share with one another the vitally important things needed to stay alive' and that 'there should also be unity of mind and feeling'). However, the present conception pits social sharing against a kind of dull autism or insensibility, which differs from the more political antithesis of ὁμόνοια versus disagreement and discord (Chrysippus, *SVF* fr. 625 von Arnim (ap. Stob. 2.7.11b) Τήν τε ὁμόνοιαν ἐπιστήμην εἶναι κοινῶν ἀγαθῶν, δι' ὃ καὶ τοὺς σπουδαίους πάντας ὁμονοεῖν ἀλλήλοις διὰ τὸ συμφωνεῖν ἐν τοῖς κατὰ τὸν βίον, τοὺς δὲ φαύλους διαφωνοῦντας πρὸς ἀλλήλους ἐχθροὺς εἶναι καὶ κακοποιητικοὺς ἀλλήλων καὶ πολεμίους).

542-3 ἀναισθήτῳ τε παλαίῃ | δυσκρασίῃ: the imprecise expression evokes the idea of old age, conceivable as a time of humoral imbalance (K. Cokayne, *Experiencing Old Age in Ancient Rome* (London, 2003), 34-7), and of both old age and death itself as a state of ἀναισθησία.[330] The natives are not necessarily old, nor yet dead, but their insensibility inclines them towards both states. The Pythagorean writer Hippon explained that the senses of the elderly were blunted precisely because of an imbalance in the constitution (38 B 11 D.-K. ὅταν δὲ ἀναξηρανθῆι, ἀναισθητεῖ δὲ τὸ ζῷον καὶ ἀποθνήισκει. διὰ δὴ τοῦτο οἱ γέροντες ξηροὶ καὶ ἀναίσθητοι, ὅτι χωρὶς ὑγρότητος).

543 καὶ ἢν φάος ὄμμασι λεύσσῃ: see on 6.44-5, 165 for 'seeing the light of day' expressions (Hes. *Th.* 451, al.); the hexameter ending first in Nic. *Ther.* 457 ὄμμασι λεύσσων, thence LGHP.

544 νεκύεσσιν ὁμοίη: the dative plural is Homeric and evokes the Homeric conception of the dead. The formula νεκύων ἀμενηνὰ κάρηνα was taken to mean ἀσθενῆ, μένος οὐκ ἔχοντα, ἢ σώματος δύναμιν (Σ *Od.* 10.521)—words which suit a state of affairs brought about by torpid stars (4.538 n.). On the other hand, it is hard to explain ἀμαθής, even by appeal to the epic trope of the lack of purposeful intelligence in Hades;[331] ἀπαθής would be more compatible with ἀναισθήτῳ two lines before. The many variations and adaptations of the cadence of *Il* 17.51 Χαρίτεσσιν ὁμοῖαι (TLG s.v. -εσσιν ὁμοι-) have long effaced any direct connection with that verse.

545-6 M^b and Θ agree that σύνδεσμος (the Moon crossing the node) takes place when she is Full. (M^a mentions σύνδεσμος in 6.601, but in a separate chart

---

[330] Thuc. 2.43.6; Epicurus, *Kuriai Doxai* 2, ap. Diog. Laert. 10.139, Aretaeus, *De Caus. et Sign. Diut. Morb.* 1.6.2, etc. ἀναισθησία is also the state from which the blood-drinking awakened the Odyssean νεκύων ἀμενηνὰ κάρηνα (which will be suggested by 4.544): Porphyry, *Quaest. Hom. ad Od. pertinentes*, 11.29-30 ... εἰ μὴ αἰσθάνονται πρὸ τοῦ πιεῖν τὸ αἷμα.

[331] Bremmer 1983, 84-5; *Il.* 23.104 ἀτὰρ φρένες οὐκ ἔνι πάμπαν; *Od.* 11.476 ἀφραδέες; Sourvinou-Inwood, 76.

involving Mars.) But M^b seems to have an additional specification concealed beneath 546 ῥυσμοῖο, which Koechly tried to remedy by introducing a reference to Saturn; he pointed out that 4.552 σὺν τοῖσι suggests that more than one entity is present. It is true that Θ p. 193.20-2 (in what corresponds to the *first* chart in this sequence) reports that the Moon is aspected by Saturn, in the absence of benefics. Nonetheless it is hard to see what a 'σύνδεσμος of Kronos' would be, and in Θ p. 193.16-17 it is simply a matter of the Full Moon at node. Hence I correct ῥυσμοῖο to κόσμοιο, and συνδέσμους to συνδέσμῳ, suggesting that it was the iota written adscript that gave rise to the accusative plural ending -ς : all the remaining four references to the Moon at node in the Manethoniana employ the singular. The redundant reference to the κόσμος is entirely in M^b's style (pp. 182, 211; κόσμοιο itself in this *sedes* in 4.482). Explaining 4.552 σὺν τοῖσι is harder. Perhaps it refers to the Sun and Moon. The two agencies were introduced at 537, and the reference to the Full Moon in 545 shows that they are both still in play.

545 πάμμηνα κέλευθα: the epithet is to be added to the epithets of phase in i. 904. The phrase refits Homeric λαιψηρὰ κέλευθα with an epithet for the Full Moon, perhaps under the influence of Dorotheus, pp. 393.18, cf. 394.8; in transforming an epithet which, in Sophocles, had meant 'throughout all the months' (*El.* 851) into an astronomical term, Dorotheus himself perhaps had impetus from Aratus, 189 νυκτὶ…παμμήνιδι (p. 218).

546 σεληνιόωντα φανείη: for the Moon-struck, see on 4.81, and for the optative i. 143. The present passage contains most of the elements in the lunacy 'bundle' (nn. on 4.78-82^a and 80-1), including divine possession (Temkin, 86-92) and prophecy, but not epilepsy (i. 357), for physical symptoms have been entirely effaced in favour of mental disturbances. 4.81 and 217 accommodate prose σεληνιάζειν by dropping the ι, the present passage (uniquely) by changing the suffix. The resulting verse pattern (and phonology) is similar to (e.g.) *Il.* 5.417 κατηπιόωντο βαρεῖαι.

547 φῦλα βροτῶν: see on 2.16.

εἰδώλοισιν ὅμοια: by adapting formulae like ἀθανάτοισιν ὁμοῖος, ἐτύμοισιν ὁμοῖα, the poet has made these persons doubly nebulous, for they are not even themselves, only 'like' something that is itself an image. For εἴδωλα as images or shades, see Bremmer 1983, 78-80; Sourvinou-Inwood, 56, 58 n. 136. The paradox (whether or not the poet was deliberately playing on it) is that the εἴδωλον is so-called because of its likeness to the real person (cf. *Il.* 5.449-50 εἴδωλον… αὐτῷ τ' Αἰνείᾳ ἴκελον, 23.107 [ψυχὴ καὶ εἴδωλον] ἔικτο δὲ θέσκελον αὐτῷ, *Od.* 4.796 εἴδωλον ποίησε, δέμας δ' ἤικτο γυναικί), whereas for these living shadows it is the other way round.

548-51 This account of inspired prophecy has echoes of the *Phaedrus'* account of the first type of madness. Prophecy is of divine origin (548 θεόληπτα ~ 244 A μανίας, θεία μέντοι δόσει διδομένης), and perhaps specifically Apolline, if φοιβητοῖς μύθοισιν can be taken at face value (265 B). It happens when the rational part of the soul is impotent (548 ἀκρατέοντι λογισμῷ; the participle also happens to evoke another familiar theme in Plato and Aristotle, the critique of weakness of the will or ἀκράτεια, and the very rare verb ἀκρατεῖν occurs twice in the form ἀκρατέεσθαι in *Σ* Arist. *EN* 1145^{b}22, a summary of Socrates' position on error in the *Protagoras*). The prophecies are ἔνσοφα but ἄβουλα (549). This recalls the motif of prophetic unknowingness, the state in which the inspired make many excellent pronouncements without their conscious will being engaged (Plat. *Apol.* 22 C, *Meno* 99 C ἴσασιν δὲ οὐδὲν ὧν λέγουσι) which is also replayed against a Platonic background in the Sibylline Oracles (Lightfoot 2007, 10), and in a comparably strong form in *Or. Sib.* 13.5 ἀέκουσαν. Finally, 4.549 προλέγοντα (cf. 551 ἐσσομένων ἔργων) recalls the wording of 244 B πολλὰ δὴ πολλοῖς προλέγοντες εἰς τὸ μέλλον ὤρθωσαν.

548 **θεόλημπτα**: see on 4.80 (and for the orthography on 6.378).

549 **ἔνσοφα**: a small divergence from Plato, who has his inspired poets (not prophets, however) speak οὐ σοφίᾳ...ἀλλὰ φύσει τινί (*Apol.* 22 B–C). Extremely rare, the adjective recurs in poetry only in a dedicatory epigram, *IGUR* i. 126 (Rome, 2nd half of 4th c. AD) ἔνσοφοι ἄνδρες, where it describes two men, one of them a *quindecimvir sacris faciundis* (Groag, *RE* s.v. Crescens, 6), who dedicate a taurobolic altar to the Mother of the Gods. Their expertise consists in τελεταί.

πολλὰ: I have resisted Koechly's emendation πάντα (as does De Stefani) because the manuscript reading is closer to *Apol.* 22 C καὶ γὰρ οὗτοι λέγουσι μὲν πολλὰ καὶ καλά, *Meno* 99 C ἐνθουσιῶντες λέγουσιν μὲν ἀληθῆ καὶ πολλά, *Phaedr.* 244 B πολλὰ δὴ πολλοῖς προλέγοντες.

κατ' ἀνθρώπους: the merits of Koechly's restoration (κατ' for καὶ) are discussed by T. Mommsen, 214 n. 55. The EGHP associations of the phrase are probably supportive: in Hes. *Op.* 100 it is used of something—in this case evils—disseminated abroad. Whether one chooses κατ' or Axtius' conjecture μετ', Platonic passages on prophecy do not claim a universal range (in *Phaedr.* 244 B the scope of the priestesses in Delphi and Dodona is Hellas), though the Sibyl does (3.812 ὥστε προφητεῦσαί με βροτοῖς αἰνίγματα θεῖα; fr. 1.1 Ἄνθρωποι; fr. 4 κλῦτε δέ μου, μέροπες).

550 **φοιβητοῖς**: see on 6.491-3. This is the only example of the verbal adjective. Agent nouns appear in 1.237 φοιβητάς (Venus enclosed by malefics, aspecting Moon and Mercury in quartile), Hesych. φ 681 φοιβήτρια, Orph. *Lith.* 389 φοιβήτορι.

ἀποφθεγκτήρια κρυπτά: obscure pronouncements. The suffix produces an exotic derivative from ἀποφθέγγεσθαι in a sense which is not completely specialised to astrology, but very characteristic of it. (Other examples are Lucian, *Alex.* 25 χρησμὸν ἀπεφθέγξατο, with a direct object never found in astrology; LXX 1 Chr. 25:1 τοὺς ἀποφθεγγομένους, which LSJ renders 'chant hymns', but which most versions of the Bible render more plausibly with the verb 'prophesy'.[332]) Makers of 'pronouncements', in its impressively opaque idiom, are seers, savants, mentioned in connection with other possessors of arcane knowledge, or else the mad, the epileptic, the hangers-on in temples (i. 359). They are born under various circumstances, but most similar to this is Valens, II 37.43 μανιώδεις, ἐκστατικούς, πτωματικούς, ἀποφθεγγομένους (the malefics in some aspectual relation with the Moon at or after Full or New). Ptolemy also involves the luminaries in producing this outcome (3.9.4, 4.4.10), while other charts have various configurations of malefics (especially in the third and ninth places).[333]

551 ζωῆς τε κελεύθων: the last instance of κέλευθος in the book is the only one used of human life. The (bounded) journey of life is a sepulchral commonplace;[334] the novelty of this passage (as also of 4.169) is that it here becomes a thing to be predicted, instead of recorded *ex post facto*. Perhaps that leap is possible because astrology itself thinks in the same way. Veyne illustrates the metaphor's suggestiveness and ability to be combined with other motifs (for instance the *cursus honorum* or stately progress), one of which is the sundial as a tomb-marker; from that it is not far to its obvious aptness for astrology, where life can be analogised to the trajectories of planets and *vice versa*. The poet's transference of his habitual use of κέλευθος for stars to life[335] represents this on the level of diction. The conceptual metaphor has already been discussed in the

---

[332] Contrast Paul in Acts 26:25 Οὐ μαίνομαι...ἀλλὰ ἀληθείας καὶ σωφροσύνης ῥήματα ἀποφθέγγομαι.

[333] Valens, II 17.49, II 37.36 ~ Θ p. 193.19–20; Θ pp. 147.15, 165.3–4, 194.3–4.

[334] W. Weber, *Die Darstellungen einer Wagenfahrt auf römischen Sarkophagdeckeln und Loculusplatten des 3. und 4. Jahrhunderts n. Chr.* (Rome, 1978), esp. 124–33; P. Veyne, 'Les saluts aux dieux, le voyage de cette vie et la "réception" en iconographie', *RA* 1985, 47–61, at 56–60; Latin examples in 58 n. 48. Not the other commonplace, that one has a choice of ways (Lightfoot 2007, 460 and bibliography in n. 40). An early comparison of life to a road (Democritus, 68 B 230 D.-K. βίος ἀνεόρταστος μακρὴ ὁδὸς ἀπανδόκευτος/'life without festivity is like a long journey without inns') lacks the idea of limit, as does περιπατεῖν in the sense 'live' (LSJ 3, though Philod. *De Libertate Dicendi*, 23.3 falls away with Olivieri's supplements; Bertram and Seesemann, *TDNT* v. 940–5, s.v. *Pateō*, sense 3).

[335] Also *TAM* III.1 590.2–3 (Termessos) ξοινὴ δὲ ἰθεῖα κέλευθος | ἔσκε βίου; *IGLS* XIII,1 9434.1–2 (Bostra) οὔποτ' [ἴση]ν βιότοιο | βροτοὶ β[αίν]ουσι κέλευθον; Greg. Naz. *AP* 8.29.4 βίου τμήξασα κέλευθον; Christodorus, *AP* 2.1.134 σφαλερὰς...βιότοιο κελεύθους, Agathias, *AP* 4.3.124 βιότοιο πολυσπερέεσσι κελεύθοις.

methods of calculating the length of life, especially the one which distributes it along an arc between an ἀφέτης, which set the ball rolling, and an ἀναιρέτης, which brings its trajectory to an end (see on 3.399–438). It is used again by a different poet at 5.242 βίοτον διοδεύει (see ad loc.).

552-9

As above, with the addition of Mars.

552 αἰθαλόεις: 4.319 n. and i. 909 n. 24.

553 I take ἐν κύκλοισι with Mars, referring to its orbit (cf. pseudo-pagan verses ap. Clem. Al. *Strom.* 5.14.107.4, where the same prepositional phrase refers to all the planets), whereas the second dative, δινήματι, refers to the entire cosmic whirl. δίνημα is new, but for δίνη and θοός see on i. 539 (θοός of the entire heavens already in 2.109). With the verse pattern, compare Planudes' version of Parmenides, 28 B 8.43 D.-K. πάντοθεν ἐν κύκλοισι φέρειν ἐναλίγκιον ὄγκον (Boethii de philosophiae consolatione, 3.52.37, a description of the Divine Essence); and with the cadence Crinagoras, *AP* 9.430.7 = Garland 1993 τερένης μυκήματι μόσχου; Nonn. *D.* 28.272 μιῆς μυκήματι φωνῆς.

554 φάσμασι δαιμονίοισι: the only use of φάσμα, 'manifestation', in an astrological outcome. On its range of meanings, see J.-P. Vernant, '«Psychè»: Simulacro del corpo o immagine del divino?', in B. Bettini (ed.), *La maschera, il doppio e il ritratto: Strategie dell'identità* (Rome, 1991), 3–11, esp. 3–6; C. Thumiger, 'Vision and Knowledge in Greek Tragedy', *Helios*, 40 (2013), 223–45, at 231–2 (specifically on tragedy); Petridou, 64–71. As illusions they belong in the company of εἴδωλα of 547 and 558, but are more specifically conceived as the ghosts of the dead (cf. Eur. *Alc.* 1127; Origen, *Cels.* 7.35). Calling them 'daemonic' recalls the hocus-pocus that Lucian sends up in the mouth of Eucrates (*Philops.* 29 ἡγεῖσθαι δαίμονάς τινας εἶναι καὶ φάσματα καὶ νεκρῶν ψυχὰς περιπολεῖν ὑπὲρ γῆς καὶ φαίνεσθαι οἷς ἂν ἐθέλωσιν), but M[b] himself is non-committal on their truth-value. ψυχῇ δερκόμενοι in the next line implies that the experience of visionaries is 'psychical', subjectively perceived, but after that the poet seems to admit that natives *do* receive divine disclosures (see on 556) and in 559 is entirely happy to talk about Hecate. His aim is achieved provided he evokes their uncanny and terrifying character.[336]

---

[336] φάσματα and fear: Dion. Hal. *AR* 5.16.3; Plut. *Solon*, 12.6, *Cimon*, 6.6; HOrph. 71.6; Greg. Nyss. *PG* 46.952.22–4, al. F. Graf, 'Serious Singing: The Orphic Hymns as Religious Texts', *Kernos*, 22 (2009), 169–82, reads the Orphic Hymns as attempts to head off encounters with real deities or apparitions—*phasmata*—in a malign mood.

555 There are two ways of interpreting this construction. The first takes νεκροειδῆ, νερτερόμορφα as the direct objects of δερκόμενοι, in which case this is the topos of seeing visions of the dead (i. 360, and 4.365 n.). The second takes them as internal or adverbial accusatives, 'look deathly', a construction possible with both singular and plural neuter adjectives (LSJ δέρκομαι, I.1). D'Orville understood the latter (303: 'non sunt umbris videndae inferorum formae, sed moribundam faciem habentes formae morticinae'), Koechly and Lopilato the former. I think this is likelier, although Koechly's own correction of L's νεκροδερκῆ introduces a very rare word which, in its other occurrences, does not refer to the dead, but to the living who approach that state (ps.-John Chrys. PG 55.632.20 and Vita Sancti Apostili Marci, 4 νεκροειδεῖς...ἐθεράπευσε). But νερτερόμορφα, which is new, looks to have been inspired by Eur. Alc. 1127 ὅρα δὲ μή τι φάσμα νερτέρων τόδ᾽ ἦι. In the play, that was an unpleasant possibility (though did not happen); ψυχῆ now locates the experience in the psyche rather than in a world-view which definitely endorsed the objective existence of ghosts (see also on 1.232).

556 The line means apparently that the natives receive divine communications (another loose use of ἐν: p. 202). D'Orville's correction μηνύμασι is as good as certain; what is meant is illustrated by HOrph. 86.16, where the hymnode asks Oneiros, the personification of prophetic dreams, to disclose θεῶν μηνύματα (the phrase is parallel to γνώμας μακάρων in the fifth line). LSJ's rendering of that passage and the present one as 'evocations' (III) is completely off the mark: what is meant are informations, indications, disclosures. It is less easy to decide between L's καταγγελίαισι and Lobeck's κακαγγελίῃσι. 'Announcements' of some sort are clearly appropriate; the Orphic Hymn called Oneiros ἄγγελε μελλόντων (2). κατ- would be neutral communications, κακ- bad ones; the somewhat similar configuration in 6.625 (luminaries in opposition, as here, or quartile, and Mars again present) where the natives cry out against the gods also involves *bad* utterance, although it goes in the opposite direction. This would be the only poetic instance of κακαγγελία, but κακάγγελος began its career in tragedy (Ag. 636–7 κακαγγέλωι | γλώσσηι, cf. Soph. Antig. 1286 κακάγγελτά μοι).

557 ὀξύγοοι: Koechly's ὀξύγοοι for L's ὀξύχολοι has advantage of introducing more tragic vocabulary (p. 216): the only other occurrence is Aesch. Sept. 320 ὀξυγόοις λιταῖσιν.

ἀθρήσουσιν: for the use of ἀθρεῖν for 'experience' or 'endure', compare 4.390 φάος σπανάδελφον ἐσαθρῶν, where the use of star-terminology for humans is even more glaring (n. ad loc.).

558 εἰδώλων στονόεντα τύπον: the reference to εἴδωλα suggests some connection with the account of Mars in right quartile to the Moon in Περὶ σχημ. 52,

Γενεαί and τέχναι 721

but the poet again employs a formulation that evades a position on their reality: what is seen is an impression (compare Valens, II 37.43 θεῶν ἢ νεκρῶν εἰδωλοποιητάς 'makers, i.e. seers, of phantoms' and nn. on 1.229-34, 232). See Livrea on Ap. Rhod. 4.1005 on the EGHP *iuncturae* of the epithet. This passage, straddling the caesura, is most like *HHom.* 27.6 and Quint. Smyrn. 6.530, 13.335 στονόεντα βέλη, Quint. Smyrn. 9.139 στονόεντα μόθον, 9.404 στονόεντα χόλον.

559 Hecate specialises in sending ((ἐπι)πέμπειν) apparitions (φάσματα/ φαντάσματα),[337] or is credited with their impetus (various words for attack, προσβολή, ἐπιβολή etc.) (Jouanna on Hippocr. *Morb. Sacr.* 1.11 n. 9), but this goes unusually far in making her fashion them, using the word for a craftsman moulding images. πλάστειρα is rare, not unique (title of Physis in *HOrph.* 10.20 and Damocharis, *AP* 16.310.1), but the basic phrase is εἴδωλα πλάσσειν/πλάσσεσθαι (Democritus, 68 B 119 D.-K.; Plut. *Sull.* 38.2; Lucian, *Dial. Deor.* 9.4, al.).

πικροῦ θαμβήματος: the expression is hybrid. The epithet is better suited to fear, which in Hecate's usual lexicon is φοβεῖν/φόβος/φοβερά,[338] but θάμβος is a word proper to divine epiphany (Petridou, 88) or to visions (including in Theodotion's version of Daniel 8:17). The LSJ entries for θάμβος and θαμβέω should single out this special sense, as *LfrgrE* does, from the basic meaning 'be amazed at'. In 4.365 θάμβησιν is once again fear that arises specifically in connection with apparitions (φαντάσματα). θάμβημα occurs here for the first time, and there are only five occurrences in all. A good parallel for ghosts—the ultimate parallel, in fact—is Romanus Melodus, *Cantica*, 42.14 οὐ ταῖς φρεσὶ θάμβημα, insisting that the vision of the resurrected Christ was *no* illusion. Less edifying is Cyril, *Comm. in Isaiam*, PG 70.621.10-11 τοῦτό ἐστι φάσμα, τοῦτ᾽ ἔστι κατάπληξις, καὶ οἷόν τι θάμβημα (the visionaries were simply drunk).

4.560-92 Aspects Across *Kentra*

Compare 3.132-226. These versions tend to be wordier. Usually each planet has a whole line to itself, whereas in book 3 it had half a line (p. 210). However, there are exceptions to both. Book 3's usual pattern is also found in 4.560, book 4's in 3.207.

---

[337] Roscher, s.v. Hekate (Roscher), 1894.19-34; Heckenbach, *RE* s.v. Hekate, 2774.27-30; M. P. Nilsson, *Geschichte der griechischen Religion*, i: *Die Religion Griechenlands bis auf die griechische Weltherrschaft* (Munich, ³1967), 724; Johnston, 203-4, and ead., *Hekate Soteira: A Study of Hekate's Roles in the Chaldaean Oracles and Related Literature* (Atlanta, GA, 1990), 34-5, 135-6; Petridou, 65-6, 209 n. 75; Eur. *Hel.* 569; Σ Ap. Rhod. 3.861; *Suda*, ε 1049; Or. ap. Euseb. *PE* 4.23.7 = Porphyry, *De philosophia ex oraculis haurienda*, p. 151.3 Wolff κόρη πολυφάσματος; Σ Lyc. *Al.* 1030 ἡ Ἑκάτη φαντασμάτων αἰτία.

[338] Hippocr. *Morb. Sacr.* 1.11; Tr. Adesp. 375 K.-S.; *Hymnus in Hecatam* (LIV Heitsch), 6 φόβον θνητοῖσι φέρουσα; Σ Ap. Rhod. 3.861; Heckenbach, *RE* s.v. Hekate, 2776.16-18.

560–6

Saturn in MC, Mars in DESC. Counter-intuitively, this is in fact a πρᾶξις configuration, though there is nothing to match in Ptolemy himself. While Θ p. 212.24–5 has only the one focus, an ethnic one (I take ἀλλοφύλους to mean that they adopt foreign customs or live overseas, not that they *are* ethnically non-Greek), M^b expands this into a portrait of the misanthrope; from this perspective, impiety towards the gods forms the natural complement to antisociality or sociopathy. Note the remarkable number of works for mentalities, which in this individual have gone very badly astray (φρεσίν, λογισμῷ, ἀλλόφρων, κακόθυμος, ἐπιθύμιος, ἀφροσύνην ἀλόγιστον). Koechly took this as a reference to Christians (p. 178), and derived from it an argument that the book was written under Julian. But the attitudes are conventional ones directed towards any non-conformist or recluse.

561–2 The combination of 'atheists' and misanthropes, easy to understand from an ancient perspective, often happens in connection with Mars and/or Saturn (2.301–3 n.; Ptol. 3.14.15 ἀθέους, ἀστόργους, 28 μισοικείους, ἀθέους, 32; Περὶ κράσ. 150 ἄθεοι, μισοίκειοι; Valens, I 20.6 ἀθέους…μισοϊδίους, τῆς ἰδίας χωριζομένους, μετὰ ἀλλοφύλων ἀναστρεφομένους. Also in Valens, I 2.67 μισάνθρωποι, ἄθεοι (under Aquarius, sign of Saturn); Θ p. 179.21–2 ἀθέους, ἀφίλους (the effect of various bright stars in daytime nativities).

561 μισέλλην: the word is unique in astrology to these two passages. I interpret it, certainly in M^b and probably also in Θ (though the lack of supporting detail makes it possible that M^b has changed the emphasis), to refer to Greeks who shun their fellow Greeks, hostile to their own race (γενέθλῃ, uniquely in the corpus in this sense), though otherwise it is used of non-Greeks who hate Greeks for ethnic reasons (LSJ + Diod. Sic. 13.43.6; Σ bT *Il*. 1.454), or of Christians hostile to pagan culture (Euseb. *PE* 14.2.7), and once of Zeus' partisanship (or otherwise) in the Trojan war (Σ bT *Il*. 8.134).

562 ἄνομος, κτλ.: one might have expected astrology, with its communitarian outlook, its conventional value-system and suspicion of the outsider, to make much of this type of delinquent, but it does not. The adjective is not found in any of the mainstream astrological texts (Ptolemy, Dorotheus, Valens, Hephaestion), and is confined to late outliers like the treatises on brontology or predictions from zodiacal signs which are written in very late Greek. Nor does Artemidorus use it. I adopt De Stefani's λήθοντι because πλήθοντι clearly will not do; the sense should be 'defective', as in 4.548 ἀκρατέοντι. If the Moon can λανθάνειν, can reason? Or might one consider πλαγχθέντι (for ἀποπλαγχθέντι)?

563 ἀλλόφρων: LSJ renders 'thinking differently', but a sense based on the usual meaning of the verb ἀλλοφρονεῖν, 'be out of one's mind', 'be deranged',

Γενεαί and τέχναι 723

would also be suitable, given the whole 'Cambyses' complex of *anomia* linked to madness (see e.g. ps.-Polemon, 9 ἔργα ἄνομα, ἅπερ αὐτῶν ἡ ψυχὴ μαινομένη ποιήσει; Plut. Mor. 1048 Ε μαίνεσθαι πάντας, ἀφραίνειν, ἀνοσίους εἶναι, παρανόμους). The adjective is unique except for Theodorus Studites (8th/9th c.), which in the context of heterodox or wavering faith is little help (Μεγάλη Κατήχησις, 21, p. 154 ἑτερόψυχον καὶ ἀλλόφρονα καὶ γνωμικῶς διασχιζόμενον).

δύσμικτος: the most influential instance of this word is undoubtedly Plat. *Tim.* 35 A, where it is used of the composite nature of the soul, and it also has physical and political applications. In an ethical sense, Galen uses it in his exposition of a Platonic passage discussing an intransigent individual (*Theaet.* 155 E σκληρούς γε λέγεις καὶ ἀντιτύπους ἀνθρώπους), proposing that this individual is μονότροπον καὶ δυσπειθῆ καὶ πρὸς ἅπαν ἀντιτείνοντα (viii. 689.11, 16-17 Kühn). Pollux includes both the adjective in a collection of synonyms for loners and misfits (3.64 δύσμικτος, μισέταιρος, μισάνθρωπος, ἀπάνθρωπος) and the adverb in the company of other words for gauche, unkind, rude, or hostile behaviour (5.139 δυσμίκτως...σκυθρωπῶς, ἀγρίως, σκαιῶς, ἀργαλέως, δυσμενῶς, σκληρῶς, τραχέως, ἀπανθρώπως). And the Hesiod scholia use it of the sociopaths of the Bronze Age (Σ *Op.* 152-6). Places, too are δύσμικτα if they are inaccessible (Pollux, 9.33).

ἀμετροεπής: the associations with Thersites (*Il.* 2.212) could not escape an ancient reader; if one accepts it (De Stefani is dubious), is it warrantable because Thersites is an outsider and (although he purports to speak for them) rejected by his community (*Il.* 2.270-7)? See H. D. Rankin, 'Thersites the Malcontent: A Discussion', *SO* 47 (1972), 36-60, at 44: 'the poet suggests that Thersites speaks for nobody but himself, and that he is isolated'; 54: 'a social outcaste [*sic*]'.

δολοεργός: see on 4.57. Although they do not use this word, many 'atheist' configurations have delinquents who practise deceit in some way: ψεύστας in 2.301 (see 2.301-3 n.) and Ptol. 3.14.32; κλέπτας, ἐπιόρκους in Ptol. 3.14.15 and Π.τ.δ. 16 (plus πλαστογράφους); also Ptol. 2.3.31 ἐπιβουλευτικοί; Valens, I 2.67 δόλιοι, ἀποκρυπτόμενοι πάντα, I 20.6 προδότας, 9 ἐπίορκοι; App. X 9 ἐπιορκοῦντας.

564 αὐτόνομος: the only other occurrence in astrology is Ptol. 2.3.19 φιλελεύθεροι δὲ καὶ αὐτόνομοι καὶ δημοκρατικοὶ καὶ νομοθετικοί, where it is a Jovian quality and describes the political temperament of the Greek nation: good for a people, dubious for an individual.

κακόθυμος ($Π^1$ κακόθοινος): L's epithet is rare, the papyrus' unique. Both are meaningful in the context. Monaco, 58 feels called upon to choose, and opts for κακόθοινος, which obviously reinforces the theme of 'bad dining' (see next note). But L's reading is defensible as well (De Stefani 2017, 26: 'scheinbar richtig'). Most of the other occurrences of the epithet are in physiognomy, in passages (i) which analogise people with a certain kind of mouth formations to dogs (Adamantius, 2.24 κακόθυμοι, ὑβρισταί, κράκται, ἐπεσβόλοι ~ ps.-Polemon, 33) and (ii) which characterise 'asthmatics' (those with heaving breath) as ἄβουλοι, κακόθυμοι, παντορέκται, παντοεπεῖς (Adamantius, 2.41)/ἄβουλοι, κακόθυμοι, παντεπίθυμοι, παντολόγοι (ps.-Polemon 30). In both cases the implication is of a lack of control, which is not exactly what the present context implies, but closer is the way Plutarch uses κακοθυμία (which is unique to him). If a single word can render the sense in all four passages, that word would be 'malevolence', and in each case it is a state of mind which sunders a person from his or her fellows (*Mor.* 465 D, 487 E, 567 B, *Lycurg.* 4.2).[339] That is exactly the case here. Once again, the recensions have equal valence.

ἀθεσμοφάγος: this epicises ἀθεμιτοφάγος, a piece of astrological jargon, which seems to signify different kinds of malpractice. One must assume that authors who use it reflect a pagan, not a Jewish or Christian perspective: they were formulated within a culture that was extremely tolerant in dietetics and in which restrictions were embraced only by certain philosophical sects or formulated for certain priests (P. Garnsey, *Food and Society in Classical Antiquity* (Cambridge, 1999), 82–99, esp. 83–91; M. Beer, *Taste or Taboo: Dietary Choices in Antiquity* (Totnes, 2010)). It is not a matter of universal food taboos or Christian asceticism. In the present passage it is about antisociality, not sharing food or sitting at the same table; this is broadly also the context in Ptol. 3.14.15 ἀθεμιτοφάγους (Saturn allied with Mars in bad places). The emphasis is on irreligion/heterodoxy in Valens, IV 15.4 τινὲς δὲ καὶ κατ' ἐκείνους τοὺς χρόνους ἀρνοῦνται τὰ θεῖα καὶ ἑτεροσεβοῦσιν ἢ ἀθεμιτοφαγοῦσιν, while the idea of eating, consumption, indulgence, suggests other sorts of corporeal (sexual) abuses in Θ p. 196.5-7 ἀσελγεῖς ποιεῖ καὶ ἀθεμιτοφάγους καὶ ἀθεμιτογάμους καὶ ἀρρητοποιοὺς καὶ λείκτας καὶ ψογιστὰς καὶ ἐμπαθεῖς καὶ ἀρρενοκοίτας καὶ ἅρπαγας γυναικῶν (Venus in first decan of Aries). The other instance is Θ p. 134.10 ἀθεμιτοφάγους...ὑπὲρ βρώματα βίου (the Sun and Venus in ASC in Leo in day birth), which sound like violations in the matter of basic foodstuffs (Erysichthon?), not just luxuries.

ἀτράπεζος: if, following Hermann's suggestion, the epithet is transposed here, it reinforces the implications of the previous word. Otherwise it occurs only in Gregory of Nyssa, with completely different implications (the Christian rejection of worldliness, the nature of true 'riches').[340]

565 ὀθνείων κτεάνων ἐπιθύμιος: this looks very much like a poetic rendering of ἀλλοτρίων ἐπιθυμητάς. The phrase is not exclusively astrological, but its occurrences there (especially Valens) outnumber those in the Church Fathers

---

[339] Otherwise *Or. Sib.* 1.318 ('sinners', on whom God brings the deluge), 7.118, epithet of the sea.
[340] *Hom.* 8 (v. p. 359.18 Alexander); *Ep.* 17.14.

Γενεαί and τέχναι 725

and lexica, the two other main sources. Lexica rank ἀλλοτρίων ἐπιθυμητής with other words for individuals who violate social norms, in Pollux 8.7 along with ἄδικον...ἄνομον, βίαιον, in the *Etymologica* and ps.-Zonaras with κλέπτης, as in Θ p. 155.19–20. Valens alone uses it eleven times, and in association with other sociopathic traits (e.g. I 2.54 μισοΐδιοι, II 41.91). It occurs in other 'atheist' configurations in Π.τ.δ. 16 and Valens, I 20.6 ἀλλοτρίων ἐπιθυμητάς, which also have other ways of formulating the predation theme (Paul. p. 67.18 λῃστάς; 2.302 κλῶπας, λῃίστορας; Ptol. 3.14.15 ἅρπαγας, λῃστάς, 32 ψεύστας, κλέπτας).

566 A different, barely interpretable, reading in $Π^1$: Monaco, 58.

567-70

Moon in MC, Mercury in DESC, Saturn in ASC.

Protasis. This is the same configuration as in 6.341–7: Moon in MC; Saturn in ASC, Mercury setting. Θ, as far as I can see, has only a scratch collection of Π- and τ- charts with similar outcomes, but no similar set-up.

Apodosis. Although their inputs are the same, M^a's outcomes are much wider-ranging than those of M^b, who focuses on makers of statues, whether carpenters or metal workers. M^a adds painters of gemstones, engravers of seals, and metalworkers in more media (silver and gold as well as bronze). *Variatio* on the basic theme of sculpture allows monumental work and divine images on the one hand, miniatures on the other.

567-8 This is one of the few occasions where $Π^1$ is superior to L, because it preserves the opening of a verse which supplies the necessary main verb; Koechly had already marked a lacuna. But because only the first half of the column is preserved, the papyrus does not solve the problem of ἄνδρας at the end of 567, which is separated from the epithets in 569 that seem to qualify it. ἄνδρας is viable only if one can accept Monaco's suggestion (59) that ἄνδρας is governed by ὡρονομῶν, which is implausible. One could accept Axtius and Rigler's suggestion (A.–R.^{c}, xliv) and reverse the order of 567 and 568, whereby ἄνδρας immediately precedes παντευχούς (in $Π^1$) or εὐξοάνους (in L), but two things are suspicious about that: (i) it would be very strange for a genitive absolute phrase to *open* an apotelesma (contrast 571–2, 577–8), and (ii) no other instance of ἄνδρας at line-end in the Manethoniana depends on enjambment to provide it with content: in M^b it is generally proceeded by a word in -τορας (183, 220, 276, 349, 397, 439, 482) or -μονας (21, 445), and has a preposition in 505. I prefer to accept the transmitted order of lines—which is supported by the order of presentation in 6.341–2—and to replace ἄνδρας in 567 with a suitable epithet. That happens to make the line a more satisfactory instance of the chiastic scheme M^a uses so often for opposition (i. 197; p. 220; Hübner 2001, 230, had noted the anomaly). A likely choice is αἰνός (at line-end in 6.64, 1.83, and before the main caesura in 6.450), or, failing that, αἰπύς. αἰνός has the (slight) merit that it would contain yet another confusion of ν and ρ in the minuscule exemplar (i. 375).

568a παντευχοὺς: another possible case of reinterpretation or even resemanticisation, since πάντευχον means 'armed tooth and nail' in the Chaldaean Oracles and here looks as if it agrees with τορν[εύτορας vel sim., meaning perhaps 'carpenters of all sorts of things' (Monaco, 59), which, with a long penultimate syllable, requires the accentuation to be oxytone (Chandler, §426). Astrological τορνευταί (Appendix II, II.7.iv) involve Venus and Mercury and have a feminine, gracious, turn.

569 Both compounds εὐξοάνους...ἀγαλμοτυπεῖς are unique, and ξόανον is not used elsewhere in astrology. In Pausanias' usage ξόανον is an ancient image,[341] not the product of modern craftsmanship, but this is not necessarily so in other sources; in any case, the poet is presumably thinking of its wooden nature (derived from ξέω or ξύω)[342] which makes these craftsmen a suitable adjunct to carpenters. παλάμῃσι in Il. 15.411 is also used of a carpenter, though also for other craftsmen (4.442 n.). The last word refers explicitly to makers of divine images. Neither ἀγάλματα nor ξόανα *need* be divine, but very often are, and the context of most instances of ἀγάλματα in astrology makes this clear (though not at 6.420).[343] When astrology talks about makers of divine images it calls them ἀγαλματογλύφους (Valens, I 1.39) or ἀγαλματοποιούς (Περὶ κράσ. 207, 'Heliodorus' on Paul, p. 84.29), and their products ἀγάλματα (Hephaestion, i. 258.17–259.3, 17; Π.τ.δ. 21): ἀγαλμοτυπεῖς is a unique variation for these contemporary craftsmen. Mercury is the expected agency, but in combination with Venus in 4.130 λιθογλυφίαισι θεῶν.

θεοπλάστας: not new in this sense (Pollux, 1.12 τοὺς δὲ ἐπὶ τοῖς ἀγάλμασι χειροτέχνας οὐκ ἀγαλματοποιοὺς μόνον οὐδ' ἀγαλματουργούς, ἀλλὰ καὶ θεοποιοὺς καὶ θεοπλάστας = Ar. fr. 828 K.–A.), but very rare (Appendix II, V.5.vi). The verb θεοπλαστεῖν is overwhelmingly attested in Philo, but a Jewish author has his own perspective, and Philo uses it to critique idolatry. Heliodorus, *Aeth.* 9.9.3 Θεοπλαστοῦσι τὸν Νεῖλον Αἰγύπτιοι, is about the creation of gods, not statues, as well. The only other attestation is indirect: Firmicus' *fabricatores deorum* (3.5.33) looks like a rendering of the Greek agent noun.

---

[341] Scheer, 19–21; J.-C. Vincent, 'Le *xoanon* chez Pausanias: Littératures et réalités cultuelles', *DHA* 29 (2003), 31–73. See also Lightfoot 2003, 293.

[342] J.-P. Vernant, 'Figuration et image', *Mètis*, 5 (1990), 225–38, at 227–8; Scheer, 19–20; Vincent (n. 341), 32.

[343] For ἄγαλμα in the sense of divine image (usually a sculpture, rarely a painting), see Hermary, 22–3; Scheer, 8–18.

570 χαλκοτύποις τέχνῃσι κολοσσοπόνους: at this date a κολοσσός will have meant something of colossal size.[344] How often sculptors received commissions for such statues is moot, but presumably when they were so engaged it was on honorific pieces. The colossus is associated with bronze.[345] In Herodotus a colossus *could* be of bronze (4.152.4) but did not have to be. Perhaps it was the massive renown of the Rhodian colossus that turned bronze colossi into a topos (cf. Sopater of Paphos, ap. Athen. 4.158 E χαλκήλατον | μέγαν κολοσσὸν). Theocritus, though he does not spell it out, has bronze in mind for his σφυρήλατος...κολοσσός in *Id*. 22.47 (Dickie 1996, 249–50), and there are bronze colossi in *MDAI(A)* 32 (1907), 243,4 (Pergamum, 1st c. BC) l. 25 ἰκόνι...χαλκῆι κολοσσικῆι and *IK* Kyme 13 (after 130 BC) l. 3 εἰκόνα χαλκέαν...κ]ολοσσιαίαν.[346]

The use of χαλκοτύπος as a decorative epithet goes back to *Il*. 19.25 (epithet of wounds inflicted by bronze), but it is also the standard trade name for a smith, attested since the fifth century; see Appendix II, II.6.i and 1.79 n. On the formation of the adjective κολοσσοπόνους, there are many other -πόνος compounds (see on 4.72), but no parallels for manufacturing (λεβητοπόνος 'working *over* the λέβης).

571–6

Jupiter in MC aspects New Moon, Sun aspects ASC. Evidently a πρᾶξις configuration, like those that surround it. It indicates the right places (ASC and MC); it involves a *synaphe* with the Moon in the MC (Ptol. 4.4.1); it specifies that the Moon is New (important on the Anubion theory of πρᾶξις, Θ p. 208.19; p. 130); and it exemplifies the rule that the planet in the MC signifies one who will share power with the king (Hephaestion, Epit. IV, ii. 234.10–13).

571 For φεγγοβολήσας see on 4.264, and for φοράδην on 4.131. I interpret ὑψοῦ to refer to the MC (p. 246) because a *kentron* is required, and because *kentra* (see on 1.26–8) and especially the MC (3.222–4, 4.93–9, 1.281–3) signify kingship. It is used of the pole in 2.25, and ὕψι together with explicit indications of the MC in 3.61, 222.

---

[344] G. Roux, 'Qu'est-ce qu'un κολοσσός?', *REA* 62 (1960), 5–40, at 36–7; Dickie 1996, esp. 237–48. See also A. A. Donohue, *Xoana and the Origins of Greek Sculpture* (Atlanta, GA, 1988), 27; Hermary, 24–7 (Herodotus).

[345] The Cypselid colossus at Olympia, made of plates of beaten gold, was exceptional. In an epigram in Photius, κ 1280, Suda, κ 2804, it describes itself with a technological emphasis not dissimilar to the present passage (χρυσοῦς σφυρήλατός εἰμι κολοσσός). See R. Gagné, 'Who's afraid of Cypselus? Contested theologies and dynastic dedications', in E. Eidinow, J. Kindt, and R. Osborne (eds.), *Theologies of Ancient Greek Religion* (Cambridge, 2016), 62–88, at 64–72.

[346] Where gold colossi are specified, presumably gilded bronze is meant (*IDid*. 217.2–3; Sardis 7,1 27 (c.75–50 BC), ll. 3–4).

572 βιοτοσκόπον: unique (and misunderstood by LSJ). See Heilen 2015, 642: the degree that is rising at the moment of birth looks upon the native's life.

αὐγάζοντος: transitive, whether the poet is rendering the meaning 'see' in a quasi-technical sense, i.e. 'aspect', or 'illumine' (LSJ II.1; HOrph. 7.10 αὐγάζοντες ἀεὶ νυκτὸς ζοφοειδέα πέπλον, of the stars). The verb is poetic (in astrology only in M^a, M^b, and Maximus), the transitive use unique to this passage.

573–4 I take κοινωνοὺς to govern γενεῆς βασιληίδος (rather than that 573, taken independently, calls the natives of kingly race).

575 Koechly's emendation restored the regular construction of μετέχειν with partitive genitive, but deeming μέγ' superfluous (which it is) and accepting the transmitted reading μετ' (L and Π^1), T. Mommsen, 214–15 considered it equally likely that the poet constructed μετέχοντας with the dative (having a share of the art of rhetoric) and that he redoubled the verbal compound with the prepositional phrase (having a share of good fortune, by means of the art of rhetoric), a misconceived ultra-prosaicism if so (p. 200). On prosperity from literary careers, see i. 344–5; p. 107.

577–81

Mercury in ASC, Moon in DESC.

Protasis. The same configuration—Mercury in ASC, Moon in DESC—appears in 6.355–6. I consider them τ- realisations of Mercury ruling πρᾶξις, which, according to both Ptol. 4.4.3 and Θ p. 210.26–7, produces money-lenders/bankers (τραπεζίτας). But it is unclear why the Moon is located in the DESC, on either Ptolemy's or Anubion's method of forecasting πρᾶξις.

Apodosis. M^b is more florid, but M^a in any case has a lacuna.

577 For the construction of ἐλθεῖν, see p. 213; no need to treat it as a choice between the two recensions (Monaco, 60).

μεροποσπόρον: most similar to 4.597 τεκνοσπόρον ὥρην, on which see n.

578 λοίσθια τέρματα γαίης: this expression for the DESC, while resembling 4.480 ἀπὸ τέρμονος αἴθρης, is erected on the foundations of Homeric πείρατα γαίης as well as Hes. *Th*. 731 πελώρης ἔσχατα γαίης, and shares its rhythm with Orph. 243 F 30 Bernabé ἔσχατα πείρατα γαίης (see Bernabé's apparatus for a roster of other πείρατα phrases), Ap. Rhod. 2.1261 ἔσχατα πείρατα Πόντου, and Greg. Naz. PG 37.532.4 (*et al.*) εὐρέα πείρατα γαίης. For ἔσχατος, the proper word for an ultimate limit in space,[347] M^b substitutes an epithet (λοίσθιος) whose

---

[347] J. S. Romm, *The Edges of the Earth in Ancient Thought: Geography, Exploration, and Fiction* (Princeton, 1992), 39–40 = id., 'The Boundaries of the Earth', in R. V. Munson (ed.), *Herodotus:*

Γενεαί and τέχναι 729

sense is *normally* temporal[348] in a clausula which enjoys modest popularity in late antique hexameter poetry,[349] sometimes used of the far east (Dion. Per. 1164) or the far west (restored in the Tabula Albana, *FGrH* 40 F 1c, l. 8; Quint. Smyrn. 10.196, of the place where the stars set). The effect is both to identify the western horizon (Hesych. τ 533 τερματίζει· τελειοῖ, ὁρίζει) and perhaps, given the frequency with which λοίσθιος describes death, to evoke the analogy between the *dodecatopos* and the course of human life (Bouché-Leclercq, 277, 286).

579 βαθυχρήμονες: see on 4.66.

τραπέζαις: see on 2.256, 3.99–100; here of a bank.

580 πιστόφρονες: unique, but πίστις is a regular adjunct to the management of private or public or royal property, e.g. Valens, e.g. I 2.50 πιστικοί, ἀγαθοὶ οἰκονόμοι, I 20.5 πιστούς…χρημάτων χειριστὰς; Firmicus, 4.14.5 *regiosque thesauros fideli tuitione custodiant*; the πιστὸς οἰκονόμος is a figure in the NT as well (Luke 12:42; 1 Cor. 4:2). The Attic orators already observed that πίστις is also the first requirement for bankers (R. Bogaert, *Banques et banquiers dans les cités grecques* (Leiden, 1968), 394, citing Isocr. 17.2, Demosth. *Or.* 36.44, 57); a banker from Cirta conspicuous for *veritas* in Tran 2013, 245. The elements that dominate Morgan's account of literary treatments of πίστις/*fides* in economic life—cynicism about trustworthiness, on the one hand, and appeal to religious sanction, on the other—are completely absent (104–8).

πόλεως: I retain L's reading in view of the Atticising tendency of this book's dialect.

ταμιεύτορες: from the verb ταμιεύω. Fraenkel, i. 134–5, notes the popularity of -ευτήρ and -εύτωρ formations in Hellenistic and imperial poetry. It possibly also does a better job than ταμίας, which astrology anyway does not use for human professions,[350] of rendering the meaning 'treasurer', 'paymaster' (or quaestor: Mason, 91); see the characterisation of the -εύειν suffix by Hübner 2001, 231 ('…in dem die personale Bedeutung eines Wesens, das eine bestimmte Funktion oder ein Amt ausübt, stärker in den Blick gerät wie etwa bei πρυτανεύω oder βασιλεύω').

580–1 ἔν τε τοκισμοῖς | καὶ χρείαις: usury, lending at interest (LSJ) (Appendix II, iv.1.iii). The prepositional phrase could reflect prose (Θ p. 166.19 ἐν δημοσίαις χρείαις ὑπουργοῦντα).

581 βίον πολὺν ὀλβονομοῦντες: the unique compound glamorises prosaic οἰκονόμους, who are frequent in combinations involving Mercury. The noun

---

Volume 2: Herodotus and the World (Oxford, 2013), 21–43, at 39–40; Or. ap. Hdt. 7.140.2 φύγ' ἐς ἔσχατα γαίης.

[348] Not, though, the reading λοισθίαν, accepted by Hornblower, in Lyc. *Al.* 246; Nonn. *D.* 4.21.
[349] *HOrph.* 11.23, 14.14, 71.11; Greg. Naz. *PG* 37.996.15.
[350] Valens, App. II 18 ψυχῆς ταμίας, of the Sun; 4.22 ταμίης, of Aquarius; see ad loc.

itself appears in 4.610 (which illustrates precisely what goes wrong when πίστις is undermined). Other expressions for managers include ἐπιτρόπους; Valens, I 20.5 χρημάτων χειριστὰς, 29 ἐπάνω χρημάτων, γραμμάτων, ψήφων τεταγμένοι, Firmicus, 3.2.14 pecuniarum custodem, 3.10.7 multarum pecuniarum aut multi auri domini; Appendix II, VII.6.ii.

582–5 + 586–8 + 589–92

Venus in IMC, Saturn in MC; with Jupiter in aspect; and with Mars in equal degrees. The sequence of charts is precisely the same as in 6.286–9 + 290–2 + 293–4, though the outcome of the last is different. M^a's charts are very obviously narrativised into a little sequence, 'told' from the point of the woman (the previous chart, in 6.285, has already established that the subjects are female). Here the sequence is reoriented from the point of view of both sexes (584 ἀνδράσι νύμφας; 588 ἀνδράσιν ἠδὲ γυναιξὶν). I wonder whether an alternative version of 4.589–92 supplied more continuity with the previous two charts by making it clearer that these homosexual men were supposedly *husbands*, as they are in Valens, II 38.82 (another collection of charts on marriage), where Mars, in opposition to the Moon and aspected by Saturn and the Sun, makes a husband who is κατηγορηθεὶς μαλακός. As M^b presents it here, these men are born homosexual and the sequence with 582–5 and 586–8 is less tightly knit and more loosely themed on the absence of (legitimate) offspring.

Jupiter's effect is to produce supposititious children, as in 4.373 (but there as an amelioration of exposure). But it is decidedly strange that a dose of Mars, of all planets, should make males homosexual (passive, to judge from 591). Saturn should be the planet of 'unclean' sexuality, and while there are homosexuality charts in which Mars is involved (Valens, II 38.82; Firmicus, 7.25.5), it is not the addition of Mars that brings the outcome about. From the comparison with M^a it looks as if M^b inherited Mars, but introduced this modification which contravenes basic astrological logic (p. 254).

582 ἕλκῃ: for ἕλκεσθαι see i. 538 and 2.11 n., but M^a does not use the active, which M^b combines with his favourite pathway metaphor. ἀστερόεντα in Homer is epithet of οὐρανόν, which is overhead, into which stars rise and towards which a person can stretch a hand. By transferring its application to a Venus invisible in the IMC, the epithet is reduced from decoration to tautology (the path is starry only insofar as it belongs to its planetary owner).

583 οὐρανίην ἀτραπὸν...βαίνῃ: for the construction of the verb see on 4.294, and for the noun-epithet phrase on 4.37.

μεσοδερκέα: for -δερκής compounds see B.–P. 718: what is unusual about this example is that the verb must be passive (3.63–4 n.).

Γενεαί and *τέχναι* 731

584 στείρας: for sterile wives, see on 2.181, adding 6.285; *Περὶ σχημ.* 98/*Περὶ κράσ.* 29.

ἀτέκμονας: 'nicht nur unerhört, sondern schlechterdings undenkbar' (Nauck). I fail to see anything wrong with it at all (women who are not characterised by childbirth, with τεκ- used, as normal, of the mother). Nauck admits that his own emendation ἀκύμονας lacks the right sense. It would ostentatiously vary ἄτοκοι (2.181 στείραις ἠδ' ἀτόκοισι, 6.264, 285 στείρας ἠδ' ἀτόκους; Ptol. 3.13.11 αἱ δὲ γυναῖκες ἄτοκοι καὶ στεῖραι; for the theme, see Hephaestion, i. 142.28–9 αἱ δὲ γυναῖκες ἄγονοι καὶ ‹στεῖραι›). In Mᵃ are born women who commit abortion, though ἀτέκμων would have to be made to work very hard indeed to mean that (not just failing to give birth, but actively intervening to prevent it).

585 Π¹ is too damaged to help remedy the corruption at the beginning of the line. All that remains is the ending -ην, which, if it is not accusative singular, could be an adverb (**ἀσποράδην, 'not sowing seed for offspring'?). But anything connected with the σπείρω root is itself difficult, not because women did not have seed,³⁵¹ but because astrology itself regards the male as the 'seeder' (Valens, I 3.23–4 στειρώδεις δὲ καὶ ἄσποροι), and when astrology speaks of sterile women (584 n.), the fault is squarely their own. I have no further suggestions for the beginning of the line. As for the end, it has a somewhat tragic cast (Eur. *Or.* 1305 τὰν λιποπάτορα λιπογάμετον; hypallage with λέχος in Soph. *Aj.* 211), while anticipating Nonnus' great fondness for the λιπό- prefix (Spanoudakis on *Par.* 11.36b; cf. the cadences of *D.* 4.63 ἐγὼ λιπόπατριν ἀκοίτην, 46.259 ἐμὸς λιπόπατρις ἀλήτης, *Par.* 12.181 ἐγὼ λιποφεγγέι κόσμῳ).

586-8 As it stands in L, this chart lacks a verb, which Koechly proposed stood in a lacuna after 588 which also contained the word παῖδας. The absence of confirmation in the papyrus does not defeat the theory. By adopting Axtius' emendation θυραίοις to make 588 to some extent self-contained, one thrusts on Mᵇ an instance of the verbless 'who whom' construction (i. 215; p. 322), which is not otherwise characteristic of this poet. At any rate, the parallel in Mᵃ, which is exactly coextensive with this, does not suggest any fresh content, so at most a missing line or lines would seem to have contained packing.

586 αἰθροπλανής: unique.

---

³⁵¹ H. King, *Hippocrates' Woman: Reading the Female Body in Ancient Greece* (London, 1998), index s.v. female seed; ead., *The Disease of Virgins: Green Sickness, Chlorosis, and the Problems of Puberty* (London, 2004), index s.v. seed, female; ead., 'Galen and the Widow: Towards a History of Therapeutic Masturbation in Ancient Gynaecology', *Eugesta*, 1 (2011), 205–35, at 213; Congourdeau, 190–5; R. Flemming, 'One-Seed, Two-Seed, Three-Seed? Reassessing the Fluid Economy of Ancient Generation', in M. Bradley, V. Leonard, and L. Totelin (eds.), *Bodily Fluids in Antiquity* (London, 2021), 158–72. Not that it was necessarily of much use in conception: Soranus, *Gyn.* 1.12.2.

587 δερχθείς: for the passive, see on 3.63–4.

ὑπόβλητα γένεθλα: see on 6.292 ὑποβλήδην. For once, M^a has the more adventurous form, for ὑπόβλητος is regular. For γένεθλα and for the cadence, see on 4.282.

588 ἀνδράσιν ἠδὲ γυναιξὶν: an uncharacteristically heavy-handed theft (*Od.* 19.408; also Mimnermus, fr. 1.5 W., al.).

στοργῇσι: see on 4.377–8.

θυραίους: the implied antithesis is between non-relative/kin, as in Eur. *Or.* 805–6 θυραῖος ... μυρίων κρείσσων ὁμαίμων and perhaps also Dicaeogenes, F 1 Snell (although the text is corrupt); non-relative/within the house: Eur. fr. 491.2 K. παῖδας θυραίους εἰς δόμους ἐκτήσατο. For other antitheses with this adjective, see on 4.526.

589 κατὰ σήματα τοιάδε: (in equal degrees) with respect to the aforementioned stars; for σήματα in this sense see on 4.109. No details are given about the aspect in M^a. The sense of κατά is unusual in this book, where κατά + acc. is usually used of location in *kentra* or signs. One possible meaning of κατά + acc. is 'over against' or 'opposite' (LSJ B.I.3), and in Firmicus, 7.25.5 (above), Mars opposes Venus; but it cannot mean that here, for Venus and Saturn are already in opposition. The best parallel seems to be 4.457, another chart involving aspect in equal degrees.

590 μάχλοι: see i. 302 and n. 22.

†διδυματόκαι†: Koechly's suggestion is suitably obscene; he explains it *qui molunt per utramque cavernam*, which is plausible if the *cavernae* in question can be called 'twins'. I wondered whether this had something to do with those born with male and female sets of genitals, but that lacks the right sense of perversion. Alternatively, with the same sense as De Stefani's διδυμέκτομοι, *διδυμά- or διδυμή-κοποι, or even -κοπαι (B.–P. 8), cf. LSJ s.v. διδύμη, διδυμαῖον = ὄρχις, supported by Ptol. 3.13.11 οἱ μὲν ἄνδρες ἀπόκοποι.

ἀρσενομίκται: this recalls Paul's ἀρσενοκοῖται (1 Cor. 6:9, along with μοιχοί and μαλακοί and others who will not inherit the Kingdom of Heaven; 1 Tim. 1:10), and confirms the reference to homosexuality which some NT scholars have tried to evade (for review of opinion, see W. D. Mounce, WBC 46, on 1 Tim. 1:10); see too *Or. Sib.* 2.73 ἀρσενοκοιτεῖν; Aristides, *Apol.* fr. 13.5 Vona ἀρσενοκοιτίας. The formation is rare (B.–P. 559).

591 μεμφόμενοι φύσεως ὀρθὴν ὁδόν: the discussion about natural and unnatural sexual practices in relation to homosexuality had been going on since at least Plato.[352] The points at issue are (i) whether the poet means that *all*

---

[352] Plato and Aristotle: K. Dover, *Greek Homosexuality* (London, 1978), 153–70 (pederasty according to φύσις in *Symp.* 189, 192 E, 193 C, D; this contrasts with e.g. *Leg.* 836 C). Judaeo-Christian

homosexual behaviour is unnatural, or only the passive role, and (ii) to illustrate the metaphor of the path (which replaces the usual παρὰ φύσιν,[353] antonym of κατὰ φύσιν).

On (i). Received opinion is that for classical peoples, Greeks and Romans, what was unnatural was the male who took the passive role. Most astrology agrees. It is the basis of the gendered luminaries scheme, according to which luminaries not in their 'natural' places produce men who do the works of women or women who do the works of men (but not active male homosexuals, who are not a stigmatised category). Other passages in the Manethoniana reflect the same attitude (1.117–18, 5.139–40). Ptolemy's discussions of sexuality among diseases of the soul (3.15.7–12; Heilen 2015, 1114–18) has nothing to say about unproblematic sexuality, only about 'perversions' (males taking the passive role and females the active one), though the system in 4.5.16–17 (Heilen 2015, 1117–1118), which is based on moderation and balance irrespective of orientation, is somewhat different. According to this, *any* form of exclusive attachment to one sex (including the opposite one) ranks as a perversion. Pederasty is counted as the first degree of perversion when the influences are masculinised (for attitudes to pederasty see on 1.25), and devotion to males of any age is the second, while exclusive heterosexuality is the first degree of perversion under excessive feminine influence (which agrees with the Roman preparedness to extend charges of 'effeminacy' to womanisers, adulterers, those whose heterosexuality was uncontrolled[354]), while passive homosexuality is its aggravation. What counts as deviation under this scheme is excessive devotion to *either* sex, though there is an asymmetry, untypical of Ptolemy, in that three of the perverted positions are assigned to homosexual sex and only one to heterosexual. Orientation as a principle of classification *per se* is absent; what counts as normal is instead the untrammelled exercise of the active drive. Insofar as M[b] implies disapproval of an orientation, his stance looks different. His ἀρσενομίκται is practically equivalent to ἀρσενοκοῖται, the word with which Christian authors condemn all same-sex relations *in toto*,[355] but in a broader context his attitude could be seen as typical of the Stoic-inflected 'new conjugiality' of the Second Sophistic period, where male identity was increasingly invested in harmonious marriage, a perspective to which homosexuality was a threat (S. Swain, *Hellenism*

---

authors: Testament of Naphtali, 3:4 '...that ye become not as Sodom, which changed the order of nature'; ps.-Phoc. 190–1; Rom. 1:26–7 (J. B. de Young, 'The Meaning of "Nature" in Romans 1 and its Implications for Biblical Proscriptions of Homosexual Behavior', *JETS* 31 (1988), 429–41).

[353] παρὰ φύσιν: Plat. *Leg.* 636 C, 841 D; Aeschin. *Or.* 1.185 (Dover (n. 352), 60–8); van der Horst on ps.-Phoc. 190.

[354] e.g. Richlin, 222; Williams, 125–59, 206; K. Olson, 'Masculinity, Appearance, and Sexuality: Dandies in Roman Antiquity', *JHSex* 23 (2014), 182–205.

[355] See Dunn, WBC 38A, pp. 65–6, on Romans 1:27; van der Horst on ps.-Phoc. 190.

and Empire: Language, Classicism, and Power in the Greek World AD 50–250 (Oxford, 1996), 122–7).

On (ii). The path of Nature is a familiar philosophical metaphor, especially Stoic,[356] but I have not found it used otherwise for sexual orientation or behaviour. It is and is not like the path metaphor for choice of life (see on 4.551). On the one hand, the binary choice of right and wrong, essential to the 'two ways' image, is implicit here as well; on the other, the correct choice is grounded in the workings of the universe itself. Pindar also connects the path metaphor with Nature—not, however, some hypothetical cosmic order to which one must align one's behaviour, but inborn talent which one must strive to realise (*Nem.* 1.25 χρὴ δ' ἐν εὐθείαις ὁδοῖς στείχοντα μάρνασθαι φυᾷ). Ethical instances of the 'road' metaphor employ both εὐθύς or ἰθύς (Pind. fr. 108a Snell εὐθεῖα δή κέλευθος ἀρετὰν ἑλεῖν; O. Becker, *Das Bild des Weges und verwandte Vorstellungen im frühgriechischen Denken* (Berlin, 1937), 64–5, 85–92; Prov. 2:13, 16; Acts 13:10; *TDNT* v. 53, s.v. ὁδός) and ὀρθός (e.g. Dem. *Or.* 18.15, 322; Philo, *Agr.* 101), with alternative directional conceptions of 'rectitude' (straight forward/straight up).

592 Perhaps the same logic that produced homosexuals (disruption to the natural order of things) now makes them live abroad, or perhaps the poet has the wandering *galli* specifically in mind (6.299 ἀλῶνται; 4.222 n.). The motifs of 'shameful speech' and 'wandering' are shared with mimes (cf. 4.445, 449), but αἰσχεόφημοι here, which is unique, must mean 'with shameful reputations'; for the αἰσχ- element, see i. 367.

4.593–626 Miscellanea

593–6

Saturn in ASC, Moon in Evil Demon, Sun cadent from MC.

Protasis. Not only are the circumstances the same as in 6.60–3 (Saturn in ASC, Moon in Evil Demon, Sun cadent from a *kentron*), but each chart devotes a self-contained line to each item, and each arranges them as parallelisms (finite verbs in M[b], genitives absolute in M[a]). The only difference is that M[b] apparently specifies the MC from which the Sun is cadent.

Apodosis. In both cases the outcome is contained in a single hexameter consisting of two antithetical clauses, both with part of ἔχειν standing at the

---

[356] e.g. Plat. *Leg.* 716 A; Musonius Rufus, *Diss.* 17 τὸ ζῆν ὁδῷ καὶ κατὰ φύσιν; Marcus Aurelius, V 3.1 ἀλλ' εὐθεῖαν πέραινε ἀκολουθῶν τῇ φύσει τῇ ἰδίᾳ καὶ τῇ κοινῇ, μία δὲ ἀμφοτέρων τούτων ἡ ὁδός; V 4.1 Πορεύομαι διὰ τῶν κατὰ φύσιν; Sen. *Ep.* 122.19 Ideo, Lucili, tenenda nobis via est, quam natura praescripsit, nec ab illa declinandum.

Γενεαί and τέχναι   735

caesura, and a part of ἐκτιθῆναι, but placed in the reverse order. All in all, the one chart looks like a reprise of the other; see p. 219.

593 ἐφέπῃ: both 'controls' or 'administers' the birth and occupies the ASC, which is the sense found in 3.32 ὥρην ἐφέπων, 6.556 ὥρην δ᾽ ἐφέπωσιν, 618 ὥρην ἐφέποντος (cf. i. 879).

Κρόνος ὡρονομεύων: Hübner 2001, 230–1: again in Dorotheus, p. 398.33, and derivable in M^b from him (p. 218) or conceivably both from 'Antiochus' (l. 23 = CCAG i. 109.19 Ζεύς … ὡρονομεύων).

594 The normal prose name of this place, the twelfth, is the Kakos Daimon (κακὸς δαίμων, sometimes κακοδαιμόνημα; i. 878). A planet or sign that occupies it is also said to κακοδαιμονεῖν. It is typical of their two approaches (p. 220) that M^a paraphrases with a poetic (Epic) synonym whereas this one offers up a differently-suffixed alternative (for which see on 4.462).

595 Ὀλύμπου: see on 4.396 for Olympus as the MC, and on 2.73 for the heavens in general.

596 ἐκθεσίην: see on 4.368.
ὑπ᾽ ὀθνείων: see on 4.371.

597–612. Slave Charts

The two main slave charts here have correspondences in the sixth book, especially close in the second case, but they were not contiguous there; M^b seems to have reworked them to make them a pair. The second worsens the first. The difference between semi-slaves (4.600) and full-slaves (4.602) is between plain aspect on the one hand, and aspect in equal degrees on the other.

597–600

Venus aspects ASC, Saturn and Mars accompanying. 4.597–600 and 6.692–4 are not identical, but both involve Venus and the malefics. M^a does not mention the ASC, nor M^b the Sun. Given their differences, it is doubtful whether M^b can be used to heal the corruption in M^a. There is nothing much to compare in Firmicus' charts of slaves. He has a chart in which Venus' hostility to Mars or Saturn is *one* of the factors that causes slaves to be freed (7.4.12 *Venus vero aut Martem aut Saturnum impugnet*), but this amounts to little.

597 τεκνοσπόρον ὥρην: see on 6.540 for the epithet and cadence. The epithet is among the poet's decorative compound epithets for the ASC (p. 246; Hübner 2001, 233), particularly like 4.577 μεροσπόρον, and in that respect recalling tragic compounds like Soph. *Tr.* 359 τὸν φυτοσπόρον. But some astrologers also use it technically for places with special responsibility for childbirth (Serapion,

CCAG v/2. 179.23; the fifth place in Paul, p. 73.10–11, 16, and 'Heliodorus', p. 80.23).

598 συνέη...σὺν αὐτῷ: the initial placement of a singular verb which coheres with the first item in a sequence, to which others are later added, is familiar from Homer and elsewhere (K.-G. i. 79; Chantraine, ii. 18–19; e.g. *Il.* 1.255 ἦ κεν γηθήσαι Πρίαμος Πριάμοιό τε παῖδες; see also on 4.171–2). The special refinement here (if refinement it is, not ineptitude) is the presence of a participle, whether dual or plural, in the next line which instead construes the nouns as a group, and not an additive sequence. The preposition is overkill (p. 200), for the verb is normally construed with a bare dative, whereas the preposition is used alone (e.g. 3.309), with παρεῖναι (2.438, 6.439, 5.178), or with verbs of motion or appearance. The only (part) parallel in the corpus is 5.62–3 Κρόνῳ συνοδεύων | σύν τ' ἄστροις πᾶσιν. Perhaps the verse pattern in *Il.* 15.353 οἳ δὲ σὺν αὐτῷ impinged.

599 λαμπομένῳ: Koechly restored the dual in his second edition. (The papyrus evidently played things differently, with a noun in this position.) It is not required by metre, unlike opportunistic uses of the dual in imperial verse (K.-G. i. 20; K. Lehrs, *Quaestiones Epicae* (Königsberg, 1837), 319; S. Mersinias, 'Notes on the *Cynegetica* of ps.-Oppian', *Minerva*, 13 (1999), 103–25, at 106; Vian, 57), but, if correctly restored, sooner implies that the malefics are seen as tightly enough knit to count as a pair, in which case it is intelligent, even elegant.

κακοεργέϊ: κακοεργός was a Homeric *hapax* (*Od.* 18.54, of Odysseus' belly) and not rare thereafter. Astrological poetry employs both second- and third-declension forms, for malefics (i. 908 n. 8, 909 n. 8), corresponding to standard prose κακοποιοί, and for adverse outcomes and maleficent characters. The third-declension form is confined to this passage and Dorotheus, p. 326.6 κακοεργέες (p. 218).

600 ἐξ ἀπελευθερίης βασιληΐδος: the adjective, describing the status of a freedman, and the verb ἀπελευθεροῦν, are much commoner than the noun, but ἀπελευθερία is in manuscripts (though deleted by Cobet) at Aeschin. *Or.* 3.41 and Dio Cass. 48.45.9.[357] Given that βασιλεύς can mean Emperor, these could be imperial freedmen, the *Augusti liberti* or Σεβάστου ἀπελεύθεροι, who boasted of their status on their monuments.[358] For imperial freedmen in the Greek East, see

---

[357] For the basic word, see A. R. W. Harrison, *The Law of Athens*, i: *The Family and Property* (Oxford, 1968), 181; Zelnick-Abramovitz, 99–120. The present passage squares rather well with the suggestion of the latter (106) that an ἀπελεύθερος is less free than an ἐξελεύθερος, and that the word indicates a state of 'protracted dependence' (110).

[358] On the status: G. Vitucci, in E. De Ruggiero (ed.), *Dizionario epigrafico di antichità romane*, iv. 29 (Rome, 1958), s.v. Libertus, V. *I liberti imperiali*, 933–46; Millar 1977, 69–83; K. Acton, 'Vespasian and the Social World of the Roman Court', *AJP* 132 (2011), 103–24, at 113–17;

Robert 1968, 440–1; J. F. Gilliam, 'Some Roman Elements in Roman Egypt', *ICS* 3 (1978), 115–31, at 126–8; P. A. Brunt, 'The Administrators of Roman Egypt', *JRS* 65 (1975), 124–47, at 140–1; Strab. 17.1.12. For freedmen in astrology, see p. 96.

ἡμισύδουλοι: otherwise only in *Epimerismi Homerici*, π 130 (without context). The word is apparently paired with πανδούλους in 4.602, another rarity, but the informality of the labels in no way closes down the question of the social situation of the natives. If it is appropriate to seek a legal category, it could lie in the interim status of *Latinus Junianus* which was created by Augustus' reform of manumission and lasted until Justinian abolished it in AD 531.[359] This status, granted to those freed below the age of thirty, left *liberti* short of full citizenship, which could nevertheless be obtained by meeting certain requirements (child-rearing) or by the procedure of *iteratio*. Alternatively, it could just refer informally to the continued dependence of freedmen on their former master, their *patronus*. In that case it is nothing to do with legal status and everything to do with sentiment, custom, and the expectation that the freedman would continue to remain under his former master's sway.[360]

Could the word be focalised? There is a risk of over-reading: half-slaves is in the first place an organising category the author has imposed to contrast with the next chart. But the narrative voice also channels social attitudes. The freeborn looked down on the freedman, and perhaps especially on imperial freedmen, whose wealth and influence they found suspect.[361] To a philosopher the deference that was paid to the emperor's lackeys, the cringing, the fawning, the toadying, looked contemptible.[362] More interesting, perhaps, is the possibility that it reflects the attitude of the freed themselves, who certainly benefited from ongoing connections with a *patronus* in terms of economic opportunities, patronage networks, a stable administrative position in the case of an imperial freedman, and sometimes even continued to describe themselves in servile terms on their tombstones,[363] but were not necessarily inured to feelings of resentment, chafing at continued limitations on their autonomy. (Parker, 8,

---

MacLean, 104–30. On titulature: L. R. Taylor, 'Freedmen and Freeborn in the Epitaphs of Imperial Rome', *AJP* 82 (1961), 113–32, at 122; P. R. C. Weaver, 'The Status Nomenclature of the Imperial Freedman', *CQ*² 13 (1963), 272–8.

[359] Steinwenter, *RE* s.v. Latini Iuniani; Millar, 486–8; H. Mouritsen, 'Manumission', in P. J. du Plessis, C. Ando, K. Tuori (eds.), *The Oxford Handbook of Roman Law and Society* (Oxford, 2016), 402–16, at 407, 409–10.

[360] Which plays a large part of the analysis of Zelnick-Abramovitz's monograph *Not Wholly Free*, although this focuses on Greek at the expense of Roman slavery; MacLean, 135 for Roman *liberti*.

[361] MacLean, 31, 107–11, on Pliny and Pallas.

[362] F. Millar, 'Epictetus and the Imperial Court', *JRS* 55 (1965), 141–8, at 143–4, 145.

[363] MacLean, 137–8, with examples of *conservus* and *contubernalis* used by those who were verifiably free.

wonders whether DVC no. 73 (420–400 BC) attests to this attitude in a possible question to the oracle at Dodona about *paramone*.)

601–7
Venus in equal degrees with Saturn. The matching 6.724–9 concentrates on multiple sales, saying nothing about their being house-born. In 6.724–5, the two planets are expressly on the ASC.

601 'If the rays of Venus are seen in equal degrees with <those of> Saturn.' ἰσόμοιρος throughout the book has been constructed with datives, which are normal with ἴσος/ἴσος; here a dative expression 'star of' must be understood.

σελάσματα: this last variant on σέλας (also 4.36 σελασμός, 189 σελάγισμα) recurs only in Σ vet. Od. 18.354 σέλας] τὸ σέλασμα, and Tzetzes, *Chil.* 5 *hist.* 1 ll. 251–2 (in an allegory, of creative fire) and 9 *hist.* 266 l. 308 (of the Sun).

602 πανδούλους: otherwise only Rufinus, *AP* 5.22.3 = *Ep.* viii. 3 Page πάνδουλον.

ὁμόζυγα λατρεύοντας: perhaps an extension of the 'yoke of slavery' metaphor, indicating slaves who work in a team, rather than that they are literally shackled, as they would be, say, in the mines, which is reserved for the aggravation in 609. The rhetoric goes contrary to the practical advice born of bitter experience *not* to have slaves too closely networked, for that would risk insurrection (Arist. *Pol.* 1330ᵃ26–8; *Oec.* 1344ᵇ18–19; Athen. 6.264 F; Varro, *Rust.* 1.17.5).

603 οἰκέτιδος γενεῆς τε πεφυκότας: this is the house-born slave, the οἰκογένης, Latin *verna*.[364] ἐκ γενετήρων (a newly-fashionable hexameter end in LGHP) allows both for double slave parentage and for unions between female slaves and their masters. The category is particularly relevant to the question of ancient slave supply. The evidence, such as it is, yields different results for different parts of the empire, though the category is well represented in Egyptian papyri, and it is surprising not to find other astrological examples of οἰκογένης (nor, in Latin, of *verna*); the house is the default location for slaves in Artemidorus (p. 100), but he does not use the term either. Ancient terminology distinguishes the house-born slave and the one bought in the market ((ἀργυρ)ώνητος/*empticius*), who was less highly prized.[365] But the present passage envisages sale, and that is amply confirmed by papyri (see too the *verna* on sale in Hor. *Epist.* 2.2.6). Straus 2004, 235–9, argues convincingly that 'house-born' means only 'born in *someone's* house', not necessarily in the house of his or her present master.

---

[364] Robert 1968, 439–41; Bieżuńska-Małowist 1961 and ead., *L'esclavage dans l'Egypte gréco-romaine*, i: *Période ptolémaïque* (Wroclaw, 1974), 49–54 and ii. 1977, 28–30, 44–9 ~ 1984, 78–9, 123–7; Herrmann-Otto; Scheidel, 306.

[365] Zelnick-Abramovitz, 27, 170. For the status of the two types, see Soph. *OT* 1123, with Finglass ad loc.; Petron. *Sat.* 47.12, with Schmeling ad loc.; ps.-Quint. *Decl.* 311.7; Kudlien 1986, 242–4, 255. On why the house-born slave was so prized, Bieżuńska-Małowist 1961, 155–62.

604 δεσποσύνων: see on 4.41–2. There are many epigraphic examples, both poetic and prose, and they include dedications by slaves to their masters (e.g. *SGDI* 4334; *GVI* 1475; *IGBulg* III,1 1391) and slave epitaphs referring to their masters (*IG* XIV 795.2).

πικρὰς...ἀνάγκας: for epithets of slavery, see i. 366 and n. 32. This one is wholly conventional.[366]

605 ἐξ ἑτέρων τε δόμων ἑτέροις: *Od*. 17.266 ἐξ ἑτέρων ἕτερ' ἐστίν; for the polyptoton expressing continuity, in particular continuity of evils, see M. Coray on *Il*. 19.290b (Basler Kommentar).

πάλι δουλεύσουσιν: the adverb gestures at various labels for the resold slave (Kudlien 1986, 253–4): παλίμπρατος (Call. fr. 203.55 Pf.); παλίμβολος (Pollux, 3.125 ὁ δὲ πολλάκις πραθείς, ὃν εἴποι τις ἂν παλίμπρατον, παλίμβολος ἂν λέγοιτο; Menand. *Sic*. 11 and fr. 379 Koerte παλίμβολος τρίπρατος); παλίνδουλος (Hesych. π 171). The implication of multiple sales is that there is something suspect about the goods (e.g. Plut. *Mor*. 4 A[367]), as opposed to the altogether more reliable house-born slave; but if the antithesis between born and bought is unreal in practice it completely collapses in this passage, which elides the one into the other.

606 κυρείαις: Origen, *De Principiis*, fr. 11 κυρείαν τὴν κατὰ δούλων.

ἑπτάκι...καὶ πεντάκι: where do these remarkably specific (and strange) numbers come from? There is no sign that the number was produced by any of the methods in Firmicus, 7.5.1–2, which purport to give the number of masters with reference to the number of signs between malefics and luminaries, neither of which is involved here. On the face of it, it seems unlikely a seller would want to advertise that his goods had been sold multiple times for fear of making them look suspect. Most documents concerned with slave sales and registrations specify only the immediate seller and buyer. Yet they do sometimes indicate that a slave had passed through several hands, even though it is impossible to know what proportion of slave sales were affected,[368] and one remarkable document (P. Vindob. Bosw. 7) even discloses an instance of a slave who had been sold no fewer than five times in the space of less than four years (Straus 2004, 313). Other instances of multiple sales are presented in the table in Straus

---

[366] TLG s.v. πικρ- + δουλ-, e.g. Eur. *Hyps*. fr. 61 + 82.8 Bond δουλείαν πικρ[ὰν, *Tr*. 964 πικρῶς ἐδούλωσ'; Plat. *Rep*. 569 c πικροτάτην δούλων δουλείαν; there are many more.

[367] Cf. W. Martin Bloomer, 'The Technology of Child Production: Eugenics and Eulogics in the *De Liberis Educandis*', *Arethusa*, 39 (2006), 71–99, at 92 = id., *The School of Rome: Latin Studies and the Origins of Liberal Education* (Berkeley, 2011), 74.

[368] Scheidel, 293: the numbers of slaves traded multiple times are 'unknowable'.

2004, 311–12;[369] add P.Oxy 1.95 (AD 129), a female slave with two previous masters; *BGU* iii. 937 (Heracl., 250), P.Euphr. 8–9 = SB XXIV 16169–16170 (Coele Syria, 251 and 252), P. Manch. inv. 10894 (Oxyrhynchus, 282–6, ed. A. Benaissa, 'A Syrian Slave Girl Twice Sold in Egypt', *ZPE* 173 (2010), 175–89), and six other documents to be published in P.Oxy. LXXXVI). Epictet. *Diss.* 4.1.7 refers to τῶν τρὶς πεπραμένων. I thank Dan Etches and Amin Benaissa for generous help with this discussion.

If πεντάκι is no mere rhetorical inflation, then perhaps the same is true of ἑπτάκι (although it sounds at first sight suspiciously like a magical number: cf. e.g. Ap. Rhod. 3.861). But the line is oddly formulated. Why put the smaller figure after the larger one if the idea is to express multiplicity? The oddity arouses sympathy for Koechly's second thoughts, or for De Stefani's ἐπί in place of καί.

καινισθέντες: the stars mete out change, and the tenth house in particular presides over καινισμός.[370] The passive verb is readily documentable in inscriptions referring to renovation of buildings, or administrative innovations, but leaves a sense of studied oddity when applied to human vicissitude.

607 Because the slave's hope was of course for eventual manumission, as the evidence of divination makes particularly clear (p. 97; Klees, 74; *Sortes Astrampsychi*, Quaestio 32 εἰ ἐλευθεροῦμαι τῆς δουλείας, and innumerable responses on the subject of being freed or not, cf. Kudlien 1986, 244–5). These unfortunates are those who fell foul of the perhaps roseate expectation implied by Cicero (*Phil.* 8.32) that diligent slaves might expect liberty within six years, those who had been unable to scrape together the funds to buy their liberty (Hopkins 1978, 129, 147–8), or those whose hard work and diligence simply failed to pay off (N. Morley, 'Slavery under the Principate', in Bradley and Cartledge, 265–86, at 281). What 'old age' means in this connection is unclear. Hopkins provided figures that showed that the majority (3/5) of those who *were* fortunate enough to be manumitted, and whose ages of death are known, had been manumitted by the age of thirty (126–7), at least in the western empire; more recently, L. Mihailescu-Bîrliba, 'Les âges d'affranchissement dans les provinces balkano-danubiennes', in A. Gonzales (ed.), *La Fin du statut servile? Affranchissement, libération, abolition: 30ᵉ colloque du Groupe international de recherches sur l'esclavage dans l'Antiquité (GIREA), Besançon, 15-16-17 décembre 2005: Hommage à Jacques Annequin* (Besançon, 2008), 493–500, at 498, found that 29 out of 57 freed slaves in the area in question had been freed before that same

---

[369] He presents the evidence in connection with the suggestion that multiple sales within a short space of time attest the presence of slave dealers: see Bieżuńska-Małowist 1975, 15–16 and Straus 2004, 309 and 313.

[370] Valens, IV 12.1; Apomasar, *De Myst.*, CCAG xi/1. 203.7; CCAG ii. 158.28–9 μεταβολῆς καὶ καινισμοῦ. Also Valens, IV 19.5 (Moon in ASC); VII 3.46 (the cosmos in general).

age (despite the Lex Aelia Sentia, which supposedly restricted manumissions to those aged 30 and above). How large or small a proportion of the slave population, though, were they?

608–11

As above, aspected by the Sun in places not its own. 6.728–9 is shorter: there is nothing about places, nor about release.

608 ἀνοικείως: the adverb only here; for ἀνοικεῖος see on 4.28.

609 νεύουσαι: see on 4.310. The probable reference of συννεύειν there is to conjunction. The parallel passage here suggests the meaning is simply 'aspect'.

δεσμούς τε κατηγορίας τε: these very common motifs are sometimes combined (Firmicus, 3.4.20 *Tunc accusationes, tunc vincula*), but rarely in slave charts. Chains, in particular, are usually associated with prison (4.486 n.), though they are sometimes (perhaps less often than might have been expected) mentioned in connection with slaves:[371] discounting 4.602 (see above) we find 6.729 δεσμοὺς ὀτλεῦσι; Critodemus, CCAG viii/1. 258.21 ὑποταγή, ὀρφανία, δεσμοί (whence Camaterus, *Introd*. 463 ὑποταγὴ δὲ λέγεται, δεσμὰ καὶ ὀρφανία); Valens, I 1.8, δεσμά and αἰχμαλωσίας separated in a list.[372] Chains are more often referred to in catarchic astrology, which is very aware of them as the destiny of recaptured runaways (p. 88).[373]

610 ἀνδράσιν οἰκονόμοισι: when astrology mentions οἰκονόμοι, as it very often does (see on 4.580, 581), it means managers or stewards. Here, given the context, they are not 'householders', 'masters of the house', but slave managers.[374] The NT presents us with at least one slave οἰκονόμος (Luke 12:42 ~ Matth. 24:45 δοῦλος), metaphorical ones in 1 Cor. 4:1–2, 9:17,[375] and possibly another in Luke 16:1.[376] This last is the most interesting, because he too faces accusations; and this is also the worry of the οἰκονόμος in Galen, *De Praecogn*. 6 (xiv. 633–5 K.).

---

[371] For chained slaves, see several of the essays in Bradley and Cartledge, e.g. J. Bodel, 'Slave Labour and Roman Society', 311–36, at 330 [*ergastula*]; Edmondson, 346; M. George, 'Slavery and Roman Material Culture', 385–413, at 386, 388, 392, 395, 400; Bradley, 120, and id., 'The Bitter Chain of Slavery', *DHA* 41 (2015), 149–76, at 157, 158. For the *compeditus*, see Kudlien 1991, 91.

[372] Also Achmet, CCAG ii. 124.4 καὶ δεσμοὺς ‹καὶ δουλείας, though not natal astrology.

[373] Dorotheus, pp. 415.16, 23, 416.24–5; Demetrius, CCAG i. 105.24, 106.10; Timaeus Praxidas, CCAG i. 98.21.

[374] See O. Michel, *TDNT* v. 149–50, s.v. οἰκονόμος; for the *dispensator*, see Schmeling on Petronius, *Sat*. 29.3–5, with references, adding Herrmann-Otto, 369–96; R. A. Baergen, 'Servant, Manager or Slave? Reading the Parable of the Rich Man and his Steward (Luke 16: 1–8a) through the Lens of Ancient Slavery', *Studies in Religion/Sciences Religieuses*, 35 (2006), 25–38, at 31–2; Plut. *Mor*. 4 B.

[375] Not, however, according to J. Byron, 'Slave of Christ or Willing Servant? Paul's Self-Description in 1 Corinthians 4:1–2 and 9:16–18', *Neotestamentica*, 37 (2003), 179–98.

[376] Slave status argued by Baergen, n. 374; *contra* Michel, *TDNT* v. 150, 'a free treasurer'.

ἔκλυσιν ἄτης: prose astrology has ἀπόλυσις for 'release' from evil; e.g. Dorotheus, p. 421.11 ἀπόλυσιν τῆς νόσου; Valens, IV 23.7 τῶν φαύλων... ἀπόλυσιν; Hephaestion, i. 206.11 ἀπόλυσιν τῶν κακῶν, pp. 207.18, 212.16, 222.3 ἀπόλυσιν κακῶν.

611 The line is shaped with irresistible similarity to 477, which suggests that what is wanted instead of the presumably corrupt ending is something agreeing with the natives (companions of, victims of, sufferers from) to govern the genitives. παρέδροις, from 477, now in the dative, would itself do. Or it could mean 'escapees from', given the second half of 610. For κρυερῶν, see on 2.175–6: this seems to be imitating a pet usage of the earlier poet (p. 219).

612

Apparently this truncated chart stayed on the same theme, but there is no help from M^a in restoring the passage, for his slave sequence ended at 6.729. It is hard to choose between Koechly's πάθος and De Stefani's σίνος to heal γένος transmitted in L. Did it refer to the condition of slavery in general (as a chronic state perhaps a πάθος), or to chains and accusations (perhaps, as adventitious events, σίνος)? The line to which Koechly appeals to justify his correction, 6.553, is preceded by the verb λήγειν, like ἀπολήγῃ here, which Koechly took very probably to refer to the Moon. But that is a blindness chart, where the Moon is entirely at home. It does not take us much further.

613–18

Saturn in IMC aspects Mars. This is one of a set of variations on the harms done when Saturn aspects Mars, perhaps from opposition, though that is not explicit. The apodosis lists three of the typical modes of violent death—(i) being eaten by animals, (ii) being crushed by collapsing buildings, and (iii) falling from a height. It is one of those charts where the differentiation might originally have been by sign, as it is in Firmicus, 6.29.10–11, with Saturn on the ASC and Mars in the IMC or DESC, with the Full Moon moving towards Mars or waning towards Saturn, and Firmicus, 6.15.4–8, with Saturn and Mars in opposition. If so, the signs have also been effaced from the list in 3.260–3 (where all aspects bar conjunction are bundled together). 5.192–6 (Saturn on ASC and Mars on DESC) mentions just wild animals.

614 However one heals the end of the line it has something to do with *Od.* 7.197–8 (πείσεται) ἄσσα οἱ αἶσα κατὰ Κλῶθές τε βαρεῖαι | γεινομένῳ νήσαντο λίνῳ or its variants (ap. Eust.) κατακλῶθες (sc. αἱ μὴ εὐτυχεῖς)/κατακλώθησι βαρεῖα. (Hence I decline De Stefani's suggestion, which disrespects βαρεῖαι.) Simply repeating the *Odyssey's* Κλῶθές τε βαρεῖαι would be uncharacteristically passive; an alternative to Koechly's proposal would be θηρόβορον θάνατον φωσὶν κλωθώ [accusative] τε βαρεῖαν, 'death from being eaten by animals *and* a heavy fate', the construction a zeugma. Either way, a line containing the main verb seems to have fallen out afterwards.

θηρόβορον θάνατον paraphrases astrological θηριόβρωτον (*Περὶ κέντρ*. 12; Hephaestion, i. 26.19; Epit. IIIb, *CCAG* vii. 114.31; Θ pp. 128.23, 184.5, 201.24). Although it is not exclusive to astrology,[377] its emotive character and vagueness well suits the idiom. Hephaestion, who ranks θηριοβρώτους alongside ἐκβολιμαίους, is thinking of exposed infants (see on 6.34 and 98), but Dorotheus, who combines them with the burned[378] and crucified, must mean victims of *damnatio ad bestias*,[379] and that is certainly also the context in Θ p. 201.24 (from ch. 77 Καθολικὰ σχήματα βιαιοθανάτων, which includes other victims of judicial condemnation, the beheaded and the crucified). Although the punishment *ad bestias* was initially used for traitors and for special categories of prisoner, by the time M[b] was writing it had been extended to thieves, murderers, arsonists, poisoners, and other types of common criminal.[380]

Among the other βιαιοθάνατοι in Θ are the θηριομάχοι (p. 201.21). The term's imprecision is illustrated by the fact that Cumont, whose beliefs about astrological texts required them to reflect the pre-Roman period, wanted it to mean simply 'hunter' (60 n. 1, 62 n. 2). Robert 1938, 79–80, corrected him. These were the gladiators known as *venatores* or *bestiarii* and/or criminals condemned to the gladiatorial schools.[381]

615–16 These are three standard species for *venationes*. Sen. *Ep*. 7.4 speaks of prisoners being thrown to lions and bears, and both—particularly bears—are represented in execution scenes in art,[382] including a mosaic from Wadi Lebda, near Lepcis, in which bears attack captives and even eat one of them (Dunbabin 2016, 193 and fig. 7.17a). Victims could be wheeled on, bound to an upright pole from which they could not escape, or thrust or whipped forward by an assistant who was himself at risk; there seems also to have been a moderately amusing sport called the *Tichobates* in which the victim had to scramble

---

[377] In Diod. Sic. 18.36.3 of victims of a military disaster; in LXX Gen. 44:28 of Joseph.
[378] For *vivicombustio*, see Callu, 337, 343, 347–8, 352–3; Kyle, 53; Ruffing 2012, 81; Ebner 2012a, 249, and 2012b, 97.
[379] C. Lo Giudice, 'L'impiego degli animali negli spettacoli romani: Venatio e *damnatio ad bestias*', *Italies*, 12 (2008), 361–95, at §§ 24–30; Ebner 2012a, 249–56, and 2012b, 97–109.
[380] Ebner 2012a, 251–4, and 2012b, 98–102, 104–8.
[381] Kyle, 79–80; Ruffing 2012, 82; Ebner 2012a, 259–61, 264–8, and 2012b, 115–16.
[382] Bears: Vismara, B 4, 6–7, 16, 18, 20–3, and Coleman, 59; lions: Vismara, B 5, 12, 14, 17, 19, and Coleman, 54, 59. For mosaics of *damnatio ad bestias* (including leopards), see also Dunbabin 2016, 191 and n. 84.

up a wall out of the reaches of a marauding bear (Vismara, 150 and figs. 8 and 16). Martial's *Liber Spectaculorum* is a particularly good literary source for bears in the amphitheatre;[383] for a boar, see 1.43.14. The poet has rendered these several species by barely concealed Homeric grab-and-snatch and a little more innovation.

615 ~ *Od.* 10.212 ὀρέστεροι ἠδὲ λέοντες (line-end). σάρκας in connection with flesh-eating lions in *Od.* 9.293.

616 ἢ σύες ἀργιόδοντες: most like *Od.* 14.532 σύες ἀργιόδοντες, but replaced from line-end to line-beginning, where the Homeric poems usually have ἀργιόδοντος ὑός, while reproducing the position of the epithet when ἀργιόδοντες ὕες straddles the main caesura (*Il.* 23.32, *Od.* 8.60).

αἱματοπώτιδες ἄρκτοι: the poet does something a little more adventurous, adding bears to the classical menagerie of blood-drinking animals (see Pfeiffer on Call. fr. 523). Attested names like *Homicida, Crudelis, Phobos* suggest he was not exaggerating (Robert 1940a, 158, 191–2; id., 'Amulettes grecques', *JS* 1981, 3–44, at 28 n. 6; id. 1982, 246–8). Lexically, the poet is offering a new variant on 'blood-drinking' compounds which go back at least to Aeschylus (*Ag.* 1478 αἱματολοιχός, epithet of ἔρως), continue with Ar. *Eq.* 198, 208 αἱματοπώτης (a serpent/dragon), and persevere into Byzantine Greek (14th c.: Ὁ Πουλολόγος, 370 αἱματοπότα λύκε, 375), taking in Greg. Naz. *PG* 37.655.2 αἱμολάπτιν (a leech) along the way. Also worth noting is αἱματοπότης, an epithet which occurs mostly in lexica and etymologica, but also in an astrological treatise on the character of those born on specified days of the week (*CCAG* x. 194.4). It seems, then, that the poet is thinking of the Aristophanic αἱματοπώτης, which is supposed to represent grand oracular style. Aeschylus' compound occurs in a chorus and establishes a suitably portentous character.

617 πτώσιας οἴκων: the Greek comparanda for Saturn in opposition to Mars simply have falling (see on 3.261–3, and note on next line). M[a] has the collapse of a building (see on 3.126–30); Firmicus, 6.15.8 *gravi ruinarum pondere oppressi* (in four-footed signs), and 6.29.10–11 *corpus cadentium culminum ruinis opprimitur...nutantium tecto‹rum› culmina impingunt* (in solid signs) with A. E. Housman, 'Ovid *Ibis* 512 and *Tristia* III 6 8', *CQ* 9 (1915), 31–38, at 36 = *Classical Papers*, ed. J. Diggle and F. R. D. Goodyear (Cambridge, 1972), iii. 905–12, at 910–11.

618 ταρβείτω: formally, the only other occurrence of this part of the verb is in Quint. Smyrn. 8.18 (same *sedes*, but 'do *not* fear'). For 'beware lest', see p. 171.

---

[383] 7.3 (Laureolus), 8, 21.7; cf. Coleman, 62, 63, 64–5; Kyle, 54; more bibliography on Laureolus in n. 144 on 4.200.

σφάλματ' ἀφ' ὑψηλοῖο μελάθρου: falling from a height when Saturn and Mars are in opposition: Firmicus, 6.31.76 (Saturn in IMC). The fall takes place in solid signs, according to Firmicus, 3.4.20, 23, and 7.23.4. Well might this qualify as violent death: in *Dig.* 29.5.1.17 the man who dies *praecipitatum* is listed among those *qui per vim aut caedem sunt interfecti*. In Firmicus the fall is sometimes from a chariot, or a horse; the building here comes from *Od.* 11.278 ἀφ' ὑψηλοῖο μελάθρου, where it is used of suicide by hanging, and the fall from a height could imply suicide as well (*Dig.* 21.1.23.3 (a slave[384]); 48.8.7). M^a had already alluded to the *first* half of the same line (ἀψαμένη βρόχον αἰπὺν) in 3.262. They seem to be playing a game of complementarity (p. 219). Astrological topos and literary *jeu d'esprit* this may be, but for a real instance in Roman Egypt where the malefics apparently did their worst, see L. A. Graumann, 'Children's Accidents in the Roman Empire: The Medical Eye on 500 Years of Mishaps in Injured Children', in C. Laes and V. Vuolanto (eds.), *Children and Everyday Life in the Roman and Late Antique World* (London, 2017), 267–86, at 278.

619–26 Explicit

619 For statements of hard determinism in astrology, see i. 9, 14, and for the Manethoniana in particular, i. 58. This book does not entangle itself in claims about the non-existence or uselessness of free will, but is typical of natal astrology's insistence on ineluctability. It is possible that Μοῖραν ἄφυκτον is a very condensed allusion to Solon, fr. 13.63–4 W. μοῖρα δέ τοι θνητοῖσι κακὸν φέρει ἠδὲ καὶ ἐσθλόν· | δῶρα δ' ἄφυκτα θεῶν γίγνεται ἀθανάτων, to which the poet may have had access in an anthology (the lines appear in Stobaeus). If so, the borrowing would show a typical pattern of transference from Olympian gods to the forces of Fate (p. 220). See on 3.259 for another Solon rewrite.

620–2 ὡς μὲν...οὕτω καὶ: only *presque homérique*, for ὡς μὲν is used of the *comparandum* in *Il.* 10.487, 17.740, while οὕτω καὶ leads in the analogy in *Il.* 9.524.

620 πόρος αἰθέρα τέμνει: compare 4.37 δρόμῳ ἠέρα τέμνῃ, and see ad loc. The earlier passage reflects EGHP ἠέρα τέμνον. The αἰθέρα variant, on the other hand, is first attested in Posidipp. 115.5 A.–B. (of a high tower), but becomes celestial in *Orph. Arg.* 303 and Nonn. *D.* 17.271 (of the Sun), and above all 'astronomised' in Callistr. *Statuarum Descriptiones*, 7.3, where it is no longer from the point of view of an earth-bound human but refers to constellations, the Pleiades and Great Bear Πλειάδες τὸν αἰθέρα τέμνουσαι.

---

[384] This must be the referent in K. Bradley, 'Resisting Slavery at Rome', in Bradley and Cartledge, 362–84, at 377.

621 †τε δικήλων: δίκηλον is a well-attested variant on δείκηλον, glossed in Hesych. δ 1820–1 and Σ Ap. Rhod. 1.745–6a by εἴδωλον, but its alternation with δείκηλον in manuscripts in the latter passage shows that the first syllable is long. For εἴδωλον = 'constellation', see i. 876. But there is a real difficulty in adopting any reading (I agree with Koechly that one cannot do without a copula linking the participles) that signifies 'constellations' ('Miscentibus-se ex ordine et absistentibus signis': Koechly 1851), for the analogy is with the wandering generations of men in 622, and it is planets, not signs, that meet and move apart again. στοιχηδόν[385] suggests orderly, sequential, linear movement (rather than that of the planets, which retrograde), but it remains that the analogy only works with planets. Indeed, there is a similar one, also using ἀφίστασθαι,[386] in Theophilus, *Autol.* 2.15 οἱ δ' αὖ μεταβαίνοντες καὶ φεύγοντες τόπον ἐκ τόπου, οἱ καὶ πλάνητες καλούμενοι, καὶ αὐτοὶ τύπος τυγχάνουσιν τῶν ἀφισταμένων ἀνθρώπων ἀπὸ τοῦ θεοῦ. Lopilato sees that there should be a reference to the planets, but his emendation τε πλαγκτῶν ('while the planets mingle or stand apart therein') is prosodically and palaeographically dreadful. πλανήτων is better on the first count and equally bad on the second. So: *aporia* for the time being.

622 μερόπων γενεή: *Il.* 1.250 γενεαὶ μερόπων.

καματηδὸν ἀλᾶται: the adverb is unique. It would be a fitting conclusion if the poet meant to combine the sense 'suffering humanity' (κάματος is a fact of the human condition, Hes. *Op.* 177) with the work theme the book has been at such pains to promote (see p. 172 and 4.293 n.). The cadence emerges in Hellenistic didactic (Aratus, 531 σφαιρηδὸν ἑλίσσων, Nic. *Ther.* 556 ῥοιζηδὸν ἵενται, *Al.* 203 μετρηδὸν ὀρέξαις, 357 μοσχηδὸν ἀμέλγοι), to become popular with Nonnus.

623 οὐρανόπλαγκτον: otherwise only HOrph. 21.1 οὐρανόπλαγκτοι, of clouds, 'roaming across heaven'. Here it seems to have been transferred to θάνατον by some sort of hypallage (it should be the human race condemned to wander by the stars), unless it is in fact corrupt for οὐρανόπλαγκτος, agreeing with γενεή; as it is, it would have to mean something like 'driven on by heaven', which is not what πλάζεσθαι really means (see on 2.15, 4.7, and on 4.9 for -πλαγκτος compounds). Hence also De Stefani's suggestion οὐρανόκραντον.

---

[385] In this *sedes* Ap. Rhod. 1.1004, 'in a row'; Dion. Per. 63, 'in sequence'; Anubion, F 2.5 'along an arc'. Nonnus is inordinately fond of this adverb, mostly in this *sedes*, less often in penultimate place in the line, generally meaning 'in a row' or 'in a line', or 'in sequence', but of regular circular movement (people dancing round someone) in *D.* 19.115.

[386] The verb is often used with planets, but usually of their distance from some point, especially the Sun, but also from the ecliptic, or *kentra*. It does not seem to be regularly used of their moving apart from *each other*, though it is used of the Moon's *aporrhoia* ('Heliodorus' on Paul, pp. 4.6, 29.17–18), and for moving out of aspect in Psellus, *De omnifaria doctrina*, 165 ἀφιστάμενοι...ἐκ διαμέτρου.

Γενεαί and *τέχναι*   747

624 The line draws the poem to its final conclusion by creating a ring with its beginning (οὐρανίων ἄστρων were its opening words; also in this metrical *sedes* in Dion. Per. 909, of Phoenician star-gazers). The tone is conversable; ταῦτά τοι occurs at the end of speeches in *Od.* 7.297, *HHom. Dem.* 433, and refers back to the previous speaker in *Od.* 11.80. It illustrates how EGHP speech words and particles are co-opted to enliven didactic poetry (i. 192). *Or. Sib.* 3.809 ταῦτά σοι also uses it in the final *sphragis*. στοιχεῖα is well chosen in its capaciousness, for it can mean planets, stars, and constellations, as well as suggesting the elements of a doctrine. Lloyd-Jones and Parsons refer to this line in their commentary on *SH* 908.28 ἄστατα γὰρ στοιχε[ῖα, from a hexameter poem on comets, where the meaning is, however, obscure; see also Perale ad loc. (= his no. 2.26).

625-6 These lines correspond to, and cap, the beginning of the poem. In 4.2, it was human life that was measured out by the stars. Now it is time itself. This is the conception from which Greek astronomy began, with Hesiod marking the seasons by risings and settings of the constellations (Maximus, *Diss.* 24.6). But it looks in particular as if the poet has tried to sign off with a (sub-) philosophical formulation, ultimately in the slipstream of the *Timaeus* (p. 181). The crucial passage is 38 B–C. Plato there claims that time came into being along with the heaven (Χρόνος δ' οὖν μετ' οὐρανοῦ γέγονεν: we now see that the epithet οὐρανίων in the previous line not only ringed with the first line but also helps broker the new allusion), and that the luminaries and planets were created as markers of time (εἰς διορισμὸν καὶ φυλακὴν ἀριθμῶν χρόνου).[387] Plato has his own view that this world is a copy of an eternal model. That is entirely irrelevant to this writer, but he has nevertheless retained enough Platonic vocabulary to leave the link still visible. The past–present–future motif reproduces what Plato had said about the divisions of time in this, the created world (37 E–38 B *passim*, and 38 C ὁ δ' αὖ διὰ τέλους τὸν ἅπαντα χρόνον γεγονώς τε καὶ ὢν καὶ ἐσόμενος). On the other hand, in the next line, εἰς αἰῶνας ὀπηδεῖ ('et in saecula comitatur' (Koechly); 'and it follows on for ever' (Lopilato)) is a relic of Plato's two-tier system, with eternity (τὸ μὲν γὰρ δὴ παράδειγμα πάντα αἰωνά ἐστιν ὄν) set against creation. The cosmology that supported it in Plato has gone, but it makes a good rhetorical filip to end the poem.

---

[387] Cf. 42 D ὄργανα χρόνου, which is taken by all interpreters to mean the stars or planets, cf. Procl. *In Plat. Tim. Comm.* iii. 306.2-5 καὶ γὰρ πάντες οἱ ἀπλανεῖς καὶ πᾶς ἐγκόσμιος θεὸς κινούμενοι κατὰ κύκλον πάντως ἔχουσι περιοδικοὺς χρόνους, καθ' οὓς ὁ πᾶς μετρεῖται χρόνος τοῦ κοσμικοῦ βίου. Later passages under the influence of these include Timaeus, *Περὶ φύσιος*, 30 (ed. W. Marg, in Thesleff, p. 215.1-3) and Plut. *Mor.* 1006 D-E. The claim about measuring time is sometimes narrowed specifically to the luminaries (ps.-Plat. *Def.* 411 B).

The precise vocabulary of measurement (μετρεῖν) seems to reflect Plato's later interpreters (e.g. Phil. Op. 55 μέτρα χρόνου, 60; Proclus, n. 387, and *In Plat. Tim. Comm.* iii. 52.24–5, on each planet's orbit having τὸ πρόσφορον ἑαυτῇ μέτρον) rather than Plato himself. Koechly's correction introduces a parechesis (ἐκμεμέτρηται | ἐκμέτροις) which seems to me superior to Magnelli's suggestion, because jingles are characteristic of the poet (pp. 213–14). It better brings out the intended paradox: the stars have measured out all time, past, present, and future, and yet the ages into which they have measured it are measureless (1851, xlviii: 'saeculis, quae metrum excedunt, i.e. immensis, innumerabilibus'). This is not an example of the 'bind with a bond' type of repetition (Fehling, 158; see too n. on 4.463–4), and goes further than other cases where repeated forms of the same root are set in opposition to one another (Fehling, 268) because they here carry antithetical meanings. If Koechly is right, the poet is trying his hand at a paradox inspired by Plato's contrast between the real and ideal universes: measured out, yet immeasurable. It is a curiosity that two very different examples of popular (sub-élite) verse—this poet, and some books of the Sibylline Oracles (Lightfoot 2007, 10)—have both turned to Platonic topoi as closural devices.

Book One

1.1–15 + 16–17 Proem

The proem opens by saluting the monarch. It then advertises the present work (*deixis* in 3), overviewing its contents (including impressively windy verbiage about Fate) and stressing the pains the author has taken over it. The stated aim is to re-render Petosiris, (i) in the interests of greater depth—or concision (see on 11–12) and (ii) into hexameters. The combination is awkward (unless one of the lines, presumably 13, is interpolated), but the claim to be revisiting a source in the interests of greater user-friendliness is readily paralleled, including in astrology.[1] The goal is for Ptolemy to become aware of Egyptian learning.

Koechly, who expresses himself with uncharacteristic lack of clarity at this point (1851, xlix), seems to be denying that Manetho's name was attached to the corpus (i.e. casually, *ex post facto*) by someone who read the proems of books 1 and 5, but to be asserting that this book's editor deliberately set out to assemble 'Manethonian' material. For the proem of this book, which is an assemblage of fragments ('qui hos flosculos composuit'), he took the proem of some older poem into which he inserted ll. 4–7 and 9–10, as can be told from their verbiage and ineptitudes (see on 4–7). Koechly is certainly right about the infelicities, but if one admits the possibility of the reuse and wadding of earlier proems the interesting possibility arises that at least some of what we have here preserves parts of M^a's original poem. The reference to Petosiris is compatible with that, for he was of course the source from which Heilen wanted the parallel material in M^a, Dorotheus, Firmicus, and Anubion ultimately to derive.

It obviously cannot be the case that the *whole* of 1–15 reproduces M^a's preface. It is impossible to believe that M^a could have misused σφετέρων as in l. 10, which presumably rules out at least 9–10 (deleted by Koechly), or all of 8–10 (deleted by De Stefani) as having any connection with M^a. However:

---

[1] esp. Firmicus 4 *Praef.* 5. Valens advertises the superiority of his method and presentation over those of his rivals, but as a practitioner and theorist who is in competition with them, rather than as mere compiler. He does boast of having published his methods (e.g. VIII 5.14) and of his explanatory clarity (e.g. IX 15.1 διασαφήσας).

(i) The address to Ptolemy makes a parade of knowledge (1.14) which would be appropriately rounded off by 6.742–4 δαέντες, δεδάσθαι, ἰδμοσύνην. In that case, there would be an escalation from *Ptolemy* knowing to men in the future knowing, balanced by a narrowing-down from wise men in Egypt to the poet himself (in other words, what Don Fowler would have called a little 'didactic plot'). In each case, testimony would be offered: at the beginning, the rendering of Petosiris would be proof that the men of Egypt are all-knowing (1.11 ὄφρα κεν); at the end, the horoscope would be proof of the knowledge and skill of the poet himself (6.742 ὄφρα καὶ...). The didactic plot would involve increase in knowledge. It would be quantitative rather than qualitative, radiating out from Ptolemy to men in the future.

(ii) The promise of accuracy in 12 and its diction is redolent of Mᵃ. ἀτρεκέως or ἀτρεκίην occurs in book 3 (ll. 4, 229), and similar promises about clarity and order are almost confined to books 3 and 6 (see i. 207–8). λέξω and καταλέξω at line-end (and elsewhere) are otherwise confined to books 3 and 6 (eight instances in all), except for 4.109 Ἄλλα δέ τοι λέξω.

(iii) 1.6 contains the miserabilist topos 'what the stars bring about for wretched mortals', which is recurrent throughout Mᵃ. Koechly objected to the reference to conception, and it is true Mᵃ does not mention this (though his imitator, Mᵇ, does: 4.577, 597), but the absence of a third-foot caesura in this line is at least compatible with Mᵃ (Mᵇ and Mᵈ do not indulge it, though there are six examples in all in this book). Lines 4–6 remain vulnerable, however, to other objections raised by Koechly, and 6 is certainly inept after βροτοῖς in the line before.

On the other hand:

(iv) There is no sign that the references to Ptolemy and Egypt in 1 would ever be developed in Mᵃ.

(v) Conversely, the proem as it stands contains no appeal to any Muse, although repeated address to a Muse or Muses are implied by 6.2 (see ad loc.) and 751.[2] (Calliope occurs in 17 in a couplet stylistically unacceptable for Mᵃ.)

---

[2] This objection loses force if, on the hypothesis that the proem contains Anubionic material, Anubion himself managed to combine a contemporary *Sitz im Leben* (Ptolemy) with Muses (see on 1.360–1, in an elegiac couplet).

One could perhaps rejoin that this was an epistolary preface separate from the rest of the work, where Muses would not be expected anyway. But it would be hard to have it both ways, as if it were possible to argue that it is both integrated into the poem (point i) and separate from it (points iv and v).

Mᵃ is not the only possible background for these lines. De Stefani (2017, 25) contemplates the possibility that 11–15 contains an adapted version of Anubion's prologue, tweaked to accommodate it to hexameters (whence the interpolation of 13), which would be at least consistent with the pentameters scattered throughout the whole. De Stefani does not say whether, or how much, of, 1–7 he also wants to be retrofitted to Anubion, but the second person addressee of 14 is presumably still Ptolemy. The references to accuracy (F 4 ii. 7 ἀτρεκέως) and to Petosiris are just as appropriate to Anubion. If he is Anubion, it is new evidence that he addressed himself to Ptolemy. Whether he is Anubion or not, provided he is *not* Mᵃ, it would illustrate how much Mᵃ has in common with *an* other poet, and thereby suggest a suite of conventions for astrological poetry. They would share the rhetoric of knowledge as well as accuracy, have a similar kind of narrator who blocks out what is to come like the author of a prose treatise, and, most interestingly, have parallel strategies of advertising their competence as both poets and astrologers (Anubion, or *n*, through the whole poem that follows; Mᵃ, through the *sphragis* of his horoscope).

1–2 By combining the self-contained formula *x y* χαίρειν, which occurs in epistolary prefaces, such as several by Archimedes, or the first, second, and fourth books of Apollonius' *Conica*, with a more florid designation of the ruler's domain (e.g. ps.-Opp. *Cyn*.1.1–15, Opp. *Hal*. 1.3 γαίης ὕπατον κράτος, Ἀντωνῖνε), the poet marries a suggestion of brisk professionalism to a more fulsome and flattering approach to the monarch.

1 Χαίροις, ὦ Πτολεμαῖε: cf. Greg. Naz. *AP* 8.11.1 Χαίροις, ὦ Βασίλειε (beginning of a sepulchral epigram). The normal prose formula of salutation is the infinitive (notwithstanding ps.-John Chrys. *Oratio de nativ.* 1 Χαίροις, ὦ βρέφος ἀληθινὸν and other Byzantine authors).

λαχὼν βασιληίδα τιμὴν: Hes. *Th.* 422 καὶ τιμὴν ἔλαχον + Hes. *Th.* 462 (ἔχοι), 892 (ἔχειν) βασιληίδα τιμήν. Hesiod's line-end is much adapted, but most similarly in *HHom.* 29.3 ἔλαχες πρεσβηΐδα τιμήν.

2 γαίης ἡμετέρης: *Od.* 16.382.

κοσμοτρόφου Αἰγύπτοιο: the earliest documentable instances of this rare adjective are in inscriptions, in one of which it applies to Rome (*IGUR* i. 251.19–20 Ῥώμῃ τῇ κοσμ[ο]-[τ]ρόφῳ; 2nd half of 3rd c. AD, semi-metrical, boasting of the achievements of a Bithynian athlete who came to Rome as a child), the other to Egypt (E. Bernand, *Inscriptions métriques de l'Égypte gréco-romaine*:

Recherches sur la poésie épigrammatique des grecs en Égypte (Paris, 1969), 19.1–2 πατρὶς Ἀλεξάνδρεια Μακηδονὶς Αἰγύπτοιο | κοσμοτρόφον δάπεδον μεγάλου Πλουτῆος ἄνακτος). The latter is an early imperial epitaph for a goldsmith and silversmith who died in Rome, but has a cenotaph erected for him by his wife in Alexandria. Bernand ad loc. connects it with Egyptian wheat which was exported across the Mediterranean from the port of Alexandria, and the Byzantine poetic recension of the Alexander Romance applies it to both Egypt and the Nile (l. 44 γῆς τῆς θαυμαστῆς, καλλίστης κοσμοτρόφου, l. 1518 ποταμὸν τὸν μέγιστον Νεῖλον τὸν κοσμοτρόφον, l. 3085 τὴν κοσμοτρόφον Αἴγυπτον (of the Nile flood)). The imperial poet describes the state of affairs in his own times, though he is (accidentally?) not wrong to project it back to Ptolemaic Egypt.[3] To look no later, Procl. *In Plat. Crat.* 170 applies the epithet to φύσις; in Byzantine poetry it describes γάλα, χάρις, Christ.

3 ἄξιά σοι τάδε δῶρα φέρω βασιληίδος ἀρχῆς: this version of the 'worthiness' motif praises the king and implicitly reflects well on the giver (compare Isocrates, *Ad Nicocl.* 2 ἡγησάμην δ᾽ ἂν γενέσθαι ταύτην καλλίστην δωρεὰν καὶ χρησιμωτάτην καὶ μάλιστα πρέπουσαν ἐμοί τε δοῦναι καὶ σοὶ λαβεῖν); elsewhere the speaker turns to self-praise outright.[4] In other versions, he feigns to doubt his own worthiness, or his ability to make a worthy offering.[5] In the Hermetic version, he mysticates his offering by a parade of having been worthy himself to receive it from a divine source, or requires the addressee to be worthy to receive it (Festugière, 352).

δῶρα φέρω: cf. *inter al.* Philicus, *SH* 677.

βασιληίδος ἀρχῆς: Ariphron, *PMG* 813.4 (4th c. BC); then a commonplace late antique hexameter ending, especially in the *Oracula Sibyllina*.

4–7 In these lines Koechly 1851, xlix took exception to the ineptitude of the connective in τε φάσεις and to the irrelevant reference to conception in l. 6, to which can be added that whole line is word-spinning on βροτοῖς in the line before. Take these lines out, and the preface becomes a vague advertisement

---

[3] D. Rathbone, 'The Grain Trade and Grain Shortages in the Hellenistic East', in P. D. A. Garnsey and C. R. Whittaker (eds.), *Trade and Famine in Classical Antiquity* (Cambridge, 1983), 45–55, at 50–3; K. Buraselis, 'Ptolemaic Grain, Seaways and Power', in K. Buraselis, M. Stefanou, and D. Thompson (eds.), *The Ptolemies, the Sea and the Nile: Studies in Waterborne Power* (Cambridge, 2013), 97–107. For the promotion of the wealth theme in Ptolemaic Egypt, see Hunter on Theocr. 17.79–80 and 95–7.

[4] Isocr. *Nicocl.* 10; Hyginus, *Astr. praef.* 6 *quod si vel optimis usus auctoribus effeci ut neque brevius neque verius diceret quisquam, non inmerito fuerim laudari dignus a vobis, quae vel amplissima laus hominibus est doctis...*

[5] Isocr. *Nicocl.* 7; ps.-Aelius Aristides, εἰς βασιλέα 57 ἐγὼ δ᾽ οὔτε χρόνου πλῆθος ἱκανὸν οὔτε λόγον οὐδένα ὁρῶ τοῦ βασιλέως ἄξιον, οὐδ᾽ ὅστις αὐτὸν ἱκανῶς ἐγκωμιάσαι δυνήσεται· ὅμως δὲ οὐκ ἀποδειλιατέον, ἀλλ᾽ ὅση δύναμις πειρατέον εἰπεῖν; Firmicus Maternus, *Praef.* 1.1.

with no announcement of subject; the same is true of book 5. Suppose these lines are not genuine; the sentiment and language of 6–7 is nevertheless very reminiscent of 1.200-2 (from Koechly's poet B) ἥ θ' ἅμα νηπιάχοις συγγίγνεται ἀνθρώποισιν, | εὐθύ τε <u>Μοιράων</u> εἱλίσσεται ἀμφὶ <u>μίτοισιν</u>, | κλώσμασιν <u>ἀρρήκτοισι</u> σιδηρείοισί τ' ἀτράκτοις). On the other hand, the repetition of the line-ending of 4 in 359, and the absence of third-foot caesura in both 6 and 359, might suggest a connection with the poet/editor who cobbled together the conclusion.

4 At least as the line is deployed here, φάσεις must be non-technical, 'appearance' (see 5.122 n.), nothing to do with φάσις in the sense of a star's proximity to the sun. ἄστρα should be constellations not stars (see on 2.3), but presumably the genitive plural necessitates the second-declension form for the sake of metre. At 1.294, 321, 327, which are lines shared with M^b, the poet uses ἀστέρες correctly, of planets. For the unfulfilled but apparently conventional pledge to talk about fixed stars, see on 4.3-4.

5 τελέουσιν: the stars do not just signify (5.244 n.), they cause (though somehow also in concert with Fate: 7). The choice of verb of course points to the genre of ἀποτελέσματα and evokes ἀποτελεῖν, the standard prose verb for the stars' effects (Heilen 2015, 777). There is a striking difference between M^a, who uses the simplex and ἐκτελεῖν—a good equivalent for ἀποτελεῖν while also having the endorsement of EGHP[6]—and some of the other poets in the corpus. In this book τελ- also occurs in 1.213, 214, 284, 311, but M^b has τελ- only in 4.363, and M^d not at all (though he does have τὰ τελέσματα at 128). ἐκτελ- otherwise occurs in the corpus only at 1.76.

ἐπιβλέψαντες: a common prose word for aspect, also used in the pinax of the third book (where, however, I am not sure I have grasped any implied difference between συμμαρτυροῦντες, συσχηματιζόμενοι, and ἐπιβλέποντες; a difference is also implied by ps.-Palchus, CCAG ix/1. 169.22-170.1 ἴδε... τίς αὐτὴν ἀστὴρ ἐπιβλέπει... καὶ τίς αὐτῇ μαρτυρεῖ). As usual (cf. Prévot, 258), the corpus uses simplex βλέπειν in the present (4.171), and compound forms in the aorist (here and 1.109).

ἐν ἀρχαῖς: at the beginnings of human lives: cf. 3.401, 416, where the meaning is made explicit by the addition of ζωῆς or ζωῆς χρόνου, and 4.474 ἄρχεται. Using his own, idiosyncratic, terminology, Ptol. 3.2.1-4 distinguishes the ἀρχή (conception) from καταρχή (birth). The next line looks precisely to those two

---

[6] Present: 6× before caesura, 8× line-end; aorist ἐξετέλεσσε/αν: 2× before caesura (sing.) and 8× line-end. Both positions for both tenses are Homeric (ἐξετέλεσσε before caesura specifically Odyssean), though epic also has other positions not reflected in M^a, esp. ἐκτελ- at line-beginning.

events, so that ἀρχαῖς here (supposing the two lines are from the hand of the same poet) might comprise both. If, on the other hand, 6 is an interpolation, ἀρχαῖς here is a poetic plural and the next line could be an explanatory expansion (I thank the anonymous reader for this suggestion).

6 As Koechly said, horoscopes from conception (not birth) are irrelevant to this book, and to the corpus in general, although *de facto* conception is the only factor involved for a foetus that never comes to term (as Lopilato notes). The moment of conception, as the true genesis of an individual, attracted the interest of astrologers from the very beginning of the discipline (see Ptolemy, cited in the previous note). Various methods are known for calculating it, including one by Nechepso and Petosiris. Equally, there are no extant examples of conception (as opposed to natal) horoscopes, so perhaps we should be surprised that the poet even promises something of which, if he delivered a formal example of it, he would be an almost unique representative in antiquity (Heilen 2015, 511–13, 525).

The verse pattern in which two parallel middle participles override a third-foot caesura goes back to *Od*. 24.163 βαλλόμενος καὶ ἐνισσόμενος.[7] M^a does not have this, though he has the commoner Homeric pattern (e.g. *Il*. 4.451 = 8.65 ὀλλύντων τε καὶ ὀλλυμένων) where just the element that overrides the caesura is a middle participle (3.18, 146, 198, 272, 382, 424; 6.22, 76, 103, 137, 195). From the point of view of authorship, other verses lacking a third-foot caesura in this book are also of the shape *x* καὶ *y*, but they involve nouns (see on 46). For a comprehensive Homeric list see Lehrs, 396–403.

7 The cliché is so familiar (Giannakis 1998, 1999) that one tends to project the whole complex back to Homer. In fact, in the Homeric poems themselves the gods are much more often the spinners than μοῖρα or αἶσα are (Giannakis 1998, 7–8, 12–13). This is therefore another appropriation of the gods' vocabulary by the forces of Fate, except that it extends well beyond astrology. The poet joins the great majority in substituting μίτος for λίνον (*Il*. 24.210; for μίτος, which is Homeric, but not used of Fate, see Giannakis 1998, 15–16). λίνον does not disappear completely, but it is hard to explain why μίτος (already in Lyc. 584–5; *IG* V,1 1186.1, Gytheion, 1st half of 1st c. BC, but mostly imperial) swamps the other to such an extent. It is banal in inscriptions, and again in the Manethoniana in 1.201, 5.8; TLG and PHI s.v. Μοιρ- and μίτ- disclose so many more that there is no point in further citations, save to say that most are epitaphic (or in references to death), whereas those in the Manethoniana refer to *everything* (so too Constantinus Manasses, *Aristandros and Callithea*, fr. 137.5

---

[7] Other parts of verbs: *Il*. 4.371 τί πτώσσεις, τί δ' ὀπιπεύεις; *Od*. 15.323 δαιτρεῦσαί τε καὶ ὀπτῆσαι.

μίτοις αἱ Μοῖραι κλώθουσι πάντα τὰ τῶν ἀνθρώπων). Unbreakability again in 1.202; the motif, which perhaps began from the idea of Fate's shackles (Il. 22.5, Od. 3.269, etc.), has been transferred to oaths in Lollius Bassus, AP 9.236.1 = Garland 1611 Ἄρρηκτοι Μοιρῶν... ὅρκοι (of the fated fall of Troy; Gow–Page are surprised). 'Law of necessity' is another fatalistic commonplace (TLG θεσμ- + ἀναγκ-; the first example is as early as Aristarchus Trag. 14 F 2.2 Snell, 5th c.). For astrological ἀνάγκη, see Zito on Maximus, 121.

8–10 Koechly 1851, xlix, deleted 9 and 10, objecting to the repetition of ἅσπερ κάμον, ἅσπερ ἔτευξα and to the catachresis of σφετέρων. De Stefani transposed 8 (which depends on the idea of labour) and 9, and took out all three. Without them, the poet still offers his work to the king, but without the *labor* motif (8 μογήσας, 9 κάμον, 10 καμάτων), which is found in connection with *belles-lettres*[8] and technical[9] and scientific[10] texts. For κάματος see further on 6.4–5; 5.11.

8 For working day and night, compare Artemidorus, 2.70.12 ἐγὼ μὲν οὖν πάντων διὰ πείρας ἐλήλυθα τῷ μηδὲν ἄλλο πράττειν, ἀεὶ δὲ καὶ νύκτωρ καὶ μεθ' ἡμέραν πρὸς ὀνειροκρισίᾳ εἶναι. Most versions of the diligence motif, however, just involve the night,[11] and that makes plausible Monteventi's suggestion that the poet is thinking specifically of Il. 9.325–6 (144–5), where Achilles refers to both sleepless nights (ἀΰπνους νύκτας) and toilsome days (ἤματα). The bizarreness is presumably outweighed by the advantage of amplifying the customary boast, which is especially frequent in proems but sometimes found in sign-offs and elsewhere. It seems to have a niche in specifically astronomical and astrological literature. It might underlie Alexander of Ephesus' soubriquet Λύχνος (A. Meineke, *Analecta Alexandrina* (Berlin, 1843), 371 n. 1; Radt on Strab. XIV p. 642C 8 ff.), and it is used as a sign-off by Firmicus Maternus, 8.33.4... *quod* (sc. the present work) *nos pervigili cura et labore animi pariter et corporis, cum maxima sollicitudine ac trepidatione perfecimus*. See too Lyne on ps.-Virg. *Ciris*, 46; Hollis on Cinna, fr. 13.1; Janson, 97–8; J. Robert, 286–7; Call. *Ep.* 27.4 Pf. ἀγρυπνίη; Monteventi, 145–6.

---

[8] Meleager, AP 4.1.4 = HE 3929 ἐξεπόνησε; Lyne on ps.-Virg. *Ciris*, 99.
[9] *Sortes Astrampsychi*, Epist. p. 1.3 πολὺν κόπον ὑπομείνας; *Rhet. ad Herenn*. 1.1.1.
[10] 'Thessalus', Epist. ad Augustum, 2 (CCAG viii/3. 135.4–5) τούτοις γε (sc. superhuman matters which no-one hitherto has been able to tackle) μετὰ πολλῶν βασάνων καὶ κινδύνων τὸ καθῆκον τέλος ἐπέθηκα; Lucr. 1.141–2, 2.730–1, 3.419–20; Hyginus, *Astr., praef.* Ptolemy praises Hipparchus for being φιλόπονος (*Synt.* 3.1 = i/1. 191.20 Heiberg).
[11] Lucr. 1.142 *noctes vigilare serenas*; Cic. *Paradoxa* 5 *accipies igitur hoc parvum opusculum lucubratum his iam contractioribus noctibus, quoniam illud maiorum vigiliarum munus in tuo nomine apparuit* (sc. the *Brutus*); Plin. *NH Praef.* 18; ps.-Virg. *Ciris* 46 *accipe dona meo multum vigilata labore*; Persius, 5.62 *at te nocturnis iuvat inpallescere chartis*; Stat. *Theb.* 12.811–12 *o mihi bissenos multum vigilata per annos | Thebai*.

9 ἅσπερ κἀμόν: LSJ I.1: the construction is epic (of weapons, garments, a sceptre, ships, furniture, etc).

10 With its dispatch formula the line combines the clinical, impersonal style of a Hellenistic scientific treatise (Janson, 21, e.g. Archimedes, *Quadratura Parabolae*, ἐπροχειριξάμεθα δὲ ἀποστεῖλαί τοι γράψαντες...; id. *De lineis spiralibus*, Τῶν ποτὶ Κόνωνα ἀποσταλέντων θεωρημάτων...τινὰς...καὶ ἐν τῷδε τῷ βιβλίῳ γράψας ἐπιστέλλω τοι; Archimedes Palimpsest, ii, p. 71.30-2 τούτων δὴ τῶν θεωρημάτων τὰς ἀποδείξεις ἐν τῷδε τῷ βιβλίῳ γράψας ἀποστελῶ σοι, 'In this book therefore I send you the written proofs of theorems') with a poetic phrase (*Od.* 4.444, *Th.* 871, *Op.* 41, 346, 822 μέγ' ὄνειαρ) which positions the treatise as a boon conferred by the giver rather than answering to the specific intellectual interests of the addressee (e.g. Archimedes Palimpsest, ii, p. 71.33-5 Ὁρῶν δέ σε, καθάπερ λέγω, σπουδαῖον καὶ φιλοσοφίας προεστῶτα ἀξιολόγως), though it might imply that he will find it practically useful.

καμάτων σφετέρων: see Syntax, p. 287.

11-15 See De Stefani 2017, 25, for the theory that these lines are a hexameter adaptation of a fragment of Anubion, and the sceptical reaction by Heilen 2017, 223-4 n. 14.

11-12 ἐπιτροχάδην...εἴρηκεν: there are two questions here, (i) whether εἴρηκεν is to be taken literally and implies that Petosiris communicated by word of mouth, and (ii) what the adverb means. The two questions are imbricated, because the phrase at first sight looks to be making some version of the claim conventional in prose prefaces that the writer is offering up something whose presentation is superior to what precedes it; but that becomes harder if the earlier authority was himself an oral source.

On the first point, I think that εἴρηκεν has to be a citation formula. While the Graeco-Roman Nechepso–Petosiris literature fathers treatises on them,[12] or has the sage addressing letters to the king,[13] Egyptian versions of the tradition seem prepared to envisage further possibilities; the Yale papyrus from Tebtunis (P. CtYBR inv. 422 verso; p. 864 n. 10) has 'Petesis' in oral exchange with the pharaoh, and P. Rylands 63 represents 'Peteesis' among Egyptian 'prophets' in dialogue with Plato (see on 5.10). But λέγω is a normal word to introduce quotations, including in passages where Valens quotes or alludes to Petosiris' writings

---

[12] The astrological writer of P.Salt (i. 55; p. 865) identifies Petosiris along with 'Necheus' among the σοφῶν ἀρχαίων from whose many books he derives his learning. Firmicus (4 *Praef.* 5) and Valens (II 29.1 ἐν τοῖς ὑπομνήμασιν ἑαυτῶν; IX 11.2) have read Petosiris' books and cite him specifically as an author.

[13] Moyer, 246-7. In one such text he is made to refer to an earlier treatise by himself (*CCAG* vii. 161.4-5 καθὰ καὶ ἐν τῷ περὶ πλανήτων ἀστέρων ὑπεδείξαμεν λόγῳ, καί, ὡς ἐνταῦθα ἀπεγραψάμεθα...).

(IX 2.7 λέγει ἐν τοῖς Ὅροις; Additamenta Antiqua, II 5 λέγουσι δὲ οἱ περὶ Πετόσιριν, cf. II 29.1 ἐξεῖπον, VII 6.35 ἔφη). So there is no objection to putting this passage in the context of other advertisements in prose prefaces. The question is what the poet is claiming to have done with Petosiris' writings.

The two Homeric precedents for the adverb point in different directions. On the one hand, *Il.* 3.213 ἐπιτροχάδην ἀγόρευε characterises the way Menelaus spoke in contrast to Odysseus, hence, 'briefly' (214–15 παῦρα μὲν ἀλλὰ μάλα λιγέως, ἐπεὶ οὐ πολύμυθος | οὐδ᾽ ἀφαμαρτοεπής). The contrast would then be between a short, or superficial, version and the informationally and poetically more adequate version now on offer. That meaning has been proposed by LSJ ('cursorily'), Gundel and Gundel (162 'die nur oberflächliche Darstellung des Petosiris'), and Heilen 2017, 223-4 n. 14, although he then develops an unsustainable and uncharacteristically 'literary' theory that the narrator implies that he stands in the same relation to Petosiris as Homeric Odysseus in relation to Menelaus (i.e. rhetorically superior). Monteventi, 188–9, cf. 197, suggests that the reference is to the quality of brevity which is in inherent in iambic verse (and for the association of the iambus with the verb ἐπιτρέχειν points also to ps.-Scymnus, 43 ἐπιτρέχουσαν ἐν ἑαυτῇ χάριν, although there the verb means something different).

I have adopted this interpretation in my own rendering ('passingly'), but if the poet means that he is offering a fuller presentation of what was brief and condensed in his source, it is the opposite of the aspiration to succinctness, and to improved organisation, which other prefaces express.[14] Consider Dionysius the son of Calliphon, 8–11 Τὰ γὰρ ἐν πλείοσιν | ὑπὸ τῶν παλαιῶν συγγραφέων εἰρημένα, | ταῦτ᾽ ἐμμέτρως ῥηθήσετ᾽ ἐν βραχεῖ χρόνῳ, | ὅπερ ἐστὶν ἱκανῶς δύναμιν ἰσχυρὰν ἔχον, and compare especially with the adverbs of diffuseness or copiousness in ps.-Scymnus, 32 πάντων ἐπιτομὴν τῶν χύδην εἰρημένων, 65-6 Ἐκ τῶν σποράδην γὰρ ἱστορουμένων τισίν ἐν ἐπιτομῇ σοι γέγραφα; Galen, *De Typis*, vii. 463.1-3 Kühn Πολλῶν πλατυτέρῳ ὑπὲρ τῆς περὶ τύπων θεωρίας πεπραγματευμένων, ἀναγκαῖον ἡγησάμην αὐτὸς ὁριστικώτερον καὶ κατὰ περιγραφὴν ἐπιδραμεῖν ταῦτα. In fact, such a contrast, conventional in prefaces, between previous discursive treatments and an offering which is more condensed and user-friendly, could be supported by the other Homeric occurrence of the adverb, *Od.* 18.26 ἐπιτροχάδην ἀγορεύει, where Irus characterises the speech of Odysseus-as-beggar as fluent or glib.

Neither interpretation is entirely satisfactory. The second seems more appropriate to a preface, but the poet's antithesis is not, strictly, between diffuseness and succinctness, but between writing ἐπιτροχάδην and writing in hexameters, which are not what one would mention if one's point were to advertise brevity.

---

[14] Fögen, 39, on συντομία.

This helps De Stefani's case for deleting line 13. Heilen 2011, 81 n. 290, had wondered whether 'glib' had in fact developed into the meaning 'prosaic', so that the contrast would indeed be between prose and verse, though that meaning is not attested elsewhere.

12 μάλ' ἀτρεκέως: i. 178, 207 n. 104; the closest is *Od.* 24.303 τοιγὰρ ἐγώ τοι πάντα μάλ' ἀτρεκέως καταλέξω.

13 The technical term for the hexameter is μέτρον ἡρωικόν (e.g. Dion. Hal. *Comp. Verb.* 20).

14–15 The present work (all of it) attests the poet's learning to the king, much as the horoscope in 6.742 testified to the poet's capacity to future generations. δαήμονες (i. 58 and n. 53) remakes Homeric δαήμονα φῶτα, δαήμονι φωτί (same *sedes*), reversing the negatives in the Homeric passages with a resounding claim to omnicompetence. Heilen 2017, 223–4 n. 14, notes a striking parallel in Antipater, *AP* 11.23.1 = *HE* 277 (where the speaker dismisses the predictions of astrologers, δαήμονες ἄνδρες), and conjectures a possible common source in (or about) Petosiris. In fact Gow–Page note another parallel in Leonidas, *AP* 9.25.1 = *HE* 2573 Ἀρήτοιο δαήμονος (a man who wrote about the stars), so there is a lineage traceable to the Hellenistic period for the epithet to be used, respectfully or otherwise, of experts in the heavens. Anyway, an attitude completely different from this proud boast is displayed by *Corp. Herm.* XVI. 2, where Asclepius writes to Ammon advising him to keep the *logos* untranslated lest holy secrets be revealed to the Greeks.

ἱερὸν πέδον Αἰγύπτοιο: Dorotheus, p. 428.25 καλὸν πέδον Αἰγύπτοιο; Dion. Per. 227 (πιαίνων) λιπαρὸν πέδον Αἰγύπτοιο; *Or. Sib.* 14.120 μέλαν πέδον Αἰγύπτοιο. The first occurrence of ἱερὸν πέδον is Ap. Rhod. 4.1396. All later examples, which are imperial, contain a genitive place-name, though they put it in the first half of the line. Those in Dion. Per. 788, Quint. Smyrn. 8.358, Lascaris, *Ep.* 63.5, involve journeys or itineraries; *HOrph. Pr.* 8 ναίεις ἱερὸν πέδον and Julius Polyaenus *AP* 9.7.3 = *Garland* 3949 are hymnic (the other example is Greg. Naz. *AP* 8.146.1). This is neither, but most like the Orphic example because of the verb. But there is also a strange parallel with *Theos. Tüb.* 34 οἳ λάχομεν περὶ κόσμον ἀλήμονα ναιέμεν αἰεί, in which Apollo speaks for pagan gods subaltern to the supreme deity.

16–17 Koechly 1851, xlix: 'Egenum frustulum...compilatoris'. The planetary order is qualitative, like the standard Seleucid one, but it puts the malefics ahead of Mercury and the benefics, which is unusual (on planetary order, see i. 44 n. 10 and 70–1 n. 23; Lopilato notes that it corresponds to planetary days of the week except for Saturn). But it is so similar to 1.203–4—save for the reversal of luminaries and of benefics—that I would attribute them to the same poet

(Koechly's 'B', the author of the *schetliasmos* of Mars and 'why sacrifice') (p. 283). But it is worth noting that a couple of lines were apparently missing from the first, lost, column of Π^3, which contained ll. 1–25; although there are other possibilities, this couplet is an obvious candidate for the absent lines. The licence in accommodating Jupiter's name to the hexameter (Ἑρμέα, Ζῆνα) was brokered by Dorotheus (see i. 232 n. 3 and p. 381).

17 καλή...Καλλιόπεια: perhaps generic, perhaps looking to the Muse-formula in *Il*. 1.603, *Od*. 24.60, Hes. *Th*. 68, HHom. Ap. 189 ὀπὶ καλῇ. (In *IGUR* III, 1305 [Rome, Hadrianic], Μοῦσα καλή is both the name of the deceased woman, Petronia Musa, and a play on her musical gifts.) Calliope was chosen presumably as chief Muse (Harder on Call. fr. 7c,4) rather than because the poet was making some statement about didactic as a species of *epos*, which feels rather pretending for a poet who was *also* prepared to sink to the entirely prosaic λέγε instead of ἔννεπε or ἔνισπε. The extended form of her name, almost always used in invocations, and often with an epithet, is first found in Stesichorus, fr. 277 Davies and Finglass δεῦρ᾽ ἄγε Καλλιόπεια λίγεια, and then at line-end in Empedocles, 31 B 131 παρίστασο, Καλλιόπεια, and Call. fr. 759 Pf. (possibly, not verifiably, from the *Aitia*); later, Triph. 4 ἔννεπε, Καλλιόπεια and Mesomedes (II Heitsch), 1.5 Καλλιόπεια σοφά. The question is what function the invocation might have served in an original context. If it was designed to preface a systematic catalogue (it adapts the traditional formula in which the Muse is asked for names; she is now already supplied with them), and if that catalogue followed the same planetary order as here, it implies a different procedure from Mᵃ, Dorotheus, Firmicus, and *Lib. Herm*., who all follow *heptazonos* order. For Venus' epithet, see i. 907 n. 14.

1.18–361 The Book Proper

1.18–25 Charts Involving Venus

Koechly held that this group was from the hand of same poet, with the possible exception of 20–1. There is a clear similarity between these lines and 258 + 261, and Koechly bracketed them. Yet apart from the catachrestic use of λάφυρα in 20 (which remains catachrestic however one treats it), exactly the same method could be used to argue that they are by the hand of his main poet, A, for 22 Ἄρης καὶ Παφίη = 42, 22 κέντρων ὅτ᾽ ἄν ὦσιν ἄνακτες = 66, and 23 ῥέζουσι γυναικῶν ~ 46 ῥέζουσι γυναιξίν. Either the lines are genuine, or the whole of 18–25 is by a pastichist; but pastiche is not a useful concept for verse which is already created out of set patterns. As a matter of fact 18 Ἦν Κρόνος also = 1.339, which for

Koechly is the *ineptus versificator*, but perhaps this is not quite substantial enough to constitute a link.

18–21

Saturn and Sun aspect Venus. Compare very approximately Firmicus, 6.31.82 (malefics and Venus in conjunction on ASC and Sun in same sign), where wives who are slaves and prostitutes are among the outcomes.

18 κατίδωσι: see on 4.362 κατιδών.

19 δυσγαμίην: see 2.179 n. ἀστασίην: see 3.81 n. ἐπὶ λέκτροις: Eur. Med. 640, Tr. 324; see on 5.102, where an allusion to Euripides is detectable, perceptible here too, though weaker, since Venus herself is not the subject of the verb.

20 For the categories or category (they could be the same) of degraded women, see n. on 2.178 + 180. For the last word L reads λαφύραις,[15] with a subsequent attempt to delete the last two letters. Koechly corrected to λαφύροις in the sense of 'slave captives', but was apparently too contemptuous of the whole couplet to bother to supply an object for διδόασι. The accusative is still catachrestic. Was the poet trying to make the point that the gifts given were themselves stolen goods?

21 κυθερείης: for metonymy, see on 3.154. Antip. Thess. AP 5.31.2 = Garland 706 is a borderline case. It is very popular in the *Cynegetica* (6×), though one would be reluctant to attribute that to the Manethoniana alone.

22–3

Mars and Venus in *kentra*. This is unremarkable. Adulterers are produced by Mars and Venus in 2.267–70; 4.304–5, 350, cf. 394; 5.136, 283.

22 Ἄρης καὶ Παφίη: also 42.

κέντρων ὅτ᾽ ἂν ὦσιν ἄνακτες: also 66: see i. 879 (on location) and 890 (on the notion of Lordship). The high point that appears at the end of this line in both editions of Koechly is presumably a mistake. There is no punctuation in the manuscript.

23 ἁρπακτῆρας: first in *Il.* 24.262 (line-end), but of animals used metaphorically for human seducers in Lyc. 147. For the metaphor see on 4.56. References to animals tend to stay at line-end, in the Homeric position, whereas

---

[15] Not *λαφύναις (M. Papathomopoulos, 'ΛΑΦΥΝΑΓ', RPh³ 47 (1973), 109).

the human/divine seducers of Nonn. *D.* 6.92 and Triph. 164 are in this *sedes* (although so is Opp. *Hal.* 1.373, which refers to dogs).

24–5

As above, with Mercury (in equal degrees?). This is the conventional coding for pederasty (Heilen 2015, 1119).

24 ἰσόρροπος ἀντήσειεν: it may have been obvious to the poet, but it is not obvious to me whether this means 'encounter' (of conjunction) (cf. 51) or 'come opposite to' (of opposition). Perhaps, if the aspect is one of concord (n. on 2.436–8), it makes no difference, but the verb implies the hostile encounter of personified agents (*Il.* 7.158 τώ κε τάχ' ἀντήσειε μάχης κορυθαίολος Ἕκτωρ; pp. 292–3). Is ἰσόρροπος intended to convey specific information, presumably as an equivalent to ἰσόμοιρος? It is not an astrological technical term (otherwise only Ptol. 3.5.11, which is used of reckoning up contributory factors).

25 χαλεπῇ ἐπὶ κύπριδι: like κακῆς... κυθερείης in 21.[16] Some astrological texts (Cumont, 181 n. 3) evince a strikingly blanket condemnation of pederasty which does not reflect what is documentable about contemporary social attitudes. It is not something to be tolerated with a certain amount of sniggering, something that only raised eyebrows if it was done to excess or if there was a suggestion that the boy was a prostitute, nor is it tolerable within limits (i.e., when directed to slaves as opposed to the freeborn), but something that is, in and of itself, deplorable.[17] In Ptol. 4.5.17 pederasts—whom Ptolemy calls pathological, νοσηματώδεις—are also the result of an imbalance (both Mars and Venus are eastern), though not as bad as when men are drawn exclusively to men of any age (Heilen 2015, 1119, who notes that Mercury is jettisoned in this system because it lacks a female counterpart to make it perfectly symmetrical). In 3.14.35, where the coding is different (Venus modified by Mercury), pederasts (διαφθορέας... παίδων) figure alongside many other kinds of reprobate. See further on 4.591 for the Manethoniana on homosexuality.

---

[16] Pressed into service from an expression for love-pangs? Theognis, 1307 Κυπρογενοῦς δ' ἔργων ἀντιάσεις χαλεπῶν, cf. 1321 ἔρος... χαλεπόν; Anacreon, *PMG* 346 fr. 4.6]. χαλεπῶν δι' Ἀφροδίτη[; Asclepiades, *AP* 12.50.2 = *HE* 881 χαλεπὴ Κύπρις.

[17] Boy a prostitute: Richlin, 221–3. Boy a slave: ead., 'Reading Boy-Love and Child-Love in the Greco-Roman World', in M. Masterson, N. Sorkin Rabinowitz, and J. Robson (eds.), *Sex in Antiquity: Exploring Gender and Sexuality in the Ancient World* (Abingdon, 2015), 352–73. For attitudes to pederasty, see T. K. Hubbard, 'Historical Views of Homosexuality: Roman Empire', in Oxford Research Encyclopedia of Politics (online).

1.26–33 Luminaries in Places of Gender

There are only two options in this passage—(i) concord and (ii) masculinisation (for females only). But it is likely that 1.115–18 supplies the counterpart of (ii), namely the feminisation of men.

The first outcome concerns status (kingship), the second sexuality. The first has some affiliation with Ptolemy, 4.3.1, who also assigns importance to the location of luminaries on angles, but who uses a different logic (see i. 703), according to which the greatest privilege comes about, not through concord, but through maximal masculinisation. The second, on the other hand, is related to our old friend Ptol. 3.15.7–12 (i. 702–5). Venus is an additional influence, as in Ptolemy and 3.387, but so is the horoscope, and what is relevant is their opposition to the luminaries, not the fact of their masculinisation. (If the poet is working with the system that the gender of signs alternates, then being directly opposite will *de facto* mean that Venus and the horoscope are masculine as well, but he does not say this directly.) The commentary on book 3 should have noted that what masculinises Venus in Ptolemy is phase as well as quality of sign, while in book 3 it is only quality of sign. Here it is neither.

26–8

Sun, centred, in male places, Moon, centred, in female. This chart is obviously similar to 1.277–80 (28 ~ 280), where both luminaries are on centres, the Moon is in sect, and the Sun is in a male place, but see pp. 282–3 for doubts on stylistic grounds about assigning the lines to the same poet. Luminaries on centres regularly produce kings (see on 2.389; 4.93–100 + 101–6; 1.278–80, 281–3 + 284–5; 5.39), and some of the sources that discuss this situation also talk about types of sign. But when it is a matter of the *gender* of signs, they use Ptolemy's system in 4.3.1, where the privileged position is two masculine signs, not concord (passages cited on 28).

26 κερόεσσα: i. 904 n. 2. A possible restoration in *SH* 909.2 (Lloyd-Jones and Parsons).

27 ἐναλλάξ: contrariwise, viz. in the type of sign appropriate to her (feminine); contrast 4.515, where ἐναλλάξωσι meant swapping polarities (Moon in masculine signs, Sun in feminine). Both are easily understood, neither depends on knowledge of the other; for the latter, see on 6.368; for the present meaning e.g. Sarapion, *CCAG* viii/4. 231.20 (the masculine planets rejoice in eastern, the feminine contrariwise in western).

28 βασιλῆας ὑπερθύμους τε δυνάστας: this glamorises a frequent astrological pairing with a multipurpose Homeric epithet, for groups and categories (including Trojans) and individuals. We find 'kings and dynasts' in other sources dealing with king-making luminaries on centres. Particularly similar is *Π.τ.δ.* 8 εἰ δὲ καὶ ὁ Ἥλιος καὶ ἡ Σελήνη ἐπίκεντροι ὄντες ὑπὸ Διὸς καὶ Ἄρεως μαρτυρηθῶσιν, καὶ μάλιστα ἐν ἀρρενικοῖς ζῳδίοις ὄντες, βασιλεῖς ποιοῦσιν ἢ δυνάστας; Camaterus, *Introd.* 2945-6. The *Dodecatopos* also uses the formula for luminaries in *kentra*, sometimes specifying sect, but not the quality of signs (Θ p. 152.2-3, Moon in IMC and Sun on ASC; 170.5-7, Moon in MC). Firmicus, 7.22.1, *reges...potentes* perhaps renders the same thing.

29-33

Luminaries in male places, opposite Venus and ASC. All the vital indicators are masculine, and the outcome is masculinisation of women. The additional stipulation about Venus in 30 is paralleled by 3.387, though there she is accompanied by Mars, here by mention of the horoscope.

29 φωστῆρες: see Heilen 2015, 857. It possibly becomes commoner in Christian astrological writers because it is LXX's word for luminaries in the creation story.

30 θηλυτέρης: the poet continues sensitive to the comparative's implicit sense of opposition (references in Garvie on *Od.* 8.324; Livrea on Ap. Rhod. 4.1345), in this case of the feminine planet to the masculine places in which she is located (contrast 4.220, with note). He also follows EGHP usage in making this an epithet (in EGHP of either γυναῖκες or θεαί), unlike Apollonius, who makes it a noun; but in EGHP it is never singular.

κατιθύ: otherwise only Hdt. 9.51.3 ('opposite', adverbial); κατιθύς in Babrius, 1.95.42 ('forth') and Quint. Smyrn. 7.136 ('facing', prep. + gen.). The new papyrus has the reading [κατ] ιθυν, which recalls the reading at 1.339 (ascribed by Koechly to his 'ineptus'): see ad loc.

31 ἀρσενικοῖς ἔργοισιν: see on 4.358.

32 μέγα θαῦμα: either intentionally or inadvertently comic, if one thinks of the contexts in EGHP (where it is often stretched across a whole line in formulae like ὦ πόποι ἦ μέγα θαῦμα τόδ' ὀφθαλμοῖσιν ὁρῶμαι, etc.), where it is used for physical impossibilities like people apparently coming back from the dead, physical disappearances, a child leading a herd of cattle; perhaps least unlike *Il.* 13.99, of the formerly cowardly Trojans becoming dominant.

γυναιμανέες: Paris' epithet at *Il.* 3.39, 13.769.

33 ἀργαλέως γαμέουσιν: this could just be the use of γαμεῖν for sexual intercourse (see on 4.311), with the active pointedly assigned to women who take the active role, but it might also recall Ptolemy's τριβάδες in 3.15.9, who, likewise under a double dose of masculinisation, openly take 'wives'. In Martial, 7.70, a *tribas* has an *amica*. The male version is more familiar (Cic. *Phil*. 2.44; Suet. *Jul*. 52.3, *Nero* 28.1, 29; Williams, appendix 2, 245–52).

1.34–44 Three Mars-Related Charts?

34–7

Jupiter in a *kentron* aspects Aries or Scorpio (Mars' signs). The natives are leaders. I have not taken the same approach to this chart as Koechly or De Stefani, who follows him. I see 37 as a pentameter following on from 34–6 and rounding them off (as again in 1.139–51 + 152 and 1.359–60 + 361). Koechly saw 34–6 as an interpolation (linked to 28 by the theme of kingship), and then created an extra hexameter based on 36 as a separate protasis for 37. He also thought of an alternative configuration in which Venus was involved (appealing to 6.478, 481), producing the leaders of youth, but that seems to me out of the question: the essential player for that outcome, Mercury, is missing. It is simplest to take all four lines as an unbroken sequence. Hephaestion has a chart in which a similar outcome is produced by the same factors (i. 211.10–11 κατόρθωσιν πάντων τῶν πραγμάτων, Mars distributing to Jupiter), which suggests that 37 should simply follow on from 34–6.

34 ἐποπτεύων: unique within the Manethoniana. Astrological usage develops the earlier poetic one, 'oversee' (Prévot, 264–5), and in Anubion, F 12.33 = 12 Perale φα[ί]νοντες ἐποπτεύοντ[αι], the planets oversee a certain kind of nativity. Of the other astrological passages where it is used of aspect, 'Antiochus', l. 7 (*CCAG* i. 108.10), is poetic, and of the four uses in Hephaestion, two are acknowledged as Dorothean by Pingree (pp. 338.8, 342.15), another one by Stegemann (i. 230.17 = fr. 66b Stegemann), and a fourth immediately precedes a passage Pingree counts as Dorothean (i. 144.23); the only other example is *CCAG* viii/1. 173.22. The poet may or may not have been directly influenced by Dorotheus.

35 σκόρπειον κυανόχροον οἶκον Ἄρηος: when references to Scorpio are decorated, it is usually with a generic word for fieriness or with reference to its sting. Black is unusual, and parallels are from neo-Latin texts: Conradus Celtis, *Quattuor libri amorum secundum quattuor latera Germaniae*, 2.5.64 *Corpore quod nigro Scorpius ater habet*; Iodocus Badius Ascensius, *In Parthenicen Catharinariam Baptiste Mantuani expositio*, Liber 1, 1.290 *scorpius niger*. (In Aelius Promotus, Περὶ τῶν ἰοβόλων θηρίων καὶ δηλητηρίων φαρμάκων, 15 μέλανος σκορπίου is classificatory, not descriptive.) For κυανόχροος, see i. 911 n. 15. The epithet σκόρπειος/σπορπήιος is otherwise only in Orph. *Lith*. 510, 622.

36 ἀνέρας ἡγεμονῆας: so too other combinations of the same planets: 3.296 ἡγεμόνας ῥέζει στρατιῆς, κτλ (conjunction or trine; see i. 693); Περὶ σχημ. 104 ἡγεμόνας (conjunction); Π.τ.δ. 8 ὁ Ζεὺς οἴκῳ Ἄρεως ἢ ὁρίοις ἡγεμόνας ἢ ἑταίρους ἡγεμόνων.

37 I take πραγματίη (the poet's Ionic for πραγματεία, common in astrology) not to be restricted to business affairs or lawsuits, but to mean all the business of life. Περὶ σχημ. 103 has ἐπιτευκτικούς. No substantial argument for Anubionic authorship can be derived from the fact that πάντοτε occurs also in F 1b 9; F 12.7–8, where it occurs in successive lines, is *incerti auctoris*.

38–9 + 40 + 41

Mercury and Mars in quartile; when setting; and without the influence of Jupiter. The position produces generally unstable and violent characters (3.339–43; Περὶ σχημ. 50–1/Dor.^ARAB II 15.27–8; Firmicus, 6.11.8–9). Insofar as this elaboration of the astrological prose phrase κινδύνους σωματικούς, vague enough to include illness and accident, implies the active courting of danger, the outcome also recalls those who put their life on the line in Θ pp. 217.24–218.2, which appears in another form in 4.230–7. These bloodthirsty and reckless types born under Leo are associable with the temperaments described by Manilius, 5.220–2, and Firmicus, 8.10.1, for those born at the rising of the Dog Star.

41 Some of the parallels for Mercury and Mars (cited on 4.230–7) suggest that we might be dealing with mercenaries, in which case the line could be dealing with death in the service of the powerful; for what it is worth, μόρον αἰνὸν[18] is also in 1.261 (A), though not in the same *sedes*. De Stefani intervened to tackle the lesser problem (substituting χόλον, of ill-effects of their masters' anger) while leaving the greater one—metre, for which I have no better solution—unresolved.

42–4

Mars and Venus on a common path aspect the Moon. Various incest charts involve these agents, but none in the same arrangement. In Oedipus', among other factors, Mars is in aspect with both the Moon and Venus (Firmicus, 6.30.1, cf. Anubion, F 4 ii. 14; 6.163–4). In Valens, II 38.18, Venus and the Moon in trine in Venus' house, especially with Mars (and Jupiter) in aspect, yield συγγενικούς...γάμους; in Firmicus, 6.24.4, a conjunction of Mars with Venus

---

[18] Also with verbs of evading in Bion, fr. 12.7 οὐ μόρον αἰνὸν ἄμυνεν (the first occurrence of this phrase) and Greg. Naz. PG 37.1243.9 ὅπως μόρον αἰνὸν ἀλύξω.

<and Mercury>, and receiving the light of the waxing Moon, makes natives publicly shamed for scandals including incest; in 6.29.22, Venus and the Moon in equal degrees with both malefics opposing them, results in father–daughter incest.

42 κοινὴν ὁδὸν ἰθύνοντες: not unlike 6.120 ξυνὴν ὁδὸν ἐξανύωσιν; from the antecedents for κοινὴν ὁδόν in Soph. *Ant.* 988 (Teiresias and his guide) and Ap. Rhod. 1.103 (Theseus and Pirithous), gentle personification is implied. For the construction with the accusative of a pathway, see K.-G. i. 312–13; with this verb it is also in ps.-Apollinaris, *Metaphr.* 118:17 πῶς νέος ἰθύνειεν ὁδόν;

43–4 The outcome combines prose astrological terminology (συγγενικοὺς ... γάμους in Valens, II 38.18–20, Epit. II = *CCAG* i. 161.27–8; see also on 4.416–17 νύμφας συγγενικάς) with poetic pieties about sexual offence (Eur. *Ion* 1092–3 ἁμέτερα λέχεα καὶ γάμους | Κύπριδος ἀθέμιτος ἀνοσίους; Mnasalcas, *AP* 9.70.2 = *HE* 2656 Τηρέος οὐ θεμιτῶν ἁψαμένα λεχέων (sc. Philomela)). For *themis* and incest see ps.-Clem. *Recogn.* 9.25/Euseb. *PE* 6.10.35 ἀθεμίτως ... γαμεῖν (of the Persian practice), and a whole chapter in Justinian's *Novellae* (12) on marriage within prohibited degrees ΠΕΡΙ ΑΘΕΜΙΤΟΓΑΜΙΩΝ. ἐφαρμόζουσι (Hes. *Op.* 76, *Il.* 19.385) adapts to the stars the simplex ἁρμόζειν, 'betroth', but the latter puts the man in the accusative when active, the women when middle.

1.45–138 Miscellanea

45–9

Saturn takes Venus into his embrace. Natives have unhappy marriages and sterile wives. There are two good parallels in Firmicus, (i) 6.22.12 and (ii) 6.31.43 (second configuration). In each case the two planets are in equal degrees. ἀγκαλίσαιτο could correspond to *aequabili societatis potestate iungantur/aequata partium societate iungantur*. It could also be a way of saying that Venus is in Saturn's house, for this, too, effects sterility (Π.τ.δ. 17). δυσγαμίην corresponds to Firmicus' *misera matrimonium infortunia*, although both of Firmicus' charts go into more detail about what is wrong with the wife. The *next* configuration yields incestuous marriages (6.31.44), like the *previous* one here, although it involves Mars and Mercury, not Venus.

45 καλὴν πολιὸς: i. 907 n. 12 and 911 n. 14.

ἀγκαλίσαιτο: if there is an innuendo it suits the context, but the metaphor masks the precise relationship (conjunction?); *synaphe* seems to be involved in 1.351 (E, lacking the innuendo). The conceit (Orlando and Torre, 305 n. 30) is not found in other astrology, but ἀμφιβάλοι in 124 seems to be a weaker version of it. The ungrammatical optative is not accounted for by earlier poetry (i. 139).

46 δυσγαμίην καὶ δυστοκίην: most like 2.179 δυσγαμίην καὶ δυστεκνίην (see ad loc.). δυστοκία is much commoner, including in astrology (4.412 n.), meaning 'difficult/painful childbirth' (as it still does as a veterinary term). Line 49 suggests, however, that in this line it means the failure to have children at all, and LSJ have a separate entry for which they suggest the meaning 'ill luck in the matter of children'. Still, the same factors as here are in play in Achmet, *CCAG* ii. 124.34-5, where Saturn and Venus in quartile produce δυσκολίαν καὶ δυστοκίαν, where δυστοκία seems to have its usual meaning. For the absence of a third-foot caesura, see on 1.6. The example in 1.219 also involves paired common nouns, which is not a Homeric pattern, nor do other Manethonian poets use it. (Homer does, very often, have paired *proper* nouns, e.g. *Il.* 18.41, 44, 46, and M[a] uses this at 3.14 Αἰγόκερῳ τε καὶ Ὑδροχόῳ, 6.695 εἰ δὲ Κρόνῳ μὲν ἰδ᾽ Ἡελίῳ.)

47 Because their husbands divorce them, or die? Unless they have both arrived at this tweak of EGHP κουριδίην ἄλοχον independently, it looks as if there is an ironic allusion to *HHom. Dem.* 136 κουριδίους ἄνδρας, where the disguised Demeter wishes for husbands and childbirth for Metaneira's daughters. If so, this somewhat expands the poet's allusive range.

48 This line remixes topoi without copying any one passage. γλυκεροῖς could qualify, and is equally apposite to, either noun (sweet children: i. 364 and n. 18; sweet lips: V. *Aen.* 12.802; the verse pattern would be as in Ap. Rhod. 4.1457 διεροῖς ἐπὶ χείλεσιν). Sweet children are a sepulchral cliché, either the children lost or the children never born; take, for instance, the gravestone of an unwed maiden, οὐ τέκνων γλυκερῶν εἰκόνα θησαμένη[ν] (*CIRB* 139.7 (Pantikapaion, 1st c. AD(?)). The second half of the line gives a powerfully *presque homérique* effect, but the best parallels I can find are Euphorion, fr. 92 P. λαρὸν δ᾽ ἐπὶ χείλεσι πρώτη | μαστὸν ἐπισχομένη (cf. Opp. *Hal.* 2.404-5 ἠΰτε κοῦρος ὑπὲκ μαζοῖο τιθήνης | χείλεσιν αὖ ἐρύει λαρὸν γλάγος), and a Hellenistic epitaph for a mother who died in childbirth, *IG* IX,2 97.4 (Demetrias) μαστῶι τε ἀρδεύσειν χεῖλος ἑοῖο βρέφους (Gourevitch 1988, 48). An intriguing parallel in Antonius Eparchus (16th c., Corfiote), *Lamentatio*, 113 Μειλιχίη γὰρ ἁπάντων χείλεσι μαζὸν ἐνῆκεν. Could he have had sight of L?

49 στειρώδεις: astrological jargon. It applies above all to signs (Hübner 1982, 164), or to degrees that produce certain effects (Saturn's in Valens, I 3.5, 23, 31, 55), but also to natives, whether male or female (Saturn involved in Π.τ.δ. 17, above; Valens, II 38.47). The exceptions that prove the rule are the only two non-astrological examples (Hippocrates, *Mul. Affect.* 2.158; Iamblichus, *Vit. Pyth.* 17.73), of which the former applies to the mouth of the womb, not the woman herself, and the latter is figurative.

50-7

Moon after Full applies to Saturn. So too Θ p. 189.10-13 and Firmicus, 8.21.7. The eventuality is covered by Π.σ.α. p. 182.14-16 (Saturn not centred and ὕπαυγος), but the outcome (wet diseases) is unspecific. For the Moon leaving Saturn, see 1.153-7.

This is unusual among astrological cases of 'elephantiasis', which usually involve signs, according to which it is classified as a scaly or watery disease (or both). For Ptol. 3.13.17 the signs are terrestrial or piscine. For Θ p. 183.3, the Moon is in scaly signs with malefics in equal degrees. A group of texts connect it with Aquarius, with jaundice, and with melancholy (Valens, II 37.18, Teucer, *CCAG* vii. 210.20, and Camaterus, *Introd.* 1573; cf. also Valens, II 41.38, Aquarius and Virgo). Lastly, precisely the same agents as here are involved in Anubion, F 12.36-7 = 12 Perale (λευκὰς...λέπρας; the Moon is Full); Valens, II 41.31 (Cancer under Aquarius, which as Valens explains are tantamount to the Moon and Saturn), cf. Firmicus, 7.20.12 (but Mars and Venus, or their signs, are also involved). For the involvement of the Moon in skin diseases among Babylonians and Hebrews, and in the Ebers papyrus, see Stol 1987-8, 28, 30, and id. 1993, 127-30.

The disease in question is actually lepromatous leprosy (for 'elephantiasis' as the ancient term for this disease, see Koelbing and Stettler-Schär, 46-8; Stol 1987-8, 26; D. Gourevitch, 'Un éléphant peut en cacher un autre, ou comment sauter du coq à l'âne peut mettre la puce à l'oreille', in A. Debru, N. Palmieri and B. Jacquinod (eds.), « *Docente natura* »: *Mélanges de médecine ancienne et médiévale offerts à Guy Sabbah* (Saint-Étienne, 2001), 156-76, at 160-4). Greek and Roman authors of the early imperial period regard it as 'new': mentions in medical literature can be traced back to Straton, pupil of Erasistratus.[19] That means astrology responds to current realities, and it admits 'elephantiasis' along with the old Hippocratic term λέπρα, which refers to scaly and flakey skin conditions like eczema and psoriasis. There is an overlap between the two diseases: λέπρα might in practice include leprosy, and leprosy may manifest itself with λειχῆνες (Aret. *De Caus. et Sign. Diur. Morb.* 2.13.15); but that is not what

---

[19] M. Wellmann, *Die pneumatische Schule bis auf Antigenes* (Berlin, 1895), 24-31; J. G. Andersen, *Studies in the Mediaeval Diagnosis of Leprosy in Denmark: An Osteoarchaeological, Historical, and Clinical Study* (Copenhagen, 1969), 18-43 (ancient sources with translation and commentary); Koebling and Stettler-Schär; S. G. Browne, 'Some Aspects of the History of Leprosy: The Leprosie of Yesterday', *Proc. Royal Soc. Med.* 68 (1975), 485-93 [13-21], at 486 [14]; Grmek, 168-71; Mark, 304-5. Also on 'elephantiasis', see W. Scheidel, 'Age and Health', in Riggs 2012, 305-16, at 311. Its enracination in Egypt led to an ancient (mis)perception that it was native there (Lucr. 6.1114-15 *elephas morbus*, Plin. *NH* 26.7-8), and it is possible (as argued by Mark) that that was the first Mediterranean land to which it was carried from India. For Egyptian osteoarchaeological evidence, see Manchester, 39-40.

The Book Proper 769

λέπρα in principle means. Scaly signs (see on 5.246–51) are also invoked as an analogical cause of the latter, but it is not classified as a watery disease, and so Aquarius is not involved.

50 φάσιν λύσασα: also 5.128 (q.v.), and Valens, II 37.43 τῆς Σελήνης φάσιν τινὰ λυούσης (Riley: 'while the moon is passing out of a given phase'), III 1.28 ἐὰν... λύῃ τὴν φάσιν ('passes out of this phase', sc. Full).

51 μὴ Κρόνῳ ἀντήσειε: this third person optative, 'beware lest', stands somewhere between 'be very afraid that' (p. 171) and 'pay attention, do not be inattentive' (5.202 n.). It belongs on the one hand in literature of formidable signs (Aratus, 822–4, 1049, 1086, among the signs of bad weather), on the other in Nicander's iology (*Al.* 335–6 (cited on 5.202), 415–16, 521), so it is appropriate that the poet uses it here precisely in a medical configuration. This configuration is a fearful prognostic, and we are all vulnerable to physical harm.

51-2 A combination of epic idiom and tragic packaging? The question is shaped especially like *Il.* 9.77 τίς ἂν τάδε γηθήσειε (of another unwelcome sight by night, indeed a situation which has elicited a famous night-sky simile involving stars around the Moon at the close of the previous book), but is combined with δύσμορος, ὅς (*Aj.* 372 ὦ δύσμορος), which adds a tragic register. κακὰ πολλὰ παθών illustrates the poet's method and intentions in using EGHP: it is so firmly associated with Odysseus that any half-literate Greek must have recognised it, but it is hard to see (in connection with disease and death) why the poet would have wanted to evoke him, unless one really stretches the point and says that Odysseus *does* suffer—temporary—physical disfigurement, which seems rather desperate; at the same time, Ἀϊδόσδε κάτεισιν is lifted from *Il.* 20.294, and there are of course other examples of κατῆεν (ps.-Hes. *Scut.* 254), κατῆλθον and βεβήκει (*Il.* and *Od.*, *passim*). See p. 293 for the technique.

53 χροιὴν μέν: complexion, a staple of physiognomy and ethnography (e.g. Hippocr. *Aer.* 15.2 τήν τε χροιήν, of the people of Phasis; Polyb. 4.21.2 χρώμασιν) and often first item in descriptions of physique (Hdt. 2.104.2 μελάγχροές εἰσι; ps.-Arist. *Physiogn.* 806^{b}3 αἱ μὲν οὖν χροιαὶ σημαίνουσιν; ps.-Opp. *Cyn.* 2.90, 383, 447, 3.332), is now listed first as a diagnostic pathological feature.

ἀμετροβίων ἐλεφάντων: the disease's name elicits a paradoxographical (and largely irrelevant) *tour de force* on the elephant from Aretaeus, *De Caus. et Sign. Diut. Morb.* 2.13, who explains, however, that the fissures on the skin are the chief point of similarity. Nonnus also uses this line-ending three times, but its presence also in *AP* App. *Epigr. Demonstr.* 55.2 (from an unknown source) suggests that Nonnus did not necessarily take it from this poet. It is also quoted without a context in Etymologica (*EtMag*; *EtSym*; ps.-Zonaras, ε p. 682.18). A variant in an epigram ap. Philostr. *Her.* 55.5 ἀμετροβίοις κοράκεσσιν.

54 This line is interesting because ulceration is not among the conditions that accompany 'elephantiasis' in most other astrological lists (which instead name 'wet' or humoral conditions like rheum, jaundice, melancholy, dropsy; a good example in Teucer, CCAG ix/2. 184.2–4). Ptol. 3.13.17, whence Θ p. 188.3, does list it besides χοιράδων and συρίγγων (scrofula, fistula). The language, instead, is medical. Both Aretaeus (*De Caus. et Sign. Diut. Morb.* 2.13.1) and Galen (*De sympt. caus.* vii. 226.18 Kühn) connect the name of the disease with its characteristic complexion (χροιά). Both also mention ὄχθους, the tumours that characterise lepromatous[20] leprosy: Galen, op. cit. 227.1–2 τῆς δέ γε μελαίνης σαρκὸς ἅμα καὶ ὀχθώδους ἀπὸ τοῦ ἐλέφαντος ἐποίησαν τοὔνομα; Aretaeus, *De Caus. et Sign. Diut. Morb.* 2.13.12 ὄχθοι...ξυνεχέες μὲν οὐδέκω, παχέες δὲ καὶ τρηχέες, 14 (on the face) σκληροί, ὀξέες, 16 (on the nose; also ἕλκεα at the base of the ears), and especially 17: with progression of the disease, patients become ἑλκώδεες τοὺς ὄχθους; on cheeks, chin, fingers, and knees are found κάκοδμα καὶ ἀναλθέα [τὰ] ἕλκεα, which come and go on different parts of the body. See also Oribasius, *Coll. Med.* 45.27.1: ἕλκη as a feature of 'elephantiasis'; 45.27.10: τὸ τοῦ δέρματος ὀχθῶδες; 45.28.3 τὰ δὲ συμπτώματα οὐκ ἄδηλα, ὄχθοι πελιδνοὶ καὶ μέλανες μώλωψι [weals] μάλιστα ὅμοιοι...τὰ μὲν πρῶτα ἀνέλκωτοι, εἶτα καὶ ἑλκούμενοι τρόπον τὸν πονηρότατον; Celsus, *De Med.* 3.25.1 *tumores*. See Manchester, 32 (skin lesions).

55 δάκτυλα σηπόμενοι λιποσαρκέα: why fingertips?[21] A clue comes in Ptol. 3.13.17, who explains that diseases of the extremities (περὶ τὰ ἄκρα) are caused by planets in the last degrees of signs, of which 'elephantiasis' as well as 'gout' of the hands and feet (χειράγραι, ποδάγραι) are examples. Aretaeus, *De Caus. et Sign. Diut. Morb.* 2.13.10, notes that while it usually begins on the face in some people it begins ἀπὸ κονδύλων χειρῶν τε καὶ ποδῶν, and Pliny, *NH* 26.7, who regards it as affecting the skin of the whole body, also notes that the fingers and toes swell up (*intumescentibus digitis in pedibus manibusque*).

Pliny's comment is interesting in the light of a possible ambiguity about the epithet. Normally it means 'skinny'. But Herodian, *Part.* 78.13 and 263.15, attempts a distinction between λιπο- and λειπο-, deriving the first from λίπος, and one wonders whether the poet could be suggesting that the fingers are, not emaciated, but 'fat' because swollen. A stronger possibility, however, is that the poet is referring to the characteristically short and stumpy fingers of advanced leprosy, which happens because the digits are eventually reabsorbed by the

---

[20] Tuberculous leprosy is different, so, contra LSJ II.1, the word 'tubercules' is probably best avoided; in any case, perhaps led astray by Koechly's *tubera*, they bizarrely interpret this passage as a reference to plants.
[21] One thinks of the necrotic fingertips of the moribunda Karen Karstedt in Mann's *Der Zauberberg*, but she is consumptive.

body—hence, not just 'lacking in flesh', but reduced in size. Rufus noted this feature of the disease (fr. 37 Daremberg-Ruelle, from Oribasius, *Coll. Med.* 45.28.3…ὥστε ἐνίοις καὶ ἄκρους δακτύλους ἀποπίπτειν; cf. Celsus, *De Med.* 3.25.2 *Ubi vetus morbus est, digiti in manibus pedibusque sub tumore conduntur*; Mark, 305), and it is even noted in the earliest certain reference to leprosy, the *Sushruta Samhita*, a Sanskrit text of *c.*600 BC (Manchester, 34, 38; Mark, 301). The epithet is usually second-declension (Nonn. *D.* 26.312), though there is a third-declension form in Macedonius, *AP* 11.374.1; at ps.-Opp. *Cyn.* 2.106 the MSS are divided between λειπόσαρκες and λιπόσαρκοι.[22]

νηλέϊ λύθρῳ: convincingly *presque homérique* (νηλέι χαλκῷ/ὕπνῳ/θυμῷ + λύθρῳ, always in dative, on the hands in *Il.* 11.169, 20.503). 'Gore', the Homeric meaning, suggests fluid. As far as I know the fingers in leprosy do not weep (like Karen Karstedt's), though they may in other skin diseases, including pompholyx (dyshidrotic eczema) which causes 'tiny itchy blisters that may weep fluid' (NHS website): in view of the terminological confusion described above, it seems possible that the poet is conflating with leprosy a symptom of another disease the Greeks would have called *lepra*. Otherwise, if he really does mean blood and not pus, perhaps the reference is to subungual haematoma (blood under the nail), which *is* sometimes seen in leprosy (I. Belinchón Romero, J. M. Ramos Rincón, and F. Reyes Rabell, 'Nail Involvement in Leprosy', *Actas Dermosifilográficas*, 103 (2012), 276–84).

56 εὐπλοκάμου: i. 907 n. 14.

57 ἀπόστροφοι: having no aspect with: otherwise a mannerism of M[a] (6.127, 295 *ex emend.*, 406, 650, 652, and not elsewhere in astrology).

58–61 + 62–5

Conjunction of Mercury and Venus. These charts are doublets: a conjunction of Mercury and Venus makes musicians, with different add-ons in each case. Both, however, involve the Moon. Ptolemy in his preamble on πρᾶξις does make the Moon a factor (4.4.1), though what matters for him is *synaphe*: he is silent about phase. Koechly considered them different poets' efforts brought by an editor, and further that they were connected to the wider context by the presence of Mercury (38 Ἑρμείας). We can rephrase and say that, like 38, these are πρᾶξις configurations (where Mercury has a starring role), though it does not explain why they have been separated from it by extraneous material on marital discord. Noting the curious construction of the first chart (which lacks a main

---

[22] λιπόσαρκες Boudreaux, from λιπόσαρξ: λιποσαρκὲς Schneider, agreeing with following δέμας.

verb for the agents in the protasis), Koechly 1851, 1, considered this the interloper: an editor, in his view, appended the work of an *imperitus* to that of A, the main poet of the book. He placed daggers beside it; De Stefani bracketed it. Both imply the idea of a restorable integrity (delete what an 'editor' interpolated and you can return to an 'original'), which is hard to square with the acceptance that the book is already essentially a compilation (De Stefani 2017, 23). Further, it is perfectly possible in principle for a poet to return to the same material (as is the case in 4.491–507). The questions would then be whether 58–61 is stylistically acceptable for A, and if it is, whether he also intended the two charts to stand together, as here, or whether this is a secondary collocation. See pp. 283–4.

58–61
Mercury in ASC with Moon and Venus, Jupiter in DESC. Boll 1898, 204, compared Firmicus, 3.12.2, where both Mercury and Venus are located in the ASC, but there is no Moon, nor Jupiter. The DESC, too, is an odd detail to find in a πρᾶξις chart. It seems to scratch together a variety of occupations individually connected with the named planets, but puzzlingly incoherent when put together. Mysteries should belong to uncanny Saturn, musicians to Mercury and Venus, and athletes usually to Mercury alone (Valens, I 1.37; Περὶ κράσ. 205 πάλη), though in the only other reference I know of to the pancratium in astrology (Firmicus, 8.8.1, ‹pam›macharios, cf. Robert 1938, 89–92), Mercury is not involved, but Mars and the Moon are. The Venus–Mercury chart in Firmicus, 3.12.2, combines high priests and *baiuli* with musicians, but lacks athletes.

59 μυστήρια δρῶσιν: not a normal collocation. In Heliodorus, *Aeth.* 6.15.3, a corpse raised by a witch accuses her of μυστήρια δρᾶν (its voice is pointed and hostile), while Dositheus, *Dodecabiblos*, 3.125.28, draws a distinction between the τελετή of the mystery and the person who performs it (τὸν δρῶντα). F. L. Schudeboom, *Greek Religious Terminology: Telete and Orgia* (Leiden, 2009), 143, lists ten verbs with ὄργια, among which δρᾶν does not figure. On references to mysteries, see nn. on 2.197–9, 205; Cumont, 155 n. 2.

60 I have no advance on the suggestions recorded in the apparatus. The final epithet looks right in some collocation (2.333 μελῶν μολπῆς εὐρύθμου), and in 6.506 ἀοιδῆς εὐρύθμοιο the spondeiazon is again preceded (as it is not otherwise in M^c(A)) by another spondee. For the metre, see p. 298.

61 πάλην φιλέουσιν ἀμύμονα: except for Hesych. φ 472, the epithet φιλοπάλαιστρος is an astrological specialism, and Firmicus/*Lib. Herm.* have Latin equivalents (Appendix II, VI.7.iv). Most often such types are born under a combination of Mars and Mercury, though Venus is again involved in Critodemus, *CCAG* viii/1. 259.28 (her terms within Libra, which is her sign). The epithet is associated with cultured leisure-time activities in *Il.* 13.637 = *Od.*

23.145 ἀμύμονος ὀρχηθμοῖο, and with those who practise them, including wrestlers, in *Od.* 8.246 οὐ γὰρ πυγμάχοι εἰμὲν ἀμύμονες οὐδὲ παλαισταί.

62–5

Mercury and Venus in conjunction, with Mercury aspecting the Full (or waxing) Moon or Venus the New (or waning). They cannot be doing this at the same time (see Lopilato), hence *either/or* rather than *both/and*.

63 Every word in the line is Mᵃ-like: the executive verb (6× in this book) is otherwise only in Mᵃ; μούσης ἐπιίστορας is in 2.331, 3.350; and εὔφρονας is otherwise only in 2.451. At a push this could refer to expertise, and/or it might suggest the pleasure and feeling of 'rightness' evoked by their compositions/performances (*IGR* I,5 1154.14 ἐπ' ἐμαῖς εὔφροσι ταῖσδ' ἀοιδαῖς, cf. *PMG* 887, conj. Wilamowitz).

65 The chiasmus suggests complementarity. φωσφορεῖν is rare in astrological prose, and when it occurs means straightforwardly 'shine', 'irradiate', 'bring light' (as it does in Philo).[23] Here it is an indication of Moon phase, 'increasing in light' as it moves away from the Sun, as opposed to λιποφεγγέα. That is apparently also true of the three other uses in this book: 1.134 (where the parallel chart in Θ indicates that it means 'Full'), 1.186 (ἔτ' ἔμπεδον), and 1.225, where it presumably adds a new detail to the bare mention of the Moon in the line before (and hence is in Focus position). So too potentially in Valens, VII 6.19 διὰ τὸ φωσφορούσῃ [sc. Σελήνῃ] συνάπτειν Ἄρεα, cf. VI 8.6 τὴν φωσφόρον Σελήνην, but neither passage is interpreted in this way by Riley. For λιποφεγγέα, poetic and new in Mᵃ, see on 3.273.

66–9

Jupiter and Saturn 'Lords of' *kentra*.

66 κέντρων ὅτ' ἂν ὦσιν ἄνακτες: see on 1.22.

67 τύχης πολυήρατα δῶρα: the poet has reshaped the cliché of 'gifts of Fortune' in a similar phrase-pattern to epic θεῶν ἐρικυδέα δῶρα (*Il.* 3.65; 20.265; cf. *Od.* 7.132), and with a nicely transvalued epithet which, in EGHP, applies mostly to youth, beauty, the bed, marriage, and occasionally to place (Thomas on *HHom. Herm.* 186 n. 238); natural running water in Hes. *Op.* 739. Fertility and the delights of nature have all been swept away by status and honour, and

---

[23] Paul, p. 96.13–14 τὰ φωσφοροῦντα σώματα = the luminaries; in Ptol. 2.9.23 τοὺς φωσφοροῦντας (sc. τόπους) are the places occupied by the luminaries.

astrology wants none of a philosopher's finger-wagging about the caprice, lability, or even irrelevance, of Fortune's gifts.[24]

68 βασιληίδας αὐλὰς: prose has αὐλὰς βασιλικὰς (LXX, Diodorus, Plutarch, Josephus, and thereafter). For the cadence see on 1.3 and 4.98–9.

70–4

Mercury and Jupiter in the MC, and with Moon in *synaphe*. The relevant parallel is Firmicus, 3.10.12 (not, *contra* Boll 1898, 204, Firmicus, 3.8.10: Φαέθων is not the Sun). Status is also the result of each of the planets individually located in the MC: compare Θ pp. 168.6–9 + 169.16–20, with stipulations about sect and phase.

71 πλούτῳ γαυρούμενον: while the two words commonly go together, exulting in wealth *always* ends badly, whether it is a matter of simply being vainglorious, enjoying ill repute, being humiliated by a wife, not looking after the poor, or being swept away by the Day of the Lord.[25] The poet is apparently entirely unselfconscious in his choice of words.

εὐτεκνίῃ τε: also 3.313 (Venus in aspect with Jupiter), but common in, and beyond, astrology.

73 καὶ δόξῃ μεγάλῃ γαυρούμενον: Jupiter's *synaphe* with Moon: Π.σ.α. p. 182.24 εὐκλείαν… ἀγαθῶν; Firmicus, 4.3.1 *gloriosos*.

73–4 Once again, an essentially technical prose expression is brightened up with a poeticism. συναφὴν… ἐπέχειν means 'sustain contact with' (Dorotheus, p. 415.19; Ptolemy; Valens; Θ p. 157.26); the subject is often the planet, but the Moon, as here, in Ptol. 4.5.2. For εὐκέραος see i. 904 n. 6. αἴ κεν ἴδηαι dresses up in an epic cadence (*Il.* 17.652) a stipulation by astrologer to adept (pp. 358–9; Anubion, F 3d εἰ δ᾽ Ἄρην ἐσίδοις, 3a ἢν δὲ Κρόνον ἐσίδῃς; *CCAG* v/3. 119.32 εἰ δὲ ἴδῃς τὸν τοιοῦτον ἀστέρα ἐν κέντρῳ; Theophilus, *CCAG* xi/1. 219.6–7 and 221.8 εἰ δὲ ἴδῃς τὸν κύριον τοῦ ὡροσκόπου).

75–7 + 78–82

Mars on a *kentron* rules πρᾶξις. We learn first about the bare effect of Mars, and then about the additional effect of the Sun, which supplies heat. The material is

---

[24] e.g. Sen. *Ep.* 8.3; 74.7–9; 87.8 (loan).
[25] Eur. fr. 661.4 Collard–Cropp (Stob. 4.22b.46); 'Eur.' fr. 1113a.2 Collard–Cropp ~ 'Menand.' *Sent.* 2.112 (Stob. 3.22.5); 'Menand.' *Sent.* 1.295; Aesop, *Fab.* 249; Hermas, *Pastor*, 1.8, 17.6; Euseb. *Comm. in Isaiam*, 1.28; John Chrys. *PG* 64.41.53–4; Cyril Alex. *PG* 77.1077.29; Romanus Melodus, *Hymn* 30.15; to cite no later examples.

ultimately Ptolemaic (4.4.5), although Ptolemy himself had strangely placed the secondary effect before the primary one, and omitted the formula τὸ πράσσειν παρέχων, which he had already used with Mercury and Venus. Θ normalises, reversing the order and restoring the formula. It is curious, however, that at this precise point Θ seems to be following a *poetic* source (pp. 140–1)—a poetic source, moreover, very like M^c, for (i) 77 reappears *verbatim* except for the first disjunctive (the epitomator has not even bothered to replace λιθοεργούς with a contracted form), and (ii) only here in ch. 83 is the planet called by its divine name alone, as opposed to 'star of *x*', which the epitomator uses for both Mercury, which precedes, and Venus, which follows, and which Ptolemy uses throughout. But does that have implications for our poet? Did the epitomator fortify himself from a poem which only had this isolated πρᾶξις configuration? Or was there once upon a time a poem which dealt systematically with the three Ptolemaic Rulers of πρᾶξις, of which we have a *disiectum membrum* here?

The source of the pentameter in 76 and subsequent hexameter is unknown. Nothing confirms that it is Anubion. Θ tells us about Anubion's method of calculating the Ruler of πρᾶξις (p. 130), which was different from Ptolemy's; nothing warrants our supposing that the poet suddenly swerved to Anubion for 75–6 when 77 itself is verifiably Ptolemaic. Koechly thought that 75–6 were a stray elegiac couplet appended close to 66 because of the reference to *kentra*, and so he posted a lacuna after 76—but for once he was wrong, as the evidence of Ptolemy and Θ shows. All of 75–82 belong together (there is no need for the restatement of Mars' name, or for the repetition of πάντοτε, before 77). Θ exactly parallels the present material, with nothing intervening between 76 and 77, nor anything to confirm the lacuna De Stefani marked after 77, hypothesising a second pentameter.

75 **Πάντοτε μὲν κέντροισιν ἐπών**: for Ptolemy, of course, πρᾶξις is above all associated with the MC. πάντοτε (1.37 n.) is deeply prosaic, but also used at the head of a configuration in Dorotheus, p. 342.10 (of location in a *kentron*) and in 1.83. κέντρῳ ἐπεῖναι is also in M^a (6.115–16, 180, 185, 410, 529, 706; the verb also with signs in 3.386, 6.256, 360, 535; houses in 6.367; terms in 6.372), but not elsewhere in the corpus.

κορυθαίολος: i. 909 n. 13, 915, 917.

76 **τὴν πρᾶξιν παρέχων**: the phrase in Ptolemy and Θ is τὸ πράσσειν παρέχων (Ptol. 4.4.6 τὰς πράξεις παρέχειν). For ἐκτελέει, see on 1.5.

77 **λαξευτὰς...ἢ λιθοεργούς**: Ptolemy has λαοξόους, λιθουργούς, immediately juxtaposed. The first is a real trade name, λα(ο)ξό(ο)s (Appendix II, II.5.iii); λαξ- alternates with λαοξ-, just as in Latin *latomiae* alternates with *lautumiae*. This is the first occurrence of λαξευτής.²⁶ It is not clear whether any distinction is being implied between the two terms (quarrymen *versus* those whose input came at a later stage of the process) or not; perhaps not, since evidence for the activity of the λαοξόος implies it, too, could reach a degree of artistry (Ruffing 2008, 622). For stone-quarrying, see further Drexhage–Konen–Ruffing (eds.), 224–8, with bibl., and for representations of stone-masons in art, see Zimmer 1982, 35–6 and 153–61, nos. 75–83.

τέκτονας: presumably carpenters, but also a general-purpose word for craftsmen which, according to the *Suda*, can itself include stone-masons (τ 251 Τέκτων: κοινῶς τεχνίτης, ὁ λαοξόος, καὶ ὁ τῶν ξύλων εἰδήμων). If the former, carpenters and stone-masons are often mentioned together.²⁷ For carpenters' tools, see Zimmer 1982, 31–3 and 149–53, nos. 70–4. This is the only use of the basic trade name (Appendix II, II.7.iv) in the corpus which is not a periphrasis.

78 πυροεργέας ἄνδρας: unique, for Ptolemy's τοὺς διὰ πυρὸς ἐργαζομένους.

79 χαλκοτύπους: a trade name (Appendix II, II.6.i) see on 4.570. Distinct from χαλκεῖς (but unclear how) in Xen. *Hell*. 3.4.17, but unclear in *TAM* V,2 936 (Thyateira) [χα]λκεῖς χαλκοτύποι.

φυσητὰς ὑέλοιο: unambiguous glass-blowers (cf. Sen. *Ep.* 90.31 *vitreari- um...qui spiritu vitrum in habitus plurimos format*; Plin, *NH* 36.193 *aliud flatu figuratur*); contrast Strab. 16.2.25, who continues to use the language of casting (χέω, χωνεία). The technique was apparently invented in the eastern Mediterranean around the mid-1st c. BC,²⁸ so this shows astrology doing more than recycling material ossified since Nechepso and Petosiris, and it attracted the attention of other imperial poets as well, Mesomedes (II Heitsch) 13 and P.Oxy. 3536 = 15 Perale. The professional terms for glassmakers were ὑα(ε)λουργός, ὑελάριος, or ὑελιάριος (Appendix II, II.7.ii), the first of which is presumably to be restored in Θ²⁹ to yield another sequence of three trade names exactly matching Mᶜ; Latin *vitrearius* (Seneca), *opifex artis vitrariae* (*CIL* xiii. 2000; Lyon, early third century). φυσητής means the blower of a bellows in Dioscor. *De mat. med.* 5.75.4 (on the industrial preparation of zinc oxide), and otherwise is used to gloss Homeric βυκτάων (e.g. *EtMag* 179.20; Hesch. β 1306).

---

²⁶ Later in John Damasc. *Passio magni martyris Artemii*, *PG* 96.1308C, and then in a handful of 12th-c. writers (TLG).
²⁷ e.g. Thuc. 5.82.6 τέκτονες καὶ λιθουργοί; Ar. *Av.* 1134; Dion. Hal. *AR* 4.44.2; Plut. *Per.* 12.6, *Alc.* 15.4; Σ Hes. *Op.* 594; Σ Thuc. 6.31.3.
²⁸ D. F. Grose, 'Early Blown Glass: The Western Evidence', *Journal of Glass Studies*, 19 (1977), 9–29; Stern; S. C. Rasmussen, 'Modern Materials in Antiquity: An Early History of the Art and Technology of Glass', in id. (ed.), 267–313, at 302–5.
²⁹ ἱερουργοὺς, 'priests', 'sacrificers' (Call. fr. 517 Pf.) do work with fire and iron, but one expects a trade name. ρ and λ both have descenders below the line.

80 βαφέας μογερούς: this is the trade name (Appendix II, II.7.viii.e). Why are dyers among the professions associated with fire? Because the vats in the dyeing process had to be heated.[30] Pliny speaks of lead furnaces used in the dyeing of purple (NH 9.133; Cardon 2007, 559–60), and remains of six dyeing workshops in Pompeii yielded evidence for forty lead kettles housed in brick or rubble and mortar surrounds, heatable from a firebox below, both with and without flues.[31] And this suggests a possible answer to the question why dyers are described as μογερούς, in contrast to the normal astrological coding for dyeing which looked, not to the process, but to its outcome (a visually pleasing effect), and hence associated it with Venus (n. on 2.325–7, and p. 59). For, over and above the smell, noted by Plin. NH 9.127,[32] and the possible insinuation that such workers were of low status,[33] there was the heat and the danger of lead poisoning, of which the Romans were certainly aware, from both lead pipes and lead derivatives used in medicine and cosmetics, although no ancient writer mentions it specifically in connection with dyeing.[34] There was also a risk of toxicity from metallic mordants other than alum.

Of course dyers still had their professional *amour propre*. A διανομή... βαφέων was one of the trade *collegia* introduced into the city of Rome by Numa (Plut. *Num*. 17.2), although the only subsequent reference seems to be by emendation of *lictorumque* in Cic. *Pro Cornelio* (see J.–P. Waltzing, *Étude historique sur les corporations professionelles chez les Romains, depuis les origines*

---

[30] J. P. Wild and P. Walton Rogers, 'Introduction', in D. Jenkins (ed.), *The Cambridge History of Western Textiles*, i (Cambridge, 2003), 28.

[31] J. P. Wild, 'The Romans in the West, 600 BC–AD 400', in Jenkins (n. 30), 77–93, at 91; H. Hopkins, 'Using Experimental Archaeology to Answer the Unanswerable: A Case Study Using Roman Dyeing', in P. Cunningham, J. Heeb, and R. Paardekooper (eds.), *Experiencing Archaeology by Experiment: Proceedings from the Second Conference of Experimental Archaeology* (Oxford, 2008), 103–18, and (same title, different paper) in K. Staubermann (ed.), *Reconstructions: Recreating Science and Technology of the Past* (Edinburgh, 2011), 21–49 [28: her experiments showed that wood, not charcoal, was the fuel used]; ead., 'The Importance to Archaeology of Undertaking and Presenting Experimental Research: A Case Study Using Dyeing in Pompeii', *Archaeological and Anthropological Sciences*, 7 (2015), 131–40; K. Kania, H. Hopkins, and S. Ringenberg (eds.), 'The Influence of Metal Kettle Materials on the Mordanting and Dyeing Outcome', in Hopkins (ed.), 99–121. Further bibliography in E. Harlizius-Klück, 'Textile Technology', in Irby (ed.), 747–67, at 754–5.

[32] Alum was the most commonly-used mordant in antiquity: Cardon 2007, 22, 24; Z. C. Koren, 'Modern Chemistry of the Ancient Chemical Processing of Organic Dyes and Pigments', in Rasmussen (ed.), 197–217, at 200.

[33] But the *murileguli* of Cod. Theod. 10.20.14–16 = Cod. Iust. 11.8.11–13 (424) and the *conchylioleguli* of Cod. Theod. 10.20.17 = Cod. Iust. 11.8.15 (427), whom the code condemns to remain in their trades and whose attempts to improve their status it stamps on (Quintana Orive, 338–40), sound more like collectors of the raw material than those who processed it.

[34] Vitruvius, 8.6.11 *Exemplar autem ab artificibus plumbariis possumus accipere, quod palloribus occupatos habent corporis colores*; A. Trevor Hodge, 'Vitruvius, Lead Pipes and Lead Poisoning', *AJA* 81 (1985), 486–91; H. J. Hopkins, 'The Supply of Water to the Dyeing Workshops of Pompeii', in ead. (ed.), 122–40, at 125.

jusqu'à la chute de l'Empire d'Occident, i (Louvain, 1895), 91–2 n. 1). For monuments (one of which may show a stirring vat for the fabric, but not the furnaces), Zimmer 1982, 29, and 130–1 (nos. 46, 46a). Further on ambivalence about dyeing in antiquity, see i. 340 and n. 79.

κλιβανέας σκοτοεργούς: another case where a banal trade name is given a little lustre with a made-up epithet. Indeed, the trade name, quite well attested in papyri (App. II, VII.1.ii), is so banal that no other literary text uses it. The κρίβανον is strictly the earthenware hood or crock that bread was baked under until the Late Republic (D.–S. s.v. Clibanus (E. Saglio); A. Cubberley, 'Bread-Baking in Ancient Italy: *Clibanus* and *sub testa* in the Roman World: Further Thoughts', in Wilkins *et al.* 55–68). The name stuck, and continued to be used even for those who were mass-producing bread in large built ovens, or furnaces, which are nicely depicted in bakers' monuments.[35] On the technology of baking, see J. Paulas, 'Cooking and Baking Technology', in Irby (ed.), 570–86, at 580–3.

81 Mars' conjunction with the Sun, which renders the planet invisible, has the effect of producing a type of worker who is active during the night and sleeps by day. γάρ proffers an explanation for an outcome: see on 4.91.

82 νύκτα μὲν ἐργάζονται: as indeed they did. For Rome, see Mart. *Ep.* 12.57.5, 14.223.1 (A. Hug, *RE* s.v. pistor, 1825.8–13); for a papyrus from Arsinoe that concerns a slave baker whose master might provisionally want her back to work at night, see Bieżuńska-Małowist 1977, ii. 89 = 1984, 195, and Straus 1988, 871 (P. Wisc. I 5, AD 186). In Firmicus, 3.8.7, baking is among trades from whom *vigiliae perpetuae ab operantibus exigantur*. Bakers' hours have been a subject of grievance well into the early modern and modern periods.[36]

ἐν ἤματι δ' ὑπνώουσιν: Opp. *Hal.* 3.237 ἐν ἤμασιν αὐλίζονται (the verse-pattern established by Theocr. 12.2 ἐν ἤματι γηράσκουσιν).

---

[35] Zimmer 1982, 20–5, and 106–20, nos. 18–32, esp. nos. 18 (Eurysaces, Rome, Porta Maggiore), 19 (Bologna), and 20 (Rome, Villa Medici); see too a panel in the 3rd-c. mosaic of the four seasons from Saint-Romain-en-Gal, now displayed in the Musée des Antiquités nationales, Saint-Germain-en-Laye, showing a baker inserting a loaf into an oven (illustrated in Dunbabin 1999, 81 fig. 80; J. Lancha, *Recueil general des mosäiques de la Gaule III. Province de Narbonnaise*, 2 (1981), no. 368, 212–13 and pl. cxiii, a).

[36] Eighteenth-century France (H. Morgan, 'Bakers and the Baking Trade in the Roman Empire: Social and Political Responses from the Principate to Late Antiquity' (MPhil. thesis, Oxford, 2015), 10 and n. 30); twentieth-century Lithuania (U. M. Andrijauskaitė, 'Taking Matters into Their Own Hands: Lithuanian Bakers in 1920s–1930s', *Istorija. Lietuvos aukštųjų mokyklų mokslo darbai*, 2 (2018), 4–18, at 10–12). In the UK The Baking Industry (Hours of Work) Act, known as the Night Baking Act, was in force between 1954 and 1986, and there is a story (not aggrieved) about a seventeen-hour shift in a bakery in King's Lynn in 2011: https://www.theguardian.com/money/2011/sep/09/a-working-life-the-baker

83–8

Saturn out of sect on MC. See apparatus for 4.251–62.

Protasis. Of the three charts which place Saturn in the MC, this configuration is most similar to Θ p. 166.22–4 (from the *Dodecatopos*), which provides precisely the same information about sect and location and no more. The other two add that Saturn is in another planet's sign. Related Π- charts involve Mars (Ptol. 4.4.5, Θ p. 211.24–31), so it is intriguing that this chart follows so soon after a generalisation about Mars as Ruler of πρᾶξις (1.76–7). But the asyndeton in 1.83 seems to rule out any connection.

Apodosis. Between them, the same three charts about Saturn parallel almost every detail. The trade names in 84 are linked specifically to Θ p. 166.22 and *CCAG* ii. 191.22 (Epit. IV),[37] although the subterranean workers of 85–6 look more like the ὑπονομευτάς born when Saturn aspects Mars as Ruler of πρᾶξις. The watery workplaces of 87 correspond to the watery trades of Θ p. 212.17, while Θ's further remark about hard labour either captures the sense of the epithets in 84–5, or corresponds to the comment about wages (86, 88), or both.

83 νυκτερινοῖσι: 'for those born in a night birth', an unusual personal application of a standard technical term (p. 312) which in prose would either refer directly to a planet or accompany a noun (usually γένεσις, cf. θέμα in 1.278; also αἵρεσις, hora).
Κρόνος αἰνὸς: i. 911 n. 2.

84–5 ἀργαλέους ὑδραγωγούς...ὑδροφόρους πολυπήμονας: the poet performs the same trick twice over, choosing words which are, or can be used as, trade descriptions, and embellishing each with an epithet which transforms a nuisance-causing adjective to one meaning 'nuisance-suffering' (see i. 367). For water-carriers see on 4.251, and add Farag Ebeid Zaki Shehata, 'The Water-Carrier in Graeco-Roman Egypt', *Journal of Association of Arab Universities for Tourism and Hospitality*, 17 (2019), 1–15 (bad English, but enlightening). Shehata well illustrates how crucial they were, in practice, to every activity in Egypt, supplying private houses, towns, agriculture, industry, mines, quarries, and military installations; if astrological texts tend to associate them with a narrow range of activities (gardening and civil engineering), that downplays their central role to the maintenance of life itself. Terracottas representing carriers with their waterskins also suggest the physical demands which elicit the pitying epithets in our poem. Both terms occur in papyri, with no clear difference in sense. When ὑδραγωγός, which usually means a water-channel,[38] or

---

[37] They are unique to these passages in astrology. In Hephaestion, ii. 281.9 ὑδραγωγούς is not a trade name, and corresponds to ποταμούς in i. 248.18.
[38] Krüger, 21.

describes a diuretic drug, serves as a job description in literary texts (it is preserved only in Epit. IV, not Θ; see Appendix II, II.3.i), it designates someone who maintains pipes and gutters or waters gardens.[39] A ὑδραγωγός also appears among other workers for a daily wage in *IG* V/1 1406.3 (Asine, AD 301), but no further details emerge.[40] As for the ὑδροφόρος, he is listed next to a digger in Lucian, *Vit. auct.* 7 σκαπανέα γε καὶ ὑδροφόρον, much as in 4.251–2.

85–6 οἵθ' ὑπὸ γαίης | κευθμῶνας δύνουσιν: corresponding, it seems, to ὑπονομευτάς, on whom see on 4.252. They could be channelling fresh water into a settlement or facility, or they could be sewer-workers channelling waste out of it. The poet reaches for solemn vocabulary to dignify them; γαίης | κευθμῶνας transforms a phrase which Hesiod, in a portentous passage about seasonal change, used in a kenning (fr. 204.130 M.–W. γ]αί[η]ς ἐν κευθμῶνι) and which reappears in oracular or eschatological material (*Or. Sib.* 1.188, 3.409, 8.413; Orph. 339.8 F Bernabé).

ἀεικέος εἵνεκα μισθοῦ: see i. 340. The phrase crosses *Il.* 12.435 ἀεικέα μισθὸν (simile of female wool-worker) with Call. *Hymn* 3.175 εἵνεκα μισθοῦ (where the point is not the paucity of the amount itself, but the implications of a very long day's work for a wage labourer).

87 παρύγροισι: Koechly and De Stefani both accept Axtius' conjecture πανύγροισι, but the parallel chart in Θ p. 212.17 (τὰς παρύγρους πράξεις) confirms that L has the right reading, as does pp. 167.33–168.1 νυκτὸς δὲ ὁ τοῦ Κρόνου μεσουρανῶν δυσπράκτους ἀποτελεῖ καὶ ἐπὶ παρύγρων τάσσει. See also Θ p. 142.19–20 τινὰς δὲ καὶ ἀπὸ παρύγρων βιοῦντας (Saturn in sect in second place); Valens, I 1.7 πάρυγρα πράσσοντας (a typical Saturnian activity), and, for the sense, 4.534 παράλοιο.

88 Daily payments of half an obol (a twelfth of a drachma) to water-carriers are recorded in Ptolemaic documents concerning ὑδροφόροι (Shehata, cited on 84–5, 1–2 and n. 3). In Diocletian's Price Edict (301), they get the same daily wage (25 *denarii communes*, plus maintenance) as other unskilled labourers (brick-maker, farm labourer, lime burner, mule/camel driver, sewer cleaner, shepherd), half as much as bakers or stone-masons (*marmorarii*), and six times less than a *pictor imaginarius*, which is at least an index of differential prestige, if not reliably of actual income.[41] An *aquatarius* (sic) commemorates himself

---

[39] Pipes: Stephanus, *In Hippocratis aphorismos*, 4.1.89 (*CMG* XI 1.3.2). Gardens: Cyril, *Comm. in Isaiam*, PG 70.841.14, cf. Σ D *Il.* 21.257, where the word glosses ὀχετηγός, ὁ τὸν τοῦ ὕδατος ὀχετὸν καθαίρων.

[40] Whatever else he is, not an 'obscure' official connected with the water supply (Y. A. Lolos, 'The Hadrianic Aqueduct of Corinth', *Hesperia*, 66 (1997), 271–314, at 296 n. 62).

[41] Groen-Vallinga and Tacoma, 105–6. For an attempt to contextualise that with other societies (in which case it is wretchedly low, lower than early modern Delhi), see R. C. Allen, 'How

The Book Proper 781

on a plaque from the Isola Sacra, Ostia, but from the scene he is clearly a shop-owner who sells drinks.[42]

89–91 + 92–5

Mercury centred, and opposite to Saturn and the Moon on the ASC; then cadent. This is a οἴνος chart. The first part corresponds to the first entry in Περὶ μαινομένων καὶ ἐπιληπτικῶν. Koechly transposed 90 and 91 to create a single distich on madness, then repeated 89 before the newly positioned 90 with 94 to serve as the first line of the apodosis. If there ever was such a version of the text, Θ knows nothing of it. Its sequence is exactly as here. I find no parallel, however, for the tweak in 92–5. The discussion of this passage by Heilen 2010, 166–8, is beside the point, for he misses the relationship with Θ and cites the wrong parallels (Firmicus and Dorotheus) which put him onto the track of speech defects.

90 κατεναντίον ὡρονόμοιο: compare 3.137 κατεναντίον ὡρονομοῦντος; for κατεναντίον, see i. 887 and Lightfoot on Dion. Per. 114.

91 ἐμμανέας is distinctive: otherwise only 231 (in an elegiac couplet), and unrelated passages in Hephaestion, i. 12.24, and 'Palchus', CCAG ix/1. 184.2 (erotic madness). There are implications for the overlap between the author of the elegiacs and A (p. 281).

92 εἰ δὲ ῥοπῆς μὴ μοῖρα τύχῃ: the idea is clearly that madness is the outcome if the planets are on kentra, but that the edge is taken off if they are declining from them. So I interpret: 'if it is not [on] the degree of the balance', i.e. poised on the very tip of the kentron before it starts to turn down and fall away. ῥοπή is otherwise only in the Manethoniana in 1.276 βίοτόν τε ῥοπῇ λείψουσι πρόμοιροι, where it clearly refers to la forza del destino.

καθέτου δ' ἀποκλίνῃ: see on 4.45.

93 Darkness and turbulence readily combine in imagery for mental disorder (Padel, 68–77 + 78–88), which strikes us as tragic in character (as also for Turnus in V. Aen. 12.666–9 aestuat . . . ut primum discussae umbrae et lux reddita

---

Prosperous Were the Romans? Evidence from Diocletian's Price Edict (AD 301)', in A. K. Bowman and A. I. Wilson (eds.), *Quantifying the Roman Economy: Methods and Problems* (Oxford, 2009), 327–45.

[42] Zimmer 1982, 218, no. 176; A. Landskron, 'The Perception of "Skills" in Ostia: The Evidence of Monuments and Written Sources', in E. Stewart, E. Harris, and D. Lewis (eds.), *Skilled Labour and Professionalism in Ancient Greece and Rome* (Cambridge, 2020), 175–201, at 187, speculating that he made a decent living in a thirsty harbour town.

*menti*⁴³), though they can also be combined to suggest pre-philosophic benightedness (Lucr. 5.11 *fluctibus e tantis...tantique tenebris*), and for Paul darkness is the state of those alienated from God (Ephes. 4:18 ἐσκοτωμένοι τῇ διανοίᾳ ὄντες). The metaphor of madness as a storm or flood⁴⁴ sounds particularly tragic (Soph. *Aj.* 206–7 θολερῷ...χειμῶνι; Eur. *HF* 1091–2 ὡς ‹δ'› ἐν κλύδωνι καὶ φρενῶν ταράγματι | πέπτωκα δεινῶι; *Or.* 279 ἐκ κυμάτων γὰρ αὖθις αὖ γαλήν' ὁρῶ; ps.-Aesch. *PV* 883–4 λύσσης | πνεύματι μάργωι and 886 στυγνῆς πρὸς κύμασιν ἄτης, where the metaphor of waves of disaster⁴⁵ is combined with mental breakdown; Sen. *Her.* 1092 *insanos fluctus animi*; one thinks of King Lear). The flood metaphor is also used of strong emotions, especially anger, which themselves border on mental illness.⁴⁶ κλεψίφρονι, which otherwise occurs only in *HHom. Herm.* 413 (see Thomas ad loc.), Greg. Naz. *PG* 37.457.12, has been co-opted into the imagery; on both other occasions it means 'deceptive' rather than engulfing, something that sweeps the mind away. μούνῳ is hard: is it supposed to suggest pre-eminence or unique intensity?

94 The line-end is simply lifted from *Od.* 20.346 (of Athena's effect on the suitors), while the first part mirrors it, curiously with a phrase which can certainly be paralleled, but only in texts of the third or fourth century and later (a good example, clearly of mental estrangement rather than a simple change of mind, in Nicephorus, *Antirrhetici tres adversus Constantinum Copronymum*, 1.313.11–12 εἴ σοι τὰ τῶν φρενῶν μὴ ἠλλοίωτο, which is eighth or ninth century). The verb alone, passive, is used of mental confusion already in Polybius: LSJ ἀλλοιόω, II.4.

95 The parallelistic jingle (p. 295) is achieved through the use of a colourful word for madness which originates as a *hapax* in *Il.* 5.882 (of Diomedes madly attacking gods) and was relocated at line-end by Democritus and then Aratus, 1123 (see Martin's note ad loc.; the passages are about swine). Together these set the tone for later uses of μαργαίνειν, suggesting hybris (Opp. *Hal.* 3.491) or animal rage (Opp. *Hal.* 4.430, 5.365).

---

⁴³ D. Hershkowitz, *The Madness of Epic: Reading Insanity from Homer to Statius* (Oxford, 1999), 74 and n. 16.
⁴⁴ Which also applies the other way round, to oceans raging (Opp. *Hal.* 1.38, using the same verb as in l. 95 here).
⁴⁵ Aesch. *Pers.* 599–600 (van Nes, 36); ps.-Aesch. *PV* 1015 (van Nes, 26, 43); Soph. *OT* 1527, with Finglass ad loc. A sea of distress: ps.-Aesch. *PV* 746 (van Nes, 41).
⁴⁶ Padel, 84–8; Hershkowitz (n. 43), 71 n. 13; Pease on V. *Aen.* 4.532 *magnoque irarum fluctuat aestu*; Fitch (excellent) and Billerbeck on Sen. *Her.* 1092. Boiling in Gow on Theocr. 20.15 and Livrea on Ap. Rhod. 4.391.

96-9

Mars ὕπαυγος; Mars aspects Sun. Two (or perhaps three, including 114: see comments below) couplets on the theme of the Sun nullifying the ill effects of Mars, a doctrine also stated by Firmicus, 2.8.2. They do not say quite the same thing, so it is not that the elegiac couplet merely reiterates the hexameter. The point of 96-7 is that the planet is nullified when it is ὕπαυγος, which is not surprising. But if καθορᾶν means 'aspect', as it usually does, 98-9 implies that any (unspecified) aspect to the Sun weakens Mars, and that is certainly not what we have gathered from 2.422-5 (not even conjunction does this).

97 The poet has simply lifted an Odyssean line-end (ὑπ' αὐγὰς ἠελίοιο) with not the slightest embarrassment about the ensuing hiatus when, with Ares at the caesura, it is left one syllable short. For hiatus after uncontracted biceps, see p. 308.

98 καθορῶν φάος Ἡελίοιο: the common EGHP formula 'light of the Sun' (8× Il., 10× Il., also in the Homeric Hymns and Hesiod) often employs part of ὁρᾶν, which the poet has simply modified to a part of the compound which astrological poets favour for aspect. It should have emerged more strongly in vol. i that καθορᾶν is almost exclusive to poetic astrology. Of aspect it is used in 6.23, 30, 72, 458, 689; 5.75, 228; Camaterus, Zod. 1075, and in the middle in 6.704; otherwise it is only in Hephaestion, ii. 228.16 (from Epit. IV).

99 κακοφροσύνην: this word only recurs twice in astrology, both times involving Mars: (i) in 2.294 and (ii) in CCAG ii. 202.28, from a chapter περὶ ἐπεμβάσεων which Cumont attributed to Anubion on the evidence of the elegiac couplets and isolated pentameters which are quoted in the course of it (= Anubion, F 10). The attribution is supported by Heilen 2010, 152, who notes that the next chapter in the manuscript is 'Par. Anub.' There is a risk of circularity in arguing that 1.98-9 are Anubionic on the unproven grounds that CCAG's chapter is as well. It is at least possible, although on stylistic grounds the parallel epithet-noun pair at caesura and line-end is not characteristic of the fragments of Anubion (p. 279).

100-5 Planets and Leadership

These are not just natives in whom the planet's character is exemplified; they are types of leader, in the specialism represented by the planet. They are all provincial worthies—high priests, holders of liturgies, in one case a consul. These are the men praised in a thousand honorific inscriptions of Asia Minor (note the homogeneity of the culture of provincial élites if the writer is Egyptian): the titles, the terms of commendation, the values, are either matched verbatim, or are gentle poeticisations of inscriptional commonplace. Take, for instance, Tiberius Julius Junianus of Ancyra (*SEG* 27.842, 2nd or 3rd c.), honoured as an ἀρχιερέα (~ 101), κτίστην τῆς μητροπόλεως (~ 5.308), πορφύραι κὲ στεφάνωι διὰ βίου τετιμημένον (~ 101), conspicuous for φιλοτιμία (~ 5.308), ἔργοις τε περικαλλεστάτοις κοσμήσαντα (sc. τὴν πατρίδα) (~ 105), κὲ μόνον τῶν πρὸ αὐτοῦ δι᾽ ὅλης ἐλαιοθετήσαντα τῆς ἡμέρας (~ 100). Or Tiberius Claudius Zelos of Aphrodisias (*IAphr.* 260, late 2nd or early 3rd c.), a κτίστην (~ 5.308), high priest (~ 101), τοῦ πολλοῖς καὶ μεγάλοις ἔργοις ἐκ τῶν ἰδίων κοσμήσαντος τὴν πόλιν (~ 105). Or Laevianus of Thyateira (*TAM* V/2 983, c. AD 200) and T. Flavius Domitianus Nestor of Prusias (*IK* Prusias ad Hypium, 46), who both conducted themselves ἐν[δό]ξως as ἀγορανόμοι (102) and adorned their cities (κοσμήσαντα τὴν πατρίδα ~ 105).

The planets are presented in three pairs, malefics, benefics, luminaries, then the unpaired Mercury. The order is unusual, with Mercury not dividing malefics from benefics, but placed last of all.

100 One might have expected Mercury in connection with the palaestra, and Jupiter for the civic benefactors of 105. Given the leadership theme, these men will be, not athletic victors, but gymnasiarchs, and that is what κρατέοντας ... παλαίστρης paraphrases. The epithet is new. It is not necessary to see the line-end as a renovation specifically of Theocr. 2.51 λιπαρᾶς ... παλαίστρας (cf. also ps.-Lucian, *Amores*, 3, 45), but for the topos, with Latin examples, see Gow ad loc. and Hollis on *Hecale* fr. 71.3. For the single rhota, compare Eur. *Bacch.* 154 χρυσορόου, Nic. *Ther.* 318 αἱμορόοι, ps.-Opp. *Cyn.* 1.116 φυλλορόῳ.

101 Venus makes high priests also in Firmicus, 3.6.1 (in the ASC), 4.21.5 (as Ruler of πρᾶξις, together with other high officers clad in purple and gold). For their costume, see i. 334, 346–7, p. 1062, and nn. on 2.234–5, 4.39, 5.258–9. Gold and purple were traditional priestly prerogatives,[47] but from the fact that these are specified as *high* priests we are perhaps to think specifically of the civic

---

[47] Examples include *FD* iii/2. 69 (Delphi, (?)117 BC), a decree of the Amphictyonic Council permitting the priests of the Athenian guild of Artists of Dionysus to wear purple(?) and gold, ll. 31–2 χρ]υσοφορεῖν τοῖς θεοῖς κατὰ πάσας τὰς πόλεις κατὰ τὰ πά[τρια, ὁμοίως τε καὶ πορφυροφ]ορεῖν (though see A. B. Kuhn, 57); the priest of Dionysus in Scepsis, *BE* 1976, 572 = *SEG* 26.1334.11–12 (2nd c. BC?); the Coan priests of Zeus Alseios, *IG* XII/4 1 328, ll. 15–18, and of Nike, ibid. 330, ll. 8–9 (both 1st c. BC; cf. A. B. Kuhn, 60); a *stephanephoros* of Heracles in Tarsus, Athen. 5.215 B–C (late Hellenistic or early Augustan); a priestess of Side, *IK* Side, 226.9 (late 3rd c. AD); Ov. *Fast.* 4.339 (a priest of Cybele, admittedly outlandish); Pliny, *NH* 9.127. The Jewish high priest wore a purple ephod, for which the LXX word is ὑακίνθινον, suggesting an amethyst tone (D.-S. s.v. Purpura, 773 (M. Besnier)): Exod. 28:31, cf. Jos. *AJ* 3.184, with A. Weissenrieder, 'A Roadmap to Heaven: High-Priestly Vestments and the Jerusalem Temple in Flavius Josephus', in R. L. Gordon, G. Petridou, and J. Rüpke (eds.), *Beyond Priesthood: Religious Entrepreneurs and Innovators in the Roman Empire* (Berlin, 2017), 157–84, at 169–70; M. Reinhold, *History of Purple as a Status Symbol in Antiquity* (Brussels, 1970), 20, 35.

or provincial high priests of the imperial cult, who borrowed and adapted traditional priestly dress (many sources, including Dio Chrys. *Or.* 35.10, cf. 34.30; Robert 1938, 78-9 n. 2 and references; A. B. Kuhn, 72; for gold in their costume, see 4.39). There is surprisingly little systematic discussion of the purple dress of pagan priests, in comparison to royal dress, but see C. Jones, 'Processional Colours', in B. Bergmann and C. Kondoleon (eds.), *The Art of Ancient Spectacle* (New Haven, 1999), 247-55, at 248-9, 251-2; Chaniotis, 50-1.

102 Across the Greek world the ἀγορανόμος was the official in charge of the market, the equivalent of the Roman aedile. In Egypt itself, the office had notarial functions.[48] The association with Saturn, close-fisted and ungenerous, perhaps sorts better with the idea of a market official (Mercury would have better suited notaries), which is also implied by their standing association in other astrological texts (despite disagreement over the planets responsible for them) with measurement and regulation (Valens, I 1.31 ἀγορανομίας, μέτρα, σταθμούς, ἐμπορίας, ἐργαστήρια, similar in App. II 30, and Rhetorius, *CCAG* vii. 220.8). Superintending weights and measures was precisely what the Athenian officials did at the turn of the millennium (Rayhab, n. 48, 45).

The ἀγορανόμος readily takes his place in a list of honoured individuals. In Egypt as throughout the Greek East the office became a liturgy, held by wealthy individuals, something to boast of; a good comparison for the present passage is the gravestone of Apollonius (Lycopolis/Asyut, 1st/2nd c. AD) recording his service as gymnasiarch, ἀγορανόμος, and high priest, among other offices (E. Bernand, *Inscriptions grecques d'Égypte et de Nubie au Musée du Louvre* (Paris, 1992), 91). Honours for ἀγορανόμοι are legion. Individuals might receive personal honours for good management (*IG* XII,5 129, Paros, 2nd c. BC), and as the post over time became a liturgy, its holders were of a status that εὐδόξως and ἐστεφάνωσεν might suit (several are both ἀγορανόμος and στεφανηφόρος). In fact, ἀγορανόμοι are often commended for having behaved ἐνδόξως during

---

[48] D.-S. s.v. Agoranomoi (E. Caillemer); J. Oehler, *RE* s.v. Agoranomoi; S. Rayhab, 'The Rise and Development of the Office of Agoranomos in Greco-Roman Egypt', *NECJ* 46 (2019), 37-61 (37-47 on the ἀγορανόμος throughout the Greco-Roman world, and 47-58 specifically on Egypt). For Egypt see also Cumont, 70-1 n. 3; M. G. Raschke, 'The Office of Agoranomos in Ptolemaic and Roman Egypt', in E. Kiessling and H.-A. Rupprecht (eds.), *Akten des XIII. Internationalen Papyrologenkongresses, Marburg/Lahn, 2. bis 6. August 1971* (Munich, 1974), 349-56, and id., 'An Official Letter to an Agoranomus: P.Oxy. I 170', *BASP* 13 (1976), 17-29 (with earlier bibl. in n. 9); H. J. Wolff, *Das Recht der griechischen Papyri Ägyptens in der Zeit der Ptolemaeer und des Prinzipats, ii: Organisation und Kontrolle des privaten Rechtsverkehrs* (Munich, 1978), 9-18; P. W. Pestman, 'Agoranomoi et actes agoranomiques: Krokodilopolis et Pathyris, 145-88 av. J.C.', in id. (ed.), *Textes et études de papyrologie grecque, démotique et copte (Pap. Lugd. Bat. XXIII)* (Leiden, 1985), 9-44. In Strab. 15.1.50 (C 707) the transmitted ἀγορανόμοι who had the task of maintaining the river and measuring the land are to be corrected to ἀγρονόμοι (see Radt ad loc.).

their office.⁴⁹ But although ἐνδόξως is the epigraphical norm, εὐδόξως occurs as well, e.g. *SEG* 25.155 (Rhamnous, 236/5), l. 15 καλῶς καὶ εὐδόξ[ω]s.

103 εὐτόλμους: Mars also involved in 2.172.

104 ὕπατον: this agrees with Firmicus, 3.5.2, where the Sun optimally placed in the ASC produces emperors, but slightly less optimally *consulares faciet ‹et› proconsulares et dat ordinarios consulatus*, and more of the same in the MC (3.5.34–5). In Greek texts luminaries in *kentra* produce any number of kings (see on 1.26–8). Consuls are not specified very often (Cumont, 44 n. 3; pp. 18–19), though in the interpretation of Pamprepius' chart (no. L 440 Neugebauer–Van Hoesen, for 29 Sept. 440) the fact that he became successively κουέστωρ, ὕπατος, πατρίκιος is attributed to the fact that he was born at a time when the Sun, Jupiter, and Mercury were in Libra (Θ p. 224.13). Jupiter produces consuls in Firmicus, 3.3.10.

ἀρχιδικαστήν: see i. 333 n. 27 and n. on 2.264–5, adding Fraser, 95, 113; L. C. Youtie, 'A Petition to an Acting Strategos', *ZPE* 46 (1982), 223–6, at 223–4; A. K. Bowman and D. Rathbone, 'Cities and Administration in Roman Egypt', *JRS* 82 (1992), 107–27, at 117, 125, 127.

105 κοσμητῆρας ἑῆς ... πόληος: the poet has adapted a standard formula of commendation. Dozens of inscriptions praise the benefactor who has beautified his homeland (κοσμήσαντα τὴν πατρίδα), usually having held at least some of the offices mentioned in the previous lines. For instance, M. Aurelius Asiaticus, a high priest, sponsor of public buildings (*SEG* 52.694, Augusta Traiana, after 212); C. Julius Epicrates of Miletus, high priest of Asia and of the Ionians, agonothete, gymnasiarch, and multiple liturgist (*SEG* 44.938/*AE* 1994, 1650, mid-1st c. AD); a successful ambassador of Tabai, who also served as an ἀγορανόμος (L. and J. Robert, 106 no. 7).

106–11 + 112–13 (+ 114?)

Venus in Capricorn or Aquarius with Saturn and Jupiter, in *synaphe* with Saturn, with Mars aspecting Moon and Venus, 'with' Saturn; and with aspect of Sun. This is fascinating. It is evidence of the use of one of the Sample Charts. It is the chart of Oedipus (as in 6.160–9), without naming him (so, like Anubion, F 4 ii. 11–16). It belongs with the other two poetic sources insofar as, like them, it lacks the extra precision Firmicus, 6.30.1, provides (Jupiter and Venus are in equal degrees and Saturn is in the second house). It shares with Mᵃ the slight

---

⁴⁹ e.g. *IG* IV 609, Argos, Roman; *IG* XII,3 1115, Melos; *IG* XII/4 2:834, Cos, c.AD 200–250; many more.

oddity that Venus receives ($\lambda\acute{a}\beta\eta/\delta\epsilon\chi\nu\nu\mu\acute{\epsilon}\nu\eta s$) the contact of Saturn (which is strange when Venus is by far the faster-moving planet). Its distinctive detail is that it names the signs of Saturn. It loses a little precision in comparison to M[a] (6.161) and Firmicus, who have Saturn following behind Venus and Jupiter, by putting Saturn in the same sign. Interestingly, though the relevant line in Anubion is damaged (11), it did not have enough room to make the same specification as M[a] and Firmicus. Obbink suggests there was room for $\mathring{a}\gamma\chi\iota$, but suppose Anubion, too, had simply said 'in the same sign as' (e.g. $\tau\hat{\omega}$ δ' $a\mathring{v}\tau\hat{\omega}$ $\tau\epsilon\tau\acute{v}\chi\eta$ vel sim.)?

There are also a couple of more certain similarities with Anubion:

(i) 1.108 $\sigma\nu\nu\alpha\phi\grave{\eta}\nu$ $\pi\rho\acute{\omega}\tau o\iota o$ and Anubion l. 12 $\kappa\alpha\grave{\iota}$ $\pi\rho\acute{\omega}\tau[\omega]\iota$ $\tau o\acute{v}\tau\omega\iota$ $\sigma\nu\nu\alpha\phi\acute{\eta}\nu$ (Obbink notes this).

(ii) l. 109 and Anubion l. 14. Mars aspects both the Moon and Venus. M[a] just puts Mars in aspect to Venus. Firmicus has a somewhat more complex formulation.

So what are the implications? That there was a hexametrised version of Anubion in circulation, or at least that this particular passage is a hexametrised rendering of a particular chart?

Lines 112–13 (+ 114?), however, are not found in any other versions of the chart, and they are certainly not in Anubion. In 112–13 we are told that the Sun modifies the outcome to stepmothers instead of full mothers. This is stated in a couple of self-contained lines; 114, an add-on pentameter, is in theory detachable. Indeed, it is not particularly happy, for the Sun's effect cannot be said to 'extinguish' the evil, only at best to mitigate it to a (slightly) lesser one which astrology still regards as a sin and an offence (for stepmothers, see on 2.187–9). Koechly carried it back and replaced it after 97, which necessitated a second, remade version of 97 in order to supply the first verse of the supposed couplet. Although the necessity of inventing a whole new line was suspect, and Koechly shows himself slightly self-conscious about that ('erunt qui vituperent'), what motivated him was the principle of like going with like: he thought that an editor had brought together three similarly-themed couplets in the earlier passage. It also has the advantage that, by decoupling 114 from 112 and 113, the passage no longer strikes so hard against the normal attitude in astrology that sex with stepmothers is not much better than with the real thing. But one must then explain what carried the pentameter to its present position, the *lectio* (or at least *locus*) *difficilior*.

Koechly, of course, did not yet know that Anubion had treated the Oedipus chart, which seems at first sight an argument for keeping the line in its approximately Anubionic environment. On the other hand there are difficulties about attributing it to Anubion. For in his Oedipus chart, he had treated stepmothers quite differently. Despite the maddening loss of l. 15b, where mothers must have been mentioned (the whole point of the chart, after all), it seems that he ranked mothers and stepmothers together, with a disjunctive (as does Firmicus, 6.30.1), taking the usual line about equal heinousness. So far from regarding stepmother intercourse as a mitigation, Anubion describes the native as αἰνότατος, and Firmicus as acting *praepostero mentis ardore*. Does that mean that we leave the line here but attribute it to a *different* elegiac poet (someone who took a curiously libertarian view of stepmothers)? It is baffling, but the case for transposition remains less than wholly compelling.

106 Αἰγόκερῳ: as normal, and as in 3.14 (same *sedes*). Dorotheus, p. 419.1, has Αἰγοκερεῖ.

108 πολιοῖο Κρόνοιο: i. 911 n. 14; the same line-ending at 4.402.

109 εἰσβλέψαντος: with straight accusative (instead of εἰς) at Eur. *Or.* 105; 'Menand.' *Sent.* 84; Machon, fr. 11.152 Gow; George of Pisidia (7th c.), *Epigr.* 81.3. An almost exclusively prosaic word, but unique in astrology. See 1.5 n.

110 Κρόνῳ βλαβερῷ: i. 911 n. 3. cf. also Valens, Additamenta Antiqua, IV 1 Κρόνος ἑαυτῷ παραδιδοὺς βλαβερὸς καὶ ἄπρακτος; Περὶ κράσ. 50 Διαμετρικῶς δὲ ὁρῶν τὸν Δία ὁ Κρόνος βλαβερὸς μὲν περὶ τὰς πράξεις; Dorotheus, p. 425.3 (Saturn aspects waning Moon) βλαβερὸς γίνεται τῷ κάμνοντι, Camaterus, *Introd.* 1753 βλαβερώτερος ὁ Κρόνος (that is, of the two malefics, which both do harm to sailors, Saturn is worse).

δυστλήμονες ἀνέρες οὗτοι: for this generalising equivalent to πολυπενθέος Οἰδιπόδαο (6.166) we may but need not look specifically to HHom. *Ap.* 532 νήπιοι ἄνθρωποι δυστλήμονες (also Soph. fr. 555.8 Radt, very damaged). To judge from P. Berol. 44 col. vi = Orph. 1 B 15a D.-K. ἄφρονες ἄνθρωποι δυστλήμονες this rare epithet was traditional in comminations/commiserations.

111 βαίνουσιν... ἐπὶ λέκτρα: varying ἐπὶ δέμνια βαίνειν (of illicit liaisons in *Od.* 8.296, 314, and especially of incestuous unions in Hes. *Op.* 328, ps.-Phocyl. 183), βαίνειν εἰς λέχος (Matron, *SH* 534.75; Theocr. 17.42).

112 Apparently referring informally to any kind of aspect; compare Menander Rhetor, p. 446.7 Sp. παρὰ σοῦ (sc. ἡλίου) καὶ σελήνη τὴν ἀκτῖνα λαμβάνει.

πυραυγέος Ἡελίοιο: i. 908 n. 4 (EGHP has ὀξέος/Ὑπερίονος/φαεσιμβρότου/ τερψιμβρότου/λαμπρὸν φάος Ἡελίοιο).

113 For these two categories, see i. 303 and 2.187–9 n. They are combined in 2.189–90 (Venus in the houses of Saturn), and the diction (stepmothers +

The Book Proper 789

μίγνυμι) corresponds to Π.τ.δ. 17 μητρυιαῖς…μιγνυμένους, Anubion, l. 16 μητρυιῇ μείξεται, 5.205 μητρυιῆσιν ἔμιξεν (Saturn and Venus in equal degrees). In none of these cases is the Sun involved.

115–18 + 119–20

Moon in female places opposite Sun, and in ASC; then with malefics in MC. This is the typical feminisation produced by both luminaries being in feminine places (not spelled out here, but necessarily so if the Sun is opposite the Moon, which it *is*). Compare 'Antiochus' (quoted on i. 702), Ptol. 3.15.10 (less closely 3.376–9). As Koechly saw, this looks very much like the male counterpart to the lesbians who were treated in 1.29–33, and the involvement of the horoscope marries up with 1.30.

This version of the gendered-luminaries chart does not appear in Θ, nor has it parallels in the section on the sterile in Mᵃ. But it is related to Firmicus, 6.30.18, of which there is a different version in 6.534–40 (the chart that closes the τέχναι). The relationships go in all directions. Mercury is absent here, but on the ASC in Firmicus and Mᵃ. The ASC is in a female sign in Firmicus and Mᶜ, but not in Mᵃ. In 1.119 and 6.536–7 both malefics are on *kentra* (albeit different ones in Mᵃ), while they are absent from Firmicus.

115 ἐπεμβαίνουσα: see Heilen 2015, 521–2; 5.80, 105nn. This is the technical sense, of entering into a new place or sign.

117 For the various ways of representing the sex of the effeminate male, see on 1.125. With this formulation compare Dio Cass. 62.6.3 ὄνομα μὲν ‹γὰρ› ἀνδρὸς ἔχει, ἔργῳ δὲ γυνή ἐστι (of Nero). In Cic. *Off.* 1.105 *sunt enim quidam homines non re, sed nomine*, the context is those who are addicted to pleasures, but the antithesis is not that of male and female, but of man and beast.

118 The line is of very similar shape to Opp. *Hal.* 1.6 καὶ βίον ἰχθυόεντα καὶ ἔχθεα καὶ φιλότητας (also about lifestyle, including love-life); the cadence is originally from Hes. *Th.* 224. For αἰσχ- of sexual misconduct, see i. 367.

119 Ἄρης τε κραταιός: i. 909 n. 14.

120 One way or another, references to castration lead backwards and forwards to Hesiod's Uranus (p. 219)—with (possibly) tragic diction to help out. As Mᵃ in 3.396 had used *Th.* 180–1 with a dash of Euripides, so too the end of this line recalls Hes. *Th.* 188 μήδεα δ' ὡς τὸ πρῶτον ἀποτμήξας ἀδάμαντι. Hesiod's verb ἀποτμήγειν was also exploited in the same context at 6.580, and will be again (together with a part of σίδηρος and an 'engendering' euphemism for the penis, but no στάχυες) by Nonnus in *Par.* 7.78–81 in the context of circumcision. στάχυν ἄρρενα reminds us of the much-quoted passage from Euripides' *Erechtheus*, fr. 360.22–3 στάχυς ἄρσην which, although it refers to offspring (6.304 n.), looks forward to Nonnus' use of the same conceit, in still more extravagant vein, for Uranus' castration (*D*. 18.228 τάμνεν ἀνυμφεύτων στάχυν ἄρσενα πατρὸς ἀρότρων). Hesiod had not used the word στάχυς itself, but he had used an agricultural metaphor for the 'reaping' of Uranus' genitals (*Th*. 181 ἤμησε; see Vian on Nonn. *D*. 18.227–8 and 25.313–18, a passage which also includes στάχυν and σιδήρῳ at line-end; Julian, *Or*. 5.168 D τέμνεται τὸ ἱερὸν καὶ ἀπόρρητον θέρος τοῦ θεοῦ Γάλλου). The same conceit is applied to the Attis cult (Julian, loc. cit.), and Pesik. R. s. 43 *qamah* ("standing crop") implies the same idea ('the standing crop of Abraham was dried up, but it became again full of ears' = his virile strength was restored): see M. Jastrow, *A Dictionary of the Targumim, the Talmud Babli and Yerushalmi, and the Midrashic Literature* (New York, 1926), s.v. קָמָה.[50]

Monaco, 41, discusses the marginal variant σταχυνον πανόδυρτον, contemplating the possibility that πανόδυρτον was the original reading, ἄρρενα a gloss, and δεινῷ a bland fill-in once πανόδυρτον was lost. Once again, the idea of an 'original' version may not be the right way of modelling the various versions of the text. Presumably the reading would have been στάχυν ὅν, not ἄν, since ἀποτμήξειε is the use of the optative for future, and ἄν is inappropriate. However the variant arose, πανόδυρτον is strongly associated with sepulchral epigram. There are instances in Posidippus (*Ep*. 37.5) and Meleager, *AP* 7.476.9 = HE 4290, but it is best attested in inscriptions (easily elicited on PHI). The poet would be using the epithet in a transferred sense to evoke the pathos self-castration usually elicits (6.537 ὀϊζυροί), applied either to the sword by hypallage or, by a particularly weird sensibility, to the member itself.

121–8

Venus in opposition to Saturn and Moon, Mars in quartile to Venus, Mercury in MC, and Saturn in aspect to the latter. Compare 6.276–81 and Firmicus, 6.30.5. The charts are all related although none is a copy of any other. All have Mercury in the MC (essential for hermaphrodites), and malefics harming both the Moon and Venus. The poet agrees with Firmicus, against Mᵃ, that Venus is opposed by Saturn, and in quartile to Mars. But they all give different reasons for the harm to the Moon (here in conjunction with Saturn; in Mᵃ quartile to Mars; in Firmicus opposed to Mars). There are also relationships with (i) 3.285–6: Venus conjunct with or opposite to Saturn, and Mars and/or the Moon

---

[50] In Artemidorus, 5.84, στάχυες symbolise male offspring (as if they could not symbolise female), and in 5.63 they again symbolise a son (who impregnates his mother).

aspected by Saturn as well (eunuchs); (ii) Camaterus, *Introd.* 2553-5: Saturn centred with the Moon, Venus, and Mercury (eunuchs); (iii) Θ pp. 134.6-9, 150.3-5: Saturn centred with the Sun when a solar eclipse happens on the birth day, along with Venus and Mercury (eunuchs); (iv) Θ p. 169.12-15: damage to both the Moon and Venus, which now occupies the MC (eunuchs and hermaphrodites). The outcome is most like that of Firmicus, in the separate mention of (*a*) eunuchs, (*b*) the sterile, (*c*) hermaphrodites. In M^a they had either no genitals, or both types.

The reasonably close relationship with one of the sample charts forms at least a basis for thinking of Anubion in connection with the two pentameters, although once again 128 exhibits the pattern of parallel epithet and noun which is not particularly Anubionic (p. 279 and 1.99 n.). Koechly took these pentameters and tried to refurbish them into a second chart containing the essence of this one, making a second version of 122 to constitute a protasis for 124, and then filling out 128 with a second version of 125 combined with 127. This was unavailing because he did so without adverting to the parallel charts and their logic, and thus missed out on the two essential characteristics noted above.

122 καλὴν Ἀφροδίτην: i. 907 n. 12.

123 κέντρον ἔχοι: the construction (though not uniquely poetic, e.g. Valens, App. XIX 4; Hephaestion, i. 114.29) is paralleled by Dorotheus, p. 432.10 κέντρον ἔχῃ (same *sedes*). Other astrologers agree that hermaphrodites are born with Mercury centred: Glycas, *Annales*, 215.10-12 (together with Venus and Saturn, and Mars in additional aspect); MC: Timaeus Praxidas, *CCAG* i. 98.37; ASC: Hephaestion, i. 327.15-16.

124 ἀμφιβάλοι: see on 45 ἀγκαλίσαιτο. This is certainly another conceit, for I do not find the verb used to notate planetary positions again except in Camaterus, *Zod.* 1116 Ἐν δ' αὖ δισώμοις ἀμφιβληθὲν πολλάκις, which lacks the implied personification and *Affekt*.

125 Astrological factors in the birth of eunuchs include the feminisation of the luminaries (5.212), harm to Venus and/or the Moon (above; Astrol. Anon. *CCAG* v/1. 207.30), and the involvement of Mercury (Ptol. 3.13.10; Timaeus Praxidas, *CCAG* i. 98.95). The present chart combines all three.

οὔτ' ἄρρενας οὔτε γυναῖκας: examples of this topos include Eur. *Or.* 1528 οὔτε γὰρ γυνὴ πέφυκας οὔτ' ἐν ἀνδράσιν σύ γ' εἶ; Phil. *Somn.* 2.184 μετανάστης μὲν τῆς ἀνδρωνίτιδος, φυγὰς δὲ καὶ τῆς γυναικωνίτιδος, οὔτ' ἄρρεν οὔτε θῆλυ; Lucian, *Eunuch.* 6 καὶ πολὺς ἦν ὁ περὶ τούτου λόγος, οὔτε ἄνδρα οὔτε γυναῖκα εἶναι τὸν εὐνοῦχον λέγοντος, ἀλλά τι σύνθετον καὶ μικτὸν καὶ τερατῶδες, ἔξω τῆς ἀνθρωπείας φύσεως; *AP* 2.1.102-3 οὔθ' ὅλος ἀνὴρ | οὐδὲ γυνή (Hermaphroditus); Colluthus, *Rapt.* 189 οὔτ' ἄρσενες οὔτε γυναῖκες (mannish women); Basil, *Ep.*

115.1 ἄθηλυ, ἄνανδρον (cited by Hopkins 1978, 195); Ov. Am. 2.3.1 nec vir nec femina (with McKeown ad loc.), Ibis 453 Deque viro fias nec femina nec vir, ut Attis; Valerius Maximus, 7.7.6...quod diceret Genucium amputatis sui ipsius sponte genitalibus corporis partibus neque virorum neque mulierum numero haberi debere; ps.-Cyprian, De Spectaculis, 6.4 unum nescio quem nec virum nec feminam (a stage performer); Augustine, Civ. 7.24 ita amputatur virilitas ut nec convertatur in feminam nec vir relinquatur; Lactantius, Div. Inst. 1.21.16 amputato enim sexu nec viros se nec feminas faciunt; cf. Claudian, In Eutrop. 1.467 alter quos pepulit sexus nec suscipit alter; Prudentius, Peristeph. 10.1073 mas esse cessat ille, nec fit femina; Anth. Lat. 129.6 Riese femina cum non sis, vir tamen esse nequis. Another negative expression for the eunuch is Clearchus, frr. 94 and 95a–b ἀνήρ τε κοὐκ ἀνήρ. The opposite of neither/nor is both/and, at 5.140 ἀρρενόθηλυς; and see on 4.220 for outright femininity.

126 The context requires these eunuchs to be sexless (the line-end comes from HHom. Aphr. 133, of Aphrodite the faux virgin). That is in flagrant contradiction to the stories, especially in satire, of eunuch lubricity (Martial, 10.52; Apul. Met. 8.26; Martial, 6.2.6, 6.39.21, 11.81; Juv. Sat. 1.22; Quint. 6.3.64). Indeed, some of these pointedly contrast smooth cheeks and sexual capacity (Lucian, Eunuch. 10 ὁ τὰς γνάθους λεῖος; Juv. Sat. 6.367 desperatio barbae). The fairly rare and always poetic ἄχνοας (heteroclite ending here unique) usually suggests youth, not effeminacy, though the first occurrence in Philip, AP 6.259.1 = Garland 2789, applies to the epicene Hermes. Otherwise on lack of facial hair: Lucilius, 1058 Marx inverbi (i.e. inberbi) androgyni; Plin. NH 11.230 (nongrowth of adult hair); Prudentius, Perist. 10.1074–5 felix deorum mater imberbes sibi | parat ministros.

127 From the un-endowed eunuch to the doubly endowed hermaphrodite. ἑρμαφρόδιτος is synonymous with ἀνδρόγυνος, but 'the term...itself indicates rather a religious and mythological context' (Graumann, 189). The adaptation of EGHP ἐπιείκελον ἀθανάτοισιν for ὁμώνυμον ἀθανάτοισιν adds a little touch of charisma.

128 In other words, they are useless. They have two sex organs, but they are functionless; in Hephaestion, i. 28.18 (source unknown) the hermaphrodite figures in a list of prodigious births which includes the albino and the δίδυμος ἢ δικέφαλος.[51] This is not how they are shown in art, however, which gives them a female body-shape and (small) breasts, but a penis. They do not have

---

[51] Also among prodigies in Ptol. 3.9.4, but the most honourable type thereof, τιμώμενον καὶ εὔσχημον, born under the aspect of a benefic.

ambiguous or double genitalia.⁵² As complement to δισσάς, εἰς ἕν is somewhat mystifying. Lopilato takes it to mean that the genitals are 'conjoined' in some way. Ptolemy lists hermaphrodites together with eunuchs and the ἄτρωγλοι καὶ ἄτρητοι (3.13.10); Robbins renders 'with no ducts or vents'. Does this mean that there is somehow a missing orifice, some anatomical divider or cleft that the hermaphrodite lacks? Perhaps so. Diodorus (32.11.1–4 cf. Graumann, 194; Doroszewska, 128–9) tells of an Epidaurian woman, Callo, who had no perforation in her genitalia except a passage to excrete urine, i.e. presumably she had no vagina (αὕτη τὸν ἐπὶ τῆς φύσεως ἀποδεδειγμένον ταῖς γυναιξὶ πόρον ἄτρητον εἶχεν). Surgery brings to light male genitalia, including a penis which also lacks a perforation (καυλὸς ἄτρητος), which is again corrected by surgery (ὁ φαρμακοπώλης...συνέτρησεν εἰς τὸν οὐρητῆρα), and eventually she transitions to a full man. More unperforated females in Plin. NH 7.69 *quasdam concreto genitali gigni*. When ancient authors remark on the absence of a perforation in male genitalia, what they seem to mean is the condition hypospadias (S. van der Gracht, 'Setting Aside the Loom: Hermaphroditism in Ancient Medicine', in *The Proceedings of the 18th Annual History of Medicine Days, March 6th and 7th, 2009 University of Calgary, Faculty of Medicine, Calgary, AB* (Newcastle, 2012), 247–62, at 252–3).

129–33

Jupiter and Mercury in conjunction and on *kentra*. This is closer to Θ p. 209.10–13 than to the bare Π- chart for Mercury as Ruler of πρᾶξις aspected by Jupiter (Ptol. 4.4.3, Θ pp. 210.30–211.2). There are many charts that bring together Mercury and Jupiter for this kind of outcome (see on 131–2), but what nails the link with this one is its reference to penmanship; the only other is in 3.97–8, where Mercury in the MC gives καλάμοιό τε γραπτῶν | πρῆξιν. What is Θ's source? It comes from the discussion of the effect on πρᾶξις of the location of planets in the houses of other planets which the epitomator derives from the *topikai diakriseis*. Anubion was cited earlier (p. 208.18; see p. 139), and the material is certainly not Ptolemaic, whatever else it is, and whatever similarities it has with 4.4.3, for Ptolemy was having nothing to do with the Lot of πρᾶξις. Are we to infer that this part of the paragraph is Anubionic, as well as what has come before? There are no pentameters to support (or even hinder) the argument.

---

[52] Graumann, 197. There is a collection of illustrations at the end of K. T. von Stackelberg, 'Garden Hybrids: Hermaphrodite Images in the Roman House', CA 33 (2014), 395–426.

129 Archly reapplying *Il.* 5.631 Υἱὸς θ' υἱωνός τε Διὸς νεφεληγερέταο from Zeus' progeny to his father's.

131-2 τεύχουσιν ῥητῆρας... γραπτῆρας πινυτούς: editors since Axtius and Rigler (not Gronovius) have punctuated after the end of 131 (there is nothing in the manuscript). That would seem to imply two types of *rhetor*, one 'from the word', the other 'from the pen', which is a poor way of making a meaningless distinction. When compared with (?)Anubion, however, it becomes clear that the poet is selecting items from his list of πράξεις... ἢ ψήφων ἢ λόγων ἢ καλάμου. This list is itself built around the astrological catch-phrase 'from numbers and words' (always with Mercury), which is sometimes found in the vicinity of part of γράπτ- or γράμμ- (Valens, I 2.50 γραμματεῖς, ἀπὸ λόγων ἢ ψήφων ἀναγόμενοι; IV 21.9 διὰ λόγων ἢ ψήφων ἢ γραπτῶν, under Jupiter and Mercury), and attaches to secretaries or accountants.[53] So I have punctuated instead after ῥήτορας (which is Ptolemaic), and taken the second half of the line with γραπτῆρας. This agent noun is unique save for Paul the Silentiary, *AP* 6.66.1 (of writing equipment, not the scribe). πινυτός (eleven occurrences in the corpus, six of them in M^d) has evolved from one of the *Odyssey*'s many 'shrewdness' and 'prudence' words to a word for grammarians/exponents of *paideia*, immediately or in their vicinity, here and in 3.101, 5.245, 265, and remains strongly associated with *paideia* in epigram (e.g. *IG* II² 7447.12 (Athens, 2nd c.) παιδείᾳ πινυτῇ, 11477.6 (Athens, 1st/2nd c.) παιδείας... πινυτῆς, XII,6 285.9 (Samos, 2nd c. BC) πινυτὰς... ἱστορίας, of a local historian). Generally an effect of Mercury.

132 πολυκερδέας ἄνδρας: not in Θ, but trading and profit go together in the aspects of Jupiter and Mercury in 3.321-2 (with knowledge of screeds a few lines later), and in Valens, IV 21.9 (partly quoted in the note above) the same two planets produce a propensity for gain (ἐπικερδής); see 5.276-7 n. As for πολυκερδής itself, it repurposes an epithet that had described the wiles of Odysseus (*Od.* 13.255) and Medea (Ap. Rhod. 3.1364) for commerce (Π.τ.δ. 46, Moon in house of Venus; 'Antiochus', l. 88 (*CCAG* i. 112.6), Jupiter in the fourth house). After all, it is only fitting that Odysseus becomes a huckster. ps.-Polemon, 8 δειλὸν καὶ πολυκερδῆ apparently does not regard the type highly.

134-8

Full Moon in *synaphe* with Mars in the sixth place. Precisely as in Θ p. 189.6-8 and Firmicus, 4.4.2-3. Π.σ.α. p. 183.1-3 does not specify the sixth place, but does mention τομάς.

---

[53] Other examples: Περὶ σχημ. 8 and Περὶ κράσ. 75 (Saturn trine with Mercury) αἱ δὲ πράξεις ἐκ λόγων ἢ γραμμάτων ἢ ψήφων ἢ ἐμπορίας; Valens, I 19.14 (Jupiter and Mercury); I 20.5 (Saturn, Jupiter, and Mercury) λόγων ἢ ψήφων διευθυντάς.

134 Ἄρεϊ συμβάλλουσα: this intransitive use, of the Moon's contacts, is found in prose, though rarely: *Π.σ.α.* p. 186.16 κακοποιῷ δὲ συμβάλλουσα κακόν; Theophilus, *CCAG* xi/1. 245.22 κακοποιοῖς δὲ συμβάλλουσα κακῇ καὶ ἀνεπιτήδειος. Otherwise: Camaterus, *Introd.* 1850-1 κρεῖσσον γὰρ, ἡ Σελήνη | ὅτε μόνη καθ᾽ ἑαυτὴν συμβάλλουσα. (In 3873-4 εἰ Σελήνη συμβάλλουσα ἐπὶ βορείων ἔλθῃ | τῶν ζῳδιων[54] and 3876, the Moon is passing through the nodes.)

135 ἕκτον ἔχοντι τόπον: the sixth place is the κακὴ τύχη (Bouché-Leclercq, 283). Mars most rejoices in it (Paul, pp. 57.15-58.1), and it causes σίνος, especially to the feet (Θ pp. 154.21-155.2; see too Firmicus, 3.4.16 (Mars in the sixth place) *claudos et gibberosos* (hunchbacks)). For Valens, II 11.2, the type of harm depends on the nature of the signs.

136 So they are not born lame. They are wounded, which is consonant with the house causing σίνος rather than (congenital) πάθος. Perhaps the deliberate aim was to make them beggars, especially given that other versions of this chart speak of poverty. The Elder Seneca attests this practice (*Controv.* 10.4.2...*huic convulsi pedum articuli sunt et extorti tali, huic elisa crura, illius inviolatis pedibus cruribusque femina contudit....* 'This child has had the joints of his feet torn, his ankles wrenched; this has had his legs crushed. Another's thighs he has smashed, though leaving feet and legs unharmed', transl. Winterbottom; cf. Parkin, 71-2, 73, 80). The *presque homérique* cadence convincingly masks a prosaic phrase (*Sent. Sext.* 324 σίδηρον ἀνδροφόνον and later, esp. in John Chrysostom). Perhaps the occasional application of ἀνδροφόνοιο to Ares (*Il.* 4.441, *Scut.* 98) was helpful.

137 The definitive treatment is L. J. Bliquez, 'Prosthetics in Classical Antiquity: Greek, Etruscan and Roman Prosthetics', *ANRW* II 37.3 (1996), 2640-76. The star examples are the Cairo toe, of leather and wood (Luxor, 950-710 BC) and the Capua leg, of bronze over a wooden core (*c.*300 BC); the latter looks like a greave and was perhaps made by an armourer rather than medical professional (Bliquez, 2667-73). There are also literary anecdotes. Hegesistratus cut off his foot to escape a Spartan jail, then made himself a wooden replacement (Hdt. 9.37.4 προσποιησάμενος ξύλινον πόδα). Marcus Sergius Silus, Catiline's great-grandfather, lost his hand in the Second Punic War and wore an iron replacement (Plin. *NH* 7.104-5). Various anecdotes and jokes suggest that wooden prostheses were nothing out of the ordinary—Plut. *Mor.* 479 B, in a comparison for man who disowned his own brother and bought a replacement, cf. Constantinus Manasses, *Aristandros et Callithea*, fr. 66; Lucian, *Adv. Indoct.* 6, a merchant who, having lost his feet to frostbite, bought expensive sandals for his prosthetic limbs; Martial, 10.100.6, *frustra crure ligneo curres*, a jibe about literary plagiarism. I find no obvious model to explain why

---

[54] The accentuation, frequent but not invariable in Camaterus, is *metri gratia*.

the poet, who could have constructed προσκείμενοι with the dative, as normal, has chosen the accusative instead. Dr Holford-Strevens suggests that it is possibly misused in place of the perfect of προστίθεμαι middle, 'having attached it to themselves'.

138 Presumably to be written down as typical astrological *dolor* rather than included in any attempt, however well-intentioned, to gather evidence for the experience of the disabled (J. Draycott, 'Reconstructing the Lived Experience of Disability in Antiquity: A Case Study from Roman Egypt', *G&R* 62 (2015), 189–205). With its image of the doleful contemplation of a disabled foot in the style of a sepulchral inscription,[55] the *de facto* effect is comical, whether that was the intention or not. παπταίνειν, with its associations of anxious peering-about on a Homeric battlefield, is an odd verb in the context as well. ἑὸν πόδα occurs in this *sedes* also five times in Nonnus, three times followed by a participle, twice of debility (*D.* 25.281, 45.60), and not otherwise in hexameter poetry.

1.139–52 *Schetliasmos* of Mars

This is constructed as a crescendo, in which a series of foils gives way to Mars' destructive effect on human life (Bouché-Leclercq, 99). It reads much as a reversal of the cosmological syllabus in Aesch. *Eum.* 904–9, in which the Eumenides are called upon to preside over a system in which earth, sea, and sky, send blessings, winds are gentle, and vegetable, animal, and human seed prospers. In 142–5, three of the elements of 140–1 are given a whole-line treatment, and with the addition of trees they culminate in types of more or less familiar astrological harm to man. Mars' culpability is both in virtue of Ares' mythological *persona* (war) and through the planet's associations with fire and violent death (including non-fiery and non-martial methods like shipwreck, wild beasts, i.e. the arena, and crucifixion).

The poet has reached to a wide range of classical poetry to heighten the effect. The listing device in 146–7 οὓς μὲν γὰρ... οὓς δὲ καὶ betrays its origins ultimately in Hes. *Op.* 162–5 (surveying how Zeus killed off the Golden Race, and therefore ultimately another reapplication of a Zeus-motif in EGHP):

<u>τοὺς μὲν</u> ὑφ' ἑπταπύλῳ Θήβῃ, Καδμηίδι γαίῃ,
<u>ὤλεσε</u> μαρναμένους μήλων ἕνεκ' Οἰδιπόδαο,
<u>τοὺς δὲ καὶ</u> ἐν νήεσσιν ὑπὲρ μέγα λαῖτμα θαλάσσης
ἐς Τροίην ἀγαγὼν Ἑλένης ἕνεκ' ἠυκόμοιο.

---

[55] SEG 28.525.1 (Pharsalos(?), 4th/3rd c. BC) [κ]ῆδος ἀεί[μν]ηστον; IK Kibyra, 104.4 (Hellenistic) ἀείμνηστον... πόθον; IG II² 11169 (Attica, 4th c. AD) πένθος ἀείμνηστον; Lucian, Pod. 316 (of Niobe) πένθος ἀείμνηστον.

There are many other signs that the poet intends this as a little *morceau de bravoure*: the parallelistic listing in 142–4 and 146–8, with characteristic change of rhythm in 149; *hapax legomena* (141 εὐρείθροις, 144 ἀνύδατοι, 145 αἰνογένεθλοι, 149 ἡλοπαγής; 146 μογερῶς possibly *proton*, and πυρικαέας a rarity), combinatory allusions (145), and borrowings from Hellenistic poetry (142, 143) beside the usual Homeric fodder (139, 150–2). As to the last of these, perhaps he was so pleased with his effort that he did not expect to be held to account over the theological implications of ventriloquising Homer's lines. What place have Zeus and Hera—Zeus with his confusing new identity as Jupiter, and his completely irrelevant consort—in the astrological universe?

The passage has common features with other examples of the genre. The last two lines specifically reference Patroclus' indictment of Achilles (see ad loc.); the list of resultant evils (Tibullus, 1.10.3–4) is here engineered into a catalogue of typical astrological causes of death (146–9). There is also a certain similarity with the *schetliasmos* of hybris in *Or. Sib.* 5.228–46 (nineteen lines as against thirteen): the apostrophe, the even more insistent messaging about harm to mankind (ἀνθρώποις, ἀνδράσι), the blame thrust in the face of the accused (233 ἐν σοί, 235 καὶ διὰ σοῦ)—as well as the generally parallelistic style.

139 ~ Ἄρες Ἄρες βροτολοιγὲ μιαιφόνε τειχεσιπλῆτα. In *Il.* 5.31 the speaker is Athena, and in 455 it is Apollo. The first epithet is replaced by a standard poetic word for malefic: see i. 909 n. 8, and add that (while malefics cause κακουργία) κακο-ποιός is the standard term for malefics in prose. In the Ersatz polar expression which ends the line, by substituting μάκαρες for θεοί[56] (and by suppressing θεοί as almost invariable complement of μάκαρες in the sense of 'gods' in EGHP) the poet defers the question who these beings, in the astrological universe, are actually supposed to be.

140–1 Line 140 consists of two polar statements or quasi-polar statements (cities and ships evoke e.g. *Il.* 20.60 Τρώων τε πόλις καὶ νῆες Ἀχαιῶν). The sea then suggests the tripartite cosmological syllabus earth, sea, and rivers (see my note on Dion. Per. 1–2), whose other elements figure in the next line. Also similar is Greg. Naz. *PG* 37.1302.8 Γαίῃ καὶ πελάγεσσι καὶ ἠέρι.[57]

141 HHom. *Dem.* 332 γῆς καρπὸν; HHom. *Ap.* 365 γαίης πολυφόρβου καρπὸν; Aesch. *Eum.* 907 καρπόν τε γαίας. In the cadence the new version of the river

---

[56] (πατὴρ) ἀνδρῶν τε θεῶν τε; also *Il.* 24.677 θεοί τε καὶ ἀνέρες ἱπποκορυσταί; *Od.* 5.194 θεὸς ἠδὲ καὶ ἀνήρ, *Od.* 16.265 ἀνδράσι... καὶ ἀθανάτοισι θεοῖσι; Hes. *Th.* 197 θεοί τε καὶ ἀνέρες, 923 θεῶν βασιλῆι καὶ ἀνδρῶν; Hes. fr. 195.28–9 M.–W. θεοῖσιν | ἀνδράσι τ' ἀλφηστῆισιν; HHom. *Ap.* 336 ἄνδρες τε θεοί τε.

[57] Earth, sea, and sky: M. L. West, *The East Face of Helicon: West Asiatic Elements in Early Poetry and Myth* (Oxford, 1997), 137–8; Hes. *Th.* 413–14, and West ad loc.; *Il.* 18.483; HHom. *Dem.* 13–14; Aesch. *Eum.* 904–5; Lucr. 5.92; Ingleheart on Ov. *Trist.* 2.53–4.

epithet ἐϋρρείτης (in EGHP always with a p.n.), matches Homeric ἐϋρρεῖος ποταμοῖο, and later Dion. Per. 848 and *Orph. Arg.* 783 ἐϋρρείτου ποταμοῖο. If L's εὐρίθροις is restored as ἐϋρρείθροις, it spares us a strange, though not impossible, verse rhythm.

142 There are suggestions of Apollonius here. εἵνεκα σεῦ recalls Ap. Rhod. 4.398, another remonstration pitched at a force threatening indiscriminate destruction (Jason to Medea)—a force, moreover, wielding, or threatening to wield, destructive fire. But εἵνεκα means, not 'for your sake' but 'in consequence of' (LSJ I.3), and in that respect is more like ἐκ σέθεν in the *schetliasmos* of Love which follows shortly afterwards (4.445–6 Σχέτλι᾽ Ἔρως... ἐκ σέθεν..., from Theogn. 1231–2). That, too, is a recrimination against a personified force to which is traced the origin of noxious things, though the similarity remains formal and there are no lexical echoes to confirm the poet had the second passage in mind. With the line-end compare Quint. Smyrn. 5.381 ὑπαὶ πυρὸς αἰθομένοιο, 13.489 καίηται ὑπαὶ πυρὸς ὀρνυμένοιο. In light of 144 (see n.), it turns out that Ares is responsible for the destruction of cities, not only as war-god, but also because he is associated, *qua* fiery planet, with the element of fire itself.

143 In itself this is a standard type of death, and sometimes even mentioned along with sacked cities (Favorinus ap. Gell. 14.1.27 *aut oppidorum expugnationibus aut eadem in navi fluctu obruti*), but unless the idea is that the ships perish in conflagrations it disrupts the equation of Ares with fire in 142 and 144. Mars is, however, involved in causing shipwrecks in 3.255–6; see ad loc. and on 4.400–1.

More Hellenistic poetry is on view (p. 293). The poet seems to have combined Call. *Ep.* 5.3 ναυτίλος ὃς πελάγεσσιν ἐπέπλεον/*Hymn* 4.36 ἀλλ᾽ ἄφετος πελάγεσσιν ἐπέπλεες with *Hymn* 4.213 ἐπιπλώουσα θαλάσσῃ, whence (or from Theocr. 17.91) he has taken the present tense of the stem ἐπιπλώ- (Homer has only the aorist participle) and the construction with the dative (Homer has the accusative). But Callimachus' smiling conceits (a sailing shell, a floating island) have been reliteralised as ships, with ὄλοντο (line-end) used of shipwreck as in *Od.* 10.132 (and of people dying at sea: 19.277).

144 For Ares to be responsible for rivers running dry (a portentous event and sometime eschatological motif) he must continue to be treated as the element of fire. One thinks of Hephaestus and the Scamander, or of the Sun and Sirius burning waterways in midsummer heat (Nic. *Ther.* 367–8; V. *Georg.* 4.426–8). Fire from heaven dries up rivers in *Or. Sib.* 7.122 καύσει ποταμούς, πηγὰς δὲ κενώσει, and by implication in 8.238 ποταμοί τε καχλάζοντες λείψουσιν, although the most famous dried-up river of all, the Euphrates in Rev. 16:12, is parched by the opening of one of the vials of God's wrath (see Aune ad loc. for the Day of the Lord motif). The Ganges and other great rivers are dried by the third of the Suns in the Buddhist apocalypse *Sattasūriya sutta* (sermon of the Seven Suns). In V. *Ecl.* 7.56 *videas et flumina sicca* the motif reverses the torrential rivers of 52 and signifies lack, absence, and desolation.

145 δένδρεά τ' ὠλεσίκαρπα: combining *Od.* 11.588 δένδρεα δ' ὑψιπέτηλα κατὰ κρῆθεν χέε καρπόν with 10.510 ἰτέαι ὠλεσίκαρποι. The salutary fruit-loss in the first passage is replaced with the less salubrious and sicklier one of the second. The epithet, *hapax* in Homer, was explained by the willow losing its flower/fruit before it was fully ripe, but also because it rendered those who ate it sterile (*Σ* ad loc.; Hesychius, ω 157; Didymus Caecus, *Comm. in Eccl.* p. 355.1-2 ὅτι εὐνουχίζει τρόπον τινὰ τοὺς πιόντας, cf. ps.-Opp. *Cyn.* 3.283), or caused abortions (*Comm. in Dionys. Thrac. Art. Gramm.* p. 235.7-8). Anyway the associations with sterility, and in its original context with the world of the dead, make it a fitting lead-in here for short-lived humans. αἰνογένεθλοι is an outright *hapax*.

146 πυρικαέας: keeping alive the fire theme. It is rare but not unique, used of fevers in Hippocr. *Epid.* 6.2.11, cf. Galen, xviiA. 946.5 and xvi. 709.2 Kühn, and for Phrygia (Katakekaumene) in Leonidas, *AP* 6.281.1 = *HE* 2239. That suggests a double application: Mars injures men (the line-end tweaks Hes. *Op.* 372) by fire itself (i. 664 n. 23; 4.614 n.; Cumont, 196 n. 2) and also by causing fevers. Sometimes these are listed together (Dorotheus, p. 381.7-8; Firmicus, 6.35.7).

147 For this fate see on 4.614, 5.192-6 (both of which involve Mars). There is influence from *Od.* 5.473 θήρεσσιν ἕλωρ. The noun–epithet pair is conventional in LGHP.[58] For the epithet itself see on 6.454.

148 ἀκλειῶς gets it exactly right: this is the hexameter rendering of Latin *infamia* (*Anth. Lat.* 415.23 *Noxius infami districtus stipite membra*). An alternative rendering uses αἰσχ-: Heb. 12:2 σταυρὸν αἰσχύνης; Cels. in Origen, *Cels.* 6.10 κἂν ᾖ δεδεμένος ἀτιμότατα ἢ κεκολασμένος αἴσχιστα; Justin, *Tryph.* 90.1 σταυρωθῆναι καὶ οὕτως αἰσχρῶς καὶ ἀτίμως ἀποθανεῖν (and many later examples, in Ignatius, Gregory of Nyssa, and elsewhere). On the deliberate shamefulness of crucifixion, see 4.200 n.; Hengel, 7, and ch. 8, 'The slaves' punishment'; M. T. Finney, '*Servile Supplicium*: Shame and Deuteronomic Curse–Crucifixion in its Cultural Context', *Biblical Theology Bulletin*, 43/3 (2013), 124-34.

---

[58] *Or. Sib.* 11.215, and of a lion in 14.317-18; ps.-Opp. *Cyn.* 4.305-6; Quint. Smyrn. 1.222, 11.300; Greg. Naz. *PG* 37.593.8, 620.1; Paul the Silentiary, *AP* 11.60.6; none arranged as here. More in prose.

μετέωρον ἀνεσταύρωσας: Koechly's emendation implies a palaeographically highly plausible ρ/ν confusion typical of L (i. 375 n. 13), although it violates Hermann's Bridge (p. 304); for the 'on high' motif, see on 5.219. In support of D'Orville's minimal μεθ' ἑὸν μόρον is that bodies *were* nailed up after death as part of the humiliation (see on 4.198 σκολοπηίδα μοῖραν ὁρῶσιν and 200; Hdt. 3.125.3). But from the next line it seems that they are dying on the cross. For crucifixion see on 4.197-8; p. 272.

149 τέτατ': the proper verb for crucifixion, or rather that part of it which consisted in having one's arms spread out and fixed to the *patibulum*, the crossbeam, is ἐκτείνειν, sometimes used of the whole person (Epict. 3.26.22 ἐκτείνας σεαυτὸν ὡς οἱ ἐσταυρωμένοι; Or. Sib. 6.26 ὦ ξύλον ὦ μακαριστόν, ὑφ' οὗ θεὸς ἐξετανύσθη), but more often specifically of the hands. Pagan and Christian authors both use it: Artemidorus, 1.76.4 κακοῦργος δὲ ὢν σταυρωθήσεται διὰ τὸ ὕψος καὶ τὴν τῶν χειρῶν ἔκτασιν; John 21:18 ἐκτενεῖς τὰς χεῖράς σου (Jesus predicts Peter's death) (see Beasley-Murray, WBC 36, and W. Bauer, *Das Johannesevangelium* (Tübingen, 1933), ad loc.); Barnabas 12:2 καὶ σταθεὶς ὑψηλότερος πάντων ἐξέτεινεν τὰς χεῖρας; Athanasius, *De Inc.* 25.3 ἐν μόνῳ γὰρ τῷ σταυρῷ ἐκτεταμέναις χερσί τις ἀποθνήσκει. Διὸ καὶ τοῦτο ἔπρεπεν ὑπομεῖναι τὸν Κύριον, καὶ τὰς χεῖρας ἐκτεῖναι (with a conceit making this a gesture of welcome). Other verbs: Dion. Hal. 7.69.2 τὰς χεῖρας ἀποτείναντες ἀμφοτέρας καὶ ξύλῳ προσδήσαντες; Lucian, *Prom.* 1 ἐκπετασθεὶς τὼ χεῖρε (also the verb in Isa. 65:2, which was interpreted as a reference to the crucifixion), cf. 2 ἀλλ' ὄρεγε τὴν δεξιάν; Sen. *Cons. ad Marc.* 20.3 *alii brachia patibulo explicuerunt*, *De Ira* 1.2.2 *alium in cruce membra diffindere*; Tert. *Adv. Jud.* 10.10 *expansis manibus* (Moses praying, as a figure for crucified Christ); 5.219 n.

ἡλοπαγὴς χείρ: this is one of a handful of passages from pagan authors, along with Plaut. *Most.* 360 *sed ea lege ut offigantur bis pedes, bis bracchia*, and Lucan, 6.547 *insertum manibus chalybem*, that might be adduced to head off any suggestion that the tradition that Jesus was nailed hand and (possibly) foot (John 20:25 Ἐὰν μὴ ἴδω ἐν ταῖς χερσὶν αὐτοῦ τὸν τύπον τῶν ἥλων; Gospel of Peter, 21 Καὶ τότε ἀπέσπασαν τοὺς ἥλους ἀπὸ τῶν χειρῶν τοῦ Κυρίου; Nonn. *Par.* 19.93-5, and E. Livrea and D. Accorinti, 'Nonno e la crocifissione', SIFC 6 (1988), 262-78 = E. Livrea, *ΚΡΕΣΣΟΝΑ ΒΑΣΚΑΝΙΗΣ: Quindici studi di poesia ellenistica* (Florence, 1993), 201-24, esp. 219) arose through the dogmatic need to 'fulfil' Ps. 21:17 ὤρυξαν χεῖράς μου καὶ πόδας as a prophecy of the crucifixion. The crucified *were*, or at least could be, nailed through the hands (or in practice, wrists: for the wider use of χείρ as '<hand and> arm', see LSJ I.2). For evidence on nailing in crucifixion, see J. W. Hewitt, 'The Use of Nails in the Crucifixion', HThR 25 (1932), 29-45 (much on visual representations); J. Blinzler, *Der Prozeß Jesu*[4] (Regensburg, 1969), 377-9 (exhaustive literary documentation).

150-2 The original version of Patroclus' reproach to Achilles is νηλεές, οὐκ ἄρα σοί γε πατὴρ ἦν ἱππότα Πηλεύς, | οὐδὲ Θέτις μήτηρ· γλαυκὴ δέ σε τίκτε θάλασσα | πέτραι τ' ἠλίβατοι, ὅτι τοι νόος ἐστὶν ἀπηνής (*Il.* 16.33–5). For αἰγίοχος Ζεύς see i. 910 n. 4. The sea obviously had to go: the fiery Mars could not be born from that. The 'rock' option is also the one Dido prefers in *Aen.* 4.366–7, and Pease ad loc. has many other examples, mostly Latin, of the topos. The point is the hardness of the substance, whether rock, iron, or adamant, and if mountains are named they are Scythian: πικρά is feeble. On the other hand, as epithet of λύσσα, στυγερὴ is not only stronger than κρατερή (*Il.* 9.239 and 21.543; otherwise 9.305 ὀλοήν), but it avoids position at word-division before mute and liquid which these days probably sounded quaintly old-fashioned (p. 306; otherwise in this book only at 273, which might count as a metrical word anyway). As for the final pentameter, its neat alignment of parallel items seems to me to speak more for its standing here as a closural device than to indicate Anubionic authorship.

1.153–95 Miscellanea

153–7

Moon leaves Saturn 'by degree'. This is the sister chart of 50–7 (Moon applying to Saturn), similar in the precise and semi-medical language of its outcome (wet diseases), and similar, too, in its concentration, or near-concentration, on one particular disease, in this case dropsy. One might have supposed that in an original collection they would have stood together, but Θ does not confirm it. It does have a partial match in p. 193.5–6 (which supplies the Moon phase which is missing here), but the harm is psychological and accordingly it appears in the chapter on madmen and epileptics.

The best match is in Firmicus, 4.15.2, from his catalogue of *aporrhoiai*, which specifies that when the waning Moon leaves Saturn for no other planet it causes various pathologies associated with coldness and wetness depending on the quality of signs. Firmicus in this passage clearly has a common source with *Π.σ.α.* p. 182.16–22, with whom he shares the little sequence on *psychrocoelii*, the phlegmatic, and the emaciated. While they otherwise offer a different selection of items on their long list of cold and wet conditions, the latter additionally agrees with M^c about weakness (154).[59] Neither specifies 'rheumatism', though that keeps company with items in other Saturnian lists.[60] As for dropsy itself

---

[59] Saturnian also in Ptol. 3.13.15; Hephaestion, i. 221.25–6; Rhetorius, *CCAG* vii. 215.21–2. Saturn and Venus: Valens, IV 20.10.
[60] Ptol. 4.9.3; Valens, II 34.16; Περὶ κράσ. 8; Hephaestion, i. 19.1–2 and Camaterus, *Introd.* 976–7. Elsewhere caused by signs (Hübner 1982, 200, §3.423.6: three watery signs + Sagittarius).

(ὕδρωψ, ὕδερος, *hydrops*), it seems to have been this poet's whimsy to single out this one disease for special treatment and subject it to extravagant artifice. It is the wet disease *par excellence*, typically caused by one or all of the wet factors, Saturn, the Moon, and Aquarius. Firmicus also lists the dropsical (*hydropicos*) when the Moon leaves Saturn for both the Sun (4.9.6) and—again when she is waning—Mercury (4.9.9).

153 κατὰ μοῖραν: apparently corresponding to Θ's κατὰ σῶμα, this is a phrase from astrological prose (and also, conveniently, an EGHP line-ending in Hes. *Op.* 765, rendered 'duly' [Evelyn-White] or 'due' [West]). In astrology κατὰ σῶμα is usually one half of the pair κατὰ σῶμα ἢ κατὰ σχῆμα. When it refers to the *synaphe* and *aporrhoia* of the Moon, it means 'in the same sign' as opposed to 'by aspect'; this is explained very clearly by 'Heliodorus' on Paul, p. 3.9–24. κατὰ μοῖραν is a poor choice to render it (if that is what is intended), since it moves up to the next level of specificity, i.e. a conjunction by degree as opposed to sign (i. 884). Lopilato therefore understands it to mean that the Moon is leaving Saturn's precise degree: technically correct, but an unusual specification.

154 ἀσθενέας κατὰ σῶμα: weakness is caused by the Moon (principle of growth) harmed by malefics in various ways (Θ p. 190.1–3 ὁ ὡροσκόπος καὶ ἡ Σελήνη ὑπὸ κακοποιῶν θεωρούμενοι ἐπινόσους καὶ ἀσθενεῖς ποιοῦσι τὰς γενέσεις; Hephaestion, i. 166.32: waning Moon in *synaphe* with malefics produces bodily weakness; Firmicus, 6.31.29: *infirmitas corporis* caused by conjunction of Moon and Saturn, opposing Mars and Sun in eighth house). Weakness and wateriness seem to go together, at least in astrological physiology (Apomasar, *De Rev.* p. 19.9–10 καὶ γὰρ τὸ ἀσθενὲς τῆς φύσεως τοῦ παιδὸς καὶ ἡ ὑγρότης (sc. reveal the Moon's predominance), sim. Anon. *De Astrologia Dialogus*, p. 22.20–2, and *De Rev.* 23.17 ἀσθενὴς γὰρ καὶ ὑγρός). κατὰ σῶμα is another EGHP line-end, containing a curious echo-cum-displacement of the same phrase in Θ, where it has a technical sense (see previous note).

155 ὑδρογάστορας: simplified Hippocrates (*Aff.* 22 ἡ μὲν γαστὴρ ὕδατος πίμπλαται; *Int. Aff.* 26 καὶ ἡ γαστὴρ μεγάλη ... ἡ δὲ γαστὴρ δίϋδρος καὶ μεγάλη ὥσπερ λαμπτήρ),[61] a visually arresting feature converted into a striking word which is grotesque, if not comic, given the ancestry of some other compounds (Ar. *Av.* 1696 γλωττογαστόρων, a skit on (ἐγ)χειρογάστορες; Epicharmus, fr. 67 ἐκτραπελόγαστρος) and the suggestion of an agent noun (was this, then, their

---

[61] A. Touwaide and N. G. De Santo, 'Edema in the Corpus Hippocraticum', *Am J Nephrol* 19 (1999), 155–8.

professional métier?).⁶² In Hadrian's chart, §49 (Heilen 2015, 882–3), dropsy is combined with breathlessness, which is at least physiologically plausible (the circulation is too poor to clear the fluid, and the lungs struggle), but normal astrological categories would have foreclosed the association of dropsy and coughing (which belongs with wasting, consumption, and hot, hence Martian, conditions—as in the next apotelesma).

156 'Their bones flabby with noxious fluid'. Perhaps extending the condition to the bones is part of the conceit, for it is the flesh that liquefies in Hippocr. *Aff.* 22 φθείρονται γὰρ αἱ σάρκες, καὶ τήκονται, καὶ γίνονται ὕδωρ. There is, however, a passage in Oribasius (*Coll. Med.* 46.22.4, from Heliodorus, an Egyptian surgeon of the 1st c. AD) discussing bone 'caries' (τερηδονισμός) which envisages the softening of the bones through noxious fluid. Heliodorus/Oribasius' word for the decayed bone is precisely χαῦνον/κεχαυνωμένον: the poet here is using medical language, and since Heliodorus/Oribasius calls the liquid ῥεῦμα, it adds meaning to the ῥευματικούς of 154 as well. For the pattern of the clausula, see Theognis, 527 γήραος οὐλομένοιο, Dorotheus, p. 397.10 ἐπὶ δαίμονος οὐλομένοιο (of the Evil Demon), Quint. Smyrn. 2.565, al. ἕλκεος οὐλομένοιο, but the fluid now is literally 'perishing', not just by way of epic cliché.

157 Exactly as in Jerome, *PL* 22.641 = *Ep.* 66.5 *alius tumenti aqualiculo* [stomach] *mortem parturit*, quoted in E. Auerbach, *Mimesis* (Princeton, 1968), 64–5, and by Susan Sontag, *Illness as Metaphor* (New York, 1977), 14, for whom cancer is a 'demonic pregnancy', opining that that was what Jerome was thinking of. And that is quite possible if the 'dropsy' was actually ascites, a cancer symptom, though Jerome is describing a horde of beggars at a rich benefactor's gate, and the repulsive physical characteristics of each one which, in their context, function as marks of poverty. Does the conceit originate with Jerome (c.347–420), which would make our text very late? It is very much in the same style as another entry in his catalogue, a man with the *morbus regius*, whom Jerome describes as having 'survived his own death'/*supravivit cadaveri suo*). Or was this a common conceit about dropsy? Whatever its origin, Auerbach's discussion shows how this passage is very much in line with Jerome's values ('opposed to generation and intent upon the annihilation of the earthly…the sombrely suicidal ethos, the immersion in horror, in distortion of life and hostility to life'). In astrology, which revels in the materiality of this world, if not exactly 'delighting' in it, the effect is very different, a moment of fascinated horror. There is grim humour as well, if we are supposed to note that the verse pattern of the second half of the line has been modelled on *Od.* 2.341 ἄκρητον

---

⁶² Also Aesch. *Sept.* 496 κοιλογάστορος κύκλου; Nic. *Al.* 344 ἐριγάστορας; Philip, *AP* 16.52.1 ταυρογάστορα; Leonidas, *AP* 6.305.3 = *HE* 2315 κυτογάστορας Toup *ex emend*.

θεῖον ποτὸν ἐντὸς ἔχοντες, describing the *pithoi* full of wine in Odysseus' storehouse, waiting for their master's return.

158–66

Moon leaves Mars. This produces hidden diseases affecting the liver, spleen, kidneys, heart (presented as seat of rational intellect), and lungs, with special emphasis on pulmonary consumption (ulcerated lung, coughing/expectoration, weakness, unalleviated by food and drink).

Mars is of course the appropriate agent for anything involving blood-loss. So too, in *Π.σ.α.* p. 183.5–11, the Moon leaving Mars has properly Martian effects (τὸ θυμικὸν καὶ ὀργίλον) which, if she is waning or 'declining in numbers', include αἵματος ἀναγωγὰς...καὶ αἱμορροΐδας. On the other hand, we may be surprised to find him associated with hidden disease (sc. of the internal organs), normally Saturn's domain. But Saturn is indeed involved in a coda, which adds (without further detail) that if Saturn aspects and the Moon is waning, περὶ τοὺς ἀπορρήτους τοῦ σώματος τόπους κρυπτὰ πάθη καὶ σίνη γίνονται. Further, lung diseases are implied by Firmicus, 4.9.4, where the waning Moon leaving Saturn for Mars causes an evil death for the mother *ut adsidue vomens sanguinem pereat*, as well as 4.11.7, where the waning Moon leaving Mars for Saturn causes haemorrhage. It looks as if the poet is simplifying a situation that had an additional factor, Saturn, in his source.

158 φορέοιτο: indicating *kenodromia* (i. 633–4). φέρεσθαι is the verb used in *Π.σ.α.* (from p. 184.18) for the Moon's motions, implying (for once) involuntary rather than purposeful movement, but it is accompanied by prepositional phrases, not used absolutely. There may be influence from Dorotheus, p. 398.3 καὶ δ' αὐτὴ (sc. Selene) ὑπερχθονίη φορέοιτο. The mood of Dorotheus' verb (after εὖτε) is legitimate, while the present instance (following ἤν) is not; the parallel suggests that 'wrong' moods could be licensed by carry-over from a source (see i. 139 and p. 289). There is no parallel for the outcome in Firmicus, 4.15.4–5.

159 ἐκτήκει: suitable for the demoisturising effect of Mars, and preparing for the description of φθίσις. Of the various words for wasting disease (also φθίνειν, μαραίνειν), this has the oldest credentials (*Od.* 5.396 δηρὸν τηκόμενος, 11.201 τηκεδόνι στυγερῇ μελέων; Meinecke, 380), and it is taken up technically, or semi-technically, in medical writers, especially Galen, *In Hippocr. Prorrh. Comm.* xvi. 552.11–553.1 Kühn τοῖς μὲν γὰρ μαραινομένοις ἐκτέτηκε πᾶν ὅσον ἐστὶ κατὰ τὸ πρόσωπόν τε καὶ τοὺς κροτάφους σαρκῶδες. The συν- compound is commoner: Aretaeus, *De Caus. et Sign. Diut. Morb.* 1.8.2 αἱ ξυντήξιες ('colliquative wasting': Adams), 1.8.3 ξυντετηκότα, 1.8.4 ξυντετήκασι...πυρετοῖσι χρονίοισι; ps.-Galen, *Introductio sive medicus*, 13.29 (p. 60 Petit; xiv. 745.1-3 Kühn) φθίσις μὲν κυρίως λέγεται ἡ ἐν πνεύμονι, ἢ εἰς τὸν θώρακα ἐπὶ τῶν ἐμπυημάτων σύντηξις τοῦ σώματος ('corporis ob suppurationes colliquatio').

ἐκ κρυφίμων: see 4.413 n. and pp. 16-17. Mars causes what are otherwise apparently Saturnian afflictions in Firmicus, 3.4.19 (in DESC), *Lib. Herm.* xxxii. 35 (in own house, out of sect), 46 (in house of Moon, with waning Moon aspecting him).

160-1 There are just too many systems of melothesia to expect a clear pattern in the organs singled out here. They certainly do not represent a single physical principle or ruler, nor even apparently two opposite ones (hot and cold, or wet and dry); nor do they seem to be divided between the domains of Mars and the Moon. There is general consensus that the spleen (which is the source of dropsy) is wet,[63] and that the heart is the source of heat, but sources can be found which contradict even that (for instance, the heart and Cancer in Firmicus, 2.24). In Ptolemy's system, Saturn rules the spleen, Jupiter the lungs, Mars the kidneys,[64] the Sun the heart, and Venus the liver; in Valens, Saturn the kidneys, Jupiter the liver, the Sun the heart, Venus the lungs, and the Moon the spleen. Rather, the collection seems simply to exemplify 'hidden organs' (cf. e.g. Valens, I 1.12 νεφρῶν καὶ τῶν ἐντὸς ἀποκρύφων; II 37.10 Καρκίνος... σπλήν... ἀπόκρυφοι τόποι; Teucer, CCAG vii. 200.15-16 καρδίας, σπληνός, ἀποκρύφων τόπων). We have the same sense of random sampling in another passage where most of them are brought together just to illustrate the harm malefics can do (*Liber ad Ammonem*, 1.8 Δῆλον γὰρ ὡς ἀκτὶς κακοποιοῦ ἐπιβαλοῦσα τούτων τινὶ φθείρει καὶ λυμαίνεται, ὁμοίως καὶ ἐπὶ θώρακος, ἢ ὁ πνεύμων ἔπαθεν ἢ τὸ ἧπαρ ἢ ὁ σπλὴν ἢ ἡ καρδία ἢ τι τῶν περὶ τὰ ἔντερα). In another source which brings together at least three—the spleen, liver, and (implied by spitting blood) the lungs—the factors involved are Sagittarius (a sign of Jupiter) and Cancer (sign of the Moon) (Valens, II 41.36, σπληνικοὶ ἢ ἡπατικοί, στομαχικοί, ἀναφορικοί, αἱμοπτυϊκοί).

161 παρέτριψε: implies physical abrasion. It is not an astrological word for causing harm. It is very frequent in medical descriptions of the preparation of

---

[63] It belongs to the Moon (Valens, II 37.10, Περὶ κράσ. 222), or Saturn (Hephaestion, i. 141.13, cf. 217.12).

[64] The kidneys are ascribed to so various a range of planets (Saturn: Valens, I 1.12; Mars: Ptol. 3.13.5; Mercury: Rhetorius, CCAG vii. 221.17) that one wonders if the astrologers had no idea they produced urine, and hence should *ipso facto* be watery. Doctors knew this (Galen; Pseudo-Galen, *Introduction*, 11.10 (p. 39 Petit; xiv. 718-19 K.: thanks to Vivian Nutton for this reference); Aretaeus, *De Caus. et Sign. Acut. Morb.* 2.9.1; Caelius Aurelianus (i.e. Soranus), *Chronic Diseases*, 5.3.54). Otherwise it is hard to demonstrate that this belief was widespread; Dr Holford-Strevens draws my attention to a comment by Michael Glycas (12th c.!) that nature has not given birds οὐρηδόχον κύστιν καὶ νεφρούς.

ingredients, but not for pathology, and it is unclear, if this is a metaphor, what it is drawn from.

μητέρα βουλῆς: while the shape of the phrase, and to some extent of the whole line, is Iliadic ('Ἴδην δ' ἵκανεν πολυπίδακα μητέρα θηρῶν (3×), Il. 9.479 Φθίην δ' ἐξικόμην ἐριβώλακα μητέρα μήλων), it gives Homeric cladding to an Aristotelian and subsequently Stoic opinion, as opposed to the cephalocentric view of Pythagoras, Plato, some parts of the Hippocratic corpus, and Galen.[65] The seeming use of dumbed-down Hippocrates for dropsy, followed by a different source for the hegemonic principle, presumably testifies to what a ragbag the thought-system(s) of astrology is/are. The switch is not explained by the Homeric poems, which have no locatable cognitive principle as such, and which, insofar as they employ the notion of an intellect, attribute it to the φρένες (e.g. Od. 21.288); the Homeric κραδίη is emotional.[66] Perhaps it was rather that astrology had more in common with the Aristotelian and Stoic world-views in general, so that this item went over as part of the package. Still, if that were so, one would expect to find Ptolemy its spokesman, and Ptolemy is not very forthcoming. In his discussion of the active, or rational, part of the soul (the vitiation of which causes mental illnesses), the ψυχή is conspicuously unembodied. He does, however, regard the heart as 'hegemonic' (2.3.25 τὸ τῆς καρδίας ἡγεμονικόν, for which reason the Sun rules it), and perhaps, like the Stoics, he simply took it as read that that principle was rational.

162–6 The poet meant this description of pulmonary tuberculosis to impress. It is a closely packed list of symptoms which, as Aretaeus said, were easily recognised even by a layman through ὄψις alone (*De Caus. et Sign. Diut. Morb.* 1.8.3). At the same time, it flaunts poeticised medical language; the tetracolon in 164, enclosed by almost-tetracola on either side, suggests a little moment of ambition. It is in step with other Roman medical writers, for whom the defining feature of what they call φθίσις or φθόη was the presence of lesions or ulceration (for which the word is ἕλκος) in the lungs. This becomes effectively its dictionary definition,[67] from which M^c begins. For what follows, the best

---

[65] Brooke Holmes, 'Disturbing Connections: Sympathetic Affections, Mental Disorder, and the Elusive Soul in Galen', in Harris 2013a, 147–76.

[66] R. B. Onians, *The Origins of European Thought about the Body, the Mind, the Soul, the World, Time, and Fate* (Cambridge, 1951), 82, notes *Il.* 3.60–3 and *Il.* 9.553–4 + 646, which imply (via the heart's location in the στῆθος) the location there of the νόος as well. But it is hard to believe that either passage was the source of κραδίην ... νοήμονα.

[67] ps.-Galen, *Definitiones medicae*, xix. 419.15–17 Kühn Φθίσις ἐστὶν ἕλκωσις τοῦ πνεύμονος ἢ θώρακος ἢ φάρυγγος, ὥστε βῆχας παρακολουθεῖν καὶ πυρετοὺς βληχροὺς καὶ συντήκεσθαι τὸ σῶμα; Celsus, *De med.* 3.22.3; Isidore, 4.7.17 *Tisis est ulceratio et tumor in pulmonibus*. For Aretaeus lesions in the lung are precisely what distinguishes the condition, which he calls φθόη, from other lung conditions (*De Caus. et Sign. Diut. Morb.* 1.8.1). Note how Galen, explicating Hippocrates, imports the notion of ulceration where the ancient text lacked it (*In Hippocr. Aphorism. Comment.*).

parallels are in Aretaeus (*De Caus. et Sign. Diut. Morb.* 1.8) and Soranus, *Chr.* 2.196-9 (for text and translation see I. E. Drabkin, *Caelius Aurelianus: On Acute Diseases and on Chronic Diseases* (Chicago, 1950), 694-7). The symptoms all find correspondences: coughing/expectoration (163-4 ~ Soranus, 197; Aret. 1.8.3-4: he adds that those who πυκνὰ... καὶ σκληρὰ καὶ ἀτελέα βήσσουσι, even if they have no lung lesions, may still count as phthisics; Cels. *De Med.* 3.22.3); bloody sputa (not here, but in Π.σ.α. p. 183.10, cf. Valens, II 33.8 ὑφ' αἵματος ἢ φθορᾶς, II 41.33 αἱμαγμοῖς, φθοραῖς, IV 22.7 αἱμαγμούς τε καὶ φθοράς, IV 23.8 αἱμαγμούς, φθοράς; Firmicus, 7.23.4 *pthisi aut nigro felle aut sanguinis reiectione* ~ Soranus, 197; Cels. *De Med.* 3.22.3); emaciation and weakness (165 λεπταλέοι, ἀδρανέες ~ Aret. 1.8.3 ἀδρανῇ, 1.8.6 ἰσχνοί, ἄσαρκοι and 1.8.5-7, Soranus, 198 *corporis tenuitas*); appetite and ingestion of food which fails to nourish the body (166 ~ Soranus, 198, 199). Aretaeus also stresses fever (1.8.2 ξύνεστι δὲ καὶ πῦρ ξυνεχές), which makes it a suitably Martian complaint although the poet does not make the point explicitly. For tuberculosis in Hellenistic sources and Roman medicine, see Meinecke; A. S. Pease, 'Some Remarks on the Diagnosis and Treatment of Tuberculosis in Antiquity', *Isis*, 31 (1940), 380-93; Grmek, 192-4 (183-92 on the Hippocratic corpus). For the incidence of tuberculosis in Egypt (Upper and Lower) in ancient and Roman Egypt, see W. Scheidel, *Death on the Nile: Disease and the Demography of Roman Egypt* (Leiden, 2001), 91-3.

162 The line does a good job of rendering the medical detail into *presque homérique*, using a verse pattern reminiscent of, say, *Il.* 15.389, and coining ἑλκήεντα, which remains unique, as an equivalent for the more prosaic ἑλκώδη. The appositional phrase at the end recalls the Chimaera, at *Il.* 16.329 πολέσιν κακὸν ἀνθρώποισιν (cf. also Hes. *Th.* 590, of the first woman, though not appositional). In less pretending language, the Hippocratic text agrees: *Int. Aff.* 11 ἡ γὰρ νοῦσος χαλεπή; Celsus calls it, of all the wasting diseases, *longe periculosissima* (*De Med.* 3.22.3).

163 ἀποπτύουσιν ὄλεθρον: a similar conceit to 157. The Homeric word for spitting (*Il.* 23.781, of Oilean Ajax spitting out dung) is still used in Hippocr. *Int. Aff.* 10-12, but the later technical term is ἀνάγειν (Aret. 1.8.1, 8 ἀναγωγῆς αἵματος).

164-5 These symptoms are brought together by Hippocr. *Int. Aff.* 10 βὴξ πιέζει ὀξείη... Ταῦτα μὲν καταρχὰς τῆς νούσου πάσχει· προϊούσης δὲ τό τε γυῖον

xviib. 796 Kühn Τὰς ἐπὶ πνεύμονι ἑλκώδεις διαθέσεις ὀνομάζει νῦν φθίσεις vis-à-vis Hippocr. *Aphor.* 5.11). Hippocr. *Int. Affect.* 10-12, describes three types of φθίσις which have sharp coughing and emaciation (10 λεπτύνεται... ἐκ δὲ τῶν ὤμων λεπτὸς καὶ ἀσθενής), but says nothing about ulceration in the lungs, or expectorated blood. *De locis* 14 is a discussion of lung diseases including φθίσις (14.7). Ulceration (τὸ ἡλκώμενον) and lesions (ἕλκεα) have been mentioned earlier in the chapter (14.5), but not as accompaniments of φθίσις.

λεπτύνεται... ἐκ δὲ τῶν ὤμων λεπτὸς καὶ ἀσθενής; ps.-Arist. Probl. 860ᵃ37–ᵇ7; Plin. Ep. 7.19.3 Insident febres, tussis increscit; summa macies summa defectio; Cassiodorus, Var. 11.10.1 qui crebra tussi retonans anhelo pectore membra tenuavit. For emaciation, see also Hippocr. Morb. 2.48 καταλεπτύνονται καὶ τὰ ἄνω μινύθει; Epictetus, 3.22.86 φθισικὸς... λεπτὸς καὶ ὠχρός; Lucr. 4.1166–7; for weakness, Hippocr. Int. Aff. 10 ἀκρασίη πολλὴ τὸ σῶμα ἔχει; Valens, IV 24.5 ἐν ἀσθενείαις ἢ φθίσεσι; Aret. 1.8.3 ἀδρανῆ.

ἀνιάτοισιν... στροφάλιγξιν: the noun has a history of being applied to things stirred up by air currents (Il. 16.775, Ap. Rhod. 4.140), or to air currents themselves (Opp. Hal. 1.446), and is now transferred to a different kind of expulsion of air. The epithet is not merely decorative. Hippocrates pronounces his first two φθίσεις fatal, though the third, for which he gives the most detailed regimen, can be cured; cf. Galen, In Hippocr. Aphorism. Comment. xviiiA. 116.3 Kühn ἐπὶ πνεύμονος ἑλκώσεσιν ἀνιάτοις and ps.-Galen, Introductio, sive medicus, 13.29 (xiv. 745.3–4 Kühn) δυσίατον δὲ τὸ πάθος, ἢ καὶ ἀνίατον. Aretaeus thinks recovery possible but difficult. Theodorus Priscianus (4th c.) considers the condition so far beyond remedy that he visits as a friend, not a doctor (Rer. Med. 2.61 phthisicos... medicina desperat... chronicos vero plena iam sub desperatione, non iam ut medicorum medelis, sed magis tantum amicorum solacio visitamus).

165 The poet has based his antithesis of body and soul on two Homeric words which were related but not in this way: in the Homeric worldview, the θυμός flew from the limbs at the moment of death, and it is only then that we hear of their relationship (Bremmer 1983, 55). Here, they have a parallel existence. The effect of giving parity to soul and body, and of describing the former with an epithet (λεπταλέος) that combines suggestions of subtlety and aesthetic finesse (whether of a sound or a fabric), anatomical slenderness (much used in this sense by ps.-Oppian) and fragility (Greg. Naz. PG 37.1005.4 Λεπταλέαις αὔρησιν ἐοικότες, of human beings), is that the poet inadvertently anticipates something of the romantic sensibility about consumption.

166 πίνοντες καὶ ἔδοντες: Soranus, Chr. 2.198 reports cibi fastidium, vel maior appetitus (loss of appetite in Hippocr. Epid. 3.3.13 ἀποσιτίη, Progn. 17 σιτίων οὐκ ἐπιθυμέουσι); on the inutility of food for a consumptive, see Cassiodorus, Var. 11.10.1 escas enim in auxilium humani corporis contributas, dum apte non transigit, reddit inutiles. nec interest talibus an sumere cibum an sustinere ieiunium.[68] It was sanatorium practice to serve up enormous meals: see not only Der Zauberberg, but also K. S. Ray and N. N. Sen, 'Diet in Tuberculosis', Indian Medical Gazette, 75(10) (1940), 603–7.

---

[68] The letter goes on to recommend the milk of Mons Lactarius. Milk has been an article in the diet of consumptives since the author of Int. Affect. 10 recommended cow's, goat's, or ass's, milk for the first type of φθίσις; Celsus, De med. 3.23.10; Plin. NH 28.129, 130; Meinecke, 383; Lane Fox, 69.

ἀειθανὲς ἦτορ ἔχοντες: or, as Aretaeus has it, τὰ πάντα νεκρώδεες (1.8.6). Perhaps in this case the reuse of the epic formula ἦτορ ἔχ- — — is more than merely opportunistic, for its associated epithets, which this pointedly reverses, are ἄλκιμον in *Il*. 16.264 and ὑπέρβιον in *Th*. 139, 898.

167–74 + 175

Mars in MC by day. The generally disastrous effect of this configuration matches that reported by Firmicus, 3.4.32, although M^c's report is too generic to furnish detailed parallels other than poverty. Various subentries in Firmicus' discussion involve the additional presence of Jupiter, so although he happens not to furnish one for this particular eventuality it is quite possible that in 175 the poet is preserving a detail from their common source that Firmicus has dropped. The single agency on a *kentron* effecting a harm instantiates the principle in Θ p. 186.5–6 ὅτι γὰρ οἱ κακοποιοὶ μόνοι ἐπίκεντροι ἢ καὶ ἐπαναφερόμενοι ἢ καὶ ἐπιθεωροῦντες τὰ φῶτα σίνη ἢ πάθη παρέχουσι δῆλον.

167 ἡμερινοῖσι: day births, not, *contra* De Stefani, the 'creatures of a day' topos: Mars, being a night planet, should have worse effects by day. L and Hephaestion, who quotes 167–9 (ἡμερινῆσι sc. γενέθλησι) both have readings which imply day births; Koechly 1851, lv, implicitly noting the similarity to 83 νυκτερινοῖσι μεσουρανέων (obviously about night births), used this as a basis to attribute both charts to the same poet; and Boll 1898, 203, understood (Mars) *per diem constitutus*. It is in Focus position, too, which one would expect to be used to communicate something contentful, not just an instance of miserabilism.

168 γονέων βίον ὤλεσε: presumably the loss of their wealth, not their life (though see Bouché-Leclercq, 394 n. 1); Firmicus has *amissionem patrimonii* for the native.

169 For the restoration of a pentameter by combining Hephaestion's line-end with L's disjunctive, see Heilen 2010, 164–5. I acknowledge the likelihood that L's hexameter is secondary; κακῷ is a feeble stop-gap. But the principle of rendering the recension that L presents rather than a composite, as if it were possible to attain an 'ideal' state of the text that way, requires it to stand. (There is thus a question whether ὄλλυσι should also be printed in 168.)

διχοστασίησιν: for Mars sundering parents, see Περὶ κέντρ. 48 ὁ Ἄρης δύνων καὶ ὁρῶν τὸν Ἥλιον ἢ τὴν Σελήνην διαστήσει τοὺς γονεῖς. The fact that they have been sundered here by a word that in archaic poetry denotes civic strife (Theognis, 77; Solon, fr. 4.37 W., both at pentameter-end; Bornmann on Call. *Hymn* 3.133) is another illustration of astrology's *embourgeoisement*. Its other appearance in astrology is Dorotheus, i. 384.20 ἔριν τε διχοστασίην τε (Stegemann, i. 23).

170 ἐγύμνασε: an intended tragic effect? To the examples in LSJ II, add Eur. fr. 344 πόνοις δέ γ' οὐκ ἀγύμναστος φρένας. But the figurative sense does occur outside tragedy, e.g. in Isocr. *Demon.* 21 Γύμναζε σεαυτὸν πόνοις ἑκουσίοις.

171 The phrase is built up around θλῖψις, which is given epic cladding. The metaphor is one of squeezing or constraint. The same or a similar idea underlies astrological συνοχή and στενότης (5.240 εἰς στεινὸν ζωῆς), and the very frequent duo θλίψεις καὶ στενοχωρίας, 'afflictions and difficulties', which is also used of difficulty and distress in LXX and of the tribulations of the present and end-times in NT (see *TDNT* s.v. θλίβω (Schlier)), but usually in the singular,[69] whereas pagan writers (including Artemidorus) mostly use plurals (p. 272). The same is true in Latin, where the exact counterpart is *angustiae*. Firmicus (though not *Lib. Herm.*) often combines this with *egestas, paupertas,* or *penuria*. The combination of θλῖψις and πενία (or πτωχεία), constraint and poverty, is also present in OT and NT writers,[70] but not elsewhere in Greek astrology, which instead couples θλίψεις with general 'affliction' words (βλάβας, λύπας, ὀχλήσεις, πόνους) as well as less unspecific harms like disease, debt, onslaughts of enemies, accusations, informers, much in the style of 172. For the development of the sense, see F. Mawet, '«Mais en ces jours, après cette détresse...»', *RevPhil* 65/1³ (1991), 169–78 and 'Du grec θλῖψις à l'arménien nelut'iwn', *Chronique d'Égypte,* 66 (1991), 245–9. On epithets for poverty, see i. 158.

172 All this is standard astrological vocabulary, with somewhat less common (more Attic, according to Moeris) βλάβος for βλάβη. For loans, see p. 79.

173 The alpha-privative jingle rams home the point about estrangement. ἄστεγον could mean literally homeless, not having a roof over one's head (cf. 4.113 ἀμελάθρους, with Mars in the DESC; for the homeless poor, see p. 75), but could, and probably does, also gesture at the themes of estrangement, exile, an unstable lifestyle (Firmicus, 4.14.15 *et qui nusquam sedem domiciliumque constituant,* 8.6.2 *Variabunt semper domicilia, domus sedesque mutabunt*), or a perverse desire for foreign parts (Firmicus, 3.4.5 *faciet enim alienari a parentibus et a domo sua et in finibus semper errare peregrinis*, where it is also an effect of Mars; 8.19.1 *domicilium suum ad peregrinas regiones transferentes*). Wifelessness and childlessness, an obvious pair, are not only piteous, but also

---

[69] Including in the Christian Achmet, *Oneir.* 146 εἰς θλῖψιν καὶ ἔνδειαν καὶ στενοχωρίαν ἥξει.
[70] See G. Le Grelle, 'La plénitude de la parole dans la pauvreté de la chair d'après Col., I, 24', *Nouvelle Revue Théologique*, 81 (1959), 232–50, at 234–8 (cf. Ps. 9:10, 43:25; Ps. Sal. 16:14; Ecclus. 4:4, 22:23). θλίψεις καὶ ταπεινώσεις (Valens, II 17.26) reappear at a little distance in Philippians 4:12 + 14.

the result of a chosen, reckless, lifestyle. Seven of the 24 instances of ἀγύναιος are astrological, and some make this point ('Heliodorus' on Paul, p. 68.28-9; Περὶ κέντρ. 14 καί τινας μὲν ἀγυναίους, τινὰς δὲ τῶν γονέων χωρίζει also suggests dislocation). The qualification about being wifeless and childless 'in youth' reads oddly (why would you expect children in youth anyway?), but perhaps means that the children come late in life. Elsewhere this is a characteristic of Saturn in combination with Venus (ὀψιτέκνους in Περὶ σχημ. 98; Π.τ.δ. 5); of Jupiter in the IMC in Περὶ κέντρ. 38.

174 Trivially Martian: also produced by Mars in the MC at 3.70. There is a case for taking στυγερῷ with either noun (for θάνατος, see Davies and Finglass on Stesichorus, fr. 19.31-2; on the other hand, consider the ornamentation of σιδήρῳ in 3.70 and 1.120; Ov. *Met.* 1.141 *nocens ferrum*). For the *figura etymologica* θανάτῳ... θνῄσκουσι see Fehling, 158 (*Od.* 11.412 ὣς θάνον οἰκτίστῳ θανάτῳ; Tatian, *Or. ad Graec.* 17.4 ὁ τεθνεὼς οἰκτίστῳ θανάτῳ).

175 This is so inept after we have been told that the man is dead that one wonders if in this case the pentameter really is a random import.

176-9

Mars in DESC.

176 Usually the construction would be the other way round, with the planet as the subject and place as the object (1.267, and elsewhere in the corpus). The parenthesis δεινὸν θεόν derives from Hes. *Th.* 933 (of Triton) and 759 δεινοὶ θεοί (of Sleep and Death), entirely unrelated deities (cf. also *Il.* 4.514 δεινὸς θεός, of Apollo, not parenthetical). With the cadence compare Nonn. *D.* 18.263, Musaeus, 8 αἰθέριος Ζεύς; for λίψ see on 3.18.

177 Most of the parallels begin with a little fanfare about awfulness: 3.51 δύνων δ' αὖτ' ἄλγεσσι βροτοὺς ἄταις τε προσάπτει; Firmicus, 3.4.17 *maxima mala et immensa pericula decernit*; CCAG viii/1. 166.24 λίαν ἐστὶν ἀηδής; Paul, p. 60.1-2 Ὁ δὲ τοῦ Ἄρεως ἐπὶ τοῦδε τοῦ τόπου τυχὼν πολλῶν κακῶν παραίτιος γίνεται.

178 θορύβους: CCAG viii/1. 166.24-5 καὶ γὰρ τὴν οἰκίαν καὶ τὸν βίον ταράσσει, καὶ μάχας ποιεῖ.

ἐγκλήματα ~ Περὶ κέντρ. 45/CCAG viii/1. 166.25 ἐπιβουλάς; Firmicus, 3.4.17 *reos*; Valens, II 10.3 (malefics in DESC) ἐξ ὀνειδισμῶν γὰρ καὶ κακῶν τὰ ποριζόμενα ἀναλώσουσιν.

178-9 καὶ σίνος αἰνόν | ἢ πάθος: Paul, p. 60.2-3 ὁτὲ μὲν σίνεσιν, ὁτὲ δὲ πάθεσι περιτρέπων.

179 Paul, p. 60.3-5 ἢ ἐν ἀλλοδαπῇ γῇ διατελοῦντας ἢ μετανάστας ἢ ξενιτεύοντας ποιήσει; Περὶ κέντρ. 45 φυγὴν πατρίδος; Dor.^ARAB II 25.9 'he [the native] will die or run away from his city'. The poet has recast this in the appropriate poetic language for leaving home (Aesch. Pers. 18, Sotades, fr. 4b.2 P.), abandoning one settlement for another (Tyrtaeus, fr. 2.14-15 W., Nicander, fr. 19 G.-S.) or just for a life of indigence (Tyrtaeus, fr. 10.3-4 W.). None of the comparanda mentions specifically sailing, but might have suggested it. Perhaps the poet is rendering a piece of astrological jargon, πλευστικούς, although it is true that anything to do with water is usually associated with Saturn (Valens, I 1.7; in I 3.52, with degrees of Venus within Saturn's sign Aquarius). If so, Wakefield's emendation ἤ‹ν› πλώωσιν would introduce unwanted conditionality. See also on 5.65.

180-4

Mercury, Venus, Saturn rule πρᾶξις; and with Jupiter in aspect. By the time the confusions in L's text are sorted out (see Monaco, 41-2[71]), this exactly matches Θ p. 213.19-22, one of the expansions of Ptolemy's πράξεις (and, like most of the rest of the supplementary material, showing no trace of a poetic source). Θ further differentiates doctors into ἐπαοιδοὺς ἢ βοτανικούς; the poet here, in contrast, cobbles together formulae suggestive of Iliadic Machaon and his anodyne arts. There is also an interesting comparison in the Anonymous Astrologer of 379, CCAG v/1. 199.9-10, in a chapter about the effect of bright stars in producing people with intellectual or artistic (or spiritual) gifts.[72] Each of the five stars in question is said to be of the κρᾶσις of Venus and Mercury, and doctors (ἰατρικῆς ἔμπειροι) are produced through the additional aspect of Saturn, so the result is the convergence of the selfsame planets as here. Doctors and druggists are also among those produced by Mars (not Mercury) and Venus sole (without Saturn) in Ptol. 4.4.8, Θ p. 212.29 φαρμακοποιούς, ἰατρούς.

---

[71] Though he misunderstands πρᾶξιν as 'influsso' exercised by the planets. It is the normal technical term in astrology for the domain of action.

[72] Also transmitted in CCAG i. 115.15-16 (from Laur. Plut. 28.33) and Θ p. 176.15-16. Julian in his Apotelesmata is cited at the top of the chapter in Θ = F17* László (L. László, 'Julianus of Laodicea and his Astrological Fragments', Mnemosyne⁴, 73 (2020), 1-20), where the asterisk registers the uncertainty about how much of the chapter goes back to Julian.

180-1 ἢν μὲν ἔχωσιν | τὴν πρᾶξιν: close to prose: Ptol. 4.4.1 Ὁ δὲ τῆς πράξεως τὴν κυρίαν ἔχων; Valens, VII 6.224 τὸν τῶν πράξεων τόπον ἔχοντος. For πολιὸς Κρόνος, see on 1.45.

181 ἀμύμονας ἰητῆρας: 3× Il. ἀμύμονος ἰητῆρος, of Machaon. The characterisation of the doctor in terms of harmlessness, and in terms of healing drugs, need not, of course, refer to the Hippocratic Oath, but the emphasis is similar, recalling, by contraries, the Oath's pledge not to administer any harmful drug (φάρμακον ... θανάσιμον).

184 In place of the sub-branches of medicine in Θ (and Firmicus) the poet has chosen analgesics, which he first renders in *presque homérique* (Il. 4.218 ἐπ' ἄρ' ἤπια φάρμακα εἰδώς, Il. 11.515, 830 ἐπί τ' ἤπια φάρμακα πάσσειν; Lane Fox, 16–17), and then glosses with a more prosaic phrase that recalls the topic of ἀνώδυνα φάρμακα, much discussed in ancient medicine, especially by Galen (e.g. *Ad Glauconem, de medendi methodo*, xi. 114.12–13 Kühn καλεῖται μὲν οὖν ἀνώδυνα φάρμακα τὰ τοιαῦτα τῷ παύειν τὰς ὀδύνας; passim throughout *De simplicium medicamentorum temperamentis ac facultatibus* and *De compositione medicamentorum secundum locos*). Plut. *Mor.* 614 c uses ἀνώδυνον to gloss Helen's φάρμακον ... νηπενθές in *Od.* 4.220-1—a drug given her by an Egyptian expert, though there is no sign that the poet is thinking specifically of Egyptian pharmakopoeia.

182 Again to his credit, Koechly 1851, lii saw that this line had been displaced before the evidence of Θ confirmed it. πολυόλβους is Mᵃ's word (2.246, 475, 3.177, 312; i. 158–9).

183 The line, precisely encapsulating the wealth–renown nexus (i. 308, and Index s.v. wealth—and renown), is repeated exactly at 228. It is distinction (rather than wealth) that Firmicus' charts for doctors generally single out: 4.9.8 *medicos cunctorum testimoniis adornatos*, 8.25.7 *medici, famosa artis nobilitate perspicui*; 8.26.12 *medici, sed quos professionis suae nobilitet ingenium*. In one case, it is the additional presence of Jupiter that confers advantage (though over a different base chart): 5.2.17 (ASC in terms of Mercury) *iuris peritos, medicos <...> ut res potentium hominum sua intercessione disponant*.

185-95

Waxing (or Full?) Moon in contact with a malefic. See the discussions on 6.46–50 + 51–2 + 53–6 + 57–9 and 4.366–71 + 372–3 + 373–8. What the poet offers here, which sticks to the fate of the mother, corresponds to Firmicus,

7.2.15, while the version in the fourth book, on the fate of the child, corresponds broadly to Firmicus, 7.2.16, and the original sequence on M^a veers from child to mother and back again, but shares the detail of the mother's cries (6.50). The difference, however, from Firmicus, is that the set-up has been cast in terms, not of aspect, but of *synaphe*, and this corresponds better to the sequence of predictions for the Moon's contact with Mars in Π.σ.α. pp. 182.29–183.12 (plus the general rule in Θ p. 186.8–9, which does not specify the malefic or type of harm), all of which concern mother and child and harms to both. (Mars is taken as the comparison here because the treatment of Saturn is altogether sketchier about both mothers and children.) The outcome that goes into gynaecological detail like this one is in fact, not for *synaphe*, but for the *waning* Moon leaving Mars (183.11–12 ἐμβρυοτομίας καὶ τῆς ὑστέρας κίνδυνον), but the sequence mother's death–mother's salvation through the redeeming power of Jupiter is most like Firmicus—as well as *Lib. Herm.* xxvi. 48, where the Moon is in the ASC and each malefic is in a house on either side. There were evidently different ways of presenting this situation, in terms of both aspect and of *synaphe/aporrhoia*, and this poet shows the influence of both. His version is not perfectly represented by either extant comparison, and does not stand in relation to them as, say, the previous chart stood to Θ.

185 The expression for moving away from σύνοδος (i.e. waxing) combines *Il.* 15.628 ὑπὲκ θανάτοιο φέρονται with ὑπὲκ κακότητα φύγοιμεν (3× *Od.*), and the line as a whole is metrically identical to *Od.* 3.175 τέμνειν, ὄφρα τάχιστα ὑπὲκ κακότητα φύγοιμεν. That, however, is a tmesis, whereas here the preposition governs a case; compare 1.351 ἐκ συνόδοιο and Dorotheus, p. 388.28–9 ἰούσης | ἐκ συνόδου. There are precedents for the double particle, which in Homer occurs with the potential optative, with ὄφρα, and in a counterfactual,[73] but post-Homerically also in temporal constructions (Marcellus (LXIII Heitsch), 72 εὖτ᾽ ἄν κε; *SH* 923.12 ἔστ᾽ ἄν ⌊κε; μέχρις ἄν κε transmitted at 6.45, but see ad loc.). A mechanical explanation is that the poet combines *Il.* 19.230 ὅσσοι δ᾽ ἄν with a construction like *Od.* 4.756 = Dorotheus, p. 393.15 ὅς κεν ἔχῃσι (or another relative: Xenophanes, fr. B 1.17 W. ὁπόσον κεν ἔχων).

186 φωσφορέουσαν ἔτ᾽ ἔμπεδον, ὀρνυμένην τε: this looks like an indication that the Moon is gaining light or Full, and in the ASC (though the verb is apparently not otherwise used of the rising Moon), details not in Π.σ.α. For φωσφορέουσαν see on 1.65. If the Moon is leaving the Sun, therefore waxing, the sense should be that it is shining steadily 'again', 'once more', although in the

---

[73] K.-G. i. 248; Janko on *Il.* 13.126–8. The potential has most take-up in astrological poetry, helped by Aratus, 562 Τὰς δ᾽ ἄν κε περισκέψαιο μάλιστα (see Kidd ad loc.), whence often in Maximus (38, 46, 107, 303, 366, 521); combined with indirect question in 6.307.

proof text, *Od.* 23.203 (different *sedes*), ἔτ' ἔμπεδον means 'still' (whence Koechly's 'adhuc firmiter'). Lopilato renders ἔτ' ἔμπεδον as 'steadfastly'.

187 For the epithets see i. 909 n. 4, 911 n. 2. Add that ἀνηλ-, first securely attested in the Hellenistic period, is a doublet of Homeric νηλ-: see Mineur on Call. *Hymn* 4.106, and for such doublets J. Wackernagel, *Kleine Schriften*, ii (Göttingen, 1955), 949–50.

188 ἔμβρυα μὲν φθείρουσι: abortion (for which φθείρειν τὸ ἔμβρυον has been in use since the Hippocratic corpus[74]) or even specifically embryotomy, which is the case in *Lib. Herm.* xxvi. 48 and in a fairly similar chart in xxxvi. 32: see on 2.288–9. Readers might remember that, of the eight instances of Homeric μινυνθάδιος, a couple are linked with the verb τίκτειν (*Il.* 1.352, *Od.* 11.307), another with γεινᾶσθαι (*Il.* 21.84–5). These embryos never even got as far as that.

189–90 These lines are not interested in ensouling as such, but they do suggest the idea that the stage prior to full humanity is a bestial one. It is hard to find an exact match for this theory. For Aristotle, the embryo acquires, or rather develops, its already potential nutritive soul, that which is shared with every living thing, including plants, then the sensitive soul, which is shared with animals, and finally the rational one, which is uniquely human (*De Generatione Animalium*, 2 ch. 3, 736ᵃ33–ᵇ8). Aristotle does not, however, state or suggest that the foetus passes through a stage prior to full humanity in which it has bestial form.[75] Galen expresses himself differently in different passages, but he draws on the analogy between an embryo and a plant, which he found in Hippocrates' *On the Nature of the Child*, 24–7, to suggest likewise a development from vegetal to an animal stage, as the embryo acquires circulation, warmth, and the capacity to move (*De Sem.* iv. 543–4 Kühn; *Foet. Form.* iv. 670–4 and 698–700 Kühn; B. Holmes, 'Pure Life: The Limits of the Vegetal Analogy in the Hippocratics and Galen', in J. Z. Wee (ed.), *The Comparable Body: Analogy and Metaphor in Ancient Mesopotamian, Egyptian, and Greco-Roman Medicine* (Leiden, 2017), 358–86); but his point is this acquisition of capacity (i.e. when the foetus becomes a ζῷον), not the bestiality or subhumanity of the foetus. Even Tertullian, who is committed to the idea that the soul enters the body on conception, is sufficiently heir to the old Aristotelian notions as to hold that the foetus only becomes fully human when its form is completed (*De Anima*, 37.2

---

[74] Ellis Hanson, 299–300 on (δια)φθείρειν.
[75] We should not be reminded of 'recapitulation theory', associated with Johann Friedrich Meckel (1781–1833) and Étienne Serres (1786–1868), according to whom 'ontogeny recapitulates phylogeny', that is, the developing embryo recapitulates the (adult) stages of its ancestors in the course of its evolution. This is nonsense, and any similarity here can only be accidental.

Ex eo igitur fetus in utero homo, a quo forma completa est), but that is certainly not to say that it is bestial until this point.[76]

I would not normally write an entry just on the history of a word, but LSJ's entry on ἐγγάστριον is entirely inadequate. It first occurs in Aristophanes of Byzantium's epitome of the *Historia Animalium*, where τὸ ἐγγάστριον is a noun (the thing conceived in the womb). Eventually it settles down, mostly as an adjective, as here, referring to human pregnancy and what sustains it, and especially to the Virgin Birth (or at the very least St John), but it is not common before Byzantine authors and the present poet stands out among the pre-Byzantine passages in using it of human pregnancy. Otherwise it refers to intestinal worms (Herodian, *Part.* 31), imposture (Origen, *PG* 12.1033.46, as in ἐγγαστρίμυθα), or gestation in animals (*Physiologus*, rec. 1, 43; rec. 3, 29; Eutecnius, *Paraphr. in Opp. Cyn.* p. 36.27). The word's only other astrological occurrence is in a pre-Constantinian Hermetic tract discussing gestation and birth (*CCAG* viii/1. 175.9–12 τὸ ἐγγάστριον = foetus).

190–1 These lines are engaging with either or both of M[a] on abortions (3.150 and especially 6.245, where ὠμοτόκοις ὠδῖσι has already occurred) and Callimachus, on the crude birth of the lioness, which has inspired the earlier poet (*Hymn* 4.120 ὠμοτόκους ὠδῖνας ἀπηρείσαντο λέαιναι); the reference to wild animal flesh suggests that the poet has gone back to his model's model, making this a window allusion. Looking to Callimachus suggests that the sense of the line-end of 190 might be that they deposit the contents of their womb as if it were animal flesh (ἀπορρίψασαι would be a suitable verb in connection with abortions: P.Bon. 4.3). But given this poet's usual style, one might expect a participle in parallel with 189 αὐξήσαντα (i.e. a neuter plural), to be broken off with a sting in the tail in 191.

191 ἐς ἠελίου φέρον αὐγάς: see on 6.20.

192 ἀνηλέα κωκύουσαι: the verb is well observed, for every Homeric instance of it not only applies to women (a distinction not always observed in later literature), but often to women bereaved, or about to be bereaved, of their children (including *Il.* 18.71 ὀξὺ δὲ κωκύσασα, the only Homeric example of the participle). See also on 6.50 ἐπ' ὀξέα κεκληγυίης. But the adverb, which obviously means 'pitiless' in 187, 263, seems to mean the opposite here, unless 'pitiless' is stretched to 'unpitied'. I take ἀμφὶ πόνοισιν to approximate to Firmicus' *in ipso*

---

[76] On ancient embryology, see J. Needham, *A History of Embryology* (Cambridge, 1959), 27–74; Ellis Hanson; Congourdeau, esp. 287–92; L. Brisson, M.-H. Congourdeau, and J.-L. Solère (eds.), *L'Embryon, formation et animation: Antiquité grecque et latine, traditions hébraïque, chrétienne et islamique* (Paris, 2008).

partu constitutae, since πόνος is the proper word for labour pains (the textbook example being Eur. *Med*. 1030): see Loraux, 175; King, 124, 125–6.

193 The line almost exactly matches the rhythm of *Il*. 13.415 εἰς Ἀϊδός περ ἰόντα πυλάρταο κρατεροῖο, while also throwing in reminiscences of (Odyssean) εἰς Ἀΐδαο δόμους and the 'whence no traveller returns' topos (Gow on Theocr. 12.19). For the epithet, which is first (?) in Tr. Adesp. 658.17 K.-S., then Antipater, *AP* 7.467.6 = *HE* 537 ἐς τὸν ἀνόστητον χῶρον ἔβης ἐνέρων, see Livrea on Nonn. *Par*. 2.104, Agosti on *Par*. 5.97. The best comparison for the present line, with noun and epithet in the same *sedes*, is Nonn. *D*. 35.65 ἐξ Ἀΐδος ζώουσαν ἀνοστήτοιο σαώσω; also Quint. Smyrn. 3.15 ἀνοστήτοιο κατελθέμεν Ἀϊδονῆος; for once, there are no epigraphical parallels.

194 μάλα πολλὰ παθοῦσαν: Homeric μάλα πολλὰ πάθον, which straddles the hexameter, does not refer to labour pains, though it does refer to Phoenix's care for the infant Achilles in *Il*. 9.492. The woman with a (presumably gynaecological: p. 854) issue of blood is also, presumably by coincidence, πολλὰ παθοῦσα in Mark 5:26.

195 (κακῶν δ᾽ οὐκ) ἔσσετ᾽ ἀρωγός ~ *Il*. 4.235 (πατὴρ Ζεὺς) ἔσσετ᾽ ἀρωγός: this is the game of repurposed Zeus language. Presumably this hints darkly at the child's death, even though the mother's life has been saved (cf. Firmicus).

1.196–207 Protreptic

Why sacrifice vainly to the gods, who can do nothing against Fate? Sacrifice, rather, to the planetary deities. There are three stages to this argument: (i) Why sacrifice to the traditional gods of paganism? (ii) Sacrifice is unavailing against the chief power in the universe, which has predetermined everything. (iii) A more appropriate object of devotion would be the powers that represent Fate, i.e. the stars.

This passage belongs in a broad tradition of criticism of petitionary prayer.[77] It goes back to Plato, *Leg*. 10.885 B, where a type of impious person thinks that the gods may be turned from their course θυσίαις τε καὶ εὐχαῖς (a belief which is, in context, false). This tradition is taken up by pagan and Christian writers alike. They allege—and often counter—various reasons why petitionary prayer is useless. Maximus, an unoriginal thinker who presents standard positions in a clear, reasoned, and popular way, gives a good survey of the objections in his fifth *Oration*; while he favours prayer as a means for the virtuous soul (like

---

[77] For ancient debate about the value of prayer, see Trapp, 41, with bibliography.

Socrates) to connect with divinity, he roundly disposes of petitionary prayer, whether the future is disposed by providence (πρόνοια), necessity (εἱμαρμένη), fortune (τύχη), or is controllable by science (τέχνη) (5.4). Sacrifice, on this view, is not misdirected, but misconceived; it treats the gods as bribable, and is in any case irrelevant. Likewise, in his commentary on the *Timaeus*, Porphyry (who himself argues strongly for the value of certain *kinds* of prayer) is aware of the various sceptical positions, beginning with the 'primary' atheists who deny the existence of gods outright, and moving on to the 'secondary' ones who deny providence or hold that everything arises from necessity (ἐξ ἀνάγκης).[78] Origen is moved to respond to those who argue that prayer is useless, either because God has foreknowledge of everything anyway, or because he has preordained it.[79] He takes his place in a long debate about determinism vis-à-vis moral responsibility.[80] A third option is the combination of steps (i) and (iii): why sacrifice to *x* when you *should* be sacrificing to *y*? This is what we find in sectarian writers, Jewish and Christian, and although the thrust of their argument may seem obvious (stop worshipping Your gods[81] and worship Ours) it is worth mentioning here because of the very close similarity of some poetic versions of anti-pagan polemic to the opening of this one (see on 196–7).

It is Porphyry, and Eusebius' own criticisms of him, that form the most interesting parallels to the present passage. Porphyry's own position was apparently complex—or the fragments are representing him in a way that is hard to make coherent. On the one hand, the passage from the *Timaeus* commentary makes clear his approval of prayer as a means of connection to divinity (συναφὴ πρὸς τὸ θεῖόν ἐστι), and his disapproval of the deniers. The *Timaeus* passage argues most strongly for prayer as a spiritual exercise, but it also envisages certain kinds of petitionary prayer as well (on behalf of rain and wind; to avert disease; and to promote fertility) (ap. Procl. *In Tim.* i. 213.20–214.8). Yet in another

---

[78] Porphyry, *In Tim.* fr. 28 Sodano (ap. Procl. *In Platonis Timaeum Comm.* 1.207.23–208.3 Diehl) οἱ καὶ εἶναι καὶ προνοεῖν αὐτοὺς (sc. the gods) συγχωροῦντες, ἄπαντα δὲ ἀπ' αὐτῶν ἐξ ἀνάγκης γίνεσθαι· τῶν γὰρ ἐνδεχομένων καὶ ἄλλως γίνεσθαι μὴ ὄντων ἀναιρεῖται τὸ τῆς εὐχῆς ὄφελος ('for if there is nothing that can take place other than it does, the benefit of prayer is destroyed'). Clem. Al. *Strom.* 7.7.41.2 associates the anti-prayer position with the Cyrenaics, who are taxed with atheism in ancient sources.

[79] *De Orat.* 5.1–3, pp. 308–9 Koetschau. Clement, likewise, manages to reconcile an all-knowing and providential God (*Strom.* 7.7.37.5) with the value of petitionary prayer (7.7.41.6 οὐ μὴν παρέλκει ἡ αἴτησις).

[80] Cumont 1912, 154. Origen's contemporary, Alexander of Aphrodisias, *On Fate* 17 (p. 188 Bruns), takes a hatchet to the notion of determinism, which would do away with providence, piety, and prophecy.

[81] Clem. Al. *Strom.* 7.7.39.2 ἐσχάτη δὲ ἀμαθία παρὰ τῶν μὴ θεῶν ὡς θεῶν αἰτεῖσθαι.

work he turns the argument about sacrificing to gods who are uninvolved (ἀπαθεῖς) against the Egyptian Anebo.[82] If there is a way of squaring the circle, it may be that he believed it pointless to make sacrifices to the (higher) gods, who were pure intellects, and not subject to passion,[83] but that prayer nonetheless had a function in placating *daimones*. On the other hand, when in his *Philosophy from Oracles* he cites the long and well-known oracle about the destruction of Apollo's temple in a lightning strike (i. 50) and has the god muse in traditional hexameter idiom about the Fates and their spindles, Zeus nodding his head, and αἶσα, he simply lays himself open to attack by Eusebius on very similar grounds to the argument mounted here: why worship the gods at all, rather than Necessity?[84]

There are in fact two passages where Eusebius confronts a pagan with the argument that he should strictly be worshipping the Fates, rather than the gods who are subject to them. One is the attack on Porphyry, the other is when he takes on the anti-Christian persecutor Hierocles and his advocacy of Apollonius of Tyana (a potential rival to Christ and therefore to be put down). A Christian writer himself could not, of course, accept the argument that the Fates deserved worship. In Christian hands the argument had to be a way of hoisting his opponent with his own petard, before the writer squared his own circle in which the Christian God was both a disposer and dispenser of Providence *and* also allowed his creatures moral responsibility.[85] But the point here is the similarity in the logical and rhetorical structure of the argument, which parallels all three steps in the present passage:

(i) 'Why in vain...', with reference to the particularities of pagan sacrifice;
(ii) The chief power is inexorable Fate;
(iii) So the power of Fate ought rather to be worshipped instead.

The passages from Eusebius are laid out in the table below. It looks as if the author of 196–207 has taken an argument of set structure—not necessarily from a Christian source, for Porphyry suggests the possibility of a tradition in which it was mounted against the Stoics—and deployed it as a positive argument for astral worship.

---

[82] *Letter to Anebo*, fr. 13 Saffrey–Segonds/1.2c Sodano (ap. Euseb. *PE* 5.10.10) μάταιαι αἱ θεῶν κλήσεις; A. Timotin, 'Porphyry on Prayer: Platonic Tradition and Religious Trends in the Third Century', in J. Dillon and A. Timotin (eds.), *Platonic Theories of Prayer* (Leiden, 2016), 88–107.
[83] R. T. Wallis, *Neoplatonism* (London, 1995), 109–10.
[84] Euseb. *PE* 6.3; Porphyry, 338 F Smith (*Philosophia ex oraculis*, 170–2 Wolff); i. 50.
[85] Thus e.g. Clem. Al. *Strom.* 7.7.42.4–8.

Euseb. *Contra Hierocl.* 45.42–50 des Places	Euseb. *PE* 6.3.2–4	1.196–207
τί δὲ καὶ οἷς νομίζεις θεοῖς τὰ μελιττοῦτα καὶ τὸν λιβανωτὸν εἰς μάτην ῥιπτεῖς, εὐσέβειάν τε ἐπιμορφαζόμενος ἐπ᾽ εὐχὰς τρέπεσθαι τοὺς ἑταίρους παρορμᾷς; αὐτός τε εὐχόμενος τί παρὰ θεῶν αἰτεῖς, ὁπότε καὶ τούτων ὁμολογεῖς τὴν εἱμαρμένην κρατεῖν;	εἰ δὲ καὶ μηδεμία ἐκ θεῶν ὑπάρχοι βοήθεια, δεῖ δὲ ἐξ ἅπαντος τετλάναι "Μοιράων ἀμετάτροπα δήνεα θυμῷ," (3) καὶ τίς ἡ περὶ τοὺς θεοὺς ματαία σπουδή; εἴποι ἄν τις. τί δὲ δεῖ "λοιβῆς τε κνίσης τε" καὶ τὸ ἐκ τούτων γέρας τοῖς μηδὲ τούτων ἀξίοις ἀπονέμειν, εἰ κατ᾽ οὐδὲν ἡμᾶς ὠφελεῖν δύνανται; ἐπεὶ μηδὲ "τῶν ἀγαθῶν δοτῆρας" οἴεσθαι (4) χρῆν αὐτούς, ἀλλ᾽ ἦν καὶ τῶν ἐναντίων ὡμολόγουν αἰτίαν. εἰ γὰρ πέπρωται ἀνθρώποις εἴτε τι ἀγαθὸν εἴτε τι καὶ ἐναντίον, ἔσται ἐξ ἀνάγκης καὶ παρέσται τοῦτο καὶ βουλομένων καὶ μὴ τῶν θεῶν.	Τίπτε μάτην, ἄνθρωπε, θυηπολέεις μακάρεσσιν; τίπτε μάτην τρισέλικτος ἀν᾽ οὐρανὸν ἤλυθε κνῖσα; ἴσχεο· οὐ γὰρ ὄνειαρ ἐν ἀθανάτοιο θυηλαῖς. οὐ γάρ τις δύναται γένεσιν μετατρεψέμεν ἀνδρῶν, ἤθ᾽ ἅμα νηπιάχοις συγγίγνεται ἀνθρώποισιν, (200)
And why do you vainly cast before those whom you consider to be gods, your honey-cake and your frankincense, and putting on the cloak of religion encourage your companions to be diligent at their prayers? And what do you yourself in your prayers ask of the gods, inasmuch as you admit that they too are subject to Destiny?	If, moreover, there is no help from the gods, but one must in any case 'Bear with brave soul the counsels of the Fates | That know no change,' what is the meaning, some one may say, of our useless zeal concerning the gods? Or what need to assign a portion 'of libation and burnt-offering,' and the honour thereof, to those who are not worthy even of these things, if they have no power to help us at all? For then we ought not to ascribe the bestowal of good things to them, but to that (destiny) which they confessed to be the cause of the evil. For if anything either good or the reverse is destined for men, it will of necessity occur, and, whether the gods will or not, it will come to pass.	εὐθύ τε Μοιράων εἰλίσσεται ἀμφὶ μίτοισιν, κλώσμασιν ἀρρήκτοισι σιδηρείοισί τ᾽ ἀτράκτοις.
καὶ μὴν ἔδει τοὺς ἄλλους θεοὺς παραμειψάμενον Ἀνάγκῃ μόνον καὶ Μοίραις θύειν καὶ τοῦ Διὸς αὐτοῦ μᾶλλον τὴν εἱμαρμένην προτιμᾶν. οὕτω δ᾽ ἄν σοι θεοὶ μὲν οὐκέτ᾽ ἂν ἦσαν καὶ εἰκότως, ἅτε μηδὲ ἀνθρώπους οἷοί τε ὠφελεῖν.		ῥέζε Κρόνῳ καὶ Ἄρηι καὶ Ἑρμῇ καὶ Κυθερείῃ καὶ Διὶ καὶ Μήνῃ τε καὶ Ἡελίῳ βασιλῆι· οὗτοι γὰρ κρατέουσι θεῶν, κρατέουσι καὶ ἀνδρῶν, (205) πόντου καὶ ποταμῶν πάντων ῥοθίων ἀνέμων τε, καὶ γῆς καρποφόροιο καὶ ἠέρος ἀενάοιο.
Nay you ought to make a clean sweep of all the other gods, and sacrifice to Necessity alone and to the Fates, and pay your respects rather to Destiny than to Zeus himself. In that case no doubt you would have no gods left; and rightly too, seeing that they are not even able to help mankind.	μόνην ἄρα τὴν Ἀνάγκην θεραπευτέον, σμικρὰ μᾶλλον δὲ τὸ μηθὲν φροντίσαντας τῶν θεῶν μήτε λυπεῖν μήτε εὐεργετεῖν δυναμένων.	
	We ought therefore to worship Necessity only, and care little, or rather nothing, for the gods, as being able neither to annoy nor to benefit us.	

That the argument is a set piece is suggested by the fact that it is sometimes couched in the form of *diceret quispiam*, a known rhetorical position to be considered and, if necessary, countered. Arnobius, who is attacking pagan worship, has the whole company of the learned (*universus ille doctissimorum chorus*) descend on the man who has the temerity to say that he offers sacrifices and other gifts (*hostias... et cetera munera*) in order to gain the gods' favour with the argument that everything is so bound by chains of necessity that gods cannot help us.[86] It is not clear that Arnobius thinks much of this argument either, and he does not go as far as to have his learned men claim that the Fates should receive worship instead of the gods (in other words he stops at step (ii)), but at least he finds it useful in putting down the naive sacrificer; he has taken over a set piece because, at this point, he finds it rhetorically convenient. And in a specifically astrological context, Firmicus puts the familiar objections in the mouth of an unsympathetic opponent (1.2.5–12)—the gods have determined the future, they have determined our moral character and taken away responsibility for our actions;[87] what, therefore, is the point of traditional religious piety? Unlike Arnobius, Firmicus shortly replies (1.6.1–2) that astrology teaches us to appreciate the majesty of the true gods; that the divine element in our minds is fortified;[88] and that, somehow, we shall be better placed to resist their 'violent decree' (*ex aliqua parte stellarum violenti decreto et earum potestatibus resistamus*).

---

[86] Arnobius, *Adv. Nat.* 7.10.3 *Si definitum et fixum est, quid optingere singulis mali debeat bonive, iam certum est.* 4. *Quod si certum est et fixum, vacant omnia deorum auxilia, vacant odia, vacant benignitates. Tam enim praestare non possunt id quod non potest fieri quam prohibere ne fiat id quod necesse est evenire; nisi quod validius premere opinionem istam, si voluerint, quibunt* [the subject has changed to the clever men whose objections Arnobius is rehearsing], *ut etiam ipsos deos frustra dicant a vobis coli et supervacaneis supplicationibus adorari. Cum enim ordinem vertere et fatalia nequeant constituta mutare, quid rei, quid causae est fatigare et obtundere eorum aures velle quorum auxiliis nequeas supremis in necessitatibus fidere?*/'If it has been determined and fixed what evil or good should befall each person, it is already certain; but if this is certain and fixed, there is no room for all the help given by the gods, their hatred, and favours. For they are just as unable to do for you that which cannot be done, as to prevent that from being done which must happen, except that they will be able, if they choose, to depreciate somewhat powerfully that belief which you entertain, so that they say that even the gods themselves are worshipped by you in vain, and that the supplications with which you address them are superfluous. For as they are unable to turn aside the course of events, and change what has been appointed by fate, what reason, what cause, is there to wish to weary and deafen the ears of those in whose help you cannot trust at your utmost need?' (Transl. H. Bryce and H. Campbell.)

[87] Abry, 43, with n. 26.

[88] *confirmata animi nostri divinitate*. This strikes us as Stoic or sub-Stoic (Cumont 1912, 155), but we also find an argument from affinity in Plotinus, who considers that prayers addressed to the heavenly bodies may be effective as a natural result of cosmic sympathy (*Ennead* IV 4.40.32–41.3).

Observe that he avoids saying that we can change it. His formulation strikes us as an evasion which is entirely characteristic, both of its author,[89] and of astrologers in general: Valens manages to have, and eat, a similar cake. On the one hand, he asserts, in his own voice, that it is impossible to alter any outcome with prayer or sacrifice: what is fated will come about anyway, and what is not fated cannot be made to come about through any effort of our own (V 6.10; Cumont, 205 n. 2). On the other, when he moves over to catarchic astrology, he seizes on the manoeuvrability that the more negotiable system offered (i. 13–15).[90] If you choose the wrong time, it is not profitable to sacrifice to the gods nor to found temples—but that implies that at other times it *can* be (V 2.24, 25).

Observe, too, that neither Firmicus nor Valens (nor Manilius, who briefly evokes the pointlessness-of-prayer motif in 4.21) go as far as step (iii). They do not assert, with our poet, that the stars deserve worship *in place of* the traditional pantheon. Is he serious? What we think of in connection with 'star worship' in the ancient world is principally one of three things. The first is the existence of various cults specifically of the Sun (Rhodian Helios, Apollo/Helios, native Italian Sol Indiges, Elagabalus' Baal of Emesa, Aurelian's Sol Invictus, the reverence of the neo-Platonists for the Sun interpreted in their own eccentric way).[91] The second is the whole formidable field of 'oriental religions',[92] such as the (in)famous cult of Sin, the Moon God, at Harran;[93] the triad of Sun, Morning Star (Azizos), and Evening Star (Monimos) in various places of northern Syria and Mesopotamia,[94] or the Arabic goddess al-ʿUzza, associated with the planet Venus.[95] Explicating all this—reaching to the temples of the seven planets which an Arabic historian attributes to the 'Sabians' of Ḥarrān[96]—would take us

---

[89] When he invokes the seven planetary deities for the protection of Constantine and his children (1.10.14) he elides Jupiter into the deity of the Capitoline temple (cf. 5 *Praef.* 5–6), somehow uniting the planet with civic cult.

[90] Maybe this was a circle impossible for a Roman to square (Cumont 1912, 157–61). Inconsistency is also the point in Suetonius, *Tib.* 69: stellar fatalism inculcated negligence about traditional religion (*Circa deos ac religiones neglegentior, quippe addictus mathematicae plenusque persuasionis cuncta fato agi*), yet Tiberius was superstitious about thunder.

[91] Heilen 2015, 734–5. Rhodes: W. Burkert, *Greek Religion* (Oxford, 1985), 175. Sol: Liebeschuetz, 281–5. Mesopotamia: Green, 63–5. Palmyra: J. Teixidor, *The Pantheon of Palmyra* (Leiden, 1979), 29–52; L. Dirven, *The Palmyrenes of Dura-Europos: A Study of Religious Interaction in Roman Syria* (Leiden, 1999), index s.v. sun god; T. Kaizer, *The Religious Life of Palmyra: A Study of the Social Patterns of Worship in the Roman Period* (Stuttgart, 2002), 154–7.

[92] Cumont 1912, 161–6; 1935, 32–3, 36–7.

[93] Green; D. Pingree, 'The Ṣābians of Ḥarrān and the Classical Tradition', *IJCT* 9/1 (2002), 8–35; on Sin, Teixidor (n. 91); H. J. W. Drijvers, *Cults and Beliefs at Edessa* (Leiden, 1980), 122–45.

[94] Drijvers (n. 93), 146–74. [95] Green, 61–2.

[96] D. A. Chwolsohn, *Die Ssabier und der Ssabismus* (St Petersburg, 1858), ii. 367 (Al-Masʿudi, c.896–956); Green, 71–2.

too far away from a useful exegesis of the present passage. Staying well inside the Roman empire we might think of Mithraism too, though we are fooling ourselves if we claim to understand the planetary and zodiacal imagery of the cult.[97] And the third, which overlaps with the second, is the biblical tradition of warning against star-worship, which in the OT is treated as a threat both external and internal to the worshippers of Yahweh, and is then refurbished for warnings against pagan habits as Christianity spread.[98] But the poet is not offering any of these as models to his reader on how to approach the stars. This is a conceit, set against the background of the astrologer's respect for the stars and reverence for their powers, in which the full panoply of pagan cult is extended in fancy to all the heavenly bodies.

196 Τίπτε μάτην, ἄνθρωπε: while there are endless permutations on the 'why in vain' motif (especially in Christian polemicists), it tends especially to be used in two relevant contexts, (i) 'why worship x in vain',[99] and (ii) 'why vainly struggle against Fate',[100] and a series of specifically poetic parallels for 'why, O man?'[101] suggest that the poet is adapting the pattern of a literary sermon/diatribe. (i) The Sibylline Oracles deploy it in the argument 'do not worship x, worship y': Or. Sib. 3.8–9 ἄνθρωποι θεόπλαστον ἔχοντες ἐν εἰκόνι μορφήν | τίπτε μάτην πλάζεσθε; cf. fr. 1.1–2 + fr. 3.21 ἄνθρωποι, τί μάτην ὑψούμενοι ἐκριζοῦσθε ... In their case, the target is Egyptian animal-worship. (ii) The argument 'why struggle vainly against Fate' is found in Palladas (4th c. AD), AP 10.77.1–2 Τίπτε

---

[97] N. M. Swerdlow, 'Review Article: On the Cosmical Mysteries of Mithras [review of David Ulansey, *The Origins of the Mithraic Mysteries: Cosmology and Salvation in the Ancient World* (New York and Oxford, 1989)]', *CPh* 86 (1991), 48–63. Celsus does tell us about seven grades of initiation associated with the seven planets (Origen, *Cels.* 6.22), and Porphyry, *De Antro Nympharum*, 24, interprets the imagery of the bull relief in astral terms (the bull is Taurus, sign of Venus, and Mithras carries the sword of Aries, sign of Mars).

[98] *Const. Apol.* 5.12 (citing Deut. 4:19 now in a warning against oaths by the stars). The *Doctrina Addai* (late 4th c.) warns the people of Edessa against the practices of their pagan neighbours, including worship of the Sun and Moon, as in Harran (Green, 61, 63).

[99] e.g. Aesop, *Fab.* 129.1: a dog asks a crow why she sacrifices in vain to a goddess who hates her (τί μάτην τὰς θυσίας ἀναλίσκεις; —but here there is an answer: the crow thinks to overcome the goddess's antipathy). Julian has a new variant on the argument from impersonal providence which he turns against the Christians: *Contra Galilaeos*, 138 B–C, p. 184 εἰ μὲν οὖν ἄνευ προνοίας μείζονος καὶ θειοτέρας ταῦτα συνηνέχθη τὰ μείζω καὶ τιμιώτερα, τί μάτην περιεργαζόμεθα καὶ θεραπεύομεν τὸν μηδὲν προνοοῦντα; Julian's main argument is 'Why should we care for a god who sends you prophets and not us?'; but the way he musters his evidence suggests rather 'Why worship the Christian god given that there is such demonstrable diversity among human races that there is no reason to suppose that there is a providence that cares for us in particular?'

[100] Paus. 4.21.10.

[101] Another group asks why we inflict so much on ourselves in this vale of tears etc., e.g. Ephrem Syrus, *Quod ludicris rebus abstinendum sit christianis*, p. 247.8 Τί μάτην ταράσσῃ, ἄνθρωπε; *Canon de requie Andreae Cretensis*, 87 (7th–8th c.), Ὦ ἄνθρωποι, τί μάτην κοπιῶμεν ἐν τῇ προσκαίρῳ ζωῇ; *Euchologia, Officia Ecclesiastica*, 23.4.654 Ἄνθρωποι, τί μάτην ταραττόμεθα; ὁ δρόμος ταχὺς καὶ τραχύς ἐστιν.

μάτην, ἄνθρωπε, πονεῖς καὶ πάντα ταράσσεις | κλήρῳ δουλεύων τῷ κατὰ τὴν γένεσιν, and *IG* II² 11267 (Attica, 2nd/3rd c. AD) τίπτε μάτην, ὦ ξεῖνε, κεναῖς φρεσὶ σαῖσι πέποιθας; | δέρκεο μὴ δαίμων ἐχθρὸς ὄπισθε γελᾶι· | οὐδὲν ἐν ἀνθρώποις γὰρ ἀριφραδές· εἴ σε μέλει σῶν, | ἴσθ᾿ ὅτι τῶν πάντων Μοῖρα κρατεῖ γε μόνη. These occurrences suggest its conventional nature, and in view of that it does not seem possible to arrange the evidence into a stemma. The Sibylline passages possibly take it back as far as Hellenistic Judaism, though their history and the relationship between them is extremely complicated,[102] and the only available date is the *terminus ante quem* for the fragments supplied by the composition of the *Ad Autolycum* apparently in the 180s.

197 ~ *Il.* 1.317 κνίση δ᾿ οὐρανὸν ἷκεν ἑλισσομένη. τρισέλικτος, *vl* for τριέλικτος, occurs in the citation of Aratus, 816 (epithet of a halo round the Moon) in *De Astrol. Dialog.* p. 68.5 and Synesius, *De insomn.* 16; MSS of Aratus all have τριέλικτος. The prefix is now a vague intensifier (G.-P. on Leonidas, *AP* 6.110.2 = *HE* 2552). For more passages see Martin on Aratus, loc. cit.

198 The beginning of the line reworks an EGHP formula of prohibition (*Il.* 2.247 ἴσχεο, μηδ᾿ ἔθελ᾿ οἶος; *Od.* 22.356 ἴσχεο, μηδέ τι τοῦτον…; *HHom. Aphr.* 290 ἴσχεο μηδ᾿ ὀνόμαινε), and the poet's sense that a negative should follow the imperative has apparently overridden any inhibition about hiatus. The end comes from Ap. Rhod. 2.156 ἀθανάτοισι θυηλάς (ῥέξαντες). It is replayed, still with the plural, in Orph. *Lith.* 743 θυηλὰς ἀθανάτοισιν (ἐξαῦτις ῥέζοντας), Musaeus, 53, and Quint. Smyrn. 12.500, but with a singular in Quint. Smyrn. 14.258 ἐς ⟨ἀ⟩θανάτοιο θυηλάς (where, however, the passage concerns a particular deity, rather than, as here with Koechly's emendation, divinity in general).

199–203 Nothing can avert the fate that is allocated to us at our birth. This is the premise of astrology, and of the Manethoniana in particular: see i. 7, 60 nn. 66 and 69, 61, and on 5.18–19 (= *Il.* 6.488–9). When the Homeric poems mention this, the point is usually the fulfilment (in death) of what was then allocated (*Il.* 20.127–8; 23.78–9; 24.209–10). *Il.* 6.488–9 declared it impossible to escape one's fate (death). This has now been reformulated as the inability to avert fate, conceived as the totality of what has been determined, and that is the point that is made over and over by the astrologers: Valens, V 6.10; Firmicus, 1.7.9 *fortunae contra se saevientis invidiam vitare non potuit* (Alcibiades), 4.20.8…*ut mors imminens vel periculum nulla possit ratione vitari*; cf. i. 13–14 and n. 42, the story of Domitian and Ascletarion; Firmicus, 1.7.14–22, on

---

[102] The fragments are cited by Theophilus, *Ad Autol.* 2.36, who locates them ἐν ἀρχῇ τῆς προφητείας αὐτῆς. The general view of the passage from the head of book 3 is that it does not belong with the rest of the book, from which it is divided by a section heading in one of the main groups of manuscripts, but see V. Nikiprowetsky, *La Troisième Sibylle* (Paris, 1970), 61–6, for an attempt to take it, along with the fragments, back to the earliest, Jewish, Sibyl.

The Book Proper 825

Plotinus' vain aspiration to control his destiny (i. 10), though this is about overcoming by strength of will (*superare*) rather than averting. On the other hand, this apparently lumpen determinism does not quite go as far as to deny that there might be other things, as the Middle Platonists said, that *are* contingent or within our power to change. It takes no position on the relation between Fate and Tyche (although Tyche had had a mention at 1.67). And it does not correspond to Stoicism insofar as the Stoics advocated suicide under certain circumstances as a way for the individual to assert control over *Fortuna* when she was hostile.

199 ~ *Od*. 3.89 οὐ γάρ τις δύναται σάφα εἰπέμεν, and for the rhythm of the end of the line *Il*. 7.36 πόλεμον καταπαυσέμεν ἀνδρῶν. γένεσις is one of the technical terms for a horoscope (Heilen 2015, 536–7), though the Manethoniana (M^a, M^b) substitute γενέθλη, as does Maximus. Conversely, γένεσις has its technical meaning neither here nor in 5.12 (q.v.); here it abridges 'the fate allocated at birth', and is not the birth chart itself. The meaning of the new infinitive (Homer has only μετατρέπεσθαι, always middle = 'pay heed to') is not quite captured by any of LSJ's entries; for 'turn in a different direction', 'divert', see Lucian, *Jup. Confut*. 11 οὐ γὰρ οἶμαι δυνατὸν εἶναι οὐδὲ αὐταῖς ἔτι ταῖς Μοίραις ἀλλάξαι τι καὶ μετατρέψαι τῶν ἐξ ἀρχῆς δοξάντων περὶ ἑκάστου. The future tense after δύναμαι is unusual to say the least, though see K.–G. i. 185, §389.5c *fin*.

200 συγγίγνεται: i. 60 n. 69, 61. The cadence is like *HHom. Aphr*. 245 παρίσταται ἀνθρώποισιν (old age).

201–2 The vocabulary is similar to 1.6–7 (see on 4–7, and for μίτ- see on 7), but the idea is a bit muddled. The fate should be threads wound around the spindles. It should not be wound around the threads themselves.

202 κλώσμασιν ἀρρήκτοισι: for the verb κλώθειν see Giannakis 1998, 7; the noun on its first occurrence means 'cord' (so Gow–Scholfield render Nic. fr. 72.1). In this sense, the thread spun by the Fates, it is the language of epitaphs (*IEpidamnos* 58, l. 4 κλώσμασι μοιριδίοις; *IG* XII/7 123.4–5 (Amorgos) ἅρπασμ' ἐγενήθην | αἰφνιδίου μοίρης, κλώσματα θεῖα τελῶν; *IGUR* iii. 1208.10–11 (Rome, n.d.) κ[λώ]σμασι μοιριδίο̣[ις]), and will duly become Byzantine novelistic cliché.[103]

σιδηρείοισί τ' ἀτράκτοις: the Fates' threads are spun on brazen spindles in Lyc. *Al*. 584–5, but for these purposes, bronze, iron, and indeed adamant are all much of a muchness (Lightfoot on *Or. Sib*. 2.227–8). They suggest (i) inexorability

---

[103] *Belthandrus et Chrysantza*, 738–9 πολλὰ γὰρ ἔνι ἀδύνατον ἄνθρωπον εἰς τὸν κόσμον τὴν εἱμαρμένην ἐκφυγεῖν καὶ τὸ τῆς τύχης κλῶσμα; Andronicus Palaeologus, *Callimachus et Chrysorrhoe*, 703–5 Κλῶσμα τῆς τύχης δυστυχὲς ἐκλώσθη μου καὶ μοίρας καὶ πάλιν ἐπικλώθει με τὸ κακομοίρασμά μου ἀπὸ δυστυχοκλώσματος πτεροῦ τῆς Ἀφροδίτης.

(Ov. Met. 15.781 *ferrea... veterum decreta sororum*, 810 *ex aere et solido rerum tabularia ferro*, inscribed with the records of Fate; Stat. *Theb.* 3.556 *ferrea Clotho*) and (ii) cosmic architecture, and are just as good at evoking thoughts of the epic heavens (Steiner on *Od.* 17.565) and Hades (*Il.* 8.15). There is an exact match in Claudian, *Rapt. Pros.* 1.53 *longaque ferratis evolvunt saecula fusis*.

203–4 For the order of the planets, which is qualitative, see on 16–17. This very order is found (minus luminaries) in a Demotic ostrakon (D 521 of the Strassburg collection); cf. O. Neugebauer, 'Demotic Horoscopes', *JAOS* 63 (1943), 115–27, at 121–2; M. Ross, 'A Survey of Demotic Astrological Texts', *Culture and Cosmos*, 11 (2007), 1–25, at 13–15 (though it is not correct to say that 'As Neugebauer notes, the text preserves the "younger" Mesopotamian planetary order': it does not, and Neugebauer did not say it did: he observed, rather, that it obeyed the same qualitative principle with Mercury separating malefics from benefics). The first editor of the ostrakon placed it in the first century AD, but the principles that it uses in its list could be older. Gundel and Gundel, 163 n. 63, report that examples are found in Egyptian tombs and temples of the 19th and 20th dynasties (1292–1069 BC), but to be strictly accurate what is found, in a list from the Valley of the Kings, is the order Saturn–Mars–Jupiter–Mercury–Venus (Boll, *RE* s.v. Hebdomas, 2564.39) which, by inverting Jupiter and Mercury, spoils what would *later* be the qualitative principle—which presumably, at this date, no one had heard of anyway. The ostrakon also contains a list of months in which the year begins with Scorpio, and Neugebauer showed that that would have held true in the Egyptian calendar for 250 BC and the following century. So in principle this could be a modification of a Seleucid planetary ordering which had reached Egypt in the Hellenistic period. As for the luminaries, there are indeed Seleucid Babylonian cases where the qualitative order of planets is followed by Moon + Sun (F. Rochberg, 'Benefic and Malefic Planets in Babylonian Astrology', in ead., *In the Path of the Moon: Babylonian Celestial Divination and its Legacy* (Leiden, 2010), 135–42, at 136–7, 142).

203 καὶ Κυθερείῃ: this hexameter-ending is strongly associated with lists. That was already the case in the first occurrence, 6.139 Ἑρμείης τε καὶ Ἄρης καὶ Κυθέρεια, and remains true in the *Dionysiaca* (3.444 Κρονίωνι καὶ Ἄρεϊ καὶ Κυθερείῃ; 8.418 Ζηνὶ καὶ Ἑρμάωνι καὶ Ἄρεϊ καὶ Κυθερείῃ, which names the same three planets as in 6.139; also Ἀδώνιδι καὶ Κυθερείῃ, Παλλάδι καὶ Κυθερείῃ, Ἄρεϊ καὶ Κυθερείῃ). The other two examples of the ending in this book are a modified form of list as well (58, 224... Μήνης μέτα καὶ Κυθερείης), and while there is no sign that Nonnus has an eye on this poet one might wonder about some sort of contact or common source with M[a].

204 Ἠελίῳ βασιλῆϊ: see i. 908 n. 10, and see on 3.219-20. The cadence is adapted from Ἠελίῳ καταδύντι or ἀνιόντι crossed with *Il.* 11.262 Ἀτρεΐδη βασιλῆϊ; *Od.* 13.62 Ἀλκινόῳ βασιλῆϊ; the poet has not bothered to heal the resulting hiatus that precedes the proper name unless one has recourse to <τε> at the caesura (p. 308).

205 Adapting predications of Zeus like *Il.* 2.669 ἐκ Διός, ὅς τε θεοῖσι καὶ ἀνθρώποισιν ἀνάσσει (Fehling, 277), *Od.* 16.265 ἀνδράσι τε κρατέουσι καὶ ἀθανάτοισι θεοῖσι (sc. Zeus and Athena), and the phrase-pattern of Hes. *Th. bis* θεῶν βασιλῆϊ καὶ ἀνδρῶν, fr. 10(a) 9 M.-W. θεῶν βασί]λεια καὶ ἀνδρῶν. The anaphora of the verb dins the message home.

206-7 For the list of the components of the cosmos, see on 140-1. They are the same here (and the earth is adorned with fruits), save for the addition of the winds, and that adds to Koechly's case for attributing them to the same poet. The winds go with the waters (cf. *IK* Kyme, 41 §39 ἐγὼ ποταμῶν καὶ ἀνέμων [κ]αὶ θαλάσσης εἰμὶ κυρία), while in other lists of cosmic elements they go with the sky (Isidore, *Hymn* 1.10 καὶ πνοιαὶ ἀνέμων καὶ ἥλιος ὁ γλυκυφεγγής) or bridge the two (Isidore, *Hymn* 4.13; Xenophanes, 21 B 30.5-6 ἀλλὰ μέγας πόντος γενέτωρ νεφέων ἀνέμων τε | καὶ ποταμῶν, which has a great deal of overlap with this passage).

206 The collocation of πόντος and ποταμός suggests cosmic lists, but no particular model (Hes. *Th.* 109 καὶ ποταμοὶ καὶ πόντος ἀπείριτος οἴδματι θυίων; Dion. Per. 1-2, 1183-4; *Or. Sib.* 1.13; Opp. *Hal.* 2.526). ῥόθιος normally goes together with turbulent water (Eur. *Hel.* 1502-3; Opp. *Hal.* 1.231-2), but with winds in Eur. *Phaethon*, l. 80 ἀνέμων τ' εὐαέσσιν ῥοθίοις (see Diggle ad loc.), and apparently again in Dionysius, *Gigantias*, fr. 51v (77v Livrea) 7 Benaissa. ῥοθίων could therefore belong to the preceding or (with easy postponement of τε: p. 286) following noun, or be impressionistically placed to suggest the turbulence of both winds and choppy waters.

207 A polar expression of sorts, but ἀήρ here, as in 140, is less 'sky' (for which the usual word in polar expressions is οὐρανός) than an element in this world which the planets rule, in other words the lower air (4.37 n.). ἀέννaos shows the typical drift away from the basic sense 'flowing'; it has extended to other elements already in Pind. *P.* 1.6 αἰενάου πυρός, cf. Williams on Call. *Hymn* 2.83, and is totally degraded in *Or. Sib.* 8.309 χθονὸς ἀενάοιο. A precedent for air in Ar. *Nub.* 275 ἀέναοι Νεφέλαι, and Hippocr. *Flat.* 3.3 ὁ ἀὴρ ἀέναος (among the *veteres*, the epithet is missing in A but present in M and Vat).

1.208–76 Miscellanea

208–14

Moon and Jupiter. There are three situations covered here and presumably one is missing:

(i) Full Moon approaching Jupiter (208–9)
(ii) Full Moon leaving Jupiter (210–11)
(iii) Waning Moon approaching Jupiter (212–14)
(iv) <Waning Moon leaving Jupiter>

Firmicus is more use here than *Π.σ.α.*, which does not deal with the contingency of Moon phase.

208 Κρονίωνι: i. 910 n. 2.

συναντήσασα: συνανταν and especially συνάντησις are entirely normal in prose for one star, especially the Moon and Sun, encountering another.[104] Here it could be set down to the prosaic lexicon of elegiacs, but at 1.245, its only other occurrence in the Manethoniana, it is in hexameters, suggesting little stylistic differentiation between the two metres.

209 With the line as a whole compare 1.352, which also involves *synaphe*, there of Saturn with the Moon. καὶ μακαριστοτάτους is also used in 2.476 of the Moon leaving Mars for Jupiter, who is there called Κρονίδη for the only time in M^a (i. 900). Might that point to an ultimately shared source, presumably poetic? As for felicity, compare Firmicus, 4.3.1 *Si Luna se Iovis applicaverit stellae et, crescens lumine, ista se societate coniunxerit vel ad Iovem feratur, faciet felices, gloriosos, divites, multorum et magnorum fundamentorum et latissimarum possessionum dominos.*

210 πλήθουσα Σελήνη: *Il.* 18.484 σελήνην τε πλήθουσαν.

211 Far more calamitous in *Π.σ.α.* p. 182.26–8. Firmicus has no parallel, because his *aporrhoia* charts involve two factors (Moon from *x* to *y*).

212 κακῶν ῥεκτεῖρα: this puts it far more strongly than Firmicus, 4.3.2, for whom the outcome is not positively bad, but the natives are adopted, or exposed, and only later reunited with their parents; they make their own livings and acquire wealth over time (provided Mars is absent). The noun is *hapax* (ῥέκτης,

---

[104] The Moon: e.g. Ptol. 3.13.12; Paul, pp. 90.3–4, 92.20, 95.7; *CCAG* i. 127.33; Apomasar, *De Myst.*, *CCAG* xi/1. 173.25. The Sun: 'Heliodorus', pp. 127.27–128.2.

a doer, a proactive individual, is first in Plut. *Brut.* 12.5, but only really common in Byzantine writers; in 4.149 ῥεκτῆρας are 'makers').

213 The least interesting of these epithets is αἰνομόρους, a bland EGHP 'misfortune' word. ἔκφρονας is unique in astrology. Of the possible meanings 'stupid' or 'maddened', the latter is likelier: even when the Moon is waxing, according to Firmicus, the natives are prophetic (*aut propria animi divinitate*...), i.e. a little crazy. νοσερούς is strange, because almost all of its occurrences in astrology (except *Π.σ.α.* p. 184.4, *aporrhoia* from Mercury, and Θ p. 139.13, Saturn in the second place) involve Mars, whose presence is explicitly discussed by Firmicus (4.3.3 *aut ipsi certe fiunt parte quadam corporis debiles*). Has the poet omitted it?

214 ἀμβλύτερόν τ': used of both stellar (Dorotheus, p. 380.11, 21; Valens, II 17.82; 2.409 n.) and psychic (Ptol. 3.14.4, 37) enfeeblement.

215–22 + 223

Mars and Jupiter in opposition; Mars on MC. See on 3.295–308. There is complete unanimity in the comparanda[105] for opposition on unevenness (3.306 ἀνωμαλίην βιότου; Περὶ σχημ. 77 ἀνώμαλον ποιεῖ τὸν βίον, Περὶ κράσ. 129 πᾶσαν ἀνωμαλίαν καὶ σκέδασιν τοῦ βίου; Firmicus, 6.16.1 *omnem vitae inaequalitatem*), which in all sources except Mᵃ tends to net loss rather than alternation. The attribution of the opposite effects to the respective characters of each planet, the one a force for good, the other for harm, is paralleled in Περὶ κράσεως, there of the rupture of friendship. None of these sources specifies that the planets are both on *kentra*, but if that detail is sound, which it apparently is, it is clearly out of place; Koechly replaced the first half of 218 before 216 ἀνωμαλίην βιότοιο and shifted the first halves of the next two lines down a line. One notes the reference to a *kentron* in the next chart (224); that this poet uses κέντρον ἔχειν more often than others in the corpus (also 123, 224, and Dorotheus, p. 432.10); and the very similar chart at 1.267–70, in which Saturn joins Mars and the locations are now specified as ASC/DESC, in which ἀνωμαλία is once again the result (see ad loc.).

215 κατεναντίον ἀλλήλοισιν: the language of purposeful movement, especially of hostile parties pitted against one another (pp. 292–3): *Il.* 11.67, *Th.* 646 ἐναντίοι ἀλλήλοισιν; *Scut.* 347 ὑπεναντίοι ἀλλήλοισιν (respectively of reapers, gods, and the horses of combatants); exactly as in *AP* 9.132.1 (Adesp.), of a head-on clash between hostile forces (Love and Chastity). For the preposition

---

[105] Interpreting Φαέθων as the Sun, Boll 1898, 203, compares Firmicus, 3.4.11; but see on 1.70.

see 90 n., 343 n. (there with genitives); again for the opposition of Jupiter and Mars in 268, which once more produces ἀνώμαλα ἔργα.

216 ἀνωμαλίην βιότοιο: i. 168. Add Kroll, *CCAG* v/2. 143.

217 ἐκ φιλίης ἐλάσουσιν: Περὶ σχημ. 77 καὶ οἱ φίλοι ἐχθροὶ γίνονται; Περὶ κράσ. 129 καὶ τοὺς φίλους ἐχθροὺς ποιεῖ; Firmicus, 6.16.1 *Sed et omnium amicorum ex ista radiatione <...> et assiduis offensis contra illos odium concitatur.* For the verb, which appears as a marginal variant for ὁδάσουσι and was independently conjectured by D'Orville, see Monaco, 42.

218b The half-line *bon mot* is shaped like *Il.* 10.45 ἐπεὶ Διὸς ἐτράπετο φρήν, Aratus, 181 ἐπεὶ Διὸς ἐγγύθεν ἦσαν.

219 The run of plurals is in the astrological idiom. δόξαι are individual honours, and πίστιες (i. 307, 312–14) individual trusts, representing astrology's habitual use of πίστις in what Teresa Morgan calls a 'reified' sense,[106] referring to institutions, employments, transactions, objects, and so on, in which confidence in, or hope of, integrity is reposed. With plural σωφροσύναι, which is more unusual, the poet regards each bestowal as a separate gift, the usage paralleled in e.g. Ptol. 2.9.9 αὐξήσεις καὶ μεγαλειότητας καὶ μεγαλοψυχίας; Valens, II 17.7 ὁ γεννώμενος ἐν ταῖς μεγαλειότησι καὶ δόξαις ὄχλων γενήσεται. Camaterus agrees with Jupiter's gift of σωφροσύνη (*Zod.* 578 Καὶ σωφροσύνην μέχρις εἰς τέλος βίου: in the ASC), but otherwise this is not a typical 'Jupiter' word. One infers it means judiciousness, intelligence, in the same way as Jupiter contributes to the ἔμφρονας ἄνδρας of 226, rather than chastity (an effect Jupiter sometimes produces in company with Venus[107]), and a facet of the dignity or σεμνότης which Jupiter tends to produce in Ptolemy. For the overridden third-foot caesura, see on 1.46.

220 πενίη τε κακή: i. 158.

221 ἐγκλήσεις: accusations (Clem. Al. *Paed.* 1.9.80.2 Ἔγκλησις δέ ἐστι ψόγος ἀδικούντων; *SB* 14 11346.15 (AD 41–54) ἐγ]κλήσεως ἀδικημάτων). The usual noun in astrology is ἔγκλημα, ἐγκλήματα (2.296–9; 5.67 nn.). This form is much commoner than LSJ implies, but the present passage would be one of its earliest literary occurrences, and one of only two in astrology, the other being in the title of a chapter in one of the epitomes of Hephaestion (Περὶ κριτηρίων καὶ ἐγκλήσεων καὶ νίκης καὶ ἥττης).[108]

---

[106] Morgan, 6, and *passim*.
[107] Ptol. 4.5.18; Apomasar, *De Myst.*, *CCAG* xi/1. 174.23 σωφροσύνην... γυναικῶν.
[108] And perhaps in the title of the original chapter as well (i. 295.4), where Pingree prints ἐκκλήτου, which makes no sense. The chapter itself has the usual ἐγκλήματα.

222 Loss of wealth: 264; 6.632–3, 668, 673; i. Index: wealth—loss of. The unanimity of the comparanda about loss of wealth confirms Koechly's conjecture, or something like it; there is no place for tortuous paradox with ἐν εὐπορίῃ. The line thus takes its place in a long tradition of gnomai, some snappily formulated in a single line, others spilling over line-divisions, which pit wealth against poverty,[109] and especially on reciprocal gain and loss: Theogn. 661–3 καί τε πενιχρὸς ἀνήρ | αἶψα μάλ' ἐπλούτησε καὶ ὃς μάλα πολλὰ πέπαται | ἐξαπίνης ἀπό τ(οι) οὖν ὤλεσε νυκτὶ μιῆι. The subject is Zeus in Theogn. 156–7, and the reciprocal antithesis somewhat recalls divine predications where gods make great and then bring low again (Hes. *Op.* 5–6; *Th.* 447; Fehling, 306), especially the repetition of the word on which the reversal pivots in the two halves of the line (~ βριάει...βριάοντα).

223 τέλος αἰνὸν ἔχουσιν: 261 μόρον αἰνόν; 6.502 θανάτοιο τέλος τετληότας αἰνόν (different circumstances); Maximus, 307 τέλος δ' ἀναδέξεται αἰνόν (not death, but a poor outcome to surgical intervention). The rhythm is like ps.-Hes. *Scut.* 227 ζόφον αἰνὸν ἔχουσα.

224–8

Jupiter on *kentron* with (non-New) Moon and Venus.

225 φωσφορέουσα: see on 1.65.

226 ἔμφρονας ἄνδρας: the only other occurrence of this word in astrology also involves Jupiter and the Moon, this time in trine (Περὶ κράσ. 144 εὐκλεεῖς καὶ ἔμφρονας). Ptolemy's Jupiter produces μεγαλόφρονας (3.14.20).

227 The στρόφιον is a twisted cloth head-band worn by priests (LSJ II, adding Fest. 410.6–9 *Stroppus est, ut Ateius Philologus existimat, quod graece* στρόφιον *vocatur et quod sacerdotes pro insigni habent in capite*, cf. 472.15–16, 473.4–5; in Pollux, 8.94, by Athenian νομοφύλακες). It is shown in religious iconography, especially, for the priests at Eleusis, in combination with a leaf wreath.[110] As a badge of distinction, when the Eleusinian Dadouchos wears one

---

[109] Differential treatment of rich and poor: Theogn. 621, 929–30; wealth distributed inequitably: Solon, fr. 15.1 W. = Theognis, 314; Theogn. 751–2.
[110] L. Robert, *Hellenica*, 11–12 (1960), 452 and pl. XXVIII, and 597, *BE* 1961, 267, and 1982, 260; D. Salzmann, 'Ein Priesterbild in Zadar', *Boreas*, 18 (1995), 101–4; E. B. Harrison, 'Eumolpos Arrives in Eleusis', *Hesperia*, 69 (2000), 267–91, at 275; M. Horster and T. Schröder, 'Priests, Crowns and Priestly Headdresses in Imperial Athens', in B. Alroth and C. Scheffer (eds.), *Attitudes towards the Past in Antiquity: Creating Identities: Proceedings of an International Conference held at Stockholm University, 15–17 May 2009* (Stockholm, 2014), 233–9, at 235–6; Thonemann 2021, 158.

in Plut. *Arist.* 5.7, a barbarian mistakes him for a king. When a painter wears one, together with a purple cloak, in Athen. 12.543 F, it is a sign of luxury.

229–34

Malefics setting; luminaries opposite. This is a variation on a number of madness charts, involving one or both malefics and one or both luminaries (at New or Full Moon; New here), sometimes a relationship of opposition, and sometimes specifically the ASC and DESC. Compare for instance, Valens, II 37.43 (malefics in various positions including in opposition to the New or Full Moon), where Riley renders θεῶν ἢ νεκρῶν εἰδωλοποιητάς 'men who see visions of the gods or the dead', and LSJ renders εἰδωλοποιητής 'seer of phantoms' (rather than a manufacturer of images).

Θ's chapter Περὶ μαινομένων καὶ ἐπιληπτικῶν begins with several charts that involve opposition across the ASC/DESC, one or both luminaries, and one or both malefics. The closest similarity is with p. 192.13–14, while pp. 193.9–10 and 193.20–2 are also relevant. Π.σ.α. p. 183.19–20, has a chart involving both malefics, though not specifying their location. A textual manipulation in 4.473 produces a similar configuration, but see my commentary on 472–7 (I reject it). Other ghostly/visionary outcomes: (i) Θ p. 194.2–3 ὑπὸ εἰδώλων φοβεριζομένους (a malefic in IMC); (ii) Θ p. 193.5 νεκυομάντεις (Mars and Mercury centred, aspected by Saturn and Moon); (iii) 4.555, visions of the dead (Full Moon at node and Mars 'with them' (sc. both luminaries?)); (iv) 4.365, nightmares of the dead (Mars in quartile to Mercury).

230 καταντίον: see i. 887 and n. 103. The phrase is similar to Anubion, F 12.36 = Perale 12 κατ{εν}αντίον Ἡελίο[ιο].

231 ἐμμανέας: see on 91.

232 νεκύων σκιοειδέα μορφήν: for visions of the dead, see i. 360, adding Cumont, 166 n. 5, and nn. on 4.554, 555. This passage is particularly interesting in connection with the suggestion of epilepsy in 234. While the cadence is suitably similar to the uncanny Homeric formula νεκύων ἀμενηνὰ κάρηνα, the epithet is used as it is in Plato's much-quoted passage in the *Phaedo* about unpurified souls which continue to cling to the phenomenal world, especially in the vicinity of tombs (Plato, *Phaed.* 81 D ψυχῶν σκιοειδῆ φαντάσματα).[111] Unlike some allusions in later authors who may no longer even mean ghosts at

---

[111] The other main way in which the adjective is used in the miserabilist view of human life (man is a shadow of a dream etc.): Ar. *Av.* 686 σκιοειδέα φῦλ' ἀμενηνά, al.

all,[112] the spirits of the dead remain, but the emphasis is on the subjective experience of the visionary, the psychological abnormality (as in 4.555 ψυχῇ δερκόμενοι); Plato's cosmology has become irrelevant. Nonnus also has a number of similar line-endings, in connection with false forms (D. 8.324 τύπῳ σκιοειδέι μορφῆς [for τύπος, see on 4.558], 43.242 σκιοειδέι μορφῇ), dreams (10.266 σκιοειδέα φάσματα μορφῆς, 29.327 νόθῃ σκιοειδέι μορφῇ); or reflections (48.586, like 10.266).

233 εὐφρονέοντες: whether to emend to ἐμφρονέοντες, as one would expect for 'sane' as opposed to mad, depends on how much respect one has for the *lectio difficilior* (Xenophanes, B 1 13 εὔφρονας ἄνδρας = right-thinking is not really a parallel). The beginning of the line is like Ὀλύμπια δώματ' ἔχοντες (with rhyme at mid-line in HHom. Dem. 135, Op. 81), and the end has a casual similarity to Quint. Smyrn. 7.279 ἀεικέα πήματα πάσχειν.

234 πίπτουσιν συνόδοισι: this adds nothing to the configuration, for we already knew from 230 that this was a New Moon. Given the strong association between epilepsy and the Moon, especially when New (i. 356 n. 54; Stol 1993, 124–5, 130: the reference in n. 29 to the magical papyrus should be Suppl. Mag. 99 recto ii τῆς ἱερᾶς λυσ[| τὴν νεομηνί[αν; P. Grunert, 'Historische Konzepte der Epilepsie aus klinischer Sicht', in J. Althoff, S. Föllinger, G. Wöhrle (edd.), *Antike Naturwissenschaft und ihre Rezeption. 21* (Trier, 2011), 89–134, at 96 n. 10; Firmicus, 4.5 *alios facit caducos*; 6.31.76, with more factors), πίπτουσιν could suggest specifically the falling sickness (Temkin, 85–6), which is not an exclusively Latin figure of speech, and which has many Greek renderings such as πτωματικούς, πτωματισμούς, and πτωματιζομένους (i. 357 n. 61; 3.55 n.; Cumont, 168 n. 5; Stol 1993, 123, 133).[113] One of the Babylonian terms for epilepsy (though neither confined to epilepsy nor the only term for it) was *miqtu*, from the verb *maqatu*, 'fall', but in the sense 'fall from heaven', or 'suddenly overtake' (Stol 1993, 9–12).

In the whole field of mental disturbance, epilepsy would be a suitable accompaniment to visions, particularly of the dead. The same nexus between mental

---

[112] Plato is quoted e.g. by Sallustius, *De Dis et Mundo*, 19.2; Origen, *Cels*. 2.60, 7.5. Clem. Al. *Protr*. 4.55.5, applies the passage to *daimones*, the same category including Olympian gods; Philostratus' Apollonius means spirits that deceive by giving a counterfeit appearance of reality (*Vit. Ap*. 6.11.6 ὅτε ψεύδοιντο εἴδη ἀνθρώπων, presumably like the spirit of the plague that he drove out of Ephesus); Iamblichus, *Myst*. 3.29, discusses, with characteristic opacity, man-made idols with no divinity in them.

[113] πτωματικούς in Valens, II 37.43 (p. 832), Θ p. 151.8–9 (Mars in IMC), Π.σ.α. p. 182.5 = CCAG v/1. 212.5 (waning Moon on empty course); πτωματισμούς in Ptol. 3.13.17, 4.9.7, Περὶ κράσ. 213; Paul, pp. 56.17–57.1 πτωματιζομένους.

disturbance and epilepsy that associated epilepsy with prophecy[114] facilitated its link with dreams and visions, which happened when the soul in its abnormal state was liberated from reason; epileptics are subject to nightmares in Aretaeus, *De Caus. et Sign. Diut. Morb.* 1.4.3 δυσόνειροι πολλοῖσι ἀλλοκότοισι, and for other Greek doctors night terrors could be a precursor of epilepsy (Stol 1993, 39; W. H. Roscher, *Ephialtes: Eine pathologisch-mythologische Abhandlung über die Alpträume und Alpdämonen des Klassischen Altertums* (Leipzig, 1990), 22). ὑπὸ ῥιπῆς well suggests onslaught—not unlike ἐφιάλτης, the demon of nightmare himself. The word has already been used of starlight (Soph. *El.* 105–6 παμφεγγεῖς ἄστρων | ῥιπάς), and is suitable for an overpowering impulse attributable to a divine power (Opp. *Hal.* 4.141, Quint. Smyrn. 3.729). Put these together, and it is a good word for light considered especially and uncannily potent (Stol 1993, 126–7; φωτοπλήξ of the Moon in *PGM* 4.2237–8).

235–44

Venus between malefics, aspecting Moon and Mercury. An interesting case. 4.214–17 and 6.491–3 have a similar situation, a conjunction of Venus and Saturn, to which Mars is appended. This situation is compatible with Θ p. 194.2–4, which locates them in the IMC. 235–44, however, exactly and impressively replicate the situation in Θ p. 192.16–18. This is the first of three charts involving ἐμπερίσχεσις of either Venus or the Moon (see on 1.250–5), almost in a row, interrupted only by 245–9.

The apodosis, as it is developed here, is remarkable. It pivots from a situation that looks characteristically Egyptian in 237–9, via self-inflicted harm, to a collection of topoi about *galli* in 241–4 (though the word is not used) which are generally, placelessly, Graeco-Roman (i. 119), but includes the motif of bloodiness which is predominantly Latin.

236 λεύσσωσι: 4.59 n.

237 φοιβητὰς: unique in literary texts, but there are φοιβηταὶ Ἀφρο(δίτης) in P.Count 3, i. 14 (229 BC, Arsinoe; W. Clarysse and D. J. Thompson, *Counting the People in Hellenistic Egypt* (Cambridge, 2006), text no. 3). The text, which is a tax register, specifies that five are female and two are male, but it does not shed much more light on their role or status, nor indeed on the identity of the 'Aphrodite' in question. Clarysse and Thompson connect their title with the verb φοιβάζω 'clean', 'purify' (i. 109, ii. 184 n. 361) rather than 'rave', 'prophesy',

---

[114] Temkin, 148–61. Temkin's discussions of visions and hallucinations become more prominent in the later stages of his book where he is discussing modern analyses of epilepsy which relate it to hysteria.

but they also render them 'prophets' of Aphrodite (ii. 200, cf. 202).[115] Anyhow, it is intriguing that they are listed immediately after παστοφόροι, for the latter are connected with dream interpretation, precisely the right context for the present passage (1.239 n.). For φοιβαζομένους see on 6.491-3.

237-8 οἴθ᾽ ἱεροῖσιν...μυθίζοντες: for dream interpreters, see on 2.206-8. What this passage tells us is that they 'sit' in temples, but not whether they are official temple staff—priests who have this role—or whether they were freelancers who congregated there because work was to be had there; nor does it tells us whether actual incubation is involved (the dreamer might in theory have had the dream anywhere and come to the shrine to have it interpreted). But there is a strong presumption in favour of an Egyptian origin for this detail, for dream interpreters are overwhelmingly a feature of the temples in Egypt, or, failing that, of temples of Egyptian deities outside Egypt (holders of official positions are known from Athens and Delos (L. Bricault, *Recueil des inscriptions concernant les cultes isiaques (RICIS)* (Paris, 2005), nos. 101/0206 ll. 16-17 and 202/0245 l. 13, respectively κρίνοντος τὰ ὁ|[ρ]άματα and ὀνειροκρί[του).[116]

Perhaps one should be struck that astrology has at this point been receptive to an Egyptian cultural practice. S. Kidd notes how, when Greek-speakers in Egyptian papyri write about dream interpretation, there is a tendency to slip into Egyptian, or at least to try to transliterate it. He also notes the enormous disparity between the representation of dream manuals in Greek and Demotic papyri (127-9): there are none in the former but ten in a ten-times smaller sample in Demotic. This leaves an impression that dream interpretation had a particularly elaborate apparatus in Demotic, although it was by no means a one-way street, for a Ptolemaic stele from Saqqara (Cairo CG 27567) in which a dream interpreter advertises his services—beautifully illustrated in Renberg, ii. 729, fig. 59—is in Greek. Obviously there is no point complaining about lack of detail here, but it is at least worth noting that astrology here apparently acknowledges popular religion, Egyptian temple-culture, and an activity that throve among Demotic as well as Greek speakers. Much more often there is occasion to note how much more air-time it gives to aspects of popular culture shared across the whole empire, or at least across the east of it (pp. 117-18).

239 Strictly, the text says that these people are 'in the detention of the gods'. This is the only occurrence in the Manethoniana of κατοχή, 'detention' or

---

[115] Ptol. 3.14.16 has φοιβαστικούς among mystics and ritual experts, though not prophets.

[116] Renberg, ii, appendix XIV, 717-34; 717 n. 1 on dream interpreters in sanctuaries outside Egypt. The Egyptian evidence suggests the existence of both priestly staff and private professionals, as well as—possibly—officials who offered dream consultation in their free time. Renberg, ii. 727 n. 29, thinks that the Alexandrian dream interpreters of Artemidorus, 4.80.1, were associated with the Serapeum.

'confinement', one of astrology's deliberately unspecific terms which can sometimes mean 'prison' in imperial texts (Delekat, 72–3), but which was chosen for its much wider potential range of reference.[117] This apparently extends in the present passage to the institution of κατοχή in temples, the nature of which has been so contested precisely because of the word's vagueness. There are several references to (ἐγ)κάτοχοι in astrological prose:[118] Ptol. 3.14.25 (Jupiter allied with Venus in dishonourable positions), Valens, II 8.4 (certain influences in the 9th house) ἐγκάτοχοι ἐν ἱεροῖς γίνονται παθῶν ἢ ἡδονῶν ἕνεκεν, II 17.49 (Mercury trine with Saturn) καὶ ἐν ἱεροῖς κάτοχοι γίνονται ἀποφθεγγόμενοι ἢ καὶ τῇ διανοίᾳ παραπίπτοντες, Θ p. 147.15 (Saturn in third place) ἐγκατόχους, ἀποφθεγγομένους, φιλοσόφους and p. 165.3–4 (Saturn in ninth place) ἐγκατόχους, ἀποφθεγγομένους, ὀνειροπόλους, φιλοσόφους. From the company they keep they seem to have two main associations. One (especially when they are associated with uncanny Saturn) is prophecy.[119] The matching chart in Θ lacks κατόχους, but it does have the ἀποφθεγγομένους with whom they are elsewhere linked; for astrological ἀποφθέγγεσθαι see 4.550 n. ('hymn-chanters' in Renberg, 732–3 n. 41, fails to capture the oracular overtone). The other is a sort of liability to pleasure or effeminacy (Valens and Ptolemy).[120] Is the implication that this kind of withdrawal is an abnegation of responsibility, that those attracted to this way of life are weak?

Detainees called κάτοχοι are best known from the Memphite Sarapeum, secondarily from Abydos, occasionally in temples of Egyptian gods outside Egypt, and very rarely in Syria.[121] The Memphis texts use both the adjective κάτοχος and the abstract noun κατοχή, as here. The association of κάτοχοι and dream interpreters has not been lost on those who have studied the institution of temple-dependence (P. Perdrizet–G. Lefebvre, *Les Graffites grecs du Memnonion d'Abydos* (Nancy, 1919), xviii; Delekat, 163–4; Legras, 16, 86); the backlash against overreading should not reduce it to mere happenstance (*contra*

---

[117] Deliberately multivalent in Valens, V 1.17 (Delekat, 166–7); studiedly vague in IV 7.5 κατοχὰς... εἴς τινας τόπους ἢ ἐπιμονάς; of wrestling holds in I 20.7; of hold-ups on a journey in Hephaestion, i. 285.5 κατοχὴν καὶ ἀναποδισμοὺς καὶ δυσχερείας.

[118] Cumont, 148–51; Legras, 89–90.

[119] Kroll, *CCAG* v/2. 147, apropos of this passage, rightly rejects the comparison with monks, but at the same time the κάτοχοι are more than 'homines aegrotos κατεχομένους (manentes) in templo et remedia morborum a dis eorumque sacerdotibus expectantes'.

[120] Reitzenstein, 85, romantically takes the παθῶν ἢ ἡδονῶν to be, not past experiences, but the pains and pleasures of askesis.

[121] Versnel, 65–6 n. 91; Alvar, 306 n. 399; Thompson, 201 and n. 12; Ahmad, 216–17. Add *RAC* s.v. Gefangenschaft (S. Arbandt–W. Macheiner), 338. Κάτοχοι of Aphrodite in Baalbek in *IGLS* VI 2733 (AD 60); Ahmad, 227–8. For temples of Egyptian gods outside Egypt, see Alvar, 306 and nn. 399, 400. On Papinius (*IK Smyrna*, 725 (AD 211–12) Παπίνιος ὁ φιλόσοφος ἐγκατοχήσας τῷ κυρίῳ Σαράπιδι παρὰ ταῖς Νεμέσεσιν), see also L. Deubner, *De Incubatione: Capita Quattuor* (Leipzig, 1900), 6–7 n. 3. For self-dedication in temples, not using the term κάτοχος, Richard Gordon (*OCD*⁴ s.v. Sarapis) adds *IG* V/2 472 (Megalopolis, 2nd/3rd c. AD: λάτρις and πρόπολος) and Apul. *Met.* 11.9 (Lucius in the temple of Isis in Cenchreae).

Renberg, 732-3 n. 41). It does not necessarily mean that these individuals were themselves dream interpreters, although that has sometimes been suggested, mainly on the basis of the archive of the best-known of them, Ptolemaios and Apollonios sons of Glaucias (172-152 BC),[122] which makes frequent reference to dreams.[123] Ptolemaios himself is likely at least to have kept company with dream interpreters, since he spent his 'detention' in the *pastophorion* in a shrine of Astarte within the Memphite Serapeum[124] and since, according to Renberg, the παστοφόροι were those priests who, among all the Egyptian cult personnel, mostly likely functioned as dream interpreters.[125] What matters more than individual situations is the simple, assumed, casual transition from the one category to the other, which does strongly support, if not guarantee, an Egyptian temple setting.

239-40 πεπεδημένοι αἰεί... ἀρρήκτοισιν: in the long debate about the status of κάτοχοι, this passage, insofar as it glosses or interprets ἐν κατοχαῖσι, lends no support to the idea that it refers to possession.[126] This is physical detention.[127] But it is self-inflicted, so neither is there any support for attempts to interpret the word and institution in terms of imprisonment for unpaid dues or desertion, or even slavery (at least, not unless it is voluntarily undergone).[128]

And apparently it is literal. One can certainly speak metaphorically of slavery, of 'bonds', in connection with religious devotion,[129] of being 'bound' by a vow,[130] and one can use πεπεδημένοι figuratively (*Or. Sib.* 1.342, 371). But it is

---

[122] Legras, 169-89.

[123] J. Ray, *Reflections of Osiris: Lives from Ancient Egypt* (Oxford, 2002), 140-6 (+ 148-52 on the priest and possible dream interpreter Hor) and id., 'The Dreams of the Twins in St Petersburg', in K. Szpakowska (ed.), *Through a Glass Darkly: Magic, Dreams, and Prophecy in Ancient Egypt* (Swansea, 2006), 189-203; W. Clarysse and K. Vandorpe, 'A Demotic Lease of Temple Land Reused in the "Katochoi" Archive (Louvre N 2328a)', *AncSoc* 36 (2006), 1-11, at 1; S. Kidd, 117-22; Legras, 91, 131, 168, 216-25, 232-3, 234-5, 256-9; Renberg, i. 398-403; G. Jennes, 'Life Portraits: People in Worship', in K. Vandorpe (ed.), *A Companion to Greco-Roman and Late Antique Egypt* (Hoboken, NJ, 2019), 473-81, at 474-5. Kidd wonders on 125 whether Ptolemaios and his brother Apollonios are using dream manuals. Consider also the significance of dreams for the quasi-κάτοχος Lucius in Apul. *Met.* 11.20.

[124] S. E. Thomas, 'The "Pastophorion": "Priests' houses" in Legal Texts from Ptolemaic Pathyris and Elsewhere in Egypt', *JEA* 99 (2013), 155-69, at 160, and 'The "Pastophorion" Revisited: Owners and Users of "Priests' Houses" in Ptolemaic Pathyris and Elsewhere in Egypt', *JEA* 100 (2014), 111-32, at 118.

[125] Renberg, ii. 726, 730, 733; cf. J. D. Ray, *The Archive of Ḥor* (London, 1976), 136.

[126] Perdrizet and Lefebvre (p. 836), xviii; Reitzenstein, 79.   [127] Reitzenstein, 79-82.

[128] Legras, 17, 18, 19-20. For κατοχή as imprisonment, see *BGU* vi. 1297.5, 248 BC.

[129] Reitzenstein, 77-8; H. W. Pleket, 'Religious History as the History of Mentality: The "Believer" as Servant of the Deity in the Greek World', in H. S. Versnel (ed.), *Faith, Hope and Worship: Aspects of Religious Mentality in the Ancient World* (Leiden, 1981), 152-92; Versnel, 65-6, 88-91; Lightfoot 2003, 530, 538; C. Hezser, 'Slavery and the Jews', in Bradley and Cartledge, 438-55, at 450, and J. Glancy, 'Slavery and the Rise of Christianity', op. cit. 456-81, at 457-9; C. Martínez Maza, 'Los lenguajes de la sumisión en los cultos egipcios', Όρμος: *Ricerche di storia antica*, 3 (2011), 180-8.

[130] Sulpicius Severus, *Vita Martini* 2.5 *catenatus sacramentis militaribus*.

hard to believe that the poet would have spoken very concretely of 'the person' (even if he were lifting a cadence from earlier poetry, which he is), if he had meant this figuratively. Both Reitzenstein, and, after him, Versnel, have taken this passage literally,[131] even though the other known pagan κάτοχοι do not seem to be behaving in so extreme a way (Ptolemaios refers to his restriction in the temple as a physical inability to leave it (UPZ I 4, verso, ll. 9–10 [ἐμοῦ δὲ χάρ]ιν [το]ῦ Σαράπιος χωρισθῆναι | [οὐ δυναμένο]υ), but gives no indication that he was literally chained up). Closer, perhaps, is a Lydian *Beichtinschrift* where a god (Men?) proclaims the release of a penitent after confinement in a φυλακή for a year and ten months (*SEG* 38.1237). A psychological element could be involved here (feelings of guilt?), but we learn nothing of the character of this confinement (G. Petzl, 'Sünde, Strafe, Wiedergutmachung', *EA* 12 (1988), 155–66, at 165). The apparently 'obvious' analogy with the chains-and-iron version of Christian asceticism is hampered by the fact that this was far more a feature of Syrian than of Egyptian Christianity, so it is not necessarily right to assume that this was simply an indigenous religious practice.[132]

240 δεσμοῖσιν...ἑὸν δέμας ἀρρήκτοισιν: I have no particular suggestions for what this was contrasted with (μέν) in the next, missing line (do they mutilate themselves as well?), but the poet evokes their constraint in the grandiose terms of divine chastisements (*Il.* 15.19–20; *Od.* 8.274–5; Semonides, fr. 7.116 W.; ps.-Aesch. *PV* 6; *Or. Sib.* 1.102, 2.289; Diog. Laert. 8.31); 'bind with a bond' (Fehling, 158; C. Watkins, *How to Kill a Dragon: Aspects of Indo-European Poetics* (New York, 1995), 457–9) is associated in EGHP with gods and heroes, and embellished with epithets like κρατερός, νηλής, ἀργαλέος. Imperial poets reproduce the cadence first found in Ap. Rhod. 3.847 ἑὸν δέμας ἰκμαίνοιτο; this one (also at 244) and ps.-Opp. *Cyn.* 2.81 retain the spondeiazon. ps.-Opp. *Cyn.* 2.106, 589 also treats the possessive as a third person plural.

241–2 This behaviour has no parallel in the Ptolemaios archive. Reitzenstein, 84, cites Jerome, *Ep.* 22.28 (on sham holy men) *viros quoque fuge, quos videris catenatos, quibus feminei contra apostolum crines, hircorum barba, nigrum pallium et nudi in patientiam frigoris pedes*; for disreputable Christian recluses see also Legras, 91–2. But the comparison is limited. Long hair is also mentioned immediately after the ἐγκάτοχοι in Θ p. 165.4 (Saturn in the ninth place[133]) ἐνίους δὲ καὶ κόμας τρέφοντας, and Cumont, 150 n. 3, adds *CCAG* viii/1. 260.6

---

[131] Reitzenstein, 84; Versnel, 90 and n. 174 for chained Christian ascetics.

[132] S. Brock, 'Early Syrian Asceticism', *Numen*, 20 (1973), 1–19, at 12–13; C. de Wet, 'Slavery and Asceticism in John of Ephesus' Lives of the Eastern Saints', *Scrinium*, 13 (2017), 84–113.

[133] Venus' effect in this place is similar, but without the κάτοχοι: Θ p. 165.15–16 ἐν ἱεροῖς ῥακενδύτας, κομοτροφοῦντας ~ Firmicus, 3.6.17 *faciet autem in templis manere sordide et sic semper incedere et qui numquam tondeant comam*.

(Saturn's terms within Scorpio) συνοχή, κομοτροφία [*ex emend.*, for the manuscripts' corrupt κωμοτροφία]. But from the next lines it appears that the poet is pivoting from a group that looks *prima facie* Egyptian to the *galli*, who are a general classical topos. What facilitates the transition is the *galli*'s own association with divination, including oneiromancy (Graillot, 306–12)—as well as their peculiar physical state. The *galli* are famously long-haired (see i. 347 and n. 5, and add Graillot, 299–300), but instead of that hair being dirty and unkempt, as it often is, here it appears as *coiffeured*—a variant on the topos which also appears in hostile Christian observers (Firmicus, *Err.* 4.2 *exornant muliebriter nutritos crines*; Augustine, *Civ.* 7.26 *madidis capillis*, with a great deal more about pampered effeminacy; *RAC* s.v. Gallos, 1021 (G. M. Sanders)). The comparison to horses reinforces the associations with grooming, couture— also, less appropriately, with the élite (Alcman's women as exotic breeds of horse; Semonides' luxurious horse-woman).[134] In other words, holy men might have cued us to expect grunge (see too Greg. Naz., *PG* 37.569.2 Κόσμος ἐμοὶ ῥυπόωσα κόμη, καὶ εἵματα λυπρά, though he speaks figuratively),[135] but what we get is a very different kind of decadence.

241 The conjuncture εἵματα μὲν ῥυπόωντα comes originally from Odyssean ἦ ὅτι δὴ ῥυπόω, κακὰ δὲ χροῒ εἵματα εἷμαι (2×), cf. *Od.* 13.434–5 εἵματ'... ῥυπόωντα, as quoted by ps.-Diogenes, *Ep.* 7.2. There might also be a link with 6.433–4 ῥυπόεντα...εἵματα. In the second half of the line, τρίχες δ' οὐρῆσιν ὅμοιαι is reminiscent of *Il.* 17.51 κόμαι Χαρίτεσσιν ὁμοῖαι, of the death of Euphorbus—all the more in that in both cases the hair is clotted with something, wax in one case, blood in another.

242 (τρίχες) **κηροπαγεῖς οὖλαι:** Firmicus and Augustine both describe the hair of the *galli* as pomaded; cf. also Erycius, *AP* 6.234.5–6 = *Garland* 2260–1 μυρόεντα | βόστρυχον (more on unguents in Gibson on Ov. *Ars Am.* 3.443). Dr Helen Ackers declined to answer a question about ancient hair wax, but if κηροπαγεῖς is not corrupt for μυρο-, it does suggest some kind of fixative (cf. also Ov. *Ars Am.* 3.434 *quique suas ponunt in statione comas*, as a type of effeminate man, and Gibson ad loc. for more on 'ordered' hair). 'Thick' is appropriate to both European and African hair (Mineur on Call. *Hymn* 4.302), and the

---

[134] M. Griffith, 'Horsepower and Donkeywork: Equids and the Ancient Greek Imagination: Part Two', *CP* 101 (2006), 307–58, at 308–17. Alcman: E. Robbins, 'Alcman's Partheneion: Legend and Choral Ceremony', *CQ*² 44 (1994), 7–16, at 8–9.
[135] Koechly's emendation πληροῦσι somewhat suggests the plenitude of hair with which miraculous Christian ascetics are credited (K. Upson-Saia, 'Hairiness and Holiness in the Early Christian Desert', in K. Upson-Saia, C. Daniel-Hughes, and A. J. Batten (eds.), *Dressing Judaeans and Christians in Antiquity* (Farnham, 2014), 155–72), but they tend to have full beards, or whole bodies covered with hair, as in the later iconography of St Mary Magdalen.

adjective usually implies curly as well,[136] though in the present case it pulls against the horse comparison which requires the locks to be flowing rather than curly. The poet is mixing and confusing his topoi. Be that as it may, the suggestion is not only of youth and attractiveness (*Od.* 6.231 = 23.158) but also of feminine indulgence (Marcus Argentarius, *AP* 6.201, where again the hair is μυρόπνουν).

243-4 ἀμφιτόμοισι σιδηρείοις πελέκεσσιν: the verse-pattern recurs in Triph. 254 ἀμφιτόμοισι διαρρῆξαι πελέκεσσιν (that passage, like others combining the epithet and noun, beginning with Ap. Rhod. 1.168-9, is military). The *galli* carry both axes and swords when they put on their displays of self-wounding in Apul. *Met.* 8.27 *adtollentes immanes gladios ac secures*. While the iron blade is presumably conventional (Martial, 3.47.2 *Phrygiumque Matris...ferrum*), 'two-edged', an epithet hitherto used for swords or lance-tips,[137] may be making the precise point that these are double axes (Vian renders Ap. Rhod. 1.168-9 ἀμφίτομόν... πέλεκυν μέγαν 'une grande hache à deux tranchants'). If so these are illustrated on a probably early third-century relief from Rome of a priest of Ma-Bellona (another self-wounding cult), who carries a pair of double axes in one hand and a sprig of laurel (to sprinkle the blood) in another.[138] More on self-wounding in Graillot, 304-6. The poet makes the effect still more lurid by opting for part of λυσσάω (λυσσ- in prose most often used for rabid animals) rather than μαίνομαι, the usual adjunct of ἔνθεος in connection with divine madness.

244 αἱμάσσουσιν: blood spilt, whether in casual displays (Apul. *Met.* 8.28 *spurcitia sanguinis effeminati, profusum cruorem*/ps.-Lucian, *Asin.* 37) or on the notorious *Dies Sanguinis* on 24 March (*CIL* 1² p. 260, for AD 354; first datable mention in Tertullian, *Apol.* 25.5...*sanguinem impurum lacertos quoque castrando libabat*, sc. the *archigallus*, in AD 180, but perhaps prefigured by Valerius Flaccus, *Arg.* 8.241-2 *quis modo tam saevos adytis fluxisse cruores | cogitet?*; cf. Alvar, 289-90). These spectacular displays became a topos predominantly, it seems, in Latin texts. The best example is on a curse tablet from Mainz, mid-1st c. AD, ed. J. Blänsdorf, 'The *Defixiones* from the Sanctuary of Isis and Mater Magna in Mainz', in R. L. Gordon and F. M. Simón (eds.), *Magical Practice in the*

---

[136] Whether naturally or artificially: the use of curling tongs is part of the decadent Phrygian image, cf. V. *Aen.* 12.99-100 *crinis | vibratos calido ferro murraque madentis*. Curls go together with unguents: Olson 2014, 188-9, 196.

[137] Axe or sword in Aesch. *Ag.* 1496, 1520 ἀμφιτόμωι βελέμνωι (see Fraenkel on 1149).

[138] A. Brent, 'Ignatius and Polycarp: The Transformation of New Testament Traditions in the Context of Mystery Cults', in A. F. Gregory and C. M. Tuckett (eds.), *Trajectories through the New Testament and the Apostolic Fathers* (Oxford, 2005), 325-49, at 338; ill. in J. Elsner, *Imperial Rome and Christian Triumph* (Oxford, 1998), 208, fig. 137.

Latin West: Papers from the International Conference held at the University of Zaragoza, 30 Sept.-1 Oct. 2005 (Leiden, 2010), 141-89, no. 16, ll. 9-10 *Quomodo galli, bellonari, magal[i] sibi sanguin[em] ferventem fundunt*..., cf. 158 on the extraordinarily vivid expression. Literary examples in Lucan, 1.566-7 *crinem... sanguineum*; Stat. *Theb.* 10.173 *sanguineos... crines*; Claudian, *Rapt.* 2.269 *sanguineis... Gallis*; Arnob. *Adv. gentes* 5.14.2 *iras sanguinem furias*; Minucius Felix, *Octav.* 22.9 *qui sanguine suo libat et vulneribus suis supplicat, non profanus melius esset quam sic religiosus?*; Lactantius, *Div. Inst.* 1.21.16 *sacerdotes... suo cruore sacrificant* [Bellona]; Prudentius, *Peristeph.* 10.1069-70 *illam revulsa masculini germinis | vena effluenti pascit auctam sanguine*.

245-9

Full Moon encountering Mars, without benefics. Harms, but not financial damage, are paralleled in Π.σ.α. p. 183.1-5 (νόσους, ἐκπτώσεις, ὀρφανίας when Mars is retrograde), and Firmicus, 4.4.1-2. This disappointingly contentless chart oddly interrupts the mini-sequence involving ἐμπερίσχεσις.

246 κακὴ κατὰ πάντα τέτυκται: cf. Π.σ.α. p. 183.6 κακὴ πρὸς πάντα (Moon leaving Mars); *CCAG* vii. 109.5 ἐναντία πρὸς πάντα εὑρίσκεται (Moon conjunct with Mars).

247-8 πλούσιον ἄνδρα πένητα | ῥηιδίως ἔρρεξε: the ease motif (placed, as so often, line-initially), combined with a polar reversal, is a marvellous example both of the astrologisation of EGHP rhetoric about gods, and of the *embourgeoisement* of EGHP values. The theme is specifically *wealth*, in contrast to the locus classicus for reversal, *Op.* 5-7, where Hesiod had avoided language that was too directly associable with social status. Hesiod's author of reversal, Zeus, is explicitly excluded here, so the redeployment of Zeus-motifs has (if the poet intended it) an added edge. For divine ease, see Janko on *Il.* 13.90; this is the destructive ease of a Homeric divinity (unlike the more benign vision of the Periegete: Kneebone, 93-4).

μινυνθάδιόν τε: parallels are not close except for Firmicus' *quosdam oligochronios, biothanatos facit* (in a day-birth).

250-5

Moon between malefics. A classic case of what astrologers call ἐμπερίσχεσις κατὰ συμπαρουσίαν; see Bouché-Leclercq, 251, and 6.657 n., where it afflicts the Sun. Most definitions cover any planet (Epit. II = 'Antiochus', *CCAG* i. 159.8-10 Ἐμπερίσχεσις δέ ἐστιν, ὅταν δύο πλάνητες ἕνα μέσον ἔχωσι καθ' οἷον δήποτε σχῆμα, μηδενὸς ἑτέρου ἐν τοῖς μέσοις ἀκτῖνα βάλλοντος ἐντὸς ἑπτὰ μοιρῶν ἐπὶ τὰ πρόσω ἢ ὀπίσω).¹³⁹ Hephaestion's definition narrows it down to the Moon or horoscope (i. 40.10–14), which makes sense, given the Moon's special susceptibility.

There are similar charts in 4.409–13 and 5.197–201. This is the fullest version, with twin outcomes, for women and men, each of which is authenticable from a separate source. The main hand had it right. The corrector, who made the masculine endings feminine, was trying to harmonise, as he saw it, the second half of the chart with the first; this was simply misconceived conjecture. Gronovius followed; Axtius and Rigler set it right from the Liber Halensis.

The outcome for women corresponds to Dorotheus, p. 324.21–4, where the Moon surrounded by malefics causes δυστοκία (4.412 n.), and less closely to 4.409–13, where the Moon is in the vicinity of Saturn, and Mars is looking on. This passage (not, *pace* Pingree, 6.237–9 + 244–5) is alluded to, under the name of Manetho, by Hephaestion, i. 330.25–331.3, who even echoes its diction (ἀργαλέα ἐστὶ ταῖς τικτούσαις), but adds additional specifications which either come from a fuller version of the poem than we now have, or which he did not mean also to attribute to Manetho (p. 271). It is interesting that one of the missing factors is the quality of signs, which seems to have been a factor in some alternative recensions of the τέχναι (p. 141): here it is a possibility among the harms as well, with the Manethoniana representing a stripped-back form of what elsewhere featured constellations too.

The outcome for men corresponds to 5.197–201 (also ἐμπερίσχεσις) and Θ p. 200.1–2. The types of death are presented as conventional pairs—hanging/ the sword (also 4.488–9) and burning/drowning; both pairs in Firmicus, 1.9.1, and 4.9.5. Fire and the sword are another Martian pairing (Dorotheus, p. 416.5; Valens, II 17.79, al.).

250 δείμαινε: the 'be very afraid' motif: see p. 171.

251 μογεραῖσι τεκούσαις: the corresponding 4.411 (subject: the μήτηρ) suggests this is supposed to be multivalent, either in the act of childbirth, or generally in their capacity as mothers. The epithet is a multi-purpose suffering word, though one could think of the pregnant hare in Aesch. *Ag.* 136 μογερὰν πτάκα.

252 κρυφίμων ἄπο: likely from gynaecological complaints, as in 1.338; 4.413 gives a little more detail.

254–5 These conventional options are clad in barely adapted Homerism, ἁψαμένους βρόχον αἰνὸν from *Od.* 11.278 ἁψαμένη βρόχον αἰπὺν (a female death now rendered male, or generic) and ἀραμένους ξίφος ὀξύ from ἐρυσσάμενος

---

¹³⁹ Similarly Porphyry, *Introd. in Tetrabibl.* 15 (*CCAG* v/4. 200.7–13); a shorter form in Epit. IIIa = Antiochus, *CCAG* viii/3. 107.28–9.

ξίφος ὀξύ/ξίφος ὀξὺ ἐρυσσάμενος. For suicide by hanging see on 4.489, and for the sword on 4.488. πυρὶ δαιομένους is a little more interesting. The poet has rewritten *Il*. 21.361 Φῆ πυρὶ καιόμενος (of the river), but has apparently chosen to replace the participle, which was entirely available to him, with a synonym that results in a very rare passive construction (LSJ II), 'be kindled' (as applied to a person, nastily reminiscent of Latimer's 'We shall this day light such a candle, by God's grace, in England, as I trust shall never be put out', or worse still, of Ridley's 'I cannot burn'). At Eur. *Heraclid*. 913–14 πυρὸς δεινᾷ φλογὶ σῶμα δαισθείς (sc. Heracles) the verb could be δαίνυμι (see Wilkins ad loc.), and in Call. *Ep*. 49.3 δεδαυμένον (which also agrees with a person, but is metaphorical) is an emendation for transmitted δεδαγμένον.

256–61

Venus between malefics. This set-up causes madness in Θ p. 192.16–18. There are several similarities with Saturn in Venus' houses in 2.177–83.

258 Slaves *or* prostitutes in 2.178–9, 5.236 (Moon flees both malefics, plus other factors).

259 ζήλῳ ἐλαύνονται κακοεργέϊ: astrological ζῆλος often attends Venus/ relations with women (2.183, 5.67, 236; Dorotheus, p. 342.23; *Hygromantia Salominis, CCAG* viii/2. 146.19). For the sense of ἐλαύνεσθαι (be hounded, dogged, persecuted), see LSJ ἐλαύνειν, I.4; Finglass on Soph. *Aj*. 274–6.

259–60 Wife-murder: see on 2.182–3. ὀργιόωντας are celebrants of ὄργια in 4.229; here, with greater licence, they are victims of ὀργή (~ ὀργῶντες, ὀργαίνοντες, ὀργιζόμενοι).

261 Although I have not adopted it, Koechly's emendation of καὶ to αἳ, which presents a less ragged sequence without sudden change of subject, is attractive. There is no direct parallel in 2.177–83, but the account of Mars in the houses of Venus canvasses alternatives in which either husbands kill wives or wives kill husbands (see on 2.271–2). When Koechly further proposed either φίλτρα (which he read) or θέλκτρα in place of λέκτρα, he presumably meant that they came to grief upon being caught meddling with drugs, rather than upon consuming them (for the trope, see Faraone, 9–10, 114–16). For μόρον αἰνὸν, see on 1.41.

262–6

Benefics in ASC, malefics in DESC.

262 λαχών: as also 6.703 (with genitive) and 5.84 (with accusative). The accusative ought strictly to mean 'having obtained by lot', and is often used in astrology in the sense of 'presiding over' (a permanent domain, an area of interest, an apportionment, e.g. of degrees in Dorotheus' *horothesiai*) or when a planet has been allocated a Lot. But it can also be used when an entity has moved into a (temporary) position (Dorotheus, p. 361.22; Paul, pp. 61.1, 74.8; 'Heliodorus', pp. 74.1, 75.16; Camaterus, *Zod.* 567–8; Theophilus, *CCAG* xi/1. 216.4).

263 ἀνηλέος: i. 909 n. 4.

264 Loss of wealth: see on 222. The situation elicits a more perfect chiasmus here than there, pivoting round the old antithesis of 'first and last' (ranks: *Il.* 11.64–5; order of precedence: Theocr. 17.3–4, *HHom.* 29.5) so as now to counterpoint the opposite stages of life.

265 The conventionality of this cluster can be illustrated from *CCAG* viii/1. 245.13 δίκας, θορύβους, αἰφνιδίους πολέμους (Mars); Hephaestion, i. 205.5 ἐν θορύβοις ἔσται καὶ δίκαις (Saturn distributing to Mercury), 218.29 θορύβους, δίκας καὶ ἐγκλήματα (Mercury as chronocrator aspected by malefic).

266 The saving clause is precisely as in prose astrological texts where a reel of disasters is predicted *unless* (εἰ μή πως) a benefic saves the day;[140] in 3.253 the if-clause is unusually placed first. The logic seems to be that Jupiter has a salvific effect if he appears at the edge of the sign, and the strongly implied personification in the verb pictures him marching to the rescue (but for μοῖραν, the phrase is rather like the chariot image in 6.738 νειατίην ἐλάων περὶ νύσσαν). For the verb ὀδεύσῃ, see i. 879 and n. 31, although this passage does not involve location in a *kentron*.

267–70

Malefics in ASC, Jupiter in DESC. This constitutes a pair with the last chart. The situation is very like 1.215–22, which strips the situation down to Mars and Jupiter in opposition: the additional presence of Saturn does not change the basic theme of ἀνωμαλία. The specifications of *kentra* are also new vis-à-vis that chart, and for these we can compare the *kentrothesiai*, 3.163–7 + 168–75, where yet again the combination of these planets produces an οὐχ ὁμαλὸν βίοτον (164). This chart, unlike that, concentrates on wealth. The logic of having wealth come at the end of life is simple: Jupiter is situated in the place that represents

[140] Valens, I 20.33, II 39.10, IV 22.8; Hephaestion, i. 209.20, 211.4, 212.1, 10, 24, 215.31, 222.31; Θ pp. 129.23, 168.2–3.

the end. Similar logic is implied at 3.135-6 (Saturn in ASC, Jupiter in DESC) and 3.175 (Mars in ASC, Jupiter in DESC: respite from labours in old age), although the way there is now a lot choppier.

268 κατεναντίον: see on 1.215.

269 The same antithesis as 1.222, but reversed, with a parallelism in place of a chiasmus.

270 ἀνώμαλα ἔργα τελοῦσιν: the phrase looks to Hes. *Th.* 89 μετάτροπα ἔργα τελεῦσι (cf. ἔργα τελείει, ἔργα τελέσσῃ), but instead of deeds turned back on their authors (in retribution) we now have the chronic instability of a mechanistic but purposeless universe. For ἀνωμαλία, see 1.216 n.

271-6

Moon in same degree as malefics. This is bound to be bad, but it is disappointingly vague. There are conjunctions of the Moon and malefics in Firmicus, 6.31.20 (in the MC), 6.31.35 (in equinoctial signs), 6.31.70 (in the eleventh house), but not in the same degree, and the outcomes are all less generic than here.

271 κερόεσσα Σελήνη: see i. 904 n. 2. The line-end is like 6.593 συνίῃ κερόεσσα Σελήνη, 640 συνέῃ κερόεσσα Σελήνη, but there may be a common background (Dorotheus, p. 328.6 κερόεσσα Σελήνη; cf. Maximus, 397 συνῇ κερόεσσα Σελήνη).

272 One could distinguish between συναφή by sign (ζῳδιακῶς) and degree (μοιρικῶς) (i. 47-8, 884), or between συναφή within a certain number of degrees and the exact degree (Antiochus, *CCAG* viii/3. 113.36-114.1), but either way this seems a *hysteron proteron*; the precise data about degree (μοίρης ἐντός) should come second.

273-4 The lack of coordinating conjunction implies that the apodosis begins in 273, but with the Moon (presumably) still as subject of ἔχει. Anaphora of ἐντός tries to persuade us of the correlation between the Moon's proximity to the malefics and the amount of harm she absorbs, and epanalepsis (unparalleled in the Manethoniana) that 273 and 274 (where the outcome proper begins) are coordinated. But the attempt to make the dread (αἰνήν) effect of the Moon parallel with the dread outcome for humans (αἰνός τ') does not really mitigate the eccentricity of the construction, which is untypically experimental for this poet.

274 ἠδ' ἐλεεινός: *Il.* 24.309, *Od.* 6.327 ἠδ' ἐλεεινόν. In the lines from which this is adapted, the speaker is praying for a favourable reception in a particular setting with a host or hosts of unknown but possibly dangerous disposition. Now the natives become generically pitiful in the miserabilist view of human life.

275 μοῖρα κακή: abridged from *Il*. 13.602 μοῖρα κακὴ θανάτοιο (Janko ad loc.: a variation on μοῖρ' ὀλοή). It is hard to be confident that with λάτρια ἔργα the poet precisely intends hired labour that is technically free, in contradistinction to slave labour, δούλια ἔργα, on which his phrase is based (Ap. Rhod. 4.38: see Livrea ad loc.; Quint Smyrn. *bis*; Dorotheus, p. 328.5, paraphrased by Hephaestion, perhaps representing Dorotheus' verse). Maximus, 474 μισθῷ ἐπὶ λατρίῳ means a labourer's hire, but the λατρεύοντας in 4.602 are *vernae*, house-born slaves. For hired labour in astrology, see p. 81.

276 A string of tropes. βίον/βίοτον λείπειν is tragic, especially Euripidean, but also in sepulchral epigram (e.g. *IG* IX/1. 234/235 (Larymna, n.d.) τὸν καὶ ἔτ' ἀκμαίην βίοτον λείποντα καθ' ἥβην), and πρόμοιροι is strongly associated with the latter, for apart from Aelian, fr. 49, the attestations—of which there are dozens—are all in epitaphs, either literary (Lucillius, *AP* 11.159.3), or in inscribed verse or prose. On the other hand, ῥοπῇ, the turn of fortune's scales, does not seem to be a topos of epitaphs,[141] but belongs especially to historians (or orators in the thick of events) meditating on unexpected or knife-edged outcomes,[142] and is properly associated with Tyche (chance) rather than Fate. Some passages employ the topos of elevation and overthrow which astrology also uses for Martian upset (see on 3.67–8; Herodian, *Ab excess*. 1.13.6; *Hist. Alex., rec.* γ 2.16 *sub fin.* ἡ γὰρ τύχη βραχεῖαν ἐὰν λάβῃ ῥοπήν, τοὺς ταπεινοὺς ὑπεράνω τῶν νεφελῶν ἀναβιβάζει καὶ τοὺς ἀπὸ ὕψους εἰς ζόφον κατάγει).

1.277–80 + 281–3 + 284–5 Royal Charts

These charts have a very similar logic to 1.26–8, including that of a luminary in places of concordant gender (1.279), save that this passage also employs the principle of sect. The curiosity is that the sect of the Moon seems to be more important than that of the Sun. The king is born *by night*, with the Moon in sect in a dominant place (cf. also Θ p. 170.5–6, on the MC), and the Sun centred in male signs (i.e. favourably placed but out of sect). On the other hand, the queen

---

[141] Interesting inscriptional example on a dice-oracle from Antiocheia ad Cragum in G. E. Bean and T. B. Mitford, *Journeys in Rough Cilicia in 1962 and 1963* (Österreichische Akademie der Wissenschaften, Philosophisch-historische Klasse, Denkschriften [DAW], 85) (Vienna, 1965), 40, (43) § 33 πάντων ἐνεργὴς ἐμ βίῳ τύχῃ ῥοπῇ.

[142] Demosthenes, *Olynth*. 2.22 μεγάλη γὰρ ῥοπή, μᾶλλον δὲ ὅλον ἡ τύχη παρὰ πάντ' ἐστὶ τὰ τῶν ἀνθρώπων πράγματα; ps.-Lucian, *Demosth*. 38; Diod. Sic. 13.24.6; a favourite of Plutarch; also in Dio, Libanius, and others.

is born *by day*, when the Moon is out of sect (but still dominating the hour of birth), even though, by the same token, the Sun is *in* sect. One might have expected the in-sect Sun to produce kings, and the Moon queens, but not so. There is a certain similarity with Firmicus, 7.22, esp. 7.22.1 (where the MC confers extra privilege), but the main principle there is the gender of the luminaries' signs (a double dose of masculinity produces kings), and whether or not it is a day or night birth is secondary.

278–80

Moon in MC by degree in night birth, with the Sun in a *kentron* in a male place (sign). Exactly as in *Lib. Herm.* xxvi. 34, which adds that the Sun is on the ASC, the Moon in favourable signs, and malefics absent.

277 μέσον πόλον ἀμφιβεβῶσα: from Homeric (ἦμος δ'/ὄφρα μὲν Ἥλιος) μέσον οὐρανὸν ἀμφιβεβήκει (2× *Il.*, 1× *Od.*).

278 νυκτερινοῦ θέματος: for θέμα, see Heilen 2015, 537–8. It is not attested in papyri, which do, however, have διάθεμα; poets find it useful, but it is also prosaic and even borrowed into Latin. This phrase is found in 'Heliodorus', p. 49.9 Εἰ μέντοι νυκτερινὸν ἦν τὸ θέμα.

κατὰ μοῖραν: presumably because the conditions have to be exactly right for so unusual a birth.

280 θεὸν βροτὸν: in theory befitting either a Ptolemy (if we are not supposed to have lost sight of Ptolemy as notional addressee) or a Roman emperor, but a commonplace either way; *Lib. Herm.* has *regem, deum existentem hominem humanitatis participem*, and compare Diotogenes, ap. Stob. 4.7.61 ὁ δὲ βασιλεὺς … θεὸς ἐν ἀνθρώποις παρεσχαμάτισται ('has been transformed into a god'); *Corp. Herm.* fr. 24.3 καὶ ὁ μὲν βασιλεὺς τῶν μὲν ἄλλων θεῶν ἐστιν ἔσχατος, πρῶτος δὲ ἀνθρώπων· καὶ μέχρις ὅτου ἐπὶ γῆς ἐστι, τῆς μὲν ἀληθοῦς θειότητος ἀπήλλακται, ἔχει δὲ ἐξαίρετόν τι παρ' ἀνθρώπους, ὃ ὅμοιόν ἐστι τῷ θεῷ (both cited by Hopkins 1978, 198 and 217; see his whole ch. 5 on the popular idea of the emperor as a god). The poet has recycled a collocation in EGHP where the two words are contrastive (e.g. *Od.* 4.397 θεὸς βροτῷ ἀνδρί); now they are paradoxically complementary, and the whole thing wrapped up in the rhythm of e.g. *Il.* 4.320 θεοὶ δόσαν ἀνθρώποισιν, *Od.* 11.274 θεοὶ θέσαν ἀνθρώποισιν. For the Greek use of θεός for the Roman emperor (unsystematic, save that it is the standard equivalent of *divus* in imperial titulature), see Mason, 124–5; S. R. F. Price, 'Gods and Emperors: The Greek Language of the Roman Imperial Cult', *JHS* 104 (1984), 79–95, especially 81–2; M. Peppard, *The Son of God in the Roman World: Divine Sonship in its Social and Political Context* (Oxford, 2011),

41–2. The phrase suggests the deference of Greek communities towards their overlords, even if it does not reflect specific courtesy-formulae, for instance that of acclamations, or of officials addressing emperors or each other.[143]

Firmicus takes a different approach. He acknowledges the divinity of the emperor, but considers that this takes him out of prognosticability altogether (2.30.5). On the other hand he includes many royal charts in which kings are presented as temporal lords, with power of life and death, formidable (frequent motif of 'death from the anger of kings'), but not divine.[144] Presumably this still reflects a popular perception, but it is that of cowering provincials rather than courteous officialdom (pp. 23–4).

281–5

Mercury in MC with Sun, Moon in ASC, in a day birth; centred, without malefics. The accompaniment of the Sun by Mercury recalls Firmicus, 3.8.1, though there the *kentron* is the ASC, and a day birth gives rise to kings.

282 καθ' ὡρονόμοιο: the genitive (as opposed to the routine accusative) is mostly a feature of M^a (p. 312), especially in book 6, and especially for *kentra* (6.69 καθ' ὡρονόμου, also of the Moon; 155–6 δυτικοῦ κατὰ κέντρου | ἢ καὶ ὑποχθονίου; 333 μεσάτου κατὰ κέντρου; 342 μεσάτοιο φαεινούσης κατὰ κέντρου; 680 κατὰ κέντρου; 716, 747 καθ' ὥρης). For other, quasi-distributive, instances, see on 4.38. This is the only instance outside M^a where it occurs with a *kentron*: imitation is possible, although the usage also occurs, rarely, in prose (Ptol. 4.5.14, 4.7.9, Valens, II 19.2), perhaps surprisingly in the light of the decline of the genitive vis-à-vis the accusative in contemporary usage (Blass–Debrunner–Rehkopf, §225; Mayser, ii/2.2, p. 428); perhaps it is a hypercorrection. I doubt there can be a strong implication of downward motion, as if the planet had come down from its course to settle temporarily on a point (which

---

[143] J. de Jong, 'Emperor Meets Gods: Divine Discourse in Greek Papyri from Roman Egypt', in M. Kahlos (ed.), *Emperors and the Divine: Rome and its Influence* (Helsinki, 2016), 22–55, esp. 29, on θεὸς Καῖσαρ in an acclamation of Vespasian, SB XVI 12255 = P.Fouad I 8, and J. Whitehorne, 'Augustus as "Theos" in Contemporary Papyri', in *Proceedings of the XIXth International Congress of Papyrology* (Cairo, 2–9 September 1989), II (Cairo, 1992), 421–34; de Jong, 38–9, on θειότατος, in papyri as an epithet of emperors from Septimius Severus onwards, before becoming a feature of imperial titulature in the sixth century; the epigraphic formula θεὸς τηλικοῦτος, on which see S. R. F. Price, *Rituals and Power: The Roman Imperial Cult in Asia Minor* (Cambridge, 1984), 244; A. Chaniotis, 'Megatheism: The Search for the Almighty God and the Competition of Cults', in S. Mitchell and P. van Nuffelen (eds.), *One God: Pagan Monotheism in the Roman Empire* (Cambridge, 2010), 112–40, at 121–2.

[144] e.g. 3.4.30 *reges, imperatores, potentes, maxime terribiles, periculosi, civitatum eversores vel fabricatores*; 7.22.1 *reges facient terribiles, potentes, regiones vel civitates maximas subiugantes*; 7.22.3 *periculosi, terribiles, efficaces, totius orbis dominia possidentes*; 8.29.1 *rex magnus, gloriosus, polychronius, omnium terrarum possidens circulum*; 8.31.9 *rex, magnus, gloriosus, religiosus, iustus, longaevus*.

would anyway contradict the idea that *kentra* are high points: 3.126–30 n.), because the alternation with the accusative in M^a is casual.

283 De Stefani's conjecture γενέθλης misunderstands that what is wanted is the geniture of a queen (correctly, Bouché-Leclercq, 440 n. 2), the counterpart of the previous one, and introduces an irrelevant distinction between a king and a king who is of royal birth. Compare Firmicus, 6.31.51, where once again the Moon on the horoscope represents a woman.

284 ταῦτα δέ τοι τελέουσιν: *Od.* 2.306 ταῦτα δέ τοι μάλα πάντα τελευτήσουσιν Ἀχαιοί.

285 Implying opposition as discord (unlike the general view of M^a: 2.436–8 n.); Firmicus, 2.22.2 *sed haec semper maligna ac minax radiatio est*.

1.286–326 Τέχναι

The main commentary is on book 4. Variants are discussed here.

290 οἰκείοις: sc. δώμασι or δόμοις (as in e.g. 4.16, 157). While M^b's adverb οἰκείως (4.139) is also found in 4.328, and the negative in 608, the present usage is also found in 4.20 ἐν οἰκείοισι. In other words, this is not an instance where each variant is uniquely characteristic of the book in which it is found.

294 Σεληναίης ἑλικώπιδος: while M^b's version characteristically uses motion vocabulary (4.146 ἑλικοδρόμος) and assigns a single noun two epithets, this one seems to be looking back to Dorotheus (i. 905 n. 21). It is not obviously a deviation or departure from M^b's version, and is equally viable in its own right (p. 275). Later: John of Gaza, *Descr.* 248 ἑλικώπιδος αἰθέρι Μήνης.

298 ζωγραφίης μεδέοντας: the -γραφ- part of the compound speaks for De Stefani's emendation in the corresponding 4.150. The reference is still to painters. Astrology has numerous references to ζωγραφία, which it ranks among the 'clean' crafts (p. 64), but sometimes also together with more 'practical' ones like carpentry (Apomasar, *De Rev.* pp. 42.23–43.1, 98.10 ζωγραφίας καὶ τορεύσεις); from *CCAG* viii/1. 208.1–2 καλὸν εἰς τοίχους ζωγραφίας ποιῆσαι it appears that it can refer to fresco work, which suits the present context well. μεδέοντας suggests, in the Homeric idiom, the mastery over their specialism of which craftsmen boasted (p. 71).

299 In this version M^b's characteristic ἔσσεσθαι construction has gone. εὐφυέας, which replaces the infinitive, means 'naturally skilful'.[145] The word is

---

[145] LSJ III, adding Isocr. *Pan.* 33 πρός τε τὰς τέχνας εὐφυεστάτους ὄντας; Diod. Sic. 13.40.2 (of a neat nautical manoeuvre); Lucian, *Parasit.* 33 πρὸς τὴν τέχνην εὐφυής.

common in astrology, and is entirely plausible in this passage; its association with skill emerges best from Ptol. 3.14.34 φιλοτέχνους, ἐμφιλοσόφους, ἐπιστημονικούς, εὐφυεῖς; here and elsewhere the quality is Mercurial (Valens, II 17.37, Περὶ κράσ. 207; Epit. II = 'Antiochus', CCAG i. 164.16; Rhetorius, CCAG vii. 222.1; Θ p. 167.3 etc.).

I do not know what to do with the line's other departure from M^b's version, whether to take the word, which is transmitted as εὐτυπέῶν, as an epithet of κανονισμῶν or (with a resulting parallelism with εὐφυέας of which this poet is certainly capable) of κοσμήτας (p. 275). But it seems that the scribes were no better off. There is no *εὐτυπής, though it is a possible formation (B.–P. 727), and it does not seem entirely out of the question that it could refer to the kinds of hammer-blow delivered by skilled masons, whether to those who aim them or to that which is struck.[146] With no criteria for judgement, and uncertainty about the meaning of κανονισμῶν (see on 4.151), I decline to enter the competition to suggest emendations, and merely observe the alternation of οι and υ in εὐτυπέων/εὐτοίχων suggesting the possibility that the one version or the other is a phonetic variant.

303-4 It is not a question of being able to determine which version, this or 4.203-4, is original (τέχνης τε λόγων and ῥητορικῆς...τέχνης are both legitimate combinations), but the parallel accusatives of 1.303 and the choice of epithet in 4.204 σκολιῶν τε λόγων seem characteristic of their respective poets. 1.303 appears as an independent line in 4.141, save that σοφίη for σοφίης removes the need for a noun in the next line on which the genitive can depend.

306 In this case M^c's reading looks secondary, and inferior, to that of M^b, which it transforms into a genitival expression in defiance of logic (p. 394). It is the Moon that moves, not its δρόμος, and why not take ἀμφίκερως into the genitive alongside Μήνης?

307-8 The reason for the discrepancy between this passage and 4.479 (which completely omits l. 308) is hard to explain, but it is notable that by offering an indication of aspect (εἰς τετράγωνα, which is slightly awkward, because Mercury can only be with or in opposition to one at a time, not both together) in place of the reference to rays (ἀκτίνεσσι) M^b adheres the better to his fairly strict policy of confining references to rays to within 4.165–365 (see p. 572).

310-11 For this author's liking for τελεῖν, see on 1.5; it substitutes for M^b's characteristic verb of generation, ἐκφύειν (4.483) (p. 275).

---

[146] εὔτυπος is a rare variant for εὐτύπωτος, 'malleable', first attested in Simplicius, In Aristot. Phys., CAG ix. 630.25 (Corollaries on Time and Place), in whom, however, it means 'well-shaped' (so the translation of J. O. Urmson).

314 ἀλύσεσσιν: for 4.486 ἀλυσηδόν. Also a hexameter-ending at Or. Sib. 2.288. This version coheres with verse-patterns like 6.525 χαρασσομένους γραφίδεσσιν, 2.430 ἐφεζομέναις στεγέεσσιν, which are ultimately Homeric (ἀφυσσόμενοι δεπάεσσιν, etc).

315 Koechly 1851, liv attempts to explain how this nonsensical line arose. To address the first problem, the combination of θάνατον with λείψει, he suggested that θάνατον had displaced βίοτον (either, suggests Dr Holford-Strevens, by polar error or by false supplementation once βίοτον had been lost by homoeoarcton after βίᾳ), but the second, the singular verb amidst plurals, is hard to explain other than on the hypothesis that the line is an intrusion from elsewhere. Some of its shaping nevertheless seems due to the main poet of the book; κακοεργέϊ θυμῷ can be compared to 1.249 βίη κακοεργέϊ Μοίρης (and to the rhythm of Hes. Th. 98 νεοκηδέι θυμῷ).

316 σφαγίοις ξίφεσιν: 4.488 φοβεροῖς ξίφεσιν: M^c's epithet is remarkable. Veins which, when severed, cause haemorrhage, i.e. the jugular, are called σφάγιοι (Maximus, 169 σύριγγες σφάγιαι uses a technical term from the Hippocratic texts, cf. I. Boehm, 'Astrologie et médecine ancienne: La description des maladies dans le Peri Katarchon de Maximus, un example d'écriture poétique?', in Boehm and Hübner, 193–207, at 198), but other than that there is only Soph. Ant. 1291 (1291–2 σφάγιον ἐπ' ὀλέθρῳ, γυναικεῖον ἀμφικεῖσθαι μόρον) where LSJ, F. T. Ellendt and H. F. Genthe, Lexicon Sophocleum (repr. Hildesheim, 1965), s.v. σφάγιος, and Kamerbeek take σφάγιον with μόρον and Griffith agrees ('probably'), though it could also be construed as the normal meaning, 'sacrificial victim', with the phrase in the next line appositional. M^b's combination is much more obvious (see ad loc.). This is a clear instance where M^c's reading is *not* banalised with respect to that of M^b (p. 395).

317 ἀγχονόωντα: the verb 'strangle' is in lexicographers (Suda, α 412, 2870, ps.-Zonaras, α p. 37.18, who gloss it with πνίξαι) and then not until Theodorus II Ducas Lascaris (13th c.), but ἀγχόνη, a noose, that which throttles, is as early as Semonides and Alcaeus. This is also a more interesting and less generic reading than M^b's ἀλγινόεντα (p. 395).

ἐνδήσαντες: M^b's ἐκδήσαντες is preferable (cf. Eur. Andr. 555–6 χέρας | βρόχοισιν ἐκδήσαντες; Σ Od. 11.278 ἀψαμένη] ἀναρτήσασα, ἐκδήσασα, ἀναψομένη βρόχον ὑψηλὸν; Phil. Spec. Leg. 3.159 ἄμμου σπυρίδα πλήρη βρόχοις ἐκδησάμενος ἀνήρτα κατὰ τῶν αὐχένων). ἐν- is used metaphorically with βρόχος, of the bonds of the flesh/sin, by Christian writers (e.g. Cyril, PG 70.1040.31–2 καὶ τοῖς τῆς ἁμαρτίας ἐνδεδέσθαι βρόχοις), but the sense is 'to be bound/hemmed in' with it.

318–20 Lines 318–19 are interpolated from 4.50–1. Here we have a kind of 'concordance interpolation' of two lines on a similar subject, their extraneous nature obvious from the disruption of the syntax (a shift from plurals to singulars and then back again), and the poet can be seen *both* purloining *and* (mal-) adapting to his own style. 1.319 ἢ ἰνίον is clearly inferior to 4.51 ἐς ἰνίον (also Quint. Smyrn. 11.83), but how did such an error arise? Could misquotation from memory have anything to do with it? Finally, discovering he needed a new coordinating conjunction after the interpolation, the poet replaced the epithet πικρὸν [λυγρὸν K] (4.490) with θ' ἑόν (1.320). M^b does not use, let alone misuse, the third-person possessive at all. M^c does, repeatedly (p. 287), so that his new version is both secondary and stylistically typical of him.

323 ὕδατος ἵστορας ἄνδρας: see on 4.397.

324 πλωτάρχας σκαφέων: see on 4.399 πρῳράρχους τε νεῶν. Both nouns are *hapax*. See also on 4.398 for the line this poet seems to have omitted; having no need for a connective, he then substituted σκαφέων (already present in 4.398) for τε νεῶν.

325 βίον σώζουσι: see on 4.400–1 ('patently absurd', which I reiterate).

326 ὑπὸ τρόμον: having decided to rescue his mariners, and needing to replace the expression for their limited lifespan in the water (4.401 βαιὸν χρόνον), the poet reached for Homeric ὑπὸ τρόμος (3× *Il.*, 1× *Od.*) to make them shiver but not drown.

1.327–33 + 334–8 Parents

Saturn in equal degrees with Sun; Moon approaches Saturn.

327 κυανοχρώτοιο: see i. 911 n. 15. In the quotation of Nechepso by Valens, VI 1.9, the *peplos* veiling the voice that addresses the king is qualified by an epithet transmitted as κυανόχρα, which Kroll emended to κυανόχρους and Pingree to κυάνεος (Heilen 2011, 49). Heilen himself (art. cit. 52) prefers Kroll's reading, in my view rightly; Nechepso's epithet would seem to have a background, like the present one, in tragic iambics. The noun-epithet combination here takes the place of EGHP μεγάλοιο Κρόνοιο.

328 ἦν: vis-a-vis 4.403, since ὁπότ' ἂν in the previous line has made way for a longer epithet than πολιοῖο, ἦν has to do duty for the conjunction (Monaco, 55). The absence of a main verb is out of keeping with the style of *both* M^b *and* M^c.

330 νεκυηπόλος Αἶσα: this misses M^b's playfulness in personifying Fate as an undertaker (4.405), and the glossing effect implied by πέμψει νεκυοστόλος, but has its own self-evident validity (p. 395): the epithet, unique, obviously

recalls θαλαμηπόλος, and such late antique cadences as Nonn. D. 42.485 θαλαμηπόλος Ἰνώ, 31.186 θαλαμηπόλον Ἥρην, al.

331 ἐκβάλλει...μέγαν: see on 4.406. The (unexciting) epithet is first in Hes. *Op.* 321, then at line-end in Theocr. 25.111, as well as in Pindar and tragic lyric, including sentiments about its loss in Soph. fr. 879a Radt, and ancestral wealth in Aesch. *Choe.* 865

333 The trivial differences between this line and 4.408 that make no difference to the sense are the sort that could have arisen through quotation from memory (*Or. Sib.* 8.72 πλοῦτον μέγαν in this *sedes*).

334–5 This is an impossible case for an editor who thinks that the text had better be treated as an entity in its own right rather than a witness to a 'better' or more original version, for as it stands it is defective. It is clear that 334–5 cannot be healed by simply converting 335 to a scannable hexameter because πελάζῃ in 334 needs an object—the point of *synaphai* is that the Moon approaches something—and as the parallel with 4.410 (and further texts documented in 402–8 + 409–13) illustrates, Saturn is also part of the scheme (cf. 335 τοῦτο, sc. τὸ σχῆμα, or even φωτὶ Κρόνου, as in 4.410). Saturn is the natural agent of hidden pains. So, do we posit a lost (?)pentameter at 334b in which, granted that the rest of the information in M^b and the papyrus is accounted for, some indication of Saturn is stretched over a single line?

336 The second half of the couplet is conventional, unlike the corresponding ἵξετ᾽ ἐς Ἀίδην in 4.411: Magnelli on his Alex. Aet. fr. 3.34 βήσεται εἰς Ἀίδην; Tyrt. fr. 12.38 and Mimnermus fr. 2.14 W. ἔρχεται εἰς Ἀίδην.

337–8 νούσου | αἱμηρῆς ἃ γυναιξὶ φύσις κρύφιμ᾽ ἄλγε᾽ ἔδωκεν: see on 4.413, where it is argued that the bloody condition represented here and in Π^1 (whose reading is here accepted) is independent of the abortions in M^b; neither was corrupted into the other.

Astrology has various kinds of bloody outcome, the special preserve of Mars. As well as wounds, he causes haemorrhage[147] and the coughing and vomiting of blood,[148] which shows that the astrologers knew about pulmonary tuberculosis (1.162–6 n.). Few cases are so clearly gynaecological as this one, but Hephaestion refers to αἱμαγμοὺς γυναικῶν (i. 216.17, with Venus ὕπαυγος and injured by a malefic), *Lib. Herm.* xxvi. 38 (Full Moon and Mars, out of sect, in

---

[147] Valens, VII 6.59; Firmicus, 5.6.2 *importuna sanguinis profusione*, 6.11.10 *profluvio sanguinis*; 8.12.2 *sanguinis iactura* (of gladiators); 8.20.13 *facient per narem aut per os aut per anum sanguinem mitti*, 8.23.11 *haemorragias, id est sanguinis eruptiones*, 8.26.13 *profusionem sanguinis*.

[148] Valens, II 37.10 ἀναφορικούς, 41.36; Ptol. 2.9.11 αἱμάτων ἀναγωγάς; Firmicus, 4.9.4 *adsidue vomens sanguinem*, 7.9.3 *sanguinem reiectans*, 7.20.11, 7.23.4.

ASC or DESC) to a birth which takes place *fluxu sanguinis*, and Maximus to bloody miscarriages in 198 αἱμορύτοισιν ἐπ' ὠδίνεσσι (see Zito ad loc.) and 241 αἱματόεντι μιασμῷ. In any case we are clearly reminded of the evangelists' woman with a bloody flux (Mark 5:25 and Luke 8:43 οὖσα ἐν ῥύσει αἵματος; Matt. 9:20 αἱμορροοῦσα). Hagner (WBC on Matthew) suggests that the flux was probably from the womb; κρύφι' ἄλγε' points the same way. But in the Gospels the condition goes into the mental category of things that are ritually defiling. Astrology puts it into that of hidden disease: see n. below.

Words include αἱμαγμοί, a term unique to astrology which often envisages injuries or acute harms, and in Valens is associated with cuttings and falls;[149] αἱμορραγίαι;[150] words for disgorging or spitting (αἱμάτων ἀναγωγαί, αἱμοπτύσεις or αἱμάτων πτύσεις); and, as in the Gospels, words for 'flow', including αἱμόρροιαι (Apomasar, *De Rev.* p. 153.7), αἱμορροΐδες, sc. φλέβες (Ptol. 3.13.15; *Π.σ.α.* p. 183.11), and ῥύσις αἱματώδης/ῥύσις αἱματώδης (Camaterus). The phrase most similar to this one is in Hephaestion, ii. 248.12 νόσους αἱματικάς, corresponding to νόσους σωματικάς in the original at i. 209.3 (and hence perhaps a corruption?). The very rare adjective αἱμηρός describes colour,[151] and it is lexica that provide the right meaning here, full of blood.[152]

338 φύσις: see on 4.413.

κρύφιμ': the text of L presents the normal form of the adjective, which L¹ corrects in the margin to the more idiomatically astrological form (see on 4.413; Nauck, *Mélanges*, v. 168–9; Monaco, 43). For an issue of blood as a hidden disease, compare Firmicus, 3.2.14 (Saturn in DESC), *latentium vero corporum dolores indicit, facit enim aemorroicos*...; Valens, V 2.4 (Saturn in an *apoklima*) σωματικὴ ἀσθένεια καὶ αἱμαγμοὶ καὶ ἐπισφαλεῖς νόσοι ἢ κρυπτοὶ πόνοι ~ *Lib. Herm.* v. 3 *effusio sanguinis seu aegritudines fallaces vel dolores absconditi*; Θ p. 155.27 (Mars ὕπαυγος in sixth place) κρυπτὰ πάθη τῶν σπλάγχνων ἢ αἱμορροίας.

1.339–58 Miscellanea

339–40

Saturn in ASC, Mars opposite. This configuration in 3.141–4 causes loss of wives, but exactly this outcome in Περὶ κέντρ. 17 (cf. 'a bad death' in Dor.^ARAB II

---

[149] I 1.22; IV 4.3, 17.5, 18.7, 22.3, 5; IX 2.11; Additamenta Antiqua, IV 19; ps.-Galen, *Progn.*, xix. p. 535.8 Kühn.
[150] Περὶ κράσ. 156; Ptol. 4.9.5; Rhetorius, *CCAG* vii. 219.9; Teucer, *CCAG* vii. 206.10 (under Scorpio).
[151] Philodemus, Περὶ ὀργῆς, fr. 6 i. 15 Indelli (the complexion of an angry man); Andromachus the Elder (LXII Heitsch), 10 αἱμηρῶν... κανθαρίδων (but αἱμοβόρων conj. Heitsch); Oribasius, *Synopsis ad Eustath. fil.* 3.20 (the stone αἱμηρή).
[152] Hesych. α 1952 αἱμηραί· αἱματώδεις; ps.-Zonaras, α p. 87.12 Αἱμηρόν· πλῆρες αἵματος; Suda, α 197, *Lex. Seguer.* α 44.25, Photius α 598 Αἱμηρόν· αἵματος πλῆρες/η.

23.5) and Firmicus, 3.2.2 *biothanatos* (with no benefics in aspect). In Firmicus, 3.4.20 and 6.29.10 (where the Moon is involved as well, moving to the one planet or the other in a specific phase), the types of violent death are specified. The lack of precise fit with 6.29.10 means that it is impossible to be certain whether this chart belongs in the following group, which, if it did, would imply that it has been converted from elegiacs.

339 κατ' ἰθύν: otherwise *vl* in 1.30 (see ad loc.) and in Maximus, 448 ἠὲ κατ' ἰθὺν ἴῃσιν, also for opposition; see Zito ad loc. This is a revival of the old Homeric noun ἰθύς, recalling prepositional phrases like *Il.* 6.79 ἐπ' ἰθύν, *Od.* 4.434 πᾶσαν ἐπ' ἰθύν, *Il.* 21.303 ἀν' ἰθύν (straight on against, upstream) and *Od.* 8.377 ἀν' ἰθύν (upwards), but with a sense closer to *Il.* 14.403 πρὸς ἰθύ οἱ, where ἰθύ is adverbial (see Janko on 14.402-8), and as in passages where one warrior goes to face another, i.e. confronts him (e.g. *Il.* 8.322 βῆ δ' ἰθὺς Τεύκρου). As elsewhere in this book, opposition is an aggressive aspect (285 n.; pp. 292-3).

340 If γε is not to seem desperate to the point of raising suspicions that the line has been converted from a pentameter (ὅστις ἀνήρ ends a hemiepes in Theognis, 744), only *males* must be at risk of violent death, a strange restriction, though De Stefani's apparatus implies this interpretation. For the adjectival use of αἴλινος he compares *GVI* 473.1 = *IGUR* 1177 (Rome, 3rd c. AD) βρέφος αἴλινον, to which add Bernand, 22 II.3 (Hermoupolis Magna, 2nd/3rd c. AD) νέκυν αἴλινον, *SEG* 26.1217.1 (Tarraco, 3rd c. AD) γόον αἴλινον.

341–52

Sequence of elegiac couplets. These charts all have parallels among the sample charts (Firmicus, 6.29 and 31), and two have parallels on papyrus, one attributed with a good degree of likelihood to Anubion.

341-2 + 343-5

A pair of charts concerning slaves. In the first, Mars is quartile to the Sun, Saturn to the Moon. Natives are slaves or parentless. In the second, expressly presented as a follow-on to the first (ἢν δ' ἔτι καί), Venus is opposite to Mars < > and Saturn (in MC?) in quartile to her (sc. the Moon). Slaves are born of slaves.

There are parallels for this mini-sequence within Anubion, F 11, and Firmicus, 6.29.3-4. In Firmicus the correspondence is clear. In the badly-damaged Anubion papyrus it is only the occurrence of ‹σ›τερέσει in l. 3 (supporting Koechly's conjecture in 1.342) which confirms that a chart corresponding to 1.341-2 stood at this point, but F 11.5 is a version of 1.344 and F 11.6 = 1.345. In neither author is the second configuration presented as a follow-on from the first as clearly as here; on the contrary, in the Anubion papyrus the second is set off by a separate (unfortunately damaged) heading. In Firmicus, they belong to a section headed *de servorum nativitatibus*, which begins with this theme and then moves to the extended one of nurture, but at least has a coherence that the present section lacks.

Firmicus' first chart features slavery and loss of parents, the second slaves born of slaves. The first abides by the principle that the harm is done by injury to a luminary, but mentions only the Moon and gives a different aspect (Anubion is too damaged to show what the protasis contained). In the second, there is a relationship of quartile or opposition between the malefics and Venus and the Moon, which confirms Koechly's guess that the Moon is what is meant by ταύτην in 1.344 after a presumably missing pentameter in 343b. If one can talk about 'primary' or 'original' configurations here, Firmicus' seems to be that, for his version makes more sense than the Manethonian one which cobbles the two charts together in a complicated way, making Venus as an add-on to the previous mention of Mars.

Anubion's is secondary too; see the discussion in Heilen 2010, 158–9; p. 277. After the title, F 11.5 has been gerrymandered so as to be self-contained. That has meant eliminating anaphoric ταύτην, and introducing a direct reference to the Moon in the first half of the line. There is nothing to correspond to Venus' opposition to Mars in 1.343.

342 καί: Firmicus has a disjunctive (*aut*), and perhaps L's original reading, ἤ, is the right one here. Hiatus at the caesura of a pentameter would be either a sign of a lack of fastidiousness, or, conceivably, a sign of a late date. See West 1982, 45 (and J. Diggle, *CR*² 34 (1984), 69), 158 (later classical and Hellenistic); for the imperial period, Kristoffel Demoen, 'The Date of the Cyzicene Epigrams: An Analysis of the Vocabulary and Metrical Technique of *AP*, III', *AC* 57 (1988), 231–48, at 245 (not a single example in the *Garland*, but more examples beginning in the third century AD).

343 κατεναντίον Ἄρεος ἔλθῃ: as in 339 (and sharing authorship?), an Iliadic phrase of martial confrontation has been converted for opposition (*Il.* 21.567 κατεναντίον ἔλθω, cf. *Od.* 14.278 ἐναντίον ἤλυθον, not hostile); for the hostility of this aspect see 1.285 n.

344 ἴδοι: this is missing in a gap in the papyrus at Anubion, F 11.5, but it is the only verb that fits, and it is unmetrical. What it implies is a deeply slapdash compiler who remade the first half of the line, but lazily took over the verb which only a slight change (λεύσσῃ or Heilen's κατίδοι) might have made to scan.

ὑψόθεν ἑστώς: in the MC. In EGHP, the adverb is used of elevation, in the sky, from the clouds, from a mountaintop; the only other possible application to the MC is Camaterus, *Zod.* 654 Ἄρης ὑψόθεν (uncertain). The verb, one of the less adventurous ones for placement, is also in 3.245 ἀντίον ἑστώς, but ordinary in prose (Dorotheus, Rhetorius/Θ, Theophilus).

345 τούσδε νόει ξυνέσει: Anubion confirms that L's τούσδε was right all along, but that should have been apparent even without the papyrus. This is the construction found in 5.212, 224, 231 (see p. 359), which is followed by the accusative of that which the addressee is being called upon to diagnose or identify. Those later passages do not, it is true, use a demonstrative. But ξυνέσει, shared with Valens' promotion of his science as a discipline that calls for sagacity and intellectual acumen (VI 8.20; IX 1.3, 19; IX 9.10), should not be accompanied by a demonstrative either, which is what A.–R. intended with τῆδε ... ξυνέσει. Nor is τῆδε any better as an adverb, 'in this way'. νόει is suitably Anubionic vocabulary: he uses it in F 2.3 νοήσας and F 5 b 3 χρὴ γάρ τοι νο‹έ›ειν (though both from sets of instructions, not an apotelesma).

346–9
Jupiter in quartile or trine to Saturn ... Mercury on ASC with the Moon. Natives are fortunate from birth. They enjoy wealth, prestige, and friendships. The outcome, at least, corresponds to Firmicus, 6.29.5 *prospere natus prosperius nutrietur* (i.e. the next chart in the sequence after the previous items), even if the items in the protasis do not. Firmicus is compatible with the location of the Moon on the ASC, but in Firmicus there is no Mercury, nor aspect of Jupiter and Saturn.

348 †εσειτε†: sense requires either a verb of causing or signifying (with the planets in the previous line as the subject) or, since scansion seems to rule that out, a didactic verb (recognise, forecast), leaving the previous line as a hanging nominative. φράζεο is the right sense. My suggestion would be ἔννεπε, which is used in a pentameter of this precise shape in Anubion, F 3a γάλλους ἢ μοιχοὺς ἔννεπε τὴν γένεσιν; it is not palaeographically implausible, with π corrupted to τ, and, in a minuscule exemplar, an ν with a descender corrupted into an ει diphthong. A second person plural is not desirable from the point of view of didactic convention. At any rate, the lack of coordination this construction implies between protasis and apodosis can be paralleled in medical sign literature. In *Prorrh.* 1.39–41, for instance, symptoms are listed in the nominative before a brief comment on their implications (κακόν); that would be the underlying structure here.

349 δόξῃ καὶ πλούτῳ: also 1.218–19 πλοῦτος καὶ δόξαι, but the wealth–renown combination is too generic to add confidently to the case for common authorship of the hexameters and elegiacs.

350–2
Jupiter, Mars, and Mercury on ASC…Moon after New embraces Saturn. If these lines (despite the possible loss of an intermediate (?)pentameter) belong together, the chart recalls Firmicus, 6.31.55, where Jupiter, Mars, Mercury <and Venus> are on the ASC, Saturn is on the DESC in Pisces, and the Moon in Aquarius. Pisces will therefore be the next sign the Moon enters; in other words, as in M^c, it is about to enter *synaphe* with Saturn. In Firmicus this is the chart of a *potentissimi imperatoris*. Heilen 2010, 178–9, remarks that the horoscope is unusually detailed (it gives the location of every planet), and could be that of a historical individual; he nominates no candidates, though 96 BC suits the data.

As with 341–2 + 343–5, there is independent papyrological evidence for the treatment of this chart by a poet who used elegiac couplets, and once again it differs from the present version. The fragment (F 7.25, P.Gen. IV 157) comes from the same Berlin roll as F 8, and belongs to the section of Anubion's poem which ran parallel with large sections of Firmicus, 6.29–31; the ascription to Anubion is thus as strong (or as weak) as that of all of F 4–6 + 8.[153] The chart stands at the end of a surviving sequence which corresponds to Firmicus, 6.31.51–5. It is badly damaged, but we can at least see that in the restorable line 25 the poet mentioned the same four planets together in the ASC as Firmicus, and in the same order.

Our poet, however, behaves differently. Whatever has been lost after 350, if indeed anything, τρίτος with the third element in 350 implies that there is nothing left to come; this should specify the last item in the series (e.g. *Il.* 12.91, 16.850, Ap. Rhod. 1.73–4, and especially Dorotheus, p. 399.10 εὖτε δέ κεν Πυρόεις Φαίνων θ' ἅμα καὶ τρίτος Ἑρμῆς). Unfortunately the damage to the papyrus is too bad to glean more; there was a reference to a *kentron* or *kentra* (26), and to the γένεσις (29). But even the one reconstructable line gives some possible insight into the relationship between Anubion and the present poet. The mere fact that the latter is using elegiacs should not automatically lead us to suppose that he is copying out a predecessor. He might well be subjecting him to the same kinds of manipulation to which he subjects M^b (or rather the poem also represented by M^b). And of course, a single poet may himself have treated the same chart twice, in a specific form for a definite historical individual (as in Firmicus?) and in a more generic way; that is possible, but completely speculative. The relationship between the different witnesses suggests the relationship of borrower to source might be a great deal more complex than models hitherto have allowed, and indeed that the very model of source and borrower is not necessarily the right one.

---

[153] Schubert, 420; Heilen 2010a, 178.

351 In Firmicus, the Moon is in Aquarius and Saturn in Pisces (the next sign). But Firmicus does not say exactly that the Moon is moving ἐκ συνόδοιο (on which expression see 1.185): for him, the Sun is in Libra (in the *epanaphora* of the horoscope). The Moon, in Aquarius, is therefore four signs ahead, and it was New Moon ten days ago.

Κρόνον φίλον ἀγκαλίσαιτο: see on 1.45. The construction here particularly recalls (accidentally?) Eur. *Cycl.* 498 φίλον ἄνδρ᾽ ὑπαγκαλίζων (cf. *Tr.* 757 ὑπαγκάλισμα μητρὶ φίλτατον).

352 The line is overall very similar to 1.209. See there for commentary on καὶ μακαριστοτάτους. Taken in itself the epithet is compatible with kings (Isid. *Hymn* 3.7–8), but in 2.476, its other occurrence in the Manethoniana, it is combined, as it is here, with the πρᾶξις theme (πρήξεις τ᾽ ἀγαθὰς τελέοντας), and shows that the chart has been bourgeois-ified vis-à-vis its incarnation in Firmicus: this is how you would describe astrology's typically successful man-about-town. For εὐπράκτους, see on 3.310, where, to the quoted parallels, add Hephaestion, i. 210.7 (Mars in own house by night), 216.22 (Venus in places of the Moon), Theophilus, *CCAG* xi/1. 239.8 (Venus on ASC or on *epanaphora* of MC), and Apomasar, *De Myst.*, *CCAG* xi/2. 190.15 (second decan of Cancer). The majority of the nine astrological passages where the word occurs involve Venus, the very planet who is *not* involved here—but maybe a pointer to the loss of Venus in a hypothetical lost line 350b, or even to the fact that the poet has suppressed her.

353–6 + 357–8

Saturn transits to the place of Mars, and Mars into aspect with Saturn. These are not perfectly complementary (or, if the poet intended them to be, his language is very sloppy), nor is it easy to follow the rationale, which is implicitly connected with the planets' physical characters, but does not seem to be producing straightforward εὐκρασία as a result of contact, as it does in 5.58–61 (see ad loc.). But the contrastive effects are at least paralleled in 2.166–76, where Saturn passing into Mars' houses is injurious (natives are low-spirited and anxious), but Mars passing into Saturn's has the opposite effect. There is a difference of detail (gain here, loss of inheritance in 2.175), but the opposite outcomes (and the difficulty of understanding why they are this way round) is similar.

353 **παρόδοισιν**: LSJ I.1.b gives 'rotation of chronocratory', but that is too complicated: this is the ordinary astrological word for a 'transit', or 'passage', the natural course of a planet. It is banal in astrological prose, which would use a prepositional expression, probably κατὰ πάροδον, or else ἐπὶ τῆς παρόδου, ἐν ταῖς παρόδοις (p. 312 n. 73). These are the only occurrences in the Manethoniana, and there are none in the poetic fragments of Dorotheus or Anubion.

355-6 For ἔσσεται ἀνθρώποις see Livrea on Ap. Rhod. 4.1105, but it may be that the poet particularly had in mind Dike's prophecies of wars (which might have formed the associative link with Mars) and sufferings after she leaves the earth in Aratus: compare 125-6 (Καὶ δή που πόλεμοι, καὶ δὴ καὶ ἀνάρσιον αἷμα) | ἔσσεται ἀνθρώποισι, κακῶν (vll κακοῦ, κακόν, κακοῖς; κακῷ Voss) δ' ἐπικείσεται ἄλγος (~ λύπας). Aratus himself is looking back to Hes. Op. 197-201, and any ongoing connection between 356 and Hesiod's τὰ δὲ λείψεται ἄλγεα λυγρὰ | θνητοῖς ἀνθρώποισι (200-1) would be a window allusion, though I suspect that is too subtle. The language of woe in 356 is a nice encapsulation of the poetics of astrology. Familiar with the basic Homeric styleme of paired 'woe' words (ἄλγεά τε στοναχάς τε, δάκρυσι καὶ στοναχῇσι, στοναχῇ τε γόῳ τε, κλαυθμοῦ καὶ στοναχῆς), the poet has, on the one hand, tilted his pastiche in the direction of inscribed epitaphs (compare *IGUR* III 1373.7 (Rome, n.d.) λύπας καὶ στεναχὰ[ς [sic], *IGUR* IV 1702.24 (Rome, 3rd c. AD) λύπας καὶ στοναχὰς) and, on the other, sprung it open by appending the prosaically ordinary astrological βλάβας.

357 κατοπτεύσας: again unique in the Manethoniana (Prévot, 264). Κρόνον αἰνὸν: i. 911 n. 2.

358 νῖκος ὀπάζει: the poet appropriates to the stars another formula of divine action, ultimately from Hes. *Th.* 433 νίκην προφρονέως ὀπάσαι (Hecate).[154] The Hellenistic and later form of the noun (which also appears in Valens, II 36.19, IX 15.1, and later texts) allows a pastiche of the EGHP verse-end κῦδος ὀπάζει.

1.359-61 Sign-Off

359 The reference to planets and fixed stars rings with the opening promise to Ptolemy (see on 4-7; also 4.3-4, 4.107-8 for the style of the expression and the irrelevance of fixed stars). Εἴρηται, summarising a previous discussion, is prosaic (e.g. Hdt. 4.31.2 ταῦτα μέν νυν τὰ λέγεται μακρότατα εἴρηται, 7.153.1 Τὰ μὲν περὶ Ἀργείων εἴρηται); also in 5.26.

360-1 The poet anticipates another book. It is less an invocation ('sing, Muse'), and more a request/prayer. 'Grant me to sing' goes back to Hes. *Th.* 104 δότε δ' ἱμερόεσσαν ἀοιδήν (see West ad loc.), now expanded with the specificity of 'volume two'. Whoever he is, the writer cannot have meant that he had written one book in hexameters (ἔπος) and was now moving on to elegiacs (τῷδε

---

[154] Thereafter applied to miscellaneous deities: Pind. *Isthm.* 2.13-14 (Poseidon), Ar. *Th.* 973 (Apollo), Hermonax, fr. 2.2 P. (Zeus), Nonn. *D.* 11.55 (Dionysius), 13.274 (Zeus).

μέτρῳ). In order to make sense ἔπος must mean a single unit of verse, which, coupled with a pentameter, adds up to an elegiac couplet; Koechly already understood this, and saw that the poet was intending to add another book consisting of 'this metre' (i.e. pentameter of 361) appended to an ἔπος. Ludwich's additional contribution (1904, 133–4) was to see that the sentiment is not that of the poet who gave the collection its final shape (since of course no elegiacs follow), but of the elegiac writer, presumably Anubion, who was announcing a transition from one book to another in his favoured metre. (In offering this interpretation he accepts the reading of L[1], where -πος appears over an erasure whose original reading, he notes (130), might have been προσέτι.) Monteventi, 196, cf. 116, 233–4, instead renders 'en utilisant ce mètre en rapport avec le propos', citing phrases like οὐδέν/μηδὲν πρὸς ἔπος, which has the slightly disconcerting implication that the poet's verse might *not* be relevant unless he expressly assures us that it is; she does not, however, question the Anubionic origin of the couplet. See p. 276 for the implications. In general I am hostile to the idea of mechanical transcription, but this looks very like an example of it.

Book Five

5.1–26 Introduction

In this rather confused introduction the speaker, who is apparently once again pretending to be Manetho, addresses himself to Ptolemy with a work which he simultaneously presents as (i) somehow deriving from a temple, (ii) an anthology, and (iii) a discovery or invention which has taken place under the stars at night.

The second mode of presentation was apparently already employed by Dorotheus in the proem of the first book, also using the bee metaphor:

> I collected the best of their sayings from the first [authorities] who were before me like the bees which gather [honey] from the trees and all kinds of plants; for from it there is the honey of medicine (transl. Pingree).

Similarly in the proem of the fifth. This may simply be a re-transcription of the first (Monteventi, 103), but nevertheless the writer of the proem (speaking of Dorotheus this time in the third person) connects it more clearly with the poet's active efforts to search out the very best works of his predecessors:

> …and he made it this book like a bee when it follows the most delicious of fruits, and the best of it is made into honey (transl. Pingree).

One can unpack the levels of signification here—labour, stylistic beauty, divinity, truth—at inordinate length, but the point here is that there is nothing specifically Egyptian or even 'oriental' about them. The bee motif is an embellished version of the regular claim by authors of epistolary prefaces to have made a judicious selection of available material,[1] although Dorotheus' transformation of honey into medicine takes the trope in a rather new direction. The motif of temple wisdom, on the other hand, is more distinctive of (i) Egypt (or an

---

[1] Cf. also Firmicus, 4 *Praef.* 5 *Omnia enim quae Aesculapio Mercurius et Hanubius tradiderunt, quae Petosiris explicavit et Nechepso, et quae Abram, Orfeus et Critodemus ediderunt [et] ceterique omnes huius artis antistites, perlecta pariter atque collecta et contrariis sententiarum diversitatibus comparata illis perscripsimus libris.*

imagined Orient), and (ii) occult literature, whose antiquity and illustrious origins it promotes.[2] Versions of this framing and authenticating device go back to at least the New Kingdom. There is no need for yet another survey of a motif which has been so well studied,[3] any more than there is to add to what Monteventi, 108–13, says about the bee motif. But the way it has been mobilised here does have some distinctive and notable aspects.

Some motifs are stock.[4] The text is linked to both temples and stelai. Each can exist without the other, but they are fairly often combined,[5] and one of the most famous of all the instances of the stelai motif—Josephus' narrative of antediluvian wisdom inscribed on pillars designed to survive fire and flood— envisages the wisdom inscribed on them as specifically concerning the heavens.[6] The wisdom has a divine origin (indeed doubly so, for two divine names are mentioned), while the inclusion of Petosiris' name waves at the idea of the famous intellectual (magician or sage). Yet at the same time, the poet is sketchy in the extreme about how all these motifs are supposed to fit together. The relationship between the stelai and the books is not clear (books should not be needed at all if the pillars are inscribed, and normally you would discover the one or the other but not both; if it is worth pressing this for literal sense at all, one might look to Bolus/ps.-Democritus (n. 5), where the writing was discovered when a pillar crumbled). And what of the books themselves? In other versions of the temple wisdom motif, the writing is discovered in the temple by

---

[2] Including in astrology: *CCAG* vii. 62, in the *incipit* of a treatise about Moon phase in cod. Berlin. 173, fo. 177ᵛ: βίβλος εὑρεθεῖσα ἐν Ἡλιουπόλει τῆς Αἰγύπτου ἐν τῷ ἱερῷ ἐν ἀδύτοις (a hieroglyphic text which supposedly came to the notice of King 'Psamichus').

[3] W. Speyer, *Bücherfunde in der Glaubenswerbung der Antike* (Göttingen, 1970), esp. 'Angebliche Buchfunde in Tempeln', 125–8; Festugière, 319–24; id., *Études de religion grecque et hellénistique* (Paris, 1972), 272–4; W. Burkert, *Kleine Schriften*, iii. *Mystica, Orphica, Pythagorica* (Göttingen, 2006), 272; J. Herman and F. Hallyn (eds.), *Le Topos du manuscrit trouvé: Hommages à Christian Angelet* (Leuven, 1999); Moyer, 245–6; Naether and Thissen, 561; R. L. Fowler, *Early Greek Mythography*, ii (Oxford, 2013), 624–5.

[4] J. Dieleman, *Priests, Tongues, and Rites: The London–Leiden Magical Manuscripts and Translation in Egyptian Ritual* (100–300 CE) (Leiden, 2005), 261–84, esp. 271–5, 282–3.

[5] Bolus/ps.-Democritus, Φυσικὰ καὶ μυστικά (Bidez-Cumont, ii. 317, fr. A 6; Festugière, 224–38, 320–1; this text asserts a physical doctrine like that of Nechepso, fr. 28 Riess, in Firmicus Maternus, 4.22.2, cf. Festugière, 232 and n. 2); *PGM* 8.42; Euhemerus, T 36, 65 Winiarczyk; Plut. *Mor.* 354 A (Thebes); Nicephorus Callistos, *Hist. Eccl.* 10.33 (*PG* 146.541–2; Speyer (n. 3), 127–8: the book is St John's Gospel). In P. CtYBR inv. 422 verso (n. 10), the document comes from a cavity in a wall in the temple rather than a pillar; in Manetho, *BNJ* 609 T 11a, the pillars come at an earlier stage in the transmission than the temple. Both texts are discussed further below.

[6] Jos. *AJ* 1.69–71, esp. σοφίαν τε τὴν περὶ τὰ οὐράνια καὶ τὴν τούτων διακόσμησιν. The narrative of Pebechios in Bidez–Cumont, ii. fr. A 16 (a Syriac source preserving a story about Persian magi which is set in Egypt) also involves pillars inscribed with astronomical/astrological lore (p. 338). Their discovery evidently prompts an enquiry by the king of Egypt, but afterwards they and/or their interpretation are inscribed on a *further* set of tablets which are in a place of astrological symbolism, enclosed in a place whose gates represent the seven planets. The whole is rather reminiscent of Nonnus' tablets (κύρβεις) in *D.* 12 and the seven πίνακες of *D.* 41.

the sage, or is taken to the sage, and he takes it to the king. These stages are not clearly delineated here. The poet has formulated his language in such a way as to avoid explicitly identifying Petosiris or the narrator as discoverer of the books; indeed, it is quite unclear what Petosiris' role is supposed to be. As for the king, he is accorded no characterisation to explain how he is an appropriate recipient for such a treatise. He shows no curiosity, no eagerness for useful or secret knowledge. Finally, in other versions of the motif, the antiquity of the material and/or a change of language or writing system poses an interpretative challenge.[7] But there is nothing here about problems of intelligibility, the need for translation, nor, conversely, any insistence on the need to restrict circulation or maintain secrecy.[8] In the frame of the first book, although there was no claim to divine origins, the 'translation' motif was retained and took the form of rendering Petosiris' scattered works into a more organised and perhaps more aesthetically satisfying form. Here we do not even get that. The material is simply served up to Ptolemy with three different and not particularly compatible versions of its origins.

It is striking, though, that temple origins are combined with *al fresco* discovery under the stars, because these are both attested—separately, not together—in the Nechepso–Petosiris literature.[9]

The first is attested in a Demotic papyrus of the second century AD from the temple library of Tebtunis. The papyrus begins with a frame story, according to which a block of stone falls from a wall in the temple in Heliopolis, revealing a papyrus which is brought to the notice of King Nechepsos. To the king's great delight it is interpreted by the prophet Petesis as an astrological treatise by Imhotep.[10] The opening section of the supposed treatise itself is then quoted, beginning 'Here is a copy of the papyrus of Imhotep the Great, son of Ptah, the

---

[7] As in the documentary fiction in the Book of Sothis (Manetho, *BNJ* 609, T 11a), where pillars are first inscribed in the sacred tongue in hiero*graphic* characters (στηλῶν ἱερᾷ... διαλέκτῳ καὶ ἱερογραφικοῖς γράμμασι κεχαρακτηρισμένων), then after the flood translated into Greek but in hiero*glyphic* characters by the second Hermes (ἐκ τῆς ἱερᾶς διαλέκτου εἰς τὴν Ἑλληνίδα φωνὴν γράμμασιν ἱερογλυφικοῖς), and deposited in book form in the temples of Egypt, and now apparently presented by Manetho (after a further process of transcription into readable Greek?) to Ptolemy. See also a Hermetic example in Iambl. *Myst.* 8.5 Ὑφηγήσατο δὲ καὶ ταύτην τὴν ὁδὸν Ἑρμῆς· ἡρμήνευσε δὲ Βίτυς προφήτης Ἄμμωνι βασιλεῖ ἐν ἀδύτοις εὑρὼν ἀναγεγραμμένην ἐν ἱερογλυφικοῖς γράμμασι κατὰ Σάιν τὴν ἐν Αἰγύπτῳ. For *Suppl. Magic.* ii, no. 72 col. i. 1–6, see Bremmer 2015, 253–4.

[8] As in e.g. Bidez–Cumont, ii. 339, fr. A 16 (Pebechios to Osron).

[9] Note also the multiple modes in the 'Book of Crates' in M. Berthelot and O. V. Houdas, *La Chimie au moyen âge*, iii: *L'Alchimie arabe* (Paris, 1893), 46: the speaker has *written* a book, *discovered* a book in the temple of Serapis, and then been carried up into the path of the moon and sun in heaven.

[10] P. CtYBR inv. 422 verso and P. Lund inv. 2058 verso; see i. 54–5 and n. 47; now published in Quack and Ryholt, Text 10–11, 161–83. It is not certain, but likely, that Petesis is identical with Petosiris (Quack, 57; Quack and Ryholt, 174).

great god.' That is important, because Imhotep (or rather his Hellenised name Imouthes) is identified as Asclepius, and Asclepius presented along with his fellow authority Hermes, in P.Salt, another member of the Nechepso–Petosiris tradition.[11] In other words, a text found in a temple, associated with the names of Hermes and Asclepius, corresponds precisely to the set-up of the first four lines of the prologue. So, perhaps, does their association with a 'wisdom' tradition. Asclepius is described here as Hermes' σύμβουλον, while P.Salt represents Petosiris and King 'Necheus' as having received instruction from Hermes and Asclepius themselves; the verb is συνήδρευσαν, presumably from συνεδρεία, council or conference or advisory meeting.[12] Hermes is named first, but Asclepius is barely subordinated to him; this corresponds to the situation in P.Salt, rather than to the set-up in Hermetic literature, where Asclepius is decidedly the junior partner and the recipient of Hermes' disclosures.

The second is attested in the well-known iambic fragment (fr. 1 Riess/Heilen) quoted at the head of the sixth book of Vettius Valens, in which Nechepso gave an account of some revelatory experience which befell him πάννυχον πρὸς ἀέρα. There can be no question here of a voice; the narrator claims to have devised (καθεῦρον) his own material. But it is intriguing that he describes his material as λάλον, and that in combination with the black night and direct contact with the heavens (7) leaves us with much the same impression as the treatment of the temple motif, as if the poet were wanting to gesture towards a motif he knew to be associated with a body of material with which he wanted to claim affiliation, and yet were unsure quite how to handle it. The author of the horoscope in P.Salt presents himself as having consulted books handed down from Chaldaeans and Petosiris and Necheus, who were themselves dependent on Hermes and Asclepius. But the 'I' in the proem is not simply a passive recipient of wisdom handed down from higher authorities. He wants something of the cachet of the Nechepso–Petosiris literature, but also to advertise his own expertise and original contribution, and he compromises by presenting Petosiris as a 'friend', a colleague or kindred spirit. He does so in terms which obfuscate the centuries between their putative pseudepigraphical personae.

Finally, we know that the motif of temple wisdom was used in the pseudo-Manethonian literature elsewhere. We know this from a letter[13] attached to the beginning of a 'Book of Sothis', quoted by Syncellus (8th/9th c.) from the early fifth-century chronographer Panodorus. That is our *terminus ante quem* for the

---

[11] P.Salt (P. Louvre 2342 *bis*); no. 137c, pp. 42–4, Neugebauer–Van Hoesen; see Heilen 2015, 265–6; i. 55–6; Monteventi, 65.
[12] συνήδρευσαν is a supralinear correction of συνυδρευσαν. Riess (T6) printed συνίδρυσαν; see *contra* Kroll, *RE* xvi. s.v. Nechepso, 2161.4–5. Heilen 2015, 548, prints συνέδρευσαν.
[13] Manetho, *BNJ* 609 F 25; bibliography on the letter in Philippa Lang's commentary ad loc., s.v. 'the sacred books', and on T 11a, s.v. 'from the books'; Monteventi, 122–5.

Book of Sothis, which has itself been dated to the fifth century[14] (in which case Panodorus cited it when it was still new). Strictly, however, we cannot be sure of the relative chronology of that pseudepigraphical letter, on the one hand, and the present passage, on the other. But it appears that the motif had entered Manethonian literature by late antiquity, and the reference to *adyta* in 4.9 suggests that it was already familiar enough to gesture at by the third century at the latest. In the letter, which is addressed to Ptolemy, Manetho describes himself as high priest and scribe of the Egyptian temples, resident in Heliopolis. It is important to be clear that this particular strand of the Manethoniana has nothing to do with astrology and nothing to do with Nechepso–Petosiris. The letter-writer postures as having translated sacred books written by Hermes Trismegistos, who is not the Hermes intended by the author of the proem. The connection with Ptolemy seems to be erected on different foundations as well. The book of Sothis itself consists largely of king-lists, and its fictive address to Ptolemy may in fact have a *better* rationale than that of the astrological material, not only because its subject is royal dynasties, but also because its supposed rendering of ancient Egyptian material might be pitched at the same monarch who was famous for commissioning the Septuagint, and for having a wide interest in other cultural traditions.[15] But the letter itself credits Ptolemy with an interest in the *future* of the cosmos (ἐπιζητοῦντί σοι περὶ τῶν μελλόντων τῶι κόσμωι γίγνεσθαι, καθὼς ἐκέλευσάς μοι...). It supplies the rationale that we find wanting in the present passage. But at the same time it seems to share with it the image of a Ptolemy who, for whatever reason, has become interested in prognostication.

5.1–24 Proem

1–11 To Ptolemy

The address to Ptolemy, repeated in 11, strikes up the epistolographic manner. The readiest comparisons are other pseudepigraphic letters from sages to kings, including Ptolemy himself, which presuppose a monarch interested in methods of divination.[16] A particularly good comparison for this whole passage is the

---

[14] Lang on T 11a, s.v. 'from the books'.   [15] Lang on T 11a, s.v. Ptolemy Philadelphos.

[16] Petosiris to Nechepso, frr. 37–9 Riess (a method to predict the outcome of illnesses, the flight of slaves, and gladiatorial combats); Thessalus to Caesar Augustus, introducing an astrobotanical tract, *Virt. Herb.* 1, Pr. 1–28, ed. H. Friedrich, *Thessalos von Tralles* (Meisenheim am Glan, 1968); alternative version in which Harpocration addresses Augustus in *CCAG* viii/3. 134–8. The Demotic text with the frame-story about King Nechepsos (n. 10) had already credited the king with interest in an astrological treatise. The letter to Augustus goes one better, in that the writer narrates how he had succeeded with the help of a Theban priest in summoning Asclepius, who explained to him why Nechepso, though a great sage, had had only partial success. See D. Pingree,

letter to 'King Ptolemy' affixed to the *Sortes Astrampsychi*. The number of motifs shared between the two texts shows their essentially stereotyped nature. It boasts of the writer's hard work (πολὺν κόπον ὑπομείνας), presents his activity as one of compilation (ἐκ γὰρ τῶν ἀδύτων ἀπανθισάμενος...), and combines the idea of remote recesses (ἐκ γὰρ τῶν ἀδύτων) with the name of an eminent predecessor (Pythagoras).

Both works in turn exploit the conventions of 'court science' treatises.[17] The speaker advertises his effort (11 οὐ βαιὸς κάματος) and expertise (8 τὸ μάθημα καθεῦρον; 9 σοφίη), while also presenting himself as, not innovator, but anthologist.[18] Sometimes the king is credited with interest in the subject. Apollonius' letter to Ptolemy at the head of a treatise on dislocations describes the monarch as φιλιάτρως διακείμενον; the *Sortes Astrampsychi* credit him with a general interest in what is useful. Manetho's letter implies rather than asserts this; subsequent addresses at pertinent points help (35-8, 207-8). Above all, we find a version of the 'belatedness' motif, whereby the addressee is assured that 'the subject matter has been treated previously and on that basis is not obscure or impractical'.[19] But while other authors (Varro, Pliny) insert themselves into a lineage of literary/scientific treatments of the theme in question, this one prefers exclusiveness and élitism (10 ἢ μοῦνος Πετόσιρις). The treatises of Archimedes and Eratosthenes open with a literary allusion, assuring the recipient that reader and writer both partake in a common culture. The culture implied here is very hybrid: the stelae point to Egyptian temple wisdom, Petosiris to an intellectual community of congenial spirits, even as the medium of the poem itself situates it in the tradition of *belles-lettres*.

1-2 Ἐξ ἀδύτων ἱερῶν βίβλων...καὶ κρυφίμων στηλῶν: the combination of pillars and temples is discussed above. Syntactical clarity is not the poet's priority: ἐξ could go with either the shrines or the books, and ἱερῶν likewise. On the former, De Stefani takes ἐξ with ἀδύτων, appealing to Plat. *Tht.* 162 A, making ἀδύτων metaphorical and βίβλων a genitive of identity, shrines consisting in books (so too Monteventi, 120). Yet there should be a strong suggestion of real temple recesses containing sacred books—abstruse, if not completely inaccessible (Lang's translation 'from the *forbidden* sacred books', *BNJ* 609 T 12b, puts it

---

'Thessalus Astrologus', in F. E. Cranz and P. O. Kristeller (eds.), *Catalogus Translationum et Commentariorum: Mediaeval and Renaissance Latin Translations and Commentaries*, III (Washington, DC, 1976), 83-6, and id., 'Thessalus Astrologus: Addenda', in V. Brown *et al.* (eds.), *Catalogus Translationum et Commentariorum*, VII (Washington, DC, 1992), 330-2; G. Fowden, *The Egyptian Hermes: A Historical Approach to the Late Pagan Mind* (Princeton, 1993), 162-5; Ogden 2002, 52-4.

[17] M. Berrey, *Hellenistic Science at Court* (Berlin, 2017), 127-39 (128 on pseudepigraphal letters to kings).
[18] Koechly 1851, lvi.   [19] Berrey (n. 17), 133.

too strongly). On the latter, Fabricius' translation manages to take ἱερῶν with both nouns ἀδύτων or βίβλων (1716, 498 = 1795, 134: *E libris, Ptolemaie, sacris, sacrisque columnis*). If with ἀδύτων (Lopilato: 'temple sanctuaries'), the reference is to the sacred temple archives, but others (Riess, 328; Festugière, 76) have referred it to sacred books, and Riess drew a further connection with *Suda*, π 1399 Πετόσιρις.... καθὰ Ἕλληνες καὶ Αἰγύπτιοι τὰς περὶ θεῶν διετάξατο ἐπιλογὰς ἐκ τῶν ἱερῶν βιβλίων, according to which Petosiris himself made selections from them (a step the present poet does not take). The 'holy books' of 2.204 βίβλων ... ἱρῶν were mentioned side by side with leaders of initiations and types of prophet.[20] In other words, they had the same traditional associations as 'secret' books, for which see on 5.304. This passage, on the other hand, connects them with abstruse knowledge, of divine origin, preserved in temples. The expression, strongly associated with Egypt (Bremmer 2010, 333–6; Henrichs, 225–7), seems to embrace a wide range of content, including not only writings about gods, but also natural science (Heliodorus, *Aeth.* 2.28.2: the sources of the Nile), divination/prognostics (Horapollo, *Hieroglyphica*, 1.38), and of course Hermetism and magic (passages in Bremmer 2010, 335).

2 ἤρατο: he 'erected' them (for which the normal word would be ἔστησε or at a push ἀνέθηκε). Koechly's correction of ηὔρατο is followed by Lang in *BNJ* 609 T 12b (but not by Lopilato). Hermes should be responsible for the content of the tablets, as he is in *Corp. Herm.* Exc. XXIII. 5 (Kore Kosmou) (see on 3), and in the Pebechios narrative in Bidez–Cumont, ii. 338 ('les stèles sacerdotales d'Hermès'), and like Hermes/Thoth in the Book of Sothis (*BNJ* 609 T 11a). He should not be their discoverer. The correction results in a *hysteron proteron* (he presumably erected them after inscribing them), but that is a lesser problem.

πάνσοφος Ἑρμῆς: in the first volume I should have made it more pointed that this formulation harmonises the traditional (if vague) Hermes/Thoth as founder of astrology, who is mentioned first, with the more specific conception of paired Egyptian sages of equal status. It is not simply the case that this *is* Hermes Trismegistos (Lopilato; Lang, in *BNJ* 609 T 12b, 'a synthesis of the Egyptian Thoth and Greek Hermes'). What is wanted here is not, or not only, a list of testimonia for Hermes as founder of the discipline,[21] but also support for the idea of Hermes' partnership with Asclepius, an implied parity of status which the latter clearly does not enjoy in the Hermetic Corpus or in Firmicus, 3.1.1 *Aesculapium et Hanubium, quibus potentissimum Mercurii numen istius scientiae secreta commisit*, 4 Pr. 5 *omnia enim, quae Aesculapio Mercurius et*

---

[20] Other astrological references to 'holy books' are in citations, e.g. Anon. *De Astrologia Dialogus*, p. 33.8; *Suda*, π 1399, s.v. Πετόσιρις... Ἐπιλογὰς ἐκ τῶν ἱερῶν βιβλίων.

[21] Housman on Manilius, 1.30; Eratosthenes, *Catast.* 43; Festugière, 103–4. Unclear why Dorotheus addresses Hermes as his son (I pr. 2).

Hanubius tradiderunt...perscripsimus. A parallel is to be found in P.Salt (p. 865), where the sources of the wisdom of Petosiris and 'Necheus' are named as Asclepius, explicitly identified as 'Imouthes son of Hephaestus', and Hermes, who can plausibly be identified as his partner Amenhotep of Thebes.[22] The association is distinctive of the Nechepso–Petosiris literature, but it is not confined to it, for the two sages were jointly worshipped in Deir el-Medina under Ptolemy VI (180–45) and in Deir al-Bahari under Ptolemy VIII (d. 116).[23] Both identities of 'Hermes' are hinted at here.

Hermes' epithet is best paralleled by an invocation in the (potentially very much later) *Hygromantia Salomonis*, CCAG viii/2. 157.2–3 ὁρκίζω σε, Ἑρμῆς πάνσοφε, λογιώτατε καὶ συνετώτατε; see otherwise 6.480 σοφὸς Ἑρμῆς, and (in an alchemical text) Zosimus, CAAG ii. 188.19 ὁ φιλόσοφος Ἑρμῆς. It seems not to reflect titulature in the Hermetic corpus (unsurprising if the god is not straightforwardly Thoth). See too CCAG vii. 62 (n. 2) which ἐγράφη [τε] ὑπὸ ἱερῶν γραμματαίων πανσόφων.

4 I accept Koechly's transposition of this and the next line, although De Stefani does not. Koechly gave as the reason the 'unbreakable tie' between ἐχάραξε (3) and ἀπομαξάμενος (5), but there is the additional advantage that the pair of Hermes/Amenhotep and Asclepius/Imhotep are thereby brought more closely together.[24] It is perhaps notable that when Imhotep figures as an astrological expert, it is often in connection with *iatromathematica*, astrology invoked to determine the correct times to prepare or administer medicines. This builds on his reputation as doctor and healer that precedes the development of astrology itself, and obviously underlies his *interpretatio Graeca* (cf. the preface of Thessalus' astrobotanical treatise *De virtutibus herbarum*, n. 16, in which Asclepius himself vouchsafes a revelation).[25] It was as healing gods that he and Amenhotep were worshipped at Deir al-Bahari. That type of astrology is obviously irrelevant to the present book, but their choice as figureheads in

---

[22] K. Ryholt, 'New Light on the Legendary King Nechepsos of Egypt', *JEA* 97 (2011), 61–72, at 71.
[23] A. Łajtar, 'The Cult of Amenhotep Son of Hapu and Imhotep in Deir el-Bahari in the Hellenistic and Roman Periods', in A. Delattre and P. Heilporn (eds.), "*Et maintenant ce ne sont plus que des villages...*": *Thèbes et sa région aux époques hellénistique, romaine et byzantine* (Brussels, 2008), 113–23; Naether and Thissen, 562; Renberg, i. 448–83.
[24] For Asclepius/Imhotep, to the bibliography cited in i. 55–6 n. 51, add A. Bernand, 104–9; J. Bingen, 'La dédicace à Imhotep-Asklèpios I.Philae I 127 (186–184 a.C.)', *Chronique d'Égypte*, 80 (2005), 277–80 (the syncretism goes back at least to the reign of Ptolemy V Epiphanes); Quack, 43–66; Sérida, 356–7.
[25] R. J. Forbes, 'Imḥotep', *Proceedings of the Royal Society of Medicine*, 33 (1940), 769–73; M. Totti-Gemünd, 'Aretalogie des Imuthes-Asklepios (P.Oxy. 1381, 64–145)', in M. Girone, Ἰάματα: *Guarigioni miraculose di Asclepio in testi epigrafici* (Bari, 1998), 169–93, esp. 173–5; Quack, 48–51, 57–60; Renberg, i. 423–34.

the Nechepso–Petosiris literature might imply that it had a significant and distinctive role there.

σύμβουλον: see p. 865.

πινυτῆς σοφίης: all the Manethoniana, especially the present poet, set great store by the quality of shrewdness (see i. 57–8 n. 52), but in connection with Asclepius/Imhotep it evokes his traditional character as sage (Egyptian rḫ-ḫt: Sérida, 356). For πινυτός see also n. on 1.131–2.

3 ἐχάραξε προνοίαις: the wording is conventional; the pillars are inscribed with the wisdom of the thinker, which is referred to with some derivative of νοεῖν. In the most influential example of the motif, Josephus' account of the pillars of astronomical wisdom inscribed by the descendants of Seth, the word for 'inscribe' is ἐγγράφειν, and for 'contrive' ἐπινοεῖν (AJ 1.69–70); προνοίαις here presumably indicates that it was specifically prognostics, rather than the science of the stars in general, that Hermes inscribed. For χαράσσειν itself see Corp. Herm. Exc. XXIII. 5 (Kore Kosmou) ὃς (sc. Ἑρμῆς) καὶ εἶδε τὰ σύμπαντα καὶ ἰδὼν κατενόησε καὶ κατανοήσας ἴσχυσε δηλῶσαί τε καὶ δεῖξαι. καὶ γὰρ ἃ ἐνόησεν ἐχάραξε καὶ χαράξας ἔκρυψε; and for other instances of χαράσσειν see Manetho, BNJ 609 T 11a (Syncellus, p. 72 Dindorf) στηλῶν ἱερᾷ... διαλέκτῳ καὶ ἱερογραφικοῖς γράμμασι κεχαρακτηρισμένων; Cyranides, Prol. 13 Συριακοῖς ἐγκεχαραγμένη γράμμασιν; Corp. Herm. Exc. XXIII. 66 στήλαις καὶ ὀβελίσκοις χαράξουσιν...67 κρυπταῖς στήλαις ἐχάραξαν.

5 ἀντιτύπῳ κηρῷ: a reasonable parallel for the formulation, although not, it seems, referring to a seal, is IGUR iii. 1167.3–4 (Rome, late 3rd c. AD?)...ἧς ἀπὸ κηροῦ | ἀντίτυπον ῥεύσει τοῖς δακρύοις χάριτα: the apparent meaning is that a copy of an epitaph was retained on a wax tablet (G. H. R. Horsley, 'The Inscriptions from the So-Called "Library" at Cremna', AS 37 (1987), 49–80, at 77 n. 75). Nonn. D. 33.295 ἀντίτυπον ποίησε τύπον τροχοειδέι κηρῷ refers to the wax linchpins that wrecked Oenomaus' chariot.

ἀπομαξάμενος (LSJ ἀπομάσσω, III): take an impression. Used of making mankind in God's own image in Or. Sib. 1.23 (see Lightfoot on 1.22–3). If Hermes is the subject, presumably the wax is a seal. The god places a seal, not on the stelai themselves, but perhaps on the doors of the adyta behind which they were kept.[26] Possible parallels for sealing a room or enclosed space, as opposed to a text, are Dan. 6:17 (the lion's den) and Matt. 27:66 (see Hagner, WBC, ad loc.); Gospel of Peter, 33 (seven seals). The effect of sealing a sacred text was, first, to stake authorship, and second, to render the text secret or

---

[26] Fabricius 1716, 498 = 1795, 134 paraphrases the passage, but not in such a way as to make it clear exactly how he understands it ('Manethon ipse poema suum cum Hermetis κηροχύτῳ γραφῇ conferens...').

exclusive (Henrichs, 230–1). An extreme version of the secrecy motif is *Corp. Herm.* XVI. 2, where Asclepius adjures King Ammon *not* to allow the teachings he has derived from his master to be translated into Greek. Keydell, however (60–1), takes the participial phrase with the first-person verb (next note) so that the user of the wax is the poet, apparently taking the impress of the engraved signs. That is right for the normal sense of the verb, but a novel detail in the hidden-stelai motif, if so.

5–6 κεκόμισμαι...δώρημα μελισσῶν: the first-person verb is Keydell's emendation. 'Loquitur poeta' (De Stefani). The middle, if that is what is meant, of the normal phrase δῶρα κομίζειν, 'present a gift' (Ap. Rhod. 1.419 δῶρα κομίσσω, 4.1705 δῶρα κομίσσειν, fr. 2.2 κομίζων δῶρα, etc.) should mean 'receive', carry away for oneself', referring to the rich stores from which the poet has anthologised (the bee metaphor). But he may be trying to have the best of both worlds by combining this with the active meaning 'present a gift' (to Ptolemy), as one might expect in a preface: διδόναι Isocr. *Ad Nicocl.* 2, Dion. Hal. *Comp. Verb.* 1, citing *Od.* 15.125; Agathias Scholasticus, *AP* 4.3.20 ἥκω προθήσων, with a banquet metaphor; *OCD*[4] s.v. Dedications, Greek (M. Silk); Janson, 151–2, has examples with *praebere*.[27] Either way, there has to be punctuation after ἀπομαξάμενος, which on my interpretation does not agree with the subject of κεκόμισμαι. De Stefani has none, presumably following the interpretation of Keydell mentioned in the previous note.

6 ἀνθολόγου Μούσης βλύζον [Rigler: βληδων L] δώρημα μελισσῶν: the poet moves on to the motif of selectivity, developing the imagery which, for the author of the *Sortes Astrampsychi*, seems to have become dead metaphor (p. 1.6 ἐκ γὰρ τῶν ἀδύτων ἀπανθισάμενος). As in the proem as a whole, the poet waves at a number of topoi—flower-picking (Janson, 80–3, on the anthology), flowers of the Muses,[28] gifts of the Muses,[29] and bees/honey/choosiness[30]—while leaving it semantically and grammatically unclear how they fit together. Logically, he ought to be saying that his composition is the result of diligent choice, like bees who cull the flowers of the Muses (cf. *AP* 9.187.1–2 (adesp.) μέλισσαι | ποικίλα Μουσάων ἄνθεα δρεψάμεναι). But the Muse's epithet also suggests she is

---

[27] Revelation rather than gift in other prefaces: 'Manetho''s preface to the Book of Sothis (*BNJ* 609 F 25 = Syncellus, p. 73) παραφανήσεταί σοι ἃ ἔμαθον ἱερὰ βιβλία; *Sortes Astrampsychi*, p. 1.7 ἤδη δῆλα ποιῶ.

[28] Sappho, fr. 55 Voigt, Bacchyl. *Encomia* fr. 5.3, al. Poems as flowers: Maehler on Bacchyl. fr. 22 + 4.63; Meleager, *ad nauseam*.

[29] Archilochus, fr. 1.2 W.; Solon fr. 13.51 W.; Theogn. 250, 1055–6; Anacreon, fr. 2.3 W.; Alcman, *PMG* 59 b; al.

[30] cf. esp. Pind. *P.* 10.53–4; Isocr. *Ad Demon.* 52; Call. *Hymn* 2.110; Janson, 152–3.

the one doing the culling (cf. *PMG* adesp. 947 (a) Ἀ Μοῦσα γὰρ οὐκ ἀπόρως γενέει τὸ παρὸν μόνον, ἀλλ᾽ ἐπέρχεται πάντα θεριζομένα), while at the same time δώρημα suggests that the poet is the recipient of the Muse's gifts, not that he has gone around making selections of his own. There is an equally unhelpful and even more nebulous nexus of Muses, bees, and selectivity in 5.272–3.

7–8 ἠδ᾽ ἀνὰ νύκτα μέλαιναν, κτλ.: Wilamowitz's correction of the manuscript's ἄρα, yet another minuscule ν/ρ confusion, is clearly right. The poet has combined EGHP διὰ νύκτα μέλαιναν (usually at line-end, but in this *sedes* at *Il.* 8.486) with *Il.* 14.80 ἀνὰ νύκτα, both in the same sense of duration. The change is only possible if the connective ends in a consonant, and given the looseness of the transition from the literary part of the narrator's claim to his hints of *al fresco* revelation, ἠδ᾽ is at least no worse in sense and palaeographically much better than anything else. What precisely happened to Nechepso in the fragment quoted by Valens is unclear (Heilen 2011, 47–8) and for the purposes of this passage anyway beside the point, but the durative sense of ἀνά can be usefully compared with Nechepso's πάννυχον: it looks rather as if the poet, once again, is casting his motivic net widely, so as to suggest both the king's all-night experience and the motif of overnight toil (see on 1.8), but also the idea of some sort of decisive moment of enlightenment (καθεῦρον). For the chorus of stars, see on 4.11.

8 The speaker now claims to have found out his wisdom for himself. This is the first of half a dozen uses in this book of the extremely (before Byzantine Greek) unusual compound καθευρίσκειν,[31] which the poet uses mainly to defamiliarise the prosaic εὑρίσκειν, for finding stars in a chart (5.211, 321), or for stars finding one another (5.120, 317, 326). The voice at this point is that of a practitioner and active advancer of the art, like Valens, VII 4.4 ἐγὼ δὲ ὅσα ποτὲ μὲν εὗρον διὰ πείρας προέδειξα, ὅσα δὲ καὶ ἐν τῷ μεταξὺ χρόνῳ ἐπεξεῦρον οὐκ ἐβουλήθην ἀποκρύψαι (other claims to discovery: III 11.1, VI 8.4, IX 19 *titulus*). What work μοιραίοισι μίτοισι is doing in his claim is not completely clear, but he perhaps implies that his very discoveries were fated (6.743 n.); for the formulation, which is best paralleled in stone epitaphs, see on 1.7, and especially Milet VI, 2 754.6–7 (perhaps 2nd c. AD) μοιραίοις [μίτ]οις and *IEph.* 2101A l. 4 [μο]ιριδίους πλήσασα μίτους. He calls his discovery a μάθημα (i. 58 n. 55), a 'hard', non-intuitive, discipline or body of knowledge. At the same time, it is an eloquent one, and λάλον is being made to do some work here too, maybe as a

---

[31] To LSJ add Galen, i. 224.6 Kühn; Cyril Alex., *PG* 69.556.19 (corrupt in Hesych. κ 1722). Otherwise in astrology only in *De septem herbis planetarum*, *CCAG* xii. 134.10–11 Ὅταν ἐν τῷ ἰδίῳ οἴκῳ ὁ Ἥλιος καὶ ‹ἡ› Σελήνη καθευρίσκηται εἰς τὸν Ταῦρον.

Introduction 873

very etiolated reminiscence of Nechepso's voice (βοή), but also apparently to characterise astrology as disseminable and open knowledge, as opposed to hermetic lore (contrast e.g. *Corp. Herm.* Exc. XXIII. 5 (Kore Kosmou) καὶ γάρ ἃ ἐνόησεν ἐχάραξε καὶ χαράξας ἔκρυψε, τὰ πλεῖστα σιγήσας ἀσφαλῶς [ἢ λαλήσας del. Scott], ἵνα ζητῇ ταῦτα πᾶς αἰὼν ὁ μεταγενέστερος κόσμου). λάλος can of course be used of unexpectedly articulate things, as in λάλον ὕδωρ (Castalia) in the much-quoted lines about the cessation of Apollo's oracle (*AP* Appendix, *Oracula*, 122), and *passim* by Nonnus.

9 σοφίη (i. 57–8 n. 52) connects the narrator with Hermes (4) and with the wider tradition about Petosiris (Heilen 2015, 560–1 and n. 915). Festugière, 76 and 102, interpreted the passage to mean that the narrator is putting Petosiris on a par with Hermes, not himself with Petosiris, but that does not seem right. The pride of the boast is clear. οὐ γάρ τις expressions in EGHP sometimes reflect on the speaker's or subject's credentials vis-à-vis other people's (see especially *Il.* 9.104 οὐ γάρ τις νόον ἄλλος ἀμείνονα τοῦδε νοήσει), while the end of the line adapts Iliadic ἤρατο κῦδος from the battlefield to intellectual dexterity *via* EGHP ἐμήσατο — ‿ ‿ — — (κήδεα λυγρά, λυγρὸν ὄλεθρον).

10 The whole is modelled on lines like *Il.* 5.378 Αἰνείαν, ὅς ἐμοὶ πάντων πολὺ φίλτατός ἐστιν, 22.233 Δηΐφοβ᾽ ἦ μέν μοι τὸ πάρος πολὺ φίλτατος ἦσθα, *Od.* 16.445 τῷ μοι Τηλέμαχος πάντων πολὺ φίλτατός ἐστιν, all involving siblings or parents and children.[32] But these are relationships between living people, and someone addressing Ptolemy can only imagine himself conversing with Petosiris in a sort of timeless communion of *savants*, whether the latter is imagined as contemporary with Necho II (reigned 610–595 BC) or with Plato ('Peteesis' in P. Rylands 63; K. Ryholt, *The Petese Stories*, ii. (*P. Petese II*) (Copenhagen, 2006), 14–16; Heilen 2015, 543; Monteventi, 60). The affective tone has been carried over from the literary model: I find no convention for φίλος to be used of or by fellow philosophers. Philostratus' Apollonius speaks of Pythagoras as master, but not as φίλος, and when, in the Hermetic discourse of Mind to Hermes, Nous calls him φίλτατε (*Corp. Herm.* XI (ii) 8, 13, 15), this is presumably because a pupil stands in lieu of a son (like Asclepius to Hermes). The narrator and Petosiris are embarked on a similar enterprise, whether as followers of Hermes or anthologists or innovators in the μάθημα of astrology or all three.

11 οὐ βαιὸς κάματος δ᾽οὗτος: sense surely requires the negative to go with βαιὸς (against De Stefani's οὐδ᾽ οὗτος), and the *deixis* with the labour; effort is

[32] Eleanor Dickey finds the vocative φίλτατε to be used in expressions of genuine and deep affection, often between family members (*Greek Forms of Address from Herodotus to Lucian* (Oxford, 1996), 135–8, and *passim*).

what the poet draws attention to, not the book *per se*,³³ nor its contents.³⁴ For the topos, see on 1.8: the labour can be that of compiling demanding technical material and/or in fulfilling a divine commission. Compare, in the correspondence between the Persians Pebechios and Osron about the rediscovered writings of Ostanes, Pebechios' lament 'Mon âme en a recueilli de l'avantage [sc. from Ostanes' doctrine]; mais mon corps s'est épuisé dans le travail nécessaire pour faire sortir de ce présent mis à notre disposition les paroles divines (qu'il renferme)' (Bidez–Cumont, ii. 338).³⁵ It is also used by the compiler of Achmet's dream book (1 πολλὰ κοπιάσας).

12–24 Sayings of Homer³⁶

Unlike the Sibyl, the narrator is not in competition with Homer, but complements him. There are three quotations (*Il.* 6.147–9, 488–9, and a fivefold repeated formula of decision-making which the narrator uses in 20 as a transition) leading to a comparison which the poet rather botches. The implication of 21–2 is that *his* words are ordinary (ἀγελαῖα) beside Homer's divine ones, *his* the bronze beside Homer's gold. But the δόγματα θεῖα of 22 must be his astrological aperçus, and at this point the terms shift, so that *his* gold offsets Homer's purple like a border on royal dress. Textual differences are trivial. L¹'s correction ὥρῃ in 16 is an ancient variant in the text of Homer (Aristophanes, and printed by West).

M^d does not make Homer into a full-blown proto-astrologer.³⁷ On the contrary, while treating him with great respect, he uses his sayings as a useful offset for his own; the only tweak to Homeric vocabulary that makes him more

---

³³ *Cyranides*, Prol. 1 βίβλος αὕτη, μυστικῶν βιβλίον τόδε, αὕτη ἡ βίβλος; Flaccus Africus, *Compendium Aureum* (quoted by Festugière, 323): 'Après les livres des antiques *Kyranides*...j'ai découvert dans la ville de Troie, caché dans un tombeau avec les ossements du premier roi Kyranos, cet opuscule intitulé "Compendium d'or"...'

³⁴ *Cyranides*, Prol. 67–8 ἐτύγχανον δὲ τὰ ἐν τῇ στήλῃ ἀναγινωσκόμενα οὕτως ἔχοντα.

³⁵ Also in the 'Imouthes Aretalogy' (Renberg, i. 427–9, P.Oxy. 1381.32–42), where the translator of a book of Asclepius/Imouthes became ill and unable to proceed, but was cured when both he and his mother dreamed of Asclepius healing him.

³⁶ On Homeric citation technique: G. M. Bolling, 'The quotations from Homer in Polyainos 1. Proem. 4–12', *CP* 24 (1929), 330–4; G. Glockmann, *Homer in der frühchristlichen Literatur bis Justinus* (Berlin, 1968) (the present passages are not discussed); J. K. Kindstrand, *Homer in der Zweiten Sophistik: Studien zu der Homerlektüre und dem Homerbild bei Dion von Prusa, Maximos von Tyros und Ailios Aristeides* (Uppsala, 1973); W. R. Kahles, *Strabo and Homer: The Homeric Citations in the Geography of Strabo* (Diss. Loyola University of Chicago, 1976); Stanley; Curta, 185–8; P. G. Lake, 'Plato's Homeric Dialogue: Homeric Quotation, Paraphrase, and Allusion in the *Republic*' (Diss. Fordham, NY, 2011).

³⁷ Unlike Chrysippus, who, as Velleius complained (Cic. *Nat. Deor.* 1.41), saw all the poets as Stoics; and unlike Lucian's naïve scholastic narrator in the *Astrologia*. For astrological interpretations of Homer, see F. Buffière, *Les Mythes d'Homère et la pensée grecque* (Paris, 1956), 593–4.

astrology-friendly occurs in the lead-in (12 γενέσεις), not in the citations themselves. But M^d's interest in Homer also seems to differ from Manilius', which is purely literary (2.1-11, at the head of a survey which concludes with the Choerilan trope of *omnia iam vulgata*); for Manilius the bard figures as the poet of *Iliad* and *Odyssey*, and there is no attempt to appropriate him for astrology. The style of citation is more like that of Valens who, like him, is likely to be drawing from an anthology. If M^d strings together three quotations here, Valens joins two in VII. 3.53 (*Il.* 19.128 + 6.488), and distributes a series of four within IX 9.12-19, concluding with further allusions to Achilles and the Doloneia and a reference to ἕτερα...τεκμήρια which imply the use of a collection of testimonia. There are also four Orphic sayings on the soul in IX 1.12-15.

Valens cites Homer for weighty material on divine dispensation, fate, and necessity, the trajectory of human lives over which humans themselves have no control, as well as about Hermes' special identity as mediator and the god who elevates the human intellect. Like M^d he cites Homer (and other poets) in discursive passages, occasionally close to the head of a book (VII 1.3, cf. IX 1.12-15), always to illustrate an argument, and often in connection with imagery and analogies.[38] Some of the quoted lines are themselves images, analogies, or can be interpreted as such.[39] Unlike the formal quotation in the present passage, however, most of Valens' nine Homeric citations are unattributed, save for IX 9.12 (κατὰ τὸν ποιητήν) and IX 9.17 (μαρτυρεῖ δὲ τούτοις ὁ ποιητὴς λέγων), and some are worked seamlessly into the syntax of the surrounding passage (V 6.14, VI 8.3, VII 1.3); for Valens, it is the non-Homeric poets who receive fanfare (IX 15.1, Hesiod ὁ παλαιὸς καὶ Μούσαις μεμελημένος σοφὸς ἀνήρ, IX 1.12-15 καθὼς καὶ ὁ θειότατος Ὀρφεὺς λέγει). M^d, on the other hand, is engaging with Homer *qua* poet, and he makes Homer's verses themselves the term of a comparison, as opposed to using them as illustrative material for something else. The relationship for him is a head to head, whichever of the two comes out better.

12 Ἀνθρώπων γενέσεις: this prepares for the quotation of *Il.* 6.147-9, rendering γενεή (*Il.* 6.149 ὣς ἀνδρῶν γενεή; also 146 οἵη περ φύλλων γενεὴ τοίη δὲ καὶ ἀνδρῶν) into more astrological language (see on 1.199 γένεσιν... ἀνδρῶν). But in the original γενεή means 'generations'. Homer's point was that the generations of men come and go. The present point is the completely different one that the individual's geniture is fixed. Insofar as γενεή can be equated with

---

[38] V 6.14 + changing parts in a play and Cleanthes, fr. 527 von Arnim (i. 12 and n. 36); VI 8.3 + a father's last commissions to his children; VII 1.3 + climbing a mountain and finding a richly endowed temple at the top: here *Od.* 4.73, which is not itself part of a simile, is enlisted to embellish what is already a simile.

[39] IX 9.17, the golden chain of *Il.* 8.19 taken allegorically; IX 15.1, on Hesiod's two Erides.

astrological γένεσις at all, it must be through its post-Homeric meaning of '(time of) birth' (LSJ II.3).

μυρίος αἰών: also Dioscorides, *AP* 7.410.5 = *HE* 1589; Porphyry, *De philosophia ex oraculis haurienda*, p. 173.5 Wolff (ap. Euseb. *PE* 5.16.1). No particular reason to think that the poet is trying to evoke the αἰών of the *Timaeus* (4.625–6 n.). G.–P. on Dioscorides give instances of μυρίος χρόνος, to which add Pind. *Isthm.* 5.28, ps.-Aesch. *PV* 94 τὸν μυριετῆ χρόνον (ps.-Plat. *Epinomis* 987 A χρόνῳ μυριετεῖ τε καὶ ἀπείρῳ), Theodectas, 72 F 9.3 Snell; μυρίοι χρόνοι a pet phrase in Eusebius.

13 ἐκ στομάτων ἱερῶν: the original lips from which sounds emerged were the Muses', which were sweet (Hes. *Th.* 40). From that passage stems a long tradition of pronouncements about bards (Aesch. *Suppl.* 696 ἁγνῶν τ' ἐκ στομάτων) and sweet vocalising (Ap. Rhod. 4.903, Theocr. 20.27). In the absence of any other information about him Homer *becomes* a mouth (Moschus, *Epit. Bion.* 71–2 Ὅμηρος, | τῆνο τὸ Καλλιόπας γλυκερὸν στόμα), and the tradition of what emerged from it included roaring (Theodorus Prodromus, *Carm. Hist.* 56a.55–6 Ὁμήρου τὸ στόμα | βρυχήσεται μέγιστον), thunder (Paul Silent. *Descr.* 617 ἐριγδούποισι... στομάτεσσιν Ὁμήρου), and vomit, in a painting by Galaton described by Aelian, *VH* 13.22, maybe or maybe not in the Ptolemaic Homereion.[40] But the present passage is a light transmutation of the cliché of θεῖος Ὅμηρος (R. L. Hunter, *The Measure of Homer: The Ancient Reception of the Iliad and Odyssey* (Cambridge, 2018), 2), which is often connected with his 'wisdom' [next note] or quality of his thought,[41] and/or gloomy pronouncements about mortality (ps.-Plut. *Mor.* 104 D).

ὁ σοφώτατος εἶπεν Ὅμηρος: 'as the wise Homer said', a standard citational formula.[42] Each author who cites him naturally appropriates Homer's wisdom for his own ends. In the present case, σοφώτατος helps perhaps to draw him into the wisdom tradition M^d pushes so hard, assigning him at least the credentials of a fatalist, if not those of a fully fledged astrologer.

---

[40] Travestying the idea of a watersource: C. O. Brink, 'Ennius and the Hellenistic Worship of Homer', *AJP* 93 (1972), 547–67, at 555.

[41] Ar. *Ran.* 1034; Plat. *Ion* 530 B; ps.-Plat. *Alcibiades* 147 C Ὅμηρόν γε τὸν θειότατόν τε καὶ σοφώτατον; Dio Chrys. *Or.* 44.1 τῷ γὰρ ὄντι πολλὰ σοφὰ καὶ θεῖα εἰρηκὼς Ὅμηρος οὐδὲν σοφώτερον ἔφη τούτου τοῦ ἔπους...; Herodian, *De figuris*, 61 Ὅρα δὲ ἐνταῦθα τοῦ θείου Ὁμήρου τὴν σοφίαν. The topos is well represented in epigraphy as well where we continue to see the same association with wisdom (*IGUR* iv. 1532 (Rome, late 2nd/3rd c. AD?), 1533 (mid 2nd c.) Ὅμηρος φιλόσοφος καὶ θεῖος ποιητής.

[42] Ar. *Pax* 1096; Dio Chrys. *Or.* 44.1; Lucian, *Parasit.* 10, 24; ps.-Clem. *Hom.* 6.3.2; Heliodorus, *Aeth.* 3.12.2; with superlative: Plut. *Mor.* 164 D (in mouth of Solon); Dio Chrys. *Or.* 80.7; Malalas, *Chron.* 1.10. Paraphrase: Dio Chrys. *Or.* 1.14, 30.8; anecdote: Heraclitus, 22 B 56 D.–K.

14 The lips and the διάνοια complement one another; the latter is the intellectual element of what emerges through the former (ps.-Plat. *Def.* 414 D Φωνὴ ῥεῦμα διὰ στόματος ἀπὸ διανοίας; for the divine Homer's διάνοια, see Plato, *Ion* 530 B). Put otherwise, this is a version of the ancient dichotomy of content and form, in which διάνοια was counterpoised to λέξις;[43] compare also the description of Homer in *Or. Sib.* 3.421 νοῦν δὲ πολὺν καὶ ἔπος διανοίαις ἔμμετρον ἕξει. The locus classicus for 'sweetness in the poet's mouth' is Hes. *Th.* 83–4, there, ἐέρσην on the lips. West's note ad loc. is about honey, but he notes that ἐέρση could be any liquid distilled from heaven, and associations are activated here, not only with the speaker's eloquence,[44] but also with his immortal or divine status (Pind. *P.* 9.63–4, of Aristaeus; Nonn. *Par.* 20.96, of Jesus), and also, perhaps, the exalted nature of his teachings (Ptolemy compares the intellectual experience of studying the heavens with supping ambrosia beside Zeus, *AP* 9.577.4 θεοτρεφέος πίμπλαμαι ἀμβροσίης). Nectar likewise suggests divinity and poesy, except that poetry is generally lyric (Pind. *Ol.* 7.7 νέκταρ χυτόν, Μοισᾶν δόσιν, fr. 6b, in which ἀοιδαῖς and νεκτα͙ρ͙έας occur in close proximity; Antipater of Sidon, *AP* 7.29.4 = *HE* 273; Meleager, *AP* 4.1.35–6 = *HE* 3960–1) or lyric-like (Theocr. 7.82); more loosely, *IG* VII 1797 (Thespiae, 2nd/1st c. BC; supposedly a dedication by Polymnia of nectar to Zeus).

15–17 This seems to be simply a quotable quote, much used in various philosophic contexts, but not germane to discussions of fate and not pointedly relevant to astrology at all except insofar as γενεή can be creatively misread. Its function is to establish a woeful picture of human life. Ancient quotations are as follows:

(i) of *Il.* 6.145–9: ps.-Plut. *Mor.* 104 E, a collage of Homeric quotations on mortality. The straightforward purpose is shared with Marcus Aurelius, *Meditations*, 10.34, who quotes *Il.* 6.147 + 149 ὡς ἀνδρῶν γενεή.

(ii) of *Il.* 6.147–9: Atticus (anti-Peripatetic philosopher, dated by Eusebius to the Olympiad AD 176–80), fr. 4.13 Baudry = fr. 2.13 des Places (ap. Euseb. *PE* 15.4.13): the transitoriness of human life apropos of Aristotle's concept of εὐδαιμονία; Clem. Al. *Strom.* 6.2.5.8, whose point is simply that Homer has supposedly purloined the sentiment from Musaeus.

(iii) of *Il.* 6.147–8: Philo, *Aet. Mund.* 132 (Posidonius, fr. 310 Theiler), without the application to human life, so that it is *merely* a statement about the life-cycle of trees.

---

[43] A. Barker, 'Shifting Frontiers in Ancient Theories of Metaphor', *PCPS* 45 (1999), 1–16, at 3.

[44] Fulsomely ambrosial Byzantine lips: Manuel Rhaul, *Epist.* 1.14 ἄκροις χείλεσι γευσαμένους τῆς ἀπὸ τῆς σῆς γλώττης γλυκίονος μέλιτος ῥεούσης αὐδῆς, ὡσεί τινος ἀμβροσίας καὶ νέκταρος; Manuel Holobolus, *Encomium in imperatorem Michaelem Palaeologum*, p. 45.24–7 ὡς ὁμιλίας ἤκουσαν γλυκυτέρας τοῦ μέλιτος, ἡδυτέρας τοῦ νέκταρος, ὡς τῆς τῶν σῶν λόγων ἀμβροσίαν [sic cod.] ἐνεφορήθησαν—ἐξεχύθη γάρ σοι πηγαία χάρις ἐν χείλεσι...

16 ἐπιγίνεται ὥρη: L¹ ὥρῃ restores the correct reading, which is that of Aristophanes (also in Clement), but the quotations of these lines by Philo, Plutarch, and Eusebius also employ ὥρη.

18-19 Hector's fatalistic words at *Il.* 6.488-9 (where ἐπὴν τὰ πρῶτα γένηται refers to the moment of birth) are much quoted, not necessarily in their original sense. Crucial to M^d's interpretation is that μοῖρα be extended from 'death', the correct meaning of the *Iliad* passage,[45] to *everything* (1.199-203 n.). A minority of authors do cite the passage in its Homeric sense.[46] More often, though, it is taken to refer to fate, not death, an interpretation which goes back to the Stoic Chrysippus,[47] and then provokes a debate about the extent to which Homer supports the notion that *all* things are predetermined, rather than that some things are within human control (which is in turn supported by a different selection of lines from *Iliad* and *Odyssey*).[48] The lines had already been appropriated by astrologers; the Homeric scholia report that 'Heraclitus' had used *Il.* 6.488-9 to make Homer an astrologer,[49] and Valens, VII 3.53, wheels out Cleanthes, fr. 527 von Arnim, quickly followed by *Il.* 19.128 and 6.488 in favour of a cheerful determinism in which one simply gets on with it.

---

[45] As noted by Eustathius ad loc. (ii. 370.28-9) and *EtMag* 589.30. Porphyry, *Quaest. Hom. ad Iliad. pertinentes*, 1.3, qualifies by noting that it means *premature* death, which would come to all in old age anyway.

[46] Ps.-Plut. *Mor.* 118 A, citing *Il.* 6.486-9 + 20.128, a similarly straightforward application to that of *Il.* 6.145-9, p. 877; Clem. Al. *Strom.* 6.2.22.3 cites 6.488 to show that Homer was the source purloined by Archinus and Demosthenes in their statements about the inevitability of death.

[47] Chrysippus, fr. 925 von Arnim, ap. Euseb. *PE* 6.8.2; cf. A. A. Long, 'Stoic Readings of Homer', in R. Lamberton and J. J. Keaney (eds.), *Homer's Ancient Readers: The Hermeneutics of Greek Epic's Earliest Exegetes* (Princeton, 1992), 41-66, at 61 n. 46. The same sentiment in Lucian, *Apol.* 8 (mock-solemnly); ps.-Lucian, *Philopatris* 14; Tzetz. *Exegesis in Homeri Iliadem*, Prol., l. 865; Bessarion, *In calumniatorem Platonis*, 2.10.3 (citing Cleanthes, fr. 527 von Arnim + *Il.* 6.488).

[48] Ps.-Plut. *Vit. Hom.* 120, cites *Il.* 6.488-9 and alludes to Odysseus' companions (cf. Hillgrüber ad loc., and pp. 51-2); Diogenianus the Peripatetic, ap. Euseb. *PE* 6.8, cites *Il.* 23.78-9, 20.127-8, and 6.488, and *contra Od.* 1.7, 32-4; Porphyry, ap. Stob. 2.8.42 (fr. 271F Smith), cites *Il.* 6.488-9 and *contra Od.* 1.32-4 [the fragment is translated in A. P. Johnson, *Religion and Identity in Porphyry of Tyre: The Limits of Hellenism in Late Antiquity* (Cambridge, 2013), Appendix 2, 342-6, cf. 345; see S. Heilen, 'Ptolemy's Doctrine of the Terms and its Reception', in A. Jones (ed.), *Ptolemy in Perspective: Use and Criticism of his Work from Antiquity to the Nineteenth Century* (Dordrecht and London, 2010), 45-93, at 82, nn. 90-1, with further bibliography]; Porphyry, *Quaest. Hom. ad Iliadem pertinentes*, 1.3, cites *Il.* 1.3 against *Il.* 6.488 + *Od.* 11.222; Aristides Quintilianus, *De musica* 3.26, uses *Il.* 6.488, 19.336, 1.3 v. *Od.* 1.8-9 to illustrate the difference between something that happens of necessity and something that is contingent; ps.-Alexander of Aphrodisias, *De anima libri mantissa*, p. 182.15 (trans. R. W. Sharples, *Alexander of Aphrodisias: Supplement to On the Soul* (London, 2004), 229), cites *Il.* 6.488-9 (without *Od.* 1.32-4) in a debate between determinism and free will, in which he is open-minded; Ammonius, cited in *Catena in Acta*, p. 401.22, refutes *Il.* 6.488-9 on the evidence of God sparing the mariners' lives for Paul's sake.

[49] Σ AT *Il.* 18.251b/Heraclitus, 22 B 105 D.-K.

20 This formula, which signals a sudden change of direction, is quoted in a posse of Byzantine writers (Procop. *Epist.* 90; Theodorus Prodrom. *Carm. hist.* 38.109, al.); this looks to be the earliest quotation. But why does the poet use it? Not because his thought has changed direction (he will not row back on the hard determinism he has just put forward), but apparently because it has suddenly struck him that his own verses are commonplace beside Homer's, and he needs to comment on that. The asyndeton at the beginning of the next line implies that that is an answer to the question he poses himself here.

22-3 A comparison of two metals, bronze and gold, precedes a simile about purple and gold cloth. Both are about poetics. 'Bronze beside gold' recalls the Glaucus/Diomedes weapon-exchange in *Il.* 6.236, which seems also to have been in the mind of the scribe who switched round the order of metals (χρύσεα χαλκείων / χρύσεα χαλκείοισιν L, corr. A.-R.). Then the juxtaposition—not substitution—of precious stuffs very much recalls the simile in *Od.* 6.232-5 = 23.159-62 where Athena beautifies Odysseus like a goldsmith gilding silver; compare χρυσὸν περιχεύεται ἀργύρῳ with κόχλῳ χρυσὸς περικείμενος; Strab. 1.2.9 had reapplied this to Homer's own method in glamourising actuality with little dabs of myth. M^d is thinking of Homer complementing another source, Strabo of Homer complementing himself; was there a wider tradition of the metapoetic use of this simile which has not (as far as one can see[50]) left traces in our surviving literary sources? But while Strabo may not have got his argument quite clear in his own mind,[51] it is at least clear how Homer is relevant to his project. That is less so here. The poet does not say that he regards Homer as the founding father of his discipline, as Strabo does for geography. Presumably his own prognostics are to be seen as amplifications of the deterministic world-view which *does* go back to Homer. It is less clear that he is making any claims about literary dependence.

22 δόγματα θεῖα: also 28, and 4.12 δόγματος ἐξ ἱεροῖο. Other astrological references to δόγματα do not call them divine, although they do mention them with respect: Valens, II 36.20 τὰ τῶν ἀρχαίων δόγματα, V 8.112 ὁ δὲ ἀπὸ δογμάτων καὶ ἀπὸ θεωρημάτων φερόμενος (a commendable character), Anon. *De Astrol. Dialogus*, p. 5.1: not divine, but foolish to reject them.

---

[50] But another case where Homeric emblems are repurposed in a metapoetic way is Plut. *Mor.* 15 c, where the φάρμακα of *Od.* 4.230 and the κεστός of *Il.* 14.216 become metaphors for the charming power of poetry (Stanley, 71).

[51] Strabo and M^d both involve themselves in conceptual muddle over the relationship between the two elements in the compound. Strabo's involves the nature of myth, whether add-on or essential factor (L. Kim, *Homer between History and Fiction in Imperial Greek Literature* (Cambridge, 2010), 68–71).

23 οἷα κόχλῳ χρυσὸς περικείμενος: astrological doctrines are like gold which ornaments a purple cloth. The comparison belongs in the context of dress metaphors used for poetic composition (Roberts, 115–16). Yet it is unusually complicated, for instead of Homeric poetry providing stylistic ornamentation (as Cicero provides the gold for Naucellius, in Symmachus, *Ep.* 3.12.2, quoted by Roberts), gold here represents the tenets of astrology which *complement* Homer's ideas, now represented by a purple cloak; the shift from the previous image, where gold represented Homer's words in contrast to the poet's workaday ones, is rather confusing. The gold is embroidered onto the purple cloth, perhaps as a border, perhaps as a superimposed pattern. Such sumptuous stuffs were fit for gods, kings, and triumphing generals (the *toga picta*); see note on 5.258–9.[52] It would be fitting if the poet were thinking of a robe embroidered with stars, like those in Appian, *Lib.* 297 πορφύραν, ἀστέρων χρυσῶν ἐνυφασμένων, and Suet. *Nero* 25.1 *in veste purpurea distinctaque stellis aureis chlamyde*.

24 κοχλίδεσσιν ἁλὸς περιπορφύροντος: the noun is κόχλος, and this diminutive is otherwise used only by Lucian, *Catapl.* 16 (κοχλίδιον is less rare). Is Koechly's conjecture περιπορφυρούσαις needed? The hypallage produces an inversion, to my sense acceptable in a poet, of the normal expression sea-purple (e.g. Diod. Sic. 17.70.3 θαλασσίαις πορφύραις; 1 Macc. 4:23 πορφύραν θαλασσίαν). The verb περιπορφύρειν (new until Anna Comnena, *Alexias* 3.1.1 περιπορφύρει τὰ πέδιλα) adds another small source of confusion, being formed from the adjective περιπόρφυρος 'having a purple border', 'edged with purple' (of the *toga praetexta*); that is precisely what the garment here is *not*.

5.25–6 Words and Thought

However this couplet has become stranded here, the distinction between words and διάνοια and the labour motif does provide some continuity with what has gone before (11, 13–14). Although there are no first-person forms, this looks to come from some authorial/narratorial announcement. εἴρηται (1.359) would

---

[52] L. B. Jensen, 'Royal Purple of Tyre', *JNES* 22 (1963), 104–18, at 115–17; Roberts, 111–14; H. R. Goette, 'Die römische ›Staatstracht‹ – *toga, tunica* und *calcei*', in M. Tellenbach, R. Schulz, and A. Wieczorek (eds.), *Die Macht der Toga: DressCode im Römischen Weltreich* (Hildesheim, 2013), 39–52, at 47–9, and C. A. Giner and M. J. Martinez, 'Purpur und Macht an den Küsten des Mittelmeerraumes', op. cit. 55–8; A. B. Kühn, 63–4 (gods and triumphing generals), 69–73 (prominent citizens in the Greek East), 82, 85–6; Courtney on Juv. *Sat.* 10.38 (triumphs). For the use of gold thread in ancient textiles, see Marquardt, 518–20; M. Gleba, 'Auratae Vestes: Gold Textiles in the ancient Mediterranean', in C. Alfaro, J. P. Wild, and B. Costa (eds.), *Purpureae vestes: Actas del I Symposium Internacional sobre Textiles y Tintes del Mediterráneo en Época Romana (Ibiza, 8 al 10 de noviembre, 2002)* (Ibiza and Valencia, 2004), 61–77, including a table on 71–5 of extant specimens of precisely the kind of textiles M^d has in mind.

sooner suggest a formal conclusion than a preface, although the advertisement of qualities (26 n.) suggests the latter.

25 At first sight the same distinction between words and thought (i.e. verbal formulation and content) as in 14; compare e.g. Dion. Hal. *Comp. Verb.* 1 Διττῆς γὰρ οὔσης ἀσκήσεως περὶ πάντας ὡς εἰπεῖν τοὺς λόγους, τῆς περὶ τὰ νοήματα καὶ τῆς περὶ τὰ ὀνόματα, ὧν ἡ μὲν τοῦ πραγματικοῦ τόπου μᾶλλον ἐφάπτεσθαι δόξειεν ἄν, ἡ δὲ τοῦ λεκτικοῦ. But the addition of ἴδιος suggests that the writer was boasting about his personal contribution and perhaps twinning that with what has been handed down to him (Hero of Alexandria, *Pneumatica* Pr. 1 τὰ παραδοθέντα ὑπὸ τῶν ἀρχαίων versus καὶ ἃ ἡμεῖς ... προσευρήκαμεν). It is hard, though, to see how to get that coherently out of ἐν πᾶσιν μύθοις, even if it were emended to ἐν πάντων μύθοις.

26 κάματος: for the 'labour' motif, see on 1.8–10.

εὐσυνθέτῳ ἔργῳ: the epithet again in 5.272, an opaque pronouncement, which LSJ construes as 'constructive', 'inventive', applied to the native. It is often applied to words in a morphological sense (well-formed), but sometimes also to rhetorical logoi.[53] Here I take it to refer to a sound and orderly composition: Eustathius on *Il.* 1.93 (i. 275.21) says that bees are comparable to poetry in various ways, including τὸ τοῦ κηρίου εὐσύνθετον.

The speaker takes pride in a well-constructed work, like writers of prose prefaces who boast of σύνθεσις (Dion. Hal. *Comp. Verb.* 1 καὶ συνθέσει ταῦτα [sc. τὰ ὀνόματα] κοσμήσειν μεμιγμένον ἐχούσῃ τῷ σεμνῷ τὸ ἡδύ; Quintilian, *Inst.* 1 Pr. 1.8 *omnia vero compositiora et quantum nos potuerimus elaborata*) or the related virtues of order[54] and definition.[55] In that case—on top of the misuse of ἐν and the hamfisted definite article, characteristic of this book—we seem to have the use of ἴδιος for the first-person possessive. There is an example in a papyrus (AD 158) in Mayser, ii/2.1. 73–4. εἰς ἰδίαν μου χρεία(ν) and ἰδίαν ἡμῶν χρεία[ν] are quite common in late (6th/7th c.) papyri, but they have a personal pronoun as well. For ἴδιος of the third person, which is much commoner in late Greek, see LSJ I.6.a; Mayser, i. 308 n. 1; Schwyzer, ii. 205; Blass–Debrunner–Rehkopf, §286.1c and n. 4.

---

[53] Gregory of Nyssa, *Epist.* 4.3 λόγος μέν τις περιηνθισμένος ταῖς καλλιφώνοις τε καὶ εὐσυνθέτοις τῶν λέξεων; Cyril of Jerusalem, *Epist. ad Constant. Imp.* 1 γραμμάτων ἀπαρχάς ... εὐσυνθέτους λόγων ῥητορικὰς πιθανότητας περιεχούσας; Euthymius (admittedly 12th/13th c.), *Orat.* 3.9 λόγους ... μετ᾽ εὐσυνθέτου τε καὶ καθαρωτάτης τῆς λεκτικῆς.

[54] Hero of Alexandria, *Pneumatica* Pr. 1 τὰ παραδοθέντα ὑπὸ τῶν ἀρχαίων εἰς τάξιν ἀγαγεῖν; Luke 1:3 καθεξῆς σοι γράψαι; Dionysius son of Calliphon, *Descr. Graeciae* l. 8 τὰς ἑξῆς πόλεις.

[55] ps.-Scymnus, 7–9 (εὐπεριγράφως); Galen, *De typis*, vii. 463.2–3 Kühn ἀναγκαῖον ἡγησάμην αὐτὸς ὁριστικώτερον καὶ κατὰ περιγραφὴν ἐπιδραμεῖν ταῦτα.

5.27–340 Charts

5.27–43 Miscellanea

28 + 27 Horoscope

The horoscope must be aligned correctly; if not, all else fails. This was basic doctrine (Manilius, 3.206-10; see Housman ad loc.), and parallel formulations once again guarantee that Koechly, who did not know them, was correct to invert the lines. Manilius also has parallels for the language of falsity (*cardinibus quoniam falsis... mentitur faciem mundus*) and collapse (*fundamenta ruunt*), while the construction 'if that fails, the rest fails with it' is also found in the anonymous commentator on Ptolemy's *Tetrabiblos*.[56] Hence the many methods of calculating the ASC (i. 47 and n. 18).

28 Ὥρῃ ἀκριβοῦται: the poet has managed to overlay the primary sense, 'by the horoscope divine decrees are ratified', with vocabulary suggesting the secondary sense 'and it is necessary to determine it accurately'. Many sources talk about ἀκρίβεια in its calculation, e.g. Valens, IX 15 Ὅτι δεῖ τὴν γεννητικὴν ὥραν πρὸς μέρος ἀκριβῶς στῆσαι; Hephaestion, i. 85.14–15 ἡ τοῦ ὡροσκόπου ἀκριβὴς μοῖρα τῆς γενέσεως, 95.5 ἐξακριβοῦν δὲ τὴν ὡροσκοποῦσαν μοῖραν; Camaterus, *Introd*. 2251 καὶ ταύτην λέξον ἀκριβῶς εἶναι τὴν ὥραν τότε.

δόγματα θεῖα: as in, and presumably by the same poet as, 22, but now grammatically incorrect.

27 John Philoponus quotes this line twice (*Op. Mund.* p. 199.23 observing that people use this as an excuse when predictions go awry, and p. 233.9, simply stating that it is basic to the alignment of a chart). He does so in the form which is grammatically expected, but unmetrical (Ἢν δ' ὥρη ψεύσηται). Ptol. 3.3.1 talks about the potential of inaccurate instruments to falsify the time of birth (πολλαχῇ διαψεύδεσθαι τῆς ἀληθείας δυναμένων), and Valens also assures us that a method is secure but can go wrong (διαψεύσεται) if luminaries and Ascendants are misaligned (VIII 7.282).

---

[56] Εἰς τὴν Τετράβιβλον τοῦ Πτολεμαίου ἐξηγητὴς ἀνώνυμος/*In Claudii Ptolemaei Quadripartitum enarrator ignoti nominis, quem tamen Proclum fuisse quidam existimant*, ed. H. Wolf (Basel, 1559), p. 90 [ad Ptol. 3.3.1 τοῦ πρώτου καὶ κυριωτάτου]: ἐπειδήπερ πρώτη ἀρχὴ πάντων καὶ ῥίζα ὁ ὡροσκόπος παρὰ τοῖς ἀποτελεσματικοῖς ὀνομάζεται, τούτου τί νυν ἡμαρτημένου μὲν ἀνάγκη πάντα τὰ ἄλλα αὐτῷ συναμαρτάνεσθαι, κατωρθωμένου δὲ συγκατορθοῦσθαι. See too Sext. *Adv. Math.* 5.50-1, esp. 51 τούτων δὲ ἀκαταληπτουμένων συναφανίζεται πᾶσα ἡ Χαλδαϊκὴ μέθοδος (if that is not understood, the whole system fails).

συνεξώλισθεν ἅπαντα: the verb is rare but not unique,[57] but neither it nor the single compound ἐξολισθαίνειν seems to be used elsewhere of a miscalculation which brings other errors in its wake. The simplex can, however, be used of falling into (moral) error (Ecclus. 3:24, trans.; cf. Plut. *Mor.* 49 c ὀλίσθημα).

29–34 Seven Planets

This has the character of a beginner's digest. Whether it once contained more of the material proper to such elementary digests (twelve signs, *kentra*, celestial spheres) can hardly be said, but a comparable self-contained passage on the seven planets is transmitted under the heading Ἑρμοῦ in Stobaeus, 1.5.14 (*AP* Appendix, *Epigr. Demonstr.* 147), and in some manuscripts at the head of the pseudo-Empedoclean *Sphaera* (Maass 1898, 170; Heitsch S 4 *Carmen astrologicum*). At thirteen lines, that passage is somewhat longer, but both are asyndetic, start with a statement about the number seven and location in the sky; both use the words αἰών, φύσις, and (although not in the same sense) γένος. This passage mentions the zones and specifies in what positions the planets rejoice. The other mentions neither. Instead, it lists them twice over, first sketching their characters with epithets, then bringing those characters to bear on human life (see on 74, where the poet seems to be reflecting the Hermetic poet's characterisation of Mars; F. Boll, *Die Lebensalter* (Leipzig, 1913), 38; Monteventi, 214).[58] Only this passage calls the stars gods, which is consistent with 5.22, 28 τὰ δόγματα θεῖα, and the definite article in 30 also suggests the hand of the same poet as the rest of the book. It may be that different poets exercised their ingenuity on a stock theme, the jingle or mnemonic on astronomical basics; the result can still be stylistically distinctive.

29 θεοὶ μὲν: the particle is presumably paired, non-adversatively, with τε in 31, placing γένος in apposition to θεοί: see Denniston, 374–6 (examples from epic, lyric, tragedy, and Attic prose).

ἀν᾽ οὐρανοῦ ἠέρα πουλύν: ἀν᾽ οὐρανὸν is established in this *sedes* in other books of the Manethoniana (6, 4, 1), but combined here with Homeric ἠέρα πουλὺν, used of mist (*Il.* 5.776, 8.50, and of the lower atmosphere by ps.-Opp. *Cyn.* 2.594, Quint. Smyrn. 2.195). For the use of ἠέρα instead of the commoner αἰθέρα (which is restored by A.–R.), see 4.37 n.

---

[57] Ps.-Martyrius, *Oratio Funebris*, p. 121.16 συνεξολισθαινόντων, of worms, a disgusting passage; Aetius, *Iatr.* 9.37.97 συνεξολισθαίνουσι τοῖς ῥοφήμασι, also of literal physical discharges; Lydus, *Magistr.* p. 44.22–3 συνεξώλισθε τοῖς ἐν γένει τὰ ἐν εἴδει, of an institution falling into desuetude.

[58] There are also prose reductions of ll. 10–12 in *CCAG* viii/1. 265.9–10 and *CCAG* xi/2. 111.11–12, listing the planets' effects as their εὐεργεσίαι.

30 οἳ ζώνας κατέχουσιν: basic dogma; for instance, the treatise Περὶ τῶν ἑπτὰ ζωνῶν, ed. R. Kunze, 'Die anonyme Handschrift (Da 61) der Dresdner Königlichen Bibliothek', *Hermes*, 34 (1899), 345–62, begins with a very elementary review of the seven spheres and their occupants; Σ vet. (Tzetzes) Hes. *Op.* 381 ἐπιτελλομενάων. The verb is appropriate to occupants (i. 879: 3.394, of a sign, and books 6 and 1, *passim*, of *kentra*; *IEph.* 3112 ψυχὴ δ' αἰθέριον κατέχει πόλον; ultimately, *Od.* 13.269 κάτεχ' οὐρανόν), but also to rulers and tutelary gods.[59]

31 αἰῶνός τε γένος: the reference to the αἰών surely betrays the influence of the *Timaeus*, and so too the verses at the head of the *Sphaera* (καὶ τοῖσιν ἀεὶ κανονίζεται αἰών, that is, time is marked out by the stars; see on 4.625–6). Both slightly misrepresent Plato, for whom the stars measured χρόνος (time in the created universe, not eternity). γένος is perhaps a badly formulated version of Plato's idea that the stars belong to the created world, which is secondary to the eternal one.

ῥίζα φύσεως πολυμόρφου: 'root', which is present in the *Tetrabiblos* commentary (n. 56), does not reflect the *Timaeus*' ideas. The idea of nature's variegatedness can be used to illustrate how topoi are in the service of utterly different world-views (e.g. Himerius, *Or.* 68.81–2 τὸ τῆς φύσεως κάλλος τῇ πολυμορφίᾳ τῶν γεννηθέντων ἐδημιούργησαν, where Prometheus and Epimetheus produce it; Chrysippus, fr. 1163 von Arnim (ap. Plut. *Mor.* 1044 D) τὴν φύσιν τῇ ποικιλίᾳ χαίρουσαν; the finger of God himself in Philo, *Migr. Abr.* 85 τῇ τῆς φύσεως ἐντέχνῳ ποικιλίᾳ).

32 σφαίρωμ' ἄνα καγχαλόωσιν: the stars rejoice, using a happy Homeric replacement for the prosaic astrological χαίρουσι (a textbook substitution, standard in lexicographers, e.g. Hesych. κ 35), in the sphere; this is not a reference to the music of the spheres (*contra* Potter on *Or. Sib.* 13.69). The singular σφαίρωμ' is Koechly's emendation for L's σφαιρώματα, which formed a hexameter ending very similar to *Or. Sib.* 3.88 φωστήρων σφαιρώματα καγχαλόωντα (spheres in which the stars are located, or spheres which *are* the stars), and especially 13.69–70 σφαιρώματα καγχαλόωντα | ζωδιακοῦ κύκλου (attached to the city of Bostra, as if this were particularly associated with astrology). The use of a main verb instead of a participle[60] requires the construction to be emended, and if one suspects Koechly's emendation for introducing an anastrophic preposition, which is insecure in this poet (p. 331), σφαιρώματι is another

---

[59] LSJ II.a, b; add a *defixio* from 4th c. Cos, *SEG* 47.1291.27 ὁ τὸν κνώδακα τοῦ οὐ(ρα)νοῦ κατέχων, also of Zeus; *Hymni e papyris magicis collecti* (LIX Heitsch), 5.15 τὸν οὐράνιον κόσμον κατέχοντα, of Raphael.

[60] In EGHP the verb occurs mostly in the form of a participle (καγχαλόωσα in this *sedes* twice in *Od.* 23); *Il.* 3.43 places a main verb before the caesura.

possibility, the construction as in e.g. Opp. *Hal.* 3.619 ἀθύρμασι καγχαλόωντες (and datives in Opp., ps.-Opp., and Quint. Smyrn. elsewhere).

35–8

On great kings. Lines 33–8 in the manuscript are punctuated as a single configuration, with a point at the end of the previous line, but without punctuation at the end of 33. That cannot be right, and Gronovius already removed the point after 32 and inserted one after 33 so that the positions specified in 33 are, properly, those in which the planets are said in 32 to rejoice. This is surely correct.

By failing to punctuate after 34 L also implies that it is the joint *synodos* of all seven planets listed there that produces the birth of kings. That is what Gronovius (for whom 34–5 are a single sentence) understood as well, despite the singular παρέχει, and it is still the way Monteventi, 223, takes the passage. If so, the point would be that having *all* the planets in conjunction simultaneously is a very improbable outcome; only the most exceptional people are born under this configuration. Apomasar countenances the possibility that the *synodos* of the five planets (minus luminaries) effects kingship, but has never seen it, and his son adds that the conjunction of the three outer planets and the aspect of the Sun ἔστι μεγάλη σύνοδος καὶ ἀποτελεῖ μεγάλους βασιλεῖς (*CCAG* xii. 97.1–7). A chart in Firmicus, 6.31.55, with a correspondence in Anubion, F 7.25 (see on 1.350–2), produces a *potentissimus imperator* when Jupiter, Mars, Mercury, and Venus are in the ASC, and Saturn opposes them. There is no guarantee that that chart is connected to this one, but Firmicus is careful to give the locations of every planet; three of the four that are located together correspond to the first three named in 34, and Anubion's line, which is damaged but restorable, also begins with Ζεὺς δ' Ἄρης (a combination which does not otherwise recur in the Manethoniana) (see Schubert, 428–9).

On the other hand, Axtius and Rigler introduced a high point after 34, breaking the connection with what follows, and the line is certainly also transmitted alone, apparently as a handy mnemonic for the names of all the planets. Koechly marked a lacuna after 34, and argued that it was not the conjunction of *all* the planets that produced the royal outcome but of certain stars which were presumably specified in a verse lost before 35. The problem seems to me, less that παρέχει is singular (for singular verbs are occasionally used in lists of proper names: K.–G. i. 81), but the fact that this configuration is being claimed, not only for Alexander, but also for Ptolemy himself, and a less ambitious set of conjunctions would be more plausible than a wholly exceptional set of all seven. Koechly guessed Mars and Jupiter, or Sun and Jupiter. Alternatively, given that σύνοδος specifically refers to the conjunction of Sun and Moon (Heilen 2015, 1094 n. 2769), the subject of παρέχει in the putative missing line was the Moon (so, perhaps Moon + Sun + Jupiter, or just Moon + Jupiter?). It is true that this author idiosyncratically applies σύνοδος to the malefics in 5.58 (for the verb συνοδεύειν see on 5.62). But ἐν συνόδῳ occurs only here (35, 36, 38; dat. pl. in 58), and in all other astrological occurrences of the phrase ἐν συνόδῳ—which is surprisingly infrequent—the subject is the Moon.[61] Whatever the solution, this method of predicting the birth of great kings, not involving *kentra*, is very different from anything else in the Manethoniana (35 and 2.389 nn.).

33 εἰν ἰδίοις ὁρίοις: also 4.177.

ὑψώμασιν: see on 3.14–15 and i. 890 and n. 119. This is the only book of the Manethoniana in which the technical term occurs, again in 173 and 261. See also p. 387, on the table of exaltations.

ἠδέ τ': i. 113 n. 8; connecting parallel parts of speech also in Maximus, 551.

34 The line reappears, alone, attributed to 'Theon' (that is, of Alexandria), in *AP* 9.491 (K. Ziegler, *RE* s.v. Theon, 15), 2080.22–36). Essentially the same line, except with the Moon shunted to the front, appears in the verses that preface the *Sphaera* (l. 7), where, as quoted in Stobaeus, 1.5.14, they are ascribed to Hermes: Μήνη, Ζεύς, Ἄρης, Παφίη, Κρόνος, Ἥλιος, Ἑρμῆς.

35 On the birth of kings, see on 2.389. The phrase 'great kings' is formulaic in astrology and not associated with any one set-up, though recurrent factors are the luminaries, the kingly planet Jupiter and his conjunctions, and *kentra*: 2.350 μεγάλους βασιλῆας (Jupiter in Leo); 3.224 (the luminaries opposing each other over ASC and DESC or MC and IMC); 3.297 (Jupiter and Mars in conjunction or trine); Valens, II 4.7 (discussed below); Apomasar, *CCAG* xii. 96.13, 97.7 (discussed above).

36 For Alexander's chart, see Heilen 2015, 759–61. This is the earliest ancient datum about it. A long and very corrupt version appears in the Alexander Romance, *Recensio* α, 1.12. It has no direct overlap with this, but a detail in it—Jupiter's location in the MC—may have been of interest to the interpreters of Hadrian's chart, which contains a conjunction of Sun, Moon, and Jupiter on the ASC. In Valens, II 4.7, too, 'great kings' are born when the Moon is on the ASC[62] (and ruling the Hour or Lot of Fortune), and accompanied by Jupiter in conjunction or in quartile. All this may help with the interpretation of σύνοδος in the previous line.

---

[61] Dorotheus, pp. 384.13, 419.24; Hephaestion, i. 284.2; Camaterus, *Zodiaco*, 1095; Anon. *De Astrologia Dialogus*, pp. 13.8, 45.20.

[62] Which has to be supplemented from other entries in the catalogue; it must just have dropped out.

Evidently there was a whole industry of Alexander charts which continued into the early modern period (and beyond), though it is not clear how much is to be gained by pursuing it. The ancient evidence is in Heilen. Early modern astrologers include (i) Andrea Argoli, *Ptolemaeus paruus in genethliacis junctus arabibus auctore Andrea Argolo* (Lyon, 1652), 180–1 (for 355 BC, 12 August 16.40 p.m., 41° N), no source given, and (ii) John Gadbury, *Collectio Geniturarum, Or, A Collection of divers choice nativities* (London: Printed by James Cottrel, 1662), p. 5, for 357 BC, 1 July, 9h 26m. p.m. (based on the birth-date given in 'Lyndholt fo. 112'). In Argoli's, the Sun and Mercury are within seven degrees of each other on the ASC, and perhaps more interestingly Mars and Jupiter are within two degrees (cf. the 'great kings' of 3.298), though not on a *kentron*. In Gadbury's, there are conjunctions of Mars and the Moon (in the MC), and of Venus and Jupiter (in the DESC).

37 Taken by De Stefani 2016, 201, to mean that the people wisely chose Alexander as king, but I take the stars as the subject of ἀνέδειξαν, just as they are the subjects of 39 ἐπιδείξει, 73 ἐπέδειξε, 220 ἐπέδειξεν, only with a different compound of the verb which is more suitable to proclaiming someone king (LSJ ἀναδείκνυμι, II). πινυταῖς πραπίδεσσιν is comitative. The Alexander tradition remodelled him as a seeker of wisdom and philosopher-king, and would eventually turn him into a figure of practical, bibliographic, cosmic, and spiritual wisdom. Although this interpretation reaches its height in oriental traditions about Alexander which are late antique or early mediaeval,[63] its basis was Alexander's association with Aristotle and his encounters with Diogenes and the naked sages of Taxila, and for all that the latter showed up his philosophical development as very much a 'work in progress', he did have an inclination (Plut. *Vit. Alex.* 8.5) in that direction; depending on the poet's date he might also have been aware of the early stages of the Alexander Romance in which Alexander becomes more tractable towards the Brahmins, and reflective (S. Asirvatham, 'Alexander the Philosopher in the Greco-Roman, Persian and Arabic tradition', in Stoneman *et al.* 311–26; 'work in progress' comes from 314). Admittedly, the phrase πινυταῖς πραπίδεσσιν implies shrewdness rather than philosophical receptivity. Otherwise it occurs in ps.-Apollinaris, *Metaphr.*

---

[63] The *Iskandarnāma* of the Persian poet Niẓāmī Ganjavī (12th c., but preserving pre-Islamic sources; H. Manteghi, *Alexander the Great in the Persian Tradition: History, Myth and Legend in Medieval Iran* (London, 2018), 71–127); chapters in Stoneman *et al.*, on the Arabic romances (F. Doufikar-Aerts, 61–79, at 74), the Talmud (O. Amitay, 349–65), early mediaeval versions, which had him investigate the heavens and the ocean's depths (F. Melville, 405–9, at 406–8); Arabic *belles-lettres*, developing the relationship with Aristotle: E. Cottrell, 'Alexander at the Buyid Court', in R. Stoneman, K. Nawotka, and A. Wojciechowska (eds.), *The Alexander Romance: History and Literature* (Groningen, 2018), 245–78, at 247–8.

72:30, 91:29 (in both cases an embellishment of the original). For the epithet see on 5.4.

38 Ptolemy's horoscope. The fabrication of a birth-chart for Ptolemy which was evidently based on Alexander's, with a different horoscope, confirms the plausibility of Heilen's suggestion that Antigonus' interpretation of Hadrian's chart was intended to bring out its similarities with Alexander's (Heilen 2015, 761). The multiplication of charts by varying the position of the horoscope also recalls the sequence in Firmicus, 6.30.22–6 of charts of famous men, although in that case the natives are not all distinguished in the same way. For comparison, the Seleucus legend also involves astrologers, but I know of no attempt to fabricate a horoscope for him. The astrologers try (and fail) to manipulate the time of the foundation of Seleucia-on-Tigris, as Nectanebo tries (and succeeds) to manipulate the time of Alexander's birth from Olympias (D. Ogden, *The Legend of Seleucus: Kingship, Narrative, and Mythmaking in the Ancient World* (Cambridge, 2017), 157–60).

39–43

Miscellanea on dynasts. This little section seems to be a collection of material related to *kentra* and *topikai diakriseis* from the same source as M^a, Dorotheus, and their other comparanda studied in the first volume. It seems to have been scraped together on the theme of powerful individuals, placed here (by an editor?) because it follows Alexander's and Ptolemy's charts. Compare also 1.100–5, another sound-bite on various types of leader, there running through all the planets rather than just a selection.

39 σατράπας μεσσουρανέων: in the parallels (3.116, Dor.^{ARAB} II 22.2; Paul, pp. 64.17–65.1; Θ p. 167.7–8; Firmicus, 3.5.34) kings and socially prominent individuals are born. In light of that, σατράπας might simply mean loosely 'big men', which is also possible in *Lib. Herm.* xx. 5 *dicimus quod parentes sunt gloriosissimorum, scilicet satraparum vel tribunorum vel eorum qui sunt sub rege*. But on the other (rare) occasions where the word is used in astrology the setting does seem to be Near Eastern: Hephaestion, i. 75.4 (Nechepso–Petosiris, fr. 10 Riess) refers to a type of comet that brings danger from satraps to the Assyrian or Persian king, and they are mentioned twice in a short section within Περὶ τῆς τῶν ἀπλανῶν ἀστέρων δυνάμεως where Cumont and Boll note traces of Arabic star-names.[64] Neither of these is a birth chart. μεσσουρανέων appears thus, with double sigma, otherwise only in 189.

---

[64] *CCAG* v/1. 221 ll. 3, 14–15 ~ Camaterus, *Introd.* 2444, 2503; cf. commentary on p. 218.

40 Perhaps retaining the same location as the previous line; for Mars in the MC, see 3.64 ἡγεμόνας; Θ p. 168.14 στρατοπεδάρχας (by night); Firmicus, 3.4.28–9 *praesides, duces* (and a good deal more); but Mars in his own houses would presumably be sufficient to bring about his own specialism anyway. The phrase στρατιῆς...ἡγήτορας is like 3.296 ἡγεμόνας...στρατιῆς, 4.471 στρατιῆς ἐπιβήτορας, 1.103 στρατιῆς ἡγήτορας, all variously involving Mars, and the last the effect of Mars generically.

41 The outcomes in 2.210–12, *Π.τ.δ.* 8, and *Lib. Herm.* xxxii. 19 involve leadership and militarism. They do not include judges, but cf. Περὶ σχημ. 14 ἡγεμόνας ἢ δικαστάς (Jupiter aspects the Moon). An ἀρχιδικαστήν is oddly associated with the Moon in 1.104.

42 This looks very much like the add-on in *Π.τ.δ.* 8. There, Jupiter in a house of Mars or in his terms makes leaders, especially military leaders; and when they aspect the luminaries, the latter in *kentra* (ἐπίκεντροι ὄντες), they make formidable kings. It suggests or reinforces suspicions that something is missing after 42. The required sense is that each of the stars, when aspecting the luminaries in *kentra*, ⟨has such-and-such an effect⟩; Koechly's τάδ᾽ ἕκαστος (sc. ἀνέφηνε) would achieve this, but he had too little faith in the poet to print it. It is not clear why he reversed the punctuation of Axtius and Rigler, who have a comma after 41 and a high point after 42; L itself has a high point after 41, and nothing after 42, but Koechly of course did not see it in person.

43 This has no connection with *Π.τ.δ.* 8. ἀτονία, ἀτονέω are especially popular with Valens (II 17.25; V 7.14, 15; VI 4.2, VI 5.1; IX 4.5; also ps.-Palchus, *CCAG* v/1. 191.7). What is it for a star to look ἀτόνως? A star might be weak because it is setting (i. 623), or retrograde (78–80 n.), or has resigned its chronocratorship; it might be in its debility (Bouché-Leclercq, 194); not all these concepts are otherwise invoked in the Manethoniana. For the Aeolic third-person ending of λεύσσειε, see i. 103. For συνεξώλισθεν ἄπαντα, see on 5.27: here it should mean 'fail of effect', not 'throw the calculation out'.

5.44–129 Good and Bad Stars

I use this label because so many entries in this section contain a comment on a star's quality, either a simple statement that a star is good or bad (62 μειλίχιος, 66 κάκιστος, 74 ἄστοργος, 76 κακός, 100 κακή, 105 οὐ καλός, 108 ἥμερος, 109 ἀγαθή, 111 καλή, 112 κακίστη, 113 ἀρίστη, 127 ὀλοώτατός), or general remarks (44–7, 78–9 πανήμερος, πονηρός, φαῦλος, 81 ἀργαλέων), or a less direct and more evocative indication (48–61). That is, a common astrological idiom, adumbration followed by precision (i. 224–5 and n. 41), nearly becomes an organising principle. That idiom is particularly well represented in the section on the *synaphai* and *aporrhoiai* of the Moon (2.438–502), whose organisation is closely related to the one here, as well as in its relative *Π.σ.α.*, which has clear overlaps with the section on the Moon.

It is not a systematic catalogue. There are glimmerings of organising principles, but the entries are sufficiently disrupted to suggest the hand of a poet who failed to apply the system consistently or an editor who failed to understand it. There is no attempt to present the section as a sequence: entries are mostly asyndetic, save for a little sequence on the Moon at the end (connectives in 109, 111, 112).

(*a*) Qualitative order (i. 633). The section begins with Saturn and Mars (48–61) and ends with the Moon (109–29). In the middle a long sequence sticks essentially to Mars (72–108) and is again approximately qualitative: because Mars and Saturn have already been coupled together, the focus is on (i) Mars with the neutral planet Mercury (72–3, 84–9, 93–9) and (ii) Mars with benefics (first, in 74–7 a note on Mars *without* benefics, then 105–8, 110). The order which places malefics first is also found in 1.203–4, and the (idiosyncratic) treatment of the Moon in 2.438–502 is organised entirely around the Moon's contact with malefics (i. 633). On the other hand, the final lines on the Moon, which is the clearest and most straightforward passage in the whole section, place benefics before malefics (omitting Mercury in between), and finish with the Sun and node. This is closer to the standard Seleucid planetary order (Jupiter before Venus), save that the latter also places Saturn (113–19) before Mars (112).

(*b*) Positional order. The entries for Jupiter (62, 63–5, 69–71) and Venus (100–2, 103–4) look as if someone (an editor?) has made a stab—a pretty half-hearted one—at imposing positional order. For if the order is positional, why the interjection of the Sun and Venus in 66–8 in the middle of a Jupiter cluster? As for 100–2 and 103–4, they have been nested inside the main Mars sequence, and reasons ad loc. are given for regarding 103–4 as interpolated.

(*c*) Extraneous matter. Why the generalisations in 78–80, 81, 82–3?

Unfortunately, the items that begin with a straightforward qualitative statement do not correspond with the items arranged in qualitative order. That would be logical and convenient, indicating that the two went together, but the 'positional' entries for Jupiter (62–5) and Venus (100–2), which disrupt the qualitative sequence, also begin with qualitative statements.

As for the sources, there are overlaps with both M^a books 2 and 3, with Firmicus, especially with 3.11 (Mercury and Mars, within a review of the *dodecatopos*), and with Π.σ.a. for the Moon. These are systematic catalogues of various kinds, organised firmly on the positional principle. It was already observed in the first volume that the same material reappears in different types of catalogue and appears to be able to travel across different organising principles.

44–7

The chiastic structure of this preamble suggests that what is meant is a contrast between bad stars that spoil good ones and good stars that redeem bad ones. (There is a fairly similar but much more straightforward parallelism in Dorotheus, p. 326.13–14 in which good places redeem bad planets and good planets redeem bad places.) The references to aspect confuse matters, not least because of the obscurity of what is meant by the 'great aspects' in 44. I find no trace of any such terminology elsewhere in astrology, but perhaps we can infer from the references in 47 to quartile and opposition (an ambivalent but potentially hostile aspect: see on 2.436–8) that the 'great' aspects are the complementary ones of conjunction and trine. In that case, the point would be that *even in* these sympathetic aspects the effect of a malefic on a benefic is bad, and that even in the antipathetic ones of quartile and opposition the benefic overcomes the malefic. That works at least some of the time. It works best for combinations of Jupiter and Mars (3.295–308).

45 The notion of the Evil Eye seems not to be otherwise applied to stars, though given their similitude with eyes it might have been, and the only star to be called βάσκανος is Venus in connection with marriage and reproduction (5.102; Περὶ σχημ. 85 ~ Περὶ κράσ. 175). ἀργαλέος refers again to malefics at 5.81, but in 1.251 to the Moon in a specific circumstance.

46 ὄμματ᾽ ἐποίσει: EGHP has eyes cast *down* (*HHom. Aphr.* 156 κατ᾽ ὄμματα καλὰ βαλοῦσα) or *aside* (*Il.* 3.427 ὄσσε πάλιν κλίνασα, 13.3 αὐτὸς δὲ πάλιν τρέπεν ὄσσε φαεινώ). Lifting them *up* seems to be a Hellenistic reflex (see on 77; V. *Aen.* 2.687–8 *oculos ad sidera laetus* | *extulit*) or a Hebraism, though the Jewish versions use a different verb (Gen. 13:10 καὶ ἐπάρας Λωτ τοὺς ὀφθαλμοὺς αὐτοῦ; Ps. 122:1 Πρὸς σὲ ἦρα τοὺς ὀφθαλμούς μου; Isa. 40:26 ἀναβλέψατε εἰς ὕψος τοὺς ὀφθαλμοὺς ὑμῶν; John 4: 35 ἐπάρατε τοὺς ὀφθαλμοὺς ὑμῶν, 11:41 ὁ δὲ Ἰησοῦς ἦρεν τοὺς ὀφθαλμοὺς ἄνω). Personification is implied.

48–61

Beware Mars and Saturn. Since this is about phase, συνάφη refers presumably to the planets' contact with the Sun, and ἀντολίην means 'rising' in the sense of escaping the immediate vicinity of the sun, not rising with respect to the horizon (see i. 623). νυκτερινός and ἑῷος look as if they should be a pair, but unless the poet is being hopelessly slovenly in his terminology, νυκτερινός (antonym ἡμερινός) can only refer to time of day, in other words be an indication of sect (1.83 n.; for dangerous Saturn in a night birth see also 5.217), while ἑῷος (antonym ἑσπέριος) must refer to the planet's eastern rising (from the vicinity of the Sun), in other words be an indication of phase. We have already seen phase and sect mixed up in the section on planets with the Sun in 2.410-38 (see i. 626-7), which the compiler of the table at the head of the book put under the general heading of φάσις even though it dealt with both factors. Saturn is to be feared at night because he is a day planet; that was made very clear in 2.412. Mars, on the other hand, is to be feared when he is ἑῷος because this is the most potent kind of rising for *all* planets (2.405 and i. 623-4), to which Mars is no exception (see 2.425: less awful when ἑσπέριος).

What, then, of the 'beginnings' in l. 50 and the 'ending' in l. 54? Perhaps Mars is to be feared at the beginning of the period of its visibility, when it is emerging from the Sun's rays, which nullified its evil effect (1.96-9). As for Saturn, taking ὄψιμος (56) to mean 'late in the season' (not 'late in the day'), he is to be feared at the end of his period of visibility: that would make a neat antithesis, with Saturn's behaviour the converse of Mars'. An alternative suggestion, however, is that the beginning and end, in both cases, is of life itself (for ἀρχή in this sense, see 1.5 and 5.121 nn.): Mars is perilous in rash youth, Saturn in sluggish old age.

49 δείμαινε: for the 'be very afraid' motif, see p. 171.

50 ἀρχαὶ...ἀηδεῖς: the adjective is not confined to, but especially associated with, Valens and Hephaestion. For statements about Mars, compare especially 'Valens', *CCAG* viii/1. 166.23-4 εἰς δὲ τὸ δῦνον ἐλθὼν λίαν ἐστὶν ἀηδής, 167.4, 168.5 (Sun moving towards Mars, which should mean that Mars is also bad when 'setting'); Valens, IV. 22.1 Ἄρης ἑαυτῷ ἐπιμερίζων ἡμερινὸς ἀηδὴς καὶ ἐπιτάραχος γενήσεται; *CCAG* xi/2. 131.32 Ὥρα Ἄρεως... ἐν πάσῃ θεωρίᾳ ἀηδής ἐστιν.

51 The first and last elements in this line have been sourced directly from Homer or taken from the Homeric poems with light adaptation. At the beginning, *Il.* 22.135 ὡς πυρὸς αἰθομένου is a comparison for Achilles' armour, but closely follows a simile comparing him to Ares; at the end, εἰσὶν ἐν ὕλῃ seems purely opportunistic (*Il.* 17.134 ἐν ὕλῃ, from a simile describing Ajax; *Od.* 13.246 ἔστι μὲν ὕλη, from Athena's description of Ithaca). That speaks for Rigler's emendation of L's φλογεραὶ (*Il.* 9.242 μαλεροῦ πυρός, 20.316 μαλερῷ πυρί, al.) rather than Koechly's στυγεραί (for which he gave no reason). The plural φλόγες is post-Homeric.

52a λάβρ᾽ ἐπιγινομένου: Koechly saw that this referred to a sudden influx of water which put the fire out (rather than the raging fire, hence not D'Orville's ἐπειγομένου). Water is described in this way in *Il.* 21.271 λάβρος ὕπαιθα ῥέων, 16.385 ὅτε λαβρότατον χέει ὕδωρ, and for a phrase of similar shape *Il.* 2.148 *et al.* λάβρος ἐπαιγίζων (of wind).

52b παρ᾽ ἀκμήν: the fire is quenched when at its height; the phrase is unique, but reminiscent of κατ᾽ ἄκρης, of the burning of Troy (*Il.* 22.411).

53 The missing lines before this presumably contained a οὕτως clause explaining the referent. Ares 'rages' (μαίνεσθαι) throughout the Homeric poems (*Il.* 5.717, 831, 15.127–8, *Od.* 11.537); see especially *Il.* 15.605 μαίνετο δ᾽ ὡς ὅτ᾽ Ἄρης ἐγχέσπαλος ἢ ὀλοὸν πῦρ. This line is also quoted by Valens, IX 9.19, not in connection with the planet Mars, but simply to illustrate the ups and downs of Hector's fate-governed career; was it in an anthology of Homeric tags useful to astrologers? That Mars' rage is stilled by Venus is certainly not supported by 3.329–34 and parallels, where, on the contrary, they produce marital uproar and infidelity, even in the otherwise favourable aspect of trine (the most positive account being that of Firmicus, 6.5.3). Given that the language is suggestive rather than scientific, it is no surprise that κενοῦται (be voided of effect) appears not to be an astrological *terminus technicus*. Astrology refers to empty signs and empty places, but does not use this verb of ineffectual agents.

54 τάρβει: p. 171. κατὰ πάντα 3× in this *sedes* in the Homeric poems, adverbial (or in tmesis).

55–6 Line 55 is catastrophically corrupt, but ψυχρός (i. 911 n. 13; 3.245 ψυχρότατον Κρόνον) shows that (even if πήγνυται is a gloss, which seems not impossible) the reference is to freezing. I had wondered whether there might also be a secondary reference to Saturn's station (στηριγμός/*statio*), the point at which a planet's motion slows to an apparent halt before it reverses direction, given Firmicus' direct connection between Saturn's speed or sluggishness and its proximity to or distance from the Sun's vivifying rays.[65] It would be hard, though, to reconcile sluggishness at the planet's furthest point from the Sun with the apparent claim that it is at its chilliest (and hence presumably most sluggish) at the end of its period of visibility, if this is what τελευτήν means, for it would then be approaching the Sun. Hesiod's ψυχρὴ γάρ τ᾽ ἠὼς πέλεται (*Op.* 547) seems to underlie the line-beginning, but does not necessarily help restore the rest.

---

[65] Cf. Firmicus, 1.4.6 *praedicimus etiam quando retrogradus ad stationem pristinam revertatur, quando tarditatis eius pigros cursus regali maiestatis auctoritate vicinum solis lumen exagitet, quando profectus ab eo solis ardor tardae agitationi quietam tribuat potestatem.*

56 δῆριν...ἔχωσιν: for special malice on *kentra*, see 3.248 (hence De Stefani's λιπόκεντροι is the opposite of what is wanted). Homeric δηριάομαι is constructed with περί + genitive of the object of contention (*Il.* 16.756–7, 17.157–8, 734); περὶ κέντρον means the place around which they contend.

57 One of many Manethonian lines that combine astrological jargon with a *presque homérique* tournure at the end. ἀκαταστασία (for which see on 3.81 ἀστασίας; Heilen 2015, 1254–5) embraces all sorts of upset, especially domestic and marital, but also legal (e.g. Valens, IV 22.5), military (e.g. Theophilus, *CCAG* xi/1. 251.25)—Mars being implicated in every one of these, and both Mars and Saturn in Hephaestion, i. 210.29, Θ p. 142.4—and environmental (*CCAG* iv. 131.12 and *Π.σ.α.* p. 182.8, famine and disease). Disasters precipitated by the malefics on *kentra* are listed in 3.249–63, mostly types of violent death after a life of poverty. The *clausula* comes from the well-known oracle in Hdt. 1.67.4, there in a transferred sense, here conveniently in its primary meaning (δεινῷ suggests a possible phonic reminiscence of κεῖται).

58–61 The cancelling effect of Saturnian cold and Martian heat is referred to repeatedly in astrology. From (i) its similarity to the doctrine that *natura alia natura vincitur* (Firmicus, 4.22.2; Nechepso–Petosiris, fr. 28 Riess) and (ii) Apomasar's claim that εὐκρασία is a doctrine of the ancients,[66] one wonders whether it goes back to Nechepso–Petosiris. The conditions under which it comes about are conjunction (Apomasar; Dorotheus, pp. 368.25–369.3; Firmicus, 6.22.5) and/or the one planet being in the house of another (Firmicus, 1.4.7 *cum ad Saturnum, cum etiam ad eius venerit domum*; *Lib. Herm.* xxxii. 29; cf. 1.354, where the encounter of cold and hot agencies when Saturn reaches Mars' 'place', i.e. presumably house, results in upset instead of mutual cancellation). Once again, the poet does not seem to have thought through the implications. How is their encounter tranquillising when, located on a *kentron*, it counted as 'strife' (and in 3.246 was disastrous under any circumstances)?

The poet uses the proper word, εὐκρασία (59). Apomasar uses it; Dorotheus suggests it with κιρναμένων (p. 369.3); Latin authors use *temperare* (Firmicus, 1.4.7, 6.22.5). The concept of εὐκρασία also occurs in Valens, although not apropos of Saturn and Mars. In IX 8.40, he speaks abstractly of the mutual interpenetration of the elements (*stoicheia*) which, left apart, would be unproductive, but which, blending with one another, become productive. This seems to betray the ultimate influence of Aristotle's *De generatione et corruptione*, which contains the idea of elements (*stoicheia*) being generated out of one another, even if he does not call it εὐκρασία; Aristotle does use the word elsewhere, but he

---

[66] *CCAG* ii. 137.5–7 Ἀπομάσαρ φησὶ ὅτι φασίν τινες τῶν ἀρχαίων ὅτι ὅτε συνοδεύουσιν ὁ Κρόνος καὶ Ἄρης, ποιοῦσιν εὐτυχίαν· ὁ μὲν γάρ ἐστι ψυχρός, ὁ δὲ θερμὸς καὶ γίνεται μεταξὺ αὐτῶν εὐκρασία.

does so in connection with the physiology and temperament of individuals, which is also the context in which Dorotheus and Firmicus will ultimately conceive of Mars' and Saturn's mutually tempering effects. Secondly, in IV 4.24-5 Valens applies the notion to signs which, being in sympathy and transmitting to one another, establish εὐκρασία. This implies a model which is similar to the one for planets, but is more complex insofar as signs are associated with elements (fire, earth, air, water, succeeding each other around the zodiac) which are *combinations* of qualities, rather than representing the primary qualities themselves (hot/cold; wet/dry).[67]

58 How are these alternatives? Is σύνοδος more or less exact than being in the same place? (Antiochus of Athens' definition of σύνοδος when it pertains to Sun and Moon locates it at between 3° and 15°: Heilen 2015, 755.) What we should expect is either conjunction or one planet in another's house (for which χῶρος can be a synonym: i. 877 n. 20)—see above—but not both in the same place.

στείχωσι δ' ὁμοῦ: the verb is more popular in this poet (also 165, 320) than in other books (6.277, 4.466). It suggests regimentation (i. 894 n. 147). Its application to heavenly bodies was prepared by *Od.* 11.17, of the Sun, and implies 'going in a line' (στίχος) or taking a specified path (*Od.* 17.204 στείχοντες ὁδόν, 23.136 ἀν' ὁδὸν στείχων), which is suitable for an army marching in file, but also to a planet in its course. For the adverb compare esp. *Il.* 9.86 ἅμα στεῖχον.

60 Compare 5.225–6; 1.354 ψυχρὸς ἐὼν θερμοῖο; Apomasar (n. 66), ὁ μὲν γάρ ἐστι ψυχρός, ὁ δὲ θερμός. The verb is used in philosophical discussion of kinds of mixture, including the mixing of elements, but the idea of εὐκρασία is quite the opposite of cases where elements share qualities but remain distinct (e.g. earth and water sharing the property of coldness[68]), and closer to, but still not identical with, the 'everyday' use where substances are blended so as to produce

---

[67] Valens gives the examples of the fiery sign of Leo and the airy sign of Aquarius, the former preventing the air from becoming icy (κρυμώδη) and dark (ζοφώδη), and the watery signs of Cancer and Pisces and the earthy signs of Capricorn and Virgo which, by entering into alliance, nurture life. To some extent this can be compared with Galen, *Quod animi mores corporis temperamenta sequantur*, iv. 783.10–784.13 Kühn, who also speaks of the tempering effect of fire and air, of which the former prevents the latter becoming too cold, save that Galen (following the Stoics, SVF ii. 787) is talking about the components of the soul. See M. Broze, 'Un jeu de mots stoïcien sur le mélange: *Eukrasia* et *Epikratein*', *RPhA* 25 (2007), 81–6; C. Mirrione, 'Theory and Terminology of Mixture in Galen: The Concepts of *Krasis* and *Mixis* in Galen's Thought' (Diss. Berlin, 2017). The difference between this and the planetary model is the idea that the qualities of two sympathetic entities enter into a creative alliance with one another—not that two opposite qualities cancel out each other's harm.

[68] Maximus, *Diss.* 9.3; Basil of Caesarea, *Homil. in Hexaemeron*, 4.5.

an intermixture (e.g. water mixed with wine, honey, or hemlock[69]), which does not include the idea of neutralisation. There is a limited background in astrology, but the passages in question deal with the transmission of influence rather than the cancellation of two opposite qualities (Geminus, 2.14 συναναχρωτίζεσθαι καὶ συνανακίρνασθαι τοῖς πλησιάζουσι ζῳδίοις of the transmission of planetary influence, here called *sympatheia*; Hephaestion, i. 252.7–8 Ἑρμῆς γὰρ κοινὸς ὢν συνανακίρναται οἷς ἂν συγγένηται, 253.9–10 πρὸς τὴν τῶν ἀστέρων αὐτῇ (sc. Σελήνῃ) συνανακιρναμένην φύσιν).

61 ὑποθάλπεται: once again there is a parallel in the passage where Valens is indeed talking about the effect of the elements on one another, but according to the Aristotelian model whereby they grow out of one another rather than cancel out their opposite (IV 4.23 ἀλλὰ καθάπερ ἐπὶ τοῦ κοσμικοῦ τὰ τέτταρα στοιχεῖα τὴν πρὸς ἄλληλα συμπάθειαν κέκτηται, καὶ ἕκαστον ἀπὸ ἑτέρου ζῳογονεῖται καὶ θάλπεται...; this is urged as an analogy for the transmission of influence from sign to sign). The verb suggests a pleasant, nurturing warmth (e.g. Aelian, *NA* 3.16, 13.12 [Aristophanes, *Hist. An. Epit.* 2.418], 14.7; Basil, *Homil. in Hexaem.* 2.6 ζωτικήν τινα δύναμιν ἐνιείσης τοῖς ὑποθαλπομένοις, of the Spirit of God in Gen. 1:2). For the use of the formal parallelism across this couplet combined with polyptoton to reinforce the sense of mutuality, see p. 343.

62–5

Jupiter in conjunction with Saturn and other planets, and with the Sun. For Jupiter's combinations with Saturn see 3.234–43: the message is wealth and influence. For Jupiter and the Sun see 2.417–22: the two passages agree insofar as they mention the ruin of πατρῴια and foreign wanderings, and that is perhaps less trivial than it seems, for the other comparanda (both versions of Dorotheus and Firmicus) (i) specify that the bad outcome happens when Jupiter is ὕπαυγος and (ii) give otherwise much thinner information. Perhaps they were versified from the same source, or M^d even reacts to M^a?

62 Μειλίχιος: only here in astrology as a qualifier of a star.
Κρονίδης: i. 910 n. 1.
συνοδεύων: the verb seems to be less restricted than the noun σύνοδος (35–8 n.) to conjunctions of Sun and Moon. It usually involves the Moon, or another planet with the Moon (Dorotheus, p. 423.7, 424.18), and/or Sun (Paul, pp. 32.30, 33.6), but in this book it also applies to the Moon and Venus (111) and Mercury and

---

[69] Sext. Emp. *Hypotyp.* 3.8.62 (μίξις distinguished from θίξις, physical contact); Athen. 1.33 E; Oribasius, *Coll. Med.* 4.11.5; al.

Jupiter (274), and other texts, not only late ones,[70] are prepared to extend it to other planets ('Par. Anub.', p. 354.4 Περὶ συνοδευόντων ἀστέρων; Saturn and Jupiter again in Serapion, CCAG viii/4. 227.30).

63 ἄστροις: planets. Here and in 81—although he uses ἀστήρ for planets in 45, 46, 78, 307—the poet overrides the distinction observed by M[a] and other authors (see on 2.3), between ἄστρα = constellations, and ἀστέρες = stars (whether fixed or wandering). See 4.1 and 1.4 nn. for further breaches.

Ἡελίου κακοεργοῦ: the Sun's epithet is unique to this passage (i. 908 n. 8), and presumably refers to its effect in combination with Saturn, since in principle the Sun is ambivalent, like Mercury (Ptol. 1.5.2).

64 πατρῴιον οἶκον: see on 6.80–1.

65 ἐν νήεσσιν: M[a] gives no help with this, though the succinctness with which seafaring is indicated bears comparison with 1.179 πλώουσιν (Mars in DESC).

66–8

Sun in conjunction with Venus. See 2.426–30. They agree on δυσγαμίη, but M[a] (like Firmicus, 6.25.1) concentrates on the status of the wives, while the present poet piles up the abstract nouns for the resultant ills.

66 κοινούμενος: 2.426 has συνοῦσ'. The participle could be construed as middle ('making common cause with') or passive ('being brought together with'), for both of which the dative is a possible construction, though the implication of this 'commonality' is presumably not the same as the mixing of properties suggested by ἀνακίρναται (5.60 n.); apparently simply they share a common space.

67 Depressing associations for marriage: ζῆλον (1.259 n.); δυσγαμίην (2.179 n.). ἐγκλήματα, a term from prose astrology (1.178 n.), are associated with other words for disturbance (cf. 1.221 ἐγκλήσεις μεγάλαι), sometimes lawsuits, and in marriage once again in Ptol. 4.5.8.

68 The nouns need not have a verb to govern them, since this poet is so fond of the 'who whom' construction (p. 322), but ἀσχήμονά τ' ἀλλοπρόσαλλον presumably agreed with a lost abstract noun in the next line. Sexual offence readily attracts ψόγον (4.506 n.). ἀσχήμων, too, is apt for lewd behaviour (5.318; Περὶ σχημ. 70 πόρνους; Περὶ κράσ. 74 πορνικούς; Astrol. Anon. 379, CCAG v/1.

---

[70] Others include CCAG v/3. 111.4, 11, 24; xi/2. 188.12; Apomasar, De myst., CCAG xi/1, and De Rev., passim; Achmet, Introductio et fundamentum astrologiae (CCAG ii. 123–37), passim; Camaterus, Introd. 2426.

206.24, 207.17, al.), and ἀλλοπρόσαλλον, which starts life as a Homeric *dis legomenon* (*Il.* 5.831, one of a string of epithets of Ares, and 889), and becomes popular in prognostic/diagnostic literature (also in physiognomy), would suit a word for promiscuity, or many other shifty, unreliable behaviours.[71] Apollonius, *Lex. Hom.* p. 22.17, glosses it ἄλλοτε ἄλλῳ φίλον; see too Nonn. D. 7.113 εἰς πόθον ἀλλοπρόσαλλον ἐπιχθονίων ὑμεναίων, of Zeus' serial philanderings (a similar context in 1.532).

69–71

Jupiter in DESC or IMC. Here it looks as if the poet shares a common source with 3.39–48, but has drawn different detail from it, ignoring the bereavements associated with the DESC and the loss of wealth that precedes its restoration in the IMC.

70 Conspicuously successful business in foreign lands and wealth ~ Firmicus, 3.3.6 (Jupiter in the IMC) *et qui cursu publico iussu principum vel ducum vel iudicum hac atque illac frequenti discursione mittuntur*.

71 ὀψίτυχόν τινα πίστιν: I have not found parallels for positions of trust (1.219 n.). But there is a consensus on good fortune late in life, for both locations. M[a] locates it on the IMC (3.48); see too for that location Dor.[ARAB] II 24.14 'or he will marry at the end of his life and [children] will be born to him at the end of his years or their middle, and he will fall in the middle of his years from his good fortune, [but] then he will get up and his affairs will prosper' and Firmicus, 3.3.7 *sed patrimonium eius circa medium aetatis tempus dissipabit et rursus postea colligit* (M[a] has the full sequence of loss and gain); Περὶ κέντρ. 38 ὀψίγαμοί τε καὶ ὀψίτεκνοι; Θ p. 151.4–5 διὸ καὶ τὸ γῆρας καλῶς διάξουσι. παραιρέτης δὲ ὢν μετρίους ποιεῖ, τοῖς δὲ κατὰ πρόβασιν χρόνοις εὐτυχεστέρους καὶ ἐνδοξοτέρους. But there is also a series of parallels for the DESC: Θ p. 159.24–5 πλουσίους περὶ τὰ ἔσχατα ~ Dor.[ARAB] II 24.10 'It indicates that in [his] old age his condition and his status will be better, and his end will be good' ~ Περὶ κέντρ. 32 κρεῖττον τῆς νεότητος τὸ γῆρας, καὶ εὐθανασίαν σημαίνει; Firmicus, 3.3.15 *locupletes divites et longae ac beatae senectutis spatia*.

72–3

Mars aspects Mercury in DESC(?). The outcome would suggest the IMC, but 'at the ends of the earth' implies the DESC, and perhaps Mercury can exercise his

---

[71] ἀλλοπρόσαλλοι: Ptol. 2.3.30 (merchants), 3.14.35 (γυναικῶν διαφθορέας καὶ παίδων a little later on), Dorotheus, p. 412.13 (thieves), ps.-Palchus, *CCAG* v/1. 185.16 (along with δόλιος). Physiognomy: Adamantius, 2.37 and ps.-Polemon, 8 (along with ἀσελγῆ).

serendipitous character irrespective of location (e.g. in Firmicus, 3.7.17, he does so in the eighth house). Firmicus, 3.11.5 (IMC), 9–11 (DESC), does not confirm either way.

72 ἐπὶ τέρματος αἴης: see on 4.578 ὑπὸ λοίσθια τέρματα γαίης (for the genitive, and in an expression of place, compare *Test. Orph.* 19 Riedweg ἐπὶ τέρματος ὠκεανοῖο).

73 For treasure trove see i. 280, 321 n. 1; add G. F. Hill, 'Treasure-Trove: The Law and Practice of Antiquity', *PBA* 19 (1933), 1–59; D. Braund, 'Treasure-Trove and Nero', *G&R* 30 (1983), 65–9. This normally takes effect in the IMC,[72] and the idea of wealth from the earth is slightly reminiscent of Aesch. *Eum.* 945–7 γόνος ‹› | πλουτόχθων ἑρμαίαν | δαιμόνων δόσιν τίοι (gifts, wealth, earth, Hermes), while not overriding the suggestion of the previous line.

74–7

Mars without aspect of benefics, but when on a *kentron* aspecting Venus... Firmicus' chapter on Mars in the *dodecatopos* (3.4) does not help with what is missing after 77 (though 3.4.4 notes the effect of the additional presence of Jupiter on the ASC). A marginal note in the Halensis on 76 already observed that material was missing ('Desunt aliquot versus, si vera est nota marginalis'). This is presumably a reference to an annotation in (?)Langermann's copy of L (i. 384). It is hard to see it as an interpretation of the asterisk in L against l. 75, which does not seem otherwise to function as a sign of missing material (p. 388; in i. 380 n. 41 it was taken perhaps to mark a generalisation or principle), but there is also a very faint pattern of three dots in a very flattened triangle directly below it against l. 76, perhaps by the main hand, and certainly not by L^1.

74 Ἄστοργος: an effect of Mars and the Sun in Ptol. 4.5.5.

θυμοῖσιν: cf. 5.280 Ἄρην... θυμούμενον. Mars' specialism according to the verses at the head of the *Sphaera*, 11 θυμὸς Ἄρης, and its paraphrase in *CCAG* xi/2. 111.12 Ἄρης θυμόν; known also to Περὶ κράσ. 129 ὁ δὲ Ἄρης ὀργῆς καὶ θυμοῦ (sc. αἴτιος); Procl. *In Plat. Tim.* iii. 69.21, 355.14 τὸ θυμοειδές; Macrobius, *In Somn. Scip. Comm.* 1.12.14 *in Martis animositatis ardorem, quod θυμικόν nuncupatur*; see W. H. Roscher, *Die Hebdomadenlehren der griechischen Philosophen und Ärzte* (Leipzig, 1906), 173. A weak clue that the poet might know, not just the planetary heptalogy (l. 34), but at least some of the rest of the lines of the poem at the head of the *Sphaera* as well (see on 5.29–34).

ὀλοώτατος Ἄρης: i. 909 n. 9.

---

[72] Περὶ κέντρ. 38; Θ p. 149.15–16, 18; Camaterus, *Zod.* 517–19, 586, 689; Firmicus, 3.3.6, 3.10.4; cf. also Valens, II 22.32.

75 εὐπλόκαμον Κυθέρειαν: i. 907 n. 14.

77 ὄσσ' ἀνέχων: for stars' eyes, see p. 339 and notes on 4.122 and 5.257 (Sun and Moon); for benefics raising their eyes against malefics (i.e. the opposite of this), see on 5.46; and for this verb, Ap. Rhod. 2.254–5 κενεὰς ὁ γεραιὸς ἀνέσχε | γλήνας; 4.697–8 οὐδέ ποτ' ὄσσε | ἰθὺς ἐνὶ βλεφάροισιν ἀνέσχεθον (presumably what is elided here, too, is the dual form); Philostr. Vit. Apoll. 8.4 ἀνέσχεν ὁ Ἀπολλώνιος τοὺς ὀφθαλμοὺς ἐς τὸν ὄροφον; Synesius, Dion, 18 αὐτὸς ἀνέχω τοὺς ὀφθαλμούς. The situations vary, but common to them is the idea of paying special attention to the object of the gaze (reverent attention, in Apollonius' case). Has Venus a transformative effect?

καταλαμπομένην Ἀφροδίτην: καταλάμπειν is proper to natural light, usually Sun or Moon, but sometimes stars (Empedocles, 31 A 33 D.-K.), and specifically Venus in Ptol. Synt. i/2. 298.14–15 (there a technical term meaning 'outshine'). The active means 'irradiate', the passive 'be irradiated' (e.g. Eur. Ion 87). The middle has been imported from poetry (δαΐδων ὕπο λαμπομενάων, τεύχεσι λαμπόμενος) and accommodated to a verse in which Ἀφροδίτην occupies final place.

78–80

Any planet is bad when retrograde. No astrologer would disagree with that. Retrogradations and settings produce poor outcomes (Bouché-Leclercq, 111–14; Valens, III 4.16, V 2.16, V 7.15), even in the case of benefics (Valens, IV 8.17). But what of the further specification that the planet is returning to its own house? Being in direct motion and being in one's own house are factors that make for strength, while being retrograde and in foreign houses make for weakness (Ptol. 3.4.7). Ptolemy does not say what happens when wires are crossed and a planet enters its own house 'backwards' (nor does the commentary elaborate), but presumably any kind of retrograde weakens or nullifies the advantage of being at home. There is an interesting parallel in Anubion, F 12.14–16 = 12 Perale, on Perale's reconstruction of the passage, where an evil effect is produced when the Rulers of the nativity are being carried retrograde in their own houses (σφετέρο[ισι δόμοισι…τοὔμπαλιν…[κατ'] ἐ[ν]αντιότητα [τ]ρ[έπωνται]). In Theophilus, CCAG xi/1. 257.11, a tyrant will stand firm provided the house-ruler is in its own house καὶ μὴ ἀναποδίζων.

78 πανήμερος: in this sense, 'altogether gentle', is unique (not even registered by LSJ) until Concilia Oecumenica, Sixth Oecumenical Council (AD 680/1), 206.20–1 and 210.4 τὸ πανήμερον ὑμῶν κράτος.

πονηρός: not a usual word for a malefic, but see 'Valens', CCAG viii/1. 167.5, 24, Additamenta Antiqua, IV 5; CCAG ix/1. 177.8, 179.13–14 καὶ εἰ μέν εἰσιν οἱ κύριοι τῶν τόπων πονηροί... Again it implies a degree of personification by imputing motivation, 'mischief-making'.

79 παλίνορσος: also 1.91. *Hapax* at *Il*. 3.33 παλίνορσος ἀπέστη, in this *sedes* (most of the many later poets who resurrect it relocate it in the line); the sudden jerk backwards of the man confronted by a snake contrasts amusingly with the stately progress of the planet, for anyone who recalls the original. Aretaeus uses it to mean a back-flow of matter (*De Caus. et Sign. Acut. Morb.* 2.5.1 Ἡ χολέρη παλίνορσός ἐτι φορὴ τῆς ὕλης) and resurgent disease (*De Caus. et Sign. Acut. Morb.* 2.7.5, *De Curat. Diurn. Morb.* 1.5.7), but the LSJ entry which describes this as 'retrograde' would have done better to reserve that term for planets, and in that sense this epithet in astrology is unique (non-technical in 91 and Maximus, 586). The poet means that the planet is carried backwards on itself (οἷ), backwards in relation to its normal forward motion, which is in fact contrary to cosmic motion (from west to east). When it retrogrades, it moves along with the rest of the heavens from east to west, which is 'forwards' from the point of view of cosmic motion; hence retrogradation is both προήγησις and ἀναποδισμός. For retrograde, astrologers generally prefer ἀφαιρετικός, 'decreasing', that is, in longitude (Heilen 2015, 1301–7), but ἀναποδίζειν, ἀναποδισμός, ἀναποδιστικός (Valens, IV 14.4, and p. 900; Dorotheus, p. 400.16; al.) conveys a similar sense of stepping back, retracing one's steps.

80 εἰς ἰδίαν χώρην: consistent with Ptolemy's terminology: ἐν ἰδίοις ἢ ἐν οἰκείοις ... τόποις.

κατ' ἐπέμβασιν: the noun is unique in the corpus, but for the sense see on 1.115 ἐπεμβαίνουσα. In this case the new place the planet is entering is its own sign.

81–3

The gifts of malefics. As Koechly noted, 81 looks like the dislocated introduction to a section on malefics. A lacuna precedes 82–3, whose original sense, accordingly to Koechly, was originally that, if malefics grant children at all, they take them away again (6.258–9); as it is, 82 was strung on after 81 simply by the verbal association of δῶρα and δοτῆρες.

81 ἀργαλέων ἄστρων is an unlikely transformation of *Il.* 4.471 ἀργαλέον Τρώων (where, as Dr Holford-Strevens notes, the ensuing καὶ Ἀχαιῶν explains the choriambus + spondee rhythm; there is no such justification here).

82 This elaborates basic astrological idiom: Ptol. 4.6.5 δοτῆρες ἔσονται τέκνων; Περὶ σχημ. 11 τέκνων ἐστὶ δοτήρ. Presumably the sense of ἀγνώμονες is 'unfeeling'; 'ungenerous' (LSJ I.3): at best, malefics grant only children.

83 Koechly hesitated to print γονῇ ἔπι, but the poet is hardly inhibited about hiatus (p. 354); the sense of the preposition with the dative is exactly right (LSJ B.III.1 especially 'with verbs expressing some mental affection'). In the verses preceding the *Sphaera*, δάκρυ is the domain of Saturn in particular. The poet need not have that specifically in mind, but anyway he clads the idea in plangent language which is both tragic pastiche (Eur. *Ion* 246 ὄμμα σὸν δακρυρροεῖ, 676–7 δάκρυα καὶ πενθίμους ‹ἀλαλαγάς›, and Euripidean examples *ad nauseam*) and reminiscent of sepulchral epigram (*IG* XIV 405.15–17 (Messina, n.d.) δάκρυσι | τέγξε λυγροῖς ὄμ-|ματα μυρόμενο[ς]), including for children (*IK* Kyzikos, 526, Cyzicene, 2nd/3rd c. AD πένθιμά μοι δάκρυα).

84–99

Mars and Mercury on *kentra* in friendly relation. These lines clearly belong together. There is a series of correspondences with Firmicus' generally much more detailed treatment of Mars and Mercury on *kentra* (3.11.1, 5, 9–11, 15–16). Firmicus' discussion is nested within his review of the *dodecatopos* (planet × place). Only for Mercury does he offer a subset of double factors (Mercury + the other planets). It is intriguing that the same agents are involved as in 5.72–3 (which also lacked an initial comment on quality), but in that case there were no Firmican parallels.

84–9

Mars and Mercury on angles in friendly relation. Firmicus mentions prison when they are on the DESC (3.11.9), and accusations on the MC (3.11.16), which there result from public office. The natives also leave home, but not under duress (3.11.15 *delectabuntur autem adsiduis navigationibus*). There is no close relationship with 3.211–14 or 339–45, save for general theme of turbulence, contention, and perhaps prison (3.343).

84 σύμφωνα τὰ κέντρα λαχόντες: one would expect σύμφωνος to apply to aspect (see on 6.106–7, 4.147), not *kentra*; the poet infringes Hermann's Bridge on the pretext of using a technical term—and then does so catachrestically. 'Occupying *kentra* in a harmonious relationship' implies not in the hostile one of quartile.

85 ὑψηλούς: only here in the corpus does this designate natives. It can be a status term ('high-up' people), which implies a focalisation from a middling point-of-view (pp. 32–3);[73] it can mean 'proud', 'haughty' (Eur. *Hipp.* 730); it can

---

[73] As in Valens, I 3.31, 50. See Artemidorus, 2.68.1 ἀεὶ δὲ ὑψηλοτέρους τοὺς εὐδαιμονεστέρους καλοῦμεν; see Klees, 57, and Thonemann 2020, 179, on Artemidorus' vertical social hierarchy, and

also suggest forward and bold (Stob. 4.11.5 Τὸ νέον ἅπαν ὑψηλόν ἐστι καὶ θρασύ; Plut. Dion 4.3 ὑψηλὸς τῷ ἤθει καὶ μεγαλόφρων καὶ ἀνδρώδης); LSJ would have done better to introduce some distinctions here. The other epithets in the line suggest the particular focus is on temperament rather than status, and so does Firmicus.

δράστας: see on 3.210 δρηστῆρας ἐν ἔργοις.

μεγαλόφρονας: also unique in the corpus, but common elsewhere. 'Great-heartedness' has Jovian associations (kingliness and liberality), but also the Martian ones of energy and mettle: Valens, I 3.35 (degrees of Mars within Libra), 36 (degrees of Mars within Scorpio), Περὶ κράς. 172 (Mars and Venus in trine).

86 πταίοντας τόλμῃ: like the violent denizens of Mars in 2.471 (also 469 βιαίους).

87-9 The poet arranges this as a parallelism with a sting in the tail (p. 327). Firmicus has no fewer than six parallel clauses (3.11.16 *aut enim impetiti aut accusati amoventur et frequenter iudiciis applicantur et falsis interdum accusationibus opprimuntur* (~ 88); *ex quibus infortuniis ita eorum patrimonia dissipantur, ut gravi fenore usurarum quatiantur; sed et sponsione aut fideiussione aliqua gravibus damnorum vel condemnationum generibus opprimuntur*), with the apparent implication that the style goes back to a common source. Both sets of repetitions pivot on a third-person plural passive verb, and the poet has worked hard to achieve the formal perfection of his version. βεβάρηνται (87) combines suggestions of literal chains (see on 4.486) with metaphorical oppression, while the metaphor in πεπάτηνται (~ *opprimuntur*), insofar as it applies to persons (rather than moral qualities, where it is common), is still bolder, though compare Plut. *Timol.* 14.2 οἷον ἐρριμμένον ὑπὸ τῆς τύχης πατήσοντες. In order to make ὑπενεγκάμενοι rhyme with συνελαυνόμενοι, the poet has had to make ὑποφέρω (LSJ II.2) middle, for which the difficulty of finding parallels bears out a certain sense of strain.[74] The phrase μέμψεις ὑπενεγκάμενοι is like Hephaest. i. 217.10 μέμψιν ὑπομένουσι, cf. Περὶ σχημ. 3 ἕξουσι γὰρ φθόνους καὶ

5.276-7 on 'ascent' as a metaphor for social advancement. In Achmet's *Oneirocriticon*, the ὑψηλοί are almost always people from whom the native receives aid (or perhaps harm), but whom he rarely joins, which is in keeping with the restricted possibilities of social mobility in that text (89.11, 111.8, 126.3, 142.68-9, 71, 145.32, 269.3, 285.18). The exception is 11.22 ὑψηλὸς ἔσται καὶ περίβλεπτος ἐν ἀξιώματι.

[74] The sense as in Psellus (11th c.), *Theologica, Opusc.* 36 (Εἰς τὰ ζητούμενα τοῦ ἑξηκοστοῦ ἑβδόμου ψαλμοῦ), ll. 30-1 ἡ μὲν γὰρ γῆ, ὥσπερ δὴ μὴ...ὑπενεγκαμένη τὸν ἄστεκτον ('not bearing the insufferable'). In Syncellus, *Chron.* p. 398.20 Mosshammer ὑπενεγκάμενος στέφανον, of Stephen bearing off for himself a martyr's crown.

μέμψεις ἐν ταῖς πράξεσι καὶ διαβολὰς καὶ ἐναντιώματα πολλά, where both Mars and Mercury are involved.

+ 90–2
With Saturn in aspect. Very different from Firmicus, 3.11.2, where the additional aspect of Saturn from quartile or opposition when they are at night on the ASC debilitates the natives.

90 τούτῳ τῷ σχήματι: see on 4.80.

91 τὸν δεσμὸν λύσας: I take Firmicus, 3.11.9 and 3.343 to support L's reading, rather than adopt Koechly's δρησμόν. For singular δεσμός = prison, see 6.208; Dorotheus, pp. 402.21, 403.14; Maximus, 558, 565.

παλίνορσον: 1.79 n. Its application to a restored moral quality seems rare.

92 For the γαλήνη metaphor[75] see van Nes, 64–5. The expression for pouring x on y (p. 340) is erected on the Odyssean formula χέρνιβα δ' ἀμφίπολος προχόῳ ἐπέχευε φέρουσα (6×), but the poet has rearranged the cases into a chiasmus (AabVB), so that the counterposed epithets suggest the contrasting state of affairs. Lucretius has a similar conception (of mental calm), but without chiasmus: *DRN* 5.11–12 *fluctibus e tantis vitam tantisque tenebris | in tam tranquillo et tam clara luce locavit* (L. van Ryneveld, 'Lucretius *DRN* V 11– A note on word order and imagery', *AClass* 29 (1986), 123).

93–9
Mercury and Mars setting together or in IMC. This corresponds to Firmicus, 3.11.5 (DESC) and 15–16 (IMC), which are connected by the theme of *fideiussio* (the giving of sureties) and attendant danger. The particular point of contact is with 3.11.16. The charts share insecurity of tenure, but M[d] has omitted anything about the nature of the natives' office or the reason for their downfall, in favour of the kind of dramatic plunge from high estate depicted in 3.67–8 (Mars alone in the MC). A lacuna before l. 95 is presumed on the grounds of syntax, but Firmicus offers no insight on how to fill it.

93 κακότεχνος: i. 906 n. 13; πυρβόλος: i. 909 n. 22.

95 ἐλπίσιν ἀπλήστοις: very like Eur. *IT* 414–15 φίλα γὰρ ἐλπὶς †γένετ' ἐπὶ πήμασι βροτῶν† | ἄπληστος ἀνθρώποις. For empty hopes see Valens VI 2.28 κεναῖς ἐλπίσι βουκοληθέντες (in unspecific circumstances).

96 This does not sound like Firmicus' public servants and administrators—more like the bodyguards armed to the gills in 3.64–5 (Mars in MC, in the

---

[75] γαλήνη = 'calm' in Critodemus, *CCAG* viii/1. 258.16; Achmet, *Oneir.* 238.29.

additional presence of benefics), who do, however, tie in with those *qui vitam suam potentibus viris aut regibus vitii cuiusdam causa vendant* in Firmicus, 3.11.15. τεύχεσι θωρηχθέντες: 6× *Il.* + one instance of τεύχεα θωρηχθῆναι.

97-8 It is surprising that Axtius and Rigler's ἐπαειρόμενοι and ψευσθέντες have not found more favour. The former is supported by 3.67 ἀείρας, and implies an ρ/ν error which is so characteristic of this manuscript, while the latter would correspond to ἔσφηλεν in the same line. On this understanding, ἐὴν διὰ πίστιν ἄπιστον does not mean that the stars are inherently unreliable, but that the man who has been buoyed up by them deludes himself about the nature of their support.

98 ἐὴν διὰ πίστιν ἄπιστον: what the poet means is not faith in the system of astrology itself (what Firmicus calls *fides*, 1.1.2, 1.3.1, al.), but what Valens calls ἐλπίς, vain hope that temporary success will remain on a permanent basis (V 6.4-9, esp. 7 ἐλπίζοντες ἃ θέλουσι πιστεύουσιν, ἐπιτυγχάνουσι δὲ ἃ μὴ προσδοκῶσιν). For the alpha-privative jingle, Breitenbach, 236-7; Fraenkel on Aesch. *Ag.* 1142; Fehling, 287-9, remarking that the device is almost exclusively tragic, and id., 'Νυκτὸς παῖδες ἄπαιδες. A. *Eum.* 1034 und das sogennante Oxymoron in der Tragödie', *Hermes*, 96 (1968), 142-55 (the paradox works in various ways: in this case, not 'trust that is not trust', but 'trust where trust is ill-founded'). The play on πιστ- also reads like a turning to account of a sophistic paradox (Ar. *Ran.* 1443-4 (parody of Euripides) ὅταν τὰ νῦν ἄπιστα πίσθ᾽ ἡγώμεθα, | τὰ δ᾽ ὄντα πίστ᾽ ἄπιστα).

98b-99 No improvement on Koechly's bold and brilliant reconstruction. Another passage in which there is an analogy between the state of a star and the enduringness (or otherwise) of the benefits it confers is Dorotheus, p. 338.30, where stars which are ὕπαυγοι, or about to become so, have an effect of fleeting radiance (εἰς ὀλίγον λάμψαντα μαραίνεται αἶψα πεσόντα).

100-2

Setting Venus, setting Mars. This is an add-on to the previous item, with obvious similarity to 3.84 καὶ δ᾽ ἔτι καὶ δύνουσα κακὴ περὶ λέκτρα γυναικῶν, which has been threaded onto a recapitulation of Mars' generally malefic quality.

100 λοίγιος Ἄρης: i. 909 n. 5.

101 For Mars and ἄλγος see also 'Antiochus', ll. 49-50 (*CCAG* i. 110.20-1) Ἢν δ᾽ Ἄρης εἰς μοῖραν ἐπεμβαίνῃ βιότοιο | ἄλγεσι καὶ στοναχαῖς καὶ πήμασι καὶ κακότησιν (sc. in ASC); 95 (112.14) ἔν τε βίῳ μόχθους παναεικέας ἀλγύνοντας (in IMC, Place of Parents). σῶμα βρότειον is also a hexameter ending in *Or. Chald.* 97.3 (body subordinate to soul), 215.6 (body a mixture of good and bad elements).

102 πικρὴ καὶ βάσκανος: for the second adjective see on 5.45. The first has no particular connection with Venus, but ever since the Odyssean suitors (πικρόγαμοι) has been the proper word for bitterness in marriage, especially in tragedy (Aesch. *Ag.* 745 γάμου πικρὰς τελευτάς, Eur. *Med.* 400 πικρὸν δὲ κῆδος, 1388, *Hipp.* 635, *Suppl.* 832, *Ion* 506, al.), but also for anything that turns out badly.

ἐπὶ λέκτροις: similar to 1.19 δυσγαμίην... καὶ ἀστασίην ἐπὶ λέκτροις, where the effect is produced by Saturn and the Sun aspecting Venus. In both cases Venus is harmed or does harm, but the present passage is rather reminiscent of the context of Eur. *Med.* 639–41, where the chorus wishes that Aphrodite (Cypris) may not promote marital strife (ἀμφιλόγους ὀργὰς ἀκόρεστά τε νείκη... ἑτέροις ἐπὶ λέκτροις). The element of *others'* beds is absent here, but the *Medea* is one of this poet's favourite tragic warhorses.

103–4

Mercury and Venus depressed in their own degrees. This represents the sudden irruption into the sequence of a τέχνη chart, and precisely the first in the Περὶ μίμων sequence (p. 217.5–7). The technical term ταπεινός, which corresponds to Θ's ταπεινούμενοι, does not recur in the corpus, and is so far out of step with the generally periphrastic approach to technical language in this section that one wonders whether an editor thrust it among the 'good and bad stars' believing it to be an adjective of quality. Is that also an argument for different authorship? Not definitely. Uncertainty whether there is a lacuna after 104 obscures whether the chart contained the 'who whom' construction (p. 322).

104 ξυρομένους: for the shaven head of the mime, see on 4.284 κορυφῇσι φαλακρούς.

ὄχλοισι: very often designating the theatre crowd (see on 4.277 ὀχλοχαρεῖς and φιλόμοχθα, θεατρομανοῦντας). Some disparaging examples in ps.-Plat. *Axioch.* 370 D φιλοσοφῶν οὐ πρὸς ὄχλον καὶ θέατρον ἀλλὰ πρὸς ἀμφιθαλῆ τὴν ἀλήθειαν; Dion. Hal. *Comp. Verb.* 11 ἐν τοῖς πολυανθρωποτάτοις θεάτροις, ἃ συμπληροῖ παντοδαπὸς καὶ ἄμουσος ὄχλος; Clem. Al. *Strom.* 7.7.36.3 ὀχλοκρασίαν τὴν τῶν θεάτρων δεσπότιν. Thonemann 2020, 162, also notes the use in Artemidorus (2.30.4, 3.62, 4.44.2, 5.57), and see too Dio Chrys. *Or.* 7.122, 32.86.

γελοίων: evoking the professional names of the μῖμος γελοῖος, μῖμος γελοίων, and/or γελωτοποιός, on whom see S. Milanezi, 'À l'ombre des acteurs: Les amuseurs à l'époque classique', in Hugoniot et al. (eds.), 183–209, at 194–5. Koechly signalled a lacuna after the line in both editions, in the first correcting γελοίων to the accusative, but in the second supposing the genitive dependent on a missing noun such as ἔργων. It could also be a direct rendering of the ancient term μίμους γελοίων (Demosth. Olynth. 2.19 μίμους γελοίων, Alciphron, 3.19.10 [3.55], Philostr. Vit. Apoll. 4.44.1, Clem. Al. Paed. 2.5.45.1 μιμηλούς ... ἀνθρώπους γελοίων, al.). See also on 4.283 αἰσχρογέλωτας.

105–7

Mars transiting Venus.

105 ἐπεμβαίνων: another technical term used in a slovenly way. The rest of the Manethoniana use this properly, for entering signs or places (see i. 893 and n. 140, and nn. on 1.115, 5.80). Here it either waves at some sort of aspectual relationship, or is an unsatisfactorily abbreviated way of saying that Mars enters one of Venus' signs.

106 φάρμακα δεινά: this combines Od. 10.236 φάρμακα λύγρ' or Hes. fr. 302.16 M.–W. ἄγρια φάρμακα (line-initial) with line-endings with φάρμακα in the fifth foot (Il. 4.218 φάρμακα εἰδώς, Hes. fr. 307.2 M.–W. φάρμακα οἶδεν, and parts of φάρμακα πάσσειν) as well as Hes. Th. 744 οἰκία δεινά. The phrase also in ps.-Lucian, Asin. 54 (of wizardry).

107 Hard to explain this. Whatever it is (it has multiple possible referents), the στόμαχος is governed and affected by so many different factors[76] that it does not seem to have a clear categorisation, e.g. as cold, or wet, or conversely as the seat of warm emotions, which it might have been, given that it can also mean anger, and that Mars in the houses of Venus causes στομάχους in that sense (Hephaestion, i. 210.20). Indeed, one might have expected 'hidden' disease not to have been produced by Mars at all, but by Saturn (pp. 16–17), although it is true that the Moon reaching Mars in Firmicus, 4.4.2, *stomachum latentium vitiorum continuatione debilitat*. As for joints, it is less that they belong in a certain domain (although various signs are said to preside over them) and more a matter of what types of harm affect them: wet factors produce evil humours, while Mars causes acute damage (Firmicus, 3.13.4 *articulorum*

---

[76] In Θ p. 189.13–14 Mars in Leo causes σίνη ἢ πάθη περὶ τοὺς ὀφθαλμοὺς ἢ ἀπὸ στομάχου ἢ σπληνὸς ἢ πλευρῶν, but without the presence of either benefic. Mercury and Mars: Hephaestion, i. 220.8. Sometimes the Moon is involved: Hephaestion, i. 209.28 (Mars in the house of the Moon), 222.9. But almost every planetary agency save Jupiter is implicated in diseases of the στόμαχος. Saturn: Hephaestion, i. 203.3, 12; Saturn and Venus: Hephaestion, i. 204.25; Saturn and Mercury: Ptol. 3.13.16, Hephaestion, i. 144.9; Saturn and the Moon: Θ p. 150.32, Hephaestion, i. 205.18, 221.20, 225.2, Firmicus, 3.2.9; Venus: Ptol. 4.9.6, Περὶ κράσ. 195, Hephaestion, i. 187.8; Mercury: Camaterus, *Introd*. 1410; Sun and Mercury: Hephaestion, i. 215.30; Sun and Moon: Hephaestion, i. 214.6; Moon: Ptol. 3.13.5, Valens, I 1.4, Περὶ κράσ. 222, App. II 24; Moon in Virgo: Maximus, 212; Leo: Hephaestion, i. 270.7, Paul, p. 10.12, Firmicus, 2.24; Cancer: Valens, IV 8.13, Camaterus, *Introd*. 607.

dolores vel eiectiones vel fracturas (Moon in second place, Mars on ASC). See too Valens, II 17.15 (Mars in opposition with Sun causes σίνος to joints).

108

Mars and Jupiter, not in a *kentron*. Mars' effect is mitigated when he is not in a *kentron*, since the latter is a position of strength. Ἥμερος is evocative, not technical; it is sometimes used to characterise signs, but not usually the quality of planets. ἄκεντρος, on the other hand, is an occasional technical term, unique in this book in the Manethoniana, found in Valens (II 23.24, 30; Appendix XI, 110) and ps.-Palchus (*CCAG* v/1. 183.24, 190.33, cf. also 189.22 ἀκεντρότητας).

109–29

Compilation on the Moon. Three organising principles are in play: (i) phase (waxing, 109; waning, 111; Full, 113, 115; New, 120) and finally node (127); (ii) leaving and approaching; (iii) planetary order. (i) is superordinate to (ii), and both (i) and (ii) to (iii). This is evident because the material on Saturn is split across these categories. And yet there are also signs of a tug of war between opposed principles: phase to begin with, but at the same time an initial (misleading) implication that this will be a review of planets, either in positional order beginning with Saturn and Jupiter, or (discounting the reference to Saturn in 110) in qualitative order taking benefics (110–11) before malefics (113–19) and then the Sun (120–6). There are little notifications on quality throughout: 109 ἀγαθὴ κατὰ πάντα, 111 καλή, 112 κακίστη, 113 ἀρίστη, 127 ὀλοώτατος.

This arrangement differs from the obvious comparanda, Π.σ.α., Firmicus, 4.2–15, and *Lib. Herm.* chs. xxvii and xxxiii. Although there are some individual differences,[77] all have separate one- and two-factor catalogues (the former for either or both of *synaphe* and *aporrhoia*, the latter for the Moon leaving *x* and joining *x*); the biggest formal difference from the present passage is that the poet or an editor presents a very confused hash of the two kinds. Conversely, while phase seems to be the superordinate principle here, the three comparanda only make incidental observations about it within a structure organised on a different basis. And finally, all three take the planets in straightforward

---

[77] Firmicus: 4.2–7 + 8 (single-factor: *synaphe*, then *kenodromia*) and 4.9–14 + 15 (two-factor: *aporrhoia*, with Moon leaving *x* for *y*, then *kenodromia*). Π.σ.α.: pp. 182.3–184.11 (single-factor: *kenodromia*, then Moon approaching then leaving *x*, then node) and 184.12–186.19 (two-factor, reciprocally arranged, i.e. Moon leaving *x* for *y*/Moon leaving *y* for *x*). *Lib. Herm.*: xxvii (*aporrhoia* + *synaphe*; the first part is lost, and it picks up with the Moon leaving the Sun for Mars) and xxxiii (*aporrhoia* from planets from Saturn to Mercury followed by *kenodromia*).

positional order, not (as is at least partly the case here) qualitative. *Π.σ.α.* sometimes gives little notifications of quality, but there are no especially striking similarities of outcome.

109–10
When the waxing Moon is good: leaving Saturn for Jupiter.

109 αὐξιφαής: also 174, 225, 257. Otherwise only in Θ p. 217.19 and Hephaestion, i. 221.8. For the terminology, see Heilen 2015, 1125–6. The Moon's waxing can be expressed with part of αὔξειν, αὐξάνειν (cf. 5.189 αὔξουσα), and αὐξάνεσθαι (cf. 2.442 αὐξομένη). αὐξιφωτεῖν, apart from one instance in Valens, IV 22.6, begins to appear only certainly in the fourth century. If αὐξιφαής is to be seen as a metrical version of that (enabling it to be accommodated to the hexameter), it implies a late date for this text. λιποφεγγής in 3.273, 275 (as well as 1.65) is one of the poet's favourite -φεγγής compounds (i. 106 n. 87), and not as a counterpart for this.

111
When the waning Moon is good: (leaving Saturn for?) Venus. If this means she is again leaving Saturn, for Firmicus the worldly success this engenders is not nullified by a certain amount of depravity (4.9.7; cf. *Π.σ.α.* p. 184.23–4, bad for marriage and children). With no reference to Saturn, success is spoiled by ill rumour (4.6.2).

112
Moon approaching Mars more or less Full. *Π.σ.α.* p. 183.1–3 agrees that the ill effects of the Moon's approach to Mars are aggravated if she is Full. Firmicus' account of the Moon's approaches to Mars concentrates on waxing and waning (4.4); all outcomes are bad except for the waning Moon approaching Mars by night.

μεῖον δ' ἢ μεῖζον μεστή: a highly unusually vague formulation, which does not owe its existence to a jingle in EGHP. The proper word for gibbous is ἀμφίκυρτος (6.575 n.; i. 892; Heilen 2015, 851–2); the poet seems to want to specify something particularly close to Full.

113–14
Full Moon approaching Saturn. Cf. *Π.σ.α* p. 182.8–9 ἀνατολική (that is, waxing) πρὸς βίον ἀγαθή. Firmicus, 4.2.1, has a different emphasis for the waxing Moon: at first, patrimony is lost, but later it is regained through the native's own labours.

113 πλησιφαής: i. 904, n. 10, and as a standalone name, Dorotheus, p. 388.24 πλησιφάεσσα.

115–19
Full Moon leaving Saturn. The best parallel is one of the σίνος charts in Θ p. 193.5–6, where this situation produces apoplexy, madness, or blindness. Mental disturbance is also the outcome in 4.552–9, which deals with the Full Moon in σύνδεσμος plus the other malefic. But in other sources—1.153–7, *Π.σ.α.* p. 182.18–22, Firmicus, 4.15.2, *Lib. Herm.* xxxiii. 2—the effects are physiological (cold and wet conditions), and in 2.445–50 economic.

116 ψυχαῖς πλαζομένους: πλάζεσθαι (LSJ πλάζειν I.2 'baffle, thwart, balk, especially mentally') approaches the sense of πλανᾶσθαι (LSJ II.5 'wander in wits'): already *HHom. Aphr.* 254 ἀπεπλάγχθην δὲ νόοιο; Tr. Adesp. 649.19 K.–S. μέμηνα[s] αὐτὴ καὶ παρεπλάγχθης φρένα[. But here, as also in Maximus, 166 πλαζομένοιο νόοιο (see Zito ad loc.), there is no implication of a stable basis from which the mind has wandered and to which it might return, rather a baseless, rootless, indurated state of distraction. Other referents are to literally wandering souls—ghosts[78] or souls in metempsychosis[79]—or minds distracted from the true focus that is God.[80] Nonn. *D.* 34.8 πλάζεται ἀλλοπρόσαλλος ἐμὸς νόος involves extreme mental turmoil, though not madness.

ἐξισταμένους διανοίης: Valens, II 17.16 (Mars in right quartile to the Sun) τῆς διανοίας ἐκστήσονται.

117 For self-harm see i. 358 and n. 64 (Koechly was reminded of Cleomenes in Hdt. 6.75.3), but *eating* one's own flesh (*degustantes* Koechly; 'taste of their own flesh' Lopilato) reaches a new level of horror. It is said to be almost unheard of, even among those who self harm (see https://www.ncbi.nlm.nih.gov/pmc/articles/PMC4162732/), so my suggestion—especially in a poet who is fond of bringing forward mythological exempla (p. 326)—is that he is evoking, even without naming him, Erysichthon, a heightened and even more culturally resonant form of the stock characters and attitudes M^a himself sometimes evokes (i. 170, 227–8). If so, it is another Greek testimonium, outside Ovid, to that part of the myth (otherwise Hollis on *Met.* 8 adduces only *EtMag* 33.17–18). Hyginus, *Astr.* 2.14, attaches the story to Triopas, certainly including the disastrous hunger, but not mentioning autophagy (what eventually saw Triopas off was a serpent, with whom he was to be translated to the heavens as the constellation Ophiouchos).

---

[78] Philoponus, *CAG* xv. 20.14–15 πῶς δ᾽ ἂν καὶ ψυχαὶ ἐπί τινα χρόνον ἐνταῦθα πλάζοιντο (sc. flitting around graves).
[79] Anon. *De Astrologia Dialogus*, p. 63.2–3 μυρίου ὄχλου ψυχῶν πλαζομένων, Cosmas of Jerusalem, *In Greg. Naz.* chh. 53–4, §§ 38–9, l. 4–5...τοῦ σώματος ἐξιοῦσα ἡ ψυχὴ πλάζεται καὶ εἰσπίπτει ἐν ἄλλῳ σώματι.
[80] Greg. Naz. *PG* 37.603.4; 986.2; 1281.3; 1356.11, 1432.1.

118 For railing madmen, see on 6.625 ἐπεσβολίῃσι and στοβέειν: again both luminaries and a malefic are involved.

θυμῷ μορμύροντας: this adaptation of *Il.* 5.599 ἀφρῷ μορμύροντα (of a turbulent river), cf. *Il.* 18.403 ἀφρῷ μορμύρων (of the Ocean), 21.325 μορμύρων ἀφρῷ (of the Scamander rising up against Achilles), entails the metaphorical transference of the verb from seething water to a turbulent spirit, for which there was obvious precedent in verbs such as πορφύρειν (*Il.* 21.551, cf. Σ *Od.* 4.427b1), ζέω (LSJ I.3b), (ἀνα)βράσσω (LSJ 1), and doubtless many others.

ἐπίψογον εἰς νόσον ὀργῆς: not easy. Are they railing at a blameworthy disease in anger (Lopilato, reading the transmitted ὀργῇ)? Are they railing in blameworthy anger at their disease (Koechly, reading νόσου ὀργήν, as if equivalent to ἐπιψόγῳ... ὀργῇ)? Or are they railing to the point where their anger becomes a disease (De Stefani, reading νόσον ὀργῆς, which he presumably construes as a genitive of identity, and taking εἰς in the sense 'usque ad')? De Stefani appeals convincingly to the rhythm of Nonn. *D.* 5.238 κυνοσσόον εἰς δρόμον ἄγρης; others include 21.309 θαλάσσιον εἰς μόθον Ἰνδῶν, 45.229 δυσέμβατον εἰς ῥάχιν ὕλης. On either his or Koechly's reading, ἐπίψογον (or indeed Dr Holford-Strevens' ἐπιψόγου.... ὀργῆς) might suggest the blasphemy incurred by the natives in 6.625.

119 *βωμολόχους θ' ἱερεῖς*: this is a grammarian's usage (passages are assembled in Stephanus). These are specifically priests. 'Secular' uses of βωμολόχος (especially in Aristophanes) use it to mean a buffoon or clown or flatterer, but grammarians derive the adjective from βωμός and λοχᾶν; this is a person who lies in wait or lurks at altars. From there grammarians suggest more specialised senses. One is a ἱερόσυλος, a temple-robber (Hesych. β 1389; Zonaras; also Philostr. *Vit. Ap.* 6.19.4). Another is someone who lurks in the hope of cadging gifts, and hence (as in the non-grammatical sources), a *parasitos*, a flatterer, buffoon, someone who is prepared to put up with anything in the hope of getting something for free (e.g. *Suda*, β 486, *EtGen*, *EtMag*, al.). Or they suggest it means a beggar (Moeris, β 31), as βωμολοχία is also explained as mendicancy (Pollux, 3.111); in which case, if the poet understood the word in this way, he might be thinking of *galli*. They keep honourable company, though: for priests and prophets and their honours, see 2.225–6, 2.317–18.

120–6 + 127–9

Moon in *synaphe* with the Sun, and Moon at σύνδεσμος. A similar pair of charts in 300–6 + 307–12 concerns σύνδεσμος at New Moon and what follows it, with associated gain and loss of wealth. The two passages are linked through technical vocabulary (127, 300 σύνδεσμος; 128, 307 λύσις) and through antitheses of πλοῦτος and πενίη in 121 + 125, 301). Both have the idea that the Moon's release from σύνδεσμος produces impoverishment (straightforward beggary in 129; in the later passage, in the presence of benefics, where a rich man spends all his money on benefactions and ends up destitute). They are obviously from the same hand.

The idea rests on analogy (122–6) which ought to be clear but is not. The Moon gives wealth and takes it back again—just as she receives light and has to render it up again. But this is a bad analogy, because the Sun is the giver, not the Moon; hence the lack of immediate clarity about whether, when she is Full, she is giving wealth to natives or rendering back what she has borrowed from the Sun, and, conversely, when she is New, whether she is taking wealth away from natives or storing up light from her proximity to the Sun which she later has to surrender. Π.σ.α. p. 185.20–2, it is clearer: at *synaphe* the native commences life in poverty, but then gets richer, suggesting that it is when the Moon is transmitting light that she is also transmitting wealth. 2.481–2 reports that *synaphe* produces loss, which again suggests that when the Moon joins with the Sun, i.e. when she loses her light, she takes away wealth. On the other hand, 5.307–12 implies that as the Moon gains in light the native disburses his acquired wealth: the Moon no longer corresponds to the benefactor, but to his beneficiaries. From this it appears that moonlight corresponds to wealth itself, rather than to a particular party in a transaction (Hübner 2003, 163): the application of the metaphor is mobile.

120–6
Moon in *synaphe* with the Sun.

120 Ἥλιον Μήνη models their propinquity. For καθεύροι, see on 5.8.

121 The line expresses initial gain and subsequent loss in a very condensed way. ἀρχαῖσιν is clarified by Π.σ.α. p. 185.19–20 ἐν δέ τε ‹πρώτῃ› [suppl. Cumont] ἡλικίᾳ: 'in first youth'/'at the inception' (of life); see too 1.5 n. ἐν ἀρχαῖς. ἐπάγειν is used by Mᵃ, sometimes in the sense 'bring something on top of, over and above, something else' (3.343), but not so as to effect radical change or reversal, as here.

122 οὐκ ἰδικὴν γὰρ ἔχει φάσιν: another redeployment of a technical term. φάσιν here means 'shining', as the verb is used of the Sun's and Moon's light (LSJ II.a; Rev. 21:23 καὶ ἡ πόλις οὐ χρείαν ἔχει τοῦ ἡλίου οὐδὲ τῆς σελήνης, ἵνα φαίνωσιν αὐτῇ).

ἡ θεός: she goes under this name in prose astrology too, for instance, in the name of the third place, ἡ θεά (e.g. Valens, II 14 Τρίτος τόπος θεᾶς Σελήνης; Bouché-Leclercq, 279, 283). Other heavenly bodies can be referred to like this too, e.g. Venus, in Valens, II 14.7, and Θ p. 130.20 ἡ θεά. On the Platonic background for stars as θεοί, see p. 181.

123 δανείζεται: quite so, but otherwise in astrology that makes the Moon pertinent to borrowing (not to loss). Not that the metaphor is always the same. The Sun may be pictured as the lender, the Moon the borrower (ps.-Palchus,

CCAG v/1. 188. 27–9); or the roles may change according to phase (Dorotheus, p. 406.33–5, cf. 395.17–19); or the Moon is imagined as the money itself, passing from lender to borrower and back again (Dorotheus, p. 395.14–16; cf. Hübner 2003, 147, 163).

οὐ μόνιμον φῶς: the Moon's light is transient, like wealth itself (Eur. *Or.* 340; see West ad loc.). For the final monosyllable, see De Stefani on Nonn. *Par.* 1.3 (6.123 means this passage). Homeric ἰσόθεος φώς paves the way for the appositional use of the phrase, for it often accompanies a personal name in the first half of the line; the apposition is now stretched further, with a different kind of, and differently accentuated, φῶς.

124 ὡς σχομένη περ: presumably 'when she is (held) in this position', i.e. in *synaphe*. The poet has imposed the verse pattern of ἀχνυμένη περ (*HHom. Dem.* 433 in this *sedes*) even though he clearly does not want the sense to be concessive.

125 The line embeds a little tournure of the poet's own (πλούτῳ πενίην ~ 301 ἐκ πενίης πλουτεῖ) within EGHP formulary (*Il.* 9.524 οὕτω καί; the hexameter endings *Il.* 3.425 κατέθηκε φέρουσα, *Od.* 1.139 al. παρέθηκε φέρουσα) implying the literal deposition of a material object (p. 337).

126 ἀντιτύπῳ νεμέσει: ps.-Aeschines, *AP* 10.123.6 ἀμοιβαίην ἐκδέχεται νέμεσιν (a portion of harm corresponding to a portion of good); Antiphilus of Byzantium, *AP* 7.631.6 = *Garland* 808 ἀντίπαλον Νέμεσιν (whence John Ryndacenos Lascaris, *Ep.* 26.4 εὐτυχίης ἀντίπαλος νέμεσις).

ἀποδωκαμένη: the middle ought to mean 'sell' (not 'render back'), while this form of the aorist (whether finite verb or participle) is vanishingly rare (ὁ δωκάμενος cited as a theoretical form in Manuel Chrysoloras' *Ars Grammatica*, 86).

127–9
Moon at σύνδεσμος, or node, where the Moon crosses the ecliptic (2.496–9 n.). Because only when the Moon is near one of the nodes do eclipses occur, it is closely related to Moon phase, and the σύνδεσμοι are mentioned among the Moon phases in, for example, *CCAG* i. 126.14, after New, first quarter, Full, and last quarter. But it is not only on the organising principle of phase that σύνδεσμος is placed last. The catalogue in 2.398–502, which is organised qualitatively, deals separately with the Moon's *synaphai* and *aporrhoiai* with the Sun (2.481–5) and treats the nodes in the penultimate entry (2.498–9), and *Π.σ.α.*, which is organised in *heptazonos* order, likewise deals separately with *aporrhoia* from the Sun (p. 183.16–17) and σύνδεσμος (p. 184.7–9).

128 κἢν λύσῃ δὲ φάσιν τὰ τελέσματά γ': both φάσιν λύειν and σύνδεσμον λύειν/λύσις συνδέσμου are set phrases. For the former see on 1.50; for the latter, e.g.

Dorotheus, 403.4–5 καὶ Μήνη σύνδεσμον ἐπὴν μέλλησιν ἄνασσα | λυέμεναι; Valens, II 37.43, III 1.28, IV 4.31, and *passim* (I am not sure why Riley consistently translates it 'make' rather than 'break off' a connection). But it is not certain that the poet means this here. The harm might be expected to occur at σύνδεσμος itself, of whose horrors we have just been told, not afterwards, and Pingree (reported in Lopilato's note) translated 'and if it gives up its appearance (in an eclipse)'. Lopilato, on the other hand, thought the reference was back to 120 and 122, and the poet means that 'the unfavourable result persists when the Moon begins to wax'. *Π.σ.a.* p. 184.7–8 has a parallel for the formulation, but is no help, because the Moon here, moving away from Full, analogically causes harm to sight (ἡ Σελήνη σύνδεσμον λύουσα καὶ ἐξ ἀποκρούσεως φερομένη λείπουσα φωτί[81]).

τελέσματα as a short form of ἀποτελέσματα is not completely unique (Camaterus, *Introd.* 1446 εἰρηνικὰ τελέσματα), but here it must refer, not to the outcome, but to the stars that bring that outcome about. It is another instance of M^d's cavalier way with technical language.

οὗτος ἔφυσεν: it is hard to feel confidence in Koechly's emendation. An executive verb is needed for L's ἔασιν, though transitive ἔφυσεν would be unique in both poet (who prefers ἔθηκεν) and corpus; see, however, n. on 4.483 ἐκφύσει. The *deixis* referring, apparently, to the σύνδεσμος is also peculiar (of planets in 4.16, 1.355, 5.76), but neither should it refer (with Axtius' οὗτοι) to natives. Given the poet's lax usage it is perhaps pedantic to object that it is not the σύνδεσμος itself that has this effect if the Moon is moving out of it.

129 χερνήτην ταλαπείριον: for the noun, see on 4.114. It replaces ξεῖνος or ἱκέτης, which the epithet in EGHP normally qualifies, but ἀλήτην, which follows, continues to evoke the original contexts.

5.130–6 Compilation on Mars' Oppositions

130–1

Mars in *kentra* in opposition to the Sun. This is confirmed by Firmicus, 7.10.1: among other situations involving Mars and the Sun, Mars on the ASC or MC, and the Sun in diametrical opposition, causes estrangements. 7.10.2 adds that the opposition of these planets when the Sun is in Mars' terms by day induces sons to kill their fathers, and 7.10.3 that a malefic in (quartile or) opposition to the Sun in the sixth or twelfth places causes disinheritance.

---

[81] ἐξ ἀποκρούσεως would seem to refer to a doctrine known from Valens, V 5, whereby the Moon performs ἀπόκρουσις when she is in the sign opposite the Sun (Neugebauer–Van Hoesen, 66).

130 Ἡλίου…διάμετρος: perhaps constructed with the genitive again in 134, but aspectual relationships normally take the dative (2.480, 3.339, 6.278, 595, 623, 717, 1.341, 5.136; accusative and dative in 4.74 and 296). There was no metrical need for this; perhaps the poet wanted to avoid two adjacent dative nouns. Unless (e.g.) ἀστέρι is to be understood, it implies a different conception from the dative (not *en face*, but on the other side and away *from*). διαφόρος can also take the genitive, again with an ablatival sense.

131 ἄστατον ὀργήν: not (in practice) the usual meaning, 'unstable', 'inconstant' (especially of marriage: see on 4.137–8), but the opposite: never resting and hence constant, the opposite of intermittent. The best matches for the cadence are Nonnian, especially ἄστατον ὁρμήν (D. 18.108, 37.696), ἄστατος οὐρή (4.415 and 26.315), and ἄστατος Ὥρη (12.90), as well as ἄστατος/-ν Ἠχώ (16.210, 32.279, 48.494) and other proper names.

132–3

Mars in opposition to the Moon in (its, i.e. Mars') degrees. Although none specifies that the Moon should be in Mars' degrees, this is compatible with Περὶ κέντρ. 6, Θ p. 149.9–11, and Firmicus, 3.4.15 (where chains and prison come about unless saved by Jupiter). In Dor.^ARAB II 25.2 (not paralleled in Περὶ κέντρ.), with Mars in the ASC, one luminary in the DESC, the other in the IMC, and Jupiter cadent, the native is imprisoned but not for long. Prison is repeatedly the outcome in Firmicus' charts on the Moon's *synaphai* and *aporrhoiai* involving Mars.

133 βρόχους: see on 4.489 (judicial punishment or suicide?).

ἀσχήμονα ζωήν: the poet extends the licence with initial zeta (p. 381) beyond proper names (as again in 5.338), accommodating what is to some extent a set phrase (Valens, IV 11.12 ἀσχήμονα βίον, cf. II 13.2 διὰ κακῶν ἕξει τὸν βίον ἀσχημονῶν; CCAG v/1. 206.24 ἀσχημόνως διάγειν). Given the context this looks more like a reference to general disgrace than specifically to lewd behaviour (for which see on 5.68; in 4.283 ἀσχήμονας of mimes; CCAG v/1. 206.24, of promiscuous females).

134–5

Mars in opposition in its own degrees, or to its own degrees, no longer in a *kentron*. Lopilato infers that Mars is still in opposition to the Moon (the Didot literal translation does not help), in which case μοιρῶν ἰδίων is genitive of place. Alternatively, Mars opposes his own degrees (constructed with the genitive as in 130): that would presumably intensify Mars' effects. The outcome is like that of a πρᾶξις configuration. The charts that bring it about in 2.355–6, 6.519, 4.123–4 = 1.288–9 (see ad loc. in all cases), Θ p. 211.13–14, all involve Mars and/or Venus, but none the Moon (which does produce fiery professions with Mars in *synaphe* charts).

134 ἀπόκεντρος: see on 3.269–70.

135 μιμηλὰς τέχνας: not the μιμητικαὶ τέχναι, the arts of music and poetry. To expand the note on 6.524–5, where μιμηλῆσι... γραφίδεσσιν are the graving tools of the encaustic painter, this phrase is used of visual and plastic arts, sometimes including metal-working (Lucian, *Jup. Trag.* 33 μιμηλῇ τέχνῃ σφραγῖδα χαλκοῦ πᾶσαν ἐκτυπούμενος, of a cast for a bronze statue; Dio Chrys. *Or.* 37.44 χαιρέτω δ' ὁ Δαίδαλος καὶ τὰ Δαιδάλου μιμηλὰ τεχνήματα, after an anecdote about portrait sculpture in wood or bronze; otherwise Lucian, *Imag.* 17 = Aeschines Socraticus, fr. 15 Dittmar, where Aeschines and Socrates are metaphorical portrait-artists (γραφεῖς δὲ καὶ δημιουργοί) of σοφία and σύνεσις, described as μιμηλότατοι τεχνιτῶν ἁπάντων). In other words, this confers an additional specification on the generic 'fire and iron' motif, which in principle could refer to something cruder and grosser and more painful. For κάματος, see on 4.293.

136

Mars in opposition to Venus. This is compatible with Θ p. 195.5–8. In the catalogue of aspects, adulterers are delineated most clearly in 3.329–34 (for conjunction, then extended to the rest). Opposition effects general marital upset in Dor.^ARAB II 16.23/Περὶ σχημ. 85 βάσκανος δὲ ἡ Ἀφροδίτη εἰς γάμον; Περὶ κράσ. 175; Firmicus, 6.17.2 *nuptias... impugnant*.

5.137–88 The Περὶ μίμων Sequence (from Θ pp. 217.5–218.8)

137–41 + 142–3

Luminaries in bent signs; Mercury in aspect to Venus. Koechly's brilliant rearrangement of the hemistichs is more or less confirmed by Θ p. 217.5–7, which has an additional reference to the paranatellon of the Ape (see on 4.271–85). It seems the poet has stripped back this further detail.

This, the first chart in the sequence that shadows Θ, is at the same time the outlier, because it matches its protasis only in respect of the agents involved; the details correspond rather to the doublet at 5.103–4. What Θ baldly labels a mime is in 140–1 presented rather as a *panto*mime. This is clear from the emendation in 141, which produces a reference to dancing in connection with the *thymele*, from their female dress, and from their sexual attractiveness. All are pantomimic motifs. It is further supported by the fact that the sister chart in 142–3 is of another type of musical performer. This double outcome for men and women, however, is better paralleled by Θ p. 169.4–8 (from the *dodecatopos*), which involves Venus with Mars, not Mercury. It does not mention bent signs, but does remark generally that the character of the signs contingently inflects the outcome. Both charts, by aligning passive male homosexuals (assuming this is meant by Θ p. 169.6 ἐπαίσχρους) with prostitutes (not with lesbians), entail an asymmetry between the sexes. In the present case, Mercury seems to operate on the man's sexuality,[82] but not on the woman's. But for both sexes, bent signs signify the willingness to 'bend over', which is not a problem of orientation, but of self-control.

137 καμπτομένοις ζῴοις: see i. 876 and n. 13, but add that there are two possible interpretations. First, according to their physical form, the curved or bent signs almost always include Capricorn, generally Cancer, Scorpio, and Pisces, and sometimes Aries and Taurus. They are usually called κυρτά or some affiliated form, but κάμπια in Ptol. 3.13.13. Second, they are the signs in which the Sun turns in its course (τροπικά; cf. modern German *Sonnenwende*), Cancer and Capricorn, which Anon. L (Ludwich, 1877, 109) calls περικάμπια (Hübner 1982, 77–8). Hübner classifies this passage under the latter category, but with a query. My guess is that the poet means the former. Curved signs produce hunchbacks by obvious analogical means (Θ p. 192.5–6), and I conjecture that their effect on sexuality is based on the same association in classical languages as in modern English 'bent'. κύπτειν, and the related κύβδα, stooped', describes the position of the passive homosexual (Henderson, 180) or indeed of the penetrated female (Archilochus, fr. 42 W.; Ar. *Pax*. 897; cf. Henderson, 181); as for Latin, Adams 1982, 191–2, illustrates the use of *incurvo* and *inclino* to describe the position of the *pathicus*. κάμπτειν itself can refer to sexual contortions (Henderson, 175, 180); the example cited, Pherecrates, F 155.15 K.–A., is used of heterosexual rape, and so the terminology chosen for the sign is suitable for perverts of any and every sex.

ὅτ᾽ ἂν εὑρήσῃς: for the addressee, see pp. 358–9. The sigmatic aorist of εὑρίσκω is occasional in late prose (e.g. ps.-Pythagoras, *CCAG* xi/2. 142.24, 28 ἐὰν εὑρήσῃς; *Physiologus*; ps.-Galen, *De remediis*; Zosimus).

ποτέ: M^d is the only poet in the corpus to use this adverb in protases (as opposed to apodoses, which is common in M^a and also in M^d himself); again in

---

[82] For Mercury and pederasty, see A. Pérez Jiménez, 'El mensajero Hermes y las propiedades astrológicas de su planeta Mercurio', in id. and G. Cruz Andreotti (eds.), *Aladas Palabras: Correos y comunicaciones en el Mediterráneo* (Madrid, 1999), 95–122, at 101.

918   *Commentary on Book Five*

300. Apparently it implies an occasionality more suited for outcomes (it *might* be this, but sometimes it is that) than for arrangements of stars.

φῶτα: Koechly posited a lacuna before this line in which mention was made of the Sun and Moon, but I suspect this poet was capable of using φῶτα alone to indicate the luminaries, even in the absence of a word for 'two' (3.376 ἄμφω; 6.146, 649 δύω) or an article (5.42, 285). φῶτα is never accompanied by their separate names in its other uses in the Manethoniana.

138-9 μεθοδεύεται...σχήματι τῆς Παφίης: this is an extremely strange expression for (presumably) 'move into aspect with' (p. 335). The simplex verb (active) is normal in astrology (i. 879 n. 31 and 895 n. 153), and outside it is sometimes found in the passive in a spatial sense to refer to ground covered or traversed (LSJ 2; Strab. 2.2.2, Hermas, *Pastor*, 22.2). The compound presumably has the force of 'move over' (into) (μεταβαίνειν is used of stars passing the zenith in *Od*. 12.312, 14.483; μετανίσσεσθαι of the Sun setting in *Od*. 9.58), but I cannot parallel it as a verb of motion, nor is this a sense recognised by LSJ. Astrologers use μεθοδεύειν (active) when discussing method and procedure (270-1 n.), while outside astrology μεθοδεύεσθαι (passive) often means 'to be managed', 'to be handled in such-and-such a way'. Perhaps the poet's rationale in using or coining a word which suggests transition was that he wanted to suggest a definite passage from one state of affairs to another, reflecting the departure from the norm in the natives' sexuality.

139 θηλυνόμενος: in the system of Ptolemy, who speaks often of planets being feminised (θηλύνεσθαι), feminisation is a matter of location (eastern or western, or location in a quadrant). Heilen 2015, 1119 argues that this is Ptolemy's innovation in the interests of symmetry, for Mercury was the usual astrological symbol of pederasty, without, however, indicating which role the native was to perform, and lacking, too, a female counterpart. Mercury again presides over a chart of ambivalent sexuality in 6.276-81, in which each feminine influence is harmed by a malefic.

140 ἀρρενόθηλυς: the intersex quality of the pantomime, which is a topos (Lucian, *Salt*. 2 θηλυδρίαν ἄνθρωπον; Anth. Lat. 111 Riese, quoted by Tedeschi 2002, 127-8), is imagined in multiple ways, like eunuchism, sometimes as a both/and, sometimes as a neither/nor, and sometimes as a depleted version of the one thing or the other. For Firmicus, 8.20.8 *pantomimi sed cinaedi*, 8.23.3 *cinaedi et pantomimi*, cf. 6.30.9 *molli corporis flexu*, they are passive homosexuals (cf. Apul. *Apol*. 74.7 *mollitia*). For ps.-Cyprian, *De Spectaculis*, 6.4, they are neither men nor women; for the motif see on 1.125. ἀρρενόθηλυς, on the other hand, puts it in terms of plenitude, like the much commoner ἀνδρόγυνος (Graumann, 188-9; ἀνδρόθηλυς is also used by Philostratus to characterise

Favorinus): it makes them hermaphrodites, on whom see on 1.121-8. But the epithet ἀρρενόθηλυς itself is associated with cosmic or cosmogonic gods (Phanes) or with planets: Venus is ἀρρενόθηλυς (Valens, App. II 30; John of Gaza, *Descr.* 224), which goes back to the old idea of Ishtar's double sex, so is the Moon (Plut. *Mor.* 368 c), and so are all of the Moon, Hecate, and Hermes (*PGM* 4.2605-6). The pantomimes are hermaphrodites in virtue of Mercury's own double quality and of the roles of Mercury and Venus in the chart. But perhaps the epithet, not the normal one for mere human beings, lifts them from freak to wonder.

πέπλοισι γυναικῶν: a *peplos* is strictly a woman's costume (LSJ II.1), but can refer to male dress, and does for the civic bigwigs in their ceremonial costumes in 2.234 = 3.37, to which this discussion should be added.[83] But against the background of common usage, the specification 'female' emphasises the violation of the norm (see also Lyc. 277 θῆλυν ἀμφὶ σῶμα τλήσεται πέπλον and Tzetz. *Carm. Il.* 1.176 πέπλους θηλυτεράων, of Achilles on Scyros; Nonn. *D.* 14.164, 46.83). For the pantomime's long, female dress, see Lucian, *Salt.* 2 ἐσθῆσι μαλακαῖς; Libanius, *Or.* 64.52; Garelli, 212-17; R. Wyles, 'The Symbolism of Costume in Ancient Pantomime', in Hall and Wyles, 61-86, at 64-5. For the stigma of males wearing female dress, see also Olson 2014, 190-3 and 2017, 140-5 (on fabric, colour, sleeve-length, and cincture).

141 The reference to the *thymele* makes it practically certain that the manuscript's ἀρχιδήμου is a corruption of ὀρχηθμός; compare 4.186 ὀρχηθμῶν ἴδριάς τε, καὶ ἐν θυμέλαις προφέροντας, and see ad loc. for ὀρχηστής as the normal term for a pantomime dancer, which is certainly what is meant here. That line could be used to restore the beginning of the verse (e.g. ἴδρις τ' ὀρχηθμοῦ), but instead I have used Nonn. *D.* 19.137 ἴδμονας ὀρχηθμοῖο on the grounds that L's reading suggests the ending -ων. With the reference to their lovers, compare Firmicus, 8.21.6 *pantomimi, sed quos multorum amoribus perspicua pulchritudo corporis semper insinuet*, and references to their *venustas* in 6.30.9, 6.31.85, 8.28.11.

142 πολύκοινον…ἑταίρην: again in 5.236 πολύκοινον; 3.85-6 πολυκοίνους… ἀλόχους. See on 4.352. This is astrological jargon, not evidence of the use of M[a] by M[d], and that could be the reason why, although it is not strictly a technical term, the poet is ready to violate Hermann's Bridge.

---

[83] Stephanus, s.v. πέπλος, 748 A-B; LSJ II.3; many more examples could be added, e.g. Ap. Rhod. 4.1294; Nonnus, *passim*. Heracles: N. Loraux, 'Herakles: The super-male and the feminine', in D. M. Halperin, J. J. Winkler, and F. I. Zeitlin (eds.), *Before Sexuality: The Construction of Erotic Experience in the Ancient Greek World* (Princeton, 1990), 21-52, at 33-40. Statuary: Amelung, *RE* s.v. Χιτών, 2317.3-32; M. M. Lee, 'Acheloös Peplophoros: A Lost Statuette of a River God in Feminine Dress', *Hesperia*, 75 (2006), 317-25.

143 μουσῳδόν: the word is unique (save for Nicetas Choniates (12th/13th c.), Or. 15.168 μουσῶδες ᾆσμα), a more precious substitute for the μουσουργός or singing-girl, whose reputation barely needs documenting.[84] They figure in astrology, too (Anubion, F 8 ii. 44 μουσ[ο]υργοί, line too badly damaged to tell whether these are singing-girls or musicians generally), but the μουσουργίαι in Valens, I 1.29; Rhetorius, CCAG vii. 220.7, are mentioned among Venus' delightful outcomes and carry no stigma. For female musicians and prostitutes, see 5.236 n.

σοβαρήν: see on 4.468. This poet associates haughtiness with women (5.305 n.), singers (5.288), and both (here). Other authors apply it to harlots (Plut. Mor. 706 B τοῦ πορνοβοσκοῦ σοβαράν τινα παιδίσκην ἐπάγοντος; ps.-Plut. Mor. 5 B ἑταίρας καὶ χαμαιτύπας... σοβαρὰς καὶ πολυτελεῖς). σοβάς is also a rare word for prostitute,[85] and σοβαρεύεσθαι is to behave like one (Hypatius, Fragmenta in prophetas minores, 3.138.15–16 ὥσπερ καὶ παιδίσκαι... σοβαρεύονται δι᾽ ἀκρασίαν αὐτῶν). For the figure of the arrogant prostitute, see Glazebrook, 180–1.

πολλοὺς τήκουσαν ἐραστάς: Love routinely does this, or people have it done to them, but the best parallel for the transitive use, and with a personal subject (as opposed to Love itself), is perhaps Nicarchus, AP 6.285.5–6 = HE 2741–2 κακῶν λιμηρὰ γυναικῶν | ἔργα (their personified handiwork), νέον τήκειν ἄνθος ἐπιστάμενα.

144–7 + 148

Mars and Venus in IMC, and with the addition of the Sun. For the various tightrope-walker configurations, see pp. 617–18 and the apparatus for 4.271–85 + 286–9. The best parallel for Mars and Venus in IMC is Θ p. 213.6–7 (from the supplements to Ptolemy among Π- charts). The entry that corresponds to this one in Θ's sequence does involve the IMC, but with different agencies (p. 217.9). Mars, Venus, and the Sun together are paralleled in Θ p. 213.1 (also among the supplements to Ptolemy) νευροβάτας... μαγγαναρίους, but the Sun does not have the effect of making them fall.

145 ἰοβλέφαρος Κυθέρεια: i. 907 n. 15.

146 καλοβάτην: for the terminology, see on 6.440. Add to the Delphic example there cited the hexameter epitaph of a κα]λοβάτης (or σκα]λοβάτης)

---

[84] Among αὐλητρίδες and ἑταῖραι: e.g. Theopompus, FGrH 115 F 114; Aelian, VH 7.2; Athen. 4.129 A; Plut. Crass. 32.3; Alciphron, 1.15.3 [1.12]; al.
[85] Many examples could be added to LSJ, e.g. Σ Ar. Pax 812a, CCAG ix/2. 164.16 (Σοβάς among names of Aphrodite, along with Χαμαιτύπη et al.), and entries in ps.-Zonaras, Photius, and Suda.

εἶτ' ὀξυβάτης (SEG 27.266, Beroia, 2nd-c.). This man was some sort of acrobat (W. Slater, 'Mime Problems: Cicero *Ad Fam.* 7.1 and Martial 9.38', *Phoenix*, 56 (2002), 315–29, at 324–5; he is described by another title as well, restorable as [κοτυ?]|λιστής, which Slater doubts). There are no literary parallels for the word except for καλοβατεῖν once in Porphyr. *Abst.* 3.15. In other words this suggests a different lexical style from Mᵃ and Mᵇ's poetic artifice αἰθροβάτας. The poet has apparently taken the liberty of lengthening the first syllable by analogy with epic κᾱλός, but why the consistent use, across all occurrences, of *o* instead of ω?

ἠερόφοιτον: Homeric ἠεροφοῖτις (*Il.* 9.571, 19.87), epithet of the Erinys, 'walking in mist', is repurposed many times over, usually in the second declension form used here, and usually removed to line-end or before the main caesura (as is the case with most of Nonnus' uses). In this respect the poet's conservative handling of the epithet is best paralleled by Oppian's ἠερόφοιτα γένεθλα, of birds (*Hal.* 3.166). De Stefani has a long discussion of the word at Nonn. *Par.* 1.215 (hosts of angels). All that needs to be added here is that it evokes the conceit of tightrope-walkers as human birds (see on 6.441–5 and 443), and that this is not the only 'air-treading' epithet that can be shared with more grandiose situations like supernatural beings suspended midair (*D.* 33.58, Eros), rapture (*D.* 10.262, Ampelos; *D.* 24.79, Aeacus; *D.* 18.32, 35.296 Tantalus), and the *Himmelfahrt* (*D.* 11.132, Abaris), for αἰθροβάτας, used elsewhere of Abaris (6.440 n.), applies to tightrope-walkers there and in 4.278.

147–8 For the comparison see on 6.443 (a spontaneous parallel in M. Bussi, *Don't Let Go: Some Holidays are Paradise and Some are Murder* (London, 2017), ch. 17: 'a gecko is creeping carefully along the beam, like a tightrope walker… An Icarus without feathers'). Only here is the comparison pressed as far as the performer's falling. The Sun's role works better on the level of the myth than in its this-worldly counterpart; the poet has preferred the conceit over any system-based rationale (why would the Sun cause the performer to fall unless, say, it was setting?).

147 δίχα καὶ δίχα: the repetition of the preposition is an affectation in itself (Fehling, 197, and Braswell on Pindar, *P.* 4.290(d)), and with *variatio* of placement still more so. It is trivially easy to find adjacent anastrophic and prepositional instances of (e.g.) μετά/μέτα, ἐπί/ἔπι, ἀπό/ἄπο in archaic poetry, but not to show that any is as self-conscious as this, in a poet who courts chiastic order.

148 Τιτὰν φαέθων: i. 908 n. 7.

149–53

Moon setting in watery signs as she approaches Saturn, or setting in northern signs. The protasis is an exact match for Θ pp. 217.10–11 and 212.23–4. The apodosis is the poet's little flourish (or the epitomator who produced Θ has curtailed it), and no help is to be had from that quarter for restoration.

149 For all the many generalising statements throughout the corpus, the use of αἰεί in a protasis cast formally as an *if p then q* construction is very unusual (in 3.72 the protasis consists only of a participle). For watery signs see i. 876; Hübner, 1982, 176–8. 'Watery' in this connection refers to *Lebensbereich*, because that is the lifestyle implication for the natives, and the signs generally include Cancer, Capricorn, Aquarius, and Pisces. The terminology varies: κάθ-, πάρ-, δί-, and ἐν- are all attested, and Hübner (178) suggests at least the possibility of reading ἐφύγροις here. Another sailor chart involving watery signs in 6.362–5.

150 δύνουσαν τὰ βόρεια: if this refers to signs, it must mean that the Moon is setting in the northern quadrant (see on 4.241 βορειοτάτην τε χορείην), which is variously defined (Hübner 1982, 50), but should at least include the watery sign of Cancer. But Θ's βορεία κατιοῦσα should mean 'setting in the north' (nothing to do with signs), and that meaning here obviates the confusing shift from quality of signs to a quadrant. The Moon can do this more pronouncedly than the Sun, since its orbit is tilted an additional 5.1% from the ecliptic (4.91 ἕλιξ n.). It can thus rise up to 28.6° north (or south) of the equator.

151 Koechly's restoration here displeases. Had the poet intended a jingle, it would have been characteristic of him to put δύνουσαν and θύνουσαν at matching positions in the line.

152–3 A little repository of IE clichés—mostly available from the Homeric poems, in particular the *Odyssey*—strung together in a style that is reminiscent of the aphorisms and conceits of the novelists, especially Achilles, and slightly, too, of the style of 4.289, but without the Gorgianic jingles of that poet.

152 For the rhythm of the line, compare 5.270 οὗ πόρος ἐστὶ φύσις, ἡ δ' αὖ φύσις ἐστὶν ὁ δαίμων.

ὧν ὁδός ἐστιν ὕδωρ: like ὑγρὰ κέλευθα; Sanskrit *Vāripatha* water-path, voyage; OE *flōdweġ, wæterweġ, lagulād* (sea-route, sea-way); kennings for the sea, including *seġlrād* (sail-road), *hronrād* (whale-road), and *hwælweġ* (whale-way). In *haswe herestrǣta* = grey highways (*Exodus* 284, Moses' description of the parting of the ways of the Red Sea), the roads are literal, and the expression also prosaic.

οἱ δ' ἀστέρες εἰσὶν ὁδηγοί: as they were for Odysseus (*Od*. 5.272–5). The Church Fathers often talk in these terms about the star that guided the Magi (e.g. Epiphanius, *Panarion*, i. 372.25–6 τοῦ ἀστέρος ὁδηγοῦντος αὐτούς; ps-Epiphanius, *Homilia in laudes Mariae Deiparae*, PG 43.500.52 ὁ ἀστὴρ ὁ τῶν μάγων ὁδηγός).

153 ἡνίοχοι δ' ἄνεμοι: a development of that most familiar IE conceit, the ship as steed (Norse *gjálfrmarr, hafvigg* and many other *vigg-* compounds[86])— or, in some Greek and Skaldic poetry, chariot (West 2007, 82-3; S. West on *Od.* 4.708; Bowie on *Od.* 13.81-5; Skaldic *hafreiðar, lǫgreiðar* [of the] sea-chariot). If the ship is a chariot the winds direct it, though more coherently the charioteer ought to be the pilot (cf. ps.-Plut. *Vit. Hom.* 231 φθέγξατο δ' ἡνίοχος νηὸς κυανοπρῴροιο). The author of the Περὶ τρόπων, who quotes this verse, points out that horses can have pilots, too (ἵππων κυβερνητῆρες).[87]

κύματα μακρὰ κέλευθα: this hybridises κύματα μακρά (5× EGHP, and in this *sedes* in *Il.* 2.144 κύματα μακρὰ θαλάσσης) with ὑγρὰ κέλευθα.

154-8

Kentra in slippery signs. This passage seems to have escaped attention in discussions of ancient diving, the main ancient sources for sponge-divers being Oppian, *Hal.* 5.612-74, and Plin. *NH* 9.152-3.[88] Sponge-divers (Appendix II, I.2.iii) are also born (i) under the 21st degrees of Scorpio and Pisces, according to Firmicus (8.26.9; 8.30.8, where the image is not a happy one), and (ii) under the 6th degree of Cancer, according to *Lib. Herm.* xxv. 4.1 *piscatores vel extractores spongiarum* (Feraboli, 219). According to Goold, the *merces...quas umor alit* in Manil. 5.248-9 include sponges, fetched up by the native born under Crater. Divers (κολυμβητάς), not specifically for sponges, are born in Teucer, II 9.6, under the constellation Delphis (paranatellon of Sagittarius).

154-5 ζῴοις ἐν ὀλισθηροῖσι...τοῖσιν ἀφώνοις: see i. 876 and n. 12. The first category is without parallel. The second one is known, and under this name (Hübner 1982, 169). Different combinations of signs are attributed to it, never again this particular one—whence Hübner reasonably takes ἀφώνοις to refer only to Pisces, which does feature in other specifications of mute signs. The muteness of fish is conventional.[89]

156 δεσμευομένους: see Opp. *Hal.* 5.634, 655, 668 δεσμόν; Plin. loc. cit.; Rodríguez-Álvarez, 75-6, interpreting a scene on an Attic *oenochoe* from Vulvi (510-490 BC), not as mythological, but as a representation of a diver with a rope

---

[86] G. Vigfusson, *An Icelandic-English Dictionary Based on the MS. Collections of the Late Richard Cleasby* (Oxford, 1874), s.v. VIGG.

[87] The conceit applies not only to mariners but also to gods: cf. West 2007, 264, 265, for IE wind-gods with chariots and winds riding horses; Ps. 104:3 '...who maketh the clouds his chariot'.

[88] F. J. Frost, 'Scyllias: Diving in Antiquity', *G&R* 15 (1968), 180-5; Rodríguez-Álvarez.

[89] Garvie in Aesch. *Pers.* 576-8, Finglass on Soph. *Aj.* 1295-7 (p. 499), Bömer on Ov. *Met.* 4.50; add e.g. Arist. *De Anim.* 421ª4, *HA* 535ᵇ14; Lucian, *Adv. ind.* 16; Athen. 8.348 A.

round his waist (in fact his pelvis, not his chest) preparing to jump from a ship. I wonder whether this detail has been included because it connects the outcome to the chain (λίνον) that joins the two fishes, and is listed as Pisces' paranatellon in Teucer I, p. 21.3, 8; Teucer, II 12.1 (cf. Boll 1903, 263)? The second Teucer text lists ἁλιεῖς ἢ καὶ συμπλοκὴν πράγματος as the outcomes. Here is a literal realisation.

157 Save for the verb, which is prosaic, and rare (Plutarch; Aelian; Pollux), the line creates a *presque homérique* setting for the sponges—suitably so, since divers (*Il.* 16.742, 747–8—not sponges, but oysters) take their place in EGHP via similes,[90] and the dolphin simile (built out of expressions like ἠΰτε νεβροί, ἠΰτε ἄρνες, ἠΰτε ταῦρος, as well as several other non-animal comparisons) acknowledges dolphin comparisons in *Il.* 21.22 as well as *HHom. Ap.* 400 δελφῖνι ἐοικώς, 494 εἰδόμενος δελφῖνι. κυανέῳ πελάγει manages an epic feel, though its best antecedents are in fact tragic and lyric: Simonides, *PMG* 567.4 κυανέου 'ξ ὕδατος; [possibly] Soph. *Ant.* 966 παρὰ δὲ κυανέων †πελαγέων πετρῶν† διδύμας ἁλός (see H. Lloyd-Jones, 'Notes on Sophocles' *Antigone*', *CQ*² 7 (1957), 12–27, at 23, for other tragic passages where κυάνεος is used of waters); Eur. *Andr.* 1011–12 καὶ πόντιε κυανέαις ἵπποις διφρεύ|ων ἅλιον πέλαγος; Grand-Clément, 126, whose rendering 'bleu sombre', sometimes with suggestions of a heavy, laden atmosphere (Bacchyl. *Ep.* 13.91), is not matched by the present, decorative, passage.

158 σφόγγους...πουλυτρήτους: the poet has repositioned the Odyssean formula σπόγγοισι πολυτρήτοισι; so has Babrius, *Fab.* 111.15 σπόγγους... πολυτρήτους, where a merchant exploits their commercial possibilities. ἐκ βυθίων (Alexander Magnes, *AP* 6.182.2 = *FGE* 1 (Page dates him to the later part of the period covered by Philip's *Garland*, 90 BC–AD 40), Greg. Naz. *AP* 8.79.7 ἐκ βυθίων...κόλπων (metaphorically); Nonnus has ἐκ βυθίων and ἐκ βυθίου, both nominal and adjectival, at the beginning of the line) both glamorises and perhaps acknowledges the depths that sponge-divers could really reach (30 metres, apparently, in the nineteenth-century Aegean). On the uses of sponges (mostly domestic, medicinal, and for personal care: Ar. *Ran.* 482–90; Pompeian lavatories!) in antiquity, see J. M. Cook, 'Bath-Tubs in Ancient Greece', *G&R* 6 (1959), 31–41, at 33; E. Voultsiadou, 'Sponges: An Historical Survey of Their Knowledge in Greek Antiquity', in *Journal of the Marine Biological Association of the United Kingdom*, 87 (2007), 1757–63; Rodríguez-Álvarez, 78–9. Mesomedes' poem on the sponge (II Heitsch), 9, ends with an intimate glimpse of the plucky diver's toil put to use in a lady's boudoir.

---

[90] Janko notes that *Od.* 5.432 ὡς δ' ὅτε πουλύποδος θαλάμης ἐξελκομένοιο implies a diver as well.

159–64

Venus in her own places with Mercury. All versions of this favourite combination, producing musicians, are formulated slightly differently. 6.366–70 + 371–2, 6.504–10 have some reciprocal element in the set-up. 1.58–61, 62–5 do not. But this situation is an exact match for Θ p. 217.12–13 and Θ p. 213.24–5 (the apodosis is more expansive). Θ locates Venus in the houses of the Sun (Leo) or Venus' own (Taurus and Libra). That suggests a link with Teucer, according to whom the second decan of Leo is associated with οἱ Φρύγιοι αὐλοί (TR, p. 18.6), and the first decan of Libra with Μοῦσα λυρίζουσα (TR, p. 19.1–2), though Taurus itself contributes little in the way of music.

The poet has expanded the list of instrumentalists into five different kinds, whether because he already knew M^a's efforts in this regard (also 2.331–5), or simply because it took his fancy. There is a comparable list in *Or. Sib.* 8.114–17 + 119, which contains practically the same instruments—cymbals, αὐλὸς πολύτρητος ~ τρητοῖς καλάμοις, pipes (σύριγμα ~ σύριγγι), the trumpet, and the lyre—except that the occasion is almost exactly the opposite of the present one, namely a list of absences in the undifferentiated world of the dead. It bears comparison, too, in its one-component-per-line parallelistic style. But its thumping anaphoras are unrelieved by *variatio*, which the poet applies here to a studied extent (p. 342).

160 τρητοῖς καλάμοις: the instrument must be the aulos, because pan pipes are mentioned separately in the next line. The καλαμαύλους who figure in the corresponding part of Θ are particularly interesting. The instrumentalists in question are known from two epitaphs, (i) a verse epigram for Theon by Hedylus quoted by Athenaeus, 4.176 D, and (ii) a funerary stele from Este for Quintus Appeus Eutychianus, καλαμαύλης.[91] Hedylus' epigram calls the same man αὐλητής, μόναυλος, and καλαμαυλήτης, and Athenaeus' discussion[92] explains that the player on the κάλαμος (singular) is called καλαμαύλης. The stele from Este is crowned by a tympanum which represents two instruments, one cylindrical, the other (a shawm?) conical. It is not clear to which instrument the term καλαμαύλης in the inscription refers, although the popular (and possibly, in this particular instance, home-made) nature of the instruments and instrumentalist has been inferred from the poor quality of the stele and the Greek name of the player. No other source parallels Θ's second-declension form, but it appears more precise than an epitomator's rendering of a poem that merely referred to κάλαμοι; in other words it adds to the likelihood that Θ is not a reduction of verse (pp. 143–4).

---

[91] F. Guizzi, 'The Oboe of Quintus Appeus Eutychianus: A Rare Representation of a Roman Single Conical Reed-Pipe', *Imago Musicae*, 18–19 (2001–2), 121–54.
[92] Cf. also Eustathius on *Il.* 18.495 (iv. 233.3), who paraphrases him.

For the epithet, see commentary on 2.334 πολυτρήτοις... ἐν αὐλοῖς, adding PSI inv. 516, i. 12 τρητοῦ δόνακος (S. Stephens and J. Winkler, *Ancient Greek Novels: The Fragments: Introduction, Text, Translation, and Commentary* (Princeton, 1995), 446, with n. on 449). In Julian, *AP* 9.365.5 ἐυτρήτων καλάμων, the pipes are those of an organ.

161 νομίᾳ σύριγγι: absent from Θ, and perhaps the poet's elaboration on his source with a conventional item. The only other astrological references to pan pipes known to me—in Manilius, 5.116–17 (*pastor*) *cui fistula collo | haereat* (cf. 4.154 *calamos*) and Firmicus, 8.6.5 *sed qui fistula rustici carminis dulces modos dicant*—are better motivated: they are born analogically under the rising of the constellation Haedi/star Haedus in the twentieth degree of Aries. (For the sentimental tone in these passages, which go back to a common source, see p. 60 and n. 104.) The cladding is poetic topos: see Ap. Rhod. 1.577–8 σύριγγι λιγείῃ | καλὰ μελιζόμενος νόμιον μέλος; Nonn. *D*. 27.227 νομίη... σύριγξ; Greg. Naz. *PG* 36.619.50–620.2 Ἄρτι δὲ ποιμὴν καὶ βουκόλος ἁρμόζονται σύριγγας, καὶ νόμιον ἐμπνέουσι μέλος; connected with Pan in Nonn. *D*. 27.294, 41.373, Himerius, *Or*. 9 l. 58.

κεφαλὴν ἐπισείει: although I have not found this motif paralleled in bucolic, swaying or shaking the head is an easily understood sign of rapt absorption or a trance-like state (Thonemann 2021, 92). It is sometimes mentioned for stage performers (Athen. 1.21 F Φίλλις ὁ Δήλιος μουσικὸς τοὺς ἀρχαίους φησὶ κιθαρῳδοὺς κινήσεις ἀπὸ μὲν τοῦ προσώπου μικρὰς φέρειν, ἀπὸ ποδῶν δὲ πλείους; of Nero's efforts as a citharode: Philostr. *Nero* 6–7 τὸ νεῦμα ἐξομοιῶσαι τοῖς μέλεσιν... νεύει μὲν γὰρ τοῦ μετρίου πλέον); Cic. *Leg.* 2.39, on the behaviour of theatre audiences, once decorous, but now (we see) *ut... cervices oculosque pariter cum modorum flexionibus torqueant*: if this is not a reference to the audiences themselves, it could be to the performers (H. Morgan, 'Music, Spectacle, and Society in Ancient Rome, 168 BC–AD 68' (D.Phil. thesis, Oxford, 2018), 72–80, proposing that it refers to *tibicines*). Two extreme examples are Maenads (J. N. Bremmer, 'Greek Maenadism', in id., *The World of Greek Religion and Mythology: Collected Essays*, ii (Tübingen, 2019), 251–77, at 262–3), where auloi are also involved, and shamans (C. Laderman, *Taming the Wind of Desire: Psychology, Medicine, and Aesthetics in Malay Shamanistic Performance* (Berkeley, 1991), 110).

162 More conventional vocabulary. ἐκ στομάτων (at line-beginning) is used for the Muses' song in Hes. *Th.* 40. Trumpets resound with the verb κελαδεῖν from as early as tragedy, and especially in epigram.[93] 'Bellowing' trumpets are

---

[93] Eur. *Phoen.* 1102 παιὰν δὲ καὶ σάλπιγγες ἐκελάδουν ὁμοῦ; Crinagoras, *AP* 6.350.1 = *Garland* 1835; ps.-Opp. *Cyn.* 4.398 σάλπιγξ μὲν κελάδησε πελώριον; epigram ap. *Suda*, κ 1281; ps.-Apollinaris, *Metaphr.* 46:9 εὐκελάδου σάλπιγγος, al.

last to be attested. Heliodorus (4th c.?) compares the bellowing of a bull to a trumpet (*Aeth.* 10.30.5 τῷ μυκηθμῷ τοῦ ταύρου καθάπερ σάλπιγγι), and Nonnus has plenty of literal or metaphorical bellowing trumpets, including the cadence μυκήσατο σάλπιγξ at D. 2.558, 6.231, 23.194, 29.290, from which we should presumably infer some common motivic background rather than direct contact with M^d. Army trumpeters are born under Venus and Saturn in Anubion, F 12.29 = 12 Perale, one of relatively few references in poetic astrology to military professions.

163 The line is of some pretension, combining the workmanlike Homeric ἐν παλάμῃσιν (tools, craftsmen: 4.442 n.) with the originally lyric motif of the singing lyre and a quasi-dithyrambic new compound. For instruments that sing, see on 2.334; *TLL* s.v. *cano*, I.A.1.d. The singing lyre is essentially a spillover from invocations, which seem to be its original context;[94] the Sibylline passage that is parallel to this (above) endows the lyre with a φθόγγος (8.119, cf. Posipp. 37.1–2 A.–B., al.), but for ἀείδειν see also Anacreontea 23.11–12 ἡ λύρη γάρ | μόνους ἔρωτας ἄιδει; *TLL* loc. cit. 266.36–9, adding Jerome, *Epist.* 27.1 *asino quippe lyra superflue canit.*[95] νευρένδετος is *hapax*,[96] but varies the stringed-lyre motif, e.g. Pind. *Nem.* 10.21 εὔχορδον...λύραν; Honestus, *AP* 9.250.6 = Garland 2427 ἑπταμίτῳ...κιθάρῃ; Tullius Sabinus, *AP* 9.410.3 = Garland 3366 νευρολάλον... χορδήν.

164 For the idea that cymbals produce ἁρμονία (not obvious), cf. *CA*, Lyr. Adesp. fr. 11.27–8 κτ]ύπον...χαλ[κῆς] κανα[χῆς], | [στυγνὸν ἀ]χόρδου μέλος ἁ[ρμονίας and Nonn. D. 46.120–1 οἷα δὲ ῥόπτρῳ | δίκτυπον ἁρμονίην κροτέων ἑτερόζυγι χαλκῷ. My restoration—for the epithet see Bacchyl. *Ep.* 14.15–16 καναχὰ | [χαλκ]όκτυπος, Diogenes, F 1 Snell χαλκοκτύπων... κυμβάλων—is based on the suggestion that χαλκῶι τε παρ in fact contains a typical confusion of ν and ρ (hence not παρ-, but -πον); the next four letters are then correct (εξετ). The change of construction in the last line, as the subject of the verb reverts to the stars, is the sting in the tail that this poet cultivates so much (p. 341). I am unconfident about the verb, which is a favourite of M^a, though not otherwise in the youngest three books. It is challenging to explain how πνεῦμα (which repeats 160) came to be here—as Koechly notes, we are done with wind

---

[94] Sappho fr. 118 V. ἄγι δὴ χέλυ δῖα †μοι λέγε† | φωνάεσσα †δὲ γίνεο†; Hor. *Od.* 1.32.3–4 *age dic Latinum,* | *barbite, carmen*; *Carmen in Nilum Crescentem* (= XXXIX Heitsch), l. 12 δεῦρο λύρη μ[ἐν ἄ]ειδε.

[95] Later: *Hist. Alex. Magn.* (Recensio Byzantina poetica) 5699 ᾄδουσα λύρα θαυμαστὴ τὸ μέλος αὐτομάτως (a wonder in the palace of Cyrus); Theodorus Prodromos, *Carm. Hist.* 69.9–10 οὐδέ τε Τιμοθέοιο καλὸν μέλος οὐδὲ κιθάρῃ | Δημοδόκου τοῖ᾽ ἄειδον; Σ Tzetz. in Lyc. Prol. ll. 96–8 πρὸς μουσικὴν καὶ φόρμιγγα καὶ βάρβιτον καὶ κιθάραν καὶ πᾶν ὄργανον μουσικῶς ᾀδόμενον.

[96] One of a small number of -ένδετος compounds (B.–P. 478), not all of which are poetic, but cf. Timotheus, *PMG* 791.22 ἀγκυλένδετος (bound with thongs).

165–8

Venus with Mercury in places of Mercury. The converse of the above. Many configurations with these agents produce this kind of outcome, but the best match for both protasis and apodosis is the next one in the Περὶ μίμων sequence, Θ p. 217.14–15. Mercury's houses are Gemini and Virgo, and placement therein might suggest a connection with the λιθοξόους and μαρμαρίους born under Theseus/Engonasin, paranatellon of Gemini, in Teucer (II 3.4), although the link is weaker than with some of the other paranatellonta. Also identical in protasis is Θ p. 213.25–7. But this self-same set-up in 6.465–71 has an outcome tipped towards intellectual enterprise. The only source to mention wax-workers is Ptol. 4.4.6 (Venus and Mercury as Rulers of πρᾶξις, especially when they have changed places)... ὑφάντας, κηροπλάστας, ζωγράφους (~ Θ p. 213.13, without wax-workers).

Less similar in protasis, but related to the outcome, is Θ p. 209.7–9 (the giver of πρᾶξις in Venus' houses) ὅσα πρὸς γυναικεῖα ἔργα ἢ μουσικὰ ἢ ὑφάντας ἢ ζωγράφους ἢ πλάστας ἢ μυροπώλας ἢ ἀνθοπλόκους ἢ βαφεῖς ἢ πορφυροπώλας καὶ τὰ ὅμοια.

165 συνοικῇ: this is the only passage cited by LSJ I.c for the verb in the sense 'be in the house of'. If there is any connection at all with Ptolemy's notion of συνοικείωσις (familiarity), which seems questionable, it is used in a far narrower way than Ptolemy intended. For Ptolemy this familiarity subsists between planets and signs of the zodiac through their houses, triangles, exaltations, and terms (1.17–23). But the relationship is between a planet and its house, not between two planets which are sharing the house of one of them. Elsewhere he indicates that two planets may be affiliated in terms of their physical properties (3.13.16), and he uses the notion throughout his chapter on the quality of the soul (3.14) where one planet is often said to be συνοικειωθείς with another, but does not properly explain it.[97] It might mean one planet being in another's house, but it is unlikely to be confined to that. And Ptolemy only ever uses the verb in the passive, συνοικειωθῆναι, never the intransitive active, as here.

---

[97] On the first occasion such a relationship is mentioned he uses the phrase κατὰ τὸν ἐκκείμενον τρόπον (3.14.12), but it is not clear what this 'aforementioned way' is (Robbins translates συνοικειωθείς as 'allied with'). He also uses συνοικείωσις of the affinity 'by nature' (κατὰ φύσιν) between planets and that on which they have an effect (3.5.1), which includes between planets and signs and the terrestrial regions they govern.

166 ἀγαλλομένη: of a happy planet already in 2.404, 501; 'Antiochus', l. 28 (*CCAG* i. 109.24) (Jupiter in MC); Camaterus, *Introd.* 2777 (Mercury on the ASC), *Zod.* 212 (Sun in the ninth house). It seems possible that ἐπὶ χώρῃ belongs with the participle, not at the beginning of the apodosis, if so reinforcing the idea of affinity between Venus and Mercury's house. ἐπὶ χώρᾳ is not otherwise used in astrology, but χῶρος is apparently sometimes used in the Manethoniana to mean a sign (i. 877 and n. 21). It is not a copycat EGHP ending save for *HHom. Herm.* 123 ἐπὶ χώρης, 'on the ground'.

167 It is clear from the comparanda what this line is about, but not how to restore it. It could be another 'who whom' configuration (p. 322), and there is no strict requirement for a factitive or executive verb. The most obvious comparison is with 2.319–27 (Venus in the houses of Mercury), where natives are weavers and embroiderers and painters in wax (as well as makers of garlands, dyers, and parfumiers), especially 323 πάντων μορφάς, 320 αἰόλ' ὑπὸ χροιῇ (αἰόλα also in connection with Venus and Mercury in 6.401), and possibly 323 δεικνύντας. It is not difficult to fabricate a line that scans, e.g. παντοίων μορφὰς τοῖς χρώμασιν οὗτος ἔδειξεν, but I do not see how to choose one reconstruction over another. Firmicus refers to makers of *colores*, manufacturers of dyes, always in connection with Venus (3.6.4) and mostly with both Venus and Mercury (4.13.2, 4.14.17, 5.5.6).

168 πολλοῖσι μίτοις: Θ's answer to this is πολυμιταρίους, which is unique in Greek,[98] but an attested loan in Latin (*TLL* x/1. 2582: Vulgate; glossographers; Venantius Fortunatus), together with *polymitus* = 'having many threads' (Pliny, *NH* 8.196; Petronius, *Sat.* 40.5; al.). M^d offers a poeticisation of a prose term, whether or not Θ at this point renders the underlying original or a re-rendering of verse back into prose, but I would guess the former (p. 145). The complex, polychrome designs envisaged here are associated with Egypt (Pliny says the technique was invented in Alexandria), Syria (Dura Europos, Palmyra), and the eastern provinces (Marquardt, 515–17; J. P. Wild, *Textile Manufacture in the Northern Roman Provinces* (Cambridge, 1970), 54–5; M. M. El-Homossani, 'Early Compound Weave Structures in Theory and Practice', *Ars Textrina*, 9 (1988), 157–90). Pliny uses the verb *texere* for the technique, though it is not necessarily a straightforward choice between weaving (which is how Cumont, 89 n. 3, takes the present passage) and embroidery, if Wild (loc. cit.) is right that ancient Gobelin technique involved darning free-hand over the basic ground weave.[99]

---

[98] *Suda*, π 3035, Hesychius, π 2720, Photius, π 1002, al. gloss ποικιλτικήν as πολυμιταρικήν (sc. τέχνην). Strictly ποικιλ- means only 'variegated' (A. J. B. Wace, 'Weaving or Embroidery?', *AJA* 52 (1948), 51–5, at 54), but it implies a web of multiple threads.

[99] The ποικίλματα of 2.320 are produced by both weaving and hand-sewing (see on 2.320–7, 321–2, 322).

πλάσμασιν: statue-makers figure in all the Θ outcomes cited above (not in 2.319–27).

169–72

Moon with Sun in *epanaphora* ⟨of Mercury and Venus⟩. So far as it goes, this is an exact match for Θ p. 217.16–18, which mentions Gemini and Taurus. Once again, there is a connection with Teucer's paranatellonta, where charioteers (ἡνιόχους) figure under Auriga, paranatellon of Taurus (II 2.3, cf. TR, p. 17.8) and Gemini (II 3.11, cf. TR, p. 17.1). Given how closely M^d usually follows Θ's protases, I suspect that a line is missing after 169 in which it was specified that the luminaries were rising after Mercury and Venus; for once, Koechly did not spot the lacuna because 169 appears to be self-contained. But if that is so, it suggests a different approach to tackling the corrupt verb ἐπαναφέρηται in 169, which does not mean simply 'carried on high' (Lopilato)/'sursum feratur' (Koechly). The fact that L reads ἦν δέ (unelided) is also suggestive. One could then read ἦν δέ τ' ἐπαμφορέοιτο μετ' (with D'Orville's optative) or ἦν δέ τ' ἐπαμφέρεται μετά (with his less-favoured indicative, adopted by Koechly), or indeed, at greater remove, ἦν δέ τ' ἐπαμφορίῃσι μετ' (an expedient already used by M^a at 6.104: see n. ad loc., and i. 882), postponing the main verb till the next line. Either way, the particle packing is entirely appropriate for a poet who has the same again in 300 (see Syntax, p. 330).

170 ἡνίοχος καμπτῆρα διερχόμενος: the poet seems to have condensed two constructions: (i) reaching, or rounding, or grazing, or being carried past, the turning-post (for which there are various verbs,[100] but note in hexameters John of Gaza, *Descr.* 258 ἀμφιθέει καμπτῆρα); (ii) proceeding through the length of the race-course. Manilius uses the same topos in his description of Auriga in 5.83 *meta currere acuta* (where Housman ad loc. explains the ablative as equivalent to *secundum metam*, and Hübner, appealing to this passage, takes *acuta* to refer to the grating sound as the chariot scrapes past it).

φιλονείκως: the language of sporting glory (-νείκ- hovering, as usual, between loving victory and loving contention): a boy pancratiast in *I. Sardis*, 7,1 78.15 (n.d.) [ἐνδόξως] κὲ φιλονείκως; a gladiator in *SEG* 55.672 (Amphipolis, n.d.) ὁ τοῖς σταδίοις φιλόνεικος (see Robert 1940a, 21, and 302–3 for the victory motif; id. *Hellenica*, 5 (1948), 77–8 no. 314); for literary references in connection with sport, LSJ φιλονικία, 2.

---

[100] Apollonius Dyscolus, *De constr.* 4.452.8–9 περὶ τὸν καμπτῆρα ἔδραμον—περιέδραμον τὸν καμπτῆρα; Anatolius, Περὶ δεκάδος καὶ τῶν ἐντὸς αὐτῆς ἀριθμῶν, p. 15.5–6 περὶ αὐτὸν γὰρ εἰλούμενοι ‹καὶ› ἀνακάμπτοντες ὥσπερ καμπτῆρα. A number of *defixiones* from Carthage mention the turning-post, in which the victim is cursed not to round them (μηδὲ κυκλεῦσαι τοὺς καμπτῆρας; A. Audollent, *Defixionum Tabellae quotquot innotuerunt* (Paris, 1904), nos. 234–40).

171 ἱπταμένων πώλων: this form of πέτεσθαι, with prothetic ι and in the simplex, though mostly imperial, begins to appear in Hellenistic poetry (and is also in 6.443, where there should have been a note).[101] There is similar vocabulary in John of Gaza, *Descr.* 275 ἱπταμένους... ἐπεσσυμένου πόδας ἵππου (and πῶλος in the next line), of the steed of one of the winds.[102] It updates the Iliadic conceit of 'flying' horses (μάστιξεν δ' ἐλάαν, τὼ δ' οὐκ ἀέκοντε πετέσθην; ps.-Hes. *Sc.* 308–9 τὰ δ' ἐπικροτέοντα πέτοντο | ἅρματα κολλήεντ'), a stronger version of which is that they barely leave tracks; Manilius uses this for Auriga (5.78–9: outstripping the winds, barely touching the track). Hübner ad loc. calls it an epic motif.

τετράζυγον ἅρμα διώκων: the epithet first attaches to chariots in tragedy (Soph. fr. dub. 1132 13.2 Radt [τε]τραζυγεῖς ὄχ[ους; Eur. *Helen* 1039–40 τετραζύγων | ὄχων), and this cadence occurs several times in late antique poetry. Closest are Nonn. *D.* 20.121 τετράζυγον ἅρμα τιταίνων (of a ἡνίοχος) and 1.473 τετράζυγον ἅρμα δεχέσθω, but the same rhythm is also in Anon. *De Vir. Herb.* (LXIV Heitsch) 6 τετράζυγον ἄντυγα πώλων; John of Gaza, *Descr.* 257 τετράζυγον ἄντυγα δίφρου (also of a charioteer who rounds the turning-post).

172 σύρδην: the two main proof-texts for the rare adverb are Aesch. *Pers.* 54 and ps.-Eur. *Rhes.* 58, of armies dragged out in long lines (the scholiasts on both passages offer the unhelpful gloss ὁμοῦ). D'Orville, whose correction this was, adduced *Il.* 23.338 ἐν νύσσῃ δέ τοι ἵππος ἀριστερὸς ἐγχριμφθήτω, the implied sense being 'grazing the surface of' (rather than strictly 'dragging'). Another possibly relevant passage is Alciphron, 3.40.1 [1.23] σύρδην φερόμενοι, of the winds: that would connect the adverb more closely with the participial phrase (admittedly leaving νύσσῃ rather stranded) and refer to the charioteer's flying course.

ἐπινίκιον ἵππον ἐλαύνων: cadged from *Od.* 5.371 (κέληθ' ὡς) ἵππον ἐλαύνων, but remodelled like Nonn. *D.* 37.252 and 43.275 ἑκούσιον ἵππον ἐλαύνων, 37.322 Μαραθώνιον ἵππον ἐλαύνων, 407 τόσον ἵππον ἐλαύνειν. I do not think the epithet need be connected with Call. fr. 54.3 ἐπινίκιον ἵππῳ[ν, but see *contra* De Stefani 2016, 181 n. 16.

173–6

Waxing Moon in her exaltation with Mercury, aspecting Sun in ASC or DESC. An almost exact match for Θ p. 217.19–20, 'almost' because there is an unusual

---

[101] Overduin on Nic. *Ther.* 456; H. Bernsdorff, *Das Fragmentum Bucolicum Vindobonense (P. Vindob. Rainer 29081): Einleitung, Text und Kommentar* (Göttingen, 1999), 140, on 65 ἵπτατο Περσεύς ((?)Bion, *Fragmentum bucolicum*); Gow on ps.-Theocr. 23.59.

[102] Implicit in *AP* 8.157.4 (but a metaphor for a soul being released from the body). The flying-horse motif was to be expected in victory epigrams, but did not appear.

extra specification that Θ does not carry, namely for the position of the Moon. Taurus is the Moon's exaltation (Bouché-Leclercq, 134, 195, 204, 227). The bird-catchers born here are presumably to be connected with the paranatellon Orion in the first decan. The second Teucer text itself gives Orion a different set of associations (II 2.5 Ὠρίων ξιφήρης στρατηγόν, στρατηλάτην, στρατιώτην), but Orion is the icon of hunting (*Lib. Herm.* xxv. 2.8, the sixth and seventh degrees of Taurus produce both animal tenders (*iumentorum nutritores*) and hunters (*ferarum persecutores*)), and fowling goes together with that (cf. 4.333–40, hunters and fowlers born with the Moon together with or in opposition to Mercury).

173 ὑψώματι: see on 5.33. Koechly's emendation is not needed, here or at 5.261: this poet does not need saving from himself.

174 αὐξιφαής: see on 5.109.

κλυτὸν Ἥλιον: i. 908 n. 13. This does not replicate any particular EGHP formula (Hes. *Th.* 927 Ἥφαιστον κλυτόν, *Op.* 84 κλυτὸν Ἀργεϊφόντην; *Od.* 9.518 κλυτὸν ἐννοσίγαιον).

Ὠκεανίτην: curious that the poet should be so vague about whether the Sun is rising or setting. Otherwise the epithet exists only as an ethnonym (Diod. Sic. 5.42.4, 44.6; Steph. Byz. p. 108.4), and in the feminine form Ὠκεανῖτις suggesting origin in, or location beside, the Ocean. The sun could be rising out of the Ocean (which is how Lopilato understands this passage), like the sunrise in Ap. Rhod. 3.1230 ὅτε πρῶτον ἀνέρχεται Ὠκεανοῖο, and as in 3.106–7. Alternatively, the poet could rely on his readers' knowledge of EGHP passages like *Il.* 8.485 ἐν δ' ἔπεσ' Ὠκεανῷ λαμπρὸν φάος ἠελίοιο, 18.239–41, *HHom. Herm.* 68 Ἥέλιος μὲν ἔδυνε κατὰ χθονὸς Ὠκεανόνδε to be able to use this as a shorthand for the DESC. The rhythm is like *Il.* 11.420 Δηϊοπίτην.

175 The individual born under this configuration is a fowler (Appendix II, I.2.iv.), the person all but lost to view under the generic activity credited to him and its stock accoutrements. The bird lime (made from mistletoe) is smeared on twigs to snare the birds; the twigs (*virgae*) are mounted on reeds (the *harundo* or *canna aucupatoria*). The two are habitually mentioned together (e.g. Aesop, *Fab.* 117; Dionysius, *Ixeuticon* (paraphrasis), *passim*; Artemidorus, 2.19; Sext. Emp. *Adv. Math.* 9.3). There have been different interpretations of how it works; this is that of Capponi.[103]

---

[103] Also Johnson, 59–60; K. Lindner, *Beiträge zu Vogelfang und Falknerei in Altertum* (Berlin, 1973), 95; G. Kron, 'Animal Husbandry, Hunting, Fishing, and Fish Production', in Oleson, 175–222, at 188–92, where the Pliny reference on 188 should be *NH* 16.248; Vendries, 120–3 (one touches the bird's wings directly with the twig; one does not just wait for it to perch). Representations on mosaics: J. Anderson, *Hunting in the Ancient World* (Berkeley, 1985), 143, 147, and 146 fig. 47.

176 Two points are made: (i) the bird is stuck fast in lime (οὔ ποτε λείπει) but also (ii) the bird is a hawk. Θ has separate listings of ἰξευτὰς and ἱερακαρίους, another illustration of M^d's secondary and Θ's presumably primary character. The poet has combined these neatly by lifting ἴρηξ ὠκύπτερος from *Il*. 13.62, but the cadence ὦρτο πέτεσθαι (the bird takes flight) is swapped for one that recalls *Il*. 10.164 οὔ ποτε λήγεις; see also *Il*. 2.396 οὔ ποτε κύματα λείπει; *Od*. 7.117 οὔ ποτε καρπὸς ἀπόλλυται οὐδ' ἀπολείπει.

177–80

Mars rising at nightfall (acronychal rising), accompanied by Saturn and Mercury. In the two most closely related charts, the agency is the same or similar but the locations differ. In 1.119–20 the malefics are in the MC (not ASC); in 6.534–40, where they conclude the τέχνη sequence, Mercury is on the ASC but Mars and Saturn are in the MC, and the Moon is also in a feminine sign. It is interesting that in both books 5 and 6 this chart, although apparently without connection to Θ, has worked its way among the τέχναι and is apparently classified as such. In Firmicus, 6.30.18, which I originally cited as a parallel for 6.534–40, Mercury is on the ASC, but other than that it is a matter of gendered signs (the luminaries and ASC are all in feminine ones). The agencies in the *galli* chart in 4.218–23 are quite different (the luminaries are involved along with Venus).

177 ἀκρονύκτιον: a poetic version of the technical term ἀκρόνυχος (sometimes ἀκρόνυκτος, of which -ιος is a poetic version). A rare specification in horoscopes (Heilen 2015, 1051–3), it nevertheless suits a poet who is interested in phase and retrogradation (79 παλίνορσος). Porphyry, *Introd. in Tetrabibl*. 3, *CCAG* v/4. 195.25–6, explains that the ἀκρόνυκτος φάσις happens when a planet is at perigee and begins to retrograde. A planet in its acronychal phase is in opposition to the Sun. Its rarity in horoscopes is perhaps surprising since—given the implication that the star is in the sky all night—it might be considered a position of particular potency; in fact sources disagree about whether the effect is to strengthen (because it is most remote from the Sun's rays) or to weaken the force of the planet (because it is about to retrograde) (Heilen, loc. cit. 1053). According to the first principle, Mars ought to be strengthened (since he is at furthest remove from the Sun, who smothers him: 1.96–9); on the other hand he is out of sect. It seems to have muted his masculinity, but not his bloodiness (self-wounding and castration is in the background here).

ὀβριμοεργόν: i. 909 n. 16.

179 ἀράμενοι…φάσγανον ὀξύ: 1.254 ἀραμένους ξίφος ὀξύ. The sword (as opposed to a knife, for which see J. N. Bremmer, 'Attis: A Greek god in Anatolian

Pessinous and Catullan Rome', *Mnemosyne*⁴, 57/5 (2004) 534–73, at 559 n. 122) is paralleled in Lucian, *DDS* 51 (see Lightfoot 2003, 507–8); 'iron' in 1.120; φάσγανα for self-woundings in Anon. *AP* 6.51.8 = *HE* 3839. The noun–epithet formula stands six times at line-end in the Homeric poems, and once elsewhere (usually with part of the verb ἐρύσασθαι).

ὑπὸ τύμπανα: of accompaniment: LSJ ὑπό, C.IV.1. For drums see Graillot, 258–60, and Lightfoot 2003, 507, on Lucian, *DDS* 51.

180 μιμοῦνται: for *imitatio Attidis*, see Lucian, *DDS* §15 Ἄττεα μιμέονται; Ov. *Fast*. 4.243f., and to some extent Firmicus, *Err*. 3.1, Minucius Felix, *Octav*. 23.4; *RAC* s.v. Gallos, 1006 (G. M. Sanders).

δυσαγῆ: irreligious. Certainly the concept was available to a pagan (Pollux, 1.33 ἐναγές, ἐξάγιστον, δυσαγές, μιαρόν, παμμίαρον, μίασμα, μύσος); earlier, δύσαγνος meant much the same thing (Aesch. *Suppl*. 751 δυσάγνοις φρεσίν of the race of Aegyptus, who reck naught of altars). And certainly, too, the cult of Cybele was already the object of attack by pagan writers (J. Latham, 'Fabulous Clap-Trap": Roman Masculinity, the Cult of Magna Mater, and Literary Constructions of the *Galli* at Rome from the Late Republic to Late Antiquity', *Journal of Religion*, 92 (2012), 84–122). Yet one wonders whether the way the attack is framed—self-emasculation not, primarily, as a threat to the sexuality of the Roman male, but as a religious offence—is to be seen against a background of pagan/Christian polemic, in which the majority of instances of δυσαγής occur,[104] and in which the cult of the Magna Mater, involving the bodily mutilation of Attis, became a particular object of attack by Church Fathers (Arnobius, *Adv. Nat.* 5.5–7, 11–17; Augustine, *Civ.* 7.24–6; Minucius Felix, *Octav.* 23.4; Tertullian, *Apol.* 12.4; A. T. Fear, 'Cybele and Christ', in E. N. Lane, *Cybele, Attis and Related Cults: Essays in Memory of M. J. Vermaseren* (Leiden, 1996), 37–50). This is not to suggest that the author is a Christian, but that he expresses an attitude, and in vocabulary, that has been shaped in encounters between the two religions. See too p. 318 and on 5.219.

Κυβελήιον ἔνθεον Ἄττιν: a late antique hexameter ending best paralleled on the one hand by an oracle ap. Euseb. *PE* 5.16.1 Μυκαλήιον ἔνθεον ὕδωρ and Nonn. *Par*. 14.116 προώριον ἔνθεον ὀμφήν,[105] and on the other by Nonn. *D*. 10.140 Κυβεληίδος ὄργανα Ῥείης, 12.395 Κυβεληίδος ἄντρα θεαίνης, 13.567 Κυβεληίδες ἔκτυπον αὐλαί, 25.319 Κυβεληίδος ἅρμα θεαίνης, 37.624 Κυβεληίδος

---

[104] Celsus, in Origen, *Cels*. 7.62 ἔθνη τὰ δυσαγέστατα καὶ ἀνομώτατα (accusations against Christians); Clem. Al. *Protr*. 12.119.1 αἱ μαινάδες, αἱ δύσαγνον κρεανομίαν μυούμεναι (Bacchants, contrasted with the true faithful); Euseb. *HE* 10.8.17 (of Licinius, portrayed as an anti-Christian); Theodoret, *Graecarum Affectionum Curatio*, 1.114 τὰ δυσαγῆ ταῦτα καὶ βδελυρὰ ὄργια, sim. 2.32, al.

[105] There are earlier, incomplete examples, e.g. Asclepiades, *AP* 9.64.5 = *HE* 1022 Ἑλικωνίδος ἔνθεον ὕδωρ.

ἀστὸς ἀρούρης. But compare also Ov. Met. 10.104 Cybeleius Attis, and similar endings (Ars Am. 1.507, Ibis 453 Cybeleïa mater), and the whole shape of Met. 10.704 Cybeleia frena leones. The epithet is very rare (not in Latin before Ovid, and in Greek the -(η)ιος ending otherwise only in Suda, κ 2588 Κυβελίοις· τοῖς τῆς Ῥέας). One thinks of a common Greek source.

181–8

ASC in scaly signs, Saturn with Jupiter in the IMC as Rulers of πρᾶξις. The corresponding chart is Θ p. 217.21–3, which involves medical practitioners. Cumont printed P's θηριοδήκτους, but noted that Epit. IIIb (Monacensis 287) read θηριοδείκτους, which had been corrected to -as by its editor, Boll (CCAG vii. 118.6–8; see Robert 1940b, 133). See too Θ p. 212.20–1, where the manuscript has θυριωδήκτας, which Cumont also (unconfidently) corrected.

The protasis in Θ specifies that the horoscope is in Cancer, Scorpio, or Pisces. The outcomes are relevant to Ophiouchos, paranatellon of Scorpio (Teucer, II 8.3 θηροφόνους ἢ καὶ καλλίστους ἰατρούς), as well as 'the two snakes' (οἱ δύο δράκοντες), paranatellon of Pisces (II 12.6 ἰατρούς, θηριοδείκτας), though I am not sure of the significance of Cancer. One further difference between Θ's version and this is the apparent presence here of Mars; given the normal closeness of protases in this section this seems suspect. My reconstruction of the corrupt lines 181–2 accordingly (i) takes Ares as a corruption for the 'hour', i.e. the horoscope; (ii) jettisons the nonsensical idea of 'lurking' (the analogy with 223 is false, for the later passage reads φωλ- and specifies where the lurking is taking place), with φολ- preserving an original reference to the technical name for scaly signs (Hübner 1982, 148–9); and (iii) upholds the reference to Jupiter in L (ζηνί), underwritten by Θ's Jupiter with Saturn in the IMC. The outcome is identical (if here elaborated): herbalists and snake-handlers.

181 For my reconstruction, compare 5.321 εἰ καὶ τὴν ὥρην ἐν τετραπόδεσσι καθεύροις (it is true that M^d uses ὥρη for the ASC far less than other poets in the corpus, especially M^a, but here is one instance); for the scaly signs see 5.246–7 Σκορπίος, Αἰγόκερως καὶ Καρκίνος ἠδ' ἄρ' οἱ Ἰχθῦς | ἐκ φολίδων πολλῶν συγκείμενοί εἰσι τὸ σῶμα (which adds Capricorn to those specified by Θ).

183 Root-cutting, charm-singing, and an obscure middle term which is not obviously ipso facto medical (Koechly renders vita-prodigos, i.e. exposing themselves to risk; Lopilato 'deceivers'), though given what surrounds it I wonder if it is supposed to mean something like 'appliers of' (medicaments). Root-cutting and charm-singing are mentioned together in 1 Enoch 7:1 φαρμακείας καὶ ἐπαοιδὰς καὶ ῥιζοτομίας and 8:3 ἐπα[ο]ιδὰς καὶ ῥιζοτομίας where, as teachings of the Watchers, they are suspect; ἐπαοιδοί are treated in the same way throughout the OT, where they keep company with μάγοι, φαρμακοί, and other kinds of diviner (a particularly long list in Deut. 18:10–11); another contemptuous reference in Epictetus, *Diss.* 3.24.10. ῥιζοτόμοι are not always charlatans (ps.-Hippocr. *Ep.* 16 purports to address one respectfully; they are listed among technicians ancillary to the ἰατρός by Galen, *In Hippocratis librum vi epidemiarum commentarii vi*, xviiB. 229.13 Kühn), but a belittling label used for Asclepius by Heracles in Lucian, *Dial. Deor.* 15.1. These characters (on whom see Schmidt, 70–3; G. E. R. Lloyd, *Science, Folklore and Ideology: Studies in the Life Sciences in Ancient Greece* (Cambridge, 1986), 120; Lane Fox, 93) are not otherwise named in Greek-language astrology, though Firmicus has several references to persons who specialise in herbal remedies (Appendix II, V.3.iv).

184 ζητοῦντας...αὔτως: Θ makes clear that these are snake-handlers (Robert 1940*b* and 1969, 934–8), a type of native also referred to in Teucer (L, p. 44.10–11; II 5.4a; II 12.6), and with remarkable frequency in Firmicus, who sometimes refers to them in specifically Italian terms as Marsi (Appendix II, V.3.vii; see Horsfall on V. *Aen.* 7.753; A. Le Bris, 'L' image des Marses chez Virgile (Énéide VII, 750-760)', in E. Oudot and F. Poli (eds.), « *Epiphania* »: *Études orientales, grecques et latines offertes à Aline Pourkier* (Paris, 2008), 369–83). M^d adopts a mock-solemn censorious stance. αὔτως presumably has the contemptuous sense that it sometimes has in Homer (LSJ I.2), 'just as they please', 'recklessly'. The same attitude is present in Ecclus. 12:13 τίς ἐλεήσει ἐπαοιδὸν ὀφιόδηκτον καὶ πάντας τοὺς προσάγοντας θηρίοις;

The combination of snake-handling with medical practitioners (or quacks) is paralleled. Beside Θ, the second and third Teucer passages combine them with ἰατρούς; Robert 1940*b*, 141–2, cites a glossary which lists them adjacent to the ἐπῳδός and βοτανικός (*CGL* iii. 433); Firmicus, 8.17.7, combines procurers of poisons and *herbarii*. They make an obvious pair. The north African tribe of Psylloi, famous snake-handlers (cf. Nicander, fr. 32 G.-S.), had remedies for snake-bites according to Dio Cass. 51.14.4–5 and Suet. *Aug.* 17.4.[106] See generally Robert 1940*b*, 137–42.

Poetically the formula for death is a remake of EGHP θάνατος καὶ μοῖρα κραταιή + θάνατόν τε μόρον τε + κακὸν μόρον, but introduces an epithet which is not normally decorative in EGHP (though see Hes. fr. 302.21 M.-W. κακοδαίμονα τέχνην) and which usually has a personal referent (Comedy's standard word for 'poor wretch').

---

[106] In Aelian, *NA* 9.62, a man described as a φαρμακοτριβής keeps snakes for show and allows one of them to bite him, but botches the remedy.

185 The thick-necked 'asp' is the Egyptian cobra with its distinctive hood.[107] The epithet, πλατυαύχην, recurs only in ps.-Eustathius, *Commentarius in Hexaemeron*, p. 745.48, on the traditional combat of the asp (τὴν Αἰγυπτίαν ἀσπίδα) with the ichneumon (Egyptian mongoose?); this becomes a topos of bestiaries after Pliny, *NH* 8.85, who also comments on the swollen neck of the asp and the deadliness of its bite (*colla aspidum intumescere nullo ictus remedio*). Authors who comment on the asp's behaviour in expanding its neck when it goes on the attack usually describe it in terms of swelling (Wick on Lucan, 9.701, mostly *tumidus* and *tumescere*; see also Jacques on Nic. *Ther.* 157–89(d));[108] perhaps closest to this passage is ps.-Opp. *Cyn.* 3.442 στήθεά τ' εὔρυνε. The asp's deadliness is also noted by Aelian, *NA* 1.54, 2.24, 6.38; Galen, *De Theriaca ad Pisonem*, xiv. 237.7–17 Kühn; it stands at the head of Lucan's catalogue, with the claim that no snake is more poisonous (9.703).

αἰνομανοῦς: because snakes are habitually irascible. Jacques on Nic. *Ther.* 157–89(d) has six examples from Nicander alone; Horsfall on *Aen.* 2.381 *attollentem iras* (and the fact that Juno's serpent kindles *furor* in angry Amata, *Aen.* 7.348, 350); Cleopatra to the asp: 'Be angry.' This epithet, which perhaps looks back at *Il.* 22.94 (simile of Hector as snake) ἔδυ δέ τέ μιν χόλος αἰνός, itself recurs only in Nonnus (14×), in both poems, always at either line-beginning or after the bucolic diaeresis; usually of crazed human beings, but of an enraged lion in *D.* 32.108.

185-6 ἠδ' ἄρ' ἐχίδνης | διψάδος αἱμοβόρου: the epithet αἱμοβόρου comes from Theocr. 24.18, epithet of the bellies of the snakes sent by Hera to kill the infant Heracles. In that passage it is proleptic (this is what they intend to do to Heracles), and the snakes are generic δράκοντας. But why link it specifically to an echidna (viper)? The echidna's domestic life was not a model of harmony; notoriously, the female bit through the head of the male in the act of mating and had revenge taken on her by her offspring.[109] Alluding to this myth, Nicander describes the species as γαστέρ' ἀναβρώσαντες (*Ther.* 134), which conceivably connects to the -βόρου part of the compound (see also *Ther.* 826 οὐλοβόροις ἐχίεσσι), though Nicander does not mention blood. Whether or not

---

[107] For the asp = cobra, see A. Tronson, 'Vergil, the Augustans, and the Invention of Cleopatra's Suicide—One Asp or Two?', *Vergilius*, 44 (1998), 31–50, at 34–5; Wick on Lucan, 9.700-7. Plutarch, *Mor.* 380 F–381 A (*Is.* 74), uses *aspis* for a kind of snake which represents the power of the gods, and Gwyn Griffiths ad loc. takes it to refer to the cobra on the royal headdress.

[108] True, swollen throats are a literary topos of angry serpents, even when not specifically identified as asps: Cic. *Vatin.* 4 *Repente enim te tamquam serpens e latibulis oculis eminentibus, inflato collo, tumidis cervicibus intulisti*; V. *Aen.* 2.381 *attollentem iras et caerula colla tumentem*, *Georg.* 3.421 *sibila colla tumentem*.

[109] Overduin on *Ther.* 134; K. D. Wilson, 'Avenging Vipers: Tragedy and Succession in Nicander's *Theriaca*', *CJ* 113 (2018), 257–80.

that passage is in play, the qualification of echidna as διψάς is certainly attested elsewhere.[110] It could be taken simply as a residue of habitual pre-Nicandrian/poetic imprecision in the use of snake-names (in Lyc. *Al.* 1114, Clytaemnestra is a δράκαινα διψάς and an echidna in 1121). Or the connection could be associative: Nicander says that the two species (physically?) resemble one another (*Ther.* 334; cf. Lucian, *Dips.* 4). But it could also be taken as a further precision, as (to speak anachronistically) 'genus' is narrowed down to 'species'. Galen qualifies at least some vipers as διψάδες in order to describe the thirsty effect of eating their flesh,[111] and the poet's elaboration of the thirsty effect of the bite in the next pair of lines suggests that this is indeed what he has in mind.

φοβερὸν θάνατον †δὲ καλούντων: not from death's standard formulary. It condenses the effect that longer-winded descriptions of the διψάς (Nicander, Lucian, Lucan) strain for. De Stefani's προκαλοῦντας is good. It would once again suggest snake-handlers (see on 5.184), in terms somehow recalling *Il.* 16.693 and *Il.* 22.297 θανατόνδε κάλεσσαν.

187 Τανταλικῇ κολάσει: because of the unquenchable thirst that was his punishment, like that of the victims of the viper/διψάς. Authors who elaborate explain that the thirst killed in two ways, by not being quenched, but also, if the victims had the opportunity to drink, to do so till they burst (Bodson, 86 and nn. 103–4). The Tantalus myth, which obviously evokes the first of these, is also mentioned—specifically in connection with the Libyan διψάς, which is said to be ἐχίδνῃ ὅμοιος rather than a subspecies of it—by Lucian, *Dips.* 6, together with the Danaids (punished by eternal water-carrying in leaky containers), and Matthew Leigh argues that the myth of Tantalus is implied in Lucan's reference to a διψάς thirsty in the middle of an oasis in the Libyan desert (9.610), followed by an account of the sufferings visited on a victim (9.737–62).[112] The epithet is new, and remains unique until Byzantine writers return to the Tantalus myth for metaphor (Theodorus II Ducas Lascaris writes of another Ταντάλικος λίθος). Rather strikingly, Theodorus Prodromos, *Carm. Hist.* 38.103–4 Ταντάλικὴν γὰρ ἄλαστον ἔχω νόσον· ὡς γὰρ ἐκεῖνος | ὕδασιν ἐν μεσάτοις πολυδίψιον ἦμαρ ἴανε... combines thirst with another raid on *Il.* 4.171 (see on the next line), though I doubt this poem was his inspiration.

187–8 ὑπὸ γαμφηλῇσιν ὀδοῦσιν | ἰὸν ἐρευγομένης ὑποδίψιον ἄσθματι δεινῷ: the poet continues to pillage Nicander, in the first place his description of another breed of viper—the Cocytos, not the διψάς—in *Ther.* 232 ἰὸν

---

[110] Bodson, 80–1; Jacques on Nic. *Ther.* 334–7 (5); G.-P. on Antipater, *AP* 7.172.5 = *HE* 316. For the multiple names of the διψάς see Wick on Lucan, 9.718.
[111] Bodson, 81 n. 56; Greg. Naz. *PG* 37.867.13 Διψάς τίς ἐστι τῶν ἐχιδναίων γενῶν.
[112] *Lucan: Spectacle and Engagement* (Oxford, 1997), 270; id. 'Lucan and the Libyan Tale', *JRS* 90 (2000), 95–109, at 99–102.

ἐρευγόμενοι[113] (same *sedes*; at the end of the same line his mate is called an echidna), but also (again) the asp/cobra, to which he is cued back by the phrase about spewing venom (*Ther.* 185 ἐνερεύγεται ἰόν); that in turn seems to have inspired the present description of the envenomed fangs (*Ther.* 182–3 ὀδόντες | ἀγκύλοι) and perhaps also the hissing (180 ἄκριτα ποιφύσσοντος). The first of these is rendered by a (fairly ham-fisted) Homeric concoction. Normally γαμφηλαί on its own is a noun, and since ὀδούς is of course masculine it would presumably be better to describe ὀδοῦσιν as appositional/a gloss, rather than (with LSJ) to call the first noun adjectival. At any rate the end of 187 is a maladroit combination of *Il.* 16.489 ὑπὸ γαμφηλῇσι λέοντος and 3× *Il.* κρατεροῖσιν ὀδοῦσιν. ὑποδίψιον is *hapax* (in the same slot as *Il.* 4.171 πολυδίψιον, epithet of Argos), though there may be some influence from yet another Nicandrian snake, the chelydros, whose bite also provokes a terrible thirst (*Ther.* 436 κακὴ δ' ἐπιδίψιος ἄτη). The line-end of 188 has the same shape as 5.57 πήματι δεινῷ. Perhaps the poet glances at *Il.* 15.10 ἀργαλέῳ ἔχετ' ἄσθματι, though this describes the winded Hector, not a malevolent beast.

5.189–312 Miscellanea

189–91

Waxing Moon in MC, Mars and Sun in IMC. The Περὶ μίμων sequence from Θ has come to a baroque climax. The snakes were the poet's most spectacular effort at intertextuality. We now move into very different territory, yet the placement of this chart straight after the διψάς suggests at least the hand of an editor who was thinking associatively, while the connective might imply the intentions of the poet (p. 330). The vocabulary continues to suit thirst (cf. φρύγεσθαι in *AP* 7.293.4). Mars no longer constitutes a link between the charts on my reconstruction of 181, though he might have done if an editor himself read 181 in its corrupt form. However that may be, it will surprise no one that fevers come when Mars unites with the Sun (Dorotheus, p. 381.7–8); also in connection with the Moon and Mars (p. 424.20); specifically when Mars opposes the Moon from the fifth house (Firmicus, 3.4.15). Natives are (literally) burned with Mars and the Sun in the MC (Firmicus, 6.31.63).

189 εἰ δ' αὔξουσα τύχῃ: see Heilen 2015, 1125 n. 2859: this must mean πλήθουσα (because the Moon is opposite the Sun). For the periphrastic tense, see on 4.384.

---

[113] Nonnus, too, is attracted to this in descriptions of the serpentine feet of the monster Campe (*D.* 18.240–1 ἐχιδναίων ἀπὸ ταρσῶν | ἰὸν ἐρευγομένων) and hair of Typho (*D.* 1.508–9 ἐρευγομένων δὲ κομάων | ἰὸν ἐχιδνήεντα).

191

I suspect D'Orville was right about the corrupt word (presumably epithet) at the end of the line, and that αἴλινος (cf. 1.340) was later replaced by πένθιμος, which glossed it. At all events one is struck by the completely different lexical approach in this line from that of the charts which precede it. The vocabulary is prosaic, indeed medical: compare e.g. Porphyry, *Quaest. Hom. ad Od. pertinentes*, on *Od.* 9.388 φρυγομένων τῶν σαρκῶν; John Chrys. *PG* 50.688.50–1 Κατετήκοντο μὲν γὰρ σάρκες, καὶ ὀστᾶ συνεφρύγετο (of a martyr); Nicetas Stethatus (11th c.), *Vita Simeonis Novi Theologici*, 115 ὡς κηρὸν ἐτηκόμην τὰς σάρκας, καὶ ὡσεὶ φρύγιόν μου τὰ ὀστᾶ συνεφρύγετο (of a severe fever). ὑποτήκεται (which is uncommon) means 'pine'/'waste away' (LSJ), or 'dissolve'/'melt'/'evaporate' (e.g. Paul, *Epit*. 2.47.1; Basil, *PG* 31.1461.23–4). The best parallels for bodily emaciation are Maximus, *Diss*. 28.2 ψυχῆς γοῦν καμούσης λύπῃ συγκάμνει τὸ σῶμα καὶ ὑποτήκεται and especially (though he is late) John Apocaucus (12th/13th c.), *Epist. ad Georgium Bardanem*, 3 l. 26 τῆς εὐσαρκίας ὑποτακείσης (of losing so much weight that his trousers no longer held up).

192–6

Mars setting, Saturn in ASC. Once again there seems to be an associative link with 5.181–8—big cats follow snakes, and claws follow fangs (5.187, where γαμφηλῇσι were anyway suited to lions)—but the subject has pivoted from what was classified in Θ under τέχναι to σίνος. This belongs to a group of configurations, discussed on 4.613–18, all of which involve violent death. All place Saturn and Mars in opposition, whether across ASC/DESC (Θ p. 201.20–2, Firmicus, 6.29.10, who adds that they are located on their respective *kentra* by degree, and that the Moon is either moving towards Mars, Full, or to Saturn, waning), MC/IMC (4.613–18), or in unspecified locations (3.260–3, with quartile as an alternative).

All these related charts except Θ list various modes of violent death; for Firmicus it depends on the kind of sign. Only M^d and Θ (κυνηγοὺς ἢ θηριομάχους ἢ κυνοβρώτους) concentrate on animals to the exclusion of anything else. Both include lions and boars. The leopard in 196 replaces bears in 4.616.

193

This line varies astrological jargon, where the usual construction is τὰ γεννώμενα + predicative adjective ('the offspring are viable', and so on). The stars now consign the native to his fate.

194

Epic has both κάπριος alone and ὗς/σῦς κάπριος in various cases, with κάπροισι (if anywhere) before the third-foot caesura; λευκὸν ὀδόντα (of a κάπριος) stands before the caesura in *Il*. 11.416, and (of a κάπρος) at line-end in ps.-Hes. *Scut*. 388. It is a similar game of reshuffle to the one in 4.616 σύες ἀργιόδοντες, though not clear exactly how the poet handled it; perhaps simplest is Rigler's ‹ὑὸς› καπρίοιο...ἀργὸν ὀδόντα (cf. *Od.* 8.60 ἀργιόδοντας ὗας, 476 ἀργιόδοντος ὑός). The verb refits epic παρίσταται in this position. I interpret that 'he (the native) is subjected to', i.e. endures. See Cumont, 60 n. 4, for Egyptian boar-hunts.

For boar, see on 4.615–16 and 616.

195-6 The heroic animals, leopard and lion (together in *Il.* 17.20 as well as *HHom. Aphr.* 70-1), located in the mountains (ὄρεσσιν at line-end in *Il.* 12.146 (boar) and 16.353 (wolves))—as opposed to the probable reality, the amphitheatre—give the strong impression of a Homeric simile, although (i) the claws most suggest Hesiod's hawk (*Op.* 205 γναμπτοῖσι πεπαρμένη ἀμφ' ὀνύχεσσι); (ii) the λαιμός is a vulnerable body-part in main-frame Homeric narrative; (iii) the dappled leopard-skin comes eventually from *Il.* 10.29–30 παρδαλέη...ποικίλη, though the particular lexicon is closer to Soph. fr. 11 Radt καταστίκτου κυνὸς | σπολὰς Λίβυσσα, παρδαλήφορον δέρος[114]; (iv) the βλοσυροῖο λέοντος comes ultimately from ps.-Hes, *Scut.* 175 βλοσυροῖσι λέουσιν, perhaps *via* Dorotheus' constellation (p. 335.2 βλοσυροῦ τ' ἐφύπερθε Λέοντος, p. 398.12 κατὰ βλοσυροῖο...Λέοντος, cf. Mᵃ 3.14), but now in any case cliché[115]; (v) διόρυξαν is not Homeric at all, and unpleasantly suggests that the claws tear right through the neck.

197-201

Moon between malefics, in equal degrees. See 4.409–13 and 1.250–5. These related charts are all embedded in their respective contexts. The fullest version is in 1.250–5, which has outcomes for both sexes. This one concentrates on violent death, in which respect it continues the theme of the previous chart and, like it, figures in Θ ch. 77 Καθολικὰ σχήματα βιαιοθανάτων.

On the types of death, this chart shares hanging and drowning with 1.254–5. It lacks the sword and fire, but adds falling and building-collapse. All are among astrology's standard mishaps (most are in 3.255–63, on the aspects of Mars and Saturn, and all are in Firmicus, 1.9.1 *Ille, cogente fato, suspenditur laqueo; at ille gladio percutitur; ille mari fluminibusque submergitur; ille, saevientibus flammis*

---

[114] κατάστικτος seems to be the normal form in this context (e.g. Strab. 2.5.33 ἐοικυῖα παρδαλῇ· κατάστικτος γάρ ἐστιν, Dio Cass. 43.23.2 τὴν δὲ δὴ χρόαν κατέστικται ὥσπερ πάρδαλις). But the simplex is best paralleled by three instances of cases of στικτὴ πάρδαλις at line-beginning in Nonnus (*D.* 9.189 στικτοῖς πορδαλίεσσιν; 15.145, 188 στικτῶν πορδαλίων). There are other more remote parallels, including Greg. Naz. PG 37.1507.4–5 στικτῇ...πάρδαλις.

[115] βλοσυροῖο λέοντος at line-end also in Antipater, *AP* 9.603.3 = *HE* 594; Quint. Smyrn. 1.5; ps.-Apollinaris, 21:42 ~ Ps. 21:22. Other variations in e.g. Archias, *AP* 9.19.5 = *Garland* 3704, ps.-Opp. *Cyn.* 2.165, Euseb. *Or. ad coet. sanct.* 20.2 (~ V. *Ecl.* 4.22 *magnos...leones*), Nonnus *passim*.

ignique traditus, in cinerem favillasque convertitur; ille per praecipitia iactatur; ille cadentium tectorum ruina comprimitur, along with poisoning, fevers, and animal attacks). The version in Θ p. 200.1–2 has a more detailed protasis (the Moon is on a centre or its *epanaphora*, and the malefics are in one and the same sign rather than in equal degrees), but reduces the outcome to its essentials.

197–8 In this paraphrase of the technical term ἐμπερίσχεσις, the genitives are presumably governed by μέση (LSJ μέσος, I.1.c).

197 ἡ βασίλεια: i. 905 n. 27; add Anubion, F 12.8 = 12 Perale M]ήνην β[α]σιλήιδα; 3.219–20 n.

198 De Stefani's emendation is obviously and brilliantly right (Heilen 2017, 227); cf. Timaeus Praxidas, *CCAG* i. 99.25–6 ἐὰν δύνῃ ὁ Ἥλιος καὶ ἀπὸ Κρόνου ἢ Ἄρεως θλίβηται. This tight relationship of equal degrees presumably implies a particularly dire outcome; the definitions of ἐμπερίσχεσις in Porphyry and 'Antiochus' (1.250–5 n.) allow for a distance of up to seven degrees.

199 For ὁ μέν... ὁ δέ in outcomes, see i. 227. Among other charts of violent death, hanging and drowning are also juxtaposed in Firmicus, 7.23.10 (Mars in equal degrees with the Moon, the Sun in watery signs, and Saturn opposing the horoscope). M^d has found a neat little jingle to combine them, neither βρόχος nor βυθός being astrology's normal word for the things denoted (the former only in Hephaestion, i. 205.7—could this reflect Dorotheus?—the latter in Valens, II 36.23, which is not an apotelesma). For hanging (suicide, not judicial punishment) see on 4.489.

200 Falling from a height (4.618 n.) and collapsing buildings (3.130 n.) are a conventional pair (Valens, II 17.59 ἀπὸ ὕψους ἢ συμπτώσεως; Ptol. 3.13.13 τῶν ἀποκρημνισμῶν ἢ συμπτώσεων; Firmicus, 6.29.10 *aut facient per praecipitia iactari, aut corpus cadentium culminum ruinis opprimitur*, the configuration discussed in the previous chart; they are separated by hanging in 3.261–3). πτῶσις is the native's own fall from a height (Valens, I 1.15 πτώσεις ἐπὶ στόμα, caused by Saturn; I 1.23 πτώσεις ἀπὸ ὕψους ἢ τετραπόδων, caused by Mars; I 20.6 ἀπὸ ὕψους ἢ τετραπόδων πτώσεις, caused by both malefics with the Sun), though it is the word used for collapsing buildings in 3.130 and 262. The Moon topples the buildings purposefully, with the same word the Synoptics used for Joseph of Arimathea sealing Jesus' tomb (Matth. 27:60 προσκυλίσας; Mark 15:46 προσεκύλισεν).

201 Rather more intelligently than M^a, whose Homerism at 3.130 κατὰ κρατός was unintentionally comic, this poet describes the effect of falling masonry by rewriting, in more prosaic vocabulary, *Il.* 5.307 θλάσσε δέ οἱ κοτύλην, πρὸς δ' ἄμφω ῥῆξε τένοντε (a wound caused by a *rock* hurled by Diomedes). He replaces κοτύλη with the more usual word for collar-bone (Homeric but not in this *sedes*), and for the simplex verbs uses more prosaic compounds (of which the second is also used by Jesus in Matth. 21:44 Καὶ ὁ πεσὼν ἐπὶ τὸν λίθον τοῦτον συνθλασθήσεται, for the man who falls *on* the corner-stone—not vice versa[116]). Perhaps he knows 3.263 ὀστέα συνθλιφθέντες, also of a building collapse. βίη, not usual in the Homeric poems for individual acts of violence (except at *Od.* 21.128, for the drawing of the bow), points to the classification of this chart under *biothanasia*.

202-8

Saturn in equal degrees with Venus. An incest configuration, reduced to its essentials. The opposition (Firmicus, 6.29.22, 6.31.25 sub fin.) or conjunction (Firmicus, 6.31.9) of these planets figures in other, more complex, incest charts.

Although it mentions him, this does not strictly belong among the witnesses to Oedipus' chart (6.160-9, 1.106-11, Anubion, F 4 ii. 11-18, and Firmicus, 6.30.1), in which—among many other specifications—the planets are moving into *synaphe*, but Saturn is behind Venus and not, therefore, in equal degrees. Nevertheless, in common with the versions of that chart in Anubion and Firmicus, it mentions not only parent–child incest (both versions of it), but also incest between stepmother and stepson (Anubion and Firmicus also have stepfathers; 1.112-13 makes stepmothers and father's concubines the result of an additional factor). Sibling incest, which enables M^d to make the link with his royal addressee, is not found in the Oedipus charts, and strictly it defies the logic whereby Saturn's effect on Venus is to cause incest across rather than within generations (Bouché-Leclercq, 450-1 n. 3).

202 Μὴ λαθέτω σε: see p. 359 for other imperatives in M^d. Prognostic literature depends on scrupulous observation (Hippocr. *Progn.* II Σκέπτεσθαι δὲ χρή, σκοπεῖν δὲ χρή...), didactic adjures its addressee to take heed, but the negative 'let it not escape you' derives ultimately from Hes. *Op.* 491 ἐν θυμῷ δ' εὖ πάντα φυλάσσεο, μηδέ σε λήθοι. Nicander is particularly fond of it (*Ther.* 574 Μηδὲ σύ γ' ἀβροτόνου ἐπιλήθεο; 583 Μηδὲ σέ γε χραίσμη πολίου λάθοι ἠὲ κέδροιο (see Overduin ad loc.); *Al.* 335-6 Μὴ μὲν ἐπαλγύνουσα πόσις βουπρήστιδος ἐχθρῆς | λήσειεν, σὺ δὲ φῶτα δαμαζόμενον πεπύθοιο), though several times he uses it to mean 'be on your guard against' in cautionary statements,[117] rather than 'don't be inattentive', i.e. this is important/take heed of this useful thing or

---

[116] And also by Aetius, *Iatr.* 16.26 l. 72 συνθλᾶν τὰ ὀστᾶ in a discussion of embryotomy.
[117] *Al.* 279-80; 397; 594-5.

fact. Hesiod's founding instance involves observation of the seasons, and Aratus uses it in his weather-signs (983–4 Μηδὲ σύ...λελαθέσθαι), thereby authorising its use by star-poets observing the cosmos. There are three instances of M^d's exact formulation in Hephaestion, of which i. 230.17 was Dorotheus, fr. 66b Stegemann; the others are i. 12.20 and 164.21, and another in Θ p. 187.6 (= Dorotheus, p. 376.7) Μή σε λαθέτω, καθὼς προεῖπον, so one might infer that it played a role in his poetry. It is also in pure prose in Paul, p. 95.11–12, and in an astrological tract Περὶ γονέων, CCAG ii. 188.8 μηδέ σε λαθέτω ὅτι....It seems much less popular in other branches of technical literature, perhaps because it is most at home in the one that *par excellence* depended on observation (hence in Xen. *De re equestri* 3.1 it is again a question of looking out for something, in this case when buying a horse). Lucretius has more long-winded formulations that admonish Memmius not to disregard his instruction (1.51–2 *ne mea dona tibi studio disposta fideli, | intellecta prius quam sint, contempta relinquas*; 4.931 *tu fac ne ventis verba profundam*).

203 The Oedipus chart evidently came from a series of charts of mythological and historical figures, in which it illustrated mother–son incest. Thyestes illustrates its complement, father–daughter incest (the epithet Πελοπήιον evokes not only Thyestes' father Pelops but also Pelopeia, the daughter he impregnated).[118] Possibly the original source mentioned both figures as counterparts, though 6.166 and Firmicus, 6.30.1 name Oedipus but leave the father–daughter situation anonymous, and Anubion, F 4 ii. 17–18, has no names at all. Or perhaps it is simply that the poet independently evokes an archetype, using big names and cultural icons (Lucian, *Salt.* 43 notes the marriage of Pelopeia as a theme in pantomime, which is just the kind of paradigm the Manethoniana evoke: see i. Index, s.v. mythological schemata).

204 The line, which is desperate, seems to represent a change of direction: we expect 'a child which is a menace to its parent', complementing τέκνῳ μὲν in the previous line, but instead we get a disjunctive (not listed among the non-adversative complements of μέν in Denniston, 374–6). Alongside Koechly's reconstruction I have simply taken the manuscript's word about a second disjunctive, which produces a better parallelism with the previous line, though the sense, 'a son impious towards some other woman or (specifically) to Jocasta', is hardly satisfactory. ἀσεβῆ appears to look directly to Sophocles, who calls Oedipus precisely this (*OT* 1382, 1441, *OC* 823).

---

[118] Sources in K. Keyßner, *RE* s.v. Pelopia; Roscher, s.v. Pelopeia (Höfer); H. L. Levy, 'Claudian's *In Rufinum* 1.83–84 and a Vatican Vase-Painting', *TAPA* 72 (1941), 237–44, esp. 238–41.

205 προγόνους: not 'ancestors', but stepsons, *privignos* (already Gronovius; see LSJ πρόγονος, III); but it is its third meaning, 'early-born' (*Od.* 9.221, of the Cyclops' flock) which authorises its placement in this *sedes*. On intercourse with stepmothers, see on 2.187-9, and i. 303, 368, 756, 763.

206 ἠδὲ κασιγνήτοις: in this *sedes* at *Il.* 6.430 ἠδὲ κασίγνητος, which may also have been recycled by Anubion, F 12.21 [ἠδὲ] κασιγνήτοις in another chart (the inner planets with the Moon) which apparently dealt with outrages within the family (the previous line mentions stepmothers).

ὁμογάστριον εὐνήν: the epithet, a Homeric *dis legomenon*, is also used of sibling incest in 6.118 (in a different configuration). In *Il.* 24.47 it is decorative, but in 21.95 it distinguishes a full brother from a half-brother (Lycaon), and that is how it is used in Θ p. 146.8. The cadence is late antique (ps.-Opp. *Cyn.* 3.375 φιλοτήσιον εὐνήν, Nonn. *D.* 11.395 πολυλήιον εὐνήν, 43.10 μετανάστιον εὐνήν, 47.347 ἀπατήλιον εὐνήν).

207-8 The use of γνωρίζειν in forecasting (from *this* you may deduce *this*: Hephaestion, i. 164.25, 167.16, 171.14; Teucer, *CCAG* vii. 213.5) is weakened or trivialised to invite the king simply to recognise his own (existing) situation, but the address is matched in (i) a treatise about the properties of the zodiacal signs, which begins (*CCAG* x. 66.2-3) Μάθε [ἀ]κρι[βῶς] καὶ γνώριζε τὰς ἐνεργείας καὶ χάριτας τῶν ζῳδίων, and (ii) a short tract about the movement of the planets which calls on its anonymous addressee Γνώριζε καὶ τοῦτο (*CCAG* xii. 108.14). 5.81 γίγνωσκε τὰ δῶρα is similar. Given that the chart began with the standard assumption of pious outrage, the effect is rather odd—a combination of Sotades, for whom the marriage was obscenely unholy (fr. 1 P.), the helpful, informative narrator of a didactic text, and the respectful courtier. γενεῇ waves feebly at the idea of consanguine marriage. I interpret the plural as poetic, referring to a single, specified, marriage; this is well matched, and at line-end, by Nonn. *D.* 1.407 Εὐρώπης ὑμεναίους, 42.366 Βερόης ὑμεναίους, 43.384 Ἀμυμώνης ὑμεναίων, 48.554 Ἀλθαίης ὑμεναίους, Adesp. *AP* 16.151.7 Ἰαρβαίων ὑμεναίων (of Dido); V. *Aen.* 7.344 *Turnique hymenaeos*. See, however, Montevcnti, 151, for the suggestion that the allusion is to Arsinoe's *two* incestuous marriages.

209-16

Luminaries in places of gender. See commentaries on 3.363-98, 4.508-36, and 1.26-33. This much-abbreviated version states the principle of alignment and adds the two outcomes that produce gender reversal, (i) both luminaries in feminine places for a man (cf. 3.376-9; different outcome in 4.519-26) and (ii) both in masculine places for a woman (cf. 3.383-5). The result is a clear and straightforward binary not matched in other books. In 3.378 the sexual implications for a man are only glanced at; women receive more attention, but other factors are involved in turning them lesbian (3.386–91). In the first book, masculine and feminine charts (1.115–18 + 29–33) have been split apart and both involve factors other than the gender of signs. As a result, this version is not a mere duplicate of any other. With Ptolemy, 3.15.7–12, the present poet shares an interest in sexual perversion, but for Ptolemy, as well as for M^a and M^c, that only comes about in the presence of additional factors (Mars and Venus; Mercury in 3.394 for emasculated men), whereas here the misplaced luminaries do it on their own. That is true of the stars of 'Antiochus' as well (quoted in i. 702). He mentions the effect on gender roles (men are μαλακούς, women τριβάδας), but it is not his sole interest.

209–10 The parallelism is nicely reinforced not only by isocolon but also by the repeated metrical pattern (p. 341). The poet finds two alternatives for ζώοις (M^a)/ζῳδίοις in the prose writers ('Antiochus' has ἠρρενωμένοις ζῳδίοις ἢ τοῖς ἠρρενωμένοις τεταρτημορίοις).

211 ἄμφω τούτους: this exact collocation does not recur before Byzantine writers (nor do τούτους ἄμφω, nor the nominative), but the Homeric poems already combine the plural with ἄμφω for a natural pair, e.g. *Od.* 11.301 τοὺς ἄμφω of Castor and Polydeuces (Chantraine, ii. 26 on plural/dual alternation).
καθεύροις: see on 5.8.

212 'Antiochus' calls his effeminates ἀποκόπους. Ptolemy's effeminate men in the first place incline πρὸς τὸ εὔθρυπτον καὶ τεθηλυσμένον τῆς ψυχῆς; with one additional factor (Venus in feminine places), they act παθητικῶς, but secretly, and with two (Mars feminised as well) their behaviour becomes flagrant. Odyssean ταλαπείριος (it is not Iliadic) is epithet of ξεῖνος and ἱκέτης, hence not inappropriate insofar as eunuchs stretch to thoughts of mendicant *galli*.

213 The poet briefly evokes yet another topos with a long history,[119] that weaving is women's work, and that the violation of the norm represents sexual deviance. Indeed, he borrows the earliest classical formulation of this idea, *Il.* 6.491 and *Od.* 1.357 ἱστόν τ' ἠλακάτην τε, where it is used by Hector and Telemachus respectively to put down a woman who is supposedly infiltrating the man's sphere (i.e. precisely the opposite way round from here).[120] It recurs

---

[119] The spindle in ancient Mesopotamia: J. Bottéro and H. Petschow, 'Homosexualität', in *Reallexikon der Assyriologie und Vorderasiatischen Archäologie*, iv (Berlin and New York, 1972–5), 463 §11, 465 §16.
[120] Conversely, when the hermaphrodite Callo (1.128 n.) ceases to be a woman, textile work symbolises everything she leaves behind (Diod. Sic. 32.11.4 τὰς μὲν ἐκ τῶν ἱστῶν κερκίδας καὶ τὴν ἄλλην τῶν γυναικῶν ταλασιουργίαν).

in the ethnographic topsy-turvy of sex-reversal in Egypt (Hdt. 2.35.2 οἱ δὲ ἄνδρες κατ᾽ οἴκους ἐόντες ὑφαίνουσι, repeated in Soph. OC 339–40 ἐκεῖ γὰρ οἱ μὲν ἄρσενες κατὰ στέγας | θακοῦσιν ἱστουργοῦντες¹²¹), where the point is as much that the men stayed at home as that they wove (curiously, the effeminates in the corresponding passage at 3.379 are precisely the opposite, longing for foreign lands). It also occurs in philosophical discussions of gender roles, when Musonius in his fourth discourse (ap. Stob. 2.31.123) counters his addressee's shock at the proposition that a man should learn to work wool (ταλασίαν) with the suggestion that each person should do what best suits him or her, which might in a few cases lead to a man's doing women's work and vice versa. That textile work is for effeminate men is both a jibe and an idea that can be entertained with philosophic seriousness. Old Comedy's stock *kinaidos*, Cleisthenes, is taxed with having a spindle (Ar. *Av.* 831 Κλεισθένης δὲ κερκίδα); Cicero tells a story about a consul teasing an epicene youth about his spindle and wool (*De Or.* 2.277 *Quid tu, Egilia mea? quando ad me venis cum tua colu et lana?*);¹²² a speaker in Juvenal draws out the conceit of male wool-workers more expert than Penelope or Arachne (*Sat.* 2.54–7; see Courtney on l. 54); the Stoic Hierocles opines that a man who is utterly confident in his masculinity may share occupations with his wife, while admitting that half-men do indeed work in the textile industry in their quest for femininity;¹²³ in the version of the Artemisia story told in the Anonymous *Tractatus de Mulieribus* (§13), Xerxes not only sends her a panoply, but complements it with distaffs and spindles (classified as τοῖς τῶν γυναικῶν ἐπιτηδεύμασιν) for the womanish Phoenicians. See also Diod. Sic. 2.45.2. The 'works of women' motif has a sexual sense in Ptolemy, 'Antiochus', and Θ p. 169.12–15 (with Venus in the MC) εὐνοῦχοι ἢ ἀπόκοποι ἢ ἑρμαφρόδιτοι... γυναικῶν ἔργα ἐπιτελοῦντες. But the formulation here is once again EGHP (*Il.* 6.289, *Od.* 7.97), where it refers to the products of the loom, and so is in more or less happy symbiosis with the first half of the line.

216 See 4.358 n. for the 'works of men'. The rhythm is thoroughly bizarre, and the violation of Hermann's Bridge is not prompted by a technical term. I am not sure whether it falls within this poet's aesthetic to imitate 'unnaturalness' by deviant metre; he breaks the Bridge too often (p. 351).

---

¹²¹ Herodotus was in fact right (see Lloyd ad loc.), but the practice looked bizarre to a Greek. On Sophocles' borrowing, see S. West, 'Cultural Antitheses: Reflections of Herodotus 2.35–36', *IJCT* 5 (1998), 3–19, at 7–8.

¹²² A. Richlin, 'Not before Homosexuality: The Materiality of the *Cinaedus* and the Roman Law against Love between Men', *JHS* 3 (1993), 523–73, at 541.

¹²³ Ap. Stob. 4.28.21 ἐπεὶ γὰρ ὡς ἐπὶ τὸ πλῆθος εὐτελεῖς ἀνθρωπίσκοι καὶ τὸ τῶν κατεαγότων καὶ γυννίδων φῦλον ὡς τὴν ἐρίων ἐργασίαν καταφέρεται ζήλῳ θηλύτητος, οὐ δοκεῖ κατὰ τὸν ἀληθινώτερον ἄνδρα τυγχάνειν τὸ εἰς ταῦτα συγκαθιέναι (H. F. A. von Arnim, *Hierokles ethische Elementarlehre, Papyrus 9780, nebst den bei Stobäus erhaltenen ethischen Exzerpten aus Hierokles* (Berlin, 1906), 62–3).

217-21

Saturn by night in IMC, with Mars in MC. Crucifixion, precisely as in Θ p. 201.22-3. In Θ this directly follows a configuration whose corresponding number is 5.192-6, on being torn apart by animals. There is another crucifixion chart in 4.193-200 (the malefics conjunct in the DESC, and Mercury in equal degrees). Birds ⟨and dogs⟩ are mentioned there; the outcome is described more bombastically.

217 Νυκτερινός: 'by night', in a night birth (Θ νυκτὸς), so that the planet is out of sect and angry.

218 ἐσίδοις: also 280. The verb is only in poetic astrology, usually of aspect, but of the observer also in Maximus, 498 εἰσορόων, and in the apodosis at 3.370.

219 The line as a whole is remarkably like *Or. Sib.* 5.257 ὃς παλάμας ἥπλωσεν ἐπὶ ξύλου πολυκάρπου (save that the Sibyl's metre is even worse than M^{d}'s). Assuming this is a pagan author, he shows himself in this line steeped in the language of his Christian environment (p. 318; see too on 5.180 δυσαγῆ), for ἐπὶ ξύλου, applied to crucifixion, seems an otherwise entirely Judaeo-Christian expression, confined to LXX (Gen. 40:19; Deut. 21:22; Joshua 8:29; Esther 8:7), and then ubiquitous in Christian writers ever since Paul (Galat. 3:13), Luke (Acts 5:30, 10:39), and other early Christian writers (Epist. Barnab. 5:13a) applied Deut. 21:22 to Jesus.

ἁπλώσας παλάμῃσιν...σῶμα: Lucilius, *AP* 11.107.4 ἁπλώσας κατὰ γῆς σῶμα is not really a parallel; it is not about crucifixion. This is remarkably reminiscent of the language of Christ's crucifixion (Lampe, s.v. ἁπλόω, A.1.a, b); compare e.g. Greg. Naz. *PG* 36.729.14-15 τὴν ἐπὶ τοῦ σταυροῦ τῶν θείων σου παλάμων ἐφάπλωσιν; *Horologium*, 79.3 σὺ δὲ ἐφαπλώσας τὰς παλάμας σου ξύλῳ σταυροῦ.[124] With other verbs: *Analecta Hymnica Graeca, Canones Aprilis*, 1.1.1.15-16 Ἔτεινεν ἐπὶ ξύλου σταυροῦ Χριστὸς παλάμας, cf. 1.149 n. for τείνειν; *Canones Septembris*, 14.22.5.17-19 Ὡς ἐξεπέτασας τὰς παλάμας σου, | Δέσποτα Κύριε, | ἐπὶ τοῦ ξύλου τῆς σταυρώσεως.

ὑψόθι: based on its famous occurrence in John 3:14 ὑψωθῆναι δεῖ τὸν υἱὸν τοῦ ἀνθρώπου, D'Orville, 669, thought it a Hebraism. In fact it is a topos expressed in varied vocabulary that goes back at least as far as Herodotus' account of Polycrates (3.124.1 ἐδόκεέ οἱ τὸν πατέρα ἐν τῷ ἠέρι μετέωρον ἐόντα, which is fulfilled when he is crucified; compare 1.148 μετέωρον ἀνεσταύρωσας

---

[124] Of other victims of crucifixion/judicial punishment: e.g. Euseb. *Hist. Eccl.* 8.7.4 τὰς μὲν χεῖρας ἐφαπλοῦντος εἰς σταυροῦ τύπον; Basil of Caesarea, *PG* 28.1060.16-17 σὺ δέ, εὐκαίρως ἐπὶ τὸν σταυρὸν τὰς χεῖρας ἁπλώσας, of the good thief; ps.-John Chrys. *In Catenas Sancti Petri*, 4 χεῖρες ἐκτάδην προσεφαπλούμεναι; *Mart. Sanct. Ignat. Antioch.* 5.1 ἁπλώσαντες αὐτοῦ τὰς χεῖρας πληρώσατε αὐτὰς πυρός, supposedly of an order given by Trajan.

Charts 949

[*ex emend.*]; and what is going on in *Or. Sib.* 5.217 ἄξουσιν μετέωρον, albeit in the context of Nero and the Isthmus?). ὑψ- also occurs in Artemidorus, 2.53.1 καὶ γὰρ ὑψηλὸς ὁ σταυρωθείς, 4.49... διὰ τὸ ὑψηλότατον εἶναι τὸν ἐσταυρωμένον. Other variants are Plutarch, *Flamin.* 9.4 Ἀλκαίῳ σταυρὸς πήγνυται ἠλίβατος; Photius, *Bibl.* cod. 94, 78 A 32 ἄνωθεν; Silius Italicus, *Pun.* 2.343–4 *vidi, cum robore pendens* | *Hesperiam cruce sublimis spectaret ab alta*; Cic. *Tusc.* 1.102. In Ptol. 4.9.13 crucifixion is caused by the placement of planets in the 'high' *kentra* (the MC or IMC) ἐπὶ δὲ τοῦ μεσουρανήματος ἢ ἀντιμεσουρανήματος σταυροῖς ἀνορθουμένους. For Achmet the height of the crucifix is an analogy for social position (*Oneir.* 89.3–4; 90.6–9).

220 On birds and crucifixion victims, see on 4.200, and for the language see on 6.98 βορήν τ' ἔμεν οἰωνοῖσιν. Other variants are Quint. Smyrn. 1.329 οἰωνοῖς δὲ βόσις, 3.211 and 6.49 οἰωνοῖσιν ἀερσιπέτῃσιν ἐδωδήν, and 14.285 ἕλωρ ἔμεν οἰωνοῖσιν. The double compound is the poet's innovation (ἀνίπτασθαι exists).

221 μοίρης νευροτόμου: like 4.198 σκολοπηίδα μοῖραν. For tragic periphrases, see on 4.52, and for the use of compound adjectives in genus–species expressions, characteristically with a verbal element, '*x* consisting in the doing of *y*', G. C. Richards, 'Greek Compound Adjectives with a Verbal Element in Tragedy', *CQ* 12 (1918), 15–21, at 19. For expressions involving fate and death, in particular, compare Lyc. *Al.* 595 οἰωνόμικτον μοῖραν (fate consisting in being turned into birds); Aesch. *Ag.* 1528–9 ξιφοδηλήτωι θανάτωι, cf. K.–G. i. 262–3, who put it in the category of expressions where a compound epithet replaces a dependent genitive; Eur. *Ion* 1237 λεύσιμοι δὲ καταφθοραί (Breitenbach, 37); Aesch. *Sept.* 681 θάνατος ὧδ' αὐτοκτόνος. The epithet is new; there is a very rare verb νευροτομεῖν, used of cattle by Dion. Hal. *AR* 20.2.5, of an enfeebled physical state by Oribasius, 10.7.9, and metaphorically of the soul by John of Damascus. As for crucifixion consisting in cutting the nerves (accurate, as a matter of fact: nails in the wrists would pierce the median nerve running up the arm, and those in the feet would cut the nerves between the metatarsal bones), see Tertullian, *Adv. Jud.* 10.9 *nervos eius suffigendo clavis desaevierunt*. Procopius, *Comm. in Gen.* 49.2 manages to interpret Gen. 49:6 ἐνευροκόπησαν (of hamstringing an ox) as a reference to the crucifixion (ἢ ἐπειδὴ ἐν τῷ σταυρῷ διέτρησαν αὐτοῦ τὰ νεῦρα).

222–4

Moon in house of Sun. Another hexameter version of this chart is quoted in Θ p. 222.12–14. The epitomator suppresses the name of the poet (φησὶν γάρ). Cumont supplied ⟨Δωρόθεος⟩, but Pingree did not include the lines in his edition. He does admit a second block of lines quoted anonymously shortly afterwards (φησὶ γάρ τις τῶν σοφῶν), but perhaps was deterred from including these by their transmission in the Manethoniana; the alternative would be to suppose that book 5 itself contains at least snatches of Dorotheus (and if here, then perhaps elsewhere?) in a slightly different recension.

The lines in Θ do not involve the Sun. They are quoted apropos of the interpretation of a chart in which the Moon is in Taurus, and opposed by Venus, and they instruct the adept to establish *whose* house the Moon is in, i.e. as a general rule. The problem is that the Moon is opposed by the planet which rules the house she occupies, her οἰκοδεσπότης, and this is restated in a couple of prose paraphrases: (i) Θ p. 183.16–17 (from ch. 59 entitled Περὶ σχημάτων Σελήνης καθολικῶν) Σελήνη διαμετροῦσα τὸν ἴδιον οἰκοδεσπότην φυγάδας, ἀτίμους, μετανάστας, ξενιτεύοντας and (ii) CCAG vii. 115.5–7 (from an abbreviated selection of the same material in cod. Monac. 7, attributed by its editor Boll to Antiochus) Σελήνη διαμετροῦσα [ἢ διαμετροῦσα] τὸν ἴδιον οἰκοδεσπότην φυγάδας ποιεῖ, μετανάστας, μετοικιζομένους. The opposing planet need not be the Sun: that is unique to the version of the chart in L. Indeed, it is a surprising presence in a miserable outcome given that in 2.395–6 we were told that the luminaries *rejoiced* in each other's houses, and Full Moon ought to be auspicious and *productive* of honour (2.500–2, 3.221–5). Lopilato's note ad loc. conjectures that L's version is not an alternative recension but a simple corruption of the lines in Θ (in other words, that Τιτῆνος is a corruption of τίνος ἀστέρος) and there is much to be said for this.

223 φωλευόμενον: given the word's zoological associations, this is a bizarre metaphor, and the middle is unparalleled, but the lines in Θ establish that this is not just a corruption.

224 ἀτιμήτους: in the same *sedes* as *Il.* 9.648 = 16.59 (and nowhere else in EGHP). Although the corresponding epithet in Θ is partly corrupt, the paraphrase on p. 183.17 suggests it read κάτιμος,[125] continuing καὶ μετανάστης; in other words the two recensions would be saluting the same Iliadic line in different ways (p. 138). διὰ πάντων, replacing μετανάστας, is an expression of distinction in *Il.* 12.104. This is the kind of variation one also finds between recensions in M^b/M^c and Π^1.

---

[125] ἄτιμος is fairly rare in astrology, and otherwise used of persons in astrological texts only outside the usual group of Manetho comparanda: CCAG v/4. 161.24 οἱ βασιλεῖς ἄτιμοι ἔσονται; Camaterus, *Introd.* 2885 δοῦλον ἄτιμον. μετανάστης is only slightly less rare (it is also in prose astrology in Paul, pp. 55.4 and 60.4), but the abstract μετανάστασιν occurs in the second set of anonymous verses quoted by Θ (those admitted by Pingree as Dorothean).

225-42

Waxing Moon fleeing Mars and Saturn in opposition, Jupiter in trine; Jupiter Lord of Bios (πρᾶξις?) or in opposition to it. An unusually complex chart. Is it that of an historical individual?

225-6 The implications of these physical notices (θερμὸν: i. 909 n. 26; ψυχρήν: i. 911 n. 13) are unclear, whether the Moon is escaping baneful influences or striking a happy medium between them.

228 τὸν βίον αὐτὸς ἔχων: different systems give this name to different houses: see Heilen 2015, 1351 (commonly the second or tenth, but also sometimes the eighth), but what is said of Jupiter in the eighth house in the system of Firmicus (3.3.16) is compatible with the outcome in 232–3 (though Θ p. 162.24–5 has eventual *gain*, and Paul, p. 61.12–13, says, more intuitively, that benefics in this position provide benefit from death, presumably in the form of inheritances). This line implies an understanding of opposition as concord (see on 2.436–8).

229-30 These sound like tokens of kingliness, presumably from the influence of Jupiter; cf. Ptol. 3.12.4, where natives are tall and (as in the next line) large-eyed; similarly Rhetorius, *CCAG* vii. 217.7–8 εὐμεγέθεις, εὐρυμετώπους, χαροπούς. They are stock components in the description of a physically impressive individual, which usually begins with a note on stature and often continues immediately or a little later with eyes.[126] Still, while Jupiter and his signs (Sagittarius and Pisces) engender tall persons in some systems,[127] in others— just as Agamemnon was not the tallest Greek in the *teichoskopia*, but the best proportioned—they produce a golden mean (*CCAG* x. 115.15, s.v. Sagittarius, γίνεται ἀνὴρ μεστός) or robust maturity (Hephaestion, i. 264.22 μέσης ἡλικίας).

229 Almost wholly composed of Homeric verse units. The swapping-in of ἡλικίη (the use is found in Dorotheus and Hephaestion) in the Homeric line-beginning *Il.* 10.29 παρδαλέη μὲν πρῶτα for the physiognomist's compulsory note on stature[128] is a good illustration of the opportunism of this kind of

---

[126] For example: Lucian, *Alexander*, 3: μέγας and, a little later, ὀφθαλμοὶ πολὺ τὸ γοργὸν καὶ ἔνθεον διεμφαίνοντες. Stature, complexion, hair, eyes, in Adamantius' sketch of the ideal Greek build (2.32); stature, hair, complexion, eyes in *Laudatio Sancti Pauli Junioris*, 53 Ἦν δὲ ὁ τῷ ὄντι μακάριος Παῦλος μέτριος μὲν τὴν ἡλικίαν, ἀναφαλαντίας δὲ τὴν κεφαλήν, οὐκ ἐπὶ πολὺ καθεικὼς τὴν ὑπήνην ἀλλὰ μᾶλλον εἰς πλάτος διήκουσαν, τὴν ὄψιν μὲν ἐπὶ τὸ ὠχρότερον νεύουσαν, τὸ χαρωπὸν δὲ πλεονεκτοῦσαν ταῖς τῶν ὀμμάτων βολαῖς... On the primacy of eyes among physiognomical signs, see Rizzini, 73.

[127] Hephaestion, i. 30.2 εὐμήκης τὴν ἡλικίαν (first decan of Pisces, sim. Camaterus, *Introd.* 1638).

[128] *Statura* an unmissable element in Suetonius' biographies of emperors: G. Vidén, 'Bodily Attributes and Authority: Descriptions of the Body in Suetonius' *Biographies*', in S. Thorsen and

composition. The readjustment of Od. 18.292 μέγαν περικαλλέα πέπλον (thence Ap. Rhod. 3.1365 μέγαν περιηγέα πέτρον) for the tall individual leaves a slight sense of awkwardness: given the invariable application of περιμήκης in EGHP (and still Apollonius) to inanimate objects (in this sedes Il. 13.63, Od. 9.487, 10.293, al.), it is as if the poet had described a tall individual as 'long'; this notwithstanding Aratus' description of Perseus as περιμήκετος (250, also of things in Homer), as his point is the extent of the constellation, not the stature of the individual.

230 ὀφθαλμοῖσι χαρωπὸν: the epithet, originally *hapax* in Od. 11.611 χαροποί τε λέοντες, has extended from animal to human and divine eyes certainly by the Hellenistic period, and Aratus, who uses it of stars and the Moon, implies both possible senses, 'brilliant' (Martin on 1152) and 'bluish' (both Kidd and Martin on 394). So does astrology, which otherwise continues to use the Homeric form,[129] and so it seems does physiognomy, which uses it as a signifier of bravery (ps.-Arist. *Physiog.* 807 B 1 ὄμμα χαροπόν), characteristic of the lion (809 B 19, cf. 812 B 5), as well as of the well-conditioned (εὐφυής) man (807 B 19).[130] This passage obviously means 'brilliant',[131] in which case, as a sign of manliness, Jupiter produces it (229–30 n.; Camaterus, *Introd.* 1392 χαροπός, of the third decan of Sagittarius, sign of Jupiter, which belongs to the Sun), but so can the fierce quality of Mars (Dorotheus, p. 412.12).

ὀφρύσιν εὖ ἀραρυίαις: this sign usually indicates masculinity.[132] The terminology varies; σύνοφρυς is commonest (e.g. in Teucer, *CCAG* vii. 199.13, where συνόφρυας are ranged alongside the dark-skinned, bearded, bald, and those with business acumen). For Adamantius, 1.19 ὀφρῦς συνεστραμμένας ('close-packed': I. Redpath, in S. Swain (ed.), *Seeing the Face, Seeing the Soul: Polemon's Physiognomy from Classical Antiquity to Medieval Islam* (Oxford, 2007), 511) or ὀφρῦς συντεταμένας ('contracted': Epit. Matrit. and ps.-Polemon, 22) are one of the signs of a bold and daring disposition, and in 2.37 such people are troublesome (οἱ δὲ σφόδρα συνόφρυες ἀνιαροί· πρέπει γὰρ αὐτοῖς ἀνία). In the story in

---

S. Harrison (eds.), *Dynamics of Ancient Prose: Biographic, Novelistic, Apologetic* (Berlin, 2018), 37–48, at 39.

[129] This is the only instance of the late variant χαρωπ-, otherwise in Herodian, *GG* iii/1. 188.4 (restored from Theognostus), then the Alexander Romance, Athanasius, and Simplicius.

[130] Adamantius also has two kinds of eyes which he calls χαροποί; the associations are good when it goes together with ὑγροί (2.32), bad (1.7, 11, 16) when it is a colour term ('dark blue': Redpath).

[131] 'Bright-eyed' (Lopilato); 'oculis superbum' (Koechly). P. G. Maxwell-Stuart, *Studies in Greek Colour Terminology*, Volume II Χαροπός (Leiden, 1981), 48, takes it in the same sense as its earlier applications to Leo (2.76, 387). I agree, but render both 'bright-eyed', rather than 'amber-coloured'. For the other meaning, see Θ p. 180.17 = *CCAG* i. 116.13 = v/1. 203.2 = 224.28, distinct from ὑπογλαύκους.

[132] But a captious disposition in ps.-Arist. *Physiogn.* 812^{b}25.

Dio Chrys. *Or.* 33.54, being σύνοφρυν should signify masculinity, but can mislead (M. Gleason, *Making Men: Sophists and Self-Presentation in Ancient Rome* (Princeton, 1995), 77). Suetonius' Augustus has this characteristic (*Aug.* 79.2 *supercilia coniuncta*), and so does a young Celtic giant called Heracles (Philostratus, *Vit. Soph.* 552 καὶ τῶν ὀφρύων λασίως ἔχειν, ἃς καὶ ξυμβάλλειν ἀλλήλαις οἷον μίαν...). Brilliant eyes and continuous eyebrows are combined, as here, in *Prognostica ex signis zodiaci, CCAG* iv. 159.1 χαροπός, δασύφριδος, for a person born under Aries, which is a sign of Mars. The line-end refurbishes a formula for gates and doors (*Il.* 7.339, 438, *Od.* 22.148, 23.42).

231 μηχανικὸν could indicate specifically a craftsman or engineer, as in 4.439 and Θ p. 217.1, 3, or it could be a character description, 'resourceful', full of μηχανή, as in Valens, I 19.21 μηχανικοὺς καὶ πολυπείρους καὶ περιέργους, sim. I 20.31, 36 μηχανικούς, ῥᾳδίως περὶ τὰς πράξεις ὁρμωμένους καὶ πολυκινήτους. The strong suggestions of Odyssean vocabulary in the second half of the line perhaps point to the latter, and imply that the poet is trying to characterise the practical, capable individual; he seems to be trying to populate verse patterns like πολύχρυσος πολύχαλκος, πολύρρηνες πολυβοῦται, πολυσημάντωρ πολυδέγμων, πολυσπερέας πολύφορβος, and so on, with vocabulary that evokes Odysseus (which will surprise anyone who recalls *Il.* 3.193 after reading 229). But πολύτλητον (itself only in *Od.* 11.38) wants to evoke adversity as well as capability; see on the next line.

232–7 We find ourselves in the world of invective. The themes that follow—squandering patrimony, prostituting oneself, and cowardice—are all staples of the genre; so too is banausic profession (oneself or one's parents), which might suggest that the invective already begins in 231, or at least that that line forms a transition to it. The particular status of 231 seems borderline, but the clustering of invective themes in 232–7 undermines Koechly's view that 231–3 are an interpolation and that 234 picks up from 230. On the contrary, the physiognomy ended with 230, and the succeeding lines stick to familiar topoi of denunciations.[133] In i. 305 n. 1 I noted the interest of comparing the themes of invective with the ethics of astrology, even though one was deployed by highly trained rhetoricians among the political élites and the latter is supposedly 'popular'. This passage shows how very close the overlap is; indeed, the formulation of the cowardice motif in 237 as cowering before one's enemies seems to be a direct reflection of accusations in more formal invectives of cowardice on the

---

[133] W. Süss, *Ethos: Studien zur älteren griechischen Rhetorik* (Leipzig and Berlin, 1920; reprint Aalen, 1975), 254; A. Corbeill, 'Ciceronian Invective', in J. M. May (ed.), *Brill's Companion to Cicero: Oratory and Rhetoric* (Leiden, 2002), 197–217, at 201 and n. 17. An early and influential example is Aeschines' *Against Timarchus*; a full-blown Roman example is Cicero's *In Pisonem*.

battlefield (e.g. Aeschin. *Timarch.* 29, throwing away one's shield; Nisbet and Hubbard on Hor. *Od.* 2.7.10, with parallels for the topos).

οἶκον μὲν φθείροντα: 2.463 οἴκων γὰρ φθείρει κτῆσιν. That happens when the Moon is joining the malefics, not leaving them. Also 6.80 and 5.64 πατρώιον οἶκον.

233 See on 228 for Jupiter's effect on wealth. The whole line is a weaker version of 309–10. Using much of the same vocabulary as M^d, Libanius, *Or.* 11.134, magnificently reverses the attitude to expenditure when it is a matter of civic ethics:

οὗτοι γὰρ διὰ μὲν εὐδαιμονίαν πατρῷα ἐκληρονόμησαν, διὰ δὲ φιλοτιμίαν πλεῖστα ἀνηλώκασι... λαμπρότητι δὲ πάσῃ πρὸς τὰς λειτουργίας χρώμενοι, προνοίᾳ δὲ τὴν πενίαν φεύγοντες, ἥδιον μὲν δαπανώμενοι περὶ τὴν πόλιν ἢ κερδαίνουσιν ἕτεροι...

(and much more in the same vein). ὃς σκεδάσας ὄλβον is plausible astrological language. Some parallels, under various circumstances: Περὶ κράσ. 69 τὰ πατρικὰ σκεδάννυνται (Sun in right quartile with Saturn), 129 σκέδασιν τοῦ βίου (Mars opposing Jupiter); 161 ὁ δὲ πατρικὸς βίος σκεδάννυται (Mars with the Sun); Apomasar, *De Rev.* p. 82.5 τὸν πατρικὸν διασκεδάσει πλοῦτον, 87.20 διασκορπίσει τὸν οἰκεῖον πλοῦτον καὶ διασκεδάσει (Mars as chronocrator), 165.9 πλούτου διασκέδασιν (an unspecified malefic). As for courting penury, this is precisely what contrarian Christian ethics thinks we should do (John Chrys. *PG* 61.296.23 διώκωμεν πενίαν, 63.136.52 τὴν πενίαν ἀεὶ διώκωμεν, 232.11–12 Τὴν πενίαν τοίνυν ζητῶμεν, ταύτην διώκωμεν).

234–5 Like the aspersions of Cicero against Antony or Piso, or the tittle-tattle about Julius Caesar and Augustus,[134] and an ongoing topos of invective in the later empire when the astrological texts were compiled (Apuleius, *Apol.* 74.7, of the youth of his foe Herennius Rufinus). This one is too brief to include the usual topoi about selling oneself for money (recycled for Alexander of Abonouteichos, Lucian, *Alex.* 5), or effeminate appearance (which would anyway gainsay the physiognomy). But it does combine homosexuality in youth and maturity which, according to Richlin, was the worst insult invective could muster: the guilty party didn't even grow out of it (Richlin, 98).

---

[134] Cic. *Phil.* 2.44; Suet. *Jul. Caes.* 49, *Aug.* 68; W. A. Krenkel, 'Sexual Allegations for Political Ends', *Ciceroniana*, 7 (1990), 183–91, at 186–7, and *passim*; Richlin, 94, 98, 101 (and ch. 4 on invective generally), 220–1, 242 n. 30; E. Eyben, *Restless Youth in Ancient Rome* (London, 1993), 235–7, and bibliography in n. 205; J. W. Knust, *Abandoned to Lust: Sexual Slander and Ancient Christianity* (New York, 2006), 35–7; J. Meister, 'Reports about the "Sex Life" of Early Roman Emperors: A Case of Character Assassination?', in E. Shiraev and M. Icks (eds.), *Character Assassination Through the Ages* (New York, 2014), 59–81, at 62–4; Thonemann 2021, 74–5.

236 ἢ ψάλτριαν, ἢ πολύκοινον: for the combination of musical entertainers and prostitutes (n. on 5.143 μουσῳδόν; L. McClure, *Courtesans at Table: Gender and Greek Literary Culture in Athenaeus* (London and New York, 2003), 21–2) see P.Oxy. 840.36 αἱ πόρναι καὶ α[ἱ] αὐλητρίδες (Jesus' riposte to a Pharisee); Gospel of the Nazoreans, no. 18 'one who squandered his master's substance with harlots and flute-girls' (a version of Matth. 24:14–15, which itself says no such thing). ψάλτριαι are on precisely the same footing as dancing-girls, flute-girls, and the rest of the sympotic rabble.[135] Other female musicians in astrology: to 5.143 add Dor.^{ARAB} II 16.11 (Saturn and Venus in opposition): 'he will marry a disgraced songstress.' For πολύκοινον, the common whore, see on 5.142 and 2.180; and for the topos of squandering patrimony on whores, Callon, 267–72.

237 Did the poet plunder Hes. *Op.* 210 ἄφρων δ', ὅς κ' ἐθέλῃ πρὸς κρείσσονας ἀντιφερίζειν directly, or did he draw on an anthology, where this and perhaps the next line were quoted (as in Stob. 3.4.3, and by George Pelagonius and Michael Apostolius; Theon, *Progymn.* p. 74.18 has just 210) as a simple *bon mot* about foolhardiness? Either way, the poet confuses standing up against a powerful foe (the hawk in the Hesiodic original) with what he presumably meant to say about cowardice. The compound ἐκπτώσσει, though *hapax*, respects the *sedes* and reflects the construction (LSJ πτώσσω, II) of the simplex in *Il.* 20.427 ἀλλήλους πτώσσοιμεν.

238 The effect of Mars at 2.420, 3.69 (exile), 1.179; Mars and Jupiter in opposition at 3.173–4; Mars and Mercury in 5.89. There is a certain similarity to 4.521–6, where natives are wanderers, and prefer living abroad to loyalty to their native lands, though the agencies are different.

239 Full of forgers though astrology is, it does not seem elsewhere to make forgery the reason for exile. This perhaps has the circumstantial detail of an individual chart. γραφαί are unspecified documents, such as wills (Hephaestion, i. 331.26), contracts (Antiochus, *CCAG* vii. 110.18), or letters (Theophilus, *CCAG* xi/1. 264.10, 12), less often mentioned in astrology than γραπτά (n. on 3.97–8), but equally usefully vague.

240–1 Reading (ἐπερείδεται) ὕψοσε γαίης in the previous line, D'Orville understood a reference to being lifted above the ground (5.219 n.), with crucifixion as a punishment for forgery. For the metaphor in εἰς στεινὸν ζωῆς, see on 1.171; as for the rest of the couplet I throw away my shield.

---

[135] Theopompus, *FGrH* 115 F 213 αὐλητρίδας καὶ ψαλτρίας καὶ πεζὰς ἑταίρας; Plut. *Agis* 33.4, *Mor.* 644 C; Tatian, *Orat.* 33.4; al.

242 εὐτράπελος means basically versatile, of persons, or words in Ar. *Vesp.* 469. εὐτραπελία can extend to wit or facetiousness (Webb 2017, 222, and *passim*; cf. Hesychius, ε 7247 εὐτράπελος· γελοιώδης), but 'shifty', 'devious', 'duplicitous', 'untrustworthy', are senses better suited to writings ('By means of dishonest documents he leads a joyous life': Lopilato).[136] Are we to think back to 231 πολύτροπον, of the individual himself? The line-ending is remodelled in 271 βίοτον μεθοδεύων, and there is a similar formulation of the path-of-life cliché in Anacreontea, 40.2 βιότου τρίβον ὁδεύειν. For the metaphor, see 4.551 n., where it was suggested to be particularly apt for astrology. διοδεύειν is indeed used of planetary motion in astrological prose, and in verse by 'Antiochus', ll. 28, 45 (*CCAG* i. 109.24, 110.14).

243–5

Moon in *synaphe* with Mercury. This is obvious enough. The outcome suggests a connection with Θ p. 208.19–23 (attributed to Anubion), though ῥήτορα and σοφιστήν are common enough.

244 σημαίνει: see i. 9, 21, 39; 4.109 and 1.5 nn.; and Heilen 2015, 1373, an important addition. In practice σημαίνειν is used diffusely in astrological texts to mean 'give signs about' a given topic, as in 6.110 (the only other use of σημαίνειν in the corpus), where a particular sign gives indications about nurture, or as when a *kentron* represents one of the actors in a catarchic prediction; or, as here, just 'indicates' an outcome. But it cannot be pressed to mean that the signs only indicate, as opposed to cause (see i. 58 and n. 56, and note on 1.5 τελέουσιν), and Heilen notes that astrological compilers become increasingly careless about the crucial distinction between signification and causation. Ptolemy, on the other hand, makes much use of ἐπι-, προ-, δια- σημαίνειν unambiguously to mean 'signify', which reflects either or both conservatism in the use of terminology (Böker, *RE* Suppl. IX, s.v. Wetterzeichen, 1619.26–7) and caution about committing to hard astrology (i. 9).

ἐν μελέταισι σοφιστήν: LSJ II.1.c 'rehearsal, declamation'. The general sense is training, practice, ἄσκησις, the third element in the triad of a rhetor's requirements along with natural talent and theoretical knowledge (Plat. *Phaedr.* 269 D; Isocr. *Antidosis*, 188).[137] The specific one is the fictitious speech ('what would *x* say') on which orators were trained (W. Kroll, *RE* s.v. Melete 1); D. A. Russell,

---

[136] Rather than the indeterminacy of the omni-applicable oracles in Aristophanes, which anyway are specifically books (i. 19).
[137] E. Fantham, *The Roman World of Cicero's De Oratore* (Oxford, 2004), 68 and n. 39, 82; L. Pernot, transl. W. E. Higgins, *Rhetoric in Antiquity* (Washington, DC, 2005), 219; Leeman and Pinkster on Cic. *De Oratore*, i. 211.

Greek Declamation (Cambridge, 1983), 10–15; Brunt 1994, 29; J. Lauwers, *Philosophy, Rhetoric, and Sophistry in the High Roman Empire: Maximus of Tyre and Twelve Other Intellectuals* (Leiden, 2015), 21 n. 21).

245 εὔγραμμον: not a new adjective, but used in the new sense of 'literate' (not 'well drawn'); so too Hephaestion, i. 16.14 εὐγράμματος (*hapax*) and *CCAG* xi/2. 125.5 εὐγραμματισμένους (among the specialisms of Mercury).

πινυτόν: n. on 1.131–2.

ἴσον Ἑρμῇ: if Axtius and Rigler's emendation is right, the hyperbole is born of rewriting Iliadic ἶσον Ἄρηϊ (2×). For Mercury and the gymnasium, see i. 700.

246–51

Saturn, Mars, Moon, Venus in scaly signs. These engender skin diseases like psoriasis that make the skin flake (possibly including leprosy, but the proper name of the latter in ancient authors was elephantiasis: see on 1.50–7).

Firmicus has a number of charts which bring about some combination of *maculae, leprae,* and *impetigines*, where the essential element is the harm done to the Moon, whether by both malefics (3.5.30, 6.31.35) or by one (4.19.35; 7.20.11, Mars alone in opposition to the Moon in the same four signs as here); some specify that the character of the signs determines the kind of affliction (7.21.4). Among Greek sources there is an almost exact match from the general chapter Καθολικὰ σχήματα περὶ σινῶν καὶ παθῶν, Θ p. 189.25–6, among charts which the compiler notes were not included by οἱ παλαιοί. This lists exactly the same planets as here, but lacks Capricorn. Other versions fasten specifically on the Moon (Epit. II = 'Antiochus', *CCAG* i. 147.4–10 (adding Aries);[138] Θ p. 183.2–3 (from Περὶ σχημάτων Σελήνης καθολικῶν) (also lacking Capricorn)). Finally, there are many lists of scaly signs (5.251 n.), from which I single out *CCAG* i. 166.15–19 (Hübner 1982, 151, §3.223.21, 197, §3.423.41), which (i) lists the same four as here (Pisces, Cancer, Scorpio, and 'in part' Capricorn), which it classifies as both ἰχθυακά and λεπρώδη, (ii) mentions their leprous effect when the Moon or ASC is located in them, and (iii) describes them for that reason also as δίχρωμα (i.e. bi-coloured, although not multi-coloured).

Although Saturn's name of Πρέσβυς is very characteristic of Dorotheus (i. 920), a definite connection with him cannot be established. No Greek fragment of Dorotheus mentions λέπρα. There is a reference to leprosy in Dor.^ARAB II 15.7, but not in the Moon + malefics type of chart.

---

[138] Of this chapter the heading alone appears in Epit. IIIa = Antiochus, *CCAG* viii/3. 105.25 Τίνα τούτων λεπρώδη καὶ ἀλφώδη καὶ ψωροποιὰ ἢ λειχηνώδη.

247-8 ἐκ φολίδων πολλῶν... καὶ λεπίδων πολλῶν: for a zoological writer, φόλις is a horny plate, while λέπις is the scale of a fish. Astrology, however, whose classification is looser, treats the two as interchangeable (Hübner 1982, 148–9). On scaly signs (λεπιδωτά, φολιδωτά), see i. 876 and n. 11, and on 5.181–8. This is our fullest list (Hübner, §3.222.11).

248 λεπτῶν I think is decorative, but πολυχρώμων not, or not merely, if it can be related to the little treatise on the character of signs that describes them as δίχρωμα (p. 957). In another group of texts (Hübner 1982, 152, §3.223.32), Pisces is singled out as ποικίλον (variegated), cf. esp. (on Pisces) Rhetorius, *CCAG* vii. 211.6 λεπιδωτόν, ποικίλον, λεπρῶδες, ἀλφῶδες, Camaterus, *Introd.* 1604–5 λεπιδωτὸν, ἀλφῶδες .... ποικίλον καὶ λεπρῶδες.[139]

249 Πρέσβυς: i. 911 n. 19.[140] λοίγιος Ἄρης: i. 909 n. 5, to which add further EGHP precedent: ps.-Hes. *Scut.* 192, 441, and Hes. fr. 10a.69 M.–W. οὔλιος Ἄρης.

250 Μήνη κεραή: i. 904 n. 1.

γλαυκιόωσα Κυθήρη: i. 907 n. 20. The appropriate meaning is 'fiery', as in the passages where the extended form in -ιόων occurs in similes describing a lion's eyes (M. Leumann, *Homerische Wörter* (Basel, 1950), 151); Russo on ps.-Hes. *Scut.* 430). The sense of blue-grey is unsuitable for a planet which, when it is ascribed a colour, is either white or golden (4.225 n.); P. G. Maxwell-Stuart, *Studies in Greek Colour Terminology*, Volume I *Γλαυκός* (Leiden, 1981), 44, connects the 'whitish glare' with the pathological outcome. Grand-Clément, 257–8, nonetheless wants blue to remain part of the implicature even of the 'fiery' meaning.

251 Literally: an itching disease, a scaly disease, diseases of whiteness, lichens. These regularly go together in medicine (e.g. Galen, *De simpl. med. temp.* xi. 874.3–4 Kühn πρὸς ἀλφοὺς καὶ λειχῆνας καὶ ψώρας καὶ λέπρας), and the association remains in astrology, which uses the descriptive labels λεπρῶδες, λειχηνῶδες, ἀλφῶδες, though for some reason not ψωρῶδες, which is common in medical writers (Hübner 1982, 196–9). The same four signs mentioned here constitute the basic core of those described as λεπρῶδες, but Cancer is mostly missing as ἀλφῶδες, and Scorpio as λειχηνῶδες. The system is not Ptolemaic: when Ptolemy mentions these diseases, he uses a different taxonomy (3.13.14,

---

[139] Catarchic astrology also refers to 'multi-coloured' signs in connection with lost objects (Hübner 1982, 152, §3.223.31: Hephaestion, i. 311.19 ποικίλα; Dor.^ARAB V 35.66 'variegated'; §3.223.32: *CCAG* i. 103.21–2 πολύχρωμα).

[140] A text cited by Bouché-Leclercq, 94 n. 2, connects seniority with Saturn's primacy among the planets, on which see n. on 4.14 παντὸς... αἰθέρος ἄρχει. Bouché-Leclercq's page reference to the anonymous commentator on the *Tetrabiblos* (cited in n. 56), however, is not correct.

tropic and equinoctial; 3.13.17, terrestrial and piscine). In the Galen passage these conditions are treated by hellebore, which has a heating effect, implying that the conditions are intrinsically 'cold'. That does not, however, seem to be how astrology regards these diseases, which does not make them specifically Saturnian, but (as discussed above) tends to involve the Moon and both malefics, or Mars alone.

252–5

Mars in a *kentron* with Mercury in house of Sun, aspecting one or both luminaries. This small tweak on the stock situation of luminaries being harmed by malefics is partly paralleled in the same chapter from which the previous chart was taken, in Θ p. 189.13–14 (from the Καθολικὰ σχήματα περὶ σινῶν καὶ παθῶν): Mars in the house of the Sun in the absence of benefics harms eyes (cf. *Lib. Herm.* xxxii. 36 and 2.354). Mars has the same effect directly with the Sun in Περὶ κράσ. 98 αὐτοὶ δὲ τοὺς ὀφθαλμοὺς βλάπτονται and 161 ἔνιοι καὶ τοὺς ὀφθαλμοὺς ἐβλάβησαν (contradicting the logic that the Sun's effect nullifies Mars' power); the correspondence with Περὶ σχημ. 115 and Firmicus, 6.24.1 (although 2.421–5 is too sketchy to retain this particular detail) suggests it had a place in Dorotheus' underlying poem. Finally, there is at least a counterpart in the protasis of Θ pp. 217.24–218.1, where Mars in the house of the Sun, accompanied by Mercury on *kentra*, produces desperadoes. This is curious, because that chart takes its place in the Περὶ μίμων sequence which was broken off after 188, and will shortly be concluded with another very altered reworking of Θ p. 218.3–6 + 7–8 in 260–73. See p. 321.

253 καθορώμενος: the lines in Θ p. 222.12 parallel to 222 (pp. 949–50) had used the active καθόρα, and the corresponding passive is found in 6.40 and 312 as well as here. For the meaning 'aspect', see on 1.98.

ἐχθρὸς ἐπ' ἐχθρῷ: normally this preposition is used in expressions of accumulation (Gygli-Wyss, 74–5, 96; Fehling, 226),[141] but the sense of juxtaposition (Archil. fr. 119 W. κἀπὶ γαστρὶ γαστέρα | προσβαλεῖν μηρούς τε μηροῖς, cf. Gygli-Wyss, 98) approaches that of confrontation, which is more useful in astrology (see i. 197–8, 220, on word-order figuring aspect). It was unexpectedly hard to find other examples at hexameter-end.

254 εἰ μέν θ' ἕνα φωσφόρον: Rigler's correction, or something very like it, is obviously right (for the one eye–both eyes pattern, see also 6.548–52 and Ptol.

---

[141] To the examples in Gygli-Wyss, 75 n. 2, add Hes. fr. 204.105 M.–W. ἄλγος ἐπ' ἄλγει and Soph. *Antig.* 595 πήματα φθιτῶν ἐπὶ πήμασι. See also on 5.57. For *Od.* 7.120–1, see also Fehling, 317 and Gygli-Wyss, 91, and for Hes. *Op.* 361 σμικρὸν ἐπὶ σμικρῷ, Fehling, 224.

3.13.7–9). Although the exact collocation does not recur, one might compare, especially in a bipartite expression, *Il*. 23.319–22 ἀλλ' ὃς μέν θ'... ὃς δέ κε; *Od*. 7.123–4 τῆς ἕτερον μέν θ'... ἑτέρας δ' ἄρα τε. φωσφόρον as a common noun = 'luminary' seems to be unique here, though M^b has used it with dependent genitives for Venus (4.55) and Mercury (4.207); more importantly, a fragment of Nechepso–Petosiris new with respect to Riess (+27 Heilen, from Theophilus, *CCAG* xi/1. 223.21) calls the Sun ὁ Φωσφόρος, which could (Heilen 2015, 653 n. 1300) preserve poetic diction (conceivably iambic, since parts of φωσφόρος occur seven times in Euripidean iambics).

255 ἀλαὸν καὶ πηρὸν ἔθηκεν: *Il*. 2.599 πηρὸν θέσαν; opportunistically, *Il*. 8.188 πυρὸν ἔθηκεν.

256–9

Waxing Moon applies to Jupiter. This is at least generically similar to Θ p. 208.19–22. The effect of the Moon's *synaphe* with Jupiter is predictably good (*Π.σ.α.* p. 182.23–4; Firmicus, 3.3.1). Purple robes are the only individuating touch.

256 For the individual epithets see pp. 363–4. The accumulation, including a cultic epithet alongside the celestial ones, is rather remarkable, and one wonders whether it is, for once, keyed into the outcome rather than being a random assemblage, if 259 is taken to mean that the natives are priests.

257 Μήνης ὑποδέξεται ἱερὸν ὄμμα: the eye of the Moon is sometimes paired with that of the Sun, an old Indo-European notion,[142] but it can be mentioned alone (Rizzini, 132), and ὄμμα Σελήνης is a LGHP hexameter ending (3× Nonn. *D*.; John of Gaza, *Descr.* 238; *AP* 14.140.2). ὑποδέξεται, which I interpret as a short-vowel subjunctive (p. 333), is fairly unusual, since the verb is normally used in astrology of a planet being received into a house (e.g. Paul, *Anacephalaeosis*, p. xxiv. 4) or sign (e.g. Valens, II 32.1, 34.1), or of a planet encountering the dodecatemories (Θ p. 195.7–8) or terms (Θ p. 214.15, 20; Epit. IIIb, *CCAG* vii. 117.16; 'Valens', *CCAG* viii/1. 240.22–3) of another. The closest parallels seem to be in Paul, for *synaphe*: p. 60.7 ('Ο δὲ τοῦ Ἄρεως) τὴν τῆς Σελήνης συναφὴν

---

[142] The Sun's eye: West 2007, 172, 199. Both Moon and Sun together: Aesch. fr. dub. 451s 75.4–5 Radt = fr. 585.4–5 Mette ἡλίου τε [καὶ φίλον | φαιδρᾶς σελήνης] ὄμμα [restored by Mette]; then securely in Plut. *Mor.* 372 в (of the Egyptians: see Gwyn Griffiths, comm. on ch. 44, p. 186,21, and Sext. Emp. *Adv. Math.* 5.31); ps.-Galen, xix. 161.12–13 Kühn οἷον ὀφθαλμοῖς ἡλίῳ καὶ σελήνῃ; Nonn. *D*. 9.67; *Catenae in Nov. Test., In Coloss.* p. 326.16–17; Theodorus Studites, *Catechesis*, 59, p. 165.18–19 ἥλιον καὶ σελήνην ὡς δύο τινὰς ὀφθαλμοὺς φωτεινούς; H. Schmedt, *Antonius Diogenes: Die unglaublichen Dinge jenseits von Thule: Edition, Übersetzung, Kommentar* (Berlin and Boston, 2020), 155.

ὑποδέξεται, sim. p. 76.1; for other aspects: p. 72.8 ὁ ὑποδεξάμενος τὸν τῆς Ἀφροδίτης ἀστέρα. One can also compare the simplex in 6.79–80 συναφήν τε Σελήνης δεχνυμένου, 6.162 δεχνυμένης αὐτοῦ συναφήν, and Apomasar, *De Rev.* p. 34.7. Still, the use is a minority one. The result is a line-end of a shape (-εται ἱερὸν — —) that is occasional (ps.-Hes. *Scut.* 99 περιμαίνεται ἱερὸν ἄλσος; Theodotus, *SH* 757.7 καταφαίνεται, ἱερὸν ἄστυ, of biblical Shechem), rather than distinctively late antique. It is mildly interesting that two uses are in oracles (*Or. Sib.* 13.96 ῥύσεται ἱερὸν ἄστυ; Or. ap. Paus. 4.12.4 ἐπόψεται ἱερὸν ἦμαρ).

258-9 The wearers of purple could be big men and/or high priests who are also distinguished by purple robes (see on 2.234–5 and p. 1062; 1.101, where the planet is Venus; 5.23).[143] Verse collocations for purple robes standardly link them to kingliness and (oriental) luxury.[144] One of the few that, like this passage, has real-life office-holders in mind is *AP* 9.383.5 Τυβὶ δὲ πορφύρεον βουληφόρον εἷμα τιταίνει, where the Egyptian month Tybi figures as the equivalent of the Roman January, when the new consuls took up office.[145]

260–73

Saturn κατέχων Mercury in Aries, aspecting the Moon in her exaltation, and ruling the ASC. This fairly complex chart has an almost exact parallel in Θ p. 218.3–6. This is the penultimate entry in the chapter Περὶ μίμων, and the only one to contain a mixture of πρᾶξις, σίνος, and ἦθος. The only difference in the protasis is that Saturn *et al.* are in the house of the other malefic: Aries is one of the houses of Mars. Taurus is the exaltation of the Moon. In the apodosis, the chief differences are that the two charts reverse the order of πρᾶξις and σίνος (or rather πάθος, disability), and that M^d has a great deal more on ἦθος.

The corresponding version in Epit. IIIb is similar:

> ἐὰν ὁ Κρόνος καὶ ἡ Ἀφροδίτη καὶ Σελήνη τύχωσιν ἐν Ταύρῳ, ποιοῦσι σοφόν [‹φιλό›σοφον Cumont], ῥήτορα, μαθηματικόν, χαριέστατον καὶ φιλόμουσον (*CCAG* vii. 118.11–12).

---

[143] In practice, despite the material in n. 52, fragments of purple fabric from the Roman garrison at Didymoi in Upper Egypt (1st–3rd c. AD) show how far down the social scale the wearing of purple had spread. The dumps contain both 'true' purple derived from molluscs (not just imitation dyes) and cheaper dyes. Recycling may come into question, but some clothes seem new, in which case they must have been affordable to the low- and middle-ranking inhabitants of this fort (Cardon *et al.*, 204–7).

[144] Aesch. *Ag.* 959–60; Bion, *Epit. Adon.* 79 εἵμασι πορφυρέοισιν (dead Adonis); *SH* 958.15 π]ορφυρέοισιν ἐν εἵμασιν (luxury the Gauls do *not* enjoy); *Or. Sib.* 14.203 πορφύρεον ῥήξουσι κλυτὸν βασιλήιον εἷμα; luxury/decadence: Greg. Naz. *PG* 37.1542.11–1543.1, 1562.4–5. Line-initial: ps.-Opp. *Cyn.* 1.356 εἵματα πορφύρεα; Greg. Naz. *PG* 37.1314.7 Εἵματι πορφυρέῳ.

[145] E. Courtney, 'The Roman Months in Art and Literature', *MusHelv* 45 (1988), 33–57, at 39, and N. M. Kay, 161, on *Anth. Lat.* 106.1 (117R), with Latin parallels.

962   *Commentary on Book Five*

Every item in the apodosis matches Θ, but Mercury is replaced by Venus, who is now in her own house and hence presumably holds particular sway. This is important because there are also elements in the charts of both M^d and Θ which strongly suggest the presence of Venus—χαριέστατον and φιλόμουσον (Θ), as well as πουλύγαμον, εὔμουσον (and more Muses in 272), and φιλοπαίγμονα (eroticism, cultured playfulness) in the present chart.[146]

Nor is this all. In Θ there is one more chart at the very end of the chapter (p. 218.7–8) in which Mars and Venus in quartile or opposition ἐν τοῖς αὐτοῦ κλίμασι produce ἰατροὺς ... καὶ φιλοσόφους. The corresponding chart in Epit. IIIb reads as follows:

ἐὰν ἡ Ἀφροδίτη ‹καὶ ὁ› Κρόνος ‹ἢ› ὁ Ἄρης ἐν διαμέτρῳ, τραυλὸν ποιεῖ καὶ ῥευματιζόμενον, μάλιστα ἐν τοῖς ‹βορείοις suppl. Boll› κλίμασι τοῦ Κρόνου βορείου ὄντος (CCAG vii. 118.12–15).

This, too, is worth mentioning because, although its protasis is now quite unlike M^d's original, this chart does add the word τραυλὸν before ῥευματιζόμενον. This is missing in Θ itself, but present in line 263 here. Given this obvious connection, one then looks back at the corresponding Θ p. 218.7–8 and wonders whether its doctors and philosophers are *also* adumbrated in M^d. Could οὗ πόρος ἐστὶ φύσις in 270 incorporate the meaning 'whose livelihood is *human* nature', i.e. 'physiology', among the various branches of ancient natural philosophy (λόγοι φυσικοί)?

We therefore have a number of complicatedly interrelated sources. Each scrambles the data differently, but the present one has essentially (i) all of the protasis and apodosis of Θ p. 218.3–6; (ii) possible shades of Θ p. 218.7–8 (doctors and/or philosophers?); (iii) lisping from the apodosis of the second chart in Epit. IIIb; and (iv) relics of the influence of Venus which is still present in the first chart in Epit. IIIb.

These data are not explained simply by omissions. It seems rather that one of two things happened. *Either* there was a chart which originally included both Venus and Mercury (which would account for both the intellectual dexterity and the charm), a chart which does not survive in full; the descendants of this chart variously omitted Venus (leaving the charm hanging, as in M^d and Θ p. 218.3–6) or Mercury (leaving the wisdom hanging, as in Epit. IIIb's first

---

[146] For the combination of charm, culture, and marital difficulties, see, for instance, Θ p. 132.16–18 Ἀφροδίτη δὲ ὡροσκοποῦσα χαρίεντας, τερπνούς, φιλομούσους, πολυκοίνους λέγει τοὺς γεννηθέντας, οὐκ εὐγάμους δέ. The combination of intellectual gifts, culture, charm, and a light touch in erotic relationships is found in Θ pp. 175.15–176.7 under the joint influence of Mercury and Venus: note especially ἐμφιλοσόφους ... φιλομούσους ... ἐπιχαρεῖς ... εὐκινήτους περὶ τὰ ἀφροδίσια. πουλύγαμον is also suggestive, since Mars and Venus in either opposition or quartile, as they are in Θ p. 218.7–8, or just opposition in Epit. IIIb, do indeed engender instability/inconstancy, as well as upsets involving children (see on 268).

chart). *Or* the original chart contained Venus, which was for some reason at some point simply replaced with Mercury, perhaps at this stage with the addition of some characteristic effects of the injury of Mercury by Saturn (deafness, dumbness). I prefer the first possibility. It may be that in the course of this adjustment, Taurus was reconceived: initially it had been included because it was one of the houses of Venus, but M^d, who has the Venus-less version, represents it as the exaltation of the Moon. Finally, it would appear that Epit. IIIb has split the Venus chart into two. The first has Saturn, Venus, Moon, no Mercury, but retains both intellect and charm. The second has a new protasis, dropping the Moon and adding Mars, and introducing the relationship of opposition, but with a reference to dumbness which continues to imply the presence of the lost Mercury.

One final point is that Koechly had intuited that this apotelesma contained interpolations. He bracketed 265-7 ['hic aliunde intrusum videtur'], 268 ['item, sed rursus ex alio loco', and 270-1 ['etiam alieni videntur']. 265 is certainly not an interpolation because it is backed by Θ p. 218.4-5 and by the first chart in Epit. IIIb. But it is quite true that the verses from that point onwards cease to find correspondences in those charts (hence, Koechly's original insight was not perfect but typically intuitive). On Koechly's model this was evidence of interpolation of verses on the part of an editor, but it could also be the result of the poet himself trying to combine some of the many related charts which were circulating (perhaps under a heading such as we find in Epit. IIIb, Περὶ ῥητόρων καὶ παιδευτῶν καὶ ἑτέρων ὑποθέσεων). Thus, the suggestions of a doctor's chart in 270-1 would come from conflating Θ p. 218.3-6 with the outcome of 218.7-8, and the suggestions of unhappy marriage/family problems in 268 suggest a chart in which Venus interacted badly with Mars, two entities present in Epit. IIIb's second chart.

260 κατέχων: normally this would be used for a planet occupying a centre, or occasionally a sign (i. 879[147]), rarely occupying degrees (Hephaestion, i. 115.7). In ps.-Palchus, CCAG viii/1. 250.25 ἡνίκα δὲ τὸ τετράπλευρον τῆς Σελήνης κατέχουσιν...οἱ ἀστέρες, it appears to mean 'be in quartile with'. The closest available parallels, where a planet is the object of the verb, seem to be Ptol. 3.15.3 ὅταν οὕτως ἔχοντες οἱ κακοποιοῦντες ἐπὶ φάσεως οὖσαν κατέχωσι τὴν σελήνην (for the passive construction, being controlled by a malefic, see Valens, II 30.21) and Anubion, F 12.22 Μήνη ὅταν Θοῦρο[ν κατέ]χηι κέν[τρ]οιο κρ[ατοῦσα] = 12 Perale. The verbs are rendered respectively by Robbins 'control' and by Perale 'take over'. This could of course be in a number of different ways,

---

[147] *Kentron*: 6.191, 672; 1.176 (see n.), 267; 'Antiochus', ll. 17, 32 (*CCAG* i. 109.12, 29); Hephaestion, i. 231.6, 325.18; Dorotheus, p. 342.10; Balbillus, *CCAG* viii/3. 103.16. Sign: 3.394; 6.274.

964   Commentary on Book Five

and Lopilato ad loc. takes the reference to be to the phenomenon of περισχέσις (Bouché-Leclercq, 251), where one planet 'blocks' another by casting rays to the signs to the left and right of it. In sum the meaning is not necessarily 'be in conjunction with', but the point is that Saturn dominates Mercury.

261 Exaltation: see on 5.33 and 173.

262 βραβεὺς τοῦ πνεύματος: apparently still referring to Saturn, not the horoscope, to which the application might have been easier (Epit. II = 'Antiochus', CCAG i. 160.16-18; Valens, IX 3.7; Paul, p. 50.17-18 Ἡ δὲ βάσις, ὅ ἐστιν ὡροσκόπος, ζωῆς καὶ πνεύματος παραιτία καθέστηκεν). A βραβεύς is a judge or umpire, including at the games (Robert 1982, 263-6; J. Vélissaropoulos-Karakostas, 'Justice and Games: The Brabeus', in R. W. Wallace and M. Gagarin (eds.), *Symposion 2001: Papers on Greek and Hellenistic Legal History (Evanston, IL, Sept. 5-8, 2001)* (Vienna, 2005), 303-15, esp. 304-7). For an attempt to explain the application to Saturn, see Bouché-Leclercq, 323 n. 1; he is also βραβευτής in Pingree[1,2]. For his primacy among the planets, see on 4.14.

263 τραυλὸν ἐνὶ γλώσσῃ: lisping; sometimes specified as the inability to pronounce a certain letter (C. Laes, 'Silent History? Speech Impairment in Roman Antiquity', in Laes *et al.*, 145-80, at 150-1, 156, 158-9; on speech defects see also n. on 2.192-3). Only here in the Manethoniana, but common in astrology, along with other sub-categories of ἄλαλοι/κωφοί (dumb) such as the ψελλοί (inarticulate, incoherent) and βραγχοί (hoarse). It comes of Saturn injuring Mercury, and happens in all aspects except trine (Περὶ σχημ. 32, 71, 99, Π.τ.δ. 21, Περὶ κράσ. 76, 78; Dorotheus, p. 375.24; more complicatedly in Ptol. 3.13.12), hence perhaps the absence of any need to be more specific than κατέχων.

χαριέστατον εἶδος ἔχοντα: given the surrounding items, A.-R's correction ἀχαρίστατον looks convincing (it is in Π.σ.α. p. 183.30, *aporrhoia* from Venus), but χαριέστατον is confirmed by Θ, and rightly retained by De Stefani. What complicates matters is that χαριέστατον in Θ accompanies φιλόμουσον, whereas in M^d it is shifted among the handicaps. The present version looks secondary, since χαριέστατον and φιλόμουσον are a natural pair (compare e.g. Hephaestion, i. 233.15 χαρίεντα, μουσικά). The formula the poet has based his new version on is, appropriately, catalogic (ἐπήρατον/πολυήρατον εἶδος ἔχουσα; see Richardson on *HHom. Dem.* 315).

264 ταῖς ἀκοαῖσι βαρὺν: afflicted in the ears (an extension of the use of βαρύς with old age, suffering, and disease); ἀκοή = ear, LSJ II.3, adding Simonides, *PMG* 595, Eur. *IT* 1496, al.; also 2.192. Deafness there a co-harm inflicted by Saturn's effect on Mercury.

καὶ τοῖς ποσὶν ἠδὲ καὶ ἄρθροις: Θ has the additional detail that feet and joints are afflicted by ῥεύματα, obviously through the agency of the wet planet;[148] there is a parallel for Saturn's harming Mercury with this effect in *Liber ad Ammonem*, 2.14 (*PMGM* i. ed. Ideler) Οἱ μὲν γὰρ ὑπὸ Κρόνου καὶ Ἑρμοῦ κατακλινόμενοι, νωχελεῖς ἔσονται καὶ δυσκίνητοι [καὶ ἀναλγεῖς] τοῖς τε ἄρθροις καὶ παντὶ τῷ σώματι ἀπὸ ψύξεων καὶ ῥευματισμοῦ. M^d's use of the definite article at this point is haywire.

265 Corresponding to Θ, save for the relocation of χαριέστατον, and swapping round the rhetor and astrologer. πινυτόν (n. on 1.131–2) is decorative, but the interesting item is φιλόμουσον, which one would expect to be the result of the gracious and cultured Venus (4.492 n.; TLG s.v. Astrologica, φιλόμουσ-: many instances), and to be the natural twin of χαριέστατον. Mercury might bring this about on a good day (e.g. Mercury's sign, Gemini, does in Valens, I 2.19), but this is *not* a good day, blighted as Mercury is by Saturn. This is a trace of the original Venus chart (see argumentation above).

266 εὔστοχον ἄνδρα: this is appropriate for stochastic activities like medicine or astrology (i. 20), or for any undertaking whose outcome is uncertain but which, embarked on with due diligence, has a reasonable chance of success. Poetry is not such an activity. I have therefore removed the comma, first introduced by Gronovius, from the end of the previous line (there is no punctuation in L); ῥυθμοῖς καὶ μέτρων ποιήμασιν becomes padding of φιλόμουσον, and εὔστοχον ἄνδρα a phrase on its own. It is a good fit for Mercury's oversight of speculative intellectual enquiry (Ptol. 3.14.36 εὐστόχους, μαθηματικούς; *Περὶ κράσ.* 207 φυσιολόγους, εὐστόχους; Camaterus, *Introd.* 992).

267 †ἀπροφίδητον†: Koechly ad loc. in the Didot edition candidly admits he was not able to emend it, and no translation is attempted. In his second edition he prints ἀπρονόητον, which De Stefani praises without adopting ('ft. recte'). Presumably 'unpremeditated' or 'unpremeditating' is meant to parallel εὐθαρσῆ, which in turn—especially when taken in connection with the stormy next line—suggests the rash, inconsiderate effect of Mars. (See p. 962 for the presence of Mars in the second chart in Θ.) It is hard to make sense either of σχήμασιν with εὐθαρσῆ (the Didot rendering is simply literal, 'figuris audacem') or of χρώμασιν with the epithet here, whatever it is. Lopilato adopts a different reading.

268 πουλύγαμον, τέκνοισιν ἐπώδυνον: this is obviously a relic of a previous incarnation of this chart involving Venus (for Venus and polygamy, see Valens,

---

[148] Θ p. 158.16–17 ῥεύματα περὶ τοὺς πόδας (Saturn in DESC), pp. 191.19–192.1 ῥευματικοὺς ποιεῖ περὶ τοὺς πόδας καὶ τὰς χεῖρας (Lot of Fortune or its Lord aspected by Saturn). Wet signs bring about the combination ποδαλγοὶ ἢ ῥευματικοί (Θ p. 191.17; Epit. IIIb = *CCAG* vii. 112.9–10).

II 38.4; Apomasar, *De Myst.*, *CCAG* xi/1. 182.19–20), but conceivably, in the suggestion of family conflict, involves Mars as well (see n. 146).[149] The resolutely prose ἐπώδυνον, 'painful', of diseases or wounds, might, applied exceptionally to a person, support either or both of the meanings 'causing pain to', or 'suffering pain by reason of'; the latter sense, reinforced by πολύτλαν, could be a version of the frequent astrological motif of λῦπαι ἐπὶ τέκνοις (poeticised in 3.159 πένθεα γεινομένοισι τελεῖ δειλοῖς ἐπὶ τέκνοις).[150] ἐπώδυνος in this sense is rare, but attested in Zenodorus, Περὶ συνηθείας, p. 256.13 Μέλεος, συνήθως μὲν ὁ ταλαίπωρος καὶ ἐπίπονος καὶ ἐπώδυνος; Theophanus Continuatus, *Chron.* p. 122.1 τὴν ψυχὴν ὁ Θεόφιλος ἐπώδυνος γεγονώς.

269 The effective repetition of εὔμουσον from 265 φιλόμουσον contributes to suspicions about the amalgamation of plural charts. The associations of εὔμουσον (4.60 n.) are with Venus (of the other testimonia, Antiochus, *CCAG* xi/2. 110.17 εὐμουσίας involves Venus and the Sun; Critodemus, *CCAG* viii/1. 258.9 εὔμουσοι, ἐπιχαρεῖς, Venus' terms within Taurus). The same is presumably true of φιλοπαίγμονα, though the closest match in astrology, strangely, associates persons of this type with the Saturnian sign of Aquarius (Dorotheus, p. 413.18); Venus in Valens, I 1.30 φιλοπαιγνίους. If λιγυρόν suggests a singer, that would indicate the influence of both Mercury and Venus (6.506; also 2.334 λιγέως μέλποντας and n. ad loc.).

270–1 Especially given the astrologers in 265, this sounds like a renewed reference to someone who makes a living from natural science (see too 6.471 ἀθανάτων ἔργων φύσιος πέρι μητιόωσιν); a connection was suggested above with the philosophers and doctors of Θ's second chart. φυσικὸς λόγος means something no less general and non-technical than 'doctrines of natural philosophy' (e.g. Plut. *Pericl.* 6.1), though the Stoics made the territory their own and drew up a formidable taxonomy of its branches (Diog. Laert. 7.132; J. Mansfeld and D. T. Runia, *Aëtiana: The Method and Intellectual Context of a Doxographer*, II: *The Compendium*, i: (Leiden, 2009), 97–100; also the title of a work in at least eight books by Posidonius, F 4–12 E.-K.).

βίοτον μεθοδεύων: perhaps not just making a living, but doing so with a metaphor appropriate to a calling that involves systematic thinking (for the verb see 138–9 n.). In Ptolemy, 3.14.31, μεθοδευταί are born when Mars is allied with Mercury in good positions (rendered 'systematic workers' by Robbins/'one who goes to work by rule' LSJ), and in a list of signs suitable for different

---

[149] Mars in opposition to Venus: Περὶ σχημ. 85–6; Περὶ κράσ. 175; Firmicus, 6.17.2.

[150] e.g. Περὶ σχημ. 36 ἐπὶ τέκνοις λῦπαι; Περὶ κέντρ. 5 διὰ γυναῖκας καὶ τέκνα λύπας; Hephaestion, i. 12.5–6, 16.19–20, 21.4, 29.23–4, 62.14–15, 203.26–7; Teucer, *CCAG* vii. 208.10. In a real chart in Valens, VII 6.88 = no. L 105 Neugebauer–Van Hoesen πένθος βαρύτατον τέκνου φιλοστόργου θάνατον θεασάμενος. Firmicus typically uses part of *dolor*.

activities and groups of people, ps-Palchus, *Dodecateris Chaldaica, CCAG* v/1. 188.1-2, has τὰ δ' αἰνιγματώδη μεθοδευταῖς; whoever these people are, the implication is that they are linked with things cognitively difficult that need brains to overcome. It is true that some of the later astrological treatises seem to use μεθοδεύειν or μεθοδεύεσθαι simply for embarking on a task, without implications of persistence or intellectual dexterity (*CCAG* xi/2. 132.31; *CCAG* iv. 138.11, 22, 27).

272-3 εὐσύνθετον: already used in 5.26, but there of a work of art; its normal application is to words and verbal compositions. Apparently the transmitted accusative still agrees with βίοτον (Lopilato: '(so as to be) well-composed of life and art'). LSJ, however, creates a separate category referring to persons, meaning 'constructive', 'inventive', which with the following infinitive produces the acceptable sense 'well constituted for understanding', although it implies an emendation to the nominative εὐσύνθετος, which no one seems to have proposed, and leaves the genitives hanging. It is interesting that Ptolemy follows μεθοδευτάς (previous lemma) with εὐσυνθέτους at a short remove, but the required sense is 'capable of keeping faith with' (Robbins; 'easy to deal with' LSJ), of relations with other people. Then: 'by means of selections that provide ⟨intellectual⟩ *pabulum*, as well as their own inspiration', apparently meaning that they make selections of the best authors for exegesis and compose their own poetry, or otherwise exquisite literary works, as well. μέλισσα is used as in Anon. *AP* 9.505.6, 'poem', or Agathias, *AP* 16.36.1 μύθων τε καὶ εὐτροχάλοιο μελίσσης (Paton: 'discourses and well-running, honeyed speech', of the sophist Heraclamon). This is the least-worst rendering of an atrocious line.

Taking the apotelesma as a whole, I suggest that the subject is simultaneously a man of science and of literature—rhetor (265), poet (266), but also reputed for knowledge of natural science (271), one of the men praised in the many inscriptions that commemorate them for their generally all-encompassing culture.[151] He could be the sort of person who gave virtuoso rhetorical displays on cosmology and cosmogony (Dio Chrys. *Or.* 33.4), and if we think that the second chart in Epit. IIIb is relevant as well he could be one of the doctor-rhetoricians known to Dio (*Or.* 33.6) and Galen (*In Hippocr. Prognost. Comm.* xviiib. 258 Kühn [*CMG* V 9.2 p. 344], those called in the high empire *logiatroi* and, from the fourth century onwards *iatrosophistai*.[152] The reference to σοφία,

---

[151] Like Marcellus, in *AP* 7.158 (i. 866); Dioscorus (*GVI* 1907; *SEG* 34.1003 [Milan, late 4th/early 5th c. AD], cf. Agosti 2008, 204–6); Heraclitus of Rhodiapolis, *TAM* II. 910 (Pleket 1995, 32); E. Samama, *Les Médecins dans le monde grec: Sources épigraphiques sur la naissance d'un corps médical* (Geneva, 2003), 77–8. There is in fact a chart for a *medicosophista* in Lib. Herm. xxvi. 21, but it locates the Sun in the ASC and Jupiter in the MC.

[152] See A. Grilli, 'Iatrosophistes', *RIL* 122 (1988), 125–8; M. Plastira, 'AP 11.281: A Satirical Epitaph on Magnus of Nisibis', *AC* 72 (2003), 187–94, esp. 192; G. W. Bowersock, 'Iatrosophist', in

the thrice-repeated Muse trope, and even χαριέστατον (in Θ's presumably original version), while they have a background in astrology's jargon, all suit the epigraphic language of praise for these men.[153] In that case, with the idea of composition implicit in εὐσύνθετος one could perhaps compare Damascius' praise for the fifth-century philosopher (though not doctor) Agapius as τετράγωνος... τὴν σοφίαν (*Life of Isidorus*, F 127a Athanassiadi; cited by Agosti 2008, n. 78). He was well accommodated to, and habituated in, all branches of wisdom.

274–81

Miscellaneous charts involving Mercury.

274–7

Mercury in conjunction with Jupiter makes a money-lender, someone whose business is money. That is not the expected outcome. The closest I find comes in Περὶ κράσ. 122 Σὺν δὲ Ἑρμῇ ὢν ὁ Ζεὺς... ἔκ τε παρακαταθήκης καὶ δανείων ὠφελείας διδοῦσιν. There it is attributed to Valens, and not included among the material which seems to come from the shared source of M^a, Dorotheus, Firmicus, *et al*.

274 Εὔσφυρος: i. 906 n. 15.
συνοδεύοι: see on 5.62.

275 εὔπορος ἀκριβής τε: in Valens, I 3.18, Mercury's degrees within Cancer produce similar types in similar vocabulary, including the ἀκριβεῖς and εὔποροι; they too are money-lovers, but as tax-collectors rather than lenders. The εὔπορος, the type who 'fares well', is common enough in astrology, influenced by both Mercury and Jupiter,[154] but not truly distinctive. ἀκριβής, however, is more unusual, and specific to Mercury: Critodemus, *CCAG* viii/1. 259.15 ἀκρίβεια; Ptol. 3.14.18 ἀκριβεῖς (Saturn allied to Mercury in honourable positions); Π.σ.α. p. 183.33 ἀκριβεῖς μαθηματικούς (Moon moving towards Mercury; perhaps there should be a comma).

κυκλῶν τὸ νόμισμα: if the native were literally coining money this could be taken literally, 'making it round', but as it is it appears to mean that he makes it

---

Les Traditions historiographiques de l'antiquité tardive: Idéologie, propagande, fiction, réalité (11th Historiae Augustae Colloquium: 2008: Geneva, Switzerland) (Bari, 2010), 83–91.

[153] Agosti 2008, nn. 78, 80; Dioscorus (n. 151) is praised for excelling μύθωι καὶ χάρισιν (l. 8). For the cliché of Muses in encomia of *literati*, see Kaster, 49, 74 n. 177, 318, 332.

[154] A Mercurial characteristic in Valens, I 3.18, Additamenta Antiqua, IV 35; under Mercury's sign Virgo in Valens, I 2.50; brought about by the Moon's *synaphe* with Jupiter in Θ p. 208.22, by Jupiter with the Sun in Valens, I 19.10.

metaphorically go in circles, circulate. If so, this seems to anticipate a metaphor which gained currency (so to speak) at the end of the sixteenth century.[155] But there are at least two critical differences. There, the point was the analogy between the lubricating effect of money and the circulation of the blood; money was the life-blood of the body politic. There is no physiological metaphor here. Second, the lender is the subject, and the verb is transitive. The idea appears to be that he makes it go round in a circle, and the next lines imply that it returns in greater quantities than it started off. The claim is not that money is in *general* circulation.

276–7 One might have expected that the penny-pinching and stinginess, and the occupation of money-lender, would be produced by a chart in which Mercury is harmed, hardly by the liberal Jupiter. For μικρολογία engendered by Mercury and Saturn, see Ptol. 3.14.11, Hephaestion, i. 148.12–13; money-lenders born under Mercury and Mars, in 2.309 and 4.330 (though just Mercury and the Moon in 4.580–1 and 6.357, but NB the lacuna after 355). Yet Jupiter's sign, Sagittarius, produces μικρολόγους in Teucer, *CCAG* vii. 208.4; Jupiter can sometimes produce money-lenders (Valens, I 19.11 δανειστικούς);[156] in Valens, I 19.15, Mercury and Jupiter ἐν χρηματιστικοῖς ζῳδίοις... θησαυρῶν εὑρετὰς ποιοῦσιν ἢ ἐκ παραθηκῶν ὠφελουμένους δανειστικούς (Riley: 'moneylenders who profit from cash deposits'); and in the only other example of φιλάργυρος that I find in an apotelesma, Θ p. 142.3, Jupiter and Mercury are both involved (along with both luminaries, Venus, and the ascending node in the House of Bios, on which see on 5.228). This is quite a surprise, but see 1.132 n.

276 ἀναβαίνει: presumably the poet is trying to signal the kind of opprobrium-free success indicated for Jupiter and the Moon by Valens, I 19.11 (good men of business), and though it does not seem to be used for social ascent elsewhere in astrology, the verb implies the same metaphor as ἀναβιβασθῆναι (Valens: i. 289 n. 20; further on the metaphorical equation of elevation and social position, see 5.85 n.). It would be useful to make a closer comparison of Greek and Latin

---

[155] J. Johnson, 'The Money=Blood Metaphor, 1300–1800', *The Journal of Finance*, 21/1 (1966), 119–22; J. Cribb, 'The President's Address: Money As Metaphor 4', *NC* 169 (2009), 461–529, at 470–1; N. T. O. Mouton, 'Metaphor and Economic Thought: A Historical Perspective', in H. Herrera-Soler and M. White (eds.), *Metaphor and Mills: Figurative Language in Business and Economics* (Berlin, 2012), at 49–76, at 62–3; C. Resche, 'Towards a Better Understanding of Metaphorical Networks in the Language of Economics: The Importance of Theory-Constitutive Metaphors', ibid. 77–102, at 84–5, 91, 92; P. Briant, 'The Debate about the Spread of Alexander's Coinage and its Economic Impact: Engaging with the Historiographical *longue durée*', in S. Glenn, F. Duyrat, A. Meadows (eds.), *Alexander the Great: A Linked Open World* (Bordeaux, 2018), 235–47, at 236–7 (Droysen had used it to describe the effect of Alexander's conquests on the economy of the former Persian empire).

[156] Bram interprets Firmicus' *generatores* (7.26.10) in this way.

usage. Some of the Greek language of social improvement cited in i. 289 n. 20 does not imply upward movement at all (καταντάω quite the opposite; 5.306 ὁδεύει progress, but not ascent), whereas Latin *ascendere*, and the idea of *gradus*, is banal (J. Onians, 'Architecture, Metaphor and the Mind', *Architectural History*, 35 (1992), 192–207, at 202–3; Apomasar's ἄνω τύχη, i. 288, implies elevation but not necessarily ascent). It would seem that the sense of hierarchy crosses back into later Greek; LSJ Suppl. gives examples of ἀναβαίνειν used of promotion in Justinian (*Codex Justinianus* and *Novellae*), and this anticipates that usage. The question is by how much. What is entirely characteristic of astrology is of course that ascent does not consist in a structured career, a *cursus honorum*, but in money-grabs.

277 ψηφῶν: accented by A.–R. as if it were an agent noun equivalent to ψηφιστής (Περὶ κέντρ. 73, Περὶ κράσ. 207, both times Mercurial, as here; these people are somehow skilled in calculation, both in the vicinity of γραμματικούς, and the former of γεωμέτρας). While the form itself is dubious, and recherché formations are not this poet's usual style, it is easy to connect the word with astrological diction in general. Valens has three instances of ψηφικὰ πράγματα (IV 18.11, 20.12, 22.14), all connected with money-matters (ἀργυρικά), while the collocation with δανειστής can be illustrated by I 20.21 ἀπὸ λόγων καὶ ψήφων ἀναγομένους, δανειστικούς. See *BE* 1979 no. 556 for ψῆφος as the science of number, a usage which is illustrated by Valens, I 1.37, App. II 35, and Περὶ κράσ. 205, and by the frequent collocation λόγοι καὶ ψῆφοι (1.131–2 n.).

278–9
Mercury in the third place from the ASC. I infer that Jupiter has been dropped since the previous chart; he is absent from the next. The native is a fisherman (Appendix II, I.2.ii; p. 57). This is the House of Brothers, also called Θεά, specially associated with the Moon (5.122 n.), and that seems to be the reason for the outcome, for in 4.333–40, hunters and fowlers are also born from a vaguely worded configuration that gives two alternative forms of contact between the Moon and Mercury. There are no parallels in *dodecatopoi* (Firmicus, 3.7.6; Θ, Valens, Paul).

278 The catachresis results from the poet's determinedly bipartite compositional technique: the prepositional phrase occupying the first half of the line would be expected to depend on an expression of location in, e.g. τυχών (5.249 ἐν τούτοισι τυχών, the normal prose use; cf. 4.157 τυχὼν κατά; 1.282 καθ' ὡρονόμοιο τυχοῦσα), but he has combined it with the verse-pattern ὑπὸ στέρνοιο τυχήσας (etc.) used for encountering or striking. χώραισιν means 'places', an extension of χῶρος in this sense (i. 877 n. 20, adding Dorotheus, p. 407.21 for a sign).

279 ἀγρευτῆρι λίνῳ: the vast majority of instances of the agent noun are in the Oppians, anticipated by ps.-Theocr. 21.6 in the sense 'fisherman' and by Call. *Hymn* 3.218 in that of 'hunter'. The fact that Oppian reserves the adjectival use for a proem (*Hal.* 3.2 ἀγρευτῆρας ἀέθλους) suggests he intended it to be something a little out of the ordinary, and coupled with the new verbal compound this seems to represent a little moment of ambition by M^d as well. Nonnus also uses it as epithet (5× κύνες/κύνας ἀγρ., before caesura).

280-1

...and with Mars in opposition. The natives are hunters with nets, precisely as in Θ p. 212.11-12 and Epit. IV = *CCAG* ii. 191.17.

280 εἰ δ' Ἄρην ἐσίδοις: see on 1.73-4.

θυμούμενον: see on 5.74.

ἐκ διαμέτρου: prose expression.

281 δολίοισι βρόχοις: βρόχος is strictly a noose, and the usual Manethonian word for the rope of suicide (4.489 n.). The poet could be using it as a metonym for hunting nets in general—nooses *could* be used in hunting (Orth, *RE* s.v. Jagd, 571.30-49; Arrian, *Cyn.* 24.4)—but perhaps likelier is that he means the mesh of which a net was composed (ps.-Opp. *Cyn.* 1.151 δίκτυά τε σχαλίδας τε βρόχων τε πολύστονα δεσμά). The formulation applies the old topos of hunting and trickery,[157] which began with the *Odyssey* calling fish-bait δόλος (see on 4.243 δολοεργούς), to nets in particular—a logical state of affairs when a plan or stratagem can itself be metaphorically 'woven' (Detienne and Vernant, 53 n. 130). For the association with trickery, see Eur. *El.* 154-5 δολίοις βρόχων ἔρκεσιν (with good reason—of Agamemnon); Arrian, loc. cit. οὐ πάγαις οὐδὲ ἄρκυσιν οὐδὲ βρόχοις οὐδὲ ἁπλῶς δόλοις καὶ σοφίσμασιν ἐξαπατῶντες τὰ θηρία; ps.-Opp. *Cyn.* 3.258-9 ἐϋστρέπτοισι βρόχοισιν... δολίοισι λόχοις.

ὀρεσίτροφα: Homeric epithet of the lion, first revived in poetry here, and then, less conservatively by Nonnus as epithet of a herdsman (*D.* 15.204) and a wood (*D.* 37.9, different *sedes*).

282-3

Venus in Aspect with Mars.

---

[157] Detienne and Vernant, index s.v. hunting; Vendries, 129-30; C. Tsaknaki, 'Ars Venandi: The Art of Hunting in Grattius' *Cynegetica* and Ovid's *Ars Amatoria*', in S. J. Green (ed.), *Grattius: Hunting an Augustan Poet* (Oxford, 2018), 115-32, at 127-8. Applications of the topos (*passim* in ps.-Oppian) wobble along a spectrum that uses language implying disapproval (Grattius' words include 88 *falsus*; 45, 91 *fraus*; 91 *insidiae*) and pragmatism.

282 περιπλεξαμένην: embraces with this verb do not necessarily, in fact usually seem not to, have a sexual element (though see Call. *Ep.* 44.3 Pf.), but the poet has adapted an occasional astrological metaphor for contact, συμπλοκή,[158] with what is, in context, an obvious innuendo. There is a fairly similar metaphor in Dorotheus, p. 326.14 ἀσπάζηται, of a place welcoming a planet (but not of one planet greeting another).

283 For the sexual harms that come about when Venus and Mars are in aspect, see on 3.329–38. M[a] there concentrates on adultery, on which all sources agree. λάγνος is the natural counterpart of the μοιχός; their combination in astrology is trivial. Grammarians say it should be applied to libidinous males (as opposed to μάχλος for females) (i. 302 n. 22). Here, as it happens, it *is*—but astrology is equally full of λάγναι and μοιχάδες. Then with παντοπαθεῖς the poet suggests the sexual damage the planets cause in conjunction and in quartile in tropic signs: Περὶ κρασ. 173 κίναιδος, μαλακός, πασχητιῶν;[159] Περὶ σχημ. 48 μαλακοί, cf. 117; Dor.[ARAB] II 15.25; Firmicus, 6.11.5, cf. 6.24.4. The 'passive' words in Περὶ κρασ. and Firmicus (*patientur*) suggest that Dorotheus may have had some such formulation as well. In his choice of epithet M[d] is preceded by Statilius Flaccus, *AP* 5.5.4 = *Garland* 3799 παντοπαθῆ κούρης αἴσχεα (so the epithet is suitable for the passive partner of either sex). Before Byzantine Greek, the word is remarkably popular in the Clementina (TLG) for the shameless and abandoned nature of pagan gods.

284–99

Jupiter in houses of Venus, with luminaries well placed. See 2.221–31: wealth and social status are the themes.

284–5 ἐπίδοξος…ἐπίδοξα: often in astrological prose of natives and the planets' role in producing distinguished persons; sometimes of the nativity itself. But here, ἐπίδοξα seems to mean 'well placed' (Lopilato: 'benefic'), unless the second instance is deliberately offering an alternative sense ('if the luminaries are likely', i.e. conducive to such an outcome).

285 Unclear how παρέχει adds to ὑπάρχει: it *is* good, but only *gives* accordingly when the luminaries are well positioned too?

---

[158] Valens, I 1.40 τὰς τῶν ἀστέρων συμπλοκὰς ἑτεροσχήμονας; V 7.19 τὰς διαστάσεις τῶν ἀστέρων καὶ συμπλοκάς ('the same intervals and configurations': Riley); VII 6.39 κατὰ συμπλοκὴν καὶ ἐναντίωσιν ('by combination and opposition': Riley); *Liber ad Ammonem*, 2.5 οὐδὲν χωρὶς τῆς συμπλοκῆς τούτων γίνεταί τι τῶν ἀνθρωπίνων; Anon. *De Astrologia Dialogus*, p. 11.12 οὐδεμία τις ἀστέρων συμπλοκὴ καὶ περίοδος, 39.27–8 τῆς τῶν ἀστέρων πρὸς ἀλλήλους συμπλοκῆς.

[159] As a desiderative, this means that they do not just play the passive role, but, what is worse, they *want* to; for a disgustingly desirous passive homosexual, see also Richlin, 138.

286-7 The fact that physiognomy has been included in a chart involving *topikai diakriseis* deserves note. It was not at all characteristic of the material shared between Mᵃ, *Π.τ.δ.*, and *Lib. Herm.* The best parallels for much of this are in fact reviews of decans (Hephaestion, i. 12.17 ξανθός, λευκός; Camaterus, *Introd.* 253-4, 572). The physiognomy itself is routine. As in 5.229-30 (see n.), the first two items are stature and eyes; complexion and hair follow.

286 περικαλλέες: this supports other indices of perfect physique in this and the next line, although in EGHP, where it originates, where it applies to human beings at all (as opposed to objects, with which it is more common), it describes females. But it also describes Odysseus' eyes at the moment when Athena transforms them in *Od.* 13.401, 433.

ὄμμασι γαῦροι: a characterisation, less of the eyes themselves, which in white-complexioned Jovians are said to be large (Ptol. 3.12.4), but more of their expression: 'haughty'. The physiognomists do not otherwise use the word, but it suggests the same manly quality as in a description of an emperor, otherwise with similar elements to this, by John Scylitzes, *Synops. hist.*, John Tzimiskes, 22 (~ Leo Diaconus, *Hist.* p. 96.18) ὀφθαλμοὶ τούτῳ ἀνδρώδεις καὶ χαρωποί. One of the other occurrences of γαῦρος in the corpus applies it to a manly woman (2.285), and Jupiter is implicated in the second (1.71-3). Other physiognomical descriptions that want to describe spirited, impressive characters call eyes γοργοί (Lucian, *Alex.* 3 ὀφθαλμοὶ πολὺ τὸ γοργὸν καὶ ἔνθεον διεμφαίνοντες; Heliodorus, *Aeth.* 7.10.4); for other descriptions of bold, daring expressions see Nesselrath, 409.

287 λευκοί: the ethical and perhaps also racial implications are as in Adamantius, for whom pure Greeks are λευκότεροι τὴν χρόαν (2.32), while 'a white and rather pale colour indicates courage and spirit' (2.33 ἡ δὲ λευκὴ (sc. χροιά) καὶ ὑπόξανθος ἀλκὴν καὶ θυμὸν λέγει)—precisely Alexander's complexion (Plut. *Alex.* 4.3) and temperament. Perhaps the positive connotation comes from the two references to the white skin of Iliadic warriors (11.573, 15.316).[160] In astrology, the nexus of pale complexion, high spirits, and Greekness, which applies all the way from kings[161] to thieves (Dorotheus, p. 412.6 Ἐὰν ὁ τοῦ Διὸς ἀστὴρ δηλοῖ τὸν κλέπτην ἔσται λευκόχρους), is connected to Jupiter, whose whiteness, strongly marked in Ptolemy (3.12.4 ὁ δὲ τοῦ Διὸς οἰκοδεσποτήσας

---

[160] Whiteness might in practice have different connotations, such as vulnerability in the Homeric passages (Grand-Clément, 197-8) or even cowardice (as noted by Eustathius, i. 720.13-14, on *Il.* 4.146-7, ὅτι λευκοὶ οἱ δειλοὶ καὶ λευκώπιοι οἱ αὐτοί, and more in the same vein).

[161] According to Apomasar, *De Myst.*, CCAG xi/2. 190.24, the second decan of Leo brings to birth an ἄνδρα λευκὸν σὺν ἐρυθρότητι προσώπου whom other versions of this chart call a king (Hephaestion, i. 14.3-10, although he drops the pale complexion; Camaterus, *Isag.* 692-7 (Alexander and emperors); Heilen 2015, 759-60).

τοὺς προκειμένους τόπους ἀνατολικὸς τῇ μὲν μορφῇ ποιεῖ λευκούς, cf. Hephaestion, i. 94.18 Ζεὺς δὲ λευκούς), goes back at least as far as Plato: Boll 1916, 20, 21, 22; Pingree 1978, ii. 248–50; add the entry in a catalogue of metals and minerals in Laur. Plut. 28.34, published by Ludwich (1877, 121.8): Διὸς κασσίτερος, βήρυλλος καὶ πᾶς λίθος λευκός; and the association of Jupiter with whitish /crystalline stone in P. Wash.Univ. inv.181., ll. 10–12 (ed. Packman).

ξανθοῖσιν ἐπαντέλλοντες ἰούλοις: for Adamantius, fair hair along with pale skin typify the northerner (2.31), the individual of good physique (2.46), and the pure Greek (2.32). This patent improbability presumably testifies to the enduringness of the archeype created by Homeric heroes (*Il.* 1.197, etc.; Grand-Clement, 306–15), perpetuated by Alexander (Aelian, *VH* 12.14), and still a requisite of the novelistic hero (Heliodorus, *Aeth.* 7.10.4 τὴν παρειὰν ἄρτι ξανθῷ τῷ ἰούλῳ περιστέφων, Arsace's description of Theagenes, with similar diction).[162] ἰούλοις suggests youth, a rather temporary state of affairs for a natal chart to signify in the absence of chronocrators. Be that as it may, the poet uses the same kind of metaphor for 'efflorescences' on the skin as in *Od.* 11.319–20 πρίν σφωϊν ὑπὸ κροτάφοισιν ἰούλους | ἀνθῆσαι. See also Aesch. *Choe.* 282, where ἐπαντέλλειν is used for skin eruptions; Garvie ad loc. notes the comparability of ἐπαντέλλειν and ἐξανθεῖν, and suggests that the former is also botanical metaphor. In ps.-Opp. *Cyn.* 3.476 ἐπαντέλλουσι (in this *sedes*, but that is common) is used of a deer's horns.

288 **εὐπρόσιτοι, γλυκεροί**: affability (i. 311). Approachability is the gift of Jupiter and Venus (Ptol. 3.14.25, the only other attestation in astrology, where accessibility is one of the redeeming characteristics of those natives born when the planets are *un*favourably placed). 'Sweetness' is more specifically Venereal (though γλυκύς is not common in prose astrology for personality-types). The scion of Venus in Camaterus, *Introd.* 2669, is γλυκερός; the Moon in quartile with Venus engenders the γλυκυλάλον (Περὶ σχημ. 58), and produces βίον εὔχαριν καὶ γλυκὺν ἐν ὁμιλίαις in Περὶ κράσ. 201.

σοβαροί: see on 5.143

χαρίεντες ἀοιδοί: the transference to singers of the traditional quality of song,[163] divested of its religious associations,[164] is suitable to the astrologers'

---

[162] Date and context poison it, but there is a useable collection of testimonia to blonde hair among Greeks and Romans in W. Sieglin, *Die blonden Haare der indogermanischen Völker des Altertums: Eine Sammlung der antiken Zeugnisse als Beitrag zur Indogermanenfrage* (Munich, 1935), 39–50 (Greece), and 50–8 (Rome). The present passage is mentioned on 44, and Adamantius on 42–3.

[163] *Od.* 24.197–8 ἀοιδήν... χαρίεσσαν; *CA*, Ep. Adesp. 8.14 P. χ[αρίεσ]σαν ἀοιδήν; cf. Euphorion, *SH* 443.12–13?

[164] Gods are pleased *by* songs, or their favour is requested *for* them (*HHom.* 24.5 χάριν δ' ἅμ' ὄπασσον ἀοιδῇ), or they even generate their charm (*Od.* 24.197–8; Pind. fr. 141 Snell); M. Scott, 'Charis in Homer and the Homeric Hymns', *AClass* 26 (1983), 1–13, at 5.

world, where so much hangs on social capital (for charming musicians, see also Manilius, 4.527–8 *dulci tincta lepore | corda*). Yet musicians/bards already have the quality in Ar. *Vesp.* 1278 τὸν κιθαραοιδότατον, ᾧ χάρις ἐφέσπετο, and especially Nicaenetus, *AP* 13.29.1 = *HE* 2711 χαρίεντι...ἀοιδῷ (sometimes included as a fragment of Cratinus, though not in the scope of the quotation in K.–A. fr. *203).

289 The first three adjectives (the first unique in astrology, the second a Manethonian favourite (see on 1.131–2), the third a common outcome for both Jupiter and Venus) describe the socially adept individual, witty, clever, well-mannered, so the job-description that ends the line really only makes sense insofar as it prepares for the quip in the next line, returning to social *mores*.

The ἀρχικυνηγοί are a minor *cause célèbre*. They appear only another three times in literary texts, in Josephus, *AJ* 16.316, of a 'master of hounds' in the court of Herod, and the others in the context of 'managers of beasts' in an amphitheatre in Christian martyrologies/wonder-stories.[165] The world is better attested in epigraphy, where it is mentioned (i) on epitaphs; (ii) as an honorific title next to 'high priest', held by Helenus governor of Cyprus under Ptolemy VIII Physcon (d. 116); (iii) in Philae and Alexandria under Ptolemy V (205–180), where three inscriptions attest a father–son pair of ἀρχικυνηγοί who are also ἀρχισωματοφύλακες and among the king's friends, whence it would appear to be a court title (A. Bernand, *De Thèbes à Syène* (Paris, 1989), 287–9, no. 314); (iv) also in Ptolemaic Egypt as a military command where it does, genuinely, denote someone at the head of a band of hunters, perhaps for wild animals for royal gazebos (see A. Bernand, *Pan du Désert* (Leiden, 1977), nos. 2 and 11, from Wadi bir el-Aïn, and for royal gazebos, Bernand's commentary on no. 4, pp. 29–30); on nos. (iii) and (iv) id. 1969, no. 9, p. 111.

To which of these types of 'chief huntsman' should we refer the present case? Observing references in Firmicus to *venatores* in the vicinity of court positions (3.6.3, 3.11.18), Cumont took this, like those passages, to be evidence of the persistence, at least textually, of the old Ptolemaic court title (62 n. 3)—spectacular confirmation, if so, of his world-view of astrological texts (i. 291). Louis Robert, on the other hand, suggested (without insisting) that it could be the type of gladiator the Romans called a *venator*, which would certainly explain the sex appeal.[166] He was followed by Versnel, 230. But given the generally polite and urbane context, is this really plausible? Or again—is it a similar type of person to Herod's employee in Josephus, in which case we are at least in a reasonably familiar imperial world of big landowners and their estate managers?

---

[165] Acts of Paul; Acta Sancti Mamantis, 22.
[166] 1938, 78 n. 1, citing the gladiatorial θηρ‹ε›ύτο‹ρε›ς ἄνδρες in the Corinthian amphitheatre (*IG* IV 365).

976   *Commentary on Book Five*

290 On predation, see 4.56 and 4.164 nn., though Jupiter and Venus are not usually the culprits. Compare also the alignment of *adulteros* and *venatores* in *Lib. Herm.* xxv. 4.12 (9° Cancer).

291 Everything about this individual is double, and the vocabulary in which this is expressed is mostly very rare. It is not astrological jargon, and has been designed for this passage. δισσολόγοι and δίγονοι are very rare in general, and unique in astrology, while the only other occurrence of διπολῖται is in an astrological text. One might have expected this insistent doubleness to be produced by double signs (Θ p. 134.1–2).

δισσολόγοι: could mean 'bilingual' (and is so taken by Koechly, LSJ, and Lopilato) = δίγλωσσος, an interesting detail if so, for astrology is interested in speech defects on the one hand, fluency on the other, but not usually in proficiency across languages.[167] If these men are Roman citizens (below), the languages in question could be Greek and Latin, but that is speculation. Another possible meaning is 'double-tongued', i.e. duplicitous, which is Lampe's interpretation of the only other occurrence, Const. Apostol. 3.5.1 (4th c.), in a list of undesirable characteristics in a woman. The context would suit that interpretation, but 'saying everything twice', i.e. garrulous, equally well; Valens' uses of δισσολογεῖν in methodological discussions means 'repeat oneself'. The interpretation of this word is also important insofar as it sets the tone for the rest of the line (neutral or judgemental?). Perhaps it even equivocates between 'bilingual' and 'duplicitous'; Latin *bilinguis* has the same potential double meaning.

δίγαμοι: the two other astrological instances (Περὶ κράσ. 201, and Θ p. 159.12) are about women, voicing astrology's concern about marrying widows (4.393 n.). That does not seem to be the point here: it is the native, not his wife, who is married twice; it is another facet of his doubleness.

δίγονοι: 'having two, or twin, children' (so Koechly and LSJ, though the latter, like Chandler, §467, make it paroxytone; Lopilato does not translate it), which logically follows reference to marriage. If this individual is inherently double, it could also mean that he is a twin. Either way it is very rare: 'twice-born' of Dionysus (Eur. *Hipp.* 560), 'double' (Eur. *El.* 1179 and Soph. fr. 129 Radt), 'bearing twice' (Empedocl. 31 B 69 D.–K.).

διπολῖται: the only other occurrence (barring 4.376, which is about adoption) is Critodemus, *CCAG* viii/1. 258.1, dated by Pingree to the early first century AD (Heilen 2015, 31 n. 148) but in a forthcoming monograph by C. Tolsa (*The Orphic Astrologer Critodemus: Fragments with Annotated Translation and Commentary*) to the late second or early first century BC. Critodemus' natives

---

[167] There are interesting references to various kinds of linguistic proficiency: a stenographer (Manil. 4.198–9); someone who teaches birds human language (Manil. 5.378–87). But no bilinguals that I can see.

are born under Jupiter's terms within Aries (corresponding to *Lib. Herm.* xxv. 1.9 *quidam prosperantur et bicives fiunt*): they are distinguished, and also ἐν ὄχλοις εὐδοξοῦσιν. High status suits the role of Jupiter in this chart as well, reinforcing what is said in 286 and 295-6. A related term, used of one enjoying rights in another state, is ἰσοπολίτης. Usually this is used where an entire citizen body shares rights with another, but one papyrus example, P.Oxy. 41.28, records acclamations (296 n.), where the honorand Dioscorus is hailed as πρωτοπολῖτα, ἰσάρχων, ἰσ[ο]πολῖτ[α]. These multiple citizenships are therefore likely to be a badge of individual honour.

The natives are citizens of more than one *polis*, or perhaps both municipal and Roman citizens (like Paul), at least in the years before 212, when the latter was still a coveted privilege.[168] I thank Georgy Kantor for the observation that in an Egyptian setting, and since the reference is specifically to *two* citizenships, the date is likely to be before 212 (or at least the date of the source that the poet is repeating) and the citizenships in question to be one municipal and one Roman.[169] In Egypt the Romans introduced a strictly tiered system of Romans, Greeks (citizens of the three, subsequently four, Greek *poleis*), and non-citizen Egyptians (everyone else, though status-differences marked out the élites in the *metropoleis*),[170] though in order to enjoy Roman citizenship you had to have citizenship of a Greek *polis* first (Pliny, *Ep.* 10.6).[171] If the reference is to municipal citizenships there were only three Greek *poleis* in Egypt anyway before the foundation of Antinoopolis (and before Severus granted city status to *metropoleis*), but the specific boast about *two* makes it look like something particularly distinctive.

At the same time, the term is informal and non-technical. It seems that it is not the norm in antiquity to speak of 'dual citizenship' (which is so natural to us). The implication of the old (obsolete?) ἰσοπολιτεία terminology is that 'you, the outsider, are to have equal citizenship with us'—not 'you are to hold joint

---

[168] A. Besson, 'Fifty Years before the Antonine Constitution: Access to Roman Citizenship and Exclusive Rights', in L. Cecchet and A. Busetto (eds.), *Citizens in the Graeco-Roman World: Aspects of Citizenship from the Archaic Period to AD 212* (Leiden, 2017), 199–220.

[169] Honorific multiple citizenships are best known outside Egypt, especially in Asia Minor and in grants of *isopoliteia* in Hellenistic mainland Greece. See P. Gauthier, *Les Cités grecques et leurs bienfaiteurs (ive–i^{er} siècle avant J.-C.): Contribution à l'histoire des institutions* (BCH Suppl. 12, 1985), 149–62; A. Heller and A.-V. Pont (eds.), *Patrie d'origine et patries électives: Les citoyennetés multiples dans le monde grec d'époque romaine: Actes du colloque international de Tours, 6-7 novembre 2009* (Bordeaux, 2012); A. Ştefan, 'The Case of Multiple Citizenship Holders in the Graeco-Roman East', in Cecchet and Busetto (eds.), 110–31.

[170] A. Jördens, 'Status and Citizenship', in Riggs (ed.) 2012, 247–59; K. Vandorpe, 'Identity', ibid. 260–76, at 262–4.

[171] Fraser, ii. 797; V. Marotta, 'Egyptians and Citizenship from the First Century AD to the Constitutio Antoniniana', in Cecchet and Busetto (eds.), 172–98, at 177–81.

citizenship'.[172] The norm is for multiple citizenships simply to be listed city by city. That is presumably a consequence of the point of view of the sources (mostly honorific or sepulchral) which tend either to enumerate multiple citizenships boastfully (e.g. Titus Julius Apolaustos, *FD* iii. 1, 551.24–8) or to record a grant from one community to an outsider; astrology is different because it adopts a distanced, non-localised, perspective which puts the two on an equal footing. Or, as Georgy Kantor puts it, 'on a theoretical level different citizenships still continue in parallel, rather than become a merged dual citizenship status'.

292 Of the various ways of emending this line the simplest (D'Orville's πᾶσιν) makes it a pentameter, the only one in this book. This sort of ethological material is quite conceivable in Anubion. For instance, one papyrus represents a series of character-types, with headings to pick them out (F 6 a–b; see i. 720–1), and although the charts there are nothing like as long as this one, they do have asyndetic lists of epithets describing characteristics, as here (a 5, b 7, 10). Yet subsequent lines in this chart look sooner to be original hexameters composed in the poet's habitual parallelistic style than gerrymandered elegiacs; their isocola and rhyme look too deliberate to be secondary. Were different recensions of this chart circulating in antiquity, of which an editor has sought to cobble together two versions? Or is this an isolated flourish (p. 280)?

293 Very like 238, from another discursive 'biographical' chart, with physiognomy at the beginning, and there is a third iteration of the 'at home/abroad' jingle in 299. Perhaps an argument in favour of the multiple citizenships of 291 being honorary and municipal? But see p. 977 and n. 169.

294 Potentially τιμῶνται extends to the wives as well, as in 3.185 τῆμος γὰρ σεμναί τ' ἄλοχοι τίουσί τ' ἀκοίτας, again the effect of Venus and Jupiter (there, over ASC/DESC).

295 Crowns: i. 347. These are honorific, but not specifically priestly. On the gradations and semantics of honorific crowns, see Chaniotis, 55–7. Friendships with big men: i. 310. To the construction of αὐχεῖν with the bare dative, rare in classical Greek (as LSJ indicate), *Or. Sib.* 4.88 could be added.

296 It is the first word in this line that gives the game away. The reference is to public acclamations, well known from Rome, Byzantium, and the dossier

---

[172] The noun ἰσοπολιτεία is the term used in Hellenistic grants to individuals (as well as in agreements about communities) from mainland Greece; it seems to go out of use in the imperial period.

from Aphrodisias for the bigwig Albinus.[173] There is no single word for such demonstrations of formalised chanting, but μαρτυρίαι is the one used in P.Oxy. 41.18, a third- or fourth-century papyrus recording the acclamations given to Dioscorus, a local benefactor, called a prytanis, in a meeting on the occasion of a visit by the prefect (LSJ renders: 'demonstrations of favour'; see the discussion by Kruse, §11: 'The acclamations consequently are a witness to how much the crowd desires honour for the Prytanis, they are thus at the same time also witnesses of the legitimacy of the honouring'). Blume, 288–9, draws attention to another example from fifth-century Sardis (*IG* IV 1756.37), where the benefactor Menogenes receives τὴν . . . τοῦ δήμου εἰς αὐτὸν μα‹ρ›τυρίαν before the formal conferral of honour on a later occasion.

On purely palaeographical grounds it was hard to understand the lack of take-up for Axtius and Rigler's κελαδοῦνται (which also occurred to me independently), where a delta–lambda confusion is surely more plausible than Koechly's σελαγεῦνται. But what clinches it is the sense: the natives are not 'irradiated' by glory, but acclaimed in resonant semi-metrical chants (Roueché 1989, 131–2; C. T. Kuhn, 297–9, 310, 311). κελαδοῦνται is a more pretentious version of the verbs used in prose accounts and inscriptions, most commonly (ἐκ-, ἐπι)βοᾶν, but also κράζειν (Acts 19:28), and is the very word used for the crowd's approval in a verse inscription commemorating a gladiator from Hierapolis (Robert 1940a, no. 124, [ἢ] τὸ πρὶν ἐν στα[δίῳ κε]λαδούμενος; cf. 302, Celadus, a gladiator from Pompeii). This is the celebratory sense so familiar from Pindar (*Ol.* 2.2 τίνα θεόν, τίν᾽ ἥρωα, τίνα δ᾽ ἄνδρα κελαδήσομεν;); the poet uses the verb again in 5.162, but of a musical instrument. ἀγαλλόμενοι is also a good word for semi-incantatory acclamations, for Hesiod uses it (same *sedes*) to describe the Muses' songs in *Th.* 68 ἀγαλλόμεναι ὀπὶ καλῇ (cf. also *HHom.* 19.24 λιγυρῇσιν ἀγαλλόμενος φρένα μολπαῖς, of Pan leading a chorus of mountain nymphs). As for δόξῃσι, this is *ipso facto* what acclamations

---

[173] Robert 1960b, 570–1; C. Roueché, 'Acclamations in the Later Roman Empire: New Evidence from Aphrodisias', *JRS* 74 (1984), 181–99, cf. Zuiderhoeck, 203–4, 208–9; ead., 2007, 190–1; P. Brown, *Power and Persuasion in Late Antiquity: Toward a Christian Empire* (Madison, WI, 1992), 149–50; C. Ando, *Imperial Ideology and Provincial Loyalty in the Roman Empire* (Berkeley, 2000), 199–205; H.-U. Wiemer, 'Akklamationen im spätrömischen Reich: Zur Typologie und Funktion eines Kommunikationsrituals', *Archiv für Kulturgeschichte*, 86(1) (2004), 27–74; A.-V. Pont, 'Rituels civiques (*apantēsis* et acclamations) et gouverneurs à l'époque romaine en Asie Mineure' in O. Hekster, S. Schmidt-Hofner, and Ch. Witschel (eds.), *Ritual Dynamics and Religious Change in the Roman Empire: Proceedings of the Eighth Workshop of the International Network Impact of Empire (Heidelberg, July 5-7, 2007)* (Leiden, 2009), 185–211, esp. 190–2, 197–202, 210–11; H.-L. Fernoux, *Le Demos et la cité: Communautés et assemblées populaires en Asie Mineure à l'époque impériale* (Rennes, 2011), 134–50; C. T. Kuhn; van Nijf 2013, 356–7; Courrier, 657–65; S. Lalanne, 'Le témoignage de Chariton d'Aphrodisias sur la pratique civique des honneurs', in A. Heller and O. M. van Nijf (eds.), *The Politics of Honour in the Greek Cities of the Roman Empire* (Leiden, 2017), 149–81, esp. 169–70.

acknowledge and enhance. The one for the prytanis in Oxyrhynchus calls him δόξα πόλεω[ς] (P.Oxy. 41.4), and although Blume's commentary (285–6) finds the expression unusual and wonders whether there are special circumstances that elicit it, one of those for the benefactor Albinus in Aphrodisias, hailing him λαμπρότατε, also contains the words καὶ δόξαν ἐκτήσω (Rouché 1989, no. 83 (xvi)). Such acclamations became a public ritual, an increasingly formalised matter of protocol and form, hence a conventional signifier of status, and papyri and inscriptions suggest that they were a matter of public record in and after the second century (C. T. Kuhn, 301). That does not, sadly, tell us anything we did not already know about the date of the present book (p. 318).

297–8 The two categories of forbidden women correspond to those in 2.268–9, wives of ἑταίρων and πηῶν, but under the more obvious influence of Mars and Venus; it is hard to understand Jupiter's role here. πενθερικοῖς δὲ δόμοισι suggests above all brothers' wives (i. 303 n. 27, 583, 764), which is supported by Lib. Herm. xxxii. 39 *muneribus decipientes amicorum suorum uxores vel sociorum vel fratrum* (the passage parallel to 2.268–9); the adjective remains without parallel until the tenth century. For the theft metaphor see on 4.56 and 164. συνέφηβος (mostly prose, but sometimes in epigram) evokes the world of young male camaraderie, dinner-parties, and courtesans (title of several comedies; in Lucian's *Dialogi Meretricum*; the novel), but this is less inconsequential. On the basis of this line, Boll restored Anubion, F 12.21 [ἠδὲ] κασιγνήτοις ὕ[βριν] τεύχουσιν [ἐ]φ[ήβοις] (under different circumstances: Venus and Mercury are in conjunction with the Moon).

299 No reason to delete this verse with Koechly and De Stefani, who however admits its stylistic plausibility (2017, 33), but there is a question whether it should be shifted nearer to 293 (for the sake of theme) or 296–7 (for the sake of the parallelism; Axtius and Rigler placed it before 297). Either way, the verbs would continue to press the visibility motif (292 φαινόμενον, probably not to be emended; 297 καθορῶνται). The implied contrast between civilian and military is unusual in astrology.

300–6 + 307–12

Moon at node when New(?), and after her release from the Sun, applying to benefics. The commentary on 120–6 + 127–9 notes the flexibility of the analogy between moonlight and wealth. What seems to be happening here is that when the Moon at node is New, the native acquires wealth, (i) through professional specialism (magic), and (ii) through the confidence of rich women, but that when the Moon is released from the Sun he disburses his wealth, spending it on public projects which leave him destitute. The Moon's increasing light equates, not with the distribution of wealth to the natives, but with the natives' disbursement of wealth to others. *Π.σ.α.* p. 186.14–15 says that the Moon after *synodos* encountering a benefic is καλὴ πρὸς πρᾶξιν καὶ δόξαν, obviously compatible with *grands projets*, but with no further details.

300 ἐπ' Ἡέλιόν: implying a verb of motion towards (the Homeric model, *Il.* 2.413 ἐπ' ἠέλιον δῦναι, involved tmesis). The Moon is at the node at the time she is moving (or rather has moved) into conjunction with the Sun.

ποτε: see on 5.137.

301 Compare 5.121, 125. ἀνακάμπτει would be especially appropriate were it also to be a technical term for planetary movement, especially for the Moon's 'bending back' towards the Sun after Full Moon, but that appears not to be the case: I find ἀνακάμπτειν only in Ptol. *Synt.* i/1. 11.18–19, for the (apparent) return of the stars to the same starting-point each day.

302 Ἑκατησίου: of two terminations, with τέχνης. Ἑκατήσιον/Ἑκατήσια normally refer to shrines, rites, or (in Stratonicea) games, and the epithet is only matched by *Lexicon Artis Grammaticae*, p. 445.3 Ἔμπουσα... φάσμα Ἑκατήσιον. Venality has been a strong and constant part of the image of mages since at least Sophocles. Following an allusion to the *OT* at 5.204, one wonders about a connection with *OT* 388–9 ὅστις ἐν τοῖς κέρδεσιν | μόνον δέδορκε (see Finglass ad loc. for the accusation[174]), only remodelled after the EGHP cadence εἵνεκα — —, several examples of which involve expressions of gain or expense (τιμῆς, ποινῆς, δώρων). There is a good parallel in Firmicus, 3.8.9 (even under different circumstances: Mercury with the Sun in the ninth house): exorcists and expellers of demons make a lucrative trade, *ut his artibus maxima illis vitae substantia conferatur*.

303–4 These lines are perfectly contextualised by the story in Acts 19:13–19 (Dickie 2003, 223–4) about wandering Jewish exorcists in Ephesus who try in vain to expel evil spirits (πνεύματα) in Jesus' name, and bring together their sacred books (τὰς βίβλους) and burn them. These people are called literally 'those who do excessive things', τῶν τὰ περίεργα πραξάντων. LSJ has two testimonia for the adjective in this sense, the other being Plut. *Alex.* 2.8 περιέργοις ἱερουργίαις (of the magic practices of Thracian women); the noun περιεργίαι means 'practices that go over and above' (an acceptable norm).[175] This passage

---

[174] And add *On the Sacred Disease*, 4; Plat. *Rep.* 364 B, *Leg.* 909 B χρημάτων χάριν. In the Derveni papyrus, col. xx. l. 9, the commentator pities those who waste money on performing rites without gaining understanding in the process, which implicitly reflects badly on the charlatans who dupe them.

[175] To LSJ add Irenaeus, *Adv. haer.* 1.7.1 and 1.16.3 (ed. Harvey); in the first passage the reference to a ποτήριον suggests lecanomancy (4.213 n.).

apparently illustrates the verb used in the same way, and Axtius' περιέργει (for L's περίεργα, retained by Lopilato) better represents this than his alternative περιείργει (accepted by Koechly, and rendered 'circumcludit'). The sense is 'over-busy, meddlesome'.

303 καὶ μαγικῇ συνέσει: the poet waves at the enormous body of tradition that associated the manipulation of spirits with magic in general as well as, perhaps, the specialism of magi in particular.[176]

πέπιθεν τὰ πνεύματα φεύγειν: as so often, the terminology partly reflects real usage: 'flee' is a formula used against evil influences in exorcistic texts. Kotansky notes its use as early as the Phalasarna tablet (SEG 42.818), which is Hellenistic (1 φεύγεμεν, 3, 5 φεῦγε) (254), again in Tobit 6:8, 7:17, 8:3 (258), and the related notion of fear in PGM 4.3013–14 (262–3). To these, add φεῦγε, πνεῦμα μεμισημένον in PGM 5b (said to be Christian), as well as use of φεύγειν throughout the Cyranides for δαίμονες, δαιμόνια, φαντάσματα, pestilences, and wild animals (in the form of the assurance φεύξεται, subj. the intimidated spirit).[177] The exorcist's methods could be violent (C. A. Bonner, 'The Technique of Exorcism', HThR 36 (1943), 39–49; 'The violence of departing demons', 37 (1944), 334–6), and the rather courteously-phrased πέπιθεν ('he persuades spirits to flee') might be euphemistic; one thinks, also, of the sort of feat performed by Apollonius, when he identified the spirit of plague in Ephesus in the form of an old man, who was duly stoned in the theatre (Philostr. Vit. Ap. 4.10). Kotansky (276) makes an interesting distinction between a 'Greek' demonology of evocable δαίμονες which can be coerced into service versus the Semitic idea of the πνεῦμα ἀκάθαρτον which called for expulsion, while pointing out that in practice these ideas and the motifs and formulas associated with them cross

---

[176] Already in the Derveni papyrus, col. vi, μάγοι (whoever they are) manipulate δαίμονες through ἐπ[ωιδή. Evocation and converse with spirits of the dead are fixtures of μαγία, μαγική: e.g. Aesch. Pers., the summoning of Darius' ghost (possibly: Dickie 2003, 29–30); Bidez–Cumont, ii: Ostanes, nos. 12 (ap. Plin. NH 30.14 umbrarum inferorumque colloquia), 13 (Tertullian); Iamblichus (in Photius, cod. 94, 75 в 24) μάγον...νεκυομαντείας; Lucian, Menippus, 6; M. Boyce and F. Grenet, A History of Zoroastrianism, iii: Zoroastrianism under Macedonian and Roman Rule (Leiden, 1991), 518–20. Magi derive their power from spirits (Bidez–Cumont, ii: Ostanes, no. 14a = Minucius Felix, Octav. 26.10–11, and Cyprian, Quod idola dii non sint, 6). On magic and δαίμονες, Boyce and Grenet, 498–9.

[177] For verbs used in narratives of demon-expulsion, see W. D. Smith, 'So-called Possession in Pre-Christian Greece', TAPA 96 (1965), 403–46, at 409; RAC s.v. Exorzismus, 52 (K. Thraede). Examples include ἐξέλκειν in Jos. AJ 8.47; ἐκβάλλειν in Matth. 8:31 and 12:24, Mark 9:18, 28, Luke 9:40, PGM 4.1227 titulus, Eunap. Vit. Soph. 4.1.12; ἐξελαύνειν in Lucian, Philops. 16, cf. Sophron, fr. 3 ἐξελᾶν, if this means exorcism. On (ἐξ)ελαύνειν, see Kotansky, 255–6. ἔξελθε is the command most often given by the exorcist (e.g. Mark 5:8, 9: 25, Luke 4:35, 8:29, PGM 4.3009), and ἐξελθεῖν is what the spirit duly does (e.g. Matth. 17:18, Mark 9:26, Acts 16:18); Kotansky, 249, 262, 268, 269, 275. Latin exi: Actus Petri cum Simone, 11.

cultures. At any rate, as Ogden puts it, 'much of the richest evidence for exorcism of individuals in the Graeco-Roman world derives from or salutes the Judaeo-Christian tradition',[178] and this is another moment, as with the legends about Apollonius, where a pagan text and early Christian literature come close.

304 κρυφίμαις βίβλοις: this supplements the note on secret books at 2.197–9 βίβλοις... κρυπταῖς. First, the usual prose phrase is βίβλος ἀπόκρυφος.[179] This variant (also in 3.294 βίβλων κρυφίμων) substitutes the corpus' favourite piece of astrological and magical jargon, κρύφιμος, for which see on 4.413. The secret books of 2.197–9 are connected with initiation, one of the earliest two associations for books in Greek religion (Demosth. Or. 18.259). The connection with φιλομάντιας ἄνδρας in 3.293 suggests the other, namely divination. Here, though, the context is magic, a mainly late antique association discoverable since the first century BC, especially in Egypt (Bremmer 2015, esp. 250–64); another relevant passage (using the same form of the adjective) is PGM 12.405–6 ἐκ τῶν πολλῶν ἀντιγράφων καὶ κρυφίμων πάντων, where the author is discussing his sources.[180] The holy books and secret pillars of 5.1–2 (see ad loc.) represent yet another late antique phenomenon, that of the work of philosophic lore, especially Hermetic (Bremmer 2015, 254). The theme is in keeping with astrology's general obsession with lack of candour or public scrutability, as opposed to that which has clear signage. Interestingly Firmicus only refers to books *at all* in citations (of himself and others), but lacks the motif of either secret or holy books in apotelesmata (in 6.40.4 *secreta libri septimi* is a transitional device at the end of the sixth book).

305 σοβαραῖς μεγάλῃσι γυναιξίν: Juvenal, *Sat.* 6.511–626, has already introduced us to the superstitious rich women into whose good graces these charlatans insinuate themselves;[181] see also Lucian, *Alexander* 6 (a woman of Pella preyed on by Alexander and his partner Cocconas), with Thonemann 2021, 78; Clem. Al. *Paed.* 3.4.28.3, on rich women accompanied by a retinue of hangers-on as they make their way from one temple to another, ἀγύρταις καὶ

---

[178] Ogden 2002, 167; on the idea of possession as new around the turn of the Christian era, Smith (n. 177); Kotansky, 246–9. Examples of exorcism in Ogden, nos. 127–32, with bibliography on 310 (= 2009, 348); add Dickie 2003, 204, 222–4; Forst, 183–5.
[179] e.g. Clem. Al. *Strom.* 1.15.69.6, of Pythagoras; Epiphanius, *Adv. haer.* ii. 82.8–9 (for secret books and heretics, see Bremmer 2015, 263); in the magical papyri, H. D. Betz, 'Secrecy in the Greek Magical Papyri', in H. G. Kippenberg and G. G. Stroumsa (eds.), *Secrecy and Concealment: Studies in the History of Mediterranean and Near Eastern Religions* (Leiden, 1995), 153–75, at 159.
[180] On magic books: Kotansky, 244–5 n. 5; Bremmer 2015.
[181] Priests of Bellona and Egyptian deities, a Jewish woman, *haruspices* from Armenia and Commagene, and Chaldaeans, i.e. astrologers, although the salient feature of that list is where the charlatans come from: they are all from the east (Courtney on 511), a point missing from Egyptian 'Manetho'.

μητραγύρταις καὶ γραίαις βωμολόχοις, purveying love-charms and incantations (φίλτρα ἄττα καὶ ἐπῳδάς; Dickie 2003, 226-7). On Greek sorcerers who insinuate themselves into the salons of wealthy patrons, not necessarily women, see Dickie 2003, 186-91 (Rome), 212-16 (the Greek East: Alexander of Abonuteichos, and others), 307-8 (post-Constantinian Rome). In Plautus, *Miles Gloriosus*, 692-4, the charlatans themselves are all female (*praecantrici, coniectrici, hariolae atque haruspicae*, and *quae supercilio spicit*, rendered by Dickie 2003, 128, 'the woman who utters incantations, the woman who interprets dreams, the inspired prophetess and the woman who divines from entrails', and 'the woman who observes the sky').

The epithet (4.468 n.) may be used of dignified (and respectable) women: Chariton, 8.1.12 ἐβάδιζε δὲ σοβαρά; of a respectable and haughty woman: Joseph and Asenath, 12.5 ἣ ποτε σοβαρὰ καὶ ὑπερήφανος καὶ εὐθηνοῦσα ἐν τῷ πλούτῳ μου ὑπὲρ πάντας ἀνθρώπους; of Tyre personified as a haughty woman: Procopius, *Comment. in Isaiam*, PG 87/2. 2185.41. But also of prostitutes: 5.143 n.

306 The note of Spanoudakis, 207-8, seems to me to tackle only half the problem. He proposes to restore the metre of L's ἐκ δὲ μικρῆς ψυχῆς by inverting noun and adjective (ψυχῆς δ᾽ ἐκ μικρῆς), but there is also a question of sense. The line describes the native's own situation, not the stinginess (μικροψυχία) of his patrons. The narrative pattern of the mage/charlatan (γόης) who starts out poor but grows in influence is familiar, e.g. from Lucian's account of Alexander, and applied to Orpheus himself in Strab. 7a.1.18 (ἀγυρτεύοντα τὸ πρῶτον, εἶτ᾽ ἤδη καὶ μειζόνων ἀξιοῦντα ἑαυτὸν καὶ ὄχλον καὶ δύναμιν κατασκευαζόμενον). The sense of τύχη, which was D'Orville's correction, is the class in which one happens to find oneself, like that found throughout Apomasar (i. 288, ἡ ἄνω τύχη, ἡ μέση τύχη, ἡ κάτω τύχη).

308-12 A modern analysis of the problems of ancient euergetism, in which financial ruin was a very real possibility (*IG* IV²/1. 65, Epidauros, 1st c. BC, ll. 5-6 βλάπτοντος τὸν ἴδιον βίον χάριν τοῦ πᾶσιν συμφέροντος; L. Robert, 'Trois oracles de la Théosophie et un prophète d'Apollon', *CRAI* 112 (1968), 568-99, at 585-6), can point to political factors like intra-élite competition (a concern analysed by Zuiderhoeck). Ethically and moralistically driven ancient analyses, both pagan and Christian, can also see that the problems were partly structural, in that the individual φιλότιμος was coerced into such ruinous behaviour,[182] but they also blame frivolous individual choices to spend on gladiators and shows (Robert 1960b, 571-3), as opposed to 'solid' and enduring things like

---

[182] See also i. 312 and pp. 11, 32, and 71 n. 155 for the painful awareness that the reciprocity of benefits might break down.

buildings. Authors both pagan and Christian describe the consequences of overreach (Plut. *Mor.* 822 A καταλύειν ἑαυτούς, 822 D; Dio Chrys. *Or.* 66.1-3; John Chrysostom, *De inani gloria*, 4-8, on which see Roskam), and do so in highly-coloured terms. John describes at length the triumph and subsequent humiliation and reduction to beggary of a man who has spent lavishly on what he calls whores and mimes (8), whores, mimes, and dancers (12), entertainments in the theatre. Whether or not he knew them, with Dio he shares the vivid visualisations of the spendthrift's state (hungry and ragged; begging in the agora), and his rejection by former toadies; with Plutarch he shares the conceit of populace as whore, and the mockery of the ruined spender. Unlike them, he blames the man's former associates for their cruelty in deserting him in his poverty (τί τούτων ἐλεεινότερον).

In the present passage, too, the problem is an ethical one. It is a matter of disposition, of behaviour which infringes astrology's basic conservatism about wealth. διαπαιζόμενοι (middle for active) may suggest the triviality and transitoriness of the expenses, the games and gladiators, inane diversions, that Plutarch, John, as well as Cic. *Off.* 2.55-6, also complain about, but it also implies that the spenders throw their money away in jest, Antony-like. For the astrologer the problem lies wholly in a faulty attitude, the natives' disposition— not, as for others, the blameworthy behaviour of the whole nexus of those involved in this culture of spending. There is a suggestion, however, shared with Plutarch and Dio, that the ruined spendthrift is ultimately to be pitied (*Mor.* 822 D οἰκτρὸν ἅμα καὶ καταγέλαστον/*Or.* 66.2 ἀθλίους καὶ πένητας).

309 σιτοδόται, κτίσται: this is almost exactly as in epigraphy. Natives engage in the traditional activities of civic benefactors, coming to the aid of their fellow citizens with corn doles and enhancing the cityscape with new buildings. Indeed, these are precisely among the benefactions that elicit acclamations (5.296 n.): Dioscorus the Egyptian prytanis (P.Oxy. 41; pp. 977, 979) and Albinus the benefactor of Aphrodisias (Roueché 1989, no. 83 (vi, viii, xv, xviii, xix)) are both acclaimed as κτίσται (Blume, 278-9; Kruse, §34), which at least in Albinus' case seems to have been literally the case, although κτίστης (as is well documented[183]) had come to take on the simple meaning of 'benefactor', εὐεργέτης. In particular, they are exactly matched in an inscription recording the erection of a statue for the benefactor Rhodopaeus in Aphrodisias (L. Robert, *Hellenica*, 4 (1949), 128; Roueché 1989, no. 87 τὸν μεγαλοπρεπέ|στατον Ῥοδοπαῖον | τὸν φιλόπατριν καὶ | ἀ‹ρ›ωγὸν τοῦ δήμου, |…καὶ σιτοδότην ὁ|μοῦ δὲ

---

[183] L. Robert, *Hellenica*, 4 (1949), 116 (an example in *À travers l'Asie Mineure: Poètes et prosateurs, monnaies grecques, voyageurs et géographie* (Athens, 1980), 254); Erkelenz; E. Meyer-Zwiffelhoffer, Πολιτικῶς ἄρχειν: *Zum Regierungsstil der senatorischen Statthalter in den kaiserzeitlichen griechischen Provinzen* (Stuttgart, 2002), 334-5; C. Begass, 'Φιλοκτίστης: Ein Beitrag zum spätantiken Euergetismus', *Chiron*, 90 (2014), 165-90, at 167, 186, 187.

καὶ κτίστην, etc.). Roueché dates Rhodopaeus to the mid-sixth century, and suggests that his position as σιτοδότης (cf. σιταρχίαις in the previous inscription in the series) was an exceptional one, ensuring food supplies in the aftermath of the plague of 541/2. The title is descriptive, rather than official (Ramsay, 443); the poet could be thinking of any or all of magistrates charged with grain provision (ἀγορανόμοι, σιτομέτραι, σιτῶναι), landowners who contribute (cheap) grain, or just rich men who put up cash for the grain dole.[184] Perhaps it even has something of the range of associations of τροφεύς, 'nurturer', another conventional term of civic commendation (L. Robert, 'Notes de numismatique et d'épigraphie grecques. 1: Sur une monnaie de Synnada', RA 3 (1934), 48–52 and Hellenica, 7 (1948), 74–81; Dio Chrys. Or. 48.10; Menander Rhetor, Περὶ ἐπιδεικτικῶν, p. 381.12 Spengel, where Russell and Wilson ad loc. cite Pliny, Paneg. 26–7 on alimenta; but also outside Asia Minor, e.g. in SEG 17.809 (Cyrenaica, AD 129) πατέρα πατρί]δος κτίσταν καὶ τροφ[έα).

μὴ φειδόμενοι φιλοτίμως: for φιλοτιμία, see 11 and i. 312. For profligate expenditure it is worth comparing the sketch of the φιλότιμος ἀνήρ receiving acclamations in John Chrysostom, De inani gloria, 4 τὸ τῆς φιλοτιμίας ἁδρὸν καὶ ἐκκεχυμένον, etc. (Roskam, 151). As for 'not sparing', there is IK Sestos 1 (133–20 BC) l. 4 οὔτε δαπάνης καὶ χορηγίας οὐδεμιᾶς φειδόμενος (and several other cases of restoration), but the commoner formulation in inscriptions is ἀφειδῶς or ἀφειδήσας, or ἀφειδεῖς agreeing with the gifts or grants or expenditures of whatever type.

308 χρυσοφορητά: hapax. χρυσοφόρος and χρυσοφορεῖν and χρυσοφορία, of course, are not. The poet alludes to the squandered wealth in terms which suggest the benefactor's honours which traditionally consist in χρυσοφορία (A. B. Kuhn).

310 The metaphor of consigning money to the depths and the winds (what Chrysostom, De inani gloria, 11, calls τοσούτων χρημάτων εἰκῇ κενουμένων) can be seen as a version, or reflex, of the trope about the benefactor's generosity being as copious and flowing as the Nile or the Ocean (Chrysostom, 4, cf. Roskam, 152; Kruse, §§22–33[185]); an early instance is Clytaemnestra's suggestion that the house's ancestral wealth is as inexhaustible as the sea in Aesch. Ag. 958, and a late and extravagant version is in Theodorus Prodromos, De

---

[184] Grain euergetism: M. Scapini, 'Studying Roman Economy and Imperial Food Supply: Conceptual and Historical Premises of the Study of the Economic Initiatives of the Emperors in the 1st and 2nd Century AD', Gerión, 34 (2016), 217–48, at 231, and n. 98; P. Erdkamp, The Grain Market in the Roman Empire: A Social, Political and Economic Study (Cambridge, 2005), 258–316 passim.

[185] Drawing attention to Ὠκεανέ acclamations for benefactors in papyri Kruse notes how well established the trope is in Egypt.

Manganis carmina, 3.1-6, where the emperor Manuel I Komnenos (12th c.) is the Ocean and the Nile, an outflow that is never spent. This is what that image looks like when it is focalised, not by grateful recipients, but by either censorious parsimony (διαπαιζόμενοι suggests traditional disapproval of the δαπανηρός, or spendthrift), or the resentful spender himself who sees his wealth dissipate. We, too, talk about a 'sea' or 'ocean' of expenditure, or, using a different liquid metaphor (4.92 n.), we could call it going down the drain.

311 περισσὰ ‹διδόντες›: like Hes. *Th.* 399 and fr. 10a.61 M.-W. περισσὰ δὲ δῶρα ἔδωκεν.

312 λείπονται πάντων: not enough to tie this specifically to Pind. *Isthm.* 2.11 κτεάνων θ' ἅμα λειφθεὶς καὶ φίλων (cited by LSJ II.2 to illustrate this post-Homeric usage), but the sentiment is a near-perfect match, for this and the texts cited in 308-12: money does indeed make the man, and to be bereft of the one is to be bereft of all status.

5.313-40 Charts Specifically for Women

The norm throughout the Manethoniana is for a chart to be neutral (but by default male), with any modifications for women appended at the end (e.g. 2.284; 6.170, 532; 5.142; p. 120). Isolated female charts are dotted throughout the collection too, but it is possible that the separate presentation of female charts reflects Egyptian practice, since Winkler 2009 (writing in 2005) reported that two of thirty then-known Demotic astrological manuals seemed to be devoted entirely to female charts. One of them even begins, in Winkler's rendering, '[the good] fate, the evil fate, and the things/matters that happen to women' (Quack, 57; Winkler 2016, 250 n. 29), which suggests that τὰ γυναικῶν, even though not exactly paralleled in the Greek astrological corpus,[186] might reflect a conventional type of heading. The Demotic material for women places 'greater emphasis... upon the personal character of women than what is found in the manuals written for males' (Winkler 2009, 372). Perhaps that is because the clientele were not the women themselves but their menfolk, those with a stake in a woman's eventual marriageability and quality as wife and mother. The same explanation is at hand here for the focus on reproductive capacity and sexual behaviour and character as a potential spouse.

---

[186] Some Zodiologia which review the implications of the signs severally for male and female births (W. Hübner, *Zodiacus Christianus: Jüdisch-christliche Adaptationen des Tierkreises von der Antike bis zur Gegenwart* (Königstein, 1983), 109) employ a separate heading for the woman (e.g. *CCAG* x. 102-21, Περὶ γυναικός, 171-92, Τῆς κόρης; x. 211-27, Ἀρχὴ τῶν γυναικῶν; Hübner, op. cit. pp. 176, 188).

313-14 δυνάμεις...προλέγω: 'I predict' (Valens, VI 2.2 προλέγειν τὰ τῶν ἀστέρων ἀποτελέσματα, 'forecast the effects of the stars', sim. 16, VII 6.204, or V 7.3 σκοπεῖν... καὶ πάντων τὰς ἐκβάσεις προλέγειν τῶν τε τόπων καὶ τῶν ἀστέρων 'look... and predict the outcomes'), or 'I announce' (Valens, VII 3.2 προλέγω δὲ πᾶσι). δύναμις is not a technical term in astrology (as opposed to medicine, where for Galen it means essential property, intrinsic function—the active side of a thing's φύσις), and here it is synonymous with Valens' ἀποτελέσματα. Even this modest narratorial assertion (where it occurs at all, προλέγειν is usually an imperative or infinitive) is unusual in the Manethoniana.

313 εἴτ' ἀνδράσιν εἴτε γυναιξὶν: Il. 9.134 ἀνδρῶν ἠδὲ γυναικῶν (at line-end) + Od. 19.408 ἀνδράσιν ἠδὲ γυναιξὶν (line-initial).

314 ὥρη δὲ φύσιν διορίζει: the point is not at all clear. In Firmicus' charts for famous persons (6.30.22–6), the position of the horoscope determines the exact character-type involved (so, the configuration of the stars is the same, but the horoscope determines its realisation in individual lives), but that is not the point here. It is hard to believe that the poet is saying that the horoscope determines whether a child is male or female (~ φύσις). But if this is just a platitude of nursery-school astrology (5.262 n.; Firmicus, 2.19.2 *Est autem cardo primus et totius geniturae compago atque substantia*; see too 5.27–8), how is it relevant?

315 ἀλλὰ καὶ ὣς ἐρέω: 3× EGHP, of which *Il*. 24.106 and *Od*. 19.171 are speakers responding to a question; the only one with an accusative object is Hes. *Op*. 661 ἀλλὰ καὶ ὣς ἐρέω Ζηνὸς νόον αἰγιόχοιο, suggesting that this poet, like the rest, may be repurposing divine material (p. 358).

316–19

Venus in her own houses, with Jupiter, Mercury, Saturn in aspect. This does not seem to be related to the *topikai diakriseis* in *Lib. Herm*. xxxii, which are (i) oriented to male births, with only haphazard coverage of female, and (ii) in *heptazonos* order. The latter is of course far more detailed, with separate treatments for planets in and out of sect, but not so detailed as to give the effects of Venus in her own houses along with the aspect of each of the other planets. The aspecting planets are arranged in Seleucid qualitative order (i. 44 n. 10). Was Mars omitted because it had the same effect as Saturn (318 n.)?

316 σώφρονας ἡ Παφίη: *Lib. Herm*. xxxii. 63 (the only treatment of *topikai diakriseis* to have Venus in her own house) is concerned only with male natives, who are not chaste at all (*inconstantes vero in mulieribus, venerei*). Other ways for Venus to produce this effect: Hephaestion, i. 176.16–18 Γυναῖκας ὁμοίως ὁ

τῆς Ἀφροδίτης ποιεῖ σώφρονας καὶ καθαρίους συσχηματισθεὶς τῷ τοῦ Διὸς καὶ τῷ τοῦ Κρόνου (!); Θ p. 158.10–11 (Venus in the DESC) εἰ δὲ Ἀφροδίτη δυτικὴ ἐκεῖ, δίχα τῆς τῶν κακοποιῶν θεωρίας, σώφρονας.

316–17 μετὰ Ζηνός | εὐμόρφους: likewise (for a male) Jupiter in the houses of Venus in 5.286–7. εὔμορφος, common in astrological prose, is above all associated with Venus, but Jupiter on the ASC produces such individuals in 4.497 (see n.).

317 καθεύρῃ: see on 5.8.

318 The closest match for this seems to be Περὶ σχημ. 70 ὁ Κρόνος Ἀφροδίτην διαμετρῶν πόρνους and Περὶ κράσ. 74 Διάμετρος δὲ ὢν ὁ Κρόνος τῇ Ἀφροδίτῃ τοὺς μὲν πορνικοὺς ‹ποιήσει›; this is the female equivalent, with Venus in her own house. Promiscuity is an obvious outcome when Venus combines with either malefic (Dorotheus, p. 343.12–13 Ἀφροδίτη οἴκοις Κρόνου ἢ Ἄρεως ὑπ' αὐτῶν θεωρουμένη ἀσελγεῖς ποιεῖ).

319 A variation on the topos of 'standing (or sitting) on the roof', i.e. in the brothel (2.430 n., to which add Kapparis, 242, s.v. *stegitis*); they now stand in full view before the door (which lies invitingly open: Philemon, fr. 3.12 K.–A. ἡ θύρα 'στ' ἀνεῳγμένη): see Dio Cass. 79.13.3 γυμνός τ' ἀεὶ ἐπὶ τῆς θύρας αὐτοῦ ἑστὼς ὥσπερ αἱ πόρναι (of 'Sardanapalus' i.e. Elagabalus); John Chrysostom, *PG* 60.505.17–18, who interprets the 'foolish woman' of Prov. 9:14 who sits ἐπὶ θύραις τοῦ ἑαυτῆς οἴκου ἐπὶ δίφρου ἐμφανῶς ἐν πλατείαις enticing people inside as a whore.[187] I take διθύροις to be from δίθυρα = double doors, while noting how rare that is (LSJ has only two examples, both in papyri), but possibly with a double entendre itself on the obscene sense of θύρα (Henderson, 137–8; Adams, 89; M. Fischer, 'Ancient Greek Prostitutes and the Textile Industry in Attic Vase-Painting ca. 550–450 B.C.E.', *CW* 106 (2013), 219–59, at 257). προϊσταμένας is used in the specialised sense of standing in front of a brothel (LSJ B.I.4, esp. Valens, I 3.27: Venus' terms within Virgo when beheld by malefics προΐστασθαι ποιεῖ), exactly like Latin *prostibulum* = 'brothel', and indeed 'prostitution' itself. The sense 'sitting' (like the woman in Proverbs) also appears in *prosedae* = 'prostitutes' (V. Rosivach, *When a Young Man Falls in Love: The Sexual Exploitation of Women in New Comedy* (London, 1983), 95 and 186 n. 83, 183 n. 41). For ἀναφανδόν see 3.331 n. M^d has the prose form (like Ptol. 2.3.25 and 3.15.9, of flagrant lesbians), in contrast to M^a's Odyssean ἀναφανδά.

---

[187] An enduring association between prostitutes and *doors*, still in the 9th- or 10th-c. compilation of laws called the *Procheiron* (35bis 4; *Procheiron Auctum*, 39.98 εἰ γὰρ θυρίδας τις κλάσει τῆς πόρνης…).

320–3

Moon and ASC in four-footed signs. Whores are born. Compare Θ p. 195.12–14 (i. 841). Θ adds Venus; otherwise it is the same.

This does not seem to have anything to do with the specific category of signs that cause lewd behaviour (Hübner 1982, 214–16), which match up only very partially with four-footed signs. The 'lewd' signs (ζῴδια ἀσελγῆ) usually include Capricorn (which is at best marginal among the *tetrapoda*), Pisces (presumably because fish are prolific and produce a lot of milt/roe), and sometimes (because its paranatellon is the Goat) Libra (which is, if anything, bipedal).

Θ's ἀσελγοπύγους is not recognised by LSJ nor supplement. It is a legitimate formation (other -πυγος compounds in B.–P. 632, several with adjectival initial components), but picturesque as it is it is presumably corrupt for ἀσελγοποιούς (with typical confusion of οι and υ). This occurs in the title of the very next section in Θ and Θ¹ (ξζ΄. Περὶ δεκανῶν ἀσελγοποιῶν τῆς Ἀφροδίτης ἐνούσης αὐτοῖς). καταπύγων and occasionally καταπύγαινα are relevant to prostitution. This is about oral sex.

320–1 τετράποσιν...τετραπόδεσσι: perhaps deliberate *variatio* rather than unthinking repetition. (The former is the prose norm, but both are present in epic.)

320 ᾗ στείχουσα: for the periphrastic tense see on 4.384.

321 καθεύροις: see on 5.8.

322 ἀρρήτοις ἔργοισι μιαίνεται: apparently ~ ἀρρητοποιός. There are other examples involving signs which qualify as both lewd and four-footed (Θ p. 196.5–7 and 11–12, with Venus in the first decans of Aries and Leo). The word applies equally to passive homosexual males (Θ p. 196.5–7; Valens, II 37.55 μαλακός, ἀρρητοποιός, cf. ps.-Lucian, *Asin.* 38 καταλαμβάνουσι τοὺς κιναίδους ἄρρητα ἔνδον ἐργαζομένους) and to promiscuous females (Θ p. 196.11; Amphilochius, *In mulierem peccatricem*, l. 8 πορνῶν καὶ τῶν τὰ ἄρρητα ἐργασαμένων, on the sinful woman of Luke 7:37); linked with promiscuity in Teucer, *CCAG* vii. 206.9 ἀρρητοποιίας, πολυκοινίας (first decan of Scorpio).

322–3 L reads ἠΰτε ἔργα. Koechly's ἐπ' ἔργοις is defensible despite the heavy-handed repetition, which is after all characteristic of the Manethonian poets (p. 341). The women are badly spoken of because of shameful *deeds*, which are readily identifiable from the fact that their male counterparts in Θ are λείκτας (the same association in Θ p. 196.5–6; for oral sex see on 4.311–12, and for αἰσχρ- in Greek terms for fellation, see Krenkel, 77). αἰσχροῖς needs a noun to qualify, and ἔργοις is that noun. They are not slandered by shameful mouths (ἐκ στομάτων αἰσχρῶν, printed by Lopilato and De Stefani). ἐκ στομάτων is lifted from Hes. *Th*. 40; if the theft was supposed to be acknowledged, then with a smile-inducing reversal, for the Muses' song was ἐκ στομάτων ἡδεῖα.

κακοφήμως: κακόφημος is not uncommon in astrology for someone in bad repute for louche behaviour which, as usual, does not distinguish between heterosexual promiscuity and passive homosexuality: Ptol. 3.14.35…γυναικῶν διαφθορέας καὶ παίδων, ἔτι δὲ καλλωπιστάς, ὑπομαλάκους, ἐπιψόγους, κακοφήμους, πολυθρυλλήτους, παντοπράκτας; Θ p. 180.11–13…ἐμπαθεῖς δὲ καὶ αἰσχροποιοὺς καὶ μαλακολάλους ἢ καὶ φιλορχηστὰς καὶ κακοφήμους δὲ περὶ τὰ ἀφροδίσια (sim. CCAG i. 116.7–9, CCAG v/1. 202.26–8); Apomasar, *De Rev*. p. 100.16 (in bad odour on account of women).

324–5

Mars in MC by day. The outcome is childlessness. So too in 6.234–6 Mars and the Sun cause childlessness on both MC and IMC; Θ p. 166.26–7 (Mars in MC) κακίζει δὲ καὶ τὸν γάμον καὶ τὰ τέκνα. This is also compatible with Ptol. 4.6.3, where malefics in the MC (or the place after it) produce childlessness, though Ptolemy adds solid signs and the absence of benefics. In the birth chart of Hadrian, who was childless, Mars is in aspect to the MC (Heilen 2015, 868).

324 ἠοῦς γε: Θ (above) has ἡμέρας, in other words, out of sect and therefore out of sorts. ἤως is better understood in its poetic sense, 'day' (LSJ I.2) than as a notation of *time* of day (Koechly: 'mane'; Lopilato: 'in the morning'), which is an irrelevant detail. Alternatively, the poet means 'eastern' (in the astrological sense of ἑῷος: i. 623), but the notation of sect seems more convincing.

λογίζου: buttonholing the addressee in the style of didactic poetry (p. 359) with a word from astrological prose; likewise Dorotheus, p. 434.25 λογίζεο; Anubion, F 12.2 λογιῇι = 12 Perale (rendered by him 'you shall calculate'); Camaterus, *Introd*. 2387–8 τοῦ πράγματος λογίζου | τὴν καταρχὴν εἶναι ⟨λαμπρὰν⟩.

325 ἢ πολλοῖς: loose remake of ἢ πολύ expressions in EGHP, where πολύ is adverbial (*Il*. 1.229 ἢ πολὺ λώϊον, *Od*. 21.325 ἢ πολὺ χείρονες, and elsewhere in line: *Il*. 4.56, 4.307, etc. ἢ πολὺ φέρτερος).

ἄτεκνος: Heilen 2015, 868.

326–31

Saturn 'finds' Venus in his own houses. The woman claims to have given birth, but any children she has are supposititious. This is related to 6.286–94, which starts off with Saturn in the MC and Venus in opposition, but then adds on (i) Jupiter and (ii) Mars to create a little domestic drama of pretence and exposure. In 2.185, Venus in Saturn's houses engenders the childless, and *Lib. Herm*. adds that the effect on females of Venus in Saturn's house is sterility (xxxii. 68 *sterilis fit vel laeditur et fessum semen viri habebit*). There is nothing about supposititious children, though the male native is said to have children by other men whom he raises as his own (66 *Fiunt enim eis filii ab aliis viris et ex adulterio et humo inventi et tamquam proprios filios ipsos nutriunt*).

326 καθεύροι: see on 5.8.

327 ἐκ νηδύος: *Il.* 24.496 (different *sedes*).

328 ψευδομένη δ' ὠδῖνας: 6.291 ψευδέσιν ὠδίνεσσι.

330 κλίνασα δέμας...ἐπὶ κλίνης: 'leaning' is used of postures adopted in childbirth: Call. *Hymn* 4.209 ἀπὸ δ'ἐκλίθη; Nonn. *D.* 41.166 νῶτον ἐπικλίνασα; the back of the birthing stool described by Soranus is to be equipped with an ἀνάκλιτον, for the woman to lean back against (*Gynaik.* 2.3.2). But on a κλίνη, which ought properly to be a couch or bed?[188] Representations of pregnant women, such as they are, show women, sometimes reclined on couches, and sometimes seated on what look like chairs.[189] Soranus, *Gynaik.* 2.3.1, describes a specially modified birthing stool which he called a δίφρος μαιωτικός (Gourevitch 1988, 45), but he also refers separately to beds (κλίνας...δύο), a hard one and a soft one, which should also be available during and after labour, respectively. A marble plaque from Ostia, 400–300 BC (London, Science Museum, inv. no. A129245, reg. nr. 17/1936), nicely shows a woman in a recumbent posture on a couch, while a Roman relief of the 2nd c. AD shows a midwife attending a semi-recumbent woman (Wellcome Library, Photo number: M0003964). The expression looks to be recycling Eur. *Or.* 311 κλῖνον εἰς εὐνὴν δέμας, which is used for a sick person, cf. *Christus Patiens*, 1838 ἀνέκλινας δέμας, of reclining in sleep, and John of Gaza, *Descr.* 700 καὶ δέμας ἀγκλίνασα.

---

[188] E. P. Baughan, *Couched in Death: Klinai and Identity in Anatolia and Beyond* (Madison, Wis., 2013), 17: 'Derived from κλίνω, "to recline," the noun literally refers to any piece of furniture on which one lies down and so can be translated as either "bed" or "couch," depending on context. From the Classical period through the Roman era, the word was used to refer to both beds for sleeping and couches for dining.' For instance, the Gospels use ἐπὶ κλίνης for the bed of the paralytic (Matth. 9:2, Luke 5:18) and of the common couch from which one man shall be saved and another cast out (Luke 17:34).

[189] N. Demand, *Birth, Death, and Motherhood in Classical Greece* (Baltimore, 1994), 121–34, and pll. 1–12; ead., 'Monuments, Midwives and Gynecology', in P. van der Eijk et al. (eds.), *Ancient Medicine in Its Socio-Cultural Context*, i (Amsterdam, 1995), 275–90, and pls. 1–6; Gourevitch 1988, 46–7, and 2011, 225–6. In her descriptions of these scenes, U. Vedder 'Frauentod–Kriegertod im Spiegel der attischen Grabkunst des 4. Jhs. v.Chr.', *MDAI(A)* 103 (1988), 161–91, differentiates between *kline*, *klismos*, and *diphros* (for what is more clearly a chair, as on the lekythos of Theophante, Athens National Archaeological Museum, NM 1055, than the more capacious supports that allow a reclining posture). See also M. M. Lee, 'Maternity and Miasma: Dress and the Transition from παρθένος to γυνή', in L. Hackworth Petersen and P. Salzman-Mitchell (eds.), *Mothering and Motherhood in Ancient Greece and Rome* (Austin, 2012), 23–42, at 31: 'the conventional composition includes the woman reclining on a kline (small bed or couch)'.

στεῖρα λοχός: like 3.278 στείρας τ᾽ ἀλόχους, produced by conjunction or opposition of Saturn and Venus, but with a rare form of λέχω, 'woman in childbirth' (LSJ; *Geoponica*, 12.22.4; late antique Christian authors, beginning with Ephraem, apply it to the Virgin Mary).

331 πλαστὴ μήτηρ: influenced by the son who is πλαστός...πατρί in Soph. *OT* 780 (whence also Sositheus, *TrGF* 99 F 2.4 παῖς παράπλαστος)?

332–40

Moon in *synaphe* with Mars and Venus in the place(s) of the Sun or houses of Mercury; Saturn in opposition. This cascade of adjectives, partly connected and partly asyndetic, is in the style of both late antique poetry (e.g. Orphic Hymns) and apodoses which characterise the ethical effects of a planet, sign, or configuration (like many of Ptolemy's, or Valens' opening characterisation of each planet), and do so in long asyndetic lists. It leavens words standard in astrological prose with tragic vocabulary (λυπρήν, λυσσάδα, γαμέτης) and some rarities (εὔκνιστον, πρόλαλον). What is striking about the former is that they are almost invariably paralleled in Ptolemy's chapter on the quality of the soul (3.14, in which he surveys the effects of the planets as sole governors and then when allied with other stars). Why? Ptolemy is talking generically, and never specifically about women. As for the characteristics imputed to the awful wife, several are depressingly familiar already from Semonides' anti-women invective, and for grim resignation to marriage, see Susarion, fr. 1 K.–A., Gell. *NA* 1.6 (Holford-Strevens, 308–9).

334 δνοφερὴν: i. 911 n. 16, and on Saturn's darkness n. 15. EGHP epithet of night (as well as earth, pitch, and water).

335 ἰσχνὴν: the adjective means thin, withered, dried-up. Semonides' dog-woman has an ἄπρηκτον αὐονήν (20) (though Lloyd-Jones reads αὐονήν and translates 'barking'), while his monkey-woman, whom he calls the μέγιστον... κακόν, is ἄπυγος, αὐτόκωλος (76) ('skin and bone', *a mere skeleton*: LSJ). She is malevolent, too (81–2 καὶ τοῦτο πᾶσαν ἡμέρην βουλεύεται, | ὅκως τι κὼς μέγιστον ἔρξειεν κακόν ~ κακόβουλον), and an association seems to persist between thinness and ill will in the physiognomists (Adamantius, 2.14 αἱ δὲ ἰσχναὶ πάνυ καὶ κεναὶ (sc. γαστέρες) δειλίαν καὶ κακοήθειαν [cf. 339] καὶ γαστριμαργίαν σημαίνουσι; sim. ps.-Polemon, 46).

λυπρήν: this is strongly Euripidean (30 instances), with another two in Aeschylus and five in Lycophron; in tragedy, it generally applies to circumstances (often βίος), and rarely to people (Aesch. *Eum.* 173; Eur. *Med.* 301).

336 All these epithets are common in astrology; M^d has just arranged them in a scannable order. All are attested in Ptol. 3.14. Taking these and other astrological occurrences into account, αὐστηρός[190] and βασκανός[191] have a particular association with Saturn; προπετής[192] generally with Mars (but with Mercury badly placed in Ptol. 3.14.36), while πολυπράγμων tends to combine the influences of Mercury (alone in Hephaestion, i. 295.21) and Mars (Ptolemy, 3.14.31 (Mars allied with Mercury in honourable positions); Θ p. 179.17, sim. CCAG v/1. 202.1, 223.27).

αὐστηρός characterises both male and female natives, and when a female chart was scrutinised from the point of view of a potential mate, harsh, crabbed, and unaccommodating was precisely what she was *not* supposed to be (Ptol. 4.5.3 γυναῖκας ἐπιπόνους καὶ αὐστηράς; CCAG x. 114.29 αὐστηρή, ἰδιόπεισμος; xi/2. 116.5 πρὸς τοὺς ἄνδρας αὐστηρά).

337 This line presents a general contrast with the previous one, in that the first three epithets are unique in astrology, and the first two very rare altogether. εὔκνιστος is altogether unique but for Dorotheus (6th c. ecclesiastic), *Didascalia*, 4.55, an adjuration not to be too easily riled; πρόλαλος is otherwise found in Aelian, fr. 22 πρόλαλον... καὶ ἰταμόν, hence a quality that goes well with προπετῆ in the line before. φιλόνεικος returns to familiar astrological jargon—very familiar indeed, given the frequency with which it deals with conflict (including sports in 5.170). It would be a bigger project to study what kinds of situation different astrological authors have in mind when they mention conflict, but it is striking how rarely, when occasions for φιλονεικία are given at all, they are expressly political (Hephaestion, i. 30.25 φιλονεικήσει δὲ πρὸς ὑπερέχοντας), or commercial (Hephaestion, i. 221.1 φιλονεικίας πραγμάτων?), let alone intellectual (Apomasar, *De Myst.*, CCAG xi/1. 174.9 σημαίνει τινὰ ἐπιμελούμενον τῶν δογματικῶν καὶ φιλονεικοῦντα ἕνεκεν αὐτῶν). Marital antagonisms, on the other hand, are trivially common.[193]

βληχρὰν: this time, for an adjective that stands outside the prose/Ptolemaic lexicon, the poet has not used the tragic register; the epithet is epic (though Homer has only ἀβληχρ-) and Ionic, including Hippocratic. What does it mean? Usually it is applied to things—elements (Alcaeus, fr. 319 Voigt),

---

[190] Valens, I 1.7, I 3.49, II 17.62 (Saturn trine with Venus), Περὶ κράσ. 1; Ptol. 2.3.36, 3.14.10, 13 (Saturn allied with Jupiter in dishonourable positions), 14 αὐστηροπράκτους (Saturn allied with Mars in honourable positions), 16 (Saturn allied with Venus in honourable positions); Περὶ σχημ. 99 (Saturn conjunct with Mercury).

[191] Valens, I 1.1, I 3.5, I 3.49, Περὶ κράσ. 76 (Saturn quartile to Mercury, Mercury superior); Ptol. 3.14.11; Π.σ.α. p. 184.29 (Moon leaves Saturn for Mercury); CCAG xi/2. 109.6.

[192] Ptol. 3.14.28, 23 (Jupiter allied with Mars in dishonourable positions); Θ p. 178.16, sim. CCAG v/1. 201.6, 222.30; Περὶ σχημ. 77 (Jupiter and Mars in opposition).

[193] Specifically of women: CCAG x. 190.11–12 Ἡ γεννηθεῖσα κόρη ἐν καιρῷ ζῳδίου τοῦ Λέοντος εἰς τὸν ἄνδρα της πικρή, οἰκονομική, φιλόνεικος, 231.4–5 ἀλλὰ τὸ ἴδιον πεῖσμα πράττουσα· ἔστιν γὰρ φιλόνεικος, 242.25–6 ...ἀποβάλεται [sic] ἢ καταρρίξει αὐτόν [sc. her husband]· ἔστι γὰρ φιλόνεικος; Achmet, *Oneir.* 294.6–7 εὑρήσει γυναῖκα εὐειδῆ μέν, φιλόνεικον δὲ καὶ δυσπρόσιτον.

currents of water, disease—whose force is blunted (see Livrea on Ap. Rhod. 4.152), which seems precisely the opposite of what is required (cf. προπετῆ), but 'slight' of build would seem to reiterate the point made by ἰσχνήν. Is M^d, in defiance of poetic usage, using the grammarians' (incorrect) notion that it means 'strong', 'in full force', according to which the Homeric form is the privative (passages cited in Stephanus, including Heraclides of Miletus, fr. 7 Cohn = Pind. fr. incert. 245 Maehler, cf. *Suda*, β 340; Orion, α p. 7 ἀβληχρόν)?

338 But for the first epithet, we return to Ptolemaic vocabulary.

λυσσάδα: again tragic/dithyrambic: Eur. *Her.* 887 (epithet of Ποιναί) and 1024 (epithet of μοῖραι); Timotheus, *PMG* 778 fr. 2b (of Artemis). Nonnus' nineteen instances apply to animals, persons in the ambit of Dionysus, Aura (only in *D.* 14.207 in this *sedes*, so too Leontius Scholasticus, *AP* 16.289.6, of Agave); for a bad-tempered wife it is hyperbolical, to perhaps comical effect.

ζηλότυπον: jealousy is caused by Mars (for strife), blighted Venus, or both, as here.[194] In Ptolemy it comes about, strikingly, when planets are in honourable positions (3.14.16 (Saturn with Venus), 29 (Mars with Venus)), which suggests that in males, at least, it ranks with spiritedness as no bad quality. In 2.3.14 and 3.14.34 (Venus with Mercury) it means 'eager', 'desirous', of homosexual relations.

ἀγνώμονα: 'hard-hearted' (Apomasar, *De Myst.*, *CCAG* xi/1. 202.2 ἀχάριστον καὶ ἀγνώμονα), or better still 'headstrong', suits the context better than 'lacking in good sense'; the problem is not stupidity (unlike with Semonides' earth-woman, who knows nothing except how to eat: 24), or inefficacy (as implied in Hephaestion, i. 150.19–21 τὸ δικαιότερον καὶ ἀνυστικώτερον versus τὸ ταπεινότερον καὶ ἐπιπονώτερον καὶ ἀγνωμονέστερον). The required sense is in Ptol. 3.14.23 (Jupiter allied with Mars in dishonourable positions), where it is near προπετεῖς, and especially in 4.5.3 θυμικὰς καὶ ἀστάτους καὶ ἀγνώμονας, where it describes Mars' effect on wives.

περίεργον: the meddlesome wife is another Semonidean archetype (his dog-woman, who wants to hear and see everything, ll. 13–14). The outcome is Mercurial;[195] wives in Θ p. 158.14 (DESC). For the word see 303–4 n.

339 πῆμα...κακόηθες: the right agencies produce malevolence in Valens (I 20.12 κακοηθείας within the family produced by Saturn, Venus, and the Moon; I 20.27 κακοήθεις, Venus and the luminaries; II 17.42, Mercury in quartile with the Moon), but the nice touch is attaching the epithet to the personified

---

[194] Valens, I 19.18 (Mars and Venus), II 38.17 (Moon and Venus quartile or opposed), Περὶ κράσ. 163 (Mars and Venus).

[195] Θ p. 140.18; Valens, I 2.19 and 50 (Gemini and Virgo, houses of Mercury), II 15.9. Mercury with Saturn: Ptol. 3.14.18; Valens, I 19.4, IV 20.12, Περὶ κράσ. 34.

πῆμα, for κακόηθες can also be used of wounds, sores, and ulcers (e.g. CCAG viii/3. 161.18 κακοήθη ἕλκη). A wizened condition indicates both a malevolent person (335 n.) and an indurated disease (Stephanus, In Hippocratis Aphorismos commentaria, 2.27 κακοήθειαν πολλὴν... τοῦ νοσήματος).

λυγρῷ γαμέτῃ: long-suffering spouse. In EGHP the epithet, when applied to persons, means 'miserable' in the sense of weak, cowardly, contemptible, but presumably the poet does not mean they are wimps; he uses M[a]'s trick of converting epithets that mean 'inflicting' grief (πήματα λυγρά: Lyc. Al. 763; Anon. De Vir. Herb. (LXIV Heitsch), 205; Maximus, 130) to the meaning 'suffering' it (3.40 n.). As for the noun, from its appearances in Hephaestion and Περὶ κράσ. 138, it looks as if the feminine, γαμέτη, was used in Dorotheus and/or the poem that Περὶ κράσ. paraphrases, one of the moderately recherché words for 'spouse' that astrological poetry likes (nn. on 2.268–9, 3.148); but the masculine, which is still more of a rarity, is attested in astrology only here. It perhaps has a deliberately chosen tragic feel (ps.-Aesch. PV 897; Eur. Suppl. 1028, Tr. 311), and put together the two words perhaps recall Eur. Med. 399 λυγροὺς θήσω γάμους, spoken by tragedy's ultimate awful wife.

συναλιζόμενον: unless the poet is playing fast and loose with quantities, this should derive from συνᾰλίζω, 'share salt with', as LSJ take it, not συνᾱλίζω, 'gather together' (Koechly, 'congregatum', taking it as passive; Lopilato: 'in forming evil associations', taking it as middle). In other words, this horror is in the very heart of the household. The verb is very rare (Acts 1:4, of Jesus sharing the board of the disciples). The metaphor is not (see Lightfoot 1999, 465, on Alexander of Aetolia in Parthenius, Narr. Am. 14 = Magnelli fr. 3.15), but it usually refers to relations of amity/sodality (and their betrayal), not marital ones.

340 What is this additional circumstance? The Moon is already in *synaphe* with Venus, so what more influence can she exert? The verb of mitigation carries across to the woman from its frequent astrological application to stars and their evil (or good) effects (1.214 n.; e.g. 2.409 ἀμβλύνοντες; Dorotheus, p. 326.6 κακοεργέες ἀμβλύνονται). Perhaps the line sounded funnier to an ancient reader than it does to us, since it continues to suggest that the wife is a (mitigable) disaster, a parcel of calamity sent by the stars.

Epimetrum

> 'For better or worse, it is the commentator who has the last word.'
> (Charles Kinbote)

Losing oneself in a morass of detail is the eternal problem with astrological poetry, just like astrological charts themselves with their endless accumulation of petty circumstances that add up to so many dots that still remained unjoined. Now that I have gone just about as far as I can go with the Manethoniana, is it possible to draw any general conclusions?

First, they are mostly a collection of a particular kind of thing, *if p then q* literature, though they also contain, largely as a result of editorial caprice, other material as well. The earliest poet elected to begin(?) his poem with a résumé of elementary doctrine about the celestial circles, more because it established his professional and Aratean and didactic credentials than because it did very much to underpin the science of μαθηματική. The first book contains snatches of polemic about the astrological deities and their superiority over the traditional gods of cult, and a *schetliasmos* of the planet Mars; the fifth book contains, after the proem, stock lines from Homer which ground the astrological world-view in the most venerable authority. It need not follow that the discursive passages are differently authored than the prognostic ones. Koechly attributed the two long passages in book 1 to an author other than that of the apotelesmata, but that is a *petitio principii* and cannot be established by metre or style. Our understanding of ancient star poetry would be transformed were we able to see these passages in their original contexts, rather than as *disiecta membra* among material given mostly over to other things. Are we to infer a corpus of poetry which was significantly more self-reflecting than the unthinking applications of unexplained postulates that constitutes the mass of apotelesmata? There is no evidence of any conscience about philosophical groundedness, such as we find in Manilius, but what all these discursive passages are dancing around instead is the question of tradition. It may be a matter of breaking with the old gods of cult in a flagrant way. Or it may be a matter of poets hitching their wagon to *literary* tradition, garnering cultural capital for their art and didactic authority for their poetry. Are we right to pick up on suggestions of technocratic aggressiveness and defensiveness? Medical didactic does not seem to throw up anything like this, either to assert and justify and place itself, or even to versify workaday lists of day-to-day prognostics, which is mostly what the Manethoniana are about. Why not?

So, astrological poetry did a great deal more than what the editors of the Manethonian corpus have decided to concentrate on, which is narrow and realised in a highly formal and rule-governed way. Maximus shows how the same format could be handled with less sclerosis and more caprice. Even so, the very restrictive formalism of the Manethoniana creates micro-opportunities of its own, and one can appreciate the poets' ingenuity within the very limited form to which they have committed themselves, especially how well it comports with the late-antique aesthetic of segmentation, *Medalliondichtung* or *Blockbildung*. Where segments are apparently preserved in an original sequence (easy enough to identify in systematic catalogues; not necessarily so easy with material of more miscellaneous content) we can appreciate the interplay of sequence, on the one hand, and the self-containment of micro-segments, on the other. Where this is not possible, we can still appreciate the pains poets have taken, especially those of the first and fifth books, to create pleasingly 'closed' structures. But the larger question is why. What was it all for?

The obvious answer is that verse has a mnemotechnic function. That does seem likely to some extent, although it has to face certain obvious, practical objections, not only the sketchiness of much of what is versified when what the human brain usually *needs* to be reminded of is hard detail, but also the impracticality of using astrological poetry actually to formulate a set of predictions, for one would need to memorise reams and reams of poetry in order to extract the precise circumstances that met the individual constellation of a given chart. Anyway, is the answer necessarily the same for each book? The fourth has a level of stylistic ambition that raises the question whether this was meant as a poem for reading for pleasure—or even declaiming, given the metrical features it shares with the declamatory poetry of Nonnus (pp. 237–8). This is the book for which most papyrus evidence survives, now in three separate papyri, although new publications from Oxyrhynchus could quickly change that picture.

Yet that evidence is complicated. It shows evidence of micromanagement on an intense scale. So much for any suggestion that versification fixes poetry and makes it tamper-proof, as Galen claimed for the medical poetry of Damocrates and Andromachus.[1] But what Galen was in fact talking about were quantitative details in recipes for drugs. Spelling numerals out in verse is an obvious defence against the kind of adulteration that could happen at the stroke of a pen with numerals represented alphabetically in prose. But Manethonian astrological

---

[1] For mnemotechnics, see Monteventi, 50–4 (Galen on 53), 197–8, 268; i. 179.

poetry is not particularly (or at all) fond of rendering numbers.² It has very different habits from Dorotheus (at least in his section on ὅρια and ὑψώματα), let alone Manilius, with his eminent aptitude (or baneful penchant) for doing sums in verse.³ On the contrary, the differences between the various recensions of the material in the fourth book show how readily manipulable it really was. This variation has been put down (presumably rightly) to the place of the Manethoniana as *Fachliteratur*; in other words, so far from verse *saving* it from the tamperings of practitioners, it was *precisely* practitioners who were gerrymandering it with the tiresomely minute and largely trivial differences that we see. And yet a lot of these fussy interventions are not about altering the astrological details. Most in fact are not. We do see changes of that kind if we compare the charts common to the Manethoniana, Anubion, and Firmicus, but these are not the main kinds of change between book 4 and $\varPi^1$, or between either and book 1. Rather, a lot of the changes are about accommodating the inherited material to a different author's style. Aesthetic qualities are important; poets have house styles; they receive material but they also, it seems, want to impose their own stylistic fingerprints on it. This is what makes astrological poetry so complicated. It is a matter *both* of the coexistence of distinct and separable poetic personae *and* of the transmission of inherited material, which can be 'owned' or reappropriated to a greater or lesser degree by superficial or more thoroughgoing stylistic interventions.

On the aesthetics of astrological catalogue poetry in general, it bears emphasising one last time that this material can be seen, not, or not only, as some minor curiosity, but as a prime expression of trends that can be found at least as early as Hellenistic poetry (the fashionability of segmentation) and continue to develop throughout the imperial period (what Michael Roberts, in his study of the jewelled style, calls *leptologia* or ἀκριβολογία⁴). If you find star-poetry rebarbative, then you may well be reacting against the very qualities that were prized most highly in the literary cultures that produced it: the high formalism which provides precisely the grid and set of constraints against which the poets demonstrate their virtuosity (including their metrical ingenuity in incorporating difficult words); the creation of a whole from independent compositional units, in which 'contiguity does not require continuity';⁵ the technique of

---

² 6.37 n., i. 736. Sections of Dorotheus have a far greater appetite for numerals; so too Anubion, F 12.1–6 = 12 Perale.
³ For Dorotheus and Manilius respectively, see M. Vogel, *Ter quinque volumina: Zahlenperiphrase in der lateinischen Dichtung von ihren Anfängen bis ins zweite Jahrhundert n. Chr.* (Münster, 2014), 68–78, 421–522; 'sums in verse' is Housman.
⁴ Roberts, 41: *leptologia* comes from the 3rd-c. rhetorical theorist Aquila Romanus, and ἀκριβολογία from Demetrius, *Eloc.* 4.209.
⁵ Roberts, 56–7; see also Agosti 2012, 375: 'composition becomes analytic; scenes are linked by juxtaposition'.

composition through the accumulation of micromanaged detail; the 'enumerative sequences'[6] consisting of carefully curated parallelisms and antitheses, in which phonetic and syntactic effects are brought to bear (anaphora, homoeoteleuton, isocolon, assonance, and occasional full-blown Gorgianic figures) in tiny clauses consisting of *kommata* or simply single words; the offsetting of parallelism against *variatio*, managed with equal care; the long lists of related items consisting of members of a single genus, whereby the 'limited differentiation of *leptologia*'[7] becomes the perfect realisation in literary terms of the endless variations on standard types produced by the actions of the stars. Some of the aspects of the style Roberts is describing emerge with particular clarity at certain points in the collection. Late-antique literary metaphors of embroidery or mosaics extend to the treatment of canonical classics, which were designed to stand out like jewels in their new setting. All the Manethonian poets create their verse out of the warp and weft, or flotsam and jetsam, of Homeric verse, but M^d's Nicandrian moment was surely designed to stand out as a *morceau de bravoure*, and called for readers who were accordingly competent. Roberts derives the elements of the style from the rules of rhetorical ecphrasis; it has wider purchase beyond that specific context, but at the same time the outcome of an apotelesma is, in a certain sense, if not an 'ecphrasis', then a 'description' of a particular state of affairs, and in the hands of M^b the ecphrastic quality is clearly demonstrable, with a kind of rhetorical *enargeia* brought about through the circumstantiality of his overblown lists. Again, Roberts' characterisation of the jewelled style as one in which individual words have 'a physical presence of their own'[8] is well instanced by M^b's extraordinary neologisms. The effect is reinforced by general metrical trends whereby the hexameter tends to fall into four increasingly clearly demarcated sections, each occupied by a significant and weighty unit of content.

Many of the poets' mannerisms are obvious at first glance—the lumberingly prosaic definite articles in the fifth book, and still more the vaporous style (which is nevertheless kept under control with more regular verbal constructions than in the other books) of the fourth, which I suspect was meant to *sound* impressive and was suitable for declamation. But each poet in the corpus has a distinct profile more finely analysable through lexical, syntactic, and other stylistic criteria, and one of the best ways of appreciating these personae is through the study of metre. M^d's hiatuses and lengthenings *in arsi* were

---

[6] Roberts uses the phrase *passim* in his second chapter, 'The Literary Tradition and Its Refinement', 38–65.

[7] Roberts, 93.

[8] Roberts, 58, 72: 'Words draw attention to themselves by their uncommonness and disproportion to the context, their deviation from standard usage.'

always as glaring an idiosyncrasy as, say, the false quantities in some of the Sibyllina. But a closer analysis throws, for instance, M^b's sprightly dactyls and feminine caesurae into sharp relief against the opposite preferences of M^d, or the nicety of both M^b and M^c about word-break against the coach-and-horses approach of both M^a and M^d. What emerges as a matter of principle is that there is no single spectrum along which the poets can be conveniently arranged for the purposes of chronology (from archaic to Hellenistic, from Hellenistic to Nonnian), supposing anyone was expecting such a thing in the first place. More interestingly, however, it also shows that poetry which is not in the slipstream of the progressives (more spondees, more masculine caesurae) does *not* simply revert to a Homeric norm. For all his indispensability as a literary model, Homer's metre is not the default for the astrological poets. Indeed, the caesura is a particularly interesting criterion, for only M^b, M^c, and Maximus have an outright majority of feminine caesurae, as was the tendency in Greek poetry ever since Homer: not even Dorotheus, with his high rates of dactyls, pushes beyond 50%.[9] (Dorotheus' headline figure is 51.61% masculine, although that is skewed by the sections on *kentrothesia* and *horia*; without those, masculine caesurae fall to 46.45%.) One wonders whether the shade of Aratus is casting an influence here, and behind him a perception that the masculine caesura was a styleme suited for a didactic/gnomic/prophetic/'authoritarian' style of verse, though it is an isolated feature if so.[10] In other words, not only does being less progressive not equate with being more Homeric or Hesiodic, but poets who have certain 'modern' tendencies (greater numbers of dactyls) do not necessarily follow through in other respects. Other poets in the corpus present features that are more reminiscent of both the Sibylline Oracles and also of the fourth-century inscribed epigram studied by Fantuzzi and Sens, who found that in some respects Hellenistic literary and inscribed verse seemed 'in a sense to reflect a greater awareness of the "norms" inherited from Homer'[11] than the fourth-century outliers. M^a and M^d are like that, particularly in respect of outer

---

[9] I am unsure of the basis of the claim (Agosti and Gonnelli, 318; Agosti 2004*b*, 69) that the Manethoniana have a ratio of 2/3 masculine to 1/3 feminine caesurae. This is not true of any single book, and meaningless if meant to represent the whole corpus.

[10] Scholars have tended to repeat the assertion of West 1982, 153, that the masculine caesura predominates in Aratus, although elsewhere is quoted a figure of somewhat less than half (47.8%, from Fr. Jaeckel, 'De poetarum Siculorum hexametro' (Diss. Leipzig, 1902), whence van Raalte, 79; Nieto Ibáñez, 147). The gnomic sections of Hesiod also have an outright majority of masculine caesurae (West on Hesiod, *Theogony*, p. 94; van Raalte, 75); for the suggestion that this helped to mould a perception of what was suited to the gnomic style, see Nieto Ibáñez, 152; Agosti 2004*b*, 68–9. If that is right, the astrological poets chose to cultivate that facet of Hesiod rather than his genealogical mode, which often places τε mid-line (and hence elevates the number of feminine caesurae), which might equally have suited a type of poem based on lists.

[11] Fantuzzi and Sens, 109.

metric (see p. 357).¹² There is no obvious rationale for the parallels between pre-Hellenistic epigram and imperial astrological poetry (presumably one would not want to hand-wave at an ongoing tradition of 'popular verse'), but both represent a state of affairs where neither is Homer the norm, nor have the refinements of high Hellenistic poetics imposed themselves. Yet even here, there are occasional features where they seem to align with the more forward-pointing members of the corpus.¹³ Metrical features do not come as a package.

Are the first and fifth books by the same author? They do seem to be related in more deep-seated ways than through their disordered state alone, which after all could be accidental. The fact that both turn out to have so much in common with the intriguing Anubion F 12 (12 Perale) may suggest that there is some deep-rooted tradition that they share (p. 281). Both arrange the planets qualitatively rather than positionally (pp. 134–5), and in the manuscript, the first book has a table which would be better attached to the fifth (p. 387). These two books are also alike in their high numbers of Attic forms (especially the dative plural feminine ending), whether that implies anything about joint transmission. But the most immediate case for connecting them (and connecting their poets, not their editors) rests on the basis of stylistic similarities, some of which De Stefani pointed out. Above all, what they have in common is their parallelistic style, their Leonine hexameters and whole-line parallelisms and isocola. Yet other mannerisms separate them. What tells most strongly against common authorship is metre.¹⁴ The lengthening of short syllables *in arsi* that becomes a fetish in M^d is only very occasional in the first book. Other dramatic differences include the numbers of spondees in the third foot and hence rates of masculine caesurae (at the top and bottom of the range respectively), and the preparedness or otherwise to violate Meyer's First and Second Laws (which M^d simply pulverises). Rates of infractions of Hermann's Bridge are a giveaway as

---

¹² They are also the two astrological poets who fall below the norm, which remains strong until the evolution of Nonnian poetics, for the average number of dactyls *per* verse to fall somewhere in the range of 3.6–3.7. Then again, if it is true, as van Raalte suggests (31), that verse on 'technical' or 'cognitive' subjects (such as Archestratus, with a mere 3.06 dactyls per verse) struggles to limit the number of spondees, perhaps what we should be remarking on instead is the effort taken by the majority of poets to keep their numbers of dactyls as high as they are.

¹³ Imperial poetry is increasingly loth to omit the third-foot caesura (Agosti 2004*b*, 65–7; Magnelli 2016, 363). It does not surprise us that M^b has no examples, but it might that M^d is the only astrological poet to join him.

¹⁴ Dr Holford-Strevens observes that some of the fifth book's peculiarities may suggest the influence of Latin, especially the neglect of Hermann's Bridge (D. O. Ross, *Style and Tradition in Catullus* (Cambridge, MA, 1969), 129–30) and Meyer's Laws, as well as the preference for word-break after the third rather than second position when either would scan (81 Ἀργαλέων ἄστρων, 86 πταίοντας τόλμῃ, 97 οὐρανίοις ἄστροις)—though not the anomalous observance of Naeke's Law. This is also the poet whose use of ἀναβαίνει of social ascent recalls Latin usage (5.276 n.). But the extent of Latin influence, if any, is sporadic and hard to quantify; see also 4.508–10 n. and i. Index s.v. Latinisms.

well. Syntactically, the first book has nothing to match the relentless use of the definite article which is so characteristic of the fifth. Formal criteria also separate them. In the realisation of the *if p then q* formula of apotelesmata M^d has idiosyncrasies that M^c does not share; in the apodosis, he is considerably *more* fond of the gnomic aorist, and *less* fond of the future. The poet of the fifth book, for some reason, has a minor fetish for calling Venus 'the Paphian' (17×), but this is much less frequent in the first book (5×), more in line with M^a. I would suggest that such similarities as the two books have are the result of (i) their external condition, i.e. the accidents of transmission, and more interestingly either (ii) imitation of one poet by another or even (iii) a house style within late antique astrological poetry (elements of which can be seen in the Sibylline Oracles as well). That is the main gain of being able to distinguish the poets. It is hardly enough to warrant talk of a 'school' of astrological poetry. But if at least two poets share certain prominent mannerisms, either one is paying homage to the other or a level of style and set of conventions have established themselves at which both are taking aim.

In some respects they point forwards to late antiquity, although it is not clear that Nonnus knows the Manethoniana themselves.[15] The closest Nonnus comes to anything like an apotelesma is in the scene where Astraios casts the nativity of Persephone, one of whose details is that the Sun is in the IMC, exactly in opposition to the Moon. This is described in remarkably Manethonian language (save that the Sun has Jupiter's epithet) in *D*. 6.76–7 καὶ Φαέθων ἰσόμοιρος ἔην ἀντώπιδι Μήνῃ | κέντρῳ ὑποχθονίῳ πεφορημένος; the parallel, moreover, is with the literary fourth book (see on 4.336), which is the one, if any, one might expect Nonnus to know. Uranus' castration is also described in rather similar terms in 1.120 στάχυν ἄρρενα...ἀποτμήξειε and *D*. 18.228 τάμνεν...στάχυν ἄρσενα, though to explain that it might be prudent to seek a common source. For the most part, however, what one finds are anticipations of (i) some isolated words and occasional phrases, especially in the fourth book, which anticipate Nonnian diction,[16] and (ii) late antique verse-patterns which are especially well represented in Nonnus simply because there is so *much* of Nonnus, but which can hardly be pressed for evidence of the impact of the Manethoniana.[17]

---

[15] V. Stegemann, *Astrologie und Universalgeschichte: Studien und Interpretationen zu den Dionysiaka des Nonnos von Panopolis* (Leipzig, 1930), 8, 9.

[16] Book 4. 74 ἀντικέλευθος; 255 ἀρνοφάγος; 347 αἰγλήεσσα; 429 στεφανηδόν; 603 ἐκ γενετήρων. Book 1. 203 καὶ Κυθερείη. Book 5. 185 αἰνομανοῦς; 196 πορδάλιος στικτῆς; 257 ὄμμα Σελήνης.

[17] Book 4. 6 ἡμιτμῆτι πορείῃ; 7 θεομήστορα κόσμον; 23 ἀμφίβιος θήρ; 42 ὀλβίστη παράκοιτις; 55 μερόπων τις ἐνέγκῃ 131 ἀστέρα πατρός; 207 Κυθερηίδος αἴγλης; 282 ἀπόλιστα γένεθλα (cf. 316 μυσαρωπὰ γένεθλα, 587 ὑπόβλητα γένεθλα); 336 ἀντώπια φέγγεα κόσμου; 496 ὡροσκόπον ὄμμα τιταίνῃ; 585 λέχη λιπόπαιδα φερούσας. Book 1. 53 ἀμετροβίων ἐλεφάντων; 138 ἑὸν πόδα; 176 αἰθέριος λίψ; 193 εἰς Ἄϊδος κατίασιν ἀνοστήτοιο μέλαθρον; 232 νεκύων σκιοειδέα μορφήν; 330 νεκυηπόλος Αἶσα. Book 5. [5.141 ἴδμων τ' ὀρχηθμοῦ my restoration]; 162 μυκήματα σάλπιγξ; 171

These verse-patterns are found throughout the fourth, first, and fifth books, but seem to be particularly concentrated in the τέχναι of the fifth, presumably because this is precisely the point at which the poet lifts his sights, as evidenced also by his combinatory allusions and above all his homage to Nicander.

There are ultimately no easy takeaways from the Manethoniana. I have not made any advances on what they were 'for', because the evidence does not bear on that; progress would require more information about their reception, and that was not forthcoming. But we can be confident that we have advanced beyond Koechly in our models of how astrological poetry was transmitted, if not how it was used. And, not by reconceptualising it, but simply by digging so much more deeply into it, we have gleaned a great deal more about its place in literary and intellectual history. The poet of the fifth book tries to make Homer the theorist of the astrological word-view, if not of its particular doctrines. That is rhetorical posturing, but carried over to poetics it is literally true that without Homer there is no astrological poetry. Hesiod's significance as didactic barely registers beside that of Homer for the building-blocks of expropriable verse, and also for snippets of sentiments on human life and fate and suffering and everyday work and business. In their allusive technique and ability to weave multiple passages together I was surprised by the extent of overlap with the technique of an undoubted sophisticate like Dionysius the Periegete. (Even the maligned poet of the fifth book has this in his toolkit.) But above all, we can better appreciate Manethonian poetry as a treasure-house of commonplace, a repository of images and cultural memories reflecting the hopes, fears, values, mental baggage, and spiritual range of *l'homme moyen sensuel* in the world of approximately the second to the fourth centuries AD. The setting is Egypt, but much of the time we would not know it; the works of Louis Robert shed as much or more light than the papyri. This is the cultural *koine* of the Greek East, and it is not a very political one, apparently, with individuals projecting themselves into public life and interacting with their peers ultimately to the ends of self-realisation and self-interest. We get introspection and solipsism from the genre, or rather, we get private desires policed by a strong and censorious normative voice which is an excellent guide to the range and limits of acceptable behaviour. These attitudes represent a middling point of view, launched from a level which turns out to have much in common with Paul Veyne's characterisation of the *plebs media* in the city of Rome. I suggested at the beginning of the book that the trope-laden Manethoniana represented a kind of poor-man's Second Sophistic, a rag-bag of cliché instead of élite self-cultivation through

---

τετράζυγον ἅρμα διώκων; 172 ἐπινίκιον ἵππον ἐλαύνων; 180 Κυβελήιον ἔνθεον Ἄττιν; 206 ὁμογάστριον εὐνήν; 208 Ἀρσινόης ὑμεναίους. Add the contentless patterns in 118 ἐπίψογον εἰς νόσον ὀργῆς and 131 ἄστατον ὀργήν.

appeal to prestigious classic texts. And there is more to be said about cultural horizons. Take music. Sadly, a seminar planned in Corfu for 2012 on the place of music in Second Sophistic texts from Philodemus to Philostratus never happened because of the Greek financial crisis. If it had, it would no doubt have shed light on the ways in which music theory and practice were adapted to the polite artifice of classicism, 'an entrée...to that elusive ancient-Greekness which was the badge of an educated person'.[18] So much for the *pepaideumenoi*, anyway, but what does astrology give us? Apart from very bland and generic references to lyres and auloi and sweet nothings in Firmicus, we get thumping theatrical effects (6.509), the heady pipe music of Cybele (6.498), singers of smutty mimes (4.184), and flute- and harp-girls (5.143, 236). If every author or genre gets the music it deserves, the Manethonian level seems to be crude effects for coarse palates—though it is also a lovely thought that Ptolemy's 'string-twisters' (4.4.6 χορδοστρόφους) are not, in fact, the virtuosi finessing their concert citharas in order to mesmerise audiences in the odeion, but the harmonic scientists who put their theories to the test on the monochord and *helikon* and other devices described in the *Harmonics*.[19] They take their place next to instrument-makers; in other words they can be seen as a species of Ptolemaic technical expert (p. 1025), theoreticians at least as soon as artists tuning their instruments.

The statues of the great and the good in the agoras and stoas look with inscrutable solemnity on all the hubbub of the ancient city that is represented by astrological texts, although at the end of the day what statues and texts alike represent are replicable types. If I have done nothing else, I hope to have cast some light on the particular image repertoire of the Manethoniana, and the ways in which they figure the world of the High and Later Empire.

---

[18] A. Barker, 'Greek Musicologists in the Roman Empire', in T. D. Barnes (ed.), *The Sciences in Greco-Roman Society* (Edmonton, 1994), 53–74, at 62.

[19] A. Barker, 'Ptolemy and the Meta-Helikôn', *Studies in the History and Philosophy of Science*, 40/4 (2009), 344–51.

Appendices

APPENDIX I

Pinakes

P: Protasis
A: Apodosis

✳: the closest correspondence among all the comparanda
*: material in Θ supplementary to Ptolemy (see p. 140)

Book Four Members of the sequence that shadows Θ <u>are underlined</u>

14–107. *Kentrothesiai*			
<u>14–27 Saturn in its own houses in ASC</u> [cf. 503–7]		P, A: 3.12–17	P, A: Dor.^ARAB II 23.1. P: Περὶ κέντρ. 14. No houses: Θ p. 135.10–16; Firmicus, 3.2.1
<u>28–34 Saturn not in its own houses in MC or ASC</u>		MC. P: 3.21–6 ASC. P: 3.8–12	MC. P, but no houses: Θ pp. 167.30–168.5. P, A, but no houses: Dor.^ARAB II 23.8;✳Paul, p. 65.13–19 ASC. P, A: Dor.^ARAB II 23.3. P: Περὶ κέντρ. 15; no houses: Θ p. 135.10–16; Firmicus, 3.2.3
<u>35–43 Jupiter in ASC or MC, and in its own degrees</u> [cf. 496–8]		ASC. P, A: 3.32–5 MC. P, A: ✳3.36–8	ASC. P, A: Dor.^ARAB II 24.1; Περὶ κέντρ. 26; Θ p. 135.17–19; Firmicus, 3.3.1 MC. P, A: Dor.^ARAB II 24.6; Περὶ κέντρ. 30; Θ p. 168.6–9; Paul, pp. 65.20–66.2; Firmicus, 3.3.18
<u>44–52 Mars in MC</u>	4.50–1 ~ 1.318–19	P, A: ✳3.61–71	P, A: Paul, p. 66.4–11 (in sect); Dor.^ARAB II 25.5; Περὶ κέντρ. 43; Θ p. 168.12–14; Firmicus, 3.4.28 (out of sect)
53–8 Venus in DESC		P, A: ✳3.84–9	P, A: Θ p. 160.8–12; Firmicus, 3.6.14. P: Dor.^ARAB II 26.17; Περὶ κέντρ. 67; Paul, p. 60.14–16
<u>59–64 Venus in ASC</u> [cf 491–5]		P: 3.72–5	P, A: Dor.^ARAB II 26.1; Περὶ κέντρ. 52; Firmicus, 3.6.1. P: Θ pp. 136.21–137.11
<u>65–8 Venus in MC</u>		P: 3.76–80	P, A: Dor.^ARAB II 26.14; Περὶ κέντρ. 64; Θ pp. 168.20–169.1; Paul, pp. 66.17–67.3; Firmicus, 3.6.21
<u>69–72 Mercury in DESC <>, ASC, MC</u>		P, A: 3.104–5, 90–5, ✳96–100	DESC. P: Dor.^ARAB II 27.9; Περὶ κέντρ. 81; Θ p. 160.13–19; Firmicus, 3.7.14. P, A: Paul, p. 60.17–18 ASC. P, A: Dor.^ARAB II 27.1; Περὶ κέντρ. 71; Θ p. 137.12–15; Firmicus, 3.7.1 MC. P: Περὶ κέντρ. 79; Θ p. 169.16–20; Firmicus, 3.7.21. P, A: Dor.^ARAB II 27.5; ✳Paul, p. 67.9–13

(continued)

Appendix I

Book Four (Continued)

+ 73–6 Mars in equal degrees or opposition	—	DESC. P: Θ p. 160.15–16, Firmicus, 3.7.14 ASC. P: Θ p. 137.17–19, Firmicus, 3.7.2 MC. P: Θ p. 169.20–2, Firmicus, 3.7.21. ∗P, A: Paul, pp. 67.13–68.4
77–82a Moon in ASC, with Mars in MC in equal degree		P: Dor.^{ARAB} II 21.1, 3; $\Pi\epsilon\rho\grave{\iota}\ \kappa\acute{\epsilon}\nu\tau\rho$. 1, 4; Θ p. 138.8–11, 22–5; Firmicus, 3.13.2 A: Θ pp. 192.18–20, 193.16–18
83b–82b Moon in IMC	P, A: ∗3.126–9	P: Θ pp. 151.28–152.1; Firmicus, 3.13.7
84–6 Moon in MC	P: 3.123–4	P: Dor.^{ARAB} II 21.2; $\Pi\epsilon\rho\grave{\iota}\ \kappa\acute{\epsilon}\nu\tau\rho$. 1, 4; Θ p. 170.5–9; Firmicus, 3.13.9. P, A: Paul, p. 65.3–8
87–92 Moon in DESC		P, A: $\Pi\epsilon\rho\grave{\iota}\ \kappa\acute{\epsilon}\nu\tau\rho$. 5; Θ pp. 158.24, 160.20–4; ∗Paul, p. 61.1–5. P: Dor.^{ARAB} II 21.7
93–100 Sun in MC or ASC in its own signs	MC. P, A: 3.114–16 ASC. P, A: 3.106–111	MC. P, A: Dor.^{ARAB} II 22.1; $\Pi\epsilon\rho\grave{\iota}\ \kappa\acute{\epsilon}\nu\tau\rho$. 8–9; Paul, pp. 64.17–65.3; Θ p. 167.6–8; Firmicus, 3.5.34 ASC. P, A: Dor.^{ARAB} II 22.1; $\Pi\epsilon\rho\grave{\iota}\ \kappa\acute{\epsilon}\nu\tau\rho$. 8–9; Θ p. 136.9–10; ∗Firmicus, 3.5.1
+101–6 Sun not in its own signs	P: 3.117–18	P, A: Firmicus, 3.5.2, 4

110–64. 'Signs of birth'

110–15 Moon in ASC, Mars in DESC		P, A: Θ p. 138.8–11, 22–5; Firmicus, 3.13.2
116–20 Mars in ASC in signs not its own	P, A: ∗6.574–7 (+ Moon setting in terms of Saturn)	P (out of sect): Dor.^{ARAB} II 25.1; $\Pi\epsilon\rho\grave{\iota}\ \kappa\acute{\epsilon}\nu\tau\rho$. 39; Θ p. 136.5–8; Firmicus, 3.4.3
121–4 Venus aspects Mars in day births	1.286–9 A: 6.518–19, 5.135	P, A: Θ* p. 211.13–14 (Venus aspects Mars)
125–30 Mercury in ASC, Venus following	4.127–8 ~ P: ∗6.480–3 1.292–3 A: ∗6.479	A: Θ pp. 210.27–8 (Mercury as Ruler of $\pi\rho\hat{\alpha}\xi\iota\varsigma$), 210.31–211.1 (and aspected by Jupiter) ~ Ptol. 4.4.3; Θ* p. 212.18–20 (malefics and the Moon in ASC or MC), 28 (Venus and Mars as Rulers of $\pi\rho\hat{\alpha}\xi\iota\varsigma$)
131–8 Jupiter in MC, above Saturn <in a wet sign>	P, A: ∗6.484–6 Jupiter in ASC in watery signs, followed by Saturn	A: Θ p. 216.17–22 (Saturn in MC in wet sign, Sun and Mars with him or in quartile or opposition) A: Ptol. 2.3.41, 4.2.2
139–45 Mercury in its own houses, Saturn in aspect	4.139–40 ~ P, A: ∗6.487–90: 1.290–1 Saturn in his own 4.141 ~ house or terms 1.303 aspects Mercury	P, A: Θ p. 210.29–31 ~ Ptol. 4.4.3 (Mercury Ruler of $\pi\rho\hat{\alpha}\xi\iota\varsigma$ aspected by Saturn) P, A: *Lib. Herm.* xxxiv. 31 (Mercury in terms of Saturn, aspected by Saturn)
146–52 Moon in harmonious aspect with Mercury, and Venus joined with Jupiter	1.294–300 P, A: 6.520–5 Moon in *synaphe* with Mercury in its own 'place', or favourably aspected by it	P, A: Θ* p. 213.22–4 (Mercury and Venus in places governing $\pi\rho\hat{\alpha}\xi\iota\varsigma$, aspected by Jupiter)
153–6 Mars beneath rays of both luminaries	P, A: 6.548–50 Mars in the sign following the luminaries	P, A: Θ p. 187.17–18

157–60 Mercury in its own houses		P, A: Θ* p. 210.26–9 ~ Ptol. 4.4.3 (Mercury Ruler of πρᾶξις)
161–4 Jupiter aspects Mercury	P, A: *3.321–2 A: 6.484–6 Jupiter on the ASC in a wet sign, Saturn following	

170–end. Γενεαί and τέχναι
170–347. Mainly
τ- charts

170–5 Mercury and Jupiter aspect Mars, or are in his terms	A: 6.511–14 Sun in terms of Mercury with Mercury itself; also with Venus; + 515–17 Saturn in opposition, quartile, or conjunction	P, A: *Θ p. 214.9–10 (Jupiter and Mercury with Mars or in Mars' terms) A: Ptol. 4.4.4 (Venus Ruler of πρᾶξις aspected by Jupiter)
+ 176–9 Saturn aspects them in his own terms	P, A: 6.515–17	P: Θ p. 214.12–13 (Saturn aspects)
180–6 Mercury aspects Venus in each other's terms	P, A: 6.366–70 + 371–2 Mercury and Venus, each in the other's houses or terms, and the same effect in conjunction, in the terms of Mercury and house of Venus P, A: 6.504–10 Venus and Mercury, each in the other's houses and terms Lib. Herm. xxxiv. 29	P, A: Θ p. 214.13–17 (Mercury aspects Venus on a kentron in quartile; or, each in the other's terms, eastern, rising, in their own or each other's houses or trigons) A: Θ p. 217.12–13 (Venus in the Sun's house or her own with Mercury, especially in kentra) A: p. 213.9–13 ~ Ptol. 4.4.6 (Mercury and Venus Rulers of πρᾶξις)
187–92 Mars in opposition to Saturn, each in the other's terms	P, A: *6.494–8 Mars and Saturn, each in the other's terms, in same sign or in opposition	P, A: Θ p. 215.8–11 (Saturn in equal degrees with Mars and Mercury, aspecting each other's 'dodecatemories' in absence of benefics) Lib. Herm. xxxiv. 4 (Saturn and Mars, each in the other's terms) A: Θ p. 212.29–32 ~ Ptol. 4.4.8 (Mars and Venus Rulers of πρᾶξις)
193–200 Mars setting with Saturn; Mercury in equal degrees; Moon in their(?) terms and in a kentron	P, A: 6.499–503 + Mercury in aspect or in the same sign	P, A: *Θ pp. 192.20–193.1 (Moon, Mars, Mercury in kentra without aspect of benefics, and with Saturn in IMC; Mars and Mercury in DESC, Moon in opposition or quartile) A: Ptol. 4.4.7 (Mercury and Mars Rulers of πρᾶξις aspected by Saturn); cf. Θ p. 201.2–5 (ascending node in eighth place, aspected by Mars, Saturn, Mercury)

(continued)

Book Four (Continued)

201–5 Mercury aspects Jupiter, each in the other's terms	1.301–5	P, A: 6.476–9 Mercury and Jupiter, each in the other's terms, or in friendly aspect	P, A: Θ p. 214.18–21 (Mercury aspects well-placed Jupiter, each in the other's terms, *exaugoi*, in *kentra* or the *epanaphora*); *Lib. Herm.* xxxiv. 33 (Mercury and Jupiter in exchanged terms, houses, or opposition) P: Θ pp. 210.31–211.2 ~ Ptol. 4.4.3 (Mercury Ruler of $πρᾶξις$ aspected by Jupiter)
206–13 Mercury aspects Venus		P, A: *6.465–71 Venus with Mercury in houses of Mercury or, each in the other's terms; cf. *Lib. Herm.* xxxiv. 29.	A: Θ pp. 214.22–215.3 (cf. 4.425–30); cf. Θ p. 210.26–7 ~ Ptol. 4.4.3 (Mercury Ruler of $πρᾶξις$) P: Θ p. 213.9–13 (Mercury and Venus Rulers of $πρᾶξις$)
214–17 Venus aspecting Mars with Saturn	(1.235–44)	P, A: *6.491–3 Saturn, Venus, Mars in conjunction A: 6.376–8 (Venus in ASC, Jupiter in DESC, Saturn in IMC)	A: Θ p. 194.2–4 (malefic in IMC), cf. p. 192.16–18 (Venus surrounded by malefics in one sign, with Moon and Mercury in quartile)
218–23 Mars aspecting Sun, together with Moon and Venus		A: 6.534–40; 5.177–80	P: Θ pp. 194.18–195.2 (Venus and Moon in DESC, esp. when aspected by either malefic)
224–9 Venus aspecting Moon or in conjunction with it			
230–7 Mars in opposition to Mercury or in conjunction in equal degrees + 238–48 + Saturn in Sagittarius, Pisces, Virgo		P, A: 6.446–9 Mars and Mercury together in human sign *6.450–5 + Saturn in a winged sign	P, A: Θ p. 193.1–3 P, A: Θ pp. 217.24–218.2, cf. Θ p. 212.2–5 ~ Ptol. 4.4.7 A: Θ p. 216.8–15 (Mercury *exaugos*, in equal degrees with the Moon, aspecting each other's 'dodecatemories', malefics opposing each other on *kentra*; Mercury and the Moon in winged signs)
249–62 Saturn approaches Moon, each in the other's signs		A: 6.422–4, 1.85–8	P, A: Θ p. 215.4–6 (Saturn aspects Moon, whose 'dodecatemory' is in Saturn's terms) A: Θ p. 166.22–4, *p. 212.16–18, Epit. IV = *CCAG* ii. 191.20–2 Saturn in MC A: Θ p. 211.29–31 (Venus Ruler of $πρᾶξις$, Saturn, in aspect) A: Ptol. 4.4.5 (Mars Ruler of $πρᾶξις$)
263–70 Saturn aspects Mars in MC, in own terms or signs, in trine		P, A: *6.456–64 malefics in MC, each in the other's terms, no benefic in aspect	P, A: Θ p. 215.8–11 (Saturn in equal degrees with Mars and Mercury, aspecting each other's 'dodecatemories', in absence of benefics); Ptol. 4.4.5 (Mars Ruler of $πρᾶξις$ aspected by Saturn); *Lib. Herm.* xxxiv. 4 (Saturn and Mars, each in the other's terms)

271–85 Sun quartile(?) with Mars, in Taurus, Leo, Aries	A: 6.441–5 Venus and Mars with the Sun, and Mercury in aspect	A: Θ p. 217.5–8 (Venus and Mercury depressed in their own or each other's degrees)
+ 286–9 + Venus	P, A: *6.439–40 Venus and Mars with the Sun	P, A: Θ* p. 213.1 (Sun aspects Venus and Mars); Θ p. 215.16–17 (Saturn in equal degrees with and aspected by Mars in four-footed signs, with additional aspect of Venus) A: Θ* pp. 213.4–7; 217.9
+ 290–3 + Saturn	P, A: 6.415–18 Mars in MC, Saturn following, in four-footed signs (lacks κεραμεῖς)	P, A: Θ p. 215.12–16 (Saturn in equal degrees with Mars in four-footed signs, aspected by Mars without benefics) A: Θ p. 213.3 κεραμουργούς
294–308 Venus and Mars in equal degrees in trine, quartile, or opposition	P, A: 6.586–90 Venus and Mars, each in the other's terms and 'on common path of the signs'	*P, A: Θ* p. 213.4–6; Θ p. 215.18–21; Θ p. 195.5–8 (Venus and Mars in equal degrees, in quartile, trine or in opposition in tropic signs, in or aspecting each other's dodecatemories)
+ 309–16 + Saturn in houses not his own	P, A: 6.591–2	P, A: Θ p. 215.21–2, Θ p. 195.8–10
317–26 Saturn aspects Venus, in presence of Mars	A: 6.415–18 Mars on a *kentron*, Saturn following, in four-footed signs + 419–21 in dry signs	P, A: Θ p. 216.1–7 (Saturn, Venus, and Mars aspect each other in male signs); Θ p. 215.12–16 (Saturn in equal degrees with Mars in four-footed signs, aspected by Mars without benefics) (~ Mᵃ) A: Θ p. 211.27–9 ~ Ptol. 4.4.5; Θ p. 213.13–14 ~ Ptol. 4.4.6
+ 327–32 + Mercury in its own house, favourably configured with Mars		P: Θ p. 216.5–6 + Mercury A: Θ p. 193.1–3; Epit. IIIb = CCAG vii. 112.15–16; Θ p. 212.4 ~ Ptol. 4.4.7
333–40 Mercury in contact with Moon, or in opposition in the same position in their respective signs at Full Moon(?)	A: 6.454	P, A: Θ p. 216.8–15 (Mercury *exaugos* in equal degrees with Moon, aspecting each other's dodecatemories, and malefics on *kentra* in opposition to each other) A: Θ p. 217.19–20
+ 341–6 both in their own terms	6.520–5 Moon with Mercury in its own 'place', or favourably aspected by Mercury	P, A: Θ p. 216.15–16 (Moon and Mars in terms of Mercury) A: Θ p. 217.14–15; p. 213.13 ~ Ptol. 4.4.6
347–65. Group on Harms		
347–50 New Moon aspects Venus and Mars + 351–3…and for women in a day birth	P, A: *6.583–5 Mars aspects the Moon with Venus (nothing about day birth)	A: Θ p. 215.19–21 (Mars in equal degrees with Venus in quartile or trine, aspecting each other's dodecatemories, no other planet in aspect); cf. Θ pp. 194.18–195.2 (Venus and Moon in DESC); Dor.ᴬᴿᴬᴮ II 7.6 (Venus in DESC, Moon in ASC)

(continued)

Appendix I

Book Four (Continued)

354–8 Mercury aspects Saturn, plus Mars, which in turn aspects Venus		P, A: Θ p. 194.17–18 (Venus, Mercury, Mars aspecting each other); Θ p. 169.4–8 (Venus in MC, aspected by Saturn, and Mars in additional aspect)
359–61 Venus in equal degrees with Mercury		
362–5 Mars in quartile with Mercury	A: 6.601–3 (Moon at node opposing or quartile to Mars)	P, A: Θ p. 193.13–15 (Mercury unrelated to ASC or Moon, with malefic in aspect) A: Θ p. 193.16–17 (Full Moon at node)

366–413. Group on Nurture and Parentage

366–71 Mars aspects Moon, in equal degrees, in MC/IMC(?)	P: 6.46–50 Moon \<above a *kentron*\> in same degree as Mars, in same sign or in opposition	P, A: M^b ~ *Firmicus, 7.2.16 (1st config.) (Moon in DESC, Mars in equal degrees in DESC or ASC, in day birth) P: M^a ~ Firmicus, 7.2.15 (1st config.); Dor.^ARAB I 7.10–11
+ 372–3 + Saturn	P, A: 6.57–9	P, A: Firmicus, 6.15.9, 6.31.19 P: 7.2.15 (1st config.)
+ 373–8 + Jupiter	P, A: 6.53–6	P, A: *Firmicus, 7.2.16 (2nd config.); Dor.^ARAB I 7.14, 19, and I 10.22
379–83 Saturn in equal degrees with Moon or in opposition	P, A: 6.57–9 Saturn aspects Moon P, A: 6.698–702 Moon in IMC or DESC, Saturn in quartile or opposition	P, A: Dor.^ARAB I 7.10; Θ p. 219.13–14; Dor.^ARAB I 10.23 For 6.698–702 cf. Firmicus, 7.4.5 (*de servili genitura*) (2nd configuration).
+ 384–5 Venus in aspect		
386–9/390 Mercury in equal degrees with Jupiter	P, A: 6.124–5	
391–4 Mars in conjunction with Venus, with Saturn in aspect		
395–401 Sun aspects malefics in MC	1.321–6 P, A: 6.362–5	P, A: Θ p. 216.17–22 (Saturn in MC in wet sign, Sun and Mars with him or in quartile or opposition) A: Ptol. 4.4.5 (Mars Ruler of πρᾶξις aspected by Saturn)
402–8 Saturn in equal degrees with Sun	1.327–33	P, A: *Epit. IV = *CCAG* ii. 189.8–12 (Sun and Saturn in equal degrees); *Lib. Herm.* xxvi. 25 (Saturn and Sun on ASC); Περὶ σχημ. 96 (Saturn with the Sun); *Lib. Herm.* xxxi. 2 (Saturn with Sun by day and night)

409–13 Moon in equal degrees with Saturn, with Mars in aspect	1.334–8	P, A: 1.250–5 P: 5.197–201	P, A: *Epit. IV = *CCAG* ii. 189.12–14 (Saturn in equal degrees with Moon, Mars in aspect); Περὶ σχημ. 100 (Saturn with Moon) P: Θ p. 200.1–2 (Moon enclosed by malefics in one sign, on *kentron* or *epanaphora*)
414–49. More τεχναί			
414–19 Jupiter aspects Mercury and Venus		A: 6.119–21.	
420–4 Sun aspects Venus in conjunction with(?) Mars		P, A: *6.431–5 (Sun and Mars aspect Venus)	P, A: Θ p. 216.23–5 (Mars and Venus together or in quartile, each in the other's terms)
425–30 Mercury approaches Jupiter and Saturn		*6.436–8 (Mercury aspects Saturn and Jupiter)	P, A: Θ pp. 214.22–215.2 (Mercury in a good place, especially the house of Saturn, *exaugos*; aspected by Jupiter, Saturn, and Mars); cf. Ptol. 4.4.3 (Mercury Ruler of πρᾶξις); 4.4.10 (waxing Moon with Mercury in the place of πρᾶξις, in types of sign)
431–6 Saturn aspects Venus and Mars		A: 6.487–90 (Saturn aspects Mercury in its terms or house); cf. on 4.139–45	
437–43 Mars aspects Venus and Moon		A: 6.401–4 (Moon in *synaphe* with Mercury which is together with Venus, and Venus aspected by Jupiter, with its counterpart Lib. Herm. xxvi. 62)	P, A: *Θ p. 217.1–3 (Mercury, Mars, Venus, Moon in *kentra* or aspecting each other in *kentra*) A: Θ* p. 211.10–11; Θ p. 211.27–9 ~ Ptol. 4.4.5; Θ p. 213.9–12 ~ Ptol. 4.4.6; Ptol. 3.14.5
+ 444–9 Mercury in unfavourable aspect		A: 5.103–4	P, A: Θ p. 217.5–7 (Mercury and Venus dejected in their own or each other's degrees) Ptol. 3.14.29 (Mars and Venus as governors of the soul)
450–90. Miscellanea			
450–6 Venus and Moon with Sun and Mercury, in aspect to one another in MC in two-bodied signs		P, A: 6.249–51 (Mercury and luminaries in two-bodied signs in MC)	A: *Lib. Herm.* xxxiv. 39 (Moon in house of Mercury, Sun with another planet in terms of Jupiter or Mercury in two-bodied signs)
457–9 Jupiter in equal degrees with Venus + 460–1 Saturn in aspect		P, A: 6.252–5 (*kaloi asteres* along with luminaries)	P, A: *Lib. Herm.* xxxiv. 40 (Jupiter, Saturn, and Mercury on *kentra*, in a double-bodied sign, when occidental and when oriental); Ptol. 3.8.3
462–5 Mars in Evil Demon opposite Moon 466–71 Mars and Moon in favourable places		—	A: cf. Ptol. 3.9.2–4

(*continued*)

Appendix I

Book Four (Continued)

472–7 (1.229–34) Saturn aspects Mars from opposition?	1.229–34	P, A: 3.244–52	P, A: Περὶ σχημ. 63; Περὶ κράσ. 62; Firmicus, 6.15.4
478–90 (1.306–20) Moon (crescent?) in quartile with Mars, with Mercury in DESC or in opposition	cf. 1.306–20	A: 6.499–503 (malefics, each in the other's terms, in same sign or opposition, plus the additional aspect of Mercury or in the same sign)	A: Firmicus, 4.14.7 (Moon leaves Mercury for Mars in a day birth); Valens, II 10.5 (Mercury and Mars in DESC); II 17.57–8 (Mars in trine or right sextile with Mercury); Valens, IV 25.11 / Critodemus, *CCAG* v/2. 112.34–8 (Mars and Mercury on, aspecting, or receiving chronocratorship) 'Trade': Π: Θ p. 211.14–16; Θ p. 212.5–6 ~ Ptol. 4.4.7; σίνος: Θ p. 192.20–3; τ: Θ p. 215.8–11 Violent death: Θ p. 201.2–5 ~ Firmicus, 3.11.12–13, 6.31.64; Θ p. 202.4–6 ~ Firmicus, 7.23.3; Θ p. 202.9–10
491–507. More kentrothesiai			
491–5 Venus aspecting ASC [cf. 59–64]			
496–8 Jupiter aspecting ASC [cf. 35–6, 38–43] + 499–502 and when aspected by (in conjunction with?) Mars			
503–7 Saturn in ASC in female births [cf. 14–27]			
508–36. Luminaries in gendered signs			
508–14 Sun in male, Moon in female signs		P, A: 3.365–8; 5.209–10 P: 1.26–8	P: Ptol. 4.3.2; Firmicus, 7.22.4
515–18 Moon in male, Sun in female signs		P, A: 3.372–5 A: 3.376–9	A: Epit. II = *CCAG* i. 145.19–20
519–26 Both luminaries in female signs		P, A: 3.376–9 P: 5.211–13	P: Ptol. 3.15.10
527–36 Both luminaries in male signs		P, A: 3.369–71 P: 1.29–33, 5.214–16	P, A: Ptol. 3.15.8
537–59. New and Full Moon			
537–44 Moon in synodos with Sun in setting sign		P, A: ✱6.599–600 P: 2.481–2 A: 2.498–9	P, A: Firmicus, 4.5 (synodos, no DESC); Θ pp. 192.13–14 (luminaries in ASC, Saturn in DESC without benefics), 193.20–2 (New or Full Moon, aspected by Saturn, no benefics)
545–51 Full Moon at node		P, A: 2.498–9	P, A: Θ p. 193.16–17

+ 552–9 + Mars	P, A: 6.601–3 (Moon at node, in opposition or quartile to Mars; 604–5 Mars in right quartile or following Moon in DESC)	P, A: Θ p. 193.17–18 A: Περὶ σχημ. 52; Π.σ.α. p. 183.19–20
560–92. Aspects across kentra		
560–6 Saturn in MC, Mars in DESC		P, A: *Θ* p. 212.24–5
567–70 Moon in MC, Mercury in DESC, Saturn in ASC	*P, A: 6.341–7	A: Θ p. 212.27–8 ~ Ptol. 4.4.8; Θ *p. 213.26–7, p. 216.7
571–6 Jupiter in MC aspects New Moon, Sun aspects ASC		
577–81 Mercury in ASC, Moon in DESC	*P, A: 6.355–6	A: Θ p. 210.27 ~ Ptol. 4.4.3
582–5 Venus in IMC, Saturn in MC	P, A: 6.286–9; cf. 3.147–57	
+ 586–8 Jupiter in aspect	P: 6.290–2	
589–92 Mars in equal degrees	P: 6.293–4	
593–618. Miscellanea		
593–6 Saturn in ASC, Moon in Evil Demon, Sun cadent from MC	P, A: 6.60–3	—
597–600 Venus aspects ASC, Saturn and Mars with her	Cf. 6.692–4 (Mars aspects Sun and Saturn; Saturn Venus)	
601–7 Venus in equal degrees with Saturn	P, A: 6.724–7	
+ 608–11 and aspected by the Sun in places not its own	P, A: 6.728–9	
+ 612– Chart referring to waning Moon(?) (broken off)		
613–18 Saturn in IMC aspects Mars	A: 3.260–3 (aspects of Saturn and Mars other than trine); 5.192–6 (Mars in DESC, Saturn in ASC)	P: Θ p. 201.22–3 (Saturn in IMC, Mars in MC), cf. Firmicus, 6.29.10 (Saturn in ASC, Mars in DESC or IMC) A: Θ p. 201.23–4

Book One

18–25. Charts involving Venus
18–21 Saturn and Sun aspect Venus
22–3 Mars and Venus in *kentra*
+ 24–5…and with Mercury (in equal degrees?)

26–33. Luminaries in places of gender

26–8 Sun, centred, in male places, Moon centred in female	P, A: cf. 1.277–80 P: 3.363–8, 4.508–14	P: Ptol. 4.3.2; Firmicus, 7.22.4 A: Ptol. 4.3.1; *Π.τ.δ.* 8; Firmicus, 7.22.1
29–33 Luminaries in male places, opposite Venus and ASC	P, A: 3.383–91, 5.214–16 P: 4.527–36	P, A: Ptol. 3.15.8–9 P: Ptol. 4.3.1; *Π.τ.δ.* 8; Firmicus, 7.22.1

33–44. Three Mars-related charts

34–7 Jupiter in a *kentron* aspects Aries or Scorpio		
38–9 Mercury and Mars in quartile		P: 3.339–43; *Περὶ σχημ.* 50–1 / Dor.ᴬᴿᴬᴮ II 15.27–8; Firmicus, 6.11.8–9 A: Θ pp. 217.24–218.2
+ 40 and when setting		
+ 41 and without the influence of Jupiter		
42–4 Mars and Venus on a common path aspecting the Moon		A: Valens, II 38.18; Firmicus, 6.24.4, 6.29.22, 6.30.1

45–138. Miscellanea

45–9 Saturn taking Venus into his embrace		P, A: Firmicus, 6.22.12, 6.31.43
50–7 Moon after Full applies to Saturn		P, A: Θ p. 189.10–13; cf. 183.2–3; Firmicus, 8.21.7 P: *Π.σ.α.* p. 182.8–16
58–61 Mercury in ASC with Moon and Venus, Jupiter in DESC	A: 6.366–70 + 371–2, 504–10; 5.159–64	A: Firmicus, 3.12.2; Θ p. 213.9–11 (musicians)
62–5 Mercury and Venus in conjunction, with Mercury aspecting the Full (or waxing) Moon and Venus the New (or waning)	A: 6.366–70 + 371–2, 504–10; 5.159–64	A: Θ p. 213.9–11
66–9 Jupiter and Saturn 'Lords of' *kentra*		
70–4 Mercury and Jupiter in the MC, with Moon in *synaphe*		P, A: Firmicus, 3.10.12
75–7 Mars on *kentron* ruling πρᾶξις		P, A: Θ p. 211.10–11 ~ Ptol. 4.4.5
+ 78–82…and with Sun with them		P, A: Θ p. 211.11–13 ~ Ptol. 4.4.5
83–8 Saturn out of sect on MC	A: 6.422–4, 4.249–62	P, A: Θ pp. 166.21–4, 212.15–18; Epit. IV = *CCAG* ii. 191.20–2 A: Ptol. 4.4.5 (Mars Ruler of πρᾶξις aspected by Saturn); Θ p. 211.30

89–91 Mercury centred, and opposite to P, A: Θ p. 192.9–11;
Saturn and the Moon on the ASC Epit. IIIb = *CCAG* vii. 112.11–13
92–5...then cadent
96–7 Mars ὕπαυγος
98–9 Mars aspecting the Sun
100–5 Planets and leadership
106–111 Venus in Capricorn or Aquarius   P, A: 6.160–9   P, A: Firmicus, 6.30.1; Anubion,
with Saturn and Jupiter, in *synaphe* with   A: 5.202–8   F 4 ii. 10–16
Saturn, with Mars aspecting Moon and
Venus, 'with' Saturn
+ 112–14 and with aspect of Sun
115–18 Moon in female places opposite   P, A: P, A: Ptol. 3.15.10
Sun, and in ASC   5.211–13
   P: 3.376–9
   A: 6.534–40   A: Firmicus, 6.30.18

+ 119–20...and with malefics in MC
121–8 Venus in opposition to Saturn and   P, A: P, A: Firmicus, 6.30.5
Moon, Mars in quartile to Venus, Mercury   6.276–81
in MC, and Saturn in aspect to the latter
           P, A: Θ p. 209.10–14;
129–33 Jupiter and Mercury in   Θ pp. 210.31–211.2 ~ Ptol. 4.4.3
conjunction and on *kentra*   P, A: Θ p. 189.6–8, cf. p. 183.4–5;
134–8 Full Moon in *synaphe* with Mars in   Firmicus, 4.4.2–3; Π.σ.α.
the sixth place   p. 183.1–3

[139–52 *Schetliasmos* of Mars]

153–95. Miscellanea
153–7 Moon leaving Saturn 'by degree'   P: 5.115–19   P, A: Π.σ.α. p. 182.16–22;
           Firmicus, 4.15.2
           P: Θ p. 193.5–6
           A: Firmicus, 4.9.6
158–66 Moon leaving Mars   P, A: Π.σ.α. p. 183.5–11;
           Firmicus, 4.11.7
           A: Firmicus, 4.9.4
167–74 Mars in MC by day   P, A: Firmicus, 3.4.32
+ 175...and with aspect of Jupiter
176–9 Mars in DESC   P, A: 3.51–2   P, A: Περὶ κέντρ. 45; Firmicus,
           3.4.17–19; *CCAG* viii/1.
           166.23–6; Paul, p. 60.1–5
180–1, 184 Mercury, Venus, Saturn ruling   P, A: Θ p. 213.19–21, cf.
πρᾶξις   213.7–8
           A: *CCAG* v/1. 199.9–11
+ 182–3...and with Jupiter aspecting   P, A: Θ p. 213.21–2
185–93 Waxing (or Full?) Moon in contact   P, A: 6.46–50   P, A: Π.σ.α. p. 182.8–13; cf.
with a malefic   Firmicus, 7.2.15; *Lib. Herm.*
           xxvi. 48
           P: Θ p. 186.8–9
           A: Π.σ.α. p. 183.11–12
+ 194–15...and with Jupiter aspecting   P, A: Firmicus, 7.2.15
[196–207 Protreptic]

208–85. Miscellanea
208–9 Full Moon approaching Jupiter   P, A: Firmicus, 4.3.1; cf. Π.σ.α.
           p. 182.23–4

(*continued*)

Book One (Continued)

+ 210–11 Full Moon leaving Jupiter			P: *Π.σ.α.* p. 182.26–8
+ 212–14 Waning Moon approaching Jupiter			P, A: Firmicus, 4.3.2
215–22 Mars and Jupiter in opposition		P, A: 3.306–8	P, A: *Περὶ σχημ.* 77; *Περὶ κράσ.* 129; Firmicus, 6.16.1
+ 223 … and Mars on MC			
224–8 Jupiter on *kentron* with (non-New) Moon and Venus			
229–34 Malefics setting, luminaries opposite	A: 4.365, 555		P, A: Valens, II 37.43; Θ pp. 192.13–14, 193.9–10, 193.20–2; *Π.σ.α.* p. 183.19–20 A: Θ pp. 193.5, 194.2–3
235–44 Venus between malefics, aspecting Moon and Mercury	P, A: cf. 4.214–17	P, A: cf. 6.491–3	P, A: Θ p. 192.16–18 A: Θ p. 194.2–4
245–9 Full Moon encountering Mars, without benefics			P, A: *Π.σ.α.* 183.1–5; Firmicus, 4.4.1–2
250–5 Moon between malefics		A: 4.409–13 (women) P, A: 5.197–201 (men)	P, A: Dorotheus, p. 324.21–4; Θ p. 125.17–19 (women) P, A: Θ p. 200.1–2 (men)
256–61 Venus between malefics			P: Θ p. 192.16–18
262–6 Benefics in ASC, malefics in DESC			
267–70 Malefics in ASC, Jupiter in DESC		P, A: 1.215–22; 3.163–7 + 168–75	
271–6 Moon in same degree as malefics			
277–80 Moon in MC by degree in night birth, with the Sun in a *kentron* in a male place (sign)		P, A: cf. 1.26–8	P, A: *Lib. Herm.* xxvi. 34 A: Firmicus, 7.22.1
281–5 Mercury in MC with Sun, Moon in ASC, in a day birth; centred, without malefics			A: Firmicus, 7.22.1

286–326. Τέχναι

286–9 Venus aspects Mars in day births	4.121–4		P, A: Θ p. 211.13–14
290–3 Mercury in its own houses, Saturn in aspect	P: 4.139–40 A: 4.127–8		P, A: Θ p. 210.29–31 A: Θ pp. 210.26–7, 210.30–211.1 ~ Ptol. 4.4.3; Θ p. 212.18–20
294–300 Moon favourably positioned with Mercury, and Venus joined with Jupiter	4.146–152		P, A: Θ p. 213.22–4
301–5 Mercury aspects Jupiter each in the other's terms	4.201–5	P, A: 6.476–9	P, A: Θ p. 214.18–21
303	> 4.141		
306–20 Moon crescent? in unspecified relation with Mars, with Mercury setting 'around' them or opposite	cf. 4.478–9, 481–90	A: 6.499–503	A: Firmicus, 4.14.7; Valens, II 17.57–8; IV 25.11 / Critodemus, *CCAG* v/2. 112.34–8; Θ p. 212.5–6
318–19	> 4.50–1		
321–6 Sun aspecting both malefics	4.395–401		P, A: Θ p. 216.17–22

327–33 + 334–8. Parents		
327–33 Saturn in equal degrees with Sun	4.402–8	P, A: Epit. IV = *CCAG* ii. 189.8–12; *Lib. Herm.* xxxi. 2; Περὶ σχημ. 96
334–8 Moon in equal degrees approaching…and Mars in aspect	4.409–13	P, A: Epit. IV = *CCAG* ii. 189.12–14; Περὶ σχημ. 100 P: Θ p. 200.1–2
339–58. Miscellanea		
339–40 Saturn in ASC, Mars opposite	P: 3.141–4	P, A: Περὶ κέντρ. 17; Firmicus, 3.2.2, 3.4.20, 6.29.10
341–2 Mars in quartile to the Sun, Saturn to the Moon		A: Firmicus, 6.29.3; Anubion, F 11.3
343–5 Venus opposite to Mars < > and Saturn (in MC?) in quartile to her (sc. the Moon)		P, A: Firmicus, 6.29.4; Anubion, F 11.5–6
346–9 Jupiter in quartile or trine to Saturn. Mercury on ASC with the Moon		A: Firmicus, 6.29.5
350–2 Jupiter, Mars, and Mercury on ASC…Moon after New embraces Saturn		P, A: Firmicus, 6.31.55; Anubion, F 7.25
353–8 Saturn transits to the place of Mars, and Mars into aspect with Saturn		

Book Five

39–43. Miscellanea on dynasts		
39 Sun in MC	P, A: 3.114–16	P, A: Dor.ᴬᴿᴬᴮ II 22.1,2; Paul, pp. 64.17–65.1; Θ p. 167.6–7; Firmicus, 3.5.34
40 Mars in own houses	P, A: 3.64	P, A: Firmicus, 3.4.28–9; Θ p. 168.12–14
41 Jupiter in Mars' houses	P: 2.210–12	P: Π.τ.δ. 8; *Lib. Herm.* xxxii. 19 A: Περὶ σχῆμ. 14
+ 42 and when the luminaries are centred		P, (A?): Π.τ.δ. 8
+ 43 in a weak position		—
44–129. Good and Bad Stars		
44–7 —		
48–52 Saturn by night, Mars eastern	2.412	
+ 53…aspecting Venus		
54–6 Saturn at every 'ending'		
56–7 Mars and Saturn on *kentra*	P, A: 3.248	
58–61 Mars and Saturn in conjunction	P: 3.246–63	P, A: Dorotheus, pp. 368.25–369.3; Firmicus, 6.22.5; Apomasar, *CCAG* ii. 137.5–7 A: Firmicus, 1.4.7
62 Jupiter in conjunction with Saturn and other planets	P, A: 3.234–43	
+ 63–5…and with Sun	P, A: 2.417–19 + 22	P: Dor.ᴬᴿᴬᴮ II 19.3–4; Περὶ σχημ. 107; Firmicus, 6.23.3
66–8 Sun in conjunction with Venus	P, A: 2.426–30	P, A: Valens, I 19.16; Firmicus, 6.25.1 P: Dor.ᴬᴿᴬᴮ II 19.25; Περὶ σχημ. 122

(continued)

Book Five (Continued)

69–71 Jupiter in DESC or IMC	P, A: 3.39–48	P, A: Dor.^ARAB II 24.10, 14; Περὶ κέντρ. 32, 38; Firmicus, 3.3.7, 15; Θ pp. 151.1–5, 159.24–5
72–3 Mars aspects Mercury in DESC(?)		P: Firmicus, 3.11.9–11 (cf. 5)
74–6 Mars without aspect of benefics		
76–7 Mars on a *kentron* aspecting Venus		
78–80 Retrograde planets		
81, 82–3 —	A: cf. 6.258–9	
84–9 Mars and Mercury on *kentra* in friendly relation		P, A: Firmicus, 3.11.9, 16
+ 90–2…and Saturn aspecting		P: Firmicus, 3.11.2
93–9 Mercury and Mars setting together on IMC		P, A: Firmicus, 3.11.5, 16
100–2 Setting Venus, setting Mars	P, A: 3.84 Venus in DESC (3.51–2 Mars in DESC)	
103–4 Mercury and Venus depressed in own degrees	A: 4.444–9	P, A: Θ p. 217.6–8
105–7 Mars transiting Venus		
108 Mars and Jupiter, not in a *kentron*		
109–10 Waxing Moon leaving Saturn for Jupiter	P, A: 2.446–50	P, A: Π.σ.α. p. 184.12–14; Firmicus, 4.9.2
+ 111 Waning Moon (leaving Saturn for?) Venus		P, A: Π.σ.α. p. 184.23–4; Firmicus, 4.6.2; 4.9.7
+ 112 Moon, more or less Full, approaching Mars		P, A: Π.σ.α. p. 183.1–3
113–14 Full Moon approaching Saturn		P, A: Π.σ.α. p. 182.8–9; Firmicus, 4.2.1
+ 115–19 Full Moon leaving Saturn	P: 1.153–7	P, A: Θ p. 193.5–6 Π.σ.α. p. 182.18–22; Firmicus, 4.15.1; *Lib. Herm.* xxxiii. 2
120–6 New Moon	P, A: 2.481–2	P, A: p. 185.18–20
127–9 Moon at node	P: 2.498–9	P: Π.σ.α. p. 184.7

130–6. Mars' oppositions

130–1 Mars in *kentra* in opposition to Sun		P, A: Firmicus, 7.10.1
+ 132–3 Mars in opposition to Moon in its (Mars') degrees		P, A: Θ p. 149.9–11; Firmicus, 3.4.15 A: Περὶ κέντρ. 6
+ 134–5 Mars in opposition to Moon in its own degrees, or to its own degrees, no longer in a *kentron*	A: 2.355–6, 4.123–4 = 1.288–9, 6.519	A: Θ p. 211.13–14
+ 136 Mars in opposition to Venus	P, A: 3.329–34	P, A: Θ p. 195.5–8; cf. Firmicus, 6.17.2

137–88. The Περὶ μίμων sequence

137–41 Luminaries in bent signs, Mars in aspect to Venus		A: Θ p. 217.5–8, Θ p. 169.4–6
+ 142–3 and in a female chart		A: Θ p. 169.6–8
144–7 Mars and Venus in IMC	A: 4.287–9; 6.440	P, A: *Θ p. 213.6–7; cf. p. 217.9 [cf. Θ p. 213.1]
+ 148 and with the addition of the Sun		
149–53 Moon setting in watery signs as she approaches Saturn, or setting in northern signs		P: Θ p. 217.10–11, cf. 212.23–4

154–8 Kentra in slippery signs		
159–64 Venus in her own places with Mercury	A: 6.366–70 + 371–2; 504–10; 1.58–61, 62–5	P, A: Θ p. 217.12–13, *p. 213.24–5
165–8 Venus with Mercury in places of Mercury	A: 2.319–27; 6.480–3	P, A: Θ p. 217.14–15, *p. 213.25–7; cf. Ptol. 4.4.6 (wax-workers)
+ 169–72 Moon with Sun in *epanaphora* <of Mercury and Venus>		P, A: Θ p. 217.16–18
173–6 Waxing Moon in her exaltation with Mercury, aspecting Sun in ASC or DESC		P, A: Θ p. 217.19–20
177–80 Mars rising at nightfall, accompanied by Saturn and Mercury	P, A: 6.534–40, 1.119–20 A: 4.218–23	
181–8 ASC in scaly signs, Saturn with Jupiter in the IMC Rulers of πρᾶξις		P, A: Θ p. 217.21–3

189–end. Miscellanea

189–91 Waxing Moon in MC, Mars and Sun in IMC		
192–6 Mars setting, Saturn in ASC	A: 4.613–18; 3.260–3	P, A: Θ p. 201.20–2; Firmicus, 6.29.10
197–201 Moon between malefics, in equal degrees	P, A: 1.250–5; cf. P: 4.409–13	P, A: Θ p. 200.1–2
202–8 Saturn in equal degrees with Venus	A: 6.160–71, 1.106–11	P: cf. Firmicus, 6.29.22, 6.31.25. 6.31.9 A: Firmicus, 6.30.1; Anubion, F 4 ii. <15b>
209 Sun in male signs	P, A: 3.363–8	
210 Moon in female signs	P, A: 3.363–8	
+ 211–13 Luminaries in female signs for a man	P, A: 3.376–9, 1.115–18 P: 4.519–26	P, A: Ptol. 3.15.10
+ 214–16 Luminaries in male signs for a woman	P, A: 3.383–5 + 386–91, 1.29–33	P, A: Ptol. 3.15.8–9
217–21 Saturn by night in IMC, with Mars in MC		P, A: Θ p. 201.22–3
222–4 Moon in house of Sun		P, A: Θ pp. 222.12–14, 183.16–17; Epit. IIIb = CCAG vii. 115.5–7
225–42 Waxing Moon fleeing Mars and Saturn in opposition, Jupiter in trine; Jupiter Ruler of *Bios* or in opposition to it		
243–5 Moon in *synaphe* with Mercury		P, A: Θ p. 208.19–23
246–51 Saturn, Mars, Moon, Venus in scaly signs		P, A: Θ p. 189.25–6; cf. Epit. II = CCAG i. 147.4–10; Θ p. 183.2–3; CCAG i. 166.15–19
252–5 Mars in a *kentron* with Mercury in house of Sun, aspecting one or both luminaries		P, A: Θ p. 189.13–14; cf. Περὶ κράσ. 98, 161 P: Θ pp. 217.24–218.1
256–9 Waxing Moon applies to Jupiter		P, A: Θ p. 208.19–22
260–73 Saturn κατέχων Mercury in Aries, aspecting the Moon in her exaltation, and ruling the ASC		P, A: Θ p. 218.3–6 + 7–8; Epit. IIIb = CCAG vii. 118.11–12 + 12–15
274–7 Mercury in conjunction with Jupiter		P, A: Περὶ κράσ. 122

(continued)

Book Five (Continued)

+ 278–9 Mercury in the third place from the ASC	A: 6.452	
+ 280–1 …and with Mars in opposition		P, A: Θ p. 212.11–12; Epit. IV = CCAG ii. 191.17
282–3 Venus in aspect with Mars		
284–99 Jupiter in houses of Venus, with luminaries well placed	P: 2.221–31	P: Π.τ.δ. 9; Dor.^ARAB II 29.3; Lib. Herm. xxxii. 23
300–6 Moon at node when New(?)		
+ 307–12 After her release from the Sun, applying to benefics		P, A: Π.σ.α. p. 186.14–15
316–19 Venus in her own houses, with Jupiter, Mercury, Saturn in aspect		
320–3 Moon and ASC in four-footed signs		P, A: Θ p. 195.12–14
324–5 Mars in MC by day	P: 3.61–71 A: 6.234–6	P, A: Ptol. 4.6.3
326–31 Saturn 'finds' Venus in his own houses	P, A: 2.184–5 A: 6.286–94	P, A: Lib. Herm. xxxii. 68
332–40 Moon in *synaphe* with Mars and Venus in the place(s) of the Sun or houses of Mercury; Saturn in opposition		

APPENDIX II

Roster of Trades

> One of the very first requirements for a man who is fit to handle pig iron as a regular occupation is that he shall be so stupid and so phlegmatic that he more nearly resembles in his mental make-up the ox than any other type. The man who is mentally alert and intelligent is for this very reason entirely unsuited to what would, for him, be the grinding monotony of work of this character.
>
> Frederick Winslow Taylor, The Principles of
Scientific Management (New York, 1911), 59

This register is intended in the first place to support this book. It saves over-burdened footnotes in the first section and encyclopaedism in the commentary. It is not supposed to be neutrally informative. It cannot guarantee to be a comprehensive list of trades and professions mentioned in every astrological text, although an attempt has been made to record those in the texts that are the most useful comparanda for Manetho (especially Ptolemy, Θ, and the other Epitomes of Antiochus/Rhetorius, Teucer, Firmicus, and *Lib. Herm.*).

In the first place, it illustrates the range of expressions used in astrological texts. If the Greek terms are true trade names (though see pp. 38–41 for the problem with this concept), a footnote gives the references in Ruffing 2008 and any other useful secondary literature. From this it can be seen that Ptolemy and Θ tend to use trade names that are attested as such in papyri and/or inscriptions, even if the attestations are mainly outside Egypt. This is the prose basis on which the Manethoniana elaborate, and the table shows where the poets are using trade names shared with prose sources (cited at the head of the list where that is the case), poetic expansions based on the same root (indicated with cf.), or freewheeling circumlocutions (indicated with 'periphrasis').

In the second place, although it cannot promise comprehensiveness, the tabulation does give a sense how well (or under-) represented certain trades and professions are, in which authors they are concentrated, how finely differentiated are the specialisms within them, and, conversely, where a particular author's interests lie. Most fields, for instance, are represented in Teucer, including some very minute specialisms (watchers for tunny-fish, operators of water-mills, entertainers called *parapalarii*), but especially the handicrafts. Ptolemy has weaker coverage of the land and animal husbandry, and barely anything military, but is more interested in various kinds of technology (the extraction and working of stone, metallurgy, medicine, divination, and the funerary business) and retail; with respect to him, it is Θ which augments the types of instrumentalist and popular entertainer. Firmicus has massive general coverage, often also highly specialised (luxuries), but it is no surprise that he stands out for his coverage of law and Roman administration (extending to a reference to an Asiarch). Paul concentrates on finance, 'intellectual' professions, and priests and prophets, and it is his commentator, 'Heliodorus', who adds some handicrafts in his discussion of Praxis.

At the same time, this index proved very, very difficult to design, so that it cannot at first sight provide answers to every question that might arise. For the format it was hard to choose between an inscrutable list of localised references and selective quotation to illustrate the handling of the theme in question. The problem with the former is that it is pointless, given the availability of the TLG for everything Greek except Teucer, and of the Library of Latin Texts for Firmicus and *Lib. Herm.* The problem with the latter is that this appendix is not supposed to be a proxy for an essay that discusses astrology's attitudes; insofar as I attempt that, it is in section I.4, and to overindulge quotation here would simply shift bulk from one section to another. And certainly one would not want to reproduce Firmicus' verbiage for its own sake. I have therefore attempted a compromise, generally giving total number of instances of the word in question for Firmicus and *Lib. Herm.* (where anyway the translation sometimes makes it uncertain whether a trade name is meant at all, as opposed to a looser description), and quoting verbatim only material that is of particular interest and/or that would not be produced by a mechanical search for the term in question. Yet problems remain. For although this inventory does provide a sense of the extent to which a given trade is represented in astrological texts, a mere count of occurrences may be misleading where passages are related (trade names are to be weighed not counted), and this inventory cannot always indicate where that is so. Sometimes it does, as with the parallels between Ptolemy and Θ, *Περὶ σχημ.* and *Περὶ κράσ.*, and Firmicus and Manilius, but it is impossible to indicate the many occasions where correspondences among the paranatellonta are close but not identical. In these cases, the trade names are simply given separately. But such an inventory as this might form the eventual basis for a closer comparison of the sources for the paranatellonta.

The point, therefore, is to show which professions are referred to, by whom, and in what terms, to provide context for the Manethoniana, but not to reduplicate what an electronic search could achieve. In the interests of further economy, I have avoided repeating author's names, so that a three-digit reference in the form 3.6.3 refers to Firmicus, and one that begins with a Roman numeral (e.g. xxv. 1.3) means *Lib. Herm.*

I. The Land

I.1. Agriculture

I.1.i. Farmers, ploughmen
γεωπόνος: 6.489 γειοπόνους, 4.433 γειοπόνοι; Valens, I 1.9, I 2.16; Camaterus
γεωργός: Ptol. 4.4.5, 8; Θ p. 211.28; Teucer, II 2.1; Valens, I 1.9
agricola: Firmicus, 4×; *Lib. Herm.* 10×; also xxv. 12.9 *agricultores*
cultor agrorum: Firmicus, 2×; also 8.11.3 ~ Manil. 5.272–5; 8.26.15 *terrae cultura quaerentes*; 8.29.10 *ex cultura terrae habebunt vitae subsidia*
arator: Firmicus, 2×
Periphrasis: *Lib. Herm.* 3× *de terra viventes*, xxv. 8.11 *amatores agriculturae*

I.1.ii. Vine-dressers
ἀμπελουργός: Teucer, II 10.5

vinearum...cultor: 8.10.6 ~ Manil. 5.238-44
vinitor: xxv. 10.25
pastinator (who prepares the soil of the vineyard): 5.4.18

I.1.III. Gardeners

κηπουρός: 1.84; Θ p. 212.17; Epit. IV; Teucer, II 5.1; cf. 6.424 κοσμηταὶ κήπων
ἐπαρδευτής(?): cf. 4.258 ἀρδευταὶ φορβῆς
Manure: 6.423 εἰνοδίην κόπρον τε καὶ ὄνθον δηθὰ φέροντες; 4.259 ὀνθολόγοι (unless street-cleaners)
hortulanus: Firmicus, 7×; *Lib. Herm.* 5×; also 3.5.25 *hortorum praepositos*; 4.14.14 *hortorum operarios*; 8.11.1 *et qui amoenis hortorum delectationibus adhaerescat* ~ Manil. 5.256-61
herbularius: *Lib. Herm.* 3×
Periphrasis: 4.256 καρποσπόροι ἄνδρες, cf. xxv. 5.1 *collectores seminis*; 4.258 λαχανηφόροι; 8.10.6 *irriguos amait campos* ~ Manil. 5.236-7
See also II.3.ii. Workers on irrigation channels

I.2. Hunting, etc.

I.2.I. Hunters

κυνηγός: Θ pp. 162.8; 201.21, 212.11, 22, 216.8, 12; cf. 5.281 καὶ δολίοισι βρόχοις ὀρεσίτροφα πάντα κυνηγεῖ
κυνηγέτης: Teucer, II 3.8 θηρίων κυνηγέτας; CCAG xi/1. 135.7; cf. 4.337 κυνηγητῆρας
θηρευτής, etc.: Teucer, II 1.1; Θ p. 212.29-30 ἱερῶν ζῴων...θηρευτάς; cf. 6.454 ὠμοβόρων θηρήτορας
venator/βηνάτωρ: Θ p. 216.12; Firmicus, 8×, incl. 8.9.1 ~ Manil. 5.184-8; *Lib. Herm.* 8×
τοξευτής: cf. 4.244 τοξελκεῖς
Periphrasis: 4.11.5 *qui quadrupedia animalia adsiduis officiis prosequantur*
Procurers of hunting gear: 8.9.3 ~ Manil. 5.199-205

I.2.II. Fishermen

ἁλιεύς, etc.:[1] Θ pp. 157.22, 166.23; Epit. IV; Teucer, II 12.1; also Θ p. 212.17 ἁλιεύοντας
Piscator: Firmicus, 11×; also 5.2.14 *ex piscationibus dabit vitae subsidia*; *Lib. Herm.* 7×; also xxvii. 11 *piscium venatores*
Specialist types: 8.9.2 *ad omne studium piscationis applicati, ut exquisitis piscationibus etiam marinas beluas capiant* ~ Manil. 5.189-92, *cetarii*; 8.12.1 *aut pisces tridente vel cuspide inter ipsa undarum spatia figat intrepidus* ~ Manil. 5.297; 8.17.5...*sed magnorum piscium. Hi enim phocas, canes marinos, xifias, thynnos, corcodillos capient* ~ Manil. 5.658-63
θυννοσκόπος: Teucer, II 4.2; also xxv. 4.3 *thynnorum excubatores*
Periphrasis: 6.452 ἰχθυβόλους; 4.243 ἰχθυοθηρευτάς; 5.279 ἀγρευτῆρι λίνῳ ἀνεφέλκεται ἐξ ἁλὸς ἰχθύν

I.2.III. Divers

δύτης: Teucer, II 3.12; cf. 5.156 δύνοντας καθ᾽ ὕδωρ δεσμευομένους θ᾽ ὑπὸ μαζῶν

---

[1] Ruffing 2008, 404-15.

κολυμβητής:[2] Teucer, II 3.12, 9.6; Dorotheus, p. 413.14
urinator: 8.15.2 ~ Manil. 5.431–5, 8.29.6
Sponge-divers: 8.26.9 *piscator, sed qui marinas spongias colligat*; 8.30.8 *legentes spongias*; xxv. 4.1 *extractores spongiarum*

I.2.iv. Fowlers
ἰξευτής: Θ pp. 157.22, 217.19; Epit. II; Teucer, II 3.8, 5.1; cf. 4.243 ἰξοβόλους; 4.339 ἰξευτῆρας; 5.175 ἰξῷ χρησαμένην τέχνην καλάμοις τ' ἀναφαίνει
ἱερακάριος: Θ p. 217.20
auceps: Firmicus, 5×; also 8.14.3 *aves capiet* ~ Manil. 5.370–3; *Lib. Herm.* 4×
Periphrasis: 6.453 ὀρνίθων τε θοῶν θηρήτορας; 8.12.1 *iaculator, sagittator, qui volantes aves speciali artificii moderatione percutiat* ~ Manil. 5.294–6

I.3. Livestock Rearing, Maintenance, Animal Training

I.3.i. Herdsmen
ποιμήν: 6.407 ποιμένας ἀγρονόμους τε βοτῶν ἀγέλας ἐλάοντας
pastor: Firmicus, 5×, incl. 8.6.5 ~ Manil. 5.115–17; xxv. 1.40 *pastores gregum et huiusmodi iumentorum*, xxvii. 11
armentarius: Firmicus, 3×
bubulcus: Firmicus, 3×; xxv. 2.5
swineherds: 6.408 ... ἠὲ συφόρβους; 3.5.23 *pastores porcarios*
Periphrasis: 4.247 κτηνῶν δ' ἀγρονόμων σημάντορας; 3.3.6 *iumentorum amatores atque cultores*; 4.14.14 *agrestium pecorum...magistros*; xxv. 1.5 *quadrupedum nutritores*, 8 *iumentorum nutritores*, 10.4 *nutrient iumenta*
stabulator: *Lib. Herm.* 4×; also 4.13.7 *et qui iumentorum stabula purgare vel mundare iubeantur*

I.3.ii. Tamers, trainers
θηριοτρόφος: Ptol. 4.4.5 ~ Θ p. 211.30; Θ p. 123.19
Periphrasis: 6.454–5 ... ἠὲ τιθηνούς | δαμναμένους τιθασοῖσιν ὑπ' ἤθεσι πρηΰνοντας; 4.245 θηροδιδασκαλίης τ' ἐπιβήτορας; 3.11.18 *nutrientes feras beluas, ferarumque praepositos*; 4.14.14 *bestiarum magistros*; 8.16.1 *Capient etiam feras pariter et domabunt*; 8.17.6 *mansuetarii ferarum* ~ Manil. 5.699–709
See also V.5.ix. Keepers of sacred animals

Of horses
ἱπποκόμος: Teucer, II 1.12
ἱπποφορβός: Teucer, II 11.4
equorum cultor, domitor, magister, etc.: 3.5.23, 8.6.3, 8.13.3 *equorum nutritor et cultor aut certe excitator*, 8.27.5, 8, 8.29.14; xxv. 9.15 *domatores...equorum*, 25 *equorum persecutores vel equorum cursores magnatum*, xxv. 11.16 *nutritores equorum*
equarius(?) 4.13.7 [ex emend. Kroll, for *equitarios*]
Periphrasis: 6.408 ἵππων τ' ὠκυπόδων σημάντορας

---

[2] Ruffing 2008, 599.

Of Birds
ὀρνιθοτροφός: Θ p. 216.8, 15; Epit. IIIa, IIIb; cf. 6.453 ὀρνίθων…τιθηνούς; 4.244 ὀρνίθων τροφοποιούς
ἱερακοτρόφους: Θ p. 216.8, 15; Epit. IIIa, IIIb
nutritor: 8.19.8; also 8.14.3 palumbos studiose nutriet ~ Manil. 5.383–4
trainer: 8.14.3 aut ingenioso studio avibus humanae sonum vocis insinuat ~ Manil. 5.386; also xxv. 9.15 domatores avium

I.3.III. Asses and mules
μουλίων/mulio: II 2.4 μουλίωνα…βουρδουναρίους; Firmicus, 4×, incl. 8.29.14 muliones… regis
mularum pastor: 8.19.9
mulomedicus: 8.13.3 ~ Manil. 5.353–4
asinarius: 8.27.10; xxv. 1.45
ὀνηλάτης: Teucer, II 1.12

I.4. Storage
horrearius: cf. 3.7.13 horreis…praepositos; 4.10.9 ex horreis…faciet vitae substantiam
See also VII.1.ii. Bakers

II. Manual Work

II.1. General Terms
βάναυσος: 3.62, 6.527 τέχνας…βαναύσους; CCAG viii/1. 177.4, xi/1. 134.6
μηχανικός/mechanicus:[3] 4.439; Θ p. 217.1, 3; Teucer, II 1.2; 3.12.20, 5.2.12; Lib. Herm. 5×
τεχνίτης:[4] Teucer, II 1.2
χειροτέχνης:[5] Valens, I 1.22; 'Heliodorus', p. 72.17–18; CCAG viii/1. 177.4; cf. 2.100 πολέσιν δὲ τέχνας ἡρμόσσατο χειρός; 4.442 ἐργοπόνους παλάμαισι
χειρουργός: Ptol. 4.4.7 ~ Θ p. 212.4–5; Θ p. 211.3; CCAG v/1. 189.4
ἐργάτης: Teucer, II 8.5, 12.8 ἐπιδιφρίους…πολυκρίτους ἐργάτας
ἐργοπόνος: 4.150
operarius: xxv. 4.11 operarios vel in ergastulis laborantes, xxv. 8.18
fabricator: 5.4.18

II.2. Portage
laturarius: 4.14.2, 8.21.4
ἀχθοφόρος: 4.251, 443

II.3. Water-Supply
II.3.I. Water-carriers
ὑδραγωγός: 1.84; Θ p. 166.22; Epit. IV; Teucer, II 2.2, 4.11; Hephaestion, ii. 281.5; cf. 4.251 ὑδρέας
ὑδροφόρος: 1.85

---

[3] Ruffing 2008, 664–5.   [4] Ruffing 2008, 792–800.   [5] Ruffing 2008, 824.

aquarius: 4.13.6; also 3.5.25 *aquarum distributores*; *Lib. Herm.* 5× *aquae ductores*
ἀντλητής: Ptol. 4.4.5 ~ Θ p. 211.30; Θ p. 212.17; Epit. IIIa; cf. 6.424 ἄντλοις ὕδωρ φορέοντες; 4.257 (ληνῶν) ἀντλητῆρες
haustor etc.: 8.21.7 *aquam haurientes perpetuis laboribus deteruntur*; 8.29.4 *aquam hauriens misero laboris onere praegravabitur*; 8.29.6 *haustor aquarum*; *Lib. Herm.* 2×; xxv. 4.38 *haustores fontium*; xxviii. 13 *hauritores*
Raisers of water: 3.9.3 *aquas ex altis puteis levantes*; 4.13.6 *Aut enim ex altis puteis cotidiano opere aquam levare coguntur*; 4.14.14 *alios ex puteis altissimis adsiduo labore aquas levare compellit*
Also xxv. 4.38 *fluminum captatores*, xxv. 5.1 *lotores arenae*

II.3.II. Workers on irrigation channels
ὑπονομευτής: Ptol. 4.4.5 ~ Θ p. 211.30
Periphrasis: 6.422 ὀχετηγοί; 4.252 ἀμαρησκαπτῆρας; Teucer, II 5.1 ἀμαρηγούς; 1.85–6 οἵθ' ὑπὸ γαίης | κευθμῶνας δύνουσιν ἀεικέος εἵνεκα μισθοῦ
Also Teucer, II 4.11 ποταμῶν διάρτας (raisers of water from rivers)
See also I.1.iii. Gardeners; see also VII.5.i. Cleaners

II.3.III. Operators of water-mills
ὑδραλετάριος: Teucer, II 4.11, 11.1
piscator: xxv. 4.38 (so Hübner on Manil. 5.189, p. 107)

II.4. Mining
μεταλλευτής:[6] Ptol. 4.4.5 ~ Θ p. 211.26–7; cf. 4.259 γαίης τε μεταλλευταί
Periphrasis: 3.7.7 *fossores auri*; 8.17.8 *metallorum inventores, qui latentes auri et argenti venas et ceterarum specierum sollertibus inquisitionibus persequantur*
Managers/foremen: 8.17.2 *ergastulis praepositos vel metallis*; 3.9.5 *metallorum praepositos*; 3.12.10 *praepositos metallorum*

II.5. Construction

II.5.I. Brick-makers
See II.7.iii πλινθευτής, etc.

II.5.II. Wood-cutters
ξυλοσχίστης: Ptol. 4.4.5 ~ Θ p. 211.29
πελεκᾶς, πελεκητής:[7] cf. 4.324 (ὕλης) πελεκήτορας

II.5.III. Stone-cutters
λα(ο)τόμος:[8] 6.416; Ptol. 4.4.5 ~ Θ p. 211.28; Θ p. 216.6; *Lib. Herm.* 5× *lapidum incisores*; cf. 4.260 οἷς λᾶες ἀπ' οὔρεος ἀκροτομοῦνται; 4.325 λαοτόμους τε πέτρης σκληρώδεος λαοξόος:[9] Ptol. 4.4.5
λαξευτής: 1.77; Θ p. 211.11
λιθουργός:[10] 1.77; Ptol. 4.4.5 ~ Θ p. 211.28; Θ p. 211.11

---

[6] Ruffing 2008, 663 μεταλλεύς, μεταλλικός, μεταλλουργός.   [7] Ruffing 2008, 712.
[8] Ruffing 2008, 623–6; Drexhage 2012, 157.   [9] Ruffing 2008, 619–22.
[10] Ruffing 2008, 639.

λιθοξόος:[11] 6.419; Ptol. 4.4.5 ~ Θ p. 211.28-9; Θ p. 216.1, 6; Epit. IIIa; Teucer, II 1.10, 3.4, 12.8
lapidarii: 3.5.23, 4.14.14
μαρμάριος:[12] Θ p. 216.7; Teucer, II 3.4
μαρμαροξύστης: Θ p. 215.7
marmorarius: 8.19.11, 8.24.8
σκληρουργός:[13] Valens, I 1.22; cf. 4.325 λαοτόμους τε πέτρης σκληρώδεος
Periphrasis: 6.522-3 δαιδάλλοντας ... ἐκ λύγδοιο φαεινῆς

II.5.IV. Stone-dressers
λιθοψήκτης: Θ p. 216.6; cf. 4.326 λιθοψώκτῳ καμάτῳ βίον ἰθύνοντας

II.5.V. Stone-carvers
λιθογλύφος:[14] Θ p. 212.28
ἱερογλύφους: Ptol. 4.4.7 ~ Θ p. 212.4; Θ p. 165.12

II.5.VI. Builders

II.5.VI.A. General terms
ἀρχιτέκτων: Teucer, II 1.2; Περὶ κράσ. 207; Valens, I 1.39
architectus: 8.24.8, 8.29.5; xxv. 1.5 architectores
structor: Firmicus, 3×
aedificator: xxv. 1.38, xxvii. 11

II.5.VI.B. Of houses
οἰκοδόμος:[15] Θ pp. 213.2, 215.12, 15; Epit. IIIa; Teucer, II 1.10; 'Heliodorus', p. 84.26; CCAG v/1. 188.3; cf. 6.415 ἐχυρῶν δωμήτορας οἴκων; 4.325 ἐγρεσιοίκους

II.5.VI.C. Of walls
parietarius: 8.24.8
τειχοδόμος: 4.291
Coping: 4.151-2 ~ 1.299-300 θριγκῶν τε καὶ εὐτοίχων [εὐτυπέων] κανονισμῶν | κοσμήτας; 4.292-3 εὐτοίχων κανονισμῶν | θριγκῶν τ' εὐθυντῆρας

II.5.VI.D. Shinglers
σκανδουλάριος:[16] Θ p. 215.15 σκανδουλαρίους ... ἢ τοιχοβάτας

II.5.VI.E. Of siege-engines
Periphrasis: 8.27.5 mechanicus qui instrumenta bellis faciat necessaria

II.5.VI.F. Of ships
ναυπηγός:[17] Ptol. 4.4.5 ~ Θ p. 211.28; xxviii. 13 navium constructores; cf. 4.323-4 ἐν ναυπηγέσι τέχναις | καγκανέης ὕλης πελεκήτορας εὐξυλοεργούς
Other: 8.20.10 fabri, architecti navium

---

[11] Ruffing 2008, 637. [12] Ruffing 2008, 657-8; Drexhage 2012, 157.
[13] Ruffing 2008, 749. [14] Ruffing 2008, 636.
[15] Ruffing 2008, 682-95; Drexhage 2012, 159-60. [16] Ruffing 2008, 747.
[17] Ruffing 2008, 673-6; Drexhage 2012, 155-6.

Makers of pitch: 4.345–6 πευκῆέν τε λίπασμα συνασκοῦντας σὺν ἐλαίῳ | μόχθον πισσήεντα πονήσοντας

Painters: 4.342 κηραγγέας, ὁλκαδοχρίστας; see also II.8.v. Workers in wax

II.6. Metal-Working

Periphrasis: 4.14.20 et qui artes metallicas exercere consueverint; 8.25.9 qui res metallicas tractet

See also II.7.i. General Terms: faber; II.8.vi. Workers in precious metals

II.6.I. Trade names with specific metals

Trades from fire and iron (πυρὸς, σιδήρου/igne et ferro): 6.519 ἐκ πυρὸς ἢ πολιοῖο τέχνας ὥπασσε σιδήρου; 4.123–4 = 1.288–9; 5.135; Ptol. 4.4.5 ~ Θ p. 211.27; Θ pp. 136.8, 160.3; 209.6–7, 15, 211.3–4, 12–13, 13–14, 212.3; Π.τ.δ. 29; Περὶ κράσ. 157; Valens, I 1.22; al.; Firmicus (actus; artes; vitae subsidia); xxv. 2.44

σιδηρεύς:[18] CCAG v/1. 189.3

ferramentarius: 3.11.18

ferrarius: 8.25.9, 8.26.9

χαλκοτύπος:[19] 1.79; Θ p. 211.12; cf. 4.570 χαλκοτύποις τέχνῃσι

χαλκεύς:[20] Ptol. 4.4.5; 'Heliodorus', p. 84.26; CCAG vii. 225.24

aerarius: 3.11.18, 4.14.13

κασσιτεροποιός:[21] Ptol. 4.4.8

μολυβδουργός:[22] Ptol. 4.4.8

Periphrasis: 6.391–2 bronze (i.e. copper), lead, iron; 1.288–9 iron, hammers, furnace

II.6.II. Specific manufactures

ὁπλουργός:[23] Ptol. 4.4.7 ~ Θ p. 212.3; xxvii. 26 factores armorum, xxviii. 10 armorum operatores

scutarius: 3.12.1

κλειδοποιός:[24] 'Heliodorus', p. 84.31; CCAG v/3. 88.26

II.7. Handicrafts

II.7.I. General terms

artifex: Firmicus, 7×, incl. 4.4.5 artifices... publicos; Lib. Herm. 3×

faber: Firmicus, 3×; Lib. Herm. 4×

opifex: 8.26.3

See also II.1. Manual Work: General terms

II.7.II. Glass-makers

ὑα(ε)λᾶς/ὑελάριος/ὑα(ε)λουργός:[25] cf. 1.79 φυσητὰς ὑέλοιο

---

[18] Ruffing 2008, 741.
[19] Ruffing 2008, 820–1; Drexhage 2012, 154; Reynolds and Tannenbaum, 118.
[20] Ruffing 2008, 814–19.   [21] Ruffing 2008, 579.   [22] Ruffing 2008, 666.
[23] Ruffing 2008, 703 ὁπλοποιός.   [24] Ruffing 2008, 593–5.
[25] Ruffing 2008, 805–6; also ὑελιάριος: Drexhage 2012, 142.

II.7.III. Workers in ceramics
κεραμεύς:[26] Θ p. 215.12, 16; Epit. IIIa
κεραμουργός:[27] Θ p. 213.3; 4.291
πλινθευτής, πλινθουργός, πλινθοποιός:[28] cf. 4.291-2 εὐτόλμους κεραμουργούς | πηλαίης πλίνθου
figulus: 8.27.11
Makers of lamps: Θ p. 215.16 λυχνοποιούς; Teucer, II 1.8 κανδηλάπτας, λαμπαδαρίους; xxv. 1.30 accensores lampadum vel lampadarios

II.7.IV. Carpenters
τέκτων:[29] 1.77; Ptol. 4.4.5 ~ Θ p. 211.28; Θ pp. 211.11, 216.1, 5; Epit. IIIa; Teucer, II 1.10; 'Heliodorus', p. 84.26; cf. 6.418 τεκτοσύνης στάθμης τ' ἐπιίστορας; 4.323 and 440 τεκτοσύνης τ' ἄρχοντας
τορνευτής:[30] Π.τ.δ. 20; Apomasar, Rev. p. 98.10; 4.568a τορν[εύτορας
Tornator: 4.13.2 tor<na>tores; xxviii. 10

II.7.V. Leather-workers
βυρσεύς:[31] Θ p. 216.1, 5; Epit. IIIa, IIIb; cf. 4.320 βυρσοτόμους ... δεροεργέας
βυρσοδέψης:[32] CCAG v/1. 189.6-7
coriarius: 4.14.13, 20; also 3.8.7 confectores coriorum, 3.10.8 coriorum confectores, 3.11.18 coriorum infectores; xxviii. 10 coriorum aptatores
σκυτοτόμος:[33] Teucer, II 12.8; cf. 4.320-1 ἔν τε καθέδραις | σκυτείῃ τέχνῃ μεμελημένα δαιδάλλοντας
sutor: Lib. Herm. 3×
caligarius: 3.10.8 caligarios [codd. callicarios]; 4.14.13 gallicarios [ex emend.: codd. calligarios; caligarios equally possible][34]
Makers of reins: Θ p. 216.5 λωροτόμους (~ lorarius);[35] Teucer, II 1.10 (P) κατασκευαστὰς χαλινῶν

II.7.VI. Manufacturers of pitch
πισσουργός:[36] cf. 4.346 μόχθον πισσήεντα πονήσοντας

II.7.VII. Furriers
pellio, pellarios: 3.11.18; 4.14.13

II.7.VIII. Textile workers

II.7.VIII.A. General terms
Teucer, II 1.10 (L) χλαινῶν κατασκευαστὰς καὶ παντοίας ἐσθῆτος

---

[26] Ruffing 2008, 582-90; Drexhage 2012, 152-3.   [27] Ruffing 2008, 591.
[28] Ruffing 2008, 719-22.   [29] Ruffing 2008, 774-91; Reynolds and Tannenbaum, 122.
[30] Ruffing 2008, 801.   [31] Ruffing 2008, 463-5; Drexhage 2012, 152.
[32] Ruffing 2008, 465-6.   [33] Ruffing 2008, 755-6.
[34] Ruffing 2008, 563-4; Drexhage 2012, 150-1; another possible Greek example in Reynolds and Tannenbaum, 120.
[35] Ruffing 2008, 648; cf. Drexhage 2012, 151-2 ἡνιοράφος; a possible χαλινουργός in Reynolds and Tannenbaum, 122.
[36] Ruffing 2008, 716.

II.7.VIII.B. Specific fabrics
λινόϋφος/ λίνυφος:³⁷ Θ p. 216.25 λινοῦφους, ὀθονιακούς; cf. 4.344 μεθόδῳ τε λινοστολίης προφέροντας
λινουργοί:³⁸ Θ p. 137.10
linteo: 3.6.4, 3.11.18, 4.14.13; cf. xxviii. 11 *lini opifices*
ἐριουργός:³⁹ Π.σ.α. p. 183.26
lanarius: Firmicus, 3×; also, 8.19.7 *textores faciet, vel qui lanas purpurasque pertractent*;⁴⁰ 3.12.10 *tinctores lanarum* [*ex emend.*]
μεταξάριος:⁴¹ Teucer, II 1.2; *siricarius/sericarius*: 8.19.12; xxv. i.5

II.7.VIII.C. Weavers
ὑφάντης:⁴² Ptol. 4.4.4; 4.4.6 ~ Θ p. 213.13, Θ p. 209.8; Περὶ κράσ. 207; Valens, I 1.39; Camaterus, ὑφαντάδας; *CCAG* v/3. 88.27 ὑφαντὰς ποικίλων ἱματίων; cf. 6.433 φάρεά θ' ὑφανόωντας
ἱστουργός:⁴³ 6.432; Π.τ.δ. 20; Π.σ.α. p. 183.26; cf. 2.321–3 τοὺς μὲν ἐφ' ἱστῶν | κερκίσιν… ἀμφί τε πέπλοις | δεικνύντας πάντων μορφὰς θηρῶν τε καὶ ἀνδρῶν; 4.422–3 τεύκτορας… ἱστοπόνους
textor, etc.: Firmicus, 5×, incl. 3.6.3 *qui magnificas vestes texant*; 3.6.4 *textores…regis textrinis…praepositos*; 8.25.9 *textor gerdius*⁴⁴
Of *tunicae*: 3.11.18 *textores tunicarum*, also 4.14.17 *pretiosas tunicas arte sua facientes*; xxv. 1.38 *aptatores tunicarum vel cuiuscumque vestis*
πολυμιτάριος: Θ p. 217.15, cf. 5.168 πολλοῖσι μίτοις
Weavers with gold thread (*barbaricarii*): 3.3.14 *eos, qui neto auro vestes pingunt*, 3.13.23 *aut ex auro vestes pingentes*⁴⁵

II.7.VIII.D. Embroiderers
πλουμάριος/*plumarius*:⁴⁶ Θ p. 213.26; 3.6.4, 3.11.18
Periphrasis: 2.320–1 αἰόλ' ὑπὸ χροιῇ ποικίλματα δαιδάλλοντας | παντοίοις ζώοισιν ἐοικότα; 2.322–3…ἠδὲ χερῶν τεχνήμασιν ἀμφί τε πέπλοις | δεικνύντας πάντων μορφὰς θηρῶν τε καὶ ἀνδρῶν

II.7.VIII.E. Dyers
βαφεύς:⁴⁷ 1.80; Ptol. 4.4.4; 4.4.8 ~ Θ p. 212.27; Θ pp. 209.9, 211.12, 19; Π.τ.δ. 20; Valens, I 1.29 πορφυροβαφίαν; cf. 2.326 ἀνθοβάφους
tinctor: Firmicus, 7×; xxvii. 30
Colours: 3.6.4 *colorum inventores*, 4.13.2 *coloris repertores*; 4.14.17 *colorum…repertores*; 5.5.6 *infectores colorum*; xxvii. 17 *artes…colorum*, 18 *operatores colorum*, xxviii. 11 *a coloribus aut tincturis…actus*

---

[37] Ruffing 2008, 642–7; otherwise λινοποιοί, λινουργοί; *lintearii*: Dumitrache, 30–1.
[38] Ruffing 2008, 641–2.   [39] Ruffing 2008, 527.
[40] Purple dealers: Pleket 1984, 20, 22–3; id. 1988, 267; id. 'Greek Epigraphy and Comparative Ancient History: Two Case Studies', *EA* 12 (1988), 25–37, at 33–4, 36; Ruffing 2004, 95; Dumitrache, 27–9: *purpurarii*.
[41] Ruffing 2008, 663.   [42] Ruffing 2008, 808.   [43] Ruffing 2008, 551.
[44] Ruffing 2008, 470–87 γέρδιος.   [45] Paraphrasing *barbaricarius* (Pruneti, 47)?
[46] Ruffing 2008, 722; Drexhage 2012, 150.   [47] Ruffing 2008, 453–9.

II.7.VIII.F. Fullers
κναφεύς:[48] Maximus, Epit. 2.15; Camaterus, *Introd.* 1736; cf. 4.422 γνάπτορας εὐσήμων πέπλων
fullo: Firmicus, 3×
Periphrasis: 6.433–4 ῥυπόεντα πλυνοῖσιν | εἵματα καλλύνοντας

II.7.VIII.G. Tailors
ῥάπτης:[49] Θ pp. 216.23, 25; Epit. IIIa; Teucer, II 1.10, 3.12 (P); *CCAG* v/1. 164.20; 4.423 ῥαπτῆρας [*ex emend.*]
Periphrasis: 6.434–5 ἰσχαλέαις βελόνῃσιν | ῥωγαλέους πέπλους ἀσκηθέας ἐκτελέοντας
annexor: xxvii. 27 *vestium honorabilium annexores*, xxviii. 11 *vestium connexores*
Retailers: see III.4. Shopkeepers

II.8. Luxury goods

II.8.I. Instrument-makers
ὀργανοποιός:[50] Ptol. 4.4.6 ~ Θ p. 213.12; cf. 6.401 ὄργανα δαιδάλλοντας; 6.483 ὄργανα θέσκελ' ἑαῖς πολυμηχανίῃσι τελοῦντας; 4.439 ὀργανοπήκτορας ἄνδρας
Also xxvi. 62 *instrumentorum annexores*
Automaton-makers: 6.402–3 ἄλλα τε θαυματόεντ' ἔργ'…τεύχοντας; 4.440–1 αὐτοδίδακτα τέχνῃσιν | θαύματα δαιδάλλοντας

II.8.II. Painters
ζωγράφος:[51] Ptol. 4.4.4 ~ Θ p. 211.19; Ptol. 4.4.5, 6; Θ pp. 209.8, 213.24, 26, 216.9, 16, 217.15; Epit. IIIa; *Π.τ.δ.* 20; Valens, I 3.34; 'Heliodorus', p. 85.8; *CCAG* v/3. 88.27, vii. 118.6; cf. 1.298 ζωγραφίης μεδέοντας (~ 4.150 ἐν γραφίδεσσιν ἀρίστους)
Periphrasis: 5.167 αἰόλλειν μορφὰς ἢ χρώμασι… [*ex emend.*]
Encaustic painters: 2.324; 6.524–5 (see II.8.v. Workers in wax), (?)4.342 ὑλογράφους ἄνδρας
pictor: Firmicus, 6×; also 8.29.1 *artem quae pertinet ad ornatum vel ad picturas*

II.8.III. Makers of mosaics[52]
musivarius: 3.3.23

II.8.IV. Sculptors
ἀγαλματογλύφος:[53] Valens, I 1.39
ἀγαλματοποιός:[54] *Περὶ κράσ.* 207; 'Heliodorus', p. 84.29 (+ μηνοποιός); cf. 6.420 ἠδέ τ' ἀγάλματα καλὰ τέχναις τεύχοντες ἔῃσιν; 4.569 εὐξοάνους παλάμῃσιν ἀγαλμοτυπεῖς
ἀνδριαντοπλάστης: Θ pp. 213.27, 217.15

---

[48] Ruffing 2008, 492–501; Reynolds and Tannenbaum, 119–20.
[49] Ruffing 2008, 731–4, cf. 538–41 ἠπητής; Drexhage 2012, 149.
[50] Ruffing 2008, 706.   [51] Ruffing 2008, 533–6.
[52] L. Robert, 'Sur Didymes à l'époque byzantine', *Hellenica*, 11 (1960), 490–504, at 493 ψηφιωτής, ψηφιστής.
[53] Ruffing 2008, 396–7; J. Diethart, 'Zu seltenen und neuren griechischen Berufsbezeichnungen vor allem aus byzantinischer Zeit (I)', *MBAH* 37 (2019), 105–26, at 107–8.
[54] Ruffing 2008, 397–8 and n. 53.

ἀνδριαντοποιός:⁵⁵ Ptol. 4.4.7 ~ Θ p. 212.2–3
γλύπτης:⁵⁶ Θ p. 213.26; cf. 6.343–4 δεικήλων ξεστῶν... γλυφέας
ζωοπλάστης: Ptol. 4.4.7 ~ Θ p. 212.4; cf. 4.343 ζωοτύπους... εἰκονομόρφους
πλάστης:⁵⁷ Θ pp. 209.8, 213.13; Περὶ κράσ. 207; Valens, I 3.34 ἐπιπλαστῶν; Lib. Herm. 3× *statuarum plasmatores*, xxvi. 44 *statuarum fabricatores*; cf. 5.167–8 αἰόλλειν μορφὰς... πλάσμασιν [*ex emend.*]
sculptor: Firmicus, 7×, incl. 4.14.20 *sculptores simulacrorum*; *see also* V.5.vi. Manufacture and care of statues
statuarius: 3.11.18
Periphrasis: 6.523 ἢ ἐκ λύγδοιο φαεινῆς; 4.570 χαλκοτύποις τέχνῃσι κολοσσοπόνους παναρίστους
For divine images, see V.5.vi. Manufacture and care of statues

II.8.v. Workers in wax
κηροπλάστης:⁵⁸ Ptol. 4.4.6; cf. 6.524–5 εὐτήκτου τ' ἀπὸ κηροῦ... χαρασσομένους; 5.167–8 αἰόλλειν μορφὰς... κηρῷ [*ex emend.*]
Periphrasis: 2.323–4, 5.167–8: wax among media for visual representations
See also II.5.vi.f. Painters of ships

II.8.vi. Workers in precious metals
Periphrasis: xxvii. 17 *artes... auri vel argenti*, 44 *per aurum vel argentum actus... et operationes*
See also II.6. Metal-working

II.8.vi.a. Goldsmiths, etc.
χρυσοχόος:⁵⁹ Ptol. 4.4.8 ~ Θ p. 212.28; Θ p. 213.24; CCAG v/3. 88.25; cf. 6.387–8 ἐν χοάνοις χρυσόν τε καὶ ἄργυρον αἰγλήεντα | τήκοντας
αὐράριος/*aurarius*:⁶⁰ Teucer, II 4.2; xxv. 4.3 *aurarios quos vulgus vocat praeenenses*
aurifex: Firmicus, 11×, incl. 8.16.3 ~ Manil. 5.506; also 3.12.9 *fabricatores auri*; xxvii. 23 *aurificia*
inaurator: Firmicus, 4×; also xxv. 6.30 *inaurizatores* (< ἐγχρυσ-?)
bratiarius/bractearius/bracteator: 4.21.6, 8.16.3, 8.19.11, 8.26.6
Periphrasis: 4.149 ~ 1.297 ῥεκτῆρας χρυσοῖο; 6.345–6 ἢ χρυσῷ δαιδάλματ' ἢ ἀργύρῳ ἐκτελέοντας | ἢ ἴκελα ζῴοισιν ὑπὸ γλαφυρῇσι τορείαις

II.8.vi.b. Silversmiths
argentarius: Firmicus, 3×; also 3.3.23 *ex argento quaedam facientes opera*; xxv. 6.30... *vel argenteis*
See also IV.1.iv. Stampers of coins

II.8.vi.c. Chasers, engravers
τορευτής:⁶¹ cf. 6.346 ὑπὸ γλαφυρῇσι τορείαις
caelator: 8.30.9

---

[55] Ruffing 2008, 420. [56] Ruffing 2008, 487–90. [57] Ruffing 2008, 719.
[58] Ruffing 2008, 592. [59] Ruffing 2008, 828–35; Drexhage 2012, 161.
[60] Ruffing 2008, 447–9; Drexhage 2012, 161. [61] Ruffing 2008, 800–1.

II.8.vii. Jewellers, workers in precious stones
καβιδάριος:[62] Θ p. 216.2, 7; Epit. IIIb
Periphrasis: 4.11.2 artes...margaritarum; 4.14.17 aut pretiosorum lapidum repertores; xxvii. 27 lapidum inventores
See also III.4.vi. Dealers in precious stones
Engravers: xxvii. 27 lapidum pretiosorum sculptores; 6.343–4 καὶ ἐπ' ἀνθηραῖς λιθάκεσσιν | σφρηγίδων γλυφέας
Painters: 4.14.20 vel qui gemmis ex vario pigmentorum genere aliam speciem coloris adpingant
Polishers: 4.14.20 politores pretiosarum gemmarum
Expressions involving monilia: xxvii. 17 artes monilium, 27 monilium...annexores, 30 tractatores...monilium

II.8.viii. Workers in ivory
ἐλεφαντουργός, etc.:[63] Θ p. 213.23; Valens, I 1.29 ἐλεφαντουργίας; xxvi. 44 eborei...operatores vel decoratores, xxvii. 30 tractatores...eboris; cf. 6.421 ἀπὸ πριστοῦ ἐλέφαντος, 523 ἐκ πριστοῦ ἐλέφαντος; 4.149–50 = 1.297–8 Ἰνδογενοῦς ἐλέφαντος | ἐργοπόνους

II.8.ix. Parfumiers
μυρεψός:[64] Ptol. 4.4.8 ~ Θ p. 212.27; Π.τ.δ. 20; CCAG v/1. 164.20; cf. 2.327 εὐόδμων τε μύρων...τεχνήτορας
Expressions involving aromata: 3.13.5 actus...de aromatibus, 4.13.1 aromatum inventores, 4.14.17 aromatum...repertores; xxvii. 17 artes...aromatum, 27 aromatum...mixtores, 30 magnis operibus, vel...aromatum; xxxii. 59 operationibus...aromatum gratia
Expressions involving odores: 3.6.3 qui odorum pigmenta faciant; 8.11.1 ~ Manil. 5.263^b–5; xxv. 4.27 viventes...ab odoribus
See also III.4.vii. Perfume sellers

II.8.x. Garland-makers
στεφανοπλόκος:[65] Ptol. 4.4.4; cf. 2.325 ἐν πετάλοις στεφανώματα ποικίλλοντας ἀνθοπλόκος: Θ p. 209.9; Π.τ.δ. 20; CCAG v/1. 212.13 ~ viii/1. 183.24
Expressions involving flores, coronae: 3.13.5 actus...de floribus, 4.21.6 et qui coronas ex florum varietate compositas festis ac sacris diebus distrahere consuerint, 8.11.1 florum et coronarum inventor ~ Manil. 5.262–3^b; xxv. 1.36 florum annexores, xxv. 10.10 coronarum annexores
Also: xxvii. 17 artes...capitis vinctionum?
See also III.4.viii. Florists

II.8.xi. Other
emplastratores? 7.26.10 [ex emend. for plastratos]; 8.16.3 [ex emend. for implastratores, implastatores, implastores]

---

[62] Ruffing 2008, 555; Drexhage 2012, 161.
[63] Ruffing 2008, 515–16.
[64] Ruffing 2008, 671; Drexhage 2012, 161.
[65] Ruffing 2008, 758.

III. Commerce

III.1. Merchants

ἔμπορος:[66] Ptol. 4.4.3; Θ p. 144.3; Teucer, II 7.9, 9.3; Περὶ σχημ. 17; Valens, II 17.55; Paul, p. 61.4 ἐμπορικὸν βίον διάγοντας; CCAG v/1. 189.11, 192.8, vii. 225.30, xii. 125.20; Apomasar, Rev. p. 186.13–14 θαλάττιος γενήσεται ἔμπορος; cf. 3.321 οἱ δ' ἄρ' ἀπ' ἐμπορίης ἐσθλῆς βίοτον συνάγειραν; 6.448 πόντον τ' ἐξανύοντας ὑπ' ἐμπορίαις θαμινῇσιν; 6.486 ἐμπορίη νηός θ' ἡγήτορα ποντοπόροιο; 4.88 ἐμπορίης ἐμπείραμος; 4.134 ἐμπορικοῦ πλοίου φορτοστόλος ἴδρις; 1.133 ἐμπορίην φιλέοντας
πρηκτήρ (poetic): 4.329, 1.133
negotiator: Firmicus, passim, incl. 3.12.9 peregrini negotiatores; 8.22.2 negotiatores, laboriosi non consistentes loco; 8.25.5 negotiator sed qui peregrinas merces advehat semper; 8.25.8 negotiatores qui peregrinas merces advehant in navibus; 8.27.12 negotiatores, sed qui ad occidentem navigent; also 3.11.17 et qui magna negotia tractare consueverunt, 3.10.8 negotiorum interpretes; xxv. 2.38 negotiatores in aquis vitam peragentes vel per aliqua humida; xxv. 3.3 negotiatores ad loca plura euntes et in alienis frequenter vitam habentes. Also: 4.9.3 et qui peregrinis negotiationibus immorentur; 4.10.10 peregrinarum mercium gratia navigantes; 5.5.6 peregrinae negotiationis officia.
mercator: Lib. Herm. 2×

III.2. Shipping

III.2.i. Ship-owners

ναύκληρος/nauclerus: Θ p. 216.20; Teucer, II 7.9, 9.3; Valens, I 20.2; Paul, p. 61.3/'Heliodorus', p. 69.11; Hephaestion, i. 20–1; cf. 4.135 ναυκλήρου τέχνας θ' αἱρήσεται; Firmicus, 6×; Lib. Herm. 3×
navicularius: 8.6.1, 8.20.10

III.2.ii. Pilots

κυβερνήτης: Θ pp. 138.21; 216.17, 20; Teucer, II 2.1; cf. 6.364 (νηῶν τε), 4.398 = 1.324 (σκαφέων τε) κυβερνητῆρας
gubernator: Firmicus, 9×, incl. 3.13.1 gubernatores maiorum navium; 8.6.1 ~ Manil. 5.41, 54; 8.30.13 periti gubernatores; Lib. Herm. 4×; also xxv. 4.1 ductores navium?

III.2.iii. Sailors

ναύτης/nauta, etc.: 2.65, 6.501; Θ pp. 166.23, 216.17, 20; Epit. IV; Teucer, II 3.12, 4.1, 5.9; Paul, p. 61.4; Firmicus, 6×; Lib. Herm. 8×, incl. xxv. 4.3 nautas ascendentes in arborem navis et significantes terram vel ventos vel civitatem
ναυτικός/nauticus: Ptol. 4.4.5 ~ Θ p. 211.30; Θ pp. 212.11, 212.24, 217.11; 4.14.14, 8.30.9
Periphrasis: 4.397 = 1.323 ναυσιβάτας (Sun and malefics); 6.364 πλωτῆρας νηῶν; 4.399 πρωράρχους τε νεῶν ~ 1.324 πλωτάρχας σκαφέων; 5.151 ναυτίλοι
For ship-building, see II.5.vi.f. Builders—of ships

III.3. Slave-Dealers

σωματέμπορος:[67] Ptol. 4.4.6 ~ Θ p. 213.12; Dorotheus, p. 342.25 σώματος ἔμπορος
Periphrasis: 6.447 παίδων πρηκτῆρας

---

[66] Ruffing 2008, 516–22.   [67] Ruffing 2008, 766.

III.4. Shopkeepers

III.4.I. General terms
tabernarius: Firmicus, 4×; *see also* VII.2. Hospitality

III.4.II. Clothes dealers, etc.
Various expressions: 4.424 πρηκτῆρας; Ptol. 4.4.4 ~ Θ p. 211.19–20 ἱματιοπώλας; Ptol. 4.4.6 ~ Θ p. 213.14 ἐμπορευομένους κόσμους γυναικείους; Θ pp. 209.9 πορφυροπώλας, 211.18–19 βαφῶν...πραγματεύτας

III.4.III. Dealers in bric-a-brac
ῥωποπώλης:[68] cf. 4.322 ῥώπου τε γυναικῶν ἴδριας

III.4.IV. Dealers in metals
Periphrasis: 4.11.2 *metalli etiam cuiusdam commercia tractabunt*

III.4.V. Dealers in luxuries
Periphrasis: Ptol. 4.4.4 ~ Θ p. 211.21 ἐμπόρους τῶν πρὸς ἀπόλαυσιν καὶ κόσμον; xxxii. 10 *emptores rerum pretiosarum regum vel principum*

III.4.VI. Dealers in precious stones
margaritarii: 4.13.1; 8.16.3 ~ Manil. 5.508, 518; also 3.12.10 *gemmarum aut margaritarum mercatores*
Periphrasis: Valens, I 1.29 τέχνας ἢ ἐμπορικὰς ἐργασίας σμαράγδου τε καὶ λιθείας; 3.9.5 *aut gemmarum aut margaritarum...praepositos*; 3.11.18 *aut gemmas aut margaritas aliqua ratione tractantes*; 5.5.6 *aut pretiosarum gemmarum merces*
See also II.8.vii. Jewellers, workers in precious stones

III.4.VII. Perfume-sellers
ἀρωματοπώλης: Ptol. 4.4.4 ~ Θ p. 211.18–19 ἀρωμάτων πραγματεύτας; 3.9.5 *aromatum....praepositos*; 3.12.10 *aromatum...mercatores*; 4.14.20 *qui aromata mercari consueverint*; xxvii. 30 *tractatores...aromatum*
μυροπώλης/*myropola*:[69] Ptol. 4.4.4 ~ Θ p. 211.17; Θ p. 209.9; CCAG v/1. 212.12 ~ viii/1. 183.24; 3.12.10, 4.21.6
See also II.8.ix. Parfumiers

III.4.VIII. Florists
ἀνθοπώλης: Θ p. 211.18
See also II.8.x. Garland-makers

III.4.IX. Sellers of incense
turarius: 8.25.9[70]

III.4.X. Druggists
φαρμακοπώλης/*farmacopola*:[71] Ptol. 4.4.4 ~ Θ p. 211.19; 4.13.2

---

[68] Ruffing 2008, 735. [69] Ruffing 2008, 671–2.
[70] I. Bonati, 'Testimonianze papiracee sulla forma commerciale dell'incenso', *MBAH* 30 (2012), 9–25.
[71] Ruffing 2008, 810.

Also xxv. 8.30 *unguentorum venditores*, xxxii. 59 *operationibus…unguentorum… gratia*

III.4.xi. Sellers of consumables
caupo: Firmicus, 3×, incl. 4.11.2 *caupones, ut ea quae ad victum et potum sunt necessaria famosis et publicis mercimoniis praeparent*; xxv. 8.30
Liquid products: 3.2.6 *ex humidis negotiis vitae subsidia largitur*, 8.10.6 *humidas merces negotiabitur*
οἰνοπώλης:[72] Θ p. 211.18
οἰνέμπορος:[73] Ptol. 4.4.4
Salted products: 8.17.5 …*et haec mercabuntur*; xxv. 10.22 *venditorem carnium et aliarum rerum huiusmodi salitarum vel talia negotiantem*; see also VII.1.v. Saline products

III.4.xii. Dealers in birds[74]
Periphrasis: 8.14.3 *aut aves mercabitur*

IV. Documents, Writing, Lettered Professions

IV.1. Finance
IV.1.i. Wealth managers
Managers of royal wealth and comptrollers of revenue: 2.152–4 (~ xxxii. 3 *collectores tributorum regalium*); 3.188–9 ἀσχολίην δ' ὤπασσ' ἀφένους βασιληίου ἀμφίς; 3.317–18 ἀεὶ βασιλήιον ὄλβον | νωμῶντας, χρυσόν τ' ἐθνέων ἄπο δασμολογοῦντας; 3.7.5, 3.12.1, 4.14.5, 8.14.1 ~ Manil. 5.360; xxxii. 25 *colligentes pecunias regias*
Involving *fiscus*: 3.5.14, 3.10.7, 3.11.6, 17, 3.13.5, 4.7.2, 4.10.8, 4.14.6, 5.2.15, 6.3.3, 12
Managers of private wealth: 3.320; 6.358 ἀλλοτρίων κτεάνων ἰθύντορας; 4.41–2 ἀλλοτρίων κτεανισμῶν | δεσποσύνους; 3.7.4 *qui alienarum curam rerum procurationemque sustineant*; also 8.24.2 *praepositi thesaurorum*
Managers of the wealth of cities: 3.189 πολίων κλήρους καὶ κτήσιας ἀμφιέποντας; 4.580 πόλεως ταμιεύτορες; cf. 6.359–60 ἑῆς πάτρης διέποντας | χρήματ' ἰδὲ ξυνὸν πλοῦτον
Managers of public funds: 3.5.14 *rationes publicas tractantes*, 3.11.6 *de publico… victus…conferantur*, 4.7.2 *rationibus praeponi…populi*, 4.14.6 *quibus publica… instrumenta credantur*, 5.2.15 *principales civitatum publici rationibus praepositos*, 6.3.12 *publicis computationibus…praeponunt*, 8.14.1 *aerarium populi* ~ Manil. 5.362, 8.28.4 *publicis vectigalibus praeerunt*

IV.1.ii. Money-changers/bankers
τραπεζίτης: Ptol. 4.4.3 ~ Θ p. 210.27; Valens, II 17.57; Paul, p. 67.13/'Heliodorus', p. 72.23; *CCAG* vii. 222.15; xi/2. 125.7, xii. 126.8; 3.7.3 *mensarum…negotia tractantes*, 13 *mensis…praepositos*; cf. 4.579 ἔν τε τραπέζαις…; 3.99–100 τοὺς δ' αὖτε τραπέζης ἀργυραμοιβοῦ | εἷσεν ὕπερ
nummularius: xxv. 1.24, xxv. 11.8
Periphrasis: 2.256 ἢ δίφρῳ ἑζομένους, ὅθι τ' ἀργύρου ἐστὶν ἀμοιβή; 6.361 ἑζομένους, ὅθι τ' αἰὲν ἀμείβεται ἀργύρου αἴγλη

---

[72] Ruffing 2008, 700–2. [73] Ruffing 2008, 695–6.
[74] ὀρνιθοπώλης: Ruffing 2008, 706–7; Reynolds and Tannenbaum, 118.

IV.1.III. Money-lenders
δανειστής: 5.277
τοκιστής: Θ p. 144.3; CCAG v/1. 188.3; cf. 580–1 ἔν τε τοκισμοῖς | καὶ χρείαις
fenerator: Firmicus, 6×, incl. 8.19.7 fenerator de mensis publicis colligens magna diutiarum subsidia; also 3.7.3 fenerationis negotia tractantes; 4.14.6 fenoris negotiationibus...praepositos; 4.15.8 fenoris... officia tractantes
Periphrasis: 6.357 χρεῶν νωμήτορας; 4.330 δεινούς τε χρεάρπαγας

IV.1.IV. Stampers of coins
ἀργυροκόπος:[75] Ptol. 4.4.8 ~ Θ p. 212.28; see also II.8.vi.b. Silversmiths
Periphrasis: 6.388–9 ἀμοιβαίοιο χαράκτας | σήματος
monetarius: 8.17.8 (or master of the mint)

IV.1.V. Taxmen
τελώνης: Ptol. 4.4.5 ~ Θ p. 212.1; Valens, I 1.10; Paul, p. 68.1/'Heliodorus', p. 73.4; cf. 4.329 τελωνητάς
vectigaliarius: 3.11.3; also 3.7.3 vectigalium...negotia tractantes, 4.9.3 vectigalium conductores, 8.12.3 publicorum vectigalium tractans officia, 8.28.4 publicis vectigalibus praeerunt
publicanus: 3.11.3; xxxii. 12

IV.1.VI. Tax-farmers
ἐργολάβος: 4.330; Paul, p. 72.13/'Heliodorus', p. 75.17–18

IV.1.VII. Accountants
rationalis: Firmicus, 5×; rationibus praepositi, etc.: 3.7.5, 7, 13, 4.14.6; also 3.5.14 rationes publicas tractantes; 3.13.5 publicarum <rationum> dispositores vel correctores; 6.3.12 actus aut ex rationibus dabunt

IV.1.VIII. Auditors
λογιστής: Ptol. 4.4.3; Π.τ.δ. 11, 22; Περὶ κράσ. 141; cf. 4.160 ἔν τε λογιστονόμοισιν ἀεὶ πολυπρήκτορας ἔργοις

IV.1.IX. Other
conductor: 3.7.24 conductores publicorum negotiorum, 4.9.3 vectigalium conductores; also 3.7.3 conductionum...negotia tractantes
discussor: 3.11.17
Master of weights and measures: 4.14.6 aut ponderibus publicis...facit praeponi, 4.21.10
In charge of annona(e): 6.3.3 sacrae...praepositos annonae; 3.9.5 annonae aut frumentorum...praepositos, 3.10.7 exactores regiarum annonarum

IV.2. Intellectual Professions

IV.2.I. Teachers
παιδευτής: 2.336; Θ p. 214.18, 21; Epit. IIIa, IIIb, IV; 'Heliodorus', pp. 84.21, 85.7; Camaterus; CCAG viii/1. 258.6

---

[75] Ruffing 2008, 422–5.

'Leaders of youth': 2.254–5 παιδείης πραπίδεσσι σοφῆς παιδεύματ᾽ ἔχοντας | παίδων θ᾽ ἡγητῆρας; 3.98–9 παισὶν ὑφηγητῆρας ἔφηνεν | παιδείης, 3.193 παίδων θ᾽ ἡγητῆρας; 3.325 παίδων ἡγήτορες; 6.351–2 ἡγητῆρας ἀρίστους | παιδείης; 6.394 παίδων ἡγήτορας; 6.478 παίδων ἡγητῆρας
διδάσκαλος: Ptol. 4.4.3 ~ Θ p. 213.16; Ptol. 4.4.6; Θ pp. 131.10, 154.9, 174.6, 179.3; Περὶ σχημ. 56; Π.τ.δ. 22 βασιλέων διδασκάλους, 49; 'Heliodorus', p. 75.18–19; Camaterus; CCAG v/1. 223.14; cf. 4.179 διδασκαλίης τε παρέδρους
χαμαιδιδάσκαλος: Paul, p. 72.15/'Heliodorus', p. 84.23; CCAG v/3. 88.24
γραμματικός/*grammaticus*: Θ pp. 131.9, 137.13, 146.16, 208.23, 214.21; Epit. IIIa; Teucer, II 3.10; Περὶ σχημ. 42, 111 ~ Περὶ κράσ. 120; Περὶ κέντρ. 73; Περὶ κράσ. 207; 'Heliodorus', pp. 84.21, 117.17; Camaterus; CCAG iv. 117.22, v/3. 88.23, ix/1. 160.9, xii. 126.8; 4.205 = 1.305 γραμματικήν τ᾽ ἄσκησιν...ἔχοντας; 4.418–19 ἔν τε καθέδραις | γραμματικαῖς; Firmicus, 11×; *Lib. Herm.* 6×
magister: 3.7.25; xxxiv. 33 *puerorum magistri*; *grammaticae/oratoriae artis*: 3.7.1, 3.9.10, 4.19.29; *publici magistri*: 3.12.1; 4.9.8 *liberalium artium publicos magistros*
paedagogos: xxv. 11.12, xxxii. 44
Periphrasis: 3.7.13 *qui, cum imperatoribus constituti, docendi habeant aliquam potestatem*

IV.2.II. Orators
ῥήτωρ/*rhetor*: 2.259; 6.350, 479; 4.127, 141 [= 1.303], 575; 1.292; 5.244; Ptol. 4.4.3 ~ Θ p. 211.1; Θ pp. 131.9, 137.13, 146.16, 208.23, 210.28, 212.19–20, 214.18, 218.4; Epit. IIIa, IV; Περὶ κράσ. 120; Valens, I 1.39, II 17.37; Heliodorus, CCAG vii. 118.12; Camaterus; CCAG v/1. 189.10; viii/1. 186.3, 259.16; xi/1. 179.28; xii. 102.20; *Lib. Herm.* 6×; cf. 4.203 ῥητορικῆς...κρατίστους, 575 ῥητορικοῖς τε λόγοισι; 1.131 ῥητῆρας
orator: Firmicus, 20×; also *oratoriae artis magistri* (above); 6.23.6 *orationis splendore fulgentes*

IV.2.III. Sophists/philosophers
σοφιστής/*sophistes*: 5.244; Ptol. 3.14.31, 4.4.3 ~ Θ p. 211.1; Θ pp. 136.23, 146.16, 147.19–20, 165.9, 214.21; Teucer, II 12.6; Περὶ σχημ. 111 ~ Περὶ κράσ. 120; 'Heliodorus', p. 84.21; Heliodorus, CCAG vii. 117.17; Camaterus; CCAG v/1. 189.10; xxvi. 63; cf. 3.102 σοφίης δεδαηκότας, 325–6 ἐν σοφίῃ τε | πολλὸν ἀριπρεπέες μύθων ὑποφήτορες ἐσθλῶν; 6.350–1 σοφίῃ τε μάλ᾽ αἰεὶ | εὐπρεπέας, 479 σοφίῃσί τε πάμπαν ἀρίστους; 4.127 ἐν σοφίῃσιν ἀρίστους, 141 σοφίῃ τε κρατίστους [~ 1.292 ἐν σοφίαισιν ἀρίστους], 203–4 [= 1.303–4] σοφίης τε κρατίστους | ζηλωτάς, 575 ἐκ σοφίης κλέος ἕξειν; 1.292 ἐν σοφίαισιν ἀρίστους
φιλόσοφος/*philosophus*: Ptol. 3.14.5; Θ pp. 137.12–13, 144.5, 147.13–14, 15, 148.3, 165.1, 4, 17, 176.22, 212.19, 218.8; Epit. IV; Paul, p. 64.1; Camaterus; CCAG i. 115.21, v/i. 199.15, 219.20, 220.16, 223.7; vii. 108.19, 109.4; Firmicus, 5×, incl. 3.2.18 *philosophos opinatos...philosophos capillatos*; 3.12.6 *philosophos et caelestia saepe tractantes*; 4.19.29 *philosopharum litterarum interpretes*; xxv. 11.9

IV.2.IV. Literary professions
φιλόλογος: Ptol. 3.14.20, 26; Θ p. 178.23–4; Περὶ κέντρ. 52; Valens, 5×; Camaterus; CCAG v/1. 201.13; vii. 212.11, viii/1. 259.2, 260.11
litteratus: Firmicus, 5×; also 3.7.4 *philologos aut laboriosarum litterarum peritos*; 4.10.9 *ex litteris...faciet vitae substantiam*; 4.12.4 *litteris quaerant vitae subsidia*; 4.24.11 *litterarum*

gratia claros; 5.1.12 *ex litteris habebit substantiae facultatem*; 5.5.6 *duplicibus litteris imbuentur*; 8.25.3 *in litteris vehementer peritos*; 7.26.1 *expertos faciet litterarum*; *litterarum officia*: 6.5.4; 6.10.8; 8.26.2; 8.30.3; xxvii. 6 *a litteris utilitatem habentes*
In royal employ: 3.5.37; 6.23.6; 8.24.1 ~ Teucer, II 6.3 εὐπαιδεύτους; see also IV.2.vi. Clerical workers

IV.2.v. Lawyers
IV.2.v.A. Judges
ἀρχιδικαστής: 1.104
δικαστής: 5.41; Περὶ σχημ. 14
iudex: Firmicus, 8×, incl. 4.14.6 *privatarum litium iudices*; 3.7.3 *potentissimorum iudicum… interpretes*; *Lib. Herm.* 6×, incl. xxiv. 36 *iudex populorum*, xxxiv. 31 *populorum iudices*. Also 8.19.2 *de rebus maximis iudicabit*; 8.24.8 *sed his frequenter iudicia credentur*; *publica iudicia*, etc.: 8.15.3; 8.21.8; 8.24.5; 8.25.4; 8.27.2; *de aliorum iudicum sententiis iudicans*: 8.26.4; 8.28.11; 8.29.3
iuridicus: 3.3.6; 3.10.1 *iuridicos et qui provinciis aut civitatibus iura restituant, sed qui iustis semper gaudent causis*
adsessor: 3.4.15 *adsessores iudicum maximorum*

IV.2.v.B. Pleaders, advocates
δικολόγος: Ptol. 4.4.6 ~ Θ p. 213.15; Valens, II 17.87; Paul, pp. 67.12, 72.15/'Heliodorus', pp. 72.22, 75.19; Camaterus
συνήγορος: Paul, p. 67.12/'Heliodorus', p. 72.22–3
Periphrasis: 2.261 ἔν τε δικασπολίῃσιν ἐριδμαίνοντας ἔπεσσιν
advocatus: Firmicus, 8×; *Lib. Herm.* 3×, incl. xxxi. 35 *advocati principum causidicus*: 7.26.5

IV.2.v.C. Legal experts
Periphrasis: 2.257 νόμων θεσμῶν τ' ἐπίστορας, 3.323–4 θεσμῶν ἐπίστορες… διὰ γραπτῶν | ἰδμοσύνης
iuris or *iure peritus*: Firmicus, 4×; also xxv. 10.12 *legisperiti*
iuris interpres: 4.10.8
Expressions involving *lex*: 3.3.6 *legum latores… legum interpretes*; 3.12.1 *legum inventores*; xxxii. 25 *legum pronuntiatores*
Other: 8.28.10 *tabellis et forensibus studiis applicatus*

IV.2.v.D. Other
νομικός: Θ p. 210.28; Valens, 4×; Paul, p. 67.13/'Heliodorus', pp. 72.23, 84.22; 'Camaterus'; *CCAG* v/1. 189.11, v/3. 88.24, vii. 222.15, xi/2. 125.7, 179.28, xii. 126.9
νομογράφος: Ptol. 4.4.3, Θ p. 211.1

IV.2.vi. Clerical workers (scribes, secretaries)
γραμματεύς: Ptol. 4.4.3 ~ Θ p. 210.26; Θ pp. 152.18, 157.26 πόλεως γραμματεῖς, 164.1 βασιλικοὶ γραμματεῖς; Περὶ σχημ. 123 ~ Περὶ κράσ. 188; Περὶ σχημ. 111 ~ Περὶ κράσ. 139 γραμματεῖς βασιλέων; Περὶ κράσ. 139, 141; Valens, 5×, incl. II 8.2 βασιλικοὶ γραμματεῖς, II 17.37 γραμματεῖς βασιλέων, II 17.50 βασιλέων ἢ πόλεων ἢ ὄχλων γραμματεῖς; Paul, p. 72.14/'Heliodorus', p. 75.18; cf. 1.132 (ἐκ λόγου ἢ καλάμοιο) γραπτῆρας

γραφεύς: CCAG iv. 93.7
ἀντιγραφεύς: Paul, p. 67.12/'Heliodorus', p. 72.22
ἐξ(σ)κέπτωρ/exceptor (shorthand writer): Teucer, II 6.4 ἐξκέπτορας; 'Heliodorus', p. 72.21 (ἐπισκέπτωρ Paul, p. 67.11); Firmicus, 4×, incl. 3.5.26 exceptores earum sententiarum quae de hominum capitibus proferuntur; 3.10.14 exceptores principum; 4.14.10 exceptores personalium causarum
νοτάριος/notarius: Hephaestion, ii. vii.14 βασιλικὸν νοτάριον, 80.1; Paul, p. 67.12/'Heliodorus', p. 72.22; Camaterus; CCAG v/3. 89.14, vii. 222.15, xi/2. 125.7; 3.10.4; Lib. Herm. 2×
σκρινιάριος: Paul, p. 67.11/'Heliodorus', p. 72.22
χαλτουλάριος (archivist): Teucer, II 6.4 ~ xxv. 6.12 chartularios
commentariensis: 3.5.26
cornicularius: 3.5.26
scriba: Firmicus, 15×, incl. 3.7.13 scribas aut iudicum <aut> auctoritatum aut senatus; 3.10.1 magnorum aut potentium virorum…scribas; 6.4.5 scribas publicis rationibus fiscalibusque praepositos; 8.12.3 scriba tabularius ~ Manil. 5.316–21; 8.27.3 magistri scribae; Lib. Herm. 9×. Royal: 3.10.14; 6.3.12; 8.25.6; 8.26.2; 8.28.9; 8.30.3; xxxiv. 30–1. Of cities: xxv. 10.11 civitatum scribas. See also IV.2.iv. Literary professions
tabellio: 4.12.4; 5.2.17

V. Technical Specialisms

V.1. Applied Mathematics

γεωμέτρης/geometres: Ptol. 3.14.26; Θ pp. 131.10, 137.13–14, 154.9, 174.6; Περὶ σχημ. 42; Περὶ κέντρ. 73; Π.σ.α. p. 183.33; CCAG v/1. 189.6, vii. 225.30; Firmicus, 4×; Lib. Herm. 2×, incl. xxvi. 21 geometra in regiis aulis intrans; cf. 6.469 μέτρα μακρῆς χθονὸς ἐξεδάησαν; 4.129 ἔν τε γεωμετρίῃσι…ἀρίστους; 4.210 γαιομέτρας
arithmeticus: xxv. 1.1, xxxiii. 10
Expressions involving pondus: 4.14.6, 4.21.10 ponderibus publicis (praeponi); 8.25.7 actus de mensuris et ponderibus; xxvii. 23 super…ponderibus statuuntur, xxxii. 25 a ponderibus vitam habentes

V.2. 'Chemistry'

Pigmentarius: Firmicus, 4×; xxv. 8.10, 30; also 3.13.5 actus…de pigmentis; artes pigmentorum: 4.10.2; 4.11.2; inventor/repertor pigmentorum: 3.6.4; 4.14.17
See also II.7.viii.e. Dyers; II.8.ix. Parfumiers; V.3.iii. Druggists

V.3. Medicine

V.3.1. Doctors

ἰατρός: Ptol. 4.4.7 ~ Θ p. 212.4; Ptol. 4.4.8 ~ Θ p. 212.29; Θ pp. 148.15, 17, 166.4; 210.27, 212.13, 213.8, 20, 218.8; Teucer, II 3.2, 10, II 5.4a, II 8.3 φιλιάτρους καὶ ἰατρικούς…ἢ καὶ καλλίστους ἰατρούς, II 12.6; Περὶ σχημ. 111; Περὶ κράσ. 207; Valens, I 1.39, II 17.57; cf. 4.158 ἰητῆρα…βροτῶν, 1.181 ἰητῆρας
archiatrus: 3.7.6; 4.21.9
medicus: Firmicus, 18×; Lib. Herm. 7×
medicosophista: xxvi. 21

V.3.II. Surgeons
χειρουργός/chirurgus: Ptol. 4.4.7 ~ Θ p. 212.4–5; Θ p. 211.3; CCAG v/1. 189.4; 4.10.3

V.3.III. Druggists
φαρμακοποιός, etc.: Ptol. 4.4.8 ~ Θ p. 212.28–9; Θ p. 211.22; cf. 1.184 ἤπια φάρμακ' ἔχοντας, ἀνώδυνα φαρμάσσοντας; 3.12.10 *pigmentorum medicinalium inventores*; 4.14.17 *medicamentorum...repertores*; 8.17.7 *vel qui venenis et herbarum pigmentis salutaria soleant remedia comparare*; xxv. 5.13 *pharmachiarii*, xxv. 7.18 *pharmachiatores*

V.3.IV. Herbalists
ῥιζοτόμος: 5.183
βοτανικός: Ptol. 4.4.9 ~ Θ p. 210.3; Θ p. 212.21; Epit. IIIb; Teucer, II 3.2
Herbarius: Firmicus, 3×, incl. 3.3.11 *herbarios faciet et plus volentes scire quam patitur humanae naturae substantia*; 8.13.3 *herbarios, qui herbas sollerti arte collectas ad medelas laborantium pecorum servent*; also 8.17.3 *medici sed qui herbis medelas hominibus pecoribusque componant* ~ Manil. 5.642–4

V.3.V. Purveyors of ointments
Expressions involving *unguenta*: xxvii. 27 *unguentorum...mixtores*

V.3.VI. Singers of incantations
ἐπαοιδός: 5.183; Θ p. 213.21
Incantatores: 8.26.1 *incantator qui latentes dolores mitiget potestate verborum*; also 3.5.32 *valitudines istas quas diximus aut remedio aliquo aut cantationibus compescit aut mitigat*; also xxv. 7.18, xxvi. 63 *praecantatores*

V.3.VII. Snake-charmers
θηριοδείκτας: Θ p. 212.21; Epit. IIIb; Teucer, II 3.8 (L), 5.4a, 12.6
Periphrasis: 5.184–8
marsus: Firmicus, 6× incl. 8.15.1 ~ Manil. 5.391–3

V.4. Divination
V.4.I. General terms
μάντις: 2.206; 6.473; 4.211; 1.237; Ptol. 4.4.3 ~ Θ p. 210.27; 4.4.10 ~ Θ p. 210.7; Θ pp. 214.22, 215.2; Epit. IIIa; Teucer, II 3.2, 10; Π.τ.δ. 6, 47; Περὶ κέντρ. 37; Περὶ κράσ. 207; Valens, I 1.39; Paul, p. 64.6; Heliodorus, CCAG vii. 117.19; cf. 3.293 φιλομάντιας ἄνδρας; 6.438 μαντοσύνας ζαθέης φαίνοντας ἀπ' ὀμφῆς; also Ptol. 4.4.3 ~ Θ p. 210.30–1 ἐν ἱεροῖς ἀναστροφὰς ποιουμένους προφάσει μαντειῶν, ἐνθουσιασμῶν ἢ μαθημάτων
προφήτης/propheta: 5.119; Dorotheus, p. 367.1; Valens, II 8.1 προφήτης μεγάλου θεοῦ, II 14.4; Θ pp. 145.5, 176.22; CCAG i. 115.21 (and parallels); Firmicus, 9×, incl. 8.13.1 ~ Manil. 5.347; *Lib. Herm.* 2×; cf. 4.217 προφητάζοντά τε θνητοῖς, 4.227 προφήτορας, 4.428 τεμενῶν τε προφήτορας
χρησμῳδός: Π.τ.δ. 47
χρησμολόγος: Περὶ κέντρ. 37
θεολόγος: Περὶ κέντρ. 77
Interpreter of oracles: Θ p. 211.24 ὑποκριτὴν λογίων

Periphrasis: 3.92–3 προδαῆναι ἐνὶ πραπίδεσσι βροτοῖσιν | πείρατα μελλόντων; 6.378 θεσπιστὰς θεόληπτα μεμηνότας; 6.493 φοιβάζοντας; Θ p. 210.9–10 ἀποφθεγγομένους, προγνωστικούς; xxxii. 16 *responsa dantes de futuris vates*: Firmicus, 4×; *Lib. Herm.* 4× *vaticinatores*; *vaticinari in templis*: 3.6.17; 4.14.3; 4.15.9; 8.20.1; xxxii. 26–7 *praevaticinantes futura/-um futura praedicere/praenoscere* etc.: 3.3.17; 3.6.1, 10; 3.8.3; 3.10.3; 3.11.4; 3.12.16 with remark on inspiration (*instinctu*, etc.): 4.3.1; 5.2.15; 5.3.34; 6.31.54; 8.26.14 in temples: 3.3.6; 3.11.4; 3.12.16; 7.20.15
omina, ominare: 3.12.16 *qui omina explicare consueverunt*; 5.2.16 *et qui omnia quae futura sunt ominare consueverint*

V.4.ii. Astrologers
ἀστρονόμος/*astronomus*: 2.206, 6.473; Θ pp. 164.3, 210.9; Teucer, II 8.2; Περὶ σχημ. 13; *Lib. Herm.* 6×
ἀστρολόγος/*astrologus*: 4.128, 142 [= 1.293], 211; 5.265; Ptol. 4.4.3 ~ Θ p. 210.27; Ptol. 4.4.10; Θ pp. 148.15, 150.19, 166.5; 211.7, 212.20, 215.1–2; Epit. IIIa, IV; Π.τ.δ. 21; Valens, II 17.57; Paul, p. 64.6/'Heliodorus', p. 70.24; *CCAG* viii/1. 259.16; Firmicus, 11×; *Lib. Herm.* 6×
μαθηματικός: 4.210; Ptol. 3.14.26, 36; Θ pp. 214.22, 215.3 ἀπαραβάτους μαθηματικούς, Epit. IIIa, IV; Π.σ.α. p. 183.33; Firmicus, 6×; xxv. 10.11

V.4.iii. Dream interpreters
ὀνειροκρίτης, etc.: Ptol. 4.4.3 ~ Θ p. 210.30; Ptol. 4.4.10 ~ Θ p. 210.10; Teucer, II 3.10; Π.τ.δ. 47; Περὶ κράσ. 207; Valens, I 1.39; Paul, p. 64.6/'Heliodorus', p. 70.25; cf. 2.206 ὀνειροπόλους; 3.94 θεσπίζειν φήμησιν ὀνείρασί θ'; 1.238 ὀνείρατα μυθίζοντες
somniorum interpres, etc.: 3.2.18; 3.6.17; 3.8.3; xxvi. 63, xxxiv. 29 *somniorum iudicatores*; also *per somnium/-a*: 5.1.16; 5.2.16
hypnocrites: xxv. 3.25

V.4.iv. Bird diviners
Periphrasis: 2.208 πτηνῶν τε ποτῆς ἄπο θεσπίζοντας
οἰωνιστής: Ptol. 4.4.8 ~ Θ p. 212.33; Θ p. 148.14; Π.τ.δ. 6, 21; cf. 6.473 οἰωνοπόλοι; 4.212 οἰωνοσκοπικούς
ὀρνεοσκόπος: Περὶ κράσ. 207; Valens, I 1.39
augur: Firmicus, 5×; *Lib. Herm.* 5×
avium indicator: xxvi. 63

V.4.v. Diviners from entrails
haruspex: Firmicus, 11×
Periphrasis: 6.206–7 προπάροιθεν | ἑζομένους θυσιῶν; 474 ἐκ σπλάγχνων…θεσπίζοντες

V.4.vi. Other types of diviner
λεκανόμαντις: Ptol. 4.4.10 ~ Θ p. 210.7; cf. 4.213 οἷς λεκανοσκοπίη πιστεύεται
νεκυόμαντις: Θ pp. 193.5, 210.8; cf. 4.213 ἢ νεκυϊσμός; xxvi. 77 *necromantes*
ἐξορκιστής/*exorcista*: Ptol. 4.4.10 ~ Θ p. 210.11; 3.4.27, 3.8.9
ὑδρόμαντις: 4.212
palmists: xxvi. 63 *palmarum exscrutatores*, xxxii. 60 *palmarum…periti*

V.5. Religious Roles

V.5.I. Builders of temples
ἱεροτεύκτης: Περὶ κράσ. 207; Valens, I 1.39
templorum fabricator, etc.: 3.5.15, 33; 4.14.19; 6.3.3
Periphrasis: 4.130 νηῶν τε θεμέθλοις; xxxii. 23 templa aedificant
Builders of panelled ceilings in temples: Manil. 5.288–9.

V.5.II. High-priests
ἀρχιερεύς: 4.39 χρυσοστέπτορας ἄνδρας ἢ ἀρχιερῆας; 1.101 πορφυρέοισιν ἐν εἵμασιν ἀρχιερῆας; Θ pp. 136.25 ἀρχιερεῖς χρυσοκόσμητοι, 138.12, 176.27; Valens, 4×; Paul, p. 66.19/'Heliodorus', p. 72.14; Hephaestion, i. 23.5; Camaterus; CCAG i. 115.27
sacerdotum princeps/sacerdotibus praepositus: Firmicus, 6×, incl. 3.6.1 faciet sacerdotum principes et qui in ipsis sacerdotiis purpureis aut auratis vestibus induantur; 4.19.18 claros et diadematibus aut aureis coronarum infulis coronatos

V.5.III. Priests
ἱερεύς: 2.225 μακάρων ἱερεῖς σηκῶν τε προέδρους; 6.437 σηκῶν θ' ἁγίων ἱερῆας; 4.427 νηοπόλους ἱερῆας; 5.119 βωμολόχους θ' ἱερεῖς; Θ pp. 145.3, 148.17, 164.23, 165.18, 166.4, 176.21–2 ἱερεῖς μεγαλοτίμους; 215.2; Teucer, II 3.2, 10, 8.8, 12.6; Π.τ.δ. 20; Valens, 3×, incl. II 14.2 ἱερεὺς θεᾶς μεγίστης ἢ ἱέρεια, II 22.47 ἱερεὺς θεᾶς; Hephaestion, ii. 79.22; 'Heliodorus', p. 70.21; CCAG i. 115.21 and parallels, v/1. 220.16, v/3. 89.7, vii. 220.29
sacerdos: Firmicus, 21×, incl. 3.2.18 sacerdotes templorum in magica semper opinione famosos; 3.13.5 antistites facit maximae cuiusdam deae vel potentissimae religionis sacerdotes; 4.21.5 Asiarchas, provinciarum sacerdotes; 8.13.1 ~ Manil. 5.343–6; 8.24.1 speciosi sacerdotes, 7 primi sacerdotes; 8.26.3 entheus sacerdos, dans responsa quaerentibus, 15 sacerdotes ex sacrificiis habentes vitae subsidia; Lib. Herm. 8×; also 3.3.17 Quidam autem et sacerdotia consequuntur
pontifex: xxvii. 22, 29

V.5.IV. Sacristans/managerial offices in temples
ζάκορος: 6.437, 4.427
νεωκόρος/neocoros: Π.τ.δ. 10; Περὶ κράσ. 207; Paul, p. 66.19/'Heliodorus', p. 72.14; cf. 4.216 ἱερῶν τε νεωκόρα; 4.430 σηκῶν τε νεωκορίῃσι μέλοντας; Firmicus, 5×
sacrista: xxvii. 29, xxxvi. 43
Periphrasis with templorum: 3.10.3 custodes templorum; 4.15.9 templorum custodias sempiternas; 6.31.54 homines templorum obsequiis deputatos; 8.21.11 aeditui custodesque templorum; 8.24.5 magnorum templorum ... rectores; xxvii. 22 templorum curam habentes; xxxii. 50 templorum praestites

V.5.V. Unspecified officia
In temples: 3.5.27; 3.12.16; 4.13.9; 4.14.19; 7.25.10
sacrorum officia: 5.1.29; 8.21.11
Other: 3.2.18 Quosdam autem faciet in templorum cultu semper perseverare; 5.2.11 et qui in templis honorum consequantur insignia; 5.3.55 in templis loca; 6.31.54 homines templorum obsequiis deputatos

V.5.VI. Manufacture and care of statues
λιθογλύφος:[76] cf. 4.130 ἔν...λιθογλυφίαισι θεῶν
θεοπλάστης:[77] 4.569, cf. 4.343 μακάρων ἀποπλάστορας; xxvi. 62, xxvii. 26, xxviii. 10 statuarum plasmatores
fabricator: 3.5.33 fabricatores deorum; xxvi. 44 statuarum fabricatores
sculptor: 3.9.5 sacrorum simulacrorum sculptores; 8.25.5 sculptor et qui deorum simulacra miro artificii splendore perficiat; xxxiv. 31 sacrorum scultores; xxxiv. 30 sacrorum sculptores
consecrator: 4.14.19 simulacrorum consecratores; 3.5.15 qui simulacra deorum per se facta religiosis consecrationibus dedicent
ornator: 3.5.33 vel ornatores deorum
vestitor: 3.9.9 vestitores divinorum simulacrorum; 3.12.5 vestitores deorum
cultor: 3.5.33 cultores divinorum...simulacrorum
baiulus: 3.9.9 baiulos divinarum caerimoniarum; 3.10.3 deorum baiulos; 3.12.1 sacrorum simulacrorum baiuli
See also II.8.iv. Sculptors

V.5.VII. Humble offices/temple slaves
servus templorum: 3.9.2; 4.15.8; 8.26.4; 8.29.10
hierodulus: 8.21.11; 8.29.10
servilia officia, etc.: 3.5.15; 3.13.8; 4.24.9; also 5.3.53 ut in ipsis templis laboriosis actibus implicentur.

V.5.VIII. Sacrificers
θύτης: 4.211 μαγικούς τε θύτας; Ptol. 4.4.3 ~ Θ p. 210.27; 4.4.10 ~ Θ p. 210.7; Θ pp. 148.14, 166.5; 211.3, 7; Teucer, II 8.8; Περὶ σχημ. 2; Π.τ.δ. 6, 20 θύτας θεοῦ; Περὶ κράσ. 207; Valens, I 1.39, al.; CCAG v/1. 189.3
θυσιουργός: Θ p. 212.1
ἱερουργός: Θ p. 211.12; Περὶ κράσ. 207
σφάκτης: Teucer, II 10.1
ῥεκτήρ: 4.229
victimarius: 3.5.27
sacrificator: xxv. 8.28
Other: 8.21.3 reges sacrorum

V.5.IX. Keepers of sacred animals
ἱερῶν ζῴων θεραπευτάς: Ptol. 4.4.8 ~ Θ p. 212.29–30
Periphrasis: 3.5.27 qui pecora sacra aut sacris aut religionibus destinata pascunt

V.5.X. Performers of initiations
Periphrasis: 2.205 παννυχίδων τελετῶν θ' ἡγήτορας, 4.129, 228 ἐν τελεταῖσιν ἀρίστους; CCAG v/1. 199.15–16 τελετῶν τινων προφήτας; 3.10.3 qui religionibus homines initient et consecrent

---

[76] Ruffing 2008, 636   [77] Ruffing 2008, 719 (πλάστης).

V.5.xi. Magi
μάγος/magus: 6.475; Ptol. 2.3.34, 3.14.32, 4.4.10 ~ Θ p. 210.9; Θ pp. 145.5, 148.17, 166.4; Valens, II 17.57; CCAG v/1. 189.6; Firmicus, 7×; xxviii. 5, xxxi. 10; also 3.2.18 *in magica semper opinione famosos*; 4.19.25 *secretarum ac magicarum artium scientes*

V.5.xii. *Galli*; beggars
Periphrasis: 5.179–80
ἀγείρειν, etc.: 6.299, 538 ἀγείροντες; 4.221 ἀγυρτῆρας
γάλλος: 4.221 γαλλομανεῖς; (*abscisi*) *galli*: Firmicus, 10×
archigalli: 3.5.24; 3.6.22; 4.13.5
cinaedi: 7.25.4 *cinaedos...templorum cantibus servientes* (for temple singers, see VI.2.iv); 7.25.10 *cinaedos felices efficiet, quibus templorum officia credantur*

V.5.xiii. Temple scribes
γραμματεύς: 4.428
Also xxxiv. 30 *sacrorum scribae*, 43 *sacer scriba*?

V.6. Funeral Industry

V.6.i. General terms
νεκροτάφος: 4.192; Θ p. 215.10, Epit. IIIb
Other νεκ- compounds: 6.530 νεκυοστόλοι; 4.192 νεκρονώμας; Θ p. 215.10–11, Epit. IIIb νεκροθάπτας ἢ νεκρεπάρτας
ἐνταφιαστής: Ptol. 4.4.8 ~ Θ p. 212.30
funerarius: Firmicus, 3×
pollinctor: Firmicus, 5×
Also xxvii. 11, xxviii. 13 *mortuorum sepelitores*

V.6.ii. Specialists in mummification
ταριχευτής:[78] Teucer, II 1.7, 12.3; cf. 4.267 νεκρῶν τε ταριχευτῆρας
Evisceration: Ptol. 4.4.5 παρασχίστας ~ 4.267 γαστροτόμους ~ 6.461 γαστέρας ἀμπτύξαντες

V.6.iii. Coffin-makers
σοροποιός(?): cf. 4.191 σορόεργα τέχνης κανονίσματ' ἔχοντας,
Periphrasis: 6.496 θήκας τεκταίνοντας ἀποφθιμένοισι βροτοῖσιν; xxxiv. 4 *mortuorum lignea diverticula facientes*

V.6.iv. Cremators
Periphrasis: 6.497 ἠὲ πυραῖς μαλερῇσι νεκροὺς αἴθοντας ἔτευξαν

V.6.v. Professional mourners
θρηνῳδός: Ptol. 4.4.8 ~ Θ p. 212.30; cf. 6.498 ἢ θρηνεῦντας ἀεὶ κεραοῖς ἐπιτύμβιον αὐλοῖς; 4.190 θρηνήτορας ἄνδρας; Periphrasis: 4.192 κλαυστῆρας ἀποφθιμένων
τυμβαύλης: Ptol. 4.4.8; see also VI.2.iii.c. Wind instruments

[78] Ruffing 2008, 770.

V.6.vi. Custodians of graves (see pp. 1064–5)

πυλωρός: 6.409 τύμβων ... πυλαώρους

Periphrasis: 6.531 φρουροὶ νεκύων; 3.5.23 *quibus sepulchrorum cura aut custodia mandetur*; 3.9.3 *custodes mortuorum cadaverum aut sepulchrorum ... ianitores*; 8.26.15 *custodes monumentorum*; 8.27.2 *monumentorum custodes*; xxvii. 11 *sepulcrorum custodes*

τυμβωρύχος (grave-robber): Ptol. 3.14.15; Θ pp. 192.22, 215.11

VI. Leisure

VI.1. Stage Artists (Generic Terms)

θυμελικός: Ptol. 4.4.6 ~ Θ p. 213.12; 'Heliodorus', p. 72.18–19; *CCAG* v/3. 88.28; also xxv. 7.19 *eos qui in ... thymele student*

σκηνικός/*scaenicus*: *CCAG* viii/1. 176.6; 3.12.17; 8.20.1; xxv. 1.6, 3.13; also 8.12.3 *scaenicas artes*

Teachers thereof: 2.336 παιδευτὰς δ' ἄλλων τοίων ἔργων

VI.2. Music

VI.2.i. General terms

μουσικός/*musicus*: Θ pp. 169.1; 211.23, 213.10, 19, 217.13; Περὶ κέντρ. 52, 76; Περὶ κράσ. 207; Valens, 5×; Hephaestion, i. 20.19–20, 21.7–8; Camaterus; *CCAG* v/1. 188.19, viii/1. 176.5, xi/1. 173.17, 203.19, xi/2. 125.2; Firmicus, *passim*; *Lib. Herm.* 5× (also *amatores musicae*, sim.); cf. 1.60 μούσης ἅπτοντ', 63 μούσης ἐπιίστορας

Also Θ p. 214.17 μουσοχόρους [μουσοχαρεῖς?]

Periphrasis: many involving μουσικά, μουσικαὶ τέχναι, etc.; Firmicus, 6.8.1 *aliis dulcem musicae sonum tradunt*; 6.30.9 *musici carminis modos dulciter flectere*; 3.12.1 *armoniae cuiusdam peritos*; al.

VI.2.ii. Composers

μελογράφος: Valens, II 17.60; cf. 2.333 μελῶν μολπῆς εὐρύθμου τεύκτορας ἄνδρας?

Periphrasis: 3.6.21 *cordarum disciplinae auctores*(?); 3.12.1 *qui musicos modos faciant*; 3.12.17 *modorum musicorum inventores*; 5.5.6 *musicae modos dulci modulatione conponunt*

VI.2.iii. Instrumentalists

VI.2.iii.a. General terms

Periphrasis: 5.2.12 *musicos organis dulcibus semper applicatos*; 7.26.7 *musicos ... organa dulci modulatione tractantes*

VI.2.iii.b. Stringed instruments

κιθαριστής: Θ p. 217.13; Teucer, II 3.10, 5.9–11; 'Heliodorus', p. 72.18; *CCAG* v/3. 88.27

κιθαρῳδός/*citharoedus*: Θ pp. 213.12–13, 25, 214.16; Firmicus, 5×; xxv. 10.7 *citharoedos magnatum*, xxxiv. 29

Expressions involving κιθάρα: 2.332 κιθάρης ὑποφήτορας; 6.370 λιγυρῆς κιθάρης ἐπιίστορας; 6.506–7 κιθάρης ... ἴδριας; 4.185 κιθάρης τε μελουργούς; 5.163 ᾧ δ' ᾄσει κίθαρις νευρένδετος ἐν παλάμῃσιν; 6.30.9 *aut citharam lyramque percutere*; 6.31.84 *qui lyrae vel citharae nervos dulci semper modulatione percutiant*; cf. 1.60 ... ἅπτοντ' ἢ λύρης εὐρύθμοιο

Roster of Trades   1051

ναβλᾶς (vel sim.): cf. 4.185 ναβλιστοκτυπέας τε χοροῖς
Periphrasis: Ptol. 4.4.6 χορδοστρόφους

VI.2.III.C. Wind instruments
αὐλητής: Θ p. 213.25; CCAG v/1. 188.8; cf. 2.334 πολυτρήτοις λιγέως μέλποντας ἐν
αὐλοῖς; 6.370 ...ἠδὲ καὶ αὐλῶν; 6.506-7 αὐλῶν...ἴδριας
καλάμαυλος: Θ p. 217.13
tibicen: 4.14.20 tibicines templorum; xxv. 5.12 Phrygii tibicines, xxv. 10.7
Periphrasis involving κάλαμος: 5.160 ἢ τρητοῖς καλάμοις ὑπὸ πνεύμασιν ᾆσμα μελῳδεῖ
Periphrasis involving σῦριγξ/fistula: 5.161 ἢ νομίᾳ σύριγγι φίλην κεφαλὴν ἐπισείει; 8.6.5
sed qui fistula rustici carminis dulces modos dicant
See also V.6.v. Professional mourners

VI.2.III.D. Trumpeters
σαλπιγκτής: CCAG v/1. 188.8; cf. 5.162 ἄλλῳ δ' ἐκ στομάτων κελαδεῖ μυκήματα σάλπιγξ
salpista: 8.21.4
tubator: xxv. 10.7

VI.2.III.E. Percussionists
Cymbal player: 5.164 ἄλλῳ δ' ἁρμονίην χαλκόκτυπον ἐξετέλεσσαν [ex emend.]

VI.2.III.F. Organists
organarius: Firmicus, 4×

VI.2.IV. Singers
Periphrasis: 2.331-2 ἀοιδοὺς | εὐκλέας; 3.351 μολπῇσί τ' ἀγαλλομένους καὶ ἀοιδῇ; 6.369
μολπῇσιν γλυκερῇσι μεμηλότας ἄνδρας; 4.183 λυρικῶν τε μελῶν μελπήτορας; 5.143
μουσῳδόν; 7.26.7 musicae sonum vocis; dulci voce, dulciter etc.: 4.14.17, 6.8.2, 8.24.8,
8.28.6, 8.30.7; Manil. 5.329-36
choricus: Firmicus, 3.12.1
hymnologus: Firmicus, 4×; also 8.25.1 hymnodici nobiles
Temple-singers: 4.14.20 in templis sacra carmina precantes; 7.25.4 cinaedos...templorum cantibus servientes; 8.29.10 in sacrorum caerimoniis hymnos dicentes
See also VI.5, s.v. φωνικός, φωνασκός

VI.3. Poetry
ποιητής/poeta: Teucer, II 3.10, 10.11; Περὶ σχημ. 124; Valens, II 17.60; Firmicus, 5×;
6.30.23 (chart of Homer); 6.30.25 (chart of Archilochus and Pindar); Lib. Herm. 2×; also
6.26.4 carmina eorum divina dicentur inspiratione conscripta

VI.4. Dance
ὀρχηστάς: Ptol. 4.4.6; Θ p. 214.16; cf. 2.335 ἄλλους ὀρχηθμοῦ βητάρμονας; 6.507 ὀρχηθμοῦ
βητάρμονας ἴδριας; 4.186 ὀρχηθμῶν ἴδριάς τε; also Teucer, II 5.9-11 ὀρχουμένους
ὁπλορχηστής: Ptol. 4.4.8 ~ Θ p. 212.28
saltator: 6.31.85, 8.29.13 (also 4.14.17 aut qui ad omne genus saltationis adfectant; 6.30.9
aut certe molli corpore flexu cum grata venustate saltare); Lib. Herm. 3×
pantomimus: Firmicus, 7×

References to effeminacy: 5.139–41; Teucer, II 5.9–11 κιναίδους; 6.31.39 *cum effeminati corporis mollitie cinaedos efficient, qui veterum fabularum exitus in scaenis semper saltantes imitentur*

VI.5. Acting and Dramaturgy

τραγῳδός/*tragoedus*: Θ p. 213.13; CCAG viii/1. 176.6; cf. 6.509 τραγικῆς τε βαρυβρόμου ἵστορας οἴμης; 8.20.7; also 8.15.5 *arte tragica carmina aut legunt semper aut faciunt* ~ Manil. 5.459–69; xxxiv. 29

κωμῳδός/*comoedus*: 4.183; 8.20.7; Valens, II 17.60 ὑποκριτὰς…κωμῳδίας

ὑποκριτής: Ptol. 4.4.6 ~ Θ p. 213.12; Θ p. 211.24; Valens, II 17.60; Paul, p. 72.14; CCAG vii. 216.1

Periphrasis: Manil. 5.477–85

δραματουργός: Teucer, II 12.6

φωνικός (voice-coach): Θ p. 213.19; φωνασκός: Valens, I 2.19, II 17.60–1

Herald: 8.20.7 *ceruces*

VI.6. Popular Entertainment

VI.6.I. Mimes

μῖμος: 5.104; Θ p. 217.7; Epit. IIIa,b; Valens, II 17.60 ὑποκριτὰς μίμων; CCAG v/3. 88.28; xxv. 10.4; cf. 4.280 μιμοβίους; also Teucer, II 3.5 μιμηλούς (L μιμικούς)…σχεδιαστάς

ἀρεταλόγος: cf. 4.447 ἔν τ' ἀρεταλογίῃ μυθεύματα ποικίλ' ἔχοντας

mimologus: 8.8.1 ~ xxv. 3.13 *mimos ioculatores*

παραπαλάριος: Teucer, II 3.5 (in the company of mimes)

Periphrasis: 4.445–6; 6.508; 4.184 μαχλικῶν τε λόγων θρασυγλωσσέας ᾠδούς

VI.6.II. Gladiators

μονομάχος: Teucer, II 5.4a; Valens, II 17.95

θηριομάχος: Θ pp. 201.21, 212.22–3; Epit. IV; xxv. 4.39 *pugnatores cum feris*

gladiator: Firmicus, 7×

(h)oplomachus: 7.26.3; 8.21.5; 8.27.3

Periphrasis: 8.12.2 *tales qui se ob alienae gratiae voluntatem nundinati sanguinis iactura ad mortis spectaculum vendant. Si vero Saturnus hoc fecerit, in ludum sententia iudicantis addicuntur.*

VI.6.III. Conjurers

ψηφοπαίκτης/*psefopaectes*: 3.7.15; Θ p. 217.4 ψηφάδας; cf. 4.448 ψηφάων παίκτας

μαγγανάριος: Θ pp. 213.1, 217.9

praestigiator: 8.8.1; 8.20.2

Ball-players: 8.8.1 *pilis ludentes* ~ Manil. 5.165–71

VI.6.IV. Tightrope-walkers and acrobats

αἰθροβάτης: 6.440; 4.278

σχοινοβάτας: 4.287; Θ p. 213.7

καλοβάτης: 5.146 καλοβάτην σχοίνων; cf. 4.287 καλοβάμονας; 8.17.4 *ex emend.*

νευροβάτης/*neurobates*: Θ pp. 213.1, 215.16, 217.9; 8.17.4

funambulus: 8.17.4 ~ Manil. 5.653–5

πεταυρίστης/*petaurista*: 8.15.2 *petaminarios…petauristarios* ~ Manil. 5.438–45; cf. 6.444 ἐπ' ἠνεμόεντι πετεύρῳ; 4.278 πηκτοῖσι πεταυριστῆρας ἐν ἔργοις

Roster of Trades

VI.6.v. Trick riders
Periphrasis: 8.6.3 *aut qui saltu quadrigas transeat, aut qui <in> dorso stans equorum mirifica se moderatione sustentet* ~ Manil. 5.85-9

VI.6.vi. Strongmen
ἰσχυροπαίκτης: Valens, I 1.39; cf. 4.276 ἰσχυρῶν ἔργων...πονοπαίκτορας ἄνδρας

VI.7. Games and Sports

VI.7.i. Agonothetes
Periphrasis: 3.38 τερπωλῆς τεύχων λαῶν ἡγήτορας ἄνδρας; 4.40 πολέων τε διθυντῆρας ἀέθλων; 3.10.3 *aut sacris certaminibus facient praepositos*; 3.12.5 *sacri certaminis principes*; 4.14.19 *aut sacris certaminibus...praepositos*; xxvii. 29 *sacrorum certaminum praepositos*

VI.7.ii. Athletes
ἀθλητής: Ptol. 4.4.9; Θ pp. 213.19, 214.12; Epit. IV; Teucer, II 5.4a; Περὶ κράσ. 164; Valens, II 17.60; cf. 6.512 ἀεθλητῆρας; 4.173 ἀθλητῆρας; also, Θ p. 214.9, Valens, 13× ἀθλητικούς
athletae: Firmicus, 20×; *Lib. Herm.* 4×; also 4.4.1 *athleticis certaminibus deputatos*; 6.8.2 *athleticae disciplinam*; 6.24.6 *athleticae disciplinae*
ἱερονίκης: Valens, II 17.60; CCAG viii/1. 259.12, 260.24; 3.12.5 *sacris certaminibus esse victores*; 6.31.3 *athletam...sed qui sacris certaminibus victor famosa reportet insignia coronarum*
Periphrasis: 3.353-4; xxv. 9.14 *certatores coronatos*

VI.7.iii. Boxers
πύκτης/*pyctes*: 7.26.4; 8.8.1 ~ Manil. 5.163-4; cf. 3.357 πυγμαχίῃσί τ' ἀγασθενέες πληγῇσί τε χειρῶν; also xxv. 3.29 *pugilatores*

VI.7.iv. Wrestlers
παλαιστής: Ptol. 4.4.7; CCAG v/1. 188.9, 189.10-11, xi/1. 183.15; cf. 3.356 παλαισμοσύνῃσί τ' ἄριστοι; 6.374 παλαίστρης ἔργ' ἐφέποντας; also 4.7.1 *palaestricam semper exercebunt*; 8.21.7 *palaestricis semper obsequiis deputati*. Leaders of: 3.7.7, 9; 8.20.4 *magister palaestrae*
φιλοπάλαιστρος: Valens, I 20.7, IV 25.6; Θ p. 214.10; CCAG viii/1. 259.27; 3.11.15 *amatores...palaestrarum*, 19 *amatores palaestrae*; 4.14.13 *amatores armorum aut palaestrae*; xxv. 5.10, xxviii. 12 *amatores luctaminum*, xxv. 7.29 *amatores luctationis*; cf. 1.61 πάλην φιλέουσιν
luctator: 8.24.4 (crowned); xxv. 3.29 *luctatores coronatos*; also xxv. 7.19 *eos qui in...luctatione student*

VI.7.v. Runners
Cursor: Firmicus, 3×; also 8.8.1 *tanta erunt levitate corporis, ut cum currere coeperint agitati <cursus> velocitate aves superare videantur* ~ Manil. 5.160-1
stadiodromus: 8.8.1 ~ Manil. 5.162; cf. 3.356 σταδίοισι...ἄριστοι; 6.517 σταδίοισι μογεῦντες
Periphrasis: 4.173 ἀθλητῆρας ἀελλόποδας

VI.7.VI. Pancratiasts
παγκρατιαστής/pancratiastes: 8.27.6; cf. 1.61 φιλέουσιν...παγκράτιόν τε
παμμαχάριος: Teucer, II 3.1 [ex emend. for παμμακαρίους]; 8.8.1 <pam>macharios <suppl. Robert>

VI.7.VII. Armed fighters
6.375 σθεναρούς ῥοπάλοισι γεγηθότας

VI.7.VIII. Habitués of gymnasia
γυμναστής: Περὶ κράσ. 164, 207; cf. 5.245 ἐν γυμνασίοις <τ'> ἴσον Ἑρμῇ
gymnasiarchas: 4.21.5

VI.7.IX. Trainers
ἀλείπτης: cf. 4.178 ἀλειπτῆρας
unctor: 8.23.2
παιδοτρίβης: Apomasar, De Myst., CCAG xi/1. 183.25; cf. 4.179 παιδότριβας (< παιδότριψ)
athletarum exercitator: 8.21.7
athletarum magister: 4.13.1; 7.26.3; 8.23.2; cf. 8.20.4 praepositus athletarum
Periphrasis: 4.232 σωματοφόρβους

VI.7.X. Charioteers
ἡνίοχος: 5.170; Θ pp. 123.18, 217.17, 178.8–9 ἡνιόχων ἐργάτας ἢ καὶ αὐτοὺς περὶ... ἡνιοχικὴν ἔχοντας; Teucer, II 3.11; Περὶ κράσ. 164
ἱππηλάτης: CCAG v/1. 222.23
ἱππόδρομος: Θ p. 123.19
auriga: Firmicus, 6×, incl. 8.6.3 ~ Manil. 5.71–84; 8.13.3 ~ Manil. 5.351; 8.17.3 curiosi aurigae ~ Manil. 5.636–9; 8.27.8 auriga regius; Lib. Herm. 3×

VII. Service Sector

VII.1. Food

VII.1.I. Butchers
μακελλάριος/macellarius:[79] Teucer, II 8.8, 10.1; CCAG vii. 225.25; xxv. 8.28, xxv. 10.1
Periphrasis: Lib. Herm. xxv. 10.22 venditorem carnium

VII.1.II. Bakers
κλιβανεύς:[80] 1.80 κλιβανέας σκοτοεργούς; xxxii. 37 clibanarios
Pistores: Firmicus, 6×, incl. 8.11.3 pistores dulciarios ~ Manil. 5.279–84
See also I.4. Storage

VII.1.III. Cooks
μάγειρος:[81] Ptol. 4.4.5 ~ Θ p. 211.26, 30; Teucer, II 8.8; CCAG v/3. 88.26, vii. 225.25
Coquus: Firmicus, 3×; Lib. Herm. 5×

VII.1.IV. Wine-producers or retailers
Periphrasis: 3.13.5 actus...de vino

---

[79] Ruffing 2008, 656–7.
[80] Ruffing 2008, 595. There is also a σκουτάριος κλιβανάριος in SEG 20.332 (Syria, Brād, 5th c.).
[81] Ruffing 2008, 649–55.

Roster of Trades

VII.1.v. Saline products
Firmicus, 8.17.5 *Habebunt etiam officia quae ex salibus sunt* (~ Manil. 5.682–92, *salinas*) *vel ex salsamentis* (~ Manil. 5.672 *mixto...sale*); xxv. 1.26 *salitores*
Garum: 6.464; 4.269; Firmicus, 8.17.5 ....*et a liquamine* (~ Manil. 5.680–1 *liquidam tabem*...)
See also III.4.xi. Sellers of consumables

VII.2. Hospitality
πανδοχεύς: Θ p. 212.1
ἐκδοχεύς: Ptol. 4.4.4
κνιπός: Teucer, II 1.7
caupo: Firmicus, 3×; xxv. 8.30
popinarius: 4.13.2; 4.21.6
See also III.4.i. *tabernarius*

VII.3. Personal Care, Personal Service

VII.3.I. Bathmen
περιχύτης: Θ pp. 211.30–1, 215.6; Teucer, II 2.2, 4.11, 6.2a; Hephaestion, i. 169.18
βαλανεύς: Θ pp. 211.31, 215.4, 6; Epit. IIIa,b; cf. 4.253 λουτρῶν τε καθαρτῆρας βαλανείων
λουτροχόος: 6.422 λοετροχόοι
balneator: Firmicus, 5×; *Lib. Herm.* 3×
Periphrasis: 4.254–5(?)

VII.3.II. Barbers[82]
tonsor: Firmicus, 4×

VII.3.III. Bodyguards
σωματοφύλαξ: cf. 4.232 σωματοφρουρητῆρας
Periphrasis: 3.64 ἡγεμόνας θῆκε φρουρούς τε τυράννων; 4.47 φρουρητῆρα σίδηρον ἔχων, φυλακάς τε κρατούντων

VII.3.IV. Doorkeepers, ushers
ianitor: 8.14.1 *domus regiae ianitores, aut quibus in palatio admittendi vel salutandi officia credantur*

VII.3.V. Entertainers
nanus, ridiculus: 8.26.1 *bis*, incl. *nani, regum vel imperatorum deliciis deputati*; 8.27.6; 8.28.7
Ministers of pleasure: 3.6.3 *faciet etiam praepositos voluptatum, sed earum quae ad delectationem regiam praeparantur*[83]

---

[82] Ruffing 2008, 85, 87.
[83] S. Viola, *Tivoli, nel decennio dalla deviazione del fiume Aniene nel traforo del monte Catillo*, i (Rome, 1848), 28 n., took Firmicus' expression as an anticipation of the *tribuni voluptatum* of later antiquity, but they were in charge of *ludi et circenses* in certain big cities, in other words were concerned with the people's pleasure, not the monarch's (R. Lim, 'The *Tribunus Voluptatum* in the Later Roman Empire', *Memoirs of the American Academy in Rome*, 41 (1996), 163–73).

Appendix II

VII.3.vi. Sex workers

Matchmakers: 4.306 μάστροπά τ' ἔργα τελοῦντες; Ptol. 4.4.8 γάμων καὶ συνεπιπλοκῶν ἑρμηνέας ~ Θ p. 212.33 ἐκγαμιστὰς ἢ μαυλιστάς
leno: Firmicus, 5×; *Lib. Herm.* 4×; also 8.28.6 *sequestres libidinum*
Periphrasis for pimp: 4.314 πορνοσύνης ἀκρατοῦς σημάντορας
ἑταίρα: 5.142; Ptol.; Valens, II 17.61
πόρνη: 4.357, 5.318; Περὶ κέντρ. 68; Θ p. 160.12
πολύκοινος: Περὶ σχημ. 109, Περὶ κέντρ. 66; Valens, II 38.85; Camaterus
ἐπὶ τέγαις, *vel sim.*: 2.430; 6.533; Θ p. 169.7; Valens, II 38.85
Periphrasis for prostitute: 6.585
meretrix: Firmicus, 17×; *Lib. Herm.* 7×

VII.3.vii. Servants

ὑπουργός: 4.259, 468; Ptol. 4.4.5; *CCAG* xi/1. 196.29, 33 ὑπουργοὺς βασιλέων
ὑπηρέτης: Ptol. 4.4.5
mediast(r)inus: Firmicus, 3×
famulus: xxv. 10.35

VII.3.viii. Tasters
praegustator: xxv. 8.30

VII.4. Communication

ἑρμηνεύς: 4.142; Θ p. 157.21; Valens, I 2.19, II 17.55; Paul, pp. 67.13, 72.15/'Heliodorus', pp. 72.23, 75.19; *CCAG* v/1. 187.22
interpres: 3.7.3 *imperatorum aut potentissimorum iudicum frequenter interpretes*, 12; 4.14.1 *ex verborum interpretationibus*; 8.27.3 *interpretes regum*; also 8.26.2 *ex magisterio vel interpretationibus habebunt vitae substantiam*
nuntius regum: Firmicus, 3×; also 3.3.16 *aut quibus nuntiandi potestas conceditur*; 3.11.2 *praenuntius*
βερεδάριος/*veredarius*: Teucer, II 1.12; 3.11.18 *veredarios regum*, 8.17.3 ~ Manil. 5.640–1
πορθμεύς: Ptol. 4.4.5; Θ p. 166.23

VII.5. Public Servants

VII.5.i. Cleaners
Street cleaners (καθαρτής?): 4.251–2 καθαρτῆράς τε κελεύθων | ἀμφοδικῶν
Sewer cleaners: 4.13.6 <*aut*> *iubentur adsidue lacunas cluacasque purgare*; 8.19.12 *latrinas semper cloacasque mundabit*; 8.20.1 *latrinas cloacasque purgabunt*; 8.29.6 *vel qui cloacas mundent*; see also II.3.ii. Workers on irrigation channels
Also 8.20.1 *baiulabunt stercora*

VII.5.ii. Prison guards
δεσμοφύλαξ: Θ p. 140.5; Teucer, II 1.7 φύλακας δεσμωτηρίων, II 12.3 δεσμοφύλακας; Valens, II 15.6; Paul, p. 67.20/'Heliodorus', p. 73.4
custos carceris, etc.: 3.5.26; 4.11.5; 4.14.1; 4.14.10; 8.17.1 ~ Manil. 5.621; 8.17.1; 8.21.4; *Lib. Herm.* 3× (also xxv. 1.14 *incarceratis praepositos super*)

VII.5.iii. Torturers
carnifex: Firmicus, 10×, incl. 8.17.1 ~ Manil. 5.625
tortor: Firmicus, 5×, incl. 8.15.3 ~ Manil. 5.413–15

VII.6. Administrators

VII.6.i. Roman governmental or provincial officials

consul: Firmicus, 3×; *consulares*: 3.3.10; 3.5.2; *consulatus*: 5×; 4.19.20 *consularium fascium...insignia*
proconsul: Firmicus, 3×; 3.5.2 *proconsulares*; 3.5.35 *proconsulatus*; 4.21.5 *consularium vel proconsularium fascium nobilitat potestate; proconsulare imperium*: 3.3.20; 4.19.21
praeses:[84] 3.4.8 *praesides riparum*, 28; 4.14.8 *civitatum*, 13 *aut civitatum vel provinciarum praesides*
defensor civitatum:[85] 4.14.18
decem primi: Firmicus, 5×
procurator: 3.10.1; 4.9.3. Of kings: 3.3.8, 16; 3.7.6; xxvii. 22, xxxii. 19. Of big men: 3.9.2, 10. Of *civitates*: 3.5.14; xxvii. 22. Of women: 3.6.19, 3.7.15, 4.13.1; xxv. 6.26, 11.18. Of minors: 4.10.10.
στρατηγός: Valens, II 14.5 στρατηγὸς ἔσται χωρῶν καὶ πόλεων
administrator: Firmicus, 18×
exactor: 3.10.7 *regiarum annonarum; fiscalium praestationum*: 3.11.17, 4.10.8, 6.3.3; *Lib. Herm.* 4×, incl. xxxii. 56 *rei publicae exactores*
minister: 8.16.2 *ministros imperatorum*; 8.28.7 *ministri regum*; xxv. 10.35, xxxiv. 43 *regum aut tyrannorum minister*
ab epistulis: cf. 3.12.2 *litteris regis praepositos*, 4.14.5 *quibus imperatorum litterae ac secreta credantur*
Eunuchs: 8.20.9 *felices nascentur eunuchi, et quibus regni tuitio credatur*

VII.6.ii. Agents

πραγματευτής: Θ pp. 210.27, 211.18–19; Camaterus; *CCAG* v/1. 189.12
πραγματευτικός: Ptol. 4.4.3
οἰκονόμος: Ptol. 4.4.3 ~ Θ p. 210.30; Θ pp. 146.17, 208.24; Epit. IV; Περὶ σχημ. 94; Π.τ.δ. 11; Valens, 4×, incl. I 19.14 πραγμάτων οἰκονόμους, II 17.44 βασιλέων οἰκονόμους; *CCAG* x. 232.10
ἐπίτροπος: Θ pp. 134.5–6, 144.4, 146.17, 150.32; 208.24; Epit. IV; 'Par. Anub.', *passim*; Valens, 4×; Camaterus; *CCAG* v/1. 189.4, viii/1. 258.6, 10
actor: 3.9.3 *actores modicarum villarum*, 10; 4.14.6; 5.2.17
dispensator: *Lib. Herm.* 6×
vilicus: xxv. 6.3, xxxii. 25

VIII. Military

VIII.1. Leaders

στρατηγός: Valens, II 12.4; Θ pp. 145.8, 152.13; Teucer, II 2.5; Camaterus; *CCAG* v/3. 88.25; cf. 3.296–7 ἡγεμόνας ῥέζει στρατιῆς νηῶν τε καὶ ἵππων | καὶ πεζῶν; 4.471 πάσης στρατιῆς ἐπιβήτορας; 1.103 εὐτόλμους στρατιῆς ἡγήτορας ἄνδρας; 5.40 στρατιῆς Ἄρης ἡγήτορας; see also VII.6.i. Roman governmental or provincial officials
στρατηλάτης: Θ pp. 151.7, 177.18; Teucer, II 2.5; 'Heliodorus', p. 84.25; *CCAG* v/1. 189.3, 200.6–7, 222.1

---

[84] Frakes, 80–1.   [85] Frakes, 79–83.

στρατοπεδάρχης: Θ pp. 136.4, 146.15, 168.14; Περὶ σχημ. 106; Valens, II 17.70; Hephaestion, i. 20.21; *CCAG* iv. 105.32, 152.4, ix/2. 183.16
princeps: 8.31.3; xxxii. 31, 49 *principes exercitus*
dux: Firmicus, *passim*; xxvi. 5. Combined with *imperator*: 3.2.20; 4.11.8 *imperiosos*; with rex: 3.2.10; 3.5.4, 5 *bis*, 6 *bis*, 36; 3.8.1; 8.19.1; 8.20.9; 8.31.2. Provincial governor: 3.4.2, 29; 4.11.8; 4.19.15. Famosus: 3.7.6; 8.19.5. (Prae)potens: 3.4.13, 29; 3.5.21; 3.8.1; 3.11.5; 4.11.8; 4.19.15; 5.4.21; 8.31.2. Power of life and death: 3.3.8; 3.4.2, 13, 28, 29. Terribiles: 4.11.8; 4.14.8; 4.19.15; 8.20.9. Leaders of armies: 3.4.2, 13; 4.11.8; 8.19.1; 8.20.9, 10; 8.21.2; 8.24.2; 8.28.1; 8.31.7; 8.31.8;[86] *Lib. Herm.* 8× *duces exercitus*. In charge of legions: 3.5.8; 4.14.13. Entrusted with *navale imperium*: Firmicus, 7×; cf. xxvi. 31 *ducet vero exercitus non solum peditum et militum ascendentium super equos, sed stoli et navalis*. References to *ducatus*: 3.5.2, 35; 3.14.1; 4.21.2; 5.2.5
tribunus: Firmicus, 10×;[87] *Lib. Herm.* 4×
Praetorian prefects: 3.2.20 *praefectos praetorio*, 3.4.8 *praefectos praetorii*

VIII.2. Soldiers

στρατιώτης: Ptol. 4.4.5 ~ Θ p. 212.1; Θ p. 136.4; Epit. II; Teucer, II 2.5, 8.1; Περὶ σχημ. 16; Περὶ κράσ. 144 στρατιῶται ἔνοπλοι, 145 αὐθεντικοὶ στρατιῶται; 'Heliodorus', p. 84.25; Camaterus; *CCAG* iv. 159.4, v/1. 185.24, 189.2, v/3. 88.25, viii/1. 176.22
ὁπλίτης: Θ p. 212.14
ὁπλοφόρος: Θ p. 211.3
(ἀ)κοντιστής: Teucer, II 3.11; *CCAG* v/1. 188.19
τοξευτής: Teucer, II 9.1
miles: Firmicus, 10×; *Lib. Herm.* 7×; also *militares*: 3.4.1, 9; 8.16.1; *militaria officia*: 6.10.2; 8.19.3
sagittator: xxv. 9.1
equitiarius: 8.13.3; also 8.6.3 *equo vectus militares armaturas exerceat*; 8.20.10 *equitibus peditibusque praepositi*
καβαλλάριος: Teucer, II 1.12
mercenarius: xxvi. 21

---

[86] Frakes, 81, thinks Firmicus' usage shows the influence of Diocletian's reforms, whereby *duces* become a type of provincial military commander.

[87] Frakes, 81, is again prepared to see the influence on Firmicus' usage of Diocletian's reforms, whereby tribunes became a middle-ranking official under the authority of the *dux*.

Addenda and Corrigenda to the First Volume

p. 4 n. 7: on the world-as-stage topos, add Halliwell, 511.
pp. 7, 61: on fate being determined for an individual at birth, see Giannakis 1998, 2–3, 8, 18–19, 22, 24–5.
p. 20 n. 20: on prognosis in medicine, add Lane Fox, 218–21.
p. 21 and n. 26: physiognomy too proceeds cumulatively: ps.-Arist. *Physiogn.* 807ᵃ1–3 ὅλως δὲ τὸ ἑνὶ μὲν πιστεύειν τῶν σημείων εὔηθες· ὅταν δὲ πλείω συμφωνοῦντα καθ' ἑνὸς λάβῃ, μᾶλλον ἤδη κατὰ τὸ εἰκὸς ἄν τις ὑπολαμβάνοι ἀληθῆ εἶναι τὰ σημεῖα.
p. 28 n. 58: on medicine and the language of mysteries, add Lane Fox, 84–5.
p. 30 n. 66: on Ptolemy's πινακικαὶ ἐκθέσεις, see Greenbaum and Ross, 117: 'a *pinax* could be the collected explanations of the components of a material *pinax*, laid out in an organised ("tabulated" or "catalogued") fashion'.
p. 35: on astrological terms that use metaphors drawn from human interactions, see Orlando and Torre, 303–5 n. 30.
p. 44 n. 10: on planetary order, add Bouché-Leclercq, 104–10; O. Neugebauer, *The Exact Sciences in Antiquity*² (Providence, RI, 1959), 169; Heilen 2005, 147–8; Monteventi, 129–30 n. 237, with further literature.
p. 47 n. 18: on twins being born at almost the same time yet having different destinies, whence the enormous implications of minute calibrations, add Favorinus ap. Gellium, *NA* 14.1.26 = fr. 3 Barigazzi.
p. 152 and n. 26. On combinatory citations, and especially passages threaded together through a link word, see C. D. Stanley, 'Paul and Homer: Greco-Roman Citation Practices in the First Century CE', *Novum Testamentum*, 32 (1990), 48–78, at 73, noting this technique in ps.-Plut. *Mor.* 114 E, conflating *Il.* 23.109 with *Od.* 1.423 through τοῖσι accompanying a present middle participle describing an emotional reaction (μυρομένοισι, τερπομένοισι). Perhaps it was taught in the rhetorical schools?
pp. 178–9: on clarity in *Fachschriften*, add Fögen, 38–9.
p. 182–3 and n. 17: on recapitulations and prospectuses, add Monteventi, 234.
p. 184 and n. 24: on 'from these examples you can work out more', see also M. Fantuzzi and R. L. Hunter, *Tradition and Innovation in Hellenistic Poetry* (Cambridge, 2004), 235 (Aratus, 1036–7, implicitly); Monteventi, 216, 275–6.
p. 192: where τοι occurs it generally stands either at the start of the protasis (2.266, 3.266) or apodosis (6.275 [*ex emend.* K]; 4.66, 80, 584), or in a general announcement (4.109, 624, 1.284, 5.209). In 4.152 = 1.300, where neither is the case, μάλα τοι πεπονημένα replicates *Il.* 23.543 μάλα τοι κεχολώσομαι, *Op.* 799 μάλα τοι τετελεσμένον.
pp. 206–7 and n. 101: on astrological boards, add S. Heilen, 'Ancient Scholars on the Horoscope of Rome', *Culture and Cosmos*, 11 (2007), 43–68, at 47–8; id. 2015, 578–80; Greenbaum and Ross, 114–16.
pp. 209–10: on φράζεσθαι, see Monteventi, 269.
p. 210: close quotation mark after 'didactic'.

p. 232 n. 3: correct to 'rescued by Hübner 2011'. There are now more Dorothean hexameters, complete and incomplete, rescued from Hephaestion and from a treatise containing a partly Dorotheus-derived chapter on the stations of the Moon, by W. Hübner, *Disiecti Membra Poetae: Neue Spuren des astrologischen Lehrdichters Dorotheus von Sidon* (Stuttgart, 2021). This book came to my attention after I had completed the manuscript of vol. ii, and the rescued hexameters involve various degrees of intervention and reconstruction (see p. 62). My statistics are therefore drawn from the same sources as in the first volume. Additional material might shift the figures very slightly but would be unlikely to change them.

p. 235: for '73.35% of the second, and 67.82% of the third', read '73.35% of the third, and 67.82% of the sixth'.

p. 246: for × – ⏑ ⏑ – – read of course × – ⏑ ⏑

pp. 291–2 n. 4: on $βασιλεύς$ = emperor, add Mason, 120–1 (inscriptional instances beginning with Hadrian); Heilen 2015, 1194–5. There is a difference between M^a and Artemidorus, in that poetry licenses this usage earlier than prose literature does (though Heilen finds it already in the astrologer Antigonus of Nicaea, 2nd c. AD).

p. 302 and n. 22: on $μάχλος$, add Kapparis, 237–8.

p. 307: correct to get-ahead.

p. 323: on meanness. Apul. *Met.* 4.9 has a brilliant characterisation of meanness, a *nummularius* called Chryseros who sits alone at home, wearing rags, *sordidus*, hoarding his wealth for fear of *officia* and *munera*. I should have considered the possibility that 2.159 (p. 577) 'not extending his wealth to others' refers to fear of liturgies.

p. 326 and n. 25: on ordure and wealth (filthy lucre), see Pomeroy, 70–1.

p. 321 n. 1: on the windfall, see Favorinus, fr. 105 Barigazzi, on $εὕρεσις$ (probably the discovery of treasure) as the second of four methods of countering poverty—ahead of work itself (see Pleket 1988, 273).

p. 345 n. 104: on un- or underemployment in Artemidorus, see Pomeroy, 62–3, 65–6.

pp. 346–7: on clothes as symbols of status in Artemidorus, see Pomeroy, 64–5; Klees, 61.

p. 355: on *phrenitis*, see Lane Fox, 243–5.

p. 356 and n. 54: on epilepsy and the Moon, see Stol 1993, 121–7, 130. On epilepsy and demons, see Stol 1993, 51–3 (demonic possession not really a Babylonian idea); Forst, 183–5.

p. 357: correct to Owsei Temkin.

p. 357 n. 56: on the association of epilepsy and madness, see Stol 1993, 49–50.

p. 360 n. 86: on terrors and epilepsy, add Stol 1993, 38–41.

p. 361 and n. on 2.367 (p. 616): on the sick congregating in pagan temples, see G. Schmitt and V. Rödel, 'Die kranken Sklaven auf der Tiberinsel nach dem Edikt des Claudius: Versuch einer rechts- und medizingeschichtlichen Interpretation', *Medizinhistorisches Journal*, 9 (1974), 106–24, esp. 107–11, and B. Gevaert and C. Laes, 'What's in a Monster?', in Laes *et al.* (eds.), 211–30, at 226, on sick slaves in Julio-Claudian Rome deposited near the temple of Asclepius on Tiber Island (Suet. *Claud.* 25.2); P. Brown, *Power and Persuasion in Late Antiquity: Towards a Christian Empire* (Madison, WI, 1993), 93 and n. 118.

p. 373: see Trapp, lviii, for the scholia in another member of Allen's scriptorium (Par. gr. 1962, containing Maximus of Tyre): those on the text of Alcinous' *Didascalicus* have been suggested to go back to the Alexandrian scholars of the sixth century.

p. 381 n. 51: on paragraphoi in Anubion, add F 7 ll. 7-8 and 24-5, cf. Schubert 2009, 412-13.

pp. 418, 419, app. crit.: correct to *Lib. Herm.* xxxii.

pp. 430-2. A new papyrus fragment of the second book from Oxyrhynchus (P.Oxy. 5589, 2nd or 3rd c. AD), overlaps with lines 363-84. Like the fragment of the first book, and unlike the earlier Oxyrhynchus fragments of the fourth, the hand is cursive. Among the interesting readings are the omission of line 376 (its alien content was noted in i. 617) and the singular verb-ending in 367, supporting those sources, other than M^a, who attach the 'recourse to temples' motif to the mother, not the native (see i. 616). The suggestions of Rigler in 364 and Axtius in 382 are confirmed, and D'Orville is vindicated in 374 in correcting οὔτ' to a positive conjunction. There are also a few new variants, including και επαιϲχεα in line 381 (see Π.τ.δ. 33 καὶ ἐπαίϲχρους). 370 μεγαροιϲι has a supralinear lambda over rho, and 377 reads (possibly) νοϲ[οιϲιν] at line-end. I thank Dr Amin Benaissa allowing me to use this information in advance of publication.

p. 439, l. 457: read wretchedness.

p. 537: on the general productivity of the root φαίν- in astronomy and astrology, see Orlando and Torre, 299-301.

p. 539: on the ϲτροφάλιγξ. Also mentioned in P.Oxy. 5349.5 = 10 Perale, probably of the spinning of the winter tropic; less likely (so Perale) of the stars of Ursa Major rotating around the Arctic Circle.

2.12 (p. 544): for this use of τυπόω, see also *SSH* 391.5 = 08 Perale, a piece which is also in Aratus' debt.

2.76 (p. 557) χαροποῖο Λέοντος: for the epithet see Grand-Clement, 304-5. The question is whether it refers to character ('fierce') and/or colour, specifically of the eyes, and, if so, whether it means blue-grey or clear brown, an amber colour. Grand-Clement is open to the suggestion that it refers to skin-colour as well, but if that is what the poet meant he would be repeating himself by separately referring to its tawny mane.

2.79-82, 126-7 (pp. 558, 568): the listing of body-parts is very much in the style of Aratus: see Bone, 45 n. 64 (Aratus, 633, 671-2, 683, 704).

2.80, 81, 89, 90, 100 (pp. 558, 560, 561-2): in each case the enjambed word is the name of a constellation. This, too, is Aratean: see Kidd on 97.

2.97-8 (p. 561): the stern, or rather poop (ἄφλαϲτον), of the Argo is mentioned in P.Oxy. 5349.10 = 10 Perale.

2.134 (p. 569): on the question of singular versus plural ears of corn, see Hübner 2010, ii. 150.

2.185 (p. 582): for alpha privative and genitive of separation, see Allan on Eur. *Helen* 524, and further references.

2.197-9 (p. 585-6): as a parallel for the restricted circulation of sacred books connected with mysteries, add that Paus. 4.27.5 says that priestly families recorded the rediscovered τελετή of Andania in books (κατετίθεντο ἐς βίβλους). Henrichs, 247, infers that 'their circulation was apparently limited to the members of a priestly clan, a measure designed to prevent their unauthorized use and to guarantee their secrecy'.

2.208 (p. 587): add Thomas on *HHom. Herm.* 544, suggesting that this passage depends on that rather than on the *Odyssey*.

2.216 (p. 588): the military sense of ἡγεμόνας, here and at 3.296, is not found in the other poets of the Manethoniana. See Mason, 150: when the Roman army is in view, it often denotes commanders who are themselves under the command of another, even if that meant the *legatus* of a legion, himself under the command of Caesar. Such a sense well fits the implied subordination here (ἡγεμόνας βασιλεῦσιν ἀρηρότας).

2.234–5 (pp. 590–1 and 346–7): for purple robes and gold crowns of priests, see L. Robert, 'Nouvelles remarques sur l'« édit d'Ériza »', *BCH* 54 (1930), 262–7, at 262–3 n. 3; Chaniotis, 52–5 (crowns).

2.256 (p. 594) δίφρῳ ἑζομένους: to my remark that these are sedentary workers, add that an ἐπιδίφριος τέχνη is precisely a sedentary trade, and an ἐπιδίφριος τεχνίτης a sedentary worker (LSJ ἐπιδίφριος; illiberal, according to Dion. Hal. *Thuc.* 50). Astrology itself does not use these terms, but Artemidorus does (2.68.7). In that passage, he explains that dreaming of flying means that such workers will no longer be confined to their benches (καὶ μὴ μείνωσιν ἐφ' ἕδρας), with which one compares the language of M^a's other reference to sedentary workers, at 6.394 ἔνδον ἐφεζομένους.

2.264–5 (p. 596): this could refer to the Roman administration of justice (in Egypt assize-courts were supplemented by standing courts of the prefect and lower-ranking Roman officials in Alexandria), but would also be comprehensible under the Ptolemies, where civic and royal jurisdictions operated side by side (Fraser, 112–13).

2.320 (p. 607) αἰόλ' ὑπὸ χροιῇ ποικίλματα δαιδάλλοντας: for the frequent association of αἰόλος and ποικίλος, see Grand-Clément, 90–1. For the connection of ποικίλος with textiles, ead., 435–9, though she notes that the proper domain of δαιδάλλειν is in fact metals.

2.321–3 (pp. 607–8): these elaborate embroideries representing human and animal shapes sound like the work of the *barbaricarii* (Marquardt, 673; H. Blümner, *Der Maximaltarif des Diokletian* (Berlin, 1858), 157; Pruneti, 47) as described by Ti. Claudius Donatus on V. *Aen.* 11.777 *Qui hanc (sc. artem) exercent barbaricarii dicuntur, exprimentes ex auro et coloratis filis hominum formas, et diversorum animalium, et specierum imitatam subtilitate veritatem* (ed. H. Georgii, Leipzig, 1906). See also Roberts, 115, on gorgeous cloth decorated with human figures and animals (his examples are from later antiquity, but M^a anticipates them by a century and a half, or more).

2.325–7 (p. 608): on perfume-making in antiquity, see N. Balasubramanian, 'Scented Oils and Perfumes', in Rasmussen (ed.), 219–44, esp. 235–7; and on retail, S. Mrozek, 'Zum Handel von einigen Gewürzen und Wohlgerüchen in der spätrömischen Zeit', *MBAH* 1/2 (1982), 15–22, and A. Händel, 'Der Handel mit Drogen und Spezereien im Rom der Prinzipatszeit in Auswertung der Inschriften (Salz und Honig, Gewürze, Medikamente, Duftstoffe, Toilettegegenstände, Farben)', *MBAH* 4/1 (1985), 30–48.

2.400 (p. 621): on κρᾶσις/*mixtura*, add Firmicus, 3.6.26 (simile of a painter mixing colours).

2.430 (p. 630): to prostitutes 'standing on the roof', add Justin, 1 *Apol.* 26.3 πρότερον ἐπὶ τέγους σταθεῖσαν.

3.37 (pp. 652 and 347): on the purple robes of the agonothete, see Robert 1982, 258–9; M. Wörrle, *Stadt und Fest im kaiserzeitlichen Kleinasien: Studien zu einer agonistischen Stiftung aus Oinoanda* (Munich, 1988), 10, ll. 56–7, and 192–3; A. B. Kuhn,

71-2; *IK Prusias ad Hypium*, 72 = Merkelbach and Stauber, 09/08/04 (3rd c. AD) l. 4 φάρεσι πορφυρέοις κοσμήσας σεμνὸν ἀγῶνα.

3.38 (p. 652): cf. Paul, p. 67.3 δημοχαρεῖς (Venus in MC). On the fictional character Demochares, see Millar 1981, 74.

3.90-105 (p. 659): see Thomas on *HHom. Herm.* 565-6, n. 639, noting a series of similarities: 92-3 ~ 565-6; 95 ὀρφναίην κατὰ νύκτα ~ 578 νύκτα δι' ὀρφναίην; 102 σοφίης δεδαηκοτας ~ 483 σοφίῃ δεδαημένος.

3.118 (p. 663) ἀκτεάνους: see 4.31 n.

3.126-30 (p. 664): on collapsing buildings, see P. A. Brunt, 'The Roman Mob', *P&P* 35 (1966), 3-27, at 12; Hasegawa, 46, 47.

3.319 (p. 697): the relevant comparisons here are Valens, I 20.3 κελεύοντας καὶ ἐνακουομένους (Saturn, Jupiter, Mars); I 20.5 κελεύοντας καὶ ἐνακουομένους (Saturn, Jupiter, Mercury); Camaterus, *Introd.* 2929 κελεῦον, ἀκουόμενον (one luminary in ASC in a male sign, Jupiter in second house, Mercury in aspect).

3.363-98 (p. 702 n. 68): on feminine signs, add Neugebauer-Van Hoesen, 9; Quack and Ryholt, 176.

p. 703 n. 70: on the Hippocratic scheme from *On Regimen*, add Graumann, 191-2; Doroszewska, 126; Lane Fox, 96.

3.399-428 (p. 711 n. 81): on the edict(s) of AD 16, see Pomeroy, 54 n. 10.

6.19-112 (p. 731 n. 26): on exposure (foundlings) and subsequent slavery, add I. Bieżuńska, 'Die Expositio von Kindern als Quelle der Sklavenbeschaffung im griechisch-römischen Ägypten', *JWG* 12/2 (1971), 129-34; Harris 1994, 2, 5-6, 9, 18-19; Scheidel, 298-9; C. Hezser, 'Slavery and the Jews', in Bradley and Cartledge (eds.), 438-55, at 442; A. Ricciardetto and D. Gourevitch, 'The Cost of a Baby: How Much did it Cost to Hire a Wet-Nurse in Roman Egypt?', in L. M. V. Totelin and R. Flemming (eds.), *Medicine and Markets in the Graeco-Roman World and Beyond: Essays on Ancient Medicine in Honour of Vivian Nutton* (Swansea, 2020), 41-69, at 41-2, and bibliography in 58 n. 13.

6.37 (pp. 736 and 899): on 'they call' to flag a technical term, add Fögen, 45.

6.46-50 + 51-2 + 53-6 + 57-9 (p. 737): for 5.15.9 read 6.15.9.

6.133-4 (p. 751): on marital πίστις, see Morgan, 47-9.

6.142 (p. 752): on δοκεύειν, see Prévot, 253-4 (he renders 'attendre en embuscade', perhaps suited for sluggish Saturn).

6.292 (p. 777): for the meaning—and reading—at *HHom. Herm.* 415, see Thomas ad loc.

6.343: on dyeing gemstones. This could be in good faith, or not (Plin. *NH* 37.197). See Bidez-Cumont, ii. 338, on the discovery in Egypt of a book of Ostanes which contains, among other lore, 'des teintures divines des pierres précieuses', which ought to mean dyeing, not natural colour. Dyeing gemstones is discussed in alchemical tracts (Schmidt, 22-3; M. Martelli, 'Greco-Egyptian and Byzantine Alchemy', in Irby (ed.), 217-31, at 222; M. Martelli, 'Alchemical textiles: Colourful garments, recipes and dyeing techniques in Graeco-Roman Egypt', in Mary Harlow and Marie-Louise Nosch (eds.), *Greek and Roman Textiles and Dress: An Interdisciplinary Anthology* (Oxford, 2014), 111-29, at 112-13), especially the Stockholm papyrus (ed. R. Halleux,

Les Alchimistes grecs (Paris, 1981), i. 110–51, cf. discussion on 47–52), which includes 79 recipes on how to dye crystal quartzes to make them look like emeralds, beryls, and jaspers. For the colourful dyes available in antiquity, see M. V. Orna, 'Historic Mineral Pigments: Colorful Benchmarks of Ancient Civilizations', in Rasmussen (ed.), 17–69, esp. 36 table 6 (the pigments named in Pliny and Vitruvius that produce certain colours).

6.381–4 (p. 797): on the low wages and generally unhappy condition of porters, see Apuleius, *Met.* 1.7 (*saccaria*, the carrying of sacks), and the wretched σκευοφόρος in an Epidaurian wonder inscription, *IG* IV²/1. 121.79–89. What were they porters of? Goods? Or perhaps their masters, in other words were they litter-bearers (for whose professional pride, in other circumstances, see Joshel, 90–1)?

On the metaphorical equivalence of haulage and slavery, see Artemidorus, 3.18: 'to be harnessed to a cart as if one of the four-footed beasts foretells slavery and toil and disease'; Achmet, *Oneir.* 235.15–16, where camels are dream symbols for slaves. Slaves are like beasts of burden: Tyrtaeus, fr. 6.1 W. ὥσπερ ὄνοι μεγάλοις ἄχθεσι τειρόμενοι (the helots). Slaves are treated as equivalent to beasts of burden in the Lex Aquilia, the basis of Roman Law on damage to property (K. Bradley, 'Animalizing the Slave: The Truth of Fiction', *JRS* 90 (2000), 110–25, at 111), though at the same time there is a moral tradition of critique of masters who exploited their slaves in this way (Plut. *Cat. Maj.* 5.1 ὡς ὑποζυγίοις ἀποχρησάμενον; Sen. *Ep.* 47.5 (*iumenta*)). For the modern trope of the black African slave as a beast (not necessarily a beast of burden or domestic animal, but also as an ape), see Bradley, art. cit. 111–12.

6.402 (p. 801): on automata arousing wonder, see B. Meissner, *Die technologische Fachliteratur der Antike: Struktur, Überlieferung und Wirkung technischen Wissens in der Antike (ca. 400 v. Chr.-ca. 500 n. Chr.)* (Berlin, 1999), 93; and on automata and the divine sphere, J. Lightfoot, *Wonder and the Marvellous from Homer to the Hellenistic World* (Cambridge, 2021), 208–14.

Correct to statuettes.

6.409 (pp. 801–2): custodians of tombs, who are well attested in Asia Minor.[1] But perhaps the most interesting evidence comes from *SEG* ii. 848 (Egypt, c. 120), which concerns an individual who did not fulfil the μνηματοφυλακία with which he was charged; proceedings are now being taken against him by the πολίτευμα Λυκίων, which may be a community of Lycians keeping up their ancestral burial practices in Egypt (discussion in Zimmermann (n. 1), 160–2). The point matters for whether this is one of astrology's placeless references, or whether (alongside other funerary

---

[1] For Lycia, see M. Zimmermann, *Untersuchungen zur historischen Landeskunde Zentrallykiens* (Diss. Tübingen, 1992), 159–62. A μνημόδουλος is mentioned (i) in *IK* Arykanda, 147 (E. Lycia, n. d.) (though Zimmermann, 160, is agnostic) and (ii) in H. Uzunoğlu and E. Taşdelen, 'Parerga zum Stadiasmus Patarensis (14): Die Strecken 35 (Arykanda-Arneai) und 37 (Arykanda-Lesei)', *Gephyra*, 10 (2013), 121–31, at 123–4 (Yeşilköy, territory of Arykanda, 3rd c. AD; ed. pr. of an epitaph which mentions a slave caretaker). ταφόδουλοι and ταφοδούλαι are mentioned in H. Engelmann, 'Inschriften von Patara', *ZPE* 182 (2012), 179–201, at 200 = *Epigraphic Bulletin for Greek Religions* 2012, no. 63 (Patara, *c.* AD 250). Zimmermann, op. cit. 160 n. 81, gives further references, including to the φύλα]ξ of a heroon (Keil–Premerstein, iii. no. 117, Tire, Lydia, 1st c. AD) and to a τηρητής in Hierapolis.

Addenda and Corrigenda to the First Volume 1065

workers) the poet is acknowledging practices in Egypt itself. Quite possibly the latter. The present passage was adduced by Youtie, 655-6, to clarify the activities of the ἐξωπυλῖται of Kysis in the Great Oasis. See too Dunand, 121-2; G. Wagner, *Les oasis d'Égypte à l'époque grecque, romaine et byzantine d'après les documents grecs: Recherches de papyrologie et d'épigraphie grecques* (Cairo, 1987), 352-3; Derda, 34-5; Bagnall 2017, 7-9. Papyri reveal these people in company with νεκροτάφοι, who may reasonably be inferred from Valens, II 15.2 νεκροφύλακες γίνονται ἔξω πύλης τὸν βίον διάγοντες ~ Θ p. 139.9-10 νεκροφύλακας ποιοῦσι καὶ τὸν βίον ἔξω τῆς πόλεως διατελοῦντας, to have been resident beyond the bounds of cities; Gundel, 355, identified those in *Lib. Herm.* xxv. 3.22 *extra civitatem latitantes, abiectiones facientes* as 'Grabwächter', though the text does not specify. The papyri do not prove that the ἐξωπυλῖται were custodians of graves, but Youtie, 655, noted *BGU* i. 34 col. ii. 31-2, where they are followed by a φρουρός.

For πυλουρός as a job-title, see Reynolds and Tannenbaum, 121-2: they suggest janitor or perhaps customs-collector (πύλη = customs-house), but do not illustrate the usage in connection with tombs.

6.410-14 + 415-18 + 419-21 + 422-4 (p. 802): correct to anthropomorphic.

6.416 (p. 803) λαοτόμους: see 4.325 n. In this passage they are clearly quarrymen (Robert 1960, 32-3 n. 4).

6.419 (p. 804): λιθοξόους are distinguished from λαοτόμους by being born under different signs, but in my commentary I should not have implied that they were stone-polishers. This is a common word for stone-mason, and was e.g. the trade of Lucian's uncle, which the infant Lucian was expected to follow (*Somnium*). On this trade-name, see Robert 1960, 30-7; Ruffing 2008, 637. It is well attested epigraphically in local associations of stone-carvers (to Robert's evidence add J. B. Ward-Perkins, 'Nicomedia and the Marble Trade', *PBSR* 48 (1980), 23-69, at 34). It is better and earlier attested than μαρμαράριος (Ruffing 2008, 657-8), for which attestations begin in the first third of the 3rd c. AD.

Robert's discussion took its departure from *Corinth VIII,1. The Greek Inscriptions 1896-1927*, ed. B. D. Meritt (Cambridge, MA, 1931), no. 245, where Robert restored it in the first line before a reference to μαρ]μαράριοι in the following line, just as the corresponding chart in Θ p. 216.6-7 places λιθοξόους and μαρμαρίους in close proximity, and so too Teucer has λιθοξόους, μαρμαρίους (II 3.4, under Engonasin, paranatellon of Gemini). Teucer in fact mentions them three times (II 1.10, 3.4, 12.8). In the first passage (for 24-5° Aries) they correspond to a *marmorarius* in Firmicus, 8.19.11, and *incisores lapidum* in *Lib. Herm.* xxv. i.38 (Feraboli, 215), and their associations (οἰκοδόμους ~ 6.415, τέκτονας ~ 6.418, λιθοξόους ~ 6.419, καὶ πάντας τοὺς περὶ σταθμία ἀσχολουμένους ~ 6.418) effectively replicate the range of interests in Mᵃ's stone-cutter chart. Teucer makes clear that their job involves the squaring of angles (II 1.10 πάντας τοὺς περὶ σταθμία ἀσχολουμένους): they are cutters, not polishers.

6.434-5 (p. 807): on cleaners and repairers of clothes, add Drexhage and Reinard, esp. 27-39; 26 on ῥυπαρός for dirty garments; 28-30 on the possible existence of professional clothes-washers based on the papyrological occurrences of words like πλυνεύς, πλύντης, πλύντρια, πλυσιμάριος; 30-1 on fulling; 31, on the repair [sometimes using the verb θεραπεύειν] of old clothes ~ 435, and 32-4 on the professional terms ῥάπτης (Appendix II, II.7.viii.g) and ἠπητής, in which case Mᵃ has chosen to paraphrase the professional term without suggesting its root. The Latin equivalent is *sarcinator*, e.g. in Plaut. *Aulul.* 515 *sarcinatores*, and in the *Monumentum Liviae* (Treggiari 1975, 54). Ruffing 2002, 42, doubts the extent of any trade in second-hand clothes, which were valuable commodities and would be patched up and kept in the same hands as long as possible, or passed on by testamentary disposition.

6.447 (p. 811). On slave-dealers and the slave trade, add Bieżuńska-Małowist 1975; Harris 1980, 125-6, 129-32; Bradley, 114-16; A. Benaissa, 'A Syrian Slave Girl Twice sold in Egypt', *ZPE* 173 (2010), 175-89, 180; Thompson, 206; Scheidel, 300-1; M. George, 'Slavery and Roman Material Culture', in Bradley and Cartledge (eds.), 385-413, at 392-4, and I. Morris, 'Archaeology and Greek Slavery', ibid. 176-93, at 191.

6.456-64 (p. 813): for other trade-names involving work with saline preservatives (pickled cucumbers etc.), see Robert 1960, 39-41 (the σαλγαμάριος, equivalent to the ἁλμευτής) and *BE* 1958 no. 452 (a name derived from τάριχος, perhaps ταρειχοπώλης or ταρειχώτης on an epitaph from Alabanda).

6.460 (pp. 813-14): malodorousness features in the Coffin Texts as one of the negative attributes of the corpse which distinguishes it from its spiritual counterpart, the *ba*: R. Nyord, *Breathing Flesh: Conceptions of the Body in the Ancient Egyptian Coffin Texts* (Copenhagen, 2009), 342.

6.461-2 (p. 814 n. 91): on the persistence of mummification, add Dunand, 123 (on Kharga Oasis).

6.470-1 (p. 817): could these be the sort of show-orators described by Dio, *Or.* 33.4 οἳ πάντα εἰδέναι φασὶ καὶ περὶ πάντων ἐρεῖν ᾗ διατέτακται καὶ τίνα ἔχει φύσιν, περί τε ἀνθρώπων καὶ δαιμόνων καὶ [περὶ] θεῶν, ἔτι δὲ γῆς καὶ οὐρανοῦ καὶ θαλάττης, καὶ περὶ ἡλίου καὶ σελήνης καὶ τῶν ἄλλων ἄστρων, καὶ περὶ τοῦ σύμπαντος κόσμου, καὶ περὶ φθορᾶς καὶ γενέσεως καὶ μυρίων ἄλλων?

6.475 (p. 818): on magian whisperings, see Bremmer 2015, 248; M. Boyce and F. Grenet, *A History of Zoroastrianism*, iii: *Zoroastrianism under Macedonian and Roman Rule* (Leiden, 1991), 558. Who are the *sacrorum sibilatores* in *Lib. Herm.* xxvii. 30?

6.489-90 (p. 820): on smallholders owning land and leasing more. There are case-studies in D. P. Kehoe, *Management and Investment on Estates in Roman Egypt during the Early Empire* (Bonn, 1992), 149-65 (the family of Kronion, mid-2nd c., Tebtunis; Aurelius Isidorus of Karanis, late 3rd/early 4th c.); A. E. R. Boak and H. C. Youtie, *The Archive of Aurelius Isidorus in the Egyptian Museum, Cairo, and the University of Michigan (P.Cair. Isidor.)* (Ann Arbor, 1960), 7-11. See also Cam Grey, 'Salvian, the Ideal Christian Community and the Fate of the Poor in Fifth-Century Gaul', in Atkins and Osborne, 162-82, at 179-80.

If γέγηθε is to be defended in 6.489, could it be that the cultivation of land, whether one's own or someone else's, is simply the best occupation (Grassl, 171-2)?

6.498 (p. 823 and n. 101): on the *elymos*, see A. Barker, 'Telestes and the « five-rodded joining of strings »', *CQ*² 48 (1998), 75-81, at 79, and id. *Euterpe: Ricerche sulla musica greca e romana* (Pisa, 2002), 80.

6.524-5 (pp. 828-9): on wax in encaustic painting, add Reinard, 232-3.

Addenda and Corrigenda to the First Volume

6.665–9 (p. 854): a part parallel is Firmicus, 4.11.6 (to add also to the register on p. 726): the <Full or waxing> Moon leaving Mars for Saturn causes loss of *patrimonium* (though there is no ASC and no Jupiter).

6.692–4 (pp. 857–8): on slaves uniting with their mistresses, see Kudlien 1991, 42.

6.727 (p. 861): on sale of infants (technically with no legal validity, but a grey area with endless potential for dispute), see Harris 1980, 124; id. 1994, 21; Grassl, 63; Scheidel, 299–300; Cam Grey, 'Slavery in the Late Roman World', in Bradley and Cartledge (eds.), 482–509, at 491.

p. 880 and n. 39: on ὡρονόμος, add Schubert 2009, 410–112.

p. 896: on the light-names of the planets (Phainon etc.), add Orlando and Torre, 302.

p. 898–9 n. 4: add Heilen 2005, 146.

p. 920: last sentence, delete 'it' (or add 'is').

p. 927: entry for S. Heilen, *Hadriani Genitura*: delete 539–62; entry for Hübner, W., 'Dorothée de Sidon: L'Édition de David Pingree', in Boehm and Hübner, 115–27: add [= Hübner 2011].

p. 991 (Index): planets—personified 589 n. 72: correct to 588 n. 72.

Bibliography

ABRY, J.-H., 'Manilius et Julius Firmicus Maternus: Deux astrologues sous l'Empire', in N. Blanc and A. Buisson (eds.), *Imago Antiquitatis: Religions et iconographie du monde romain: Mélanges offerts à Robert Turcan* (Paris, 1999), 35-45.

ACKERS, H., 'Portrait Busts of Roman Women in the Third Century AD' (D.Phil. thesis. Oxford, 2016).

ADAMS, J. N., *The Latin Sexual Vocabulary* (London, 1982).

—— *Bilingualism and the Latin Language* (Cambridge, 2003).

AGOSTI, G., *Nonno di Panopoli: Le Dionisiache, Volume Terzo (Canti XXV–XXXIX)* (Milan, 2004) [= 2004*a*].

—— 'Alcuni problemi relativi alla cesura principale nell'esametro greco tardoantico', in F. Spaltenstein, O. Bianchi, M. Steinrück, and A. Lukinovich (eds.), *Autour de la césure: Actes du colloque Damon des 3 et 4 novembre 2000* (Bern, 2004), 61-80 [= 2004*b*].

—— 'Literariness and Levels of Style in Epigraphical Poetry of Late Antiquity', *Ramus*, 37 (2008), 191-232.

—— '*Eisthesis*, divisione dei versi, percezione dei *cola* negli epigrammi epigrafici in età tardoantica', *S&T* 8 (2010), 67-98.

—— 'Greek Poetry', in S. F. Johnson (ed.), *The Oxford Handbook of Late Antiquity* (Oxford, 2012), 361-404.

—— and GONNELLI, F., 'Materiali per la storia del esametro nei poeti cristiani greci', in M. Fantuzzi and R. Pretagostini (eds.), *Struttura e storia dell'esametro greco* (Rome, 1995), i. 289-434.

AHMAD, T., 'The *katochoi* of Zeus at Baitokaike (Hoson Sulaiman, Syria)', *JAH* 6 (2018), 215-33.

ALSTON, R., *The City in Roman and Byzantine Egypt* (London, 2002).

ALVAR, J., *Romanising Oriental Gods: Myth, Salvation and Ethics in the Cults of Cybele, Isis, and Mithras* (Leiden, 2008).

ARBANDT, S., and MACHEINER, W., *RAC* s.v. Gefangenschaft, 318-45.

ARNOLD, P. J., 'The Pornoboskos and Leno in Greek and Roman comedy' (D.Phil. thesis, Oxford, 1998).

ATKINS, E. M., and OSBORNE, R., *Poverty in the Roman World* (Cambridge, 2006).

AXTIUS, C. A. M., and RIGLER, FR. A., Μανέθωνος Ἀποτελεσματικῶν βιβλία ἕξ (Cologne, 1832).

BAGNALL, R. S., 'Slavery and Society in Late Roman Egypt', in id., *Later Roman Egypt: Society, Religion, Economy and Administration* (Aldershot, 2003), 220-40.

—— *The Undertakers of the Great Oasis (P.Nekr.)* (London, 2017).

BASSETT, S. E., 'Versus Tetracolos', *CP* 14 (1919), 216-33.

BÉAL, J.-C., 'La dignité des artisans: Les images d'artisans sur les monuments funéraires de Gaule romaine', *DHA* 26 (2000), 149-82.

BENAISSA, A., 'Greek Language, Education, and Literary Culture', in Riggs 2012, 526-42.

Bergamasco, M., 'Le διδασκαλικαί nella ricerca attuale', *Aegyptus*, 75 (1995), 95–167.
Bernand, A., *Les Inscriptions grecques de Philae*, i: *Époque ptolémaïque* (Paris, 1969).
Bernard, S. G., 'Workers in the Roman Imperial Building Industry', in Verboven and Laes, 62–86.
Bidez, J., and Cumont, H., *Les Mages hellénisés: Zoroastre, Ostanès et Hystaspe d'après la tradition grecque*, 2 vols. (Paris, 1938).
Bieżuńska-Małowist, I., 'Les esclaves nés dans la maison du maître (οἰκογενεῖς) et le travail des esclaves en Égypte romaine', *Studii clasice*, 3 (1961), 146–62.
—— 'La traite d'esclaves en Égypte', *Proceedings of the XIVth International Congress of Papyrologists (Oxford, 24–31 July, 1974)* (London, 1975), 11–18.
—— *L'Esclavage dans l'Égypte gréco-romaine*, ii: *Période romaine* (Wrocław, 1977) = *La schiavitù nell'Egitto greco-romano*, prefazione di Pierre Lévêque (Rome, 1984).
Biliński, B., 'Elogio della mano e la concezione ciceroniana della società', in *Atti del I Congresso internazionale di studi ciceroniani*, i (Rome, 1961), 195–212.
Blass, F., Debrunner, A., and Rehkopf, F., *Grammatik des neutestamentlichen Griechisch* (Göttingen, [14]1975).
Blümner, H., 'Fahrendes Volk im Altertum', *SBAW* 1918, Abh. 6.
Blume, M., 'À propos de *P.Oxy.* I 41: Des acclamations en l'honneur d'un prytane confrontées aux témoignages épigraphiques du reste de l'Empire', in L. Criscuolo and G. Geraci (eds.), *Egitto e storia antica dall'ellenismo all'età araba. Bilancio di un confronto. Atti del Colloquio Internazionale Bologna, 31 agosto–2 settembre 1981* (Bologna, 1989), 271–90.
Bodson, L., 'Introduction au système de nomination des serpents en grec ancien: L'ophionyme *dipsas* et ses synonymes', *Anthropozoologica*, 47(1) (2012), 73–155.
Boehm, I. and Hübner, W. (eds.), *La Poésie astrologique dans l'Antiquité* (Paris, 2011).
Boll, F., rev. of W. Kroll and F. Skutsch, *Iulii Firmici Materni Matheseos Libri VIII*, Fasciculus Prior (Leipzig, 1897), *Berliner Philologische Wochenschrift*, 1898, 199–207.
—— *Sphaera: Neue griechische Texte und Untersuchungen zur Geschichte der Sternbilder* (Leipzig, 1903).
—— 'Antike Beobachtungen farbiger Sterne', *ABAW* 30.1 (1916), 1–164.
—— 'Kronos–Helios', *Archiv für Religionswissenschaft*, 19 (1919), 342–6.
Bone, P., 'The Multipartite Muse: Sectioned Composition in Hellenistic Long Poems' (D.Phil. thesis, Oxford, 2021).
Boswell, J., *The Kindness of Strangers: The Abandonment of Children in Western Europe from Late Antiquity to the Renaissance* (New York, 1988).
Bottéro, J., *Mythes et rites de Babylone* (Paris, 1985).
Bouché-Leclercq, A., *Histoire de la divination dans l'Antiquité*, 4 vols. (Paris, 1879–82, repr. New York, 1975).
—— *L'Astrologie grecque* (Paris, 1899) [cited as Bouché-Leclercq].
Bradley, K. R., *Slaves and Masters in the Roman Empire: A Study in Social Control* (Brussels, 1984).
—— and Cartledge, P. (eds.), *The Cambridge World History of Slavery, Volume 1: The Ancient Mediterranean World* (Cambridge, 2011).
Bram, J. R., *Ancient Astrology, Theory and Practice: Matheseos libri VIII by Firmicus Maternus* (Park Ridge, NJ, 1975).

Breitenbach, W., *Untersuchungen zur Sprache der euripideischen Lyrik* (Stuttgart, 1934).
Bremmer, J. N., *The Early Greek Concept of the Soul* (Princeton, 1983).
—— 'From Holy Books to Holy Bible: An Itinerary from Ancient Greece to Modern Islam via Second Temple Judaism and Early Christianity', in M. Popović (ed.), *Authoritative Scriptures in Ancient Judaism* (Leiden, 2010), 327–60.
—— 'From Books with Magic to Magical Books in Ancient Greece and Rome?', in D. Boschung and J. N. Bremmer (eds.), *The Materiality of Magic* (Paderborn, 2015), 241–70.
Brunt, P. A., 'Aspects of the Social Thought of Dio Chrysostom and of the Stoics', *PCPS* 19 (1973), 9–34.
—— 'The Bubble of the Second Sophistic', *BICS* 39 (1994), 25–52.
Callon, C., '*Adulescentes* and *Meretrices*: The Correlation between Squandered Patrimony and Prostitutes in the Parable of the Prodigal Son', *Catholic Biblical Quarterly*, 75 (2013), 259–78.
Callu, J.-P., 'Le jardin des supplices au Bas-Empire', in *Du châtiment dans la cité: Supplices corporels et peine de mort dans le monde antique: Table ronde organisée par l'École française de Rome avec le concours du Centre national de la recherche scientifique (Rome 9-11 novembre 1982)* (Rome, 1984), 313–59.
Cannata, M., 'Funerary Artists: The Textual Evidence', in Riggs 2012, 597–612.
—— *Three Hundred Years of Death: The Egyptian Funerary Industry in the Ptolemaic Period* (Leiden, 2020).
Cantarella, E., *I supplizi capitali in Grecia e a Roma* (Milan, 1991).
Capponi, F., 'Le rôle de l'*arundo* dans l'oisellerie', *Latomus*, 18 (1959), 724–41.
Carcopino, J., *Daily Life in Ancient Rome: The People and the City at the Height of the Empire*, transl. E. O. Lorimer (London, 1941).
Cardon, D., *Natural Dyes: Sources, Tradition, Technology and Science* (London, 2007).
—— and Nowik, W., Granger-Taylor, H., Marcinowska, R., Kusyk, K., and Trojanowicz, M. 'Who Could Wear True Purple in Roman Egypt? Technical and Social Considerations on Some New Identifications of Purple from Marine Molluscs in Archaeological Textiles', in C. Alfaro, J.-P. Brun, Ph. Borgard, and R. Pierobon Benoît (eds.), *Textiles y Tintes en la Ciudad antigua (Purpurae Vestes III)* (València, 2011), 197–214.
Casson, L., *Ships and Seamanship in the Ancient World* (Princeton, NJ, 1971).
Cavenaile, R., 'Quelques aspects de l'apport linguistique du grec au latin d'Égypte', *Aegyptus*, 32 (1952), 191–203.
Cecchet, L., and Busetto, A. (eds.), *Citizens in the Graeco-Roman World: Aspects of Citizenship from the Archaic Period to AD 212* (Leiden, 2017).
Chandler, H. W., *Greek Accentuation* (Oxford, ²1881).
Chaniotis, A., 'Griechische Rituale der Statusänderung und ihre Dynamik', in M. Steinicke und S. Weinfurter (eds.), *Investitur- und Krönungsrituale: Herrschaftseinsetzungen im kulturellen Vergleich* (Cologne, 2005), 43–61.
Coleman, K., 'Fatal Charades: Roman Executions Staged as Mythological Enactments', *JRS* 80 (1990), 44–73.
Congourdeau, M.-H., *L'Embryon et son âme dans les sources grecques (VIᵉ siècle av. J.-C.-Vᵉ siècle apr. J.-C.)* (Paris, 2007).

Cook, J. G., *Crucifixion in the Mediterranean World* (Tübingen, 2014).
Courrier, C., *La Plèbe de Rome et sa culture (fin du IIe siècle av. J.-C.-fin du Ier siècle ap. J.-C.)* (Rome, 2014).
Csapo, E., 'Star Choruses: Eleusis, Orphism, and New Musical Imagery and Dance', in M. Revermann and P. J. Wilson (eds.), *Performance, Iconography, Reception: Studies in Honour of Oliver Taplin* (Oxford, 2008), 262–90.
Cumont, F., *Astrology and Religion among the Greeks and Romans* (New York, 1912).
—— 'Les Noms des planètes et l'astrolatrie chez les Grecs', *AC* 4 (1935), 5–43.
—— *L'Égypte des astrologues* (Brussels, 1937) [cited as Cumont].
Cupcea, G., and Varga, R. (eds.), *Social Interactions and Status Markers in the Roman World* (Oxford, 2018).
Curta, F., 'Atticism, Homer, Neoplatonism, and *Fürstenspiegel*: Julian's Second Panegyric on Constantius', *GRBS* 36 (1995), 177–211.
Curtis, R. I., *Garum and Salsamenta: Production and Commerce in Materia Medica* (Leiden, 1991).
Delekat, L., *Katoche, Hierodulie und Adoptionsfreilassung* (Munich, 1964).
Denniston, J. D., *The Greek Particles* (Oxford, ²1954).
Derda, T., 'Necropolis Workers in Graeco-Roman Egypt in the Light of the Greek Papyri', *JJP* 21 (1991), 13–36.
De Stefani, C., 'Per il testo dei Manethoniana', *Prometheus*, 42 (2016), 178–206.
—— *Ps.-Manethonis Apotelesmatica: Einleitung, Text, Appendices* (Wiesbaden, 2017).
Detienne, M., and Vernant, J.-P., transl. J. Lloyd, *Cunning Intelligence in Greek Culture and Society* (Chicago, 1991).
De Zorzi, N., 'The Omen Series *Šumma Izbu*: Internal Structure and Hermeneutic Strategies', *Kaskal*, 8 (2011), 43–75.
Dickie, M., 'What is a Kolossos and How Were Kolossoi Made in the Hellenistic Period?', *GRBS* 37 (1996), 235–57.
—— 'Mimes, Thaumaturgy, and the Theatre', *CQ*² 51 (2001), 599–603.
—— *Magic and Magicians in the Greco-Roman World* (London, 2003).
Doroszewska, J., 'Beyond the Limits of the Human Body: Phlegon of Tralles' Medical Curiosities', in G. Kazantzidis (ed.), *Medicine and Paradoxography in the Ancient World* (Berlin, 2019), 117–40.
Drexhage, H.-J., '*Λάχανον* und *λαχανοπῶλαι* im römischen Ägypten (1.-3. Jh. n. Chr.)', *MBAH* 9/2 (1990), 88–117.
—— 'Einige Bemerkungen zu den *ἔμποροι* und *κάπηλοι* im römischen Ägypten (1.-3. Jh. n.)', *MBAH* 10/2 (1991), 28–46.
—— 'Garum und Garumhandel im römischen und spätantiken Ägypten', *MBAH* 12/1 (1993), 27–55.
—— 'Zu den Berufsbezeichnungen mit dem Suffix -âs in der literarischen, papyrologischen und epigraphischen Überlieferung', *MBAH* 23/1 (2004), 18–40.
—— 'Wirtschaft und Handel Westkilikiens in römischer und frühbyzantinischer Zeit (1.-6. Jahrhundert n. Chr.). 1: Land- und Forstwirtschaft', *MBAH* 26 (2008), 1–48.
—— 'Wirtschaft und Handel Westkilikiens in römischer und frühbyzantinischer Zeit (1.-6. Jahrhundert n. Chr.). 2: Handwerk und Gewerbe sowie Handel', *MBAH* 30 (2012), 139–74.

—— and REINARD, P., 'Vom Wert der Dinge: Verschlissene, getragene und ausgebesserte Kleider und Textilien im papyrologischen Befund: Überlegungen zum Verwertungskreislauf und Second Hand-Markt', *MBAH* 32 (2014), 1–70.
—— and KONEN, H., and RUFFING, K. (eds.), *Die Wirtschaft des Römischen Reiches (1.-3. Jahrhundert): Eine Einführung* (Berlin, 2002).
DUMITRACHE, I., 'Latin Occupational Titles in Roman Textile Trade', in Cupcea and Varga, 23–45.
DUNAND, F., 'Les nécrotaphes de Kysis', *Cahiers de recherches de l'Institut de Papyrologie et d'Égyptologie de Lille*, 7 (1985), 117–27.
DUNBABIN, K. M. D., *Mosaics of the Greek and Roman World* (Cambridge, 1999).
—— *Theater and Spectacle in the Art of the Roman Empire* (Ithaca, 2016).
EBNER, C., 'Die Konzeption der Arenastrafen im römischen Strafrecht', *ZRG* 129 (2012), 245–85 = 2012a.
—— 'Hinrichtungen in der Arena', in Rollinger et al. (eds.), 95–127 = 2012b.
EDMONDSON, J., 'Slavery and the Roman Family', in Bradley and Cartledge (eds.), 337–61.
EIDINOW, E., *Oracles, Curses, and Risk among the Ancient Greeks* (Oxford, 2007).
—— '"What Will Happen to Me if I Leave?" Ancient Greek Oracles, Slaves and Slave-Owners', in S. Hodkinson and D. Geary (eds.), *Slaves and Religions in Graeco-Roman Antiquity and the Modern Americas* (Cambridge, 2011), 244–78.
ELLIS HANSON, A., '*Paidopoiïa*: Metaphors for Conception, Abortion, and Gestation in the *Hippocratic Corpus*', *Clio Medica*, 27 (1995), 291–307.
ELSTER, J., *Alchemies of the Mind: Rationality and the Emotions* (Cambridge, 1999).
ERKELENZ, D., 'Keine Konkurrenz zum Kaiser: Zur Verleihung der Titel Κτίστης und Σωτήρ in der römischen Kaiserzeit', *SCI* 21 (2002), 61–77.
FABRICIUS, J. A., *Bibliothecae Graecae Liber III: De Scriptoribus qui claruerunt a Platone usque ad tempora nati Christi* (Hamburg, 1716), 498–503.
—— *Bibliotheca Graeca, Sive Notitia Scriptorum Veterum Graecorum, Editio Nova*, curante G. Ch. Harles (Hamburg, 1795), iv. 133–9.
FANTUZZI, M., and SENS, A., 'The Hexameter of Inscribed Hellenistic Epigram', in A. Harder, R. F. Regtuit, and G. C. Wakker (eds.), *Beyond the Canon* (Leuven, 2006), 105–22.
FARAONE, C. A., *Ancient Greek Love Magic* (Cambridge, MA, 1999).
FEHLING, D., *Die Wiederholungsfiguren und ihr Gebrauch bei den Griechen vor Gorgias* (Berlin, 1969).
FERABOLI, S., 'Ricerche sulle monomoiriai di Firmico', *SIFC* 82 (1989), 213–40.
FESTUGIÈRE, A. J., *La Révélation d'Hermès Trismégiste*, i: *L'Astrologie et les sciences occultes* (Paris, 1944).
FINLEY, M., *The Ancient Economy* (London, 1973).
—— *Ancient Slavery and Modern Ideology* (London, 1980).
—— 'The Elderly in Classical Antiquity', *G&R* 28 (1981), 156–71, repr. in J. de Luce and T. M. Falkner (eds.), *Old Age in Greek and Latin Literature* (Albany, NY, 1989), 1–20.
FLOHR, M., 'Exploring the Limits of Skilled Craftsmanship: The *Fullonicae* of Roman Italy', in Monteix and Tran (eds.), 87–100 [= Flohr 2011].
—— *The World of the Fullo: Work, Economy, and Society in Roman Italy* (Oxford, 2013).

FÖGEN, T., 'Metasprachliche Reflexionen antiker Autoren zu den Charakteristika von Fachtexten und Fachsprachen', in M. Horster and C. Reitz (eds.), *Antike Fachschriftsteller: Literarischer Diskurs und sozialer Kontext* (Stuttgart, 2003), 31–60.

FORST, A., 'Exorzismus, Heilschlaf oder Versöhnung eines Dämons? Die *incantatio* des Apuleius in *Apol.* 42–52', *MH* 75 (2018), 173–93.

FOUNTOULAKIS, A., 'Punishing the Lecherous Slave: Desire and Power in Herondas 5', in Serghidou (ed.), 251–64.

FRAENKEL, E., *Geschichte der griechischen nomina agentis auf -tēr, -tōr, -tēs(-t-)*, 2 vols. (Strassburg, 1910–12).

FRAKES, R. M., *Contra potentium iniurias: The Defensor Civitatis and Late Roman Justice* (Munich, 2001).

FRASER, P. M., *Ptolemaic Alexandria*, 3 vols. (Oxford, 1972).

FREU, C., 'Apprendre et exercer un métier dans l'Égypte romaine (Ier–VIe siècles ap. J.–C.)', in Monteix and Tran (eds.), 27–40.

GALJANIC, A., 'Three and Then Some: A Typology of Poetic Enumeration in Greek and Related Indo-European Traditions' (Diss. Harvard, 2007).

GARELLI, M.-H., *Danser le mythe: La Pantomime et sa réception dans la culture antique* (Louvain, 2007).

GARNSEY, P., *Social Status and Legal Privilege in the Roman Empire* (Oxford, 1970).

—— *Non-Slave Labour in the Graeco-Roman World* (ed.) (PCPhS, suppl. vol. 6. Cambridge, 1980).

—— 'Non-Slave Labour in the Roman World', in id. 1980, 34–47.

—— *Ideas of Slavery from Aristotle to Augustine* (Cambridge, 1996).

GIANNAKIS, G., 'The "Fate-as-Spinner" Motif: A Study on the Poetic and Metaphorical Language of Ancient Greek and Indo-European (Part I)', *IF* 103 (1998), 1–27.

—— 'The "Fate-as-Spinner" Motif: A Study on the Poetic and Metaphorical Language of Ancient Greek and Indo-European (Part II)', *IF* 104 (1999), 95–109.

GLAZEBROOK, A., 'The Making of a Prostitute: Apollodoros's Portrait of Neaira', *Arethusa*, 38 (2005), 161–87.

GOUREVITCH, D., 'Grossesse et accouchement dans l'iconographie antique', *Dossiers de l'Archéologie. Document Archeologia*, 123 (1988), 42–8.

—— *Pour une archéologie de la médecine romaine* (Paris, 2011).

GRAILLOT, H., *Le Culte de Cybèle, mère des dieux, à Rome et dans l'Empire romain* (Paris, 1912).

GRAND-CLÉMENT, A., *La Fabrique des couleurs: Histoire du paysage sensible des Grecs anciens (VIIIe–début du Ve siècle av. n. è.)* (Paris, 2011).

GRASSL, H., *Sozialökonomische Vorstellungen in der kaiserzeitlichen griechischen Literatur: 1–3 Jh. n. Chr.* (Wiesbaden, 1982).

GRAUMANN, L. A., 'Monstrous Births and Retrospective Diagnosis: The Case of Hermaphrodites in Antiquity', in Laes *et al.* (eds.), 181–209.

GREEN, T. M., *The City of the Moon God: Religious Traditions of Harran* (Leiden, 1992).

GREENBAUM, D. G., *The Daimon in Hellenistic Astrology: Origins and Influence* (Leiden, 2016).

—— and ROSS, M. T., 'Various Renderings of Πίναξ in Greek and Demotic at Medīnet Māḍī', in N. Campion and D. G. Greenbaum (eds.), *Astrology in Time and Place:*

Cross-Cultural Questions in the History of Astrology (Newcastle-Upon-Tyne, 2015), 109–29.
GRMEK, M. D., *Diseases in the Ancient Greek World* (Baltimore, 1989).
GROEN-VALLINGA, M. J., and TACOMA, L. E., 'The Value of Labour: Diocletian's Prices Edict', in Verboven and Laes, 104–32.
GUNDEL, W., *Neue astrologische Texte des Hermes Trismegistos: Funde und Forschungen auf dem Gebiet der antiken Astronomie und Astrologie* (Munich, 1936).
—— and GUNDEL, H. G., *Astrologumena: Die astrologische Literatur in der Antike und ihre Geschichte* (Wiesbaden, 1966).
GYGLI-WYSS, B., *Das nominale Polyptoton in älteren Griechisch* (Göttingen, 1966).
HAHN, I., *Traumdeutung und gesellschaftliche Wirklichkeit: Artemidorus Daldianus als sozialgeschichtliche Quelle* (Konstanz, 1992).
HALL, E., and WYLES, R. (eds.), *New Directions in Ancient Pantomime* (Oxford, 2008).
HALLIWELL, S., *Greek Laughter: A Study of Cultural Psychology from Homer to Early Christianity* (Cambridge, 2008).
HARPER, K., *Slavery in the Late Roman World, AD 275–425* (Cambridge, 2011).
HARRIS, W. V., 'Towards a Study of the Roman Slave Trade', in J. H. D'Arms and E. C. Koppf (eds.), *The Seaborne Commerce of Ancient Rome: Studies in Archaeology and History* (Memoirs of the American Academy in Rome, vol. 36, 1980), 117–40.
—— 'Child-Exposure in the Roman Empire', *JRS* 84 (1994), 1–22.
—— (ed.), *Mental Disorders in the Classical World* (Leiden, 2013) [=2013a].
—— 'Greek and Roman Hallucinations', in Harris (ed.), 2013a, 286–306 [=2013b].
HARRIS-MCCOY, D. E., *Artemidorus' Oneirocritica: Text, Translation, and Commentary* (Oxford, 2012).
HASEGAWA, K., *The Familia Urbana during the Early Empire: A Study of the Columbaria Inscriptions* (Oxford, 2005).
HEILEN, S., 'Zur Deutung und Datierung des, Löwenhoroskops' auf dem Nemrud Dağı', *EA* 38 (2005), 145–58.
—— 'Anubio Reconsidered', *Aestimatio*, 7 (2010), 127–92.
—— 'Some Metrical Fragments from Nechepsos and Petosiris', in Boehm and Hübner 2011, 23–93.
—— *Hadriani Genitura: Die astrologischen Fragmente des Antigonos von Nikaia*, 2 vols. (Berlin, 2015).
—— Review of C. De Stefani, *Ps.-Manethonis Apotelesmatica*, in *MHNH* 17 (2017), 220–38.
HENDERSON, J., *The Maculate Muse: Obscene Language in Attic Comedy* (New York, 1991).
HENGEL, M., *Crucifixion in the Ancient World and the Folly of the Message of the Cross*, transl. J. Bowden (London, 1977).
HENRICHS, A., '*Hieroi Logoi* and *Hierai Bibloi*: The (Un)written Margins of the Sacred in Ancient Greece', *HSCP* 101 (2003), 207–66.
HERMARY, A., 'Les noms de la statue chez Hérodote', in M.-Cl. Amouretti and P. Villard (eds.), Εὔκρατα: *Mélanges offerts à Claude Vatin* (Aix-en-Provence, 1994), 21–9.
HERRMANN-OTTO, E., *Ex ancilla natus: Untersuchungen zu den „hausgeborenen" Sklaven und Sklavinnen im Westen des Römischen Kaiserreiches* (Stuttgart, 1994).

HOLFORD-STREVENS, L., *Aulus Gellius: An Antonine Scholar and his Achievement* (Oxford, 2003).
HOLLERAN, C., *Shopping in Ancient Rome: The Retail Trade in the Late Republic and the Principate* (Oxford, 2012).
HOLMAN, S. R., *The Hungry are Dying: Beggars and Bishops in Roman Cappadocia* (Oxford, 2001).
HOPKINS, H. J. (ed.), *Ancient Textiles, Modern Science: Re-Creating Techniques through Experiment: Proceedings of the First and Second European Textile Forum* (Oxford, 2013).
HOPKINS, K., *Conquerors and Slaves* (Cambridge, 1978).
—— 'Conquest by Book', in C. Kelly (ed.), *Sociological Studies in Roman History* (Cambridge, 2017), 363–90.
HOUSMAN, A. E., 'Dorotheus of Sidon', in *The Classical Papers of A. E. Housman, Collected and Edited by J. Diggle and F. R. D. Goodyear, ii: 1897–1914* (Cambridge, 1972), 740–57.
HUBBARD, T. K., 'Hieron and the Ape in Pindar, *Pythian* 2.72–73', *TAPA* 120 (1990), 73–83.
HÜBNER, W., *Die Eigenschaften der Tierkreiszeichen in der Antike: Ihre Darstellung und Verwendung under besonderer Berücksichtigung des Manilius* (Wiesbaden, 1982).
—— 'Manilius als Astrologe und Dichter', *ANRW* II 32.1 (1984), 126–320.
—— 'Zur Verwendung und Umschreibung des Terminus ὡροσκόπος in der astrologischen Lehrdichtung der Antike', *MHNH*, 1 (2001), 219–38.
—— *Raum, Zeit und soziales Rollenspiel der vier Kardinalpunkte in der antiken Katarchenhoroskopie* (Leipzig, 2003).
—— 'Δωδεκατημόριον', in S. Harwardt and J. Schwind (eds.), *Corona Coronaria. Festschrift für Hans-Otto Kröner zum 75. Geburtstag* (Hildesheim, 2005), 189–217.
—— *Manilius, Astronomica, Buch V*, 2 vols. (Berlin, 2010).
HUGONIOT, C., HURLET, F., and MILANEZI, S. (eds.), *Le Statut de l'acteur dans l'Antiquité grecque et romaine* (Tours, 2004).
HUNTER, R., *The Measure of Homer: The Ancient Reception of the Iliad and the Odyssey* (Cambridge, 2018).
HUTCHINSON, G. O., 'Read the Instructions: Didactic Poetry and Didactic Prose', *CQ*² 59 (2009), 196–211.
HUTTUNEN, P., *The Social Strata in the Imperial City of Rome: A Quantitative Study of the Social Representation in the Epitaphs Published in the Corpus Inscriptionum Latinarum, Volumen VI* (Oulu, 1974).
IRBY, G. L. (ed.), *A Companion to Science, Technology, and Medicine in Ancient Greece and Rome*, i (Chichester, 2016).
JAMES, A. W., *Studies in the Language of Oppian of Cilicia: An Analysis of the New Formations in the Halieutica* (Amsterdam, 1970).
JANSON, T., *Latin Prose Prefaces: Studies in Literary Conventions* (Stockholm, 1964).
JENNISON, G., *Animals for Show and Pleasure in Ancient Rome* (Manchester, 1937, repr. Philadelphia, 2005).
JOHNSON, L. R., 'Aviaries and Aviculture in Ancient Rome' (Diss. Maryland, 1968).

JOHNSTON, S. I., *The Restless Dead: Encounters between the Living and the Dead in Ancient Greece* (Berkeley, 1999).
JONES, A. H. M., 'The Cloth Industry under the Roman Empire', *Economic History Review*, 13/2 (1960), 183–92.
JONG, A. DE, *Traditions of the Magi: Zoroastrianism in Greek and Latin Literature* (Leiden, 1997).
JOSHEL, S., *Work, Identity, and Legal Status in Rome: A Study of the Occupational Inscriptions* (Norman, OK, 1992).
KAPPARIS, K., 'The Terminology of Prostitution in the Ancient Greek World', in A. M. J. Glazebrook and M. M. Henry (eds.), *Greek Prostitutes in the Ancient Mediterranean, 800 BCE–200 CE* (Madison, WI, 2011), 222–55.
KASTER, R. A., *Guardians of Language: The Grammarian and Society in Late Antiquity* (Berkeley, CA, 1988).
KAY, N. M., *Epigrams from the Anthologia Latina: Text, Translation and Commentary* (London, 2006).
KEIL, J., and PREMERSTEIN, A. VON, *Bericht über eine Reise in Lydien und der südlichen Aiolis; Bericht über eine zweite (dritte) Reise in Lydien (und den angrenzenden Gebieten Ioniens)* (Vienna, 1908–14).
KEYDELL, R., *Kleine Schriften zur hellenistischen und spätgriechischen Dichtung (1911–1976)*, ed. W. Peek (Leipzig, 1982).
KIDD, D. A., *Aratus: Phaenomena. Edited with Introduction, Translation and Commentary* (Cambridge, 1997).
KIDD, S., 'Dreams in Bilingual Papyri from the Ptolemaic Period ', *BASP* 48 (2011), 111–30.
KING, H., *Hippocrates' Woman: Reading the Female Body in Ancient Greece* (London, 1998).
KLEES, H., 'Griechisches und Römisches in der Traumdeutung Artemidors für Herren und Sklaven', in C. Boerker and M. Donderer (eds.), *Das antike Rom und der Osten: Festschrift für Klaus Parlasca zum 65. Geburtstag* (Erlangen, 1990), 53–76.
KNEEBONE, E., *Oppian's Halieutica: Charting a Didactic Epic* (Cambridge, 2020).
KOELBING, H. M., and STETTLER-SCHÄR, A., 'Aussatz, Lepra, Elephantiasis Graecorum: Zur Geschichte der Lepra in Altertum', in H. M. Koelbing, M. Schär-Send, A. Stettler-Schär, and H. Trümpy (eds.), *Beiträge zur Geschichte der Lepra* (Zurich, 1972), 34–54.
KOTANSKY, R. D., 'Greek Exorcistic Amulets', in M. W. Meyer and P. A. Mirecki (eds.), *Ancient Magic and Ritual Power* (Leiden, 1995), 243–77.
KRAUSE, J.-U., *Gefängnisse im Römischen Reich* (Stuttgart, 1996).
KRENKEL, W. A., 'Fellatio and Irrumatio', *WZRostock*, 29 (1980), 77–88.
KRÜGER, J., 'Terminologie der künstlichen Wasserläufe in den Papyri des griechisch-römischen Ägypten', *MBAH* 10/2 (1991), 18–27.
KRUSE, T., 'The Magistrate and the Ocean: Acclamations and Ritualised Communication in Town Gatherings in Roman Egypt', in E. Stavrianopoulou (ed.), *Ritual and Communication in the Graeco-Roman World* (Liège, 2006), 297–315.
KUDLIEN, F., 'Empticius servus: Bemerkungen zum antiken Sklavenmarkt', *Historia*, 35 (1986), 240–56.
—— *Sklaven-Mentalität im Spiegel antiker Wahrsagerei* (Stuttgart, 1991).

Kuhn, A. B., 'The Chrysophoria in the Cities of Greece and Asia Minor in the Hellenistic and Roman Periods', *Tyche*, 29 (2014), 51–88.

Kuhn, C. T., 'Emotionality in the Political Culture of the Graeco-Roman East: The Role of Acclamations', in A. Chaniotis (ed.), *Unveiling Emotions: Sources and Methods for the Study of Emotions in the Greek World* (Stuttgart, 2012), 295–316.

Kyle, D. G., *Spectacles of Death in Ancient Rome* (London, 1998).

La Roche, J., 'Zur Prosodie und Metrik der späteren Epiker', *WS* 22 (1900), 35–55.

Laes, C., Goodey, C. F., and Rose, M. L. (eds.), *Disabilities in Roman Antiquity: Disparate Bodies, A Capite ad Calcem* (Leiden, 2013).

Lane Fox, R., *The Invention of Medicine: From Homer to Hippocrates* (London, 2020).

Larsson Lovén, L., 'Women, Trade, and Production in Urban Centres of Roman Italy', in Wilson and Flohr (eds.), 200–21.

László, L., 'Rhetorius, Zeno's Astrologer, and a Sixth-Century Astrological Compendium', *DOP* 74 (2020), 329–50.

Lau, O., *Schuster und Schusterhandwerk in der griechisch-römischen Literatur und Kunst* (Bonn, 1967).

Legras, B., *Les Reclus grecs du Sarapieion de Memphis: Une enquête sur l'hellénisme égyptien* (Louvain, 2011).

Lehrs, K., *De Aristarchi Studiis Homericis* (Leipzig, ²1865).

Lhôte, E., *Les Lamelles oraculaires de Dodone* (Geneva, 2006).

Liebeschuetz, J. H. W. G., *Continuity and Change in Roman Religion* (Oxford, 1979).

Lightfoot, J. L., *Parthenius of Nicaea* (Oxford, 1999).

—— *Lucian: On the Syrian Goddess* (Oxford, 2003).

—— *The Sibylline Oracles: With Introduction, Translation, and Commentary on the First and Second Books* (Oxford, 2007).

—— *Dionysius Periegetes, Description of the Known World: With Introduction, Text, Translation, and Commentary* (Oxford, 2014).

Lis, C., and Soly, H., 'Work, Identity and Self-Representation in the Roman Empire and the West-European Middle Ages: Different Interplays between the Social and the Cultural', in Verboven and Laes (eds.), 261–89.

Loraux, N., 'Ponos: Sur quelques difficultés de la peine comme nom du travail', in *Annali del seminario di studi del mondo classico* (Sezione di Archeologia e Storia antica), 4 (1982), 171–92.

Ludwich, A., *Maximi et Ammonis carminum de actionum auspiciis reliquiae. Accedunt anecdota astrologica* (Leipzig, 1877).

—— *Aristarchs Homerische Textkritik nach den Fragmenten des Didymos dargestellt und beurtheilt*, ii (Leipzig, 1885).

—— 'Das elegische Lehrgedicht des Astrologen Anubion und die Manethoniana', *Philologus*, 63 (1904), 116–34.

Ma, J., 'The Two Cultures: Connoisseurship and Civic Honours', *Art History*, 29 (2006), 325–38.

Maass, E., *Commentariorum in Aratum Reliquiae* (Berlin, 1898).

McGinn, T. A. J., *The Economy of Prostitution in the Roman World: A Study of Social History and the Brothel* (Ann Arbor, MI, 2014).

MacLean, R., *Freed Slaves and Roman Imperial Culture: Social Integration and the Transformation of Values* (Cambridge, 2018).
Magnelli, E., *Studi su Euforione* (Rome, 2002).
—— 'The Nonnian Hexameter', in D. Accorinti (ed.), *Brill's Companion to Nonnus of Panopolis* (Leiden, 2016), 353–71.
Manchester, K., 'Leprosy: The Origin and Development of the Disease in Antiquity', in D. Gourevitch (ed.), *Maladie et maladies: Histoire et conceptualisation: Mélanges en l'honneur de Mirko Grmek* (Geneva, 1992), 31–49.
Mark, S. E., 'Alexander the Great, Seafaring, and the Spread of Leprosy', *Journal of the History of Medicine and Allied Sciences*, 57/3 (2002) 285–311.
Marquardt, J., *Das Privatleben der Römer*, i (Leipzig, 1879).
Martínez-Hernández, M., 'El campo léxico de los sustantivos de dolor en Sófocles: Ensayo de semántica estructural funcional, I', *CFC* 13 (1977), 33–112.
Mason, H. J., *Greek Terms for Roman Institutions: A Lexicon and Analysis* (Toronto, 1974).
Massimilla, G., 'Sul testo dello pseudo-Manetone, *Apotelesmatica* 4.420-424', *Prometheus*, 46 (2020), 264–71.
Mavroudi, M., *A Byzantine Book on Dream Interpretation: The Oneirocriticon of Achmet and its Arabic Sources* (Leiden, 2002).
Mayer, E., *The Ancient Middle Classes: Urban Life and Aesthetics in the Roman Empire, 100 BCE–250 CE* (Cambridge, MA, 2012).
Mayser, E., *Grammatik der griechischen Papyri aus der Ptolemäerzeit: Mit Einschluß der gleichzeitigen Ostraka und der in Ägypten verfaßten Inschriften*² (Berlin, 1935–); i/1 rev. H. Schmoll (Berlin, 1970).
Meinecke, B., 'Consumption (Tuberculosis) in Classical Antiquity', *Annals of Medical History*, 9/4 (1927), 379–402.
Merkelbach, R., and Stauber, J., *Steinepigramme aus dem griechischen Osten*, 5 vols. (Stuttgart, 1998–2004).
Millar, F., *The Emperor in the Roman World (31 BC–AD 337)* (London, 1977).
—— 'The World of the *Golden Ass*', *JRS* 71 (1981), 63–75.
Mommsen, T., *Beiträge zu der Lehre von den griechischen Präpositionen* (Berlin, 1895).
Mommsen, Th., *Römisches Strafrecht* (Leipzig, 1899).
Monaco, D., 'Il *Laur*. 28. 27 e il testo degli *Apotelesmatica* di Manetone: Pluralità testuale e attività esegetica', *BollClass* 34 (2013), 37–76.
Monteix, N., and Tran, N. (eds.), *Les Savoirs professionnels des gens de métier: Études sur le monde du travail dans les sociétés urbaines de l'Empire romain* (Naples, 2011).
Monteventi, V., *La Poésie astrologique dans la littérature grecque et latine* (Basel, 2020).
Morgan, T., *Roman Faith and Christian Faith: Pistis and Fides in the Early Roman Empire and Early Churches* (Oxford, 2015).
Morley, N., *Theories, Models and Concepts in Ancient History* (London, 2004).
Moyer, I., *Egypt and the Limits of Hellenism* (Cambridge, 2011).
Naether, F., *Die Sortes Astrampsychi: Problemlösungsstrategien durch Orakel im römischen Ägypten* (Tübingen, 2010).
—— and Thissen, H.-J., 'Genesis einer Aretalogie: Anmerkungen zu einer Neuedition von P.Oxy. XI 1381', in P. Schubert (ed.), *Actes du 26ᵉ Congrès International de Papyrologie: Genève, 16–21 août 2010* (Geneva, 2012), 559–63.

NELSON, M., 'Narcissus: Myth and Magic', *CJ* 95 (2000), 363–89.
NERI, V., *I marginali nell'Occidente tardoantico: Poveri, 'infames' e criminali nella nascente società cristiana* (Bari, 1998).
NES, D. VAN, 'Die maritime Bildersprache des Aischylos' (Diss. Groningen, 1963).
NESSELRATH, H.-G., *Lukians Parasitendialog: Untersuchungen und Kommentar* (Berlin, 1985).
NEUGEBAUER, O., and VAN HOESEN, H. B., *Greek Horoscopes* (Philadelphia, 1959).
NIETO IBÁÑEZ, J.-M., *El hexámetro de los Oráculos sibilinos* (Amsterdam, 1992).
NIJF, O. M. VAN, *The Civic World of Professional Associations in the Roman East* (Amsterdam, 1997).
—— 'Inscriptions and Civic Memory in the Roman East', in A. E. Cooley (ed.), *The Afterlife of Inscriptions: Reusing, Rediscovering, Reinventing and Revitalizing Ancient Inscriptions*, BICS Suppl. 75 (2000), 21–36.
—— 'Affective Politics: The Emotional Regime in the Imperial City', in A. Chaniotis and P. Ducrey (eds.), *Unveiling Emotions*, ii: *Emotions in Greece and Rome: Texts, Images, Material Culture* (Stuttgart, 2013), 351–68.
—— 'Civic Mirrors: Honorific Inscriptions and the Politics of Prestige', in A. B. Kuhn (ed.), *Social Status and Prestige in the Graeco-Roman World* (Stuttgart, 2015), 233–45.
OGDEN, D., *Greek and Roman Necromancy* (Princeton, 2001).
—— *Magic, Witchcraft, and Ghosts in the Greek and Roman Worlds: A Sourcebook* (Oxford, 2002, ²2009).
OLESON, J. P., *The Oxford Handbook of Engineering and Technology in the Classical World* (Oxford, 2008).
OLSON, K. 'Masculinity, Appearance, and Sexuality: Dandies in Roman Antiquity', *Journal of the History of Sexuality*, 23 (2014), 182–205.
—— *Masculinity and Dress in Roman Antiquity* (Abingdon, 2017).
ORLANDO, C., and TORRE, R., 'Lessico astronomico-astrologico greco', in P. Radici Colace and M. Caccamo Caltabiano (eds.), *Atti del I seminario di studi sui lessici tecnici greci e latini (Messina, 8–10 marzo 1990)* (Messina, 1991), 291–309.
OSBORNE, R., 'Introduction: Roman Poverty in Context', in Atkins and Osborne, 1–20.
OVERDUIN, F., *Nicander of Colophon's Theriaca: A Literary Commentary* (Leiden, 2015).
PACKMAN, Z. M., 'Instructions for the Use of Planet Markers on a Horoscope Board', *ZPE* 74 (1988), 85–95.
PADEL, R., *In and Out of the Mind: Greek Images of the Tragic Self* (Princeton, 1992).
PALMER, L. R., *A Grammar of the Post-Ptolemaic Papyri*, i: *Accidence and Word-Formation*, 1: *The Suffixes* (London, 1945).
PANCIERA, S., and ZANKER, P., 'Il ritratto e l'iscrizione di L. Licinius Nepos', *RPAA* 61 (1988-9), 357–84, repr. in S. Panciera, *Epigrafi, epigrafia, epigrafisti: Scritti vari editi e inediti (1956–2005) con note complementari e indici* (Rome, 2006), 377–97.
PANGAS, J. C., 'Birth Malformations in Babylonia and Assyria', in *American Journal of Medical Genetics*, 91 (2000), 318–21.
PARKER, R., 'Seeking Advice from Zeus at Dodona', *G&R* 63 (2016), 69–90.
PARKIN, A., '"You Do Him No service": An Exploration of Pagan Almsgiving', in Atkins and Osborne, 60–82.

PATLAGEAN, E., *Pauvreté économique et pauvreté sociale à Byzance, 4ᵉ–7ᵉ siècles* (Paris, 1977).
PERALE, M., *Adespota Papyracea Hexametra Graeca (APHex I): Hexameters of Unknown or Uncertain Authorship from Graeco-Roman Egypt* (Berlin, 2020).
PETRIDOU, G., *Divine Epiphany in Greek Literature and Culture* (Oxford, 2016).
PETRIKOVITS, H. V., 'Die Spezialisierung des römischen Handwerks, I', in H. Jankuhn, W. Janssen, R. Schmidt-Wiegand, and H. Teifenbach (eds.), *Das Handwerk in vor- und frühgeschichtlicher Zeit*, i: *Historische und rechtshistorische Beiträge und Untersuchungen zur Frühgeschichte der Gilde* (Göttingen, 1981), 63–132.
PINGREE, D., 'Antiochus and Rhetorius', *CP* 72 (1977), 203–23.
—— *The Yavanajātaka of Sphujidhvaja*, 2 vols. (Cambridge, MA, 1978).
PLEKET, H. W., 'Urban Elites and the Economy in the Greek Cities in the Roman Empire', *MBAH* 3/1 (1984), 3–36.
—— 'Labour and Unemployment in the Roman Empire: Some Preliminary Remarks', in Weiler and Graßl, 267–76 [= Pleket 1988].
—— 'The Social Status of Physicians in the Graeco-Roman World', *Clio Medica*, 27 (1995), 27–34.
POBLOME, J., 'Comparing Ordinary Craft Production: Textile and Pottery Production in Roman Asia Minor', *Journal of the Economic and Social History of the Orient*, 47 (2004), 491–506.
POMEROY, A. J., 'Status and Status-Concern in the Greco-Roman Dream-Books', *AncSoc* 22 (1991), 51–74.
PRÉVOT, A., 'Verbes grecs relatifs à la vision et noms de l'œil', *RPh*³ 9 (1935), 133–60, 233–79.
PRUNETI, P., 'Frammento di "didaskalike" ', *MPhL* 2 (1977), 43–8.
PURCELL, N., 'Eating Fish: The Paradoxes of Seafood', in Wilkins *et al.* (eds.), 132–49.
QUACK, J. F., 'Imhotep—Der Weise, der zum Gott wurde', in V. M. Lepper (ed.), *Persönlichkeiten aus dem Alten Ägypten im Neuen Museum* (Berlin, 2014), 43–66.
—— and RYHOLT, K. S. B., *Demotic Literary Texts from Tebtunis and Beyond* (Copenhagen, 2019).
QUINTANA ORIVE, E., 'CTh.10.20: Acerca del régimen jurídico de los *gynaeciarii, murileguli, monetarii* y *bastagarii* en época postclásica', *Revue internationale des droits de l'Antiquité*, 53 (2006), 335–43.
RAALTE, M. VAN, *Rhythm and Metre: Towards a Systematic Description of Greek Stichic Verse* (Assen-Maastricht, 1986).
RAMSAY, W. M., *Cities and Bishoprics of Phrygia, Vol. 1 Part II: West and West-Central Phrygia* (Oxford, 1897).
RASMUSSEN, S. C. (ed.), *Chemical Technology in Antiquity* (Oxford, 2015).
REDEN, S. VON, 'Arbeit und Zivilisation: Kriterien der Selbstdefinition im antiken Athen', *MBAH* 11/1 (1992), 1–31.
REINARD, P., '... et ceras mille ad usus vitae': Wachs und seine ökonomische Bedeutung nach literarischen und papyrologischen Quellen', *MBAH* 37 (2019), 225–59.
REITZENSTEIN, R., *Die hellenistischen Mysterienreligionen nach ihren Grundgedanken und Wirkungen*² (Leipzig, 1920).

Renberg, G., *Where Dreams May Come: Incubation Sanctuaries in the Greco-Roman World*, 2 vols. (Leiden, 2016).
Reynolds, J., and Tannenbaum, R., *Jews and God-Fearers at Aphrodisias: Greek Inscriptions with Commentary* (Cambridge, 1987).
Richlin, A., *The Garden of Priapus: Sexuality and Aggression in Roman Humor* (New York, ²1992).
Ricl, M., 'Legal and Social Status of *Threptoi* and Related Categories in Narrative and Documentary Sources', in H. M. Cotton, R. G. Hoyland, J. J. Price, and D. J. Wasserstein (eds.), *From Hellenism to Islam: Cultural and Linguistic Change in the Roman Near East* (Cambridge, 2009), 93–114.
Riess, E., 'Nechepsonis et Petosiridis fragmenta magica', *Philologus Supplementband*, 6 (1892), 325–94.
Riggs, C., *The Beautiful Burial in Roman Egypt: Art, Identity, and Funerary Religion* (Oxford, 2005).
—— (ed.), *The Oxford Handbook of Roman Egypt* (Oxford, 2012).
Rizzini, I., *L'occhio parlante: Per una semiotica dello sguardo nel mondo antico* (Venice, 1998).
Robert, J., 'Épigramme de Chios', *REG* 80 (1967), 282–91.
Robert, L., 'Epigraphica VIII. Au théâtre de Delphes', *REG* 42 (1929), 433–8.
—— 'Ἀρχαιολόγος', *REG* 49 (1936), 235–54.
—— *Études anatoliennes: Recherches sur les inscriptions grecques de l'Asie Mineure* (Paris, 1937).
—— *Études épigraphiques et philologiques* (Paris, 1938).
—— *Les Gladiateurs dans l'Orient grec* (Paris, 1940) = 1940*a*.
—— 'ΘΗΡΙΟΔΕΙΚΤΗΣ', *Hellenica*, 1 (1940), 132–42 = 1940*b*.
—— 'Épigramme d'Égine', *Hellenica*, 4 (1948), 5–34.
—— 'Épitaphes et acclamations byzantines à Corinthe', *Hellenica*, 11–12 (1960), 21–52 [= 1960*a*].
—— 'Addenda aux tomes i–x', *Hellenica*, 11–12 (1960), 542–95 [= 1960*b*].
—— 'Enterrements et épitaphes', *AC* 37 (1968), 406–48.
—— 'Noms de métiers dans des documents byzantins', Χαριστήριον *An. K. Orlandos*, I (1964), 324–47 = *OMS* ii. (Paris, 1969), 915–38.
—— 'Documents d'Asie Mineure', *BCH* 102 (1978), 395–543.
—— 'Une vision de Perpétue martyre à Carthage en 203', *CRAI* 126 (1982), 228–76.
—— and Robert, J., *La Carie*, ii: *Le Plateau de Tabai et ses environs* (Paris, 1954).
Roberts, M., *The Jeweled Style: Poetry and Poetics in Late Antiquity* (Ithaca, NY, 1989).
Rodríguez-Álvarez, E., 'The Hidden Divers: Sponge Harvesting in the Archaeological Record of the Mediterranean Basin', in E. Emery (ed.), *The Global Life of Sponges: Proceedings of the International Sponges Conference [SOAS, University of London], Island of Hydra, Greece, 19–20 May 2018* (London, 2020), 69–83.
Rollinger, R., Lang, M., and Barta, H. (eds.), *Strafe und Strafrecht in den antiken Welten: Unter Berücksichtigung von Todesstrafe, Hinrichtung und peinlicher Befragung* (Wiesbaden, 2012).
Roskam, G., 'John Chrysostom on Pagan Euergetism: A Reading of the First Part of *De inani gloria et de educandis liberis*', *Sacris Erudiri*, 53 (2014), 147–69.

ROUECHÉ, C., *Aphrodisias in Late Antiquity: The Late Roman and Byzantine Inscriptions Including Texts from the Excavations at Aphrodisias Conducted by Kenan T. Erim* (London, 1989).
—— 'From Aphrodisias to Stauropolis', in J. F. Drinkwater and R. W. B. Salway (eds.), *Wolf Liebeschuetz Reflected: Essays Presented by Colleagues, Friends, & Pupils* (London, 2007), 183–92.
RÜEDI, E. H., 'Vom ἑλλανοδίκας zum ἀλλαντοπώλης: Eine Studie zu den verbalen Rektionskomposita auf -ας/-ης' (Diss. Zurich, 1969).
RUFFING, K., 'Die Berufsbezeichnungen auf -πώλης und -πράτης in der epigraphischen Überlieferung', *MBAH* 21/1 (2002), 16–58.
—— 'Die Selbstdarstellung von Händlern und Handwerkern in den griechischen Inschriften', *MBAH* 23/2 (2004) 85–102.
—— *Die berufliche Spezialisierung in Handel und Handwerk: Untersuchungen zu ihrer Entwicklung und zu ihren Bedingungen in der römischen Kaiserzeit im östlichen Mittelmeerraum auf der Grundlage griechischer Inschriften und Papyri* (Rahden, 2008).
—— 'Körperstrafen und Gesellschaft im Römischen Reich', in Rollinger *et al.* (eds.), 77–93 [= Ruffing 2012].
SEAFORD, R., 'Politics of the Mystic Chorus', in J. Billings, F. Budelmann, and F. Macintosh (eds.), *Choruses, Ancient and Modern* (Oxford, 2013), 261–80.
SCHEER, T. S., *Die Gottheit und ihr Bild: Untersuchungen zur Funktion griechischer Kultbilder in Religion und Politik* (Munich, 2000).
SCHEIDEL, W., 'The Roman Slave Supply', in Bradley and Cartledge (eds.), 287–310.
SCHERBERICH, K., 'Zur sozialen Bewertung der Arbeit bei Cicero, De officiis 1. 150f.', in D. Dormeyer, F. Siegert, *et al.* (eds.), *Arbeit in der Antike, in Judentum und Christentum* (Münster, 2006), 86–97.
SCHMIDT, A., *Drogen und Drogenhandel im Altertum* (Leipzig, 1924, repr. New York, 1979).
SCHUBERT, P., 'Le papyrus de Genève inv. 268: Un nouveau fragment du poème astrologique d'Anoubion, précurseur de Firmicus Maternus', *CRAI* janvier-mars 2009, 399–432.
SERGHIDOU, A. (ed.), *Fear of Slaves—Fear of Enslavement in the Ancient Mediterranean/ Peur de l'esclave—peur de l'esclavage en Méditerranée ancienne (discours, représentations, pratiques): Actes du XXIXᵉ colloque du Groupe international de recherche sur l'esclavage dans l'Antiquité (GIREA), Rethymnon, 4–7 novembre 2004* (Besançon, 2007).
SÉRIDA, R., 'Cultural Memory and Motifs of Magician Heroes from Ancient to Islamic Egypt', in R. Nyord and K. Ryholt (eds.), *Lotus and Laurel: Studies on Egyptian Language and Religion in Honour of Paul John Frandsen* (Copenhagen, 2015), 351–72.
SISTAKOU, E., and RENGAKOS, A. (eds.), *Dialect, Diction, and Style in Greek Literary and Inscribed Epigram* (Berlin, 2016).
SORIGA, E., 'A Diachronic View on Fulling Technology in the Mediterranean and the Ancient Near East: Tools, Raw Materials and Natural Resources for the Finishing of Textiles', in S. Gaspa, M. Cécile, and M.-L. Nosch (eds.), *Textile Terminologies from the Orient to the Mediterranean and Europe, 1000 BC–1000 AD* (Lincoln, NE, 2017), 24–46.

SOURVINOU-INWOOD, C., *Reading Greek Death: To the End of the Classical Period* (Oxford, 1995).
SPANOUDAKIS, K., 'Manethoniana', *Yearbook of Ancient Greek Epic Online*, 1 (2016), 206-9. https://brill.com/view/journals/yago/1/1/article-p206_9.xml?language=en
STANLEY, C. D., 'Paul and Homer: Greco-Roman Citation Practice in the First Century CE', *NT* 32 (1990), 48-78.
STEGEMANN, V., *Die Fragmente des Dorotheos von Sidon*, 2 vols. (Heidelberg, 1939-43).
STERN, E. M., 'Roman Glassblowing in a Cultural Context', *AJA* 103 (1999), 441-84.
STOL, M., 'Leprosy: New Light from Greek and Babylonian Sources', *JVEG* 30 (1987-8), 22-31.
—— *Epilepsy in Babylonia* (Groningen, 1993).
STONEMAN, R., ERICKSON, K., and NETTON, I. R. (eds.), *The Alexander Romance in Persia and the East* (Groningen, 2012).
STRAUS, J. A., 'L'esclavage dans l'Égypte romaine', *ANRW* X/1 (1988), 841-911.
—— *L'Achat et la vente des esclaves dans l'Égypte romaine: Contribution papyrologique à l'étude de l'esclavage dans une province orientale de l'empire romain* (Leipzig, 2004).
TEDESCHI, G., 'Lo spettacolo in età ellenistica e tardo antica nella documentazione epigrafica e papiracea', *Papyrologica Lupiensia*, 11 (2002), 87-187.
—— *Intrattenimenti e spettacoli nell'Egitto ellenistico-romano* (Trieste, 2011).
TEMKIN, O., *The Falling Sickness: A History of Epilepsy from the Greeks to the Beginnings of Modern Neurology* (Baltimore and London, ^{2}1971).
THESLEFF, H. (ed.), *The Pythagorean Texts of the Hellenistic Period* (Åbo, 1965).
THOMPSON, D., 'Slavery in the Hellenistic World', in Bradley and Cartledge (eds.), 194-213.
THONEMANN, P. J., *An Ancient Dream Manual: Artemidorus' The Interpretation of Dreams* (Oxford, 2020).
—— *Lucian: Alexander or the False Prophet* (Oxford, 2021).
TRAN, N., 'Les gens de métier romains: Savoirs professionnels et supériorités plébéiennes', in Monteix and Tran (eds.), 119-33 [= Tran 2011].
—— *Dominus Tabernae: Le Statut de travail des artisans et des commerçants de l'Occident romain (Ier siècle av. J.-C. – IIIe siècle ap. J.-C.)* (Rome, 2013).
—— '*Ars* and *Doctrina*: The Socioeconomic Identity of Roman Skilled Workers (First Century BC-Third Century AD)', in Verboven and Laes (eds.), 246-61 [= Tran 2017].
TRAPP, M. B., *Maximus of Tyre: The Philosophical Orations* (Oxford, 1997).
TREGGIARI, S., *Roman Freedmen during the Late Republic* (Oxford, 1969).
—— 'Jobs in the Household of Livia', *PBSR* 43 (1975), 48-77.
—— 'Urban Labour in Rome: *Mercennarii* and *Tabernarii*', in Garnsey (ed.), 1980, 48-64.
TYRWHITT, T., Περὶ Λίθων. *De lapidibus, poema Orpheo a quibusdam adscriptum, græce et latine, ex editione Jo. Matthiæ Gesneri. Recensuit notasque adjecit Thomas Tyrwhitt. Simul prodit Auctarium dissertationis de Babrio* (London, 1781).
VARGA, R., 'The Professionals of the Latin West: Encoding the Occupational Titles', in Cupcea and Varga (eds.), 9-21.

VENDRIES, C., 'L'auceps, les gluaux et l'appeau: À propos de la ruse et de l'habileté du chasseur d'oiseaux', in J. Trinquier and C. Vendries (eds.), *Chasses antiques: Pratiques et représentations dans le monde gréco-romain* (Rennes, 2009), 119–40.

VENTICINQUE, P., *Honor among Thieves: Craftsmen, Merchants, and Associations in Roman and Late Roman Egypt* (Ann Arbor, MI, 2016).

VERBOVEN, K., and LAES, C. (eds.), *Work, Labour, and Professions in the Roman World* (Leiden, 2017).

VERNANT, J.-P., *Myth and Thought Among the Greeks* (New York, 2006).

VERSNEL, H. S., *Inconsistencies in Greek and Roman Religion: 1. Ter Unus: Isis, Dionysos, Hermes: Three Studies in Henotheism* (Leiden, 1990).

VEYNE, P., transl. A. Goldhammer, *A History of Private Life, I: From Pagan Rome to Byzantium* (Cambridge, MA, 1987).

—— 'Histoire de Rome', *Annuaire du Collège de France*, 1990–1, 721–7.

—— 'La "plèbe moyenne" sous le Haut-Empire romain', *Annales. Histoire, Sciences Sociales*, 55 (2000), 1169–99.

—— *L'Empire gréco-romain* (Paris, 2005).

VIAN, F., *Les Argonautiques orphiques* (Paris, 1987).

VISMARA, C., 'Sangue e arena: Iconografie di supplizi in margine a *Du châtiment dans la cité*', *Dialoghi di archeologia*, ser. 3, 5 (1987), 135–55.

VOGT, J., transl. T. Wiedemann, *Ancient Slavery and the Ideal of Man* (Oxford, 1974).

WEBB, R., *Demons and Dancers: Performance in Late Antiquity* (Cambridge, MA, 2008).

—— 'Mime and the Dangers of Laughter in Late Antiquity', in M. Alexiou and D. Cairns (eds.), *Greek Laughter and Tears: Antiquity and After* (Edinburgh, 2017), 219–31.

WEILER, I., and GRASSL, H. (eds.), *Soziale Randgruppen und Außenseiter im Alterum: Referate vom Symposion „Soziale Randgruppen und antike Sozialpolitik" in Graz (21. bis 23. September 1987)* (Graz, 1988).

WELBORN, L. L., 'μωρὸς γενέσθω: Paul's Appropriation of the Role of the Fool in 1 Corinthians 1–4', in *Biblical Interpretation*, 10 (2002), 420–35.

—— *Paul, the Fool of Christ: A Study of 1 Corinthians 1–4 in the Comic-Philosophical Tradition* (London, 2005).

WEST, M. L., *Greek Metre* (Oxford, 1982).

—— *Ancient Greek Music* (Oxford, 1992).

—— *Indo-European Poetry and Myth* (Oxford, 2007).

WIEMKEN, H., *Der griechische Mimus: Dokumente zur Geschichte des antiken Volkstheaters* (Bremen, 1972).

WILKINS, J., HARVEY, D., DOBSON, M., and DAVIDSON, A. (eds.), *Food in Antiquity* (Exeter, 1995).

WILLIAMS, C. A., *Roman Homosexuality: Ideologies of Masculinity in Classical Antiquity* (New York, 1999).

WILSON, A., and FLOHR, M. (eds.), *Urban Craftsmen and Traders in the Roman World* (Oxford, 2016).

WINKLER, A., 'On the Astrological Papyri from the Tebtunis Temple Library', in G. Widmer and D. Devauchelle (eds.), *Actes du IXe Congrès international des études démotiques, Paris, 31 août–3 septembre 2005* (Cairo, 2009), 361–75.

—— 'Some Astrologers and their Handbooks in Demotic Egyptian', in J. M. Steele (ed.), *The Circulation of Astronomical Knowledge in the Ancient World* (Leiden, 2016), 245–86.

YOUTIE, H., 'Notes on O. Mich. I', *TAPA* 71 (1940), 623–59 = *Scriptiunculae*, i (Amsterdam, 1973), 63–104.

ZELNICK-ABRAMOVITZ, R., *Not Wholly Free: The Concept of Manumission and the Status of Manumitted Slaves in the Ancient Greek World* (Leiden, 2005).

ZIMMER, G., *Römische Berufsdarstellungen* (Berlin, 1982).

—— 'Römische Handwerker', *ANRW* II 12.3 (1985), 205–28.

ZITO, N., *Maxime, Des Initiatives* (Paris, 2016).

ZUIDERHOECK, A., 'The Ambiguity of Munificence', *Historia*, 56 (2007), 196–213.

Index of Passages Discussed

GREEK AUTHORS

Apollonius Rhodius
Argonautica
1.1099 517
2.254–5 900
4.398 798
4.697–8 900

Aratus
Phaenomena
11 512
90 518
97 685
125–6 860
189 716
202–4 160 n. 91
364–6 160 n. 91
401 157 n. 78
460–1 573
532–3 510–11
607 518
773 551
816 824
983–4 944

Artemidorus
Oneirocriticon
1 Praef. 2 102
1.35.5 105
1.53 108
1.64.6 104
1.74.3 104
1.76.4 800
1.78.5 93 n. 50
2.20.3 36 n. 8
2.24.4 104
2.30.4 32
2.33.2 102
2.42 104
2.53.1 949
2.68.1 902 n. 73
2.70.12 755
3.30 104
3.54 104
4.30.3 105
4.49 949
4.77.1 121 n. 57
5.25 104
5.63 790 n. 50
5.84 790 n. 50

Callimachus
Fragmenta (ed. Harder, Pfeiffer)
7c.5–6 507
67.8 682
54.3 931
383.10 551
533 648

Epigrams
5.3 798
55.3–4 690

Hymns
3.59–61 556
3.175 780
4.36 798
4.120 816
4.213 798
4.311 646

Dio Chrysostom
Orationes
7.110 63, 64
7.118 68
7.122 70
7.125 63
33.4 1066
66.2 985

Dorotheus
p. 324.21–4 670, 842
p. 326.6 736
p. 326.13–14 891, 972
p. 328.6 845
p. 335.2 941
p. 338.30 905
p. 342.25 72 n. 160
pp. 368.25–369.3 543, 894, 895
p. 383.8 519
p. 386.11–12 538
p. 386.19 542, 558
pp. 389.21–390.3 89
p. 394.6 361 n. 96
p. 394.9 538

1088 Index of Passages Discussed

p. 395.14–19 913
p. 398.3 804
p. 398.12 941
p. 398.15 685
p. 399.10 858
p. 403.33–4 695 n. 294
p. 406.33–5 913
p. 413.28 81
pp. 416.19–417.10 88
p. 417.5–10 88–9
p. 428.25 758
p. 428.102 594
p. 428.121 603
p. 430.124 591
p. 431 130

HEPHAESTION

Apotelesmatica
i. 3.29 518
i. 14.4 18–19 n. 2
i. 14.5 23
i. 14.7 20
i. 25.27–26.1 561
i. 28.9–11 20–1
i. 28.18 792
i. 68.9 603
i. 102.9–11 270–1, 276, 809
i. 155.12 21 n. 10
i. 240.3 121 n. 37
i. 256.3–6 22
i. 330.25–331.3 842
i. 330.25–6 271

HESIOD

Opera et Dies
5–7 841
151 556
162–5 796
177 746
197–201 860
210 955
230 706
307 549
315 562
383–4 158 n. 83
473 680
491 943
661 988

Theogony
40 337 n. 47, 876, 926, 991
83–4 877
89 845
104 860
180–1 219, 595, 790

188 789
433 860

HOMER

Iliad
1.5 588
1.255 736
1.317 824
2.212 723
2.217 554
2.224 555
2.599 960
2.669 827
3.11 694
3.33 901
3.213 757
4.235 817
4.441 795
4.471 901, 938, 939
5.31 = 455 797
5.73 527
5.307 942
5.599 911
5.631 794
5.639 710
5.882 782
6.147–9 874, 875, 877
6.236 336, 879
6.488–9 824, 874, 875, 878
6.491 946
7.158 761
7.221 639
9.63 530
9.77 769
9.325–6 755
9.544 582
9.648 = 16.59 950
10.11 690
10.29–30 941
10.491 714
11.416 940
12.433 552
12.435 780
13.6 552
13.62 933
13.602 846
14.80 872
14.403 855
15.325 605
15.411 726
15.605 893
15.628 814
16.33–5 801
16.160 674

Index of Passages Discussed

16.329 807
16.352 610
16.489 939
17.20 941
17.51 839
17.136 23
17.547, 551, 582
17.558 588
18.474 613
18.484 828
18.549 679
19.25 727
19.128 878
19.374 704
20.294 769
20.483 527
21.22 924
21.257–9 219, 608
21.361 843
21.445 689
22.72 669
22.94 937
22.135 892
22.209 509
22.263 610
22.335–6 588
22.411 893
23.261 556
23.338 931
23.422 550
23.589 644
24.210 754

Odyssey
1.7, 8–9 878 n. 48
1.32–4 878 n. 48
1.204 694
1.357 946
2.306 292 n. 35, 849
2.341 803–4
4.150 556
4.220–1 813
4.248 215, 596
4.404 648
5.240 640
5.250 640
5.270–1 666
5.272–5 922
5.371 931
5.473 799
6.232–5 = 23.159–62 336, 879
7.197–8 215, 742
8.246 773
9.120–1 605
9.144–5 523

10.11 631
10.212 744
10.510 799
11.17 895
11.38 953
11.278 219, 745, 842
11.319–20 974
11.588 799
11.611 952
12.27 534 n. 37
12.252 604
13.255 794
14.39 15
14.278 856
14.532 744
15.343 596
16.265 827
17.266 739
17.322–3 94
17.597 668
18.26 757
18.54 215, 736
18.292 952
19.408 732
20.346 782
22.448 574
23.350 524
24.163 754
24.303 758

Homeric Hymns
To Aphrodite
133 292 n. 36, 792

To Apollo
532 788

To Demeter
136 767
383 522

To Hermes
413 782
511 625
544 1061

Maximus
13 706
145 620
166 910
169 851
198 854
209 713
220–1 315
258 702
380 87

448 855
474 846
498 948
552 519

NECHEPSO-PETOSIRIS

fr. 1 Riess 865
fr. 12 Riess 73 n. 4
fr. +27 Heilen 960
fr. 28 Riess 863 n. 5, 894
frr. 37-9 Riess 866 n. 16

NICANDER

Theriaca

134 937
182-3 939
232 938
334 938
436 939
677 615
923-4 556

NONNUS

Dionysiaca

6.76-7 647, 1003
18.228 790, 1003

PLATO

Charmides

163 B-D 176

Ion

530 B 877

Leges

6.777 D-E 91
10.885 B 817

Phaedo

81 D 832

Timaeus

35 A 723
37 E-38 B 747
38 B-C 747
41 A 575

PTOLEMY

Tetrabiblos

2.3.19 723
2.3.38 95, 689
2.3.41 559, 561
2.9.11 29
2.9.14 12
3.2.1-4 753-4
3.3.1 882
3.4.7 900
3.8 684
3.9.2-4 684, 688
3.9.4 792 n. 51
3.12.4 951, 973
3.12.7 537
3.13.5 537
3.13.10 791, 793
3.13.11 731, 732
3.13.14 958-9
3.13.17 701, 768, 770, 959
3.14 334, 993
3.14.5 590, 592, 678
3.14.11 621, 969
3.14.15 616, 722, 723, 724, 725
3.14.25 836, 974
3.14.28 689, 690, 722
3.14.29 678, 995
3.14.31 966, 967, 994
3.14.32 636, 722, 723, 725
3.14.34 709, 850, 995
3.15.5 13, 691
3.15.6 594
3.15.7-12 131, 733, 762, 946
3.15.9 653, 763-4
3.15.10 789
4.2.2 532, 558
4.3 131, 704
4.3.1 762
4.4.1 727, 771, 813
4.4.3 562, 568, 570, 592, 675, 728, 793
4.4.4 38, 54, 68, 574 n. 105, 617, 672
4.4.5 559, 606, 613, 614, 637, 641 n. 234, 664, 678, 689, 775, 779
4.4.6 569, 578, 590, 638, 645, 678, 775, 928, 1005
4.4.7 584, 638, 691
4.4.8 555, 637, 672, 676, 812
4.4.9 613, 617, 627
4.4.10 539, 591, 593, 598, 675
4.5.3 995
4.5.16-17 733
4.5.17 761
4.9.11 665
4.9.13 949

STRABO

1.2.9 879
15.1.50 785 n. 48

TEUCER, I

p. 18.6 114 n. 34, 925
pp. 19-20 645
p. 19.1-2 925
p. 20.3, 6 618
p. 21.1-2 645

p. 21.3, 8 924
p. 44.10–11 936

TEUCER, II

1.2, 8, 10 627
1.10 53 n. 72, 55 n. 77, 637
2.2 55 n. 79
2.3 930
2.4 114 n. 36
2.5 932
3.4 928
3.5 113 n. 33
3.10 114 n. 34
3.11 930
5.1 608
5.4a 936
6.3 114 n. 34
8.3 935
9.5, 8 645
9.6 923
10.9 618
12.1 924
12.6 936
12.8 63 n. 115, 638–9

Θ

ch. 56 (pp. 125.21–126.11)
  p. 125.26–7 527
ch. 57 (pp. 126.12–182.26) 138
  p. 131.12–13 536
  p. 132.16–18 962 n. 146
  p. 132.17 531
  p. 133.3 553
  p. 133.22–3 660
  pp. 133.24–134.1 660
  p. 134.1–2 976
  p. 134.6–9 791
  p. 134.10 724
  p. 135.18–19 522
  p. 136.9–20 546
  p. 136.10 548
  p. 137.7–8 605
  p. 137.13–14 590
  p. 138.8–11 553
  p. 138.12 523
  p. 138.22–5 553
  p. 139.9–10 1065
  p. 139.13 829
  p. 142.3 969
  p. 142.19–20 780
  p. 145.5 597
  p. 145.29 532
  p. 146.8 945
  p. 147.3–4 669

p. 147.15 836
p. 148.14–15 598
p. 148.19 532
p. 149.9–11 915
p. 150.3–5 791
p. 151.4–5 898
p. 151.7 138, 601, 605
pp. 151.28–152.1 540
p. 152.18 535
pp. 154.21–155.2 795
p. 155.19–20 725
p. 155.24 702
p. 155.27 854
p. 156.9–10 553 n. 63
p. 156.26–7 691
p. 157.12–13 664
p. 157.14 670
p. 157.24–5 569
p. 158.10–11 989
p. 158.14 995
p. 158.16–17 702, 965 n. 148
p. 158.24 541
p. 159.12 976
p. 159.16–17 664
p. 159.24–5 898
p. 160.15 633
p. 160.16 537
p. 160.18–19 535
p. 160.20 541
p. 160.23 541
p. 162.24–5 951
p. 163.6–7 664
p. 165.3–4 836
p. 165.4 838
p. 165.15–16 838 n. 133
p. 166.4–6 590
p. 166.8 532
p. 166.19 729
p. 166.22–4 138, 606, 612, 779
p. 166.22 141 n. 36, 267, 268, 607, 779
p. 166.26–7 991
p. 167.6–8 546
p. 167.7–8 888
p. 168.6–9 774
p. 168.8 540
p. 168.13–14 526
p. 168.14 889
p. 168.20–1 534
p. 169.4–8 652, 917
p. 169.12–15 791, 947
p. 169.16–20 774
p. 170.5–6 846
p. 174.5–6 569
p. 175.1 598

pp. 175.15–176.7 962 n. 146
p. 175.19 540
p. 176.4–5 709
p. 176.13 541
p. 177.3 541
p. 179.15–24 598–9
p. 179.17 994
p. 179.21–2 722
p. 179.21 600
p. 180.11–13 991
p. 180.12 639
ch. 59 (p. 183.1–22) 138
    p. 183.2–3 957
    p. 183.3 768, 770
    p. 183.14–16 600
    p. 183.16–17 138, 913, 950
ch. 60 (pp. 184.1–185.21)
    p. 185.6 671
    p. 185.18–19 108 n. 10
ch. 61 (pp. 186.1–190.18) 138–9
    p. 186.5–6 139 n. 32, 809
    p. 186.8–9 313, 814
    p. 187.2–5 566 n. 86
    p. 187.6 944
    p. 187.17–18 566 n. 86
    p. 187.18 267
    p. 187.28–9 567
    p. 189.6–8 794
    p. 189.10–13 768
    p. 189.13–14 907 n. 76, 959
    p. 189.25–6 957
    p. 190.1–3 802
ch. 64 (pp. 191.14–192.7)
    p. 191.15–192.1 702
    p. 191.17 965 n. 148
    pp. 191.19–192.1 965 n. 148
ch. 65 (pp. 192.8–194.8) 139
    p. 192.5–6 917
    p. 192.13–14 263, 832
    p. 192.14 265, 267
    p. 192.16–18 263, 594, 834, 843
    p. 192.18–20 538
    p. 192.18 268, 594
    pp. 192.20–193.1 253, 264, 584
    p. 192.20–3 691, 692
    p. 192.21 265, 267
    p. 192.22 616
    pp. 192.24–193.1 265
    p. 192.24–5 585
    p. 192.24 265
    p. 193.1–3 264, 536, 598
    p. 193.3 266, 267, 600, 638
    p. 193.5–6 801, 910

p. 193.5 593, 832
p. 193.13–15 654
p. 193.13 242
p. 193.16–18 538
p. 193.16–17 598, 716
p. 193.16 267
p. 193.17 267, 268
p. 193.20–2 263, 716, 832
p. 194.2–4 263, 832, 834
p. 194.2–3 832
p. 194.2 594
p. 194.3 248 n. 209
p. 194.7 139, 711
ch. 66 (pp. 194.9–195.14) 139
    p. 194.17–18 139, 652
    pp. 194.18–195.2 139 n. 34, 263, 595, 651
    p. 194.18 240
    p. 195.5–10 264
    p. 195.5–8 628, 916
    p. 195.6 629
    p. 195.7–8 960
    p. 195.8 267
    p. 195.9 629
    p. 195.12–14 990
ch. 68 (pp. 196.3–198.21)
    p. 196.5–7 724, 990
    p. 196.11–12 990
ch. 77 (pp. 199.1–202.10) 139, 691
    p. 200.1–2 842, 942
    p. 201.2–5 253, 584, 692
    p. 201.4–5 267
    p. 201.10–18 692
    p. 201.20–2 940
    p. 201.22–3 264, 585 n. 133, 587 n. 143, 948
    p. 201.22 240
    p. 201.24 267, 743
    p. 202.2–6 692
    p. 202.6 267
    p. 202.9–10 692
    p. 202.10 267
ch. 78 (pp. 202.11–210.21)
    p. 202.14–15 76 n. 23
ch. 82 (pp. 207.25–210.19) 139
    p. 208.2–8 137 n. 28
    p. 208.19–23 956, 960
    p. 208.19 727
    p. 209.6–7 31 n. 65
    p. 209.7–9 928
    p. 209.10–13 793
    pp. 209.17–210.4 557
    p. 210.1–2 558
    p. 210.7 593

p. 210.8   593
p. 210.10   598
ch. 83 (pp. 210.20–213.34)   139–41, 144
   p. 210.26–7   263, 728
   p. 210.26   568, 592
   p. 210.27   266
   p. 210.29–31   263
   pp. 210.30–211.2   793
   p. 210.30   264
   p. 211.1–2   570
   p. 211.1   264
   p. 211.11   140–1, 266, 678
   p. 211.12–13   264
   p. 211.12   141
   p. 211.13–14   263, 916
   p. 211.14   266
   p. 211.15–16   267, 689
   p. 211.24–31   779
   p. 211.26–7   266
   p. 211.27   266
   p. 211.28   266, 268, 678
   p. 211.30   264, 266, 609
   p. 211.31   267
   p. 212.2–5   264
   p. 212.4   266, 638
   p. 212.5–6   691
   p. 212.5   266
   p. 212.11–12   971
   p. 212.15–18   606
   p. 212.17   264, 265, 601 n. 167, 603 n. 171, 779, 780
   p. 212.18–20   557
   p. 212.18   267, 606
   p. 212.19–20   264
   p. 212.20–1   935
   p. 212.20   266
   p. 212.23–4   921
   p. 212.24–5   722
   p. 212.25   267
   p. 212.28   266
   p. 212.29–32   676
   p. 212.29   812
   p. 212.30   265
   p. 213.1   242, 618, 920
   p. 213.3   267
   p. 213.4–6   629
   p. 213.5   629
   p. 213.6–7   920
   p. 213.6   265, 267
   p. 213.7   618, 626
   p. 213.9–13   262, 590
   p. 213.10   266
   p. 213.11   578
   p. 213.12–13   265
   p. 213.12   264
   p. 213.13   266, 268, 928
   p. 213.14   266
   p. 213.15–16   569
   p. 213.19–22   812
   p. 213.22–4   262, 563
   p. 213.23   253, 264
   p. 213.24–5   925
   p. 213.24   266
   p. 213.25–7   928
ch. 84 (p. 214.1–17)
   p. 214.9–13   242, 574
   p. 214.9–11   263
   p. 214.12   242
   p. 214.13–17   262, 578
   p. 214.13–14   242
   p. 214.13   267
   p. 214.15   268, 960
   p. 214.16   265
ch. 85 (p. 214.18–21)   262, 588
   p. 214.21   264, 267, 268
ch. 86 (pp. 214.22–215.3)   147 n. 50, 263, 590, 675
   p. 215.1–2   266
   p. 215.2–3   590
   p. 215.2   265, 268
   p. 215.3   267
ch. 87 (p. 215.4–7)   264, 606
   p. 215.4–5   247–8
   p. 215.5–7   143
   p. 215.5   267
   p. 215.6   265, 267
   p. 215.7   563
ch. 88 (p. 215.8–11)   142 n. 39, 263, 581, 614
   p. 215.9   247–8, 267
   p. 215.10   267
   p. 215.11   54, 264
ch. 89 (p. 215.12–17)
   p. 215.12–16   141, 627, 637
   p. 215.13–14   240
   p. 215.13   619, 627
   p. 215.15   53, 141, 144 n. 42, 267, 268, 564 n. 80, 638, 641
   p. 215.16–17   263, 617
   p. 215.16   265, 267, 626
ch. 90 (p. 215.18–22)   264
   p. 215.19–21   263, 651
   p. 215.20   247
   p. 215.21   265, 267, 651
   p. 215.22   629
ch. 91 (p. 216.1–7)   264, 637, 641
   p. 216.1–6   141

p. 216.4 241
p. 216.5 141, 267, 637
p. 216.6–7 1065
p. 216.6 253, 267, 268, 613
ch. 92 (p. 216.8–16) 644
p. 216.8–15 141, 142 n. 39, 147 n. 50, 263, 601, 644
p. 216.11 247
p. 216.12 267
p. 216.13–15 240
p. 216.14–15 645
p. 216.15–16 263, 644
p. 216.15 267, 645
p. 216.16 266, 644
ch. 93 (p. 216.17–22) 147 n. 50, 262, 263, 555, 559, 664
p. 216.18–19 240, 242, 248 n. 209
p. 216.18 241, 264
p. 216.20 265, 266
ch. 94 (p. 216.23–5) 263, 672
p. 216.24 242
p. 216.25 268
ch. 95 (p. 217.1–4)
p. 217.1, 3 953
p. 217.4 678
ch. 96 (pp. 217.5–218.8) 142
p. 217.5–23 150
p. 217.5–8 618
p. 217.5–7 141, 142, 143, 678, 906, 916
p. 217.7 267
p. 217.7–8 31, 141, 143
p. 217.9 142, p. 144 n. 42, 920
p. 217.10–11 921
p. 217.12–13 141, 925
p. 217.13 144, 265
p. 217.14–15 141, 928
p. 217.15 144, 145, 266, 267
p. 217.16–18 141, 930
p. 217.19–20 141, 144, 644, 931
p. 217.19 267, 649, 909
p. 217.21–3 141, 935
pp. 217.24–218.8 143
pp. 217.24–218.2 141 n. 37, 143, 264, 598, 765, 959
p. 217.21–3 141, 935
p. 218.1–2 598
p. 218.2 266, 267, 600
p. 218.3–6 143, 959, 961, 962, 963
p. 218.4–5 963
p. 218.7–8 962, 963
chs. 97–108 (pp. 218.9–221.9) 145
p. 219.13–14 659
ch. 113 (pp. 221.1–223.2)
p. 221.2 35, 79 n. 47

p. 221.5–6 19
p. 222.12–14 949–50
p. 222.12 959
ch. 117 (p. 224.1–20)
p. 224.13 19, 786

VETTIUS VALENS

I 1.10 642
I 1.29 67 n. 135, 564
I 1.39 620, 622, 679, 682
I 1.40 643
I 2.38 28–9
I 2.42 619
I 3.18 712, 968
I 3.40 600
I 18.79 629
I 19.11 969
I 19.15 969
I 20.2 711
I 20.8 530
I 20.13 708
II 4.7 886
II 4.9 633
II 9.5 79 n. 46
II 17.57–8 692, 694
II 17.60 579
II 17.68 595, 653
II 17.69 23
II 22 121
II 23.25 76
II 35.6 84 n. 3
II 37.8 701
II 37.43 718, 721, 832
II 37.50 702
II 37.51 655
II 38.16–20 671
II 38.45 663
II 38.73 671
II 38.82 730
II 41.55 527
IV 4.23 896
IV 4.24–5 895
IV 13.6 626
IV 15.3 24 n. 32
IV 15.4 724
IV 16.22 30, 32
IV 16.26 658
IV 21.3 29 n. 56
IV 21.9 794
IV 22.7 670
IV 25.10 703
V 6.4–9 905
VI 1.9 852, 865
VI 3.10 537

VII 3.53 878
VII 4.4 872
VIII 7.282 882
IX 1.12–15 875
IX 2.14 32
IX 8.40 894
IX 9.19 893
IX 15.1 81 n. 64, 875

XENOPHON

Oec.
4.2 64, 640

LATIN AUTHORS

CICERO

De Divinatione
2.89 249 n. 212, 508, 511

De Officiis
1.150–1 65–70, 71

FIRMICUS MATERNUS

1.2.5–12 + 1.6.1–2 821, 822
1.4.6 893
1.4.7 894
1.7.14–22 824
1.9.1 697, 941–2
2.8.2 783
2.19.2 988
2.30.5 848
3 34, 514
3.1.1 868
3.2–7 and 13 138
3.2.14 854
3.3.6 898
3.3.16 951
3.4.17 811
3.4.32 278, 809
3.5.1–11 546, 547
3.5.1 240
3.5.2 786
3.5.33 726
3.5.34 888
3.6.1 531, 532
3.7.15 682
3.8.1 848
3.8.7 778
3.8.9 981
3.10.12 774
3.11.15 905
3.11.16 903, 904
3.13.2 553, 693

4 34, 131, 278, 908 n. 77
4 *Praef.* 5 749 n. 1, 756 n. 12, 868–9
4.2.1 909
4.3.1–2 278, 828, 829
4.4.2–3 794
4.5.1 713
4.9.4 804
4.9.7 909
4.11.7 278, 804
4.13.6 612
4.14.7 132, 692, 693, 695
4.15.2 801
4.22.2 894
6.15.6 666
6.15.9 656, 657
6.16.1 829, 830
6.22.5 894
6.22.12 766
6.24.1 959
6.24.4 765
6.29–31 132, 259, 277, 858
6.29.3–4 855, 856
6.29.5 857
6.29.10 940, 942
6.29.22 766, 943
6.30.1 147 n. 51, 765, 786, 787, 788, 943, 944
6.30.5 277, 790, 791
6.30.13 694
6.30.18 595, 789, 933
6.31.9 943
6.31.19 656, 657
6.31.43 766
6.31.51 849
6.31.55 858, 859, 885
6.31.79 652
6.31.82 760
7.2.15–16 132 n. 22, 656
7.2.15 656, 657, 814
7.2.16 133 n. 24, 240, 656, 814
7.4.5 132 n. 22, 660
7.5.1–2 739
7.6 85 n. 7
7.9 667
7.10.1 914
7.20.12 768
7.22 154, 847
7.22.1 763
7.23 692
7.23.10 942
7.26.7 132 n. 22
8 34, 112–14
8.6.5 926
8.6–17 262

8.8.1 112 n. 29, 772
8.10.4 112 n. 29
8.14.3 645
8.15.2 112 nn. 29–30
8.15.5 618
8.17.4 617 n. 199
8.17.7 936
8.19.12 607
8.21.6 919
8.21.7 768
8.24.4 114
8.24.8 563
8.27.3 114
8.28.2 114
8.29.6 607

LIBER HERMETIS DE TRIGINTA SEX DECANIS

xxv
  1.6 112 n. 30
  1.9 977
  1.38 55 n. 77
  2.8 932
  2.13 114 n. 36
  3.13 113 n. 33, 622
  3.29 114 n. 34
  3.34 665
  4.1 923
  4.12 976
  4.26 66
  6.14 114
  9.14 114
  9.16 114 n. 34
  10.7 114
  10.13 619
  12.1 645
xxvi 516
  25 667
  34 847
  38 853–4
  43 609
  48 815
  62 269, 678
  70 516
  71 516, 520
xxvii 908
  11 612
  48 814
xxxii 988
  19 889
  29 894
  39 980
  63 988

xxxiii 908
xxxiv 148, 260
  4 268, 269, 581
  29 268, 269, 590
  31 268, 269
  33 269, 588
  39–40 683–4, 687
  39 240

MANILIUS

3.106–7 28 n. 47
3.206–10 882
4.21 822
4.368 645, 648
4.527–8 975
4.549 24 n. 28
5.78–9 931
5.83 930
5.116–17 926
5.220–2 141 n. 37
5.288–9 565 n. 84
5.654–5 626

PLAUTUS

Aulul. 508–21 38 n. 13, 144 n. 44, 1066

PAPYRI

ANUBION

F 2
  6 541
F 4 ii
  4 93 n. 47
  11–16 786–8, 788, 943
  14 765
  17–18 944
F 6 978
F 7.25 858, 885
F 10 783
F 11 855
  5 289, 855–6
  6 857
F 12 281, 999 n. 2, 1002
  2 991
  8 942
  14–16 900
  19 539
  21 945, 980
  22 963
  26–7 87 n. 13
  29 927

30 634
33 764
36–7 768
36 832
38 591

P.Salt 756 n. 12, 865, 869

DEMOTIC TEXTS

P. CtYBR inv. 422 verso and P. Lund inv. 2058 verso 756, 863 n. 5, 864 n. 10

Index of Greek Words

ἀγκαλίσαιτο 289, 313, 766
ἀγορανόμος 9, 118 n. 50, 119, 271, 784, 785, 786, 986
ἀήρ 181, 522, 827
ἀθρεῖν + prep. 690
αἰθήρ 181, 522–3, 602
αἰθροβάτης 265, 597, 618, 921, 1052
αἴλινος 119, 294, 855, 940
αἱμαγμός 527, 670, 807, 853, 854
αἱμηρός 392, 395, 670, 853, 854
αἰσχρός 115, 990–1
αἰών 181, 876, 883, 884
ἀκαταστασία 561, 894
ἀκρίβεια, ἀκριβής 882, 968
ἀκριβολογία 999
ἀκτινοβολία 189, 220, 248–9, 615
ἀλείπτης 576–7, 1054
ἀλλότριος 651
ἀμβλυωπία 567–8
ἀμβλωσμός 395, 397, 670
ἄμμιγα 201, 242, 594
ἀμυδρός 713
ἀναβαίνειν 969–70
ἀνάγκη 508, 818
ἀνοικεῖος 241
ἀντλητήρ 264, 610–11
ἀνωμαλία 76
ἀπόκρουσις 914
ἀρεταλόγος 681, 1052
ἀρετή 524
ἀρχή 753–4
ἀρχιδικαστής 117, 271, 786, 889, 1043
ἀρχικυνηγός 318, 975
ἀστήρ / ἄστρον 508, 753, 897
αὐξιφαής 325, 909

βασιλεύς 18, 20, 1060
βίοτος 549, 667, 851
βρόχος 697, 842, 942, 971

γαμεῖν 635, 763
γαμέτη(s) 996
γάρ 543
γενεά 184–5, 875–6
γενέθλη 251, 663, 722, 849
γένεσις 243, 779, 825, 875–6
γλυκερός 767

δαιδάλλειν 173, 639, 679, 1062
δείκηλον 746
δέκτης 215, 596
δέρκεσθαι 698, 720
διάνοια 335, 877
δίπολις 658
διωνυμία 658
δύναμις 988
δυστοκία 669–70, 767, 842
δωδεκατημόριον 211, 247, 573

εἴδωλον 716, 720–1
ἔκδυσις 643
ἐκτελεῖν 753
ἐλθεῖν 213, 663, 704
ἕλιξ 181, 538, 543–4, 630
ἐμβασίκοιτος 605
ἐμπερίσχεσις 242, 263, 361 n. 95, 584, 594, 667, 834, 841, 842, 942
ἐναλλάγδην 262, 268, 578
ἐναλλάξ, ἐναλλάσσειν 251, 578, 582, 588, 706, 762
ἐπαγωγή 655
ἐπεμβαίνειν 789, 907
ἐπέμβασις 629, 901
ἐπίμοχθος 605, 612
ἐπιτροχάδην 757
ἐποπτεύειν 764
ἐργολάβος 643, 1041
ἔργον 174, 175, 176
εὐκρασία 360, 859, 894–5
εὔστερνος 548
ἑῷος 892

ζῷον 180, 705, 706

ἡγεμών 548, 1062

θηλύτερος 595, 702, 763
θηριόβρωτος 743
θλῖψις 74, 80 n. 54, 272, 810
θρεπτοί 658–9
θυμός 25, 714, 808, 809

ἴδιος 881
ἰθυδίκαιος / ἰθύδικος 706
ἰσχυροπαίκτας 620, 1053

κάθετος 525
καθορᾶν 783, 959
καλοβάτης 340, 920-1, 1052
κάματος 172, 177, 628, 690, 746
καταθρεῖν 673
κατοχή, κάτοχοι 117, 271, 835-7, 838
κελαδεῖν 328, 926, 979
κέλευθος 718
κηδεμών 705-6
κοινωνικός 31, 561, 714
κοσμεῖν 786
κοσμικῶς 243 n. 169
κοσμοκράτωρ 21
κόσμος 92, 100 n. 79, 182, 211, 245-6 n. 195, 394, 511, 647, 693, 701, 716
κοσμοτρόφος 751-2
κρᾶσις 218, 242, 1062
κρύφιμος 671, 854, 983

λαξευτής 140, 775-6, 1030
λαοξόος 775-6, 1030
λαοτόμος 613, 641, 1030, 1065
λέπρα 769, 957
λιθοξόος 641, 928, 1031, 1065
λιθοψήκτης 641, 1031
λογιστής 180, 268, 568-9, 1041
λοξός 544

μαρμαρυγή 645
μαστροπός 542, 633
μάχλος 578, 580, 1060
μεθοδεύειν 335, 918, 966-7
μεσόβιος 36
μετά 288, 332
μεταλλευταί 266, 612-13, 1030
μετέωρος 304, 677, 800, 948-9
μίγα 242, 595
μίγδην 242
μιμηλαὶ τέχναι 916
μίτος 754, 872
μοῖρα 878
μόχθος 172, 177, 605, 621, 705

νεκρονώμας 584
νυκτερινός 312 n. 74, 779, 892, 948

ξυλουργός 641

ὀθνεῖος 657
οἰκεῖος 241-2, 516
οἰκονόμος 729, 741, 1057
ὁμογάστριος 945
ὀπυίω 635
ὀρχηστής 116, 581, 919, 1051

ὄχλος 10, 13, 26-7, 29-30, 32, 82, 83, 91, 115, 682
  and theatre 620, 906
  in Valens 8 n. 12

παλάμῃσι 61 n. 106, 332 n. 29, 680, 726, 927, 948
πανόδυρτος 15 n. 41, 119, 790
πάροδος 859
παστοφόροι 271, 835, 837
πένης 73
περισσομελής 687
πίστις 710, 729, 730, 830, 1063
πολυμιτάριος 53, 145, 318, 929, 1034
πόνος 72, 173, 174, 179, 220, 535, 705, 817
πρᾶξις 3, 8, 34, 71, 130, 133, 137, 138, 139, 140, 147-8, 176, 178, and passim
πτωχός 73-4

ῥαπτήρ 674
ῥεμβηδόν 683
ῥομβηδόν 550
ῥόμβος 601-2
ῥῶπος 640

σῆμα 551, 573
σημαίνειν 956
σίνος 76, 130, 137 n. 28, and passim
σκληρώδης 180, 641
σοφία 870, 873
στειρώδης 767
στείχειν 244, 895
στεφανηδόν 676
στοιχεῖον 747
στρατηγός 18, 19, 24 n. 28, 99 n. 74, 569 n. 99, 932, 1057
στρέφειν 636, 653
στρόφιον 831
σύγκρασις see κρᾶσις
σύν 201, 288
συναφή 361 n. 94, 774, 845
σύνδεσμος 321, 715-16, 911, 913-14
συνοδεύειν 324, 332, 361 n. 94, 736, 896-7
σύνοδος 361 n. 94, 814, 885-6, 895, 896
συνοικείωσις 928
σφάγιος 851
σχοινοβάτης 618, 626, 1052

τάξις 120-1, 576
ταριχευτής 191, 193, 212, 615-16, 1049
τείνειν 272, 800
τέκτων 640, 776, 1033
τελεῖν 653, 753, 850
τελευτή 156, 892
τετράγωνος 619

τέχναι 130, 137, 141, 142, 147, 175, and passim
τέχναι καθάριοι 64
τῆμος 220, 525
τηνίκα 538
τριβάς 653, 763, 946

ὑδραγωγός 55 n. 79, 141 n. 36, 607, 779–80, 1029
ὑδροφόρος 779, 780, 1029
ὕπαυγος 88, 257 n. 230, 566, 905
ὑπέρ 200, 559
ὑπονομευτής 606, 607, 608, 779, 780, 1030
ὑψηλός 902–3
ὕψωμα 387, 886, 932

φάντασμα 655, 721, 832, 982
φάσις 753, 892

φάσμα 719, 721
φέρεσθαι, φορεῖσθαι 244, 804
φιλοτιμία 11
φοιβητής 271, 834–5
φωσφορεῖν 773, 814
φωσφόρον 960

χαμαιτυπίη 651
χιλιάρχης 533
χῶρος 970

ψηφοπαίκτης 621, 682, 1052
ψυχή 539, 714, 719, 720, 806

ὡρονομεῖν, -εύειν 218, 246, 735
ὡρονόμος 848, 1067
ὡροσκόπος 246, 534, 698

General Index

abortifacients 699
abortion 313, 660, 670, 731, 799, 815, 816; *see also* embryotomy; miscarriage
acclamations 11, 318, 848, 977, 978–80, 985, 986
accountants 56, 568, 794, 1041; *see also* λογιστής
accuracy 750, 751
 of Ascendant 360, 882
 see also ἀκρίβεια; clarity
Achilles (hero) 555, 755, 797, 801, 817, 875, 892, 911, 919; *see also* Thersites
Achmet 5–6, 101
 and charity 75 n. 20
 and debt 80 n. 54
 and the economy 81 n. 64
 and labour 874
 and scripture 106
 and slaves 45, 100, 104, 1064
 social hierarchy in 19, 25, 26, 73–4, 902–3 n. 73, 949
 see also Artemidorus; δυστοκία; θλῖψις
acrobats 5, 112 n. 30, 115, 116, 621, 626, 921, 1052; *see also* mimes; petauristae; theatre—popular entertainers in; tightrope-walkers
actors 69, 111 n. 25, 115 n. 39, 578, 622, 681
 comic 579
 see also mimes; theatre
adoption 658–9, 828
adulterers, charts for 651, 760, 916
 perfumed 632
 see also husband—complaisant; μάχλος; pimps; wigs; wives
adultery 14, 528, 530, 633–4, 699, 733, 972
 and divorce 664
 as rapine 214, 218, 529, 976, 980
adumbration-precision 543, 889
affability 704, 974
agonothetes 212, 522, 523, 786, 1053, 1062;
 see also priests—high; purple
agriculture 49, 1026
 attitude of astrologers 47, 55, 60–1, 63, 72
 and Hesiod 174, 680, 790
 only activity for a gentleman 63
 and Saturn 22, 60, 563

and slaves 45 n. 37, 87, 99
and wealth 60 n. 100, 63
 see also gardeners; leasing land; metaphor—agricultural
alchemy 1063
Alexander of Abonouteichos 88 n. 16, 954, 983, 984
Alexander of Aetolia 347
Alexander of Ephesus 218, 511, 755
Alexander the Great 969 n. 155
Alexander Romance 593, 752, 887; *see also* Nectanebo
 complexion 973, 974
 horoscope of 326, 341, 358, 885, 886–8
Alexander Severus 178
Alexandria 33, 42, 43 n. 29, 44, 57, 625, 752
 administration 569; *see also* λογιστής
 courts 1062; *see also* ἀρχιδικαστής
 industry 929
 scholars 1060
 Serapeum 835 n. 116
Amenhotep 869; *see also* Imhotep
amphitheatre 115, 744, 941, 975; *see also* Laureolus; *venatio*
analogy 103, 241, 543, 558, 969, 980
 in catarchic astrology 88, 361 n. 96, 543
 with dodecatopos 729
 in dream interpretation 949; *see also* Artemidorus—method
 with location and motion of planets 701, 714, 718, 746, 905
 in medicine 815
 with Moon 708, 912, 914
 in physiognomy 723–4
 reinforced by style 163, 342
 with signs 60, 553, 687, 701, 769, 917, 926
 of stars with eyes 556
 in Valens 875, 896
anaphora 159 n. 85, 162 n. 99, 295, 296, 827, 845, 925, 1000
anger 25, 29, 160, 710 n. 326, 711, 765, 782, 848, 907, 911
animal trainers 601, 604, 605, 1028–9
anthologies 534, 602, 648, 745, 862, 867, 875, 955
 bee metaphor 339, 862, 871
 of Homer 336, 893

1104 General Index

Antigonus of Nicaea 18 n. 2, 35 n. 1, 888, 1060
'Antiochus', astrological poet 129, 237, 246, 363
  inner metric 226, 227, 229, 301, 352, 382
  outer metric 222, 224, 300
  prosody 233, 306, 307
Antiochus of Athens, astrologer 89 n. 26, 135, 136, 138, 145, 146, 261, 895
Anubion
  addressee 155, 312, 359, 774
  definite article 287
  on incest 277; *see also* Oedipus; stepmothers, intercourse with
  and M^c 131, 146, 154, 276–81, 282, 283, 313, 315, 327, 765, 775, 783, 791, 793, 794, 801
    and final couplet 284, 311, 861
    and proem 750 n. 2, 751, 756
  marginal signs 1061
  and Nechepso–Petosiris 133, 277, 749, 999
  parallel word-ending 279, 296, 783, 791
  particles 287
  on πρᾶξις 34, 130, 137 n. 28, 139, 147–8, 260–1, 727, 728, 775
  prosody 280, 307
  'sample charts' 132
  tenses in 290
  and Θ 139, 141
  topike diakrisis 141 n. 36
Ape (constellation) 31, 141, 143, 618–19, 916; *see also* Cepheus
Apollonius of Perga 751, 867
Apollonius of Rhodes
  allusions 216, 798
  metre 383
  source of verse patterns 217, 647
Apollonius of Tyana 819, 833 n. 112, 873, 900, 982, 983
Apomasar
  on the birth of kings 885
  on social class 61 n. 105, 970
  see also εὐκρασία
Aquarius 607, 768, 786, 858, 859
  classification
    airy 895 n. 67
    see also zodiac, signs of—watery
  house of Saturn 16 n. 46, 516, 517, 537 n. 40, 634, 722, 768, 812, 966
  'steward' 517, 729 n. 350
  see also Cepheus
Aratus 110, 216, 217
  circles 510–11, 573
  notes to addressee 359, 551, 769, 944, 1059
  organisation 150
  segmentation 155, 157
  style 158–9, 160 n. 91, 342, 1061
  third-foot caesura 383, 1001
  see also Libra—Claws; Virgo
Archimedes 42 n. 25, 751, 756, 867
Ares
  declension 187, 285, 329, 664
  formulary 638, 639, 795, 898
  schetliasmos of 280, 291, 293, 294, 296, 796, 798
  simile 336, 892
Argo 1061
Aries
  classification, *see* zodiac, signs of—bent, four-footed, male, tropic
  decans and terms 977, 990
  exaltation of the Sun 516, 517, 547
  'head of the universe' 518
  house of Mars 21 n. 13, 764, 823 n. 97, 953, 961
  in MC 518
  monomoiriai 55 nn. 77 and 79, 112 n. 30
  paranatellonta 59, 627, 637, 926
  and spring 518, 620; *see also* Cancer—start of year
Aristarchus 588, 596
army, the 144, 1057–8
  commands 23, 24, 525, 526, 548, 889, 1062; *see also* ἀρχικυνηγός, στρατηγός, χιλιάρχης
  low profile of 59, 1025
  supplies 56, 638, 640, 673
  trumpeters 927
  see also slaves—prisoners of war
Artemidorus 16, 98 n. 73, 835 n. 116
  and Achmet 6
  on crucifixion 585, 800, 949
  date 5
  on debt 80 n. 54
  on donations 32
  dream symbolism 25–6, 32, 790 n. 50, 1060, 1062
  on gods 59 n. 94
  on letters 108
  method 6, 99, 101
  and musicians 579
  on πρᾶξις / ἀπραγία 62 n. 110, 71, 80, 1060
  and shame 8 n. 11
  and slaves 45, 88 n. 24, 90 n. 30, 93 n. 50, 96, 99–105, 738, 1064
  on social hierarchy 902–3 n. 73
    on kings and big men 18 n. 2, 20 n. 6, 24 n. 31, 25–6, 1060
    on the masses 29, 682, 906
    on the 'middling' 36 n. 8

on the poor 73, 74 n. 6, 80 nn. 58–9, 95–6 n. 60
see also army, the; burning; crucifixion; sedentary trades; slaves; τάξις; θλῖψις
Ascendant
and birth 181, 183, 213, 246
symbolism 89
see also accuracy—of Ascendant
Asclepius 866 n. 16, 869, 936, 1060
and Hermes 865, 868, 869
in Hermetic Corpus 758, 865, 871, 873
see also Imhotep; Imouthes
asp (cobra) 117, 338 n. 49, 937, 939; see also Nicander; snakes
astrologers 1046
birth of 557
and their clients 533
and divine will 558
and doctors 568
and foundation of Seleucia 888
and jargon 57, 119, 211, 334, 516, 527, 561, 589, 605, 643, 662, 680, 687, 724, 787, 812, 894, 919, 940, 968, 983, 994
as technical experts 590
in temples 117
see also determinism; Homer—as astrologer; σοφία
astrologers' boards 518 n. 18, 597, 1059
astrology
as imaginary xi, 4, 36, 41, 42, 57, 176, 613–14
catarchic 218, 361 n. 96, 822, 956
see also analogy—in catarctic astrology; debt; marriage—in catarchic astrology; Moon—in catarctic astrology; slaves—in catarchic astrology; Sun—in catarchic astrology
as open knowledge 873
stochastic character 965
use of metaphor 148, 313, 339, 718–19, 972, 1059
Moonlight and wealth 76, 912–13
see also metaphor; θλῖψις
atheists 722, 723, 725, 818
athletes 34, 43 n. 30, 59 n. 94, 114, 548, 622, 772, 1053
(un)crowned 574, 576
formulae for 119 n. 53, 576 n. 111
see also charioteers; gymnasium; pancratiasts, pancratium
athletic trainers 63 n. 115, 577, 599

Attis 318, 326, 340, 341, 790, 792, 934–5;
see also Cybele; galli
Augustales 123; see also freedmen; Trimalchio
aulos, auloi 925, 926, 1005
automata 678, 679, 1035, 1064
aviaries 604
axe 680, 695–6, 840; see also beheading; sword

bakers 41, 47, 50, 57, 543, 778, 780, 1054;
see also Eurysaces, M. Vergilius
Balances, see Libra
banausic trades 45–6 n. 40, 61 n. 105, 67 n. 138, 68 n. 143, 69 n. 152, 525, 637, 639, 953
banks, bankers 38, 56, 728, 729, 1040
barbaricarii 1034, 1062
baths, bathing 609–10
attendants at 606, 608, 609, 1055
cleaners of 607
'be very afraid' 171, 312, 314, 323, 359, 769
bear 743–4, 940; see also Laureolus
bee 339, 862, 863, 871, 872, 881
industry 104, 172 n. 120
beggars 83, 272, 803, 985, 1049
and the employed 81
mutilated 795
vocabulary for 73–4, 215, 596, 911
wandering 75
see also galli
beheading 527–8, 692, 695, 743; see also axe; sword
benefactors 22, 23, 31 n. 68, 578, 705–6, 784, 786
of grain 986
'labour' 179, 535
not rewarded 32
profligacy 11, 912, 984–5, 986–7
see also acclamations; Augustales
Berufsbezeichnung 39; see also Tätigkeitsbezeichnung
'best in show' 173, 202, 220, 332, 526, 680
biaiothanasia, see death—violent
bile 537
bilingualism 976
birds 648, 933, 949
catchers of 141, 144, 253, 601, 603, 644, 645, 649, 932, 970, 1028
comparisons to 623, 921
dealers in 1040
diviners from 1046
rearers of 604, 644
as symbols 104, 105

birds (cont.)
    trainers 601, 976 n. 167, 1029
    see also aviaries; dogs and birds; Hawk, the;
        Sagittarius—*monomoiriai*,
        paranatellonta
birth, see Ascendant—symbolism
birthing stool 992; see also midwives
blindness 78, 742, 910; see also eyes—harm to
Blockbildung 149, 998; see also
        Medalliondichtung
blonde hair 974; see also physiognomy
blood 579, 771, 804, 839, 853-4
    circulation of 969
    drinking 744
    issue of 17 n. 54, 670, 804, 817, 851, 853,
        854
    spitting 805, 807
    symbolism of 103
    see also consumption; disease—bloody; *galli*
boar 338, 744, 940, 941
bodyguards 130 n. 12, 250, 526, 533, 598,
        904, 1055
Book of Sothis 864 n. 7, 865-6, 868, 871 n. 27
books 106-7
    and magic 107, 868, 983
    in mystery religions 107, 1061
    in P.Salt 865
    sacred 866, 867-8, 983, 1061
    secret 16, 62, 106-7, 117, 671, 868, 982, 983
    suspicion of 122
    see also temples—discovery of writings in;
        grammarians; preface, conventions of
boxers, boxing 111 n. 25, 113 n. 31, 576 n. 111,
        1053
brick-makers 41, 50, 51, 565, 627-8, 780,
        1030
bronze 50 n. 61, 613, 725, 795, 825, 874, 879,
        1032
    statues 650 n. 250, 727, 916
brothers
    death of 254, 667
    elder 254, 667, 669
    House of 970
    shortage of 254, 662-3
    wives of 980
    see also incest—sibling; siblings
builders 43, 52, 53, 254, 563-4, 565, 617-18,
        627, 628, 641, 1031
    of houses 53, 173, 565, 638, 1031
    of ships 45 n. 40, 53, 59 n. 94, 637, 640, 680,
        1031
    of temples 557, 558, 1047
    tools 565

of walls 565, 627, 1031
see also coping; shinglers
buildings, collapse of 337, 742, 744, 941, 942,
        943, 1063
buildings, sponsors of 4, 786, 984-5
burglars, see thieves—housebreakers
burning 88 n. 24, 842

Callimachus 110
    and M^b 217, 682, 690
    and M^c 293, 315, 798, 816
    and M^d 317 n. 5, 551
    inner metric 227, 230
    outer metric 222
Calliope 750, 759; see also Muses
cancer 17 n. 54, 803
Cancer 593, 702, 768, 805
    and bodily organs 805, 907 n. 76
    classification, see zodiac, signs of—
        amphibious, bent, scaly, tropic,
        watery
    decans 859
    home of Praesepe 567 n. 90
    monomoiriai 923, 976
    paranatellonta 527, 935
    start of year 117, 518
    and the summer tropic 602
    terms 21 n. 13, 968
Capricorn 567 n. 89, 593, 664 n. 268, 671, 786
    classification
        see zodiac, signs of—amphibious, bent,
        earthy, four-footed, lewd, scaly,
        tropic, watery
    house of Saturn 516, 517, 634
    monomoiriai 112 n. 30, 114, 619
    number of stars 519
    paranatellonta 143, 618
carpenter, carpentry 41, 45 n. 37, 50 n. 61,
        565, 639 n. 230
    in astrology 39, 118, 849, 1033
    in EGHP 172 n. 120, 173, 174
    in Manethoniana 53, 61, 231, 726, 776
    charts for 254, 637, 678, 725
    in Ptolemy 613, 617, 640
    tools 583, 776
    see also builders—of ships
cedar oil/wood 117, 581, 583
Cepheus 112 n. 30, 618; see also Ape
    (constellation)
chains 694, 903; see also slaves—chained
    and imprisonment 88, 393, 692, 694, 695,
        741, 915; see also prison
    of Pisces 160 n. 91; 924

charioteers 56 n. 80, 111 n. 26, 113, 114 n. 36,
  141, 143, 655 n. 257, 923, 930, 931,
  1054
charity 73, 75, 83
charm-singers 568, 905, 1045
Chelae, *see* Libra
'chemical' industry 54
chiasmus 162
  in Aratus 159
  in Hesiod 158 n. 83
  in M^b 161, 207, 208, 220, 536, 684, 701, 725
  in M^c 294, 295, 773, 844, 845
  in M^d 341, 342, 343, 904, 921
  in Orphic Hymns 162 n. 99
  see also parallelism
child exposure 14, 587–8, 730, 743, 828
  foundlings become slaves 86, 90, 254, 656,
    659, 1063; *see also* slaves
  of slave offspring 660
children
  birth 185, 337, 557, 661, 669, 731, 735, 767,
    814, 842, 992, 993; *see also* abortion;
    δυστοκία; miscarriage
  custodians of 598
  few 663
  foster- 92, 656, 657, 659
  of happy man 12
  late-born 811, 898
  loss of 767, 816, 901, 902
  love for 658, 767
  multiple 684, 685–6, 687, 976, 1059
  none 767
  only 901
  power over 24 n. 28, 91 n. 37
  separation from 90 n. 31
  supposititious 730, 991, 992
  see also adoption; beggars—mutilated;
    incest; siblings
chiliarch 533
chorus 83 n. 71, 578, 580
  of stars 181, 508, 513, 602, 872
Christianity 364, 602, 633, 722, 823, 851, 954
  anti-pagan polemic 839, 934
  asceticism 838, 839 n. 135
  bathing, attitude to 609 n. 183
  on homosexuality 732, 733
  martyrologies 975
  overlapping motifs 179, 271, 272, 318,
    585–6, 611, 624, 948
  on petitionary prayer 817, 818, 819
  pseudepigrapha 395–6; *see also* Sibylline
    Oracles
  references to 178, 722

  see also charity; Constantine, the Great;
    crucifixion; dietary taboos;
    Egypt—Christianity in; exorcism;
    Jerome; John Chrysostom; labyrinth
Chrysippus 67 n. 138, 715, 874 n. 37,
  878, 884
citharodes 69, 578, 926; *see also* Mesomedes
cities 4, 25, 30, 119, 658, 977–8
  economy of 4, 42, 44; *see also* shopkeepers
  founding, overthrowing 23, 24 n. 28, 798
  and honours 9–10, 26, 784; *see also*
    benefactors
  outsiders from 62, 96, 623, 812, 1065
  see also Alexandria; Corycos; *decuriones*;
    κηδεμών, λογιστής; Oxyrhynchus;
    plebs media; Pompeii; Rome
citizenship 28, 318, 658, 737, 977–8
clarity 239, 749 n. 1, 750, 1059; *see also*
  accuracy
Claws, *see* Libra
Cleanthes 65, 67 n. 138, 536, 610, 875 n. 38,
  878
clothes 961 n. 143, 1060
  cleaners of 1065; *see also* fulling
  repair of 38 n. 13, 120 n. 56, 253, 672,
    1065–6
  vendors of 4, 33, 38 n. 13, 66, 253, 1039
  see also dyeing; embroidery; purple; tailors;
    weavers, weaving
cobra, *see* asp
coffin-makers 39, 54, 565, 581, 583, 1049
coinage, coiners 56, 968, 1041
colossi 54, 173, 727
columbaria 49, 51
comitative expressions 201, 217, 242, 588,
  594, 595
complexion 769, 770, 854 n. 151, 951 n. 126,
  973; *see also* physiognomy
conception 246 n. 200, 677, 731 n. 351, 750,
  752, 753–4, 815
conjurers 111, 113 n. 31, 617, 621, 622, 682,
  1052; *see also* ψηφοπαίκτης
Constantine, the Great 318, 659, 696 n. 304,
  822 n. 89
constellations, *see* zodiac, signs of and s.vv.
  individual signs, *monomoiriai* and
  paranatellonta
consul 115, 546, 783, 786, 961, 1057
  consular rank 569
consumption 295, 305, 313, 537, 803, 804,
  806–9; *see also* disease—wasting;
  Mann, Thomas
coping 53, 565, 628, 1031

copper 613
Corpus Hermeticum, *see* Hermetic literature
Corycos 42 n. 24, 48, 57, 108 n. 11
professions 47 n. 47, 50, 144 n. 46
cosmic lists 797, 827
coughing, *see* consumption
courtesans, *see* prostitutes, prostitution
craftsmen 42, 63, 81, 953
astrology's interest in 50, 70, 72, 177, 682
charts for 141, 253, 644, 678
in Homer 172 n. 120, 173, 174
masters of their trade 63 n. 115, 173, 640, 641, 849; *see also* 'best in show' and wonder 679
see also banausic trades
crafts, *see* automata; carpenter, carpentry; coinage, coiners; embroidery; engravers; florists; fulling; glass-blowers; goldsmiths; instruments, makers of; ivory-carving; luxury products; metal-working; mummification; painters; perfumes; precious stones; sculpture, sculptors; silversmiths; stone-masons; weavers, weaving
crafts, clean 64, 147
cremation 54, 581, 1049
cripples 701
crowns 534, 978
of martyrs 903 n. 74
of priests 523, 1062
of sportsmen 114, 523, 574, 576
see also purple
crucifixion 162 n. 97, 695, 743, 796
charts for 253, 584, 948
cutting nerves 949
exposure to predators 587, 949; *see also* dogs and birds
language used for 179, 272, 318, 341, 585, 586, 800, 948
nailing of hands in 800
'on high' motif 800, 948–9, 955
replaced by hanging 696 n. 304; *see also* impalement
shame 587, 799
of slaves 88, 101, 105, 587
Cumont, Franz
and Egyptian sources of astrology ix–x, 118, 318, 743, 975
and the origin of astrological doctrines 131, 314
custodians of tombs 1050, 1064–5

Cybele 934–5, 1005; *see also* Attis; *galli*
cymbals 111 n. 25, 580, 925, 927, 1051

Daedalus 45–6 n. 40, 69 n. 148, 639
damnatio ad bestias 743; *see also* gladiators—*bestiarii*; wild animals
dancers 35, 68, 69–70, 111 n. 25, 578, 619, 622, 985; *see also* pantomimes
daughters, birth of 540–1; *see also* incest—parent–child
deafness 963, 964
death 272, 715, 729, 797
of child 817
and Fate 292 n. 35, 626, 754, 824, 842, 878, 949
formulary of 936, 938
of master 101
of parents 136, 145, 254, 267, 667, 804, 814
and the soul 808
violent 15, 136 n. 27, 139, 241, 254, 295, 296, 525, 526, 527, 548, 553, 584, 691, 692, 696, 742, 745, 796, 855, 894, 940, 941, 942; *see also* buildings, collapse of; burning; crucifixion; drowning; falling from a height; hanging; impalement; kings—lords of life and death; poison; shipwreck; sword; wild animals
see also brothers—death of
debt 76 n. 29, 79, 80, 560–1, 810
declamation 238, 255, 956–7, 998, 1000
decuriones 70, 123
Deir al-Bahari 869; *see also* Amenhotep; Imhotep
determinism 745, 818, 824, 825, 878, 879
dietary taboos 724
Diocletian's Price Edict 53 n. 71, 673 n. 274, 780
Dionysius Periegetes 841
allusive technique 109, 293, 338, 1004
break-off formula 551
metre 224, 300
Dionysius son of Calliphon 757, 881 n. 54
διψάς, *see* viper
disease 34, 537, 818, 911, 995, 1064
bloody 670, 854; *see also* miscarriage
hidden 16–17, 62, 671, 804, 853, 854, 907
and Moon 34, 153, 313–15, 959
of nerves 701–2
psychic 733; *see also* madness; mental defect; mental disturbance
sacred, *see* epilepsy
scaly 135, 958

shameful 13
  of skin 17, 340, 768, 771, 957, 958–9, 974;
    see also leprosy
  vocabulary of 810, 901, 964, 966
  wasting 78, 701, 803, 804, 807, 940; see also
    consumption
  wet 768, 769, 801–2; see also dropsy
  see also blood—issue of; druggists;
    drugs; epilepsy; eyes—harm to;
    famine; gout; jaundice; melancholy;
    poison
dithyrambic style 209, 216, 527, 630, 927, 995
divers 143, 923–4, 1027–8; see also sponges
divination 47, 868, 983, 1025, 1045
  Ptolemy's interest in 866
  used by masters and slaves 84, 87, 97, 98,
    102, 105, 740
  see also astrology; books—secret;
    galli—and divination; prophecy;
    Sortes Astrampsychi; Sortes
    Sangallenses
diviners 120, 151, 178, 253, 269, 590, 591, 592,
    675, 936, 1046; see also astrologers;
    birds—diviners from; dream
    interpreters; lecanomancy;
    necromancy; prophets
doctors 42, 49, 52, 87 n. 13, 623 n. 204,
    805 n. 64, 808, 834
  in astrology 59, 295, 568, 812, 813, 962,
    963, 966, 1044
  rhetoricians and 967
  see also druggists; Hippocratic corpus—
    oath; iatrosophist; Imhotep
dodecatemories 200, 261, 263, 561 n. 78, 614,
    628, 644, 701, 960
  'signs' 247–8, 571, 572, 582, 591, 606, 629,
    646
dodecaoros 117, 141, 618, 645
dodecatopos 91, 96, 138, 551, 553, 629, 729
  in Firmicus 34, 86 n. 11, 278, 514, 891,
    899, 902
  in Θ 136 n. 27, 514, 664, 763, 779, 917
Dodona 84, 85, 96–8, 717, 738
dogs and birds 587, 609, 948
dolphin 924
Dorotheus
  addressee 868 n. 21
  on debt 79
  formulary of planets 139, 255, 256, 315,
    362, 559, 591, 654, 849, 957
  and M^a 133, 134
  and M^b 218, 246, 514, 516, 570, 691 n. 288,
    716
  and M^c 277–8 n. 14, 289, 764, 804

  and M^d 360, 361, 959, 996; see also
    anthologies—bee metaphor
  on masters and slaves 89
  metre 237, 309
    inner metric 226, 227, 229, 230, 303,
      304, 1001
    outer metric 222, 224, 225, 300, 301,
      349, 352
    prosody 233, 236–7, 280, 307, 308, 357,
      381, 382
  and numbers 999
  on πρᾶξις 130, 139, 260
  in Θ 136, 138, 139, 145, 146
  traces of hexameter diction 7 n. 4, 138,
    550, 942, 944
  words for pauper 73 n. 3
  words for populace 26
  words for slave 100
dream interpreters 562, 598, 984, 1046;
    see also Achmet; Artemidorus
  in temples 117, 119, 271, 835, 836–7;
    see also παστοφόροι
dreams 874 n. 35
  in Memphite Serapeum 837
  revelation in 720
  see also epilepsy—and visions; visions
dropsy 17, 295, 313, 770, 801–2, 803, 805, 806
drowning 545, 665, 842, 852, 941, 942
druggists 38, 59, 68, 568, 812, 1039, 1045;
    see also doctors
drugs 54 n. 76, 568, 713, 780, 813, 843, 988,
    998; see also medicine
dual, use of 203, 736, 900, 946
dumbness 963, 964; see also speech defect
dyeing 38, 43 n. 31, 53, 54, 56 n. 81, 68, 69,
    640, 1034
  gemstones 1063–4
  trades pleasant 59, 68, 69, 564, 929; see also
    purple
  trades unpleasant 59 n. 96, 777–8

echidna, see viper
eclipses 47 n. 44, 312 n. 74, 522, 543, 597,
    791, 913, 914
ecliptic 181, 183, 510, 523, 544, 573, 630, 693
  Moon and 88 n. 17, 538, 543–4, 922
  see also Aratus—circles; nodes
efficacy 11, 20 n. 4, 176, 533, 704, 705, 714;
    see also inefficacy
Egypt 97, 613, 700, 813
  absence of local detail 106, 116–19, 783,
    834, 1004
  adoption in 658
  animal-worship 823

Egypt (*cont.*)
  astrological texts 987; *see also* Tebtunis—texts from temple library
  beer 47
  calendar 518, 961
  Christianity in 838
  citizenship in 977
  divination, *see* hydromancy; lecanomancy; export of wheat 751–2
  Herodotus on 118 n. 52, 615–16, 947
  leprosy in 768 n. 19
  local colour 180, 271, 318, 641
  and magic 699, 983
  second marriage in 664
  slaves in 44–5, 100
  temples 271 n. 6, 358, 864 n. 7, 866, 867; *see also* dream interpreters—in temples; κάτοχοι
  textiles 53, 929, 961 n. 143
  trades in 48, 608, 610; *see also* painters—encaustic
  tuberculosis in 807
  wet-nurses 57 n. 90
  wise men in 271, 750, 862–3, 868, 870; *see also* Amenhotep; Imhotep; Nechepso(s) and Petosiris; Petosiris
  see also ἀγορανόμος; Alexandria; ἀρχικυνηγός; asp (cobra); books—sacred; Cumont, Franz—and Egyptian sources of astrology; custodians of tombs; *dodecaoros*; funeral industry; garum; λογιστής; Oxyrhynchus; παστοφόροι; Thoth
elephant 26 n. 39, 605, 769; *see also* ivory-carving
elephantiasis as name of leprosy 768, 957; *see also* leprosy
embalmers 54, 117, 581, 583 n. 131, 614, 615–16; *see also* necrotaphoi
embassies 22, 28 n. 47
embourgeoisement 33 n. 74, 809, 841, 859
embroidery 53, 54, 68, 929, 1000, 1034, 1062
  with gold thread 42 n. 23, 51, 53, 523, 880
embryotomy 815, 943 n. 116; *see also* abortion; miscarriage
encaustic painting, *see* painters—encaustic
engravers 51, 68 n. 143, 725, 1036; *see also* gems
enslavement, self- 84, 95; *see also* Mariandynoi; slavery
epigram, sepulchral, *see* epitaphs
epilepsy 13, 17
  and madness 137, 538, 691, 711, 718, 801, 1060; *see also* mental disturbance
  and the Moon 538–9, 716, 832, 833, 1060
  and visions 833–4
  see also possession, divine and demonic
  epitaphs 14, 15, 119, 276, 524, 526, 697, 718, 751, 767, 790, 796, 846, 902
Erysichthon 326, 724, 910
euergetism, *see* benefactors
Eurysaces, M. Vergilius 43–4, 778 n. 35
excess body-parts 687–8
exorcism 318, 981, 982–3, 1046
expenditure 30, 980–1, 985; *see also* benefactors; metaphor—liquids
eyebrows 337 n. 40, 629, 952–3
eyes 135, 958, 1061
  harm to 137, 566–8, 959; *see also* ἀμβλυωπία; blindness
  and heavenly bodies 339, 556 n. 70, 891, 900
  and luminaries 341, 543, 555, 566, 900, 960
  in physiognomy 16, 951, 952, 973
  and rays 339, 556, 647, 700

Fachliteratur 149, 270, 390, 396, 999
falling from a height 742, 745, 941, 942
famine 27, 79 n. 49, 686 n. 282, 894
farming, *see* agriculture
Fate 1059
  balances of 508–9
  literary expressions involving 292 n. 35, 509, 526, 697, 825–6, 852, 949
  resistance is futile 817–25 *passim*
  and the stars 204, 289, 509, 753, 940; *see also* 'Olympian' motifs transferred to stars
  see also death—and Fate; Fortune; Homeric poems—on Fate; spindles, spinning—and Fates; Tyche
father
  concubines of 943
  death of 146, 254, 667
  paternal affection 91 n. 36
  power over children 24 n. 28, 91 n. 37
  slaves love master like 92
  sons kill 914
  status of 540, 546, 659, 660
  see also adoption; incest—parent-child; slaves—as parents; stepfathers
fellatio, *see* oral sex
fingertips 701, 770
Firmicus Maternus
  on agriculture 60, 63
  on the army 59 n. 99
  on astrologers 558
  on books 983

General Index

and citizenship 28 n. 47
daily bread 71, 81
on doctors 813
legal terminology 56, 1025
on letters 107, 108
life and times 42, 86
on music 1005
on pantomimes 112, 918
on performers 112–14
'poor in spirit' 82 n. 66
relatedness to the Manethonianan poets 133
on skin diseases 957
and smells 617
on status 63
on trades 40–1, 43, 47, 49 n. 56, 50, 51, 52–7, 63 n. 115, 66–71 *passim*, 144 n. 43
value-judgements 62 n. 111, 64, 65, 80 n. 53
'why sacrifice?' 272, 821
see also falling from a height; kings—lords of life and death; Marsi; Rome—setting for astrology?; slaves—prisoners of war
fishing, fishermen 55, 57, 59 n. 94, 565, 601, 603, 604, 970, 971, 1027
florists 53, 68, 1039; *see also* dyeing; perfumes
forgers 109, 536, 599, 955
Fortune 24 n. 28, 818, 825, 846
gifts of 773–4
Lot of 60 n. 100, 121, 130 n. 5, 527, 545, 558, 692, 886, 965 n. 148
see also Fate; Tyche
fowlers, fowling, *see* birds—catchers of
freedmen 44, 46, 84, 96, 97 n. 72, 121–2, 736–7
imperial 85 n. 7, 736, 737
Latini Juniani 737
see also Augustales; Eurysaces, M. Vergilius; slaves; Trimalchio
friends 22 n. 15, 82 n. 67, 808, 857
ingratitude of 71 n. 155
of kings and big men 151, 546, 549, 679, 978
and the *plebs media* 110, 111, 122
and trust 7, 28 n. 47, 710
fulling 51 n. 64, 53, 59, 69, 118, 120 n. 56, 216, 673, 674, 1035, 1065; *see also* smells
funeral industry 42, 50, 54, 58, 1049; *see also* coffin-makers; embalmers; mourners, professional; mummification; necrotaphoi

galli 119, 143, 271, 341, 834, 933, 1049
and divination 839
drums 934
effeminate 595
hair 632, 839

mendicants 596, 734, 911, 946
self-wounding 595, 840–1, 934
see also Attis
Ganymede 517
gardeners 52, 212, 780
in Corycos 57 n. 88
in Egypt 118 n. 50, 119, 180, 610
literary treatments of 179, 219, 608, 611
in Pompeii 57 n. 89
representation in astrology 47, 60, 62, 605, 606, 610–12, 779, 1027
see also vegetables
garum 48, 55, 57, 123 n. 68, 581, 609, 616–17, 1055
Gemini 519, 702
classification, *see* zodiac, signs of—double-bodied, winged
house of Mercury 928, 965, 995 n. 195
monomoiriai 113 n. 33, 114 n. 34
northern 603
paranatellonta 928, 930, 1065
and the Sun 547, 548
gems, *see* precious stones
geometers, geometry 64 n. 122, 253, 265, 557, 558, 590, 591, 1044
ghosts 654, 655, 719, 720, 721, 832, 910, 982 n. 176; *see also* visions
gifts 9, 25, 28, 633, 760, 821, 871, 911; *see also* benefactors; expenditure; Muses—gifts of
gladiators 67 n. 140, 87 n. 13, 111 n. 26, 621 n. 202, 853 n. 147, 866 n. 16, 984, 985, 1052
bestiarii 743, 975
conventions of commemoration 114, 576 n. 111, 930, 979
glass-blowers 120 n. 56, 175, 776, 1032
gnomic aorist 168, 170, 204, 208, 289, 290, 333, 334, 1003
gold, wearing of 42, 523, 784–5, 880; *see also* crowns; embroidery—with gold thread; purple
goldsmiths 50 n. 61, 51, 54, 55 n. 77, 59 n. 96, 64, 65 n. 123, 68, 564, 725, 752, 879, 1036; *see also* coinage, coiners; metalworking—precious metal
Gorgianic figures 160 n. 90, 180, 214, 238, 342, 542, 626–7, 700, 922, 1000
gout 34, 137, 241, 701–2, 770
grammar 589; *see also* rhetoric, rhetoricians
grammarians 35, 79 n. 47, 107, 109, 122, 794; *see also* books
gymnasiarch 784, 785, 786, 1054
gymnasium 576 n. 112, 577, 957, 1054

Hadrian, horoscope of 35 n. 4, 803, 886, 888, 991
haemorrhage, see blood—issue of
hair
  curly 840
  facial 792
  fair 974
  long 838, 839
  in physiognomy 951 n. 126, 973
  scented 632, 839
  thick 839
  thin 554
  see also eyebrows; wigs
hallucinations, see visions
handicrafts, see crafts
hanging 318, 696, 745, 842, 843, 941, 942; see also impalement
hatred 600
Hawk, the 141, 645
hawkers, see birds, catchers of
Hecate 540, 544, 622, 719, 721, 919
Hector 526, 878, 893, 937, 939, 946
helmsman 666
Hephaestion, quotes Manetho 270–1, 276, 317, 809
Heracles 680, 710, 784 n. 47, 843, 919 n. 83, 936, 937
  and *labor* 172, 621
hermaphrodites 292 n. 36, 790, 791, 792–3, 919
Hermes 131, 314, 864 n. 7, 865, 868, 869, 870, 873, 875, 886; see also Amenhotep
Hermes Trismegistos 866, 868; see also Thoth
Hermetic literature 107, 508 n. 2, 752, 864 n. 7, 865, 868, 869, 873, 883, 983
high priests, see priests—high
Hippocratic corpus 802, 806, 807, 808, 1063
  language of 530, 567, 767, 768, 815, 851, 994
  oath 813
Homer
  as astrologer 358, 874, 875, 876, 878, 879, 1004
  διάνοια/ideas of 877, 880
Homeric poems
  basis of Manethoniana 109, 1000, 1004
  citations of 874 n. 36, 875, 876, 877–8, 893
  combinatory allusions to 216, 293, 338, 653, 657–8, 842, 939, 951
  on the dead 715, 832
  on Fate 754, 755, 819, 824, 875, 878, 893
  hapax legomena 214, 527, 674, 736, 782, 799, 901, 952
  heroes, physique of 974
  location of hegemonic principle in 806
  in M^a 578, 942
  in M^b
    formulary 209, 292, 523, 532, 547, 562, 639, 648, 650, 669, 690, 716, 728, 730, 744
    presque homérique 216, 589, 613, 616, 653, 745
  in M^c 291–3
    formulary 758, 798, 816, 817, 847
    presque homérique 288 n. 25, 293, 767, 771, 795, 807, 813, 860
  in M^d 336–8, 797
    formulary 883, 921, 934, 971
    presque homérique 894, 924
  metaphor 545
  metre 1001, 1002
    inner metric 226 n. 141, 227, 230, 303, 352, 383, 754
    outer metric 298, 345, 357 n. 81
    prosody 307, 354, 355
    tetracola 517
  morphology 191, 192, 512, 521, 575, 600
  pathos 14
  phrase patterns 526, 527, 542, 551, 851
  similes 23, 552, 879, 892, 941
  on the soul 714, 808
  syntax 507, 665, 675, 736, 798, 814, 894, 981
  vocabulary astrologised 249, 313, 361, 693, 736, 855, 884, 913
  see also Calliope; dogs and birds; dual, use of; Muses; naming formulae; 'Olympian' motifs transferred to stars; παλάμῃσι
Homeristes 116; see also mimes
homicides, see murderers
homoeoteleuton 157, 159 n. 86, 1000
homosexuals 14, 137, 179, 730, 732–3, 734, 954, 995
  passive 254, 634–5, 653, 730, 733, 917, 918, 972 n. 159, 990, 991
  see also Christianity—on homosexuality; husband—homosexual; lesbians; oral sex; pederasty; wives—homosexual
horizon 510, 693, 729, 892
horoscope, the, see Ascendant
horoscopes
  casting of 510
  from conception 754
  Old Coptic 35 n. 1
  of M^a 117, 157, 750, 751, 758
  royal 26, 154, 846–8, 858(?)
  slave 99

see also Alexander the Great; γένεσις;
  Hadrian, horoscope of; Oedipus;
  Ptolemy, king of Egypt
hunters, hunting 59 n. 94, 111 n. 26, 141, 644,
    648, 1027
  combined with fowlers 253, 601, 932, 970;
    see also birds—catchers of; fishing,
    fishermen;
  hard life 177 n. 140, 605, 649
  nets 971
  weapons 604
  see also ἀρχικυνηγός; gladiators—*bestiarii*;
    Orion; wild animals
husband 767
  complaisant 633; *see also* adulterers;
    wives
  homosexual 730
  shares occupation with wife 947; *see also*
    wives—take on husband's
    businesses
  and wife, relations of 91 n. 37, 92 n. 40,
    661, 664, 843
  see also wives
hydromancy 592; *see also* lecanomancy
hypallage 536, 651, 652, 713, 731, 746,
  790, 880

iatrosophist 119 n. 53, 318, 967
Icarus 326, 340, 921
if p then q 922, 997, 1003
illness, mental, *see* madness
Imhotep 864–5, 869, 870; *see also*
    Amenhotep; Asclepius
Imouthes 865, 869, 874 n. 35
impalement 586, 587, 696
incest 133 n. 24, 152, 250, 253, 254, 339, 671,
    765–6, 788, 943
  parent-child 326, 766, 944; *see also*
    Oedipus, Thyestes
  sibling 671, 943, 945
  see also father—concubines of; stepfathers;
    stepmothers
inefficacy 176, 707, 995; *see also* efficacy;
    planets—debility/depression
inheritance 686–7, 1066
  legacies 96, 254, 596 n. 158, 667, 669, 951
  loss of 78 n. 42, 667, 859, 914
instruments, makers of 61, 254, 678, 679,
    1005, 1035; *see also* automata
invective 78, 953–4, 993
iron 60 n. 100, 613
  blade 527, 840, 934; *see also* axe
  chains 694
  in cosmic architecture 825–6

  epithets 556–7, 614
  fire and 39, 40, 59 n. 94, 61, 217, 555, 776 n.
    29, 916, 1032
  wounds 527
Ishtar 919
isocolon 158, 160 n. 89, 162, 1000, 1002
  in M^b 208
  in M^c 294
  in M^d 163, 342, 343, 946, 978
ivory-carving 51, 253, 563, 564, 639, 1037
  retail 67 n. 135
  see also luxury products

jaundice 537, 768, 770
Jerome 272, 803, 838
Jesus 623; *see also* crucifixion; φάντασμα
Jocasta 326, 340, 944; *see also* Oedipus
John Chrysostom 624, 985, 986, 989
judges 24 n. 28, 116, 546, 695, 706, 889, 964,
    1043; *see also* law courts
justice 21–2, 24 n. 28, 179, 509; *see also*
    judges; law courts

kennings 217 n. 116, 645, 648–9, 780, 922
kidneys 16 n. 51, 804, 805
kings 18–24, 25–6, 32, 74, 152, 515
  and big men 32, 122, 533, 679, 762–3, 961;
    see also purple
  birth of 341–2, 548, 885–6, 889
  in the 'gendered luminaries' scheme 131,
    762, 846–7
  on *kentra* 546–7, 786, 848, 888
  lords of life and death 23, 24 n. 28, 526,
    848, 1058
  see also Alexander the Great; friends—of
    kings and big men; horoscopes—
    royal; Necho II (Pharaoh);
    physiognomy—of kings; Ptolemy,
    king of Egypt; satraps
Koechly, Hermann
  method 149–55 *passim*
  view of M^b 178, 182, 184, 237, 550, 553,
    571, 697
  view of M^c 133, 164, 270–6, 281–3 *passim*,
    296, 310, 311, 323–4
  view of M^d 317, 319, 320, 321, 325–6, 327

L (Laur. Plut. 28.27)
  asteriskos 388, 899
  marginal variants 387–8
  tables of contents 387
labyrinth 214, 646
Latinisms 144, 191, 664, 970, 1002 n. 15
Latinus Junianus 737

Laureolus 587 n. 144, 744 n. 383
law courts 21, 56, 1062; *see also* judges
lawsuits 22 n. 15, 76, 79, 120 n. 55, 122, 364, 765, 897
lead poisoning 777
leasing land 677, 1066
leather workers 53, 65, 637, 638
   disdained 67, 639
   in Homer 172 n. 120, 173
   trade names 41 n. 18, 1033
   see also shoemakers
lecanomancy 118 n. 50, 180, 590, 592–3, 981 n. 175, 1046; *see also* diviners; necromancy
legacies, *see* inheritance
Leo 598, 602–3, 765, 886, 907 n. 76, 973 n. 161
   classification, *see* zodiac, signs of—four-footed, male
   fiery 519, 895 n. 67
   formulary 548, 619, 952 n. 131
   house of the Sun 516, 517, 519, 547, 724, 925
   monomoiriai 114 n. 36
   number of stars 519
   paranatellonta 608
Leonine hexameter 162, 163, 1002
   in M^c 294, 295, 296
   in M^d 341, 342, 343
leprosy 295, 313, 768–71, 957
leptologia 999, 1000
lesbians 131, 305, 651, 653, 763–4, 789, 917, 946, 989; *see also* homosexuals; τριβάς
Libra 21 n. 13, 47 n. 44, 93 n. 51, 509, 519, 555, 653, 786, 859
   and Augustus 24 n. 28
   Balances 508, 516, 603
   Claws 516, 518–19
   exaltation of Saturn 516, 517
   house of Venus 772, 925
   paranatellonta 603, 925, 990
   terms of 903
   see also zodiac, signs of—tropic
lion 26 n. 39, 596, 743, 744, 941
   characteristics 548, 952
   Homeric formulary 23, 940, 958, 971
   see also venatio
lioness 816
literacy 107–8, 110, 957; *see also* Pompeii
Lots
   of daughters 541
   of farming 47
   of Fortune 60 n. 100, 121, 130 n. 5, 527, 545, 558, 692, 886, 965 n. 148
   of πρᾶξις 140, 793
love-charms, *see* magic—love

luxury products 639, 832, 961, 1035
   moralists and 68–9, 81, 564, 614, 961 n. 144
   valued by élites 68, 70
   well represented in astrology 41, 50, 51, 106 *see also* crafts, clean

madmen 137, 259, 538, 654, 691, 711, 801, 911
madness 781, 843, 910
   divine 594, 717, 840
   literary treatments of 216, 293, 295, 782
   and the Moon 713, 832
   see also epilepsy—and madness; *galli*; mental defect; mental disturbance; possession, divine and demonic; visions
maenads 926
magi 592, 863 n. 6, 982, 1049
magic 119, 577, 713–14 n. 328, 980, 981, 982, 983
   love 699, 843, 984
   see also books—and magic; prostitutes, prostitution—and magic
managers 44 n. 33, 45 n. 37, 60 n. 100, 729–30, 741, 1030; *see also* οἰκονόμος
   of farms and property 61, 562
Manetho, priest of Heliopolis 866; *see also* Book of Sothis
Manilius 37, 997, 999
   on the generation of animate beings 694
   on Homer 875
   on poverty 83
   on the transmission of astrology 558
   used by Firmicus 14 n. 39, 52, 55, 60, 69, 112, 113, 262
   on *visus* 249
   see also Cepheus
Mann, Thomas 770 n. 21, 808; *see also* consumption
Mariandynoi 95
marriage 133 n. 24, 145, 259, 677, 730, 987, 993
   in catarchic astrology 664
   euphemism 635
   happy 12, 122, 733
   incestuous 253, 671, 766, 944, 945
   second 664, 976
   with slaves 92, 93 n. 51, 760
   unhappy 891, 897, 906, 909, 963
   unstable 561–2, 915
   virgin 662, 663
   see also husband; prostitutes, prostitution; widows; wives; women

General Index

Marsi 117, 936, 1045; *see also* snake-handlers
matchmakers 633, 1056
Maximus, astrological poet 109, 998
  metre 237, 309
    inner metric 226, 227, 229, 230, 231, 302, 303, 305, 349, 1001
    outer metric 222, 224–5, 300, 301, 345
    prosody 234–5, 237, 307, 308
  planetary names 255, 382
  on slaves 89, 92, 93 n. 51
Maximus of Tyre 1060
  on luxury 68–9
  on petitionary prayer 272, 817–18
meanness 13, 1060
Medalliondichtung 128, 148, 998
medicine
  astrology's treatment of 54, 59
  see also analogy—in medicine; bile; disease; doctors; druggists; drugs; δύναμις; garum; Hippocratic corpus; madness; midwives; physiognomy; sponges
melancholy 16, 594, 768, 770
melothesia 805
Memphite Serapeum 836, 837; *see also* Ptolemaios archive
Menelaus 757
mental defect 94, 95, 153
mental disturbance 95 n. 58, 295, 314, 654, 677 n. 277, 714, 716, 781, 782, 806, 910; *see also* epilepsy; madness
mercenaries 250, 689, 765, 1058
merchants 38, 295, 560–1, 674, 1038
  individual 110, 123 n. 68, 541 n. 45
  literary image 66, 177 n. 140, 210, 677
  sailing 541, 545, 561, 665
Mesomedes 175, 924
metalworking 628, 725, 916, 1032, 1036
  precious metal 50, 66, 614; *see also* coinage, coiners; engravers; goldsmiths
  trade names 41 n. 18
metaphor
  agricultural 677–8, 790
  conceptual 339, 718–19
  liquids 544–5, 911, 986–7
  in M^b 509, 511, 529, 570, 646, 672, 707; also s.vv. agricultural, liquids, pathway, sexual
  in M^c 760, 782; also s.vv. sexual
  in M^d 339–40, 361, 903, 904, 950, 955, 968, 974, 996; also s.vv. liquids, metapoetic, pathway, sexual
  of social hierarchy 902, 969–70

  pathway 214, 244, 508, 522, 578, 619, 629, 718–19, 730, 734, 956, 966
  poetological 862, 871, 880, 1000
  sexual 629, 766, 972
  see also adultery—as rapine; astrology—use of metaphor; slavery—metaphorical, yoke of
metonymy 251, 577, 604, 650, 670, 714, 760, 971
midwives 57, 992; *see also* birthing stool
mimes 5, 70, 111, 210, 985, 1005, 1052
  and the Ape 31, 618, 619
  charts for 113, 141, 142, 143, 151, 254, 617, 618, 620, 678
  in competitions 581
  costume 625
  disdained 69, 115, 179, 578
  in Egypt 116
  fool (μῶρος) 624, 681
  gives enjoyment 111 n. 23, 578
  itinerant 622, 734
  laughter 622, 624
  obscenity 578, 580, 624, 915
  shaven head 624–5, 906
  and song 579, 1005
  and speech 530, 622, 680, 681
  types of 578–9, 621–2; *see also* Homeristes
  see also acrobats; ἀρεταλόγος; conjurers; Laureolus; pantomimes; strongmen
mining 613–14, 738, 1030
misanthropes, *see* sociopaths
miscarriage 152 n. 59, 295, 296, 313, 670, 671, 854; *see also* abortion; embryotomy
miserabilism 15, 43, 65, 91, 92, 94, 95, 243, 272, 552, 594, 621, 690, 750, 809, 846
misogyny 839, 993
Mithras, Mithraism 59, 515, 823
mnemonics 159, 213, 883, 998
money 970
  circulation of 968–9
  working for 65
  see also accountants; coinage, coiners; debt; inheritance; metaphor—liquids; Moon—and money
money-changers 56, 1040
money-lenders 56, 728, 968, 969, 1041
Mons Claudianus 641
Moon 538–45, 908–14
  anomaly 646
  and the birth of children 814, 842
  and the birth of daughters 540–1
  in catarchic astrology 79, 88; *see also* —and money

Moon (cont.)
  chariot of 543
  dodecatemories of 247 n. 205
  epithets 257–8, 315, 316, 363, 520, 538, 543, 544, 630, 651
  eye of 960
  kenodromia 804, 908 n. 77
  and mental illness 538–9, 713, 716, 801, 910; *see also* epilepsy—and madness, the Moon
  and money 76, 543, 911–12, 912–13, 980–1
  and the mother 146
  phase 130 n. 9, 140, 243, 313, 704, 769, 771, 774, 801, 828, 855, 908
    crescent 538, 693
    Full 200, 647, 950
    gibbous 909
    see also—and money, epithets, in catarchic astrology; φωσφορεῖν
  and places of gender 789, 846–7
  and πρᾶξις 139, 140, 147, 771
  in royal trigon 22
  and skin diseases 768, 957
  synaphe and *aporrhoia* 86 n. 11, 91, 130 n. 5, 131, 132 n. 20, 134, 153, 164, 278, 313, 314, 746 n. 386, 802, 814, 890
  twisted course 88 n. 17, 181, 214, 244, 538, 543–4, 564, 646, 922; *see also* ecliptic—Moon and
  wandering 66, 255, 257, 541, 543, 560, 708
  see also analogy—with Moon; Anubion—on πρᾶξις; blindness; eclipses; ἕλιξ; ἐμπερίσχεσις; nodes; planets—order; sect—Moon; Sin, Moon God; spleen; σύνδεσμος; σύνοδος; terms—of Moon
mother 842, 987
  death of 146, 656, 667, 767, 804, 813–14
  sexual history of 661
  status of 540, 659, 660
  see also abortion; birthing stool; embryotomy; incest—parent–child; miscarriage; slaves—as parents; stepmothers, intercourse with
mourners, professional 54, 117, 581, 582–3, 1049
mummification 48, 180, 582, 583, 609, 616–17, 1049, 1066
  see also cedar oil/wood; funeral industry; garum; necrotaphoi; smells; ταριχευτής
murderers 130 n. 12, 253, 585 n. 133, 692, 695, 743

Muses 115, 979
  gifts of 871, 872
  lips/mouths of 876, 926, 991
  in M^c 311, 507, 750–1, 759, 860
  in M^d 962, 968
music, musicians 52, 64 n. 122, 69, 116, 975, 1005, 1050–1
  associated with Mercury and Venus 59, 153, 578 n. 117, 590, 771, 772, 925
  see also aulos, auloi; citharodes; mimes—and song; prostitutes—musicians; singers
muteness, *see* dumbness
mysteries 531, 597, 598, 772, 1059
  see also books—in mystery religions

nabla 111 n. 25, 580–1, 590
naming formulae 204, 257, 337, 515, 528
Nechepso(s) 852, 864, 865, 866 n. 16, 872–3
Nechepso(s) and Petosiris 117, 180, 756, 776, 869
  and astrobotany 869–70
  doctrines 131, 248, 314, 754, 894
  iambi? 852, 865, 960
  revelation 511, 864–5
  source of Anubion, Dorotheus, Firmicus, Manetho 130, 133, 277, 691 n. 288
  writings 20 n. 8, 756–7, 866 n. 16, 960
  see also Petosiris; P.Salt
Necho II (Pharaoh) 873
necromancy 590, 592, 593, 1046
necrotaphoi 50, 54 n. 74, 66 n. 134, 118 n. 52, 180, 583, 1049, 1065
  see also funeral industry; mummification
Nectanebo 591, 593, 888; *see also* Alexander Romance
nectar 877
Nemesis 509, 697
neologism 221, 521, 1000
Nicander
  M^d and 110, 317 n. 5, 338 n. 49, 1004; *see also* snakes
  narrative voice 171 n. 117, 217, 315
  style 155 nn. 72–3, 157 n. 77, 342
  see also comitative expressions
night 933
  birth 779, 809, 846, 847, 892, 904, 909, 948
  revelation by 865, 872
  turned into day 631
  work by 543, 755, 778
  see also thieves—by night
nodes 130 n. 9, 132 n. 20, 543, 692, 795, 890, 908, 913, 969, 980, 981

General Index

Full Moon at 539, 712, 715, 716, 832
Nonnus 863 n. 6, 1003
  anticipated by M^b 179, 186 n. 17, 237–8, 676, 731, 746, 769, 998
  anticipated by M^c 796, 826, 833
  anticipated by M^d 927
  aspects of style 232 n. 155

Ocean 361, 932, 986–7
Odysseus 757, 769, 794, 804, 879, 953, 973
  as craftsman 172, 173, 177, 680
Odyssey
  metre 224, 225
  on slaves 91
  and wandering 75, 596, 683, 922
Oedipus 147 n. 51, 216, 277, 279, 765, 786–8, 943, 944; *see also* incest; Jocasta
old age 568, 715, 740, 845, 878 n. 45, 898
  formulary of 964
  impoverished 80
'Olympian' motifs transferred to stars 15, 293, 522, 668, 670, 697, 745, 754, 796, 817, 827, 831, 841, 860, 988; *see also* Homeric poems—vocabulary astrologised
opposition
  as concord 588, 761, 951
  as discord 849, 891
  Homeric expressions for 292–3, 313, 761, 829, 855, 856
  in *Timaeus* 180
  modelled by chiasmus 220, 536, 725
oracles 79, 204, 530, 549, 961
  Apolline 586, 675, 676, 819
  Chaldaean 317, 726
  dice 846 n. 141
  see also Dodona; Sibylline Oracles
oral sex 210, 634, 635, 637, 990
Origen, on prayer 818
Orion 603, 644, 932
Orphic Hymns 162 n. 99, 232, 598, 993
Oxyrhynchus 42 nn. 23–24, 57, 116, 569 n. 100, 980, 998; *see also* papyri

painters 68–9, 564, 649–50, 832, 849, 1035
  encaustic 54, 118, 649, 916, 929, 1035, 1066
  of ships 53, 649, 1032
  see also crafts, clean; precious stones—painting
palaestra, *see* wrestlers, wrestling
pancratiasts, pancratium 576 n. 111, 772, 930, 1054
pantomimes 70, 111, 113, 115, 581, 619
  androgyny 916–17, 918–19

  in Firmicus 112, 113, 114 n. 36
  themes 944
  see also mimes
pan pipes 925, 926
papyri
  of Anubion 277–80
  of Manetho 178–9, 234, 270, 274–6, 279, 283, 389–90, 395, 396, 397, 998, 1061
parallelism 158, 159, 160–1, 162, 163, 272, 1000, 1002
  in Aratus 157
  in M^b 161, 206, 207, 208, 222, 238, 540, 664, 684, 734
  in M^c 163, 275, 294, 295, 296, 298, 845, 850
  in M^d 321, 325, 327, 341, 342, 343, 891, 896, 903, 944, 946, 980
  in *Or. Sib.* 160 n. 90, 342
  see also chiasmus
paramone 97, 738
paranatellonta, *see* Ape (constellation); Teucer; and s.vv. individual zodiacal signs
'Par. Anub.' 26 n. 41, 138, 514, 783
  see also planets—order
Paris (Trojan hero) 173, 562, 632, 653, 763
pearl-dealers 53, 66; *see also* precious stones
pederasty 652, 732 n. 352, 733, 761, 917 n. 82, 918; *see also* homosexuals
Pegasus 644, 645
peplos 852, 919
perfumes 38, 42, 54, 64, 66, 564, 617
  decadent 69, 630, 632
  manufacture of 51, 57, 929, 1037, 1062
  sale of 67, 69, 1039
  see also dyeing; smells
periphrastic expressions
  for occupations 212, 542, 579, 612, 633, 639, 640, 674, 776, and Appendix II, *passim*
  for technical terms 246, 247, 256, 361, 559, 603, 906
  tragic 211, 335, 528, 586, 648, 685, 687, 949
periphrastic tenses 323, 660–1, 663, 939
petauristae 111, 113 n. 31, 621, 1053
  charts for 254, 617, 618
  itinerant 622
  motifs 114, 626
  in theatre 620
  see also acrobats; tightrope-walkers
Peteesis 756, 873
Petesis 756, 864

Petosiris 868
   and M^c 311, 749, 750, 751, 756–7
   and M^d 319, 358, 863, 864, 867, 873
   wisdom 873
   see also Nechepso(s) and Petosiris
phase, see Moon; planets
physiognomy 723, 769, 898, 952, 954, 973, 978, 993, 1059
   of kings 19, 548, 951
   of slaves 45 n. 40
   see also complexion; eyebrows; eyes; hair; Thersites
pigmenta 54, 59, 69, 1044
pillars, in temples 117, 511, 863, 864 n. 7, 867, 870, 983
pimps 14, 632–3, 636, 651, 653, 703, 1056; see also prostitutes, prostitution
Pisces 545, 601, 602, 603, 620, 671, 702, 858, 859
   chains 160 n. 91, 924
   classification
      variegated 958
      see also zodiac, signs of—bent, double-bodied, lewd, mute, scaly, watery
   decans 951 n. 127
   house of Jupiter 516, 559, 951
   monomoiriai 63 n. 115, 923
   paranatellonta 617 n. 199, 638, 644, 645, 924, 935
pitch 61 n. 106, 605, 650, 1032, 1033
places
   of birth 183
   eighth 692
   fifth 22 n. 19, 574 n. 105, 736
   fourth (of Parents) 905
   for 'house' or 'sign' 894
   ninth 590, 836
   second 780, 829, 908
   sixth (κακὴ τύχη) 691, 794, 795, 854
   tenth 740
   third (θεά) 836, 912, 970
   twelfth (Evil Demon) 199, 243 n. 174, 683, 684, 734, 735, 803
planets
   colour of
      Jupiter 973–4
      Mars 581–2
      Mercury 537
      Saturn 993
      Venus 597–8, 958
   debility/depression 516, 714, 889, 900, 906
   exaltation 387, 516, 517, 546, 547, 626, 886, 928, 931–2, 961, 963
   gender of 763, 918
   and gods 180, 181, 511, 574–5, 797, 883, 884
   lists of 883, 885
   names and epithets 255–8, 315–16, 362–4
   order 134–5, 886, 1059
      heptazonos (positional) 132, 134, 259, 314, 514, 759, 890, 908–9, 913, 988
      qualitative 132, 134, 117, 155, 283, 314, 758, 759, 826, 890, 908–9, 988
   personified 180, 242, 245, 708, 791, 901
      implied by verbs of motion 293, 313, 595, 761, 766, 844, 895
      implied by verbs of vision 556, 654, 891
   phase 653, 762, 891–2, 933
   pursuit 638
   retrograde 88, 361, 746, 841, 889, 900, 901, 933
   see also dodecatemories; *dodecatopos*; sect; terms
Plato
   cephalocentrism 806
   on ἔργα and πρᾶξις 176
   on homosexuality 732
   on inspired prophecy 717
   on petitionary prayer 817
   on the souls of the dead 832
   Timaeus 180–2, 575, 747–8, 884
   see also ἀήρ; αἰθήρ; αἰών; Peteesis; planets—colour of—Jupiter
plebs media 36–7, 53 n. 72, 70–1, 109, 110, 113, 115, 121–3, 1004; see also Veyne, Paul
Plotinus 821 n. 88, 825
poison 24 n. 29, 220 n. 131, 526, 528, 942; see also lead poisoning; snakes
poisoners 16, 743, 936
poles 508 nn. 2–3, 518 n. 17, 727
Pompeii 123 n. 68, 635, 924, 979
   economic life 51, 57 n. 89, 639 n. 230, 652, 674 n. 275, 777
   literacy in 108 n. 11
Porphyry 140 n. 35, 272, 818–19, 878 nn. 45 and 48, 933
porters 50, 173, 174, 1064
possession, divine and demonic 716, 837, 983 n. 178, 1060; see also epilepsy; exorcism; visions
potters 45 n. 40, 51, 627, 648 n. 247, 680, 1033
poverty 73–83, 521, 809, 894, 912
   absolute and relative 75
   caused by faulty temperament 77, 78, 82
   and manual work 80–1, 552

General Index

philosophical attitude to 82–3
structural and conjunctural 76, 95
vocabulary of 74, 810
vs wealth 36, 295, 343, 546, 831, 841;
  see also wealth
see also beggars; benefactors—profligacy;
  charity; lawsuits; old age;
  prostitutes, prostitution
prayer, petitionary 272, 817–22
precious stones 53, 54, 66, 1037
  cutting 68 n. 143
  dealing in 1039
  dyeing 1063
  engraving 50 n. 61, 53, 145, 1037
  painting 725, 1037
  see also crafts, clean
preface, conventions of 358, 751, 752, 756,
  757, 862, 871, 881
priesthood, high 22 n. 15, 35 n. 2
priests 532, 837 n. 123, 911, 960, 1047
  of Cybele 784 n. 47
  dietary rules 724
  of Eleusis 831
  eunuch 35
  high 522, 523, 772, 784–5, 786, 866, 961,
    975, 1047
  of Ma-Bellona 840, 983 n. 181
  of Syrian Goddess 596
  see also agonothetes; crowns; dream
    interpreters; *galli*; Manetho;
    παστοφόροι; Petosiris; purple—
    robes; στρόφιον
prison 208, 695, 836, 837, 902, 904, 915;
  see also chains—and imprisonment
prophecy 168, 594, 716, 717, 818 n. 80, 836
  apocalyptic 33 n. 73, 160 n. 90; *see also*
    Sibylline Oracles
  see also epilepsy—and visions
prophets 593, 598, 756, 829, 868, 911, 1026,
  1045
  inspired 594, 717, 984
  in temples 117, 676
  φοιβηταί 834–5
  see also diviners; Petesis
prosthetic limbs 15 n. 41, 795
prostitutes, prostitution 176 n. 139, 917, 990,
  1056
  in Athens 698, 703
  boy 761
  'common' 651, 955
  economic condition 652, 702, 703
  haughty 920, 984
  and magic 636, 698
  musicians 920, 955

slaves 45 n. 37, 633, 843
squandering money on 955, 985
standing/sitting 989
as wives 93, 760
see also χαμαιτυπίη; pimps
pseudepigrapha 271 n. 4, 395–6, 865, 866,
  867 n. 17
ps.-Scymnus 757, 881 n. 55
Ptolemaios archive 837, 838; *see also*
  Memphite Serapeum
Ptolemy, Claudius
  epigram on astronomy 877
  Tetrabiblos
    on ἀήρ 522
    commentary on 882, 884, 958 n. 140
    date of material 52, 140, 146, 260,
      261, 559
    on location of hegemonic principle 806
    on miscarriage 314
    and Posidonius 95
    on πρᾶξις 3, 34, 48, 130, 138, 140, 141,
      147–8, 252, 771, 1025; *see also*
      'chemical' industry
    on relations between masters and
      slaves 89–90
    on retail 67
    on sexuality 131, 653, 733, 761, 763–4,
      918, 946
    on types of sign 558, 617, 619, 627, 687,
      768, 917, 991
    words for citizenry 26
  see also accuracy—of Ascendant;
    Mariandynoi; hatred; melothesia
Ptolemy, king of Egypt
  addressee
    of Book of Sothis 866
    of 'court science' treatises 867
    of Manetho 117, 118, 272, 319
      M^c 271, 311, 749, 750, 751, 860
      M^d 318, 320, 326, 862, 864, 866, 871
    of *Sortes Astrampsychi* 867
  god-man 847
  horoscope of 341, 885, 888
pure *vs* impure arts, *see* crafts, clean
purple 157
  dealers in 65 n. 123, 67, 541 n. 45
  dyeing 43 n. 31, 777, 1034
  robes 42, 53, 111, 336, 832, 879,
    880, 960
  of priests 523, 784–5, 961, 1062
  on toga 587, 880
  see also agonothetes; crowns; dyeing

queens, birth of 846–7, 849

Regulus (α Leonis) 548
retail 41, 42, 47, 49, 66, 67, 176 n. 139, 1025;
    see also shopkeepers, and s.vv.
    specific industries
rhetoric, rhetoricians 576 n. 112, 589, 666,
    728, 881, 953, 956, 1042; see also
    grammar
  charts of 238, 318, 557, 794, 965, 967
  respect for 109
Rhetorius xxv, 135 n. 25, 136
rheumatism 701, 801
rivers running dry 798–9
Rome 123, 658, 674, 699 n. 308, 751, 752
  collegia 777
  labour market 43 n. 29
  Sacra Via 70, 106 n. 1; see also shopkeepers
  setting for astrology? 37, 42, 44, 55
  work inscriptions 48–9, 50, 51; see also
    columbaria
  see also acclamations; Eurysaces, M.
    Vergilius; Firmicus Maternus; *plebs
    media*; Sacra Via; shopkeepers
root-cutters 141, 568, 935
runners 112 n. 30, 113 n. 31, 575, 1053;
    see also athletes, charioteers

sacrifice, vanity of 152 n. 59, 154, 272, 273,
    291, 295, 296, 759, 817–22
sacrificer 776 n. 29, 1048
Sagittarius 567 n. 89, 601, 602
  classification, see zodiac, signs of—four-
    footed, male, winged
  house of Jupiter 516, 805, 951, 952, 969
  monomoiriai 114
  paranatellonta 645, 648, 923
  and the Sun 547
  see also Hawk, the
satraps 888
Saturn
  chief of the planets 515, 964
  star of the Sun 515
schetliasmos 154 n. 65, 273, 291, 296, 759,
    796, 797, 798, 997
Scorpio 518, 567 n. 89
  begins year 826
  classification 957; see also zodiac, signs
    of—bent, scaly
  decans 990
  dodecatemories 561 n. 78
  formulary 764
  house of Mars 764, 854 n. 150
  monomoiriai 55 n. 78, 923
  paranatellonta 935
  terms 16, 600, 839, 903

  see also Libra—Claws
scribes 24, 38, 56 n. 80, 534, 535, 583, 1043
  temple 676, 1049
  see also Manetho, priest of Heliopolis
sculpture, sculptors 41 n. 18, 69, 565, 649–50,
    1035–6, 1048; see also colossi;
    goldsmiths; ivory-carving;
    precious stones—cutting
seals, sealing, see engravers; wax—seals
Second Sophistic xi–xii, 109, 733, 1004–5
secretaries 56 n. 80, 794, 1043
sect 555, 706, 709, 763, 774, 988
  Mars 805, 853, 933, 991
  Mercury 535
  Moon 67 n. 139, 523, 540, 656, 846–7
  Saturn 516, 517, 520, 601 n. 167, 779, 780,
    892, 948
  Sun 546, 547, 846–7
  Venus 651
sedentary trades 64, 638, 639, 1062; see also
    shoemakers; teachers
segmentation 128, 238, 998, 999; see also
    Medalliondichtung
Seleucus legend 888
self-harm 710, 910
Seneca, the Younger 67, 68 n. 143, 70, 91, 112
sepulchral epigram, see epitaphs
sewers, sewer-cleaners 55 n. 79, 220, 606, 607,
    780, 1056
shinglers 53, 145, 628, 1031
ship, as steed 649 n. 248, 923
shipbuilding, see builders—of ships; wax—on
    ships
shipwreck 210, 393, 665, 666, 796, 798;
    see also drowning
shoemakers 34, 50, 53, 61 n. 107, 176 n. 139,
    640, 672
  female 120 n. 56
  trade names 144 n. 46
  see also leather workers; sedentary trades
shopkeepers 4, 43, 45 n. 40, 51, 59, 70, 175,
    781, 1039
  difficulty of identifying 42, 639, 650
  see also Pompeii; Rome—Sacra Via
siblings 145, 685, 873
  number of 546, 662
  see also brothers; incest—sibling
Sibylline Oracles 5 n. 8, 204, 396, 823,
    824, 874
  metre 224, 345, 347, 348, 350, 357, 948,
    1000–1
  style 160, 161, 162, 210, 752, 1003
  use of Plato 717, 748
signs, see zodiac, signs of

silversmiths 50, 59 n. 96, 68, 122, 752, 1036;
    see also coinage, coiners; goldsmiths
Sin, Moon God 822
singers 111 n. 25, 579, 920, 966, 974, 1051;
    see also charm-singers; mimes—and
    song
slave-owners 24 n. 28, 44, 102, 659; see also
    Valens, Vettius—on
    slave-ownership
slavery
    metaphorical 837
    'natural slavery' 78, 94
    and wage labour 65
    yoke of 214, 220, 656, 657, 659, 738
    see also enslavement, self-
slaves 69, 84–105, 594
    acquisition of 86; see also child exposure;
        slave trade, slave traders
    agricultural 87, 99
    as beasts of burden 1064
    and beggars 73, 75
    in catarchic astrology 85, 86, 87, 88, 96, 98,
        99, 741
    chained 87, 88, 608, 738, 741, 742
    charts for 133 n. 24, 185, 659, 735–42, 855–7
    commemoration of 46
    consulting astrologers 88, 89
    as custodians of graves 1064 n. 1
    in dream interpretation 98–9, 102; see also
        Achmet—and slaves;
        Artemidorus—and slaves
    house-born 86, 738, 846
    in household 45, 87, 91–2, 99–100, 103
    iconography of 45 n. 40, 625
    juridical status of 43–4, 45, 85, 91, 94, 96,
        106, 173, 846
    manumission of 84 n. 1, 85, 86, 89, 90, 96,
        97, 101, 102, 105, 735, 740–1;
        see also freedmen
    multiple sales of 739–40
    number of masters 85
    occupations 44, 45 n. 37, 49 n. 56, 51 n. 62,
        52, 85, 87, 104, 650, 778; see also
        Eurysaces, M. Vergilius
    as parents 90, 659, 660, 856
    and the poor 95
    as possessions 11, 91, 92
    prisoners of war 86, 91
    public 87, 104, 607
    runaway 84, 86, 88, 89, 90 n. 30, 92, 97,
        102, 120, 683, 741, 866 n. 16
    sexual relations with 86, 90, 92–3, 761,
        1067; see also wives—consort with
        slaves, slave

stewards 104, 741
    in temples 1048, 1060
thieves 86, 89
    see also agriculture—and slaves; burning;
        child exposure; crucifixion—of
        slaves; divination—used by masters
        and slaves; Dodona; Dorotheus—on
        masters and slaves, words for slave;
        Egypt—slaves in; enslavement, self-;
        father—slaves love master like;
        horoscopes—slave; marriage—with
        slaves; Maximus—on slaves;
        Odyssey—on slaves; physiognomy—
        of slaves; prostitutes—slaves;
        Ptolemy, Claudius—Tetrabiblos—on
        relations between masters and
        slaves; Stoicism—on slavery;
        torture—of slaves; weavers,
        weaving—slaves
slave trade, slave traders 66, 72 n. 160, 86,
    658, 740 n. 369, 1038, 1066
smells 69, 617, 639, 777, 1066; see also dyeing;
    fulling; garum; leather workers;
    mummification; perfumes
snake-handlers 117, 141, 144, 326, 337, 568,
    935, 936, 938, 1045; see also Marsi
snakes 338, 341, 342, 937, 938, 939
    in similes 901, 937
    see also asp (cobra); Pisces—monomoiriai,
        paranatellonta; viper
social capital 82, 121, 975
sociopaths 14 n. 40, 16, 28, 62, 231, 600, 722,
    723, 725
Sortes Astrampsychi 79, 88 n. 16, 97–8, 171,
    390 n. 4, 740, 867, 871
Sortes Sangallenses 88 n. 16, 171
speech defect 781, 964, 976; see also
    dumbness
Spica 60, 510, 565 n. 84; see also Virgo
spindles, spinning 672
    and Fates 509, 754, 819, 825
    and women's work 58, 946, 947
spleen 16 n. 51, 804, 805
sponges 175, 923, 924; see also divers
stars
    as causes/signs 551, 753, 956; see also
        determinism
    fixed vs wandering 182–3, 509–10, 513,
        573, 598–9, 753, 860, 897
    see also planets; Plato—Timaeus; zodiac,
        signs of
stepfathers 943
stepmothers, intercourse with 787–9, 943,
    945; see also incest

sterility 94 n. 55, 185, 789, 791, 922; see also
    wives—sterile
Stoicism 682, 819, 821 n. 88
    on brotherhood of man 93
    on location of the hegemonic principle 806
    on marriage 733, 947
    on natural philosophy 966
    on Nature 734
    on the philosophic life 67
    on slavery 95 n. 58
    see also Chrysippus; Cleanthes; suicide
stone-masons 41 n. 18, 42, 53, 117, 565,
        641–2, 776, 850, 1025, 1030–1,
        1065
    pay of 642, 780
    tools 583
street-cleaners 607, 612, 1056
strongmen 111, 254, 535, 618, 620, 622, 1053;
        see also acrobats; mimes
suicide 80 n. 54, 162 n. 97, 587, 745, 825;
        see also hanging
Sun
    ambivalent 897
    in catarchic astrology 88; see also
        Moon—and money
    chariot of 619
    cults of 822, 823 n. 98
    and euergetism 22
    eye of 960
    and fathers 146, 540, 546, 667
    formulary 654, 693, 704, 783, 918, 960
        epithets 257, 315, 362, 547, 1003
    Julian on 508 n. 3
    and kings 546, 762, 763, 786, 846–7
    as lamp 647, 675
    and Mars 783, 933, 939, 991
    and the Ocean 361, 932
    and πρᾶξις 130 n. 5, 140
    see also Cancer; ecliptic; ὕπαυγος; Leo;
        melothesia; φάσις; σύνοδος
swimming 392, 665
sword 692, 695–6, 790, 840, 842, 843, 933,
        941; see also axe; beheading

tailors 34, 50, 173, 1035; see also clothes
Tantalus 326, 338, 340, 921, 938
Tätigkeitsbezeichnung 39, 212; see also
    Berufsbezeichnung
Taurus 593, 617, 701
    classification, see zodiac, signs of—bent,
        four-footed
    exaltation of Moon 932, 950, 961
    formulary 619

house of Venus 823 n. 97, 925, 963
    monomoiriai 55 n. 79, 114 n. 36,
        607, 932
    paranatellonta 644, 930
    terms 966
tax-collectors 65, 710, 968
    of harbour taxes 712
tax-farmers 56, 1041
teachers 49, 52, 671, 1041
    sedentary 577, 672
    shepherd metaphor 672
    see also grammarians; rhetoric, rhetoricians
Tebtunis 108 n. 11, 1066
    texts from temple library 271 n. 6,
        756, 864
technai, see crafts
temples 862
    Apollo's 819
    Capitoline 822 n. 89
    craftsmen in 565 n. 84
    devotees in 718, 983, 1060, 1061
    discovery of writings in 117, 180, 508, 511,
        863–6, 867–8
    Egyptian 117, 118, 119, 358, 826, 836, 837;
        see also Tebtunis
    founders of 822, 1047
    in Harran 822
    of imperial cult 24 n. 32
    personnel of 271, 532, 569 n. 99, 594,
        675–6, 1047–9, 1051; see also
        κατοχή, κάτοχοι
    robbers 911
    see also astrologers—in temples; dream
        interpreters—in temples; Egypt;
        Manetho, priest of Heliopolis;
        pillars, in temples; priests;
        prophets—in temples; scribes—
        temple; slaves—in temples;
        Tebtunis
    terms 148, 262–3
        language used of 615, 642, 960; see also
            ἐναλλάγδην; ἐναλλάξ, ἐναλλάσσειν
        in Lib. Herm. 148, 562
        in M^b 184, 199, 241, 242, 243, 244, 571,
            572, 585, 591
        in M^d 332 n. 28, 343
        of Moon 644, 649
    tetracolon 157, 158, 162
        in M^b 231, 238, 517, 527
        in M^c 157, 305, 309, 806
        in M^d 157, 320, 352
Teucer, of Babylon xxv, 34, 55, 136, 138, 144,
        148, 565, 1025

General Index

source of Firmicus 52, 112, 262
underlies Θ 113, 141, 645
textile workers, *see barbaricarii*; clothes;
    dyeing; embroidery; fulling; purple;
    tailors; weaving
theatre 116, 622, 985
   audiences 926; *see also* ὄχλος
   popular entertainers in 620-1, 624; *see also*
    mimes
Thersites 554-5, 723
Thessalus 866 n. 16, 869
thieves 96, 253, 254, 600-1 n. 166, 642, 643,
   691, 695, 743, 973
   house-breakers 689, 692, 694
   by night 694
   see also slaves; tomb-robbers
Thoth 513, 868, 869; *see also* Hermes
   Trismegistos
throat-cutting 210, 527
Thyestes 326, 340, 944
thymele, thymelic artists 111 n. 25, 578, 579,
   580, 917, 919, 1050
tightrope-walkers 111, 115, 340, 621, 626,
   1052; *see also* acrobats; *petauristae*
   charts for 143, 147, 254, 617-18, 627, 920
   in Firmicus 112 n. 30, 113 n. 31
   itinerant 622
   motifs 921
tin 613
Titan (title of Saturn) 515
tomb-robbers 66, 616, 1050
torture 179, 586, 587, 695 n. 296, 1056
   of slaves 101
tragedy 618
   M^b and 209, 211, 216, 540, 541, 544 n. 50,
    559, 647, 675, 685, 690, 704, 708,
    709, 714, 731
    epithets 527, 528, 533, 549, 568, 626,
     648, 691, 713, 720, 735
   M^c and 293, 294, 769, 781-2, 789, 810, 846,
    853
   M^d and 338-9, 340, 902, 905, 926, 996
    epithets 334, 906, 924, 931, 949, 993, 995
   see also periphrastic expressions
tragic playwrights 113 n. 31, 1052
treasure, *see* wealth—acquisition of—windfalls
Trimalchio 69 n. 148, 123, 280 n. 19
triplets, *see* children—multiple
triplicity, royal 548
trumpets 111 n. 25, 580, 925, 926-7, 1051
tuberculosis, *see* consumption
twins, *see* children—multiple
Tyche 509, 825, 846

Uranus 789, 790, 1003
usury 729; *see also* money-lenders

Valens, Vettius
   charts for historical individuals 35, 90 n. 32,
    93 n. 50, 120, 643 n. 240, 966 n. 150
   on (in)utility of prayer 822
   quotations of Homer 336, 875, 893
   self-advertisement 749 n. 1, 857
   on slave-ownership 92, 100
   source of Θ 136, 138
   use of metaphor 76
   words for pauper 73 n. 3
   words for populace 26
   see also ἀπόκρουσις; εὐκρασία; κοινωνικός;
    melothesia; μεσόβιος; μετέωρος;
    Nemesis; τάξις
vegetables 606, 610, 612; *see also* gardeners
veins, jugular 851
venality 554-5
venatio 604, 743; *see also* amphitheatre
Veyne, Paul 36-7, 71, 109, 110, 121, 122, 718,
   1004; see also *plebs media*
viper 338 nn. 49-50, 937, 938-9; *see also*
   Nicander—M^d and; snakes
visions 593, 654, 719, 721, 834
   of the dead 231, 655, 720, 832-3; *see also*
    epilepsy—and visions; ghosts
Virgo 601, 602, 603, 653, 664 n. 268, 768,
   907 n. 76
   classification, *see* zodiac, signs of—double-
    bodied, earthy, winged
   formulary 218, 685
   house of Mercury 794, 928, 968 n. 154,
    995 n. 195
   monomoiriai 114, 563
   number of stars 519
   Scales 508
   terms 989
   see also Spica

wages, wage labourers 43, 65, 173, 174, 689,
   779, 780, 1064
wandering 82 n. 69, 95, 520, 570, 574, 710,
   746, 896, 910
   performers 622-3, 678, 683, 734; see also
    galli—mendicants; mimes—
    itinerant; *petauristae*—itinerant;
    tightrope-walkers—itinerant
   see also beggars; birds—comparisons to;
    merchants—sailing; Moon—
    wandering; *Odyssey*—and
    wandering

watery occupations 137 n. 29, 231, 295, 544, 561, 605, 612, 628, 704, 710, 711, 779; *see also* gardeners
water-carriers 606, 607, 779, 780, 1029
water-drawers 610–11, 1030
wax 253, 644, 645, 649, 928, 1036
  on hair 839
  seals 870, 871
  on ships 180, 649
  see also painters—encaustic
weakness
  mental 79 n. 46
  moral 717
  physical 690, 701, 713, 801, 802, 804, 807, 808
  see also planets—debility/depression
wealth 534, 540, 898
  acquisition of 77, 254, 543, 828; *see also* Moon—and money
  from kings and big men 19
  late in life 844
  windfalls 17, 899, 1060
  from women 531, 980, 983–4
  see also merchants
  enduring 538
  exulting in 774
  formulary of 516, 531, 540
  imagery of 76; *see also* metaphor—liquids; Moon—and money
  Jupiter and 560, 954
  loss of 77, 82, 254, 259, 516, 667, 809, 831, 841, 844, 853; *see also* Moon—and money; poverty
  and renown 8, 11, 295, 515, 813, 857
  restoration of 898
  and social status 36, 82, 857, 896, 972
  theme in Ptolemaic Egypt 752 n. 3
  true 724
  see also agriculture—and wealth; expenditure; freedmen; inheritance; meanness; money; poverty; prostitutes—economic condition
wealth-managers 56, 1040
weavers, weaving 38, 53, 64, 68, 644, 649, 672, 674, 929, 1034
  in apprenticeship contracts 42
  in Homer 174 n. 130, 679
  master 56, 173
  slaves 45 n. 37
  women's work 120 n. 56, 673, 946
  see also embroidery
weirdness 15, 119, 211, 243, 790

'who whom' construction 169 n. 115, 170, 322, 675, 731, 897, 906, 929
widows 664, 976
wigs 631–2; *see also* adulterers; hair
wild animals 25, 101, 338, 343, 742, 796, 816, 975, 982; *see also* bear; boar; lion
window allusion 816, 860
wine 38, 47 n. 44, 48, 54, 59, 1054
  containers 104, 611, 804
  selling 50, 67, 68, 82
wives 104, 633, 648, 677, 766, 774, 897, 987
  adjunct to male charts 120 n. 55
  consort with slaves 86, 90
  death of 854
  elderly 664
  happiness in 12 n. 31, 978
  homosexual 764
  of kinsmen 980
  murder of 305, 843
  none 810, 811
  shrewish 993, 995, 996
  slave, *see* marriage—with slaves
  sterile 731, 766; *see also* sterility
  take on husband's businesses 120 n. 56; *see also* husband—shares occupation with wife
  unchaste 528, 633, 702
  virtuous 119, 122
  see also adulterers; husband—and wife, relations of; husband—complaisant; prostitutes—as wives
women 595, 639, 640, 843
  adornment 637
  bereaved 816
  charts for 117, 120, 184, 358, 842, 917, 987–96
  déclassé 570, 760, 990
  foreign 654
  haughty 920, 984
  meretricious 634, 703
  old 663
  pregnant 992; *see also* abortion
  survival 664
  women-only cults 532
  women's quarters 103
  'women's works' 337, 733, 946–7
  in workforce 58, 120 n. 56, 173, 174 n. 130
  see also inheritance; lesbians; magic—love; metaphor—agricultural; misogyny; prostitutes; slaves—sexual relationships with; sterility; wealth—acquisition of—from women; widows; wigs; wives

work scenes 37, 45, 123 n. 67, 639
wrestlers, wrestling 111 n. 25, 112 n. 30, 114, 115 n. 39, 173, 773, 1053

Zeus
  in Aratus 512
  formulary 363–4, 794
  in mythology 509, 662, 697, 722, 797, 898; *see also* Ganymede
  see also Homeric poems; 'Olympian' motifs transferred to stars

zodiac, signs of
  amphibious 517
  aquatic, *see* watery
  bent 148, 553, 916, 917
  double-bodied 240, 683, 684, 685
  earthy 895 n. 67
  equinoctial 557, 845, 959
  female 634, 660, 704, 706, 707, 789
  four-footed 240, 254, 619, 627, 687, 744, 990
  human 598, 687
  lewd 990
  male 241, 242, 546, 637, 660, 706, 710, 846, 1063
  multi-coloured 958 n. 139
  mute 148, 923
  scaly 143 n. 40, 148, 162 n. 97, 341, 768–9, 935, 957, 958
  slippery 148, 923
  solid 685, 744, 745, 991
  terrestrial 60, 563, 768, 959
  tropic 29, 31 n. 63, 60 n. 100, 557, 620, 685, 703, 959, 972
  watery 60, 240, 262, 263, 541, 559, 560, 606, 664, 666, 711, 801 n. 60, 802, 895 n. 67, 921, 922, 942
  winged 240, 559, 601, 602, 603, 644, 645
  see also ecliptic and s.vv. individual signs

zodiac, *vis* in 249 n. 212, 508, 511